ISBN 978-0-282-93757-7
PIBN 10873924

This book is a reproduction of an important historical work. Forgotten Books uses state-of-the-art technology to digitally reconstruct the work, preserving the original format whilst repairing imperfections present in the aged copy. In rare cases, an imperfection in the original, such as a blemish or missing page, may be replicated in our edition. We do, however, repair the vast majority of imperfections successfully; any imperfections that remain are intentionally left to preserve the state of such historical works.

# 1 MONTH OF
# FREE
# READING

## at

## www.ForgottenBooks.com

By purchasing this book you are eligible for one month membership to ForgottenBooks.com, giving you unlimited access to our entire collection of over 1,000,000 titles via our web site and mobile apps.

To claim your free month visit:

www.forgottenbooks.com/free873924

English
Français
Deutsche
Italiano
Español
Português

# www.forgottenbooks.com

**Mythology** Photography **Fiction**
Fishing Christianity **Art** Cooking
Essays Buddhism Freemasonry
Medicine **Biology** Music **Ancient**
**Egypt** Evolution Carpentry Physics
Dance Geology **Mathematics** Fitness
Shakespeare **Folklore** Yoga Marketing
**Confidence** Immortality Biographies
Poetry **Psychology** Witchcraft
Electronics Chemistry History **Law**
Accounting **Philosophy** Anthropology
Alchemy Drama Quantum Mechanics
Atheism Sexual Health **Ancient History**
**Entrepreneurship** Languages Sport
Paleontology Needlework Islam
**Metaphysics** Investment Archaeology
Parenting Statistics Criminology
**Motivational**

# BREEDER & SPORTSMAN

VOL. 1—No. 1
No. 508 MONTGOMERY STREET. } 147795 SAN FRANCISCO, SATURDAY, JULY 1, 1882. { SUBSCRIPTION FIVE DOLLARS A YEAR.

## NOTABLE HORSES OF CALIFORNIA.

## DUCHESS OF NORFOLK.

We promised Mr. Winters that if Duchess of Norfolk did not win, her portrait should be withheld. While we intend to keep promises religiously, in this instance there are good reasons for breaking it, and circumstances which will warrant the violation. As the intelligence of her defeat did not reach here until after midnight Thursday, there was not time to confer with Mr. Winters before the form would have to go to press. We had another cut to take the place of the one selected for the opening of the series in case it was required, but from the meager telegraphic account we feel well assured that the filly is still entitled to rank as one of the "Notable horses of California," and that it would be rank injustice to defer her claims.

Her running at the May meeting here demonstrated that she was the possessor of rare powers, and until she has another trial, under circumstances which show that she is "at herself," we cannot believe that she is otherwise than the Nonpareil we have rated her to be, being well acquainted with the peculiarities of the climate of Chicago at all seasons, and more particularly the drawbacks attending the peculiarities that are so prevalent during the latter part of June and the first of July. At these times there are violent rain storms, in some cases followed by a lowering of temperature very many degrees; at others, there is increased heat, murkiness, climatic revulsions, which induce languor, if not actual debility.

The track is rendered dangerous, as the rich, unctuous, dark prairie soil, when wet, affords no foothold, and the careful trainer is fearful that if he attempts strong work he will take chances of crippling, and, it may be, beyond recovery. ? revert : Duchess was leading the three-quarter pole means it was in advance of the others

when a mile and a quarter had been made. In the same condition she was in when she won the Pacific Cup, after running a mile and a quarter at any pace, the least judicious rider would make, Jim Renwick could not beat her through the stretch.

In she goes, the first of the series of the grand horses of California, and if her owner takes us to task for the breaking of troth, all right. We will call him to account for going contrary to his own convictions, and changing a line of policy, which, if followed according to his original intentions, might have changed the result. Again, we have faith that before this number of the paper reaches the "City on the Lake," the Illinois Derby will be placed to her credit.

Shotover won the Two Thousand, but was beaten in the One Thousand. She then won the Derby and did not start for the Oaks. I you think what make the odds. Duchess will win the Derby. Queen sake.

## NEW YORK CORRESPONDENCE.

NEW YORK, June 19, 1882.

MR. JOSEPH CAIRN SIMPSON—DEAR SIR: Your esteemed favor of 30th ultimo is received, and you have my best wishes personally and for the new enterprise with which you are identified. "Hark Comstock" thanks you for remembering him in your invitation to write for your new journal, but he has somewhat cooled down in that author' steam for the horse and his breeding which formerly impelled him to write frequently for the press, not from any lack of interest in the subject, but because the views which it used to seem important to him to have disseminated and considered have gradually become familiar to most of the reading minds who, by example, sway the action and plans of others. Younger enthusiasts are taking up the work, and putting more energy and surplus vitality into it than springs readily from those who have reached mid-life, and as one who is constitutionally inclined to take things easy, he finds himself tempted to look on and become a listener rather than a writer. Young blood tells, and in that fact lies one of the best assurances of the success of your journal.

Now, Mr. Editor, it hardly seems in place for me to tell so experienced a writer and journalist as yourself anything about conducting a newspaper, but an observer may occasionally notice things that an experienced worker overlooks or fails to estimate at correctly. Whatever force and training of the mind an individual may have, the world at large will surpass him in elaborating any subject that may be raised. Only in the sense of starting the ball in motion can he be considered the originator or leader in the thought, principle or theory. I said, a good many years ago, that all writers upon the subject of the horse (I was quite active in that direction myself at that time) were confirmed egotists. I think so still, and probably the rule applies in equal force to writers upon many other subjects. Most people, who voluntarily take pen in hand to place their views before the public, assume that upon the subject discussed they are more valuable than the average. This implies a certain degree of conceit, which may or may not be well founded. I have noticed that, while almost every theory put forward draws some adherents, there is scarcely one that does not excite opposition. Until a sufficiently broad statistical basis can be reached from which to generalize any theory of breeding, training, feeding, or in any manner manipulating the horse, no solution of the theory can be obtained that will be accepted as a practical principle by the mass of horsemen. I think, therefore, that the most useful and successful editors are those who sufficiently bury their personality as not to permit their journals to become partizan for or against any theory that is widely disputed or combatted, no matter how clearly the editor may think he is able to demonstrate the correctness of one side or the other. If he must be a partizan, let him not make his journal one. This may be scouted as conservatism by some, but what is the use of radicalism in such a position, if its effect is to bar out discussion from one side or the other. Let the correspondents hammer away, so long as they do so in a good tempered and gentlemanly way, and lucky is the editor who, by impartiality, keeps the good will of both sides, and thus brings up before his readers a full and free discussion. Let him keep in mind that it is not the editorial dictum that is to decide which practical shall be followed. It is the conclusion arrived at in each individual case by his mass of readers. For this reason, if an interesting topic fails to be sufficiently discussed by direct correspondence, let him quote both sides of the argument from other papers, striving to give forth clear-cut thought and argument impartially before the two sides, and let him not be too anxious to add the official weight of his editorial pen to one side or the other of the argument, for in this case he will draw the opposition of one-half his readers against his journal that would otherwise have rested only against his correspondent, while, on the other hand, he will scarcely have more fully convinced those who were inclined to side with him. In this way he may hold the attention of a far greater number of readers, educate them just as thoroughly, convince them just as surely upon all theories that are well grounded, and accomplish far greater results, than by a partizan course. Most correspondents are sensitive at being snubbed or opposed in the editorial columns, and fail to continue their contributions. It is only the old stagers like myself and you, Mr. Editor, who are not particularly strenuous on that subject. Being just as conceited as the editors themselves, we are wont to keep right on without the slightest idea that we are worsted in the fray, and, if anything, rather glad that we have succeeded in getting the best of the editor before his own readers. But that is not the feeling with most writers, and many readers who side with the theories of their favorite writers are apt to take his grievances to themselves, and to look upon the editorial interference as wrongful, and to drop the journal for a more congenial one. Hence, there is in journal or magazine in this country, in which the horse is a special feature, that is radical and conducive in its editorial management, that has much circulation or carries much influence. While the combative course generally claims for itself the quality of courage, it is cowardly, in the fact that it seldom dares to let all opposing facts come unabridged before its readers, without attempting to thwart their force by editorial detraction. Such editors seem to think that they control the minds of their readers, and that eternal vigilance is the price of the possession. They are unwilling, because afraid of the result of permitting free thought to weigh the merits of the question, lest what they consider heresy undermine their pet theories. And in this they show a lack of confidence either in the stability of their theories, or in the intelligence and discernment of their readers, and either interpretation lowers their journal in public esteem. When arguments are based upon a misstatement of statistics, it is the editorial duty to point out the errors, and leave the rest to the intelligence of the reader. If the editor rates his readers as incompetent, and treats them as such, he will soon have only that kind to deal with. I venture the prediction that twenty years hence that class of the newspaper business pertaining to the interests of breeders and sportsmen which has survived will be conducted in a much less personal way, both as to the nature of the matter published, and the individuality reflected from the editorial pen. The world is fast losing, its need of individual promises. Intelligence is

## WISCONSIN CORRESPONDENCE.

JANESVILLE, WISCONSIN, June 21, 1882.

JOSEPH CAIRN SIMPSON, ESQ.—DEAR SIR: Your esteemed favor of May 30th received. I am very much pleased to learn that you are about to engage in an enterprise for which your abilities so eminently qualify you. For many years I have been a close and interested reader, a student, in fact, of your writings, deriving great benefits, in a practical way, from the many valuable lessons and suggestions that you have given from time to time to the reading world. Your writings have possessed unusual interest to me, as I knew they emanated from the cultured mind of a practical horseman—no mere theorist with his whims, fancies and vagaries. Not among all the Turf writers of America can be found one that so thoroughly understands the true science of breeding, and, at the same time, thoroughly informed in the science, as well, of developing the speed inheritance of a colt, no matter whether trotting bred or racing bred, as Joseph Cairn Simpson.

The field which you have chosen in which to labor is one wherein many golden harvests have been garnered, and I hope and believe that your efforts will soon place you among the successes of your adopted home, for which you have formed so strong attachments.

Although the BREEDER AND SPORTSMAN is to be published so remote from the great breeding interests of the Eastern and Middle States, we are confident that the paper will find the extensive circulation among our intelligent breeders and horsemen that it is sure to merit. Your able papers on breeding, the horse in motion, the horse's foot, etc., gained for the California Spirit of the Times a wide circulation in the East, and to these old subscribers of the California Spirit of the Times, I am sure will be added a greatly increased number.

Breeding in your section of the country has been a revelation in the development of the speed of the youngsters. But remarkable and wonderful as has been the performance of your colts, what would it have benefited the breeding world but for the able pen of one who could, in giving an account of the wonders performed, give us also at the same time a correct analysis of their breeding, and the combination of blood forces producing such happy results?

Mr. Stanford, Mr. Rose, and your numerous successful breeders, no doubt feel a justifiable pride in their glorious triumph, as breeders. At the same time, we trust they all fully appreciate the fact that the able pen is a very important factor in the problem of success, as a business proposition, in a breeding enterprise. Producing a wonderful colt is a gratification to the breeder, but his pride is that the world shall learn of his wonderful colt and the name of the successful breeder; also, the blood forces that have blended so kindly in producing marvelous results.

Basking and frolicking in the sunny field of your golden clime, while our young things are seeking the loss of a friendly straw stack to protect them from the driving snows and sleet of our rigorous winters, has given you an advantage unmeasured of in early development. Of course, we are now all watching with deep interest the improvement made in later years may bring; whether the advantage gained at one and two years may be maintained at five or six, the age we feel safe in putting our trotters to the severe tests of circuit campaigns. Our Eastern breeders shall look upon Kentucky as the great nursery of trotters, and heavy and successful drafts are being constantly made from their fashionable blood.

Tennessee is occasionally heard from, sending a fast pacer, Little Brown Jug, and a few trotters of merit. It has always seemed a great surprise to me that Tennessee with its unrivalled advantages of climate and grasses has not so much neglected as a breeding State. Its advantages over Kentucky in climate are as great as Kentucky over Wisconsin.

The improvement in breeding in Wisconsin the past few years has been remarkable. Thanks to the liberality of the millionaire lovers of the horse they have placed at the disposal of our breeders the very best blood in the land. Hon. J. I. Case, of Racine, has given us to breed from not only Governor Sprague, for which he paid what was at the time of purchase a remarkable price, $27,500, but he has several sons of Dictator of rare individual merit and great promise as sires. We will mention, as a "sample," Phallas, by Dictator, full brother to Jay-eye-see, by Dictator, 3d by

trot in 2:25, five years old; his full brother Tyrant and many others. Of Gov. Sprague we have the most extravagant faith in the get of Sprague. We are happy in the possession of two—filly and colt—both please me. Sprague has proven a valuable acquisition to our State, and from the class of mares served has been a remarkable success. Had he remained in Kentucky no sire in America would have shown a handsomer list of fast ones. I have four, and like them. One of the best bred sons of Hambletonian, Milwaukee, full brother to Curtis Hambletonian, is owned by Chas. T. Bradley, of Milwaukee; he is also a most successful sire and a favorite with our breeders; from number of mares served he has begotten many very fast and level-headed trotters. Mr. Bradley has by him one of the finest four-year-old fillies in the country, so good that last week he refused for her $5,000. We have several well-bred sons of Almont in Southern Wisconsin, and all growing successful sires. I have a three-year-old gelding by Athlete, son of Almont, owned by Dr. H. P. Strong, that is the best three-year-old I have ever owned. They say "the best three-year-old in Wisconsin." I am just informed that a filly, two years old, 15¾ hands, by Swigert, and a good one, has a hind leg broken between pastern and gambrel joints; evidently from a kick in pasture. Now, this is one of those little episodes in breeding, which, while it may furnish variety, is not so very pleasant. You may ask, kill her? Not if veterinary skill can save her. Sired by Swigert, I saw him trot a full mile four weeks from service of 50 mares in 2:26, half in 1:10½; dam by Mambrino Star, 2:28½; 3d dam Reed's Morgan Messenger, by Hill's Black Hawk, dam by Lady Messenger, by American Messenger, &c., 3d dam by Evans Backus, &c. She could trot faster than any two-year-old I have ever handled, If I can save her I shall prize her for a brood mare. Sold her full sister, coming four, for $1,500; her full brother, coming three, for $750, and was offered $900. I will console myself by saying, "glad it was no worse."

You have written many interesting articles on various themes; a very interesting article might be written on "My Experience in Buying Horses for Friends."

With my best wishes for a golden harvest, I am, very truly yours,     MAMBRINO.

## LOS ANGELES CORRESPONDENCE.

SUNNY SLOPE, SAN GABRIEL, CAL., June 26, 1882.

MR. JOS. CAIRN SIMPSON—DEAR SIR: I received your letter, also your circular, from which I see that you are going to publish a sporting paper in San Francisco. Inclosed please find five dollars for subscription, I am much pleased with your new enterprise, and if good wishes will avail you it will be prosperous.

I am much flattered by your good opinion about my capacity, and would be much pleased to do anything in my power to help along. For the present, time will not permit me to do much, but hope some future day to avail myself of your request. My young trotters are doing well, all trotting finely, but I do not have many in training as yet. This year I have a large number of foals, and not only numerous, but the best bred lot and the best "lookers" I ever saw. This year my colts have run largely to males. Minnie-ha-ha leading off, and followed by sister to Beautiful Bells, sister to a Rose, Georgiana, by Overland, dam Maggie Mitchell, by Clay Pilot, g. d. by Dr. Spaulding's Abdallah; bay mare Sampson, son of Hambletonian, dam by Sealy's American Star, Blonde by Tecumseh, dam by St. Clair, Peg Woffington, Souvenier by The Moor, dam Lulu Jackson, a thoroughbred, by Jack Malone, and two Echo fillies out of a mare by Langford. All these are stallion colts, and all but one by Sultan, and these are not all.

You can see from this that there are several mares by The Moor, and Sultan being by the Moor, it makes very close in-breeding. It has ever been a favorite theory with me, this in-breeding, yet I have seen so many failures that I began to have misgivings about it. For myself I have had no opportunity until this year that would give me a line of facts to go by. This year I have four two-year-olds that I am training; all are perfect in conformation, large size and fast. From this I am led to believe that in-breeding will stand the test with The Moors. The best yearling (stallion) in my stable is an in-bred Moor. He is the largest, has more speed and as much style and beauty of form as any of my stock, whether in-bred or otherwise.

I am for the first time handling yearlings for speed; I have three at work now and then, and so far, it all goes well. I have ever believed that judicious handling can never be done too young, but that is the exact point: What is judicious handling? and it takes much experience and good sense to determine. Nine men in ten will do too much if they are believers in the theory; and again, nine men in ten will do too little if they believe that early development is an injury.

The breeding and training of trotters present an endless school of valuable lessons. Every year adds experience, and every new colt is different from all before it, requiring, in some particulars, a change of treatment. There are many blunders committed, and many colts are ruined by a want of judgment or sense; and again, many fail by accidents or some inherent weakness. But this is not confined to young things. How many old horses are trained and hunged from year to year, and how many ever come to a race, but drop out of existence and are never heard of again? Yet some phenomenal youngster appears as a two-year-old, something happens to him, and the world's finger is pointed at him, and all is laid to early training. Whereas, if the colt had not been trained while young, it is also chances in ten he would have never been heard from at all. Old horses fail too. St. Julien was laid up all summer, Santa Claus has to be retired too this year, Maud S. had to be withdrawn from the turf for last part of last season; yet there is a Trinket So-So, and others, who were fast when young, and are fast yet. It is true there have been three and two-year-olds that were fast when young, and are not heard from now. Part of these were injured while being worked. The others of some small result, but have not improved on their young form. It is a fact, that some colts, and I believe it runs in families, or rather follows the sire, will trot when young as fast as they ever can. This may be fast or it may not be better than a four-minute or a three-minute gait, and the trotting, whether fast or slow, must get them to 'not' at 'all. It is ....

from many different stallions, and this has been my experience. Each stallion seemed to have a given capacity to get trotters, which would vary some small degree with different mares, yet there was a stubborn uniformity that would make itself felt, and could not be overcome. Yet I could learn colts to trot while young much quicker, with less trouble or toil, and with less liability of hurting or injuring them, than Ic ould older ones of the same families. A stallion may get fast young trotters that will improve with age, or he may get fast young trotters, or slow young trotters, that will not improve with age. Some stallions who get fast young trotters, it turned out for any length of time, say a year, will lose their gait; others again you can turn out for any time, and when you hitch them up you find them where you left them, and ready for improvement.

You speak about the closing of the Embryo having been good. I think the Embryo has had its day as it now stands. The nature of the stake is such that there can be no success without a large entry list, and this cannot be got, in my opinion, with Gov. Stanford and myself to enter. There should be a class of colt stakes got up in this State as they have in the East, barring the get of certain stallions, and the quickest way out of it would be to bar Gov. Stanford's and my stable. I have no doubt that there will be other colts in this State the equal, and even superior, to anything we may raise, but it is generally believed that by some mode of early training, or a peculiarity of our stock, that we would carry off such prizes, and there will be no entries. Whereas, if we were barred it would lead to the training of hundreds of youngsters, many of which, or, at least some, would make fast horses, and which their owners would be willing to enter in other stakes, which are free to all, like the Stanford and the Occident stakes, or purses given at the different district and State fairs.

You see I did not think of writing when I sat down, but start "horse" and a man never knows when to stop. Hoping, however, that it may please you and your readers,

I am yours truly,
L. J. Rose.,

## OREGON CORRESPONDENCE.

Breedville, Or., June 12, 1882.
Jos. Cairn Simpson, Esq.—Dear Sir: Your favor of the 5th inst. together with circular calling attention to the Breeder and Sportsman, came to hand in due time.

It gives me great pleasure to hear of your contemplated enterprise. I know of no one so eminently qualified to conduct a journal in the interests of the breeders and sportsmen of the Pacific coast as yourself, and hope it will meet with a liberal patronage from the great number of people on this coast interested in such matters, and feel confident that it will.

Although your State has eclipsed the world in the breeding and training of trotting horses, we in Oregon have not lost heart; and when the direct railroad connection is made will meet you halfway and try to beat you. I am satisfied we have the blood, but our climate is not so favorable for the development of young trotters as yours. I think that will be obviated before two years pass, by having covered tracks to work under during the rainy season. There is a great interest manifested here now in the breeding and training of trotters, and the lovers of thoroughbreds are numerous. Everything indicates that we shall have some of the grandest contests of speed during the coming summer and fall ever witnessed in the world. When a lot of such horses as Conner, Trade Dollar, Red Colllier, Caddie R., Jim Renwick, Jo Howell, Premium, Billy C., Jim Merritt, Mayflower, Lulu Riggs, and a lot of others that can run to the half-mile stake in 48 or 49 seconds, there is likely to be a horse-race. All of the above horses are now at the Washington County Fair Grounds, where the first meeting takes place, commencing July 3d, and continuing five days. There are about twenty-five trotters entered for the trotting races at the same meeting. The next meeting will be at Portland, the 18th of July, then to Vancouver, W. T., the last of the same month; from there to Olympia, W. T., some time in August, and then to the Oregon State Fair, commencing September 18th. The entries closed there April 1st, with 53 entries for the trotting races. If you could possibly arrange to attend the coming State Fair in Oregon you would never regret it, as you would see the handsomest fair grounds in the United States, and an Agricultural Fair, with the agriculturists in attendance. From twenty to forty thousand people meet there every year, and at least half of them camp on the grounds. All of the farmers, their wives and their children assemble there, get acquainted, exchange views, report their experiences on farming matters, and have a good time generally. Everything indicates that we shall have the most successful fair this year we have ever had. If you should then pay us a visit I don't think you will go home and publish in the Breeder and Sportsman that the Oregonians are the meanest people you ever met, Yours truly,
L. B. Lindsey.

## STOCKTON CORRESPONDENCE.

Editor Breeder and Sportsman—Dear Sir: The good people of this coast invariably manage to come to the front once a year, and especially the people of this valley make a week's holiday of the Fair. They depend on the Managers of the San Joaquin Valley Association to decide on the merits of their running, trotting and pacing horses, well assured that they will have a fair deal and as good a show as the most exacting could desire. At the present time owners are at work in dead earnest to produce a winner, and though the finishing polish of the "grand preparation" will come hereafter, there is enough shown now to warrant high anticipations.

The running comes first, and the opening race of the programme is a district purse of $800, for three-year-olds and upwards, which closed on the 1st of April with six nominations. The contestants are, G. W. Graham's Kate Carson; J. Shepherd's Minnie Bell; W. Ash's colt. Colonel Dorsey

has two in, and C. McGlashin one. Nearly all are by Joe Daniels, and that he is a grand stock-horse no one will dispute when they see such fine-lookers and speed from flint-look mares. His opportunities on thoroughbred, proved mares have been limited to so few that he is practically debarred from anything like a show, and yet some of his get have shown well. He stands to-day in the center of a farming community, speaking his piece all alone, and had he been favored with an ordinary share of the mares of the State, Joe Daniels to-day would rank second to no stallion on the coast for first class runners. It seems strange that such a performer and one so well known receives no more encouragement from breeders. The time is not distant when breeders, who desire to rank in the first class, will have to drop their one-pet family system, and the sooner the better. When we have so many other pure strains of the strictest thoroughbred blood, equally rich, there is a desire to make the happiest cross of all, and then we will have first class race horses in numbers.

The second race is a district purse of $400, for two-year-olds, dash of a mile; the entries to which close on the 15th of July. Many parties are boasting of what they possess, and the prospect of strong competition in this race is good. The third is a district purse of $500, mile and repeat; boots barred; the entries to which also close on the 15th of July. Next comes the district trotting: a two-year-old race for a purse of $800, closed April 1st, ten nominations, get of Reliance, Membrino, Wilkes, Argois, Pearly's Echo and Nephew, and the blood of Byedyks' Hambletonian, Alexander's Abdallah. Membrino Chief, George Wilkes' Almont, Patchen, Hambrino, Black Hawk, Belmont and Chieftain, crops out in the above race, and it would be difficult to guess the winner. The colts are all doing well, and every owner has a right to claim first money, just now.

The following colts are entered:

G. W. Trahen's blk f Baby Mine, by Nephew.
L. U. Shippee's b f, by Echo.
Fred. Arnold's Ha Ha, b c, by Nephew.
L. M. Moss' b g, by Membrino Wilkes.
D. Visbe's b f, by Pserless.
Warren's b c, by Membrino Wilkes.
C. Giddings ——, by Angora.
S. F. Gilmore's ——, by Argola.
I. M. Gearnnt's b c, by Reliance.
W. Murray's blk f, by Nephew.

"This race is much thought of, and not only the owners are looking forward to the final result, but the owners of Stallion, whose get are represented in this race, feel uneasy. District yearling trotting one-mile race; purse, $300. Entries close July 15th.

In future, we must cultivate the idea of colt races at home, for the time has come when it is all nonsense for us to think we can make a decent showing in the Bay District Embryo races, and we are satisfied that Palo Alto colts are dangerous and we place ourselves accordingly.

District trotting, 2:50 class; purse, $500. There are many eyes craving a bead on this race. The competitors will be named by our committee. Entries close July 15th. District trotters that never beat 2:38; purse $600. We have upwards of twenty that have a right to contend for this race, which closes July 15th. Our trotters are being handled by John Williams, W. H. Parker, W. E. Morris, John Donohoe, Fred. Vail and John McCloud, and we have a right to expect loud reports.

Our State Races. The entries close at the usual time, August 1st, for running, trotting and pacing. The programme we have now is frame, and when the proper time comes we shall throw it to the breeze. I promise you it is loud and liberal, and will pay all who take part in it. Our scale for State trotting races will run throughout the entire line, from 2:40 to free for all. We give the pacers a show. Also, a first-rate assortment of State running races. In all, we hang up $12,000 for speed, forc moneys.
Respectfully, Ha Ha.

## OAKLAND CORRESPONDENCE.

Oakland, June 28, 1882.
Editor Breeder and Sportsman—It would not be according to the eternal fitness of things for the second city on the Pacific Coast not to be present at the launch of your fair bark on the great sea of journalism, and bid you Godspeed; so put Oakland down as "present" on the muster-roll of your friends, and hear her say with a right good will all manner of pleasant things about the new captain, and listen to her anguries of the brightest success for the new venture. Please accept from us who have known you so well and so long our profoundest faith in the future of your new journal, and receive our congratulations for your hosts of readers who are to have a long felt want supplied. You have done me the honor to intimate that something from my pen would be acceptable to you, and I do myself the pleasure to respond by this letter. If it pleases your editorial mind to write above it " From Our Regular Correspondent," by way of caption, so be it, and I will do my best endeavor to keep your readers posted, in a gossipy way, about men and things—that may seem to jump with your mood—only excuse me, please, from the writing of many statistics after the manner of the world's Gradgrinds. I trust that I shall write facts, but I much prefer to sandwich them in between something more appetizing—sugar-coat them with words of my own conceit and fancies of my own brain. It may be that I am something like a hunting friend of mine, who quaintly remarked on an occasion, that one good will snipe would afford him an admirable day's sport, so one good fact will sometimes last a long time, and give a good pretext for a good deal of imagination. I could tell you that Oakland contains fifty thousand people, but I shan't put in bald figures between ruled columns, for then it would probably be skipped, while, as narrow stands, you have got it anyway, whether you like it or not: and thus I might go on to tell you how many columns we occupy within our extremest limits, but it suits my modesty better to say that she is a city of magnificent distances; that for beauty of situation she is without a rival in this beautiful world of ours; that all her streets are magnificent boulevards; that no spot in vaunted Italy has fairer villa sites; that it is her just and proud boast that her universities, colleges, schools and seminaries are second in

rank to none; that her sons are manly and her daughters beautiful and virtuous; that her citizens are prosperous and happy, and that, having all these things, we are content.

Now, while these are facts, I submit that they are more readable than they would have been if I had dished them up in figures and labeled them "statistics." Perhaps it will have struck you that I have said nothing about the climate of Oakland. Well, to tell you the truth, I couldn't enthuse much over the climate that has been meted out to us by the gods so far this year. Ordinarily, the climate of our city is admirable—much less harsh and cold than that of San Francisco, across the bay. But this spring has been exceptionally cold, windy and disagreeable. We seemed to have shared in the general elemental disturbances that have played such sad havoc on this mundane sphere this year. But, like most of Nature's evils, there has been a compensating good, and that is, that the cool weather has been very favorable to the farmers and the ripening grain crops, so that in view of the whitening harvests, doubt and gloom have given place to hope and smiles. But I started out to say something about our horses, and, as I think over what has been written, I seem to have told about them after the manner of old widow Bedott. Well, among our other attributes of greatness we are not much behind in the mattee of horses, whether we speak of speed, style or breeding. It is true, we can not boast of any such breeding establishments within or near our borders as Palo Alto or Sunny Slope, but for all that, we have several ambitions and discriminating breeders whose names are on our Great Register, a large number of very fine carriage teams, not a few speedy double teams, and more than several single roadsters whose owners take no man's dust up to a $40 gait, and some that will go you better by 10 seconds. Our streets are very favorable for road driving, barring a little hardness of our macadam, and our fast roadsters are daily increasing to the shards of our wealthy citizens, who do not affect a runner's gait on the thoroughfares of life. It will be my pleasure to give them greater prominence and individuality on another occasion. But I see that I must call a halt and try no further generalizing while I tell you something of the trotters and runners in training at Oakland Trotting Park. The horses have been a little backward in getting into training quarters on account of the backwardness of the spring, but there are more animals taking their work at the Park than there have been in any previous season in the month of June, some eighty odd in round numbers, and some important stables on the way.

The first stable that we approached, pencil in hand, was L. H. Titus', from Los Angeles, or, more accurately speaking, San Gabriel, and we had the good fortune to meet the owner, Mr. Titus, himself, who very kindly chaperoned us among his string of trotters. To our first question, "How is Belle Echo?" he threw open the door of her box, and curtly said, "See for yourself." Belle has greatly improved on her last year's form and for the better, and it was easy to see that she is the pet and the pride of her owner. And when you look her over carefully and critically, and hear Titus say, with an emphasis, "She is second to no animal top of earth, sir!" it does not seem extravagant or hard to believe. She is symmetry itself, and to our eye, and we have seen a good many horses, she is the very perfection of trotting form, and she, with her royal breeding, and the speed and gameness she displayed last year as a four-year-old, we venture the prediction that in the near future she will score in the first rank of great trotters. Titus says that she is all right and as sound as a bullet. She is a beautiful bay, by Echo, and her dam by old Belmont.

The next we come to is a new one to us, a bay stallion, named Exile, six years old, by Echo, dam Belle Mason, by Belmont. You will travel a long way before you will see the superior of this fellow in looks. A beautiful bright bay in color, with black points, about 15 hands 3 inches, a flowing mane, and a tail like a Pasha's standard, a form superior to his celebrated sire and a perfect disposition. He should make his mark high up on the roll of fame; and we add that he can beat 2:30 any day in the week when in trim (and how much less we are not at liberty to say). You will all say that this is a good green horse.

The other members of this stable are the old favorite Echora, who is looking remarkably well, Bullet, Grasshopper, a natural pacer, by Echo, dam a Royal George mare; Battle Johnson, a large, likely looking bay mare, and a full sister to Gibraltar; and an unnamed Echo filly, that looks like the family.

Mr. Titus has sold the well known trotter Joe Hamilton to G. Valensin.

We pass along, and come to M. Salisbury's stable, under the general superintendence of John H. Goldsmith, the rising trainer and driver.

And some way it comes natural for us to place at the head of this stable the young gray stallion Romeer. This now celebrated 5-year-old has shaped up a good deal since last season, and is looking and feeling well, and when he and Belle Echo come together in the 2:22 class, this season, there will be music in the air, and it will be a battle royal and worth going a long way to see. We may refresh failing memories by saying that he is by A. W. Richmond, and his dam is Gretchen by Membrino Pilot.

Goldsmith says, with a complacent look, that he is all right.

In the next box stands the old favorite Gibraltar, known among all the boys as "Old Gib." He is looking well after his season in the harem, and will make the rounds of the circuit.

Alongside of him stands Buteman, who needs no description and no introduction to your readers. He is in good condition.

We next come to one who is comparatively a stranger, one of the new purchases of Mr. Salisbury, the blk. s. Director, 5 years old. This horse is 15 hands 2 inches high, and has about him a business look that may seem trouble along the line when the order comes to march. He is by Dictator, a full brother to Dexter, and his dam is by Membrino Chief, and is also the dam of Thorndale (2:22½) and Onward (2:25½), so that he takes speed by right of inheritance. Director's own record is—3-year-old, 2:30; 4-year-old, 2:27¼. What his 5-year-old may be—quien sabe?

Another stranger is Sweetness, b. m., 9 years old, by Volunteer; dam by Edward Everett, 2d dam by old Harry Clay. This is a mare of great substance, 16 hands high, and was very speedy, getting a record of 2:20, and then went lame, and got a long let-up. She is now all right, and will be no mean opponent for the best.

And then comes another stranger, a full brother to Little Brown Jug, also a pacer, like his famous brother. All we can say is that he is a dark roan in color, hard looking nails, and as big a little horse as a man ever looked at. If he isn't speedy, we give it up, and pass.

Then comes Dashwood, b. s., by Legal Tender, dam by Volunteer, another green pacer.

Goldsmith is also breaking a full brother to Romero, and has in his stables a yearling colt by Santa Claus, dam Sweetness by Volunteer, and a yearling Nutwood colt out of a mare by Volunteer, and that was a full sister to Powers with a record of 2:21.

A. Waldstein's stable is in charge of James Duane, and contains only three animals: Albert W., b. s., by Electioneer; dam full sister to Aurora. This horse has a record of 2:32 as a three-year-old, but this does not tell his speed. He is doing well, and will be entered in the Circuit.

Nelly W., three-year-old, by Electioneer, out of the dam of Albert W. This filly is entered in the Occident and Stanford Stakes, and will probably be entered in the Circuit.

Also, a chestnut filly by Nutwood, out of Albert W.'s dam, that looks well and ought to trot.

Martin Rollins, of Santa Rosa, has quite a stable of horses, the most of which are without public records.

The first in order on our list is a chestnut five-year-old mare by Capt. Webster; dam, the dam of Terry, and owned by Myron Dusenburry, that is a pacer and quite promising.

Ch. g., 7 years old, by Patchen, without a record.

A bay Patchen mare, very promising, and that Rollins says can trot in 2:30, and will be entered through the Circuit.

He also showed us a big bay gelding, sire Capt. Webster, dam by Belmont, that Rollins says is the best green horse on the coast. As this is pretty large talk, we hereby put Mr. Rollins on record, in order that horsemen may have an opportunity to test his judgment before the season closes.

He is also working a 5-year-old Echo filly owned by Andy Ryder, our popular County Clerk. We hope she is a good one for the owner's sake.

He has also a gray pacing gelding, owned by John Thomas, by Washington, dam a thoroughbred mare, that he thinks well of, and that will be entered in the pacing classes.

Henry McConn's stable consists of—

Maggie C., br. mare, with a record of 2:25, by Whipple's Hambletonian, and owned by P. Canavan of Virginia City.

Bay colt by Electioneer, dam Stockton Belle, owned by Morrow of San Francisco.

Contractor, 4-year-old, b. c., by Dick Taylor, dam Amy, with record of 2:22, and owned by James McCord of San Francisco, who also owns Blackmoor, in an adjoining box, by Patchen, record, 2:30½.

In the same stable is the b. g. Majors, with a record of 2:34, and owned by Covarubias of Los Angeles.

Pete Williams' stable consists of eight animals: Frank, ch. g., nine years old, by Moscow, and owned by A. B. Cooper of Alameda; Cinderella, ch. m., by Whipple's Hambletonian, dam Belle, by Belmont, and owned by Martin Carter, of Newark, that is said to be very promising; Dick, b. g., four years old, by imported Hercules, dam a Lomax mare, and owned by Evans of Milpitas; Goldnut, ch. c., two years old, by Nutwood, dam the dam of Lady Sherman, which can trot a '50 gait; also, a gray Nutwood filly, two years old, from a mare by Gen. Taylor, owned by Mr. Carter of Newark, that Williams thinks very highly of; a three-year-old Elmo filly, dam by Niagara, and owned by Mr. Storms of Oakland; a Billy Hayward filly, and a blk. g. by McCracken's Black Hawk.

H. A. Mayhew has three good ones at the Park: Setting Sun, ch. g., by Billy Hayward; Bertie Hayward, by Hayward, from the dam of Poscora Hayward; and a gray two-year-old filly, "Angerstein," all of which have the a fmily look and share the family speed.

Lee Shaner has in his stable Terry, the pacer; Rowdy Boy, a four-year-old gray gelding, by Rustic; and a gray three-year-old Rustic colt. He has also a few runners—Night Hawk, by Haddington; Haddington, Jr., by Haddington; a Daniel Boone filly, and two Haddington fillies.

John McConnell has in training Poscora Hayward and the Grand Moor, both owned by Mr. Hammond, former partner of Andrew Newland. Rumor has it that Poscora is an extraordinary good horse this season, and that it will take a clinker to beat him.

Gus Walters has the dun pacer Johnny Wiegle, and two or three good ones.

Cox has Dom Pedro, Pauline, and several others without records.

Sawyer has Emperor, out of old Katy Tricks, and another one.

A. L. Hinds has the gray stallion Alonzo Hayward, by Billy Hayward, with a record of 2:30, and five or six young things of more or less promise.

Mathew B. Storn has charge of J. B. Chase's stable, consisting of Wheatly, ch. s., aged, by War Dance; two-year-old filly, by Hubbard; two-year-old, by Shannon; and a four-year-old black gelding, owned by Dr. Taliaferro, of San Rafael, by Shannon, dam Velveteen, by Lodi.

Besides the horses stabled at the Park, there are a number of promising ones in outside stables that take their work at the track. Among this number are the three-year-old Electioneer colt Anteo, owned by Joseph Cairn Simpson, and a yearling, full brother to Anteo, and named Antevolo. I saw Anteo take a little sharp work at the Park on Tuesday morning, and he marks a trotter without doubt. His way of going is very fine, and his ability to stay the distance is already demonstrated, proving the old adage that blood will tell, and that the Electioneers will *not* quit. And his younger brother is even finer, if possible, and already gives promise of sustaining the very high reputation of a famous family. They are both by Electioneer, from Columbine, now owned at Palo Alto, and she is from Columbia, by imported Bonnie Scotland, and her dam again was Young Fashion, by imported Monarch. Here is rare breeding, and a union of lines famous the world over.

Hoping that I have not trespassed upon good nature in the way of space, I will defer other matters until next week.

INDEX.

## SAGEBRUSH TROUT-LIARS.

Either fish are biting more wildly and foolishly this spring than ever before since the days of the Apostles, or those who are doing the fishing are the biggest liars that ever packed a pole and line. Not a man goes forth to the smallest puddle, horse pond or duck pond, that does not report having hauled in from 80 to 250 trout in two hours. They always do it in from two hours to two hours and a half. It is beginning to be strongly suspected by our inland people that there is a band of liars working the lakes from Lundy on the south to Independence on the north.—*Virginia Enterprise.*

# THE TURF.

Saratoga, Jerome Park, Long Branch, Coney Island and Baltimore are the fashionable places of Turf sports in the East. Lexington, Louisville, St. Louis and Chicago is what is called in that country "the West." The Coney Island Jockey Club has one of the best appointed courses in the country, and the attendance rivals Saratoga and Jerome Park, not alone in numbers, but also in regard to the brilliancy of the assemblage. Convenient to New York, managed by men who rank high in the world, and a favorite place with owners and trainers, it could not well be otherwise than popular.

We copy an account of the opening day, Tuesday, June 13th, from the New York *Herald*, as the general description will be of interest to our readers on this Coast, and give epitomized summaries of the racing. The summaries are abbreviated, so as to give the names of those only which obtained a place, as it would occupy too much space to give the names and pedigrees of all of the starters.

The plan followed hereafter will be to give the most prominent events which occur at the chief meetings, as even a brief synopsis of all the races would take room which can be more advantageously used in other ways. It will be noticed that "old Parole" won a good race, defeating a strong field, in fast time.

## CONEY ISLAND JOCKEY CLUB.

The Coney Island Jockey Club yesterday opened the season's racing upon the Sheepshead Bay course by a most enjoyable programme of races. Those who had been present at the dusty opening day of two years ago, or the moist and muddy one of a year past, were loud in their praises and thanks for the excellent weather. Each year improves the property of the Club, and whether the visitor is an enthusiastic horse lover or merely bent on an afternoon's outing, the run down to the Sheepshead Bay track, and the lounge of a few hours upon the grand stand, or, better still, upon the sloping green turf before it, is sure to send the excursionist home with renewed health and a lively appetite. The means of access to the course from the city left nothing to be desired yesterday. The pleasant sail down the bay on a swift moving steamboat enabled those bound to the races to make close connections with the waiting trains, and, speeding over the narrow gauge railroad toward Manhattan Beach, the trains stopped within a few yards of the entrance to the racing enclosure. Stop-over tickets were given to the many who wished to finish off the view of the races with a visit to the beach and a dinner by the seaside.

Few changes have been made in the arrangements of the Coney Island Jockey Club grounds. None were needed, for the original plan was so carefully considered, and the structures erected on so liberal a scale, that thousands may be accommodated and yet not give the individual sightseer any feeling that there is not enough elbow room. Everything was, of course, in the best of order, and the ground in all its appointments as neat as the best kept suburban estate. In its weather conditions the day could not have been improved. The foliage in and about the premises had no parched look, but rather the rich verdancy of early spring. The lopped trees in the track enclosure did their best to look graceful, but with all their lower limbs cut away to give clear views of the track, they would hardly be styled things of beauty. The trees over the grand stand extension running toward the club house were, however, charming to sit under, and fulfilled their natural function of shade givers admirably. Each year shows a marked improvement in the turf of the lawns. That before the grand stand has now put on a velvety surface, and bids fair to stand the wear and tear of the many restless boot heels that go tramping over it. The track bore evidence of careful attention, and was in the best of order for the runners.

The opening day did not bring a crush of spectators, yet there were a sufficient number present to bring the attendance up into the thousands and give the grand stand, the quarter stretch, the side paddock and especially the area set apart for the odd and even speculators a very animated appearance. The grand stand was comfortably filled, the annex to the right, toward the club house, was crowded, while not a box along the entire line was noted as vacant. The toilets were charming and the display of early summer finery worth the trip to the track to witness. The members of the club were out in force and their quarters, over the weighing room, were crowded at all times. The arrangements for the booking fraternity, who afford profit for the few at the expense of the many and the pleasurable excitement of anticipations for all, were, as before, upon the shaded platform to the right of the stand. It was crowded at all times, and the opening day brought everybody down to their wagering instincts whetted by the winter's rest The managers of the pools were too busy to be noisy, being kept engaged either making or meeting bets. The admirably systematized scheme enabled the public to reduce its opinions, hopes, suggestions or hints to the concrete form of pool tickets with the least possible trouble and later, in some instances, to reconvert these tickets into good coin of the Commonwealth with equal dispatch and readiness. Such of the spectators as did not care to take a ticketed interest in the races did not have their attention distracted by the traffic in odds. Upon the track the races were close enough to be interesting, without enough uncertainty to make them worth seeing. They were punctually started, and the jockeys were generally careful not to have too many breakaways and false starts. In the first race the favorite did not win, and the holders of the tickets were well rewarded. In the next the ladies were delighted to see the little boy jockey, in his rich costume of cherry and black and gold, force Itaska to the front. The P. Lorillard colors had not been favorites in the mutuals, which accordingly paid over $70 when the race was over. In the mile and a half race for allages, international Parole was a starter, and though on the first rush past the grand stand with one-third of the race over, the old brown horse appeared to be lost in the rift of flyers, Feakes knew the animal he was striding, and in the last third of the race the P. Lorillard colors again came to the front and another victory was added to the long list of Parole triumphs. Too many friends and backers, however, did not make the victory a very profitable one to the army of Parole ticket-holders. The Tidal Stakes, for three-year-olds, did not bring out such a great race as the Hindoo-Crickmore struggle of last June, but a fair field of starters gave a satisfactory race.

The races over, the crowd dispersed in many directions. The drive up the ocean parkway and thence to the city via Prospect Park and the suburbs of Brooklyn tempted many, who found a capital road in the best of driving condition. The railroad travelers took trains in either direction, depending whether dinner was to be taken at the shore or in town. The day had been one of exceptionable enjoyment, with such air, sky and foliage as the ordinary June day does not always bring.

The following gentlemen were the officers of the day:

Judges—Messrs. J. H. Bradford, J. G. K. Lawrence and J. G. Heckscher.

Timers—Messrs. C. Fellows and W. M. Conner.

Dismounting Judge—Mr. W. K. Vanderbilt.

Starter—Mr. J. Sheridan.

The following are the details of the racing:

FIRST RACE.—Purse $500, for all ages. Five furlongs.
Preakness Stable's b f Bonnie Lizzie, 4 yrs, by Hurrah—Bonnie Kate; 113 lbs.................(Fisher) 1
Morris & Patton's b g Fellowplay, 4 yrs, by Longfellow—Platina; 115 lbs.................(Brown) 2
H Welch's b g Wakefield, 5 yrs, by Wanderer—Australia; 117 lbs.................(Jones) 3
And thirteen others ran unplaced.
Time, 1:02¾.

SECOND RACE.—Purse $500, for three year-olds and upward; winner to be sold at auction. If entered to be sold for $5,000, to carry weight for age; $4,000, allowed 5 lbs.; $3,000, allowed 10 lbs: one pound allowed for each $100 less down to $1000 One mile and a quarter.
P. Lorrillard's b g Itaska, 3 yrs, by Saxon—Betty Washington; to be sold for $1,000; 70 lb.................(P. Hyslop) 1
lbs.................(J. McLaughlin) 2
J. Daly's b c Strathspey, 4 yrs, by Glenelg—Polka; $1,000; 98
Dwyer Bros' b g Warfield, aged, by War Dance—Florae; $2,500 104 lbs.................(F. McLaughlin) 3
And six others ran unplaced.
Time, 2:11¾.

THIRD RACE.—Purse $600, for all ages. Winners of any race of 1882 of the value of $1,000 to carry weight for age; of two such races, 3 lbs.; of three or more, 5 lbs. extra; other horses allowed 5 lbs.; maidens allowed 12 lbs. extra. One mile and a half.
P. Lorrillard's br g Parole, aged, by Leamington—Maiden; 115 lbs.................(Feakes) 1
Oden Bowie's b g Compensation, 4 yrs, by Catesby—Australia; 110 lbs.................(Brophy) 2
G. L. Lorrillard's ch g Monitor, 5 yrs, by Glenelg—Minx; 115 lbs.................(Costello) 3
And three others ran unplaced.
Time, 2:36¾.

FOURTH RACE.—The Tidal Stakes, for three-year-olds; a sweepstake of $100 each, half forfeit, and $20 if declared out before July 1, 1881, for foals of 1879, with $1,000 added. The second to receive $200 out of the stakes. One mile. Closed with 78 subscribers, of which 18 declared out.
Dwyer Brothers' br c Runnymede, by Billet—Mercedes; 118 lbs.................(J. McLaughlin) 1
D. D. Withers' ch c by Stonehenge—Julietta; 118 lbs.(Barbee)
W. Lakeland's ch c Babcock, by Buckden—Ethel Sprague; 118 lbs.................(Owner) 3
Spellman & Co.'s c c Hilarity, by Bonnie Scotland—Beulah; 118 lbs.................(Spellman) 0
L. C. Bruce's ch c Timbucktoo, by Lever—Evangeline; 118 lbs.................(Brophy)
Time, 1:43¾.

FIFTH RACE.—Purse, $500. One mile.
G. L. Lorrillard's ch c Volusia, 3 yrs, by Pat Malloy—Vandalia; 103 lbs.................(Ural) 1
Preakness Stable's ch c McBeth, 3 yrs, by Macaroon—Jersey Belle; 103 lbs.................(Fisher) 2
Dwyer Brothers, b g Blenheim, 3 yrs, by Billet—Keno; 100 lbs.................(J. McLaughlin) 3
W. Jennings' b f Farewell, 3 years old, by Lisbon—Fairy; 98 lbs.................(O'Hara) 0
Mr. Somerville's La Belle N., 3 yrs, by Reform—Megara; 98 lbs.................(Blaylock) 0
Time, 1:43½.

STEEPLECHASE.—Purse $550, of which $100 to the second, and $50 to the third horse. Horses which have not won a steeplechase in 1882 allowed 7 lbs.; those which have never won a steeplechase allowed 12 lbs.; winners of one steeplechase in 1882 to carry weight for age; winners of two or more steeplechases of 1882 to carry 7 lbs extra. Three horses, two of which shall be the property of different owners, to start, or no race. The short steeplechase course.
Geo. Sutliff's ch h Day Star, aged, by Star Davis—Squeeze 'em; 144 lbs.................(Fitzpatrick) 1
J. N. Ackerman's b g Ohio Boy, aged, by Hurrah—Charmer; 144 lbs.................(Nolan) 2
James McMahon's b h Ike Bonham, aged, by Bonnie Scotland—Viola; 141 lbs.................(Harley) 3
R. Bradley's ch m Lilly Morson, 5 yrs, by Brennan—Unknown; 133 lbs.................(Dickens) 4
Stanley Williams' ch g Woodcock, 5 yrs, by War Dance—Miss Grey; 140 lbs.................(Holmes) 5
C. Reed's b h Turfman, 5 years old, by Revolver—Regards; 138 lbs.................(Meany) 6
Dr. Lynch's g h Derby, aged, by Eugene—Kate Sovereign; 144 lbs.................(McBride) 7
Time, 5:09¾.

On the second day there were five events, and the usual steeple chase, a dangerous kind of racing that, however, is now very popular at the East. The chief interest of the day was centered in the Foam stakes, which is one of the most valuable two-year-old stakes run in the country. There were 61 subscribers, of whom eleven appeared at the post, and E. V. Snedeker's filly Soubrette, by Alarm from Susan Beane, was made the favorite on the strength of her winning a two-year-old purse at Jerome Park, in the excellent time of 49 sc., with 107 pounds up, on which occasion Parthenia was second. On this occasion, however, the latter, a fine filly, bred by P. Lorillard, turned the tables on Soubrette, and won a fine race in 1:03¾, the Dwyer Brothers' colt George Kenney being second and G. L. Lorillard's Magnate being third. Parthenia is by Alarm from Maiden, and is thus a half sister to that celebrated horse Parole, and she promises well for her many future engagements. In the Coney Island stakes, a dash of a mile and a quarter for three-year-olds and upwards, there were forty-seven subscribers, but Hindoo frightened them all away save Barrett, and with five to one on him, the great son of Virgil and Florence won in a canter in 1:57¾, having made the first mile in 1:42. The steeple chase was won by Disturbance, who appears to be the best horse across country that is to be found at the East.

On the third day there were again five races, and some very heavy investments were made on the result of the Mermaid stakes and of the selling race. The former is a great three-year-old filly stake, and, notwithstanding that Hiawasse had beaten Rica in the Ladies' stake, a mile and a half, at Jerome Park, the latter was made a favorite, as it was believed a mile and a furlong would suit her better. The race, however, was won by Hiawasse, with Rica second and Francesca third, in 1:58½. The winner is owned by P. Lorillard, and is by imported Saxon, her dam being the whilom famous racer Vandalite; Rica is by Kingfisher from Lady Mentmore, and Francesca is by Leamington from Maggie B. B., and thus an own sister to Iroquois. The selling sweepstakes have become very popular, as by this method owners have the privilege of handicapping their own horses. In this race horses entered to be sold for $5,-

000 carried weight for age; if for $4,000, allowed five, and if for $3,000, then ten pounds weight off; and one pound for each $100 down to $1,000. There were twelve horses ran, and the winner was Barrett, the favorite, entered to be sold for $2,500, and P. Lorillard had to pay $4,100 to bring back this son of Bonnie Scotland and Sue Washington to the Rancocus stable.

The fourth was the Cup day, and, as is the case at Ascot and Goodwood, the assemblage was the most numerous and fashionable of any day of the meeting. The weather was delightful, the course in capital condition, and the five events afforded racing of the most exciting character. The chief interest was centered in the Coney Island Cup, two miles and a quarter, which had closed with the pick of the best horses in the country, but the prowess of Hindoo again reduced the field to three starters, Eole and Parole being the only two contestants. At one time it was hoped that Thora would put in an appearance, but as she would have had to carry a ten-pound penalty for winning the Baltimore and Westchester Cups, she was wisely withheld for the Monmouth Cup at Long Branch, where she will yet have to carry five pounds extra, while Hindoo is penalized three pounds. This was a remarkable race, and the following short but graphic account is taken from the New York *World:*

The Coney Island Cup, for three-year-olds and upward; a sweepstakes of $50 each, half forfeit, with $1,500 added; the second to receive $300 out of the stakes; three-year-olds to carry 90 lbs.; four-year-olds, 108 lbs.; five-year-olds and upward, 114 lbs.; sex allowances; the winner of the Baltimore or Westchester Cup of 1882 to carry 7 lbs. extra; of both, 10 lbs. extra. Two miles and a quarter.

*Starters.*

Dwyer Brothers' br. c. Hindoo, by Virgil, dam Florence, 4 years old, 108 lbs............(J. McLaughlin) 1
F. Gebhard's b. c. Eole, by Eolus, dam War Song, 4 years old, 108 lbs............(Barbee) 2
P. Lorillard's br. g. Parole, by Leamington, dam Maiden, aged, 111 lbs............(Feakes) 3

Time, 3:58.

The Betting.—Hindoo, in the pools, sold for $300; Eole, $75; Parole, $30. In the books there were 3 to 10 against Hindoo, 7 to 2 against Eole, 10 to 1 against Parole. The mutuals paid $6.75.

Exactly to the minute for which the race was fixed—5 P.M.—the three moved up for the flag with Eole on the outside. They got an even start, and as they came to the turn Barbee took the lead with Eole, and as the horse ran somewhat sluggishly up the stretch, Barbee "bustled" him right along at the lower end of the stand, which gave him such a lead that as they passed the judges' stand Eole lead by five lengths, with Parole third, six lengths behind Hindoo. In the run round the quarter turn McLaughlin moved Hindoo up a trifle, so that Eole led by only four lengths at the quarter. There was no change in the run down the back-stretch, nor in the run round the turn, Eole leading at the end of the mile by four lengths, Parole ten lengths behind Hindoo. They ran up the stretch in the same position, there being no change until they were well into the last mile. Then Hindoo began to gain slowly, and at the quarter was but two lengths behind Eole. They continued to run two lengths apart to the five furlongs, after which Hindoo gained at every stride, and amid the greatest excitement and cheering, the two went past the half-mile post as nearly even as they could run. They stayed together until nearly opposite the Dwyer stables, when McLaughlin cut loose and letting Hindoo go right along he quickly led, first by a length, then by two lengths, until, when the two miles were finished, having been run in 3:29¾, he lead by four lengths, with Parole rapidly closing in upon Eole.

In the run round the turn Hindoo increased his lead to six lengths, but when well into the stretch so strong did Eole respond to Barbee's call that half-way up the stretch the distance was reduced to three lengths, which for an instant raised the hopes of the admirers of Eole, so that some began to claim the race. Their hopes were quickly dashed as Hindoo drew away, and, amid the cheers of nearly all present, passed the post an easy winner by four lengths, with Eole a dozen lengths in front of Parole, on whom Feakes took things very easily when he found that he could not reach either of the leaders. The time, 3.58, although very fast, is a trifle slower than was expected, some few bets having been made that the famous dead-heat record of 3.56¼, made by Preakness and Springbok at Saratoga in 1875, would be beaten. This probably would have been the case had Eole been able to push Hindoo in the run up the stretch, for it will be seen from the time of the several quarters that the last quarter was very slow.

*Quarters.*

1st—28.
2d—25¼; half mile............0.54
3d—26; three quarters............1.20
4th—25½; mile............1.45½
5th—25¾; mile and a quarter............2.11¼
6th—26¾; mile and a half............2.38
7th—26¼; mile and three quarters............3.04¼
8th—25½; two miles............3.29¾
9th—28¼; two miles and a quarter............3.58

The other races of the day call for no special comment, save that in the steeple chase the mare Lilly Munson fell at one of the fences and threw her jockey, Dicken, who had his collar bone broken and was otherwise badly shaken, but not in the manner to seriously disable him. Another example of the danger of steeple chasing.

Again lovely weather and grand sport was the verdict of the immense assemblage that witnessed the fifth and sixth days of the meeting. It was poor betting for the talent, for when the backers of the favorites get two or three facers they are apt to plunge on the outsiders, that, in case they win, will give them a more liberal return on their investment. The chief event on Tuesday was the two-year-old stakes; and in this the previous performances of the favorites were eclipsed.

In the Foam Stakes, five furlongs, of the sixty-five subscribers there were eleven that sported silk, and P. Lorillard's Pizarro and the George Kenney of the Dwyer Brothers, were made first choice, while the winner, Jacobus, was only in the middle division, although he made a favorable impression at Jerome Park. Jacobus is by Ill-Used from Nellie James, and was purchased by J. E. Kelley from Mr. Belmont, for $10,000, with other untried colts included. This was the first time the Blue and Canary was sported, and the result augurs well for the success of the new colors. Mr. Kelley is well known here in sporting circles in connection with the famous four mile and repeat race won by Foster some six years since, in which he is said to have landed a good stake.

On Wednesday there were six races, and they were generally disastrous to backers, the first race for all ages resulting in the victory of Mr. Withers' Stonehenge-Julietta colt, selling for $30 against $50 for Fellowplay and Barrett, the former winning from the latter a sharp race of a mile by a short head, in 1:43½. The next and prominent event of the meeting was the Coney Island Derby, in which it was thought that Runnymede and Apollo would fight their western battles over again, and try to gain the best of the day against Forester, that had hitherto been classed as the first three-year-old of the season. On the strength of the latter having won both the Withers and the Belmont, he was made first favorite at $200 against $85 for Runnymede and $15 for Carley B., Apollo being absent. Forester made the running, but Runnymede closed on the favorite on the home-stretch, making the mile and a half in 2:37, the best time made in a three-year-old stake this season. Runnymede is by imported Billet, from Mercedes, is owned by the Dwyer Brothers, and in this colt it really appears as if they had a formidable successor in the three-year-old stakes, to Luke Blackburn and Hindoo.

## THE CAPITAL TURF CLUB.

The Spring meeting of this association was held at the Agricultural Park, Sacramento, commencing on Wednesday, June 14th, and continuing the three remaining days of the week. The following is the official record of the proceedings:

### FIRST DAY, JUNE 14.

FIRST RACE.—Running stake, three-quarters of a mile dash; $20 entrance; $10 forfeit; $100 added; second to save stake.

Theo. Winters names Duke of Norfolk............ 1
James McM. Shafter names Haddington............ 2
H. C. Judson names b. h. Belshaw............ 3

Time, 1:16.

SECOND RACE.—Running stake, mile dash; $25 entrance; $15 forfeit; $150 added.

H. C. Judson names s. m. May D............ 1
James McM. Shafter names Night Hawk............ 2
A. Miller names b. h. Boots............ 3
Theo. Winters names ch. f. Atalanta............ 0

Time, 1:43¼.

THIRD RACE.—Running race, half mile dash; $20 entrance; $10 forfeit; $75 added.

A. Miller names filly, by Monday, from dam of Douglas............ 1
Theo. Winters names b. f. Clara W............ 2

Time, :51.

### SECOND DAY, JUNE 15.

FIRST RACE.—Trotting purse, for the three-minute class; $250; $150 to first, $75 for second, and $25 to the third horse.

| | | | | | |
|---|---|---|---|---|---|
| Wilbur Smith names b. m. Adalia | 3 | 2 | 1 | 1 | 1 |
| Charles Shear names b. s. General | 4 | 4 | 2 | 2 | 2 |
| M. W. Hicks names b. m. Pearl | 1 | 3 | dis | | |
| C. Coward, by consent, names b. g. Starr | 2 | 1 | 3 | 3 | dis |

Time, 2:32¼, 2:34½, 2:37, 2:36, 2:36.

SECOND RACE.—Trotting purse, of $400, for the 2:30 class, of which $240 to the first, $120 to the second, and $40 to the third horse.

| | | | | | |
|---|---|---|---|---|---|
| J. H. Goldsmith names b. s. Inca | 2 | 1 | 1 | 2 | 1 |
| Wilbur Smith names b. g. Clairmont | 1 | 2 | 3 | 3 | 2 |
| Henry McConn names g. g. Blackmore | 3 | 3 | 2 | 1 | 3 |

Time, 2:30¼, 2:32¼, 2:30¼, 2:30½, 2:34¼.

### THIRD DAY, JUNE 16.

FIRST RACE.—Running stake for two-year-olds; five-eighths of a mile dash; $25 entrance; $10 forfeit; $150 added.

A. Miller names b. f. by Monday, from dam of Douglas............ 1
Theo. Winters names b. f. Clara W............ 2

Time, 1:07.

SECOND RACE.—Selling race; $40 entrance; $10 forfeit; $150 added; one and one-quarter miles.

James McM. Shafter names Haddington ($800)............ 1
W. L. Appleby names b. h. Belshaw ($800)............ 2
H. Schwartz names b. f. Sister to Lottery ($500)............ 3

Time, 2:14.

THIRD RACE.—Running stake, one mile and repeat; $50 entrance; $15 forfeit; $150 added.

| | | | |
|---|---|---|---|
| James McM. Shafter names Night Hawk | 3 | 1 | 1 |
| H. C. Judson names s. m. May D. | 2 | 3 | 2 |
| A. Miller names b. h. Boots | 1 | 2 | 3 |

Time, 1:45¼, 1:47, 1:46½.

### FOURTH DAY, JUNE 17.

FIRST RACE.—Trotting purse, three-minute class; $250.

| | | | | |
|---|---|---|---|---|
| Wilbur Smith names b. m. Adalia | 2 | 1 | 1 | 1 |
| H. G. Cox names b. s. Don Pedro | 3 | 2 | 2 | 3 |
| M. W. Hicks names b. m. Pearl | 1 | 3 | 4 | 4 |
| Charles Shear names b. s. General | 4 | 4 | 3 | 2 |

Time, 2:33, 2:35, 2:38, 2:35¼.

SECOND RACE.—Gentlemen's buggy stake; $10 entrance; $50 added; two miles out; winner to receive whole amount.

J. D. Young names b. g. Colonel............ 1
M. Toomey names b. g. Robin Hood............ 2
J. H. McNassar names b. m. Mollie A............ 3

Time, 5:48.

THIRD RACE.—Pacing; purse of $200; heats of a mile.

| | | | |
|---|---|---|---|
| Nelse McDonald names r. g. Brince | 3 | 1 | 1 |
| S. C. Tryon names b. g. Prince | 2 | 2 | 2 |
| Charles Shear names b. s. Revenue | 2 | 3 | 3 |
| M. Toomey names b. g. St. Valentine | 4 | dis | |

Time, 2:43½, 2:43, 2:42¼.

It is pleasant to announce that the proceedings passed off without a single hitch, and that they gave great satisfaction to the many visitors at the track. The financial result was also quite favorable, when it is considered that this was the first meeting held under the auspices of the association; for, after all the accounts were paid, there was a surplus of $4,100. This success must be attributed to the energy and zeal of the executive officers, as also to the liberality of the citizens of Sacramento, whose subscriptions warranted the announcement of the programme on an enterprising scale. A committee, consisting of Messrs. J. H. Miller, J. McNassar and Ed. F. Smith, has been appointed to effect a perfect organization, with Mr. Chris. Green as President, Mr. J. W. Wilson as Vice President, Mr. W. P. Emery as Secretary, and Mr. E. L. Billings as Treasurer.

The following is the list of the present members; and as nothing succeeds like success, it is probable that within a short period there will be such an accession to the list as to place the Capital Turf Club on a solid financial basis: Messrs. Chris. Green, J. W. Wilson, E. L. Billings, A. L. Frost, E. Walters, Robert Allen, H. S. Beals, W. O. Bowers, S. S. Bede, J. H. McNassar, E. G. Blessing, Henry Grice, W. A. Henry, A. Weiman, A. J. Rhoades, Isidore Townsend, John Mackey, Phil Seibenhaller, G. Valensin, J. H. Miller, Ed. F. Smith, John McFetrish, and J. W. Houston. We wish the Capital Turf Club every success.

## THE TRACK.

There is so little transpiring at the present time, in the way of trotting, to our readers on this coast, and also being so hurried to get our paper out at the date fixed, that this Department will be left blank for this number. At the best there would be a meager showing, and the following week there will be a full allotment of space to the sports of the Track. In that will be an account which can be depended upon as accurate, from the meeting at Salt Lake, and we hope to receive reports from the main Eastern Meetings which came off last week.

## TURF AND TRACK.

For Blanchard's $10,000 Purse, for the 2:17 Class, that will come off at Beacon Park, Boston, on September 14th, next, there are thirteen entries, as follows: Commodore N., W. Kitson, St. Paul; J. E. Turner, Philadelphia; H. S. Russell, Milton, Mass.; G. W. Sanders, Cleveland; J. H. Phillips, Philadelphia; E. L. Norcross, Manchester, Maine; J. Monroe, Chicago; J. E. Stewart, Boston; Gus Wilson, Philadelphia; James Golden, Medford, Mass.; L. B. Brown, Providence, R. I.; W. P. Balch, Boston, Mass., and Charles S. Green, Babylon, N. Y. The conditions of the race are 10 per cent. entrance, of which 2½ per cent. at the time of nomination, and a like amount on the first days of July, August and September. The entrance money is to be forfeited on failure of any of these regular payments, and the horses are not to be named until August 31st. This is a new departure in Trotting stakes, and assimilates in a slight degree to the Post matches that were so popular in England a century since, when the respective horses were named at the Post.

From the Washington County Fair Grounds, in Oregon, the advices are very favorable for the meeting that commences there July 3d, continuing throughout the week. The track is admirably situated, within easy reach of Hillsborough, and with the many improvements made, the buildings present a handsome appearance, and the grounds, almost surrounded by umbrageous trees, form as pretty a picture as can be found on the Pacific Coast. Although sixty new stalls have been built, the arrivals are so large that doubts are expressed if even now the accommodations will be sufficient. This fact speaks volumes for the future prosperity of the turf in Oregon.

On July 5th, a Running programme has been arranged at San Diego, the first race being half mile and repeat, for $100; the second, a half mile dash, for $75, for three-year-olds, raised in the county; then a purse of $50, for two-year-olds, owned in the county; and the last is a handicap, for beaten horses. Among other attractions, there is a slow mule race, that is very amusing, as, contrary to the general rules, the prize is given to the last animal under the wire, that has not come to a stop during the race.

The Citizens of Galt, Sacramento County, are making great preparations for the celebration of the Fourth of July, and, among other attractions, they offer a varied programme of races, consisting of trotting, running and pacing, that will doubtless lead to a lively competition among the fast horses around that district.

Algona, a son of Almont, has been purchased by Mr. J. B. Haggin, and has been sent to that gentleman's stock farm in Sacramento County; as also a two-year-old filly, by Algona, bought from Mr. E. Giddings, of Lemoore, Tulare County.

The First Meeting of the Mexican Jockey Club, that was held a few weeks since at Mexico, was a pronounced success, both in regard to the attendance and the financial result. All the wealth, beauty and fashion of the city graced the race-track with their presence, and the principal trotting purse was won by Halcon Negro, an American horse. The running races did not show such large fields as might have been expected, but, with improved facilities of transportation, California will surely be represented, and our thoroughbreds will quickly follow the iron horse, to try conclusions with Mexico's purest and finest strains of trotting stock.

At Mr. Claus Spreckel's Aptos Ranch, a great loss has been felt in the death of that noted brood mare, Ashcat. She was by Rysdyk's Hambletonian, her dam by American Star, and her grand-dam by Abdallah. Ashcat was the dam of Ajax, Hambletonian, Jr., and Grapevine. The mare died foaling, but the colt was saved, and is doing well. Mr. Spreckels has four colts by Speculation, all of which are of a very promising description.

The Tulare Valley Agricultural Association has made arrangements to lay out a fine race track at Visalia, with a grand stand, stalls and the usual buildings required in a first-class race course. The contract for these has been given to Messrs. Fox and Wild, but the executive officers have decided to lay out the track by day work, as the bids were too high, and by keeping the operatives under their own supervision, they will see that the work is completed in the best and most efficient manner.

Two of our legal gentlemen—Judge R. E. Warren and A. J. Gifford—went to Butte Creek yesterday evening for a quiet fish. The game they were after was catfish, and they yanked them out as fast as they could bait their hooks and throw in. They did not fish over an hour, but when they tied up their lines each had a splendid string. Persons who live along Butte Creek are of the opinion that in a few years the tules even will be filled with these fish. We hear that a party of fishers will go to Butte Creek on Sunday evening, build up a rousing camp-fire on the bank, and spend the night there. Boarders at the hotels can expect plenty of brain-food for breakfast on Monday morning.—*Butte Record.*

Yesterday afternoon, says the *Butte Record*, about a dozen of our German citizens went down to the river for an afternoon's sport at fishing, and they really had good luck and a "bully" time. Some, who did not care to angle, spent a greater portion of their time at bathing in the river, but they were promptly on hand when the lunch hour arrived. Before going to lunch, all the hooks were well baited and the poles set. During the progress of the meal, E. Jacobs, who is a constant practical joker, slipped to the river, hauled up one of the lines, and attached to it a fish made of canvas filled with sawdust. It was painted and fixed up to resemble a large salmon. Its weight was twenty-six pounds. After the feed, all hands rushed to the river-bank to make a haul. Every line with one exception came out easily, there being only a water-haul. One young fellow tugged and jerked and raised the sawdust fish to the surface. He was wild with excitement, and thought he was about to land a whale. He couldn't land his game with the pole, so he pulled off his boots and jumped into the stream, and thus secured his catch. It was brought ashore, but goodness! he was mad as a hornet, and threatened to pulverize the whole gang. He was finally pacified, and stood treat for the whole party when they returned home.

## THE PADDOCK.

There is usually a surprising neglect among breeders in sending a list of their foals for publication. The compilers of stud books are not only put to a great deal of unnecessary trouble, but there are quite a large number of breeders who never send the desired intelligence, and hence they are omitted from the volumes. We would like to obtain every foal which has any pretensions to breeding—thoroughbred or trotting—which has been dropped on the coast this year, so as to complete the record, and will be obliged if the owners will furnish them. It is not a great deal of trouble. If many a letter can be sent, if one or two, a postal card will bring the information. We make a grand start with the Palo Alto foals, and hope to add to this list until all are placed on record. This will give a better idea of the magnitude of the breeding interests of the coast than volumes of general information:

### LIST OF PALO ALTO FOALS FOR 1882.

#### TROTTING BRED.

Jan. 6—Lady Ellen, by Mohawk Chief; bay colt by General Benton.
Jan. 10—Cleopatra, by Fred Low; brown colt, by General Benton.
Jan. 15—Cornelia, by Fred Low; bay filly, by Gen. Benton.
Jan. 18—Alvoretta, by George Lancaster; bay colt, by Electioneer.
Jan. 25—Norma, by Alexander's Norman; bay colt, by Electioneer.
Jan. 23—Piney Lewis, by Longfellow; bay filly, by Electioneer.
Jan. 26—Alameda Maid, by Whipple's Hambletonian; bay filly, by Electioneer.
Jan. 28—Maria Pilot, by Mambrino Pilot; bay filly, by Electioneer.
Jan. 28—Mamie C., by Imp. Hercules; bay colt, by Electioneer.
Jan. 29—Eliza Dolph, by Wild Idle; bay filly, by Electioneer.
Jan. 30—Barnes' Idol, by Idol; bay filly, by Electioneer.
Feb. 3—Lady Kline, by Mohawk Chief; bay filly, by Gen. Benton.
Feb. 3—Glendale, by Messenger Duroc; bay filly, by Gen. Benton.
Feb. 6—Electa, by Electioneer; bay filly, by Gen. Benton.
Feb. 8—Americquita, by Mohawk Chief; brown colt, by Gen. Benton.
Feb. 9—Nellie Walker, by Thorndale, or son of Edwin Forrest; bay filly, by Gen. Benton.
Feb. 15—Dame Winnie, by Planet; bay colt, by Electioneer.
Feb. 16—Fannie Lewis, by Imp. Buckden; bay colt, by Electioneer.
Feb. 18—Texanna, by Foreigner; bay filly, by Gen. Benton.
Feb. 20—Alameda, by Langford; bay filly, by Fallis, son of Electioneer.
Feb. 20—Blarney, by Blarney Stone; bay colt, by Bentonian, son of Gen. Benton.
Feb. 21—Daisy C., by The Moor; brown colt, by Gen. Benton.
Feb. 25—Mayflower, by St. Clair; bay filly, by Electioneer.
Feb. 25—Mollie Shelton, by Rifleman, brown filly, by Electioneer.
Feb. 28—Maggie Mitchell, by Clay Pilot; bay filly, by Electioneer.
March 4—Aurore, by John Nelson; bay filly, by Electioneer.
March 6—Sallie Hamlet, by Hamlet, son of Volunteer; bay colt, by Electioneer.
March 6—Beautiful Bells, by the "Moor;" brown colt, by Electioneer.
March 7—Prussian Maid, by Signal; bay colt, by Shannon.
March 8—Glencora, by Mohawk Chief; brown colt, by Electioneer.
March 10—Lizzie Collins, by Stanzifer's Woful; bay filly, by Electioneer.
March 17—Waxana, by General Benton; bay filly, by Electioneer.
March 18—Abbie, by Almont; bay colt, by Electioneer.
March 18—Tippers, by Tipperrary; bay filly, by Electioneer.
March 19—Sister to Irene, by Mohawk Chief; bay colt, by Gen. Benton.
March 19—Juniatta, by Fred Lowe; bay colt, by Gen. Benton.
March 21—Ashland Mare, by Ashland; bay filly, by Gen. Benton.
March 25—Mamie, by Hambletonian, Jr.; bay colt, by Electioneer.
March 26—Lillian, by Lodi; bay filly, by Gen. Benton.
March 26—Blooming, by Messenger Duroc; chestnut filly, by Shannon.
March 28—Mabell, by Electioneer; bay filly, by Gen. Benton.
March 28—Winona, by Almont; bay filly, by Electioneer.
March 31—Esther, by Express; bay colt, by Electioneer.
April 1—Ada, by Messenger Duroc; bay filly, by Gen. Benton.
April 3—Amy, by Messenger Duroc; bay filly, by Electioneer.
April 4—Lady Morgan, by Rysdyke's Hambletonian; chestnut filly, by Gen. Benton.
April 4—Lilly, by Mohawk Chief; brown colt, by Electioneer.
April 5—Wilhelmina, by Messenger Duroc; bay colt, by Gen. Benton.
April 6—Frolic, by Thunder; black colt, by Electioneer.
April 9—American Girl, by Toronto Sontag; bay colt, by Electioneer.
April 10—Elaine, by Messenger Duroc; chestnut filly, by Gen. Benton.
April 14—Bijou, by Electioneer; bay filly, by Gen. Benton.
April 15—Lilly Roberts, by Mohawk Chief; bay filly, by Shannon.
April 16—Clara, by Mohawk Chief; bay colt, by Shannon.
April 17—Consolation, by Dictator; bay filly, by Shannon.
April 21—Lady Thorn, Jr., by Williams' Mambrino; bay colt, by Electioneer.
April 27—Adelaide, by Donald; bay colt, by Electioneer.
April 27—Lady Dooley, by Black Hawk; bay filly, by Electioneer.
May 2—Maimabe, by St. Clair; bay filly, by Electioneer.
May 2—Irene, by Mohawk Chief; chestnut filly, by General Benton.
May 3—Dixie, by Billy Townes; bay filly, by Electioneer.
May 2—Juliet, by Mohawk Chief; bay colt, by Electioneer.
May 3—Mohawk Waxey, by Mohawk Chief; bay filly, by General Benton.
May 3—Columbine, by A. W. Richmond; bay colt, by Electioneer.
May 10—Emma Robson, by Woodburn; bay colt, by Electioneer.
May 11—Alice, by Almont; bay colt, by Electioneer.
May 17—Idabelle, by Rysdyk's Hambletonian; chestnut filly by Shannon.
May 17—Wildred, by Mohawk Chief; bay filly, by General Benton.
May 19—Sprite, by Belmont; bay colt, by Electioneer.
May 23—Mayflower Mohawk, by Mohawk Chief; bay filly, by Electioneer.
May 23—Prima Donna, by Mohawk Chief; bay filly, by General Benton.

#### THOROUGHBRED FOALS.

1882.
January 17—Riglin, by imp. Glengarry; brown colt, by Shannon.
January 24—Boydena, by imp. Knight of St. George; bay filly, by Shannon.
February 3—Robin Girl, by Enquirer; bay colt, by Shannon.
February 6—Hattie Hawthorne, by Enquirer; brown colt, by Flood.
February 15—Sallie Gardner, by Vandal; bay colt, by Shannon.
February 16—Planetia, by Planet; chestnut colt, by Flood.
February 28—Lizzie Whipa, by Enquirer; chestnut filly, by Shannon.
March 8—Miss Peyton, by imp. Glengarry; bay colt, by Shannon.
March 22—Katharion, by Harry of the West; bay filly, by Flood.
April 2—Battle Bishop, by imp. Buckden; bay colt, by Shannon.
April 18—Florence Anderson, by Enquirer; bay colt, by Shannon.
April 16—Frou Frou, by Asteroid; bay filly, by Flood.
May 5—Rivual, by Rivoli; bay filly, by Flood.
May 16—Oubet, by imp. Australian; bay filly, by Shannon.

## THE HERD.

Our contributors in the Cattle Department of the BREEDER AND SPORTSMAN have not been as prompt as those who make other fields a specialty, though we have the assurance that when the busy season of haying and harvesting is over there shall be no lack. The breeders of these valuable animals are somewhat skeptical that a paper which gives much consideration to horses will find room for a race over which there cannot be so much excitement. Still, we can assure them that it rests with those who are the most interested in this branch of rural economy whether it shall be so or not. We will gladly give the room, though from the nature of things it depends more on correspondents to give life to the subject than anything editorial labor can accomplish. There, are scores of breeders in California who can send interesting communications, and about the only time their names are mentioned is during the fairs. Should these take the trouble to write relative to their experiences, they will benefit that branch of the breeding interests of the Pacific Coast, and be of direct service to themselves. All we can do is to solicit the favors of communications, which we will be pleased to publish, and do everything in our power to forward the business. There are herds here of Shorthorns, Jerseys, Ayrshires, Herefords, Holsteins, Devons, Guernseys, etc., which will rank as high as those of any country, and in the acknowledged superiority of this coast for the production of the best specimens of the equine race, it will be singular indeed if there are not the same advantages for the bovine.

### HOLSTEINS AS BUTTER COWS.

To THE EDITOR OF THE GAZETTE: During the past winter and early spring we have tested a few of our cows, and quite a number of our young heifers, for butter. Considering all the circumstances, the very young age of most of the heifers, the fact that they were imported last fall and dropped their calves soon after coming out of quarantine, and before they were acclimated, also that these tests were made in winter on winter feed, corn fodder not cut long hay with grain feed or bran, and ground oats, with not over a quart of corn meal per day—a feed not calculated to produce butter—we are very much gratified with the result:

| | lbs. oz. |
|---|---|
| Jenuek, 8 years old, tested last season | 19 15 |
| Ægis, 3 years old, last February, 4 months after calving | 11 13 |
| Topaz, 4 years old | 13 3½ |
| Rarity, 4 years old | 13 12 |
| Netherland Queen, before she was 3 years old | 14 4 |
| Netherland Queen, at 3 years old | 14 11½ |
| Oriana, before she was 3 years old | 13 3½ |
| Frolicsome, 3 years old | 13 10 |
| Meadow Lily, 3 years old | 12 10 |
| Carlotta, 3 years old | 12 1 |
| Clothild, 3 years old | 19 3½ |
| Isadora, 33 months old | 10 13½ |
| Meadow Maid, 22 months old | 9 4½ |
| Careno, 2 years old | 9 7 |
| Amazon, 2 years old | 9 5½ |
| Catalpa, 2 years old | 8 14½ |
| Hernestein, 2 years old | 8 10 |
| Kitty, 22 months old | 8 5½ |
| Marjorie Daw, 22 months old | 8 13½ |
| Mistletoe, 22 months old | 8 5 |

A few of the above were tested for 4 days, and a few others for 8 days, but we share given the rate per week, in order to have all uniform. We again call the attention of the reader to the very young age of these heifers, and the fact that they are not yet acclimated; also that these records were made on winter feed. Our cow, Netherland Queen, has just closed her four-year-old milk record, 15,641 lbs. in one year. Last Autumn she was shipped to the State and other fairs, being away two weeks, during which time she shrank 40 per cent. on her milk, and did not again recover, which on an estimate, would reduce her record over 1,000 lbs. Our three-year-old heifers are now milking from 54 to 60 lbs. per day, each; many of our two-year-olds, over 40 lbs., and some about 50 lbs., although not acclimated.

Syracuse, N. Y.     SMITH & POWELL.
—*Breeders' Gazette.*

### SALES OF JERSEY CATTLE IN NEW YORK—COOMASSIE AND HER DESCENDANTS.

From the *National Live Stock Journal* the following is copied, and to those who are not posted in the capacity of these popular cattle, the story of such a yield of butter will appear incredible:

The public sales of Jersey cattle, conducted by Messrs. P. C. Kellogg & Co., in New York city, commencing May 9th, and continuing four days, were remarkable, not only for the very high prices paid for several animals, but also for the satisfactory average on the large number sold. As will be seen by the detailed report elsewhere in this issue, two hundred and fifty animals brought $108,400, an average of $433 each. Fourteen of them sold at prices ranging from $1,000 to $4,800, realizing a total of $29,585, being an average of over $2,100 each. Instead of, as was anticipated by many, the market being overloaded by offering so many at one time, the demand seemed to increase as the sale progressed, and the average of the last day was the best of all. Fifty head belonging to the late firm of Cooper, Maddux & Co. were sold on that day for $38,886, an average of $761.86 each. The cup which is given each year at Messrs. P. C. Kellogg & Co.'s combination sales to the breeder making the highest average on five or more animals was won by Mr. A. B. Darling, of New York city, who consigned six head that brought $854.17 each. The result of these sales is certainly most encouraging to breeders of this popular race of cattle. There were about 200 people in attendance each day, a large proportion of whom were breeders. On the first day some disappointment was manifested that higher prices were not reached, but on the second day this feeling was dissipated; and when Princess 2d, a descendant of Coomassie, was sold for $4,800, there was great excitement. This cow, five years old, was consigned by Mr. S. M. Burnham. There were four or five competitors for her, but Mr. Pierce, of Boston, and Mr. Moulton, of Vermont, made the highest bids next to Mr. Shoemaker, of Baltimore, who secured her. Our representative, Mr. E. T. Blois, attended these sales, and through him we have some interesting particulars in reference to the famous cow Coomassie, the grand-dam of Princess 2d, who has the honor of having been sold for the highest price ever paid for any animal of this breed.

Mr. Burnham purchased Coomassie two years ago, paying for her $210, a little over $1,000. Her prize-winnings had become so uninterrupted that by common consent the cow was admitted to be the type of the Jersey, and competition at last practically ceased, but one aspirant for championship honors appearing against her in each of the last two years, these only to be easily vanquished. Her prizes at the Royal Jersey Agricultural Show were, in 1876, 1st prize in young cow class; in 1877, 1st prize in old cow class; in 1878, 1879 and 1880, 1st prize in champion class; in 1880, 3d prize for richest milk, in a class of 16; also from 1874 to 1877, four 1st parish prizes. But the cow was something more than a prize-winner. She was destined to be the founder of a butter family whose certainty of transmission of dairy qualities stands unrivaled in this country to-day. Not only was the cow herself good, but she had the power of sending down through two and three generations her great qualities, generally intensifying them. This ability, so rarely found in great cows, of multiplying and retaining the butter yield, she possesses to a remarkable degree, as will be seen from the list below.

The importation of Coomassie was not only the result of Ona's remarkable test, and the fact of the cow being champion over Jersey, but the desire as well, on the part of her owner, to have a distinctive strain of his own. Starting with the test of Ona, and that of the old cow herself, he sought for confirmation of his belief in the powers of the strain from the descendants of the first three sons, those being the only ones that have contributed to the increase of the stock. One son was represented in Ona. The next example was sought in an inbred great-granddaughter Island Star, tracing to another son. The butter came again. At two years of age she made 1 lb. 5 oz. per gross alone, and ten months later made equal to 11 lbs. 6 oz. in 7 days. Remarkable as this was, it was the more so from the fact that at this time the heifer was six and a half months in calf. To complete the chain, a test was needed from a daughter of the third son. This was soon furnished by La Rouge, who made, at four years, 14 lbs. 2 oz. in seven days. Thus the butter power of Coomassie was traced through each of her first three sons, from whom have sprung all the living Koffee, her inbred son, just entering service. New examples of this quality were not wanting, and the list, as far as is known, shows a degree of certainty which is indeed remarkable. The strain is in its infancy, and those interested have had to rely upon young animals for the tests they needed to confirm their opinion of its merits. The list is as follows:

Coomassie, 16 lbs. 11 ozs. in 7 days.
Tracing to Koffee, the oldest son, are:
Island Star, 11 lbs. 6 ozs. in 7 days, 10 months after dropping calf, at 2 years old; 6½ months in calf.
Queen of Ashantee, 10 lbs. 14 ozs. in 7 days, 6½ months after calving, at 3 years old; 8 lbs. 12 ozs. in 7 days, 11 months after calving, at 3 years old.
Auntybel, 9 lbs. 3 ozs. in 7 days, 7 months after calving, at 3 years old; 5½ months in calf.
Mabel of Trinity, 9 lbs. 10 ozs., at 2 years, 3 months after calving.
Fancy Fawkes, 8 lbs. 3 ozs. 7 months after first calf.
Morning Star, 7 lbs. 14 ozs. 10 months after first calf, at 3 years old; 6½ months in calf.
Tracing to Khedive, the second son, are:
Ona, 17 lbs. 4 ozs in 7 days, at 3 years old; 11 lbs. 4 ozs. in 7 days, 7 months after.
Princess of Ashantee, 11 lbs. 13 ozs. in 7 days, at 3 years, and 16 quarts per day.
Princess 2d—her share given 42 lbs., made by Coomassie, Ona and herself, in one week, on short winter feed; Coomassie being 11 years old, and 3 months in milk, Ona 5 months in milk, and Princess 2d 10 days after calving.
Tracing to Vertumnus, the third son, are:
La Rouge, 14 lbs. 2 ozs. in 7 days, at 4 years old.
Lady Velvetine, 15 lbs. 12 ozs. in 7 days, at 3½ years old.
Le Gros' Lily of the Valley, 8 lbs. 12 ozs. in 6 days, at 2 years old.
Punchinello, 15 quarts of milk on first calf.

The scale of points for a Jersey cow has of late been considered an excellent thing to judge prize winners by, but not useful as an indication of any essential dairy qualities. A greater mistake was never made. It is not claimed that from it can be told how much butter and milk a cow will produce, but that one should be able to tell comparatively whether his animal will be useful for these purposes. Look at it carefully and see how many points are given for fancy characteristics, and how insignificant they are to the number that indicate the splendid capacity to turn food into milk and butter, without adding flesh to the carcass or undue size to the bony structure. Of this we think Coomassie an excellent exemplification. She scores extraordinarily high, and has the dairy quality and potency to transmit it. More prize winners in Jersey trace to Coomassie than to any other one individual animal known there.

The splendid udder development of all the tribe is worth noticing, and seems as invariable as their butter qualities. In almost every instance they have enormous udders, running well forward and back, with yellow skins and well-spread teats. Their escutcheons are uniformly good. Princess 2d, that sold for $4,800 is the first of the blood that Mr. Burnham ever offered for sale.

### GUERNSEY CATTLE.

The following first rate description of the Guernseys is by a correspondent of the *London Field*. This justly celebrated breed of cattle has not yet met with the favor in America they so richly deserve, but are becoming better appreciated. One of the finest herds of Guernseys in the United States belongs to H. Pierce, of San Francisco:

This race of cattle seldom get the name and credit they deserve, being often coupled with the Jersey or Alderney. Comparatively few people know that there is any difference between the Guernsey and Jersey, most being frequently ignorant of the fact that the Guernseys are a distinct breed, and, in reality, very different from the Jersey. One great advantage is that they are altogether a more fleshy animal, without the exceedingly bony frame that, though good for converting a small amount of food into milk, gives no protection from hard weather, and will not fatten. There is little doubt that this race of cattle could be well acclimatized and bred to a very hardy, useful breed. Size could be cultivated; they could be in time brought to a larger animal than they are at present, though there are many fair-sized Guernseys to be seen now. The English farmer has ordinarily nothing to fall back upon but "market value." He has no breed that combines quality as well as good milking properties. The "better" he breeds his stock, so to speak, the less chance he has of having a good dairy. His down-calving heifers are of no special value; whereas, if they were thoroughbred and had quality, whether Short-Horn, Devon, or, in fact, any breed, he would have a considerable chance of obtaining high prices for them. The Guernsey heifers are of high value, and will always obtain a price, especially now the Americans have taken them up.

The Guernsey cow is a long, deep animal, her depth being carried on all through—wide pins, and lots of room behind, and gradually forming into a light dairy-looking forehand; narrow shoulder tops, and a thin neck and head, the legs short and clean, with no daylight at all under the body. The fawn and white patches, cream-colored nose, and general orange gloss denote the true breed. They are not the small cow they are generally supposed to be. Mr. James, whose name is well known as a breeder of first-class Guernsey stock, both for show and good milkers, says: "Some of our cattle will come very little short in weight of an *ordinary* Short-Horn at three years old." Then he goes on: "I farmed for many years in the South of Scotland, and bred Short-Horns. I had the opportunity of comparing the two breeds." This surely speaks well for the Guernsey.

Though different in many ways, there is a great similarity between the Jersey and Guernsey, both breeds being essentially butter-maker's cows, giving similar amounts of butter, and of the same quality. This butter, as is well known, is of superb quality, color and taste, and always fetches the highest price. The Guernsey gives more milk, often three to four gallons to the two or two and a half of the Jersey. In fact, a dairy of Guernseys would give more milk than the average of ordinary Short-Horns, especially if selected and bred for it. The first-prize Guernsey cow at the Royal Counties' Show at Salisbury in June last, gave one an excellent idea of what the breed should be. She was deep, long and wedge-shaped, with a splendid bag, and was then giving four gallons per day of milk of good quality, which is not very wonderful for the breed. A Guernsey heifer, after her first calf, was only the other day giving four gallons a day. This was not a prize animal. A Guernsey will yield 350 pounds to 400 pounds of the finest butter in the year.

There is a structural limit to the production of every cow—that is, in the actual mechanism of the animal itself. There are no two animals made exactly alike, inside or out. Any difference in the formation of the internal structure might make a difference of many gallons yield in the course of the year. This does not infer that the anatomy of cows is in any way different; but there are undoubtedly structures better formed for produce than others.

As regards the breeding of good dairy cows, it is always allowed that like, to a certain extent, produces like, externally and internally. Then, again, there is the law of variation, against which the breeder of good stock always has to struggle. Be it as it may, the only safe road to certainty, or, we might say, success, in breeding good milkers, is to breed from pedigree milking stock. This seldom can be obtained where a pedigree Short-Horn bull is used. You cannot have the milking type unless you breed from animals which have been milkers. The Guernseys, both bull and cow, are descended from stock which have been esteemed for their large produce of milk and butter for generations. With regard to bulls for producing good milkers, it is sometimes argued that the milking properties of a cow invariably descend through the female line; but this gives no ground for any rule, as there are, and have been, many bulls which have produced good milkers. For instance, the Earl of Dublin and the Jamestown bull had this milking propensity.

The structural economy of a Guernsey allows her to convert the food she eats into produce far more perfectly than the ordinary dairy cow. Of course there are advantages in having massive-framed animals, in order to attain great weight when fatted out; but massive frames require a good deal to support life during the time they are in milk, leaving the remainder for the production of milk.

It is easier to infuse flesh into a milking breed of cattle than to create a "milking prepotency" in a fleshy breed. By selecting the large ones, and feeding the calves well, there is no doubt this breed might be made fit for any tenant farmer.

### AYRSHIRE STATISTICS.

Ed. Gazette: The following statistics of Ayrshires were recently sent me. Perhaps they may be of interest to publish: Alonzo Libby, Saccarappa, Maine, reports a daily weight of milk, as follows: Queen of Ayr 4th 4465, from March 24 to April 23, 1882, 31 days, gave 1,377 lbs.; from April 24 to May 23, 1882, 30 days, gave 1,350½; and Queen of Ayr 5th 4466, for the same time, gave for 31 days 1,541 lbs.; for 30 days, 1,520½. Norman Gourlay, Victor, N. Y., reports: Guess 2d 3120 as giving, for the 30 days of June, 1881, 1,258 lbs., and for 7 days, from the 12th to 18th of same month, she averaged 53 lbs. a day, and made from the milk 14 lbs. 6 oz. butter before salting.

Wm. Fairweather, McLane, Pa., states that he has butchered Nonesuch 3018, aged 12 years. Live weight, 1,150 lbs.; dressed, 732 lbs. beef. C. M. Winslow.

—*Breeder's Gazette.*

## ATHLETICS.

### THE GROWTH OF ATHLETICS.

The first attempt to introduce amateur athletics on the Pacific Coast was made by a few members of the Olympic Club, in 1875, at the Recreation Grounds in this city. The track was of macadam, about one-third of a mile in circumference, with sharp corners, and a fall of about six feet diagonally from the north to the south corner. The few enthusiasts of that time struggled manfully to create an interest among the members of the club and the public in purely amateur and honorable sports, but up to this year the want of suitable grounds for the purpose has made it an arduous and disheartening undertaking. The Recreation Grounds and Bay District Track, unprotected from the chilling and fog-laden winds for which San Francisco is noted, were of little encouragement to beginners in training; and spectators were not anxious to put themselves to the discomfort of viewing a second meeting through the clouds of dust prevailing at almost any time of the season when it is possible to give a meeting here, especially as every event was at such a distance from them that it was impossible to know anything of the outcome until it had been reported from mouth to mouth. Dissensions in the club and the want of an intelligent report of meetings by the newspapers prevented any combined action toward the support of athletics. Being virtually isolated from the rest of the world, home athletics were of small moment. The meeting of the Bay District Track last Thanksgiving Day passed off very well, but the audience was too far from the track to fully understand and appreciate all the events. The Olympic Athletic Club is now in possession of grounds of its own, corner Fourteenth and Center streets, Oakland. They have put in a good track for running and bicycle riding, good dressing rooms, and everything of necessity, both for training and convenience at athletic meetings. All of their events are usually open to amateurs. Other clubs can easily obtain the use of grounds for their members, and by opening most of their events and holding their meetings there, the interest in athletics will rapidly increase, and the stimulating effects of an enthusiastic and appreciative audience will, undoubtedly, develop among us numerous first-class athletes in all branches of manly sports. We have enough material, in embryo, we brag about our climate and horses, and there is no longer any reason for hanging back on account of poor accommodations. A new departure and combined action by all friends of the cause will insure success.

### THE CHAMPIONSHIP.

The defeat of L. E. Meyers at the Championship meeting on June 10th has had a most disastrous effect on his newspaper admirers, and such backing and filling to frame excuses for the champion is seldom indulged in by independent sporting journals. He has been credited this season with beating several records, both at shorter and longer distances than the event in which he was defeated, and his friends were anxious to back him as a winner to the tune of several thousand dollars, for which they have since duly repented in sack-cloth and ashes. There was no hint of lack of condition before the race, but immediately afterwards it was suddenly realized that, record breaking to the contrary notwithstanding, he was far below last year's form. His conqueror slept but two hours the night before while journeying to New York, and still eclipsed any time made by Meyers at the same distance when compelled to breast the tape to obtain a record. And Brooks was not allowed to go over the mark three times without being even penalized. It is a long time since Meyers has been started by a man not under the glamour of his fame, and independent enough to insist that the pistol should decide the start. The innovation is a wholesome one, and will undoubtedly encourage athletics who of late have been compelled to put up with wretched starting for the sake of beating a record. Of late it had become a common occurrence in amateur handicap meetings in the East, for scratch man to creep over the mark two or three yards before the pistol was fired, and the only penalty was to be sent back to scratch without being penalized. Such culpable carelessness should be frowned on by all handicappers, whose efforts to equalize the chances of competitors are entirely frustrated. Fortunately for athletics on this coast thus far, the starter in all events has attended to his duties without showing the least favoritism; and the unusually large audience at the championship meeting was no doubt partly due to the knowledge that enough money was at stake on the important event to ensure an honest start by the pistol, or an enforcement of the penalty, as well as the fact that the event would be closely contested.

Mr. Meyers undoubtedly deserves all honor for what he has accomplished by sheer perseverance and pluck, and we wish there were more amateurs as enthusiastic as he has shown himself to be; but still, why the penalty should be ignored for a couple of years on account of one individual, is more than the heathen in this benighted region can comprehend.

Annexed are the entries, and a synopsis of the race. Those who appeared at the starting post were: H. S. Brooks, Jr., Yale College, 1; S. Derickson, M. A. C., 2; A. Waldron, M. A. C., 3; A. C. Cooper, W. A. C., 0. Cooper did not start, and Derickson ceasing to persevere, Brooks trotted to the tape in 30 4-5s. Second heat—Entries: L. E. Myers, M. A. C., 1; W. C. Wilmer, N. Y. A. C., 2; J. B. White, M. A. C., 3; B. H. Tobey, W. A. C., 0; E. J. Wendell, N. Y. A. C., 0. Neither Wendell nor Tobey started, and Myers won by two yards, in 23¾s. Final heat—Brooks, 1; Myers, 2; Derickson, 3. Wilmer did not start. Brooks stood like a statue on the mark, but the others were very nervous, and got put back once for their stealing propensities; but when the pistol was fired they both gained the lost yard, and all then ran side by side for 25 yards; but at the turn it was plain to be seen that the Yale man had the pride of place, and he was never headed throughout, but had Myers beaten 50 yards from home, while Derickson was out of the hunt altogether. Time—22 3-5.

The following are the records beaten at the same meeting: Throwing the hammer—F. L. Lambrecht, P. A. C., 93 ft. ½ in., W. L. Condon having held the best record for four hours, with 89 ft. 10⅛ in. Putting the shot—F. L. Lambrecht, 39 ft. 9⅝ in. The hurdle race, 120 yds., over 10 hurdles, was made by J. A. Tivey, W. A. C., in 16 4-5s, the best record for American amateurs. Throwing of the 56 lb weight resulted in the victory of H. W. Best, Boston Y. M. A. C., with 24 ft. 10¼ in., the best on record.

In connection with the above, we annex the following from the *N. Y. Clipper*: "The defeat of L. E. Myers by H. S. Brooks, in the 220-yards race at the championship meeting, naturally gave rise to a general desire to see the men engage in a match race at the same distance, for which each should undergo a special preparation. With a view to bringing about such a meeting, a retired amateur runner decided to offer a silver cup of the value of $150, and having readily gained the consent of Myers, addressed a communication to the Yalencian, notifying him of his intention, and that the choice of ground was left to him (Brooks). Promptly replying thereto, the latter says: 'It will be impossible for me to meet Mr. Myers, as I have broken training for the season. My time is not my own, as I am just in the midst of my annual examinations. I leave for home (San Francisco) in a few days, and have made all my arrangements. I will be most happy to meet Mr. Myers at some future time, and I am sure I am very much obliged to you for your very kind offer of a prize.' That settles the matter for the present, but it is probable that the coming Autumn will witness the wished-for race. Until which time it is to be hoped that both men will continue well."

The Olympic Athletic Club Handicap Meeting, at their grounds, at Oakland, announced for July 8th, has been postponed for two weeks, in order to allow competitors to enjoy the coming holidays—and recover from the usual effects. It is to be hoped that entries and competitors will be plentiful, as the events are open to all amateurs, and the grounds are the only ones on the coast suitably arranged for the proper management of an athletic meeting. The officers will make it a point to keep the inner grounds clear, in order that every event shall be in full view of the spectators.

At the Half-Mile Track, last Sunday, a match between M. Geary and John Larkey, of 100 yards, for an alleged stake of $100 a side, was won in a jog by Geary. The time, with almost a gale of wind at their backs, was 10¾ seconds. Larkey has been credited with numerous trials in even time, and could almost immediately repeat in 10¼, but even with the wind directly behind him, was beaten in the most hollow manner in the above time.

## THE GUN.

The Cosmopolitan Shooting Club.—This Club held its annual session in Police Court No. 1, on Tuesday last, Judge Hale Rix in the chair. The following officers were elected to serve for the ensuing term: President, Judge Rix (unanimously re-elected); Vice-President, George W. Shorten; Secretary and Treasurer, Jerry Browell, Jr. Board of Directors—A. Ault, F. Maskey and F. Putzman, Jr. Probably in the last week of this month the Cosmopolitan will shoot their fourth match with the California Club for the diamond trophy. The latter Club has but one match to its credit, so that if the Cosmopolitan wins in the coming event, they will count the diamond trophy among their spoils.

Dove Shooting.—The close season for this favorite bird with our wing shots, expires to-day, and many of our local sportsmen have gone into the country to spend their Fourth of July vacation hunting these fleet wingers. The last legislature very wisely classed the dove as a game bird, and made it unlawful to shoot or trap it between January first and July first. The wisdom of this course is shown by the increased number of birds this year.

There are young ducks about the size of quail up in the breeding grounds, up river. The little fellows are very difficult to catch, as they run and hide in the tules and get out of the way. The old one will almost allow herself to be caught in saving the young ones. One old mallard was seen with nine little ones.

Up on the Suisun marshes it is stated that there is more feed for the ducks than for years past. The hunters may expect a fine season this year.

Charles W. Kellogg, of Oakland, will to-day unstrap his gun-case at Summer Home Farm, Santa Cruz Mountains, for a four-days' dove hunt.

There are a good many ducks up in the Suisun marshes now. Many teal and mallard breed there during the Summer.

J. H. Jellett will open his dove shooting practice to-morrow, at Soquel, Santa Cruz County.

Ben Brown and Robert Liddle, of Liddle & Kaeding, have gone dove shooting in the neighborhood of San Jose.

Sam Platt will open dove season to-day, at San Mateo.

J. V. Coleman, of Menlo Park, will shoot doves in the neighborhood of his residence.

Judge Rix, Dr. Leavitt, Philip Funcke and John Muller, will scour the fields around Pleasanton and Sunol for doves to-day.

Fine dove shooting can be had near Cloverdale, Sonoma County.

Messers Wm. Lindsey and Wm. Golcher, Sr., leave to-day for Novato, Marin County, dove hunting.

There were two or three inches of water covering the Suisun marshes during the high tides of last week.

Wild celery is very plentiful in Suisun marshes. [illegible] will make it good for the canvasbacks this Winter.

THE

# Breeder and Sportsman.

PUBLISHED BY THE

BREEDER AND SPORTSMAN PUBLISHING CO.

THE TURF AND SPORTING AUTHORITY OF THE
PACIFIC COAST.

**OFFICE, 508 MONTGOMERY STREET**
P. O. Box 1333.

*Five dollars a year; three dollars for six months; one dollar and a
half for three months. Strictly in advance.*
*Money should be sent by postal order, draft or by registered letter.*
*Communications must be accompanied by the writer's name and address
not necessarily for publication, but as a private guarantee of good faith.*

JOSEPH CAIRN SIMPSON, - - - Editor

SAN FRANCISCO, - - SATURDAY, JULY 1, 1882

## GREETING.

To those who prefer the sunny side of life, who appreciate the many enjoyments the Great Creator has placed within our reach, who are not held in bondage by fanaticism to see merit in gloom, and to consider all diversions frivolous, if not absolutely wicked; to those who can discover the golden edging to the blackest cloud, and who have faith that there is always a silver lining within the shadow; to those who seek to make the bright days brighter, and who are earnest in their endeavors to increase the happiness of all, our greeting is presented.

There is implanted in every human being a desire for enjoyment. In place of trying to eradicate it as a pernicious propensity, our effort will be to direct it so that it may be beneficially indulged. Believing that there is little virtue in austerity, or salvation in asceticism, our aim will be to follow paths which lead in other directions.

By the side of the mountain brook, when the Spring flowers are blooming, and the linnets and robins are singing their liveliest notes;

Through the forests, when there is quiet and fragrance, and where the interlocking branches form giant arches, and the music of the breeze soughing through the twigs;

Among verdant fields, where foals are gamboling around their dams, and the lowing of cattle and the bleating of sheep welcoming the herdsman and shepherd;

Over the glad waters, where the spray is sparkling in the sunshine, and the white sails are in a tremor, and the masts quivering in the excitement of motion swift, and as graceful as the flight of the seagull;

By the side of the racecourse, when there is an eager strife for mastery, and the blood bounds through the veins and arteries, and there are shouts and cheers, and an intensity of feeling indescribable;

On the plains, where the fleet courser flits by like the shadows of cloudlets over a waving grainfield when there is a brisk wind driving the fleecy figments of vapor between earth and sun;

Under the lea of the coppice, when the flag-tailed setter or staunch pointer is transformed into a statue, and then the whirr of wings, the sharp report, and the puff of smoke vanishing in the clear air;

Through orchards, crimson with the flowers of the peach and almond, white with the bloom of the pear, and rich with the perfume of orange blossoms;

Meandering among the vines, green as emerald when the hills are sere and brown, and the clusters hang embowered in the abundant foliage, shining in purple, red, topaz-colored and luscious;

Winding among fields, when the grain stalks are bending beneath the bearded heads, and there is the rattle of the reaper and the hum of the thresher;

Halting at the grounds where the young men are developing activity and strength to fit them for the sterner battles of life, and there is a fierce emulation to excel—determination, the antithesis of irresolution—health against the flaccidity of indolence and luxury;

Quiet walks in the evening, to weep and laugh over the sorrows and joys, so skilfully counterfeited as to appear actual; lessons burned into the mind with the red-hot iron of realistic effect;

Visits to the family circle, when there is a glow on the hearth; devotees bending over the figures of kings, queens, bishops and knights; eager parties debating the last hand at whist:

This is the merest sketch of the route we intend to compass, a hint of the long journey contemplated.

While the course is marked through a country of sunshine and flowers, enlivened with the song of birds, and which Nature has clothed with a gay garb, there is instruction on either side of the road. There are learned professors among the travelers to proffer lessons which will benefit, and illustrators who will picture from practical results.

Far from recommending that men—even those who can afford to do so—should spend their whole time in sport, our desires are that they should blend amusement with labor, so that each may have its appropriate place in life. Sport alone is like wearing garments made entirely of decorations, like a meal of condiments and sauces. Ornaments add beauty to the dress, sauces give relish and piquancy to the repast. But there must be strong warp and woof to support the lighter fabrics, and substantial food to produce brain, muscle and bones which will endure the strains which active life imposes. To withstand this strain, it is necessary that there should be a proper apportionment of work and a fitting time for recreation. Labor—constant, unremitting labor, especially that work which compels sedentary habits, or long hours of in-door confinement—will speedily wear out the strongest constitution, and there is absolute necessity for relaxation and change. The racehorse, with sinews and muscles of the truest kind, endurance perfected by breeding from the best for a score of generations, can not stand being "keyed up" for long periods. There must be a cessation in the exercise, a change from the track to the roads or fields, else there is a waste which can never be repaired. Man, though capable of undergoing more severe training without permanent injury than animal of any kind, is still amenable to natural laws; and, besides physical loss, the greater danger is from the strain on the brain, and consequently the failure of nerve force.

To aid in adjusting the proper balance between labor and sport, to remove the obstacles which are in the way of a better understanding of the relation between sport and good morals, and to assist in advancing the interests and increasing the enjoyments of all, are our fervent desires.

---

## THANKS.

We return our sincere, heartfelt thanks for the kind notices which our contemporaries have given the BREEDER AND SPORTSMAN. They have been so manifold that to acknowledge separately would appear vainglorious, and hence we make the return general.

The Eastern turf and rural papers, the press of the Pacific Coast, have been lavish in good words and kind wishes for our enterprise, and we shall do our utmost to render the paper worthy of the encomiums, the flattering prognostics which have been awarded. There is a feeling of responsibility, arising from these friendly greetings, which at times impresses us with the fear that we will not be able to meet the expectations; and then there is the stimulus of good wishes, so copiously offered, which will nerve us to continued exertion, to prove in a measure at least worthy of the trust. Should there be, at any time, a desire for ease, a sort of a hankering for a break in the work, an anxiety to escape from the self-imposed task, the remembrance of the encouraging "send-off" will brace us up and the struggle be renewed with a determination to last out the race.

But were it not for the assistance we have been so fortunate in securing, the misgivings would be increased, and sanguine as we are, there might be at times doubt and despondency.

Beside the regular forces ready for duty, however arduous, and who can be depended on to carry out the plans to a successful issue, there are volunteers which complete a grand army, and make the certainty of ultimate victory. It is only necessary to refer to the names, which are given in another place, to show that at the head of every division are generals who are eminently capable, and there is an *esprit*, collectively and individually, as well as knowledge, which insures the departments being handled in a way which must be satisfactory. We can scarcely overestimate the important aid which those gentlemen lend who favor us with presenting to our readers such a wealth of varied information as their contributions will show. With these co-adjutors comes confidence, and a reliance that our journal will merit the plaudits, for which we again thank our brethren of the press.

## THEN AND NOW.

When good old Isaak Walton used to wander along the umbrageous banks of his favorite streams he never had any misgiving about being able to fill his creel because there were no fish left in the waters. His philosophic meditations were not disturbed by intrusive thoughts of vengeance and mental curses against those vandals who deplete the water courses of their inhabitants. The sky, the clouds, the air, the wind, the water, the shadows; and the momentous question as to colors and shape of fly, were subjects which had the bearing on the result of the day's sport.

His prophetic mind gave no hint as to the possibilities of time, soap root or *cocculus indicus*. He never dreamed of giant powder, and all his philosophic musings never wrought up his imagination to the point of supposing it possible that such agencies would almost destroy the sport which made his name famous. "The Compleat Angler, or the Contemplative Man's Recreation," tells us how to catch fish, but not how to catch the man who kills the fish and sweeps the streams.

If Sir Isaak was "behind the times" through the accident of having lived in the seventeenth century, he had the advantage of us in some respects. If he did not have a split bamboo pole with nickeled fittings, and improved gut leaders or casting line, he could make his cast where a dozen or two others had not already done so the same day. If he had no hundreds of varieties of ready-made flies, waterproof line and automatic reel, he had a chance to catch something with a rude home-made tackle. If he knew nothing about the breeding and hatching of trout by artificial means, or the stocking of streams, he had the satisfaction of "working" those stocked by nature. In short, had our venerable father of the gentle sport lived now-a-days, the "Contemplative Recreation" would not have been written, for instead of sitting on a bank "contemplating" and waiting for bites, he would have put in his time swearing at the Portuguese woodchoppers who blasted out the pools and destroyed the fish. The man who sits by on many of our streams must sit by them and wait for the fish to grow.

## OUR CORRESPONDENTS.

We must say that there never was a paper which commenced with a more brilliant array of correspondents than the BREEDER AND SPORTSMAN, and the pages of the first number afford the best proof of the correctness of the statement.

It is superfluous to say more than to call attention to the contributions, and request for them a careful perusal. It is, in fact, all that we can do at present, as individually and collectively they are worthy of so high praise that it would require a great deal of room to do them justice. Still better, we have an assurance of a continuation of the favors, especially when the busy racing season is over. Then will come the discussion of topics which are of paramount interest to breeders, trainers, the disciples of Nimrod and Walton, and all others who are interested in the various fields this paper covers.

Exciting as the Summer exploits are, there will be no lack of interest when the long evenings give more time for the consideration of questions of so much importance. In the meantime there is no news from the race courses, from the breeding farms, from the woods and streams, from the rifle grounds, from every place, in this busy season of sport. And again we have to thank our correspondents for the favor which are beyond prices.

### EDITORIAL DUTIES.

The letter of Mr. Kellogg, in calling attention to the editorial management of a journal the main topics of which are breeding and sport, will naturally lead to an expression of our views on the subject; and there could not be a more appropriate place than in the first number of the BREEDER AND SPORTSMAN.

No one can value correspondence more than we do. In a paper of this kind, it is a feature which does not yield in importance to any other department, and we regard ourselves as being extremely fortunate in securing such an array of talent as these columns will show. But the idea that the editor is merely a clerical officer, gathering and arranging the contributions, printing them without comment, unless statistical errors are to be corrected, is far different from what we hold the duties of a manager to be. Mr. Kellogg is right in advising that partisanship be avoided. We have an utter abhorrence of "organs," when that term means the adhering, right or wrong, to a party, or any pre-arranged course of action which is marked by those who control for the organ to follow. In that case the editor is a servitor, wearing the collar of thraldom inscribed with the name of his owners, and as much a chattel as though he were a dog. It matters not whether the ownership is vested in a party or an individual, the slavery is the same. There is such a thing as independence in turf journals, however, as well as in those which have the most potent influence in the political world, though independence can not be real without opinions to sustain it; and these opinions must not be kept in the background, but supported publicly, manfully, and in accordance with convictions. There are numerous topics which elicit differences of opinion in a paper which makes the breeding, rearing, training, racing and trotting of horses one of the prominent features of its columns. It will not answer for the paper to ignore these questions in the editorial pages, no matter how capably they are handled by correspondents; and the editor does not fulfil his trust, when, from motives of expediency, he keeps aloof from the discussion.

The contributors stand in the position of attorneys, doing the best they can to forward the interests of their clients; the editor has judicial duties, which he must not shirk. This does not compel him to take sides with either of the contestants, or to turn the duel into a triangular battle. By such a course, he would lower the dignity of his position, and incur the charge of favoritism to one or other of the disputants. But it is seldom, indeed, that the editor is called upon in a controversy between correspondents to decide any of the points at issue, especially when the disagreement is in relation to the places which should be awarded rival families of horses.

The readers generally care little about the individual preferences of the editor, so far as his fancies in that direction go, though they have a right to expect that he will not give an undue prominence to any particular strain. Fancy has a great deal to do with preferences in the breeding of horses of every description. One man favors the Normans for heavy draft, another the Clydesdale, and still another is sure that the "Shire horse" is the proper animal for the moving of heavy loads. With fast trotters, there is the greatest disparity in the views of breeders, and every family of note has enthusiastic advocates. These advocates are prone to disparage the families which are outside of their favorites; and, unfortunately, many think that decrying those which come in competition exalts the race that is their particular hobby. There is a jealousy among owners as well as writers, and, like the youngster who has become hopelessly smitten with some fair damsel, praise of others is a bitter poison to their minds. We presume that this is the feature which our esteemed correspondent had in his mind while giving the advice, and the fear of raising any animosities what he counsels avoiding. This is very well. But to pander to the absurd jealousy of those who are so thin-skinned, by avoiding editorial articles which have a bearing on the important questions of breeding, will not be

our course. Egotistical though it may appear, we have a good deal of confidence in the judgment which has come from many years of experience, and a close observation; and we shall not hesitate to present our views whenever we deem the occasion requires that they shall be given.

There are other questions which demand still more emphatic handling on the part of the editor. There are practices to commend or reprobate; in the management of courses, there are points to praise, errors to condemn; and there is scarcely a fair or meeting which does not present salient characteristics.

We would much rather write words of commendation than censure—and the turf millenium will be close at hand when there is little necessity for rebuke. When the necessity arises, when castigation is the only remedy, the lash must be laid on with a will.

To return to the letter of Mr. Kellogg. We think our readers will coincide with us in hearty commendations, if even there are points of difference of opinion. One portion of his advice we shall follow, viz., giving both sides a full hearing irrespective of our belief.

From discussion comes knowledge, and if we are wrong in the premises, no one will more cheerfully concede the error, and just as cheerfully adopt contrary views to those which have been promulgated. Again, the advice to avoid personalities and partisanship is as sound as "heart of oak," and is well worthy of being kept in constant remembrance.

### OUR ASSOCIATES.

We are indeed fortunate in the Field Marshals who are at the head of the various departments, and this good luck is shared by our readers.

Piercy Wilson, who has had long experience in journalism, closely identified with all pertaining to papers of the stamp of the BREEDER AND SPORTSMAN, is a valued general auxiliary.

Charles G. Yale has charge of the Yachting and Fishing columns, and it is supererogatory to state that there is no one better qualified to handle these important departments, East or West.

T. T. Williams is an enthusiast in all pertaining to Dogs, and in England, Australia and this country the love for "man's best and truest companion" has never wavered. When joined to such a complete knowledge of all varieties of the species, Mr. Williams is peculiarly well fitted for the place.

Athletics are under the charge of Dwight Germain, and again we will have the endorsement of every one who is acquainted with Mr. Germain, that better could not be obtained.

Boating is under the supervision of as competent a man as there is on the coast, but for the present, at least, he desires to remain incognito. We have not the least hesitation in promising that there shall be no lack, and in this department the work will show that the tiller is in good hands.

Bicycling requires a person who has the right knowledge of this popular exercise, and in obtaining the aid of Geo. H. Strong to oversee the department, we feel that it is on a par with the others.

These gentlemen, and others outside of the ranks of journalism, as it may be termed, who aid in the various departments, are equally as proficient, and thus we can safely say, that there never was a paper which had a brighter prospect.

### THE EARLY TRAINING OF COLTS.

In the admirable letter of Mr. Rose he makes a strong point when writing of the early training of colts. The idea is novel, and much as has been printed and said on the subject, we never heard it advanced before. That is, if two men are training colts, one a firm believer in the system, the other of a contrary opinion, in a great majority of instances the former will do too much, the latter too little. The point would be a guard in the one case fearful of doing injury, the confidence in the powers of the animal might tend to overwork. With a very prom-

ising colt the danger is increased, especially when the aim is to develop phenomenal speed. So far as our experience has gone, there is a guide which will do to rely upon, provided due care is taken in noting the indications. If the colt does his allotted task cheerfully, eats with a relish, has no heat or swelling of the limbs, and there is a bright look in his eyes, it is safe to say that the work is proper. But then there are colts of such high spirit that they never exhibit fatigue until their powers have been completely exhausted, while others are so sluggish that it requires continual urging to get them along from the first. As Mr. Rose says, there is constant necessity for careful handling, and it is impossible to lay down rules which can be depended upon in all instances. The impetus which the wonderful performances of the California colts has given to the trotting of youngsters makes this one of the most important questions for the consideration of breeders at the present time, and we hope that it will be fully discussed.

### CLOSING OF STAKES.

As will be learned from the advertisement, the "Fixed Events" of the Pacific Coast Blood-horse Association close on the first of August. There is scarcely a doubt that every one of the stakes will have the largest number of nominations ever made on the Pacific coast. The fact is, that every one who owns a thoroughbred yearling can not afford to leave it out; and though he may think that the larger breeders have the pull over him in numbers, the history of the turf will show that those who have bred on a small scale have gained their full share of the good things.

The classification gives the opportunity for the nominator to select, and as the stakes range from half a mile to two, the distances can be chosen according to the anticipated merits. Scan the advertisement, weigh well the necessity for every man, who is in a position, to name, and then—why, name in every stake on the bill.

### THE FAIRS.

In the hurry of getting out the first number, we are forced to postpone a subject which properly should have been given a place. It does not require an apology, however, as no matter how little a person may know of the newspaper business, the truth is evident that one number would not suffice to write proper acknowledgments, or call attention to every advertisement. As the weeks come, due attention will be given to these prominent matters.

The Fairs of California deservedly rank high among the agricultural exhibitions of the country, and we will take pleasure in presenting their claims—in the first place, to those who must assist in keeping them up to the mark; in the second, to the public, by giving such a description as they are so well entitled to. Give us time to get properly "warmed up," and we will endeavor to do this part in a way that will be satisfactory.

### THE FIRST OF AUGUST.

The first of August is an important day in the diary of a turfman. Following the Eastern practice, the prominent California stakes close on that day, and the Fairs have generally adopted that date for the entries to close in the trotting purses. Between this and that time there will be many questions asked, and as nearly as we can learn there is a likelihood of favorable answers being returned, as the horses are generally doing well. So far the classification appears to be very satisfactory, and there is a certainty of numerous entries. As a majority of the Fair programmes are advertised, owners and trainers can see what there is before them. There is certainly quite a variety, and it looks as though a horse which has any pretensions can find a place which will suit him.

### CROWDED OUT.

Proofs everywhere. There is an avalanche of matter, every line of it timely, every paragraph worthy of a place. Sixteen pages are a bagatelle. Four times sixteen would be necessary to do justice; and were it not that we are determined to start at a pace we feel confident of bettering, other form would have been sent to press.

## ROWING.

The action of the Fourth of July Committee in appropriating a small sum of money for a regatta at Long Bridge on the National holiday, will do much to increase the public interest in rowing. San Francisco should be preeminent in aquatic sports, as the opportunities for amusement on the water are numerous. For yachting, our magnificent bay offers unrivalled attractions. During several months of the year the most adventurous yachtman can enjoy the delights of a half gale any afternoon by soul hankers for the excitement of scudding under reefed canvas. These stiff winds are not as acceptable to oarsmen as to the yachting fraternity, but they are not solvent or changeable enough to prevent rowing in racing craft, or even to mar the sport. The mornings are almost invariably beautiful. For four hours in the forenoon the most timid oarsman can enjoy the pleasures of a row on a sheet of water as bright as a mirror and as smooth as a hill pond. The winds come up with the regularity of clockwork, and blow in the same direction with a conscientiousness that speaks volumes for the steadiness of the clerk of the weather. During the afternoon gale the sheltered water along the wharves offers a course of three miles which is rarely so rough that an ordinary shell twelve inches in beam can not go through it without much discomfort to the occupant. In other parts of the world, is it possible to do as much rowing in a year as on San Francisco Bay? The sun never shines so fiercely that a row is not possible and pleasant, and the rigors of frost and ice are unknown. Except when a fierce southeaster or icy norther lashes the tide into the semblance of a sea, a moderately expert sculler can dance over the bay in a light practice boat with safety and comfort. For fully ten months in the year the bay is fit for ordinary racing craft, and there do not occur more than three weeks in the twelve months, when a resolute oarsman would be compelled to take his exercise on land. For some inexplicable reason, however, regattas are generally held at the time of the year least favorable to racing. The Fall is by far the best season for rowing on San Francisco Bay. In September the trade winds die away, and until the southeasterly gales begin in Winter, the bay is generally as calm as a duck pond. If the present custom of holding regattas during the existence of the trade winds should prevail, a modification in the class of boats used for racing would be most desirable. These matters, however, generally accommodate themselves to circumstances, and already a class of racing boats, designated as "barges," has established itself in favor. The weatherly qualities of the barge makes it available on any day during the Summer months, and in this respect the rough boat is preferable to the shell, which often makes the postponement of an important race necessary. The wind never blows strong enough during the Summer to deter a barge, and crew from making the trip over the stiff course from Long Bridge to the Rolling Mills, and to the spectators the contest is just as interesting as if the crews were in paper shells. Among scullers the same tendency to rough boats is observed, and the "wherry" has become very popular, and promises to become more so. The narrow racing shell may in time undergo the process of evolution, and give place to a class of boats with more beam and less length. On a fine morning a thirty pound single scull of eleven or twelve inch beam may show to great advantage; but for every afternoon during six months of the year, a boat with a few inches more beam would lead her a merry dance over the white caps.

For the first time in some years we are to have a first-class four-oar shell race. For this contest on the Fourth of July, the South End, the Golden Gate, the Pioneer and the Ariel Clubs have each entered a crew, and if they all come to the line as promised a good race is sure to result. Four-oar shell racing has gone out of fashion somewhat since the Pioneer Club won the McKinley Cup and the championship. The St. George Club made a desperate attempt to revive the sport, and died in the attempt. Since then the Pioneer Club has had a monopoly of shell rowing, and has improved the opportunity by keeping its boat where it could gather dust and cobwebs. The younger clubs have devoted much of their energy to barge racing, and with two of them the contest on the Fourth will be a debut in fine boats. The Pioneer crew should win, as they have a really fine paper boat that has done some hard work. It is very dubious, however, if, even with this advantage, the Pioneers come first to the stake. In their initial pulls they showed up very badly. L. C. White, the sculler, is in the bow, and seems altogether out of place there. The rig of the boat evidently disagrees very badly with him, and he labors hard at the oar without doing effective work. B. Crowley, at forward waist, has a reprehensible habit of hooping his back, and nearly smiting his knees with his chin every time he reaches for the stroke. B. C. Lyne, at No. 3 seat, pulls a vigorous oar, but his style differs from that of the two men in front of him. John Sullivan, the sculler, is stroke oar, and pulls in good form, but is out of place. The stroke seat is not his best position. The crew is, therefore, anything but a strong one. It needs a good deal of practice to become fast, and not having the opportunity to get it, must expect a hard race in slow time. The Ariel four have had a few spins, and though a lighter crew, do far better work than the Pioneer men. Fred. Smith is stroke, and while not the loveliest in the world, pulls hard, and does fully his share of the work. Sam. Watkins, the sculler, is in the bow, and steers well. The crew is handicapped in boats, but in lumpy water will make the Pioneer men row the whole distance. The Golden Gate crew will use the paper shell formerly owned by the St. George Club, but so far have not appeared in anything but their barge. If they show up to equal advantage in the paper boat they will be the strongest crew in the list, as the South End men are also handicapped in a wooden boat of uncertain age and speed.

The Fourth of July Regatta will commence at 9 A. M., and the course will be from Long Bridge, running south, one mile and return. The disadvantage of Long Bridge is that it offers very poor accommodations for spectators, and if the wind blows with all its accustomed vigor in the afternoon the less enthusiastic admirers of aquatic sport will have their endurance severely tested. The committee having charge of the

regatta is, however, experienced and competent, and will doubtless arrange matters to the best advantage for competitors and spectators. The single scull race will be rowed at 9 A. M., before the procession. All other races will be rowed after the procession. For the single scull race the possible entries are: Henry Peterson, John Sullivan, Louis White, Denis Griffin, Sam Watkins and B. Crowley. Peterson, of whom great things have long been expected, is regarded as the favorite, and it is intended that he will row the course nearly a minute faster than it has ever before been rowed in a public trial. Out of such a large field there ought to be some one to keep him company, and there are several who fancy they can, even if the extra minute is annihilated. In some respects Peterson's sculling is very good, but he has a few very grave faults which will tell against him when he meets a man with force enough to rush him from the start, and stamina enough to row stroke for stroke with him over the course. While he is not in proper fix for a hard race, having been recently under the doctor's care, Sullivan is also comparatively untrained, and Griffin has had insufficient practice and will very likely find himself outclassed in such company. The boy sculls in better style than most of the Long Bridge men, but he lacks the weight. With ten or fifteen pounds to help him over a stiff course he would make a first class sculler, but it is very doubtful if an oarsman of his inches can get in the front rank. Watkins will come to the post in better trim than any man in the race, but will have a heavy contract on hand to keep Peterson, White or Sullivan company. Samuel is a very game and cool sculler, but he is troubled to a considerable extent with the "slows," and when it comes to a contest of good force and nerve pluck the fast man is very likely to give the plucky one his wash. In speculations on sculling matches one generally hears a great deal about the "gameness" of the race, but the result generally shows that pace is the great desideratum. Any man can be game when he finds himself drawing away from his opponent. Of course, it is not denied that gameness is an essential qualification for a sculler. A man who gets into his boat in fear and trembling had better stay on shore; but so may he if his sole reliance is on pluck. A good many game men have tried conclusions with Hanlon, but none of them have found that rowing a stern chase was a profitable business.

In this Fourth of July regatta it looks as if some of the scullers were arranging a fat contract for themselves, by entering in several races. One man is booked for four races, expecting, of course, that he will capture a few prizes. It is respectfully suggested to the Committee of Arrangements that, in the interest of rowing, the men who take part in the first class single scull race be debarred from competition in the wherry race. There are a number of young scullers on the bay who would gladly enter for the wherry race, and make a spirited contest if left to themselves, but who will either form the tail end of a procession if pitted against old scullers, or else will fail to come to the post. The Nautilus Club ought to push forward two entries for the wherry race, the Tritons and the Dolphins two or three, and the Ariel, Golden Gate and Pioneer Clubs four more. All these entries would be genuine junior scullers, and a competition between them would be lively and interesting. The barge race will bring the South End and Golden Gate crews into rivalry once more. The Pioneer Club has a new barge crew in training, with Captain Brannan stroke, Al Tobin sculler, H. Flynn forward waist, and Long bow. The Club is rather badly off for fast barges, and unless the crew can get a new boat before the Fourth, they will be shown the way over the course. The Dolphin and Triton Clubs will enter for the junior barge race, having an objection to competing with professionals, which is not generally shared by the other clubs. In fact, since the collapse of the Amateur Rowing Association, the regard for amateur rules has died out almost entirely, and among the better oarsmen it would be hard to find one who has not rowed for a money stake. It is somewhat significant, too, that the interest in rowing has greatly increased since the dismemberment of the Amateur Association. It would not be well to infer from this that an amateur association is undesirable. On the contrary, it is most desirable, but its management must be intelligent or liberal, or it will defeat the good object of its organization. The trouble with the Pacific Amateur Association was that its professed object was to place professional rowing, which was a grievous mistake, as there is no antagonism between the men who row for money stakes and those who row for mugs. The only thing necessary is to keep them apart, and let each row in his own class, and by such an arrangement advance and maintain the popularity of a most admirable pastime.

On the Standing of the Rowing Clubs on the Pacific Coast we have received many questions, especially in regard to the rules of all Eastern amateur rowing and athletic clubs. We would respectfully refer all questioners to some one of authority among the shells. So far as we can see, there is no particular and general restriction enforced in regard to the amateur standing of members of such clubs. Well known professional athletes are unhesitatingly elected to membership, and, after becoming members, are even encouraged to make matches for any amount of money, to be rowed Sundays, without any hint of its being for a prize, and pools and bets on the event are freely quoted several days in advance. Amateurs who have been disqualified by Athletic Associations should by all means join a Pacific Coast Rowing Club.

### THE LONG BRIDGE REGATTA.

The Executive Body of the Fourth of July Committee has proposed the following programme for the regatta on Tuesday next at Long Bridge:

First—Single shell race; first prize, $40; second, $20.
Second—Wherry; first prize, $30; second, $15.
Third—Four-oared shell; first prize, $50.
Fourth—Four-oared shell, laperseal; $30.
Fifth—Barge, for seniors; first prize, $40; second, $20.
Sixth—Barge, for juniors; first prize, $30; second, $15.
Seventh—Whitehall, double scull, 19 feet; first prize, $20; second, $10.
Eighth—Ships' boats, not over 24 feet; first prize, $25; second, $15.

Entries must be made at the rooms of the Committee, No. 235 Kearny street, not later than to-day, and are subject to the following conditions:

If not more than two boats enter for any one race, there shall be but one prize; and if only one entry, there shall be no race.

The single scull race will take place at 9 A. M., and all

other races at 12:30 P. M., or immediately after the procession. Judges, Captain Charles Nelson, Captain C. L. Dingley, M. Price. Referee, Charles Yale. A band will furnish music during the regatta.

## YACHTING.

Mr. P. Lorillard's steam yacht, Radha, is credited with a very high comparative speed. She has steamed seventeen miles an hour, and yet it is the opinion of all hands on board that what is in her has not been exhibited up to the present time. Since she was launched she has had three different propeller wheels, each of different types, and with each one has her speed been improved. At present her four-bladed screw, said to be an improvement on all former ones, is of a type made on the Hudson River, but a Philadelphia firm are now making a screw propeller for her that they claim will improve her speed. The steam yachting fraternity are much interested in the matter

There are four new steam yachts nearing completion in New York.

The new keel schooner Varuna, built at Noak, Conn., by G. L. Davoll, is 94 feet over all; 85 feet water line; 22 feet 6 inches beam; 10 feet deep, and 9 feet draught. She is owned by Mr. Geo. B. B. Hill, former owner of the Prospero. No expense has been spared in construction or outfit.

If anybody wants a fine, large, steel center-board, they will find it up on the Petaluma flats. The only trouble is the flats are wide and the board was not buoyed.

The sloop Ella, which was wrecked on Mare Island, a couple of weeks ago, is being repaired at San Quentin.

The Yacht Cruise.—The Yachts of the San Francisco Yacht Club leave to-day on a cruise up river.
The following orders have been issued by Commodore Harrison:

Yachts of the S. F. Y. C. will assemble at Front street wharf, previous to 8 P. M. on Saturday, July 1st, and at 2 P. M. sharp, the preparatory gun will fire, and five minutes later, the starting gun, when the fleet will get under way, and proceed to Martinez, anchoring outside of the line of the wharves.

On Sunday, at 11 A. M., the preparatory gun will fire, and five minutes later, the starting gun, when the fleet will get under way, and proceed to Antioch, making fast there alongside of each other at the wharf.

On Monday, at 6 A. M. the preparatory gun will fire, and five minutes later the starting gun, when yachts will get under way and proceed to Benicia, anchoring close to the steamboat wharf.

On Tuesday, July 4th, at 8 A. M., the fleet will dress ship. There will be a regatta while the fleet is at Benicia. At 2 P. M., the preparatory gun will fire, and five minutes later, the starting gun, when yachts will get under way and try rate of sailing to San Francisco.

On May 17, the steam yacht "Bandices" was launched from the works of Messrs. John Elder & Co., on the Clyde, for the head of the firm, Mr. William Pearce. The new yacht is 180 feet in length, 24 feet 3 inches beam, and 13 feet 11 inches deep (moulded), with a yacht measurement tonnage of 446. The new yacht, which is expected to be propelled at the rate of 15 knots per hour, is built of steel, and her engines are of the most recently improved type, having cylinders of 23 inches and 46 inches diameter by 2 feet 6 inches stroke, to indicate 660 horse-power. The boiler is to carry 110 lb. pressure, and is constructed with a shell of the best soft steel and corrugated furnaces. The propeller is of manganese bronze.

The Whitewing has had an accident with her board. The staple broke on the chain barrel and they lost the end of the chain. The board was a new one, heavier than that of the Chispa.

The Nellie will take Mr. Bowie, Mr. Harlow, Mr. Edgar, and several friends to Santa Cruz. She will stay in Monterey Bay about two weeks.

The sloop Nellie has gone on a three day's cruise up river.

Four gentlemen, three of them owners of yachts, have purchased the residence on the beach road, in the rear of the San Francisco Yacht Club at New Saucelito, and will fit it up as a private club house.

There is talk of a new yacht club, to be called the "California." There are to be no officers, and all the members are to have their own way, each one bossing his own boat, and having nothing to say about those of others; but, come to think of it, that is the way in all clubs. It is difficult to see the use of another yacht club in this bay, when the two now in existence are far from being in strong financial condition. There are a number of rich men belonging to them, but they do not make, unfortunately, rich clubs. The clubs owe their houses and are out of debt, but when entertainments are to be given, the club treasuries cannot be called upon to any extent. Charges have to be made or subscriptions given. With this condition of things, we think a third club seems not only unnecessary but possibly dangerous to the yachting interests of San Francisco.

The Fisherman's Regatta, at Benicia, promises to be an aquatic event of considerable interest. Mr. John Eckley, formerly Commodore of the San Francisco, who resides at his farm on Carquinez Straits, was the originator of the idea, and has done most in getting up the race and arranging the details. There are some 800 boats in the straits, bays and rivers, engaged in salmon fishing, and it is thought that from 150 to 200 of them will enter the race. Of course, there will be a great many collisions, and possibly, some capsizes. So large a fleet under way will, however, make a spectacle worth seeing. The race is comprised of boats engaged in salmon fishery, so it is, of course, and a "yachting" event, but the yacht fleet will, on its return from Antioch, remain a day in Carquinez Straits, and the yachtsmen will be on hand to see the fishermen race.

## MISTAKE.

The added money in the Winters Stake is $300 in place of $500, as it appears in the advertisement. This error came from using the old bill and over-looking the change that was made at a late meeting of the Trustees. At the same time the added money in the Pacific Cup was reduced from $1,000 to $600.

## THE RIFLE.

We are fortunate, indeed, in securing the valuable assistance of Dr. E. H. Pardee in this department, and feel that this addition to the force makes it invincible. Dr. Pardee will extend his communications through several numbers, showing the successive steps in progressing from the sling and bow to the latest improvements which make so terrible and effective a weapon of the modern rifle. There is not one more capable, having continued practice and study, joining field and target practice, and never suffering the most minute point to escape.

There is a fascination in shooting which none but the ardent sportsman can understand. Apart from the fierce excitement in the pursuit of the larger species of game, there is the satisfaction of excelling in target practice, and even the mere "shooting at a mark" alone, and with the stimulus of excelling previous efforts, is a pleasure. The rifle plays an important part in the sports of the Pacific Coast. The grizzly and cinnamon bears, more to be feared than the "man-eaters" of India, the California tiger, the panther, the buffalo, elk, deer, antelope, &c., gain a field for the use of the single bullet which no other country can equal. California has developed talent at the butts which ranks with the foremost of the world, and altogether the columns under the caption of "The Rifle" will be of exceeding interest.

### ANCIENT AND MODERN ARMS.

MR. EDITOR:—As we turn over the pages of ancient history, we find from the earliest ages of the world, a proneness, a disposition of mankind, to disagree, which not only holds good in the individual, but communities have risen against communities, and nation against nation, resulting in bloody war. While it is not in the province of this article to speak of the causes of the sanguinary conflicts, it will be but proper to speak of war as a science, and the ingenuity of man to invent the most deadly instruments for the destruction of his fellow-men. Arms, therefore, may be regarded to mean every imaginable weapon that the ingenuity of man could contrive both for defensive and offensive, for "self-preservation" in all ages has been regarded "the first law of nature." And the great study of the civil engineer, is to invent some method in developing the ruling passion to injure, slaughter and kill, while remaining himself in comparative safety.

The first weapons that were recognized in the infancy of the world were the "sling" and the "bow," which in those primitive days were manipulated with such wonderful precision, and power, that large armies was decimated, until the dieing and the dead, upon the battlefield in many places would be as thick as sardines in a box, and the earth saturated and fertilized with human blood. The sling and bow were the recognized weapons, for centuries, when the fertile brain of some inventive genius introduced the battleax, the spear, the sword, and javalins, as auxiliaries to the sling and bow, and were used with terrible slaughter in close engagements.

The biblical account of the tragical death of Goliath, with a stone from the brook, only proves that David was a "dead shot," and that Goliath had understood the ability of the young chieftain boy, in the art and essence of trajector, ies as practiced in those antiquated days.

From authentic and reliable sources we are led to believe that an immense force was given to the stone from the sling, and with a precision that to us appears almost incredible, and can only be equaled or excelled by our system of modern gunnery. Leaden balls were used as projectiles, and the account given by Seneca of their great velocity appears to be fabulous, for even with our modern gunnery no theory has ever been advanced whereby the leaden missile is melted by the atmospheric friction in its passage through the air. And, I think, if the spirit of Seneca could be communicated with by some man of the present day who understands the principles and laws of gunnery, he could be made to see that his philosophy when in the flesh was false, and would be glad to issue a contradiction of his former statement, and say that no sling could impart sufficient power to a leaden ball whereby its great force and velocity through the atmosphere would cause it to become so heated by friction that it would fuse and melt.

The strongest advocates and the greatest experts in the use of the sling is given to the Phœnicians, or the inhabitants of the Balearic Islands, where it was regarded by all classes and sexes one of the necessary accomplishments, and their fame in the use of the sling became universally acknowledged, which grew up from a spirit of emulation and assiduity in its use. The children of the Island, in the sling days, were not allowed breakfast until they struck the food, which was perched upon the top of a high pole, with a stone from a sling. Like the man digging after the woodchuck, he had to get him, as he had no meat for breakfast. I will dismiss the sling by saying, like many men, it outlived its usefulness, and the last account we have of it as an instrument of war was in the Huguenot campaign in 1572.

The bow dates back in the dimness of the past to remote antiquity, and the first account given of it may be found in the 61st chapter of Genesis and 20th verse, when the ruler in speaking of Ishmael, says: "And God was with the lad, and he grew and dwelt in the wilderness, and he became an archer."

History tells us some remarkable and almost incredible stories regarding the abilities of the bygone expert archers. And not being very credulous myself, I must confess I feel a little sensitive about taking the dose, though I am free to admit that the general shape and contour of the arrow is much better fitted to pass through the atmosphere with less resistance than the old spherical ball; but with all that advantage, when we compare the power of a man's arm to that of the expansive power of gas produced from the combustion of gunpowder, the argument is like the handle of a jug, all on one side. And in some future article I will endeavor to give the power and quantity of gas generated from one hundred grains of rifle powder; the result of which will be almost incredible to those who have never given the subject thought and attention. History is prolific with Roman and Grecian authority in giving detailed accounts of this little engine of war, which, if true (and who can doubt history) the battles fought during the existence of the Roman Republic were more sanguinary and bloody than those fought with our more modern implements of war. But when history tells me that battles have been fought with the crossbow at 700 yards, I must confess that our archery clubs here are but lilliputians in their feeble attempt to cope with the brown-arm, scar-worn veteran of the bow one thousand years ago.

[To be continued.]

### SNAP SHOOTING.

About three years ago, Colonel Horace Fletcher, of San Francisco, published a pamphlet of about forty pages, entitled "The A B C of Snap Shooting," in which the author advocated a method of practice with rifles of 22-caliber at moving globes, as the simplest, quickest and most economical method of acquiring proficiency in shooting.

The "A B C" met with immediate favor with the most practical shots in this country and Europe, where it went, particularly the officers of the Regular Army, and the United States Cartridge Company acquired the right of publication and distributed thousands of copies gratuitously.

Numbers of examples of splendid results from this practice having come to our knowledge, we propose to devote space occasionally to notice of this branch of sport.

Col. Fletcher has promised contributions on the subject, which will be valuable to those interested in learning to shoot.

An English gentleman who has lived in Germany much of his life, and who won no less than a dozen first prizes at different rifle meetings in Germany, Austria and Switzerland last season, in two of which more than eight thousand riflemen competed, writes to say, that all his skill with both rifle and pistol was acquired in two seasons by following the course prescribed by Col. Fletcher in the "A B C," and he expresses the opinion that his acquisition of skill was due to the method, and not to the man, because, at beginning, he was as clumsy as possible for any one to be.

There is undoubtedly a one-two-three method of practice which is applicable to shooting, as there is to everything else, and which, if followed as prescribed, will unravel the difficulty of learning as easily as the practice of the scales in music will take the kinks out of clumsy fingers.

Perfect acquaintance and sympathy is necessary between the gun, muscles and eye, which can be acquired in one-tenth the time, and at one-tenth the expense, by using the minimum caliber of rifle in a systematic manner.

We would be very glad to receive communications from gentlemen who practice snap shooting with the rifle.

Deer shooting, to-day, marks the opening of the deer shooting season, and many an enthusiastic hunter, spread before his camp-fire built on mountain sides, anxiously awaited last night the coming of dawn. Deer this year are plentiful throughout the State, and residents of few cities in the world possess such opportunities as San Franciscans to enjoy the pleasures of deer hunting without the loss of much time. A four-hours' ride from this city will take them to ground where the game can be had.

Deer are quite plenty on the hills near Pescadero, San Mateo County, and as soon as the season opens hunters hope for big hauls of fine game. A farmer saw a bind of five deer in his grain field a few evenings ago.

## TRAP AND WING.

### THE ALAMEDA CLUB.

The muster of the Alameda County Sportsman's Club at Bird's Point, on Saturday last, was not so large in numbers as had been generally expected. The chief event was the match at 10 birds, 21 yards rise, State Sportsman's Association rules, in which the high wind and the good flyers so bothered the shooters that on the average the birds beat the guns. Following is the score:

| | | | | | | | | | | | |
|---|---|---|---|---|---|---|---|---|---|---|---|
| A. W. Havens..... | 1 | 0 | 0 | *0 | 1 | 1 | 1 | 0 | 0 | 1—5 |
| W. W. Mosehll..... | 1 | 1 | 0 | 1 | 1 | *0 | 0 | 1 | 1—5 |
| E. E. Bell..... | 0 | 0 | 1 | 1 | 0 | 0 | 1 | 0 | 0 | 0—3 |
| J. G. Edwards..... | 1 | 0 | 0 | 0 | 0 | 1 | 1 | 1 | 1—5 |
| Wm. McCHnary*..... | 0 | 1 | 1 | 0 | 1 | 1 | 1 | 1 | 1—7 |
| C. Tuttle..... | 0 | 1 | 1 | 1 | *0 | 1 | 1 | 1 | 0—6 |
| Besser Prince..... | 1 | 0 | 0 | 0 | 1 | 1 | 1 | 0 | 0—5 |
| West..... | 0 | 1 | 1 | 1 | *0 | 0 | 0 | 0—4 |
| Mayhew..... | 0 | 1 | 1 | 0 | 1 | 1 | 1 | 0 | 1—8 |

*Shot out of bounds.

There being a tie between Messrs. Tuttle and Mayhew, they shot off at five singles, and the former gentleman was the victor, killing three out of five. There was then a five-bird match at 26 yards, in which Mr. Havens was the winner by a clean score, and this was followed by two other matches on the same terms, in which Messrs. Adams and Galindo divided the honors. There were some speculative matches shot between individual members, and some contests on the freeze out principle, and it was only when darkness set in that the five irons were relegated to their cases, and the members and visitors returned to their homes.

### THE CALIFORNIA CLUB.

On Sunday last there was a contest for the several trophies of this club, represented by three medals. There were thirteen entries, and, as will be seen, the shooting was close and exciting to the finish. The conditions were twelve birds at twenty-one yards rise, under the California Club rules, and the score was as follows:

| | | | | | | | | | | | | | |
|---|---|---|---|---|---|---|---|---|---|---|---|---|---|
| J. Burns..... | 1 | 1 | 1 | 1 | 0 | 1 | 1 | 0 | 1 | 1 | 1 | 0—9 |
| D. Barwise..... | 1 | 1 | 1 | 1 | 0 | 1 | 1 | 1 | 0 | 1 | 0—9 |
| A. Held..... | 1 | 1 | 1 | 1 | 1 | 1 | 1 | 1 | 1 | 1 | 1—10 |
| Dr. Slade..... | 1 | 0 | 1 | 1 | 1 | 1 | 1 | 1 | 1 | 1—10 |
| Dr. Hays..... | 1 | 0 | 1 | 1 | 0 | 1 | 1 | 1 | 0 | 1 | 1—9 |
| J. F. Jackett..... | 1 | 1 | 0 | 1 | 1 | 1 | 1 | 0 | 1 | 1—10 |
| C. Robinson..... | 0 | 0 | 0 | 1 | 1 | 1 | 1 | 0 | 0 | 0—6 |
| S. E. Knowles..... | 0 | 1 | 0 | 1 | 1 | 1 | 1 | 1 | 1—11 |
| F. A. Pembton..... | 1 | 1 | 1 | 1 | 1 | 1 | 1 | 1 | 1—11 |
| J. Held..... | 1 | 0 | 1 | 1 | 1 | 0 | 1 | 1 | 1—9 |
| H. F. Bogart..... | 1 | 0 | 0 | 1 | 1 | 1 | 0 | 1 | 1—0 |
| O. W. W. Rocke..... | 1 | 1 | 1 | 1 | 1 | 1 | 1 | 1—11 |
| H. Chisnore..... | 1 | 0 | 0 | 1 | 0 | 0 | 1 | 1 | 1—9 |
| C. Robinson..... | 1 | 1 | 1 | *0 | 1 | 1 | 1 | 1—11 |

*Shot out of bounds.

A match of four doubles was next shot, with the following result:

| | | | |
|---|---|---|---|
| Dr. Hays..... | 10 | 11 | 10—8 |
| Jackett..... | 10 | 11 | 11—7 |
| Robinson..... | 10 | 11 | 11—7 |
| Pinton..... | 10 | 10 | 11—7 |
| Burns..... | 11 | 10 | 11—8 |
| Bogart..... | 11 | 10 | 11—8 |
| Chismore..... | 11 | 11 | 11—8 |
| Loan..... | 11 | 00 | 11—6 |
| Weeks..... | 11 | 11 | 11—8 |

Dr. Chismore and T. Weeks divided first and second money, the ties on seven kills taking the fragments.

A match at six birds for three prizes—$33 50, $19 50 and $13—followed. J. A. A. Robinson and P. Welch divided first and second money, and Roche and C. Robinson divided third.

Several other matches followed, the shooting lasting until daylight gave way. The best contested match was the last one, at five birds, Huntingham rules, resulting in clean scores for all competitors, as follows:

| | | | | | | |
|---|---|---|---|---|---|---|
| Bogart..... | 1 | 1 | 1 | 1—5 |
| Roche..... | 1 | 1 | 1 | 1—5 |
| Loan..... | 1 | 1 | 1 | 1—5 |
| Frech..... | 1 | 1 | 1 | 1—5 |
| Weeks..... | 1 | 1 | 1 | 1—5 |
| Walsh..... | 1 | 1 | 1 | 1—5 |
| Pinton..... | 1 | 1 | 1 | 1—5 |
| Robinson..... | 1 | 1 | 1 | 1—5 |

In the off-shoot at two birds four fell out, leaving the contest between Messrs. Pinson and Robinson, which resulted in favor of Mr. Robinson.

The Occidental Club held their first meeting at South San Francisco, on Saturday. The match was at clay pigeons, and terminated in a victory for F. J. Walsh, who scored 9 out of 12, thus winning the gold medal. F. Miller took second prize, with a score of 8.

The Ligowsky Flying Clay Pigeon and Trap form an excellent substitute for pigeons, both in practice and in match shooting. The trap is of very ingenious device, and the pigeon is light pottery clay, weighing about 1¼ ounce, which on being thrown by the spring, imitates exactly the flight of that bird. There are many features in these imitations that will recommend them to the popular favor, the chief one being that it enables a person to become a crack shot on the wing without the expensive use of pigeons. Pierce & Co., 1209 Broadway, Oakland, are the sole agents for the Pacific Coast, and from them circulars, containing all necessary information, can be obtained.

## FISH.

Mr. Horace C. Ladd, of the W. U. Telegraph Co., is about starting on a three weeks fishing trip to Gualala River.

Last Sunday Messrs. Green and Sellers caught 525 trout from the San Lorenzo creek, Santa Cruz county, Mr. Green catching 300 of them.

On Sunday last, the Cyante creek, Santa Cruz county, yielded a number of trout to aspiring anglers. Mr. Swan caught 100, Mr. Mastick 37, Mr. Reynolds 35, Mr. Sloane 85, and Mr. Mastick 83.

Mr. Fred. A. Walton, of Novarro River, Mendocino county, was in this city recently for a few days. Fred. is acknowledged to be one of the best handlers of a rod on the coast.

Mr. Fred. S. Butler, who used to be an enthusiastic angler, has hung up his rod for several seasons past because the fish he caught did not bend it enough. He wants pounds, not ounces. We all like big fish, but we cannot all walk, like Fred. is doing, for them to grow.

Eugene Gaylord and T. W. Sigorney, of Nevada City, have been up on a fishing excursion to Bowman's dam.

Wm. Magee and Mr. Johnson, while on a fishing trip on the Mokelumne river, above West Point, saw a bear and succeeded in killing it.

Several large carp were caught in Butte creek the other day.

The Butte Record has reports of 16-inch trout having been caught in two-inch streams. At that rate trout fishing ought to be pretty good up in that region.

Some 1700 pounds of trout were shipped from Truckee to San Francisco, one day last week. The trout were all from Tahoe.

It does not follow that because a fly does well in a creek on a certain day, the same fly will always succeed there. Lots of time is sometimes wasted trying to make trout take flies they don't like. And a hard thing to coax is a trout. After a man has tried an hour or two unsuccessfully it is time to try a new color, and keep on experimenting until the "killer" is found.

The case of S. P. Taylor, who was convicted of failure to provide a fish ladder at his dam, in Paper Mill Creek, will undoubtedly be appealed. It is hoped that the decision of the lower Court will be sustained.

Governor Perkins, ex-Governor Booth, Hon B. B. Redding, President Reed, of the State University, and James McClatchy, editor of the Sacramento Bee, will spend the Fourth of July fishing on the McCloud River.

W. W. Taylor is rusticating at Lake Tahoe, but will soon leave for his favorite fishing grounds, Weber and Independence lakes. He sent fifty fish to this city on Monday last from Tahoe. They ran from one-half to three pounds in weight.

That enthusiastic fisherman, Bill Battams, has got a holiday at last—the first two weeks in over twenty years. True to his instincts, he left for Weber and Independence lakes on Saturday last.

Messrs. Green, Ziegler and Searles leave to-day for Salmon Creek, Sonoma County, to remain until the fifth inst. These same well-known fishermen took twenty-six fish from this stream early in the season. The fish are reported now as taking the fly readily, and affording royal sport.

The Los Gatos Creek, Santa Clara County, is well supplied with fish this year, and of good size. Mr. Wilcox, Superintendent of the San Jose Water Works, caught forty in a morning's fishing, five of them weighing a pound each. W. D. Tisdale, Cashier of the Farmer's and National Bank of San Jose, caught fourteen punds of the speckled beauties in one day. J. C. Harvey, of San Jose, also caught one hundred and thirty-one in one day's fishing. J. W. Ainsworth, of San Francisco, who has been stopping at Alma the past week fishing city for enough to supply his table, averaged thirty a day, working the stream about two hours each morning. The best part of the stream lies between Wright's and Alma. The Los Gatos Creek is one of the finest in the State, and easy of access. Its many ripples, fine holes and clear space for fly casting, invite the admiring disciple of Izaak, as the train whirls him along its banks, to streams more remote and less worthy of his attention.

That portion of the St. Helena Creek passing through Pope Valley, Napa County, abounds with trout this season. Some fine creels are reported to have been made by visi. from St. Helena.

## THE KENNEL.

### FIELD DOGS IN CALIFORNIA.

A few years ago, when gold hunting was the leading pursuit in this State, few men cared for the pleasures of the field. Mining was such an uncertain business, that most of those who followed it demanded for recreation something in the nature of gregarious hilarity. The race track, theaters and saloons were resorted to most frequently for amusement. When commerce, agriculture, vine culture, fine stock-raising and kindred industries began to assume respectable proportions, a taste for field sports was more generally cultivated, until, I think, I am safe in saying that ten sportsmen are afield now on any general holiday to where there was one ten years ago.

With the desire for field sports came the desire for the best of field accoutrements, for Californians never like to be outdone in anything they undertake, and they have to-day probably as fine guns as the sportsmen of any other State.

Next to the gun, in order of importance, comes the sportsman's best and dearest friend, his dog.

I know that all sportsmen will agree with me when I say that a day spent in upland shooting (and it is of this kind that I shall speak) without a staunch, good-nosed dog, would be very unsatisfactory and lonesome work. Upland shooting requires more physical exertion than any other sort, and for that reason is to be most recommended to gentlemen following sedentary pursuits; it also requires more skill in both master and dog.

Let me say to any young sportsman who is going to hunt quail, and that is the *ne plus ultra* of hunting, that he had better not waste time and money breaking or having broke a *cold blooded* dog. I tell you, it requires the stamina and courage of the blue blood to travel for eight or ten hours on a hot September day.

There are two breeds of dogs, viz: the setter and pointer, which, if pure bred, may be depended on to stand up to the rack if in condition.

Of the two breeds I prefer the former, although the latter requires the least water when hunting.

There are three prominent breeds of setters, which I will name, as I think, in the order of their merits—the English, Irish and Scotch, or Scotch setter.

I prefer the setter to the pointer for the reason that the former has far more pluck, style, generally more speed, and is much more affectionate.

If one wants to take a day at fowl or snipe shooting, the setter is better fitted by Nature to stand the water, though he should never be used to any great extent in the water, as that will give him rheumatism and other diseases. If the sportsman hunts most of the time for water fowl, the best dog for him is an Irish water spaniel.

In a country where game is extremely abundant, a person would probably get as large a bag without as with a dog, but, sincerely, I would sooner kill one bird from a staunch, handsome "point" than to fire into a flock and kill a dozen. I don't think that there is anything that equals in point of beauty, barring a beautiful woman and a thoroughbred horse, a handsome setter pointing. No artist that ever lived can reproduce the expression, poise and attitude of the animal. I have seen sketches by artists of world-wide reputations, and I have never yet seen one that did half justice to the subject. I have seen men tremble all over with excitement on seeing a dog on point, and be so pleased and carried away with pleasure at this evidence of breeding and nose that they could almost hug their pet.

We in this State are fast acquiring a fine lot of thoroughbred. There is not in the only sort (thoroughbred) a gentleman should own of any breed. It don't cost any more to feed such a one than it does to feed a cur.

It may cost from twenty to fifty dollars to secure a fine puppy, but after you once own a thoroughbred, my word for it, you will never waste time on a mongrel.

When I say thoroughbred, I don't mean a dog said to be by somebody's dog out of somebody else's bitch, and above all things, deliver me from a dog that has been "stolen from off an English ship." That dog is ubiquitous, he is a dog of fabulous imaginary value, he is possibly descended from Royal ancestors; covered with canine glory, but I prefer to patronize some reputable dog breeder, pay a good price for a dog whose pedigree is unquestioned, break him myself, for that is not a heroicless task, but, on the contrary, to me a pleasure, so that when I go to the field I know I have a companion who is intelligent and "game," who will stay by me from sun to sun, and do his part in making the day pleasant and securing a fair bag of game.

It is not generally known outside of a small coterie that the breeding of sporting dogs has become a scientific business. Nor is it generally known that large sums of money are invested in kennels of dogs.

Mr. A. H. Moore, of Philadelphia, in the neighborhood of twenty thousand dollars so invested, and the following gentlemen have from two to ten thousand dollars laid out in similar enterprises: J. C. Goodsell, Brooklyn, N. Y.; Mr. Snellenburg, New Brighton, Penn.; J. O. Higgins, Wilmington, Del.; John Boine, Wooster, Ohio, and G. W. Campbell, Tennessee. The St. Louis Kennel Club, composed of wealthy gentlemen, residents of that city, have disbanded, the members retaining such dogs as they desired for their own use and disposing of the rest. They imported from England at least ten thousand dollars' worth of pointers. "Faust," who stood at the head of their stud, cost $1,500. Their other stud dog, Bow, cost $900. Mr. Goodsell refused $1,000 for his Llewellin setter puppy, Plantagenet, 14 months old, after he had run in the Eastern Field Trials last fall. Countess Bear, the dam of Mr. Llewellin's cracks, Dashing Bondhu, Dashing Beauty and Burgess Dashing Berwyn, was imported to this country from Mr. Llewellin's kennels in England by the Montview K. Club. When that association dissolved she was advertised for sale at $750, and as soon as Mr. Llewellin received that information he cabled across the Atlantic and claimed her at that price. He has since taken her back to England to add more bench and field prize winners to the long list already produced by the incomparable strain of setters that bear his name. This same gentlemen paid $1,650 for Dash II, the sire of the three pups I named from Countess Bear. He also refused

Mr. Moore's offer of $3,750 for his great winner Count Wind'em. Nor is it generally known what rich stakes are contended for in the Eastern States every year at field trials. Mr. Sanborn's Llewellin setter Count Noble, by Count Wind'em out of Nora, won first, $435, and Daisy Laverack second, $290, in the Derby of 1880, at Vincennes, Ind.

You see, dear reader, that dogs cost and represent money, and when a gentleman who owns a fine bitch and has paid, possibly $50, to have her warded to a suitable mate, charges a reasonable price for her puppies, don't elevate your nose in a contemptuous manner and say, "Nice fellow; wants money for a dog!" for dog-breeding is just as honorable and becomes any gentleman just as much as horse or cattle breeding, and I apprehend that no one would think of going to Governor Stanford, or any other breeder, and asking him to give them a colt, or a calf, as the case might be. I have heard some talk of a Bench Show in San Francisco this fall, and hope that one will be held and conducted so as to make it a success.

The Gilroy Rod and Gun Club are going to hold a Field Trial in October, and have selected grounds near that place for it. A number of owners of good dogs throughout the State object to meeting the Gilroy dogs right at home, and Folsom and Vacaville have been suggested as better places. I think Folsom the best place that could be selected, and if the Gilroy Club cannot be induced to change the location of their trials I suggest that the Folsom Sportsman's Club hold a Field Trial there any way. I think they could count on twenty entries at least. Let those interested in these matters come forward and through your columns give expression to their opinions.     C. N. Post.

Sacramento, June 25, 1882.

### COURSING IN CALIFORNIA.

Before many years have elapsed, coursing is destined to hold a rank second to none among the field sports of California. One of the most ancient of all pastimes, and the especial sport of Greece and Rome, it has vastly improved both in practice and popularity, until to-day it is chief among all the field sports in England and Ireland. In the second century of the Christian era Arrian published a defense of coursing. Oppian, in the Cynegetics, attributes to Pollux the practice of the chase with dogs about 200 years after the Levitical law was made. A greyhound was the especial pet and inseparable companion of Alcibiades. Alexander the Great built a city in honor of a greyhound, and the Emperor Hadrian declared solemn rites and sacrifices to another for his endurance and sagacity. The *celeres*, the dogs of speed, as greyhounds of all kinds were classed in contradistinction to the *pugnaces* (fighting) and *sagaces* (intelligent), who used cunning to capture their prey, were originally from the Celtic nations. The vertragi, *canes celeres*, or dogs that hunted by sight alone, are spoken of by Zenophon as Celtic novelties, just introduced into Greece. So it may fairly be presumed that the earlier greyhounds possessed nose, as well as sight and speed. It is not the intention of this article to enter further into the ancient history of the greyhound, and the above facts are simply given to show that the oldest sports are popular to-day, and that coursing, like horse racing, is as ancient as it is popular. The modifications made in the sport since it was first made a pastime instead of an ignorant savage's means of obtaining food, are but few and extremely simple. The early Norman kings found the greyhound in England, and used him for their sport. The race between the dog and his quarry was all the sport they needed, until at last a rivalry sprang up between gentlemen as to who owned the gamest and fleetest dog, and some rude rules to guide the judges were first introduced. These prevailed, with more or less local alterations, until the reign of Queen Elizabeth, when good old Thomas, Duke of Norfolk, at the special request of the virgin Queen, drew up a set of rules for the better determination of coursing matches. These rules, with some very trifling additions instead of respecting nominations for stakes, are precisely the same as are in vogue to-day, and control the great match for the Waterloo Cup, as well as all coursing matches in England, Australia and California. On all the vast Continent of America, in all parts of which hare or jack rabbits are plentiful and coursing grounds unexcelled, the State of California alone possesses coursing clubs, and here alone is the sport of coursing carried on.

Officers stationed at the Presidio have from time to time taken a few greyhounds from this State to the great northwestern plains, but no further attempt has ever been made to introduce this noble sport among that class of people. General Custer got his celebrated greyhound from Captain Lord, who, when stationed here, procured a brace of pups from Tom Tunstead, one of the most active members of the old Pioneer Club. Of the original founders of the sport of coursing in California, where it has from the very first been carried on according to rule, but few are left. Prominent among them is Clem Dixon, by no means young in years, but a very boy for sport and his love for the unrestrained fun of a meet in the country. Clem may fairly be said to be the father of coursing in America, being the first man who ever slipped a pair of dogs and judged a race in the State of California. What the sport is here to-day, is more owing to the enthusiastic efforts of Clem Dixon than of any other man.

By purchase and importation, he, with others, has improved the breed of greyhounds in this State until they are not only the equal of any in the world, but are superior in point of bottom and endurance to any that can be brought from the British Isles. Since the importation of Franklin's old blue dog Speculation—a winner in several English matches—by Captain Bingham, no dog has been brought to this coast capable of improving the breed, or in any way excelling the dogs already here. When Speculation arrived, a new stain was needed to mix with the blood of Underwriter, Factor, Cartwright, Thornhill and Jones, who were then dominating all the kennels in the State. By good fortune Speculation was just the needed cross, and to-day every coursing-match shows one or more winners who trace their lineage back to the old blue dog. To tell of the past and gone glories of California coursing matches at Merced, and Livermore, and Banban, and Ellis, and Benicia, and Sacramento, and Stockton, and Folsom, would fill a paper as large as a blanket and having as many pages as Webster's Dictionary. It warms one's heart and makes one long for the cool days of early winter, when the dogs will once more wake up the lazy shepherds on the Ruy Blas, to call to mind the fearful leap of Quicksilver, the like of which was never made before or since by any animal, the three successive victories of Tom Tunstead's pet Minnehaha, and her final defeat by Ruler. How the writer's hand trembles, and his blood grows turgid with in-

dignation when he calls to mind the sad fate of the three time victor, by poison administered by a callous beast in human shape, whom it were base and fulsome flattery to call a smuggler, and upon whose ignoble head may the scorching curses of all good sportsmen rest. It makes one long for the leash once more when he thinks of the deeds of Kitty Clover, Jennie, the lordly Monarch, Paul Jones, Pride of the Canyon and her son, Chief of the Canyon, old Thornhill, Master Joe, and a hundred others whose names do not as readily come to mind. The game of that plucky son of California, McGrath, who, less than two years ago, lay down to die of exhaustion on the plains of Merced, beside the hare whose speed had cost him his life, is a theme better fitted for the poet or novelist than for the prosaic writer on sports, who occasionally contributes to the papers.

Coursing in California is not confined to any particular spot or section. It is becoming general, owing to the efforts of the several clubs, whose membership rolls include most of the ardent coursers in the State. Six years ago there was only one club worth mentioning—the Pioneer Club—now there are many.

The Pacific Coast Coursing Club is really an offshoot from the old Pioneer Club, and was formed by a few gentlemen who left the parent organization because they thought it was not sufficiently progressive. At the time of its organization the club decided that all the matches held under its auspices should be decided by three judges, and has enforced this rule ever since. In this respect the club is unique, for the law all over the world is one judge, and only one. The members of the club find that the rule works well, and so far have shown no disposition to go back to the old plan of letting one judge decide the matches.

Next in age, though by no means second to any other in strength and importance, is the California Coursing Club, formed last year. This young organization has shown a surprising amount of life and vigor, and bids fair to outstrip its older competitors unless they bestir themselves.

The youngest club in the city is the Occidental Coursing Association, which owes its existence to the efforts of D. L. Levy.

Outside of San Francisco, the Capital Coursing Club, of Sacramento, is the oldest organization devoted to the noble sport of coursing.

The Stockton Coursing Club comes next, while the Folsom Club, Willows Coursing Club, San Jose Club, Alameda Club, Santa Rosa Club, Winters Club, Galt Club and several others are about coequal in the date of formation.

All of the San Francisco clubs hold an open meeting in the Spring of the year, generally at Merced, and a club meeting, for members' dogs only, in the Fall. Generally from twenty-four to thirty-two is the size of the stake, and the prizes run for, about $200 in money and plate. These matches are generally attended by several hundred people, in spite of the distance from home at which they are held. They have been so often described that little need be said about them here. The plains of Merced cannot be equalled as a coursing ground by any place in the world. This phrase may seem vain and meaningless, but it is strictly in accordance with the truth. The writer has seen the hare at Altcar and the pen at Plumpton, as well as the best known coursing grounds in Australia, and has never seen a place where both hare, dogs and spectators, had so good a show as at Merced.

In a future number the present state of California kennels and the records of a few of the old heroes of the leash will be spoken of.

### THAT COURSING TOURNAMENT.

The Occidental Coursing Association, by Mr. D. L. Levy, advertises a "grand coursing tournament, to take place at the Half Mile Track, on July 2d and 3d." The circular speaks of England's choicest sport being brought to the doors of the people, and mentions the fact that a number of trapped hares have been procured from the plains of Auburn and Merced. It also announces that the great Baron Waldken and Tempete will compete for $500 a side. There are so many things about this so-called tournament which do not commend it to the esteem of sportsmen, that we had almost decided to let the affair go by default, and merely state that it would simply be a miserable travesty upon the sport which it pretended to represent. It occurs to us, however, that the non-sporting reporters of the daily press, who, with few exceptions, are not familiar with coursing, will not be likely to put the affair in its true light, and that to prevent people from gaining an incorrect idea of a noble sport, it is our duty to go more fully into the matter. The projector of the enterprise may be, and doubtless is, desirous of providing the public with a certain amount of amusement in exchange for the gate money he will receive, but it is utterly impossible for him to keep his word and show the public a coursing match. Again, the match between Baron Waldken and Tempete is not a bona fide affair, in that the stake is not put up as alleged, and further, no man not an idiot would back a dog in the condition in which Waldken appears on the streets for 500 cents, let alone 500 dollars. This match is regarded by all coursing men as simply a bait to catch spectators, and they object vigorously to have the sport they admire burlesqued by one who does not understand the difference between a "wrench" and a "turn." Trapped hares will not and cannot run, and Mr. Levy will find that the dogs entered, poor in condition, as they all will be, will gobble up his Auburn and Merced hares as quickly as they would as many cotton-tail rabbits. Even if the hares would run, the confined limits of the race track are dangerous to the dogs and death to the hares, who should at least be accorded what every sportsman gives his game—a chance for its life. If Mr. Levy called his affair a hare-killing match and took down that sign about a match, for $500 a side, the matter would concern no one but the public, who paid to see it, and the Society for the Prevention of Cruelty to Animals, but so long as he has chosen to dignify it with the name of a sport that it only burlesques, it becomes our unpleasant task to protect the sport of coursing from the disgrace about to be thrust upon it.

### CLEVELAND BENCH SHOW.

Cleveland has just closed its first dog show, held under the auspices of the Cleveland Bench Show Association, so San Francisco dog fanciers can proudly point to the fact that in the matter of dog shows this city is far from being ahead of the city of Cleveland. The Cleveland Bench Show was a grand success financially, in which respect it cuts out a trifle ahead of those held in this city. Eight thousand persons paid admission during the week the show was open. The show was managed by Charles Lincoln, the Secretary of the Westminster Kennel Club, and in spite of his good sense and tact, left behind the usual amount of heart-burning and kicking on the part of the losers. Setters were well represented, as were also most of the different types of field dogs, but in the fancy classes, in which this city excels, Cleveland made but a poor showing. The greyhounds were poorly represented and few in number, and the same may be said of the mastiffs, St. Bernards, Newfoundlands, collies and field dogs. The show of toy terriers was also poor and small. A Mexican hairless dog which won the first prize in the miscellaneous class at the last San Francisco dog show, obtained a precisely similar honor at Cleveland.

## LAVERACKS AND LLEWELLINS.

The verbal fight between the champions of the Laverack and Llewellin setters is raging with great force in the East and in England. Llewellin, Arnold, Burgess, E. A. Herrberg and a dozen other well posted gentlemen, are now in the fight, and fairly fill the sporting papers with arguments and assertions. The question of field qualities is an important point, and if some of the readers of the BREEDER will favor us with their experience of the relative work done by these two breeds in this State, valuable information will be added to the large fund already gathered by this discussion.

## ANSWERS TO CORRESPONDENTS.

Under this head will be found replies to all questions that may be of the Kennel Editor in relation to breaking, breeding, or enforcing dogs, feeding or curing them of any ordinary disease. Correspondents must state plainly what are the peculiar symptoms of the malady for which they seek advice, and in all cases, especially when desiring to know the best way to correct a dog of a fault, must be careful to state the age and sex. No answers will be sent by mail and all questions must be marked Kennel—Editor WEEKLY BREEDER AND SPORTSMAN, San Francisco, Cal.

A few questions have already been received, to which answers will be found below:

GEORGE, SAN JOSE.—Sore and inflamed feet. If neglected, are liable to become a bad ... [illegible] ... and too ... [illegible]

C. F., SAN FRANCISCO.—No case of rabies has ever yet been heard of in the State of California. Cats and other animals are sometimes afflicted with rabies in England and in the Eastern states. The disease is liable to be imported here at any time. Statistics prove that only about one in thirty persons bitten by rabid dogs suffer fatal consequences. As all rabid dogs, unless in an extremely scarce and late disease, and frequently the symptoms of poisoning are mistaken for rabies. In nearly twenty-five years' experience with dogs, seventeen of which were spent in England, the writer has only seen one genuine case of rabies, though he has seen fifty dogs slaughtered under the supposition that they had hydrophobia, when the fact is that they had nothing of the kind.

H. J. W., SAN FRANCISCO.—Mix. Area, freshly powdered, is thought to be a specific cure for all except rage worms, and will remove even them in many cases.

## BICYCLING.

This most exhilarating amusement, although of but recent date in its present improved form, has grown with such rapidity, that it fairly overshadows all other athletic sports. The reason is apparent in the ease with which it is mastered, and the large proportionate return, in speed and distance traversed, for the comparatively small outlay of strength. The ease of motion, consciousness of power, and the perfect independence of the rider, render it a most fascinating sport to those who have the patience to master it, and are not too indolent or timid or any moderate exertion. For its being [illegible] perfectly smooth road, like that of a park, may be considered essential, although it may be questioned if the monotony would not in time tire the rider more than a variety of hill and dale, with occasional irregularities, requiring greater watchfulness.

So much has been written about it, that it is hardly necessary now to go into its history at length. Suffice it to say that, from the clumsy device of a hundred years ago, having two slow wheels, united by a perch, with a saddle, upon which the operator could all but propel himself by striking his feet against the ground at intervals, the development has been gradual. The addition of cranks to the driving wheel, and the riveting of this wheel so that the machine could be turned, was made in 1866 by a Frenchman, and from this grew the velocipede of a dozen years ago. The machine yet lacked something to fit it for outdoor use, and again fell into disuse, but a few English mechanics saw in it the germ of a useful vehicle and an important industry. The enlarging of the front wheel and the reduction of the rear one, the adoption of the suspension or spider wheel, the use of hollow metal for the different parts, to produce lightness and rigidity, and, perhaps, more than all else, the application of the rubber tire, by which the greater part of the vibration and unpleasant jar of the road are absorbed, have finally accomplished the result, and made the bicycle a practical and a beautiful reality.

Any good, ordinary country road is suitable for a bicycle, provided it is not so rough as to be disagreeable (or riding in any vehicle, or is not deep with loose sand or gravel. A speed of from eight to twelve miles per hour is easily attainable, and may be kept up by a seasoned rider for hours. Fifty miles inside of three hours, one hundred miles upon an ordinary road in a little over seven hours, and two hundred and twenty miles in twenty-four hours, have been accomplished, while the number of riders who have accomplished one hundred miles and upwards in a day is legion. It is estimated that 250,000 bicycles are now in use in England, 75,000 of which are used in London alone.

Everybody, as the saying goes, rides a bicycle in England, and the Governments of both France and England provide them for the mail carriers, while, in some instances, the Park policemen are also mounted. The number in use in this country was estimated at upwards of 10,000 before this season, but they are increasing so rapidly that it is difficult to give the number with much accuracy.

A New York physician says: "If we could only get every professional man, bank presidents, brokers and writers, and the rest of the community, to patronize the bicycle, the majority of the doctors in New York would be given an indefinite vacation. It is better than ball playing, swimming or shooting, as no one runs the risk of being injured. The coming man will ride the bicycle."

At the Crystal Palace Grounds, London, in the early part of June, H. L. Curtis rode one mile in 3 min. 43 1-5 sec., being the fastest on record by about 3 seconds.

There will be a number of interesting bicycle races on the 22d of July, upon the grounds of the Olympic Athletic Club in Oakland.

## THE STAGE.

"Caryswold," the drama in which Miss Ada Ward made her debut at the Baldwin Theatre, appears to have been condensed from one of those curdling and pathetic stories that have made the success of the London Journal and other famous London penny periodicals. The plot, although lacking in constructive sequence, is still quite interesting, and at times rises to a high dramatic plane, but the somber incidents require more lighting up to make the play acceptable, although it must be owned that the first scene, as depicted at the Baldwin, is one of the most lurid, sensational effects ever produced in a theater. Miss Ada Ward made an immediate favorable impression, and her entrance was greeted with a round of applause, that is so appreciated, especially by those who make their first bow before a foreign audience. Miss Ward has many natural qualifications for an actress, and they have evidently been improved by careful study in the modern English school. Endowed with a winsome, mobile and expressive countenance, a well formed, svelte and willowy figure, she is ever graceful and appropriate in gesture, and with a soft, well trained, melodious voice, Miss Ward appears capable of occupying an important niche in the society drama of the day. Naturally this judgment will have to be ratified by future efforts that may develop the strength and versatility with which she is credited by the foreign press. "Caryswold" was very well cast, and under the careful stage management of Dave Belasco and with the excellent scenic effects by William Porter, the drama met with a favorable reception and was continued throughout the week to good business. Mr. Colson played the principal part, a gentlemanly villain of the deepest dye, in a somewhat too expressive manner, and the remainder of the cast included Messrs. Grismer, Bradley and Jennings, Miss Phebe Davis, Miss Lillie Owen, Belle Goosman, and Miss Constance Murielle, the latter meeting with a warm reception on her return from the East.

In regard to the future management of the Baldwin Theatre, matters appear still to be involved in great doubt. Finding that the theatre was let for intermediate dates, thus preventing any continuity of action, Mr. Gus Frohman retires from the management, but he can make any satisfactory arrangement, he will secure a lease and will engage a good stock company, playing stars and small combinations. Mr. Frohman has conducted the theater, during his short regime, in a very liberal and efficient manner, and should he resume the reins of management and secure proper attractions, he will be sure of meeting with liberal support. The Rial "Uncle Tom's Cabin" Combination commences a week's engagement on Monday next, and if successful at the usual popular prices, the piece may remain on the boards for a fortnight.

On the 17th we shall see the Hanlon-Lees in their athletic and acrobatic absurdity, "La Voyage en Suisse," but whether or not under the management of Tom Maguire, remains to be seen. There is little doubt but that the veteran secured a refusal of this theater for that date, but it is said that he allowed the contract to run beyond the specified time, and that is is thus annulled. Under whatever management they appear, it is to be hoped that the terms will be such as to allow some margin of profit, and in that case the Hanlon-Lees will be almost the first to break the spell of ill-luck that, outside of "Uncle Tom," has attended the combination system this season.

At the California, J. K. Emmet enters on the third and last week of his engagement, which has not met with the success that the undoubted merits of the star so well deserve. There is not on the stage a more natural and sympathetic actor than Emmet, but with his experience he surely might have known that he could not secure in San Francisco paying audiences, in one piece, to a three weeks' run. It is this egregious error that causes so much theatrical sore-headedness among stars and combinations on their return to the East, when, ignoring the true causes of their lack of success, they abuse San Francisco and its people and swear they will never be caught here again. Not for one moment alluding to J. K. Emmet, who will always be a favorite here, there are certain stars and combinations whose absence will always be greatly preferred to their company in this self same misguided city that is yet so appreciative of true musical and dramatic talent.

At the Standard Theatre the amusing burlesque of "Our Goblins," will be replaced this evening by a similar absurdity entitled "My Brudder In-Law," in which it is said that the Mitchell's Pleasure Party will strengthen the favorable impression they have created. Of its kind this is one of the most talented and versatile troupes we have ever seen on the road, and if opportunities are given in the new piece it is sure that the comedians will avail themselves of the advantage. There was some talk of their resuming their old standpoint at the Bush Street Theater, which would then pass under the management of William Emerson, but the negotiations to this effect, at this time of writing, have not arrived at a satisfactory conclusion. In case of success Mr. Emerson would devote the theater to light comedy, burlesque and negro minstrelsy, and under his liberal and experienced management the Bush Street would certainly become one of the most popular establishments in the city.

The Gardens continue to be well patronized, and during the coming week the attractions will be "The Voltigeurs," by Robert Fanquette, the composer of the "Belle of Corneville" at the Tivoli, and a grand spectacular opera by John Barnett, with the romantic title of "Æolia, or the Mountain Sylph" at the Winter Garden. These are great holiday cards.

Mdle. Sara Berndhardt made her re-appearance in Paris, under the joint mantle of financial sympathy and of Figaro supervision. It was a benefit for Maisnot Cheret, the widow of the man kindly and talented Parisian scenic artist, and what with the great newspapers' puffs, and the many excellent actors who volunteered their services, it was a monied and artistic success. This was her first appearance in Paris after breaking with the Theatre Francais, and fault, still

graver in Parisian eyes of getting married to Mr. Damala, who possessed the aspirations of being a first-class actor rather than a third-class broker in the Levant trade. The most fabulous sums were paid for the stalls and boxes, the total receipts amounting to some $12,000. The house was crammed with the beauty, fashion and finance of the gay capital, the play was "Camille" and when Bernhardt made her appearance there was a subdued murmur of chilly import, when a voice from the gallery interrupted her opening lines with—

*Ho-la,*
*La-a'-la,*
*La-femme-à,*
*Damala,*

which in a free translation meant: "Here she is, Whoop-la, the wife of Damala." A tremor ran around the house, the celebrated artiste faltered in her words, and at one moment it seemed as if she would break down, but she re-rallied, and after a well fought battle she re-conquered the suffrages of that fickle constituency, and is now the reigning sensation of Paris. Her husband was simply credited with a mild success, due more to his good looks than to his good acting.

It appears that Mrs. Langtry will come to this country in October, under Henry Abbey's management. Her repertoire as yet consists of "She Stoops to Conquer," "The Unequal Match," and "As You Like It." The Jerseys have always commanded outrageous prices, but whatever the Jersey Lily demands, for Abbey "There's millions in it."

Miss Jeffreys Lewis lately left for England, but will return early in August, to star in "La Belle Russe," which drama, despite the almost general condemnation of the New York critics, had proved to be a great popular success. After stigmatizing it as a plagiarism, and an obscene production unworthy of the first theater in America, it must be rather obnoxious to these gentlemen to see the piece, instead of "going to the dogs," run further into the dog days of any regular season at Wallack's for the last decade. "La Belle Russe" will be the great success of the coming season.

Max Freeman appears never to know when he is well off. It is but a short time since he secured the position of Stage Manager at the Union Square Theatre, with the privilege of playing eccentric parts. This was a great step in the profession, but in a weak moment, at Boston, he undertook to try Charles Thorne's part in "The Banker's Daughter," and thus imperilled the success of the Union Square Company. This led to an angry discussion, and Max Freeman was released from his engagement, and now goes on the road to play a character with a few lines, the waiter in the comedy of "Divorcons." Such are the ups and downs of dramatic life.

The Union Square Company will appear at the California Theatre in the first week of August, and after playing their usual repertoire, will produce "The Lights of London," with a strong cast, new scenery and novel effects, that made the drama such a success last season in New York. Miss Eleanor Carey comes as the leading lady, and as she is a great favorite here, she will doubtless meet with a generous and well-merited reception. Mr. da Belville also returns to the scene of his former successes. Both these artists came from the Australian Colonies, and made their first appearance at the Baldwin, and they are now at the head of their profession. It is probable that Miss Ada Ward will follow suit although if Mr. Gus Frohman should form a stock company, we should be pleased to see him secure this lady for the leading position.

King Headly, a well known aspirant for Thespian and Athletic renown, has branched off with the world of letters, sending to the N. Y. Clipper a very pretty and pathetic poem entitled "A Broken Life" which was much admired. Unfortunately Mr. Willie Winter, some fifteen years since, was seized with the same inspiration and told the story in the self same verse. King Headly is evidently as unreliable in his lyric feet as he was with his pedal extremities in this city.

Miss Bessie Darling announces her intention to star the coming season in a drama entitled "A Perfidious Woman," alleged to be founded on the same story that furnished the main plot for "La Belle Russe." And, by the way, Amory Sullivan and Miss Adaline Stanhope were recently enjoined in the Vice-Chancellor's court from producing a drama entitled "A Beautiful Wretch" which was simply "Forget Me Not," copies of which were sold openly in this city at $25 each. At the time Miss Stanhope was making a success of Stephanie in the English provinces.

Rossi recently appeared as King Lear, in London, supported by an English speaking company, and met with no better success than when here. The critics pronounced it an insult to English dramatic art. On subsequent nights he played the fourth and fifth acts in English, and met with a more cordial reception, but if the great tragedian's vernacular was as strong and varied as when he pouted forth in regard to his broken engagements an avalanche of verse and imprecations in Manager Kelley's ears, the English public were treated to a rare and artistic exhibition.

It is said that J. H. Haverly has the idea of incorporating all his theatrical ventures into a joint stock company. This is no startling innovation, as the London Alhambra, the largest and handsomest music hall in the world, has for years been conducted on this principle, and efficient management has made good returns on the investment. But the difficulty is to find the managers who combine the qualities of prudence, enterprise, energy, judgment and liberality. They who possess such attributes generally elect "to paddle their own canoe," and not to be at the beck of every disgruntled stockholder. We think the project will not prove a success.

James O'Neill recently produced a new drama at Chicago entitled "The Two Brothers" and the play was another failure to be added to the many dramatic disasters registered so early in this season. O'Neill will star during the next season with Miss M'Caull's company, and the managers hope to smooth away all obstacles. John Malone as his leading man. The latter gentleman is said to be rapidly improving in his newly adopted profession.

Miss Constance Murielle made quite a hit as Mrs. Blythe in "The Colonel" in the Eastern and Canadian tour of that eccentric play. This is in surprise as the lady possesses the dash, vim, grace and pleasing face that are requisite for the charming foil to the female æsthetic cranks. Outside the large cities "The Colonel" has not scored a great success.

[FOR THE BREEDER AND SPORTSMAN.]

## OUT-DOOR GAMES.

The surest of all natural prophylactics is active exercise in the open air. This being an admitted fact, the next consideration is how to invite and encourage it. It is said that air is a part of our daily food, and a most important part. The purity of our blood depends greatly on the quality of the air we breathe. Now if a person be confined to the counting-room or workshop all day, and returning to his or her home at evening to spend the time until the hour of retiring for the night, in an ill ventilated dwelling or close room, as do a majority of both old and young, we may naturally look for precisely what we get, viz: an aggregation of diseases, and as a restorative the sagacious adopt the panaceas prescribed by some sensible and good friend—exercise in the open air and an indulgence in some healthful and invigorating out-door game.

It has been said by a writer in the *Medical Review* that out door life is both a remedy and a prevention of all known disorders of the respiratory organs; consumption, in all but its last stages having been conquered by transferring the battle-ground from the sick-room to the wilderness of the next mountain range. Whether this be the case or not, it is beyond controversy that out-door games and out-door air and exercise contribute to health.

In England out-door games are universal in adoption, and the same in Germany and Switzerland, and, in fact, in most European countries. The United States introduced them into prominence about twenty years' ago, commencing with an improvement on the old-fashioned system of playing base-ball, and culminating, after cricket, quoits, croquet and polo had severally been revived or introduced, in the fascinating game of lawn-tennis.

It is my purpose, at this time, only to allude in general terms to these various games, as possessing in each a peculiar attraction for exercise and healthful attendants, and to urge their more universal adoption in the promotion of health, beneficent recreation and delightful amusement.

We should be glad to see base ball extended beyond the limits of professional clubs, when, as in times of old, school holidays found the pupils engaged in unlimited numbers in this invigorating game, and the public playgrounds were made to ring with the joyous notes of glee and satisfaction of the participants. Nor was the game confined to the "boys," for young men, middle aged and old men, married and single, took part with as much gusto and satisfaction as the juvenile. And then we had more sturdy, rosy, healthful boys, and hardier and more elastic men.

Cricket is particularly English, and though there was a time when it seemed likely to flourish in the United States—and principally through the action of some English gentlemen at New York City and Philadelphia, who induced the cricketers from Canada to visit them in friendly contests during a few years—yet the game at this time finds its popularity at the seaboard, with Philadelphia as the nucleus. It has many attractions and is filled with the right kind of exercise, and is now making a bid for popular favor.

Quoits, once universal in almost every town and hamlet in the United States, and a game which expanded the chest, strengthened the limbs, and called into requisition the muscular force of the whole body, and which to-day has no superior as a game for exercise, amusement and healthful attendants, is now almost unheard of; and in this neglect or forgetfulness or indifference to a noble game, how much is lost to young and old, both of extreme pleasure and delightful recreation. If any of the olden games deserve to be restored to popular favor, it is decidedly the game of quoits.

Polo is played on horseback—introduced by Bennett, of the New York *Herald*—and has found no favor except in the few intimates of this gentleman, who after a limited number of exhibitions or games, surfeited with it and dropped it into insignificance. It is an out-door game, and I mention it in that connection and nothing more.

Lawn tennis is a recent importation, and our young men and misses who understand and can play the game go in ecstacies over it. That it is a cheery, rollicking game none can deny, and that skill is required to make a good play is equally undeniable. That it will become popular, however, is a question, simply from the lack of zeal manifested by our young people in spreading the game.

---

Croquet, once the favorite among old and young, has been suffered to drop of late years, and partially abandoned, until the present season, when a revival of this fascinating, mirthful and controversial game seems to have taken place. A recent visit to the Southern portion of San Francisco and to Oakland and Alameda, developed a large number of private grounds freshly prepared for this delightful, invigorating game, and we recognized the screams of old, as they came thick and fast on our ear: "You are out of position." "You can't hit me until you have gone through a wicket." "Loose racquet him." "Send him down to the end." "You have not hit the stake." "I am a rover." "Come down here and help me." "You can't play on my ball." "I can." "You can't," and followed by a battle of wild clamoring for and against, until a sharp whack and a flying ball proclaims the point settled, and a chorus of merry voices, coupled with ringing laughter and shouts of joy attest the merry fun and rare delight experienced by the players. Sometimes, it is true, little misunderstandings will arise, but over croquet they are only transient.

Heads of families, the young ladies and gentlemen and the boys and girls even down to the little children can understandingly engage in this game, with little or no instruction. It is attractive, it is healthful; it is innocent, and pure, and no wonder that it finds renewed favor with the masses, especially as it is within the reach of all.

I have called attention to the various games connected with out-door exercise, and have not forgotten archery or bicycle exercise, as being connected with out-door exercise, though not of course classed with games. They commend themselves as beneficial and amusing.

It is more particularly my purpose at this time to call attention to these games as aids to health and sources of pleasure and amusement, and to impress, if possible, the advantages that will accrue by their introduction and increased adoption.

As it is the purpose of the BREEDER AND SPORTSMAN to give particular attention to all out-door games and pastimes, I trust those who are interested will join in making this department of the paper complete. There is a grand field in California for sports of this class, as the Winter time is favorable, with few interruptions, as well as Spring, Summer and Autumn, and much depends on correspondents, their assistance being an indispensable adjunct to editorial labor.

SAN FRANCISCO, June 25th, 1882.     T. W. H.

---

## ECCENTRICITIES OF SALMON AND TROUT.

ROBERT B. ROOSEVELT.

I was fishing the Nipisiquit River in New Brunswick many years ago. The weather was warm and dry, the water clear and low, and the salmon, although they could be seen from the overhanging cliffs lying thick in the pools, were shy and would not bite. My friend and myself had exhausted the resources of our fly-books: no lure, however tempting, would entice another fish to the surface, and the standard and accepted flies were at a total discount. Finding ordinary methods vain, I proceeded to test one of my theories. I always carried my box of fly-making materials with me on every excursion after salmon, and unusual as it seemed, I proceeded to manufacture so strange and unnatural an insect as had never braved the air of heaven—a thing so unnatural that it could not be known to the finny foe. The result justified my hopes. When I tried it the following morning the salmon were moved to wonder and curiosity, if not to appetite. Fish after fish rose at it and two rewarded my enter prise by taking it. The same success attended me in my evening's fishing, the pools being rested during the heat and glare of the day. Next day that fly was, as I had anticipated, useless, but I had manufactured another. The first was pure green, the next was light yellow. It brought one or two victims to the gaff, and was followed by a series of strange and contrasted devices until even my stock of out-of-the-way material, which was as rare as it was extensive, for it was the cullings from Dr. Andrew Clark's unrivaled resources that he had kindly placed at my disposal, was exhausted. But I had had fair sport and managed to supply the table at a time when by no other method could a fish be obtained. I had a modified renewal of this pexrience the present Spring. I was fishing for trout on a Long Island preserve, which is remarkable for the size and shyness of the fish. They were breaking here and there over the pond quite freely, but would not touch the fly, although it was cast over immediately and where they had risen. I had changed fly after fly—had imitated the natural flies perfectly. Beside the gnats there were two flies on the water, the American May fly—much smaller than the English, but of the same color—and the cowdung. Of course I had the thes

---

in my book, and of several sizes, but they were in vain; the red ibis and the black gnat were equally useless, and I could find nothing which would tempt the dainty palates or va. grant fancies of my longed-for victims. I had with me a book, of which Mr. Holberton had just made me a present as a specimen of his handiwork, and among its contents I noticed a large cinnamon fly, too large for our Long Island waters, and intended probably for Maine or Canada. I made up my mind at once that I would astonish these exacting Long Island species, and I did. I put it in for a hand fly, and when I cast, could see it in the water fifty feet off. It looked like a small bird, but it stirred fish hunger or curiosity to the caudal fins. I got rise after rise at it. It was simply irresistible, and although of course many that rose only looked at and did not take it, I managed to make a fine catch and had splendid sport. So much for trying to meet, the eccentricities of trout by diversity of lure and method, a good thing to do whenever ordinary methods fail.—*Turf Field and Farm.*

SAD DAY FOR THE FROGS.

Specimen of off-hand drawing by Tata Sao, special artist for icon Sao. Our artist and our celebrated art embroiderers can be seen at work daily, dressed in their native costumes, at icon Sao. The great Fine Sale Exhibition of Japanese and Oriental Wares, 20 and 24 Geary Street. The largest in the world. Special Agents of the Imana Kroku of the Japanese Government. Wholesale and Retail.

CLAY PIGEONS—PERFECT IMITATION OF A QUAIL'S FLIGHT

EVANSVILLE ARGUS

SPORTSMEN! SEND FOR CIRCULAR TO

**PIERCE & CO., - - - - - OAKLAND, CAL.**

SOLE AGENTS FOR THE PACIFIC COAST.

# REVISED SPEED PROGRAMME
## FOR 1882.

### FOURTH ANNUAL MEETING
OF THE
## SONOMA COUNTY
### Agricultural Park Association,
AT SANTA ROSA.

**FIRST DAY—Tuesday, Aug. 22, 1882.**

No. 1—TROTTING RACE—Free for all two-year-olds owned in the District. Mile heats, 2 best in 3; purse, $200. First horse, $150; second, $60; third, $30. Closed on the first day of May with the following entries:

E. Conway names ch. s. Abbotsford.
A. Foster names s. m. Clara Patterson, by Grey McClellan.
G. C. Lawrence names blk. f. May Day, by Eugene Casserly.

J. Shafter names g. h. Greyson, by brother to Rustic.
Steve Crandall names b. f. no name, sire unknown.

No. 2—TROTTING RACE—Free for all horses that never beat 2:35; purse, $400. First horse, $240; second, $120; third, $40.

**SECOND DAY—Wednesday, Aug. 23.**

No. 3—RUNNING RACE—Half mile heats, 2 best in 3, free to all; purse, $200. First horse, $150; second, $75; third, $25.

No. 4—PACING RACE—Free to all horses that never beat 2:26; purse, $300. First horse, $200; second, $75; third, $25.

**THIRD DAY—Thursday, Aug. 24.**

No. 5—TROTTING RACE—Free for all three-year-olds owned in the District; purse, $300. First horse, $150; second, $90; third, $60. Closed May 1st, with the following entries:

C. Brugell names b. f. Debby Mott, by Grey McClellan.
W. J. Starr names blk. f. Starr, by Nutwood.
E. B. Conley names b. c. Magnet, by Brigadier.
J. M. Foster names br. s. Monte Foster, by Gen'l Dana.
J. M. Wood names b. c. Red, by Overland.
L. H. Boggs names b. s. Warwick, by Milton Medium.

No. 6—TROTTING RACE—Free for all that never beat 2:25; purse, $400. First horse, $240; second, $120; third, $40.

**FOURTH DAY—Friday, Aug. 25.**

No. 7—TROTTING RACE—Free to all horses that never beat 2:40; purse, $500. First horse, $300; second, $150; third, $50.

No. 8—RUNNING RACE—Free for all; single dash; one mile; purse, $250. First horse, $150; second, $60; third, $40.

No. 9—TROTTING RACE—Free for all horses that never beat 2:30; purse, $500. First horse, $3; second, $150; third, $40.

**FIFTH DAY—Saturday, Aug. 26.**

No. 10—RUNNING RACE—Free for all three-year-olds; one mile and repeat; purse, $300. First horse, $150; second, $90; third, $60.

No. 11—TROTTING RACE—Free to all that never beat 2:31; purse, $700. First horse, $400; second, $200; third, $100.

## ENTRIES.

1 Entries must be made in writing and dated, and give sex, color and marks of horse; also name and residence of owner.
2 State number of the race in which you wish to enter.
3 State names of sire and dam of horse entered. If known; if unknown, state the fact.
4 State name and postoffice address of party entering the horse.
5 If names of horse has been changed, state former name.
6 Send entrance fee to all nominations.

## CONDITIONS.

1 Entries to all races, except Nos. 1 and 5, to close with the Secretary at 12 o'clock m. on Monday, the first day of August, 1882.
2 Entrance fee to the above races will be 10 per cent. of the purse, and must accompany the nomination.
3 In all races five to enter and three to start. Any horse distanced or not starting will forfeit his entrance fee. No money will be paid for a walk over.
4 Rules of the Pacific Blood Horse Association to govern running races, and of the National Trotting Association to govern trotting.
5 No horse entered in a purse can be withdrawn except by consent of the Judges.
6 All trotting and pacing races, except No. 1, will be mile heats, 3 best in 5.

J. P. CLARK, President.
CHARLES HOFFER, Secretary.

## Pacific Breeders' Association.
### Embryo Trotting Stakes, 1882.

Sweepstakes for foals, 1882, $100 each; $25 forfeit; $10 declaration; $5 nomination fee.

There are three stakes under the denomination of Embryo for 1885, viz., for yearlings, two-year-olds and three-year-olds. The nominator chooses whether he will name in one or all of them. The one horse to trot a dash of a mile; two-year-old, heats of a mile, 2 in 3; three-year-old, 3 in 5—all in harness. Five dollars must accompany the nomination; the declaration, $10; or at before the 1st of September of the year she is to trot.

No. 1—RUNNING RACE—For all maiden horses owned in the state on the day of race, which is two days previous to the date fixed for the race. If the declaration or forfeit is not paid at the specified time, the subscriber will be held for the full amount of the stake. Pedigree, color, marks, and date of foaling must be given, and the following will be the formula for making the nomination:

Say Pacific Breeders' Association. I name in Embryo Stake of 1882, the ——— colt (or filly), foaled ———, 1881, by ———, dam ———, by ———, to run at (the nomination being to enter in the race, specify which year). The $5 fee covers the entrance of the foal in named in one or all of the races, specify which part. The $5 fee covers the entrance of the foal named in one, two or all of the races, and the following will be the formula:

## PAUL FRIEDHOFER,
### Pathological Horse Shoer.
PRACTICAL IN ALL ITS VARIOUS BRANCHES.

No. 118 Commercial St.

HOOF EVILS, such as Toe and Quarter Cracks, Uneven Growth of Wall, Contraction, Thrush, Quittors and Lameness, treated with radical success.

# SECOND
## ANNUAL EXHIBITION
OF THE
# SAN MATEO AND SANTA
# CLARA COUNTY
# AGRICULTURAL ASSOCIATION
## NO. 5,
### TO BE HELD AT
# SAN JOSE, CAL.
......FROM......
## Sept. 25th to 30th, '82, inclusive

### SPEED PROGRAMME.

**FIRST DAY—Monday, Sept. 25th, 1882.**

No. 1. TROTTING—2:40 class. Purse, $500.
No. 2. SAME DAY—TROTTING—2:25 class. Purse, $750.

**SECOND DAY—Tuesday, Sept. 26th.**

No. 3. RUNNING—For two-year-olds; three-quarter mile dash; $50 entrance; $15 forfeit; $250 added. Second horse to receive his entrance and one-third of added money.

No. 4. SAME DAY—RUNNING—For all ages; mile dash; $50 entrance; $15 forfeit; $250 added. Second horse to receive his entrance and one-third of added money.

No. 5. SAME DAY—RUNNING—For all ages; mile heats, 2 in 3; $50 entrance; $15 forfeit; $250 added. Entrance five per cent. to third horse. Horses entered to be sold for $1,000 to carry entitled wt. $500. Two pounds off for each $500 under fixed valuation. Winner can be claimed by any one.

**THIRD DAY—Wednesday, Sept. 27th.**

No. 6. TROTTING—2:26 class. Purse, $600.
No. 7. SAME DAY—BUGGY HORSE RACE—For horses owned in the District to be driven by owner in buggy. Two miles and repeat. Purse to be hereafter offered.
No. 8. SAME DAY—Ladies' Riding Tournament—Bicycle Race, etc.

**FOURTH DAY—Thursday, Sept. 28th.**

No. 9. RUNNING—Three-year-olds, 1¼ mile dash; $50 entrance; $15 forfeit; $275 added. Second horse to receive his entrance and one-third of added money.
No. 10. SAME DAY—PACING—For four-year-olds. Purse $400.

**FIFTH DAY—Friday, Sept. 29th.**

No. 11. RUNNING—1¼ mile dash. Free for all; $50 entrance; $15 forfeit; $500 added. Second horse to receive his entrance and one-third of added money.
No. 12. SAME DAY—TROTTING—2:17 class. Purse $600.
No. 13. SAME DAY—TROTTING—For two-year-olds. Purse $400.

**SIXTH DAY—Saturday, Sept. 30th.**

No. 14. TROTTING—2:22 class. Purse $750.
No. 15. SAME DAY—TROTTING—2:30 class. Two miles and repeat. Purse $500.

## REMARKS AND CONDITIONS.

All trotting and pacing races are the best three in five, except the two-year-old trot, unless otherwise specified; five to enter and three to start. Entrance fee ten per cent. on purse, to accompany nominations. Purse divided at the rate of sixty, thirty per cent to second, and ten per cent to third.

# Pacific Coast Blood Horse As'n.
## PROGRAMME.
FIXED EVENTS—SPRING & FALL MEETINGS
## 1883 and 1884.
# BALDWIN STAKE FOR 1882
### SPRING MEETING.
#### FIRST DAY.

WINTERS' STAKE—For three-year-olds, to be run the first day of the Spring Meeting; dash of one-and-a-half miles; $100 each, $25 forfeit, $500 added; second to have $100, third to save stake. Nominations above to be made for 1883.

SAME DAY—CALIFORNIA STAKE—For two-year-olds, $50 each, $25 forfeit, $250 added; to be run on the first day of the Spring Meeting; second to save stake; dash of half a mile. Nominations above to be made for 1883.

#### SECOND DAY.

PACIFIC CUP—Handicap of $100 each, $50 forfeit, $20 declaration, $1,000 added; second to receive $300, third to save stake; two and-a-quarter miles; to be run on the second day of the Spring Meeting. Will close the 1st of March, 1883.

#### THIRD DAY.

"SPIRIT OF THE TIMES" STAKE—Dash of one-and-three-quarter miles for all three-year-olds; $100 each, $25 forfeit, $500 added; $150 to second, third to save stake. Nominations to be made for 1884.

SAME DAY—GANG STAKE—Handicap of three-quarters of a mile for two-year-olds, $50 each, $25 forfeit, $250 added; second horse to have stake. When any California two-year-old beats the time of Connor, 1:15 for three-quarters of a mile, the Stake to be named after the colt which beats it. Nominations to be made for 1884.

### FALL MEETING.

LADIES' STAKE—For two-year-old fillies; $50 entrance, $25 forfeit, $250 added; three-quarters of a mile; second to save entrance. Nominations to be made for 1883.

SAME DAY—THE VESTAL STAKE—For three-year-old fillies, one-and-a-quarter miles; $50 h, p. $300 added; second to receive $100, third to save stake. Nominations to be made for 1884.

#### SECOND DAY.

STALLION STAKE—Conditions—Only those three-year-old get eligible which are the get of stallions named in this State. The stallions have to subscribe the amount charged for their services to the fund; privilege of the State of their foal season, and those which have not made a subscription, so pay $25 that can bestate within the meaning of the State. The stake to be the get of a stallion to complete the stake for the colts nigel to $100 each, $25 forfeit; stake or money added in the discretion of the committee; distance, 1¾ miles. To close for 1882 on the 1st of August next, at which time both the stallion and colts (progeny) must be named.

#### THIRD DAY.

THE BALDWIN STAKE—Post stake for all ages; dash of four miles; $250 each, p. p.; $1,000 added; second, $200; third to save stake. Will close on the 1st of August, 1882, for this year.

SAME DAY—PIMICAN STAKE—For two-year-olds; dash of a mile; $50 each, $25 forfeit; $250 added; second to save stake. Nominations to be made for 1883.

SAME DAY—FAME STAKE—For three-year-olds; dash of two miles; $100 each, $25 forfeit; $500 added; second to have $150; third to save stake. Nominations to be made for 1884.

All of these Stakes close on the first of August next. The colts racing now as yearlings, foals of 1880. Nominations to be made by 1st day of June. Assistant Secretary, P. O. Box 1,061. S. P. F. C. S. M. A. To be valid they must be plainly instructed on the back. Entries not up to the rules.

THEO. WINTERS, President.
C. M. CHASE, Ass'y Sec'y.

## SPEED PROGRAMME
FOR THE
## First Annual Meeting
OF THE
# SANTA CRUZ COUNTY
# Agricultural Fair Association,
### At SANTA CRUZ,
Commencing - Tuesday, August 15th,
# $3,500 IN PURSES!

**FIRST DAY—Tuesday, Aug. 15, 1882.**

No. 1—TROTTING RACE—Purse $500 for horses that have never beaten 2:40. Owned in the District.
No. 2—TROTTING RACE—Purse $500. For horses that have never beaten 2:25.

**SECOND DAY—Wednesday, Aug. 16.**

No. 3—RUNNING STAKE—For two-year-olds; $30 entrance; $10 forfeit; $250 added. Dash of three-quarters of a mile.
No. 4—RUNNING STAKE—Free for all; $60 entrance; $10 forfeit; $100 added. Second to have entrance. Dash of a mile.
No. 5—TROTTING RACE—Purse $500. For double teams owned in the District by one team.

**THIRD DAY—Thursday, Aug. 17.**

No. 6—TROTTING RACE—Purse $400. For horses that have never beaten 2:30.
No. 7—TROTTING RACE—Purse $600. For horses that have never beaten three minutes. Owned in District.

**FOURTH DAY—Friday, Aug. 18.**

No. 8—RUNNING RACE—Selling Purse, $300; $50 to

second horse; entrance 5 per cent. to third horse. One mile and repeat. Horses entered to be sold for $1,000 to carry their entitled weight. Two pounds off for each $500 under fixed valuation. Winner can be claimed by any one.

No. 9—RUNNING STAKE—Free for all; $50 entrance; $10 forfeit; $75 added. Second to save entrance. One mile and repeat.

No. 10—TROTTING RACE—Purse, $500. For horses that have never beaten 2:36.

**FIFTH DAY—Saturday, Aug. 19.**

No. 11—TROTTING RACE—Purse $600. Free for all.
No. 12—TROTTING RACE—Purse, $400. Free for all two-year-olds. Mile and repeat.

## Remarks and Conditions.

All trotting races are the best three in five, except the two-year-old trot; five to enter and three to start. Entrance fee 10 per cent. on purse, to accompany nomination. Purses divided at the rate of sixty per cent. to first horse, thirty per cent. to second, and ten per cent. to third.

National Association Rules to govern trotting; but the Board reserves the right to trot heats of any two classes, alternately, if necessary to finish a day's racing, or to trot a special race between heats.

To fill running races, three or more subscribers are necessary.

All two-year-olds, when running in their classes, shall carry one hundred pounds, with the usual allowance for mares and geldings.

All three-year-olds, when running in their classes, to carry one hundred and ten pounds, with the usual allowance as above.

Those who have nominations in stakes MUST name to the Secretary, in writing, the horse they will start on Tuesday, the 14th day previous, and on Thursday the Tuesday next on Monday previous; and on Wednesday previous, by twelve o'clock M. This rule is obvious, and must be strictly adhered to.

No added money paid for a walk-over.

Horses entered in purses can only be drawn by consent of the Judges.

Rules of the Pacific Coast Blood-Horse Association hold weight to govern running races, except when conditions named are otherwise.

Special racing will be run by the Southern Pacific Railroad and South Pacific Coast Railroad, and excursion tickets sold by both companies from all points on their lines, good from August 14th to August 20th, inclusive.

J. D. CHACE, President.
JAMES O. WANZER, Secretary.

## SPEED PROGRAMME
OF
# Mount Shasta Agricultural
### Association,
## TO BE HELD IN
# YREKA, SISKIYOU CO.,
——ON——
## Wednesday, - - October 4th, 1882.

For racing purposes this District shall comprise Siskiyou, Shasta, Trinity, and Modoc Counties, Cal., and Jackson and Lake Counties, Oregon.

No horse shall be eligible to any of the following District Races unless owned in the District prior to October 1882.

**FIRST DAY—Wednesday, Oct. 4.**

No. 1—TROTTING—Free for all; 3 in 5; purse, $300. First horse receives $400; second horse, $150. Entrance 10 per cent. of purse, to enter, 5 to start. Entries close September 1st.

No. 2—RUNNING—Dash of a mile and a half; free for all horses owned in the District; purse, $100; entrance $20, added.

**SECOND DAY—Thursday, Oct. 5.**

No. 3—TROTTING—Free for all matched horses owned in the District; 2 in 3; purse $75; entrance $5, added.

No. 4—RUNNING—Half mile and repeat; free for all horses owned in the District; purse, $75; entrance $5, added.

No. 5—TROTTING—Free for all three-year-olds and under, owned in the District; 3 in 5; purse, $75; entrance $5, added.

**THIRD DAY—Friday, Oct. 6.**

Grand parade of Stock.
No. 6—TROTTING—Free for all in the District; 3 in 5; purse, $200; entrance $20, added.
No. 7—FOOT RACE—75 yards and repeat; purse, $30; entrance $5.
No. 8—RUNNING—Free for all three-year-olds and under owned in the District; dash of three-quarters of a mile; purse, $75; entrance $5, added.

**FOURTH DAY—Saturday, Oct. 7.**

No. 9—RUNNING—Free for all; 3 in 5 dash. Entries close Sept 1st. Expiration. Entrance $5.
No. 10—TROTTING—Free for all horses in the District that have never beaten three minutes; 3 in 5; purse, $150; entrance $5, added.

## Rules and Regulations.

1st. No others purses will be given without discount.

2nd. Entries to be placed in the entry box half an hour before the opening of the Fair.

3rd. Horses must give name, pedigree, and description of horse entered.

4th. All District Races two or more entries make a field.

5th. No horse to start in more than one race per day prior to race.

6th. Rules of Pacific Coast Blood-Horse Association Rules to govern trotting running races.

7th. Rules of the Pacific Coast Blood-Horse Association Rules to govern running races.

J. H. MAGOFFEY, Secretary.
A. SWAIN, President.

# SAVE MONEY!
BUY DIRECT FROM THE MANUFACTURER.
## James Wylie,
20 & 22 Seventh St., nr. Market,
MANUFACTURER

**Light Carriages, Buggies and Wagons,**

Guarantees First-class Work and Low Prices. Repair ing, Painting and Trimming with promptness and a reasonable rates.

# For Sale!
A BRACE OF
# FINE FOX HOUNDS!
Training and Breeding guaranteed. Address for particulars,
TOM TUNSTED,
Nicasio, Marin.

# Golden Gate Fair.

## SPEED PROGRAMME FOR 1882.

## $10.000

### IN

## Stakes and Prizes

**FIRST DAY—SEPT. 4, 1882.**

No. 1.—RUNNING—GOLDEN GATE STAKES.—For two-year-olds; three-quarter mile dash; $25 entrance; $15 forfeit; $150 added; second to save stake; winners a penalty.

No. 2.—SAME DAY — RUNNING. — ALAMEDA STAKES.—For three-year-olds; one and one-half mile dash; $25 entrance; $25 forfeit; $175 added; second to save stake.

No. 3.—SAME DAY — RUNNING — PARDEE STAKES.—Free for all; one mile and repeat; $75 entrance; $50 forfeit; $250 added.

No. 4.—SAME DAY—TROTTING.—2:30 Class; purse, $600; first horse, $400; second, $150; third, $50.

No. 5.—SAME DAY—SPECIAL TROT AGAINST TIME.—Able to beat will be awarded any stallion that beats best time.

No. 6.—SAME DAY—SPECIAL TROT AGAINST the best time; a trial to harness; no entrance fee.

**SECOND DAY—SEPT. 5.**

No. 7.—TROTTING.—2:30 Class; purse, $800; first horse, $600; second, $200; third, $50.

No. 8.—SAME DAY—PACING.—Free for all. Purse, $600; first horse, $400; second, $150; third, $50.
Washington and Johnny Weight, to wagon.

**THIRD DAY—SEPT. 6.**

No. 9.—RUNNING.—Free for all; 3-mile dash; $100 entrance; $50 forfeit; $300 added; second horse to save stake.

No. 10.—SAME DAY—TROTTING.—Free for all three-year-olds; purse, $600; first horse, $400; second, $150; third, $50.

No. 11.—SAME DAY—TROTTING.—2:23 Class purse, $600; first horse, $400; second, $200; third, $50.

**FOURTH DAY—SEPT. 7.**

No. 12.—TROTTING.—Free for all two-year-olds; one mile and repeat; purse, $400; first horse, $200; second, $150; third, $50.

No. 13.—SAME DAY—TROTTING.—Free for all four-year-olds; purse, $600; first horse, $400; second, $150; third, $50.

No. 14.—SAME DAY—RUNNING.—SELLING RACE.—Purse, $300; free for all; 1-mile dash; second horse to save $50; horses entered to be sold for $1,000, to carry entitled weight; 3 pounds off for each $100 under that value.

Any person has the right to claim when the winner shall be put up at auction; the surplus to go—one-half to the second horse, one-half to the Society.

**FIFTH DAY—SEPT. 8.**

No. 15.—RUNNING — CONSOLATION PURSE.—$250 for beaten horses; mile-and-a-quarter dash; second horse to save $75. If per cent entrance.

No. 16.—SAME DAY—LADIES' RIDING TOURNAMENT.—There will be several very choice and elegant prizes offered, to be competed for, contributed by the merchants and citizens of Oakland and San Francisco; the lady who may desire to contend for these premiums in this department, and so as well as the prizes are distributed. Ladies wishing to contend for these prizes will send their names to the President or Secretary on or before the last day of September, 1882, indorsed by at least two gentlemen of the Society. Conditions will be published in the daily papers.

No. 17.—SAME DAY—TROTTING.—2:26 CLASS.—Purse, $600; first horse, $400; second, $150; third, $50.

**SIXTH DAY—SEPT. 9.**

No. 18.—COMPETITIVE CADET DRILL.—PRIZE, $100 Gold Medal. Competition open to all educational institutions in the State.

No. 19.—SAME DAY—COMPETITIVE MILITARY DRILL.—A prize of the value of $250 will be offered by the Association to the best drilled Military Company in the State of California. Rules and conditions to be published hereafter. It is the intent of the Directors to have the first competing companies determine when the prize or trophy shall be, and to have the same annually competed for, until it shall have been won three times by the same company; when it shall become the absolute property of the winning company.

No. 20.—SAME DAY—GRAND BICYCLE TOURNAMENT, for the Association's Gold Medal to first, Silver Medal to second, and Bronze Medal to third; [mile dash;] open to all bicyclists.

No. 21.—SAME DAY—TROTTING.—Free for all; purse, $600; first horse, $400; second, $150; third, $50.

No. 22.—SAME DAY—A SET OF HARNESS of the value of $125, will be offered for sportsmen's roadsters; best two in three; owner to drive.

For a "scrub-race," or a match among any animal owned and driven on the road by any gentleman for his own private pleasure.

## CONDITIONS.

Entries to all running stakes, trotting and running races, to be made to Secretary Wilcox, on or before August 1, 1882. Forfeits in running stakes, and the entrance fee of 10 per cent. in the trotting and pacing races, should in all cases accompany the nominations and entries.

All trotting and pacing races are the best three in five. In all, five to enter, and three to start.

Entrance fee, ten per cent. on purses.

When there are eight or more starters in a trotting race, the parties may be entitled to a distance.

National Trotting Association rules to govern trotting, but the Board reserves the right to trot heats with any two classes alternately, if necessary to finish any day's racing, or to trot a special race between heats.

All eligible offers in trotting races confined to horses on the Pacific Coast May 22, 1882.

In running races, three or more entries required to fill.

Those who have nominations in stakes MUST name to the Secretary, in writing, the horses they will start on Monday, on the Saturday previous; and on Wednesday, the Monday previous; and on Friday, the Wednesday previous. For added money will be paid for a walk-over.

Horses entered in purses can only be drawn by consent of the Judges.

Rules of the Pacific Blood Horse Association to govern running races, except as above specially provided.

All entries to be made in writing, to give sex, color and marks of horse; also, name and residence of owner; and in running races colors to be worn by the rider. And in all, any other particulars that will enable the spectators to distinguish the horses in the race.

Write "Entries to races" on outside of Envelope.

L. WALKER,     A. C. DIETZ,
Secretary.     Preside[nt]

---

# $12,500
## In Purses and Stakes.

## CALIFORNIA
# STATE FAIR
## SPEED PROGRAMME

### FOR 1882.

**FIRST DAY—MONDAY, SEPT. 11.**

No. 1.—RUNNING—INTRODUCTION STAKE.—For all ages, three-quarters of a mile dash; $50 entrance, $15 forfeit; $200 added, second to save stake.

No. 2.—RUNNING—SWEEPSTAKE STAKE.—For foals of 1879; one and a half mile dash; $50 entrance, p. p.; $250 added. Closed March 1st with nominations.

No. 3.—RUNNING—SELLING RACE.—Purse, $250. Free for all; one mile and repeat; second horse to save $50. Entrance five per cent to third horse. Horses entered to be sold for $1,500 to carry entitled weight; one pound off for each $100 under fixed valuation.

No. 4.—TROTTING.—2:40 class; purse, $1,000.

**SECOND DAY—TUESDAY, SEPT. 12.**

No. 5.—TROTTING.—2:23 class; purse, $1,500.

No. 6.—TROTTING—Purse, $600; for three year olds and under.

No. 7.—TROTTING.—Purse, $600; mile heats for two year olds.

**THIRD DAY—WEDNESDAY, SEPT. 13.**

No. 8.—RUNNING—FILLY STAKE FOR TWO YEAR OLD FILLIES.—Five-eighths of a mile; $50 entrance; $25 forfeit; $200 added; second to receive $75; third, $25.

No. 9.—RUNNING—CALIFORNIA DERBY STAKE.—For three-year-olds; one and one-half mile dash; $100 entrance; $25 forfeit; $300 added; second horse, $100; third, $50.

No. 10.—RUNNING—SELLING RACE.—Purse, $300; one and one-eighth miles; second horse, $100; entrance five per cent. to third horse. Horses entered to be sold for $1,000, to carry entitled weight. Two pounds off for each $100 under fixed valuation.

No. 11.—TROTTING—2:30 class; purse, $1,000.

**FOURTH DAY—THURSDAY, SEPT. 14.**

No. 12.—TROTTING.—2:35 class; purse, $1,000.

No. 13.—TROTTING.—2:26 class; purse, $800.

No. 14.—TROTTING—Two miles and repeat; 2:40 horses; purse, $800.

**FIFTH DAY—FRIDAY, SEPT. 15.**

No. 15.—RUNNING—COLT AND FILLY STAKE.—For two year olds; dash of one mile; $50 entrance, $15 forfeit, $300 added; second horse, $100; third, $50.

No. 16.—RUNNING—SELLING RACE.—Purse, $300; for all ages; dash of one and a quarter miles; $150 to second horse; entrance five per cent. to third; horses entered to be sold for $1,500, carry full weight; for $1,200, three pounds off; for $1,000, five pounds off; for $800, seven pounds off; for $600, ten pounds off.

No. 17.—RUNNING.—Dash of three miles; free for all $400 entrance; $200 added; third, $100. Purse to second horse, $100; entrance five per cent. to third horse.

No. 18.—RUNNING—CONSOLATION PURSE.—$250 for beaten horses; one mile and repeat; entrance free; second horse to receive $50.

**SIXTH DAY—SATURDAY, SEPT. 16.**

No. 20.—TROTTING—2:19 class; purse, $1,500.

No. 21.—TROTTING.—Purse, $800; for double teams of 2:40 horses.

No. 22.—TROTTING—OCCIDENT STAKE FOR 1882, closed in 1881 with twelve nominations.

No. 23.—SPECIAL TROT AGAINST TIME.—$250 to state will be awarded to any stallion that beats Santa Claus time (2:21½).

Entries for the following events for 1883-4 were ordered to be closed with the above races:

No. 1.—RUNNING—CALIFORNIA DERBY STAKE, for foals of 1880, to be run at the State Fair of 1883. One and one-half miles dash. $50 entrance, p. p.; $300 added; second horse, $100; third, $50.

No. 2.—Same stake, for foals of 1881, to be run at State Fair of 1884. Same conditions.

No. 3.—TROTTING—MATURITY STAKE.—Three mile dash, for four year olds, in 1883. $100 entrance; $50 forfeit; $500 added; second horse, $150; third, $50. To be run at the State Fair of 1883.

No. 4.—TROTTING — CALIFORNIA ANNUAL STAKE.—For two-year-olds in 1881. Dash of one mile; $50 entrance; $25 forfeit; $250 added; second horse, $100; third, $50. To be run at the State Fair of 1883.

## REMARKS and CONDITIONS.

All trotting and pacing races are the best three in five, except the two year old trot, unless otherwise specified; five to enter and three to start. Entrance fee ten per cent. on purse, to accompany nomination. Purses divided at the rate of sixty per cent. to first horse, twenty-five per cent. to second and ten per cent. to third.

National Association Rules to govern trotting; but the Board reserves the right to trot heats of any two classes alternately, if necessary to finish any day's racing, or to trot a special race between heats.

To fill running races, three or more subscribers are necessary.

All two-year-olds, when running in their classes, shall carry one hundred pounds, with the usual allowance for sex and position.

All three-year-olds, when running in their classes, to carry one hundred and ten pounds, with the usual allowance for age and sex.

Those who have nominations in stakes MUST name to the Secretary, in writing, the horses they will start on Monday, on the Saturday previous; and on Wednesday, the Monday previous; and on Friday, the Wednesday previous, by twelve o'clock M. This rule is arbitrary, and horses not so named must be simply adhered to.

No added money paid for a walk-over.

Horses entered in purses can only be drawn by consent of Judges.

Rules of the Pacific Coast Blood Horse Association hold weighted to govern running races, except when conditions named are otherwise specified.

Mile heats; best three in five.

Open to all comers; pay entrance.

Winner to receive $1,500 second, two-thirds of Sweeps and Entrance Fees, and third, one-third. Entrance 5 per cent.; five to enter and three to start.

Entries must be in the hands of Secretary at or before 8 P.M. on WEDNESDAY, 8th December, 1882.

The Victorian Trotting Club holds membership in the National Trotting Association of the United States, under which Rules the races will be performed.

Any further information desired can be obtained from July 26th, or Dr. JOHN WEB, Rabbit's Hotel, San Francisco.

EDWIN P. SMITH,     HUGH M. LARUE,
Secretary.     President.

---

# BREEDER AND SPORTSMAN

VOL. I—No. 1.
No. 508 MONTGOMERY STREET. }  SAN FRANCISCO, SATURDAY, JULY 8, 1882.  { SUBSCRIPTION FIVE DOLLARS A YEAR.

## NOTABLE HORSES OF CALIFORNIA.

### ROMERO.

A beautiful dark grey, neither dappled or iron, but between the two shades. A handsome horse in either way the phrase is accepted. Not only handsome, but standing the first of his age, and entitled to the foremost place in the record of four-year-old stallions. We present him with an additional feeling of pride, inasmuch as we brought his sire to California, and never met a horse he could not beat on the road. There was a long stretch of straight work on the boulevard, and we always took delight in driving "Alf" along it. He went so squarely as well as fast that there was pleasure in driving him, and there never was any hitching, single-footing or any other of the provoking propensities which road horses are some times prone to indulge in. Straight, honest trotting, never clambering, never making a mistake, and when his competitor would lock him, there was always a link to let out and a reserve of speed for an emergency. Those who take delight in the peculiar American custom of road-driving will understand the pleasure there is in having a horse of this kind to handle, and appreciate the eulogy of a good sire to a worthy son. Sterne, in writing the biography of Tristam Shandy, dated

the origin of his hero rather further back than we will that of Romero, and yet pedigree is everything in a horse. His sire, A. W. Richmond, was by Linford's Blackbird, and the dam of Richmond was a white mare brought from Ohio to Iowa by Thomas W. Pope, a Methodist clergyman, with the proverbial love of a horse which the cloth are celebrated for. She was a great old mare, capable of making her three-quarters of an hour, and coming home something faster. She was by a thoroughbred horse owned near Cleveland, and her dam was said to be by an Arabian. From the peculiar markings, however, this was doubtless an Opelousas horse, and these horses being called in Northern New York, Ohio and Pennsylvania Arabians, this was the reason for the nomenclature. Which of the Barb or Arabian horses which came to the United States was the progenitor of these spotted horses is in doubt. Alberoni, or Spanker, or Spottee are each credited with the paternity, though there is little question that the blood was from the Orient. At all events these rat-tailed, ragged-hipped horses had great powers of endurance, and some of the best horses

were of the blood. The dam of Romero, Gretchen, can claim to be one of the great brood mares of the United States. With two sons in the 2:30 list, and another which is only a trifle outside of that mark, she is entitled to place, and there is a good prospect of others of her progeny coming into the charmed circle. There are reports that her two-year-old daughter, Zeluska, is still faster than any which have preceded her, and that there is a strong probability that the record for this age will be beaten by her. Gretchen was by Mambrino Pilot, the sire of Hannis, Mambrino Gift, and others of renown, and her dam was by Canada Chief, her second dam by Fanning's Tobe, and her third dam by imported Leviathan. Thus the pedigree on both sides is good, showing a preponderance of the blood which Fanny Kemble said "only did it quite well," and therefore there was reasonable expectation that Romero should make a good showing. Still to take the first place in the calendar was more than could be anticipated; and that a colt with so little work as he had, should make a bound to the top of the ladder, scarcely to be looked. He was not broken until after he was three years old.

ran with a band of mares on Charley Thomas' ranch, near San Diego. He was bred by Hancock M. Johnston, at Los Angeles, and only driven six weeks when he was thrown out of training. In that time he showed 2:36, and his owner was confident that he could show still faster, though a slight injury to his leg necessitated his being thrown out of work. The winter before he was four years old Mr. Salisbury purchased him, and he was placed in the hands of John H. Goldsmith. From the first there was great improvement, and it was evident that he must make a fast horse, with the usual proviso that there should be no mishap befall him. His first race was trotted at Santa Rosa, and in this he was beaten by Alex. Button. The fastest heat was 2:26¼, and from the way he trotted it was palpable that even this fast work for a four-year-old was no measure of his powers. Button won the fast heat, though when they met at Oakland the following week Romero scored 2:22½ to his credit, which gave him the pride of place in the four-year-old stallion race. This mark he seemed easily to accomplish, making it again on the Bay District Course, and at the same time going so easily that it appeared to be much within his rate. Still he had a tough customer in Belle Echo, and in every race they met it was doubtful to the last which would prove the victor. This made the races when they came together of the highest interest, and gives additional zest to those which are before them for this year. As Belle will doubtless be the next illustration of the "Notable Horses of California," the comments can be deferred, though it will suffice to say that there will be fierce battles before the fight is ended.

In saying that Romero is a handsome gray, does not quite express the beauty of his form. He is a trifle over fifteen hands two inches in height, and a lengthy horse, that is, he is somewhat longer than he is high. Apart from the symmetry of his formation he has the "points" which will please the eye of a horseman. The very best kind of legs and feet. A good head, showing intelligence of a high cast, and this in a trotter is now duly appreciated. Without sense the trotter is of little account, and a "level head" is a recognized essential feature. This is what gives the determination to stick to the trot under any circumstances, and pulls races out of the fire when they appear to be hopelessly lost. His action is nearly perfect. Last year there was an excess of motion in knee and hock; this year there is more ease, while he has not lost the freedom which is so necessary to give the proper stride. Altogether he is very nearly a model of the American trotter, and should there be the improvement which can rightly be anticipated, he will be a very hard one to beat. The cut is capital, giving the points as exactly as can be shown in a picture, and the artist, Mr. Wyttenbach, has done the famous horse due credit in the portraiture. We are not prone to predict, though we must say that if Romero does not lower the five-year-old record, we will be disappointed.

## TROUT FISHING ON WIND RIVER.

The following account of fishing on Wind river is copied from the New York Herald, the correspondence being inscribed "Fort Keogh, M. T., May 16th, 1882." The fish are almost too plentiful in that country to make the sport an enticing as when it requires some time to fill a fair-sized creel, and the loading down a Government ambulance in a few hours with real "speckled beauties" is rather a tough story for those to believe who are only conversant with the Eastern trout streams. Californians who make trips to the streams of the upper country, and those of the Argonauts who had a fancy for the gentle sport, will not dispute Mr. Brisbin's statement; and before long, when the letters come from the parties visiting the happy fishing of the North, there may be something as exciting as that which is so graphically portrayed in the following:

My first experience at trout fishing out West was in the Wind River country. We had camped late one night on the Big Popoagie River, and the guides told me it was a famous trout stream. In the morning I rose at reveille, and taking my rod, went down the stream and cast the line, baiting with a grasshopper. Hardly had the bait touched the water before it was taken under by a trout. Another and another was taken until I had six, when I went back to camp to have them cooked for my breakfast. These trout were one to one and one-half pounders, red speckled, and their meat hard, firm and sweet. They were as good as any brook trout I had ever eaten.

Next day we camped at three o'clock on the Little Popoagie, and all hands turned out to fish. The soldiers caught enough for the companies, and Major Jackson and I took forty and thirty-seven respectively. They were smaller than the Big Popoagie trout, and even better, I thought. The guide said there was a lake at the head of the stream, about six miles distant, and Jackson and I rode up to it. The trout were enormous—one taken weighing nearly three pounds. Nelson, my guide, told me over on the North Fork of the Wind River I would find still better fishing and very large trout. Jackson and I one day took an ambulance and went over. Almost at the first cast I hooked a monster. I tried to land him, but in vain. "Drown him!" cried Jackson, and I gave him the line. Whisk! whirl went the reel, and he ran down the stream like a race horse. Turning short about, he came up again.

"That will never do!" cried Jackson. "He will go under a log or get the line fast! Reel him in, man!" I did reel him in, coming back a few steps to gain line. But it was too late. He went under a cottonwood tree which had fallen into the stream, and parted my line with a snap.

"That's as bad as Bob Roosevelt would do," cried Jackson, and I felt humiliated.

"I'm going to wade," continued Jackson.

"And take a mean advantage of your superior," I added, "knowing he has the rheumatism and can't go in."

"Never mind," responded the little man, and in he went. "Come out, Jackson," I said. "you will catch your death of cold; besides the water is full five feet deep." The little man waded out until he was waist deep and cast his line. There was a nibble, and if some one had thrown a stone into the river, and under the line went. I laid my rod down and watched Jackson. First, out went the reel and the play was enormous. Slowly Jackson drew him up until we could see his back, and then off he went again, Jackson following him. Again and again he wound him up and let him out until I could see his head, and saw he was drowning. Jackson came on shore and we landed him, a full four-pounder, undressed.

I repaired my line, and in an hour we had a full string—fifty pounds at least—and returned to camp. Jackson well wrapped up in the ambulance driver's blanket to prevent him from taking cold.

Two days later we crossed the divide and encamped in a beautiful cottonwood grove on the banks of Little Wind River. I had often heard of the trout in this river, and at once made arrangements for a general fish. Part of the officers were to go up the stream and part fish down, while Jackson and myself, advised by Crutcher, the guide, had determined to fish in a little stream called Trout Creek. The one who took the greatest amount of trout in pounds was to have a feast, and the one who secured the largest single trout to be given a fine buffalo robe. The sun was just rising when we set out up the beautiful valley. Parting at the forks of the trail with our friends, they went down to the river while Jackson and I turned toward the hills.

"Remember," cried Jackson, after the throng of retreating horsemen and ambulances, "the man that is late don't count: four o'clock sharp, gentlemen, if you please, at Crutcher's house."

A sharp drive of an hour across the open country brought us to a large meadow through which Crutcher said the stream we were in quest of ran. It was an insignificant little affair, very crooked, but full of deep holes and enticing shallows. It was the veritable picture of the famous "Willows," and as the trout sang all day:

    Down in the dark holes I keep
    And there in the moonlike I float and sleep,
    By cottonwood log and the springing bog
    And the aching willows I lie loeng.

We were soon at work lifting out the speckled denizens. Taking my post behind a leaning cottonwood tree I let my line drop over the bank, and hardly had it touched the water before there was a splash, a jerk, and I landed a half-pounder.

"A good beginning," cried Jackson, who was still fixing his rod.

"Take him off." I said, "for I am afraid to move. The water is very clear and they are wild, so we will have to keep under cover."

Jackson took my fish off, and calling to a soldier to assist me, hurried down the stream. I could see the old fisherman was being 'consumed' by a desire to begin the sport. What is it in a man that makes him so love to shoot birds and catch fish? How we dream in the spring of the glorious summer days, when we shall linger along the green banks of the bright flowing streams or wander through the valleys that conduct them toward their ocean homes, listening to the whirr of the wing that is to be broken by our swift flying shot. There is, indeed, an earthly bliss in hunting and fishing known only to the true lovers of field sports.

But I forgot quite. From my perch behind the cottonwood stump I cast again and again, each time hooking my nimble victim until eleven had been landed from one hole. They were not large trout, perhaps from half to three-quarters of a pound. Just right for table use and very fat, their sleek sides and deep vermilion spots glistening like silver in the sunlight. Half an hour later I overtook Jackson and found him with a full string. We emptied our strings twice into the ambulance, and then we lunched under the shade of a wide spreading cottonwood tree.

Two hours later the driver came to say if we intended to ride home in the ambulance we must stop fishing, as we had all the springs with our own weight would bear. Every one who has seen a government army ambulance knows the seats run lengthwise, and sure enough the space between the seats was well filled with trout. I could hardly realize that we had taken so many; but there they were.

It was not yet quite three o'clock when we arrived at Crutcher's house, but some of the party were there before us, each having taken great abundance of fish. Lieutenant Dinwiddie had the largest trout, having taken a three-pounder. Jackson and I had by far the largest number and the greatest weight, he claiming seventy-six pounds when they were divided. I had sixty-four.

I longed to catch one of the big trout in the Wind River, and Jackson, Russell and I agreed to go out alone next day and try the deep water for some of the monsters reported to be hidden in the dark green pools. I found a glassy looking place and whipped it vigorously, but the hermit, if there, would not rise. Russell was more fortunate and raised a three-pounder, but could not land him. Jackson, after some patient angling, hooked his prize and called loudly for help. We found him playing the largest trout I had ever seen in the country. Up and down the stream they went, Jack doing his best to drown him. He threshed the water into a foam, and now and then showed a head that looked as large as a sheep's head. After a long fight he was safely brought to shore, and was a full three-and-a-half pounder.

We took a great many small ones, but it was late in the day and I had almost begun to despair of getting a hermit, when, while whipping the water near a cottonwood log, I felt a sudden jerk. I did not see him, but I knew he was there all the same, and he pulled like a yearling calf. I let him run, and called to Jackson to come and help me. We were soon playing him, and got him away from the log. He started down the river, and the stream being clear we let him run. He carried out nearly one hundred feet of line before he stopped. "Now wind him up carefully," said Jackson. "and see he don't double back under the log or he will break the line, certain."

He lay so still and was so heavy I thought him dead, but just as I raised his head and he got a sniff of fresh air away he went, taking with him a cottonwood log.

"Run him into the shallow," cried Jackson, "and we will drown him." I tried it, but found the task more difficult than I had anticipated. I was sure he would part my line, and, asking Jackson to hold the rod and net a moment, I waded in behind him and pounced upon his back. The line parted almost immediately, and I was afraid he would escape.

"Lie down upon him," said Jackson, and I did. He struggled under me like a young whale, and to make sure of him I thrust my hand into his mouth and seized him through the gills. Drawing his sleek carcass from the water I held him up, as fine a specimen of an old hermit as ever was seen. He bit me horribly, and made the blood run, but what did I care for that so I had my prize safe? What sportsman would not stand a bite on the hand for the honor of capturing such a monster trout? I have taken many fine trout since in western streams, but none finer than this one from the Wind River.

The next day Crutcher, our guide, announced that he would give us a frontier dinner at his house, or rather cabin, up the valley. Crutcher had for a wife a Sioux squaw, a

fine looking woman, and said to be a good cook. The following is, as near as I can remember, the bill of fare served:

    SOUP.
    Green pea and bean.
    FISH.
Baked trout and boiled whitefish.
    MEATS.
Rocky Mountain sheep, roast; elk, roast; fried antelope.
    ENTRÉES.
New potatoes, peas, radishes, mashed turnips and lettuce.
    DESERT.
Pumpkin pie, wild raspberry pie, cream on canned peaches, wild sweet raspberries in cream.

The fresh bread and sweet new butter were the best part of the dinner, and I never ate better anywhere.

There are hundreds of fine trout streams out west, and I could fill a side of the Herald with descriptions that would make the mouths of your New York sportsmen water. What I have said, however, will be sufficient, and the description of the Wind River will answer for a hundred other streams equally as good for trouting. We actually catch the hermit trout and not in our dreams:

    When the streams with moonlight beams,
    Sparkle all silver and starlight gleams,
    Then, then look out for the hermit trout,
    For he springs and dimples the shallows about,
    While the tired angler dreams.

           JAMES S. BRISBIN.

## THE CALIFORNIA TROUT.

Dr. T. H. Bean, a well-informed ichthyologist of the Smithsonian Institute, writes to Mr. E. G. Blackford of the New York Commission a letter, which is published in Forest and Stream, in which he says the trout found in California are the following:

1. Salmo irideus, Gibbons.—California brook trout, rainbow trout, occurs west of the Sierra Nevada, throughout California and northward to Oregon. I have collected a young trout at Sitka which is so nearly like iridea that I referred it to that species in my "Preliminary Catalogue of Alaskan Fishes." Young iridea cannot be distinguished from young gairdneri by one who is little acquainted with fishes.

2. Salmo gairdneri, Rich.—Steelhead, hardhead, salmon trout, ah shut (Sitkas.) Sacramento River to Kodiak, Alaska. The adult bears a striking resemblance to the salar or Maine salmon, and reaches a weight of twenty pounds or more. I found gravid females at Sitka, in June, 1880. As already remarked, it is very difficult to distinguish the difference between the young of this and the last, though the adults are easily enough separated.

3. Salmo purpuratus pallas. Columbia River salmon trout, Rocky Mountain brook trout, lake trout, "the salmon trout of the Rocky Mountain region," "not common south of Mount Shasta in California." Abundant in Washington, Oregon, British Columbia and Southern Alaska. This is a black spotted species, with red patches on the lower jaw, and is readily distinguished from the two preceding. You remember the pair which was sent you from the museum over a year ago, marked Sitka, L. A. Beardslee and T. H. Bean.

4. Salmo purpuratus, var. Henshawi, Gill & Jordan.— Lake Tahoe trout, silver trout, black trout found in Lake Tahoe, Pyramid Lake and streams of the Sierra Nevada. Considered by Prof. Jordan to be a variety of S. purpuratus. This trout is regularly brought to San Francisco market.

Two of the above species (irideus and purpuratus), were included in the lot which we received from you April 6, 1882. You have also sent us the Lake Tahoe trout at another time. With the trout forwarded April 6th there was a species of California salmon from Willow Brook, Minnesota.

The only species of red-spotted trout so far known on the whole west coast is the Salvelinus malma (Walbaum) Jordan & Gilbert. This is the Dolly Varden trout, bull trout, red-spotted trout, salmon trout, Galets (Russian), Ahn Chuck, (Kodiakmut); it is found west of the Cascade Range, from Northern California to, at least, Colville River in Alaska. In other words, throughout the mainland and islands of Alaska. This trout has received a great many scientific names, but the one here given is apparently the oldest. The sea-run individuals lose their red spots, and are then called so the Salmo immaculatus of H. R. Storer. This is much like the common brook of the East (S. fontinalis), reaching its greatest size in cold, northern waters. At Kodiak it forms an important article of export under the name of salmon trout. Now, as to the question: "Is there any difference between the California mountain or rainbow trout and the McCloud River trout?" In my opinion the two species are applied to the same fish (Salmo irideus), and I think there is no other black-spotted trout in California but the irideus, there is the red-spotted species (Salvelinus malma.) I have the impression that we have never received any other black-spotted species from the McCloud than irideus. However, I will look up the records and inform you if I find that I am in error. "McCloud River trout" is a bad name, because you cannot know whether reference is made to the red-spotted or the black-spotted one. Salvelinus is a good descriptive term for S. irideus.

OUR FIRST BEAR STORY.—From the Calaveras Chronicle we learn that two men, named William Magee and William Johnson, were out fishing recently on the Mokelumne River, above West Point, and beside their fishing outfit had provided themselves for a hunt as well, so as to take in all the sport that might offer on their trip. While on their way home, and within four miles of West Point, their attention was attracted by the fierce barking of one of their dogs in the woods a short distance from the road. On going to ascertain the cause, they found that the hound had treed a very respectable sized cinnamon bear. Magee leveled his rifle on the animal and lodged a ball in his shoulder, which caused the bear to let go his hold and drop to the ground, a distance of about twenty feet. The hound immediately fastened on to the bear as he landed, but would have paid dearly for his temerity had not another dog belonging to the party come up and attacked the enemy in the rear about the same time, getting a hold that made the bear weaken at once and let go the hound and turn upon his new adversary. No sooner was the hound free than he retired precipitately, having had enough of the fight. The other dog, seeing he was to be alone in the contest, also beat a hasty retreat. Once free from the dogs, the bear ascended the tree with wonderful rapidity, and did not stop until he had reached some large branches at least seventy feet from the ground. Magee fired twice at the animal, and only at the second shot did he leave his lofty perch, and struck the ground with tremendous force. The animal, though mortally wounded, having just emerged from the snow of the mountains, weighed 400 pounds dressed. One of the fore paws was brought to this place and shown to us, and it was no small one either.

## HONOLULU CORRESPONDENCE.

HONOLULU, June 13th, 1882.

MR. JOSEPH CAIRN SIMPSON—DEAR SIR:—Your favor of May 30th duly came to hand, and in answer, please first to put my name on your list, and then believe that I will do my best to add to your subscribers on the Islands. As to racing information I shall be at all times glad to give you every information in my power, the more so as there is no paper published here that shows any interest in racing or breeding, or indeed any other sport; but for the past six months there is little that has transpired here in this line that would be interesting to your readers. The plain fact is that racing here is not in a very healthy condition, as there appears among a certain clique an evident desire to scoop in the winnings through transactions of questionable character, rather than run the risk of competition all open and above board. The result of the races that have just taken place fully justifies these remarks, as there was marked evidence that in some cases the programme of winners was planned out in advance, although there are many victims among those who lost their money who still think that their money was lost on the square. Following is the list of races and entries:

*Kamehameka Day.*

KAPIOLANI PLATE—$100. Free to all Hawaiian-bred horses; catch weight. Mile dash.

J. A. Cummins' b g B. G. Stanford ... 1
G. Lucas' b g Stranger ... 2
G. B. Kelly's ch m Venus ... 3

Time, 1:48¼.

KING'S PLATE.—$125. Open to all three year-olds; to carry 100 pounds. Mile and repeat.

W. H. Cornwell's gr h Garfield ... 1
G. B. Kelly's b h Hancock ... Dist.

Time, 1:50¼.

These colts have been pitted against each other several times with varying results, but the general impression is that Hancock is the best horse when in condition, but it was a notable fact that he had been ailing for the ten days previous to the race. Still, for a time he made a good showing, and the winner was received with cheers, which he would have deserved had he beaten Hancock on even merits, the latter being weak and weighted down with a surplus impost of 35 pounds.

QUEEN EMMA PLATE.—$100. Free to all. A dash of three-quarters of a mile.

G. A. Cummins's b g B. G. Stanford ... 1
O. Stillman's b h Mark Twain ... 2
G. B. Kelly's ch m Venus ... 3
M. E. Allbaugh's ch m Romping Girl ... Dist.

Time, 1:20.

In this race the betting was principally on Stanford against the field, it not being generally known that Mark Twain was the only true contestant, the others being entered merely as a blind. Thus, the Romping Girl is a fine speedy mare, and I have seen her run three-quarters of a mile in 1:17½, and on this occasion it would have been dollars to cents on her had she been meant, but she was withdrawn on the plea of acting ugly at the post, and such a serious breach of the racing laws was allowed to pass unnoticed.

LEAHI CUP.—Mule race; a mile dash; free to all, at catch weights.

C. A. Bailey's Nigger ... 1
G. A. Dick's Kate ... 2
H. N. Crabbe's Minnie ... 3
L. J. Aylette's Coco Head ... 4

REGENT'S PLATE.—$100; free to all Hawaiian-bred horses; mile and repeat, at catch weights.

J. A. Cummins' b. g. Stanford ... 1
G. B. Kelly's ch. m. Venus ... Dist.
G. Lucas' b. g. Stranger ... Dist.

Time, 1:49¼.

RECIPROCITY PLATE.—$100; trotting; best three in five, to harness, for all horses that have not a better record than 2:40 in any public race in the Kingdom.

M. E. Allbaugh's ch. m. Coquette ... 1
James Dodd's ch. g. Thomas H ... dr.

Time, 2:39¼.

Thos. H. having pink-eye, the handlers of Coquette asked the judges to let them trot Coquette against the time, 2:40. They consented. The money was there and did not belong to them, and it was an easy thing. According to the terms of this race, Barns or Goldsmith Maid could have entered, or even Maud S. Coquette has a record of 2:28¾.

PARK CUP.—$75. Three-quarters of a mile. Free for all three-year-olds bred in Kingdom; catch weights.

W. H. Colburn enters Unnamed ... 1
J. F. Colburn enters Equal Rights ... 2

Time, 1:24¼.

EXPRESS CUP.—$75. Trotting race; one mile. Free to all horses driven in a public hack six months.

Keopuhiwa enters b m Dolly ... 1
Manuel Reis enters b m Mollie ... 2

Time, 3:51¼.

This was the most enjoyable race of the day. The horses were driven by their owners, one a native and the other a Portuguese. No jockey tricks, but a good square race.

PONY RACE.—$50. One mile dash, for ponies bred in the Kingdom; not over 13¼ hands; catch weights.

J. Lishman enters Why Not ... 1
O. J. Holt enters Tyrnat ... 2
J. Kaanaana enters Mokulehua ... 3
J. H. King enters Bushwhacker ... 4

Time, 2:05.

KAMEHAMEHA PLATE.—$200. Free for all trotters; best three in five, to harness.

W. H. Cornwell's b g Oliver ... 1 2 1 2 1
M. E. Allbaugh's ch m Coquette ... 2 1 2 1 2

This was a queer sort of a race, in which a great deal of money changed hands. The best time was 2:35, and to an unprejudiced mind it appeared as if the heats were trotted to suit the betting.

LUNAMAKAAINANA PLATE.—$100. Free for all; a mile and a half dash; to carry 100 pounds.

W. H. Cornwell's gr h Garfield ... 1
G. Kelly's b h Hancock ... 2

Time, 2:45.

KAIULANI CUP.—$75. Hurdle race; a mile dash, over four hurdles; free for all, at catch weights.

C. Lucas' b g Stranger ... w. o.
M. E. Allbaugh's ch m Romping Girl ... dr.

Time, 2:19¼.

For some unknown reasons Romping Girl did not start, but the judges allowed Stranger to walk over for the cup. But, then, had they adhered rigidly to the rules, there would have been fewer races. There is naught to be said of the Racing Committee in the way of blame. They made some errors, but, then, they were chosen principally to ward off the idea that anything but square racing would be allowed, and as far as they were concerned such was the case; but when it came to fine racing points and decisions, they knew as much about them as I do about elephants.

Send us some horses that can not be controlled by any clique, and we shall have better sport next time.

Yours, KAAMAINA.

## BREEZES FROM MOUNT AND DELL.

HIGHLAND SPRINGS CAMP,
Lake Co., July 2, 1882.

EDITOR BREEDER AND SPORTSMAN: 'Tis the figure above that follows the eight, which speaks the truth; there is one notch more cut in the stick that stands recorded to our allotted time. And then why not be industrious and persistent and wait not for a more favorable opportunity, but grasp the occasion to enjoy every pleasure that nature's bountiful store has conceived for man, and which only health of mind and body can appreciate? Lay down the hammer and trowel, the needle, book and pen, and bid good-bye to the city's dust, the poisonous gases, the destroying malaria that causes typhoid, the excruciating neuralgia and rheumatism, dyspepsia and biliousness, and let every man, woman and child leave that ocean fog, the summer winds, that heavy damp atmosphere, at least once a year, and go to the mountains, where there exists no malaria, no ache or pain, if only but for a few days, there to inhale the pure mountain air and drink the water that glows and sparkles with the elixir of life. You then can return, refreshed and restored, with mind and body strong, and for every day so spent years will be added to your life. You can become more useful to yourself and a pleasure to your friends, and then fit to live. Each year I can notice a greater desire for the people of the city to avail themselves of this very important change and pleasure. The watering places are this year well patronized—the pleasure seekers are taxing the stage lines to their full capacity. Lake county has been specially favored, and that justly, as I do not think that any county in the State offers a finer climate, a greater variety of mineral waters and springs, picturesque mountain scenery, abundance of game and fish, and a great variety of beautiful mountain songsters, various flowering shrubs and trees that are interwoven with the wild climatis and grapevine. Each county, however, has its special attractions, and one cannot go astray without realizing sufficient pleasure to well repay him for the trip.

There are times, however, when the traveler in the mountains becomes wearied and tired, and he whiles in a half doze hours in a stage coach, climbing the steep winding road over the rugged mountains, in midday, when the full rays of the noonday sun are reflected from the parched brown surface, which is generally void of all moisture or vegetation, especially on the southern slopes; the dust rising from under the horses' feet and curling up in dense volumes settles in the coach so thick that you can scarcely recognize your traveling companions. Yet you soon forget the tedious part, for when the summit is reached a gentle refreshing breeze fans you to consciousness. As from a dream, you become spellbound and speechless, suddenly beholding before you as if by magic a panorama so grand and beautiful, and extending so far that part is lost from view; as the eye cannot follow the vast extent of the valleys beneath you—so charming and beautiful—frescoed with waving grasses, wild flowers, vines, fields of grain and corn, which are varied and blended in many shades and colors as to their near aproach to ripening; with orchards and their golden tropical and semi-tropical fruits well defined; the rivers and streams, having their curves and angles outlined with the foliage of massive oaks and cottonwood trees; lakes, with their placid waters so clear and still that they resemble immense mirrors placed there, which are reflecting the sun's rays in obedience to nature's laws, which provide nourishment and warmth to both animal and vegetable life. With herds of fat and silky-coated cattle, horses and sheep quietly feeding, their shepherds near at hand, dreaming away a lazy existence. The vulture and turkey buzzard, with outstretched and motionless wings quietly drifting with the currents in a deep blue and cloudless sky, the sun's rays reflecting upon their purple and bronzed feathers, which cast a moving shadow upon the earth. For the moment you are startled—'tis the shadow of death—for their bright piercing eyes are feasting and fattening their feathered carcasses, and transmitting a thanksgiving feast to their naked and wistful young, who are securely nestled on some rugged projecting cliff that overlooks the dying struggles of some poor creature beneath them. In astonishment you look and move not, and still look again at the grand panorama, and think of the strange workings of Nature. With one full breath of the mountain elixir and another you feel as though the depths of unlimited space in the heavens could be explored; you advance, and in the twinkle of an eye you are lost, and know not where you stand. WHETSTONE.

## A CHALLENGE FROM M. W. HICKS.

EDITOR BREEDER AND SPORTSMAN: This is a country exceptionally free in its speech; a fact with which I have no quarrel, merely claiming the right to "talk back." Mr. John Mackey, Superintendent for Messrs. Haggin and Tevis, has made the public declaration that my stock all "duffed." As I have stallions asking public patronage, and am breeding trotters for sale, this declaration, if unanswered, would be prejudicial to my interests. Now, as I have representatives of the Hambletonian, Mambrino and Bashaw families, backed up by stout thorough blood in the distance, if they are quitters it must be the fault of their management. It is true that most of my stock have a pacing cross, but pacing blood did not hurt Lady Thorn, Maud S., or Santa Claus, and ought not to prove an injury in regard to mine. But this talk does not refute the gentleman's charge, nor will it convince the public; so I will make Mr. Mackey a friendly proposition that will settle the question, in which the public as well as ourselves are interested. The firm for which Mr. Mackey is employed are older breeders than myself, and probably breed fifty colts to my one. Now, I will match a one-year-old, a two-year-old, a three-year-old, and a mature horse, of my breeding, against like classes bred by Messrs. Haggin & Tevis, for two hundred dollars a race; and to make the test of staying qualities more thorough, I will make the yearling race mile heats; the two-year-old race, best three in five; and the three-year-old race two mile heats. Races to be trotted at any agreed time between now and November, on the Sacramento track. M. W. HICKS.

Florin, June 29, 1882.

## CORRESPONDENCE.

LEMOORE, Tulare Co., July 5, 1882.

EDITOR BREEDER AND SPORTSMAN: This is the Upper San Joaquin, or perhaps we had better say the Tulare Valley. Ordinarily a fair grain country, a most excellent stock country, as well as the very best part of the State for raising most kinds of fruit. But this is our dry year; consequently a small allowance of grain. This immediate section—Mussel Slough country—will produce about half a crop of grain, but as irrigation is the order here, summer crops follow. Those, with the frequent cutting of the alfalfa fields, will make quite a busy and prosperous season.

In your Stockton correspondence, last issue, there seems to be a little mistake in the name of the sire of the colts from this county entered in the two-year-old race, Stockton District, to be trotted next week. The name of the horse is *Algona*, a son of Almont, not "Angora" or "Argola," as published. Algona was bred and raised by Gen. Withers, of Kentucky, and introduced here by S. F. Gilmore, in the spring of 1879. Since which time he has been kept here till April of this year, when he was sold to J. B. Haggin and taken to Sacramento county. He was really the first trotting stallion ever introduced here. As might have been expected few, if any, mares here were well enough bred to produce trotters. Such as they were, however, a fair number were bred to him. Consequently we have in and around Lemoore a number of half-bred trotting colts. Among those, two or three only have been handled at all for speed, one of which has been sold, the other two have been entered to trot at Stockton this fall. Your correspondent, in speaking of the race and colts, says "they are all doing well." This is likely true so far as the colts at Stockton and vicinity are concerned. But if I am correctly informed, three of the colts for this race are in this county, two of them in training at Visalia. The colts at Visalia are s. c. Almoore by Algona, named by H. Robinson, not S. F. Gilmore, as stated by your correspondent, and a nephew filly named by Mr. Murray and being handled by him, Robinson & Gambling have their stable of horses at Visalia; among them is the colt Almoore. It is said he is doing well and going fast. Likely the same could be said of the nephew-filly being worked by Mr. Murray. The other colt from this county is by Algona and kept on the farm of the owner, Mr. E. Giddings, near Lemoore. He was handled a little as a yearling and showed quite well for an alfalfa raised colt and one handled only by the boys on the farm. But, unfortunately, soon after he was entered in this race, he went lame, and has been entirely laid up till within a few days. He is now much better, and hopes are entertained that he will be able to work a little from now on, and *possibly* be able to start in the race.

Yours, E.

# ATHLETICS.

Harmon, the well-known sprinter, is reported as anxious to concede McComb some yards in a short distance sprint.

There are rumors of a five-mile match between P. McIntyre and G. Guerrero for a stake of $500 a side. Mc. don't love the distance, and Guerrero's backers are not very plentiful. We hardly think the match will come off this season.

H. S. Brooks, who defeated L. E. Myers at the championship meeting, is expected to arrive in this city in a few days. R. S. Haley, of the O. A. C., is anxious to meet him in a dash of 100 or 220 yards. If Mr. Brooks is able and willing to accommodate him, the event will be a treat to our local athletes. Two years ago Mr. Brooks could not be induced to compete in the O. A. C. handicaps, in which Haley was scratch man. And he would undoubtedly have needed a liberal handicap at that time. Since then Brooks has gained the reputation of being a first-class amateur at Bob's favorite distances, and will not need the services of the handicapper.

### A BRILLIANT PERFORMANCE.

In the Civil Service sports that opened in London June 3d, there was an event to which we desire to call the attention of our athletes. This was the handicap in which all the cracks were entered, and, as may be seen by the following description, was a brilliant triumph for W. G. George:

"His magnificent running really made the race no race, for he was the only one in it. Going off with a wonderfully easy stride, he slipped along without in any way revealing the pace he was going at, and it was only when the watch showed 1m. 17⅘s. for the first lap that one commenced to realize what was going on. When, however, he got amongst his men, going up the back stretch for the second time, and ran through them as though they were so many ordinary limit markers instead of aspiring champions, the excitement grew apace, and waxed stronger when he took the lead at the half mile. As he came down the straight for the second time, forty yards or more ahead of every one else, cheering set in, but some old hands thought he must be going too fast, and screamed at him to take care. As the watch showed 2m. 45s. for two laps, there was some reason for their fears, but George kept on. Up the back he, not unnaturally, began to get slower, and Birkett (50 yards), putting it on along the top, got nearer, and improving his position until he had no more spurt left, finished 18 yards only behind George, who broke the worsted in 4m. 19.2-5s., not by any means so much exhausted as one would expect, although we do not join in the belief (shared by himself) that he could have done very much better. At the outside, he might have knocked off the odd 2-5, had he been pressed. The quarter-mile time was not taken, but the half was completed in 2m. 4⅕s., and the three-quarters in 3m. 8⅗s. Birkett ran quite up to his form, and would have done 4m. 32s. for the full distance."

Our athletes, who lead an easy life six months, then enter a mile run without previous training, and are badly beaten in much worse time than five minutes, will probably not be comforted by reading the above. A hundred yards dash, with a sufficient handicap to insure the winning of the medal, without having to exercise half a dozen times to fit themselves for the event, seems to be the height of their ambition.

Several members of the O. A. C. are anxious to beat some of the Club records, and would like to see a few good medals offered as an encouragement to go into active training for the purpose. They should by all means be accommodated. The best part of the season for athletics on this coast is still before us, and the athletes who have survived the holidays propose to go to work in earnest on the new track. It behooves the officers of the Club to give them as much encouragement as possible.

## THE TURF.

### THE CHICAGO RACES.

Similar to the Coney Island Jockey Club, of whose brilliant meeting at Sheepshead Bay, Long Island, we wrote at such length in the last issue, the Chicago Driving Park Association seems at once to have attained to a pinnacle of success that in less liberal and enterprising hands it would have taken a decade to achieve. Following in the steps of the Chicago Jockey Club, that commenced operations in 1877, the present Association was formed about the commencement of last year, with a capital of $100,000 and an executive committee of wealth, experience, liberality and social standing—a combination so devoutly to be wished for in an enterprise of this character. Under these favorable auspices two successful meetings were held last year, and the programmes for the running races commencing Saturday, June 24th, and for the trotting races that begin on July 15th, are of such a varied and brilliant character as to enlist the largest number of entries ever registered in a western city, including horses of finest quality from almost every State of the Union. At both these meetings California is well represented, and although our hopes in the promise of our horses have not been fully realized, in their running there is much to be proud of, considering the unfavorable conditions that marked their first appearance on the Eastern Turf.

There was no secret about the fact among the Californian owners and trainers, that if a violent rain storm came on during the meeting, the consequent heavy track would greatly impede the chances of our horses. Surely enough, as luck would have it, a heavy storm came up on Saturday, continuing the Sunday, and necessitating the postponement of the races to the 26th of June. On that day there was a fair attendance, with rather warm and sunny weather, but the track was yet heavy, and the time made was therefore slow.

The first race was the "Inaugural Rush," for a purse of $300, for all ages, which was won by Bootjack, the favorite, with Gus Matthews second and Clarissima third, with Ranger and Good Night unplaced.

The second race was the Ladies' Stake, three-quarters of a mile, for two-year-old fillies, $50 each, half forfeit, with $800 added. This was won easily by Miss Woodford, the favorite, with Vis-a-Vis second, and Blue Grass Belle, Orange Blossom and Olean in the order mentioned. Time, 1:20¾.

The third was the Board of Trade Handicap, a mile and a-half dash, in which there was some heavy wagering at the following odds and weights: Bend Or, 4 years, 117 pounds, $400; John Davis, aged, 108, $350; Monogram, 3 years, 107, $85; Mr. Baldwin's Sunday, 3 years, 91, $75; Aliunde, 5 years, 108, $65, while $80 was given for the field, in which were Blazes, 4 years, 117 pounds; Annie G., 5 years, 110; Babee, 4 years, 101, and Intrinsic, 4 years, 96 pounds. With a good start, Babee and Sunday took the lead, and held it for a mile, when they gave place to Blazes and John Davis, followed by Bend Or. The last named waited until well up the stretch, when he passed the leaders, and, keeping the lead, won without special exertion by half a length from John Davis, with Aliunde third, two lengths further off. Time, 2:46½.

The fourth race was mile heats, over four hurdles, which was won by Guy, he winning the first heat in 1:58½. Judge Burnett taking the second heat in 1:55¼, and Guy securing the final heat in 1:58¾.

The last race was an extra purse for horses that had not run this year, a mile and a furlong, in which there were ten starters. It was won by Stanton in 2 min.

On the Tuesday, the proceedings commenced with the Flash Stakes, in which our California crack, Gano, made his *debut* on an Eastern track. The weather was fine and the attendance large. The Flash is for two-year-olds, five furlongs, in which there were forty-seven subscribers. Punster was the favorite at $225, Ascender next choice at $185, Barnes $75, and the field $50, comprising Barnes, Slocum, Atzec, April Fool and Pearl Thorne. To a good start, Barnes and Ascender took the lead, which they held, with the others bunched and well up, until well round the turn. It was a good race home, Ascender beating Barnes by half a length in 1:03, he being three lengths in front of Pearl Thorne, who was followed by Gano, Slocum, Punster, April Fool and Aztec. The defeat of Punster was a great blow to some of the Kentuckians present and to some of the Chicago speculators, but the majority of the local betters backed Captain Cottrill's colt. The winner is a bay gelding, by imported Buckden, dam Ascension, and promises to be very useful to the Mobile stable.

The second race was the Selling Purse, of $300, for all ages, a mile and an eighth, which was won by Flash in 1:57¼, Tom Barlow second, Churchill third, and nine others unplaced.

The next was the Green Stakes, a mile and a quarter, for three-year-olds, that did not win last year, for which there were fifty-six nominations. Harry Gilmore was the favorite at $100 against $70 for Mistral, $40 for Plunkett and $50 for the field, in which were Gunnar, Washburd, Glenarm and Gus Matthews. Gilmore and Gus made the running until well in the homestretch, when Tom Plunkett and Gunnar came to the front, the former winning by half a length, with Gilmore third. Time, 2:13¼.

The last race was a Club Purse of $300, for all ages, heats of five furlongs, and was run in a heavy rain storm. There were eleven starters. Bell Boy took the first heat in 1:04, Mamie W. the second in 1:08½. In the third heat the filly was favorite at $100 to $30, and won easily in 1:11¾. The Mutual pools paid $50 for every $5 invested.

On the Thursday, in the first race, a Club Purse of $350, for all ages, was won by the favorite, John Davis, Metropolis being second, Madame Rowett third, with five other starters. Time, 2:11.

The next was the Illinois Oaks, a mile and a half, for three-year-old fillies, $50 each, half forfeit, with $800 added, and in this the Duchess of Norfolk made her first appearance. On the faith of her reputation here, she was made equal favorite at $225 with Belle of Runnymede, Pearl Jennings and Pinafore selling for $135 each, and Lizzie McWhirter and Katie Creel $25 each. The two favorites made the running for a mile, and in the deep mud, then pumped themselves out, and Katie Creel, judiciously ridden, came to the front and beat the Belle out, Lizzie McWhirter securing the third position. Time was 2:54, and the Mutual pools paid $117 20, an excellent $5 investment.

In the Merchants' Stake, for all ages, a mile and a quarter, Checkmate won handily in 2.22, with Blazes second, Bootjack third, and six others unplaced, including Mr. Baldwin's filly Sunday, who apparently found herself in too good a company.

The Steeplechase was won by Guy, and the final race was an Owners' Handicap, in which there were eleven starters, including Gano, who sold for $150, against $175 for Mary Corbett, and the field $325. The affair was very one-sided, Saunterer taking the lead, and winning easily in 1:19½, with Jack Haverly second and Arno third. The French pools paid $70, another good turn for the outsiders.

It rained almost all the night on Thursday, and then there was another down pour an hour before the races, making the track so muddy and disagreeable that the attendance was very slight. The first race was "The Criterion," a dash of three-quarters of a mile for two-year-old colts, which closed with forty-one nominations. Of these there were but five that came to the post; Ascender bing a great favorite at $100, against $30 for the field, in which were the two Californians, Lucky B. and Grismer, Idle Pat and Atzec. The start was pretty even, and Lucky B. made the running with Ascender, the latter having slightly the best of it at the distance, but Lucky B. rallied and won by a short head in 1:28½. In the selling purse, $300 for all ages, a dash of a mile and a quarter, Ecker won in 2:31½, with Bailey second and Barlow third, with Edison, John Happy and Third Out unplaced. The third was a handicap purse, which was taken by Metropolis, Tosco second, Startle third, and Windrush last. Time, 3:42½. The fourth was a blub purse, for all ages, mile heats, in which there were only two starters, Lizzie S. and Force, the former winning two straight heats in 2,01½ and 2:05¼. The fifth race, a dash of a mile for beaten horses, was won by Farragut, with John Sullivan second and John Henry third. Time, 2:04. With the exception of the Criterion stake the proceedings were voted as somewhat slow.

On Saturday the day was fine, the attendance good, and the track was improving rapidly under a strong breeze, though still it was pronounced very heavy and slower than when the mud was thinner. The first race was the Chicago Stakes for three-year-old colts, one and one-half miles. Bengal was the favorite, at $275; Monogram, $200; Stanton, $180. There was an exciting race at the finish, Stanton winning under persuasion of both whip and steel. The second race was the Chicago Cup, and the Californians spiritedly stuck to Clara D., although Checkmate was the favorite at $420, John Davis selling the next choice at $200, Blazes bringing $65 and Clara D. $65. There was little variation in the race, as John Davis took the lead at the start and never relinquished it, while Clara D. appeared to be watching Checkmate; and though she ran into the second place very handily, she could not reach the victor, John Davis coming in without even having his position in jeopardy. To beat Checkmate was held to be a full measure of glory for the California mare, and the predictions are rife that she will yet place a good race to the Occidental contingent.

The next event was the club purse of $400, 1½ miles. Just before the race, Topsy was the favorite in the pools at $130; Duchess of Norfolk, $100; and Madame Rowett, $25. Topsy got the best of the start, and led to the lower turn, the Duchess next coming round the turn. The Duchess then took the lead and won easily by two lengths, Topsy second, Rowett third. Time, 2:12¾. For the second heat, in the pools Duchess brought $100, field $25. The Duchess went to the lead at once, and was never headed, winning in a canter by half a dozen lengths, Rowett second. Time, 2:16½.

The fourth race was a hurdle handicap, two miles. In the pools Judge Burnett brought $100, field $100. The three ran well together to the fourth hurdle, where Nora fell and rolled directly over her rider, injuring him quite severely. After passing the fifth hurdle, Burnett won easily by half a dozen lengths. Time, 1:20.

The fifth race was a selling purse, one and a half miles, all ages. In the pools Sam Recker brought $100, John Sullivan $70, Jack Haverly $40. Sullivan and Haverly ran head and head for seven furlongs, when Haverly began to fall away and Recker to move up, but Sullivan held the lead and won by four lengths. Recker second, Haverly third. Time, 2:52.

The sixth race was three-quarters of a mile, all ages. In the pools Bell Boy brought $165, Saunterer $125, field $25. The finish was between Goodnight and Saunterer. The former won. Saunterer second, Intrinsic third. Time, 1:22.

On the Monday the promise of good weather was not fulfilled. The rain fell in the night and early in the morning, making the track quite heavy. Just before the first race a drizzling rain set in, and increased to a heavy down-pour before the second race was run, making the track deep in mud and compelling a postponement of the day's programme at the conclusion of the second race. For the first event, Nursery stakes, mile dash, Lucky B was the favorite in the pools. He got away badly, and an effort to make up lost ground and force the pace over such a heavy track was too much for him, and Ascender, who ran a waiting race, three-quarters of a mile, came in a rush in the last furlong, and won. Time, 1:58, Lucky B dropping to third place. With a good track he would give the Mobile crack a very lively race for that distance. In the two-mile heats, Clara D had everything her way, settling the pace throughout and winning at will, under a strong pull, in two straight heats. She demonstrated that she is a good mud horse, as at the conclusion of each heat she scarcely took a long breath, while the others were dead tired. Time, 4:05¼, 4:11.

On Tuesday the first race, three-quarters of a mile for maidens of all ages, John Henry won by half a length, Intrinsic second. Time, 1:27. In the second race, one mile, for three-year-olds that have not run first or second this year, colts 103 pounds, fillies 98 pounds, Boatman won by a length, Jesse James second. Time, 2:01½. In the third race, Selling Purse, half a mile, for two-year-olds, Virgil (filly) won by half a length, Early Bird second. Time, 0:56¼. In the fourth race, one mile and one-eighth, for no winners at this meeting, Lizzie S. won by half a length, Tom Barlow second. Time, 2:11½. The fifth race was the Illinois Derby, for three-year-old colts and fillies. In the pools Duchess of Norfolk sold for $700; Stanton, $450; Anglia, $320; Gunnar, $340; Bengal, $325; Monogram, $200. Gunnar won, hands down, by four open lengths, Stanton second, Bengal third. Monogram, Anglia and Duchess of Norfolk were beaten off, and pulled up, finishing as named. In the sixth race, two miles, for all ages, Bootjack won by a nose, Lida Stanhope second. Time, 4:07½. The seventh race was mile heats, best three in five, for all ages. The starters were Force and Metropolis. Metropolis took the lead and hold it to the finish in each heat. Best time, 2:00. The eighth race, handicap steeplechase, for all ages, about two and a half miles, was won by Edison by a quarter of a mile, Strychnine second, Bailey third. The ninth race, selling purse, for all ages, one and a quarter miles, was won by Dodette in a canter by half a dozen lengths, Amazon second. Time, 2:24½. The tenth race, Owners' handicap, for all ages, three-quarters of a mile, was won by Good Night by half a length, Lizzie S second, Reybee third. Time 1:21½. The eleventh race for all ages, maiden allowance, one and a half miles, was won by Flander in a canter by a dozen lengths, Pope Leo second. Time, 3:55½. The twelfth race, for maiden two-year-olds, five-eighths of a mile, was won by Idle Pal by two necks, Slocum second. Time, 1:09.

Wednesday was an extra day. The attendance was light, but the day was bright and warm and the track heavy. The first race was 1¼ miles for non-winning three-year-olds. In the pools Belle of Runnemede brought $125, the field $50. From the start Flone made the running with John Sullivan lagged on her; Viron, third; Belle of Runnemede, fourth. At the half-mile post Runnemede joined the leaders and at the three-quarter mile post she and Sullivan were together and at distance, and both got the whip, but Sullivan won by a neck; the Belle second, four lengths before Willansee, third; Flone, fourth; Tricks, fifth; Viron, last. Time, 2:18. The Mutuals paid $45 10. The second was three-quarters of a mile for non-winning three-year-olds at this meeting. In the pools Grismer brought $100, Baritone $90. The start was even and Baritone led to the half-mile post, when Grismer went to the front and won handsomely by a length. Time, 1:22½.

The third race was a selling purse, 1¼ miles, for all ages. In the pools Mammorist brought $200, Farragut $165, Bailey $110, the field $65. At the start Farragut, Mammorist and Jack Haverly were together in front, and led without material change for three-quarters of a mile. On the far side, Bailey, running alone, in fourth place, drew up to a length from the leaders, and at the three-quarter post the whole field ran into a bunch, from which Bailey emerged in the lead and won easily by two lengths; Jack Haverly, second, half a length before Katie B., third; Farragut, fourth; Mammorist, fifth; Ed. Reardon, last. Time, 2:17.

The fourth race was mile heats, all ages, allowance for beaten horses. In the first heat pools sold, Clara D. $250, the field $71. Athelstane and Tom Barlow had a little the best of it at the start. Around the first turn Clara D. and Clarissima went forward, At the half-mile Tom Barlow ran into second place and lapped on Clara D. After a driving finish Clara D. won by a length: Clarissima, third, three lengths away; Amazon, fourth; Athelstane, distanced. Time, 1:49½. In the second heat pools Clara D. brought $175, the field $25. Clara D. was never headed, winning by two lengths; Tom Barlow, second, two lengths before Clarissima, third; Amazon, last. Time, 1:48.

## TURF AND TRACK.

The July stakes for two-year-olds at Newmarket, England, five furlongs one hundred and thirty-six yards, was won by Macbeth, Fulmen second, and Lyndell third. The maiden plate, two-year-old colts and fillies, five furlongs, was won by Couleur de Rosa, Canon second and Bisserta third. P. Lorillard's Winonah ran.

Mr. P. Lorillard has recently purchased of Messrs. McIntyre & Swiney, of Kentucky, the chestnut colt foaled in 1881 by Wanderer, dam Katie Pearce, by imp. Leamington, out of Stamps, by Lexington. The colt has been named Wonder. This is close inbreeding to strong and swift stock, as Katie Pearce was a good racer, and Wanderer a famous son of Lexington, second almost to none.

The Breeders' Stakes at Monmouth Park, New Jersey, filled well, but not up to expectations, there being a decided falling off when compared with the figures of previous years. In 1881 the stake had 142 nominations, the present year 166; the stake which has just closed (to be run in 1883) has only 110. This is to be regretted, as the Association have gone to great pains to form the best stake ever constructed. The principal entries are G. Lorillard, 13; P. Lorillard, 17; D. D. Withers, 10; L. Stanford, 12; A. Belmont, 5; Dwyer Brothers, 5; Whitten Brothers, 4; R. W. Walden, 6; Preakness Stable, 5; Mr. Kelso and B. G. Thomas, 3 each. This proves that Ex-Governor Stanford is not content with owning the best young trotting stock, but that he will as well enter the lists against all the best Eastern thoroughbreds. We wish him success.

Judge Mee has two promising fillies this summer, both sired by Thad Stevens. The one from Katie Pease is handsome, lusty, and as playful as a kitten, and she promises well. The other is from Mistake—a daughter of Katie Pease sired by Wildidle—and she, being a first and late foal, is delicate, although prettily formed. Katie and her progeny are the pets of the household, and Judge McKinstry, a fine three-year-old, her only son, by Grinstead or Thad Stevens, will at once go into active training for the fall campaign; making his first appearance probably at the Golden Gate Fair. Katie this year was sent to Wheatley who, although a famous son of War Dance, has as yet had but few opportunities at the stud.

In the Brighton Beach stakes at Long Island on the 16th of June, there was a pretty big bid at a fraud, Laura Glass being doubly pulled so as to allow her stable companion, Aurelius, to win, he being a rank outsider in the betting. They came in first and second, and were both disqualified, the race being given to Florimel, the third horse. At a recent meeting of the Executive Committee it was resolved that the two jockeys, Brophy and Hughes, be exonerated, as they rode to instructions, that, when examined, they at once disclosed; that Frank McCabe, the trainer of both horses, be censured by the President; that Dominick Colaizzi, who named Laura Glass, be suspended for the season; that Wm. Lovell, who entered Aurelius, be expelled, and that both Laura Glass and Aurelius be ruled off the track. This is a severe and summary punishment that puts an end to the racing career of two useful horses, but such solitary examples are necessary to prevent frauds of a similar description.

From Honolulu we hear that there is a notable increase in the demand for good trotting strains. In a few years King Kalakaua will have some fine young stock from Boswell, by Almont and Triumph, by C. M. Clay, owned by his Majesty. There are also several fine mares there with foals by Patchen, Vernon, King William and Boswell, as also some fine youngsters, the produce of Waterford, Gloster and Bantwood. A mare from the Winters' ranch called Rosewood, although she was a failure there, is much thought of by Mr. James Campbell, her present owner. She is now in foal to Gloster, who was sired by Jack Rowatt, a grandson of Lexington, the dam being Lady Fairfield by Bonnie Scotland. This is a rare cross. Mr. H. A. Agnew has also some ten head in his stable, and among them several fast ones. Among the principal ones are mentioned a bay colt by Corbett's Irvington from Lady Hamilton, and another one by Irvington from Kate, a fast pacer; a bay mare, Maude Bowley, and some other good stock.

A telegraphic dispatch tells of a sad occurrence that is said to have taken place at Sheepshead Bay on the 27th of June. It appears that in a private race between two well known sporting gentlemen, one of the horses dropped dead at the conclusion of the contest. An eye-witness of the affair said that Pierre Lorillard and Carroll Livingston appeared on the track hours before the races on Tuesday morning. Lorillard, who weighs about 240 pounds, was mounted on a magnificent bay; Livingston, whose weight is some fifteen or twenty pounds less than Lorillard's, rode a smaller bay. The gentlemen bantered each other for a short race, each feeling confident that he could win. A dash of a quarter of a mile was agreed on for a sweepstakes of 25 cents. Starting at the three-quarters pole, just below the turn into the home-stretch, Lorillard soon gained the lead, while Livingston dashed on at his flanks until near the judge's stand, where Lorillard opened a slight gap, winning the race by about a length and a half, in the fast time of '28 seconds. Livingston's horse carried him a few rods beyond the stand, when he fell and expired. It is supposed from the bursting of a blood-vessel. The racers had been used by the gentlemen as saddle-horses.

Although the grand meetings of the circuits at the East have not yet commenced, it is extraordinary to note the number of horses that are working themselves into a forement position, as already the following horses have dropped into the 2:30 class during the past year:—

| | |
|---|---|
| Buffalo Girl, b.m., converted pacer, by Pocahontas Boy | 2:24 |
| Charley Hood, b. g., by Pearsall | 2:29¼ |
| Clara M., b. m. | 2:29½ |
| Clara Cleveland, ch. m., Fall 1881 | 2:29½ |
| Commander, b. h., by Blue Bull | 2:26½ |
| Cornelia, bl. m. | 2:26½ |
| Clarement, b. h., by Fred Low | 2:29 |
| Dou, gr. g., by Idol (Akers' or Peck's) | 2:24½ |
| Douglas, gr. g., by son of Woful, dam by Henry Clay | 2:26 |
| Elmer, br. g., by Gooding's Champion | 2:24¾ |
| Estelle, b. m. | 2:26½ |
| Florence M., ch. m., by Blue Bull, dam by Red Buck | 2:26½ |
| George M., br.g. | 2:26 |
| Gipsey, b. m. | 2:28½ |
| H. W. Beecher, br. h. | 2:28¼ |
| Highland Stranger, b. h., by Mambrino Patchen | 2:26½ |
| Hudson, b. g., by Tippoo | 2:29 |
| Ina G., b. m., by Blue Bull | 2:29 |
| Jack Sailor, b. g., by Sweepstakes | 2:27½ |
| Keno, b. g., by Mack | 2:29½ |
| King William, blk g. | 2:26½ |
| Lillian, ch. m., by Almont | 2:26 |
| Lola P., b. m., by Ericsson | 2:29 |
| Maud I., b. m., by Hamlin's Almont, Jr. | 2:28 |
| Overman, ch. g., by St. Elmo | 2:28¼ |
| R. P., br. h., by Happy Medium | 2:23 |
| Vivid O., b. g. | 2:28¼ |
| Young Fullerton, ch. h., by Edward Everett | 2:29¾ |

We append a few of the records that call for special attention:

At Poughkeepsie, on the 27th June, Early Rose won the 2.23 purse, she winning the first, third and fifth heats in 2:22¼, 2:22, and 2:23. The second heat was a dead-heat between Early Rose and Tariff in 2:30½; and Pickard won the fourth heat in 2:22¾. The three-minute purse was won by Crown Point Maid in three straight heats; time, 2:30¾, 2:30½, and 2:30½. On the 28th, George M., in three straight heats, won the 2:23 class. Time, 2.24, 2:26½, 2.27. Frank won the 2.33 class in three straight heats. Time, 2.27, 2:27¼, 2.26½.

At Grand Rapids, on the same day, the 2:20 class race, purse $800, two starters, was won by Annie W., William H. second. Time, 2.27, 2.24½, 2.25½. The three-for-all pacing race, purse $600, four starters, was won by Bay Billy, Buffalo Girl second, Sweetser third. Time, 2:23½, 2.23½, 2.24.

On the 15th, Californians will be more directly interested in three events, as at Chicago the State will be well represented.

At the Hillsboro, Oregon, races, on the 3d, the trotting, 2:50 class, was won by Maggie Arnold, Stranger second. Time, 2:39¼, 2:39½, 2.37, 2.39, 2.40. The three-quarter dash was won by Jim Merritt, Joe Howell second, Renwick third. Time, 1:17, fastest ever made on the track. On the following day, Collier won the mile and a quarter dash, beating Joe Howell and Trade Dollar, in 2:13½. Pedro won the trotting race, beating Tempest and Maggie Arnold. Best time, 2.33½.

### THE CONEY ISLAND RACES.

On Saturday, July 1st, in the one-mile race, Frankie B and Nellie Peyton made a dead heat. Colnage third. Time, 1:44½. Frankie B. and Nellie ran the race off, and the former won by a head. Time, 1.45. In the mile and one-eighth race, Talisman won, Bedouin second, Edwin A. third. Time 1.57½. A claim of foul against the winner was not allowed. In the seven-furlong race, Carrie B. won, Nonplus second, Tittlebat third. Time, 1:31½. In the mile and one-eighth race, Astonish won, Marchioness second, Baton Rouge third. Time, 1.57½. In the hurdle race, a mile and a half, King Dutchman won, Harry C. second, Gift third. Time, 2:53½. Drigasand fell.

On the Monday, the seven-eighths mile was won by Lalisa, Mary Warren second, Belle of the North third. Time, 1:30½. In the three-quarters mile, Prosper won, Ida D.

second; Monk third. Time, 1:16½. In the one-mile, Vanguard won, Bonheur second, L. B. Sprague third. Time, 1:45½. All the horses except Vanguard and Bonheur got off on a false start, and run over the whole course. In the hurdle race, a mile and a quarter, Gift won, Delaware second, Dalgsaian third. Time, 2:24½.

At Coney Island, on the 4th of July, the three-quarters of a mile race, Tittlebat won; Elector second. Time, 1.18. The seven furlongs race Bedouin won; Brideoake second. Time, 1.32. The mile and furlong race Capias won; Oakdale second. Time, 1:58. The mile and a quarter race Brambalatta won; Militia second. Time, 2:10¾. The three-quarters of a mile race Owen Bowling won; Mary Warren second. Time, 1:19¼. The Independence stakes, steeplechase over the short course, Kittie Clark won; Ike Bonham second. Time, 2:40.

### AT MONMOUTH PARK.

At this, the favorite race track of Long Branch, on the 4th of July, the first race, the ¾ mile race, was won by Iarrett easily; Greenland second. Time, 1:56¼. The ¾-mile race Pizarro won; Clonmel second. Time, 1:53¼. The Lorillard stakes race, 1½-mile, Runnymede won by a head; Forester second. Time, 2:40. The Screwsbury handicap, 1¾-mile, Glenmore won; Oidelia second. Time, 3:08¾. In the auction race, 1½-mile, Mary Anderson and Strathgsey ran. The former won. Time, 2.26½. In the race for the Wether cup for gentlemen riders, ¾-mile, Corsair, ridden by Mr. Holmes, won; Arsenic, Mr. Ward in the saddle, second. Time, 1:19¾. The steeplechase, full course, Frank Short won; Bernardine second. Time, 5.30.

On Monday, the five-eighths mile, for two-year-olds, was won by Blackman, Fairfield second, Marc Antony third. Time, 1.04. In the one mile, three-year-olds, Amazon won, Bonheim second, Bouthier third. Time, 1:46¼. In the mile and an eighth, Sweet Home won, Warfield second, Duplex third. Time, 1.58. In the mile and three-eighths, Parole won, Hilarity second, Francisco third. Time, 2:26¾. In the seven-eighths mile, Little Phil won, Sir Hugh second, Clarence third. Time, 1:26½, the best on record. In the hurdle race, a mile and a quarter, Frank Short won, Bernardine second, Ohio Boy third. Time, 2:24½.

### SCENES AT CONEY ISLAND RACES.

"Here's your winners in all the races," are the hopeful words which fall upon the ears of the sports as they flock through the entrance to the course at Sheepshead Bay. An investment of twenty-five cents secures a sealed envelope indicating a slip of paper on which are the names of the "sure winners." The selections are either based on the betting at Brighton Beach or Hunter's Point the night before, or on the judgment of the enterprising vendor of "tips," which is very probable not a whit better than that of the buyer. One of the slips, bought for curiosity by the writer on Wednesday last, did not bear the name of a single winner. But then that day was declared by veterans to be "one of the worst ever seen on the turf." Last year the sale of selections in envelopes was confined to an individual who had lost a small fortune in backing his selections, and who sought to recover it by selecting for others. In a few cases his judgment was followed in opposition to that of the "knowing ones" with probable result, but as a general rule he did no better than the average sport who follows the favorites. This year his place has been taken by a dozen or more "envelope touts," mostly youths in need of the means of betting.

Two dozen bookmakers all in a row make of the covered platform devoted to betting purposes a perfect pandemonium. Kelly & Bliss own the entire privileges, and sublet them, retaining only the mutual and auction pools and two book-stands. The auction pool is falling more and more into disfavor. Either in the books or mutuals the fraternity can get much more for their money. In a few years the pari-marly American style of betting will have entirely given place to the French and English styles.

How much bettors are controlled by signs and omens is illustrated by the following narration, made to the reporter the other day:

"'I was in the line going up to buy Barrett, intending to put $20 on him, although I had a strong affection, born of past winnings, for the Julietta colt. The man ahead of me called for two tickets on Barrett, and the absent-minded ticket-seller called out to the marker, 'Withers' colt two.' I don't want the colt; I want Barrett,' exclaimed the buyer impatiently, and the mistake was instantly corrected. That incident put nearly $200 in my pocket, for, impelled by a sudden impulse, I took the rejected tickets and two more, and exchanged them after the race for $300.'"

Rev. Justin D. Fulton has been dilating on the growing female appetite for alcoholic liquors. If he was to visit Sheepshead Bay on a race day he might find a subject for another discourse. The women who come down to the sea to "bet their money like little men," are neither few nor far between. From the handful of two years ago they have grown into a very considerable section of the patrons of the course. And their judgment, not by any means based on a knowledge of the horses, is generally better than that of the men. One lady who sat in the immediate vicinity of the reporters on Blue Wednesday last, "picked" tout of the five winners, a feat which none of her male friends, judging from their expressions, were able to accomplish.

"'If she were playing poker,'" said one of these gentlemen afterward, "'and were to go in on a shutter, she'd draw a house and lot sure.'"

The female choice is often dictated by the name of the horse or the color of the rider. And the dismay of 'cold uns' when a winner is thus chosen can be better imagined than described.—New York Star.

### THE SPRING MEETING OF THE BLOOD HORSE ASSOCIATION.

OFFICIAL REPORT.

The races were held at the Bay District Track. The weather was fine and the attendance fair in numbers, while the track was in fine order, and the time, in many cases, was fast.

First Day, April 26th.

FIRST RACE—California stakes for two-year-olds; $30 each, $15 forfeit with $250 added; the second to save his stake; a dash of half a mile. 30 subscribers, of whom 16 paid forfeit.

| | | |
|---|---|---|
| E. J. Baldwin's b c Gano, by Grinstead—Santa Anita | 130 lbs. | 1 |
| T. Conlin's c (nameus, by Shannon—Ladle w. | 100 lbs. | 2 |
| P. Weber's b f Clara W., by Norfolk—Ballerina | 100 lbs. | 3 |

The following ran together, Theodore Winters starting: S. J. Baldwin's ch f Precious, by Norfolk... E. J. Baldwin's ch f May B., by Shannon...

... (remaining race results illegible) ...

SECOND RACE—The Cooper stake, for all ages, $50 each, $25 forfeit with $300 added; the second to save stake. A dash of a mile and a quarter free for all.

| | | |
|---|---|---|
| T. Winters' ch f Atlanta, 3 yrs, by Norfolk—Lady Jane | 97 lbs. | 1 |
| Palo Alto Stable's b f Precious, 3 yrs, by Lever—Frolic | 97 lbs. | 2 |
| J. J. Shafter's b m Right Hawk, 5 yrs, by Haddington—Napa Queen | 117 lbs. | 3 |

THIRD RACE—The Winters Stake, $100 each and $25 forfeit with $5 added; $150 to the second and the third to save his stake—a dash of one mile and a half for three-year olds—closed with 15 subscribers, of whom 16 paid forfeit.

| | | |
|---|---|---|
| T. Winters' b f The Duchess of Norfolk, by Norfolk—Marion | 108 lbs. | 1 |
| P. Coutts' br c Forest King, by Monday—Abbie W. | 105 lbs. | 2 |

FOURTH RACE—The Cosgroson Stakes, $50 each and $25 forfeit, with $200 added; the second to save stake. A dash of a mile and an eighth for maiden fillies.

| | | |
|---|---|---|
| Geo. Hearst's ch f Marta F., by Leinster—Flush | 112 lbs. | 1 |
| T. Winters' ch f Hattie E., by Norfolk—Maggie Dale | 115 lbs. | 2 |
| J. & H. C. Judson's ch f Lottie J., by Wildidle—Little Brown | 115 lbs. | 3 |

Second Day, April 27th.

FIRST RACE—The Hearst Stake, $50 each and $25 forfeit, with $150 added; second to save stake. A dash of three-quarters of a mile, free for all. Five subscribers, of whom two paid forfeit.

| | | |
|---|---|---|
| A. G. Wood's ch g Jim Renwick, 4 yrs, by Jos Hooker—Big Gun | 118 lbs. | 1 |
| T. Winters' ch f Atlanta, 3 yrs, by Norfolk—Lady Jane | 101 lbs. | 2 |
| P. Siebert's b m Right Hawk, 5 yrs, by Haddington—Napa Queen | 118 lbs. | 3 |

SECOND RACE—The Trial Stakes. $50 each, $25 forfeit with $75 added; the second to save his stake. A dash of a mile and two-eighths for maiden three-year-olds, the winner of the Cosgroson Stakes to carry seven pounds extra. Four subscribers, of whom two paid forfeit.

| | | |
|---|---|---|
| Geo. Hearst's ch f Marta F., by Leinster—Flush | 105 lbs. | 1 |
| T. Winters' ch f Hattie E., by Norfolk—Maggie Dale | 115 lbs. | 2 |

THIRD RACE—Selling Purse, $200 to first; second to save; entrance to be sold at $1,000, to carry weight for age, 2 lbs allowed off for every $100 under that condition; winner to be claimed by any one, and if the sum is in excess of the amount named, then half the surplus to second, and half to the association. One mile and a furlong. Eight subscribers, of whom two paid forfeit.

| | | |
|---|---|---|
| Nettie Brn's b m Minnie Norris, 4 yrs, entered to be sold for $400, by Leinster, her dam by Bellfield | 101 lbs. | 1 |
| J. & H. C. Judson's b g Wheel, 4 yrs, $550, by Wildidle—State W. | 105 lbs. | 2 |
| J. N. Harris's ch g Geo. Bender, aged, $400, Sam Super Plant | 107 lbs. | 3 |

FOURTH RACE—The Pacific Cup, a handicap of $100 each, $30 forfeit $20 if declared, with $1,000 added, of which $300 to the second, and the third horse to save stake. A dash of two miles and a quarter. Eight subscribers, of whom two declared out and two paid forfeit.

| | | |
|---|---|---|
| C. McLaughlin's b h Bootn, 4 yrs, by imp. Hercules—Emma Barros | 100 lbs. | 1 |
| C. McLaughlin's b h Booth, 4 yrs, by imp. Hercules—Emma Bro | | 1 |
| T. Winters' ch f Atlanta, 3 yrs, by Norfolk—Lady Jane | 101 lbs. | 2 |

Third Day, April 28th.

FIRST RACE—The Oxford Stake for two-year-olds; $20 each, $25 for fest, with $250 added; the second to save his stake. A dash of three-quarters of a mile. 15 subscribers, of whom 10 paid forfeit.

| | | |
|---|---|---|
| J. B. Haggin's Nubia, by Leinster—Addie A. | | 1 |
| E. J. Baldwin's b c Gano, by Grinstead—Santa Anita | | 2 |
| J. B. Haggin's b f Frolic, by Lever—Frolic | | 3 |

SECOND RACE—The Spirit of the Times Stake, $50 each; $25 forfeit, with $300 added; $50 to the second and the third to save its stake. A dash of a mile and three-quarters for three-year-olds. Closed with eighteen subscribers, of whom sixteen paid forfeit.

| | | |
|---|---|---|
| T. Winters' b f The Duchess of Norfolk, by Norfolk—Marion | 108 lbs. | 1 |

THIRD RACE—A handicap purse of $300 to first; second to receive $50 and the entrance, free for all. A mile and three-quarters.

... (remaining entries illegible) ...

FOURTH RACE—Member's Cup, of $100 valuation, presented by Theo. Winters, Esq., to be ridden by members only. A dash of a mile.

FIFTH RACE—The Consolation Purse, $100; the second horse to receive $25. A mile and an eighth.

Fourth Day, May 2d.

FIRST RACE—The Sequel Stakes, for three-year-olds; $25 p. p. with $150 added. A mile and a furlong.

SECOND RACE—The Junior Stakes, for beaten two-year-olds; $25 p. p. with $100 added. Five furlongs.

THIRD RACE—A handicap for all ages; $10 each with $250 added. A mile and a quarter.

FOURTH RACE—Purse $250, for horses that have started and never won. Mile heats.

JOSEPH CAIRN SIMPSON, Sec'y. THEODORE WINTERS, Pres.
G. M. GRANT, Assistant Sec'y.

## ROWING.

The city regatta at Long Bridge, on Tuesday, was far more successful than there was reason to expect. The prizes were, to use the least offensive word "small." The entries and the attendance were however in the inverse ratio to the trophies, and several of the contests were close enough to be exciting. As usual at rowing matches on our harbor the length of the course was guessed at. No two races were started from the same point in consequence of the wind and tide, so that the time taken was worthless as a test of comparative merit. Even had the course been properly surveyed, the time would have been still valueless, as the timer did his work with an ordinary watch and in such a manner that in two races he was most undoubtedly several minutes wrong. When the glaring error was observed by one of the judges, who is a rowing man, the time was shaved down to reasonable proportions and in its reconstructed form given to the press as an honest record. The management of the regatta was by no means good, but considering that the regatta was only an experiment, it might have been worse. There was no police boat and the course was kept as clear as a lot of boys in small boats chose to make it. Several times when a race was about to be started some pestiferous boat-sailer came booming over the course in his scow or plunger and the oarsmen had to wait until the defiant trespasser had been blown out of the way. The yacht Ariel also contributed to the disadvantages of rowing by anchoring right on the course and allowing her boat to swing out at the stern at the full length of a long rope. Considering that the Ariel is owned by a gentleman who takes a lively interest in aquatic sport, the disposition made of the yacht on this occasion seemed very strange. The only explanation is that Mr. Lloyd was not a party to it, and would have speedily corrected the trouble had he been present. The stiff wind blew across the course all day, and made it impossible to give the competing boats a fair flying start. Had the committee taken the precaution to stretch a line across the course and start the boats from an anchored skiff, the difficulty of sending the competitors off on even terms would have been greatly lessened, and the patience of the spectators would not have been so sorely tried. The honesty and earnestness of the contest compensated however for the shortcomings of the hasty arrangements, and an annual city regatta may now be regarded as a fixture. Every member of the Fourth of July Committee who witnessed the races and observed the large crowd in attendance expressed the belief that the five hundred dollars given in prizes were well spent, and should have been doubled. It would be a good idea to put a premium on promptness in the next regatta by starting all races on time. Let the Committee of arrangements advertise that the races will be started in their regular order, and that ten minutes after each signal gun the men or crews must be on the line. This will prevent the delays that are sure to occur when men know that the race will not be started until they have completed their slow and careful preparations, and pulled up to the line as if time was of no object.

The first event of the regatta was the single scull-race and to oarsmen was one of the most important. The question of superiority among the young scullers has been in dispute for some time, and this was the first occasion on which they all met on very even terms; Griffin, who seems to row under a lucky star, won the choice of positions, and took the sheltered station under the wharf. Watkins was next with White. Peterson and Sullivan, who always drawn the outside position, lying in the stream. The outside stations were about as good as the inner ones, however, as the tide was running in swiftly, and except a strip of lumpy water near the stakeboats, the course was pretty smooth. Griffin and White had the best of the start. White, who rowed a fine boat recently built by Waters & Co., was expected to lead in the first quarter, but Watkins and Peterson held him well, and he passed the cattle wharf without much advantage. The rowing men watched Peterson closely, as it was his debut as a sculler in shells, and were not surprised to see him display a great turn of speed. It is very doubtful if his boat was rigged as well as she might be. She seemed a little down at the stern, but despite this disadvantage he sent her flying along at a tremendous pace, with a powerful stroke of thirty to the minute. He rowed with great steadiness, and in view of his great strength, he looked a winner half way to the stakeboat. Meantime Sullivan had steered himself out of the race, and Griffin had gone inshore unobserved and was diligently working his passage through the smooth water. Peterson came toward the stakeboat like a quarter-horse, but the wind had carried him to leeward and he had to turn his boat at right angles and row forty yards toward shore to make the turn. He rowed those forty yards in such a lively manner that he got around first, and started for home with enough in hand to make him a winner by two hundred yards if he had been pushed. The race for second place fully demonstrated the abilities of White, Watkins and Griffin. White turned better than Watkins, and Griffin got around a few moments after. Coming home, Griffin steadily forged ahead, and half way to the wharf the three boats were in line once more. It then became a question of stamina, and White let go suddenly. Watkins and Griffin continued the battle to the very end. On the last hundred yards Watkins made a desperate effort to get to the front, but Griffin held him and finished a clear length ahead and in good fit for another mile. The race demonstrated the fact that Peterson was by all odds the best sculler on the bay at present, while Griffin possesses abilities far higher than he has been accredited with. He rows in good form and improves over a long distance. Watkins had the advantage of him a boat's length and should have beaten him. White was the best boated man in the race, but his hard

style of rowing proved too much for his condition when he had men alongside who could make the pace and keep it. In smooth water he may have done better, but nobody but Peterson could have won. Peterson is little more than a boy, though a giant in size, standing nearly six feet and weighing 185 pounds in his boat. He has been almost raised on the water. Griffin is the lightest sculler on the bay, weighing 135 pounds, but hard as a rock and full of pluck.

The four oar shell race, which ought to have been the best contest of the day, was a very miserable exhibition. The Pioneer crew rowed a fine paper boat, while the Ariel and South End crews used a couple of old wooden shells nearly a minute slower. The race was not rowed until the afternoon, by which time the wind was very strong. When the word was given, the Ariels, who had the middle station, struck off evenly and headed straight for the stake-boat. The Pioneers, who had the outside, rushed inshore, and the stroke side being evidently stronger than the bow, they ran up straight in the wind and fouled the South End boat. The foul was most unmistakeably accidental. For a moment both crews stopped rowing, and then the Pioneers turned back and went for their stake-boat, and the South Enders followed rowing very badly, and evidently having all they could do to manage their boat in the rough water. The Pioneers did not do the liveliest rowing in the world, but the excellence of their boat helped them along, and they got to the stake-boat close behind the Ariels. The latter made a bad turn, but the Pioneers got around in good style and started for home with the race in hand. Towards the finish they nearly ran into the yacht Ariel and lost so much way that the Ariel crew went by and gained a length. The race then became exciting. The Pioneers, by a spurt, got ahead of the Ariels once more, but the effort had taken so much out of them that they began to fall away and finally crossed the line with only a few feet to spare. It looked as if in another hundred yards they would have been beaten, and only for the superiority of their boat that result should have certainly followed their bad steering. After their hard race, however, they deserved the prize, but the referee disqualified them, although the South Enders waived all claims to the money and declined to enter a protest. Considering the manner in which the regatta was conducted, this interpretation of the rules was very severe and hardly fair. In any event, the South Enders could not have won, and the foul did not interfere with the Ariels, who were beaten on their merits. Under the circumstances the Pioneers should have had the race, but the referee was probably disposed to hold them to strict account, as a moment before the start he warned White to avoid a foul, and was promised that nothing of the kind should occur.

The amateur wherry race for a cup presented by Colonel Andrews was a tame affair, owing to the inability of Mr. Haughey to sit his boat properly on the rough water. If W. Tuckey, the other contestant, rowed a weak stroke throughout, and won by half a mile. Both gentlemen were of the Triton Club. The professional wherry race which followed was even more ridiculous than the amateur contest. The entries were Thomas Murphy and R. C. Lyne, of the Pioneer Club, and B. Kehrlein, of the Triton Club. Murphy and Lyne, after carefully considering the matter, arrived at the conclusion that the race lay between them, and accordingly did nothing but watch each other from the start. The result was that while Kehrlein was steadily pulling up the course towards his stake-boat, Lyne and Murphy were going at a terrific pace towards the scene of the literary exercises on Mission street. But for the frantic shouts of Mike Price, whose new boat Lyne was rowing, the determined rivals would have knocked a hole in the Point of Rocks, but seeing this obstacle at the last moment, they veered off sixteen points, and began to look for the stake-boats. By this time Mr. Kehrlein was turning homewards. He finally reached the post without mishap or fatigue, and took first money, much to the disgust of the veterans, who had already pocketed the purse in their minds. Murphy, after a hard tussle with his old wherry, which looked like a monitor beside the racing craft of his antagonists, gave up the struggle, and when last seen was dancing over the white caps in the direction of San Jose.

The four-oar lapstreak race between the Golden Gate and Ariel crews was a tame affair, and was won easily by the Golden Gate men. The Stroke of the Ariels had much to do with their defeat, as he has a bad habit of giving his knees together and swinging diagonally across the boat instead of fore and aft. Besides, he pulls too low a stroke for a racing four. They ought to have beaten the Golden Gates, for their rowing was not beautiful. The most praiseworthy exhibition of the day in crew rowing was given by the new South End crew, in the Senior barge race, in which two crews from the Ariel Club also entered. The South End men are the most taking four that have appeared this year on the water, and ought to have the championship within their grasp. They are a very powerful four, and row with a dash that is particularly attractive after one has watched the listless exhibition of some of the other crews. They rowed right away from the others. In the Junior barge race, the Dolphins won easily. It is hardly creditable for such a heavy crew as the Dolphin four to be always ambitious of "Junior" honors. They are heavy enough and have practice enough to row in any company.

The Whitehall boat race demonstrated how easily Smith and Watkins could row away from professional Whitehall men.

The Ariel lads row very evenly together, and not having the "kink" in their arms that Whitehall pullers think is indispensable, get up a fine pace without much labor. Their new boat, which was built for the race last Sunday, seems light, and draws little water, but she has a great deal of side, and will be a heavy load when the wind bears on her amidships. She was built by Twigg, and as far as workmanship goes, is a creditable production.

The disadvantage of the constant and almost unvaried practice in heavy boats is the carelessness in style which many of the crews acquire. When four strong men pull in a heavy barge with some regard for time but none for any other essential, the boat is sure to make fair headway. The oarsmen, however, are the very opposite. Their good qualities experience no development, while their bad points grow with discouraging rapidity. This fact was particularly noticeable from Long Bridge the other night, when several crews were practicing for the regatta on the Fourth. There was not of the entire lot a single "four" that would have passed muster in a first class crew. Not that there were no first class men in the crews. On the contrary, the material seemed of a good quality, but the method of its preparation had evidently been very hasty and ill-judged. The men

seemed to have been thrown together without regard to their peculiarities or those of their boats. Some men were sliding short and others were using twenty-four inches of slide at every stroke. In one boat the bow-oar was swinging back until his head threatened to knock a hole through the deck while the after waist was trying to butt the stroke oar every time he slid up for the stroke. The complete and lamentable absence of coaching was very vigorously exemplified, and must have been a sorry spectacle for the experienced captains of several clubs, who looked on in gloomy silence. There is no danger of the records being broken at the regatta on the Fourth, and it would be a gross misrepresentation of facts to assert that there is a really formidable four on the bay at present. That out of several of the clubs a first class crew could easily be got is plain enough, but, owing either to the disinclination of the proper men to sit together, or their aversion to reasonable practice and training, they have not so far organized and shown themselves on the water.

## THE CITY'S REGATTA.

The contestants and result of the Fourth of July regatta at Long Bridge were as follows:

Single scull race—H. Peterson, G. G. B. C., 1 by ten lengths; D. Griffin, G. G. B. C., 2; Sam Watkins, A. R. C., 3; L. C. White, P. R. C., 4; J. Sullivan, P. R. C., 0.

Four-oar shell race—Pioneer crew, L. C. White, B. Crowley, R. Lyne, J. Sullivan, 1; Ariel crew, Sam Watkins, Oscar Branch, Alfred Branch, Fred. Smith, 2; South End crew, J. Dougherty, J. Daly, I. Cleary, Fred. Smith, 0.

Amateur wherry—H. Tuckey, Triton B. C., 1 by half a mile; J. Haughey, 2.

Professional wherry—Ben. Kehrlein, Triton B. C., 1 by six lengths; R. C. Lyne, P. R. C., 2; Tom Murphy, P. R. C., 0.

Four-oar lapstreak—Golden Gate crew, D. Griffin, J. D. Griffin, P. Connors, John Walthown, 1 by five lengths; Ariel crew, W. Well, Jeff. Blake, Ben. Smith, Thomas Maher, 2.

First-class barge race—South End crew, W. Thomas, J. Wilder, S. Dupleass, M. O'Nell, 1 by five lengths; Ariel crew, Sam Watkins, Alf Branch, Oscar Branch, Fred. Smith, 2; Ariel crew, Jas. Ward, W. Welch, R. Ranton, Jos. Cochrane, 3.

Second class barge race—Dolphin crew, T. T. Frazer, G. Van Graw, F. Moss, E. Peterson, 1 by three lengths; South End crew, D. Dougherty, E. Quigley, W. Turner, J. J. Barrett, 2; Golden Gate crew, John Flynn, Wm. Smith, John Lamb, Dan. Griffin, 3.

Whitehall double scull—Sam. Watkins and Fred. Smith, 1; John Engels and Wm. Pinkley, 2.

Referee—Chas. G. Yale. Judges—Captain C. L. Dingley, Captain C. Nelson, Mr. Pierce.

Stevenson, of the Ariel Club, and Flynn of the Pioneer Club, will row over the Long Bridge one-mile course on Sunday, the 16th, for $200. Each man backs himself and the race is play or pay. The only proviso is smooth water, which Stevenson demands. The Pioneer man would rather have it a little rough.

Last week the Neptune Swimming and Rowing Club elected the following officers to serve for the ensuing year: President, A. E. McDowell; Vice-President, J. W. F. Plat; Secretary and Treasurer, L. Osborne; Captain C. Pennell, R. B. Cunningham and N. J. Smith, Directors.

The performance of Peterson on Tuesday last led to speculations on his ability to row Austin Stevenson, and it would not be surprising if a match should result. The Long Bridge lad seems to have more pace than the Vallejoite, but whether he can stay the distance is to be yet demonstrated.

The Hillsdale crew have entered for the race for the senior fours in the Marlow regatta. Only two local crews—the Cockham and Marlow—have entered against them. The course is one mile long and is rowed down stream.

A match between Watkins and Griffin is talked of, but no money is up so far. Over a three-mile course Griffin will make it very interesting for the Ariel man, if properly boated.

## YACHTING.

SIGNALS AND PENNANTS.—The by-laws of the N. Y. Y. C. have been changed to read as follows: "The distinguishing signal of the club shall be a pointed flag; the device a white five-pointed star in the centre of two red stripes, they being in width one-fifth of that of the signal, one running lengthwise through it in the middle, the other running crosswise through it at one-third the length of the signal from its head, all on a blue field. Each yacht shall have a distinguishing signal flag and shall show it when signalled by another yacht. The Commodore shall display a broad pennant, with a foul anchor encircled by thirteen five-pointed stars in white on a blue field; the Vice-Commodore, a broad pennant with a similar device on a red field; the Rear Commodore, a broad pennant with a similar device in red on a white field. The Acting Commodore, under chapter 10, shall display a broad pennant, blue field, without device. These pennants shall be burgees—viz., tapering, swallow-tailed flags. All the foregoing mentioned flags shall be, in length, one-half of one inch for each foot of height of truck from the water, and, in width, two-thirds the length. Each yacht shall also have a blue pennant—in length, at the head, three-quarters of one inch to the foot, as aforesaid; in width, one-tenth the length; to be used as a day or night pennant. Each yacht shall have a set of signal flags, such as may be ordered by the club, to be not less than four feet long. Single masted yachts, while cruising in squadron, shall display their private signal when under sail and the club flag when at anchor."

NEW YORK MEASUREMENT.—In the New York Yacht Club the rule of measurement for time allowances has been changed as follows: The actual load water-line of each yacht shall be divided into four equal parts and a section taken at each point of division, making five sections. The area in square feet of each section shall be taken as follows: From the bottom of keel to a line which is three per cent. of the length of the load water line, as above, and parallel with it. In case the plank sheer at any section or sections be below this predetermined line the actual height at the plank sheer of such section or sections shall be used to obtain the square contents of the same. The cubical contents shall then be obtained by the formula taken from "Chapman's Rules for Measuring Vessels."

The sloop Nellie had to be left up at Mayberry slough on Tuesday by a party of gentlemen who had hired her. When it became necessary to loosen the centre board and the wrench was turned, the chain flew off the barrel, letting the board go by the run. It is of iron, and weighs 1,600 pounds. The chain pennant was only secured to the barrel by a piece of worn-out wire rope in a very careless manner. After two days' work trying to get it raised back into the case, the yacht was left with the boat keeper. Two more men have gone up to see what can be done about it. Men who keep boats to hire ought to keep the gear in order above all things. The Nellie's rigging does not work particularly neat of late, and probably a good overhauling would be an improvement. The fun of the trip was spoiled by the accident to the board, all because a little care was not exercised in shankling the pennant to the board.

The fishermens' boat race at Benicia brought to the front 33 starters. There would have been more, but many imagined they would have to get new sails and go to considerable expense. The boats that went to the south shore got worsted. Those that kept on the north light did best, as the adverse tide was strong and the wind fell light. No. 16 rounded the stake-boat first. Mr. Gutte was patriotic enough to place his fine yacht Chispa at the disposal of the Committee for stake-boat. The first boat won $100, a fine marine glass, and the prize flag. After the first few rounded the stake-boat the others squared away. The San Francisco Yacht Club fleet was expected to be present, but left at 6 A. M., much to the disgust of the people of Benicia, who had extended hospitalities to the gentlemen the evening previous in the expectation of their presence at the regatta next day. Having ladies aboard the yachts, they decided to start early to get home before dark.

Mr. Bowie has his fine yacht Nellie down at Monterey, and will keep her there for several weeks. The passage down was monotonous, the wind being light and ahead. In fact, they had to beat down from Pillar Point. Off New Year's Point they met a very rugged sea, which turned things up; but the Nellie is a most beautiful sea boat and handles well in any weather. The lead on her keel makes her rather quick in her motions, however. From Santa Cruz Mr. Bowie cruised to Aptos and Soquel. On the night of the 4th they gave from the yacht a fine display of fireworks. Mr. Bowie is one of the few San Francisco yachtsmen who enjoys blue water sailing. He has a fine large yacht and can indulge his tastes.

The yacht Chispa took quite a party of ladies and gentlemen from Commodore Eckley's ranch, on Carquinez Straits, to a sail up Suisun Bay last Sunday. The yacht went up Suisun Creek six or eight miles, a style of sailing very enjoyable. The water was very smooth and the wind strong but warm and balmy. The party did not get back until 6 P. M., and enjoyed a most delightful sail. Mr. Gutte has the happy faculty of making all his friends thoroughly at home on his yacht, so that the invitations to join the Chispa for a sail are always in demand and eagerly accepted.

Mr. Ed. Munfrey was out in his plunger on the 4th. She is a dandy little craft, just launched by Farmer, the Oakland boat-builder, and is as stiff a boat for her inches as any in the bay. She has a steamboat stern and rather a high house, with small cockpit. She carries her sail well, and, like all boats that do that, is fast. Farmer models his boats so well, that all of them are speedy and safe.

## CRUISE OF THE YACHT CLUB.

The cruise of the San Francisco Yacht Club to Antioch was very much enjoyed by all who participated. The yachts Frolic, Stardust Emerald, Rambler, Lillie, Fleur de Lis and Whitewing left on Saturday afternoon for Martinez, staying there all night. At 11 A. M. the next day they went to Antioch, returning on the following day to Benicia. That evening (Monday) the party attended the ball of the Olympic Club. It was the intention to remain at Benicia until after the regatta of the fishermen in the afternoon. A meeting of the yacht owners was held, however, and it was decided to get under way at 6 A. M. on Tuesday, sail up the Club House, at Saucelito, and have a dance there, getting back home by night. This programme was carried out, and the yachts got down to Saucelito by noon. Calms and baffling winds scattered the fleet, and the last one down Pablo Bay got into Saucelito first, so the Frolic had the honor once of having sailed down from Benicia first. The Whitewing remained up there. The Fleur de Lis had returned previously. Altogether the trip was highly enjoyable. They had pleasant weather, just suitable for a ladies' cruise. It was voted the best cruise of the season by all the participants.

Stone is working on a new plunger.

The sloop Fleetwing was at Martinez last Sunday.

The new yacht for Mr. John D. Spreckels will be eighty feet long.

The new Yacht Club has under consideration a design for a flag.

No new large yachts this season until Mr. Spreckels' boat comes out.

The Clara was not out during the holidays, Mr. Hamilton and Mr. Few both being away.

The Whitewing party came down from Benicia by rail, leaving the yacht up there.

The Angel Dolly had a large yachting party out on the 4th. They went to Glen Cove, in Raccoon Straits.

Some of the yachts had to anchor in Raccoon Straits the other day, while others went around the island.

The schooner Ariel has not yet been put on the ways, but will soon be, and will then receive a thorough overhauling.

Dr. Merritt is still cruising down the coast in his yacht, the Casco. After his southern cruise, he will go north to Puget Sound.

The steamer Pride of the River backed into the yacht Frolic at Martinez, and her wheel damaged the Frolic's rail, badly frightening the ladies aboard the yacht. No serious harm was done, however. The steamer will pay damages, as the yacht was at anchor when the collision occurred.

The yawl Ariel was up Napa Creek during the holidays. She found more creeks than Napa, and had a series of adventures, but got home all right.

The "Evolution of the American Yacht," an illustrated article in the July Century, will interest all yachtsmen. It is clearly written and correct.

The little Rambler is one of the prettiest yachts on the bay. It is a pity there are not more of her size about. She is of a type which should increase here.

Mr. Tevis having other engagements for the 4th, placed his yacht Whitewing at the disposal of some of his friends, who enjoyed the trip to Antioch very much.

The yawl Enid is lying at Martinez, but looks dilapidated. No one would recognize her as the yacht taking the prize for neatness at Napa four years ago, under another owner.

The yacht Aggie is down at Monterey. Mr. Macdonough says he sailed from Santa Cruz to Monterey in one hour and fifty minutes. They had a slow passage to Santa Cruz from this place, owing to baffling and light winds and fog.

## TRAP AND WING.

THE PACIFIC GUN CLUB met at George Bird's grounds, Alameda Point, last Sunday. Although the attendance was not large, probably owing to the dove fever which is now raging, the record of 86 per cent. shows of what material the Club is composed. The following is the score:

| Lambert | 1 1 1 1 1 1 1 1 1 1—1½ |
| Fowler | 1 1 1 0 1 1 0 0 0 1 1—7 |
| Fnhis | 1 0 0 1 1 1 1 1 1 1 1—11 |
| Galindo | 0 0 1 1 0 0 1 1 1 1 1—10 |
| Moyes | 1 0 *1 1 1 1 1 1 1 1 0—10 |
| Haines | 1 0 1 1 1 1 1 1 0 1 1—10 |
| Adams | 1 0 1 1 1 1 1 1 1 3—1¼ |
| Velleau | 1 1 1 1 1 1 1 1 1 1 1—11 |

* Dead out of bounds.

Lambert, as shown above, won the medal for the second time, and first money. Precht and Tom Velleau, President of the Club, shot off for second place at three doubles, the result being in Velleau's favor, he killing five birds against four scored for Precht.

## CLAY PIGEON TOURNAMENT.

A very interesting tournament was held Saturday last, at Littlefield Range, on the grounds of the Alameda County Sportsman's Club. The proceedings were under the management of that veteran Sportsman, Frank Eastman, and the whole programme was carried out to the satisfaction of all those who participated, and among them were some of the crack shots around the bay. The conditions of the match were fifteen birds each, at fifteen yards rise, and some trial scores were made. There were fourteen entries at $5 each, divided as follows: First money, $28; second money, $21; third money, $14; fourth money, $7. Total, $70. As told by the score the shooting was close and exciting to the finish. Mr. Crellin breaking fourteen of fifteen, won first money. Messrs. Tuttle and Schnabel tieing on thirteen birds each, divided second and third money. Mr. Adams breaking twelve birds, won the fourth money. The following was the score:

| Mayhew | 0 1 0 1 0 1 1 1 0 1 1 0 1 1 1—10 |
| Wash | 0 0 1 1 1 1 1 0 0 0 1 1 1 1 1—10 |
| Lambert | 1 1 1 0 0 1 0 1 0 1 1 0 1 0 1—8 |
| Adams | 1 1 1 1 1 1 1 1 1 0 0 1 0 1 1—12 |
| Adams | 1 1 1 1 1 0 1 1 0 1 1 1 1 1—11 |
| Galindo | 0 1 0 1 1 1 0 1 1 0 1 1 0 1 1—10 |
| Schnabel | 1 1 1 1 1 0 1 1 1 1 1 0 1 1 1—13 |
| Marlott | 1 1 0 0 1 0 1 1 0 1 1 1 0 1 0—9 |
| Toose | 0 0 1 1 1 0 0 1 0 1 1 1 1 1 1—10 |
| Crellin | 1 1 1 1 1 1 1 1 1 1 1 1 1 1 0—14 |
| Bowman | 0 1 1 1 1 1 1 0 0 1 1 0 0 1 1—10 |
| Tuttle | 1 0 1 1 1 1 0 1 1 1 1 1 1 1 1—13 |
| Wash | 0 0 1 0 1 1 1 0 0 1 0 1 0 0—6 |
| Vaughn | 1 1 0 0 1 1 0 0 0 1 1 1 1 1—11 |

## THE GUN.

Dick Brooks and Charley Dahl have gone down shooting near the Mission of San Jose.

John B. Orr and party celebrated the Fourth in deer-hunting on the Shatter Ranch, Oiema. They are credited with having killed three bucks.

Deer are reported exceedingly plentiful in the neighborhood of the Gualula River, Mendocino County. There being few ranches, the game is therefore little disturbed. For camping parties, the country spoken of is one of the finest in the State and very easy of access.

Payne's Ponds, at Tule Station, do not seem to have so much feed as those ponds which have just been flooded with fresh water. This is probably due to the fact that these ponds had ditches dug to them some time since, and during the winter a great deal of salt water found its way into them.

James Payne, the well known market hunter, has sold out the lease of his boats, scow, and all his traps, to a new shooting club. Some of the members of this club are Messrs. Hopkins, G. Frank Smith, R. S. Floyd, Whittier, Fuller & Co., and others. Payne received $2,000, and will remain in charge at $100 a month.

Teal Station, up in Suisun Bay, will not be accessible to outsiders this season. All the ponds above and below the track are preserved for private parties. The best shooting place near the city for those desiring a day or two's shoot, where all the conveniences can be had, is therefore closed to the public.

## GAME PRESERVES.

It seems somewhat strange to speak of game preserves in California, but the time has already arrived when it has become a necessity for gentlemen who desire to have surety of a good day's sport to establish preserves. This is more particularly the case with respect to the duck shooting, for the feeding grounds are each year becoming narrower and narrower, and the number of persons hunting increase in proportion.

A thie cities increase in population the "market hunters'' become more numerous, and instead of the hunting being confined to Saturdays and Sundays, as it used to be, the birds are blazed away at every day during the season. And this is not the worst of it; out of season there is more or less shooting going on. Up in the marshes there are crow lots

of fishermen who kill ducks now and then, and who care very little for seasons. And people who live near the fords and streams also shoot when they like.

The idea of preserving game is somewhat repugnant to the average American; but the true sportsman transfers the repugnant feeling to the people who render it necessary for him to keep shooting grounds.

In localities remote from the more thickly settled centers of the communities, there is yet plenty of game. But people of the city, who are mainly those who will keep preserves, can not afford the time, as a general thing, to travel great distances.

In our "up-river" marshes there are now several preserves maintained by gentlemen who are fond of duck-shooting, and lately a number of leases have been made of available grounds. It will not be long, it seems, before all opportunities for a day's duck-shooting will be denied all persons not interested in a preserve of some kind.

We shall have more to say on this subject at a future time.

THE DOVE-SHOOTING SEASON opening on Saturday last gave many of our local sportsmen an opportunity to enjoy the first day of the season. Birds are plentiful this year and the sport was keenly relished after the enforced idleness of the past four months. We have heard of many good bags having been made. Among the number: John McDougall, at Pleasanton, one hundred and three birds; Messrs. Liddle and Brown, at Mountain View, seventy-two; and Wm. Walker, near Redwood City, sixty-five; Judge Rix and party, near Pleasanton, between three and four hundred birds; Dr. Leavitt, Sunol, about two hundred, and Philip Faneke, in same neighborhood, about one hundred. Messrs. Walker, Liddle and Brown only shot a half day each.

The Cordelia Shooting Club, which has leased the "Spring Ponds" and others, in Suisun Marsh, has been having the ditches enlarged. A ditch 800 feet long, 4 feet wide, and 2 feet deep, has been dug to let the fresh water into the ponds so as to start them first. At this time of year the water through these marshes is all fresh. In fact, it is fresh down as far as Pablo Bay. By thus letting the fresh water into the ponds a good stock of feed is insured for the coming season, and the shooters will not be bothered with barren ponds. Raising feed for wild ducks is something of a novelty, but it is necessary to insure good shooting ground.

## CHESS.

No event in the history of chess tourneys since the days of the advent of the American chess champion Morphy has excited such widespread interest in chess circles throughout the world as the international meeting of chess champions at Vienna, which is now nearing its close. Especially is the tourney at Vienna of interest to American chess players, in view of the fact that we have at least one legitimate representative of American chess in the lists, while two others as quasi representatives, viz., the Scotch-American chess champion, Captain Mackenzie, and the Boston player, Ware, who created such a decided sensation in the Chess Congress Tourney of 1880, in New York. But Mason is the strongest native American player sent to Europe since Morphy's time, and all American players feel gratified that Mason is well up in lead. Up to the close of the first half of the tourney, which was reached on the first instant, the leading players were: Winawer, 12 victories and 4 defeats; Mackenzie, 12 victories and 5 defeats; Steinitz, with 11 victories and 5 defeats; Blackburne, with 10 victories and 5 defeats; and Mason, with 10 victories and 6 defeats—these being the only players who had scored double figures. Afterwards, however, quite a change was made in the order of the contestants, the position in victories up to June 10 being as follows: Steinitz, 18; Winawer, 17; Mason, 17; Zuckertort, 15½; Mackenzie, 15½; Englisch, 15; Blackburne, 14½; Bird, 9½; and Ware, 8. One of the amusing incidents of the tourney, especially to the American players, was the result of the meeting between the German champion, Steinitz, and the American, Ware. It will be remembered that in the American Chess Congress Tourney of 1880, Ware introduced a novel opening of his own construction, which he termed the Meadow Hay opening.

A press dispatch states that the tournament closed on June 21st, and the prizes were awarded as follows: Steinitz and Winawer, first and second, each winning 24 games; Mason, third, with 23 games; Mackenzie and Zukertort, fourth and fifth, with 22½ games each; and Blackburns sixth, with 21½ games. The ties will be played off.

There is no more indefatigable sportsman than Mr. B. B. Redding, the able Fish Commissioner of the State. He is always on the alert to guard our game and fish from wanton and illegal destruction, as also to increase the variety of our game birds. Through his agency there are now on the way from China some sixty pheasants, which assimilate close to the English stock, and that will be distributed carefully among native woodland dells under the auspices of the California Sportsmen's Association. Mr. John K. Orr has already half a dozen females at his ranch, but the males exhausted their vitality in tireless attempts to escape from confinement. In this instance the birds will will probably be released to the woods, and with ample supplies of straw, seed foliage and water, they may become attached to their homes, as in the English preserves.

A Practical Party—Tourist Fisherman No. 1: Any fish about here, my man? Scot: Nae! ye'll get nae fish about here. Tourist Fisherman No. 2: But this must be the place a little fat man in a kilt directed us to as a good swim. Scot: Eh! that's Sandy Macintosh, an' he's a liar. A mon that can tell a deleeberate lie, wi'out it's in the way o' gain, is a maist immoral character.

That political antagonism does not interfere with social relations among sportsmen is evident from the fact that Mr. Arthur went on a fishing excursion, a short time since, with Gen. Hampton, of South Carolina. For the time being they dropped politics and devoted themselves to piscatorial pursuits, in which both are experts.

The Duke of Edinburgh, while fishing recently near Bayons, hooked a large fish. In his attempts to haul in the fish, he lost his footing, and was dragged into water sixteen feet deep. He was carried under four times. After strug-gling for half an hour, he at last succeeded in reaching

THE

# Breeder and Sportsman.

PUBLISHED BY THE
BREEDER AND SPORTSMAN PUBLISHING CO.
THE TURF AND SPORTING AUTHORITY OF THE
PACIFIC COAST.

**OFFICE, 508 MONTGOMERY STREET**
P. O. Box 1396.

*Five dollars a year; three dollars for six months; one dollar and a half for three months. Strictly in advance*

*Money should be sent by postal order, draft or by registered letter.*

*Communications must be accompanied by the writer's name and address not necessarily for publication, but as a private guarantee of good faith*

JOSEPH CAIRN SIMPSON,　- - - EDITOR

SAN FRANCISCO, - - SATURDAY, JULY 8, 1882

## CONGRATULATORY.

Every mail brings us something which is worthy of record, only that it may be considered too eulogistic. In some of the letters it would be "We like the looks of the paper, and it seems as though California had a paper of which Californians need not be ashamed." In another we like the "Greetings," and your idea of "editorial duties" meets our approbation. We are glad to hear the indorsements and hope to continue to merit the good wishes. We shall certainly do our best to be worthy of the encomiums and shall endeavor to continue to be worthy of the credit. The turf journalist has a task before him which is anything but easy. There are errors to correct, abuses to remedy. There are unpleasant tasks which cannot be shirked, and duties which must be performed. Yet there are many things to commend and these we take pleasure in noting. Being much in this branch of journalism gives us pleasure, and to record the breeding of a performer which has become distinguished is a joy. There are lessons to be learned from pedigrees, and the genealogy of a winner is instructive to those who make a study of lines. The winner gives a clue to the future winners, and the strains in his pedigree are a source of information. All this is a pleasant part of the journalism of the turf. To write of lines which have proven victorious, to delineate the genealogical tree, the branches of which are marked with names which are renowned in hippic animals is a pleasant interlude. But to censure, to find fault, to castigate, easy as it may appear, always brings sorrow, and we wish that there was only a bright side to picture. To bring out the sunny side it may be necessary to show the darker, and in the portrayal of that which is faulty there may be an opportunity to gild the sombre edge. This is the side of the picture we would fain look at. We have always the desire to put glowing colors on the canvas, and if it rests with us there always will be a brilliant daub of color. It may be a daub, the red shawl on the dark-eyed gypsey, and yet there is life in the coloring, and something to relieve the monotony of every day life. And thus we feel pleasure in the congratulations we have noted, and will endeavor to merit the continuance of the good wishes.

## WASTING TIME.

Why it should be considered as a neglect of manners because one manifests an interest on some of the out-door sports, is to us inexplicable. As "self-preservation is the first law of Nature," the young man who neglects his physical welfare does not obey this law. If he holds his nose so close to the grindstone that he gradually wears it and himself away, there are more noses and more grindstones, but his personality is no longer interested. The great system of modern civilization is grand in the extreme, but is apt to be rather rough on the individual; and the man who allows himself passively to be crushed beneath the ever-moving Juggernaut wheels of "business," receives no pity, even from those whose influence causes the sacrifice.

We all need rest; we all need change; we all need recreation. The employer, who is getting rich, does not seem to care for a change. He wants to keep right on. But the man who does the work and isn't getting rich, does need the change and ought to have it.

But if a young man happens to have a hobby, such as shooting, fishing, rowing, sailing, bicycling, or any other out-door sport, he has, in most places here, to keep the liking hidden like a skeleton in a closet. It does not behoove him to say much about it or to let much be known about it. He must keep it dark the same as he would if he gambled or did any other disreputable thing. This is not as it should be by any manner of means. The young men should be encouraged to take up some manly pastime and follow it. The employers can exercise a wholesome restraint which will prevent any undue allegiance to it; but they need not frown down everything connected with man's hobby.

Some men are fond of music, some of gardening, some of taking care of chickens, some run to secret societies and others to church festivals and the like; all of which are very good in their way. And o none of these can any objection be made. But let a man want to handle an oar, rod or gun, take a tiller or the lines, and an outcry is raised that he is wasting his time and endangering his business prospects.

The writer knows of men who are ardent lovers of these sports but never let themselves think of them for fear of the displeasure of their employers; who forego these pleasures and lead humdrum lives of changeless rounds because some tyrannical employer, too fat or lazy to take exercise, too old to enjoy pleasure, and too rich to afford to spend money for amusement, decrees that all persons who are under him shall "stick to business."

We have no patience with the utter selfishness that condemns men to treat their employees in his way. Time spent in health-giving recreation is time well spent. The pecuniary feature of our short lives is prominent enough at all times, but ought not to stand in the way of everything.

Men who waste their employers' time are to be blamed of course. But they are to blame, too, if without an effort to enjoy themselves in some rational manner when and how they can.

## THE DOG.

One of the aims of the BREEDER is to popularize the breeding and breaking of well-bred dogs for use in the hunting field. While we admire the points of a well-bred bull terrier or bull dog, we are among those who hold the opinion that man's best friend among the animals can be put to a better use than by affording the means to carry out the brutal and degrading sports of the dog pit and the rat pit. For this reason the doings of dog fighters will find no space in these columns. This exclusion may give offense to a few, but we beg them to remember that dog fighting and rat killing are not now considered gentlemanly sports, and while we presume to dictate to no man as to what course of conduct he shall pursue, yet we hold it our right and province to condemn the acts of those who set at defiance the laws passed for the protection of the brute creation. A celebrated writer has said that the finest sight in the world is a beautiful girl seated on a thoroughbred horse. To our mind, an equally fine sight is a trace of fine setters or pointers quartering their ground or standing their game. Another right that ranks in point of beauty with either is a pair of fleet greyhounds just slipped after a hare. Yet another fine sight is a pack of fox or buck hounds on a hot scent or in view of their game, and none of these glorious visions of animal beauty take precedence of the handsome appearance presented by a noble St. Bernard or Newfoundland dog taking charge of its master's children. But few artists have ever lived who were able to do even common justice to any of these charming illustrations of the beauty of canine life, and the greatest of them all, Sir Edwin Landseer, made a sad and irreparable blunder. In attempting to delineate the perfect Newfoundland, he produced a halfbred animal which, though noble enough in appearance as a dog, was a perfect failure as a Newfoundland, and would not claim a second glance in a bench show. The general public can learn much about the kennel, and as yet the art of breaking dogs is not an exact science. New ideas and new rules will be spoken of in the BREEDER as fast as they come up, and it will ever be our pleasure to cater to the special demands of our friends in these matters. Dog thieves and dog poisoners will find the BREEDER their unrelenting foe, as will also those scoundrels who impose worthless dogs at high prices upon credulous and unsuspecting purchasers. We shall always be ready and willing to advise our readers as far as possible in all matters pertaining to the breeding, rearing, purchase and cure of man's best friend, the dog.

## FISH AND GAME.

It is a common saying among yachtmen that "boat builders do not know anything about boats," because, as a general rule, they do not sail them, and the improvements come from the users and not the constructors. We have all of us, no doubt, had experience of the fact that many people who hire out as cooks know nothing about cookery; and that the average servant whose mission in life is to keep house, and who makes a living by it, knows nothing about housekeeping.

These apparent contradictions are not confined to the walks in life in which professionals are concerned, by any means, nor to any class of persons, or any branch of business; and, to tell the truth, it would be hard to find a class where a more evident illustration can be shown than among lovers of the rod and gun.

How many fishermen know anything about fish? How many hunters know anything about game? They know where to catch the fish and how to do it. They know where to hunt for game and how to shoot it. That is, some of them do. They pick up just enough knowledge about the habits of game as is useful to them in hunting it. About the families, varieties, species, history, habits, etc., they know nothing. As to the structure of a fish, bird, or animal, not one sportsman in a hundred knows a single thing. They can tell a fish which has a good, tender and juicy taste; but can not always tell this. Sturgeon disguised as tenderloin of sole, or as baked sea-bass, or any one of the many things that much maligned but useful fish is made to do duty for, will continue to fool people for years to come. Mighty few can distinguish the species of trout. They can not tell the salmo irideu from the salmo fontinalis, unless some one says the stream has been stocked with Eastern trout. Whether the salmo purpuratus is any relation to the salvelinus malma is to them a profound mystery. And they can not tell which of these scientific names means in the vernacular rainbow trout, salmon trout, brook trout, lake trout, silver trout, black trout, red-spotted trout, Dolly Varden trout, bull trout, or any other trout.

They can tell quail when they see it in the market with its feathers on, or, when broiled, it reclines on its native toast, because, then the toast is what prospectors call an "indication."

As to ducks—those universally hunted birds—every sportsman considers himself an expert. Yet, as little is known about them as can possibly be. Every hunter thinks he knows their habitat better than any other. Pin him down to facts and details, and he will tell you how they hover over the marshes up at Teal Station, in the "String Ponds," at the Hard Ground Club rendezvous, at Mayberry Slough, at Bowlder Island, or in the Sherman Island tules, which are protected by the ægis of the Tule Belle Club; or else he will refer to the Alvarado Creeks, where the Pelican Club used to reverse the ancient legend of that capaciously throated and pocketed bird by the older ones "drawing blood" from the younger by means of poker, and where pot-hunters always found markets for their game on Sunday afternoons, when the Club returned home after its all-night work. This is the idea of habitat in the mind of the average hunter—strictly local in its character; and as to distinguishing species, all the knowledge of the combined sporting clubs of this coast would not be sufficient to judicially decide the difference between blue-winged teal and cinnamon teal; whether they are the same or different species; or one or the other the male or female of the same species. In fact, we do not believe there is one sportsman in a hundred who knows whether a duck is of the family *Anatidae* and order *Anseres*, or of the order *Anseres* and family *Anatidae*, or which of the sub-families, *Anatinae* and *Fuligulinae* is the fresh water and which the sea duck. There are very few of them who know whether *Anas boschas* is a common domestic, or a wild canvas-back duck. Some of them even make the mistake of confounding the species in practice, when game is scarce and the man not around.

Some hunters have even doubled their stock of natural history knowledge since the invention of the "clay pigeon," by learning to distinguish the live pigeon from that one, and finding that a new species is added to the genus *Columba*.

It is by no means to be inferred from these remarks that we consider it necessary for a hunter or fisherman to be a scientist as well. But we feel assured that the additional pleasure which will be derived from at least a slight knowledge of natural history will repay any sportsman who gives it slight attention. All prominent sporting papers now give space to natural history items, and the BREEDER AND SPORTSMAN intends following the excellent example. Without having a special department for this purpose, we intend giving, from week to week, such items of general interest concerning natural history as will, we hope, lead our readers to pursue the subject further.

## CORRESPONDENCE.

There was some fault in the mails, and many of our letters came as the printer insisted on locking the forms up. Fortunately they were of a kind which will keep, and so the next week's issue will contain them. Then there came from Highland Springs an account of the first deer hunt of the season; and within a few minutes thereafter a letter from Hanford. We can scarcely find words to express the obligations we are under to "Our Correspondents." And we have not the least hesitation in stating that in this foremost essential the BREEDER AND SPORTSMAN will not be second in the race to any paper. In fact, it brings to our remembrance the histories of the long past many years ago, so many that we will have to acknowledge more seasons passed than an observer—that is, a casual one—would credit; and we place the contributors the equal of those who made the old *Spirit of the Times* so readable in its palmiest days. This will be granted when both numbers are looked over, and then the next will clinch the argument. We state, without fear of contradiction, that the BREEDER AND SPORTSMAN starts out with a more brilliant corps of correspondents than any paper in the United States, and this we hold to be the main feature.

Again we say that our correspondents are the chief upholders of the paper, and with their aid we have no fears of ultimate success.

## THE EMBRYO STAKE.

The advertisement of this stake appears in the appropriate column. Heretofore it has closed on the 1st of March, at which time many of the foals were not dropped. This season it was thought best to postpone until the first of August in order that those who desired to make nominations could see how the foals looked before entering into the engagement. We cannot agree with our correspondent that it should be passed over or that any should be barred from participating. While it is true that there was a general scare when the Palo Alto and Sunny Slope colts made such a terrible break in the records, there is now a disposition to keep trying, in hopes that others may have the same good fortune.

Then the Pacific Breeders' Association can scarcely take upon itself to say that the stock of all the other breeders are inferior, and always will be,

to those of these two celebrated breeding farms. The Embryo gives the opportunity of making engagements at a very small cost, and the engagement encourages training. The training gives purchasers a line to base a valuation upon, and those which are, perhaps, several grades below first-class bear a greatly enhanced value over what it would have been if they had not been educated

## THAT CHALLENGE.

In racing parlance, challenges are always in order, from the time of the Crusaders when the courtly knight was ever ready to break a lance on his Flemish or Spanish charger; or when the first noblemen in England would test the power of their best strains of thoroughbreds by challenging for the Whip over the Beacon course; or among our sporting and financial magnates who shall possess the King or Queen of the turf. Imbued with a similar spirit, Mr. M. W. Hicks enters the trotting arena with a challenge to be found in another column. There is evidently somewhat of the character of Faulconbridge in Mr. Hicks' personality. He does not soften his phrases. "Soft" to his idea is euphonious, but has not the power or expression of "duffer." Messrs. Haggin and Tevis may accept the conditions, but there is one of them to which many objections may be urged, and we deem that the gentleman has gone rather beyond the bounds of discretion in his stipulation of mile and repeat in the yearling form. A mile dash is surely sufficient to test speed and endurance at so tender an age.

## SACRAMENTO LETTER.

DEAR SIMPSON; Admiration and Respect—"These are my sentiments," which expressed at the present time not only denote their usual definition, but may be used in the sense of Dryden and our old friend Shok—namely : "Your boldness I with admiration see," and "In one respect I'll assist thee." Therefore you will find my name with the usual fee in the hands of your gentlemanly solicitor. I made an ineffectual attempt to have something ready for your introductory number, but owing to a pressure of business in another direction I did not complete it in time; and then again I do not know but I had rather write after having seen the make-up of your excellent paper. I am more than surprised at its neat and dressy form. I received it Saturday night, took it home, and exhibited it to the family first, who likewise admired the "make-up." I remarked to my wife that the first thing we would read was the "Greeting." So I read it aloud to her, after which she casually remarked, "Why, he writes like a young man who intends to settle here and grow up with the country." I explained that she hit it exactly, that the writer was young in every way except that of experience with topics of this character, and that in almost every paragraph written in that salutation he had received a schooling upon the subject, which fact should be readily recognized by all interested in the innocent sports that make up a holiday ; and give recreation to both brain and mind that should be indulged in by those who think of it the least, but could be induced by the perusal of a journal of this character, conducted in such a manner as to be independent of politics and interests outside of its line of policy set forth in the beginning, and to which it must adhere.

Healthful sports and good morals have a relation which could be intermingled with society had we at all times the proper devotees of them. But when morality is completely frowned down by the intrusion of brutal performances, by many called Sport, then recreative and innocent sports, of which we are all, individually and collectively, more or less fond of, falls with it. The association of immoral practices with that of innocent amusement should be discountenanced by journals of this character, of which I have no fear in your case. There is no doubt but what your list of subscribers in Sacramento will be large, as the citizens of this city are noted for their liberality, and contribute handsomely, whether for charitable, religious, political or sporting occurrences. For instance: The Capital Turf Club of this city concluded to give a spring meeting. Their funds were low, and a soliciting committee was appointed. They started out, and in three days had the magnificent sum of $1,300 subscribed. Upon their heels came the Fourth of July Committee, who succeeded in raising, in about the same time, about $3,000. Thus you will see that our city gave for sport and recreation alone $4,300 in less than two weeks. We had our Spring meeting, which, in every particular, was a success. This club is now upon a substantial footing, and will, during each succeeding year, give their Spring meet, wich will, in all probability, follow the blood-horse meeting. So we will be enabled to have two meetings each Spring, the value of which will be recognized by the breeders who desire to "repeat " the colts that did pot suit them in their

first run. The indications for a lively Fall meeting clear through the circuit are good, both for running and trotting. It is rumored that many of the horses that took part in the races this Spring at Salt Lake will come to this coast, as the season will be too short for them to go East. George Hearst's stable will return from there this week, to which has been made an addition of one or two good ones. He will be a formidable competitor for all this Fall.

There is a general dissatisfaction at the results of the Chicago races respecting the performances of California horses, which we know were better than many who won when they last here. But, as I have often remarked, the only way to properly compete with the Eastern horses is to go there in the Fall and train with them in the mud. Trained as they are upon spring-board tracks, where the rebound exhilarates instead of deadening, is the greatest drawback we have in competing with them. When our horses strike the Eastern tracks in the midst of a thunder shower, which keeps up for two or three weeks, and undertake to work on a track that is almost impossible for a man to run on, it is not to be supposed that we can win. This kind of a track will make a horse log-weary before he has attempted to exert himself in the way of speed. The Duchess of Norfolk we know to be a fast and game filly. We know she has run in her trials barefooted almost a minute faster than she ran the two miles at Chicago—with more weight up too. We know that she is a mare that runs altogether on her courage, and never was hit with whip or spur up to the day she left. Her defeat at Chicago at the Derby must be attributed to weather and track—not that we are trying to explain away our defeat, but to show those who are always ready to ridicule our Eastern attempts that it is the fault of those having them in charge, and not our breeding; not but what they believed they were doing right, but they erred in their judgment. Gentlemen, you must Winter there before you can come to the post in condition such as is needed in that climate. But I would advise the losers to stand by the little mare, as she will pull them all out when they least expect.

Word has been received here that Mr. Thomas Delaney has accepted a proposition made by Mr. Jack Glimer to take charge of his stable, and that he will be with us this Fall with a string of fast ones. Munro Johnson is coming for the Duke of Norfolk, Atlanta, Clara W., a yearling and two year-old from Mattie A., and the little Prince of Norfolk, a full brother to the Duke and Duchess. Mr. Winters wants them all to look out, for he is still coming. Willis Hull is working up Mr. Pritchard's stable, eight in number, at the head of which stands Frank Rhoads, the handsomest Leinster get; also the Leinster filly that won the five-eighths at Oakland last Spring. She is a very promising filly, and in the Breeders stake at the State Fair she will start with the Duchess, Maria F., Duke of Monday, Judge McKinstry, Precious and Idler. The distance is one mile and a half, and the pace, I imagine, will be faster than we have ever seen on this Coast—each will make the other run to win it. No canter nor hands down in that field will win. Frank Dupoister is working on his stable with the intention of being first at the finish in more than one race. He has Schwartz's Lottery filly, Robson's May D., and one or two green ones. Miller is working up old Boots, with his eye on the $1,000—that will be in the Post stake of three miles this Fall. He is also keying up the Monday filly, sister to Douglass, who is liable to carry off the two-year-old stakes. Charley Shear says he has a lot of trotters, mostly colts, about his age that he intends to land in first-class order. His says he has one for every class clear through the circuit. Being that he is the only one of the old guard left, he intends to make reparation for all their follies and go to the front every time. He says there is no money in being a good second. He must and will be first.

The sorrel horse Thump Winston, formerly Kent, is showing up better than ever; he is likely to be troublesome in both the twenty-five and thirty class this Fall. McIntyre is working Reavis' stable of Blackbirds and promises to be ready when the bell taps. Wilbur Smith has been driving Clairpoint and Adalia double, having in view probably the capture of the double-team purse. Dr. Hicks, Valensin Cochran, Jim McDonald and other suburban stables are quietly at work sharpening up and feeling of their respective favorites. The report from all is—good as could be accounted. Another breeder of some magnitude has sprung up in our midst in the person of the genial Col. J. McNassar, ably assisted by his son, John B.

They have purchased the Kleinkans place, about five miles down the river. It contains about 650 acres of good bottom land. Besides the usual amount of hay and grain, they intend to raise a few trotters. To commence with, they have sixteen as fine looking brood mares as the next man; in size they range from 15-3 to 16 hands; in weight from 900 to 1,300 lbs.—well-bred, rangy-looking mares. At the head of these stand Ensign, a beautiful chestnut stallion, about 15-3 hands, well proportioned and speedy. He is by Gold Dust. Next to him is Silver Cliff, who is by Lexington Gold Lust. This stud of horses were brought to this country by the Colonel, from Colorado.

His pride and his joy, Bob Newton, met with a mishap while en route, which resulted in his death, by which we lose a valuable acquisition to our trotters of this State. His public record was 2.10½, made over the figure 8 track at Peoria, Ill., previous to which he trotted the fifth heat in 2.24½, making the last half in 1.06, after which the Colonel sold him for $16,000 and repurchased shortly after for the same amount. His loss is irreparable to the Colonel, but he says he has some coming that wont be very slow.

We hail his appearance in the Breeder's circle; in his case as with many others, it is done for the sport and love he has for the Turf, more than for the pecuniary returns, which are of slow growth. But then, here I should be stopped, as my letter is fast assuming proportions entirely inadequate to your liberality of space. Wishing you any amount of success in your new enterprise, and that admiration and respect will be rendered by all,

I remain, sincerely your friend,
MILE-AND-A-QUARTER.

SACRAMENTO, July 6, 1882.

## THE KENNEL.

### FIXTURES.

BENCH SHOWS.—Western Pennsylvania Society's English Setter Bench Show Derby, Pittsburgh, Pa., for English setter puppies whelped on or after March 1, 1882. Entries closed December 1, 1882. I. R. Stayton, Allegheny City, Pa., secretary.

FIELD TRIALS.—National American Kennel Club's trials on prairie chickens, Fairmont, Minn., September 4. Entries to American Field Derby closed July 1; to All-Age Stake, September 4. Joseph H. Dew, Columbia, Tenn., special secretary for these trials.

Gilroy Rod and Gun Club's trials on quails, near Gilroy, Cal., October 26. Open to dogs owned in California, Oregon, Nevada and Arizona. E. Leavesley, secretary, Gilroy, Cal.

Eastern Field Trials Club's trials on quails, near High Point, N. C., November 17. Entries to Derby close July 1; to All-Age and Members' Stake, November 1. Fred. N. Hall, secretary, P. O. Box 884, New York.

National American Kennel Club's trials on quails, Grand Junction, Tenn., December 4. D. Bryson, Memphis, Tenn. secretary.

### SUNDAY'S RABBIT KILLING.

The time has come for the sporting press of America to point out to the public, in the plainest possible language, the difference between real sport and the so-called sporting exhibitions gotten up for gate money. Speculators, who, without any knowledge of the sport which they pretend to illustrate, make of it, by their burlesque travesties, a bye word and a reproach. While the true sportsmen are laboring hard to popularize their favorite amusements, these speculators in the art of humbuggery cause hundreds of people, who do not know what true sport really is, to class it with the miserable gate money affairs presented to their notice by the speculators. The sporting papers which announce themselves as gentlemen's papers, devoted to the interests of manly and respectable sport, are false to the cause they claim to represent, and recreant to their trust, when they fail to show up in their true light all performances and exhibitions given under the name of sport, and which are liable to bring discredit upon an honorable and respectable amusement. A full knowledge of this moral responsibility and obligation, called forth in these columns last week an exposure of the hollow and fraudulent pretenses of the so-called coursing tournament given under the auspices of the Occidental Coursing Association. Strangely enough, the BREEDER AND SPORTSMAN was the only one of the many papers published in San Francisco that did not maintain a financially discreet silence about that tournament, or else behave it with fulsome and unwarranted flattery.

One paper said, that the trapped hares procured by Mr. Levy were in fine condition, and that splendid sport was anticipated. Another said that the tournament afforded a splendid chance for the general public to witness the noble sport of coursing almost at their very doors; and so on, and so on through an endless variety of sickening changes.

The BREEDER AND SPORTSMAN spoke of the affair as follows:

"This match is regarded by all coursing men as simply a belt to catch spectators, and they object vigorously to have the sport they admire burlesqued by one who does not understand the difference between a 'wrench' and a 'turn.' Trapped hares will not and cannot run, and Mr. Levy will find that the dogs entered, poor in condition, as they all will be, will gobble up his Auburn and Merced hares as quickly as they would as many cotton-tail rabbits. Even if the hares would run, the confined limits of the race track are dangerous to the dogs and death to the hares, who should at least be accorded what every sportsman gives his game—a chance for its life. If Mr. Levy called his affair a hare-killing match, and took down that sign about a match for $500 a side, the matter would concern no one but the public, who paid to see it, and the Society for the Prevention of Cruelty to Animals, but so long as he has chosen to dignify it with the name of a sport that it only burlesques, it becomes our unpleasant task to protect the sport of coursing from the disgrace about to be thrust upon it."

The task was really an unpleasant one, for not only is it a violence to our feelings to censure any one, but many personal and some intimate friends of the Kennel Editor had allowed their names to be used in connection with the match, and had especially asked as a favor that the affair either be let alone or spoken of as a first-class, bona fide coursing match.

The result of the exhibition on Sunday last showed that all the anticipations of this paper were correct, except that the miserable, unsportsmanlike nature of the affair had not been stated in sufficiently strong terms of condemnation.

A very few lines will suffice for a description of the exhibition, the like of which it is to be hoped will never again be permitted in a civilized country. About three-fourths of an acre of ground, at the eastern end of the Half Mile Track, had been cleared of shrubbery, and was set aside for the hare killing. Around this contracted space was a slight fence, over which leaned a close row of spectators. Behind the spectators was the track, and behind that the high, close fence that environs the track. The lower end of the centre of the track is full of a coarse growth of lupins and stunted shrubs; consequently, as all sportsmen well know, was utterly inaccessible to the hare as a place of refuge, for instinct teaches the hare always to keep to the open ground when pursued. More than half of the open ground is sandy, which means certain capture to any hare that chanced to venture on it. Under these circumstances, had the hares provided by Mr. Levy been the freest and fleetest animals that ever traveled sixteen miles for water on the great San Joaquin plains, and unincumbered by any deprivation of their liberty, they would still have no chance to escape, and it would fall an easy prey to any yelping terrier that fancied a hare lunch. What must be thought, then, of men who would attempt to give a coursing match on such grounds, and use for game poor, miserable hares that had been half

killed by their first capture, and utterly deprived of the ability to run by weeks of confinement and improper feeding?

Before the brutality commenced, the two thousand spectators were regaled with music by a remarkably aggressive brass band, which looked like a relic of the last female "pedestrian tournament," and was fully in accord with the other surroundings of the "coursing tournament."

About half-past one o'clock the Secretary of the Occidental Association ordered the first pair, Baron Waldken and Pacific Life, to be placed in the slips.

The band ceased playing, the various keepers of "ease games" and other devices to catch the unwary stopped their requests to "gentlemen sportsmen" to try their luck, and all was hushed and still for the first chapter in the great brutality of the 19th century. The dogs were put in charge of Joe Staddeldt, the "slipper," and F. Conlon, who appeared to be the master of ceremonies, came out of a tent, bearing in his hands a poor, miserable crying leveret. After manding the animal around until the little life it originally had was nearly squeezed out of its body, Conlon took it about forty yards and then let it loose. At the same time Staddeldt slipped the eager dogs. Baron Waldken did not seem to care about the business, but the dog substituted for Pacific Life, which was drawn, dashed off at full speed, and before the hare had traveled 90 feet, had caught and killed it. Time and again this miserable burlesque on sport was repeated. As the BREEDER AND SPORTSMAN stated, "the dogs did one of them succeed in eluding the dogs a distance of 300 yards. Even the saplings that had never seen a hare before ran down and killed these poor frightened things as easily as a terrier catches and kills a rat. One or two of them ran into the crowd of spectators, and were kicked to death by the boys. The sight was sickening, and before half a dozen courses had been run most of the respectable visitors left the track in disgust. Further description of the affair is unnecessary, and could only cater to morbid appetites. The official record of the tournament is as follows:

FIRST TIES.—Levy's Baron Waldken ran a bye.
Con Shay's Lady Lyons beat O. Mooney's Kitty Clover, who got unslipped.
R. Brock's Jeff Davis, beat F. F. Lord's Sam. Tilden.
John Egan's Star beat John Shay's Lady Mary.
R. Bell's Cherokee beat J. Kelly's Con Hollow.
John Grace's Parnell beat D. L. Levy's Prairie Girl.
SECOND TIES.—Lady Lyons beat Baron Waldken.
Star beat Jeff Davis.
Parnell beat Cherokee.
FINAL TIES.—Lady of Lyons beat Star.
Cherokee ran a bye.

PUPPY STAKES.
S. King's Maude beat Thomas Brady's Lady Mac.
J. Kelly's Lily of Killarney beat J. Shay's Carig Baun.
SECOND TIES.—Maude beat Lily of Killarney.

SAPLING STAKES.
P. J. Jacoby's Cassie Mara beat F. Conlon's Maid of the Mill.
M. Galvini's Bingo beat J. Whelan's Spotted Ida.
SECOND TIES.—Cassie Mara beat Bingo.

The prizes were awarded as follows: 'Old Dogs—First prize, Lady of Lyons; second prize, Cherokee; third prize, Star; fourth prize, Jeff Davis. Puppies—First prize, Maude; second prize, Lily of Killarney. Saplings—First prize, Cassie Mara; second prize, Bingo.

The Judges were J. Sillery, H. Boscough, and J. L. Rivers. Stewards, John Shay, F. Conlon. Slipper, Joseph Staddeldt.

### STANDARD MEASUREMENT OF DOGS.

EDITOR BREEDER AND SPORTSMAN.—DEAR SIR: For a long time I have given considerable thought to the subject of Bench Shows. I have written the Eastern and Western sporting papers to publish the measurements of prize winners, and have collected quite a number of measurements, but not sufficient to warrant a basis for the proper shape at different weights of sporting dogs. Stonehenge was the first to collect and publish a gradation of points as a guide for judges. Tileston placed them in a much more compact form, and is an excellent little book, but nowhere have I found yet it seems such an easy thing to do, with so many Bench Shows taking place all over the country. A standard of excellence might be arrived at, with very little trouble, that can be used by every judge. It might also be used to advantage by those wishing to enter dogs, thereby preventing many dogs utterly inferior being placed upon exhibition, and also raise the standards, making it easier for judges and the exposés to patrons. I placed by themselves, first, the dogs of the different breeds, then bitches, so that after a while I can average. For instance, Lavarack dogs, Lavarack bitches, Gordon dogs, Gordon bitches.

I would suggest, so that measurements may be taken uniformly, that they come under the following heads:

1.—Length of head.
2.—Length of body.
3.—Length of tail.
      From which you have—
4.—Length from tip to tip.
5.—Height of shoulder.
6.—Height of forearm.
      From which you have—
7.—Height to shoulder.
8.—Girth of muzzle midway between eyes and tip of nose.
9.—Girth of neck midway between head and shoulders.
10.—Girth of skull at apex.
11.—Girth of chest.
12.—Girth of loin.
13.—Girth of loin.
14.—Girth of forearm one inch from elbow.†
15.—Corner of eye to end of nose.
16.—Width of head between ears.
17.—Spread of ears.
      From which you have—
18.—Length of ears.
19.—Weight.
20.—Age.

Making a maximum of twenty points to go by, and sufficient to take in all the principal measurements of the dog in question.

If the judges of the different Bench Shows, at the time the winners are announced, will hand to the Secretary, or

duly authorized member, the measurements of said winners, and should they be published in the American Field or Forest Stream, the BREEDER AND SPORTSMAN will compile them, and as soon as a sufficient number of prize winners are obtained, an average will be made, and the information will be given to the public.

I write the foregoing for the purpose of helping to raise, in my small way, the standard of American sporting dogs, and uphold it as an honorable a calling as that of breeding horses or cattle. All have their votaries, but from lack of, say the gentleman, the one who finds a pleasure with the dog, is not looked upon with as much respect as are the others.

No country can excel ours for pleasure with the dog and gun, and if by striving for a standard of excellence for the dumb animal would bring about a higher order for the others, I shall not have taken up my pen in vain. There is luck in old numbers. Starting with the Forest and Stream on the Atlantic, midway the American Field, and here on the Pacific we open the Golden Gate to the BREEDER AND SPORTSMAN.                     Respectfully yours,

SAN FRANCISCO, CAL., July 5, 1882.                     SUDS.

* I do not consider it of sufficient importance to make a separate head for measurement of height of hock.
† Measure, drawing feather close to forearm, and not outside of feather tips, as some have.

### A WELL TRAINED DOG.

The writer once knew a dog dealer who always named his dogs Mike. When asked the reason for this fancy he replied in a burst of confidence "Oh you see my own name is Mike, and when buyers come and ask me if my dogs are well trained I always reply, 'What Mike well trained?' he's broke sir, he is, and when you say he's broke you say it all." This always used to satisfy Mike's purchasers and eased the conscience of the human Mike. It must have been a lineal descendant of Mike that presented Mrs. Coit with a splendid looking sleuth hound with which she started on deer hunting last week. This celebrated animal was called Bill, and was warranted by his owner to trail deer as long as he had a leg to stand on, and also to show a most thorough indifference to any other kind of game. Said the original possessor of Bill to his first friend, "That dog could wade through a whole ocean of jack rabbits or foxes, and would never for an instant lose scent of a deer that had passed over the bed of the ocean a year before. Mrs. Coit believed this Modern Munchausen and the day after Bill came into her possession, and in company with a friend started out on a hunt; for be it known to the uninitiated, Mrs. Coit, though a delicate looking lady, is an unerring hunter and a splendid shot. The parties had not gone far when Bill commenced to show by his actions that he had struck a scent. After a few undecided sniffs he put down his nose in good style and started off for a clump of brush at a twelve-mile gait.

"What style, what pace," whispered Mrs. Coit to her companion. "I really believe that Bill is one of the best as well as the handsomest dogs I ever saw."

"Ah, he's sighted now," said Mrs. Coit, as the melodious music of William's wrinkled throat was heard coming up the ravine. "But where is the dog? Bill is driving this way and the game must surely be ahead of him."

"Well, I don't know where the deer is, but I can see a jack-rabbit a few jumps ahead of Bill," replied Mrs. Coit's companion.

When the horrible truth dawned across Mrs. Coit's mind that the great William had disgraced himself and her by chasing a miserable rabbit, she turned and went home without speaking another word, and when Bill came home about two hours later with the blood of the rabbit on his chops, she positively declined to allow him to enter the house.

### ANSWERS TO CORRESPONDENTS.

Under this head will be found replies to all questions that may be asked of the Kennel Editor in relation to breeding, breaking, or entering dogs, feeding and curing them or any ordinary disease. Correspondents must state plainly what are the peculiar symptoms of the malady for which they need advice, and in all cases, especially when desiring to have their dog treated, a day of the fault must be careful to state the age and sex. No answers will be sent by mail, and all questions must be marked Kennel Editor BREEDER AND SPORTSMAN, San Francisco, Cal.

J. C. MARSHEVAN—Your dog is evidently suffering from dirt or canker. Wash once a day with warm water and carbolic acid soap. Bed on new dried or hardwood shavings instead of straw, and change bed every day. Give the animal a coat of chloride of lime at least twice a week. Avoid heating food, and especially salt meat. If the irritation does not disappear in a few days, give a mild dose of castor oil or Epsom salts. Avoid any application of a stimulating nature to the sore places.

CAVE, SAN FRANCISCO—Dew claws are not an injury to a dog, and there is not any need to remove them. They can be taken off without leaving a scar by carefully cutting open the skin at the base of the claw and then removing the excrescence at the joint. That can be done with a sharp knife or pair of scissors. Some sportsmen bend the claw off at the joint with their fingers. After removal, put a small piece of plaster over the incision in the skin and bandage carefully. Care must be taken not to bandage too tightly or inflammation is liable to set in and cause strictu trouble.

A. T., SAN FRANCISCO—The best cure for common muscular rheumatism in a dog, caused by wet exposure and damp bedding, is warm baths, warm bedding, an occasional purge of blue mass and aloes, and the following liniment, which never fails to give immediate relief when rubbed into the skin, whether in dogs, horses or human beings, provided the disease has not gone too far: "Spirits Wine, one ounce; Chloroform, one ounce; Vinegar, four ounces. Rub in whiskey thirty dry, and repeat the operation when there are evidences of pain.

B. B., SAN JOSE—A dog has of teeth—six upper and lower incisors, twelve upper and fourteen lower molars. Occasionally extra or supernumerary teeth are found, in some cases as many as six.

### THE PADDOCK.

March 13—Lightfoot, by Flaxtail, s. f. by Prompter.
March 24—Violin, by Flaxtail, c. f. by Prompter.
March 24—Lady Buckner, by Tom Hal, b. f. by Blackbird.
March 30—Meany, by Flaxtail, b. c. by Prompter.
April 11—Lady Nariy, by Marion, br. f. by Singleton.
April 11—Rachel, by Wayland Forest, b. c. by Prompter.
April 14—Starlight, by Wayland Forest, b. c. by Prompter.
May 7—Gazette, by Buccaneer, c. c. by Prompter.
May 26—Venis, by Vanderbilt, c. f. by Prompter.
May 26—Mahaska Belle, by Flaxtail, br. f. by Singleton.
                                                M. W. HICKS.

FISH RANCH.—The Reno (Nev.) Journal says: "At Lake Anna, near Fort Bidwell, Henry Woodson has started a fishery. He commenced operations three years ago with 3,000 common trout. Now he has realized so handsomely from them that he has sold 30,000, and 12,000 spawn have been sent to different places. The trout obtained a weight of seven pounds in thirty-one months, which is remarkably rapid growing. He supplies the whole Bidwell county with fresh fish. The lake is forty-five acres in extent. He has also a small lake stocked with catfish. Mr. Woodson has made it a profitable business, and every year adds to his wealth."

## THE HERD.

BEEF AND STOCK CATTLE.—Last week Mr. Hemler got back from Pitt River; he bought four hundred head of stock cattle on the trip and will have most of them brought to his place at Pete's Valley and fatted for this market. He reports that young beeves will be ready for market about the beginning of July. Copious rains have fallen all over that country; grass is very good and cattle coming on rapidly. Nearly all the animals that will be offered for beef will be from one to two years younger than in previous years. During the past season, all over Eastern Oregon and Nevada the Eastern demand for beef has been so great that fully matured animals have all been sold off, and now younger stock must be taken to supply the demand; these being of less weight each than older animals, greater numbers are needed to make the usual quantity. At present beef cattle cost only about one cent per pound more than last year's price. Stock cattle sell readily at an advance of from three to four dollars per head. The present prospect for stockmen is very favorable; the feed never looked better, and the demand for beef is constantly increasing, both at home and in the foreign markets.—Greenville Bulletin.

### HOW TO JUDGE SHEEP.

The day has come when the loose and methods of old fashioned farmers will no longer be found profitable. All the resources of science are rapidly being opened to the agriculturist, while the open pages of the Stud Book elevate the calling of the stock raiser almost to a science. What the Stud Book has done for the thoroughbred horse, the Devonshire, Ayrshire, Jersey and other standard breeds of cattle, could be equally well done for the various fine breeds of sheep. The importance of grading their flocks up to a higher standard of wool and mutton excellence, is daily becoming more pressing to the California sheep raiser, and like energetic men they are quick to seize upon every scrap of information which may tend to increase their profits. Hence the sale of graded and thoroughbred Cotswolds, Leicesters and Merinos, for breeding purposes, is rapidly advancing to huge proportions. Sellers are always able to protect themselves, but the buyers are too often in the dark. For that reason the publication in the BREEDER of the following scale of points of excellence, prepared by a special committee of the Indiana State Wool Growers' Association, should prove a valuable assistance to the wool growers of our State:

In bringing the matter before the Indiana Association, the committee having it in charge said:

In presenting this knowledge to the Wool Growers' Association of the State of Indiana, your committee has been to a great deal of trouble and bother in summing up what we consider to be the greatest benefit to the Association.

The scale of points to be taken into consideration in the breeding of all the different breeds of sheep, is the blood of the sire and dam; this must be ascertained before we commence to breed our sheep up to standard, or otherwise we had better not try to breed to any given point, for without pure blood being infused into our flocks, it would be useless to make the trial.

SCALE OF ONE HUNDRED POINTS FOR COTSWOLD SHEEP.

BLOOD.—Thoroughbred, purely bred from one or more importations of Cotswold sheep of some reputable breeder from England. Seven points.

HEAD.—Not too fine; moderately small and broad between the eyes and nostrils, but without a short thick appearance, and in young animals, covered on crown with long lustrous wool. Seven points.

FACE.—Either white or slightly mixed with grey, or white dappled with brown. Four points.

NOSTRILS.—Wide and expanded; nose dark. One point.

EYES.—Prominent but mild looking. Two points.

EARS.—Broad, long, moderately thick and covered with wool. Four points.

COLLAR.—Full from breast, and shoulders tapering gradually all the way to where the head and neck joins. The neck of rams should be short, thick and strong, indicating constitutional vigor. The neck of ewes should be fine and graceful, and free from coarse and loose skin. (Collar five points with ewe.) Six points.

SHOULDERS.—Broad and full, and at the same time join so gracefully to the collar forward, and the chin backward, as not to leave the least hollow in either place. Seven points.

FORE LEGS.—The mutton on the arm or fore thigh should come quite to the knee—leg upright, with heavy bone, being clear from superfluous skin, with wool to fetlocks, and may be mixed with grey. Four points.

BREAST.—Broad and well formed, keeping the legs wide apart. Girth on chest full and deep. Eight points.

FORE FLANK.—Quite full, not showing hollow behind the shoulder. (Four points with ewe.) Five points.

BACK AND LOIN.—Broad, flat and straight, from which the ribs must spring with a fine circular arch, and scrotum of rams well covered with wool. Ten points.

BELLY.—Straight on underline. (Five points with ewe.) Three points.

QUARTERS.—Long and full with mutton quite down to the hock. Eight points.

HOCK.—Should neither stand in or out. Two points.

TWIST.—Or junction inside the thighs should be deep, wide and full; which, with a broad breast, will keep the legs open and upright. Four points.

FLEECE.—The whole body should be covered with long lustrous wool. Eighteen points.

ONE HUNDRED POINTS OF EXCELLENCE FOR MERINO SHEEP.

BLOOD.—Thoroughbred—i. e., purely bred, from one or more of the direct importations of Merino sheep from Spain, prior to the year 1812, without admixture of any other blood. One point.

CONSTITUTION.—Indicated by form of body; deep, large breast cavity, broad back, heavy quarters, with muscular development forming capacious abdomen. Skin thick, but soft, of fine texture, and pink color; expansive nostril; brilliant eyes, healthful countenance, and good size, age considered. Fifteen pounds.

SIZE.—In fair condition, with fleece of twelve months' growth, full grown rams should weigh not less than 150 pounds, and ewes not less than 100 pounds. Seven points.

GENERAL APPEARANCE.—Good carriage, bold style, elastic movement, showing in particular parts, as well as general outline, symmetry of form. Three points.

BODY.—Throughout, heavy bones, well proportioned in length, smooth joints, ribs starting horizontally from back bone and well rounded to the breast-bone, which should be

wide, strong and prominent in front; strong backbone, straight and well proportioned as to length. Heavy, muscular quarters, deep through and squarely formed behind and before, with shoulders well set on, neither projecting sharply above the backbone, nor standing so wide and flat as to incur liability to slip shoulder. Folds on the ribs should be larger than on the ewes. Large and pendulous folds from the chin or jaws succeeding each other down the neck to the brisket, ending with large fold or "apron," and extending up the sides of the neck, but higher if at all extending over top of neck, also behind the fore-leg or shoulder. one on front of hind leg, hanging well down across the flank, also on rear of hind legs, or quarters, extending upward toward the tail, with one or two on and around the tail, giving the animal a square appearance on the hind quarters, and straight down as may be from end of tail to the joints and hind feet. Eighteen points.

HEAD.—Wide between the ears, and between the eyes and across the nose; short from top of head to tip of nose; face straight; eye clear and prominent; ears thick, medium size, and, together with face, nose and lips, white and covered with soft fur or downy wool. Ewes should give no appearance of horns; while upon rams the horns should be clear in color, symmetrically curved, without tendency to press upon the side of the head or to extreme expansion. Six points.

NECK.—Medium length, good bone and muscular development; and especially with the rams, heavier toward the shoulders, well set high up, and rising from that point to the back of the head. Five points.

LEGS AND FEET.—Legs medium or short in length, straight and set well apart forward and back, heavy bone, smooth joints, with large muscular development of the fore-arm; thick, heavy thighs, wide down to hock joints, and from knee joints downward covered with short wool, or the soft furry covering peculiar to the ears and face; hoofs well shaped and of clear color. Five points.

COVERING.—Tendency to hair and gare upon any part of the sheep, is to be avoided. Evenness of fleece in length, quality, density, luster, crimp, trueness, strength and elasticity, covering the entire body, belly and legs to the knee; head well covered forward, squarely to a line in front of the eyes; well filled between the eyes, ears or horns, and well upon the cheeks; muzzle clear, with small opening up to and around the eyes. Scrotum of rams covered with wool free from tendency to hair. Fifteen points.

QUALITY.—Medium, but such as is known in our markets as fine delaine and fine clothing wool, distinctly better in quality, luster, crimp, and elasticity, than the wools of same length grown upon the common grade sheep. Five points.

DENSITY.—Shown by the compactness of the fleece throughout, which should open free but close, showing very little of the skin at any point, even at the extremities. Ten points.

LENGTH.—At one year's growth not less than two and one-half inches, and as near as may be uniform in length to the extremities of the fleece. Five points.

OIL.—Evenly distributed; soft and flowing freely from skin to surface; medium in quality, and of a light color. Five points.

ONE HUNDRED POINTS OF EXCELLENCY FOR THE DOWN SHEEP.

BLOOD.—Purely bred from one or more of direct importation from Great Britain. Ten points.

CONSTITUTION.—Constitution and quality indicated by the form of body; deep and large in breast and through the heart, back wide, straight, and well covered with flesh and meat or muscle; wide and full in the thigh, deep in flank; skin thick but soft and of a saffron color; prominent, brilliant eyes and healthful countenance. Twenty-five points.

SIZE.—In fair condition, when fully matured, rams should weigh not less than 200 pounds, and ewes not less than 175 pounds. Ten points.

GENERAL APPEARANCE.—General appearance and character, good carriage; head well up, elastic movement, showing great symmetry of form and uniformity of character throughout. Ten points.

BODY.—Well proportioned, small bones, great scale and length, well finished hind quarters, thick back and loins, standing with legs well placed outside, breast wide and prominent in front, brisket wide and extending well forward. Ten points.

HEAD.—Head short and broad; wide between the ears and between the eyes; short from top of head to tip of nose; ears short, of medium size and covered with downy wool; head should be well covered with wool to a point even with eyes, without any appearance of horns; color dark brown in some families and fawn color in others without speck of spot; light muzzle not objectionable. Ten points.

NECK.—Short and heavy, especially towards shoulders. Five points.

LEGS AND FEET.—Broad and short and well set apart, color same as head and wooled to the hoof, which must be well shaped. Five points.

COVERING.—Body, belly, head and legs well covered with fleece of even length and quality. Scrotum of rams well covered. Ten points.

QUALITY OF WOOL.—Medium such as is known in our markets as "medium-delaine" and "half-combing wool," strong, fine, lustrous fibre, without tendency to mat or felt together, and at one year's growth not less than three and one-half inches in length. Five points.

### BICYCLING.

BICYCLES AND TRICYCLES.

In England, the more sociable and less dangerous tricycle is fast gaining in popularity upon the more rapid bicycle. As yet the tricycle only numbers its hundreds where its elder rival counts its thousands, but before long the proportion may be reversed. The recent meet of four hundred tricyclists at Barnes has given great stimulus to the demand for three-wheelers. The extent to which the tricycle is being used by ladies, may possibly lead to the gradual introduction of the much talked of but seldom seen dipiht garment which figures so largely in the dress of the future. For tricycling it ought to be quite as much a matter of course as the riding-habit is for riding. But according to a very pleasing picture in a recent number of Punch, the ladies can enjoy this pastime without having to resort to such methods. The cut represents two charming girls seated in a tricycle, working the treadle in sewing-machine manner, while accompanying them are two handsome youths on bicycles, with whom they are engaged in pleasant conversation. It is pounds to shillings that those same young gallants have some steel wire about them, so that if their fair companions become tired, or were puzzled by a rising slope, they could hitch on and draw them out—of their difficulties.

Bicycling is advancing with rapid strides in England. It is much indebted for its popularity to Royal favor, quite a number of machines having been ordered by the English and other European Royal houses.

The annual 100-mile road race of the London Bicycle Club (Eng.), from Bath to London, took place last month, and was won in seven and one-half hours. There were between sixty and seventy entries for the race.

In view of the immense impetus given to this healthful and invigorating pastime, that is now acknowledged as so essential to the preservation of health to those whose occupations are of a sedentary character, we advise all such to join the army of wheelmen who now make the smooth, level roads across the bay so lovely with their swift and graceful vehicles.

LEAGUE RIDING REGULATIONS.

Members should keep as much as possible to the right side of the road. It is illegal to ride on any path set aside for foot passengers, and the practice must be avoided.

The rules of the road should be most strictly followed out.

In meeting keep to the right. In overtaking pass to the left.

In passing a vehicle or foot passenger notice should be given at a sufficient distance by whistle, bell, or otherwise. Never pass between two vehicles or riders when overtaking them.

If any vehicle or rider wishes to pass keep well over to the right.

It is considered advisable to avoid, as much as possible, the use of the voice when passing foot passengers or vehicles.

In meeting or passing restive horses, a dismount should only be made if requested, as sudden dismounts often have the worst effect. A slow pace, and a few words, from the best course. A rider should always keep as far away from the horse as possible.

Riders should not take the ground in front of a horse until at least forty feet ahead.

The above rules should be observed in every particular by wheelmen, and thus avoid the possibility of accidents.

Ride slow around curves, and under no circumstances indulge in racing. Wheelmen are welcome steeds by drivers to try their metal with their horses, but this must be avoided.

The famous old Julia, one of George Steers' best boats, has been put all in order after her original design. She was built in 1854, and sailed many matches, several of which were with the Rebecca, the most noted one being that of twenty miles to windward, outside of Sandy Hook, in a stiff southeast breeze. She beat the Rebecca about twenty minutes in this race. The Julia's dimensions now are: Length over all, 78 feet 8 inches; length on water line, 70 feet; extreme breadth, 20 feet 6 inches; depth of hold, 6 feet 8 inches; draft of water, 6 feet 4 inches. Her new center-board, which replaces the old keel, is 14 feet in length. It is of oak, working in a yellow pine case. Although this famous yacht was built in 1854, and many changes have been made in her since, still the carpenters found her timbers and planking sound, showing little evidence of age and none of decay. Her keel, keelson, deadwoods, stem, sternpost, frames, wales, top timbers, deck beams, deck beams and rails are all of oak. She is ceiled with yellow pine and her decks are of clear white pine. She has a counter stern and will steer this year with a diamond screw wheel. Following are the dimensions of the "sticks" that have been put in her: Mainmast, 73 feet out of deck to hounds, 50 feet; length of mast-head, 7 feet 9 inches; topmast, 39 feet in length; mainboom, 63 feet; maingaff, 30 feet; bowsprit, 26 feet; centerboard, 14 feet.

The blue fishing of Monterey Bay is said to be excellent just now. A party of gentlemen caught 89 of these fish on the 4th. One of the fish was the largest of the kind ever caught there, being over 18 inches long and weighing somewhat over three pounds. The party consisted of George Cope, John Pew, E. B. Young and Mr. Delamaidi. They were in a fisherman's boat and made fast to the kelp about two miles from the lighthouse. Sand fleas were used for bait, and small hooks with light sinkers were employed. The party fished with poles and had good sport. In addition to the blue fish some sea trout and one sea gopher was caught; the latter was found in deep water. The bluefish are increasing in numbers each year in Monterey, this being the third year since they first put in an appearance there.

The Guardian Angel Roman Catholic Church, in close proximity to the Brighton Beach, Brooklyn, race track, for some time past has been in a straightened pecuniary condition. On learning this, the executive officers of the track offered to donate one day's receipts to the church, and on June 26th the result was $1,700 from the gate and $500 from the purse money, an aggregate of $2,300 that passed into the treasury of the religious institution. Is it not time for a certain straight-laced Brooklyn divine to enlarge on this last fearful kink of the sporting community?

ABOUT two miles south of McDenney's, or Sugar Pine Point, Lake Tahoe, says the Oroville Mercury, there puts into the lake from the west a fine mountain stream, which heads among the craggy, snow-laden peaks of the western summit of the Sierra. Like the water of the lake, that of the stream is translucent—as clear as it is possible for water to be, and so soft and pure and cold. At the mouth for several hundred yards it meanders through a nice little meadow with willows and tall grass, and is deep, though where it enters the lake it shoals and somewhat widens. This stream is a favorite breeding ground for trout, and at certain seasons of the year they fairly throng its waters. Up the little creek, a few score of yards from the mouth, is a corral in the water into which the trout ascending the stream can enter, but cannot pass down again without the aid of the keeper, and consequently an abundant supply of trout is almost always attainable. Spawn is here collected in quantities as called for, and carefully packed in moss and sent abroad for propagation to stock other streams and ponds.

PERSONAL.—Charles Kaeding of the firm of Liddle & Kaeding, who has been in Europe some months purchasing for the firm, left Queenstown on July 4th, on his return to this city.

## THE STAGE.

The season that has just passed has certainly been the most quiescent of a series of annual disasters, for it may be safely averred that, outside of the Gardens, there has been a great deal more lost than made in theatrical enterprises in this city, but the losses have not been so large as in previous years. Now, all the possible changes of the Thespian bells have been rung, and it yet remains to be said what is the true, popular and managerial keynote. There is no doubt but that we have had liberal and enterprising managers in our midst, who have brought forward the most expensive talent that figured in the stellar system, and that sometimes great returns have been made from these extraordinary outlays; the Booth, Nielson, "Diplomacy" and "Hazel Kirke" engagements forming the red letters of the few past years, but the failures are, in the words of Bardwell Slote, "in a large majority." Manager Maguire has sunk a small fortune in trying to run a stock company at the Baldwin that was not to be excelled outside of New York, and there only by the Union Square and Wallack's Theatres. Manager Locke has played a series of novelties at the Bush Street Theatre, and the Comic Opera Company, with Miss Emily Melville at the head, was scarcely to be surpassed by any organization in the East. The Grand Opera House has been closed save for special occasions, and thus, by charging special rates, has probably made more money than any of the other theatres. The California Theatre has been conducted under the Haverly regime on somewhat vacillating principles, but with a good, honest faith towards the public that merited better returns. It is sincerely to be desired that the coming attractions will show such a balance to the good that will justify that enterprising Manager in continuing to cater for our fickle yet liberal-minded public during the Winter months, when that drama was so in demand at the East. At the Standard, William Emerson has made a bold and successful bid for popularity with his Minstrels, but it is doubtful if his later ventures have added to the exchequer. He it was who, for a season, first appealed to the masses with his moderate charges of admission, and although the example was followed by the Rial Combination at the California, and by Mr. Gus Frohman at the Baldwin, it is very doubtful if a good entertainment can possibly be offered, in the long run, at a first-class theatre at such prices as 75 cents, 50 cents and 25 cents entrance. In solving such a problem, Mr. Frohman certainly came closest to the solution, but even with him it was, we opine, somewhat like squaring the circle.

Alluding to the recent successful production of George R. Sims' melodrama at the Princess' Theatre, the *Times* remarks: "The Ruming Rye," contains, along with much that is clever and that gives promise of better things, all the vices of the transpontine drama in its most objectionable form. It reeks of the slums, and the tone of it is such as can only commend itself to the minds wholly destitute of artistic sentiment. It is difficult to say which is its more conspicuous feature—the exaggerated virtue which throughout the piece invariably accompanies poverty or the equally exaggerated wickedness which is the unfailing concomitant of wealth and education. All this is the more deplorable from its being presented with much dramatic ingenuity and resource. There is not a scene or passage from the beginning of the first act to the end of the fifth which is not full of life and movement. Indeed, dramatic situations of the most startling kind follow each other with a bewildering rapidity that must make even the gallery long for a moment's repose. Through five crowded acts the fight between villainy and virtue goes on—success inclining now to the one side and now to the other. There are at least three attempts at murder—by bullet, by poison and by drowning. There is a burglary with violence, there are two attempts at abduction, and there is a wreck at sea and a perilous rescue. Interspersed with these events are picturesque, but irrelevant sketches of gypsy life and of the interior of the old thieving dens of Seven Dials. Here and there Mr. Sims deepens his colors, until the sombreness of the picture is both appalling and even repulsive, as it is where he shows us murder carried on not as a "fine art," but distinctly as a trade in the lowest river-side slums of Ratcliffe highway. The morbid dwelling upon horrors which goes to make up the fourth act is positively loathsome. It is matter for surprise and also matter for regret that a dramatist of Mr. Sims' standing should not have turned his talents into a worthier channel than the writing of this bad, mischievous play."

Mr. Gye has had a serious altercation with Mme. Christine Nilsson once more, in connection with a broken contract. The matter passed into the hands of her lawyers, and among other indiscreet things, Mr. Gye said that the fair songstress, a short time since, was very eager to make an engagement, and that this time he desired a "guarantee of good faith." The solicitor replied that he was amused by Mr. Gye's picture of his client "going cap in hand to him for an engagement," and is sure that "no such exciting chase has yet fallen to her experience." To close the case, he puts his client's position in a nutshell with these words: "With Mme. Nilsson it is not a question of formal contract, but one of contract at all. There was a negotiation for a contract, the form of contract was tendered and rejected, and thereupon the abortive negotiation was closed."

It would really appear as if Sara Bernhardt in her marriage had stolen a few leaves from the happier life of "Camille." She looks better, acts better, and behaves better than ever before. Her solemn-looking Greek husband, either through his strength of will, or her weakness through love, has succeeded in transforming her whole nature. "He is the first man," said she to a friend, "who ever made love to me of whom I am afraid. He can make me do what he likes."

On the 17th instant the celebrated Hanlon-Lees open at the Baldwin Theater in their amusing acrobatic absurdity entitled "Le Voyage en Suisse." In their recent engagement in Chicago, the piece was a great success, drawing so well that their stay might have been prolonged, but their opening having been arranged here for the above date, they were obliged to refuse the flattering offers made to them. The company numbers twenty-seven persons.

Miss Genevieve Ward is seriously ill in England. She was never famous in any character except her last creation, Stephanie, in "Forget-me-not."

Wallack's Theater closed last Wednesday, with the fiftieth representation of "La Belle Russe." The drama was a great financial success, and during the next season it promises to be the best drawing card in the road, as the cast is small and easily controlled. Miss Jeffreys-Lewis, will assume her original character as "La Belle Russe."

A new domestic drama, by Charles Reade, entitled "Single Heart and Double Face," was produced at the Princess Theatre, Edinburgh, and was well received. The plot is interesting, but appears to be rather tame in comparison with the blood, thunder and carpenter drama so much in vogue at the present time.

Mrs. Langtry, as a beauty, was deemed a trifle fast, and now that she has adopted the stage as a career, she keeps up this reputation. At the conclusion of her engagement at Glasgow, she, in company with her maid, took a special train at midnight, and arrived in London at 9:30 A. M., in order to meet a large number of her friends at dinner at Mrs. Labouchere's, who wished to congratulate her on the great success she had achieved in the English provinces. The trip cost the lady £103 15s., and, in the way of advertising, was cheap at the price.

Miss Maud Granger is suffering from illness and poverty, and application has been made to the Executive Officers of the Actors' Fund for her relief, but as yet apparently without result. Miss Granger was the original Dora in "Diplomacy," when that drama was produced at the California, and it is astonishing the number of misfortunes that have befallen those who took part in that play. A benefit for Miss Granger would be in order, but unfortunately the weather in New York is not propitious for such an undertaking.

Melodrama with startling, lurid scenic effects will have full sway next season. "Taken from Life," "Mankind" and "Romany Rye" are among the novelties promised. McVickers' Theatre, Chicago, where "Taken from Life" will have its first American representation, is now being altered and refitted. The regular season will open with "Taken from Life," and the scenery and mechanical effects to be introduced in it, Mr. Colville says, will be the most expensive and intricate ever used in this country. Genuine gypsies will be introduced in the encampment scene. The inaugural performance will be given July 31.

Edwin Booth met with a flattering reception on his first appearance at the Adelphi, in London, on the 25th of June last. This Theatre has always been identified with the melodrama, "The Green Bushes," "Oliver Twist" and "The Colleen Bawn" showing the range of its, multifarious successes and it was deemed hazardous to test the legitimate on this stage. The play was "Richelieu" and Mr. Booth made the most marked effect in the famous scene in which Richelieu draws the awful circle of the power of Rome around Julie, but his unquestionable success according to the general impression was a success of declamation, rather than of tragic art.

As a comment on popular criticism *The Score* states that the following incident recently occurred in a village not thirty miles from Boston: An Irish laborer was taken to a concert for the first time and was asked how he liked it. "Well," he replied, "I loiked it all ixcept a piece called quartiet. They didn't know that at all. Furrust the two ladies begun singing, and the min waited for them to stop, but thin they got tired of waitin' and started in anyhow. But the ladies kipt on, as it was quite roight they should, and thin whin they all stopped singin' the guril at the piany she didn't know the piece was done and just kipt on a whoile by herself. They spoilt it intirely; but I didn't loike the piece anyway."

At a recent meeting in London for the promotion of the Actors' Benevolent Fund, Henry Irving spoke as follows: "You must distinctly bear in mind that this proposed scheme is not one of charity; it is one of aid—aid of which we might all of us at some time be in need. When brother or sister in fortune helps brother or sister in distress, we cannot call it charity. We must all bear in mind this one thing—that we do not ask charity or accept it. We help each other and ourselves. It is the accident of our lives or our calling which may make such help as we can give welcome or even necessary, but it is needful that we have some actual scheme, perpetual in its aim, comprehensive in its scope, large-hearted in its workings, which may enable us to give that aid while we can, and to accept it should we fall on evil times."

At the present the outlook is more promising than it has been for months past. At the California, Haverly's Mastodon Minstrels ought to crowd the house through a good three weeks' engagement, as they are favorites here, and come re-inforced with new faces and new songs and interludes. At the Standard, "My Sweetheart's-in-Law" will probably give place on Thursday, to "H. M. S. Pinafore," that it properly produced is never lacking in popularity. At the Baldwin, a new drama will be produced entitled "American Born," in which there are, it is said, many thrilling effects accompanied by a volcanic eruption, and in this scenery William Porter is an expert, he having made a study of this specialty in all its phases in the Hawaiian Islands. The cast includes Miss Ada Ward, Miss Ada Gilman, and the old favorites of the theatre. The Gardens continue their programme to the delight of their countless visitors.

A most distressing accident occurred at the hippodrome in Paris recently. During the race of the Roman chariots the one that was leading came in contact with a post, and, overturning with violence, the charioteer, Mlle. Dupre, was thrown out and dragged along by her dress, which had become entangled. The material was on the point of yielding to the strain, when the next chariot, before its conqueror, Mlle. Carro, could pull up, passed over the body of the unfortunate girl, who was thought to be dead when picked up. She was carried in a perfectly insensible condition to the infirmary attached to the building, where her wounds were dressed. Her collar-bone was broken, and she sustained internal injuries. She was subsequently removed to a hospital, and, it is said, the physicians have some hopes of saving her life.

The gentlemen interested in the J. H. Haverly Amusement Company, with a capital of $300,000, which recently filed a certificate of incorporation, are J. H. Haverly, Henry Mann,

C. H. McConnell, A. Hayman, Edward Keyes, and E. G. Gilmore. Mr. Haverly's idea appears to be to bring good English attractions to this country and to send good American attractions to England. We like anything that is thoroughly and characteristically English, and English audiences liberally patronize everything which is really American, in the theatrical line. The company will control Mr. Haverly's theatres, which are the California Theater, San Francisco; the Chestnut Street Theatre, Philadelphia; the Brooklyn Theatre; Haverly's Theatre, Chicago, and the Fourteenth Street Theater here. It is said that the Olympic Theater, in London, has been secured, and also a theatre in Manchester, and that other theaters are being negotiated for. Mr. Haverly is expected to return from Europe in the course of this month.

## FEEDING EXPERIMENTS.

In considering the following scale it must be borne in mind that Canada has a vastly different climate to California, and that the day has not yet come in this State when manure is worth $2.80 per ton at any distance from the large cities.

The superintendent of the model farm at Guelph, Canada, gives as below the results of some experiments made there in cattle-breeding:

1. A steady frosty winter is better than an open one in feeding cattle.

2. An average 2 or 3-year-old steer will eat its own weight of different materials in three weeks.

3. Two or 3-year-old cattle will add one-third of a pound more per day to their weight upon prepared hay and roots than upon the same materials unprepared.

4. It is 30 per cent. more profitable to premature and dispose of fattening cattle at two years old than to keep them up to three years.

5. There is no loss in feeding a cattle beast well upon a variety of materials for the sake of manure alone.

6. Barnyard manure from well-fed cattle, 3-year olds, is worth an average of $2.80 per ton.

7. A 3-year-old cattle beast, well fed, will make at least one ton of manure every month of winter.

8. No cattle beast whatever will pay for the direct increase to its weight from the consumption of any kind or quantity of food.

9. On an average it costs twelve cents for every additional pound of flesh added to the weight of a 2 or 3-year-old fattening steer.

10. In Canada the market value of store cattle can be increased 26 per cent. during six months of finishing by good feeding.

11. In order to secure a safe profit, no store cattle beast, well done to, can be sold at less than 4½ cents per pound (live weight).

12. In the fattening of wethers, to finish as shearlings, the Cotswold and Leicester grades can be made up to 200 pounds, the Oxford-down 180 pounds, and the South-down (grade) 160 pounds each (live weight).

13. A cow wintered upon two tons and a half of hay will produce not far from five tons of manure, provided that she be well littered and none of the excrements be wasted.

## THE HORSE IN AMERICA.

It has been generally believed that the horse was introduced in America by the Spanish. Professor Marsh, on the other hand, has found abundant remains of probable ancestors of the horse in our Western geological formations; so that, if there were no horses before the Spanish came, there must have occurred a failure of the race. Mr. E. L. Berthoud, of Golden, Colorado, believes that he has evidence that the Spaniards found horses in South America when they first visited it. Among the maps which he has recently received from Paris, in a collection of the fifteenth and sixteenth centuries, is one which Sebastian Cabot drew for the Emperor Charles V., representing his explorations of the La Plata and Parana rivers, and containing symbols of the horse and plants that he found. Among these symbols was that of the horse represented near the plains of the Grand Chaco, where the immense herds of that animal range to-day. He claims that this affords a fair presumption of the native origin of the race, for neither the Spaniards nor the Portuguese had then been long enough in the country (in 1527) for their horses to have escaped from Peru to the head of the Paraguay and Parana rivers and to have increased in numbers sufficiently to attract attention.—*Popular Science Monthly.*

Tom Tunstead has carefully laid out his hunting camp at Nicasio, Marin County, and will be ready for full operations when this journal makes its appearance. He has two fine box hounds for sale; the particulars of which are to be found in our advertising columns.

## THE VICTORIAN TROTTING CLUB.

We take pleasure in calling attention to the advertisement which appears in another part of the paper, and which informs our readers that the Victorian Trotting Club offers a prize of $2,500 for the trotting to contend for on some day in January next. There is no country which is as much interested in trotting in Australia as California. There is a surplus of trotters here and the outlook for them is in that country. The purse of $2,500 is certainly very liberal, and restricting it to few procreative animals is a move in the right direction. It is not only the winning the purse which should be an enticement, as it is sure that the stallion or mare lucky enough to win will sell for a round sum. Dr. Weir will furnish all the intelligence to those who are desirous of making entries.

# FISH.

## PRESERVATION OF FISH.

There are men in this city, ardent lovers of the rod and line, whose rods have hung in the covers, for two or three years. And this, not from apathy or inability to get away, but simply from disgust with experiences in the coast streams, and the impossibility of getting a good day's sport without traveling a hundred miles or so to reach the spot.

There is no place in the world where there are better facilities in the way of streams than with us. There are trout streams, creeks and brooks in every direction. And such streams, too, as furnish good waters for the finny tribes.

But if those fond of the rod and creel are content to lay away their outfits, and give it up as a bad job, simply because a few weeks' good sport, then the vandals will have it all their own way.

On general principles, monopolies and combinations of all kinds are distasteful, but it is absolutely necessary that the fishermen among us must combine in a united effort to prevent a destruction of fish, and must take an active part in the measures which are adopted.

It will not do to get together and pass a lot of resolutions. A "whereas" and "resolved" may scare off a political candidate, but it will not in any degree intimidate the class of men who use Giant Powder to catch fish. As a general thing, they do not understand that kind of language.

But who is to take the first step towards a rigorous prosecution? Surely it must be the sportsmen, who are to reap its benefits. For $5 a man can go to a stream and make his cast where he will get no fish. It costs him $50 to get to one where his fly will be taken. Why not spend the $45 in going for the fish killer, and then the $5 trip can be taken with more satisfaction and some chance of success.

The men who hang up their rods and put away their reels, fly books and baskets, ought take them down again and make up their minds to cast them once more. They ought to make up their minds, too, to lend aid, countenance and practical help to whatever efforts are inaugurated to bring about a reform.

Trolling on Twin Lakes gives good rewards.

The trout on the San Lorenzo creek are pretty small.

There is said to be very good trout fishing in Donner Lake.

Fishing parties on Lake Lundy, Mono County, have good sport.

Fishing is good on Willow creek, near Jacksonville, Oregon.

The Weber Lake House, which has been closed during the winter, was opened on the first instant.

Bay fishing is reported as being good—large numbers of rock cod, sea trout and perch being caught.

There are said to be good trout streams in Indian Valley, Plumas county, and hotels convenient to the streams.

As to flies, every man thinks he knows the best ones for certain creeks. And probably he does if he knows the creek.

Edward Bosqui and party have gone to the Little Seour and adjoining streams in Monterey county.

A large party of railroad attaches spent the Fourth in fishing Donner creek and lake, and speak of the fishing being unusually good.

Excellent fishing is to be had this year in Independence Lake. Good. Bedding, and many other San Franciscans, being late visitors there.

If the Truckee Republican is not misinformed, S. T. Burton caught over 1400 Lake Tahoe trout two weeks ago, and shipped them to this city to the market.

A sturgeon weighing 487 pounds was caught at Red Bluff the other day. It measured eleven feet nine inches in length, and three feet six inches around the body.

At Catalina Island, in the Santa Barbara Channel, there is fine fishing. A party caught 885 barracouta, thirteen "yellow tails" weighing 40 pounds each, and a lot of rock cod, in ten days. The catch aggregated 4000 pounds.

A Chico editor went fishing the other day, and by accident fell into the river, but he was not at all alarmed, because he had his life insured; he said he "never had anything happen to him by which he could make any money."

Lundy Lake, Homer Mining District, Mono county, in this State, is said to abound in fish. Mill Creek, near by, is also good fishing ground. A new hotel was opened there recently, so there is now accommodation for anglers.

A large number of fish are being caught in Santa Cruz county streams. The Monday morning boats show a goodly number of excursionists returning from Sunday trips. A great many people are camping out about Felton, Glenwood, etc.

The Sonoma Index, of June 24th, says: "On Wednesday of last week a party of fishermen, consisting of Capt. N. Carriger, Geo. S. Tule and others, made a big catch of 245 catfish in the Laguna, near Mark West." They brought 75 to town alive.

Geo. H. Maxwell has returned from a two weeks' vacation, spent in fishing the streams between Lakeport and Ukiah. He found good fishing in the streams, but the contrary at Blue Lakes, where a large number of San Francisco people are sojourning.

Messrs. J. H. W. Riley and Joseph Shain have returned from an angling trip of ten days. During this period they fished the Navarro, Garcia, Russian and Grallala rivers. They report the latter, from which they sent several boxes of trout to this city, as being much the best stream.

The Reno Gazette is responsible for the following: "A few days ago a man caught a 16-pound trout in Pyramid Lake. Inside the trout was a 4-pound sucker, and in the sucker was a half-pound chub. There was nothing inside the chub but worms. This is no fish story. It is an actual fact.

---

The Salt Lake Tribune says, "Trout fishing is good in all the mountain streams, and the size of the fish is gauged by the imagination of the city fisherman. The more exaggerated the imagination the bigger the fish, and now white whales are caught in the Cottonwoods while the air swims with white lies."

There are more ways than one of fishing, and this is the way the barbarians of Mono County do it, according to the Bodie Free Press: "The enthusiastic fisherman quickly slides into the hardware store and fills his pockets with giant-powder cartridges, and then takes to the streams. Once on the banks of a trout stream it is but the work of a moment for him to blow out a hundred or more trout. Satisfied with his splendid luck, he returns home and tells the boys all about his trip and how the fish took the hook with an eagerness that denoted enthusiasm."

Mr. Benjamin Burling, who was so severely injured in the sad accident in Santa Cruz county, is one of the most skilled anglers and shots on the Coast. He is an ardent sportsman, and has few equals in handling a rod. knowing all the streams and frequenting them often. With the shotgun he is an expert, and is well known as such to all the hunting fraternity. During the duck season, Mr. Burling is a constant shooter in the Scisen or Sherman Island marshes. His many friends anxiously hope for a speedy recovery.

Carp.—The biggest carp yield, by a large majority, is that of Wm. Gilson. William has a fine place on Date Creek, with abundance of water. About a year ago he procured eight carp, from which he now has 8,000 or 10,000 head, with more spawn to hear from. All this has occurred in Yavapai County waters. William says his carp are great feeders, as well as breeders ; that they have great confidence in him, will almost take bread crumbs out of his hand, and never fail to come to the surface when he calls them.—Prescott (Arizona) Courier.

The Monterey Argus says: "W. W. James was out fishing in the Carmel River, above the head of the Laureles ditch. He had two hooks on his line, and while fishing in a big hole, hooked a trout sixteen inches in length, and while trying to land it, another one about the same size grabbed the other hook. He succeeded in safely landing the two of them. Carter Wadhams, who was an eye-witness, says it was better than a circus.

# THE RIFLE.

[Continued.]

The story of Robin Hood and Little John, who could do effective work with the crossbow a measured mile, is a good one, and could I be credulous enough to believe this "Robin Hood Story," it would make me a truly happy man ; but I am unkind enough to believe that historians sometimes "draw the long-bow" with such striking imagination that to take the whole dose would be as fatal as barbed shafts would be when sent from the cross-bow by the well-trained arm of the skilful and ancient archer. The almost tragical story of "William Tell" is a good one, too, which I need to read when a great deal younger than I am now, with eye-balls protruding from their sockets and hair standing on end ; 'like quills upon the fretful porcupine," but as nature ago came upon me I classed it as a twin brother of poor old Rip Van Winkle, whose sleep for twenty years has been deeply impressed upon the young of America, so that every schoolboy can repeat the sad ordeal that the old man passed through during his long and eventful sleep. For five hundred years after the battle of Hastings, which was fought on the 14th of October, 1066, the archers of England formed a national guard, whose constant practice made them so efficient that all of Europe recognized their power, and the most vigilant care was taken by the government to maintain the advantage they had gained. It was obligatory for every able-bodied man, between the ages of 19 and 60 years, under a severe penalty, to have a bow of his own length and a quantity of arrows, and to do a certain amount of practice each week in target shooting, butts and targets being established by the Government in every parish at the distances regulated by law.

Holidays were always celebrated by prize shooting, under the supervision of government officials, and every effort was used to create a popular feeling in this national sport until it became the universal recreation on which the power and even the very existence and solidity of the nation depended. England is indebted much to the cross-bow for the power that the possessors to-day among the nations of the earth, and I have often thought that the cross-bow would be a better and more appropriate national emblem, or insignia, than that of the snapping and roaring lion. But the lion in all ages has been considered the king brute of the jungle and the forest, while England for centuries, by her well-conducted commercial relations among the nations of the earth, has been regarded as the king of the seas.

In the isle of Bruce, written by Barker, we are informed that guns were used by the English in the year 1327, at the battle of Merewater; but their clumsy and uncouth forms made them little better than the sling and bow. Therefore the use of guns as implements of war only dates back some five hundred years.

And the antiquated specimens that are preserved among the English curiosos, with their drawings and designs, are preserved with the utmost care, and their examination, and comparison, with fire-arms of the present day, must convince any one that they were almost worthless, and one wonders how they could have been used to any advantage. The old English musqueteer was so burdened with phantastic and accoutrements, that it weighed him down, and made him an encumbered soldier. Besides being forced to pack or carry his cumbersome and unwieldy weapon, he had his can of coarse powder for loading his musket, his horn of fine powder for priming in a touch-hop, his bullets in a leathern bag down deep in his pocket, which faxen slings to draw to get to them, while in his hand was his ram-rod, his gun rest, and burning match; and getting on his knees to sight and level his piece, he would apply the torch made from tar or pitch, then rising to go through the same manipulation in reloading, not knowing what kind of execution, the spent bullet had done. It must have been unsatisfactory and discouraging at least to the feigned soldier. Hence it was a long time, in deciding the superiority of the musket, over the natives' favorite weapon, the cross-bow.

But slowly the change took place, and by each improvement after improvement of the firearm was accomplished, did its unwieldy proportions gave place to a more symmetrical and easily manipulated piece. But even then it took a great display of oratory upon the rostrum, and annual exhibitions of the musket, by the best practical mechanics of the time, to get the disciples of the cross-bow to admit the superiority of the musket over their long-cherished and long-admired bow; and it required two centuries of hard work for the devotees of the musket before it became universally acknowledged as a more destructive engine of war; and for four hundred years the quivers of Cloth-yard shafts have been supplanted by bright bristling bayonets, festooned, as it were, upon the muzzles of the muskets.

Many splendid exhibitors of mechanical ingenuity have been left us to study and ponder over, consisting of rational and complex ideas, from which much of our present and improved firearms took their origin. We find in many instances the laws of mechanism closely observed, and even scientific principles are manifest in many of the early productions, that now govern the laws that regulate and perfect our present system of gunnery. A more perfect knowledge of what has been done by our predecessors would prove a great boon to our race, and, especially, our generation. Europeans nations, more especially France, have made ample provisions for this by their museums of antiquated arts—the like of which we want—a museum of progression, an epitome of the great mechanical minds of the present age, handed down from generation to generation, so that no man would be assigned the laborious task of pulling, by night and by day, on an endless rope. Thanks to those men who have deemed the science and value of gunnery of sufficient importance to warrant them to engage in the laborious undertaking of compiling facts and data; and I will say, the greatest benefactor in this important matter will be he who will have the ability to blow away the cobwebs of mystery, rendering each improvement to him who is entitled to it.

Nothing now remains of the once beautiful machinery of the old flintlock—the tens of thousands that were used by our Fathers in the Revolutionary war; but one can be seen. In its day it was a great improvement, and the whole world looked upon it as the ne plus ultra of a lock. The fancy cock and hammers have given place to a "Simple" hammer striking on a little thimble containing fulminates seated in the butt of the breech-loading cartridge.

(To be Continued.)

## ROWING NOTES.

Talking about Hanlon reminds us of the champion's sickness, which is evidently genuine. The doctor's certificate has been produced to show that the invincible Canadian is suffering from typhoid fever. It would seem that, under the circumstances, Ross would have relinquished his claims in the champion's purse and consented to a postponement of the race. The Brunswicker prefers, however, to hold the Toronto man to the strict letter of the articles, and has wired him that he will claim forfeit and the championship unless the invalid leaves his sick bed to run. This is a very ungraceful proceeding for Mr. Ross, and the indignation which his action has aroused in Toronto will be generally shared by all honest, manly admirers of aquatic sport. The Brunswicker's threat that he will claim the championship does not appear to trouble Hanlon much. "Let him take it," said the prostrate champion; "when I get well I'll beat him." And beat him he will. It ought to be no trick to beat a man who would seek to make glory by dragging a fever patient out of his bed to run. Besides, there is nothing in Mr. Ross' record to show that he can keep within halling distance of Hanlon over a full championship course. He has been beaten twice by the champion. It is said that since then Ross has improved. Any one who thinks that while Ross has been making this improvement Hanlon has stood still, or fallen off, will make a grievous mistake. The best judges of rowing think that he is to-day incomparably superior to what he was when he defeated Courtney at Lachine.

The fact that Ross beat Hanlon on the Hop Bitters Regatta proves nothing. The defeat of a professional oarsman in a race where he has not a cent staked and has not spent a dollar in training is of no importance. It is far more significant that in each match with Ross the champion has won easily. One would think that the result of the recent race between Hanlon and Trickett would have discouraged the supporters of Ross. The Australian rowed the Brunswicker two very hard races, and will at any time extend him, whereas in his races with Hanlon, Trickett each time brought up the rear of a very uninteresting procession. Another point which is generally overlooked is the fact that in the regatta in which Ross astonished the rowing world and himself by beating Hanlon, he did not show such tremendous pace at the start. Both Boyd and Hanlon led the Brunswicker for a distance, and it was not until the race between the Englishman and the Canadian was over, that Ross forged up and went ahead. Many Eastern oarsmen think that the interest taken in Ross by Davis and Kennedy shows that the Brunswicker must have been doing some terrific private trials. Perhaps he has, but who knows what the private trials of Hanlon have been like?

Moreover, even the ingenious Mr. Davis is liable to be mistaken. He had for a long time and perhaps even yet cherished the belief that he could have beaten Courtney in his best and most popular days—but he never did it.

THE HILLSDALE CREW.— The London *Sportsman* says: It is difficult to believe that the Hillsdales are the best amateur crew America can produce. In rowing under favorable circumstances, on Wednesday last, they got a pace on the boat, but the time of the oars was lost and irregular, and the work was left entirely to the arms.

[New York Spirit of the Times.]

**Meanderings in the Metropolis.**

With the departure of Winter, and the return of the longed-for days of Spring, there will come, no doubt, unwonted activity in the market for fine animals. This, at least, is the general impression, based upon the large and profitable business done in every line during the past year, and the consequent tendency on the part of gentlemen of taste to gratify their ideas and fancy by investing in horse-flesh. With these impressions upon his mind, the writer sauntered into the commodious New York Club Stables, 15 and 17 East Twenty-eighth street, between Fifth and Madison avenues, owned and managed by Mr. Calvin M. Priest, whose genial manners and finely stocked stalls have attracted to him a valued and appreciative constituency. The fact that his rare experience with horse-flesh gave him charge of Mr. Robert Bonner's stock years ago is sufficient guaranty of his responsibility. During this time we had gone the round of the stable, and turning we came upon a fancy cupboard, pointing to which the writer asked its purpose. "Oh!" said Mr. Priest, "that contains something of especial value to us horsemen; no doubt you've heard of it, but you shall see it." And opening the door, which should greet our sight but an ample supply of St. Jacobs Oil. "Do you have much faith in that?" we asked of Mr. Priest. With a look that signified much more than words, he deliberately said: "We keep our stables constantly supplied with St. Jacobs Oil, buying a case at a time; and it gives us pleasure to bear testimony to its marvelous healing and pain-relieving properties. In rheumatic affections, cuts, bruises and similar painful ailments, so frequently occurring among horses and human beings, we have yet to find anything equal to the 'Great German Remedy.'" Thanking Mr. Priest, the writer withdrew, and walking a few steps, came to the popular Empire Stables, 4 and 6 East Twenty-eighth street, kept by Mr. S. H. Mason, at whose mammoth establishment are to be found the finest carriages in New York. Speaking with Mr. Mason upon the matter, still in our mind from the conversation with Mr. Priest, Mr. M. freely and strongly endorsed all that Mr. Priest had said regarding the Great German Remedy. Pointing to a fine looking animal, Mr. Mason observed: "There stands a good illustration of the efficacy of St. Jacobs Oil. He was cut severely a few days ago, and by daily application of the Oil he has recovered, without a scar, and we will work him to-morrow. Calling at the Sturtevant House to see a friend whom should we meet there (how strange the coincidence of names!) but Mr. W. B. Sturtevant, of Newport, Vt., who is sojourning in the metropolis at present. Knowing the interest Mr. Sturtevant took in fine stock, we naturally drifted into that subject, and as naturally touched upon the ailments of the horse. After expatiating upon the numerous means and remedies employed at various times and under various conditions, Mr. S. added: "Having owned a large number of trotting horses, as well as carriage and driving horses in great numbers, (such valuable stock as Vermont Boy, Junot, Kit Carson, black gelding General, Thunderbolt, and many others) it gives me pleasure to testify to the curative qualities of St. Jacobs Oil for all the afflictions that man or horse is heir to, and to state that, in all my experience among horses with the Great German Remedy, I have never yet seen its equal." Continuing at some length, Mr. Sturtevant cited case after case where the St. Jacobs Oil had certainly effected remarkable results in diseases of, and accidents to horses. Mr. L. H. Durr, of Milwaukee, Wis., who was also stopping at the Sturtevant House, and who happened to join us during the above narration of Mr. S., volunteered the experience that he had used St. Jacobs Oil for a very stubborn case of rheumatism in his family at home with eminent satisfaction, and had seen it used on one of the largest stock farms in Wisconsin, with most gratifying success. The writer learned all that he started out to discover, and vastly more beside, and could not, with a superabundance of evidence before his eyes, feel otherwise than impressed with the surpassing value of a substance whose virtue and record could boast such endorsers as those who were testifying, the country over, to the magical efficacy of the article above referred to.

---

**J. A. McKERRON,**

Manufacturer of Fine Harness, Horse Boots a Specialty.

NO. 227 SUTTER STREET,

Between Dupont and Stockton.    San Francisco.

REPAIRING NEATLY AND PROMPTLY EXECUTED

---

**THE BALDWIN THEATER.**

ONE WEEK ONLY, COMMENCING MONDAY, July 10.

The Grand Drama,

**AN AMERICAN BORN.**

---

**The CALIFORNIA THEATER**

MONDAY, JULY 10, AND DURING THE WEEK,

**HAVERLY'S**

**MASTADON MINSTRELS.**

---

**EMERSON'S**

**STANDARD THEATER.**

MONDAY, TUESDAY AND WEDNESDAY,

**MY BRUDDER-IN-LAW.**

Thursday and remainder of the week,

**H. M. S. Pinafore.**

---

**THE TIVOLI GARDEN.**

Monday..........................July 10th

Grand Production of the Romantic Opera

**DER FREISCHUTZ.**

---

**THE WINTER GARDEN.**

MONDAY, July THIRD, AND DURING THE WEEK,

The Grand Spectacular Opera,

**ÆOLIA;**

Or, THE MOUNTAIN SYLPH.

---

# J. O'KANE,

MANUFACTURER AND IMPORTER OF

**Harness, Saddles, Whips, Blankets, Boots, Etc.**

767......MARKET STREET......767

SAN FRANCISCO, CAL.

Special attention given to the manufacture of "Boots" of all kinds for horses. Can refer to all the principal trainers and horsemen on the Pacific Coast.

N. B.—My acknowledged superiority in this branch of business is largely due to the careful observation and the Valuable suggestions of the most skillful "horsemen" in the United States. The benefits of which redound to the public in the shape of a GENUINE WELL-FITTING ARTICLE. Sole agent for Dr. A. H. Dixon's Condition Powders and McKinney's patent "Everka" and "Eclipse" Toe Weights. Repairing done with neatness and dispatch. Always on hand with the latest assortment of English Ladies and Gentlemen's saddles, bridles, whips, spurs, bits, and all horse sundries.

JOHN O'KANE

---

I. LANDSBERGER.      J. M. CURTIS.

# LANDSBERGER & CURTIS,

123 CALIFORNIA ST., S. F.,

**GENERAL BROKERS AND COMMISSION MERCHANTS**

For the sale and purchase on commission of all kinds of merchandise, and especially of

**California Wines and Brandies.**

Agencies for Eastern houses in good standing, for the sale and purchase of goods, solicited.

---

**Cobb, Bovee & Co.,**

Real Estate and General Auctioneers

OFFICE AND SALESROOM

**No. 321 Montgomery Street,**

ODD FELLOWS' BUILDING.

Real Estate Sale Day, Thursday.

Sales at Public or Private Sale of Real Estate, Estate Sales, Receivers', Assignees, Trust and Administrators' Sales, Merchandise, Furniture, Stock and outdoor Sale of all description solicited and carefully attended to. We assume charge of property, collect rents, attend to Taxes, Insurance, street work, improvement and building.

---

# REVISED SPEED PROGRAMME

## FOR 1882.

FOURTH ANNUAL MEETING

OF THE

SONOMA COUNTY

**Agricultural Park Association,**

At SANTA ROSA.

**FIRST DAY—Tuesday, Aug. 22, 1882.**

No 1—TROTTING RACE.—Free for all two-year-olds owned in the District. Mile heats, 2 best in 3; purse, $300. First horse, $150; second, $100; third, $50. Closed on the first day of May with the following entries:

J. P. Conwar names B. &c., b. bball, by J. Abbotsford.
E. P. Foster names &c. m. Clara Patterson, by Grey McClellan.
G. C. Fountain names blk. f. May Day, by Eugene Casserly.

...

**SECOND DAY—Wednesday, Aug. 23.**

No 4—PACING RACE.—Free to all horses that never beat 2:20; purse, $300. First horse, $200; second, $75; third, $25.

**THIRD DAY—Thursday, Aug. 24.**

No 5—TROTTING RACE.—Free for all three-year-olds owned in the District; purse, $300. First horse, $150; second, $100; third, $50. Closed May 1st, with the following entries:

...

**FOURTH DAY—Friday, Aug. 25.**

No 7—TROTTING RACE.—Free to all that never beat 2:30; purse, $500. First horse, $250; second, $150; third, $100.

...

**FIFTH DAY—Saturday, Aug. 26.**

No 10—RUNNING RACE.—Free for all three-year-olds one mile and repeat; purse, $300. First horse, $150; second, $100.

No 11—TROTTING RACE.—Free to all that never beat 2:25; purse, $500. First horse, $400; second, $300; third, $100.

**ENTRIES.**

...

**CONDITIONS.**

...

CHARLES HOPPER, Secretary.

---

# Pacific Breeders' Association.

**Embryo Trotting Stakes, 1882.**

Sweepstakes for foals, 1882, $100 each; $25 forfeit; $10 declaration; $5 nomination fee.

...

N. T. SMITH, Treasurer.
JOS. CAIRN SIMPSON, Secretary pro tem.

---

# PAUL FRIEDHOFER,

**Pathological Horse Shoer,**

PRACTICAL IN ALL ITS VARIOUS BRANCHES.

No. 105 COMMERCIAL ST.

Hoof evils and Malformations in their earliest stages treated with radical success.

---

**CLAY PIGEONS—PERFECT IMITATION OF A QUAIL'S FLIGHT**

EVANSVILLE ARGUS

SPORTSMEN! SEND FOR CIRCULAR TO

**PIERCE & CO., ----- OAKLAND, CAL**

SOLE AGENTS FOR THE PACIFIC COAST.

## Pacific Coast Blood Horse As'n.

### PROGRAMME.

FIXED EVENTS—SPRING & FALL MEETINGS

1883 and 1884.

---

### BALDWIN STAKE FOR 1882

---

#### SPRING MEETING.

First Day.

WINTERS' STAKE—For three-year-olds, to be run the first day of the Spring Meeting; dash of one-and-a-half miles; $100 each, $25 forfeit, $300 added; second to half $100, third to save stake. Nominations to above to be made for 1883.

SAME DAY—CALIFORNIA STAKE—For two-year-olds, $50 each, $20 forfeit, $250 added; to be run on the first day of the Spring Meeting; second to save stake; dash of half a mile. Nominations to above to be made for 1883.

Second Day.

PACIFIC CUP—Handicap of $100 each, $60 forfeit, $20 declaration, $600 added; second to receive $300, third to save stake; two and-a-quarter miles; to be run on the second day of the Spring Meeting. Will close the 1st of March, 1883.

Third Day.

"SPIRIT OF THE TIMES" STAKE—Dash of one-and-three-quarter miles for all three-year-olds; $100 each, $25 forfeit, $300 added; $150 to second, third to save stake. Nominations to above to be made for 1884.

SAME DAY—GANO STAKE—Dash of three-quarters of a mile for two-year-olds; $50 each, $20 forfeit, $250 added; second horse to save stake. Nominations to above to be made for 1884.

FALL MEETING.

Second Day.

STALLION STAKE—Conditions—Only those three-year-olds are eligible which are the get of stallions owned in this State. The stallions have to subscribe the amount charged for their services to the fund.

Third Day.

THE BALDWIN STAKE—Post stake for all ages; dash of four miles; $300 each, p. p.; $1,000 added; second, $400, third to save stake. Will close on the 1st of August, 1883, for that year.

SAME DAY—FLYINGAT STAKE—For two-year-olds; dash of a mile; $50 each, $20 forfeit, $250 added; second to save stake. Nominations to be made for 1883.

SAME DAY—JAMES STAKE—For three-year-olds; dash of two miles; $100 each, $25 forfeit, $300 added; second to have $150, third to save stake. Nominations to be made for 1883.

THEO. WINTERS, President.
JOS. CAIRN SIMPSON, Secretary.

---

### SPEED PROGRAMME

FOR THE

## First Annual Meeting

OF THE

### SANTA CRUZ COUNTY

## Agricultural Fair Association,

### At SANTA CRUZ,

Commencing - Tuesday, August 15th.

### $3,500 IN PURSES!

FIRST DAY—Tuesday, Aug. 15, 1882.

No. 1—TROTTING RACE—Purse $250 for horses that have never beaten 2:40. Owned in the District.

No. 2—RUNNING RACE—Purse, $500. For horses that have never beaten 1:26.

SECOND DAY—Wednesday, Aug. 16.

No. 3—RUNNING STAKE—For two-year-olds; $50 entrance; $25 forfeit; $150 added. Second to save entrance. Dash of three-quarters of a mile.

No. 4—RUNNING STAKE—Free for all; $50 entrance; $25 forfeit; $150 added. Second to have entrance. Dash of one mile.

No. 5—TROTTING RACE—Purse $100. For double team owned in the District by one man.

THIRD DAY—Thursday, Aug. 17.

No. 6—TROTTING RACE—Purse $100 for horses that have never beaten 7:40.

No. 7—TROTTING RACE—Purse $100 for horses that have never beaten three minutes.

FOURTH DAY—Friday, Aug. 18.

No. 8—RUNNING RACE—Selling Purse, $300; $50 to

---

second horse; entrance 3 per cent to third horse. One mile and repeat. Horses entered to be sold for $1,000 to carry their entitled weight. Two pounds off for each $100 under fixed valuation. Winner can be claimed by any one.

No. 9—TROTTING STAKE—Free for all; $25 entrance; $15 forfeit; $75 added. Second to save entrance. Half-mile and repeat.

No. 10—TROTTING RACE—Purse, $500. For horses that have never beaten 2:26.

### FIFTH DAY—Saturday, Aug. 19.

No. 11—TROTTING RACE—Purse, $600. Free for all two-year-olds. Mile and repeat.

No. 12—TROTTING RACE—Purse, $600. Free for all two-year-olds. Mile and repeat.

### Remarks and Conditions.

All trotting races are the best three in five, except the two-year-old trot, five to enter and three to start. Entrance fee 10 per cent. o a purse to accompany nomination. Purses divided at the rate of sixty per cent. to first horse, thirty per cent. to second, and ten per cent. to third.

National Association Rules to govern trotting; but the Board reserves the right to trot heats of any two classes alternately, if necessary to finish a day's racing, or to trot a special race between heats.

To all running races, three or more subscribers are necessary.

All two-year-olds, when running in their classes, shall carry one hundred pounds, with the usual allowance to mares and geldings.

All three-year-olds, when running in their classes, to carry one hundred and ten pounds, with the usual allowance as above.

Those who have nominations in stakes MUST name to the Secretary, in writing, the horses they will start on Wednesday, on the Monday previous, and on Friday the Wednesday previous, by twelve o'clock M. This rule is obvious, and must be strictly adhered to.

No added money paid for a walk over.

Horses entered in purses can only be drawn by consent of Judges.

Rules of the Pacific Coast Blood-Horse Association hold weights to govern running races, except when conditions named are otherwise.

Special trains will be run by the Southern Pacific Railroad and South Pacific Coast Railroad, and excursion tickets sold by both companies from all points on their lines, good from August 14th to August 20th, inclusive.

JAMES O. WANZER, Secretary. J. C. CHACE, President.

---

### SPEED PROGRAMME

OF THE

## Mount Shasta Agricultural

### Association,

TO BE HELD IN

## YREKA, SISKIYOU CO.,

— ON —

Wednesday, - - October 4th, 1882.

For racing purposes this District shall comprise Siskiyou, Shasta, Trinity, and Modoc Counties, Cal., and Jackson and Lake Counties, Oregon.

No horse shall be eligible to any of the following District Races unless owned in the District prior to October, 1881.

FIRST DAY—Wednesday, Oct. 4.

No. 1—TROTTING—Free for all; 3 in 5; purse, $500. First horse receives $600; second $200. Entrance 10 per cent. of purse; 5 to enter, 3 to start. Entries close September 1.

No. 2—RUNNING—Dash of a mile and a half, free for all horses owned in the District; purse, $100; entrance $5, added.

SECOND DAY—Thursday, Oct. 5.

No. 3—TROTTING—Free for all untried horses owned in the District; 3 in 5; purse, $75; entrance $5, added.

No. 4—RUNNING—Half mile and repeat; free for all horses owned in the District; purse, $75; entrance $5, added.

No. 5—TROTTING—Free for all three-year-olds and under, owned in the District; 3 in 5; purse, $75; entrance $5, added.

THIRD DAY—Friday, Oct. 6.

Grand match of Bands.

No. 6—TROTTING—Free for all in the District; 3 in 5; purse, $100; entrance $5, added.

No. 7—FOOT RACE—75 yards and repeat; purse, $50; entrance $5.

No. 8—RUNNING—Free for all three-year-olds and under owned in the District; dash of three-quarters of a mile; purse, $75; entrance $5, added.

FOURTH DAY—Saturday, Oct. 7.

No. 9—RUNNING—Free for all; 3 in 5; purse, $600. First horse receives $400; second horse, $200; the remainder of purse; 5 to enter, 3 to start. Entries close Sept. 1st.

No. 10—TROTTING—Free for all three-year-olds in the District that have never beaten three minutes; 3 in 5; purse, $100; entrance $5, added.

### Rules and Regulations.

1st. The above purses will be given without discount.
2d. In all District Races the second horse to save entrance.
3d. Entries to be placed in the entry box, kept for that purpose at the Pavilion, prior to 9 o'clock P. M. on the day prior to race.
4th. Entries must give name, pedigree, and description of horse entered as far as known.
5th. In all District Races two or more entries make a field.
6th. All trotting races must be in harness.
7th. National Trotting Association Rules to govern trotting.
8th. Pacific Coast Blood-Horse Association Rules to govern any running race.
9th. Free for all, in races 1 and 9, means just what it says, and all entries to these races must be made with the Secretary on or before September 1st.

L. SWAIN, President
J. H. MAGOFFEY, Secretary.

---

## SAVE MONEY!

### BUY DIRECT FROM THE MANUFACTURER.

## James Wylie,

20 & 22 Seventh St., nr. Market.

MANUFACTURES

#### Light Carriages, Buggies and Wagons,

Guarantees First-class Work and Low Prices. Repairing, Painting and Trimming with promptness and at reasonable rates.

---

### For Sale!

A BRACE OF

## FINE FOX HOUNDS!

Training and Breeding guaranteed. Address for particulars,

TOM TUNSTEAD,
Nicasio, Marin County.

---

---

---

# Golden Gate Fair.

SPEED PROGRAMME FOR 1882

—

## $10,000

IN

## Stakes and Prizes

FIRST DAY—Monday, Sept. 4, 1882.

No. 1—RUNNING—GOLDEN GATE STAKE—For all two-year-olds; three-quarter mile dash; $50 entrance; $15 forfeit; $250 added; second to save stake; winners 5 pounds extra.

No. 2—SAME DAY—RUNNING—ALAMEDA STAKE—For three-year-olds, one and one-half mile dash; $75 entrance; $35 forfeit; $375 added; second to save stake.

No. 3—SAME DAY—RUNNING—PARDEE SCALE—Free for all; one mile and repeat; $75 entrance; $30 forfeit; $300 added; second to save stake.

No. 4—SAME DAY—TROTTING—2:40 Class; purse, $500; first horse, $300; second, $150; third, $50.

No. 5—SAME DAY—SPECIAL TROT AGAINST TIME.—$150 to plate will be awarded any stallion that beats Santa Claus' time (2:17½).

SECOND DAY—Tuesday, Sept. 5.

No. 6—TROTTING—2:30 Class; purse, $800; first horse, $480; second, $240; third, $80.

No. 7—SAME DAY—PACING—Purse, $500; first horse, $300; second, $150; third, $50. Washington and Johnny Wiegle, to wagon.

THIRD DAY—Wednesday, Sept. 6.

No. 8—RUNNING—Free for all; mile dash; $100 entrance; $25 forfeit; $300 added; second horse to save stake.

No. 9—SAME DAY—TROTTING—Free for all three-year-olds; purse, $600; first horse, $360; second, $180; third, $60.

FOURTH DAY—Thursday, Sept. 7.

No. 10—TROTTING—Free for all two-year-olds; one mile and repeat; purse, $300; first horse, $180; second, $90; third, $30.

No. 11—SAME DAY—TROTTING—For all four-year-olds; purse, $600; first horse, $360; second, $180; third, $60.

No. 12—SAME DAY—RUNNING—SELLING RACE—Entries, &c.

FIFTH DAY—Friday, Sept. 8.

No. 14—RUNNING—CONSOLATION PURSE—$250 for beaten horses; mile-and-a-quarter dash; second horse to receive $75; 10 per cent. entrance.

No. 15—SAME DAY—LADIES' RIDING TOURNAMENT. There will be several Very choice and elegant prizes to be competed for contributed by the merchants and citizens of Oakland and San Francisco; the lady winning first prize to have first choice, the second prize winner second choice, and so on; all the prizes are distributed. Lady riders competing for these prizes will send their names to the President or Secretary on or before the first day of the meeting; $10 must be sent to the Secretary in all cases.

No. 16—SAME DAY—TROTTING—2:25 Class. Purse, $600; first horse, $360; second, $180; third, $60.

No. 17—SAME DAY—SPECIAL TROT AGAINST TIME—A purse of $50 will be given the yearling making the best time; a full mile in harness; no entrance fee.

SIXTH DAY—Sept. 9.

No. 18—COMPETITIVE CADET DRILL.—PRIZE, Gold Medal. Competition open to all educational institutions in the State.

No. 19—SAME DAY—COMPETITIVE MILITARY DRILL.—A prize of the value of $400 will be offered by the Association to the best drilled Military Company in the State of California. Rules and conditions to be published hereafter. It is the intent of the Directors to have the first competing companies determine what the prize or trophy shall be, and to have the same annually competed for, until it shall have been won three times by the same company, when it shall become the absolute property of the winning company.

No. 20—SAME DAY—GRAND BICYCLE TOURNAMENT, for the Association's Gold Medal to first, three-fourths value to second; a Bronze Medal to third; 1-mile dash; open to all bicyclists.

No. 21—SAME DAY—TROTTING—Free for all; the value of $125, will be offered for gentlemen's roadsters; best two in three; owners to drive.

No. 22—SAME DAY—A SET OF HARNESS, of the value of $125, will be offered for gentlemen's roadsters; best two in three; owners to drive.

To a "gentleman's roadster," is meant any animal owned and driven on the road by any gentleman for his own private pleasure.

### CONDITIONS.

Entries to all running stakes, trotting and pacing races, to be made to Secretary before, on or before August 5, 1882. Forfeits in running stakes, and the entrance fee of 10 per cent. on the trotting and pacing races, should in all cases accompany the nominations and entries.

All the trotting and pacing races are to be best three in five. In all, five to enter, and three to start.

Entrance fee, ten per cent. on purse.

When there are eight or more starters in a trotting race, 300 yards to be added to distance.

National Trotting Association rules to govern trotting, but the Board reserves the right to trot heats with any two classes alternately, if necessary to finish any day's trotting, or to trot a special race between heats.

To fill running races, three or more subscribers are necessary to distinguish the horses from the race.

In running races, three or more entries required to fill.

Those who have nominations to make must come to the Secretary, in writing, the horses they will start on Monday, on the Saturday previous; and on Wednesday the Monday previous; and on Friday, the Wednesday previous. No added money will be paid for a walk-over.

Horses entered in purses one daily to be drawn by consent of the judges.

Rules of the Pacific Coast Blood Horse Association to govern running races, except when conditions named are otherwise.

All entries to be made in writing, giving name, sex, color, and marks of horses; also, name and residence of owner. In running races, full colors to be worn by rider; and drivers in trotting races are respectfully requested to wear a cap or cap of distinguishing colors, so their horses will be designated upon programmes by colors worn by drivers. This is necessary to enable spectators to distinguish the horses in the race.

Entries to all the above races to close with the Secretary on Tuesday, August 1, 1882.

Write "Entries to races" on outside of Envelope.

L. WALKER,     A. C. DIETZ,
Secretary.     Pres't.

---

# $12,500

## In Purses and Stakes.

---

### CALIFORNIA

## STATE FAIR

### SPEED PROGRAMME

FOR 1882.

FIRST DAY—Monday, Sept. 11.

No. 1—RUNNING—INTRODUCTION STAKE—For all ages; three-quarters of a mile dash; $20 entrance; $15 forfeit; $300 added; second to save stake.

No. 2—RUNNING—BREEDERS STAKE—For foals of 1879; one and a half miles dash; $50 entrance, p. p.; $300 added. Closed March 1st with nineteen nominations.

No. 3—RUNNING—SELLING RACE—Purse, $300. Free for all; one mile and repeat; second horse to receive $75. Entrance ten per cent. to third horse. Horses entered to be sold for $1,500 to carry entitled weight, one pound off for each $100 under fixed Valuation.

No. 4—TROTTING—2:40 class; purse, $1,000.

SECOND DAY—Tuesday, Sept. 12.

No. 5—TROTTING—2:23 class; purse, $1,200.

No. 6—TROTTING—Purse, $600; for three year olds and under.

No. 7—TROTTING—Purse, $800; mile heats for two year olds.

THIRD DAY—Wednesday, Sept. 13.

No. 8—RUNNING—Three-year-old STAKE FOR TWO YEAR OLDS FILLIES—Five-eighths of a mile; $50 entrance; $25 forfeit; $300 added; second to receive $75; third, $25.

No. 9—TROTTING—2:35 Class; purse, $1,000; first horse, $600; second, $300; third, $100.

No. 10—RUNNING—JENNIE B. STAKE—For all ages; dash of one mile; $50 entrance, $25 forfeit; $300 added; second horse, $75; third, $25. Stake to be named after winner, if Jennie B. trots 1:30½ or faster.

No. 11—RUNNING—SELLING RACE—Purse, $300; one and one-half miles dash; second horse to receive $75; horses entered to be sold for $1,000 to carry entitled weight. Two pounds off for each $100 under fixed Valuation.

No. 12—TROTTING—2:20 class; purse, $1,200.

FOURTH DAY—Thursday, Sept. 14.

No. 13—TROTTING—2:22 class; purse, $1,500.

No. 14—PACING—2:25 class; purse, $500.

No. 15—TROTTING—Two miles and repeat; 2:40 horses; purse, $500.

FIFTH DAY—Friday, Sept. 15.

No. 16—RUNNING—COLT AND FILLY STAKE—For two year olds; dash of one mile; $50 entrance, $15 forfeit; $300 added; second horse to receive $75; third, $25.

No. 17—RUNNING—SELLING RACE—Purse, $300; for all ages; dash of one and one-quarter miles; second horse to receive $75; horses entered to be sold for $1,200 to carry entitled weight, two pounds off for $100, five pounds off for $750; seven pounds off for $500, ten pounds off.

No. 18—RUNNING—POST STAKE—Dash of three miles; free for all; $100 entrance; $300 added; weight 100 pounds; three-year-olds, 90 pounds; second horse to receive $75; third, $25. Starters to be named to the Secretary Wednesday evening, at or before 8 o'clock p. m.

No. 19—TROTTING—CONSOLATION PURSE—$250 for beaten horses; one mile and repeat; entrance free; second and horses to receive $50.

SIXTH DAY—Saturday, Sept. 16.

No. 20—TROTTING—2:19 class; purse, $1,500.

No. 21—TROTTING—OCCIDENT STAKE FOR 1882, closed in 1881 with twelve nominations.

No. 22—SPECIAL TROT AGAINST TIME—$250 to plate will be awarded to any stallion that beats Santa Claus' time (2:17½).

Entries for the following events for 1883-4 were ordered to be closed with the Secretary July 1st.

No. 1—RUNNING—CALIFORNIA DERBY STAKE, for foals of 1880, to be run at the State Fair of 1883. One and one-half miles dash; $100 entrance, p. p.; $300 added; second horse, $300; third, $60.

No. 2—RUNNING—Purse of 1881, to be run at State Fair of 1884. Same conditions.

No. 3—RUNNING—MATURITY STAKE—Three miles dash, for four-year-olds, in 1885; $300 entrance; $50 forfeit; $500 added; second horse, $150; third horse, $100. To be run at the State Fair of 1885.

No. 4—RUNNING—CALIFORNIA ANNUAL STAKE—For two-year-olds, foals of 1881. Dash of one mile; $100 entrance; $25 forfeit; $250 added; second horse, $100; third, $50. To be run at the Fair of 1883.

### REMARKS and CONDITIONS.

All trotting and pacing races are the best three in five, except the two-year old trots, unless otherwise specified; five to enter and three to start. Entrance fee ten per cent. on purse, to accompany nomination. Purses divided at the rate of sixty per cent. to first horse, thirty per cent. to second, and ten per cent. to third.

National Association Rules to govern trotting; but the Board reserves the right to trot heats of any two classes alternately, if necessary to finish any day's trotting, or to trot a special race between heats.

To fill running races, three or more subscribers are necessary to distinguish the horses from the race.

In two-year-olds, when running in their classes, shall carry one hundred pounds, with the usual allowance for mares and geldings.

All three-year-olds, when running in their classes, to carry one hundred and ten pounds, with the usual allowance as above.

Those who have nominations to stakes must name to the Secretary, (P. Wright), the horses they will start on Monday, on the Saturday previous; and on Wednesday the Monday previous; and on Friday the Wednesday previous, by twelve o'clock m. This rule is obvious, and must be strictly adhered to.

No added money paid for a walk-over.

Horses entered in purses can only be drawn by consent of the Judges.

Rules of the Pacific Coast Blood Horse Association (old weights) to govern running races, except when conditions named are otherwise.

All entries to be made in writing, giving name, sex, color, and marks of horses; also, name and residence of owner. In running races, full colors to be worn by rider; and drivers in trotting races are respectfully requested to wear cap of distinct colors, to be named in their entries, so their horses will be designated upon programmes by colors worn by drivers. This is necessary to enable spectators to distinguish the horses in the race.

Entries to all the above races to close with the Secretary, on Tuesday, August 1, 1882.

Write "Entries to Races" on outside of envelopes.

EDWIN F. SMITH,     HUGH M. LARUE,
Secretary.     President.

---

### SPEED PROGRAMME.

## $13,000 Gold Coin

### IN PURSES.

## The Largest Purses Offered in the State.

—

## STOCKTON,

Sept. 19th to 23d inclusive, 1882.

TUESDAY, Sept. 19th.

No. 1—DISTRICT—RUNNING—For two-year-olds; purse $400; mile dash; 3 to enter, 2 to start. Four moneys.

No. 2—DISTRICT TROTTING—For yearlings; purse $300; half mile; 3 to enter, 2 to start. Four moneys.

No. 3—PACIFIC COAST TROTTING—2:30 Class; purse $1,000, and $300 added if more than ten entries. Four moneys.

WEDNESDAY, Sept. 20th.

No. 4—PACIFIC COAST NOVELTY RUNNING—½ mile dash; purse $500. The first horse to each half mile to win $100, and the horse first to two and two-and-one-half mile posts to win $50 each more; $300 additional will be added to the purse, two rats, if more than ten entries.

No. 5—DISTRICT RUNNING—For three-year-olds; purse $500. Closed with six entries.

No. 6—PACIFIC COAST TROTTING—2:35 purse $1,000, and $300 added if more than ten entries. Four moneys.

No. 7—DISTRICT—TROTTING—For named horses; purse $500; 7 to enter, 4 to start. This race is intended for horses that can trot in three minutes or a little better. Four moneys.

THURSDAY, Sept. 21st.

No. 8—PACIFIC COAST TROTTING—Mile and repeat; purse $500, and 3 added if more horse making the low set record will receive $200 additional. Four moneys.

No. 9—DISTRICT TROTTING—For two-year-olds; purse $800. Closed with six entries.

#### Ladies' Equestrianism.

FOUR PRIZES IN GOLD COIN. $40, $30, $20, $10.

No. 10—DISTRICT—TROTTING—2:36 Class; purse $800; 7 to enter, 4 to start. Four moneys.

FRIDAY, Sept. 22d.

No. 11—PACIFIC COAST RUNNING—Free for all; two miles and repeat; purse $600, and $200 added if more than ten entries. Four moneys.

No. 12—PACIFIC COAST RUNNING—For three-year-olds and over; purse $500; best two in three; 7 to enter, 4 to start. Four moneys.

No. 13—PACIFIC COAST TROTTING—For horses owned on the Pacific Coast, July 1st, 1882. 2:22 Class; purse $1,500; and $500 added if more than ten subscribers. The nominator not required to name his horse, but simply send his cash ($150) as his own entrance money. He has then earned the right to start any horse eligible that he may fairly control, provided the horse he starts is named to the Secretary, September 1, 1882. Four moneys.

No. 14—PACIFIC COAST TROTTING—2:26 Class; purse $1,000, and $300 added if more than ten entries. Four moneys.

No. 15—PACIFIC COAST PACING—2:25 Class; purse $400, and $200 added if more than ten entries. Four moneys.

#### REMARKS AND CONDITIONS.

All Trotting Races best three in five, except numbers 3 and 8.

In all these Races (Pacific Coast Novelty Race excepted) FOUR moneys, 50, 25, 15 and 10 per cent. of purse. Entrance fee, 10 per cent. of purse, and MUST accompany the nomination. District Races will close with the Secretary at 8 o'clock p. m. of July 15, 1882. Pacific Coast Races to close with the Secretary August 1, 1882.

When there are eight or more to start in a Trotting Race, 100 yards shall be allowed to distance.

Rules of the National Trotting Association to govern trotting, except as specified; but the Board of Managers reserve the right to trot heats of any two classes alternately, or to start a special race between heats.

All two-year-olds, when running in their classes, shall carry 100 pounds, with the usual allowance for mares and geldings.

All three-year-olds, when running in their classes, to carry 110 pounds, with the usual allowance as above, either to geldings.

For a walk-over in any race a horse shall only be entitled to his own entrance fee and one quarter of the entrance fee received from the other entries for said purse; and a horse winning a race entitled to first money only, except when distancing the field, then entitled to first and third moneys only. A horse winning any race not distancing the field, and third moneys only.

Money earned in purses can only be drawn by consent of the Judges.

The Board reserving the right to change the day and hour of any race, if they deem it necessary.

Unless otherwise ordered by the Board, no horse shall be qualified to enter in any District Race that has not been owned in the District six (6) months prior to the day of the race; and any entry by any person of any horse so disqualified shall be held liable for the entrance fee so contracted without any right to compete, and the Board liable to exclude therefrom, or refusing the Judges of the National Trotting Association and explusion from the Association.

Rules of the Pacific Coast Blood Horse Association to govern Running Races (including additions to rules, except as especially provided).

All Running Races orders to be worn by riders, and in all other races, and other particulars that will enable spectators to distinguish the horses in the race.

In all the Coast Races noted above, NO ENTRIES are required to fill, and three horses to start but the Board RESERVES THE RIGHT TO CLOSE ANY RACE WITH A LESS NUMBER.

The track is first-class, having been improved. Stable hay and straw free to competitors.

#### ENTRIES.

1st. Entries must be made in writing and dated.

2nd. State number of the race in which you wish to enter.

3rd. State colors of horse, and marks if necessary.

4th. State whether the horse is a STALLION, MARE OF GELDING.

5th. State NAME OF SIRE AND DAM if known; also the date of the entry.

6th. State NAME and P. O. ADDRESS of the owner of the horse entered.

7th. Sign with P. O. address of the party entering the horse.

8th. If the name has been changed, give former name.

9th. Report by mail, all entries made to the Secretary at, Agricultural District No. 1 (California, comprises the counties of San Joaquin, Calaveras, Tuolumne, Stanislaus, Mariposa, Merced, Fresno, Tulare, and Kern).

J. L. PHELPS, Secretary.     J. H. SHIPPEE, President.
P. O. Box 130, Stockton, Cal.

---

### SECOND

## ANNUAL EXHIBITION

OF THE

### SAN MATEO AND SANTA CLARA COUNTY

## AGRICULTURAL ASSOCIATION

### NO. 5,

TO BE HELD AT

## SAN JOSE, CAL.,

......FROM,......

## Sept. 25th to 30th, '82 inclusive

---

### SPEED PROGRAMME.

FIRST DAY—Monday, Sept. 25th, 1882.

No. 1. TROTTING—2:40 class. Purse, $500.

No. 2. SAME DAY—TROTTING—2:36 class. Purse, $750.

SECOND DAY—Tuesday, Sept. 26th.

No. 3. RUNNING—For two-year-olds; three-quarter mile dash; $50 entrance; $15 forfeit; $250 added. Second horse to receive his entrance and one-third of added money.

No. 4. SAME DAY—RUNNING—A Selling Race—For four-year-olds; $15 forfeit; $300 added. Second horse to receive his entrance and one-third of added money.

No. 5. SAME DAY—RUNNING—Free for all; mile dash; $50 entrance; $15 forfeit; $250 added. Second horse to receive his entrance. Two pounds off for each $100 under fixed Valuation. Winner can be claimed by any buyer.

THIRD DAY—Wednesday, Sept. 27th.

No. 6. TROTTING—2:30 class. Purse, $600.

No. 7. SAME DAY—RUNNING RACE—For horses owned in the District to be driven in buggy. Two mile heats. Purse to be hereafter offered.

No. 8. SAME DAY—Ladies' Riding Tournament—Bicycle Race, etc.

FOURTH DAY—Thursday, Sept. 28th.

No. 9. RUNNING—Three-year-olds, ½ mile dash; $50 entrance; $15 forfeit; $300 added. Second horse to receive his entrance and one-third of added money.

No. 10. SAME DAY—PACING—Free for all horses. Purse, $400.

No. 11. SAMEDAY—TROTTING—For four-year-olds. Purse $400.

FIFTH DAY—Friday, Sept. 19th.

No. 11. RUNNING—½ mile dash. Free for all; $50 entrance; $15 forfeit; $300 added. Second horse to receive his entrance and one-third of added money.

No. 12. SAME DAY—TROTTING—2:27 class. Purse $600.

No. 13. SAME DAY—TROTTING—For two-year-olds. Purse $400.

SIXTH DAY—Saturday, Sept. 30th.

No. 14. TROTTING—2:22 class. Purse $700.

No. 15. SAME DAY—TROTTING—2:36 class. Two miles and repeat. Purse $600.

#### REMARKS AND CONDITIONS.

All trotting and pacing races are the best three in five, except the two-year-old trot, unless otherwise specified; five to enter and three to start. Entrance fee ten per cent. on purse, to accompany nominations. Purse divided at the rate of sixty per cent to first horse, thirty per cent to second and ten per cent to third.

National Association Rules to govern trotting; but the Board reserves the right to trot heats of any two classes alternately, if necessary to finish any day's racing, or to trot a special race between heats.

To fill running races, three or more subscribers are necessary.

In two-year-olds, when running in their classes, shall carry one hundred pounds, with the usual allowance for mares and geldings.

All three-year-olds, when running in their classes, to carry one hundred and ten pounds, with the usual allowance as above.

Those who have nominations to stakes must name to the Secretary, in writing, the horses they will start on Saturday previous to the first day; and on the Monday previous; and on Thursday the Tuesday previous, and on Friday the Wednesday previous, by twelve o'clock m. This rule is obvious, and must be strictly adhered to.

No added money paid for a walk-over.

Horses entered in purses can only be drawn by consent of the Judges.

Rules of the Pacific Coast Blood Horse Association (old weights) to govern running races, except when conditions named are otherwise.

All entries to be made in writing, giving name, sex, color, and marks of horses; also, name and residence of owner. In running races, full colors to be worn by rider; and drivers in trotting races are respectfully requested to wear cap of distinct colors, to be named in their entries, so their horses will be designated upon programmes by colors worn by drivers.

Entries to all the above races to close with the Secretary on Tuesday, August 1st, 1882.

Write "Entries to Races" on outside of envelope.

R. KING, President.

T. S. MONTGOMERY, Secretary.

VOL. 1.—No 3
No. 508 MONTGOMERY STREET. }

SAN FRANCISCO, SATURDAY, JULY 15, 1882.

{ SUBSCRIPTION
FIVE DOLLARS A YEAR.

# NOTABLE HORSES OF CALIFORNIA.

## BELLE ECHO.

There is a pleasure in writing histories of horses, when the scribe feels that each is entitled to be ranked among the "notable horses of California." This gives them a rank which even the hypercritical will have to acknowledge; and when the portrait is on the first page of the BREEDER AND SPORTSMAN, it is well known that there is merit behind that which will not be questioned. There may be explanations needed of the Duchess of Norfolk, as the placing in the Illinois Derby did not warrant the predictions so confidently made. Still, there is the utmost confidence among her admirers that she will yet do something to merit the place given her, and that the future will show that she was entitled to the place awarded. But no one will question the right of Romero to a place, standing as he does in the foremost rank of four-year-old stallions; and when Belle Echo succeeds him in the list of the notables, it would be a supercritical mind which denied her the place.

The portraiture is done with the fidelity which marks our artist's sketches. It is not an ideal horse which he represents, but the actual, tangible equine which he so skillfully portrays. The Belle of California stands on the page lifelike, a drawing of what she is, not a fanciful representation. the life and blood fac-simile of the horse. There are points, however, which the pencil does not do justice to. Standing handsomely out on the page, even the the casual observer would notice that the outlines marked a beautiful animal, and that the black and white lines had all the curves which Hogarth claimed to be the marks of grace and beauty. With all this, there is the necessity for more accurate portrayal. It is not enough to point to the page and say "there is a true representation." Every one who ever saw Belle Echo, and paid enough attention to her to remember her salient features, would recognize the picture. After all, there is a good deal to say. For instance, she is now nearly sixteen hands in hight. the handsomest shade of bay conceivable, with just white enough to relieve the monotony of the whole color. From nose to heel she is beautiful—scarcely a point which could be found fault with by one who is a competent

judge of the form of a horse. But better still than form are performances, and Belle can show a grand record from the time she was first brought on the track. Her first race was at Sacramento, September 21, 1881, when, then a threeyear-old, she won a stake in 2:48¾, 2:48¼, 2:49¾. At the same meeting, and the next day, she was beaten, Alexander Button getting the first money, Annie Laurie the second. She made a great race at San Jose, and, though defeated, showed that she was worthy of the place she has been given in these annals. She won the first heat in 2:28¾, the fastest time made by a three-year-old during that year, and she showed a capacity far within the recorded time, by going some parts of the route so much faster that it was evident that there was a reserve of force which would be sure to tell when the actual warfare came on.

It is needless to reiterate that the race at San Jose, fast as the mile was, showed that she was one of the notable horses. So sick that a competent veterinarian gave the opinion that one more heat would be likely to destroy he the owner took the chances in his determination to give those who supported her the best he could do for their money. She nearly died the night after the race, and there were grave doubts whether she would ever be the mare she gave the promise of. In her four-year-old form, however, she more than came up to the expectations of her friends.

The first race she trotted in 1581 was at the Golden Gate Fair, Romero, Alex. Button, Honesty and Annie Laurie being her competitors; and in the race she gained the record of 2:23¼, which is now to her credit. It is scarcely necessary to recapitulate the races between her and Romero. There were five heats in the race at Oakland, Belle winning the second and third heats, Romero the others; time 2:27, 2:23¾, 2:26, 2:22½, 2:24½. This race alone gives a value beyond the mere presentation of minutes and seconds, when it is compared with others in which colts of the same age contended. When Trinket trotted at Louisville, Kentucky, in 1879, a mile in 2:19¾, it was held by many to be as good a performance, reckoning of course on the age, and though a California two-year-old and a three-year-old bred in Kentucky have come within 1¾ seconds of trotting as fast, it has yet the first place. But the time of the five heats in the Oakland race has never been equaled by colts of that age, and this was followed by her winning in three straight heats at Sacramento, the time 2:27¼, 2:25½, 2:25. Honesty, Alex. Button, and Annie Laurie were her competitors, and a short time afterwards she beat Romero on the Bay District Course, the colt winning the first heat in 2:24½, the slowest of the four being 2:26. Romero reversed the decree a few days after, though she was close on him at the finish of every heat, and the three were made in 2:22½, 2:25½, 2:24, and then at San Jose she was again only beaten by a trifle by the grey, in 2:25½, 2:23, 2:22¾. To lose in such fast time as every heat showed when she was beaten, was no discredit, and it could scarcely be held that Romero was greatly her superior, if even he had been the victor in a majority of the races in which they met. It is not necessary, however, to award a decided preference between the two cracks, numbers two and three of the notable horses of our coast. Her pedigree is a capital one by Echo, who is also the sire of Gibralter, Echora, Bullet, Joe Hamilton and others; her dam by Belmont, the thoroughbred which has done so much for the stock of California.

## OAKLAND LETTER.

OAKLAND, July 14, 1882.

BREEDER AND SPORTSMAN: To say tha we in Oakland, whom you so accurately described in your Salutatory, are pleased with the new candidate for popular favor, THE BREEDER AND SPORTSMAN, would be to state it very mildly indeed. It does every man good once and again to hold the mirror up to himself to see what manner of man he is; and so we will read your "Greeting" once more: "To those who prefer the sunny side of life, who appreciate the many enjoyments the Great Creator has placed within our reach, who are not held in bondage by fanaticism to see merit in gloom, and to consider all diversion frivolous, if not absolutely wicked; to those who can discover the golden edgeing of the blackest cloud, and who have faith that there is always a silver lining within the shadow; to those who seek to make the bright days brighter, and who are earnest in their endeavors to increase the happiness of all, our greeting is presented." That's us, Mr. Editor! Upon that platform we will plant our feet boldly for all the future, and bide our victory over asceticism and gloom with patience and joy Thank you much that you aim from the start to create and develop a love for the higher and purer pleasures that Mother Nature can give her loving children, and invite such a noble following, when you send special greeting to all "who are earnest in their endeavors to increase the happiness of all."

All hail, most royal missionary, upon whom the Great Father of all has set His seal!

Man's happiness is the final end and aim of all God's plans in all religions in all worlds, and just so far as you call man to true happiness, you are in harmony with the Divine plan of human development. And your paper shall be more potent than all pulpits, if you can plant an everlasting hunger in the hearts of your thousands of subscribers, to leave the deadly lowlands of the great cities' slums and sloughs, and flee with glad cries to the verdure of fields inviting the weary to rest, and to the still waters whispering of hope and peace to the despairing.

When you have withdrawn a man from muck-raking after gold, and led him to bathe in the fountains of "glad waters, where the spray is sparkling in the sunshine," and made him to rejoice over every pleasant and glad thing that the good God has planted along every step of life's highways, that man is being "born again;" and although some men may take a good deal of "borning," yet you have got him in the right path, and he may finally be saved if he is not *too* big an idiot.

I should be more than glad to know that your paper was a regular visitant to the counting-room of every business man, and was weekly welcomed on every minister's study table, for I think he would be the better for the reading of it, as I am sure his hearers would be the better for listening to a preacher large-minded and broad enough to read its lessons aright.

Let him but catch the fragrance of the fields in its columns, his sermons would fall on his world-weary listeners like the breath of new mown hay, and they would depart refreshed as from a glad communing.

Need I apologize to you, Mr. Editor, for writing this? I confess that when I began I didn't intend it, but I glanced at your cheerful "Greeting," and my pen took the bits in its teeth and started off after you, so you are really responsible for the bolt. Well, I have pulled up my Pegasus at last, perhaps to the relief of some, who thought they sighted a sermon, and prepared to break themselves.

I do not know that I have much that is really new since my last letter. There are several new roadsters on our Oakland thoroughfares, and I had it in my mind to describe a few of them and their genial owners, who sit behind them and look as happy as if they held the reins of all power, as they speed along apparently oblivious of hard times and broken banks, but I'm afraid the pleasant task must be postponed until "a more convenient season." But I must be allowed to say that there are two men in our city who greatly delight men when they tackle each other on the road and struggle for the mastery, and the one begins his name with Dr. E. H. Pardee, and the initials of the other's name are Francis Blake. These two are numbered among our solid and representative business men, and while they can-not be called "fast" they are by no means *slow* when they start up their family horses for an airing. Mr. Blake is the happy owner of several good ones, but I judge his prime favorite, when business is on hand, is old Stockton well known to horsemen, while the Doctor rejoices in the ownership of a ranger chestnut gelding, yet in his youth, a son of Billy Hayward, and a good one, and whenever these good men meet, there is a very pretty rivalry for a front seat in the orchestra. They don't intend to try to beat each other. O, bless you, no; they are too good friends for that; but it always happens, when they kinder meet by chance on a good road, you know, one has a business engagement, which he is in a tremendous hurry to keep, and calls on old Stockton who winks his off eye, and says, "Here goes;" and then the Doctor suddenly remembers that *he* has got to meet a friend, and is a little late already, and the chestnut gets a hint to quicken his speed, and these good business horses just paw the dust for a few minutes, and sometimes one sees his friend before the other can keep his engagement, and then the other will be prompt on time, before the other can catch sight of his friend. They are both capital business horses, but the Doctor told me on the sly that he could see his friend oftener than Blake could keep his engagements; and when I asked the latter gentleman about it, he smiled and said that he had kept his business engagements more times than Blake had seen his friend. Well, gentlemen, to reconcile these little discrepancies, you had better take the Secretary along next time to record the minutes.

Your correspondent jogged out to Oakland Park, last Saturday morning, to see some of the horses take their work, and although he arrived a little late, he felt well repaid. As we landed on the steps of the hotel, Titus was just driving out Belle Echo, and Jimmy Duane was behind Albert W., both going in company for the second mile trial. They were looking remarkably well, and moving with elastic, limber motion, denoting fine condition. They both jogged up the stretch and, turning, came down and passed under the wire well together, and both going very fast, while several watches were started to catch the time. It was a very pretty sight, and both drivers were going faster than they thought, for when the quarter was reached, the watches marked 35 *seconds*, a 2:20 gait. Evidently Titus was a little surprised that he didn't shake off the colt, for he said afterwards that he knew he was driving Belle pretty sharply, but from this on, Albert W. slowed his gait, and Belle took the lead, both going very steadily and apparently within themselves. The mare made the half mile in 1:10½, and the mile in 2:24, with all ease; while Albert W. was not far behind, making the mile in 2:26¾—Pretty good for a 4-year old.

And now here are two more appearing to drive in company for a little fast work. One is the big brown gelding Bateman, piloted by his owner, Mr. Salisbury, and the other the bay mare Sweetness, owned by the same gentleman, and driven by her trainer, John Goldsmith. As Sweetness is a new mare to us, we take a good look at her as she moves along. She does not impress one at first as an animal of exceptional speed. She has great substance, and not the slightest sign of nervousness or flightiness as she jogs along, carrying her head rather low than otherwise. She shows in harness great depth at the girth, with grand propelling powers, and is thoroughly good all over, but still looking to our eyes more like a real fair business mare than a speedy trotter. But all this time they are moving up the stretch, and presently they turn and come down for the start, Sweetness well in hand and Bateman gathering himself for fast work; and as they pass us at about a three-minute gate, we can see that Sweetness's way of going is perfection itself—not a hitch nor a waver, but legs playing as true as piston-rods in perfect line, and going with a most resolute gait, straight as an arrow from a bow. And now the strides quicken, and Bateman begins to tiptoe, and finally goes overboard as he rounds the first turn; but Salisbury sends him right on, the mare going as steady as clock-work. Goldsmith slows up a little, however, and Bateman regains his trot; and away they go again, down the back stretch, until the pace gets too hot, and Bateman is on the run again, with not a falter or a wobble on the part of the rightly named mare. And so, with Bateman sometimes running and sometimes trotting, they passed under the wire, and the watches mark 2:27¼.

Salisbury says in his quaint way that the boys are not going to play any more slow horses on him, when he drives, but must give him something that will enable him to keep in speaking distance. If Sweetness stands training she will make a record that is low down, or I am unable to read the signs aright. Before the buzz about the fine mare dies away, there appears a big slashing stallion, and I recognize Alonzo Hayward, driven by A. L. Hinds. He has just been taken up, and looks big and off form; but for all that I remember some of his performances, and I know that he is a right good one, and dead game in a race, as are all the family of Haywards; and it occurs to me here that as there are a good many of this family of horses on the track and in the hands of gentlemen as roadsters, it may be as well to say a word about their origin, for the information of those who own good ones and are not quite familiar with their history. The sire of them all is the grey stallion Billy Hayward, bred and owned by H. A. Mayhew, of East Oakland, and a well-known grain broker of San Francisco. His sire was Geo. M. Patchen, Jr., commonly known in this State as old Patchen, and sometimes as California Patchen, and as everybody is familiar with his pedigree and performances, nothing further need be said by way of description. A few words, however, about Billy Hayward's dam may not be uninteresting. She was a grey mare brought to California from Janesville, Ill., in 1863, by a man of the name of Frost, and at that time called Grey Lize, but was afterwards known as Peanuts. Her true breeding is a little obscure, and although a good many enquiries have been made, it is more than probable that it never will be positively known. It is claimed by some that she was by a Messenger Horse, that Frost brought from Baltimore, and others are just as positive that she was by the Morse Horse. In any event she was a very remarkable mare, and showed a great deal of breeding, and for invincible gameness has never had a superior. She both trotted and ran races, and was speedy in either way of going. She trotted one 20 mile race, but in what time we have no information. She was the mother of Young Peanuts, the dam of Sweet Brier. Billy Hayward himself has been a remarkably enduring horse, as well as a horse of great speed. With all due deference to his owner, I think, and always have thought, that the horse has never hed the opportunities on the turf, or at the stud, that his true merits entitled him to. He has not always been in the best of hands, and has been used too many times with an eye to what could be captured, rather than to his highest development as a trotter.

He has stood more bruising races, coming out unscathed, than any horse we know. He was always a very dangerous horse in a hard race, when the heats were broken, for that was his opportunity, as he could trot all day, and the next day following. He won a great majority of the races in which he was entered, and has a record to his credit of 2:31 and a two-mile record of 5:13. His colts all trot, and many of them are very fast. Poscora Hayward, now the property of Hammond, is about the speediest, trotting a fourth heat as a four-year-old in 2:30, and the fifth heat in 2:31, and he is still a-coming.

All this time Hinds has been driving Alonzo, only jogging him, however, as he is hardly far enough along to set going. His best record is 2:30, and he has all the gameness of his family, trotting a fifth heat in 2:32½. He trotted a race of three-mile heats, in 1879, against Red Cross and Bullet, trotting the first two miles in the first heat in 5:06. He ought to be a good horse this season in his class. I intended following Hinds into his stable, and to give your readers a pen-picture of two or three that deserve special notice, particularly a beautiful bay three-year-old Nutwood filly, the property of Mr. Requa, of Piedmont, but this letter has lengthened to such proportions that I fear to provoke your editorial frown. There are several animals in Mart Rollins' stable that I purposed noticing a little more in detail, and many other good ones, but I must bid them wait until another time. W.

## DEER SHOOTING.

HIGHLAND SPRINGS CAMP, July 4th, 1882.

EDITOR BREEDER AND SPORTSMAN: After patiently waiting for the season to come around, and being fully prepared for the opening deer hunt of the season, four of us in the party, were well mounted on experienced mountain horses, that can keep a trail the darkest night or pack a "buck" and ride over the roughest country where the deer is found in Lake county, and with hounds fresh and eager for the chase. We left camp at 3 o'clock P. M. on the 1st instant, and took a trail that leads directly west from our camp-ground, and followed over a rough range of mountains, well covered with chaparral, the gulches being timbered with oak, madrone, laurel and black alder. After keeping the trail for fully one mile, I concluded to follow a gulch leading to a bluff to our left, and instructed the balance of the party to keep the trail and meet me about a half mile distant on the top of a high ridge. The hounds had now become divided, the two oldest following in my direction, and by their actions indicated that there had been deer passing in the direction I was taking. The gulch soon became so steep that it was with the greatest effort that I could master my task. But, dismounting and taking the lead, my pony, with his usual experience, struggled till the top was reached. It never occurs, however, with the hunter to say "back" when every moment anticipating the starting of a deer. I had no sooner got there when I espied the Captain coming directly towards me in double-quick time, the balance of the party remaining behind about one hundred yards distant. The full pack of hounds had now come together and was moving through the chaparral in a rapid and anxious manner, indicating without a doubt that they meant business. We now left our horses and made for positions, as it was quite evident from the actions of the hounds that there was a deer close at hand. We had just gained positions when the old hound, "Rough," gave tongue, and the balance of the pack quickly joined in the music. The deer, it was now evident, had left his hiding place and was making up a very dense point, and could not be seen, owing to the thick growth of brush. The music was up now to a high key, every hound doing his level best, and making the mountains ring with that heavenly music which the hunter so much enjoys. Now the chase was excitement in the extreme. The dry twigs were cracking and the boughs yielding at every bound of the deer, the hounds apparently close up and running rapidly. All was excitement, and every eye watched with an anxious look for the first glimpse of the deer, the horses seemingly enjoying the chase as well as the hunters and hounds. Their heads were elevated and ears extended, and they were anxiously looking in the direct course. The deer changed his course, for, instead of running to the top of the ridge where we could have plainly seen him, he kept the brush and was making for the gulch. Now our only chance left for a shot was that he would cross the cañon, as there was an opening on the other side. Crack went a rifle. One of the party had got a snap shot as he was darting through the brush. He missed the mark, as onward flew the deer. This stimulated the hounds still more, for they gave extra tongue, and each one could be distinctly heard. The deer's quick bounds soon gained him the opposite side, and within fifty yards of where the Captain stood, but, owing to the deer being down the hill, he could not get to see him. I soon got a glimpse of him as he was rising up the ridge in double-quick time. I drew up my rifle, and with steady aim, fired. The deer dropped, but no sooner had I announced the fact than up he jumps, and with apparently new vigor, changing his course and running directly back for the gulch. Two more shots were fired, but without effect, as he soon gained the thicket. He was evidently wounded badly and could not run very far, as the hounds were close up and running very fast. He kept the gulch and out of sight, crossing the lower spur of the ridge and through a dense thicket, and was evidently making for Donovan Creek, which was fully half a mile distant, and almost an impossibility for man to reach. The dogs soon came to a stop, and all was quiet.

While viewing the situation and studying how to get through the thicket, the dogs returned, well fagged out, and apparently content that the chase was ended. It was now evident that the deer was caught, but not one of us dare venture to find him. It was finally decided to continue the hunt, although we much regretted to leave the deer behind. After a short rest, we started for a glen on the opposite ridge, and with much difficulty it was gained. The hounds hunted well, but could not raise a deer, and they soon returned. We followed down to a point where there had been a burn, and near at hand a thicket of scrub oaks. As soon as the point was reached, the hounds led forward, indicating the scent of a deer which was near at hand. Each hunter runs for a position, the hounds immediately giving tongue, and starting, but their course was directly down the gulch. There was an opening, however, at the bottom, and the deer would have to cross, which would bring him in full view. All were anxiously looking at this point, and expecting every moment to see the deer cross, but, much to our disappointment, he had crossed before we got in a position to see. The chase was now a hot one, and evidently the deer would make his run well out of our reach. The hounds ran well, and for a short time were quite out of hearing, but the deer had made a turn towards us. We could now hear the hounds distinctly. We now directed our attention to the top of the ridge to our right, when the deer made his appearance in full view. It was a fine large buck. Now commenced the fire, and fully ten shots were made, at a distance of about two hundred and fifty yards. Two of the party were inexperienced, and they were more anxious than discreet, for many shots fell wide of the mark. Soon the deer was out of sight in the thicket. The hounds in their run had evidently started the second deer, as one came in full view, and from a different point from where the first one was last seen. The same fire was now opened on him, and it sounded as though a company of soldiers was having a skirmish, as the shooting was so rapid. I said, "Boys, go slow, you are wasting ammunition." The deer now began to stagger, and from a rapid run had settled down to a walk. He soon reached a clump of brush, and was out of sight, and the fire ceased; but for a moment only, for up starts the third deer, and was making for a gulch. Again the fire commenced, but his run in open ground was short, as he was soon out of sight. The dogs had evidently gone astray and got divided, but most of them were still after the first deer seen, which was running directly from us, and out of sight and hearing, the wounded deer still remaining in the thicket. After a consultation, I concluded to cross the gulch, while the balance remained in their positions, and I went to see whether he was dead. After considerable effort, I reached the other side of the gulch, but was somewhat winded, as it was much steeper and rougher than I expected. Before I could get in position, one of the hounds that come across with me scented the deer and in he went. The deer made a break and intended to reach the gulch below, but unfortunately for him he ran in my sight, and was now only about fifty yards distant from me. It was now dollars to cents that he was my deer. At the report of my rifle he fell dead. He had made a brave run for his life, but fate was against him. The balance of the party soon reached where the deer lay, and it was found that several balls had hit him. After preparing him for the pack, he was carried to the top of the ridge, where he could be put upon a horse. He was a fine young buck, and very fat. When the top of the ridge was reached, we all sat down in the shade of a projecting cliff, and the first syllable spoken was, "Pass around the vial, and we will drink to the first hunt of the season." WHETSTONE.

---

### WHITE SULPHUR SPRINGS.

In old times this fashionable resort was frequented by the high political aspirants of the country. The F. F. V.'s of the Old Dominion were reinforced by the men in the whole country (the whole country of old days) who were looking for political preferment, and many an election was settled on the broad veranda of the hotel long before the votes were placed in the ballot-boxes. It was an ultra-aristocratic resort. The blue bloods held the sway, and it was sure that any person who was recognized at the social gathering had something more than a big bank account to recommend him. It was a quiet place withal, and to introduce the excitements of Broad Rock, Tree Hill and other places where the thoroughbreds figure, would have been thought derogatory. Not derogatory in the usual sense, as the Virginians and their visitors thought highly of the thoroughbred, but their ideal was a quieter place than where the blood-horse came in to startle the pulse from its regular beats; and politics in the day time, and a quiet game of loo or brag at night, was thought to be all that was necessary. Of course there were flirtations among the younger, and gay riding parties and picnics under the grand old oaks in the lee of the mountains. "Race week" and the "race ball," however, were held to belong to busier worlds, and no one thought that there was any necessity for them at the White Sulphur. Now, in the march of events, it has become evident that these accessories to a fashionable watering place shall be incorporated, and from the following account, which we copy from the New York Herald of the 3d instant, the great desideratum has been accomplished. The writer is evidently a little rusty in matters pertaining to the turf, and makes a few blunders which do not detract from the interest of the description. But the point from which others can gain knowledge which will be advantageous is that every watering place at the present day, which makes any pretensions to cosmopolitan attractions, must have a race track. Saratoga, Long Branch (even Cape May has races on the beach) show a congregation of thoroughbreds, and there are no other features which are so powerful in attracting visitors:

The season of '82 is destined to be one of the most memorable in the annals of the White Sulphur. It will supply the long needed attraction of a beautiful race course, and by the natural charms of this famous watering place will be added that of a lovely artificial lake, covering an area of some twenty-five or thirty acres. These two features have been talked about and craved by the visitors for years and years, but owing to the peculiar legal embarrassments of the property, their construction never could be attempted until the present company obtained complete control and began its series of extensive improvements. Virginians are noted for their sporting proclivities. They are fond of "old sledge" and "draw poker," and they even gambol with the animal on the green; but what they most glory in is a horse race. In ante-bellum times they boasted of having some of the finest blooded stock in the country, and the Virginia turf laid claim to some of the greatest exhibitions of power, endurance and speed by Virginia horses of the day. But though the war will nigh swept away the stock, as well as the means for keeping it up, the passion for horse racing remains all the same. Nor are Virginia turfmen extinct. The names of McDaniel and Doswell are well known in sporting circles to-day and their stables sustain the ancient prowess of old Virginia racers. To those devotees of the turf represented here every season must be added the steady and increasing influx of their more vigorous progeny from Kentucky and the West. Then throw in a very fair admixture of English gentlemen who have settled here and throughout the Old Dominion and you have all the elements conducive to the formation of a first-class enthusiastic racing association. It was to the clamor—I may almost say demands—of this class that the Springs company promptly responded in building a race track, and their fondest anticipations are at last about to be realized.

Every visitor to the Springs will recollect the lovely patch of meadow, about one hundred acres in extent, lying over in the valley just beyond Howard's Creek, and the old laundry buildings on the west side of the Spring grounds. It is the most charming spot that could have been selected for a race course. The meadow is oblong in shape, so will be the track. On the east it is bounded by the limpid waters of the creek, on the west by the Greenbrier range of mountains. Directly back of the creek, on the Spring side, are the overhanging bluffs of "Lovers' Leap," the windows of the Bath House and the wide verandas of the new club building, from all of which there can be an unobstructed view of the entire course, from the 'start to the finish. The races will invariably take place late in the afternoon, when the course is hidden from the rays of the declining sun by the deep and lengthened shade of Greenbrier Mountain. The track is one mile in length. The curves are north and south, the stretches east and west. About midway on the west side of the track is a beautiful little knoll at the base of the mountain, on which will be erected the grand stand, and which of itself commands a view of the whole course. Stabling for the accommodation of 100 racers will be built in the sugar grove under "Lovers' Leap," and not far from the old laundry on the bank of the creek, where exercising ground is protected by the shade, both in the morning and afternoon.

The building of a race track involves a great deal more time and expense than one would at first suppose. It has to be graded, then spread over by a fine mould, then sodded to make it springy, and then moulded again and rolled. The grading, which is of itself a heavy job, is now nearly finished, and by the latter part of August, when it is proposed to hold the first meeting, the track, buildings and all the necessary appointments will be complete and in the most thorough working order. It is now understood that the course and racing will be under the supervision of Major J. B. Ferguson, of Baltimore, who has charge also of the Pimlico course at that city. A programme of five days' racing, on alternate days, has been arranged, commencing on August 29th and ending on September 7th. Several turfmen have expressed their willingness to bring their stables to the "White" this fall for the purpose of inaugurating the races, and others have liberally offered to contribute to purses and cups. During the season it is proposed to form and incorporate the White Sulphur Racing Association, under the auspices of such prominent gentlemen as W. W. Corcoran, of Washington; Governor Mathews, of West Virginia; Major Thomas W. Doswell, of Virginia; Senator Camden, of West Virginia; Senators Hampton and Butler, of South Carolina; W. A. Grainer, of West Virginia; Senator Vest, of Missouri, and Lewis Baker, of Wheeling, W. Va. The latter gentleman offers a handsome purse on his own responsibility. In addition to the regular fall meetings at the "White," there will be numerous flat and hurdle contests between gentlemen during the spring season, which will be sources of amusement to the visitors.

JOHN NO SABBEE MELICAN WAYS.—One night recently the electric lights at the Collender billiard hall were a little late in starting, and the proprietor notified his Chinaman to go up and start them. After getting a step-ladder and finding that he could not reach the lamp, to the surprise of all present the Chinaman disappeared and in a short time appeared again upon the top of the bean to which the lamp is attached, with a gas-lighter in his hand. John had made his way to the back yard and climbed to the roof of the building. Then he opened one of the side windows of the sky-light and crept inside. When discovered he was crawling cautiously along one of the beams. Stopping in the middle he struck a match and lit the taper and then reached down to the electric light and tried to "touch it off." After fumbling about the apparatus for a minute or more he gave up the job in despair and retired by the same route he came. Presently he appeared by the scared and baffled hall again, and with an expression of disgust and baffled ingenuity on his face, approached the proprietor and said: "No can lighter 'lectec; no passee; no can catches." The proprietor kindly endeavored to explain to the Chinaman the difference between gaslight and electricity, and after a half hour's tedious lesson gave up the task, almost prostrate with nervous exhaustion.—Denver Tribune.

---

### HORSE SALE.

We call attention to the advertisement of a large sale of trotting, harness and work horses that will take place by order of Dan McCarty, at the corner of Taylor and Eddy streets, to-day (Saturday) at 10:30 a. m. The catalogue comprises some very useful and valuable stock, as also a lot of sulkies, skeleton wagons, harness, boots, etc., which merit the attention of buyers.

---

## THE TURF.

### RACING IN CANADA.

TORONTO, July 3, 1882.

EDITOR BREEDER AND SPORTSMAN: I send you a report of the annual spring meeting, held under the auspices of the newly formed Ontario Jockey Club, over the beautiful course known as the Woodbine, on Saturday, July 1st, and Monday, the 3d. This track is situated about three miles from the city, over a good road, and for natural facilities cannot be excelled in any country. The races should have commenced on Friday, but the inexorable clerk of the weather willed it otherwise, as there was a constant downpour of rain, making it absolutely impossible for a horse to stay on his feet. On Saturday, however, we had a beneficent change, and the weather was lovely, although the track was necessarily slow; but the sport that was offered thoroughly pleased everybody. Not without good reason, as every event on the programme was carried out without a single failure, to the perfect satisfaction of the general public—a thing that can seldom be said nowadays.

The programme was as follows:

The First Stakes, $150, for all ages, of which 250 went to second horse. Maidens allowed: if 3 years old, 3 pounds; 4 years old, 10 pounds; 5 years and upwards, 5 pounds; foreign-bred horses, 7 pounds extra. Distance, three-quarters of a mile.

Abingdon's Disturbance, 6 years .................................................. 1
Chaplin's Mindefull, 6 years .................................................. 2
Silvey Chipola, 5 years .................................................. 3
Ward's Victoria, 3 years .................................................. 0

Time: 1:35½.

Book-betting: Disturbance 8 to 15; 20 to 9 against Chipola; 25 to 5 against Broderick.

THE ONTARIO DERBY.—$200 for 3 year olds added to a sweepstakes of $50 each. Half forfeit for foals of 1879 filled, filled, owned and trained in the province of Ontario or Quebec. $150 to first horse; $50 to second. 1¼ miles. Colts 118 pounds each; fillies and geldings 113 pounds each.

Burgess's J. Barbee, 3 years .................................................. 1
D. O'Campbell's b c, Walkover, 3 years .................................................. 2
Smith's b f, Bonnie Vic .................................................. 3

Time: 2:34.

Betting: 3 to 10 on Barbee; 20 to 8 against Marquis; 9 to 1 against Bonnie Vic.

Md. BREWSTER PLATE.—$200, open free. Handicap. Distance, $200, $75 and $25. 1½ miles.

Johnston's Tullamore, 5 years .................................................. 1
Abingdon's Long Tow, aged .................................................. 2
Dr. Smith's Viet, 4 years .................................................. 3
Davies' Kismet .................................................. 0
Forbes' Bonnie Bird .................................................. 0
Magee's Bell Labelle .................................................. 0
Ward's Eva .................................................. 0

Time: 2:54.

Betting: 25 to 8 against Tullamore; 20 to 10 against Kismet; 20 to 10 against Long Tow; 30 to 8 against Bonnie Bird; 40 to 5 against Viet; 50 to 5 against Labelle; 80 to 5 against Eva.

THE WOODBINE STEEPLE CHASE.—$275 divided; $200, $75, $50. Distance about 3 miles.

Davies' ch m, Rose, 6 years, 160 pounds .................................................. 1
Godson's b m, Flora, 6 years, 156 pounds .................................................. 2
Milliken's b g, Alarm, 6 years, 158 pounds .................................................. 3
H. D. Grand's Lady Reveller, 5 years old, 136 pounds .................................................. 0
Campbell's b g, William, 4 years, 130 pounds .................................................. 0
Nelson's b g, Bruno, 20 to 15 against Lady Reveller; 25 to 5 against second .................................................. 0

Time: 5:35.

5th. Railway Purse—$250—For Dominion bred horses; $175 to first; $50 to second; and $25 to third.

Abingdon's Disturbance .................................................. 1
Dr. Smith's Lady T'Arff .................................................. 2
Campbell's King Labelle .................................................. 3
Second Day—Purse for all ages—$150; $175 to first; $50 to second; three-quarters of a mile.

Abingdon's Disturbance, 6 years, 120 pounds .................................................. 1
Dr. Smith's Viet, 4 years 122 pounds .................................................. 2
Johnston's Tullamore, 5 years, 118 pounds .................................................. 3

Time: 1:55½.

Betting: Disturbance favorite.

THE Hotel Stakes—$450—$350 to first; $100 to second. Mile heats.

Davies' Kismet, 3 years, 130 pounds .................................................. 1
Abingdon's Long Tow, aged, 136 pounds .................................................. 2
Dr. Smith's Lady T'Arff .................................................. 3
Kinsoff won two straight heats.

Time: 1:48½.

Betting: Disturbance favorite.

Steeple Chase Handicap—$250—$200 to first; $50 to second. Top weights 166 pounds. Distance 2½ miles.

H. D. Grand's Lady Reveller .................................................. 1
Davies' ch m, Rose .................................................. 2
Gordon's Flora .................................................. 3

Betting: 3 to 1 on Rose; 10 to 5 on Lady Reveller.

Time: 6:4.

The Oak Handicap—$250—For Dominion-bred horses; $175; $50; and $25.

Abingdon's Disturbance, 130 pounds .................................................. 1
Campbell's William, 106 pounds .................................................. 2
Forbes' Kismet, 98 pounds .................................................. 3

Betting: Little or none. Disturbance being a hot favorite, notwithstanding the weights.

Time: 2m. 4s.

The Welter Cup—$100 to winner. Entrance $5, two-thirds of which went to second horse. Distance 1½ miles.

H. D. Grand's Lady Reveller, 105 pounds .................................................. 1
Milligan's Alarm, 172 pounds .................................................. 2
Gordon's Flora, 152 pounds .................................................. 3
Grand's Sarah B, 160 pounds .................................................. 0
Beatty's Cornelia, 150 pounds .................................................. 0
Ward's Dan, 166 pounds .................................................. 0

Betting in this race was very even; it was very exciting and keenly contested but the race was run very hard by Lady Reveller.

The Selling Stakes, $120, for beaten horses; $25 to second horse, brought out Viei, Labelle and Dan; and after a sharp run, was won handily by Viei, and brought the meeting to a satisfactory conclusion. JAMES LENG.

---

### THE MONMOUTH PARK RACES.

Again is there a change of venue, and after many a well fought contest the horses have left Sheepshead Bay and Jerome Park; their numbers being about equally divided between these two delightful watering places, Long Island and Saratoga. These are about the best race tracks in the country, as they are safe, fast and of sufficient width to accommodate the large fields of horses that are now to be found on every race course where special inducements are offered. There is one drawback to Monmouth Park, and that is the four-mile drive to the track, and the scarcity of hacks and the rapacity of their drivers, but the railroad runs special trains to the gate, and a short walk brings the visitor to the spacious stands and inclosures, while farther on, past the winning post, is the Club House, one of the most delightful boxes in the country.

On the first of July the inaugural race of the very liberal programme was a mile dash for all ages, with penalties and allowances, that was won by Jim Farrell, in 1:47¾, against five competitors. The second was the Hopeful Stakes, for two-year-olds, which has been a favorite race since it was first inaugurated some ten years ago. For the last four years the famous blue and orange of that staunch sportsman George Lorillard was always in the van, but this year the prize was carried off by George Kenner, belonging to the Dwyer Brothers, after a most beautiful finish with Heel-and-Toe and Jacobus, the latter carrying 5 pounds extra, as in future be the case with all important races. We append the summary:

Hopeful Stakes, for two-year-olds, at $100 each, half forfeit; only $20 if declared by January 1, 1882, and $30 if declared by June 25, 1882, with $1,000 added; the second to receive $250 out of the stakes; winners of a stake (handicaps excepted) of the value of $1,000, to carry 5 lb.; of two such stakes, 7 lb.; and three such stakes, 12 lb. extra; closed with 59 subscribers; five furlongs.

Dwyer Bros.' b. c. George Kenney, by Bonnie Scotland, dam Kathleen, 10 lb. ........ 1
Mr. Kelso's b. f. Heel-and-Toe, by Glenelg, dam La Polka, 107 lb. (Evans). 2
J. E. Kelly's br. c. Jacobus, by Ill-Used, dam Nellie James, 115 lb., including 5 lb. penalty........(Hughes) 3
G. L. Lorillard's ch. c. Trafalgar, 110 lb., carried 112 lb........(Costello) 0
G. L. Lorillard's br. f. Swift, 107 lb........(Ural) 0
P. Lorillard's b. c. Pizarro, 110 lb........(Feakes) 0
D. D. Withers's br. c. Buckstone, 110 lb........(Sparing) 0
D. J. Bannatyne's b. c. Little Minch, 110 lb........(Gallagher) 0

Time—1:06¾.

Pools.—George Kenney, $60; G. L. Lorillard's pair, $80; Pizarro, $25; Heel-and-Toe, $20; Jacobus, $20; the field, $20.

The third race was the Ocean Stakes, for all ages, a mile and a furlong, in which Runnymede, the three-year-old crack, was made a hot favorite at $300 against $100 for the field, composed of Barrett and the Stonehenge-Julietta three-year-old colt, both fast and strong runners. Barrett made a sad example of the other two, and won by a hundred yards, in 2:02.

The fourth race was the Long Branch Handicap, a mile and a quarter, which was taken by that excellent weight carrier Monitor, belonging to G. L. Lorillard, beating Glidelia and three others in 2:20¾, this being another overturn for the talent, as the mare was a great favorite.

The fifth race was a Selling Purse, of a mile, which was won handsomely be G. Lorillard's Itaska, with Clarence second and Blenheim third, in 1:49. The winner was entered to be sold for $600, and was bought in by his owner at $960; leaving $240 and $120 to the second and third horses.

The final race was the Steeplechase over the short course, which ended in favor of Bertha at the last stride, Ohio Boy second, leading Frank Short by a length at the winning post. This exciting race brought the programme to a conclusion.

It being evident that most of the New Yorkers would make a holiday of the day preceding the 4th, the Association resolved to give an extra day's racing, when with fine weather and a better track there was an increased attendance and more attractive sport. The first race, a dash of five furlongs for $500, with allowances, G. L. Lorillard's Black Gal won in 1:04, with Fairfield second and Marie Armstrong third; Adalgisa, the favorite, getting a very bad start. The next was a handicap of a mile for three-year-olds, $25 each with $500 added, and was taken by P. Lorillard's Amazon, 100 lbs., in 11:46½, with Blenheim, 106 lbs., second, and Bouncer, 96 lbs., third. The third race was also a handicap, $25 each with $500 added, a mile and a furlong. The starters were Warfield and Victim, at 114 lbs., Wyoming and Sweethome, 105 lbs. each, and Duplex, 100 lbs. The race was so close that many speculators thought it was a dead heat between the three leading horses, but the judges placed Sweethome first, Warfield second, and Duplex third. Time 1:58. The next was also a handicap, on the same conditions, but at a mile and three-fourths, in which old Parole carried 123 lbs., and was a great favorite, and he won handily in 2:26¾; Hilarity, 100 lbs., second, and Francesca, 98 lbs., third. The latter is a three-year-old sister to Iroquois, and appears to possess none of the traits of her illustrious brother, making no show whatever in her races. But from her breeding she ought to make a fine brood mare. The next was a selling race of $500, at seven furlongs, and was won by Little Phil, the favorite, by a short head, he carrying 111 lbs., Sir Hugh, 88 lbs., being second, and Clarence, 97 lbs., third, with some others unplaced. The time, 1:28¾, is fully a second and a quarter faster than the record, which was 1:30, made at Brighton Beach last year, the first time by Reporter, carrying 94 lbs., and subsequently by Brambaletta, carrying 92 lbs. In the hurdle race, $500, a mile and a quarter, Frank Short was first in 2:21¾, with Bernardine second and Ohio Boy third. Altogether, it was a good day's sport.

On the national holiday there was the largest attendance ever seen at the track, with the exception of the day on which the great contest between Harry Barrett and Longfellow took place in the Westchester cup. Unfortunately the weather was not propitious, as it rained all day, but the sport was so good that but few of the spectators were driven away by the storm. There were six races on the card, the first being a purse of $500 for three year olds and upwards, a mile and a furlong, with penalties and allowances, and was captured by Barrett, the favorite, with 118 lbs.; Greenland, 113 lbs. second; Dan K., 114 lbs. third; and Fatinitza, 108 lbs. fourth. Time 1.56¾. The second was a purse of $500 for two year olds, with penalties and allowances, five furlongs, and was also won by the favorite, P. Lorillard's Pizarro, 107 lbs.; Clonmel, 107 lbs. second; Fairwater, 104 lbs. third; and Uisie, Black Gal and Cheerful unplaced. The next race was the event of the day, in which Runnymede and Forester met again to test their supremacy as the Champion of the three year olds. The betting was pretty even between them, with the former the choice at $115, $100 for Forester, and $35 for the two other starters, the Stonehenge-Julietta colt and Hilarity. It was the finest struggle ever seen on the track so celebrated for so many a close finoish There were many variations in the lead for the first mile but at three furlongs from home, the two favorites came to the fore with Forester half a length ahead, and he continued to hold this same advantage, until within an eighth of a mile from home.

But here Runnymede closed up, and then began a most exciting head to head finish, the two horses, under whip and spur, changing apparently their positions of advantage at every stride, and Runnymede won at the wire by the shortest of necks, amid a scene of the wildest enthusiasm and excitement. Following is the summary:

The Lorillard Stakes for three-year-olds, at $250 each, half forfeit, only $25 if declared by August 1, 1881, and $50 if declared by June 30, 1882, with $2,500, the gift of Mr. P. Lorillard, the association adding $1,000 for the second, closed with 97 subscribers; mile and a half.

Dwyer Bros.' br. c. Runnymede, by Billet, dam Mercedes, 118 lbs. ........(J. McLaughlin) 1
Appleby & Johnson's ch. c. Forester, by Ill-Used, dam Woodbine, 118 lbs........(C. Holloway) 2
Spellman & Co.'s b. c. Hilarity, by Bonnie Scotland, dam Beulah, 118 lbs........(J. Spellman) 3
D. D. Withers' ch. c. ——, by Stonehenge, dam Julietta, 118 lbs. ........(Sparling) 0

Time—2:40.

The fourth race was the Shrewsbury handicap for all ages, $100 each, h. f. with $750 added, a mile and three-quarters. Glenmore, 117 lbs. and Girofle with like weight, were even favorites at $100, and the former won in 3:03¼, with Glidelia, 112 lbs. second, and Girofle third, while Aelia, 103 lbs. and Monitor, 122 lbs., including 15 lbs. extra, ran unplaced.

The next event was a dash of a mile and three-eighths, for a purse of $500, in which Mary Anderson, 85 lbs, to be sold at $500, and Strathspey, 100 lbs, to be sold at $1,000, were the only stallions. The race was won by the latter in 2:26¼ and he was bought in for $1,455, and as the surplus over the $1,000 went to the second horse, she got $455, while the winner outside the bets was only $45 to the good for his race.

The fifth was a Welter Cup for gentlemen riders, three-quarters of a mile, that was won by Corsair, with Mr. Holmes in the saddle, Arsenic second, with Mr. Ward, and Traveler third, ridden by Mr. Sharkey, with Hospodar, Mr. Purdy, Knightly King, Mr. Hunter and Mrs. Chubbs, Mr. Easton, were unplaced. The finish was close and the time 1:19¾.

The proceedings closed with a handicap steeple chase over the field course that was won by Frank Short, with Bernardino second, and Bertha third. The day's sport was excellent, and the Lorillard Stakes and Shrewsbury Handicap of 1882 will be long remembered by those who saw those races.

## THE RACES AT SALT LAKE.

The Utah Jockey Club opened their inaugural meeting at Salt Lake City on June 24th, under favorable auspices, a good many from San Francisco going on to back Maria F. and the Duke of Monday, the latter being looked upon as one of the best horses in this State. Considering it was their initial attempt, the Executive Officers made a very successful bid for popular favor, and the result shows that the Summer meeting at Salt Lake may be looked upon as one of our permanent fixtures.

On the first day the races were Club Stakes, running, for three-year-olds, $25 entrance, $500 added, one mile—Won by Maria F. Time, 1:49½. Purse $500, one mile and a half—Won by Longstride; Chantilla second, Duke of Monday third. Time, 2:47. Purse $200, half a mile and repeat—Won by Euchre, Ben Anderson taking second heat. Time, 0:52¾, 0:50, 0:51½. Trotting, $700, class 2:30—Won by Ewing; Teazer (won first heat) second, Bicksford third. Time, 2:31½, 2:37½, 2:32, 2:34½. Purse $300, one mile—Won by Chantilla; Euchre second, Ben Anderson third. Time, 1:47¾. Juvenile Stakes, two-year-olds, $25 entrance, $200 added, six furlongs—Won by P. Lorillard; Miss Trump second. Time, 1:21¾. Purse $400, a mile and an eighth—Won by Red Boy; Norton second, Belle of the West third. Time, 1:59. Trotting, $700, class 2:35—Won by Ewing; Milo G. second, Mary Emery third. Time, 2:43, 2:41½, 2:37. Novelty race, horse leading at half mile to receive $100, one mile, $150, and mile and a half, $250. Half mile purse won by Ben Anderson in 0:51, mile by Maria T. in in 1:47, and mile and a half by Longstride in 2:47½. Purse $250, six furlongs—Won by Duke of Monday; P. Lorillard second, Sisterly third. Time, 1:18½. Trotting, $400, class 2:40—Won by Milo G.; Maggie C. (won first and second heats) second. Time, 2:44½, 2:37¾, 2:39¼, 2:40½, 2:40¼.

On July 6th was decided the great match race between Wildmoor and Euchre, mile heats, 3 in 5, for a purse of $2,000, which was won by Wildmoor. Time, 1:46, 1:48¼, 1:49½. The running race, mile heats, two in three, Norton won the first heat in 1:46½, and Chantilla the next two in 1:47½ and 1:50. This closed the Spring meeting of the Utah Jockey Club. Wildmoor is matched against Red Boy in a race for $5,000 a side, mile heats, three in five, to be run on the Salt Lake track August 16th.

The Conny Island Races.—Owing to the political excitement, the Press dispatches of the races at the East during the past week have been of a meagre character, but following are curt details of two days' races at this track. On July 7th, in the three-quarter-mile race, Mary Warner won. Time, 1:17½. The one-mile race Ida B. won in 1:46. The five-eighths-of-a-mile race Brambletta won in 1:0¾. The Coney Island Stakes for three-year-olds, 1⅛ miles, Barney Lyon won in 2:15. The Hurdle Race, 1¼ miles, five hurdles, King Dutchman won in 2:28. On the 11th, in the Palace Hotel Stakes, for two-year-olds, three-quarters of a mile, Baron, the favorite, won. Time, 1:20¼. The three-quarters of a mile race Bedouin won in 1:16½. The seven-furlongs race for three-year-olds Bonheur won in 1:32. The mile and a half race Joe Murray won in 2:36½. The Hurdle Race, one mile and a quarter, Gillie Monson won in 2:20½.

In England, the Summer Cup at Newmarket was won by Isabel after a magnificent finish with Mr. Keene's Golden Gate, with Credo third. The Chesterfield, one of the important two-year-old stakes, was won by Gaillard, with Export a good second. The next principal meeting will be at Goodwood, when Foxhall will probably appear, as well as Iroquois, if the latter can be got into good racing trim by the third week of this month.

Another very important race at the July meeting, at Newmarket, was the Exeter Stakes, over the new T. Y. C. (5 furlongs, 136 yards). Out of the twenty-seven subscribers, seven started, including Mr. Pierre Lorillard's bay colt Comanche, by Virgil or Glenlyon. He was not placed, Lord Ellesmere's Highland Chief, by Hampton, winning, with Lord Falmouth's Britomartis, by Wild Oats, second, and Mr. Lefevre's Bon Jour, by Rosicrucian, third. Highland Chief was bred by Ellesmere, and made his *debut* in the race for the Stud Produce Stakes, at the Newmarket First Spring Meeting, when he was second, being beaten a length by Prince Soltykoff's Songless, by Balfe.

Tristan promises to become in England one of the four-year-old "cracks" of the year. He has already won the Queen's Plates at Northampton and Chester, the Epsom Stakes at Epsom in May, and the Epsom Gold Cup at the same meeting. At Ascot, after winning the Queen's Vase on the first day, he took the New Biennial Stakes on the third, and the Hardwick Stakes on the fourth day, and last week he won the July Cup at Newmarket. There will be great interest if Tristan and Foxhall come together on even terms at Goodwood.

The famous French breeding stable that was backed by the late Emperor of the French in so liberal a financial manner is to be dispersed under the hammer. Count La Grange, who has managed the confederacy in so striking a manner in by-gone years, announces the sale at Tattersall's, in London, during the first week of September, and the catalogue will comprise 45 foals, 29 yearlings, 77 mares and 11 stallions. This is sending a heavy cargo of French coals to Newcastle.

Despite the very unfavorable weather, we are pleased to see that the Chicago Association have a balance of from $6,000 to $7,000, arising from their recent race meeting. There were in all forty-five events on the programme of the eight days' racing; the pool selling averaged $50,000 a day, and the attendance was uniformly good, and we wish the Association a far more successful showing in their next venture.

Mr. R. W. Cameron, of New York, who has made by far the largest importation of thoroughbreds to this country, including Leamington and Warminster, has recently sold a sister to Foxhall to Mr. Finley, in the Colony of Victoria. Before being shipped to her destination, she will probably be bred to one of Leamington's famous sons.

The English mare Lady Audley, by Macaroni, out of Secret, the dam of Pilgrimage, Pellegrino, St. Louis, etc., recently met with an accident at the Chamant Stud, and had to be destroyed. She was foaled in 1867, and last September was purchased by M. Lefevre for £1,200.

Luke Blackburn, "The Little Giant," and but two years since the champion racer of the country, has been sold to General W. F. Harding, and will in future be one of the main supports of the Belle Meade farm. He is admirably bred, being by Bonnie Scotland from Nevada, and combines the great Queen Mary blood with that of our grand horses Glencoe and Lexington. He ought to be a great success at the stud.

# THE TRACK.

## FIXED EVENTS.

Portland, Or. Summer meeting, July 18th.
Santa Cruz County Fair Association. First annual meeting at Santa Cruz, Aug 15th, 16th, 17th and 18th.
Sonoma County Park Association, at Santa Rosa, Aug. 22d, 23d, 24th, 25th and 26th.
Sonoma and Marin Agricultural Societies. Annual Fair at Petaluma, Aug 29th and four following days.
Golden Gate Fair to be held at Oakland from September 4th to the 9th inclusive.
California State Fair. Annual meeting at Sacramento from Monday, September 11th to the 16th inclusive.
The San Joaquin Valley Association Fair at Stockton, from September 19th to the 23d inclusive.
Oregon State Fair at Salem, from September 18th and during the week.
The San Mateo and Santa Clara County Agricultural Association Fair at San Jose September 25th to the 30th inclusive.
Mount Shasta Agricultural Association Fair at Yreka, October 4th, 5th, 6th and 7th.

## FAIRS AT THE EAST.

Kentucky State Fair at Lexington, August 9th to September 2d inclusive.
Mi[illegible] State Fair at Farmington, August 31st to September 8th inclusive.
Iowa State Fair at Fairfield, September 1st to the 8th inclusive.
Minnesota Agricultural Association, at Minneapolis, September 4th to the 9th inclusive.
Nebraska State Fair, at Omaha, September 11th until the 16th inclusive.
Rhode Island State Fair, at Providence, September 12th to the 15th inclusive.
Pennsylvania State Fair, at Pittsburg, September 7th to the 21st inclusive.
Wisconsin State Fair, at Fond du lac, September 11th to the 16th inclusive.
Ontario Provincial Fair, at Toronto, September 18th to the 23d inclusive.
Connecticut State Fair, at Meriden, September 18th to the 22d inclusive.
New Jersey State Fair, at Monroe, September 18th to the 22d inclusive.
West Virginia Central Fair, at Clarksburg, September 19th to the 21st inclusive.
Indiana State Fair, at Indianapolis, September 25th to the 30th inclusive.
Western Michigan Fair, at Grand Rapids, September 25th to the 30th inclusive.
Texas State Fair, at Austin, October 17th to the 21st inclusive.

## THE GENTLEMEN'S DRIVING ASSOCIATION.

This club represents the wealthiest patrons of trotting interest in the United States. Their track is the old Fleetwood race course, about half a mile from McComb's bridge and close to Jerome avenue, along which, every fine day, may be seen the finest trotters owned by amateurs in the country. The association gave an entertainment to the members and their friends on the 29th July, of which the following account is from the N. Y. *World:*

"Every effort was made by the committee to make the day a success. In the first place, a day was fixed when there were no counter attractions in the way of racing, either trotting or running, elsewhere than at Brighton Beach, and, in the second place, the conditions were made as to bring about two races—one, the slow class, to be driven by gentlemen drivers to road wagons, and the other, for fast horses, to be driven by professionals to sulkies, or, in other words, in harness. The prizes for both classes were elegant silver punch bowls. Unfortunately, neither race obtained more than three entries. That for members to drive was limited to horses that had never beaten 2:40, and the entries were A. De Cordova's bay mare Julia D., Mr. David Bonner's chestnut gelding Banjo, and Mr. C. A. Willis's brown horse Wellington. Mr. De Cordova's Julia D. was withdrawn early in the day, which left the race apparently an easy task for Banjo. He won the first heat in 2:42½, so easily that many thought that if Mr. Bonner had tried he could have distanced Wellington; but as the race was between gentlemen there was no necessity for any such exhibition. The second heat, however, completely ended Mr. Bonner's chances. The word was given with Banjo scarcely well settled down. He broke badly on the turn, and from that time out a series of most annoying accidents followed. First, the left trace became unhitched, so that for safety Mr. Bonner had to lean over the dash-board and temporarily fasten it. Next, the boot on the horse's left fore leg became unfastened and at every step flapped down so that the horse stepped on it. The final result was that Banjo was distanced, Wellington winning the heat and race in the very excellent time of 2:38¾.

The second trot was for horses that had never beaten 2.22; members to drive their own horses or to allow professionals to do so. The three entries were Mr. J. W. Shaw's bay gelding Charley Champlin, Mr. J. Collinfield's chestnut mare Helene and Mr. W. B. Ridebock's bay gelding Dan Smith, and as Dan Mace appeared as the driver of Dan Smith, his brother Ben Mace, as the driver of Charley Champlin and John Murphy as the drixer of Helene, not a few expected to see a close and well-contested race. But Helene was in so much better condition and trotted so much steadier than either of the others that she won the punch bowl for her owner, in three straight heats, without any special exertion. The first heat was trotted in 2.21, the second in 2 23¾ and the third in 2.21¾. Dan Smith secured second honors by finishing second in the second and third heats. Additional attractions were given by Mr. Vanderbilt driving Bay Dick and Lysander Boy and Mr. Frank Work driving Dick Swiveller and Edward. Several other exhibitions took place by horses of less repute, while, to make the afternoon's entertainment as a whole enjoyable, Grafulla's band, with Francis X. Duler as director, filled in the time with a programme of well-selected music.

Trotting at Island Park Albany.—This track is becoming very popular in the extreme Eastern States, and at the recent meeting the entries were large and the contests on the average were fairly contested. On July 3d, in the purse of $1,000, Clemmie G. was a great favorite, and won without being extended to her utmost, in three straight heats in 2:24, 2:23½ and 2:25. The second money was taken by Mars, the third by R. P. and the fourth by King Almont. The second race was the Nolan Stakes for a purse of $1500 for the 2:23 class, which was won by Ealy Rose, she taking the first, third and fourth heats, Naiad Queen gaining second money in the second heat, Unolala and Buzz Medium figuring in the third and fourth positions. Time 2:24¾, 2:21, 2:24½ and 2:24.

On July 4th, there was the Clay Stakes of $3,000 for the three-minute class, in which there were fourteen starters, of which six appeared on the track. Young Fullerton was the favorite, and although to Walnut was given the first beat—Guess Not being placed last for running—Fullerton won the three successive heats, Guess-Not being third in the full summary, Cornelia fourth, Bertha Clay fifth, and Lulu sixth in their positions. Time 2:27, 2:20¼, 2:27¼ and 2:30. The pacing purse of $500 was taken by Estella, with the second, third and fifth heats, Jim Jewell taking the second money, and Felix the third, while Hawk was credited with barren honors. On the 7th, Driver won the 2:20 class. Best time 2:21, in the fourth heat. Douglass won the 2:34 class. Best time 2:26¼. The attendance would have been far greater with favorable weather.

Additions to Palo Alto.—There is nothing like going away from home for news. Ex-Governor Stanford returned a few days since from the East, and while there we learn from *The Turf, Field and Farm* that "he strengthened the Palo Alto stud by a select purchase from Mr. Joseph Harker, of New York. Lulu is by Alexander's Norman, out of Kate Crockett, by imp. Hooton. She trotted a trial at Rochester in 2:14¾, and has a record of 2:15. The produce sold with her were a filly one year old by Governor Sprague, and a filly by George Wilkes dropped last Spring. Gazelle is by Rysdyk's Hambletonian, out of Hattie Wood, by Harry Clay, and her record is 2:21. Two of her daughters go with her—a four-year-old by Hambletonian Prince, and a suckling by Governor Sprague. Brunette is by Rysdyk's Hambletonian, out of Major Morton's famous Kate, and she was a great pole mare. Mattie is by Rysdyk's Hambletonian, out of Lucy Almack, by Young Engineer, and her record is 2:22½. A few days ago she trotted at the Gentlemen's Driving Park a half mile in harness, in 1:07¾, and Charley Green will handle her this Summer with the view of lowering her record. Mr. Harker will ship the above-named mares and fillies to California in the Fall, and they will be bred in due season to Electioneer and Piedmont. There can be no mistake in breeding to blood as thoroughly tried on the track as that in the veins of Gazelle, Lulu, Mattie, Brunette, George Wilkes and Governor Sprague. Mr. Harker has retained May Queen, a yearling colt out of her, and colts out of Gazelle and Brunette.

Racing in Michigan.—The June races of the Michigan, Ohio and Kentucky Circuit began at Grand Rapids, Michigan, June 27, and continued three days. Results: Class 2:40, $700 purse, won by H. M. Strong in three straight heats; time, 2:31, 2:30½, 2:32¼. Class 2:30, purse $700, won by Mattie Graham; time 2:23, 2:29¼, 2:27. Class 2:20, won by Annie W.; William H. second, Sweetzer third; time 2:23½, 2:23¼, 2:24. The Ladies' Ten-mile Race, between Miss Lizzie Williams, of Topeka, Kansas, and Miss Nellie Burke; of Omaha, Nebraska, was won by the latter in 21:15, Miss Williams arriving at the wire 45 seconds later. Class 2:26, $700, won by Jerome Eddy; Aldine second, Sue Grundy third, Largess fourth; time 2:25¼, 2:24¾, 2:27¼. Class 2:30, purse $700, won by Dr. Norman; Mattie Grasham second, King William third; time 2:26¾, 2:25½, 2:26¾. Pacing race, 2:23 class; High Jack and Joe Bowers each won a heat, but when the third was called, Jack failed to respond. His owner reported that the horse was very sick, and that he beheved it had been poisoned. All bets and pools were declared off, and the race was left unfinished. Mach dissatisfaction was expressed over the occurrence.

The Board of Stewards of the National Trotting Association have offered a special purse for the Cleveland, Buffalo and Rochester races of $4,000, open to all; $1,000 if St. Julien and Trinket enter and start, and open to all other horses; $1,200 is to go to the first; $800 to the second; $500 extra to the fastest horse trotting in 2:14 or better; $500 additional extra to the horse trotting in 2:12 or better; $1,000 additional to the horse trotting in 2:10¾ or better. No entrance is required or added to the money. In the mean time the Chicago Driving Park Association have offered a special purse of $2,500 for a match between St. Julien and Trinket, to be trotted on Thursday, July 20th, during the regular meeting. The conditions so far as arranged are mile heats—three in five, both to go to sulky. Secretary Hall will handicap the horses; it is understood, however, that St Julien is not to exceed twenty-five pounds more than Trinket.

Brighton Beach Races.—There was a goodly assemblage at this track on Monday, July 3d, when the events resulted as follows: Purse $200, for non-winners during 1882, catch-weights, seven furlongs—Irving and Co.'s Malise first, in 1:34¾; Mary Warren second, by a neck; Belle of the North third, by a length. Purse $200, selling allowances, six furlongs—R. Bradley's Prosper first in 1:16¾ Ida B. second, by a length; Monk third, by a like distance. Purse $200, one mile—W. C. Daly's Vanguard first, in 1:45¾. Bonheur second, by a head; L. B. Sprague a bad third. Purse $200, hurdle race, welter-weights, a mile and a quarter—W. C. Daly's Gift first, in 2:24½; Delaware second, by our lengths; Dailgasian third, by eight lengths.

Miss Myrtie Peck, of Michigan, aged 14, rode on the Rochester Driving Park, July 8th, twenty miles in 43 minutes 24½ seconds, beating the best recorded time by two minutes. She rode seven horses, none of them considered fast, and two or three considered slow. The time was taken by reliable parties.

The Chicago Trotting Meeting.—In regard to the races that are to be decided to-day at the City by the Lake, *The Turf, Field and Farm* makes the following remarks:

"Nevada and Second Love have been declared out of the three-year-old stake at Chicago. This leaves five to start, Garfield, Butterfly, Ernest Maltravers, Code and Eva. The great fight, doubtless, will be between the California filly and the Kentucky colt. Code is fashionably bred, being by Dictator, out of Crop, by Pilot, Jr., and he is a ripper. Eva as a two-year-old gained a record of 2:26, and the stable thinks well of her. In fact we heard an offer of $5,000 made that she would win the race, which is to be trotted on Saturday, July 15th. In the four-year-old stake, to be decided the same day, only Belle of Coldwater and First Love have declined to make the second payment, due June 1st. This leaves nine in, Farce, Jayejesee, Adelaide, Ottawa Chief, Waiting, Brouze, Jim Booman, Code and Sauveur. Farce, by Princess, out of Roma, has trotted a trial in 2:23½, and Joyeyesee, by Dictator, out of Midnight (dam by Noontide), by Pilot, Jr.; second dam Midnight, by Lexington, is reported very fast. Sauveur is moving well, and Ed Geers was rapid in his three-year-old form. Code has the disadvantage of a year, but his owner has great confidence in his ability. We know little of the others, but presume they must be good ones. Farce, very likely, will start the favorite, but favorites do not always win. The horses which have drawn out of the open to all stallion race, to be trotted Monday, July 17th, are Robert McGregor, who is lame, Alexander, who is doing stud duty in Kentucky, and Santa Claus, who is at Philadelphia and out of training. This leaves for starters Von Arnim, Voltaire, Monroe Chief, and J. B. Thomas. If Monroe Chief is as good a horse as he was two years ago, first money will go to him, but as he was a failure last year, he may not develop winning form in July. Next to him J. B. Thomas is the dangerous horse, albeit Von Arnim is speedy and Veltaire a stayer. The Summer trotting meeting at Chicago will attract visitors from all parts of the country."

According to the last dispatches the meeting will last for seven days, $52,000 in premiums and purses being offered. The list of entries includes all the best horses in the country. Among the most interesting events will be the attempt of the pacer Little Brown Jug to beat Maud S's trotting record on Saturday. The sensational event of Monday is a race open to all stallions, with Von Arnim, Voltaire, Monroe Chief and K. B. Thomas as the probable starters. On Tuesday there will be a race open to all pacers, for which there are eight entries. On Wednesday there will be a special handicap race between St. Julien and Trinket, St. Julien to draw 150 pounds to Trinket's 135 pounds. The purse is $5,000. Thursday has a 2:19-class race, with seven entries, and Friday has a 2:17-class race, with four entries, and purse race, open to all four-year-olds and under. This is intended for Sweetheart and Phil Thompson.

A Large Importation of Percherons.—The steamer France, of the National line, which arrived in New York July 2d, brought 197 French Percheron horses consigned to Mr. Dunham, of Chicago, Mr. Cook, of Charleston, Ia., and others. This is said to be the largest consignment of horses ever imported by one vessel at New York. An officer of the vessel said that the animals, which are of very large frame and great strength, were imported for breeding purposes. A large number of this importation will be transported several hundred miles beyond Chicago. They were kept in separate stalls and arrived in good condition.

Com. N. W. Kittson, of St. Paul, Minnesota, has invested some $200,000 in horseflesh, among the most noted of which are Revenue (formerly Pilgrim), by Smuggler, dam by Daniel Lambert, for which he paid $13,000; Von Arnim (2:22), by Sentinel, dam by Blood's Black Hawk, $10,000; Lady Rolfe (2:22), by Tom Rolfe, dam a pacer, $10,000; So So (2:17¼), $10,000; Fanny Witherspoon (2:19¾), $8,000; and many others ranging from $200 to $5,000. Mr. Kittson's stables have been fitted up at a cost of $50,000, while his residence cost in the neighborhood of $100,000.

There are eighty-four entries for the Cleveland Club July races. They show a greater number and faster horses than were ever before collected at a meeting here. The only California horse entered is Overman, in the 2:29 class. The other trotters entered in this class are Kate, Taylor, Rollo, Dick Ergen, Largess, Willis Wood, Big Ike, Valiant, London and Strero. In a special race, Clingstone, Edwin Thorn, J. B. Thomas, So So and Alley will contest. Little Brown Jug will pace to beat his record—2:11½.

The Grand Central Trotting Circuit opened at Pittsburg, Pennsylvania, on the 11th of July, and continued till the 14th. The Chicago meeting opens on the 15th July. Then comes Cleveland, O., July 25th to 28th, inclusive; Buffalo, N. Y., August 1st to 4th; Rochester, N. Y., August 8th to 11th; Utica, N. Y., August 15th to 18th; Poughkeepsie, N. Y., August 22d to 25th, and closes at Hartford, Conn., August 29th to September 1st.

The enormous value of first-class trotting stock is almost beyond belief. Thus it is estimated that the produce of Miss Russell, dam of Maud S., consisting of nine sons and daughter, would readily command upwards of $160,000 cash if offered for sale in open market. Her daughter, Cora Belmont, gained a record of 2:24½ at Hartford recently, and it is said she can beat 2:20.

The races that were held at Galt, Sacramento county, on the Fourth of July, passed off very successfully. The first was a trot between two district horses, Bird and Senator—Bird won the first heat, and Senator the two final heats and race. Best time, 2:58 and 3:01. A half-mile dash was then arranged between Mary Ellen and Eittle George, which was won by the latter in 56 seconds.

## LUCKY B.'S DAY.

It was very unchristian-like in the Chicago *Times* to remark that "the track and all the surroundings (on the 30th of June) were afloat. A life preserver was almost a necessity for the unfortunates who were compelled to ride on a West Division street car, as the water was little less than neck-deep in the ditch between the landing and the gate. After that seaport had been reached, eleven policemen, part of them belonging to Pinkerton, and the remainder, perhaps, to the city, inspected the ticket or badge, and then the journey to the grand stand or club house began. For some portion of the distance the planks had not floated away, but as the approach to the grand stand was made the footing was very uncertain. Large sections of the walk were floating hither and yon, and a misguided step would cause the mixture of rain and mud to fly between the crevices and all over the horseman's raiment. Then, as a matter of necessity, profanity prevailed, and when the entire crowd, if crowd it could be called, was finally mustered, it is doubtful whether a careful census would have brought the number of noses up to one thousand. There was a solitary single carriage in the field, the occupants of which cared little about the pool-box, but the majority of the spectators were composed of professional sports and gentlemen from Senegambia.

A reporter for the *Times* asked a well-known Chicago gentleman, who is a great admirer of horses and the owner of several good ones, why it was that the people of the Northern States—the business men—could not be induced to take an interest in running horses; and why Chicago people would not drive to the race track to see the flyers, despite the weather.

"My friend," was the response, "the answer is very easy. North of the old imaginary Mason and Dixon's line the people are thoroughly practical. They want something they can use when they invest their money, and do not propose to pay something for nothing. Now, why, they argue, should we take an interest in a running horse? Blood is good enough, in its way, but a running horse is of no account only on the track. He is a vicious, unmanageable, treacherous brute, requiring constant attention, and, when the season is over, can you tell me what he amounts to? On the other hand, the trotter is always good. He may be broken down as a purse winner, but after that he can be used as a family horse, and then, perhaps, he may be attached to a delivery wagon; but until he goes the way of all horseflesh, a trotting horse can always pay his feed. That is why, I think, the practical Northern sense does not take kindly to an animal that can be beaten by a greyhound or a jack-rabbit, that is always vicious, and takes 'two niggers' to hold it, one to ride it, and three to groom it."

After listening to this oracular exposition of the reasons why only a thousand people were present to witness four good races, the reporter wended around and looked at the pool buyers. The Chicago man is not as numerous as he was. Only two days ago he drove out tandem and placed his money on Punster. Yesterday he was more mild-mannered, and came along in a plain hack, without a liveried driver, and wagered the bulk of his remaining wealth on Ascender. Ascender won the other day. He did not yesterday. To-day, if these same reports come out, any one of the private carriages of Superintendent Lake, of the West Division Railway, will be good enough. Unprejudiced people will always have a fear, however, that Ascender was a straight winner, though he was ridden veey carelessly on the home-stretch, and even then it was head and head. From the reporters' outlook over the wire, he was a square head in front, but the good judges thought otherwise. The California colt, undoubtedly one of the finest horses on the turf, made a wonderful burst of speed on the home run, but the decision was far from satisfactory, nevertheless. In the pools, Ascender brought $100 and field $30.

## ANSWERS TO CORRESPONDENTS.

Editor Breeder: Will you to please state in your paper the amount of Areca to be given for worms, and what it should be mixed with, and oblige A. Reader.

Ans.—The dose for a young dog should be 3 grains of the freshly powdered nut for each 12 pounds of the dog's weight. The best plan is to put the powder in some savory broth and give at once. If left to stand the bitter taste of the nut impregnates the broth and the dog will refuse to touch it. In case your dog will not take broth, place the powder in the center of a thin piece of meat. Roll it up in the form of a small ball and allow the dog to bolt it about two hours. After giving the nut give an average dose of castor oil. This is a sure cure for all small worms.

A bets B that Ross will get more votes in the Democratic Convention than Sharpstein, for the position of Judges of the Supreme Court:

| | First Ballot. | Second. | Third. |
|---|---|---|---|
| Ross | 154 | 176 | 233 |
| Sharpstein | 154 | 187 | 211 |

On the 4th ballot, Sharpstein, 247.
229 will elect.
B wins.

Sacramento, June 26, 1882.

Editor Breeder and Sportsman: The last paragraph of Rule 52, Page 47, P. C. B. H. Rules, is somewhat ambiguous. Supposing my horse has the best of it for second money up to the last heat, thus:

A—3....1....1
B—1....2....dist.
C—2....3....2

The above summary relates to second and third place. Must distance be waived in this case, or only when they are equal up to the last heat? Who is entitled to second money in above summary? Yours, E. F. S.

B is entitled to second money.

Mr. Seth Green, the famous fish culturist, asserts that an acre of water can be made to pay as much as an acre of land.—*City and Country.*

We should smile! A milkman, for instance, would make $44,935.27 out of an acre of water without making any visible inroad upon the supply, while a cock-tail contractor could discount him and run a saw-mill besides.—*Columbus Sunday Capital.*

Many of the interior clubs are taking to the clay pigeons instead of the bird itself, as the imitation gives as much excitement to the shooter and the spectators without entailing an extra expense and the mutilation of the birds. The demand has been so large that the supply is not equal to the occasion, but the agents, Messrs. Pierce & Co., of Oakland, now expect a consignment that will enable them to meet all orders.

At the Alameda County Sportsman's Club at Littlefield on Saturday last, there was a series of clay pigeon matches that ended only with the giving out of the birds. In the first shoot there were fourteen entries, fifteen birds each, fifteen yards rise. Mr. Crellin won first money, Messrs. Tuttle and Schnuble tying on thirteen birds each, divided second and third, and Mr. Adams broke twelve birds and secured fourth money.

# ROWING.

In professional rowing this week the noticeable event was the Whitehall (double scull) race on Sunday last between Peter Burns and J. Desmond and Fred Smith and Sam Watkins, for $100 a side. The course was from the Oakland ferry slips, around Goat Island and return. No stiffer pull could be desired, as the ebb tide was running strong and the water in the stream was choppy. Burns and Desmond, being professional boatmen who have been pulling Whitehall boats all their lives, it was regarded by the watermen as a foregone conclusion that the South End boys would be disgraced. It was not even taken into account that Smith and his mate had had a very light and fast boat made for the occasion. A week before the race two to one was freely offered on the watermen, but the betting dropped to more rational figures before the morning of the race, and was even, when the men took their places for the start. John F. Sullivan, of the Pioneer Club, acted as Referee. The start was fair. In the first 100 yards Smith and Watkins drew away half a length from their opponents, but the watermen, by a spurt, caught and passed them. They never got clear water between the boats, however, and at the end of the first quarter began to fall back again. The rowing of the South End boys was incomparably superior to that of their opponents, who indulged in that peculiar method of feathering their sculls so dear to the hearts of professional Whitehall boatmen. The race was a fine illustration of the well-known fact that a man may be all his life on the water and know very little about racing. Instead of steering southeast so as to weather the Island, toward which the tide was running with great force, Burns and his mate kept directly east, and the result was that off the Island they had to stem the full force of the current. Smith and mate allowed for the tide and made a fine turn, the current just carrying them past the rocks and giving them such an advantage that the remainder of the affair was a procession. On the last half mile Smith stood up in his boat several times, but whether for the purpose of making his opponents ridiculous or merely to stretch his legs, he did not state on landing. The Whitehall men were beaten a full hundred yards. After the race there was some talk of changing boats and making another match, but so far nothing has come of it. A change in the style of rowing would be more essential to the success of the watermen than a change in their boat, though they evidently were not as well boxed as their opponents.

Mr. Yale, who kindly acted as Referee in the city's regatta on the 4th of July, defends himself against the criticism on his decision which appeared in these columns last week. The Rowing Editor of the BREEDER AND SPORTSMAN has no hesitation in repeating the criticism of Mr. Yale's action, which comment only went to the moderate degree of condemning the decision as "very severe and hardly fair." It was very severe, because had the race been a regular professional match for the championship of the world, Mr. Yale's interpretation of the rules could not have been more rigid. It was "hardly fair" for several reasons. In the first place, the South End crew, which was the one fouled, not only neglected while in their boat to lodge a complaint against the Pioneer crew, but actually, in the hearing of the writer, stated that they did not wish to urge any objections against the Pioneers. A majority of the judges, if not the whole number, were in favor of giving the race to the Pioneers, and under these circumstances Mr. Yale's decision could not have been regarded as anything else than "hardly fair." The reasons might be multiplied, however, in support of the mild criticism to which the Referee objects. Mr. Yale will not deny that the object of the regatta was not to give any crew a prize by the virtue of technical objections. The affair was intended to be a popular pastime, and it was the wish of the citizens connected with it that the best crews should carry off the trophies. That the Pioneers proved themselves the best crew in the disputed race, could not have been doubted for a moment. The yacht Ariel lay right across the course and the Pioneers had the outside section in the full face of the wind when it was blowing with sufficient force to make the outside station a heavy handicap. To have gone outside the yacht would have been equivalent to throwing away the race, and the bowman accordingly allowed the two rival boats to shoot ahead and then steered inshore for the smooth water. The stroke side of the Pioneers' boat being stronger than the bow side, the boat ran up into the strong wind, and went straight towards the South End men, who, instead of avoiding a collision, pulled straight across the course, so as to cut off the Pioneers. A collision was thus rendered unavoidable and the boats came together. After the disentanglement the Pioneers, who were a hundred yards behind the Ariel boat, rowed strongly to the stakeboat, turned it ahead of the Ariels, and came home in the lead. Once more the yacht Ariel obstructed them, and nearly brought the race to a sudden and disastrous end for the Pioneers. The bowman just managed to clear the yacht, but in doing so his crew lost so much time that the Ariels once more shot to the front a clear length. Again the unlucky Pioneers gave chase, and after a desperate race crossed the line winners by a few feet. There was considerable money wagered that the Pioneers would beat the Ariels, for it was conceded by all oarsmen that the South Enders were out of the race. That the Pioneers did beat the Ariels, and beat them under extraordinary disadvantages, there could be no question, and when Mr. Yale, after seeing the race, disqualified the Pioneers, though not solicited to do so by the South Enders, he did an injustice to a plucky crew, and to a lot of people who put their money on a square contest without any consideration of technicalities. Mr. Yale says that he visited the South End boat house after the race, and examined the injured boat before giving his decision. It is difficult to see why he should have taken that trouble after the crew in the injured boat had rowed up to the Judge's launch, and plainly announced that they had no charge to lodge against the winning crew. The fact of any member of the crew holding up his hand at the moment of the collision does not outweigh what the whole crew stated after it had been called up by the Referee, and asked whether it wished to claim another race. It is hard to see how, under a strict construction of the rules, Mr. Yale can defend his decision, which was in antagonism to that of a majority of the Judges. It does not seem to be required by the rules that a Referee shall follow up a crew, and almost insist on their preferring a claim of "foul" against a rival crew, when they voluntarily decline to take that advantage. The great hardship, however, lies in the fact that the race was judged as if had been a well-conducted match race, when, in fact, it was only a helter-skelter affair. None of the boats started on strictly even terms. Without anchored skiffs to hold the sterns of the racing crafts, it was impossible to give them a fair send-off in the strong wind and tide. When they were sent off, they had to work their way around a vessel lying straight in their path, and to hold a crew to strict account for a plainly accidental foul under such circumstances is certainly, in the opinion of the Rowing Editor of the BREEDER AND SPORTSMAN, "very severe and hardly fair."

Hanlan is again able to walk about. His confidence in himself has evidently not been much shaken by his fit, for he issues the following challenge:

"I will row any five men in the world two miles straight away, or two miles and turn from $1,000 to $2,000 aside. I will row these five men after lapse of forty-eight hours (two full days) of each other on any suitable water on the continent of America. The challenge is open to the whole world." Hanlan further adds, if he could get on these matches in America, he would forego for the present his intended visit to Australia.

The London Sportsman of the 28th ult. says it is difficult to believe that the Hilsdales are the best amateur crew America can produce. In a row under favorable circumstances yesterday, they got no place on the boat, the time of the oars was most irregular, and the work was left entirely to the arms. Notwithstanding the peculiarities which offend the critical British eye, the various regatta committees continue to bar the Hilsdales.

London, July 6.—The Sportsman says of the preceding: "We are utterly astonished at the action of the Committee of the Amateur Rowing Association in passing a resolution touching the status of the Hilsdale crew. It feels with pain almost the degradation of the Association in not affording simple justice to the visitors. The entries of the Hilsdales in one or two regattas have been duly accepted, and now they find themselves thrown out of the entire category of amateurs, though they have held the proud position of amateur champions of America for four successive years. It would be surprising if the resolution should debar them from rowing in regattas for which they are entered. If so, the framers of the resolution will incur a heavy odium and reproach. The Sportsman specially appeals to amateur oarsmen generally to decline to share the shame.

At the Marlow regatta the Hilsdale crew beat the Marlow crew by a clear length. Directly after the start the Hilsdales fouled the Marlows badly. The latter, however, did not claim a foul. The Hilsdales went rapidly ahead, and after leading at one time by a hundred yards, won easily by a length and a half. The Referee did not insist on the foul being preferred.

"It is pretty safe to predict that the new Yale stroke will not cause the promised revolution in boating," remarks the New Haven Palladium, "for a graduate of sixteen years' standing writes: 'Tell the boys it served 'em right for taking up that old, exploded, short-clipping stroke. The moral of Harvard's victory is simply that Yale tried an experiment and failed. She deserves credit for her pluck, but the less said of her discretion the better. She had the skill, muscle and endurance requisite to success, but her powers were misapplied. It was a pretty race, nevertheless.'" According to the Hartford Times, "Yale, notwithstanding its supposed superiority in weight and muscle, was beaten in the race this year by the better stroke of the Harvard crew."

## THE DECISION ON THE SHELL RACE.

ROWING EDITOR BREEDER AND SPORTSMAN: In accordance with the usual custom in rowing circles, I see you consider it necessary to criticize the referee in the late race as well as the contestants. It accords with my former experience in this direction that those against whom a decision rests are those who complain or feel aggrieved, so it is scarcely worth while to enter into an argument on every occasion. The referee interprets the rules to the best of his ability in as fair a manner as he can, and in this instance, as in others, I have endeavored to do strict justice to all.

As the criticism this time comes from an oarsman and writer, I should be pleased to have him give his interpretation of the rules which would admit of a decision being given in any other way than it was in the case of the four-oared shell race on the 4th.

I have not the slightest objection to giving my reasons for ruling as I did. Three boats started; Pioneers outside, Ariels in middle, South Ends inside.

Rule 5 of the laws of boat racing says: "Each boat shall keep its own water throughout the race, and any boat departing from its own water (when racing) shall be responsible for all damages she may occasion."

Rule 6 says: "A boat's own water is the straight course parallel with those of the other contesting boats from the station assigned to it at the starting to the finish."

According to these rules all departure of a competitor from his own water and proper course is at the peril of instant disqualification if touched while out of his true course. When the Pioneers came in collision, they had rowed diagonally out of their line—gone past (astern) of the Ariels and rowed into the water of the South Ends, who had inside station, while the Pioneers belonged outside. Therefore, no matter what the other circumstances of the collision, according to Rules 5 and 6, which contains the vital principles of the improved code of boat racing, the Pioneers were at fault.

Rule 8 says: No fouling whatever shall be allowed; the boat committing a foul shall be disqualified.

Now, the foul was unmistakable and the boat committing the foul was unmistakable. A man in the South End boat threw up his hand as the usual signal that a foul was claimed. The boats went on, the Pioneers came in first, Ariels a few feet behind, and South Ends far behind. I decide that the Pioneers are disqualified for the foul, and that the Ariels and South Ends row over at a future day to decide the race. You think the Pioneers ought to have had it, because the foul "did not interfere with the Ariels, who were beaten on their merits, and in any event the South Ends could not have won."

You say the South Enders waived all claim to the money and declined to enter a protest. You are mistaken. They protested when their Captain threw up his hand at the moment of collision. They stopped and asked me if there was second money in the race when they came in. I said no, and they rowed off. The Ariels protested and claimed first money on the ground that the Pioneers rounded the wrong stake. This the rules allow them to do, so that claim was disallowed.

I understand your criticism, I was wrong because no formal claim of foul was made by the South Ends before they left their boats. They held up their hands at the collision; they asked if there was a second prize. But I maintain no claim is necessary where there is unmistakable evidence of a foul where it influences the race. Rule 8, above quoted, makes it imperative on the umpire to disqualify the fouling boat.

At first I thought the race belonged to the Ariels, the Pioneers being out, but I reserved my decision in order to look at the South End boat. After all the races were over I did look at the boat. Her rail-beading was broken, the cloth cover torn and the boat bruised. A hole was in her bottom on the other side. The crew claimed this was done by the collision; that the after compartment had filled with water; that the steering wire had caught in the broken moulding, and that the boat would not steer.

I had seen the collision, which was evident to all. I saw the marks on the boat, and I saw water poured out of the hole where she was struck. The hole in the bottom on the other side may have been made by the Pioneers' boat, or may not; but that in the canvas was, without doubt.

Now, there is no doubt the race was influenced by this collision. The South Ends boat was made to leak and their steering gear disarranged through no fault of their own. Therefore they did not row with equal chances with the Ariels. As to the ability of the men to row the other crews, that's none of my business—the result decides those questions. Nor have I a right to say the leak would not let in water or the mouldings would not catch the wire. The fact remains that the boat sprung a leak after the collision.

In view of all these facts, I ruled that the Pioneers had committed a foul and were disqualified. The South Ends had been wronged, and should have a right to a fair contest. That the foul was accidental, is admitted, but it was none the less a foul. You think "considering the manner in which the regatta was conducted, the interpretation of the rules was very severe and hardly fair."

I do not know what you mean by the first part of that sentence. The regatta was conducted, as far as I know, under rowing rules. As to delays and all that, I express no opinion, but with interpretation of the rules I should decide according to the rules fairly criticized. If in my decision is unjust, please point out where it is so. All rowing men are interested in a fair discussion of such subjects as this, for their elucidation serves as precedent. Had I given the Pioneers the race because they came in first, it would have been unjust to the South Ends, whose boat had been damaged so as to leak by the first boat in. Had I given it to the Ariels, it would have been unjust to the South Ends, who had been interfered with by the Pioneers. I could not give it to the South Ends because of the collision, because that would have been unjust to the Ariels and contrary to rule. I could not let the Pioneers join in the second race, because Section B of Rule 13 says: "To order the boats engaged in the race, other than the boat committing the foul, to row once again on the same or another day."

You may maintain that I should not decide a foul unless appealed to. But I say an appeal may be by either signal or word of mouth, and signal was made. Again, read Rule 8, given above, and tell me, for my own instruction and the benefit of others, what else could have been done, all the circumstances being considered. I am willing to rest under an accusation of error of judgment, but not one of unfairness, for I considered this question from all its bearings, and decided according to the arguments I give herewith.

Respectfully,　　　　　CHAS. G. YALE.

# YACHTING.

The Lively is once more in commission.

Mr. Blakiston was out in the Virgin last Sunday.

The sloop Nellie has been brought back from up river.

No more races announced just now.

There is a Yale Yacht Club now at New Haven.

The Sunnyside is a new Yacht Club of Winthrop, Mass.

Two of our fleet are still "outside." The Casco and Nellie are both south yet on a cruise.

A. B. Spreckels, of the Bohemian Yacht Club, has gone to the Sandwich Islands.

Mr. H. B. Underhill, Jr., of the S. F. Y. C., has gone to Puget Sound on a trip for his health.

The Aggie made the trip up from Monterey in twenty-four hours.

The Solita is back from up river. Captain Chittenden is the most enthusiastic sailor among the yachtsmen.

The Frolic got becalmed Sunday, an unusual thing at this season of the year.

The New York Yacht Club Schooner Intrepid is coming back from Europe, on account of all health of the owner.

The famous schooner Dauntless has changed hands, and her new owner will go to Europe on her.

Between sunset and colors yachts should carry a night pennant.

When yachts pass each other the juniors should salute first.

When squadrons of different clubs meet on a cruise salutes should be exchanged only by the commanding officers.

The American cat boat Gleam was beaten by the Britisher on British waters.

A 35 ft. keel and 45 ft. over all cutter being built in Boston, is to have $3,000 pounds of lead on her keel.

Ingalls', new plunger, built by Stone, has the historic name of Restless. She is a fine boat.

The Ariel has not been put in proper trim yet. Captain Turner is very busy.

The Whitewing came out with a new set of sails on Sunday.

There, we knew it was coming! A South Carolina man has named his yacht "Oscar Wilde." She ought to have a lead keel to stand up well under such a name.

The yawl Fleetwing has been carried on a ship's deck to New Tacoma, Puget Sound, where her owner, Mr. Cook, now resides.

Berry's Elia will be all right again pretty soon. Jack Caswell, her builder, is at work on her The cushions, mattresses, etc., were saved without being injured.

Yachts in commission should hoist their colors at 8 A. M., and haul them down at sunset, taking time from the senior officer present.

The famous old sloop Julia never took kindly to a schooner rig She sailed better when swinging a 64 ft. boom and a jib 40 ft. on the foot.

A cutter being built East is described as being as deep in the hold as an artesian well. Yes, and she will draw almost as much water.

Instead of large schooner yachts being built now-a-days, the tendency is to steam yachts· With small yachts however, sailing yachts will always remain the favorites.

The Larchmont Yacht Club has taken in more new members this season than any of the Eastern clubs. She has a large membership and fine headquarters on Long Island Sound.

During the yacht races East there are in danger of thunder squalls, something we never think of here. We have downright good strong breezes, but no provoking thunder squalls in which to douse everything and scud under bare poles.

In order to add an iron keel of 4380 pounds to the sloop yacht Guandeline, a full set of new floor timber was put in to strengthen the boat. We have heard of lots of lead added lately in this way, but have heard of no new floor timber. Indeed we have heard of numerous leaks.

At the Ladies' Day Regatta of the Atlantic Yacht Club a prize was awarded to the winning yacht in each class, the prizes being all alike. They consisted of neat gold lace pins, with the flag of the club attached in enamel, and were presented to the favorite lady in each winning yacht.

It is not generally understood. but it is a fact, that the American cup when won does not belong to the owners of the vessel winning it, but to the club she represents, and the condition of keeping it open to be sailed for by all organized yacht clubs, of all foreign countries, is forever attached to it, thus making it perpetually a challenge cup for friendly competition between foreign countries.

One of the handsomest boats ever built in this city has just been completed to order of Mr. I. Gutte by Burns & Eneas, the Mission street boat builders. She is for a custom house boat for a new Mexican custom house on the Gulf of Tehuantepec—Tonalá. She is 30 feet long, 8 feet beam, and is coppered. She has two masts and sails. She is copper fastened, has a brass keel-board half-inch thick, and has knees, rowlocks, yoke, etc. She is to be propelled by six oars. She looks like a regular little dandy yacht, and is the best built craft we have seen for many a day.

The match between the Gleam and the Mocking Bird was decided on the Solent on the 3d inst., and resulted in the success of the English boat. The Gleam is a center-board Rhode Island cat-boat, 25 feet 6 inches long and 11 feet 2 inches beam. The Mocking Bird is a new boat, built almost on purpose to race with the Gleam, by Stockham & Prickett, of Southampton. She is 30 feet long, with a beam 10 feet 6 inches, is a keel boat, with a large spread of canvas. If the above match was sailed without time allowance the extra length of the English boat gave her a decided advantage.

The one gun start has been tried by the Atlantic Club, but according to the *Spirit of the Time*, does not seem to have been satisfactory. It says:

"The advocates of the 'one-gun start' will be delighted to know that the gentleman in charge of the race, Mr. H. C. Wintringham, adopted it on this occasion in order, as he said, to avoid the trouble of timing the yachts as they started, and possibly for the purpose of seeing how it would work; but they will not be as well pleased to learn that the result showed, as it always will show, its extreme unfairness. Of the seven yachts in the first four classes who were sent off at 3.39, only five had got across when, at 3.44, the signal for the rest to go was given, and of the nineteen which were included in the four last classes who were sent off at 3.39, only five had got across when, at 3.44, the signal for the rest to go was given, and six got over inside of five minutes."

A CLOSE FINISH.—The Seawanhaka Yacht Club, of New York, is naturally a Corinthian club, and has set a good example to the other clubs of the United States in the matter of amateur racing. Its Corinthian regatta came off on the 7th ult. We have not space for details, but the following were the results:

**SCHOONERS.**

| Name. | Start. | Finish. | Elapsed Time. | Corrected Time. |
|---|---|---|---|---|
| | H. M. S. | H. M. S. | H. M. S. | H. M. S. |
| Albatross | 11 35 00 | 4 55 15 | 5 20 15 | .... |
| Clytie | 11 35 00 | 4 33 40 | 4 58 40 | .... |
| Louisa | 11 35 00 | Not timed. | | |

**FIRST CLASS SLOOPS.**

| | | | | |
|---|---|---|---|---|
| Gracie | 11 36 00 | 4 16 15 | 4 41 15 | 4 41 15 |
| Fanny | 11 36 00 | 4 24 12 | 4 49 12 | 4 42 03 |

**SECOND CLASS SLOOPS.**

| | | | | |
|---|---|---|---|---|
| Eclipse | 11 35 00 | 4 32 10 | 4 57 10 | |
| Clytie | 11 32 37 | 4 39 15 | 5 06 48 | 5 06 48 |
| Vixen | 11 35 00 | 4 40 57 | 5 14 57 | |
| Vixen | 11 35 00 | 4 35 15 | 5 00 15 | |

**THIRD CLASS SLOOPS.**

| | | | | |
|---|---|---|---|---|
| Wave | 11 32 48 | 4 05 17 | 4 32 33 | |
| Schemer | 11 32 22 | 4 05 44 | 4 33 22 | |
| Volante | 11 33 32 | 4 34 00 | 5 00 47 | |

**FOURTH CLASS SLOOPS.**

| | | | | |
|---|---|---|---|---|
| Gael | 11 32 30 | 3 30 00 | 3 45 20 | |
| Amazon | 11 35 00 | 3 31 40 | 3 56 40 | |
| Vivien | 11 32 00 | 3 36 00 | 4 01 00 | |

The winners are the Clytie, Eclipse, Schemer, Gael and the Gracie. A protest was filed against the Gracie for carrying a balloon jib contrary to rules. A feature was the close contest between the well known Wave and Schemer, for under a fresh breeze the Wave crossed the finish line 27 seconds in advance of the other, but the elapsed time put the Schemer at the front by 13 seconds.

## THE GUN.

AMENDMENTS TO THE GAME LAWS.—The Secretary of the California State Sportsman's Association has had printed the proposed amendments to section 628 of the Penal Code, which will be enclosed to the Supervisors of every county in the State. The amendments are designed to rectify an oversight of the Legislature in failing to pass a law for the protection of female deer and does, and reads as follows:

Section 1. Every person who shall, after the passage of this ordinance, pursue, hunt, take, kill or destroy any female deer or doe, shall be guilty of a misdemeanor, and upon conviction thereof shall be punished by fine of not less than $50, nor more than $300, or imprisonment in the County Jail for not less than thirty days, nor more than six months, or by both such fine and imprisonment.

Sec. 2. Every deer in possession, exposed or offered for sale shall show conclusive evidence of its sex, and proof of failure to comply with the provisions of this section shall be prima facie evidence in any prosecution for a violation of Section 1 of this ordinance, that such deer in possession, exposed or offered for sale was a female deer or doe.

Sec. 3. Sections 1 and 2 of the ordinance shall not have the effect to repeal any of the provisions of Chapter 1, of Title 15 of the Penal Code of the State of California, which provisions were in force at the date of the passage of this ordinance.

VERY QUESTIONABLE "SPORT."—Dove shooting is all the go at this time, and everybody that owns or can borrow a gun is out on some pass or other. The birds are very numerous in some places, and bags of from 75 to 150 a day to the gun have been made since the 1st. One party of four young men went up beyond Folsom on Sunday and killed 380 birds, which rotted in their pockets and had to be thrown away. We hear of other parties killing quite as many, and do not doubt it, as one may shoot from daylight till dark on a good dove pass, almost without cessation. On both Saturday and Sunday last there were not less than seventy-five men and boys banging away at the birds along the roads and in the grain fields between this city and Alder Creek. A desire to hunt is very natural and proper, but the exertion that some make to kill game they cannot use, is certainly reprehensible. It is about equivalent to granting a stranger the privilege of picking a handful of fruit from your orchard and then for him to cut down the tree or scatter its load upon the ground to decay. Or for the traveler—after having slaked his thirst—to empty the well and turn the water to waste. One of these days the class of shooters will be compelled to hunt sparrows, if at all, for they will have nothing else to kill. We trust they may live long enough to realize how senseless, to use a mild term, had been their course.

"Mr. Peter Reid, of Pauquier county, says that a few days ago as he was talking to a friend, he noticed a little snake, about a foot long, and before killing it he turned it over with the muzzle of his gun. To his surprise the snake ran up the gun-barrel, and he could not get it to come out, so he let it remain. As he was going home he saw a hawk flying overhead and raised his gun and fired at it. The hawk was not hurt, but seeing the snake in the air, started toward it and caught it on the fly. Mr. Peter Reid is a brother of a magistrate and a church member." The above, taken from a Virginia City paper, suggests the inquiry as to whether Sam Davis, Esq., is not on a visit to his former haunts. The story is well worthy of his imaginative pen.

A FUNNY POINTER'S JOKE.—The dog had pointed at snakes without ever once making a mistake for three years, when one day last September he accompanied his master on a walk through a particularly stony field, where snakes were known to be plentiful. Suddenly the dog, who was walking just in front of the huntsman, stopped and pointed so earnestly that it was evident he had almost stepped on a snake. The huntsman sprang back with immense celerity—for he was a very nervous man—and in so doing tripped and fell with a tremendous crash. The dog, merely glancing around to see what was the matter, resumed his point until his master had picked himself up, calmed his mind, and resolved·to kill the snake. Advancing with that direful purpose, he discovered, not a snake, but a cast-off snake's skin at which the dog had pointed. The moment the man discovered the trick the dog threw himself on his back, rolled over and over in an uncontrollable fit of laughter, and finally sitting down on his haunches, laughed till the tears rolled down his cheeks. He knew a snake's skin from a live snake perfectly well, and his purpose in pointing at the snake was simply to give his master a good fright.

The picturesque mountain peak above Santa Rosa is a favorite haunt of the grizzly, and is their incursions from St. Helena into Knight's Valley they have played such havoc with the lambs and sheep, that the ranchmen have organized a regular hunt for pelts and bears' grease.

From the *Photographic News* we learn that M. Marey presented recently to the Royal Academy of Sciences at Paris, some pictures of birds on the wing, secured in the camera with an exposure, it is said, of 1-700 of a second. Mr. Muybridge's "Animals in Motion" includes birds on the wing, and he shows, what we believe, has never before been depicted, a bird in the air with its wings below its body. We have not seen M. Marey's apparatus, but it is cleverly constructed like a rifle, so as to be capable of being raised to the eye to take aim and expose. It is on the principle of M. Janssen's revolver, which makes a series of rapid exposures one after the other, and with this M. Marey is able to secure the bird in various positions. A chronograph regulates the periods of exposure, which may be as brief as 1-1,500 of a second. M. Marey proposes to combine a series of the photographs thus taken, after the manner of Maybridge, and in this way to analyze a bird's movements and demonstrate it in motion, as the American photographer has done with his galloping horse.

Messrs. Robert Liddle, J. M. Bassford and F. J. Bassford, in two hours' shooting, near Vacaville, on Saturday last put part of the succeeding day, succeeded in bagging 232 doves.

The Cosmopolitan Club will indulge in pigeon-shooting, at San Bruno, on Sunday next.

J. D. Lucas, of St. Louis, Missouri, and who is a crack wing shot, is on a visit to this city.

H. A. Hahn and J. F. Simms, in hunting at Pleasanton, Sunday last, found doves very scarce.

## THE RIFLE.

SNAP SHOOTING AT MONTEREY.

A number of gentlemen, who spend their Saturdays and Sundays at Hotel Del Monte, have taken up snap shooting with 22-calibre rifles, and under the direction and encouragement of Col. Fletcher are making rapid progress in the art of hitting. Carey Friedlander, Austin Tubbs, Alfred Tubbs, Will Tubbs, Capt. R. C. Hooker, Dick Hammond, Major Hammond, J. W. Brown, and others are among the number, with the greatest amount of enthusiasm centered in Friedlander, Austin Tubbs, Hammond and Brown. More than fifty per cent. of hits have been attained, and all the gentlemen are infatuated with the facility of aim which the practice gives them. Pistol practice also is in favor, and any of the gentlemen named would be dangerous antagonists to open fire on with the revolver. Numbers of the ladies also find pleasant recreation in both rifle and revolver practice, and healthful, invigorating exercise combined with it. As we propose to make snap shooting a feature of this paper, we again invite correspondence on the subject from gentlemen who are interested in it.

## THE HUNT.

Frank Cooper killed a large panther or California lion in Bear Valley, Mariposa county, about a week since. Cooper had gone out one morning on a hunt, taking a valuable hunting dog with him. The lion jumped from the limb of a tree onto the dog's back, and after a short tussel with the canine demolished him. Cooper then killed the lion with a shot from his rifle. The beast measured nine feet and a half from the nose to the tip of its tail. The skin is of a light-brown color.

ANOTHER PANTHER STORY.—Last week we made note of the fact that Henry Meckel passed three panthers—or California lions—on Rush Creek, and that the animals seemed quite tame and made no attempt to get out of the way. The following regarding one of this species of animals is certainly a most remarkable occurrence and is vouched for by Supervisor F. Bates, an authority which no one will doubt: Recently in the vicinity of Minesville, Trinity county, California, some neighboring Chinese called at the cabin of Jonathan Smith and wanted to borrow a rifle to shoot a dog, which they said had been killing their chickens. Mr. Smith had no gun, and so informed them. Next day the Chinese again visited Smith's cabin and wanted him to "come quick; look see, dog eatee chicken!" Mr. Smith went with them and to his surprise found a large panther in the brush devouring a chicken and which refused to leave its dainty meal. Smith grabbed the panther by the tail and wanted the Chinamen to hit it over the head with a shovel, but they either did not understand or were too cowardly to tackle the beast. Mr. Smith let go his tail-hold with one hand, still gripping firmly with the other, stooped and picked up a rock with which he succeeded in breaking the animal's body. It was a daring deed and one which deserves to go on record. The apparent harmlessness of the panthers at this time is accounted for on the supposition that the animals are nearly starved.—*Trinity Journal.*

### SOMETHING ALWAYS HAPPENED.

I recently met an old friend, and we were relating bygone reminiscences to each other, when he said:

"Did I ever tell you my snake story ?"

"No."

"Well, then, I will tell it now. You are aware that I am a great sufferer from asthma, and to obtain relief from it I have been everywhere that I ever advised to go, except to heaven. Amongst other places, the lower part of the State of Georgia, out in the 'pine country', was recommended to me, so thither I went. I always kept a few hounds about me, and at that time had a bitch, and two puppies, about twelve months old, that were beauties. My new neighbors praised their looks, and said: 'Maybe you can kill three old foxes that have been in this section for twenty years, have been run at least ten thousand times, but something always happens to facilitate their escape.'

"After much boasting of the good qualities of my dogs and my prowess as a hunter, and a promise to furnish them some venison from the aforesaid foxes, I decided to try my luck the first leisure moment. This occurred in a short time, and I found a good trail, jumping my deer in a short time. Putting spurs to my horse, I made for a stand, but in crossing a flat my horse stepped in an old stump hole and threw me about forty feet. This was 'something always happened,' number one.

"However, I had found exactly where they ran, and said to myself, I would be sure of them next time. I did not wait long for the next trial, just long enough for them to come back, when I started after them again. I put the dogs in at the same place, and they soon struck the trail, while I made for the stand, a few minutes after reaching which, the dogs passed me, but no deer. Upon examining the trail, I discovered the deer had slipped out as soon as they heard the dogs. 'Something always happened,' number two.

"It was a week before I got the chance to go again. I determined to put the dogs in, say not a word, and slip out for the stand. There was a little gall berry flat, near the middle of which the path run, and close by this path was a high bunch, near to a steep root. I got there in a hurry, jumped into the gall berries, and squatted. Listening intently, I thought I heard the hounds, and parting the gall berry bushes, I looked steadily up the path. As I did so, I felt something move under me, but thought it the movement of the bushes. About this time I heard the dogs, and saw the deer coming down the path. I got my gun all ready, and moved cautiously forward, when I felt a peculiar and unmistakable movement under me, and shouting: 'Snakes by thunder!' I leaped out. I looked over my shoulder as I went, and Mr. B., as I hope for heaven, I had been sitting upon a half bushel of the largest rattlesnakes in the state."

"Well, how about the deer ?"

"The deer! Oh, yes. Well, as soon as I could hold my gun on that pile of snakes, I emptied both barrels into it, and left, having come to the conclusion that 'something always happened,' and I never went back after those deer any more."—[C. A. B. in the American Field.

THE

# Breeder and Sportsman.

PUBLISHED BY THE

BREEDER AND SPORTSMAN PUBLISHING CO.

THE TURF AND SPORTING AUTHORITY OF THE
PACIFIC COAST.

**OFFICE, 508 MONTGOMERY STREET**
P. O. Box 1836.

*Five dollars a year; three dollars for six months; one dollar and a
half for three months. Strictly in advance*
*Money should be sent by postal order, draft or by registered letter.*
*Communications must be accompanied by the writer's name and address
not necessarily for publication, but as a private guarantee of good faith*

JOSEPH CAIRN SIMPSON,  - - -  EDITOR

SAN FRANCISCO,  - -  SATURDAY, JULY 15, 1882

## THE RACE TRACK AT MONTEREY.

When the Hotel Del Monte was built at Monterey, it was officially promulgated that a race course was to be one of the improvements. This was welcome intelligence, not merely to the devotees of the turf, as the people who frequent a Summer resort are more especially interested in the sport than those who have a more intimate connection with it.

There never was a finer natural location than is in the immediate vicinity of the hotel. The plateau, which extends from the northern front of the house, is admirably adapted for a course of a mile in circuit. In fact, the course could be made to rival that in Goodwood Park, and the famous ducal grounds are not a whit more attractive than those at Monterey can be made for racing.

The characteristics of an English course could be preserved, and, in place of the stereotyped American track, with the brown surface of plowed and harrowed earth, there could be a variety of courses. One by the side of the creek, which has worn a channel deep below the general lay of the ground, the banks umbrageous with shrubbery, and decked with a wealth of flowers such as Southern California can only show, would be just the thing for a two-year-old course. Straight running for three-quarters of a mile, with just enough of it hidden to add to the excitement when the sprinters were in sight. Then, afar off on the eastern side, there could be a Cup course marked, the horses vanishing from view under the pine and cypress trees, coming into sight in the vistas between the oaks, hidden for a time among the manzanitas, and then rushing into the stretch, and ending the race in plain sight of veranda and balcony.

There is a park-like picture in the foreground of the Hotel Del Monte. Lawns and parterres in the immediate vicinity of the house, wildness and repose only a short distance beyond. With training grounds such as could be marked out there, the morning gallops would be actually more interesting than the races of the evening. There would be flitting pictures in the early dawn which would entice the laziest from the couch. Even those who think that the night was made for something besides sleep would be compelled to await the morning gallops before retiring, and there would be an eager assemblage looking at the exhilarating brushes.

The grandest training ground in the world could be made on the plain which extends from the lawn in front of the hotel, between the creek which is on the west and the rivulet on the east. It could be marked into different courses, and without much outlay there could always be turf to gallop upon. And yet there is a question whether turf or harrowed ground is the best for horses to work over. The green, elastic turf compels the belief that it must be the best, and the differences of opinion will gain a score of supporters, but there are good reasons why the harrowed earth should not be so severe as the harder sod, and, with all due deference to the original ideas, we must give our preference for the disintegrated soil. Cut down to a depth which takes the jar off from the limbs, there is the least chance for concussion, and the only argument in favor of the other is that there is less sinking, and, consequently, less strain on the tendons. This can be obviated by harrowing to a

less depth, and, with the requirements of a better foothold, there can be little question of the benefits following. In either case, there can be courses made at Monterey which will meet the fancies of all parties, and either turf or track made suitable. But the whole cannot be bettered, and whether there is ground or turf to gallop over, there is a certainty that either will be good. Still more sure it is that there is not a place from Maine to Oregon which shows better facilities for a race course than Monterey, and the carrying out of the idea to build one there will conduce to the attractions. There is a grand chance in any event. The location could not be excelled. So far, the natural advantages have been improved, and with a race course such as will be built whenever it is determined to construct it, it will be the attraction of this famous watering place.

## THE STATE'S FAIRS.

The annual State and County Fairs which flourish so well in California are institutions modelled on the best features of the European and Eastern holiday gatherings, and are yet something entirely different from any gatherings for profit and pleasure that take place at stated periods in the older settled parts of the world. In England the old fairs are rapidly dying out, their places being filled by the grand expositions constantly taking place, and the great metropolitan and provincial cattle shows. The old English fair was either a horse fair, or a sheep fair, or a cattle fair, or a cheese fair, or an onion fair, or a miserable collection of gypsey wagons, roundabouts, "Old Aunt Sally," and all the other games by which the sharpers depleted the yokels' pockets of the spare cash earned at harvesting. One of the great horse fairs was held at Barnett, near London, and usually gathered together from eight to ten thousand head of horses of all grades, from the lordly Clydesdale and Shire horses to the miserable Shetland and Welsh ponies, not eleven hands high. The great sheep fair was held at Arnham, near Salisbury, and there it was no uncommon sight to see well filled sheep pens covering in all, not less than one hundred acres of ground. These fairs were not so much for exhibition and competition as for sale and exchange of cattle, sheep and other farm produce. They were not enlivened by horse races or athletic games, unless the impromptu trials of skill between rival herders can be dignified with the name of sport. The boxing and wrestling booths, run by some enterprising pugilist, afforded the people all the fun they wanted, and it was by putting on the gloves against all comers at county fairs that Jem Mace gained the skill and endurance that made him the foremost boxer in the world. Bartering all day and drinking all night were the rigidly adhered to programmes of English country fairs. It is a good job that they are things of the past. On the continent of Europe, the lace fairs, the glove fairs, the servants' hiring fairs, were all, as their names imply, gatherings for specific business, and not for sport or competitive exhibition. Here in California is where the county fairs flourish above all other places. The homes of the farmers are far apart, and the interchange of social pleasures consequently difficult. At the county fairs, people who have not seen each other for months meet and talk upon the subjects nearest to the farmer's heart. There they engage in friendly rivalry as to whose cattle, or sheep, or horses, or crops are the best, and there they learn much that is of great value in their business. There they see the newest inventions in labor-saving machinery, and keep level with the inventive genius of the entire world. Better than all this, they and their families have a pleasant period of rest and recreation. The horse races amuse and instruct the farmer, while his wife and daughters find pleasure in the pavilion, inspecting the handiwork of their friends and neighbors. The California county fair is an epitome of all that is purest and best in the lives of the people, and is the most admirable institution for business recreation and instruction that this country has ever seen. It is the direct result of the needs of the people,

and so well it fills those needs that we question if it will ever be superseded. It will enlarge and improve and extend its influence for good as the State becomes more thickly settled, and will ever be found in the van of popular thought and knowledge.

## THE CLOSING OF ENTRIES.

The first of August is not far off, and those who have horses to engage must soon make up their minds where they will place them. The trouble will be in the great number of classes to select among, where the trotters are to be provided for, and in the numerous stakes for the youngsters, racers and trotters, there can be little difficulty in finding a suitable place. It is rather a difficult thing at times to tell where the best places are, and whenever there is likely to be a bother on this score, our advice will be to stick them in every place there is an opening. The most acute turfmen are apt to make mistakes in selecting the classes for their horses to figure in, and it is nearly certain that those which are thought to be the hardest places prove the easier. It is not very rare for the slower classes to turn out faster than the others which are marked by several seconds difference, and the "2:40" to be filled by a gang which could more easily win in the races gauged by a dozen seconds of increased speed. Not unfrequently the "three-minute" proves a rare exhibition of speed, and the "2:30" about the slowest on the bill. Under all of these considerations, it appears to be the safest plan to make as many entries as there are places to engage, and to give every Fair in the circuit a trial. In the California programmes there are a variety of purses and classes. Racing, trotting and pacing are all provided for, and it must be rather bad luck if expenses cannot be got out of the trip. There is one thing which all will acknowledge, that there is no chance to win if entries are not made, and therefore the first step towards success is to make engagements.

## "DISTANCE WAIVED."

As will be seen from the query in another column, there is a question concerning the meaning of one of the rules in the Code of the Pacific Coast Blood-Horse Association. There can not be a doubt, however, as the waiving of distance in a final heat means that the distance-flag has no part to play in the last heat of a race. The wisdom of that provision will be evident when the question is given a little consideration. There can be nothing gained by the horse which distances the others in a final heat, excepting that there might be money depending upon it which he would not get under the present rule; and often it would deprive a horse of the benefits which should follow a meritorious performance. The case cited presents a forcible illustration of the justness of the rule. "B" makes a valiant struggle to win, and scores the first heat to his credit, and then runs second to "A," which wins the next. It might be that "C" had never made an effort in the first and second heats, coming in with the ease which the extra number of yards afford.

From the comparative freshness which this gives him he is able to push "A" fast enough to "shut out" the winner of one heat and the "runner up" in another, and under the old schedule this would give him a better place. It would be equally as defensible to have a distance in a dash race as in the final heat of a repeating race, and if there is any difference it would be in favor of making it the former. According to the Eastern rules, "C" could not have started in a third heat under the same circumstances, and would have been sent to the stable, leaving "A" and "B" to continue the race by themselves. This is even more effective than the waiving of distance in a final heat, inasmuch as there is a chance for "C" to win the race when he has the opportunity to contend in a third heat.

We write this explanatory of the justice of the rule, as there cannot be a question under it of "B" being entitled to the second money.

The summary sent is defective, as the placing in the last heat should have been, "A, 1; C, 2; B, 3." This does not make any difference, however, as there cannot be "dist." in such a situation.

## LEAVE THE SMALL ONES.

It is by no means sportsmanlike to fill a creel with fingerlings simply to "make count," but neither is it a rare thing for even experienced anglers to do. In fact, "old hands" are not much better than new ones in this respect. A man likes to come from a stream and catch 100 to 150 fish—or say he did—rather than to say he only caught half a dozen. Even if he brings back the fingerlings he can call them "pan fish," and eke out with them the camp fare, whatever it may be.

But if the true sportsman is sincere in his belief, he will throw back into the stream all the small unfortunates he may hook, leaving them to grow up, mayhap, for others. It takes courage to do this, of course, especially when several men are at a stream together, and comparative counts are made at the evening camp fire. But if, when men start out in company, they will agree among themselves to "bar" all below a certain specified size, there will be no inducement to basket the little fellows that ought to be allowed to attain size sufficient to give sport to some one.

There are streams which have become entirely depopulated by the conscienceless fishing they have undergone. If anglers will only keep the fish that are of respectable size, and return to freedom those they take which are too small for sport, the stream will furnish amusement for others in time to come. We have no patience with the man who will talk wisely of laws to preserve the fish, and make a boast at the same time of having caught from 150 to 300 fish a day in a brook, for it is evident the quarter and half pounders are rare in such cases. A little forbearance on the part of individual anglers will help the whole fraternity. If these words serve to remind only a few, they will have served a purpose.

## OUR HUNTING GROUNDS.

As regards facilities for wild fowl shooting, the city of San Francisco is happily located. Both north and south from it extend wide expanses of marsh lands, intersected in every direction by navigable creeks and sloughs. On both sides of the bay for thirty-five or forty miles south are marshes from one to two miles wide, where there is not a single habitation of any sort and where the land is as wild as if there was no city of two or three hundred thousand inhabitants within hundreds of miles. On the inner edge of the marsh on this side of the bay a railroad passes, and on the opposite shore two lines of rail give opportunity for the sportsmen to come and go readily.

In the midst of these marshes are streams and ponds where the aquatic birds swarm in their season. When the tide runs out these birds follow the water down and are way out a mile or more from the edge of the marsh, on the edge of the mud. When the "flights" begin, numerous flocks fly overland, and then the sport begins.

Then, going north, the great Petaluma and Sonoma marshes present good fields, though game is not now as abundant there as formerly.

But passing through Carquinez Straits, one comes to the great Suisun bay and marshes and to the tule islands, where is a sportsman's paradise. The Suisun marsh is a salt one, but the ponds are fresh in winter. Through the waters of this marsh a railroad passes, with but one small station—Teal—and that for sportsmen alone. There is not a better place in the country for shooting, but this is preserved.

The Montezuma marshes, with the long Montezuma creek passing through them from Suisun bay into the Sacramento river, are also good sporting grounds, but they are little used because there is no way to get at them except by boat, and there are no hotels to stop at.

Then comes Sherman Island, an immense tract of land abounding in ponds, and half flooded, the tules forming shelter for millions of wild fowl in the season. Bouldin Island, Brannan Island, Union Island, and dozens more to be named, all are good places for shooting. Mayberry Slough, Potato Slough, Iron Horse Slough, and fifty more, make good places to resort for wild fowl shooting.

When it is remembered that all these grounds are within one to two and a half hours' travel from the city, it will be seen that San Francisco is well situated for lovers of the gun.

Of course the nearer places are soon "laid waste" by hunters who have a Sunday's trip every week during the season. The better places "up river" are to an extent preserved, but there are such ranges of marsh and tule land where very little shooting is done, all within a radius of say 50 miles of San Francisco. Sportsmen here have no cause of complaint that there is not territory enough, for the marshes are extensive and widespread, and as a general thing, during winter, all of them bear more or less game.

## CORRESPONDENTS OF THE BREEDER AND SPORTSMAN.

There is not a particle of necessity for calling attention editorially to the correspondents of this paper, otherwise than to present our acknowledgments for their valued contributions, as the most stolid can scarcely fail to give them a careful perusal. We claim with the fullest confidence in establishing the position, that there never was a paper devoted to the same pursuits which could show a more brilliant array. And when we take this ground, it is also with the fullest knowledge that this class of journals has always been favored in respect to contributors.

From the days when the *Spirit of the Times* first made its appearance, over fifty years ago, until the present, the turf, breeding, shooting, fishing, and other kindred topics have brought out a succession of powerful writers, and the galaxy which gave such a cordial support to the "Tall Son of York" has had successors well worthy of wearing the mantles of the pioneers in this branch of American literature. It may be that only a few now remember the "Old Spirit Guard," or, at least, those which first came to the support of that paper. "Observer," "An Old Turfman," "N., of Arkansas," "Egus," "A Young Turfman," a host of others of equal celebrity, gave a tone to this species of writing which has fortunately been retained. It would be difficult to find a more vigorous style, happier powers of description, keener humor, and a better argumentative display than the "old-timers" presented, and this has been the standard accepted by those of later days.

The three numbers of this paper now published present the most conclusive testimony that there is no falling off, and we may be permitted to say that those who have favored the BREEDER AND SPORTSMAN will rank with the best of any period. Strong as was our faith from before the start that this would be one of the most valued departments of the paper, the result has exceeded our most sanguine expectations. It would take pages to pass upon their merits, and, as we have heretofore written, there is not a single contributor who will fail to attract the attention of our readers.

## THE HAPPY HUNTING GROUNDS.

The Pacific Coast is surely the hunter's paradise. In the long stretch of shore line, the valleys covering an area equal to a European kingdom, and, above all, the mountains and the cañons between them, there are opportunities such as no other country presents. Some of our friends are now camping in Lake County, and there are a constant succession of eventful days and repose at night which is denied to the denizens of the city. There are pleasant interludes to the pursuit of game, and the mountain streams afford libations of pure water, but, according to a correspondent, it presents the best effects when mixed ever so little, however, with double-distilled. All of the campers are enthusiastic over the climate of that

Much as one would like to share in the delights of camp life, we are very partial to the cooler air region, and express a condolence for those who have to endure the fogs and trade-winds of the Bay, which is met on our diurnal transit on the ferry boat. The hunting must be a deferred pleasure, and the kind invitations we will be forced to decline. There are hopes, however, for the future, and 1883 may be more propitious.

## HORSES IN TRAINING.

There are probably double the number of trotting horses in training in California over what there were two years ago. There are so many at work on private tracks that the fact is only apparent to those who are familiar with the changes which have been made in the last few years. From the letters which have already appeared it is evident that there are lively times on the public tracks, and that as a rule the horses are doing well. To those who have paid much attention to the training of trotters it is palpable that casualties are not nearly so frequent. Trainers have acquired more skill, and the bootmaker has had a good deal to do with the immunity from injury. Then there have been changes in shoeing, though to note even the most prominent will require columns. To give anything like a fair account of the progress which has been made in the past decade will occupy a great deal of space. This space can be well afforded, and after the very busy season is over our readers shall have no reason to complain of any lack.

## MARKET REPORT.

We are pleased to present such complete reports of the market. These are prepared expressly for the BREEDER AND SPORTSMAN by a gentleman who has unusual opportunities for making them perfect, not a single sale of any magnitude with which he is not acquainted. There is not a point of information wanting, and the column must be appreciated by a large majority of our readers.

ACROSTIC.

## COLUMBIA TO HER HEROES.

Dauntless they died where the ice King dwells;
Eternal the fame their Valor won;
Loudly my song of sorrow swells,
Over the graves of my daring sons:
Nations and kings may fade away—
Glory like theirs cannot decay.

## THE BULL'S HEAD BREAKFAST.

Last Sunday at San Rafael that jovial organization known as the Bull's Head Club of San Francisco, gave their regular monthly feast. To give the names of all who were present would simply be to give the names of all the prime good fellows in San Francisco who were honored with invitations and could spare the time for a day's enjoyment. Colonel William P. Barnes presided over the festivities, while Senator T. McCarty fairly outvied himself, and added an extra lustre to his already brilliant reputation by the manner in which he presided over the culinary department. William T. Coleman was there, beaming smiles and genial nature on all, and especially devoting himself to explaining the mysteries of a Bull's Head feast to a number of Eastern tourists who were his guests. The square and dignified Mr. Cheeseborough filled the responsible post of head waiter with considerable eclat, and literally brought down the house by the manner in which he handed refreshments to the hungry guests. It was a blending of anxiety to please, a desire to live up to the light of his exalted office, and a good-natured attempt to fill six orders at once, to which the pen of a Dickens or the pencil of Dore are alone competent to do justice. Frank Murphy, the genial Secretary of the Club, was, of course, on hand, and performed the arduous duties of his office with his usual aplomb. The pièce de resistance was a bull's head, cooked in its natural covering, and baked in a trench dug in the ground, in the old fashion first introduced into America by the Spanish brave who accompanied Cortes on his swash-buckler expedition against the Incas. Good eating deserves good drinking, and as soon as the cloth was removed, Colonel Barnes announced that the literary execution of the day were in order. Then the jinks commenced. Senator McCarty told a story, and so did William T. Coleman, and Colonel Barnes, and nearly all of the other gentlemen present. To pay due honor to the day, all the stories were of a deeply moral character, and highly edified the listeners. The punch circulated freely. As Senator McCarty put it, "the cup was filled to overflowing, and even the saucer had as much as it could hold." There was no sloping, as singing seldom goes well after a hearty meal. The pleasures of the day may be summed up by saying that it was the happiest, jolliest, nicest time the Bull's Head Club ever had, and if any one fancies that the Bull's Head Club does not know how to make the time pass pleasantly, he don't know enough to wear a solemn face at a funeral. That's all.

# THE KENNEL.

## FIXTURES.

National American Kennel Club's trials on quails, Grand Junction, Tenn., December 4. D. Bryson, Memphis, Tenn. secretary.

Louisiana Field Trials near New Orleans, La., beginning Dec. 11, under the management of the New Orleans Gun Club.

Bench Shows.—Western Pennsylvania Society's English Setter Bench Show Derby, Pittsburgh, Pa., for English setter puppies whelped on or after March 1, 1882. Entries closed December 1, 1882. I. R. Stayton, Allegheny City, Pa., secretary.

Field Trials.—National American Kennel Club's trials on prairie chickens, Fairmont, Minn., September 4. Entries to American Field Derby closed July 1; to All-Age Stake, September 4. Joseph H. Dew, Columbia, Tenn., special secretary for these trials.

Gilroy Rod and Gun Club's trials on quails, near Gilroy, Cal., October 28. Open to dogs owned in California, Oregon, Nevada and Arizona. E. Leavesley, secretary, Gilroy, Cal.

Eastern Field Trials Club's trials on quails, near High Point, N. C., November 17. Entries to Derby close July 1; to All-Age and Members' Stake, November 1. Fred. N. Hall, secretary, P. O. Box 884, New York.

## JUDGING BY MEASURE.

Editor Breeder and Sportsman: I noticed in your last issue a communication from a gentleman who desired the adoption of a regular system of measuring prize dogs, for the purpose of creating a reliable standard for the determination of excellence on the show bench. I think the plan is a good one in many respects, but is open to the objection that it is liable to result in the adoption of an arbitrary and fictitious standard, which cannot possibly provide for the due consideration of some of the most important points of excellence in a dog. The principal of these points is what is often termed by fanciers "quality," and can only be defined by the French expression, "the tout ensemble."

The nearest definition in English that occurs to me is "general appearance," and as every fancier knows the general appearance of the animal is the strongest point in its favor or against it. A dog may measure exactly what the best authorities agree is the correct amount in every part of its body, it may have exactly the right shade of color and the proper length of coat, and yet its general appearance is called bearing, and if a man or woman's bearing or carriage is good, it covers up a multitude of bad points. The points which go to make up perfect bearing or general appearance are so minute, and undefinable, that it is impossible to introduce them into any schedule of excellence. Like the electric current, the effects are seen and felt, but no one can state exactly what they are. They fill the eye in an instant, and while it is hard to find a man who can pick out the best of twenty dogs by a separate examination, the merest tyro can select with ease the finest looking when all the batch are together. I have occupied the unfortunate position of judge at bench shows several times, and like every other judge have had my decisions soundly condemned.

When exhibitors have come to me to demand why I placed A.'s dog above B.'s, I have invariably asked them to examine both animals side by side and in a general way, without regard to special points—of course presuming that neither dog had any serious blemish. The result has always been that the exhibitors, unless, as in one or two cases, they were so blinded by prejudice as to be unable to find even the approach to excellence in any dog except their own. "Quality," as I first called it, is the most apparent and at the same time the most indescribable of all things. It always the opinions of all judges largely, and, as I believe, correctly, and is apparent alike to the expert and the uninitiated. Dog judgment is not and can never be an exact science, and any attempt to make it one will result in a failure.

The distribution of awards at a dog show calls for exactly the same qualifications as the awarding of prizes for an exhibition of pictures, and has exactly the same results. Before awards are made, the judges are honest, expert gentlemen, and every one expresses himself as willing to accept their decision as final. After the awards, the judges are accused of dishonesty or incompetency, simply because the decisions they made did not satisfy the expectations of all the exhibitors. Nothing would please judges better than to have an arbitrary scale by which they could judge and of which the results would admit of positive demonstration; but all judges know that this is impossible for the reason above stated, and similar to the abuse showered upon them as a testimony to the ignorance of the abusers.

I met with a good instance of this in a bench show at San Francisco last year. An estimable gentleman had a fine looking St. Bernard dog, which he had entered as a New-foundland. In passing through the show I noticed the mistake, and though I was not the judge of that class, I took the liberty to call the exhibitor's attention to the error. After he had consulted several others, he became convinced that he had classed his dog wrong, and that the animal he had for months regarded as a Newfoundland was really a St. Bernard. He was loth to confess his ignorance, but at last had his dog, reclassed and put where it belonged, in the St. Bernards. The judge passed over his dog when awarding prizes, simply because there were better animals present. One would imagine that the man who did not even know the breed of his dog would accept the decision in silence at least. This gentleman did not do that, and next day I heard him tell a circle of friends that the judge of St. Bernards was a scoundrel or a fool for passing over his dog.

He bragged of his knowledge and experience of St. Bernards, and abused the judges so badly that I ventured to remind him that he had originally entered his dog as a Newfoundland.

Turning on me a look full of surprise, shame, hate and indignation, he blurted out, "Oh, that's what I expected.

All you judges stand in with each other." Having discharged this shot he marched proudly away, leaving his friends with the impression that he was a wonderful judge of a dog, and that I was a perjured villain.

When he had cooled off I got him to compare his dog, side by side, with the winner, and then he acknowledged that the judge was right, and much to my surprise pointed out several points of superiority in the other dog.

It is this opportunity for intelligent comparison of "quality" that in my opinion makes bench shows valuable in a town like San Francisco, where a majority of the people speak of spaniels, setters, pointers and hounds as "hunting dogs," and do not know the distinction between the various breeds. Measurement is well enough in its way, but judging dogs, like judging pictures, has to be done by "the rule of thumb."     Edwin.

## GET UP DOG CLUBS.

It is a matter of surprise to eastern sportsmen who visit this State that there are no dog clubs here, except the coursing clubs, composed exclusively of lovers of the greyhound. There is no better way to carry out any desired aim than organization and co-operation, and those persons interested in the breeding and training of any particular species of dogs will find that individual effort, though good in its way, entails a greater cost of time and money than any one man can afford. It must be admitted by all candid sportsmen, that while Californians boast the possession of many superb specimens of the canine race, the average of dogs in this State is very low. For every thoroughbred dog owned in this State there are twenty nondescript animals, whose owners, for want of knowledge, regard them as the most valuable. They are not to blame for this ignorance, and should by no means be ridiculed. They have not had the opportunity to learn what constitutes a first class dog, and readily accept the statement of the person from whom they obtain their canine curios, that they are thoroughbred. Again, the really good judges of dogs here are not very plentiful, and many of them are so prejudiced in favor of a certain class, or breed, as to be unable to give an unbiased opinion of the merits of other and perhaps better strains of blood. A man who has any article to sell is a bad adviser as to the merits of the different kinds of that particular article, whatever it may be. The gentleman who breeds Lavericks, , they are far the best kind of setter, while the one who rears Llewellyns is sure that the crossed dog is the superior of the more inbred strain. The best way for gentlemen who take an especial interest in any breed, to improve their stock, and at the same time improve their knowledge of the breed, is to form clubs, having for their object the improvement of the breed and the dissemination of information in regard to it. Say, for instance, that the setter men—if such an expression may be used towards those who are interested in that noble breed—form a club. A small entrance fee could be charged and laid away for club use. Monthly meetings could be held at which papers might be read by members giving their views upon particular strains and the best way to rear and break them. At stated periods the members of the club could engage their dogs in a trial on quail, and judge for themselves how their precept was backed up by practice. No expenditure of money would be needed for these trials, for which a simple medal, or diploma, would constitute the prize. When the funds of the club justified such a procedure, the club could import some extra fine specimens of the strain acknowledged to be the best suited to the wants of its members, and place it in the stud for the use of members, and as many outsiders as might feel disposed to pay an agreed fee. Or course the club would refuse the use of the dog to any kitchen-cur of a pure strain. This idea might be followed out by the fox and deer-hound men, the pointer men, the spaniel men, and so on to the very fanciers of the various toy breeds.

## THE FIRST COURSING CLUB.

The publication of certain articles in the Breeder and Sportsman has given rise to an animated discussion among the prominent members of San Francisco Coursing Clubs, as to who was really the first to introduce the sport of Coursing into America. So far as can be ascertained from parole evidence, Dr. Starkey and James Adams shipped a pair of dogs for a course in this State as far back as 1856. Subsequent to that, many lovers of the dog were wont to take their animals up to John Scarlett's place, at Dublin, or to Pacheco, Benicia, Newark and other convenient spots, and give them a run after any game that turned up. These affairs were entirely impromptu, and were not run according to the rules of Coursing. In February, 1867, the Pioneer Coursing Club was formed, and Mr. Clement Dixon thereupon drew up from memory a very good set of rules to govern the sport as nearly as he could recollect the same as those in use in Great Britain. Those were the first rules ever used in this State. He then sent to England for a copy of the Waterloo rules, and in September, 1867, the first regular coursing match ever held in America took place on the plains of Santa Clara. The winner belonged to James Adams, and Clem Dixon owned the "runner-up." A gentleman familiarly spoken of as Whiskey Kelly was the judge. The next match was held on December 30th, at Pacheco, and was again won by Mr. Adams' dog, Mr. Dixon owning the runner-up. This match was the first reported at length in the daily papers of the State, and was specially telegraphed to the Morning Call. It was also reported in Bell's Life. This subject will furnish food for future articles.

The second volume of the N. A. K. C. Stud Book is in press, and will be issued at an early date. As previously announced, the work is in the hands of Dr. N. Rowe ("Mohawk"), Chicago, Ill.

The setter breeders of America will regret to learn of the death of the well known blue belton dog, Prince Taxis, by Aldershot—Kate the II. Mr. Cooper writes: "Prince Taxis died on June 12, of distemper, contracted at the Westminster Kennel Club Show."

After the close of the National Trials at Grand Junction, Tenn., the Louisiana Field Trials will take place, beginning December 11, near New Orleans, La., under the management of the New Orleans Gun Club. The events will be the New Orleans Gun Club Stakes, for a solid silver cup, open only to members; the Opelousas Derby, for dogs whelped on or after April 1, 1881; first prize, $150; second, $100; third, $50; and the Free-for-All: first prize, $300; second, $150; third, $75. The last two stakes are open to the world. The entrance fee is $5, and must be made on or before Dec. 10. The Secretary is Mr. J. K. Renaud, New Orleans.

# THE HERD.

## BREEDING MERINO SHEEP.

From the Rocky Mountain Husbandman we take the following letter in regard to this important subject in the ranch, as the proper condition of the fleece is a matter of serious interest when placed on the market in competition with other growths. It would be pleasant to have the opinion of some of our sheep breeders on this matter:

Many breeders of thoroughbred Merino sheep insist upon producing sheep that will yield wool containing the greatest possible quality of oil or yolk, and they stoutly assert that it is for the interest of wool-growers in the Territories to breed of such sheep. Here in Montana we have all learned that very greasy sheep cannot stand our winters; that not only is there no warmth in oil or yolk, but that it is a great source of weakness. As this oil or yolk has no commercial value, the question arises where is the advantage of greasy sheep? The breeding of such sheep arose, and has been perpetuated in the United States from a desire to palm off upon the buyer or manufacturer this yolk or worthless material for wool. Had our woolen manufacturers always adopted the test of the scoured weight in buying wool, the excess of oil or yolk would have been unknown even in Vermont flocks. To such an extent have our manufacturers lost from heavy shrinking wools that they are now almost universally adopting the clean or scoured fleece as a basis for wool buying. Every well regulated woolen mill now keeps an exact record of the shrinkage of all wools they purchase, and upon this record is based, to a full extent, the relative of the wools of the country. The agent of one of the leading cassimere mills of New England, writes me as follows: "It is very important that the wool-growers of your country understand that wool must be sold here at a price based upon the scoured fleece. It is possible for wool-growers to cultivate only the thick growth, and long stapled, fine wool without the grease, as we have abundant evidence in this country, and will instance among others the efforts of Mr. Campbell, of Westminster, in this State, as being a grower worthy of imitation. The Australian wool-growers, who now produce more than four hundred million pounds annually, are constantly improving wool in this respect, and shy one who follows the course of the market will see that unwashed Australian is sold the present season freely in Boston, from 40 to 47 cents per pound, showing that the buyers do appreciate wool that is free from grease. To-day we are buying heavenly stapled wool in this State (Vermont) at from 15 to 23 cents unwashed, simply because it contains so large a per cent. of grease,"

At the East the prejudice against greasy wool is rapidly increasing. On a dull market it is always the last to sell, and it is difficult now to obtain its actual value. Can we, here in Montana, afford to grow such wool ? Shall we not make greater gains by breeding our flocks to Merinos, more like those used by the English colonies in Australia ?

## THE CROSSES IN SWINE.

It has only been a few years, comparatively, since swine of the improved breeds have been brought to this country in any considerable numbers, and so far as crossing upon our common stock is concerned, there was hardly stock to build upon, and the upward grade has been ascended with becoming speed. The result of all this is, that an enormous quantity of well-bred, shapely hogs are shipped forward each winter; and it is rare that any other than good ones are seen in market, either East or West. This is a most desirable state of things, and is quite sure to continue, because the foundation, resting upon the old-time brood sow is not yet run down to a low state of vitality by in-and-in breeding.

The timber lots of the country are still prolific in the hardy white oak sort, by crossing upon which the farmer of ancient views may keep close to his first love. As we have before taken occasion to say, for what is commonly understood to be the rough-and-tumble life of the hog upon the farm, kept for breeding feeding stock, a roomy grade sow, of good quality is better than an inbred thoroughbred. She is likely to bring more pigs at a litter, and to suckle them better.

But while care is needed to maintain a profitable feeding stock, there is more critical care required that degeneracy in vigor of constitution may not make too rapid progress in our herds. Hogs stand some in-and-in breeding, but it should be borne in mind that this has been indulged in at the fountain head, upon the other side of the water, until we can hardly indulge in it here with any degree of safety. What may be supposed to be out-crosses, probably contain full as much consanguinity of blood as they do of that which is distinct; hence too much care cannot be taken when searching for new blood.

Breeders of the best of high-bred swine quite commonly adopt a source of supply to which they adhere, and in this way it is quite easy to drift into a stock that has been largely inbred. There are so many advocates and apologists for close breeding, that men resort to it many times against their own judgment; partly, perhaps, as a matter of convenience, having the stock at hand in their own herds, and partly because breeders are liable to become wedded to their own stock, that which they themselves have bred and reared. This, with care, is dangerous practice, because the ratio of increase is rapid ; and while with cattle we approach the practicability of inbreeding very slowly, with swine we have new opportunities every few months. In fact, it requires the utmost vigilance to prevent the coupling of animals close of kin.

Amateur breeders, not generally very deeply versed in the art, are not competent to give due weight to the principles necessary to be observed, hence venture to mix blood which is not sufficiently distinct. It would be the wiser plan to seek a new source of supply, so far as it is possible to do this, even though it be remote. It has been so much proved that new blood gives a new lease of life, as it were, imparting vigor and a tendency to long life, that the benefits likely to accrue will be ample remuneration for the necessary outlay of time and cash.—[National Live Stock Journal.

A. C. Dietz and family, accompanied by Capt. E. W. Travers, are camping at the old camp ground near the Highland Springs, Lake County, Cal. Al. Stilwell, of Oakland, intends joining them for a few days, for the purpose of a deer hunt in the mountains.

## FISH.

P. McShane is still enjoying himself at Independence Lake.

Tom-cods are exceedingly plentiful in the bay at present. The waters around Saucelito abound with them.

Wm. Battams has returned from his fishing trip to Weber and Tahoe Lakes. He is enthusiastic in praise of them.

Archibald McKinley, agent Bank of British North America, left yesterday for a trout fishing trip to Weber Lake.

Santa Ana, Mill Creek, Plunge Creek, and many other of the mountain streams of San Bernardino County, are said to be good fishing grounds.

Seth Green, the noted fish culturist, tersely says: "There is no simpler way to practice fish culture than on paper, and it requires but a slight movement of the pen to convert thousands into millions."

A party of gentlemen connected with the Central Pacific Railroad, fishing in Lake Tahoe, near Tahoe City, on the 3d and 3d instant, found the fish numerous. Nearly 300 were taken, ranging from one to three and one-half pounds.

To become good anglers, the ladies are generally lacking in one essential element, and that is patience. In England and Scotland there are several very expert amateurs, among them the Princess Louise, the Ladies Lennox, and the late Countess of March. Our ladies are not much addicted to the "gentle craft," but there are exceptions, and Mrs. John Fifield, of Galt, who is on a visit to Boston, to the astonishment of her friends, recently landed from the Merrimac, in fine style, a gamey black bass of 2¾ pounds.

There is very good rock-cod fishing in the bay of San Francisco at certain points. There are places along the Angel Island shore, especially in Raccoon straits, where they may be taken in abundance. The points of Hospital cove, the tank, the quarry, Tiburon point, etc., all offer good fishing grounds. If one can strike the reef off Point Blunt, Angel Island, and get the right stage of tide very large rock-cod may be taken. When fresh from their element, and properly cooked, these fish are very good. Half dried and poorly cooked they have no flavor.

A salmon was caught at Bay Point, Contra Costa county, the other day, that weighed 187 pounds. This is supposed to be the largest caught on the coast this season, and being caught on exhibition attracted considerable attention from the professional fishermen. This fish was caught in a net in the usual way the Sacramento fish are taken. If these fish would only take the hook, what a jolly chance for some expert with an 8 ounce rod to distinguish himself, by going up and heading off one of these big fellows. The 8 ounce rod man always takes the biggest fish, if his stories are to be believed, but this 187 pounds would give a split bamboo all the work it wanted. It will be well to remember this weight for an expert fisherman can speak of having caught such fish without having to go outside the record. Hereafter 187 pounds is the limit.

A gentleman recently from that resort, says that the fishing at Lake Tahoe appears to be growing better day by day. No one can recollect when the Tahoe trout were caught with so little troubles as at present. One can scarcely drop a line into the water without at once finding a trout at the submerged end. The success is alike in trowling and still fishing. It is no great feat for the merest novice to hook fifty splendid trout during one afternoon. At Tallac the fish are carted off by the wheelbarrowful. I cannot doubt whether there is as good trout fishing in any other part of the United States as at Lake Tahoe this season.—*Polo Mail.*

The San Bernardino *Index* says: From the days of the disciples in Galilee to the present hour, there has been found no human amusement so exhilarating, so exciting, and so restful to tired brains and bodies. Let those who will lay in the shade at fashionable summer watering places, read yellow-backed literature during the day, and hop at night to the soft strains of music; but if strength of body and mind are desired, our advice is to hunt some purling stream, where trout are idling and birds are singing, in the deep woods or the placid waters of some inland lake, where the black bass and pickerel will make such strikes that it will send life and vigor to body, brain and mind. A man who loves to fish and practices the art, never swindles, he is never a defaulter, he is full of generosity, he loves his home, he is patriotic, and as a rule has but one fault, and that is, he will lie a little about the size of his catch. But as everybody expects it, as Joe Jefferson would say, "It don't count."

OYSTERS IN ITALY.—From the report of Consul Depuis, the Italians would appear to have solved the problem of how to obtain a cheap supply of native oysters. The most extensive ground of all, and that from which most of the oysters consumed in Southern Italy are obtained, is known as the "Mare Piccolo," or little sea, near Taranto, at the land's-end of the peninsula, familiarly known as the "heel of the boot." An immense number is said to be reared there, and the consumption of the produce of these beds alone is estimated to average 7,000,000 to 8,000,000 annually, the price being from 2s. 6d. to 3s. a hundred. The system of cultivation appears to be as successful as it is simple. From April to November bundles of brushwood are submerged in the oyster sea, and to these the spawn is found to readily attach itself. They are afterwards raised, and those on which the tiny oysters have settled are submerged in the "Mare Piccolo," where in about two years they attain their full size.

SEND SOME OF THEM ALONG.—From the Troy, N.Y., *Times* we learn that during the past four weeks at least 200,000 young eels have been captured at the State dam and forwarded to the Fish Commissioners of Michigan and Ohio to replenish the streams and rivers of those States. Robert Brodi, an uptown boatman, has annually captured and shipped to the Michigan Commissioners probably millions of these tiny members of the finny tribe during the last five years. This season Ohio applied for a supply for the first time, and with Michigan has been so generously furnished that orders have come from both States to stop further shipments. Troy is called upon to provide eels for the waters of Ohio and Michigan for the reason that the fish are remarkably abundant about the dam, and such large shipments can be made at a time that but a small percentage die during the journey. Until the last few days the "catches" have averaged fifteen quarts, or about 15,000 every morning.

---

A bundle of twigs from hickory trees is tied, and at night set near the raceway of the Green Island sawmill, a few yards south of the dam. At daylight the branches are alive with the squirming objects, which are quickly turned into a box with a sieve bottom. Mr. Brodi stated that the yearly demand made upon the Hudson at this point had reduced the stock of eels wonderfully, and was slightly noticeable during the past several days, when the number captured fell off to five quarts at each "catch."

## TROUT FISHING ON WEBER LAKE.

EDITOR BREEDER AND SPORTSMAN:—SIR: Among the many pleasant resorts of the Sierra Nevadas frequented by the angler, Weber Lake holds a prominent place, and, to judge from the accounts given by a party of disciples of the gentle Izaak, who visited this charming spot during the recent holidays, it is likely in the present season to retain if not increase its reputation as a fisherman's Paradise. The party above alluded to consisted of Ed. Davenport and Mrs. Davenport, George Redding, Wm. Hoelm, Frank Commins and Leon D. Smith, all of whom left the city on the Overland train of Saturday, the 1st instant, bound for Prosser Creek Station, and though the train was bristling with fishing-rods and dip-nets, and the smoking rooms of the sleeping cars redolent of fishy stories—the narrators of the latter all being bound for some one of the mountain lakes—this little band of piscatorial adventurers were the only ones who cast their lot on the pleasant pine-clad shores of Weber. Arriving at Prosser Creek shortly after sunrise, a good breakfast proved a most satisfactory prelude to the twenty-five-mile drive across the mountains. No better road, or prettier and more varied scenery, is to be met with in the wide area of the Sierras than that through which the route to Weber leads; and this fact, coupled with the many novel incidents of a mountain drive through bracing mountain air, fragrant with the perfume of wild flowers and tamarack, all combined to make the journey seem as short as a drive to the Cliff House. The lake is situated in a plateau about 7,000 feet above sea level, and is overlooked by some of the highest peaks of the mountains, Weber Peak being the king pin, its summit scoring some 9,400 feet. The last half mile or so of the road leads along the side of a ravine, through which the cold let from the basin rushes, in one place forming a beautiful fall 150 feet high. On the northern shore of the lake (which in not much more than a mile square) is situated the hotel, and there a hearty welcome awaits all visitors at the hands of the courteous host, Doctor Weber, who is assisted by his equally attentive and hospitable nephew and his good lady. The fishing is superb. In the morning a good basket can be easily filled, by still fishing in the inlet to the lake. Later in the day trolling is in order, and it well repays the rower for his exertions, to see his colleague in the stern of the boat reel in his line every few minutes with a pound or one and a half pound trout at the end of his leader. Towards evening they begin to rise to the fly, and the man who can select a combination of wing and hackle to suit the fastidious taste of the finny beauties is sure of good sport. The trout in the lake are the feather River fish, and game fish never beat a rod. They run almost evenly about a pound weight each, but make a harder fight than many heavier fish the writer has killed. The largest fish taken weighed a pound and a half—the smallest not more than three-quarters of a pound, and very few of the latter. The catch of the party during their brief stay was about the best made in the lake for some time, and for this satisfactory result they are in no small measure indebted to the kindness of Mr. A. P. Williams, who with Mrs. Williams is making his annual visit to Weber, and who supplied many useful points as to the best fishing ground and most enticing colors to lure the victims to their doom. A more enthusiastic party never entered the city than that which returned from Weber to the fogs and wind of old Frisco by Tuesday's overland train, with but one regret, and that was that they were unable to prolong their visit.

Yours,    EED IDES.

## TRAP AND WING.

### THE GUN CLUB SHOOT.

Fifteen members of the Gun Club participated in the regular match held at Bird's Point, Alameda, on the 8th inst., shooting from five ground traps. Huntingham rules. The gold medal fell to Mr. Babcock in shooting off the ties, but was captured by Mr. Orr for him, as he, with others, was compelled to leave before the result was finally known. Mr. Fuller was unfortunate in losing two birds out of bounds on the start, a rather discouraging beginning. The day being warm the birds were not as lively as usual, but were far from being squabs, as reported by several non-shooters. Mr. Butler did the best shooting of the day, having several hard flyers to contend with, but he succeeded in getting all but a comparatively safe right quarterer in the ties, and it is undoubtedly owing to his opponent securing easy birds, that he was finally overcome. All shot at 30 yards, excepting Messrs. Gordon, Fox, Coleman and Barrell, 26 yards each. The official score is as follows:

| | | | | | | | | | | | | | | |
|---|---|---|---|---|---|---|---|---|---|---|---|---|---|---|
| F. S. Butler | 1 | 1 | 1 | 0 | 1 | 1 | 1 | 1 | 1 | 1 | 1 | | | —11 |
| A. W. Havens | 1 | 1 | 1 | 0 | 1 | 1 | 1 | 1 | 1 | 1 | | | | —11 |
| G. W. Randall | 1 | 0 | 1 | 1 | 1 | 1 | 1 | 0 | 1 | 1 | | | | —9 |
| M. Babcock | 1 | 1 | 1 | 1 | 1 | 1 | 1 | 1 | 1 | 1 | | | | —11 |
| R. Wilson | 1 | 0 | 1 | 1 | 0 | 1 | 1 | 1 | 1 | 0 | | | | —8 |
| W. Golcher | 1 | 0 | 1 | 1 | 0 | 1 | 0 | 1 | 1 | 0 | | | | —9 |
| Henry May | 0 | 0 | 1 | 1 | 1 | 1 | 1 | 0 | 1 | 1 | | | | —8 |
| Thos. Ewing | 1 | 1 | 1 | 1 | 0 | 1 | 1 | 1 | 1 | 1 | | | | —11 |
| C. P. Gordon | 1 | 1 | 1 | 1 | 1 | 0 | 1 | 0 | 1 | 1 | | | | —9 |
| H. L. Fox | 0 | 1 | 1 | 0 | 0 | 1 | 0 | 1 | 1 | 0 | | | | —6 |
| A. Orr | 1 | 1 | 1 | 1 | 0 | 1 | 1 | 1 | 1 | 1 | | | | —10 |
| J. V. Coleman | 0 | 1 | 1 | 1 | 0 | 0 | 1 | 0 | 1 | 0 | | | | —6 |
| M. Fallen | 0 | 1 | 1 | 0 | 1 | 1 | withdrawn. | | | | | | | |
| J. Bharell | 1 | 1 | 1 | 0 | 1 | 1 | 0 | 1 | | | | | | —6 |
| J. K. Orr | 1 | 1 | 1 | 1 | 0 | 1 | 1 | 0 | 1 | 1 | | | | —10 |

FIRST TIES 4 BIRDS EACH.

| | | | | | |
|---|---|---|---|---|---|
| F. S. Butler | 1 | 1 | 1 | 1 | —4 |
| M. Babcock (Shot by Orr) | 1 | 1 | 1 | 1 | —4 |
| T. Ewing | 0 | 0 | 0 | 0 | —0 |
| M. Black | 1 | 1 | 0 | 1 | —3 |

SECOND TIES 4 BIRDS EACH.

| | | | | | |
|---|---|---|---|---|---|
| F. S. Butler | 1 | 0 | 1 | 1 | —3 |
| M. Babcock (Shot by Orr) | 1 | 1 | 1 | 1 | —4 |

Gold Medal, M. Babcock. Second Prize, $10, F. S. Butler. Third Prize, $5, M. Black.

After the regular match several freeze-outs were shot Messrs. Butler, Ewing, Orr and Black being the fortunate ones interested. A match at 30 yards, Eurlingham rules, is being arranged between teams of men each from the Coemopolitan and Gun Clubs, and in the above match it was understood that the Gun Club team would be chosen from the best scores made.

---

## BICYCLING.

THE ROAD CHAMPIONSHIP OF AMERICA.—The fifty-mile bicycle race was run off around the lake at Druid Hill Park, Baltimore, on July 8th, and was won by Charles H. Jenkins, of Louisville, in 3 hours, 35 minutes and 34¼ seconds. The following were the conditions of the match: 50-Mile Race, Road Championship of America, under the auspices of the Badgeless Brotherhood of Baltimore Bicyclists. Druid Hill Park Lake. Baltimore, Md. First prize, $50 gold medal and the title of Road Champion of the United States; second prize, gold medal; third prize, silver medal. Entrance, $1; three starters to make a race. At a meeting of the B. B. B. B.'s it was resolved that: Whereas, The members of this club protest against the usual methods of obtaining long distance bicycle records, on specially prepared board floors, inside buildings, etc., and claim that the bicycle is a road vehicle, and its records should be made on the road; and whereas, Baltimore has the finest road course in this country, dead level, one mile and a half lap, 50 feet wide, smooth, and with half-mile straightaway homestretch; Resolved, That we offer to the amateur bicyclists of America a $50 gold medal and the title of "Road Champion of the United States," and a gold medal to second, and a silver to third, for a 50-mile race to take place under the auspices of this club, and we will guarantee the medals and title, and will offer a similar competition every year in connection with our club races, to be ridden over the Druid Hill Lake course, at the appointed time, rain or shine, take both road and weather as they are on that day and hour. As it is a public park, no gate money can be charged, and subscriptions are solicited for the purchase of the medals. The time of preparation is limited, to bar "special training," as this is a general rider's road race. Entries and subscriptions close July 1st, the race to take place on the 8th. It would be as well for our own wheel roadsters to inaugurate a similar contest at 20 miles over the most suitable road in the vicinity.

## CHESS.

A NEWSBOY CHESS PLAYER.—Fifteen years ago, or thereabouts, a bright-faced youngster "established himself in business," as he was fond of telling his customers, on board the Fulton ferryboats. His business was selling the morning and evening papers. In line, he had a list of regular customers, who waited till they were on the boat to buy papers from him. The youngster's name was James Mason. In those days Otis Field, well known to New York billiard players, kept a billiard room in the basement at the corner of Fulton and Nassau streets. On the Nassau street side he had tables for chess and draughts. The newsboy had to pass the place four times a day, and, as the windows were open in warm weather, could not fail to see the chess games with their curved men. One day, while he was watching the pieces with boyish interest, an old gentleman at one of the tables beckoned him down stairs. He had observed the boy's interest in the game, and offered to teach him the moves. The boy learned very rapidly, and in a few days was able to cope with his instructor. In a fortnight he could give the old gentleman the odds of a queen and beat him. The "boy phenomenon" began to be talked of. The best players that came into Otis Field's were pitted against him and beaten. Finally, when he was scarcely fifteen, young Mason's fame spread among the up-town players. With two years he improved so greatly that none but the best players would engage him, and before he was twenty his admirers were anxious to match him against Captain McKenzie, then the acknowledged champion of New York. They played no public game, so far as known, but it is stated that Mason held his own with McKenzie in friendly encounters. He is now second in the Vienna match for the championship of the world.

## HANFORD CORRESPONDENCE.

HANFORD, July 9, 1882.

EDITOR BREEDER AND SPORTSMAN: While there is not much going on in this part of the great State in the way of horse sports, there are animals in this section of the valley which are likely to make their mark whenever they come in competition with those which have had the advantage of the "glorious" climate of the Bay District. While willing to concede that Sunny Slope, Dew Drop, Canadá La Grandé, and Palo Alto are entitled to the laurels, it may be that there will be successful claimants before many other seasons elapse. There is the progeny of a highly bred son of Almont, which show that they are worthy descendants of an illustrious sire; and though he has been transferred to the upper country, the owners have high expectations that they will make a good mark. Conceding that the equines are not as yet up to the mark in those in your section, we think that there is a boy here who can successfully compete with the conqueror of the world-renowned Myers. At all events, if Brooks and he were to meet, many dollars would be intrusted on the horse champion, and from his performances there are good grounds for the belief. Winning the previous race with so much ease that it scarcely had the appearance of a race, he supplemented this with a performance on the 4th which stamps him as the possessor of extraordinary powers. In place of the spiked shoes which are held to be so indispensable to the outfit of a pedestrian, he ran with a pair of carpet slippers, insecurely fastened to his ankles, and then made the 100 yards in 10 1-5 seconds. Though this was accomplished with a flying start the time, I can assure you, is beyond question; and the impression on the mind of every one who saw the race was that there was a little left in him at the finish. Myrick is only eighteen years old, and without training, which would be considered necessary to bring out his full powers.

The Knights of Pythias had their annual picnic on the Fourth. In addition to the regular games, there was base ball playing; and it is safe to say that the large attendance was gratified by a fine display of skill.

The first number of the BREEDER AND SPORTSMAN was duly received, and the universal impression is that California has now a paper of the class that will be satisfactory.

Truly yours,    C. A. McVEY.

## FOX-HUNTING IN AMERICA.

The following interesting account of early fox-hunts is from the Riding's correspondence of the *Turf, Field and Farm:*

From the little conversation I this day held with an English gentleman now engaged in extensive travel here, who said from his travels in this country he had reason to believe, that America was not suited to fox-hunting, consequently that fox-hunting is not one of the prevailing pastimes of its people. Still we would remind him of the fact that it was one of the favorite pursuits of the father of the nation—the great General George Washington, whose doings in the field and chase are thus technically described in records kept at Mount Vernon and at the time the then President presided over the hunt of the St. George Club of 1793:

"The time which General Washington could spare from his other avocations between the years 1759 and 1794, was considerably—or as far as possible devoted to the chase. His kennel was situated about one hundred yards south of the family vault, in which now repose its venerated remains. The building was a rude structure, but afforded comfortable quarters for the hounds, with a large enclosure paled in, having in the midst of it a spring of running water. The pack was very choice and numerous—Colonel (i. e. General Washington) visiting and inspecting his kennel and its select dogs morning and evening, after the same manner as he did his stables. It was his pride, and a proof of his skill in hunting, to have his pack so critically crafted, as to speed and bottom, that in running if one leading dog should lose the scent; another was at hand immediately to recover it; and thus when in full cry, to use a sporting phrase, you might cover the pack with a blanket.

"During the hunting season Mount Vernon had many sporting guests from the North, the kennel neighborhood, Maryland, Delaware and elsewhere. The gentlemen's visits were not of days, but weeks, and they were entertained in the good old style of Virginia's ancient hospitality.

"Washington, always superbly mounted in true sporting costume of blue coat, scarlet waistcoat, leather breeches, top-boots, velvet cap and whip with long thong, took the field at day dawn with his huntsman, Will Lee, his friends and neighbors; and none rode more gallantly the chase from end to end, nor with voice more cheerily awakened echo in the moorland, than he who was afterwards destined, by voice and example, to cheer his fellow countrymen in their glorious struggle for independence and empire, commemorated this day.

"The custom was to hunt three times a week, weather permitting. Breakfast was served in these mornings by candle light, the General always breaking his fast with an Indian-corn cake and a bowl of milk; and ere the cock had done saluting the morn, the whole cavalcade would often have left the house, and a fox frequently unkenneled before sunrise.

"The vicious propensities of horses were of no moment to this skillful and daring rider." He always said that he required but one good quality in a horse, "to go along," and ridiculed the idea of its being even possible that he should be unhorsed, provided the animal kept on its legs. Indeed, the perfect and sinewy frame of this admirable man gave him such a surpassing grip with his knees, that a horse might as soon disencumber itself of the saddle as of such a rider.

"The General usually rode in the chase a horse called Blueskin, of a dark iron-gray color, approaching a blue. This was a fine but fiery animal, and of great endurance in a long run.

"Will Lee, the huntsman, better known in revolutionary lore as 'Billy,' rode a horse called Chinkling, a surprising leaper, and made very much like his rider—low but sturdy, and of great bone and muscle.

"Will had but one order, which was to keep with the hounds; and mounting the animal with his spur in his flank, this fearless horseman would rush at full speed through the break or tangled wood, in a style at which modern huntsmen would stand aghast.

"There were roads cut through the woods in various directions, by which aged and timid hunters and ladies could enjoy the exhilarating cry without risk of life or limb; but Washington rode gaily up to his hounds through all the difficulties and dangers of the grounds on which he hunted, nor spared he his generous steed, as the distended nostrils of Blue-skin often would show; always in at the death, and yielding to no man in the honor of the brush.

"The horse hunted in those days were gay foxes, with one exception; this was a famous black fox, which, differing from his brethren of 'order gray' would flourish his brush, set his pursuers at defiance, and go from ten to twenty miles end and, distancing both dogs and man; and what was truly remarkable, would return to its place of starting the same night, so as always to be found there the ensuing morning.

"After seven or eight severe runs, Billy recommended that the black Reynard should be left alone, giving it as his opinion that he was very near akin to another sable character inhabiting a lower region, and as remarkable for his wiles.

"The advice was adopted from necessity; and ever thereafter, in throwing off the hounds, care was taken to avoid the haunt of the unconquerable black fox.

"The chase ended, the party would return to the mansion house, where, on the well-spread board, and with cheerful glass, the feats of the leading dogs, the most gallant horses, or boldest rider, together with the prowess of the famous black fox, were all discussed; while Washington, never permitting even his pleasures to infringe upon the order and regularity of his habits, would, after a few glasses of Madeira, retire to his suppertless bed at nine o'clock."

Our doubting traveled English friend may take the above substantial facts with him on his intended visit to Mount Vernon and the South, where many of our Southern hunting friends will be made happy to convince him of the errors of his convictions.

We would likewise inform our distinguished English traveler that he will find in the States upward of an hundred organized Fox Hunt clubs, with an average membership of fifty each.

In his able account of fox hunting the New York writer unintentionally omitted to speak of the great fox hunting clubs of Virginia City and Reno, Nevada, and the daring deeds of Jim Orndorf, "Kettle-belly" Brown and the mighty heroes of the Comstock. Neither did he refer to Bill Henderson and Ike Brannan, the great hunters of Alum Rock, or to Sheriff Meaney and Tom Tunstead, who once ran down and lassoed a fox on the Merced plains. We shall endeavor to supply these deficiencies in a future number.

## THE STAGE.

Never in the history of San Francisco has there been such a dearth of dramatic novelty as is the case at the present time. During the past week there was not one theatre by which the drama was represented—the others being devoted to the minstrels, to burlesque and to opera. In such a state of affairs it is a difficult matter to entertain our readers with the details of the week's business without wearying them with a repetition of platitudes, the changes of which have been rung without ceasing for the two last years. With the establishment of the Tivoli and other places of light amusement, as also with the rage for private theatricals, the patronage of the higher priced theatres has gradually diminished, and now it is a very risky business to bring any combination to this city, on account of the heavy expenses, that include not only the fares but also the salaries of the people while on their way from, and back to, the East. There is only one way in which the dramatic taste could apparently be revived, and that is by the engagement of a company of some ten excellent artists, such as do not aspire to the stars, and who would devote their attention, and talents to the service of the public in the presentation of modern dramas and comedies and such original pieces as would be likely to attract attention and patronage. With a talented company who would strive to please by the production of novelties, such a theatre as the Baldwin, at popular prices, ought to prove to be a most successful venture; and it would indeed be pleasant to record the fact that Gus Frohman and his associates had secured that pretty theatre for the next season, and we should then be sure of having at least one temple devoted to the dramatic art.

The novelties last week were the re-appearance of Haverly's Mastodon Minstrels at the California, and the production of a drama originally entitled "British Born," at the Baldwin. The Minstrels have been greeted by large and enthusiastic audiences, showing conclusively the hold they have obtained in the popular favor. It may be safely said that never has there been such a combination of vocal merit, musical ability and mirth-provoking talent in any minstrel troupe that has visited this Coast, and they well deserve the patronage so liberally bestowed upon them.

The drama "American Born," produced on Monday last, at the Baldwin, was produced in such a perfect manner, both as regards the cast and scenic effects, as to merit the encomiums so liberally bestowed upon it. The plot is interesting and the characters in the hands of such good artists as Miss Ada Ward, Miss Ada Gilman, John Dillon, Jennings, Bradley, Osbourne, Kennedy and Grismer were delineated in a manner that showed both study and ability. It is to be hoped that such a company of artists will not be entirely dispersed, and we should be pleased to see them, with the addition of Mr. Wheatleigh, produce some of those sterling old comedies and farces in which the latter gentleman and Mr. Dillon have achieved such remarkable successes. If the Bush St. Theatre could be obtained; we feel convinced that such an entertainment, at popular prices, would meet with public favor.

For the coming week the Hanlons appear at the Baldwin in their far-famed musical acrobatic absurdity called "Le Voyage en Suisse," which, according to impartial reports, is unique in character, mirthful in incident and sensational in effects. We should not be surprised to see it at once achieve a success, and that the very favorable encomiums of the Eastern press will be ratified in this city. As the California minstrels will continue to attract crowded and delighted audiences, and at the Standard the very pleasing musical satire "H. M. S. Pinafore" will hold the boards. At the Winter Garden the spectacular opera of "Aeolia" will court the public patronage, and the Tivoli will probably announce "Standing room only," the attraction being "Der Freischutz," produced in a style that merits ample approval. So that even in the absence of dramatic presentations there is plenty of amusement to be found in the city.

"The Wreck of the Pinafore" an operatta by Luscombe Searle, the libretto by William Horace Lingard, was recently produced in London and achieved an instantaneous failure that the author and compositor attribute to a conspiracy among the London critics. We have heard this same complaint before made by John Raymond and others who have taken their wares to an English market. The same grievance exists among our own aspiring dramatic authors in regard to the New York critics, it being claimed that criticism in that city is ruled by a prejudiced clique. It may be so, but in either city they cannot form, but can only sway public opinion, and we thoroughly believe that "The Wreck of the Pinafore" was wrecked on its own demerits. Was there not an operetta by the same name that was originally produced here at the Tivoli Gardens? But if so the libretto and music were said to be the work of a lady, and surely William Horace was not guying us with one of his choice travesties. In that case the word would take on a new and expressive meaning

A strike of a most unique and perplexing nature was recently organized in Paris that threatened at one time to surpass in interest the crisis on the Eastern question. At the Chatelet the reigning success has been a spectacular extravaganza entitled "The Thousand and One Nights," in which some 250 danseuses and figurantes appear in the dances, evolutions and processions. According to his agreement the manager announced a reduction in their salary during the three summer months, when there was a strike organized on such a grand scale as recalled the battles of the Amazons. Relying on their arms, clad in dazzling armor and marching in serried phalanx, they took possession of the stage, and guarding all the approaches they summoned the recreant chief before their august tribunal, as it were, only that the outbreak occurred in June. The manager appeared and would certainly have been intimidated by the assault of 250 pretty menacing arms, flashing eyes and heaving bosoms, but when doubled in number as they were on this occasion, he realized the force of the expression, "woe to the vanquished." Guided by prudence, he demanded a parley, accompanied by the offer of re-enforcing their military supplies with sundry boxes of cakes and kegs of foaming beer. The peace offering was received with acclamation, the ranks were broken and when an hour afterwards is impressed on their memory the risks of a summer season, and that he was merely making a scaling reduction that but little affected the poorer employes, the strike was at an end and happily for Paris "The Thousand and One Nights" resumed its brilliant career.

When Critics Disagree.—As it is a the beauty rather than as the actress that Mrs. Langtry has succeeded and is likely to succeed, it may not be amiss to collide some of the descriptions of her. Mr. G. W. Smalley—who, however, always goes into hysterical descriptive whenever a foreign star like Nielson or Bernhardt is about to dawn on America—raves about her "delicate ripe splendor," and her "peach-colored cheek," and vows that no actress of modern days is able to hold a candle to her in the matter of looks. "The purity of her complexion," he says, in his coldly critical way, "has not been matched anywhere, nor perhaps the soft fullness of her violet eyes, which can only be described by the epithet which Homer bestowed on the Queen of the Gods—ox-eyed. The setting of the eye and the moulding of the temples, over which the dark brown hair falls far, are equally fine; the lines of that part of the head are pure Greek, passing into a more modern type below. The profile is a little irregular, the mouth and jaw strongly shaped, the teeth perfect, the head elegantly set on the shoulders, which are possibly high, but rounded and full, as is the bust and the whole figure." "She possesses wonderful eyes of a limpid, transparent blue, which always wear a winning expression," says another correspondent. "I don't think her pretty," says a third, "her hair is dark, and her eyes are blue—an unusual combination, which is effective. Her lips are thick, denoting, they say, kindliness and love of life." Says still another, "She is of medium size, regular features, rosebud mouth, large blue eyes, low forehead, nice creamy complexion, dark-brown hair, squared shoulders, flat bust, and long, classical arms." Says still another—an American actress, by the way: "She is not strictly beautiful, but has a fair skin and large round dark eyes, which she uses very expressively and with a great deal of art in conversation. The natural color of her hair is chestnut, but she is as often seen with very light or reddish frizzes, which enhance the effect of her really handsome eyes." Finally, a more critical observer describes her as "quiet-looking, somewhat pallid, large-eyed, high-shouldered and wasp-waisted," and a friend of mine—who adds that you could pick out a dozen handsomer women on the streets of Chicago or New York of a Summer day—says she has very large, wistful, liquid eyes, and a soft creamy complexion, and makes a body think of a Jersey—heifer!

When Bernhardt made her re-appearance in Paris was for the benefit of Madame Cheret, the wife of a celebrated scenic artist. The play was "Camille," and the receipts were upwards of frs. 70,000. In claiming his authors' rights of ten per cent., Alexander Dumas has aroused public indignation to such a point as to cause an aspiring journal to start a public subscription to avert this lawsuit on the widow's mite. It is a cheap and imprudent bid for notoriety, as there was no justice in demanding that the author should contribute a hundred fold more to the fund than the countless guineas of the Bourse who were present on the occasion. And had he consented, he knew perfectly well that at every benefit he would be importuned for the gratuitous use of his dramas that represent as much his stock in trade as do the tiaras of diamonds so lavishly displayed by the jewellers of the Boulevards and of the Palais Royal.

A somewhat similar incident occurred in this city on the occasion of a benefit that was arranged for some charitable institution. The advertising in a leading daily journal amounted to about fifty dollars, and the most persistent efforts were made to induce one of the proprietors to make a reduction. This proposition met with no response and the money was paid with little grace, that we changed for gladness when he pulled from his pocket a hundred dollar bill and remarked, "I never allow my charitable feelings to interfere with my business; but as I really think the cause you advocate is a very deserving one, allow me to contribute this offering."

In a letter to a friend in this city, the popular comedian, C. B. Bishop, states that he had intended to pay a visit to San Francisco this season, but that he is so busy in making his arrangements for the next campaign, that he is obliged to abandon the idea. He has a new play by A. C. Gunther, entitled "Strictly Business," and he writes that "it is now finished and reads remarkably well; in fact if one can judge of how a piece will go with the public by the way it reads, I should say that I have a very strong melo-dramatic comedy, and one that is sure to be a big success; but—and alas for those buts—I have seen so many failures that I am afraid to brink any expectations, feeling that they will be on aerial foundations. Let us wait and see how it will go." The genial Doctor also states that "La Belle Russe" was a very great hit at Wallack's, "and only yielded to extreme hot weather. It saved the season and could have run for three months longer but for the extreme temperature. Master Dave has scored a great triumph." Mr. Bishop has a host of friends in San Francisco who take an interest in his career and his future success.

Samuel of Posen has returned to the East, and has given a glowing description of his success in this city. In this case he must be borrowing some of the imperturbable cheek of Samuel of Posen, or be drawing strongly on his imagination. The piece was a failure here, being received as a gross exaggeration in artistic effects, and his was the last combination that completed their disgagement, previous to the closing of the Bush Street Theater.

And, by the way, what funny stories the Eastern dramatic papers concoct aren't this same city of 'Frisco, as they do light to call it. Thus we find it announced seriously that E. J. Baldwin is a General, and that his hotel and theater cover an entire block on Market street. If it were true, we should have much pleasure in congratulating the gentleman on this grand accession to his rank and riches.

At a recent trial at Paris, Mme. Judic, who appeared as a witness, gave her age as "almost thirty-two." Once upon a time Mlle. Mars made her appearance before the court at Rouen as a witness, and was asked the customary questions: Madamy years!" mumbled the star. "She says fifty," remarked the judge to the clerk. "Forty!!! Put it down forty!" screamed the actress, with no hesitation or whispering this time.

# ATHLETICS.

## MYERS AGAIN BEATS THE RECORD.

The fifth annual summer games of the American Athletic Club were held July 2d, at the Polo Grounds, near New York. The games opened with a dash of 100-yards handicap, for which there were thirty-eight entries. It was divided into eight heats, the winners of which and those coming in second were allowed to compete in a second trial heat, and the winners in the second heat were allowed in the final heat. The winner of the dash was A. Doremus, who made the 100 yards in 10⅕ seconds, with F G. Abbott, of the Manhattan Athletic Club, second, and S. A. Safford, of the American Athletic Club, third. There were twenty-nine entries and twenty-one starters in a half-mile handicap run. H. Jacquelin, of the American Club, won the race in 2 minutes, with J. J. Hoff, of the Staten Island Athletic Club, second, and T. J. Murphy, of the Park Athletic Club, third. For a one-mile handicap walk for persons who have beaten the record of 7 minutes 45 seconds there were ten entries. J. J. Raynes, of the Pastime Athletic Club, who had been given twenty-five seconds, won the race in 7 minutes 15⅖ seconds, W. S. Hart, of the Williamsburg Athletic Club, was second, and W. H. Perry, of the same club, who was scratched, third. A handicap hurdle race of 220 yards was won by S. A. Safford, of the American Athletic Club, in 27⅖ seconds. A handicap run of a mile, in which thirty persons had entered, was won by T. F. Delany, of the Gramercy Athletic Club, in 4 minutes 40⅕ seconds. C. L. Jacquelin, of the Manhattan Athletic Club, distanced fifteen competitors in a 300-yard handicap run. His time was 33 seconds. The event of the day was a 600-yard run, in which L. E. Myers, the amateur champion, had entered for the purpose of attempting to beat the best previous record at this distance, which was 1 minute 14⅖ seconds. He ran away completely from the six others in the race, and lowered the record to 1 minute 11 2-5 seconds. G. D. Baird, of the Y. M. C. A., won a two-mile walk in 15 minutes 45 2-5 seconds. In a handicap race of two miles on bicycles, E. A. Thompson, of the Lenox Bicycle Club, beat four others. He covered the first mile in 3 minutes 22 seconds, and the whole distance in 7 minutes 3⅖ seconds.

## THE SCHUHL-TOPLITZ MATCH.

The relative merits of R. L. Toplitz and M. Schuhl, in a five mile match for a $20 medal, was decided at the O. A. C. grounds a few days since, to the mutual satisfaction of both gentlemen and their friends and admirers. Mr. Toplitz kicks the beam at something over 200 pounds when in fine condition for the distance, and his opponent was probably about forty pounds lighter when he toed the mark for the start. They started on their long journey by the word, and neither of the contestants spurted for the lead. Toplitz, however, was unable to restrain his ardor, and before the first turn was made had taken the lead and set the pace with an advantage of about five yards. In two laps he had bettered it by about 20 more, and not hearing anything of his rival, ventured to look around to see what had become of him, and he found that he had time to take a good look, too. Schuhl, attired in a pair of heavy, high-heeled shoes, white loose-fitting tights, dark trunks, flaming red shirt, and a white handkerchief in lieu of a cap, with feet well forward, shoulders back and head erect, had settled down to a six-day, go-as-you-please gait, expecting Toplitz to break down at three miles. Having been trained for the event by his friend McIntyre, Toplitz was highly amused at the spectacle, smiling audibly to his friends and slackening his pace for company. For a couple more laps the positions of the two men were unchanged; but tiring of this jog, Toplitz let out a link, and at two miles passed Schuhl, having gained a lap without exerting himself in the least. Schuhl soon after hung out signals of distress, and tried square heel and toe for relief. Soon reviving, he put on a flat-footed spurt, but Toplitz easily kept the lead, which he had meanwhile increased by another half of a lap. After a couple more laps, Schuhl remarked that as the day was remarkably warm he would postpone his interest in the event to some day later in the season; and to prevent ill feeling, order a handsome medal for his tireless opponent. Toplitz, however, was not satisfied with so hollow a victory, and for the sake of a little exercise kept on and finished the full distance, running the last seventy-five yards at a hundred yards gait, with an ambitious, would-be sprinter. The time was not taken with a stop-watch, and what the winner can do at the distance is still a problem to all but himself and his trainer. Schuhl realizes his mistake in underrating his opponent and starting out of condition, and is reported to have expressed a determination to redeem his laurels at an early day.

## THE THREE-HUNDRED-YARD RECORD LOWERED.

At the Ninth Annual Summer Meeting of the Mosely Harriers, held at Birmingham, England, on June 10th, there was some good running, although in a damp, disagreeable day. C. S. Johnstone lowered the 300-yard record, of which we have the following account:

Three-hundred-yard Handicap Run (Members).—C. S. Johnstone, scratch, 3 1-5; S. Ingerthorp, 5 yards, 2, by half a yard; L. Ball, 8 yards, 3, by 1 yard; E. Cumming, 9 yards, 0; J. S. Doughty, 13 yards, 0; Herbert Reeve, 14 yards, 0; George H. Ryall, 16 yards, 0; W. E. Breakwell, 18 yards, 0; J. L. Jones, 22 yards, 0; W. J. Gregory, 22 yards, 0; W. R. Davis, 22 yards, 0. This beats the best previous performance, which was 31⅘ seconds. These are the same grounds on which, July 16, 1881, Myers made the fastest amateur quarter-mile record in the world, and Johnstone was beaten by Myers the same day, in the first trial heat of the 100-yard run. The course is hardly a fair one for short distance races, as the final 250 yards is down hill.

A Sad Showing.—M. C. Geary, a local sprint runner, has been arrested, the affair being an outgrowth of the recent athletic meeting at the Half-mile Track, in which Geary was matched to run 100 yards against John Larkey. Geary's statement is to the effect that when he entered the race South offered to back him as the loser, provided that Geary would consent to throw the race, in which event he was to receive one-half the winnings. Geary also claims to have consented to the agreement, but, subsequently learning that South proposed to fleece his friends, he resolved to win the race, which he did, thereby causing South to lose considerable money. This gives a good idea of the style of *matches* the public are expected to encourage with their money and presence. Jobs are the rule in almost all professional events, and in a genuine match, the contestants have to labor under the suspicion of its being conducted under the same system of despicable trickery.

The Swim for the Championship. — Captain Mathew Webb, the champion swimmer of England, and George H. Wade, of Brooklyn, who has heretofore claimed to be the champion ocean swimmer of America, swam a match on July 1st for the championship of America and $1000 in money, starting from Brighton Beach, near Coney Island, New York Bay. The course was one mile out to sea from the bathing pavilion and return. John Y. Fitcheet acted as referee, G. H. Richey as stakeholder and Frank Ogden and William Smart as umpires. At 6:10 A. M. Webb and Wade dropped into the water, Wade immediately taking the lead. At the turning point, which was designated by a row-boat, Wade was fully 200 yards in advance, but showed plainly that he was fast losing his breath by repeated efforts to swim with one arm. After turning the boat Webb rapidly reduced the lead of Wade and succeeded in completely closing the gap when within half a mile from the shore. For nearly a quarter of a mile the two swimmers were side by side, but Webb gradually forged ahead, winning by about fifty feet. Webb's time was 1 h. 7m. for the two miles, with Wade about 30 seconds behind him. Both swimmers claim that in all they covered four miles, being carried out of their course by the tide.

Swimming with Hands and Feet Tied.—Upon the third attempt Marquis Bibbero recently succeeded in swimming across the East River with his feet tied together and his hands pinioned behind him. Two men took him up and pitched him into the water. The swimmer started off with a wriggling motion. He gave two or three violent kicks with both legs together, and at intervals of about once in half a minute the swimmer's head would appear above water. He spouted like a whale and continued to kick with his feet. In response to signals, tugboats and ferryboats kept out of the way and gave the swimmer a chance. Bibbero was thrown into the water at 11:10 A. M. At 11:20 he was exactly under the middle of the Brooklyn Bridge. Eight minutes later the phenomenal swimmer was in danger of bumping his head against the spiles of the Roosevelt street ferry, when his attendants, who were following him in a rowboat, reached out and pulled him in. He had been in the water but twenty minutes. Bibbero has issued a challenge to any professional swimmer in the world.

A large crowd of spectators were present at Yonkers, on July 3d, to witness the annual athletic games held under the auspices of the Yonkers Caledonian Society. The principal event of the day was the contest between Donald Dennie, of Scotland, the champion of the world, and Duncan C. Ross, of Louisville, Ky. Ross defeated the champion in the two principal contests of the day, as follows: Putting the heavy stone—Ross, 44 feet 9½ inches; Dennie, 43 feet 7½ inches. Throwing the heavy hammer—Ross, 102 feet 10½ inches; Dennie, 101 feet 7 inches.

Wm. M. Sime leaves us for the mountains in a few days, and does not expect to return in time to take part in any of the coming events of this season. Business duties will deprive Horace Hawes of the pleasure of throwing dirt in the eyes of the majority of our athletes. E. S. Emmons, however, has been caught running wild on the track, and will bear watching. Mr. Sime will be on hand in the next handicap, and is liable to finish stronger than ever. B. S. Haley is also in active training again, and flatters himself that he will show the limit man a splendid lot of spikes on the finish.

Richard K. Fox has arranged a six-day go-as-you-please match to begin at Boston on July 31st. Entrance fee, $100, all to go to the winner, with the international championship, and a special prize for lowering the record. After the expenses are divided from the gate money, the remainder is to be divided among those covering 500 miles.

# BASE BALL.

## THE HAVERLY AND NIANTICS.

It cannot be claimed that the Niantics and Haverleys are evenly matched, but when not at a disadvantage through accidents they can both turn out a nine that may be relied on to make the game interesting to the spectators. Thus in the Recreation grounds on Sunday last there was a full and appreciative attendance, and as, through the unavoidable absence of two or three of the usual Haverly team, the contest was of a most spirited and equal character, until the ninth innings, when the theater boys made some fair batting to a poor defence, and scored a victory of eight to six. A few such interesting games like this would revive the public interest in the Diamond field. Following is the score:

HAVERLY.

| | T.B. | R. | 1B. | P.O. | A. | E. |
|---|---|---|---|---|---|---|
| Meegan, 3d b | 4 | 1 | 1 | 2 | 3 | 1 |
| Levy, l. f. & c. f | 4 | 1 | 1 | 1 | 0 | 0 |
| McDonald, 1st b | 4 | 1 | 3 | 5 | 1 | 0 |
| Carroll, p | 4 | 0 | 0 | 1 | 10 | 0 |
| Lawton, c | 4 | 1 | 1 | 10 | 1 | 0 |
| Gagus, 2d b | 4 | 0 | 0 | 3 | 2 | 0 |
| McCord, s. s | 4 | 1 | 1 | 2 | 0 | 4 |
| Pope, r. f | 4 | 2 | 0 | 0 | 0 | 0 |
| Moran, l. f. & c. f | 4 | 1 | 0 | 3 | 0 | 1 |
| Totals | 36 | 8 | 7 | 27 | 17 | 6 |

NIANTICS.

| | T.B. | R. | 1B. | P.O. | A. | E. |
|---|---|---|---|---|---|---|
| Emerson, s. s | 4 | 2 | 2 | 0 | 2 | 1 |
| Sweeney, p | 4 | 0 | 0 | 0 | 9 | 0 |
| Finn, c | 4 | 1 | 1 | 11 | 1 | 1 |
| Eagan, 1st b | 4 | 0 | 0 | 12 | 0 | 0 |
| Sullivan, l. f | 4 | 1 | 0 | 0 | 0 | 2 |
| Incell, r. f | 4 | 0 | 0 | 0 | 0 | 0 |
| Arnold, c. f | 4 | 1 | 0 | 0 | 0 | 1 |
| McElroy, 3d b | 4 | 1 | 0 | 0 | 0 | 2 |
| Fogarty, 2d b | 3 | 0 | 0 | 2 | 3 | 0 |
| Totals | 35 | 6 | 3 | 25 | 14 | 7 |

| Innings | 1 | 2 | 3 | 4 | 5 | 6 | 7 | 8 | 9 | |
|---|---|---|---|---|---|---|---|---|---|---|
| Haverly | 1 | 0 | 0 | 2 | 1 | 0 | 0 | 1 | 3 | —8 |
| Niantic | 0 | 0 | 4 | 1 | 1 | 0 | 0 | 0 | 0 | —6 |

Earned runs, Emerson 1, McCord 1—Home runs, Emerson, McCord and Moran—Three base hits, Finn—First on balls, Haverly 4, Niantic 4—Left on bases, Haverly 0, Niantic 2—Struck out, Haverly 6, Niantics 5—Passed balls, Lawton 1—Wild pitches, Carroll 2.

Swanton, of the Renos, officiated as umpire.

And now it is claimed that the Mastodon Minstrels can turn out a team that can beat any of the old League Clubs, and it is in order that the Haverlys should represent our local interests. It is stated, however, that the minstrels were so fatigued with the effects of their promerade and flattering reception on Monday last, that they will be unable to take the field at least for some period of time.

## THE LEAGUE CHAMPIONSHIP.

The appended table gives the relative standing of the League Clubs in their struggle for championship honors to July 4, inclusive:

| Clubs. | Boston | Buffalo | Chicago | Cleveland | Detroit | Providence | Troy | Worcester | Games Won | Games Played | Games to Play |
|---|---|---|---|---|---|---|---|---|---|---|---|
| Boston | .... | 4 | 2 | 4 | 3 | 2 | 2 | 4 | 21 | 41 | 19 |
| Buffalo | 2 | .... | 4 | 3 | 1 | 3 | 2 | 4 | 19 | 39 | 21 |
| Chicago | 4 | 1 | .... | 4 | 4 | 4 | 3 | 4 | 24 | 39 | 21 |
| Cleveland | 2 | 3 | 1 | .... | 1 | 2 | 4 | 6 | 9 | 30 | 30 |
| Detroit | 2 | 4 | 2 | 5 | .... | 2 | 4 | 6 | 25 | 40 | 20 |
| Providence | 4 | 3 | 2 | 3 | 4 | .... | 4 | 4 | 24 | 40 | 20 |
| Troy | 4 | 4 | 2 | 2 | 2 | 2 | .... | 3 | 19 | 41 | 19 |
| Worcester | 2 | 1 | 2 | 0 | 0 | 1 | 3 | .... | 9 | 30 | 30 |
| Games Lost | 20 | 20 | 15 | 21 | 15 | 16 | 22 | 21 | 160 | 300 | 180 |

## THE AMERICAN CHAMPIONSHIP.

There is a hard tussle for supremacy in this series of games, but the Cincinnati Club has reconquered its position, but is closely followed by the Athletics and St. Louis Browns. Following is the record to July 3d, inclusive.

| Clubs. | Allegheny | Athletic | Baltimore | Cincinnati | Eclipse | St. Louis | Won |
|---|---|---|---|---|---|---|---|
| Allegheny | .... | 1 | 0 | 5 | 1 | 4 | 11 |
| Athletic | 3 | .... | 3 | 3 | 5 | 4 | 18 |
| Baltimore | 0 | 1 | .... | 1 | 0 | 1 | 3 |
| Cincinnati | 7 | 5 | 9 | .... | 1 | 0 | 22 |
| Eclipse | 4 | 3 | 4 | 1 | .... | 3 | 15 |
| St. Louis | 2 | 4 | 9 | 0 | 6 | .... | 21 |
| Lost | 16 | 14 | 25 | 10 | 13 | 12 | 90 |

## THE AMERICAN COLLEGE ASSOCIATION.

The final game was played at New Haven, on July 3d, with the Yale against Princeton, the New Haven boys winning by a score of 9 to 5, Yale thus taking the pennant after a series of remarkably well played games, all the contesting clubs showing up in splendid form. The following is the record:

| Clubs. | Yale | Princeton | Harvard | Brown | Amherst | Dartmouth | Games Won | Games Played |
|---|---|---|---|---|---|---|---|---|
| Yale | .. | 2 | 1 | 1 | 2 | 2 | 8 | 11 |
| Princeton | 1 | .. | 2 | 1 | 1 | 2 | 7 | 11 |
| Harvard | 1 | 0 | .. | 2 | 2 | 0 | 5 | 10 |
| Brown | 1 | 1 | 0 | .. | 0 | 2 | 4 | 10 |
| Amherst | 0 | 1 | 0 | 2 | .. | 1 | 4 | 10 |
| Dartmouth | 0 | 0 | 2 | 0 | 1 | .. | 3 | 10 |
| Games lost | 3 | 4 | 5 | 6 | 6 | 7 | 31 | .. |

Haverly's Mastodon Minstrels and the Reno base-ball clubs will play a match game of base-ball at the Recreation Grounds next Sunday. The minstrels will play the following nine: Dan Thompson, Andy Piercy, Pete Mack, Tom Sadler, Frank Cushman, Joseph Garland, John Gasman, Lew Dockstader and George Gorman.

A game was arranged last Sunday at the Olympic Athletic Grounds at Oakland, between a picked nine from the players of the old League Clubs, and the team of the Olympic Club, which resulted in a victory for the Olympics by a score of 15 to 4, showing a lack of unity in the fielding of the other team.

## THE ARCHERY TOURNAMENT.

In the Chicago archery tournament the competition for the National Championship medals was completed on July 12th. The National round for the ladies' championship was won by Mrs. Gibbs of Newark, N. J., with 101 hits, the value of the score being 449. Miss Morrison of Cincinnati, was second with 94 hits, value 374. The York round for gentlemen was won by H. S. Taylor of Highland Park with 168 hits, value 678. D. A. Nash of Brooklyn, N. Y., was second with 197 hits, value 713. John P. Wilkiuson shot the longest flight, 213 yards. Mrs. Frye of Brooklyn shot the longest ladies' flight, 172 yards. At the meeting at night Colonel S. A. Whitfield of Dayton was chosen President; Major O. G. Constable of New York, Mr. Frye of Lycoming, Pa., and J. P. Allen of San Francisco, Vice Presidents; C. R. Wild of Cincinnati, Secretary; K. W. Pyle of Cincinnati, Corresponding Secretary. The next annual tournament will be held at Cincinnati on the first Monday in July, 1883.

An immense rattle snake, measuring four feet and ten inches, was killed by Chas. L. Dietz, near the Highland Springs Hotel, Lake County, Cal., while out dove shooting. When first seen he was in a coil ready to strike, when he shot his head entirely off. He measured seven inches in circumference, and had thirteen rattles and a button. His skin has been prepared, ready for exhibition. When brought to camp every male adult partook of a liberal dose of the antidote as a precautionary measure.

Successful Dog Show.—The Alexandra Palace Dog Show turned out a grand affair, having no less than 1,241 exhibits on its benches. Mr. E. S. Spratt, for the first time, undertaking the benching as well as the feeding of the dogs, using Spratt's patent polished wood in the place of bare boards, These benches all fit in together and can be taken up and down with the greatest ease. The hoops and rings are all arranged so as to be adjusted without the slightest trouble. This plan should be tried here.

Mr. Jesse D. Carr, the President of Salinas City Bank, and one who is well known as one of the most enterprising breeders of stock in the State, is now on a visit to this city.

## MARKET REPORT.

WHEAT—So far only two consignments of the new crop have been received here, but free deliveries are reported at Vallejo and Port Costa. It is not expected that growers will be over-anxious to market their grain at an early date, as present indications are favorable for higher prices in the near future. During the past week the English and Continental markets have shown a material appreciation in values, and in Chicago and New York prices are higher—this owing to an improvement in European markets. Here the speculative element has been free bidders, but holders have shown little disposition to dispose of their grain, so legitimate transactions are unimportant, though speculative transactions on call show a fair aggregate—settlements to be made on the basis of current quotations at the time of supposed delivery. For spot lots of No. 1 White $1 75 is bid, both for local and Port Costa delivery. It is not probable that really choice milling could be had for less than $1 77½ per ctl.

BARLEY—In our last report we noted free arrivals of the new crop, and a consequent depressed feeling in the market, but during the week under review the deliveries have been meagre, and speculators have caused quite an advance in rates. Many well informed operators assert that the probable yield of this season's harvest will be materially less than was anticipated at the beginning of the current month, and back their assertion by being liberal purchasers of parcels for future delivery. Considerable sales of No. 1 Feed were made at the close at $1 24@1 26 for spot or July delivery; No. Feed, $1 17@1 18, August. Transactions in New Brewing are unworthy of note, but the local brewers and maltsters are ready purchasers of choice old at, say, $1 90@2 per ctl.

OATS—As yet no consignments of the new crop have been received, though it was expected that such would have been received from the Salinas Valley before the close of last week. Under light receipts, the market shows more strength, and holders are confident that higher prices will rule. For No. 1 $1 85 is the asking price for spot lots. For No. 2 $1 89½ per ctl was paid at the close, seller 1882.

CORN—There has been no movement worthy of note. Holders of spot lots are firm in their demands for full figures, say $1 70 per ctl for No 1 Large Yellow. The bids and offerings in open call show that buyers and sellers are weak in their propositions.

RYE—No definite information is in possession of dealers as to the amount of old on hand, and reports of the new crop are meagre. A sale of a small parcel of No 1 was made at $2 per ctl.

BUCKWHEAT—No transactions have recently been been recorded. Quotable at $1 40@$1 50 per ctl.

BRAN—For spot lots $13 35@$13 50 is a fair range. Speculators show less interest in the trade, and, consequently, the market is quiet.

FEED—Shorts, $16@$17; Middlings, $25@$26; Oil Cake Meal, $32 50; Ground Barley, $25@$30 for new, $32@$34 for mixed, and $36@$38 for old; Feed Cornmeal, $39 per ton; Oatmeal, 5c; Buckwheat Flour, 4c; Cracked Wheat, 3½c per lb.

HAY—Receipts of choice kinds are very light, and the same command higher prices than was expected at the opening of the harvest. Wheat Hay is, as a general thing, very coarse, or short, and strictly choice. Cargoes would command fancy figures. Alfalfa is in more liberal supply. For all kinds the range is $11@15 per ton.

STRAW—Recent arrivals have been free, and prices have declined; quotable at 60@70c per bale, as to quality and condition.

SEEDS—There is an active demand for Mustard at 4@4½c for Brown, and 2@3½c per lb for Yellow.

BEANS—The market is dull and quotations nominal. Pea and Small White, $4 25, Butter $3 75@4 25, Bayos $3@3 25, Limas $4@4 50, Pink and Red, $2 50@3 per ctl

ONIONS—Receipts are free and the market weak. Silverskins, 75@87½c; Reds, 37½@50c per ctl.

POTATOES—Arrivals are free, but the demand is sufficient to cause prices to be steady. Quotable at $1 00@1 25.

POULTRY—Arrivals are light and the market is firm. So far during the current year prices have been higher than for several years past, and consignees are encouraged to further extend their product. Turkeys; 18@20c; ducks, $5@6 50; hens $7@8; geese, $1@1 75 for old and young respectively; young roosters, $7 50@10; old, $6@7; broilers, $3@6.

GAME—Venison is in free supply and the market is overloaded with doves. We quote: Doves 50@75c per doz; Venison, 10@12½c per lb; hare, $2@2 25; rabbits, $1@1 25 per doz.

EGGS—Strictly choice ranch meet with ready sale at 30c, while fair to good are quoted at 28@29c per doz.

CHEESE.—Stocks are moderate and with a good demand; prices are firm. California product sells for 12½@14c per lb.

BUTTER—Choice fresh ranch roll is scarce at 31c; fair to good, 27½@30c per lb.

HONEY—The market is steady at 8@9c for extracted and 17@18c for comb, as to kind and quality.

HOPS—Petty consignments are received from Oregon and Washington Territory. The market is firm, but quotations are nominal at 28@35c per lb.

PROVISIONS—The demand is active; market strong, and prices show an advancing tendency, especially for bacon. We quote breakfast bacon 16½@17c for Eastern, and 15½@13c for California, for heavy to medium; for light and extra light 16½@17c is the jobbing price; sides, 15½@16c. Hams—Eastern, 17@17½c; California, 14½@15½c. Clear pork, $24 50@25; extra clear, $25@26; extra prime, $21 50@22; mess, $24@24 50 per bbl. Smoked beef, 14½@15c per lb. Lard, 14@16c per lb, as to kind and packages.

TALLOW—The demand is active at 7½@8c per lb for rendered.

HIDES—Market quiet. Dry calf, 20c; kips, 19c; sheepskins, 25c@$1; long wool, $1@1 50; salted steers, 9@11c.

WOOL—Stocks are unusually heavy and trade is unimportant, yet the inquiry shows an improvement. Calaveras and foot-hill, 22@24c; northern, 23@26c; southern coast, 15@22c; San Joaquin, 16@20c; Oregon, 22@27c per lb. Receipts of the Oregon spring clip continue free.

BAGS—The market shows an improvement. Calcutta, $9 27½ for spot lots, and $9 35 bid, buyer July. For Dundee $8 75 is bid.

FRUIT—Supplies of all seasonable varieties are large and prices rule low. Peaches, 35@50c in baskets, and 40@85c in boxes; Apples, 30@75c in boxes and 30@50c in baskets; Pears, in boxes $1, baskets 25@30c; Cherries, $12; Strawberries, $10@13; Blackberries, $9@10 per chest; Figs, 50c@$1 per box; Watermelons, $3@5 50; Cantaloupes, $3@3 50 per doz; Grapes, 50c@$1 50 per box; Apricots, 37½@75c per box.

VEGETABLES—Supplies are free. Squash, 25@50c; Asparagus, $1; Tomatoes, 40@50c; Cucumbers, 35@50c per box; Peppers, 5@6c; Okra, 12@15c; Egg Plant, 5@6c per pound; Green corn, 4@9c per doz; Beans, 2@2½c; Green Peas, 1½@2c per lb.

MEATS—Beef is firm at 4½@8c; Veal, 6½@9c; Lambs, 4@6½c; Mutton, 3½@4½c; Pork, 7½@8½c for hard, and 6@7c for soft, and 10½c per pound for dressed.

"BEAR AND FORBEAR."—An amusing anecdote in the spirited brochure entitled "Summer on the Shores of Lake Superior," gives a new application to the well-worn phrase above quoted, thus: We had heard that bear had been found on the rocky ridges, and Mr. Kellogg, whose instinct prompted him to win renown as a mighty Nimrod, went forth to see and conquer. In a dense thicket he was startled by the apparition of a large black form which, on Mr. K.'s approach, instantly rushed out. Firing both barrels of his gun, charged with buckshot, the sportsman fled, nor paused to look back until he arrived among his companions, battered and torn from contact with bush and briar. His story, interspersed with convulsive gaspings for breath, was told, and soon the whole party made for the scene of conflict, to find—what? A huge black porker well riddled with buckshot! This porcine venture cost poor Kellogg $10, which went to appease the righteous indignation of the provoked pig proprietor. To this day our staid friend likes not to hear of bear hunting. His invariable response to all banter on the subject is a shake of his head and the dissyllabic warning—pregnant with meaning—"For-bear."

THE NEW YORK STATE FISH COMMISSION, under the supervision of Seth Green, has done the following excellent work:

Shad hatched from 1870 to 1881, 58,609,000.
Salmon trout from 1870 to 1881, 10,090,000.
White fish from 1870 to 1880, 2,438,000.
Brook trout from 1876 to 1881, 5,375,000.
California trout from 1879 to 1881, 1,288,700.
California Salmon from 1873 to 1879, 678,000.
Kennebec salmon 82,000; land-locked salmon 21,000.
Mature bass, including black bass, rock bass, Oswego bass and strawberry bass, from 1871 to 1880, 82,849.
Mature yellow pike from 1871 to 1880, 2,882.
Mature bullheads from 1871 to 1880, 5,750.
Mature yellow perch from 1871 to 1880, 2,341.

There have also been distributed at different times 93,000 eels, 900,000 frost fish, 780,000 fresh water shrimps, 155,500 sturgeon, 610 carp and 18,000 crawfish.

## REVISED SPEED PROGRAMME FOR 1882.

FOURTH ANNUAL MEETING

OF THE

SONOMA COUNTY

Agricultural Park Association,

AT SANTA ROSA.

**FIRST DAY—Tuesday, Aug. 22, 1882.**

No. 1—TROTTING RACE.—Free for all two-year-olds owned in the District. Mile heats, 2 best in 3; purse, $200. First horse, $120; second, $60; third, $20. Closed on the first day of May with the following entries:

E. B. Conway names ch. c. Ideal, by Abbotsford.
J. E. Foster names s. m. Clara Patterson, by Grey McClellan.
G. C. Fountain names blk. f. May Day, by Eugene Casserly.
P. J. Shafter names g. h. Greyson, by brother to Rustic.
Steve Crandall names b. f. no name, sire unknown.

No. 2—TROTTING RACE.—Free for all horses that never beat 2:35; purse, $400. First horse, $240; second, $120; third, $40.

**SECOND DAY—Wednesday, Aug. 23.**

No. 3—RUNNING RACE.—Half mile heats; 3 best in 5, free to all; purse, $250. First horse, $150; second, $75; third $25.

No. 4—PACING RACE.—Free to all horses that never beat 2:25; purse, $300. First horse, $200; second, $75; third, $25.

**THIRD DAY—Thursday, Aug. 24.**

No. 5—TROTTING RACE.—Free for all three-year-olds owned in the District; purse, $300. First horse, $180; second, $90; third, $30. Closed May 1st, with the following entries:

C. Stingell names b. f. Debby Mott, by Grey McClellan.
W. J. Starr names blk. f. Starr, by Nanbuck.
E. B. Conley names b. c. Magnet, by Brigadier.
J. E. Foster names br. s. Buck Foster, by Gen'l Dana.
W. M. Wood names b. c. Ned, by Overland.
L. H. Boggs names b. c. Warwick, by Milton Medium.

No. 6—TROTTING RACE.—Free for all that never beat 2:25; purse, $500. First horse, $300; second, $150; third, $50

**FOURTH DAY—Friday, Aug. 25.**

No. 7—TROTTING RACE.—Free to all horses that never beat 2:40; purse, $500. First horse, $300; second, $150; third, $50.

No. 8—RUNNING RACE.—Free for all; single dash; one mile; purse, $200. First horse, $120; second, $60; third, $20.

No. 9—TROTTING RACE.—Free for all horses that never beat 2.30; purse, $500. First horse, $300; second, $150; third, $50.

**FIFTH DAY—Saturday, Aug. 26.**

No. 10—RUNNING RACE.—Free for all three-year-olds—one mile and repeat; purse, $200. First horse, $120; second, $60; third, $20.

No. 11—TROTTING RACE.—Free to all that never beat 2:21; purse, $700. First horse, $400; second, $200; third, $100.

### ENTRIES.

1. Entries must be made in writing and dated, and give sex, color and marks of horse; also name and residence of owner.
2. State number of the race in which you wish to enter.
3. State name of sire and dam of horse entered if known; if unknown, state the fact.
4. State name and postoffice address of party entering the horse.
5. If name of horse has been changed, state former name.
6. Send entrance fee to all nominations.

### CONDITIONS.

1. Entries to all races, except Nos. 1 and 5, to close with the Secretary at 12 o'clock M. on Monday, the first day of August, 1882.
2. Entrance fee to the above races will be 10 per cent. of the purse, and must accompany the nomination.
3. In all races five to enter and three to start. Any horse distanced or not starting will forfeit his entrance fee. No money will be paid for a walk over.
4. Rules of the Pacific Blood Horse Association to govern running races, and of the National Trotting Association to govern trotting.
5. No horse entered in a purse can be withdrawn except by consent of the Judges.
6. All trotting and pacing races, except No. 1, will be mile heats, 3 best in 5.

J. P. CLARK, President.
CHARLES HOFFER, Secretary.

## Pacific Breeders' Association.

### Embryo Trotting Stakes, 1882.

Sweepstakes for foals, 1882, $100 each; $25 forfeit; $10 declaration; $5 nomination fee.

There are three stakes under the denomination of Embryo for 1882, viz., for yearlings, two-year-olds, and three-year-olds. The nominator chooses whether he will name in one or all of them. The yearling distance is a dash of a mile; two-year-old, heats of a mile (2 in 3); three-year-old, 3 in 5—all in harness. Five dollars must accompany the nomination; the declaration, $10; on or before the 1st of September of the year the race is to be trotted; the forfeit, $25, on or before the day, which is ten days previous to the date fixed for the race. If the declaration or forfeit is not paid at the specified time, the subscriber will be held for the full amount of the stake. Pedigree, color, marks, and date of foaling must be given, and the following will be the formula for making the nomination:

Sec'y Pacific Breeders' Association. I name in Embryo Stake of 1882, the —— colt (or filly), foaled ——, 1882, by ——, dam ——, by ——, in the Stakes of 1883, 1884, 1885, if the nominator desires to enter in all of the Stakes. If he desires to name in one or more, specify which years. The $5 fee covers the first expense if the colt is named in one or all of the races; payment of the declaration $10 absolves from further payments. The race to be trotted on the first Saturday of November of each year, if good day and track, and on the track named by the officers of the Association. If the day or track is not good, on the first good day and track following the date. The winner shall receive six-ninths of the whole sum, stakes, forfeits, and other sources of revenue; the second, two-ninths; the third, one-ninth. National Trotting Association Rules of 1882 to govern. Nominations to be made to JOS. CAIRN SIMPSON, Secretary pro tem. of Pacific Breeder's Association, office of BREEDER AND SPORTSMAN, 508 Montgomery Street, San Francisco.

JAMES McM. SHAFTER, President.
A. P. WHITNEY, Vice-President.
N. T. SMITH, Treasurer.
JOS. CAIRN SIMPSON, Secretary pro tem.

The BREEDER AND SPORTSMAN is printed with Shattuck and Fletcher's Ink.

July 15

## Pacific Coast Blood Horse As'n.

### PROGRAMME.

FIXED EVENTS--SPRING & FALL MEETINGS
1883 and 1884.

### BALDWIN STAKE FOR 1882

#### SPRING MEETING.

FIRST DAY.

WINTERS' STAKE—For three-year-olds, to be run the first day of the Spring Meeting; dash of one-and-a-half miles; $100 each, $25 forfeit, $500 added; second to have $100, third to save stake. Nominations in above to be made for 1883.

SAME DAY—CALIFORNIA STAKE—For two-year-olds, $50 each, $25 forfeit, $250 added; to be run on the first day of the Spring Meeting; second to save stake; dash of half a mile. Nominations in above to be made for 1883.

SECOND DAY.

PACIFIC CUP—Handicap of $100 each, $50 forfeit, $20 declaration, $600 added; second to receive $300, third to save stake; two and-a-quarter miles; to be run on the second day of the Spring Meeting. Will close the 1st of March, 1883.

THIRD DAY.

"SPIRIT OF THE TIMES" STAKE—Dash of one-and-three-quarter miles for all three-year-olds; $100 each, $25 forfeit, $300 added; $150 to second, third to save stake. Nominations in above to be made for 1883.

SAME DAY—DERBY STAKE—Dash of three-quarters of a mile for two-year-olds; $50 each, $25 forfeit, $250 added; second horse to save stake. When any California two-year-old beats the time of Game, 1:15 for three-quarters of a mile, the Stake to be named after the colt which beats it. Nominations to be made for 1883.

#### FALL MEETING.

FIRST DAY.

LADIES' STAKE—For two-year-old fillies; $50 entrance, $25 forfeit, $250 added; three-quarters of a mile; second to save entrance. Nominations to be made for 1884.

SAME DAY—THE VESTAL STAKE—For three-year-old fillies, one-and-a-quarter miles; $25 p. p.; $250 added; second to receive $100, third to save stake. Nominations to be made for 1884.

SECOND DAY.

STALLION STAKE—Conditions—Only those three-year-olds are eligible which are the get of stallions owned in this State. The stallions have to subscribe the amount charged for their services to the mare; private stallions at the price of their last season, and those which have not made a public season to pay $50, that sum being the minimum price. The owner of the get of a stallion is compelled to name the mare for the male stated he filled in; $25 forfeit; stake or money added at the discretion of the Committee; distance, 1 mile. To close for 1883 on the 1st of August, 1883, at which time both stallions and colts (progeny) must be named.

THIRD DAY.

THE BALDWIN STAKE—Post stake for all open dash of four miles; $250 each, p. p., $1,000 added; second, $500, third to save stake. Will close on the 1st of August, 1883, for this year.

SAME DAY—SWIGART STAKE—For two-year-olds; dash of a mile; $50 each, $25 forfeit; $250 added; second to save stake. Nominations to be made for 1883.

SAME DAY—FAME STAKE—For three-year-olds; dash of two miles; $100 each, $25 forfeit, $500 added; second to have $150; third to save stake. Nominations to be made for 1883.

All of these Stakes close on the first day of August next, the colts riding new or yearlings, foals of 1881. Nominations to be made to J. N. Chase, Assistant Secretary, P. C. B. H. A. To be valid they must be plainly postmarked on that day, 1st of August.

THEO. WINTERS, President.
Jos. Cairn Simpson, Secretary.
G. M. Chase, Ass't Sec'y.

### SPEED PROGRAMME

FOR THE

## First Annual Meeting

OF THE

SANTA CRUZ COUNTY

## Agricultural Fair Association,

At SANTA CRUZ,
Commencing — Tuesday, August 15th.

## $3,500 IN PURSES!

FIRST DAY—Tuesday, Aug. 15, 1882.
No. 1—TROTTING RACE—Purse $250 for horses that have never beaten 2:40. Owned in the District.
No. 2—TROTTING RACE—Purse, $500. For horses that have never beaten 2:30.

SECOND DAY—Wednesday, Aug. 16.
No. 3—RUNNING STAKE—For two-year-olds; $50 entrance, $25 forfeit, $150 added. Second to save entrance. Dash of three-quarters of a mile.
No. 4—RUNNING STAKE—Free for all; $50 entrance; $25 forfeit; $100 added. Second to have entrance. Dash of a mile.
No. 5—TROTTING RACE—Purse $100. For double team owned in the District by one man.

THIRD DAY—Thursday, Aug. 17.
No. 6—TROTTING RACE—Purse $400. For horses that have never beaten 2:40.
No. 7—TROTTING RACE—Purse $600. For horses that have never beaten three minutes. Owned in the District.

FOURTH DAY—Friday, Aug. 18.
No. 8—RUNNING RACE—Selling Purse, $200; $50 to

second horse, entrance 3 per cent to third horse. One mile and repeat. Horses declared to be sold for $1,000 to carry their full net weight. Two pounds off for each $100 under fixed valuation. Weight can be claimed by any one.
No. 9—RUNNING RACE—Free for all; $25 entrance; $10 forfeit; $250 added. Second to save entrance. Half-mile and repeat.
No. 10—TROTTING RACE—Purse, $600. For horses that have never beaten 2:26.

FIFTH DAY—Saturday, Aug. 19.
No. 11—TROTTING RACE—Purse $600. Free for all two-year-olds. Mile and Repeat.
No. 12—TROTTING RACE—Purse, $600. Free for all two-year-olds. Mile and Repeat.

### Remarks and Conditions.

All Trotting Races are the best three in five, except the two-year-old trot; five to enter and three to start. Entrance fee 10 per cent, no entry to accompany nomination. Purses divided 60, the rule of suite per cent. to first horse. Entry per cent. to second, and ten per cent. to third.

National Association Rules to govern Trotting; but the Board reserve the right to trot heats of any two classes alternately, if necessary to finish a day's racing, or to trot a special race between heats.

To fill running race, three or more subscribers are necessary.

All two-year-olds, when running in their classes, shall carry one hundred pounds, with the usual allowance for mares and geldings.

All three-year-olds, when running in their classes, to carry one hundred and ten pounds, with the usual allowances as above.

Those who have nominations to make must attend to the Secretary, in writing, on the horses they will start on Wednesday, on the Monday previous, and on Friday the Wednesday previous, by twelve o'clock a.m. This rule is obvious, and must be strictly adhered to.

No added money paid for a walk over.

Horses declared in purses can only be drawn by consent of Judges.

Entries to the Pacific Coast Blood Horse Association (old weights) to govern. Running Races, except when conditions named are otherwise.

Special Races will be run the Southern Pacific Railroad and South Pacific Coast Railroad; and excursion tickets sold to both compounds from all points on their lines, good from August 14th to August 20th, inclusive.

J. D. CHACE, President.
JAMES O. WANZER, Secretary.

## SPEED PROGRAMME
OF THE
## Mount Shasta Agricultural Association,
TO BE HELD IN
## YREKA, SISKIYOU CO.,
— ON —
Wednesday, - - - October 4th, 1882.

For racing purposes this District shall comprise Siskiyou, Shasta, Trinity, and Modoc Counties, Cal., and Jackson and Lake Counties, Oregon.

No horse shall be eligible to any of the following District Races unless owned in the District prior to October, 1881.

FIRST DAY—Wednesday, Oct. 4.
No. 1—TROTTING—Free for all; 3 in 5; purse, $500.
First heats—three-minute heats; $100. Entrance 10 per cent of purse; 5 to enter, 3 to start. Entries close September 1.
No. 2—RUNNING—Dash of a mile and a half; free for all horses owned in the District; purse, $300; entrance $25 added.

SECOND DAY—Thursday, Oct. 5.
No. 3—TROTTING—Free for all unbeat horses owned in the District; 3 in 5; purse, $75; entrance $5 added.
No. 4—RUNNING—Half mile and repeat; free for all horses owned in the District; purse, $75; entrance $5 added.
No. 5—TROTTING—Free for all three-year-olds and under owned in the District; 3 in 5; purse $100, entrance $10 added.

THIRD DAY—Friday, Oct. 6.
Great match of Free.
No. 6—TROTTING—Free for all in the District; 3 in 5; purse $100; entrance $5 added.
No. 7—RUNNING—Dash of all three-year-olds and under owned in the District; dash of three-quarters of a mile purse, $75; entrance $5 added.

FOURTH DAY—Saturday, Oct. 7.
No. 8—RUNNING—Free for all; 3 in 5; purse $500. First horse over the field; second horse $100; entrance $10 added of purse; 5 to enter, 3 to start. Entries close Sept 1st.
No. 9—TROTTING—Free for all three-year-olds and under owned in the District; 3 in 5; purse $100; entrance $5 added.

### Rules and Regulations.

1st. The above purses will be given without discount.
2nd. In all District Races the amount added to stand each purse.

3rd. Entries to be placed in the entry box, kept for that purpose, at the Pavilion, prior to 9 o'clock p. m. on the day prior to race.

4th. National good, green purses pedigree, and description of horses entered, so far as known.

5th. In all purses any three competitors can make a race.

6th. All trotting shall must be in harness.

7th. National Trotting Association Rules to govern trotting Races.

8th. Pacific Coast Blood-Horse Association Rules to govern Running Races.

9th. Free for all, in races 1 and 9, unless read what it says, and all entries to these races must be made with the Secretary on or before September 1st.

J. H. MAGOFFEY, Secretary.

## SAVE MONEY!
BUY DIRECT FROM THE MANUFACTURER.

## James Wylie,
20 & 22 Seventh St., nr. Market.
MANUFACTURER
Light Carriages, Buggies and Wagons,

Guarantee First-class Work and Low Prices. Repairing, Painting and Trimming with promptness and at reasonable rates.

## For Sale!
A BRACE OF
## FINE FOX HOUNDS!

Training and Breeding guaranteed. Address for particulars,
TOM TUNSTEAD,
Nicasio, Marin County.

## C. P. R. R.

## TIME SCHEDULE.

MONDAY, May 15th, 1882.

Trains leave, and are due to arrive in San Francisco, as follows:

| LEAVE S. F. | DESTINATION | ARRIVE FROM |
|---|---|---|
| | Antioch and Martinez. | |
| | Benicia. | |
| | Deming, El Paso | Express |
| | Gait and Martinez. | Emigrant. |
| | Gait and l via Livermore. | |
| | Knight's Landing | |
| | [Sundays only] | |
| | Los Angeles and South | |
| | Livermore and Pleasanton. | |
| | Madera and Fresno. | |
| | Marysville and Chico. | |
| | Niles and Haywards. | |
| | Ogden and l Express | |
| | Sacramento, l via Livermore | |
| | Redding and Red Bluff. | |
| | Sacramento, l via Livermore | |
| | Colfax and l via Benicia. | |
| | Niles. l via Benicia. | |
| | Sacramento, via Benicia. | |
| | Sacramento River Steamers | |
| | San Jose. | |
| | Vallejo | |
| | [Sundays only] | |
| | Virginia | |
| | Woodland | |
| | Willows and Williams | |

### LOCAL FERRY TRAINS.
VIA OAKLAND PIER.

From "San Francisco," Daily.

To EAST OAKLAND
To ALAMEDA
To BERKELEY
To WEST BERKELEY

To "San Francisco," Daily.

From BROADWAY OAKLAND
From ALAMEDA
From BERKELEY
From WEST BERKELEY

### CREEK ROUTE.
From SAN FRANCISCO
From OAKLAND

All trains run daily except night trips (Sundays excepted). Trains marked thus (†) run via East Oakland. Sundays only.

"Standard Time" furnished by Randolph & Co., Jewelers, 101 and 103 Montgomery St.

A. N. TOWNE, Gen. Supt.
T. H. GOODMAN, Gen. Pass. & Tkt. Agt.

### The Victorian Trotting Club,
(L'd)
MELBOURNE, Australia,
...OFFER...

## PRIZE OF 2,500 DOLLARS,

With Entrance Fees and Sweepstakes of $50 each from Starters added.
Open to all comers, to be run. Open to all comers, top geldings. Winner to receive $2,500 added, two-thirds of $5,000 and Entrance Fees, and Second, one-third. Entrance 5 per cent. First to finish and three to start.
Entries must be in the hands of Secretary at or before 5 p.m. WEDNESDAY 2nd December, 1882.

The Victorian Trotting Club holds subscription in the different Trotting Associations of the United States, and all particulars can be procured.

Any further information desired can be obtained, on full application, to Dr. JOHN GIBNEY, 523 Sacramento St., San Francisco, Cal.
R. J. GIBNEY, Secretary.
Kifk Street, Melbourne.

# Golden Gate Fair.

**SPEED PROGRAMME FOR 1882**

## $10,000

IN

## Stakes and Prizes

FIRST DAY—Monday, Sept. 4, 1882.

No. 1—RUNNING—GOLDEN GATE STAKE—For all two-year-olds; three-quarter mile dash; $50 entrance; $25 forfeit; $150 added; second colt to save stake; winners 5 pounds extra.

No. 2—SAME DAY — RUNNING — ALAMEDA STAKE — For three-year-olds; one and one-half mile dash; $75 entrance; $25 forfeit; $175 added; second to save stake.

No. 3—SAME DAY — RUNNING — PARDEE STAKE — Free for all; one mile and repeat; $75 entrance; $25 forfeit; $250 added; second to save stake.

No. 4—SAME DAY—TROTTING—2:40 Class; purse, $600; first horse, $350; second, $150; third, $100.

No. 5—SAME DAY—SPECIAL TROT AGAINST TIME—$250 to plate; it will be awarded any stallion that beats Santa Claus' time (2:27½).

SECOND DAY—Tuesday, Sept. 5.

No. 6—TROTTING—2:30 Class; purse, $600; first horse, $400; second, $200; third, $100.

No. 7—SAME DAY—PACING—Purse, $600; first horse, $350; second, $150; third, $100.
Washington and Johnny Weigle, to wagon.

THIRD DAY—Wednesday, Sept. 6.

No. 8—RUNNING—Free for all; 2-mile dash; $100 entrance; $50 forfeit; $250 added; second horse to save stake.

No. 9—SAME DAY—TROTTING—For all three-year-olds; purse, $600; first horse, $350; second, $150; third, $60.

No. 10—SAME DAY—TROTTING—2:23 Class; purse, $800; first horse, $450; second, $240; third, $50.

FOURTH DAY—Thursday, Sept. 7.

No. 11—TROTTING—Free for all 3-mile and repeat; purse, $1,000; first horse, $600; second, $250; third, $50.

No. 12—SAME DAY—TROTTING—For all four-year-olds; purse, $600; first horse, $350; second, $150; third, $60.

No. 13—SAME DAY — RUNNING — SELLING RACE—Purse, $300; for all; 1-mile dash; second horse to receive $75; horses entered to be sold for $1,000, to carry entitled weight; 3 pounds off for each $100 under fixed Valuation.

FIFTH DAY—Friday, Sept. 8.

No. 14—RUNNING — CONSOLATION PURSE — $300 for beaten horses; mile-and-a-quarter dash; second horse to receive $75; 10 per cent entrance.

No. 15—SAME DAY—LADIES RIDING TOURNAMENT. There will be offered Very choice and elegant prizes to be competed for, contributed by the merchants and citizens of Oakland and San Francisco; the lady winning first prize to have first choice, the second, second choice, and so on until all the prizes are distributed. Ladies wishing to contest are requested to forward their names to the President or Secretary on or before the first day of September, 1882, indorsed by at least two gentlemen of the Society. Conditions will be published in the daily papers.

No. 16—SAME DAY—TROTTING—2:18 Class—Purse, $800; first horse, $450; second, $240; third, $90.

No. 17—SAME DAY—SPECIAL TROT AGAINST TIME—A purse of $250 will be given the yearling beating the best time; a full mile to harness; to entrance fee.

SIXTH DAY—Saturday, Sept. 9.

No. 18—COMPETITIVE CADET DRILL—PRIZE, $150 Gold Medal. Competition open to all educational institutions in the State.

No. 19—SAME DAY—COMPETITIVE MILITARY DRILL—A prize of the Value of $250 will be offered by the association to the best drilled Military Company in the State of California. Rules and conditions to be published hereafter. It is the intent of the Directors to have the first competing companies determine what the prize or trophy shall be, and when the same shall be competed for, until in shall have been won three times by the same company, when it shall become the absolute property of the winning company.

No. 20—SAME DAY—GRAND BICYCLE TOURNAMENT for the Association's Gold Medal to Sun Silver Medal to second and Bronze Medal to third; Golf as open to all bicyclists.

No. 21—SAME DAY—TROTTING—Free for all; purse, $800; first horse, $450; second, $240; third, $90.

No. 22—SAME DAY—A SET OF HARNESS of the Value of $125, will be offered for gentleman's roadster; best two in three; owners to drive.

By a gentleman's roadster is meant any animal owned and driven on the road by any gentleman for his own private pleasure.

## CONDITIONS.

Entries to all running stakes, trotting and pacing races, to be made to Secretary Walker, on or before August 1, 1882. Forfeits in running stakes, and the entrance fee of 10 per cent. on the trotting and pacing races, should in all cases accompany the nominations and entries.

All the trotting and pacing races are the best three in five in all, five to start, and three to start.

Entrance fee, ten per cent. on purse.

When there are eight or more starters in a trotting race, 100 yards to be a distance.

National Trotting Association rules to govern trotting, but the Board reserves the right to trot heats with any two classes alternately, if necessary to finish any day's racing, or to trot a special race between heats.

All others in trotting races are confined to horses on the Pacific Coast May 15, 1882.

In running races, three or more entries required to fill.

Those who have nominations in stakes must name to the Secretary, in writing, the horses they will start on Monday, on the Saturday previous; and on Wednesday, the Monday previous; and on Friday, the Wednesday previous. The added money will be paid for a walk-over.

Horses entered in purses can only be drawn by consent of the judges.

Rules of the Pacific Coast Blood Horse Association to govern running races, except as above specially provided.

All entries to be made in writing, giving name, age, color and residence of owner, also name, age, color and marks of horse; also, name and residence of owner; and in running races colors to be worn by the rider. And in all, any other particulars that will enable the spectators to distinguish the horses in the race.

Write "Entries to races" on outside of Envelope.

L. WALKER,     A. C. DIETZ,
Secretary.     President.

---

# $12,500
## In Purses and Staks.

### CALIFORNIA
### STATE FAIR
### SPEED PROGRAMME
#### FOR 1882.

FIRST DAY—Monday, Sept. 11.

No. 1—RUNNING—INTRODUCTION STAKE—For all ages; three-quarters of a mile dash; $50 entrance, $15 forfeit, $250 added; second to save stake.

No. 2—RUNNING—BREEDERS STAKE—For foals of 1879; one and a half mile dash; $100 entrance; p. p.; $500 added. Closed March 1st with eighteen nominations.

No. 3—RUNNING—SELLING RACE—Purse, $250. Free for all; one mile and repeat; second horse to receive $75. Entrance five per cent. to third horse. Horses entered to be sold for $1,500 to carry entitled weight, one pound off for each $100 under fixed Valuation.

No. 4—TROTTING—2:40 class; purse, $1,000.

SECOND DAY—Tuesday, Sept. 12.

No. 5—TROTTING—2:24 class; purse, $1,500.

No. 6—TROTTING—Purse, $600; for three year colts and under.

No. 7—TROTTING—Purse, $600; mile heats for two year colts.

THIRD DAY—Wednesday, Sept. 13.

No. 8—RUNNING—FILLY STAKE FOR TWO YEAR OLD FILLIES—Three-quarters of a mile; $50 entrance; $15 forfeit; $200 added; second to receive $75; third, $25.

No. 9—RUNNING—CALIFORNIA DERBY STAKE.—For three-year-olds; one and one-half mile dash; $100 entrance; $25 forfeit; $300 added; second horse, $100; third, $50.

No. 10—RUNNING—JENNIE B STAKE—For all ages; dash of mile; $25 entrance, $15 forfeit; $250 added; second horse, $75; third, $25. Stake to be named after winner of Jennie B.'s time, 1:43¼ in heats.

No. 11—TROTTING—SELLING RACE—Purse, $250; one and one-eighth mile; second horse, $75; entered five per cent. to third horse. Horses entered to be sold for $1,500, to carry entitled weight. Two pounds off for each $100 under fixed Valuation.

No. 12—TROTTING—2:30 class; purse, $1,500.

FOURTH DAY—Thursday, Sept. 14.

No. 13—TROTTING—2:22 class; purse, $1,500.

No. 14—PACING—2:25 class; purse, $600.

No. 15—TROTTING—Two quikes and repeat; 2:40 horses; purse, $600.

FIFTH DAY—Friday, Sept. 15.

No. 16—RUNNING—COLT AND FILLY STAKE—For two year olds; dash of one mile; $50 entrance; $15 forfeit, $300 added, second horse, $90; third, $50.

No. 17—RUNNING—SELLING RACE—Purse, $300; for all ages; dash of one and a quarter miles; $100 to second horse; entrance, five per cent. to third; horses entered to be sold for $1,500 carry full weight; for $1,200, three pounds off; for $900, five pounds off; for $750, seven pounds off; for $500, ten pounds off.

No. 18—RUNNING—POST STAKE—Dash of three miles; free for all; $100 entrance; $500 added; second, $150; third, $100. Starters to be named to the Secretary Wednesday evening, at or before 6 o'clock p.m.

No. 19—RUNNING—CONSOLATION PURSE—$250 for beaten horses; one mile and repeat; entrance free; second horse to receive $50.

SIXTH DAY—Saturday, Sept. 16.

No. 20—TROTTING—2:19 class; purse, $1,500.

No. 21—TROTTING—Purse, $600; for double teams of 2:40 horses.

No. 22—TROTTING—OCCIDENT STAKE for 1882, closed in 1881 with twelve nominations.

No. 23—SPECIAL TROT AGAINST TIME—$250 to plate; will be awarded to any horse that beats Santa Claus time (2:27½).

Entries for the following stakes for 1883-4 were ordered to be closed with the State Fair, 1882:

No. 1—RUNNING—CALIFORNIA DERBY STAKE for foals of 1880, to be run at the State Fair of 1883. One and one-half miles dash; $50 entrance, p. p.; $300 added; second horse, $100; third, $50.

No. 2—Same stake, for foals of 1881, to be run at State Fair of 1884. Same conditions.

No. 3—RUNNING—MATURITY STAKE—Three mile dash, for four-year-olds, in 1883; $100 entrance; $50 forfeit; $500 added; second horse, $100; third, $50.

No. 4—RUNNING—CALIFORNIA ANNUAL STAKE—For two-year-olds of 1881. Dash of one mile; $100 entrance; $25 forfeit; $250 added; second horse, $100; third, $50. To be run at the Fair of 1883.

## REMARKS and CONDITIONS.

All trotting and pacing races are the best three in five, except the two year old trot, unless otherwise specified; five to enter and three to start. Entrance fee ten per cent. on purse, to accompany nomination. Purses divided at the rate of sixty per cent. to first horse, thirty per cent. to second, and ten per cent. to third.

National Association Rules to govern trotting; but the Board reserves the right to trot heats of any two classes alternately, if necessary to finish any day's racing, or to trot a special race between heats.

To fill running races, three or more subscribers are necessary.

All two-year-olds, when running in their classes, shall carry one hundred pounds, with the usual allowance for mares and geldings.

All three-year-olds, when running in their classes, to carry one hundred and ten pounds, with the usual allowance for sex.

National Association Rules to govern running. In all but the one day previous and on Wednesday, the Monday previous and on Friday the Wednesday previous, by twelve o'clock m. This rule is obvious and must be strictly adhered to.

No added money paid for a walk-over.

Horses entered in purses can only be drawn by consent of Judges.

Rules of the Pacific Coast Blood Horse Association told weighted to govern running races, except when conditions named are otherwise.

All entries to be made in writing, giving name, age, color, residence and marks of owner; and in running races full colors to be worn by rider; and in running races all the particulars that will enable spectators to distinguish the horses. In the one day previous and on the second day's race, in their entries; the horses they will start on; a second the first day, the second on the third day; the third on the fourth day. If it is necessary to enable spectators to distinguish the horses in the race.

Entries to all the above races to close with the Secretary on Tuesday, August 1, 1882.

Write "Entries to Races" on outside of envelope.

EDWIN F. SMITH,     HUGH M. LARUE,
Secretary.     President.

---

## SPEED PROGRAMME.
## $13,000 Gold Coin
### IN PURSES.

### The Largest Purses Offered in
### the State.

## STOCKTON;
### Sept. 19th to 23d inclusive, 1882.

TUESDAY, SEPT. 19TH.

No. 1—DISTRICT—RUNNING—For two-year-olds; purse $600; mile dash; 1 to enter, 3 to start. Four moneys.

No. 2—DISTRICT—TROTTING—For yearlings; purse $600; mile dash; 3 to enter, 3 to start. Four moneys.

No. 3—PACIFIC COAST TROTTING—2:30 Class; purse $1,000, and $500 added if more than ten entries. Four moneys.

WEDNESDAY, SEPT. 20TH.

No. 4—PACIFIC COAST NOVELTY RUNNING—¾ mile dash, purse $600. The first horse to each half mile to win $100, and the horse first to two and two-and-one-half mile posts to win $50 each. Extra $200 additional will be added to the purse, pro rata, if more than ten entries.

No. 5—DISTRICT RUNNING — Two-year-olds; purse $600. Closed with six entries.

No. 6—PACIFIC COAST TROTTING—2:25 Class; purse $1,000, and $500 added if more than ten entries. Four moneys.

No. 7—DISTRICT — TROTTING — For named horses; purse $300; 7 to enter, 4 to start. This race is intended for horses that can trot in three minutes or a little better. Four moneys.

THURSDAY, SEPT. 21ST.

No. 8—PACIFIC COAST TROTTING—Mile and repeat; purse $500, and if 1:40 in beaten, the horse making the low record will receive $200 additional. Four moneys.

No. 9—DISTRICT — TROTTING — For three-year-olds; purse $600. Closed with ten entries.

### Ladies' Equestrianism.

FOUR PRIZES in Gold Coin — $40, $30, $20, $10.
7 to enter, 4 to start. Four moneys.

No. 10—DISTRICT—TROTTING—2:28 Class; purse $600; 7 to enter, 4 to start. Four moneys.

FRIDAY, SEPT. 22D.

No. 11—PACIFIC COAST—RUNNING—Free for all; two mile and repeat; purse $600, and $300 added if more than ten entries. Four moneys.

No. 12—DISTRICT—RUNNING—For three-year-olds and over; purse $500; best two in three; 1 to enter, 4 to start. Four moneys.

No. 13—PACIFIC COAST TROTTING—For horses owned on the Pacific Coast, July 1st, 1882; $25 Class; purse $1,000, and $500 added if more than ten subscribers. The nominator not required to name his horse, but pledged his cash $100, with the entry of his horse, August 1, 1882. He has until August 1, 1882, to start any horse eligible that he may fairly control, provided the horse be starts be named to the Secretary, September 1, 1882. Four moneys.

SATURDAY, SEPT. 23D.

No. 14—PACIFIC COAST TROTTING—2:22 Class; purse $1,000, and $500 added if more than ten entries. Four moneys.

No. 15—PACIFIC COAST PACING—2:25 Class; purse $400, and $200 added if more than ten entries. Four moneys.

## REMARKS AND CONDITIONS.

All Trotting Races best three in five, except numbers 7 and 8.

In all these Races (Pacific Coast Novelty Race excepted) more moneys, 30, 20, 15 and 10 per cent of purse. Entrance fee, 10 per cent. of purse, and must accompany the nomination. District Races will close with the Secretary at 5 o'clock p.m. of July 15, 1882. Pacific Coast Races to close with the Secretary August 1, 1882.

When there are eight or more to start in a Trotting Race, 100 yards shall be a distance.

Rules of the National Trotting Association to govern trotting, except as specified; but the Board of Managers reserve the right to trot heats of any two classes alternately, or to start a special race between heats.

All two-year-olds, when running in their classes, shall carry 100 pounds, with the usual allowance for mares and geldings.

All three-year-olds, when running in their classes, to carry 110 pounds with the usual allowance as above, otherwise, and weights to go Post.

For a walk-over in any race a horse shall only be entitled to his own entrance fee and one-quarter of the entrance received from the other entries for said purse; and a horse winning a race entitled to first money only, except when distancing the field, shall be entitled to first and second money only. A horse wins that our money under any other circumstances.

Horses entered in purses can only be drawn by consent of the Judges.

The Board reserves the right to change the day and hour of any race, if they deem it necessary.

Unless otherwise ordered by the Board, no horse shall be qualified to enter in any District Race that has not been owned in the District six (6) months prior to the day of the race; and any entry by any person of any horse so disqualified shall be held liable for the entrance fee to be contested without any right to compete, and the same shall be held liable to penalties prescribed by the Rules of the National Trotting Association and expulsion from this Association.

Rules of the Pacific Coast Blood Horse Association to govern Running Races, including additions to rules, except as especially provided.

In all Running Races colors to be worn by riders, and in all other races, any other particulars that will enable spectators to distinguish the horses in the race.

In all the Coast Races noted above, all entries are required to fill, and three horses to start; but the Board RESERVE THE RIGHT TO CLOSE ANY RACE WITH A LESS NUMBER.

All entrance fees paid, as I deduct, in short.

This race is first-class, having been improved. Stables, hay and straw free to competitors.

## ENTRIES.

1st. Entries must be made in writing and dated.
2nd. State number of the race in which you wish to enter.
3rd. State COLOR of horse, and name if necessary.
4th. State whether the horse is a STALLION, MARE or GELDING.
5th. State NAME OF SIRE AND DAM if known; if unknown, state the fact to the best of your knowledge.
6th. State NAME and P. O. ADDRESS of the owner of the horse engaged.
7th. Sign with P. O. address of the party entering the horse.
8th. If the name has been changed, give former name.
9th. Entries by telegraph will be recognized if the party telegraphing is responsible, and entry confirmed by letter and fee forwarded by mail the same day.

Address all communications to San Joaquin, Calaveras, Tuolumne, Stanislaus, Mariposa, Merced, Fresno, Tulare Agricultural Association.

J. L. PHELPS, President.
P. O. Box 183, Stockton, Cal.

---

### SECOND
### ANNUAL EXHIBITION
OF THE

### SAN MATEO AND SANTA
### CLARA COUNTY
### AGRICULTURAL ASSOCIATION
### NO. 5,
TO BE HELD AT
## SAN JOSE, CAL.,
.....FROM......
### Sept. 25th to 30th, '82 inclusive

## SPEED PROGRAMME.

FIRST DAY—Monday, Sept. 25th, 1882.

No. 1. TROTTING—2:40 Class. Purse, $500.
No. 2. SAME DAY—TROTTING—2:25 Class. Purse, $750.

SECOND DAY—Tuesday, Sept. 26th.

No. 3. RUNNING—For two-year-olds; three-quarter mile dash; $50 entrance; $25 forfeit; $250 added. Second horse to receive his entrance and one-third of added money.

No. 4. SAME DAY—RUNNING—Selling Race—Purse, $300; mile and repeat. Second horse to receive his entrance and one-third of added money.

No. 5. SAME DAY—RUNNING — Selling Race — Purse, $300; mile and repeat. Horses entered to be sold for $1,000 to carry entitled weight. Two pounds off for each $100 under fixed Valuation. Winner can be claimed by any person.

THIRD DAY—Wednesday, Sept. 27th.

No. 6. TROTTING—2:30 class. Purse, $500.
No. 7. SAME DAY—BOOT HORSE RACE—For horses owned in the District to be driven by owner in buggy. Two mile heats. Purse to be hereafter offered.
No. 8. SAME DAY—Ladies' Riding Tournament — Bicycle Race, etc.

FOURTH DAY—Thursday, Sept. 28th.

No. 9. RUNNING — Three-year-olds; 1½ mile dash; $50 entrance; $25 forfeit; $275 added. Second horse to receive his entrance and one-third of added money.
No. 10. SAME DAY—PACING—Free for all. Purse $400.
No. 11. SAME DAY—TROTTING—For four-year-olds. Purse $400.

FIFTH DAY—Friday, Sept. 29th.

No. 11. RUNNING—½ mile dash. For all ages; $50 entrance; $25 forfeit; $250 added. Second horse to receive his entrance and one-third of added money.
No. 12. SAME DAY—TROTTING—2:37 class. Purse $600.
No. 13. SAME DAY — TROTTING—For two-year-olds. Purse $400.

SIXTH DAY—Saturday, Sept. 30th.

No. 14. TROTTING—2:22 class. Purse $750.
No. 15. SAME DAY—TROTTING—2:30 class. Two miles and repeat. Purse $800.

## REMARKS AND CONDITIONS.

All trotting and pacing races are the best three in five, except the two-year-old trot, unless otherwise specified; five to enter and three to start. Entrance fee ten per cent. on purse, to accompany nominations. Purses divided at the rate of sixty per cent. to first horse, thirty per cent. to second and ten per cent. to third.

National Association Rules to govern trotting; but the Board reserves the right to trot heats of any two classes alternately, if necessary to finish any day's racing, or to trot a special race between heats.

To fill running races, three or more subscribers are necessary.

All two-year-olds, when running in their classes, shall carry one hundred pounds, with the usual allowance for mares and geldings.

All three-year-olds, when running in their classes, to carry one hundred and ten pounds, with the usual allowance as above.

Those who have nominations in stakes must name to the Secretary, in writing, the horses they will start on Tuesday, on the Monday previous; and the horses they will start on Thursday, the Tuesday previous; and on Friday, the Wednesday previous, by twelve o'clock m. This rule is obvious, and must be strictly adhered to.

No added money paid for a walk-over.

Horses entered in purses can only be drawn by consent of the Judges.

Rules of the Pacific Coast Blood Horse Association told weighted to govern running races, except when conditions named are otherwise.

All entries to be made in writing, giving name, age, color and marks of horse, also name and residence of owner. In running races full colors to be worn by rider; and in all, any other particulars that are respectfully requested to those entries, as these entries will enable spectators to distinguish the horses in the race.

If the entry has been changed, give the former name. If not so the horse will be disqualified upon programmes by colors worn by drivers.

Entries to all the above races to close with the Secretary on Tuesday, August 1st, 1882.

Write "Entries to Races" on outside of envelope.

E. S. MONTGOMERY, Secretary.     A. KING, President.

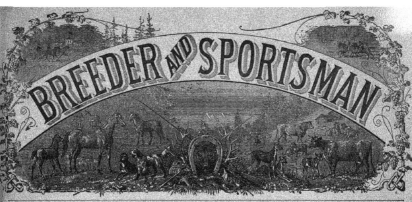

# BREEDER AND SPORTSMAN

VOL. I.—No 4
No. 508 MONTGOMERY STREET.

SAN FRANCISCO, SATURDAY, JULY 22, 1882.

SUBSCRIPTION
FIVE DOLLARS A YEAR.

## NOTABLE HORSES OF CALIFORNIA.

## ELECTIONEER.

No one who has the smallest knowledge of the great horses of the time will question the right of Electioneer to a prominent niche in the Temple of Hippie Fame, if he does not figure in the list of winners. That he is still more eminently entitled to be ranked among the "Notable Horses of California," if not born or raised in this State, is undeniable. Like many of the greatest names in the human race, his fame rests on what has been accomplished in the land of adoption, and after coming here comparatively unknown, a short five years has given him a place among trotting sires of the highest grade. In one respect he takes precedence of all, and can show a succession of young prodigies, any one of which would be a measure of glory to a progenitor. The remarkable "prepotency," as writers are now so partial to calling the power of transmitting qualities he has shown would scarcely have been credited before he gained the distinction he enjoys. A few years ago the prophet

who ventured the prediction that any stallion would show in one season a yearling with a record of 2:36½, a two-year-old with 2:31 to her credit, another two-year-old with 2:24½, and several more of the latter age which gave a public exhibition of speed much below a 3:30 gait, would have been held demented. Even after Fred Crocker trotted in 2:25½ the most acute observers held that it was a phenomenal performance which, in all probability, would not be reached in years. Had it not been that Sweetheart was so near the same point, there would have been still greater doubt, though as it was, the likelihood of still more marvellous feats speedily following, there was general incredulity.

Though Electioneer has never trotted in public, he gave evidence of possessing his share of the well known speed of the family, and it was only the "worst run of bad luck" imaginable which prevented him from leading the noted progeny of Green Mountain Maid, great as the feats of

Prospero, Dame Trot, Elaine, etc., have been. Probabilities, however, are not required, and the glory which Electioneer has obtained through his progeny is far beyond what individual capacity would merit, though that capacity were of the highest class. Individual merit in horses ends with the active life of the performer. He who has the faculty of perpetuating the desired qualities lives in future generations, and in the case of the horse under consideration there are already as many of his sons and daughters which are endowed, that it is sure he will take the place of a founder of a family, and the Electioneers be known through several generations by this distinctive appellation. Even when broken up into several branches the "head of the clan" will be remembered as the founder of the dynasty, and the banner emblazoned with the colors of the chieftain. As has been stated, there was a succession of prodigies to his credit after the fruits of his first season in Califorcame upon the track. Though he had made some seasons in the East, he was so completely overshadowed, in the estimation of his former owner, by his stable companion, Messenger Duroc, that he occupied an inferior position. Not so humiliating as the Godolphin Arab occupied at Gog Magog, but restricted in his opportunities and his colts given no chance.

When Governor Stanford visited Stony Ford and the stallions were paraded for his inspection, his companions were enthusiastic over the fancy of the owner. Messenger Duroc was the only horse in the world, and to show another after he had been on the stage was like displaying the daubs of a village pothouse in juxtaposition to a gallery of the grand masters of the art. He was not to be misled, however, by the acclamations. First he saw that the form of Electioneer was superior—much superior, according to his idea,—and then the next thing to consider was the breeding. Both were by the same sire. Messenger Duroc's dam Satinet by Roe's Abdallah Chief, and the dam of Electioneer was Green Mountain Maid by Harry Clay.

Messenger Duroc, at that time, owed all of his celebrity to Prospero and Dame Trot, both from the dam of Electioneer, and to Hogarth, the dam of which was also by Harry Clay. To a man who had a knowledge of breeding, in the habit of forming his opinions from his own knowledge, and not easily influenced by the enthusiastic notions of others, there could be little question when a choice had to be made, and though the "big horse" was priced at a figure at least four times as much as the other, the more highly formed and better bred was taken. Price had nothing to do with the choice. The intention was to buy the best regardless of cost, and fortunately for the breeding interests of California the son of Green Mountain Maid was the selection. It is not the intention to make this series of articles a dissertation on breeding. The plan is to accompany the picture with a short sketch of the animal portrayed; but this must, of course, depend on circumstances. When the title of "notable" depends on the progeny, then the ancestry also comes in for a share of the notice. It is superogatory to say anything of the sire of Electioneer, Rysdyk's Hambletonian. His fame is so great, and so deservedly great, that it cannot be questioned with any logical argument to support the questioner. His dam, Green Mountain Maid, stands so nearly at the head of the list of trotting broodmares that Miss Russell is the only one which can dispute the claim that she should be the premier. Prospero 2.20, Elaine 2:20, and Dame Trot 2:22, are a trio of jewels of which the highest might be proud. There are assuredly "speed lines" enough here to suit the most fastidious sticklers for this essential part of a pedigree, and to add still greater force we find that the second generation is likely, and we believe sure, to better the showing. We have not the least doubt that there will be grandsons and granddaughters of Green Mountain Maid which will show far faster, and of this sort not a few.

For the proof, a brief recapitulation of what has already been done will be all that is necessary, and that we will rest the case: On the Bay District Course November 13, 1880, Fred Crocker was matched against 2:30. He then was a two-year-old, and had trotted a race in Sacramento, when he was beaten by Sweetheart in 2:31½–2:32¼ This he won very handily in 2:28¾ One week afterwards he was again asked to beat his own time, and he accomplished it with a margin of 3¼ seconds, placing 2:25¼ on the blackboard. Sweetheart had trotted in 2:26½, and the performances by two California-bred two-year-olds set the Eastern world ablaze. The fastest time for years, and it still ranks the fastest for that section, was 2:31, and to have it lowered so much was scarcely to be credited. There were chapters upon chapters in the Eastern papers. Some questioned the accuracy of the timing, others the length of the track, and never before was there such a hubbub unless, perhaps, when Goldsmith Maid trotted in 2:17 at Milwaukee. Anno Domini 1881, increased the surprise, or rather so completely established the superiority of the California colts that the Eastern breeders were in dismay. At a meeting of an association, composed of the prominent breeders of the East, it was gravely debated whether the Occidentals should be barred, handicapped, or some other plan adopted which would save from impending danger. A resolution was offered that the distance should be increased to 220 yards in colt races, and then an amendment was offered that it should be 150 yards. The cause for all of this tribulation was the trotting of another lot of two-year-olds, and was as follows: At the State Fair at Sacramento there was a stake for two-year-olds, the starters Wildflower by Electioneer, and Eva by Sultan. The latter was a sister to Sweetheart, Wildflower nearly a sister in blood to Fred Crocker, both of their dams being by St. Clair. Eva won the first heat in 2:33¾, Wildflower the second and third in 2:33-2:37. This was good, if not up to the standard of the preceding year, but the owners were well aware that it was well within the rate of the two fillies, and means were taken to put it to a test. The race at Sacramento was on September 22d, and on the Bay District Course, on October 22d, there were two prizes given for two-year-olds to beat the once celebrated time of So-So, 2:31. The track was in good order and the day fair. The attendance was good, a large number of those who take delight in the sports of the track, but who are prone to verify the time of the judges with their own watches. Wildflower came out first. She moved up and down the stretch a few times to "warm up," going so smoothly and easily that it was evident that 2:31 was nowhere, and some were sanguine enough to predict that the time of Fred Crocker might be equalled.

She started with the daisy-cutting stride for which she is noted, and the very best judge of speed, with his eye merely to guide, would have thought that a "forty gait" was about the measure. Thirty-five and a quarter seconds was the tale told by the watches when the quarter pole was made, and there were many of those who held timing watches who doubted the accuracy of the report and thought that their "old reliables" had failed them at a critical moment. Acting as Clerk of the course, which gave the best opportunity to see every portion of the track, and the position of the fractional posts being such that there is no difficulty in "catching the time" correctly, with as good a split-second watch as ever came from the hands of the best maker, we were prepared to be accurate, and from our coin of advantage were prepared to verify the official time. Each of the judges had a watch, and the figures of the regular timers, stationed immediately opposite the judges' stand, agreed with ours as to the fractions, and there was a remarkable unanimity in officials and "outsiders" regarding the time. But this break in the description is very different from the trotting of Wildflower. She swept down the backstretch at such a flight of speed that the galloper which accompanied her was put to a racing stride, and at the half mile 1:09 was the record. This was surely far too fast, and any animal not yet forty months old could not withstand the strain. There was a slight slackening of the speed around the further turn, whether owing to tiring, which appeared inevitable, or strategy on the part of the driver in order to enable her to come home, was, of course, unknown to the spectators. With all the evident slowing, she reached the three-quarters in 1:44¾, and yet there was not the rush which marked her progress in the backstretch. Mr. Covey ran up the track shouting and signalling her driver to come on. He did not understand the mandate until nearly opposite the 150 yard mark, when for the first time she was touched with the whip. The response was such an accelleration of the rate that the "teaser" was forced to extend herself for the rest of the journey, and she swept under the wire in 2:21. The explanation of the slackening on the upper turn and down the stretch was this; Frank Covey drove the galloper, carrying a chronograph in his hand. When he saw that the half mile was made in 1:09 he was startled, and fearful that a break might render all that had been done of no avail. He was satisfied that any previous three-year-old time would be beaten easily if there was no mishap, and very judiciously he directed McGregory to "take a pull." It is unnecessary to speculate what would have resulted from a different course, and it is sufficient that the best time of the East had been beaten ten seconds, and when that time was "hung out", there was a shout which might have been heard in the city. There are few men who would have started another filly after such an exhibition of speed, but Mr. Rose, with the feeling of a true sportsman, determined that Eva should fulfill her part of the programme, and a grand effort she made, accomplishing the mile in 2:26. On the 5th day of November there was another wonderful exhibition of speed by the youngsters. There were special prizes for yearlings, and after what the two-year-olds had shown, some were sanguine enough to predict that the time of Memento would be beaten. This grand record for a yearling was held to be so superlatively good that our old and esteemed friend "H. B.," of the *Turf, Field and Farm* wrote "that it would be a long time before we saw such a wonderful baby trotter." Doctor Hicks' bay filly Pride, by Buccaneer, made the first essay, and left the Kentucky time 12¾ seconds behind, trotting in 2:44½. This was a "hard stent," and as in the preceding day it took some nerve to make a trial after such a "breaking of the record." Mr. Covey, however, was not easily discouraged, and Hinda Rose, by Electioneer, her dam Beautiful Belle by The Moor, was selected to battle for Palo Alto. She proved victorious by the small margin of a second, 2:43½ being the mark. This disposed of the question that Electioneer could only get trotters from St. Clair mares, and when Azol, another yearling by him, with a still different cross in the dam, trotted a quarter in 41¾ seconds, the "prepotency" of the sire was established.

On the same day there was a further exhibition of the quality of the stock of Sunny Slope and Palo Alto. Eva trotted a mile in 2:26½, and her two-year-old sister, Sweetheart, a mile in 2:22, only one second below that of the champion, Phil Thompson. We venture to say, quoting our old friend again, that it will be a long time before we will see sisters two and three years old which will show such time on the same day, or for that matter in the same season.

*Five* of the Palo Alto two-year-olds made an exhibition of a quarter of a mile. Three by Electioneer, two by General Benton. The two Bentons, Bonnie and Bertha, each made the quarter in [illegible] seconds, and the Electioneers as follows: Eros, [illegible] seconds: Bonita, 32¾ seconds; Wildflowert, 32 seconds.

It is not surprising that the Eastern people doubted the length of the track, the accuracy of the watches, the age of the colts. The wonder is that they did not set the whole thing down as a fiction, a moon hoax story, akin to the traveling stories of Gulliver, and that all Californians were in a conspiracy to humbug with stories which underrate the common sense of any one who would give them credit for truth.

But on the 24th day of November was accomplished, in our opinion, the greatest feat of them all. Two medals were offered, the first being for a yearling that would beat 2:43½, the second for a two-year-old to rub out any record for that age, save that of Wildflower. The figures are the most eloquent commentary. The yearling, Hinda Rose, went to the quarter in 40½ seconds, to the half-mile pole in 1:18¾, and made the mile in 2:36½. She made a break on the home stretch and the "middle half" was trotted in 1:15½. That a filly taking rank as a yearling, lacking several months of being two years old, should show so much speed and endurance, the speed especially, is the most marvellous illustration of the improvement of the American trotter which has ever been shown.

It seemed a fitting tribute to the two prominent breeding farms of California, and that the union of the forces was irresistible. Bonita took the second place in the record by making the mile in 2:24½. Electioneer, St. Clair, Fred Crocker, Wildflower, Bonita. One of the earliest strains of California and one among the latest, it is certainly a great "trick." There are not many Electioneer's outside of Palo Alto, but the few there are show the family characteristics. Albert W., by Electioneer, his dam a sister to Aurora, promises to conquer a place in the gallery of notables before long. Last year as a three-year-old he was very successful. He won a stake for three-year-olds at the Golden Gate Fair. At the State Fair he walked over for a stake, and won another, trotting the second, third and fourth heats in 2:38½, 2:36¼, 2:39; Flight winning the first in 2:42¾. At Stockton he and Flight again met. He won the first heat in 2:37; she the second in 2:35; he the third in 2:35 and the fourth in 2:32½. This was a very good showing for a colt of his age with as little training as has been given him. Antero, by Electioneer from Columbine by A. W. Richmond, won the Embryo stakes of 1880 and 1881, when he was a yearling and two-year-old.

Making actual performances the text, we will not add the "trials" of the Electioneers, though these would add to his renown. Not private trials but performances made as much in public as when the money is "hung up" and judges in the stand. It may be added, however, that an Electioneer which cannot trot would be considered an anomaly, and every one that has had any training can trot fast.

Our engraving is such an admirable picture of Electioneer that written description is almost unnecessary. We never saw a more faithful likeness of a horse, and if the color was added it would be as perfect as an artist could draw, if he took a year to perfect his work. Some who have seen the "proof" say, "Why that is a tremendously powerful horse." That is one of his main features. Quarters and loins are immensely so, and the gaskins are very full. The shoulders are well clothed and the neck very strong. With all this power there is a finish, more quality than is usually seen in the sons of Hambletonian, and a majority of his colts, particularly those from highly bred mares, are still finer. There are several at Palo Alto which it would be difficult to tell from thoroughbreds. His color is very fine, a deep, rich bay, with white hind feet.

## A REPLY TO EDWIN.

EDITOR BREEDER AND SPORTSMAN—DEAR SIR: I was much pleased to see "Edwin's" article on "Judging by Measure" in your issue of July 15th, and would add, by way of parenthesis, that if all who differ in opinion would treat their opponents with equal courtesy, acrimony would be expunged from our sporting papers, more harmony exist in our Clubs, and far more good ensue to our fraternity. "Edwin" has had more practical experience in the matter of judging than I have, and your correspondent defers much to his assertions; but having thought seriously upon the above subject, and seen and read of the wide divergence of one judge from another on the same dog, within the same month, and the dog in the same condition, I feel as if there was something radically wrong in the base upon which our judges work. There was no reason to impugn the opinion of either judge as to their fitness for the office, or their action as gentlemen. We all know how many different schools of art there are, and how tenacious of opinion is the advocate of one over the opinions of another as to their relative merits; therefore, in many instances, the widespread dissatisfaction among the artists over each exhibition; and for that reason alone, I do not think the citation carries strength sufficient to convince me that my proposition is untenable.

A dog is a tangible object, and can be got at from all sides; an object that has size and body; a picture is not, but is the offspring of one's imagination, and its degree of merit depends upon the artist's technique.

You may take a yacht—each line is drawn upon a true scale and mathematically correct; each curve, from rail to keelson, and stem to stern, proportioned exactly. Science has taught us that certain shapes increase the speed, others the carrying capacity, from which the craftsman knows how to plan for pleasure or business. So upon the subject of "judging my measure." In the earlier stages of Bench Shows, judging by the "rule of thumb" was the only method, and each judge did the best he knew how. The first advance and only forward move, up to date, was the standard points, as alluded to in my article of July 8th, and laid down as follows:

We will take for illustration the one hundred points given by Stonehenge for the Irish Setter. Each point is lucidly described in his work: Skull, value, 10; nose, 10; ears, lips and eyes, 4; neck, 6; shoulders and chest, 15; back, quarters and stifles, 15; legs, elbows and hocks, 12; feet, 8;

fiSs, 5; symmetry and quality, 5; texture of coat and feather, 5; color, 5.

Now, out of those 100 points I am firmly of the opinion that, with proper care in the selection of measurement of prize winners, and patience, an average can be arrived at that will arbitrarily fix a standard size under the proper weight of dog for the skull, nose, ears and lips, neck, shoulders and chest, back, quarters and stifles, legs, elbows and hocks, feet, thus compiling a standard for symmetry.

Eyes, flag, texture of coat and feather, and color, quality, or *tout ensemble*, must be judged by "rule of thumb," the same as paintings.

I should very much like to have brother sportsmen offer their views, and if my position is untenable I will gracefully and cheerfully—although I would think it rough on the dog—step down and out. It is only by a pleasant, serious, and friendly interchange of ideas that reforms are brought about—that causes pleasure to the "accomplisher" and leaves no sting to the "extinguished."

The 100-point system has by custom become established, and although Stonehenge advocates the judging by "positive and negative marks," which is an excellent arrangement, yet usage has so firmly rooted the 100 points I would not now try to break it up in favor of the positive and negative system, but would suggest that some sporting house get up a book that would carry the advertisement of said house and contain the printed points of each class of dogs, and have them for sale, or gratuitously distribute to each Judge of each Bench Show, and request said Judge to fill up the same for publication, in the BREEDER AND SPORTSMAN, *Forest and Stream*, or *American Field*.

SUDS.

## INTERESTING HISTORY OF ROMERO'S COLTHOOD.

ELA HILLS, Los Angeles County, July 5, 1882.

EDITOR BREEDER AND SPORTSMAN—DEAR SIR: Your letter dated May 31st received, and as your paper is to be exclusively for stockmen, with no politics in it, I will take pleasure at all times in adding my mite. Please find $5 enclosed, my subscription for one year.

Romero's history, up to the time of his sale to M. Salisbury, is about as follows: In 1876 I bought Gretchen, by Mambrino Pilot, dam Kitty Kirkman, from L. J. Rose, Esq., of Sunny Slope, bred her to A. W. Richmond February 28, 1877; she foaled the grey colt Jo Romero, since called Romero for short. Mr. M. S. Patrick, from whom I purchased Richmond, wanted a Richmond colt, and as I only had five colts I would not sell him any, but agreed to give him a half interest in one that he should select, on condition that he should pay for training and trotting him in all two and three-year-old purses; he was also to keep him entire and not change his name. Mr. Patrick failed in his engagement, as he left the colt for me to take care of until he was 18 months old, when I insisted upon his taking the colt, as he was bothering the mares. Mr. Patrick then gave the colt to Charles Thomas to break and to take care of. Mr. Patrick died shortly afterwards, and I told Thomas to keep the colt on the same conditions, which he agreed to. I made no points with him about the conditions not having been complied with in his two year old form, as Len Rose, the colt I kept, had done more than well, but insisted upon something being done to prepare him for his three-year-old races. Thomas' ranch is 130 miles from here in the San Jacinto Mountains, and he made first one excuse then another for not bringing the colt in for all that fall; said the colt was sick, and so on. I was informed, however, that the colt was running with a lot of mares on the Temecula Mountains all the fall and winter of 1879, and I am told has left several colts in those parts. Finally, in the spring, about the last of May, 1880, Thomas sent the colt to Los Angeles, and he looked as though he might have wintered almost anywhere, as his hair looked dead and long and he was very poor. Thomas gave the colt to Durfee to work and train for three months, but when we hitched him up it was evident that he had never looked through a collar. As we had been told the colt was broken to harness, we took no precautions to prevent him from injuring himself, and he came very near battering his brains out in the stall before the harness could be removed. This was about June 1, 1880. July 4th, 1880, we gave our horses a trial, and Romero trotted his mile in 2:41, and could brush Len Rose down the stretch, who had trotted in 2:32½ at that time. Before the entries closed at Sacramento, Romero showed that he was as fast as Len, but as he had no seasoning work and was soft, I was afraid of injuring him, and concluded to let him rest and feed him some grain until the next spring; besides I thought Len Rose would be fast enough. At this time Charles Thomas sold Charles Durfee his half interest in Romero for $220, I think. Before I sent my horses to Sacramento, Romero showed a 2:32 gait, but pulled up a little lame, having stepped in a hole; so his shoes were pulled off and he was turned out. He was not driven again until towards winter, when he was hitched up and speeded half a mile for John Mackey's entertainment, when he trotted in 1:17 or 1:17¼, I forget which. We thought it wonderful, as the horse had been kept in a box stall with no exercise for three or four months. Mackey thought him a wonderful colt, and we were much amused by his remarking that "the colt made him know that he wanted a car-load of Mambrino Pilot mares," and he intended to get them to breed to Echo. I told him that if Haggin bought them he had best buy Richmond to go with them, if he wanted to breed colts like Romero.

In December, 1880, I offered my stock to Mr. Salisbury, and as Mr. Titus had told him about Romero, he came to look at them; he wanted me to set a separate price upon Romero, and I did, putting him at $2,500, which he thought too much. I then offered to let him buy Durfee out, and leave me my half. He refused, and I then told him that I was anxious to sell the stock, and I had already had two trades broken by Romero, so, in order to get him out of the way, I would make him a present of my half and he could buy Durfee out; he would not have it so, and left. Next day Mr. McKibben offered Durfee $1,100 for the colt, and I told Durfee to consult his own necessities and feelings upon the subject—that anything would satisfy me. Durfee went away, saying that he did not want to do it, but was very much in need of money, and finally went to McKibben and took the money. I wanted him to give us a contingent $2,000 more upon condition of his beating 2.25 within the year, but could not get him to agree upon it. Mr. Salisbury bought Romero solely upon Mr. Titus' representations, and we did not even lead the colt for him to see his action, although we offered to work him next day for him. Mr. Titus told me long before Mr. Salisbury bought the colt, and after Button had beaten us all around the circuit, that though he was positive that Belle Echo could beat Alex Button, he felt nervous about that green fellow of mine, meaning Romero, and time has proven that Mr. Titus is not so blinded by his preference for his own stock as not to recognize a good horse wherever he sees him.

I have been trying to make this a short story, but find it impossible to leave out the story of my trying to do right by this colt and failing. The whole thing in a nutshell is, that Romero was allowed to raise himself, just like a $30 mustang, and ran with mares and was allowed to serve them, and never ate a sack of grain altogether, I venture to say, up to the spring he was three years old. If my partners had trotted him with Len Rose when two years old and again when three, I am sure it would have made a difference of $50,000 to me. As long as I was in funds to train and work colts I never asked odds of any one as to bars, and I believe I was the first man in this State to show yearlings in harness. I took first prize for Josie Coles and Bessie Bell, one by The Moor the other by Overland. There was no race, but I showed a four-minute gait with them in front of the grand stand at S. D. A. S., at the fall meeting of 1873 or 1874, I forget which. I am not in favor of barring, that is, punishing a stallion for having the best get; we are all striving for excellence and not for second best, all the time having an ideal in our mind to breed to. I am of the opinion that all the older breeders of trotters in California, with two or three exceptions, are too poor to afford to train eight or ten colts at a time, and don't consider the fight equal when they have to select one mare's produce and stick to it on account of the entries having been made, though he may have better ones in the herd, the poor breeders preferring to wait and select before risking much money. But I say to the rich ones who have already trotters, go ahead; we enjoy and glory in your records, and we will give you a racket at three and four years old. But there are Hearst, Haggin, Valensin, and other new breeders of trotters, who all have some young fast ones, if we only give them a little time, and it would not be fair to give them a reserved seat among us second-class, fellows until they have a shy at the best. Nobody ever heard of Lexington's, or Boston's, or Bonnie Scotland's, or King Alfonso's, or Hambletonian's get being barred on account of their parentage, although their lists of winners are legion. No; I say double and triple the purses even, if the get of one stallion rakes in the pile every time. No man should be rewarded for producing the worst article.

Yours truly, H. M. JOHNSTON.

# PADDOCK.

## HORSES BELONGING TO COLONEL McNASSER.

Colonel James McNasser, of the Golden Eagle Hotel, has lately imported from his former home in Colorado some very valuable horses. Our correspondent "Mile-and-a-Quarter," gave a sketch of them in his letter published in the number of the 8th of July, and also the information that the Kleinhaus place, containing 650 acres, had been purchased for a breeding farm. Sixteen mares were brought and two stallions, the following being a partial list:

Probably the premiership in the stallions should be awarded to Ensign Goldust, golden chestnut stallion, bred by L. L. Dorsey, Jefferson county, Kentucky, foaled 1872; by Goldust. 1st dam by Vermont Black Hawk. 2d dam a thorougbred mare. It is almost unnecessary to say that Dorsey's Goldust was one of the most successful trotting sires, having got Lucille Goldust, record 2.16¼; Fleety Goldust, 2.20; Rolla Goldust, 2.25, and Saddle, 2.21, and others of celebrity. He was by Vermont Morgan, his dam by the imported Arabian horse Zilcadi, and his grandam by imported Barefoot. The near Vermont Black Hawk cross in Ensign Goldust is valuable, as there are very many of the fast trotters of the present day which have one or more strains of the blood. The other stallion, Silver Cliff, is also a golden chestnut. He was bred by J. W. Hornsby, of Eminence, Kentucky; foaled 1872; by Lexington Goldust. 1st dam Clara Bell by Wide Awake. Lexington Goldust was a very highly bred horse. He was by Dorsey's Goldust, his dam the thoroughbred mare Eugenia by Lexington. 2d dam Attala by Ruffin, and his 3d dam the celebrated Duchess of Marlboro by Sir Archy. There has been very little of the Goldust blood in California, and the son and grandson are valuable acquisitions. Among the mares are Belle Watts by Dorrell's Blue Bull, and she has a yearling filly and horse foal by Ensign Goldust. She was bred in Indiana. Silver Spray is a dark chestnut, 15¼ hands, foaled in 1868, bred by A. J. Reed, of Fayette county, Kentucky; by Mambrino Columbus (son of Mambrino Chief), her dam by Blood's Black Hawk. This mare's suckling by Ensign Goldust is a very fine one.

Maud Furney, chestnut, bred by Phil. Warren, of Springfield, Ill., by Harry Bluff, her dam by the Arabian Fyzaul, imported by A. Keene Richards, and her grandam Argentile by Bertrand. Her foal by Ensign Goldust is large and shows a great deal of quality.

Susie, bay, foaled 1870; by Blanco, the sire of Smuggler, her dam by Ethan Allen. Her foal by Ensign Goldust is alo fine.

Mollie A., bay, foaled in 1871; by American Eagle (son of Cassius M. Clay), her dam Mollie by Weasel. She has a foal at her side by Ensign Goldust, and her yearling filly by the same horse is an extra one.

Lady Jackson, mahogany bay, by Stonewall Jackson (son of Iron Duke) his dam of Woodpecker blood.

Moroza, bay, foaled in 1868, bred by C. S. Dole, of Chicago, Ill.; by Autocrat, her dam Idlewild by Peck's Idol, a son of Mambrino Chief.

Little Belle, bay, bred by John T. Magman, Montgomery county, Ky., foaled 1872; by Belmont, the sire of Nutwood, her dam by imported Trustee.

Nanette by Peck's Idol, her dam Nancy.

Lady Estabrook by Flying Morrill, dam by Signal, grandam the Benney mare.

Julia B., bred by J. T. Hea, of Freeport, Illinois, by the Beaumont Horse (the sire of Molford Zena and others) dam a fast pacing mare of Canadian origin.

Dora by Young General Buford, her dam by Rysdyke. Besides these are the broodmares Lucy Hartman, Bell Phillips and Messenger, and many very fine yearlings and two-year-olds.

Those who are conversant with pedigrees will not require to be told that the blood of most of these animals is a high class, and as we have written before cannot fail to be of vast service in improving the trotting stock of this coast.

# THE TURF.

## CLOSING OF ENTRIES.

**On the first day of August next the stakes of the Pacific Coast Blood-Horse Association, the Embryo Stakes and the Purses and Stakes at the California Fairs will close.**

**The advertisements in this paper will give the particulars. Do not forget the date—TUESDAY, AUGUST 1st, 1882.**

## MONMOUTH PARK RACES.

The concluding days of the summer meeting by the sea were very enjoyable, as the weather was delightful and the sport good, the only drawback being the heavy state of the track arising from the storm that went over Long Branch on the fourth and continued during the following day. In the first race, a handicap for all ages, $25 each with $500 added, a mile and a furlong, the imported mare Sweet Home by Knight of St. Patrick, from Bittern, was looked on as the winner, being 4 years old with 107 lbs., her two contestants being Priam, 4 years, 103 lbs., and Fatinitza, 4 years, 105 lbs. In the deep mud the favorite was all at sea, and finished last, Priam winning in 2:06¼. The second race was the important July stake for two-year-olds, a dash of three-quarters of a mile, in which nine of the entries came to the post, and owing to George Kenney carrying extra weight, the Kelso pair brought $125, Kenney $55, Clonmel $50, the Marshal $40, P. Lorillard's pair $40, and the field $25. There was some delay at the post, and it was only at the sixth attempt that they got way, Fairfield and Inconstant first showing in the front, but at the turn into the home stretch, where the leaders were running wide, George Kenney came up, and although from sheer distress he swerved to the right, he was skilfully got in hand and won by two lengths.

The July Stakes, for two-year-olds, at $100 each, half forfeit, only $20 if declared by January 1, 1882, and $30 if declared by June 25, 1882, with $1,000 added, the second to receive $250 out of the stakes; winners of a stake (handicaps excepted) of the value of $1,000, to carry 5 lbs; two such stakes, 7 lbs, and three such stakes 12 lbs extra; closed with 58 subscribers; three-quarters of a mile.

| | | |
|---|---|---|
| Dwyer Bros.' b. c. George Kenney, by Bonnie Scotland, dam Kathleen; 115 lbs, including 5 lbs penalty | (J. McLaughlin) | 1 |
| Mr. Kelso's ch. c. Fairfield, by Bullion, dam Alumina; 105 lbs. | (O'Hara) | 2 |
| G. L. Lorillard's b. c. The Marshal, by Pat Malloy, dam Magenta; 105 lbs | (Holloway) | 3 |
| P. Lorillard's b. f. Inconstant; 102 lbs | (Shauer) | 0 |
| D. J. Bannatyne's br. f. Winna Ding; 102 lbs | (Gallagher) | 0 |
| J. E. Kelly's b. c. Clonmel; 105 lbs | (Hughes) | 0 |
| Mr. Kelso's b. f. Heel-and-Toe; 107 lbs | (Evans) | 0 |
| P. Lorillard's b. c. Nimrod; 105 lbs | (W. Donohue) | 0 |
| D. D. Withers' br. c. Buckstone; 105 lbs | (Sparling) | 0 |

Time—1:22.

In the next race, the Monmouth Oaks; P. Lorillard's pair, Amazon and Hiawasse, were held at $160; Rica $150, and the field $30; and as Rica has apparently lost entirely her fine two-year-old form, it proved to be an easy victory for the Rancocas Stable.

The Monmouth Oaks, a sweepstakes for three-year-old fillies, at $100 each, half forfeit, only $10 if declared by August 1, 1881, $20 if declared January 1, 1882, and $30 if declared by June 1, 1882, with $1,000 added, the second to receive $300 out of the stakes; closed with 62 subscribers; mile and a quarter.

| | | |
|---|---|---|
| P. Lorillard's br. f. Hiawasse, by Saxon, dam Vandalite; 113 lbs | (Feakes) | 1 |
| P. Lorillard's b. f. Amazon, by Moccasin, dam Aspasia, 113 lbs. | (Shauer) | 2 |
| C. H. Raymond's b. f. Bonella; 113 lbs | (Holloway) | 3 |
| Mr. Kelso's b. f. Rica; 113 lbs | (Evans) | 0 |
| Dwyer Bros.' b. f. Francesca; 113 lbs | (J. McLaughlin) | 0 |

Time—2:23.

The fourth was a selling race, with penalties and allowances, three-quarters of a mile, that was won by a two-year-old, Battledore by Glenlyon, belonging to P. Lorillard, beating Sir Hugh and five others. The time was 1:19, weight 69 lbs., and the winner was not claimed at $1,000. The last was a hurdle race of a mile and a half, and was won by Felix in 3:07, three others figuring in the field.

The first Summer Meeting was brought to a close on the Saturday, when there were eight races on the card that would have given general satisfaction, save that in the two-year-old race the start was delayed for three quarters of an hour through the usual cause, and that is, not taking advantage of a fair send off at the first attempt, and then getting the youngsters and their jockeys in a tremor of anxiety and excitement through a long succession of false starts. The first was a sweepstake handicap of $600, a dash of a mile and a half, in which Captain Conner's Glidelia showed she had in some measure recovered the favor that at one time foretold a most prominent position on the American turf. As a five-year-old, Glidelia carried 115 pounds, but equal in the betting with her was Fair Count, an aged horse with 116 pounds; Ballast and Blumen, each four-year-olds, carrying respectively 110 and 88 pounds. The result was simply a walk-over for Glidelia in 2:41½. The second was a match for $1,000 a side, one mile, gentlemen riders, which was regarded as a kind of international affair. Mr. Holmes, an Englishman on Corsair, giving two stone, or twenty-eight pounds, to Hospador, ridden by one of the best amateur jockeys, Mr. Hunter. The latter was an immense favorite for the talent, but made too strong a play for the first three quarters of a mile, and was beaten out easily at the finish in 1:46¾. The third was a purse for two-year-olds, which shows great talent in the way of bringing together a number of entries on even terms. It was, however, a somewhat one-sided affair, Woodflower, the favorite, winning easily and scoring another victory for her sire, the Ill-Used the Second, Carlyle being also by the same sire. Fortune does not appear to favor the colors of James E. Kelly, who with a fine stable is unfortunate enough to have to content himself with second or third honors.

Purse $500, for two-year-olds; entrance, 5 per cent of the purse ($25 each) to the second; winners of any stake of the value of $1,000 to carry 7 lb.; of two or more stakes of any value, 10 lb. extra; winners of $500, selling races and handicaps not counting, to carry 3 lb. extra; the winner of the two-year-old purse on the second day, if not then a maiden, to carry 5 lb. more than he then carried; maidens not having run second for a stake of the value of $1,000 allowed 3 lb.; 10 entries; five furlongs.

| | | |
|---|---|---|
| A. Belmont's ch. f. Woodflower, by Ill-Used, dam Woodbine, 107 lb | (Barbee) | 1 |
| J. E. Kelly's b. c. Carlyle, by Ill-Used, dam Caroline, 107 lb. | (Hughes) | 2 |
| P. Lorillard's b. f. Battledore, 107 lb | (Shauer) | 3 |
| G. L. Lorillard's ch. f. Gift, 104 lb | (Ural) | 0 |
| Preakness Stables' b. f. Vintage, 104 lb | (Holloway) | 0 |
| H. T. Howard's ch. f. Fairwater, 104 lb | (J. Donohue) | 0 |
| T. M. Fleming's ch. c. Ganymede | (Blaylock) | 0 |
| L. A. Ehler's ch. c. Circassian, 107 lb | (Sparling) | 0 |
| E. V. Snediker's b. f. Touch-Me-Not, 104 lb | (W. Donohue) | 0 |

Time—1:04½.

The fourth race was a handicap sweepstake of $500, a mile and a half for three-year-olds, which was won by W. Jennings' Infanta, 100 lbs., Duplex, 100 lbs., being second, Bouncer, 90 lbs, being third, with Macbeth, 115, and Buxom, 87 lbs., unplaced. Time, 2:04. The next was the famous Monmouth Cup, in which there have been recorded such brilliant performances, and among them the first and great struggle for supremacy between Longfellow and Bassett. This year, owing to the multiplicity of their engagements, a great many were declared out of this important race, and in the absence of such cracks as Thora and Hindoo, Eole was spotted by the talent as the winner, they paying $600 for him against $300 for Girofle and $105 for Monitor. The race was pretty evenly contested until within a furlong of the wire, but Eole stayed the longest and won in 4:07¾, which is slow time, Monitor winning the same race last year in 4:06½.

The Monmouth Cup, a sweepstake for all ages, at $50 each, play or pay, with $1,000 added, the second to receive $300 out of the stakes; the winner of the Baltimore, Westchester or Coney Island Cup in 1882 to carry 3 lb. extra; of two of them, 5 lb.; of three of them, 7 lb. extra; 16 subscribers; two miles and a quarter.

F. Gebhard's b. c. Eole, 4, by Eolus, dam War Song, 118 lb.... ....(Barbee) 1
E. V. Snediker & Co.'s Girofle, 5, by Leamington, dam Ratan, 117 lb.... ....(W. Donohue) 2
G. L. Lorillard's ch. g. Monitor, 6, by Glenelg, dam Minx, 120 lb.... ....(Costello) 3

Time—4:07¾.

The next was a selling purse of $500, one mile, that was captured cleverly by Marathon, 4 years, 104 lbs., beating Jim Farrell, 3 years, 95 lbs., second; Constantina, 4 years, 94 lbs., third, and Strathspey, 4 years, 107 lbs., and Krupp Gun, aged, 106 lbs. The time was 1:45¼, and there was no bid for the winner. Then came the Corinthian Stakes for gentlemen riders, $25 each, p. p., with $300 added, a dash of a mile, which was won by Arsenic in 1:48½, who being the first choice in the betting as a four-year-old, with 158 lbs., and ridden by Mr. Hunter, beating Bonnie Oaks, 5 years, 145 lbs., and Baby, 6 years, 140 lbs., piloted by Mr. Holmes and Mr. Ward. The last was a steeplechase, over the full course, in which the talent got a facer. Felix, an extreme outsider, beat Kittie Clark, Ohio Boy, Bertha, Joe Hunt, Bethune, Victim and Coinage. A fine field and a good race, and a grand finale to those who scratch up the remnants, the mutual pools paying $70 to each $5 investment. This brought the Summer meeting to a close.

Between the first and second Summer meetings it was resolved to have some extra racing each Wednesday and Saturday. On the 15th, in the inaugural race of a mile and a quarter, Sunday, a three-year-old representative of the Baldwin stable, could only gain the second position—the race being won by that famous old reliable horse, Parole; time, 2:15. The mile and five-eighths was won by Forester, Macbeth second, Volusca third; time, 2:54. In the three-quarter mile Parthenia won, Inconstant second; time, 1:16¼. In the mile and three-eighths Prima won, Monitor second; time, 2:25. In the mile dash Hospodar won, Babcock second; time 1:43¾. In the three-quarter mile Corsair won, Godiva second; time, 1:19¾. In the steeplechase Ohio Boy won, Felix second; time, 3:18¼.

On Wednesday, the 19th, in the first dash of a mile, Jack of Hearts was the victor, while Constantine and Yorkshire ran a dead heat for second place; time, 1:43½. For the Red Bank stake, three-quarters of a mile, Pizarro and Inconstant ran a dead heat, Renegade third; time, 1:16½. In the mile-and-a-half race Monitor was first, Eole second, Baton Rouge third; time, 2:42. The seven-eighths-of-a-mile race Strathspey won, Constantine second, Hospodar third; time, 1:29¾. The steeplechase over the full course Felix won, Ike Bonham second, Joe Hunt third; time, 3:17.

From the above telegraphic dispatches it would appear as if the California horses were being held in reserve for the second Summer meeting.

On Wednesday, the 12th, the first day of the intervening season, there was a pretty match race, a mile and three furlongs, for a purse of $500, for all ages, in which Parole, with 112 pounds, beat Aolia with 101 pounds, in 2:26. The next was the Atlantic stakes for two-year-olds, a dash of three-quarters of a mile, that was won in 1:18½ by Pizarro, Renegade second, and a field of nine others. Then came the Raritan stakes, a mile and three furlongs, that was taken by Turco in 2:29, with Macbeth second, Duplex third, and three in the field. The fourth was a handicap of a mile and a quarter, in which Monitor was to the fore, with Jack of Hearts second, and Fair Count third, and six unplaced. The fifth race, a mile and a furlong, for all ages, was won by Dan K. in 1:57, with Strathspey second, Babcock third, and four others, and the hurdle race went to Kitty Clark, with Ohio Boy and Frank Short, second and third.

## THE SARATOGA RACES.

Of all the watering places in this country and in Europe, Saratoga holds pre-eminence in the way of racing. The track is beautifully laid out, and within easy access from the Springs. The buildings, although somewhat old fashioned, are large and commodious, and the liberal purses offered attract a large number of horses, principally from the West and South. A few years since the Saratoga meeting was recognized as the most important of the season, all the cracks of the country meeting there in friendly rivalry, and many are the well fought battles that have been seen on its classic grounds; but from the desire to extend the programme from two weeks to two months, thus clashing with the second meeting at Monmouth Park, there has been lately a terrible falling off in the entries, as, from appearances, such patrons of the turf as the Lorillard Brothers, Mr. Belmont, Mr. Withers, and other prominent members of the American Jockey Club, have thrown their influence in favor of the Long Branch track, rather than of that of the queen of watering places. Thus, in the vicinity of New York there are three places where races are held through the two Summer months continuously, Saratoga, Monmouth Park and Brighton Beach, and as to the latter, it would appear as if the meeting lasts from early Spring until late in the Fall. It is not surprising, therefore, that the attendance at Saratoga was light at the opening of the meeting, and the unavoidable absence of some of the best horses made the proceedings somewhat tame in comparison with previous years.

The first race on the opening day, July 11th, was a scramble of five furlongs, for all ages, for a purse of $400, entrance free, in which there were nine entries, with Fellowplay and Bounce great favorites, but Saunterer, a fine four-year-old son of Leamington and Lemonade, took first honors in 1:06¼.

Then came the most important race of the meeting, the Travers Stake, that in years gone by brought together the best three-year-olds in the country, but the race was shorn of its attractions this season when it became known that both Forester and Runnymede would be forced absentees, on account of the punishing race they had run together the previous week at Long Branch, and at a late hour the Western horse, Apollo, who had beaten Runnymede, was also scratched, leaving a beggarly quartet only to fight out for one of the most valuable stakes in the East. These were Carley B., a great favorite in the betting, Tom Plunkett, Mandamus and Boatman, and the race was a hollow victory for Carley B.

Travers Stakes, for three-year-olds, at $100 each, half forfeit, with $1,000 added by the association and $500 in plate by W. R. Travers; the second to receive $300 out of the stakes; closed with 56 subscribers, of which 5 were rendered void by the death of H. P. McGrath and E. A. Clabaugh. Mile and three-quarters.

A. Burnham's blk. g. Carley B., by Virgil, dam Ladylike, 115 lb.... ....(Quantrell) 1
W. L. Cassidy's ch. c. Tom Plunkett, by Glenelg, dam Kate Mattingly, 118 lb.... ....(Murphy) 3
C. Reed's br. c. Mandamus, by John Morgan, dam Duet, 118 lb.... ....(Brophy) 3
M. Young's b. g. Boatman, by Bonnie Scotland, dam Valerian, 115 lb.... ....(Walker) 0

Time—3:28¾.

The Excelsior Sweepstakes came next, a dash of a mile and a quarter, $50 each, play or pay, with $1,000 added, that attracted a fine batch of twenty-two entries, but the redoubtable Thora frightened a great many away, and as it was, the betting was limited as to who should get the $250 that was given to the second horse, Bend Or selling for $150 against $110 for Crickmore. The race was altogether between Crickmore and the favorite, but after a pretty close contest down the home-stretch Thora came away and won easily by two lengths in 2:20. The last race was one of those popular selling races, in which owners are allowed to handicap their own horses by placing on them a certain valuation, and it was won by Warfield, an aged horse, entered to be sold for $1,000, and he came an easy winner in 1:53, only two horses, Explorer and Mattie Rapture, being pitted against him. There was no bid for the winner, and a very tame day's sport was brought to its conclusion.

Following are the telegraph records of the past week:

On July 17th, in the first race, one mile, Ada Glenn was first, Bootjack second, Jennie V. third. Time, 1:42. In the second race, one mile, 500 yards, Warfield was first, Fellowplay second, Granger third. Time, 2:13½. In the third race, five furlongs, Ascender was first, Pearl Thorn second, Blue Grass Belle third. Time, 1:03½. In the fourth race, three-quarters of a mile, Wapakonette was first, Lute String second, Morgan Spy third. Time, 1:17.

On the 18th, in the first race, one and one-eighth mile, Good Night won, Pinafore second. Time, 1:55½. In the second race, five furlongs, Miss Woodford won, Tarantella second. Time, 1:03½. In the third race, one mile, Ben d'Or won, Monogram second. Time, 1:45. In the fourth race, one mile and a half, Boatman won, Mamie Fields second. Time, 2:37½.

On the 19th, in the first race, five furlongs, Bounce won, Brambaletta second. Time, 1:06½, 1:05¼. In the second race, one and three-fourths miles, Glendelia won, Spark second. Time, 3:12½.

## RACING IN ENGLAND.

From the following cablegram to the *Evening Telegram* of July 8th, it seems that the American two-year-olds are not likely to make any very brilliant running this season. The running of Golden Gate is another proof that the American horses show better over a distance of ground than in the shorter races. Golden Gate won one race last year, the Granby stakes, and ran well in others. He is by King Alfonso from Mollie Ward by Lexington, and was doubtless christened by Mr. Keene from recollections of California life.

LONDON, July 8th.—The Newmarket July meeting was productive of brilliant racing, several of the principal contests having quite an international character. The two-year-old racing was very interesting, the July Stakes and the Chesterfield Plate being won respectively by two of the best youngsters seen out this season—Macheath and Galliard—who both won in a gallant fashion.

Great disappointment was caused by the absence of any worthy American representative for these important races, one of which—the Chesterfield Plate—Iroquois won so cleverly and forshadowed his memorable Derby triumph. Lorillard's two-year-olds are a very moderate lot, I am afraid, and washy looking. The chestnut filly, Touch-me-not, is fast for half a mile only, and the same may be said of Wenonah. Paregraph, Comanche and Massasoit do not make the improvement anticipated, the last named having been withdrawn from the Princess of Wales Cup on Friday because his chances were hopeless even against the moderate lot entered for the race.

We do not hear good accounts of the racing ability of Mr. Keene's two-year-olds. Day, the veteran trainer, advised that none of them should run at all at the July meeting. With a little extra time they may be found in better trim.

Golden Gate ran well for the Summer Cup—one of the longest distance races in England, being over three miles and a half.

The contest was one of the most interesting of the week, and many thousands of pounds were bet on it, Isabel having a slight call over Golden Gate. Fordham and Cannon vied with each other in magnificent riding to literally the last stride. Isabel won by a short head. The enthusiasm was intense.

Clark, the judge, said it was the grandest finish he had ever witnessed. Golden Gate ran so gamely that his chances for the Goodwood Stakes are considerably enhanced, tens being taken freely. His stable companion, General Scott, is engaged in the race at 82 lbs., but is not yet mentioned in the betting.

On the 17th inst. there was an extra day's racing at the track of the Utah Jockey Club of Salt Lake City, the first race being a single dash of a mile for a purse of $1,500, which was won by Euchre, Belle of the West second. Time—1:45. The second race, a dash of a mile and a quarter, between Pearl Jennings and Maria F., for $5,000 a side, was won by Pearl Jennings. Time—2 13.

From Portland we learn that the Northwestern District Agricultural Association races at City View Park began on the 19th inst. Lou Spencer won the running race, five-eighths of a mile, for two-year-olds, in 1:05¼, beating Nevella and Rosa A. Blackhawk won the trotting race for three-year-olds, beating Edna J., Charles Albert and Zelophone. Best time, 2:59¾.

# THE TRACK.

## CLOSING OF STAKES AND PURSES.

**On the first day of August next, the Stakes of the Pacific Coast Blood-Horse Association, the Embryo Stakes and the purses and stakes at the California Fairs will close.**

**The advertisements in this paper will give the particulars. Do not forget the date, TUESDAY, AUGUST 1st, 1882.**

## FIXED EVENTS.

Santa Cruz County Fair Association. First annual meeting at Santa Cruz, Aug 15th, 16th, 17th and 18th.

Sonoma County Park Association, at Santa Rosa, Aug. 22d, 23d, 24th, 25th and 26th.

Sonoma and Marin Agricultural Societies. Annual Fair at Petaluma, Aug 29th and four following days.

Golden Gate Fair, to be held at Oakland, from September 4th to the 9th inclusive.

Butte District Fair at Chico; from September 5th to September 8th, inclusive.

El Dorado District Fair at Placerville, from September 5th to September 8th, inclusive.

California State Fair. Annual meeting at Sacramento, from Monday, September 11th to the 16th inclusive.

The San Joaquin Valley Association Fair at Stockton, from September 19th to the 23d inclusive.

Oregon State Fair at Salem, from September 18th and during the week.

The San Mateo and Santa Clara County Agricultural Association Fair at San Jose, September 25th to the 30th inclusive.

Humboldt and Mendocino District Fair at Rhonerville, September 19th to September 22d, inclusive.

Modoc, Plumas and Lassen District Fair at Greenville, from October 2d to October 5th, inclusive.

Monterey District Fair at Salinas City, from October 2d to October 6th, inclusive.

Mount Shasta Agricultural Association Fair at Yreka, October 4th, 5th, 6th and 7th.

## FAIRS AT THE EAST.

Kentucky State Fair at Lexington, August 9th to September 2d inclusive.

Minnesota State Fair at Farmington, August 31st to September 8th inclusive.

Iowa State Fair at Fairfield, September 1st to the 8th inclusive.

Minnesota Agricultural Association, at Minneapolis, September 4th to the 9th inclusive.

Nebraska State Fair, at Omaha, September 11th until the 16th inclusive.

Rhode Island State Fair, at Providence, September 12th to the 15th inclusive.

Pennsylvania State Fair, at Pittsburg, September 7th to the 21st inclusive.

Wisconsin State Fair, at Fond du lac, September 11th to the 16th inclusive.

Ontario Provincial Fair, at Toronto, September 18th to the 23d inclusive.

Connecticut State Fair, at Meriden, September 18th to the 22d inclusive.

New Jersey State Fair, at Monroe, September 18th to the 22d inclusive.

West Virginia Central Fair, at Clarksburg, September 19th to the 21st inclusive.

Indiana State Fair, at Indianapolis, September 25th to the 30th inclusive.

Western Michigan Fair, at Grand Rapids, September 25th to the 30th inclusive.

Texas State Fair, at Austin, October 17th to the 21st inclusive.

## THE WASHINGTON COUNTY FAIR.

For some time past great preparations have been made at Hillsboro, Or. for the County Fair that opened there on the 3d inst. Although a large number of new stalls had been built, the accommodations were scarcely equal to the demand. So numerous were the number of entries, the purses and stakes were arranged on a very liberal basis. The weather was bright and warm and the attendance large and enthusiastic, all being pleased with the pleasant surroundings and the sport that was offered in the programme. Promptly at 1 o'clock the four following horses were called up for the 2:50 class: James Misner's b. g. Stranger, James Mohr's ch. g. Hector, Henry Smiley's ch. h. General Crook, and the b. m. Maggie Arnold, entered by Jay Beach. The mare was a great favorite, but seemingly was not allowed to show her best paces at first, as Stranger and Crook fought out the two initial heats, with the former a victim on each occasion. The mare then went in and won the race in three successive heats:

Purse $600, for 2:50 class, mile heats, 3 in 5, in harness.

| | | | | | |
|---|---|---|---|---|---|
| Jay Beach's b. m. Maggie Arnold | 4 | 4 | 1 | 1 | 1 |
| J. Misner's b. g. Stranger | 1 | 1 | 3 | 4 | 3 |
| P. J. Martin's ch. h. Gen. Crook | 2 | 2 | 2 | 2 | 2 |
| H. P. Isaac's ch. g. Hector | 3 | 3 | 4 | 3 | 4 |

Time—2:39½, 2:39½, 2:37, 2:39, 2:40.

The second was a running race of three quarters of a mile, in which the big horse Jim Renwick was the first chosen, owing to his having made this distance in 1:15 at the Bay District this spring, with 112 pounds up, but his owner was not very confident that he would repeat the trick. The entries were Jem Merritt, by Langford from Sweetwater; Joe Howell, by Bonnie Scotland, and Jim Renwick by Joe Hooker. Jim Merritt got the best of the start, but at the turn they were all bunched, and then the leader maintaining his position won a fine race by a neck, amid much excitement:

Purse $300, $100 to the second; three-quarters of a mile.

W. G. Scoggin's b. h. Jim Merritt, 5 years, 114 lbs.... 1
C. Mulkey's b. g. Joe Howe, aged, 115 lbs.... 2
A. G. Wood's ch. g. Jim Renwick, 4 years, 104 lbs.... 3

Time—1:17.

On the National holiday the weather was again very propitious, but the track was hard for the running horses, the result again showing the advisability of giving the outer part of the circle a better harrowing, so that advantage might be taken of it by horses who are not quite sound on their pins. The first race was for the 2:30 class, and there were but two entries, Dexter and Milton Medium, the former being a great favorite at almost $20 to $10; and he won handsomely in three straight heats.

Purse $700, for 2:30 class, mile heats, 3 in 5.

| | | | |
|---|---|---|---|
| Jas. Misner's b. h. Dexter, by Bellfounder | 1 | 1 | 1 |
| H. Smiley's br. h. Milton Medium | 2 | 2 | 2 |

Time—2:30, 2:29½, 2:26½.

The next race was the Novelty Stake for all ages, to run a single dash of a mile, with the purse of $900 subdivided into three equal parts: $300 to the first horse ahead at the half-mile, $300 to the head horse at the three-quarters pole, and $300 to the first horse under the wire. The entries were the Idaho mare Premium, Fred Collier and Jim Renwick. Premium was first choice for the half mile, Renwick for the three-quarters, and Fred Collier for the mile; so that there was a great diversity of interest in the race. Premium made the running for the half, with Renwick close up; but the mare scored the first honors by a length, and then again put the three-quarters to her credit, when Collier, who had been waiting a little too long, came up with a rush and made a desperate effort for victory, but in vain, the mare winning by a neck, Jim Renwick a poor third.

Novelty Race, running. Purse $900, $300 to first at ½, $300 to first at ¾, $300 to first at mile.

Mulkey & Marsh's ch. m. Premium, 111 lbs. by Custer, dam Flying Cloud.... 1
Foster Bros.' b. Connor, 114 lbs, by Norfolk, dam Ada C.... 2
Stemler & Ayers' s. g. Jim Renwick, 105 lbs, by Hooker, dam Big Gun, by Old George.... 3

Time—½, 50 sec.; ¾, 1:17; mile, 1:47½.

The last race was for two-year-olds, in which Lou Spencer, from the Winters' stable, was a hot favorite, and she took the lead and won cleverly.

Purse $300, for two-year-olds. Half a mile.

| | |
|---|---|
| I. A. Stemlar's b. f. Lou Spencer | 1 |
| R. E. Brxber's ch. f. Ney Allen | 2 |
| Foster Brothers' ch. f. Gold Wire | 3 |

Time, 52s.

On the third day the weather was delightful and the track, roads and grounds were in finer order through a good shower that had fallen during the previous night. The first race was for the 2:38 class, in which were entered Tempest, Pedro and Maggie Arnold, the latter being first choice in the pools at $20, Tempest bringing $10 and Pedro $5. In the first heat Maggie trailed until well into the straight, when she passed Pedro and won cleverly. In the succeeding heat Pedro trotted very steadily and soon had the mare in trouble, for when she found herself out-speeded she broke and thus lost all chance for the race, Pedro winning in three successive heats, Tempest being last on each occasion.

Purse $300 for the 2:38 class. Mile heats, 3 in 5.

| | | | | |
|---|---|---|---|---|
| L. B. Lindsay's blk. g. Pedro | 2 | 1 | 1 | 1 |
| Jay Beach's b. m. Maggie Arnold | 1 | 2 | 2 | 2 |
| H. S. Hogoboom's ch. g. Tempest | 3 | 3 | 3 | 3 |

Time—2:37¾, 2:35, 2:33½, 2:33½.

The last race of the day was a dash of a mile and a quarter, in which were entered Fred Collier, Joe Howell and Trade Dollar, and in the result there was a great deal of speculation, each one being first choice and favorite in the pools. Howell and Trade Dollar raced together until they had gone three-quarters of a mile, when the latter had shot his bolt, and Fred Collier, who had been making a wasting race of it, moved up and challenging Howell at the distance, beat him out after a fine finish by a short length.

Purse $400, for all ages. One mile and a quarter.

| | |
|---|---|
| W. M. Ayers' ch. g. *Fred.* Collier, by Joe Hooker—Puss by Norfolk, 4 yrs | 1 |
| Cy. Mulkey's b. g. Bowers, by Bonnie Scotland—Etta Shipper by Sovereign, aged | |
| Jerome Porter's ch. m. Trade Dollar, by Norfolk—Eva Ashton, 6 yrs | |

Time, 2:13½.

Fred Collier was looked upon here as one of our best racers last year, and at one time was first favorite in the Pacific Cup, but getting badly beaten at the same distance in the Coutts' Stake, won by Atalanta in 2:11, on the first day of the Spring meeting in this city, he did not start again, and his trainer, A. J. Stemlar, deserves credit for getting him again in condition at so short an interval. This fine race concluded the day's programme.

On the fourth day the weather was pleasant and the attendance good, exceeding in numbers that of the previous day. The first race was a trot for three-year-olds, which resulted in an easy victory for Edna J., Sheriff being the only other starter of the four entries that remained to the end. The time was slow, but this was easily accounted for by the fact that it was late in the season before the horses went into training. Before the campaign is over they will make a better account of themselves.

Trotting race for three-year-olds, 3 in 5, to harness; purse $300—$200, $70, $30.

| | | | | |
|---|---|---|---|---|
| E. J. Jeffrey's br. f. Edna J., by Kisber, dam Fly-by-Night | 1 | 1 | 2 | 1 |
| Jos. Buchtel's b. c. Sheriff, by Kisber, dam by Red Buck | 2 | 2 | 1 | 2 |
| L. B. Lindsley's br. f. Jane L., by Hambletonian, Mambrino, dam Mollie Welch | dist. | | | |
| John Pender's b. f. May Wintler, by Rockwood, dam by St. Louis | dist. | | | |

Time—3:05, 3:14, 3:11, 3:12.

The second race was a half mile dash, in which Lulu Riggs was a great favorite, and she won quite easily.

Running race, free for all Oregon, Washington and Idaho bred horses—purse $500—a half-mile dash.

| | |
|---|---|
| Foster Bros.' ch. m. Lulu Riggs, by Humboldt | 1 |
| W. Hefner's b. g. Honest John, by Dr. Lindsay | 2 |
| Matt White's s. g. Tabago | 3 |
| R. S. Perkins' b. m. Mayflower, by Luther | 4 |
| Glenger & Son's g. g., by son of Old Dan | 5 |

Time—51½.

On the concluding day the principal event was a mile and repeat race, in which were entered Joe Howell, Connor and Trade Dollar; the former selling for $20 against $15 for the others combined. The two heats were very similar, Joe Howell running well within himself and winning handily on each occasion.

Running mile and repeat, free for all; purse $300—$250, $50.

| | | |
|---|---|---|
| Mulkey & Marsh's b. g. Joe Howell, aged, by imp. Bonnie Scotland | 1 | 1 |
| Foster Bros.' ch. h. Connor, 5, by Norfolk | 2 | 2 |
| J. A. Porter's ch. m. Trade Dollar, aged, by Norfolk | 3 | 3 |

Time—1:46¼, 1:46¼.

The consolation purse did not fill, and the officers offered a special purse of $200, so as to eke out the day's amusement. The entries were Tempest, Nellie Russell, Hector and Oleander. The latter was found to be lame and was withdrawn, and Nellie Russell being distanced in the first heat, the contest was restricted to the two horses, which was won by the favorite, Tempest.

Special purse, trotting, 3 in 5, purse $200—$150, $150.

| | | | | |
|---|---|---|---|---|
| H. S. Hogoboom's ch. g. Tempest, aged, by Bellfounder | 1 | 2 | 1 | 1 |
| J. W. Morh's ch. g. Hector, aged, by Billy Wilson | 2 | 1 | 2 | 2 |
| Mr. Crow's b. m. Nellie Russell, 5, by Bellfounder | dist. | | | |

Time—2:45, 2:45 2:39, 2:39½.

There was a fine display of stock, to which we will refer more fully in a later issue, and a Ladies' Riding Tournament, in which Mrs. J. W. Scroggin won the first, Miss Jane Imbrie the second, and Miss Laura Fowler the third purse. Barring a heavy shower, the proceedings of the Washington County Fair were brought to a satisfactory conclusion, the financial result showing a balance of about $1,000 to the good side of the ledger. This fact may safely be attributed to the skill and energy shown by the Executive Officers of the Washington County Agricultural Society.

## THE CHICAGO TROTTING MEETING.

This meeting has created great interest in turf circles from the fine purses given, as also for the special inducements offered for a fine display of speed by such noted horses as St. Julien, Trinket, Little Brown Jug and Phil Thompson, while it was well known that in the several classes there were certain horses of the dark division who, at their first appearance, would earn a most enviable repute. On July 15th, the opening day, the weather was warm, but cloudy, the track was in good condition, and the attendance fair in numbers. The first on the card was the three-year-old colt race of $1,500, in which, of the original seven entries, there were but four that put in an appearance—Garfield, Butterfly, Code and Eva. The latter, the own sister to Sweetheart, was made a favorite on the faith of some telling private trials, but unfortunately she came into an unavoidable collision with Code in the first heat that entirely destroyed her chances in the race, for although the judges, under the rules, placed her on the outside when she was beyond the flag, the filly is of so excitable a disposition, that afterwards, despite Orrin Hickock's efforts, she could not make her undoubted speed tell in the final result. Code won in three straight heats, in 2:31¼, 2:33 and 2:31, which, in the way of time, is no great showing for the winner, who has been cracked up as the fleetest youngster of his age at the East. Eva took the second money, Butterfly third, and Garfield was distanced. In the next race, for $1,500, four-year-olds and under, there were twelve entries and five starters, and some very good trotting and exceedingly close finishes. The race resulted in favor of Waiting, Bronze second, Jayeye-See third, Jim Bowman fourth, and Adelaide fith. The time was 2:28¼, 2:25¾, 2:25¼, 2:26½, 2:22¾, 2:23½ and 2:30, showing among them a speed and endurance that stamp the leading horses as fit aspirants of the free-for-all class when their powers are more fully matured. The pacing wonder, Little Brown Jug, then tried to beat 2:11¼ for a special purse of $2,000, with $500 extra if he reduced his record to 2:10¼. He made the first heat in 2:15, the second in 2:22, with a bad break at the five-furlong pole, and repeated 2:15 in the third. The season is as yet too early for these wonderful exhibitions of speed.

The meeting was continued on Monday with the 2:23 class, for a purse of $2,500, in which there were originally ten entries. Buzz Medium was the favorite, but he was nowhere in the race, as it was won in an easy manner by Minnie R., who would have gained the prize in three straight heats but that in the second she broke badly and only gained third position, Tariff winning that heat and second money, Unalala third and Buzz Medium fourth. Time—2:18, 2:20¾, 2:19½, 2:20. The second race was open to all stallions, for a purse of $5,000, with $1,000 extra to beat 2:15¼. Von Arnim, the favorite, won in straight heats, though Monroe Chief trotted to a head in the first and third, and was only beaten a length in the second, J. B. Thomas being third and Voltaire last on each occasion. Summary: Von Arnim, 1, 1, 1; Monroe Chief, 2, 2, 2; J. B. Thomas, 3, 3, 3; Voltaire, 4, 4, 4. Time—2:30, 2:20¾, 2:20. Distance was waived in this race. The last race was the 2:35 class, in which there were originally thirty entries. It was admirably contested, Walnut taking the two first heats, Clara Cleveland the third and Hardcastle the fourth, when proceedings were postponed by darkness, and on the succeeding day there were three more heats trotted before Clara was declared the victor, Hardwood second, Rigolette, King Wilkens, Maud T. and Defender ruled out for not winning one heat in five, and Walnut distanced. Time—2:23¼, 2:24½, 2:27, 2:27½, 2:23¼, 2:24¾, 2:23,

On Tuesday the first race on the programme was the 2:25 class, for a purse of $2,000, with $500 extra to beat 2:22. Rosa Wilkes was the winner in three straight heats; Forest Queen second, Early Rose third, Big Soap fourth money. Time—2:20¼, 2:18¼, 2:20¾. The third race was open to all pacers; purse $2,500, with $500 extra to beat 2:11¼. There were six heats, and Bay Billy won the last three; Buffalo Girl second, Mattie Hunter third. Time—2:14¼, 2:14½, 2:15¾, 2:18, 2:20½, 2:21¼. The fourth race was the 2:30 class, for a purse of $2,000, with $500 extra to beat 2:22. Mattie Graham took the first, second and fourth heats, Bliss second, Mag third, Red Cross fourth. Time—2:21½, 2:21¾, 2:21½, 2:23½.

On July 12th, at Sioux City, Iowa, there was a large attendance at the track to witness the match between R. T. Krebs's b. s. Elthwood Chief and John T. Fisher's b. m. Hampton Girl. The match was two-mile heats, best three in five, for a purse of $2,000: The Chief won easily in three straight heats. Time, 5:32½, 5:28½, 5:32. Great interest was felt in the race, and probably $10,000 changed hands on the result. The Girl disappointed her friends, while the Chief fully retrieved himself from the suspicion that he was not a stayer.

On the Wednesday the day was cloudy and cool and the track fast. The first race was the 2:27 class, for a purse of $2,000, with $500 extra to beat 2:21. It was won easily by Jerome Eddy, who had greater speed than any of the others, and only lost the first heat because of a bad break. Mattie Graham took second money; Aldene third; Largesse fourth; Catchfly and Naiad Queen distanced. Time, 2:21¾, 2:22, 2:21, 2:23¼. There was to have been a special handicap race between St. Julien and Trinket for a purse of $5,000, but unfortunately the King of the Turf has of late been slightly off, and during his stay at Point Breeze he was only indulged with slight exercise. It is now reported that his ailment is of a more serious character, and that he will not be able to make an appearance before some weeks have elapsed. This is a serious loss as special large purses had been arranged for these pair, all through the circuit. In his absence a special purse of $1,000 was offered to Phil Thompson, in three trials, $500 extra to beat 2:19¾, and $500 additional to beat 2:17½. The colt was evidently out of form. At the first trial he broke at the first turn and did not go around. At the second attempt he broke again and did the time in 2:36¼. In the third trial he trotted, without breaking, but could do no better than 2:23½. C. H. Raymond of New York, his owner, who was present to see him trot, stated that on the previous Thursday he showed a mile in 2:13. The third race was the 2:21 class, for a purse of $2,500, with $500 to beat 2:17½. It was a struggle throughout between Black Cloud, William H., Unalala and Scott's Thomas, all the heats being finely contested and the finishing close and exciting. Summary—Black Cloud 1, William H 2, Scott's Thomas 3, Unalala 4, Pilot R 5, Annie Robinson 6. Time—2:20½, 2:18½, 2:19¾, 2:21½.

## PITTSBURGH RACES.

The Summer meeting of the Pittsburgh Driving Park commenced on July 11th. The attendance was fair, the weather fine, and the track good. The first race was for a purse of $1,500, with the following result:

| | | | | |
|---|---|---|---|---|
| King Wilkes | 1 | 5 | 1 | 1 |
| Rurie Neville | 2 | 2 | 5 | 2 |
| Fannie Irwin | 3 | 3 | 3 | 3 |
| Hotspur Chief | 4 | 1 | 2 | dis. |
| Mattie H | 5 | 4 | 4 | 4 |

Time—2:26½, 2:29, 2:26½, 2:28½.

The second race, 2:23 class, was for a purse of $2,000:

| | | | |
|---|---|---|---|
| Buzz Medium | 1 | 1 | 1 |
| Unalala | 2 | 2 | 2 |
| Mattie Graham | 3 | 5 | 4 |
| Abdallah Boy | 4 | 4 | 3 |
| J. Witt | 5 | 5 | 5 |
| Bliss | 6 | 6 | 6 |

Time—2:20½, 2:20½, 2:22.

Th esecond day, on the 12th, the attendance was fair, the weather fine, and the track in first-class condition. The first race was for the 2:29 class; purse, $1,500:

| | | | | |
|---|---|---|---|---|
| Young Fullerton | 3 | 1 | 1 | 1 |
| Largesse | 1 | 2 | 3 | 4 |
| Dick Organ | 2 | 4 | 6 | 3 |
| Mercutio | 4 | 3 | 4 | 5 |
| Effie G | 5 | 5 | 2 | 6 |
| Walter | 6 | 6 | 7 | 7 |
| Kate Taylor | 7 | 7 | 5 | 2 |

Time—2:25, 2:23, 2:25, 2:22½.

Second race, free-for-all, pacing; purse, $1,500:

| | | | | | | |
|---|---|---|---|---|---|---|
| Lucy | 4 | 2 | 1 | 1 | 3 | 1 |
| Mattie Hunter | 2 | 1 | 4 | 2 | 1 | 2 |
| Ben Hamilton | 1 | 4 | 3 | 3 | 2 | 3 |
| Charley H | 3 | 3 | 2 | 4 | 4 | 4 |

Time—2:18, 2:15½, 2:17½, 2:16½, 2:18½, 2:20.

## A SUNDAY MORNING AT FLEETWOOD.

[N. Y. Herald, July 10th.]

Yesterday morning was one of unusual interest at the grounds of the Gentlemen's Driving Association. A large number of gentlemen who enjoy a Summer morning's drive and take an interest in trotting matters assembled and were well repaid for their trouble in witnessing the numerous and very creditable performances which took place. Among the number we noticed Messrs. S. Knapp, Phyte, Bailey, Barron, Stillings, I. Cohnfeld, Lange, Lichtenstein, Humphreyville, Ridabock, Riley, Waite, Parker, Madden, Barnett, Jones, Chandler, Brown and many others.

It was a lovely morning, and a southerly breeze swept the broad piazza of the club house and tempered the somewhat too ardent sun. The first to appear, with John Murphy behind him, was Mr. S. Lichtenstein's bay gelding, by Waldo, a son of Messenger Duroc, dam Effie Deans. This horse has no record, but left a mile behind him in grand style in 2:25¾.

Mr. Nathan Strauss drove the Boston horse Joe Ripley (record 2:25) a half mile in 1:00½, and another half later in 1:12¾.

Mr. Isidor Cohnfeld drove his bay road team a half in 1:17, and a repeat in 1:18¼. That is a very improving team, and are matched to trot a mile within a week in 2:39.

John Murphy drove Gabe Case's horse Big Fellow (record 2:26) a mile in 2:29, and, keeping right on, another hals in 1:10¼.

Then the same driver appeared behind the chestnut mare Helene—Mr. Cohnfeld's late purchase—and going down to the half-mile pole in 1:07½, to the three-quarters in 1:43, finished the mile in 2:19½ in an easy and creditable manner, with her long, daisy cutting stroke playing like the piston rod of a locomotive. This performance elicited hearty applause and caused the ordering and drinking of several bottles in hearty congratulation to Helene's owner.

Still Murphy came again, this time behind a black mare and running mate. Watches held on them, and they made the mile in 2:21½.

Mr. J. D. Brown's bay mare Lady Allen, by a son of old Ethan, driven by Cleveland, a very clever driver, trotted a half mile in 1:11¼.

Murphy then put his runner beside Mr. Matthew Riley's bay mare Silver, and they made the half mile in 1:12¾ and the mile in 2:26¼. A very nice performance for a horse off the road and made without a skip on the part of the mare.

The figures 2:23 hung out on the blackboard of the judge's stand for Mr. Frank Work's performance of Saturday, when he drove his team in that time. It was done to an open road wagon.

Mr. Madden brought out a green mare from Northampton county, Pa., a few days ago, and she trotted a mile in 2:25, the half in 1:10, driven by a country lad to fame unknown.

Rowdy Boy, the pacer—record 2:13¾—showed some fast work through the stretches.

The stallion Clara Bassett appeared on the track, and Jimmy Stewart drove Palma and several others, who showed well.

Mr. A. R. Phyfe drove his Startle gelding, dam Jessie Kirk, which can trot in about 2:30.

John Rogers, John Moore and Cleveland showed up some fast stock which they have in training.

Mr. Straut drove his black mare Lady Emma, one of the best road horses in New York, and can trot in 2:25 when called on.

The final was a race of great interest, being the slowest ever trotted over Fleetwood Park. Mr. G. C. Barnett drove the black mare K. P., a half mile to top wagon in 2:04 for a bottle of wine. This performance provoked another wager of the same nature, and Mr. George Jones getting behind the mare drove her without a break a half mile in 1:57¼. This was conceded to be the performance of the day, as it was supposed by those interested and looking on that the mare came to a dead stop several times, she went so slowly.

The track was in good condition.

The veteran Judge Fullerton seemed in good fettle; also the great two-mile gray gelding Steve Maxwell, who is as fine as silk and faster than he ever was.

All present left the track highly pleased with the impromptu performances they had witnessed.

## REPLY TO THE CHALLENGE OF M. W. HICKS.

EDITOR BREEDER AND SPORTSMAN: I notice in your issue of the 8th instant Mr. M. W. Hicks' challenge to trot a yearling, a two-year-old, a three-year-old, and a mature horse of his breeding, against like classes bred under my charge. In reply, I would like to accept his challenge, but have no stock to meet the requirement. Mr. Haggin has not been breeding trotting stock until within the last year. Echo was purchased by him in the fall of 1880, and placed under my charge at Rancho del Paso. His colts are therefore only sucklings. Algona was purchased this spring for Rancho del Paso, and his colts have not yet come. But if Mr. Hicks wants to compete with any of this stock he will find plenty of the get of Echo already on the track, belonging to other parties, and he can no doubt get plenty of races against them. Algona, too, has a few that are entered at Stockton and elsewhere, and competition with them is doubtless open to him. He will have full opportunity of proving whether his stock are all *duffers* or not, and when he does prove it I shall be as ready as any one to acknowledge it.

JOHN MACKEY.

Rancho del Paso, July 11, 1882.

H. D. McKinney, of Janesville, Wis., has bought the Messenger filly Bronze, which won the third and fourth heats in the four-year-old race on the first day of the Chicago meeting, for $7,500. It is stated that Robert Bonner was negotiating for her by telegraph, offering $15,000. Horsemen pronounce her the best four-year-old of the year, but she has yet to meet such horses as Sweetheart and Phil. Thompson.

CLINGSTONE.—At the conclusion of his race in the 2:19 class at Chicago, on Thursday last, which he won in three heats in 2:17, 2:18 and 2:20, his owner, Mr. Gordon, offered to match him against any horse in the world for $5,000 a side. This is a rare chance for our princes of the turf.

# ATHLETICS.

## THE OLYMPIC CLUB GAMES.

The Olympic Athletic Club games, which take place at their grounds in Oakland to-day, promise a good afternoon's entertainment to all lovers of out-door sports. The entries for the events are not restricted to members of the Club, and include several outsiders of much promise. All the events being handicaps, the wise ones are unable to pick the winners, and close, well contested finishes will probably be the order of the day. R. S. Haley, the most prominent sprinter of the O. A. C., is entered in the 100 and 440 yards events. Having been out of training since last November, he is not up to his best form, and will need to put his best foot forward to maintain his past reputation. He undoubtedly has speed, but has been in poor health for some time, has had little preparation for the events, and lacks strength for a hard finish. Haley is anxious to compete with H. S. Brooks, who defeated Myers, the American amateur champion, at the championship meeting last month, but will need to take good care of himself if he expects to defeat Brooks before the end of his vacation. A match between the two would be the most interesting event of the season, and Haley's friends are confident that three or four more weeks' training will enable him to represent the Club against all comers. Much improvement is noticed in several other members, and before the season is over the Club will probably develop more than one 10⅕ second sprinter. Since Thursday the grounds have been closed for the purpose of putting the track in first-class condition, and if the day is pleasant, the events will be well worth the attendance of all lovers of athletics. The bicycle events, of which there are several, are also handicaps, and will excite the enthusiasm of all who witness the two-mile contest, in which the best wheelmen of the coast are entered. Games will be called promptly at 2:45 P. M., and from the Grand Stand an unobstructed view will be obtained of all events, as the officers make it a point to keep the inner grounds clear of a crowd. The admittance at the gate is a nominal sum of twenty-five cents for gentlemen, for the purpose of defraying the expenses of the meeting, and no charge will be made for ladies. To witness the first event, it will be necessary to take the 2 P. M. Oakland boat, and all the events will be finished in time to take an early return boat for dinner in the city.

The following is the order of events, with list of entries and handicaps: 1.—One mile handicap and bicycle race—1. J. C. Quinn, scratch; 2. J. H. Spring, 40 yards; 3. C. Burkhalter, 70 yards; 4. W. C. Lowden, 82 yards. 2.—100 yards handicap run; trial heats; first trial heat—5. R. S. Haley, scratch; 6. D. Eiseman, 10 yards; 7. Arthur Harris, 11 yards; 8. Joseph Green, 11 yards. 3.—Second trial heat—9. E. S. Emmons, 6 yards; 10. W. C. Brown, 7 yards; 11. D. B. M. Woolley, 9 yards; 12. J. H. Anderson, 11. 4—880 yards handicap bicycle race—13. C. L. Leonard, scratch; 2. J. H. Spring, scratch; 15. R. F. Verrinder, 40 yards. 5.—100 yards handicap run; final heat. 6—Two-mile handicap bicycle race—16. H. C. Finkler, scratch; 1. J. C. Quinn, 140 yards; 17. G. L. King, 180 yards; 4. W. H. Lowden, 310 yards; 3. C. Burkhalter, 310 yards. 7.—440 yards handicap run—5. R. S. Haley, scratch; 10. W. C. Brown, 22 yards; 7. Arthur Harris, 40 yards; 6. D. Eiseman, 37 yards; 11. D B. M. Woolley, 37 yards; 18. Harry Germain, 45 yards; 12. J. H. Anderson, 55 yards.

QUEER TIMING.—The London *Athletic Review* states: "We are continually being questioned, both verbally and by letter, as to the time made by George at the intermediate distances in his great mile performance. As what is now printed in athletic and sporting papers will, in future times, be consulted as authoritative statements, it is well to have everything as clearly set out as possible. The official timekeeper was Jack White, whom every one knows as a man who, on all occasions, conscientiously does his best, whatever the capacity he is called upon to fill. The representatives of the press within the enclosure, who also timed the race, were three in number. Watch 1 marks eighths, and is stopped and started by an arrangement in which we, speaking with some knowledge of horological mechanism, have not a very strong faith, and we do not here quote it. The two other watches mark fifths, and we believe are, in themselves, quite trustworthy. The holder of watch 2 is a man who has, probably, as much practice at foot-race timing as any man in England, and we would as soon trust him as anybody. The official watch we know nothing about, except that it was borrowed for the occasion—a circumstance in no way very likely to strengthen confidence in its rate of going. This watch was only used for timing the full distance. The quarter mile was not taken, but the first lap was registered by watch No. 2 as 1m. 17⅕s., and by watch No. 3 as 1m. 17s., the time being read off the dial. The position of the half mile starting post cannot be accurately seen from the finish, some 150 yards distant, so that the times (watch No. 2, 2m. 4⅕s., watch No. 3, 2m. 3 2-5s.) are only valuable as showing that half the distance was run inside 2m. 5s. The second lap (two-thirds of a mile) was given by watch No. 2 as 2m. 45⅕s., and by watch No. 3 as 2m. 45s.

"The watch-holders were a hundred yards or so away from the quarter-mile post, so the three-quarters was not taken with any greater accuracy than was the half. This was given by watch No. 2 as 3m. 8⅘s., and by the same allowance as with the half, and say that it was done in about 3m. 9s. As this three-quarter mile time is so astonishingly in advance of anything else that has ever been done previously, it should command our serious attention and investigation. As it happens, the more we go into figures the more we become convinced that the watches were only a little out. Up to the conclusion of the second lap George had been traveling at the rate of 7 yards (7 yards and 4 inches, to be correct) per second. The difference between two-thirds of a mile and three-quarters is 146 yards 2 feet, and this distance, at 7 yards per second, George would have covered in an inappreciable shade inside 21s., which taking the longest time given for two laps, 2m. 45⅕., would make his three-quarter mile time 3m. 6⅕s. The watches show that he was actually some two seconds longer, which is exactly in accordance with the natural slackening of pace that would occur after two such laps. We must also remember that everything we add on to the time of the three-quarter we have to deduct from the last quarter. Taking it at 3m. 9s., we only allow the jaded runner 70 4-5s. for his last race, 440 yards; and all who saw the performance know in which half of the race the pace was made. We, ourselves, unhesitatingly say that the half was done inside 2m. 5s., and the three-quarters inside 3m. 9s.; but we think no one will have the temerity to say, to a fifth of a second, what the exact time was. As regards the full time of the mile, we feel inclined to accept that given by watch No. 2, viz, 4m. 19 4-5s."

# ROWING.

## BREEDER AND SPORTSMAN'S ROWING CUP.

Although within the past year a number of races between the various Rowing Clubs have taken place, it is still an open question which Club is entitled to consider itself the holder of the Championship. The Pioneer Club, by its victories, under the rules of the Pacific Amateur Rowing Association, and its possession of the McKinley Cup, is undoubtedly the holder of the Amateur Championship. With the dissolution of the Amateur Association, however, the title which the Pioneer Club can justly claim has lost much of its value. All the important races rowed during the past year were professional contests for money. None of them, however, could be considered as deciding the Championship, and were, in fact, nothing more than ordinary match races in specified classes of boats. The Golden Gate Club, for example, beat the South End Club, but the contest took place in barges, and it was stipulated that only that class of boat should be used in the competition. The arrangements have been similar in other races. There have been lapstreak contests, barge races, etc., but no genuine competition in best boats for the Championship of the Pacific Coast. Under these circumstances any club can lay claims to superiority, and several of them do with some show of justice. Desiring to settle the matter in the only formal manner, the BREEDER AND SPORTSMAN will offer a valuable trophy, to be known as the BREEDER AND SPORTSMAN CUP, and the possession of which will carry with it the championship of the Pacific Coast. The contest for the cup shall take place in best boats, and the trophy must be won twice before it can become the property of any club. The first competition shall take place on Thanksgiving Day, and the only stipulation made by the donor of the trophy is that at least three clubs shall be represented. Out of the large number of rowing clubs on the Bay, as well as in the State, three entries for a really valuable cup would not be large. On this score, however, there is not any probability of trouble, as at least four clubs profess anxiety to settle the question of superiority, and need only the opportunity to decide it. Between this date and Thanksgiving Day there will be ample time for all clubs to prepare crews and boats for the contest, which should prove close and exciting.

The desire of the donor of the trophy is that the victorious Club may earn its laurels only after a stubborn contest, and that the best crew may be to the front at the finish. Having no other interest than the promotion of a manly sport and the furtherance of fair play, the BREEDER AND SPORTSMAN shall take pains to make the race such a fair competition that the result must be accepted by oarsmen as an evidence of true merit. The length of the course and the appointment of officials are matters for future discussion. All that is necessary at present is to announce that the BREEDER AND SPORTSMAN CUP will be the most valuable trophy ever offered for an out-door sport in San Francisco, and the donor has no fears that the contest will do credit to the competitors.

## THE FLYNN-STEVENSON MATCH.

The race between Leander Stevenson of the Ariel Club and Thomas Flynn of the Pioneer Club took place Sunday morning, over the Long Bridge course, and contrary to expectation ended very tamely. The race was to have been rowed at an early hour on smooth water, but the usual delay in placing stakeboats occurred, and the breeze was blowing freshly across the course before the men got into position. Stevenson won the choice of stations and of course took the inside. After a few attempts the men were sent off, Flynn catching the water first. There was little change in the positions of the men until the first quarter had been covered, when Flynn began to draw away from his opponent and soon had a length the advantage. Immediately after, however, the Pioneer man got into serious difficulties in the rough water and fell a length behind. Leaving the stakeboats, the men were again on about even terms, but again misfortune attended the Pioneer man whose boat instead of being forty yards from the other as prescribed by the articles was fully eighty yards out in the stream. Stevenson made a good turn and shot inshore into the smooth water at once, while his opponent turned widely and rowing with the full force of the flood tide, which was running like a millrace, lost at every stroke. Coming back again through the stretch of rough water below the Rolling Mills, Flynn got into difficulties once more, and was beaten with great ease. The time for the race, 17 min. 43½ sec., was slow enough to have been made in wherries. Flynn's friends attribute his defeat to the position of his stakeboat. Nearly every man who gets the inside station on the Long Bridge course wins with comparative ease, and so often has this been demonstrated that scullers who know the eccentricities of the course are opposed to racing over it for money. It is likely, however, that Flynn's failure was due as much to his lack of preparation as to the position of his stakeboat. He had been very careless in his training, while his opponent attended strictly to his preparation for some weeks. The result was that the Pioneer was after making the pace for a mile did not have enough left to combat with any disadvantages of rough water, and had to give way.

A CONTRAST OF STYLES.—The late race between Harvard and Yale was remarkable for more than the fast time of 20 min. 47⅕ sec. in which the four miles were made. The styles of the crews and the rig of the boats afforded a strong contrast. Yale used a Spanish cedar boat ten feet longer than the Harvard craft. Her dimensions were 66 feet long, 23¾ inches beam, 9 inches depth. The crew were seated in pairs, the bow oar being well up toward the stern of the craft, and the diminutive coxswain seated near the stern. The Harvard men were distributed in the old fashioned way. Both boats were fitted with swivel rowlocks. Harvard used 12-foot oars with 6½-inch blades, and Yale 11-foot 6-inch oars, with crooked blades 7 inches wide. The difference between the strokes of the crews was also marked. Harvard adopted a long, steady swing, dipping its oars deep into the water with almost monotonous regularity, using legs, arms and backs in about equal proportion—in fact, bringing into play nearly every set of muscles, and sending its frail craft dancing along like a fairy by the side of its more bulky antagonist. Yale, sitting almost bolt upright at each recovery from the rapid rush forward, dishing out the water with its broad oar blades, dipping the latter so frequently that it was difficult to count the strokes with exactitude; using legs and arms for all the power that could be got out of them, letting backs take care of themselves. Yale led for the first mile, when the crew got in difficulties and Harvard forged past and gained a commanding lead of 100 yards on the second mile. Yale then worked its way out of the slack water into the strong current, and gradually closing the gap, finished within three seconds of the remarkable time of the Harvard boat.

THE PERENNIAL PLAISTED.—Plaisted, formerly of San Francisco, and lately the factotum of Hanlon, has a very poor opinion of Wm. Elliott, the ex-champion of England, who was beaten so badly by the Toronto sculler. In a recent talk with the *Boston Herald* aquatic writer, Plaisted gave vent to the following: "What is Elliott shooting himself off about? He comes over here from England and challenges Johnson, Hosmer and Riley, and they don't say anything to him. What's the matter with them? Elliott has no license with them. Why, I don't call myself as good as Hosmer or Jim, but I'll row Elliott. He comes over here and gives us all bluff; but I think he can be beaten by a 'duffer.' That's what they call me at Creve Cœur Lake, where Trickett beat me. Now, Elliott challenges Riley and Hosmer, but he doesn't say anything to me, and although they say I'm a duffer, I'll row Elliott for $500 or $1,000 a side, and I'll give him expenses to row at Toronto, or I'll take expenses to row at New York. The idea of challenging poor, sick Frenchy I'll give Elliott all the racing he wants, and I'll put up dollar for dollar with him."

ENGLISH SNOBBISHNESS REBUKED.—The London *Sportsman*, the *Athletic News*, the London *Referee*, and other independent sporting journals, condemn in unqualified terms the action of the Henly, Steward and other regatta committees that have debarred the Hillsdale crew from competition. The *Athletic News* says: "The Hillsdales are represented as young men of irreproachable character and antecedents, the *bona fides* of whose amateurship is unimpeachable; why, therefore, should they be deprived of the privilege for which they are prepared to sacrifice so much of their time, money and conveniene? The answer that will be given to this question, both in England and America, is likely to be that these blue-blooded young gentlemen of the Thames are afraid of their Transatlantic rivals. Time was when Englishmen liked nothing better than to meet and overcome all foreign rivalry in everything relating to manly sports and exercises; but that appears to be fast becoming nothing more than a legend among the supercilious snobs who now represent the country which erstwhile claimed to be the nursing mother of heroes."

HANLON'S MOVEMENTS.—It is impossible to judge from the various newspaper reports what the champion sculler of the world intends to do professionally this year. The telegraph describes him issuing challenges to row any five men in the world, and Ross accepting the cartel and modestly announcing his willingness to take the entire contract himself. It is not likely, however, that Hanlon will row any races before next year. Ross will soon go to Europe, and the champion is likely to come to California and proceed to Australia for the benefit of his health. Hanlon was taken sick while returning from New York to Toronto after his European trip. On his arrival in Toronto he was taken to his home in a feverish condition, and then for the first time learned that his young daughter was dead. Immediately after his arrival home, Dr. McFarland was sent for and an examination was made, when it was found that he was suffering from typhoid fever. During sickness he was reduced to 132 pounds, having lost 46 pounds. At times he was delirious, and nurses were in constant attendance.

THE PACIFIC COAST CHAMPIONSHIP.—The Fourth of July Regatta at Long Bridge having demonstrated the superior powers of young Peterson as an oarsman, his friends are now talking of a match with Austin Stevenson, the present holder of the Pacific Coast Championship. It is not likely that Stevenson will throw any obstacles in the way of a match, as he has been for some time looking for a race with Cotsford of British Columbia. Peterson is as yet untried over a long course, but he possesses great strength and good pace, and should be a formidable competitor at any distance. His friends would rather try him at two miles, but when it comes to putting up the money it is not likely that they will let the match fall through for the sake of an additional mile to the course. Peterson is rather young, being not yet 19 years of age, while Stevenson is 26, and has the experience which only hard races can bring.

BOYD'S DEFEAT.—The scullers' match arranged some time ago between Elias C. Laycock, of Sydney, N. S. W., and Robert W. Boyd of Middlesborough, England, for one thousand dollars a side, was decided over a course of three miles and a half, straightaway, on the Tees, England, on Monday, July 3d. Several thousand persons arrived in town by excursion trains to witness the race. The weather was fine and the water in good condition. The betting before the race was six to four on Boyd. After the first two hundred yards it became manifest that Laycock would be the winner. At half the distance he was leading by six lengths, and he finished twelve lengths ahead. The winner was thirty-six years of age last May, stands 6 feet 2 inches in height, and his weight in condition is about 177 pounds. Boyd was born September 20, 1854.

GRIFFIN AND WATKINS.—These scullers are determined to settle the dispute as to superiority which in the opinion of their friends was left undecided by the Fourth of July regatta. The course on that occasion was short, and no doubt Griffin profited much by the inside station. The race home between the men was close and gamely contested, and it seemed as if Griffin displayed the best staying powers. He certainly showed the best form. Watkins had the advantage in boats and was in good fix. When the men meet under the more even conditions of a match race they may be expected to give an interesting exhibition. The race will be for $500 a side and will take place at Saucelito. Griffin will use the new paper boat which White procured from Waters & Co. of New York, and which seems to suit him admirably.

WILLAMETTE ANNUAL BOAT RACE. — Friday, July 7th, being the date for the annual regatta of the Willamette

Rowing Club, quite a crowd visited the starting point, while a number of boats were in the river filled with spectators. About 7:30 the Vida struck out with a regular and slow stroke; 2 minutes and 20 seconds later the Cressid slid out, the crew pulling in fine style; 40 seconds later the Willamette glided away at a rapid and quick stroke, till it paid well on the start but counted against the paper shell on the outcome. The barge Vida led all the way, and any and all attempts to pass her were fruitless. The time occupied in going the two miles was as follows: Vida, 16:3; Cressid, 13:58; Willamette, 14:38. T. N. Dunbar won the single scull race by half a length, defeating J. S. Dunbar and J. Hart; time 7:39.—*Rural Spirit, Portland, Or.*

THE BOSTON REGATTA.—The Professional Scullers' Race on the Charles River, Boston, July 4, ended in the defeat of some old favorites. George W. Lee, of Newark, New Jersey, was the winner of the first prize, $150, and A. Hamm, of Halifax, won the second prize of $75. The other starters were: James M. Riley, of Saratoga; Fred A. Plaisted, of Toronto; George H. Hosmer, of Boston; and P. H. Conley, of Halifax. The Halifax Rowing Association preferred to win with Hamm, and Conley understood that he was not to force the pace, but was to hold for the double-scull race. Lee won in 20 min. 48 sec.; Hamm second, in 21 min. 17 sec.; Conley third, in 22 min. 23 sec.; Plaisted and Riley even for fourth position, and Hosmer sixth.

COLUMBIA'S EASY VICTORY.—Referee R. C. Watson has decided that the Harvard crew, by refusing to row the Columbia crew on July 3d, at New London, lost the match. Mr. Watson, in a letter to the Captain of the Columbia crew, says: "The original agreement was that the race should be rowed upon a fair ebb tide—that is, when the tide has run out for at least two hours. The tide was high July 3d at noon, and in requesting Harvard to row at 2 P. M. you were simply asking to have the agreement carried out. Moreover, the challenge sent by you and accepted by Harvard stipulated that the time of the race should be 'mutually agreed' upon, and neither party had any right to insist upon any particular hour, and, in refusing to compromise, Harvard assumed a position which was not in accordance with the agreement."

Elliott declines to row Courtney, for he says: "The American people consider Courtney as good as Hanlon, and the latter gentleman outrowed me easily. But I will row any of the following men four miles, for $500 a side, six weeks from date of first deposit, viz.: George Hosmer, Ten Eyck, J. Riley, E. Morris, Warren Smith, Frenchy Johnson, Lee (of North River), or any of the Ward Brothers."

## YACHTING.

### NO CAPSIZES IN CALIFORNIA.

To San Francisco yachtmen it sounds somewhat strange to hear of the numerous capsizes of yachts during regattas in the Eastern States. There this is an accident that happens quite frequently; here there never has been an instance of the kind. Yet in San Francisco bay we have strong and puffy winds, sharp seas, swift currents, and many of our races are sailed in breezes which Eastern men confess they could not start their boats in. This is of course due to our rig and model. We build and spar our boats for strong breezes and jumpy water; they are intended to carry full sail in winds that blow from 25 to 30 miles an hour. These winds are not stormy, but regular daily visitors in Summer. As we have to sail in them or not at all, our boats must comply with the requirements. We therefore model our yachts with a view to great sail carrying power; for here the boat that carries sail best is the one that wins.

On some other occasion we shall discuss the question of type more fully, as it is a matter of interest to all lovers of aquatic sports. Now we simply refer to the subject to say, we never have capsizes here, and it is not because we are afraid to carry sail, or because we do not got out in strong breezes. The capsizing of two yachts in one race in New York waters the other day—one a broad, beamy, shallow, skimming deck sloop; the other a deep, lead keel cutter—has been the subject of considerable talk among yachtmen. The deep boat, even with the lead keel, capsized and sank; the other one spilled out her sand bags and floated. This shows that lead keel yachts, if not properly handled, have some elements of danger as well as the other type.

The men who sail yachts here are used to sailing with rails awash and with plenty of wind. They are accustomed to handling their vessels in all sorts of circumstances. The boats they have faith in, because they know what they will do on a sea way, and danger of capsize never enters their minds. As we have before stated no yacht can capsize in this harbor during a race; and no regular yacht can capsize here at any time. Our boats are as good as there are in the world for the work they have to do.

The Folie has been at Saucelito all the week.

The Fawn was on the beach at Oakland this week.

The Emerald lies in Oakland Creek during the week.

Mr. Boone sailed the Nellie up from Monterey himself.

There were more yachts out last Sunday than for a long time.

Ingall's new boat, the Restless, is the largest plunger in the bay.

The new sails of the yacht Whitewing seem to shove her ahead faster.

The Salt Jake yacht fleet has gone into a decline like Uncle Sam's Navy.

The Chispa and Clara were in company in Hospital Cove last Saturday night.

All the ocean cruising yachts are back again in yellow water once more.

That big Lillie seems to get through the water pretty lively for a boat of her size.

The la Viva has come into service once more, and is now "wrecking" the Escambia.

Mr. Berry will soon have the Elia in commission again. There is not so very much to do on her now.

The Ariel has been on the ways this week. She is to have a bigger jib, and 5,000 pounds of lead on her keel.

The Fleur de Lis has had her masts shortened very recently. They ought to have been shorter during the race with the Nellie.

Last Sunday was an exceedingly fine day for sailing, and a small fleet of yachts kept company for an hour or more out in the channel.

The Rambler is out on the ways being painted and generally overhauled. She will go up river before very long. The boys intend going as far as Stockton in her.

If we had not promised to say nothing about the Lolita losing her jib-boom while caressing Jackson street wharf, we would have made a good item of the occurrence.

Bill Stone, the builder of the yacht Peerless, Startled Fawn, Lolita, Magic, Thetis, Rambler, Whitewing and others, hurt his hand the other day in launching the Mischief, and has had to knock off work. He is going to take an enforced rest for a while, and will go up river. Stone builds good boats, and is always kept pretty busy.

Collins, the Long Bridge boat builder, has just turned out a very handsome boat like a man-of-war's gig. She is 25 feet long, 6 foot beam, has fancy gratings, and is very finely finished. She is for Mazatlan, for a custom house boat. She is built of cedar and eastern oak, with black walnut gratings, and there is a good deal of brass work on her. She has cushions, awnings, and everything complete. She is the "Candidest" boat turned out here for some time.

LIVE START.—Concerning the start from an anchor revived by the Boston Y. C. in their great match June 17th, the Boston Herald has this to say: "The start was made in a new and novel manner, entirely out of the general rule, the yachts being required to start from an anchor with all sails down, thus giving an excellent exhibition of the efficiency of the crews in making sail. When the word was given a most exciting scene was witnessed, each crew naturally vieing with the others to 'masthead' their sails and gain whatever supremacy they might by their celerity. In some cases the halliards were led through snatch blocks, and a 'walk away' was made with the slack, running the sails up with almost lightning rapidity."

MISS MARY ANDERSON'S YACHT.—Miss Anderson, when not galloping over the country roads on her big black Kentucky horse, is on the water, and her fondness for out-door life is attested by her very brown complexion. She has been looking forward anxiously for the completion of her boat, and yesterday made a trial trip in it. The boat is a very handsome one, 52 feet long, 10 feet 10 inches wide, and draws 3 feet of water. It is furnished with all modern improvements. It has two cabins, one fore and the other aft of the engine-room. The after cabin, measuring 12 feet by 7 feet, is furnished in hard woods, and leading from it is a retiring room and lavatory. The forward cabin is finished in white ash and black walnut. Next to the engine-room, which contains a Herthan engine, there is a cook's galley and pantry. There is ample room on the deck for a party of twelve or fifteen persons.

While Dr. Merritt, of Oakland, was at Santa Barbara last week, he gave a sail on his fine yacht Casco to a number of the guests at the Arlington. Mr. Dixey Thompson, the proprietor of the hotel, is an old salt, and a jolly one, and he and all hands enjoyed themselves greatly. The trip brought out the following suggestion by the Santa Barbara Press: "The pleasure excursion of the yacht Casco, yesterday, caused a revival of the oft repeated question, why does not Santa Barbara have a yacht club. Never was a sea more inviting to sailing parties, that to the channel. The wind is steady, gentle, and can be relied upon almost every day of the year. There are many wealthy residents who could well afford to keep private yachts, but if this were not thought desirable, a few could club together and support a few yacht in elegant style. Nothing could contribute more to the attractions of our city as a tourist resort, than occasional excursions along the coast, or toward the islands. The cost of keeping the vessel in order would be merely nominal, and the return, in the way of sport and healthful recreation, would be full compensation. We have a number of wealthy gentlemen in our city, who were formerly interested in ocean vessels, as captains and owners, and it would seem as though they would enter heartily into any plan for the organization of a yacht club. Mr. J. Doutiou's Dashaway has proven an entire success, and should stimulate others to follow the example, and own private yachts, but in any event clubs should be formed, and at least one large first-class yacht should be placed on the channel."

HIGH SPEED STEAM YACHT.—The Herreshoffs have delivered the Siesta, a new high speed steam yacht to her owner, H. H. Warner, of Rochester, N. Y. Like all their handiwork, the Siesta presents numerous features original with the Bristol builders. In point of model she is totally different from the usual run of overgrown launches still built, about New York in the clumsy fashions of our forefathers. The Siesta is sharp as a knife, with U frames throughout, and moderate hollow to her lines. Her speed is derived from a very light displacement and small wet surface, owing to the use of composite construction and the Herreshoff coil boiler and their light weight engines. She is lightly built but of selected material, well-fastened, and therefore tough and able to withstand far rougher usage than the heavier boats with the old style oak frame, yellow pine plank and iron spike fastening. She is 98 feet long over all, 17 feet beam, and 6 feet deep. Her great beam in mainly across deck, her sides have considerable flare. These proportions were determined upon by Mr Nathaniel Herreshoff after extended experiments made a year ago. The boiler is of the circular coil pattern, already fully described in this journal, and occupies but 6 feet 8 inches. measured from out to out of casing. The engine is compound condensing, with cylinders 10½ and 18 inches diameter by 18 inches stroke, and develops 200 horsepower upon 300 pounds coal per hour. A performance which is highly satisfactory. The screw is 56 inches diameter with 96-inch pitch, four bladed. The hull has an angle iron frame 2x3 inches, with reverse frames, and floor plates 3-16 inch thick. She is planked with oak and pine, screwbolted to the frame. Rudder, screw and skeg are of bronze. Rigged as a pole schooner, has a gig, dingy and a 20x4½ foot steam cutter at davits, the latter capable of making nine miles an hour. As the Siesta is designed for the St. L—rence river, she has been given ample head room and ventilation below by a deck house fore and aft with a pilot house and dining saloon at the forward end, the saloon being 9x12 feet, with the kitchen beneath, and a pantry, forecastle, etc., forward of

the latter. The main saloon is reached by a companion from aft and is 15x11 feet, finished in very stylish and tasty design in birdseye maple and cherry trimmings. Two large and two small staterooms lead off from the saloon, fitted with numerous small devices for comfort and convenience, all characterized by that peculiar and pleasing originality for which the Herreshoffs have become famous. The same builders have just finished a sister ship, called the Orient, and both are sure to maintain the credit of America as progressive, even in the darkest hours of prostration which have overcome our nautical interests.—*Forest and Stream.*

## BASE BALL.

### THE RENOS AND THE MINSTRELS.

The first appearance of the Haverly Minstrels on the diamond field, in a friendly game with the Renos, attracted a very good attendance last Sunday at the Recreation Grounds, and considering that the home team are now in good working trim, the visitors gave them a pretty hard tussle, and the game would have been still closer if the Minstrels had been in better practice in their fielding. On some future occasion they will give a better account of themselves.

| RENOS. | | | | | |
|---|---|---|---|---|---|
| | T.B. | R. | B.H. | P.O. | A. | E. |
| Bigelow, 1b. | 5 | 5 | 1 | 9 | 0 | 0 |
| Barnes, 1b. | 5 | 7 | 1 | 9 | 0 | 0 |
| Swanton, c. f. | 5 | 1 | 1 | 0 | 0 | 0 |
| Cushigan, s. f. | 5 | 1 | 0 | 1 | 0 | 1 |
| Lake, l. f. | 5 | 2 | 1 | 1 | 0 | 0 |
| Riordan, p. | 5 | 3 | 1 | 0 | 3 | 2 |
| Sheridan, 3b. | 5 | 0 | 1 | 2 | 3 | 3 |
| Bianchi, s. s. | 6 | 1 | 1 | 1 | 2 | 1 |
| Oregan, c. | 4 | 1 | 1 | 12 | 2 | 2 |
| Totals | 44 | 15 | 12 | 27 | 11 | 9 |

| MINSTRELS. | | | | | |
|---|---|---|---|---|---|
| | T.B. | R. | B.H. | P.O. | A. | E. |
| Thompson, 2b. | 5 | 3 | 0 | 0 | 1 | 2 |
| Garcand, 3b. | 5 | 2 | 1 | 0 | 1 | 3 |
| Piercy, l. | 5 | 1 | 2 | 1 | 0 | 0 |
| J. Gorman, 1 f. | 5 | 1 | 1 | 1 | 0 | 1 |
| Pete Mack, r. f. | 5 | 0 | 0 | 0 | 0 | 1 |
| Cushman, s. s. | 4 | 1 | 2 | 1 | 1 | 1 |
| Rice, c. | 4 | 1 | 1 | 7 | 1 | 1 |
| O. Gorman, 1b. | 4 | 0 | 0 | 14 | 0 | 1 |
| Sadler, s. f. | 4 | 2 | 2 | 0 | 1 | 1 |
| Totals | 41 | 10 | 7 | 24 | 17 | 10 |

| Innings | 1 | 2 | 3 | 4 | 5 | 6 | 7 | 8 | 9 | |
|---|---|---|---|---|---|---|---|---|---|---|
| Renos | 0 | 6 | 3 | 0 | 2 | 1 | 2 | 0 | x | —16 |
| Minstrels | 1 | 1 | 0 | 4 | 0 | 0 | 1 | 3 | 0 | —10 |

Home Runs—Sadler, Lake. Three base hits—Lake. Two-base hits—Mischie, 1. Left on Bases—Renos, 8; Minstrels, 4. First Base on Errors—Renos, 8; Minstrels, 4. Double Plays—Piercy and O. Gorman, and Cushman and Thompson. Struck Out—Renos, 5; Minstrels, 8. Passed Balls—Oregan, 4; Rice, 1. Umpire—Charles Oeffin. Scorer—Walter Wallace. Time of Game—One hour and thirty-five minutes.

On next Sunday we are promised, at the same grounds, one of those travestie games which excite so much merriment among the spectators.

### THE AMERICAN CHAMPIONSHIP.

For the week since our last report the Cincinnatis continue to hold their lead, with St. Louis second, and the Athletics and Eclipse Club in a close contest for third position. Following is the record to the 11th instant:

| Clubs. | Allegheny | Athletic | Baltimore | Cincinnati | Eclipse | St. Louis | Won. | Lost. |
|---|---|---|---|---|---|---|---|---|
| Allegheny | | 1 | 1 | 3 | 1 | 1 | 13 | 23 |
| Athletic | 3 | | 5 | 3 | 1 | 5 | 22 | 20 |
| Baltimore | 7 | 7 | | 1 | 1 | 7 | 24 | 22 |
| Cincinnati | 2 | 2 | 3 | | | 2 | 32 | 10 |
| Eclipse | 4 | 5 | 5 | 7 | | 2 | 22 | 22 |
| St. Louis | 4 | 4 | 3 | 6 | 3 | | 27 | 17 |
| Lost | 16 | 16 | 27 | 19 | 14 | 17 | 104 | |

### THE LEAGUE CHAMPIONSHIP.

There has been a notable change in the records of the League games. The Chicago teams having assumed the lead, with Detroit and Providence almost tying them, it is still an open question as to naming the first and second in the series, as may be seen from the following record up to July 11th:

| Clubs. | Boston. | Buffalo. | Chicago. | Cleveland. | Detroit. | Providence. | Troy. | Worcester. | Games Won. | Games to Play. |
|---|---|---|---|---|---|---|---|---|---|---|
| Boston | | 4 | 4 | 4 | 4 | 3 | 9 | 5 | 23 | 41 | 19 |
| Buffalo | 5 | | 2 | 5 | 4 | 4 | 4 | 4 | 20 | 41 | 16 |
| Chicago | 5 | 8 | | 4 | 4 | 2 | 4 | 5 | 30 | 45 | 15 |
| Cleveland | 4 | 5 | 3 | | 2 | 2 | 5 | 4 | 26 | 41 | 19 |
| Detroit | 4 | 5 | 4 | 5 | | 4 | 6 | 5 | 28 | 42 | 16 |
| Providence | 5 | 5 | 4 | 5 | 5 | | 4 | 2 | 29 | 42 | 15 |
| Troy | 3 | 4 | 2 | 3 | 3 | 5 | | 4 | 19 | 40 | 18 |
| Worcester | 4 | 4 | 1 | 3 | 1 | 3 | 5 | | 18 | 40 | 18 |
| Games Lost | 20 | 21 | 13 | 21 | 17 | 17 | 24 | 25 | 168 | 336 | 144 |

A most remarkable game was played at Providence, R. I., on last Wednesday, which was won by the home team—the Boston Club having to content themselves with a duck's egg.

## SHOOTING NOTES.

The California and Cosmopolitan Clubs will shoot a match at San Bruno, on Sunday, the 30th inst., for the Diamond Medal. The Cosmopolitans have won it twice and the Californians once. Should the Cosmopolitans again succeed in winning it on Sunday week, the trophy will be theirs.

One of the chief attractions to our pigeon matches lies in the fact that after the regular club shooting is finished, pool shooting is inaugurated, in which outsiders indulge.

A private pigeon shooting match will be held to-day, Saturday, at Bird's Point, Alameda.

Dove shooting is little indulged in by our wing shots at present.

To-morrow, Sunday, the California Club will shoot at San Bruno.

# THE
# Breeder and Sportsman.

PUBLISHED BY THE

BREEDER AND SPORTSMAN PUBLISHING CO.

THE TURF AND SPORTING AUTHORITY OF THE
PACIFIC COAST.

**OFFICE, 508 MONTGOMERY STREET**

P. O. Box 1386.

*Five dollars a year; three dollars for six months; one dollar and a
half for three months. Strictly in advance*

*Money should be sent by postal order, draft or by registered letter.*

*Communications must be accompanied by the writer's name and address
not necessarily for publication, but as a private guarantee of good faith*

JOSEPH CAIRN SIMPSON, - - - EDITOR

SAN FRANCISCO, - - SATURDAY, JULY 22, 1882

## SUNDAY MORNING AT THE OAKLAND TROTTING PARK.

In another part of the paper is a description of Sunday morning at the Gentlemen's Driving Park (formerly Fleetwood), in the vicinity of New York, and it is nearly a perfect transcript of what was formerly the practice here. There is a change now at the Oakland Trotting Park In place of the bustle, the merry spins, the brushes, the verandah and stands crowded with spectators, a hundred timing watches in view, the track lively, on every turn there is quiet. In place of taking that day as the especial one to move the trotters and breeze the racehorses, it is a day of rest. The shouts of the drivers and the cadence of the foot-falls of the flying steeds are wanting, and beyond some sheeted animals, lazily walking about under the charge of the grooms, there is nothing to remind of the tumult of the Sabbaths of the past, nothing which the most ultra pro-Sunday-law advocate could take exception to.

Last Sunday we strolled from the house to the track, the morning as lovely as could be. A light breeze, so light that, though it could scarcely be felt, there was enough to carry northward the smoke from the chimneys of the ferry steamers, and give a tremor to the flags on the pavilion at Shell Mound. The sun shone with a subdued radiance, warm without brightness, adding softness to the atmosphere.

What a grand morning to "scrape out," we mentally ejaculated, or to give any sort of judicious work, with as little danger of "soreness" following as is possible. Looking over the fence of the track the surface was smooth, but a glance showed that it was not prepared for an extra day. When there is a general desire to give fast exercise, great care is taken in the preparation. It is nicely sprinkled in the evening, so that the water may not be evaporated, and early in the morning the light harrow mellows the surface to just the right depth to take off the jar, without making it so deep as to be laborious for the horses. Inside of the track, all over the oval, the haycocks were thick, and in some portions it looked as though the yellow mounds covered the whole of the ground.

The Easterner, when for the first time he sees a California hayfield, is astonished that these straw-colored heaps are called hay. His recollections are of the green timothy and sweetly scented clover, and he imagines that it is a "guy" when told that it is the best forage for horses in training, and that the whole of the field will average four tons, at least, to the acre.

It lends a rural appearance to the scene, and were it not that the high fence, the stands, and the long rows of stables dispel the illusion, it would be mistaken for a "ranch." Two or three men are sitting on the veranda listlessly smoking, and the only occupant of the bar-room is the one waiting for customers, which are not likely to come. The rattle of the Berkeley train is heard, and as this is the one which leaves San Francisco at eight o'clock, in the olden time there would have been a throng of passengers. There are three arrivals. A gentleman from Virginia City, fond of trotters, and expecting to see a host of them at speed. He had learned that an unusual number were domiciled at the track, and, of course, so near the opening of the circuit, there would be lively work. A friend accompanied him, and the third was a trainer from Vallejo, who had made the journey with the same fond anticipations. There is a blank lock, a sort of puzzled stare at the small group and the silent course. "What's the matter?" says the Virginian. "Where are the horses?" inquires the trainer, almost at the same instant. "Oh! the boys all work out Saturday now," was the answer. That it was not a satisfactory one was evident, and even the visit to the bar did not appear to revive their spirits. In place of the fizzing champagne which followed the performance of Helene at the Gentlemen's Driving Park, a light cocktail or two was imbibed, fresh cigars lighted, and almost disconsolately the seats were resumed on the veranda. There was the usual horse talk, of course, but not the vivacious speeches of the days of yore. The trainers joined the group at intervals, every one of them arrayed in his best clothes, and with cleanly shaven faces and freshly polished boots. In the stalls the horses were "bedded down," and in some of the larger there were congregations of "rubbers" putting the time in with reading the morning and sporting papers.

There is no necessity for elaborating further to show the contrast between the scene which the Herald describes, or that which was witnessed on the same ground a couple of years ago, and the picture presented. There will be a difference of opinion which is the best, and arguments on both sides. For the old plan the advocates will say that many men who have trotters trained cannot afford to leave their business on week days, and the pleasure they take in seeing their horses exercised is the only thing which induces them to keep them. Leaving out of the discussion the morality of the question, and the advantage of gaining the good opinion of those who do not approve of any breach of the Sabbath, there are other things that have a bearing, not the least of which is, that generally it gives the trainer a better opportunity of getting the horses in order. The "Sunday Matinees" draw a large assemblage. At many of them the concourse would be as great as at an ordinary race. The owners of the class alluded to are always anxious to have their horses make a good showing, and there were contests after contests of horse against the watch, the latter invariably getting the best of the fight if the battle was a long one. Stimulated by applause when the animal made a good mile, there was a desire to beat it, and if it did not work up to expectations it must be kept going until it did. In lieu of waiting for the races to come, there would be races every Sunday, and these given long before the animal was in condition to endure the rigor of the many trials.

Beaten, as they inevitably must be after this course of treatment, the blame was laid on the trainer, and he was declared utterly incompetent, when the failure arose from the owner being desirous to entertain his friends by a display of his horse's capacity. The larger the gathering, the greater the excitement, the more imminent the danger. If this view be correct, and we are confident that it is, the abrogation of fast work on Sunday is an advantage to all who are concerned in the horses, and though it drops one of the exciting episodes, there are enough left to give plenty of animation and life to the race course.

## OUR ILLUSTRATIONS.

The pictures of the "Notable Horses of California" which have appeared on the title page of this paper are the very best which we have seen; that is, they are portraits, not the fanciful idea of the artist, but representations of the animal, exact and admirable. As a general thing, the horses which artists draw are ideal, or rather an erroneous conception of what they should be. It does not appear to vary the case a great deal whether the animal is at rest or in motion, save that in the latter case the absurdity is heightened. Our artist has divested himself of the notions of the schools, and, studying from nature, has acquired the capacity to depict a horse truthfully. Let these pictures be carefully and closely scrutinized, and the verdict must be that they are faithful portrayals of the animals, and without the usual discrepancies and divergences from nature.

## A VALUABLE REINFORCEMENT—THE BREEDING FARM OF COLONEL M'NASSER.

We heartily welcome Colonel James McNasser to the ranks of California breeders. It is an accession which will be of vast benefit, as the stock he has added to the home strains is of the right stamp. In some of them there are new elements, the blood being different from any previously owned in this State; and individually they are highly praised by men who are good judges. Very judiciously has Colonel McNasser located his breeding farm, and this is another consideration in arriving at success. The proprietorship of the Golden Eagle Hotel made Sacramento his home again, as in the early days of California he was a resident, and though he transferred his domicile to Denver for a time, the old hankering for the banks of the Sacramento came over him, and he was not fully satisfied until he returned. The hotel alone would not do, as he had a number of horses in Colorado, and he had a love for fine horses which must be gratified. A pair to drive, a carriage team, and an extra saddle-horse was not enough; the greater fascination of breeding must be added; and to accomplish this, a farm must be purchased.

The east side of the Sacramento contiguous to the city is one of the fairest spots in California. There is a rich soil, undulating enough to give dry pasture land, which is so essential in the breeding of fine horses, and plenty of pure water. It is conceded that the finest drive on the Pacific Coast is that which extends from Sacramento to Riverside—a wide boulevard following the bank of the river, and shaded with grand old oaks, which would be the glory of an English park. The roadway is kept in as good order as a trotting track, and from the start to the finish there is "brushing ground." Six miles straight out there is a chance for the exhibition of bottom as well as speed, and on these glorious Summer evenings it is thronged with the fleet roadsters of the Capital City. Such a drive in the vicinity of San Francisco would double the value of every trotter in the State; and old residents of Sacramento whose business compels them to live in the metropolis are constantly bewailing being deprived first of the climate and next of their favorite drive. Any one who is acquainted with the Colonel could easily have foretold that his farm would not be far off from this famous boulevard, as he dearly enjoys a friendly contest on the road, and, then, it is so handy to the hotel. The farm is located within a mile of the terminus. Our correspondent, "Mile-and-a-quarter," gave a sketch of it two weeks ago, but we must insist on a rechristening, and that "Kleinhaus place" be replaced with something more euphonious. Nevertheless, any name will not interfere with a drive between lunch and dinner, and leave an hour or two to look at the horses and colts. With his son John to leave in charge of the hotel, it is more than an even bet that the Colonel will spend most of his time among the horses, and very many of the guests of the Golden Eagle will participate in the enjoyments of a jaunt to the farm.

We have written of a trip between lunch and dinner, but the intention is to time our visit to Sacramento when the harvest moon is showing its full orb above the Sierras, soon after the sun is sinking behind the brown summits of the Coast Range; and then the hotel dinner, good as it always is, will not entice us. Our friends know that we fully appreciate the good things of this world, and without claiming the distinction of being called a *gourmet*, will pass for a good feeder. But with a moonlight drive in the balance—well, we will take the chance of there being something left in the larder, and prolong the stay among the weanlings, yearlings, etc., until Luna is well up in the firmament.

A partial list of the stock of Colonel McNasser -will be found on another page, and what we have said about the value of the blood will be concurred in by those who are acquainted with the strains. Morosa is an old acquaintance. She was bred by C. S. Dole, of Chicago, and when owned by S. Lasher, of Elgin, Illinois, gave us a drubbing in a three-year-old race. She was a slashing, square-gaited, big filly, and the "Governor" was in great glee that he had taken us into camp.

## THE EARLY DAYS OF ROMERO.

There is a spice of romance in the young days of Romero, and the history which his breeder gives is proof that he is a "borned trotter," as the Kentucky darkies say. We know that his sire was of that class, and his dam, having also the honor of producing Inca, Del Sur and Zeluska, no one can question her title to being one of the noble matrons of the track. Those who argue, however, that good feeding and good care are, if anything, detrimental to the horse, must not lay too much stress on the example, but rather ascribe the size and activity of Romero to a vigorous constitution that neglect could not shatter. Again, California is a wonderland in the respect of providing sustenance, when to the eye there is nothing but a barren waste, and in the sections where the native grasses have not been obliterated by overstocking, there is an abundance of rich food, excepting in the season of the year when the old crop is rotting and the new too watery to afford much nourishment.

But that a colt should overcome the drawbacks which fell to the lot of Romero, is one of the remarkable instances so rarely met. And who can say, authoritatively, that the ill treatment did not affect him? With care and proper training from youth, without ailments, the 2:22½ at four years old might have been lowered several seconds.

The history which our correspondent so kindly has furnished finishes the history, and makes it complete until he makes his next appearance in public. That he will continue his victorious career we have the utmost confidence. That Mr. Johnston may have other "Richmonds in the field" which will make amends for the disappointments we sincerely hope, and we have full faith in that too. With two such colts as Len Rose and Romero from a season which was limited to five to choose from, is an exemplification which is a safe guide for the prediction, though the prophecy is not based on that alone. Richmond only got a few colts in the East, and not one of them which had not a good share of the fast-trotting inheritance.

## THE HERD.

There is an immense field to explore, over the gateway of which are the two little words which form the caption to this article and stand at the head of one of the departments of the BREEDER AND SPORTSMAN. Shorthorns, Herefords, Devons, Jerseys, Guernseys, Ayreshires, Holsteins, Polled Angus, Kerry cattle, the little black fellows from the Highlands of Scotland, Grades, Natives, Brahmins, the French breeds, the names of which we dare not attempt to spell without a reference for every letter, are all roaming in it, and not one of them which has not some characteristic which is worthy of notice. Each, too, has some valuable quality, as the Hindoo has oddity of appearance as well as the reverence of millions of people to fall back upon, and the Natives can be made good use of to cross with the more valuable. It would have been a grand oversight to omit the Spanish, as they not only contributed to the amusement of aristocratic and plebeian spectators, as their long legs and lithe bodies enabled them to make the journey on foot from Texas to the North before the days of railroads, and brought beef within the reach of the masses, who otherwise would have rarely tasted the knightly roast, the juicy steak, maybe not even the porter-house cut from close behind the ears.

Colonel W. P. B. assures us that since the long-horns have become so nearly extinct, the bull's head, cooked after the old-time fashion, has lost some of its flavor, though this may arise from our friend not being so young as he was twenty-five years ago, as he also swears that there is no such nectar to wash down the monthly breakfasts of the club as regaled the palates of the Argonauts. We should not be surprised if he were to aver that Tamalpais had lost a thousand feet or so of its height, and that the trees which have shaded their camping-ground ever since the club was formed were not so umbrageous.

The first drove of Texas cattle which came to Chicago attracted more attention than a score of Jumbos would now, and the comments of farmers and stock-buyers were strangely discordant. With all due deference to the gastronomic taste of the Colonel, we must acknowledge a preference for a prime cut from some of the breeds which do not carry such magnificent antlers; and never yet have enjoyed the pleasure of tasting the covering of the cranium of Taurus, cooked in the manner described in the B. and S. two weeks ago, either in the old days or new, we can not demur from his conclusions.

But we have wandered from the track, the intention being to inform our readers that we have the promise of communications from practical men as soon as the busy season is over. These articles will be of great value, embodying the views of men who are intimately acquainted with the various breeds and their adaptability to the Pacific Coast. In this wide extent of territory, with such a dissimilarity of topography, soil and climate, it is evident that there is room for, and need for, more than one race.

## THE RIFLE.

In tracing the progress of arms which propel projectiles, especially those which use an explosive force to effect the object, is an interesting topic to those who have an interest in gunnery; and the essays of Dr. E. H. Pardee will give a clearer insight of the subject than any save those who have made it an especial study possess. To the rifle-shooter the lessons will be of the greatest importance, as ultimately the Doctor will impart lessons his long practice so eminently fit him to give. In this practice he has not only aimed to make a good score, but to investigate all the theories, and select those which he found correct.

## CLOSING OF STAKES AND PRIZES.

**On the first day of August next, the stakes of the Pacific Coast Blood-Horse Association, the Embryo Stakes and the Purses and Stakes at the California Fairs will close.**

**The advertisements in this paper will give full particulars. Do not forget the date, TUESDAY, AUGUST 1st, 1882.**

## THE ALMONTS ON THE PACIFIC COAST.

There are several fine Almonts on the Coast. It could scarcely be otherwise when the well-deserved reputation of the strain is taken into consideration, and being so highly prized, it is equally certain that our liberal breeders would determine not to be without the blood. Writing from memory some may be overlooked, but among the sires, there are the following: Jay Beach, at Linkville, Oregon, has Altoona, J. B. Haggin, at the Rancho de-Paso, has Algona, J. J. Gosper, of Prescott, Arizona, has Gosper's Almont, formerly Exemplar, and at Palo Alto is Piedmont. Some years ago, a very fine Almont yearling, from a mare by Prophet, was taken to Santa Barbara, but we have not heard from him lately. Mr. Beach has several fine Almont mares, and there are a number of them among the matrons of the Palo Alto stud. We have oftentimes claimed that California was as well supplied with trotting strains as any state in the Union, and now the impression is strong that she will take precedence of any of her sister states. To substantiate the claim, measures will be taken to obtain the necessary information, and when that is in, there will be a good show to establish the proposition. The Almonts are a potent factor in the calculation, as every one mentioned is from the right sort of a dam, and this is as essential as the male side of the parentage.

## PURCHASE OF BRONZE.

This great filly, which made so good a showing in the race for four-year-olds at Chicago, trotting seven heats, the third and fourth in 2:25½ and 2:26½, was purchased after the race by H. D. McKinney, of Janesville, in consideration for $7,500. That it was a judicious investment is proven by the offer of Robert Bonner of $15,000, though the telegraph does not give the information whether the offer was accepted or not.

We are not violating confidence in stating that Mr. McKinney is one of our corp of correspondents over the signature of "Mambrino," as he has written over that nom de plume for so long a time and made it so popular, that there are few readers of the Eastern papers who are not aware of the fact. Mr. McKinney is not only a graceful and forcible writer, but a first-rate judge of a horse, and as he has given us a half promise to write for the BREEDER AND SPORTSMAN "My Experience in Buying Horses for Friends;" and should he do so, we can promise our readers an entertainment which will please the most exacting.

The experience of "Mambrino" extends over a longer period than any one would imagine from reading his communications, and although in this respect we may "give away" his age, he has seen all the famous trotting horses from the days of the old-time celebrities, we will not say which—to the present time. Better still, he has owned many, can drive them as well as the old professors of the art, and has done more to educate trainers in the proper use of the toe-weight than any ten men in the country.

The consideration of those useful adjuncts in training the trotter will come more appropriately when the racing and trotting season is at an end. In the meantime, we congratulate Mambrino on his purchase.

## BEEF AND MUTTON.

Butchers' bills are a dreaded portion of the household expenses, though the good fortune is that when these are heavy the bills of the doctors are correspondingly light. Light or heavy, all of our readers are interested. To guard these interests, arrangements have been made to secure reliable reports of the Live Stock Market on this Coast, and in another part of this paper will be found the first of the series. It rests with stock-breeders to assist us in making this complete, and this they can do by sending reports of all sales with which they are acquainted. By joint effort all of the sales of any magnitude will be reported, and it does not require a great deal of argument to show the advantages which will result.

## WONDERFUL STORIES.

As the time approaches for the closing of entries, there are always wonderful stories of what the horses are doing.

In some cases the trainers are a party hoping to reduce the fields by promulgating big stories of what their horses are doing, and in other cases it is only necessary to start the ball in motion, when the natural accumulations will give it sufficient size.

Our advice is: If you have a good horse for the classes he is eligible to make the entry, and the chances are that when the races come off, some of the swans will lose their plumage.

## TYPOGRAPHICAL ERRORS.

It is not astonishing that proof readers who are not versed in the technical terms of the turf and track should make blunders. Some of them appear so senseless to any except the initiated, that there appears to be an absolute necessity for a change. Thus: "Nick" is changed into "trick," and "forehand" into "forehead." The use of the dash in denoting the combination of blood is troublesome, and "Electioneer—St. Clair" is so ambiguous, that a comma takes the place of the mark intended. Until compositors and proof readers are "well up" in the phraseology, there is no help for it, and sometimes we think fewer mistakes are made than could be expected.

# THE KENNEL.

## FIXTURES.

National American Kennel Club's trial on quails. Grand Junction, Tenn., December 4th. D. Bryson, Memphis, Tenn., Secretary.

Louisiana Field Trials near New Orleans, La., beginning Dec. 11, under the management of the New Orleans Gun Club.

Irving Brown.—Western Pennsylvania Society's English Setter Bench Show Derby, Pittsburgh, Pa., for English setter puppies whelped on or after March 1, 1885. Entries closed December 1, 1885. J. H. Stayton, Allegheny City, Pa., Secretary.

Field Trials.—National American Kennel Club's trials on prairie chickens, Fairmont Minn', September 4th. Entries to American Field Derby closed July 1st; to All-Age Stake, September 4th. Joseph E. Dew, Columbia, Tenn., Special Notes any for these trials.

Gilroy Beef and Gun Club's trials on quails' near Gilroy, Cal., October 29th. Open to dogs owed in California, Oregon, Nevada and Arizona. E. Leavesley, Secretary, Gilroy, Cal.

Eastern Field Trials Club's trials on quails, near High Point, N. C., November 17th. Entrance to Derby close July 1st; to All-Age and Members' Stakes, November 1st. Fred. N. Hall, Secretary, P. O. Box 604, New York.

## ANSWERS TO CORRESPONDENTS.

Under this head will be found replies to all questions that may be asked of the Kennel Editor in relation to breeding, breaking, or entering dogs, feeding or curing them of any ordinary disease. Correspondents must state plainly what are the p 'culiar symptoms of the malady for which they seek advice, and in all cases, especially when desiring to know the best way to correct a dog of a fault, must be careful to state the age and s x. No answers will be sent by mail, and all questions must be marked Kennel-Editor WEEKLY BREEDER AND SPORTSMAN, San Francisco, Cal.

E. BROWN, ALAMEDA.—The best way to keep kennels free from fleas and lice is to sprinkle a little coal oil around and rub a little in the dog's hair occasionally. A mere trace is all that is needed. The widely advertised Persian insect powder is a specific.

J. A. W., SUISUN.—The symptoms you describe are those of bronchitis. Rub spirits of turpentine into the chest once a day and give a tablespoonful of the following mixture three times a day; Syrup of tolu, 3 oz.; syrup of squills, 3 drams; tincture of aconite, 15 drops; water, 3 oz.

## STILL HUNTING.

A correspondent, who neglects the customary courtesy of signing his name to his letter, writes to the Kennel Editor, requesting him to denounce what the anonymous correspondent is pleased to designate as the "cowardly and unsportsmanlike practice of running deer with hounds." The writer referred in complimentary terms to the stand taken by the BREEDER AND SPORTSMAN on the hare killing brutality a few weeks since, and suggests that buck running is a far more brutal sport. As this question has often been raised before, the Kennel Editor feels justified in speaking of the matter, though the communication hardly deserves notice. As an individual he has often followed a pack of hounds chasing a deer, and considers the sport the finest and fairest that this glorious sportsman's paradise affords. In his opinion it is as far above the pot hunter's practice of killing deer at a pond by moonlight as quail shooting is above trap killing; therefore he cannot denounce it as cowardly and cruel and laud still-hunting to the skies. In this as in all other matters, there appears to be a decided difference of opinion, and as the columns of the BREEDER AND SPORTSMAN are always open to gentlemen not afraid to sign their names (as a guarantee of good faith only and not necessarily for publication, correspondence on the subject is respectfully invited. Experience is of more value than theory, and it is to be hoped that some gentlemen who have had some experience in either style of deer hunting will favor this paper with its results.

## A BOLD CHALLENGE.

Judge Mee has allowed it to be stated in various newspapers that he is willing to match a seven-months-old pup against any greyhound of similar age in the State of California. The statement leaves the impression that the Judge is willing to waive all his rights as to the time, place, and other conditions in favor of the acceptor. The pup that the Judge will run in case his challenge is taken up is by California Boy, a dog which as yet has not made any special mark in the stud, and who when in the field was the worst in and out runner ever seen. Tom Tunstead, who if not the first owner of California Boy, was the first person to run him in a public match, always had a great faith in his speed and pluck, and in spite of repeated defeats ran him in match after match until he finally divided a first prize in the Pioneer Club with another of Tunstead's entries. On that occasion it was generally thought that the bad luck of Murphy's black dog, War wick, who was one of the fleetest hounds that ever went out of slips, helped California Boy to his victory; but leaving that question on one side there is no doubt but the white dog showed marvelous form and was quite a surprise to all except Tunstead, who from the first said he was sure to win. California Boy was once owned by J. C. Murphy, who to disgust at his being badly beaten by a fourth-rate dog, either gave him away or sold him for a nominal sum. He was afterwards raffled and fell into the possession of Dougherty, who on account of lack of kennel room sold him for a mere song. The price paid ($25) was thought at the time to be fully as much as he was worth. If he has bred a world-beater for Judge Mee, those who had the refusal of him at that price will doubtless feel sorry they did not snap up the offer. If, however, his pups are as unreliable runners as their father, the Judge will perhaps regret his purchase. Judged by a breeder's standard, there should be many pups able to beat the produce of California Boy, no matter how fine they may look, unless they inherit some special merit from the dam. Under favorable conditions, the get of Gentleman Jones seems to develop earlier than those of most other dogs. At ten months Paul Jones and his brother, Master Jones, said to be out of Branch, by Jones, were as well grown as many fourteen months old pups and were excellent runners. Too much loose coursing around Point of Timbers made the objects of suspicion, but judicious handling later corrected any tendency to lurch. Coronoway, by Jones and Lady Amanda, was as fine a young dog as this State has ever seen. The get of Speculation from well selected bitches also show remarkable form when young. Monarch, Warwick, Chinchilla and many others are evidences of that fact. The get of all the Cartwright stock develop early, and then seem to die away until they are quite old. In fact, as a general rule, all greyhounds in this State show better form when young than those raised in England, perhaps owing to climatic influences. Seven months is rather too young to run a dog, especially in the heat of summer; but if the progeny of California Boy are equal to the task, there should be no lack of opponents able to give them a race and doubtless Judge Mee will soon be accommodated with a match.

## THE COCKER SPANIEL.

The full standard of points for a Cocker Spaniel, as defined by the Cocker Spaniel Club of America, is as follows:

A cocker spaniel must not weigh more than 28 pounds nor less than 18 pounds.

GENERAL APPEARANCE, SYMMETRY, etc. (value 10).—A cocker spaniel should be eminently a well built, graceful and active dog, and should show strength without heaviness or clumsiness. Any of the spaniel colors is allowable, but beauty of color and marking must be taken into consideration.

HEAD (value 15) should be of fair length, muzzle cut off square, tapering off gradually from the eye, but not snipy. Skull rising in a graceful curve from the top, and with the same outline at the occiput, the curve lines being flatter but still curving at the middle of the skull. The head should be narrowed at the eyes and broadest at the set-on of ears, and, viewed from the front, the outline between the ears should be a nearly perfect segment of a circle. The stop is marked and a groove runs up the skull, gradually becoming less apparent, till lost about half way to the occiput. This prevents the domed King Charles scull, and there should not be the heaviness of the large field spaniel, but a light, graceful, well-balanced head. Jaws level, neither undershot nor pig-jawed, teeth strong, regular and free from canker.

EYES (value 5) round and moderately full. They should correspond in color with the coat.

EARS (value 10) lobular, set on low, leather fine, and not extending beyond the nose, well clothed with long silky hair, which must be straight or wavy—no positive curls or ringlets.

NECK AND SHOULDERS (value 10). Neck should be sufficiently long to allow the nose to reach the ground easily; muscular, and running into well-shaped sloping shoulders.

BODY (value 15). Ribs should be well sprung; chest of fair width and depth; body well ribbed back, short in the coupling, flank free from any tucked up appearance, loin strong.

LENGTH (value 5). From tip of nose to root of tail, should be about twice the hight at shoulder, rather more than less.

LEGS AND FEET (value 15). The fore legs should be short, strong in bone and muscle; straight, neither bent in nor out at the elbow; pasterns straight, short and strong; elbows well in down; the hind legs should be strong, with well-bent stifles; hocks straight, looked at from behind, and near the ground. Feet should be of good size, round, turning neither in or out, toes not too spreading; the soles should be furnished with hard, horny pads, and there should be plenty of hair between the toes.

COAT (value 10) should be abundant, soft and silky, straight or wavy, but without curl; chest, legs and tail well feathered. There should be no top-knot or curly hair on top of head.

TAIL (value 5) usually docked, carried nearly level with the back. At work it is carried lower, with a quick nervous action which is characteristic of the breed.

SCALE OF POINTS.—General appearance, 10; head, 15; eyes, 5; ears, 10; neck and shoulders, 10; body, 15; length, 5; legs and feet, 15; coat, 10; tail, 5. Total, 100.

## SAN FRANCISCO DOG SHOW.

During the past two weeks several members of the old Kennel Club have been canvassing the possibility of arranging for a bench show, to take place in this city on or about September 5th. The BREEDER AND SPORTSMAN would welcome such an exhibition in as hearty a manner as it knows, and beg to extend every assurance of aid and comfort to the projectors. It is generally understood that a well known coursing man who was connected with the last bench show held in this city will be at the head of affairs inside the hall. His name will be such a guarantee of care and skill in the charge of the animals exhibited as would induce the most timid to send their pets to the show. Last year the Kennel Club, under whose auspices the show was held, selected all the judges for the various classes, and the plan was found to work far better than the plan once adopted here of allowing the exhibitors in each class to select their own judges. Experience unfortunately teaches that when exhibitors elect judges, it often happens that the strain that has the most friends gets all the prizes, simply because a majority select a man who is known to have a preference for such a strain. Prizes have been given to shortcoins such as double-nosed setters, because an elected judge imagined that this deformity was the apex of canine grace. The Kennel Club is still in existence, though not very active, and would doubtless be pleased to take the judging in hand.

AMERICAN FIELD DERBY.—The American Field Derby, open to all setters and pointers from and after March, 1881, closed with 44 entries, of which 40 are setters and 4 are pointers.

## DEER HUNTING.

HIGHLAND SPRINGS CAMP.

EDITOR BREEDER AND SPORTSMAN: Since my last letter to you we have had several enjoyable as well as unsuccessful deer hunts. The hounds are now well seasoned, and ours to make no false starts. The weather, however, has been extremely warm, and much to our disadvantage, the thermometer marking ninety-five degrees in the shade, and when placed in the sun the instrument was not long enough to indicate the heat. Early dawn or one hour before sunset is about the only time that a good run can be had. Water is not very plentiful in the mountains, and only occasionally to be found. There is water in the gulches, but it is very difficult to reach. The bucks, at this season of the year, owing to their horns being in the velvet, are well up on the tops of the high ridges, and away from timber or underbrush. They will soon seek the thickets, and commence rubbing their horns to clear them of the velvet. When this takes place they are hard to drive from the brush, and it requires extra work to get a sight or shot at them. A very amusing occurrence, as well as a remarkable one, happened in one of our chases the other day, which afforded a variety of scenes. We all started out at daylight on horseback, with the hounds, for a hunt, and when about three miles from camp and well on the summit, a deer was started, and, it being quite early and cool, the hounds ran very steadily and rapidly. The deer was cunning enough to keep well out of our reach, and could be seen only at a distance, and then only at such times as he was crossing

the point of some high ridge. We were well divided, and had stationed ourselves at several different prominent points, but for no purpose, as the deer kept well out of bounds. The hounds ran steadily and sure, and the deer had no time to rest. The hounds' notes gradually grew fainter and fainter, and finally were entirely out of hearing. We patiently waited in our positions, and then gathered in a group in the shadow of a high, projecting cliff. We regaled ourselves with a sociable smoke, and discussed the prospects of our day's hunt. One hour and a half was spent quietly and patiently waiting for the return of the hounds, but not a sound could be heard; all was quiet, with the exception of the morning song of the birds and the trowing of the mountain quail perched on a rock and keeping guard over his mate that was quietly feeding with their young. Our situation was most certainly not without pleasure, as the scenery was grand in the extreme. Clear Lake, with its smooth, clear, reflecting waters, lay beneath us; the rising sun gliding the purple peaks of the mountains; the several valleys indicating their culture and vines in miniature beauty; the morning's fragrant air, pure and exhilarating; every care left behind us; saddle-bags well filled with fried ve-ison and biscuits divided with layers of sweet butter; our pocket flasks yet untouched, full of glowing delight; the horses quietly feeding from the sweet, tender grasses that grew around the rocks and fern. With all this we were happy, but not contented, our anticipations in doubt, knowing by sad experience that the hounds were running the deer in the direction of our camp, and should they become tired they would not again climb the steep mountains, and at the distance of several miles to again reach us. Hours had passed and no signs of the hounds returning. It was dollars to cents that they had gone to camp, and that the day's hunt had ended. It had by this time grown so warm that we had concluded to abandon the day's hunt and return to camp. We could easily see our camp in the distance, but it was far beneath us; but to the old trail it would be a long, tedious ride in the hot, burning sun; so we located a more direct and apparently pleasant course. We started on our new projected journey, but before we reached the camp we concluded that the longest way around was generally the nearest way home. Our camp was finally reached, but we were not specially pleased or in love with the new route. On our arrival we were greeted with much excitement by the colored cook. He had much to tell us, all of which was corroborated by our legal friend whom we had left in camp and who intended, that morning, to have taken the stage on his homeward mission. The facts were, summed up, that the hounds had run the young buck into camp, creating great excitement. The cook armed himself with a huge carving knife, our legal friend with a broom, and then a fierce attack was made; the buck had run so far that he was completely fagged out; the hounds were close up, but so tired that their services were of little account. The excitement was now intense and more than the members in camp expected to realize. Such dodging, striking, running, tumbling, rolling, yelling, never was heard before in a mountain camp. The buck seemed to gain new life over the change of scene and the noise, for, rallying, he made a break for the brush and creek, which he crossed, closely pursued by lawyer, cook and hounds, the broom and carving knife flourishing above their heads. The chase was desperate and for dear life and blood, the scent universal; up the grade they went, giving tongue at every jump. The buck now gaining, darted for the brush, and was out of sight; the lawyer quits—all broke up and surrendered the case to the cook, who had now lost sight of the deer, but continued the chase with ardor. The hounds coming up took the scent of the cook, and fresh music filled the air. The cook rallied, but no use; the up grade was telling on him, and the hounds close at his heels. Realizing their mistake and his situation he breaks down the hill, yelling, "no hire, no hire;" but no use, they were closing on him. The situation was growing still more serious, and his only salvation was to climb. Fortunately a tree was near at hand, and at one bound he was securely hanging in the branches of a scrub oak. The hounds' mistake was soon discovered; for the cook's familiar voice pacified them, and by their actions regaled him to come down. This he was well pleased to do, though he swore a huge and heartfelt oath. He will never give chase to any more deer. The hounds being much demoralized gave up the chase, and walked quietly with the cook to the camp.
　　　　　　　　　　　　　WHETSTONE.

# THE HERD.

A REMARKABLE HEIFER.—Wm. Corbitt, Esq., is the owner of an Ayrshire heifer, 13 months old on the 23d of this month, who is the mother of a fine healthy calf, now three weeks old. Can any of your breeders give us an example of earlier maturity?

## JERSEY, GUERNSEY AND ALDERNEY.

The Channel Islands, from which originally came and still come the Jersey and other cattle known by their respective names, are but little known to the farmers of this country; hence a brief description of them, their people and products may not be uninteresting to our readers. Of the different routes from England to all the Channel Islands, the popular one is via Southampton, from which port no fewer than 12,881 passengers traveled to Jersey in the summer months of 1881.

Jersey is the most important island of the group, and it is the farthest from England, being 132 miles distant from Southampton. Agriculture is the chief pursuit followed by the inhabitants, and a good portion of the grain, as a staple of commerce, devoted to a description of the best little farm houses which are so numerous in the country, and to the modes of life of the people. The land is generally speaking, of good quality; it does not seem to require liming, but it is regularly manured; and the crops enjoy a comparative immunity from insect pests. The farmers are, however, something more than mere agriculturists; they are also market gardeners, florists, and dairymen, and by their frugality and industry—which is a marked characteristic of this Norman race—they can on a small patch of ground live comfortably and save money. In the Island of Jersey, there are 2,600 farmers. Out of 28,717 acres, there are 19,436 und-r crops of various kinds; 4,302 acres being pasture, 2,714 wheat, and 1,546 being turnips. Cattle are not reared for fattening, and sheep being also few, the inhabitants are chiefly dependent on France and Spain for their supply of beef and mutton. Potatoes are the farmers' most important crop, and early varieties is a good spring are field in some cases to realize no less than £50 a ton, while £15 is a common figure. But it is to the breed of the former generally looks on his select source of income, the harvest being most prolific, and the fruit of the best quality. It rests in the Channel Islands are poor cow-Herewere," being almost entirely cast of animals from France and England. The good milking qualities of the Jersey cows, and the richness of their butter, are well-known, but of late years the distinctive points of the breed have been greatly improved, an agricultural society having been formed with this object. Previously severe penalties were imposed for the importation of foreign animals for breeding purposes, and great care was exercised, by branding on the horn and the granting of certificates by magistrates, to guarantee the purity of the breed, but the Jersey Herd Book is now intended to give every security necessary in this respect. The cows are petted and hand-fed, and when the pasturage in the orchard gets bare, the animals receive extra feeding, in the shape of mangolds and cabbages, under which treatment they yield a bountiful return, from 10 to 12 pounds of butter in the week being not unusual, and this is sold at from 1s 4d to 1s 8d per pound. The quantity of milk from each cow ranges from 5 to 7 gallons a day, but it would appear that the adulteration of milk and butter is not altogether unknown there. From the stalks of the tall Jersey cabbages which are grown in every cottage garden, and which will shoot up to a great height, handsome walking sticks are made and sold at good prices, while the leaves serve as valuable feeding for pigs and cows. Something similar to a peasant proprietary is established in Jersey, the land being either in the actual possession of the occupier, or there is a security of tenure which prevents expulsion or raising of rents.

In Guernsey, the land, although very rich, is not so much so as in Jersey, but the system of husbandry pursued is the same, potatoes being the mainstay of the farmer; fruit, however, being also an important crop. Rents for the land are as high there as in Jersey, but there is a greater proportion of second rate land. £8 to £12 per acre is paid for good land, but most of the farms are occupied by the owners, and when a sale takes place, from £100 to £200 an acre is obtained for the land, and in the town of St. Peters Port it brings from £150 to even £400 an acre. In Alderney a much larger breadth of land lies in permanent pasture than in either Jersey or Guersey, and potatoes are extensively grown.

## THE MARKET PROSPECTS FOR CATTLE.

The present high price of beef in the East, and on the Pacific Coast promises a profitable year to the cattle raiser. The price of beef has been gradually increasing for the last two years, until at last it has became the cause of alarm in the East. This has been brought about partially by bad seasons, the high price of corn and other fattening products, and principally by the large shipments of cattle to Europe, which were bound to have their effect on the country at large.

The cattle exported to foreign countries were prime, large beeves, so for every ten head sent away we may reasonably state that it will take from fourteen to fifteen of our ordinary ones to replace them. Thus it will be seen that although we may have only sent a half a million the effect on this country is equal to at least seven hundred thousand. This extra deficiency, most likely, was not counted upon during the last feeding season in the Western States, for we find during last Winter Eastern men coming to Winnemucca and Reno, Nevada, after beef cattle for Denver and other Eastern cities—in fact only a week or so ago parties were negotiating with Oakland butchers for a large drove of beef cattle on the San Joaquin, to be delivered in Chicago at we may say a fancy price. But the liability of loss from the extreme hot weather on the line of the railroad prevented the consummation of the sale. Our butchers on thiscoast will undoubtedly have all they can do to keep up a supply for the local consumption during the coming Fall and Winter. Thus far the season has been a very late one and a large number of cattle have been killed that were only half fat, and the coast counties have been called upon to such an extent that in many of them they will not have retained enough for local demands. We have then only the San Joaquin and Nevada to look to. On the San Joaquin the cattle are mostly all held by Miller & Lux, and other large dealers, who have no necessity to crowd the market, knowing that before the year is out the surplus will be entirely consumed by the coast and neighboring towns, at even or better prices than can be obtained in this city.

In Nevada the past Winter was a disastrous one to the cows and young stock, many ranches losing fully fifty per cent., and some as high as seventy per cent. The present high price of cattle in Oregon, as parties who went there to buy on speculation and returned empty handed will testify to, will prevent the importation of the usual number. This, coupled with the chance thatthis Winter, as last, they may be called upon to send a few to the East, will most likely keep the price firm in the sage brush State.

We intend to devote a part of each number of this paper to the cattle and stock raisers' interests, and shall furnish reports not only of the weekly slaughterhouse prices but of all large sales of which we can receive information. It will be to their advantage and we will be obliged to all stock raisers in California, Oregon or Nevada, to send us a reliable report of any large sale made in their neighborhood.

In our next issue we will present a view of the "sheep and hog" market. We here give the present market prices from the wholesalers to the retailers:

Beef—Firm at quotations. Steers, extra prime, 8½c; prime, 8c; fair, 6½@7½c. Cows, prime, 7@7½c; fair, 6@7c.

Veal—Choice, small, 8@9c; large, 6½@7½c.

Mutton—Weathers, choice, 5c; fair, 4½c. Ewes, 4@4½c. Lamb—6½@7c.

Pork—Scarce and firm. Hogs, dressed, prime hard, 10¾@11c; do. do. soft, 9¾@10¼c; live, prime hard, 7¾@8¼c; do. do. soft, 7@7¼c.

## VARIETIES OF POULTRY.

Brighton, Sacramento Co.,
July 17th, 1882.

Editor Breeder and Sportsman: I am pleased to see that among the other questions to be dealt with in your columns the raising and proper handling of poultry is not to be neglected. For my part I think that the barnyard is one of the most profitable accessories of a farm, when conducted in a liberal and intelligent manner, and I receive many letters in regard to the subject, the majority asking my opinion as to the best variety of chickens to keep. My experience prompts me to answer that for egg-producing, for size and for quality, the white Leghorn is to be preferred. I have made lengthy and expensive trials both with the white and brown Leghorn, as also with the silver-spangled Hamburgs, and I find the latter very good layers, with the disadvantage that the eggs are rather small. For the table, my choice is the Plymouth Rock, and as they run very high in weight, some of them going to eleven pounds, the hens about two pounds less, I am going to give this variety a fair trial, and have imported from Charles Matthewson, of Rhode Island, some of his finest stock, and in time I will inform you of the result.

In regard to feeding, it depends largely on the climate, and as you are well aware this is very varied and changeable throughout the Pacific coast. For the warm temperature of the interior I recommend bran and sour milk noon and night, with wheat in the morning. For winter feed, scraps of meat and wheat are excellent, and a mess of scalded bran will keep the poultry in fine condition. A little corn is good for laying hens, but not too much, even in winter. A careful examination of the stock now and then will aid greatly in these experiments, but when judiciously handled, I am convinced that nothing on a farm pays better than a hundred thoroughbred Leghorns or Hamburgs. Some sound the praises of the pig in this respect, but my experience with the Berkshire and other strains proves that the poultry are the most profitable. Some get discouraged on account of sickness among the young growing chickens. In that case, first carefully examine the food, water and chicken house, seeing that everything is of a character to stimulate growth and health. That failing to make an improvement, there is some inherent fault in the breed, which may have been kept too far in the same family. Change your male birds, choosing the very best blood. Two five-dollar cockerels will pay a good percentage on the outlay, not only in the healthy condition of your fowls, but also as regards the egg-producing capacity. Some maintain that the white Leghorns are difficult to raise. So, indeed, is every variety, unless some means are taken to see that the mother is in a normal state of health. During the incubation, and while the young ones seek the warmth of the parent's breast, lice are the great enemies that have to be contended with. Go to your drug store and get twenty-five cents' worth of carbolic powder and sprinkle your hens and their nests with it freely, and be careful to keep your hen house in a cleanly condition. Then with the slight precaution necessary in wet or damp weather, you can raise every variety with but a trifling loss. A few words as to setting will bring my letter to a conclusion. From careful observation, I am convinced that the Spanish speckled and white and brown Leghorns of pure blood are non-setters, as I have never had a hen of either variety that would set on the nest over night. Therefore, to those who purpose starting in to keep a few fowls, I would recommend Leghorns and Plymouth Rocks, using the large birds of the latter variety for hatching purposes. The Plymouth Rocks are good winter layers, and with that good quality combine the still better one, as some think, of excellence for table use.

Thomas Waite.
Brighton Poultry Yard.

The Black Langshan.—Of this splendid variety there are but few to be found in the State, and indeed Mrs. Raynor, of this city, claims that she alone possesses the true Croad strains, imported by her from England at great expense, the other specimens exhibited here showing more or less a cross of the black Cochin. They are certainly of beautiful appearance, and Mrs. Raynor possesses a curiosity in an egg from one of these birds measuring seven inches by nine, and weighing originally six ounces, and within the outer shell is another egg of the ordinary pullet size. These Langshans, if exhibited at the fairs, will doubtless create a favorable impression.

## FISH.

W. W. Lapham has left for Truckee.

Hon. W. W. Traylor has returned from Weber Lake.

Messrs. Frank Whittier and party leave for McCloud river next week.

Anglers lately returned from McCloud river report trout-fishing exceedingly good there.

A lady caught a number of tom-cod in Hospital cove, Angel Island, last Sunday.

The black bass are being removed from Crystal Springs Lake to San Andreas, where good fishing is looked for.

This year the trout in Lake Tahoe appear to be ravenously hungry, and anyone can haul them in by the dozen.

A thirteen pound trout was caught near Tahoe, the other day; also another weighing eight and three-quarter pounds.

Black bass fishing at Temescal Lake is good, although the fish are small as yet. The Sportsman's Club control the fishing in this preserve.

Quite a number of persons from this city and Sacramento have gone up to Bowman's dam, on the Yuba river, sixteen miles from Emigrant Gap.

Tom-cod fishing is very lively along the Saucelito wharves in the shoaler water and on Richardson's bay. People are catching them there by the hundreds.

Fishing on north fork of the American river, near Alta, is reported good. The stream is rather high for this time of year, but in August it will be in fine shape for fishing.

Reports from the Sacramento river are that catfish are so numerous as to be a positive nuisance. With mouth agape they lay in wait for every hook that is dropped. No other fish has a chance.

Tom cods are plentiful all over the bay, but abound particularly in the neighborhood of Union-street bulkhead, Mission street new wharf and foot of Second street. They are also numerous at Saucelito.

The French Government is making experiments with the electric light as a means of luring fish into nets. The light is placed inside of a glass globe and sunk to the desired depth. The fish flock to that part of the sea thus brilliantly illuminated.

Washoe Lake is said to be now well filled with fish, native and planted. The catfish planted in the lake are said to have multiplied at a wonderful rate, and the California perch are also becoming plentiful. The natives are suckers and what is called white fish, both very small and rather soft.

Lake fishing within convenient distance of San Francisco is now exceedingly poor, where but a couple of years ago they afforded royal sport and recreation. Pillarcitos, San Andreas, Merced, Chabot's and Coleman's are now hardly worth visiting.

We see by the *Mountain Messenger* (Downieville, Sierra county) that Andy Steele brings into town a fine lot of river trout nearly every evening. The boys, too, during school vacation, are now trying their hand with the rod, but they have not stocked the market, as Andy finds ready sale so far for all he can catch.

Big Fish.—John Burns, who has been at work at the Four Hills, came to town this week, says the *Mountain Messenger*, bringing some of the largest trout we have seen in this section, one weighing 3¼ pounds, and 20¼ inches in length, caught out of upper Spencer Lake. He says there is but little snow at the Hills, and that is fast disappearing.

Miss Jean Parker, principal of one of the public schools, is to be credited with and complimented for having caught and landed without assistance, a *Dolly Varden* trout, weighing four and one-half pounds. The fish was caught in the McCloud river while the lady was enjoying her vacation a couple of weeks ago.

Bishop Bissell, here on a visit from the Eastern States, and a veteran fly fisher, has just returned from a trip to the McCloud river. He is enthusiastic in his praises of the *Red Banded trout* of those waters, considering them far superior to the *salmo iridea*, or *Dolly Varden*. The *Red Banded trout* is a gamey fish, and runs from one-half to four pounds in weight.

The big bed of hard clams recently discovered in Long Island Sound, off the mouth of Hempstead Harbor, N. Y., is apparently inexhaustible. More than one hundred vessels from Long Island, New Jersey, and Connecticut are constantly working the bed, making on an average $150 per day per boat. It is estimated that over 300,000 bushels of clams have already been taken from the bed.

Rock Cod.—A party residing on Alcatraz Island discovered on Wednesday last a fine fishing ground about two hundred yards from the island and in a line between the Alcatraz fog bell and Selby's lead works. The fishing was done between tides and in about one hundred and twenty feet of water. He caught a large number of rock cods, some of them running as high as three pounds in weight. At suitable tide good cod-fishing is found at Saucelito.

The steward of Dietz Camp, Lake County, has changed his vocation, much to the surprise of the campers, stealing an opportunity, when not manipulating venison chops and dove pies, to angle for the spotted thoroughbred. He returned to camp with forty good-sized terrapin. The campers and epicures have since smiled each day at seven P. M. over his success, as it was a welcome addition to their fare.

At Lake Ann, near Fort Bidwell, Henry Woodson has started a fishery. He commenced opperations three years ago with 2000 common brook trout. Now he has realized so handsomely from them that he has sold 30,600 and 12,000 spawn have been sent to Germany. The trout attained a weight of seven pounds in thirty-one months, which is remarkable rapid growing. He supplies the whole Bidwell country with fresh fish. The lake is forty-five acres in extent. He has also a small lake of six acres stocked with catfish Mr. Woodson has made it a profitable business, and every year adds to his wealth.

Through some unaccountable source the waters of Schuylkill have become impregnated with a poisonous substance that has played a tremendous havoc with the finny tribe in that stream. At first it was attributed to an overflow from land where Paris green had been used in large quantities, but now the general theory is that the water is heavily charged with sulphur from the mine water of the Schuylkill Company, and that this coming in contact with the limestone causes the strange color. The reason of so many fish dying is that a white substance lodges in the gills, which smothers them. What forms this substance has not as yet been fully demonstrated.

James McClatchy, of the Sacramento *Bee*, is of a happy disposition, and at the best of times is unmindful of the severe castigation he now and then receives from the hands of his contemporaries. In answer to a recent tirade addressed against his chief, the editor retorts that as Mr. McClatchy "is and has been for some time fishing beneath the shadow of Shasta and returning to camp every evening with a suspiciously large string of fish and a suspiciously small amount of pocket money, these little love-taps are wasted upon the vacant air. Buried in the bosom of Nature, he is blissfully unconscious of our esteemed contemporary's effort to canonize him."

The Reno *Journal* states that at Lake Ann, near Fort Bidwell, Henry Woodson has started a fishery. He commenced operations three years ago wirh 2,000 common brook trout. Now he has realized so handsomely from them that he has sold 30,600, and 12,000 spawn have been sent to Germany. The trout attained a weight of seven pounds in thirty-one months, which is remarkably rapid growing. He supplies the whole Bidwell country with fresh fish. The lake is forty-five acres in extent. He has also a small lake of six acres stocked with catfish. Mr. Woodson has made it a profitable business, and every year adds to his wealth.

At Gloucester, Maine, there is considerable excitement among the fishery owners and fishermen, caused by a threatened innovation in mackerel catching. Preparations are making to put a steamer into the business, the fish to be manufactured into oil and guano, and diverted from their use as food. There are now one hundred menhaden steamers, and if the experiment is successful they will engage in mackerel catching. The employment of these steamers has undoubtedly driven off the menhaden, and the same effect will be produced on the mackerel. There is a general feeling that stringent laws should be at once enacted for the protection of the mackerel fishery, which gives employment to thousands, and is an important food industry.

Billiard Tournament.—The first of a series of contests is announced to take place in the billiard rooms of the Union Hotel at Sacramento, commencing on the 20th, and W. O. Bowman expects to see a large number of entries, as there are a goodly array of amateurs in the capital city. The conditions are the old four ball American game for a purse of $100, one half to the first and the remainder to be divided between the next two.

## BICYCLING.

The joint exhibition of the Olympic Athletic Club and Pacific Wheelmen takes place at their new grounds, corner of Fourteenth and Centre streets, Oakland, Saturday, July 22d, commencing at 2:45 sharp. Not the least interesting of the events will be the bicycle races, of which there are three—a half-mile, one-mile and a two-mile race. The entries for these events embrace the best racing talent of both the San Francisco and Oakland clubs, including some new men, and if the finishes are as close as they were at the former meeting, it will be a treat which no one should miss seeing.

In order to pay expenses, the small charge of twenty-five cents will be made for gentlemen. Ladies free.

We append the racing rules as adopted by the League of American Wheelmen, May 30th, 1882:

### L. A. W. RACING RULES.

AS AMENDED AND ADOPTED AT THE ANNUAL MEETING HELD 30 MAY, 1882.

1. Entries and awards will be confined strictly to amateurs; and persons entering for these races, who are not members of bicycle or other athletic clubs whose rules of membership exclude professionals, must satisfy the judges that they are not professionals, either by their own statements in writing, or otherwise. Any wheelman competing in races other than those held under the auspices of the League, or of a League club in good standing, or of an organization whose games have not received the written sanction and endorsement of the League racing committee, will be disqualified from competition in future League races, unless this disqualification shall be subsequently removed by the board of officers of the League.

2. (a) An amateur is a person who has never competed in an open competition, (b) or for a stake, (c) or for public money, (d) or for gate money, (e) or under a false name, (f) or with a professional for a prize, (g) or with a professional where gate money is charged, (h) nor has ever personally taught or pursued bicycling or any other athletic exercise as a means of livelihood.—*L. A. W. Rule 25.*

3. Any competitor making a false entry will be disqualified.

4. Choice or change of machine, and choice of costume, are not limited.

5. Each competitor will receive from the judges, before the start, a card bearing a number, which must be worn during the race.

6. The position in each race will be drawn by the games committee and printed in the programme of entries.

7. All starts will be from a standstill, and the machines are to be held in position until the signal is given by the starters. Any contestant starting before the word is given shall be placed one yard behind the starting line, and an additional yard for each repeated false start.

8. Riders must pass on the outside (unless the man passed be dismounted), and must be at least a clear length of the bicycle in front before taking the inside; the inside man must allow room for his competitor to pass on the outside.

9. Any competitor guilty of foul riding will be disqualified.

10. Any protest against a competitor respecting his qualification as an amateur must be lodged with the judges before the start is effected; and any protest respecting foul riding or breach of rules must be made to the judges immediately after the heat is finished.

11. Competitors may dismount during a race at their pleasure, and may run with their bicycles if they wish to; but they must keep to the extreme outside of the path whenever dismounted.

12. The right is reserved to the judges of refusing or cancelling any entry, if necessary, before the start, of adjudicating any questionable entry, of deciding any other point not provided for, and of making any alteration in the programme that they may deem necessary.

13. The decision of the judges and referee will in all cases be final.

14. All championship races shall be held under the immediate supervision of the League or its constituent clubs. No trotting, athletic or other non-League organization shall be allowed to hold State or other bicycle championships in which League members shall compete.

15. Championship races shall be run in one heat, or should the number of starters be too large, in trial heats, and a final in which the winners and seconds in trials shall compete.

16. In handicap races the handicaps must be drawn up by a League member or committee of the same, and written reports of the handicaps and results must be sent to the racing committee L. A. W. for reference. No handicap races shall be run in heats.

17. No League member will be permitted to race under trotting rules; and no prize won or time made with a flying start will receive the sanction of the League.

18. The rules of the National Association of Amateur Athletes shall be sanctioned by the League, and no League member competing in the games of the Association or of its associate clubs, shall be debarred from competition in the League races or from enjoyment of any of its privileges.

19. The racing committee L. A. W. shall be empowered to appoint at its discretion a League handicapper, who shall, for a stated remuneration, frame the handicaps of the League and of such of its associate clubs as shall desire his services.

E. C. HODGES, Boston, Mass.,
A. A. HATHAWAY, Milwaukee, Wis.,
CLYMER WHITE, Baltimore Md.,
*Racing Committee L. A. W.*

WELL-MATCHED WHEELMEN.—A bicycle race for the twenty-five-mile champion belt took place June 17, at Leicester, Eng., the contestants being F. Wood and R. James, who in a previous race for the trophy, May 27 (John Keen, G. W. Waller and C. R. Garrard also competing), made a dead heat. It was expected that the race of the 17th ult. would have settled the question between them, but, to the surprise of the spectators, the result was another dead heat. The finish is thus described in *The Sporting Life:* "Just before entering the last lap, James made his effort with a well-timed spurt, which evidently took Wood by surprise, for in less than a twinkling the Birmingham man was soon six yards ahead (the greatest distance that ever separated them), and, holding this lead to the top of the hill, the race appeared a foregone conclusion for him. At about three hundred yards from home, however, Wood, spurting pluckily, began to gain inch by inch, and finally making the turn into the straight he was not more than three yards behind. Keeping up the spurt, he still gained, and ten yards from home their wheels overlapped, and by a desperate effort Wood just managed to draw up dead level on the post, amidst great excitement. Thus for the second time the two finished a dead heat, a thing unprecedented in the annals of long-distance racing. The friends of both were disappointed at the result, and each claimed the victory, but the judges' verdict was received without a murmur from the spectators, and gave general satisfaction. After the race it transpired that both of them were a little 'off' in condition, hence neither cared to force the pace from start to finish."

The difficulty of propelling tricycles up-hill, which formerly militated against their general adoption, is now fairly overcome. It was long ago seen that it would be most desirable for hill-climbing purposes to be able to substitute power for speed when ascending inclines, and several clumsy attempts to accomplish this were made; but the heavy, cumbersome differential gear applied was too complicated and too easily disarranged to meet with much favor among wheelmen, and moreover the great cost of the machines prevented their general adoption. Now, however, there are two or three ingenious arrangements by which a turn of the wrist will change speed for power, and *vice versa.* All the best tricycles are now fitted with the latest bicycle improvements, such as ball bearings to all wheels, etc.; and when I mention that I have seen a tricycle driven at the rate of fifteen miles per hour, it will be seen that the modern tricycle is no mean competitor of the bicycle, while its greater safety and baggage-carrying capabilities mark it out as the favorite travelling vehicle. Last year the Prince of Wales made tricycling very popular by purchasing a Salvo for his own use; and the Duke of Teck and other members of the royal family having copied his example, a regular rage for three-wheelers has set in. There are about sixty distinct makes now to be had, and the number is increasing daily. "Sociable" machines to carry two, three, four, and even more riders are to be had. The government has recognized the utility of the tricycle by supplying machines to many country mail-carriers; and in short, the three-wheeled machine bids fair to eclipse its two-wheeled rival in popularity. Nearly twenty-five per cent. of the riders are ladies.

It appears to be pretty difficult this season to win a twenty-five-mile professional champion bicycle race in England, each of the last two attempts we have heard of to date having resulted in a dead heat in 1h. 26m. 15s. and 1h. 29m. 34s., respectively.

One of the things to be remarked on the streets of London is the numerous bicycles. They are quite the fashion, not to say the rage, just now. One meets them everywhere. Many of them are elegant and costly. Their right to the street is recognized, as well and as much as that of any other vehicle. In the evening they carry a blue light. The manner of riding them has evidently been made a study, for the riders sit gracefully, and seem to drive them with great ease. There was an exhibition of bicycles and bicycle riding this week at Hampton Court, and a procession was formed numbering 2,350 bicycles with their riders. The procession was five miles long, two abreast. You can perhaps imagine the fine sight presented by such a procession, all the men experienced riders, all the bicycles of the most elegant kind, and all the riders in uniform. Then there was a great race, over a course of one hundred miles, the course being from London to Bath. Twenty-four men entered the race, and of these fourteen made the distance of one hundred miles in nine hours, and two made the distance in seven and one-half hours. Is has become with the young men a favorite mode of travel, and tours are being made by them to every part of England every week. What the donkey is in Egypt the bicycle is becoming to England.

The President of the Fairfield County Agricultural Society (Conn) wants to put a fast trotting horse against J. S. Prince, the American pro-champion bicyclist, twenty miles run, for a purse of $300 or $500. Prince has expressed his willingness to make the race.

### THE LARGEST BICYCLE MANUFACTORY.

The enquiry came from Sacramento: "Which is the largest manufactory of bicycles in America, and also the largest in England?"

Answer: The largest manufacturing establishment of bicycles in the United States is at the Weed Sewing Machine Co.'s Works, Hartford, Conn. It manufactures partly from *home* stock, but imports the most important parts from England. They claim to have facilities for turning out upwards of fifty per day if the demand requires it. These machines are made for the Pope Manufacturing Co. of Boston, and are called Columbias. There are a few other makers in a small way, but this is the only large factory.

There are upwards of 200 considerable makers in England, but the largest establishments are at Coventry, Birmingham, Nottingham, Leeds and London.

The oldest establishment is at Coventry, and probably the largest is the Excelsior Works of Bayliss & Thomas, who in addition to a large home and foreign demand are the manufacturers of the Harvard, made solely for the American market, and the most popular machine in the United States. This factory turns out upwards of fifty complete machines per day during the season, and filled one single order this year from the United States agents for 250 machines.

### THE CHAMPION TEAM.

There has long existed a great rivalry among our rich amateurs of trotters to possess the best double team in the country. Until the recent performance of Dick Swiveller and Edward, it was generally conceded that a steady 2:18 gait might be expected this season, and among the candidates for first honors were named W. H. Vanderbilt's Small Hopes and Lysander, that had already shown 2:20; T. C. Eastman's Glendale and Captain Jack, 2:24; W. J. Gordon's Clingstone and William H.; and I. Cohnfeld's Helene and mate. But it is probable that the performance of Frank Worth's team, 2:16¼, at the Gentlemen's Driving Park, New York, on July 14, will remain the top notch of the season. The contest was against time, and was of an impromptu character. Shepherd F. Knapp offered to wager Frank Work $1,000 that the team could not trot in 2:20. Mr. Work accepted the wager, and put John Murphy behind the team, in a road wagon. The judges were Messrs. Bush, Morgan and Alley, and over one hundred gentlemen prepared to time the trot. The horses were in tiptop condition, and everything was favorable for fast time, but few were willing to bet that the teams would trot in 2:20. When everything was in readiness Murphy let them out, and they whizzed by the wire at a rattling pace. Murphy carried 153¾ pounds, which was overweight. The first quarter was made in 33¼; the half in 1:05; the three-quarters in 1:40; and the full mile in 2:16¼—by long odds the fastest in the world by a team. Great excitement prevailed among the spectators, many of them insisting that the team did better than 2:16¼. Dick Swiveller is by Walkall Chief, from Madam Swiveller by Sayre's Harry Clay, with a record of 2:18, and Edward is by Fisk's Hambletonian Starr, dam by Magna Charta, and his best time 2:19. On the very day that this trot was made, Mr. Cohnfeld, in order to promote gentlemanly sport between road teams, challenged with Helene and mate to trot any team in the country for $1,000 a side, the match to take place at the track of the Gentlemen's Driving Park, and this may perhaps lead to an exciting contest for the championship of the double teams.

### ANSWERS TO CORRESPONDENTS.

SAN FRANCISCO, July 18th, 1882.

EDITOR BREEDER AND SPORTSMAN: Is it possible to have one card in hand which will count three with the starter, according to cribbage count? If so, explain. ANSWER—Jack in hand; starter, five of the same suit.

SAN FRANCISCO, July, 1882.

EDITOR BREEDER AND SPORTSMAN: During a game of crib a dispute arose between the players regarding the number of points contained in a hand consisting of three trays and two nines. The result was a wager, with an agreement to abide by the decision of your paper. Respectfully, B. B. ANSWER—Twenty.

DOVE SHOOTING.—There is an enquiry from an Eastern Sportsman where to find a day's dove shooting, the main consideration being within such a distance of San Francisco as will not compel staying away over night. Fair shooting can be had in the neighborhood of Mountain View, and from San Mateo South, and West of the railway there may be a chance for some sport.

## THE STAGE.

Very pleasing and attractive were the entertainments offered at the Baldwin and the California theatres last week, and their bright and mirthful incidents artistically portrayed leave but little regret for the drama that has now almost definitely fizzled out at the pretty Market street theatre. One might as well try to analyze an *omelette souffle* in a scientific manner as to render a strict description of the ever-varying scenes and startling changes that are to be seen in *Le Voyage en Suisse.* It is really a pantomime of the olden time cleverly adapted to these latter days. There is the same story of the thwarted loves of Harlequin and Columbine, owing to the persecutions of aged Pantaloon, but by the aid of the Clown and his friend the Sprite, the lovers, in the end, are united and nothing is wanting but the transformation scene of the Realms of Bliss, a sort of glorious United State to which our youths and maidens so ardently aspire. The Hanlons are not only excellent acrobats, but possess mimic powers that are very telling in such a piece as this, and through their agility, nerve and humor, aided by many good artists in their specialties and by a series of mechanical *mises-en-scene,* they give an entertainment that has already taken a firm hold in the minds of theatre-goers. And yet it must be owned that in the old pantomime there was always some relief from the rattling sensational scenes in which both Clown and Pantaloon were bothered out of their wits by the power of Harlequin's magic wand, there was a little *pas de deux* between Harlequin and Columbine, and the scene-shifters and stage-carpenters were hurrying like a pack of demons to prepare the next tableau. Now, this relief to a pleased and excited brain is wanting in the *Voyage en Suisse.* It is all bustle, movement and surprise, and it would be a good thing for the Hanlons to take a lesson from "The Purveyor of Sausages to H. M., the Queen of England," who was called as an expert in a case recently decided in England, where he testified that in the best sausages the meat had to be mixed with bread crumbs, or otherwise they were too rich for the table. This "*Sausage en Suisse*" is too meaty for the average digestion.

The Mastadon Minstrels continue their successful career, varying and adding to their programme every week. The principal artists get almost all the praise, but the songs are wonderfully well backed up in their execution by the many agreeable voices that have not as yet been deemed of sufficient timbre and compass to promote to solo importance. The groupings, too, are very well done and show the hand of a skillful stage manager, but the sketches could be improved upon by the outlay of a small sum of money among the writers who devote themselves to this eccentric style, and it would be but a drop in the bucket of these mastedonic expenses.

The gardens continue to draw immense crowds, and such is the growing interest taken in these well conducted establishments that it must lead to a great competition for this valuable patronage, and we shall not be surprised to see within a short time the Grand Opera changed into halls of dazzling light where light opera and ballet will be produced on a scale as yet unequaled on the Pacific Coast.

Henry Labouchere, of *Truth,* almost always likes to side with the minority, and as the London critics are very unanimous in their condemnation of the new drama, "The Romany Rye," he alludes in his notice to "certain doubtless very earnest gentlemen, who are beating their breasts and tearing their hair because Mr. Sims' play is not what it never professed to be. When these critical gentlemen talk of intellect, and taste and art, and ennobling influences, the higher purpose of the drama, and so on," says Henry, "let them remember what honest John Ryder said the other day about blank verse—the public do not want it." In the meantime the drama continues to draw large and enthusiastic audiences.

On Monday last there was a tempest in a teapot among the theatrical critics, owing to the fact that the strictest orders were issued that no one should be admitted to the Baldwin unless furnished with a ticket. These orders of admission, according to the idea of Colonel Brown, had been sent in sufficient quantities to the different leading journals, and the critics, as usual, had distributed them without regard to self. Their surprise was great, therefore, and on a par somewhat with the pantomime that was going on inside, when they found the portals closed against them, and themselves, in a figurative point of view, all agog on the sidewalk. The remarks on the play in the journals on the succeeding morning were of the tersest description, and as the doyen of our critics mentions, "the prospect is for a *bon voyage,* but much depends on the man at the helm."

Londoners are still indebted to foreign players for the only dramatic productions calling for comment. Adeline Ristori at Drury Lane and Celine Chaumont at the Gaiety, are struggling against the cheerless climatic influences and delighting large audiences in "Macbeth" and "Divorcons" respectively, Ristori being in addition burdened with a strange language. Her impersonation of Lady Macbeth has created a deep impression, notwithstanding the feebleness of the support. Mr. Rignold's career as Macbeth has been brought to a sudden end by Mr. Barnes as Macduff, who accidentally gave the Thane of Fife half an inch of cold steel full in the chest.

The author of the play entitled "The Two Brothers," recently produced at Chicago with James O'Neill in the principal character, has sued Mr. Gardiner for damages, inasmuch as that gentleman, as the manager of the company, allowed the drama to be put on the stage in an inefficient manner. This is quite a novel point, and if the plea holds good, it will not conduce to the production of new plays, it being already a peculiar task to get a manager even to unroll a manuscript.

Octave Feuillet is to read, August 15th, to the company of the Gymnase, Paris, his new play, "Un Roman Parisien," with which the season at that theatre is to be re-opened the latter part of that month. This author is well known in this country, by his delightful drama, "The Romance of a Poor Young Man," and if this is as good a play, it will prove to be a relief to the trashy melodramas with which we are seemingly to be plagued and pestered during the next season.

## THE RIFLE.

### ANCIENT AND MODERN ARMS.

#### BY DR. E. E. PARDEE.

[*Continued From No.3.*]

The Match Lock was a unique and ingenious piece of mechanism in its day, but time, the great leveler of all things, made it give way to a little better, and more easily manipulated mode of firing. The match lock made it necessary to carry one of different kinds of materials for igniting the powder. The one most universally used was several yards of slow match, wound round the body and the piece, and in a rainy day, it could not be used, and the prime being exposed the wind would blow it away, so that the match lock found its admirers for but a short time, when it was superseded by the ingeniously combined wheel lock. This curious piece of mechanism generated the sparks, and simultaneously uncovered the priming fuse, so that the danger of rain and wind was averted. But before, firing the apparatus required to be wound up like a clock, therefore the discharges could not be frequent. It possessed, however, the superiority over all other locks in its day, and was used for a long period of time in Germany and France. In the course of time Spain turned out a more simple and easily manipulated lock called the Snaphaunce or Asnaphan lock, which acting by means of a spring outside of the lock-plate, produced fire through the concussion of a flint against the ribbue top of the powder pan. It did not meet the expectations of the people, and about the middle of the seventeenth century the flint-lock was invented, combining in a great measure the action of the match and wheel-lock and snaphaunce, making it greatly superior to either of the above-named locks. After much fuss and feathers, it became universally used in the armies of Western Europe in the early part of the eighteenth century. With successive improvements, the flint-lock continued in general use until the introduction of the percussion, which was about sixty years ago, and among Eastern and barbaric nations, the flint-lock is still in demand. Its great superiority over the snaphaunce consisted in the "tumbler" and "scear" appliances still retained in the best percussion locks, which enabled the positions of half and full cock to be taken up without the intervention of pins, always uncertain in their actions. The principle of the percussion lock is familiar to the present generation, and does not need any particular explanation. It is simply the production of fire by the falling of the hammer upon the detonating powder, the explosion of which is conducted through the "cone" or "nipple" to the powder in the breech of the gun.

To keep the works of the lock in position a metallic shield, called the "bridle," is fastened over them and held securely by screws. The percussion lock was adopted in the British army about the year 1840, and it now used on large ordnance as well as small arms, by all the civilized nations of the earth. The usual formula for the percussion cap is thus given: Fulminating mercury $HgO$, $O_2O_2$.

However the original fulminating powder, patented by the Rev. Mr. Forsyth in 1807, consisted only of chlorate of potash, sulphur and charcoal. In the manufacture of the percussion cap a drop of mucilage is dropped in the bottom of the cap, when the fulminate is dropped in upon it, and then a coating of varnish is applied, to prevent dilequessence, in moist and rainy weather. In order to show the great demand for the percussion cap, it was represented by an exhibition at the London fair in 1851—thirty years ago—1,300,000,000 were manufactured yearly in that city, and that, too, for sporting purposes, which necessarily involved an annual consumption of copper of 396,000 pounds; and that, too, at a time when nothing, as a rule, but muzzle-loading guns were in use. One can hardly estimate the number of pounds of powder that was burned annually by the consumption of almost a billion and a half of caps that were manufactured in only one city of Europe. And were I disposed to make an estimate of the number of caps made by the civilized world from the number of the population of London, I would almost come to the conclusion that the whole population of the world were sportsmen, and the greater part of their time occupied in the use of the firearm, in order to consume the number of caps manufactured. But I will leave the reader to use his own power of imagination, or to make his own mathematical calculations and deductions, which must prove both interesting and instructive.

One-half of the present generation will remember the many landstions and encomiums that were given to Mr. Coit for his revolving cylinder, repeating pistol and rifle. Thirty years ago it was considered the perfection of a weapon, and all Americans rejoiced at the result of Mr. Coit's unparalleled success, and justly claimed that Mr. Coit had made an advance that placed America in the van of all other nations in the mechanical ingenuity displayed in the perfection of his masterly weapon.

While the theory of a revolving cylinder applied to a gun barrel dated back in the mist and cobwebs of two hundred years, it remained for Mr. Coit to simplify and bring into practical use that which others failed to do. Anyone going to Europe who is interested in the science and mechanical skill displayed upon this interesting subject, will be most highly interested by making a visit to the "Musée d'Artillerie" of Paris, and there satisfy himself of the many meritorious works of art, kept in a high state of preservation by the French Government. Here, if he is a lover of the gun, he will find employment for his active mind for days, in gazing and admiring the display of inventive genius of men of a former generation. Here he will find revolving pistols, revolving rifles, swords and revolving pistols combined in one, and many of them bearing the inscription of the maker's name and date of 1632 and 1700. Therefore, the revolving pistol and rifle did not originate with the present generation, notwithstanding many think and claim that it did.

In that Museum can be seen four, five and six chambers, though in all there is an absence or want of genius displayed, as there is no concentric movement of cylinder in the cocking of the lock. And under the undisputed titse of the flint-lock, I cannot see, for my life, how they could have utilized the percussion principle in conjunction with the flint-lock, for at every revolution of the cylinder the fine priming-powder of the chamber going downwards would necessarily be lost. But with the advent of the percussion cap, says the fertile

brain of Mr. Colt, this objection can be overcome. And by the application of a little lever or crank, as applied by Mr. Colt, the whole world took it up, and a national spirit of emulation began, ending in our present, and apparently perfect breech-loading firearms; proving the old proverb,

"Tall oaks from little acorns grow,
Large streams from little fountains flow."

But Mr. Colt had great difficulty in securing his letters of patent, so near was he upon the infringement of mechanical skill displayed by others who were dead and rotten in their graves. The whole right of patent being upon this simple point: Did Mr. Colt, for perfecting the revolution of his cylinder by a crank or lever during the cocking of the lock, or did he not? that was the rub. And after a long and tedious trial it was declared that he did; and letters of patent were issued. Hurrah for Colt! But for all that can be said, the invention of revolving cylinders originated with our progenitors, and to "render unto Cæsar things that belong to Cæsar" is but a righteous judgment.

[ *To be continued.* ]

---

**THE SCHUETZEN CLUB.**—This Club met at Schuetzen Park last Sunday for a match and prize shooting contest, the best centers in twenty shots, which resulted as follows: 1st, Freese; 2d, Hoz; 3d, Streeke; 4th, Haake; 5th, Werthsimer, 6th, Jacoby; 7th. Hatje; 8th, Rochel; 9th, Bertelson; 10th, Adams; 11th, Keeth; 12th, Rohlffs; 13th, Beckman; 14th, Eckman; 15th, Brener; 16th, Krahman; 17th, Fisher; 18th, Baerwald; 19th, Zecher; 20th, Stroeven; 21st, Rapp; 22d, Schulte; 23d, Thompson; 24th, Utschig; 35th, Bertrand; 26th, Peters. The first class medal contest resulted in the following order: 1st, Zecher, 407 rings; 2d, Hatje, 396 rings; 3d, Hoz, 319 rings. In the Turners' Sharpshooters contest Burmeister won the championship medal and first prize by making 348 rings; D. Schoenfeld, gained the first class medal and prize by a score of 310; Lorich second class medal and prize, 266; Hubert, second class medal of the second class and prize, 299; third class medal and prize, R. Finking, 305; Charles Sagehour, second medal, 262.

**THE INTERNATIONAL MATCH.**—A recent telegram received from London states that those officially connected with the arrangements of the rifle team for America are well satisfied with the average made in practice by the competitors for places in the team. They consider them larger than the Americans appear capable of. The team will be finally selected in a week. Competitors for places in the American team in the international rifle match will be required to average 152 points; not less than 55 at the 200, 500 and 600-range, nor less than 67 at the 800, 900 and 1,000-yard range, on three distinct occasions. The time for making these scores has been extended from August 1st to August 15th.

Al. Stillwell, of Oakland, the expert in handling single as well as double sheet posters, while on his maiden deer-hunting trip at Camp Dietz, Lake County, declares that he shot at and mortally wounded the largest deer that he ever saw, stating that it was as large as the horse that he rode. His mount, he swears, was a hard rider, and there must have been some truth in it, as he competed for the prize for nine clement when he arrived in camp. After dismounting, it was discovered that the hostler had carelessly placed an old Spanish spur in the seat of the saddle, and he had neglected to place it on his boot. To prove that he had hit the deer and drawn blood, he gathered a battul of blood stained leaves, but on examination they proved to be, much to his disappointment, the autumn leaves from the madrone tree.

---

## TRAP AND TRIGGER.

### COSMOPOLITAN CLUB MATCH.

The delightful weather of last Sunday was the strongest possible temptation to city folks to take a trip into the country, and as no more pleasant spot within easy reach can be found on this peninsula than San Bruno, it is little wonder that there was quite a large gathering there to witness the shoot of the Cosmopolitan Club for the championship medal. Many of the shooters and spectators went down by the South Pacific Railroad, which line, though commonly supposed to be a "bloated, soulless corporation," pays a good deal of attention to the comfort and convenience of the Sunday outing public, and charges so little for the round trip that it is positively most distressingly plebeian to patronize the road. Others went down by road—that is, if the public highway space between this city and San Bruno can be dignified by the name of a road, when, as an actual fact, it is only to be distinguished from the surrounding rough country by being a great deal rougher, and-having its naturally aggressive roughness made still more painfully apparent by the system of road mending adopted by the persons who have that matter in charge. In mending books, one often comes across an allusion to "breaking stones on the public roads," and a certain hazy idea floats in the minds of most people that stone-breaking is an essential part of road-making. On the road to San Bruno, this order of things is reversed. The stones are not broken, and like the ungrateful, flinty-hearted things that they are, they repay this kind treatment by breaking the heads of every person who drives over them, and at the same time breaking the wheels of his vehicle and the legs of his horses. The "Roady road to Dublin" and the cobble laid streets of San Francisco, are down-covered beds of roses, smooth as billiard tables, and soft as an undegradate's head in comparison to the broad highway-between Mission street and Dick Cunningham's cosy retreat at San Bruno. However, the sport-loving people who visited San Bruno, last Sunday, were not of the kind to grumble and feel sore, because the trip down had made soft cushions an absolute necessity for the following week, and, when the match commenced every one was in excellent spirits. The weather was warm, in fact to be accurate, it was a red-hot, blistering, tropical, one hundred and fifteen in the shade, sunstroke-giving kind of a day, until a bit of a sea breeze sprang up in the afternoon to cool off the spectators, and give the pigeons ambition and life enough to get up and leave the traps without pulling the trapper to the trouble of assisting their flight by heaving at them mammoth geological samples from the San Bruno road. Frank Maskey was the first to shoot, and he easily killed his bird as did also the other twelve gentlemen who competed in the

match. Twenty-one birds were killed without a miss, and the charm of success was first broken by a gentleman who shoots under the name of H. Nelson, and who only succeeded in knocking a couple of feathers out of a hard twisting "three-o'clock bird." Muller, who followed him, also made a miss. On fifth round, Maskey made his first miss, being the only one, except Tallant, Liddle and Graham, who had not missed before that time. Graham was the only one who made five straight kills in the first part of the match. Golcher kept on even terms with Maskey until the 12th round, when he succumbed to an easy five-o'clock bird. Maskey killed all the remainder of his birds, and won the match. The score was as follows:

| | | | | | | | | | | | | | | | |
|---|---|---|---|---|---|---|---|---|---|---|---|---|---|---|---|
| F. Maskey | 1 | 1 | 1 | 1 | 0 | 1 | 1 | 1 | 1 | 1 | 1—11 |
| A. Brownel | 1 | 1 | 0 | 0 | 1 | 1 | 1 | 1 | 1 | 0 | 0—8 |
| A. Higgins | 1 | 1 | 0 | 0 | 1 | 0 | 1 | 1 | 1 | 1 | 1—9 |
| W. Golcher | 1 | 1 | 1 | 0 | 1 | 1 | 1 | 0 | 1 | 1 | 1—10 |
| B. Tallant | 1 | 1 | 1 | 1 | 0 | 1 | 0 | 0 | 1 | 1 | 1—9 |
| B. Brown | 1 | 1 | 1 | 0 | 1 | 0 | 0 | 0 | 1 | 1 | 1—8 |
| F. Buckley | 1 | 1 | 1 | 0 | 0 | 0 | 1 | 1 | 0 | 1 | 1—8 |
| R. Liddle | 1 | 1 | 1 | 1 | 0 | 0 | 1 | 1 | 1 | 0 | 0—7 |
| B. Robinson | 1 | 0 | 0 | 1 | 1 | 0 | 1 | 0 | 0 | 1 | 1—7 |
| G. Muller | 1 | 0 | 1 | 0 | 0 | 0 | 1 | 0 | 1 | 1 | 1—5 |
| C. H. Graham | 1 | 1 | 1 | 1 | 1 | 0 | 1 | 0 | 1 | 1—10 |
| B. Rover | 1 | 1 | 1 | 1 | 0 | 1 | 0 | 1 | 1 | 1—9 |
| J. Ferguson | 1 | 0 | 0 | 1 | 1 | 0 | 1 | 1 | 1 | 1 | 1—8 |

The ties on ten were then shot off at three double birds, with the following result:

| | | | | | | |
|---|---|---|---|---|---|---|
| Golcher | 0 | 1 | 1 | 1 | 0 | 1— |
| Graham | 1 | 0 | 0 | 1 | 0 | 0— |
| Rover | 1 | 0 | 0 | 1 | 1—6 |

Maskey having won the medal three times running, is entitled to hold it perpetually. Rover won second money, and Golcher third money.

The next match was at six birds open to all comers, and for which there were 19 entries. Brovell, Nelson, R. Bass, ford and R. Liddle, killed all their birds and divided the money. J. Ferguson, R. Tallant, C. Robinson and F. Beasford tied on five each.

Then followed a match at three doubles, which was won by Frank Maskey, who made the only clean score. The score was as follows:

| | | | | | |
|---|---|---|---|---|---|
| W. Nelson | 0 | 0 | 1 | 0 | wn—1 |
| F. Maskey | 1 | 1 | 1 | 1 | 1—6 |
| A. Higgins | 1 | 1 | 1 | 1 | 0 | wn—1 |
| R. R. Blade | 0 | 0 | 1 | 0 | 0—2 |
| L. W. Hayne | 0 | 0 | | wn | —0 |
| F. Beasford | 1 | 0 | 1 | 0—2 |
| J. Stowell | 1 | 1 | 0 | 0 | 0—2 |
| H. Beasford | 1 | 0 | 1 | 0 | 1—3 |
| C. Robinson | 1 | 1 | 1 | 1—4 |
| J. Buckley | 1 | 1 | 1 | 1—4 |
| R. Liddle | 1 | 0 | 1 | 0—1 |
| L. Frank | 0 | 0 | 1 | 0—0 |
| P. J. Walsh | 1 | 0 | 1 | 1—0 |
| J. Quin | 1 | 0 | 0 | 1—2 |
| B. Rover | 1 | 1 | 1 | 1—6 |
| J. Kempson | 1 | 1 | 0 | 1—2 |
| J. Ferguson | 1 | 1 | 1 | 1—6 |
| D. Rover | 1 | 0 | 0 | 1—2 |
| C. H. Graham | 1 | 1 | 1 | 1—6 |

H. Rice acted as trapper to the satisfaction of all. The judges were Messrs. Conrad and Beasford.

**THE ALAMEDA COUNTY SPORTSMAN'S CLUB.**—The members of this organization met on Saturday last at Littlefield range to compete for the Club medals and blue sweepstakes. The sweepstakes resulted in a victory for Mr. Bassett, Mr. Spaulding taking the second prize. Both these gentlemen are excellent shots. The trap worked very well, and the clay pigeons gave general satisfaction, bothering many of the shooters by their swift and erratic flight. Following is the score, the conditions being ten birds at eighteen yards rise:

| | | | | | | | | | | |
|---|---|---|---|---|---|---|---|---|---|---|
| Fraser | 0 | 1 | 1 | 0 | 1 | 0 | 1 | 0 | 0—6 |
| Williams | 0 | 1 | 0 | 1 | 1 | 1 | 1 | 1 | 1—7 |
| Bennett | 1 | 1 | 1 | 1 | 1 | 1 | 1 | 1 | 1—10 |
| Claringe | 0 | 1 | 0 | 1 | 1 | 1 | 1 | 1 | 1—7 |
| Bell | 0 | 1 | 1 | 0 | 1 | 1 | 0 | 1 | 0—6 |
| Havens | 0 | 1 | 1 | 0 | 1 | 0 | 1 | 1 | 1—6 |
| Cahill | 0 | 1 | 1 | 1 | 1 | 0 | 1 | 0 | 1—7 |
| Perce | 0 | 1 | 1 | 1 | 1 | 0 | 1 | 1 | 1—8 |
| Taylor | 0 | 1 | 1 | 0 | 1 | 1 | 0 | 0 | 1—5 |
| Norton | 0 | 0 | 1 | 1 | 1 | 0 | 1 | 0 | 0—5 |
| Bassett | 1 | 0 | 1 | 1 | 0 | 1 | 1 | 1 | 1—7 |
| Bacheus | 1 | 1 | 0 | 1 | 1 | 1 | 0 | 1 | 1—7 |
| Spaulding | 1 | 1 | 1 | 1 | 1 | 1 | 1 | 0 | 1—8 |
| Mayhew | 1 | 0 | 1 | 0 | 1 | 0 | 1 | 0 | 0—4 |
| Jacobs | 0 | 1 | 0 | 0 | 0 | 1 | 0 | 0 | 0—2 |

TIE AT 15 YARDS.

| | | | | | |
|---|---|---|---|---|---|
| Bennett | 1 | 0 | 1 | 1—4 |
| Spaulding | 1 | 1 | 0 | 1—4 |

SECOND TIE AT 18 YARDS.

| | | | | | |
|---|---|---|---|---|---|
| Bennett | 1 | 1 | 0 | 1—3 |
| Spaulding | 1 | 0 | 0 | 1—2 |

The present surpasses all former seasons for dove shooting. Captain E. W. Travers surprised the camp, the other evening, after an afternoon's hunt, by bringing in four full-grown-doves. The appearance of each bird was positive proof that it had been badly shot. He was in ecstasies over his new hammerless, choke-bore gun, made to order by Claybrough & Co. He is much in love with the choke-bore gun, but thinks it a great nuisance to pack along a rest for such small game.

**NORWEGIAN GULLS' EGGS.**—A melancholy account comes from Tromsoe, in the north of Norway, to the *Gazette* of Drontheim. It is said that there has been a strange mortality among the gulls and sea-birds which habitually visit this part of the coast to build in the summer months, and that a sort of famine is thereby likely to be caused among the inhabitants. In order to understand this dispiriting message it is necessary to explain that on these coasts of Finmark and Nordland the sea-birds, and especially the highly prized eider duck, come and take up their annual abode in vast numbers on the rocks and cliffs, where they lay their eggs. The most notable "bird mountain" is the Spoetholthishen, in Finmark, but many other favorite spots are regarded with almost equal respect by the owners of them, who, so far from killing the goose with the golden egg, take extreme care to encourage the birds by saving them from destruction as they build and lay. Thus in the pairing time even the flocks of sheep and their attendant dogs are driven back from the coast to inland pastures, where they cannot alarm the feathered strangers. The ducks and gulls very quickly build their nests, and the eiders are careful to line theirs with the valuable feathers taken from their own bodies. Then the eggs are laid in such abundance that in some places it is difficult to walk about on the rocks without stepping on them. A grand collection is made at the proper time by fishermen, who carry away whole boat-loads and sell them to the Norwegians, by whom eggs are highly esteemed as articles of food. But this year the collectors have come back with very short supplies, and declare that there is an amazing diminution in the number of the nests. It is now supposed that large numbers of the birds were unable to contend against the violent and protracted storms of the past winter, and that they actually perished in their struggle with the adverse elements.

## MARKET REPORT.

FLOUR—The market is unsettled, and quotations are more or less nominal at $5 50@6 00½ for city extras, and $4 60@5 25 per bbl for the product of the inferior mills.

WHEAT—European advices are less favorable, and prices here show a downward tendency. The report of the San Francisco Produce Exchange shows that on July 1st we had on hand 2,353,902 ctls of old crop wheat, against 13,416,578 ctls for the corresponding time in 1881. Current quotations for spot lots of No. 1 range in the neighborhood of $1 75½; and for future deliveries of the same, $1 73½ is about the obtainable figure. For parties for immediate delivery the market is quiet, but few future months trade is made inquiry. The first full seller of the new crop is now on board of ship and will be despatched during the current week.

BARLEY—New crop brewing is little inquired for, but choice old is in active demand. Chevalier is inquired for at $1 40 for present and future months, but at such higher handsome and growers are not sellers. The first consignment of the season of the new crop of Chevalier came to hand during the past week, and was sold, at price withheld, for export to New York, per steamer. There continues to be a little speculative demand for feed, and on "call," $1 25 is freely offered for July delivery, and $1 22 is offered for August and September, and $1 30 for October and November. Trade in futures on the Produce Exchange call is active, and the future of the market is a question of serious importance to both buyers and sellers.

OATS—The speculative demand for lots for future delivery continues quite active, but the difference in sellers' and buyers' views is such that trade is restricted. Continued already made on call are of considerable magnitude and there seems to be a disposition on the part of sellers to hedge. No. 1 is in demand at $1 73½ for spot lots, and extra choice would, probably, command $1 90 per ctl. Consignments of the new crop have already been received, and further arrivals are expected within the current week.

CORN—There is a decided disinclination on the part of would-be buyers to become purchasers at present selling prices, and, as a consequence, the market is inactive. For choice large Yellow $1 70 is asked for spot lots, and $1 60 per ctl is bid for the same.

RYE—It is well known that the stock of old is unusually light, but information in reference to the new crop is meagre; as a consequence trade is light. For choice old rye is asked, while for the same grade, seller 1882, $1 65 per ctl is the top price bid.

BRAN—There is considerable speculative inquiry on call, but transactions are light. For spot lots $14 50@ $14 75 per ton is a fair quotable range.

FEED AND MILLSTUFFS—Shorts, $17@$18; Middlings, $22@$25; Ground Barley, $21 for new, $24 for milled, and $26 for old; Oil Cake Meal, $27 50; Cracked Corn, $29; Cornmeal, $29 per ton.

HAY—Receipts continue large, but an active demand causes steady prices. For all kinds the range is $10@$15 per ton.

STRAW—Recent receipts have been free and the market is weak at 70@75c per bale.

SEEDS—Mustard is scarce at 2@2½c for Yellow, and 4@4½c for Brown; Alfalfa, nominal; Canary, 2½c per lb. Supplies of the latter are light, and holders are firm for full figures.

BEANS—The market is quiet, and quotations more or less nominal. Pea and Small White, $4 25; Butter, $3 25@$3 50 for Small and larger; Bayos, $2@$2 25; Pink and Red, $2 50@$3 00; Limas, $4@$4 50 per ctl.

ONIONS—Receipts are free, and market dull sp week at 60@75c for Silverskins, and 35@40c per ctl for Reds.

POTATOES—The demand is active, but receipts are of sufficient magnitude to cause a weakening in prices. Quotable at 75@$1 15 per ctl, as to kind and condition.

HONEY—Comb is quotable at 15@17c, White Extracted sells for 8@9c per lb.

EGGS—Choice fresh ranch are in demand at 30@32½c per doz.

CHEESE—Though supplies are free, the market is steady at 12½@14c per lb for California manufacture.

BUTTER—The market is very firm and has an advancing tendency. Choice fresh ranch Roll is scarce and wanted at 30½c; While good sells for 30c; fair, 25@27c; Calif Eula firkin, 27½@30c per lb.

GAME—The market is poorly supplied with Venison, and quotations for the same range from 15@18c per lb; Hare, $1 75@$3 00; Rabbits, $2@$2 25; Doves, 50@75 per doz.

POULTRY—Turkeys are scarce at 18@21c per lb; Hens, $6 00@$8 00; Young Roosters, $7@$8 00; Old do, $6@$7 00; Broilers, $4@$5 00; Ducks, $4@$5 00 per doz; Young Geese, $1 50@$1 75; Old do, $1@$1 25 per pair.

HIDES—The market is steady. Dry, 16@20c; Sheep-skins, 50@300c for shearlings; $1@$2c for short Wool; 60c@$1 for medium and $1@$1 50 for long hair; Deerskins, 20@30c; Salted steers, 7@11c per lb.

TALLOW—There is a good demand for desirable parcels at 7½c per lb.

PROVISIONS—There is considerable excitement in the market and prices are on the ascending scale. California bacon, 16@17½c for smoked; Sides, 14@16c; California hams, 15@16½c; Eastern do, 17½@21½c; Calif formia lard, 14@16½c per lb, according to package; Clear pork Eiln Extra prime, $21 50@$27; Extra clear, $23@$25 50; Mess, $21@$22; Mess beef, $19@$19 50; Extra do, $21@$21 50 per bbl; Smoked beef, 14@18½c per lb.

HOPS—Spot quotations are largely nominal. For future delivery the bids are 15@17c for Oregon and Washington Territory, and 50@25c per lb for good to choice California.

WOOL—There is an improved inquiry, and the market is in a more acceptable condition for choice grade of Northern, Humboldt, Sonoma and Mendocino, which sell at 24@27c; San Joaquin, 11@20c; Coast, 18@29c; Oregon, 20@27c per lb. Recent receipts from Mendocino and Sonoma Counties have been of considerable importance.

FRUITS—The market is fully supplied with all seasonable kinds. Peaches, 50@75c per box; Apricots, 75c per box; Pears, 75c@$1; Nectarines, $1 75@$1 75 per box; Figs, 50@$1; Grapes, 75c@$1 25 per box; Cantaloupes, $3@$5 50; Watermelons, $7@$8 per doz; Currants, $3 50@ $4 per box.

---

4 50; Strawberries, 6@$12; Blackberries, 25@$4; Raspberries, $10@$11 per chst; Plums, 2@4c per lb. VEGETABLES—Malt, wild Squash, $1@$1 50 per ton; Summer Squash, 27½@65½ per bx; Peas, 2½@6c; String Beans, 2c per lb; Cucumbers, 50@60c; Tomatoes, 75c@ $1 50 per bx; Green Corn, 10@15c per doz; Rhubarb, 50@75c; Okra, 10@12½c; Egg Plant, 5@6c per lb; Green Peppers, 75c@$1 per lb.

MEAT—Beef, 8@9c; Mutton, 4@5c; Lamb, 6@6½c; Veal, 5½@6c; Dressed Pork, 8@11½c; Live do, 6@6½c per lb.

¶The Delta has received a copy of the Breeder and Sportsman, publish-d at 508 Montgomery street, S.F. It announces itself to be the best and sporting authority of the State. Joseph Cairn Simpson is the editor. The very name of this gentleman is sufficient to guarantee a paper pre-eminently devoted to the interests of that class of sporting men who take an interest in the discussion of sporting events. It is sixteen pages, and can be had for five dollars a year, in advance.—[The Nevada Slough Delta, July 14.

## CALIFORNIA'S EXPOSITION.

THE 29TH ANNUAL

# STATE FAIR

BEGINS AT—

### SACRAMENTO, CAL.,

ON THE 11th AND CLOSES ON THE 16th OF SEPTEMBER.

The Premium List embraces liberal awards for all kinds of Live Stock, Machinery, Implements, etc., Textile Fabrics, Mechanical, Agricultural and Horticultural Products, Fine Arts, etc.

Any further information may be had upon application to the Secretary, from whom Premium Lists may be procured.

HUGH M. LARUE, President.
EDWIN F. SMITH, Secretary.
P. O. Drawer J, Sacramento, Cal. July 15 t4

## SPORTING GOODS.

BOXING GLOVES, FOILS,
COMBAT SWORDS, MASKS,
INDIAN CLUBS,
HUNTING KNIVES,
Our Own Manufacture,
DOG COLLARS AND CHAINS,
Fine Assortment in the City.
WILL. & FINCK,
Leading Cutlers. 769 Market Street

## DAN. McCARTHY,

LIVERY, BOARDING AND SALE STABLE,

606 Howard St., near Second.

Largest stock of fast livery teams in the State. First class boarding. Horses bought and sold. Cash advanced on horses, buggies, sheds, harness or anything connected with the business.

## LANGSHANS.

I guarantee a pure Langshan, Grand Strain, from healthy Chicks, not related, for sale of this magnificent breed, for September delivery.

MRS. J. RAYNOR,
1416 Folsom St., S. F

## Specimen of Our Artist's Humor.

THE MUSIC LESSON.

# HUNDREDS OF DELIGHTED ONES

See, for the First Time in their Lives, the

## JAPANESE ARTIST AND EMBROIDERERS

AT WORK IN THEIR NATIVE COSTUMES, AT

# ICHI BAN, 22 and 24 Geary Street.

The Breeder and Sportsman is printed with Shattuck and Fletcher's Ink.

## Pacific Coast Blood Horse As'n.

### PROGRAMME.

FIXED EVENTS—SPRING & FALL MEETINGS

1883 and 1884.

### BALDWIN STAKE FOR 1882

#### SPRING MEETING.

FIRST DAY.

WINTERS STAKE—For three-year-olds, to be run the first day of the Spring Meeting; dash of one-and-a-half miles; $100 each, $75 forfeit, $300 added; second to have $100; third to save stake. Nominations in above to be made for 1883.

SAME DAY—CALIFORNIA STAKE—For two-year-olds, $30 each, $25 forfeit, $300 added; to be run on the first day of the Spring Meeting; second to save stake; dash of half a mile. Nominations in above to be made for 1883.

SECOND DAY.

PACIFIC CUP—Handicap of $100 each, $50 forfeit, $500 declaration, $600 added; second to receive $200; third to save stake; two and-a-quarter miles; to be run on the second day of the Spring Meeting. Will close the 1st of March.

THIRD DAY.

SPIRIT OF THE TIMES STAKE—Dash of one-and-three-quarter miles for all three-year-olds; $100 each, $75 forfeit, $300 added; $150 to second; third to save stake. Nominations to above to be made for 1884.

SAME DAY—GANO STAKE—Dash of three-quarters of a mile for two-year-olds; $60 each, $25 forfeit, $300 added; second horse to save stake. When any California two-year-old beats the time of Gano, 1.10 for three-quarters of a mile, the Stake to be named after the colt which beats it. Nominations to be made for 1883.

#### FALL MEETING.

FIRST DAY.

LADIES STAKE—For two-year-old fillies; $50 entrance, $25 forfeit, $250 added; three-quarters of a mile; second to save entrance. Nominations to be made for 1883.

SAME DAY—THE VESTAL STAKE—For three-year-old fillies; one-and-a-quarter miles; $25 p. p.; $300 added; second to receive $100; third to save stake. Nominations to be made for 1883.

SECOND DAY.

STALLION STAKE—Conditions—Only those three-year-olds are eligible which are the get of stallions owned in this State. The stallions have to subscribe the amount charged for their services to the fund; private stallions at the price of their last season, and those which have not made a public season, to pay $50, that sum being the minimum price. The owner of the get of a stallion is competent to name. The stake for the colts shall be $100 each, $25 forfeit, plate or money added as the discretion of the Committee; Entrance, 1⅛ miles. To close for 1883 on the 1st of August next, at which time both stallions and colts (progeny) must be named.

THIRD DAY.

THE BALDWIN STAKE—Post stake for all ages; dash of four miles; $250 each, p. p.; $1,000 added; second, $400; third to save stake. Will close on the 1st of August, 1883 for that year.

SAME DAY—FINDLAN STAKE—For two-year-olds; dash of a mile; $50 each, $25 forfeit; $250 added; second to save stake. Nominations to be made for 1883.

SAME DAY—RAILROAD STAKE—For three-year-olds; dash of two miles; $100 each, $25 forfeit; $300 added; second to save stake. Nominations to be made for 1883.

All of these Stakes close on the first day of August next, the colts ruling now as yearlings, foals of 1881. Nominations to be made to C. M. Chase, Assistant Secretary, P. O. box 1,961, S. F., P. C. B. H. A. To be valid they must be plainly postmarked on that day, 1st of August.

THEO. WINTERS, President.
C. M. CHASE, As't Sec'y.

---

### SPEED PROGRAMME

FOR THE

### First Annual Meeting

OF THE

SANTA CRUZ COUNTY

### Agricultural Fair Association,

**At SANTA CRUZ,**

Commencing - Tuesday, August 15th.

## $3,500 IN PURSES!

FIRST DAY—TUESDAY, AUG. 15, 1882.

No. 1—TROTTING RACE—Purse $350 for horses that have never beaten 2:23. Owned in the District.
No. 2—TROTTING RACE—Purse, $500. For horses that have never beaten 2:28.

SECOND DAY—WEDNESDAY, AUG. 16.

No. 3—RUNNING RACE—For two-year-olds; $50 entrance; $15 forfeit; $150 added. Second to save entrance. Dash of three-quarters of a mile.
No. 4—RUNNING STAKE—Free for all; $50 entrance; $15 forfeit; $150 added. Second to have entrance. Dash of a mile.
No. 5—TROTTING RACE—Purse $500. For double team owned in the District by one man.

THIRD DAY—THURSDAY, AUG. 17.

No. 6—TROTTING RACE—Purse $300. For horses that have never beaten 2:40.
No. 7—TROTTING RACE—Purse $400. For horses that have never beaten three minutes. Owned in the District.

FOURTH DAY—FRIDAY, AUG. 18.

No. 8—RUNNING RACE—Selling Purse, $200; $30 to second horse; ent and 5 per cent to third horse. One mile and repeat. Horses entered to be sold for $1,000 to carry their entitled weight. Two pounds off for each $100 under fixed valuation. Winner can be claimed by any one.
No. 9—RUNNING STAKE—Free for all; $25 entrance; $10 forfeit; $75 added. Second to save entrance. Half-mile and repeat.
No. 10—TROTTING RACE—Purse, $300. For horses that have never beaten 2:30.

FIFTH DAY—SATURDAY, AUG. 19.

No. 11—TROTTING RACE—Purse, $500. Free for all.
No. 12—TROTTING RACE—Purse, $400. Free for all two-year-olds. Mile and repeat.

#### Remarks and Conditions.

All trotting races are the best three in five, except the two-year-old trot; five to enter and three to start. Entrance fee 10 per cent. p. purse, to accompany nomination. Purses divided at the rate of sixty per cent. to first horse, thirty per cent. to second, and ten per cent. to third.

National Association Rules to govern trotting; but the Board reserves the right to trot heats of any two classes alternately, if necessary to finish a day's racing, or to trot a special race between heats.

To fill running race, three or more subscribers are necessary.

All two-year-olds, when running in their classes, shall carry one hundred pounds, with the usual allowance to mares and geldings.

All three-year-olds, when running in their classes, to carry one hundred and ten pounds, with the usual allowances as above.

Those who have nominations in stakes must name to the Secretary, IN WRITING, the horses they will start on Wednesday, on the Monday previous, and on Friday the Wednesday previous, by twelve o'clock m. This rule is obvious, and must be strictly adhered to.

No added money paid for a walk over.

Horses entered in purses can only be drawn by consent of Judges.

Rules of the Pacific Coast Blood-Horse Association (old weights) to govern running races, except when conditions named are otherwise.

Special plates will be run by the Southern Pacific Railroad and South Pacific Coast Railroad, and competitors tickets sold by both companies from all points on their lines, good from August 14th to August 20th, inclusive.

J. D. CHACE, President.
JAMES O. WANZER, Secretary.

---

### SPEED PROGRAMME

OF THE

### Mount Shasta Agricultural

Association,

**TO BE HELD IN**

### YREKA, SISKIYOU CO.,

— OR —

Wednesday, - - October 4th, 1882.

For racing purposes this District shall comprise Siskiyou, Shasta, Trinity, and Modoc Counties, Cal., and Jackson and Lake Counties, Oregon.

No horse shall be eligible to any of the following District Races unless owned in the District prior to October, 1881.

FIRST DAY—WEDNESDAY, OCT. 4.

No. 1—TROTTING—Free for all; 3 in 5; purse, $600. First horse receives $400; second horse, $150. Entrance 10 per cent. p. purse; to accompany nomination.
No. 2—RUNNING—Dash of a mile and a half, free for all horses owned in the District; purse, $300; entrance $5, added.

SECOND DAY—THURSDAY, OCT. 5.

No. 3—TROTTING—Free for all yearling horses owned in the District; 2 in 3 purse, $75; entrance $5, added.
No. 4—RUNNING—Half mile and repeat; free for all horses owned in the District; purse, $250; entrance $5, added.
No. 5—TROTTING—Free for all three-year-olds and under, owned in the District; 3 in 5 purse, $75; entrance, $5, added.

THIRD DAY—FRIDAY, OCT. 6.

Grand parade of Stock.
No. 6—TROTTING—Free for all in the District; 3 in 5; purse, $400.
No. 7—FOOT RACE—75 yards and repeat; purse, $60; entrance $5.
No. 8—RUNNING—Free for all three-year-olds and under owned in the District; dash of three-quarters of a mile; purse, $75; entrance $5, added.

FOURTE DAY—SATURDAY, OCT. 7.

No. 9—RUNNING—Free for all; 3 in 5; purse, $300. First horse receives $400; second horse, $150; entrance 10 per cent of purse; 2 to enter; 3 to start. Entries close Sept. 1st.
No. 10—TROTTING—Free for all horses in the District that have never beaten three minutes; 3 in 5; purse, $150; entrance $5, added.

#### Rules and Regulations.

1st. The above purses will be given without discount.
2d. In all District Races the second horse to save entrance.
3d. Entries to be placed in the entry box, kept for that purpose at the Pavilion, prior to 9 o'clock p. m. on the day prior to race.
4th. Entries must give name, pedigree, and description of horse entered as far as known.
5th. In all District Races two or more entries make a field.
6th. All trotting races must be in harness.
7th. Free, for all, to races 1 and 2, names must start 24 days, and all entries to these races must be made with the Secretary on or before September 1st.
8th. Pacific Coast Blood-Horse Association Rules to govern running races.
9th. National Trotting Association Rules to govern trotting races.
10th. National Trotting Association Rules to govern trotting races.

J. H. MAGOFFEY, Secretary.    E. SWAIN, President.

---

# SAVE MONEY!

**BUY DIRECT FROM THE MANUFACTURER.**

## James Wylie,

**20 & 22 Seventh St., nr. Market.**

MANUFACTURES

**Light Carriages, Buggies and Wagons,**

Guarantees First-class Work and Low Prices. Repairing, Painting and Trimming with promptness and at reasonable rates.

---

## For Sale!

A BRACE OF

### FINE FOX HOUNDS!

Training and Breeding guaranteed. Address for particulars,

TOM TUNSTEAD,
Nicacio, Marin County

---

# Golden Gate Fair.

## SPEED PROGRAMME FOR 1882

## $10.000

IN

## Stakes and Prizes

### FIRST DAY—Monday, Sept. 4, 1882.

No. 1—RUNNING—GOLDEN GATE STAKE.—For all two-year-olds; three-quarter mile dash; $50 entrance; $15 forfeit; $150 added; second colt to save stake; winners 5 pounds extra.

No. 2—SAME DAY.—RUNNING.—ALAMEDA STAKE.—For three-year-olds; one and one-half mile dash; $75 entrance; $25 forfeit; $175 added; second to save stake.

No. 3.—SAME DAY.—RUNNING.—PARDEE STAKE.—Free for all; one mile and repeat; $75 entrance; $25 forfeit; $200 added; second to save stake.

No. 4—SAME DAY.—TROTTING.—2:40 Class; purse, $600; first horse, $360; second, $180; third, $60.

No. 5.—SAME DAY.—SPECIAL TROT AGAINST TIME.—$150 in plate will be awarded any stallion that beats Santa Claus' time (2:17½).

### SECOND DAY—Tuesday, Sept. 5.

No. 6.—TROTTING.—2:30 Class; purse, $800; first horse, $480; second, $240; third, $80.

No. 7.—SAME DAY.—PACING.—Purse, $500; first horse, $300; second, $150; third, $50.

Washington and Johnny Wiegle, to wagon.

### THIRD DAY—Wednesday, Sept. 6.

No. 8.—RUNNING.—Free for all; 2-mile dash; $100 entrance; $25 forfeit; $250 added; second horse to save stake.

No. 9.—SAME DAY.—TROTTING.—Free for all three-year-olds; purse, $600; first horse, $360; second, $180; third, $60.

No. 10.—SAME DAY.—TROTTING.—2:22 Class; purse, $800; first horse, $480; second, $240; third, $80.

### FOURTH DAY—Thursday, Sept. 7.

No. 11.—TROTTING.—Free for all two-year-olds; one mile and repeat; purse, $400; first horse, $240; second, $120; third, $40.

No. 12.—SAME DAY.—TROTTING.—For all four-year-olds; purse, $600; first horse, $360; second, $180; third, $60.

No. 13.—SAME DAY.—RUNNING.—SELLING RACE.—Purse, $250; free for all; 1-mile dash; second horse to receive $75; horses entered to be sold for $1,000, to carry entitled weight; 2 pounds off for each $100 under fixed valuation.

### FIFTH DAY—Friday, Sept. 8.

NO. 14.—RUNNING.—CONSOLATION PURSE.—$250 for beaten horses; mile-and-a-quarter dash; second horse to receive $75; 10 per cent. entrance.

NO. 15.—SAME DAY.—LADIES' RIDING TOURNAMENT. There will be several very choice and elegant prizes to be competed for, contributed by the merchants and citizens of Oakland and San Francisco; the lady winning first prize to have first choice, the second, second choice, and so on until all the prizes are distributed. Ladies wishing to compete for premiums will send their names to the President or Secretary on or before the first day of September, 1882, indorsed by at least two gentlemen of the Society. Conditions will be published in the daily papers.

NO. 16.—SAME DAY.—TROTTING.—2:25 CLASS.—Purse, $800; first horse, $480; second, $240; third, $80.

No. 17.—SAME DAY.—SPECIAL TROT AGAINST TIME.—A purse of $50 will be given the yearling making the best time; a full mile to harness; no entrance fee.

### SIXTH DAY—Saturday, Sept. 9.

NO. 18.—COMPETITIVE CADET DRILL.—PRIZE, $150 Gold Medal. Competition open to all educational institutions in the State.

NO. 19.—SAME DAY.—COMPETITIVE MILITARY DRILL.—A prize of the value of $250 will be offered by the Association to the best drilled Military Company in the State of California. Rules and conditions to be published hereafter. It is the intent of the Directors to have the first competing companies determine what the prize or trophy shall be, and to have the same annually competed for, until it shall have been won three times by the same company, when it shall become the absolute property of the winning company.

No. 20—SAME DAY—GRAND BICYCLE TOURNAMENT, for the Association's Gold Medal to first, Silver Medal to second, and Bronze Medal to third; 1-mile dash; open to all bicyclists.

No. 21.—SAME DAY.—TROTTING.—Free for all; purse, $800; first horse, $480; second, $240; third, $80.

No. 22.—SAME DAY.—A SET OF HARNESS, of the value of $125, will be offered for gentlemen's roadsters; best two in three; owners to drive.

By a "gentleman's roadster," is meant any animal owned and driven on the road by any gentleman for his own private pleasure.

### CONDITIONS.

Entries to all running stakes, trotting and pacing races, to be made to Secretary Walker, on or before August 1, 1882. Forfeits in running stakes, and the entrance fee of 10 per cent. on the trotting and pacing races, should in all cases accompany the nominations and entries.

All the trotting and pacing races are the best three in five.

In all, five to enter, and three to start.

Entrance fee, ten per cent. on purse.

When there are eight or more starters in a trotting race, 150 yards to be a distance.

National Trotting Association rules to govern trotting, but the Board reserves the right to trot heats with any two classes alternately, if necessary to finish any day's racing, or to trot a special race between heats.

All offers in trotting races are confined to horses on the Pacific Coast May 22, 1882.

In running races, three or more entries required to fill.

Those who have nominations in stakes MUST name to the Secretary, in writing, the horses they will start on Monday, on the Saturday previous; and on Wednesday, the Monday previous; and on Friday, the Wednesday previous. No added money will be paid for a walk-over.

Horses entered in purses can only be drawn by consent of the judges.

Rules of the Pacific Coast Blood Horse Association to govern running races, except as above specially provided.

All entries to be made in writing, to give sex, color and marks of horse; also, name and residence of owner; and in running races colors to be worn by the rider. And in all, any other particulars that will enable the spectators to distinguish the horses in the race.

Write "Entries to races" on outside of Envelope.

L. WALKER, Secretary. A. C. DIETZ, President.

---

## $12,500

## In Purses and Stakes.

CALIFORNIA

## STATE FAIR

## SPEED PROGRAMME

FOR 1882.

### FIRST DAY—Monday, Sept. 11.

No. 1—RUNNING.—INTRODUCTION STAKE.—For all ages; three-quarters of a mile dash; $50 entrance, $15 forfeit; $200 added; second to save stake.

No. 2—RUNNING.—BREEDERS' STAKE.—For foals of 1879; one and a half miles dash; $50 entrance, p. p.; $300 added. Closed March 1st with nineteen nominations.

No. 3.—RUNNING.—SELLING RACE.—Purse, $250. Free for all; one mile and repeat; second horse to receive $75. Entrance five per cent. to third horse. Horses entered to be sold for $1,500 to carry entitled weight, one pound off for each $100 under fixed valuation.

No. 4.—TROTTING.—2:40 class; purse, $1,000.

### SECOND DAY—Tuesday, Sept. 12.

No. 5—TROTTING.—2:25 class; purse, $1,200.

No. 6.—TROTTING.—Purse, $600; for three year olds and under.

No. 7.—TROTTING.—Purse, $500; mile heats for two year olds.

### THIRD DAY—Wednesday, Sept. 13.

No. 8.—RUNNING—FILLY STAKE FOR TWO YEAR OLD FILLIES.—Five-eighths of a mile; $50 entrance; $15 forfeit; $200 added; second to receive $75; third, $25.

No. 9.—RUNNING.—CALIFORNIA DERBY STAKE.—For three-year olds; one and one-half mile dash; $100 entrance; $25 forfeit; $250 added; second horse, $100; third, $50.

No. 10.—RUNNING.—JENNIE B. STAKE.—For all ages; dash of one mile; $50 entrance, $15 forfeit; $200 added; second horse, $75; third, $25. Stake to be named after winner, if Jennie B.'s time—1:42¾—is beaten.

No. 11.—RUNNING.—SELLING RACE.—Purse, $250; one and one-eighth miles; second horse, $100; entrance, five per cent. to third horse. Horses entered to be sold for $1,000, to carry entitled weight. Two pounds off for each $100 under fixed valuation.

No. 12—TROTTING—2:30 class; purse, $1,200.

### FOURTH DAY—Thursday, Sept. 14.

No. 13.—TROTTING.—2:22 class; purse, $1,200.

No. 14.—PACING.—2:25 class; purse, $800.

No. 15.—TROTTING—Two miles and repeat; 2:40 horses; purse, $800.

### FIFTH DAY—Friday, Sept. 15.

No. 16.—RUNNING.—COLT AND FILLY STAKE.—For two year olds; dash of one mile; $50 entrance, $15 forfeit, $200 added; second horse, $50; third, $25.

No. 17.—RUNNING.—SELLING RACE.—Purse, $300; for all ages; dash of one and a quarter miles; $100 to second horse; entrance, five per cent. to third; horses entered to be sold for $1,500, carry full weight; for $1,200, three pounds off; for $1,000, five pounds off; for $750, seven pounds off; for $500, ten pounds off.

No. 18.—RUNNING.—POST STAKE.—Dash of three miles; free for all; $100 entrance; $500 added; weight 100 pounds; three-year-olds, 90 pounds; second horse to receive $150; third, $100. Starters to be named to the Secretary Wednesday evening, at or before 8 o'clock P. M.

No. 19.—RUNNING.—CONSOLATION PURSE.—$250 for beaten horses; one mile and repeat; entrance free; second horse to receive $50.

### SIXTH DAY—Saturday, Sept. 16.

No. 20.—TROTTING.—2:19 class; purse, $1,200.

No. 21.—TROTTING.—Purse, $800; for double teams of 2:30 horses.

No. 22.—TROTTING.—OCCIDENT STAKE FOR 1882, closed in 1881 with twelve nominations.

No. 23.—SPECIAL TROT AGAINST TIME.—$250 in plate will be awarded to any stallion that beats Santa Claus' time (2:17½).

Entries for the following events for 1883-4 were ordered to be closed with the above races:

No. 1.—RUNNING.—CALIFORNIA DERBY STAKE, for foals of 1880, to be run at the State Fair of 1883. One and one-half miles dash; $50 entrance, p. p.; $300 added; second horse, $100; third, $50.

No. 2.—Same stake, for foals of 1881, to be run at State Fair of 1884. Same conditions.

No. 3.—RUNNING—MATURITY STAKE.—Three-mile dash, for four-year-olds, in 1883; $100 entrance; $25 forfeit; $500 added; second horse, $150; third horse, $100. To be run at the State Fair of 1883.

No. 4.—RUNNING—CALIFORNIA ANNUAL STAKE.—For two-year-olds, foals of 1881. Dash of one mile; $100 entrance; $25 forfeit; $250 added; second horse, $100; third, $50. To be run at the Fair of 1883.

### REMARKS and CONDITIONS.

All trotting and pacing races are the best three in five, except the two year old trot, unless otherwise specified; five to enter and three to start. Entrance fee ten per cent. on purse, to accompany nomination. Purses divided at the rate of sixty per cent. to first horse, thirty per cent. to second, and ten per cent. to third.

National Association Rules to govern trotting; but the Board reserves the right to trot heats of any two classes alternately, if necessary to finish any day's racing, or to trot a special race between heats.

To fill running races, three or more subscribers are necessary.

All two-year-olds, when running in their classes, shall carry one hundred pounds, with the usual allowance for mares and geldings.

All three-year-olds, when running in their classes, to carry one hundred and ten pounds, with the usual allowances as above.

Those who have nominations in stakes MUST name to the Secretary, IN WRITING, the horses they will start on Monday, on the Saturday previous; and on Wednesday the Monday previous; and on Friday the Wednesday previous, by twelve o'clock M. This rule is obvious, and must be strictly adhered to.

No added money paid for a walk-over.

Horses entered in purses can only be drawn by consent of Judges.

Rules of the Pacific Coast Blood Horse Association (old weights) to govern running races, except when conditions named are otherwise.

All entries to be made in writing, giving name, sex, color, and marks of horses; also, name and residence of owner. In running races, full colors to be worn by rider; and drivers in trotting races are respectfully requested to wear caps of distinct colors, to be named in their entries, as their horses will be designated upon programmes by colors worn by drivers. This is necessary to enable spectators to distinguish the horses in the race.

Entries to all the above races to close with the Secretary on Tuesday, August 1, 1882.

Write "Entries to Races" on outside of envelope.

EDWIN F. SMITH, Secretary. HUGH M. LARUE, President.

---

## *SPEED PROGRAMME.*

## $13,000 Gold Coin

### IN PURSES.

The Largest Purses Offered in the State.

## STOCKTON,

### Sept. 19th to 23d inclusive, 1882.

#### Tuesday, Sept. 19th.

No. 1—DISTRICT—RUNNING—For two-year-olds; purse $400; mile dash; 5 to enter, 3 to start. Four moneys.

No. 2—DISTRICT TROTTING—For yearlings; purse $300; mile dash; 5 to enter, 3 to start. Four moneys.

No. 3—PACIFIC COAST TROTTING—2:36 Class; purse $1,000, and $200 added if more than ten entries. Four moneys.

#### Wednesday, Sept. 20th.

No. 4—PACIFIC COAST NOVELTY RUNNING—3½ mile dash, purse $600. The first horse to each half mile to win $100, and the horse first to two and two-and-one-half mile posts to win $50 EACH extra; $200 additional will be added to the purse, pro rata, if more than ten entries.

No. 5—DISTRICT RUNNING—For three-year-olds; purse $800. Closed with six entries.

No. 6—PACIFIC COAST TROTTING—2:25 Class; purse $1,000, and $200 added if more than ten entries. Four moneys.

No. 7—DISTRICT—TROTTING—For named horses; purse $500; 7 to enter, 4 to start. This race is intended for horses that can trot in three minutes or a little better. Four moneys.

#### Thursday, Sept. 21st.

No. 8—PACIFIC COAST RUNNING—Mile and repeat; purse $500, and if 1:43 is beaten, the horse making the lowest record will receive $200 additional. Four moneys.

No. 9—DISTRICT—TROTTING—For two-year-olds; purse $800. Closed with ten entries.

**Ladies' Equestrianism.**

☞ FOUR PRIZES IN GOLD COIN. $40, $30, $20, $10.

No. 10—DISTRICT—TROTTING—2:38 Class; purse $800; 7 to enter, 4 to start. Four moneys.

#### Friday, Sept. 22d.

No. 11—PACIFIC COAST—RUNNING—Free for all; two miles and repeat; purse $800, and $200 added if more than ten entries. Four moneys.

No. 12—DISTRICT—RUNNING—For three-year-olds and over; purse $500; best two in three; 7 to enter, 4 to start. Four moneys.

No. 13—PACIFIC COAST TROTTING—For horses owned on the Pacific Coast, July 1st, 1882; 2:22 Class; purse $1,500, and $500 added if more than ten subscribers. The nominator NOT required to name his horse, but simply send his cash ($150) with his OWN NAME, August 1, 1882. He has then earned the right to start any horse eligible that he may fully control, provided the horse he starts be named to the Secretary, September 1, 1882. Four moneys.

#### Saturday, Sept. 23d.

No. 14—PACIFIC COAST TROTTING—2:28 Class; purse $1,000, and $200 added if more than ten entries. Four moneys.

No. 15—PACIFIC COAST PACING—2:25 Class; purse $400, and $200 added if more than ten entries. Four moneys.

### REMARKS AND CONDITIONS.

All Trotting Races best three in five, except numbers 2 and 9.

In all these Races (Pacific Coast Novelty Race excepted) FOUR moneys, 50, 25, 15 and 10 per cent. of purse. Entrance fee, 10 per cent. of purse, and MUST accompany the nomination. District Races will close with the Secretary at 5 o'clock P. M. of July 15, 1882. Pacific Coast Races to close with the Secretary August 1, 1882.

When there are eight or more to start in a Trotting Race, 150 yards shall be a distance.

Rules of the National Trotting Association to govern trotting, except as specified: but the Board of Managers reserve the right to trot heats of any two classes alternately, or to start a special race between heats.

All two-year-olds, when running in their classes, shall carry 100 pounds, with the usual allowance for mares and geldings.

All three-year-olds, when running in their classes, to carry 110 pounds, with the usual allowances as above, otherwise, old weights to govern.

For a walk-over in any race a horse shall only be entitled to his own entrance fee and one quarter of the entrance received from the other entries for said purse; and a horse winning a race entitled to first money only, except when distancing the field, then entitled to first and third moneys only. A horse wins but one money under any other circumstances.

Horses entered in purses can only be drawn by consent of the Judges.

The Board reserves the right to change the day and hour of any race, if they deem it necessary.

Unless otherwise ordered by the Board, no horse shall be qualified to enter in any District Race that has not been OWNED in the District six (6) months prior to the day of the race—and any entry by any person of any horse so disqualified shall be held liable for the entrance fee so contracted without any right to compete, and the same shall be held liable to penalties prescribed by the Rules of the National Trotting Association and expulsion from this Association.

Rules of the Pacific Coast Blood Horse Association to govern Running Races, including additions to rules, except as especially provided.

In all Running Races colors to be worn by riders, and in all other races, any other particulars that will enable spectators to distinguish the horses in the race.

In all the Coast Races noted above, SIX ENTRIES are required to fill, and three horses to start; but the Board RESERVE THE RIGHT TO CLOSE ANY RACE WITH A LESS NUMBER.

Races to commence each day at 1 o'clock P. M. sharp.

The track is first-class, having been improved. Stables, hay and straw free to competitors.

### ENTRIES.

1st. Entries must be made in writing and dated.

2nd. State number of the race in which you wish to enter.

3rd. State COLOR of horse, and marks if necessary.

4th. State whether the horse is a STALLION, MARE or GELDING.

5th. State NAME OF SIRE AND DAM if known; if unknown, state the fact in the entry.

6th. State NAME and P. O. ADDRESS of the owner of the horse entered.

7th. Sign with P. O. address of the party entering the horse.

8th. If the name has been changed, give former name.

9th. Repeat by mail all entries made by telegraph.

Agricultural District No. 2, California, comprises the Counties of San Joaquin, Calaveras, Tuolumne, Stanislaus, Mariposa, Merced, Fresno, Tulare, and Kern.

L. U. SHIPPEE, President.

J. L. PHELPS, Secretary,
P. O. Box 135, Stockton, Cal.

---

## SECOND

## *ANNUAL EXHIBITION*

OF THE

## SAN MATEO AND SANTA CLARA COUNTY

## AGRICULTURAL ASSOCIATION

### NO. 5,

TO BE HELD AT

## SAN JOSE, CAL.,

......FROM......

### Sept. 25th to 30th, '82, inclusive

### *SPEED PROGRAMME.*

#### FIRST DAY—Monday, Sept. 25th, 1882.

No. 1. TROTTING—2:40 class. Purse, $600.

No. 2. SAME DAY—TROTTING—2:25 class. Purse, $750.

#### SECOND DAY—Tuesday, Sept. 26th.

No. 3. RUNNING—For two year-olds; three-quarter mile dash; $50 entrance; $15 forfeit; $150 added. Second horse to receive his entrance and one-third of added money.

No. 4. SAME DAY—RUNNING—For all ages; mile dash; $50 entrance; $15 forfeit; $125 added. Second horse to receive his entrance and one-third of added money.

No. 5. SAME DAY—RUNNING—Selling Race—Purse, $200; mile and repeat. Second horse $75. Entrance five per cent. to third horse. Horses entered to be sold for $1,000 to carry entitled weight. Two pounds off for each $100 under fixed valuation. Winner can be claimed by any one.

#### THIRD DAY—Wednesday, Sept. 27th.

NO. 6. TROTTING—2:30 class. Purse, $400.

NO. 7. SAME DAY—BUGGY HORSE RACE—For horses owned in the District to be driven by owner in buggy. Two mile heats. Purse to be hereafter offered.

SAME DAY—Ladies' Riding Tournament—Bicycle Race, etc.

#### FOURTH DAY—Thursday, Sept. 28th.

No. 8. RUNNING—Three-year-olds, 1¼ mile dash; $50 entrance; $15 forfeit; $175 added. Second horse to receive his entrance and one-third of added money.

No. 9. SAME DAY—PACING—Free for all. Purse $300.

No. 10. SAME DAY—TROTTING—For four-year-olds. Purse $400.

#### FIFTH DAY—Friday, Sept. 29th.

No. 11. RUNNING—1¼ mile dash. Free for all; $50 entrance; $15 forfeit; $200 added. Second horse to receive his entrance and one-third of added money.

No. 12. SAME DAY—TROTTING—2:27 class. Purse $700.

NO. 13. SAME DAY—TROTTING—For two-year-olds. Purse $400.

#### SIXTH DAY—Saturday, Sept. 30th.

No. 14. TROTTING—2:22 class. Purse $750.

No. 15. SAME DAY—TROTTING—2:30 class. Two miles and repeat. Purse $500.

### REMARKS AND CONDITIONS.

All trotting and pacing races are the best three in five, except the two-year-old trot, unless otherwise specified; five to enter and three to start. Entrance fee ten per cent. on purse, to accompany nominations. Purse divided at the rate of sixty per cent to first horse, thirty per cent to second and ten per cent to third.

National Association Rules to govern trotting; but the Board reserves the right to trot heats of any two classes alternately, if necessary to finish any day's racing, or to trot a special race between heats.

To fill running races, three or more subscribers are necessary.

All two-year-olds, when running in their classes, shall carry one hundred pounds, with the usual allowance for mares and geldings.

All three-year-olds, when running in their classes, to carry one hundred and ten pounds, with the usual allowances as above.

Those who have nominations in stakes must name to the Secretary, in writing, the horse they will start on Tuesday, on the Monday previous; and on Thursday the Tuesday previous, and on Friday, the Wednesday previous, by twelve o'clock M. This rule is obvious, and must be strictly adhered to.

No added money paid for a walk-over.

Horses entered in purses can only be drawn by consent of the Judges.

Rules of the Pacific Coast Blood-Horse Association (old weights) to govern running races, except when conditions named are otherwise.

All entries to be made in writing, giving name, sex, color, and marks of horses; also, name and residence of owner. In running races full colors to be worn by rider; and drivers in trotting races are respectfully requested to wear caps of distinct colors, to be named in their entries, as their horses will be designated upon programmes by colors worn by drivers.

Entries to all the above races to close with the Secretary on Tuesday, August 1st, 1882.

Write "Entries to Races" on outside of envelope.

A. KING, President.

T. S. MONTGOMERY, Secretary.

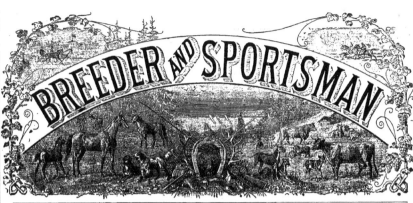

# BREEDER AND SPORTSMAN

VOL. I.—No. 5.
No. 508 MONTGOMERY STREET.

### SAN FRANCISCO, SATURDAY, JULY 29, 1882.

SUBSCRIPTION
FIVE DOLLARS A YEAR.

## NOTABLE HORSES OF CALIFORNIA

## ECHO.

In taking stallions which have become notable through the performances of their offspring for illustration, it necessarily extends the history to several in place of one. This spreading, as it may be termed, of the good qualities, is manifestly superior to concentration, and the victorious blood disseminated to the advantage of breeders. There have been many striking examples of the benefits following the use in the breeding stud of one animal, and it is not necessary to go outside of this country to prove the truth of the position. Sir Archy has been termed the "patriarch of the American turf," and certainly there never has been another American sire which has shown so many celebrities in near and remote descendants. Messenger has been awarded the same prominence as a trotting progenitor, though the difference was that Sir Archy got race horses while Messenger cannot show fast trotters in his immediate progeny. The main cause for the lack was that in his day fast trotters were not valued,

and, consequently, no pains were taken to produce them. His son, Mambrino, has the honor of founding two of the great lines, the Hambletonians and Mambrino Chiefs. A son of Mambrino, Abdallah, acquired some distinction as the sire of trotters, and his son Rysdyk's Hambletonian wears the undisputed title of the greatest of trotting sires. It would be far beyond the limit of these sketches to give reasons why there was a regular progression in the generations, but there is one feature which is ever present, and that is the influence which a certain combination of blood possesses in fixing the standard. Thus the Hambletonian and Clay has proved a "happy nick;" but before that was found to be so good, the potency of the Hambletonian and American Star was fully acknowledged. From this combination came Dexter, Jay Gould, Aberdeen and many others, and the subject of this paper is further proof of the efficacy of the cross. The blood of Echo was the main inducement

for his purchase by Mr. Titus, and that his judgment was correct, and the wisdom of the selections has been established by the performances of the colts.

Echo was bred by Jesse T. Seely, Warwick, Orange county, New York; foaled, 1866. His sire Rysdyk's Hambletonian, his dam Fanny Felter, by Magnolia, a son of Seely's American Star, second dam by Webber's Kentucky Whip, third dam by Shakespeare, a son of Duroc. He was purchased of Jesse T. Seely, in the fall of 1870, by L. H. Titus, of Dewdrop Farm, Los Angeles county, California, and brought here the January following. His stud services have been limited, the first season being restricted to nine mares, two of which were taken away, and Mr. Titus could never learn anything about them or their produce. Of the seven remaining five had foals, and every one of them could trot inside of 2:40, Gibraltar and Echora being among them. Before his importation to California he served a few mares but, as he was only a three-year-old when bought, his opportunities were necessarily limited. If ever he had been awarded a full share of mares, he would be regarded as one of the very successful sires, and, as in these sketches we do not intend to base reputation on hypothetical conditions, it will be very seldom that surmises will come into consideration. Echo himself was a good performer, trotting a mile in 2:35, and winning a race of heats of two miles against such strong competitors as The Moor and Vaughn. The first of his get to appear on the track was Echora, and this was in a stake for three-year-olds trotted at Sacramento at the State Fair of 1875. It was a short race, as she distanced both of her competitors, Arabia and Beautiful Bells, in the first heat; time, 2:42, the fastest ever made up to that date by a three-year-old in California. This was her only appearance in 1875. In 1877 she won a very good race in which were Rustic, Nemo, Gladstone and Amanda Murray. Rustic won the second and third heats in 2:30½, 2:33; Echora the first, fourth and fifth in 2:32¼, 2:33, 2:31. The time of the fifth heat proved that she could stay, and this capacity she has exhibited in every race she has been in. It is unnecessary to follow Echora through the many races she has trotted, and a few more instances will suffice to show that she is worthy of a good place in the records. In 1880 she won at Oakland, beating Gus (who won the first heat), Volunteer, Startle, and Captain Jenks—the time, 2:26¾, 2:26¼, 2:27¾, 2:28¾; and last season she trotted six races, of which she won four, one of them at heats of two miles, and reducing her record to 2:25. This was in a race with Crown Point and Del Sur, and a very hot one it was. She won the first heat in 2:25½, the second Del Sur got in 2:26. The third was to Echora's credit in 2:25, and then Crown Point got a heat in 2:28, when the mare scored another victory. There was nothing to start against her in the two mile heat race at the Bay District Course, and previous to that she had stubbornly contested a race at Sacramento, one of the hardest fought battles ever seen on a track. There were eight heats; Echora won the first in 2:25, Del Sur the second in 2:24, then Crown Point the third and fourth in 2:26, 2:26¾; Ashley came in first on the fifth in 2:29, and then Echora got the sixth in 2:30; the seventh Ashley won in 2:25½, when on account of the Garfield obsequies the concluding heat was postponed from Saturday until Tuesday. The heat was in doubt even after the horses passed the winning score, and whether it would be given to Ashley or Echora a matter of question until the judges rendered their decision in favor of Ashley; the time, 2:26¾. In 1877 there was another very promising Echo came out—one of those unfortunate horses which appear to have been foaled under the influence of some malign star, and though possessed of a world of speed and unquestionable endurance, casualty followed casualty, and the "brackets" are still in reserve for him. This was Jo Hamilton, his dam a thoroughbred mare by Belmont, and his best effort in public was at Chico, when he forced Brigadier to trot a third heat in 2:30 to beat him, both at that time being four years old.

One of our especial favorites among the trotters of California is Gibraltar, by Echo, his dam at one time claimed to be by Owen Dale, and his breeder, Mr. Tiffany, of Los Angeles, had a good deal of faith in that being correct. It may be so, though the only reliable information is that she was a large mare taken from Sonoma county to Los Angeles. Gibraltar is rather coarser than any other Echo we ever saw, but he has the thoroughbred characteristic of "gameness," and will finish up a heat and a race with as much determination as need be. He will keep trotting under punishment as severe as the driver can administer, and, like Monsieur Tonson, will "come again" and keep coming. One of his notable races was in 1878, September 12th. The contestants were Abbotsford, Echora, Alice, Barney, Bickford, Prophet and Hayward Chief. Abbotsford won the first heat in 2:25—Gibraltar the second, third and fourth, in the capital time of 2:26, 2:27, 2:24½. 1879 was rather a blank year for him, and in 1880 he only trotted two races, second to Elaine in Sacramento, and a winner at Stockton. He had then been bought by Mr. Salisbury, and last year he lowered his record to 2:22½, and made a performance which, under the circumstances, was more creditable than even the fast time shown. It was at the Golden Gate Fair—the starters Ashley, Echora, Del Sur, Tommy Dodd and Crown Point. Gibraltar had a bad leg, and what is worse in a trotter, it was a hind leg was ailing. The ankle was much enlarged, the swelling extending half way to the hock, and though the lameness was slight at the time, the following week it was so bad as to stop him trotting at Sacramento. He won in straight heats, the time 2:24, 2:23½, 2:22½. Owing to the bad leg, he was unable to fulfill his other engagements, and that was the only race he participated in during the year.

In 1880 Echo showed two of the best three-year-olds of the year. Belle Echo made the fastest time for the age during the season, and Annie Laurie equaled the best Eastern record. Belle Echo has been awarded a place among the notabilities, and the capital likeness which appeared in the Breeder and Sportsman of the 15th instant will convey a good idea of her form; but the grace and rapidity of her movements are beyond the pencil of artist to depict. Although her owner, Mr. Titus, is enthusiastic over the stock of the horse in the aggregate, we are of the opinion that he regards Belle as the bright particular star of the family, and there cannot be a question that she is entitled to rank with the stars of whatever tribe. Annie Laurie also exhibited a great deal of promise in her three-year-old form. The race between her and Alex. Button, at the State Fair, was a hot contest from end to end. Button won the first heat in 2:34¼, Annie Laurie the second in 2:30, Button the third in 2:29. The fourth heat was a "dead" one between the two in 2:30¾, Button winning the fifth, which decided the race. Belle Echo, Len Rose, Honesty and Glencora also trotted, Belle being evidently "off," and in all probability suffering from the complaint, in its incipient stages, which affected her at San Jose.

While not entirely beyond the scope of these articles to include performances which do not constitute a technical record, public deeds are rightfully entitled to the first place. It is manifest, however, that a horse may be a stock-getter of undoubtful superiority without a single one of his get appearing in public. Horses show so much speed and endurance on the road that they are highly valued, would sell for a large amount of money, and that without ever having the benefit of regular track training. It is important then that all performances be considered, and while giving the appropriate weight to actual records, it is also a legitimate subject of inquiry what else there is to give value to the stock? In a "gentleman's road-horse" there must be other qualities beside speed—soundness, form, godd temper and good looks being important factors in the composition. The faculty of "going the route" is imperatively demanded. To our eye one of the finest types of a road-horse in the country is Exile, a son of Echo, and a "full brother" (as horsemen term colts from the same parents) to Jo Hamilton. While Belle Echo is very nearly a model, this horse, of three-quarters the same blood, has rather more finish. He can show a rate a good deal inside of 2:30, and at times a flight of speed which would keep Belle moving. Both are bright bays with black points, and the horse especially, with flowing manes and tails which our correspondent "Index" not inaptly compared to the standard of a Pasha.

As in the other illustrations the engraving is a capital likeness of the horse, and it is only necessary to add that like a majority of his colts he is a bright bay, and there is a further similarity in all of them being of the best disposition. He was sold by Mr. Titus the Fall of 1880 to J. B. Haggin, and is now at the head of the trotting department of the Rancho del Paso stud.

## THE EMBRYO STAKE.

Owing to the novel features of the Embryo Stake, the conditions appear to be puzzling, and in answer to many inquirers the following explanation is given:

It is a stake for foals of 1882; that is, any colt or filly foaled on or since January first of this year. There are three different races in the stake, viz: for yearlings, two-year-olds and three-year-olds. The subscriber elects whether he will name in one, two, or all of them, and his purpose must be declared at the time of making the nomination. The race for yearlings is a mile, for two-year-olds heats of a mile, best 2 in 3, and for three-year-olds, heats of a mile, best 3 in 5. Five dollars must accompany the nomination, and this is the first payment to be made, whether one or all the stakes are entered in. It may be clearer to illustrate with an example. In the first place, the nomination should be made something in this form:

San Francisco, August 1, 1882.

Jos. Cairn Simpson, Secretary pro tem. Pacific Breeders' Association:

I name in Embryo Stake of 1882, my colt Ajax; bay, white hind feet, star in forehead, no other marks; foaled April 5th, by Ajax, his dam Flora by Signal, in all three of the stakes. Enclosed find $5. John Smith.

Should the subscriber, John Smith, desire to declare him out of the yearling race on the first day of September, 1883, he notifies the Secretary and pays $10. If he does not declare out at that time he is liable for a forfeit of $25, and if this is not paid ten days before the day fixed for the race he is then held liable for the whole amount of the stake, $100. In this respect the two and three-year-old races are the same as the yearling. The whole liability incurred if a subscriber names in them all is $35. If he names in two $25; and if in one, $15. The object of the declaration of $10 was to make the liability as light as possible, so that if the foal turned out poorly the expense would be small. Should it be satisfactory on the 1st of September, there is nearly two months more to continue the training before determining whether to pay the forfeit of twenty-five dollars or risk the whole amount of the stake. The nominating fee of $5.00 is credited to the races in which the colt is named. If, as in the example, it is named in all three, $1.66 will go to the credit of each; if in two stakes, $2.50; if in one, that race will be credited with the whole amount. Should the subscriber desire to name in the races to be trotted when the colts are two and three years old, the entry will be made in races of 1884 and 1885; if in the three-year-old alone, in the race of 1885. In order to prevent confusion, the stakes are named after the year the foals came. Thus, in the Embryo of 1879, the yearling and two-year-old have been decided, and the three-year-old is to be trotted on the first Saturday in November of this year. The Embryo of 1880, the yearling race, has been scored, and the two-year-old of that year will be decided on the same day. That of 1881, the yearling, will come off, and from this time out, should there be no lapse in the stake, there will be three races on the same day. On the first Saturday in November, 1882, the programme will be: Embryo Stake 1879, three-year-old race; Embryo Stake 1880, two-year-old race; Embryo Stake 1881, yearling race.

From the above explanation a proper understanding will be obtained; bearing in mind that there are three races embraced in the stake, and that one nominating fee is all that is required, and that there is a chance to "draw out" on the first of September of the year the race is to be trotted for $10; ten days before the day fixed for trotting a forfeit of $25 will absolve, and these conditions apply to each one of the races. To make it still plainer, we will carry the case of the imaginary entry of Ajax through the several stages. His owner concludes on the first of September, 1883, that he will not trot Ajax in that year. He notifies the Secretary as follows:

San Francisco, Sept. 1, 1883.

Secretary Pacific Breeders' Association: I declare out of the yearling race, Embryo 1882, my bay colt Ajax. Enclosed find $10. John Smith.

Should he have thoughts of trotting him on Sept. 1st, but something goes wrong, or he does not come up to expectations, and he desires to pay forfeit, the notice will be:

San Francisco, October —, 1883.

Secretary Pacific Breeders' Association: Enclosed find $25 forfeit on my bay colt Ajax, which I delare out of yearling race, Embryo 1882. John Smith.

If he resolves to trot, no notice is necessary, paying the stake, $100, the Friday before the race is to come off. The same formula, of course, applies through all the races.

---

Danville, July 25, 1882.

Editor Breeder and Sportsman—Dear Sir: I received three numbers of your new paper, and am pleased to learn that you are engaged in this enterprise, for it is what is really needed on this Coast very much. As long as I can get five dollars a year you can count on me as a subscriber. I am delighted with it, indeed, and inclose subscription for one year, and then I shall have all the sporting papers. You have my best wishes for your new enterprise.

I noticed in your issue of July 1st a letter from Sunny Slope, saying that the Embryo has had its day, and that it is Mr. Rose's opinion, with Palo Alto and Sunny Slope in the field, it would stop others from entering in stakes with them. I doubt that either of these two named places has shown enough in any one race to prevent or frighten others from entering to trot against their nominations in a three-year-old stake. Let the associations give a large three-year-old stake two years from this Fall, and I think you will see five entries, and that three will start. It is not the speedy horse or colt that always wins the race, and the fast colt is not always at himself, and even then he may see a bird on the fence. The Thompson started last in a race, and trotted third heat in 2:21, and as a four-year-old went for a fast mile, and could only make 2:32. You can't always tell. Don't bar anybody's colt, how great his repute, for it is not right, and I maintain that there are five persons on this Coast that are raising colts that will enter against Palo Alto or Sunny Slop. If they think that no one will enter with them, let the associations make the distance 150 yards. We will enter with them in the three-year-old farm, and the distance may be 100 yards. George Wilks sired a faster horse than he was himself; Governor Sprague the same, Echo the same, Sultan the same, Electioneer the same; and if Steinway sires one as fast as I have seen him trot, I will be certain to enter and start one of his colts, and I know that there are others on this Coast that think the same way. Now, dear Editor, I have spoken my piece, and want it published, for I am Steinway's beau. Truly yours,

Sam'l Gamble,
Supt. Cook Farm, Danville.

---

Military Marksmen.—Orders have been issued from general headquarters at the Presidio directing each post commander in the Department of California to ascertain by a competitive trial, on or before August 12th, the most suitable marksmen of each company, troop or battery, and one from each non-commissioned staff or band at his post, and report their names to Department Headquarters, with the scores made during the contest and on the four previous practice days. The marksmen thus reported will be ordered to the Presidio August 16th, to compete on August 24th, 25th and 26th, for the honor of a place in the Department Team of 12. Two alternates will be added to the team. The several Department Teams will assemble at the Presidio of San Francisco, Cal., about August 26th, to compete on the 7th, 8th and 9th of September, for the honor of places upon the Division Team of 12, and for the twelve prizes awarded by the War Department. The four best marksmen on the Division Team will represent the Military Division of the Pacific in the Army Team, and will proceed to Fort Leavenworth October 9th, to prepare for the competition which is to take place at that post October 25th, this year.

---

Sportsman's Paradise.—If the young man of the Chico *Record*, who produced the following, had only added a bison or so to the game quadrupeds that abound in his "sportsman's elysium," and now and then thrown in an albatross with his water-fowl and woodcock and wild turkey, he'd been fairly entitled to the prize jack-knife. Hear him: "Big Meadow can be called the sportsman's elysium of California, at least of the northern part. The vast forests in its neighborhood, which as yet have never been fully explored, abound with black bear, deer, wild turkey, ruffled grouse or pheasants, rabbits, squirrels, quails and all the infinite variety of water-fowl that hatch their brood amid its numerous beautiful lakes. Snipe and woodcock are found in countless numbers, and occasionally in the deep shades of the pine woods a lordly elk is seen. All the streams swarm with the finny tribe—trout, salmon, bass, pickerel, pike and perch, which are caught mostly by the Indians, but a white angler sometimes finds his way into this paradise."—*Exchange.*

---

Breeder and Sportsman.—Such is the title of a new journal published in San Francisco, the first issue of which appeared July 1st. The object of the Breeder and Sportsman will be "to advance the breeding interests of the Pacific Coast, and to elevate and popularize out-door sports." The editor is Mr. Joseph Cairn Simpson, for so many years connected with the sporting press, and recognized as one of the ablest writers of the day on turf subjects. Mr. Simpson has always been independent and bold in expressing his opinions, and has not hesitated to expose fraud whenever and wherever he found it. With an editor so thoroughly competent, and possessed of so many friends, the success of the Breeder and Sportsman may be considered assured. It is sixteen pages, neatly gotten up, published weekly, and the subscription is five dollars a year.—[*The American Field.*

## ROWING.

**GRIFFIN AND WATKINS.**—On Sunday last the backers of D. Griffin and Sam Watkins met at Long Bridge to arrange for a sculling match between their men. Bob Goble, on behalf of Watkins, insisted that the race should take place over the Long Bridge Course. Griffin's friends were equally positive in their wish to have the match decided at Saucelito, and the result of the difference was that the negotiations were suspended. The *Call*, in commenting on the affair, last Monday, stated that Watkins was so anxious for the match that he was willing to concede the choice of position to Griffin, if the latter would but agree to have the race take place at Long Bridge. Such a concession would be very liberal, as the outside station on the Long Bridge Course is a heavy handicap at certain stages of the tide, and especially when the wind is blowing freshly. Griffin is not, however, desirous of accepting any concessions from Watkins, and professes and seems to be as anxious for a match as his rival's magnanimity would seem to indicate. The intimation conveyed by the *Call's* article is that Watkins will be compelled to force Griffin into a match. This we think will be shown to be erroneous. The Golden Gate man is perfectly right in holding out for any course most agreeable to him, but when he finds that he cannot draw his opponent to Saucelito, he will consent to a match over the Long Bridge Course. The three-mile course at Long Bridge is not so unfavorable as the two-mile course, for there is a long stretch of smooth water at the start and finish, so that the choice of stations is not as important as in the shorter distance, where the whole race is over an exposed sheet of water and through strong currents. Considerable interest is taken in the proposed match, as the men are believed to be nearly equal in speed, and both are undeniably game. A good deal of money will be bet on the result.

### INSULT TO INJURY.

It looks as if the Hillsdale crew is doomed to bring back from England nothing but the evidence of innumerable snubs. The American oarsmen have been reviled and rejected until they ought to be heartily sick of their trip and eager to return to the right side of the Atlantic. The last gratuitous slur on the Hillsdale four, of which we have official notice, came in the shape of a resolution proposed by Captain Hornton of the London Rowing Club, seconded by President Lambert of the Cambridge University, and unanimously adopted at a meeting of the Amateur Rowing Association, presided over by Rev. Mr. Lisley, of the Oxford Boat Club. The dispatch says that the captains of the Thames and Kingston Rowing Clubs and well known members of other amateur clubs were present. This insult is as follows: "Taking into consideration the vagueness of description of several members of the Hillsdale crew, the committee would not be justified in recognizing the crew as amateurs in accordance with the English definition of the term, and cannot, without further evidence, advise the acceptance of their challenge." The Hillsdale crew has been given unmistakable evidence that its presence on England waters is not desired, and if it has as much dignity as it is supposed to have speed it ought to pack up its oars and come home. For our part we are not particularly aggrieved that the Hillsdale crew has had such poor luck, for its experience will be valuable to all other ambitious American crews that may seek fame in English waters. The Hillsdale four have chiefly themselves to blame for the slurs and snubs so freely administered. They ought to have profited by the experience of the Cornell crew, and if their common sense was commensurate with their aquatic prowess they would have taken the valuable lesson to heart. The English oarsmen showed, by their action toward the Cornell crew, that they had a prejudice against American amateur crews and would lose no opportunity to display their unfriendly feelings. Knowing this, the Hillsdale acted in a most precipitate, unbusiness-like and senseless manner. They rushed off to England without having arranged a programme and gave the adverse parties an opportunity to exhibit their hostility by stupid mistakes in the entries. The proper course for the Hillsdale crew to have pursued and the one which would have suggested itself to any but a committee of hot-headed amateurs was to have arranged for a race or a series of races with representative English crews. When the arrangements were completed and there was no possibility of any slips or excuse for slurs the American crew could have crossed the ocean to practice in confidence and row with credit. By such a proceeding the Hillsdale crew would have shown itself a dignified and able representative of American amateur oarsmanship, whereas by lunging round the edges of small regattas and fighting for a chance to carry off pewter pots and tin medals it has placed itself in the humiliating position in which insults can be administered with impunity.

**ROWING ON PAPER.**—Hanlan and Ross are doing so much rowing through the columns of the sporting press that some good judges think they will never row against one another anywhere else. Ross, in reply to Hanlan's challenge to row any five men in the world, has aroused the indignation of Ross, who publishes a card, in which he says: "As Hanlan has distinctly named me as one of those he is ready to meet, I am willing to row him five races on five consecutive days, each race for $1,000 a side; distance to be from three to five miles; the races to begin on a Monday and end on a Friday, and no postponement to be permitted on account of the weather. As Hanlan is the originator of this idea of five races, I hope he will not now attempt to back out. Let him name his date in September, and let the races take place at Winnipeg, whose people went to great expense, in anticipation of the race to have rowed there on June 20th, only to be disappointed owing to Hanlan's absence.

"One thing I wish Hanlan and the public to understand and that is that he ran away to England without rowing me last Winter, putting up only a check to bind a race. If he ever intended to row he did not prepare himself for it, and was not fit to row within three weeks of his Atlantic voyage. He is not now to be allowed to skip off to Australia, going there as champion of the world, unless he shows that he is willing to row for that title. When Hanlan puts up $500 in cash, not a check, in the hands of some responsible party, I will cover it to bind a race, which Mr. Hanlan seems to desire, and which a great many people would be glad to see rowed."

Hanlan has signified his willingness to give Ross the race he so much desires, and there is a faint possibility that the men may come together next year. The Boston *Herald*, which is a great authority on boating, announces that if the men do not row very soon, the public will have some justification for believing that the postponements and delays are agreeable to both parties, and that neither is ready to row

a match race for the world's championship. If Hanlan has a desire to row a boat race with Ross, and will make a deposit of $500 in good hands to bind a match, he can have a race any time this Fall for $1,000 a side, over a four-mile course, to be mutually agreed upon. This statement is made substantially.

**THE HILLSDALE CREW CRITICISED.**—The London *Sportsman* says of the Hillsdale crew and a recent practice pull of the Michigan oarsmen: We "glassed" them carefully all the way from the Soap house to the creek, and their style was as irregular and defective as the subsequent row up. The row up home commenced from the aqueduct, 46 being tried the first minute, to be increased to 48 directly after. Without diminishing the latter rate of striking the crew rowed the between-bridges course, Putney and Hammersmith, but got no pace out of their boat. It taking them 1m. 58s. to reach the Creek. Admitted that the tide was sluggish, the time occupied in covering the ground was bad and could have been done by several of our scullers. The time of the oars was most irregular, and that of the men's bodies not at all in accord, the bow men appearing to work on his own account. Body swing is ignored altogether, and the pulling is left entirely to the arms, an ugly, jerky action, with no beginning or finish, the blades "catching" at right angles with the riggers, while the water displacement is very trivial. We are inclined to think that the Hillsdale themselves have seen better style with our own amateurs now practicing for Henley than they anticipated.

The aquatic editor of *Bell's Life* in London says the oarsmen of the Hillsdale crew slide indifferently, do most of their work with their arms, and, rowing 46 to 48 strokes a minute, only get pace enough on their boat (having been timed from Putney to the Creek in 1m. 58s.) to keep level with a good sculler.

**HANLAN'S RESPONSE.**—To a correspondent of the New York *Herald* Hanlan stated on the 16th inst. that his challenge had been misinterpreted. He was not in condition to row now, nor would he be this year. He had not been in a shell since his sickness. He said: "My challenge to row any five men in the world still holds good, as I only want to arrange my programme for next Summer. I will row Wallace Ross anywhere between here and New York any time next year for $5,000 a side. I don't see why Ross wants to row five races. It is ridiculous. I will row him from one to five miles, and if he beats me will row him a second race. Ross talks about my putting up money this time and not of checks. I wonder how he got on in Boston with his checks? He did not act squarely down there and dare not go back there now. I can't say if I will go to Australia before I arrange with Ross. He says I want to run there with the championship. If he is a better man he may have it. Next year I will leave my favorite element and row no more at all. He may take the forfeit money and welcome this time if I don't row. I don't know my future movements further than my trip to Detroit on the 9th of August and to Montreal same month. I will put up $500 forfeit any day to row next season, only let him arrange to row before next September. I am tired holding the trophy. You see there is a great deal of bother consequent on being champion oarsman of the world."

A FRIEND IN NEED.—One sporting journal has been found which can say a kind and complimentary word for Plaisted. The journal is the New York *Sportsman*, and in commenting on Plaisted's acceptance of Wm. Elliott's challenge it says: "Plaisted's races with Hanlan show that he is a good man, possessed of both speed and gameness, and he is one of the very few who can boast of having defeated the champion of the world, in a rowing contest. This fact has been pointed out, as many people may think, that Plaisted is not of important class enough to justify matching him against the sculling pitman of Newcastle, but the American's record shows that he is good enough to row anybody, and, furthermore, that he has a reasonable chance of proving victorious when he meets the only Englishman who was able to give Hanlan any kind of a race at all." Plaisted is in training at Massahesis Lake, near Manchester, N. H., with George Hosmer of Boston. Both men take from 10 to 15 miles of walking and rowing every day, and vary the monotony of their training by cutting grass.

ENGLISH CONSERVATISM.—Regarding the defeats of English athletes in England, and the 'newspaper comments thereon, the London *Sportsman* says: "Judging by the tone of the majority of effusions, the prevailing sentiment seems to be that our overweening confidence and exceptional pride in our own ability has largely contributed to our downfall. Now, we are not prepared to say that our critics are altogether unjustified in their accusations. Our oarsmen, we fear, for years neglected to keep such a sharp eye on the doings of rivals in other countries as might profitably have been the case. Some heard of improvements being effected in the construction of racing skiffs, and of new styles of boat propulsion being adopted. They evidently regarded these matters, however, as new-fangled notions, quite unworthy of attention, and it was not until they received a severe reminder or two that they began to imagine that their own mode of procedure might be open to a little alteration.

ROSS AND LAYCOCK.—By this time Laycock ought to be on his way to the antipodes. Some days before his intended departure was announced an interesting newspaper correspondence occurred between him and William Spencer, the latter representing Wallace Ross, and Spencer had by far the best of the argument. Laycock declined to row Ross in England, but invited the New Brunswicker to the antipodes. He wrote: "As I have to row there about the end of September for a prize of £500, it would not pay me to stop, even were Ross or his backers to make me a present of £300. In conclusion, I beg to state that, if Ross likes to pay Australia a visit, it will afford me great pleasure to give him a spin over the championship course on the Parramatta river for from £300 to £500 a side. At the same time he can row for the £500 prize given by Mr. Punch, which would be killing two birds with one stone, and if he can win the two, the trip ought to pay."

ELLIOTT AND KENNEDY.—John A. Kennedy, of Portland, has challenged William Elliott, ex-champion oarsman of England, at present living in New York, to a scullers' race, distance two or three miles, for $1,000. Elliott has replied that he will row Kennedy a four-mile race on Flushing Bay, and allow Kennedy expenses. To this proposition Kennedy answers that he will accept, provided $200 be allowed him for expenses; or he will allow Elliott $250 expenses to row in the East. The Portland sculler is now only waiting to hear from Elliott to close the match.

NAVAL OARSMEN.—A race has been arranged between the gigs of the Ranger and Alert, for the sum of $300, to come off to-day, weather permitting, at the Navy Yard, Mare Island.

SMITH ACCEPTS.—Warren Smith of Halifax, N. S., has accepted the challenge issued by William Elliott, with the understanding that the race shall be one of three miles, for $500 a side, the time and place of rowing to be here-after agreed upon. He has deposited $200 forfeit with W. L. Lowell & Co., bankers, of Halifax.

The entry of the Hillsdale crew for the Barnes and Mortlake regatta has been accepted. The Thames and London clubs are also entered.

Wallace Ross says English scullers, in preparation for their races, drink too much beer.

The champion Hanlan began his 28th year Wednesday.

## BASE BALL.

### THE OLYMPICS AND REDINGTONS.

These Clubs played a good game last Sunday at the grounds of the Olympic Club, at Oakland, and it looked at one time a certain victory for the Redingtons, they scoring seven to one at the conclusion of the fifth innings, but the Olympics batted very effectively towards the close, and won easily at last. Leman at first and Lewis at left were a valuable acquisition to the Redingtons, while with the exception of substituting Leonard for Boswell, the Olympics played their regular nine.

| OLYMPIC. | T. B. | R. | 1b. | P.O. | A. | E. |
|---|---|---|---|---|---|---|
| Sanders, p. | 1 | 2 | 2 | 3 | 8 | 0 |
| Eltner, 3d b. | 2 | 2 | 2 | 1 | 1 | 2 |
| Van Dyke, l. f. | 3 | 3 | 3 | 1 | 0 | 0 |
| Burr, 1st b. | 1 | 1 | 1 | 5 | 0 | 2 |
| Leonard, c. | 2 | 0 | 1 | 2 | 0 | 1 |
| Sumner, c. f. | 0 | 1 | 2 | 0 | 1 | 3 |
| Kelly, 2d b. | 0 | 0 | 2 | 3 | 3 | 0 |
| Barton, s. s. | 1 | 1 | 1 | 1 | 1 | 0 |
| Van Bergen, r. f. | 0 | 0 | 2 | 2 | 0 | 0 |
| **Totals** | **47** | **18** | **10** | **27** | **14** | **13** |

| REDINGTON. | T. B. | R. | 1b. | P.O. | A. | E. |
|---|---|---|---|---|---|---|
| Dillon, 2d b. | 1 | 1 | 1 | 3 | 2 | 3 |
| Ewart, l. f. | 1 | 0 | 0 | 0 | 0 | 1 |
| Lewis, 3d b. | 1 | 0 | 1 | 0 | 2 | 0 |
| Leman, 1st b. | 2 | 0 | 2 | 10 | 1 | 1 |
| Moran, p. | 3 | 0 | 2 | 0 | 12 | 2 |
| Pope, c. | 2 | 3 | 2 | 10 | 7 | 1 |
| Nolan, c. f. | 0 | 0 | 0 | 0 | 0 | 1 |
| Dickey, s. s. | 0 | 0 | 0 | 0 | 0 | 0 |
| Mullin, r. f. | 0 | 0 | 0 | 0 | 0 | 0 |
| **Totals** | **40** | **7** | **8** | **27** | **21** | **14** |

Innings ... 1 2 3 4 5 6 7 8 9
Olympics ... 1 0 0 1 0 3 5 3 —13
Redingtons ... 1 0 2 3 0 0 0 0—7

Second Base Hits—Elliott 1, Ewart 1, Lewis 1. Scorers—M. Hutton and C. S. Riggins, Jr. Umpire—W. V. White. Time of Game—Two hours, ten minutes.

THE MASQUERADE GAME.—On Sunday last, at the Recreation Grounds, there was a masquerade game between teams chosen from the Minstrels and the local clubs, and the affair drew out a large attendance. The costumes were neither very humorous or expensive, but the public was evidently amused, as but few people left before the end of the game, which was won by the Cushman side, according to the following score:

| CUSHMAN. | T. B. | R. | 1b. | P.O. | A. | E. |
|---|---|---|---|---|---|---|
| Sadler, 3d b. | 5 | 2 | 3 | 1 | 2 | 1 |
| Casey, c. s. | 5 | 2 | 1 | 0 | 1 | 8 |
| Grimshaw, c. f. | 3 | 1 | 1 | 1 | 0 | 0 |
| McCord, 2d b. | 5 | 1 | 1 | 3 | 2 | 0 |
| Creegan, l. f. | 4 | 1 | 2 | 0 | 0 | 1 |
| J. Carroll, p. | 5 | 2 | 1 | 1 | 1 | 1 |
| Larry, c. f. | 4 | 1 | 0 | 0 | 2 | 2 |
| Lawton, c. | 4 | 1 | 2 | 5 | 13 | 3 |
| Pratt, 1st b. | 5 | 1 | 2 | 11 | 0 | 0 |
| **Totals** | **40** | **12** | **13** | **27** | **20** | **6** |

| THOMPSON. | T. B. | R. | 1b. | P.O. | A. | E. |
|---|---|---|---|---|---|---|
| Keagan, p. | 5 | 1 | 2 | 1 | 7 | 0 |
| Thompson, s. s. | 4 | 1 | 1 | 0 | 0 | 2 |
| F. Carroll, c. | 5 | 1 | 1 | 1 | 1 | 1 |
| Gorman, 1st b. | 4 | 1 | 1 | 12 | 0 | 1 |
| McDonald, 3d b. | 4 | 1 | 2 | 1 | 1 | 2 |
| Mack, r. f. | 4 | 0 | 0 | 0 | 0 | 1 |
| Gagan, 2d b. | 4 | 0 | 1 | 1 | 1 | 2 |
| Ackerman, c. f. | 4 | 0 | 0 | 0 | 0 | 0 |
| Scher, l. f. | 4 | 0 | 0 | 0 | 0 | 0 |
| **Totals** | **38** | **7** | **9** | **24** | **15** | **8** |

Innings ... 1 2 3 4 5 6 7 8 9
Cushman ... 1 1 0 1 1 0 3 4 x—12
Thompson ... 1 0 1 0 0 2 3 0 0—7

Home Runs—Lawton 1. Three Base Hits—Carroll 1, Grimshaw 1. Base on Balls—Thompson 1, Sadler 1. Catches off Base on Errors—Thompson 4, Cushman 3. Passed Balls—Creegan, abt. 2 Struck Out—Thompson 9, Cushman 5. Passed Balls—F. Carroll 4. Lawton 1. Umpire—Dan Webster. Scorer—T. Malone. Time of Game—2:06.

### THE LEAGUE CHAMPIONSHIP.

The games of Saturday, July 19th, ended the third week's play of the League Clubs in July and the first week's work of the Eastern and Western Clubs in their home games together. The Providence team has done the best at home in the East, and the Clevelands in the West, as each won three games out of the four played. The Troy team lost all three of the games it played. Detroit was the least successful in the West, losing three out of the four games. Thus far in the July games the Cleveland and Chicago teams head the League Clubs with six victories each out of eight games. Buffalo is third, with six out of nine, and Providence fourth, with five out of nine, all the rest losing more games than they have won. Troy being last on the list, with only one victory out of seven games. Thirty-three games have been played up to July 15th, of which the four Western Clubs won twenty-one out of their Eastern Clubs four victories. The present race to date, Chicago heads the list by having the best percentage of victories, as the team has won twenty-seven games and lost seventeen, while Providence has won twenty-seven and lost eighteen, Detroit being third, with twenty-six victories and nineteen defeats. The defeat of the Chicago champions by the Detroit and Buffalo teams will help Providence, provided Providence can keep its own end up in the East.

| CLUBS. | Chicago. | Providence. | Detroit. | Boston. | Cleveland. | Buffalo. | Troy. | Worcester. | Games Won. |
|---|---|---|---|---|---|---|---|---|---|
| Chicago | | 4 | 6 | 4 | 5 | 4 | 4 | 4 | 27 |
| Providence | 4 | | 5 | 5 | 3 | 2 | 3 | 4 | 27 |
| Detroit | 1 | 3 | | 5 | 4 | 3 | 2 | 4 | 26 |
| Boston | 3 | 2 | 3 | | 3 | 3 | 3 | 4 | 24 |
| Cleveland | 2 | 4 | 4 | 4 | | 4 | 4 | 3 | 23 |
| Buffalo | 4 | 4 | 5 | 4 | 2 | | 2 | 4 | 22 |
| Troy | 2 | 2 | 2 | 3 | 1 | 4 | | 1 | 15 |
| Worcester | 1 | 2 | 2 | 2 | 3 | 1 | 2 | | 11 |
| Games Lost | 17 | 18 | 19 | 21 | 22 | 22 | 23 | 28 | 170 |

There are now four strong co-operative teams in New York and its vicinity, in the nines of the Atlantics of Brooklyn, the Alaskas of New York, the Domestics of Newark, and the Olympics of Paterson. A series of championship matches is shortly to be arranged between them, to be played alternately on each other's grounds, two games each.

# THE TURF.

## CLOSING OF STAKES AND PRIZES.

**On the first day of August next, the stakes of the Pacific Coast Blood-Horse Association, the Embryo Stakes and the Purses and Stakes at the California Fairs will close.**

**The advertisements in this paper will give full particulars. Do not forget the date, TUESDAY. AUGUST 1st, 1882.**

### SARATOGA RACES.

On Thursday, July 13th, at Saratoga, were decided two races that in days gone by attracted a great deal of attention, but that drew this year but a small attendance, and these were the Flash and the Alabama Stakes. The Flash Stake has been noted for the thirteen years it has been established, for the excellence of its entries and the fast time made, and among the winners were such flyers as Remorseless in 49¾ scs., Tom Bowling and Regardless in 50½ scs., the speedy Otilipa, who made the half mile in 47¾ scs., the best record; then came Faithless, Zoo Zoo, in successive years owned by P. Lorillard, and followed on the list by the Duke of Magenta, Harold and Sensation, all belonging to George Lorillard, who again took it last year with Me neuto. Owing to the conflicting elements existing between Saratoga and Long Branch, the popular colors of these gentlemen are absent this season from the Springs, and the interest in the racing is thereby greatly diminished. Thus, in the Flash Stake there were but six who faced the starters, and the betting was all between George Kenney and Henlopen, the filly being the first choice in the pools, but she was not evidently at herself, and George Kenney won a very easy race, thus adding this stake to the Hopeful and July he had already carried off at Monmouth Park.

The Flash Stakes, for two-year-olds, at $100 each, half forfeit, with $800 added, the second to save its stake; 36 subscribers; half a mile.

Dwyer Bros.' b. c. George Kenney, by Bonnie Scotland, dam Kathleen, 110 lb., carried 112 lb. ....(J. McLaughlin) 1
O. Bowie's br. f. Empress, by Narragansett, dam Maudine, 107 lb. ....(Brown) 2
Bowen & Co.' br. f. Miss Woodford, by Billet, dam Fancy Jane, 107 lb. ....(Stovall) 3
C. Reed's ch. f. Henlopen, 107 lb., carried 109 lb. ....(Brophy) 0
A. Burnam's b. c. Tocsin, 110 lb. ....(Quantrull) 0
J. A. Grinstead's ch. f. ——, by War Dance, dam Tarantella, 107 lbs. ....(Hovey) 0

Time—0:53.

Pool —Henlopen, $200; George Kenney, $150; Miss Woodford, $150; field, $75.

The Alabama Stake, for three-year-old fillies, has also been very celebrated in the annals of our turf, and among the winners may be counted Regardless, Olitipa, Merciless, Susquehanna, Ferida, Glidelia and Thora, the latter winning last year. Bonella was made a great favorite on account of her good showing in the Monmouth Oaks, won by Hiawassa; but the Dwyer Brothers sent their second string, Francesca, to make the running with Bonella, and when they were both pumped out the Belle of Runnymede came up and won easily.

The Alabama Stakes, for three-year-old fillies, at $100 each, half forfeit, with $8.0 added, the second to receive $800 out of the stakes; 51 subscribers; mile and a furlong.

Bowen & Co.'s b. f. Belle of Runnymede, by Billet, dam Fancy Jane, 113 lb. ....(Stoval) 1
C. H. Raymond's b. f. Bonella, by Bonnie Scotland, dam Dora, 113 lb. ....(Brophy) 2
G. B. Bryson's b. f. Olivia, by Ill-Used, dam Olitipa, 113 lb. ...(Walker) 3
Dwyer Bros.' b. f. Francesca, 113 lb. ....(J. McLaughlin) 0
O. Bowie's br. f. Wildfire, 113 lb. ....(Brown) 0
R. H. Owens' ch. f. Ißsie, 113 lb, carried 115 lb. ....(Murphy) 0

Time—2:08¼.

Pools—Bonella, $350; Belle of Runnymede, $320; Issie, $180; Wildfire, $120; Olivia, $75, Francesca, $30.

The next race was a purse of $600, a handicap for all ages, a mile and five hundred yards, that was won by the favorite, Belle of the Highlands, 4 yrs., 105 pds., in 2:25¼, beating Oakleaf, 4 yrs., 94 pds., second; Mamie Fields, 6 yrs., 100 pds., Nellie Peyton, 3 yrs., 85 pds., and Bounce, 5 yrs., 105 pds.

The last race was a steeplechase handicap over the short course, in which Turfman beat Judge Burnett, his only antagonist.

Friday, the 14th, was the first extra day, and although the weather was fair and the programme attractive, there was again but a poor attendance. The proceedings opening with a $350 purse for all ages, 1 mile, in which Ada Glen, 6 yrs., 103 pds., was almost equal favorite with Perplex, 3 yrs, 102 pds., the former winning in 1:50, with Lutestring, 3 yrs., 92 pds., second, and Navarro, 4 yrs., 111 pds., Wanoulla, 3 yrs., 100 pds., and Morgan Spy, 3 yrs, 92 pds., all unplaced. The favorites had been winning quite steadily for some time, but the next race was one that, in turf parlance, is called a facer to the talent. It was a purse of $600 for all ages, with penalties and allowances, a mile and five furlongs, and John Davis, on the strength of his Western performances, including the winning of the Garden City cup, was made a hot favorite at $180, although as a six-year-old he carried the steadying weight of 122 pds.; Creosote, 4 yrs., with 113 pds., Nettle, 3 yrs., 95 pds., Lizzie McWherter, 3 yrs., 81 pds., Granger, 4 yrs., 103 pds., and Ella Warfield, 5 yrs., $60 each, with $30 for Glenarm, 3 yrs., and 95 pds.; Ella Worfield cut out the running and won easily in 3:01, with Nettle second and Lizzie third. The mutual pools paid $61.70 on each five dollars invested. The next was a purse for all ages, three quarters of a mile, that was taken in 1:18¼ by Saunterer, 4 yrs., 115 pds., with Square Dance, 3 yrs., 97 pds., second; Antrim, 2 yrs., 80 pds., third, and Buccaneer, 3 yrs., 102 pds., Pearl Thorne, 2 yrs., 81 pds., Northland, 3 yrs., 102 pds., and Minnie D., 4 yrs., 106 pds, unplaced. The last was a selling purse of $350, a mile and a furlong, in which again the favorite won. Boatman, 3 yrs., entered to be sold at $1,500, with 97 pds., being first; Mamie Fields, $800, 6 yrs., 101 pds., second; Sam Ecker, $800, 6 yrs., 103 pds., third; Mandamus, $500, 3 yrs., 85 pds., Rochester, $1,000, 6 yrs., 107 pds., Linchpin, $300, 6 yrs., 93 pds., and Explorer, $500, 4 yrs., 95 pds., were unplaced. There was no bid for the winner.

Saturday, July 15th, was the famous Cup Day at Saratoga, but this year that classic event was shorn of all its interest, as it was a mere walk over for Thora. The weather was fine, but the attendance only moderate. First on the cards was a dash of six furlongs for $400, in which Saunterer, 115 pounds, proved himself to be the best horse, in 1:16¾, with Maggie Ayer, 108 pds., second, and Fellowplay, with 115 pds., third, with Pearl Thorne, Good Night, Appollo, Bonnie Lizzie, Fairview and Wapakoneta, unplaced. The cup, a dash of two miles and a quarter, was won easily by Thora in 4:05½, with Carley B. second, Alta B. third. In the selling race, a mile and a furlong, for $500, Warfield, 112 pds., was first, in 1:59¾, Churchill, 103 pds., second, Morgan Spy, 77 pds., third, Major Hughes, 94 pds., and Blumen, 93 pds., last. The hurdle handicap, a mile and a quarter, for $5·0, was won by Judge Burnett, with Turfman second, Glasgow third, with Strychnine that did not go the course.

On the 17th, there was a good day and fine track, and a large attendance. The programme of races included thirty-six entries, a large number for an extra day. For the first purse, $350, mile dash, Bootjack and Saunterer were the favorites. There was a close contest, won by Ada Glenn (115 pds.) by a head, Bootjack (115 pds.) second, four lengths in front of Jennie V. (88 pds.), third; the order of the others being: Saunterer, Minnie D., Martinique, Nellie Peyton, and Wild Fire; time, 1:42; mutuals paid $36 60. The second race, purse $500, mile and five hundred yards; had seven starters, and was won with hands down by the favorite, Warfield (117 pds.), in 2:13¼, three lengths better than Fellowplay (115 pds.), second, a length in front of Granger (108 pds.), third, followed by Square Dance, Lizzie C., McWhirter, Metropolis, and Strychnine; mutuals paid $10 80. The third race, purse $300, for 2-year-olds, five furlongs; had nine starters. Ascender (107 pds.), the favorite, won handily by three lengths, in 1:03½; Pearl Thorn (102 pds.), second, and a length better than Blue Grass Belle (97 pds.), third; the order of the others being: Standiford Keller, Hattie M., Baritone, Olivette, Patrick Dennis, and Talleyrand; time, 1:03½; mutuals paid $7 90. The fourth and last race of the day, purse $300, three-quarters of a mile; had twelve starters, with Bancroft the favorite at the start. It was a close and exciting race, won by Wapakoneta (99 pds.) by two lengths, Lutestring (100 pds.) second, and a length in front of Morgan Spy (82 pds.), third, followed home by Bancroft, Blenheim, Antrim, Mattie Rapture, Maj. Hughes, Bell Boy, Intrinsic, Explorer, and Buccaneer; time, 1:17; mutals paid $1,078 20, the largest dividend ever declared on this track, the odds being more than two hundred to one against the winner.

In the first race on July 25th, one mile, Wedding Day was first, Maggie Ayer second, and Bruno third; time, 1:4½. In the second race, three quarters of a mile, Barnes won, Kenny second; time, 1:15. In the third race, one mile and 500 yards, Ben D'Or won, Ida Glenn second; time, 2:10½. In the fourth race (hurdle), one and one-eighth miles, Raven won, Judge Burnett second; time, 2:06.

On the 18th, the first race was $500, for all ages, with penalties and allowances, a mile and a furlong, which was won by Goodnight (120 pds.) in 1:55½, Pinafore (93 pds.), Maggie Ayer (106 pds.) third, with Crickmore, Oakleaf and Carissima, unplaced. The second was the Spinaway stake for two-year-olds, a dash of five furlongs, that closed with 27 subscribers, at $100 each, $800 added, that was won by the favorite, Miss Woodford (103 pounds), in 1:03½ by a head from the filly by War Dance from Tarentella (95 pounds), Empress (100 pds.) third, and Fairwood, Tea Rose and Hollyrood, unplaced. The next was a Welter sweepstakes, $25 each (p. p.) with $500 added, in which Ben Or (149 pds.) was first in 1.45, Monogram (130 pds.) second, Navarro (146 pds.) third, with Spark, Tocsin and Liatunah, unplaced. This was a firm and stubbornly contested race, the conditions being for gentlemen riders; but, as usual, they backed out and professionals had to ride, taking up three pounds extra. The last race was a selling race, $500, a mile and a half, which was taken by Boatman (103 pds.), in 2:37½, with Mamie Fields (97 pds.), second, Katie Creel (108 pds.), third, Helen Wallace, Rochester, Churchill, Sam Ecker and Explorer, unplaced. Boatman was the favorite, and he won in fast and good style.

On the 19th the card was very meagre and afforded but poor amusement to a slight attendance. The first was a race of five furlongs and repeat for a purse of $500, which resulted in the victory of Bounce (113 pds.) in two straight heats in 1:06½ and 1:05½, Brambeletta (113 pds.), a great favorite in the pools, being second on each occasion, Northland (104 pds.), being third, with Navarro, Jim Nelson, Reardon and Intrinsic in the order mentioned. The second was a purse of $500, for all ages, a mile and three-quarters, in which Glidelia (116 pds.) was first, Spark (103 pds.) second, Compensation (105 pds.), third, and Warfield (114 pds.), last. Time, 3:12½. Then came a selling purse of $350, for all ages, one mile, which was taken by Blenheim, valued at $700 (83 pds.), in 1:47; Perplex, $1,100 (91 pds.), the favorite being second; Buccaneer, $1,000 (92 pds.), third, and Balance Wheel, $500, fourth. The last was a handicap steeplechase for $400, about a mile and a half, which resulted in a very easy victory for the favorite Turfman, with Lighthorse second, and Edison a poor last.

On July 20th, in the first race, one mile, Francis B was first, Bootjack second, and John Davis third. Time, 1:44½. In the third race, a mile and five hundred yards, Pinafore won, Laura second. Time, 2:11½. In the race for three-quarters of a mile George Kenney won, Barnes second. Time, 1:16½. In the fourth race, a steeplechase, Trouble won, Judge Burnett second. Time, 3:02½.

On July 21st, in the first race, a mile and a furlong, Jennie V, won, and Springfield was second; time 1:57. In the dash of five furlongs Ascender won, Exeter second, Faurot third; time 1:03¼. The three-quarter mile was won by Bancroft, Mamie Field second, Lutestring third; time 1:16.

On July 22d, in the first race, five furlongs, Blue Grass Belle won, Buricarian, second, Carlisle third; time 1:04. In the second race, one and one-half miles, Bootjack was first, Boatman second; time 1:54¾. In the third race, mile and five furlongs, Thora won, Frankie B. second, Sullivan third; time 1:51. In the fourth race, three-quarters of a mile, Iota won, Autumn second; time 1:16.

On July 24th, the first race, three-quarters of a mile, Square Dance won, Buccaneer second; time 1:16¾. In the second race, for a mile and 500 yards, Ada Glen won, Compensation second; time 2:11. In the third race, one mile, Rochester won, Blenheim second; time 1:43. The fourth race, steeplechase, one and a half miles, Rose won, Turfman second; time 2:52.

In the first race, on July 25th, one mile, Wedding Day was first, Maggie Ayer second and Bruno third. Time, 1:41¼. In the second race, three-quarters of a mile, Barnes won, George Kenny second. Time, 1:15. In the third race, one mile and five hundred yards, Ben d'Or won, Ada Glenn second. Time, 2:10½. In the fourth race, hurdle, one and one-eighth miles, Raven won, Judge Burnett second. Time, 2:06.

On the 26th, in the first race for five furlongs, Stande Nord was first, Charley Johnston second. Time, 1:03. In the second race, one mile, Warfield won, Little Phil second. Time, 1:41. In the third race, three-quarter mile, Wildfire won, Mandamus second. Time, 1:16¾. In the fourth race, a steeplechase, about 2¼ miles, Rose won, Postguard second. Time, 4:26½.

### THE PORTLAND RACES.

The second annual meeting of the Northwestern District Association commenced on the 19th inst. at the City View Driving Park, which is very favorably situated about three miles up the Willamette river, near Portland, Oregon. The weather was very favorable, the attendance was good, and the races gave general satisfaction. The first race was a dash of five furlongs for two-year-olds, in which Lou Spencer was a hot favorite, although she had to carry seven pounds extra, and she won very easily from Nev. Ella, Rosa May being a bad third.

City View Driving Park, July 19th.—Juvenile Stakes.—Five furlongs for two-year-olds; $400 added to a sweepstake of $50 each; colts to carry 100 pounds, fillies 97 pounds; non-thoroughbreds allowed 10 pounds; Colts and fillies brought from the East and from California since February 1, 1882, to carry 7 pounds extra.

Theodore Winters' b. f. Lou Spencer, by Norfolk, dam Ballerina ....1
R. E. Bybee's b. f. Nev. Ella, by California dam Laura Barnes, 97 lbs ....2
W. G. Scoggin's ch. f. Rosa May, by Napa, dam Rosa Rogers, 87 lbs ....3

Time—1:05½.

The next race created a great deal of interest, as it was a contest between the get of noted Oregon stallions, and again the favorite won easily, this time in two straight heats, the trot for second money being well fought out.

Same Day.—The Kisber Stakes for three-year-olds raised in Oregon or the Territories of Washington or Idaho; two in three; purse, $750; $500 to first, $250 to second.

| | | |
|---|---|---|
| L. P. W. Quimby's Blackhawk, by Rockwood, dam Nelly | 1 | 1 |
| E. J. Jeffery's br. f. Edna J., by Kisber, dam Fly-by-Night and Morgan | 2 | 2 |
| S. S. Cook's bl. g. Charles Albert, by Ben Franklin, dam Kitty Brimus and Stranger | 3 | 3 |
| Jay Beach's b. c. Zilophone, by Altamont, dam Nellie Price, by Doble | dis. | |

Time—2:59½, 3:00.

On the 20th there were three races on the card. The first for the 2:40 class eliciting a good deal of unfavorable comment, not solely on account that the favorite, Maggie Arnold, was beaten, but there was some curious driving, Misner being fined $25 for foul driving, and Stranger being set back for running.

City View Driving Park, July 21st.—Trotting.—2:40 class; purse, $400; $150 to second horse.

| | | | | | |
|---|---|---|---|---|---|
| H. S. Hogoboom's br m. Walla Walla Maid, 5, by Millman's Bell-founder, dam Grey Eagle | 2 | 2 | 1 | 1 | 1 |
| Jay Beach's br. m. Maggie Arnold, aged, by Almont Mambrino, dam Alice Drake | 3 | 1 | 2 | 0 | 2 |
| Misner Bros.' b. g. Stranger, aged, by Signal, dam by George M. Patchen | 1 | 3 | 3 | 0 | 3 |

Time—2:40, 2:38, 2:39, 2:39, 2:39½.

The next race was a dash of a mile and a quarter, in which Fred Collier and Joe Howell at $60 and $40, with $20 for the other two horses combined. At about these prices there was a great deal of betting, the Oregonians backing their flyers, while large amounts were placed on the California horses. Fred was in fine condition and scored an easy victory over his opponents.

Same Day.—Running.—Mile and a quarter. Purse, $400; $100 to second horse.

Stemlar & Ayres' ch. g. Collier, 4, by Joe Hooker, dam Puss ....1
Mulkey & Marsh's b. g. Joe Howell, a, by Bonnie Scotland, dam Etta Shippen ....2
W. G. Scoggin's br. h. Jim Merritt, 5, by Langford, dam Sweetwater, by Volcano ....3
J. A. Porter's br. m. Caddie R., 7, by Bayswater, dam Sally Wallace ....4

Time—2:12.

The last race was a half-mile handicap, in which Jim Renwick, the favorite, showed that he had lost none of his speed, for he won after a grand rush with the two mares.

Same Day.—Half Mile Handicap. Purse, $300; $90 to second horse.

Stemlar & Ayers' ch. g. Jim Renwick, by Hooker, dam Big Gun, by Old George, 4, 109 lbs ....1
Judge Hamilton's br. m. Blue Mountain Belle, 7, by Napa, 104 lbs ....2
Mulkey & Marsh's s. m. Premium, aged, by Caster, dam Flying Cloud, 115 lbs ....3
Foster Bros.' s. m. Lulu Riggs, by Humboldt, dam the mother of Crooked River, 106 lbs ....4
W. Hefner's b. g. Honest John, aged, by Dr. Lindsey, dam Dasher ....5
W. R. Johnson's ch. g. Tallago, aged, by a son of Dr. Lindsey ....6

Time—0:48½.

On the 21st there was not so large a crowd present as might have been expected, although the withdrawal of Stranger from the trot, and the certainty almost that Maggie Arnold would win, might easily account for the diminished attendance. The first race was very well contested until the finish, and was certainly the most exciting one of the meeting, the mare losing the deciding heat through leaving her feet at a critical moment.

City View Park, July 21.—Purse $400, for 2:50 class.

| | | | | | |
|---|---|---|---|---|---|
| P. J. Martin's ch. h. Gen. Crook | 2 | 1 | 1 | 2 | 1 |
| J. Beach's br. f. Maggie Arnold | 1 | 2 | 2 | 1 | 2 |

Time—2:41, 2:35, 2:41½, 2:42¾, 2:40½.

The second race was a dash of two miles, that appeared almost as a walk over for Fred Collier, who looked in the finest fettle.

Same Day.—Purse $600; a dash of two miles.

Wm. Ayer's ch. g. Fred Collier, by Hooker, dam by Norfolk, 4 yrs. 1
C. Mulkey's b. g. Joe Howell, aged ....2
G. R. Buchanan's ch. m. Trade Dollar, aged ....3

THE PORTLAND RACES.—At the City View Park races, July 25th, the trotting race for the 2:30 class was won by Milton Medium, in three straight heats, Dexter second, Derigo distanced; time 2:29½, 2:27, 2:25¼. The last heat was the fastest ever trotted in Oregon. The mile and repeat was won by Joe Howell, Fred Collier second, Caddie R. third; time 1:46½, 1:45¾. The three-quarter dash was won by Jim Renwick, Premium second; time 1:16½. These races closed the meeting, which was in every way successful.

### MONMOUTH PARK RACES.

The intervening season was continued on July 20th, with the following results: The first race, three-quarter mile, Bedouin won; time, 1:16¼. In the three-quarter mile for two-year-olds, Maiden Bell was first, Fan Fan, colt, second, Magnate, third; time, 1:17½. In the one-mile dash Mary Anderson was first, Corsair second, Sweet Home third; time, 1:44. The Mutuals paid $96. In the mile and a quarter, Adla was first, Giroffla second, Hilarity third; time, 2:13¼. In the mile and a furlong Hospodar and Marathon started, and the former won; time, 1:58. In the hurdle race, one mile and a half, Felix was first, Kitty Clark second, Bernardine third; time, 2:51¼.

On the 22d the first race, a mile, Parole won; Clara D, second; time, 1:43¾. In the second race, three-quarters of a mile, Bella won; Woodblower second, La Petit Duc third; time, 1:16¾. In the third race, one and one-quarter miles, Jack-of-Hearts won, Griddle second, Alaska third; time, 2:11. In the fourth race, three-quarters of a mile, Fair Count won; Monitor second, Mallz third; time, 3:06½. In the fifth race, three-fourths of a mile, Constantine won; Sir Hugh second, Memento third; time, 1:16. In the sixth race, seven-eighths of a mile, Hospadore won; Vampire second, Victory third; time, 1:33. In the seventh race, a hurdle race, one and one-fourth miles, Kittie Clark won; Frank Short second, Joe Hunt third; time, 2:22¾.

On the 26th, the optional stakes, three-quarters of a mile, Disdain won; time, 1:16. The mile-and-a-quarter race Girofle won; Bye-and-Bye second, Clare D third; time, 2:11¼. The Neversink handicap, one mile and a half, Monitor won, Eole second; time, 2:37½. The mile-and-an-eighth race, Marathon won; time, 1:57⅛. The steeple-chase over the short course, Ingomar won; time, 3:12½. At the conclusion of the races James E. Kelly, bookmaker, made a complaint that Walton, "the plunger," had caused the pulling of Marathon in the Hospodar-Marathon race on Wednesday. Walton indignantly denied the charge. The matter will be investigated. The rider of Marathon denies that any improper means were used to cause the defeat of Marathon.

A dispatch from Saratoga states that Runnymede broke down hopelessly, having broken a tendon in the hind leg. Runnymede is by Billet, from Mercedes, and was the most promising three-year-old of the season. Unfortunately, he had a great many engagements in all the principal races, and meeting many with whom he was pretty evenly matched, finally he was run off his legs, and the turf loses an excellent horse.

At the Woodbine Park, Toronto, a match was run on the 14th inst. for $200 a side, between Mr. Wilson's b. g. Jonathan Scott, by Harry Bassett, from Adeline Carter, and Sheppard Brother's b. m. La Belle, by Reveller, dam unknown, and the former won by a length in 1:47¾.

# THE TRACK.

### CLOSING OF STAKES AND PURSES.

**On the first day of August next, the Stakes of the Pacific Coast Blood-Horse Association, the Embryo Stakes and the purses and stakes at the California Fairs will close.**

**The advertisements in this paper will give the particulars. Do not forget the date, TUESDAY, AUGUST 1st, 1882.**

### FIXED EVENTS.

Santa Cruz County Fair Association. First annual meeting at Santa Cruz, Aug 15th. 16th, 17th and 18th.

Sonoma County Park Association, at Santa Rosa, Aug. 22d, 23d, 24th, 25th and 26th.

Sonoma and Marin Agricultural Societies. Annual Fair at Petaluma, Aug 29th and four following days.

Golden Gate Fair, to be held at Oakland, from September 4th to the 9th inclusive.

Butte District Fair at Chico, from September 5th to September 8th, inclusive.

El Dorado District Fair at Placerville, from September 5th to September 8th, inclusive.

California State Fair. Annual meeting at Sacramento, from Monday, September 11th to the 16th inclusive.

The San Joaquin Valley Association Fair at Stockton, from September 19th to the 23d inclusive.

Oregon State Fair at Salem, from September 18th and during the week.

The San Mateo and Santa Clara County Agricultural Association Fair at San Jose, September 25th to the 30th inclusive.

Humboldt and Mendocino District Fair at Rhonerville, September 19th to September 22d, inclusive.

Modoc, Plumas and Lassen District Fair at Greenville, from October 2d to October 5th, inclusive.

Monterey District Fair at Salinas City, from October 2d to October 6th, inclusive.

Mount Shasta Agricultural Association Fair at Yreka, October 4th, 5th, 6th and 7th.

Eastern Oregon Fine Stock Association at Union, from October 9th to the 14th inclusive.

#### FAIRS AT THE EAST.

Kentucky State Fair at Lexington, August 9th to September 2d inclusive.

Minnesota State Fair at Farmington, August 31st to September 8th inclusive.

Iowa State Fair at Fairfield, September 1st to the 8th inclusive.

Minnesota Agricultural Association, at Minneapolis, September 4th to the 9th inclusive.

Nebraska State Fair, at Omaha, September 11th until the 16th inclusive.

Rhode Island State Fair, at Providence, September 12th to the 15th inclusive.

Pennsylvania State Fair, at Pittsburg, September 7th to the 21st inclusive.

Wisconsin State Fair, at Fond du lac, September 11th to the 16th inclusive.

Ontario Provincial Fair, at Toronto, September 18th to the 23d inclusive.

Connecticut State Fair, at Meriden, September 18th to the 22d inclusive.

New Jersey State Fair, at Monroe, September 18th to the 22d inclusive.

West Virginia Central Fair, at Clarksburg, September 19th to the 21st inclusive.

Indiana State Fair, at Indianapolis, September 25th to the 30th inclusive.

Western Michigan Fair, at Grand Rapids, September 25th to the 30th inclusive.

Texas State Fair, at Austin, October 17th to the 21st inclusive.

### CHICAGO TROTTING MEETING.

Thursday, July 20th, was the fifth day of the meeting. The weather was cloudy and cool and the track fast. The first race was the 2:25 pacing class, for a purse of $2,000, with $500 extra to beat 2:15. Flora Bell, the favorite, won without difficulty. Flora Bell 1, Winder 2, Princess 3, Joe Bowers 4, Keno distanced, Wonderful distanced. Time, 2:19¾—2:18—2:22—2:18¼. The second race was the 2:19 class, for a purse of $2,500, with $500 extra to beat 2:16. Clingstone was the hot favorite, and won without urging, the general opinion being that he could have beaten 2:16 if driven for it. Fanny Witherspoon was a good second in every heat, and in the first lapped Clingstone out to the shoulders. Clingstone 1, Fanny Witherspoon 2, Driver 3, Annie 4, J. B. Thomas 5. Time, 2:17—2:18—2:20. The third race was the 2:40 class, for a purse of $2,000, with $500 extra to beat 2:25. Neta Medium was the favorite, but owing to rumors as to the speed of Golden Rule and Douglas, the judges suspected that they were not being driven to win, so after the second heat a new driver was put up behind Golden Rule and Douglas' driver was cautioned. It was a very close race throughout, none of the finishes being more than a length. In the third heat the five horses came under the wire so close together that not more than a length separated the first and the last. Neta Medium 1, Lilian 2, Golden Rule 3, Douglas 4, Florence M 5, Logan B distanced. Time, 2:22¾—2:22½—2:26¼.

On the sixth day of the meeting the weather was clear and warm with a light breeze blowing across the quarter stretch. The track was fast. There were only two events and both were won in straight heats with great ease. The first race was the 2:25 class, stallions, purse $2,500, with $500 extra to beat 2:20. Fred Douglas won, Corbin's Bassaw second, Little Billy third, Abdallah Boy fourth, Red Cross fifth. Time, 2:20¼—2:23—2:21¼. The second race was the 2:17 class, for a purse of $2,500, with $500 extra to beat 2:14. So So was the favorite before the race was started, but Edwin Thorne was never headed in either heat, Kate Sprague second, So So third. Time, 2:16½—2:20—2:21.

Saturday was an extra day that brought the meeting to a close. The weather was bright and warm, with no wind. The track was fast and the attendance good. The first race, sweepstakes $250 each, with $1,000 added by the Association, was won by Croxie with ease. Croxie 1, Overman 2, Abe Downing 3, King William 4. Time, 2:28—2:22¼—2:25.

Second race, Stallion sweepstakes, $250 each, with $1,000 added by the Association. Monroe Chief was the favorite, Scott's Thomas being second choice. The race was short and sharp. Black Cloud showed himself a very speedy horse, getting a record surpassed by but one stallion in the country. In the last heat Monroe Chief was lapped on the winner, showing he had lost none of his speed, for he certainly beat his record of 2:18¼. In point of sustained speed for three heats it was one of the best stallion races in the history of the trotting turf. Black Cloud 1, Monroe Chief 2, Scott's Thomas 3. Time, 2:19—2:18¾—2:17¼.

Third race, three minute class, purse of $1,000, Jim Bowman, 1, 1; Reel, 3, 4, 2; Billy R, 5, 2, 3; The Sheppard, 2, 5, 5; Henderson, 4, 3, 4. Time, 2:30½—2:30¼—2:29½. Jim Bowman was bought during the race by Budd Doble for $3,000.

### PITTSBURG RACES.

Continuing from our last issue we find that on the 13th there was a couple of very interesting races that elicited much enthusiasm among the crowd of spectators who were attracted to the grounds.

Homewood Park.—Purse $1,500, for the 2:23 class.

| | | | | | |
|---|---|---|---|---|---|
| B. G. Gonover's b. m. Adele Gould | 3 | 2 | 1 | 1 | 1 |
| Robt. Steel's b. m. Neta Medium | 1 | 1 | 3 | 2 | 2 |
| W. P. Maxwell's gr. g. Big Ike | 4 | 4 | 2 | 3 | 3 |
| A. Goldsmith's b. g. Barrett, by Chester Chf. | 2 | 5 | 4 | 4 | 5 |
| H. P. Wade's b. h. Reveille | 5 | 3 | 6 | 6 | 6 |
| H. Daws' b. h. Lookout, jr. | 7 | 7 | 7 | 5 | 4 |
| G. W. Saunders' b. g. Tom B | 6 | 6 | 5 | 7 | 7 |

Time—2:25¼, 2:23¼, 2:21, 2:23¼, 2:24.

Same Day.—Purse $1,500, for the 2:26 class.

| | | | | | |
|---|---|---|---|---|---|
| R. P. Stetson's b. g. R. P | 1 | 1 | 4 | 2 | 1 |
| W. A. Forth's blk. g. Dick Organ | 3 | 4 | 1 | 1 | 2 |
| H. Daws' ch. m. Clara J | 2 | 2 | 2 | 5 | 3 |
| John Call's b. m. Mollie Kistler | 6 | 3 | 3 | 3 | 4 |
| John Splan's ch. m. Belle of Lexington | 5 | 6 | 6 | 4 | 5 |
| C. H. Stile's gr. m. Tola | 4 | 5 | 5 | 6 | dr. |
| D. F. Bowman's br. m. Sue Grundy | 7 | 7 | dr. | | |

Time—2:23¾, 2:24¾, 2:25¾, 2:26, 2:25.

On July 14th the last day of the summer meeting at the Homewood Driving Park attracted a good crowd. The weather was variable, rain falling a portion of the time, which made the track heavy. In the first race there was nothing especially interesting, but the pacing race was hotly contested and very exciting.

The first race, 2:20, was for a purse of $2,000, as follows:

| | | | |
|---|---|---|---|
| Early Rose | 1 | 1 | 1 |
| Driver | 2 | 2 | 3 |
| William H. | 3 | 3 | 2 |
| Leontine | 4 | 4 | 4 |

Time—2:21¼, 2:23¼, 2:22.

Early Rose is one of the sensations of the season. She is by Almont, and is owned by J. Elliott, a vegetable dealer in Philadelphia, and was bought by him near Lexington, Kentucky, in 1879, as a four-year-old, for $400. In 1880 she trotted in 2:35, last season her time was 2:25, and now she can cut under 2:20 with ease. She is valued at $20,000.

The second race, 2:35 class (pacing), was for a purse of $1,000, as follows:

| | | | | | | |
|---|---|---|---|---|---|---|
| Bay Jim | 3 | 4 | 2 | 1 | 1 | 1 |
| Princess | 4 | 1 | 1 | 3 | 2 | 2 |
| Felix | 1 | 2 | 7 | 3 | 3 | 3 |
| Eddie D. | 2 | 3 | 6 | 7 | 6 | r. |
| Rostraver | 5 | 7 | 4 | 5 | 5 | r. d. |
| Capt. Jack | 6 | 6 | 5 | 4 | 4 | r. d. |
| Estella | 7 | 5 | 3 | 6 | | dr. |

Time—2:24¼, 2:23¼, 2:20¼, 2:21¼, 2:27¼, 2:29.

### CLEVELAND RACES.

The twelfth annual meeting of the Cleveland Club began July 25th. It was bright and warm, an excellent track, and there was a good attendance. In the 2:38 trot, purse of $1,500, Wilson won, Rockton second, May Thorne third. Time, 2:22½, 2:24¼, 2:25¼. In the 2:23 trot, purse of $2,000, Jerome Eddy won, Mattie Graham second, Unolala third, Minnie K. fourth. Time, 2:19, 2:18, 2:19.

On the second day there was a large attendance, a fast track and fair weather, varied with slight showers. In the 2:25, pacers' purse, for $1,000, Warrior and Mattie Bond were favorites. Joe Bowers won; Fuller second. Warrior, Princess, Reno, Estella and Mattie Bond also paced and gained positions in the order named. Time, 2:17½, 2:18, 2:19¾, 2:20¼. In the 2:29 trotting purse for $1,500, Big Ike and Owen Hickok's Overman were favorites. Six heats were trotted, London winning the first, second and last; Overman the fourth and fifth, and Kate Taylor the third, Willis Wood, Big Ike and Dick Organ were ruled out, and Largess was drawn. Time, 2:20½, 2:21¾, 2:23¾, 2:24½, 2:25, 2:27¾. The free-for-all pacing purse was unfinished. Buffalo Girl was the favorite before the start. Mattie Hunter took the first and second and the third heats. Time, 2:18½, 2:17, 2:20¾.

As a sequel to the big poker game at Newburg, N. Y., in which Mr. Weed lost $150,000, Judge Fullerton of New York, and Mr. Trude of Chicago, on the 19th inst., acting for Mr. Weed, attached the stable of M. M. Hedges, who won the money from Weed. The stable consists of the horses J. B. Thomas, St. Remo, Bay Billy and Novelty, and is valued at $15,000. A bond was furnished by friends at the Driving Park. Scott, Hedges' partner in the game, was also taken into custody, although sick at the Briggs House.

Harvard University has established a professorship of veterinary medicine, in connection with the medical school. An animal hospital will soon be established. Two veterinary schools exist in New York and two in Canada, and are well patronized. The college has been influenced in part to take this new course by the fact of the great increase of the number of horses used both for laboring and pleasure purposes, and by the fact that so large a portion of the country's export consists of cattle and meats.

At the Rochester (N. Y.) Driving Park on the 17th inst., W. H. Brown drove Colonel Pearson's team, St. Cloud and Valley Chief, one mile in 2:22¾. The trial was timed by the watches of five prominent horsemen.

We are sorry to hear from Chicago that St. Julien has a bad leg and is under the care of a veterinary surgeon, who has caused him to be thrown out of training, but it is to be hoped that he will yet be able to trot this Fall, and thus recoup in a small degree for the heavy loss made through his non-appearance in the grand circuit. It appears now an open question between Clingstone, Trinkett, Edwin Thorne and Black Cloud for supremacy on the turf.

After the team rivalry come naturally the four-in-hand tests, and last Tuesday, at Cleveland, Ohio, W. J. Gordon's team trotted against the best record, 2:56¼, and in the first heat made 2:56, and in the second 2:48. The English will not feel jealous of this performance, as with their stage coaches the coachman prefers a good three-mile gallop to vary the monotony of the drive.

# THE PADDOCK.

Property of James Mee, of San Francisco:

Jan. 10th, 1882.—Mischief, chestnut filly, by Thad. Stevens, from Katy Pease, by Planet.

March 11th, 1882—Mistake, chestnut filly, by Thad. Stevens, from Mistletoe, she by Wild-Idle, from Katy Pease.

Both these mares have been bred to Wheatley this season.

### A DEER HUNT.

Editor Breeder and Sportsman — Dear Sir: A few weeks ago I received an invitation from an old friend to spend a few days at his home in Marin county. As I needed a little recreation, it did not take me long to make the few preparations necessary for a trip to the country. Saturday afternoon found me, with my gun and gamebag, on the San Rafael ferry boat skimming over the muddy waters of the bay toward the blue hills that loom up against the western sky back of the town of San Rafael. As I stepped off the boat I was greeted with the outstretched hand and hearty welcome of my friend, Frank DeLong, who, knowing my love for hunting, promised me, even before we reached the wagon, all the fun I could wish for in that line. In a few hours' easy travel we arrived at the house, and after supper we sat down and talked of old times as well as the topics of the day. My friend's place is known as the Novato Ranch. This ranch is well watered and contains several hundred acres. It is situated about thirteen miles from the town of San Rafael. Mr. DeLong showed his good taste in selecting this place for a home.

Of course a deer hunt was the first thing on the programme, so early next morning, with my rifle on my shoulder and high hopes of pleasure and sport, I started out, accompanied by a young gentleman named DeFreege, who, by the way, is a fine huntsman. As Mr. DeLong was harvesting, we did not have the pleasure of his company. We struck across the hills to a spring, about three miles from the house, where my companion said that deer were in the habit of coming to water. On arriving at the spring, as we could find no fresh deer tracks, we concluded that the deer had not come to drink yet; so we secreted ourselves in a clump of bushes, about forty yards from the stream. We had not waited more than a quarter of an hour before the breaking of a dry twig on the other side of the spring caught our ears, and which, I acknowledge, made my heart beat faster. We waited a minute longer when the noise was repeated; and presently a large buck—a perfect beauty—pushed his way through the brush that grew on the edge of the opening around the water. Cautiously we raised our rifles, took a "dead center" sight at his head, and waited for him to come closer. Hardly had he advanced five steps toward us when a doe and her pretty young fawn joined him, and together they came to drink. "Shoot only at the buck," whispered DeFreege. I nodded. "Ready?" "Yes." Two sharp rifle reports rang out as one. The doe and fawn sprang across the opening and bounded away to the hills, but the buck lay at the water's edge pierced by our two "leaden messengers of death." He was a big fellow, and in fine condition.

The rest of the day I amused myself by driving several game poachers off from the Novato tract. These poachers insist not only on breaking the State Game Laws by killing doe and fawns, but also in infringing on the personal rights of the land-owners who have forbidden them to hunt on their premises.

The next morning we shot and crippled a buck, that gave us a merry chase over rocky hills and brushy cañons before we succeeded in bringing him down. In the evening I killed a plump little buck, which made the second; and on the final day of my visit, the eve of the first of July, when the Game Law regarding the killing of bucks goes into effect, I resolved to have one more hunt.

Mr. DeLong, DeFreege and myself tramped over the ranch for several hours without getting a shot, for, though we saw half a dozen or more, we could not get within distance of them. The wildness of these animals was owing, no doubt, to the fact that the trespassers before alluded to had hunted many of them down with hounds. Late in the afternoon I brought down a fine buck, and considered myself fortunate in doing so, as he was at a greater distance than any I had shot at before while on this expedition. This made the fourth deer that I had shot in three days.

The second of July, with a good supply of deer meat for my friends in the city, I bade "good bye" to my friend and host, and returned once more to 'Frisco, in time to take part in the dusty 4th of July procession. I shall retain the memory of the pleasure I had on Frank DeLong's ranch for many a day. Yours, respectfully, H. H.

*The Tuolumne Independent* states that a monster grizzley bear was shot last week, at Jo. Lord's place, above Lake Elnor, by his son, Wm. J. The bear was not captured, as he ran down a steep, rocky cañon, where it was impolitic for the hunter to follow. The old fellow must have been shot through and through the body, as every jump he made down the declivity the blood spurted out on either side. Lord said he was as big as a mule—and the Lord is above prevarication. Two cinnamon or brown bears have also been killed by the same party this Spring.

## THE HORSES IN TRAINING AT SACRAMENTO.

SACRAMENTO, July 26th, 1882.

EDITOR BREEDER AND SPORTSMAN: Having just returned from a delightful drive down the Riverside road, I feel somewhat imbued with a desire to write you a few lines respecting the horses in training here and their condition. No one but a Sacramentan, who has enjoyed a drive on the Riverside at times when it was enjoyable, can imagine the pleasure it is after dinner to light a fine cigar and jog down behind an animal that has a record of 2:35. Such was my privilege this evening. One of Sacramento's redeeming features are her evenings; no matter if the mercury has touched 95 degrees during the day, the delightful trade wind up the valley from the South is almost sure to be felt after old Sol has disappeared under the western horizon—then one can "cool out" as nicely as though he was "rubbed" and "walked." It is the custom among gentlemen here who have roadsters—and they are quite plentiful—to drive about six, then a pleasant jog down to Nick Doles at the end of the road—a game or two of shuffle-board beneath the sweet-scented locust trees, with a cool breeze sighing through them—refreshes one abundantly; by the time the games are ended, the moon is well up; then comes the "brush" home. I know of no one who can enjoy such pleasure better than your humble servant, unless it is you. Were you here, I would willingly relinquish my place when invited to you, and you would have a chance to guess the best one on a home brush. Should any of your friends express a desire to bring a roadster along this Fall for the purpose of speeding, be sure to advise them to come with their best, as it will require one that can pull a buggy in .40 to beat either Hamilton, Caswell, Wachhorst, Locke, Arnold, McNasser, Wilson, or Taylor home. Well, we have enjoyed our ride; now to business. I know your readers will be more interested in the following than that which has preceded.

At the Park everything looks well; the track is in the best condition—so expressed by those who, I might say, almost live upon it. The number of runners at work is thirty-four, and I can assure you one requires assistance if he wishes to "catch" all of them. Their cooling-out places are stationed at almost every eighth post, and the scene from 4 o'clock until ten is a busy one. Theo. Winters has returned and brought out a new trainer, Dudley Allen of Lexington, Kentucky. He is a colored one, of the new school, and seems to understand his business.

We noticed him at work with the two year olds and observed that he did not run them "against the watch," but gave them such preparatory work as will not injure their muscles, but still at the same time harden their flesh. He was engaged by Mr. Winters at Chicago. Having just left the employ of Mr. Robt. Johnson of Lexington, he is highly recommended by such men as Jno. Clay of Kentucky, in whose service he was five years. He expresses himself well pleased with our country and says he has come here to stay. He is agreeably surprised at our race horses, which he thinks are "as good as any body's horses;" and the track is pronounced by him to be the "best in America." He is well satisfied with Mr. Winters' stable, and thinks after having felt of them he will land one or two at the front. The following is a list of the race horses that are receiving their work here.

JIM DOUGLASS—Bay stallion, by Wild Idle, dam full sister to Tom Atchison, owned by Densdale and Howson; in the stable of Geo. Howson. In his past performances he has achieved success, as will be seen by the following record: In his two year old form he ran two races winning one. In his three year old form he ran sixteen faces winning eleven. Thus it will be seen that during his short career he has run eighteen races winning twelve. He is now four years old, sixteen hands and one-quarter in highth, and weighs about 1,100. The past season was his first in the stud; the number of mares served was 24, and he came out apparently none the worse for it. His best performance, notwithstanding his many good ones, George thinks was his one and one-eighth mile run in San Francisco in his three year old form, with 104 pounds up, which he ran in 1:55½. He is looking fine and taking his work well.

AUGUSTA E.—Brown filly, by Monday, dam same as Jim Douglass—owned and trained by Geo. Howson. She is only two years old. Her maiden rece was run during the meeting of the Capital Turf Club this Spring, at Sacramento, in which she defeated Clara W., one-half mile, in .51½ and five-eighths in 1:07. She is about 15-3, weighs about 950, and is a very promising filly.

JUDGE MCKINSTRY—Beautiful bay, by Thad Stevens or Grinstead. We might as well state right here that there is no doubt in our mind but that his sire is Grinstead. His form, color and head show Grinstead plainly. His dam is the speedy little queen Katie Pease, this being her third colt, and the first one that has ever been trained. Her first colt was by Joe Daniels, and being injured while a suckling it was found necessary to destroy it. Her second colt was by Wild Idle, a filly, and for some reason was never trained. Her last colt, at present by her side, is by Thad Stevens, whom it favors in form, and in color the mare. Judge McKinstry, as well as his dam and colts mentioned is the property of Judge Mee, and is being handled by Mr. Matthew Storns. He is a powerful built horse, three years old, stands about 15-2, will weigh 950. He is deceiving in that respect as he is "low on the ground." We have seen him in his work and he resembles old Grinstead in every particular. He is entered in the Breeders' Stake, to be run at the State Fair of 1882, which stake amounts to $1,250, with such horses as the Duchess, Maria F., Frank Rhoads, Duke of Monday and Idler. Mr. Storns takes great pride in showing him, and thinks he will be able to start a race horse this Fall. The Judge's stable companion is the small Scotch terrier "Aleck," who curls up and goes to sleep as comfortably on the Judge's back as in his kennel.

MARION—Bright bay filly, by Hubbard, dam Electra, she being full sister to Warwick and half sister to Winnifred—owned by J. B. Chase of San Francisco. She is a very handsome two-year-old, and, as will be observed, is bred for a runner. She will probably run her maiden race this Fall.

LADY CLARE—A ch. filly, by Joe Daniels, dam by Owen Dale, g. d. Bonnie Bell, by Belmont—owned by J. B. Chase of San Francisco. She is three years old, 15½ hands high, will weigh 900 lbs. In form she resembles her sire, in color her dam. She is a strong, compact built filly, and if she does not show speed when turned loose we will be deceived. She is entered in the Winters Stake, to be run this Fall.

LAURA—Ch. filly, by Shannon, dam Folly, by Planet—owned by J. B. Chase. She is a handsome two-year-old. Her maiden race was run this Spring over the Bay District with Gano, Lucky B., and eleven others. Although last to get off, she finished well up in the bunch. It is said she has shown a half better than 50 seconds. She will be started with a few fast ones this Fall, when we will be able to witness her performance.

EBONY—Black gelding, by Shannon, dam Velveteen, by Lodi—owned by Dr. Taliferro. He is four years old, ran second in the Gentleman's race this Spring. The above are trained by Mat. Storn.

FRANK RHOADS—Bay stallion, by Leinster, dam Addie A.—owned by W. L. Pritchard, trained by Willis Hull. He is four years old, a short, pony-built horse, will weigh about 900; has run two races, one in his two-year and one in his three-year old form. He, with the others belonging to Mr. Pritchard, wintered in Nevada, and when brought over last May was very high in flesh. Mr. Hull is steadily working on them, and hopes to be among the winners this Fall.

CAPT. KIDD—Bay stallion, by Leinster, dam Tibbie Dunbar, by Bonnie Scotland. He is also owned by Mr. Pritchard and worked by Mr. Hull. He is three years old, and will start in the Breeders' Stake this Fall, which is 1½ miles, and just about his distance.

LIZZIE P.—By filly, full sister to Rhoads—owned by Mr. Pritchard; in the stable of Mr. Hull. She is built exactly opposite in form to Rhoads, being longer and more rangy. She is three years old, ran at Oakland in 1881, in her two-year-old form, beating Maria F., Winnifred, Rosemary and Belle S. She will probably meet some of them again this Fall. She is in fine form and taking her work with ease.

CY MULKEY—Bay stallion, by Leinster, dam Irene Harding—owned by W. L. Pritchard, being trained by Mr. Hull. He is three years old; a very promising colt; will run his first race this Fall; well bred, and should make a racehorse.

VILA RANDLETT—Gray filly, by Waterford, dam Little Sophie—owned by Pritchard, worked by Hull. She is four years old, has run one race at Oakland, in which she failed to get a place. She will probably show some good ones her heels this Fall.

SORREL FILLY—By Leinster, dam Lotta Lee—owned and worked by same parties. She is a fine, large, good gaited filly, shows considerable speed, and will be entered through the circuit. Mr. Hull has also in training two two-year-olds that he says will not be slow.

JIM BROWN—Ch. stallion, by Foster, dam Flush, by Hiawatha—owned by Geo. Hearst, in the stable of Mr. Thos. Delaney, who has just returned from Salt Lake. He tells many funny stories about his exploits there, but is perfectly willing to return, as he believes there is no place like California. Jim Brown is four years old, has run nine races, winning five. His best race was at Sacramento last Fall, when he beat Fred. Collier 1½ miles, with 110 up, in 2:36¾. Delaney says he will fetch him up all right, and that he will be as good if not better than ever he was.

NUBIA—Brown filly, by Leinster, dam Addie A., by Asteroid—owned by J. B. Haggin; being worked by Thos. Delaney. She is two years old, ran her maiden race this Spring.

IRENE—Chestnut filly, by Leinster, dam Irene Harding—owned by J. B. Haggin; in charge of Mr. Delaney. Two years old. Will run her first race this Fall.

YOUNG FLUSH—Dark chestnut, by Leinster, dam Flush—owned by J. B. Haggin; trained by Thomas Delaney. Two years old. Has never run. She is a handsome filly. Is bred right, and should be a fast one.

SOPHIE—Light chestnut filly, by Bazaar, dam Sophie Jennison—owned by J. B. Haggin, worked by Delaney. She is two years old. Ran her first race this Spring. Unplaced

MY LOVE—Brown yearling filly, by Virgil, dam Lightfoot, by Lexington. This is one of the yearlings purchased by Mr. Haggin at the Swigert sale this Spring. Also, a bay colt, by imported Billet, grand dam Leon. These are being carefully handled by Mr. Delaney. We would say that Maria F., Red Boy, Pearl Jennings, Wildmoor, and a couple of fast two-year-olds, are expected to arrive soon. They have engaged stalls at the Park, and will prove quite an addition to the turf of California. They are at present quartered at Salt Lake City, where they have had engagements during the last meeting there.

MAY D.—Chestnut filly, by Shannon, dam Jessie R.—owned by Put Robson; in the stable of Frank De Peyster, who is doing well with her. She is but two years old, and showed up very fine at the Spring meeting.

SISTER TO LOTTERY—Bay, by Monday, dam Virginia—owned by Henry Schwartz, of San Francisco; in the stable of Frank De Peyster. She is three years old, and is doing nicely.

LADY PARTISAN—Bay filly, by imported Partisan, dam Jule, by Nena Sahib—owned and trained by A. Miller. She is three years old. Never ran, but is bred and has the action of a runner.

In Mr. Winters' stable, under the care of Dudley Allen, is found Duke of Norfolk, Atalanta and Clara W., all of whom are well known. They are in fine order, and will be entered throughout the circuit. The Mattie A., two-year old, is a very promising filly, and will surprise some this year. She is doing well.

The trotters are gathering at the Park, and as a general thing are doing well. Buccaneer is a dark brown stallion, by Iowa Chief, by Green's Bashaw, dam Tinsley Maid, by Flaxtail, supposed to be by Blue Bull—owned by G. Valensin of Hicksville, and in the stable of Wm. Donathan. Buccaneer is 15-3, will weigh over 1,100 in stud shape. During the past season he has covered 19 mares and passed through his season well. In reference to his progeny we would say that Buccaneer has proven himself to be a model stock horse; as to size and speed he excels many of our finer and closer bred horses. The only two colts of his that have ever been shown up and handled for trotters are Flight and Pride. The former in her three-year-old form, without being in condition, got a record of 2.35, and was well up in .32½. As to Pride much has been written, suffice it to say that she trotted as a yearling in 2:44½, being beaten by the renowned Hinda Rose by one second only—the last half she trotted in 1:19. Buccaneer has been handled this year with the intention of trotting him clear through the circuit. But owing to a mishap which required him to be severely blistered, it is now not known whether or not he will be able to go the route. He will at all events be entered. Six of his colts will be in the Embryo Stakes this Fall. Crown Point and Flight are worked in the same stable. The former, with a record of 2:24½, will be entered in the 22 and 25 classes. The latter is doing nicely, having shown a mile in 2:28¼, the last half in 1:12 and last quarter in .35¼.

TUMP WINSTON (formerly Kent)—Ch. gelding, by Primus, dam Lady Dow—owned by the Winston estate, in the stable of Elijah Downer. He is nine years old, 15½ hands, weight 930. He has trotted six races, winning four. His record is 2:33. He is in fine form and doing better than ever. He has shown Mr. Downer 26½ this year. He will go through the circuit.

NED FORREST—Chestnut gelding, by Blackbird, dam by Jno. Morgan, g. d. by Glencoe—owned by D. M. Reavis; in the stable of Jno. McIntyre. He is six years old, has never trotted in public. He has proven himself a very handy horse to Mack, who will send him clear through.

WILLIAM D.—Iron grey stallion, by Blackird, dam Flora, said to be by Taylor—owned by D. M. Reavis. She is but two years old, has shown 2:55, and will, under McIntyre's schooling, lower that considerable, it is thought.

JAMES DUANE—Dark brown gelding by Blackbird, dam by Signal—owned by D. M. Reavis; in the stable of Mc. Intyre. He is four years old, a green one that will bear working up.

Mr. Wilbur Smith has charge of Mr. E. H. Miller's stable, in which are quartered the well known horses:

Claremount, Adalia, Berlin, Adair, Hamil and Adina, being the get of Fred Low and Electioneer principally. They are all doing splendidly under Wilbur's tuition. Adina is entered in the Embryo Stakes for '82-3-4, in all her forms up to that age. She is now a yearling, a beautiful bay, by Electioneer, dam Addie Lee.

COMO—Dark chestnut stallion, flax mane and tail, by Elmo, dam Juno, by Pat Malloy—owned by C. D. Hastings of Suisun; in the stable of Worth Ober. This colt is 4 years old; trotted two races in 3-year-old form. Has no record.

GOOD BYE—Dark iron grey gelding, dam a thoroughbred mare—owned by Jos. Beaks of Suisun; in the stable of Worth Ober. He is 3-years old—a green one.

SULTAN FILLY—Bay, by Sultan, dam Katy Did, by Fireman. She is two years old, a beautiful filly; resembles Eva very much in her form and action. She is owned and trained by Worth Ober.

I WONDER—Brown gelding, by Young's Henry Belmont, dam a Blackhawk mare—owned by C. H. Merrill of Willows, Colusa Co.; in the stable of W. R. Merrill. He has never trotted yet; is a handsome gaited horse, and will be entered through the circuit in both the 40 and 30 classes.

BOXER—Ch. g., by Young's Henry Belmont, dam a thoroughbred mare—owned and worked by W. R. Merrill. He is five years old; has never trotted. The same gentleman has a roadster pacer, which he claims is not very slow. He calls him "Finnigan."

GREENVILLE—Brown gelding, by the Tyler hose, dam a thoroughbred mare. He is owned by A. G. Bechtel, of Greenville; in the stable of Chas. Shear. Will be entered in the 30 and 40 classes through the circuit.

BILLEY LYLE—Bay stallion, by Roach's American Star, dam by McCracken's Blackhawk—owned by M. Ryan of San Francisco; in the stable of Chas. Shear. He will be in the two mile race.

Yours, etc., MILE-AND-A-QUARTER.

## NATIONAL ASSOCIATION OF TROTTING-HORSE BREEDERS.

*Sixth Annual Meeting, Gentlemen's Driving Park, New York, Oct. 3, 4 and 5, 1882.*

The following are the payments and nominations made, as per condition annexed, in stakes, July 1:

2. *Third Renewal of the Annual Nursery* (*Declaration Stakes*) for foals of 1879, to be trotted (when three years old) at the Fall meeting of 1882; $50 entrance, payable as follows: $10 to accompany the nomination, May 1, 1880; $15 additional July 1, 1882, and the remainder twenty days before the meeting, after which the whole becomes play or pay. Closed May 1, 1880, the final payment of $25 forfeit will be due on Sept. 13, 1882.

W. H. Taylor's b. f. Lizzie Taylor, by Abdallah Duroc, dam by King's Champion.
W. H. Wilson's blk. f. Martha W., by Arnold—Edna.
C. Stanford's br. f., by Knox—Laura Keene.
C. Stanford's br. c., by Victor Mohawk—Lady Clay.
J. D. Willis' b. c. Rosewood, by Norwood—Rosemary.
C. S. Burr's b. c. Comac, by Kentucky Prince—Atlanta, by Messenger Duroc.
C. S. Burr's b. c. Conflict, by Messenger Duroc—Madeline.
C. Backman's ch. c. Chestnut, by Messenger Duroc—Romance.
G. K. Sistare's b. f. Thalia, by Messenger Duroc—Lady Bryant.
B. F. Tracy's b. c. Alroy, by Peacemaker—Monson Girl, by Arabian Girl.

4. *Atlantic Stakes*, for foals of 1877; $250 entrance; payable in the following forfeits: $50 to accompany nomination, May 1, 1882; $50 additional July 1, 1882, and the remainder ($150) Sept. 13, 1882, twenty days before the meeting of 1882.

J. D. Willis' b. g. Jupiter Norwood, by Norwood—Rosemary, by Jupiter.
A. Goldsmith's b. h. Barrett, by Chester Chief, dam by Houston's Clay.

This stake re-opened to name and close July 1, received the following additional nominations:

B. J. Treacy's b. g. McLeod, by Hemphill's Patchen, dam by John Dillard.
J. L. Russell's b. m. Lotta, by Florida—Kate Foster, by Daniel Lambert.

5. *Pacific Stakes*, for foals of 1878; like conditions.

R. Steel's b. f. First Love, by Happy Medium—Mary A. Whitney, by Volunteer.
R. Steel's b. f. Souvenir, by Happy Medium—Lydia Mon[illegible]gue, by Tippoo Bashaw.
W. H. Wilson's gr. g. De Soto, by Administrator—Sil[illegible] Foil, by Jackson's Flying Cloud.

6. *Initiation Stakes*, for stallions that have never bea[illegible] 2:30; like conditions.

J. O'Rorke's b. h. Daniel O'Rorke, by Dr. Syntax—Eri[illegible], by Volunteer.
E. Buck's b. h. Red Cross, by Brigand—Fanny, by Do[illegible] Magna Charta.
A. C. Green's b. h. Gen. Greene, by Ajax—Lady Sheeh[illegible], by American Star.
S. Condit's b. h. Patrician, by Thos. Jefferson—Sylph, by Dunbarton.
S. C. Well's b. h. St. Gothard, by Geo. Wilkes—Nor[illegible], by American Clay.

. *Confirmation Stakes*, for stallions that have never beaten 2:20; like conditions.

By consent of the nominators this stake was withdrawn, a stake for stallions that have never beaten 2:23 substituted upon like conditions to name and close June 10. It ring failed to receive any additional nominations and the original nominators having forfeited in second payments, a stake is declared off.]

8. *Hopscell Stakes*, for stallions that have never beaten 2:40; conditions same as "Atlantic."

D. Willis' b. h. Norwood Star, by Norwood—Voluntary, by Volunteer.

O'Rorke's b. h. Touchstone (formerly John O'Rorke), by Knickerbocker—Spring Day, by Lapidist.

W. McKee's ch. h. Young Fullerton, by Edward Everett—Flora, by Jupiter.

B. Tracy's b. h. Oxmoor, by Princeps—Lindora, by Hambletonian.

Goldsmith's b. h. Walnut, by Florida, dam by Messenger Hambletonian.

9 (1). *Everett House-Stakes*, for foals of 1879, by stallions whose get have never beaten 2:45, at three years old or der; $50 entrance, payable in the following forfeits: $10 accompany the nomination, May 1, 1882; $15 additional ly 1, 1882, and the remainder ($25) Sept. 13, 1882, twenty ys before the meeting of 1882.

aker & Harrigan's b. c. Hugo, by Ashland's Patchen—Belle of Pawlet.

oulton Bros.' ch. f. by Vermont Messenger—Fanny Sleight, by Ethan Allen.

. Strahan's (for owner) b. f. Bergen Belle, by Sweepstakes, dam by Post Boy (Barclay's).

Ruddell's ch. g. Johnny Walter, by Sir Walter— Lady Darling.

. P. Pond's b. c. Thornewood, by Woodlawn—May Strader, by Mambrino Clay.

. Stanford's b. c. Victor Clay.

. C. Hubbard's b. f. Alice Owen, by Metropolitan—Flora, by Yankee.

. Conditt's b. f. Bessie Parke, by Patrician—Betsy Wood, by Knickerbocker.

. D. Kitredge's br. c. Volmer, by Gambetta—Ulster Queen, by Hambletonian.

. B. Tracy's b. c. Alroy, by Peacemaker—Mason Girl, by Arabian Chief.

. Kilpatrick's b. f. Jennie Walter, by Sir Walter—Semonita, by Sentinel.

. Kilpatrick's b. f. Lucy Walter, by Sir Walter, dam by Hambletonian.

10 (2). *Union Stakes*, for foals of 1878, by stallions whose have never beaten 2:40 at four years old or under. Conditions same as (1).

. H. Kerner's b. f. Daisy, by Flatbush Abdallah—Lady Waldron, by Norwood.

. P. Boylan's b. f. by Warwick Boy, dam by Bay Billy.

. Yearance's ch. g. Sir Charles, by Beaustire, dam by Former-man's Warfield.

. J. Willis' b. f. Mary Archita, by Warwick Boy—Loveless Mare, dam of Bonnie Kate.

aker & Harrigan's b. g. Humbert, by Bona Fide—Belle of Pawlet.

G. Stanford's br. c. Lurline Boy, by Victor Mohawk—Lurline, by Hambletonian.

E. G. Doolittle's br. c. Jessie, by Metropolitan—Flora, by Yankee.

W. H. Wilson's gr. g. Dunklee, by Selim, dam by Indian Chief.

11 (3). *Manhattan Stakes*, for foals of 1877, by stallions whose get have never beaten 2:35 at 5 years old or under. Conditions same as (1).

. Goldsmith's b. h. Barrett, by Chester Chief, dam by Houston's Clay.

. Haner's gr. g. Don Carlos, by Highland Gray—Dolly Daly (Florence's dam).

*Consolation Stakes*, for four-year-olds (foals 1878), non-inners as three-year-olds, and under only; $100 each, h. f., $50 to accompany nomination July 1 next; $50 additional orfeit 20 days (Sept. 17) before the coming Fall Meeting of 1882, when the stakes will be trotted for.

). H. Kerhar's b. f. Daisy, by Flatbush Abdallah—Lady Waldron, by Norwood.

2. Steel's b. f. Souvenir, by Happy Medium—Lydia Montague, by Tippoo Saib.

3. Steel's b. f. First Love, by Happy Medium—Mary Whitney, by Volunteer.

*Combination Stakes*, for mares and stallions only that have [ever beaten 2:30, $100 each, h. f., $50 to accompany nomi-[ation July 1, 1882, and the remainder $50 (forfeit) 20 days before the above meeting. Received only one nomination, ind is declared off.

In addition to the foregoing the Executive Committee an-[ounces the designation of the "Juvenile Stakes" for the [nnual Nursery Stakes (fifth renewal) for foals of 1881, to [e trotted as three-year-olds; by stallions whose get have [ever beaten 2:30 at three years old or under, which closed [ay 1, 1882, and the fifth renewal of the Annual Nursery Stakes, for foals of 1881 (to be trotted for when three years [d] at the Fall meeting of 1884); $150 entrance, payable in he following forfeits: $25 to accompany nomination July , 1882; $25 additional May 1, 1883; $25 additional May 1, [884, and the remainder ($75) 20 days before the meeting f 1884.

3. J. Treacy's b. f. Carrie Wilkes, by George Wilkes—Carrie Prince, by Black Prince.

2. J. Treacy's rn. g. Freeland, by Abdallah West—Alice White, by Denmark.

3. J. Treacy's b. c. Western Sprague, by Gov. Sprague—Mamie, by Allie West.

3. S. Burr's b. g. Niketa, by Belmont—In Nose, by Wm. Welch.

4. S. Burr's b. g. by Kentucky Prince—Belinda, by Hambletonian.

5. S. Burr's b. c. by Kentucky Prince—Friendship, by Messenger Duroc.

2. Backman's ch. f. by Messenger Duroc—Antoinette, by Shepherd's Rattler.

3. Backman's b. f. by Meredith—Annie Seely, by Gifford Morgan.

3. Backman's blk. f. by Kentucky Prince—Lady Dexter, by Hambletonian.

3. Backman's b. f. by Kentucky Prince—Queen of May, by Hambletonian.

3. Backman's b. c. by Kentucky Prince—Starbeam, by Hambletonian.

J. D. Willis' b. f. Ella Clay, by Henry Clay—Lady Winfield, by Ed. Everett.

Palo Alto Stock Farm's br. c. Magenta, by Electioneer—Nancy, by John Nelson.

Palo Alto Stock Farm's b. c. Will Crocker, by Electioneer—Melinche, by St. Clair.

Palo Alto Stock Farm's b. f. Chiquita, by Electioneer—Pearl, by Geo. Lancaster.

Palo Alto Stock Farm's b. f. Argo, by Electioneer—American Girl, by Toronto Sontag.

Palo Alto Stock Farm's b. f. Martinique, by Electioneer—Marti, by Whipple's Hambletonian.

Palo Alto Stock Farm's br. f. Alta Bella, by Electioneer—Beautiful Bells, by the Moor.

Palo Alto Stock Farm's b. c. Allen, by Gen. Benton—Lady Morgan, by Hambletonian.

Palo Alto Stock Farm's b. c. Ione, by Gen. Benton—Irene, by Mohawk Chief.

Palo Alto Stock Farm's b. c. Edos, by Gen. Benton—Sontag Mohawk, by Mohawk Chief.

Palo Alto Stock Farm's b. f. Aragon, by Gen. Benton—Alice, by Almont.

H. W. T. Mali's ch. f. Helena—Helen, by Messenger Duroc. *Mali Stakes*, for foals of 1880 (now two-year-olds), to be trotted for when three years old: $250 each; $500 added by Mr. H. W. T. Mali; $50 forfeit to accompany nomination, July 1, 1882; $50 additional forfeit May 1, 1883, and the remainder, $150 forfeit, 20 days before the meeting of 1883, when the stakes will be trotted for.

M. E. Cunningham's ch. c. Marc Antony, by Sir Walter—Susie L., by Hambletonian Abdallah.

T. Loughran's ch. c. Sparticus, by Kentucky Prince—Dolly Everett, by Edward Everett.

J. W. Mackey's b. f. Ruby, by Sultan, dam a Hambletonian mare.

G. K. Sistare's b. f. Marion, by Messenger Duroc—Starbeam, by Hambletonian.

R. Steel's b. c. Leon Lamar, by Happy Medium—Lydia Montague, by Tippoo Sahib.

R. Steel's b. c. Puritan, by Happy Medium—Lady Mambrino, by Puritan.

R. Steel's b. c. Warlock, by Belmont—Waterwich, dam of Scotland.

O. B. Lowell's b. f. Uletta, by Warwick Boy, dam by the Lee horse, son of Wood's Hambletonian.

L. D. Parker's b. c. Prepotency, by Solicitor—Red Bird, by Alexander's Norman.

H. W. T. Mali's br. f. Perdita, by Messenger Duroc—Annie Cook, by Bowman's Clark Chief.

Hunting & Nicholas' blk. g. Gurnee, by Leland—Rosena by Young America.

J. H. DeMott's b. g. Intuition, by Kentucky Prince—Friendship, by Messenger Duroc.

J. H. DeMott's b. f. Impression, by Mambrino Rattler—Lottie, by Grand Bashaw.

C. Backman's b. c. by Messenger Duroc—Green Mountain Maid, by Harry Clay.

C. Backman's blk. c. by Messenger Duroc—Hattie Hogan, by Henry Clay.

C. S. Burr's b. f. Kentucky Prince—Bess, by Hambletonian.

C. S. Burr's b. g. by Messenger Duroc—Antoinette, by Shepherd's Rattler.

S. F. Knapp's b. f. Sweetness, by Messenger Duroc—Fanny Clay, by Henry Clay.

Palo Alto Stock Farm's b. f. Helen, by Gen. Benton—Almeda Maid, by Whipple's Hambletonian.

Palo Alto Stock Farm's b. f. Nellie Benton, by Gen. Benton—Norma, by Alexander's Norman.

Palo Alto Stock Farm's b. c. Alfred, by Gen. Benton—Alice, by Almont.

Palo Alto Stock Farm's br. f. Hinda Rose, by Electioneer—Beautiful Bells, by the Moor.

Palo Alto Stock Farm's b. f. Wave, by Electioneer—Waxey, by Lexington.

Palo Alto Stock Farm's b. f. Flower Girl, by Electioneer—Mayflower, by St. Clair.

**NOTICE.**

The Secretaries of the different District Fair Associations should send a list of their entries to this office, so that they can be printed in our next issue.

# THE GUN.

### THE GUN CLUB.

Last Saturday several members of The Gun Club, on invitation from Mr. T. Ewing, met at Bird's Point, near Alameda, to enjoy the sport of an afternoon's pigeon shooting. The day was very pleasant, a little cloudy, with just enough wind to help the birds fly well. For the first match a purse of $10 was offered for the best, and $5 for the second best shot in twelve points, at thirty yards raise from ground traps. The following are the names of the gentlemen and their score in the first match:

| | | | | | | | | | | | | |
|---|---|---|---|---|---|---|---|---|---|---|---|---|
| Babcock | 0 | 1 | 1 | 1 | 1 | 1 | 1 | 1 | 1 | 0 | 0—9 |
| Y. Butler | 1 | 0 | 1 | 1 | 1 | 1 | 1 | 1 | 1 | 1 | 1—11 |
| W. Havens | 1 | 1 | 1 | 1 | 1 | 1 | 1 | 0 | 0 | 1 | 0—9 |
| Jos. Murphy | 1 | 1 | 0 | 0 | 0 | 1 | 1 | 1 | 1 | 1 | 1—8 |
| R. Wilson | 1 | 1 | 1 | 1 | 0 | 1 | 0 | 0 | 0 | 1 | 1—8 |
| R. Liddle | 1 | 1 | 1 | 1 | 1 | 1 | 1 | 1 | 0 | 0 | 1—11 |
| T. Ewing | 0 | 1 | 1 | 1 | 1 | 1 | 1 | 1 | 0 | 1 | 1—11 |
| E. Orr | 1 | 1 | 1 | 1 | 1 | 1 | 1 | 1 | 1 | 1 | 1—12 |

Messrs. Butler, Ewing and Orr having made a tie on 11 points, it was agreed that the $10 and $5 purses be divided equally among the three gentlemen. There was some very good shooting done, taking into consideration the difference in the pigeons—some being very quick, while others were slow and hard to raise.

The next match was for purses of $10 and $5 for the best and second best shots respectively, at the same distance, and C. V. Colman, who was one of the judges in the first match, took part in this match. The score made was:

| | | | | | | | | | | | | |
|---|---|---|---|---|---|---|---|---|---|---|---|---|
| Colman | 0 | 1 | 1 | 1 | 1 | 1 | 1 | 0—5 |
| Babcock | 1 | 0 | 0 | 1 | 1 | 1 | 1 | 1—5 |
| Butler | 0 | 1 | 0 | 1 | 1 | 0—3 |
| Havens | 1 | 1 | 0 | 0 | 0 | 1—3 |
| Murphy | 1 | 1 | 1 | 0 | 1 | 1—5 |
| Wilson | 1 | 1 | 1 | 0 | 0 | 0—3 |
| Liddle | 1 | 1 | 1 | 1 | 1 | 1—6 |
| Ewing | 0 | 1 | 1 | 0 | 1 | 1—4 |
| Orr | 1 | 1 | 1 | 0 | 1 | 1—5 |

Mr. Liddle killed his six birds and took the first prize. Messrs. Colman, Murphy, Wilson, Ewing and Orr "tied" on 5 points, and in shooting off the second prize was won by Mr. Murphy.

The third match was the most exciting of all, a pair of birds being thrown from the plunge traps placed eighteen yards from the shooter. The pigeons were lively ones, and it required quick moves to bring down two birds flying in opposite directions, and away from the shooting point. The following score speaks well for the sportsmen:

| | | | | |
|---|---|---|---|---|
| Colman | 0 0 | 1 0 | 1 1—3 |
| Murphy | 1 0 | 0 1 | 1 1—4 |
| Wilson | 1 1 | 1 0 | 1 0—4 |
| Ewing | 0 1 | 1 1 | 0—4 |
| Babcock | 1 1 | 1 1 | 1 0—5 |
| Liddle | 1 1 | 1 1 | 1 1—6 |
| Havens | 1 1 | 1 1 | 1—5 |
| Butler | 0 1 | 1 1 | 1 1—5 |

The last match was the same as the second—distance 30 yards, 4 ground traps, 6 points. The score was as follows:

| | | | | |
|---|---|---|---|---|
| Colman | 1 | 1 | 1 | 0—4 |
| Babcock | 1 | 1 | 0 | 1—3 |
| Butler | 1 | 1 | 1 | 0—5 |
| Havens | 1 | 1 | 1 | 0—5 |
| Murphy | 1 | 1 | 0 | 0—3 |
| Liddle | 1 | 1 | 0 | 1—5 |
| Ewing | 1 | 1 | 1 | 1—6 |

But few birds escaped outside of the 100-yard bounds, and Mr. Liddle missed less pigeons than any one else. Messrs. Butler, Ewing and Orr proved themselves to be more than average shots. Mr. Murphy made several very pretty shots; in fact, all of the gentlemen are perfectly familiar with, and very quick in, the handling of their guns. At 6 o'clock a homeward movement was made, every one expressing satisfaction with the afternoon's sport. The members of "The Gun Club" meet again for practice about the middle of August.

### THE CALIFORNIA CLUB'S SHOOT.

Last Sunday was a pleasant day at San Bruno, and there was quite a large attendance at Dick Cunningham's shooting grounds to witness the contest for the California Club's medal. The match was at 12 birds, 21 yards rise, 100 yards boundary, and 7 traps. An additional incentive to extra good shooting was the desire on the part of many contestants to keep up the average and secure a place in the club team, which will shoot against a team from the Cosmopolitan Club for the diamond medal, on Sunday next. The weather seemed to suit the birds well enough, and there were but few instances of shooting on the traps. Some of the birds flew in the most baffling manner, which accounts for the poor scores made by such excellent shots as Dr. Knowles, Stackpool, Walsh and Berwick. Robinson, who was the first man at the trap, opened the ball by missing an easy incomer. Pearson's miss was also an easy bird, while Eilon cannot be blamed in the least for allowing the eleventh to get over the fence to attend to some family affairs that it had awaiting its presence on top of Cunningham's dove cote. The score was as follows:

| | | | | | | | | | | | | | |
|---|---|---|---|---|---|---|---|---|---|---|---|---|---|
| C. Robinson | 0 | 1 | 1 | 1 | 1 | 1 | 1 | 1 | 1 | 1 | 1—11 |
| Dr. Knowles | 1 | 0 | 1 | 0 | 1 | 0 | 1 | 0 | 1 | 1 | 1—7 |
| C. Blackpool | 0 | 1 | 1 | 0 | 1 | 1 | 0 | 1 | 0 | 1 | 1—7 |
| R. Berwick | 0 | 1 | 1 | 1 | 0 | 1 | 0 | 1 | 0 | 1 | 1—7 |
| J. B. Jellett | 1 | 1 | 0 | 1 | 1 | 1 | 1 | 1 | 1 | 1 | 1—10 |
| A. Burbank | 1 | 1 | 1 | 0 | 1 | 1 | 1 | 1 | 1 | 0 | 0—8 |
| Dr. Hays | 1 | 1 | 1 | 1 | 1 | 1 | 1 | 1 | 1 | 1 | 0—11 |
| T. A. Pearson | 1 | 1 | 1 | 0 | 1 | 1 | 1 | 0 | 1 | 1 | 1—9 |
| S. Elion | 1 | 1 | 1 | 1 | 1 | 1 | 1 | 1 | 0 | 1 | 1—10 |
| J. Kerrigan | 1 | 1 | 1 | 1 | 1 | 0 | 0 | 0 | 1 | 0 | 1—7 |
| D. McEvoy | 1 | 0 | 0 | 1 | 1 | 1 | 1 | 1 | 1 | 1 | 1—9 |
| O. Johnston | 1 | 1 | 1 | 1 | 1 | 1 | 1 | 1 | 1 | 0 | 1—10 |
| G. F. Bogart | 1 | 1 | 1 | 0 | 1 | 1 | 1 | 1 | 1 | 1 | 1—10 |
| J. Brussell | 0 | 0 | 0 | 1 | 1 | 1 | 1 | 0 | 1 | 0 | 0—5 |
| P. J. Walsh | 0 | 1 | 1 | 1 | 1 | 1 | 0 | 1 | 1 | 0 | 1—8 |

The three gentlemen who tied on 11 kills each then shot off at double birds, with the following result:

| | | | |
|---|---|---|---|
| Robinson | 1 | 1 | 1—4 |
| Pearson | 1 | 0 | 0—2 |
| Elion | 0 | 0 | —0 |

This gave Crittenden Robinson first prize, T. Pearson second and R. Elion third.

A match at six birds followed, for prizes of $20, $12 50 and $5. The score was as follows:

| | | | | | | |
|---|---|---|---|---|---|---|
| Robinson | 1 | 1 | 1 | 1 | 1—5 |
| Pearson | 1 | 0 | 1 | 1 | 1—4 |
| Harvey | 0 | 0 | 1 | 0 | 1—3 |
| Walsh | 1 | 0 | 0* | —1 |
| Clary | 0 | 0 | 1 | —1 |
| Hays | 1 | 0 | 1 | 0—2 |
| Chismore | 1 | 1 | 1 | 1—4 |
| Berwick | 1 | 1 | 1 | 1—5 |
| Slade | 0 | 1 | 1 | 1—4 |
| Bogart | 1 | 0 | 1 | 1—5 |
| Jellett | 1 | 1 | 1 | 1—5 |
| Shedberg | 1 | 1 | 1 | 0—4 |
| Knowles | 1 | 1 | 1 | 1—5 |
| R. Brown | 0 | 0 | 0 | 1—1 |
| J. Kerrigan | 0 | 0* | —0 |
| * Withdrew. | | | | | | |

Robinson, Chismore, Slade, Jellett and M. Brown having tied on clean scores, shot off at three pair. Slade and Jellett tied again, and divided first and second money, M. Brown winning third.

A five bird match which followed was won by Robinson, who tied with Pearson and Jellett and beat them in shooting off. Robinson also divided a four bird match with Dr. Hays. The day's shooting resulted in upwards of 75 per cent of kills—not high figures for good shots, but good work for an all day club match.

### MATCHES AT SACRAMENTO.

On the 21st inst. a couple of matches were shot at the Agricultural Park, which drew together a fair assemblage of amateurs. The first was a contest between C. H. Todd and George Wittenbrock for $40 a side, each killing ten birds in the dozen. In the tie at three pairs of double birds they each scored four birds, but on the second tie the victory resulted in Mr. Wittenbrock's favor by a score of six to one. The Capital Club shoot was at clay pigeons, William Nesbit and Charles Flohr tieing on 12 straight, and in the shoot-off at live birds Nesbit won the first medal with five straight kills.

The Diamond Medal Trophy will be competed for by the Cosmopolitan and California Clubs at San Bruno on Sunday next. It will be a twelve-bird match, and each team comprise fifteen men.

# THE
# Breeder and Sportsman.

PUBLISHED BY THE

BREEDER AND SPORTSMAN PUBLISHING CO.

THE TURF AND SPORTING AUTHORITY OF THE
PACIFIC COAST.

**OFFICE, 508 MONTGOMERY STREET**
P. O. Box 1338.

*Five dollars a year; three dollars for six months; one dollar and a
half for three months. Strictly in advance*

*Money should be sent by postal order, draft or by registered letter.*

*Communications must be accompanied by the writer's name and address,
not necessarily for publication, but as a private guarantee of good faith*

JOSEPH CAIRN SIMPSON,  - -  EDITOR

SAN FRANCISCO, - - SATURDAY, JULY 29, 1882

## CLOSING OF ENTRIES.

On the first day of August next the stakes of the
Pacific Coast Blood-Horse Association, the Embryo
Stakes and the Purses and Stakes at the California
Fairs will close.

The advertisements in this paper will give the particulars. Do not forget the date—TUESDAY, AUGUST
1st, 1882.

## A GRAND DRIVE FOR SAN FRANCISCO.

There is a report current that there is a chance
for the construction of a drive in San Francisco
which will be a great boon to the citizens of the
metropolis, and which will be a benefit to the
breeders of road-horses and trotters in every portion of the State. The good results will not be
confined to owners, sellers and buyers of horses;
the advantages will be general, and the city an
equal shareholder in return for the investment.
This without cost to the corporation, as it is contemplated to build it with individual subscriptions.
There are other things required than commercial
advantages to make a great city. It must have the
elements of pleasure as well as adaptability for
business to attract; and when there is a combination of pleasure and exercise conducing to mental
and physical health, the two great essentials of life
are joined. From mid-life to old age there is a
greater necessity for exercise than youth or early
manhood demands. The buoyant spirits compel
exertion. The blood is mercurial, and that which
causes colts to gambol and run in the pasture-field
drives the young man to athletic sports of some
kind to work off the superabundant energy. Business cares do not engross the faculties. The work
accomplished, and it is banished from the mind.
The older are debarred from the same relief. If
the inclinations are bent in the same direction,
they dare not follow them. Dignity, propriety,
all the senseless shams of social and business life,
forbid the indulgence. Were a man of fifty years
or upwards to engage in a rowing match, a foot
race, or bestride a bicycle in a contest with others,
his business and social standing would be in serious
jeopardy. There are few, however, of that age
who have the least desire to engage in these active
sports. The truly American recreation of road-
driving comes to their aid. In the whole range of
exercises suitable for men of business in the cities
and large towns, there is none other which is so
well adapted to counteract the wear of sedentary
and exciting pursuits. There is a counter excitement, turning the thoughts into other channels,
relieving the mind from a strain which is destructive if not overcome, and with sufficient exercise
to restore the physical functions. Any one who
has been in the habit of road-driving, and who is
immersed in the cares of business, will acknowledge
how great the relief is. From the moment the
horses are "set going," especially if the speed is
called out by a contest with others, the weariness
is gone. There is a magical influence in the swift
motion and the struggle for victory. The driver
is intent on winning, and the thoughts which tormented him vanish like a dream. Debarred from
the favorite pastime, and he will tell you that he
is entirely out of sorts. The close of business
hours finds him gloomy and despondent, and he
goes to bed still under the shadow. He is languid
when he arises in the morning, tired when he commences the labor of day.

But in order to obtain the benefits, there must
be an opportunity. With such drives as there are
in the vicinity of San Francisco at present, there
is no chance for the exhilarating amusement. Since
the Cliff House road has been rendered unfit for
fast driving, there is no place suitable, and it is a
well known fact that road-horses have depreciated
fully fifty per cent. on account of there being no
suitable drive. The plan which is now proposed
is to construct a driveway skirting Golden Gate
Park. The former Superintendent, Mr. Hennessy,
had a survey made on the north side of the Park,
and he estimated that a mile in length, two hundred feet in width, with fifty feet of the center
macadamized, could be built for $25,000. The
grade would only be thirty feet in the mile, which
would be little if any impediment. With seventy-
five feet on each side of the macadamized portion,
there would be ample room for the fast work, and
less danger from collisions than if there was a par-
rower dirt road and no macadam. Without the
broken stone in the center, and a dirt roadway of
one hundred or one hundred and twenty feet, the
probable cost would not be over $15,000. Either
of these amounts can certainly be raised by subscription, if the Park Commissioners decide to take
it in hand; and there may be other locations than
the one surveyed which will offer equal advantages.
Now that the trees have grown to a guarding height,
there is protection from the wind, and in a few
years more the barrier will be complete. Where
previously the sand drifted, piling up in huge
heaps, there is no trouble from that source now,
and, every year adds to the efficacy of the living
guard. There are no serious obstacles to overcome, and we hope to announce ere many weeks
have passed that the preliminary steps have been
taken.

## THE EMBRYO STAKE.

Owing to the somewhat complicated conditions,
the Embryo Stake is not easily understood by those
who intend making nominations. In "The Track"
department will be found an explanation which we
hope will be a sufficient information to guide those
making entries.

The wonderful performances of the Palo Alto
and Sunny Slope youngsters have caused such a
trepidation among some of the breeders, that there
is a disposition to "stay out," but we think that if
the faint-hearted will take a good look at it they
will come to the conclusion that such a course is
not the proper one. In the first place, it is a direct admission of inferiority, for no matter how
plausible the excuses offered, there will be a general verdict that the owners have no confidence in
the animals they are rearing. Any person who is
engaged in breeding trotting horses cannot afford
to lie under this imputation, and there are certainly limited numbers who are enabled to give a
few the same chances which the many are granted
on the big breeding farms. The amount is so
small to risk that no one can claim it is beyond
their means, and for this small sum there is a
chance for a large gain.

Apart from the question of dollars and cents,
dependent on winning the stake, there are interests of far greater moment.

It is important to show that California has advantages for breeding and rearing fast trotters
outside of the farms which are so largely stocked,
and that a man with a single mare of the right
stamp can cope with the owner of scores of them.
There are the same climatic advantages, the
same natural aids for development; and though
some of the adjuncts for the education of a large
number are lacking, this is not an essential when
only a few have to go through the course. The
Embryo Stake gives the small breeder an opportunity which he should not neglect. The bugbear
of injury arising from the early training of colts is
no longer dreaded, and that old-time prejudice is
fast giving way to a more enlightened knowledge.
We hope to receive enough nominations to convince the Eastern people that there are breeders in
California who do not share in the belief that the
colts on one or two farms are all that there are
here, and that even the wonderful deeds of the
past have not demoralized them.

## BROOKS VS. MYERS.

From a private letter which the editor received
from a friend in New York there was a likelihood
that Mr. Myers, the "Champion of the World,"
would visit California, provided he could get the
opportunity to have another bout with his conqueror. It is needless to state that his coming
would have awakened a vast deal of interest on
this Coast, and the enthusiasm which a contest
between the two would excite greater than anything else in pedestrianism. We laid the matter
before Mr. Brooks, and the following letter was
his reply:

> SAN FRANCISCO, July 24, 1882.
> EDITOR BREEDER AND SPORTSMAN—DEAR SIR: This morn-
> ing I received your favor, having just come in from the
> country. I would have answered it before if I had received
> it sooner, and must beg your pardon for the seeming delay.
> In regard to running: I am not going to run out here, for
> various reasons. I have gone out of training, and I ex-
> plained to Mr. Myers (and to his satisfaction) that I could
> not run until late in the Fall. I am here on a vacation, and
> am enjoying it as such, which I could not if I had to train.
> Therefore, I shall not run while I am here with any one.
> Thanking you for your courtesy towards me,
> I am, yours,     HENRY S. BROOKS, JR

This is a straightforward, manly reply, and much
as the people here would like to see the two come
together, the reasons on the part of Mr. Brooks
for declining are sufficient, and will be considered
an excuse which is valid, and which should free
him from the annoyance of further challenges.
Were he to run anyone he would be in duty bound
to give Mr. Myers the first opportunity; and if the
meeting were to take place here, there would be
widespread desire to see it.

## THE MEETING ON THE BAY DISTRICT COURSE.

As will be seen by the advertisement, the initial
meeting of the series will be held on the Bay District Course on the 5th and 12th proximo, and it
must not be forgotten that the entries to the purses
close on Monday, July 31st. It was necessary to
close them as soon as then in order to do away
with the risk of delay in the mails. Under the
new Trotting Rules an entry legibly post-marked
on the day of closing is valid, and hence, as in
some cases, the better part of a week is taken in
bringing postal missives from Oakland, it was
necessary to look out for the rapid transit through
Uncle Sam's agents. The entries should be numerous.

The week intervening between the two days
will give the horses ample time to recover, and
those which participate in the 2:40 class can have
another "fling for fame and fortune" in the 2:30
the Saturday following. The 2:25 and the 2:22
present the same good features. By engaging in
and trotting in these purses, the finishing touches
will be put on for the circuit, and then for Santa
Cruz, etc. There is a misapprehension with some
in regard to the 2:40 races at Santa Cruz. There
are two of this class, the first on August 15th, for
district horses, the second on the 17th, the open
race. The 2:25 open race at Santa Cruz is on the
15th, and the 2:30 on August 18th.

Every horse eligible in this section of the country
should be named in the Bay District races. A good
showing at this meeting will ensure that which it
is contemplated to hold in October. We have not
the least doubt of there being a hearty response.

## PACIFIC COAST BLOOD-HORSE ASSOCIATION---
## FIXED EVENTS.

There can scarcely be a question of the stakes
of the Pacific Coast Blood-Horse Association showing a large increase in the nominations over those
of previous years, and though last year there were
thirty in some of these, we expect to see this large
number exceeded. Men who are breeding thoroughbred colts "cannot afford" to leave them out.
Should the desire be to sell, the colts will bring
double the amount, and if retained there is the
chance to win a large sum from a small investment.
The stakes are well arranged, offering a variety of
races in the two and the two and three-year-old
form. Do not overlook the time of closing, Tuesday next, August 1st. Direct nominations to C.
M. Chase, P. O. box 1961, S. F. See advertisement
for particulars.

## THE ROWING CHAMPIONSHIP.

Of all out-door sports, in California, rowing has within the past two years most rapidly advanced in popularity. There are now in San Francisco bay half a dozen clubs capable of putting forward representative crews on a first-class regatta, while in various parts of the State rowing associations have sprung into vigorous existence. It is to be regretted that the rowing clubs of interior cities are not more animated by a desire to compete with the San Francisco organizations. Nothing would so rapidly or effectually increase the interest in this healthiest of all sports than competitions of the clubs of one part of the State with those of another. In times past Sacramento and Vallejo were accustomed to dispute the laurels with the oarsmen of the Bay, but of late years the athletes of the Capital and the naval headquarters have been conspicuous by their absence from our harbor. One reason of this retirement of the clubs of the interior has been the lack of attractions on our bay. The regattas held here have not been sufficiently rich in trophies to tempt a crew at Sacramento or Vallejo to undergo the discomforts and expense of training, and submit itself to the possibility of defeat. It is not an inviting prospect for a crew to travel from a distant part of the State to compete for a cheap medal representing nothing but its small intrinsic value. Where there are no rewards for athletic prowess there will be very little of it displayed, and to this fact may be ascribed the termination of the rivalry between the oarsmen of the metropolis and those of interior cities and towns.

The BREEDER AND SPORTSMAN hopes that by the offer of its challenge cup the old spirit of emulation will be revived, and that at the regatta on Thanksgiving Day we shall see once more on home waters the representatives of the country club which formerly boasted some of the best athletes in the State. There is nothing in the air of the metropolis or the water of our bay to invest the oarsmen of San Francisco with superior ability. On the contrary they achieve excellence in the art of rowing under grave disadvantages, which are entirely unknown to the rowing men of Vallejo, Stockton and Sacramento. Training in our harbor is made a veritable hardship by the winds, fogs and tides, while on the waters of the interior it is a pleasant and healthful undertaking. It may be argued that owing to the number of oarsmen on the bay, the chances of a strange crew carrying off the championship are too remote to be pleasant. This does not follow. The competition for the BREEDER AND SPORTSMAN'S cup will be club contest. Entries will be limited to established clubs, and no combination of picked oarsmen will be permitted to swoop down and appropriate the prize and the championship.

A club in Stockton having as many members as the Golden Gate or Pioneer or Ariel clubs of San Francisco should stand an equal chance with these organizations. The number of actual rowing men in each of the San Francisco clubs named is not large and should certainly not be formidable enough to discourage any strange club from aspiring to the championship. The BREEDER AND SPORTSMAN'S cup will be the handsomest and most valuable trophy ever offered on the Pacific Coast. As the contest for the cup will decide the championship of the Pacific Coast, there will be no limitation as to boats. The competitors can row whatever suits them and will naturally seek the best boats. So much rowing has been done here in heavy-working boats that some of the most powerful clubs have no four-oar racing shells, but the time which will elapse before the first race for the cup will enable all competitors to equip themselves properly for the competition. So far the indications are that four first-class metropolitan crews will meet to decide the vexed question of superiority. This will insure a grand race, and if only a few entries from the country could be obtained the match would assume a degree of importance never before reached by a regatta on the Pacific Coast.

## A RACING CAMPAIGN.

Theodore Winters has returned from the Eastern trip, and in a conversation with him a few days ago he outlined a campaign for California horses at home and in the East, which appears to us to have many points to recommend its adoption. The plan is for the Pacific Coast Blood-Horse Association to hold the Spring meeting in April, a little earlier, perhaps, than that of this season; follow that with a meeting at Sacramento, and then at Salt Lake. From there horses could be taken to any Eastern point desired, or return home. The advantages of such a course will be apparent when consideration is given. In the first place, it is evident that our horses taking part in the Eastern meetings will increase the interest taken in them at home. In order to make the breeding of racehorses properly remunerative in California, it is absolutely essential that there should be outside fields for them to display their powers, outside markets to sell. With all the encouragement possible at home, there must be a surplus from the breeding farms now established, and when this supply is augmented by the natural produce the trouble will be increased.

The impetus to breeding which an Eastern outlet will give is of the greatest importance to the well-doing of turf sports at home. There will be large fields to contend for the home stakes and purses, as the owners will be desirous of making the best selections, which can only be done through public trials, emphatic trials, which actual races alone afford, and the people will have an additional incentive to attend, knowing that there is more at issue than the mere winning of so much money. There will be an anxiety to see the contention which is to decide which are the most worthy to represent California in the far-off courses, and this anxiety will largely increase the gate receipts.

The oldest race course in the United States is at Lexington, Kentucky. That is the oldest, where there has only been one slight break in the meetings for upwards of half a century. The purses and stakes are comparatively small, and yet there is always a good attendance and a large number of starters. This arose from it being the home trial, the touchstone which was to determine the character, the crucible which would separate the gold from the dross, for it has long been an axiom that the colt which wins his stakes there need not be apprehensive of defeat in any company.

The meeting of the Pacific Coast Blood-Horse Association, held as early in April as is thought advisable, followed by one at Sacramento, with a week to intervene, will give plenty of time for a gathering at Salt Lake; and this is just the point which will come in best on the way East. It will break the long journey, making it one of two stages in place of a long stretch without interruption. Mr. Winters informs us that the Jockey Club at Salt Lake will co-operate heartily in this plan, and arrange the meeting so that it will be satisfactory. The first thing to do is for the Capital Turf Club to open stakes similar to those of the Pacific Coast Blood-Horse Association, and have them close at the time of the State Fair. There is scarcely a question that there will be as many nominations as those of the older association when the time of running will not interfere with an Eastern campaign, and a successful meeting result. At all events, we cannot see any objections to giving it a trial. It may be claimed that by having the Spring meetings earlier than usual that trainers cannot get the horses in order, and that there is more risk to run of unfavorable weather during the meeting. Racehorses can be got in condition at any time of the year in California, if the trainers will follow the system which is compulsory in the East; and if not afraid of a gallop through the mud, there is rarely a day when proper exercise cannot be given. There was better weather last year than at any of the previous Spring meetings, though it was held two weeks earlier; and another good feature, it anticipates the picnic season.

## RUNNING IN THE MUD.

There is scarcely a doubt that the main cause for the defeat of the California horses at Chicago was the heavy track—not what our folks would call a heavy track, but such a one as never was seen in California. "Imagine," says Mr. Winters, "a black adobe soil of six inches, and beneath that a stratum of yellow clay. Let it rain two-thirds of the time, and have two or three hundred horses galloping on it, mixing the black and the yellow, and then, when it is partially dry—not enough to keep them from sinking, but sticky and holding—run the race." Horses accommodate their action, in a measure, to the ground they are accustomed to run upon. Thus a majority of the horses here have a low, easy, "daisy cutting" style, induced by the courses being adapted for that kind of action; and when first called upon to run on such a track as there was at Chicago during the late race meeting, they necessarily must become tired. Round, even high, action is the sort of progression which comes into play, and the "good mud horse" beats the crack capable of giving him twenty pounds when the conditions are favorable for the one which does not labor so much. It does not depend on strength or size so much as the "way of going;" and as a general rule, the very fast animals have not the right method of handling their limbs for the contingency.

### BARRING FROM COLT STAKES.

From all we can learn there is a general concurrence in the opinion that there should be nothing like a bar in colt stakes. If one or two breeders are fortunate enough to rear the winners for years in succession, the only thing to do is to try still, harder to reverse the decision of superiority. In all the conversations we have had with men who are engaged in breeding trotters, there are few who desire any bar being incorporated in colt stakes. They are not willing to admit a superiority based on the result of a couple of years, and desire further opportunities of testing the question before acknowledging defeat. This is exactly our view; but to convince people that they are sincere in the desire to do battle they must make entries. We can scarcely credit a man with sincerity when his actions do not "back up" his word, and should he decline to enter in the stakes, the declination will carry more weight than a volume of statements. When there is so little to risk as there is in the Embryo or any of the California, excepting the Stanford stake, it cannot be truthfully said that the amounts are too large. Show your faith, gentlemen, by making engagements, take the best care of your colts, train them early and thoroughly, and the chances are you will make a good showing.

### THE ENTRIES FOR THE FAIRS.

As the advertisements give all the necessary information, the only thing to be done is to call attention to the closing of the entries on the 1st of August, so that every one interested will be aware of the fact. It is manifestly a waste of space to urge owners to enter into engagements which are so much to their own interest, but it may be as well to reiterate that little attention must be given to the reports of the wonderful performances on tracks at a distance. These stories are always rife about the time of closing of entries, and some are promulgated with an intention to deceive, others from the universal tendency to increase from repetition. Thus a colt trots on the Oakland track in 2:38, at Petaluma in 2:33, at Sacramento 2:28, and probably at Chico fifteen seconds have been subtracted and 2:23 given. Then, a horse under the most favorable circumstances on a track which is "as fast as chain-lightning" trots in 2:22, and people are sure that he will reach 2:17 in a race. Our advice is, if you have a good horse for the classes in which he is eligible enter him regardless of what you hear. Study the programmes and you will find plenty of places where you can have a chance.

## STAKES OF THE NATIONAL TROTTING HORSE BREEDERS' ASSOCIATION.

Elsewhere the stakes for the Fall meeting of the Trotting Horse Breeders' Association will be found, with those who have made the payment which was due July 1st. It will be seen that California figures largely in them, and in one of the twenty-five making the second payment, ten are from Palo Alto, and J. W. Mackay's filly, by Sultan. There is not a doubt of California figuring prominently hereafter in the Eastern events. There will be others who will join in entering into Eastern engagements, and as has been shown in relation to the racing, to the great advantage of home sport.

## YACHTING.

### SHARPIES.

During last Summer there was considerable interest manifested here on the subject of sharpies. It was the intention of several gentlemen to build a fifty-foot sharpie, but one after another backed out until only one was left, and he could not afford the expense alone. Then a sharpie was built in Oakland, and, as usual, experiments were made to "improve" the experience of others, and the results were not satisfactory. She was given lead ballast instead of bricks; an iron centre-board instead of wood; had a skag and deadwood put on aft, contrary to custom, and had a keel put on also. Then she was rigged with heavy, stiff spars instead of the pliable "sliding-gunter" rig experience has proven the best. The boat was, therefore, not a success. This was unfortunate, since it prevented other people from trying the type of boat, which is, no doubt, well suited to our upper bays and rivers, and for hunting purposes cannot be excelled.

The whole subject of sharpies was pretty well discussed before the San Francisco Yacht Club last year, and Mr. Thomas Clapham, of Roslyn, Long Island, contributed a paper describing their peculiar qualities.

It will interest many, therefore, to give the experience of a New York Yachtsman with one of these boats, and we take from *Forest and Stream* a letter of Mr. Robert B. Roosevelt, describing his sharpie and what he did with her:

About a year ago I wrote a letter to *Forest and Stream* to inquire about the true qualities of the sharpie, a boat about which I had heard much from my youth up, and which had been equally praised and dispraised with unstinted enthusiasm. The replies then furnished were a continuation of my previous experience, one writer contending that perfection alone was to be found where another could discover nothing but faults and shortcomings. Interspersed with this information was a mass of valuable advice concerning Barnegat sneak boxes, Newport pleasure boats, Long Island gunning skiffs, and the regulation catboats, till I felt at the end of my efforts as though I knew almost everything in the nautical way—except just what I wanted to know; so I announced my intention of finding out for myself what no two other persons seemed to be able to agree upon, and I have fairly accomplished and now will lay before your readers.

I wanted a roomy, comfortable, safe boat for shoal waters, something with a cabin of which the earlins would not be at perpetual war with my skull, a private hotel, with spring beds, and a chance to turn over in sleep without getting jammed between the timbers; a big table for visitors and unlimited lockers for stores; a good forecastle and a coal stove; and all this adapted for the Great South Bay of Long Island, where the bottom for the most is only two or three feet below the top of the water. In other words, I wanted a yachting canal-boat with a hall in it. I did not ask for speed, intending to take Mr. Seth Green along with me and devote the entire summer to studying the piscatorial capacities of our salt-water inlets and bays. I engaged Mr. Clapham to build me a "Nonpareil" sharpie, 56 ft. long over all and 15 ft. extreme beam, with 6 ft. head room in the cabin and about 4 ft. 6 in. under the deck. As my correspondence had, as I have explained, failed to produce a very clear comprehension of such vessels, I worried the builder somewhat with numerous suggestions, but in the end produced the boat which I am about to describe.

The first item to consider was, naturally, the cost, for I take it that a great deal depends upon how much boat you get for your money. Twenty-five hundred dollars covered that, including anchors, sails, patent blocks, and everything of the best, the cabin and staterooms being tastefully finished inside with hard woods.

On the south side of Long Island we have a beautiful insect, or small bird, as it might almost be called from the delicacy of its sung note. This comes to us in great abundance at times, and makes the air fairly rejoice with its hum. It is called, popularly, the mosquito, and to prevent its getting lost in the intricacies of the cabin, the windows, which were kept to make double, half glass and half of mosquito netting, while there were a pair of swinging mosquito net doors in the companionway. There are five berths in the main cabin, each on spring slats, and all under the deck, so that they cannot be sat upon during the day and reduced to the consistency of flint. Sleeping on them is a luxury, and instead of turning out at 5 A. M., as we have always done heretofore, we sleep till 10. Curtains on rods in front of them shut them out of sight during the day.

But if these are luxuries, what will be thought of those in the two staterooms where they are still wider and deeper and softer, and will at a pinch almost accommodate two. In one of these staterooms is a w. c., without which no yacht, large or small, is suitable for the use of ladies. There are then seven berths, besides two in the forecastle for the men; and the centerboard table will seat twelve on chairs having backs and arms to them, not on bunks which are subsequently to belie beds. There is no door between the cabin and forecastle, only a sliding panel large enough to pass dishes; and under the berths are shelves and boxes for clothes, and so forth. The forecastle is roomy, except in

matter of height. Under the cockpit are two water-casks, one of which connects with a coil of pipe in the ice chest with a faucet in the cabin, so that ice-water can always be had without the waste of a cooler. Further aft there is much room for boxes, spare rigging, and the thousand and one things which make up a yacht's furniture. In fact, as one visitor remarked, "she is all boat," every inch of space being utilized. In the way of comfort, she is perfection; and she only draws twenty inches of water.

When she was finished and launched, we—myself and my seafaring friends, some of whom had become converts to the cutter theory—tried her sailing qualities with many doubts and misgivings. None of us knew anything of the handling of such a craft with a bottom like a bridge turned upside down, and no keel or skag to keep her on her course, and a rudder with a nose to it. But to our pleasurable disappointment she worked as easy as a catboat, never missed stays, and seemed to get to the windward somehow, at least as well as the merchant vessels we met. The sails were small, the mainsail had a twenty-eight foot boom, and thirty-five feet in the hoist, the foresail was only twenty feet on the foot, and the jib about twenty-six. One man could hoist them all without too much exertion. There were no topsails and no flying jib. She was a handsome craft, dashing and rakish looking, with the one fault of a bad stern, and made to appear almost like a man-of-war with her lozenge-shaped windows for ports. We took her around to Fire Island Inlet after a severe storm. The Montauk made her trial trip the following day, and monster as she is by comparison, came in reporting a very heavy sea. We noticed the old ground swell, but minded it so little that we had our dinner in perfect comfort while under way. We had all sorts of wind, from half a gale to a dead calm, close hauled and dead aft, and we ran out of sight astern every working vessel that went out when we did, and we overhauled vessels that were out of sight ahead when we started. These were working vessels only, big and little, schooners, sloops and catboats, but then the sharpie was not built for speed.

We have beaten every working vessel (and some of these are quite fast) we have yet met. Since then I have had her in the South Bay. Seth Green has run her into one pound net and on to three sand flats, but when she grounds she grounds astern, so that we have only to push her head around, and she goes off as she came on. We have carried sail all through all the heavy weather of this Summer, except when we had ladies aboard, and have rarely had her gunvale under, and there is no sea that ever gets up in the South Bay that troubles her at all. She is most remarkable in this particular when lying at anchor, for when other vessels around her were scooping up the seas with their noses, she was so quiet the carpenters could fit up the inside joiner work.

As to single-handed cruising, I was left alone on her by the sickness of my man, and ran her by myself, without aid of any kind for several days. It was under these circumstances that I met the Orion, a sloop five tons larger. She beat me; but I had no one to help me start sheet or trim in, or handle the board, and I got out of the channel. She had a topsail set and a fair topsail breeze, whereas my boat paddled more wind. Still, probably the Orion can beat me. You know her record; and my yacht was not built for speed.

In United States patents it is the custom to wind up with what is claimed as new and valuable, and so will I do. I claim therefore that the sharpie is the cheapest boat built and probably the strongest, for a veritable canal boat loaded with coal, drew in alongside of my boat, and at the side fell leaned against her and crushed her against the dock. When the tide rose again three men were very busy pumping away at that canal boat, while the Heartsease only needed a new fender strip. I claim further that the sharpie is without comparison the roomiest and most comfortable vessel and next in point of safety to the cutter. That she will work like a top, stand any sea and will prove fairly fast when sparred for that object without losing her wonderful stability. I claim the berths in the wings and wholly under deck as a public boon, the swinging mosquito net doors as an original invention, the coil in the ice chest and water barrels as a decided improvement, the mosquito net windows as a capital arrangement, and the sharpie yacht for all inside work as an unqualified success.

The Virgin is very little used now-a-days.

Ingalls' new plunger, Restless, sails well.

The sloop Lillie has gone up river for a week.

The Chiquita is kept at Saucelito now during the week.

The Lively, though her sails are bent, is very little used.

The Magic is off up river, with Wm. Stone and family aboard.

Bob Goble has taken his family off on a cruise up the bay.

The Clara and Annie both lie at Saucelito during the week.

Mission Bay is so shoal that it is a poor place to lay a boat up in.

The Casco is going up to the Puget Sound waters before very long.

The sloop Bessie comes out of Oakland creek for a short sail occasionally.

Commodore Harrison has been cruising for a week up river in the Frolic.

Vice-Commodore Oliver is cruising up river in the Emerald in company with the Frolic.

A good many yachts are cruising now-a-days. This makes better yachtsmen than racing does.

The improved sailing of the Ariel caused the Chispa to be put on the ways for cleaning.

The old yacht Mermaid is in commission yet, lying at Saucelito. She is old as the hills, but is a good boat yet.

The Whitewing had her full new suit of sails on last Sunday and looks well. What is more to the purpose, she sails well.

The yacht Turner is to build for the Spreckels boys will be 80 feet long, 21 feet beam, 9 feet draught, and will have a 30,000-pound lead keel.

Lots of boat sailing going on in Lake Merritt now-a-days. It is a good place to practice on, as the water is so shallow one can wade ashore if upset.

To-day the Rambler starts for a two weeks' cruise, her first port being Stockton. She will return down river and go up Napa creek a few days before coming home.

Vice-Commodore Floyd's Ariel is very much improved since lead was put on her keel and she was overhauled. She now swings a big single jib instead of three of them.

The Chispa and Clara, flying the Bohemian Yacht Club flag, went up to, Commodore Eckley's place on Carquinez straits last Saturday. They went up to Martinez also, where the party attended a concert.

Charley Kellogg is blossoming out into an ocean sailor, piloting the Lolita out through the Golden Gate and across the bar. If they all had this gentleman's love of sailing what a fine lot of yachtsmen there would be here in this bay.

Because one of the dailies complimented the yacht Clara on her fine appearance some of the boat-keepers of other yachts feel jealous. This is as it should be. Anything which will make them jealous is good, as it will arouse a spirit of emulation and all the yacht-owners will be benefited by seeing their yachts in better order. As a general thing the men on the yachts get pretty lazy after a month or so in service, and something is needed to stir them up in order to keep them at their duty properly.

## FISH.

### BLACK BASS.

Of all the varieties of fish that inhabit the waters of this and the Eastern States, there is none that deserves our notice more than the black bass. The first scientific notice taken of this fish was by a French naturalist, about the year 1800. The native waters of black bass are the St. Lawrence and Mississippi rivers, with their lakes and tributaries, but then they readily adapt themselves to any water or climate. Some that were placed in the lakes and rivers in England have increased wonderfully, so that in a few years they will be considered as one of England's principal food and game fish. There are two varieties of the species, the small mouth and the large mouth bass. The former inhabit the Northern lakes and rivers, and are smaller than their large mouth brothers that bask in the stagnant pools and shallow marshes of the sunny South. As may be supposed from their names, they differ greatly in the size of the mouth, as well as in habits and size. The small mouth bass of the North, when full grown, weighs on an average five pounds. Their meat is perfectly white, and is of a very fine grain and flavor. Their body, too, is not quite so bulky, and as they inhabit the clear, swift-running streams, their movements are more lively, greatly resembling those of the trout. The large mouth bass spend most of their time in the shade of logs or among the submerged roots of trees that grow on the water's edge. In the warm waters of the South, which preserve a more equal temperature than those of the Northern States, the black bass grow to be very large, weighing as high as twelve and fourteen pounds.

Black Bass will thrive and multiply where many other fish would die. They are hardy, not easily affected by change of climate, and have an appetite like an ostrich. They subsist largely on other fish, and when hungry will devour the smaller ones of their own kind. Frogs and snakes stand a poor chance around water inhabited by these fish. They multiply faster than many other fish, as they lay their eggs on the under side of logs or on the pebbles at the bottom of a deep pool, and there the parents remain, fighting away other fish, until the eggs are hatched and the young able to swim; then the young ones must look out for themselves, as they are liable to be devoured by their own parents; whereas many other kinds of fish deposit their spawn in shallow streams, where the young fall easy victims to ravenous watersnakes and birds. The mouth of an ordinary Black Bass is so large that it can easily devour a fish two-thirds of their own size. As a game fish, they are unexcelled. If the angler is not very expert with his rod the fish will get away from him, as the tricks that he will resort to to free himself from the hook are astonishing. He will dart hither and thither with the rapidity of lightning, and if there is a root, log or rock near by, he will entangle the line every time. Another trick of the fish is, when he is hooked, to spring out of the water and strike the line with his tail close to his mouth. This cunning movement will, nine times out of ten, free the finny rascal from the hook. The best snare one can use in fishing for this kind is live bait of most any sort—minnows, shrimp, small trout and small frogs.

Before the State Fish Commissioners interested themselves in black bass, there were none of the kind west of the Rocky Mountains, although there is a kind that somewhat resembles them that is caught in the vicinity of Monterey and Tomales. About twelve years ago the Commissioners brought from the East a lot of sixty or seventy small-mouth black bass, which they placed in the waters of the Napa and Alameda creeks. As very little has been heard of this lot, it is supposed they were nearly all killed off after being placed there. Since then the Commissioners have brought out other lots which they placed in the Spring Valley Water Company's lakes; these fish have multiplied so fast that they are being placed in other lakes and rivers, that they may stock as much of our water as possible. The Sportsman's Club of California have interested themselves in this fish and have taken great pains to bring them from the East and introduce them to the waters of Russian and American rivers. Three years ago they brought out one hundred black bass that averaged about ten inches in length, which they placed in Lake Temescal, back of Oakland. Now the lake is over-stocked and the club are making arrangements to stock Santa Rosa, Vallejo creeks, John K. Orr's lake and many private lakes and ponds with the surplus stock of Lake Temescal. It is the opinion of several sportsmen that black bass will do well in the brackish water of Lake Merced and several lakes that lie close to the ocean. If their ideas are correct and the fish will thrive in brackish water, we see no difficulty in the propagation of this valuable fish.

J. C. Woodbury, the agent of the California Fish Commissioners, arrived in this city on last Monday night, bringing with him, in twelve transportation cans, a select lot of three hundred young striped bass. They were taken from the Shrewsbury River, at Red Banks, N. J., on Monday, the 17th instant. Over four hundred were placed in all. A few died before leaving, and over seventy-five were lost at Council Bluffs, owing to the discourtesy of a railway

1882 79

official. On the road the fish required the constant attention of Mr. Woodbury and one assistant, an agent of Seth Green, the Superintendent of the New York Fish Commissioners. It was necessary to change the water every few hours and add the requisite amount of salt. The fish were fed several times a day. Crossing the plains good water was obtained from artesian wells at Fremont, Laramie, Antelope and Humboldt. In size these fish average about seven inches in length. They were taken to Benicia the night of arrival and set loose in the Carquinez Straits, at Army Point. Here the water is nearly the same as that to which they have been accustomed in their Eastern homes in the waters of the Atlantic Ocean and tributaries. This lot cost the Commissioners about $3.50 each, and when placed in the water the fish were in splendid condition; and if they can on y succeed in escaping the close nets placed by the Chinese in the neighborhood of Pinole Point, and thus reach salt water, we may confidently look forward to some splendid salt water fishing in future years. But one importation of striped bass has been made before this. It was four years ago last June, when one hundred and seventy-five were brought across the continent, and put in the water near Martinez. Only two adult fish of this lot have been taken, so far as known. One in this bay, the first season after being put in the water, weighing one and a half pounds, and the other was captured at sea, off Bolinas, the succeeding year, weighing four pounds.

The striped bass is one of the best known and most appreciated of all Eastern salt-water fish. They are eagerly sought after by enthusiastic anglers, and are an excellent food fish. Every summer sportsmen from the Eastern cities flock to the New England coast. Here among the many islands and about the mouths of the rivers striped bass are abundant. They are extremely cautious and wary, and the angler is often discouraged before his prize is finally secured. The striped bass is a native of salt water. It is found in all stages of growth, from the size of a smelt to seventy pounds weight. In form they are something similar to the salmon, but the head is larger and the body fuller. In color the bass is a bluish-brown above and white below. From the head to the tail, on a well-developed fish, are from seven to nine narrow dark stripes, which give to this variety its name. In the Spring they run far up the fresh water rivers after smaller fish. In the Autumn they spawn, and in the Winter are found in muddy salt water bays or about the mouths of rivers.

Congress not having, up to the present time, made any appropriation for the United States Fish Commission, no action has been taken by Professor Baird to put the hatchery on the McCloud River in order for this season's work. Ever since the establishment of this hatchery—a period of about ten years—from seven to ten millions of salmon eggs have been taken yearly, of which one-half to two and a half millions have each year been hatched out and placed in the McCloud River. By this means the supply of salmon in the Sacramento River for canning purposes has steadily increased—one hundred and thirty-seven thousand cases having been produced last year. If this supply is not kept up artificially, it is probable that the run of fish in the Sacramento will not be equal to the demand, and one of the great industries of the State thereby crippled. It has been suggested that in the absence of any action by the United States Fish Commission, the Fish Commissioners of this State obtain the use of the hatchery buildings on the McCloud River, and take and hatch out the salmon spawn on their own account. This will have to be done quickly, as all the arrangements will have to be made by August 15th to be of use.

The close season for salmon commences August 1st and terminates September 1st, during which time it is unlawful to take or have a salmon in one's possession. It is to be hoped that the close season will be religiously kept, as the supply of salmon during the month in the upper waters of the Sacramento and McCloud rivers is not one-tenth that of former years. The necessity is so urgent that it is expected that the Fish Commissioners will take extra measures to protect the salmon in their run.

Bay fishing during the past week has been good. Rock Cod have been especially plenty, and unusually large party of three fishing in the steam launch Wilson, off Lime Point, on Saturday last, caught sixty-three in a couple of hours—the largest weighing five pounds. Equally large catches are reported in Raccoon Straits and neighborhood. Toncods and smelts can be caught in all parts of the bay.

Near Colusa is Butte Slough, a lake about two miles long, and from 75 to 60 yards wide, which is well stocked with fish, particularly catfish. Any one who knows how to handle a hook and line properly can catch several hundred in a day. Some of the catfish weigh two pounds apiece, but there is not much pleasure in the sport. Pike, perch and chub are also taken there.

Of the twenty-one lobsters brought here four years ago and placed in the sea off Point Bonita, no authentic information has been received. They were all full of spawn, but being brought all the way from New York in the same water they started in, it is surmised that the spawn must have lost its vitality while on the way.

Serious complaints are made of a dam on the Mokelumne river near Lancha Plana which prevents the fish from ascending the stream. The river swarms there with catfish and salmon to such an extent that catching them is not attended with very great sport.

Black bass and catfish are now to be found in the mountain streams above Butte creek. The catfish are beginning to be looked upon as a nuisance, as they increase so rapidly in numbers that they will almost exterminate the other species in the same stream.

The fishing is reported as very good this season at Santa Monica and the sea-wharves are crowded daily with the devotees of the gentel art, who are generally rewarded with good catches of fish, with mackerel among the number.

There has been a very heavy mortality among the fish lately at Donner Lake, large number of club being washed ashore dead. It is attributed to some dynamite fluid, who ought to be prosecuted to the full extent of the law.

The Reno Gazette is informed that W. B. Todhunter has sent to market this season over 6,000 head of beeves. He is said to be the largest stock raiser in the country. There are others who send more cattle to the markets, but they buy them instead of raising them. He has over 20,000 head of stock cattle on 100,000 acres of land.

## THE HERD.

### THE ART OF BREEDING.

Farmers are prone to breed in a haphazard, careless sort of way. It is not given to everyone to be a Bates or a Booth, an I'Anson or an Ellesmere. To excel in the art of breeding the closest observation is needful. Darwin put it thus: "Not one man in a thousand has accuracy of eye and judgment sufficient to become an eminent breeder. If gifted with these qualities, and he studies the subject for years, and devotes his lifetime to it with indomitable perseverance, he will succeed and make great improvements, and if he wants any of these qualities he will assuredly fail." Breeding is an inborn art, an inspiration, as much as statesmanship, generalship, painting, poetry, music, mechanics. The germ must be there, ab initio. In such splendid specimens as are to be seen in our show-yards and sale-rings, the student has presented to him models which, aided by a close and discriminating study of our stud and herd books, can teach and develop the great principles and lines of breeding, so far as they have been disclosed to us. All are not destined to shine, but one and all have the command laid on them to make goodly use of even the one talent entrusted to their care. Do not, therefore, because you are not possessed of large capital, or, doubtless, your ability to create a Blair Athol or a Young Duchess, shirk and venture. Strive to learn from the often dear-bought experience of others; take up their results, and though you may never carry off the blue rosette, you may effect many improvements in your time and generation, and more than pay your way. Life is rarely long enough for a man to make his mark as the founder of a new and distinctive breed, and to see success in his own days, although he may effect vast improvements in existing breeds, and add many rungs to the ladder placed to climb the summit of perfection. Remember that over a century has sped away since Sir William St. Quinton (write his honored name in letters of gold), of Scampson-in-Holderness, and Mr. Michael Dobinson, of Durham, imported the Hollanders, to which breed our Short-horns owe their origin.

Some of the breeders' greatest successes have sprung from modest beginnings. The matron of the Duchess tribe of world-wide fame cost but 13 guineas. The dam of Oroñifs with her peerless filly-foal at foot, changed hands for forty sovereigns. Pocahontas, till she bore the Emperor of Stallions and his four distinguished brethren, was in obscurity. Queen Mary would have ranked as a common plater but for her pale-faced son Blair Athol. Laura, too, was of little repute in her own country till the elegant Petrarch showed his quality, and Phaeton, the grandsire of imp. Foxhall—the sensational horse of his year—was picked up at Tattersall's for an old song. Per contra, some of the best, as reproducers, have turned out heart-breaking failures. The plums are within the reach of all.

Gentle manners and quiet patient ways mark the successful breeder and his men. The fascinating ascendancy women obtain over the secondary animals is because of the tenderness and winningness of their approach. A rough master may upset all the virtues of generations.—Live Stock Journal.

Mr. A. B. Darling's three-year-old cow Bomba, 10,330, by Duke of Darlington, 3,460, out of Beauty of Darlington, 5,736, tested for the week ending July 15th, at his farm in New Jersey, gave 21 pounds 1 ounce of butter, which is the largest recorded week for a cow milking with her second calf. She came in June 16th, and is to be tested for a year if she persists at a rate that promises to reach 600 pounds or over. She is a grand-daughter of Eurotas, 2,454, that in her prime made the highest test yet recorded of an in-calf cow, viz., 778 pounds in a year.

## THE STAGE.

There is nothing in the way of novelty to announce, either in the past or during the present week that merits mention, save the phenomenal success of the Hanlons in La Voyage en Suisse and the production of a comic romantic opera, entitled Nemon, at the Winter Garden, that will be noticed more fully in our next issue.

It is generally understood that William Emerson will shortly take charge of the Bush-street Theatre, and with his tact, liberality and enterprise, he 'is' bound 'to make a brilliant season in this pretty and popular establishment. The only difficulty at the present moment appears to be in the elevation of the improvements made by Mr. Locke during his leasership.

At the Tivoli, the opera of "Der Freischutz" continues on its successful career; but other novelties are in active preparation. Save as regards a series of benefits, in which the acting is of a very secondary consideration, the drama appears in a comatose state; but with the advent of the Union Square Theatre in about a fortnight, we hope to chronicle a most successful season at the California Theatre.

The Baldwin Company, with the exception of Messrs. Jennings, Grismer and Bradley, and Miss Phoebe Davies, proceeded on Thursday last to Denver, to play an engagement of two weeks during the Exhibition there. The company will be under the management of Mr. Gus Frohman, and will doubtless meet with a good reception. At the conclusion of this engagement, a majority of the artists will go on to the East in search of pastures new, and we shall be glad to hear of their success, for such artists as Miss Ada Ward, Mr. Wheatleigh and Mr. John Dillon will be most valuable artists in any company in which they may be engaged.

The Haverly Minstrels, by a judicious change of programme, continue to draw large audiences, and from present appearances they will make the time as brilliant a season as they had on their previous visit. There is a hum of busy preparation at the Baldwin with the production of a spectacular piece that will partake more of the pantomine order than does the present attraction. Our theatre goers who remember the glories of The Red Gnome, with its spectacular scenes, bright incidents and clever acrobatic feats, will gladly welcome a piece of that kind to our boards, especially as the Hanlon Brothers strive in all they do to impart an originality to their tricks that excites both astonishment and approval.

Two sons of Harry Irving played Charles and Joseph Surface in the screen scene of "The School for Scandal" at a Liliputian Fair in London June 30 and July 1.

## THE MARKET PROSPECTS FOR LIVE STOCK.

Last week we gave a short article on the beef prospect of the Pacific Coast. From what we have learned during the past few days, we have no reason to change our opinion as to the steady price of beef during the coming month. The Coast feeders have sent us all they could spare, and the chances are that this Winter they will have to call on us for some of them back, as elated by the high price received during the Spring months, they have not reserved enough for home consumption. Nevada now comes to hand with a few; and by the middle of August that will be our main supply. But, judging by the price which butchers have been paying for large droves, the rates are firm, and no disposition is shown to let go of any short of paying prices.

From all accounts it would appear as if the cattle men of the Pacific slope have seen their worst days, as regards the price of beef. The greatest drawback in the past to beef has been the abundance of sheep, which have been thrown upon the market regardless of price. This was necessary, as should the herders hold them the ranges would soon be overstocked; but the last Winter was a hard one on sheep in California. Thousands upon thousands died from want of feed, and almost the entire increase had to be killed in order to keep the ewes alive. This, combined with the Eastern demand which at present exists for ewes for Montana and Texas, has kept the price steady all Spring, and will continue to do so during the Fall, as the Texas men are ready and willing to buy all that are offered them at less than the present market value. From this and various other reasons, some of which we have mentioned previously, it will be seen that both cattle and sheep men have cause to be jubilant.

Pork is very scarce, and packers have great difficulty in keeping up a supply; and at the present it looks as if it will be still harder before the year is out. Wars, and rumors of wars, have always been a point as to the holding of grain and corn for better prices, and in none of the Western States the corn crop is reported at about a 'one-half crop.' If such should be the case, it would prevent any crowding of our markets by Eastern packers. The latest intelligence is that the hog cholera has broken out in a virulent form at Bloomington, Ill., and that will also have an effect on California markets. Even should these changes not have their immediate effect on pork, as we look at it, there will be no great change in price during August. We give with our weekly slaughter-house report the price of wool, as taken from an exchange: Beef 6½m at quotations: steers, extra prime, 8½c; steers, prime, 8c; steers, fair, 6½@7½c; cows, extra prime, 7½@8c; cows, extra fair, 6 to 7c; veal, small 8 to 10c, large 7 to 8c; mutton, wethers, choice, 5c; fair, 4½c; ewes, choice, 4½c; fair, 4c; lamb, 6½ to 7c; pork, very scarce; prime hard, 10¾ to 11¼c; prime soft, 9¾ to 10½c; live hogs, hard, 7¾ to 8¼c; live hogs, soft, 7 to 7½c. Wool, sales limited: Humboldt and Mendocino, 25 to 26c per pound; Sonoma, 25 to 28c; Southern Sacramento Valley, 20 to 24c; Siskiyou and Modoc, 20 to 24c; Calaveras and foothills, 20 to 24c; San Joaquin, 15 to 20c; San Joaquin, defective, 15 to 18c; Southern Coast, burry and seedy, 15 to 18c; Eastern Oregon, fine, 25 to 26c; Eastern Oregon, poor to fair, 20 to 23c; Valley Oregon, fine, 25 to 27c; Valley Oregon, coarse, 22 to 24c.

## MARKET REPORT.

FLOUR—There is an active demand from local consumers, but the export inquiry is light. The best city extras sell for 65@$6 75 ⅌ bbl for jobbing lots.

WHEAT—During the past week there has been a material shading off in prices quoted in the foreign and foreign markets, and here buyers are shy. Considerable purchases of the new crop are reported to have been made in the interior by shippers, for forward delivery, principally for Port Costa, Benicia or Vallejo, and prices to paid are said to be relatively higher than buyers offer in this market. Spot lots of extra choice milling should be had for less than $1 70@1 75 for No. 1 while $1 70 is freely offered for August delivery at No. 1 of September delivery at Port Costa, with $1 70@1 72 asked; No. 2 while, $1 60@1 65; No. 2 while to fair, $1 55@1 60 for August delivery at Port Costa.

BARLEY—Owing to the lack of facilities for transportation, the arrivals are comparatively light, but it is expected will be more abundant in the near future. For feed there is an active speculative demand for future deliveries, and transactions on Call at the Produce Exchange have averaged about $1 20 per cental per sack. Early in the week the market was firm, but at the close holders are far from confident. Choice of bay brewing is scarce, and must have been sold at $1 40@1 45; No. 1 $1 30@1 35; feed, choice and fair, $1 15@1 20; ordinary $1 10@1 12; for No. 1 to best; bid $1 20 per ctl for No. 2.

OATS—Consignments of the new crop are increasing, and the market is bare from the tendency. Quotable at $1 65@1 85 per cental, as to kind and quality.

FEED—Jobbing lots from the city mills are quotable as follows: Ground barley, new, $31; old, $31½ coarse, $32; old, $32½; bran, $18; Middlings, $25@$27 80; Shorts, $18@17; Cornmeal, $36½ per ton.

HAY—Receipts are large, and the market continues steady. Wheat, $14@16; Wild Oat, $12@15; Barley, $10@12; Stock, $10@12; Alfalfa, $9@11; Compressed, $14@16; Clover, $9@11.

STRAW—Supplies are fair, and steady at 70@75c per bale.

BEANS—Quotations are largely nominal. Limas, $4@4 50; Pea and small white, $4@4 25; Bayos, $3@3 50; Butter, $3 75@4 25; Pink and Red, $2 00@3 25 per ctl.

ONIONS—Arrivals are less free, but low prices rule; Reds, 40@50c; Silverskins, 50@75c per ctl.

POTATOES—New crop sweets are now becoming forward, but have a stiffly face, selling for 3@3½c; Garnet Chile, 75@85c; Early Rose, 90@95c per ctl.

POULTRY—Live Turkeys, 15@18 per lb; Hens, $6 50@$7 50; Ducks, $4@5 per dozen; Broilers, $3@4 50 per dozen; Geese, $6@11 per pair.

GAME—Venison is now plentiful though at 11@14c per lb; Doves 50c of 75 at $6@$7 50; Hare, $1 25@1 50; Rabbits, $1@1 25 per doz.

EGGS—The demand is active and market firm at 30@32c per doz for store, good to choice fresh ranch.

HONEY—Market is dull at 7@8½c for extracted, and 17@18c ⅌ lb for comb.

BUTTER—Strictly choice fresh ranch roll is scarce at 31@32½c; common, 25@27c; mixed lots 22@27½c; firkin, 25@30c ⅌ lb.

CHEESE—Steady at 11@12½c ⅌ lb for California.

HIDES—Hides, dry and salt, 19@20c; steers, 20@21c; sheepskins, long wool, $1 50@2 25; medium, 75@1 50; short, 30@50c; goatskins, shearlings, 25@40c per skin; Calfskins, 12@15c per lb.

TALLOW—The demand is active and market well cleaned up. Rendered, 7½@8½c; refined, 8@8½c per lb.

WOOL—Receipts are light, and nearly all the spring clip has been forwarded to market. Choice Sonoma, Siskiyou, Humboldt and Mendocino product is quotable at 24@27c, as to condition; Great Valley, San Joaquin, free, 18@20c; defective, 14@17c; Calaveras and Foothill, 22@25c ⅌ lb.

FRUITS—Arrivals of all seasonable kinds are free and consignments meet with ready sale, for all kinds excepting lemons, which are a drug in the market, at jingles: German Prunes, 6@7½c ⅌ box; Pears, common, 50@75c per box; Apples, choice, 75@1 00 per box and 1 00@1 50 per ton; Blackberries, $2 25@2 50 per chest; Nectarines, 75@1 25 ⅌ box; Peaches, 50@75c ⅌ box; Crabapples, 75@1 25 per box; Cherries, 6@10c ⅌ lb; Apricots, 50@75c ⅌ box; Watermelons, $10@15 per 100; Cantaloupes, $1 75@2 50 ⅌ doz; Currants, $4 00@4 50; Raspberries, $3 00@3 50; Strawberries, $6 50@12 50 per chest.

VEGETABLES—Marrowfat Squash, $10@15 ⅌ ton; Egg Plant, $1 00@1 25 ⅌ box; Okra, 10@12½c ⅌ lb; Green Corn, 75@90c per doz; String Beans, 1½@2c ⅌ lb; Tomatoes, Vacaville, 50@75c; River, 50@75c; Oakland, 50c ⅌ box; Peppers, 50c ⅌ lb and 75c@1 25 ⅌ box; Asparagus, 6c ⅌ lb.

# THE KENNEL.

## FIXTURES.

National American Kennel Club's trial on quails, Grand Junction, Tenn., December 4th. D. Bryson, Memphis, Tenn., Secretary.

Louisiana Field Trials near New Orleans, La., beginning Dec. 11, under the management of the New Orleans Gun Club.

BENCH SHOWS.—Western Pennsylvania Society's English Setter Bench Show Derby, Pittsburgh, Pa., for English setter puppies whelped on or after March 1, 1882. Entries closed December 1, 1882. I. R. Stayton Allegheny City, Pa., Secretary.

FIELD TRIALS.—National American Kennel Club's trials on prairie chickens, Fairmont, Minn., September 4th. Entries to American Field Derby closed July 1st; to All-Age Stake, September 4th. Joseph H. Dew, Columbia, Tenn., Special Secretary for these trials.

Gilroy Rod and Gun Club's trials on quails near Gilroy, Cal., October 28th Open to dogs owed in California, Oregon, Nevada and Arizona. E. Leavesley Secretary, Gilroy, Cal.

Eastern Field Trials Club's trials on quails, near High Point, N. C., November 17th. Entrance to Derby close July 1st; to All-Age and Members' Stake November 1st. Fred. N. Hall, Secretary, P. O. Box 834, New York.

## ANSWERS TO CORRESPONDENTS.

Under this head will be found replies to all questions that may be asked of the Kennel Editor in relation to breeding, breaking, or entering dogs, feeding or curing them of any ordinary disease. Correspondents must state plainly what are the peculiar symptoms of the malady for which they need advice, and in all cases, especially when desiring to know the best way to correct a dog of a fault, must be careful to state the age and sex. No answers will be sent by mail, and all questions must be marked Kennel-Editor WEEKLY BREEDER AND SPORTSMAN, San Francisco, Cal.

J. L., MARYSVILLE.—We will shortly publish an article on breeding dogs to retrieve, which will give you all the information you need. Space will not permit of a full answer this week.

L. JONES, TURLOCK.—An injection of warm water and soap is frequently found to be a valuable remedy for cases of mechanical constipation, such as you speak of.

T. C., SAN FRANCISCO.—We do not know of an Irish Water Spaniel pup for sale. If any of our readers have one and will forward the particulars to this office, we will advise you.

MISS M., SAN FRANCISCO.—Japanese pug dogs are utterly useless except as pets. They are very scarce in Japan and China now, and a well-bred one, possessing all the special marks of the breed, will command a good price. In England and the East they are rarer than in San Francisco, and often bring as much as $200. Any of the officers of the Chinese steamers would doubtless be able and willing to procure one for you from Yokohama

P. S., SACRAMENTO.—Ergot of rye given in three-grain doses, at intervals of two hours, will generally be found a great aid in cases of difficult parturition.

## NEW COURSING GROUNDS.

One of the principal reasons that the glorious sport of coursing has not yet taken its proper place at the head of the field sports of California is, that to enjoy a first-class run one has to go a greater distance from the principal cities than can well be accomplished within the limited time at the command of gentlemen engaged in business. When one looks around for a suitable place, well stocked with hares, in which to enjoy a day's coursing he calls to mind the plains near Lodi, Point of Timbers near Mount Diablo, Merced, Whitcomb's Ranch near Sacramento, the Santa Clara Valley, San Jose, and other places still farther afield, but can hardly name a spot any closer to home. Of all these places Point of Timbers is the only one that can be visited in one day, and then the time for sport is not sufficient to pay for the trouble and expense of making the trip. Under these circumstances it cannot be doubted that lovers of the leash will hail with delight a scheme to furnish coursing grounds at Newark on the line of the S. P. C. R. R., less than one hour's journey from the city and which can be reached at a merely nominal expense.

Mr. John Dugan is the projector of this splendid place, and has already matured it so far that ere the cool weather makes coursing practicable the coursing grounds at Newark will be complete, and ready for all who have dogs to run and love to see them in chase of an active jack rabbit. The land Mr. Dugan has set apart and laid out for the sport is but a hundred rods from the railway station at Newark. It is about a quarter of a mile square, and will soon be increased by the addition of nearly a quarter of a mile more. On the land there are about 35 acres of trees and underbrush, which will form a fit and natural home for the hares to breed. Beets, lettuce and turnip food, of which hares are inordinately fond, will be planted in spots widely apart to insure the game taking plenty of natural exercise in their search for food. In fact, we use the words of that ardent courser, Clem Dixon, "it is the best natural spot for coursing and for breeding hares that I have seen in all my travels."

There are already a few hares on the land. Years ago they swarmed there, but the constant practice of the persistent pot hunter has thinned them out, and to fill up, Mr. Dugan has made arrangements for the capture and shipment of a large number from the San Joaquin plains. As soon as they arrive they will be turned loose within this spacious inclosure to breed and enjoy life as they please, free and unmolested, until the greyhounds are brought up in the Fall to see how fast they can run. When all Mr. Dugan's plans are complete, and they soon will be, for he has the liberal aid and help of the South Pacific Coast Railroad in his scheme, a new era will dawn for coursing in this State. Gentlemen in San Francisco who, for the reasons above stated, have held aloof from the sport, will commence to keep and breed greyhounds. Those who have dogs already will increase their kennels when they find that they can always get a run at a few hours' notice. Private matches will be arranged. Ladies will take an interest in the sport when they find they can witness it without a three day's trip to Merced or Stockton. Dogs being in greater demand will increase in value and importations will be more frequent than at present.

Perhaps the new grounds for a time will be found inadequate to run off the great Spring matches, but they certainly will be all that is needed for the club meetings, as there will be an unlimited number of hares. The increased interest in coursing will add largely to the number of dogs run at the open meetings, so that there will be no loss to Merced, and the day is not far distant when as in England it will be esteemed a valuable favor to secure a nomination in an open meeting.

Mr. Dugan owns some fine dogs himself, and is fully alive to the requirements of a coursing ground. Teams will hardly be needed at his place, but he will doubtless always be able to supply as many good sound horses as the judges need. His hotel at Newark furnishes excellent accommodations, and altogether, when complete, it will be no exaggeration to speak of Newark as the courser's paradise. The grounds are far larger than the Plumpton grounds or the far-famed flats at "Altcar," and as the hares will be in a wild and natural state the sport will be not a jot less exciting than on the almost boundless plains of Merced. The proprietor will find no lack of patronage from the start, and the only trouble he will have is to keep away the murderous pot-hunter and his little gun. His plans are entirely practicable. They have been found successful in several instances in England, and here, where the supply of hare is unlimited, they cannot fail of being a grand success.

One of the greatest advantages they will afford is that they will enable gentlemen to properly train and test their dogs before a big match.

Time and again the owners of dogs have lost valuable prizes simply because the dogs have not been trained to work in slips. This can only be properly taught by actual practice, which heretofore could not be given in the city. It is also necessary to success to give a dog an occasional chase after a hare, that it may learn to watch its game for a "turn," and not run blindly and give the spectators the idea that it needs more ground in which to get around than a forty acre field affords. A little coursing is necessary, though too much on the same ground always makes a dog "lurch" and ruins him for a match. The grounds will also serve to educate judges, and that good judges are somewhat needed here no one will deny. A judge who only sees a course twice a year is apt to lose confidence in his riding; also in his judgment, and as judging is, to a great extent, a matter of a quick eye and good nerves, practice is indispensable. It is also well for slippers to take a little practice other than what they get in the actual performance of their duties in a match. Practice makes perfect all around, and the new grounds will give to all a splendid chance to practice.

The following table may be found of interest to the gentlemen who are commencing to found a standard of measurement to guide judges at bench shows. The measurements are taken from celebrated dogs that have won distinction at bench shows:

| | Gordon Heavy Weight. | Light weight dog. | Light weight bitch. | Light weight bitch. |
|---|---|---|---|---|
| Height | 22 inches. | 22¾ inches. | 21½ inches. | 21 inches. |
| Length of head | 9¼ " | 9¼ " | 8½ " | 6¼ " |
| Girth of chest | 27½ " | 27 " | 25½ " | 24¾ " |
| Round cranium | 16 " | 15½ " | 15 " | 15 " |
| Round forearm | 14 " | 12 " | 10 " | 10½ " |
| Length of tail | 15 " | 16 " | 15 " | 13¼ " |
| Nose to end of stern | 48 " | 39¾ " | 37½ " | 38¼ " |
| Lower corner of eye to end of nose | 4½ " | 4¾ " | 4 " | 4 " |
| Weight in condition for work | 60 pounds. | 50 pounds. | 47 pounds. | 45 pounds. |

## THE GORDON SETTER.

The following letter to the *American Field* from the pen of Harry Malcolm is well worthy of careful perusal by all persons interested in that most beautiful of all sporting dogs, the "Gordon," or black-and-tan setter:

EDITOR AMERICAN FIELD: I wish to lay before the breeders of this grand field dog, the Gordon setter, a standard by which I think they should be judged at future shows, as my experience in hunting these dogs for many years has proved to me conclusively that the present standard by which they are judged is an abortion. Stonehenge evidently selected the largest dogs ever seen in the Gordon setter family, and while they may have looked well upon the bench, they are of very little service in the field, either in America or Europe, for I have always seen them succumb, after a day or two's work, to those of lighter frames, the latter made dog lasting for as many weeks, and enduring just as much hardship as dogs of any other strain. The Gordon setter of former days was evidently of a light, racy frame; was a merry worker and good stayer, which we find to be the case to-day. Stonehenge, in making his standard from the large, heavy dog, has been mainly responsible for the present misconception about him, and we at present are suffering from that error. The original Gordon setter was anything but heavy or clumsy.

I agitated this change of standard several years ago, and was in hopes some person would get up a new one. After having waited in vain, I now take upon myself the task, and will request the breeders of these field beauties, if this standard meets with their approval, that they indorse the same through the *American Field*, and at the same time request the officers of the different shows to adopt it. If the breeders of the black-and-tan setters wish to have a separate class for their dogs, they have the same right as the Laverack or Llewellin setter, but by no means should a breeder of Gordon setters allow the two classes to be mixed as they are now at our bench shows; allow no dogs to win in the Gordon setter class unless they can show by pedigree on side of sire and dam that they trace back to Gordon setter dogs of undoubted purity. Now the following is what I suggest as a scale of points by which these dogs should be judged:

| | |
|---|---|
| Skull | 10 |
| Nose | 10 |
| Ears, lips and eyes | 4 |
| Neck | 6 |
| Shoulders and chest | 15 |
| Back, quarters and stifles | 15 |
| Legs, elbows and hocks | 11 |
| Feet | 9 |
| Stern | 4 |
| Flag | 4 |
| Symmetry and quality | 4 |
| Texture of coat and feather | 4 |
| Color | 4 |
| Total | 100 |

The skull should be very nearly like the English setter, with the exception that the Gordon setter's head should be a shade heavier and wider; the heavy heads they have now must be gotten rid of. The nose should be moderately long and wide, no fullness allowed under their eyes; from corner of eye to end of nose should be from four to four and one-half inches; there should be a slight depression between the eyes; the nostrils should be a shade wider than in the English setter, and a shade larger in the openings; the nose should be moist and cool, and the end of the nose should be of a black color. The jaws should be perfectly even in length; a "swine nose" or "pig jaw" is a decided blemish. With regard to ears they should be a trifle longer than the English setter, but in other respects they must resemble them, and must be thin in leather; they should be set low, and should lie closely to the cheeks without showing any of the inside; they should be well covered with hair with as little wave as possible. The lips should be like the English setter, and must not be so full and pendulous as the present type. The eyes must be full of animation, of medium size, and of a rich color, between brown and a gold, or like the ovary of the Italian bee. The neck must be like the English setter, it must not be throaty, but must be clean and racy; it should show well back into the shoulders. The chest, and herein lies one of the great faults of many of our present show Gordon setters, must be gotten rid of at once; I mean his wide bull-dog chest, and heavily loaded fore shoulder. On the contrary, he should have a narrow, deep chest, a nice racy front. What would one think of seeing a thoroughbred racer coming on the track with a Percheron horse's chest? Many of our present Gordon setters look to me just as ridiculous as the racer would look thus bred. He must have well sprung ribs behind the shoulders, a straight back, and a good depth of back ribs. The shoulders should have plenty of liberty, with sloping deep shoulder blades, the elbows well let down and a moderately arched loin. Beware of stooping hindquarters, they show weakness and want of pace. The hindquarters should be well guarded; they must be as strong or stronger than the front. The tail should be well put on, and carried in very nearly a straight line, and be string-like at the end; a crooked tail at the end, or better known as a "tea-pot" tail, is a decided blemish, and though many Gordon setters are seen with it, it must be gotten rid of. The thighs must be long from hip to hock; the hocks must be straight, and the stifles moderately well bent, and set wide apart to allow the hind legs to be well brought forward, which will allow ease in his movements. See that the loins are not slack, for if they are, endurance in the setter is lost. The elbows and toes should be set straight, for otherwise you will confine the dog in his movements by their close attachments to the ribs. The feet should be well looked after, for without good feet any setter is useless. Many differ as to how the foot should be formed. My preference is always for a "cat-foot;" it looks better, is handled by its possessor with more ease and grace, and when well filled in with hair between the pads, you will not require a stronger or stouter foot, nor one with more endurance than such a foot possesses, either to hunt on the hills or prairies. Any foot, either cat or hare shaped, bare of hair between the toes, is almost useless to the dog possessing it. Symmetry and quality in character the Gordon setter should display an amount of, or, in other words, the general outline must be good and at a glance taking to the eye of a sportsman. The coat should be softer, flat and close. A number of Gordon setters have wavy or curly coats; the curly coat is an abomination, and should be bred out; the wavy coat should be treated in the same manner, but it is the lesser evil of the two. The coat should be straight and flat, and should not be as long as the English setter's. The back and ribs should be well coated with softer, flatter and straighter hair than the present Gordon setter; it should be very glossy looking, and in color be of a rich plum black. The Gordon setter should only show setter coat on his profile, legs and tail; the latter should be shorter than the English setter's, and of graceful form, being bare of hair two inches from root of tail, with flag flat and scanty, tapering to nothing at the end. The tan markings should be of deep, sienna color, and should show on lips, cheeks, throat, spot over eyes, under side of ear, but not to show except faintly in upper corner edges nearly at skull, to show nearly to elbows, hind legs up to stifles, and on the under side of flag but not running into its long hair. A Gordon setter with a white frill or a white toe or two should not be cast aside as has too often been done in the past, but always aim to breed them with as little white as possible.

The Gordon setter should not weigh less than fifty nor more than fifty-five pounds, and should not stand at shoulder higher than twenty-four nor more than twenty-four and a half inches. This will give a nice sized dog; he will look well, will not look by any means squatty, but stand well up, with nice straight legs and they must not be too short or too long.

If the above is followed you will see Gordon setters worth looking at on the bench, and a pride and glory to their masters in the field.

HARRY MALCOLM.

# THE RIFLE.

THE INTERNATIONAL MATCH.—Among the twenty-three gentlemen selected to participate in the final competition for places in the team to go to America are the following well known shots: Caldwell, of Renfrew; Gibbs, of Gloucester; Goodyear, of the Sixth Lancashire; Goodsell, of the Second Bucks; Major Humphreys, of the Cambridge University Regiment, who was second among the competitors for the Albert jewel; Corporal Mullineaux, of the Sixth Lancashire; Mr. Vatie, of Dumfries; Major Parsee, of Devon, former winner of the Queen's prize, and Colonel Woodrow, of Devon. The team will sail for New York in the steamer Alaska on the 26th of August. They will take up quarters at the Garden City Hotel, Long Island. The scores so far made by the team are no criterion of their strength, as none of the men will use the Martini rifle, but most of them will shoot with the Metford rifle.

## A NOVEL MATCH.

The Rod and Gun Club of Santa Barbara celebrated their organization by a grand hunt on the 19th inst. A match was formed, sides chosen by the leaders, C. F. McGlashan and Chet F. Brown, each of whom was desirous his side should be victorious in the day's doings. O. Kaeding, L. A. Holmberg and James F. Barron were appointed judges to decide who are the victors getting the most points on the following basis:

Bear, 1,000; California lion, 500; wild boar, 500; lynx, 500; deer, 250; coyote, 100; wildcat, 100; eagle, 50; road-runner, 25; crane, 25; yellow-hammer, 15; hare, 15; magpie, 15; rabbit, 10; gopher, 10; bee-martin, 10; hawk, 10; crow, 10; dove, 5; trout, 5; lark, 5; squirrel, 5; curlew, 5; woodpecker, 5; linnet, 2; blackbird, 1; snipe, 1.

The following were the teams as chosen: C. F. McGlashan's—Israel Miller, Charles B. Greenwell, J. W. Ogad, Harry Stoddard, A. Silva, J. J. Elizalda, S. S. Fisk, L. D. Lilley, N. McCloskey, E. M. Hoit, J. H. Ogan, W. W. Hollister, Jr., John Spence, F. L. Birabent, Fred. A. Moore, Manuel Garcia, C. W. Gorham, A. Goux, A. Hayman, E. C. Roeder, J. A. Maguire, John Reed, Thomas Nixon and Al. Crane. C. F. Brown's consist of—L. A. Holmberg, F. C. Foster, John Baillard, J. T. Barron, George A. Culbertson, E. C. Durfee, James P. Vance, Tracy L. Warn, Ed. Breck, A. C. Rynerson, C. Aug. Thompson, Ed. C. Tallant, J. M. Hunter, Thomas A. Cravens, G. A. Lloyd, J. M. Short, Otto Kaeding, A. M. Ruiz, S. C. Hicks, I. K. Fisher, John Longawa, P. L. Moore, H. F. Maguire and John T. Hope.

Each member was expected to strictly regard the game laws; he was allowed to start as early as possible, and to hunt when he pleased. The whole day was to be devoted to hunting, and every one was expected to be at the headquarters by sunset.

The result, as the Santa Barbara *Independent* remarks, was very one-sided, but in giving the score, as follows, that journal omits mention of the game killed.

"For Captain Brown's credit, let it be said, several of his best shots failed from some cause to put in an appearance, which, together with the fact that they selected unfortunate ground, reduced his showing by hundreds more than it should have been. For this reason Captain McGlashan and his men have not felt they could hoist the traditional rooster so common to party victories, especially as the probabilities are that the other side will win the belt at the next bout, and the boot will then be on the other leg.

"Those who arrived at the rendezvous at sundown, and whose scores were counted, were as follows: Chet Brown's side—J. R. Vance, 735 points; C. F. Brown and Tracy L. Warne, 527; Joseph Bates, 250; John Longawa, 242; John T. Hope, 149; I. K. Fisher, 56: total, 1,959. Their total number of points were 1,224; divided by six, the number of hunters, gave 204 as an average. McGlashan's side—Israel Miller, 884 points; C. F. McGlashan, 611; F. A. Moore, 598; S. S. Fiske, 461; Al. Crane, 420; John Spence, 397; A. Silva, 283; N. McCloskey, 283; R. R. Fullington and L. D. Lilley, 175; E. M. Hoit, 40; C. W. Gorham, 30: total, 4,182. The total number of points of these was 1,883; divided by eight, makes an average of 235⅜. May there be many returns of the day."

It is said that bear, both cinnamon and grizzly, are plentiful this year in the mountains and that experienced hunters have been known to kill three within the week.

In Key West, Florida, sheep will lose their wool in the second year that they are on that island. No matter where they are brought from, they will become as woolless as goats. Lambs dropped there will retain wool just about the same length of time, when their woolly coats become nothing else but a soft, short hair, like in every respect to that of the goat. It is well known that there are woolless sheep, but it was doubtful whether an importation of any kind to a strictly tropic clime would result as above.

# ATHLETICS.

## OLYMPIC ATHLETIC CLUB HANDICAP MEETING.

This meeting, which took place at the grounds of the Club, in Oakland, last Saturday, deserves more than a passing notice. The Club is the most prominent one on the Coast. The grounds are excellent, and were well prepared for the occasion. The attendance for a handicap meeting in this part of the world was unusually large, numbering about three hundred, all very orderly, respectable and enthusiastic. Everything passed off smoothly and pleasantly. The inner grounds were kept clear of all intruders, and an unobstructed view was obtained of every event. The day was not bad, but still was not what could be called a favorable one for speed, as the wind was directly in the face of the competitors on the back-stretch. The atmosphere was moist, cold and heavy, and the sun, as usual at this season of the year, was obscured by heavy clouds. Still, these were slight drawbacks compared with the lack of competitors in the events. The Club boasts a membership of over seven hundred, almost all young and energetic, and many among them of much promise as athletes. These should have been represented by at least thirty members in the 100 yards, and almost as many in the 440 yards; instead of which, four only appeared during the day to uphold the reputation of the Club, and but two of the four were in condition to make an effort if hard pushed. As we predicted last week, R. S. Haley showed poor form. His trial heat was won by a fine burst of speed in the last twenty-five yards, when his friends had given up all hope of his winning a place in the final. His time from scratch was given as 10⅕, the slowest taken on the grounds. Harris was beaten about half a yard, and Eiseman, being out of condition, was third, a yard and a half behind. In the second trial heat Brown was awarded first, but it could not have been by more than three inches, and Emmons was only shut out by half the thickness of his breast, and every inch from the start to the finish was a bitter contest between the three contestants. The time, 10¾ seconds, was a poor showing for Brown and Emmons, considering their handicaps, 7 and 6 yards respectively, but was good for Anderson, who won second and a place in the final.

Haley, Brown, Harris and Anderson were the starters in the final heat. Haley, even if not in the best of condition, can do a single dash of 100 yards in 10⅕. Harris and Anderson are not better than 11⅕ from scratch. Brown should have won first, but was left on his mark at the start, and made very little effort to win, seeing that his case was hopeless. Haley's want of preparation was very apparent in this heat. He weakened at seventy yards, and undoubtedly ran three yards slower than in his trial heat. The time given was 10 seconds. Harris ran a game race, and deserves the medal which he won, but that he could cover the distance in the time reported is too much to believe of him yet. In the 440 yards Brown, although in the best form, for some unknown reason made no effort whatever. Haley, realizing that he could not do the full distance, started from scratch at a 220 gait, and stopped as soon as he saw the dressing rooms. Eiseman, not having had any preparation, naturally failed in the last 100 yards, and ran a hopeless race. Anderson was liberally handicapped, as it was known that he never had ran before, and was never in danger at any point in the race, and won first by fully twelve yards. The struggle for second place between Harris and Germain was closely contested up to within fifteen yards of the finish, but Germain was done up, and Harris added a second medal to his maiden first in the 100 yards. The Club members failed to secure either a first or second medal in either event. It is to be hoped that some of them will make a more favorable showing at the next meeting.

The following is a summary of the events:

One Mile Handicap Bicycle Race.—W. H. Lowden, 82 yards, 1; C. Burkhalter, 70 yards, 2; J. H. Spring, 40 yards, 0. Time, 3:17¼.

One Hundred Yards Handicap Run.—First Trial Heat.—R. S. Haley, scratch, 1; Arthur Harris, 11 yards, 2; D. Eiseman, 10 yards, 0. Time, 10¼. Second Trial Heat.—Wm. C. Brown, 7 yards, 1; J. H. Anderson, 11 yards (penalized 1 yard), 2; E. S. Emmons, 6 yards, 3. Time, 10¼.

Eight Hundred and Eighty yards; Handicap Bicycle Race.—J. H. Spring, scratch, 1; C. L. Leonard, scratch, 2; R. F. Varrinder, 40 yards, 0. Time, 1:37.

One Hundred Yards Handicap Run.—Final Heat.—Arthur Harris, 11 yards, 1; J. H. Anderson, 11 yards, 2: R. S. Haley, scratch, 0; Wm. C. Brown, 7 yards, 0. Time given, 10 sec.

Two Mile Handicap Bicycle Race.—C. Burkhalter, 310 yards, 1; G. L. King, 180 yards, and W. H. Lowden, 310 yards, tie for second place; H. C. Finkler, scratch, 0. Time, 6:42.

Four Hundred and Forty Yards Handicap Run.—J. H. Anderson, 55 yards, 1; Arthur Harris, 40 yards, 2; Harry Germain, 45 yards, 0; D. Eiseman, 37 yards, 0; R. S. Haley, scratch, 0; Wm. C. Brown, 22 yards, 0. In this event a penalty of 1 yard was inflicted on all but Germain. Time, 60 sec.

## THE OLYMPIC ATHLETIC CLUB.

The members of the Olympic Athletic Club are anxious to have an important Fall meeting on their new grounds, open to all amateurs on the Coast. It is suggested, also, that special gold medals be offered for breaking club records. R. S. Haley would undoubtedly attempt to beat the 220 yards record, and possibly the 100 or 440 yards. Hawes, Emmons, O'Kane, Doolan and Searle of the Club, and Frick and Dwyer of the University, would make an interesting contest at 100 yards, all starting from scratch. The wheelmen would certainly do their part towards making the meeting one worth attending. The Golden Gate Athletic Club is praying for an opportunity to compete with the Olympics in a tug of war. Admission day will probably be a holiday, and at that time we are almost certain of being favored with the pleasantest weather of the season. The following are standard events, and, with perhaps three or four additional ones, would fill the programme for an entire afternoon's entertainment:

100 yards, handicap run, open; 100 yards, scratch run, open; 100 yards, handicap run, juvenile class; 220 yards, handicap run, juvenile class; 220 yards, handicap run, open; 440 yards, handicap run, open; one mile, scratch run, open; 220 yards by R. S. Haley, to beat club record; putting 16lb weight; running high jump; running wide jump; pole vaulting; 440 yards bicycle race, without hands; 880 yards bicycle race, handicap; one mile bicycle race, handicap; two mile bicycle race, handicap.

There is ample time to talk the matter up, *enthuse* the athletes, and make such a meeting a success.

## HOW TO SAVE THE DROWNING.

It may be well just now to make some suggestions to residents at the seashore in regard to the proper course to be pursued in cases of danger by drowning, and, in the first place, to offer a few words of advice to those who may be called on to swim to the aid of persons struggling in the water. It is most important that the drowning person be assured in a cheery voice that he is safe, and urged to cease struggling, for the more he struggles the more water he swallows, and the more dangerous it is to attempt a rescue. It is sheer madness to seize a man struggling in the water, for he will blindly grasp his would-be rescuer and drag him down; but when he has become quiet, the swimmer should catch him by the hair of his head, turn him quickly on his back, giving him a sudden pull, which will cause him to float, and then start for the shore. Those who have tried this plan say that it is very easy of execution, and instances are on record where one man has swam ashore with four persons, whose hair he grasped and whom he then threw on their backs. In case of a strong outsetting tide the rescuer should, however, throw himself on his back and float until help arrives, for he will soon exhaust himself by batting against the current. And it may be said, in passing, that a lone swimmer, when caught by the undertow, will do far better to float than to wear himself out in uninterrupted struggling for the shore. When a body has sunk to the bottom, and bubbles indicate that life is not extinct, a person may dive in the direction indicated by the bubbles; but he should seize the hair with one hand only, using the other hand in conjunction with the feet in raising both himself and the drowning person to the surface. When the rescued person has been landed, the first thing in order is to arouse him by wiping his body dry, and by slapping smartly the stomach and chest. The jaws should be separated if they are clinched, and kept apart with a cork or small piece of wood. The person should be turned on his face, and the stomach kneaded as long as water flows from the mouth. Then the throat should be wiped with a rolled handkerchief, and the patient turned on his back, with the pit of the stomach elevated above the rest of the body. The waist should then be squeezed with great pressure, as if to force the contents of the chest into the mouth, and suddenly let go. This process, which is an imitation of natural breathing, should be repeated at momentary intervals, but with regularity, until the person's breath is restored; but if satisfactory results do not follow after three or four minutes, the patient should be again turned on his stomach, but in the opposite direction from before, for the purpose of expelling any water remaining in the air passages. Then the artificial respiration should be resumed, and continued until the patient revives or until death is beyond doubt. The process of drying and rubbing should be all the while continued, soon after the breath returns. These simple rules are old, but every one who reads them may this very Summer have cause to put them in practice.

Recent advices from London state that the English pedestrians are already preparing for the foot race which is to come off in New York next October. Rowell has been there for two weeks, with Peter Duryea. The pedestrian takes a run of ten miles every morning, just to keep his muscles flexible. In the afternoon he and Duryea drive a team of American trotters through Hyde Park. They are going to Paris for a week; after which Rowell will go into regular training for the race. He has a private track on his country place near Chesterton, of seven laps to the mile. Rowell promises to be in better condition than he was last Spring. He has an unknown pedestrian that will train him for the race. They will start for New York in the Alaska, August 26th. Hazael is training steadily at a quiet retreat a few miles out of London. He looks in excellent condition, and says that he will make the man who beats him go a long ways beyond six hundred miles. George also drives an American trotter. Weston is giving temperance lectures in England, and it is said he may start in the October race.

# BICYCLING.

## BICYCLING IN OAKLAND.

The weather on Saturday last was unusually pleasant and favorable for the athletic meeting at the Club Grounds in Oakland. The first race was a mile handicap, the contestants being J. H. Spring, 40 yds., 52-inch wheel; C. Burkhalter, 70 yds., 54-inch wheel; W. H. Lowden, 82 yds., 52-inch wheel. Spring went to work immediately to overtake the leaders, but it was not until the fourth lap that he succeeded in coming up with Burkhalter, who had also about closed the gap between himself and Lowden. In this manner the contestants crossed the line and commenced the last lap, in which all were closely lapped in their original order. Spring coming with a rush on the last turn would have crept into second place, but was pocketed between the two others and did not get out until too late, the line being crossed in the original order, Lowden leading by a length, and Spring lapping Burkhalter's wheel; time, 3m. 17s.

The next race was a half mile handicap, with three entries, as follows: C. L. Leonard, scratch, 50-inch wheel; J. H. Spring, scratch, 52-inch wheel; R. F. Verrinder, 40 yds., 46-inch wheel. Verrinder held his own splendidly for nearly a lap, when Leonard closed upon him and passed into the lead, finishing the lap well ahead. On the last lap Spring made his effort and passed into first place in spite of Leonard's efforts, winning the race by about eight yards in 1m. 37s.

The last race was two miles, and promised to be the most interesting of all, but the scratch man was so heavily handicapped that he lost heart and never attempted to overtake his man and the following were the starters: W. C. Franklin, scratch, 52-inch wheel; G. L. King, 180 yds., 54-inch wheel; W. H. Lowden, 310 yds., 52-inch wheel; C. Burkhalter, 310 yds., 54-inch wheel.

Burkhalter took the lead at once, and gradually increased it over Lowden to the finish. King set out at once to overhaul the leaders, and had cut down Lowden's lead in the third lap of the second mile, but Burkhalter was too far ahead to be caught, and King finished more leisurely in Lowden's company, making a dead heat with him. Finkler, after one lap, without much effort, increased his pace and began to cut down the leaders, but at the end of six laps, finding the task hopeless, gave it up and ran out at a slower pace. Time of race, 6:42.

The Twenty-five Miles Championship.—F. Wood, of Leicester, and R. James, of Birmingham, met for the third time at the Leicestershire Cricket Ground, June 24th, to decide who was to be the first twenty-five miles champion. It will be remembered that the same riders ran the same distance on the 17th, and after a splendid race the referee was unable to separate his men at the finish, and therefore wisely gave in for a dead heat. James, of course, remained in Leicester, in view of to-day's race, and during the week both men took the greatest care of themselves. Unfortunately, however, when Wood went for a spin on the Friday previous, his shoe came off, and, being thrown from his machine, he was severely shaken. Receiving every attention, the mishap did not interfere materially with his condition, and, upon appearing at the mark, both seemed in good fettle, and considerable interest was evinced in the issue. The weather was fine. There were over three thousand spectators present, and the utmost enthusiasm prevailed. At the start, at five minutes to seven, James went off with the lead, and made the running considerably faster than the previous race. The first five miles was recorded in 15 minutes 58 seconds, nearly three minutes better than the last race. Two laps later, James made a tremendous spurt, but Wood was fully equal to the occasion. James made another determined effort to get away in the twenty-second lap, but Wood objected. The ten miles was hoisted in 32 minutes 10 seconds, and great excitement prevailed when, four laps later, James made a determined effort to get away. Both were still proceeding at a capital pace, and the fifteen miles time was made in 48 minutes 12 seconds. In the forty-third lap another splendid spurt was made by the local man, who, for the first time, assumed the leadership. During the ensuing few laps Wood took his man along at a merry pace, and twenty miles was covered in 1 hour 3 minutes 48 seconds, the best on record. From this point to the finish the issue was stubbornly contested, and towards the finish the excitement grew intense. Amid loud cheering, Wood, just previous to entering the last lap, dashed away from his man, and, half a lap from home, six yards separated the pair. After this, however, James made his final effort, and, gradually drawing on his rival, got upon even terms a dozen yards from the tape, and secured the verdict by a length. Time, 1 hour 20 minutes 15 seconds, beating the previous best—1 hour 20 minutes 55 seconds, by J. Keen, on the Surbiton Grounds, August 23, 1880.

The Hon. I. Keith Falconer, formerly a noted racing man, whose time, 5:36 for two miles, still remains unbeaten, has recently made a notable journey from Lands End, England, to John O'Groat's House, at the extreme northern point of Scotland, 994 miles, in a little less than thirteen days, making nearly 77 miles per day, although a great deal of wet weather and strong head winds were encountered.

Dick Turpin's famous ride from London to York has often been beaten by bicyclists. During the early part of July the distance, 196¾ miles, was accomplished by H. R. Reynolds of the London Bicycle Club, in 21 hours 43 minutes. The same gentleman also won the annual road race from Bath to London, 100 miles, May 29th, in 7 hours and 26 minutes.

Tricycles have not as yet become common or frequent in the United States, but one has recently been ordered by a lady in a neighboring town for short trips about town, shopping, etc., and it will be found far more convenient than walking and less troublesome than a horse, where the roads are reasonably good.

The question is often asked whether tricycles are not slow. This is best answered by the time of a mile race which recently took place in England, where the full mile was made in 3:16, and three miles were ridden in 11 minutes.

Game-Bag Filled at One Shot.—H. J. Sheldon left his camp at Cooper City, on the Pecos, last Saturday afternoon in search of game. Saturday night he camped at the upper forks of the river, and Sunday, bright and early, was again on the march. About four o'clock in the afternoon the burro, which had wandered ahead, came running back, apparently in great terror, ears and tail erect, eyes glaring, making that peculiar mournful sound for which his species is noted, and refusing to be caught or comforted. Not being able to make out from the report of the confused burro just what had happened, Mr. S. cocked his gun and advanced slowly and cautiously on the unknown enemy. Crawling along on his hands and knees for about a quarter of a mile, he at length doubled a bend in the river, and there, standing in full view in the meadow, and not more than 150 yards away, he saw a huge grizzly bear with three cubs, and, just beyond the bear and in direct range with her, an animal that he at once recognized as the long-sought-for elk. Neither of the beasts was aware of his approach, so, quietly rising upon one knee and resting his rifle across the other, which is Mr. S.'s favorite position in shooting, he took deliberate aim. Bang went the gun, away sped the bullet and down fell two animals—in fact, three—the bear, the elk and Mr. S. himself. The bullet had cut the backbone of the bear completely in two, and, passing on through, had lodged in the heart of the elk; and the extraordinary task to which the rifle had been subjected produced such a violent recoil that the hunter himself was stretched flat upon the ground. Recovering himself speedily, Mr. S. advanced upon the prey, hunting knife in hand, but life was extinct in both animals. The little cubs on hearing the report of the gun, fled; but, being only a few weeks old, were speedily captured, tied in bags and fastened on the back of the horse.—*Santa Fe News.*

Worse than Fishermen's Yarns.—Sanders Hyatt, of Covington, some years ago shot the head off a rattlesnake which was coiled ready to spring. Noticing that the snake looked uncommonly large, Hyatt cut it open with his knife, and a fox squirrel jumped out and ran up a tree, where he shot it. His dog had chased the squirrel, which, running close to the snake, had been snapped up just before Hyatt arrived on the scene. An immense water moccasin was killed recently near Albany, Ga., having in its mouth a catfish eight inches long. The snake had seized the fish by the head, unfortunately for him. There are two big fins on the head of a catfish, and this fish stuck these fins into each jaw of the serpent, which was thus rendered powerless to either swallow or relinquish its prey.—*Atlanta* (Ga.) *Constitution.*

## ANSWERS TO CORRESPONDENTS.

Salinas City, July 26, 1882.

Breeder and Sportsman.—Please inform me whether Bertrand and Cherokee were by Sir Archy? If they were not, inform me through the Breeder and Sportsman what horse was their sire. W. O. Hatch.

Answer.—Bertrand, by Sir Archy, his dam, Eliza, by imported Bedford, grand-dam, imported Mambrina. Cherokee, by Sir Archy, his dam, Roxana, by Hephestion, grand-dam, Roxana, by imported Marpiot.

## BAY DISTRICT ASSOCIATION.

**RACES!**    **RACES!**

Saturday, August 5, 1882.
.....AND.....
Saturday, August 12, 1882.

☞ **Notice for Entries.** ☜

FOR SATURDAY, AUGUST 5, 1882.

*(race conditions and purse details)*

SAME DAY.

FOR SATURDAY, AUGUST 12, 1882.

SAME DAY.

☞ Five or more to enter; three or more to start. Entrance 10 per cent. National rules to govern. Entries to close with Secretary, Monday, July 31st.

T. W. HINCHMAN, Secretary.
1435 California street.

## POSTPONEMENT OF ENTRIES

The time for making entries at the

## CHICO FAIR

Has been extended from

### July 22d to August 1st.

The weights in races Nos. 4 and 8 as per Speed Programme will be announced August 10th.

J. H. KRAUSE, Secretary.

## Pacific Breeders' Association.

### Embryo Trotting Stakes, 1882.

Sweepstakes for foals, 1882, $100 each; $25 forfeit; $10 declaration; $5 nomination fee.

*(stake conditions)*

N. T. SMITH, President.
JOS. CAIRN SIMPSON, Secretary pro tem.

## CALIFORNIA'S EXPOSITION.

THE 29th ANNUAL

## STATE FAIR

BEGINS AT

### SACRAMENTO, CAL.,

ON THE 11th AND CLOSES ON THE 16th OF SEPTEMBER.

The Premium List embraces liberal awards for all kinds of Live Stock, Machinery, Implements, etc., Textile Fabrics, Mechanical, Agricultural and Horticultural Products, Fine Arts, etc.

Any further information may be had upon application to the Secretary, from whom Premium Lists may be procured.

EDWIN F. SMITH, Secretary.
P. O. Drawer A, Sacramento, Cal.      July 15 44

## The Victorian Trotting Club,

(L'd)

### MELBOURNE, AUSTRALIA,

.....OFFER.....

### PRIZE OF 2,500 DOLLARS,

With Entrance Fees and Sweepstakes of $50 each from Starters added.

---

## Pacific Coast Blood Horse As'n.

## PROGRAMME.

FIXED EVENTS—SPRING & FALL MEETINGS

### 1883 and 1884.

## BALDWIN STAKE FOR 1882

### SPRING MEETING.

FIRST DAY.

WINTERS' STAKE—For three-year-olds, to be run the first day of the Spring Meeting; dash of one-and-a-half miles; $100 each; $25 forfeit, $500 added; second to have $100; third to save stake. Nominations to close for 1883.

SECOND DAY.

PACIFIC CUP—Handicap of $100 each, $50 forfeit, $20 declaration, $500 added; second to receive $100, third to save stake; two-and-a-quarter miles; to be run on the second day of the Spring Meeting. Will close the 1st of March, 1883.

THIRD DAY.

"SPIRIT OF THE TIMES" STAKE—Dash of one-and-three-quarter miles for all three-year-olds; $100 each, $25 forfeit, $500 added; $100 to second, third to save stake. Nominations to close for 1883.

### FALL MEETING.

SECOND DAY.

LADIES STAKE—For two-year-old fillies; $50 entrance, $25 forfeit, $500 added; three-quarters of a mile; second to have $100, third to save stake. Nominations to be made for 1883.

THIRD DAY.

STALLION STAKE—Conditions—Only those three-year-olds are eligible which are the get of stallions owned in this State.

## SPEED PROGRAMME

OF THE

## Mount Shasta Agricultural Association,

TO BE HELD IN

## YREKA, SISKIYOU CO.,

—ON—

### Wednesday, - - October 4th, 1882.

For racing purposes this District shall comprise Siskiyou, Shasta, Trinity, and Modoc Counties, Cal., and Jackson and Lake Counties, Oregon.

FIRST DAY—WEDNESDAY, OCT. 4.

SECOND DAY—THURSDAY, OCT. 5.

THIRD DAY—FRIDAY, OCT. 6.

FOURTH DAY—SATURDAY, OCT. 7.

### Rules and Regulations.

C. M. CHASE, Ass't Sec'ty.

## SPEED PROGRAMME

FOR THE

### First Annual Meeting

OF THE

### SANTA CRUZ COUNTY

## Agricultural Fair Association,

At SANTA CRUZ,

Commencing - Tuesday, August 15th,

## $3,500 IN PURSES!

FIRST DAY—TUESDAY, AUG. 15, 1882.

SECOND DAY—WEDNESDAY, AUG. 16.

THIRD DAY—THURSDAY, AUG. 17.

FOURTH DAY—FRIDAY, AUG. 18.

## REVISED SPEED PROGRAMME

FOR 1882.

### FOURTH ANNUAL MEETING

OF THE

### SONOMA COUNTY

## Agricultural Park Association,

At SANTA ROSA.

FIRST DAY—TUESDAY, AUG. 22, 1882.

---

SECOND DAY.

FIFTH DAY—SATURDAY, AUG. 19.

### Remarks and Conditions.

JAMES O. WANZER, Secretary.

J. D. CHACE, President.

### SECOND DAY—Wednesday, Aug. 23.

### THIRD DAY—Thursday, Aug. 24.

### FOURTH DAY—Friday, Aug. 25.

### FIFTH DAY—Saturday, Aug. 26.

### ENTRIES.

### CONDITIONS.

CHARLES HOFFER, Secretary.
J. P. CLARK, President.

## THIRD FAIR

OF THE

## Ninth District Agricultural Ass'n

TO BE HELD ON

### September 19, 20, 21 and 22, '82

AT

### Rohnerville, Humboldt Co., Cal.

SPEED PROGRAMME

FIRST DAY.

SECOND DAY.

THIRD DAY.

FOURTH DAY.

### Remarks and Conditions.

OFFICERS OF THE BOARD.

G. C. BARBER, Ferndale ............................ President
R. M. CHALFERS, Rohnerville .................. Secretary
MORRIS LEVINGER, Rohnerville .............. Treasurer

# Golden Gate Fair.

**SPEED PROGRAMME FOR 1882**

## $10.000

IN

## Stakes and Prizes

FIRST DAY—Monday, Sept. 4, 1882.

SECOND DAY—Tuesday, Sept. 5.

THIRD DAY—Wednesday, Sept. 6.

FOURTH DAY—Thursday, Sept. 7.

FIFTH DAY—Friday, Sept. 8.

SIXTH DAY—Saturday, Sept. 9.

### CONDITIONS.

L. WALKER,     A. C. DIETZ,
Secretary.     President.

---

## $12,500

## In Purses and Stakes.

CALIFORNIA

# STATE FAIR

## SPEED PROGRAMME

FOR 1882.

FIRST DAY—Monday, Sept. 11.

SECOND DAY—Tuesday, Sept. 12.

THIRD DAY—Wednesday, Sept. 13.

FOURTH DAY—Thursday, Sept. 14.

FIFTH DAY—Friday, Sept. 15.

SIXTH DAY—Saturday, Sept. 16.

### REMARKS and CONDITIONS.

EDWIN F. SMITH,     HUGH M. LARUE,
Secretary.     President.

---

## SPEED PROGRAMME.

## $13,000 Gold Coin

### IN PURSES.

## The Largest Purses Offered in the State.

## STOCKTON,

### Sept. 19th to 23d inclusive, 1882.

TUESDAY, SEPT. 19TH.

WEDNESDAY, SEPT. 20TH.

THURSDAY, SEPT. 21ST.

FRIDAY, SEPT. 22D.

SATURDAY, SEPT. 23D.

### REMARKS AND CONDITIONS.

#### Ladies' Equestrianism.

### ENTRIES..

J. L. PHELPS, Secretary.
P. O. Box 133, Stockton, Cal.

---

SECOND

## ANNUAL EXHIBITION

OF THE

## SAN MATEO AND SANTA CLARA COUNTY

## AGRICULTURAL ASSOCIATION

### NO. 5,

TO BE HELD AT

## SAN JOSE, CAL.,

......FROM......

### Sept. 25th to 30th, '82, inclusive

## SPEED PROGRAMME.

FIRST DAY—Monday, Sept. 25th, 1882.

SECOND DAY—Tuesday, Sept. 26th.

THIRD DAY—Wednesday, Sept. 27th.

FOURTH DAY—Thursday, Sept. 28th.

FIFTH DAY—Friday, Sept. 29th.

SIXTH DAY—Saturday, Sept. 30th.

### REMARKS AND CONDITIONS.

K. KING, President.
T. S. MONTGOMERY, Secretary.

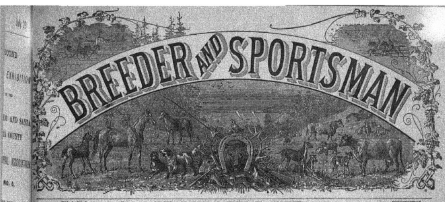

VOL. I—NO. 5.
No. 508 MONTGOMERY STREET
SAN FRANCISCO, SATURDAY, AUGUST 5, 1882.
SUBSCRIPTION
FIVE DOLLARS A YEAR

# NOTABLE HORSES OF CALIFORNIA.

## ABBOTSFORD.

So far the illustrations of trotting horses have been confined to two families, Romero being a scion of the Simpson Blackbirds on the male side of the house, Belle Echo, Electioneer and Echo Hambletonians. The dam of Romero was of the Mambrino Chiefs following the sire; and this week we presents distinguished son of the same great clan. Though many years ago there were bitter controversies over the position which Mambrino Chief was entitled to fill in the trotting records, every man who is conversant with the subject, and not swayed by prejudice, must acknowledge the great merit of the descendants of this horse. The blood mixes kindly with others of the great families of trotters, and though we claim that every one of the trotting families are greatly benefited by a direct strain of thoroughbreds, few will question the advantage which has followed incorporating it with the Mambrinos. Thus the first which gave the highest celebrity was the great, truly great, mare Lady Thorn. Her dam was by Gano, a thoroughbred son of American

Eclipse, and her grandam by a son of Sir William, a thoroughbred horse by Sir Archy. Those who had the best knowledge of the capacity of Lady Thorn, men thoroughly posted in regard to the fast trotters of the past and present, rank her as being the peer of the best, and Dan Mace had the utmost confidence that the accident which disabled her was the sole reason she did not make a mark which would have been close to the best on record now. The Mambrino Chief stallions which have gained distinction have been from highly bred mares. The sire of Black Cloud, who made so capital a race at Chicago, is Ashland Chief, by Mambrino Chief, the dam of Ashland Chief being a mare by imported Yorkshire, and his grandam imported Flounce, by Mulatto. The sire of Abbotsford was Woodford Mambrino, by Mambrino Chief, and his dam Woodbine was by the thoroughbred horse Woodford. She was also the dam of Wedgewood—record 2:19; and this gives additional value to her offspring, showing that she had merit as the progenitress

o' trotters in her own inheritance. Woodford Mambrino, though not trotted in public until he was fifteen years old, made a record of 2:21¼; and his got make a fine showing in the calendar—Abbotsford 2:21½, Convoy 2:22¼, Magenta 2:24½, etc.

Illustrations of the value of the Mambrino Chief blood could be multiplied until the space occupied would be far beyond the limit of these sketches. A few more will show the potency of it when coupled with many other strains. Croxie—record 2:19¼—was by a son of Mambrino, Clark Chief, and this horse was also the sire of Woodford Chief, 2:22¼; Blanch Armory 2:26; and several others in the 2:30 list. The dam of Protoine—2:18—was by Mambrino Chorister, a son of Mambrino Chief, and another son, Mambrino Patchen, has five, with records running from 2:23 to 2:30; and still has another son, Mambrino Pilot, a large number of fast ones to his credit, from Hannis, 2:17½, and Mambrino Gift, 2:20, up. Santa Claus and Piedmont have each two crosses of Mambrino Chief, so that the four stallions next to Smuggler, with records of 2:17¼, 2:17¼, 2:17½, 2:17¼, are strongly imbued with the blood.

Mambrino Chief bears the same relationship to the thoroughbred Mambrino as Rysdyk's Hambletonian, both being grandsons, the sire of Mambrino Chief, Mambrino Paymaster, the dam of which was by imported Paymaster. Thus on the side of the sire, Abbotsford has many near kindred of the greatest distinction, and his dam Columbia, by Smith's Young Columbus, is also honored by a relationship to many of the celebrities of the tracks. Her sire also got Myron Perry, 2:24½, Sea Foam 2:24¼, Commodore Vanderbilt 2:25, Harry Harley 2:25¾, Phil Sheridan 2:26½, Ben Smith 2:27, Farmer Boy 2:28, Jim Ward 2:28½, and Fitzgerald 2:30. Columbia was also the dam of Dido, a very fast pacer and now in the Sunny Slope stud.

Abbotsford was foaled in 1872, bred by J. W. Knox, and sold by him to C. W. Smith of San Francisco, when five years old. His first race was trotted in Sacramento, August 14th, 1878, and we were very much amused at a conversation in which a Mr. —— of San Jose, George Treat and William Hendrickson participated. It was during the journey to Sacramento, and the informer was anxious to impress them with the merit of a young brown horse which Mr. Knox was training. He was sure that he would win the race he was engaged in, but in response to the cross-questioning of Hendrickson he would not give any reasons for his belief, but at least fifty times between San Francisco and Sacramento he reiterated that the "brown colt would win sure." This was not satisfactory to Messrs. Treat and Hendrickson, and when they found that Harry was largely the favorite before the start, their investments went with those of the majority. The starters were Harry, Corisande, Tamarack, Granger, Lady Emmet and Abbotsford, and after Harry won the first heat in 2:29½, it was thought to be so great a certainty for him to win that in the pool sales he brought $20 to $5 on all the others. The second heat, however, turned the tables. Abbotsford trotted fast from the start, took the lead in a few strides, went to the half-mile in 1:12, and won the heat handily in 2:27. He won the other two with the greatest ease in 2:29, 2:29¼. His next appearance was on the Oakland Trotting Park at the Fair of the Golden Gate Association, when he defeated Corisande (who won the third heat), Harry, Lady Emmet, Proctor and Goldfinder, the time 2:31¼, 2:29¼, 2:27½, 2:27. This was on September 10th, 1878, and the next day he was called upon to try conclusions with Gibraltar, Echora, Alice, Barney, Bickford, Prophet, Hayward Chief and Harry, in the 2:31 class, and from the good showing he had made in his previous races he was the favorite in the betting, bringing more in the pools than all the others. He won the first heat in 2:25, but Gibraltar proved a far better horse than was anticipated, as he won the second, third and fourth, in 2:26, 2:27, 2:24½. In the last heat there was a grand struggle between Gibraltar and Abbotsford. One hundred yards from home Abbotsford led by a neck, "Old Gib." managing to get his nose to the score first.

At the State Fair, in the 2:40 class, it was held that Abbotsford "could not lose," and a compromise was effected whereby he got one-half of the purse, $500, and left the other $500 for the other entries to fight for.

His great race for this year was at San Jose, and a queer feature of it was the attempt of Mr. Knox to withdraw Abbotsford, claiming that he was lame. While it was evident that there was a trifle of "dodging" on one foot the judges did not consider it enough to interfere with his trotting, and the result proved that their estimate was correct. The other starters were Gibraltar and Monarch, Gibraltar the favorite in the betting, though quite a number gave Abbotsford strong support, and after the first heat, which Abbotsford won in 2:25¼, the premiership was reversed and the odds changed to $10, to $8 in favor of Abbotsford. The second heat was a remarkably fine showing for so young a horse, especially in his first season on the track. The quarter-pole was reached in 35¼ seconds, and the half-mile made in 1:10. There was a splendid race down the stretch, Gibraltar had drawn up when the straight work was entered, and all the way from the three-quarters to within one hundred yards of the score it was hard to say which had the best of it. Gibraltar broke at the critical time and Abbotsford won the heat in 2:21½. The third heat Abbotsford went to the half-mile in 1:10½, and had opened a gap of five lengths on Gibraltar, and it seemed as though the race was at an end; but on coming into the stretch something went wrong with him, as nearly we can remember a shoe or weight out of place, he broke, changed into a pace, broke again, Gibraltar winning in 2:27½. The fourth heat proved that there was something wrong in the third, as Abbotsford won in 2:24½. This race took place on October 2d, and on the 26th of the same month he won a $2,000 match with Corisande, the mare getting the first heat in 2:26, Abbotsford the others in 2:30, 2:26¼, 2:28. That this season's performances were a notable showing for a horse which was first put in training in April, few will deny. Owing to an injury which he received, 1879 and 1880 were almost blank years for him on the track. In 1880 we saw him trot a trial on the Oakland track in 2:20, and from the ease with which he made it the impression was general that two or three seconds could be subtracted whenever it was necessary. But the leg again was injured at Petaluma, and one race was all that he participated in. This was at Petaluma, on the old half-mile track; he won the first heat in 2:27½, hurt himself in the second, which was won by Brigadier in 2:27¼, and was then withdrawn. His first race in 1881 was at Santa Rosa, in a race won by Brigadier in 2:25, 2:25, 2:25¾, Abbotsford and Bateman dividing the honors for second place. From what he had shown in his work both owner and trainer were disappointed, and the only explanation which seemed to cover the case was that the old injury still troubled him. There is no necessity for following him through the races which he participated in after the race at Santa Rosa. They gave rise to considerable feeling, and if anything more than a mere mention at all was made, it would involve questions which are now settled, and we hope satisfactorily. It is sufficient to say that he came within one quarter of a second of duplicating his fastest record, trotting at San Jose in 2:21¾ in a second heat, after making the first in 2:22.

As to the form of Abbotsford the engraving is admitted to be one of the best likenesses ever published, and those who are intimately acquainted with his form pronounce it such. There may be a trifle of too much fineness given to the limbs from the knees and hocks down, as Abbotsford has more bone and greater width of leg than it is usual to see in a horse of his size. In size he is medium, and in color a rich, rosewood brown, and though it may be thought that the picture is an exaggeration as to the exuberance of mane and tail shown, it is exactly represented. He is a handsome, without being a "showy" horse, and those of his colts which we have seen are of very high form. Better than that, they show that they have inherited the fast-trotting step, and their owners are of the opinion that they will not be found wanting when the trial comes. Jasmine, by Abbotsford, her dam Sweetbriar, won the yearling Embryo last year, and as this is the first of his get which ever started, and we are under the impression that he has none which are older than two years, it is a good beginning. From his blood, his own performances, action, temper, etc., there is a strong guarantee that "notable" as he is, the future will show him still more worthy.

## SOME OF THE ROADSTERS OF SACRAMENTO.

SACRAMENTO, August 2, 1882.

EDITOR BREEDER AND SPORTSMAN: I wish to devote a few lines of your space to a description of the beautiful Riverside drive of the Sacramentans, and of the fine gentlemen's roadsters which one can see almost daily there. There is probably no amusement that could be conceived of that is so conducive to health, that will so quickly and completely restore a man to his normal condition after the cares and perplexities of a hard day's work at the desk or behind the counter or in the shop, as a drive behind a fast trotter, especially if there are a number of good roadsters on the road all eager to have a brush. It braces a man up, sets his blood to circulating with fresh vigor, and removes the cares of business from his tired brain so effectually that it is impossible for it to return until the following day. There is probably not another drive in the country that is equal to the Riverside drive of Sacramento for this kind of amusement. Four miles out of road, made of as good material and kept in as perfect condition as any race-track in the world, gives them a chance which is unequaled for testing the speed and endurance of their nags. At the end of the road the genial Nick has ample facilities for refreshment of man and beast, and a game of shuffleboard. I would suggest the propriety of having other amusements—a bowling alley, for instance, and a croquet ground, so that the ladies could have a way of amusing themselves instead of sitting in the buggy while their escorts are having all the fun. Every night after business hours you may see them out here by the dozens, each one thinking he has the boss. This is hard to decide, as one gets the advantage one night and another the next, according to the condition of their horses or the position one gets in the crowd. But I will inform you of one fact: if any outsider comes here thinking he can get away with the laurels, he must bring something that can pull a buggy faster than a 2:40 gait.

I give a brief mention of some of the roadsters that are to be seen during the week in this beautiful drive: John T. Carey's matched pair of blacks, Forrest and Buck, half brothers, by St. Clair; W. R. S. Fay's matched pair, full brothers, by Challenge from a Morgan mare, and two single ones, Friday by Morgan, dam of Messenger blood, and Lady Grace by Signal, her dam Morgan; Dr. M. Gardner's roadster, bright bay, by Young Rattler, dam by Belmont; B. McCreery, of Sacramento Flouring Mills, large bay mare Madge, by Fred Low, from Fanny King by Rysdyk's Hambletonian, Jr.; C. H. Hubbard's matched pair of ponies, Lady and Buck, formerly owned by Mr. Tubbs of Oakland, can pull a phaeton in three minutes; Henry Gerber's bay mare Kitty, by Chieftain from a Kentucky Whip mare; Mr. Gilman, of the Red House, has the old and well known gray pacer Prince; Gus. Hart, Attorney-General, fine bright bay roadster by Keokuk; Dr. N. A. Hughran has a handsome pair of chestnut roadsters, Dick and Jo, Dick by Young David Hill, dam by Gold Dust, Jo by Young Kentucky Hunter; A. L. Frost, Internal Revenue Collector, black mare Fannie by Black Hawk; W. H. Govan's Danger, by Young Nelson, dam by St. Clair; C. H. Eldred, of the State House Hotel, pair of sorrel roadsters, both by Black Hawk, dam by Belmont: H. J. Kilgariff has a fine bay mare that but few of them can beat; E. L. Billing's Joker, by Black Ralph, from a St. Clair mare; S. H. Todhunter's brown mare, by Young Rattler out of Skaggs' mare, Lady Washington; Capt. J. D. Young's roadster, Colonel, by Bellfounder, dam by St. Clair; Ed. F. Taylor, of the U. S. Land Office, has a good one, a big gray; Mr. G. M. Locke, of the firm of Locke & Lavenson, bay mare Mollie, by Rattler, dam by Sir Harry; H. Wachhorst, jeweler, has a very fine speedy mare by Butterfield's St. Clair, dam by Geo. Moore; Samuel Jelly, jeweler, chestnut, Jim Nelson, by Old John Nelson; W. O'Brien's Splendor, gray mare, by Tecumseh, dam by Messenger Duroc, she and Wachhorst's mare are among the fastest on the road; Ed. R. Hamilton's bay gelding, Henry, by Mambrino Chief, from a thoroughbred mare; J. D. Smith has a fine roadster by Tecumseh; Wm. Beckman, of the People's Savings Bank, drives a good one, and Frank Mitchell, owner of the Golden Eagle carriages, gets out among the fast ones occasionally.

H. P. M.

# TURF AND TRACK.

## FIXED EVENTS.

Santa Cruz County Fair Association. First annual meeting at Santa Cruz, Aug. 15th, 16th, 17th and 18th.

Sonoma County Park Association, at Santa Rosa, Aug. 22d, 23d, 24th, 25th and 26th.

Sonoma and Marin Agricultural Societies. Annual Fair at Petaluma, Aug. 29th and four following days.

Golden Gate Fair, to be held at Oakland, from September 4th to the 9th inclusive.

Butte District Fair at Chico, from September 5th to September 8th, inclusive.

El Dorado District Fair at Placerville, from September 5th to September 8th, inclusive.

California State Fair. Annual meeting at Sacramento, from Monday, September 11th to the 16th inclusive.

The San Joaquin Valley Association Fair at Stockton, from September 19th to the 23d inclusive.

Oregon State Fair at Salem, from September 18th and during the week.

The San Mateo and Santa Clara County Agricultural Association Fair at San Jose, September 25th to the 30th inclusive.

Humboldt and Mendocino District Fair at Rhonerville, September 19th to September 22d, inclusive.

Modoc, Plumas and Lassen District Fair at Greenville, from October 2d to October 5th, inclusive.

Monterey District Fair at Salinas City, from October 2d to October 6th, inclusive.

Nevada State Fair, at Reno, from Monday, October 2d, to the 7th, inclusive.

Mount Shasta Agricultural Association Fair at Yreka, October 4th, 5th, 6th and 7th.

Eastern Oregon Fine Stock Association at Union, from October 9th to the 14th inclusive.

### FAIRS AT THE EAST.

Kentucky State Fair at Lexington, August 9th to September 2d inclusive.

Minnesota State Fair at Farmington, August 31st to September 8th inclusive.

Iowa State Fair at Fairfield, September 1st to the 8th inclusive.

Minnesota Agricultural Association, at Minneapolis, September 4th to the 9th inclusive.

Nebraska State Fair, at Omaha, September 11th until the 16th inclusive.

Rhode Island State Fair, at Providence, September 12th to the 15th inclusive.

Pennsylvania State Fair, at Pittsburg, September 7th to the 21st inclusive.

Wisconsin State Fair, at Fond du lac, September 11th to the 16th inclusive.

Ontario Provincial Fair, at Toronto, September 18th to the 23d inclusive.

Connecticut State Fair, at Meriden, September 18th to the 22d inclusive.

New Jersey State Fair, at Monroe, September 18th to the 22d inclusive.

West Virginia Central Fair, at Clarksburg, September 19th to the 21st inclusive.

Indiana State Fair, at Indianapolis, September 25th to the 30th inclusive.

Western Michigan Fair, at Grand Rapids, September 25th to the 30th inclusive.

Texas State Fair, at Austin, October 17th to the 21st inclusive.

## THE GREAT FOUR-YEAR-OLD TROT AT CHICAGO.

For this race six colts of the twelve nominations answered to the bell-call, and a remarkable lot they were—Jay Eye See, Adelaide, Waiting, Bronze, Jim Booman, and Ed. Geers. In the pools Bronze sold for $50, Jay Eye See bringing $45, Waiting $42, and the field $21.

*First Heat.*—On the fourth scoring an even send-off was effected, Waiting having the pole, Jim Booman second place, Adelaide third, Bronze fourth, Jay Eye See fifth, and Ed. Geers the outside. Waiting evidently had the speed of the party, as he shot to the front as soon as the word was given, going around the first turn a length in advance of Bronze, who led Jay Eye See a like distance. Before the quarter-pole was reached, however, the Racine colt had passed Bronze, Waiting constantly going away from the others. Down the backstretch the entire lot was well strung out, but at the half-mile pole, in 1:14, Adelaide had trotted into third place, and was rapidly overhauling Jay Eye See, Waiting being now ten lengths ahead of the black colt. Adelaide made a break soon after entering the homestretch, which enabled Jay Eye See to retain second place easily. Waiting was pulled to a jog at the distance-stand: and walked under the wire a length ahead of Jay Eye See, Adelaide a poor third, and the others as per summary.

*Second Heat.*—In spite of Waiting's easy victory, the pool-selling after the heat was livelier. Jay Eye See soon became prominent in the pools, and so rapidly did he advance that before the start for the second heat he was selling even against the field. The start was a good one, but before the turn was reached Jay Eye See broke and fell back to fourth place, Waiting leading Bronze a length to the quarter-pole, in 39 seconds. He maintained his advantage down the backstretch, Adelaide trotting into third place, with Jay Eye See a poor fourth, and the rest strung out. The Racine colt made another break near the half-mile pole, and a third at the lower turn, Waiting and Bronze being still in the lead. Waiting seemed to have the heat won at the distance stand, but from this point to the wire Bronze came very fast, being beaten a head only, in 2:25¾, Jim Booman third, Jay Eye See fourth, Ed. Geers fifth, and Adelaide last.

At the conclusion of the second heat the crowd had become deeply interested in the race, and Bronze finishing so easily rather demoralized the pool-buyers, who, having received the "correct tip," had played their money freely on Jay Eye See. The Michigan delegation shifted the cut and backed Bronze heavily.

*Third Heat.*—Hickok was selected as their best man to pilot Bronze safely into port. The driver was removed from behind Bronze and Orrin took his place. In the meantime, Budd had been secured to drive Jay Eye See. As Jay Eye See had acted unsteady in the previous heat Budd, at the risk of losing the heat and race to Waiting, determined to go an easy heat and feel of his colt, the race being considered virtually lost to him, but "desperate case, desperate remedies." Bronze took the lead when the word was given, and was never headed, although Waiting got within a length of her in the homestretch. The filly won in 2:25½, Jay Eye See a good third, the others as per summary.

*Fourth Heat.*—The betting now ruled: Bronze, $100; field, $60. The scoring showed evidently that Budd now meant business, as he brought his horse up at every score. The word was given on the fifth score, when Bronze, lapped by Waiting, showed at the turn, Budd trailing Bronze closely. Midway of the turn Waiting made one of his grapevine breaks, ran in, and crowded Budd back. Then Budd tried to go around him on the outside, and the grapevine twist was still at it. Rounding into the backstretch Budd succeeded in getting by, after the sitting down process had caused him to lose ten open lengths. Bronze passed the quarter-pole in 37 seconds. Down the back side she was sent for blood, but the grand shout from the grand stand evidenced the fact that the Doble's black beauty was gradually closing on Orrin, who passed the half going smooth as a bird, 1:15½. Rounding the turn nearer and nearer drew the black phantom, rounding into the straight, every motion, every effort of man and horse was watched. Nearer they come; the crowd are silent. Will he catch her? Will he stand the pinching at the finish without breaking? If so, Budd has her beaten surely. At the distance-stand they are on even terms, and ch driver and horse strain every nerve; a rousing shout d yell. Budd has won! but in a flash, and the long cheer hushed, and "Oh! Isn't that too bad," with the deep-hing crowd. It was not only too bad, but painful—parularly to a fellow that had his money that way, you know the rousing welcome to victory had frightened the little ck beauty, and he bounded into the air like a frightened r. The grand bay mare beats him for the heat in 2:26½. tting home in 1:11, and Jay Eye See in 1:09; but for the thusiasm of the crowd he would have won this heat sure, spite the unfair work of Waiting's driver. Bronze won, t the terrific finish is beginning to tell.

At the conclusion of this heat there was more dismay among oling speculators, the manner in which Budd was bringing is colt nearer to the front each heat, and the colt showing distress, made the Bronze party shaky; still they stuck Bronze as favorite at long odds before the horses were ng up.

*Fifth Heat.*—Mr. Dow, the Judge, requested the crowd to ease refrain from shouting at the finish, as it frightened e colts. When the word was given on the fourth scoring, e start was a good one to all. Hickok went away fast, but is time Budd lay up painfully close to him. Bronze led a length at quarter-pole in 38 seconds, and position out same at half-mile. Rounding the turn Budd began to ose on the mare, and as they shot past the three-quarter-le at a 2:19 gait, a long, frenzied shout went up from the owd, with wild exclamations, "Budd has him!" But Budd sn't got him yet. At a terrific pace they come thundering the stretch, nearer, closer. Budd is on even terms at the stance. A suppressed murmur, "Don't shout," passes ong the line; all are silent; they are within ten yards of e wire; Budd is leading nearly a neck, and as the crowd itness the artistic manipulations of these two great horse-en, in this desperate struggle for the finish, they will con-ol themselves no longer, and the old Goldsmith Maid-nuggler shout goes rolling out from the thousands of roats as Budd fairly rolled, as well as lifted the grandest ur-year-old in the world under the wire in the unprece-ented time, for the fifth heat, of 2:22¾, the wonderful are beaten but a neck, the last half of this fifth mile, by vo four-year-old colts in 1:09¼. As Budd returns to weigh rousing welcome is given him, and his friends rush around im to congratulate him as in the pleasant days of memory hen Dexter, the uncle of this black colt, was king of the arf, as we may yet see this worthy representative of the amily a ruler again.

*Sixth Heat.*—Pools were selling Jay Eye See even against ie field, and many of the timid "boys" "shifted the out" nce more; but the friends of Jay Eye See stuck to him to ie last, as Budd assured them he could not lose. Orrin, ho had heretofore considered the race sure to him and his iends, began to look a little shaky. The word was given n the fourth, with Jay Eye See, who now had the pole and hould have been protected, fully a length behind. Orrin as quick to take advantage of the favor, and rushed his are at once to the pole, and, going on with a great burst f speed for a four-year-old in the sixth heat, he showed at ie quarter in 36s., leading Budd not more than a length. he positions were maintained to the half-mile in 1:10½. the back quarter in 34½s., a 2:17 gait (if this would not stop a four-year-old in the sixth heat, every one of which had been a horse race, nothing but a club would). Rounding the turn the terrific pace began to tell on the mare, and perpetual motion—Jay Eye See—keeping up the clip, soon placed himself on even terms with Orrin, who, seeing that he was beaten, carried Doble so far out that it looked as though he headed for the gate out of the park. This proved a delusion, as they were soon discovered making for the home plate at a killing pace. Midway of the stretch, when Budd had the mare beaten, his horse left his feet, and a prolonged "Oh!" and "He's beaten" by the crowd. Budd in his skillful manner pulls him together, but finds himself ten lengths behind, and everybody concedes the race to Bronze. A less stout-hearted and inexperienced driver would have fainted right there; but not Budd. Gathering the little fellow well together he came with a wet sail, and right here gave the assembly one of the finest exhibitions of driving ever witnessed on a racetrack. The wonderful little gamecock, responding to his demands, came with a marvelous burst of speed, and, in spite of Orrin's best efforts, amid the rousing cheers of the crowd, won the heat by a neck in the wonderful time of 2:23½, for a sixth heat by two baby trotters, Waiting barely saving his distance, many claiming him shut out. At the conclusion of this heat the backers of Bronze were paralyzed, for the mare was quite tired, and, strangely enough, Jay Eye See as fresh as a daisy.

*Seventh Heat.*—Jay Eye See was a great favorite, and the race was all over but the announcement, but right here came the bowlder that crushed the Jay Eye See party, showing once more the mutability of human affairs and the many contingencies arising to make racing quite "unsartin." The word was given, with Doble more than a length behind and tumbling all to pieces in a break. This caused many a face wreathed in smiles to change to a sort of funeral expression, and at least a hundred good fellows came near falling down dead. The horse was so tangled up before recovering that he was out of the race, and Bronze apparently the winner, as she went along at a merry clip, Waiting making his usual running break around the turn. When he did recover he trotted fast, but he was unsettled in his gait, hadn't got "his right foot forward," which in his case is literally true. Bronze continued her lead of several lengths from Waiting down the stretch, and passed the half-mile pole in 1:14½. Budd, in the meantime, had come so fast into the backstretch that he would have overhauled the mare before reaching the three-quarter pole, but he made a break midway of the stretch, and another at the head of the homestretch. When he struck his trot at the head of the stretch he was for the first time square and level, and came home with a handsome finish, in time to finish well up. Waiting finding a very tired mare, beat her out in 2:30, and the race went to a good horse, but he got in and won his race by "crawling under the canvas." Previous to the heat I understand he was begging the others not to distance him, as he would lose his third money. The start caused much unfavorable comment. It was certainly most unfortunate, beating a colt that had made the most gallant fight to win ever witnessed on a race-track; and then it burnt up the money of the grooms and their friends, who had so long concealed the possibilities of the handsome pet, that they might win a few dollars at Chicago.

This ended the best colt race ever witnessed, owing principally to the two great drivers having backed each his own horse to win, and, funny enough, both were drowned by a horse not considered in the race at all, but a great gelding nevertheless. Before starting for the deciding heat a ticket on Waiting calling for $178 was offered for $2.

It must be remembered that the track to-day was by no means at its best. The three-year-olds were unable to beat 2:30, and Little Brown Jug, in the three trials, could pace no faster that 2:15. Had the track been velvet there would have been a pretty fast colt record to record. Jay Eye See finished the seventh heat showing no evidence of tiring. This was really wonderful, for it was the first time his head was ever turned to face a starting judge.

SAME DAY.—Stakes for four-year-olds and under, $100 entrance, $25 forfeit, with $1,000 added, with $500 additional to the winner of the fastest heat, if trotted better than 2:19¾.

| | | | | | | | |
|---|---|---|---|---|---|---|---|
| Barry & Fox's b. g. Waiting, by Lexington Chief, Jr. | 1 | 1 | 2 | 6 | 3 | 3 | 1 |
| J. N. Dickerson's b. f. Bronze, by Morgan Messenger | 4 | 2 | 1 | 1 | 2 | 2 | 2 |
| E. Bither's blk. g. Jay Eye See, by Dictator | 2 | 4 | 3 | 2 | 1 | 1 | 3 |
| Simons & Maxwell's b. g. Jim Bowman | 6 | 3 | 4 | 4 | 4 | r. o. | |
| V. L. Shuler's b. f. Adelaide | 3 | 6 | 5 | 3 | 5 | r. o. | |
| E. Geers' b. c. Ed. Geers | 5 | 5 | 6 | 5 | 6 | r. o. | |

Time—2:28¼, 2:25¾, 2:25¼, 2:26½, 2:22¾, 2:23½, 2:30.

The breeding and development of these colts presents many features of interest to the student of the great problem of breeding the American trotter. Space only forbids my writing fully upon this interesting topic. I will first introduce Jay Eye See, as all things considered, I believe him the grandest four-year-old on earth, and when at the finish of the sixth heat, I asked a prominent horseman, "What do you think of the black colt now?" he replied, "He can beat Phil Thompson for my money any race horse trot." This was placing possibly a too high estimate upon the colt. In judging of the wonderful qualities of this colt, one must follow him throughout all his heats and quarters, from the start to his wonderful finishes up the homestretch.

Jay Eye See was purchased in Kentucky, in April, 1880, from Col. Richard West, at Edge Hill Farm, where he was bred by Mr. J. I Case, of Racine, along with five other two-year-olds, all sired by Dictator, the full brother of the mighty Dexter. He was the last colt selected, as he was considered rather small. Your special commissioner accompanied Mr. Case, and rather urged his purchase, as I think, without any exception, he was the fastest colt at the trot I ever saw in a poddock or small field. I had also seen his full sister, Noontide, in races, and this, with his natural action, gave me assurance of the coming trotter, and he was placed among the purchases. As before remarked, his sire was Dictator, dam by Pilot Jr. (Old Midnight), out of Twilight, by Lexington, out of Daylight, by Glencoe, out of a mare by Wagner, etc. Well, the thoroughbred lines come pretty direct here, certain. In Dictator we find the Hambletonian blood and the thorough blood of American Star. To say the least, all the blood lines indicate speed. He is now 15¼ hands, black, and (what a pity) gelded. In his conformation he is level and even, about the same height forward as behind. He has a clean-cut, intelligent head, full eye, neatly-pointed ear, neck of fine proportions, a little longer than the average Hambletonian; his back straight, and smoothly coupled; a well-rounded barrel, slightly sloping rump; his quarters, stifles, and gaskins, remarkably developed, give him a blocky appearance; in fact, when in road form, he is in the form of the handsome Ethan Allen Morgan–Black Hawk. While he has powerful propelling powers, his almost brother in blood, Code, who is a much faster colt than he has shown, is rather of a light hamed horse.

Jay Eye See, in his jogs, has the nod of Maud S., Darby, Maze-Manic, and many other celebrities, but he is as sound as a dollar, with the best of legs and feet, his tendons and muscles are cat-gut and case-hardened steel; in his disposition he is docile and tractable, and has always been a pet with Mr. Case and his family, as well as with his careful and painstaking driver, Mr. Bither. He wears no toe-weights, simply an eleven-ounce shoe forward and five-ounce behind, and has full free knee action. Code differing here again as he carries a six-ounce toe-weight. Mr. Wallace may become interested in Jay Eye See, as he will here find a double cross to the pacing Pilots, a cross to the pacing Hambletonians. "Explain?" I will sometime; and he must admit a strong infusion of the thoroughbred, and yet no toe-weights to make him trot, no toe-weights to make him overcome the lack of knee action, so claimed for the thoroughbred.

Jay Eye See was taken to Wisconsin after his purchase, was hardly broken in the fall, being a two-year-old, and run out until April, 1881; his breaking was then completed, and inside of six weeks he trotted a half mile in 1:18. Mr. Case, who has watched the development of this colt carefully, ordered him turned out to grass at once. "I am afraid you will hurt him," he would often remark to Mr. Bither. He was taken up Oct. 1; in the last of the month trotted a half mile in 1:14½, when Mr. Case requested "Ed." to stop his fast work and prepare him for his winter's jogging. He was jogged to the pole all winter beside Edwin B., went to the track May 23, and the first week in July trotted Mr. Case's half-mile track in 2:23, the last half in 1:06. No horse ever owned by Mr. Case, Gov. Sprague not excepted, had been able to equal this performance. We next find him here, and selling in pools: Bronze, $50; Waiting, $18; Jay Eye See, $15; field, $15. Of course those that knew did, and why not! And they would but for the judges' stand. So you see they did not, and I know how it is myself. Jay Eye See has been developed, and made a trotter by the careful watching and handling of Edward Bither, who has had excellent success in developing the colts of Mr. Case. "Ed." says, when he shows up Phallas, the five-year-old son of Dictator, and Betsy Trotwood, the people will begin to think that the Dictators are quite a trotting family. Phallas can beat 2:30 by several seconds at any time—has, in fact, recently. His favorites, however, are two colts by Gov. Sprague, that are "doing splendidly."

Well, I had better not enthuse over Bronze, for she is now the property of your commissioner. For her I paid $7,500, and I think in a race with the crack four-year-olds of the country she would sell "even up." In the fifth heat, trotted in 2:22¼, she was beaten a neck only. She is a beautiful bronze bay, 15¾ hands high, very blood-like, and exquisitely formed. She is a Goldsmith Maid in type, only a size larger, and a little higher on the withers, giving a handsome finish. She went into this race sadly out of form, having lost a very easy race for her a week ago. Her gait is not high and showy, but she glides along with a well-measured pace, in a rapid, stealing manner that gets the best of a watch, instead of like too many high-actioned laboring horses that go much slower than the watch. She has magnificent legs and feet, not a puff nor a pimple, and is of the improving sort. She wears a 12-oz shoe forward, and 6-oz. behind. This will seem very remarkable when I state all I know of her breeding. She was bred at the cross-roads town of Pleasant Valley, Switzerland Co., Ind., near the Ohio River, by a Mr. Hart, in August, 1881. When three she was ridden into North Vernon, and paced a half mile to saddle in 1:17. Buck Dickerson then purchased her for $175. Shortly after she paced in a race in 2:37, and George N. Dickerson purchased her from his brother. In the Fall she seemed inclined to trot, and he trotted her to a road wagon at the fair in 2:47. She ran out all last Winter, and in February was placed in the hands of Thomas Dickerson, another brother, to be handled. She took at once kindly to trotting, and in May, at Maysville, Ky., could have won her race, and, if necessary, trotted in 2:23; she did show in the race in 2:27. From there she can be followed through her campaign to Chicago. She has not only been carefully trained by Thomas, but another brother, Scott, has acted as groom.

Her breeding? Well, she was by Morrison's Morgan Messenger, Jr., he by Curtis' Morgan Messenger, he by Green Mountain Morgan. Her dam will in time be fully traced, as well as the blood lines of sires. Her sire, now dead, was a fast pacer—record 2:27—and has left a speedy progeny behind him. Now we find here a mare by a pacing horse, her dam a trotting mare, a natural pacer for three years, changing her gait without any of the appliances now used—toe-weights, etc. In form she knocks all the anatomical structure theories into a "cocked hat," for she is as clean cut and handsomely turned as any model race or trotting horse. She will be heard from hereafter.

Waiting is a large-growthy gelding, considerably over 16 hands, and a trotter of merit, but greatly outclassed yesterday, although a winner by a most unfortunate scratch—fortunate to him, however. He will very likely improve in his speed, and may develop into a phenomenal horse, for his lines of breeding just suit me, having double lines to that royal blood for staving up the trotter, Lexington Chief, Jr, being by Fisk's Lexington Chief, he by Kentucky Clay, and Lexington Chief, Jr.'s dam by Fisk's Mambrino Chief; and the dam of Waiting was by the same horse. Waiting inherits the size, and plain but powerful frame, of the Mambrino Chief family. His driver handled him well for the interest of his owner, but the manner in which he "sat down" on Doble, rounding the turn in the fourth heat, was distressingly unpleasant to your commissioner, who saw these little irregularities with "jaundiced eyes."—*N. Y. Spirit of the Times.*

## THE PORTLAND RACES.

The second annual meeting of the Northwestern District Association was brought to a close on Saturday, July 22d, and although the card was quite attractive, the attendance at the City View Park was not as large as might have been expected, especially when it is mentioned that every business house in Portland was closed to celebrate the day. It has been claimed by the local press that there was a lack of skill shown in the arrangement of the programme, inasmuch as on the opening day the card was not attractive enough to draw visitors from the country who would have stayed throughout the week, and also that the best people in Portland do not give the sport that patronage it so well merits. It is to be hoped that the financial result will show an increase on the receipts of the previous year, and that at the next meeting there will be greater care shown in getting up the programme, while the interest of the best society in Portland will be enlisted to aid the efforts of the Association.

There were three races on the card, the first being a purse of $800, free for all, in which Dexter was the favorite at $40 against $35 for Milton Medium, and $6 for Dirigo. The race was hotly contested by the two favorites, but Milton Medium was in the best form and won in three straight heats.

City View Park, Portland, July 22, 1882. First race—Trotting. Purse of $800, free for all. Mile heats, three in five.

| | | | |
|---|---|---|---|
| H. Smiley's b. h. Milton Medium | 1 | 1 | 1 |
| Jos. Misner's b. h. Dexter | 2 | 2 | 2 |
| P. McMann's b. g. Dirigo | dist. | | |

Time—2:29¼, 2:26¾, 2:25¼.

The winner is a bay stallion, by Happy Medium, his dam by Hackett's Mambrino. He was brought to this coast and was trained for some time in Oakland, when it is said that in a private trial he made a mile in 2:26. He did not show in public in 1880, and last July, at the same meeting, Dexter won a purse, Milton Medium taking the first heat in 2:31¾ and Dexter the remaining three, his time in the second heat being 2:30. It is evident that with these two fine horses Oregon will in the future have some staying and speedy stock.

The second race, a dash of three-quarters of a mile, between Jim Renwick and Premium, that was a fair race for half a mile, when the old man relinquished the contest.

Second race—Running race for purse of $——, three-quarters of a mile.

| | |
|---|---|
| Ab. Stemlar's ch. g. Jim Renwick, by Hooker, dam Big Gun | 1 |
| Cy. Mulkey's ch. m. Premium, by Castor, from Flying Cloud | 2 |

Time—1:16½.

The last race was a mile and repeat, in which Howell and Fred. Collier met again, with Caddie R. as the third contestant. In consequence of Collier's victory on the previous Thursday he was made an immense favorite at $50 against $10, and $8 for Howell and Caddie R. combined; but this was a very disagreeable wind up to the meeting for those who pinned their faith on the favorite, as after a finish in both instances of a fierce and punishing character, Joe Howell won the race in the best time ever made in Oregon with the usual weights for age.

Third race—Purse $450, mile heats:

| | | |
|---|---|---|
| Cy. Mulkey's b. g. Joe Howell, by Bonnie Scotland, aged | 1 | 1 |
| Wm. Ayers' ch. g. Fred Collier, by Joe Hooker, 4 years | 2 | 2 |
| Jerome Porter's br. m. Caddie R., by Bayswater, aged | 3 | dis |

Time—1:46½, 1:45¼.

## THE SARATOGA RACES.

The intermittent season has continued to fair sport, but the attendance and the number of entries show a great falling off as compared with the previous seasons.

On Thursday, July 27th, the first race, three-quarters of a mile, was won by Bonnie Lizzie, Saunders second, Martinique third; time, 1:15. In the second race, one and three-quarter miles, Boatman won, Frankie B. second; time, 3:05½. The third race was a walk-over for Thora. In the fourth race, one mile, Blenheim won, Mattie Rapture second; time, 1:41¾. In the fifth race, one mile and a half, Glidelia won, Monogram second, Tom Plunkett third; time, 2:36¾.

On the 28th, in the first race, one mile, Springfield won, Patti second; time, 1:42¼. In the second race, one mile and 500 yards, Spark won, Square Dance second; time, 2:14¾. In the third race, three-quarter mile, Referee won, Lytton second; time, 1:17. In the fourth race, three-quarter mile, Little Phil won, Iola second; time, 1:15½.

On the 29th, in the first race, three-quarters of a mile, Teresin won, Ascender second; time, 1:15¾. In the secon race, a mile and a half, Bend Or won, Theora second; time, 2:35. In the third race, one mile, Checkmate won, Tom Plunkett second; time, 1:43. In the fourth race, steeple chase, two and three-quarter miles, Post Guard won, Trouble second; time, 5:23.

On the 31st, in the first race, one mile, Buccaneer won, Lutestring second; time, 1:42½. In the second race, one and one-quarter miles, Compensation won, Warfield second; time, 2:08¼. Third race, three-quarter mile, Saunterer won, Bonnie Lizzie second, Little Phil third; time, 1:15. Fourth race, one and one-eighth miles, Jennie V. won, Blenheim second; time, 1:36¼.

On the 1st of August the first race, five furlongs, was a dead heat between Empress and Barbarian, the Farantella filly next; time, 1:04. The second race, one and a half miles, was won by Glidelia, General Monro second; time, 2:35½. In the third race, one mile, Bootjack won, Tom Plunkett second; time, 1:42½. In the fourth race, steeple-chase, two and three-quarter miler, Rose won, Echo second; time, 6:02.

On August 2d, in the first race, one mile, Morgan Spy was first, Elector second, Francisca third; time, 1:44½. In the second race, one mile and 500 yards, Warfield was first, Long Taw second; time, 2:12½. In the third race, five-eighths of a mile, Fairview won, Referee second; time, 1:02¾. In the fourth race, three-quarters of a mile, Blenheim won, Little Phil second; time, 1:15¼.

## THE MONMOUTH PARK RACES.

The usual meetings on the Wednesday and Saturday were continued at Long Branch, and the racing on the 29th July was as follows: In the first race, one mile, Yorkshire won, Corsair second; time, 1:44. In the second race, three-quarters of a mile, Queen won, Marc Antony second, Foxglove third; time, 1:18¾. In the third race, one mile, Wyoming won, Macbeth second, Freegold third; time, 1:45½. In the fourth race, one and one-eighth miles, Girofla won, Duplex second, Ella third; time, 1:59¼. In the fifth race, one and five-eighth miles, Priam won, Faircourt second, Mary Anderson third; time 2:58. In the sixth race, a mile and half a furlong, gentlemen riders, Sir Hugh won, Duke of Kent second, Lute Fogle third; time, 1:55. In the steeple-chase, full course, Bonham won, Felix second, Bertha fell at the water jump; time, 1:52.

The California horses have not upheld their home reputation, which may be ascribed to the change of climate, but possibly also to the fact that they have to compete with a better class of horses than is to be found on this coast. Both Grismer and Lucky B. have run in their engagements, but have failed to get even a position. The first was the Red Bank Stakes in which Mr. Lorillard's pair were great favorites, the chances of Lucky being held at twenty to one. The California colt ran well for half a mile, but here the pace was too severe and the Lorillard pair achieved a handy victory.

Monmouth Park.—The Red Bank Stakes, a sweepstakes, for two-year-olds, of $50 each for starters, with $1,500 added, of which $500 to second; a winner of a stake of the value of $1,800 to carry 5 lbs.; twice, 7 lbs.; thrice, 12 lbs. extra; maidens allowed 7 lbs.; extrance, $15 (the only liability), to go to the race fund; 69 nominations; Value to winner, $1,200; three-quarters of a mile.

| | |
|---|---|
| P. Lorillard's imp. b. c. Pizarro, by Adventurer—Milliner, by Rataplan, 115 lbs. (including 5 lbs. penalty)..........(Feakes) | 1 |
| P. Lorillard's b. f. Inconstant, by Glenlyon—Lizzie Berry, 100 lbs..........(W. Donohue) | 2 |
| D. D. Withers' ch. c Renegade, by King Ernest—Revolt, 103 lbs..........(J. Sparling) | 3 |
| G. L. Lorillard's ch. f. Gift, by Glenlyon—Hilda, 100 lbs.(Ural) | 0 |
| E. J. Baldwin's b. c. Lucky B., by Rutherford—Maggie Emerson, 115 lbs. (including 5 lbs. penalty)..........(Holloway) | 0 |

Time—1:16½.

The race in which Grismer appeared was the Seabright Stakes, in which P. Lorillard's couple were again the favorites, and Grismer's chance was thought very lightly of in the betting.

Monmouth Park.—The Seabright Stakes, a sweepstakes, for two-year-olds, of $50 each for starters, with $1,500 added, of which $500 to the second; a winner of a stake of $1,000 (handicaps and selling races excepted) to carry 3 lbs.; twice, 6 lbs.; thrice, 7 lbs. extra; those not having won more than $500 when carrying weight for age or more allowed 3 lbs.; maidens allowed 7 lbs.; entrance, $15 (the only liability), to go to the race fund; 60 nominations; Value to winner, $1,500; three-quarters of a mile.

| | |
|---|---|
| P. Lorillard's b. f. Parthenia, by Alarm—Maiden, by Lexington, 110 lbs..........(Feakes) | 1 |
| P. Lorillard's b. f. Inconstant, by Glenlyon—Lizzie Berry, 100 lbs..........(Onley) | 2 |
| J. E. Cook's b. c. Le Petit Duc, by The Ill-Used—Countess, 108 lbs. (carrying 106 lbs)..........(Barbee) | 3 |

The following ran unplaced: Renegade, Maid of Athol, Touch-me-not, Heel-and-Toe, Fan Fan colt, Bella Fairfield and Grismer, who was not persevered in as he was probably out of condition, and he came in last.

There was great interest shown in the mile and a furlong purse that was run on July 26th, in which that veteran racer Parole suffered one of his few defeats. He was the favorite at $100 against $30 for Jack of Hearts, and $15 for the field. It was a fine contest between the two named horses, but the extra weight told on Parole, and although Clara D. made a fine finish, she could not reach Jack of Hearts, who won by a length.

Purse $500, for three-year-olds and upwards; entrance, 5 per cent. of the purse ($25 each), to the second; winning penalties and maiden allowances; the winner of the first race on the fourth day (P. Lorillard's Parole) to carry 7 lbs. more than he then carried; 4 entries; mile and a furlong.

| | |
|---|---|
| Appleby & Johnson's b. c. Jack of Hearts, 4, by Ill-Used, dam Nellie James, 103 lbs..........(Evans) | 1 |
| E. J. Baldwin's b. m. Clara D., aged, by Glenelg, dam The Nun, 100 lbs..........(Carter) | 2 |
| P. Lorillard's br. g. Parole, aged, by Leamington, dam Maiden, 114 lbs..........(Feakes) | 3 |
| J. R. Graham's ch. g. Haledon, 5, by King Lear, dam Redowa, 102 lbs..........(Farley) | 0 |

Time—1:56½.

It is probable that the stable will return at once so that those who are in condition may take part in the Fall races on this coast.

Buffalo Races.—On the 2d August Overman won the 2:24 class, Abe Downing second, St. Cloud third, Rolla fourth; time, 2:20¾, 2:20¼, 2:23½, 2:24½. The 2:25 class race Limber Jack won, Joe Bowers second, Fuller third, Warrior fourth; time, 2:18½, 2:19¼, 2:21, 2:20½. The race free for all pacers, two heats, Gem won the first in 2:19, and Buffalo Girl the second in 2:27.

## THE CLEVELAND RACES.

Continuing from the previous issue, we find that the third day of the Cleveland Club races was conspicuous by a large attendance, fair weather and fast track. The free-for-all pace purse, $1,500, which was unfinished on the 26th, was first on the card, and following is a summary: Lucy first, Mattie Hunter second, Bay Billy third, Gem fourth, R. O. Ben Hamilton, Buffalo Girl, Sorrel Dan all ruled out for not winning one heat in five. Soto Lucy was awarded the first and fourth moneys. After the race, in order to close an estate, the winner was sold to O. A. Hickok for $6,000; time, 2:18½, 2:17, 2:20¼, 2:18, 2:17, 2:19¾, 2:22, 2:33. The trotting purse, $1,500, Adele Gould, the favorite, won in three straight heats, without being pushed. Summary—Adele Gould first, Harwood second, Waverly third, Nett's Medium fourth, Tom B, fifth; Time, 2:23, 2:21¼, 2:26. In the 2:26 trot for a purse of $1,500, Aldine was the favorite against the field. Summary: Aldine first, King William second, Mamie third, Joe Bulker fourth, Phillis fifth, and H. M. Strong sixth; time, 2:20¾, 2:20¾, 2:19½ and 2:21.

The 28th was the last day of the races. The weather was pleasant, and there were a fine track and a very large attendance. The principal interest was centered in a special race, which for two heats was a remarkably stubborn contest between Clingstone and Edwin Thorn, those two horses being lapped from wire to wire, creating intense excitement. The exertion was too much for Thorn, and Clingstone won the deciding heat with the greatest ease, jogging the last half mile. The average time of the twenty-eight heats trotted at this meeting was a fraction over 2:21¼. The average of the eleven pacing heats was less than 2:19. In the 2:20 trot, for a purse of $2,000, Rosa Wilkes was favorite, and won in straight heats with ease, J. P. Morris second, Fannie Witherspoon third, Wm. H. fourth, Early Rose fifth; time, 2:18½, 2:18¾, 2:18¼. By the breaking of one line in the last heat, Calmar steered against the inside fence and jumped over, throwing out but not seriously injuring his driver, Caton. In the special named race for a purse of $3,000, Clingstone sold in the pools $100 to $30 for the field. Clingstone won, Edwin Thorn second, J. B. Thomas third. So-So was distanced on the second heat; time, 2:14, 2:16¾, 2:23½. Time of the first heat by quarters—First, 34 seconds; half-mile, 1:05; three-quarters, 1:40½. Second heat—First quarter, 32¾ seconds: half-mile, 1:05; three-quarters, 1:40½. In the three-minute trot Wilson, the favorite, three to one against the field, won handily in straight heats, Howard Jay second, Golden Rule third, Secret fourth; time, 2:23¾, 2:25½, 2:25.

## THE BOSTON RACES.

At Mystic Park, on July 25th, two trots were decided, it being the first day of the July meeting. The track was in excellent condition, but the attendance light. The first race was for 2:50 horses, and was won by Zelda in three straight heats, with Belle Mahone second, Red Bird third and Edwin fourth; time, 2:33¼, 2:33¼, 2:33½. Two others started. The second race, for 2:26 horses, took five heats to decide. Camors won the first and third, and Gipsy the other three heats and the race; time, 2:25¼, 2:24¼, 2:25¼, 2:25½, 2:25½. Five started.

On the 26th the meeting was continued with excellent weather and good attendance. The first trot of the day was for 2:32 horses, and was decided in five heats. Ilka won the first and third heats and Dick Dample the second, fourth and fifth; time, 2:32¼, 2:34, 2:33¾, 2:31½, and 2:33. Achilles was third and Bay Lambert fourth. The second race was for gentlemen's road-horses to road-wagons, and was won by Alsie F. Ned Jackman was second and Jessie third, while Lady Hawes and Jim B. were drawn in the third heat; time, 2:43¾, 2:39¼, 2:41½.

## CANADIAN NOTES.

Toronto, July 24, 1882.

Editor Breeder and Sportsman: As things among horsemen here are very quiet just at present, I will content myself this week with giving you an outline of some anticipated good sport to come off over our justly celebrated "Woodbine Park Race Course," under the management of a newly-formed club entitled "Toronto Trotting Association," on August 14th and 15th, on which dates it is proposed to give two races each day for 3-minute and 2:26 classes; purses $750 for each event on first day, and 2:37 and free-for-all stakes on second day, with $250 added for 2:17 or better.

From the well-known good standing and integrity of the gentlemen composing the Committee of Management, our people are looking forward with every confidence in expecting a thoroughly enjoyable meeting, full particulars of which I shall forward in due course.

### CANADIAN HORSES FOR SARATOGA.

W. E. Owens, the well-known Canadian trainer, is taking his stable of horses to Saratoga, comprising Mr. Abingdon's brown horse Disturbance, by Terror, dam Lucy, and Long Tom, well known to American turfmen; also Sheppard Bros.' Empress, by Harry Bassett.

## SUMMER MEETING OF THE CLARKE COUNTY, W. T., ASSOCIATION AT VANCOUVER.

This meeting commenced on Tuesday, July 25th, and continued three days. Owing probably to the fact that farmers are engaged in their hay harvest the attendance was light, but the sport was enjoyed by those present. From the *North Pacific Rural Spirit*, of Portland, we take the following description of the track, together with the summaries of the races:

"To those who have lived here to see this city grow up from a little village to its present proportion, it is interesting to be comfortably seated on board so fine a steamer as the Lurline (in place of the once glorious steamer Eagle of twenty-five years ago), and swing out into our Willamette, where can now be seen a mile of costly buildings, and almost hundreds of vessels, large and small, busily engaged in the commerce of our city. Twelve miles down the river, as Oregonians know, we leave the clear, still notes of the Willamette, and rush out into the grand Columbia current, which always greets a steamer by giving her a kind of friendly shake off. Six miles up the Columbia we hauled up alongside the dock, and riding up through one of the principal streets we could not be otherwise than favorably impressed. Activity and a wholesome condition of things seemed to meet the eye in all directions. A fifteen minutes' drive in a north-easterly direction brought us to the Fair Grounds, that is situated on an eminence, from which Fort Vancouver, where the oldest civilized settlement in the North Pacific Territory was made, as well as a sweeping view of the old Columbia can be had. The grounds are favorably located, and being situated in one of the richest agricultural counties in the Territory, and being under the control of gentlemen who have no more than a common interest, these grounds at no distant day will be one of the attractions of the Northwest."

Clarke County A. & M. Fair Grounds, July 25, 1882. Trotting, 2:38 class, 3 in 5; purse, $400; divided, $225, $125, $50.

| | | | |
|---|---|---|---|
| H. S. Hogoboom na. br. m. Walla Walla Maid, by Millman Bellfounder.......... | 1 | 1 | 1 |
| Jay Beach names. b. m. Maggie Arnold, by Almont.......... | 2 | 2 | 2 |
| H. Smiley names. s. h. Gen. Crook.......... | 3 | d. | |

Time—2:48¾, 2:48, 2:48.

Same Day.—Second race, 1¼ miles; purse $300, divided $250, $50.

| | |
|---|---|
| Cy Mulkey names b. g. Joe Howell, by imp. Bonnie Scotland, 119 | 1 |
| J. A. Porter names br. m. Caddie R., by Bayswater, 115.......... | 2 |
| Mulkey & Marsh name br. h. Billy Coombs, by Shannon, 122.... | 3 |

Second Day, July 26th, 1882.—Three-quarter mile handicap; purse $250, second horse $50.

| | |
|---|---|
| W. G. Scoggin names br. h. Jim Merritt, 5, by Langford, 116.... | 1 |
| R. E. Bybee names b. f. Ney Ella, 2, by California, Ford, 87.... | 2 |

Time—1:22.

Third Day.—Trotting, for three-year-olds, 3 in 5; purse $400, divided $225, $125, $50.

| | | | | | |
|---|---|---|---|---|---|
| L. B. Lindsly names br. f. Jane L., by Hambletonian Mambrino, dam Mollie Welch.......... | 3 | 3 | 1 | 1 | 1 |
| John Pender names b. f. May Wintler, by Rockwood, dam by St. Louis.......... | 1 | 1 | 2 | 2 | 2 |
| E. J. Jeffery names br. f. Edna J., by Kisber, dam Morgan.......... | 2 | 2 | 3 | 3 | 3 |

Time—3:17, 3:16½, 3:12½, 3:09, 3:07.

Same Day.—Pacing; purse $100; mile and repeat.

| | | |
|---|---|---|
| Mr. Mismer names Captain Arnold's Dan.......... | 1 | 1 |
| Mr. McManus names Captain Arnold's Pete.......... | 2 | 2 |

Time—3:02, 2:45.

Same Day.—Running, mile and repeat; purse $250, divided $200, $50.

| | | |
|---|---|---|
| Cy Mulkey names b. g. Joe Howell, 9, by imp. Bonnie Scotland, 111.......... | 1 | 1 |
| J. A. Porter names s. m. Trade Dollar, 7, by Norfolk, 111.... | 2 | 2 |

Time—1:51, 1:52.

There was a trot on the second day, in which were engaged Medium, Dexter and Gold Foil. The first heat was given to Medium in 2:32½ (with Gold Foil distanced), as also the second in 2:34½. Dexter took the third heat in 2:33, and Medium the fourth and race, but the judges now announced that the heat as well as all pools and bets were declared off, and placed Mr. L. B. Lindsey behind Dexter. Mr. Smiley thereupon took Medium to the stable, and when time was called, Mr. Lindsey drove Dexter around alone in 2:42. This was the point that marred the pleasantness of the meeting, and the judges would have done well to announce their reasons for the course they pursued.

## THE DOUBLE-TEAM RIVALRY.

The absorbing question of the hour is, how fast will a team yet trot, this having been precipitated upon the minds of the *cognoscenti* by the performance of Edward and Dick Swiveller. The proposition that a pair, well matched, can go faster than either of them single, which was rather startling until lately—we believe Mr. Robert Bonner was the first to give the idea prominence—has already become generally accepted as an axiom. When the test of common sense is applied to it, it seems to be one of those things that goes without saying, however it may shock oldfashioned notions. A single trotter draws driver and sulky, weighing at a minimum 190 pounds, while a pair draws a driver weighing 150 pounds and a wagon weighing 70 pounds, being only 110 pounds for each horse, if they work well up to the collar evenly. This is a handicap of 80 pounds in favor of the team, more than five times as much as was considered would equalize the speed of St. Julien and Trinket. Besides, when going to the pole the horses are constantly neck-and-neck, and striving to out-do each other. If they are steady, evenly matched in speed, and do not make mistakes, why should they not go faster double than single? The difficulty is not in making the speed, but in obtaining and educating the team to do it. The success of Edward and Swiveller leads us to believe that the great team of the future will be a pair, not brought together at random, but that have long been trained in unison; and it is only a question of time when two of much greater individual speed than either of Mr. Work's pair will be so brought together, and, under favorable conditions, on some exceptionally fast track, will eclipse even the 2:10¾ of Maud S. We are quite convinced that people who read these lines will live to see the day when 2:16¾ by a double team, wonderful as the record is, will be as far eclipsed, taking into fair consideration the greater relative value of seconds as a rate of two minutes to the mile is approximated, as has been the almost forgotten 2:27¾ of Jessie Wales and Darkness; and we never yet made a prediction on the bull side of the trotting-speed market that failed to be verified. And in the great rivalry that is certain to ensue among our wealthy road-drivers, the business of breeding and training horses to meet the demand cannot fail to be vastly stimulated.

## SHORT RACING IN IDAHO.

Bellevue, July 22, 1882.

Editor Breeder and Sportsman: It has been quite a time since our races have been written up in proper shape, as we have certainly had some this season, which certainly deserved a great deal of space in some journal; but now that I have taken the responsibility of trying to fairly represent our town, as well as to give you and your readers a fair shake, I will try and do what is right. To-day was a day some of our sports looked forward to with great interest, but most of them got left, as the backers of the horses were not present, although no cause was assigned for their absence. However, to-day's race proved very interesting for those who thought they were getting on the right horse, but who found out different after the race. The race was 600 yards and repeat, and three of our best repeat horses were entered, namely, Pierce's "Johnny," Luther's "Ten Cents," and Blackwell's "McGee." Johnny is known to be a repeater, and was the favorite. Ten Cents has many backers, but most of them have weakened on him since his owner strained him in running a half mile and repeat not long ago; and to-day he weakened entirely on the third heat. McGee was second choice in the pools, but came out victorious

The first heat was the best start had, and Ten Cents came in first, McGee second, and Johnny third.

Second Heat.—The start was not as good as before, and quite a difference was made in the outcome, as Johnny was first, McGee second, and Ten Cents third.

Third Heat.—The start was very bad, and Ten Cents stopped short 50 feet from the start. McGee came in first, and Johnny second.

Fourth Heat.—Many were surprised at the race coming to a fourth heat, as most every one thought Johnny, having won the second, would also win the third and money; but McGee surprised them, and came in an easy winner of the race and money.

SUMMARY.

| | | | | |
|---|---|---|---|---|
| Pierce enters Johnny.......... | 3 | 1 | 2 | 2 |
| Luther enters Ten Cents.......... | 1 | 3 dist. | | |
| Blackwell enters McGee.......... | 2 | 2 | 1 | 1 |

Our sporting fraternity will probably get up a 50 mile race some time during the next two weeks, and a foot race of 100 yards, with a short horse race thrown in, as such is the outlook at present.

The hunting people of our vicinity are very anxious for our game laws to run out, as the game most desirable for our crack shots are plenty, and deer, bears, grouse, ducks, geese, doves and all small game of this kind are plenty hereabouts. Fishing for the past three weeks has been magnificent, and many parties have recently been formed for a week's fishing with good results.

Yours, till more news,     PHONOGRAPH.

### THE LOS ANGELES FAIR.

The District Fair last year at Los Angeles was not very successful, owing to the late date at which it was held and to the small purses, that were insufficient to attract horses so far away from their stables. This season organized efforts, through local subscription, have been made to place the association on a sound financial basis, and thus far they have been so successful that the executive officers now announce that the fair will be held at Los Angeles on Monday, October 16th, and will continue throughout the week. A committee has been appointed to arrange the speed programme, and the Park and buildings will be put in thorough order for the occasion. The Sixth District is composed of the Counties of Los Angeles, San Diego, Santa Barbara, San Bernardino, Ventura and Inyo, and in view of the immense impetus given to trade and travel through the opening of the Southern Pacific Railroad, we predict that the Fall fair at Los Angeles will be a success and a great benefit to the counties therein represented. Mr. F. J. Baretto is President and Mr. R. H. Hewett is Secretary of the Association.

### THE JOCKEYS OF THE DAY.

Symptoms abound on every side of us to show that the Jockey Club is losing its hold upon the supporters of that great and favorite pastime which no other sport is likely to dethrone from its pride of place in this country. The fact is, that, as history abundantly teaches us, no body which springs spontaneously into existence and becomes the repository of power can retain that power unless it includes among its members men of fearless independence, of strong character, and of impregnable integrity. Since the death of Admiral Rous, the Jockey Club had boasted no member who took an active part in its affairs, and who also possessed the indispensable attribute of a strong backbone. The consequence is, that while the Jockey Club is withering in influence, its subjects, whether they be the officials of the race-course, the jockey, or merely what are commonly called " racing men," have slipped their bits and emancipated themselves more and more from control. The recent race meeting at Manchester furnished a case in point.

It was an axiom with Lord George Bentinck and with Admiral Rous that no class connected with the turf is more insubordinate, or more inclined to be insolent unless kept in order by the strong hand, than successful jockeys. Who that is admitted behind the scenes of a race-course can doubt that at this moment half a dozen prominent jockeys are more powerful than the Jockey Club and its stewards? It is customary to speak of the times through which we are now passing as the " Falmouth era of the turf." Would it not be wise to tear the scales from our eyes, and to denominate them what they really are, as " the Archer era?" For this unseemly result the Jockey Club has itself to thank. Many of its most exalted members have set the example of consorting with their favorite jockeys upon terms of intimacy to which Lords Glasgow, Zetland and Eglinton, Admiral Rous and General Peel would never have stooped. The pernicious example has naturally been imitated by the friends and backers of the jockeys. Descanting, in his " Race-horse in Training," upon the " effects of lavish gifts to children," William Day remarks: " I am bound to say, that in my opinion much of the misbehavior of our light-weight jockeys has its rise in the extravagant presents made to them." Worse even than the disproportionate remuneration of which jockeys are the recipients, is the close familiarity with which they are treated by their betters. As a tree is known by its fruit, so were the results of this displacement of ranks made apparent at Manchester, when the jockeys insolently refused to give heed to the official starter, and treated a member of the Jockey Club who rode down to the starting post with equal disrespect. Appealed to by the starter, the stewards of Manchester races refused to support his authority, and the jockey triumphed over the humbled official, whose resignation their audacity necessitated. In such a state of affairs, lovers of the turf may well ask themselves whether there is any member of the existing Jockey Club at whom the jockeys of to-day would not scoff, if, like Lord George Bentinck, he ever ventured to take the starter's flag in hand.—*London Field.*

### RACING IN ENGLAND.

The meeting at Goodwood during the past week has suffered from the existing political complications. The racing was good, but the American horses were either withdrawn from their engagements, or failed yet again to break the spell of ill luck that has attended their running all through the season. On July 25th, the Goodwood Stakes, a handicap, for all ages, was won by Mr. J. Davis's Fortissimo, with Mr. Jardine's Reveller second and Mr. Tidy's Iachetta third. Eleven started, and the post betting was 3 to 1 against Fortissimo, 7 to 1 against Iachetta and 25 to 1 against Reveller. On the following day the two most important races were the Sussex and Lavant Stakes. The former was for three-year-olds, with 95 subscribers, £25 each, £10 forfeit, with £500 added. The race was won by a French horse, Count Alfred, belonging to Mr. Lefevre, with Battlefield second, Dutch Oven third, and Mr. Keene's Romeo and Mr. Lorillard's Sachem unplaced, thus tending, to prove that Dutch Oven, the best performer out last season, has not recovered her form, and that the American three-year-olds in England this season are of a mediocre character. The Lavant Stakes was won by the Duke of Hamilton's Export, with the Nuneham colt second and Ladislas third. From present appearances the outlook for the two American stables is not of a rosy character, but perhaps they will be favorably weighed in the Fall handicaps and thus retrieve the heavy losses incurred this year,

A TURF SCANDAL.—The German turf has been disturbed by a most remarkable scandal. The following are the particulars of the affair, which occurred in the Irople-Wurden-Rennen at Hoppegarten: The parties to the scandal were M. Tepper-Laski, M. Oelschlager, Prince Hatzfeldt and Mr. J. Beasley. The former gentleman, a partner of M. Oelschlager, started two horses—Siegespalme, ridden by Prince Hatzfeldt, and Prinz Eugen, mounted by Mr. J. Beasley. Two other horses ran, Basta and Rainfarn. These two were beaten before two-thirds of the distance had been covered,

and then a ding-dong race ensued between the stable companions, to the great astonishment of the public present. Mr. Beasley rode as hard as he could, and beat Prince Hatsfeidt. On the return to the paddock a crowd surrounded Prinz Eugen and his rider, and would probably have used him very roughly had he not been well protected by his friends and a number of Englishmen present. M. Tepper-Laski, Prince Hatzfeidt and Mr. Beasley were called into the stewards' room, and, without going into the charge of foul riding and fraud, the stewards decided to disqualify Siegespalme and Prinz Eugen, awarding the stakes to Rainfarn and submitting the case to the Union Club. The inquiry held by the Union Club, under the presidency of Count Lehndorf, has been brought to a conclusion, and the Berlin and Vienna journals loudly assert that the indulgence with which the matter has been treated is due in a great measure to the high position occupied by M. Tepper-Laski, who assumed the entire responsibility of the affair, alleging that the orders he gave to Mr. Beasley were not sufficiently clear and explicit. The disqualification pronounced by the stewards at Hoppegarten has been maintained. MM. Oelschlager, Tepper-Laski and J. Beasley have each been severely censured and fined £50, the two former as owners for having omitted to give explicit instructions to their jockey in accordance with the winning declaration they had made to the stewards, and the latter for having neglected to take cognizance of the declaration made and for having ridden with incomplete and unintelligible instructions.

It is stated that there is a prospect that at no remote day a racecourse surpassing in beauty and completeness of appointments anything of the kind in this country, will be established on the South Side, in the vicinity of Jackson Park, Chicago. It is proposed to devote the new enterprise exclusively to running meetings, and in the course of an informal talk concerning the matter at the Chicago Club one night last week, a few gentlemen connected with that organization pledged themselves to take $950,000 worth of stock in the enterprise. The estimated cost of the land and buildings is $600,000, and the gentlemen interested claim that this amount can be secured in twenty-four hours.

Since Shotover won the two thousand and the Derby, Geheimniss the Oaks, and with other prominent fillies to his credit, Hermit, once so neglected, is now looked upon as the most promising sire of the English turf. Mr. Chaplin owns the great Derby winner, as also a dozen choice mares, and he disposes of their produce at an annual sale, and on the 10th of July at Newmarket there were ten colts and fillies, the get of Hermit, which brought a total of $57,500, making an average of $5,750 per head, the best average ever attained at a public sale in England. Among them was a yearling filly out of Adelaide, $18,000, and another filly by Hermit out of sister to Adelaide brought $10,000.

The poolrooms of the Parole Club were recently raided by detectives and policemen, under Anthony Comstock, who, armed with warrants, arrested the reputed proprietor, John Hackett, and a number of clerks and others employed in the place. They also carted away to police headquarters all the paraphernalia of the place, including twenty-eight blackboards, twenty-five record books, a vast quantity of tickets, and over seven hundred dollars in cash. The prisoners were taken before Recorder Smyth, who committed nine of them to the tombs in default of $1,800 bail each. No charges were made against the others.

The announcement is made that a sale of over fifty brood mares, the property of Mr. William Blenkiron, will take place at the Middle Park, Eltham, Kent, England, on Saturday, October 7th. The sale includes many of the best brood mares to be found in the English Stud Book. A large majority are either the dams of winners or by winning sires out of dams that were winners, while nearly all are supposed to be in foal to such famous stallions as Scottish Chief, Doncaster, Rosicrucian, Dutch Skater, Macaroni, Coltness and Exminster. There will also be sold about forty foals by the same sires.

The ch. f. Clipsetta, foaled 1880, by Springbok, dam Eclipse, by imp. Eclipse, out of Avis, by imp. Sovereign, the property of the Hon. T. J. Megibben, Cynthiana, Ky., died recently at Cincinnati, O., from lockjaw, brought on by an injury to her hoof. Clipsetta was one of the best two-year-old fillies of the year, having won the Ladies Stakes at Lexington, five furlongs in 1.03¼. The Tennessee Stakes same place, three-quarters of a mile, in 1.20¾, and the Coquette Stakes, at St. Louis, three-quarters of a mile, in 1.17¾.

Cleveland is the home of W. J. Gordon, and on the third day of the meeting there his span of blacks, belonging to his four-in-hand team, were trotted tandem on exhibition, making the mile in 2:42, and repeated in 2:40¾. This gentleman denies the statement that he trotted those Cliftons spots against any trotter in the world. He says he never wagered a dollar on any race, and never will; that he trots his horses to develop them and furnish honest trials of speed, and that his drivers have instructions to win every race when they can without injuring the horses.

Little Ida, the dam of So-So, with a record of 2:17½, is dead, after foaling a colt by Alexander, that is one of the brightest bays of the day. Little Ida was bred by Wm. C. Goodloe, of Kentucky, was sired by Alexander's Edwin Forrest, her dam Ida May by Red Jacket, second dam Anna by Kirkhead's St. Lawrence, and third dam by Trustee, and was one of the most valuable stud mares in the country.

Phil. Thompson was given into the charge of Orrin C. Hickok by Mr. Raymond, so that clever driver can easily find out which of Phil. or Sweetheart is the best four-year-old, but from present appearances they both seem to be somewhat off.

One of if not the oldest racing fixtures still in existence is the race at Paisley, Scotland, for the "Silver Bells," dated 1620, given by the Magistrates and Town Council of Paisley, with 100 guineas added from the race funds. It is a handicap for three-year-olds and upwards.

The celebrated Clydesdale stallion Johnnie Cope died lately in Monmouth county, Illinois. He weighed 2,500 pounds and was accounted the finest Clydesdale in America.

*Dunbar's Hoof and Healing Ointment.*—This specific cure meets with hearty support on the part of owners of horses, and when, as is the case, its healing qualities are vouched for by such experts as James McCord, Samuel Gamble, A. Goldsmith, O. B. Crittenden, Captain B. E. Harris, Budd Doble, O. A. Hickok and many others, it would be well to give the Cure a fair trial.

body, etc., be Joe Hooker; his dam Too Soon, by Norfolk, grandam Lady Davis, by Red Bill. In race of 1868.

There may be other nominations delayed in the mails, and also corrections in some which were ambiguous.

## ENTRIES FOR P. C. B. H. A. STAKES.

### FIRST DAY.

WINTERS STAKE—For three-year-olds, to be run the first day of the Spring Meeting; dash of one and a half miles; $200 each, $25 forfeit, $500 added; second to have $100 third to save stake. Closed with the following nominations for 1884:

No. 1. J. K. Gries, San Buenaventura, names b f Mettie Hill, by Joe Daniels, dam Mary Wade.
No. 2. E. J. Baldwin, Santa Anita, names b c, by Rutherford, dam Maggie Emerson.
...

## ROWING.

### THE PACIFIC COAST CHAMPIONSHIP.

The offer of a Challenge Cup by the BREEDER AND SPORTSMAN has awakened the interest in crew rowing, and already several clubs are preparing to compete for the emblem of the Pacific Coast Championship. The Ariel Club has two crews in which it reposes confidence, and has already intimated a desire to give the Pioneer four a brush for a good cup. The Pioneer Club has determined, however, to keep itself in reserve for Thanksgiving Day, and devote all its energies to winning the Challenge Cup, and thus regaining some of the laurels that have lately been falling from it thick and fast. Last week a crew from the Pioneer Club, composed of J. Sullivan, R. C. Lyne, Robert Crowley and L. White were out in their paper shell. This four will probably represent the club in the race for the cup. They did not seem to have improved much on the four shown by them previous to the Fourth of July Regatta, and the comments of the critics on the bridge were not favorable. Nevertheless the fact remains that the crew showed good pace in the City Regatta, and rowed a game race from start to finish. The Golden Gate Club has not yet indicated what crew it will put forward to represent it. The probabilities are that at least four boats will start; and should this expectation be realized, the race for the BREEDER AND SPORTSMAN Cup will be the best rowing contest ever witnessed on San Francisco Bay.

PETERSON AND STEVENSON.—The friends of Henry Peterson, of the Golden Gate Rowing Club, having sounded the praises of that young sculler rather loudly since his achievement on the Fourth of July, Austin Stevenson's backers have announced their readiness to accommodate the Long Bridge man with a match for $500 whenever he desires to make it. Stevenson's backers talk as if they meant business, and if to our meeting takes place, it can be accepted as a fact that Peterson's confidence in his unclouded ability as an oarsman has not reached that stage in which he thinks himself good enough to try for the championship. His backers think he is too young, but Boyd rowed races for large stakes when younger, and Hanlan beat the best men in America and England when no older.

### SCULLING IN INK.

The two champion scullers of the world are showing great force in the columns of the respective newspapers most friendly to them. Says Mr. Ross: "If Hanlan wants to row me, and really means business, why did he," etc., etc., etc., ad nauseam. Says Mr. Hanlan, on reading the slanderous insinuations against his prowess and honesty: "Ross knows as well as I do that my doctors have forbidden me to train, and I am compelled to obey them," etc., etc., etc. Ross seems to have adopted the aggressive style of journalism, and Hanlan the mild and apologetic. Both oarsmen ought to know by this time that the public cares very little about their literary abilities. What is desired is a race, and the sooner they make it, and the quieter the manner in which it is arranged, the better for the reputations of both oarsmen. It would be an excellent idea for the editors of the country to combine and pledge themselves to close the columns of their journals to all professional athletes until they should have actually ratified a match by depositing seventy-five per cent of the stakes with some responsible person. As long as two professional oarsmen can use the columns of a newspaper, the water seems to lose much of its attraction for their backers. This peculiarity is not altogether a foreign one, for on our own waters several exhibitions of the fondness for rowing on paper have lately been given. First we hear of a bitter rivalry between some ambitious young watermen. The question of superiority has to be decided, and must be settled with the greatest possible expedition. A meeting of the backers takes place, and it looks as if a writ of injunction from the Supreme Court could not prevent the principals from putting up their money. In the midst of these enthusiastic preparations for the contest, the chilling fact is developed that there is an insurmountable barrier to a match. One man wants a two mile course, while the other feels that nothing short of forty furlongs would enable him to extend his muscles to their full capacity. A woeful disagreement about the location of the course complicates matters. One oarsman hankers after the turbulent tides of Long Bridge, and the other yearns for the turbulent tides of Long Bridge, and the natural, inevitable and not disagreeable result is the announcement that the match is "off." The match is not the only thing "off" in each cases. A very superficial surgical examination of the rival athletes would show that an evaporation of courage had as much to do with the disagreement as any regard for the prosperity of Milpitas or the glory of Long Bridge. Whenever two men are really anxious to meet in an athletic contest of any kind, and feel reasonably confident, it is easy to arrange the preliminaries of the match. When the negotiations develop unexpected difficulties about time, place and distance, and are broken off with great unanimity by the rivals, it is safe to say that their hearts have slipped down and that, in the beautiful words of the poet, "One word, and the other darsent." It is to be hoped that one of our local oarsmen may profit by these kinds words of wisdom, and preserve a reasonable silence about their ambitions intentions until they have made their matches, and bound them by the production of their good gold coin.

THERE WAS NO FOUL.—Of the race in which the American crew first made their appearance in England, at the Marlow Regatta, on July 8th, *The Sportsman* has the following report, from which it will be observed that there was no foul, as had been stated in a cable dispatch:

Special interest was felt in the gathering from the fact of the American Hillsdale crew having entered for the senior fours. Owing to a decision of that august body known as the Amateur Rowing Association, though, none of the crack clubs had the manliness to allow a crew to compete against them, and thus when the time came for the race there were only two fours left to antagonize the visitors, these hailing from Cookham and Marlow. Even these were not permitted to follow the bent of their inclinations, as some irrepressible busy body buttonholed them and set forth the evils that would befall should they engage against the Yankees. This had the desired effect on Cookham, whose members mostly hail from metropolitan clubs also, and thus Hillsdale had but to encounter the Marlow four, whom they naturally beat easily, although their form is scarcely taking, and we doubt whether they would have a chance against a trained crew such as they would have met at Henley. The Americans seem to have taken their treatment here much to heart; but at the same time with a patience and dignity which form a rather striking contrast to the vulgar caste-prejudices which have been brought to bear against them. In the course of a conversation with our representative, Mr. Teawilliger, their captain remarked that they were of course very sorry and disappointed at the result of their visit, but that as chief concern they felt was at the slight thrown upon the Amateur Rowing Association of America, whose credentials they bear, and whom they of course represented.

First stroke—Hillsdale R. C., U. S. A.: C. W. Terwilliger (bow). H. F. Mead, L. F. Bockhardt, E. B. Van Valkenburgh (stroke) ... 1
Second station—Marlow R. C.: B. F. Mead (bow), J. S. Kitchpatrick, C. E. Vaisé, W. T. Shaw (stroke) ................... 2

Hillsdale went away with the lead from the outset, and, holding their opponents easily all the way, won by rather over a clear length. Their style, however, was short and snatchy, and they scarcely pulled together like men who have been so long together. They were excellently boated in their paper shell, which carried them well, and it is just possible that their rough style may be more effective than it appears to the eye.

ENGLAND'S GREAT REGATTA.—On July 6 and 7, the dates of the Henley Regatta on the Thames, London, England, the weather was, to use the language of an English contemporary, "vile enough to spoil the business of boat polling for the pleasure of looking on; to take all the life and go out, and destroy the value of form in the racing, and make what is, under average surroundings, one of the brightest and most enjoyable of all sporting gatherings, dull, depressing and miserable."

In the first heat of the race for the grand Challenge Cup, eight oars, Exeter College, Oxford, beat Kingston R. C. and London R. C. crews by a length and a half, the same distance between second and third. In the second heat the Thames R. C. had a walk-over. In the final heat Exeter won by five lengths over Thames.

The first heat of the Diamond Challenge Sculls was a walk-over for A. Lien, of the Paris R. C. Sir C. Adam, of Oxford, won the second heat by ten lengths over E. B. Martin, of Evesham; J. Lowndes the third heat by a dozen lengths from W. Liddell, of the Twickenham R. C.; W. R. Grove, of London R. C., the fourth heat over J. Foley, of Cork, by half a length. In the second round Lien beat Adam and Lowndes beat Grove, and in the final heat Lowndes was first by two lengths in front of Lien.

HANLAN THE JOURNALIST.—Mr. Hanlan, of Toronto, who is rapidly acquiring a fine reputation as a newspaper writer, says in his latest novel: "My business requires all my attention just now. Last year I attempted to run my business and my rowing affairs together, and I discovered it was impossible to give to both the attention they required. If Wallace Ross is as anxious to get on a race with me as his words would imply, let him be the first to accept my challenge to the five best oarsmen in the world. Perhaps, if he starts the ball rolling, there will be no difficulty in getting four others to follow him. I shall have to await answers to my challenge until September next, and if it is not accepted, I shall be ready to meet Wallace Ross alone. I would like Ross to know, however, that the stakes must not be higher than $2,000 a side, for I do not wish to ask again contributions to the total amount awaiting the issue of the race. The money which I shall deposit will be my own. Regarding the Winnipeg regatta, I have a letter in my possession, received from Ross, in which he proposed to abandon the idea of a contest at that place."

CENSURING THE SNOBS.—The amateur rowing associations of the East, instead of treating with silent contempt the snobs who barred the Hillsdale crew from English regattas, are showing how much the offence has hurt them. The Schuylkill navy at Philadelphia has adopted the following:

WHEREAS, In consideration of the fact that the Hillsdale crew is the only one ever sent abroad that has received the indorsement of the National Association of Amateur Oarsmen of the United States—

*Resolved*, That the action of the Amateur Rowing Association of England in debarring them from rowing there in amateur regattas is an insult for which we have no redress, but can only condemn and deplore.

This is a poor sample of condemnation. The better way would be to ignore the contemptible action of the English committees; but when censure is indulged in it should be given in the sledge-hammer style in which the *New York Spirit of the Times* imparts it. It remarks editorially: "Those people who have been unable to decide whether the Henley Highwaymen and English Amateur Rowing Association are altogether knaves or part knaves and part fools will have no further doubt. This disreputable gang, who object to the amateur standing of the Hillsdale crew, accepted at Henley and rowed against the Aliens of Paris, whom the London *Field* proposes, from its own columns, to prove have rowed and won five money races since 1880."

ENCOURAGING OARSMANSHIP.—Several gentlemen of Saratoga, admirers of single sculling, propose to offer a purse of $1,000 for a single-scull race, either three miles straightaway or the same distance with a turn, to be rowed on Saratoga Lake within the next month, for which Elliott, Lee, Riley, Courtney and others will be asked to compete. A committee has been formed, and the following announcement was issued to the professional single-scullers of the United States and Canada: "Free purse $1,000, for all professional single scullers, of which $100 to the second; three miles with a turn; to be rowed on Saratoga Lake at four P. M., on August 25th, in good water; entries to close August 10th, to be addressed Charles Reed, Saratoga, N Y.; three to start or no race; the referee to be appointed by the committee representing the subscribers to the purse, and all conditions as to the race shall be left to him; also, if in the opinion of the referee selected that the race is not fairly rowed and won, the money will be given for charitable purposes at Saratoga."

A MOST INGENIOUS PARADOX.—The *Turf, Field and Farm* has the following remarks on the paradoxical fact that while the Hillsdale crew does not know how to row (in the opinion of the English critics), it can beat anything on the water propelled by four oars: "One of the London papers, soon after the Hillsdales began practice in England, said it was difficult to believe that they were the best of American amateurs, for they could get no pace on their boat. But an American amateur crew, much less thought of, defeated the crack four of the London Rowing Club at Philadelphia, and the Marlow oarsmen found, the other day, that the Michiganders could make their boat go."

AND STILL MORE OF HANLAN.—The telegraph, which seems to devote a large amount of its energy to Hanlan and Ross, announces that, upon the receipt of a dispatch from St. John saying that Wallace Ross would claim the championship if Hanlan refused to row him this year, Hanlan was interviewed by a New York *Herald* correspondent, and said Ross could have the championship for this year if he wanted it, as under no consideration could he (Hanlan) row this year. Wallace Ross is in steady practice at St. John, N. B. A correspondent says he has improved considerably in style and finish, his rowing, even although the water is often quite choppy, being faultless.

## YACHTING.

### A COMMOTION.

One day this week there was quite a commotion in Old Saucelito Bay, where there was a set-to between three prominent yachts of the fleet. The yacht Annie was sent over to Saucelito by her owners in charge of Peter, the "man," and John, the steward of the Pacific Yacht Club-house, John being at the helm. The yacht was under short canvass, as the wind was blowing very strong. On reaching Saucelito Cove the heavy puffs prevalent in that region were coming down fierce and sharp. In attempting to make her moorings, the Annie went raking down across the bowsprit of the schooner-yacht Nellie, and the Nellie's jibboom cut the Annie's handsome new mainsail right in two. Another puff of wind freed the Annie from the Nellie's jibboom, the topping lift and bolt rope swinging clear of the jibboom. The Annie then made a straight wake for the big Aggie, which lay at her moorings close by. She struck the Aggie on the quarter with her stem, and, strange to say, while doing slight injury to herself, damaged the Aggie to the extent of $400 or $500. She cut through and down the rail of the Aggie, through the heavy water-ways, and broke three of the heavy planks. She also carried away the cockpit rail and badly damaged the companion-way and slide. In fact, she rose right up on the Aggie, her forefoot being way out of water. The only wonder was that the Annie was not crushed like an egg-shell. As it was, only her stem was injured, so far as is known at present, but a new mainsail has had to be ordered. The Annie was insured for $2,000, and all above $200 the insurance companies will have to pay. This accident was a somewhat curious one in its results, since the Annie is very old, indeed, and not supposed to be very strong, while the Aggie is a new boat, and an unusually strong one. The Aggie's water-ways are almost heavy enough for a ship, yet the great, heavy timber was broken by the Annie's stem. The water-way of the Aggie was a single piece, and all her planks were single pieces. It would be a great expense to take these all out, and therefore the broken planks will be pieced, and so will the water-way. Captain Hall is repairing the Aggie, and Captain Turner is at work on the Annie.

It was too bad for that new mainsail of the Annie's to be spoiled.

The Chispa was cruising outside last Sunday. The wind was light out there.

Captains Freeman and Rogers had a party out on the T. H. Allen this week.

Vice Commodore MacDonough, of the Pacific Yacht Club, is out of town for a couple of weeks.

If the Chispa, Nellie, Aggie, Fleur de Lis, O'Connor and Whitewing go in one race, what a spectacle it will be.

Commodore Harrison, of the S. F. Y. C., has gone to the mountains for a month. The Frolic lies in Oakland creek.

This is the month for annual regattas of the Clubs, but none are announced, and it is not probable they will come off.

The American schooner Actæa, Mr. David Sears, arrived at Cowles, Isle of Wight, on June 19th, after a voyage of twenty-four days from Boston, Mass.

In Butte slough and creek the Chinese are catching fish by means of nets made of grain sacks. No wonder hook and line only bring out little fellows.

There are now two American topsail schooners afloat; Wanderer, 197 tons, E. D. Morgan, Jr., N. Y. Y. C., and Nokomis, 116 tons, W. A. W. Stewart, S. C. Y. C.

Frank Thibault, a well-known member of the S. F. Y. C., returned from Europe this week. He has seen the cutters sailing on the English Channel, and says they sail fast but look all under water.

The Lillie took the Golden Gate Club out recently, and in coming back from McNear's yard, with an ebb tide and southwest wind, some of the party got a pretty good wetting in the sea way of the upper channel.

The Viva was out with a fishing party the other day. She fished off the Powder Works near California City, and as she lay far enough off to be over mud bottom instead of rocks, it is not certain that a very large catch was made.

The Lolita has gone up to Montezuma slough with Capt. Eckley, John Lewis, Capt. Moody, Mr. Hines and Capt. Chittenden. With this lot of old salts there will be no danger of getting ashore. But won't the milk and fruit ranches suffer along the route.

The attempt of the Royal Cinque Ports Yacht Club, in England, to introduce steam yacht racing into their regatta, failed, as only Mr. Arabin's Celia was entered. This is scarcely to be wondered at, as the race was to be under no regulation for rating whatever beyond the condition that the competitors were not to exceed seventy feet in length.

A movement is on foot for a regatta of big yachts for a $500 prize. If all the big yachts will compete, it will be a fine race. But it will be hard to get the owners all to agree. One has stipulated that the race be finished within four hours or be considered not a race, We hope to see the race come off. Anything is better than the dullness now pervading yachting circles.

The Seawanhaka rule of measurement upon which time allowance is based is as follows: Add the length over all and length on the water line together, and divide the sum so obtained by two to get the mean length: Length over all will be measured from the after end of the planksheer, at the middle of the stern, to a point perpendicular to the forward end of the load water line at the upper line of the planksheer, or a point corresponding thereto, if the planksheer does not extend so far.

The new steamer Pilgrim is to run between New York and Fall River. Her hull is of iron. She is 374 feet long by 88 feet over the guards. She cost $1,000,000. Her depth is 18 feet 6 inches, and the measurement from the top of her dome to the base line is 60 feet. Afloat she will draw 11 feet of water, and her measurement will probably be registered at about 3,500 tons. She has a double hull, the first ever constructed for a steamer of this class. The engine is nominally 6,500-horse power but can furnish 8,000-horse power if required, while only 3,500 horse power need be ordinarily used.

Mr. James Gordon Bennett and his steam yacht Namouna arrived at Constantinople on July 12th. The Namouna, with the exception of two or three days when it blew a heavy gale, had a very pleasant passage to the Canaries. The yacht behaved very well and showed fine weatherly qualities. She left New York on the morning of June 5th, making 150 miles that day. The next days' runs were as follows: 270 miles, 267, 270½, 271½, 262½, 238, 241, 259, 269½, 276 and 180 miles more brought the Namouna to the Canaries. Here she remained three days, and then paid a flying visit to the Madeiras.

By the Seawanhaka Corinthian Club rules only one man is allowed for every five feet of length on deck and one for every additional fractional part of five feet, not including the owner. Each boat must be manned by amateurs exclusively. Any infringement of this rule will forfeit all claim to the prize. Before the owner of a winning boat shall receive the prize he, or in his absence the club member representing him on the boat, must sign a certificate stating that all the sailing regulations were complied with on such boat during the race. Each boat must be steered by her owner, a member of the Seawanhaka Club, or a member of the club from which she is entered.

The new 500-ton auxiliary steam yacht Gitana, just completed for Mr. Henry Jameson, of Dublin, Vice Commodore of the Royal Irish Yacht Club, had a most successful trial trip on the Firth of Forth, Scotland, on June 22d. Heavily rigged as a three-masted fore-and-aft schooner and designed in every other respect as a powerful sailing yacht, her engine power is only auxiliary, yet, on the measured mile at Gudane, says the London *Field*, the Gitana attained a mean speed of ten and a half knots—a most favorable result, taking into consideration that, besides sixty tons of lead ballast, she had eighty tons of coal in her bunkers, and a full equipment of stores for a Mediterranean cruise.

A PRUDENT MEASURE.—The Toronto *Mail* having become quite an authority on rowing and other sports, has lately achieved considerable notoriety as the stakeholder in several important matches. Some surprise was felt therefore when Hanlan, after challenging any five men in the world to row him five races within forty-eight hours of each other, deposited $1,000 with the Mayor of Toronto. A card from Wallace Ross explains the preference of the Canadian sculler. Ross states that the sporting editor of the *Mail* has skipped out with $1,000 of his money, which he had put up to bind the match with Hanlan. The average citizen will think that between the honesty and financial integrity of a politician and a journalist there is little to choose; but Hanlan has evidently a different opinion.

YIELDING MASTS.—A yielding mast for yachts, invented by Mr. Inchead, has been attracting much attention at the East. The mast, instead of being, according to immemorial usage, a fixture, has its lower end fixed between two powerful springs under the deck, allowing it to bend to either side. Thus, when a sharp gust of wind catches the sail, the boat is not capsized, but the mast bends and allows the surplus wind to escape over the top of the sail. The amount of pressure required to bend the mast can be regulated by an arrangement of nuts and screws. It is also claimed that by the new invention a great gain in speed is made, as all the luffing and shaking are avoided, and, as the sail does not offer so much resistance to the wind, the boat does not plunge through the waves in a rough sea, but glides over them.

A SOUTH SEA YARN.—"Here's a garfish," continued the skipper, hauling out a slender, silvery, long billed fish from the great pile. "They don't look very dangerous, but about ten years ago I was down the South Pacific on a trading schooner, and saw a man killed by one. The kind they have there have a long upper bill, like a swordfish, and grow four or five feet long. We were lying right inshore, where half a dozen natives were in the water, when all at once they began to make a big powpow and to drag one of their crowd ashore. I thought of sharks, and jumped into the dingy and pulled ashore. I found that a school of big garfish had been chased by some fish, and had jumped out of the water among the men. One of them struck a native, its bill going completely through his chest. The fish was over five feet long, and weighed about eighty pounds. I brought away its bill as a curiosity."—*New York Herald*.

## ATHLETICS.

### THE SEPTEMBER MEETING.

A Fall meeting in September, with every event open to all athletes, seems to meet with general favor. The Summer vacations being over, active training will now be in order, and no doubt the Oakland ground will be well patronized, and much quiet work be done on other quiet tracks.

The events that have already taken place this season have been a disappointment to most of the competitors, and they seem determined to make a better showing before the rains set in. Many entries for every event are already assured, and a repetition of the enthusiasm of last Thanksgiving Day, with grounds on which an audience can see and appreciate the merits of every contest, will insure the success of all future meetings. The grounds will be put in condition to warrant good performances if the contestants are fit, and the officers will undoubtedly attend to the comfort of the audience, and September is the most favorable time of the year for good weather. A little hearty enthusiasm will surely make the affair a success.

ONE HUNDRED YARDS AGAINST TIME. — This (Saturday) afternoon, on the O. A. C. Grounds in Oakland, about 4 P. M., R. S. Haley will run 100 yards for a record. It is to be hoped that good timers will be present with first class fifth second watches. Pacific Coast timing is under a cloud, and great care should be taken to prevent any question as to the correctness of the timing. As Mr. Brooks is not in condition to run with him, Old Father Time is the only amateur on the coast by whom any approximate gauge of his speed can be obtained. He feels confident of doing even time. We hope he will accomplish the feat. At the same time and place Messrs. Lowden and King will run off the tie for second place in the two-mile handicap, the contestants starting from the same marks as they did in the race on the 22d of July. No admittance will be charged at the gate. We would suggest that Harris should also attempt to do 10 seconds from the 89 yards mark. But perhaps he is out of condition now and would prefer to postpone the event a week or two.

L. E. Myers seems to be very anxious to meet Brooks again at 220 yards. Next time it will be in good taste to say nothing before the race about looking over his shoulder and calling for him to come on. He has yet to break the tape in as good time as was made by Brooks at the Championship Meeting, and he ought to do it without making four false starts. On this side of the Rockies three disqualifies everyone—even a champion.

## BICYCLING.

Great preparations are being made in bicycling circles for races to take place at the Fall Athletic meeting, which will probably be held September 9th, Admission Day, as this holiday falls early enough to insure dry weather and a good track. Most of the old riders and several new ones will enter the races, and the programme will be very attractive.

But little touring can be engaged in at this season, as the roads in the interior are much cut up by heavy traffic and extremely deep with dust, as is always the case in the dry season.

On Saturday, the 5th, the dead heat between G. L. King and W. H. Lowden, for second place in the two mile race of the 22d ult., will be run off at 4 P. M., at the grounds of the Olympic Club, Oakland. At the same time Finkler and Spring will run a half mile, both starting from scratch.

# THE
# Breeder and Sportsman.

PUBLISHED WEEKLY BY THE

BREEDER AND SPORTSMAN PUBLISHING CO.

THE TURF AND SPORTING AUTHORITY OF THE
PACIFIC COAST.

## OFFICE, 508 MONTGOMERY STREET

P. O. Box 2303.

*Five dollars a year; three dollars for six months; one dollar and a
half for three months. Strictly in advance.*

MAKE ALL CHECKS, MONEY ORDERS, ETC., PAYABLE TO ORDER OF
BREEDER AND SPORTSMAN PUBLISHING CO.

*Money should be sent by postal order, draft or by registered letter, ad-
dressed to the "Breeder and Sportsman Publishing Company, San Francisco, Cal."*

*Communications must be accompanied by the writer's name and address,
not necessarily for publication, but as a private guarantee of good faith.*

JOSEPH CAIRN SIMPSON,  -  -  -  EDITOR

SAN FRANCISCO,  -  SATURDAY, AUGUST 5, 1882

## NOTABLE HORSES.

In the six illustrations of the "Notable Horses
of California," there has been one picture of a
thoroughbred and five of trotters. This must not
be accepted as a token that the harness division
comprises five-sixths of the equine notabilities in
our estimation, or that there is such a preponderance of merit in those which are celebrated for
celerity of motion that all other kinds of horses
must be ignored. Horses which come prominently
before the public are like the stars of the theatrical
profession, attracting increasing attention as they
become still faster; and there is little doubt that
W. H. Vanderbilt, though the possessor of nearly
a hundred millions of dollars, controls more miles
of railway than any man in the world, builds palaces for himself and family, has not nearly the wide
celebrity of his mare Maud S. James R. Keene
was comparatively unknown until Foxhall won the
Grand Prix; and when Iroquois scored the "double
event" of Derby and St. Leger, scarcely a hamlet
in the civilized world where his name was not
heard. The reduction of the records by the yearlings and two-year-olds bred here turned attention
to California, and it is safe to assert that since the
days of the gold excitement there has been nothing in California history which was so widely
heralded.

Recognizing that a journal must follow the bent
of the public, presenting subjects which a large
majority of its readers demand, it does not follow
that all of our proclivities range on the side of
"fast horses." We shall present the claims of
every race, and not a single family in the wide
range of equine life which will not be brought forward in due time. From the diminutive Sheltie—
the delight of children—to the ponderous draft-
horse, all shall have due notice, though it is evident
that these will have to be treated in classes, and
types in place of individuals be the points to picture. We shall make the paper as comprehensive
as the "heading," and as our artist has so happily
grouped the illustrations of the main features of
the BREEDER AND SPORTSMAN in the vignette, our
aim shall be to follow with the pen that which the
pencil has depicted.

The Pacific Coast is well supplied, so far as the
right procreative animals go, with nearly all kinds
of horses, and large interests are pending in breeding others than horses which are reared for road
and track purposes. If there is a lack it is in
coach horses. The combination of blood which
has been found in England well adapted for the
production of these animals, is three-quarters
thoroughbred and the other portion Clydesdale;
but the thoroughbreds used must have the requisite
size and proper shape. It is not essential that
there should be high racing form, and "points,"
objectionable when great speed at the gallop is the
aim, are not so essential for the coach. So far as
our observation has gone, Oregon has taken the
lead of California in this class of horses, and also
in the better class of draft horses, though in the
exhibitions of the California State Agricultural
Society there are manifest improvements in these
classes in the last few years. Enterprising men in
some portions of the State are making strenuous
efforts to improve the breed of draft horses, and
many very fine animals have been imported.

It will not be many years when there will be a
marked superiority in this branch of horse-breeding, and notable specimens more frequently seen
than is the case at present. There is a sure remuneration for those who pursue the business intelligently. A haphazard, careless system will fail
in this as well as in the production of race horses
and fast trotters. Although size is always a marketable quality in a horse which is required to
draw heavy loads, there are other requisites to
consider. When we find a horse which comes
nearly up to what we consider the right model for
a draft horse, he shall have a place among the
"notables." This will be typical of the family to
which he belongs; and in the course of time we
hope to present a representation of the various
breeds. Clydesdales, Norman Percherons, Shire-
horses, the Suffolk Punch, etc., have points of excellence well worthy of consideration, and it may
be that in this climate, so favorable for physical
development, there will be produced a California
draft horse which will be the superior of any of
them. We write "may be," although the faith is
strong that in the not very far-off future the supposition will be changed into certainty, and *has*
take the place of expectancy.

When the breeding of coach horses receives the
same attention here as has been awarded to the
production of race horses and fast trotters, there is
scarcely the least doubt of the same success resulting. All over the United States the same unaccountable neglect has been shown, and among the
many breeders of our personal acquaintance, we
only know one whose aim is in that direction.
Districts which forty years ago were celebrated for
the production of this class of horses are now barren, and the most careful search fails to discover
a pair which have any pretensions to rank in the
category, or fit to be compared with those of the
past. The coach horse, too, shall have a place in
the portrait gallery of the BREEDER AND SPORTSMAN,
and we know of one which is not far off from the
standard. In short, the intention is to illustrate
every phase of breeding with the best portraits of
the best animals, and whether those which are
selected are renowned individually or present the
desired type of a family, in due time there will appear the notables of the breeds to which they belong.

## THE SPEED BOULEVARD.

The question of the drive for San Francisco,
where the truly American proclivities for fast trotting can be gratified, is of so much importance
that it is unnecessary to apologize for frequent recurrence to the subject. The benefits following
the construction of a road which will permit fast
driving are not limited to San Francisco, as there
is scarcely a county in the State which will not
share in the advantages, and though the direct
profits will fall to the breeders of horses adapted
for the purpose, other breeds will appreciate in
value from the "roadsters" being drawn from
places which can be filled with those which do not
possess the requisite speed. There is little necessity for argument as to the advantages which will
accrue. We have yet to meet a man, with whom
we have conversed, that does not acknowledge the
good results which are sure to follow the completion of the proposed drive. Some are sceptical
about raising the means by subscription, and
others claim that the ground is not suitable. As
to the first objection, we have full faith that in a
very short time after it is known that want of funds
is the only obstacle the subscriptions will be
ample.

The first step is to lay it before the Park Commissioners, and from the well-known public spirit
of these gentlemen there cannot be a doubt of obtaining their sanction. Petitions left in suitable
places would receive signatures enough to prove
that the public was interested, and that there was
a general desire for the construction of the drive.
After that surveys should be made, as it is probable that the expense attending this part of the
preliminary work would be met by those having
property which would be increased in value by the
road being located according to their desires.

From these surveys—the more of them the better
—estimates could be made of the cost, and the location which was found the most suitable selected.
That proper ground can be gotten is beyond question. Those who remember the difficulties which
were overcome in building the Bay District Course
cannot be sceptical on that point. Hills were cut
down, ravines filled. When this was accomplished
there was a bed of sand which called for laborious
efforts to walk upon, and he who made the circuit
of the track when it was at this stage needed rest
at the completion of the mile. The upper stratum
of clay with which the sand was covered gives a
firm foothold and the yielding foundation gave
elasticity, and now it is generally conceded that
the Bay District Course is the "fastest" in the
State.

The proper material for covering is found contiguous to the Park in many places, and the expense of coating to the requisite depth will not be
as heavy as many imagine. There is another advantage in having a foundation of sand for a road-
bed besides the springiness resulting. This is the
capillary attraction of the minute particles bringing the moisture from below nearer the surface,
and economizing the water supply. The natural
impediments to building the contemplated road in
the vicinity of the Park, in place of being so momentous as some are inclined to think, are triding
when compared with what has been overcome in
other cities. Excavations and embankments are
easily made in sand, and when the "cuts" and
"fills" are balanced, as is likely to be the case in
the project under consideration, the cost is less
than when there is a superabundance of material
to be got rid of. Then, again, it is not necessary
that there should be a level road, as, in fact, it will
be preferable on some accounts if there are undu-
lations, which give variety and bring out keener
contests. Down the grade one horse is victorious,
when the ascent brings his competitor upon even
terms, and the contest is a changing scene in lieu
of a one-sided affair.

But the main point at present is to bring the
project into tangible shape by getting the question
as soon as possible before the Commissioners.
After that is done, and with favorable action on
their part, the discussion of the various points at
issue will more appropriately follow. We would
strenuously urge that petitions be gotten up and
circulated without delay. In one week names
enough can be obtained, and in a shorter time than
even the sanguine supporters imagine, we hope to
chronicle that the grand drive is an assured fact.

## AMATEURS OR PROFESSIONALS.

There appears to be a never-ending jangle in regard to what really constitutes an amateur, and
the dividing line which marks the difference between that and a professional, like the line of no
declination, constantly changing. It is a bone of
contention among the followers of all kinds of
sport, and there are a succession of difficulties to
overcome whenever there is a chance for a clashing
of interests. The committees which have charge
of these affairs in England have narrowed it down
to a point where all can understand, and the meaning given there is, that wherever there is the remotest chance of being beaten, the parties shall be
excluded, as not coming up to the English standard.

We are not sorry that our crews and athletes are
snubbed. By offering to participate they practically acknowledge the correctness of the assumption of superiority, and join hands with those who
claim that all who are in a position to live without
abor are of a race which cannot brook fellowship
with those who do. The snob who has not brains
enough to learn to make a pair of shoes looks with
contempt on a man who is his superior in everything pertaining to real manhood, and the copying
snobs of this country adopt the habit as they do
the fashion of their trousers. But it is not the intention at present to discuss the intricate question
as it is presented in athletic sports.

Not long ago there was a jangle at the races at the
Gentleman's Driving Park, New York, over the

meaning of an amateur driver, and it was decided that any one who had ever driven for money, "purse, stake or wager," was a professional. This is an absurd definition. Too absurd for argument, were it not that it was coincided in by so many as to give it more weight than it was entitled to intrinsically. The Trotting Rules give the judges the power to order any professional driver to mount the sulky, and if he fails to respond to the imperial mandate, they have also the authority to punish to the full extent of the code. It is an arbitrary, despotic rule, which never should have been placed on record; but there it is, and as long as it is the law due deference will have to be awarded.

Should the definition alluded to be sustained, any man who has ever driven for money is amenable, liable to be ordered to drive a horse when the solons in the stand take a fancy to show their power. There is an easy solution of the meaning of professional, so far as regards the driving of trotters, and we cannot see why there should be any objections to the same construction in athletics. The definition should be, any person who makes the driving of trotters a business, followed it in whole or part as the means of making money, and this class should alone be amenable to the rule which empowers the judges to compel their services. In order that the degree of skill which is supposed to follow an active pursuit, stimulated by the hope of reward, should not come in competition with inferior ability; add, or who at any former time has engaged in it as a business. This appears to us like a common sense view, and one which would end the bickerings that are now so annoying.

### TROTTING ON THE BAY DISTRICT.

To-day the Fall season opens, and the 2:40 and 2:25 classes will be decided on the Bay District Course. In the former will meet a trio of aspirants for track fame, and as even the "touts" are puzzled to select the winner, there is a likelihood of a contest which will prove exciting. Five of the six entries in the 2:25 are well known to be very "close together," and Del Sur, Crown Point, Starr King, Cairo and Ashley, a quintet of so nearly equal capacity that the problem of which is the superior is difficult of solution. Sweetness makes her first appearance on a California track, and the "boys" at the Oakland Trotting Park are very "sweet" on her chances. She is by Volunteer, the sire of St. Julien *et al.*, her dam by Edward Everett, the same inbreeding to Hambletonian as there is in Clingstone, and her grand dam by Harry Clay, the sire of the dam of St. Julien, Electioneer, Hogarth, etc.

### SUNNY SLOPE.

The colts from Sunny Slope have arrived at the Bay District Course, and it is safe to say that it is rare to see as fine looking a lot. Mr. Rose ascribes the defeat of Eva to too gentle treatment. She had a peculiar waywardness, or, more properly, obstinacy, which required heroic treatment to overcome, and on several occasions Donathan had to be quite severe in order to make her do what he wanted. There was a very general impression that Donathan was too harsh, but the fact that she trotted in 2:26 as a two-year-old, and was beaten in 2:33 when she ranks as a year older, is good proof that his was the correct handling. No one discovers a mistake sooner than Hickok, and we shall look for her to show her old form in her future races.

### THE STALLION RECORD.

Little by little the gap between Smuggler's 2:15¼ and the next fastest stallion record is lessened. Piedmont and Black Cloud divided the honors for the second place, and now the telegraph brings the intelligence that Black Cloud took a second off his previous time, and at Buffalo last Thursday trotted a heat in 2:16¼. This grand representative of the Mambrinos appears to be capable of taking the first place, and though Smuggler is mainly of thoroughbred blood, Black Cloud can show one grandparent without a stain. In this he resembles Maud S., the difference being that her maternal grandam was thoroughbred, while it is on the paternal side in Black Cloud.

### THE EMBRYO STAKE.

We must confess that the Embryo has been a double surprise. In the first place, that the owners of forty-three colts are under the impression that they are breeding colts which are fit to cope with any one who may choose to come in, after all the talk there has been about advantages which were confined to a few. This was a more liberal response than we anticipated, and must acknowledge extreme gratification with the result. The second surprise was the absence of the Palo Alto nominations, and until Thursday supposed that it was due to some blunder of Uncle Sam's post-office officials. A search was instituted, a messenger despatched, when we learned that none had been sent. We are just as much in the dark as any of our readers, though, of course, there are imaginings which may be far from the truth. In such a case, it would be a waste of time to give opinions which are without foundation. That there was no intimation of the purpose is a certainty, and those who subscribed did so with the full expectation of encountering the stars of the great breeding farm on the banks of the San Francisquita. For this we award them a full measure of praise. It is a practical illustration of the value of California as the nursery of trotters, and that even the smaller breeders have confidence in rearing animals which have merit. That the wonderful performances of California-bred trotting colts have stimulated breeders to endeavor to rear those which will prove worthy of comparison is beyond question, and the impetus given will gather force as the years come. It turned the attention of purchasers to California, and increased the value of the stock all over the State. The fact that so many colts were named, in the face of a competition which some were craven enough to fear, will add to the value. The list of nominations which is given may not include all, as there has not been time enough to hear from distant points, and even those that are nearer may be delayed in the mails.

### THE RACING STAKES.

The long list of nominations in the stakes of the Pacific Coast Blood-Horse Association is a gratifying testimonial of the progress which has been made in the breeding of thoroughbreds in California. It is not given as perfect, as it is always a work of time to get the entries in shape; but knowing the interest that our readers felt in knowing what were "in," publication was resolved upon. There was another trouble, arising from a typographical error, which was overlooked in the proof as printed in this paper, and also in the slips when sent in the letters. The error was in the Fame Stake, where 1883 was printed for 1884. This would not mislead any one conversant with the matter, as it is well known that the colts are entered when yearlings, and in this stake run in their three-year-old form. Mr. Chase, however, has collated the nominations according to the wishes of the subscribers, and whenever there is a doubt in regard to the intention, the parties will be notified to clear it up. The official publication will follow as soon as possible, though there is scarcely a probability of change.

The Stallion Stake did not receive the requisite number of subscribers, though all the others show remarkably well. That there should be such an array of names from the limited number of breeders in California is an augury for the future which does not require a Vates to read correctly. When the measures are perfected which were outlined a week ago, it will not be long afterwards when there will be a largely increased production of thoroughbreds, and a corresponding augmentation in the nominations. There is little necessity for long comments on the breeding of the youngsters engaged. There are many of them as fashionably bred as the most exacting stickler for blue blood could desire, and from what we have seen, the form is in keeping with the genealogy. We heartily congratulate the Association on the success which is sure to follow, and also the lovers of the "royal sport" upon the bright prospects of the future.

### ANOTHER ALMONT ON THE COAST.

From E. Giddings of Lemoore, California, we obtain the information that in a short article which appeared two weeks ago, we omitted Altimont from the list of Almonts on this coast. It was not supposed to be absolutely correct, being written without other reference than memory afforded. Altimont is well worthy to be classed with those which were given, as his first dam is Belle Miller, by Blackwood, second dam by Mambrino Chief, third dam by Hickory (thoroughbred), fourth dam by Camden, and his fifth dam by Cherokee. The Camden is stated to be the horse of that name which was a son of imported Sarpedon, but this horse was castrated, though it may have been that the operation was performed after he had gotten progeny. There were three Camdens, two of them foaled in 1836, the other in 1835. Camden by Shark, from imported Invalid, made some seasons in Kentucky, and it may be that there is an error. At all events, both he and the Camden by Sarpedon were from well-bred mares, the latter being from Cherokas by Cherokee, and the combination of Almont, Blackwood, Mambrino Chief and thoroughbred in Altimont, should please the most fastidious.

There is no question that Mr. Giddings is also right in thinking that Altimont is the colt we had reference to as the yearling which we saw at the Oakland Park in 1875 or 1876. He went to San Luis Obispo, in place of Santa Barbara, and his dam, Theresa B., by Prophet, Jr.

On the card which Mr. Giddings sent giving the pedigree of Altoona, there is also the pedigree of A. T. Stewart, which we suppose to be the horse which accompanied Altoona from Kentucky. He is by Mambrino Patchen, his dam by Mambrino Chief, so that he is a double Mambrino, and his grandam being by Young's Pilot, Jr., there is a mixture which will please many breeders.

### OVERMAN A WINNER.

The telegram brings the intelligence that Overman won at Buffalo last Wednesday, trotting in either 2:20½ or 2:20¾. He has always been a great favorite with us and from the time he was broken never lost confidence in him, or waivered in the belief that he would eventually gain high distinction. That his sire Elmo would take a prominent place as the progenitor of fast trotters, whenever his colts were given a chance, has also been our belief from the time we first saw his colts, and this idea has never been abandoned. A horse of such grand size and appearance, so well bred, so purely gaited, so very fast and with unquestionable endurance, must reproduce himself when proper opportunies are awarded him. He has shown colts, many of them, that in our opinion only required the right education to equal if not surpass Overman, but Mr. Seale has had too many other irons in the fire to grant them the chance. The success of about the only colt of Elmo's which has been trained may stimulate to give others an opportunity. We hope so.

### THE GREAT FOUR-YEAR-OLD RACE.

We have copied from the New York *Spirit of the Times* an account of the great race in Chicago, and in which two four-year-olds greatly distinguished themselves. The race is admirably described by "Mambrino," and the pedigree of the colts given. The "glorious uncertainty of racing" is forcibly exemplified, and a chapter of accidents, or rather a series of misfortunes, attended the favorites. Such races as the one described will do more to advance the trotting of colts than pages of argument, and when the main features of the trotting meetings are the doings of the youngsters, breeders will find that their interests are proportionately advanced. The lines of blood being given in the account, there is no necessity for recapitulation.

## FISH.

Wild Cat Creek, Alameda County, used to be a first-rate fishing place. Now it is too near civilization.

Indian Creek, Mendocino county, is said to be a first-class trout stream. A friend lately had fine sport there.

Mr. H. A. Wilson was at Saucelito last Sunday, and reports splendid fishing in the waters in that vicinity.

Many persons who went to the lakes in the north, have returned disgusted, as trout fishing there is very poor.

A squall at Astoria on the 24th of July capsized fourteen fishing boats and drowned two men of the twenty-eight.

At Independence Lake, in this State, there is said to be good trouting. There are boats there which can be hired.

Capt. Douglas and a party of gentlemen have gone on a fishing expedition to the Farallone Islands, and will probably be gone for two or three days.

Fly-hooks, creel, rubber boots, split bamboo and inclination has many an angler, who has not the only other requisite for fine sport—time.

The Gualala river, Mendocino county, is another of those beautiful fishing streams so far from the city that one can only wish he had time to go there.

Large numbers of deer are being killed in Mendocino county. Many persons, it is said, are slaughtering them for their hides alone. It is to be hoped that this is not true.

The streams are all getting lower, and no longer does the angler have to climb to the headwaters for a chance to fill his creel. As the waters recede the big fish come down stream.

Fraser River is full of salmon, and all the canneries are taxed to their entire capacity. Forty-five thousand salmon were delivered to the six canneries along the river, recently, in one day.

Some parties have had excellent sport along the streams in the Santa Cruz Mountains, where they say trout fishing is very good. Trout are also plentiful in the vicinity of Monterey.

There have been more tomcod, rockcod and smelt caught around the bay this year, than have been caught for many years previous. For two or three days, or while the "small tides" last, the bay fishers expect considerable sport, as the fish usually come in great numbers during these tides.

Passengers on the French steamer Labrador, which arrived recently at New York, state that on several mornings before reaching the Banks of Newfoundland they observed shoals of flying-fish rise out of the water before the vessel's bow—an unusual spectacle in the North Atlantic Ocean.

Mr. Ben Burling, one of the party that met with the accident near Felton, was in town last week. He is recovering slowly. His physician advises him to take a trip to the Sierras, where he will remain enjoying the cool mountain breezes and beautiful scenery until he has fully recovered.

The Alameda Sportsmen's Club intend stocking a large lake in the neighborhood of Niles and Washington Corners with choice fish. The lake, of course, will be kept as a reserve for the club, but nevertheless it will be so much gain to the general wealth of the State and will redound greatly to the credit and add to the attractions of the club.

Wm. Goulcher, in the years 1876 and 1877, placed a number of California salmon minnows in the lakes and streams of Minnesota. He has been informed lately that California salmon have been caught in the headwaters of the Mississippi River, that weigh 5½ and 6 pounds. Mr. Goulcher was Fish Commisioner of Minnesota for many years.

Rope Valley, in the Sierra Nevadas, is said to be a region good for fishing. The Virginia *Enterprise* says that the brooks in that section swarm with trout. These are so accommodating that they are almost ready to come ashore to take the hook. This cannot be beaten at any other place, except, perhaps, at Donner Lake, where the trout are said to swim about with the strawberries in their mouths.

W. A. Spence, a fish dealer in California Market, was tried before Judge Rix, on Thursday last, and found guilty on two charges of misdemeanor, one for having had in his possession shad out of season, and the other for exposing the same for sale. The prosecution was instituted by Crittenden Robinson, of the Sportsman's Club of California. The fish, as shown by the evidence, were caught with a net in the Sacramento River, and the accused was stealthily selling them.

During the storm Thursday evening a number of good-sized fish rained down in the road near Ike Hamilton's, and could be seen there yesterday. One active fellow about four inches long survived the night, and was picked up and put into a pan of water, where he showed up as lively as ever. The fish were of the "chub" variety, and varied in size from two to four inches in length. It is the first shower of the kind experienced in this section.—*Scott Valley News.*

Colonel Charles Ledyard Norton, editor of the *American Canoeist*, after protracted search for an efficient drip stop for paddles, advises the following: "If you have no babies of your own, call at the drug store, pick out two—well, call them rubber nozzles, much sought after in raising the new generation in its earlier stages—slice off the small ends, slip over the paddle and they will fit like cups, an effective preventive to dripping."

Peter Lubiens, a fish dealer on Stockton street, was arrested on Wednesday last on a charge of selling salmon out of season. The open manner in which laws for the protection of fish and game have been violated in this city and State has been disgraceful to not only the officers of the law but to those who have formed themselves into clubs, for the avowed purpose of seeing that all violators were arrested and brought to punishment. The growing scarcity of game, and more especially of fish, is opening the eyes of fish commissioners, sportsmen's clubs, and all lovers of the rod and gun to the necessities of the case, and we are promised prompt arrests and vigorous prosecutions hereafter. We sincerely hope that such will be forthcoming.

## THE GUN.

### THE MATCH FOR THE GOLD MEDAL.

Last Sunday, two teams, composed of fifteen members in each, from the Cosmopolitan Pigeon Shooting Club and the California Pigeon Shooting Club, competed for the diamond medal and the championship of the State at "Dick" Cunningham's shooting grounds, San Bruno. The terms of the match called for twelve birds for each shooter, members of the oposing team to alternate shots; 21 yards rise, 80 yards boundary; H and T traps, five in number. Charles Nouges was unanimously selected to act as referee. J. Stack judged for the Cosmopolitan club, and J. Burns for the California Club. D. M. Pyle kept time and D. Rice trapped. Frank Maskey captained the Cosmopolitan team and retrieved wounded birds, while Crittenden Robinson performed similar offices for the California Club. The California Club won the toss and Crittenden Robinson went first to the score. He killed an easy incomer and was followed by Frank Maskey, who was equally successful. Ferguson, the third man in the Cosmopolitan team, scored the first 0, but his bird, a hard flying, right hand quarterer from the right trap, fell dead a few inches out of bounds. Hub. Parker was the first man to miss on the California side. This equalized matters, but Golcher Sr,. followed with a miss, and left the score one in favor of the California team. Bogard and Pearson on the one side, and Card on the other, all missing, made the score at the end of the first round even with 12 kills for each. In the next round the Cosmopolitans shot very steadily, scoring 14 kills out of 15. The other team was less fortunate. They made five misses, which put the California four ahead. From this time to the end of the match the Californias led right along. Once their lead was reduced to one, but they soon picked up, until the last shot was fired, when they had nine more to their credit than their opponents. In the tenth round the wind commenced to blow in violent gusts from the west. This had the effect of making the round the poorest one shot. The Californias made 9 misses; Crittenden Robinson missing for the first time, and the Cosmopolitans' having five scored against them. In the fifth round Ellon shot at and winged a bird which was going out of bounds, when one of the spectators struck at it with his cane. On a complaint by Burns, the referee under rule 26, gave Ellor a fresh bird, which he missed. In the following round a precisely similar thing occurred to one of the Cosmopolitan team. A new bird was ordered, under the same rule, which the shooter killed. Thus the California Club, which raised a technicality seldom claimed, was really loser one bird by the operation.

Though the averages made in the match were far above the usual work done by teams, Mr. Robert Tallant, of the Cosmopolitan Club, was the only gentleman who made a clean score. This he did in the face of conditions as adverse as fell to the lot of any shooter. Some of his birds were perfect demons, but he shot steadily and killed them all without the assistance of the retriever. Johnson and Kerrigan would have made clean scores but for birds dying out of bounds. The birds missed by Maskey, Robinson and Spencer got clear away though feathers flew from all three of them. Several kills were made at a great distance, Dr. Knowles' kill at 68 yards, with a 16 bore Greener gun, being the longest shot of the day. The Cosmopolitan Club only missed 35 out of 180 birds, or an average of 81 per cent. of kills. Their opponents missed 44, or an average of 75½ per cent. of kills. At the conclusion of the match President J. H. Jellett, of the California Club, presented the diamond medal to the Cosmopolitan Club in a neat speech. During his remarks he said that the rivalry was of a most friendly nature, and he hoped that ere long the two clubs would have another tussle for supremacy. President Rix replied on behalf of the winners. He paid a tribute of respect to the skill and courtesy of the vanquished, and reciprocated the previous speaker's wish for a future match. The medal is now the private property of the Cosmopolitan Club, they having won it three times. The club has given it into the custody of Mr. Robert Tellant, thinking that he alone having made a clean score in the match was the rightful custodian. It is likely that the club will put the medal up for competition among its members. The trophy is one that any man might well be proud to wear. It is a small, round gold medal, about the size of half a dollar, having in the center a two-carat diamond of exquisite water.

Following is the complete score of the match:

THE SCORE.

The following are the scores of the two teams:

COSMOPOLITANS.

| | | | | | | | | | | | | | |
|---|---|---|---|---|---|---|---|---|---|---|---|---|---|
| F. Maskey | 1 | 1 | 1 | 1 | 1 | 0 | 1 | 1 | 1 | 1 | 1 | 1 | 11 |
| J. Kelly | 1 | 1 | 0 | 1 | 1 | 1 | 1 | 1 | 1 | 1 | 0 | 1 | 10 |
| J. Ferguson | 0 | 1 | 1 | 0 | 1 | 1 | 0 | 1 | 1 | 1 | 1 | 1 | 9 |
| H. Rover | 1 | 1 | 1 | 1 | 1 | 1 | 0 | 0 | 1 | 1 | 0 | 1 | 9 |
| G. H. Graham | 1 | 1 | 1 | 0 | 1 | 1 | 1 | 1 | 1 | 0 | 1 | 1 | 10 |
| W. Golcher | 0 | 1 | 1 | 1 | 1 | 0 | 1 | 0 | 1 | 1 | 1 | 1 | 9 |
| A. Higgins | 1 | 1 | 1 | 0 | 1 | 0 | 1 | 1 | 1 | 0 | 1 | 1 | 9 |
| F. Johnson | 1 | 1 | 1 | 1 | *0 | 1 | 1 | 1 | 1 | 1 | 1 | 1 | 11 |
| F. H. Putzman | 1 | 1 | 1 | 0 | 1 | 1 | 1 | 1 | 1 | 0 | 1 | 1 | 10 |
| P. Funke | 1 | 0 | 1 | 1 | 1 | 1 | 1 | 0 | *0 | 1 | 1 | 1 | 9 |
| R. Liddle | 1 | 1 | *0 | 1 | 1 | *0 | 0 | 1 | 1 | 1 | 1 | 1 | 9 |
| R. Tallant | 1 | 1 | 1 | *1 | 1 | 1 | 1 | 1 | 1 | 1 | 1 | 1 | 12 |
| J. Browell | 1 | 1 | 1 | 1 | 1 | 1 | 0 | 0 | 1 | 1 | 0 | 1 | 9 |
| W. H. Carr | 0 | 1 | 0 | 1 | 1 | 1 | 1 | 1 | 1 | 0 | 1 | 0 | 8 |
| M. Ault | 1 | 1 | 0 | 1 | 1 | 1 | 1 | 1 | 1 | 0 | 1 | 1 | 10 |
| Total | | | | | | | | | | | | | 145 |

*Died out of bounds.

CALIFORNIAS.

| | | | | | | | | | | | | | |
|---|---|---|---|---|---|---|---|---|---|---|---|---|---|
| C. Robinson | 1 | 1 | 1 | 1 | 1 | 1 | 1 | 1 | 1 | 0 | 1 | 1 | 11 |
| G. W. W. Roche | 1 | 1 | 0 | 1 | 1 | 1 | 1 | 1 | 1 | *0 | 0 | 1 | 9 |
| G. W. Downey | 1 | 1 | 1 | 1 | 1 | 1 | 1 | *0 | 1 | *0 | 1 | 1 | 10 |
| A. E. Burbank | 1 | 1 | 1 | 0 | 0 | 0 | 1 | 1 | 0 | 0 | 1 | 1 | 7 |
| H. Spencer | 1 | 0 | 1 | 1 | 1 | 1 | 1 | 1 | 1 | 1 | 1 | 1 | 11 |
| H. G. Parker | 0 | 0 | 0 | 1 | 1 | 1 | 1 | 1 | 0 | *0 | 1 | 1 | 7 |
| P. J. Walsh | 1 | 1 | 1 | 1 | 1 | 1 | 1 | 0 | 1 | 1 | 1 | 0 | 10 |
| W. H. Bogart | 0 | 1 | 0 | 1 | 1 | 0 | 1 | 1 | 1 | 0 | 1 | 0 | 7 |
| I. W. Hays | 1 | 0 | 1 | 0 | 1 | 1 | 1 | 1 | 1 | 0 | 1 | 1 | 9 |
| J. Kerrigan | 1 | 1 | 1 | 1 | 1 | *0 | 1 | 1 | 1 | 1 | 1 | 1 | 11 |
| Dr. Berwick | 1 | *0 | 1 | 1 | 1 | 1 | 1 | *0 | 1 | 1 | 1 | 0 | 9 |
| R. Ellon | 1 | 1 | 1 | 1 | 0 | 1 | 0 | 1 | 1 | 1 | 0 | 1 | 9 |
| S. E. Knowles | 1 | 1 | 1 | *0 | 1 | 0 | 1 | 1 | 1 | 0 | 0 | 1 | 8 |
| S. W. Pearson | 0 | 0 | 1 | 1 | 0 | 1 | 1 | *0 | 1 | 1 | 1 | 1 | 8 |
| J. H. Jellett | 1 | 1 | 1 | 1 | 1 | 1 | 0 | 1 | 1 | 0 | 1 | 1 | 10 |
| Total | | | | | | | | | | | | | 136 |

*Died out of bounds.

### THE ALAMEDA SPORTSMAN'S CLUB.

The members of this club met at Bird's Point, Alameda, on Saturday last, to contest for the club's gold and silver medals. The day was windy and cold and the pigeons rather a poor lot. Before all the members who were going to shoot had arrived, an outside match was shot of four birds, twenty-one yards, for a purse of $7 and $3, for first and second best. A. Lambert killed his four birds, so did Adams and Spencer, T. Muroney killed two. The first three shot off the ties, Spencer missed his first only and Lambert and Adams divided the money. Then came the contest for the medals, in which thirteen members took part. In this match Messrs. Spencer and Kerrigan were the judges, F. Eastman the referee, and the "veteran bird trapper," Harry Bird, was at his post as trapper. Ten birds were shot at, at twenty-one yards rise. The score stands:

| | | | | | | | | | | | |
|---|---|---|---|---|---|---|---|---|---|---|---|
| W. Winter | 1 | 0 | 1 | 0 | 1 | 0 | 0 | 1 | 0 | 1 | 5 |
| T. Bennett | 0 | 0 | 0 | 0 | 1 | 1 | 0 | 1 | 0 | | 3 |
| W. Haskell | 1 | 0 | 1 | 1 | 0 | 1 | 1 | 0 | 1 | 1 | 7 |
| — Crelin | 1 | 0 | 1 | 1 | 1 | 0 | 1 | 1 | 1 | 1 | 8 |
| R. Risdon | 0 | 1 | 1 | 1 | 1 | 1 | 1 | 1 | 1 | 1 | 9 |
| C. Tuttle | 1 | 1 | 1 | 1 | 0 | 0 | 1 | 0 | * | | |
| C. Pierce | 1 | 0 | 1 | 0 | 1 | 0 | 1 | 0 | 1 | 0 | 5 |
| A. Mayhew | 1 | 0 | 1 | 1 | 1 | 0 | 0 | 1 | 1 | 1 | 7 |
| C. F. Schell | 1 | 1 | 0 | 1 | 1 | 0 | 0 | 1 | 1 | 1 | 7 |
| N. Williams | 0 | 1 | 1 | 1 | 1 | 1 | 0 | | | | |
| F. Norton | 1 | 1 | 1 | 0 | 1 | 1 | 1 | 1 | 1 | 1 | 9 |
| S. Baker | 0 | 0 | 1 | 1 | 1 | 1 | 1 | 1 | 1 | 0 | 7 |
| H. Fritsch | 1 | 1 | 1 | 0 | 0 | 0 | 1 | 1 | 0 | 1 | 6 |

*Withdrawn.

The tie between Mr. Risdon and Norton on nine birds was shot off, the distance being extended from 21 yards to 26 yards. There were five birds shot at; Mr. Norton killed four and Mr. Risdon two. Mr. Norton took the gold medal for first-class shooting, and Mr. Crellin the silver medal for the second-class. Risdon hit the only bird he lost, but it died out of bounds. Several quick shots killed some of their birds before they recovered from the throw of the trap. After the club match, several small purses were shot for, which added to the afternoon's enjoyment. The 7 o'clock train took the last of the shooters home, well satisfied with the day's sport.

### SPORTING ON DITS FROM THE CAMPS.

Since the first of July, several hunting parties have returned from various parts of the State, with more or less to say of their trips. The Golden Gate Rifle Club had many representatives scattered through the country. The President, L. A. Bauer, together with Messrs. Behlow, Slackpool, Dr. Richter, Henry Hoffman, and Mr. Dresel of Sonoma, spent two weeks in camp at Ward Creek, on the Russian River, and appear delighted with their hunt. They had seen very many does and fawns, but found bucks scarce, yet, thanks to their splendid hounds, they had some exciting runs, and, being more for sport than slaughter, were much pleased with their success. Smith, Jr., of the same club, and party of friends, made a tour from Cloverdale to Mendocino, and by the coast to Fort Ross, thence via Ingram's to Petaluma, and back to the city, making remarkably good time. Mr. J. Stanton, with a few others, visited Lake Tahoe, and report some splendid fishing and deer hunting. Dr. Boysen had quite a time at the Rawles Ranch, Boonville, with Rawles, Murray and some others. The home of the cinnamon, on Indian Creek, was invaded, and a splendid run with the bear hounds was the result. The Doctor, to keep pace with his country friends, engaged a diminutive broncho at the hotel, and beihg rather heavy weight—228 pounds—the poor animal had its native genius sorely tested to get along. But with mustang pluck he stuck to his task, and after spilling the Doctor seven times finally got relieved, and returned riderless to the hotel. After the bear was dispatched, one of the country hunters came upon the Doctor, seated, or listed, somewhat like the Escambia before she went over, on an open hillside, where he and the mustang dissolved partnership, and asked what the matter was, or why he did not follow up the hunt. The Doctor, leaning his left hand upon the ground, and placing his right gently upon an unmentionable part of his anatomy, forcibly replied, "I be d—d if I go another foot." Since his return to the city he has entertained the members of the G. G. R. C. with reminiscences of his trip, and says he is tired of bear and deer hunting—he'll go after Lions in future.

Jacoby and four others camped about seven miles from Cloverdale. They were most liberally supplied with the necessaries of camp life, from the "Post Keller," and they had the good fortune to get one spiked buck, which had been caught by a rancher's dog close to their camp. The rancher generously donated the catch. Mr. Bet packed it in, and a dozen Budweiser was uncorked to celebrate the event. Mr. B. was declared "Champion of Camp Jacoby," and they enjoyed themselves wonderfully well.

Crittenden Robinson, Tom Pearson and some other members of the California Wing-Shooting Club, were guests of one of the interior clubs belonging to the State Sportsman's Association, for a few days, and report most favorably of the entertainment. Bob says Tom's Winchester made short work of a rancher's hog, for which hog practice he had to pay $4. Tom says it was an unavoidable mistake, as he took it for a bear as it stood by a log, and made a good shot any way.

Messrs. Tubbs, Shorten, O'Connor, and Bill Nolan, of the "Æsthetic Whisker Club," had a lively time at Skaggs' Springs. They whiled away the hours with dancing, music and hunting. They killed two deer one day, and after carefully dressing them, hung them on a pepper tree for safety. On going to the place next morning with a pack-horse, to their utter astonishment they found skeletons hanging from the ropes, and not a particle of flesh on the bones. After searching about for the cause of this extraordinary state of affairs, they came upon a yellow-jackets' nest, from the size and appearance of which they were satisfied that it contained the flesh of their two deer. They returned to Skaggs', and were so disgusted they would not take even the horns. They say, anybody who doubts the story may go to the place, and there the evidence still hangs.

One of the many mistakes made by city hunters, when they go in search of game with which they are not acquainted, was evidenced by Dr. D. I. Hays, of the California Wing Club, in the neighborhood of San Jose, last week, when he shot a billy-goat of a brownish hue, which he thought was a spiked buck, until the merriment of his companions convinced him of there being something wrong. Even then he could not see where all the hilarity came in.

Golcher, Spencer, Lackey, etc., were located at Highland Springs. Mr. Lackey is a most expert croquet player, and vanquished his adversaries in every game. He and Spencer, with shotguns, etc., sallied forth for a day's sport among the redwoods. Lackey hailed Spencer some way up the hill, calling his attention to a pretty black-and-white animal which he saw about twenty-five yards off. Spencer said it was a very rare specimen of the California Mountain Squirrel, and to shoot it. Bang went the gun, and Mr. L. in a few strides reached his game. Well, the messenger who went to the hotel for a fresh suit of clothes, and the mound under which Lackey's hunting rig lies buried, as well as the decomposing carcass of a skunk, tell the whole story. Spencer said "he'd never give it away." * * *

## THE SAN FRANCISCO POLICE TEAM.

Very little interest had been taken in pistol shooting by the members of our Police Department until about two years ago, when they received a challenge from colonel Beaver, in behalf of the Citizens' Team. The challenge was accepted. At this time there were not a dozen men on the force that could make over 104 or 105 points out of a possible 125. Since then these two teams have met three times in friendly contests for honors, medals, etc. Last Spring Colonel Dickinson, President of the California Rifle Association, offered as a trophy to the best pistol team, a beautiful silver bowl, that cost no less than $125. This was the first trophy ever shot for by pistol teams on this coast. The only teams contesting for this prize were the Police Team, under Capt. Douglass, and the Citizens' Team, under Col. Beaver. The trophy was won by the Police Team, which made 472 points of a possible 500. Colonel Beaver's Team scored 471 points of a possible 500, losing only by one point. This match came off last June, and was one of the closest contested pistol matches that ever took place on this coast.

Last Saturday closed the shooting for the Police Department's gold and silver medals. The gold medal was won by Lawrence Whitworth for first class shooting, and the silver medal by Mr. Gillispie for second class. The twenty contestants of the first class and their scores are as follows: First class, first division of Company A—P. D. Linville, 488; D. A. Peckinpah, 485; H. Hook, 485; J. Glann, 484; P. J. Sirbkes, 481; H. A. Robertson, 474; O. R. Erskin, 474; I. W. Gillin, 471; H. Monahan, 462; M. J. Conboy, 469; J. Lowery, 458; Dan Leahy, 458; J. D. Bodwell, 456; M. Fitzgerald, 455; C. W. Ertine, 445; A. B. Asher, 441; A. Sharp, 436; W. E. Flynn, 433; J. H. Stanley, 429, and C. G. Simons, 427. These and the following are all of a possible 500 points:

First class, second division, Company B.—L. Whitworth, 491; J. C. Lane, 484; J. Clark, 483; G. H. Purdy, 474; J. T. McCarthy, 473; N. T. Field, 471; G. L. Gano, 471; J. L. Baills, 471; O. O. Waln, 470; T. Flanders, 467; P. Holand, 465; E. R. Harper, 464; R. Scott, 465; M. Behan, 460; W. M. Briggs, 480; G. D. Harper, 460; T. J. Duggan, 452; S. H. Rankin, 437, and C. Hash, 425. The grand total of the second class, first division of Company A, is 8,545 of a possible 10,000 points; and of the second class, second division of Company B, is 8,229 points of a possible 10,000. Though these scores show good shooting, still the private practice of many of the members of these teams far exceed those put on record. D. A. Peckinpah has recently made 87 consecutive bulls-eyes, followed by J. C. Lane, who made 86; P. D. Linville made 25, while Harry Hook made his 25, which is the largest number of consecutive bulls-eyes on record. The Supervisors have granted these teams the privilege of shooting on a range at North Beach. The Board of Police Commissioners and the Chief of Police have encouraged pistol practice on the force. The members of the teams have purchased two regulation Creedmore targets, each target weighing 3,084 pounds. The pistols used are Smith & Wesson's large size 45 caliber; the usual distance for shooting is 30 yards. Seeing the improvements in shooting that the teams have made within the last year and a half, it is no wonder that they and their captains are proud of the results. It certainly shows that the Police Teams are second to none on the coast.

A novel shooting match is reported on the tapis, in which an archery club and a pistol team are to shoot at distance of sixty yards for a small purse and honors.

Deer are reported exceedingly plentiful in the neighborhood of the Gualala river, Mendocino county. There being few ranches, the game is therefore little disturbed. For camping parties the country spoken of is one of the finest in the State, and very easy of access.

## SPORTING NOTES FROM NORTHERN CALIFORNIA.

Susanville, Lassen County, Cal.,
July 31, 1882.

Editor Breeder and Sportsman: Lassen County is almost an unknown world to the city sportsman. Situated as it is ninety miles from the railroad, few come here for pleasure alone; but those who enjoy its fishing and hunting facilities are amply repaid for their pains. A few San Francisco people are now camped at Clear Creek, twenty miles from Susanville, one of the many charming places with which nature has gifted Northern California, where a pure mountain stream, filled with speckled beauties, winds through a country redolent with pine and fir trees, and romantic by its very isolation. There is a hotel, famous for its trout dinners, at this place, and when a party of excursionists go that way word is sent ahead to Rose, the proprietor, and the delicious treat, smoking hot and cooked to perfection, is placed before the hungry traveler. Ex-Surveyor-General Wagner recently visited Clear Creek and performed mighty exploits with the rod. Indeed, it is said that on one of his excursions he caught sixteen trout and climbed seventeen trees in order to perfect his title to them. But this may be a mere rumor circulated for political effect.

Clear Creek has deer, too, but at this season of the year stockmen herd sheep in that vicinity, driving the deer farther up in the mountains, and when the visitor, weary with a day's sport, is enjoying his smoke at the evening camp fire, the inhabitant comes around and tells wild tales of "them sixty feller," who last season pursued the hilarious sheep through the woods and exultingly brought his remains to camp as their first deer.

Probably no county in the State has more streams abounding in trout than this, from the game little brook trout to salmon whose weight often reaches five pounds. Clear Creek, Willow Creek, Pine Creek, Gold Run and Susan River, afford the disciple of Walton all the sport he wishes. Eagle Lake, a large sheet of water at about the center of the county, is fine fishing ground. During the Fall and Winter it is the rendezvous of myriads of ducks and geese, and there are plenty of deer in the surrounding woods.

There are quantities of wild fowl on Honey Lake during the season. This lake is twelve miles wide and twenty miles long. The water is brackish, and is populated by only the peaceful sucker.

The Devil's Corral is a pretty little spot, worthy a choicer name, on the Susan River, where Susanville people go to picnic and fish. Here the worthy citizen takes his wife, children and lunch-basket, and spends a day of quiet enjoyment.

Grouse, sage hens, quail, snipe and curlew, are found in abundance in all parts of the county. Antelope come in droves on the mountain ranges during the Winter, and black, cinnamon, brown and grizzly bear make the Sierras their home.

The jack rabbit attains a luxurious size in Lassen. There is not much sport in chasing the tender-eyed creature over sage brush and waste of sand, but the pursuit has a peculiar excitement, and it is remarkable for the intense interest which both the pursuer and his extensively eared victim take in the affair.

Susanville has an excellent race track. It is not likely that any races will be held here this Fall, as District No. 11 Fair—in which district this county is included—will be held at Greenville, Plumas County, in September, and for which a fine speed programme has been arranged.

On account of the distance from the railroad but few theatrical representations are given here, and seldom does a "barn storming" company of merit reach us. Two variety troupes have played at Peysen's Hall this Summer. A company usually gives two performances to good houses, fifty cents admission being charged. A dance is invariably given after the last performance, and forms the attraction of that evening. Each gentleman present puts a dollar in the hat that is passed around, and goes home well satisfied with the world in general and traveling minstrel troupes in particular. Juniga.

## THE RIFLE.

### THE WIMBLEDON MEETING.

In view of the International Rifle Match, a great deal of interest is felt at the East in the result of the different competitions at the annual Wimbledon meeting. The principal event is the Queen's Prize, which entitles the winner to be the premier marksman of the year. It was won by Sergeant Lawrence, of the First Dumbarton Regiment. The event next in importance is the Elcho Shield, for which there is always an intense rivalry [between England, Scotland and Ireland, the beautiful emblem being confided for the year by the winners to the Chief Magistrate of London. Dublin or Edinburgh. This time the English team will deliver the shield to the Lord Mayor of London, and the splendid emblem will form part of the rich plate owned by the city, its reception forming one of the gala days at the Mansion House. The following are the teams and the total scores: England—Sir Henry Halford, Gilder, Humphrey, Godsall, Whitehead, Mellish, Gibbs and Edge. The last five are candidates for places in the military team that is to come to America. Scotland—Thorburn, McKerrel, Fraser, Shields, Murray, Boyd, Caldwell and McVittie. The last three are also candidates for places in the team for America. Ireland—J. Rigby, Braithwaite, W. Rigby, Maxwell, Young, Cogian, Barnett and Ganley. The total scores at the 800 yards, fifteen shots each, stood as follow: Ireland, 595; England, 519; Scotland, 510. Some of the individual scores were: Godsall, 66; Whitehead. 67; Mellish, 65; Gibbs, 65; Edge, 63; Boyd, 70; Caldwell, 66; and McVittie, 67. At 900 yards the scores were: England, 508; Scotland, 485; Ireland, 470. Godsall made 68; Whitehead, 68; Mellish, 58; Gibbs, 56; Edge, 61; Boyd, 64; Caldwell, 62; and McVittie, 54. At 1,000 yards the scores were: Ireland, 510; England, 509; Scotland 499. Godsall made 67; Whitehead, 66; Mellish, 66; Gibbs, 62; Edge, 61; Boyd, 63; Caldwell, 62; and McVittie, 65. England won, the grand total standing as follows: England, 1,536; Ireland, 1,505; Scotland, 1,494.

The following marksmen have been selected as members of the British team to compete in the rifle match: Bates, of the First Warwick; Boulter, of the Second Cheshire; Caldwell and Doda, of the First Berwick; Godsall, Goodear and Heap, of the Sixth Lancashire; McVittie and Mellish, of the Second Notts; Oliver, of the third Kent; Parry, of the Second Cheshire, and Major Pearse.

In the Bass match at Wimbledon, shot at 800, 900 and 1,000 yards, under conditions corresponding with those of the second stage of the International match, the following scores were made: Caldwell, 73; Doda, 65; Godsall, 69; Goodear, 65; Heap. 70; McVittie, 73, and Parry, 66; and if we take the following military practice at 200, 500, 600, 800, 900 and 1,000 yards, shot recently at Creedmoor, we find that the match is likely to be well contested:

| | 200, 500 and 600 | 800, 900 and 1,000 | |
| --- | --- | --- | --- |
| | Yards. | Yards. | Total. |
| Captain S. A. Day................ | 93 | 98 | 191 |
| Captain T. Wilson............... | 94 | 79 | 169 |
| Sergeant J. L. Day............. | 90 | 77 | 166 |
| Sergeant J. L. Pauling......... | 90 | 75 | 165 |
| A. B. Van Hansen.............. | 85 | 65 | 150 |
| Corporal A. L. Frich........... | 82 | 66 | 147 |
| Captain J. L. Frich........... | 89 | 90 | 159 |
| Sergeant J. McVevia........... | 79 | 89 | 159 |

The winners of the seven prizes for the month, with their scores, were Captain Day, 175; Captain Wilson, 169; Sergeant Dolan, 160; Sergeant Paulding, 159; Sergeant Van Hansen, 151; Private Smith, 147, and Private Alder, 144.

Prize Rifle Shooting.—The third quarterly prize shooting match of the San Francisco Fusileers, Company C, Second Artillery Regiment, N. G. C., was held yesterday at Shell Mound Park. The company was divided into three classes, each marksman firing ten shots. Following is the score and the name of the winners: First Class—First prize, Corporal H. J Mangels, 40; second prize, Sergeant O. Lemke, 39; third prize, Private C. Schanrze, 36; fourth prize, Lieutenant John Brewer, 38; fifth prize, Private J. C. Plagemann, 36.

Second Class—First prize, Private H. Warnkiu, 43; second prize, Private C. Geoss, 38; third prize, Corporal Charles Haske, 37; fourth prize, Sergeant D. Walbern, 37; fifth prize, Private L. Haake, 37.

In the third class, the first prize was won by Corporal C. F. Repenze, the second by Private J. C. Schancon, the third by Private H. Schueblern, the fourth by Private H. Schuebner, and the fifth by Captain H. Wobber.

## BILLIARDS.

The Sacramento Billiard Tournament.—The games for this tournament commenced on Saturday, July 29th. The purse was $100, divided into three moneys, $50, $30 and $20, and there were five entries. Lloyd Amsden and Edward Robbins, from their well known proficiency with the cue, being handicapped at 400 points, while Messrs. Johnson, Chapman and Stroup either received 300 points from the above players or in the contests among themselves they played 300 points up. The tournament excited a great deal of interest among local amateurs, and Mr. Bowman, the proprietor of the rooms, was assiduous in his attentions to make the affair a success. The chief interest was centered in the third game, when Amsden and Robbins came together, but its former showing some brilliant play, including a run of 123 points, ran the game out in twenty-three innings, while his adversary had only scored a third of the number. It was the four-ball American game, and the following was the score:

| Players. | Games Won. | Games Lost. | Number of Points Scored. | Best Average in Single Game. | General Average. | Best Run. | Amount of Prize |
| --- | --- | --- | --- | --- | --- | --- | --- |
| Amsden...... | 4 | 0 | 1600 | 17 9-23 | 11 1-5 | 123 | $50 |
| Robbins..... | 3 | 1 | 1203 | 18 3-11 | 12½ | 98 | 30 |
| Johnson..... | 2 | 2 | 617 | 6 5-7 | 5 | 21 | 20 |
| Chapman... | 1 | 3 | 689 | 4½ | 5 | 16 | 00 |
| Stroup...... | 0 | 4 | 412 | 3½ | 5 | 19 | 00 |

## BASE BALL.

### THE RENOS AND NIANTICS.

The match game between the Renos and Niantics at the Recreation grounds last Sunday calls for but little comment, save in a critical view, for the attendance was light and the game throughout was so one-sided that the old time enthusiasm was entirely lacking on this occasion. The Renos are either lacking sadly in practice or the selection of the team has been very unfortunate. In any case a few more exhibitions like that of Sunday and they will not draw a corporal's guard to witness the games in which they are engaged. The errors made were so numerous that the Niantics got tired of taking advantage of them, and playing well together they achieved a hollow victory, with the following score:

NIANTICS.

| | T.B. | R. | B.H. | P.O. | A. | E. |
| --- | --- | --- | --- | --- | --- | --- |
| Emerson, 3d b.... | 7 | 0 | 1 | 0 | 0 | 0 |
| McVey, 1st b..... | 7 | 5 | 3 | 10 | 0 | 0 |
| Donahue, s. s.... | 7 | 5 | 1 | 0 | 0 | 0 |
| Arnold, c. f...... | 6 | 2 | 3 | 1 | 0 | 0 |
| Egan, l. f........ | 6 | 3 | 1 | 4 | 0 | 0 |
| Finn, c.......... | 6 | 3 | 2 | 12 | 0 | 0 |
| Incell, p. f...... | 6 | 2 | 1 | 0 | 0 | 0 |
| Sweeney, p....... | 6 | 5 | 2 | 1 | 11 | 0 |
| Fogarty, 2d b.... | 6 | 4 | 2 | 3 | 2 | 0 |
| Totals........ | 57 | 33 | 16 | 27 | 21 | 1 |

RENOS.

| | T.B. | R. | B.H. | P.O. | A. | E. |
| --- | --- | --- | --- | --- | --- | --- |
| Swanton, c. f.... | 4 | 0 | 0 | 0 | 0 | 1 |
| Lake, l. f. & s. s. | 4 | 1 | 1 | 0 | 1 | 4 |
| Riordan, p....... | 4 | 1 | 0 | 0 | 3 | 2 |
| Calogan, c. f.... | 4 | 0 | 1 | 1 | 3 | 1 |
| Sheridan, s. s. & l. f. | 4 | 1 | 1 | 2 | 1 | 7 |
| Malloy, 1st b.... | 4 | 0 | 0 | 10 | 0 | 2 |
| Sturt, 3d b...... | 4 | 0 | 0 | 0 | 2 | 2 |
| Crosgan, c....... | 3 | 1 | 0 | 8 | 2 | 1 |
| Hamilton, 2d b... | 3 | 0 | 0 | 1 | 2 | 2 |
| Totals........ | 34 | 4 | 4 | 27 | 22 | 12 |

Innings........ 1 2 3 4 5 6 7 8 9
Niantics....... 5 4 7 5 4 3 5 0 0
Renos.......... 1 0 0 0 0 0 3 0 0

Earned runs—Niantics 3, Reno 1. Home runs—Fogarty, McVey, Riordan. Three-base hits—Riordan. Two-base hits—Emerson. Bases on errors—Niantics 13, Reno 6. Bases on balls—Niantics 2, Reno 2. Struck out—by Sweeney 9, Riordan 7. Double plays—Sheridan, Hamilton and Stürt. Passed balls—Finn 3, Crosgan 5. Umpire—Eaa. Scorer. Boyce. Scorer F. E. Hanney. Time—Three hours and ten minutes.

### THE YATES AND THE OLYMPICS.

On the same day these two nines played a well contested match at the grounds of the Olympic Club in Oakland. The batting at the commencement was not equal to the fielding, and the Yates were the first to score a run in the third inning; but from that time out the Olympics were more successful, and at the end they proved to be the victors by a score of 9 to 4.

OLYMPICS.

| | T. B. | R. | B.H. | P.O. | A. | E. |
| --- | --- | --- | --- | --- | --- | --- |
| Neal, p.......... | 5 | 1 | 1 | 0 | 0 | 0 |
| Ehoer, 3d b...... | 5 | 2 | 1 | 1 | 2 | 0 |
| Van Dyke, l. f... | 5 | 0 | 1 | 1 | 0 | 0 |
| Sumner, c....... | 4 | 1 | 1 | 8 | 3 | 2 |
| Bart, 1st b....... | 4 | 2 | 1 | 12 | 0 | 0 |
| Barton, c. f...... | 4 | 1 | 1 | 1 | 0 | 0 |
| Peterson, s. s.... | 4 | 1 | 1 | 2 | 4 | 0 |
| Kelly, 2d b....... | 4 | 0 | 1 | 1 | 3 | 2 |
| Boswell, r. f..... | 4 | 0 | 1 | 1 | 0 | 3 |
| Totals........ | 40 | 9 | 13 | 27 | 15 | 7 |

YATES.

| | T. B. | R. | B.H. | P.O. | A. | E. |
| --- | --- | --- | --- | --- | --- | --- |
| Stephens, r. f.... | 4 | 1 | 0 | 0 | 0 | 1 |
| Cully, p......... | 4 | 1 | 1 | 0 | 6 | 2 |
| Smith, c.......... | 4 | 0 | 1 | 10 | 5 | 4 |
| Clement, 3d b.... | 4 | 1 | 1 | 2 | 2 | 2 |
| Shannon, s. s.... | 4 | 0 | 1 | 1 | 0 | 2 |
| Dunn, 1st b....... | 4 | 0 | 1 | 4 | 0 | 0 |
| Conner, c. f...... | 4 | 1 | 1 | 0 | 0 | 0 |
| Hanly, 2d b....... | 4 | 0 | 1 | 3 | 1 | 0 |
| Rogers, l. f...... | 4 | 0 | 1 | 3 | 0 | 1 |
| Totals........ | 34 | 4 | 7 | 27 | 13 | 11 |

Innings........ 1 2 3 4 5 6 7 8 9
Olympics....... 0 0 0 1 3 0 4 0 1—9
Yates.......... 0 0 1 0 0 0 0 3 0—4

Umpire—E. Van Court. Time of game—One hour and fifty minutes.

The Haverly California Theatre Club visited Antioch last Sunday, and tried conclusions with the Antioch ball tossers, whom they defeated by a score of 32 to 6.

To-morrow a regular League game will be played at Recreation Park between the Niantics and Haverly California Theatre Club, which promises to be of a very interesting character.

### THE CONTEST FOR THE CHAMPIONSHIP.

As the League season is now half over, a comparison of the season's work by the League clubs in the championship arena with that of the other seasons is in order, if only to discover what improvement the clubs have made. Looking over the record of seven of the eight clubs which were in the arena in 1880, it will be seen that the first three clubs in the race at the close of the third week in July in 1880 were the Chicago, Cleveland and Providence teams. In 1881, at the corresponding time, the first three were the Chicago, Buffalo and Cleveland, while this year the first three are Chicago, Providence and Detroit. The record of the games won and lost up to the close of the third week in July during 1880, 1881 and 1882 is as follows, the clubs being given each year in the order in which they stood in won games.

| | 1880. | | 1881. | | 1882. | |
|---|---|---|---|---|---|---|
| | Won. | Lost. | Won. | Lost. | Won. | Lost. |
| Chicago | 49 | 7 | 31 | 16 | 30 | 13 |
| Cleveland | 26 | 18 | 22 | 26 | 24 | 25 |
| Providence | 28 | 20 | 18 | 27 | 29 | 20 |
| Boston | 22 | 20 | 19 | 27 | 26 | 22 |
| Worcester | 21 | 24 | 21 | 24 | 11 | 37 |
| Troy | 19 | 25 | 21 | 24 | 22 | 26 |
| Buffalo | 17 | 30 | 27 | 19 | 24 | 21 |
| Detroit | .. | .. | .. | .. | 26 | 21 |

The Detroit Club was not in existence in 1880. In 1881 Detroit stood second to Chicago by 31 victories to 22 defeats up to the last week in July, while this year the Detroits stand there by 26 victories and 21 defeats up to date, July 23. It will be seen how steadily Chicago has declined each season, from 7 defeats in 1880 to 16 in 1881 and to 13 in 1882. Providence was last at this time last year, while Boston was next. In order to show the contrast between the positions of the clubs at the close of the last season, the record of the finish in 1880 and 1881 is appended as follows:

| | 1880. | | | 1881. | |
|---|---|---|---|---|---|
| | Won. | Lost. | | Won. | Lost. |
| Chicago | 67 | 17 | Chicago | 56 | 28 |
| Providence | 52 | 32 | Providence | 47 | 37 |
| Cleveland | 47 | 37 | Buffalo | 45 | 38 |
| Troy | 41 | 42 | Troy | 39 | 45 |
| Worcester | 40 | 43 | Boston | 38 | 45 |
| Boston | 40 | 44 | Cleveland | 36 | 48 |
| Buffalo | 23 | 53 | Worcester | 32 | 50 |

Detroit in 1881 was fourth on the list with a credit of 41 victories and a charge of 43 defeats. It remains to be seen what changes the next two months' play will make in the League record. Following is the score up to July 24th:

| Clubs. | | | | | | | | | Games Lost. |
|---|---|---|---|---|---|---|---|---|---|
| Boston | | | | | | | | | 22 |
| Buffalo | | | | | | | | | 21 |
| Chicago | | | | | | | | | 13 |
| Cleveland | | | | | | | | | 25 |
| Detroit | | | | | | | | | 21 |
| Providence | | | | | | | | | 20 |
| Troy | | | | | | | | | 26 |
| Worcester | | | | | | | | | 37 |
| Games Lost. | 24 | 26 | 13 | 20 | 21 | 20 | 20 | 38 | 195 |

## THE AUSTRALIAN CRICKETERS.

The Australians played their first game during the present season at Lord's Ground, London, England, on July 6 and 7, when they defeated Middlesex, with eight wickets to spare. The respective totals were: Middlesex, 104 and 91; Australia, 136 and 61, for the loss of two wickets. Murdoch made 51, the highest score of the match. The Australians next met on Lord's Ground a very strong batting 'team, representing the Marylebone Club. Rain fell during a day and a half of the period set apart for this game, and it consequently ended in a draw. Marylebone had scored 205 and Australia 188 in the first inning, so that the former eleven, so far as the game had progressed, had decidedly the best of the situation. C. T. Studd batted remarkably well for 114, made without a chance, and was well seconded by W. G. Grace, Hornby, and A. P. Lucas; with their respective contributions of 45, 45 and 45. Horan, with 42, was the chief scorer on behalf of the Australians. Since then they have played several games, and their success in defeating some of the strongest English elevens is causing the attendance of thousands of spectators at their matches; and the Australians take two-thirds of the gate receipts at each match. At Sheffield there were 18,877 people present the first day and 13,484 the second, rain then stopping the match. At the match against the Gentlemen of England, at the Oval, 11,028 paid admission the first day, 13,540 the second, and 18,050 the third. From present appearances they will return through this country, and arrangements are being made for them to play in New York and Philadelphia. If our local clubs were in practice, and under a better state of organization, we might have an opportunity of seeing this splendid team in a match; but even as it is, some efforts might be made to afford them an opportunity of showing their skill, by dividing their twelve and choosing ten of our best local players to complete the eleven. There is no doubt that the affair would be a success.

## THE STAGE.

Aside from the benefit offered to Thomas Maguire on Thursday last, there has been nothing during the past week to disturb the monotony of theatrical affairs. The veteran manager had an old-fashioned bumper, showing clearly that the public do not forget the many expenditures he has incurred and the pains he has taken for the past thirty years in catering to the artistic requirements of our population. The Hanlons announce a change of programme, the entertainment to consist of a two-act comedietta and a forty minute pantomime. They continue to do a very good business. At the California the Union Square Company replace the Mastodon Minstrels, opening on Monday with "The Banker's Daughter." Among the number of the new arrivals are two or three favorites, chief among them being Miss Eleanor Carey and Frederick de Belville, both of whom have at different intervals made their first appearance in this country at this Baldwin Theatre. They accordingly start with all Baldwin Theatre. Our genial old president and play Miss Carey has achieved the enviable position of being considered one of the best artists on our boards, and San Francisco will doubtless accord to her a hearty welcome, and will indorse the favorable impression she has created wherever the Union Square Company has appeared. The troupe is very evenly balanced, and possesses two novelties in the shape of "Odette" and the drama "The Lights of London." It is sure to meet with an artistic and financial success. The theatre will in future be under the management of Fredrick Bert, who will be well remembered as having made several theatrical ventures in this city, showing a liberality and enterprise that merits better recognition than he received. We trust that in his new position he will succeed much better.

At the Tivoli Gardens "Der Freischutz," after a lengthy career, will be replaced by the comic opera "Cogueloed," which will be a pleasing novelty, as the libretto and music are said to be both lively and interesting. At the Winter Garden the new opera "Sinona" continues to attract a large attendance. It appears strange to our Eastern visitors that such excellent entertainments given by these houses, can be maintained with such a moderate scale of admission.

## THE KENNEL.

### FIXTURES.

National American Kennel Club's trial on quails, Grand Junction, Tenn., December 4th. D. Bryson, Memphis, Tenn., Secretary.

Louisiana Field Trials Club's trial on quail, New Orleans, La., beginning Dec. 11, under the management of the New Orleans Gun Club.

Derby Show.—Western Pennsylvania Society's English Setter Derby Show Derby, Pittsburgh, Pa., for English setter puppies whelped on or after March 1, 1882. Entries closed December 1, 1881. T. S. Barton, Allegheny City, Pa., Secretary.

Field Trials.—National American Kennel Club's trials on prairie chickens, Parkhurst, Minn., September 4th. Entries in American Field Derby closed July 1st, in All-Age Stake, September 4th. Joseph H. Dew, Columbus, Ohio, Special Secretary for field trials.

Oliver Rod and Gun Club's trials on quail, Gilroy, Cal., October 30th. Open to dogs bred in California, Oregon, Nevada and Arizona. E. Leavesley, Secretary, Gilroy, Cal.

Eastern Field Trials Club's trials on quails, near High Point, N. C., November 13th. Entrances to Derby close July 1st; to All-Age and Members' Stake, November 1st. P. H. Bryson, Memphis, Tenn.; F. C. Horr, New York.

### LAVERACK PUPS.

In our advertising columns will be found a notice of Llewellyn and Laverack pups for sale. The gentleman whose property they are forwarded to us the pedigrees and proofs of genuineness of the stock he advertises, with a request that we examine the same. We have examined them and find the dogs all that they are represented to be, and feel sure that no reason except the one he gives—lack of room—could induce him to part with them at the exceedingly low price offered. Daisy F. and Hazel K. are from Luke Laverack by Macgregor, that is they are of three-fourths pure Laverack blood, the other fourth being what is known as the celebrated Duke Rhoebe cross' Rob Roy-Queen Mab, making them Llewellyns according to the strictest definition of the term. In the East, and where there is a demand for such fine stock, they would readily bring $100 each, providing, of course, that they are free from blemish. We can only indorse their pedigree, which we do freely. As to their appearance, size, etc. all we know is that they are black, white and tan in color, and that Daisy is the larger of the two. The owner pledges himself to take them back and pay all expenses if they are not exactly as represented, and he is a gentleman whose word is beyond all doubt and whose judgment in such matters is second to none. The unwhelped pups for which he offers to book orders are pure Laveracks without a taint of any foreign blood, and we believe from the only pure Laveracks in California. We find on examination that the sale of Prince Laverack, duly recorded in American Kennel Club Stud Book, was made from Jos. J. Snellenberg to J. N. Aldrich for the sum of $800. Mr. Aldrich was acting for the present owner, who submits all necessary proofs. Prince, when out of condition, took third prize at the Pittsburg show. Luke, purchased as a weanling by her present owner for $100 from J. C. Higgins, has never been exhibited. One of her litter sisters, owned by Mr. Goodsell of New York, has taken several prizes. Snellburg's Thunder, the sire of Prince Laverack, divided first at the Pennsylvania field trial, 1880. He is by Pride of the Border and Fairy II. Pride of the Border has a standard pedigree, to which no reference need be made. Fairy II is pure Laverack, being by one-half Laverack's Moll III and one-half Laverack's Dash II. Peeress is also pure Laverack, and is sister to Phantom, Puzzle, Petrel, Pearl and Princess, all prize winners in England and America. Such an opportunity to secure pure blood may not occur again for some time, and we commend it to the notice of our many readers.

### HUNTING DEER WITH HOUNDS.

The anti-hound deer hunters are waging quite as hard a newspaper war in the East as they did here about two years ago, when they were decidedly worsted in the argument. The latest contribution to the anti-hound literature of the day is from the pen of S. T. Murray, and published in the American Field, in reply to a defence of the practice, which was published a few weeks ago. He discourses as follows:

"The practice of killing deer out of season in any way is wrong, and should not be tolerated; 'crusting' deer is wrong, and should not be allowed. In times gone by not a Fall came that I did not go deer hunting, and the remark made in my address before the delegates of the New York State Association was true then as now. The exact language, referring to the Adirondack region, in put. State, is this: 'The practice of chasing deer with hounds should be strictly prohibited by an effective law. If this is continued, it is but a matter of a short time before that kind of game will be extinct in our State.'

"I have been deer hunting where they were plenty, and one day's run with dogs drove them so that we were obliged to break camp and move across two counties into Canada in order to start a deer. This, or a similar state of things, I have often observed. If my friend, Mr. E. E. Gillman, of Detroit, Mich., will induce all the still hunters to procure hounds and follow his example for a year or two, his camp will necessarily have to be pitched in some other State than Michigan, in order to start a deer.

"My friend cannot excuse, or successfully defend, the practice of running deer with dogs by saying as he does, 'That hundreds of deer are killed by still hunters where one is killed before dogs.' I do not deny this assertion, nor do I entirely subscribe to it. The answer, to my own, unbiased mind, is this: 'The still hunter leaves in the locality what he does not kill; the sportsman with hounds frightens away to distant localities those not driven to a runway or lake and captured.'"

### REMARKABLE PRECOCITY.

We wonder if any of our readers can furnish an instance of precocity that equals the following given by Arnold Burgess in the American Field: "In your issue of the 15th, W. H. M. mentions the performance of a six months' puppy, and asks if such quality is not unusual at that age. He has certainly a promising youngster, but I see no reason to consider her a wonder. In the old days when we shot over natives, I have had many a six months' dog that worked as well as the old ones; except lacking in experience. The last native I owned was shot to at the 4th of July when but five months old, and did grand work. I have now in my kennel four puppies by Dashing Berwyn, out of Queen Dido, that will gallop as fast as their legs will carry them, hunt perfectly and point steadily too, and are but three months old. Their sister of the former litter, owned by Mr. Waterhouse, was mentioned by him in one of your late issues as doing all that W. H. M. claims for Maggie O. at the same age, and last year I shot for three full consecutive days over Mr. Bill's Druid's Girl, when she was seven months old, and never saw any dog do better work at the

opening of her first season. She was essentially 'a cracker,' and had she lived would, in my opinion, have held her own with any dog in the country. The only reason, in my opinion, that more Llewellyns do not show work at six months is that they are not given a chance to do so, from the absurd idea that early breaking will break their spirit or reduce their speed. With decent treatment they have courage for breaking any time after they are three months old, and precocity of development equal to any dogs I have ever

### CALIFORNIA COURSING CLUB.

A meeting of the California Coursing Club was held at their club room August 2d, John Hughes presiding. J. F. Carroll, Treasurer, reported that the club financially was in a flourishing condition, having on hand, after all expenses of the last match, a surplus fund. The next coursing meeting of the club will be held at Merced, on November 15th, 16th and 17th. The members and friends will leave on Tuesday, the 14th of November, at 4 P. M.

November 15th is a long time ahead to look forward to, but we have already seen enough to be able to say that the next meeting of the young and vigorous California Club will eclipse all its previous matches. J. F. Carroll, J. C. Murphy, J. Farraday, C. Mooney, the gentleman who so honors the nom de guerre of "Mercedito," J. Keating and several other members of the club we have spoken with say that they have an extra fine lot of youngsters to run this Fall, and all the old dogs are reported as doing well. With the new training ground at Newark there is no excuse for a first-class dog being shot out of the first race by breaking out of slips, as happened at the last meeting of this club. We rather think that the club have made the date of the meeting so late that they have taken big chances of wet weather, and of all the mean things that can happen to a man, to be in Merced on a wet day is the meanest.

FIELD TRIALS IN THE SOUTH.—Colonel Hoge, President of the Georgia Sportsmen's Association, proposes to call a meeting of the association soon, and it has been suggested to make arrangements at that meeting for the first annual State field trial this Fall, as Georgia contains a fine lot of dogs to form the nucleus of a successful contest. The State has long needed a first-class, reliable kennel, where the best strains of dogs could be properly bred and trained and Judge Hopkins has established such an institution in Thomasville, one of the most delightful Winter resorts in the South, where he will breed pointers, setters, beagles, hounds and Scotch collies. There are smaller and less important kennels at Bainbridge and Atlanta, but Judge Hopkins has spared no expense to make his kennel first-class in all respects, and will use every effort, through the Georgia Sportsmen's Association, to have its influence felt in the State, in improving sporting and shepherd dogs.

A BAD CUT.—In the last issue, the publishers of the American Field presented their readers with a cut of the well-known pug dog George, owned by Mrs. Edwin A. Poe, of Philadelphia. The cut represented an animal with the head and tail of a pug dog, the body of a sheep and the legs of a mastiff, slightly shortened in the second joints. Worse cuts have been published, but not of late years, and it certainly does not look well for the Field, which is by far the best kennel paper published in America, to present such poor work to its readers. It is liable to give ignorant persons a wrong impression of what a first-class, handsome pug-dog really is. The expression of the face is excellent, but that is about the only redeeming feature in the picture.

At Aldridge's, St. Martin's Lane, London, June 23d, was sold the following, the property of Mr. G. K. Smith, Colney Hatch first season:

| | |
|---|---|
| Surprise, by Don't-be-Headstrong—Pearl | $90 00 |
| Stripper, by Wolverhampton | 350 00 |
| Singer, by Stamp Duty—Little Wonder | 70 00 |
| Spoilt, by Doncaster—Blooming Heather | 130 00 |
| Sunbeam, by Stamp Duty—Bacchantes, February | 75 00 |
| Saucy, by Roy—Fly | 75 00 |
| Six Oar, by Hermit—Strong Ray | 5 00 |
| Whelp, by Marquis—Swift | 8 00 |

Colonel A. Blaine, of St. John, New Brunswick, has just imported from the kennel of Mr. Hicks, Birmingham, England, Spring and Nellie, a pair of bull terriers. They are pure white, and are said to be the best pair of dogs of this variety ever brought to this side of the Atlantic. Spring, the dog, weighs twenty pounds, and is by Old Spring, out of Gipsey; Old Spring by Bill, out of Kit; she by Prince. The bitch, Nellie, weighs eighteen pounds, and is by Rebel out of Kit II; Rebel by Eclipse out of Rose, by Turk out of Brute; Kit II out of old Kit.

At the recent show held at Belfast, Ireland, champion setter, red Irish, 1st, Mr. Gilltop's Garryowen. The Irish setters and Irish spaniels were the best of the class shown. Irish water spaniels, 1st, E. Doyle's Larry Doolin; bitches, 1st, R. B. Carey's Molly Brallaghan.

By our London exchanges we note that Mr. Badger had the great misfortune to lose by death his famous greyhound stud dog Great Gable on the 10th June last. He was bitten by a mad dog, and it was found necessary to destroy him just three weeks afterward.

### ANSWERS TO CORRESPONDENTS.

J. B., SAN FRANCISCO.—To remove color from gun barrels, use pumice stone or fine emery paper. A piece of pomice stone with a little water is the only article used by the leading gunsmiths here. Use no acid or any kind of detersive substances, simply friction and some kind of clean polishing substance. To re-brown, the barrels must be steeped in slacked lime for some time to remove all the grease before the color is applied.

Rabbits are more likely to be out in the early morning, or about sunset. The ravines in the foothills where there is plenty of cover are favorite resorts, and when far enough away from houses, are usually well stocked.

SUB. S. F.—Shannon ran second to Lady Washington in a two-year-old stake at Sacramento, in 1874, and second to Bradley in 1875. He ran in another race when three years old, and these are all that we can find in the records.

It is difficult to say what the average height of a thoroughbred 18 months old filly is. About 14½ hands would be our idea.

"L."—Mr. F—— says that the time is 2:36 and a fraction. If it is as you imagine, he must be at least 20 years old.

## THE HERD.

### OUR CATTLE PROSPECTS.

General James S. Brisbin, writing from Fort Keogh, says: While the manufacturing and cereal and vegetable interests of the United States have advanced fairly, the stock interests have comparatively stood still. We are to-day raising beef for only 40,000,000 of people, whereas we should be raising beef for 80,000,000. The reason for this are various, chief of which is the fact of the scarcity of land in the East. Farmers have found that in heavily populated districts it does not pay them to raise cattle. The large number of acres required for grazing purposes is incompatible with small farms, and to stall-feed in large numbers is not practicable. So the Eastern farmer devotes his land to cereals and vegetables, and often buys his own beef. The distance of the Plains from the East and the danger from Indians have heretofore deterred Eastern capitalists from seeking investments in stock raising out West. Happily that difficulty is now removed. The railroads have opened up the West, and the Indians, with the exception of a few in Arizona, have been conquered. The pastoral lands of the West have never been understood nor appreciated by the people of this country, or the Government. The day will come when the national treasury will derive more taxes from the grazing country than from the best agricultural regions. These arid plains, so long considered worthless, are the natural meat-producing lands of America, and in a few years fifty million people will draw their beef from them. Where are the great grazing grounds, do you ask? They are in Texas, Colorado, New Mexico, Dakota, Wyoming, Montana, Washington and Idaho.

The whole United States contains 3,603,884 square miles, of which 1,500,000 square miles is set down as grazing lands. The best ranges are on the Rio Grande, Nueces, San Antonio, Guadalupe, Colorado, Brazos, Trinity, Main Red, Washita, Canadian, Cimaron, Arkansas, Smoky Hill, Saline, Solomon Fork, Republican, North and South Platte, Loup Forks, Niobrara, White Earth, Big Cheyenne, Little Missouri, Powder River, Tongue, Rosebud, Big Horn, Wind River, Yellowstone, Milk River, Musclesheil, Marias, Jefferson, Missouri, Madison, Gallatin and Columbia. Of the smaller streams on the eastern slope of the Rocky Mountains, we have the Blue Waters, Cold Water, Hill Creek, Raw Hide, Muddy, Willow, Shawnee, Slate, Sweetwater, Ash, Pumpkin, Laramie, Carter, Cottonwood, Horseshoe, Elkhorn, Deer Creek, Medicine Bow, Rock Creek, Douglas, Lodge Pole, Big Laramie, Little Laramie, Horse Creek, Beaver, Pawnee, Crow, Lone Tree, Big Beaver, Bijou, Kiowa, Bear Creek, Big Thompson and Cache la Poudre. The grazing lands on the Plattes, Powder and Tongue, amount to over twelve million acres, and are the best I know of. For at least ten years yet I look for high prices in beef. Eastern capital is so conservative it will be slow to come West and engage in stock-raising, and only Eastern capital can raise beef in sufficient quantities on the plains to reduce the price.

A good many cattle companies have been formed of late years, and so far as I know, all are doing well. We have several here in Montana, and they are able to declare an annual dividend of 25 per cent., besides reserving a handsome surplus for increasing the herds. It is a remarkable fact that there is more English capital at present invested in cattle-growing in the United States than American money. This year the Englishmen are reaping a rich reward for their enterprise, and are selling Americans beef at 5 cents per pound, live weight, which costs them less than 2 cents to raise. There is really no immediate occasion for alarm about a cattle famine, as cattle are not yet so scarce as to create any great stress in the meat market. But the speculators have got hold of the fact that there are too few cattle in America for the population, and they are using it to fill their pockets. We must have more cattle, more cattle raisers, and more capital with which to raise cattle.

For the next ten years I believe cattle raising will be one of the most lucrative callings in the United States, and those who have the good fortune to be able to engage in it, will rapidly grow rich. The best way is to associate capital and raise cattle in large numbers. It costs no more to take care of three thousand steers than it does one thousand, and the profits are more than three times as large. In starting it is simply a question of money to buy cows and bulls for stock purposes. In 1840 there were 4,837 milch cows in the United States; in 1850 there were 6,385,094; in 1860, 8,728,863; in 1870, 11,000,000, and in 1880, 15,000,000. There cannot now be less than 15,000,000 cows in America, and these, if properly handled, will soon stock the country with sufficient beef to bring the price within the reach of the poorest man and his family. The first step is to stop killing female calves. Every female calf should be saved. The Western stock men have begun this, and already it is almost impossible for farmers to purchase calves for veal. In the west it is not so difficult to raise cattle for beef as in the east. The cattle run out all Winter long, and no matter for food is required for them, except that which nature provides. Every year the stock men start the story east for the benefit of the "tenderfeet," that the stock business is overdone, and the good ranges all taken. This is done to prevent new men from going into the business. The stock men know they have a good thing, and wish to keep it as long as possible. They would like to see beef $1 per pound, and would ask $100 for a steer worth $10 without the slightest compunction of conscience if they thought they could get it. If I had two or three thousand head of cattle I doubt if I would write this letter, but unfortunately, not having any herd of my own, I am only interested in getting beef as cheaply as possible from those who have herds. I hope soon to see more people and more capital engaged in cattle raising, and beef brought to some reasonable price by reason of its abundance, and I have no hesitation in saying that associated capital engaged in beef-raising out west, will pay an annual dividend of 24 per cent. if it is at all properly managed.—*Chicago Times.*

### ORIGIN OF THE AYRSHIRE CATTLE.

The Ayrshire cow, as we have her, is a native of County Ayr, Scotland, where we can trace her history back for about a century. Mr. William Aiton of Hamilton, in a communication made to the *British Farmer's Magazine*, in 1826, says: "The dairy breed of Scotland have been formed chiefly by skilled management within the last fifty years, and by crossing and extending to other counties. Till after 1770 the cows in Cunningham were small, ill-fed, ill-shaped, and gave but little milk. Some cows of a larger breed and of a brown and white color were about that time brought to Ayrshire from Teeswater and from Holland by some of the patriotic noblemen of Ayrshire; and these be-

ing put on good pasture, yielded more milk than the native breed, and so their calves were much sought after by the farmers." The *Magazine* goes on to say: "We are verbally assured by old breeders who had known the Ayrshires since 1780 that they had received improvement from crosses with Short-Horn bulls for the last half century, and although they may now be considered a good established breed in themselves, they are in reality merely high grade Durhams." Youatt, in his history of British cattle, says, writing in the year 1833: "The origin of the Ayrshire cow is even at the present day a matter of dispute; all that is known about her is that a century ago there was no such breed in Cunningham or Ayrshire in Scotland." Through several pages of speculation as to what crosses have compassed the breed known as "Ayrshires," at the time he wrote, and an elaboration of their remarkable yields of milk and butter in the Ayrshire dairies, he leaves the impression that the present breed has sprung from a succession of crosses by Short-Horn bulls upon the native Scotch cow; that the produce of these crosses were interbred among themselves with care and an eye to improvement both in form and dairy quality, which finally resulted in an animal eminently fitted to the climate and soil of southwestern Scotland, and the best of all they have for dairy purposes. The effort appears first to have been to introduce Short-Horns and substitute them as a dairy cow, which failed, but the cross was successful, and hence the breed. Mr. Youatt proceeds to say: "On a first view, by a judge of the different varieties, the Ayrshire would be called a diminutive Short-Horn, so nearly in figure, color and prominent characteristics do they approach them. They are about the size of our common stock, compact in form, exactly built for a dairy cow, light forward and heavy behind, with an exceedingly home-like, domestic appearance. In color they vary from a brown, running in lighter shades up to red, and into a pale yellow, alternating more or less with white, in distinct patches, rarely mingling into roan. There is scarcely that uniformity of appearance with them that there is in the Short-Horns, yet they appear to hold true to their dairy quality throughout, which, like the gentle voice in woman, is an excellent thing in a cow." A much later article in the *American Agriculturist*, 1868, says: "The Ayrshires have been bred from milk in a country where quantity and quality were both wanted, where the pastures were only moderately rich, and where rapid fattening for the shambles was also a desideratum. The result is a breed of no more than ordinary size, many being decidedly small, but hardy, easy keepers, yielding a large quantity of excellent milk, rich both in butter and cheese. The claim set forth for these cows is, that they will give more and better milk, on the same feed, than cows of any other breed. This, we believe, is not disputed. Ayrshires have been known in this country since 1833, when, we believe, they were first imported. The stock was kept pure, however, only a few generations, as it became blended with the Short-Horns, and the blood now flows in some of our registered Short-Horns. In 1831, other animals were brought over, and ever since that time the breed has grown in favor. The animals are prevailingly of medium size. The cows have great digestive capacity, as indicated by their deep, full bodies. The colors are usually red, spotted with white, the spots being very well defined, often fine and sprinkled over the body in patches."

### GREAT SALE OF GUERNSEYS.

A great auction sale of imported Channel Island cattle was held recently in Philadelphia. The catalogue comprised thirty-nine head of Guernsey cows and calves, which were allowed to be among the best ever imported. The competition at times was quite brisk, but the collection as a whole did not realize the amount expected from stock of such quality. There were thirty-two head of cows sold for $11,370, and seven calves for $486, the latter being dead cheap the price. Following are the principal lots with the names of the buyer:

| | |
|---|---|
| Cottage Maid, of St. Martins, 5 years old; Dr. Borland, New London, Conn. | $440 |
| Pickle La Chevaliere, 3 years old; John Doyle, Camden, N. J. | 360 |
| Celeste, 4 years old; I. Walter, Philadelphia. | 360 |
| Empire of Carre, 34 years old; Dr. Borland. | 400 |
| Bull Calf, mate Winox, Delaware County, Va. | 45 |
| Beauty of St. Peter's Fort, Franklin Co., Philadelphia. | 375 |
| Lily Martin, 7 years old; Dr. Borland. | 300 |
| Cow calf, Sunflower Martin, Conn. | 100 |
| Dolly La Poiderie, 7½ years old; Alex Wood, Jr., Conshohocken | 400 |
| Bull calf, Harry Lombard, Abbottson, N. J. | 40 |
| Omega, the Vain, 3½ years old; Alex Wood, Jr. | 400 |
| Dewey Maid II, 3 years old; Edward Norton, Farmington, Conn. | 400 |
| White Rose No. 4, 3 years old; Dr. Borland. | 350 |
| Type No. 3, 44 years old; Alex Wood, Jr. | 400 |
| Nora Robin, 3½ years old; James Moore, Philadelphia. | 410 |
| Rosie La Pepe, 4 years old; Dr. Borland. | 330 |
| Rose of Ontario, 3 years old; Silas Betts, Camden, N. J. | 360 |
| Fairy Maid, 4 years old; Dr. Borland. | 400 |
| Pride To meet II, 3 years old; I. Walter, Philadelphia. | 315 |
| Spotty, 4 years old; W. Shaw, New Brunswick, Md. | 240 |
| Daisy La Pepe, 4 years old; Mr. Hollis, Philadelphia. | 370 |
| Bessie, 3 years old; Major Warner, Pomfret, Conn. | 320 |
| Rose Bonheur, 3½ years old; Dr. Borland. | 300 |
| Snowdrop, 4½ years old; George Slight, Philadelphia. | 500 |
| Duckey, 3 years old; William B. Bullock, Philadelphia. | 350 |

The two day's sale realized in all $43,426, a sum that was considered low for such a number of fine stock.

SAN FRANCISCO, August 3, 1882.

EDITOR BREEDER AND SPORTSMAN: It may interest some readers to know that in the Yerba Buena herd of Jerseys and Guernseys is to be found some of the best blood known. "Fairy of Yerba Buena," a heifer, with her second calf, keeps up the reputation of her grandam. "Coomassie," and on the place are two of her heifer calves, sired by "Visitor of Yerba Buena." They are handsome and very promising, and when we see that seven head of this blood sold lately in New York at an average of $3,000 apiece, and "Formost Glory," the grandsire of "Fairy," sold for $3,950, these animals may be considered valuable. "William of Sitnose" (grandson of "Jersey Bell of Sitnose," the cow that made twenty-five pounds of butter in a single week and was valued at $30,000), which came from Boston last Spring by Wells, Fargo & Co., is doing finely. He is a beauty, and may get a prize in the show this Fall.

Some of the imported Guernsey heifers have come in, and make a showing that may dispute the prizes with the Jerseys at Sacramento in September.

The interest in these valuable animals seems to be growing. Sixty-two head of Jerseys just sold in Philadelphia at an average of $457 58, and thirty-two head of Guernseys sold at $355 31 per head, showing that the fools are not all dead, or these animals have value.

Truly yours,     JERSEY AND GUERNSEY.

### CATTLE BREEDING AND MARKETS.

John T. Raymond says: "Buy mules. There's millions in it!" Well, he is not far from right, provided you can raise enough of them. But we do say, and that with no proviso, that for a safe and profitable business, no better opportunity exists to-day than " cattle raising." What better encouragement do we want than to see our exception-ally slow and calculating cousins from the other side of the Atlantic coming over here and investing in the business? Not one nor two, but many. Single individuals and large corporations, equally as anxious to obtain the right place. Only a week or so ago the large cattle ranch at Merced, owned by the Nevada Bank, was sold to an English company for nine hundred thousand dollars, and that same week was completed of the Pablo Montoyo Ranch in New Mexico to an English syndicate for one million five hundred thousand dollars. Here we have, in two purchases, the large sum of two million four hundred thousand and invested by foreign companies, and had we knowledge of the many minor transactions, we would undoubtedly be surprised by the large amount of capital which they have invested in cattle and ranches on our continent. In a future number we shall have an interesting article on the " Increase and Profits " of a cattle ranch.

The conjecture regarding the Eastern demand on Nevada this Fall have been verified rather early, as two or three days ago twenty-two cars, equal to about four hundred head, were shipped from Pine Point and we have also information as to a large herd of something over three thousand being delivered for Eastern account. The call for sheep in this State is also very strong, and high prices are being paid in the southern counties for large droves of ewes. We know of one drove of five thousand yearlings being sold in Ventura County, a short time since, at two dollars and a quarter ($2 25) per head, to Montana men, and it is said that the Texas buyers cannot be accommodated to the extent of their desires without paying a fancy price. This week we have little or no change to note in our weekly slaughter-house price list.

BEEF—Steers, extra prime, 8⅜c; do. prime, 8c; do. fair, 7@7⅝c. Cows, extra prime, 7½@8c; fair, 6@7c.

VEAL—Large, 6½@7½c; small, 8@10c.

MUTTON—Wethers, 4½@6c; ewes, 4@4½c.

PORK—Hogs, live, 7¾@8¾ for hard; do. do. 7@7¼ for soft; do. dressed, 11%@11¼ for hard; do. do. 9¾@10¾ for soft.

WOOL—San Joaquin and Southern Coast, free, 18@21c; do. do. burry and defective, 15@18c; Northern counties range from 20@25c; Oregon, 22@27 for valley, and 20@26 for Eastern.

### MARKET REPORT.

FLOUR—The general demand is good. Best City Extra $5.50@5.64; Superfine, $4.50@4.75; Interior Extra, $4.75@5.25; Interior Superfine, $3.75@4.00 per bbl.

WHEAT—The firmness of the British grain market has but little influence on the local situation. The sales on the Produce Exchange have been, No. 1 Bench, August, Fort Costa, $1.71½; No. 1 White, September, $1.72; for No. 1 October $1.73½ was asked, $1.73½ was asked; No. 1 August, $1.66 asked, $1.62 bid.

BARLEY—In the Produce Exchange the sales of Barley seem to be dragging of late. Spot lots of Feed are bought for $1.28, but $1.30 is the purchasing limit. Such inflections is paid in Brewing and Chevalier.

OATS—The new crop coming in is being sold from $1.70@1.85 per ctl.

FEED—Ground Barley sells at $36 for old, $33 for new, and $34 per ton for mixed; Oilcake Meal, $31.50 per ton; Middlings sell in lots as milk for $30.00@37.50 per ton; Shorts, $19@17 per ton; Cornmeal, $30 per ton.

HAY—Wheat, $14@16; Wild Oat, $12@16; Alfalfa, $11@12; Stable, $16@21 per ton.

STRAW—Quoted at 70@75c per bale.

BEANS—Bayos of the new crop are being brought into the market in small lots. We quote old Bayos, $2.75@3; Butter, $2.50 for small, and $4.15 for large; Limas, 5@5½c; Pea, $3.50 to $3.65; Red, $2.50@3.62½ small White, $4.50c; and Pink, $3.50 to $3.65.

ONIONS—$2@$2½c for Bodega and Sonoma by the channel.

POTATOES—Sweet are steady as the pay in; Early Rose, in sacks, 90@85c; boxes, $1@1.10 per ctl; Garnet Chili, 70@60c per ctl.

POULTRY—All kinds of poultry are in good demand, especially young Roosters, which readily sell at $6.50@8.00 per doz. Young Broilers, 15@22c; Hens, 16@17c; Roosters, $5@6 per doz.; Fryers, $4@6; Ducks, $8@9, according to size; Ducks, $5.50@6.50 per doz; Geese, $1.50@2 per pair; Goslings, $1.50@2.00 per pair.

GAME—is quoted at: Hare, $1.75@2; Rabbits, $1@1.25 per doz; Doves, 50@75c per doz; Venison, 8@12c per lb.

PROVISIONS—Quite firm. Eastern Hams, 17@18½c; Breakfast Bacon, 15½@16c; sides 13½@14c for sugar cured and smoked; Eastern Breakfast Bacon, 15½@16c; California Smoked Bacon, $16@16½c for heavy and medium and 17½@17½c for light and extra light; China Lard, 17c; Pork, $22@25 for the Extra Prime, $24@25 for Prime Mess, $20@21 for Clear and $27@28 for Extra Clear; Pigs' Feet, 10@12½ per lb; Mess Beef, $14 for bbls and $7 for ½ bbls; Extra Mess Beef, $14@15 per bbl.

EGGS—California Choice, 30@32c; Interior, 28@27c; Eastern, 25@27c; Western, 22@26c ₱ doz.

BUTTER—Market is rather dull. Extracted mills at 7@8c per lb. Comb, 13@17c per lb.

BUTTER—The choice lots are being sold at fancy prices and are quoted: Fancy 32@35c; choice 30@32c; fair to good 27@29c; mixed lots from country stores 20@25c; firkins 28@30c per lb.

CHEESE—Is in fair demand and is quoted: California, 13@14c for choice; 12@13c for fair to good; Eastern, 16@17c; Western, 11@12c per lb.

HIDES AND SKINS—Steady and unchanged. Dry—paying the following rates for heavy, 18@19c, light and medium, 19c; culls one-third less, and Mexican Hides 1c per lb less; Dry Kip, 18c; Dry Calf, 20c; Salted Steers, over 55 lbs, 11c per lb; Steers and Cows, medium, 10c; light do, 8c; Salted Kip, 15 to 30 lbs, 10c to 10½c; Salted Calf, 11½c; Dairy Calf 40c to 70c each; Sheepskins, Shearling for Shearlings, $2.50c for short, 60@80c for medium, and 75@95 apiece for long wool; wool skins, Butchertown Green hides bring higher prices. Tallow—In demand; quoted at 6½@7c for rendered; for refined 11½c per lb.

WOOL—Moderate trade reported at current rates. We quote: Humboldt and Mendocino, 26@27c; Sonoma, 20@23c; Sacramento Valley, 19@22c; Joaquin and Mono, 20@23c; Calaveras and Foothills, 18@22c; San Joaquin, free, 18@20c; San Joaquin, defective, 15@18c; Southern Coast, burry and seedy, 15@18c; Eastern Oregon, choice, 26@29c; Oregon, fair, 22@26c; Valley Oregon, fine, 26@27c; and Valley Oregon, coarse, 22@25c per lb.

FRUIT—The market is well supplied, and the demand is fair. Oranges and Watermelons are very plentiful. The quotations are: Apples, 50c to 90c and $1 per box; Pears, 50@90c per box; Peaches, 40@60c per box; Plums, 25@60c per box; Nectarines, 40@50c per box; Apricots, 50@90c and $1 per box; Watermelons, $8@15 per hundred; Figs, $1.50@2.00 per box; Grapes, 40@75c per box; Blackberries, 5@8c per lb. Quinces, 80@90c per box; Huckleberries, 8@12c per lb; Cantaloupes, $1.50@3.50 per dozen; Lemons, 80@85 per box for Sicily and $2.50 for California; Limes, $7@8 per box for Mexican; Bananas, $2.50 per bunch; Tamarinds, 12@16c per lb; Bananas, $2@3 per bunch; Pineapples, $6@9 per dozen.

VEGETABLES—Prices show no material variation. The market is well supplied. We quote: Marrowfat Squash, 2@2½c per ton; Artichokes, 25@50c per doz; Turnips, 75c; Beets, 75c; Carrots, 80@90c; Parsnips, 75@80c per sack; Cauliflower, 50@75c per doz; Cabbage, 50@60c per ctl; Garlic, 10@12c per lb; Cucumbers, 25@40c per box; Green Peas, 2@4c per lb; Green Corn, 1@1½c per doz; String Beans, 2@3c per lb; Dried Okra, 50c per lb; Summer Squash, 30@40c per ton; String Beans, 2@3c per lb; Green Corn, 10@12c per doz; Okra, 3@5c per lb; Egg Plant, 6@8c per lb.

MEATS—Following are rates for whole carcasses from slaughterers to dealers:

BEEF—Prime, 7@8c; medium grades, 6c to 6½c; interior, 5@6½c per lb.

VEAL—Large Calves, 6@7c; small ones, 8@10c per lb.

MUTTON—Wethers are quoted at 4@6c, and Ewes at 4@4½c per lb, according to quality.

LAMB—Quotable at 8@7c per lb.

PORK—Live Hogs, 7@8½c for hard, and 6½c to 6c for soft; dressed do 11@11½c per lb for hard grade hogs.

## OTTER HUNTING IN ENGLAND.

During my last days in merry old England, just after the close of the fox-trot season, I was invited to take part in a week's hunt of the otter, a sport that was comparatively new to me, and surely to most of our American friends, who enjoy a run at hounds in the fox-hunt season only. On Monday, May 15th, the Kendal Otter Hounds meet was at Kendale Bridge, West Cumberland. Taking the stream close to a mill, the hounds were uncoupled and immediately gave tongue to a drag. Working down stream for a half-mile, the rising tide was here wet, so heads were turned and the drag taken upwards, carefully, foot by foot, almost, was the scent made out by the grand dogs of the hunt. About a mile from the starting point, bent by the mill-dam side, our drag became somewhat hotter, and Music, working alone at the foot of a steep bank "marked" first in an old root surrounded by sticks and a lot of rubbish close to a deep pool. Testers, a little terrier, found her way under ground, and got up to the otter, and in the subsequent proceedings the otter (punished his opponent terribly. However, in due course, the "Sel-otter" sprang out of his holding almost over the hounds, and dived into deep water. Now a most exciting hunt was enjoyed, and the game was kept moving for over an hour, every hound in the pack working eagerly and well. The water being deep, and becoming very muddy, happily at this point the animal took up stream, where the river flowed clearer. Here grand old Music spied her prey, and made a ferocious lunge at it, but the otter turned round, and the good old hound got decidedly the worst of the struggle. Up stream the otter swam, and soon showed signs of exhaustion, repeatedly coming to the top of the water. This it did once too often. Several of the hounds being near at hand, it was simultaneously seized in powerful jaws, in mid stream, where the water was three feet deep. The fight was hard, and lasted full twenty minutes before the otter was dragged to the bank dead.

Think, gentlemen of the Hunt Clubs of America, of a pack of six couple of hounds and a brace of wiry-looking terriers after a "fish-diver," who, to a considerable extent, thins out the numbers of the speckled beauties of our ponds and streams. Now imagine the laying on of the hounds in a few moments after. Mark then, to the deep-toned notes of the dogs as they proclaim the "puncher" at hand. Think of the pretty sight afforded as the hounds enter on the otter drag laid by this animal's movements over night across the meadows, down into a bed of spires at yonder brookside, while engaged in its bloody work in the night. After dwelling there a short time they hunt the varmint merrily out up the water course, and beautifully mark it to a drain. Here the sport begins. Spades are sent for, your Grip and Venom, the plucky little terriers, are introduced and from the row inside, evidently a war is going on. After thirty minutes of digging, stamping and bustling by the terriers, during which they get fearfully punished, the otter bolts and makes a brilliant run for over an hour. When this is accomplished in the country too much praise cannot be given to the gentlemen who have the honor and satisfaction of enjoying this plucky and exciting branch of sport in the States.—Turf, Field and Farm.

The BREEDER AND SPORTSMAN is the name of a new paper just established in San Francisco, by Joseph Cairn Simpson. The initial number is a very creditable one, and indicates a determination to make it a reliable exponent of all honorable sports. We hope it will prove a successful venture.—Gridley Herald.

## J. A. McKERRON

Manufacturer of Fine Harness. Horse Boots a Specialty.

NO. 367 SUTTER STREET,

Between Dupont and Stockton     San Francisco.

REPAIRING NEATLY AND PROMPTLY EXECUTED

---

---

Trains leave, and are due to arrive in San Francisco, as follows:

| LEAVE | DESTINATION | ARRIVE |
|---|---|---|
| | | |

---

---

## Specimen of Our Artist's Humor.

THE MUSIC LESSON.

### HUNDREDS OF DELIGHTED ONES

See, for the First Time in their Lives, the
### JAPANESE ARTIST AND EMBROIDERERS

AT WORK IN THEIR NATIVE COSTUMES, AT

### ICHI BAN, 22 and 24 Geary Street.

The BREEDER AND SPORTSMAN is printed with Shattuck and Fletcher' Ink.

**BREEDER AND SPORTSMAN**

VOL. 1.—No. 7.
No. 508 MONTGOMERY STREET. }
SAN FRANCISCO, SATURDAY, AUGUST 12, 1882.
{ SUBSCRIPTION,
FIVE DOLLARS A YEAR

# NOTABLE HORSES OF CALIFORNIA.

## WILDFLOWER.

2:21!!!  FOALED 1879, BY ELECTIONEER, HER DAM MAYFLOWER BY ST. CLAIR.  2:21!!!

We are much pleased to be able to present to our readers an accurate representation of the animal which has probably elicited more remarks than any other horse bred in California. From the trotting view point there is no doubt of her being entitled to the precedence, unless Hinda Rose be granted the first place, for, although 2:36½ in yearling form leaves a greater gap between that and the second in the record, 2:21 for two-year-old is so close to the fast of any age that three and a quarter seconds may be accorded as much weight as when the difference is between 2:36½ and 2:44¾. It would be mere guess work, a difference of opinion which can only be determined in the future, which is the most creditable, and speculations regarding the hereafter are not necessary in this connection. The portrait and accompanying description of Electioneer, which was published a few weeks ago, is sufficient in relation to the paternal side of the house, and as her races were also given

there is also no necessity for repetition. On the maternal side, however, nothing has yet been written in the history of the "notables," excepting the casual mention of the "happy nick" in the combination of Electioneer and St. Clair blood. Among the old-time horses of California two, in our opinion, are entitled to the highest distinction, the couple being Belmont, whose genealogy is well known, and St. Clair, the pedigree of which is sealed so completely that conjecture is the only guide. There are physical laws which give a clue to relationship, and men of science can tell from a few of the bones of a skeleton the class to which the animal belonged. There are peculiarities in animal and plant life determining the family to which they are allied, and in all the varieties of horses there are striking features enabling the acute observer to give a shrewd guess regarding their origin. As St. Clair had a highbred appearance, as his descendants exhibit the same quality

through successive generations, the logical presumption is that he was strongly imbued with the blood of the thoroughbred. At all events, no one of any candor can deny what the records show, and that in the first and second removes from the founder of the family there have been distinguished performers. A few illustrations will suffice to prove the tenability of this position. In writing that the name of Wildflower was better known throughout the civilized world than any other California-bred horse is owing to the greater interest which is taken in the sports of the track than was the case ten years ago. At the latter mentioned date there was nothing like the general interest that is now exhibited. Comparatively little attention was given to trotting in the press of the country, outside of the journals that made a special feature of racing and trotting, paragraphs being held sufficient where columns are now awarded. Yet one of the sensations of the day was t...

trotting of Occident, and, before he had been awarded a distinctive appellation, the "California Wonder" was the text for many articles. That he was worthy of the renown we firmly believe, and we have also implicit faith that, under more fortunate circumstances, he would have taken a place in the calendar that might still be at the top. As it was, he had the "fastest time" of the day, and this is no small honor. Though, when it was done, 2:16¾ ranked the best on record, in the opinion of his owner and those who had the same opportunity to know what he could do, it was a long way beneath his rate, and the flight of speed in his brushes was a token that several seconds were lost through the turn of bad luck which persistently pursued him. He has been timed quarters faster than thirty seconds, and such speedy pacers as Billy Mayo and Dan Voorhees could not stay with him for a hundred yards. It is too long a story to rehearse in these outline sketches, and to give our readers his history from colthood will require more space than can be allotted at present. From the time he was broken until purchased, on account of his trotting capacity, there was scarcely a day when he escaped ill-usage, and, in fact, the treatment he received in his early life could better be termed brutality. Compelled to draw loads far beyond the powers of most horses of his size, flogged, starved, etc., until his temper was soured, and yet the hauling of loads of sand for months at a stretch had not stiffened his joints or taken the elasticity from his muscles.

When showing the great rate of speed he had a stride of over twenty feet, and we draw our information from a source which is eminently trustworthy, that at times he would cover twenty-four feet. In his later races, owing to his feet being injured, he fell back to eighteen and nineteen feet, without a corresponding quickening of action.

The name of Occident, however, is familiar to a great majority of those who know anything of trotting affairs, though comparatively few have any knowledge of other St. Clairs, which are well worthy of a place in horse history.

Mayflower, the dam of Wildflower, was one of the notabilities of the St. Clair clan. She is a small mare or rather on the long and low order in her formation, and like nearly all of the St. Claire we have seen, showing a great deal of quality. Very unfortunately for this little mare she was tutored when there was the slightest knowledge among the professors as to the methods which should be employed to correct errors in the action. The boots of the period were clumsy contrivances, illy adapted for the purpose, worse even than the primitive guards of bandages and sheepskin which the old old-time trainers used. The softer material did not afford the necessary protection from hard blows, but they soon became shaped to the parts and did not interfere with the movements of the joints and play of the tendons, which the more obdurate material impeded, and the abrasions, chafings, etc., were as bad as the wounds. At that time the problem of weight on the feet and its effect on the action was a maze to those who had given it study; to those who had not pondered over the intricacies attending the use it was inscrutable. Men reasoned that if a moderately heavy shoe was found to be advantageous a still heavier would be better. Weight was applied in a loaded quarter-boot or in rolls filled with shot buckled around the pastern. The first was bad enough, the second infinitely worse. In accordance with the general belief of the period Mayflower was shod with shoes weighing two pounds each on her fore feet, and these were supplemented by rolls of shot, each foot carrying two added pounds. Four pounds on each fore foot! and with all this hindrance to speed she obtained a record of 2:30½, and showed quarters in 34 seconds. There is not an intelligent trainer who will deny that to keep up a rate which would compass a mile in 2:30½, thus encumbered, was a wonderful performance, and that under a system which would have the same effect in controlling the action, and at the same time reduce the weight of shoe and appendages to from 12 to 18 ounces, the animal showing such a rate would trot fully fifteen seconds faster. This is somewhat hypothetical, however, and yet it has a great bearing in arriving at a just conclusion regarding the merits of the animal. Mayflower made the record of 2:30½ at Sacramento, May 7th, 1872. It was for a purse of $1,500, 2:34 class, and there started against her Mattie Howard and Hiram Woodruff. Mayflower won in "straight heats," the time of which was 2:39, 2:35, 2:30½. The year previous she trotted several races, but only one in 1873, and we suppose the heavy weights had done the job.

There is another St. Clair mare which is entitled to very nearly the same place as Mayflower; by the record, she takes precedence of her. This was the mate of Mayflower, very much of the same style of an animal, and the only difference in the name is that she is called Mayfly. She is the dam of Bonita, who takes the second place in the record for two-year-olds, and there are those who regard her as the fastest of the two. Mayfly trotted on the same track three days after the race of Mayflower, and emulating her half-sister, she also won in straight heats, beating Hiram Woodruff and Jerome in 2:32, 2:30¼, 2:30½.

When to these illustrations of the value of the St. Clair blood are added the performances of Lady St. Clair, Ben Butler, Pat Hunt, Fred Low, Clay, Captain Smith, etc., the efficacy must be acknowledged, but the history of this noted California family will come more appropriately at a season when there is more leisure.

It is almost supererogatory to add a written description, the pictorial being so perfect, other than to say that she is a very handsome shade of bay. She has grown a great deal since she made her memorable trot, both in height and length. The most striking point, or rather points, is the immense sweep from the whirlbone to the stifle, and from the stifle to the hock. The great length of the tibia throws the hock back, for the femur being also long, the stifle is "well let down," and the angles are such as to give the fullest scope to the play of the limb. Though very finely formed all over, we deem this the important part of her configuration, enabling her to cover the most ground in the stride with the least exertion.

## HIRAM HAPPY'S LETTER FROM THE CITY OF MONUMENTS.

BALTIMORE, Md., July 31, 1882.

EDITOR BREEDER AND SPORTSMAN: Judging from what I have heard here and elsewhere the high expectations which lovers of stock and sport entertained respecting the BREEDER AND SPORTSMAN have been fully realized by a perusal of the initial numbers. The style of the paper, the quality and variety of its contents, its general make up, give very good satisfaction. The *Morning Herald*, of this city, which has recently made rapid strides towards a place in the foremost ranks of Baltimore journalism, paid a handsome and well merited tribute to its distant contemporary.

From extended personal observation I can say that there is certainly no State in the Union, there is no section of country which can compare with the Pacific Coast in point of natural advantages for stock raising and as a place for the enjoyment, all the year round, of outdoor sports and pastimes of every kind. Not only to the horseman and breeder, but to the hunter and fisherman, to the seeker of recreation, health and, I may say, wealth, the State of California presents inducements which I know are not possessed by any other State. As these facts are daily becoming more known and recognized in the East, I can see for the BREEDER AND SPORTSMAN a most promising future—substantial success, coupled with an enviable position and a national reputation. And I trust that when it shall again be my pleasure to take advantage of the excellent advice tendered by the late philosopher of the New York *Tribune*, and "Go West," I may learn that my hopes and wishes are being realized by you.

By the residents of other large cities Baltimore is very generally voted *slow* in more respects than one. This applies among other things to our trotting and breeding interests, and is, no doubt, merited with but one or two conspicuous exceptions, so far as breeding is concerned, to which I will refer in this letter. While this city is possessed of decided advantages as a place of residence and business, among which may be mentioned its usual mild winters, clear sunny atmosphere, fine markets and its importance as one of the great railroad and shipping centers, the hot summers, cobble stone paved streets, open sewers and hard, stony, dusty, hilly roads in the suburbs prevent the Monumental City from being set down as a paradise for the enjoyment of fine horses. And while it can boast of what is unquestionably the finest park (Druid Hill) in the country, there are fewer elegant family equipages to be seen there, and one meets fewer gentlemen's fine turnouts and trotters on the road, and more lamentable exhibitions of horsemanship than any other city of its size in America. Whether this scarcity of well equipped turnouts is due to the reasons above given, or to the tastes of the people—to their economical home habits of living—I will not attempt to say, but the fact no doubt remains that as a whole our horseflesh is below the average. Again, the only trotting race course we have is "several miles away from nowhere," and unfortunately for it and for the public, the same has long been regarded by respectable horsemen as decidedly peculiar—"for ways that are dark," as was Bret Harte's famous Heathen Chinee. The mystery which still shrouds the identity of the individual who committed an assault upon William Patterson, Esquire, is not greater than that which characterized some of the by-gone struggles on the aforesaid track. While the trotting interests are suffering severely, the running races which take place at the regular Spring and Fall meeting of the Maryland Jockey Club at Pimlico have of late years been quite successful and enjoyed the patronage of our better class.

In this connection simple justice demands a tribute to an organization to which Baltimoreans are at present largely indebted for their enjoyment of outdoor sport. I approach this subject with feelings of the profoundest variety. Cities like Pittsburgh, Cleveland and Buffalo may have their trotting clubs; but what place can boast of a base ball organization like Baltimore? The pride of our people! The glory of our city! The heroes of many well earned defeats! And while the residents of the other cities named are enjoying the dying echoes of the trotters' musical footsteps at eventide (patent applied for), our inhabitants are sipping fishy water on their marble doorsteps and discussing the distant possibility of our base ball club winning a first-class game before the leaves begin to turn. To see those nine artists vainly struggling with some small-sized enemy, and submit to the whitewashing process, would impart grace and flexibility to the intellect of an Oregon hackman. While "our boys" may be very clever young men on general principles; while, with proper "handling," they might even make first-class hands in a corn field, when it comes to playing base ball, I have in my mind a lot of trained horses which I saw in California, and which could—but no, I shall not be guilty of so unjust a reflection upon the stock of your glorious country.

This being the City of Monuments, the propriety of erecting, at the close of the current season, a suitable memorial to commemorate the glory of our base ball club has been agitated by a number of our public-spirited men. The *Herald* is to be custodian of the fund to be raised for this purpose, and the people will doubtless respond nobly. The proposed monument is to have for its base a huge *ball*, constructed of petrified *whitewash*, upon which is to be placed a miniature freight car filled with imitation goose eggs made of plaster of Paris and bats (brick-bats). This beautiful design and sentiment, emblematic, as it were, of our boys' record, was suggested by a young lady from Boston, who was recently induced to witness a game of ball here, but who desires her name withheld on account of respectable connections.

To return to the equine race. The most extensive horse-breeding farm in this section is Montebello, the magnificent suburban home of Mr. John W. Garrett, President of the Baltimore and Ohio Railroad. Most charmingly situated on high, rolling ground, commanding a splendid view of the city, the Chesapeake Bay and Fort Carroll, Montebello, with its 2,000 acres of choice meadows, forests, groves, and farming lands, its stock, stables, race track, and general improvements, is no doubt one of the grandest homes in America.

While enjoying a visit to Palo Alto some time ago, through the kindness of the editor of the BREEDER AND SPORTSMAN, I was forcibly reminded of the apparent similarity in the lives and tastes of the proprietor of that grandly appointed and stocked establishment and the owner of Montebello. Each of these gentlemen has long occupied the exalted position of chief executive of one of the great railroads of the world; each enjoys the reputation, at home and abroad, of having contributed more to the growth and prosperity of his own city and State than any other individual; and each is an ardent lover and extensive breeder of the horse. As with ex-Governor Stanford, the horse interests of Mr. Garrett are purely a matter of enjoyment and pride, a labor of love. The Arab steed has ever been an especial favorite with Mr. G., and Montebello can no doubt boast of the finest specimens of Arabian horses in this country. The beauty of outline, graceful carriage and elastic movements of these animals certainly appeal most powerfully to the eye and tastes of every visitor. Among the more noted the produce of the pure Arabian mare Esnea, a fine light bay, with white face and three white feet, imported from Damascus, Syria, by the late William McDonald, of this city, for a long time owner of Flora Temple, deserves particular mention. Two of her sons, Saladin, a magnificent bay stallion, by Daniel the Prophet; and Damascus, a highly finished, royally crested chestnut, are among the chief attractions at Montebello; as is also her daughter, the bay mare Zoe, by imp. Bonnie Scotland. Adniack, a beautiful, substantial silver grey stallion, 15½ hands high, by Burlington, out of the imported Arabian mare Saieda (dead), is frequently used by Mr. Garrett as a pole horse, and although twenty years of age, he carries himself like a four-year-old.

But the glory of Montebello, the most brilliant star among its two hundred and odd horses, is Maryland Volunteer, another worthy son of the world-renowned sire of the king of the turf, St. Julien. This horse was purchased by Mr. Garrett about two years ago, and the splendid lot of yearlings of his get now at the farm would be a credit to any stock horse in the country. The dam of Maryland Volunteer was the phenomenal mare Jennie, by Red Eagle, with a record of 2:22 and private trial of 2:16 to her credit.

The subject of our sketch is in color a very rich brown bay, with black points, full 16½ hands high, seven years old. He is a well finished, powerful horse, evenly balanced, and possessing a pure, bold, open gait. These qualities, together with his charming disposition, he seems to transmit to his offspring. The horse's speed was never developed, but he can readily trot a mile in better than 2:40, and he does this of his own will, without urging and without boots or weights. Mr. Garrett has permitted the service of this grand stallion to a limited number of outside stock, greatly to the improvement of the breeding of this section.

Among the brood mares at Montebello, the following struck me as being entitled to special reference, by reason of their choice breeding, fine size, color and form. A number of these were purchased of Col. R. P. Pepper, proprietor of the South Elkhorn farm in Kentucky, and they are certainly worthy representatives of the famous blue grass regions:

Euchre, b. m., 16¼ hands, foaled 1875, by Ericsson (four-year-old record, fourth heat, 2:30½), dam Cachuca, by Almont.

Rachel, b. m., 16½ hands, foaled 1874, by Almont; dam by Gray's Mambrino, son of Mambrino Chief.

Winetta, b. m., 16 hands, foaled 1875, by Administrator; dam by Iron Duke, son of Cassius M. Clay.

Mambrina, br. m., foaled 1874, by Lothair, son of Woodford Mambrino (2:19); dam fast pacing mare, by Jeff Davis.

Canton, b. m., foaled 1875, by Alcadne (sire of Enigma, 2:26, Hylas 2:24½), son of Mambrino Chief; dam by Lever, son of Lexington.

Flirt, b. m., sired by Abdallah Prince, by Vorhees Abdallah; dam by Black Bashaw.

Beulah, blk. m., foaled 1865, sired by Royal George; dam by Seely's American Star.

Blue Grass, b. m., by Blue Grass, by Rysdyk's Hambletonian; dam by Hunter's Glencoe, Jr., by imp. Glencoe.

With such "blood," backed by the opportunities and means which Mr. Garrett possesses, Montebello will, no doubt, very soon rank among the great breeding establishments of the land.

Meadow View Farm, the charming home of Mr. H. B. Holton, near Powhatan, Maryland, about six miles west of Baltimore, is another place where the horse has not been neglected. Orange Blossom (2:26¼) the great son of Middletown, and Meadow Chief, by Hamlet, are owned here, and their get are showing up remarkably well. It is greatly regretted by our horsemen that Mr. Holton's business matters preclude his bestowing upon the breeding interests that active attention which his tastes, judgment and ample means would under other circumstances prompt him to give.

The fleet little chestnut stallion, Hannis, by Mambrino Pilot, who a few years ago advanced so rapidly towards the place of a world-beater, is also owned in this city. He has been retired from the turf and is doing stud service.

So much for the horse in "My Maryland." At some future day it will afford me pleasure to give your readers an account of our "canvas-backs, terrapin and oysters," in which three luxuries we are as far ahead of the rest of the world as we are behind in horse and sporting matters.

HIRAM HAPPY.

We have received the first number of the BREEDER AND SPORTSMAN, published at San Francisco, and edited by Mr. J. C. Simpson, and it presents a fine appearance. It is the kind of a paper which has long been needed on the Pacific Coast, and it is to be hoped that it will meet with generous support. Its discussion of breeding topics will rouse interest in that subject and add to the value of the products of breeding farms, and its treatment of the turf will swell the receipts of racing parks. The journal, which is devoted to breeding and sport, and which is conducted with enterprise and ability, frequently puts more money into other people's pockets than its own, but we cannot believe that such will be the result of Mr. Simpson's venture. If the breeders and track managers of the Pacific Coast do not sustain him, they will not deserve to reap the benefits which will grow under the fostering care of a vigorous home organ. —*Turf, Field and Farm*.

# THE PADDOCK.

## MILLIMAN'S BELLFOUNDER.

We were much pleased to find the following in the *Oregonian* of the 30th ult. There is no mistaking the authorship, and handiwork of our old friend, Tom Merry, was evident before the first paragraph was read. The blood of Bellfounder is quite prominent on the Pacific Coast, and the short history will be interesting to many in California. Four of his get in the 2:30 list, with the limited opportunities he was awarded is a very good showing, and from what we hear the progeny of his son Gus. is likely to add to the reputation of the family.

In the Summer of 1855 Alexander Gamble of Menlo Park, California, who had accumulated considerable money in mining enterprises in Nevada, commissioned his brother, residing in the East, to buy him a trotting stallion, with a record better than 2:40. Gamble had the celebrated gray pacing mare Unknown, which had beaten Fillmore, Honest Ance and a nubmer of others at heats of two and three miles, and into this new horse he was putting the profits of her victories. The horse arrived in California in good season and in excellent health. He was not very large, but highly formed and possessed of quick and spirited action. He was a rich rosewood bay, with black points and a fine mane and tail. He had a rather large head, but it was clean and bony, with a great breadth between the eyes, indicating the highest order of gameness and ability to "go, the pace and stay the distance." Milliman's Bellfounder, as this horse will henceforth be known in the history of the trotting turf, was by Bellfounder, out of a daughter of Engineer, grandam by Bishop's Hambletonian, he by imported Messenger out of Pheasant by Shark, son of Medley. His sire, Bellfounder, was by the Morse Horse, he by European out of a daughter of Harris' Hambletonian, grandam Mozza by Peacock, son of Messenger. The horse was strongly inbred to Messenger, the very head and front of American trotting blood. Soon after his arrival in California Bellfounder was matched for $2,500 a side, half forfeit, to trot against Robert F. Morrow's brown stallion Latham, already having a record of 2:33. The race was to come off in August, at Sacramento, and Bellfounder placed in charge of George N. Ferguson, a reputable and skillful driver, who has since become wealthy and retired from the turf. Whether it was that he got too lame, or that he did not show a satisfactory trial, we have never known; but he was taken back to Mr. Gamble's farm and kept there until the great smash up of the mining stock market in 1867. This bankrupted Mr. Gamble, who caused all his horses to be sold at auction during the Summer. A merchant bought Bellfounder, but the old horse had become irritable and he soon parted with him for $800 to William Bigham, then of Rock Creek, Oregon, but now residing at or near Spokane Falls. Bigham took Bellfounder out into the wilderness of bunch grass, and there it was that he sired the gelding Mark Twain, which was afterwards sold to Rockwell, the trainer, and drowned on the steamer Pacific, wrecked off Cape Flattery in 1875. Previous to his coming to Oregon he got the stallion Gus., with a record of 2:26½. Dr. C. H. Mack of Walla Walla, subsequently purchased the horse from Mr. Bigham for $1,000, and while the doctor himself never reaped any great amount of pecuniary gain from the purchase, the county of Walla Walla probably gained at least $150,000 by his removal thither. The first of his get showed well and sold for good prices. Belleflower, bred by William Glassford, was sold for $5,000 to Col. Eyre of San Francisco, and Startle, a younger brother, is now the property of the Robertson brothers of this city. We append the records of the most noted ones:

| NAME. | OWNER. | RECORD. |
|---|---|---|
| Gus | M. Mooney | 2:26½ |
| Dexter | V. B. DeLashmutt | 2:26½ |
| Belleflower | E. E. Eyre | 2:29 |
| Sweet Home | H. S. Hogoboom | 2:30 |
| Goldfoil | William Glassford | 2:32½ |
| Startle | Robertson Bros | 2:33¾ |
| Belle Foster | Jas. W. Foster | 2:34¾ |
| Walla Walla Maid | H. S. Hogoboom | 2:35½ |
| Billy Nelson | H. Nelson | 2:35½ |
| Susy Mack | Dr. C. H. Mack | 2:37 |
| Tempest | Chas. H. Russell | 2:39 |

## ANOTHER ALMONT.

We hear of still another Almont on the coast. Alwood is owned by Dr. Mack of Oregon, and the appended description is given by Tom Merry in the *Oregonian:*

Before us stands a mighty looking horse, about sixteen hands and two inches high. In 1878 he became blind through epizooty, and the following year he came to Washington Territory. He resembles the pictures of Alexander's Abdallah (sire of Goldsmith Maid) more than any other of his ancestors, though a larger horse. His neck is a trifle short and his nose Roman, showing the Mambrino Chief characteristics very plainly in this respect. His shoulders are very oblique, raking well into a good back piece, and his chest is fairly enermous. The loins arcn finely but the hips droop considerably Yet in this respect he resembles both Almont and Alexander's Abdallah, two of the most famous sires of trotters in the world. Hence it cannot at this late day be regarded as a defect. His legs are splendid, and we doubt if a heavier boned horse ever stood over iron. His pedigree comprises the best trotting blood to be found anywhere. For twenty years there has been a rivalry between New York and Kentucky as to which could breed the best trotters. New York's favorite stock was the get of Rysdyk's Hambletonian, he by Abdallah, he by Mambrino, and he by imported Messenger. The Kentucky sire was Mambrino Chief, by Mambrino Paymaster, and he by Mambrino, son of Messenger. Both these rival strains of blood are to be found in Alwood, together with other less noted strains of scarcely less merit. He is by Almont, his dam by Blackwood (sire of Protine, 2:19), her dam by Alexander's Abdallah. Blackwood was by Alexander's Norman (sire of Lulu, 2:15), and he by the Morse Horse, also to be found in the pedigree of Bellfounder. Thus Alwood combines four of the great trotting lines—Hambletonian, Mambrino Chief, Pilot, Jr. and Blackwood, or rather, the Morse Horse.

The Mentmore yearlings, the property of Lord Roseberry, were sold publicly at auction on Thursday, July 6th, at Newmarket, England, consisting of nine head that brought $15,326, or an average of $1,714 per head. The highest priced one was the bay colt by Macaroni, dam Queen Marion, by King Tom, $5,100.

# TURF AND TRACK.

## FIXED EVENTS.

Santa Cruz County Fair Association. First annual meeting at Santa Cruz, Aug. 15th, 16th, 17th and 18th.

Sonoma County Park Association, at Santa Rosa, Aug. 22d, 23d, 24th, 25th and 26th.

Sonoma and Marin Agricultural Societies. Annual Fair at Petaluma, Aug. 29th and four following days.

Golden Gate Fair, to be held at Oakland, from September 4th to the 9th inclusive.

Butte District Fair at Chico, from September 5th to September 8th, inclusive.

El Dorado District Fair at Placerville, from September 5th to September 8th, inclusive.

California State Fair. Annual meeting at Sacramento, from Monday, September 11th to the 16th inclusive.

The San Joaquin Valley Association Fair at Stockton, from September 19th to the 23d inclusive.

Oregon State Fair at Salem, from September 18th and during the week.

The San Mateo and Santa Clara County Agricultural Association Fair at San Jose, September 25th to the 30th inclusive.

Humboldt and Mendocino District Fair at Rhonerville, September 19th to September 22d, inclusive.

Modoc, Plumas and Lassen District Fair at Greenville, from October 2d to October 5th, inclusive.

Monterey District Fair at Salinas City, from October 2d to October 6th, inclusive.

Nevada State Fair, at Reno, from Monday, October 2d, to the 7th, inclusive.

Mount Shasta Agricultural Association Fair at Yreka, October 4th, 5th, 6th and 7th.

Eastern Oregon Fine Stock Association at Union, from October 9th to the 14th inclusive.

### FAIRS AT THE EAST.

Kentucky State Fair at Lexington, August 9th to September 2d inclusive.

Minnesota State Fair at Farmington, August 31st to September 8th inclusive.

Iowa State Fair at Fairfield, September 1st to the 8th inclusive.

Minnesota Agricultural Association, at Minneapolis, September 4th to the 9th inclusive.

Nebraska State Fair, at Omaha, September 11th until the 16th inclusive.

Rhode Island State Fair, at Providence, September 12th to the 15th inclusive.

Pennsylvania State Fair, at Pittsburg, September 7th to the 21st inclusive.

Wisconsin State Fair, at Fond du lac, September 11th to the 16th inclusive.

Ontario Provincial Fair, at Toronto, September 18th to the 23d inclusive.

Connecticut State Fair, at Meriden, September 18th to the 22d inclusive.

New Jersey State Fair, at Monroe, September 18th to the 22d inclusive.

West Virginia Central Fair, at Clarksburg, September 19th to the 21st inclusive.

Indiana State Fair, at Indianapolis, September 25th to the 30th inclusive.

Western Michigan Fair, at Grand Rapids, September 25th to the 30th inclusive.

Texas State Fair, at Austin, October 17th to the 21st inclusive.

## TROTTING ON THE BAY DISTRICT COURSE.

On Saturday last the Fall circuit of 1882 was informally commenced on the Bay District track. Though not one of the regular California Fairs, the horses which came together have engagements throughout the circuit, and hence there was quite an interest taken in the opening battle. The interest, however, was mainly confined to those who have more than a transient fondness for the trotter, and, consequently, the attendance was nothing like what two such contests should have called out. Still there was quite a concourse of people, the balconies of the hotel and Club House having a fair representation of the fair ones of San Francisco; the upper stand contained a goodly number, while around the pooling quarters there was a dense crowd anxious to invest on the horses they fancied. As usual, there was a variety of opinions. In one group it was held that Sweetness could not be beaten, in another there was no end to asservations that Starr King would win in a jog, and still others who had implicit faith in the prowess of Crown Point; Ashley, Cairo and Del Sur. There had been so many stories told of the immense speed which some of them had shown in their exercise that it was not surprising that great deeds were anticipated, and the very sanguine marked figures for their favorites which, if they had been capable of accomplishing, would have ended the race in one heat. Starr King, it was stated, had gone in 2:21½ at one time and in 2:19 at another, and this so easily that it was sure he could reduce it four or five seconds without any trouble. Sweetness was certain to trot as fast as her driver desired, according to the dogmatic promulgations of those who are so good at figuring, for she had done a half mile on the Oakland Trotting Park in 1:08½—"a seventeen gait, you know; and the Volunteers go the route." Cairo was also reported to be doing well, greatly improved by his absence from the track, and entirely different, "steady as an eight-day clock," his patrons claimed, and had entirely given up his old habit of diving and breaking, as he was accustomed to do of yore. Crown Point, Ashley and Del Sur having been trained at a distance from the city, very little was known as to what they had been showing, though some good judges quietly picked up "the field," composed of all the starters excepting Sweetness and Starr King, and these were rewarded with a liberal return for the investment. Nearly all the speculation was confined to the 2:25 race, and at least nine-tenths of the comments were restricted to the horses engaged in it. It was generally conceded that Vanderlynn was so much superior to Freestone and Frank Moscow that there was not much likelihood of a contest; and although the favorite proved to be the victor, one of the games of the long-rubber was lost, and his competitors displayed qualities which are almost certain to ripen into excellence in course of time. Being all new performers, Saturday's race being their first appearance, a short description will be in place. The winner, Vanderlynn, is a very handsome bay, with fine action and a great turn of speed. He is a nice size for a trotter, and appears to have the other qualities as well. He is by George M. Patchen, Jr. (California Patchen), and his dam was by the thoroughbred horse Joseph, brought to this State by A. Mailliard. The success of Patchen as the progenitor of trotters has been such as to award him a high place in the Trotting Stud-Book; and when matched with highly bred mares, his offspring show well in form as well as in speed. Thus there is Sam Purdy, from a dam by Illinois Medoc; Susie, from a mare by Owen Dale; Starr King, from Mary Wonder, a fast quarter mare. And Billy Hayward and Alexander exhibit so much "quality" that there is a strong probability that their dams had a good share of "blood." Joseph was by Hermes, a son of Mariner and the great Fashion, from Patsey Anthony, by imported Priam, grandam by Virginian.

Freestone is a large fine looking horse, a darker bay than Vanderlyun "Rangeier", and taken altogether a fine specimen of the fast-trotting American roadster. He has the thoroughbred on both sides. His sire, Captain Webster, by Belmont (Williamson's), his dam by Owen Dale, a son of the same Belmont. This gives him a double cross of that favorite California blood, and as there is another noted family of Belmonts it is necessary to explain that the Eastern Belmont, the sire of Nutwood, Wedgewood, etc., is a grandson of Rysdyk's Hambletonian; and on the other side of the mountains a Belmont is accepted as one of that family, whereas on this coast it is the thoroughbred which is meant. Contrary to the general belief where there is so much thoroughbred blood, Freestone has high action, and still further from what many suppose is a thoroughbred characteristic, he is steadier than an "eight day clock." He never broke during the four heats, and that in situations which would be trying to an old campaigner. He trotted behind, in front and alongside of a horse with a greater development of speed, and though on different occasions he was on the verge of disaster recovered without "leaving his feet." Of course his driver is entitled to great credit for his part being played so well. We have not the least hesitation in predicting that Freestone will surely make a fine trotter.

The third in this triangular contest, Frank Moscow, is also above the usual size, still larger than Freestone, and not as highly finished as the other, though a horse of good style, and a manner of going which indicates an increase of speed in the future. He is an Eastern-bred horse, his sire being of the same name, and doubtless belonging to the family of Moscows, the members of which were mainly bred in Michigan. In both races a majority of the horses were driven "artistically," and one, two or three as far from it as is usually seen. Still it is difficult to tell whether the driver or the horse is the party in fault, and as Pete Brandow surrendered his seat behind one of them after the short experience of one heat, in that instance it may be safely set down the horse was to blame. It is the first time on record when Brandow gave up the reins, and the boys were marking the date on the stable doors. It cannot be (at least we hope not) that the luxuries of the mining camps have so far enervated our friend that he has lost his determination; but a repetition will surely lead us to that way of thinking. One of the horses was driven in a way that is very reprehensible, and though the judges penalized him by giving him the last position, this was a small sentence for the work he performed.

The following is a detailed account of the races:

The first race was for the 2:40 class, in which through his private trials Vanderlynn was made a great favorite in the pools, selling for $50 against $25 for the two other entries combined, they being Freestone and Frank Moscow. Vanderlynn showed himself quite worthy of the confidence of his backers, as, with the exception of a bad break in the third heat, he trotted in an even and determined manner. In the first heat Moscow got a slight advantage at the start, and at a moderate gait he led the two others to the half-mile in 1:16¼, but Vanderlynn was trotting squarely within himself, and overhauling the leader on the turn, he won handily in 2:32, with Moscow second and Freestone last. In the second heat Vanderlynn outspeeded his two adversaries and was an easy winner in 2:29, the half being made in the same time as in the preceding mile. In the third heat the two out made a bolder bid for victory, and at the second turn they carried Vanderlynn off his feet to such a tune that when he regained his stride his driver saw that his chance for the heat was hopeless, so he left it to the other two, who came down the homestretch side by side, so much so that on the judges' stand it seemed like as if it would be a dead heat; but Freestone passed the wire a neck in front of Moscow, the quarter being made in 37½s., the half in 1:14¾, and the mile in 2:29. There was but little change in the betting, as the result seemed to be a foregone conclusion, and so it proved to be; but Freestone made a gallant fight of it, though Vanderlynn had a trifle the best speed, and won the heat and race in 2:27, the half being made in 1:13½. Vanderlynn will be a very useful horse in his class throughout the circuit, but he will be likely to find himself in still better company than was the case on Saturday. Pat Farrell deserves credit for the manner in which he brought the horse to his first race, and for the careful way in which he guided him to victory.

SUMMARY.

Bay District Track, Aug. 5th, 1882.—2:40 class—Purse $400; $200 to first, $100 to second, and $50 to third horse.

| | | | | |
|---|---|---|---|---|
| P. Farrell names b. h. Vanderlynn | 1 | 1 | 3 | 1 |
| M. Rollins names b. g. Freestone | 3 | 2 | 1 | 2 |
| A. B. Cooper names s. g. Frank Moscow | 2 | 3 | 2 | 2 |

Time—2:32, 2:29, 2:29, 2:27.

Then came the big event of the day, the 2:25 class, on the results of which the pools had been selling in an ever-varying manner since the previous evening at the Arion, and from the arrival of the first visitors at the track, Sweetness, the newcomer, disputed with Starr King for the supremacy as the favorite, while Cairo, Ashley, Crown Point and Del Sur were sold as the field, the only absentee among the entries being the Echora of Mr. Titus. The odds kept changing with every pool, but the average was between the following extreme quotations: Starr King $25, Sweetness $21, the field $12; and with the mare as first choice at $40, Starr King would fetch $30, and the field $25. An effort was made to get a heat through between the final one of the 2:40 class, but the scoring was so wild that after half a dozen ineffectual attempts the horses were sent to the stable.

There was a great deal of jockeying in order to obtain a favorable start, but at the fifth attempt the gong was tapped to a pretty even start, save that Starr King was more than a length behind his horses. His was the second position, while Cairo was at the pole and Sweetness on the extreme outside. From the start Ashley and Cairo went to the front, with Sweetness close up, and the quarter was reached in 36½ seconds. Down the back stretch Sweetness improved her position, with Starr King on a slight break and Crown Point in the extreme rear. On the further upper turn Sweetness passed Cairo, and when Tim Kennedy saw that the mare was at his heels, he urged Ashley to a break, and the horse ran quite a distance without being brought to his proper gait, and yet, despite this perversion of the rules, Sweetness beat him out by a good neck, he being three lengths ahead of Starr King, and then came Del Sur and Crown Point, but Ashley was properly set back last for running, and his driver was cautioned. The half was made in 1:11 and the mile in 2:25.

There was but very little change in the betting, as Starr King was still strongly backed by his adherents, as was Sweetness by her admirers. The drivers were cautioned not to delay the race by their manoeuvres, as the postponement of such an important event detracted so much from the enjoyment of the race. After three ineffectual attempts the horses were ordered to score by Starr King, and they were tapped off with Starr King two lengths behind them all and on a wabble that immediately became a bad break that took away all his chances for the heat. The quarter was made by Sweetness in 37 seconds, with Crown Point close up and Ashley at his wheel, and in a few strides the latter was again on the lead with the mare, both making a speeding half in 1:11, but this being too hot a pace for Ashley he broke and surrendered his position to Crown Point, who closed up with Sweetness, and after a fine struggle he beat her out by half a length in 2:24, the mare being three lengths ahead of Cairo, driven by Mr. Hughes; then came Del Sur, Ashley and Starr King last—some timers on the outside made the heat faster.

As might naturally be supposed, there was now a great revulsion in the betting, and as he was known to be a good stayer, Crown Point was made the favorite at $60 against $30 for Starr King and $30 for the field. Pete Brandow took charge of Starr King, and again there was a great deal of tedious scoring, owing to the difficulty of getting that horse up to his position. It was thus that only at the seventh trial were they tapped off, and Crown Point, leaving his feet, lost the pole in the few first strides, and again Ashley and Sweetness were contesting for the lead and reaching the half-mile in 1:13, with Crown Point some six lengths behind and Starr King last of all. The pace was too strong for Ashley, who was whipped into a break and then allowed to run as in the first heat, an action that was very much adverse to the chances of Sweetness. Crown Point made another break on the upper turn, but, on regaining his stride, he trotted very rapidly, and passing Ashley near the three-quarter pole, he gradually overhauled Sweetness, and after a fine contest, won the heat in 2:27 by a length from the mare, she leading Starr King by thrice that distance, and then came Ashley, Del Sur and Cairo in the order mentioned. Ashley was again placed last for running, and his driver might consider himself lucky that that was the only penalty he incurred for his conduct.

It was now $100 to $30 on Crown Point, and at these terms a great deal of money went into the box, the long odds being given by those who had pinned their faith on the favorites at the early stages of the race. Pat Farrell now resumed his place with Cairo, and Chauncey Kane took the reins over Starr King. Again was the start delayed by tedious scoring, and as the weather was turning cold and windy, a great many visitors left for home. More than half an hour was wasted in attempts to get the horses together, but it was only at the tenth time that the bell was tapped to a pretty fair start. Up to the second turn they were still pretty even, but there Crown Point took a decided lead, Star King being the only one near him by six lengths at the half in 1:12. Some of this advantage was lost by the leader by a break near the three-quarter pole, and apparently had the heat safe, when he made a double break within the draw-bridge, which would have cost him the heat had Star King possessed his usual speed, but Crown Point being admirably caught by Donathan he won by half a length in 2:27, the second money going to Sweetness and the third to Starr King. This brought to a conclusion the first of the series of contests of the 2:25 class that promise to furnish some of the best races throughout the circuit.

SUMMARY.

Same Day—2:25 class—Purse, $500; mile heats, three in five, in harness, $250 to first, $100 to second, $50 to third horse.

| | | | | |
|---|---|---|---|---|
| G. Valensin names s. s. Crown Point..(W. Donathan) | 5 | 1 | 1 | 1 |
| J. A. Goldsmith names s. m. Sweetness..........(J. A. Goldsmith) | 1 | 2 | 2 | 3 |
| Chas. W. Welby names ch. g. Starr King.....(Owner) | 2 | 6 | 3 | 2 |
| John Hughes names b. g. Cairo.... ..........(Owner) | 3 | 3 | 5 | 5 |
| L. J. Rose names b. s. Del Sur..... (Walter Maybee) | 4 | 4 | 4 | 6 |
| Jackson Cochran names ch. g. Ashley (Tim Kennedy) | 6 | 5 | 3 | 4 |

Time—2:25, 2:24, 2:27, 2:27.

The Chicago Fall Trotting Meeting.—The programme for the coming horse fair, September 16th to the 23d inclusive, announces premiums aggregating upward of $15,000. The prizes are fifty-seven in number, including the following: A $1,000 purse for the 2:45 class, for the 2:25 class, for the 2:21 class; for the 2:25 class pacing, for the 2:29 class, for the 3-minute class, for the 2:33 class, for a free-to-all pacing and for a 2:17 class. Also a $2,000 purse open to all stallions, and a special four-year-old stake, open to Phil. Thompson, Farce, Bronze, Fred. Crocker, Jay Eye See and Waiting, and any other four-year-old and under; entrance, $250. If two of those named above start, the Association adds $1,000. If three or more, $2,000. A special Consolation purse will be announced for the two last days, about September 1st. The entries close on Monday, August 28th, at 11 P. M.

## AN AMATEUR STEEPLECHASE.

One of the main features of the race meeting at Saratoga, was the Grand National Hunt Steeplechase, with amateur riders, and from the following account of the race, as given in the *N. Y. World*, it would appear as if our horses and riders both lacked training in this difficult cross-country riding: "There were five starters, and Rose was a great favorite, many being willing to bet that she would be the only one to go over the course: Probably a steeplechase never was run in this country which created so much fun and amusement. At the start Mr. Holmes took the lead with Lennox, attended by Mr. Strathey on Rose. Mr. Purdy on Trojan was third, but, gradually dropping back, was passed by Mr. Penniston on Echo. Barrister began the fun by refusing at the first jump, Rose and Lennox meanwhile making a pretty race in the run round the last turn, both horses jumping well up to, and including the north section of the water. At the first of the rails into the fractional track Lennox tripped and fell, throwing Mr. Holmes, and this was the beginning of one of the most uproarious scenes of fun ever witnessed on a race-track. What with Barrister refusing each jump until he reached the water, which he refused a dozen times, the buck-jumping of Echo, the occasional falls of Mr. Penniston and the slow and deliberate jumping of Trojan, it needed half a dozen pairs of eyes to see all the fun, which was finally supplemented by Mr. Clem Alloway remounting Lennox and in his shirt-sleeves and black silk hat started over the course. Although the horse could not throw him he stopped, bolted and hung at every jump. In the meantime Mr. Strathey was rating along alone at a very fair pace, Rose jumping in fine style. The final outcome of the race was that Rose won by half a mile in 6:02. Echo was second three furlongs in front of Trojan, he "pacing" in five furlongs in front of Lennox. As Barrister could not be got over the water-jump the first time, his career in the race ended there." The following is a summary:

August 1, 1882.—Grand National Hunt Steeplechase Sweepstakes, for qualified half-bred hunters, at $10 each, with $750 added, of which $250 to the owner of the second horse, the third to receive $100 out of the stakes; to be ridden by members of any regularly organized Hunt Club in the United States and Canada; minimum weight, 160 lbs.; 10 subscribers; full course, about two miles and three-quarters.

| | |
|---|---|
| J. P. Dawes' ch. m. Rose, 6, by Helmbold, dam by Niagara (h.-b.), 160 lbs..........(Mr. Strathey) | 1 |
| Hy. Drysdale's ch. g. Echo, 5, by Judge Curtis, 160 lbs..........(Mr. Penniston) | 2 |
| S. Berkley's ro. g. Trojan, aged, 160 lbs..........(Mr. Purdy) | 3 |
| R. Craik's ch. g. Lennox, 6, by West Roxbury, dam by Joe Stoner, 160 lbs..........(Mr. Holmes and Mr. Alloway) | 0 |
| J. R. Harper's ch. f. Barrister, aged, by Judge Curtis, 160 lbs..........(Mr. Hunter) | |

Time—6:02.

Pools—Rose, $105; Lennox, $55; field, $50. Mutuals paid $11 30.

## ON THE ROAD.

There is not a city in the Union that possesses more natural requisites for good and safe driving than San Francisco, and yet that is so poorly provided for in that respect. We have an open road of easy access to the Park, and thence a fine drive to the ocean shore, but it appears that the expenditures needed for the preservation of the Golden Gate Avenue are largely in excess of the supplies, and that the necessary outlay on the Park and buildings does not admit of the disposal of a sum that would keep the roadways in fine order. This is parsimony that will not meet with the approval of our citizens, who all take a natural interest in the Park, rescued as it has been from arid, sandy dunes that border its pleasant, leafy, grassy mounds on either side, and who will witness its decay and ruin with feelings of intense disgust. The Golden Gate Park is an object of pride to both rich and poor. Alike they enjoy the view and fragrance of the lovely parterres of flowers, the green slopes of emerald, the leafy bowers, the fresh, balmy breeze, and in the distance, across the bay, the bold mountains bathed in a light, golden vapor, while far beyond are the dark blue tints of the ocean, speckled with the white wings of the world's commerce, hastening to and from the Golden Gate of the far West. There are two or three coigns of vantage from which one of the most lovely views, combining sea and landscape, can be seen, and on favorable days these are crowded with ladies and children, who, with their bright costumes, give bits of color to the rural scene of dwarfed trees and bosquets that are greatly pleasing to the eye. When they are tired of viewing this wealth of nature, they descend the hillocks, and seated on the grassy plats beneath the welcome shade of bright foliage, they watch with beaming eyes the various equipages that dash by with their merry occupants to and from the ocean shore.

The ladies who drive or ride prefer the morning hour, as then the wind is not so rough as it is likely to be in the afternoon; and from about 11 to 1 in the day may be seen skillful drivers and graceful equestriennes that might be compared successfully with their foreign sisters in Hyde Park or the Bois de Boulogne. In the afternoon, about 3 o'clock, the scene becomes very animated, especially on Saturday and Sunday, when countless teams of all kinds and descriptions come dashing around the curves with the ribbons held by men who are undisguised lovers of the speedy horse, and who are not reluctant now and then to have a friendly brush with a rival team when the lynx-like eyes of the officials are closed and the road is clear for the tussle.

It would be impossible to give a full account of the habitues of the road, but at random we note a few as they pass us at a clipping gait to and fro on the roads that are too hard for good driving:

Here comes Andrew Smith with his fine chestnut mare by Irvington, that can show 2:50, followed by William Cunningham, a slashing mare by Fred. Lowe, that although pleasant to drive, is yet somewhat faster. Next is John Hanna, with a big, stylish pair of bays to a neat rockaway, and then William Alvord, with his brown team that almost every day are so well known and admired on the drive. Driving quietly along, as if contented with himself and his surroundings, is Ned Fry; but look well at the points of that big bay mare before you test her speed in a brush, for although she is young and has no record, she can trot, so rumor says, well within the forties. Here is another clipper, one of the nicest on the road, a big brown horse, and Joe Marks is his proud possessor. Next comes the skillful amateur driver of the Pacific Coast, P. A. Finigan, who does not hesitate to enter the lists against the most noted professionals, and we cast an admiring glance at Don Elipher and mate as he dashes by. Another habitue of the drive is J. H. Tobin, with his bay and chestnut favorites, Sam and Dick, and then there is W. M. Starr, with his handsome and even-gaited mares, Black and Flora. Here are a trio that in speed are pretty evenly matched, showing about 2:40; D. E. Root with his chestnut mare by Inauguration; Charles Howe with a fine bay horse, and Mr. Bibbins with a brown slashing mare who can pull a road wagon at about the same gait. William Brown has a fine team in the Captain and the Major, but as they have not been seen on the road for some little time, the horses, like their chief, are probably on a furlough in the country. Lewis Nathan has a nice bay by Chieftain, that is as speedy as he is kind; in fact, he is the lady's horse of the road. Ex-Governor Stanford drives Occident and mate, he having disposed of Abe Edginton, and Charles Crocker has Lulu McCord and a gray colt that are fast and very stylish in appearance. One of the handsomest and best teams on the road are the chestnut and bay mares by Chieftain and St. Elmo, owned by Edward Barron, who is rather proud of the 2:40 they can show on a good road. There are Thomas Bailey and Charles Hendry, with nice and fast road mares; and E. J. Baldwin drives St. James and mate, fine looking horses, to a road buggy, when not speculating on the chances of Gano and Lucky B. at the City by the Lake. A change of description is necessary for the elegant Kentucky-bred saddle horse of C. H. Moore, that, bright white in color, is said to be one of the handsomest horses in the State. And so on for columns could we write down the finest and prettiest and fastest horses of San Francisco, but space forbids; and in conclusion we state that James G. Fair drives a pair of Chieftain bright bays; that Morris Smith has a brown mare and a black horse that he drives to a rockaway; that Mr. Wilkinson has a speedy mare, and that in Carrie F., by Irwin Davis, M. E. Gonzales has a young animal of great promise. Should the new road be laid out adjoining the Park, the number of private teams and driving horses would be quadrupled, so innate is the love of our rich citizens for animals of speed and lineage.

## THE SARATOGA RACES.

The latest dispatches from this delightful watering place state that owing to the absence of the principal Eastern stables, the racing there is very dull, and the attendance has fallen off to such an extent that for the interests of the turf the rivalry between Monmouth Park and Saratoga should cease at the conclusion of the present meeting. On August 3d, in the first race, one mile and an eighth, Bootjack was first; John Davis second; time, 1:55½. In the second race, three-fourths of a mile, George Kinney was first; Barnes second; time, 1:15. In the third race, one and a half miles, Frankie K. was first; Apollo second; time, 2:40½. In the steeplechase, full course, gentlemen riders, Post Guard won; Rose second; Charlemange third; time, 5:20.

On August 4th, in the first race, a mile and furlong, Monogram won; Tom Picket second; time, 1:57½. In the second race, for a mile and 500 yards, John Davis won; Creosote second; time, 2:13¾. In the third race for a mile, Terror won; Navarre second; time, 1:46½. In the fourth race, five furlongs, Baron, Favorst and Tarantalla (filly) ran a dead heat; time, 1:02¼.

On August 5th, in the first race, three-quarters of a mile, Little Phil won, Disturbance second; time, 1:15. In the second race, one and three-quarter miles, Glidelia won, Ben d'Or second; time, 3:01. In the third race, one and one-eighth miles, Charley B. won, Jenny V. second; time, 1:55. In the fourth race, steeple chase, one and a half miles, Turfman won, Tom Bush second; time, 3:05½.

On August 7th, in the first race, a three-quarter mile, Disturbance won; Minnie second; time 1:15. In the second race, one and one-quarter miles, Jim Nelson won; Faence second, Long Taw third; time, 2:11½. In the third race, one mile, Baby won; Churchill second. In the fourth, a hurdle race, one mile and five furlongs, Turfman won, Raven second, Bailey third; time, 2:16.

On August 8th, in the first race, three-fourths of a mile, Tocsin won; Bessie second; time, 1:18. In the second race, 1⅝ miles, Blazes won; Grange second; time, 2:52¼. In the third race, ¾-mile heats, Bonnie Lizzie won; Frankie B. second; time, 1:16½, 1:16. In the fourth race, one mile, Jennie won; John Sullivan second; time, 1:44½.

On August 9th, in the first race, one mile, Monogram was first, Stanton second, Crickmore third; time, 1:45½. In the second race, one mile and 500 yards, Warfield won, Force second; time, 2:21½; only two started. In the third race, three-fourths of a mile, Saunterer won, Col. Watoon second; time, 1:17. In the fourth race, one and one-eighth miles, Jennie V. won, Farragut second; time, 2:20¼.

On August 10th, in the first race, three-quarter-mile, Little Phil won, Springfield second, Square Dance third; time, 1:16. In the second race, two miles, Boatman was first, Apollo second; time, 3:34. In the third race, one and one-eighth miles, Adellen won, Monroe second; time, 1:55¾. In the fourth race, 1¼ mile, Bailey won, Annette second; time, 2:19.

The Olympia Fair and Races.—The Directors of the Washington Industrial Association announce that the annual fair to be held at their grounds, near Olympia, W. T., will commence on the 29th of August and continue through the week. The programme of races is as follows:

Tuesday, August 29th—Running race—Washington Territory stock; half-mile heats, best two in three; purse $150. First horse $120, second horse $30. Same day, trotting race for Oregon and Washington bred three-year-oles; half-mile heats, best two in three; purse $150. First horse $120, second horse $30.

Wednesday, August 30th—Running race—Single dash of a mile; $100; free for all. First horse $60, second horse $30, third horse $10. Trotting race same day—Three minute class; purse $100. First horse $75, second horse $25.

Thursday, August 31st—Parade of stock—Slow race—Pony purse race.

Friday, Sept. 1st—Grand running race, International—Free for all; mile heats; best two in three; purse $200. First horse $125, second horse $50, third horse $25. International trot—Free to all; best three in five; purse $200. First horse $150, second horse $50.

All entries for trotting races to close August 15th, at noon, by paying one-half the entrance money, the other half to be paid the day before the race. All entries to running races to close at 12 o'clock M. the day before the race. Ten per cent. entrance to each of the above races. In all cases three to enter and start. Non-thoroughbreds are allowed 10 lbs in all running races when thoroughbreds are running.

## THE AMERICANS IN ENGLAND.

Although our American friends carried off so many of the most coveted prizes of the English Turf last year, they, too, seem to have realized the fact of being born to trouble this year, for Foxhall's victory in the Gold Cup at Ascot can hardly be termed a symposium sufficiently satisfying to atone for disappointments experienced, even supposing that the interests of Mr. Keene and Mr. Lorillard were identical. As a matter of fact, however, a thoroughly sportsmanlike rivalry exists between them, and the blue and white spots as carried by Foxhall and Golden Gate, have thus far this season made a greater mark than the black and red hoops of the Iroquois stable. Gerald was a great disappointment, and Sachem, although he battled bravely in the Derby, has not, so far, proved a worthy substitute, judging by the two-year-old form of the pair. Mistake has been sold out of the stable, Iroquois has not been deemed fit enough to do battle, and the two-year-olds are either abiding their opportunity or are not as good as was hoped of them. Still the time may come, for our American cousins are as patient as they are astute, and we may find them "knocking about" to a merry tune as the back end draws nigh. When their day comes nobody will begrudge it them. Meanwhile Mr. Lorillard has marshalled his forces in another way in joining issues with our countrymen. This time, however, in the way of commerce rather than in sport, and though born to trouble this season, he seems determined to make the sparks fly upwards, independent of Gerald's bad temper, Iroquois' enforced retirement and the weakness of the two-year-olds. He, or rather I should say "they," for it is Pierre Lorillard & Co. of New York have joined forces with the famous firm of Cope Brothers and Hignet Brothers, Liverpool, and the Richmond Cavendish Company of the same little seaport town, for the supply of manufactured tobacco, cigars, snuffs, cigarreetes, etc., for home trade and exportation, and their works in Columbia Market, Bethnal Green, are a triumph of combined enterprise. So if Mr. Lorillard cannot make sparks fly upwards in one way this year, he means doing it in another, by the aid of that nicotine abounding plant, which a rough and ready poet in the days of Sir Walter Raleigh sang about in anti-Tennysonian strains as follows: "Tabacco is a curious weed; grows green in the morn and is cut down at eve. It shows our decay that our bodies are but clay."—*The Sporting Life.*

Charles Reed's yearling sale took place at the Saratoga race-track on July 31st. Eight lots realized an aggregate of $2,925, the highest price being paid for Queen of Hearts, by Highlander out of Countess, for which P. J. Flynn of Albany, N. Y., gave $925. The same gentleman got Jack of Clubs, by Highlander out of Helen, for $200. Milton Young's Lighthorse Harry, three years, by Enquirer out of Alice Wagner, was also sold to Mr. Flynn for $525; and his Lost Cause, three years, by King Alfonso out of Nellie Knight, to J. Donohue for $330; and B. McClelland's Explorer, four years, by Enquirer out of Slipper, to W. L. Cassidy for $175.

C. T. Harris, for some years connected with *Wallace's Monthly*, and a well known writer on horse topics, under the *nom de plume* of "Luke Clay," has taken charge of the trotting department of the *New York Sportsman*.

## RACING AT MONMOUTH PARK.

The racing season has been very prosperous thus far this ason at Long Branch, owing to the liberal purses that are ered by the management with such penalties and allowces that allow some of the second-rate horses to secure a tory now and then. The misfortunes of the California ble still continue as can be seen by the perusal of the oceedings on the 3d inst. This was the day on which re was a hope that at last there would be a turn in the g lane of their ill-luck, but the fates were once more inst our representatives.

The first race on the card was a handicap for two-years, a dash of three-quarters of a mile, for $500, in which re were eight runners, and as neither Gains, Grismer nor cky B. were entered, it may be supposed that they are der the weather. It was won by Maid of Athol in 1:20, th Bella second and Felicia third. The next race was a ndicap for a purse of $500, a dash of a mile, that was ten by Barney Lyon, with Victim second and Corsair rd; time, 1:50. Then came the important race of the y, of which we give the following description from the Y. *World:*

"The third race was the Elizabeth Stakes, for three-year-l fillies that had not won $1,000 at weight for age when o years old, the distance being a mile and a quarter. The e had winning penalty ond maiden allowance clauses, d five started at the following weights: Infanta and Amon, 113 pounds each; Sunday and Laura Glass, 110 pounds ch, and Miss Lumley, 106 pounds. Laura Glass was a ong favorite in both the books and pools. A good start s made, with Sunday in the lead, followed by Amazon, ura Glass, Infanta and Miss Lumley. As they passed the and Infanta had taken the lead, being three lengths before nday, who was a head in front of Laura Glass, she two ngths from Amazon, with Miss Lumley last. Rounding e turn Sunday had reduced the lead between the leader d himself to a length, and at the quarter was running a ngth behind Infanta and half a length in front of Laura lass. Sunday made strong play for the leader running wn the backstretch, and at the half mile was leading by lf a length, with Infanta second, four lengths in front of iss Lumley, while Laura Glass, who seemed unable to and the heavy going, had fallen back last. On the turn the three-quarters Sunday was leading by three lengths. t Infanta began closing up, reducing the distance to two ngths at the three-quarters and one length at the sevenriong pole. Infanta was rapidly closing up, and the two ere drawing away from the field. Infanta reduced the distance just enough to catch Sunday at the wire, the two aking a dead-heat, eight lengths ahead of Miss Lumley, ho was ten from Amazon; time, 2:21½. The owners deded to run the race off, which was done just before the eeplechase, Feakes being substituted for Gibbs on Sunday. nday got away first, but Feakes pulled her back, and ing around Infanta made the turn to the stand so wide at at that point six lengths separated them. From this int all interest in the race ceased. Some of the lost ound was made up, but Sunday was never afterwards able o appear even dangerous, Infanta winning easily by two lengths in a quarter of a second faster time than the deadheat, 2:21¼."

SUMMARY.

The Elizabeth Stakes, for three-year-old fillies that had not won a stake valued at $1,000 (handicaps and selling races not counting) when two years old, at $50 each for starters, with $1,500 added, of which $500 to the second; winning penalties and maiden allowances; entrance, $25 each, to the fund; 28 subscribers; mile and a quarter.

W. Jennings' b. f. Infanta, by King Alfonso, dam Queen Victoria, 113 lb, carried 115 lb ........................................(Costello) 1
E. J. Baldwin's b. f. Sunday, by Monday—Pell, 110 lb..(Gibbs and Feakes) 2
Snedecker & Co.'s b. f. Miss Lumley, by Leamington or Reform, dam Lady Lumley, 106 lb..............................(W. Donohue) 3
P. Lorillard's b. f. Amazon, 113 lb..............................(Feakes) 0
D. Colaizzi's ch. f. Laura Glass, 110 lb..............................(Ural) 0

Time—2:21¼.

Pools—Laura Glass, $35; Amazon, $19; Infanta, $16; the field, $10. Deciding heat: Pools.—Infanta, $110; Sunday, $100. Betting—2 to 1 on Infanta, and 6 to 5 against Sunday. Mutuals paid $45 90 and $7 75.

Of this same race the N. Y. *Tribune* remarks: "In the Elizabeth Stakes the notorious Laura Glass, an instrument of swindling at Brighton recently, was thought almost sure of success, but it is possible that her owner had had an inside view of some one's pocket before the race, for the filly ran as if she had drank too much water. Jennings' Infanta and E. J. Baldwin's California filly Sunday, made a close finish. Every one but the judges thought Sunday's head was in front, but it is the unexpected that always happens with judges' decisions at Monmouth, and it was declared a dead heat. For eccentricity in placing horses Monmouth has made a record this year never equalled anywhere. This extraordinary dead heat was run off and Infanta won."

This was not the only piece of ill-luck, for in the next race, the valuable Freehold Stakes, a mile and a half, the ground was so heavy from rains of the previous day that it is probable that Clara D. was not sent to the post on that account. It was won by Girofle, Eole second, Barrett third, and Monitor and Glenmore unplaced; time, 2:42. The other races deserve no further mention than was already given in the telegraphic dispatches of our last issue. Our horses may go to Sheepshead Bay, Coney Island, but if this wretched bad luck still continues it would be better to bring them back here where their presence will be so much missed.

---

Buffalo Races.—On August 3d, in the stallion race, Jerome Eddy and Black Cloud contested for a special purse to beat Smuggler's time, 2:15¼. Black Cloud took the first and second heats. Jerome Eddy was first in the third heat, but it was declared a dead heat, Jerome having run. The fourth heat was a dead one; time, 2:16¼, 2:18½, 2:20. The time of the third heat was not taken. The first heat was the fastest ever trotted by a stallion, except Smuggler. On the succeeding day they trotted two more heats, resulting in a victory for Black Cloud; time of the five heats, 2:16½, 2:18½, 2:19, 2:20, 2:18¼. Of this finely contested race the full description comes too late for our present issue. In the 2:20 class Adele Gould won, Fannie Wetherspoon second, Annie W. third. Early Rose—driver, Fred. Douglass—Humboldt and J. B. Morris also trotted; time, 2:20½, 2:19¼, 2:19, 2:19, 2:20½, 2:23¾. A special purse for named horses was won by Clingstone, Edwin Thorne second, Minnie R. third, J. B. Thomas and Kate Sprague distanced; time, 2:14¾, 2:16, 2:17¼. Edwin Thorne showed well in the race, and finished each heat close up. Little Brown Jug was brought out for exhibition at the close of the stallion race, but not being in the best condition, paced for half a mile, making it in 1:04.

## GROWTH OF COLTS.

In order to winter a colt well and have him come out a fine, showy, sturdy animal in the Spring, particular attention must be paid to his growth during the first Summer and Autumn. If the mare's milk is at all deficient to keep the colt in good flesh and thriving steadily, it is best to have recourse at once to cow's milk. Skimmed milk answers very well for this purpose, especially if a little flax-seed jelly, oil or cotten-seed meal is mixed with it. A heaped tablespoonful, night and morning, is enough to begin with, when the colt is a month old. This can be gradually increased to a pint per day, by the time it is six months old, or double this if the colt be of the large farm or cart-horse breed. Oats, also, may be given as soon as they can be eaten. Begin with a half-pint, night and morning, and go on increasing, according to the age and size of the animal, to four quarts per day. These, together with the meal above, should be supplemented with a couple of quarts of wheat bran night and morning. The latter is excellent to prevent worms, and helps to keep the bowels in good condition. Colts should not be permitted to stand on a plank, cement, paved, or any hard floor the first year, as these are liable to injuriously affect the feet and legs. Unless the yard where the colts run in the Winter has a sandy, or fine, dry, gravelly soil, it should be well littered, so as to keep their feet dry. Mud, or soft, wettish ground, is apt to make tender hoofs, no matter how well bred the colts may be. One reason why the horses in one district grow up superior to those in another in hoof, bone, muscle and action, is because it has a dry limestone or siliceous soil. When the mare is at work do not let the colt run with her; and if she comes back from her work heated, allow her to get cool before suckling the colt, as her over-heated milk is liable to give the foal diarrhœa.—*National Live Stock Journal.*

---

Was it a Cruel Hoax?—F. E. Pond, one of the editors of the *Turf, Field and Farm,* who was reported recently to have been drowned in Wisconsin, has returned safely to New York. Speaking of the report of his death, he said: "I do not understand how the story originated. One of the explanations that I have heard, though I cannot vouch for its accuracy, is that a guide named Dubois found a canoe that had been left on the banks of the Flambeau River by a man who had gone back into the woods. The canoe floated out into the stream and overturned in the rapids. I have heard that the man who left the canoe was named Bond, and it is possible that the name in passing from mouth to month got converted into Pond. At the time of the occurrence I was at Ashton, on Chequamagon Bay, seventy-five miles from Flambeau. I am still trying to arrive at the origin of the story, and if it was malicious I think the author should meet with some severe punishment. It was a serious matter for me, as my mother was ill at the time and the news might have proved fatal to her. My friends were very generally alarmed."

The American horses in England are not doing well, and a glance at their performances at the recent Goodwood meeting, as compared with former years, is not encouraging. In 1880 the Americans were in nine races and secured three firsts, viz: The Lavant Stakes, won by Iroquois; the Racing Stakes, won by Nereid; and the Molecourt Stakes, by Paw Paw. In 1881 they started in nine events, but won none, obtaining four seconds and one third. This year has been worst. Although Romeo, Sachem, Bookmaker, and Golden Gate all started, none got a place.

The duke of Hamilton is having a great run of luck on the turf in England this year, even if he is obliged to sell off all his pictures, library, and articles of vertu. At Ascot he won the valuable Alexandra stakes, beating Foxhall. At Goodwood recently be captured the much coveted Goodwood cup, with a despised outsider, Friday; the Corinthian plate with Thora, and the Lavant stakes with Export, and now he has won the Brighton cup with Fenelon.

From Milwaukee we learn that Dr. Ormond, who has St. Julien under treatment, says he was brought there while a little sick, but without any attempt at secrecy, four weeks ago, for treatment of a slight injury to the sheath of a ligament. The animal has been at work on the track every day but two since then, and to-day is as good as ever. Recently the owner refused an offer of $40,000 for him.

In consequence of its increasing circulation *The Breeders' Gazette* has enlarged its form, and now gives every week some timely illustrations. Mr. Otto Holstein, who was for a long time connected with the *Turf, Field and Farm,* has taken charge of the horse department, and as that gentleman is well acquainted with the subject, he will prove to be a valuable addition to the staff of the paper.

Messrs. Pulsifer & Scott's colt, Gunnar, the winner of the Illinois Derby, has temporarily broken down at Saratoga. Gunnar was to have run at Monmouth Park, August 15th, in the Omnibus Stakes, and he was much fancied for it. It is expected that he may be got ready for the Dixie Stakes to be run at Baltimore. Gunnar overreached himself, and is very lame.

On August 4th, at the Jockey Club track, in the race between Red Boy and Wildmoor for $10,000, for the best three in five, mile heats, Wildmoor won in three straight heats; time, 1:43½, 1:48, 1:46¼. Red Boy is engaged in some of the races during the circuit, and will meet our own best horses together with those of Oregon.

The best stallion records now are Smuggler 2:15¼, Jerome Eddy 2:16½, Piedmont 2:17¼, Black Cloud 2:17¼, Santa Claus 2:17½, and Robert McGregor 2:18, while Black Cloud has the three fastest consecutive stallion heats, 2:19¼, 2:18¼, and 2:17¼.

New York, Aug. 10.—At the Coney Island races to-day the three-quarters mile was won by Luke Fogle, Garfield second.

## ANSWERS TO CORRESPONDENTS.

PEDIGREE OF BELLE MASON.

In answer to several queries, we give the full pedigree and her foals up to 1877: Belle Mason, b. m., bred and owned by F. M. Slaughter, by Belmont; first dam Lucy Johnson, by The Pony (son of Leviathan); second dam Catalpa, by Frank; third dam by John Richards.

Produce: 1871—ch. f. Polly Lee, by Ten Broeck (son of Cosmo).
1872—b. c. Palisade, by Sacramento.
1873—b. c. Jo Hamilton, by Echo.
1874—b. f. Amanda Fortune, by Sacramento.
1876—b. c. Exile, by Echo.
1877—b. c. ——, by Echo.

Jo Hamilton is owned by G. Valensin of Arno Farm, Sacramento County, and Exile by J. B. Haggin, Rancho Del Paso.

---

Compton, Los Angeles County,
August 3, 1882.

Editor Breeder and Sportsman: Being a subscriber to your paper, will you kindly answer in your paper, under "Answers to Correspondents," the following question: In your paper of July 29, 1882, under "Echora," you mention Del Sur winning a heat against her at Sacramento in 2:24. Now, how can he start in the 2:25 race, August 5th, at the Bay District Races? Please answer and oblige

Yours, truly, Thos. S. Day.

Del Sur is credited in the "Trotting and Pacing Record" of 1881 as the winner of the second heat in the 2:25 class at Sacramento in 2:24. We were under the impression that .24 was his record, and in many instances have credited him with that figure. On making inquiries, we learn that the heat was given to Del Sur through Echora, who came in first, and Ashley second, being set back for running. This being the case, there was "no time" in the heat, and Del Sur stands with his record of 2:25, which he obtained when a four-year-old.

---

## A BULL'S HEAD BREAKFAST.

There are many ingenious methods by which a change from the usual dull routine of life is effected, without having recourse to a long voyage from our city haunts, and among them all the most enjoyable and amusing are the monthly festivities held by the Bull's Head Club. In almost every country we find stag parties organized, at certain intervals, to feast on the produce of the chase or stream. In Southern France the wild boar is yet chased, run down by hounds, and the head is considered a great dainty at the hunt dinners. In Switzerland and the Tyrol the chamois is allowed to be the delicacy of their huge repasts. In Belgium, at St. Hubert in the Ardennes, there is held every year a festival in honor of the Patron Saint of all good huntsmen, and there a young buck from the royal preserves is roasted whole, as unfortunately Rosalind, in the days of "As you like it," hunted down the last lion that haunted the ever-pretty glades of the Ardennes Forest. In England the boar's head was also esteemed a great delicacy, and the Bird of Paradise was arranged with such art and ingenuity that it appeared on the table cooked to a turn and yet clad in its gayest plumage.

From time immemorial great public or private hospitality was shown by roasting sheep and oxen in their entirety, on spits that revolved slowly over live coals. In this country the clam bake at Rhode Island forms the most enjoyable picnic of the season. In South Carolina the chief attraction of the reunion is the wild turkey, wrapped in wet mud and baked until the feathers come off. In Virginia the opposum is treated in the same manner, while in Kentucky and Tennessee the hunters disport themselves at huge barbecues, where all manner of game is offered in hospitable profusion. These meetings, with their traditions, are lost in antiquity, and it was thought that any novelty in this connection was not to be dreamt of. But here in San Francisco has been revived a custom that was very popular among the early settlers in California, and that is a Bull's Head Breakfast. In the vicinity of San Rafael, in one of the loveliest valleys of the State, is situated Laurel Grove, the headquarters of the Bull's Head Club. There are many traditions about this delightful place, of which the trees show conclusive evidence of antiquity, and for many years past the place was known for its exquisite Spanish cooking, as also for the dainty dish from which the club takes its name.

On Sunday, the 6th inst., there was the usual reunion held once a month through the Summer season, and about a hundred gentlemen assembled at the grove in acceptance of the hospitality of the members of the club. By some mischance or misunderstanding the *piece de resistance* was lacking, and no bull's head was to be watched with care, as it was cooking slowly among the bright embers in a small pit fitted up for this express purpose. Generally when the head is sufficiently cooked the pelt falls off and the flesh is found to be of the most juicy and tender flavor, and when accompanied by the hot Spanish sauce for which the cooks there are so celebrated, it is a repast fit for the monks of old, who were celebrated for their good cheer. In the absence of the usual bull's head, there were some huge joints on iron bars above the fire that were zealously basted, and these in conjunction with chicken fricassee cooked in the same Spanish mode, and large bumpers of an excellent vintage, were thoroughly enjoyed by all the gentlemen present. A novel feature in the rules of the club is that the members carve the viands and wait on their guests, and that with an assiduity and courtesy that deserve all praise. After the repast there was the usual round of songs and stories, and the pretty grove, with the sunlight glinting through the heavy foliage, rang again and again with merriment and applause. By the last boat the picnicers returned to the city delighted with their entertainments and profuse in their acknowledgments to their hosts, among whom Colonel W. P. Barnes, the President, Frank Murphy, the Secretary, ex-Senator T. McCarthy and N. Stiner, were prominent in their attention to the wants of their guests. The following were among the gentlemen invited on this occasion, together with the members, who were present, and in the future we predict that the reunions of the Bull's Head Club will be the most popular of any held on the Pacific Coast:

Hon. T. J. Bowers, Gustav Reis, Daniel Taylor, Hon. W. S. Hughes, Col. Daniel Norcross, Jno. W. Shaeffer, Col. A. H. Wands, Dr. Geo. Hubbard, Wm. T. Coleman, Jno. H. Gray, C. Van Dyck Hubbard, B. Hamilton, Wm. Kreling, R. E. Kelly, Col. A. Neumann, John Scott Wilson, John Kreling, Gen. Geo. Stoneman, Chas. A. Sumner, Chas. Sonntag, Harry Dam, Jas. A. Roach, Capt. Smith, Hy. Schmeideil, Charles Gildea, E. P. McCarthy, Capt. Williams, T. G. Cockrill, Wolff Falk, Messrs. Waterman, Eckert, Johnson, Walz, Dorcy, Wm. T. Porter, R. Hunt, Councilman More of Los Angeles, Mr. Dixon of Honolulu, Mr. McGrothy of London, Mr. Neilson of the *Examiner,* Henry Neiman, Percy Wilson, Mr. Gobe, Chas. Waters, Mr. Milne, Jno. R. Glasscock, A. Cheseborough, E. C. Marshall, and Mr. Greenberg.

# ROWING.

## AN AMBITIOUS WHERRY ROWER.

Tom Murphy of the Potrero has caused a flutter among the Long Bridge wherry rowers by his recent movements. For some time Thomas was lost in the seclusion of the neighborhood contiguous to Butchertown, and it was feared that the Select Beach had seen the last of his famous rowing craft. Last Sunday, however, Bob Goble, who was sweeping the Long Bridge course with his glass observed a strange oarsman flying down against the tide, and presently the figure developed into the once familiar presence of the Potrero sculler. Mr. Murphy was seated in his famous wherry, the Merrimac, but a year's hard work had effected a wonderful change in the proportions of that remarkable specimen of naval architecture. Her jib-boom, on which Thomas was wont to seek a Bermudan windsail, was gone, and her hurricane deck had disappeared. Her bulwarks had been cut down, and such a transformation accomplished in her general appearance that Henry Hussey fainted when informed that the abbreviated and dismantled craft was the once proud trophy of his skill. As the Potrero oarsman rushed down to the flock of the Pioneer boat-house, it was observed that the Merrimac had lost three feet of her beam, and was as thin as Louis White after six weeks' training. In answer to the excited inquiries, whether the celebrated racer had been run over by a freight train or flattened out by one of the rolling mills steam hammers, Mr. Murphy lifted up his somewhat husky voice towards the wharf.

"If any of you fellows think you can beat her trot out your wherries!" shouted Mr. Murphy, as he mopped his brow with his sleeve, and gasped after his hard pull against stream.

"I don't bar anybody," continued the Potrero oarsman, addressing the fringe of defeated Pioneer scullers that were dangling their legs over the stringer.

The bold challenge caused a flutter, but despite the presence of the Call's aquatic reporter, who stood, note-book in hand, ready to record the acceptance of the defi, none of the ex-champions offered himself as a sacrifice. White declined on the plea that Jim Roach had gone East to see Tug Wilson and taken his bottle of tincture of iron with him. Flynn cast a mournful look in the direction of the Ariel boathouse and muttered something about the exhausting labors of the "Fall campaign." Sullivan said he had determined to accept no challenger until a course with only one side to it (an inside) could be found:

"But there is Lyne," exclaimed all the defeated scullers; "He will row you too quick."

"There ain't a man on the bridge can row me too quick," retorted the modest Potrerian, as he dipped his sculls into the tide and flew towards home, the Merrimac leaving a streak of foam behind her that looked like the track of the big Transit.

The hopes of the Pioneer Club now rest on Mr. Lyne, but that sculler has so far resisted all efforts to get him into the race. His objection is that he has so far been unable to find any boat fast enough for him to "warm himself in." It has been explained to him that the great object is not to warm himself but Mr. Murphy; but still he hesitates.

DESERVING OF CREDIT.—The Ariel Rowing Club of San Francisco is not a very large or wealthy organization, but it is always to the front when there is anything to be rowed for. Some of the more pretentious clubs would add to their popularity if not to their laurels by following the example of the Ariels, who take defeat as quietly as they do victory, and never remain on shore because there is a doubt of their winning. The Ariel Club has already announced its intention of competing for the BREEDER AND SPORTSMAN'S Cup, which will be offered on Thanksgiving Day, and the possession of which will give the winners the title of Champions of the Pacific Coast. The Ariels have no boat fit to compete in the match, but will supply the want before the day of the race. There is a possibility of the Alert Rowing Club of Vallejo sending down a champion four to wrest the trophy from the metropolitan oarsmen. In former days Vallejo was famous for its oarsmanship, and can now, doubtless, get together a crew that will keep the best of our champions at full tension over a three-mile course. The two Stevensons would make the nucleus of a heavy crew and two other good men ought not to be impossible to find in a town so partial to aquatic sport. The appearance of a strange crew on the Bay would greatly increase the interest in the race, and make it by far the most important event of the kind ever decided on this coast. The Golden Gate crew have not decided whether to take part in the competition, but they talk of rowing the winners for $1,000. These high priced races rarely take place, and the oarsmen who show partiality for them place themselves under a reasonable suspicion of being more anxious to pose as champions in a newspaper column than to pull for the title in a boat. If four crews enter for the BREEDER AND SPORTSMAN'S Cup, any one of the competitors can easily invest $1,000 or twice the amount at advantageous terms, and if it should win, will, in addition to the bets, have the satisfaction of holding the Championship of the Coast, and a handsome trophy emblematic of the title. The Stockton Boat Club will, at its meeting to-morrow, consider the possibility of being represented in the regatta. The Pioneer Club, at its meeting last Sunday, decided to take part in the competition, and has already a crew in preparation.

## MORE KICKS THAN COMPLIMENTS.

It now appears that the American Amateur Association has decided to pay the expenses of the Hillsdale crew in England, and the Hillsdale Club has so informed its representatives. The indications now are that the Hillsdale four will remain in England all Summer, if necessary, and continue to submit themselves to metaphorical kicks, in their foolish eagerness to get in a match with some representative crew. It would be in far better taste for the Hillsdale crew to have quietly returned home, after the English Amateur Association had given such unmistakable evidence of its narrow-minded prejudice against Americans. It has been argued that the English Amateur Association is not a representative body, and that therefore the Americans are right in refusing to abide by its decision and refrain from thrusting themselves into regattas where they are not wanted. The facts at hand fully disprove this theory. If the Amateur Association be not a representative body, it has influence enough to keep every representative crew out of any regatta for which the Americans enter. On the 29th of July the Hillsdale four entered for the Barnes and Mortlake regatta, and the committee accepted the entry. It was then expected that at last the Americans were about to achieve their ob-

ject, by getting an opportunity to race with a representative English crew. On the 29th of July, however, the following item arrived by cable:

"The Hillsdale crew has withdrawn its entry for the Barnes and Mortlake races on account of the Thames and London Clubs refusing to row. The committee of the regatta has not changed its decision in regard to the acceptance of the Hillsdales' entry, and would have stated another crew, but the Hillsdales, under the circumstances, preferred to withdraw."

It is useless to argue in the face of such unpleasant facts that the English Amateur Association is not a representative body. It is unmistakably the exponent of the highest authority which English amateurs respect, and having set its face against the American four, the wisest and most dignified course for that crew to follow is the course across the Atlantic. It is not gentlemanly for any amateur to thrust himself into company where he is not welcomed, and the English association has shown that the room of the Americans is more desired than in their fellowship. Of such boorishness, if not cowardice, there can be but one opinion among all honorable sportsmen, and the Americans would only have strengthened the sentiment by returning home long since.

SUPPOSE THEY LOSE.—The cable brings the intimation that at last the hopes of the Hillsdale crew are to be crowned by admission to the charmed circles of English amateurism. The Sportsman reports a meeting of the English Amateur Rowing Association, to consider the replies from America relative to the status of the Hillsdale crew. The Association reported that satisfactory assurances in regard to the Hillsdale's position as amateur oarsmen were received as far back as Tuesday of last week. The answers being satisfactory and the over-sensitive Association being satisfied that the Hillsdales are not in the long category of the disreputables, our champions may soon be expected to show their mettle on English waters. And now comes the oppressive fear that, after all the recriminations and bandying of insulting epithets, the Hillsdales may row behind some inferior boat-load of Britishers. The race is not always to the swift, and stranger things than the defeat of a first-class by an ordinary crew have been written in the records of rowing. Racing on English rivers is very different from racing on American lakes, and it is quite within the range of possibility that the Hillsdales may not win their first important race, badgered and discouraged as they have been. While defeat under ordinary circumstances would not be disgraceful, defeat after all the howling and importunity that have been indulged in, would be little short of a calamity to American amateur oarsmen. Again we have to repeat that the management of the Hillsdales' interests in England has been very bad, and that American amateurs would have been the gainers in reputation had the champion crew packed up their oars and returned home the moment the English Association showed its unmanly determination to insult and discourage competitors from the other side of the Atlantic.

HANLAN SCULPING.—In the races between Boyd and Laycock, on the Tees, the first mile is alleged to have been rowed in 4 minutes and 45 seconds, and the full three and a half miles in 17 minutes and 38 seconds. Hanlan never put anything like this to his credit, and the London Referee says of the remarkable affair: "Were it not for his last race upon the Thames, we should now think Laycock was a worthy opponent for any one but Hanlan. Eighteen months or so ago it used to be said that if Laycock only possessed a turn of speed during the first mile or so, his wonderful force at the finish would enable him to hold his own with anybody. But theorists have had the ground cut from under their feet by means of the "challenge cup" competition, which casts considerable doubt upon what was done upon the Tees during the present week. If Boyd was the Boyd we used to know—and there is no reason whatever to doubt the fact—and if both were trying, then Laycock must have been poking fun at the Londoners the week before last. Boyd was admirably well served by the length of the Tees course and the swiftness of the current. It was supposed by those who knew best about rowing that he would jump away with the lead, and, served by the natural liveliness of the stream and the no less natural ease of the work, keep there until the goal was reached. As it happened, Laycock was there or thereabouts with him from the first dip of the sculls, was able to play with him before half a mile had been covered, and to go in front whenever he wanted. Here is a show of pace which I have no hesitation in saying Laycock has never made in this country upon any previous occasion."

IS HE A FRAUD?—The English sporting journals intimate pretty broadly that Laycock was mixed up in considerable "crookedness" during his late professional visit to England. Laycock's ill performances as honest races, they seem wholly inexplicable. On the Thames Laycock was rowed down by Largan, although Pearce and Laycock both appeared to be trying to pocket the English sculler, and beat him in that unfair style. The Referee, which is one of the most wide-awake of English sporting journals, comments as follows on the Australian's marvelous performance with Boyd: "On the show given by Laycock for the 'challenge cup' he could have had no possible chance against Boyd. If we are to judge by public displays, Boyd is a very much better man than Largan. Yet Largan rows Laycock to a complete standstill, though Laycock's great form is staring; and immediately afterwards Laycock completely outpaces Boyd in the first mile, though Boyd's best form is sprinting. Laycock had become heat that he has lost his previous staying power. Anyhow, a man who can row as he rowed Boyd on Monday last, providing everything was as it appeared to be, is a very different man from the man that even outsiders used to slip at the outset—a still more different man from the man who could not live a couple of lengths by the side of Largan."

DISPOSING OF THE DELINQUENTS.—The Pioneer Rowing Club, which has long been most lenient in the matter of collecting monthly dues, has taken a new departure. At the meeting last Sunday half a dozen members were expelled for non-payment of dues and at the next meeting the black list is likely to be again curtailed. Considering how moderate the fees of the rowing clubs are the penalty of expulsion is not too severe for highly pecunious individuals who attempt to use a club property without paying a cent for its muscles. There is always a lot of such barnacles attached to every rowing club, and as their presumption is generally proportionate to their uselessness, the sooner they are lopped off the better for the organization. Another club on Long Bridge was to have adopted the heroic method of dealing

with delinquents, but the absence of a quorum at the last meeting saved the close-fisted athletes for another week.

STEVENSON AND PETERSON.—Austin Stevenson, the present holder of the Pacific Coast Championship, and Henry Peterson of the Golden Gate Rowing Club, are likely to meet this year on the bay to decide the question of superiority. As far as Stevenson is concerned there is no trouble, his money is ready and it only needs the consent and the coin of the young waterman to bind the race. There is talk of having the race take place over the Long Bridge two mile course on the second Sunday in September.

# YACHTING.

## ENGLISH AND AMERICAN TYPES.

Under the head of "Shall we Burn our Yachts" the New York Spirit of the Times has a very sensible article from which we quote a few paragraphs, premising that we are sorry want of space forbids the whole article being reproduced.

The British cutter Maggie has won two races—one on July 4, at the Boston City regatta, when she defeated the Hesper by 1m. 56s. actual, and some 4m. corrected, time, and again at the regatta of the Eastern Yacht Club, when she was beaten by some seconds by actual time, and won by allowance of time. On the strength of these small margins of victory the cutter advocates have raised a wild shout of triumph, and our yacht-owners are adjured to sell their sloops for clam-boats and build cutters. Let us see if the advice is sound; and in the first place we will admit that in yacht-building speed should be the great desideratum; that cutters are no more to be called racing-machines than are our centreboard yachts; that racing-machines are most to be desired, and that as soon as it can be shown that the cutter is a more speedy racing-machine than the centreboard sloop we are prepared to throw our cap in the air, and hurrah for the cutter with the most noise. We have no pet theories to establish, no national prejudice to overcome, and simply desire the fastest and best yachts for American yachtsmen. Our native production of cutters has not as yet gained a record for speed sufficiently brilliant to warrant its continuance, but a couple of these boats imported from England have won a few races. Do these successes warrant the continued production of these boats? We think not. The Madge came last year, raced with our boats over courses unsuited to them, and when they were by no means in first class racing trim, and beat them. That these victories could not be repeated this year has been practically conceded by those who had the Madge in charge, in that they have refused to put her in commission or allow her to meet again her opponents of last year, although they knew that the owners of these boats had been put to great expense in getting them in condition expressly with a view to race with the Madge, and that this decision on the part of the Madge's agents was a sound one, is proven by the splendid performance of the Wave during the Seawanhaka Corinthian Club cruise, the sailing of the Schemer in the Seawanhaka match, and the performance of the Shadow at the recent regatta of the Eastern Yacht Club.

It may then fairly be assumed that in the opinion of those who had charge of the Madge, either of the boats which she defeated last year could this season have beaten her, and in this opinion we fully coincide. Surely this experience of the Madge will not warrant us in building cutters, a type of craft notoriously unsuited to our waters, uncomfortable and extremely expensive. While prepared to advocate their wholesale production, if it can be shown that they are the fastest boats, we must insist that, unless it can be shown that they are most speedy, the manifest advantages of our beamy centreboard boats in other respects are so great that we ought by no means to change or search for the Madge. Now for the Maggie. She came to this country with the reputation of being "the best fifteen-tonner that ever flew a racing flag in British waters." So fast was she that for a long time no fifteen-tonner would sail against her, and she has had to sail in the twenty class, or sail against some of the recently built ten-tonners, classed such by a jugglery of measurement, but which are really fifteens, and to whom the Maggie had to give so much time that they were able to compete with her.

Now she beats the Hesper, a boat which, according to her designer, was but in cruising rig, a minute and fifty-six seconds in a twenty-mile race. All experienced yachtsmen know that the Vixen, the Fanita, or the Regina could have beaten the Hesper much more than that, and if the record of the Maggie proves anything, it proves that she could have beaten every other fifteen-tonner of Great Britain more than she beat the Hesper. What, then, is proved by this race? Clearly, that the Hesper, a second rate, could have beaten every fifteen-tonner in Great Britain except the Maggie. Surely then the argument against our building cutters on account of their speed is conclusive by as much as the whole number of cutters in Great Britain is to one.

We were not present at this race. We are not advised as to the time allowance, except that it was based on load line length, which, of course, was in favor of the cutter, her overhang, which was not taken into account, being much greater than that of the Hesper, but we are willing to assume that it was a fair and square race in every way, and that the Maggie, the best fifteen-tonner that ever beat in England, beat a second-rate American boat in 50s. All that has been shown by this race, or that of the Eastern Club, is that the Maggie, the best fifteen-tonner that ever was in England, is about as good as our second-rates of our size. Surely this is not very encouraging to the cutter building business, nor is there, we humbly submit, anything to justify the panic of triumph which has been raised by the Anglophobists, who lose no opportunity of sneering at the honest work of American mechanics, and praising to the skies all that is English.

At a recent meeting of the New York Yacht Club, Mr. Charles Minton, the Secretary, made a statement regarding the financial condition, from which it appeared that, notwithstanding the extraordinary expenses of last year's cruise and for defending the America's Cup, the Club was out of debt and had a large balance in the treasury. Mr. Minton was earnest in recognizing the necessity for a club house on the bay and a common club anchorage, and believed an inexpensive plan could be devised to meet this want. His remarks on this topic evidently met with much favor from the members present, and there is no doubt but that a committee will be appointed at the next meeting to report a plan by which this result may be effected.

The Chispa has been having her trunk, etc., painted.

The Virgin now has her moorings below bridges in Oakland Creek.

The "one gun start" does not seem to be as popular East as some of its advocates hoped it would be.

At the pennant race of the Larchmont Yacht Club, last week, some $4,000 or $5,000 was wagered on the result.

The frame of Spreckels' new yacht will be up in a few days at Capt. Turner's yard. The keel is set and timbers being prepared.

The Lillie was out on Saturday night with a party of ladies from Oakland, Capt. Cummings being in charge. They returned Sunday afternoon.

In the New York Yacht Club, steam launches of forty feet water line and over, belonging to members, may, upon application to the Secretary, obtain authority to carry the Club signal, but they shall not be entitled to any other privileges. Such application shall contain style, dimensions and horse-power of engines.

The Bohemian Yacht Club will open its club-house at New Saucelito shortly. The paper hangers and decorators are at work there this week. When the opening arrives all the yachtsmen will be invited, and a general good time is expected. The "owl flag" will float from the flagstaff surmounting the club-house.

A good sign of prosperous Eastern yachting is that yachtmen who really love the sport have taken to the open sea. This class of yachtmen will want a "ship" to go in, able to stand the sea and not run for the nearest port upon the approach of bad weather. This accomplished, and yachting becomes a sport worth indulging in. On this coast we have always had boats of this sort.

The schooner Ariel is creating a great deal of talk by her improved sailing since Capt. Turner took her in hand. He has made various improvements, and she has been walking away from some of the flyers since then. Last Sunday she astonished a good many yachtsmen. She now carries a Bermudian mainsail, the long gaff having been taken down.

Arrangements are being made for a race on Admission Day, September 9th, by the Pacific Yacht Club. They hope to have all the large yachts in the bay compete. There is no reason why a first-class regatta could not be arranged except the apathy of owners of yachts. Those with the fastest yachts are willing to go into regattas, but those with second-rate speed do not care to take the trouble. It is to be hoped the Pacifics will succeed in getting up a good race.

Commodore John Eckley is going from his ranch on Carquinez Straits up to Sacramento in the little Dolphin, but is going as a passenger. His boys, Johnny, Frank and Henry, are the yachtsmen of the party, and invite their father to join them on the cruise. The accommodation of the Dolphin being somewhat limited, the party will camp out at night ashore, but this is readily done when once past the lower part of the river. They will go up by way of the old river, where there is plenty of fruit, and expect to have a jolly time. The Dolphin is 16 feet long only, but is a smart little boat.

The Lolita has gone to Oakland Creek to be cleaned. Capt. Chittenden keeps his tidy little yacht moving so much she does not get a chance to foul much, but still needs an occasional cleaning. The Lolita does as much cruising as all the rest of the fleet together. Her owner thinks no more of a sail up to Antioch than most people do of going to Saucelito. He will start at a moment's notice for Napa, Suisun or Sacramento, and be all ready for it too. The boat's accommodations and rig are for convenience, and the Lolita is a favorite with those who sail in her. During the Winter months she is kept in Suisun marshes, in the duck hunting grounds.

A Good Rule.—The New York Yacht Club makes the yacht owners give a model of their boats to the club. The rule is as follows: "The model of every yacht entered for a regatta shall be the property of the club and retained in its possession, and no person other than a United States naval constructor shall be permitted to copy it, except he shall have obtained written authority from the owner of the yacht, nor shall it be removed without authority from the secretary of the club, who shall keep in a book provided for that purpose a record of same with full particulars relating to each model and to any changes that may be made. All models to be on a scale of three-eights of one inch to the foot for all yachts of eighty feet water line and over, and of one-half of one inch to the foot for all yachts under eighty feet water line; but this rule as to scale shall not necessarily apply to any model in the possession of the club at the time of the passage of this by-law."

# ATHLETICS.

## THE FALL MEETING.

At the meeting of the Board of Management of the O. A. C. last week, it was decided to give an athletic meeting September 23d, most of the events to be open to all. It was deemed unadvisable to set the date for the 9th, as other attractions were too numerous on that day to warrant a good audience or a sufficient number of entries in the events to make the day as interesting as it should be. The officers, however, have demonstrated their ability to carry out the programme of twenty-five events in less than two hours and a half, and as Saturday afternoon is virtually after business hours with the admirers of athletics, it is not necessary for the club to wait until the next holiday (Thanksgiving Day) to give a meeting. The list of events will be posted in the club shortly, and it is hoped that entries will be numerous from all the clubs on the coast. Members of the club are very anxious to meet the University athletes, either in scratch or handicap events, and as almost every event will be open, and necessarily a handicap to ensure a large number of entries, the odium of being faint hearted will fall on the absentees. Judged by the performances of the athletes at the last few meetings, the University leads at weight putting, and in the one mile run, and possibly at hurdle racing; but the O. A. C. can give them long odds in all sprint races, jumping and pole vaulting. The Golden Gate Club is anxious to enter for the tug of war, but it is doubtful if there is backbone enough in the other clubs to compete against them. There is material enough in the O. A. C. from which to select teams of either of the three standard weights capable of defeating anything on the Coast, but the ambition to do the work and sustain the reputation of the club seems to be lacking among the members of the present day. The Lacrosse Club has been organized but a short time, but their entries promise to be more numerous, in proportion to membership, than any other club on the Coast. Before the meeting takes place, an election will be held in the O. A. C. for a new Board of Management, and the next year's officers will have but little time to prepare themselves for the event, but they will undoubtedly realize the importance of the occasion, and attend to their duties with an enthusiasm that will ensure an entertainment that will sustain the past reputation of the Club.

Haley's Attempt to Beat the Record.—R. S. Haley failed to do even time last Saturday. The day and track were good, and Bob watched the starter very carefully. The starter also watched Bob carefully, and the numerous attempts to beat the pistol were useless. The entire management of the event was very bad. Of the three watches provided for the occasion, only one was reliable. Haley was allowed three trials, and in each one he went over the mark two or three times, and was not once penalized. He ran the first trial alone, and was credited with doing 10¼. In the second and third trials Wm. C. Brown, with a liberal handicap, coached him up to within a few yards of the tape, dropping back each time at the finish to allow Bob to get the time. However his running showed very plainly that he lacked preparation, and he is probably well satisfied that he did not do better than 10 1-5. With proper training, he will be in better form at the September meeting, and may possibly do even time then. *Quien sabe?*

Another World Beater.—An athlete in Bodie is reported as having put a weight of 13½ lbs., 45 feet 1 inch easily, and is confident of doing much better with a little training. That is within the possibilities; but when we hear of his putting 21½ lbs. 35 feet 8 inches without much effort, we scent a country performance. As a friend at our elbow remarks, "the woods are full of them." It is like the 9¾ sprinters all over the coast. They are invariably beaten in a jog by 11 second men when the watches are held by competent timers.

# BICYCLING.

The Emblems of Success.—Considerable discussion has been going on both in England and in the United States during the present season, as to the propriety of giving expensive prizes for bicycle racing and other athletic sports, many holding that the prizes should be of a nominal value, and that the honor of winning should be sufficient for the aspiring athlete. It is, however, contended upon the other side that in order to attract the best talent when a race meeting is held, it is necessary to make the prizes of such a value that it will be worth the effort to win them. The expenses of training, too, are somewhat heavy, and the traditional laurel wreath is not thought by the present generation to be a sufficient compensation for the fatigues they undergo in the preparation or contest.

It may, however, be very pertinently asked, what difference can the value of the prize matter to the amateur, since he is not allowed to sell it? The fact that he has a finer medal to wear or piece of plate for his side-board does not help out his training expenses; and we cannot help thinking that there must be passing through the minds of those who argue from the contestant's standpoint, the possibility of realizing the coin value at some future time. We are very much afraid that, beneath all, there is a more or less pronounced mercenary or professional view, which is only held in check and prevented from actively cropping out by the social ostracism threatened by a strict amateur law. There is at least one sport pursued in this city in which the participants do not attempt to disguise the fact that they contend for money prizes, and hardly one of the numerous challenges which are published weekly but states a sum of money to be put up.

A Mr. and Mrs. Williams rode a double tricycle 102¾ miles in a day recently in England. Good proof of the practicability of the vehicle.

From appearances the champion who has this season been reposing on his laurels will soon have to come out of his retirement or give up the position.

The Fall meeting of the Athletic Club and the wheelmen promises to bring out some speedy riders, and is likely to show some seconds less than last year's record.

Lincoln Park has been opened to Chicago wheelmen probationally for thirty days, and there is practically no restriction against them to-day in that city. Last year at this time they had only the streets.

New England bicyclists find that the trip to the White Mountains in New Hampshire is feasible, and that even in that mountainous country there is much good wheeling; and the leisurely trip allows plenty of time to enjoy the scenery.

One of our most successful racing men is also one of the most unfortunate in his practice, having recently met with a severe accident while speeding through the Park in company with a fast horse. A sprained knee and an extensive gravel rash are the result.

On the final day of the Golden Gate Fair at Oakland Park, Saturday, September 9th, the management announce a bicycle race, a dash of ½ mile, free for all, for a purse of $50, of which $35 to the first and $15 to the second rider. Nominations to be made with the Secretary on the first day of the Fair.

The monthly run for the gold and silver medals of the Salt Lake Bicycle Club took place recently, when the gold medal was won by Wm. Jennings, who rode one mile in 3m. 20s. The silver medal was won by James Woods, in 3m. 36½s. A ten-mile race the same day was won by Jennings in 40 minutes.

Bicycle riding is again coming into vogue for exhibition purposes. Mr. Charles A. Merritt, the proprietor of the Sea Beach Palace Hotel, Coney Island, has made arrangements for a six-day bicycle race, to take place on the hotel grounds, beginning to-day. Mlle. Louise Armaindo and Miss Elsa Von Blumen will ride alternately for six hours each day against William J. Morgan, the champion bicycle rider of Canada.

Miss Lulu Montrose, an equestrienne claiming to hail from Colorado, on the afternoon of July 29, rode twenty miles on a half-dozen horses, being allowed to change at will, against R. G. Beazely and J. S. Mellon, both riding bicycles alternately, at the Park Garden, Providence, R. I. The soft track was much better for the horses than it was for the machines, and consequently the bicyclists found themselves badly handicapped, Miss Montrose completing her twenty-five miles in the announced time of one hour and thirty-four minutes, which was probably correct. The bicyclists were beaten twenty-six laps.

# BASE BALL.

## THE HAVERLYS AND THE NIANTICS.

With the exception of a somewhat too boisterous wind the weather was quite favorable at the Recreation Grounds last Sunday, and the match between these two clubs attracted a very good attendance. Owing to the fact that two of the best men in the Haverly team were absent the Niantics indulged in the idea that for once they could get away with their redoubtable antagonists; but the theatre boys started with six runs in the first two innings, and although the Niantics scored four in third inning, the Haverlys finally won by ten to nine. The game was wonderfully well contested, and to the last it appeared doubtful on which banner victory would perch, and the interest was so well maintained by the general good play that there will be a far better attendance when the same clubs again come together on the diamond field.

CALIFORNIA.

| | T.B. | R. | 1.B. | P.O. | A. | E. |
|---|---|---|---|---|---|---|
| Meegan, p | 5 | 1 | 1 | 1 | 13 | 0 |
| J. Carroll, s. s | 4 | 3 | 1 | 1 | 1 | 1 |
| Lawton, l. f | 4 | 2 | 0 | 0 | 0 | 1 |
| Levy, c. f | 4 | 1 | 1 | 1 | 0 | 1 |
| F. Carroll, c | 4 | 0 | 0 | 13 | 0 | 1 |
| Corbett, r. f | 4 | 0 | 0 | 2 | 0 | 0 |
| McCord, 3d b | 4 | 1 | 1 | 1 | 2 | 0 |
| Gagus, 2d b | 4 | 1 | 1 | 1 | 0 | 2 |
| Pratt, 1st b | 4 | 1 | 0 | 7 | 1 | 0 |
| Totals | 37 | 10 | 5 | 27 | 17 | 6 |

NIANTICS.

| | T.B. | R. | 1.B. | P.O. | A. | E. |
|---|---|---|---|---|---|---|
| Emerson, 3d b | 5 | 1 | 1 | 0 | 2 | 2 |
| McVey, 1st b | 5 | 1 | 0 | 1 | 1 | 0 |
| Donahue, s. s | 5 | 1 | 1 | 1 | 2 | 0 |
| Arnold, c. f | 4 | 2 | 0 | 0 | 0 | 2 |
| Egan, l. f | 4 | 0 | 0 | 1 | 0 | 1 |
| Finn, c | 4 | 1 | 1 | 13 | 3 | 3 |
| Incell, r. f | 4 | 1 | 3 | 0 | 0 | 1 |
| Sweeney, p | 4 | 2 | 2 | 1 | 14 | 1 |
| Fogarty, 2d b | 4 | 0 | 0 | 1 | 0 | 2 |
| Totals | 39 | 9 | 8 | 18 | 22 | 12 |

| Innings | 1 | 2 | 3 | 4 | 5 | 6 | 7 | 8 | 9 | |
|---|---|---|---|---|---|---|---|---|---|---|
| California | 2 | 4 | 0 | 0 | 1 | 0 | 3 | 0 | 0 | —10 |
| Niantic | 0 | 0 | 4 | 0 | 0 | 2 | 0 | 2 | 1 | — 9 |

Earned runs—Niantic 1. Home runs—Incell and McCord. Three-base hit—Levy. Two-base hits—Gagus and Emerson. Bases on errors—Niantic 8, California 6. Base on balls—Niantic 1, California 1. Left on bases—Niantic 1, California 1. Double plays—Pratt 1, Gagus and Carroll. Struck out—Niantic 9, California 8. Wild pitch—Sweeney 1, Meegan 1. Passed balls—Carroll 2, Finn 2. Umpire—Piercy of the Renos. Scorer—Waller Wallace. Time of game—Three hours.

The Renos and Haverlys will try conclusions next Sunday at the same grounds.

On the same afternoon, at the Oakland grounds, there was a very one-sided match between the Underwriters Club and the Olympics, in which the former had to enter on their books "wrecked, and a total loss," the scores being thirty-seven to five. The Olympics are improving rapidly, their batting especially deserving notice; but they never could have scored so rapidly if the fielding of their adversaries had been of a less demoralized character. There is some excellent material among the members of the Underwriters Club that would be speedily developed with more practice.

## THE LEAGUE CHAMPIONSHIP.

With July ends the first three months of the League championship campaign. Three of the eight League Clubs are closer in the pennant race than in any other League campaign since the association was organized. Up to date, July 31, two hundred and thirteen games have been played of the championship series. In 1881 the first three clubs on the list at this date were the Chicago, Buffalo and Detroit, Cleveland being next, Providence fifth, Boston sixth, Worcester seventh and Troy last. The two last clubs are still at the tail end, but Buffalo has lost ground considerably, while Providence has gained in proportion. Up to date Chicago holds the lead by having the best percentage of games, having one defeat less than Providence, while Detroit is two victories behind both Chicago and Providence.

The full record of the championship to July 31 is as follows:

| Clubs. | Chicago | Providence | Detroit | Boston | Cleveland | Buffalo | Troy | Worcester | Won |
|---|---|---|---|---|---|---|---|---|---|
| Chicago | .... | 4 | 8 | 4 | 7 | 2 | 4 | 4 | 33 |
| Providence | 2 | .... | 4 | 5 | 3 | 3 | 8 | 8 | 33 |
| Detroit | 4 | 2 | .... | 2 | 6 | 7 | 4 | 6 | 31 |
| Boston | 2 | 5 | 4 | .... | 4 | 4 | 2 | 5 | 28 |
| Cleveland | 2 | 3 | 3 | 2 | .... | 6 | 4 | 6 | 26 |
| Buffalo | 6 | 3 | 2 | 2 | 5 | .... | 2 | 5 | 25 |
| Troy | 2 | 3 | 2 | 6 | 2 | 4 | .... | 6 | 25 |
| Worcester | 3 | 1 | 0 | 5 | 0 | 1 | 3 | .... | 12 |
| Games Lost | 20 | 21 | 23 | 26 | 27 | 27 | 28 | 41 | 213 |

Thus far it will be seen that the Chicago, Providence and Detroit Clubs are the only ones that have won a majority of their series with all of their opponents, Providence leading in this respect, having won eight games out of twelve with the Troy and Worcester Clubs. Chicago has won eight out of twelve with Detroit thus far, and seven out of twelve with Cleveland; and Detroit seven out of twelve with Buffalo.

One of the best games of the contest was played at Cincinnati on the 31st of July between the Cincinnati and St. Louis teams. The Cincinnatis scored one run in the first inning, and that run won the game for them, as not another was scored, the score standing 1 to 0 at the close of the ninth inning.

# BILLIARDS.

One of the chief attractions of the coming Fair at the Mechanics' Institute will be a billiard tournament for prizes offered by the Brunswick & Balke Co. It will greatly revive the interest in this pretty and healthful game, as the best players on the coast will be represented on this occasion.

# Breeder and Sportsman.

PUBLISHED WEEKLY BY THE

BREEDER AND SPORTSMAN PUBLISHING CO.

THE TURF AND SPORTING AUTHORITY OF THE PACIFIC COAST.

OFFICE, 508 MONTGOMERY STREET

P. O. Box 1886.

*Five dollars a year ; three dollars for six months; one dollar and a half for three months. Strictly in advance.*

MAKE ALL CHECKS, MONEY ORDERS, ETC., PAYABLE TO ORDER OF BREEDER AND SPORTSMAN PUBLISHING CO.

*Money should be sent by postal order, draft or by registered letter, addressed to the "Breeder and Sportsman Publishing Company, San Francisco, Cal."*

*Communications must be accompanied by the writer's name and address, not necessarily for publication, but as a private guarantee of good faith.*

JOSEPH CAIRN SIMPSON, - - - - Editor

SAN FRANCISCO, - SATURDAY, AUGUST 12, 1882

## THE FAIRS.

The entries in the purses of the California State Agricultural Society, Golden Gate, San Joaquin Valley, San Mateo and Santa Clara Fairs will be found in this paper. The others, we have, do not come when the last forms were sent to press, but from the grand showing which is made by those which are given the inference is that all will make a good display. Santa Cruz is the only fair which will take place until after another issue of this paper, and we learn that in the 2:25 class are Starr King, Del Sur, Crown Point, Sweetness and Cairo. It is not safe to predict what the outcome of this race will be, though it is absolutely certain that the race will be a good one. It is to be decided on the opening day of the meeting, and on the next day there is a running race, dash of a mile, and in it are May D., Kitty Cromwell, Sister to Lottery, Mollie H. and Night Hawk. This is also sure to be a lively affair, and on the following day the trotters Rowdy Boy, Slim Jim, Frank and Big Lize will contend in the 2:40 class.

The fourth day is the red-letter one of the series; as two running races are on the card, the first heats of a mile, with Belshaw, Trouble, Kitty Cromwell, Sister to Lottery and Haddington in. As it is a selling race, the weights are likely to equalize the chances, and bring them all in a ruck in every heat. The second race is heats of half a mile, with Quien Sabe, Bay Charlie, Mollie H. and Night Hawk in. In the 2:30 are Poscora Hayward, Blackmore and Sweetness. This is all that we have learned regarding the Santa Cruz purses, though, doubtless, if any of them have not filled others will be substituted.

The other exhibitions will be subsequent to the issue of the next number of the BREEDER AND SPORTSMAN, and in that we will give a description of the most noted of the entries, with a synopsis of their previous performances. That the list foreshadows a series of brilliant meetings is beyond dispute, and we have not the least hesitation in predicting the finest sport ever witnessed on this coast, and this without a break, as many of the horses in the various classes are so nearly balanced that it is more than probable that there will be fluctuations, and such close contests that the winners at one place will be forced to take rear positions at others. Occasionally a horse comes out which is so far superior to his class that he goes clear through the circuit without suffering defeat. Overman gives promise of being one of that description, and after defeats in the Spring, he trots second in Cleveland and wins at Buffalo and Rochester. It was prophesied that Vanderlynn would never lose a heat in the classes he was eligible for, and yet in his first race he is forced to succumb in a third heat to a horse which was rated many degrees below him. And so the chances are favorable all through the circuit for kaleidoscopic changes. Though the 2:22 class is restricted to three entries, who can say which of them is entitled to the preference? And from the best of all tests, viz., that which each has shown in public, it would be a confident man who would back one and give any odds against the others. Already there has been an intimation of the glorious uncertainty in the 2:25, and before the sun of

Saturday sinks beneath the Pacific, the question may be still more complicated. All through the list the same blindness prevails, and the only place we would hazard a prediction is—is—is, well, Wildflower, in the Occident Cup; and as there is an old saying that "there is many a slip between the cup and the lip," even that might be an unverified prediction.

By the way, the last payment in the Occident Stakes must be made to-day. The conditions are that the last $50 must be paid thirty days before the Fair, and as that opens on the 11th of September, the 12th of August is the date to make good the previous payments. Scan the entry list, and there will be few who will differ with us that there could scarcely be a more auspicious showing.

## THE PARK DRIVE.

Coming from the races on the Bay District Course on Saturday evening last, the beauty of portions of it made a vivid impression, probably far greater than the regular visitor feels, although the quiet loveliness could not fail to afford pleasure to any one save perhaps those who had backed Sweetness and Starr King. The sun was half buried in the far-off western horizon when we turned to come to the eastward, and there was a broad path of glory on the smooth surface of the Pacific. A few hours before there was a lively breeze. A fog bank was settling to the north of the Straits, and Mount Tamalpais was crowned with a hood of pearl-colored vapor. With the going down of the sun came calmness, and the eager and nipping air of midday had given place to a milder atmosphere. The grass was greener in the softened light, and the bevys of quails were twittering under the evergreens. There was an aroma from the flower-beds which added to the gratification; and if the horse had not been so anxious to reach the quarters where his night feed awaited him, there would have been nothing to mar the harmony of the drive. Five hours in the sheds had whetted his appetite, and as we had delayed starting until the throng had gone, the roads were clear; the policemen had vanished, and the horse seemed to be aware that there was nothing in the way to prevent him going at a forty gait, if even he was incumbered with the avoirdupois of two "middle-weights." Clank, clank, came the steel-shod hoofs on the hard surface, the sound as clear as is heard from the anvil when the shoes are forged, echoing from among the shrubbery a regular cadence, distinct as metal coming in contact with nearly as hard a surface could produce. It is not surprising that there was a shortening of the stride, and that the long, open gait became quickened, the stroke accelerated, for there was a high spirit impelling the rapidity of motion, if even there was a stinging pain in consequence of the concussion.

What a grand place for a saunter among the green knolls, and the bright colors of the flowers, the chirruping of quails, and the background of placid water! This is eminently the proper ground for the stately coach-horse, or the one staid animal with a ton weight of humanity in the family wagon; but for the pride of the whole country wherever the Stars and Stripes are the emblem, the peerless American trotter, it is a snare and a delusion. The red, smooth surface appears favorable; the wheels glide over it without a jar, and not a great deal of strength is necessary to move the load at a fast pace. The penalty is sure to come, however, and the spirited horse of yesterday leaves his stable on the following day with swollen limbs and fevered feet.

While the horse was beating the Anvil Chorus in his homeward flight, we ruminated over the change which would follow the building of the proposed drive. Several gentlemen were discussing the scheme on the balcony of the Club House, and we were pleased to hear that the project met with the heartiest approbation—not a dissenting voice to throw cold water on the project. One who has abundant means to gratify every wish, stated that when the drive was determined upon he would be on hand with as fast a team as any one, provided

they could be bought. There will be the same emulation to excel as there is in the Eastern cities, and ten horses purchased where one is all that the market demands at present. Those who desire to enjoy fast driving are only a *small* proportion of the numbers which will be benefited, and though breeders, dealers and stablemen will obtain the most direct pecuniary benefit, the advantages will be shared by thousands who are outside these ranks. In fact, it will be of such general benefit that all will feel the good effects. This portion of the question will require an article, or rather a series of them, to properly demonstrate how general the accruing benefits will be.

## YACHT RACING.

People often ask the question why we do not have more yacht races here. Why, with a fine bay, steady, strong breezes, a good course and fine yachts, no more races are announced.

There are several reasons for this. In the first place, it is a very expensive thing to get a yacht in order for a race. The expense goes up into the hundreds of dollars and sometimes to the thousands. A fine large yacht, with a reputation for speed, must have new sails for a race, new gear, must be overhauled, have a professional crew, go on the dry dock, and have money spent right and left on her. Expenses of running a yacht are heavy enough at any time, but on such occasions they are largely increased.

Again, the comparative standing of the yachts is pretty well known. If a general regatta of all yachts on the bay were to come off all the yachtsmen know that either the Nellie, Chispa or Aggie would take the first prize. These three yachts would be the first three in at all events. The interest of the spectators would be centered on them. Now, owners of other yachts do not care to swell the procession to the glory of others. They do not want to go to the expense and trouble of preparing for a race when they know they have no chance to win. Some go in for the sake of the people who get up the regatta, but any reasonable excuse will be taken advantage of to keep out if possible.

A very potent reason, too, among yacht-owners for not entering their craft is the free criticism indulged in. A man may enter his yacht to oblige his club in filling up a regatta, knowing well beforehand she cannot hope to win. When he comes in behind he has the doubtful pleasure of seeing his yacht and himself freely criticized by the would-be critics, and his favorite vilified as a mud scow or wood barge, while his skill is ignored, and all manner of fun poked at him by men who can handle a pencil, but do not know starboard from port. One or two seasons give the most enthusiastic as much as he wants of this. On regatta days, therefore, he saves himself the expense, annoyance and trouble, and goes as a looker on instead of a participator.

We know this is not the general understanding of these things, but it is true nevertheless. Again, the owners of speedy yachts do not care to risk the reputation of their boats unless there is good reason for it. Some will not sail unless there is money up. Others will not sail if money is up. Some will not let their yachts sail unless certain men will sail them. Others will not enter if other yachts are sailed by professionals.

And so it goes. There are objections of all kinds brought. And after all the arrangements for a regatta are made one after another backs out, and the committee are forced to see half a dozen yachts start, when more than double the number ought to go. This is true in the East as well as here, and these statements may furnish some of the reasons why yacht racing is on the decline and cruising in the ascendancy.

## PURCHASE OF EXILE.

L. H. Titus has sold to J. B. Haggin the six-year-old stallion Exile, by Belmont, his dam Belle Mason, the pedigree of which is given in Answers to Correspondents. He is one of the handsomest trotting stallions in the State, and before the circuit is ended, he may conquer a place among the "Notables."

## FOUL DRIVING.

If there is one rule in the Trotting Code which hould be rigidly enforced, it is that which relates o foul driving. The term is well applied, as unair advantages are anything but sportsmanlike, isgusting those who are the chief patrons of the ports of the track. The only escape from the vils which are sure to follow if unchecked, is for 1e judges to enforce, with inexorable firmness, e penalties for every breach. When the offence so palpable that there cannot be a doubt of the tention of the guilty party, the extreme punishent must be awarded. The most flagrant cases e those when the perpetrator commits the foul 1 purpose to assist others, not caring for the ight punishment he receives, so long as he can complish the task he has undertaken. He cares out the nefarious compact, being well aware at the crime will be condoned in such a majority of instances that the risk is small; and if he be given the last place or his horse distanced, he chuckles over the success and plumes himself on the smartness he has sh wn. Were he conscious that he stood an equal chance of being heavily fined, suspended or expelled, there would be more hesitancy in undertaking the job; and an example or two will surely put a stop to the practice.

As all frequenters of the tracks are aware, there are a variety of misdeeds which are termed "fouls." The particular and specific offence which we desire to call attention to now is of the kind that often occurs, and which will require heroic treatment to overcome. One horse trots steadily, and another keeps in close company by indulging in a few breaks which are not very far outside of the rule. But on the back-stretch the trot is forsaken, and, partially screened by being hidden from the judges, he is lashed into a run, though skillfully handled, so as to keep the trotter up to the fastest pace without showing in front. Other runs are given during the heat, and when the lead is obtained, then there is swinging to the right and left in order to retard the one behind. When so close to the score that the judges cannot fail to take cognizance, the trot is resumed, and, between trotting and running, the winner is forced to open a gap on all the others. The winning has entailed, however, exertion which would not have been necessary if the other had trotted, and the one "hard heat" has a more potent effect than two or even three would if a trifle slower. With many horses, the excitement following a horse galloping by their side is far greater than when the contestant trots. Even a steady run is not so trying to them as when there is a change from the trot to the gallop, a succession of leaps, which rests though there be no absolute gain, discouraging the staunchest, and completely demoralizing those which have soft spots in their composition. There may be some excuse for a driver who, in his eagerness to win, exceeds the latitude which the laws allow; but when the object is merely to defeat to aid another; when he is merely a helper, a hired tool to assist in wearing out a dreaded competitor, there must be no temporizing. If fines will not remedy, try suspension. If ostracism for a limited period does not afford a remedy, let the sentence be for life. Should the clods prove useless, try what virtue there is in stones.

## THE EMBRYO STAKE.

Owing to a misconception in a few, carelessness on the part of others, and still another class, who had a dread of meeting with colts they had no hopes of beating, the Embryo Stake did not receive the number of nominations which was expected. In order to give these a chance, there is a desire on the part of the subscribers who have seen to permit the entry of others, and there is little doubt that the concurrence of the remainder can be obtained. This concurrence it is necessary to put in writing, and we will be much obliged if the subscribers will send their acquiescence in the following terms : " I hereby agree that nominations can be made in the Embryo Stake up to and including September 15th." By keeping the stake open to September 15th, the opportunity will be given to all those who have colts at the State Fair.

## THE PLUNGER'S ACCOUNT.

The imbroglio between Theodore Walton and James E. Kelly, and the charges brought by the latter against the heavy operator in the chances of horses, has raised so much of an excitement in New York that the *Herald* has published long accounts of the case. To a reporter of that paper Mr. Walton submitted his book for the time when it was charged he was engaged in the fraudulent transactions; and taking that as a true exhibit, he has not much success as the corrupter of trainers and jockeys. The nineteen days in July show as follows:

|  | LOSERS. |  | WINNINGS. |
|---|---|---|---|
| July 4 | $7,542 50 | July 1 | $7,557 00 |
| July 4 | 1,467 50 | July 19 | 854 50 |
| July 6 | 7,634 00 | July 22 | 1,848 00 |
| July 6 | 12,685 00 | July 26 | 13,800 00 |
| July 15 | 4,318 62 |  |  |
| July 18 | 625 00 |  |  |
| July 20 | 4,754 50 |  |  |
| Total | $37,022 12 | Total | $23,789 50 |
| Net loss | | | $13,232 62 |

He was particularly charged with bribing Snedeker, and his losses on the horses in that stable foot $12,893; and, as Walton truly states: " Now, do you suppose if I wanted to corrupt jockeys I would have lost that $24,830 ?"

To prove the animus of Kelly, he submits his account, that standing:

|  | LOSERS. |  | WINNINGS. |
|---|---|---|---|
| July 15 | $900 | July 18 | $1,250 |
| July 20 | 200 | July 18 | 1,300 |
|  | | July 22 | 1,100 |
|  | | July 26 | 3,250 |
| Total | $800 | Total | $6,800 |
| Net winnings | | | $5,900 |

Another strong point Mr. Walton makes is the query, why did Kelly bet with him when he knew he had trainers and jockeys corrupted ? Including in his charges prominent trainers and jockeys, Mr. Kelly should have seen that these were supported by evidence which would carry conviction. Failing to do this, he stands in a bad position.

## BALTIMORE LETTER.

Hiram Happy writes very happily of affairs in the Colony which ranked so highly in the horse world a century and a half ago. At that period it was held to be indispensable for a Maryland gentleman of means to keep a stable of race horses, and some of the best of the old-time turf celebrities were owned there. Virginia and the "Eastern Shore" then held undisputed sway on the racecourse, and the tug of war between the two sections was oftentimes a contest of the most stubborn kind. It is a great pity that the spirit has died out in the descendants of the Cavaliers.

Maryland Volunteer, which our correspondent thinks so highly of, is one of the very best bred trotting stallions. His dam was nearly thoroughbred, and one of the greatest performers of the season. She was the first animal wearing toe-weights we ever saw, and, as is recorded of Mayflower, these and the shoes were so ponderous that it was surprising that she could trot at all—three and a half pounds on each foot; and thus encumbered, she trotted fourteen races in 1871, and obtained a record of 2:22. Mr. Salisbury bought her, and (a great misfortune to him) she died last Winter, when in foal to Gibraltar. She had " missed " for several years, and her colt was nearly due at the time of her death. We shall be much pleased to hear of the Maryland delicacies which never go out of fashion; and there is little danger of the terrapin, canvas-back or oyster following the fate of the high-mettled racer.

## TROTTING ON THE BAY DISTRICT COURSE.

There should be two very good races on the Bay District Course to-day, as Crown Point, Starr King, Cairo and Ashley try conclusions again, Sweetness, Poscora Hayward and Blackmore composing the second set. The track is in capital order last Saturday, and will be in the same fine condition to-day. There is every prospect of two good races and a large attendance to see them. The friends of Starr King were greatly put out by his defeat, and do not think it was a true line. The race was the work which all of them needed to give a keen edge on for the second contest, and

there is scarcely a doubt of the race being fully as interesting as the one decided on the 5th instant, notwithstanding the speed which Sweetness showed in the first and second heats in the 2:25. Should the others be all right and capable of repeating what has been shown in their exercise, there is no telling how the 2:30 race will end. The greys will keep coming, and as many realized after the former trial, three heats are essential to winning when " best 3 in 5 " are the conditions.

## A GRACEFUL REMEMBRANCE.

When General Grant visited San Jose, the Managers of the old Santa Clara Valley Fair Association were anxious to show him something which would be worthy of their guest. Those who were supposed to have the horses which were the most worthy of being paraded before the great commander, were inexorable in their demands that they should be paid a sum beyond what the Association could afford. Arguments were of no avail, but fortunately P. A. Finigan was made acquainted with the situation, and at once he made a proposal which overcame the dilemma. " There is Santa Claus," he replied, " with the fastest record of any colt of his age in the world. You can command his services."

The offer was thankfully accepted, Santa Claus was brought out, and gratified every one who witnessed the display of speed, duplicating the 2:18 which he had made at Sacramento. It still stands at the head of the list, and in commemoration of that, and as a token of the appreciation which was still cherished, the Society had a gold medal struck. On the face is the title: " Santa Clara Valley Agricultural Association;" on the obverse, " To P. A. Finigan, for his public spirit on the occasion of General U. S. Grant's visit, September 28, 1879." It is a graceful return for a ind act.

## HORSES FROM OREGON.

There landed a few days ago the horses that A. J. Stemler took to Oregon, and with which he made a very successful campaign. Those taken to the north were Fred Collier, Jim Renwick and Lou Spenser, and accompanying them is Joe Howell, an old veteran of the turf, who has run in more States and Territories in the last seven years than any horse we are acquainted with. Lou Spenser met with an injury which will incapacitate her for some time. The others look remarkably well. The injury to the filly was occasioned by the steamer having to lie to, on account of the fog, before she could safely cross the bar; and the filly getting frightened at a Chinaman carrying his luggage preparatory to landing, jumped over a rail and injured her hock. She had shown very good form in her races in Oregon, and the mishap is very much to be regretted. The other horses will take part in the circuit, and the two sons of Joe Hooker, with the aid of the Bonnie Scotland, are likely to play a prominent part.

## OVERMAN WINS AT ROCHESTER.

Overman is doing good work, and performing his part well, indeed, to keep up the reputation of the California horses in the East. He has won at Buffalo and Cleveland, in both cases beating very strong fields. At Buffalo he got a record of 2:20½, and though the track was very heavy at Rochester, owing to rain, the time of the heats was 2:21½, 2:23, 2:23½, 2:27½, 2:27½. The telegraph does not say which of the heats was won by Overman, but inasmuch as he won the last, he " outstayed " his competitors. The fifth heat of the pacing race on the same day was made in 2:27½, and the sixth in 2:31. Overman is likely to set well down in the teens before the season is ended.

## THE 2:36 CLASS AT SAN JOSE.

The entries for the 2:36 Class at San Jose will close on Wednesday, the 16th instant. This is before the 2:40 " open " trot at Santa Cruz comes off, though it excludes the winners of heats on the Bay District last Saturday, and renders Vanderlynn and Freestone ineligible. With these redoubtable " green ones " out of the way, there should be a full entry list.

## FISH.

The streams are a good deal warmer to wade in than they were earlier in the season.

Parties returning from Nevada say that there is splendid trout fishing in Lake Tahoe, Weber Lake and streams in the vicinity.

Fishers at Harbor View are getting their fifty to one hundred tom cod, rock cod, etc., in an afternoon from the wharf and boats.

A camping party on Salmon Creek, Marin County, recently caught two hundred trout, varying in weight from one-fourth to five pounds.

More black bass are being put into Lake Merced. This lake is capable of sustaining a great many fish, and it will be a long time before it is overstocked.

Liver fed trout most readily take flies with some red in them; even a red ibis is killing at times, but even at best these trout give but little or indifferent sport.

There are nearly 100 fish preserves on Long Island. Little by little the wealthy classes have purchased or leased nearly every water worth fishing over in this region.

John Carlson who had a place on the road between Auburn and Forest Hill, Placer County, some time since reserved a fish pond for carp, and the waters are now filled with them.

Anglers along the trout streams near the Big Trees, Calaveras County, have to use small dark flies for bait, as the trout, though plentiful, seem to care but little for anything else.

Smelt fishing at the Oakland Wharf is excellent. Large numbers are caught by set lines. Several persons have been catching red-tail perch from this wharf, that weigh from one to two pounds.

The California Sportsman's Club have caught two hundred and fifty black bass from Lake Temescal, which are to be distributed over the State. These fish weigh about 1¾ pounds.

Trout, now-a-days, have to be educated to understand the varieties of flies offered to them. Those raised at fish hatcheries are the only ones that comprehend some of the gaudy bait thrown to them.

A general rule about flies is to use dark flies on bright days and light flies on dark days. The maxim of an old sport in this connection is worth remembering. He used to say, "go day on your hand dropper, and copper the day with the nuddle dropper and stretcher."

Salmon fishing closed on the 31st July. The catch on the Columbia is estimated at 500,000 cases, 50,000 less than last year. This season thirty-four canneries engaged in fishing on the Columbia. Four vessels are loading at Astoria with salmon for the United Kingdom.

Lieutenant Winslow, of the United States Navy, has recently planted, as an experiment in the artificial propagation of oysters, 10,000,000 young oysters upon a bed in Long Island Sound, near New York. The oysters planted were only two days old, and could only be discerned by the aid of a strong magnifying glass.

When the water was pumped out of the dry dock, on Monday last, after admitting the City of Chester, two curious fish were found in the bottom of the dock. They were about six inches long, and closely resemble the Eastern catfish, only they have no "feelers," or the sharp, stiff spike on either side of the mouth. The Italian fishermen pronounced them to be specimens of the "music fish," which are very rare in these waters.

Flounder fishing has commenced again on Lake Merritt. It will be remembered that some little time since it was discovered that flounders were plenty in the lake, and hundreds of people fished there daily. Sometimes about a ton a day of these fish came out of this small sheet of water. Of course this could not last long, and after a few weeks the fish became so scarce that very few were caught. Some Chinamen caught about 100 pounds this week, near the food-gates.

Steps should at once be taken to investigate the cause of the great mortality among the finny tribe in Donner Lake. It is probably some epidemic that is so fatal, as the club appear to be the only sufferers, and the same mortality was observable last year while the trout are not affected. It would surely pay the hotel proprietors to institute such an investigation with its attendant theories, as now the stench arising from tons of decaying fish is unbearable, and drives many visitors away from this pretty lake.

FOR FISH TRANSPORTATION.—The Government is now building in Delaware a fine new iron steamship for the special use of the Fish Commissioners. It is to cost $200,-000, to be named the Albatross, and to be ready in about four months. Its dimensions will be: Length, 200 feet; beam, 37 feet 6 inches; depth of hold, 16 feet 9 inches; tonnage, 800 tons. Among the many appliances fitting the vessel for its purpose will be a deep-sea dredge and eight miles of wire rope. One of the first important services of the Albatross will be the transportation to London of the collection which will represent this country in the great Fish Exposition next May.

A FISHING PARTY AT THE FARALLONES.—On last Wednesday a party of gentlemen, composed of P. Crowley (Chief of Police), Sheriff Sedgwick, Captain Douglas, Sergeant Bonner, G. Shoe, George Carlisle and Mr. Ellison, started for the Farallone Islands, on a fishing and pleasure expedition, in the pilot boat "Lady Mine," commanded by Captain Out. As soon as they passed the Golden Gate a dense fog set in, accompanied by a strong, cold wind, which made the sea very rough, and it continued blowing during the thirty hours that the party were out. There were only two members of the whole party (Captain Douglas and Mr. Ellison) who did not feel that inexpressible something which commonly known as sea-sickness. Mr. Ellison never feels the effect of wind or wave, and Captain Douglas, it is said, would go to sea on a shingle and not get sick. Chief Crowley, though more under the weather than any one else, is now feeling better from the trip. Most of the fishing was done near the islands, in about forty fathoms of water. There were thirty large rockfish and innumerable flounders caught by the members of the party. The next time these gentlemen go fishing, some of them no doubt will brave the "depths" of a quiet mountain lake, and leave the salt water for those who do not get sick.

---

Fishing with a pitchfork is a queer way of having sport, but the writer saw this being done at the head of Oakland Creek last week in the broad sheet of water known as Brooklyn Basin, immediately in front of East Oakland. It was high tide and the water was just lapping over the edges of the marshes. Two men, in rubber boots, were walking along the edge of the marsh looking carefully down into the water. Suddenly one of them who is carrying a common pitchfork, makes a "prod" and up comes a fine flounder weighing a couple of pounds. Notwithstanding the long rubber boots the man in his excitement had waded into water deeper than their tips, for he was wet above his waist. It looked like rather live sport, and most people would prefer a boat to get in and hooks and lines to handle while catching flounders. We have heard of people pitchforking salmon out of streams, but this is the first time we ever heard of flounder fishing with a pitchfork.

## THE GUN.

### THE PACIFIC GUN CLUB.

On last Sunday, at Bird's Point, the Pacific Gun Club met to hold their fourth shoot for the gold medal, Messrs. H. Cameron and George W. Downey officiating as judges, and T. R. Hart as referee. Only eight of the members participated. The shooting was a little above the average, and resulted in A. Lambert winning the medal for the third consecutive time, it now being his property. The birds were a very ordinary lot, and Lambert was very fortunate in having all easy ones to shoot at, with no chance of showing any brilliant shooting, of which he is capable. The shoot-off with Mr. Adams, who had also made a clean score, was very interesting. They tied on three pairs of double birds, and on the second Lambert won by one bird. The shooting of Precht and Haines was very good. They killed their birds clean, the former being unfortunate in missing his first, and the latter his fourth, or the result might have been different. They showed themselves to be good shots in the matches following at $2 50 entrance. The first was at four birds, divided between Precht and Brown; the second was at six birds, and was divided between Precht and Adams, and the third, at six also, was won by Precht after shooting a three-cornered tie with Lambert at five pairs double birds. The distance was as usual, 31 yards rise for the single birds, with 80 yards boundary, and 18 yards rise and 100 yards boundary for the double birds. Following is

THE SCORES:

| | | | | | | | | | | | | |
|---|---|---|---|---|---|---|---|---|---|---|---|---|
| C. Precht | 1 | 1 | 1 | 1 | 1 | 1 | 1 | 1 | 1 | 1 | 1—11 |
| A. Lambert | 1 | 1 | 1 | 1 | 1 | 1 | 1 | 1 | 1 | 1 | 1—11 |
| J. Meyer | 0 | 1 | 1 | 1 | 1 | 1 | 1 | 1 | 1 | 1 | 1—10 |
| L. Guldde | 1 | 0 | 1 | 1 | 1 | 1 | 1 | 1 | 1 | 1 | 0—10 |
| G. Adams | 1 | 1 | 1 | 1 | 1 | 1 | 1 | 0 | 1 | 1 | 1—10 |
| T. Haines | 1 | 1 | 1 | 0 | 1 | 1 | 1 | 1 | 1 | 1 | 1— 9 |
| J. Brown | 1 | 1 | 1 | 1 | 0 | 1 | 1 | 1 | 1 | Withdrawn. | — |
| W. Stewart | 0 | 1 | 1 | 1 | 1 | 1 | 1 | 1 | 0 | 0 | 0— 5 |
| A. Lambert | | 1 | 0 | 1 | 1 | 1 | 1 | | | | — |
| A. Adams | | 1 | 0 | 1 | 1 | 1 | 0 | | | | — |

Shot out of bounds.

On the second match the ties were shot off at two birds each.

| | | |
|---|---|---|
| Precht | 1 0 wdn. | — 1 |
| Brown | 1 1 1 1 | — 4 |
| Ferguson | 0 0 | — 0 |
| Roche | 0 1 0 | — 1 |

| | | |
|---|---|---|
| R. Brown | 1 1 1 1 | — 4 |
| Nelson | 1 1 1 | — 3 |
| A. Adams | 1 1 1 | — 3 |

On the second match the tie was shot off at two birds each.

| First Match. | | | | | | | Second Match. | | | | |
|---|---|---|---|---|---|---|---|---|---|---|---|
| Lambert | 1 1 1 1 1 | — 5 | | | | | 1 1 1 1 1 | — 5 |
| Precht | 1 1 1 1 1 | — 5 | | | | | 1 1 1 1 1 | — 5 |
| Nelson | 1 Withdrawn. | — | | | | | 0 1 1 1 1 | — 4 |
| Adams | 1 1 1 1 1 | — 5 | | | | | 1 1 1 1 1 | — 5 |
| Brown | 1 1 1 1 1 | — 5 | | | | | 1 1 1 1 0 | — 4 |
| Roche | 1 1 1 1 0 | — 4 | | | | | 0 1 1 0 1 | — 3 |
| Ferguson | 1 1 1 1 1 | — 5 | | | | | 0 1 1 1 1 | — 4 |
| Meyers | | | | | | | 1 1 1 1 1 | — 5 |

| | | |
|---|---|---|
| Precht | 1 1 1 0 1 1 1 1 | — 7 |
| Lambert | 1 1 1 0 1 1 0 1 | — 6 |

| | | |
|---|---|---|
| Adams | 0 0 | — 0 |
| Meyers | 0 1 | — 1 |

Quail are said to be very numerous throughout the country.

In the vicinity of Hollister rabbits, quail and other small game, are so numerous as to be looked on as pests by the farmers.

At the Schuetzen Park, Alameda, on Sunday, the San Francisco Schuetzen Verein held a rifle contest, which resulted in the following marksmen carrying off the first ten prizes: Philo Jacoby, F. Freese, K. Wertheimer, W. Ehrenpfort, C. C. Rohlfs, G. Adams, Boekman, J. Horstman, William Heber, J. Waller.

The members of the California Rifle Club competed Sunday at the Alameda Schuetzen Park for three medals, with the following result: First-class medal, Zecher, 301 rings; second-class medal, K. Wertheimer, 376 rings; third-class medal, Utschig, 337 rings.

We understand that good authority that quail are being shot out of season. A gentleman was taking supper with a friend the other evening, and noticed that quail was on the table, and on inquiring he was informed that they were purchased at the market. This matter should be looked into by the California Sportsman's and other clubs.

The Alameda Sportsman's Club met to-day at Littlefield range, near Oakland, to have their last clay pigeon shoot of the season. Nearly all the members will be present. The Piedmont street cars run by the range. The last live pigeon shoot of the club comes off on the last Saturday of this month.

PIGEON SHOOTING AT WATSONVILLE.—On Sunday, August 27th, there is to be a large pigeon shooting match at Watsonville, Santa Cruz County, the shooting to take place in Camp Goodall Driving Park. The entrance fee is $2 50, open to all; entrance fee to be paid to J. H. Besse, Watsonville. The entries will be closed August 20th. The entrance money is to be divided into three coin prizes, as follows: First prize, 50 per cent; second, 30 per cent; third, 20 per cent. A sack of shot is offered by the management as the fourth prize. Birds extra. Plunge traps are to be used, and the match is to be governed by the California State Sportsmen's Rules. The full particulars can be had by writing to A. C. Wood, Manager, Watsonville.

A NOVEL MATCH.—In our last issue was the announcement that a match between an archery club and a pistol team was to come off in the near future. This match will take place at 2 or 3 p. m. Saturday, 19th instant, at Bird's Point, Alameda. J. P. Allen, representing the California Archery Club, sent a challenge to Captain Douglas, of the Police force, with the following conditions: That four archers will shoot against any four officers of the Police force; the archers to use bows and arrows, and the Police

---

to use regulation revolvers off hand; the distance to be sixty yards; twenty-five or fifty shots, as may be agreed; both teams to use Archer's targets. Captain Douglas accepted the challenge as soon as it was received. As Colonel Beaver, of the Citizens' Team, interested himself considerably in bringing about this match, he is to shoot as one of the four of the Police team. The four archers are J. P. Allen, of San Francisco; O. M. Button, of Santa Cruz; T. C. Havens and A. S. Brownell, of Oakland.

## THE RIFLE.

On the 31st July the weekly shoot of the Carson Guard took place at Treadway's Park, Reno. The scores deserve mention. James Chesley made 44 at the 500-yard range, and 41 at the 200-yard range. At the 200-yard range James Crawford made the highest score with 45 points. Fourteen of the Carsons were in the contest, and they made an average of 41.10-14ths. Five men of the Emmet Guard of Virginia were at the park and shot at the ranges, making a total of 207. Haskell, of the Emmets, shot at both ranges, making 47 points at 200 yards and 46 at 500.

THE INTERNATIONAL MATCH.—Mr. G. J. Seabury, Secretary of the National Rifle Association, said that since reading the scores of the British team in the Bass match at Wimbledon, which was recently cabled over, he felt very confident that the American team would win the international match. He mentioned that the following scores, at the long-range distances, had been reported to him within the last week: T. J. Dolan, Twelfth Regiment, 93; Captain Day, 83; C. W. Hinman, of Boston, 83; P. J. Lawritzen, of the National Rifles, 82; Captain Wiltt, of Pennsylvania, 71; Capt. J. H. Griffith, of New Jersey, 79; Sergeant Van Orden, of Binghamton, 83; Captain Barnes, of Oswego, N. Y., 75; G. Hines, of Binghamton, 77; Captain Adkinson, of Pennsylvania, 81. In the Bass match the highest scores were those of Caldwell and Dods, who both made 73.

RAPIDITY MATCH AT CREEDMOOR.—The weather at the Creedmoor Range, on the 31st July, was favorable to good shooting, the sky being slightly overcast and the wind very light. The principal event of the day was the second competition in the "rapidity" match for a gold medal presented by Mr. Pierre Lorillard, Jr. The prize has to be won three times (not necessarily consecutive) before it becomes the personal property of the winner. The match is open to all comers and any rifle with open sights can be used. The distance is 200 yards. At the sound of a bugle the competitor opens fire and continues firing until the bugle again sounds, sixty seconds after the first signal. The number of shots fired during that interval must not exceed twenty, but no competitor has yet reached that limit. It will thus be seen that the match affords a test of both accuracy and dexterity, and also of the efficiency of the weapons used for rapid firing. The scores made were as follows:

| | |
|---|---|
| R. T. Mars (Botchkiss military rifle), 19 shots | 83 |
| M. W. Bull (Honorable military rifle), 19 shots | 82 |
| A. y. Day (Lee single-shooter rifle), 15 shots | 67 |
| J. C. Dolan (Sharp military rifle), 14 shots | 46 |
| Fred. Oyler (Remington rifle) | 40 |
| J. C. Mulcy (Springfield rifle) | 40 |
| F. P. Lewett (Stevens rifle) | 30 |
| R. J. Shepherd (Peabody rifle) | 30 |

In the first competition, July 1, S. A. Day was the victor with a score of 82 points.

AIMLESS HUNTING.—The deer law, relative to their killing, is out of force from July 1st to November 1st, during which time there is nothing to prevent their indiscriminate and reckless slaughter. Perhaps this is just as it should be; but we are perfectly cognizant of the fact that all summer long the hills are full of aimless hunters, who are rambling around just for the fun of the thing, and killing any number of deer for no object at all more than the sport and excitement of hunting, and believe that it is all wrong. A law that don't fit such a case is out of joint, and should be remedied, if a possible thing. This class of sportsmen are from below, who have no use for the deer after it is killed, but have an insatiable thirst for the deer hunter's fame. It will take but a very few years, at the present rate of slaughter, to exterminate the beast entirely from our hills.—Bulls Record.

The mountains near Oroville, especially the Big Meadows, afford hunting grounds, and there is this year a great increase in the number of camping parties that go out with ample supplies for a change of scene and the pleasant episodes of a sporting life in forest and stream. To-day a party consisting of R. W. Smith, George W. Stevens, W. J. Morgan, C. G. Mathews and Dr. D. W. Wanley, prominent members of the Oroville Sportsmen's Club, start for a month's trip through the same part of the mountains.

THE POLICE PISTOL TEAM OF COMPANY B.—This team is composed of the officers of Captain Short's division. They have a good range at North Beach, where they go on certain days for practice. On the 4th of last June, in competing with three other pistol teams for a trophy, Captain Short's men made the following scores, out of a possible 75 points: P. Fox 71, W. L. Coles 70, J. Smith 69, J. B. O'Connor 69, C. Reynolds 69, R. L. Cockrill 69, D. J. Paddock 68, J. Laakures 68, S. M. Thompson 66, and J. J. Hayes 60 points.

The members of Sergeant Kingsberry's watch have been shooting for the possession of two medals; the first, a fine gold medal for the best shot, cost no less than $25; the other, for the second best, is a silver medal, and is worth about $20. Officer Paddock won the gold, and Officer Pugh the silver medal. As a score of 73 points out of a possible 75—Through Paddock, Pugh and Cockrill tied on 72 points, the judges decided, according to Creedmoor rules, that Paddock was entitled to first prize, and Pugh to the second. The score of the watch in this shooting match: D. J. Paddock 73, J. Pugh 73, R. D. Cockrill 72, F. Fox 71, J. Laakree 71, S. M. Thompson 69, J. J. Hayes 69, J. B. O'Connor 68, C. Reynolds 68, J. Casey 66, J. Burk 66, J. S. Poole 66, J. Wallace 65, H. M. Gardner 65, T. P. Kingsberry 61, M. Nielsen 61, M. D. Baranced 58, J. S. Cahill 57, J. O'Donnell 55, J. H. Brigerts 43. According to the old custom, the winner of either of the medals could retain the prize as long as he continued to be the best or second best shot, but now, when one person has won a medal for the third time, it becomes his own property. If Captain Short's pistol team continue to improve in their shooting, as much in the future as they have in the last year, it will not be long ere they will rank as second best to none.

# THE KENNEL.

## FIXTURES.

National American Kennel Club's trial on quails, Grand Junction, Tenn., December 4th. D. Bryson, Memphis, Tenn., Secretary.

Louisiana Field Trials near New Orleans La., beginning Dec. 11 under the management of the New Orleans Gun Club.

BENCH SHOWS.—Western Pennsylvania Society's English Setter Bench Show Derby, Pittsburgh, Pa., for English setter puppies whelped on or after March 1, 1882. Entries closed December 1, 1882. I. E. Slayton, Allegheny City, Pa., Secretary.

FIELD TRIALS.—National American Kennel Club's trials on prairie chickens, Fairmont, Minn., September 4th. Entries to American Field Derby closed July 1st; to All-Age Stake, September 4th. Joseph H. Dew, Columbia, Tenn., Special Stakes any the three trials.

Gilroy Rod and Gun Club's trials on quails, near Gilroy, Cal., October 25th Open to dogs owned in California, Oregon, Nevada and Arizona. R. Leavesley, Secretary, Gilroy, Cal.

Eastern Field Trials Club's trials on quails, near High Point, N. C., November 17th. Entrance to Derby close J 49 1st; to All-Age and Members' Stakes November 1st. Fred. N. Hall, Secretary, P. O. Box 606, New York.

## FIELD TRIALS AT GILROY.

A valued correspondent, himself a thorough sportsman, sends the following communication. The idea that this State cannot handle more than one field trial is different from our own views expressed elsewhere, but we admit freely that our correspondent's opinion is as valuable, if not more so, than our own. The subject is open to discussion.

"Parties are advocating the holding of the field trials this year in some more central or northern portion of the State, and one suggests that if Gilroy will not consent to that movement, to get up an independent field trial. This is always the way, as soon as anything is started and made a success of, every one wants to rush into it. One field trial is enough for California at present, when all the sportsmen of the State can congregate to see each other's dogs work, and which shows best style and nose. The actual winning will not be much, as the prizes are more honorary than valuable, and the entrance is low enough ($5.00) to permit all who own a dog to enter. Sportsmen living north talk of the expense of sending their dogs to Gilroy. If they attend themselves, which, of course, they will, the dogs will cost nothing.

"Is not this feeling against Gilroy as much actuated by jealousy as anything else? A true sportsman should be the embodiment of everything that is noble and generous, and be above these petty jealousies about their dogs, which is so common among them. The fact is, California sportsmen do not know enough yet about dogs nor their performances, and have a great deal to learn both from field trials and bench shows. We know many so-called sportsmen who really do not know a pointer from a setter, but call everything a hunting-dog. Talk to them about Laveracks and Llewellins and Gordons, and you might as well talk Chinese, and yet if they do not get a prize at a bench show they set the judge down as an ass, while they know it all.

"The Gilroy Rod and Gun Club have taken field trials in hand, and have done the work well. A great many first-class dogs from Oregon and elsewhere have been sent there for training, chiefly on account of the trials being held there, and to expect them to move them up to Folsom, or Colusa, or Marysville, appears to us absurd, and we cannot suppose that Gilroy will entertain the idea for a moment. There are many dogs from San Francisco that will run in the trials —and Gilroy is as good for them as any place north. Go on, broker sportsmen; put your shoulders to the wheel; eschew all jealousy, and send your dogs, good or bad, and let us see them. We don't want to hear what your dogs can do— we prefer seeing them for ourselves."

## WAIT FOR THE SEASON.

Accounts have come to hand recently of private coursing matches held in various parts of this State. It is not the province of this paper to dictate to gentlemen how and when they shall practice their favorite sports, but perhaps a few suggestions will not be taken amiss. There can be no difference of opinion among gentlemen who understand the sport of coursing as to the evil effects of running dogs during the extreme hot weather that prevails in the interior of the State at this time of the year. It is positive cruelty to allow a dog to chase a hare when the thermometer stands 100 degrees in the shade. The cruelty is intensified when the dogs are taken from the cold climate of San Francisco. Experience has demonstrated that in case a dog is not in the most perfect health, a run in hot weather is almost certain death. Last year a party of gentlemen from this city took several greyhounds to Donohue's Landing in the month of August, and had several courses. One dog died, and three others were so seriously injured that they have been no good ever since. Two years ago, on November 1st, it was so warm at Merced that two dogs engaged in the Pacific Coast Coursing Club's match died shortly after they had finished their runs. Berry's Swindler and Fowler's Spirit of the Times died at Merced in that way, and the ill effects of the heat were so apparent that shortly after noon the club adjourned the meeting and waited tor cooler weather. Apart from the danger to the dogs, other serious objections can be urged against coursing at this season of the year. The young hares are not big enough to make a decent run, and as the chances of starting a young hare are about twice as great as starting an old one, it may safely be said that every other run will prove a failure. Then, too, some consideration is always shown by the true sportsman to female game when with their young. About the middle of May most of the leverets are born, and but few of them leave their mothers until late in September. At such times the doe ceases to seek safety from her natural enemies by flight as she does during that part of the year when her young are able to shift for themselves. By a beautiful provision of nature the doe at the season abandons her usual "form" or seat on the bare plains, and seeks a secluded place in some thickly wooded opening or brush covered patch, where her chief foes, the squirrel hawks, cannot approach. On a fine sunny day she will venture out a short distance, only to rush back to cover the instant danger is sighted. She does not seek the vast expanse of the open plain, whereon to distance her pursuer, but, knowing that her young one cannot run, she hides away. In Nevada and in the Territories the Indians run down and capture alive in nets vast numbers of jack rabbits at this season of the year, while in the Fall and every Spring the offer of $35 a head will not procure a live jack from Fresno to Round Valley. It is to be hoped that sportsmen will be more merciful than are the Indians, and will give the hares a rest until the cold weather comes. At the present time there is no need for any protection for hares. The damage that they do to the crops makes them a pest to the farmers, when they are found in large numbers, and it would be very bad policy for local sportsmen to ask that they be included in the game laws, which are already a little irksome to the grangers, though absolutely necessary for the protection of wind game there is left in the State. One predatory pot hunter, with his little shotgun, will kill more hares in an hour than would suffice for game for the largest coursing meeting in the State, but for all that if the coursing men do not protect the hares around San Francisco, where they are very scarce, they will find that in a few years they will have to dispose of their greyhounds for lack of game.

## SACRAMENTO GREYHOUNDS.

A Sacramento correspondent sends the following notes of coursing matters at the Capital City:

Around Sacramento are owned many well bred greyhounds, several of which have won fame at the large coursing matches. First in point of honor comes Bradley, owned by Michael Hanrahan. Bradley has defeated all the local dogs, and also all the dogs that have been brought against him from other parts of the State. The list of those he has vanquished includes Blue Jacket and Dakota, though I believe that in one of the last named matches the judgment was very unsatisfactory to the coursing gentlemen from San Francisco. P. Kelly of Sacramento owns several fine dogs, including Raven, a three times winner. Joe Powers of Brighton has a kennel full, and so has his neighbor Mr. Hull, whose string includes Snow Bah. M. Howard still owns the well known slut Amy Howard, who won third prize last Fall in an open stake. Mr. Shaw's slut Whitney has a fine litter of pups, by Kelly's Black Jack of the Cartwright strain. M. Keenan, E. Mohan and J. Fagan are also among our coursing men, and last, but by no means least, comes A. J. Woods, the owner of the celebrated slut Kitty Woods, who ran second at the open meeting held by the Pacific Coast Coursing Club, in the Spring of 1880, and also took second at Sacramento. The Sacramento coursers have a considerable distance to go to find good running ground, but there are many gentlemen in your city who can testify that Whitcomb's ranch, about 15 miles from here, will afford as good sport as any ground in the State.

## MORE FIELD TRIALS.

Several gentlemen have recently written to various papers giving it as their opinion that the Gilroy Club ought in fairness to hold their next trials at Folsom or Sacramento. These suggestions, though perhaps if adopted they would tend to popularize these trials, are not very logical. It is about the same as asking that the Bay District Association should hold its races on the Ohio track. It is a fact that dogs brought from a distance may suffer a little from the journey, but it should be, and doubtless is, a matter of honor with the Gilroy Club that no dog be allowed to hunt over the ground selected for the trials before the trials take place. The necessity of preserving enough game for the trials is of itself sufficient reason for the enforcement of this rule. Doubtless a declaration from the Gilroy Club that they allow no hunting over the ground—which, by the way, is private property—in advance of the trials, will entirely dispose of all talk about fairness. The objection to distance cannot be met, but sportsmen must remember that the Sacramento or any other Club has the same chance to inaugurate these trials as did the Gilroy Club, and for their own convenience can arrange trials to take place as near home as they please. There cannot too many clubs take hold of this matter, and this paper will do all in its power to foster not only the trials of the Gilroy Club, but of any club that has enterprise enough to arrange others.

## BURGESS ON LEAVESLEY.

At a recent meeting of the State Sportsman's Association of California, Mr. E. Leavesley, of Gilroy, read a paper on sporting dogs, which was published a short time since in the columns of the American Field. In the course of his remarks, Mr. Leavesley indicated a reference for the Laverack setters over the Llewellin strain. This aroused the anger of Mr. Arnold Burgess who is the great American promoter of the Llewellin strain, and who has a large setter kennel full of this stock. Mr. Burgess is a contributor to the American Field, and in the last issue of that paper makes a savage attack upon Mr. Leavesley which certainly passes the limit of those restrictions of courtesy and good breeding usually observed among gentlemen in argument. Mr. Burgess' criticisms of Mr. Leavesley's letter are all based on the assumption that Mr. Burgess and his friends are all right and that certain English authorities, as for instance "The Setter," are all wrong. Mr. Leavesley certainly should not be abused for accepting as an authority on such matters a work published in England, and they almost universally believed, and which was positively stated to be accurate by Mr. Laverack himself. If Mr. Burgess' assertions are as incorrect as his use of the English language, then they are more utterly worthless than he would have the public believe are the views of Mr. Leavesley. We have not space to print all his errors; one instance will suffice. He says:

It is evident that Mr. Leavesley has been inoculated with the Laverack phobia, and like other sufferers of those days tries to make each a case for them by quoting all that can be said in their favor, and carefully concealing all facts that militate against them. [They the gentlemen, the other Laverackphobists, would denounce in forcible terms the man who dared ask what is the use of keeping the so-called Laverack blood pure; but that, of course, principles differ with different cases.

The contest shows that Mr. Burgess intended to convey the idea that Mr. Leavesley had been inoculated with a love of the Laverack. His use therefore of the coined words "Laverackphobia" which means a hate of the Laverack, and the word "Laverackphobists," which means haters of the Laverack, is an unpardonable inaccuracy in a critic. Some of Mr. Burgess' criticism are probably correct enough, but they are so obscured by his misuse of the English language that they are difficult to understand. In our opinion, Mr. Burgess' criticism of Mr. Leavesley's paper detracts only from the former's reputation as a writer, and adds nothing to the world's store of information.

## DOG STEALING IS LARCENY.

In the case of the State of Ohio vs. Michael Moran, Judge Tilden recently decided that dogs were personal property under the law in the State of Ohio. The conclusion of his decision is as follows: "There are some decisions to be found in this country where the common law rule is adhered to that there can be no larceny in the feloniously taking and carrying away a dog, but I venture to affirm that no decision can be found in any State with a statute similar to our own that declares that the stealing of a dog is not larceny. I therefore decide that a dog is property—a thing of value, and that the stealing of a dog in Ohio is larceny. The motion in arrest is therefore overruled."

## A CANINE CHAMPION.

At the recent dog show in Paris, France, the Prix d'honneur, which was competed for by setters of all breeds, was won by the Llewellin setter dog, Kars, owned by Mr. Ivan P. Pranishnikoff, an artist, and formerly connected with Harper's Weekly. Kars was bred by Mr. L. H. Smith, and is by his Paris out of Pearl, formerly owned by Mr. Smith, but now the property of Mr. A. S. Bishop of Pittsburg, Pa. Kars is a blue belton, and was whelped July 6, 1877, and is a litter brother to Mr. A. E. Moore's Lass O'Gowrie, and to Dr. S. Fleet Speir's Wanda.

GORDON STANDARDS.—Samuel J. Dixon, in the American Field, gives the following scale of points as in his opinion the fairest and most comprehensive by which Gordon Setters can be judged:

| | |
|---|---|
| Skull | 15 |
| Nose and lip | 5 |
| Eyes | 5 |
| Ears | 5 |
| Neck | 5 |
| Shoulders and chest | 15 |
| Back, quarter and stifles | 15 |
| Legs, elbows and hocks | 5 |
| Feet | 5 |
| Stern and flag | 5 |
| Coat and feather | 5 |
| Color | 5 |
| | |
| Total | 100 |

Mr. Edmond Orgill has sold the following lemon and white pointers to Mr. M. O. Lonsdale, of Portland, Oregon, viz.: Rocket, by imp. Claude, ex imp. Champion Bang; Rhyl, by Rome, ex Champion Kelly and Rosalie, by Champion Rush, ex imp. Dart. Mr. M. O. Lonsdale is said to have the finest kennel of sporting dogs on the Pacific slope. If the above selection is a fair specimen of Mr. Lonsdale's judgment, he certainly is a gentleman possessed of rare stock.—Turf, Field and Farm.

GREYHOUND PUPS.—The imported greyhound bitch Prairie Girl, belonging to D. L. Levy, 39 Third street, on July 31st, gave birth to eight pups. The pups are by Baron Walkden, imported by Mr. Levy at the same time as the bitch. All the litter take strictly after the Baron, not one resembling the mother. In such cases as this it generally happens that when the pups all take the form of one parent, they all take the spirit and energy of the other.

# THE HERD.

Fred. Brubner, the noted cattle man, recently brought 200 head of fine beef cattle, from his cattle range in Calaveras county for Gerlach & Fisks of the El Dorado and Avenue markets, Stockton. Mr. Brunner has been long noted for raising fine, fat cattle, and which always command the highest price in the market.

The Grass Valley Tidings is informed by a gentleman from the rural districts near that locality, that there is a scarcity of beef cattle in Nevada and adjoining counties, and that there will scarcely be enough to supply the demand this Fall and Winter. Every day men on horseback visit the different farmers in this part of the country, and buy up everything that is purchasable, and that can be converted into meat. This has not occurred before for years.

Very many people desire to raise hornless cattle. It is asserted that this can be easily done, no matter what breed the cattle may be. A correspondent of the Country Gentleman tells the manner of it: "When the calf is old enough for the horn to start, a very small protuberance is felt upon the head. Take a knife and cut a small cross over this little horn, and lift out the incipient horn, press the edges of the wound together and put an adhesive strap over it, and there is no more trouble, and you have hornless cattle."

ENGLISH SHORTHORN BREEDERS.—During the late show of the Royal Agricultural Society at Reading the Shorthorn Society held a meeting, at which Earl Bective presided. The report of the Council stated the Society now consists of 495 life members, and 623 annual members, making a total of 1,118. The life compositions paid during the year, amounting to £165, have been invested; and the Society's reserve fund now amounts to £3,369 in three per cent. consols. The report stated that the 29th volume of the Herdbook will be ready for issue about October next. The report concluded by observing that, alike with all other branches of agricultural pursuits Shorthorn breeding has suffered from the depression experienced of late throughout the country; the Council, however, trusted that by the individual efforts of every breeder, the important characteristics of the Shorthorn breed will not only be maintained, but that it will become still more widely known and appreciated throughout that and other countries.

LARGE PRICES FOR JERSEY CATTLE.—The St. Helliers herd of Jersey cattle, owned by Mr. T. L. Hughes of Long Island, N. Y., was sold in New York, on the 31st July, and the prices fetched considered good, the total sum realized from thirty-three head being $8,385, or an average of $254.13. The highest price paid for any one of the lot was $625 for Lady La Grise, an imported cow, three years old, by Pilot, out of Fragrance, bred by Nicholas Noel, St. Saviours, Island of Jersey, bought by James Monaghan for Congressman A. S. Hewitt. Lady Rose, three years old, and a bull calf, by the Duke of St. Helliers, went for $610 to Mr. F. C. Havemeyer. Mr. Watson paid $525 for Lady Gypsy, three years old. Mr. A. B. Colgrove, of Middletown, Conn., paid $600 for William the Conqueror, by Pilot, out of Lady La Grise. Pilot is by Gray Coat, whose sire was Khedive, a son of the famous Coomassie. Pilot's dam, Rose, was a daughter of Khedive, so that this young bull gets a close double cross of the blood of Coomassie through his sire, and as Lady La Grise is by Pilot he gets three crosses of Coomassie. Khedive got Princess II., who at the sale in May last brought $4,800, the highest price ever paid for a Jersey.

## DAIRY SHORT-HORNS.

Not long since Mr. Ashburner read a paper before the British Dairy Farmers' Association on the above topic, from which the subjoined extracts are taken:

"I have a Short-horn descended from Mr. Collin's dairy, that gave sixteen quarts of milk per day after calving her first calf in September, 1879; twenty-two quarts per day after her second calf, in August, 1880; and a similar quantity after her third calf in July, 1881. The three calves are all remarkably healthy, and I had one hundred guineas offered for her second calf before a year old. I ask you...

gentlemen, is this a bad sort of Short-horn dairy cow? I have also a daughter of a wellbred Short-horn that won the first prize for the dairy three years in succession against cattle of any breed, and took the silver cup at the same time for the best cow and her offspring. Is it not enough that animals descended from recorded ancestors of upwards of half a century are so noted for the dairy as well as breeding good cattle?

The speaker proceeded to criticise the system of high feeding practiced in the youth of Short-horns which he said is ruinous to the development of the milking propensities, because it gives the animals such a tendency to fatten. His plan is not to feed to excess so as to injure the animal as a breeder or milker, nor on the other hand to aim at being too economical in feeding to injure the growth of an animal when young. The happy medium is the one needed to make a good Short-horn dairy cow, but even to get at this requires a little experience. Our aim should be an animal well formed, of good quality, of sufficient size, and in a fair healthy condition; one that will do good to any farmer by breeding similar animals, and concludes by saying that this can be attained by rearing stock in a natural way, and by selecting male animals of good descent, from good parents, from a dam with a good udder and the sire from a dam with a good udder; at the same time not forgetting the constitution of the animal, by looking entirely to the dairy properties.

## POULTRY.

### THE POULTRY EXHIBIT AT THE STATE FAIR.

It is to be hoped that all those who make a specialty of breeding poultry of the best class, as well as others who, as amateurs, take a pride in raising rare and valuable species of European extraction, will take the trouble to make the Poultry exhibition at the State Fair more of a success, both in quality and quantity, than has been the case in previous years. The fact vouched for by Mr. Thomas Waite of Brighton in his letters to the *Journal*, that there is more profit in a well conducted poultry yard than in raising pigs, is open to discussion and this result may be based on the superior experience of the manager of the Brighton poultry yard as well as on his energy and enterprise in selecting, at any price, the very best breeds. If France the raising of poultry is carried to perfection and thousands of peasants gain a good livelihood by themselves and families from this source only. In England, the barnyard is the pride of the farmer, for within its boundaries he sees the care and forethought of his wife and daughters, who, as in the dairy, take a pride in their occupation, for it is generally from these two sources that they get their pin money for all their clothes and extras. We should like to see this example followed in this country, and for that purpose we suggest a full exhibition of all varieties at the State Fair, and that the managers have a small pamphlet written to be distributed gratuitously describing the various breeds and the qualities for which they are celebrated.

By such simple means we may get our ladies on the farm more interested in the subject than is the case as now; with the facilities afforded by the canning establishments, we may start an immense trade that will enable us to get rid of our surplus stock at very remunerative prices. Canned terrapins and frogs are esteemed as great delicacies, and we have just the climate to carry out the French plan of raising and fattening poultry on the most extensive scale. The managers of the State Fair guarantee that the birds shall be carefully provided for, and they offer the following premiums, so let us hope that the exhibition will be the best ever held in the State: Best pair Brahmas, $5; best pair Cochins, $5; best pair Games, $5; best pair Hamburgs, $5; best pair Leghorns, $5; best pair Black Spanish, $5; best pair Dorkings, $5; best pair Dominiques, $5; best pair Plymouth Rocks, $5; best pair Polish, $5; best pair French Fowls, Hudson, Crevecoeur, or La Fleche, $5; best pair Seabright Bantams, $5; best pair Game Bantams, $5; best pair White Bantams, $5; best pair Black Bantams, $5; best pair turkeys, $10; best pair ducks, Rouen, Aylesbury, Pekin, or Cayuga, $5; best pair geese, Toulouse, Bremen, or China, $5. All fowls will be judged according to the American standard of excellence.

### GOOD BREEDS FOR GENERAL USE.

Fowls that combine the properties of both flesh and egg production are difficult to find and yet are frequently inquired for. It is nearly useless to try to unite the two qualities of flesh and eggs in one bird—it cannot be done in perfection. Fowls that attain the largest growth are slow in maturing, and before maturity is reached, it is unreasonable to expect any eggs. The large fowls require the whole season for development, and when cold weather sets in, it is difficult to force them up to egg production. Feed accomplishes something, but nature will take its course. For this end, however, the Houdan fowl may answer a good purpose where the breed is understood. They will make much flesh, and that which is prized by epicures, and are what might be termed good layers, unless when compared with the laying of the Brown Leghorns. The Houdans are non-sitters.

The Dorking is an excellent fowl, and unites size and quality of flesh with a pretty good yield of eggs for the season. They are sitters. Where size is not required, there is no bird that equals the Brown Leghorn for any purpose. At all seasons of the year they give a bountiful supply of rich, medium sized eggs, and the flesh, being sweet and fine grained, is greatly prized for early broilers. Size is demanded by the majority of poultry seekers, and it is only to be attained at the expense of quality and egg production. The Asiatic fowl has for many years been the meat producer for the multitude. Epicures choose the Game and other choice-bred birds, but most poultry consumers take the feather-legged bird.

For a roast there is no fowl equal to the Dorking. It grows to a compact shape, of good quality of flesh, with small offal, and is sweet and juicy. The Asiatic fowl is oily and strong, more like aquatic fowls: Next the Dorking may be reckoned the Crevecoeur fowl. In size it is a little below the Dorking, but the quality of the flesh is choice and fine. They are of a fair size, hens weighing from four to five pounds, and cocks from six to eight pounds. They have black plumage throughout, and are very handsome, ornamental fowls when nicely bred. They are good layers of large, fine, white eggs, and do not sit. They are rather tender.

One great drawback to good success with poultry results from not understanding the breed kept. The Houdans are what is termed hardy fowls, but require careful treatment. They should not be herded with other fowls. Their im-

---

mense crests obstruct the vision, except one way, and this renders them helpless against attacks of other fowls which they might in fair and open combat easily repel. They cannot withstand wet or dampness, but are not so sensitive to cold, providing it be dry, as some other varieties. The Dorkings are very tender, and so are the Crevecoeurs. The Dorkings must have a warm place in winter. They are even more sensitive than the large combed varieties, but will compete with them in egg production if well fed during the winter. There is no fowl more hardy, after fully grown, than the Leghorns. They will withstand great cold without injury, but no breed will endure gross neglect. Leghorn chicks are delicate when young, but soon get out of the way. They are rapid growers and mature early.—*C. B. in Country Gentleman.*

### ANCIENT AND MODERN ARMS.

#### BY DR. N. D. PARDEE.

*[Continued From No. 4.]*

Without the invention of gunpowder there would necessarily be no firearms, and were we unable to generate steam we would have no steam engines, for as a matter of fact, the ponderous guns made by Krupp or the engine made by Fulton would never have been constructed for either ornament or use. But the application of fire has made them both servants to the ingenuity of man; the one as the modus operandi forte exchange and carrying trade of the products of the earth, and the other as the great engine of war, by which man may slaughter and kill his fellow man by the hundreds of thousands, and that, too, in accordance with the most approved and scientific principle of civilized warfare. Without the steam engine, the commerce of the world would be conducted by the slow process of the sail, as it was one hundred years ago. Without the chemical compound of gunpowder, the belligerent nations of the earth would settle their little difficulties with the same implements of war that were used four hundred years ago. But as soon as the propellant force of gunpowder was established, the inventive mind of man began to devise means to make it subservient to the will of man, and to what extent it will be carried nothing but the revelation of time can tell.

Who can say what one hundred years will bring forth? Even fifty years from now, it may be, there are those now living that will see the gas of gunpowder bottled up and utilised as the motive power to take the place of the steam engine.

The history of gunpowder is contradictory. Some historians give it to the Chinese, or an explosive powder similar to gunpowder, which they use in the manufacture of fireworks. There can be no doubt of its existence in India during the life of Alexander, who showed a little cowardice when marching his army between the Hyphasis and the Ganges, a land occupied by the Oxydracians—a people possessed of superhuman means of defense. " For," it is said, " they come not out to fight those who attack them, but those holy men, beloved by the gods, overthrow their enemies with tempest and thunderbolts shot from their walls." And when the Egyptian warriors, Hercules and Bacchus, invaded India, they attacked those people with an army flushed with victory, " but were repulsed with storms of thunderbolts and lightning hurled from above." This I regard as the first evidence on record of the existence of an explosive material, and I am fully convinced that from this circumstance the real phrase of " home-made thunder" took its origin. How applicable it is to the American demagogical politician, " cheap political thunder," a great big noise emanating from some windy politician, replete with the personal pronoun I and filled with high-sounding phrases of what he has done for the poor people. Enough of these fellows live in Oakland to keep the clear people most thoroughly enlightened upon all issues of the day by their " cheap political thunderings" on the street corners. And I know of two or three men, if a record or tally had been kept of the number of big pronoun I's that they have vomited from their brazen political throats, they would fill a volume 6 x 6 feet with ten thousand pages. And the little o's, well—" what's the use talkin'—

Roger Bacon, one of the greatest philosophers and alchemists of his day, who was born in 1214, is credited with having made the discovery of gunpowder; but there is so long a stretch of time between the historical account of a combustible material used by the Oxydraceans in the days of Alexander, when he led the Macedonian army to victory, was some 330 years B. C.; while the birth of Roger Bacon was 1214 years after Christ. From these statements a deduction can be drawn that there was an explosive material that was used in the form and purpose of " hobgoblin," but not as an agent of war, and as no particular use was made of it in the arts and sciences, it became obsolete and forgotten, and until Roger Bacon made the discovery of gunpowder, we can find no authentic record of its existence. However, a German monk, by the name of Schwartz, claims the discovery, but not till the year 1320, nearly a century after the discovery made by Bacon. In the " Antiquated Arts," by Scott, reference is given, that beyond all doubt the Arabs possessed a knowledge of gunpowder, and through the Saracens in unimportant parts were introduced into Europe about the middle of the 13th century, and it is also an admitted fact that it was not used as a projectile force but for fireworks only.

In the epistles of Roger Bacon, in his " Secret Arts," I quote the following, which ought, to a great extent, settle the important event beyond all cavil: " For sounds like thunder and flashes like lightning may be made in the air, and they may be rendered even more horrible than those of Nature herself. A small quantity of matter, properly manufactured, and not larger than the human thumb, may be made to make a horrible noise; and this may be done in many ways, by which a city or an army may be destroyed, as was the case when Gideon and his men broke their pitchers, and exhibited their lamps, the issuing out of them with great force and noise, destroying an infinite number of the army of Midianths." And in a subsequent chapter of the same work occurs the following, which is almost positive proof that to Roger Bacon, the monk, belongs the honor of making known the ingredients of the combustible compound. He says: " Mix together saltpeter with *lura nove qup urbe*, and sulphur, and you make thunder and lightning, if you know the method of mixing these."

It will be at once seen that all the ingredients of gunpowder are spoken of here save that of charcoal; which, in my opinion, is covered up under the almost unintelligible inscription of " *lura nove qup urbe*," and it may be that *Anagram* was converted into *Curboum pulvere*, which would make the whole thing, as far as old Roger is concerned, " sub rosa."

---

And as it is known that Roger Bacon was an " Arabic Scholar," the supposition is but fair that he got the explosive combination, both quantitative and qualitative, from some Arabian writer, with whom I don't profess to be on intimate terms, but claim him as a distant relative, through the most singular coincidence the world has ever chronicled, the incubation, the birth and propagation of my greatest grandfather *Adam*.

I have little doubt when old Roger Bacon gave to the world the invention of this simple and wonderful compound, that he never once thought of the greatness and grandeur that future ages would impart to it. Little did he think that he was putting into the hands of the civilized world an agent by far the most powerful that skill has ever devised or accident presented. Possessing, as it does, a power more terrible in every succeeding age, and subserving all the progressive resources of the arts and sciences invented by the genius of the human intellect for the extermination of man. kind, which, as I write, appalls me with a feeling of incredulity hard to describe, at the future prospects of my kind, with a spontaneous sensibility to reconcile the developing strides that this engine of war may take in the sure approaching future, with the mysterious dispensation, with the benevolent order of Providence.

*[To be continued.]*

[SAN FRANCISCO (CAL.,) CALL.]

### BELOW ZERO— THE JEANNETTE— WHY PAST EFFORTS TO FIND HER FAILED.

LIFE-SAVING STATION NO. 7, 12th DISTRICT, OCEAN BEACH, POINT LOBOS, CAL.

A reporter has just had an interesting interview with Henry Bohn, keeper of the above station, the details of which are of such profound interest as to warrant their full publication for the readers of the *Call*.

Mr. Bohn was a member of the crew of the Corwin, which left San Francisco, May 22, 1880, in search of the Jeannette, returning October 16, 1881, after an unsuccessful search for the lost steamer. The Corwin crew numbered forty-two, all of whom returned sound and well from the Arctic expedition. They could gather no information from natives along the coast in regard to the missing Jeannette.

" But," added the plucky explorer, " I am sure we would have found her had we not been frozen out at Wrangel Island." And then he went on to give further details. He said: " It is true we all got back safely, but a number of us suffered intensely on account of the extreme weather. I had a fearful cold on my lungs, and should not have been here to-day telling the tale, but for a wise provision before our departure from this city. I feel as if I desired everybody to know what did some of us so much good during this terrible voyage. We had taken a good supply of St. Jacob's Oil on board, and to this I owe my life. Two others of our crew, named Boltzen and Wilson, were in a dreadful condition from neuralgia and rheumatism, and this wonderful remedy saved them. There isn't a scintilla of doubt about it. See here," he added warmly, pointing to a box close at hand, " see here, we have a supply right here at the station. It is a grand thing to use after exposure. It is the enemy of all disease. It is the king of pain. It is the destroyer of sickness. It is the glad harbinger of health. It is the ablest physician that never fails to cure his patient. It is the evangel of blessing. But I am getting eloquent over it, and ought to do so, for it saved my life. Of course men in my vocation must meet all weathers. We cannot stand on the order of our going, storm or no storm. During the sixteen months that I have been here we have saved thirteen lives. The last day of October, 1880, the entire crew of a brigantine were saved by this station. The Great German Remedy did good work time and again, I assure you. It was like a messenger of mercy. It is a great thing to have—the right remedy at the right time. For the lack of it many valuable lives are lost. There's no denying this fact."

Mr. Bohn, who related this, is a very intelligent German—a native of Hamburg—courteous and obliging in the extreme, a genuine man, as any one can see from a brief interchange with him. He strikes one as being the right man in the right place—a candid, honest, outspoken man, who states things as they are, and who " would not flatter Neptune for his trident, or Jove for his power to thunder."

## REVISED SPEED PROGRAMME
### FOR 1882.

### FOURTH ANNUAL MEETING
OF THE

### SONOMA COUNTY
### Agricultural Park Association,
AT SANTA ROSA.

**FIRST DAY—Tuesday, Aug. 22, 1882.**

No. 1—TROTTING RACE—Free for all two-year-old owned in the District. Mile heats, 2 best in 3; purse, $200. First horse, $120; second, $60; third, $20. Closed on the first day of May with the following entries:
E. B. Conway names sb. c. May Day, by Abbotsford.
J. E. Foster names s. m. Clara Patterson, by Greg McClellan.
G. C. Fountain names blk f. May Day, by Eugene Casserly.
P. J. Shafter names g. h. Greyson, by brother to Rustic.
Steve Crandall names b. f. no name, sire unknown.

No. 2—TROTTING RACE—Free for all horses that never beat 2:20; purse, $400. First horse, $240; second, $120; third, $80.

**SECOND DAY—Wednesday, Aug. 23.**

No. 3—RUNNING RACE—Half mile heats; 2 best in 3, free to all; purse, $250. First horse, $150; second, $75; third, $25.

No. 4—PACING RACE—Free to all horses that never beat 2:30; purse, $300. First horse, $200; second, $75; third, $25.

**THIRD DAY—Thursday, Aug. 24.**

No. 5—TROTTING RACE—Free for all three-year-olds owned in the District; purse, $300. First horse, $180; second, $90; third, $30. Closed May 1st with the following entries:
W. J. Barr names blk. f. Sunny Mott, by Gray McClellan.
W. J. Barr names blk. f. Starr, by Raybourd.
E. B. Conley names b. c. Marton, by Brigadier.
J. E. Foster names br. s. Black Foster, by Gen'l Dana.
W. M. Wood names b. c. Red, by Overland.
L. H. Boggs names b. s. Warwick, by Milton Medium.

No. 6—TROTTING RACE—Free for all that never beat 2:25; purse, $600. First horse, $360; second, $180; third, $60.

**FOURTH DAY—Friday, Aug. 25.**

No. 7—TROTTING RACE—Free to all horses that never beat 2:40; purse, $300. First horse, $200; second, $100; third, $50.

No. 8—RUNNING RACE—Free for all; single dash; one mile; purse, $200. First horse, $120; second, $60; third, $20.

No. 9—TROTTING RACE—Free for all horses that never beat 2:30; purse, $600. First horse, $360; second, $180; third, $60.

**FIFTH DAY—Saturday, Aug. 26.**

No. 10—RUNNING RACE—Free for all three-year-olds one mile and repeat; purse, $300. First horse, $180; second, $90; third, $30.

No. 11—TROTTING RACE—Free to all that never beat 2:21; purse, $700. First horse, $420; second, $200; third, $100.

### CONDITIONS.

1st. Entries to all races except Nos. 1 and 5, to close with the Secretary at 10 o'clock p. m. Monday, the first day of August, 1882.

2d. Entrance fee to the above races will be 10 per cent. of the purse, and must accompany the nomination.

3d. In all races five to enter and three to start. Any horse distanced or not starting will forfeit his entrance fee. No money will be paid for a walk over.

4th. All trotting and pacing races will be governed by the rules and regulations of the National Trotting Association now in existence.

5th. No horse entered in a purse can be withdrawn except by consent of the Judges.

6th. All trotting and pacing races, except No. 1, will be mile heats, 3 best in 5.

J. P. CLARK, President.
CHARLES HOFFER, Secretary.

## SPEED PROGRAMME
OF THE
### Mount Shasta Agricultural
### Association,
TO BE HELD IN
### YREKA, SISKIYOU CO.,
— ON —
**Wednesday, - - - October 4th, 1882.**

For racing purposes this District shall comprise Siskiyou, Shasta, Trinity, and Modoc Counties, Cal., and Jackson and Lake Counties, Oregon.

No horse shall be eligible to any of the following District Races unless owned in the District prior to October, 1881.

**FIRST DAY—Wednesday, Oct. 4.**

No. 1—TROTTING—Free for all; 3 in 5; purse, $500. First horse receives $400; second horse, $100. Entrance 10 per cent. of purse, 5 to enter, 3 to start. Entries close September 1st.

No. 2—RUNNING—Dash of a mile and a half free for all horses owned in the District; purse, $100; entrance $5, added.

**SECOND DAY—Thursday, Oct. 5.**

No. 3—TROTTING—Free for all matched horses owned in the District; 2 in 3; purse, $75; entrance $5, added.

No. 4—RUNNING—Half mile and repeat free for all horses owned in the District; purse, $75; entrance $5, added.

No. 5—TROTTING—Free for all three-year-old and under owned in the District; dash of three-quarters of a mile; purse, $75; entrance $5, added.

**THIRD DAY—Friday, Oct. 6.**

Grand parade of Stock.

No. 6—TROTTING—Free for all in the District; 3 in 5; purse, $300; entrance $5, added.

No. 7—FOOT RACE—(1) purse and repeat; purse, $50; entrance $5.

No. 8—TROTTING—Free for all three-year-old and under owned in the District; dash of three-quarters of a mile; purse, $75; entrance $5, added.

**FOURTH DAY—Saturday, Oct. 7.**

No. 9—RUNNING—Dash of a mile; free for all horses owned in the District; purse, $100; entrance 10 per cent. of purse; 5 to enter, 3 to start. Entries close Sept. 1st.

No. 10—TROTTING—Free for all horses in the District that have never beaten three minutes; 3 in 5; purse, $100; entrance $5, added.

### Rules and Regulations.

1st. The above purses will be given without discount.

---

## SECOND
## ANNUAL EXHIBITION
OF THE
### SAN MATEO AND SANTA
### CLARA COUNTY
### AGRICULTURAL ASSOCIATION
## NO. 5,
TO BE HELD AT
## SAN JOSE, CAL.
......FROM......
### Sept. 25th to 30th,'82, inclusive

### SPEED PROGRAMME.

**FIRST DAY—Monday, Sept. 25th, 1882.**

No. 1—TROTTING—2:40 class. Purse, $500.
C. Van Buren, of Mayfield, enters Peter Coutts' b m Manotte, by Nutwood, dam Addie.
Louis Duncan, Santa Clara, enters b g Louis D.
G. Bernard, San Francisco, enters g f Alice Roy, pedigree unknown.
W. Z. Price, San Mateo, enters b m San Mateo Belle, by Speculation, dam Young Lady Vernon.
M. F. Miller, San Rafael, enters b s Marin, by Patchen, dam unknown.
W. H. Henderson, San Jose, enters b m Big Lize.
H. B. Cooper, Alameda, enters s g Frank Moscow, by Frank Moscow, dam unknown.
Patrick Farrell, San Francisco, enters b h Vanderlynn, by George M. Patchen, dam a Joseph mare.

No. 2—SAME DAY—TROTTING—2:28 class. Purse, $750.

**SECOND DAY—Tuesday, Sept. 26th.**

No. 3, RUNNING—For two-year-olds; three-quarter mile dash; $50 entrance; $25 forfeit; $100 added. Second horse to receive his entrance and one-third of added money.

No. 4, SAME DAY—RUNNING—For all ages; mile dash; $50 entrance; $25 forfeit; $125 added. Second horse to receive his entrance and one-third of added money.

**THIRD DAY—Wednesday, Sept. 27th.**

No. 6, TROTTING—2:30 class. Purse, $600.

No. 7, SAME DAY—BUGGY HORSE RACE—For horses owned in the District to be driven by owner to top buggy. Two mile heats. Purse to be hereafter offered.

**FOURTH DAY—Thursday, Sept. 28th.**

No. 9, RUNNING—Three-year-olds. In the District; mile dash; $50 entrance; $25 added. Second horse to receive his entrance and one-third of added money.

---

## THE SAN MATEO AND SANTA
## CLARA COUNTY
## AGRICULTURAL ASSOCIATION, No. 5
— OFFER A —
# PURSE OF $400,
For 2:36 Class.

Entries will close August 19th, 1882.

---

## SPORTING GOODS.

BOXING GLOVES, FOILS,
COMBAT SWORDS, MASKS,
INDIAN CLUBS,
HUNTING KNIVES,
Our Own Manufacture.
DOG COLLARS AND CHAINS.
Fine Assortment in the City.
WILL & FINCK,
Leading Cutlers, 769 Market Street

---

## TURF EXCHANGE.
### FARRELLY & MITCHELL,
435 CALIFORNIA ST.
FINE
### Wines, Liquors & Cigars.

---

## $12,500
## In Purses and Stakes.

## CALIFORNIA
## STATE FAIR
## SPEED PROGRAMME
FOR 1882.

**FIRST DAY—MONDAY, SEPT. 11.**

No. 1—RUNNING—INTRODUCTION STAKE—For all ages; three-quarters of a mile dash; $50 entrance, $15 forfeit; $300 added; second to save stake.

No. 2—RUNNING—SERENDIBE STAKE—For foals of 1879; one and a half mile dash; $50 entrance, b. f. $250 forfeit; second to save stake.

**SECOND DAY—TUESDAY, SEPT. 12.**

No. 5—TROTTING—2:23 class; purse, $800. Mile heats, 3 in 5.

THIRD DAY—WEDNESDAY, SEPT. 13.

No. 4—RUNNING—CALIFORNIA DERBY STAKE.

FOURTH DAY—THURSDAY, SEPT. 14.

FIFTH DAY—FRIDAY, SEPT. 15.

SIXTH DAY—SATURDAY, SEPT. 16.

## REMARKS and CONDITIONS.

EDWIN F. SMITH,
Secretary.

HUGH M. LARUE,
President.

# Golden Gate Fair.

## SPEED PROGRAMME FOR 1882

## $10,000

IN

## Stakes and Prizes

FIRST DAY—MONDAY, SEPT. 4, 1882.

SECOND DAY—TUESDAY, SEPT. 5.

THIRD DAY—WEDNESDAY, SEPT. 6.

FOURTH DAY—THURSDAY, SEPT. 7.

FIFTH DAY—FRIDAY, SEPT. 8.

SIXTH DAY—SATURDAY, SEPT. 9.

## CONDITIONS.

L. WALKER,
Secretary.

A. C. DIETZ,
President.

## GOLDEN GATE FAIR.

## RACES! RACES!

OFFER A PURSE OF $900,

FREE FOR ALL

TROTTERS AND PACERS.

Oakland Trotting Park Course,

Saturday, September 9, 1882.

L. WALKER, Secretary.
Lock-box, 1032, Oakland.

## STATE FAIR RACES!

(EXTRA!)

RACE No. 30. (Substituted.)

RACE No. 6. (Substituted.)

Gentlemen's Saddle Horse Race.

EDWIN F. SMITH,
Secretary.

H. M. LARUE,
President.

## GOLDEN GATE FAIR.

## BICYCLE RACE!

ON SATURDAY, SEPTEMBER 9TH,

FREE FOR ALL.

ENTRANCE FREE!

Monday, September 4, 1882,
by 3 P. M., at the latest.

L. WALKER, Secretary.

## GEO. H. STRONG,

## BICYCLES

AND TRICYCLES,

MARKET STREET.

Parse error: illegible marginal column text.

VOL. I.—NO. 8.
No. 608 MONTGOMERY STREET }
SAN FRANCISCO, SATURDAY, AUGUST 19, 1882.
{ SUBSCRIPTION
FIVE DOLLARS A YEAR.

# NOTABLE HORSES OF CALIFORNIA.

## PIEDMONT.

Of the seven illustrations published four have been of horses bred in California and three reared on the far off side of the mountains. Two of these have acquired renown through the performances of their offspring, the other Eastern-reared shares with the natives the celebrity which arises from individual capacity for speed and endurance. As has already been stated, the faculty of producing excellence in progeny is a higher order of merit than individual characteristics however brilliant, though the possession of the qualities desired is a favorable augury for perpetuation in the progeny. When the breeding is of the right kind, the formation in accordance with the standard, it is rare, indeed, that the animal possessing all these qualities, united with a "good record," fails in the stud. There are instances to the contrary, and the trite maxim that "exceptions prove the rule to be correct" is received as a truism, though it would be more logical to say—in horse breeding

at least—that the exceptions are owing to some hidden cause which in all probability man can never fathom.

In taking Piedmont for the eighth pictorial representation of the "notable horses of California," few will dispute his claim to the position. He is a great horse from every point of view. In the first place his breeding is of the most fashionable kind; in the second, his form is about as nearly perfect as can be found in a trotting bred stallion, and his performances are in keeping with his breeding and form. Piedmont was bred by H. A. Ferguson of Lexington, Kentucky; foaled 1871. He is by Almont, his dam Mag Ferguson by Mambrino Chief, grandam by Grey Eagle, with a strong probability that she was a mare of very high breeding. His sire Almont is by Alexander's Abdallah, dam by Mambrino Chief, grandam by Pilot, Jr. and the next dam claimed to be thoroughbred. Alexander's Abdallah was by Rysdyk's Hambletonian, his dam Katy Darling. Thus it

will be seen that the sire of Piedmont combined three great trotting strains, and his dam brought in a reinforcement of another line of Mambrino Chief, and with the very desirable addition of more thoroughbred blood. That this had a potent effect will be shown by the following description:

We have oftentimes been asked the question: "What sort of a looking horse is Piedmont?" To many it would be sufficient answer to reply: A grand, big horse, chestnut in color and handsome all over. There are others more exacting, however, and the trotting cognoscenti, especially, require a full description of a horse which has shown the capacity he exhibited in his races of last season, and not contented with the admirable portrayal of our artist, demand a recital of the "points." He is a deceiving horse as to his size, and, at the first glance, the observer is prone to think that when his height is given at sixteen hands the stature is over-rated, though the standard shows that he is a trifle over the mark, and the justness of proportion takes away from the actual measurement when the eye is the criterion. In color he is a chestnut of the finest shade. Rather lighter than bronze, a trifle deeper than gold. Lustrous, not the metallic sheen which is seen in the plumage of birds—livelier in hue and softer in the shading. With the exception of some small white spots on the right quarter, the rich chestnut is only broken by where the girths have left a few streaks, and those on the hip look like tiny splashes of froth flung from the bit in the excitement of fast motion. The mane and tail are nearly of the same shade, and the hair is as fine as in those which trace their descent through generations of aristocratic blood. On the whole, he is a picture admirable from any point of view, standing erect on every limb, and with an air of conscious superiority. The most fastidious æsthetic could scarcely find fault with the justness and harmony of proportion he exhibits when thus posed by himself. When examined in detail the over-critical horseman will be troubled to find a single faulty point, or rather to pick a flaw which he can sustain with arbiters who are competent judges of form. "From the ground up" he is well balanced. The feet are naturally of good shape, though the errors of the shoeing forge occasioned a quarter crack and an elevation of the horn above it on the left fore foot. This rather mars the appearance by interfering with the true circle of the coronet on that one foot. The hoofs are dark, saving a narrow strip on the right, and they have the proper angle. The pasterns are of good length, and have just the right slope to obviate concussions and give elasticity to the stride without indicating weakness. The cannon bones, metacarpels and metatarsals, are short, and the tendons are prominent without blemishes of any description, giving a width and flatness to the limbs which insure strength. The knees and hocks are broad, without the least tendency to coarseness, and yet afford room for the ligamentary attachments. The arms and gaskins are muscular and long from the elbow and stifle to knee and hock. The upper arm, humerus, is long, set at the proper angle with the scapula, and well clothed with muscles. There is a corresponding length in the femur, from the stifle to the point of articulation at the haunch, and the covering of muscles fills this portion of the frame to an immense size. The shoulder-blade is long, rising nearly to the top of the withers, wide, falling well back into the sway, and with plenty of muscle. The slope of the innominatum is sufficient to throw the stifles well down without giving any approach to the "pacing quarter," and the muscular development, of course, must correspond with the power shown in the upper thigh and gaskin. The "middle piece," as it is termed, that portion lying between shoulders and hips, is extraordinarily good. There is plenty of room for heart and lungs, and the back ribs are long and have the proper curve. There is plenty of evidence that the vertebral column is large, and toward the loin the muscles on either side of it rise above the bone. The neck is of good length, strong and tapering to the setting off of the head. The crest is moderately arched, and the throttle distinct. The head is rather below the medium size, with great width between the jaws, the eyes as good as can be imagined, the ears somewhat short and pointed. Standing so as to have a side view he exhibits a good length of body, on legs which are well-proportioned to his size. The "speed angles," as some call the degrees of obliquity between the haunch-bone and stifle, and the angle formed by the hock, are such as will suit a majority of horse fanciers, though this is part of the configuration which gives rise to divergent opinions. One favors a straight quarter, after the Arabian model; another likes the ultra slope of some pacers. Between these extremes is the most satisfactory for a fast trotter, and a medium such as Piedmont presents the best. A straight or crooked hind leg elicits the same amount of argument, and the formation of the hock the subject of frequent disputes. In these respects there is a mean, the hock being wide enough to insure a proper degree of strength, without the excessive width like that of the ox, and the bend is just right to give freedom of motion. The outlines from this side view are nearly faultless, and the filling-up would be difficult to excel. From a position behind him, the most striking part of his configuration is the immense width of the stifles and fullness of muscle. The quarters are deep and powerful. The inside of the gaskin is moderately heavy, the hamstrings large. In front, the intelligent countenance is the attractive feature from that point of view. There is plenty of breadth between the eyes, the forehead broad and prominent. The muzzle is cleanly cut, the edges of the nostrils thin, and the superficial facial veins showing through the thinness of the skin. The fore legs "come to the ground" exactly right, converging sufficiently to assure his action being straight, without the knees being so closely together as to be in danger of injury from the passing foot. The "fork" is capital, the elbow far enough from the chest, and the brisket is prominent. It is rare, indeed, to see a trotting-bred stallion with so much quality, and he comes very near to the type of the thoroughbred throughout his whole conformation. He has size, style and finish, and would rank high as a progenitor for carriage horses, if he did not possess speed, and with weight enough to give value for general use. In the right condition to go into training he weighed 1,140 pounds, and, as there is no grossness, that weight means the capacity to perform any task.

Another very essential feature in a stallion is the action. Those who have seen him move extol that of Piedmont as being very nearly perfect; but what the particular features are we cannot say. There has been a great change in opinion regarding the proper action for a fast trotter in the last twenty years, and at the present time a majority of the best judges prefer that which insures sufficient length of stride with the least muscular exertion. "No waste of force" is the maxim, every motion in the right direction, progression rather than show, and this we understand is the kind which Piedmont possesses. The races he won last season show that he has the gift of endurance as well as speed, and we are creditably informed that there is every reason to anticipate a lowering of his record whenever he appears again on the track, the conditions being favorable. He has shown such a flight of speed in his work that a person who saw him move informed us that the idea was firmly fixed in his mind that he can beat any horse in the world, irrespective of sex. Previous to last season his fastest record was 2:21¼, made in a second heat at Chicago in 1880, and that year he trotted nine races, winning eight of them. In 1881 he trotted seven races and won five, the most noted of them being the $5,000 purse, free for all stallions, at Chicago, July 19th. The starters were Piedmont, Santa Claus, Robert McGregor, Hannis, Wedgewood and Monroe Chief—the grandest field of trotting stallions which ever appeared in a race. Robert McGregor won the first heat in 2:18, Santa Claus and Piedmont close up; Santa Claus won the second in 2:17½, the head of Piedmont almost at his throatlatch; Robert McGregor won the third in 2:18½, Piedmont again close at the finish, and then he won the fourth in 2:17¼, the fifth in 2:19½, and the sixth in 2:21. This was enough to render him famous, but all of the races he started in were notable performances.

## A LADY'S VISIT TO MAUD S.

By far the sweetest, prettiest, daintiest thing here is Maud S. The other morning I went down to Vanderbilt's private stables, just back of Congress Hall, to see this beautiful creature, that can clip it faster than an express train on a down grade. The head groom, after surveying me, concluded that I was a harmless atom, and invited me in. "I want to see Maud S.," said I. "Do you show her to strangers?" "Oh, yes," he answered, good-naturedly, "lots of 'em come in here, and they all want to see her." He led the way to her stall, which is about ten feet square and as dainty as a lady's boudoir, and there, with a light horse-cover to keep the flies off her, was the great mare. She seemed delighted to have company, and, like all other well bred creatures, was good-natured and affable and devoid of airs. Her coat was softer than satin, and she has the most earnest and intelligent eye ever seen in an animal's head. She sniffed around complacently, and rubbed her slender nose against me as if we had been old acquaintances. In three minutes we had established intimate relations. The groom took off her cover and turned her around, to show her off to my inexperienced eyes, when, her hind legs coming a little too close to me, I made a bolt for the door of the stall. "Come back," said he, laughing, "she never did an ill-natured thing in her life. She would no more think of kicking or biting you than you would think of striking her. She is so kind and well disposed you'd think she was human;" and I suspect that the groom did have a half belief that she was human. He was evidently delighted to have an appreciative listener, and was ready enough to talk about the Queen of the Turf. Mr. Vanderbilt is not driving her at all now. She is in training for the Fall races, and every morning at 10 o'clock her trainer takes her out for a spin down the road. Mr. Vanderbilt is not half so proud of her as the stable-men are; and she is indeed a creature so gentle, so lovable, and so altogether the ideal horse, that anything could love her. After awhile I tore myself away from her, to take a look at the other horses. First was Lysander, a pretentious beast, who eyed me superciliously, and treated all my advances with lofty indifference. This animal resembles the ideal New York editor, being a cold and haughty creature, with an icy smile and an inscrutable brow, and evidently has no time to waste on triflers—no triflers need apply. Then I was shown another horse, Lysander's mate, whose name I really forget, but with Mr. Vanderbilt's permission I will call him Abdallah. Well, Abdallah offended me as much by his flippancy as Lysander by his hauteur. As soon as he beheld me, without the formality of an introduction, he wanted to play pitch and toss with me, to which I objected and left him to his reflections. The two horses for Mrs. Vanderbilt's victoria were also shown. One of them, having a plebeian fondness for straw in his stall, and a disposition to paw and dash it around, was in disgrace, with his meddlesome nose fastened to an iron ring, where he had to remain for an hour or two until he was thought to be sufficiently punished. I could not leave without another look at the "Bride of the Wind," and she asked me to come again, as plainly and as intelligently as if she had the gift of speech.—*Saratoga Cor. N. Y. World.*

After the poor exhibition made by Phil Thompson in his attempt to beat his own record, it is doubtful if his owner will hold to the challenge he issued for a match with any four-year-old. But should he still hold to his opinion, Budd Doble, who has charge of Jay Eye See, is ready at any moment to accept the challenge with that horse. If they were both in good order it would be a good race.

Buffalo Girl, the pacer, has a record of 2:14, but she is very unsteady. She is a daughter of Pocahontas Boy, a son of Tom Rolf. She began last season without a record and paced in eleven races of which she took one, winning heats in two others, and finishing the season with a record of 2:21¼. A member of the same family of pacers is the noted Sleepy Tom, 2:12¼, who was sired by Tom Rolf.

Both J. B. Thomas and Black Cloud, two conspicuous performers in the stallion class at Chicago, have permanent afflictions, the former having the stringhalt and the latter being stone blind. Each, however, can trot a mile in 2:18 or better.

Goldsmith Maid, the old Queen of the Turf, is now 25 years old. She has two foals, a colt and filly, by General Washington, son of General Knox and Lady Thorne, the eldest being two years old. She missed this year, and has been bred to Jay Gould.

# TURF AND TRACK.

## FIXED EVENTS.

Sonoma County Park Association, at Santa Rosa, Aug. 22d, 23d, 24th, 25th and 26th.

Sonoma and Marin Agricultural Societies. Annual Fair at Petaluma, Aug. 29th and four following days.

Golden Gate Fair, to be held at Oakland, from September 4th to the 9th inclusive.

Butte District Fair at Chico, from September 5th to September 8th, inclusive.

El Dorado District Fair at Placerville, from September 5th to September 8th inclusive.

California State Fair. Annual meeting at Sacramento, from Monday, September 11th to the 16th inclusive.

The San Joaquin Valley Association Fair at Stockton, from September 19th to the 23d inclusive.

Oregon State Fair at Salem, from September 18th and during the week.

The San Mateo and Santa Clara County Agricultural Association Fair at San Jose, September 25th to the 30th inclusive.

Humboldt and Mendocino District Fair at Rhonerville, September 19th to September 22d inclusive.

Modoc, Plumas and Lassen District Fair at Greenville, from October 2d to October 5th inclusive.

Monterey District Fair at Salinas City, from October 2d to October 6th inclusive.

Nevada State Fair, at Reno, from Monday, October 2d, to the 7th inclusive.

Mount Shasta Agricultural Association Fair at Yreka, October 4th, 5th, 6th and 7th.

Eastern Oregon Fine Stock Association at Union, from October 9th to the 14th inclusive.

## FAIRS AT THE EAST.

Kentucky State Fair at Lexington, August 9th to September 2d inclusive.

Minnesota State Fair at Farmington, August 31st to September 8th inclusive.

Iowa State Fair at Fairfield, September 1st to the 8th inclusive.

Minnesota Agricultural Association, at Minneapolis, September 4th to the 9th inclusive.

Nebraska State Fair, at Omaha, September 11th until the 16th inclusive.

Rhode Island State Fair, at Providence, September 12th to the 15th inclusive.

Pennsylvania State Fair, at Pittsburg, September 7th to the 21st inclusive.

Wisconsin State Fair, at Fond du lac, September 11th to the 16th inclusive.

Ontario Provincial Fair, at Toronto, September 18th to the 23d inclusive.

Connecticut State Fair, at Meriden, September 18th to the 22d inclusive.

New Jersey State Fair, at Monroe, September 18th to the 22d inclusive.

West Virginia Central Fair, at Clarksburg, September 19th to the 21st inclusive.

Indiana State Fair, at Indianapolis, September 25th to the 30th inclusive.

Western Michigan Fair, at Grand Rapids, September 25th to the 30th inclusive.

Texas State Fair, at Austin, October 17th to the 21st inclusive.

## TROTTING ON THE BAY DISTRICT COURSE.

The second day of the meeting which was given by the Bay District Association came off last Saturday. The 2:22 race on the original programme did not fill, and the 2:25 on the preceding Saturday was such a close contest that the managers concluded that a repetition of it, or so much of it rather as would embrace Crown Point, the previous winner, Starr King, Ashley and Cairo, would be a satisfactory offering to the sport-loving public. That and the 2:30 was certainly a very liberal bill, and should have attracted a large concourse of spectators. The San Franciscans, however, appear to have lost interest in sports of the track, and there was a meager showing when a comparison is made with Eastern towns of not half the size. In some of the small cities of the East, with a population of not over forty thousand, such races as took place on the Bay District last Saturday would bring out several thousand people. Still, there were about as many as on the opening day, and a gratifying feature was the number of ladies on the balconies of the hotel and Club House. The track was in capital condition—a trifle too hard, perhaps, for every-day work, but assuredly fast. The afternoon was not as fine as was desirable, there being too much breeze for real comfort; and after the first heat was trotted, the fog clouds obscured the sun.

A full description of the race is given in the detailed account which follows. They were eminently satisfactory, excepting the unfortunate decision in the last heat of the 2:30. Starr King proved that the reputation he had acquired in his private trials was not altogether illusory, and there is plenty of evidence to warrant the belief that he will be a "hot horse" in still faster classes.

The decision which awarded Sweetness the fourth heat in the second race was as has been stated a truly unfortunate finale. The account given of the heat which was taken from Poscora Hayward does not give all the evidence in regard to whether he lost or gained by the breaks. That the mare and Blackmore lost ground when he was trotting and gained when he broke was palpable. But fully as strong proof was furnished by the third and fourth heats. The third Poscora won in 2:25. In this he made two breaks, with a long distance between them. The fourth heat in 2:29¼ showed one of two things—that he was tiring, or that he lost ground equivalent to four and a half seconds in time. Admitting that he could not make a fourth heat as fast as a third, there is a discrepancy which can scarcely be reconciled on that hypothesis alone. According each argument full weight, the logical conclusion is that the main falling off in the time was ascribable to the four breaks, beside the last near the score. Three of them occurred in a space of about three hundred yards, almost as bad as the "double-break," which all drivers know to be such a drawback. There was then corroborative proof of the facts shown in the heat, and which should have been taken into the calculation. That the driver of Poscora endeavored to the best of his ability to bring him back at once to the trot was palpable. When the horse broke in scoring he would invariably fall back, and in the breaks under discussion not one of them covered much ground. Neither was it a "revolution," a changing of feet in order to get the right one foremost, nor could it be said to be a "tangling," "falling to pieces" affair, when the animal appears to have lost use of its legs, and is on the point of tumbling down or turning a somersault. The perusal of the following description, however, will be more satisfactory than further discussion:

The first race was a purse of $400 for the 2:25 class, in which were entered the same horses as on the previous Saturday in a similar race, save that Sweetness was reserved for the second event and Del Sur was an absentee. On the previous evening there had been a good deal of betting on the event, with Crown Point the first choice, but many who had judged that the previous race would key Starr King up to a better encounter, stood so steadfastly to his chances that there was not much difference between them. On the race track, just previous to the first heat, Crown Point sold for $45, Starr King $30, and Ashley and Cairo combined $20. In drawing for positions Ashley had the pole, with Cairo next and the favorite on the outside. The horses were called up very promptly, but there was too much ineffectual scoring and it was only at the eighth attempt that the horses were tapped off to a fair start, with Ashley having slightly the best of it. Ashley took advantage of his position, and made the place hot for the outsiders, reaching the quarter-pole a length ahead of Starr King, and then speeding down the backstretch with a light skip he reached the half in 1:10½, with Starr King on his wheel, while the other two left the leaders to worry it out between them. On the further turn Ashley seemed to slightly increase his advantage, but when once in the homestretch the chestnut monarch came with a fine burst of speed that soon carried Ashley off his feet, and although he was quickly caught Starr King won handily by two lengths in 2:22, Crown Point being a poor third. Those who in the pools had belittled the chances of the big chestnut, were now eager to hedge and as they were not particular to a shade, they invested freely at $75 for Starr King against $40 for Crown Point and $15 for the field. There was some neat scoring for a favorable position, and it was only at the sixth trial that they could get the word to a fair start. At the first turn Ashley was at his old tricks, and galloped some fifty yards before he could be brought to his gait, and yet he was but two lengths behind Starr King at the quarter-pole, the time being 36¼ seconds; and then the leader opened out the gap to four lengths at the half-mile, in 1:10½, and as Ashley could not stand the pace and was again in the air, and Crown Point made no decided demonstration for the lead, Starr King held his position and won easily in 2:23½, with Ashley second, Cairo third, and Crown Point last; but on account of the breaks, Ashley was relegated to the outside position. It appeared now to be almost a certainty that Starr King would win the race in straight heats, and $100 to $25 was freely wagered in his favor. Probably there had not been enough scoring to suit Starr King, as Cairo, evidently meaning business, kept to his wheel so persistently as to carry Starr King off his feet at the second turn, and he ran for such a long spell that he was ten lengths in the rear at the mid backstretch, and seemingly out of the heat. In the meantime Cairo had kept increasing his advantage, and led Ashley by three lengths at the half-mile in 1:12½, with Crown Point almost abreast, but the latter had the most speed, and passing Ashley, he made for Cairo, and on entering the stretch carried him off his feet, and after a pretty struggle won by a head and shoulders in 2:27, with Cairo two lengths ahead of Starr King, but the latter was placed last for running.

Starr King was still a favorite, and sold for $50 against $25 for Crown Point and $5 on the other two. With a level start on the third trial, Starr King was in difficulties shortly after the gong had sounded, and he was far, and, from appearances, hopelessly in the rear, when Cairo passed the quarter-pole, with Ashley and Crown Point close in attendance. On the backstretch Cairo made a bad break, and seemingly left the matter to be decided between Ashley, when Starr King was seen rapidly decreasing the gap, and amid great applause the big chestnut got even with Crown Point, and as he left his feet, Starr King won the heat and race easily by two lengths, with Ashley a poor third. Starr King showed that he had greatly improved since his last appearance, and perhaps a change in the shoes of Crown Point for a heavier description militated somewhat against his chances. It was a good race and very well contested.

The 2:30 race was called after two of the heats in the 2:25 had been decided, but owing to the delay in scoring, the horses were sent to the barn until the third heat of that was decided. This was regarded so sure a thing for Sweetness that she was an immense favorite; and the injury to Albert W., which necessitated his withdrawal, was thought to take away the only chance of defeating her. Poscora Hayward was not supposed to be in proper condition, and that it would require a race or two before he could show his capacity; and Blackmore was not credited with the speed he exhibited in the latter part of the race. Sweetness sold for $100 in the pools to $25 on both the others, and after the first heat there were none to venture at even these odds; and when the second was scored to her credit, it appeared that it was "a tan-yard to a shoe-string" that she would prove the victor.

For the first heat a very good start was effected at the third score; Blackmore had the pole, Poscora second, Sweetness on the outside. Poscora went off rapidly, and though he made a break soon after the word was given, he led at the quarter in 36¾; Sweetness second, Blackmore several lengths in the rear. Going down the back-stretch Poscora again broke, and the mare passed him and opened quite a gap at the half mile in 1:02½. From that point home she had it all her own way, for, though the two greys closed the gap somewhat on the home-stretch, they could never reach her, and she won in 2:26; Poscora second.

The second heat, another good start was given them, on the fifth score, the mare going away with the lead, reaching the quarter in 37½ seconds. Poscora drew up a little closer on the back-stretch, and his nose was on her wheel as the half mile was made in 1:13, but he broke on the further turn, fell back, and the mare came in a "handy winner" in 2:26, Poscora about as far behind her as Blackmoor was in the rear of him, a little more than open length marking the difference between each of them.

The third heat was one of those startling episodes which add so much to the pleasure and excitement of turf and track sports. There was scarcely a man who had any knowledge of trotting affairs who did not think the race was over, unless the driver of Poscora Hayward cherished the hope. The owner certainly considered it the most forlorn kind of an expectation, as he knew that his horse was not in the proper condition, and though he showed a fair degree of speed at times, he could not hold without breaking. There were numerous false starts. Thirteen times they came up for the word without avail. Blackmore, on the outside, would break into a mad run despite the efforts of his driver to restrain him. Then Poscora would follow, though his tantrums were more after the dancing order, while Sweetness, acting as though the trot were her fastest gait, came steadily and fast every time, and, when all were trotting, generally in the lead. For this the judges fined Goldsmith $10, and at the fourteenth effort the gong sounded, Sweetness having rather the best of the start. It was evident that Goldsmith was determined to "go for a record." The mare has a bad leg which may incapacitate her at any time, and she is the dam of a fine colt by Santa Claus, which will be greatly increased in value by his mother's record being very fast. She has speed enough to trot in the teens, and with sire and dam below 2:20, the youngster would fall heir to an estate well worthy of a severe trial to obtain. Laudable as the intention was, there is scarcely a doubt that it was the cause of the loss of the heat, and, worse than that, led to a bitter end, as the sequel will show. Sweetness was first at the quarter in 37 seconds, and after leaving that point and when the curve merged into the straight, she was showing a grand flight of speed. Thirty-four seconds was the time for the second quarter, and the half-mile in 1:11, left the others far in the rear. Poscora had broken about midway of the first turn, though after that he trotted steadily and without a mistake until a short distance beyond the three-quarter pole. Some of the space between him and the leader had been closed, and when he recovered he came again with great resolution, while the fast work had told on the mare. He was surely gaining very rapidly when the seven-furlong pole was passed, and at the long distance he was almost level with her. There was excitement among the spectators, and the ringing cheers appeared to animate him, while the mare, who had gamely struggled until the brain could not endure further strain, and the muscles were without elasticity, could not respond to the punishment—fagged, dispirited, beaten—as the successful horse passed under the wire in 2:25, Blackmore a fair third.

The tiring of the mare was so evident that there was a rush for the pool-stand to "get out." The first pool sold it was $70 on Poscora to $20 on the other two; the next it was $60 to $27, and after there was time to consider that her driver would not again make the mistake he had in this heat, and the desire to hedge by those who stood to win on the horse from the start the odds were reduced to $60 on Poscora to $40 on the others. There was a large amount of money went into the poll-box between the close of the third heat and the start for the fourth. Had the scoring been prolonged the pools and bar would have shown a better dividend. But as it was, the signal was given the first time the horses came up, and a capital start it was. Blackmore broke at the further end of the stables, Poscora trotted fast, and when within one hundred yards of the quarter-pole had obtained a good lead of Sweetness. He broke and she closed some of the intervening distance. About the same number of yards beyond the quarter-pole he broke again, and she ranged alongside. A hundred yards further there was another break, and she passed him, and there was open daylight between them. He regained some of the lost ground, though she still led at the half-mile. His nose was on her wheel as he steadily gained, when half way round the upper turn he broke again. She drew away, Blackmore gained on him. The fractional timers had left the reporters' stand, and the time at quarter, half and three-quarters was lacking. Soon after getting into the homestretch the whip of Goldsmith could be heard, and the whish through the air and the thud as it struck was evidence that Sweetness was again succumbing. At the ⅞ mark they were abreast. At the two-mile distance Poscora was three lengths in the lead and his driver apparently more intent to keep him from breaking than desirous of increasing the gap. He was on the outward side of the track nearly as far away as he could get to escape the irritating sound of the lash, but just before coming to the score Poscora broke, lost at least a length, recovered and came in two lengths in the lead; the time 2:29½.

There were complaints entered by Green, the driver of Poscora, that Goldsmith had placed the but of his whip in the spokes of the wheel so as to cause Poscora to break when they were going down the backstretch. This was corroborated by McConn, the driver of Blackmore, and Green was confident that the sulky spokes would show the abrasure. Goldsmith denied the charge, and countered by claiming that Poscora had run. There was some consultation between the judges, the bell was rung, Sweetness declared the winner of the heat and race and Poscora given second place. The announcement was received with the applause of those who had unexpectedly won, the groans and hisses of others. Elsewhere there is a review. In this place the heat is reported as nearly correct as the writer is capable of giving it without prejudice or favor to either party. The reporters' stand on the Bay District Course is not favorable for an uninterrupted view as it were on the outside of the course, but this disadvantage is also shared by the judges. When the horses first come on to the homestretch it is troublesome to tell their positions or to notice a skip, and the going around the tunnel which incloses the stairs which lead to the upper story is a serious obstruction. It is one of the hardest jobs, however, to get people out of the old-time ruts when horses or race-tracks are the questions at issue, and it will, probably, be another generation which will see the judges' stand universally on the right side of the course. The following are the

SUMMARIES.

Bay District Course.—Saturday, August 12, 1882.—Purse, $400; mile heats, 3 in 5, in harness: $250 to first, $100 to second, $50 to third horse.

| | | | | |
|---|---|---|---|---|
| C. W. Welby names ch. g. Starr King | 1 | 1 | 4 | 1 |
| G. Valensin names s. s. Crown Point | 3 | 3 | 1 | 2 |
| P. Farrell names b. g. Cairo | 4 | 2 | 2 | 4 |
| J. Cochran names ch. g. Ashley | 2 | 4 | 3 | 3 |

Time—2:22, 2:23½, 2:27, 2:27.

Same day.—2:30 class; purse, $500; mile heats, 3 in 5, in harness; $350 to first, $100 to second, $50 to third horse.

| | | | | |
|---|---|---|---|---|
| J. A. Goldsmith names s. m. Sweetness | 1 | 1 | 2 | 1 |
| W. D. Hammond names g. h. Poscora Hayward | 2 | 2 | 1 | 2 |
| Hy. McConn names g. g. Blackmore | 3 | 3 | 3 | 3 |
| A. Waldstein names b. s. Albert W | Drawn. | | | |

Time—2:26, 2:26, 2:25, 2:29½.

## TWO FINE RACES AT CLEVELAND.

The meeting at Cleveland showed some excellent trotting, and many of the horses lowered their record. The attendance was large, and in some of the races that were closely contested, the enthusiasm was very great. Of the contests, that for the 2:20 and the special purse were the most exciting, and we take the following interesting account of them from the N. Y. *Spirit of the Times:*

All the horses entered in the 2:20 class started, except Tariff, and, judging from their achievements, a close and memorable race was anticipated, but Rosa Wilkes showed so much superiority that the struggle resolved itself into a question of who would win second and following premiums. Rosa won the first and second heats without being pressed, and the betting dragged, there being difficulty in finding pool-buyers for the field at $15 to $30. Suddenly the short-enders took new courage, and the field rates firmly advanced at $20 to $50, and the backers of Rosa Wilkes put up their money with confidence, saying: "If it is a job, she has so much speed and steadiness they will not get through with it." In the evening an explanation leaked out that two heavy pool-buyers lost $3,000, and were courageously putting up on what they considered a "sure thing," as an arrangement was entered into for Rosa Wilkes to, as Turner puts it, "step on her ear," but it seems they did not make their words or money strong enough, for, to their dismay, Rosa and her driver came along as steadily in front the third heat as in the others, to the admiration of all supporters of honest trotting. If all tamperers with owners and drivers were served in this manner, the jobbers would seek other fields of scheming to turn a dishonest penny.

But, coming to a particular account of the races. The judges of the day were: Messrs. Edwards, McClosky and David Bonner. Timers, H. D. McKinney and J. W. Shaw. The first event disposed of was the 2:20 race, and the speed the various starters showed in warming up indicated that fast time would be made.

First Heat.—The favorite drew the pole, Forest Patchen second position and Wm. H. third, with Witherspoon on the outside. They scored several times, and when the word was given both Forest Patchen and J. P. Morris were off their feet. Rosa showed she had the foot of the party from the start, and Wm. H. and Fanny Witherspoon drew out from the others as they rounded the first turn, closing with the leader at the quarter in 35s, and Early Rose was a good fourth. On went Rosa Wilkes as if confident of the heat, and a length separated her from Witherspoon at the half in 1:10¼, with Wm. H. at the latter's wheel. He fell back on the third quarter, but Witherspoon brushed for the lead, and Rosa shook her easily in the stretch, winning in hand by two lengths from Witherspoon, Wm. H. a good third, and Morris, who trotted the stretch very fast, was lapped on him; time, 2:18¼. The others came along one by one, as per summary.

Second Heat.—Rosa Wilkes was now an established favorite at $100 to $40. They were sent off fairly on second trial, with Rosa in the van and Driver doing his best to get to the front. He was a good second at the quarter in 35s., and Wm. H. was making it hot for him, Morris going strong in fourth position, the others strung out. Rosa maintained the lead and reached the half in 1:10, and Morris got within a length of her, with Driver still leading Wm. H. Fanny Witherspoon began to show some of her noted speed on the last turn, and passed both Wm. H. and Driver, but could not reach Morris, who came along steadily and won second position as easily as Rosa did first. He was a length behind at the wire in 2:18¾.

Third Heat.—A good send-off was secured after a few attempts, and Rosa led as usual to the quarter in 35s. Morris broke on the first turn and dropped in behind the leader. Wm. H. went into second place, and Driver managed to work up to his wheel, but at the quarter Early Rose had passed Driver and trotted neck and neck with Wm. H., two lengths behind Rosa, at the half in 1:09¾. Driver, Witherspoon, Early Rose and Wm. H. were bunched as they reached the three-quarter pole, and they had an exciting race down the stretch for position. Morris outfooted them all but Rosa, and finished a length behind her, with Early Rose close to him and Fanny Witherspoon on her wheel, the others as per summary; time, 2:18¼. One of Calmar's reins parted, and he jumped over the fence. Caton righted him and jogged in behind the flag.

Cleveland, July 28.—Purse, $2,000; 2:20 class

| | | | |
|---|---|---|---|
| A. R. Cook's b. m. Rosa Wilkes, by George Wilkes | 1 | 1 | 1 |
| G. Wilson's br. g. J. P. Morris | 4 | 2 | 2 |
| D. W. Woodmansee's ch. m. Fanny Witherspoon | 2 | 3 | 4 |
| G. W. Saunders' b. g. William H | 3 | 4 | 5 |
| J. Elliott's ch. m. Early Rose | 5 | 7 | 3 |
| J. McEwen's ch. m. Annie W | 8 | 5 | 6 |
| A. Goldsmith's b. g. Driver | 9 | 7 | 7 |
| J. F. Duntling's br. g. Forest Patchen | 7 | 8 | 8 |
| S. L. Caton's b. g. Calmar | 6 | 9 | dis. |

Time—2:18¼, 2:18¾, 2:18¼.

Between the heats of the above race the bell summoned the starters for the Grand Special, and all answered, but Alley. The movements of Clingstone and Thorne were closely scanned, for it was felt that the issue lay between them. They were received with applause, and the excitement, especially about the pool-stands, was intense, old speculators, who rarely compare notes with by-standers, asking, "What do you think of it? Will Clingstone be able to stand the pressure that Thorne will bring to bear on him?" The answer was that money talked to the tune of $100 to $40 at first, and finally $100 to $30, on Clingstone against the field.

Posting myself in the ladies' stand, which affords a capital view of the homestretch, I watched and waited to see how the first round would be fought.

First Heat.—A novice could see that Turner had determined to use all his peculiar arts to strip the laurels from his great adversary. He scored behind him merely as a boxing-master would feint, and when he meant business would turn in front, wheeling suddenly toward Clingstone, who was in second position, with So-So at the pole and J. B. Thomas outside. After several plays of this kind Thorne got a little the best of the send-off, but Clingstone, with remarkable coolness and steadiness, took him by the throat-latch as they rushed by So-So, who broke shortly after the word was given. It was a sight to see the battle of these giants as they went locked to the quarter, in 34s.; faster and faster they went to the half, in 1:07, neither of them wavering or faltering, although from the advantage of the pole Clingstone was slightly in the lead at this point. On reaching the three-quarter pole, in 1:40¼, by a supreme effort, Thorne showed a head in front, and the cry arose, "He's got him," but as they rounded into the stretch Clingstone had placed the length of his body in advance of Thorne. Turner now made his rush, and Saunders had his whip ready for an emergency, and, as Thorne closed with him just beyond the distance, he tapped Clingstone lightly. He responded like a trump, and his stroke was as true and steady as at the start. Turner took both reins in one hand at the distance, and struck Thorne sharply with the whip, lifting him and shaking him at the same time, he made a feeble effort, but on being struck again and again dropped his tail and gave up the chase within a few strides of the wire, Clingstone beating him half a length, in 2:14, amid the cheers of the multitude gathered from all parts of the State. Thorne, too, received great praise, as it is believed that none but St. Julien or Maud S. could trot such a mile as he did in second position all the way round, and they would have to be to an edge to do it.

Second Heat.—The friends of Thorne said "We think more of his chances of winning now than we did before the start." So, instead of h d ing they continued betting $.0 against $100 very freely; when the horses appeared for the word neither exhibited any signs of distress. Clingstone is a cool customer, and a person who did not know him might think that Thorne was the fresher of the two, but the latter is a very resolute scorer, and there was more generalship displayed in scoring for this heat than any other of the meeting. Turner's horse came up faster, which gave him hopes that Clingstone was getting tired of it, but it was simply a cool calculating horse and his driver biding their time. Finally, after eleven false attempts, President Edwards said, "go," with the rival horses exactly even, but Thorne was under the most headway and dashed off a neck in the lead as they made the first turn, midway of it he showed a trifle more in advance, and he was so anxious to get the pole that he struck Clingstone's sulky, but that did not "rattle" the latter; he seemed to say, "I'll trot my legs off before you get this pole." At the quarter in 32¾s., Thorne showed his nose in front. From this point to the half the pace was terrific, Clingstone was evidently all out and moving like a piece of machinery, while Thorne, whose gait is more laborious, by indomitable pluck would gather his strength and make a rush, showing, for a stride or two, a nose ahead, and in the next few strides lose this advantage, but quickly recover it again. Men, women and children gave vent to their excited feelings by suppressed applause, while this hand-to-hand encounter was going on. They were at the half in 1:05, and it was evident that one or the other must soon succumb, as the pace was a killing one. Shortly afterwards Thorne could not stand the strain longer; he fell back hopelessly beaten; Nature was exhausted. "The spirit was willing, but the flesh was weak." Thorne is like the race-horse Monitor, he will go as fast as he can without whip or spur, and never gives up unless he is over-matched. Clingstone swept on, fighting time as resolutely as he did his late competitor, reaching the three-quarter pole in 1:39½, but as Thorne was far to leeward Saunders took back his horse, and Turner seeing this shook up Thorne again, but it was a forlorn hope, for Clingstone won as he pleased by several lengths in 2:16¾, and Thorne was so badly off for speed that he had all he could do to beat J. B. Thomas; time, 2:16¾. So-So distanced.

Third Heat.—Everybody, including Turner, considered the race was virtually over, for he nodded for the word on first score, when two lengths behind, and made no effort for the heat, as he allowed Thomas to finish second. Clingstone, I dare say, could have shut out both of them, but he went an easy mile to the quarter in 35½ seconds, the half in 1:10, three-quarters in 1:46½, and mile 2:23½. So ended one of the most remarkable races of the period, a race which entitles Clingstone to take rank with the best trotters of the age.

Same Day.—Purse, $3,000; special class.

| | | | |
|---|---|---|---|
| W. J. Gordon's b. g. Clingstone, by Rysdyk | 1 | 1 | 1 |
| E. Thorne's ch. g. Edwin Thorne | 2 | 2 | 3 |
| M. M. Hedges's b. s. J. B. Thomas | 4 | 3 | 2 |
| N. W. Kittson's b. m. So So | 3 | dis. | |

Time—2:14, 2:16¾, 2:23½.

Of Clingstone we give elsewhere an extended description. Rosa Wilkes began the season of 1880 at Augusta, Georgia, in the three-minute class, and won three out of the five races in which she was engaged. Last season she began with a record of 2:41¾, and she trotted in eleven races, of which she won five, taking heats in two others, and reducing her record to 2:25¼ at Lexington, Kentucky, on October 5th. Rosa Wilkes is a bay mare, nearly 15¾ hands, very blood-like in appearance. She has a neat head, a little-dished faced, very full eye, denoting courage and resolution, blood-like ear, good length of neck, good at throat-latch, rather long in her coupling, with short rump, but has fully developed quarters and stifles, legs and feet seem excellent, but she jogs as though sore forward, yet always goes strong and sound in her speeding, like Maud S., Darby, Mazo-Manie, Idol, and many others. She has wonderful speed, with a pure, level gait, with considerable knee action. In her breeding, she comes of the blending of the blood of the great trotting families Hambletonian and Mambrino Chief, and of the best representatives of both families; dam by Mambrino-Patchen, he full of thorough blood. When we find such lines of breeding, we invariably find what we all admire—gameness.

Following are the principal winners at Pittsburg and Cleveland, together with their best time made at the two meetings:

| Winner. | Sire. | Class. | Amount won. | Best Time. |
|---|---|---|---|---|
| Adele Gould | Jay Gould | 2:23 | $750 | 2:21½ |
| Aldine | Almont | 2:26 | 750 | 2:19½ |
| Bay Billy (pacer) | Shawhan's Tom Hal | Free for all. | 225 | 2:18 |
| Clingstone | Rysdyk | Special. | 1,500 | 2:14 |
| Fuller (pacer) | Clear Grit | 2:25 | 250 | 2:17½ |
| Gordon's team, four-in-hand | | Special. | 500 | 2:40½ |
| Jerome Eddy | Louis Napoleon | 2:23 | 1,000 | 2:18 |
| Joe Bowers, Jr. (pac'r) | Joe Bowers | 2:25 | 700 | 2:18 |
| King William | Wash'ton Denmark | 2:26 | 375 | 2:20½ |
| London | Mambrino Patchen | 2:29 | 750 | 2:20½ |
| Lucy (pacer) | | Free for all. | 750 | 2:19½ |
| Mattie Hunt'r (pac'r) | Prince Pulaski | Free for all. | 375 | 2:17 |
| Overland | Elmo | 2:29 | 375 | 2:14½ |
| Rosa Wilkes | George Wilkes | 2:20 | 1,000 | 2:18½ |
| Wilson | George Wilkes | 2:38 | 750 | 2:22½ |
| Wilson | George Wilkes | 3:00 | 750 | 2:22½ |

An announcement has been made by telegraph that Col. William Edwards, of Cleveland, has accepted the challenge of John W. Shaw to trot Trinket against Clingstone for $25,000 a side, the race to be trotted at Hartford. It is doubtful if this report is correct, as Mr. Gordon, the owner of Clingstone, recently stated that he would allow Clingstone to appear soon in regular races; but if it be true, the match would create intense interest, as Clingstone has never yet lost a race, and both horses have a record of 2:14.

## SARATOGA RACES.

Towards the middle of August the season at Saratoga is at its height, and the latest reports state that the attendance was very large at that place, and that the races were of a much more interesting character. Especially was this the case in the race for the Grand Prize of Saratoga, which was a magnificent struggle from the start to the finish, and we take the following interesting account from the New York *World*:

The racing began with a dash of three-quarters of a mile, for horses of all ages, with an allowance of 7 pounds for those that had been beaten and had not won a race here since the racing began, on the 10th of July, and with maiden allowances of from 10 to 22 pounds. The starters were Little Phil, at 118 pounds; Baby, 113 pounds; Disturbance, 111 pounds; Stand-Off and Mammonist, 108 pounds each; Gus Matthews, 101 pounds; Wauculla, 99 pounds, and Martinique, 9‹ pounds. So even were the lot supposed to be in merit that the field was made the favorite, with Gus Matthews, Little Phil and Mammonist selected out. The start was delayed fully forty-five minutes, principally by the temper of Gus Matthews, which was made even worse by the wilful disobedience of Frank McLaughlin and Heard, on Waucnlla and Stand-Off, both repeatedly breaking away. When they did get the flag Gus Matthews was in front, with Mammonist and Little Phil close up. The next were Martinique, Disturbance, Waucnlla and Baby, with Stand-Off behind. Matthews held the lead down the fractional track, attended by Little Phil and Waucnlla. They passed the half together and continued so until well around the turn, when Disturbance closed up and at the three-quarters was on nearly equal terms with the leaders. Gus Matthews remained in front until within a few lengths of the seven furlong pole, when James McLaughlin cut Little Phil loose and, coming right away, won an easy race by a length and a half. In the race in from the pool-stands Disturbance beat Gus Matthews and captured the place money. Gus Matthews was third, followed by Martinique and Mammonist, with Bady, Stand-Off and Waucnlla bringing up the rear; time, 1:15.

The second race was that now known as the Grand Prize of Saratoga, a handicap for all ages, at a mile and three-quarters, which was first run in 1879, when it was known as the Grand Union Hotel Purse, but since the proprietors of that establishment withdrew their contribution to a special event named after the hotel, the name has been changed to the Grand Prize of Saratoga. Although its history is brief, it is among the most popular races with owners and the public, the several contests having been among the best of the season. In its first year Danicheff, then a four-year-old, with 113 pounds, ran the distance in 3:07 and beat a field of seven. The next year, 1880, Luke Blackburn won after one of the grandest races ever run by that (then) great three-year-old. He was handicapped at 116 pounds, and gave "lumps" of weight to all the others, One Dime (4) running second with 110 pounds, Glenmore (5) third with 118 pounds, followed by Clemmie F. (5) at 103 pounds, General Phillips (6) at 105 pounds, Chimney Sweep (4) at 103 pounds. Blackburn won by two lengths in 3:07. Last year Checkmate, at 124 pounds, ran the distance in 3:01¼, beating by a scant half length Bushwhacker, to whom he was giving no less than 28 pounds, while to each of the others he was giving more or less weight. From this it will be seen that the stake has not only brought out first class horses, but has been won by the best horse in the race. Judged by the weight imposed by the handicapper, there was no exception to the rule in the character of the starters to-day. The weights were only announced a few days ago, and, as expected, Reed's Thora, Churchill's Bend Or and Williams' Checkmate were on equal terms at the head of the list, each at 122 pounds. All three would have started had Checkmate not been sent to Monmouth Park. The starters, however, were an excellent lot, viz: Thora, Bend Or, Glidelia, Bushwhacker, Compensation, Ella Warfield and General Monroe. As to what the handicapper thought of them the following table shows:

| Name and Age. | Weight for Age. | Handicap Weight. | Difference. | Excess against Thora. |
|---|---|---|---|---|
| Thora, 4 | 113 | 122 | 9 on | .... |
| Bend Or, 4 | 118 | 122 | 4 on | 5 lb. |
| Glidelia, 5 | 115 | 116 | 1 on | 8 lb. |
| Compensation, 4 | 115 | 108 | 7 off | 16 lb. |
| Bushwhacker, aged | 118 | 101 | 17 off | 26 lb. |
| Ella Warfield, 5 | 115 | 96 | 19 off | 28 lb. |
| * General Monroe, 4 | 118 | 96 | 22 off | 31 lb. |

* General Monroe carried 3 pounds overweight, which reduced the excess against Thora to 28 pounds

Although Bend Or beat Thora last Saturday for the Summer Handicap, and the latter still had so much the worst of the weights, Thora was the favorite in the pools, with Bend Or and Glidelia filling the second places. The latter was ridden by Costello, whom Mr. G. L. Lorillard had kindly allowed to come from Monmouth Park for the express purpose of riding for Captain Conner. No time was lost in any preliminary gallops, none of the colors being shown in front of the stand, the horses going direct from the paddock to the post. There was but little delay at the post, and when the flag was dropped Glidelia and Ella Warfield were in front, with Bend Or and Thora close up, followed by General Monroe, Compensation and Bushwhacker. Before they had run fifty yards Thora took the lead, and being joined by Bend Or, Glidelia and Ella Warfield, the four ran into the main track lapped. When well into the track Thora drew away, and being joined by Ella Warfield on the turn, the two raced together to the three-quarters, followed a scant length behind by Glidelia and Bend Or. In the run up the stretch Costello moved Glidelia up, and lapping Thora on the outside, the pace became very fast as they ran past the judges, the three-quarters having been run in 1:19½. Close up was Ella Warfield, a trifle in front of Bend Or, with Compensation in front of General Monroe and Bushwhacker, they being literally suffocated in the dust raised by the leaders. In the run round the turn Costello kept Glidelia at Thora's saddle-skirts, and gradually forcing the pace Glidelia took the lead opposite the Belmont stable, and at the half was half a length in front of Thora, the half-mile from the judges' stand having being run in 51 seconds. Close up to the two mares was Compensation, running on the inside, lapped by Bend Or, with Ella Warfield and General Monroe close in behind them, and with Monroe holding the outside position. When well round the turn Thora dropped back, seeing which the shouting began; but so intense was the interest of the crowd in the struggle between Glidelia, Compensation and Bend Or that General Monroe was at Glidelia's saddle skirts and Thora fairly lost in the dust before the threatening aspect of Monroe's position was realized. Glidelia and Monroe turned into the stretch nearly together, with Bend Or following close up, lapped by Compensation. The instant they were straight the struggle became a terrific one. Inch by inch General Monroe gained, and as the two were running wide of the rails, not a few hoped to see Walker bring Bend Or through, but as they reached the seven-furlong post it was evident that he was unequal to the occasion, and the whole attention was turned to the leaders. On they came, both Costello and Quantrell riding in fine style and using both whip and spur. Forty yards from the end the contest looked as if the result would certainly be a "dead heat," but with one grand rally Costello again got Glidelia to fully extend herself, and as she did so her head showed a few inches in front, and as she was again able to repeat the exertion, she landed the stake, by a short head, with General Monroe second, a length in front of Bend Or. Six lengths away was Compensation, followed by Bushwhacker, Ella Warfield and Thora; time, 3:01, which beats the record by just one-quarter of a second, Checkmate's 3:01¼ for the same race last year being the best previous performance. Owing to the dust the timers were unable to take the time at the end of the mile, but they timed the other quarters as follows:

| | | | |
|---|---|---|---|
| First quarter | 0:26 | Half mile | 0:54½ |
| Second quarter | 0:28½ | Three-quarters | 1:19½ |
| Third quarter | 0:24 | Mile and a quarter | 2:10½ |
| Fourth and fifth quarters | 0:51 | Mile and a half | 2:35½ |
| Sixth quarter | 0:25 | Mile and three-quarters | 3:01 |
| Seventh quarter | 0:26 | | |

On the return to the scales a complaint of foul riding was made against Quantrell, the rider of General Monroe, by Walker, the rider of Bend Or, who alleged that he was run into by Monroe in coming round the last turn. After some delay the judges admitted the complaint, and disqualified General Monroe for any part of the race, giving Bend Or second place and Compensation the third place.

SUMMARY.

August 5, 1882.—The Grand Prize of Saratoga, a handicap sweepstakes, for all ages, at $30 each, half forfeit, only $10 if declared out by July 1, with $1,200 added, the owner of the second to receive $250 and of the third $100 out of the stakes; closed with 54 subscribers, of which 23 declared out; mile and three-quarters.

| | |
|---|---|
| W. M. Conner's ch. m. Glidelia, 5, by Bonnie Scotland, dam Waltz, 116 lbs. (Costello) | 1 |
| Churchill & Johnson's b. c. Bend Or, 4, by Buckden, dam Kate Walker, 122 lbs. (Walker) | 2 |
| O. Bowie's b. g. Compensation, 4, by Catesby, dam Australia, 108 lbs. (J. McLaughlin) | 3 |
| G. B. Bryson's b. g. Bushwhacker, aged, 101 lbs. (Stoval) | 0 |
| Davis & Hall's b. m. Ella Warfield, 96 lbs. (F. McLaughlin) | 0 |
| C. Reed's b. f. Thora, 4, 122 lbs. (Brophy) | 0 |
| E. J. McElmeel's b. c. General Monroe, 4, 96 lbs, carried 99 lbs. (Quantrell) | dsq. |

Time—3:01.

Pools.—Thora, $225; Glidelia, $140; Bend Or, $135; Ella Warfield, $40; Bushwhacker, $35; field, $35. Mutuels paid $20 50. General Monroe finished second, but was disqualified for a foul.

On Friday August 11th, in the first race, five furlongs, Fairview won, Verd second, Tennyson third; time, 1:04. In the second race, one mile and 500 yards, Warfield won, Granger second, Aluindo third; time, 2:14. In the third race, three-fourths of a mile, Bootjack won, Col. Watson second; time, 1:15½. In the fourth race, one mile, Valparaiso won, Duke of Mont Albans and Amazon ran a dead heat for second place; time, 1:43.

On the 12th, in the first race, three-quarters of a mile, George Kenny won, Barnes second, Tocsin third; time 1:15. In the second race, mile and a half, Bend Or won, General Monroe second; time, 2:36½. The third race, one mile, was a dead heat between Col. Watson and Julesburg, Nortland next; time, 1:44½. In the fourth race, three-quarters of a mile, Amazon won, Martinique second, time, 1:15½.

On the 14th inst., the first race, one mile, Fellowplay won, Bruno second, Stanton third; time, 1:41½. In the second race, 1¼ miles, Jennie V. won, Fatinitza second; time 2:09. In the third race, three-quarters of a mile, Bounce won, Bride second; time 1:15. In the fourth race, one mile and a furlong, Farragut won, Baby second; time 1:56.

On the 15th, in the three-quarter-mile race, Bootjack won, Waponeketa second, Copias third; time, 1:18. In the second race, a mile and a quarter, Francis won, Square Dance second; time, 2:14. In the third race, one mile and five furlongs, Lord Warfield was first, General Monroe second; time, 2:14½. In the fourth race, a steeplechase, two and a half miles, Post Guard won; Annet second; time, 5:26.

On the 16th, in the first race, five furlongs, Punster was first and Northana second; time, 1:03½. In the second race, 1½ miles, Granger won, Farragut second; time, 2:38¼. In the third race, a mile, Jennie V won, Stanton second; time, 1:42. In the fourth race, three quarters of a mile, Molosine won, Blenheim second; time, 1:15.

## THE UTICA RACES.

The meeting at Utica is the third of the great western trotting circuit, and of the races on the opening days. We have but the curt dispatches:

On Tuesday the 15th, in the purse for $1,500 for the 2:38 class Wilson won; Eva second, Topsy third, time, 2:21—2:22—2:23¼—2:23¾. In the purse of $2,000 for the 2:23, class Unalola won, R. P. second. Lucrece, Mattie, Gloster, George M. and Cora Belmont also trotted; time —2:23—2:22½—2:23¼—2:22¾—2:24.

On the second day in the 2:38 class race, Wilson won, Eva second, Topsy third, Maytheme fourth; time, 2:21¼—2:23½—2:23¾. The 2:23 class race Unalola won, R. P. second, Sucreel third, Mattie fourth; time, 2:23—2:21¼—2:22½—2:22¾—2:24.

On Wednesday the 16th in the 2:29 class, Hollow Dock won; St. Cloud second, Rigolette third; time, 2:21½—2:20¾—2:21¼. The free-for-all pacers, barring Little Brown Jug, was unfinished. Flora Belle took two heats, Buffalo Girl two, Lucy two and Gem one; time, 2:14¾—2:15¼—2:19¼—2:18—2:18¾—2:18¾.

## THE ROCHESTER RACES.

In consequence of the rain the first day's programme was postponed until Wednesday, the 9th inst., when Wilson, Rockton, May Thorne, Eva, Golden Rule, Topsy and Neville started for the $1,500 purse in the 2:38 class. Wilson took the first, second and fourth heats and Rockton the third; time, 2:24½, 2:24, 2:25½ and 2:24½. The second race was a purse of $2,000 for the 2:23 class, in which Unalala, R. P., Mattie, Lady Rolfe, Jewett, George M., Flora F. and Lucrece started. R. P. won the first and second heats so handily, each in 2:24, that the betting crowd considered him almost a certain winner. Unalala, however, captured the third heat after a sharp fight with Jewett, and, starting with the lead in the fourth and fifth heats, she outfooted all competitors, and was never headed, winning the trot with ease; time, 2:24¼, 2:24¾, 2:25½; R. P. took second money, Mattie third, and Lady Rolfe fourth.

Following are telegraphic dispatches in connection with the races on the succeeding days:

On the 10th the rain seriously interfered with the races. In class 2:25, pacing, Joe Bowers won, Limber Jack second. Fuller won the first heat and was distanced in the fifth; time, 2:18, 2:20, 2:20, 2:26¼, 2:27¾, 2:31. In the 2:29 class Overland won, Abe Downing second. Yellow Dock, Rigolette, Little Billy, Kate Taylor, London, Rolla and Big Ike also trotted; time, 2:21¾, 2:23, 2:23½, 2:27½, 2:27½. The free for all pacing race was next on the programme, but it was postponed unt[illegible]

)n the 11th the track was excellent and the attendance was ;e. Little Brown Jug, in his attempt to lower his record, de a mile in 2:18. The free-for-all pacing race was hotly tested and there was great excitement over the result. lowing is the summary: Lucy 4, 4, 1, 1, 1; Flora Belle, l, 2, 2, 2; Mattie Hunter, 2, 2, 4, 3, 3; Gem, 3, 3, 3, 4, 4; e, 2:16, 2:18½, 2:17½, 2:17¼, 2:19. Following is e summary of the 2:23 class: Barbara Patchen, 2, 1, 2, 1, Gladiator, 1, 5, 1, 2, 3; Barrett, 3, 3, 3, 4, 2; Allegheny oy, 4, 2, 4, 3, 4; Hattie Pearce, 6, 6, 5, 5, drawn; Kittie ood, 5, 4, 6, drawn; Captain Lewis, Secret and May iorne were drawn; time, 2:24½, 2:28, 2:24¾, 2:24½, 26½. Two heats were trotted in the 2:26 class, and then at event was also postponed.

On the 12th the final day of the meeting there was again very large assemblage. Aldine won the last heat and the ce, in the postponed 2:26 class; Minnie second, King ilkes third, Cornelia fourth; time, 2:23¼, 2:21, 2:21¼. r the special purse of $3,000 the result was as follows: ingstone, 2, 1, 1, 1; Edwin Thorne, 1, 2, 2, 2; Pickard, 3, 3, 4; Minnie R, 6, 4, 4, 3; Kate Sprague, 4, 6, 5, 5; J. Thomas, 5, 5, 6, 6; time, 2:19, 2:18, 2:20, 2:21¼. In e thre-minute class Wilson won; Golden Rule second, 'a third, Topsy fourth; time, 2:25, 2:22¼, 2:21¼. In e 2:20 class Von Arnim won; Early Rose second, Driver rd, Fred Douglass fourth; time, 2:20¼, 2:21¾, 2:19½.

## MONMOUTH PARK RACES.

The races continue at the pleasant watering place by the aside, and attract a large and fashionable attendance. On aturday, August 12th, in the first race, three-quarters of a ile, Pizzaro won, Magnet second; time 1:18¾. In the cond race, one and three-quarters miles, Forester won, uplex second; time 3:13½. In the third race, one mile, trathspey won, Laura Glass second; time 1:45¼. In the ourth race, one and five-eighths miles, Monitor won, Girofle cond, Checkmate third; time 2:45½. In an extra race, ve-eighths mile, Felicit won, Yorkshire second; time 1:04¼. the steeple chase, short course, Frank Short won, Harry ow second, Guy third; time 3:20. John T, the favorite, ll at the water jump and broke his leg.

On the 15th, among the valuable stakes run was the Omibus, in which there were some hundred and sixty subribers, among them Judge Mels and Judge McKinstrey. the first race, a mile, Miss Lumley was first, Gussie M. cond; time 1:48. In the Criterion stakes, three-quarters a mile, Fairfield won, Nimrod second, Inconstant third; me 1:17¾. The Omnibus stakes a mile and a half, Harry ilmore first, Wyoming second, Tom Plunkett third; time :44¼. In the mile and a quarter Mary Anderson won, Parole cond, Hospador third; 2;14¾. In the mile and an eighth orkshire won easily, beating Rochester; time, 2:02¼. In he steeplechase, whole course, Ed. Bouham won; Bernardne second. The other horses got off the course. No time was taken.

In the Breeders" stakes, somewhat similar to the Omnibus, only it is for two instead of three year olds, Mr. P. Lorillard ran first and second with Battledoor and Inconstant, both being by Glenlyon.

## THE SANTA CRUZ RACES.

The season is now at its height in this pretty watering place by the sea, and with the additional attraction of the races, the beach and drives have presented a most animated appearance during the past week. The Executive Officers to whom was entrusted the arranging of the speed programme made a happy selection for the different classes, but, as might naturally be imagined, they met with many difficulties on this their first essay for an annual meeting, and the nominations were not so numerous as they will undoubtedly be when the Association can profit by the experience gained in former meetings. In one respect Santa Cruz has a great advantage over all the county and district fairs, as it possesses the most charming site for a race track within easy distance, by a smooth and well-kept road, from the centre of the town. Situated on a slight plateau, the view of the bay is very pretty, while the track is also well shaded from the boisterous winds that now and then sweep from the ocean. There are evident signs that the inhabitants are bent upon making Santa Cruz the queen of the watering places on the Pacific Coast. New buildings are being erected, the roads in every direction are in splendid order, and there is a project to continue the pretty drive on the sands, some five miles by the ocean side, which will be an unequaled attraction.

Tuesday, the 15th, was the opening day of the races, the first event reducing itself to a match between Nell Briody and Joe Deans, in which the mare was a great favorite at $20 to $10. The track was not in as good order as might have been expected, being somewhat heavy and cuppy, as horsemen style it. The attendance was good, and judging from the spirited pool-selling, a great deal of interest was taken in the proceedings. Joe Deans won the first heat, and then the betting was reversed in his favor, but the mare proved herself the better horse, and won the three successive heats and race in very handsome style.

The second race was a renewal of the old time battle between Crown Point, Starr King and Del Sur, in the 2:25 class, the two former having each scored a victory recently at the Bay District track. The betting was $25 for Starr King, $15 for Crown Point, and $5 for Del Sur. In the first heat Starr King indulged in some of his running, and Del Sur made it hot for Crown Point, who, however, managed to score the heat to his favor. Still there was but little change in the betting, save that Starr King and Crown Point sold almost as equal favorites. To the latter, however, was accorded the second heat, and although Starr King took the third, Crown Point was the steadiest of the two, and won the fourth heat and race in a handy manner.

SUMMARIES.

Bay View Driving Park, Santa Cruz, August 15, 1882.—Purse, $175, for district horses; best 3 in 5, to harness.

| | | | | |
|---|---|---|---|---|
| E. J. Swift names b. m. Nell Briody | 2 | 1 | 1 | 1 |
| Mr. Ford names g. g. Joe Dean | 1 | 2 | 2 | 2 |

Time—2:45½, 2:43¾, 2:45, 2:44¼.

Same day.—Purse of $500 for the 2:25 class; best 3 in 5, to harness.

| | | | | |
|---|---|---|---|---|
| G. Valensin names Crown Point | 1 | 1 | 2 | 1 |
| C. W. Welby names Starr King | 3 | 3 | 1 | 2 |
| L. J. Rose names Del Sur | 2 | 2 | 3 | 3 |

Time—2:25, 2:29½, 2:27½, 2:31.

On the Wednesday, the programme was devoted chiefly to running races, and the attendance showed an increase on that of the preceding day. The first was a purse of $100, a dash of three-quarters of a mile, which was won easily by Pat. Robson's May B. in 1:20¼, she being a great favorite in the pools, with B. S. Clark's Viola R. being her sole contestant. The second event was a mile dash, $50 each, $10 forfeit with $100 added, in which were entered W. L. Appleby's May D., P. J. Shatter's Night-Hawk and W. Boots' Mollie H. The former was the favorite, the two others selling in the field, and she won after a pretty struggle, with Night-Hawk second, in 1:44¾, which was a fast run considering the state of the track and the stiff breeze that was blowing at the time. The proceedings closed with a well contested race for a purse of $80, on which the pool-selling was very brisk. Following is the

SUMMARY.

Santa Cruz, August 16th.—Purse $80, with $10 entrance; best three in five, to harness.

| | | | | | |
|---|---|---|---|---|---|
| W. E. Peck names Leland Stanford | 2 | 1 | 1 | 3 | 1 |
| J. M. Ferguson names Soquel Jim | 3 | 3 | 3 | 1 | 2 |
| D. W. Evans names Pajaro Chief | 1 | 2 | 2 | 2 | dis |

Time—3:05, 3:04, 3:03, 3:02, 3:03¼.

On Thursday the attendance was again good. The first was a trotting race, best three in five, for horses of the 2:40 class, between Slim Jim and Frank, which was won by Frank in three straight heats; time, 2:40, 2:37¾, 2:39. The second race was for double teams, E. J. Swift's Frank and Nell Briody being matched against Dr. Chas. Ford's Joe Dean and Boy Dan. The first heat was won by Dean and Dan, and the last three by Frank and Nell; time, 2:57¾, 2:53¾, 2:56¾, 2:54¾.

A great influx of visitors was expected on the Friday and Saturday, the concluding days of the meeting, and it was the general opinion at Santa Cruz that it would prove to be a relative success for a first attempt by the Association.

## GRAND CIRCUIT WINNERS OF HEATS AND RACES.

PITTSBURGH.

| Winner. | Sire. | Class. | Amount won. | Best Time. |
|---|---|---|---|---|
| Adele Gould | Jay Gould | 2:33 | $750 | 2:21 |
| Bay Jim (pacer) | | 2:25 | 750 | 2:21¼ |
| Ben Hamilt'n (pacer) | De Witt's Norman | Free for all. | 225 | 2:18 |
| Buzz Medium | Happy Medium | 2:23 | 1,000 | 2:20½ |
| Dick Organ | Commodore | 2:26 | 750 | 2:25½ |
| Early Rose | Almont | 2:20 | 1,000 | 2:21¼ |
| Felix (pacer) | Dictator | 2:25 | 150 | 2:24½ |
| Hotspur Chief | Hotspur | 2:38 | 150 | 2:29½ |
| King Wilkes | George Wilkes | 2:38 | 750 | 2:26½ |
| Largesse | Scott's Thomas | 2:19 | 750 | 2:25 |
| Lucy (pacer) | | Free for all. | 750 | 2:15½ |
| Mattie Hunt'r (pac'r) | Prince Pulaski | Free for all. | 375 | 2:15¼ |
| Neta Medium | Happy Medium | 2:33 | 375 | 2:23½ |
| Princess (pacer) | Pocahontas Boy | 2:25 | 250 | 2:20½ |
| R. P. | Happy Medium | 2:26 | 750 | 2:23¼ |
| Young Fullerton | Edward Everett | 2:19 | 750 | 2:22¼ |

## HORSES OF BUTTE COUNTY.

CHICO, BUTTE Co., August 16th, 1882.

EDITOR BREEDER AND SPORTSMAN: I send you to-day per Wells, Fargo & Co's. Express $20.00 for four subscriptions to your truly sporting paper, a journal of which this Coast has stood in need for a long time.

Our District Fair commences on the 5th of September, and lasts during the week, and the prospects are good for a big turnout. There was a good attendance last year and closely contested races, and as our President will stand no pulling, every one feels that the best horse will win. I have not had time to visit the ranch of D. M. Reavis, the home of old Blackbird, but hope to in the near future, and will let you know how his colts are getting along. I hear some of them were moving fast while McIntyre was handling them. I was out to the ranch of J. T. McIntosh the other day, and saw some very fine stallions, mares and colts. The first name in my notes is that of the brown stallion, Singleton, four-year-old by Willie Schepper by Rydsyk's Hambeltonian, 1st dam Nellie by Son of Vermont. Black Hawk, 2d dam by Busiris. Singleton's dam is Lightfoot, the dam of Pride. Singleton is a rich brown tinged with tan, white hind feet; stands full 15¾ hands high; a head and eye that show nerve and intelligence; a fine rangy neck well set into a pair of sloping shoulders; long, powerful arms; wide, flat legs; splendid feet; a middling long back, strongly coupled, deep through the heart; deep ribbed barrels, but not inclined to be slabsided, and, I think, as well shaped and powerful hind quarters as I ever saw on a horse. The next is La Harpe; three years old; bright bay, hind legs white, nearly to hocks, large star; fully 15 hands, and weighs 1100, and looked to me as I saw him move in his paddock as if some day he might make a trotter. His sire is Fame, by Alexander's Belmont. The sire of Nutwood, La Harpe's dam Prairie Bird by Flax Tail, by Blue Bull. Mr. McIntosh has some fine brood mares. Kate Signal, by Old Signal, her dam by Illinois Medoc. She has a colt by her side by Singleton, and I tell you he is a beauty. Bessie, brown mare, by Reavis' Blackbird; record 2:34¾. Trotted five miles out as a three-year old in 14:21¼. Stinted to Singleton, as are all his mares. Susie Brown, by Blackbird, dam by son of Vermont Black Hawk, record 2:42, three-year-old; dark bay mare. Rena, by Gen. Reno, trotted trial when three years old, 2:35; was bred on account of a bad leg; her dam, Kate Signal. Ch. mare Elaine, by Blackbird, dam Hattie Bay by Billy Cheatham, by Cracker, he by Boston; Hattie's dam Mary Butte, by Belmont, by American Boy; surely there is enough blue blood in her. Gray mare, Lady Emma, by Easton's David Hill, dam Dolly McNeil, by Hoagland's Messenger. This mare was bred by Yank Sessions and sold to Mr. Ralston. At the track Jas. Hasty has a three-year-old Prompter; also a two-year-old by the same horse; two yearlings by Buccaneer; two sucklings by Singleton. Mr. Chas. Sherman has a two-year-old by Plumas, and a yearling filly by Brigadier.

Mr. McIntosh is working Singleton, a two-year-old filly. Exact, by Prompter, a yearling by Prompter, dam Susie Brown; this filly is matched against Mr. Sherman's Brigadier for $200 a side, to come off Nov. 11th, and the way the Prompter moved when I saw her, there will be music in the air. The race is half a mile and repeat. There are a few good road horses up here. Lawyer Lusk drives a nice pair of Blackbirds that can beat fifty any day. Dr. Mason drives a very nice and useful pair of grays. Gen. Bidwell drives a pair of large browns, by Rattler, a fine carriage team. N. D. Rose takes the evening air behind a little bay to the time of three minutes. Mr. Burnham of the White House drives the old trotter Dutchman. And now, Mr. Editor, if you can find time to pay our little city a flying visit, you will meet with good friends and true; and if on your departure you find anything to grumble at as to hospitality, you can make your visits as I write letters—

OCCASIONALLY.

## THE PLUNGER REMAINS.

The Monmouth Park Association, after a careful investigation, has dismissed the charges made by J. E. Kelly, the bookmaker, against F. T. Walton, the decision being as follows:

"In the matter of the charges by J. E. Kelly against F. T. Walton that he had bribed the jockeys of Marathon and Inconstant to pull those horses in the race specified, the Executive Committee of the Monmouth Park Association find that the charges are not supported by proof or probability. But in the course of the investigation it was admitted by Mr. Walton that he frequently gives large sums of money to trainers and jockeys. That these gifts are made out of pure liberality is not credible. If not intended to corrupt, their tendency is corrupting. One object unquestionably is to obtain information which belongs exclusively to owners.

"In the hope of arresting the evils growing out of similar practices without having recourse to more stringent measures, the following clause is inserted in and made the fourth paragraph of the seventeenth Rule of Racing, the violation of which is punishable by ruling off the course:

" 'If any person give or offer to any trainer, jockey or employee, or if any trainer, jockey or employee accept or offer to accept any gratuity, whether in the form of money, share in a bet or other benefit, without the previous specific and written consent of the owner whose horse gives occasion to the gratuity, and to whom the trainer, jockey or employee is engaged; or' "——

The rule then continues in its various sections to provide against corruption and bribery among employees and officials of a race track.

Mr. Kelly said in reference to the decision that the action of the committee would be felt in racing before another year was passed, as it placed a premium upon dishonest practices. He claimed to have done his share to protect the interests of the turf, and said he could afford to abide the result if others could.

Mr. Walton was found among the bookmakers, with whom he was anxious to wager large sums that Frank Short would win the steeplechase. He had nothing to say except that the decision was a complete vindication of his character as a sporting man. He said that he would sue Mr. Kelly for defamation of character.

"Krik," the able correspondent of the New York *World*, from which paper we make the above excerpt, makes the following remarks, which are very pertinent to the matter:

"The Walton-Kelly decision at Monmouth Park caused some talk among the racing men here, and several had to pay bets they had lost that 'Peety' would be ruled off. The decision is generally held to be right, and only those criticise it who want Walton ruled off all courses, without regard to the evidence, on the principle that he is dangerous to the interest of the turf. The amendment to the rules, prohibiting presents to jockeys and others connected with the stables without the written consent of owners, gives satisfaction. There is certainly more legislation required in regard to jockeys and stable boys. Of late there has been much disobedience among the younger jockeys, and starts have been seriously delayed thereby. They have no punishment to fear. If they are fined, the men they are riding for will have to pay the fines; if they are suspended, it simply means to many of them that they will get just as much to eat as ever, and that they will have to do just as much work around the stables to which they are attached. The only difference is they cannot ride in a race for a certain number of days. Of course, to riders like Hughes, Fisher, Walker and others of that class, suspension is something of a punishment, but to the smaller boys like Heard, Stone, Harrison and Frank McLaughlin, it is none. If the owners by whom they are immediately engaged happen to want a light boy, there are plenty that can be borrowed for the occasion.

"Some racing men, who see the need of a change, think that jockeys should be licensed, as in England; but who shall issue the license? Another suggestion is that in the case of long meetings like those at Saratoga, Monmouth Park and Brighton, owners or trainers should be required to report to the secretary the names of their riders, with a statement of their weight and ability to ride, which statement should be submitted to the stewards, who should issue permits to ride, the permits to be revoked either for bad conduct or on proof that the boys have not the strength or ability to manage a horse. If done at one place this should be sustained elsewhere. In fact, there is no better field for true missionary work than the stables at large race tracks, if for nothing else than to teach the boys that 'cleanliness is next to godliness.' Of course this does not apply to all stables. There are a number where the boys are watched with some care, but in others they are simply left to herd together with less care bestowed on them than would be if they were so many dogs."

A PROPOSED GRAND MEETING AT NEW YORK.—There is a talk of the Gentlemen's Driving Association arranging a two days' meeting at their park, to come off at the latter part of September. It is claimed that a purse of $5,000, free for all, would secure all the first-class celebrities, and a $2,000 purse for the 2:21 class would be an attractive item on the programme. A race under the saddle and a pacing race might complete the fixtures for the two days of rare sport. Mr. Frank Work would undoubtedly be on hand with his grand team and give an exhibition mile, and Mr. William H. Vanderbilt would allow the dainty Queen of the Turf, Maud S, to appear; and perhaps Mr. Robert Bonner might be induced to send from the Westchester hills some of his choice stock. There is no doubt but that such a list of attractions would attract the largest assemblage ever seen on the Fleetwood track.

The horse Raven, by Monday from Camilla Urso, that was owned by C. M. Chase and showed such excellent ability here as a hurdle racer, is now owned in Canada. On the 8th inst., at Saratoga, he started in a handicap hurdle race, in which he was almost even favorite with Turfman, but as he was deliberately pulled, the judges immediately ruled McBride, his rider, off the course, as also Phair, the rider of Bailey, another Canadian horse, for the same offence.

The owners of Monroe Chief announce their readiness to match him for $2,500 a side on any mile track west of Cleveland with Von Arnim, who beat him on the Chicago track this year. There has been much talk about such a race between the fast and even-matched stallions.

DEATH OF CAMBUSCAN.—The Vienna and Pesth papers chronicle with regret the death of Cambuscan, the sire of Kincsem and Kamballo, who, next to Buccaneer, was the most successful stallion at the Kisber stud. For a year past Cambuscan had been blind. Owing to the fear of the disease becoming hereditary, he had not been used for stud purposes since the affection assumed a permanent form, and accordingly he has been killed. Cambuscan, by Newminster out of The Arrow, was foaled in 1861, at Hampton Court. In 1863 he ran twice, viz., in the July Stakes and the Croome Stakes, both which races he won. He ran in the Derby of 1864, and in a field of thirty horses he finished fifth. During his racing career he ran nineteen times, winning on nine occasions, including two walks over. As a five-year-old he ran twice, and after being beaten at Newmarket at the first October Meeting he was withdrawn from the turf, and put to the stud at 25 guineas each mare. In 1872 he was bought for £4,000 by Mr. Cavaliero for exportation to Austria. The first of his stock that went to the post was Kincsem in 1874. Since that time a number of his produce have run annually in Germany and Austria, the total winnings up to the end of last month being £87,000. The stakes in those countries are, it is needless to say, comparatively small judged by the English standard. This sum therefore represents a great success for his immediate descendants on the Austrian and German turf.—London Sportsman.

Pearl Jennings, Wildmoor and Belle of the West have been sent to Saratoga from Salt Lake City, where Pearl won a match of $5,000 from Red Boy. She is a three-year-old and won the Missouri Oaks at St. Louis, and ran in the Illinois Oaks with the Duchess of Norfolk, that race being taken by Katie Creel. At one time she was running to Sacramento in company with Red Boy and Euchre, who have already arrived there, but the superior inducements offered at Saratoga, changed her destination.

James A., by Leamington from Maiden, and a full brother to Parole, died last Tuesday in Pennsylvania. He was a fairly good race horse, but despite his fine breeding he had but few chances given to him at the stud. His owner recently refused $4,000 for him.

## THE PADDOCK.

### NAME CLAIMED.

STOCKTON, Aug. 16, 1882.

I claim the name Voucher for brown colt, by Nephew, dam Fanny, by Vernon Patchen, foaled the 29th of March, 1881.　　　　G. W. TRAHERN.

### ANSWERS TO CORRESPONDENTS.

I. C. C., S. F.—All we can learn of the pedigree of Alice Garrett at present is that she is by Reuben, a son of Vermont Black Hawk. The fastest record we find in the Trotting Calendar is 2:34. Perhaps the information can be obtained from some of our Stockton readers, and we will be obliged if some one will acquaint us with the breeding of this mare, and if she has trotted faster than 2:34.

EDITOR BREEDER AND SPORTSMAN—DEAR SIR : Please inform us, 1st, if the State law now exists prohibiting the killing of doe or spotted fawn ? 2nd, if so, and I should kill a spotted fawn, and it prove to be a buck, am I guilty of an offence? 3rd, when does the season expire under the present laws, if any ?　Respectfully,　　W. J. McCLANE.

ANSWER.—As nearly as we can learn the State law has expired, though at the request of the California State Sportsmen's Association, county laws protect does and spotted fawns. As a male colt is called a foal, a buck, as long as the coat is spotted, will rank as a fawn.

## ROWING.

### A REFEREE COMPLIMENTED.

MR. CHARLES G. YALE—Sir: Recognizing the difficult and unthankful task you undertook in consenting to act as referee in the Rowing Regatta held on the 4th of July last, and knowing the active interest you feel in the success of the sport of rowing on our midst, we, as the representatives of rowing clubs in San Francisco, feel that it is our duty to make some public acknowledgment of our appreciation of your efforts to further our interests.

In the last regatta, we regard your decision as just and equitable to each and all contestants, and have seen with regret all efforts which have been made to question their fairness. It is a well-known fact that every one cannot be satisfied, especially where personal interest is concerned; but we wish to state publicly that we disapprove of the ungentlemanly and unprofessional manner used by some of the disappointed oarsmen in expressing their disagreement with official decisions.

We have noted with considerable attention the discussion over the result of the four-oared shell race, and while we are inclined to sympathise with the debarred crew, which certainly rowed a game race under adverse circumstances, still we cannot see how you could have decided otherwise by any recognized code of rules for amateur rowing.

We sign ourselves, yours sincerely: Haml, H. Dobbin, President Golden Gate Rowing Club; James W. Frize, Secretary Golden Gate Rowing Club; Chas. E. Lipp, President Ariel Rowing Club; B. Smith, Secretary Ariel Rowing Club; F. M. Deucher, President Dolphin Club; W. H. Bymer, Secretary Dolphin Club; Val. Kehrlein, Jr., Secretary Triton B. and B. Club; Ed. Booremans, President Triton Club.

THE CHALLENGE CUP.—The Golden Gate Club has announced that it will not allow the Pioneers to carry off the BREEDER AND SPORTSMAN cup on Thanksgiving day without giving them a race. The Ariel Club is equally determined to win the title of champions of the Pacific coast, and if the old club obtain the trophy, it will be fully entitled to it. Both the Ariels and Golden Gate Clubs are capable of putting forward very strong crews. The Ariels will row in the paper boat imported by the St. George Club. The Pioneers feel confident of beating the Ariels in any boat, as they have once before defeated them in the St. George's shell. The boat at that time, however, was rigged according to the peculiar ideas of some amateurs, and was wholly unsuited to the Ariel crew.

THE AMATEUR CHAMPIONS.—The refusal of Mumford to meet Holmes in the recent regatta at Detroit has raised doubts of the amount of sand ballast carried by the former sculler, who has had pretensions to the title of Amateur Champion of America. R. G. Mosgrove, of New Orleans, who is a sculler of note, writes to the Turf, Field and Farm: "I had a presentiment that Mumford would not willingly cross oars with Holmes, for he never had a better opportunity than he had at Creve Cœur Lake, St. Louis, on the 23d of June. I stated to Holmes a week before the race that I was satisfied in my own mind that Mumford would withdraw the day of the race, and, as it was, my prognostications proved true. Mumford has had more luck in building up a reputation than any sculler I know. In 1879, at Saratoga, he won the championship on a foul; and at Philadelphia, in 1880, he only had two contestants who had no reputation; and Holmes having withdrawn, this gave him an easy victory. Mumford knows very well that Holmes is a fast sculler, consequently he does not wish to risk the cheap reputation he has won. I have rowed several times against Holmes, and have also rowed double with him, and I am satisfied that he is the fastest amateur single sculler in America. I do not wish to run down Mumford, but his withdrawing from the races in St. Louis last month, and his refusing to row at Detroit next month, is simply a clear back down on his part."

THE HILLSDALES AGAIN.—H. W. Garfield, Treasurer of the National Association of A. O., is now receiving donations for the "new Hillsdales fund." It will be remembered that when the American crew left for England, the total amount subscribed by the amateur boat clubs and individuals was $1,613, of which sum $413 was paid for boats, cars, etc., $400 for passage money, and the $800 remaining given in charge of Captain Terwilliger to defray the European expenses of the crew. The long sojourn of the crew in England has, it is claimed, absorbed the latter part of this item, and a movement has been started for a new fund "to enable the Hillsdales to remain long enough abroad to force the English to acknowledge the sufficiency of their credentials and the eligibility of the crew under the strictest amateur definition." The Analostan Boat Club, of Washington, has headed the new fund by subscribing $25. The movement does not please the Turf, Field and Farm, and that journal remarks: "Now why should the boat clubs of America or individuals be called upon to contribute to such a fund? At this late day nothing is to be gained by the Hillsdales being recognized by Englishmen as amateurs. They, as an amateur crew in the strictest sense of the American definition, went abroad, and were repeatedly refused admission to all the prominent boating events in which they desired to compete. At this stage when all those events are over, what good will it do the Hillsdales to be recognized as amateurs by the English snobs? Instead of contributing to a new fund, let Americans who have the good of amateur boating at heart sign a petition for the Hillsdales to return home, leaving the English amateur oarsmen branded by their own press as cowards."

A SCALY SCULLER.—For some time the exploits of John Largan, the English sculler, have been an enigma to the English sporting journals. They have been unable to classify the astute oarsman, as at times he showed form which led them to consider him the best man in England, and again exhibited poor ability that made them doubt his fitness for second class. Latterly the feelings of the puzzled critics have been crystalizing into a well-grounded suspicion that Mr. Largan is a remarkably tricky individual, who will bear much watching. This suspicion has been strengthened by his latest performance, of which Bell's Life of July 22d says: "When Largan rowed and defeated Pearce, the Australian, a short time since, it will be remembered that there was some delay in handing over the stake money on the part of the gentleman to whom it was intrusted, because he was instructed by some one not to do so. So long a time elapsed that the matter found its way into print, and the stakeholder, not being exactly pleased with that sort of thing, forwarded the money to a contemporary, deducting £5 for his trouble. Largan, who alone had the power to receive the cash, being the winner, it appears very soon applied for and received the check. As soon as this could be converted into gold, Largan took ship for Australia with Laycock and Pearce, and they are all now on the high seas. Largan's backer, who offered him £50 for winning the race, which was refused, now has cause to complain, as he is left entirely minus, and Bubear, who trained Largan, bit was away at Hereford, also lives in hopes."

A CANDID CRITIC.—A writer in Land and Water, commenting on the unfair treatment of the Hillsdale crew in England, makes some interesting allusions to the privileges granted so-called amateur crews that have rowed for money. He says: "The Americans have certainly a fair case against us, and I am surprised none of the University crews have the courage and pluck to ignore the recommendation of the association, and offer to accept a challenge from the Hillsdales. I don't fancy any portion of disqualification would lie against any college crew who chose to waive the question of status, and engage in a friendly match with the hardly-used strangers. I do not, like other writers, attempt to make out that the association is not representative. The members of the committee are sufficiently well known and capable to be thoroughly trusted with the conduct of all aquatic matters; but in this case I think a vote of want of confidence would be fairly carried, and they might alter their bill or resign. We are content to acknowledge the custom of the country, and allow Frenchmen, Germans and Irishmen who have rowed for money in their own regattas to compete as amateurs in England. Why strain to its utmost extent the amateur law in dealing with an American representative amateur crew? Their visit is under very different auspices from that of the "Shoe-wae," and they certainly have a right to more courteous and fair treatment.

THE HILLSDALE CREW.—The cable is kept busy recording the movements of the Hillsdales in England. On Saturday the London Sportsman announced that owing to a satisfactory answer from the Yale Boat Club, the Thames Rowing Club has accepted the challenge of the Hillsdale crew. Their passage home has already been booked, but it will be canceled if necessary. The match, if it comes off, will take place about a month hence. Watts, who is President of the Amateur Oarsmen's Association of America, has arrived from Liverpool. He says the real objection to the Hillsdales personally was stated to him by Chatters, the President of the English Amateur Rowing Association. He said that the two last crews from America, Cornell and the Shoe-wacenettes, proved ungentlemanly, and it was determined to guard against giving another crew an opportunity to display their vulgarity. This prevented their acceptance of the Hillsdales' challenge.

ASHAMED OF THEIR COUNTRYMEN.—The London Athletic Review thus comments on the so-called English rowing association which barred the Hillsdales: "The action is in opposition to the wishes and feelings of the best of English amateur oarsmen. It is an insult to the amateur oarsmen, that men who are recognized by the National Association as amateurs; and who are sent here as the accredited representatives of that association, should be presumed to be professionals without any direct evidence. We should advise that a public meeting of oarsmen be held in some central position in London within the next few days, and a vigorous protest be made against the action taken at the late meeting at Henley. Adjectives fail when one begins to discuss this disgraceful action, which, no matter how it terminates, will always prove a black and ineffaceable mark on English amateur records. If ever one would be justified in taking a great big D, it would be in this connection.

SHE COULD ROW.—According to the St. John Sun, considerable comment was recently excited at Indiantown by a couple of women getting into a boat, one of them seizing the oars and pulling out from the wharf. A bystander's curiosity prompted him to ask her how far she had to go. She replied ten or twelve miles, and that she pulled down that distance in the morning. She seemed to think nothing of the long pull in the hot sun that was before her, and when some one in a spirit of aquatic banter asked her if she was not a relation of Hanlan's, she said no, but expressed a desire to meet "Pompey" on any occasion and row him for any money. When the joke was got through with, she started off, pulling a stroke very few of the loiterers on the wharf could have equaled. She was said to be a Miss Clark, of Kings County, New Brunswick.

THE HALIFAX REGATTA.—A regatta is to be held at Halifax, N. S., on Wednesday and Thursday, September 6th and 7th, when prizes amounting to about $3,000 will be given. The programme decided on is as follows: Single-scull race for championship of Halifax Harbor; single and double-scull and four-oared shell races, open to all; double-scull wherries, fishing-flats, fishing-whalers, ship's jolly-boats, man-of-war gigs, cutters and pinnaces, canoes, fishing sail-boats, and a consolation race for oarsmen not winning a prize in single sculls. A yacht-race will probably be arranged also. The amount to be given for each race has not yet been decided on, but for the single and double-sculls it will probably be about $500 to the first and $200 to the second. It has been proposed to invite Hanlan to be the guest of the city during the regatta.

WILL NOT ROW.—The prospects of a match between Watkins and Griffin are not very bright. The Long Bridge oarsmen seem to think that Watkins has had the best of the discussion, if that be any credit for a professional sculler. While a victory of jaw-bone is not to be despised, a triumph of muscle is always more commendable in aquatics. It would have been more satisfactory to have seen the rival scullers expend their breath in a contest on the water than on the profitable discussion on the bridge. Griffin professed great willingness to row, but the offer of Watkins to give him the choice of positions strikes the Long Bridge men as the best guarantee of willingness, and their confidence in Samuel has been strengthened.

BOATING AT STOCKTON.—Ralph P. Lane, of the Amity Boat Club, of Stockton, writes in reply to an inquiry about the prospects of boating in Stockton, that the boys are in no great hurry to commence operations before Spring. The club has resolved to build a floating boat-house, 60x30 feet, and two stories in height. The second floor will be used as a club room, and will contain baths and other comforts for the oarsmen. The San Francisco oarsmen find the Winter the pleasantest season of the year for practice, as, with the exception perhaps of a few weeks the climate is most favorable for out-door exercise, and the water in condition for the finest boats.

The New York Sportsman says: "Charles Courtney has gone out of rowing, and is now aspiring to the championship honors of being poisoned. Wednesday's episode is his best on record."

According to present indications the single scull race on the 25th of August, at Saratoga Lake, will be a great success. The first prize of $1,000 will go to the winner, and the remaining $100 to the second. The course will be three miles and a turn. Wallace Ross, Elliott, Hosmer and other noted scullers will compete.

ROSS AND HANLAN.—Wallace Ross is particularly anxious, it seems, to get a race with Ed. Hanlan this year, and that the object in view has placed a deposit of $500 with the Daily Telegraph, St. John, N. B., and issued the subjoined challenge:

ST. JOHN, August 5th, 1882.

I hereby challenge Edward Hanlan to row me a five-mile race, two and a half miles and return, for one thousand dollars a side and the championship of the world, the race to be rowed within six weeks from the date of signing articles, and this challenge to remain open for three weeks from the 5th of August. If not accepted in that time I will claim the championship of the world, and be prepared to defend it against all comers.　　WALLACE ROSS.

Ed. Hanlan proposes giving one thousand dollars for a sculler's race, open to all, barring Wallace Ross, to take place on Toronto Bay, Ont., about the first week in September.

## YACHTING.

### YACHT CRUISING.

Yacht cruising seems to be growing in favor in the East while racing seems to be confined among a few. That is, a few fast boats have all the racing to themselves, while those who have yachts of medium speed content themselves with cruising and sailing, leaving out the exciting elements of the race. As we stated in our editorial of last week there are several reasons for this. The expense of maintaining a racing yacht is very great, and few care to keep in racing trim yachts which are not as speedy as some others in the same fleet. The fast ones are kept up for racing and the others cruise.

Cruising is really the sport of yachting, which in better liked as it is longer practiced. When a fine fleet starts off on a cruise with a lot of yachtsmen and guests, everybody is in for a good time. The good time for one does not mean defeat and chagrin for another, as in the case in a race. There are no hard feelings engendered in any way. The scrub races" which take place when going from port to ort afford amusement for all and give the racing gentlemen a chance to enjoy the contests, while the absence of rires and the general freedom from rules, etc., make the cing pleasant for all.

Within the past month the large clubs in the East, the ew York, Seawanhaka and Atlantic, have had extended uises, and judging from the published reports all hands sem to have pretty thoroughly enjoyed themselves. The sly thing to mar the pleasure has been that the yachts ave drifted from place to place without any wind. It seems as if this drifting business was rather the rule than ie exception. Here we never have any trouble on this ore, although the writer remembers several occasions hen too much wind prevented the return of a portion of a fleet.

People who own yachts and cruise about for short trips f more out of their boats than any other class. They invite a few friends and go for a day or two to some favored pot, where they fish or lounge, enjoying the sail to or from he place, and in fact the whole trip. Others can see no njoyment in this, but must have the excitement of the race r there is no fun in it for them.

When two or more yachts cruise in company a great deal f pleasure is experienced. Mutual interchange of visits, he pleasant evening in company, good natured rivalry to be t anchor or under way first, all combine to make such trips smembered. Of course, in cruises in squadron there is ore or less formality, and there is a certain submission to ders expected, which is irksome to many. Yet fleet cruising does more to create an *esprit du corps* than anything lse. Though our grounds here are comparatively limited, here are many pleasant places to go. Of these we shall speak more anon.

### AN INTERNATIONAL REGATTA.

The managers of the International Regatta Association of Nice, France, whose races have come to be considered among the principal European events, have issued its programme for the matches of 1883, which are to take place on March 27, 28 and 29 next. The President d'Honneur of the association is the Prince of Wales, President of the Yacht Racing Association, who heads a committee composed of French officials of prominence. In addition to the honorary committee, there is also a working one, members of the principal French yacht clubs. The programme embraces races for sailing and steam yachts, miniature sailing and steam yachts, and races for amateur oarsmen. Besides these, there are events for the boats of the men-of-war of the French Navy; also for yacht boats and steam launches. The prizes are large and numerous. The main features of the programmes are:

Prix de Nice, for yachts of 30 tons and over—6,000f and gold medal to first; 2,000f and a gold medal to fourth; 1,000f and a medal to third, and 500f and a medal to fourth.

Prix du Yacht Club de France, for yachts of 15 tons and under 30 tons—5,000f, divided into four prizes, with a medal accompanying each.

Prix de la Baie des Anges, for yachts of 5 tons and under 15 tons—2,900f, divided into four prizes, with medals.

Prix des Alpes Maritimes, for yachts of 2 tons and under 5 tons—1,900f, divided into three prizes, with medals.

Prix de Monte Carlo, for steam yachts of 30 tons, register tonnage, course 30 miles. Prizes the same as offered for the Prix de Nice.

The rowing races for amateurs have prizes. Four oars, with 4 coxswain, cash, or an object of d'art of the same value, as follows: 3,000f to first, 2,000f to second, 1,000f to third, 500f to fourth, and 250f to fifth. For pair oars, with coxswains, the prizes total 9,850f; and for single scullers, 1,100f.

Entries close on March 15, with M. Androit Saôtone, Secretary of the Regatta, and an entry fee of one per cent. on the amount of the first prize.

Yachting matters are rather dull in San Francisco Bay just at present.

As far as racing is concerned, yachting matters here are dull.

In the East very little yacht racing has been done this year.

Mr. Bennett's steam yacht Namoura fell a knot short of the promised speed.

Chief Justice Waite went yachting, on the schooner Ruth, with the New York Yacht Club.

The new schooner Montauk "got away with" Mr. Cook's Tidal Wave during the recent N. Y. Y. C. cruise.

The American Yacht Club, in the East, tried to have a race the other day, but did not succeed, for lack of wind.

Before the cruise of the N. Y. Y. C. the yachts were taken out of water, cleansed and prepared for the "scrub races," sure to occur.

Ex-Governor Lippit, who is Commodore of the Narragansett Yacht Club, invited the N. Y. Y. C. squadron to a grand dinner at his place on Narragansett Bay during the recent cruise of the club.

The steam yacht interest is a growing one, and such prominent gentlemen as Messrs. Lorillard, Bennett, Osgood and others have initiated proceedings toward forming a steam yacht club which shall advance the interest of the American steam yacht owners.

It is said that James Gordon Bennett has ordered a 1,100-ton steam yacht from English builders. It is also said he has ordered one from a Philadelphia firm. The Namoura does not suit him. Mr. Bennett is bound to have the finest yacht afloat, and, as he spends his money royally, will have what he wants, no doubt.

THE LOLITA YACHT CLUB.—Last Sunday this Club had their last excursion of the season. At 9:30 A. M. the yacht cast off from the sea wall with about forty ladies and gentlemen. Near mid-channel the Club's new flag was hoisted with three hearty cheers. A landing was made on the Marin shore at noon, and a substantial lunch spread for the hungry excursionists, after which sail was again set and the Lolita's prow was turned toward the Golden Gate. The party sailed several miles outside the heads and returned to Saucelito at sundown. Here they had supper, after which all tripped the light fantastic for two or three hours, and at 11:30 P.M. they were safely landed at the sea wall, well pleased with their excursion. Everyone contributed something to

the pleasure of the party, and music, songs and amusing stories were the order of the day. The Lolita Yacht Club was organized June 7th, 1880, and in these two years many good times have been had on the waters by the members. The Club rooms are on the corner of Powell and Jackson and are nicely furnished with billiard table, piano, pictures, etc. There is some talk of their holding a reception before long.

### ATHLETICS.

#### THE OLYMPIC ATHLETIC CLUB.

The following is a list of the events selected by the Committee for the meeting to be held on September 23d, on the Grounds of the Club at Oakland:

Putting 16-pound weight, scratch, open.
Throwing baseball, scratch, open.
Running high jump, scratch, open.
Running wide jump, scratch, open.
Pole leaping, scratch, open.
Tug of war, teams of 600 pounds, open.
320 yards hurdle race, 10 hurdles, 3 feet 6 inches, scratch, open.
100 yards officers' race, scratch.
100 yards juvenile race, handicap, open.
220 yards juvenile race, handicap, open.
440 yards juvenile race, handicap, open.
1 mile scratch, open.
100 yards, scratch, open—B. S. Haley barred.
880 yards bicycle race, handicap, open.
1 mile bicycle race, handicap, open.
2 mile bicycle race, handicap, open.
1-5 mile bicycle race, without hands, open.
Gold and Silver medals for first and second in each event, except the officers' race.

The Committee reserves the right to reject any entry.
Competitors not members of the O. A. C. will be charged an entrance fee of 50 cents in each event.
beThe Grounds will be open at 12 M., and the games will, called at 1 P. M., sharp.
Gold medals will be awarded for beating the Club or Pacific Coast records, from scratch, in several of the eve nts which will be named by the Committee at a later date.

#### C. S. JOHNSTONE'S 300-YARD RUN.

We published, July 1, a full report of this athlete's remarkable 300-yard race at Aston Lower Grounds, Birmingham, England. The path is 500 yards in circuit, and 250 yards of the 300 yards course is down hill. It now appears that the measurement of the path is open to suspicion. We have received from Mr. N. L. Jackson, editor of the *Midland Athlete*, a letter in which this and other matters of interest are treated as follows:

Thanks for your kindness in sending me the allegations for records, etc., but beg to report of that grand performance of Myers at 600 yards. Truly he is a wonder. I should think that he and George crippled could beat the World at all distances. Brooks included. . . . I have little news of interest. R. E. Ball, who won our championship quarter, is a really improved man, and I shall expect him to beat 50s on his day. He easily defeated C. S. Johnstone (who was credited with such fast time for his 300 at Aston) in a late 300 last Saturday, and when running the champion ship quarter he covered the first 300 in 33s, which equals our best. I shall not accept Johnstone's 300, for, although I was present, I stupidly missed timing, and only Oliver had the watch on. He is a very reliable timer, but the distance was not verified afterwards. On the 3d inst. I saw Johnstone run a quarter on the same ground in three equal to 48.1-5 or 2.5s. I felt sure it couldn't be right, and on measuring the course it was found to be about 10 or 12 yards short. Therefore, "taking one consideration with another," I do not think it safe to accept his record, although I believe on his day he is quite equal to it.

Under these circumstances it seems wise to reject Johnstone's performance.—*N. Y. Clipper*.

THE OLYMPIC CLUB.—At a meeting held on Wednesday last, Messrs. Mark Tromboni, George Barton, C. H. Slater, George McCord and William D. O'Kane were elected as a nominating committee. On Monday, September 4th, polls will be open for the election of officers from 2 to 9 P. M., and on Monday, the inauguration of officers will take place and the annual reports will be heard.

A HAND-BALL MATCH.—At the Racquet Court, No. 733 Howard street, on Sunday next, will be played a game of hand-ball between two sides for a purse of $100. The Court is very well adapted for the game, and there are a great many amateurs who are quite proficient in these athletic amusements.

### BICYCLING.

THE LOWDEN AND KING MATCH.—On Saturday, August 5th, W. H. Lowden and G. L. King met at the grounds of the Olympic Athletic Club, in Oakland, for the purpose of deciding the ownership of the second medal in the two-mile race, they having made a dead heat on the occasion of the races on July 23d. Shortly before 4 o'clock the men appeared and were placed as in the former race, Lowden at 310 yards and King at 480. At the pistol fire both got off well, and King commenced to cut down the distance which separated him from the leader, gaining so rapidly that he had overtaken him by the time the first mile was completed; after which he contested himself with following within a few yards until the last half of the last lap, when he put on steam, and, passing to the front, crossed the line ten or fifteen yards in advance, in 6 min. 39 sec., which was three seconds better than the time made in the first race. Both men used heavy roadsters. Lowden a 52-inch and King a 54-inch Harvard.

During the month of September it is the intention to hold a grand meeting, when most of the prominent riders of the coast will be represented in the different events.

Bicyclers have had much trouble in the Eastern States on account of the extortion of baggage masters wherever it has been necessary for them to take trains for any point. The following order, issued by J. Van Sneich, general baggage agent of the Baltimore and Ohio Railroad, is a sensible one, and it is hoped will be generally followed by other lines, as it will cause an increased patronage by those who would like to make as long a trip as possible and having but limited time, would return by rail: "In future bicycles will be carried free in baggage cars between any stations on this line, when accompanied by owner or rider, upon presentation by him of his passage ticket. Care must be taken in handling them to prevent damage or breakage."

The English Bicycle Union hold a series of championship meetings each year, the distances run being one, five, twenty-five and fifty miles. Two of these events usually take place in London, and the others upon some provincial track. The one and twenty-five mile races took place July 8th, at the Astor grounds, Birmingham, and were won by F. Moore of the Warstone B. C., in 2 m. 47 2-5 sec., for the mile, and 1 h. 25 m., 8 1-5 sec. for the twenty-five miles. The five miles was run at the Crystal Palace track, London, July 22d, and was won by J. S. Whatton, Cambridge University, in 15 m., 12 4-5 sec.

A twenty-mile race is announced to come off shortly upon a trotting track in Brockton, Mass., between an un-named bicycler and some trotting horses. No bicycler has yet accomplished twenty miles in as good time as that of the best trotting horses, even upon the best track which could be had. It is hardly possible, therefore, that the bicycle would stand any chance against any fair twenty-miler upon the rough soft surface of a trotting track. The only fair way would be to make a separate bicycle track inside the trotting track with a good, hard, smooth surface.

Amateur riders of bicycles and tricycles are becoming restive under the burden of the duty charged upon imported machines, which being thirty-three per cent, brings the price to high figures. The only American manufacturers own patents which enable them to add ten dollars to the cost of each imported machine, and they put the price of their own machines up to the same high figures, which should certainly give them a good profit.

### BASE BALL.

The weather was rather chilly at the Recreation Grounds last Sunday, and in consequence many of our pleasure-seekers went across the bay in quest of milder climes. The attendance was therefore only fair at the match game between the Haverly California Theatre team and Renos. The contest was a very one-sided affair, for in the third innings the Theatre Company had scored nine points to the one of their opponents, and they had such an advantage at the finish that they did not even play their ninth inning. Despite this fact, there was some good play shown on both sides, and McElroy, who took the pitcher's position, vice Riordan, relegated to third base, showed a capacity that with practice and confidence will add greatly to the strength of the Reno team. Then Creegan, as catcher, was unusually sure and alert, and the two played well into one another's hands. The Renos' fielding was much closer, but their batting needs improvement, compared with that of their adversaries, Levy especially gaining rounds of applause for his effective hits. On the side of the Theatre nine, Carroll acted as pitcher and Lawton as catcher. The former also fielded with skill and precision, as did also McDonald and Riordan in their respective positions. Following is the score:

| RENOS. | T.B. | R. | 1.B. | P.O. | A. | E. |
|---|---|---|---|---|---|---|
| Swanton, c. f.......... | 4 | 0 | 0 | 1 | 1 | 1 |
| Riordan, 3d b.......... | 4 | 0 | 0 | 1 | 1 | 0 |
| Lake, r. f............. | 4 | 0 | 1 | 0 | 0 | 0 |
| Cadogan, l. f......... | 4 | 1 | 1 | 0 | 0 | 0 |
| Starr, 2d b............ | 4 | 1 | 2 | 1 | 1 | 0 |
| Hamilton, s. s........ | 4 | 1 | 1 | 0 | 0 | 1 |
| McElroy, p........... | 4 | 0 | 1 | 10 | 10 | 0 |
| Creegan, c........... | 4 | 0 | 0 | 14 | 2 | 0 |
| Sheridan, 1st b....... | 4 | 0 | 1 | 7 | 0 | 1 |
| Totals............. | 37 | 3 | 7 | 34 | 19 | 3 |

| HAVERLY. | T.B. | R. | 1.B. | P.O. | A. | E. |
|---|---|---|---|---|---|---|
| Meegan, 3d b......... | 5 | 0 | 1 | 1 | 1 | 1 |
| J. Carroll, p......... | 5 | 2 | 2 | 1 | 10 | 1 |
| McDonald, 2d b...... | 5 | 1 | 1 | 3 | 5 | 1 |
| Lawton, c........... | 5 | 2 | 2 | 11 | 1 | 1 |
| Levy, s. f........... | 4 | 3 | 3 | 1 | 0 | 0 |
| McCord, s. s......... | 4 | 1 | 1 | 1 | 2 | 1 |
| Nugent, 1st b........ | 4 | 1 | 1 | 6 | 0 | 0 |
| Pope, r. f........... | 4 | 1 | 1 | 0 | 0 | 0 |
| Pratt, 1st b......... | 4 | 0 | 0 | 2 | 0 | 0 |
| Totals............. | 38 | 10 | 9 | 27 | 17 | 4 |

Innings............. 1 2 3 4 5 6 7 8 9
Haverly............. 0 0 3 0 2 0 0 5 0 — 10
Renos............... 1 0 1 0 0 1 0 0 0 — 3

The Haverlys played only eight innings.

Earned runs—Renos 1. Home runs—Pope. Three-base hits—Starr. Base on errors—Renos 3, Haverlys 4. Left on bases—Renos 5, Haverlys 4. Struck out—Renos 7, Haverlys 5. Base on balls—Haverlys 3. Wild pitch—Carroll 1. Umpire—M. Fine, Niantion. Time—One hour and forty-five minutes. Scorers—Hennessy and Wallace.

A ONE-SIDED GAME.—A match game of base ball was played Sunday between nines from Held Bros. & Co. and F. Toplitz & Co., resulting in the defeat of the latter in two innings by a score of 26 to 1. The game was played at Recreation Park. Following is the score:

| Held Bros. & Co. | Runs Outs. | | F. Toplitz & Co. | Runs Outs. |
|---|---|---|---|---|
| L. T. Smith, 3d b... | 4 | 1 | M. Stone, c......... | 1 | 2 |
| M. O'Donell, 1st b... | 5 | 2 | J. Greenberg, 2 b.. | 0 | 3 |
| E. Gramsbey, 3d b.. | 4 | 0 | L. L. Befael, 3d b.. | 0 | 1 |
| A. D. Stone, s. s.... | 4 | 2 | B. Rosenbetz, 3d b.. | 0 | 3 |
| J. Bolm, p......... | 4 | 0 | F. Flaherty, p..... | 0 | 1 |
| C. Sennesley, r..... | 4 | 3 | S. Ashton, 8. f.... | 0 | 1 |
| K. Urttis, c. f.... | 3 | 1 | J. Sharp, l. f..... | 0 | 1 |
| M. Heidburn, l. f.... | 3 | 0 | D. Livingstone, 1st b. | 0 | 0 |
| A. Adler, s. s....... | 3 | 0 | G. Walterboett, s. s. | 0 | 1 |
| Totals........... | | 6 | Totals........ | 1 | 6 |

Only one man was out in the second inning; Toplitz men giving up the game before Held Bros. had completed their inning. The batting of the Held nine was very heavy, four home-run being made in the first inning. Their fielding, also, was very good. One of the features of the game was the curve pitching of T. Holm, which greatly baffled the Toplitz nine.

At the Olympic Grounds, on Sunday last, the weather was much more agreeable, and there was a very good attendance to witness the match between the Olympic nine and the Nationals. The former played an open, rollicking game at the bat, which, with poor fielding on the part of their adversaries, placed the Olympics in the sixth innings at 17 to 1, but the Nationals then added 9 more to their score, the Olympics winning by 13 points.

On next Sunday the match at the Recreation Grounds will be between the Renos and the Niantics, and the Haverly California team will play at Concord against the Stars of that place.

On the 27th of this month there will be a very interesting match between the Haverly nine and the Athletics of 1878 and 1879. It will be a pleasure to see some of these popular players back on the diamond field, and, as the match is for the benefit of L. N. David, formerly the captain of the Athletics, with fair weather there is sure to be a large and appreciative assemblage.

# Breeder and Sportsman.

### PUBLISHED WEEKLY BY THE
BREEDER AND SPORTSMAN PUBLISHING CO.

THE TURF AND SPORTING AUTHORITY OF THE
PACIFIC COAST.

### OFFICE, 508 MONTGOMERY STREET
P. O. Box 1883.

*Five dollars a year; three dollars for six months; one dollar and a
half for three months. Strictly in advance.*

MAKE ALL CHECKS, MONEY ORDERS, ETC., PAYABLE TO ORDER OF
BREEDER AND SPORTSMAN PUBLISHING CO.

*Money should be sent by postal order, draft or by registered letter, ad-
dressed to the "Breeder and Sportsman Publishing Company, San Francisco, Cal."*

*Communications must be accompanied by the writer's name and address,
not necessarily for publication, but as a private guarantee of good faith*

JOSEPH CAIRN SIMPSON,   -   -   -   EDITOR

SAN FRANCISCO, - SATURDAY, AUGUST 19, 1882

## "HORSES BREAKING."

Very properly the code of the National Trotting
Association inflicts severe penalties when horses
infringe the rule which comes under the above
heading. If the driver when his horse breaks fails
to pull him back at once, he is debarred from winning the heat; and if the judges deem the case a
flagrant one, they can distance the horse, fine the
driver to the amount of $100, or suspend him for a
year. If, in spite of his best endeavors, he fails to
bring his horse to the trot or pace, twice the distance
gained is deducted at the "outcome." In case of
any horse (in a trotting race) repeatedly breaking,
or running, or pacing, he is to be placed last in
the heat. This is a synopsis of the rule bearing
on the subject, and though there may be instances
where it is difficult to determine how much a horse
has gained in a series of breaks, this is the only
troublesome thing to determine, provided the
judges have field glasses to aid them, when the
horses are at a distance from the judges' stand, in
noting what the drivers are doing.

When a horse loses by breaks, a penalty cannot
be inflicted unless there is a repetition beyond
what can be reasonably expected. This clause was
incorporated to cover the case of several horses
which were on the track when it was adopted.
These were in the habit of making a "revolution"
whenever a competitor was likely to get in front of
them, the revolution consisting in one or two racing
bounds, changing their gait while in the air, and
trotting faster than ever for a few yards, when up
they would go again. We saw a wager won at Fleetwood Park, the offer being a bet of $100 that one
of the horses in the race would make fifteen breaks
from the time the word was given until the heat was
ended. An umpire was provided with a field glass,
and he reported twenty-three distinct changes from
the trot to the run. The same horse was in a race
at Buffalo, New York, when he indulged in the
same freaks, and his owner, Commodore Vanderbilt, was so indignant that the deciding heat was
taken away from him, though he was only a neck
in front, that in the height of his dudgeon he left
the grounds—ordered the special train which
brought him to return at once; and the irate Commodore was not mollified, though the train sped at
"a mile a minute gait" on the homeward journey.
We are always reluctant to reprehend judges for
any mistake they may make. To "judge" a trotting race is at the best a disagreeable task, and
when that is likely to be followed by virulent
verbal abuse and newspaper criticisms, it requires
a bold man to run the risk. But there are instances
when the press must perform a duty, and though
it is an irksome task, it cannot be shirked without
injury following.

As will be learned by a perusal of the account of
the 2:30 race which took place on the Bay District
Course last Saturday, there was a great deal of
dissatisfaction over the award of the fourth heat to
Sweetness. That it was a wrong decision we firmly
believe, though we cannot for an instant entertain
the opinion that it was done through ulterior influences. It was far more probably a mistake from
not giving attention enough to whether the rule
was violated or not by Poscora Hayward, and from
the tendency to lean towards the "honest trotter"

which never "leaves its feet" during the pendency
of the race. There is a praiseworthy sympathy for
the horse which struggles and tries its utmost to
win, trotting and still trotting under all circumstances; but laudable as this feeling is, it must not
be allowed to do injustice. Had the rule been
followed as closely as the code directs, there should
have been noted the breaks which the horses made.

The judges can direct the Clerk of the Course
to prepare diagrams representing the track. When
a horse breaks make a note of it, by using the initial of the name and an l. or g. to denote whether
there was loss or gain. This is the general practice among reporters, excepting that no note is
made of losses or gains. A reporter may overlook
some occurrence when he is jotting down his notes;
the judges can dictate without taking their eyes off
the horses, and thus have as nearly a perfect transcript of what has been done as can be taken.
With this before them there is little chance for
disagreement, still less for making an erroneous
decision. Depending entirely on memory, for
even so short a period as the time of a heat,
there is a likelihood of mistakes being made. Two
breaks are magnified into several; a decided loss
has been transformed into a gain of several lengths.
It is not surprising that men who think they have
been greatly wronged give vent to their feelings,
and use terms which are to be regretted by every
one who has the continued welfare of the sport at
heart. No good can arise from this course. If it
can be proved that the judges have done wrong
knowingly, that they have been interested in any
way so that there is the least chance for pecuniary
benefit to them, the laws afford the remedy; not
so potent, perhaps, as to make good the losses,
but a fearful punishment to any one who has a
spark of honest, manly feeling. And in this connection we crave permission to offer advice to the
Associations regarding the selection of judges. If
possible do not appoint men who make a practice
of betting on the races. Not that there is any
danger of a large number of these doing wrong,
for in all our experience we have found the right
ones of this class the very best judges from every
point of view. But people are prone to accuse
them of having pecuniary interest at stake, and
though they are aware of the falsity of the accusation, adhere to it to carry a point. Whenever
practicable the President should occupy the position of first judge, always providing that he is
qualified. The Directors should supply the others,
and it is long odds that there will be more satisfactory rulings than when the judges are selected
on the ground.

## THE RACES AT SANTA CRUZ.

At the time of going to press there is little to
offer in regard to the races at Santa Cruz, and the
full account will be delayed until the next issue of
the paper. Our Special Commissioner reports
that the track was slow on the day which Starr
King met with an ignominious defeat. There
must have been some cause outside of a moderately heavy track, as we cannot conceive the Santa
Cruz course being so bad as to bring a horse from
3:22 on Saturday to worse than 2:30 on the following Tuesday. The journey may have affected him
prejudicially, or the former race taken away his
speed. Whatever was the trouble, it is to be regretted, as people are prone to ascribe wrong-doing
in such cases, and that when parties are clearly
innocent. We sincerely hope that the whole circuit will be made without cause for reproach on
the part of the drivers. There are numbers who
always cry robbery when they lose money, but unless these chronic denunciators have something to
base their charges upon which is apparent, not
much credit will be given to their noisy declamation. Those who did not witness the race at Santa
Cruz are certainly incompetent critics, as the mere
fact of disparity in the time there and that which
was made on the Bay District Course is not a convincing argument.

We are of the opinion that the time of holding
the Fair was not opportune. Owners of horses
are averse to taking risks before the main fairs are

held, especially when it involves a direct return.
After the San Jose Fair, with entries closing when
the State Exhibition has come to an end, would
ensure a more liberal support from the horsemen,
and with good fields, resulting from a new classification, there would be a corresponding attendance.
It is very important to the breeding interests of
California that new points be established, and
there are natural advantages at Santa Cruz which
ought to ensure the popularity of the sport at that
place. But natural advantages will not win
without the aid of good and liberal management.
The experience gained, however, is something
towards success in the future, and we have strong
faith that Santa Cruz will yet take a prominent
place in the California Circuit.

## THE PROPOSED DRIVE.

San Francisco is destined to become a great Summer resort for the people of the East. Metropolitan
pleasures are joined to a climate which will be duly
appreciated by those who live where July, August,
and part of September are almost unendurable
from the extreme heat. Eventually the Summer will be the "fashionable season," as it is now
in London, The theatres will do the most profitable business of the year; every place of amusement will have plenty of visitors; and not a trade,
profession or handicraft but which will reap some
of the benefits. There is no one project which
will be so potential in attracting the class of people
who have money enough to indulge in a Summer
vacation as the proposed drive. Those who have
been in the habit of pursuing the truly American
recreation of fast driving, can then follow their
favorite custom, and where these thing others
are sure to follow. Before many years the road-
drivers of New York and other Eastern cities will
look to California for the choicest animals. A few
may ship their teams, as they do now to Saratoga
and Long Branch; many will be on the lookout for
something to suit their fancy, and which will also
have the charm of novelty when they get back home,
as another inducement to purchase. When that
time comes, and it surely will, the breeding farms
of the State will be taxed to supply the demand.
There are scores of men here who have the means
who will not be outdone by the transient visitors,
and the result will be that this city will become
celebrated above all others of the like population
for the superior quality of the road horses. In the
great centre of America, where millions of dollars
are invested in fast animals for road-driving, there
is a limited season when these can be used with
pleasure.

In the New York Herald of the 10th instant appeared the following sentences: "The city was
filled with weary men yesterday. Women were
worried, children were dying, and animals wilted
in the heat. Here and there a ripple of excitement
was caused by a popular breeze, but it lasted a
moment only." Contrast that with a week ago
Wednesday in San Francisco. In the early morning there was just the right degree of warmth, the
sun shining brightly, and from that time until
midday there was only a gentle breeze. There
could not be a lovelier time for a morning drive, a
time when horses would feel that it was a pleasure
to go faster than they ever did before. There
were no heat-wearied men, heat-worried women,
heat-dying children; neither were there animals
wilting in a close, murky atmosphere, made intolerable by an overly fervent sun. From noon until
evening-tide a light overcoat was required by those
who are peculiarly sensitive to thermal changes,
but as the sun drew towards the Pacific even these
could dispense with its use. Mornings and evenings, during the greater part of the Summer, are all
that could be desired for a drive. Those who like
the excitement attendant on rapid motion could
select either portion of the day with ample opportunity to gratify the desire, unaccompanied by any
drawback.

Business men are prone to think that a morning's indulgence interferes with the business of
the day, and from a hygienic point of view it is
well for them to think so. There is no such a

acea to banish cankering cares as driving fast tters furnishes; still better when there are wds of people bent on the same errand. It is erly impossible for a man who is engaged in the dable endeavor to beat some one in a brush on road to think of anything else. He must give horse or horses every attention he is capable of stowing, and if the match is a close one, there fervency of feeling, an intensity of purpose, ich only those who have gone through the experience can realize or understand. It is the indest medicine in the world for an overtasked in. It is worth all the medical nostrums compnded from the days of Galen to the present e. No matter how despondent a man is, no ds how deep a hold "the blues" has upon him, load is lifted from the heart, the grapevine lock despair is broken, he returns to dinner with an petite which needs no sauces nor stimulants to ish his food, sleeps the sleep of contentment, d rises in the morning as gay as a two-year-old.

But the pleasure-seekers are not restricted to rtain hours. Morning or evening are alike to em, and we know of numbers of men in the East 10, in such a climate as this, and with a road to ve upon such as is projected, would utilize both riods of the day; that is, when visiting San rancisco on a Summer tour, in the same situation when the periodical trips are made to places hich have not a tithe of the attractions. It alys puts us in a bad humor when we cogitate over e anomalous feature of Californians so lightly preciating advantages which no other people in e world possess. To reduce the querying to the pic under consideration: the apathy which preails in regard to providing a suitable place for entlemen who have a fondness for fast driving, nd when it can be done with so little comparative utlay, and at the same time promote the interests f the whole people, is a state of affairs which we annot comprehend. We have faith, however, hat it will not be long before the stigma is reoved, and in place of San Francisco being noted for the worst roads of any city on the continent, it will be celebrated as the antitheton of its former self in this respect. This the climate guarantees, for in no other country can there be the same happy combination, viz., the best horses in the world and the best opportunity to use them, apart from a proper drive.

## EFFICIENT OFFICERS.

Only those who have been brought intimately in connection with fairs and race-meetings are aware now much depends on the Secretary for the smooth running of these exhibitions. There may be a high grade of executive ability in the President; he may be supported by a directory every way competent; and if the Secretary is not up to the equirements of his office, there are annoyances and serious drawbacks. There is a great knack in carrying out the minutiæ, the happy talent of looking after the small things, the keeping of trifles rom assuming large proportions, in managing all he details so that there is harmony all through. The correspondence is a big feature. A hundred or more silly questions will be sent through the postoffice, and inquiries which argue a want of common sense in the investigator. A curt answer nay develop an antagonism which will be detrimental, a failure to reply a slight which cannot be overcome. So far as we are acquainted, the Secretaries of the different fairs in California are capable and courteous. Those we are the most intimately acquainted with are emphatically the right men in the right place. We always admired the manner in which Major Beck managed the affairs f the State Agricultural Society, and he has a worthy successor in the present incumbent. Affable, courteous, of ready conception, methodical, untiring and industrious, he is eminently fitted for he duties of his position; and we do not hesitate o give him a place in the very foremost rank, no matter where or in what country the comparison made. The Golden Gate is equally fortunate, and the Bay District Association can be given the same compliment without there being the least chance for an accusation of undeserved flattery. It may be thought invidious to make selections from the corps, all of the members being entitled to consideration. We speak, of course, of those with whom we are the most intimate, without a doubt that a more intimate acquaintance would furnish equally as bright examples.

And now we have a request to make, that may appear as though the former remarks were on the "soft sawder" order, a touch of blarney to carry our point. But the answer will benefit the various associations more than it will the Breeder and Sportsman, as the compliance will give them the opportunity to disseminate intelligence that will be to their future advantage. The request is that the respective Secretaries will send us official summaries of the racing and trotting as soon as it can be done conveniently after the close of the fairs. There never has been a complete record of the racing and trotting on the Pacific Coast; in fact, it has been impossible to present anything further than a report of a few of the most prominent. It does not matter how perfect a representation is made by correspondents of papers, there must be official sanction to give due weight; and we sincerely hope to be enabled to give a full synopsis of all that has taken place. We will furnish the Secretaries, in return, with enough copies of the paper to supply those who are interested, or proof-slips, should they desire to mail them. There may be penalties which require immediate notice to render effective, and this will be the easiest method of giving the proper publicity.

## OUR PORTRAITS.

We are pleased to receive many testimonials indorsing the finish and accuracy of the pictures of the notable horses which have been published. As the bias may govern that causes every mother to think her own baby the handsomest, or the breeder to estimate his colts as superior to all others, the corroboration of disinterested individuals is extremely gratifying. A. B. Allen, of the firm of R. H. Allen & Co., Water street, New York, writes of the Breeder and Sportsman: "The work is nicely gotten up, and the horse portraits the finest and most truthful I have ever seen—really handsome." Mr. Allen has an intimate acquaintance with all the agricultural and turf journals for the past fifty years; has been a contributor to many of them, American and English; and therefore is well qualified to judge. Those who are familiar with the originals of the portraits unanimously concur in pronouncing them truthful representations. The aim has been to give the horses, as nearly as can be, with fidelity, and not, as is usually the case, marred by the conceptions of the artist as to what they should be. Mr. Wyttenbach is certain to take high rank as a delineator of animals. In due course there will be other illustrations—portraits of carriage, "all-work," and draft horses, the various breeds of cattle, sheep, dogs, etc. These will be as faithful as the ones which precede them.

## EDITORIAL NOTES.

Santa Rosa takes up the measure after Santa Cruz, and Tuesday next will be the opening day. A correct list of the entries will be found elsewhere, and there is a very fair list of names. The initial race is for district two-year-olds, with four in it, and the second race is for the 2:35 class.

On Wednesday there are a special race and a contest between the pacers, Washington and Johnny Weigle. On Thursday six of the district three-year-olds, and the same day the 2:25 brings together Starr King, Echora, Del Sur, Cairo, Director and Crown Point. This will be the first appearance of Director in California in a public race, and those who saw him in the East will be anxious to learn what the California climate has done. He has a record of 2:27¼, made last year when he was four years old. He and Echora will bring a new element into the 2:25, and add greatly to the interest of the race. On Friday there is the 2:40, with a fine lot to contend, and on Saturday the 2:30 is of great promise for sport, inasmuch as Poscora Hayward, Blanche, Nellie R., Inca, Albert W., and Blackmore are the entries. The closing race of the meeting is the 2:21 class, the entries to which close to-day. With the fine track at Santa Rosa, the contiguity to this city, and other favorable considerations, the meeting should attract a large attendance.

Petaluma is the next on the list, and the entries are also published in this number. Now that Petaluma has a mile track, which we understand is as good as it is possible for a newly built one to be, there should be nothing in the way of the most successful exhibition ever held there. Unfortunately, few of those who were interested were aware of the improvements which have been made, and the dread of the old track undoubtedly deterred many from putting in an appearance.

Santa Claus, the telegraph says, won the special stallion race at Rochester, last Wednesday. It was a great victory for him, as he defeated Black Cloud and Jerome Eddy; the latter the horse which trotted in 2:16¼, at Buffalo, and Black Cloud has been doing so wonderfully well that many thought he could reduce the time of Smuggler when the proper occasion came. Black Cloud won the first heat and was second in the others; the time, 2:21¼, 2:25, 2:19, 2:20¼. As Santa Claus was third in the first heat, it is probable that he did not try to win the first game of the rubber. He is evidently coming around again, and before the season is ended, he may show very prominently in the stallion record.

And now the pinkeye has fastened its unwelcome grip on a large number of horses which are expected to take part in the coming fairs. Fortunately it is in so mild a form, that in all probability very few of those attacked will be incapacitated from fulfilling their engagements. It does not seem to interfere with their appetites, and only those which are the worst off appear to lack their ordinary spirits. The cough is severe, though it seems to arise from an irritation in the throat rather than from the lungs being affected. Occasionally there is a trifle of smelling in the limbs, but, were it not for the cough, in a great many instances there would be nothing to indicate that anything was the matter.

Trotting Catalogues.—During the week we have received catalogues of the trotting stock of B. J. Treacy, Ashland Park, near Lexington, Kentucky; of the Woodburn trotting stud of A. J. Alexander, Spring Station, Kentucky; and of W. R. Nims, Lexington, Michigan. Not the least part of the trotting literature of the period is the information embodied in these catalogues. Woodburn and Ashland Park are among the noted breeding farms of the continent, and the stock of Mr. Nims are certainly of the right stamp so far as breeding goes. In the future we will have a good deal to say about the stock on the breeding farms of the East as well as California.

The accident to Albert W. suggests the propriety of following the English custom of using protecting boots on the knees of valuable horses whenever they are led, ridden or driven on the road. Horses which are given nearly all their exercise on the track are very liable to trip on an unequal surface, and when the road is hard a fall entails "broken knees." We have the pair which came across the ocean with Bonnie Scotland, and not a few have been puzzled to know what they were intended for. Though the injury to this fine son of Electioneer is slight, it is serious enough to throw him out of training at a critical period.

Overman made a great display of speed in his race at Buffalo, coming from the half-mile pole in 1:07. This is a good omen for the future, and if nothing befalls him he is sure to take a place among the top-sawyers of the tracks. There are few finer looking horses, and still more rare are those who have the same happy combination of size, form and speed.

The Yearling Race, for a purse of $300, which is to be trotted on Tuesday, at the State Fair, closes to-day. As the first gets 60 per cent., the second 30 per cent., and the third 10 per cent. of the purse, the entries should be numerous. The distance is a dash of a mile, and this is certainly easier for colts of the age than heats of half a mile.

By the way, Mr. Finigan has a yearling by Santa Claus, and from a mare by Blondin, a son of imported Sovereign, which is over fifteen hands high and of admirable form. The Santa Claus from Sweetness is a very highly finished colt, and better than good looks, he shows a gait which is a token of future excellence.

## BILLIARD TOURNAMENT.

One of the chief attractions at the Mechanics' Fair is the billiard tournament at the three-ball games for purses of $100, $75, $50, and $35, offered by the J. F. Brunswick and Balke Manufacturing Co. The entries comprise Charles Saylor, champion of the Pacific Coast, Ben. F. Saylor, L. A. Gates, W. F. Lowry, William Terrill, W. Roach and J. B. F. McClearly. This necessitates the playing of twenty-two games, the first of which came off last Wednesday, and was between Benjamin Saylor and W. Roach. The former won by a score of 300 points to 232, and his best run was 42, while his average showed 5 5-9 points.

The second game, played on Thursday evening, was between W. F. Lowry and L. A. Gates, and was won by the former with a score of 300 to 223 points of his adversary. The winner's highest runs were 14, 28, 44, 21, and his average was 8 5-37, while the best runs of Gates were 40, 15, 18, 35, and his everage was 6 7-36. A noticeable part of the entertainment was the exhibition of the fancy shots made by J. B. F. McCleary. The tournament will be continued every evening, and is well worthy of attention.

## THE GUN.

CLAY BIRD MATCH.—The last clay pigeon match of the Alameda County Sportsman's Club came off on Saturday afternoon at Littlefield Range, near Oakland. Owing to the swiftness and uncertainty of flight of the pottery birds, it was very difficult for even the best shots to make good scores. This shooting was for the Club's gold and silver medals at clay pigeons. There are also medals for shooting live pigeons, but these will be competed for on the last Saturday of this month. Twenty-five entries were made, distance fifteen yards, at ten birds, with the following results:

| | | | | | | | | | | | | |
|---|---|---|---|---|---|---|---|---|---|---|---|---|
| Tuttle..................... | 1 | 1 | 1 | 1 | 1 | 1 | 1 | 1 | 1 | 0 | — | 9 |
| Nagle...................... | 0 | 1 | 0 | 1 | 0 | 1 | 0 | 1 | 0 | 1 | — | 5 |
| Morineas.................. | 1 | 1 | 1 | 1 | 1 | 0 | 1 | 1 | 0 | 1 | — | 8 |
| Haven...................... | 0 | 1 | 0 | 1 | 0 | 1 | 1 | 1 | 1 | — | — | 6 |
| Crellin.................... | 1 | 1 | 1 | 1 | 1 | 1 | 1 | 1 | 0 | — | — | 8 |
| Pierce..................... | 1 | 1 | 1 | 0 | 1 | 1 | 1 | 1 | 0 | — | — | 7 |
| Vuillok.................... | 1 | 0 | 1 | 0 | 1 | 0 | 0 | 0 | 0 | 1 | — | 4 |
| Bell........................ | 0 | 1 | 0 | 0 | 0 | 1 | 1 | 1 | 1 | 0 | — | 5 |
| Vaughn..................... | 1 | 1 | 1 | 1 | 0 | 0 | 0 | 0 | 0 | — | — | 4 |
| Strickland................ | 1 | 1 | 0 | 0 | 0 | 0 | 0 | 1 | 0 | 1 | — | 9 |
| Tuttle..................... | 1 | 0 | 0 | 1 | 0 | 0 | 0 | 0 | 1 | 1 | — | 5 |
| Collin..................... | 0 | 0 | 1 | 1 | 0 | 0 | 0 | 1 | 1 | — | — | 4 |
| Taylor..................... | 0 | 0 | 1 | 1 | 0 | 0 | 0 | 0 | 1 | — | — | 4 |
| Rector..................... | 0 | 1 | 1 | 0 | 0 | 0 | 0 | 0 | 0 | 1 | — | 5 |
| Batchelder................ | 0 | 0 | 1 | 1 | 1 | 1 | 0 | 1 | 0 | 0 | — | 5 |
| Schell..................... | 0 | 1 | 1 | 1 | 1 | 1 | 1 | 0 | 0 | — | — | 7 |
| Jacobus.................... | 0 | 1 | 1 | 1 | 0 | 0 | 0 | 0 | 0 | 0 | — | 4 |
| Haskell.................... | 0 | 0 | 1 | 1 | 1 | 1 | 0 | 0 | 0 | 0 | — | 7 |
| Spaulding................. | 1 | 1 | 1 | 1 | 1 | 0 | 1 | 1 | 1 | 0 | — | 8 |
| Morton.................... | 1 | 1 | 1 | 0 | 0 | 0 | 0 | 0 | 0 | 1 | — | 4 |
| Shoes...................... | 1 | 1 | 1 | 0 | 1 | 0 | 1 | 1 | 1 | — | — | 7 |
| Froyer.................... | 0 | 0 | 0 | 1 | 0 | 1 | 1 | 1 | 1 | — | — | 5 |
| Eschbram................. | 1 | 0 | 1 | 0 | 0 | 1 | 1 | 1 | 1 | 0 | — | 6 |
| Strickland#.............. | 1 | 1 | 1 | 1 | 1 | 1 | 1 | 1 | 1 | 1 | — | 9 |
| *McKillican.............. | 1 | 0 | 0 | 0 | 1 | 1 | 1 | 0 | 0 | — | — | 4 |
| Williams.................. | 1 | 1 | 1 | 1 | 0 | 1 | 0 | 1 | — | — | — | 8 |

* Second class.

Mr. Strickland won the gold medal for the day, but as Mr. C. Tuttle has made the best scores of the season, it will at the next meeting become his property permanently. Crellin and Pierce shot off the tie at five birds, twenty yards. Crellin having won three times, the silver medal of the second class, it becomes his property. After this, six or eight matches for small purses where shot. Many members who made poor scores with clay-pigeons will have a chance at the live bird match to make a far better record than that of last Saturday.

THE PRIZES FOR THE COSMOPOLITAN CLUBS.—The "Champion" Cosmopolitan Shooting Club will hold their last shooting match of the season at San Bruno, on Sunday, Aug. 20, 1882. The committee having the shoot in hand are using every endeavor to make this the crowning shoot of the year. Admirers and members of the Club have donated the following prizes for the day: Ben Brown, ½ doz. ladies' silk under shirts; J. J. O'Brien, ½ doz. pair kid gloves; J. Browell, Jr., 1 dps. handkerchiefs; F. Putzman, Jr., 1 case wine; Dr. Rover, 1 pair stuffed canvas back ducks; F. Funcke, 1 pair best calfskin boots; J. Ferguson, 1 case wine; J. H. Orr, 1 scarf; Geo. Muller, 1 box crackers; W. Fulton, 2 ¼-kegs choke bow powder; Hazard Powder Co., 2 ½-kegs powder; C. H. Graham, 1 pair hunting boots; Stack & Lacombe, 1 hat; M. Luehman & Co., 1 velvet rug; Clabrough & Golcher, 1 Victoria leather gun case; Liddle & Kaeding, 1 hunting suit; F. Johnson, pair leather leggings; P. Murphy, pair hunting shoes; J. Pollack, box cigars; P. Mayer, barrel flour; L. Reynolds, $6.00 coin; A. H. Higgins, leather cartridge case; J. H. Ments, handsome meerschaum pipe; N. Cunningham, "something handsome;" Gen. Nelson, $20 piece.

PRAIRIE CHICKENS FOR SOUTHERN CALIFORNIA.—D. H. Hites, of Gibson, Neb., has written the following letter to the Santa Barbara Rod and Gun Club: "I wish to make a few suggestions to you in regard to game birds, for consideration. I suppose you have no prairie chickens or grouse in your valleys. It is one of the best of game birds, and will do well anywhere that quail will. Ten years ago we had no quail here. We imported a half dozen; now the country is covered with quail. If your members wish it, I will send you the wildest one dozen prairie chickens. That is, I will give the birds and you pay the transportation charges. Another bird you need is the wild turkey. He is the king of game birds. We have none here, but in Western Missouri they are abundant, and could be bought for a trifle. You may be able to get these much nearer home, and could thus save expense, but let me advise you by all means to get them. My interest is this: I expect to come to Santa Barbara shortly to make a home; I can shoot a little, and if the birds were plentiful, I might be able to buy some, even if I could not kill any. You may have these birds to the manner born, in which case I ask your pardon for this intrusion, but as I have never seen any mention of them, I come to the conclusion that you do not have them." The prairie bird affords good sport and is delicious eating, so we shall be pleased to see Mr. Hites' generous offer accepted; as it might lead to the bird becoming thoroughly acclimated on this coast. As to the wild turkey, it will be a more difficult matter, as they require a combination of forest where insect life abounds. Their favorite home is in the Carolinas.

On Sunday, Sept. 3d, next, there will be a wing shooting tournament at San Bruno. This match is open to all California, and will be under the government of the State Rules, except that shooting in squads will be adopted. The conditions are twenty-five birds each, at twenty-one yards rise, and the entrance fee is $25. The prizes are 40, 30, 20 and 10 per cent. of the entrance money, in the order of the score.

An excellent chance for our sportsmen who are in pursuit of fiercer game than the deer, is presented around Caneda Rancundo, in San Mateo county. It is reported that there are two or three California lions prowling about the hills there, committing sad depredations among the sheep and cattle of the neighborhood. An organized hunt would be in order.

Mr. John K. Orr is always taking a keen interest in the future of the State as regards the introduction of foreign game birds, and by the Oceanic he lately received three copper-colored cock pheasants to replace those that died some time since. He intends to turn these loose on his place, near San Rafael with the seven hane he has already in his possession.

Mr. M. M. Lytle, one of the Directors of the California State Sportsman Club, returned the other day from Santa Clara county, with his game bag filled with doves. These birds are quite plentiful at Menlo Park and vicinity.

---

Another case of game-law breaking has come to the notice of the California State Sportsman's Association. A person in Marin County was found with a spotted fawn in his possession. Five persons in all are implicated in this affair, and arrangements are being made to prosecute them to the full extent of the law.

On last Sunday, 30th, the Cosmopolitan Club meet at San Bruno, for their last pigeon shoot of the season. On Sunday, 27th, the Cosmopolitan Club will also finish their season's shooting at San Bruno.

Near Healdsburg, two gentlemen, C. W. Randell and Mr. O'Keef, in one day's shooting bagged 207 doves, Mr. Randell killing 140 and Mr. O'Keef 67.

A man at Tracy, San Joaquin County, has recently been convicted on a charge of killing fawn out of season.

Good curlew and plover shooting is to be had on the marshes near San Pablo.

## THE RIFLE.

THE N. G. C. RIFLE TEAM.—The monthly competition of the N. G. C. rifle team for class medals came off at Shell Mound range on the 6th inst. The team is divided into three classes; those of the first class shooting two and five hundred yards. The medal of the first class was won by Lieut. J. E. Klein, who made 90 out of a possible 100 points. Corporal Hampton made 40 out of a possible 50 and won the second class. The third medal was taken by Serg't. Elder in 40 out of 50 points. The second and third class shoot at two hundred yards only. Messrs. Merry, Hinchman and Campbell received the leather medals. The officers of the team are: President, Major A. T. Kloss; Secretary, Sergeant E. N. Snook; Treasurer, Lieutenant H. T. Sime; Shooting Master, Lieut. J. E. Klein. This team was organized fifteen years ago, and claims some of the best rifle shots on the Pacific Coast.

## DEER HUNTING FOR PLEASURE VS. DEER HUNTING FOR MEAT.

EDITOR BREEDER AND SPORTSMAN : In reading the letter of a deer hunt in the BREEDER AND SPORTSMAN of July 29th, signed H. H., I could help but but blush to think that where there is so much pleasure in deer hunting, if done in in a proper and sportsmanlike way, how a hunter could enjoy or take pleasure in the mere slaughter of deer for their meat, and that the sportsman with hounds was to be censured. Instead of reading a descriptive deer hunt, an exciting chase with hounds and gun, it culminated in the crimson-stained slaughter-pen, where the warm, red blood flows from the deep gash inflicted by the sharpened knife, and the brains were oozing from beneath the bludgeon which was steadily aimed by a strong muscular arm that falters not in taking life.

If such is to be the style of hunting, and to be pictured and praised; why not form societies and clubs that will take a solemn oath that no deathly poison shall remain unadministered as long as there is a deer bound in the land? Then foster and well pay a set of instructors that will educate the young sportsmen to crawl upon their bellies in pursuit of game, regardless of rocks or thorns, and so practiced and drilled that their bellies are tough and calloused; which the fangs of a rattlesnake or the sting of a tarantula could not penetrate. They should be trained to hold their breath for fear of alarming the game, and till their eyes should protrude and become dead to the enjoyment of any scenery in their scope or vision, no matter how grand. Make their arms bare and muscular, that they could sling a bludgeon and bury it deep in the brain of their victim. Instruct them to load their guns to the muzzles; callous their shoulders, that they may resist the recoil; inflict a severe penalty should they ever draw a bead upon their game outside of forty paces, and then for them to take deliberate aim at their heads, await their near approach, and when close to the muzzle, shut their eyes and blaze away; Should the deer's skull bone be entirely removed at the first fire, and the bludgeon not come in play, drop their guns, if still in their possession, and plunge their hands in the cavity made, draw from it the quivering brain, and besmear their faces at a token of the masterly art and their extreme enjoyment. Always have ready between their teeth the blade of a blood-stained and well-sharpened knife, that they could sever the main artery in the neck of the deer, and as the warm blood flows, feast themselves upon it till their thirst is quenched. Also, instruct the young sportsman that after being sumptuously entertained, if so fortunate, by the host and hostess, and attired in their hunting suit, their entire nature must undergo a change, and from the smiling face that is full of thankfulness and pleasure, and their manly form that stands erect, they must become changed to a sneaking appearance; their heads must drop and project forward; their eyes protrude; brows droop; back become humped; knees bending, and then, bring their countenance in as mean an expression as possible, prone forward, sloth and crouch in the shadow of every clump or object in sight, and should they near a water-hole, or by chance a salt lick, then make themselves as small as possible, and drag themselves upon their bellies till a clump or hole is reached. Then conceal themselves and quietly await the favorable opportunity, although swarming with ants and tormented with mosquitos, there patiently await the approach of the deer. Such is the pleasure of a descriptive still hunt.

Now draw the comparison with the sportsman well equipped and mounted on the back of a proud stepping horse, with a fine pack of well trained deer hounds leading the way, their bright eyes and glossy backs shining in the sunlight, their musical voices filling the air and making the mountains echo and ring, and as they move forward, impatiently nearing the hunting ground, the horn is sounded, away gallop the hounds, eager for the chase. The huntsman's blood grows warm, his pulse quickens, his countenance glows with excitement, his muscles grow with restless delight, his lungs expand and new life appears. Draw the comparison, and imagine the angler after the finny thoroughbred, equipped with a delicate rod, silken line, dainty colored flies and a neat straw basket hanging from his shoulders, when he quietly follows the winding brook that is overhung with the branches of various trees and vines, the sunlight seldom reaching the ripling waters that sparkle and fall from rock to rock. Casting his line in the ripples, and when the tempting bait has scarcely reached the water before there is fastened a fish that darts like a flash, only to be landed on the bank by the feet of the angler. Such is pleasure! Now, the fish hunter, with his pockets filled with giant powder cartridges, his sneaking form and guilty step hidden with an old potato sack, plods along the stream and at every hole he whirls in his cartridge and awaits the result; to see every living fish there dead? He gathers up the fish and drops them in his sack, chuckling over his spoils. Or, for instance, the quail hunter, that has for weeks baited the young brood with food in some secluded spot, and as soon as the law will shield him he skulks quietly alone through the brush at the break of day, secreting himself near at hand awaits the return of the birds to feed, and when they are gathered together feeding he blazes away with some old rusty gun that roars like distant thunder; then sneaking up he gathers together the dead and mangled birds—from twelve to twenty—and crowds them in some old sack, while reckoning their cash value in market. Two or three more similar explosions and he returns home delighted with his day's sport. The true sportsman with a fine brace of well-trained setters, the latest model of a fine breech-loading gun, and all the appliances that can add to his pleasure. He proudly watches his dogs as they beat over the meadow, and when the scent of the game is taken, which is quickly discovered by the sportsman, who is watching every move, and as they are working and drawing upon the birds more cautiously every step till a full point is made, each dog is staunch and firm as a model of brass. The sportsman watches every move and pictures their attitude with delight. The bird is flushed, and when at a proper distance is shot on the wing; the dogs drop at the report, and await the word "fetch." When brought in the dead bird is closely examined and admired, his feathers smoothed and then laid with care to his game bag. One bird thus taken has contributed more pleasure and sport than one hundred ground-sluiced at a single shot.
WHETSTONE.

## DEER HUNTING IN MARIN COUNTY.

EDITOR BREEDER AND SPORTSMAN: Last Friday noon I received an invitation from a friend in Oakland to participate in a deer hunt with himself and two other gentlemen of San Francisco. Our destination was over and through the lofty hills and deep cañons of Marin County, where the redwood and the pine extend their topmost branches toward the heavens, and the hunter with his gun and dog retire to quench their thirst for game. Saturday morning I shouldered old Winchester once more, and proceeded to San Francisco, where I met my three companions, Messrs. D. R., W. R. and M. C., at 1:35 P. M. on the little steamer Sag Rafael. Three hours later I reached my destination, it being the residence of an old Scotch mountaineer, who has witnessed sixty-six Summers of mountain life. His residence is about five miles southwesterly from San Geronimo. My three companions, having to come from Point San Quentin in a two-wheeled conveyance, did not arrive until about 10 P. M., after which a brief nap was taken by all hands. At 6 A. M. Sunday the cupboard was ransacked and the intruders decamped for the happy hunting grounds, about one mile distant, accompanied by Old Scotty and six fine hounds. At 7 o'clock we succeeded in starting a young buck at which I got two shots in quick succession, at about four hundred yards distance, but without success. A moment later they were answered by two more from the rifle of W. R., who was within seventy-five yards of his victim, both bullets having penetrated the body of the unfortunate buck and laid his lifeless upon the ground. After a few moments' rest, we concluded to search in another ravine near by. We had hardly reached our stations when a huge old buck came bounding up the hill toward us. I took deliberate aim through my peep-sight, and missed him. The old buck, becoming excited from dogs on all sides of him, threw his optics in my direction and came bounding like wildfire toward me. When at a distance of about one-hundred yards, I raised my rifle to take a peep-sight, but my eyes grew so immense and the sight appeared so small, not a deer could be seen. I then took the open sight, and planted a ball in the bosom of my would-be assailant, which laid him low with the death-look upon his eye. I then proceeded to the opposite side of the hill, where I spied a large four-pronged buck walking leisurely down the ravine. I immediately fired upon him, causing him to go across on to the side hill on which I was stationed. One of our dogs, hearing the report of my gun, came directly over the hill from where we had strung up our second deer, and meeting the buck directly face to face, caused him to rebound into the valley, at which time I fired, wounding him in the loins severely. He then decreased his speed very rapidly, and after climbing the hill to a reasonable distance he entered a small sandslide, whereupon he stood and fought for dear life with the dogs. I advanced toward him, and while doing so I saw my old banker, W. R., close by, who fired, breaking one of his fore legs. But our antagonist proved game to the last, having been pierced by four bullets. On retiring homeward our dogs trailed a young buck about fifteen months old, which was brought to bay by my friend W. R. at 9:05 A. M. we had our four bucks strapped upon our horses, the whole hunt occupying a little less than four hours' time. Had we attempted, we could have shot two doe with but little work. At 2:30 P. M. we proceeded homeward with a glad and gallant load, leaving Old Scotty to dream once more of a deer hunt. My next will likely be a black bear hunt in the locality of Mt. Tamalpais. Yours, respectfully,
Oakland, Aug. 14th.     PEEP-SIGHT.

THE BREEDER AND SPORTSMAN is the name of a new weekly paper, conducted by Jos. Cairn Simpson, and published in San Francisco, Cal., at five dollars per annum. The first copy is at hand. For beauty of typography, extent and variety of matter, and general make-up, it is unexcelled by its contemporaries. Mr. Simpson is author of a popular book, called Horse Portraiture, and for more than a quarter of a century has been a popular writer on horse and sporting matters. He is admirably qualified to conduct such an enterprise, and the breeders of the Pacific Coast are to be congratulated upon having so able and gifted a champion of their interests.—St. Louis Rural World.

# FISH.

Tomcod are caught in great numbers all around the bay.

Ben Brown and Chas. Carter were fishing at Lagunitas Lake and caught many trout ten to fourteen inches in length.

Bay fishing ought to be good this coming Sunday, as this is one of the three days of the first quarter of the moon when the tides are small.

Lon Zugler was up to Bodega Corners and caught 216 trout that measured from eight to twelve inches. The stream is alive with fish.

W. H. Lawrence, of the Spring Valley Water Co., says that the black bass in Crystal Springs Lake weigh two and three pounds and take either fly or spoon.

Strange to say, the Tussarora *Times-Review* finds fault with the Tussarora people who go fishing because they won't fish. They come home without any fish, sadly say so, and quietly take a back seat.

People who go to Donner Lake fishing should confine themselves to the lake, and not try to "work" any private fish-ponds on the outside. Somebody got chased with a shotgun for that kind of a mistake the other day.

To a good many, half the fun of a fishing excursion is in the anticipation. They talk of it, plan for it, and arrange all the details with the utmost nicety. Then comes the expedition. The other half of the fun is talking it over after it has happened. The excursion itself is of secondary consideration.

Mr. A. Badlam has just returned from Lake Tahoe and reports fine trout fishing in the lake; these trout weigh from one half to three pounds each. He thinks that his success was owing to a peculiar spoon that he used, as several who were with him did not have as good luck. Brook trout along the Truckee river are quite plentiful.

For years it has been a mooted question whether the shad takes the fly intentionally or not, the theory of some observers being that, as the fish congregate in crowds at their favorite resorts, they accidentally breathe the fly into their mouths, and are hooked. They are seldom angled for in Eastern streams, even when the run is strong in numbers.

Anglers predict that in a very few years the trout will all disappear from the valley streams of Montana, owing to the immense numbers carried out into irrigating ditches and into the fields. Screens at the heads of ditches would prevent this.

An enterprising looking countryman with a creel full of fine brook trout, was standing in the doorway of the railroad station at Nameless Springs. A passenger accosted him, and after admiring the fish remarked: "Going to take them home for supper, I suppose?" "Not if I can help it," said the rustic with a grin. "There be a party of city bloods as went fishing from here this mornin'. They're 'spected back soon, and I'm sorter lyin' round waitin' to save their feelin's."

It does not always pay for people in the country to try and claim a whole region. It does not pay either for them to threaten decent people who are quietly hunting or fishing. Here is an example cited from the *Tuolumne Independent:* "About ten days ago a crowd of young men from Sonora went to R. J. Kennedy's cattle range, situated about sixty-one miles east of Sonora, for fishing. Kennedy has a fence around a cañon and claims ten miles square from that line on unsurveyed Government land. He objected to the boys going through the fence for fishing. Sonora boys don't scare very badly at mountain bear. He followed them on horseback seven miles where they were pulling out the speckled beauties in a lively manner. He pulled his six-shooter and said that if they did any more fishing they must do it over his dead body, etc., and otherwise threatened their lives. The eight boys were well armed —especially with fish, when they returned to Sonora. Deputy Sheriff McQuade brought Kennedy to Sonora Thursday evening to answer charges before Justice Miller on Friday. He pleaded guilty of misdemeanor and paid a fine of $75. It will be remembered that Kennedy damned the river last year at his premises, causing much trouble."

A Curious Fish Story.—Some time since one of the Eastern papers published a lot of "fish stories," where each man attempted to tell the longest yarn. Here is one we take from the *Gridley Herald* (Butte County), of last week, which ought to have gone with the other batch. "Fred McCarty, an attache of the *Herald*, met with a singular adventure while fishing in Thresher's Slough, Sunday. He had caught a small catfish, weighing probably a quarter of a pound, and was swinging it into shore when a huge pelican swooped down, gobbled the fish, hook and all, and started to fly away. The sea-grass line proved too strong for the bird and, after a hard struggle, Fred succeeded in pulling the varmint of the air to terra firma, where he speedily dispatched it with a club and got his fish. The bird measured three feet six inches from tip to tip of its wings and weighed about nine pounds and a half. That is one way of hunting birds, but Fred says he'd rather use a gun, as he received several severe raps by the bird's wings before the battle terminated in his favor. Having witnessed the scene, we can vouch for the truth of this item."

A Salmon Weir.—The following is a description of a salmon trap built by Indians near the mouth of the Spokane river: The Indians have built a solid net work of willow twigs from one bank to the other. Poles were first placed at a distance of some four feet apart, upright in the water. Through these the willow twigs were woven until across a distance of 80 yards there is not a hole large enough to admit the passage of a good sized salmon. This weir is built in such a way that it forms a V, the point down stream. At either bank small wicket doors are hinged in the weir. The salmon comes up the stream and follows one or the other of the sides of the V up to the door, pushing with his nose all the time against the willows. The door opens as he pushes against it and passes through into a small pen, and the force of the current closes the door again ready for the next comer. It is then an interesting sight to see the small boys get into that pen with their spears and take out the salmon. Sometimes as much as 1,000 pounds are taken daily, during a good run, and fish may be seen in the pens at any minute. The fish are cut into slices about 8 inches long and hung over poles to be smoked and dried. The smoking process is only used to keep the meat free from insects while the drying process is going on.

---

A Generous Owner.—The *Oroville Mercury* states that Joel Flinn, at his place, situated upon a tributary of Berry Creek, has four fine fish ponds, three of them averaging about a half acre each in superficial area, and the other being about one acre in extent with a depth of water ranging from zero to six feet. Two years ago Mr. Flinn conceived the idea of stocking these ponds with carp, and sent to Sonoma County for his plant, and received twenty-two fish therefrom—German carp, that all arrived at their destination without mishap, and in good condition. Consigning them to his ponds, Mr. Flinn has let them take their chances in breeding, and so well has his plant thriven that the four ponds are fairly alive with fish of various sizes—thousands of them being twelve inches long, while the old ones are more than two feet in length, weighing six or eight pounds apiece, and can be seen lazily disporting themselves in the water as great salmon were once in the clear waters of the California streams. This abundance has induced Mr. Flinn to give the public a chance to angle for carp without cost. This Fall he proposes to drain his ponds, so he can place all of the larger sized fish that are suitable for table use into one of the ponds, excluding therefrom the small fry, and next season let any one who chooses cast their lines and keep to themselves their catch free.

## ON RAISING TROUT.

There is no doubt that many make fatal mistakes in stocking streams and turning the fry loose in the swift current. The fish being young are at once swept down the stream and generally settle at the bottom in the eddies and still pores where they are at once gobbled up by other fish of the brook. Mr. P. A. M. Van Wyck suggested this plan to Mr. Seth Green, the superintendent of the N. Y. State Fish Hatchery, as a method of preventing this loss. He says: In stocking brooks with trout fry I always place the young trout in small rills or feeders that empty in the main brook. These rills or feeders always proceed from a fountain-head or spring, and the water in them is always cold and no shiners or small fish are found in them, as the water is too cold for them to live. There the trout fry will stay nearly a year; at the same time they get their natural food from the water, and it is not necessary to feed them, and when they run into the main stream they are large and strong enough to take care of themselves. Last Spring I procured from the New York State Hatchery, at Caledonia, 5,000 California mountain trout fry, and as I had heard so much of this aquatic stranger and had been a long time trying to get a stock I concluded to take extra pains with them. I found a suitable stream in the mountains of Duchess County. On going well up to the head of the stream I found three small springs. Each spring had an outlet, and all three outlets discharged in one basin which communicated with the main stream. I dammed up the basin where the water entered the main stream by pinning down a couple of slabs and filling in with mud on both sides of the slabs. This backed the water and made quite a nice little pond. In it I put my fry and employed a man living on the grounds to look after them during the Summer. They have done splendidly, never being fed since I planted them.

---

# THE KENNEL.

## GILROY FIELD TRIALS.

Following are the stakes which will be run at the Gilroy Field Trials, commencing on October 23d:

All-Aged-Stakes.—Entrance fee, $5. First prize, silver cup; second, gold medal; third, silver medal.

Puppy Stakes.—For dogs whelped on or since January 1, 1881. Three prizes, same as in All-age-Stakes.

Brace Stakes.—Each brace of dogs entered to be the property of one owner. Three prizes, same as in All-Aged-Stakes.

In addition to the above prizes, others are expected to be added—donations from leading sportsmen.

Entries to close at 8 o'clock on the evening before the trials.

All entries must be accompanied by the entrance fee; also a full description of the dogs entered, with name of sire and dam (if known); age, color and markings.

Applications for entry to be made to the Corresponding Secretary of the Gilroy Rod and Gun Club, who will furnish on application a copy of the rules governing the trials.

For the convenience of our readers we append the rules under which the trials will be run:

### DOGS RUNNING.

1. The dogs shall be run in braces, and the order of their running shall be decided by the Executive Committee by lot, and announced the night previous.

2. Dogs may be handled by the owner or his deputy, but when once put down, they must be handled by the same person throughout.

3. Every dog must be brought up in his proper turn, without delay. If absent more than a quarter of an hour, except it be from some unavoidable accident, he shall be disqualified from running and ruled out.

4. Any owner entering two or more dogs, or any trainer having two or more dogs entrusted to his handling, may run them in braces of his own selection.

### HANDLERS OF DOGS.

1. Handlers of dogs may speak, whistle, work by hand and use their ordinary method of training, except shooting game, which shall be left to the judges. A handler may be called to order by the judges for making any unnecessary noise, and if he persists in doing so, they may order his dog to be taken up and ruled out of the stake.

2. Dogs must be handled quietly, and their handlers must walk within a reasonable distance of each other. After a caution, the judges may have power to disqualify the dog whose owner persists in neglecting this rule.

### GENERAL RULES.

1. The length of a trial shall be determined by the judges. When they are satisfied, the trial should end.

2. An undecided trial is when the judges cannot agree upon the merits of any dogs, which shall be decided by another trial, and shall stand first in order for the next day.

3. No subscriber or member of the club shall openly impugn the decisions of the judges, nor make any remarks about the dogs within their hearing during the trials.

4. An objection to a dog may be made to the Executive Committee at any time before the conclusion of the trials, upon the objector lodging $5 in their hands, which shall be forfeited if the objection prove frivolous. Should an objec-

---

tion be made which cannot be proved at the time, the dog may be allowed to run under protest, the Executive Committee retaining his winnings until the objection has been withdrawn or decided. If the dog be disqualified, the prize, if any, to which he would have been entitled, shall be given to the next dog below him in points.

5. Should any dog be considered by the Executive Committee unfit to run, by reason of being in heat, or other cause, such dog shall be disqualified.

N. B. In the foregoing rules the term dog is understood to mean both sexes.

6. No dog is to be considered a puppy that was whelped before the first of January of the year preceding that of his competing.

7. All entries of dogs shall contain the names of sire and dam (if known), with age, color and markings, and in the puppy stakes, with date of whelping.

8. Any subscriber taking an entry in a Stake, and not prefixing the word "names" to a dog that is not his own property, shall forfeit that dog's chances of the Stake. He shall likewise deliver in writing to the Executive Committee the name of the bona fide owner of the dog named by him; and this communication is to be produced should any dispute arise in the matter.

## LEVY ACQUITTED.

Last Wednesday afternoon, D. L. Levy. was tried for cruelty to animals before Judge Rosenbaum and a jury in Police Court No. 2. The prosecution grew out of the coursing tournament, so-called, given at the Half Mile Race Track, on July 2d, and was carried on by Officer Hooper, representing the Society for the Prevention of Cruelty to Animals. Considerable evidence was taken, all of which tended to show that the affair was marked by most unsportsmanlike practices and a good deal of unnecessary cruelty, but it was not proven that Levy was responsible for what took place, and the jury returned a verdict of not guilty without a moment's consideration. Had Officer Hooper, who was at the trial, arrested the parties that illtreated the hare right on the spot, he could doubtless have obtained a conviction. Levy showed that he simply gave the prizes and provided the hares, and that the details were left entirely to the gentlemen whose dogs participated. As they all claim to be coursing men they have not the excuse of ignorance which Levy, who never attended a coursing match, might have made. The effect of the prosecution will be to prevent such fiascos in future, and in this respect it has done as much service to sport as though conviction had resulted.

## BREEDING NOTIONS.

The following article is by Arnold Burgess, in the *American Field:*

With all the care which in other respects is now given to breeding, it seems very strange to me that so little importance is attached to the adaptation of the dogs bred for each other. By adaptation I mean that comparative proportion of both physical and mental or instinctive qualities which renders one individual a fitting mate for another.

All of our present breeds of animals have been brought up from the original stock by breeding from selected specimens. In a state of nature this is provided for by the law of physical strength, which insures the survival of the fittest, and thus prevents the depreciation which would otherwise follow that inbreeding which is so often quoted as authority for a similar course with domesticated animals. In the cure which run the streets and receive no attention because of no value, the same law of force prevails; but with dogs of more worth, breeding is regulated by the care and theories of the master, and consequently here is just where the necessity for adaptation should be recognized, since without it the law of the fittest is not enforced, and naturally there can be no improvement of the species even if there is no actual depreciation.

The best of our strains of sporting dogs are interbred, and with such, adaptation is specially needed to prevent depreciation as the result of consanguineous unions. The more closely inbred animals are, the more deeply family characteristics are impressed upon them to a certain point, and for this reason inbreeding to a certain extent is necessary, to develop and form a breed possessed of individual attributes which will entitle it to a distinct name. There is a point, however, beyond which inbreeding cannot be carried without loss of even family characteristics. Properly controlled by appropriate unions it produces the best results, but ill con-trolled or ignorantly followed it is ruinous.

A majority of the men who own single bitches which they breed occasionally, seem to care nothing for adaptation, but select stock dogs simply by their reputations. A light bitch should be sent to a dog of substance, with dash and strength to carry it off; and any particular defect must be corrected by seeking a mate, that is specially strong in the opposite. With a well formed and approximately perfect bitch, great care should be taken to mate her with a dog fully her equal, that the good qualities of each may be intensified in the progeny.

The principle which applies to correction of form holds equally good in respect to the higher qualities, the less being supplied from the superabundance of the greater.

In making inquiries respecting a dog, three things should be regarded: First, his own form; next, that of his parents; and last, that displayed by a majority of his progeny. The first is a description of the dog himself; the second shows his hereditary tendencies, which will be intensified by association with a bitch of the same characteristics as his parents, or the one he most resembles; the last shows his abilities as a stud dog, and whether he has the power to transmit his own attributes or not.

As dogs are supposed to be kept for work the field qualities of a stud dog should be rigidly investigated where they have not been publicly shown. What greater blunder can be perpetrated than to send a fine field bitch to a dog that is not a fielder, simply because he is well bred and handsome? The progeniency of good blood will, it is true, produce a large number of good working dogs from even such unions, but it is also true that some of the progeny will display the lack of field quality of their sire, as surely as they would inherit any other deficiency from him. To breed to a dog that is not a fielder is to perpetuate a race of dogs that are not fielders, and for this reason this quality should be a *sine qua non* with all who seek the services of stock dogs.

By such inquiries as I have indicated the adaptation of proposed unions can be determined and the law of nature observed. We cannot violate any law without incurring a penalty that will certainly be exacted. It may not be recognized at first, but it will ultimately manifest itself and prove the folly of the act which called it into existence. Nature compensates or punishes all who obey or disobey her laws, and as the *summum bonum* is an approximation to perfection, this can be most quickly and certainly reached by observance of those principles upon which depend the influences which control the development of races.

## FIELD TRIAL ENTRIES.

The first of the great American Field Trials is the American Field Trial Derby, open to all setters and pointers born on or after March 1, 1881, to be run on pinated grouse or prairie chickens, commencing September 4, 1882, at Fairmont, Minnesota. Purse $450: of which $200 to first, $125 to second, $75 to third, $50 to fourth; $5 forfeit, $10 additional for starters. Closed July 1st with forty-four entries, as follows:

SETTERS.

Mr. R. B. Morgan's Prairie Wonder, by Prairie Joe—Prairie Queen.
Sportsman's Kennel's Prairie Molly, by Prairie Joe—Prairie Queen.
Mr. D. C. Sanborn's Gus Bondhu, by Dashing Bondhu—Novel.
Mr. D. C. Sanborn's Gaze (late Blaze), by Count Noble—Spark.
Mr. D. C. Sanborn's Countess Magnet, by Count Noble—Spark.
Mr. D. McKinney Lloyd's Count Dad, by Count Noble—Nellie.
Mr. J. A. Thoomb's Old Wah, by Lincoln—Dairy Dean.
Mr. Jos. R. Dee's American Dan, by Lincoln—Dairy Dean.
Messrs. S. F. Wilson and J. J. Snellenberg's Josephine, by Don—Cora.
Mr. J. Otto Donner's Dashing Belle, by Dashing Dash—Beatie.
Mr. J. Otto Donner's Mabe, by Paris—Fairy Belle.
Mr. J. J. Snellenberg's Queen Lavernak, by Tory—Meg Merrilies.
Mr. J. J. Snellenberg's Prince, by Count Noble—Nellie.
Mr. H. Widdicomb's Countess Nellie, by Count Noble—Nellie.
Mr. W. C. Berringer's Monte Cristo, by Thunder—Bess.
Mr. J. Palmer O'Neil's Acme, by Thunder—Bess.
Messrs. Willard Bros.' Rescue, by Rip—Fuss.
Mr. W. B. Gates' Carrie J., by Count Noble—Peep o' Day.
Mr. W. B. Mallory's Pink B., by Gladstone—Countess Kay.
Dr. C. H. Thiel's Minnie, by Fred—Aileen May.
Mr. R. A. Clock's Dot, by Fred—Aileen May.
Mr. A. M. Weichard's Davy Crockett, by Sam II.—Pan.
Mr. E. E. Hardy's Rizz, by Drake—Countess May.
Mr. W. G. Dean's Sarien, by Druid—Magnolia.
Mr. W. J. G. Dean's Zuda, by Druid—Magnolia.
   George O. Marsh's Gilderoy, by Druid—Princess Draco.
   S. R. Turrill's Doctor, by Pembroke—Royal Gift.
   H. Turrill's Frank, by Blue Dash—Pipp.
   John D. Ladd's Countess Mollie, by Count Noble—Spark.
   Howard Hartley's Daisy Queen, by Rock—Flora.
   F. J. Hayward, Jr.'s Count Campbell, by Joe Jr.—Belle of Nashville.
   Mr. Ariel Low, Jr.'s Windfall.
   S. W. W. Straight's Dashing Rip, by Obes—Nancy.
   Mr. A. G. Bishop's Flirt, by Thunder—Minerva.
   Wm. Wil. Davidson's Bob Cardi, by Bill—Meldum.
   Dr. E. Pfeel Spaly's St. Elmo IV, by St. Elmo—Clio.
   Mr. B. B. Hurd's Kitty Dick, by Guy Mannering—Fairiwind.
   Mr. J. H. Henrick's Dashing Dick, by King Dash—Sally.
   Mr. Luther Adam's Countess May II, by Drake—Countess May.

POINTERS.

Mr. J. J. French's Prairie Rose, by Rival, Jr.—Queen Hamlet.
Mr. James Stinson's LaValse, by Little Sufful—Flight.
Mr. James Stinson's Dove, by Sefton—St. Glasor.
Mr. George E. Poysser's Buster, by Bang—Jean.

GORDON MEASUREMENTS.—Below are the measurements of a Gordon setter in good working condition. They may be accepted as the representative of a first-class dog, more likely to shine in the field, however, than on the bench:

| | |
|---|---|
| Height | 24 inches |
| Length of head | 10 inches |
| Girth of chest | 29 inches |
| Round muzzle | 4 inches |
| Round forearm one inch below elbow | 7 inches |
| Length of tail | 11 inches |
| From nose to end of stern | 41 inches |
| From eye to end of nose | 4½ inches |
| Weight | 50 pounds |

DEATH OF DR. ATEN'S GLEN.—Dr. Aten's Glen died at Centerport, Long Island, on Thursday, July 20th, from poison administered by some miscreant whose life would be considered by many of much less value than that of his victim. Glen's age, at the time of his death, was eight years, and he had been a faithful companion both at home and in the field. He was thoroughly broken, and few canines could add more to a man's pleasure than he, coupled with Ned, also gone to the happier hunting grounds. He was winner of first in the Brace Stakes, at the inaugural trial of the Eastern Field Trials Club, at Robin's Island in 1879; and in 1880 divided with Sensation the third and fourth prizes in the All Aged Stakes of the same club. Though not a bench show dog, he was always considered by the different judges before whom he was shown as worthy of a V. H. C., and his skull was always surrounded by many admirers. He was also the winner of two silver medals given by the Westminster Kennel Club in 1880 and 1881, for the best black and tan with a field trial record. His disposition was of the best, and his loss will be greatly deplored by his many friends, as well as his owner, who has my heartfelt sympathy. "Peace to his ashes." F. N. H.—*American Field*.

## THE HERD.

### SHEEP AND IMPROVED FARMING.

Sheep have played a most important part in the improvement of the soil in all civilized countries. At an early period sheep were kept mostly for their wool in all countries; but as population increased, and greater demand was made upon the soil to furnish food, mutton became the principal object of sheep farming and wool the incident. During this transition state skilful breeders made a long, careful and practical study in improving the carcass and its early maturity. Instead of keeping sheep to their full age as breeders and producers of wool, the most persevering effort was made to mature them for a profitable market at the earliest date. This was done by judicious selections in breeding and the most generous feeding. The sheep, like other animals, was found plastic in the hands of a skilful breeder and feeder. It was soon found that the improved Southdown and Cotswold could be fitted for the most profitable market at from six to fifteen months old, except those required for breeders, and these were most profitably turned at four to five years old, instead of at seven to ten years.

This transition to the strictly mutton breeds was first accomplished in England, in the perfection of the Leicester, Cotswold and Southdown. France is succeeding in transforming the Merino into a profitable mutton breed, by the most generous system of feeding. This transformation was produced at the breeding establishment of Rambouillet. At this establishment, the small-bodied, short-fibered, thin-fleshed, slow-maturing Merino has become of larger size, carries a slightly coarser and longer fiber, a heavier carcass, and a heavier fleece, more readily takes on flesh, and matures much earlier. Our American Merinos, in the hands of skilful breeders and feeders, are undergoing the same transformation. But still these sheep are not as well adapted to the production of mutton as the English mutton breeds; and, in this country, a cross between the Cotswold and the Merino has given satisfaction to some skilful breeders who have made it.

---

The consumption of mutton is increasing in this country, especially in our large cities, and it has become profitable to supply this demand. It is profitable, first, because the price is remunerative; and secondly, because it is promotive of good husbandry—the improvement of the soil.

The various cereal crops are depleting, rapidly exhausting to the soil; but a crop of mutton or wool takes but an imperceptible fraction, and, under the best management, adds to its fertility.

The mineral matter taken from the soil by a five-pound fleece of wool is only 1.6 ounces in a year, and 5 ounces of nitrogen. In order that the reader may see what part of the food is stored up in the body of the sheep, and what is passed in the solid and liquid excrement, we will quote from the German tables of experiment: It was found that when sheep consumed 100 lbs. of nitrogen in their food, (being barely meat), 16.7 lbs. was voided in the solid excrement, 79 lbs. in the liquid excrement, and 4.3 lbs. was stored up as increase of the body. Thus 95.7 per cent. of the nitrogen of the food was voided in the excrement, leaving as a loss to the soil (stored up in the body) only 4.3 per cent. Of the mineral or ash constituents of the food, it was found that sheep voided in the excrement 96.9 per cent., and used in the body only 3.8 per cent. When sheep were fed upon good clover and meadow hay, the solid excrement contained, of ash 3.5 per cent., of nitrogen 0.7 per cent.; whilst the urine contained, of ash 5.6 per cent., of nitrogen 1.4 per cent.

The clover crop is believed to accumulate nitrogen in the soil, by absorbing it from the air, and, as we see, it is nearly all recovered in the excrement of the sheep. If, then, clover and other grasses are fed off upon the land by sheep, the fertility is even increased. This explains the Spanish proverb, that "the foot of the sheep is golden." We wish, also, to call the reader's attention to the important fact found in these experiments, that the urine is much more valuable than the solid excrement. This also holds in the excrement of other stock. What a tremendous loss, then, occurs when the liquid is allowed to wash off into the nearest stream! How very important that farmers should prevent this loss.

Large cities are now growing up all over the country, and mutton production is to be one of the most profitable of farm industries in the near future. Let farmers study and understand the whole question.—*National Live Stock Journal.*

### IMPROVING DAIRY BREEDS.

Mr. I. K. Felch, who acquired celebrity as a poultry breeder, seems to be blossoming out in dairy cattle. In a communication to the *American Cultivator*, he advocates the crossing of dairy cattle. He says it is far safer to use a sire from remarkable ancestry with ordinary cows, than to breed cows at excellence with ordinary bulls. The former practice produces the best and most prolific progeny, in the ratio of sixty to forty.

There is no doubt about this proposition, but it is not new with Mr. Felch, neither is the statement which follows, of the transmission of quality by sire, and quantity by dam, altogether new; but these qualities are not constant. He states what he considers a remarkable circumstance, in which the progeny of a Jersey bull and an Ayrshire cow made 356 pounds of butter in twenty-seven weeks, besides furnishing milk for household use in a family of seven, who were not stinted in quantity consumed nor confined to skim milk.

The gist of the article is that a Jersey and Ayrshire cross will produce the best possible butter cow of the country. It is not at all likely. There are differences between the two breeds that will not blend kindly. The Ayrshire is superior in the yield of milk—not so much so, however, as the Holsteins. The Jersey excels in the quality of her milk. The first cross may be valuable, but it by no means follows that the succeeding progeny would follow to the line. The fact they would not. They would "strike back" through heredity to one or the other of the parents, and in the hands of the ordinary breeder would rapidly deteriorate. 'In the hands of the most successful and scientific breeders, it would take long years of breeding to produce animals that would uniformly and constantly combine the peculiar excellence of each, and then only relatively. In fact, practically, it cannot be done, if we judge by the results obtained by eminent breeders in the direction of beef. Neither has it yet been done in the dairy breeds. In other words, it is not in animal nature, no more than in human nature, to combine all known excellences in individuals as a rule. As the results of the most careful and long continued breeding, the highest excellence is only attained at rare intervals, and then not covering the greatest excellence in quality and quantity of beef, or the greatest quantity and best quality of milk.

Our advice to Western dairymen is to stick to breeds of known capability rather than to seek after something better by crossing pure breeds. In crossing upon common stock, use bulls of the breed known to inherit the qualities you seek. Here you cannot err. You must inevitably breed up. Not uniformly, of course, yet you will seldom get an animal inferior to the dam. In crossing pure breeds with a view to improvement, the result will not be so favorable. Therefore, improve the common stock of the country by using pure males on selected females, but don't waste time in improving pure breeds by crossing one another pure breed.

## POULTRY.

### FOWLS FOR BREEDING PURPOSES.

Where uniformity of size, general health and vigor, as well as color and beauty, are desired, great care must be exercised with the breeding stock. It matters little whether the chicks to be reared are for renewing the stock or for market. If a pure breed is desired in full perfection, the stock fowls must not only be well bred, but strong, vigorous, full of health, and of uniform size and markings. Nothing great or fine may be expected from low origin. Highly bred fowls may deteriorate from lack of keeping. I have seen that fact fully illustrated. That chicks hatched from well bred, highly bred birds require better keeping and care, I am compelled to believe, from experience, while at the same time I am fully able to testify to the fact that they are far more profitable and pay the keeper better.

In procuring fowls for stock purposes, either by means of eggs or the birds themselves, sufficient attention should be given as to whether the origin is good, in the first place, and in the second, if they have been well kept. Good feeding brings out the fine points in full perfection, and this is what is desired. If the blood is not there, then the points can not be brought out. There is no loss in full feeding of any kind of poultry. Any one observant of their habits knows

---

that fowls are regular and persistent feeders. The more feed the more profit, either in eggs or flesh. Egg farmers, those who keep poultry for the eggs, have no mean calling; but it is a mistaken idea that it is done without labor. For this reason, it is better to begin with good standard stock. The advantages and satisfaction are always greater. It is folly to obtain good stock and afterwards treat it with neglect, and then, because it did not come up to expectations, berate the breed.

If eggs are obtained from first-class, highly-fed and cared-for stock, reason teaches us that the chicks, in order to arrive at the perfection of their parents, must have similar care. The eggs have been produced under certain circumstances, and the chicks must have similar treatment. This is why breeders ask and get full prices under all circumstance. It is just; it keeps the stock out of the hands of all except those prepared to give the best care, thus securing the good reputation of the breed. Finely bred chicks, while hardy, are like hothouse plants, and will not bear neglect. Uniformity is not always obtainable in the broods that are reared. There are exceptions to every rule. For stocking up purposes the finest should always be selected, and only those bred from. Thus the vigor and thrift of the flocks is kept up, as well as the markings of the breed. Breed is an excellent thing, and care and feed are also good. All united bring about grand results. Where only a few fowls are kept for breeders, and the whole attention is given to those few, the chicks are much finer. Fowls that are producing hatching eggs, however, should not be forced, as in that case the eggs are produced too rapidly, and are not sufficiently fertilized. Breeds differ greatly as to the number of hens allowed to a cock. It also makes a difference whether the fowls are at large or in confinement. Fowls should have a long run when laying the hatching eggs.—*Country Gentleman.*

A new paper from the Pacific Coast makes its appearance here, the San Francisco BREEDER AND SPORTSMAN, the first number of which was issued July 1st. It is well got up and printed, and although taking general notice of sporting matters, is devoted largely to breeding and trotting interests. The Toronto correspondent of the SPREEDER is Mr. James Lang, who is well qualified to attend to its interests.—*Toronto Mail.*

## MARKET REPORT.

FLOUR—Prices keep steady. The export inquiry is fairly active. We quote Best City Extra, $5 50@5 62½; Superfine, $4 50@4 75; Interior Extra, $4 75@5 25; Interiot Superfine, $3 75@4 per bbl.

WHEAT—But little change has taken place in the market this week. As the season advances operators think that wheat will command better prices. No. 1 White September sellsat $1 69. Millers pay $1 70@1 71¼ for suitable parcels.

BARLEY—Transactions in Brewing and Chevalier are almost nominal, so far as public business is concerned. Feed is anything but active. Nobody is forcing spot parcels, fortunately for sellers, as the demand appears to be limited. At the Produce Exchange the recorded sales included 50 tons No. 1 September, $1 24½; 200 do No. 2 August, $1 21½; 150 do, $1 22 per ctl.

OATS—Market moderately active, while supplies are slowly increasing. Trading is confined wholly to legitimate business, there being no speculative feeling of consequence. Sales are negotiated within a range of $1 60 @1 70 per ctl.

CORN—Market shows but little activity, quotable at $1 65@1 70 per ctl.

FEED—Ground Barley, new, is quoted at $30, and small parcels mixed at $33@35 per ton. Middlings, $28 per ton at mill. Shorts selling at $17@18 per ton.

OILCAKE MEAL—The oil works sell to the trade at $22 50 per ton, less usual discount.

CORNMEAL—$36 per ton.

HAY—We quote: Alfalfa, $11@13; Wheat, $14@15; Wild Oat, $12@13; Stable, $10@12 per ton.

STRAW—Quotable at 55@65c per bale.

BEANS—The prices are the same as last week, quoted as follows: Bayos, $2 50@$2 75; Butter, $3 50@$3 75 for small and $4 for large; Lima, $3 75@$4; Pea, $4@$4 25; Pink, $2 40@$2 45; Red, $2 40@$2 45; Small White, $4@$4 25; Large White, $3 25@$3 60 per ctl.

ONIONS—Quotable at 60@75c ℘ ctl for Silverskins and 30@40c ℘ sack for Red.

POTATOES—In good supply. Wharf rates are as follows: Early Rose, in sacks, 50@80c; boxes, 75c@$1; Garnet Chile, 80c@$1 ℘ ctl; Sweet, 2½@3c ℘ lb.

POULTRY—Prices are well sustained. We quote prices as follows: Live Turkeys, Gobblers, 18@20c; do Hens, 16@18c; Roosters, $5.50@$6.50 for old and $6@$8 for young; Hens, $6.50@$8; Broilers, $3.50@$5 50, according to size; Ducks, $4@$6 ℘ dozen; Geese, $1@$1.25 ℘ pair; Goslings, $1.75@$2.25 ℘ pair.

GAME—We quote: Hare, $1.75@$2.25; Rabbits, $1@1.50 ℘ dozen; Doves, 50@75c ℘ dozen; Venison, 8@12c ℘ lb.

PROVISIONS—In good general request. Eastern Hams, 17½@18½c; California Hams, 16@16½c for plain, 16½@17c for sugar-cured canvased; Eastern Breakfast Bacon, 17@18c; California Smoked Bacon, 16½@16¾c for heavy and medium, and 17½@18c for light and extra light; Clear Sides, 16½@16¾c; Pork, $21.50@$22 for Extra Prime, $24@$25 for Prime Mess, $25@$25.50 for Mess, $27 for Clear and $23@$28.50 for Extra Clear; Pigs' Feet, $16@$18 ℘ bbl; Mess Beef, $14 for bbls and $7 for half bbls; Extra Mess Beef, $14.50@$15; Family Beef, $16@$16.50 ℘ bbl; California Smoked Beef, 14½@15c per lb.

HONEY—Very quiet. Comb, 14c to 17c; extracted, 7@8c per lb.

BUTTER—Market steady. Choice grades are in good demand at full figures. We quote prices as follows: Fancy, 35@37½c; choice, 32½@34c; fair to good, 25@30c; inferior lots from country stores, 23@25c; firkin, 29@31c for good to choice new, and 25@27½c for ordinary; pickled roll 30c to 32½c; Western, 18@25c per lb.

CHEESE—Fair business. We quote prices: California, 12½@13½c for choice; 10@12c for fair to good: do, factory, in boxes, 15@16c; Eastern, 16@17c; Western, 11@14c per lb.

EGGS—A steadier tone prevails of late. We quote jobbing lots as follows: California, choice, 28@32c; Interior, 24@26c; Western, 22½@27½c per dozen.

HIDES AND SKINS—No lack of supplies. Dealers are paying the following cash rates for lots in order: Dry Hides, usual selection, 19@19½c; culls one-third less, and Mexican Hides 1c per lb less; Dry Kip, 19@19½c; Dry Calf, 20c; Salted Steers, over 55 lbs, 11c ℘ lb; Steers and Cows, medium, 10c; light do, 9½c; Salted Kip, 15 to 30 lbs, 10@10½c; Salted Calf, 11@12½c; Dairy Calf, 65c to 70c each; Sheep Skins, 20@25c for Shearlings, 25c to 50c for short, 60@80c for medium, and 75c@$1 apiece for long wool and wool skins. Butchertown Green Skins bring higher prices.

TALLOW—Quotable at 8@8½c per lb for rendered and 10½@11c for refined, both in shipping order.

WOOL—Business very light. We quote nominally as follows: Humboldt and Mendocino, per lb, 26@27c; Sonoma, 25@26c; Siskiyou and Modoc, 22@25c; Calaveras and Foothills, 20@23c; San Joaquin, free, 18@19c; San Joaquin, defective, 16@17c; Southern Coast, burry and seedy, 15@17c; Eastern Oregon, choice, 23@24c; Eastern Oregon, fair, 20@23c; Eastern Oregon, poor, no sale; Valley Oregon, fine, 25@27c; Valley Oregon, coarse, 23@24c.

FRUIT—The market is profusely furnished. Grapes are making a liberal display. We quote lots: Apples, 25@50c ℘ bskt, and 50c@$1 ℘ box; Pears, 25@40c ℘ bskt, and 40c to 60c ℘ box; Bartlett do, 40@50c ℘ bskt, and 75c@$1 ℘ box; Nectarines, 75c@$1 ℘ box; Strawberries, $10@$12; Raspberries, $8@$11 ℘ chest; Peaches, 25@50c ℘ box and 25@30c ℘ bskt for common and 35@60c for Crawford; Figs, 50c@$1 00 ℘ box; Grapes, 50@75c for common, 60@85c for Black Hamburg, 50c@$1 25 for Rose of Peru, and 75c@$1 50 ℘ box for Muscat; Plums, 35@50c ℘ box; Blackberries, $1@$5 ℘ chest; Apricots, 1½@2c ℘ lb; Watermelons, $4@7 ℘ hundred; Cantaloupes, 60c@$1 00 ℘ crate; Lemons, $9@$10 ℘ box for Sicily, and $2@$2 50 for California; Limes, $7 50@$8 ℘ box, for Mexican; Bananas, $2.50@$4 ℘ bunch; Pineapples, $6@$8 ℘ dozen; Tahiti Oranges, $45@$50 ℘ thousand.

VEGETABLES—Pumpkins sold to-day at $20 ℘ ton. No particular change in other descriptions. We quote prices: Marrowfat Squash, $7@$10 ℘ ton; Artichokes, 10c ℘ dozen; Parsnips, 75c; Beets, 75c; Carrots, 50c@65c; Turnips, 75c@$1 ℘ ctl; Cauliflower, 60@65c ℘ dozen; Cabbage, 50@75c ℘ ctl; Garlic, 1@1½c ℘ lb; Cucumbers, 15@30c ℘ box; Green Peas, 2@3c ℘ lb; Green Peppers, 50@75c ℘ box; Tomatoes, 25@40c ℘ box; Spinach, 25c ℘ sack; Celery, 75c ℘ dozen; Summer Squash, 30c to 50c ℘ box; String Beans, 1½c@2c ℘ lb; Green Corn, 5@15c ℘ dozen; Okra, 50@75c ℘ lb; Egg Plant, 50c@$1 ℘ box.

MEAT MARKET—Following are rates for whole carcases from slaughterers to dealers:

BEEF—Prime, 7½@8c; medium grades, 6c to 6½c; inferior, 5@5½c per lb.

VEAL—Large Calves, 6½@7c; small ones, 8@10c per lb.

MUTTON—Wethers are quotable at 4½@5c, and Ewes at 4@4½c per lb, according to quality.

LAMB—Quotable at 6@7c per lb.

PORK—Live hogs, 5@5½c for hard, and 6¾c to 6½c for soft; dressed do, 11@11½c per lb for hard grain hogs.

# REVISED SPEED PROGRAMME FOR 1882.

FOURTH ANNUAL MEETING OF THE

SONOMA COUNTY

## Agricultural Park Association,

AT SANTA ROSA.

Commencing Tuesday, August 22d, and ending Saturday, August 26th.

### FIRST DAY—Tuesday, Aug. 22, 1882.

No. 1—TROTTING RACE.—Free for all two-year-olds owned in the District. Mile heats, 2 best in 3; purse, $200. First horse, $120; second, $60; third, $20. Closed on the first day of May with the following entries:

E. B. Conway names ch. c. Ideal, by Abbotsford. early.

J. E. Foster names s. m. Clara Patterson, by Grey McClellan.

G. C. Fountain names blk. f. May Day, by Eugene Cas-

P. J. Shafter names g. h. Greyson, by brother to Rustic.

Steve Crandall names b. f. No Name, sire unknown.

No. 2—TROTTING RACE.—Free for all horses that never beat 2:35; purse, $400. First horse, $240; second, $120; third, $40. Closed August 1st with the following entries:

Steve Crandell names Mat Doyle's b. g. Boss, by Gladiator, dam unknown.

S. Sperry names Toboas Bros.' g. g. Ralph.

James Garland names g. g. Rowdy Boy, by Rustic, dam by Belmont.

Wm. Bourke names b. g. Johnny, by Auctioneer Johnny, dam unknown.

### SECOND DAY—Wednesday, Aug. 23.

No. 3—TROTTING RACE—2:50 Class—for horses to be named by the Executive Committee, and owned in the District; mile heats, best 3 in 5. Purse, $400; first horse, $240; second, $120; third, $40. Entries to close August 19th.

No. 4—PACING RACE—Between Johnny Weagle and Washington.

### THIRD DAY—Thursday, Aug. 24.

No. 5—TROTTING RACE.—Free for all three-year-olds owned in the District; purse, $300. First horse, $180; second, $90; third, $30. Closed May 1st, with the following entries:

C. Stingell names b. f. Debby Mott, by Grey McClellan.

W. J. Starr names blk. f. Starr, by Naubuck.

E. B. Conley names b. c. Magnet, by Brigadier.

J. E. Fosternames br. s. Buck Foster, by Gen'l Dana.

W. M. Wood names b. c. Ned, by Overland.

L. H. Boggs names b. c. Warwick, by Milton Medium.

No. 6—TROTTING RACE.—Free for all that never beat 2:25; purse, $500. First horse, $300; second, $150; third, $50. Entries closed August 1st with the following entries:

C. W. Welby names ch. g. Starr King, by George M. Patchen, Jr., dam May Wonder.

L. H. Titus names br. m. Echora, by Echo, dam the Young Mare.

L. J. Rose names blk. s. Del Sur, by The Moor, dam Gretchen, by Mambrino Pilot.

John Hughes names b. g. Cairo, by Chieftain, dam unknown.

J. A. Goldsmith names blk. s. Director, by Dictator, dam by Mambrino Chief.

G. Valensin names s. s. Crown Point, by Speculator.

### FOURTH DAY—Friday, Aug. 25.

No. 7—TROTTING RACE.—Free to all horses that never beat 2:40; purse, $500. First horse, $300; second, $150; third, $50. Closed August 1st, 1882, with the following entries:

Steve Crandell names B. F. Miller's b. s. Marin, by Geo. M. Patchen, Jr., dam by Hambletonian.

L. H. Titus names b. s. Exile, by Echo, dam Bell Mason, by Belmont.

Pat Farrell names b. h. Vanderlynn, by Geo. M. Patchen, dam a Joseph mare.

G. Bernard names g. g. Allan Roy. Pedigree unknown.

A. B. Cooper names s. g. Frank Moscoe, by Frank Moscoe, dam unknown.

M. Rollins names J. McCord's b. g. Freestone, by Captain Webster, dam Owen Dale mare.

Chas. H. Shear names A. S. Bechtol's blk. g. Slim Jim, by the Tyler horse, dam unknown.

No. 8—To be filled by the Association.

### FIFTH DAY—Saturday, Aug. 26.

No. 9—TROTTING RACE.—Free for all horses that never beat 2:30; purse, $500. First horse, $300; second, $150; third, $50. Closed August 1st, 1882, with the following entries:

W. D. Hammond names g. s. Poscora Hayward, by Billy Hayward, dam Lady Poscora.

Steve Crandell names Wm. Bihler's b. m. Blanche, by Gray McClellan, dam by John Nelson.

S. Sperry names J. & W. S. Fritche's ch. m. Nellie R., by Gen McClellan, Jr., dam Susie Rose.

J. Goldsmith names br. s. Inca, by Woodford's Mambrino, dam by Mambrino Pilot.

A. Waldstein names b. s. Albert W., by Electioneer, dam by John Nelson.

H. McConn names g. g. Blackmore.

No. 10—TROTTING RACE—2:21 Class, reopened. Purse, $500; not less than four to enter. To close August 19, 1882.

### CONDITIONS.

1. In all races five to enter and three to start. Any horse distanced or not starting will forfeit his entrance fee. No money will be paid for a walk over.
2. Rules of the Pacific Blood Horse Association to govern running races, and of the National Trotting Association to govern trotting.
3. No horse entered in a purse can be withdrawn except by consent of the Judges.
4. All trotting and pacing races, except No. 1, will be mile heats, 3 best in 5.

J. P. CLARK, President.

CHARLES HOFFER, Secretary.

# SONOMA & MARIN

*DISTRICT*

## AGRICULTURAL ASSOCIATION

# RACES!

### TUESDAY, AUGUST 29TH.

No. 1—RUNNING RACE.—Purse $500; free for all, five to enter, three to start. Entries extended to August 23d, 1882.

No. 2—TROTTING RACE.—2:50 class; purse $400, with the following entries:

E. B. Conley enters b m Placeda.
S. S. Drake enters s f Huntress.
C. F. D. Hastings enters s h Como.
H. G. Carrillo enters b m Lady Zane.
M. O'Reily enters br m Emma Taylor.
S. Sperry enters s g St. Patrick.
W. G. Atkins enters b h No Name.
S. P. Taylor enters b g Little Jim.
J. B. Chase enters Mohawk Chief.

### WEDNESDAY, AUGUST 30TH, 1882.

No. 3.—TROTTING—2:25 Class. Purse, $700, with following entries:

J. Hughes enters b h Cairo.
G. Valensin enters ch s Crown Point.
Chas. W. Welby enters ch g Starr King.
J. Goldsmith enters b m Sweetness.

No. 4.—TROTTING—Three-year-olds; purse $350, with following entries:

W. M. Wood enters b g Ned, by Overland, dam unknown.

E. B. Conley enters Whitney's b c Magnet, by Brigadier, dam Gazelle.

S. Crandell enters Stingle's b f Deby Mott, by Gray McClellan, dam by John Nelson.

J. E. Foster enters Bihler's b c Buck Foster by Gen. Dana, dam by John Nelson.

W. J. Starr enters blk f Lady Starr, by Naubuck, dam unknown.

S. S. Drake enters br f Sister, by Admiral, dam Black Flora.

### THURSDAY, AUGUST 31ST.

No. 5.—RUNNING—Purse, $300; free for all; half-mile heats, 3 in 5; 5 to enter, 3 to start. Entries extended to August 23.

No. 6.—TROTTING—2:40 class. Purse, $500, with following entries:

Jas. Garland enters g g Rowdy Boy.
Pat. Farrell enters b h Vandarlyan.
B. T. Miller enters b s Marin.
Wm. Bourke enters b h Johnny.
A. B. Cooper enters ch g Frank Mosco.
J. Mackey enters b s Exile.

No. 7.—TROTTING—Yearling's Purse, $150, with following entries:

I. C. Reardon enters b c Blue Gown, by Gus, dam by Geo M. Patchen.

E. B. Conley enters Whitney's ch c Dawn, by Nutwood, dam Countess.

Wm. Bourke enters g c Dublin, by Admiral, dam by Bell Alta.

John Pfau enters b c Young Eureka, by Eureka, dam Fairbank's mare.

P. J. Shafter enters g c Viking, by Rustic, dam by Lawyer's Stockbridge Chief.

J. E. Foster enters Bihler's b c No Name, by Gen Dana, dam by John Nelson.

F. Needham enters b c Conemara, by Volunteer, dam by Speculation.

### FRIDAY, SEPTEMBER 1ST.

No. 8—TROTTING RACE.—Consolation Purse; purse $250.

E. B. Conley enters b m Placeda.
S. S. Drake enters s f Huntress.
C. F. D. Hastings enters s h Como.
H. G. Carrillo enters b m Lady Zane.
M. O'Reily enters br m Emma Taylor.
S. Sperry enters s g St. Patrick.
W. G. Atkins enters b h No Name.
S. P. Taylor enters b g Little Jim.
J. B. Chase enters — Mohawk Chief.

No. 9—TROTTING RACE.—Two-year-olds: purse $300 with following entries:

G. C. Fountain enters blk f May-Day, by Eugene Casserly, dam by Toronto Chief.

E. B. Conley enters Whitney's ch c Ideal, by Abbotsford, dam Countess.

John Pfau enters dk b g Mike, by Eureka, dam Hippedback Mare.

P. J. Shafter enters Grayson, by Norman Rustic, dam Olema, by Whipple's Hambletonian.

S. S. Drake enters b c Standard, by Admiral, dam unknown.

J. E. Foster enters s f Clara Patterson, by Gray McClellan, dam by Gen. Dana.

### SATURDAY, SEPTEMBER 2D.

No. 10—PACING RACE.—Purse $500, with following entries:

G. Valensin enters br m Ouida.
E. P. Dennison enters ch m Lady Hayes.
S. Sperry enters blk s Washington.

No. 11—TROTTING RACE.—2:30 clas; purse $500, with the following entries:

A. Waldstein enters b s Albert W.
W. D. Hammond enters g s Poscora Hayward.
J. A. Golsmith enters br s Inca.
Henry McCoun enters — Blackmore.

W. E. COX, Secretary.



The BREEDER AND SPORTSMAN is printed with Shattuck and Fletcher's Ink.

## The Victorian Trotting Club,

### MELBOURNE, AUSTRALIA.

......OFFERS......

The undermentioned Prize, to be competed for on a day to be named early in January next, 1883.

### PRIZE OF 2,500 DOLLARS,

With Entrance Fees and Sweepstakes of $50 each from Starters added.

---

# SECOND
## ANNUAL EXHIBITION
### OF THE
# SAN MATEO AND SANTA CLARA COUNTY
## AGRICULTURAL ASSOCIATION
### NO. 5,
### TO BE HELD AT
# SAN JOSE, CAL.,
......FROM......
### Sept. 25th to 30th, '82, inclusive

### SPEED PROGRAMME.

FIRST DAY—Monday, Sept. 25th, 1882.

---

# THIRD FAIR
### OF THE
# Ninth District Agricultural Ass'n
### TO BE HELD ON
## September 19, 20, 21 and 22, '82
### AT
# Rohnerville, Humboldt Co., Cal,

### SPEED PROGRAMME.

FIRST DAY.

---

## SPEED PROGRAMME
### OF THE
# Mount Shasta Agricultural Association,
### TO BE HELD IN
# YREKA, SISKIYOU CO.,
—ON—
Wednesday, — October 4th, 1882.

---

# $12,500
# In Purses and Stakes.

## CALIFORNIA
# STATE FAIR
## SPEED PROGRAMME
### FOR 1882.

### FIRST DAY—Monday, Sept. 11.

SECOND DAY—Tuesday, Sept. 12.

THIRD DAY—Wednesday, Sept. 13.

FOURTH DAY—Thursday, Sept. 14.

FIFTH DAY—Friday, Sept. 15.

SIXTH DAY—Saturday, Sept. 16.

REMARKS and CONDITIONS.

# Golden Gate Fair.

## SPEED PROGRAMME FOR 1882

## $10,000

IN

## Stakes and Prizes

FIRST DAY—Monday, Sept. 4, 1882.

SECOND DAY—Tuesday, Sept. 5.

THIRD DAY—Wednesday, Sept. 6.

FOURTH DAY—Thursday, Sept. 7.

FIFTH DAY—Friday, Sept. 8.

SIXTH DAY—Saturday, Sept. 9.

## CONDITIONS.

L. WALKER,     A. C. DIETZ,
Secretary.     President.

## GOLDEN GATE FAIR.

### BICYCLE RACE!

ON SATURDAY, SEPTEMBER 9TH.

FREE FOR ALL.

ENTRANCE FREE!

Nominations to be made on
Monday, September 4, 1882,

L. WALKER, Secretary.

# BREEDER AND SPORTSMAN

Vol. I. No. 9.
No. 508 MONTGOMERY STREET }

### SAN FRANCISCO, SATURDAY, AUGUST 26, 1882.

{ SUBSCRIPTION
FIVE DOLLARS A YEAR.

## NOTABLE HORSES OF CALIFORNIA.

## ELMO.

We have waited, not too patiently, perhaps, for Overman to verify the predictions we so confidently published from the time he was first broken. The belief was never shaken, however, and from the time he trotted his first race until the present day, the favorable impression never grew faint. Elmo was already notable, and his capacity, breeding and form were sufficient to award him a place in our gallery. But from the time the entries in the Grand Circuit were announced, we felt positively certain that before the end came, he would "show a trotter" of his get which would entitle him to a more prominent place. Overman is in reality the only colt which had any chance granted him to make a trotter, and he has been unfortunate ever since he was a three-year-old. Mr. Seale has bred many which gave just as good promise as Overman did at the same age, but owing to other pressing business and the difficulty of obtaining men whom he could entrust with the entire management,

the education was neglected. Again, when a colt showed speed it would be sold for road uses, and thus Overman is the only Elmo colt that we know of being worked on a track, excepting one or two youngsters at Mr. Seale's place. The size, style and fine appearance, which is nearly a universal characteristic of the stock, give a value for the road and carriage which ensures a ready sale. This, manifestly, interferes with the proper development of track speed; and then Mr. Seale holds that road horses should not be subjected to track usages when their destiny is so different. There is a great deal of sound logic in the arguments he advances to support this view of the question. There is the danger of causing them to "pull," and other bad habits arising from the main desire of the trainer being to increase the speed irrespective of consequences. The curves of the track necessitate boots; their heads at times are thrown into an unnatural position, and the smooth surface tends to

careless habits which are found inimical. His plan is to take the colts on the road, and in lieu of every effort to increase the speed, let the teachings be to make them pleasant drivers, square-gaited, of proper style, and above all, of good behavior. As has been previously stated the Elmos are natural roadsters. The gait is a pure, square trot, generally long striders and moving with little "friction." Elmo himself was nearly perfect in his action, and at one time so fast that a former owner, Mr. Van Giessen, informed us that he had timed him quarters in thirty seconds. He belongs to a trotting family. His sire, Mohawk, was by Long Island Black Hawk, one of the famous old-time trotters, and he was by Andrew Jackson, the founder of the great tribe of the Clays. Andrew Jackson was by Young Bashaw, a son of the imported Barb Grand Bashaw, and the dam of Young Bashaw was a very highly bred mare, Pearl, by First Consul (Bond's), grandam Fancy, by imported Messen ger, and his third dam by imported Rockingham. From this horse come the Bashaws, so that two of the prominent trotting families spring from the union of Barb and thoroughbred. The dam of Elmo was by Sir Richard, a son of the thoroughbred of that name. The sire of Elmo has proved his capacity as the progenitor of trotters, as Clark's Mohawk, Jr., had a record of 2:25, made in Cleveland, Ohio, ten years ago; Hall's Mohawk, Jr., record of 2:26, and Elmo, 2:27. Fast trotting was not the only valuable characteristic, as both of the Mohawk, Jrs., were large, fine-looking horses, of about the same size as Elmo, and with the same kind of action. Clark's Mohawk was thought to be the most promising stallion of the day. He was only six years old when he trotted in 2:25, and died when ten years old. The Mohawks—as is shown by the duplication of names—are very popular in Ohio, their size and symmetry giving them value outside of the possession of trotting speed. Elmo's trotting in California was limited to three matches. One against Ajax for $5,000; one against Jerome for $2,000, and one with May Howard for $2,000. All of these he won with the greatest ease, as he never lost a heat in the series. That with Ajax was heats of a mile, best 3 in 5, and he won in 2:30½, 2:31½, 2:31½. With Jerome the distance was heats of two miles, the time, 4:58¼, 4:59, and the match against May Howard was won in 2:27, 2:27, 2:29. In the race with Jerome he showed his old-time flight of speed, making a half mile in one of the heats in 1:08. Elmo is one of the most commanding horses in appearance which we ever saw. The engraving gives a capital idea of his form, and the likeness is as nearly perfect as can be conceived. It is not only a faithful transcript of his configuration, but the artist has caught the spirit of the scene and transferred the horse exactly as he stood on the bright morning we accompanied Mr. Wyttenbach to the Rancho San Francisquita. The color cannot be represented in an engraving, and the size requires words to express, but in every other respect the picture is a model of the horse. Elmo is sixteen and a quarter hands in height, and is a "long horse" as well as a high one. He is as sound as it is possible for a horse to be, not a swelling on any joint, not a tendon puffed or a blemish as large as a pea on any part. His color is a deep chestnut, nearly the shade that bronze assumes when long exposed to the atmosphere. It is one of the very handsomest shades of chestnut, and the light mane and tail, the white stripe in the face, the white markings on the near legs, and the brilliant light hazel eyes, are in fine contrast to the darker hue. The coat is as smooth and glossy as that of a thoroughbred, and the hairs in the mane and tail are soft and fine. Altogether he is a horse which will attract attention in any circumstance. A pair of the same appearance would command a large price for the carriage—a team of the same proportion bring the "top of the market" for general purposes. As a further proof of the high estimate we have always placed on Elmo, the following account, written in March, 1877, is given:

A deep bronze chestnut, with silver mane and tail, and of such size and symmetry of proportion, that a person is forced to exclaim, "A grand horse, truly." His color is rare, and when relieved by the light colored mane and tail, handsome in the extreme. He is remarkably well formed for so large a horse, and moves with the agility and sprightliness of an Arab. He was running in a loose box, of ample size, but in addition to this he had the freedom of a paddock adjoining, where he could inhale the perfume of the lilac, and hear the merry songs of the linnets and thrushes in the trees which shaded it. Although considerably over sixteen hands in height, there is nothing clumsy in his appearance, and he strikes out with a bold, free gait, although the limits of his paddock are somewhat circumscribed. Having a large share of the best blood, it would be singular if his looks did not comport with his pedigree. The change we noted since we first sam him was in the increased size of his body, being very much deeper through the chest, and longer from the point of the hip to the quarters.

He was only a colt when brought from Ohio to Chicago, and was somewhat leggy and light in the carcass then. A very handsome, striking looking colt withal, but as his owner did not claim much speed for him, he failed to find a purchaser in the "city on the lake," and took him to Wisconsin. He was owned there by a gentleman, Mr. Van Giesen, who still tells marvelous stories of the great speed he displayed in his exercise, and the writer has at several times awakened his ire by looking incredulous when he told of his beating a fair race mare through the stretch, she running and he trotting. That he exhibited wonderful speed is beyond question, and Messrs. Bently, Taylor and Hickok purchased him and "carried" him East. His overgrown, and at the same time rather large, frame was inimical to his showing his full capacity in races. Yet his performances were very creditable; we saw him in a race at Buffalo shut up a wonderful gap, contesting with very fast horses, and had the stretch been a little longer he would have won. He was brought to California with Goldsmith Maid and Lucy, and his races here with Ajax and Jerome stamped him as an animal of great merit. He belongs to a family which is greatly distinguished in equine history, on the sire's side tracing his genealogy to the imported Barb, from which has descended the family of Clays, the Long Island Black Hawks, the Jacksons, etc.

## OVERMAN'S GREAT PERFORMANCE.

As a fitting accompaniment to the full description of Elmo, we give the following account of the trot won recently at Buffalo by Overman, a worthy son of so great a sire, and merely add that he since has won in the 2:29 class at Rochester and Poughkeepsie. The description of the race was taken from the letter of the special commissioner of the New York *Spirit of the Times*.

"In the purse of $1,500 for the 2:29 class, there were Overman, Abe Downing, St. Cloud, Rolla, Little Billy, Kate Taylor, London Rigolette, Yellow Dock and Big Ike. The pools sold steady at $25 for London, $13 for Overman or Yellow Dock, and $25 for the field.

First Heat.—Vexatious scoring was indulged in, and at last the word was given, with Big Ike and Rolla "left at the post." St. Cloud trotted fast from an outside position, and took the pole around the turn, leading Abe Downing a length to the quarter, in 34¾ seconds, with Rigolette third, and the others bunched. St. Cloud, by aid of a few handy skips, managed to keep the lead to the half, in 1:10, with Downing at his throat-latch, Overman third, and Kate Taylor fourth. Shortly afterward Downing passed St. Cloud, and drew away from him to the three-quarter pole. Overman came very fast on third quarter, ranged alongside of Downing, and they had a close race down the home-stretch, Downing finally landing a neck in front, with St. Cloud two lengths behind and Kate Taylor on his wheel, the others as per summary. Big Ike and Rolla had a close race with the flag; time, 2:20¾.

Second Heat.—The result of the previous heat made Overman or Downing the choice. Pools, $45 for the field and $25 for Overman or Downing. There was considerable delay in scoring, and when the word was given, Downing and Overman were being steadied back, while the outside horses were under way; per consequence, Overman lost his place, and Downing had to make an extra brush to save himself from being cut off. Rolla had the best of the send-off, and lapped Downing at the quarter in 34½ seconds. He outfooted the latter to the half in 1:10½, but from this point Downing took the lead, St. Cloud spurted into second place, and Overman, having picked his way through the ruck at the quarter pole, trotted very fast along the back-stretch. Closing with the leaders around the upper turn, he passed both St. Cloud and Rolla, and got within a length of Downing at the three-quarter pole. The pace here was very hot, and they began to draw away from the others. Overman slowly but surely drew up on Downing, and the brush down the home-stretch was so well contested that ready bets were exchanged on every hand. "I'll bet $10 Overman wins it;" "I'll take you," was frequently heard, while the spectators cheered their favorites. They were even within a few yards of the wire, but Downing broke at the critical moment and caught quickly, but Overman beat him by half a length, in 2:20½. The others finished in the order named in summary, but were not close to the leaders. Johnson and Hickok both complained of the send-off, the former charging the loss of the heat to it, and Hickok asserting he could have won it easier had he not been interfered with as soon as the word was given.

Third Heat.—Overman's chances were now considered twice as good as the field's, and pools sold on him $50 to $25. Scoring was long and tedious, and, notwithstanding the drivers of Big Ike and Rolla were fined $10 each, Brown continued to show in front with St. Cloud, and when the word was given he had a length the best of it, passing immediately in front of Overman and Downing, and taking the pole on first turn, and opening a gap of two lengths to the quarter-pole, in 35½ seconds, with Overman second, and Rolla, Downing, and Kate Taylor all together, the balance of the field out of the contest. Overman, having now found clear sailing, quickly overhauled St. Cloud to the half in 1:12, but he managed to keep the pole by the aid of an occasional "dip and dive," but, as they approached the three-quarter pole, Overman crowded all sail, and carried him to a break; he settled, but could not catch Overman, who passed under the wire with plenty to spare. St. Cloud was set back to third place for running, and Rolla, who had finished on his wheel, was given second position. The others did not cut any figure in the heat, and were placed as per summary; time, 2:23½.

Fourth Heat.—A few scratch players at this stage of the race wagered $10 against $50 that Overman would not win, but pool-selling was virtually at an end. After a few vain attempts they turned close together, and Rigolette's sulky collided with that of Rolla's, throwing out Barney Stanford, his driver, who gamely held on to the reins until succor came. No serious damage or injury was done, and the horses scored up again, with McCarthy behind Yellow Dock. A good send-off was obtained, and St. Cloud had a trifle the best of it, but did not interfere with Overman on the first turn, and the latter kept the pole throughout the heat, going to the quarter in 35½ seconds, with St. Cloud second, on his wheel. Yellow Dock, for the first time in the race, appeared to dispute the lead. She drew up on the inside of Overman, but broke badly near the half, and that settled her chances. The leaders continued to draw away from the party, going to the half in 1:13. Overman left St. Cloud on third quarter, and, coming along with a big, raking stride, finished very strong in 2:24½. St. Cloud was second, under a vigorous application of the whip, and Little Billy a length behind him. The others never looked dangerous.

Buffalo, August 2, 1882.—Purse, $1,500; 2:29 class.

| | | | | |
|---|---|---|---|---|
| O. A. Hickok's ch. g. Overman, by Elmo | 2 | 1 | 1 | 1 |
| P. V. Johnson's b. s. Abe Downing, by Joe Downing | 1 | 2 | 5 | 9 |
| H. W. Brown's b. g. St. Cloud | 3 | 4 | 3 | 2 |
| J. P. Schatz's ch. g. Rolla | 9 | 5 | 2 | 8 |
| I. Hidgins' b. g. Little Billy | 7 | 3 | 4 | 3 |
| H. G. Conover's b. m. Kate Taylor | 4 | 9 | 6 | 5 |
| A. Bashford's ch. g. London | 6 | 8 | 10 | 4 |
| R. G. Pate's b. m. Rigolette | 5 | 7 | 7 | 7 |
| Mr. Morse's ch. m. Yellow Dock | 8 | 6 | 8 | 6 |
| Roop & Sewbourne's b. g. Big Ike | 10 | 10 | 9 | 10 |

Time—2:20¾, 2:20½, 2:23½, 2:24½.

Overman fulfilled my last week's estimate of him sooner than I expected. He is a high-strung fellow in a large field of horses, and Orrin Hickok drove him to-day with rare skill. He felt elated that the horse is recovering his form again, as he was severely attacked by the pink-eye in the Western Circuit, and was not fit to stay up and win, but I can see he is as game as his sire, Elmo, who beat the best long-distance horses of California, and received forfeit from others. Ten years ago Orrin trotted Elmo over the Buffalo Park, and now returns with a son of his own breeding to keep the sire's name green. Overman is seven years old, a light chestnut, with strip in face, stands 16¼ hands high, a long, easy-gaited horse, with a true, even stride, noble carriage, and no waste of action; with the day and track to suit him, I think he can trot in 2:17 or 2:18. His dam was by Billy McCracken, son of Hill's Black Hawk. Billy was at one time owned in Buffalo, and was a noted horse in his day. Overman is owned by Capt. Wm. Cole, of San Francisco, who is at present residing in Philadelphia."

## HORSES IN TRAINING ON THE STOCKTON TRACK.

Editor Breeder and Sportsman: There is quite an array of runners and trotters at work here; some of them have established reputations, some have yet to make their mark. There are seven stables. The trotters are in the hands of Fred Vail, John Williams, W. H. Parker and J. Donahue. The runners are under the management of Joe Stimpson, Sam See and J. Q. Anderson. Fred Vail has Johnny Weigle, owned by Walter Mead of San Francisco; Blacksmith Boy, bay gelding, nine years old, by Chieftain, from the McCracken mare, record 2:38, owned by F. S. Hatch of Stockton; Dick Kent, bright bay colt, three years old, by Electioneer from Gilletta, owned by Perkins Brothers of Stockton; Josh Whitcomb, bay colt, two years old, by Mambrino Wilkes, dam by Kentucky Hunter, also the property of Perkins Brothers; bay filly, two years old, by Peerless, dam by Chieftain; Peerless by General Knox. These three are very promising youngsters. A fine chestnut filly, three years old, by Priam, dam by Hill's Black Hawk, owned by Lewey Gerlach of Stockton; Felix, bay horse, by McClellan, owned by N. Randall; Black Diamond, black stallion, by Black Boy from a Hambletonian mare; Black Boy, by Black Hawk, owned by Charles McMurry; bay filly, one year old, by Abbotsford, dam by Winthrop, owned by S. M. Morse. This is a fine filly and very promising. Bay colt Gus, by Mambrino Wilkes from a Hambletonian mare, owned by Charles Yalland; two very fine sorrel fillies by Priam, owned by Mr. Silas T. Adams, and a fine bay mare, seven years old, by McClellan, dam by Jim Crow. John Williams has Tom Stout, who is too well known to need a description; a fine Nutwood colt from mare by Chieftain; bay gelding, six years old, by McClellan, dam by Chieftain; gray horse, six years old, by Speculation, dam by Gray Eagle; bay gelding, six years old, by McClellan, owned by Mr. H. Harris of Stockton; a handsome chestnut colt by Nutwood, dam by a son of David Hill's Black Hawk, owned by H. C. Smith, and a bay colt, two years old, John O'Brien, by Mambrino Wilkes, dam by Chieftain, owned by S. M. Morse. In Parker's stable there are some good ones. At the head of the list is Honesty, a finely proportioned chestnut horse, five years old, owned by Mr. J. H. Dodge. Honesty is by Priam; his dam by Chieftain. As a four-year-old he took second money in a race with Romero and Sweetheart, in 2:25¾, Romero taking first money. Ha-Ha, brown colt, two years old, by Nephew, dam by McCracken's Black Hawk, owned by Fred Arnold. This is a fine colt, with good action, with mane and tail nearly as long and heavy as Abbotsford's. Mr. Parker has another by Nephew, a handsome bay, owned by Mr. Hall, near Modesto, and two beautiful fillies, owned by L. U. Shippee; a bay by Echo, dam by Don Victor, the other a chestnut, one year old, a full sister to Honesty. A handsome roan horse, Upright, five years old, owned by Walter Morris, by Whipple's Hambletonian, out of Gilroy Belle, by Lodi. Upright has a record of 2:25 as a two-year-old and is working up nicely, and promises to make some of them step lively this Fall. Mr. Morris also has a fine gray filly, by Priam, two years old, from Gilroy Belle. The next stable of trotters is John Donahue's, his horses all being owned by Trahern & Dudley. The first one I saw was the black horse Revolution, five years old, by Prince of Orange, from Cricket, by Long Island Black Hawk. He has a record of 2:45½, and is entered in the 2:36 class. Nephew, a beautiful bay horse, eight years old, good size and fine action, with a record 2:36, and a brown filly, two years old, Baby Mine, by Nephew, dam by David Hill. This is all of the trotters. The runners are being worked by Joe Stimpson, Sam See and Anderson. Stimpson has the well-known runner George Bender, who has a record of 1:47; he is owned by Seth Peyton. Joe Daniels, Jr., owned by John Randall; Joe is by Joe Daniels, his dam by Nena Sahib; he is entered for races at Sacramento, here and at San José. Sam See has the black stallion, Frank W., two years old, by Monday, dam Babe, by Nena Sahib, owned by Thomas Williams. Reel Terry, bay colt, three years old, by California, from Laura Barnes, owned by Billy Ash; and Jack Douglass, chestnut horse, six years old, by Wildidle, dam Lady Clare, by Norfolk, owned by Jack Douglass. J. D. Anderson's stable, which has gone to Sacramento, consists of five good ones. The first is a handsome chestnut colt, two years old, by Joe Daniels, dam by Woodburn, owned by Judge Terry; chestnut stallion, six years old, by Norfolk, dam by Belmont, owned by William Butterick; dapple gray colt, three years old, by Joe Daniels, dam by Norfolk, owned by Jas. A. Sheppard of Lathrop (this colt, as a two-year-old, made a record of 1:48); Kate Carson, chestnut filly, three years old, by Joe Daniels, dam by Norfolk, owned by Wash Trahern (ran as a two-year-old three-fourths of a mile in 1:19); sorrel colt, two years old, by Joe Daniels, dam by Norfolk, owned by Mr. Trahern.

August 19th, 1882.—Since my letter descriptive of the stables at the Stockton race track, there has been added the stable of J. A. McCloud; May Boy, bay colt, two years old, by McCloud's Chieftain, dam by Henry Clay, owned by J. Heller; Hattie B., bay filly, three years old, by McCloud's Chieftain, dam by Odd Fellow, owned by Noyes Bailey; chestnut colt, one year old, by Hawthorne, from the dam of May Boy, owned by Noyes Bailey. Mr. McCloud has one of the best Nutwood colts I have seen—dark bay with black points, and small star in forehead, one year old, dam Daisy, by Chieftain. He also has a very handsome two-year-old, out of the same mare, by Nephew, named Judge Patterson. Also, Billy Robinson, brown gelding, eight years old, by Black Reuben, by Black Hawk.

After you received the description of horses in training at Sacramento there was an addition of W. M. Murray's stable: Bird Catcher, a full brother to Modoc, owned by Caleb Dorsey, also the owner of Sam Stevenson, four years old, by Thad. Stevens, dam by Rifleman; J. Stewart's Harry Hill, sorrel colt, three years old, by George M. Patchen, Jr., dam by Belmont; William M., bay colt, two years old, by Whipple's Hambletonian, dam by Black Hawk, owned by Murray; bay colt Osceola, by Monday, owned by Flemming & Tellick of

Fresno.

Mr. J. B. Haggin has suffered a great loss in the death of his promising two-year-old racer Nubia, by Leinster from Addie. She was frolicking in the lot last Friday at the Agricultural Park, at Sacramento, when she strained herself badly, and died soon after. She was well worth $1,200, and had several engagements in the coming fairs.

# TURF AND TRACK.

## FIXED EVENTS.

Sonoma and Marin Agricultural Societies. Annual Fair at Petaluma Aug. 29th and four following days.

Golden Gate Fair, to be held at Oakland, from September 4th to the 9th inclusive.

Butte District Fair at Chico, from September 5th to September 8th inclusive.

El Dorado District Fair at Placerville, from September 5th to September 8th inclusive.

California State Fair. Annual meeting at Sacramento, from Monday, September 11th to the 16th inclusive.

The San Joaquin Valley Association Fair at Stockton, from September 19th to the 23d inclusive.

Oregon State Fair at Salem, from September 18th and during the week.

The San Mateo and Santa Clara County Agricultural Association Fair at San Jose, September 25th to the 30th inclusive.

Humboldt and Mendocino District Fair at Rhonerville, September 19th to September 22d inclusive.

Modoc, Plumas and Lassen District Fair at Greenville, from October 2d to October 5th inclusive.

Monterey District Fair at Salinas City, from October 2d to October 6th inclusive.

Nevada State Fair, at Reno, from Monday, October 2d, to the 7th inclusive.

Mount Shasta Agricultural Association Fair at Yreka, October 4th, 5th, 6th and 7th.

Eastern Oregon Fine Stock Association at Union, from October 9th to the 14th inclusive.

Los Angeles Agricultural Association, at Los Angeles, from October 17th to 21st inclusive.

### FAIRS AT THE EAST.

Kentucky State Fair at Lexington, August 9th to September 2d inclusive.

Minnesota State Fair at Farmington, August 31st to September 8th inclusive.

Iowa State Fair at Fairfield, September 1st to the 8th inclusive.

Minnesota Agricultural Association, at Minneapolis, September 4th to the 9th inclusive.

Nebraska State Fair, at Omaha, September 11th until the 16th inclusive.

Rhode Island State Fair, at Providence, September 12th to the 15th inclusive.

Pennsylvania State Fair, at Pittsburg, September 7th to the 21st inclusive.

Wisconsin State Fair, at Fond du lac, September 11th to the 16th inclusive.

Ontario Provincial Fair, at Toronto, September 18th to the 23d inclusive.

Connecticut State Fair, at Meriden, September 18th to the 22d inclusive.

New Jersey State Fair, at Monroe, September 18th to the 22d inclusive.

West Virginia Central Fair, at Clarksburg, September 19th to the 21st inclusive.

Indiana State Fair, at Indianapolis, September 25th to the 30th inclusive.

Western Michigan Fair, at Grand Rapids, September 25th to the 30th inclusive.

Texas State Fair, at Austin, October 17th to the 21st inclusive.

## SANTA CRUZ RACES.

The attendance on Friday, the 18th inst., showed a large increase, and the races were generally well contested and afforded a great deal of amusement. The first on the card was a selling race, a purse of $200, in which Haddington had the call at $20 against Sister to Lottery and G. H. Trouble. This was an easy race for the favorite, who was not claimed at an advance over $800, the sum at which he was entered to be sold. The next race was a running stake, half mile and repeat, which Night Hawk, as first choice, placed to his owner's credit. There was a pretty struggle in the first heat between the winner and Mollie H., the latter being beaten only by a neck, but in the final heat the favorite won in a handsome manner. The third race was a trot for a purse of $20, in which Nutmeg, on account of his local reputation, was considered a certain winner, and he showed himself wothy of the confidence of his backers by winning in three straight heats.

SUMMARIES.

Santa Cruz, August 18th.—Running Race.—Selling purse, $200; $50 to second horse; five per cent to third horse. One mile and repeat. Horses entered to be sold for $1,000; to carry their entitled weight—2 lbs. off for each $100 under fixed valuation. Winner can be claimed by any one.

| | | |
|---|---|---|
| P. J. Shafter's b. h. Haddington, valued at $800, 110 lbs.... | 1 | 1 |
| H. Schwartz's b. f. Sister to Lottery, $1,000, 92 lbs......... | 2 | 2 |
| A. Irvin's gr. h. G. H. Trouble, $800, 91 lbs................ | 3 | 3 |

Time—1:50½, 1:50.

Same Day.—Running Stake.—Free for all; $25 each, $10 forfeit, with $75 added; a half mile and repeat; the second to save his entrance.

| | | |
|---|---|---|
| P. J. Shafter's b. m. Night Hawk, 111 lbs.. ............... | 1 | 1 |
| C. H. Watts' b. h. Bay Charley, 111 lbs.......... ... ..... | 3 | 2 |
| W. Boots' b. m. Mollie H., 111 lbs......................... | 2 | 3 |

Time—51s, 52s.

Same Day.—Trotting.—Purse of $20; entrance $10, with $10 added; best three in five; to harness.

| | | | |
|---|---|---|---|
| J. W. Scott names r. g. Nutmeg............................ | 1 | 1 | 1 |
| D. W. Grover names b. g. Pajaro Chief.................... | 4 | 2 | 2 |
| W. E. Peck names b. g. Leland Stanford................... | 2 | dis. | |
| J. M. Ferguson names b. g. Soquel Jim.................... | 3 | dis. | |

Time—2:50½, 2:53, 2:56.

On Saturday, there was a still better attendance, with two races on the card; the first, a trotting purse of $500, free for all, and the last, a novelty running race of one mile. In the former race Frank Moscow was the favorite, previous to the first heat, over Poscora Hayward and Blackmore, but the betting changed about after the first heat was decided. The second heat was very stubbornly contested, Moscow being all the time close up, and the time 2:28¾ shows that it was trotted very fast for this class of horses as, in the opinion of good judges, considering the heavy state of the track, it was equal to a 2:26 gait. In the final heat Chauncey Kane drove Blackmore, but he could do no more for him than his predecessor and as Mr. McCord sold him to Mr. E. Barron, of San Francisco, to drive double on the road, it is presumed his short career on the turf is at an end.

The second was a Novelty Race, a dash of a mile, with purse of $200, of which $50 to the first horse at each quarter of a mile, in which Haddington was a great favorite at $20 against $10 for Millie H. and $6 for the field, in which were Quien Sabe, Bay Charley and Stumbling Dick. The race was a very exciting one, as Quien Sabe, who is known as a very fleet half miler, went away with the lead and captured the $50 at each of the first three-quarters, but then she began to tire, and Haddington, under whip and spur, managed at last to overhaul him, and won the mile out by a short neck, but it was far too close a thing for those who had recklessly wagered at such extravagant odds on the success of the favorite. This brought the meeting to a conclusion. The visitors were much pleased at the sport offered to them, and the people of Santa Cruz were delighted to find that their first attempt at an annual race meeting had met with such appreciation.

SUMMARIES.

Santa Cruz, August 19th.—Trotting Race.—Purse of $500; free for all; best three in five; to harness.

| | | | |
|---|---|---|---|
| W. D. Hammond names g. h. Poscora Hayward......... | 1 | 1 | 1 |
| P. Williams names s. g. Frank Moscow.............. ... | 2 | 2 | 2 |
| Henry McCann enters g. g. Blackmoor ................ | 3 | 3 | 3 |

Time—2:30 2:28¾, 2:29½.

Same Day.—Novelty Race.—One mile dash; purse, $200; entrance, ten per cent; five to enter and three to start; $50 to first horse at each quarter mile.

| | |
|---|---|
| L. Shaner names b. s. Haddington.................. ......... | 1 |
| S. Duncan names b. g. Quien Sabe........................... | 2 |
| Wm. Boots names b. m. Mollie H............................. | 3 |
| O. H. Waters names b. g. Chestnut Charley..... ............ | 4 |
| Alfred Imus names b. g. Stumbling Dick...................... | 5 |

Time—1:48.

## MONMOUTH PARK RACES.

The second Summer season has been quite successful in the way of attendance, but the racing was not up to an average merit, the interest being mainly centered in handicaps, in which figured some of the old-time favorite performers. The fact is, that in the great two-year-old stakes at Monmouth Park the stable of P. Lorillard is not to be approached, and in those for three-year-olds, Forester holds the same position. It is now generally conceded that the three-year-olds are all of moderate quality in the East, with the exception of Runnymede (broken down) and the above mentioned Forester. It must therefore be looked upon as a pity that the Duchess of Norfolk could not be brought into condition to test the relative merits of the Eastern and California horses. Another chance was lost at the same meeting, as in the great Omnibus Stake, of which we give the following description from the New York *World*, there was a California-bred horse entered, being the three-year-old colt Judge McKinstry, owned by Judge Mee of this city. Judge McKinstry was a late colt, and his owner thought it better to delay his active training until the Summer, so that the project—once entertained for a short time—of sending him East with the Baldwin-Winters stable was abandoned, and now it is probable that he will make his first appearance on the turf in the Breeders' Stake and in the Derby during the State Fair. Following is the account of this race, so popular with owners and breeders:

While the Omnibus Stakes was no doubt a disappointment in not bringing out a superior class of three-year-olds—something impossible considering that there are really none left to do battle for the cause—it was in no measure a failure. In other words, the secondary character of the starters proved the success of the association's plan—a plan that will, without doubt, bring about a series of stakes for which the death of the nominator will not disqualify, and for which the winner will not have fully half the reputed value of the stakes paid in so many pieces of paper which he must collect, either from the subscribers direct or through the secretaries of some other association, neither idea having ever worked with success. Under the conditions of the Omnibus, the original subscribers paid a small entry, which accrues to the race fund, the association adding an amount of money to the race; and that there is no wish to profit by having the money paid direct to the association is amply proved in the present instance, for while the association received $2,500 it paid out just $5,000. As to the success of the plan, Mr. Clifton Bell of Denver, Colorado, purchased Harry Gilmore from Captain Cottrill, Mobile, and as he won, Mr. Bell takes the stakes and the first money, $2,500, the sum of $1,000, under the conditions of the stake, going to Captain Cottrill. As to the second horse, Mr. Pierre Lorillard, the owner and nominator of Wyoming, receives $1,500, namely, $1,000 second money and $500 as the nominator. But the strongest point in favor of the stake is shown in the case of Tom Plunkett. He was nominated by Mr. R. W. Cameron, who transferred the nomination to Mr. Noah Armstrong. The latter has drifted into turf bankruptcy, and is in the forfeit list, which stands as a penalty against the horses nominated by him. But under the conditions of the Omnibus Stakes, Mr. Cassidy had only to pay the starting entry to qualify his horse to start, and had Plunkett finished first or second, Mr. Cassidy would have been paid the amount due under the conditions of the stake, conditions which are so liberal and easy to breeders and owners that they must eventually become popular.

The third race on the card was the Omnibus Stake, the conditions of which are such that the actual owner of any of the horses nominated could start on payment of $100, no written transfer being necessary, nor would the death of the nominator disqualify the horses, as in other States. The only conditional qualification was that the person starting the horses must himself be eligible under the rules. To cover the stake, the association made the entrance $25 each, to go to the race fund, and to be paid when the nomination was made; under which conditions 100 subscriptions were made to the stake, which brought to the fund just half the added money. But as a further inducement for owners and breeders to enter for the stake, the $5,000 was divided so as to give the owner of the winner $2,500, the owner of the second $1,000, the nominator of the winner $1,000, and the nominator of the second $500. Like most of the stakes run at Monmouth Park, winners of other stakes were penalized, of one of the value of $2,000, 5 pounds; of two such stakes, 7 pounds; while horses that were maidens were allowed 5 pounds. Under these conditions a horse like Forester would have carried 125 pounds, but as Messrs. Appleby's "crack" had been lame since Saturday they could not start him, which left the issue to the following of the 100 subscriptions made to the stake: The Preakness Stable's Macbeth and W. L. Cassidy's Tom Plunkett, each at 118 pounds; D. D. Withers' Duplex, Clifton Bell's Harry Gilmore, and P. Lorillard's Wyoming, each at 115 pounds. The last named was the favorite both in the pools and books, with Harry Gilmore second. At the start, which was made after one breakaway, Macbeth was in front, followed by Tom Plunkett and Harry Gilmore, with the favorite last. Before they reached the five-furlong starting post Wyoming took the lead, and quickly opened a gap of two lengths, by which he led to the three-quarters, with Tom Plunkett second, Macbeth, Harry Gilmore and Duplex close up. The run up the stretch was slow and uninteresting, the only changes being that Macbeth and Harry Gilmore improved their places, they following Wyoming past the stand three lengths behind the favorite. As they made the turn by the old Club-house, Tom Plunkett, by hugging the inner rails, got to be second, and at the quarter held that position a length behind Wyoming, half a length in front of Macbeth, who was lapped by Harry Gilmore, with Duplex two lengths away. There was no change until reaching the stables, where Billy Donohue, on Harry Gilmore, moved up on the outside, and reaching Wyoming, the two ran half a length apart for nearly a furlong, with Tom Plunkett in close attendance. As they reached the railroad turn Gilmore headed Wyoming the two running a sharp race round the turn to the three-quarters, where Gilmore still held the advantage by a head, with Wyoming half a length in front of Plunkett, he closely followed by Duplex and Macbeth. They remained in that order nearly to the seven-furlong pole, reaching which, Duplex for a few strides looked dangerous, but the threat almost instantly vanished, as Gilmore gradually drew away from Wyoming, and with the greatest ease won by two lengths, followed by Wyoming a head in front of Tom Plunkett. A length away followed Duplex, two lengths in front of Macbeth; time, 2:44¼, the slowest time made at the distance since the season began on the 1st of July. In fact, although the idea of the association was carried out to the letter in affording buyers of horses a chance to win a good stake, and breeders to sell their horses and yet reap some reward by their subsequent success, it cannot be said that the race was a success, it failing to produce a grand race, which the amount of added money should have made it.

By telegraph, it is stated that on Thursday, the 17th inst., in the first race, a dash of three-quarters of a mile, Buckstone won; time, 1:21. The one-and-one-half-mile race Laura Glass won in 2:56½. The mile-and-three-eighths race Keno won in 2:19¾. The mile race Bell Boy won in 1:57½, 1:51½. The mile hurdle race Guy won in 2:07¼.

By telegraph, we learn that on last Saturday in the first race, three-quarters of a mile, Buckstone was first, Fairview second; time, 1:18½. In the second race, a mile and a furlong, Wyoming won, Gussie second, Infanta third; time, 2:00¼. In the third race, one and a quarter miles, Girofla won, Sweethome second, Della third; time, 2:16¼. In the fourth race, three-quarter mile, Carmelite won, Breese second, Disdain third; time, 1:16¾. In the fifth race, one and three-quarter miles, Monitor won, Priam second, Glengore third; time, 3:07½. In the sixth race, one mile, Marathon won, Hospodar second, Queen third; time, 1:44¾. In the steeplechase, full course, Ike Bonham won, Guy second, Joe Hunt third; time, 2:16½.

## GRAND CIRCUIT WINNERS OF HEATS AND RACES

BUFFALO.

| Winner. | Sire. | Class. | Amt. Won. | Best Time. |
|---|---|---|---|---|
| Aldine................ | Almont............... | 2:26 | 750 | 2:19¾ |
| Adele Gould........ | Jay Gould........... | 2:20 | 1,000 | 2:19 |
| Annie W............. | Bostick's Almont... | 2:20 | 300 | 2:20 |
| Abe Downing....... | Joe Downing....... | 2:29 | 375 | 2:20¾ |
| Black Cloud......... | Ashland Chief...... | Stallions. | 750 | 2:18¼ |
| Buffalo Girl (pacer)... | Pocahontas......... | Free for all. | 375 | 2:12½ |
| Captain Lewis....... | Spink................ | 2:23 | 750 | 2:22¼ |
| Clingstone........... | Rysdyk.............. | Special. | 1,500 | 2:14¼ |
| Cornelia.............. | Son of Henry Clay.. | No record. | 1,500 | 2:23 |
| Flora F............... | Clear Grit........... | 2:23 | 300 | 2:29 |
| Flora Belle (pacer)... | Stucker's Rainbow.. | Free for all. | 750 | 2:16¾ |
| Fanny Witherspoon.. | Almont.............. | 2:20 | 500 | 2:19 |
| Gem (pacer)......... | Tom Rolfe.......... | Free for all. | 225 | 2:19 |
| Jewett................ | Allie West.......... | 2:23 | 500 | 2:22¼ |
| Joe Bowers, Jr. (pacer) | Joe Bowers........ | 2:25 | 200 | 2:21 |
| Jerome Eddy........ | Louis Napoleon.... | Stallions. | 375 | 2:16½ |
| Lucrece.............. | Robert Whaley..... | 2:23 | 1,000 | 2:23½ |
| Limber Jack (pacer).. | ..................... | 2:25 | 500 | 2:18½ |
| Overman............. | Elmo................ | 2:29 | 750 | 2:2 |
| Wilson................ | George Wilkes...... | 2:33 | 750 | 2:24½ |
| Walnut............... | Florida............. | No record. | 750 | 2:22¼ |

## AN OLD-FASHIONED ENGLISH TROT.

The love of the trotting horse is to be traced to England, where these matches have been popular for centuries, but chiefly among the young farmers and dealers in stock, who all like to boast of possessing a fast nag. But these old-fashioned contests were generally made for a dinner and wine for selves and friends, and perhaps a £20 note. But in the absence of any trotting track the affair generally came off on the turnpike road, so many miles out and return. Of course the horses could not for a moment compare with the American trotting horse, even a quarter of a century since, and the fact is they were mostly ponies of a little more than fourteen hands high, but famous for their speed and gameness. An amusing anecdote is told respecting Goldsmith Maid and her trainer, when there was talk of sending that famous mare to England to give some exhibitions of her then unrivaled speed. A wealthy dealer in live stock from Smithfield Market, London, came to New York with a view to increase his shipments of fresh beef and cattle, and by chance was introduced to that famous driver who inquired as to the probable success he should meet with in this venture across the ocean. After receiving a description of Goldsmith Maid and of her performances, the dealer smiled incredulously, remarking that 2 minutes 14 seconds a mile meant ten miles in less than 23 minutes, and that no horse in the world could do it. When the explanation came that this was the time for one mile only, he laughed and proposed that they should bring the Maid over, and he would drive one of his ponies against her, ten miles out and return, on a turnpike road, to a butcher's cart, for $1,000, or £1,000 a side, the horses to come to a stand-still and to turn round at every break. The idea of the Queen of the American turf submitting to such a peculiar ordeal was so funny that it was received with shouts of laughter, in which the Englishman heartily joined. That same dealer visited some of our tracks and has tried to introduce the American trotting plans into England, as he was one of the first to aid in building the Alexandra Park track, near London. But as yet these trials have met with but little success, as the English still prefer their old fashioned ways, a specimen of which was given recently at the above park when there was a large and enthusiastic attendance to witness a match in which Hall's black horse Jim was backed to trot 16 miles in an hour, in harness. All the parties connected with the match belong to the "lemonade and ginger-beer trade," and the horse was driven to a sulky by Malcolm McLachlan, who has gained a high reputation across the Atlantic as a trotting-driver. The first five miles were accomplished in 15m. 55s., eight in 25m. 7s., and the full distance in 49m. 57s., the horse thus winning with 10m. 3s. to spare. An extra mile was then covered, increasing the time to 53m. 21s. C. Bastien was starter and referee. It has been the opinion of many who have judged the bent of the English people in regard to this sport, that such a horse as Controller, who trotted twenty miles to wagon at the Bay District track in 58:57 (the match being against an hour's time), will prove in England to be a far greater attraction than would the performances of such horses as St. Julien, Trinket or Clingstone. It will take a long time to educate the English up to the American standpoint as regards trotting.

Flies and Horses.—There is no feeling man but would like to do something to relieve his horse from the annoyance of flies. Horses are goaded almost to madness by the insects. In England flies are prevented from troubling the animals by the application to the latter, before harnessing, of a mixture of one part crude carbolic acid with six or more parts of olive oil. This should be rubbed lightly all over the animal with a rag and applied more thickly to the interior of the ears and other parts most likely to be attacked. This application may need to be repeated in the course of the day, but while any odor of the acid remains the flies decline to settle, and the horse is completely free from their annoyance.

## BOOK-BETTING.

The following are the odds now offered by Killip & Co. against the nominations in the stakes and purses at the State Fair. While the odds are given now they are, of course, subject to change, and, in fact, there may be cases when "the book is full" and no more money will be laid against the horse in which the limit has been reached. As is well known to those who have a slight acquaintance with this system of betting, the wagers are "play or pay," which means that the money is lost if the animal "backed" does not start. There are many arguments in favor of this system of betting. It is the only kind that meets with favor in England, and in combination with auction and mutual pools gives the best opportunity to support those the acceptor fancies.

No. 1. Introduction Stake, ¾ of a Mile.

Thirteen to one against Kate Carson.
Five to one against Forest King.
Ten to one against Bob.
Ten to one against Joe Daniels, Jr.
Fourteen to one against May B.
Nine to one against Atalanta.
Two to one against Jim Douglas.
Three to one against Duke of Monday.
Five to one against Premium.
Two to one against Jim Renwick.
Twelve to one against Ella Doane.

No. 2. Breeders' Stake, 1½ Miles.

Ten to one against Capt. Kidd.
Seven to one against Lizzie P.
Eight to one against Cy Mulkey.
Nine to one against Hattie Ball.
Nine to one against Belle S.
Six to one against Maria F.
Two to one against Duke of Monday.
Six to one against Duchess of Norfolk.
Thirteen to one against Judge McKinstry.
Fourteen to one against Annie Lawrie.
Eight to one against Cornucopia.
Seven to one against Conquest.
Five to one against Precious.
Eight to one against Mattie A Filly.
Fifteen to one against Idler.
Nine to one against Evangeline.

No. 3. Selling Race, Mile and Repeat.

Six to one against Patrol.
Eight to one against Shiner, weight 100 pounds.
Twelve to one against Sister to Lottery, weight 82 pounds.
Eight to one against Villa Randlett, weight 100 pounds.
Two to one against Joe Howell, weight 105 pounds.
Six to one against Inauguration.
Nine to one against Jack Douglass, weight 104 pounds.
Six to one against Haddington, weight 109 pounds.
Four to one against Euchre, weight 105 pounds.

No. 8. Filly Stake, Two-Year-Olds, ⅝ of a Mile.

Five to one against Flou Flou.
Three to one against Satinet.
Five to one against Rosa B.
Three to one against Satanella.
Five to one against Lou Spencer.
Two to one against Augusta E.
Seven to one against Irene.

No. 9: California Derby Stake, 3-Year Olds, 1½ Miles.

Three to one against Precious.
Four to one against Capt. Kidd.
Three to one against Maria F.
Six to one against Judge McKinstry.
Four to one against Hattie Ball.
One to one against Duke of Monday.

No. 10. Jennie B Stake, Free for all, Dash of a mile.

Four to one against May D.
Eight to one against Bob.
Nine to one against Night Hawk.
Six to one against Atalanta.
Six to one against Frank Rhoades.
Two to one against Duke of Monday.
Four to one against Forest King.
Eight to one against Fortress.
Ten to one against Duke of Norfolk.
Seven to one against Lizzie P.
Three to one against Jim Douglass.
Three to one against Red Boy.

No. 11. Selling Race, 1⅛ Miles.

Six to one against Belshaw, weight 93 pounds.
Eight to one against Lady Partisan, weight 92 pounds.
Twelve to one against Sister to Lottery, weight 82 pounds
Five to one against Cy Mulkey, weight 95 pounds.
One to one against Joe Howell, weight 107 pounds.
Six to one against Joe Daniels, Jr.
Nine to one against Jubilee.
Seven to one against Villa Randlett, weight 105 pounds.
Two to one against Euchre, weight 106 pounds.

No. 16. Colt and Filly Stake, 2-Year Olds.

Six to one against Panama.
Nine to one against Certiorari.
Five to one against May B.
Two to one against Augusta E.
Nine to one against Irene.
Six to one against Flou Flou.
Three to one against Satanella.
Six to one against Lou Spencer.
Eight to one against Young Flush.

No. 17. Selling Race, 1¼ Miles.

Nine to one against Ella Doane, weight 108 pounds.
Ten to one against Idler, weight 90 pounds.
Nine to one against Shiner, weight 101 pounds.
Fourteen to one against Sister to Lottery, weight 82 lbs.
Seven to one against Villa Randlett, weight 100 pounds.
Four to one against Euchre, weight 107 pounds.
Six to one against Belshaw, weight 95 pounds.
Twelve to one against Geo. Bender, weight 101 pounds.
Ten to one against Jubilee, weight 104 pounds.
Nine to one against Haddington, weight 109 pounds.
Five to one against Cy Mulkey, weight 90 pounds.
Two to one against Joe Howell, weight 101 pounds.

Books now open at Arion Halle, N. E. corner of Sutter and Kearny streets.

Address all communications as above to Killip & Co.

## THE SARATOGA RACES.

There are loud complaints at Saratoga about the poor sport that is offered on the race track in comparison with that of previous years. This is all owing to the fact that the Saratoga Association insisted on having a continuous meeting during the season, which interfering with the second Summer meeting at Monmouth Park, the gentlemen interested in the latter organization have withdrawn their stables from Saratoga, and have thus sadly diminished the attractions of the pretty watering place, as the financial exhibit of the Saratoga Association will disclose when they make their annual declaration of dividends. During the past week there is nothing that calls for special mention, the attendance being generally not up to the average, considering that the village was crowded and that the season was at its height.

On Thursday, the 17th, the first race, one mile, was won by Baron Faurst, Colonel Sprague second; time, 1:47⅕.

In the second race, two miles, Eole was first, General Monroe second; time 3:42⅕.

On the 18th, in the first race, three-quarters of a mile, Stanton won, Stand Off Second, and Patti third; time, 1:15-¾. In the second race, one mile and 500 yards, Blenheim won, Farragut second, Apollo third; time, 2:13⅕. In the third race, 1 mile, Disturbance won, Botherem second, Sir Hugh third; time, 1:47¼. In the fourth race, three-quarters of a mile, Lytton won; time, 1:18.

On the 19th, in the first race, one mile, Jennie won, Gus Matthews second; time 1:42¼. Second race, three-quarter-mile, Woodford won, Tarantella second; time, 1:16. Third race, one mile and five furlongs, Bend Or won, Creosote second; time, 2:49. In the fourth race, one and three-quarter miles, seven hurdles, Annette was first, Revenge second; time, 3:18¾.

On the 21st, in the mile-and-a-quarter dash, Tom Plunket won, Force second, Helena Wallace third; time, 2:09. In the one one-eighth miles, Baby won, George Hokes second, Startle third; time, 1:55¾. In the steeple chase, one-and-a-half miles, Rose won, Turfman second, Woodlock third; time, 2:55.

On the 22d, in the first race, three-quarters of a mile, Monarch was first, Bootjack second. There was a dead heat between Fellowplay and Little Phil for the third place; time, 1:14. The second race, mile and five furlongs, Charley B. won, Boatman second, Kite third; time, 2:54. In the mile dash Buccaneer won, Amazon second, Malasan third; time, 1:42⅕.

On the 23d, in the first race, three-quarters of a mile, London won, Pride second, Patti third; time, 1:15¼. In the second race, one mile and 500 yards, Lina Stanhope won, Kenesaw second, Bushwhacker third; time, 2:13⅕. In the third race, one mile, Force won, Jake White second, John Sullivan third; time, 1:43. In the fourth race, one mile and a half, over hurdles, Revenge won, Charlemagne second, Glasgow third; time, 2:48⅕.

---

Shetland Pony Ranch.—Baron Von Raub, Leon Springs, Bexar County, Texas, has 5,000 acres all under fence properly sub-divided and stocked with beautiful Shetland and spotted ponies. His breeding stock consists of seven stallions and forty-five mares, all thoroughbred, and 200 small spotted pony mares. He is breeding a race of striped and spotted ponies to please the children. He sells the increase to persons all over the world, and the supply is not equal to the demand. These little ponies range over the prairies like sheep or goats, and present a novel appearance—very gentle, every one is as docile as a cat and can be caught anywhere on the range.

With the publication of the entries for the Cesarewitch and Cambridgeshire handicaps the 3d inst., the English Autumn season may be said to have begun. The Cesarewitch received 104 subscribers, including P. Lorillard's Iroquois, Aranza and Nereid, J. R. Keene's Foxhall, Don Fulano, Bushman, Bookmaker, Seminole, Golden Gate and Romeo, Lord Rossmore's Passaic, Lord Ellesmere's Wallenstein, C. Archer's Abbotsford (late Mistake)—all American bred. The Cambridgeshire has 137 subscribers, for which the Americans are Iroquois, Sachem, Nereid, Aranza, Wallenstein, Abbotsford, Foxhall, Don Fulano, Bookmaker, Bushman, Golden Gate and Romeo. The English entries include the very cream of the stables in training. The Americans are also represented in several of the Nursery Handicaps, Great Eastern Railway Handicap, the Newmarket October Handicap, and the Houghton Handicap.

The Louisville Fair Association has issued a liberal programme for a five-days meeting, commencing on September 17th, in which special inducements are offered for colts and fillies. This will be about the time the Palo Alto draft may be on their way East for their engagements, and if it suited the plans of Ex-Governor Stanford they might perhaps make their first appearance at the Louisville meeting. The "perhaps" means that it is as yet uncertain whether the youngsters will be sent East at all, as they have been suffering more or less from a mild form of pink-eye, which has greatly retarded their training at this important stage of the season.

From Chicago we learn that the challenge issued by Messrs. White and Budd Doble, the owners of Monroe Chief, has been accepted by Commodore W. N. Kitson, and that Monroe Chief and Von Arnim will trot in a match for $2,500 a side at Minneapolis during the fair week in September. To this amount Colonel King adds $2,500, showing that that gentleman has an implicit faith in this being a drawing card, and certainly the race promises to be a sensational one, on account of the noted character of the horses concerned and the prominence of their owners.

The nominations for the two great English events, the Epsom Derby and Oaks, comprise fifteen American entries. For the Derby Mr. P. Lorillard has six entries, Mr. J. R. Keene three, and Mr. Harry Keene one. For the Oaks Mr. Lorillard has nominated four and Mr. J. R. Keene one. For the Grand Prize of Paris Mr. J. R. Keene has four nominations and P. Lorillard six. Amongst Mr. Keene's entries is a sister to Foxhall, who may emulate her brother's exploits, and again place this trophy, with its attendant shekels, to the credit of the American turf.

The Allan steamship Buenos Ayrean has brought out 110 Clydesdale and Cleveland bay horses and Shetland ponies. They were selected from the studs of the principal breeders in Scotland by the Messrs. Bullocks & Harding, of Indiana, the Messrs. Powell Bros., of Pennsylvania, Galbraith Bros., of Janesville, Wis., and others. They are all intended for breeding purposes, and part are to be exhibited in Canada and the United States. Some of the batch are noted prize-winners, and all are of meritorious quality.

The premium list of the Chicago Horse Show, to take place Sept. 16 to 23, is now ready, and may be had by applying to D. L. Hall, Secretary, 116 Monroe street, Chicago, Ill. The premiums aggregate about $30,000, which will be awarded to trotting and road horses, also thoroughbred draft, carriage and saddle stock. There will also be liberal purses for trotting and pacing races. It is the intention of the management to make this the greatest horse show ever held.

To show the immense difference there is in betting in the mutual pools and with the bookmakers, it may be mentioned that when on the 16th inst. Malasine won a selling purse, the highest odds procurable in the books were twenty-five to one against her chances, whereas in the mutual pools each $5 ticket brought $284.60, making a difference of much more than a hundred per cent.

Messrs. Dwyer Brothers, of Brooklyn, have sent the two-year old filly Red-and-Blue, by Alarm, dam Maggie B., the dam of Iroquois, to Tennessee, to be bred to Luke Blackburn. The result of this experiment will be watched with interest.

## DRAFT HORSES.

The Clydesdales are improved Scotch draft-horses. They have been extensively imported into the United States, and form a competent part of our working force. They originated in Scotland The Duke of Hamilton perfected the breed, and produced a more shapely animal than the old English cart-horse. He bred in all the bone and muscle that constituted the strength and power of the horses of the old style, and bred out the superfluous flesh that encumbered their action. Other breeders have modeled them over into that perfect form that commands their strength to the best advantage, and bred in that activity that gives them force of character to perform more than the old kind in the same length of time. Substance is the measure of power. A horse 16 hands high, with a powerful, close-coupled, compact form, will perform more labor, and can be kept on less food, than one 17½ hands high, whose ponderous weight tires out his legs to carry about an overgrown body. The Clydesdales are highly prized in Scotland, where they are extensively raised.

The English Shire-bred draft-horses somewhat resemble the Clydesdales. Dealers frequently sell them for Clydesdales, because the latter command a higher price in the market. The English Shire-horses are powerfully-built, strong-limbed, heavy-boned, compact, close-coupled, muscular-formed animals, weighing from 1000 to 2000 lbs. They are well adapted for large drays or lumber wagons, where great weight and power are required to steady and move large loads of merchandise or minerals at a moderate pace. The English Shires have been crossed with the Scotch Clydesdales, and this is claimed to have produced a family superior to either breed. The cross of the Scotch sire with the English mare is claimed to have bred an excellent draft-horse, superior to either sire or dam. Both breeds were originally founded upon the union of lines of powerful draft-horses. The reunion of lines long separated might be expected to culminate in a superior family. The good qualities that either possessed, single-handed, when combined together would give additional force of character to the issue, and improve the breed. It is the way that all breeds are founded, and their progeny raised up to a higher standard of excellence.

The Percheron-Norman draft-horse has been imported into the United States in great numbers. They are imported from La Perche, a district in the interior of France, where they are extensively raised. They are generally grey. The color must have been bred in for many generations, till it became a fixed inheritance, to be transmitted so uniformly to the offspring. The Percheron is claimed to have descended, at an early day, from a cross of Arab sires with Norman dams. The return to the Arab cross has restored the original type and character of the Percheron, whence they sprang. As late as 1820, Godolphin and Gallipoli, two grey Arabian stallions, were imported into France, and extensively used with Percheron mares.

The re-infusion of Oriental blood has kept up the beautiful form of the Arabian without diminishing the size the Percheron acquired from the Norman. Norman dams crossed with Arab sires will breed larger than the sire. It is found, when the Barbs of Arabs are taken from their native soil and crossed with foreign dams, they will breed a larger class than the Oriental steeds of the desert. The parched-up sands of the desert have stunted the race. When taken to a more congenial climate and fruitful soil, the young scions expand and grow larger than the diminutive Arab from which they sprang.

The Percherons are among the best-formed horses that can be found anywhere. Their shoulders exactly fit the collar. Their close-coupled, compact form gives them more strength, in proportion to weight, than any other form could possibly possess. They are not only powerful, but active; possessing a fine constitution, overflowing with robust health, which lays the foundation of physical endurance. Stout form, superior strength and activity, are the characteristics of the breed. They will work hard, keep fat on little food, and live to an advanced age.

We have several grades of horses formed from a cross of the draft with native breeds, and converted into distinct families, such as the French-Canadian. They have preserved the form and substance of their Norman ancestors for generations, except slightly diminished size, caused by scanty fare and cold climate. We have also the half-bred Clydesdale, Percheron, and Sampson, graded up with home-bred stock. These grades are the most useful stock for all work to be found in the catalogue of breeding. They are appropriately named horses-of-all-work. They are adapted for all kinds of farming, for marketing the productions of the soil, for lumbering, for use in express wagons, and various other occupations where great strength is required, combined with a good rate of speed. They supersede the heavy draft-horse for ordinary work, because they are well suited for the family carriage. They are hardy, easily acclimatized, accustomed to the food produced on their native soil, inured to hardships and privations, and possess a powerful constitution, that will stand the wear and tear of hard work through a long life. They will stand more labor on less food than the overgrown draft horse. There is no other breed that can fill their places in a rough, hilly country, for all kinds of work.—*Observer, in National Live Stock Journal.*

---

We are in receipt of a new paper, The Breeder and Sportsman, Joseph Cairn Simpson, editor and proprietor. Its typographical appearance is excellent, and it is devoted to the interest of stock-raising as well as to a variety of other matters interesting to sportsmen. It is edited with marked ability, published in San Francisco, and we commend it to breeders, sportsmen and others.—*Lower Lake Bulletin.*

## THE SANTA ROSA RACES.

On Tuesday last, was the first day of the annual Santa Rosa meeting, and the attendance was fair, when it is considered that threshing time is the busiest of all the year for our farmers. The park on all sides showed evident signs of improvement and prosperity, and the track was both fast and safe.

The first race on the programme was a trot, mile and repeat, purse of $200, free for all two-year-olds owned in the district. This closed with five entries, but Steve Crandall's bay filly, No Name, failed to appear, and Paine Shafter's gray colt, Greyson, after being speeded in front of the stand, was withdrawn with the consent of the judges, on account of lameness. This left three contestants—J. E. Foster's sorrel mare, Clara Patterson, J. C. Fountain's black filly, May Day, driven by Joseph Edge, and E. B. Conway's chestnut colt, Ideal, driven by George Bayliss. These were given positions for the first heat in the order named. In the pools on the previous night and just before the race, May Day was a large favorite, selling for $20 against $8 for Ideal, and $2 for Clara Patterson. On the third score the word was given to a good start. Clara broke badly a few yards from the stand and repeated the performance during the entire heat. The contest between the other two was exciting until the ⅝ mark was reached, when Ideal indulged in a few skips and fell behind. May Day was three lengths ahead at the ¾ pole, but left her feet while going easy, and was overtaken by the colt. From this point home they trotted neck and neck, until within fifty yards of home, when both broke and came under the wire running. The judges were unable to determine which was the victor, and decided it a dead heat, with Clara Patterson distanced; time, 3:01½.

Between heats pool-selling was lively, at even figures, until just before the start, when May Day again became a favorite, selling for $20 against $8 for the colt. For the second heat a good start was given, but Ideal soon broke and fell behind. At the half the mare broke and was passed by the colt; before the ¾ pole was reached they both indulged in jumps, but here the colt steadied and came in an easy winner; time, 3:05. Ideal was now the favorite at $20 to $5. After tedious scoring they got an even start. May Day went to the front, but broke at the quarter-pole, and from here the colt had everything his own way, winning by five lengths in 3:04.

The second race was for the 2:35 class; purse $400. Closed with four entries, but James Garland's Rowdy Boy being sick with the pinkeye was withdrawn. The starters were, Taboas Bros.' gray gelding Ralph, driven by S. Sperry; Wm. Bourke's bay gelding Johnny, driven by Fred Vail; and Mat Doyle's bay gelding Boss, driven by Steve Crandall. In the betting before the horses appeared on the track Johnny was favorite, bringing $20 against $14 for Boss and $2 for Ralph. During the scoring Johnny showed an inclination to pace, and acted so rank that it frightened the betting sharps, and Boss sold up even. A good start was given, with Ralph at the pole, Johnny next, and Boss on the outside. Soon after the word was given Boss broke, and despite Steve's efforts he never struck a square trot during the heat. Ralph and Johnny went close together for the first three-eighths, when Ralph made a disastrous break, and before Sperry could bring him to a trot Johnny had opened a gap of 200 yards. Vail seeing his advantage sent the horse for all he was worth, and succeeded in leaving the gray outside the flag, Boss being nearly a quarter of a mile behind; time, 2:33½.

SUMMARIES.

Santa Rosa Course.—Tuesday, August 22, 1882.—Purse, $200; first horse, $120; second, $60; third, $20; free for all two-year-olds owned in the district.

| | | | |
|---|---|---|---|
| E. B. Conway names ch. c. Ideal | 0 | 1 | 1 |
| G. C. Fountain names blk. f. May Day | 0 | 2 | 2 |
| J. E. Foster names s. m. Clara Patterson | dis. | | |
| P. J. Shafter names g. h. Greyson | drawn. | | |
| Steve Crandall names b. f. No Name | drawn. | | |

Time—3:01½, 3:05, 3:04.

Same day.—2:35 class; purse, $400; first horse, $240; second, $120; third, $40.

| | |
|---|---|
| Wm. Bourke names b. g. Johnny | 1 |
| Taboas Bros. names g. g. Ralph | dis. |
| Mat Doyle names b. g. Boss | dis. |
| Jas. Garland names g. g. Rowdy Boy | drawn. |

Time—2:33½.

On the second day, the first was a trotting race, 2:50 class or a purse of $400. Huntress, St. Patrick, Placida, Lady Zane and Emma Taylor started. Huntress was the favorite. Placida took the first heat in 2:45; Huntress the second, third and fourth, in 2:41, 2:41¾, 2:44½. Placida got the second money and St. Patrick third. In the third heat Lady Zane and Emma Taylor were distanced. The second race was a pacing match for $250 a side, $150 added by the association, mile heats, best three in five, between Johnny Wiegle and Washington. Wiegle sold favorite in the pools all the way through. Washington took the first heat in 2:31½; Eagle the second, third and fourth, in 2:34, 2:25¼, 2:32½.

On the Thursday there was a great increase in the attendence and the races were by far the best, and excited more enthusiasm than either of the preceding days. The first was a trotting race, free for all three-year-olds owned in the district, for a purse of $300, best three in five, with Deba Mott, Starr, Buck, Foster, Ned, and Warwick entered. Ned was the favorite in the pools at five to one, and took three straight heats in 2:56, 2:50¼ and 2:54¾, Deba Mott getting second money and Warwick third. The event of the day was the trotting race, free for all that never beat 2:25, for a $500 purse. Welby's Starr King, Titus' Echora, Rose's Del Sur, Hughes' Cairo, and Goldsmith's Director started. Del Sur got the first heat in 2:24½, Echora getting the next three in 2:25, 2.25¼ and 2:29, and winning the first money, Del Sur and Director getting second and third money. The San Francisco delegation backed Starr King heavily at $20 against $15 for Director and $12 for the field, and therefore made a heavy loss.

The Chicago Driving Park Association are certainly decided on making a success, as they now announce a Fall racing meeting that commences on Tuesday, October 3d, and lasts throughout the week. There are three two-year-old stakes, a like number for three-year-olds—the Northwestern Stake, a mile and three-quarters, and the October handicap, a mile and a furlong, the last named being for all ages. The nominations for these events close on September 1st with D. H. Hall, the secretary, at Chicago, and about the same time a liberal programme of purses will be offered, that, with the above stakes, will provide for not less than four races on each day. It is more than probable that the California horses will take part in these races, as they will then be on their way home for the Winter.

## ROWING.

### A CARD FROM L. C. WHITE.

Editor Breeder and Sportsman—Sir: In the issue of your interesting paper of the 19th inst. several representatives of San Francisco rowing clubs took occasion to compliment Chas. G. Yale for his kindness in acting as referee of the Fourth of July Regatta. Six weeks is a long time to spend in the composition of a card a few inches long, but perhaps the courteous scribes write as reluctantly as several of them row, and not much faster. As far as the compliment to Mr. Yale for his kindness in acting as referee is concerned, the card is acceptable to me. Mr. Yale has always been willing to assist in popularizing the sport of rowing, and needs no certificate of his enthusiasm or courtesy from the Golden Gate or any other club. His reputation as an honorable gentleman cannot be affected in the slightest degree by all the ink which Mr. Griffin and the tail of his literary kite could swing in a year. I would be surprised to learn that Mr. Yale has not felt more hurt by the publication of the card than the men who are aimed at over his shoulder. I am one of these targets, having been in the crew of the Pioneer Club which won the four-oar shell race on the Fourth of July, and was disqualified by Mr. Yale for fouling. Our chivalrous opponents of the Ariel Club, who were not fouled and who nevertheless were only able to row second, now unite in the condemnation of our action.

This is what is said of us by these high-toned critics, who can come to the front better in a newspaper column than in a row-boat:

It is a well known fact that every one cannot be satisfied, especially where personal interest is concerned; but we wish to state publicly that we disapprove of the ungentlemanly and unprofessional manner used by some of the disappointed oarsmen in expressing their disagreement with official decisions. We have noted with considerable attention the discussion over the result of the four-oared shell race, and while we are inclined to sympathize with the debarred crew, which certainly rowed a game race under adverse circumstances, still we cannot see how you could have decided otherwise by any recognized code of rules for amateur rowing.

Now what was the ungentlemanly and unprofessional manner used by the disappointed oarsmen to express their disagreement with official decisions? They did not fill the air with blasphemy and vituperation as some of our critics have done when official decisions did not suit them. They did not scare the referee off the bridge as has been done in other cases where some of the high-minded moralists were interested. All that the defeated oarsmen did was to row quietly to their boat-house; peacefully and silently await the decision of the referee, and promptly pay their bets when the race was given to the second crew. I do not think that such conduct comes under the definition of ungentlemanly behavior, but it is not surprising that our critics should be mistaken in the matter. The ability to judge of what is gentlemanly always presupposes the possession of some of the characteristics of a gentleman. It is interesting to compare with the conduct of the defeated oarsmen the actions of our critics. These chivalrous individuals waited until five weeks after the discussion in the newspapers had ended and in which the defeated crew took no part whatever. Then our high-minded moralists surreptitiously circulated the card complimenting Mr. Yale, and had neither the manhood nor honesty to submit it to the two clubs most interested—the Pioneer Club, which lost the disputed race, and the South End Club, which owned the boat that was fouled. The South End Club was as much interested in the matter as any other club on the bay, and would readily have joined in complimenting Mr. Yale for his disinterested activity. That was not what was wanted, however. The real purpose was to place the Pioneer Club in a discreditable position, and the means taken are entirely worthy of the projectors of the scheme. In conclusion, I beg to suggest that, as the Pioneer crew is now in training for the valuable trophy offered by the Breeder and Sportsman, the energies of the Golden Gate and Ariel Clubs could be better applied on a sheet of water than a sheet of paper. A reputation supported by printer's ink is very unsubstantial. Apologizing for trespassing so much on your valuable space,

I remain, yours,

L. C. White,
Capt. Pioneer Crew.

History of the Hillsdale Crew.—In 1877 so little was known of boating in Hillsdale that the introduction of a single scull shell caused a sensation. A small club was organized, and in 1879 the now celebrated crew was sent to Toledo, O., to row the Undine crew. The Hillsdales scored such a success that they were next sent by their townsmen to Saratoga to take part in the National Regatta. As they were about to start, the officers of the club advised them merely to "feel their way," and not to hope for success in their first race. They promised to "feel their way" as instructed, but said also they would win if they could, whereupon they were told that, if they had that much good luck, the club would defray all their expenses. At Saratoga they met the best crews in the country, and their success created the greatest excitement in their town. On receipt of the news places of business were closed, church and fire-bells were rung, houses were illuminated, bonfires were built, the people gathered in the streets and cheered themselves hoarse and the bands made music in honor of the champions. Since that time Hillsdale has been a lively boating place, and the crew has been one of the institutions of the town.

The stroke adopted by the Hillsdale crew was taught them by Capt. Terwilliger. At first he was laughed at for giving the crew the stroke which has since made it successful and famous, and he was advised by many well known boating men and members of his club to change the stroke, but he claimed that it made the boat go, and did not overtask his men, and he purposed following out his own ideas as long as he remained captain. The crew had never gone into training for a race until within a week or ten days before the time they were to row, and the only concessions they received from the club, or anybody in or out of Hillsdale, were payment of their legitimate traveling expenses by the club, and the keeping open of their positions by their employers during their absence. The time and labor they gave were their personal loss.

He Fancies the English Crews.—An impression having prevailed that the cowardly action of the British oarsmen was due in a great measure to an opinion expressed by the champion Hanlan while he was in England last Spring, Hanlan was asked on the press boat, while the races of this week were in progress on Detroit River, what he had to say about the matter.

"What is the statement about me?" he asked.

"It is charged," was answered, "that before you left England your opinion of the Hillsdale crew was asked by some of the English amateurs, and you said the Hillsdales could easily beat any amateur four in England, and advised the English oarsmen not to have anything to do with them. Is that a fact?"

"No, it is not," said Hanlan. "My recollection of it is that my opinion was asked, and I said that from what I had read and heard the Hillsdale crew could beat any amateur crew in America nearly half a minute. That's all I said. I didn't say they could beat the English crews."

"Because he doesn't think they can," put in Fred. Plaisted.

"But I haven't said as much as that," rejoined Hanlan.

"Well, I know," said Plaisted.

The subject was then dropped, and those interested in it became engrossed in a race which had just been started.

Courtney's Latest.—The *Turf, Field and Farm* announces that Charles E. Courtney is acting as prosecutor in a remarkable case where nearly 70 persons were poisoned by tartar emetic in the ice-cream served at a Methodist Church festival at Union Springs on the 4th of July. The Church began the investigation soon afterwards, as many of the victims vomited blood and narrowly escaped death. But Courtney swore out a warrant and had J. H. Robertson arrested for the offense and taken before a Justice of the Peace, just as the Church investigation was about to reach a climax in the arrest of Courtney himself.

The Early Birds.—The Pioneer Rowing Club seems to be testing the value of the proverb of the early bird, for already it has a crew in training for the Thanksgiving Day Regatta. The crew is comprised of the same men who represented the club on the Fourth of July, L. C. White, bow, R. Crowley, R. C. Lyne and John Sullivan, stroke. They were out for a practice spin on Sunday afternoon, and received considerable praise from an old Thames orsman who was of the crowd on the bridge that watched them row the half mile to the mail dock. They showed a great improvement over their form in July, and with proper training will make a fine race in November. Lyne has abandoned some old and not valuable tricks, and will soon be almost faultless in his style. If White would slide up a little more and reach less he would conform more to the style of his comrades and help the boat along many lengths in a mile. Mr. Crowley, though the most conscientious of oarsmen, needs a little coaching. He shows much improvement, however, and as he never shirks his work will be a valuable member of the crew on the day of the race. The four rowed in good time on Sunday, and kept the boat on an even keel right through the choppy water. They got a very creditable pace on their craft, and by their exhibition did much to strengthen the confidence of their club that if beaten on Thanksgiving Day they will be very far from being disgraced.

The Ariel Club.—Charles Lipp, President of the Ariel Club, states that on Thanksgiving day his Club will be represented in the race for the Breeder and Sportsman's cup. The Ariel Club will use the paper shell now owned by the St. George Rowing Club of Oakland. The boat is one of the best on the coast, and if the Ariel four fail to win in her it will not be through any handicap in boats. Fred Smith, Watkins and the Branch brothers will in all probability represent the Ariel Club. This would be a strong crew, but if the Pioneer crew continue to improve, will hardly win the championship. The Pioneer four will be under the disadvantage, however, of training half the time with a substitute for Louis White, whose business will keep him out of town at intervals. Hopes are entertained by the Ariel Club that the Alerts of Vallejo can be prevailed on to take part in the Thanksgiving Day regatta. So far the Vallejo oarsmen have not indicated their determination to compete with the Metropolitan Clubs.

Fell Through as Usual.—The Golden Gate Club is either very unfortunate or fainthearted in making matches. For some time the Golden Gate Club was anxious to arrange a match in lap-streak boats with the Ariel Club. Large stakes were talked of. The Ariel Club rather dodged the match, but the persistency of the Golden Gate champions proved too much for the prudent oarsmen, and last week they announced their intention of taking up the gauntlet. A meeting of the rivals was held on Long Bridge last Sunday, but the air of that resort had its usual depressing effect, and the negotiations fell through. The Golden Gate champions wanted to make the match for $100, while the other side would think of nothing less than $250 or $500. It is whispered that if the Golden Gate men had set their heart on a $1,000 race the Ariels would have prescribed $250 as the only acceptable figure, and *vice versa*.

Eastern Comments.—The *Turf, Field and Farm* furnishes the following paragraph from its correspondent here relative to rowing in California:

"It is quite probable that the various rowing clubs will hold a consultation with a view of getting up a regatta for next Thanksgiving Day. The success of the last Fourth of July races has considerably stimulated our representative scullers, and they may thereby be said to be experiencing a boom. The sport has been dormant for the past two years, but lately a certain interest has been manifested that bids fair to end in a number of races between rival crews and ambitious single scullers. I have already announced in this column that a valuable cup would be offered for competition between crews. The race, which is open to the State, is to be rowed in best-and-best boats, over a three-mile course, with a turn. It would certainly be a feature if the outside clubs could be induced to participate, as both the Vallejo and the Stockton Clubs are reported as having skilled manipulators of the oars."

Hanlan and Ross.—The Boston *Herald* remarks that Hanlan's characterization of Ross as a coward does not appear to be relished much by boating men of Boston, and some of them go so far as to say that perhaps the boot fits the other leg. It is urged that, if there has been no race between these worthies the last two years, the fault is not that of the New Brunswick sculler, but rather that of Hanlan himself. Ross has done all he could to bring about a race, and Hanlan, it is contended, has been glad enough, on any pretext, to escape having one.

Holmes, the amateur champion sculler of America, will retire from regatta competition this year.

The Golden Gate Rowing Club contemplates several improvements in its boat-house.

The Pioneer Boat Club held a special meeting last Sunday, and authorized Messrs. White, Crowley, Lyne and Sullivan, to represent the Club in the Thanksgiving Day races.

The racing crew of the steamer Ranger, now anchored at Mare Island, is ready to row any six men in Vallejo a boat race three miles straight away, or with a turn, for from $100 to $300 a side.

The old boat in which Dan Leahy rowed so many races and made such remarkable time, has come to grief. Rob Crowley while taking a spin in her last Sunday came in collision with one of Sam Vincent's sloops, and both Robert and Samuel mourn the collision. There is about half a foot of the shell missing, and the side of the sloop looks as if she had passed the Egyptian batteries at Fort Mex.

## YACHTING.

### THE CUTTERS BEATEN.

Cutters have not fared well of late. The little American cat boat Gleam beat a lot of them on English waters the other day. Then in the match of the Eastern and New York Club, run off Marblehead, the cutters Oriwa and Maggie were both beaten in their classes by American sloops, one in the first and the other in the second class. Both the Gracie and Fanny beat the Oriwa; and the Vixen and Hera beat the Maggie. This was on the 14th. Then on the 15th another race was sailed in which the New York sloop Vixen outsailed the much-vaunted cutter Maggie in a thirty-mile race at Marblehead, the cutter being outsailed from start to finish, both to windward and down the wind. The course was fifteen miles dead to windward, and return. The wind was light during the weather work but increased somewhat on the run home. The water was smooth for the whole course and the weather extremely fine. The contest was a perfectly fair one, the boats keeping together and having the same wind throughout. The result proves conclusively that in a fair sailing breeze the Maggie, whose reputation is that of the best fifteen-tonner that ever flew a racing flag in British waters, is no match for the Vixen, the best boat of her size in American waters.

The wind was very light and the sea smooth. Mr. Lawrence, the owner of the Vixen, having been recalled to New York by business engagements, the Vixen was under the charge of Mr. J. Frederick Tams, and on board to assist in sailing her was Captain Haff, of the sloop Fanny, and some of his crew. On board of the Maggie were ex-Commodore Peabody, of the Eastern Yacht Club, Mr. O. Goddard, the measurer of that club, and other friends of her owner, Mr. Warren. Both boats were about the same length on the water line and the match was boat against boat without time allowance. Much money was wagered on the result at the club-house, previous to the boats leaving the harbor, many enthusiastic cutter advocates being of the opinion that in the race the Maggie had been purposely held back, while the New Yorkers were firm in their confidence in the Vixen, which had never yet disappointed them, and they were willing to put their money on her to any extent. As the two yachts reached in to the westward it soon became apparent that the Vixen in light weather was the faster boat. She not only forereached on the Maggie, but held a better wind, and each moment the gap between them grew wider. The direction of the match was in charge of all the members of the Eastern Yacht Club. From the accounts in the Eastern papers it seems the crew on the cutter were demoralized by their beating and did not handle their sails well. The Vixen beat the Maggie 19 minutes. Now, we shall be interested in reading why this was, as the cutter advocates will, of course, say it was anything rather than the other was fastest. They may say it was the light winds, but as they gloried over the Oriwa a few days before, sailing in light winds through a crowd of sloops, they cannot stand on that; especially as the Oriwa was badly beaten when a good breeze came.

### FLYING STARTS.

Several clubs have this year, says Forest and Stream, conceded the necessity of reforming our slothful methods of starting by shortening the periods of graze to cross. Where ten minutes has been the custom the period has been reduced to five as a first step, and in the East anchor starts are becoming the rule to put more life and smartness in the initial portion of the race. Quite a number of slow skippers have found themselves handicapped in consequence of the change to five minutes, and some are inclined to lay the blame to the limited period. It is, however, due to the want of tact displayed, for most yachts are in the habit of knocking about without aim before the start and without thought of what is in store. Naturally they get "left." It is just this kind of baby's play we wish to see brought to a stop by the flying start to one gun after a preparatory signal has given all hands a warning to look out for a position. There is no reason why yachts should be excused from displaying the same amount of acumen at the start as in any other portion of the race, or it might properly be asked that bad seamanship at any time in the race should be met with the same tender consideration shown at the start.

Our present methods do not fit the rest of the race. If seamanship and judgment enter into the result in one part of the match, they should in another, and it is a sop to the clumsy and slothful that an excuse is made for them at the start. The only time a one-gun start can work really unfairly is when the elements step in to mar the skipper's plans. But a calm or too light airs work just the same harm throughout the race, and no legitimate ground exists for exempting the start from accidents to which the whole course is liable and yet receives no such exemption. A yacht becalmed five minutes after five miles has been sailed receives no allowance, yet the damage to her chances are not a bit different than if becalmed the same after the gun has been given to start. This is a very plain matter, and we have no doubt that in time our starts will partake of the life and snap to be witnessed in matches abroad. Cutting down starts are much to be preferred to the unfair and slipshod ten minutes hitherto observed by the slow fashion set by one of the older clubs in which smart seamanship has ever been held too lightly.

## A MODEL SCHOONER.

To show what fine yachts they are building in Boston waters, we give a brief description of a new schooner launched this month by D. J. Lawler of Chelsea, Mass., for Wm. J. Weld, and called the Gitana. Length over all, 109 ft.; on load line 92 ft. 9 in.; beam, 20 ft. 6 in.; depth of hold, 10 ft. and 11 ft. draught. Keel of white oak 15 in., sided at center, tapering to 6 in. at stem and 5 in. at heel. Width across bottom amidships 6 in., with slight taper towards ends. Frames spaced 22 in. between centers. Sided at floors 7 in. and 5 in. at head; molded 10 in. at floors, 7 in. at first futtock, and 4 in. at head. Keelson of oak, sided 16 in. in center, tapering to 6 in. at ends, and secured with 1¼-in. composition bolts. Clamps are 78 ft. long, two strakes 3 and 2¾ in. thick, bolted with ¾-in. yellow metal. Garboards and lower strakes of oak, 3 in. tapering up to 2 in., and at boodends 2 in. thick. The frame is thoroughly kneed throughout, all fastenings of copper and composition, no iron being used for that purpose in the hull. Ceiling of selected yellow pine 3 in. thick amidships, tapering to 2 in. at ends. Plank in long lengths of 80 feet. Wales of oak, 5x3 in.; bottom plank of oak 2½ in. thick, and deck 3¾-in. square white pine. Stanchions of locust, rail of white oak, and fittings of mahogany. The schooner carries 60 tons of lead ballast, 15 of which are outside on the keel. Accommodations consist of ladies' saloon aft 14x12 ft., finished in oak and cherry, Queen Anne style, with berths for six. Forward of this the companion way, then the main saloon, 18 ft. square, finished in solid mahogany and supplied with tile fireplace and grand piano. A door on the starboard hand leads to Mr. Weld's private room, 10x10 ft., finished in polished ash and cherry, with bath-room and conveniences attached. On the port hand, opening into the main saloon is the passageway forward, leading into the captain's room, icehouse, state-rooms for passengers, and galley and pantry. The forecastle contains eleven berths and is neatly furnished throughout. Eight tanks for water, holding 2,200 gallons for a long cruise.

## A MOSQUITO RACE.

Last September a race of small yachts was sailed on this bay under the auspices of the San Francisco Yacht Club. It was the best race of the season, and very great interest was taken in it. This was the first race of the kind here, but it is to be repeated next month—schooners, sloops, plungers, yawls, or boats of any rig can enter. They must not be larger than thirty-five feet long on deck, or shorter than fifteen feet. Any boat, whether belonging to a club or not, or whether in trade or not, can come in. No entrance fee is charged, and the Club furnishes plenty of prizes, two or three to each class. The boats are divided up into classes, with no time allowances. Each five feet forms a class. That is, boats between 20 and 25 feet form one class, and above 25 and less than 30 feet form another class. Prizes are for each class; no boat in one class competing with a boat in another. The course is a short one and does not go out into the channel where there is any rough water; but it will take about two or three hours to go around. Among other things the whitehall boats will be represented. No doubt a couple of dozen of these will go in, but they will be under sail of course. Boats will be confined to plain working canvas, no light sails being allowed. The object of this is to prevent some persons with more money than others from outfitting their boats specially for the race. The regatta will probably be sailed on September 9th, or if not on the following Saturday. Upwards of fifty boats will be in the race, and it will be well worth seeing.

YACHTING ETIQUETTE.—At Newport, Rhode Island, where the yacht squadrons are together, the "Commodores" of the New York and Boston Yacht Clubs are engaged in a go-as-you-please match of "commodoring." The Commodore of the Eastern Yacht Club writes to the Commodore of the New York Yacht Club that he, the Commodore of the Eastern Club, will have the honor of saluting the flag of the New York Yacht Club. The Commodore of the New York Yacht Club informs the Commodore of the Eastern Club that he will have the honor of returning the salute at four bells. And these important documents between the respective commodores are carried to and fro by boats and boats' crews, and the salutes are fired and returned and heard by the respective commodores in full uniform on their quarter-decks, and all the commodores feel themselves almost real commodores. "For it's the young navee of our jeunesse dorée whose praise our elite doth loudly chant."

The Bohemian Yacht Club is to be formally opened on September 2d.

It is getting on now towards the end of the season, which has been a very uneventful one in all respects.

The new yacht building by Turner for the Spreckels Brothers is all in frame so that her shape can be seen. She will soon be planked up and will be ready for use before very many weeks.

A yacht in racing has a perfect right to luff to prevent another passing her to windward, but must not bear away to prevent her passing to leeward—the lee side being considered that on which the leading vessel carries her boom.

A member of a yacht club owning a part of any uncalled yacht, and carrying the club flag, is the person who is responsible that the other owners shall respect and obey the regulations of the club, so long as the signal shall be carried on her.

The regatta for the big yachts, about which there has been more or less talk for some weeks, has been given up. The gentleman who was arranging for it spent a great deal of time and talk in trying to get all to agree, but was unable to get sufficient representation for the race.

## ATHLETICS.

THE HANDICAPS OF THE FALL MEETING.—In the list of Olympic Club events for September 23d, published in last week's issue, two events did not appear (probably the fault of the printer). The events omitted are very important ones, being 100 and 220 yards, both handicaps, and open to all amateurs. They are favorite distances with all novices, and the competitors in each event will probably be comprised of almost all competing athletes of the day. As R. S. Haley is still anxious to run 100 yards for a record he is not likely to start in the handicap, and the honor of being scratchman will doubtless grace the shoulders of some other ambitious printer. Sime is away; Doolan does not expect to enter. This will be a grand opportunity for Hawes. He claims to be a first class amateur, and no doubt thinks he can do 10½ with very little preparation. If the handicapper is of the same opinion, Hawes will be again able to say that he started from scratch. But the handicapper must be very careful. There is more than one in this vicinity capable of disputing the honors with Hawes.

AN EXHIBITION AT THE MECHANICS' FAIR.—There is a proposition before the Olympic Club to give an exhibition in the Mechanics' Pavilion before the Fair closes. The club would not be under any expense, and could undoubtedly get up an evening's entertainment at short notice that would sustain its past reputation as a gymnastic and athletic club. Since the meeting in the old Pavilion on Mission and Eighth streets, in June of 1881, the club has not been able to organize a tug-of-war team that had sand enough to meet all comers on equal terms. Let them gather themselves together, now, if there are enough of them that have the requisite courage, select a representative team, and show the old members of the original San Francisco Olympic Club that the club of the present day has not degenerated.

William Alkin, the well known chicken fancier, has taken possession of the premises 846 Howard street, where he has a ball court, the special attraction being the hand ball games that are played there every Sunday.

Captain Webb, who achieved the feat of swimming from England to France at Dover Straits, is giving exhibitions in this country. On Tuesday last, at Boston, he won a match of $1,000 and the championship of the world, from Thomas Rule, the champion short-distance swimmer of America.

## BICYCLING.

HOW A LITERARY MAN KEEPS WELL.—I live in the country; my general health is and has been good—that is to say I have never had any serious illness—but I am a writer by profession; my "way of life," as Dr. Jaeger says his was before he gave his attention to gymnastics and woolen clothing is "sitting," and for years I have suffered from occasional bilious headaches, which, although not very severe, were sufficiently acute to stop all literary work—sometimes for two days in succession—while they lasted. As I am very abstemious, never walk less than four or five miles every day, and faithfully observe the maxim of "early to bed and early to rise," I concluded that my headaches were constitutional, and under the belief that I should never get rid of them, bore the trouble as I best could. It did not occur to me that the two or three cigars a day that I was in the habit of smoking could do me any harm, or that, with more exercise, I should have better health. But it came to pass that some three months ago I abandoned smoking and bought a tricycle. I was led to give up smoking by reading an article in Knowledge, by Dr. Muir Brown, on the "Effects of Smoking." One of the observations particularly struck me. Replying to the argument that smoking is good because it checks waste of tissue, he observed that that is precisely the reason why smoking is bad, and that the only possession which it is a man's duty to waste is his body, new tissue being in every respect better than old. The tricycle made up this direction. It wasted tissue. You can get more exercise for an hour's tricycling, and with less fatigue, than by three hours' walking. There is an exhilaration about it, too, that a pedestrian never knows, and which can only be compared to that enjoyed by riding a good horse. As for perspiring, you perspire enough, especially if the day be warm, to satisfy Dr. Jaeger's most rigid requirements, and make your flesh as hard as the hide of a German soldier after two years' experience. When I gave up my cigars and took to tricycling, I had no idea of curing my headaches. But they are cured. I have hardly had a headache since, and I eat almost twice as much as I used to eat. I sleep well, and my general health could not easily be better. In conclusion, let me recommend all my literary brethren who are conscious of not taking sufficient exercise, all whose muscles are flabby, livers torpid, and nights restless, to try tricycling and drop smoking and any other habit which may tend to check waste of tissue, and retard that rapid renewal of the body which is the condition of physical soundness.

THE FIFTY-MILE CONTEST IN ENGLAND.—In our last issue we gave the results of the English Bicycle Union's championship races of 1883 for one, five and twenty-five miles. The fifty-mile race, which was the last of the four events, took place July 29th, on the new Crystal Palace Grounds. There were eighteen entries, of which four did not start, and seven stopped at various distances before the finish. Seven men ran the full distance inside of 3 hours and 23 minutes, and were entitled to medals, and six of these beat the previous amateur record, which was 3 hours 23 minutes and 50 and two-fifth seconds. The winner was the Hon. Ion Keith-Falconer, whose ride of 994 miles from Land's End to John O'Groat's House, inside of thirteen days, we chronicled a few weeks since. His time for the fifty miles was 3 hours 48 minutes 55 and one-fifth seconds.

A GREAT TWENTY-MILE PERFORMANCE.—Another wonderful performance took place upon the same track on the 27th of July, when H. L. Cortis made the attempt to ride twenty miles within the hour. The weather was favorable, there being not a breath of wind, and the task was accomplished in 59 minutes 28 and one-fifth seconds. The rider kept on, and when the pistol fired had covered 297 yards more. This is likely to remain the record for some time to come, unless beaten in the twenty-mile race, which was to take place August 3d, between Cortis and Keith-Falconer, of which we have not yet received the report. This was to be Cortis' last appearance upon the path, as he was to be carried upon the 3d, and to start for Australia on the 17th of August.

Philadelphia proposes to make a bicycling tournament one of the leading features of the bicentennial anniversary celebration. The response to the proposition have been so enthusiastic, that it now appears probable that four hundred wheelmen will participate. Since the Park commissioners threw open Fairmount Park for the use of wheelmen, the exercise has acquired an extraordinary impetus in that city.

## BASE BALL.

### THE RENOS AND NIANTICS.

The match on Sunday last between the Reno and Niantic Clubs drew but a slight attendance, as the beautiful weather sent a great many of our pleasure seekers across the bay where the swimming baths are the main attraction. It was a well-contested game and until the very last inning, but after a good display of batting and fielding the Renos won the game by 8 to 7 points. Following is the score:

RENOS.

| | T.B. | R. | B.H. | P.O. | A. | E. |
|---|---|---|---|---|---|---|
| Barnes, 1st b.......... | 3 | 0 | 1 | 9 | 0 | 1 |
| Swanton, s. f.......... | 5 | 1 | 1 | 1 | 1 | 1 |
| Lake, l. f............. | 5 | 1 | 0 | 1 | 0 | 0 |
| Riordan, 3d b......... | 5 | 2 | 1 | 0 | 0 | 1 |
| Start, 2d b............ | 5 | 2 | 1 | 2 | 2 | 1 |
| Cadogan, c. f......... | 5 | 1 | 1 | 0 | 0 | 0 |
| McKinney, p.......... | 5 | 1 | 1 | 0 | 13 | 0 |
| Creegan, c............ | 5 | 0 | 0 | 13 | 4 | 2 |
| Hamilton, s. s........ | 3 | 0 | 1 | 0 | 0 | 0 |
| Totals............. | 45 | 8 | 7 | 26 | 22 | 6 |

NIANTICS.

| | T.B. | R. | B.H. | P.O. | A. | E. |
|---|---|---|---|---|---|---|
| Emerson, 3d b........ | 5 | 1 | 0 | 0 | 3 | 0 |
| Donahue, s. s........ | 4 | 2 | 0 | 0 | 2 | 2 |
| Fine, c............... | 4 | 0 | 0 | 11 | 1 | 5 |
| Inzell, l. f........... | 4 | 2 | 2 | 0 | 0 | 0 |
| Arnold, c. f.......... | 4 | 0 | 3 | 1 | 0 | 1 |
| Sweeney, p........... | 4 | 1 | 1 | 3 | 10 | 0 |
| F. Carroll, c. l....... | 4 | 0 | 0 | 0 | 0 | 1 |
| Robinson, 1st b...... | 4 | 0 | 0 | 10 | 0 | 3 |
| Fogarty, 3d b........ | 4 | 1 | 1 | 2 | 1 | 2 |
| Totals............. | 37 | 7 | 6 | 27 | 17 | 15 |

| Innings | 1 | 2 | 3 | 4 | 5 | 6 | 7 | 8 | 9 |
|---|---|---|---|---|---|---|---|---|---|
| Renos | 0 | 0 | 0 | 4 | 3 | 0 | 0 | 1 | 0—8 |
| Niantics | 0 | 2 | 1 | 0 | 0 | 4 | 0 | 0 | 0—7 |

Earned runs—Renos 1. Home runs—Sweeney, Inzell and Riordan. Three-base hit—McElroy. Two-base hit—Cadogan. Bases on balls—Niantics 3. Struck out—Renos 6, Niantics 11. Left on base—Renos 7, Niantics 3. First base on errors—Renos 5, Niantics 2. Passed balls—Fine 1, Creegan 1. Wild pitches—Sweeney 1, McElroy 3. Umpire—J. Carroll of the Haverlys. Scorer—J. Hennessey. Time of game—Two hours and a half.

## FISH.

### THE OREGON SALMON SEASON.

An Astoria correspondent of the *Oregonian* says that had the salmon fishing boom lasted five days longer, the pack would have been the largest on record. It will not fall short of $950,000 cases, and the fish put up have been fine and fat. The average catch per boat was forty fish per day for the last ten days. On Friday night one cannery got 2,340 fish from 38 boats, which is over 60 fish to the boat. Of these, of course, one-third goes to the cannery for use of nets and boat, and the other two-thirds are bought at 60 cents, although 70 was paid to the men who had boats and nets of their own. This left a fisherman $24 as his day's work, most of whom divide equally with the boat pullers, as some of them got tired of paying their boat pullers by the month.

The cost of nets is the greatest expense attendant upon this business. There is hardly a cannery which has less than 30 boats, which cost on an average $250. To make a net takes two hundred and ten pounds of Irish twine, worth $1.25 per pound, making $262.50 for twine; the ropes for this net cost $70 more, and the labor of making the net cost 22½ cents per fathom, or $130 for the net, so that the total cost of a net averages about $450. At the end of a season this net is useless and cannot be sold in one case out of a hundred. Kinney's establishment has about 90 boats. Hence his nets cost him over $4,000 for a single season before he can make a single fish. Everything is expense at the start. The whole river with its 1,000 boats caught only enough to pack 30,000, or less than 1,000 cases to each of thirty-five canneries during the month of April.

The fishery law of Oregon is in need of great amendment, and even then it is of no good unless more rigidly enforced than at present. Now all the cannery boats are laid up, yet there are now not less than 300 boats on the river catching salmon to pickle in barrels. To punish these fellows would be uphill work, as they would all swear if caught that they were catching them for their family use.

Again, the law works wrong, because its dates are wrong. The close time is from March 1 to April 1, whereas it should be from March 1 to April 30 or 25. Let the law be changed in this respect and let it be properly enforced so as to punish any man who runs at that time, and the fisherman would make as much, while the canneries would make more. Meanwhile what fish did get into the river would be undisturbed, and being strong, fat fish, could work their way up to their hatching grounds on the Spokane or Umatilla rivers, or even to the Malad or Pen d'Oreille, without fear of molestation. This would save the expense of a Government hatchery on the river. With a sea on extending from April 20th to August 10th, the product would be as large, while the supply would hold out longer.

Most of the Chinese laborers employed at the canneries have been paid off and are leaving for Portland. Some of them will get work on the railroads and a few will go up the Columbia and Snake to work the bars for fine gold. Astoria looks lively and there appears to be plenty of money in circulation.

THE BOSS FISHERMAN.—A number of mill boys stopped along the flume at China Switch, in Iron Cañon. They were after fish, and landed several handsome trout and pike from Chico Creek. Doubtless they would have brought home enough fish to supply the town had they not had the life almost scared out of them by a monster snake, which is described by Cado Sweepson, a colored man, as being eight feet in length and as thick as a man's leg. Cado said the reptile was taking his ease on some rocks along the stream, and was catching fish for his breakfast. The snake would apparently peer sharply into the stream, and suddenly dart into the water. When he came out he would bring a large fish. The men made no effort to kill the snake, which was of a crimson color. His snakeship was the boss fisherman of the day, and his neighborhood will be given a wide berth in the future. All the men who were in the fishing party belong to the Good Templars, so the above is a temperance snake story. A sober man can't have 'em in his boots.—*Butte Record.*

A NOVEL EXPERIMENT.—Mr. Henry House of Corinne, Utah, has sent to New York for two barrels of seedling oysters, with the intention of making an attempt to cultivate them in the Great Salt Lake. These two barrels contain about six thousand seedling oysters, and the cost, together with freight charges, would be about $60. This is the first attempt made to plant oysters in the Great Salt Lake, and no doubt the experiment will have a satisfactory result, provided a proper feed for the oysters can be found where the minute animal life upon which the young oysters feed is plentiful. The oysters will live until they reach Utah, and the water of the Great Salt Lake is without doubt suited to them. In a year's time the young oysters, if they do live and thrive, will be fit for food, and, it is said, should the experiment result successfully, many more will be planted next season.

There are 278 species of fishes found in California waters.

A great many tom cod and smelt are being caught from Long Bridge.

Arizona has three Fish Commissioners and appropriates $500 for expenses.

It is a bottom fact that fish will take a worm almost any time in preference to a fly.

The fishing in Lake Independence is very good; the trout average one-half pound each.

In Austin Creek there are lots of trout, but there are lots of fishermen too. Still good sport may be had there.

They have a $300 fine, with an alternative of three months in jail, for fishing with giant powder in Arizona.

At the Lakes San Andreas and Pilarcitos the fishing is very poor; not that there is a scarcity of trout, but they will not bite.

Speaking of nomenclature of fishes, one fish has received nineteen different names within a few hundred miles on the Atlantic Coast.

Last Sunday a party of gentlemen went to Raccoon Straits in the barge Restless and caught twenty to thirty fish each —several rock-cod weighed five pounds.

At Gualala a gentleman caught 250 trout in one day and sent a mess of two or three dozen to Mr. J. H. W. Riley, of this city. Many of these fish were from eight to ten inches in length.

Anglers in Montana predict that in a very few years trout will all disappear from the valley streams, owing to the immense numbers carried out into irrigating ditches and thence into the fields.

Intermittent streams and the great heat has killed many fish, but a few trout are found in the northern tributaries of the Gila. The Colorado produces a hump-backed sucker of soft meat and insipid flavor. Carp are being introduced in the Territory.

There is not as good fishing in Weber Lake this season as in former years, but then anglers cannot complain, as the trout make up in weight what they lack in numbers, those that have been caught average one pound each and take the spoon quicker than the fly.

The "Painted Sea Trout" is not at all common in the San Francisco market, but becomes more abundant in higher latitudes. It is often beautifully colored when fresh with blotches of bright green upon a dark brown ground. These blotches become purple when the specimen is placed in alcohol.

It is stated that in consequence of the cessation of hydraulic mining and the consequent absence of debris, the streams tributary to the Sacramento are gradually being restocked with fish, some fine specimens of good size and flavor having been caught up as far as Folsom on the American River.

Fish-culture has become one of the laws of our civilization, and is to be, if it is not already, one of the fixed industries of the country on the same plans as sheep husbandry or any other legitimate calling. The spirit of the same laws which now protect the sheep-fold, the pasture and the cattle-yard, should extend to the pond, lake or stream.

There is a species of fish locally known as "hardmouth" in Austin Creek, although they are very like suckers. They will walk off with bait specially intended for trout, and will do it with great regularity too. A man would spend an hour in catching a little bait in the shape of grass-hoppers, and the hardmouth will have the hard cheek to eat them in twenty minutes, if one is not careful.

Rock bass are abundant in bays from Point Conception southward, especially at San Diego, where they are taken in seines, and also with hook and line from the wharves. It is not found in deep water nor about islands. It feeds chiefly on crustacea and squid. It reaches a length of 15 inches and a weight of from two to three pounds, and is considered an excellent food fish. This species is prettily spotted all over with small round purple spots, and across the body, overlying the spots, run several irregular darker transverse bands.

The red-banded trout of this State (the *salmo iridea*) is called by the Indians "syoo-loot." The band extends the whole length of the body and about as wide as one-fourth the depth of the fish. In the lower McCloud River the band is visible in June, and continues to grow deeper colored until the middle of August, when it entirely disappears, and does not show itself in September and October. At the head-waters of the Sacramento the golden band is bright the year round, and the trout are very abundant and easily taken with fly or bait.

As we predicted, last Sunday proved to be an exceptionally good day for bay-fishing, owing to the small tides on the first quarter of the moon. Thousands of fish were caught, and from Fort Point to the rivers fishermen could be seen in boats and on the wharves drawing the finny tribe from its natural element. There were no disappointed fishermen, and all had a greater or smaller string to show as the result of the day's sport. This season salt water fish have been more plentiful than for many previous years.

In the early part of the month the late Fish Commissioner, Mr. B. B. Redding, made an arrangement with the canning companies and fishermen that the latter should patrol the rivers during the close season where illicit salmon fishing was likely to be carried on. These agreements have been complied with, as fishing boats patrolling the rivers nightly. A number of parties have been caught violating the laws, and in every instance their nets were destroyed and the fish were thrown back into the river. No arrests were made owing to the difficulty of obtaining a conviction in the counties bordering on the rivers.

The International Fish Exhibition to be held in London in May, 1883, is to be under the patronage of the Queen of England, the President thereof being no less a personage than the Prince of Wales. The exhibition will continue until November, 1883. The United States will have a good display, and be well represented. The Hon. Spencer F. Baird, of the United States Fish Commission, will probably be one chosen to go from this country. It is to be hoped that the Pacific Coast will be represented, even if it be on a limited scale. There are many fishes that would form an interesting addition to the general exhibit, among them being the pomponeau, the rock cod, the tomcod, the mountain trout, our various species of salmon and salmon trout, and especially the Dolly Varden, that possesses now a world-wide reputation.

## ANSWERS TO CORRESPONDENTS.

SAN FRANCISCO, August 2, 1882.

EDITOR BREEDER AND SPORTSMAN—DEAR SIR : Please answer the following questions : 1st. Did the running mare Mayflower, by Norfolk, out of Hennie Farrow, ever win or run a race ? if so, please give some of her performances. 3d. Also, give about six of Monday's principal victories.

SUBSCRIBER.

ANSWER.—Mayflower was by imported Eclipse. We cannot find any record of her running in races. As Joe Hooker was foaled when she was four years old, it is not likely that she ran as a three-year-old.

At Jerome Park, Spring meeting, 1869, Monday won a purse, free for all, dash of a mile, beating Luther, Onward, Dot, Enchantress, Richmond and Mittie. Time, 1:45¼. At the same meeting he won a purse, 1½ miles, for all ages, beating Loadstone, Satinstone and Onward. Time, 3:11. When we have more leisure we will give all of Monday's races. The Racing Calendar was not published while he was running.

## POULTRY.

### THOROUGHBRED POULTRY.

It is to be regretted that there are so many among whom the impression seemingly prevails that pure-bred poultry is not more so, if as profitable, as that of the mongrel class, and that in consequence it is not to be indulged in by those who can afford to keep it, without any reference to gain being derived therefrom. No more fallacious notion could be entertained, as the many thousands can testify whose experiences range all the way from the common dunghill up through the different stages of improvement, to the highest type of our present pure-bred poultry. We have now our non-sitters, and our varieties best adapted where meat is the object, with which, in either line, the old-fashioned fowls are not to be compared.

Throughout all periods of the world's history there have been those seemingly content to not only live in the shade of progress, but to hold fast to the old-fashioned notions and ideas, to the utter exclusion of anything in the line of advancement, and it is for this class more particularly that this article is intended. To may tell them that horses are bred to certain points in order to accomplish an object— the greatest speed, endurance, strength, or some other valuable quality, and that they are far ahead of the low-bred scrub as can well be imagined; that the skill of the breeder has developed characteristics in our cows that make them of inestimable value as compared with our common stock, and perhaps they will concede that a part of this is true, but chickens—oh, that is a different thing ! How readily they present the very (to them) exhaustive argument that a chicken is a chicken, and that is all there is about it. Well, that is all very true; a chicken is a chicken, but in the same sense that a horse is a horse; and no one can fail to see the great contrast between the finely-bred race-horse and the scrub. There is just as great a difference between fowls of our improved varieties and the old-fashioned dunghill, as in the case of the horse, but it is a little less generally noticed from the fact that a horse ministers to the wants of man in such a capacity as to bring him more under observation.

When improvement is effected, whether in horse, chicken, or other animals, several good things are brought out— beauty, symmetry, fineness and gloss of hair or plumage, greater nerve, force, endurance—all these seem to come together in the blooded stock. Ten years ago scrub fowls were vastly more common than at the present time, and although the people of this coast are not yet apace with those in the East and West, it is a matter of congratulation that the past two years have witnessed gigantic strides in poultry culture. The most enterprising farmers have cleared out the stock of their forefathers, and now keep only the improved breeds; others more conservative have introduced pure bred males, which has resulted in improvement in size, health and productiveness. If, then, the addition of a little good blood works such a vast improvement, why will the introduction of all pure blood not improve it still more ? Excellence is what we want. How much better it is to have a pure breed of poultry that excels in something, as a Jersey cow does in producing rich milk. —*Rural Press.*

AN EXPERIMENT IN BREEDING.—Mr. Tegetmeier, one of the most noted of English breeders and writers on poultry matters, some three or four years ago took some very fine-feathered brown-red game hens, and placed with them a full-breasted Dorking cock. The hens were given the fullest liberty, and allowed to sit in an entirely natural manner. They were not cooped even after hatching out their young, but brooded under any shelter they chose. With the exception of a little custard made of equal parts of egg and milk, the little ones were fed no soft food, and this custard for only two or three days. Just before bed time they were fed a little small wheat and cracked maize. This was given again in the morning. The chickens grew rapidly, and when they were six months old four of them were sent to the Crystal Palace show. The four birds weighed thirty-two pounds, and had never been forced in the least. They took the first and second prizes as the best table fowls on exhibition. They did not look large, their feathers were close, but they were full-breasted, and their meat solid all over. It was further found that the yield of offal was much lighter than from the large pure breeds, a seven-pound bird only giving one-fourth of a pound of offal. The game character was very predominant in color, hardness of feathers and general form, while most breeders would have supposed that the characteristics of the Houdan cock would have been present more strongly.

# THE
# Breeder and Sportsman.

PUBLISHED WEEKLY BY THE

BREEDER AND SPORTSMAN PUBLISHING CO.

THE TURF AND SPORTING AUTHORITY OF THE PACIFIC COAST.

**OFFICE, 508 MONTGOMERY STREET**
P. O. Box 1333.

*Five dollars a year; three dollars for six months; one dollar and a half for three months. Strictly in advance.*

MAKE ALL CHECKS, MONEY ORDERS, ETC., PAYABLE TO ORDER OF BREEDER AND SPORTSMAN PUBLISHING CO.

*Money should be sent by postal order, draft or by registered letter, addressed to the "Breeder and Sportsman Publishing Company, San Francisco, Cal."*

*Communications must be accompanied by the writer's name and address, not necessarily for publication, but as a private guarantee of good faith.*

JOSEPH CAIRN SIMPSON,   -   -   -   EDITOR

SAN FRANCISCO, - SATURDAY, AUGUST 26, 1882

## THE PROJECTED DRIVE IN THE WINTER TIME.

Last week we showed a few of the advantages which California presents for road driving in the Summer over the Eastern country. There are some who might question the claim which gives it such a decided preference in Spring, Summer and Autumn; not one, who had the least knowledge of the subject, who would refuse to grant that in the Winter there can be no comparison. The Eastern idea of a California Winter is a season of downpouring, and that to live in any degree of comfort a person must be amphibious. Rain from above, mud below. The terms which are in use to designate the seasons have led to the misconception. The dry is supposed to be an endless succession of arid days, the wet a sky which is continually overcast, with scarcely an interval of sunshine, gloomy, disconsolate, despondent weather, worse than an English November, the only place endurable where there are pavements and indoor amusements to occupy the leisure hours. Tell these people that December and January are counterparts of April and May, that the sun's rays are the most brilliant if even they do strike the earth at a more acute angle, that heavy overcoats are an incumbrance, and that it is the grandest time to enjoy fast driving, and they credit it to what they call California bombast.

When the rains of the late Autumn come in the East they are succeeded by frosts. The muddy roads are frozen, and there are sharp "hubs" which the noonday may soften into slush, again to be frozen. They may be frozen so hard and so little warmth in the interval from morning to evening that the hubs are worn down and the roadway is smooth. Smooth, though it is hard as a Belgian pavement, and then there are icy spots on which the horses slip and strain themselves. The change comes, and in what are termed favored localities the snow falls, and the "merry sleighbells" ring out a tintinnabulary strain. There is so great an improvement over the hubby roads that the "beautiful snow" is hailed with delight. We have fancied there was enjoyment when there were icicles hanging from moustache and eyelashes, and the horses were enveloped in hoarfrost, and their breath congealed into frozen vapor within a few feet of their quivering nostrils. Ears and cheeks frozen, fingers, though protected with heavy fur gauntlets, feeling like sticks, feet—ugh! we can realize the sensation now after eight years of relief—like the feet of a dead man, and yet with a sensitiveness acute and terrible as the pangs of torture inflicted by the merciless engines of the inquisition. The long wished-for Springtime comes at last. There is neither wheeling or sleighing, snow and mud conglomerated into a mixture in which the horses sink to their knees, and the wheels are laden from hub to felloe. After that the frost is "going out of the ground," and the bottom of the road has gone out as well.

There is little necessity to amplify the discomforts to those who have experienced them, and yet the contrast is necessary to show how greatly we are favored. With a properly graded speed-drive there are comparatively few days in the Winter when it would be unfit for use. The substratum of sand insures the most perfect drainage, and by incorporating a portion of it in the top-covering only a few hours would be required after the rain had ceased to put it in condition. That this would follow the construction of a drive in any of the localities mentioned is certain, as even the Bay District Course dries very quickly notwithstanding that the soil chosen for the top-covering has very little sand in it, and the half-mile track is in tolerably good condition soon after a rain ceases.

To our readers who have a knowledge of the Winter climate of San Francisco there is no need of a comparison with that of the East; those who are not familiar with the advantages can scarcely credit the wide difference. Not one of the drawbacks alluded to is found here. It is rare, indeed, when there are rains which last the whole of the day, and the temperature is never sufficiently low to class them as cold rains. There may be slight frosts during the Winter, never more severe than to blanch the sidewalks in the early morning, never hard enough to touch the tips of the grass-blades. There are flowers and plenty of sunshine, and rarely a day when there is more than a gentle breeze. In place of the perspiration being transformed into a coating of frost on the ends of the hairs, horses can be s''craped" and got in condition the same as in the Summer.

But all these advantages, as indulging in the health-giving recreation of road-driving, cannot be made available. Bumping over pavements, broken and uneven; bouncing about, now over slivered planks and then into pitch holes; Belgian blocks with patches sunk far below where the surface should be; cobbles, concrete, Nicholson, with now and then a patch of asphaltum; and after all of these are passed, not a furlong of road fit to drive upon.

## SANTA ROSA.

It is a pleasant sail up the bay, if even there is tribulation for those who are so ignorant as to start for Santa Rosa at half-past two post meridian. There is the fresh ocean breeze when opposite Golden Gate, and the milder air when under the lee of Tamalpais; but when the knowledge comes that those who leave the city two hours and twenty minutes later will arrive at the same time, even the picturesque scenery is somewhat tiresome. There is little satisfaction under the circumstances of watching the unloading of freight at Sonoma, and it may be called truly tiresome as the trucks jangle along the wharf at Donahue. Still there was a glorious evening to ride from the landing to Santa Rosa, and if the delay had used several hours which we hoped would be spent more in accordance with anticipations, there was no help for it, and we could only blame the obtuseness which led into the blunder.

In lieu of seeing the place on the first evening, the shadows were falling before the cars rattled away from Petaluma, and the sun had sunk many degrees below the summits of the Coast Range ere the landing was made. A race between the "bus" and the street cars ended in victory for the "diligence" which carries passengers to the Occidental Hotel, and then there was dinner none the worse for the delay. There was a little satisfaction in winning a bottle of Sonoma hock, and likewise another of Roederer, of a fellow-passenger, the wager being based on which would be the favorite in the pools in the 2:25; and as this was supplemented by capturing the "Havanas" on another simple proposition of our companion who led us into the mistake of taking the Donahue route in place of the San Rafael, the acerbity engendered by making the mistake was in a measure mollified by success in the minor matters.

Very early we were astir the following morning. The day had "broke," but the sun was not yet up when the shutters were thrown open. This was the first glance of Santa Rosa. Luckily, the window was high, and the view as nearly "birdseye" as can be obtained from the top floor of a four-story hotel. Below were roofs and branches, a wealth of verdant leaves; and the panorama disclosed a lovely scene. There were streaks of radiance mounting skyward, and directly the crest of Mount Hood was glowing in refulgence. The sun crowned it with a glory which did not require an imaginative fancy to liken it to the Gates of Paradise, portals of a sphere where there was nothing but brilliance: the fable, if it be a fable, of the fire-worshipers,—not an incongruity—as the dullest soul could scarcely fail to bend in adoration, and, with all the devotees' fervor of spirit, exclaim:

> " And see—the Sun himself! on wings
>    Of glory up the East he springs.
> Angel of Light, who, from the time
> Those heavens began their march sublime,
> Hath, first of all the starry choir,
> Trod in his Maker's steps of fire! "

But there is more than to admire the sun driving the shadows into the deep cañons and gulches of the mountains from an upper window of the Occidental; and after an early breakfast, more enjoyable from the companionship, and inevitable argument on horse matters with A. P. Whitney and Payne J. Shafter, who were making ready for the morning train, we were prepared to see Santa Rosa. Mr. Byington had a pair of greys harnessed to a barouche, and in the caller air, fairly saturated with a perfume from garden and lawn, the drive was ultra-enjoyable. There are many substantial business blocks, well built, and more pretentious than a person would expect in a town of the population of Santa Rosa. But there is a rich country on all sides to supply, and every year adds to the producers, extends the list of consumers, so that the merchants are taxed to keep pace with the increase of trade. Again we were surprised at the character of the hotels. Good buildings which present an attractive appearance and in keeping with the other portions of the town. Like a majority of California places, Santa Rosa is a village of homes. Some of them pretentious. Villas which will compare favorably with those in the larger cities, snug cottages embowered among trees, vines, shrubbery and flowers. There are some splendid drives, and early as it was in the day, McDonald avenue was sprinkled and the surface nearly as smooth as a well-kept race track. Although the course has been highly extolled by those we have heard speak of it, we were not prepared to see so fine a track as the Santa Rosa Association possesses. A mile in circuit, the shape that which meets with the highest approval, viz., the stretches parallel, connected with semicircles, each an exact quarter of a mile. Though the natural soil is not bad for the purpose, a still better material was carted upon it and a depth of eighteen inches of the coating applied. The curves are thrown up to the right angle, and with the single exception of being a trifle wavy, it can be regarded as one of the very best and fastest tracks in the State. The buildings are good, the grand stand being commodious, the stalls a good size and well built. There is a neat judges' and timers' stand of three stories, the lower a weighing room, the second for timers and reporters, the upper for the judges and clerk of the course. It is an octagon and the style of architecture pleasing; but it is on the wrong side of the track, and the judges are placed too high to get the best view of the horses. Looking down on them from such an elevation is nothing nearly so favorable for a correct knowledge of what the horses are doing as when viewed from nearly the same level. As there is only one course in California with the judges' stand on the outside of the track, Santa Rosa cannot be harshly criticised for following the nearly universal example.

The sprinkling had been so thorough that on the morning of our visit there was not much of an opportunity for fast work until the day was well advanced. The jogging, however, brought out a lot of fine-looking horses, and not one of them appeared to be the least lame or even going short. There was plenty of the peculiar cough denoting that "pinkeye" was a visitor to this genial climate as well as on the shores of the bay where the breezes are harsher, and one or two so much affected as to interfere with the training. This was the cause of Crown Point being withdrawn from the 2:25 class, and placed Director in a position he could not show his usual speed. It is certainly a singular disease. The coughing fits are so severe that there is almost strangulation, and yet the animal is never "off its feed," and many are in good spirits. The feature in the morning's exercise which attracted the most attention was a "brush" between Johnny and Vanderlynn. The horse with the dreadfully plebian name was too much for the crack green horse of the season, carrying him to breaks, and at no time seeming to be exerting himself to his fullest capacity. He is the sensation of the meeting so far, as he wound up his race by distancing the field in the first heat, and brought to a summary close a contest which it was thought before the start would be a very close one.

Our stay in the afternoon was restricted to seeing too heats in the colt-race, which were won so easily by Ned, a son of Overland, that there was scarcely a shadow of a fight. The ride home was by the San Rafael route, and was a decided improvement over the sail up the bay which entailed the loss of much time.

## EDITORIAL NOTES.

The Stanford Stake, the big three-year-old stake—so far as trotters are concerned—is to be decided the thrd Saturday in October, and the last payment of $100 is due thirty days before that date. This is coming still better for the colts which have had the pinkeye. The third Saturday being the 21st, the same date in September will be the last day when the engagement can be perfected. This will be the day before the Occident Stake is trotted, therefore there will be no disturbing influences come from that. There is scarcely a doubt that all the colts which made the second payment will stay in.

The Petaluma Fair commences Tuesday next. The great bugbear of a bad track, which has formerly been such a disastrous handicap to Petaluma being now done away with, there can be nothing lacking to make the speed department satisfactory. Had the owners of horses been aware that the course was so much of an improvement over the old, there would have been, in all probability, as full an entry list as in other places. As it stands, there are enough to insure capital sport, and if there are any breaks, other races will be substituted. In the first race, the winner of the same class, 2:50, at Santa Rosa, Huntress, will come into competition with a very strong field, and on Wednesday the 2:25 class will again try conclusions. Thursday will give another opportunity for Johnny to show his capacity, and the field he has to meet will sorely try his mettle. In it are Vanderlynn, Rowdy Boy, Marin, Frank Moscow and Exile, and notwithstanding the fine showing he made at Santa Rosa, he will be fortunate indeed should he "get away" with his competitors. All through the list there is a chance for very exciting sport, and the ease with which the trip can be made should warrant a large attendance from the city.

At the same time we would advise those who go to Petaluma, not to be led astray in taking passage on the Donahue boat in the afternoon, when their destination is Petaluma. Elsewhere it will be seen the trouble which arose from making the mistake, and though we are inclined to throw the onus of the blunder on Mr. Hicks, that does not make amends for the time lost. Trusting to his known skill as a traveler, famous for never getting left or taking the wrong route, we had implicit faith in his management, and now we scarcely know how to reconcile the balk with his well-known acumen, unless under the hypothesis that he had a scheme to carry out, which may become apparent by-and-by. It is certain that he did not have the inclination to while away the time with a game of pedro, but we will not say who got off the boat at the Sonoma landing. There was a waiving of plumes and a fluttering of perfumed handkerchiefs, but that might have been the effects of the breeze which was drawing through the straits.

The Free-for-all at the State Fair did not fill, and its place will have to be taken by something else. If Brigadier, Romero and Piedmont could be induced to put in an appearance, it would be a grand card for the Society. It may be asking too much for these two with records of 2:22 and 2:22½ to enter the lists with such an adversary as the hero of 2:17¼, and yet from all we can learn, they would come out of the contest without disgrace. With a promise of this trio to start, the Association can give a purse of magnitude enough to give the second and third a remuneration, and we shall be much pleased to hear that such an arrangement has been made.

The French Pools at times show a big margin of profit. Thus many years ago at Saratoga every $5 invested on Nickajack returned something over $1,100, and this season there have been instances of over a hundred-fold coming back to the lucky ones. There is scarcely a race that there is not a marked difference between the rates in the auction and mutuals, and a ready reckoner, with some money at command, might make his skill at ciphering bring him in a fair salary. In that case he would have to ignore all the "points" proffered, depending entirely on arithmetical calculations.

Echora comes prominently to the front now by winning the 2:25 at Santa Rosa. Del Sur, too, has shown that he is "getting at himself;" and now the hitherto intricate problem is still more complicated when the question is to designate the future winners of the class through the circuit. Crown Point two victories, Starr King and Echora each one, and Del Sur and Sweetness winners of heats. The new names are likely to involve other figures in the calculation, and Captain Smith, Honesty, Reliance, etc., leave the whole matter in a labyrinth of conjecture. This race is sure to be one of the most "open" of any on the programmes, and whoever can select the winner or winners of two consecutive races will surely be the champion vaticinator.

The state of the odds, not on the St. Leger but the stakes and purses of the State Fair, will be found on another page. The only explanation necessary, further than is given, is that there is a good chance to win some money if the acceptor only makes the right guess. More than that, those who are of an arithmetical turn of mind can invest in the books, hedge in the auction and mutual pools, so that if their calculations are correct they can make a "sure winning." Thus by investing something at the odds offered on what is likely to be the favorite, there can be supplemental purchases in the pools the contrary way, and if the whole work has been skilfully performed, and a share of luck withal, there will follow a balance on the right side of the account.

The Occident Stake, which is to be trotted on the last day of the State Fair, has five in it which have paid the last installment. These are Anteeo, Adrian, Nellie W, Bertha and Benefit. This insures a good race, and the time of trotting being three weeks off, will give the opportunity for the colts to recover from the pinkeye.

Everything is progressing favorably for the Golden Gate Fair. Never before has there been such a demand for stalls, and the prospects could not be better for a good meeting. It is almost supererogatory to say that the track will be better than it ever was before. The thorough incorporation of the material that has been added with the natural soil has made a perfect composition, and it is safe to assert that no one can find fault with that essential feature. The stalls are being renovated, and everything possible done to make it satisfactory at all points. Captain Mayhew having been installed Superitendent is a guarantee that all in that department will be satisfactory.

That California is well supplied with stallions by Almont is fully apparent from the list heretofore published, and yet there are additions to be made, as will be seen from the communication from Colusa County. The publication has effected a good purpose if even the list was incomplete, by calling out corrections from those who had a better knowledge than we possessed. When the fairs are over, we intend to publish as full a list of the stock of California (race horses and trotters) as can be obtained. As the breeders here have not published catalogues of their stock, excepting the thoroughbreds at El Arroyo and those of auction sales, the public knowledge of the stock of the State is limited. A full list will demonstrate that this State can show more really valuable animals in the trotting studs than any other in the Union, excepting perhaps Kentucky; and the stallions here will not lose in comparison with that great horse-breeding State. The same can be said of the thoroughbreds as to quality, and in numbers there will not be such a discrepancy as many think.

Princeton, Aug. 23, 1882.

Editor Breeder and Sportsman: In your list and notice of the Almonts in California, you have omitted one of the best and most highly bred of that noted strain of trotting horses—I refer to Tilton Almont, bred by Gen. Withers, and imported to this State the Fall of 1878, by Dr. Beltan of Colusa. His pedigree is as follows: By Almont, dam by Clark Chief; second dam by imp. Hooton, sire of Lulu's dam; third dam by Halcorn, by Virginian, by Sir Archie. Clark Chief by Mambrino Chief, dam Little Nora, by Downing's Messenger, grand dam Mrs. Caudle, dam of Ericsson. Tilton Almont is a large brown horse, fine style, with heavy bone, and powerful form, and has many of the characteristics of the Mambrino Chief branch of the family, of which he has a double cross. Without training he can easily trot in 2:35, and his colts, the oldest now 3 years old, are very large and fine and promise to be very speedy.

Respectfully yours, B.

# THE LATEST RACES.

## THE LOS ANGELES FAIR.

The last fair of the Sixth District Agricultural Association was not so great a success as might have been anticipated, and this result was due to the lateness of the season at which it was held, and also that sufficient preparation had not been made for a good speed programme and a creditable exhibition. This year the executive officers have shown a praiseworthy evidence of zeal in promoting the interests of the Association, in appointing a committee to solicit subscriptions in aid of the funds of the Association, and the citizens of Los Angeles heve responded liberally to the appeal, as the sum will probably amount to about $4,000. This accession to the funds will greatly strengthen the hands of the executive officers, and it is expected that the fair will in all respects be worthy of the counties represented. It will commence on the 16th of October and will last until the 21st, and the speed programme is well devised to attract entries from the owners of district horses, as well as from those of a higher type. On the first day there is a purse of $300 for the three-minute district class, and also another of $400 for the 2:38 district class, concluding with a purse of $200 for all district two-year running colts, a dash of half a mile.

On the Wednesday there is a purse of $500 for the 2:30 class, and a mile and repeat running for a purse of $250.

On the Thursday there will be a grand stock parade, and a purse of $350 for three-year-old district horses and under, with a long-distance riding match.

On Friday we find a purse of $400 for the 2:45 district class, and three-quarters of a mile dash for district runners, for a purse of $200.

On the concluding day of the meeting, there is a purse of $500, free for all; a district running race free for all, three quarters of a mile for a purse of $250, and a dash of two miles and a quarter, free for all runners, for a purse of $350. The entries to the above races close with the Secretary on Saturday, September 30th. Mr. F. J. Barretto, of Downey, is President of the Association; Mr. E. T. Spence is the Treasurer, and Mr. R. H. Hewitt is the Secretary and Superintendent, while the Executive Committee is composed of Messrs. Wm. Niles, L. Lichtenberger and F. J. Barretto. The programme is a good one; the exhibition of stock and produce promises well, and there is every appearance that the fair will be a great success.

## TROTTING AT THE EAST.

At Rochester, on the 17th inst., there were two special races which resulted in the division of the purses, in the following order: Limber Jack first, Fuller second, Bessie M. third, Warrior fourth; time, 2:23, 2:21½, 2:21, 2:22. Following is a summary of the special stallion race: Santa Claus, 3, 1, 1, 1; Black Cloud, 1, 2, 2, 2; Jerome Eddy, 2, 3, 3, 3; Von Arnim, drawn; time, 2:21¼, 2:25, 2:19, 2:20¼.

At Utica, on the same day, in the unfinished pacing race, in which six heats had already been decided, Flora Belle having taken two heats, Buffalo Girl two, Lucy two, and Gem one, Flora Belle won, with Gem second, Lucy third, Buffalo Girl fourth; time, 2:14¼, 2:15¼, 2:19¼, 2:18, 2:18¾, 2:18¾, 2:18¾. The 2:23 class race Captain Lewis won, Barbara Patchen second, Allegheny Boy third, Barrett fourth; time, 2:25¼, 2:25¼, 2:24¼. On the 18th, the unfinished race in the 2:26 class was won by Cornelia; time, 2:21¼, 2:24½. The special purse was won by Edwin Thorne, Clingstone second; time, 2:18½, 2:20½, 2:21. The 2:20 class was won by J. P. Morris, Fanny Witherspoon second; time, 2:26¼, 2:20, 2:23¾, 2:24½.

At Poughkeepsie, on August 23d, in the 2:29 class, Overman won, Independence second, Rigolette third; time, 2:25¾, 2:23½, 2:21½, 2:27¼, 2:24½, 2:30¼. In the free for all pacers except Little Brown Jug, Flora Bell won, Buffalo Girl second, Gem third; time, 2:15½, 2:18¾, 2:18. The 2:21 class was unfinished. J. P. Morris won two heats and Clemmie G one; time, 2:26½, 2:26¼, 2:24½.

On the 24th there were about 3,000 people present at the races. The unfinished race, 2:21 class, J. P. Morrison won, Clemmie second; time, 2:26¼, 2:26¼, 2:24½, 2:22¼, 2:21¼. The 2:33 class race May Thorn won, Manhattan second, Wiry Jim third and Bertha Clay fourth; time, 2:28, 2:26½, 2:29. Little Brown Jug paced four times against time to beat 2:11¼. His best time was 2:18. The 2:26 class race Owen won, Cornelia second, Phyllius third and Amber fourth; time, 2:21, 2:23½, 2:23, 2:23¼, 2:24.

The pinkeye is again quite prevalent in Sacramento, although in a comparatively mild form. Fred Collier and Jim Renwick are both suffering from its effects, as are also three two-year-olds in Matt Storn's charge, belonging to Mr. J. B. Chase; Judge Mee's three-year-old colt, Judge McKinstry, in the same stable, has thus far escaped the malady that seems to be running its course through the entire country.

Mr. W. A. Caswell of Sacramento, has suffered a severe loss from lock-jaw of his well-known roadster, Starr. This horse has trotted in several purses and gained a record of 2:34½ at Sacramento in the past Spring races, and he was altogether a valuable animal. The lock-jaw was produced by his rolling violently against a box, from which he received a wound on the hip that proved fatal.

E. J. Baldwin's horses at the East have not earned the "Lucky" name of their owner this season. They have been very unfortunate, some in their races and others being laid up with the pinkeye. They are now at Long Branch, but will soon move to Sheepshead Bay, for the Fall meeting.

L. R. Martin, at last accounts, was at Saratoga, taking the measure of some of the Eastern cracks for future operations.

The celebrated four-year-old trotter Phil. Thompson, who at one time was thought able to beat the time of Maude S, for that age, 2:17½, has been so seriously ill at Buffalo that his life was dispaired of. The inflammation of the lungs has now subsided, but it is doubtful if he will be able to start again in a race during this season.

Mr. Winters has two very promising yearlings in the Prince of Norfolk and Callie Smart that are now being broken in at Sacramento. The one is a brother to the Duchess of Norfolk, and the filly is by Norfolk, from Mattie A. They are entered in several of the biggest stakes at Jerome Park, Monmouth Park and Saratoga in their two-year and three-year-old form.

Hanlan has issued a challenge to Ross to row four or five miles over any course between Toronto and New York, in June next, for $5,000 and the championship of the world.

About 10,000 head of cattle, bought by Ryan & Lang, have been marketed at the stock-yard of Robert Mays, near the Dalles, Oregon, this season. They have been driven East.

A Fine Exhibit.—The attention of all admirers of good, sound, and at the same time elegant workmanship, is called to the fine display made at the Mechanics' Institute from the manufactory of Mr. M. J. McCue, of 1317 and 1319 Market street. Mr. McCue gives his personal attention to all points, thus ensuring the thoroughness of all the details of his large and increasing business.

# THE GUN.

### THE COSMOPOLITAN'S LAST MATCH.

On Sunday last the "Cosmopolitan Shooting Club" held their last shoot of the season, and well they sustained their reputation as the champion club of the State. The birds were a very fine lot, and the shooters did not have long to dwell on them, as they nearly all left the trap with their tails to the shooter. "His Honor," Judge Rix, President of the club, astonished himself and all members of the day by doing the finest shooting of the day, killing his birds very handsomely—some of them very hard ones. In fact, the shooting of every member of the club, with one or two exceptions, was very good indeed; and the exceptions did much better in the matches following the main shoot. The day was splendid, just wind enough to give the birds a good send-off when the trap was sprung. The match was at twelve single birds, twenty-one yards rise, eighty yards boundary. Messrs. Buckley and Kelley were the only ones making a clean score, though seven had killed eleven; Maskey and Judge Rix among the number being so unfortunate as to have each one fall dead out of bounds, Rix losing his seventh and Maskey the tenth. Twenty-six members came to the score, and three hundred and twelve birds shot at with two hundred and forty scored and twelve dead out of bounds, the average being nearly seventy-seven per cent.

After the match the president of the club made a few appropriate remarks, and then came the distribution of the many prizes, twenty-eight in number, donated by different parties, leaving a prize for every shooter with two to spare. After that there were several matches for two and a half entrance, the first being divided between Tallant and Slade; the next was won by Judge Rix with a clean score, and the third and last was divided between Muller and Downey, with clean scores. On Saturday the Gun Club will have their last shoot of the season at Bird's Point, Alameda, and the California Club on Sunday, at San Bruno.

#### THE CLUB SHOOTING.

| | | | | | | | | | | | | | |
|---|---|---|---|---|---|---|---|---|---|---|---|---|---|
| F. Maskey....... | 1 | 1 | 1 | 1 | 1 | 1 | 1 | 1 | 0 | 1 | 1 | 1 | —11 |
| M. Axtt........... | 1 | 1 | 1 | 1 | 0 | 1 | 1 | 1 | 1 | 1 | 1 | 1 | —11 |
| W. Golcher...... | 1 | 1 | 1 | 0 | 1 | 1 | 1 | 1 | 1 | 1 | 1 | 1 | —11 |
| F. H. Putnam.... | 0 | 1 | 1 | 1 | 1 | 1 | 1 | 1 | 1 | 1 | 1 | 0 | —10 |
| J. Browell....... | 1 | 1 | 0 | 0 | 1 | 0 | 1 | 1 | 1 | 1 | 0 | —8 |
| A. Higgins...... | 1 | 1 | 0 | 1 | 1 | 1 | 0 | 1 | 0 | 1 | 1 | 1 | —9 |
| P. Funk......... | 1 | 1 | 1 | 1 | 1 | 1 | 1 | 0 | 1 | 1 | 1 | —11 |
| C. H. Osmsan.... | 1 | 1 | 0 | 0 | 1 | 1 | 1 | 0 | 1 | 1 | 1 | 1 | —9 |
| D. Rover........ | 1 | 1 | 1 | 1 | 1 | 1 | 0 | 1 | 1 | 0 | 1 | —11 |
| C. A. Emerson... | 1 | 1 | 1 | 0 | 0*| 0 | 1 | 1 | 0 | 1 | 0 | —5 |
| Judge Rix....... | 1 | 1 | 1 | 1 | 1 | 1 | 0*| 1 | 1 | 1 | 1 | 1 | —11 |
| S. Muller....... | 1 | 0 | 1 | 1 | 1 | 0 | 1 | 1 | 0 | 1 | 1 | 1 | —9 |
| B. N. Brooks.... | 0 | 1 | 1 | 1 | 0*| 1 | 0 | 1 | 0 | 1 | —6 |
| L. Tallant...... | 1 | 1 | 0 | 1 | 0 | 1 | 1 | 1 | 1 | 1 | 1 | 1 | —10 |
| J. Ferguson..... | 1 | 0 | 1 | 1 | 0 | 1 | 1 | 1 | 1 | 1 | 0 | —7 |
| K. Edwards...... | 1 | 1 | 1 | 0 | 1 | 1 | 0*| 1 | 1 | 1 | —8 |
| J. Buckley...... | 1 | 1 | 1 | 1 | 1 | 1 | 1 | 1 | 1 | 1 | 1 | 1 | —12 |
| M. Lachman...... | 1 | 1 | 0 | 1 | 0 | 1 | 1 | 0 | 1 | 1 | 1 | —9 |
| Ben Brown....... | 1 | 1 | 1 | 0 | 1 | 1 | 1 | 0 | 1 | 1 | 1 | 1 | —11 |
| G. W. Storben... | 1 | 0 | 0 | 0 | 0 | 1 | 0 | 1 | 0 | 1 | 1 | —5 |
| J. Kelley....... | 1 | 1 | 1 | 1 | 1 | 1 | 1 | 1 | 1 | 1 | 1 | 1 | —12 |
| J. Behan........ | 1 | 1 | 1 | 0 | 1 | 0 | 1 | 1 | 0 | 1 | —8 |
| W. Fulton....... | 1 | 0 | 1 | 0 | 1 | 0 | 0 | 1 | 0 | 1 | 0 | —6 |
| W. H. Card...... | 0 | 1 | 1 | 1 | 1 | 1 | 1 | 1 | 1 | 1 | 1 | —11 |
| F. Johnson...... | 1 | 1 | 1 | 1 | 1 | 1 | 0 | 0*| 0 | 1 | 1 | 1 | —9 |
| R. Liddle....... | 1 | 1*| 0 | 1 | 1 | 1 | 0 | 1 | 1 | 1 | 1 | 1 | —10 |

* Dead out of bounds.

#### FIRST HANDICAP SWEEPSTAKE.

| | | | | | |
|---|---|---|---|---|---|
| Rover, 24 yards............. | 0 | 1 | 1 | 1 | 0 —3 |
| Graham, 24 ............... | 1 | 1 | 1 | 1 | 1 —5 |
| Brown, 24 ................ | 0 | 1 | 1 | 1 | 0 —3 |
| Slade, 25 ................. | 1 | 1 | 1 | 1 | 1 —5 |
| Funk, 22 ................. | 1 | 1 | 1 | 1 | 1 —5 |
| Muller, 22 ................ | 1 | 1 | 1 | 0 | 1 —4 |
| Ferguson, 22 .............. | 1 | 0 | 0 | Withdrew—1 |
| Liddle, 18 ................ | 1 | 1 | 1 | 1 | 1 —5 |
| Judge Rix, 22 ............. | 1 | 1 | 1 | 1 | 1 —5 |
| Emerson, 24 .............. | 1 | 1 | 1 | 0 | 1 —4 |
| Tallant, 24 ............... | 1 | 1 | 1 | 1 | 1 —5 |
| Brooks, 22 ................ | 1 | 1 | 0 | 1 | 0 —3 |
| Buckley, 25 ............... | 1 | 1 | 1 | 1 | 1 —5 |

* Dead out of bounds.

#### SECOND HANDICAP SWEEPSTAKE.

| | | | | | |
|---|---|---|---|---|---|
| Funk, 22 yards............. | 1 | 1 | 0 | 0 | drawn—2 |
| Brown, 24 ................ | 0 | 0 | 0 | 0 | 1 — 3 |
| Downey, 24 ............... | 1 | 1 | 1 | 0 | 1 —4 |
| Graham, 24 ............... | 1 | 1 | 1 | 0 | 0 —3 |
| Liddle, 18 ................ | 0 | 0 | 1 | 1 | 0 —2 |
| Slade, 25 ................. | 0 | 1 | 1 | 1 | 1 —4 |
| Rover, 24 ................ | 0 | 0 | 0 | 1 | 0 —1 |
| Judge Rix, 22 ............. | 1 | 1 | 1 | 1 | 1 —5 |
| Muller, 23 ................ | 1 | 0 | 1 | 1 | 1 —4 |
| Carter, 21 ................ | 1 | 0 | 0 | 0 | drawn—1 |

* Dead out of bounds.

· DEFENCE OF THE MODEST WOLF.—The French Chambers having voted a sum of $20,000 for the extirpation of wolves, M. Charles Monselet, in L'Evenement, has undertaken the defence of that modest and much maligned animal as follows: "The wolf is a calumniated animal. He is ignorant, haughty, prudent and retiring. He keeps his own company, aloof from man, because he knows that he is a victim of prejudice and that his company is not attractive. He is not a flatterer, like the dog, nor is he a stupid slave like the ass. With great good sense he understands that he is not fitted to shine in society, to amuse an audience like a monkey or impress it like the elephant. He is misanthropic, but who shall blame him? He is reproached with a partiality for spring lamb. In the first place, he likes it. Vainly shall a whole faculty of philosophers counsel him to adopt a vegetable diet; for all reply he will point to the teeth given him by all-wise Nature. We, too, like spring lamb, and we have the innocent young of the sheep butchered by licensed slaughterers and exposed for sale at a mercenary price. The wolf, unable to buy, has to kill for himself, and this he does in person, after a hundred hesitations, and when impelled by the pangs of famine. 'Hunger,' says the proverb, 'brings the wolf out of the wood,' and this saying, extorted from the reluctant conscience of man, conveys the highest praise of the wolf, implying a mental struggle, a previous repugnance. Being unable to deal with the butcher and opposed to the exactions of middlemen, the wolf has to address himself in person to the lamb. He transacts his business with celerity, his good breeding making him averse to causing public scandal. As for the lamb, destined to be eaten anyhow, it can make very little difference to him how it is exterminated; indeed, it is altogether probable that if the lamb's tastes could be ascertained it would be found that he prefers the healthful excitement of death by the wolf's jaws to the tedious and debasing formalities of the slaughter-house."

· A few weeks ago three gentlemen shot a pigeon-match at Niagara Falls, one of them standing 64 yards from the traps and the others at 26 yards. The former killed 9 out of 10 birds and won. He shot a Parker gun.

---

THE ROOSEVELT CLUB.—The Roosevelt Game Protection Club held its annual meeting for the election of officers on Sunday last, at the Six-mile House, at which J. G. Hite was elected President; Wm. L. Willis, Vice-President; C. E. Mack, Jr., Secretary; J. P. Harrison, Treasurer; Wm. L. Willis, Corresponding Secretary. For the Executive Committee—H. W. Reith, S. Bodge and C. E. Mack, Jr., and on By-Laws, etc., F. M. Shepler, Wm. L. Willis and C. E. Mack, Jr. The club is now 29 strong, including two honorary members, and there is room but for one more. The club is financially healthy and proposes to keep so. It has leased the Sims Lake, back of the Union House, where the members can go and enjoy a day's sport now and then when the ducks and snipe come in. This lake affords splendid canvasback-shooting in the proper season, and as the market-hunters and bushwhackers will not be allowed to interfere with the game, the members of the club will have grand sport there.—Sacramento Bee.

NOTICE TO SPORTSMEN.—The undersigned having sold his lease to the CRAMBERLAIN TRACT, in the Suisun marshes, together with his ark, boats, etc., to a private club of gentlemen, who will hereafter strictly preserve all the premises for their own shooting only—hereby notifies his late patrons, and all persons who have been in the habit of visiting "TEAL STATION," that it will be IMPOSSIBLE to accommodate them, or in any way afford them shooting facilities, and they are therefore respectfully requested not to stop at that station.
JAMES PAINE, (Late of Teal Station.)

The Teal Shooting Club is the organization that has control of the above property, and compliance with the provisions of Mr. Paine's notice is earnestly requested, as trespassers will be dealt with according to law.

### · THE SACRAMENTO CLUB.

The Pacific Sportsman's Club, of this city, held its regular contests for the gold and silver medals at the Agricultural Park on last Sunday, the match being at single birds. Following are the scores:—

| | | | | | | | | | | | | |
|---|---|---|---|---|---|---|---|---|---|---|---|---|
| A. Graves, 21 yards......... | 1 | 1 | 1 | 1 | 1 | 1 | 1 | 1 | 1 | 1 —10 |
| F. Trommell, 21 yards....... | 1 | 1 | 1 | 1 | 1 | 1 | 1 | 1 | 1 | 1 —10 |
| P. Kunz, 21 yards.......... | 1 | 1 | 1 | 1 | 1 | 1 | 1 | 1 | 1 | 1 —10 |
| W. Naughton, 21 yards...... | 1 | 1 | 1 | 1 | 0 | 1 | 1 | 1 | 1 | 1 —9 |
| C. Flohr, 26 yards......... | 1 | 0 | 1 | 1 | 1 | 1 | 0 | 1 | 1 | 0 —7 |
| G. D. Hopper, 26 yards..... | 1 | 0 | 0 | 0 | 1 | 1 | 1 | 1 | 1 | 1 —7 |
| F. Nesbit, 26 yards........ | 1 | 0 | 1 | 0 | 0 | 1 | 0 | 1 | 1 | 1 —6 |

Ties on 10 were shot off at three pairs of birds as follows: Graves 5, Frommell 1. Ties on 9, for the silver medal, were decided at clay pigeons, freezeout: Pedler 6, Naughton 5, Kunz 0. Ties on 6 were shot off as follows at clay pigeons: Hopper 5, Nesbit 5, Flohr 4. This match decided the right of Flohr to wear the leather medal.*

Next followed a free-for-all match at five clay pigeons, in which Hopper, Pedler, Flohr and Nesbit tied on clean scores and shot off at five more birds. Flohr and Nesbit again tied on full scores, and divided first and second moneys.

Several other pool matches were shot, in which Hopper and Pedler were winners. In the match for the medals Flohr lost three birds which died beyond the flags, and Hopper and Nesbit two each.—The Bee.

Hare and doves are very plentiful in the vicinity of Antioch.

The San Jose Club is having a new shooting box constructed on the Alviso Marsh for the accommodation of its members.

· The Benito Club has arranged for a grand hunt to take place on the 15th September next, and they propose to be out two or three days.

The Pacific Gun Club will meet at Bird's Point, Alameda, on the first Sunday in September, to finish their season's shooting. About forty dollars' worth of prizes will be competed for.

Among the sportsman's clubs now being organized for the protection of game and fish, we may mention that of Nevada City, in which Tom Marker and other residents are taking great interest.

When the fishing season closes, which will be at the end of the month, a number of small boats will patrol the Sacramento, and a strict guard will be kept to prevent a violation of the law.

Country stores are sending in large orders to the wholesale ammunition dealers. As the game laws expire on the 15th of September a great demand is expected for ammunition and hunting outfits.

It is reported that the Carson sportsmen are pledging themselves not to vote for a single peace officer who will not arrest and assist in the conviction of persons who are breaking the game laws of the State.

In Marin county the game laws have been well observed this year, as the large numbers of quail and other game will show. In many localities the quail are raising their second broods. The season has been open and good for game all over the State.

Messrs. Sampson, Felker, Paine and Mitchell, in gunning last Sunday near Menlo Park met with a series of mishaps, that have almost convinced them of the ill luck attending such Sunday recreations. An injured horse, a broken shaft, a shattered ramrod, a bursted gun, and an expulsion from the hunting grounds in which they ranged have led them to contemplate the advisability of changing their mode of spending the Sabbath. They returned with five dozen doves.—San Mateo Journal.

## THE RIFLE.

PISTOLS AND ARROWS.—The match between four officers of the Police Pistol Team and four members of the California Archery Club came off at Bird's Point, Alameda, last Saturday afternoon. The distance shot was 50 yards, at archers' targets. The Police used Smith & Wesson's 45-caliber-pistols, and the Archers used bows and arrows. The match terminated in favor of the Police, who, after having fired 25 shots each, found that they had beat the Archers' points, the Archers having already shot their fifty arrows each. One great disadvantage the men of the bow labored under was the uncertainty of the wind, which blew across the range in fitful gusts, often carrying well directed arrows wide of the mark. Col. S. E. Beaver and S. H. Daniels were the judges, and Col. H. J. Burns acted as referee. The following scores were made:

Police—P. H. Linville, 107; J. C. Lane, 106; H. Hook, 106; L. Whitworth, 102. Total, 421.

Archers—J. F. Allen, 138; E. F. Murray, 101; A. S. Brownell, 98; F. C. Havens, 75. Total, 412.

Lane and Hook tied on 106 points, but according to Creedmoor Lane is entitled to second place in the team. Owing to the sickness of one of the archers, Mr. Button of Santa Cruz, Mr. Murray took his place, which he filled very creditably. It is claimed that these teams cannot be beaten by any of their classes on the coast.

THE CALIFORNIA SCHUETZEN CLUB held their regular monthly shooting for prizes, last Sunday, at Schuetzen Park. Each contestant had twenty shots off-hand at a target thirty-six inches in diameter that contained a six-inch bulls-eye. The shooting was done on the 200-yard range. When a shot struck the bulls-eye a red flag was shown, the bulls-eye taken from the target and numbered, and at the stand a corresponding number put opposite the name of the shooter; so that when the match was completed and the bulls-eyes counted and measured, one could easily tell who were the best shots. The prizes were won in the following order: 1st prize, Philo Jacoby; 2, K. Wertheimer; 3, Stroeven; 4, A. Shrecker; 5, Zecher; 6, Eckmann; 7, Bertlesen; 8, Brenner, Sr.; 9, A. Rahweiler; 10, F. Freese; 11, Brenner, Jr.; 12, Rochel; 13, Boeckmann; 14, H. Heeth; 15, Fischer; 16, Bertrand; 17, F. Greiner. This club will hold a grand rifle tournament, open to all comers, at Schuetzen Park, on the first Sunday in October. Three hundred and fifty dollars in cash will be competed for, together with forty-five valuable prizes.

The Directors of the California Rifle Association held a meeting last Wednesday afternoon to decide on the time and to arrange a programme for their Fall tournament. The shooting will take place at Shell Mound Park on the 27th, 28th and 29th days of October. The programme is the same as that of last Spring, except that the Governor's trophy will take the place of the Cosy trophy. Two rifle teams from Nevada, one from British Columbia and about six from the California Militia, will enter for the Pacific Slope Trophy. Two pistol teams, one from Carson and the other from Virginia City, will be here to shoot for the trophy that was won last Spring by the Police Team. This will be the largest tournament of its kind ever held on this coast.

On invitation of Major Heskin, the members of Company C, First Regiment, met the regulars at Fort Point in a friendly rifle contest at the Presidio Range, last Sunday. The distance was three, five and six hundred yards. The scores made were: Company C—J. E. Klein, 80; H. T. Sime, 75; H. D. Merryweather, 86; A. P. Baye, 77; L. G. Perkins, 91. Regulars—Nelson, 65; Poneeon, 74; Allen, 83; Paddin, 71; Brown, 75; Cannama, 80. These scores were of a possible 100 points, making for the first team 77.9 per cent., and for the second team 71.11 per cent.

Last Saturday, the Garde Fusiliers held a prize shooting at Shell Mound Park. The prizes were won by Messrs. Kuhls, F. Hagemann and F. Rohdefeld.

### THE INTERNATIONAL RIFLE MATCH.

The great match that is to be shot next month at Creedmoor, near New York, is exciting great attention at the East. The British team leave Liverpool to-day in the Alaska, and will arrive about September 3d. Following are the conditions of the match:

The shooting at 200 yards is to be performed "off-hand," that is, from a standing position. The target for this range will be 6 feet high by a wide, with a bull's-eye 8 inches in diameter. At 500 and 600 yards the prone position may be adopted, and targets 6 feet square, with a 22-inch bull's-eye, will be used. At the long distances any position will be permitted, and the target is that rendered familiar to the public through the old "Palma" contests. At all ranges the firing will be conducted in regular military fashion, the men being paired, and two taking their positions together on each side of a firing post and shooting alternately until their strings are complete. The weapons to be used must be bona fide military rifles with ramrods and slings, having open sights and no wind gauges or spirit levels, and the bullet must be inserted into the cartridge a distance equal to two-thirds of its diameter. The weapons must not be cleaned except between ranges, and no sighting shots at any distance will be permitted. All the arrangements at Creedmoor are already completed. The competitors, or as many as may desire it, will be lodged and boarded on the spot at the expense of the National Rifle Association. Special trains will run to Creedmoor station each day for the accommodation of those coming from the city. Five targets on the west range will be used at 200 yards, and those on the left of the old range for the mid-ranges. The long-range firing will be done against the targets on the extreme end of the field, which have borne the brunt of every international contest that Creedmoor has seen. Shelters, markers, score-keepers and all other paraphernalia of practice will be on hand in abundance, and though the first shot will not be fired until eleven o'clock or later, it is confidently hoped that the entire ground can be covered each day.

The question of weapon is still a disputed one, though the difficulty is likely to take the form of an embarras de richesse. There are, to be sure, a few men who may, or "Let every fellow choose for himself." If he shoot his way on to the team with an old brass moulded blunderbuss let him shoot through the match with it if he wants to." This sort of opinion meets with little favor from the majority. Uniformity, they argue, is the essence of team shooting, and we cannot afford to give the British the least point by allowing any man to separate himself from the rest. As it stands now the team, its captain and the committee of the National Rifle Association in charge of the selection of rifles, are to decide by a joint vote what piece or pieces are to be used, and all the members of the team are to be bound by the decision. Here the difficulty of deciding comes in. The choice will be entirely between the two new guns that have been specially designed and manufactured for the match. Of these ones—the Hepburn—is already in use, and some of the most brilliant shooting of the season has been done with it. It is already high in favor, and is admitted to be adequate to the requirements of the occasion. The second gun

—the Hotchkiss—has only just been perfected, and only on the 19th inst. it was for the first time submitted to experiment by the committee of the National Rifle Association. The practical work was intrusted to Gen. J. O. P. Burnside and Mr. D. A. Pollard of Washington, both of them riflemen of the highest reputation and skill. They fired over a hundred shots without cleaning from the piece submitted for trial, and found it as true at the end as at the beginning. There was no leading or serious defect, and altogether they considered it quite reliable in case it should be selected for use in the match. Mr. Pollard made 33 points out of a possible 35 with it at 900 yards, and the average at every range was well above an average of centres. Altogether there seems so far to be little on which to base any preference, and it is likely that no decision will be made until the teams themselves are able to experiment for a few days with both weapons. Only one thing is certain—that is, that the great danger which beset the riflemen of this country when the contest was first arranged, of losing the match through inferiority of armament, has been completely obviated, just as a similar difficulty was previous to the first international long range match with the Irish team in 1874.

There is naturally great emulation among the marksmen of the National Guard in all the states to represent our country on this occasion, and the National Rifle Association have arranged a four days' competition; at the conclusion of the practice, a team will be chosen from the men who make the highest average, none scoring under one hundred and fifty-two points being eligible. Following is the account of the first day's shooting at all ranges:

| | 200 yards. | 500 yards. | 800 yards. | 900 yards. | 1000 yards. | Totals. |
|---|---|---|---|---|---|---|
| 12th N. Y.—A. B. Van Hensen | 20 | 34 | 34 | 33 | 32 | 193 |
| 21st sep co., Dion, N. Y.—S. C. Islam | 27 | 30 | 31 | 30 | 30 | 188 |
| 8th N. Y.—Captain J. W. Griffith | 31 | 31 | 27 | 30 | 47 | 178 |
| 20th sep. co., Bingham's—D. H. Ogden | 31 | 33 | 34 | 30 | 50 | 167 |
| 6th N. Y.—J. Smith | 23 | 30 | 35 | 37 | 17 | 165 |
| 7th N. Y.—Fred Adler | 31 | 29 | 30 | 33 | 34 | 167 |
| 12th N. Y.—J. J. Dolan | 31 | 33 | 36 | 10 | 27 | 162 |
| 12th N. Y.—I. L. Spaulding | 30 | 31 | 35 | 30 | 38 | 185 |
| 71th Pennsylvania—Captain R. Atkinson | 33 | 37 | 37 | 30 | 27 | 161 |
| 8th N. Y.—J. L. Price | 30 | 28 | 33 | 27 | 46 | 17 |
| 10th separate company—M. D. Blieda | 27 | 30 | 37 | 29 | 30 | 126 |
| 1st Div. Pa.—Major E. O. Shakspeare | 33 | 20 | 33 | 27 | 31 | 181 |
| 1st Brigade, N. J.—Colonel Howard | 30 | 29 | 30 | 34 | 30 | 120 |
| 69th N. Y.—A. Kerin | 26 | 32 | 31 | 33 | 30 | 12 |
| 11th N. Y.—D. Ward | 31 | 30 | 33 | 25 | 41 | 17 |
| 26th sep. co., Catskill—G. F. Tolley | 30 | 30 | 34 | 19 | 18 | 125 |
| 10th sep. co., Bingham's—G. A. Morris | 26 | 30 | 32 | 32 | 22 | 169 |
| 1st Massachusetts—G. W. Hinman | 31 | 21 | 19 | 33 | 41 | 124 |
| Nat. Rifles, Washington—M. Pollard | 17 | 18 | 31 | 30 | 37 | 133 |
| Nat. Rifles, Washington—W. J. Johnston | 30 | 30 | 32 | 22 | 31 | 90 |
| Newport Art'y, R. I.—D. M'Hon Farrow | 28 | 31 | 31 | 18 | 26 | 129 |
| 1st Brig. Staff, N. J.—Maj. J. N. Denman | 30 | 24 | 33 | 31 | 17 | 160 |
| Nat. Rifles, Washington—J. J. Lauritzen | 30 | 35 | 22 | 18 | 18 | 117 |
| Governor's Guard, Ct.—R. Lower | 33 | 15 | 17 | 17 | 33 | 15 |
| 1st Connecticut—G. A. Barnes | 33 | 33 | 30 | 21 | 8 | 10 |
| 1st Connecticut—J. E. Williams | 36 | 18 | 4 | 32 | 14 | 80 |

## THE KENNEL.

Words—Words—Words.—For some time past the *American Field* has freely admitted to its columns communications from each and every gentleman who fancied that he knew a little more than his neighbors about the various détaine of dogs. The result is rather confusing to those good old fashioned folks who believe that all which appears in print is true, and perhaps may have muddled some folks of greater discernment. An old California sportsman writes to the editor as follows:

Gilroy, Cal.

Editor American Field:—

Gobbo. "Master, young gentleman, I pray you, which is the way to the Master Jew's?"

Launcelot. "Turn up on your right hand at the next turning, but at the next turning of all, on your left; marry, at the very next turning, turn of no hand, but turn down indirectly to the Jew's house."

Gobbo. "By God's sonties, 't will be a hard way to hit."

Launcelot's directions for finding the Jew's house are something like the articles from the various sporting writers in your paper on the subject of thoroughbred dogs. Some time ago I felt happy in the fancied possession of a pure Laverack setter, descended from Pride of the Border, and now comes a wretch of an iconoclast, who howls him over, and offers to produce evidence to prove that he was not descended from Ponto and Moll. I next purchased a pure Llewellin, and now I am told that he contains other blood than Duke—Rhœbe and Laverack—consequently, sold again. My next venture was a setter of "field trial breed," and another writer tells me that there is now no such breed. Becoming disgusted, I went into the Irish straits of setters, and obtained a beautiful dog, by Berkley, confident that I had at last hit purity itself, when, to my horror, appears a very learned disquisition which proved to my satisfaction that Berkley was not a typical Irish setter—that means, I suppose, that he is not an Irish setter at all.

My next experiment was a very beautiful, and, as I thought, perfect specimen of a Gordon setter, by Grouse, also one from Blossom, and I thought, in my simplicity, that now I had a brace of perfect dogs; when out comes another wretch and says: "They are too lumbering," and that we "must get up a new type."

I next commissioned a friend to purchase me a brace of prize winners at an English bench show, and the week after they arrived appeared an article from an English writer, saying that bench show dogs were of no account in the field; in fact, neither they nor their immediate ancestors had ever pointed a bird.

Being of a sanguine disposition and not easily discouraged, I commissioned another friend to attend the next field trials in England and purchase me a brace of winning dogs, and no sooner had I received them, and was congratulating myself upon the envy I intended to excite among my sporting friends when I showed my new dogs on game, than out comes another English writer and says: "Winners at field trials cannot be relied on;" that he had known dogs "put up to win, who were not de facto worthy."

However, I don't intend to get discouraged, and just as soon as any gentleman finds the least fault with my dogs, or throws any slur or doubt upon their pedigrees, I intend at once to discard them, and try, try again; although I begin to think like Gobbo: "By God's sonties, t'will be a hard way to hit."

A Lover of Dogs.

## COURSING AT NEWARK

Now that the mornings and evenings are getting cool San Francisco coursers are beginning to resort to Newark to give their greyhounds an occasional run on Saturdays and Sundays. Thanks to Dugan having restocked the place hares are plentiful. The early morning at this season of the year is the best possible time to train young greyhounds. The hares are not quite fullgrown, and consequently a chase is not so exhausting as in the height of the season when they are at their best. A badly trained dog is a nuisance alike to his owner, Judges and slipper, and is sure to beat himself out of his chances, when otherwise he would have a good show to win. Dogs that fight in slips and dogs that do not get down to business until they see their opponent chasing the hare a hundred yards away, are utterly worthless, and would never be seen on a coursing ground if the following plan of breaking was adopted. It is universally used in England, and the writer can safely say that it will never be found to fail: When the pup is about eight months old it should be taught to lead without hanging back in the collar or tugging ahead. To teach this the best plan is to put it in a double collar with some steady old dog, who will soon cure it of any desire to tow the trainer or be dragged along. Firmness and gentleness are at all times necessary, and care must be taken never to attempt to teach a fresh lesson until the old one is mastered. When the pup has been taught to lead he should be exercised regularly on the road about three times a week to harden his feet and improve his wind. This should be limited to a walking gait or slow trot, and occasionally he should be turned loose on soft ground where he will give himself all the galloping exercise necessary. After a few weeks of this kind of exercise he should be trained to go into slips with an old dog. To do this the feeder should go a short distance ahead and get some one to hold the dogs in the slips, taking care that the pup does not pull. Then the trainer calls to them, and instantly they should be loosed to gallop towards them. When this is learned the pup should be put in slips with an old dog and taken to the coursing ground where a hare can be found. The instant the hare is sighted the dogs should be loosed. The old dog will see it and the young dog will follow his companion. When the kill is made the pup should be allowed to mouth it but not to taste the blood. Some trainers allow their pups to chase and kill a cotton-tail rabbit, to familiarize them with the game. As soon as the pup shows eagerness to, chase, his education is complete, and after that he should be allowed with an old dog to chase a hare about once a week, not oftener; but always on soft ground. At first, when the hare doubles, he will be thrown out badly, but in time he will learn to steady himself as he goes up to the game and will greatly improve in his "working" qualities. His feet and nails should be carefully inspected for sores and cuts after a chase, and while in this period plenty of nourishing food should be given. Lean mutton and oat-cakes are the best kind of food. Dogs trained by certain persons in this city invariably pull n the slips, and are nearly choked before they sight their game. That is the fault of the trainers, and if not too far gone they can be broken of the trick by means of a spiked collar.

## HOW TO MAKE A DOG RETRIEVE

The first thing to be done with a young dog is to teach him to fetch and carry. He will probably do this of himself if well broke of a good kind, but he must learn to bring correctly; that is, quickly, and straight to you, releasing his grasp as you take hold; and you should receive from him directly he reaches you, allowing him no time to mouth or play with the article, whatever it may be. You should put on him a short cord about twenty yards long, and accustom him to bring a ball to you, or a rabbit skin, stuffed on purpose, drawing the dog steadily towards you with the cord. Short lessons, a few minutes daily, will soon make him perfect, and fond of bringing to you; and if he is inclined to be slow in coming up to you, run from him, and he will hasten to overtake you.

If he shows no inclination to bring or lift what is thrown for him, by keeping him hungry he will be inclined to lift hard biscuits or bread, and morsels to eat will reward him each time you receive from him, drawing him to you with the cord.

Great care must be taken to keep his mouth tender when under excitement; and a boy, or anybody else out at the time, will help you greatly by turning your dog gently to you with a whip, if he lingers to play with the bird's feathers.

If he lets go too soon, step back a pace or two and encourage him to carry up to you. If, on the other hand, he holds too tight, take hold of his cord with one hand and jerk it, as you receive the bird with the other, saying 'Softly" to him all the time, till he releases his hold. 'Softly" is a very important word, to be constantly used with a dog, as he may be punished if he be in any way rough with a wounded bird at any future time of his life. This is only one of the many plans adopted by breeders. Its chief merit is simplicity.

## BULL BLOOD IN THE GREYHOUND.

We have been asked to give the full particulars of the crossing of bull-dogs with greyhounds, and the result. The earliest instance of such a cross is found in Youatt's work on the dog. The author says: "The breed had begun to degenerate, and lacked courage, from inbreeding and other reasons. About 1780 Lord Orford, a nobleman enthusiastically devoted to coursing, imagined, and rightly, that the greyhound of the day was deficient in courage and perseverance. He bethought himself how this could best be rectified, and he adopted a plan which brought upon him much ridicule at the time, but ultimately redounded to his credit. He selected a bull-dog—one of the smooth rat-tailed species—and with him crossed one of his best greyhound bitches. He kept the female whelps, and crossed them with some of his fleetest greyhounds, and the consequence was that after the sixth or seventh generation there was not a vestige left of the form of the bull-dog, but his courage and indomitable perseverance remained, and having once started after his game, he did not relinquish chase until he fell exhausted, or perhaps died. This cross is now universally adopted. It is one of the secrets in the breeding of the greyhound. A favorite bitch of this breed was Czarina, bred by Lord Orford, and at his decease purchased by Col. Thornton. She won every match for which she started, and they were no fewer than forty-seven. Two of her progeny, Claret and Young Czarina, challenged the United Kingdom, and won their matches."

## TRAINING SHEPHERD DOGS.

Darwin thus describes the training of shepherd dogs: "When riding it is a common thing to meet a flock of sheep, guarded by one or two dogs, at a distance of some miles from any house or man. I often wonder how so firm a friendship had been established. The method of education consists in separating the puppy while very young from its mother and accustoming it to its future companions. A ewe is held three or four times a day for the little thing to suck, and a nest of wool is made for it in the sheep pen. At no time is it allowed to associate with other dogs, or with the children of the family. From this education it has no wish to leave the flock, and just as another dog will defend his master, man, so will this dog defend sheep. It is amusing to observe, when approaching a flock, how the dog immediately advances barking and the sheep all close in his rear, as if round the oldest ram. These dogs are also easily taught to bring home the sheep at a certain hour in the evening. Their most troublesome fault when young is their desire to play with the sheep, for in their sport they sometimes gallop the poor things most unmercifully. The shepherd dog comes to the house every day for his meat, and as soon as it is given him skulks away as if ashamed of himself. On these occasions the house dogs are very tyrannical, and the least of them will attack the stranger. The minute, however, the latter has reached the flock, he turns round and begins to bark, and then all the house dogs take quickly to their heels. In a similar manner, a whole pack of hungry wild dogs will scarcely ever venture to attack a flock guarded by one of these faithful shepherds. In this case the shepherd dog seems to regard the sheep as his fellow brethren and thus gains confidence; and the wild dogs though knowing that sheep are not dogs but are good to eat, yet when seeing them in a flock with a shepherd dog as their head, partly consent to regard them as he does."

FIELD TRIALS IN GERMANY.—There will be an international field trial in Germany in September next, on the shooting ground of Prince Albert Solms, who is one of the promoters of the trials. There will be an All-aged Setter and Pointer Stake, a stake for Setter and Pointer Puppies, and special stakes for German dogs. In spite of much grumbling at the Kennel Club for requesting its members to abstain from exhibiting or taking part in any show not held under their rules, that body is steadfast in its opinion that it is acting wisely, and its members for the most part are satisfied to absent themselves from shows not willing to guarantee them the protection which their rules afford them. No particular fault is found with the rules, but certain shows seem fearful of the power likely to accrue to the Kennel Club by an adoption of its code.

THE LAVERACK FUND.—Subscriptions to the fund for erecting in America a monument to the late Edward Laverack, the founder of the breed of setters of that name, have reached nearly $100.

Frank Noble, of Sacramento, has sold his Llewellin pup, Rob, to Judge W. S. Mesick, for the handsome price of $100.

The members of the Dog Fanciers' Association, Montreal, Canada, are making efforts to awaken an interest which shall warrant them in holding a dog show during September.

Mr. Chas. A. Schieffelin has presented to Mr. Edmund Orgill his lemon and white pointer bitch Juno, out of "old Juno," dam by Flake, by W. K. C. Sensation. She will be bred to champion Rush.

Mr. Edmund Orgill of Brooklyn, has recently sold to Mr. J. A. Wright of Austin, Lander Co., Nevada, two very promising pointer puppies, viz., dog pup Babdom, or Romp II., and bitch pup Rush, or Juno.

James H. Corbin, of Sacramento, lost his fine young Llewellin setter Roscoe, a couple of days'since, by poisoning. Some miscreant administered the deadly drug to him while he was fastened in his master's yard. Roscoe was sired by Elmore's imported dog Regent, one of the best bred Llewellins that ever came to the coast. Mr. Corbin had refused $100 for him on the very day he was poisoned. Well bred dogs are so scarce on this coast that the loss of one is to be deeply regretted.—*Sacramento Bee.*

## THE HERD.

### BEEF PACKING ESTABLISHMENT.

Enormous as has been the increase in the amount of beef sent alive to Europe, America could never have supplied the demands of the foreign markets for, beef had her exports been confined to cattle of the higher qualities required by that trade. Prices for beef of all kinds would have been much higher than they have been had there not been grazing on the plains of the West thousands of herds fattening on the rich, natural grasses, drinking the sweet waters, and breathing the pure air. These cattle are known to be the healthiest in the world, and losses from any cause except accident, or from exposure to severe storms, is practically unknown. But these cattle of the plains, healthy as their flesh is known to be, cannot be profitably sent alive across the Atlantic, for they are not heavy enough, except when fully fattened on corn, nor are they good enough in style to please the taste of John Bull. But by putting the meat of these cattle, properly prepared, in tightly-sealed tin cases or cans, and leaving here all the less desirable parts, the beef can be profitably sent to the consumer, and will keep pure and wholesome for an indefinite period.

A few years ago there were but two or three canning establishments in operation in North America, but since that time, favored by low prices of cattle, quite a number were opened, more perhaps in Chicago than in all other cities in the country; at least half a dozen important canning factories having been in active operation at one time. St. Louis had one which suspended work last year, but, it is said, will begin again this year. In South America, in Texas, and in California the very extensive business can be best profitably failed. After many failures, Chicago enterprise and skill succeeded in winning the appreciation of the civilized world, and its patronage by proving the superiority of American methods. One Chicago firm alone has shipped over 40,000 cases per month, and last year sent abroad 519,065 cases, a large number having been of cans containing 14 pounds each. This firm began business in 1868, killing only about fifty cattle per day. Now, 1,000 to 1,200 per day are killed during the busy season of the year. Of 45,000 cases per week used in England in 1878, nearly 40,000 were from one Chicago house.

## BERKSHIRE SWINE.

The Berkshire has been a favorite breed of swine for fifty years. In that time however many important changes have occurred in their make-up, so they now stand among swine where the blood horse does in the equine race, and where Short-horns do among cattle, combining elegance with symmetry of form and high breeding. Yet in all this they have preserved usefulness in the highest degree, and have been used within the last twenty-five years probably more extensively than any other breed of swine, in improving newer breeds, giving elegance, firm bone, great muscularity, and good constitutional vigor.

In reference to the history and general make-up of Berkshires, *The American Encyclopedia of Agriculture* says:

They are more uniform in color than any of the white and black breeds, the fashionable color now being white feet, tips of tails, and a little white in the face, the rest of the body being jet black.

More than forty years ago, as we then knew and bred them, there were many upon which a sandy color would appear. And they were larger boned and coarser in their make-up, but nevertheless, perhaps, containing more lean flesh (muscle) than at the present day; not so kindly in fattening, neither did they contain so much lard, but their hams, shoulders and bacon were, we think, superior to the more modern Berkshires, or those of to-day.

The best type of their breed now have short noses; slightly dished faces; small, fine, erect ears; eyes wide apart; straight back, preserving its width from the neck to the rump; muscular hams and shoulders; the bacon pieces well broken with strips of lean, fine hams, short legs, excellent hoofs, and in killing showing but little offal. Their vigor makes them excellent gleaners, to follow cattle fattened in the field, and their weight, from 300 to 600 pounds, renders them sought after by the packers, especially those of hams and bacon.

They have been with us always a favorite breed on account of their muscular development, as among the middle breeds, as the Essex have been among the small breeds. It is, however, not to be denied that they will not stand starving. They require strong feed and plenty of it, to reach the best development, and what animal does not? Nevertheless, we do not think they assimilate quite as much of their food, when the bulk of it is corn, as do some of the breeds more inclined to lard. Yet, no breed will reach good development on scant food, and when muscle as well as fat is wanted, the breeder or feeder would have to seek far for a hog better combining good qualities, and full medium weights.—*Prairie Farmer.*

## AGRICULTURAL SHOWS—THEIR ABUSES.

An experienced stockman, Colonel Weld, puts officers, exhibitors and spectators of Fairs on their guard. He writes in the August *American Agriculturist* as follows: "Influence is brought to bear upon the jury of awards in various ways. One man will openly address a judge in praise of his competitor's exhibit, and loudly call attention to the best points, but quietly regret certain defects, or express doubts about the age or breeding of the animals, or other points affecting the competing exhibit. Sometimes a third party discusses matters with a judge in a disinterested, friendly way, talking up his friend's stock of goods and trying to prejudice him against other exhibits. It is very hard to guard a jury against such influence. I have known the principal officers of Agricultural Societies take judges to one side and indicate how in their judgment the awards should go, by calling special attention to certain entries of those who were known to be on terms of personal friendship with them, and disparaging others—or damning them with faint praise. There are many men appointed as judges who are unfit to serve, and who know it themselves. These are wide awake to watch and listen and find out what practical men think, and it is very easy, if it is known that they are not strong, to influence them. An exhibitor who goes to the show to get prizes, by fair means or foul, will measure such a man at the first glance, and "go for him," as the saying is. A weak judge is of no account in any way. A jury of two judges works better than one of three, and a single good judge better than either; but he must be a man to be depended upon. The system, especially prevalent in small societies, of distributing the prizes about so as to "encourage" all exhibitors, and make everybody happy, is most pernicious. At such shows it matters very little who the judges are. The prizes are worth nothing any way as honors, and very little in money, and so long as such a system is in vogue, they will be worth no more."

THE DEMAND FOR CATTLE is on the increase, and in consequence of the advance in prices there is a great deal of speculative buying, sometimes for future delivery. But generally speaking, cattle owners on the coast are not anxious to sell before gathering in their bands for winter, as feed is plentiful and the stock is in good condition. The cattle from Nevada and the Pacific Coast is wanted to fill the void made in the new States and Territories by the immense demand from Chicago, the central point of supply for the great export trade to the British Isles. To show how this demand is stimulated we may mention that in Glasgow good American steers are selling at 17 to 18 cents per pound, medium at 15 to 16 cents per pound. Sheep are worth 15 to 18 cents per pound. In Liverpool prices are about one cent per pound lower than in Scotland. The above prices are on the basis of sinking the offal. Freights on cattle from Boston or New York to Liverpool are from $7 to $8 per head.

THE LONDON TIMES ON AMERICAN BACON.—A correspondent of the London *Times*, who visited this country last season, commenting on the quality of our bacon, says that, excepting in price, it cannot compare with the best Irish, Wiltshire or Yorkshire, but that it is steadily improving in this respect. He thinks that if our hogs were finished off, as they might be, with a daily meal of barley instead of all corn, the bacon would be firmer and less liable to shrink when cooked. He says that it is not so fat as good English bacon, and that it is better boiled than grilled. It is realized in England that, with the exception of the higher grades, the American bacon is tough, but then that is easily accounted for, as the English swine almost always live in pens, and thus do not get the exercise that hardens the flesh.

THE GROWTH OF THE WOOL INTEREST on the Pacific Slope is something marvelous. California is now the foremost sheep-breeding State in the Union. The census statistics

for 1880 show a grand total of 42,381,389 sheep in all the States and Territories, California's share being 4,152,349, or nearly one-tenth. The next highest State is Ohio, with 3,902,000. New Mexico had 2,088,831, and Michigan 2,189,-380. The Pacific States and Territories stand credited as follows: California, 4,152,349; Oregon, 1,083,162; Washington, 292,883; Nevada, 123,696; Idaho, 27,326; Colorado, 746,443; Arizona, 76,522: total, 6,512,380. That is over 15 per cent. of all the sheep in the Union; and the production of them has been the work of less than 25 years.

A NEW CATTLE COMPANY.—The Canadian Fresh-Meat Importation Company has recently issued its prospectus. The company, with its office situated in London, will import only the first quality of fresh meats of all kinds from Canada into the United Kingdom. The capital stock of the company is £50,000 in shares of £1 each. The directors also draw attention in their prospectus to the well-known superiority of Canadian cattle over those exported from the United States. [Sic.] The company will be their own importers and sell direct to the consumer from their own depots. The average cost of meat, delivered in England is five pence per pound.

One circumstance which has helped materially to make Chicago packers successful when others have failed, is that they have the advantage of the greatest live-stock market in the world, to which are brought vast numbers of cattle suited to their needs. There is no waste here. The cattle goes to makers of commercial fertilizers, and for the bones, the blood, the entrails, the hides, hoofs and horns, there are plenty of buyers at fair figures. The tallow is fresh and clean, and therefore brings a good price. Even the marrow is carefully saved for use in toilet and other goods—the average amount of marrow rendered exceeding 100,000 pounds per month, while of tallow over 1,000,000 pounds per month are rendered.

As an evidence of the immense increase in the cattle trade in that city it is stated that the four direct rail lines between Chicago and Kansas City are delivering a daily average of about one hundred car-loads of cattle in Chicago city. This average has been steadily maintained during July. The shipments thither for the month amounted to 2,800 car-loads. The same roads delivered in July, 1881, only 800 car-loads. For the month of June, 1882, the deliveries by the rool lines at Chicago were 1,439 car-loads, and for the corresponding month last year they were under 400 car-loads. The railroad companies are realizing large earnings from the cattle traffic and at the same time are fostering and developing this important interest of Arizona and Colorado.—*The Breeders' Gazette.*

From Montana we learn that the Cochrane Cattle Company have purchased 6,000 head of cattle from Poindexter & Orr, of Beaverhead county, paying at the rate of $25 per head for the entire herd. The range of the Cochrane Cattle Company is at Bow river, 180 miles north of Fort Macleod. During the past year the above company have purchased over 10,000 head of cattle in Montana, and their purchases alone have had a great tendency to raise the price of cattle in the territory. It made a market upon the range where the cattle were grazing, and entire bands were purchased.

From the Idaho *Avalanche* we learn that Mike Hyde has completed his cattle pen out in the junipers, near Silver City, and is now buying beef cattle and placing them in it until he is ready to drive them to the railroad. The pen or field contains about 3,000 acres of good grazing land, well watered, and is just the place to put cattle until ready to drive to Winnemucca. Mr. Hyde is buying for the San Francisco market, and will probably distribute something like $30,000 in the Jordan Valley, Bruneau, Catharine and Meadow Creeks, by the 10th of September.

## A SENSATIONAL SALE.

If ever there was a piece of matter on four legs, that peripatetic bit of adultery is to be found in Hermit. If ever there was a horse who had a history more sensational or more illustrious than any other, that horse is Hermit. From the day of his birth up to the present his career has been one blaze of glory. As a yearling he fetched 1,000 guineas—being bred by the late Mr. Benkiron; and his dam, Seclusion, when subsequently submitted to auction, brought the highest price ever, I believe, realized by a brood mare. Old Seclusion is still alive, and resuming fresh and well in the Eltham pastures, while Hermit's sire, Newminster, has rendered abundant proofs of his having been the veriest aristocrat of equine aristocracy. Hermit's Derby was one of the most sensational ever known. It was run in a snow storm, and so hopeless was the chance of the chestnut considered that 1,000 to 15 was laid against him to the fall of the flag, although he was decidedly the best two-year-old of his season, and won the Winter favorite, having been backed for immense sums. In a trial with Rama, however, after the First Spring Meeting, he broke a bloodvessel, and hence his retrogression for the Derby. It is computed that Mr. Chaplin, his owner, won close upon £100,000 over him in wagers on that memorable day, and there was one big bet he had with Sir Joseph Hawley of £50,000 that Hermit beat The Palmer, and another of £5,000, with Mr. Merry, that Hermit beat Marksman. The last named was second, and many think that Jemmy Grimshaw ought to have won. As a matter of fact, however, the race was a terrific finish between the pair.

Hermit's success at the stud has eclipsed, perhaps, that of any horse that can be mentioned, not forgetting that "Emperor of Stallions" Stockwell. This year the victories of his get have been something marvelous, including the Two Thousand Guineas and Derby with Shotover, the first three in the One Thousand, and that top-sawyer at present in training, Tristan, to say nothing of others. Never, perhaps, has a horse had such a year in all kinds of races, and to wind up comes the richest sale of yearlings by his get ever attributed to one sire at the same time. I allude to the auction of the Blankney stud at Newmarket. The sale took place in Lord Rosebery's paddock, and resulted in an average of nearly 1,380 guineas, in so far as the nine yearlings by Hermit are concerned, while the whole thirteen, including those by the Earl of Dartrey, Blue Gown, Sterling and Sesame, made an average of about 1,014 guineas. This is extraordinary, indeed, and is plain proof that there is plenty of money in the market when the goods are tempting enough. By this sale Hermit has indeed set the seal upon his fame, or, if I may be allowed to perpetrate a most horrible joke, his fame is now Hermitically sealed.

The 3,600 guineas given for Hermit's chestnut daughter out of Adelaide, is the highest price ever tendered for a yearling, with the exception of Maximilian, bred by Mr. Waring, and for whom Mr. Robert Peck gave 4,100 guineas at one of the Cobham sales. As a kind of "luck-penny" on that occasion La Merveille was "chucked in" for her racing career; but, whereas Maximilian turned out a great disappointment, La Merveille did all sorts of useful things, including winning a Cambridgeshire. By a curious piece of unintentional satire, Maximilian's name figures in connection with the lowest-priced lot disposed of later on the same day. This was a bay mare (pedigree unknown) with a filly foal by Maximilian, and covered by Philammon, who was sold to Mr. John Percival for the fleabite of 20 guineas. It will doubtless be noticed that the 'mares who have thrown such high-priced yearlings to Hermit are for the most part of the late Lord Glasgow's breed, and hence the result of the sale is a great triumph to the eccentric earl's judgment in blood stock. Faraway, Adelaide, Sister to Adelaide, and the dam by Musket out of Adelaide's dam, have all Glasgow pedigrees.

The late Lord Wilton's stallions (Seesaw and Wenlock) were both purchased by Lord Rosslyn, the breeder of Tristan, who is frequently but erroneously described as a French horse. The average of the Blankney yearlings would have been still further increased had one, not sold, fetched the reserve price of 3,000 guineas. As it was, Mr. Chaplin was desirous of keeping him himself, and was consequently not disappointed.—*The Sporting Life.*

## MARKET REPORT.

[Franklin (Ohio) Chronicle.]
**A TWENTY YEARS' SIEGE.**

Twenty years of uninterrupted happiness would, we think, render life almost monotonous; but what must twenty years of suffering be to the average mortal? Think of it; twenty consecutive years of misery, years wherein the mind must constantly dwell upon the suffering of the body, because of the body's incapacity to labor, and therefore forget its suffering. The following official presentation of a case covered by the foregoing considerations is worthy of attention:

*State of Ohio, Tuscarawas County, ss:*
Before me, a Justice of the Peace, within and for the township of Franklin, Tuscarawas county, Ohio, personally appeared Isaac Fulk, who being duly sworn, according to law, deposeth as follows, to wit:—That for the past twenty-eight years I have been afflicted in both knee joints with that most dreadful disease, scrofulous white swelling; that I used and tried various remedies and took treatment of the best physicians during that time, but without receiving any benefit whatever, the disease constantly growing worse. Some time ago I was induced to try St. Jacobs Oil, and I am most happy to say that after using one and one half bottles there is great change for the better in my case, and that I can now walk better and can perform more labor than I could at any time in the past twenty years, being daily employed at hard manual labor. I feel as nearly cured as it is possible to cure such a disease.
ISAAC FULK.
Signed and sworn to by the said }
Isaac Fulk, before me, this }
28th day of April, A. D. 1882. }
PHILIP A. GARVER,
JUSTICE OF THE PEACE

Mr. Garver, in his letter conveying the foregoing, thus speaks of Mr. Fulk: "I send herewith the affidavit of Mr. Isaac Fulk, with reference to the benefits derived by him from the use of St. Jacobs Oil. I would say that the statement is true and reliable in every particular. Mr. Fulk is an honest, hard-working man, and is greatly delighted at the benefit derived from the remedy, and I thought his statement might be of some service to you, as well as to those afflicted in a similar manner with him. Hoping that the sales of your justly popular remedy may continue to increase, and everywhere give the same satisfaction as it has in this community,
I am truly yours,
PHILIP A. GARVER.

A new journal is to be established in San Francisco devoted to the interests of stock-breeding and out-door sports. Of course the breeding of horses, and especially race horses, both trotting and running, will receive most attention, but valuable information will be given on the breeding and management of all kinds of stock. A paper of this kind could be made of very great value to all farmers and stockmen, and if the proposed journal shall prove to be ably managed, it will be very likely to gain a liberal support among them. The first number of the paper will be issued on the first of next month, and will contain sixteen pages of reading matter. It will be called the BREEDER AND SPORTSMAN. The paper will be issued weekly, and will cost five dollars per year. The manager of the enterprise is Joseph Cairn Simpson.—*Greenville Bulletin, June 21st.*

The BREEDER AND SPORTSMAN is the title of an elegant sixteen-page weekly journal, published in San Francisco, the initial number of which has just made its appearance. The engraved heading of the BREEDER AND SPORTSMAN is the prettiest piece of work in that line that we have ever seen. The artist has won a genuine triumph, for he has not only incorporated in his beautiful design water and foliage, fruit and blossoms, fine horses, cattle and dogs, but all the emblems and symbols of sporting life. Joseph Cairn Simpson, the veteran turfman and accomplished gentleman, is the proprietor of this new venture in the field of journalism. He is supported by an able corps of writers, all of them well trained in the several departments over which they have been called to preside. The BREEDER AND SPORTSMAN deserves and will achieve success. Its field is large and remunerative. Each of the San Francisco and Sacramento dailies dishes up a weekly potpourri of sporting news. Then there's the *California Spirit of the Times*, the *Pacific Life* and the *Olympians*—all specially devoted to the subject and making for-tunes rapidly for their owners. The thirst of the California public for sporting intelligence, however, remains unappeased, and Mr. Simpson's splendid journal comes in to relieve the stress. An attractive feature of the new paper is the appearance each week of a drawing of some one or other of the "Notable Horses of California."—Mr. Winters' Duchess of Norfolk leading off in the first number. The breeders of the Pacific Coast, from the Columbia to the Colorado, and from the Sierras to the sea, should now stand in with Joe Simpson and make this journal a financial success. He has done more than any other man in America to elevate the turf and advance the breeding interests of the Pacific Coast.—*Territorial Enterprise.*

## J. A. McKERRON

Manufacturer of Fine Harness, Horse Boots a Specialty.

NO. 227 SUTTER STREET,

Between Dupont and Stockton.　San Francisco.

REPAIRING NEATLY AND PROMPTLY EXECUTED

---

## P. DOYLE,

1011 Market St., San Francisco,
California.

## Harness, Collar, Saddle

—AND—

### Horse Boot Manufacturer.

All work made of best materials by hand and warranted.

**SEND FOR PRICES.**

## PAUL FRIEDHOFER,

Pathological Horse Shoer

PRACTICAL IN ALL ITS VARIOUS BRANCHES

No. 105 COMMERCIAL ST.

## J. CONDON'S

### HAND BALL COURT,

733 HOWARD, bet. Third and Fourth.

Match Game Every Sunday.
Fine Wines and Liquors.

# BUY DIRECT

—FROM THE—

# Manufacturer!!

## Carriages.

## Buggies,

## and Wagons

Any Style
MADE TO ORDER.

### SULKIES A SPECIALTY.

Personal attention given to
Painting, Varnishing, Alterations and Repairs.

Office and Factory:
1317 and 1319 MARKET STREET,
Between Ninth and Tenth Streets.　San Francisco
M. J. McCUE, Proprietor.

### No Pay in Advance.

## Great Electric Hair Tonic!

The only sure remedy that will restore the hair.
LABORATORY AND SALESROOM, 130 Tyler Street.
For sale by all Druggists.

# SPORTING GOODS.

BOXING GLOVES, FOILS,
COMBAT SWORDS, MASKS,
INDIAN CLUBS.
HUNTING KNIVES,
Our Own Manufacture.
DOG COLLARS AND CHAINS,
Finest Assortment in the City.
WILL & FINCK,
Leading Cutlers,　769 Market Street

## Turkish and Russian STEAM BATHS.

No. 722 Montgomery Street,
Near Washington, San Francisco.

Russian Baths Cure Rheumatism.
Turkish Baths Cure Heart Disease.
Sulphur Baths Cure Skin Diseases.
Officinalia Baths Cure Poison Oak.
Steam Baths Cure Intemperance.
Medicated Vapor Baths Cure Catarrh.
Nasal, Throat and Lung Troubles.
These Baths Cure Constipation, Piles, Liver and Kidney Diseases, Fever and Ague and Biliousness, acting as a perfect Rejuvenator for all Nervousness and Debility, and to recuperate the system after long continued sickness, when all other remedies have failed. Connected with this establishment is a Medical Sanitarium, where patients will receive every attention and home comforts, including pleasant rooms and Hygienic board. Send for circulars giving full description of these celebrated Baths and Cost for a course of treatment.

DR. JUSTIN GATES,
Late of Sacramento, proprietor of the Turkish and Russian Baths, Medical Sanitarium and Steam Bath Drug Store, 722 Montgomery street, San Francisco.

## T. G. Parker & Co.,

The American Tailoring Establishment,
237 Kearny St., near Bush.

Business Suits.......................$25 to $35
Dress Suits............................$40 to $60

No Chinese labor employed or shoddy trimmings used.

---

## J. O'KANE,

MANUFACTURER AND IMPORTER OF

Harness, Saddles, Whips,
Blankets, Boots, Etc.

767——MARKET STREET,——767
SAN FRANCISCO, CAL.

Special attention given to the manufacture of "Boots" of all kinds for horses. Can refer to all the principal trainers and horsemen on the Pacific Coast.
N. B.—My acknowledged superiority in this branch of business is largely due to the careful observation and the valuable suggestions of the most skillful "horsemen" in the United States. The benefit of which revert to the public in the shape of a GENUINE WELL-FITTING ARTICLE. Sole agent for Dr. A. H. Dixon's Condition Powders and McKinney's (called "Karn's" and "Eclipse" Toe Weight Receiving done with neatness and dispatch. Has always on hand the finest assortment of English Ladies and Gentlemen's saddles, bridles, whips, spurs, bits, and track saddles.

## TURF EXCHANGE.

### FARRELLY & MITCHELL,

435 CALIFORNIA ST.

FINE

Wines, Liquors & Cigars.

## G. H. STRONG,

BICYCLES and TRICYCLES

252 MARKET STREET.

Repairs to order.　Elevator, 12 Front street

## DAVID L. LEVY,

39 THIRD STREET,

Jeweler, Designer of Medals
and Testimonials.

Repairing neatly done.

# Fine Thoroughbreds

## FOR SALE.

## Sacramento State Fair,

1882.

The subscriber has a lot of thoroughbred horses which will be offered at

## Auction Sale

During the State Fair Week at Sacramento. The lot consists of

### Brood Mares — four-year-olds three-year-olds, two-year-olds and yearlings.

Comprising some as finely bred and promising animals as there are on the Coast.

## W. L. PRITCHARD.

---

## BALL COURT,

846 Howard Street.

Fine Wines, Liquors and Cigars.
WM. ATKINS, Proprietor.

## DAN. McCARTHY,

LIVERY, BOARDING AND SALE STABLE

608 Howard St., near Second.

Largest stock of fast livery teams in the State. First-class boarding. Horses bought and sold. Cash advanced on horses, buggies, sulkies, harness or anything connected with the business.

## MDME. EXILDA LA CHAPELLE,

SPORTSMEN'S HEADQUARTERS,

N. E. Corner Post and Central Avenue.

Refreshments and Ladies' Sitting Room.

## H. H. WILSON & SON,

Importers and Dealers in

GUNS, PISTOLS, CUTLERY, FISHING
TACKLE, AMMUNITION, ETC.

SEVENTEENTH

# INDUSTRIAL EXHIBITION

—OF THE—

# Mechanics' Institute

WILL OPEN TO THE PUBLIC ON
TUESDAY, AUGUST 15, 1882,
—AT THE—

# NEW PAVILION,

Larkin, Hayes, Polk and Grove Sts.,

AND CONTINUE UNTIL SEPT. 16th.

PREMIUMS of Gold, Silver and Bronze Medals, Diplomas and Cash, will be awarded to meritorious exhibits in Art, Manufactures and Natural Products.
Full information will be given or sent by applying at the office, 27 Post St.

P. B. CORNWALL, President
J. H. CULVER, Secretary.　J. H. GILMORE, Supt.

## T. McGINNIS,

MANUFACTURER OF

SADDLES, HARNESS, WHIPS, COL-
LARS, BRIDLES, AND HORSE
CLOTHING.

Repairing carefully done. Only first-class material used
775 Market st., bet. 3rd & 4th.

*For a Cool, Refreshing Drink,*

## SAMPLE'S HEADQUARTERS,

231 Kearny st.,

Bet. Bush and Sutter.　San Francisco.

S. S. SAMPLE.

## Specimen of Our Artist's Humor.

THE MUSIC LESSON.

# HUNDREDS OF DELIGHTED ONES

See, for the First Time in their Lives, the

## JAPANESE ARTIST AND EMBROIDERERS

AT WORK IN THEIR NATIVE COSTUMES, AT

# ICHI BAN, 22 and 24 Geary Street

The BREEDER AND SPORTSMAN is printed with Shattuck and Fletcher's Ink.

SATURDAY, SEPT. 23d.

FRIDAY, SEPTEMBER 1ST.

SATURDAY, SEPTEMBER 2D.

**REMARKS AND CONDITIONS.**

## SONOMA & MARIN
### DISTRICT
## AGRICULTURAL ASSOCIATION

# RACES
### AT
# PETALUMA

TUESDAY, AUGUST 29TH.

WEDNESDAY, AUGUST 30TH, 1882.

THURSDAY, AUGUST 31ST.

---

# SECOND
## ANNUAL EXHIBITION
### OF THE
# SAN MATEO AND SANTA CLARA COUNTY
## AGRICULTURAL ASSOCIATION
### NO. 5,
TO BE HELD AT
# SAN JOSE, CAL.,
......FROM......
### Sept. 25th to 30th, '82, inclusive

## SPEED PROGRAMME.

FIRST DAY—Monday, Sept. 25th, 1882.

SECOND DAY—Tuesday, Sept. 26th.

**REMARKS AND CONDITIONS.**

A. KING, President.
T. S. MONTGOMERY, Secretary.

---

## The Victorian Trotting Club,
### (L'd.)
MELBOURNE, AUSTRALIA,
......OFFER......

### PRIZE OF 2,500 DOLLARS,

---

## California's Exposition for 1882.
Sacramento, California.

Opens Monday, September 11th,
Closes Saturday, September 16th.

A Holiday Week of Recreation and Sport.

### $40,000 IN CASH
To be awarded in Premiums.

B. J. GREEN, Secretary.
EDWIN F. SMITH, President.

---

### $12,500
## In Purses and Stakes.

## CALIFORNIA
# STATE FAIR
## SPEED PROGRAMME
FOR 1882.

FIRST DAY—Monday, Sept. 11.

**REMARKS AND CONDITIONS.**

## SECOND DAY—Tuesday, Sept. 12.

## THIRD DAY—Wednesday, Sept. 13.

## FOURTH DAY—Thursday, Sept. 14.

## FIFTH DAY—Friday, Sept. 15.

## SIXTH DAY—Saturday, Sept. 16.

### REMARKS and CONDITIONS.

All trotting and pacing races are the best three in five, except the two year old trot, unless otherwise specified; two to enter and two to start. Entrance ten per cent on purse, to accompany nomination. Purses divided at the rate of sixty per cent to first, thirty to second, and ten per cent to third.

National Association Rules to govern trotting; but the Board reserve the right to trot heats of any two classes alternately, if necessary to finish any day's racing, or to trot a special race to fill a day, and to change the order of the programme.

All two-year-olds, when running in their classes, shall carry one hundred pounds, with the usual allowance for mares and geldings.

All three-year-olds, when running in their classes, to carry one hundred and ten pounds, with the usual allowance as above.

Those who have nominations in stakes MUST name to the Secretary, IN WRITING, the horses they will start on Monday, on the Saturday previous; and on Wednesday the Monday previous; and on Friday the Wednesday previous, to prevent delay in drawing positions. Purses can be strictly adhered to.

No added money paid for a walk over.

Horses entered in purses can only be drawn by consent of Judges.

Rules of the Pacific Coast Blood Horse Association (old system) to govern running races, except where conditions named are otherwise.

EDWIN F. SMITH, Secretary.  HUGH M. LARUE, President.

---

# Golden Gate Fair.

## SPEED PROGRAMME FOR 1882

## $10,000

### IN

## Stakes and Prizes

### FIRST DAY—Monday, Sept. 4, 1882.

### SECOND DAY—Tuesday, Sept. 5.

### THIRD DAY—Wednesday, Sept. 6.

---

## FOURTH DAY—Thursday, Sept. 7.

## FIFTH DAY—Friday, Sept. 8.

## SIXTH DAY—Saturday, Sept. 9.

### CONDITIONS.

All the trotting and pacing races are the best three in five, when there are eight or more starters in a trotting race, 100 yards to be a distance.

National Trotting Association rules to govern trotting, but the Board reserve the right to trot heats with any two races alternately, if necessary to finish any day's racing, or to trot a special race between heats.

Those who have nominations in stakes MUST name to the Secretary, in writing, the horses they will start on Monday, on the Saturday previous; and on Wednesday the Monday previous; and on Friday the Wednesday previous. No added money will be paid for a walk over. Horses entered in purses can only be drawn by consent of the Judges.

Rules of the Pacific Coast Blood Horse Association to govern running races, except as above provided.

Write "Entries to name" on outside of Envelope.

L. WALKER, Secretary.  A. G. DIETZ, President.

---

## GOLDEN GATE FAIR.

### BICYCLE RACE!

ON SATURDAY, SEPTEMBER 9TH,

FREE FOR ALL.

A dash of a mile, for a purse of $50, of which $35 to the first and $15 to the second rider.

ENTRANCE FREE!

Nominations to be made on Monday, September 4, 1882, by 3 P. M., at the office.

L. WALKER, Secretary.

# BREEDER AND SPORTSMAN

NO. 508 MONTGOMERY STREET.

## SAN FRANCISCO, SATURDAY, SEPTEMBER 2, 1882.

Vol. I., No. 10.

SUBSCRIPTION
FIVE DOLLARS A YEAR.

# ANTEVOLO.

### FOALED MAY 12, 1881. BY ELECTIONEER, HIS DAM, COLUMBINE, BY A. W. RICHMOND.

The portraiture above is not given as being the representation of a "notable" but rather as a type of an animal which can be expected from analogous breeding. And yet there might be a wide divergence. When coupling animals that have various strains of blood, it is difficult to say which will predominate. "Reversion" "atavism," "revolution," all of the terms which writers have used, may appear appropriate to the animal under discussion, and the reversion to one parent, the following a recognized type, a revolution of an individual in the genealogy upset all recognized theories, and leave the diligent student in a maze of conjecture. There is scarcely a position which cannot be sustained from the records. The calendar will sustain the thousand and one theories; who in bolstering their claims point to a combination that has been successful, and these are highly indignant when any one questions the accuracy of their statements. "Figures will not lie" is a favorite dogma, and though that "twice two are four" is a proposition which scarcely admits

of denial, there are numbers who will dispute the accuracy of the multiplication which interferes with their figuring. The illustration of the yearling colt which is though worthy of being placed on a page which has contained the presentiment of actual notabilities is a lesson which is not entirely trustworthy. It presents very nearly our ideal of the proper form of a trotting-bred youngster, and still without displaying objectional points worthy of correction. But as proof that these do not arise from the conjunction of blood, or the making of individuals, he has an older brother which is nearly perfect in points which the younger lacks, deficient where the junior is superior.

One of the chief elements in causing the breeding of horses to be so fascinating is the uncertainty. The "glorious uncertainty" of racing affords the charm which entices all who have enjoyed in the pursuit, and in breeding this is so highly intensified that a man with a spark of feeling becomes infatuated. Like the pall which hangs over the future—es-

pecially the far-off future beyond this world—there is the ever-present doubt. The overshadowing doubt which fruition can remove, only and to which previous failures give a sombering color. The next is to be the bright spot, and the hope which springs from the shadow constantly cheers.

Now as to the breeding of the subject of the sketch. His sire, Electioneer, is so well known that there is scarcely a necessity for further comment. His breeding is of the ultra-trotting stamp. By Rysdyk's Hambletonian, his dam by Sayre's Harry Clay, there are united the lines which stand second on the list. It would still be a greater waste of time amplifying on the Hambletonian. A man who does not give them the foremost place in the trotting galaxy of wonders, is either bigoted or nonsensical. There may come up another strain which will deserve equal prominence, and he would be a rash man who asserted that there would be no changes. On the side of the dam there are lines which are not so well known. All on that side are thoroughbred, so far as they ar-known, with the exception of one strain, and that "missing link" is a race which have, at least, the merit of peculiarity.

According to the formula of the stud book, the pedigree will run:

1st dam Columbine, by A. W. Richmond.
2d dam Columbia, by imported Bonnie Scotland.
3d dam Young Fashion, by imported Monarch.
4th dam Fashion, by imported Trustee.
5th dam Bonnets o' Blue, by Sir Charles.
6th dam Reality, by Sir Archy.
7th dam by imported Medley.
8th dam by imported Centinel.
9th dam by Mark Anthony.
10th dam by imported Monkey.
12th dam by imported Silvereye.
13th dam by Spanker.

This pedigree has a close resemblance to those which follow the winners of some of the big events on the legitimate, and after the first dam it would be difficult to compile a more fashionable line of dams. There would be no need of further comment if the queries were restricted to the turf, but now the question is, what is there outside of the Hambletonian to make it desirable in a trotting pedigree? A. W. Richmond was by Simpson's Blackbird, his dam by Rattler—claimed to be thoroughbred, and his granddam by Spotted Range, in the language of the bills an Arabian, though more properly an Opelousas horse. There was a race of horses in Ohio, western New York, and Northern Pennsylvania called Arabians. They were singularly marked horses, many of them spotted, with light manes and rat-tails. They were noted for gameness on the road, going long distances with little fatigue, and serviceable, though with tempers which could scarcely be called serene. In the Southern States they are denominated Opelousas horses, and their origin has been credited to the early Spanish importations. The singular markings which a majority of them show substantiates this view, and even with as little of the blood as Antevolo possesses is there, the slim tail and light mane, which are tokens of the inheritance.

A. W. Richmond is the sire of Romero, San Diegeo, Len Rose, Mavis, etc. He has enjoyed the smallest opportunity in the stud never having made a "regular season" until his importation to California, and then restricted to a few mares. Had he never done more than to get Romero, with the fastest four-year-old stallion record 2:22¼ it would scarcely be called a poor showing. On this side of the house are California Blackbird record 2:22, Little Fred, 2:20. T. Nourmahal, who beat Lady Mac in Chicago and forced her to make the fastest record for five miles, here is a sister of A. W. Richmond, and we always regarded her as one of the most perfect, pure-gaited trotters. The grandam of Antevolo, as the pedigree shows, is thoroughbred. Her sire, Bonnie Scotland, is too well known to require more than an allusion to him as the progenitor of race horses. He had the first place in the list of winning sires in 1880, his get showing winnings aggregating $135,700, and he is also a standard sire, as his sons Scotland and Dan Donaldson have respectively records of 2:22¼—2:24¾. The fourth dam of Antevolo, Fashion by imported Trustee, is generally credited with being the best race mare ever bred in America; she was certainly one of the best, and took altogether the most prominent place in the turf history of her day. Revenue, the sire of Planet, and others of the get of "Honest Trustee" kept up their reputation on the turf, and as the first horse to make twenty miles within the hour trotting was also got by him there came a trotting inheritance. In California the reputation of the family has not suffered, as John Nelson by imported Trustee is the sire of Nerea, 2:23½; Aurora, 2:27, and Governor Stanford, 2:27½. The third dam of Antevolo was by imported Monarch; and a son of this horse, Strawn's Monarch, is the sire of Monarch Rule, 2:24½, and Monarch Jr. with the same record. The sixth dam, Reality, by Sir Archy, was claimed to be the best race horse which her owner, Colonel W. R. Johnson, ever had, and as he was recognized to be the most acute turfuman of his time, his classification is sure to be nearly correct. The daughter of Reality, Bonnets o' Blue, was a fair race-mare and as she was by Sir Charles there was a "double Archy" cross and, of course, a double infusion of imported Diomed, which is generally accredited with being a potent mixture in a trotting pedigree.

The strains of thoroughbred blood in Antevolo have been demonstrated as a proper admixture for the trotting tracks, and with it there is a degree of quality which only comes from a strong infusion of the royal lines. There is so little necessity for written description accompanying the graphic representation of our artist, that it seems a waste of space to add to the penciled delineation. There may be an addenda, however, in giving the color and size. Antevolo is a brown with mealy nose and light tan in the flanks. He is nearly fifteen hands over the withers, rather more than that over the loins. He is fine as well as muscular and in a stable of thoroughbreds would not appear out of place. His disposition could scarcely be improved—docile as his companion the terrier, and with intelligence beyond what is usually seen in so young an animal. Trotting is nearly as natural to him as the gallop, and his action as good as need be. The fifth time he was driven on the track he trotted a quarter of a mile in fifty seconds, and the first time he was driven a mile he showed 3:12. This rate of speed, while far below what our California colts of the same age have shown, prove that the fast-trotting step has been inherited, and as he was only a few days over fifteen months when the trial was given, there is a chance for him to make a reduction while he is still in his yearling form.

## Breeding of Coach Horses.

CINEGA RANCHO, August 26, 1882.

EDITOR BREEDER AND SPORTSMAN:—Your leading article of the 5th of August refers to the breeding of coach horses, and says: "The combination of blood which has been found in England well adapted for the production of these animals is three-quarters throughbred and the other portion Clydesdale; but the thoroughbreds used must have the requisite size and proper shape." You are, I think, rather indefinite, and this statement might mislead some of your readers. You don't specify that the Clydesdale blood must be on the dam side—and this is, I think, essential. Here in California any such enterprise on a large scale is not within reach of the ordinary farmer and stock-raiser. To begin with, the class of thoroughbred sire would, to say the least of it, be very hard to find. Secondly, the Clydesdale mares are very expensive; and thirdly, the first cross from Clydesdale to Thoroughbred is a most unequal animal. By unequal, I mean the produce is neither level as a lot, nor are the individual specimens, what every judge so much admires, level made horses. To continue breeding these mares, the cross of the Clyde and the thoroughbred, you should have a large choice of thoroughbredsires, as thus the mares from their very inequality could not, successfully, be all rated to the same stamp of sire. This choice of thoroughbred sires cannot be found in the State. This irregularity also makes the geldings from this first cross very unsaleable.

So much for my complaint, and no one should publicly find fault without having, at least, a supposed remedy.

Look out for shape, action and bone in your mares, and don't hanker so much after size to commence with. Such mares can be picked up much cheaper than the worst made Clydes in the country. Breed these to an even-made, well boned, thoroughbred horse. Few know, however, how the first cross of thoroughbred on medium-sized, cold blooded mares increases size. Your fillies from this stock will be a much larger stamp than their dams, more rangy; breeding strongly after the horses, even as a lot and level made individually. The geldings will surely sell well as first class saddle horses or fair light road horses. In the next choice of stallion much judgment will be required. Some of these half-breed mares may require another crop of thoroughbred, but the majority should be fit to breed to a full, large, true-actioned, well-bred trotting sire; shape, size and action being more requisite than great speed. This crop will, I think, give you fine coach horses in the majority of cases, and the few that fall short should, at least, be large, useful road horses. I do not offer these suggestions to the large capitalist, who can afford to be out of his money and any return therefrom for an indefinite period, but I write to caution the ordinary farmer, who yearly expects a return on his money and trouble, against these sudden jumps in breeding, which produce clumsy nondescripts in the majority of cases. Small bodies, big legs and heads, or, worse again, large bodies, large heads, short necks, and small legs. They, in fact, ring the changes in every conceivable form.

BROAD ARROW.

## Late Importations of Percherons at Petaluma.

PETALUMA, Aug. 29.

EDITOR BREEDER AND SPORTSMAN: Upon my arrival here on the morning of the 27th I met Mr. H. Wilsey and accompanied him to his ranch about four and a half miles from this place. There are ten fine Percheron stallions lately imported by himself and Mr. H. T. Fairbanks from France. They were selected by Mr. Wilsey himself from the best to be found in France and are as fine a lot as I have ever seen. They are from three years to six years of age, perfectly sound and in fine condition. Julius Cæser was the first shown, a dark iron gray; Marshal Ney, a dapple gray; Murat, black, DeLesseps, dark dapple gray; Bob Ingersol, dapple gray; Knight of Normandy, iron-gray, is nearly black; Bonaparte, dark bay; Robespiene, nearly black; Dumas, gray, and Emperor, dark brown. These horses range in weight from 1450 to 1800 pounds, perfectly formed, of fine action and all of them so nearly perfect as to make it difficult to choose between them. Sonoma county is taking the lead for this class of stock, and previous to this latest importation there were many very superior animals of this popular breed. The show at the fair of the various draft breeds will demonstrate that this is the business county of the State for heavy horses.

H. P. M.

CHICO, Aug. 29.

EDITOR BREEDER AND SPORTSMAN: Since my last letter the following horses have arrived at the track to take a hand in the races to come off next week during the District Fair. Mr. Ab Ellis has the the following: Fred Hunter, bay, by Norfolk, dam by Lodi. Entered in 1¼ mile running race. Also Tilton Almont, by Almont. I saw an extended pedigree in your issue of last week. He is a fine, powerful looking horse. Also Kate Almont, by Tilton Almont, 3 years old. Mr. John Spurgeon's three-year-old bay colt Telegraph, by Tilton Almont. He won the three-year-old race Saturday, August 26th, for all Tilton Almont colts; best heat 2:55; by horse Shiner, by Norfolk, dam by Rifleman. Tom Haslep has ch. g. by Norfolk, dam by Rifleman. There are several draft horses on the ground, but all I had time to look at was British Stallion Sir Tom, sired by an imported Clydesdale horse.

OCCASIONAL.

SETH GREEN ON THE FINNY TRIBE.—Why talk about reasoning powers! The perseverance and instinct of these little creatures is wonderful. People go out to fish. They splash around, stand up in their boat, drop their lines three feet away, and wonder because they don't catch trout. They forget that trout can see. Fish learn that tackle, and fish are, as a rule, local in their habitation. There are not as many gypsies among fish as among men. Any man who will take the pains to study fish—or who will remember a tithe of what he reads about them—can catch them. They are smart, but our brains will beat them. I remember once of fishing for salmon trout for a long time and taking nothing. Finally I concluded to get down and look into the water, and so, throwing my coat over my head, I got the required shade and peered down. The salmon would sail up and look at the minnow. Then, with a quick dart, he would close his teeth round one-half the minnow and open them again like a flash. He did not attempt to eat the minnow, and half of the severed body would drop to the bottom. When it had fallen to the bed of the lake the salmon would go down and leisurely eat it. The next time when I dropped my hook and felt the quick bite of the trout I let out enough line to send the hook to the bottom, and the result was that when the salmon went down for his meal he was fooled and I had him.

# TURF AND TRACK.

## Fixed Events.

Golden Gate Fair, to be held at Oakland, from September 4th to the 9th inclusive.
Butte District Fair at Chico, from September 5th to September 8th inclusive.
El Dorado District Fair at Placerville, from September 5th to September 8th inclusive.
California State Fair. Annual meeting at Sacramento, from Monday, September 11th to 16th inclusive.
The San Joaquin Valley Association Fair at Stockton, from September 19th to the 23d inclusive.
Oregon State Fair at Salem, from September 18th and during the week.
The San Mateo and Santa Clara County Agricultural Association Fair at San Jose, September 25th to the 30th inclusive.
Humboldt and Mendocino District Fair at Rhonerville, September 19th to September 22d inclusive.
Modoc, Plumas and Lassen District Fair at Greenville, from October 2d to October 5th inclusive.
Monterey District Fair at Salinas City, from October 2d to October 6th inclusive.
Nevada State Fair at Reno, from Monday, October 2d to the 7th inclusive.
Mount Shasta Agricultural Association Fair at Yreka, October 4th, 5th, 6th and 7th.
Eastern Oregon Fine Stock Association at Union, from October 9th to the 14th inclusive.
Los Angeles Agricultural Association, at Los Angeles, from October 17th to 21st inclusive.

FAIRS AT THE EAST.

Minnesota State Fair at Farmington, August 31st to September 8th inclusive.
Iowa State Fair at Fairfield, September 1st to the 8th inclusive.
Minnesota Agricultural Association, at Minneapolis, September 4th to the 9th inclusive.
Nebraska State Fair, at Omaha, September 11th to the 16th inclusive.
Rhode Island State Fair, at Providence, September 12th to the 15th inclusive.
Pennsylvania State Fair, at Pittsburg, September 7th to the 21st inclusive.
Wisconsin State Fair, at Fond du Lac, September 11th to the 16th inclusive.
Ontario Provincial Fair, at Toronto, September 18th to the 23d inclusive.
Connecticut State Fair, at Meriden, September 18th to the 22d inclusive.
New Jersey State Fair, at Monroe, September 18th to the 22d inclusive.
West Virginia Central Fair, at Clarksburg, September 19th to the 21st inclusive.
Indiana State Fair, at Indianapolis, September 25th to the 30th inclusive.
Western Michigan Fair, at Grand Rapids, September 25th to the 30th inclusive.
Texas State Fair, at Austin, October 17th to the 21st inclusive.

## The Hartford Races.

The circuit meeting of Hartford, Con., opened on Wednesday last at the Charter Oak Park, with the largest attendance known anywhere in the circuit. The weather was delightful and the track perfect. In the 2:28 class Gladiator was first, Eva second, May Thorne third, Topsey distanced. Time, 2:22¼, 2:23¾, 2:26. Of the 2:25 class, pacers, Fuller came in first, Warrior second, Mattie Bond third, with Limber Jack fourth and distanced. Time, 2:17¼, 2:25¼, 2:22, 2:27, 2:18. In the 2:23 class Aldine was first, Flora F. second, R. P. third, and Cora Belmont fourth. Time, 2:20, 2:20, 2:22.

On the 30th there was a notable increase in the attendance, among whom were W. H. Vanderbilt and party. In the 2:29 class, Overman won, Morse's Yellow Dock second, Rigolette third, Independence fourth, Dave Young distanced. Time—2:21½, 2:23½, 2:23½. In the special race for $3,000, Edwin Thorne won, Clingstone second. Time—2:17, 2:19¼, 2:21½, 2:21. In the pacing race, open to all pacers, Buffalo Girl won, Gem second, Lucy third, Flora Belle fourth, Mattie Hunter distanced. Time—2:16, 2:19, 2:16, 2:16½, 2:17¼. In the 2:21 class, Clem McG. won, Brandy Boy second, Adell Gould third, Forest fourth. Time—2:23¾, 2:21½, 2:23¾.

## The Blanchard Purse.

On the 14th of this month will be decided the sensational trot of the season, the great purse of $10,000 for the 2:17 class offered by D. H. Blanchard of Boston, the race to come off at Beacon Point, near that city. The conditions of the race were that the entries should be divided into four different payments of $250 each, at stated periods, and that the non payment of any of the sums would amount to a forfeit and release the nominator from any further liability. There were thirteen entries, and all the number have paid up their quota, the proviso being that at the final installment, due on Aug. 31st, the horses must be named that represent the interests of each nominator. As may be supposed, the relative performances of all the first-class horses throughout the circuit have been eagerly scanned by those who are interested in this great event, and on the other side, the horses that have shown first-class speed are looking around to secure a nomination on the best procurable terms. The horses intended when the first payments were made have, in several cases, gone to the bad; but on the other hand, there are such flyers as Black Cloud, Jerome Eddy, Clemmie G., Rosa Wilkes, Mattie Graham, and half a dozen others that were not expected to be in the field, whose services may be available. It is said that the owner of Clemmie G. has been offered $1,000 for the use of her for this race, and various other negotiations are in progress for other stars of the season. It is claimed that never in the annals of the turf has there been such a grand selection of trotters on a track together as will figure among the starters of the great Blanchard Purse.

H.

## A Turf Scandal in England.

That excentric sportsman Sir John Astley, who had that serious quarrel with Mr. Watson the plunger last fall at Newmarket, has come to the fore again, having laid charges against Lord Ellesmere before the Stewards of Goodwood that his horse Lowland Chief was pulled in his races at Newmarket and Ascot so that he might be favorably weighted in the handicaps at Goodwood, where this same horse carried off one of the principal events with long odds against his chances. No one for a moment entertains that Lord Ellesmere would allow any such practices, but the owners of horses are greatly in the hands of their trainers, and there is no doubt but that there are many dubious deeds committed that would lead to the withdrawal of the stable from their care, if honest and capable public trainers were not so scarce in England as they are in this country. On this much mooted point as to wheather an owner or trainer has the right to start a horse in a race, which he is not intended to even try to win, that clever writer, Bendracon, in the London *Referee* makes the following remarks: "General opinion is to the effect that if the owner or the trainer is to be brought before the stewards every time a horse practically contradicts what he has done before either at the same meeting or at previous meetings, no owner or trainer will be safe from annoyance. To put the situation in its mildest form, if you do away with public airings, you are very likely at the same time to do away with public racing. Experts will be the first to understand that, in the event of such inquiries becoming the rule instead of the exception, an owner would oftener be annoyed by accusation when his horse was really amiss, or when it had not recovered from being amiss, than when it was doing a shunt, or when, having done a shunt, it was going for the pieces. If you call a man, no matter whether peer or commoner, before the stewards because his horse wins though the betting is against him, surely you will have to call him before the stewards because his horse doesn't win though the betting is in his favor. It is only now and again that a carefully planned good thing has to be carried out with anything like barefacedness. A short-distance race and a young and impulsive trainer may bring about a difficulty. But, as a rule, the people equal to arranging a "moral" are anxious not to excite unpleasant observation. In a good many cases where it looks as if the horse had been roping, or is roping, appearances, and appearances only, are against the supposed sinner. Now and again, of course, we get a flagrant case. Either a horse is stopped, and everybody knows it, or, having been stopped at one place, he gets his head loose at another.

"This is where the difficulty is with judicial interference. A great deal more evidence than is obtainable is necessary to ensure a conviction, although the judges, the witnesses, and everybody else may be as certain as they are certain of their very existences that the accused parties are guilty. Often enough when an inquiry would otherwise be held, stewards, who are above all things men of the world, allow the undoubtedly nefarious transaction to slide without notice. More harm than good is done by commencing inquiry without being able to carry it out thoroughly.

"Let us argue this matter in whatever way we will, and let us go on as long as there is any room for argument, we are always brought back to the old and hackneyed statement, which is none the less true because it is both old and hackneyed, that racing resolves itself entirely into a question of winning or losing money. This being admitted, cup races have at once no reason for existence. No man in his senses would enter a horse in a cup race while he could do anything else with him. Let us suppose that Mr. Crawford or Mr. Gretton or Lord Stamford or the Duke of Westminster or Brown or Jones or Robinson or Smith, or anybody else the reader may choose to fix upon, possesses a youngster who is, according to the kindly feelings of his owner and trainer, a good half-stone better than an average Derby winner. This horse does not happen to have been entered in any of the "classic races," (that is the great two-year-old and three-year-old stakes) but the cups and one or two other weight-for-age events are open for him. Of course an owner who had nothing but the interests of the turf at heart, and who raced for glory and for glory only, would at once enter this paragon where he would have an opportunity of showing his undoubted merit. Somehow or other no owner or trainer has yet been found to do anythiug of the sort. The temptation to win a valuable handicap, and the large amount of money that is to be got by means of such handicap, is too great for one or other of them, and so it is only after this same youngster has for a time been made to appear of the most ordinary caliber, that we at last discover what are his real merits. Millionaires and men to whom money cannot be the least object have owned horses similar to the one I have imagined, but they all go the same way to work—the way of getting money. This goes to prove that the honest and honorable owner is often enough the weakest man in the stable—is often enough but an instrument in the hands of his trainer."

## The Oregon State Fair.

From all accounts this annual fair will be a great success. It opens at Salem on September 18th and lasts throughout the week, and it is pleasant to note that the press and the public appear more than willing to aid the executive officers in their efforts to make this meeting a credit to the great State the progress and prosperity of which these fairs ought so well to represent. Mr. E. M. Waite, the Secretary of the Association, in a recent letter, remarks: "The time for holding the annual state fair is rapidly approaching, and I am making preparations for it with better spirit than for years past. Everything points to a grand financial success if the weather is favorable. The posters will be exhibited throughout Oregon, Washington Territory and Idaho in a few days. The exhibition of cattle, sheep and swine will be unusually good, especially the former, in Jerseys and Shorthorns, while the Pavilion exhibit promises to be equal to any former year. If all arrangements can be perfected as now desired by the executive committee, our receipts will be much larger in some departments than they have been for two years. Of course the public understand that the society offers no money this year for racing, but notwithstanding that, the best trials of speed ever seen at any fair will be witnessed this year. I look for a fine display of fruits, vegetables and farm products, and for a general exhibition of unusual interest and attraction."

The Goodwood Cup for 1882.—The subject of the chief prize at the Goodwood meeting is the parting of Hotspur and Lady Percy, and the pair are represented as they might have stood at the moment when, to his wife's question: "What is it carries you away?" Percy answers: "Why, my horse, my love—my horse." He forms the center of a group, wearing his armor, with his gauntlets hanging at the hilt of his sword, the right hand held out towards the head of the roan. His lady is on his left, her head bent towards him, and she holds his little finger in both her hands, as if about to carry out her half playful, half shrewish threat:

In faith, I'll break thy little finger, Harry,
An if thou wilt not tell me all things true.

The group is in oxidized silver, and the detail is most elaborately wrought out in raised and chased work, the trappings and housings of the horse bearing the motto of the Percys, "Esperance en Dieu," and the cognizances of the house, while the armor of the noble youth and the costume of his lady have been minutely worked over. The group, from the bottom of the silver base to the top of the highest figure is about twenty inches in height, and when placed on the ebony stand the trophy will be nearly a yard high. On a silver plate in front of the ebonized block is the passage from Shakespeare's play (Henry IV., Part I., act 2, scene 3) which the group illustrates.

A Famous Mare.—Glidelia, the victress in the Grand Prize at Saratoga, where she beat Thora, Bend Or and other good horses, pulled up lame a few days after that race, and was found to be incapable of further training. She now retires to the paddock and next season will be mated to Sensation, and the progeny, if they take after their sire and dam, ought to hold the van on the American turf. Her reputation was second to none of her age. As a two-year-old she started four times, winning once, when she beat Carita, Luke Blackburn and four others. As a three-year-old she won five out of nine races, and ran a dead heat with Grenada for the Breckenridge Stakes at Baltimore. Owing to sickness, her four-year-old career was a failure, but as a five-year-old up to the date of her breaking down she had won eight out of eleven races. Glidelia is by Bonnie Scotland from Walz, representing some of the very best English and American strains.

## The Crack Two-year-old at the East.

Our opinion of Pizarro is greater than ever, as his performance in winning the August stake is one that few, if any, two-year-olds in our experience would have been capable of accomplishing. He was not intended to win, and was allowed to do so only because his stable companion could not. At that juncture he was last of all, and only 400 yards from the post. Straight as an arrow he shot through them and came up the stretch as strong as a lion. At the furlong pole he was at Jacobus' head. In a few strides further he was clear, and Feake pulled him up a winner in front of the stand. It was an extraordinary bit of racing, for, in addition to the speed needed to accomplish it, we should not forget that he was conceding weight to all of his competitors—2 lbs. to Jacobus, 5 lbs. to Magnate, and 7 lbs. to Heel-and-Toe. We regard the now-acknowlekged superiority of Pizarro as a sort of vindication of our judgment, expressed in The *Spirit* when he made his first appearance at Sheepshead Bay in June. Then, and at each favorable opportunity afterward, we ventured the opinion that he would develop form of the highest class. We felt justified in doing so. Pizarro is the finest two-year-old we ever saw, unless Sensation be the exception. Moreover, we had met him at the dock when he arrived—a small, rough-coated little brute—from England, in company with the great Mortemer, and were amazed at the improvement eighteen months had made in him. Again, his ancestry was the most distinguished, and he formed a link between our early reading of English racing literature and the present, for he was bred by the widow of the late Rev. John King.

Mr. King was the rector of Ashley de la Laude in Lincolnshire, and raced over the *nom de course* of "Mr. Laude," though it is possible he is dearer to English hearts as "the sporting parson." He was born to wealth and an attachment to the turf, and, like the late Lord Glasgow and Sir Joseph Hawley, loved to breed almost exclusively from "his own blood." What "Maid of Masham," and "General Peel's dam" were to the eccentric old sailor Earl, Manganese and her daughter were to "the sporting parson." From this daughter of Birdcatcher came The Miner, Mandragora, Mineral, Thorsday, Minaret, In Memoriam and Milliner. The Miner defeated Blair Athol at York, and it only requires a cold winter's night, and a social party within, with pipe and decanter, to induce George Sutcliffe to break his reser e and tell how "the dark chestnut caught old Blair," and how "Johnny," on The Miner, "flapped his wings a little," and beat the Derby winner on thé post. Mandragora produced Mandrake, one of the best distance horses of his day; Agility, who, as a five-year-old, won five Queen's Plates at distances of two miles, and beat Albert Victor for the York cup, and her sister, Apology, won the One Thousand, Oaks, St. Leger, and Ascot Gold Cup. Mineral was equally distinguished as a brood-mare, having foaled Wenlock, who won the St. Leger, and Kisber, who won the Derby. Wenlock has sired Quicklime, and was recently sold in England for $19,330. Probably there is no instance afforded in history where the love for the blood-horse, for which Englishmen of all conditions are noted, exceeds that presented in the case of the late Mr. King. His family was one of the old-fashioned English, who saw no harm in breeding and racing their horses, but envious clergymen prompted Dr. Wordsworth, the Bishop of Lincoln, to offer the old vicar the alternative of choosing between the turf and his pastorage. The correspondence between the two forms the most lively reading, but with a beautiful consciousness of rectitude and an Anglo-Saxon inflexibility, which commands the warmest admiration, he regretfully but firmly refused. It was but shortly after this that he named a full sister to The Holy Friar, Hypocrisy. Mr. King became famous, the people sided with him against the Bishop, whose intrusion they regarded as unwarrantable. At this time Apology was at the flood-tide of her renown. The One Thousand Guineas, the Oaks and the St. Leger, fell to her, but when Royal Ascot came, the following year, with its spring flowers and fashions, and Apology reached the apex of racing glory, by succeeding West Australia, Gladiateur and Blue Gown; as winner of the Gold Cup, the fatal escutcheon had hung over the door of the Lincolnshire home, and the old Vicar was at sleep with his fathers.

Pizarro, as we have stated time and again, is a brother in blood to Apology, they being by the same sire, and their dams were full sisters. They are somewhat the antipodes of each other. Apology was a dark chestnut like their grandsire, Rataplan. She was not above 15:2, and girthed 53 inches, with not the best shoulders, and drooping quarters. Pizarro is a rich bay, of great size and substance and quarters not unlike Sensation's in their length and rotundity. His combination of blood is exquisite, possessing as he does the double Birdcatcher cross on Touchstone, which has produced more good horses in England than any other. Mr. Pryor says he remembers Adventurer as an exceedingly handsome horse, and a better racer than he gets the credit of being, but has his doubts of Pizarro's stamina. It is notorious, however, that his relations, Agility, Apology, Wenlock, and Mandrake, were thorough stayers, and his pedigree is a handsome combination of staying blood, for in addition to those noted he has crosses of Beeswing, Partisan, Glencoe, and Tomboy, five of Waxy, and as many more of Orville.—*"Vigilant" in the N. Y. Spirit of the Times.*

## On Unruly Scoring.

Mr. John Splan is reported as addressing the following winged words to Mr. C. J. Hamlin, of Buffalo: "There is nothing that so worries the people and the horses as all these long waits to get a lot of cranky horses off. There was never a time yet, so far as I can remember, that the horse making the most fuss about getting away did the best at the finish. I think it radically wrong to keep a field of well-ordered horses dodging backward and forward for forty or fifty times to suit some horse that hasn't any intention of doing work. I think the starter, after half a dozen scores at the utmost, should send the horses which are ready away, and let those which were up to funny business take their chances. Under such a rule well-ordered horses would not be fretted, and the public would be better pleased." This language scarcely possesses the well-known Splan style, and we suspect it of not being reported by a stenographer, but the fact that a representative driver advanced the idea is the important point. There is no more essential reform in the conduct of trotting races than the one indicated. It is positively monstrous that a bad actor or two should be allowed so frequently to waste the time and exhaust the patience of thousands of spectators, and the true remedy seems to be, in aggravated cases, for the judges to take the responsibility of giving the word, and letting the unruly ones take their chances. Mr. Splau might have gone farther, and said that he did not remember many cases where the horse that "made the most fuss about getting away" won any part of the purse, unless it had as few slices as there were trotters, and, therefore, no damage would result to the bad actor by being sent on a break or in the rear. It is worth considering whether it would not be well to invest the judges with explicit authority in this matter. They possess the power already, but a plain provision of the rules would support their exercise of it, and inform drivers what they might expect. It is fair to assume, if a reasonably good start cannot be effected in three trials, that some horse, or horses, are to blame, and the judges cannot be at a loss to note which ones are in fault. Give them then, in so many words, in the rules, the power to start the field in their discretion after the third trial, and their discriminating use of this power will very speedily abolish the nuisance of tedious scoring. And in advance of any change in the rules, we advise judges that they are already invested with this authority, and that its exercise will redound to their credit in every way.—*N. Y. Spirit of the Times.*

## Santa Rosa Races.

On Wednesday, the 23rd of August, there was a better gathering at Santa Rosa and more interest shown in the races. The first was a trot for a purse of $400 for district horses in which were Placeda, Huntress, St. Patrick, Lady Lane and Emma Taylor. St. Patrick was first choice in the pools, but although he held the first position, he relinquished it at the start to both Huntress and Placeda and between these two all the interest of the heat was centered. They trotted very evenly to the three quarter pole when Huntress had slightly the advantage but shortly after she broke, as did also Placeda, a feat that the latter repeated near the distance pole, but she was quickly caught and passed the wire in 2:45, half a length ahead of Huntress with St. Patrick a poor third. St. Patrick still was favorite at $20 against, Placeda selling almost even with him, while the field brought but $6. In the second heat there was a good deal of running in which both Huntress and Placeda showed to the least advantage. Huntress took the lead and maintained it to the three quarters where St. Patrick drew up to her and carried her off her feet, as was also the case near the wire, but in both cases she was handily caught and won the heat in 2:41 by three lengths from St. Patrick, with Placeda third. It was certainly a strange betting race, as despite the fact that St. Patrick could not show the speed with which he was credited, he still led in the pools, selling for $20 against $12 for Placeda and $6 for the field in which was Huntress, the winner. This heat was well contested by Huntress and St. Patrick, the other ones being badly scattered through a succession of bad breaks. Huntress took the lead, closely followed by St. Patrick, and thus they trotted until well in the homestretch, the mare being always able to hold her own, and St. Patrick making a very bad break, the mare jogged past the wire in 2:41½ with Placeda a poor third and Lady Lane and Emma Taylor distanced. Huntress was now made a great favorite and in the concluding heat she showed that she possessed that day, as although she left her feet badly at the start, on the back stretch she gradually reduced the gap and passed successively both Placeda and St. Patrick and won easily the heat and race in 2:44¼, Placeda taking the second and St. Patrick the third money.

The second race was a match between the two pacers, Johnny Wiegle and Washington, for $250 a side, with $150 added by the association. Wiegle was the favorite at $20 to $10, but Washington took the first heat after a very pretty struggle, the two horses being lapped nearly the entire mile, and the close finish in 2:31½ aroused some degree of enthusiasm, Wiegle being beaten by only half a length. Those who had accepted the odds about Washington thought that with a horse in the stable they could hedge their bets to advantage but this was evidently looked on as a good thing by the talent, for they ran up the quotations to $40 to $10 on Wiegle's chances and the results showed that their confidence was not misplaced. In the second heat Wiegle at once assumed the lead and, Washington making a bad break, Wiegle jogged in at his leisure in 2:34. In the third heat Washington barely saved his distance and the final one was taken by Wiegle as he liked, the time of the two last heats being 2:25¼ and 2:32¾.

SUMMARIES.

Santa Rosa, August 23, 1882. Trotting Race. 250 Class—for horses owned in the district. Purse of $400; first horse, $2:40; second, $120 and third $40.

| | | | | |
|---|---|---|---|---|
| Mr. Drake names ch. m. Huntress | 2 | 1 | 1 | 1 |
| Mr. Whitney names b. m. Placeda | 1 | 3 | 3 | 3 |
| Mr. Sperry names St. Patrick | 3 | 2 | 2 | 2 |
| Mr. Lane names b. m. Lady Lane | 5 | 4 | dis. | |
| Mr. Crandall names br. m. Emma Taylor | 4 | 5 | dis. | |

Time—2:45, 2:41, 2:41¾, 2:44¼.

Same day. Pacing match for $250 a side with $150 added by the association.

| | | | | |
|---|---|---|---|---|
| Walter Mead names dun g. Wiegle | 2 | 1 | 1 | 1 |
| H. A. Von Aminge names blk. s. Washington | 1 | 2 | 2 | 2 |

Time—2:31¼, 2:34, 2:25¼, 2:32¾.

Thursday's races attracted a much larger attendance than the two previous days; the weather was all that could be desired. The first race was the free for all three-year-olds owned in the district for a purse of $300. The entries being Debby Mott, Lady Starr, Buck Foster, Ned and Warwick, while Magnet was drawn. After a little scoring they got a good send off, Ned at the pole. Ned led from the start and at the half mile had opened up a gap of several lengths between himself and the rest who were all in a bunch. As they drew into the home stretch Ned still held his advantage and the rest were trailing with Debby in advance; down the stretch Debby drew up on Ned and when he passed under the wire she was a good second, with Warwick third, Buck Foster fourth and Lady Starr last. Time 2.59. After this heat Ned who had all the time been the favorite in the pools sold for five to one against the rest in the field. The second heat was almost a repetition of the first, Ned having it all his own way, winning the heat in 2.50½, Debby second, Starr third, Warwick fourth and Buck Foster fifth. The third heat the colts received a good send off, Ned at once taking the lead, holding it to the end. Coming down the home stretch there was a sharp struggle between Debby and Buck Foster for second place, but Debby was too much for the colt and came in second, Buck third, Warwick fourth and Lady Starr fifth. Ned took first money, Debby second and Warwick third.

The next race, for the 2:25 class, was the great event of the meeting thus far, in which entered Starr King, Echora, Del Sur, Cairo and Director. Starr King was largely the favorite in the pools, although he had been defeated at Santa Cruz. After some scoring they got a fine send off, with Del Sur at the pole, Echora second, Starr King third, Director fourth and Cairo outside. The favorite at once took the lead, which he maintained until the horses were well down the home stretch, but closely followed by Del Sur and Echora, the others not far behind; when half way down the stretch Starr King went all to pieces and before Welby could get him together again both Del Sur and Echora had passed him, Del Sur coming out ahead, Echora second, Director fourth and Cairo behind; time 2.24½. Although this heat ended so disastrously for Starr King, he was still largely a favorite in pools, selling nearly three to one, but the end proved the fallacy of human hopes on horse racing, as Mr. Titus' gallant little mare Echora, although quite lame, took the race on the three following heats. The second heat was an exciting one, Echora taking the lead and never once being headed, although Del Sur and Director crowded her very hard, while Starr King was acting badly all the time. Director was a dangerously close second, with Del Sur lapping him, Starr King fourth, Cairo behind. After this heat Echora became a favorite, selling about even against the other horses that were in the field. In this third heat Starr King acted badly again, and Echora and Del Sur had a fire-fight for the lead until entering the home stretch, when the brave little mare drew away; but at this time Starr King, who had gathered himself and settled to work, came up at a tremendous rate, passed Director and Del Sur, and was only a nose behind when Echora passed the wire in 2:25½.

After this heat the hopes of Starr King's friends began to revive, particularly as Echora was quite lame, and they again made him favorite; but it was useless, for the little mare's gameness proved indomitable, and she took the heat and race in 2:29. The racing in this heat was between Director and Del Sur, who made a gallant struggle for second place, Director winning by a neck, Starr King fourth, and Cairo, as usual, bringing up the rear. And so ended one of the best races of the season, in which those who pride themselves on their talent of discovering the best horse were badly cinched.

SUMMARIES.

Santa Rosa, August 24th. Trotting Race for all three-year-olds owned in the district. Purse, $300, of which $150 to the first, $90 to the second, and $30 to the third.

| | | | |
|---|---|---|---|
| W. M. Wood names b. c. Ned | 1 | 1 | 1 |
| C. Stingell names b. f. Debby Mott | 2 | 2 | 2 |
| L. H. Boggs names b. c. Warwick | 3 | 4 | 4 |
| J. E. Foster names br. s. Buck Foster | 4 | 5 | 3 |
| W. J. Starr names blk. f. Lady Starr | 5 | 3 | 5 |
| E. B. Conley names b. c. Magnet | dr. | | |

Time—2:59, 2:50¼, 2:54¾.

Same day.—Purse of $500 for the 2:25 Class, of which $300 to the first, $150 to the second, and $50 to the third horse.

| | | | | |
|---|---|---|---|---|
| L. H. Titus, names br. m. Echora | 2 | 1 | 1 | 1 |
| L. J. Rose names blk. s. Del Sur | 1 | 3 | 4 | 3 |
| J. A. Goldsmith names blk. s. Director | 4 | 2 | 3 | 2 |
| C. W. Welby names ch. g. Starr King | 3 | 4 | 2 | 4 |
| John Hughes names b. g. Cairo | 5 | 5 | 5 | 5 |
| G. Valencia names sch. s. Crown Point | dr. | | | |

Time—2:24½, 2:25¼, 2:25, 2:29.

On Friday the attendance was fair, and the only race on the programme was the trot free to all that never beat 2:40, for a purse of $500. Valderlynn, Moscow, Marin and Freestone started, Valderlynn a long way the favorite in the pools. The first heat Moscow won in 2:32; Freestone a head behind, Vanderlynn third, Marin last. Before the second heat Vanderlynn was still the favorite, but Moscow won in 2:32½, Vanderlynn second and Marin third. Before the third heat Vanderlynn was selling at $20 to $13. It was a rattling struggle between Moscow and Freestone, with Moscow visibly ahead. But the judges gave the heat to Freestone. Time 2:32; Vanderlynn second, Moscow third (for running), and Marin last. Before the fourth heat there was much dissatisfaction at the decision of the third heat. Vanderlynn was selling at $20, Moscow at $11. Vanderlynn and Moscow came in close together. The judges gave the heat to Vanderlynn, in 2:33, which caused more dissatisfaction. Moscow was second, Freestone third, and Marin last. Before the fifth heat Moscow was selling for twenty dollars to twenty dollars for the field and down to seventeen dollars. Vanderlynn got the heat in 2:34; Marin second, Moscow third, Freestone last. In the sixth heat Marin was out of the race rules, Moscow took the heat in 2:32½, and first money; Vanderlynn second, and Freestone third.

SUMMARY.

Santa Rosa, Aug. 25th—Trotting.—Purse of $500 to the 2:40 class.

| | | | | | | |
|---|---|---|---|---|---|---|
| A. B. Cooper names ch. g. Frank Moscow | 1 | 1 | 3 | 2 | 3 | 1 |
| Pat Farrell names b. h. Vanderlyn | 3 | 2 | 2 | 1 | 1 | 2 |
| M. Rollins names J. McCord's blk. g. Freestone | 2 | 4 | 1 | 3 | 4 | 3 |
| Steve Crandall names R. P. Miller's b. s. Marin | 4 | 3 | 4 | 4 | 2 | ro |

L. Titus' b. s. Exile, G. Lenard's gr. g. Allan Roy, and A. S. Bechtol's blk. g. Slim Jim, were also entered, but did not start.

Time—2:32, 2:32½, 2:32, 2:33, 2:34, 2:32½.

On the final day of the meeting, the first race was a purse of five hundred dollars for the 2:30 class, in which were Poscora Hayward, Tuca, Albert W., Blackmore, Blanche and Nellie R. Dhe two latter were withdrawn, much to the disappointment of the spectators, who were eager to see a well contested race with a large field of horses. Albert W. and Poscora sold even in the pools for twenty dollars, and the remainder in the field brought ten dollars. Tuca took the first heat evenly in 2:27 from Poscora, with Albert W a poor third, nevertheless he was then made, first favorite at twenty dollars against twelve dollars for Poscora and ten dollars for the field. The grey this time went to the front but nearing the half Tuca was at his wheels and the two sulkies collided, without much damaging effect. Albert W won in 2:27, after a good finish with Tuca down the home stretch. With the odds of 50 to 25 on his chances, Albert W disappointed the hopes of his backers during this heat by his unruly behavior, and consequently Tuca beat him out in 2:27½. Again there was a change in the betting in favor of the field, where Blackmore still figured but always coming in last. This time it was all through a close struggle that resulted in a dead heat between Albert W and Poscora Hayward in 2:28½. There was a great deal of scoring, much to the disgust of the spectators, and it took about a dozen trials before the horses could be brought up on even terms. Albert W was again the favorite and after a pretty struggle with Poscora beat him out in 2:32, showing that the protracted struggle was telling upon the horses. Blackmore not having won a heat in five was sent to the stable, and Tuca showing signs of weariness, and Poscora scarcely possessing the speed of his adversary, Albert W started with the odds of three to one on his chances and won cleverly from Poscora in 2:33, Tuca being a fair third.

There was then a match race, half mile and repeat, between James Clark's Estell C and T. D. Hoskin's Texas Boy, that was easily won by the former in two straight heats with no time given.

SUMMARY.

Santa Rosa, Aug. 26th—Trotting Race—Purse of $500, for the 2:30 class.

| | | | | | | |
|---|---|---|---|---|---|---|
| A. Waldstein names b. s. Albert W | 3 | 1 | 2 | 0 | 1 | 1 |
| J. A. Goldsmith names br. s. Inca | 1 | 2 | 1 | 4 | 4 | 3 |
| W. D. Hammond names g. s. Poscora Hayward | 2 | 3 | 3 | 0 | 2 | 2 |
| H. McConn names gr. g. Blackmore | 4 | 4 | 4 | 3 | 3 | ro |

William Bihler's b. m. Blanche, and J. and W. S. Fritch's ch. m. Nellie R, were entered, but did not start.

Time—2:27, 2:27, 2:27½, 2:28½, 2:32.

This race brought the meeting to a close, and it is to hoped that the financial results were satisfactory to the association. The Executive officers were indefatigable in their efforts to insure success, and now with all the improvements made and projected, the meeting of Santa Rosa will gain every year in usefulness and propriety. Following are the officers of the association; James P. Clark, President; Geo. P. Noonan, Treasurer; Charles Hoffer, Secrectary. Board of Directors: James P. Clark, Robert Ross, James P. Noonan, Henry Baker, John S. Taylor, Wyman Murphy. We wish the Association every success.

---

A new paper from the Pacific Coast makes its appearance here, the San Francisco BREEDER AND SPORTSMAN, the first number of which was issued July 1st. It is well got up and printed, and although taking general notice of sporting matters, is devoted largely to breeding and trotting interests. The Toronto correspondent of the BREEDER is Mr. James Lang, who is well qualified to attend to its interests. — *Toronto Mail.*

## Saratoga Races.

The race meeting at these fashionable springs closed on Saturday, the 26th August, after a season of some forty days, which is without a parallel in this country or Europe, barring always the Brighton Beach races on Coney Island, near New York, which are looked on in the majority of cases as contests for the money raised from the gate money, the pool and refreshment privileges. The season has been far from a success as regards the elevation of the turf, the management having had the poor sense to quarrel with the best patrons of the turf, that is, the prominent owners of horses who do not race entirely for money. There has been some strange in and out running during the season, but there have also been some half dozen days when the racing was of a sufficiently interesting character to draw a large and fashionable attendance. Such was the case on August 22d, when there were five good contests, two of which we take the following good discription from "Kirk's" letter in the New York *World:*

A more perfect day for racing could scarcely have been had than to-day. The weather was bright and cool, with but little wind, and as the track was good and the number of starters not too large in any of the races to prove embarrassing either to the starter or to the spectators, the day will long be remembered by those present. It was also a day to be remembered both by those who lay and those who take the odds. In the first place all four of the favorites were beaten and the Mutuals paid on the first race $83.30, on the third $125 and on the fourth $105.20—an average never before known since the introduction of the system into this country.

The racing began with a dash of three-quarters of a mile, for all ages, with the usual non-winning and beaten allowances, the entrance for which in the matter of horses specially fast for the distance have rarely been equalled. Four of the horses had each run during the present season over the same course in 1.15 viz: J. Abingdon's Disturbance, C. Reed's Bounce, E. Heffner's Little Pull and W. L. Cassidy's Saunterer. Another, the Dwyer Brothers' Bootjack, had won over the same course in 1.15½, while of the others Morris & Patten's Fellowplay had won over the mile course in 1.41½, and Fatinitza in 1.43½. The other entries, Monarch and Sir Hugh, were known to be very fast, and as none was overloaded in the matter of weight, admirers of fast time naturally expected to see the record nearly reached. The starters and weights carried were as follows: Bootjack, 114 pounds; Disturbance, Fatinitza and Little Phil, each 108 pounds; Fellowplay, Sir Hugh and Saunterer, each at 105 pounds, and Monarch at 91 pounds. Bounce, of whom many expected a good race, was scratched at 10:55 A. M. In the last of the pools sold Bootjack was the favorite, with Fellowplay a strong second choice. The horses appeared promptly at the post and they certainly presented a very handsome appearance, decorated, as all were, in the colors of their several stables. After several small skirmishes the flag was dropped to a good start to all except Saunterer, who, by some unaccountable mystery, was left at the post. The instant the flag was down McLaughlin showed a trifle in front, with Bootjack lapped by Fellowplay and Monarch and Disturbance, Little Phil close up in front of Sir Hugh and Fatinitza. The instant it was possible McLaughlin took Bootjack to the rails, and with Monarch second and Little Phil third they made it a driving race to the five-furlong post and thence to the half, which they passed as they swung into the main track each a neck apart, followed by Disturbance and Fellowplay together. When well into the main track both Bootjack and Monarch drew away from Little Phil, and as they reached the east turn Little Phil dropped back behind Fellowplay, who closed upon the leaders so quickly that at the 500-yard post Fellowplay was at Monarch's saddle skirts. He improved at every stride, as also did Monarch, so that as they turned into the homestretch Bootjack (lying in close to the rails) only lead by a head, while the others were as even as they could run. Half way between the three-quarter and seven-furlong posts both Monarch and fellowplay got up even with Bootjack, which caused McLaughlin to bring his whip into play, an example which was followed by O'Leary on Monarch, and Frank McLaughlin on Little Phil. The three kept together to the pool stands, when, amid screaming applause, Monarch got his head in front and as Stone got Fellowplay up on the outside at the same time it looked still to be anybody's race, but the light-weighted Monarch could not be reached and from a head he increased his lead to half a length by which he won, with Bootjack second, a head in front of Fellowplay and Little Phil. A length away was disturbance, with Fatinitza and Sir Hugh. Time, 1:14, which, although it beats all the previous three-quarter time over the course, only equals the record.

After the racing the judges held a meeting and investigated the failure of Saunterer to start with the other horses for the first race, and deeming that George Barbee, the rider, was solely to blame, they decided to suspend him for the remainder of the season. The decision is thought by many to be very harsh and entirely unprecedented.

The second race was the third renewal of the Relief Stakes, for three-year-olds, at a mile and five furlongs, the conditions of which were that colts should carry 110 pounds, geldings 107 pounds and fillies 105 pounds; that winners of any race the year the stake is run should carry 7 pounds extra, and that non-winners and maidens should be allowed 7 and 12 pounds. Under these conditions Green Morris won with Goldbug at 105 pounds in 1880, and Mr. Reed with Thora at 112 pounds last year. The starters to-day were Burnham's Charley B. and Young's Boatman, each at 114 pounds, and Bryson's Kite at 95 pounds. Boatman was a big favorite. Kite was the first away, followed by Charley B. and Boatman. For the first three furlongs the pace was very slow, but when Charley B. took the lead at the three-quarters, the pace became fairly fast. Charley led by a length at the seven furlongs and by a length and a half at the end of the five furlongs, with Kite and Boatman running head to head. There was but little change until they reached the turn to the backstretch, when, as Charley B. sailed away, Boatman followed, the two running down the backstretch two lengths apart and leaving Kite at every stride. As they made the east turn Boatman closed up to just about a length, which was the best he could do until they were well-nigh into the stretch. Under the whip Boatman got up with Charley and the two ran together to the pool-stands, at which point the race ended, for Charley B. came away from Boatman and won with considerable ease by two lengths; with Kite ten lengths behind Boatman. Time, 2:54. The last mile was run in 1:45. The time, as a whole, however, is somewhat slow compared with Bend Or's 2:49 last Saturday, while it is also three seconds slower than Thora beat Crickmore in last year.

As Boatman had beaten Carley B. for the Sequel and Kenner stakes and as Carley B. had defeated Boatman for the Travers Stakes there was some interest in this their fourth meeting, and as it resulted in Carley's success the question of superiority is more than ever unsettled, although Carley B. to-day in the hands of Jimmy McLaughlin certainly ran a very good race. Unfortunately he is not in either the September Stakes at Sheepshead Bay or the Dixie at Baltimore, although he may prove a dangerous customer for the Breckenridge. As Boatman has none but western engagements, the two cannot meet unless they should come together in some race to which they are both eligible at Sheepshead Bay.

The following are the telegraphic dispatches giving an account of the last days' races:

On Thursday August 24th, in the first race, three-quarters of a mile, Lord Raglan won; Baron Fauceret second, Barnes, the favorite, third. Time—1:19. In the second race, 1½ miles, Pinafore won; Farragut second, and Thorn third. Time—2:43½. In the third race, one mile, Creosote won; Vera second, Gus. Matthews third. Time—1:46½. In the fourth race, steeplechase, 2½ miles, Post Guard won; Annette second, Rose third. Time—5:20.

On the 25th, in the first race, three-quarters of a mile, Jake White won; Patti second, Lutestring third. Time—1:14½. In the second race, a mile and 500 yards, Fellowplay won; Tom Plunket, second, Fannie B. third. Time—2:43½. In the third race, one mile, Jake White won; Valparaiso second, Malasine third. Time—1:43½. In the fourth race, hurdle, one and a quarter miles, Revenge won; Charlemagne second, Glasgow third. Time—2:19.

On the 26th, in the first race, one mile, Monarch won. Wedding Day second, Farce third. Time, 1:44. In the second race, three miles, Lydia Stanhope won; Etta Warfield, second, Bushwhacker third. Time, 5:25. In the third race, one and one-eight miles, Patti won; Standoff second, Kennesaw third. Time—1:57½.

---

## The Petaluma Fair.

In the center of a large and valuable farming district, that yearly increases in value and productiveness, Petaluma is one of the most flourishing towns in the vicinity of the coast, and the visitor cannot fail to admire the many improvements projected and carried out by its thriving and public-spirited citizens. The annual fair of the Sonoma and Marin District Agricultural Society has always proved to be very popular among the farmers who take a pride in their excellent stock and produce, and so recognizing the value of fostering these important branches of stock-raising and agriculture, this association resolved on purchasing a new track, and on furnishing it with all the grand stands, stalls and exhibition buildings required for fairs of ever increasing magnitude. The tract of land is admirably suited for the purpose, being situated within three-quarters of a mile from the center of the the town, the only drawback being, that those who do not have their own carriages must walk a long distance from the entrance to the race track. The grounds are about seventy-five acres in extent, twenty-five of which are laid out with walks and drives, along which is planted trees in rows and groves, that when they attain their growth will make one of the prettiest driving parks in the state.

At the entrance, facing on the main street of East Petaluma, is the pavilion, a three-story wooden building, with a tower on each side of the entrance. The building is 100x158 feet, constructed with great care, with an eye to durability as well as architectural beauty. On the left as one enters the building are the offices, dressing-rooms for the ladies and meeting-room for the officers and directors. On the right is a spacious hall for exhibits, which is decorated with the national colors. In the center plays a beautiful fountain, overhung by singing birds and surrounded by ferns and flowering shrubs.

The track is well laid out, a full mile in length, with the first turn, as at Sacramento, a little too close to the starting point, especially when there is a large field of horses. It is built on good soil, and when properly cared for will be one of the fastest and safest in the State. There is an ample grand stand with a bar and restaurant and all the details have been carried out under careful and efficient supervision. The stalls and pens are in excellent order, but ample as the accommodations appear to be, they were found inadequate to the demand and while the races were in progress additional space was being prepared on every side. The land and improvements have cost upwards of $40,000, and with judicious and liberal management, the Petaluma park will be the finest show place of its kind in the vicinity of San Francisco.

### The Races.

The early train on Tuesday from this city took up a large deputation, and the town was filling fast with visitors from every quarter and shortly after dinner there was a lively display of vehicles on their way to the track. The weather was very agreeable, save that the wind was somewhat cool on the grand stand, and the ladies, preferring comfort to display, gathered in pretty groops in the topmost benches where they were quite shielded from the breeze. The attendance was excellent for a first day and promised auspiciously for the first fair held by the Association in their new pleasant and commodious grounds.

The first race on the programme was a purse of $500, free for all runners, a half-mile and repeat, but as the association only offered two purses for the thoroughbred horses, it was not sufficient inducement for them to put in an appearance, much to the disappointment of those who have a fondness for this style of racing. As there was thus only a trot remaining on the card, there was a long delay in ringing the horses for the start; but there was not much complaint made on this subject, as the visitors were mostly strolling through the grounds, and marking the improvements made on every side.

The race was for the 2:50 class, and the entries were Placeda, Huntress, Como, Emma Taylor, Roscoe, Lady Zane, St. Patrick, No Name and Little Jim, but only the first five in the above list entered an appearance on the track. On the previous evening, Como had been a good favorite in the pools, but just at the start he and Huntress sold about even at twenty against four for the remainder, and even at that small evaluation the three horses composing the field were rated far too high, as two of them were distanced before the race was over. At the fourth attempt they got away with Placeda in the lead, she leading Huntress half a length at the quarter, but she broke shortly after, and thence the heat was between Huntress and Como, and the latter leaving his feet, Huntress jogged past the wire in 2:40½, Emma Taylor and Roscoe being distanced. The betting now veered round, Huntress bringing $25 against $15 for the two others. Placeda had the best of the start and as Huntress broke at the first turn, Como played so close attendance on the bay mare that she got off her feet in mid back stretch, and Como coming away won handily by a length from Huntress, who was never able to close up the gap made by her bad break. The time was 2:39½. There was a good deal of scoring in the third heat and it was only at the sixth attempt that the horses were tapped off with Huntress slightly in the lead, the odds being $20 on Como, against $10 for the other two. This heat was admirably contested and the pace was so hot that both Huntress and Como left their feet two or three times, but in each instance although they lost ground, they were speedily brought to their gait by their skillful drivers. Up to the half mile Huntress had the advantage by some two lengths, but from that point he closed on the mare and when well in the home stretch he carried her off her feet, but she was speedily closing up the gap and it looked like a dead heat when again she flew in the air, a few yards from the wire, and Como won by a length in 2:38, with Placeda just escaping the distance flag. It now looked such a certainty for the chestnut stallion that there was no betting. For the fourth heat the scoring was very tedious out at last on the eighth trial they got off and Huntress showed such a burst of speed that she took the pole somewhat too soon, and Placeda trotting side by side with Como, his driver found himself in a pretty pocket, a pleasant position that was in a measure due to his lack of foresight at the start. Luckily Placeda broke in the middle of the back stretch and drew out and alongside of the mare, but her speed was not to be gainsaid and she gradually opened out a gap and won in a jog in 2:39½. The betting in the first heat was $20 on Huntress and Placeda against $15 for Como. Huntress again got slightly the best of the start and going at a merry clip she opened out a gap of two lengths at the quarter, but down the back stretch Como moved up and then broke, repeating the trick on the turn into the home stretch. but even when nearing the draw gate the race seemed undecided, as Huntress broke and ran twenty yards before she was brought to her feet, she finally beating Como but by a length. It was the general opinion that the most experienced driver won and not the best horse.

SUMMARIES.

Petaluma, August 29.—Trotting Race.—$400, best three in five to harness.

| | | | | |
|---|---|---|---|---|
| S. S. Drake names ch. f. Huntress | 1 | 2 | 2 | 1..2 |
| C. F. D. Hastings names ch. h. Como | 2 | 1 | 1 | 2..2 |
| E. B. Conley names b. m. Placeda | 3 | 3 | 3 | 3..3 |
| J. B. Chase names Roscoe | dist. | | | |
| M. O'Rielly names br. m. Emma Taylor | dist. | | | |

And the following were drawn: H. G. Carrillo's b. m., Lady Zanne; S. Sperry's ch. g. St. Patrick; W. G. Atkins' b. h. no name and S. P. Taylor's b. g. Little Jim.

Time.—2:40¼ 2:39¼ 2:38 2:39¼ 2:39.

Between the two final heats there came up a novel race for decision, it being a trial of skill and judgment to make the nearest time to three minutes for a sum of $40, offered by a gentleman interested in the success of the Association. There were four entries, Roscoe, Rustic, Plough Boy and Lady Starr, and the contest was so close that even the best timer had to await the decision of the judge, who gave the purse to Rustic with 2:59½, Roscoe being credited with 3:01. The affair created a great deal of amusement, and it might be a telling part in our programmes, if collision between the drivers and outsiders could be prevented during the time of the heat, but this is almost an impossibility.

The first race on the second day was a purse of $700 for the 2:25 class, in which were entered Starr King, selling for $25, Sweetness for $20, Crown Point $15, and Cairo, $2. The track was in excellent condition, and there was every promise of a close contest and of fast time, save by some it was claimed that Starr King was a trifle lame, while Crown Point appeared to be somewhat overtrained. After a few false starts, the horses got off on fair terms; but at the first turn Starr King was not on his good behavior, making a disastrous break and falling far into the rear, while Sweetness reached the half-mile in 1:14, with Crown Point in attendance. The position was unchanged until the three-quarter pole was reached, when Starr King was seen coming at a rapid gait, passing both Cairo and Crown Point, but he could not overtake Sweetness, who won easily by a length, in 2:27½. There was a good deal of scoring for a favorable position in the next heat, and it was only at the eighth attempt that they got the word, Starr King contenting himself with a quiet send-off when in the rear, but in trying to improve his place he broke at about the same spot as in the previous heat, and Crown Point following suit, it was left to Cairo to join conclusions with the favorite, she reaching the half mile first in one 1:13. Along the upper turn it was apparent that Sweetness could outfoot Cairo, and would surely take the heat, when Starr King was seen coming up with a fine turn of speed and at the head of the stretch he was in the second position but he could not overtake the bay mare who finished an easy heat in 2:25½, the others occupying the same relative position as in the previous mile.

As may be supposed, there were great efforts made by those who had pinned their faith on Starr King to retrieve their losses, but no one could be induced to go against the mare's chances, and betting as to the result was at an end. There was again a great deal of jockeying for a position, which appears in the eyes of the drivers to be absolutely necessary in the 2:25 class, all through the circuit, but when they come to Oakland, Sacramento and Stockton, those parties who pride themselves on their 'cuteness may find themselves "left," under a more rigid interpretation of the rules. There were fully a dozen false starts, before the drivers would deign to come up together, but at last they were well in line, and shortly after the bell was tapped the race was at an end, as all three of the horses broke in succession around the first turn, leaving the mare to show her speed to the half mile in 1:14½, when Starr King was seen once more coming up for a close brush, that for a moment revived the hopes of his backers; but this day "the mare was the better horse," and, with plenty of speed left in her, she won the heat and race in 2:24½, without a skip all through, Cairo being distanced.

The second race was for a purse of $350, given for three-year-olds owned in the district. There were six nominations, of which but three came to the start. Ned, a son of Overland, was a prominent favorite in the few pools that were sold of two to one for the other two, Sister and Deby Mott, odds that there were no ways equal to his advantage in speed and endurance, by which he was an easy and unexciting winner in straight heats.

SUMMARIES.

Petaluma, August 30.—Trotting for the 2:25 class for a purse of $700, best 3 in 5 to harness.

| | | | |
|---|---|---|---|
| J. A. Goldsmith names b. m. Sweetness | 1 | 1 | 1 |
| Charles W. Welby names ch. g. Starr King | 2 | 2 | 2 |
| G. Valensin names ch. s. Crown Point | 4 | 4 | 3 |
| J. Hughes names b. h. Cairo | 3 | 3—dist. | |

Time—2:27¼, 2:25¼, 2:24¼.

Same day—Trotting. Purse of $350 for three-year-olds owned in the district.

| | | | |
|---|---|---|---|
| W. M. Wood names b. g. Ned | 1 | 1 | 1 |
| S. Crandall names Mr. Stingle's b. f. Deby Mott | 3 | 2 | 2 |
| S. S. Drake names br. f. Sister | 2 | 3 | 3 |

Mr. Whitney's b. c. Magnet Mr. Bihler's b. c. Buck Forster and W. J. Starr's blk. f. Lady Starr were entered but withdrawn.

Time—2:56, 2:47¼, 2:45¼

The first of the three events on the programme for the second day was the trotting dash of a mile by yearlings in harness and to run for a purse of $150, for which there were the following entries: I. C. Reardon's Blue Gown, by Gus, dam by Geo. M. Patchen. Whitney's ch c Dawn, by Nutwood, dam Countess. Wm. Bourke's g c Dublin, by Admiral, dam by Bell Alta. John Pfau's b c Young Eureka, by Eureka, dam Fairbank's mare. P. J. Shafter's g c Viking, by Rustic, dam by Lawyer's Stockbridge Chief. Bihler's b c No Name, by GenDana, dam by John Nelson. F. Needham's b c Conemara, by Volunteer, dam by Speculation. Dawn, Blue Gown, Viking and Conemara the starters. Long before the hour of starting the grand stand and every available space for viewing the race was completely packed with anxious and excited men, women and children to see the babies trot. So far no race of the week has created such interest, and from the reliable and interesting character of these juvenile contests, it is now becoming quite apparent that they, in the future, are destined to become the leading feature in sporting circles. When the excitement first began over this race, rumor had it that the chief contest lay between the Volunteer and Gus colts, but when the pool test was applied the dark one soon came to light, and in spite of the efforts of owner and driver of Dawn he was booked the favorite over all the rest at long odds. That his owner was confident of success, is evident from the fact of his having given the driver of Dawn unlimited credit in the box on that race, a circumstance well calculated to establish a favorite at any time in the absence of any known merit in the animal so backed.

Although it might be expected that such youngsters would be difficult to manage in a race it was agreeably surprising to see how examplory their performance proved, even for some of the oldest quadrupeds in the business. In the third effort they were sent off on an even start, all going steadily, but Dawn, who broke badly and fell off thirty yards but at the first quarter he had regained his place and led by four open lengths in 51 seconds. When the half was reached he had gained to an open gap of 50 yards in 1:38, followed in long and open order by Blue Gown, Viking and Conemara. These positions were but little changed, except by Viking, who made a close contest with Blue Gown for second place, at the finish, which, after a break in the homestretch was first reached by Dawn, fully 30 yards in the lead. Conemara being far behind the draw gate. Time, 3:08½.

The 2:40 class for a purse of five hundred dollars was the next race called. For this there came the following closely matched contestants, who made the race a hot one from beginning to end: Rowdy Boy, Vanderlynn, Marin, Johnny, Frank Moscow. In the pools, Vanderlynnn was a rising favorite from the beginning to the finishing of the first two heats, which he won seemingly at ease, in 2:31½ and 2:32½; Moscow and Rowdy Boy alternately claiming the lead throughout the first part of each heat, both succumbing to Vanderlynn at the finish. At the close of the second heat Johnny made a fine brush and got second place, although after a hard struggle between all but Vanderlynn for the third heat, which was won by Rowdy Boy in 2:31½, Vanderlynn was still a strong favorite at 20 dollars against all the rest at 8. In the fourth heat Johuny again became troublesome, and despite the skill of contending artists, and speed of the other horses, he made a handsome finish, working his way through all adversities from the head of the stretch home, and winning the fastest heat of the race in 2:30½. Up to this time each half mile was made as reported by timers, in 1:18 or the fraction thereof, and at no time did Johnny lead at that point, hence he must be accredited with some of the best qualities of a moneyed horse. The betting was now much duller on Vanderlynn, as he had power to be unsteady, and a looser when breaking, though his friends and backers still thought he would pull through on his speed, consequently they were badly caught in the fifth heat in which he was shut out for running to save his distance, while Johuny scored another beautiful heat in 2:34, Rowdy Boy again being a very close second, Moscow third, Marin fourth, Vanderlynn being distanced. Moscow and Marin having gone to the stable, under the rules, for not winning a heat in five, the contest was left to the frolicsome Boy and Johnny. The latter being the favorite at varying odds caused some speculation among the betters who were principally losers on Vanderlynn. The sixth heat was a close and well contested trot from the go to the finish; Johnny's driver and owner, being evidently a little excited, let him stagger and lose the heat, when within twenty yards of the wire; Goldsmith seeing this quickly seized the only chance for the heat, by virtually becoming a part of his horse, and with a most beautiful effort helped him over the score, a winner of the heat by an open length in 2:35½. The betting now changed again in favor of Rowdy Boy, and once more the boys from the Bay had a double bank. The seventh heat was much like the sixth, except in the closeness of the finish, this time Rowdy Boy broke when a foot in the lead and within no more than ten feet of the score, and for which the heat race and money were given to the son of Auctioneer.

SUMMARY.

PETALUMA, Aug. 31st.—Purse of $500 for the 2:40 class.

| | | | | | | | |
|---|---|---|---|---|---|---|---|
| W. Bourke enters b. h. Johnny | 3 | 2 | 4 | 1 | 1 | 2 | 1 |
| James Garland enters gr g Rowdy Boy | 4 | 4 | 1 | 2 | 2 | 1 | 2 |
| A. B. Cooper enters c g Frank Moscow | 2 | 3 | 2 | 3 | 3 | r o | |
| B. F. Miller enters b s Marin | 5 | 5 | 3 | 4 | 4 | r o | |
| Pat. Farrell enters b h Vanderlynn | 1 | 1 | 5 | 5 | dist | | |
| J. Mackey enters b s Exile | Withdrawn | | | | | | |

Time—2:31¼, 2:32¼, 2:31¼, 2:30¼, 2:34, 2:35¼, 2:35.

The day's sport wound up with a running race, heats of half a mile for a purse of 300 dollars, in which Haddington was a great favorite at 20 dollars against 10 dols. for Estella C. The latter took the first heat, and Haddington the two next, winning the race. Time, 49½, 51 and 50½ secs.

### Entries of Stock.

S. S. Drake, graded stallion four years old or over, Admiral; stallion two years old, Argenta; colt; mare four years old or over, Eve; mare three years old, Elaida; five colts.

I. F. Cook, draft stallion three years old, Prince.

Sylvester Scott, Cloverdale, thoroughbred Durham bull four years old or over, Mazourka's Royal Oxford; yearling, Royal Oxford; two years old Loanjo; calf, Wily Oxford; cows four years old or over, Alice Gray; three years old, Sadie Maynard; calf, Maynard's Gem; jack, Monarch; jennet, Fanny.

F. W. Loeder, roadster stallion and six colts; Whippleton and six colts; graded yearling mare; single buggy horse.

J. Gallagher, draft stallion two years old, Robert Emmet.

J. Phillipini, draft stallion three years old, Rollin.

Fred Kuhnle, graded stallion two years old, Billy Wilson; yearling stallion, Black Prince; mare four years old or over, Mollie K.; yearling mare, Lotta Wilson; mare colt, Reni.

Francis De Long, thoroughbred Jessie, cow 4 years old or over, Fashion; graded bull calf Washington.

A. C. Shelton, Berkshire boar.

Horse Breeders' Association, draft stallion and six colts; horse of all work and six colts, Crown Prince and six colts.

Thos. Skillman, draft stallion, 4 years old or over, Tornado; draft mare 1 year old, Gertrude; horse of all work, 2 years old, Monarch.

S. Gilmore, draft stallion, 2 years old, Pollack II; draft colt. Pride of the West; draft mare, 4 years old or over, Queen.

J. Conway, saddle horse, Boney Boy.

A. J. Pierce, horse of all work, mare 4 years old or over, Mollie; colt; Flora; roadster stallion 4 years old or over; Hawlet, and six colts; roadster mare 3 years old, Nellie.

G. Pacheco, thoroughbred mare 4 years old or over, Cartie C; yearling mare.

L. W. Walker, two Cotswold rams.

Willis Faught, horses of all work, mare 2 years old, Peggy; mare 4 years old or over, Dolly; stallion colt, Billy; roadster stallion and family, Little Mac and six colts.

J. P. Rodehaver, draft stallion 4 years old or over, Time o'Day; horse of all work, 4 years old or over, La Fayette.

P. Hennelly, horse of all work, 3 years old, Petaluma Prince.

Wm. Bihler, roadsters, Grey McClellan and family; stallion, 3 years old, Buck Foster; yearling stallion John; mare 4 years old or over, Blanche; mare 3 years old, Mary Wallace; 2 years old, Sally; draft mare 4 years old or over, Doll; draft horse colt Ned; thoroughbred mare 4 years old or over, Jeannette.

Devon cow 4 years old or over, Young Curly.

J. Davener, draft stallion 3 years old, Cognac; mare colt; mare 4 years old or over.

John King, graded horse colt, Norman Star.

I. R. Jewell, draft stallion 3 years old, Rolla; graded bull 4 years old or over, Duke.

Pat Carroll, thoroughbred mare, 2 years old, Alice; saddle horse, Black Jack.

### Poultry.

W. D. Freeman enters pair buff Cochins, pair brown Leghorns, pair Guinea fowls, pair Rumples, pair Toulouse geese, pair white China geese.

J. K. Fix, pair Muscovy ducks.

C. S. Gibson, pair Bremen geese.

E. C. Newton, pair brown Leghorns, pair buff Cochins, pair Plymouth Rocks.

Mrs. Wm. Hill, pair buff Cochins.

Morris Bros., pair light Brahmas, pair dark Brahmas, pair Partridge Cochins, pair black Cochins, pair white Cochins, pair Plymouth Rocks, pair white Leghorns, pair brown Leghorns, pair white faced black Spanish, gold spangled Polish, black and white Crested Polish, silver spangled Polish, black Hamburgs, Houdans, black breasted game, seabright Bantams, bronze turkeys, wild turkeys, Toulouse geese, Bremen geese, Guinea fowls, peacocks.

Mrs. A. H. Patty, pair Bantams.

G. F. Ward, pair gray China geese, pair brown Leghorns.

### Pavilion Items.

The Morris Bros. deserve praise for the interest they take in improving their orchards and vineyards. On their table were found thirty-five varieties of grapes, besides oranges, walnuts, persimmons, figs and almonds, all of which were raised on their farm in Sonoma county. They also exhibit at the chicken coop twenty-five varieties of fancy fowl.

Mrs. T. T. Ennis' special exhibit was plums, of which she h as fourteen different kinds. An inspection of her tables prove there is no finer plum growing country than the vicinity of Petaluma.

Bush & Co. of San Francisco, had on exhibition Bailey's "California Chief" Grain Cleaner. The operation of this machine excited the admiration of all who take any interest in agricultural implements.

Standing close to the end of the pavilion was J. W. Cassidy's fruit drier. The superiority of this drier to many others is, that a drawer may be moved without any loss of heat, and in removing no other drawer need be disturbed.

L. A. Hardin, of Vallejo township, exhibited several sheaves of Egyptian and Smith wheat, whose plump, well-filled heads guarantee it to be a good flour grain.

Mr. Geo. Wagner manipulated the working of a miniature gate. This is a very ingenious piece of mechanism, and is opened or shut by the simple pulling of a cord. It ought to work as well on a large scale as it does before the sightseerers at the fair.

Wm. Zartman & Co., of Petaluma, had several neat, durable-looking carriages and wagons on exhibition.

D. W. C. Putnam had four breaking carts, of his own design and manufacture, which excited favorable comments from the criticising public. Mr. D. R. McLennan also exhibited two good breaking carts.

The sixteen Southdown sheep of C. H. Crane's are as fine-looking lot of mutton stock as one could wish to see. These annuals, when full grown, weigh about 250 pounds. Mr. Crane has also one Poland-China boar, one year old, that weighs about three hundred pounds, and a fine breeding sow with four pretty pigs.

Mr. L. W. Walker, of Petaluma, exhibited two Cotswold rams, two years old, that weigh about two hundred and thirty pounds each. They are covered with coats of very fine soft wool, and though they are a mutton sheep, their fleece is very much admired.

E. W. Woolsey & Son had a band of thirty-five thoroughbred merino sheep. The fleece on these sheep is unequalled by any on the ground. One large ram, claimed to be the best of his kind in the State, took the premium at the State fair in 1880, as the most promising lamb.

From the first day the numbers that attended the Fair increased until the Pavilion would hardly hold the throng. A perfect stream of people poured through the gateway into the exhibition hall and out on the track. Though the races attracted great numbers still they were hardly missed from the other parts of the grounds.

The last article entered at the Pavilion was A. La Jeunesel's Automatic Harrow. It is so constructed that by working a lever the teeth can be set at any desired depth; or if choked up with grass or clods the same lever frees it from the rubbish and transforms it into a sled by lowering the runners that guage the depth of the tooth.

D. M. Osborne & Co., of San Francisco, run a self-binding reaper by means of a stationary engine placed on the outside of the building, also an independent mower and a combined reaper and mower.

U. Warnekrons displayed a general assortment of hunters' and sportsmen's goods.

The stand that attracted the most interest was that of J. L. Dias' "Petaluma Incubators" which hatched out chickens daily in open view of the visitors. Nine hundred chickens will be brought to light by the last day of the Fair. Everyone who is a judge says that this is the best incubator ever invented. The mother and brooder that goes with his machine took the highest honors at the Sonoma and Marin Fair in 1881.

The success of the fair up to Thursday was beyond the most sanguine expectations, the receipts amounting to 3,788 dollars, 50cts., in the following order: Monday, 323 dollars; Tuesday, 1,017 dollars; Wednesday, 1,018,50 dols.; Thursday, 1,430 dols. The grand parade of stock was to be held on Friday, but on Wednesday there was a preliminary parade, when the animals took up the entire track. It was a display that has never been equalled in the two counties, and all through the week the commodious pens and stalls have been crowded with visitors, comparing notes on the merits of the stock. On Friday the premiums were awarded to-day the prizes will be distributed, of which the fullest details will be given in our next issue. We hope the association will realize the truth of the old adage: "Nothing succeeds like success."

## BASE BALL.

### The Haverlys and the Athletics.

It seems difficult to establish base ball in the city on such a sound financial basis as would allow the strengthening of our local teams with some of the efficient players from the East so that we should see a higher state of proficiency than is now the case. Last Sunday's game between the above clubs shows the truth of these remarks, for although the attendance was again very large, the visitors took but little interest in the game, as it was of the most one-sided description, it appearing at the end of the seventh inning as if the Athletics would be Chicagoed. In the eighth inning, however, they managed slightly to retrieve their fallen fortunes, but the Haverlys won in eight innings by a score of ten to six. It is a pity that the Athletics could not improve even on their former efficiency. It was a popular club, but the lack of public patronage has induced a supineness among its members that does not augur well for its success in the future. Following is the score:

HAVERLY.

ATHLETIC.

*Haverlys umpire[...] foul catching.
Left on bases—Haverly 1; Athletic 1. Absence 1, Haverlys 2, Struck out—Haverlys 2, Athletic 1. Bases on balls—Athletic [...] Haverlys 1. Wild pitches—Morgan 1, J. Carroll 1, Cummings 4. Passed Balls—Depaugher 3, Carroll 1.*

THE CHAMPIONSHIP LEAGUE.—Since the commencement of the last tour of the Western clubs to the East, Providence has made an important advance; and now, with the August games nearly at an end, Providence leads Chicago by five victories and Detroit by seven, the two nearest clubs in the race. Of the Western clubs Buffalo has made the most progress while in the East, and that team now stands next to Boston. The record to August 20 shows the clubs occupying the following relative positions in the pennant race:

CLUB.

### The American Championship.

The pennant success of the American Association clubs this season is specially noteworthy. One result of this success is the assured fact of the permanent existence of the association. Better club management, however, will be necessary in the future in the selection of a more desirable class of players than the majority of the clubs have had this season. The association championship contests have thus far been interesting, but now that the success of Cincinnati is assured the interest is falling off. The record to date shows the six clubs occupying the following relative positions in the pennant race:

| Club. | Games won. | Games lost. | Games played. | Games to play. | Possible victories. |
|---|---|---|---|---|---|
| Cincinnati | 38 | 17 | 55 | 15 | 53 |
| Athletic | 32 | 22 | 54 | 16 | 48 |
| Eclipse | 28 | 22 | 30 | 20 | 48 |
| St. Louis | 28 | 32 | 60 | 10 | 38 |
| Alleghany | 22 | 30 | 52 | 18 | 40 |
| Baltimore | 14 | 39 | 53 | 17 | 31 |

It will be seen that Baltimore is now out of the race and so also St. Louis, and Alleghany is nearly so. The best managed clubs takes the lead.

THE EAST vs. THE WEST.—It will be seen that thus far the East leads the West by one victory. The Providence leads the Eastern teams in their games with Western teams, and Buffalo leads the West as against the East. A summary of the victories and defeats of the month thus far shows the eight clubs occupying the following relative positions:

| Club. | Games won. | Games lost. | Games played. |
|---|---|---|---|
| Providence | | | |
| Buffalo | | | |
| Boston | | | |
| Troy | | | |
| Cleveland | | | |
| Chicago | | | |
| Detroit | | | |
| Worcester | | | |

There was another one-sided game at the Oakland grounds on Sunday last, between the Olympics and the Stockbrokers club, resulting in a victory for the Olympic club by a score of twenty to six.

The game to-morrow at the Recreation Grounds will be between the Niantics and the Haverlys, and it is probable that at the Oakland Grounds the Olympics will try conclusion with the Reddington Club.

### A Bold Challenge.

Dob's Lightning Salve Co. challenges all other hoof and healing ointments, not alone in this State, but in all other places, to a competitive test to take place in the city of Sacramento during the State fair. The wager of $500 will be put up that Dob's Lightning Salve is far superior for sore shoulders, collar galls, horses cut upon barb wire fences, burns and bruises, also cracked heels, and quarter cracks. The decision shall be left to prominent horsemen. Very Respectfully,

DOB'S LIGHTNING SALVE CO.
Lodi, San Joaquin Co., Cal.

## THE RIFLE.

### The International Rifle Match.

The National Rifle Association has issued a circular setting forth the terms of the international rifle match to be shot at Creedmoor, September 15th and 16th, between the teams of the British Volunteers and the National Guards of the United States. The distances will be 200, 500, 600, 800, 900 and 1,000 yards, with open-sighted military rifles, without wind-gauges or Vernier sights. The weapon used is strictly a military rifle, similar to that used by the National Guard or militia. The members of the teams will appear in the uniform of the organization to which they belong. The States having a militia organization have all encouraged its members to compete for places on the team, and it is therefore thoroughly national in its composition.

The National Rifle Association has agreed to shoot a return match with the British Volunteers at Wimbledon next year, and to do this it is necessary to raise $6,000. The funds now in the treasury of the association are entirely inadequate to meet the expenditures of the proper entertainment of the British visitors in the coming match, being barely sufficient for the cost of the rifle practice of the American troops at Creedmoor. Therefore the association, as in former years, is compelled to appeal to the public for contributions. The association hopes that the contributions may exceed the necessary $6,000, as the surplus would be devoted to the purchase of an international trophy, to be shot for alternately at Wimbledon and Creedmoor. Contributions to the amount of $1,500 have already been received.

The preliminary shooting at Creedmoor to decide on the team to represent this country was terminated on the 18th of August with the selection of the twelve volunteers who made the highest scores, while Ward and Shakespeare, the thirteenth and fourteenth are assigned to the reserve. There were three trials at which the aggregate was as follows:

| | Three highest scores. | | | Aggregate. |
|---|---|---|---|---|
| A. B. Van Heusen, 12th N. Y. | 169 | 182 | 158 | 509 |
| S. C. Islam, 31st co., Ilion, N. Y. | 163 | 180 | 160 | 505 |
| T. J. Dolan, 12th N. Y. | 163 | 165 | 175 | 505 |
| Captain J. W. Griffith, 9th N. Y. | 165 | 176 | 160 | 501 |
| J. L. Paulding, 12th N. Y. | 164 | 169 | 155 | 488 |
| Fred Adler, 7th N. Y. | 167 | 151 | 163 | 481 |
| M. D. Elinda, 10th separate company | 152 | 163 | 166 | 481 |
| D. H. Ogden, 20th sep com, Bingham'n | 166 | 167 | 144 | 477 |
| Capt. R. Atkinson, 73d Pennsylvania | 164 | 169 | 155 | 477 |
| J. Smith, 7th N. J. | 167 | 156 | 154 | 477 |
| C. W. Hinman, 1st Massachusetts | 146 | 188 | 168 | 475 |
| J. McNevin, 93d N. Y. | 150 | 156 | 164 | 460 |
| D. W. Ward, 1st N. Y. | 150 | 146 | 151 | 455 |
| Major R. C. Shakspeare, 1st Div. Pa. | 134 | 151 | 169 | 454 |

On the announcement of this selection, the team was called together and they elected Colonel Bodine to the responsible position of Captain, who in returning thanks for the honor conferred upon him said that in reference to the question of what rifle or rifles would be used by the American team, the committee would content itself with merely recommending a weapon, and that every member of the team would be free to use the weapon that suited him best.

Colonel Bodine won the sobriquet of "Old Reliable" at Dollymount in the contest with the Irish team in 1874. On the part of the American team one center was required to make a tie, and a bull's-eye to win. It fell to Colonel Bodine to fire the last shot. The result was a bull's-eye and victory for the American team. Colonel Bodine shot at Dollymount again in 1876 in the American team, and also in the contest of 1877. He was captain of the American team that gained another victory over the Irish team at Dollymount in 1880. His record as a marksman both with the smoothbore and the military rifle is not surpassed by that of any man in America. He has been a member of the National Guard for four years as Colonel and Inspector of Rifle Practice for the Fifth Division, New York State.

### Oakland vs. Nevada City.

A rifle match came off last Saturday afternoon, when Messrs. H. Cardew and S. Curnow of Virginia City, Nevada, shot against N. Williams and Col. Kellog of Oakland 50 shots, 200 yards. The former gentlemen made at Virginia city 433 points of a possible 500, or 86·6 per cent. while Williams and Kellogg shot at the Shell Mound range and made 440 points of a possible 500, or 88 per cent. Following are the scores:

| H. Cardew | 4 | 4 | 4 | 5 | 4 | 4 | 5 | 4 | — 44 |
|---|---|---|---|---|---|---|---|---|---|
| | 4 | 5 | 4 | 4 | 4 | 4 | 5 | 4 | — 43 |
| | 4 | 4 | 5 | 4 | 5 | 4 | 4 | 5 | — 45 |
| | 4 | 5 | 4 | 4 | 4 | 4 | 5 | 4 | — 43 |
| S. Curnow | 4 | 4 | 4 | 4 | 4 | 5 | 5 | 5 | — 44 |
| | 4 | 4 | 4 | 4 | 5 | 4 | 4 | 4 | — 43 |
| | 4 | 5 | 4 | 4 | 5 | 5 | 5 | 4 | — 45 |
| | 4 | 5 | 4 | 4 | 4 | 5 | 4 | 4 | — 41 |
| Total | | | | | | | | | 433 |
| Col. Kellogg | 4 | 5 | 4 | 4 | 4 | 4 | 5 | 4 | — 42 |
| | 5 | 5 | 5 | 4 | 4 | 4 | 4 | 4 | — 41 |
| | 4 | 5 | 4 | 4 | 4 | 4 | 4 | 5 | — 44 |
| | 5 | 5 | 5 | 4 | 5 | 4 | 4 | 5 | — 46 |
| | 5 | 4 | 4 | 4 | 4 | 4 | 5 | 4 | — 44 |
| Sergt. Williams | 5 | 5 | 4 | 4 | 4 | 4 | 5 | 4 | — 46 |
| | 4 | 5 | 4 | 4 | 4 | 5 | 4 | 4 | — 44 |
| | 5 | 4 | 5 | 4 | 4 | 4 | 5 | 5 | — 44 |
| | 5 | 4 | 5 | 4 | 4 | 5 | 5 | 5 | — 45 |
| Total | | | | | | | | | 440 |

### The San Francisco Fusileers.

The 11th annual picnic and target-excursion of the San Francisco Fusileers, Company C, Second Artillery, took place last Sunday at Shell Mound Park. This organization has prize shooting every quarter, and every member must practice with his rifle two or three times before each quarterly shooting, in order to be able to compete for prizes. There were three targets; one for the company, another for the honorary members and the third was the public target. The distance was 200 yards, the shots off-hand with Springfield rifles. Of the 39 members the following gentlemen are winners of prizes, with their scores, of a possible twenty-five points. 1st prize, Charles Gloss, 29 points; 2nd, Corporal H. J. Mangels, 22; 3rd, F. Kuhla, 21; 4th, D. Schonfeld, 21; 5th, Chas. Fischer, 21; 6th, John Flagemann, 21; 7th, Louis Haarke, 21. Though the last five mentioned tied on 21 points, their place on the prize list was decided by Creedmoor rules. At the honorary members' target the winners are: 1st prize, Chas Thurbach, 22 points; 2nd, John Shaertzer 20; F. Hagermann 19; and Capt. L. Siebe 18. The prizes for the company and honorary members shooting will be distributed on the 3d Sunday in September. The public target contained twenty-four rings and each competitor and two shots. The first prize, $15, was won by Corporal H. J. Mangels, 22 points; 2nd, $10, Fred Kuhla 20; 3d, $7, C. Thurbach 20; 4th, $6, Sergeant Otto Lemke 20; 5th, $4.50, Mr. Carr 20; 6th, $3, F. Hagermann 19; 7th, $2, F. Boeckman 18; 8th, $1.50, L. Haarke 18; 9th, $1, George Dobber 17. The place on the prize list for those who tied on twenty and eighteen points was decided by Creedmoor rules. The Fusileers may justly feel proud of the company's shooting.

Last Sunday, Mr. Philo Jacoby, of the California Schuetzen Club, made a remarkably good score. Of twenty shots at a twenty-five ring target at 200 yards, he made: 19, 22, 21, 24, 20, 24, 24, 17, 23, 24, 23, 23, 26, 19, 25, 24, 22, 21, 22, 22, 22; total 442, or 88·4 per cent.

## THE GUN.

### California Wing Shooting Club.

The last shoot of the "California Wing Shooting Club" took place at San Bruno on last Sunday, only thirteen members putting in an appearance. The day was very fine, a little too warm for the birds and very much in favor of the gun, as the average was over seventy-nine per cent., only thirty-two birds getting out of bounds out of one hundred and fifty-six birds shot at. Mr. Robinson killing ten, giving the best average for the season, killing 64 out of 72 and taking the first medal. Mr. Roche killed 8 and having second best, 62 out of 72, and Dr. Hayes with 11 kills and 59 out of 72 for the season taking the third medal. The match was at 12 single birds, 3 plunge traps, 21 yards rise and one hundred yards boundary. After the main shoot there were several matches, the first at five birds, 250 entrance with six-teen entries, which proved to be very interesting six of them making clean scores, and was divided between Mr. Maskey and Mr. Walch, after killing 14 birds strait. The second was at 3 pairs double birds, $5 entrance with 5 shooters, Mr. Pearson killing his three pairs and taking first money and Locan and Jellett dividing second money. The next at 3 pairs double birds, Maskey winning first money, Precht, second and W. Golcher Jr., the third:

| Robinson | 0 | 1 | 1 | 1 | 1 | 1 | 1 | 1 | — 10 |
|---|---|---|---|---|---|---|---|---|---|
| Pearson | 1 | 0 | 1 | 1 | 0 | 1 | 0 | 1 | — 8 |
| Roche | 0 | 1 | 1 | 0 | 1 | 1 | 0 | 1 | — 8 |
| Jellett | 1 | 1 | 1 | 1 | 1 | 1 | 1 | 1 | — 10 |
| Chesmore | 1 | 1 | 1 | 1 | 1 | 1 | 0 | 0 | — 10 |
| Hays | 1 | 0 | 1 | 1 | 1 | 1 | 1 | 1 | — 11 |
| Parker | 1 | 1 | 1 | 1 | 1 | 1 | 1 | 1 | — 11 |
| Walsh | 1 | 1 | 1 | 1 | 1 | 1 | 1 | 1 | — 11 |
| Knowles | 1 | 1 | 0 | 1 | 1 | 0 | 1 | 0 | — 7 |
| Rice | 0 | 1 | 0 | 0 | 1 | 1 | 1 | 0 | — 7 |
| Russ | 1 | 1 | 1 | 0 | 1 | 0 | 1 | 1 | — 8 |
| Locan | 1 | 1 | 1 | 1 | 1 | 1 | 1 | 1 | — 10 |
| Bogart | 1 | 1 | 1 | 1 | 1 | 1 | 1 | 1 | — 10 |

FIVE-BIRD MATCH.

FIRST TIE. END. 3RD.

THREE-PAIR MATCH.

| Chesmore | 0 | 1 | 1 | 0 | 1 | 0 | — 3 |
|---|---|---|---|---|---|---|---|
| Jellett | 1 | 0 | 1 | 1 | 0 | 1 | — 4 |
| Locan | 1 | 1 | 0 | 1 | 0 | 1 | — 4 |
| Pearson | 1 | 1 | 1 | 1 | 1 | 1 | — 6 |
| Brown | 1 | 1 | 0 | 0 | 1 | 0 | — 3 |

THREE-PAIR MATCH.

| Slade | 0 | 1 | 1 | 1 | 0 | 0 | — 3 |
|---|---|---|---|---|---|---|---|
| Walsh | 1 | 1 | 0 | 0 | 1 | 0 | — 3 |
| Precht | 1 | 1 | 1 | 0 | 1 | 1 | — 5 |
| Locan | 1 | 1 | 0 | 0 | 1 | 0 | — 3 |
| Russ | 0 | 0 | 0 | 1 | 0 | 0 | — 1 |
| Golcher | 1 | 1 | 1 | 1 | 1 | 1 | — 6 |
| Locan | | | | | | | |
| Hays | 0 | 1 | 1 | 1 | 1 | 1 | — 5 |
| Chesmore | 1 | 1 | 1 | 1 | 1 | 1 | — 6 |
| Jellett | 0 | 0 | 1 | 1 | 0 | 1 | — 3 |
| Pearson | 1 | 1 | 1 | 1 | 1 | 1 | — 6 |
| Brown | 1 | 0 | 0 | 0 | 1 | 0 | — 2 |

Trapping Bears is favorite sport with the stockmen while pasturing their stock in their mountain ranges. On James Moore's range, above Last West Point, they set a bear trap, and fastened it securely to a good-sized sapling, thought to be strong enough to resist the tugging of any animal that might become entangled in its clutches. One day the stockmen managed to find tree and trap shifted from their wonted place. A bear of enormous size must have got nipped, and in its violent efforts to get away, although up the tree by the roots. The trap was found a little distance off, the brute having succeeded in tugging himself loose. On one occasion bruin left his toes in the grip of the trap; another time an entire foot was left behind. The region is also a favorite haunt of California lions.—Amador Sen.

Last Sunday Messrs. A. F. Adams and W. W. Haskell bagged twenty-one curlew and plover on the marshes near East Oakland. They say that the curlew were the fattest they had ever seen.

## Gun-Club Shooting at Bird's Point.

Saturday last the Gun Club held their last shoot of the a, fourteen members answering to the call. The days ery fine, and just wind enough to favor the birds, which a very good lot, and the second barrel was often required ng them to grass. The match was at twelve single , five ground traps, thirty yards rise, use of both barand 100 yards boundary. The shooting of several members of the club was very good, Mr. Tom Ewing, the winof the medal, killing all, but the last one was so unacnodating as to fall just outside the bounds. Mr. H. k lost his eighth bird, but killed all the rest, and in the t with Mr. Ewing, at four single birds, he lost one, Mr. ng making a clean score, and taking the medal, with the es of every member of the club. After the main shoot i was a freeze-out, divided between Mr. Golcher and ock, each killing ten straight birds.

| | | | | | | | | | | |
|---|---|---|---|---|---|---|---|---|---|---|
| . Butler . . . | 1 | 1 | 1 | *0 | 0 | 1 | 0 | 1 | 1 | 0 1 — 8 |
| . Havens . | 1 | 1 | 1 | 0 | 1 | 0 | 1 | 1 | 1 | 1 0 — 9 |
| nicher, Jr. | 1 | 1 | 1 | 1 | 1 | 1 | 1 | 1 | 1 | 1 0 — 10 |
| Wilson . . | 1 | 1 | 1 | *0 | 1 | 1 | 1 | 1 | 1 | 1 — 10 |
| abcock . . . | 1 | 1 | 0 | 1 | 0 | 1 | 1 | 1 | 1 | 0 0 — 8 |
| ring . . . . | 1 | 1 | 1 | 1 | 1 | 1 | 1 | 1 | 1 | 1 *0 — 11 |
| Shane . . | 0 | 1 | 1 | 1 | 1 | 0 | 1 | 1 | 0 | 1 0 — 7 |
| King . . . | 1 | 1 | 1 | 0 | 0 | 1 | 1 | 1 | 1 | 1 0 — 9 |
| ndall . . . | 1 | 1 | 0 | 1 | 1 | 1 | 1 | 1 | 1 | 1 1 — 11 |
| Gordon . . | 1 | 1 | 0 | 0 | 1 | 0 | 0 | 0 | 0 | 0 1 — 3 |
| ler . . . . . | 0 | 1 | 1 | 0 | 0 | 0 | 0 | 0 | 0 | 0 1 — 2 |
| Orr . . . . . | 0 | 1 | 0 | 1 | 1 | 1 | 1 | 1 | 1 | 1 0 — 10 |
| Wakefield | 1 | 1 | *0 | *0 | 1 | 1 | 1 | 1 | 1 | 0 1 — 9 |
| lack. . . . . | 1 | 1 | 1 | 1 | 1 | 1 | 0 | 1 | 1 | 1 1 — 11 |

Dead out of bounds.

TIES SHOT OFF AT FOUR BIRDS.

| | | | | |
|---|---|---|---|---|
| wing. . . . . . . . . . . . . . . . . . . . . . . . . . | 1 | 1 | 1 | 1 — 4 |
| lack. . . . . . . . . . . . . . . . . . . . . . . . . . | 1 | 0 | 1 | 1 — 3 |

FREEZE-OUT.

| | | | | | | | | | | | |
|---|---|---|---|---|---|---|---|---|---|---|---|
| cock. . . . . . . . . . . | 1 | 1 | 1 | 1 | 1 | 1 | 1 | 1 | 1 | 1 — 10 |
| cher . . . . . . . . . . . | 1 | 1 | 1 | 1 | 1 | 1 | 1 | 1 | 1 | 1 — 10 |
| ng . . . . . . . . . . . . | 1 | 1 | 1 | 1 | 1 | 1 | 0 | | | — 7 |
| ier . . . . . . . . . . . . | 1 | 1 | 1 | 1 | 0 | | | | | — 4 |
| don . . . . . | 0 | | | | | | | | | — 0 |
| o . . . . . . . | 0 | | | | | | | | | — 0 |
| dall . . . . . . . . | 1 | 0 | | | | | | | | — 1 |
| ler . . . . . . . . | 1 | 1 | 1 | 1 | 1 | 1 | 0 | | | — 8 |
| he. . . . . . . . . | 0 | | | | | | | | | — 0 |
| . . . . . . . . . . | 1 | 1 | 1 | 1 | *0 | | | | | — 4 |

Dead outside.

CLAY PIGEON MATCH.—On Saturday the members of the meda Sportsmen's Club held the first of a series of four obes. The trophy to be shot for was a handsome gold lal presented by Mr. F. E. Eastman and the conditions fifteen pigeons at eighteen yards rise. Of the dozen conants Mr. Crellin was the last but not least as he won with ore of thirteen as shown by the following table

| | | | | | | | | | | | | | | | |
|---|---|---|---|---|---|---|---|---|---|---|---|---|---|---|---|
| ton . . . . . . . | 1 | 1 | 1 | 0 | 0 | 1 | 1 | 0 | 1 | 1 | 0 | 1 | 1 | 0 — 9 |
| uer. . . . . . . | 1 | 0 | 0 | 1 | 1 | 1 | 0 | 1 | 1 | 1 | 0 | 0 | 0 — 6 |
| ckland . . . . | 1 | 1 | 0 | 1 | 0 | 1 | 0 | 0 | 1 | 1 | 1 | 0 | 1 — 9 |
| pton . . . . . . | 0 | 1 | 0 | 1 | 0 | 1 | 0 | 1 | 1 | 1 | 0 | 1 | 0 — 7 |
| opkins . . . . | 0 | 0 | 1 | 0 | 0 | 1 | 1 | 1 | 1 | 1 | 1 | 1 | 1 — 9 |
| illiams. . . . . | 1 | 1 | 1 | 0 | 1 | 0 | 0 | 1 | 1 | 1 | 0 — 9 |
| nroe . . . . . . | 0 | 1 | 1 | 1 | 1 | 0 | 1 | 1 | 0 | 1 | 0 — 9 |
| ihee . . . . . . | 0 | 1 | 1 | 1 | 0 | 1 | 1 | 0 | 1 | 1 | 0 — 8 |
| arrage . . . . . | 1 | 1 | 1 | 1 | 0 | 0 | 1 | 1 | 1 | 1 | 1 — 10 |
| ttle . . . . . . . | 1 | 1 | 1 | 0 | 0 | 1 | 1 | 1 | 1 | 1 | 1 — 10 |
| uln. . . . . . . . | 0 | 1 | 1 | 0 | 1 | 1 | 1 | 1 | 1 | 1 | 1 — 9 |
| ellin. . . . . . . | 1 | 1 | 1 | 1 | 1 | *0 | 1 | 1 | 1 | 1 — 13 |

Mr. Crellin was warmly congratulated on his adding another the many emblems of success that are already in his session.

## Trifling with a She Bear.

C. and W. Masters, of Polk County, Or., while hunting the headwaters of the Santiam last week, captured two ar cubs. While on their way to the camp with their prize, a mother of the cubs suddenly attacked them and with one ow of her paw knocked Charles out of time, sending his p out of reach and freeing one cub. She then turned upon Stlliam, who discharged his Winchester rifle, inflicting a gh wound in her shoulder. She threw him down, releasf the other cub, and dragged him 50 yards down a ravine. harles had recovered his gun, but was afraid to shoot for r of killing his brother. The bear finally gave William a ow on the head, tearing his scalp fearfully, and then made f after her cubs. Charles succeeded in getting his brother camp and dressed his wounds as well as possible, but it a two days before they were able to start for home. Charles eived scratches of so severe a nature that they were h unhealed at the expiration of five days, and his brother s confined to his bed for two weeks. Bear hunting is all ght enough, but when the bear turns hunter there is not much p in it.

It is stated that jackrabbits, which were recently so abund4 in the vicinity of Bakersfield that an ordinary sportsman ight easily kill a hundred before breakfast, have nearly all sappeared, and that the late extremely hot weather has lled them.

Fifty dollars has been offered for the scalp of a very large ld very bad grizzly bear, said to weigh 1800 pounds, that s been troubling stock men on Bailey Creek, Shasta unty, killing many cattle and driving the herds from their astures.

The Pherscer Gun of Sacramento have issued their programme of the trap shooting tournament at the Agricultural ark during the State Fair. The shooting will commence on uesday, Sept. 12th, the first, or main match, being at twelve rds each, $10 entrance, under the rules of the club. The ntrance money will be divided into ten prizes. Following e main match there will be shooting for several days at igeons, bats, balls, etc.

The Prince of Wales won three first prizes at the Norfolk attle show—one for a Short-horn bull and two Southdown heep. A case of farming by proxy.

Dr. Ellis, of Russell county, Kansas, offers to pay ten nts per head for sheep pastured upon his fields. He knows he sheep's foot is golden.

Subscriptions to the Laversck monument fund have already ached $100, with several counties yet to be heard from.

# THE PADDOCK.

## Breeding Coach Horses.

As will be seen from the letter of "Broad Arrow" and the following article, copied from the Sunday Oregonian, the remarks about breeding coach horses which appeared in a late number of this paper have attracted attention. It is one of the most important questions in relation to horse breeding, and well worthy of being made the topic for the fullest discussion. The views of our correspondent are sound, through we 're of the opinion that the great consideration is how to increase the size of our horses, and how to preserve the desired characteristics. The Clydesdale was mentioned as having proved a successful admixture in giving the required stature, and the preponderance of thoroughbred blood, adding the quality. There are families which are, perhaps, better than Clydesdales, aud, in fact, we frequently see mares at work in the heavy teams of the city, far nearer the desired type than any of the draft breeds. That an augmentation of .ize can be obtained from the coupling of medium thoroughbred sizes with the ordinary mares of the country, and by liberal feeding of the offspring, is certain, and that in two or three generations the increase will surprise those who have not witnessed the effects of well-directed care.

In the article from the Oregonian, the writer makes a great mistake in classing Abbotsford and Stienway as below 15½ hands and less than a thousand pounds in weight. Stienway is a big horse and will come very nearly to the standard for the coach horse, and not one of them that is not above the height mentioned. Mr. Finigan has a yearling by Santa Claus, which is nearly 15½ hands, and all the Abbotsfords we have seen are larger than the ordinary run of colts of their age. Very many of the descendants of Belmont, in the second and third generation, are larger horses, though the patriarch of the family was of medium size, and the Owen Dales are invariably of powerful frames and great substance. That Oregon has taken a prominent place in the breeding of fine horses cannot be questioned, though we think the credit is due to an intelligent system of breeding rather than the possession of a superior climate and soil to California. 'And yet the reasons given may have some force and a longer season of greener food desirable:

The BREEDER AND SPORTSMAN, edited by Joseph Cairn Simpson probably the ripest scholar in horse lore now connected with the American press, says in the 'course of a leading article upon coach horses that "Oregon, so far as our observation has gone, has taken the lead of California in this class of horses, as well as in the better class of draft horses." Now the talented author of "Horse Portraiture" was never in Oregon in his life, but he judges from the horses shipped here for sale in the California markets, and his judgment is eminently correct. Onceftal as is his concession, we cannot believe it was done wholly from the desire to show himself a man of greater liberality of opinion than usually falls to the lot of most writers. There must have been some good ground for so positive a declaration, or the writer quoted above would never have made it. He is an observing man and is never hasty in expressing his opinions. We have long been of the belief that breeders cannot afford to breed for the race track alone, whether they keep running or trotting stallions for hire. Men of scant means who own good mares, must have something else to look forward to beyond the peradventure of getting a racehorse or a crack trotter. The old thoroughbred horse Owen Dale, which died in San Jose nearly twenty years ago, was a "poor man's horse," in this respect. But three of his get were ever trained to run and all got a better record than 1:47 for a mile. Yet it was not in this respect alone that this great horse, with his fine size and incomparable good temper, showed how valuable a piece of taxable property he was to the now wealthy county of Santa Clara. the garden of the Golden state. It was in the graded stock, bred from ordinary mares owned by men of moderate means. They comprised roadsters, carriage horses and workhorses, scattered all over that beautiful valley and adding to its material wealth. Just how the value originate on property of this sort, we are not prepared to say, but you will agree with us that any man will want a big price for an animal which he cannot readily replace. So it was with these great lengthy Owen Dale colts of which the noted Copperhead was such an example. He could trot in 2:38 with two men in a roadwagon, and could not get below 2:36 with one man in a sulky. It was therefore evident that ability to pull weight, rather than speed itself, was the prominent characteristic of Copperhead, who was big enough to pull logs to a saw-mill. Take it within the past few years, and you will see that this important consideration has been overlooked somewhat in Oregon, but to a far greater extent in California. To be of any service on a farm, a horse ought to be at least fifteen and a half hands high and weigh about one thousand pounds. How many of the great trotting sires of California will come up to this standard of excellence? Santa Claus (2:17¼), Steinway (2:23 at four years old), Echo (2:35), and Abbotsford (2:6l), all fall far below it, while Nutwood, Alexander and Brigadier were the only ones that went over it. In searching for speed they have forgotten that the true place for the trotting horse was on the road instead of the race track.

And now if the reader will pardon the digression of the past few minutes we will go back to the discussion of coachhorses in general. The coach-horse mast trot; a gallop will not do. The trotting blood of some standard-bred sire must be the foundation on one side, which it does not matter; though we prefer it through the sire. Shape and quality become naturally the next consideration and should be derived through the dam rather than the sire. Now we suppose that a man has a mare sired by some running horse like Monte Christo or Ossoolo, with no further authenticated blood on the dam's side; which would pay him best to breed the mare to another running horse or some good reliable trotting sire? It does not admit of a moment's hesitation, and he would breed to the trotter every time because trotting-bred horses are the most useful and therefore the most saleable. Our own belief is that the coach horse of the future must have an infusion of thoroughbred blood, but because of the house, because the thoroughbred horse has a longer neck, a more shapely head and generally speaking a finer coat of hair, but the trotting blood is indispensable and therefore it must be there, on one side or the other. For reasons already given, we prefer it through the paternal line. Hugh Fields, of Umatilla, a man well situated to commence the breeding

of fine carriage-horses, as he has been breeding from thoroughbred sires for nearly twenty years and must therefore have some very high-formed mares. He should now get a standard bred trotting sire and breed for the coach, not overlooking the stout blood of Mambrino Chief, which has the ability to pull weight. At four year old Ericsson, Mambrino Chief's son, trotted a fourth heat in 2:30 to wagon, on six weeks' work and trained by an amateur. We don't believe Maud S. was any better horse, but we do think that training is progressive and that the lowering of the trotting record in twenty years from 2:19½ to 2:10] is the result of education based on study and experience. Hiram Woodruff was the greatest driver and trainer of his day. He said $2000 for the pacer James K. Polk to convert him' into a trotter and could not get him below 2:40. Now every farmer's boy from Maine to Oregon can put toe-weights on a pacer and make him trot, while dear old Hiram never once thought of it.

Oregon will always breed good horses for the coach, if men will only take proper care of their colts from weaning time to maturity. The day has gone by when a man can. lie in his dirty blankets and hope to get rich by the mere spontaneous increase of dumb beasts. But for the active and studious breeder, the man who will develop and educate his horses up to a real value, there will be dollars in ten years hence where there are coppers to-day. Oregon can never hope to rival California in the development of early trotters, because the training season is so short that that a California three-year old is as thoroughly gaited as an Oregon horse of five. But for horses of ten or twelve years of age, the golden state will not surpass us much. Oregon has eight months of grass to California's five, and it is the silica in grass that makes the bone. Flesh and muscle do not give a horse. stamina and endurance. He must have the bone to enable. him to stand the hard work. We believe that the work. horses grown in eastern Oregon have more bone than those produced in the Willamette valley, because there is more. silica in the bunch grass than in the native grasses of this valley. And whenever the right men undertake their production, Oregon coach-horses will be in demand in San Francisco and at heavy prices.

Last week W. C. Moyan, living near Albany, Oregon, lost a horse, the fifth since Christmas. Desiring to know what ailed the horse, he, assisted by others, made a post-mortem examination. They were somewhat surprised to find in the. stomach enough binding wire to fill one of the hands. They were the small pieces twisted together and clipped off on threshing, and rolled together had worked themselves through the mucous membrane of the stomach in several places, of course causing death.

# FISH.

FINED FOR CATCHING SALMON.—Last week an Italian fisherman was arrested by several men engaged in the same business for violating the State fish law, he having been guilty of catching salmon since August last when the close season commenced. He with others had caught and shipped ten barrels of salmon, weich in the absence of a market in the canneries, were salted and packed for shipment. The offense was committed just below Courtland, and the case came up for trial before Justice Thomas Hodgdon, of Washington, Yolo county. I. S. Brown conducted the prosecution and I. S. Taylor was the defendant's attorney. The evidence was convicted and fined $50 and paid that sum. Mr. Brown then had half a dozen of the fishermen about Courtland appointed Deputy Constables so that they can have the power to arrest, and it is understood that anyone found violating the law will be punished to the utmost extent. The largest fine that can be imposed is $500, and imprisonment is also allowable. It is said the fishermen generally are desirous of having the law enforced.—The Bee.

A SCREW LOOSE SOMEWHERE—It will be very hard to make people obey fish and game laws when such things as occurred in Police court No. 2 in this city this week happen. A fish dealer was tried for having in his possession salmon out of season. The guilty man confessed, the Judge properly instructed the jury, and the jury brought in a verdict of "not guilty!" We know that it was considered impossible to punish the law-breakers in the counties bordering on the river where salmon are caught, but it seemed possible that San Francisco juries would convict when the guilt was proven. There is a screw loose somewhere.

Jacob Vetter, while fishing at Prince's Bay, New York, one day last week hooked a turtle that weighed 126 pounds.

Fishing on the Bear River in Calaveras county is not good. Either the fish are seeking new haunts, or they were too lazy to bite during the recent hot spell.

During the past week great numbers of dead weak-fish have been floating the lower bays of New York. The fishermen say that the fish were killed by the attempts made to blow up the sunken hull of the steamer Nankin in Swash Channel.

It is stated that mullet are running up the Pajaro and Elkhorn sloughs. These fish appear annually for a few weeks, and then suddenly disappear. They do not appear further north than the Bay of Monterey. It is said they come from the Mexican coast, and are among the best table fish caught.

The Mariposa Gazette says the water in the Merced River has become so hot that it has caused all the salmon fish to die. Tons upon tons of dead fish are daily drifting down the river, which is creating a terrible stench, and the like was never known before. Much uneasiness is felt among people along the river, who fear it will cause sickness.

Manzanita Lake is about three-quarters of a mile long and half a mile wide, and is fed by Manzanita Creek, a stream heading in the snow of Lassen Butte, six or eight miles above. From its borders, some of the projecting crags of Mount Lassen seem to tower above, yet they are in reality six miles distant. The surrounding scenery is grand beyond description. The water of the lake, pure as crystal, reflects surrounding objects. It is very deep in places. Where the bottom can be seen the clearness of the water renders the depth very deceptive. People camping there lately report excellent fishing and pretty good hunting.

The sale of several Llewellin setters at Aldridge, London, Aug. 4th, resulted thus: Noble Windem, purchased by Mr. Lidderdale, 23 guineas; Nimble Windem, purchased by Mr. Cunningham, 36 guineas; Royal Windem, purchased by Col. Makins, 36 guineas; Sydney Bondhu, to Mr. J. A. Platt, for 34 guineas, and Champion Baffle, a Birmingham winner, to the same gentleman, for 26 guineas.

# THE
# Breeder and Sportsman.

PUBLISHED WEEKLY BY THE
BREEDER AND SPORTSMAN PUBLISHING CO.

THE TURF AND SPORTING AUTHORITY OF THE
PACIFIC COAST.

### OFFICE, 508 MONTGOMERY STREET
P. O. Box 1928.

*Five dollars a year; three dollars for six months; one dollar and a
half for three months. Strictly in advance.*

MAKE ALL ORDERS, MONEY ORDERS, ETC., PAYABLE TO ORDER OF
BREEDER AND SPORTSMAN PUBLISHING CO.

*Money should be sent by postal order, draft or by registered letter, ad-
dressed to the "Breeder and Sportsman Publishing Company, San Fran
cisco, Cal."*

*Communications must be accompanied by the writer's name and address,
not necessarily for publication, but as a private guarantee of good faith*

JOSEPH CAIRN SIMPSON, - - - EDITOR

San Francisco, Saturday, Sept. 2, 1882.

## THE GOLDEN GATE FAIR.

Although the horses have already distinguished themselves on the Bay District, at Santa Cruz, Santa Rosa
and Petaluma, the great interest to the people of San
Francisco centers in the performances at Oakland.
There are many who make a practice of "following the
circuit," and to those who have the necessary time at
their disposal, a very good practice it is. But there are
a large number who cannot afford to visit all the places,
pleasant though it would be, and they are restricted to
attending the grounds, which are a practical suburb of
San Francisco. It is one of the pleasantest short trips
imaginable. Thirty-five minutes from the foot of Market street lands the passengers at Shell Mound, and
twenty-five cents is all that is required for that much of
the expense, there and back. There is only one change
from the boat to the cars, and only two stopping places
between the wharf and the park. Although for eight
years we have made daily trips across the bay, the journey is never tiresome. There is always a freshness in the
air, there is always something new to interest. To those
who make occasional trips there must be still more pleasure. But the attractiveness of the trip is only a small
part of the pleasure which awaits those who attend the
fair. In the first place there is an assurance of a fine
display in the stock ridge. The entries of cattle and
horses will be larger than ever before, and very many
notable specimens of all the breeds come into competition. Notwithstanding the great interest which is taken
in this department of the fair, the contests on the track
are the lodestones which draw ninety per cent., at least,
of the sightseers. The speed ring is always a potent
magnet when the entries give the assurance that every
contest will be a sharp struggle for supremacy, and it is
safe to assert that, every race on the programme will
prove of absorbing interest. The first day of the fair,
Monday, the 4th of September, is given principally to
running, there being two trots; one the 2:40 class, and
the other a special purse against-time. It is needless to
repeat all of the entries which appear on the programme
elsewhere, and a reference to which will show that there
can scarcely be a lack of sport in any of them. The
first is a dash of three quarters of a mile for two-year-
olds, and the few which are engaged are sure to make a
lively spin. The second race is the Alameda stake for
three-year-olds, one and a half miles, and as Precious,
Fostress, Forest King, Duke of Monday and Maria F.
come together, there must result a capital race. The
Pardee stake is heats of a mile for all ages, and there are
six engaged in it, the Salt Lake horse, Red Boy, taking
part. Night Hawk, Fred Collier, Sister to Lottery, Precious and Fostress will give him some trouble, and if the
scion of the house of War Dance gains the victory, all
who witness it will know that there has been a race.
There are twelve entries in the 2:40 class, some of them
which have already figured, with enough new names to
give spice and variety. From all the indications in previous races the classes this year bring together horses
which are so nearly matched that there will be surprises,
startling episodes which will lend zest to the proceedings.
Vanderlynn after his victory on the Bay District course
was thought to have this class at his mercy. In that
race Freestone demonstrated a capacity scarcely inferior,
and at Santa Rosa Frank Moscow "downed" the band.
Marin got a heat in the last race, and now when Manon,
San Mateo Belle, Rowdy Boy, Louis D., Exile, Edwin
Forrest and Big Lize come into the calculation, the
ciphering will give a good deal of trouble to those who
are endeavoring to select a winner. But it will be tiresome to go all through the bill of the Golden Gate Fair,
and even a succinct statement of the entries a mere
repetition of names. There is no question, however, that
there will not be a blank day throughout the week, and
while those who attend on the first day will be loth to
lose any of the succeeding, each one of the six will be

well worthy of seeing. There is not a dull day in the
lot. The racing and trotting are not the only attractions.
There are to be bicycling and military drills, and to take
part in the latter are the St. Patrick Cadets which exhibited such marvelous skill in the tactics at Sacramento
a couple of years ago. It is a pity that the programme
is so arranged that the boys can only compete with those
of the same grade, the general impression being that they
could play their part, with companies longer under arms
than their years from birth. There is scarcely a question that the Golden Gate Fair of this year will be superior to any which have preceded it, and those who miss it
will regret the omission. The track was never in better
order. In fact, the thorough incorporation of the loam
and sediment has left nothing more to be desired in the
soil.

## THE QUAIL SEASON.

The California sportsman's cup of happiness will
shortly be full. The close system for quail will expire
on the 15th, and the valleys and mountains will resound
with the crack of the breech-loaders. The dogs, so long
pent up in back yards and between brick walls, will
scamper round, mad with enjoyment. They know by the
loading of shells and the cleaning of guns that their
happy time has at last returned. Have patience with
them, ye sportsmen, and don't blame them if they flush
a few birds at starting. They are not worth much if
they do not. Remember how long they have been kept
from their favorite passion, and keep your temper; they
will be all high, before the day is through, and when they
have worn off their wire edge they will make you some
fine points, and with a full bag you will return to business refreshed and invigorated, to enjoy an appetite and
sleep the sleep that only the quail-hunter enjoys. If you
are a novice in quail hunting, do not overload yourself
with a heavy gun. A gun that feels light in a gunmaker's store will weigh pretty heavy before you get
through with a long day's tramp over the difficult
ground you have to travel to follow quail successfully.
Seven pounds, unless you are as tall and strong as Sullivan, is heavy enough, and will be quite as effective as
more metal. Remember there is much walking to little
shooting, and you have to kill birds whose flight resembles in speed the arrow from a bow, and quickness of
shooting is of more consequence than heavy loads. When
Demosthenes was asked what was the first requisite in
oratory, he replied: "Action." The second ?" "Action."
The third? "Action." If you ask for the first requisite
in quail shooting, the reply is: "Legs." The second?
"Legs." The third? "Legs." Therein lies the great
value to the city man. He will take more exercise after
quail in one day, than he could be induced to take in any
other way in a month. And then the value to the lungs
and digestion, to say nothing of dropping a brace right
and left, down a deep ravine, and seeing your well-
trained dog go down where you could not go yourself,
and bring one up and then the other, to lay them down
at your feet, more pleased than you are yourself. Now
show your appreciation by making much of him. But
don't make your bag too large; leave some for your
brother sportsmen; and for yourself another time. Don't
shoot the half-grown birds, for at the commencement
of the season there always are such; but when an old
cock gets up, bring all your San Bruno skill into play
and drop him—there is more satisfaction in that, than
the slaughter of a dozen innocents. Do not trouble
about the number of your birds. You can go back to
the city with a clear conscience that your bag, such as it
is, has been obtained in a sportsmanlike manner, and
not with what these diabolical pot-hunters call "rakes,"
whereby they maliciously wound more than they kill.
After you have found your covey, and they take wing,
keep your eye well on the direction of their flight. You
will find them in the next ravine, generally near the top.
Then "comes the tug of war," the real science of quail
shooting. You will follow them with your dog—a brace
is better, too much hard work for one dog—you beat
round, not a quail there. You are positive they came
there. Your dog, by his action, appears to be of the same
opinion. Presently, at the foot of a small bunch of
poison oak, he comes to a stand point, tail erect, himself
like a statue—beautiful sight, then which nothing is more
gladdening to a sportsman. You poke into the brush,
hardly large enough to hide a quail. You see nothing,
and begin to wonder what he is pointing at; but give it a
kick, and whirr! out goes a hen quail—they always lie
closer than the cocks. You shoot, and most likely miss
from being over excited. Best again, they are all there,
and lying like stones. Your dog finds another. You
are cool this time. Whirr!—a bunch of feathers. Seek
dead. And if you will persevere and beat that ground
thoroughly, going over it two or three times, you will
find them all, and get your afternoon's shooting out of
that flock, besides giving your dog a lesson on the tricks
of quail that he will never forget.

## THE SONOMA AND MARIN FAIR.

Those who have had horses at the fair of the Sonoma
and Marin Agricultural Association are delighted with
the new track and the stabling. Heretofore there have
been complaints. The track was anathemized. Whatever casuality happened was ascribed to the
course, and the maledictions over accidents that
that are likely to happen on the best of tracks were laid
to the shorter courpers which a half mile imposes. The
trainers of horses in California are exacting in their demands. They are, in a measure, spoiled by the uniform
excellence of the tracks throughout the State, and insist
on what would be considered in the Eastern States conditions which could not be fulfilled. Even those who
date their advent on the Pacific Coast to a few years ago
are worse than others who have been accustomed to the
benefits of this climate for a score of seasons, and they
rail at the weather and the state of the track, when in
all of their previous experience they never were so well
served. A foggy morning is held to be a grievous drawback, when in their old homes they might be compelled
to wallow through the mud for a week at a time. When
at Petaluma they had to trot over a half-mile track they
were in the doldrums. The track was accorded the
mishaps which may have arisen from their own want of
care. But now the whole circuit of the most important
fairs does not present the overrated obstacles, and at every
place the tracks are such as to disarm adverse criticism.
It is well that the directors of the Sonoma and Marin
took steps to do away with the objections, and there cannot be a shadow of doubt that in the future the entry
list will compare favorably with those of the other fairs.
When horses trot as fast as they have done at Petaluma
this week it is the best evidence that the course is all
that is claimed for it. With the rains of one winter to
give solidity it is probable that the track will be as fast
as any of the others in this State, and that will be fast
enough. A fast and safe track are not the only improvements which have followed the change. In a very few
years it will be one of the most beautiful of fair-
grounds; and the ornamentation which judicious care
has provided will be one of the most attractive features.
No matter how good the track may be there are surroundings which a fair-ground must have to make it
popular, and this needed characteristic has been duly
provided for by bringing the arts of the landscape
gardener to assist. Henceforth Petaluma will not be
behind adding one more to the first-rate courses of California.

## DEATH OF B. B. REDDING.

B. B. Redding, one of the California Fish Commissioners, died suddenly on Monday of last week. In this
death this State loses a most valuable public-spirited
citizen, and one who devoted great energy to any task
he undertook.

Mr. Redding has been for some years the leading
spirit in the Fish Commission; the man of affairs who
took an absorbing interest in all questions relating to
fish and fishing; and to whose activity and intelligent
direction the success of the commission is mainly due.
An ardent lover of the rod and line, and one who
thoroughly enjoyed the angler's pleasures, he was at the
same time imbued with a desire to advance the economic
features of fish culture, and to encourage habits of
scientific observation among those with interest in the
finny tribes.

Mr. Redding made an annual pilgrimage to the Cloud
River where he spent his vacation along its streams, rod
in hand. At all other times, his interest in the fish was
devoted to the public, and his efforts were directed
toward replenishing the supply of streams and ponds, and
stocking new waters.

His attention was not confined alone to the fish interest, but he also did a great deal toward experimenting
with the acclimatization of foreign game birds in California. Whenever he heard of any species which he
thought ought to do well here, he wrote for information,
and obtained specimens. This with fish and game.

Mr. Redding had a scientific knowledge of fishes, and
strove to impart a taste for it in others. Although in a
position where his time was greatly occupied and holding several honorary places of public trust, he directed
the greater space of his spare hours to his duties as Fish
Commissioner. In the Commission it will be exceedingly
difficult to fill his place. One with his knowledge, energy, affability, and unflagging interest, it will be hard
to find.

Mr. Redding was a warm friend, a genial companion,
an earnest worker, and a studious thinker. Such men
as he are rare. And when they are willing to devote
their energies to the public good, without fee or reward,
they are rarer still. The sportsmen of California owe a
debt of gratitude to the late Mr. Redding for his labors
on their behalf, which will keep his memory green
among them for many a year to come.

## The 2:40 Class.

Again at Petaluma there has been a change in the 2:40 class, and with only five starters, seven heats more necessary to decide the race. Vanderlynn has been unfortunate ever since his first appearance, and it will take some hard work to "rehabilitate" him in the estimation of his admirers. But green horses are proverbially uncertain. At rare intervals one will appear which has the qualities of an old stager, trotting as steadily as a veteran of a hundred fights, coming to time with the exactness of an old-fashioned clock and never disappointing those who back him. These are generally of the "leadheaded" class. Never unduly excited, always showing better in a race than in their work, and bettering the trials which are shown in private. From the work we saw in Santa Rosa when Johnny and Vanderlynn were exercised in company, it was evident that the latter was not in the same order he was in his race at the Bay District. He could not speed with the son of the Auctioneer and in the attempt would go in the air. There are disturbing influences this season which are likely to upset all previous calculations, and which are not usually met. The pinkeye is the black demon which is constantly making an appearance to mar all the carefully laid schemes. He comes in a shape to mislead. While there is a strangling cough at times so bad as to endanger choking down, the animal attacked does not get off his feed and is apparently in good spirits. But all at once the speed is gone. A 'move through' the stretch entails as much distress as formerly followed the full mile, and the work heretofore given is found to be too violent a strain. There is only conjecture to warrant the ascribing the defeat of Vanderlynn to pinkeye, but as the disease has extended all over the country, some of those attacked giving scarcely an indication of its presence, it may be that this peculiar form of 'spizooty has had something to do with the result. Whatever the cause are for the changes there is an appearance that this class is on a par with the 2:25 for startling changes, and that the interest is not likely to diminish through the whole of the circuit.

## DEATH OF AN ANGLER AND JOURNALIST.

Wm. E. J. Hooper, who died at the ripe age of 79 years, in this city this week, was a most enthusiastic disciple of the rod and line, and ardently followed his chosen sport up to the last few years of his life. Mr. Hooper was a close observer and wrote gracefully of what he saw. Wherever he had the opportunity he walked the banks of the trout streams readily accessible, and worked harder for a day's sport than many much younger men. He was a true lover of angling; was perfectly familiar with all its appliances, and skilful in their use. The writer well remembers his enthusiasm when the girdles were first found to be in the vicinity of Oakland pier. And when they were gone and the trout season over, Mr. Hooper would spend much of his spare time on the pier in quest of the humbler smelt. As a handler of the rod he had few equals, and his genial nature, good humor, ready wit and pleasant conversational powers made him a sought-for companion even by much younger men.

The Shooting Season, as all true sportsmen know, opens on the 15th. Between now and then the shooters will overhaul their guns, bring out their outfits, load up their cartridges and otherwise prepare for "the fifteenth." Longing looks have for some time been thrown on the tried breechloader and as the time draws near when it can be aired it becomes of greater importance than any other thing in the household. The opening of the season marks an era in the lives of many men. They look forward to it with eager expectation for many months. The quail will be the first sufferers but it will not be long before the ducks come in for their share too. Already there are some ducks in the marshes, but it will not be until the first rains that they will be abundant.

The Pacific Yacht Club regatta which is announced for next Saturday is expected to draw out quite a fleet. The Aggie, Ariel, O'Connor, Fleur de Lis, Whitewing, Annie and Clara at least will enter and perhaps more. The course includes a stake boat at Hunter's Point and the annual prizes including the annual prize flag will be given. We have had no regata on the bay this year, and it is even now somewhat late for one of the big prizes; August being the last month. It is to be hoped however, that the Pacific will have a good day with plenty of wind for all hands.

Men who have visited the Fair grounds at Petaluma the present week are delighted with the new arrangement. The track is not only accorded a prominent place among the grand courses of California, but the general appearance of all the appurtenances are highly extolled. The arrangement of pavilion, stalls and other necessary buildings is commendable and after a few years the trees and shrubbery will finish the beauty of the picture. Better than all this, as we learn, is the management, and probably no awards have been made that were not satisfactory to those who can look at things from this correct standpoint. Had the one missing link been

introduced there would have been nothing lacking. This gap was the neglect to furnish the information of what had been done, and, consequently, the owners of horses were ignorant in relation to the changes. There will be a remedy in the future for the only lack, and henceforward the Sonoma and Marin will come into the line showing the same liberal list of entries as marks the fairs of Oakland, Sacramento, Stockton, San Jose, etc.

Billy McCracken, the sire of the dam of Overman, we would like to hear something about. In the report copied from the N. Y. Spirit of the Times it was stated that Billy McCracken was at one time owned in Buffalo, and other information is that he was brought here when a suckling colt by Mr. McCracken. We will be much obliged for any intelligence regarding this horse, and also of the California stallion, David Hill. There are many of the get of these two horses in California, and the breeding is an essential feature which should not be overlooked. We are under the impression that the Eastern horse is not the one which was the sire of the dam of Overman.

We have missed the fairs so far. With all the yearning to enjoy the festivities there has been a "cruel fate" placing an interdict on participation. It may be that we cannot attend a single one this season. The Eastern people have very little idea of what the exhibitions are in this State. The County fairs of the country east of the Rockies are no measure. There are State fairs back home which will not compare with the smallest of the District fairs of this Coast, and some of them show a display which the whole Eastern country cannot equal.

The trouble is to get away from home farther than the busy side of the bay. Living on the Christian shore of the water, there are enticements to spend the Sunday which are hard to overcome. There are visits to the stables when everything is as quiet as a due observance of the Sunday law entails, and it may be, a drive to points of interest makes an afternoon's work, or rather enjoyment. Then again the colts have to be considered. It may be, with all due regard to the enactments of the State, that an experiment has to be tried; a new form of tip or shoe to be put on, and then the clang of the anvil reverberates from the stable, to the utter disgust of those who, with us, were duly christened in the auld kirk. Many Sunday trips have been outlined, and a few of them carried out. Those we have disappointed must place the onus on circumstances that are hard to control, and, if possible, give us absolution.

A Grand Picnic is one of the peculiar features if the fair at Petaluma. The residents of the two counties embraced in the district make a point of attending the "harvest home." The grounds from early morning until the last excites are thronged. There is a constant stream of wagons passing through the gates and there are ranged so that the best profitable view of the races can be obtained. At noon time the lunch baskets are opened and a stranger who has the least hungry look in his visage is importuned to partake. And a better luncheon could hardly be gotten up. Chickens roasted to a turn, wine of vintage which is far superior to any imported, and rolls and bread baked in a home oven. there is nothing like the average lunch put up in a ham house The chickens have never been cooped, the eggs are gathered the same morning they are put in the pot, the sliced tongue and dried beef, the boiled ham, the fruit, everything perfect. The city delicacies are nowhere. The most delicate taste does not require condiments and sauces, and there is a relish, a gout, which it is hopeless to explain.

## BICYCLING.

### Cortis' Last Ride.

Herbert L. Cortis made his last public appearance as a bicycle rider at Surbiton near London on August 2nd., and in so doing left a record not likely to be soon forgotten. The occasion was the evening race meeting of the Wanderers B. C., at which Cortis had announced his intention of endeavoring to beat his own wonderful hour's ride of a few days previous. The Hon. Ion Keith-Falconer attended the ride for the first few miles, but soon retired. Several other riders also assisted as pace-makers, to such good purpose that when time expired Cortis had covered 20 miles, 323 yards, or twenty-eight yards better than his recent performance at the Crystal Palace. En route Cortis cut all previous records from three miles upwards, both professional and amateur, except the five miles amateur time.

Of this race we take the following interesting account from the New York Spirit of the Times: "Surbiton, where the meeting was held, is some distance from London, for such purposes; but there were, nevertheless, several hundreds of spectators—indeed, more than I remember seeing on any previous occasion, the sides of the course being crowded. The course is exactly 400 yards in circuit, and is specially prepared for bicycling, the surface being hard and the corners eased off. He also makes the duty of timing tolerably easy. This office was undertaken on the present occasion by Messrs. Coleman and Atkinson (Sporting Life), and a third watch was running with theirs, as a check.

It was already past 7 o'clock, the time, when the pistol fired. Woolnough, the pace-maker, went off at his best, followed by Cortis, Falconer lying last. The time of the ride was 3 minutes, dead, but the second, with Hamilton in place of Woolnough, was a clinker, viz., 2m. 52 1-5s., the fastest of the match. The third mile was much slower, but the next two were both inside 3m.55s. In the sixth mile the pace-maker was not fast enough for Cortis, who screamed at him to go on, whilst Falconer seemed to think otherwise. Completing this mile, the Honorable was left twenty yards in the rear, as if by magic, and, not feeling comfortable, eased up; but the cheers of the spectators caused him to on again, although only for another half mile, when he stopped for good. The seventh mile was done in 2m. 55.,

exactly, He eased a good deal in the next three, and the 11th, 12th, 13th, 14th, 15th, and 16th, were all outside the 3 minutes. The whole distance occupied 59m. 20. 1-5s. and, but for the wind, would have been even better than that. After passing the post Cortis eased a good deal, but still ran 294 yards over the 20 miles in the hour. It was quite dusk when he finished, and people were very glad it was all over without a mishap. The difficult task of pace-making was splendidly done throughout, and it was wonderful to see how Cortis tired out the different riders, one after the other, although they were, most of them, doing performances which would have entitled them to championship honors only a few years before. Cortis was married the next day and is now on his way to Australia, where he intends to settle, and to devote himself to his profession. What England loses, Australia gains, the possession of the most famous bicyclist that has ever entered for honors.

The following table shows how the miles were made, all above the sixth being the best on record.

| MILES. | M. SEC. | MILES. | M. SEC |
|---|---|---|---|
| 1 | 3 0 | 11 | 22 30 |
| 2 | 5 52 1-2 | 12 | 35 30 4-5 |
| 3 | 8 51 1-5 | 13 | 38 35 3-5 |
| 4 | 11 46 1-5 | 14 | 41 36 |
| 5 | 14 40 2-5 | 15 | 44 37 2-5 |
| 6 | 17 37 | 16 | 47 37 1-5 |
| 7 | 20 32 | 17 | 50 22 2-5 |
| 8 | 23 31 1-5 | 18 | 53 27 3-5 |
| 9 | 26 31 3-5 | 19 | 56 22 3-5 |
| 10 | 29 30 2-5 | 20 | 59 20 1-5 |

### The Twenty-five Mile Championship.

The Leicester trials for this championship coming to afford the most sensational spirit. It will be remembered that the directors of the Aylestone grounds offer a prize of £25, with added money to like amount. The winner becomes the holder of the trophy (which must be won three times in all), and receives in addition £15; second, £6; third, £3; fourth, £1; while an additional sovereign is given to the leading competitor if record be beaten for ten, twenty, and twenty-five miles. The first competition was decided on the Saturday previous to last Whitsuntide, and resulted in a dead heat between R. James of Birmingham and F. Wood of Leicester. Upon-running off, another dead heat resulted, but when meeting a week later for the third time, James beat the Leicester man by a good yard. For the race under notice the following were the competitors:—R. Howell, Coventry; G. W. Waller, Newcastle; F. De Civry, Paris; A. E. Derkinderin, Coventry; F. Wood, Leicester; and C. B. Garrard, Uxbridge. Unfortunately for James he met with an accident while training some few weeks since, and consequently he was not sufficiently recovered to take part in a race of so long a distance. The track on the Aylestone grounds had been well looked after, the weather was fine, and 4,000 persons were present. At the start, Garrard went off with the lead, followed by Waller, Derkinderin, De Civry, Wood, and Howell bringing up the rear. After completing two of the sixty-six laps, the Frenchman rushed to the front, and for a couple of miles took his field along at a tremendous pace. Afterwards, Waller, Derkinderin and Wood each took a turn at the lead. The five miles was registered in 17 min. 19 sec. Positions, Derkinderin, Wood, Waller, Garrard, Howell, and De Civry. A lap later the mile champion rushed to the head of affairs, and at nine he took his opponents along at a merry rate of speed. At ten miles—33 min. 45 sec.—Howell was in front, Waller, Derkinderin, Wood, and De Civry following in the order named. A mile later Garrard went ahead, going away at a rattling pace, the Frenchman forty yards behind. Six laps later, De Civry was among his field again, and shortly afterwards rushed to the front. But one or two laps further on—at fifteen miles, 50 min. 13 sec.—Wood was leading Waller, Derkinderin, Garrard, and Howell next, with De Civry fifteen yards in the rear. The six men travelled in close company for the following thirteen laps. At the twentieth mile being hoisted, in 1 h. 7 min. 59 sec., the lot eased up, nobody seeming inclined to force the pace. Eight laps from the finish Howell got to the front, followed by Garrard and Wood, the others close up. Nearing the finish the pace rapidly increased, and just over a mile from home De Civry cried content. The others went ahead at a rattling speed, but a lap and a half from the finish Waller eased up, and when the bell signalled the last lap Howell held a yard's advantage from Garrard, Derkinderin third, and Wood close up. Half a lap from home Garrard took the lead, but getting on the straight Howell came again, followed by Derkinderin. Another splendid struggle ensued, resulting in favor of Howell by half a yard, Derkinderin beating Garrard by a few inches, with Wood just in the rear. Time, 1 h. 24 min. 15 sec. Tremendous excitement prevailed. —The Referee.

The Springfield Bicycle Club, of Springfield, Mass., will hold its first annual meet and tournament at Hampden Park on Wednesday afternoon, and at the Springfield Skating Rink on Wednesday evening, September 20th. The bicycling fraternity of the United States have been invited to attend. All the races will be held under League rules, with the sanction of the League of American Wheelmen. The programme as now arranged consists of a twenty-mile professional race for a purse of $500, by J. S. Prince, of Boston, the champion of the United States, against Thomas Harrison and James Mellen, who will alternate every five miles; a five mile professional ladies' race for a purse of $200; also the following races open to all amateurs: Five-mile race, three prizes, value $125; two-mile race, best two in three heats, three prizes, value $125; one-mile race, best two in three heats, three prizes, value $75; half-mile race, three prizes, value $50; slow race, 100 yards, three prizes, value $25; one mile, without hands, three prizes, value $50; half-mile race for boys under fifteen years of age, three prizes, value $20. At the skating rink in the evening, for the best drilled club of not less than eight members, three prizes, value $100; best single fancy riding, three prizes, value $75; best double fancy riding, three prizes, value $75. The entries are free and should be made with or with Mr. C. K. Ferry, Secretary Springfield Bicycle Club; on or before September 15.

The San Francisco B. C. shows considerable activity, turning out for frequent runs through the park, to the beach and Cliff House, and in the Presidio Reservation. Both the park and reservation roads are kept in good repair and give many miles of superb wheeling.

Dr. A. Hubbard, G. W. Davis, Judge Bowers, Tim Crowley and Frank Sweetner have returned from a two weeks hunt at Exalcott Beach, Marin county, near Bolinas bay. They found game very plenty, several deer and many doves were killed by the party, and they report many quail and good ground for the shooter when the season comes.

# THE HERD.

## Merino Sheep.

This variety of sheep were imported originally into France and Spain. They were placed upon the government farm at Rambouillet, where every care was given them, and the greatest attention paid to increasing their produce of fleece. After years of experimenting, the animals were increased in size and weight nearly one hundred per cent., and the wool from twenty to twenty-five. The fiber did not improve as was desired, but the attempt to combine in the same animal meat qualities as well as wool-bearing ones was assigned as the reason. During these experiments the sheep grew very large, were enormous feeders, but they lost those character istics of wool bearers, and they were no longer as robust. Subsequent breeding has however not only restored them to their original excellence, but improved their wool growth on the lamb's wool seventy-five per cent., and the ewes sixty-six. It required good management and about ninety years to ac complish this feat. The French were the first to produce a Merino combing wool, though subsequently they found it vain in America, Germany and Australia. The only differ ence between the breeds in the several countries is that the French ones still have larger carcasses.

D. C. Collins, of Connecticut, was the pioneer importer of the Merino sheep in America. Stock breeders eagerly sought the new variety, hoping to improve their flock, but were in most cases disappointed on account of the imported stocks being selected from those flocks which had been bred to in crease their weight and carcass, and not from those where that policy had not been followed. Later importations dis approved any prejudice that the first one might have cre ated against the breed. Numbers of them have found their way to California, where their success has been unparalleled. A Mr. Robert Blackard, of Calaveras county, clipped from one of his a sixteen months fleece which weighed 51½ pounds, the same animal clipped a 46-pound fleece at two years old. It is only just to say however in this connection that the climate of California being so dry, the wool retains a greater amount of oil than in other countries where the rainfall is large.

Mr. J. B. Bay, in an address to the New York Merino Sheep Breeders' Association, had the following to say on the points of Merino sheep: But few persons would prefer a staple of more than two and one-half inches for a ram, while many would be contented with a two-inch staple of highly crimped wool provided the maximum density of fleece had been reached. Comparative evenness of fleece with as little glare as possible is an important point reached by our west ern breeders. Experience has fully demonstrated that great weight of fleece can be combined with the highest physical development, constitutional vigor and other points of per fection as indicated above. As to the point of oil, or yolk, the greatest amount that can be secreted without impairing the vitality of the animal is admissable in a ram. Most breeders prefer a coloring bordering on a buff, while a thin, sticky oil of a greenish cast is highly objectionable. As to folds or wrinkles, which is a distinctive feature of the American Me rino type; there might be a diversity of opinion as to size, location and number. Still it would be difficult to find a ram of such heavy pendulous neck, tail and flank as would disqualify him as a stock animal in any flock, while many would prefer that with the above he should have a large fold extending across the point of the shoulder, a considerable number on the sides extending in massive proportion well under and nearly across the belly, yet diminishing well in size and lost to view in full fleece before reaching the back, with numerous large folds lengthwise across the hips and sides.

Those who fancy the delaine type are aiming in the main to secure the same points of American Merinos, while at the same time securing a longer staple of high quality of wool. As to folds or wrinkles, a good neck, tail and flanks are about all that is desirable, with little or none on the body. Thus we have before us a pen sketch of our ideal rams of the American and delaine Merino types.

## The Milk of Ruminants.

In all probability there has not been sufficient attention, thinks Dr. Brush, drawn to the differences existing between the milk of animals which ruminate, as the cow, and those which do not chew their cud, as the sea and horse; and it would divide milk into two classes—that which is the pro duct of non-cud-chewing, and that which is the product of end-chewing animals. The milk of the cud-chewers contains a variety of casein, which, under the action of the digestive process, coagulates into a hard mass. Contrary to the often expressed belief, he declares that this coagulation takes place in the ordinary process of digestion in the calf. He has one cked up cud of the reach of any food, and had it fed with freshly-drawn cow's milk. Half an hour after the meal, he always found it badly chewing its cud. After many in quiries, he has ascertained that the same takes place with the sheep and goat; and from these facts he is inclined to ex plain the difficulty often experienced by the human stomach in properly digesting the milk of ruminating animals. The other variety of milk to which human, equine, and sea' milk belongs, does not, under the action of acids, in the same way coagulate into the hard mass that is found in cow's milk, but coagulates rather into small granules or flocculent masses, which are easily diffusible. This would explain why Koomiss prepared from cow's milk is found to agree better with children than cow's milk itself; the Koomiss has been, so to speak, already chewed. In the milk of the cud chewers there is but a small amount of sugar and a large amount of casein, while exactly the reverse of this is the case with the milk of the non-cud-chewers; and in this fact there is again a reason why the milk of the latter, at least in the case of children who cannot get their natural supply, is to be preferred. It will be remembered that Koomiss is a beverage prepared by the people of Yakuts from the mare's milk, and found to be highly nutritious, but that the bever age referred to by Dr. Bauch is a product artificially pre pared from cow's milk.—Veterinary Journal.

## Feeding Pigs.

Pigs dropped this spring that are to be marketed this year should be pushed hard from the beginning, in order to insure the largest percentage of profit. They cannot be permitted to go back, or even stand still, in the accumulation of flesh any day, without loss. The utmost skill of the feeder is often taxed with the little fellows when they are about a month old; for at that period the milk of the dam ceases to be sufficient to meet the wants of the growing pigs; and if they have not been permitted to learn to eat before that time, and if abundance of highly nutritious food, in liquid or semi-liquid form, be not furnished from this time on, it will be impossible to keep up the rapid growth that has been attained by simply feeding the sows properly up to that pe riod. Ground oats and corn, mixed, or ground corn with wheat middlings, will make a good slop for the pigs; soaked corn will also be highly relished, and will be found well adapted to keeping the pigs in high flesh; but as soon as the new corn is fairly in milk, that will be found the best of all fattening foods. "Make hay while the sun shines," is the embodiment of sound doctrine in that department of hus bandry; but the injunction "Make pork before cold weather comes," is equally as sound a maxim for the government of swine raisers.

But if pigs are to be kept over the winter, and fed off for the next spring or autumn markets, we would recommend less of the forcing process; less of the stimulating, fattening grain diet; and would urge the importance of clover and grass as a means of keeping the pigs in a good growing con dition, and at the same time keeping them healthy. Pigs cannot long stand up under the forcing system—the high pressure plan of feeding that produces the enormous weights sometimes attained at six to nine months—and while this is perhaps, after all, the most profitable method in the breeder and feeder, we very much doubt whether it is the course that produces the best quality of bacon and hams. In these ex tra-heavy pigs the weight is largely made up of fat—there is no corresponding growth of bone and muscle, and the pork is soft and oily. On the contrary, when pigs are given the run of the clover field during their first summer, with only a small allowance of grain, the bone and muscle is developed by the food and exercise; and when they come to be fattened off for market, there will be found a much greater proportion of "lean meat" than in the earlier matured pigs.

We regard the latter method—this reliance largely upon pasture during the first summer—as an essential in raising healthy breeding stock, whether males or females; and we would never buy one of those forced, exceptionally heavy, and fat show pigs for breeding purposes, no matter what might be his recommendation otherwise. Our breeders have done too much of this thing in the past. It has shown itself all over the country in a loss of constitution and a lack of vitality which has made our stock an easy prey to disease, and we are glad that there are indications of a reform in this particular.—Live Stock Journal.

## Origin of the Ayrshire Cattle.

The Ayrshire cow, as we have her, is a native of County Ayr, Scotland, where we can trace her history back for about a century. Mr. William Aiton of Hamilton, in a communi cation made to the British Farmer's Magazine, in 1836, says: "The dairy breed of Scotland have been formed chiefly by skilled management within the last fifty years, and they are still improving and attending to other countries. Till after 1770 the cows in Cunningham were small, ill-fed, ill-shaped, and gave but little milk. Some cows of a larger breed and of a brown and white color were about that time brought to Ayrshire from Teeswater and from Holland by some of the patriotic noblemen of Ayrshire; and these being put on good pasture, yielded more milk than the native breed, and so their calves were much sought after by the farmers." The Magazine goes on to say: "We are verbally assured by old breeders who had known the Ayrshire since 1780 that they had received improvement from crosses with Shorthorn bulls for the last half century, and although they may now be considered a good established breed in themselves, they are in reality merely high grade Durhams." Youatt, in his history of British cattle, says, writing in the year 1833: "The origin of the Ayrshire cow is even at the present day a matter of dispute; all that is known about her is that a century ago there was no such breed in Cunning ham or Ayrshire in Scotland. Through several pages of speculation as to what crosses have compassed the breed known as "Ayrshire," at the time he wrote, and an elabora tion of their remarkable yields of milk and butter in the Ayrshire dairies, he leaves the impression that the present breed has sprung from a succession of crosses by Short-horn bulls upon the native Scotch cow; that the produce of these crosses were interbred among themselves with care and an eye to improvement both in form and dairy quality, which finally resulted in an animal eminently fitted to the climate and soil of southwestern Scotland, and the best they have for dairy purposes. The effort appears first to have been to introduce Short-horns and substitute them as a dairy cow, which failed; but the cross was successful, and hence the breed. Mr. Youatt proceeds to say: "On a first view, by a judge of the different varieties, the Ayrshire would be called a diminutive Short-horn, so nearly in figure, color and prom inent characteristics do they approach them. They are about the size of our common stock, compact in form, exact ly built for a dairy cow, light forward and heavy behind, with an exceedingly home-like, domestic appearance. In color they vary from a brown, running in lighter shades up to red, and into a pale yellow, alternated more or less with white, in distinct patches, rarely mingling into roan. There is scarcely that uniformity of appearance with them that there is in the Short-horns, yet they appear to hold true to the dairy quality throughout, which, like the gentle voice in woman, is an excellent thing in a cow." A much later article in the American Agriculturist says: "The Ayrshires have been bred for milk in a country where quantity and quality were both wanted where the pastures were only moderately rich, and where rapid fattening for the sham bles was also a desideratum. The result is a breed of no more than ordinary size, many being decidedly small, but hardy, easy keepers, yielding a large quantity of milk, rich both in butter and cheese. The claim set forth for these cows is, that they will give more and better milk, on the same feed, than cows of any other breed. This, we believe, is not disputed. Ayrshires have been known in this country since 1822, when, we believe, they were first imported. The stock was kept pure, however, only a few generations, as it became blended with the Short-horns, and the blood now of a number of our registered Short-horns. In 1831 other animals were brought over, and ever since that time the breed has grown in favor. The animals are prevailingly of medium size. The cows have great digestive capacity, as is disclosed by their deep, full bodies. The colors are usually red, spotted with white, the spots being very well defined, often fine and sprinkled over the body in patches."

## The Question of Prices.

The frequent sales of choice animals—horses, cattle, sheep, swine—at liberal prices, serve to employ the thoughts of cer tain students of events, between search for the cause of a sea son that places them in the category of a rule rather than the exception; and speculations upon the probable effect of such a condition upon the future of blood-stock transactions. These convictions have found encouragement among the more conservative writers and breeders for many years. The one has steadily predicted, and the other has as constantly feared, that not only would personal disaster overwhelm the promoters and payers of these high prices, but that general confusion and distrust would result, greatly to the detriment of live-stock interests generally. With the few exceptions that are traceable to personal imprudence, the prophecies of the one and the fears of the other have happily gone unful filled. Men of aspiring and intelligent breeders is unabated; prudent men, who have learned the value of money by earn ing it, pay "four figure" prices for animals that most nearly suit their several requirements—oftener duplicating such purchases than stopping with the first—realizing that the in satiable demand of a steadily widening field and an advanc ing intelligence will not long leave the owner of really meritorious stock searching for a purchaser for his prod ucts. But the prices demanded and paid for breeding ani mals of exceptional merit are not too high, when measured by proper standards. Such animals are not the result of chance or experimental breeding. The world is as certainly indebted to the intelligence, the study and the labor of man for the highest type of its domestic animals as it is to the science of architecture for St. Peter's, or to the engineering skill that tunnels its mountains and spans its rivers with bridges of iron or steel. The patient study necessary to a reasonable comprehension of the science of breeding and the experience required for the successful application, added to the investment of capital in parent stock, are considerations that call for a fair return as surely and as rightfully here as in any other business or profession. And until it is shown that the rewards secured by those who have devoted them selves to advancing the standard of domestic live-stock are disproportioned to the results achieved, when measured by what is conceded to other professions, this occasional protest against prices will meet with little response outside the echo of its own feeble wall.

As a rule, the men who pay liberal prices for breeding animals are those who have enjoyed a reputation for ability to discern the better side of a business transaction, as well as sufficient nerve to back their judgment with their capital. This fact should go for something. Men of discernment and business capacity are no more likely to part with these attri butes on the threshold of live-stock investments than else where and any argument predicated on an assumption of the contrary only betrays the weakness of the position it seeks to defend. In a careful study of the so-called fancy-priced sales, with due consideration of cause and subsequent circumstances, will be found such vindication of the wisdom of buyers as will entitle their purchases to be recognized as coming within the category of prudent investment—with as few exceptions as belong to the majority of business transac tions.—The Breeders' Gazette.

---

THE CHICAGO FAT STOCK SHOW.—Commenting on this com ing exhibition, the English Live Stock Journal states: "If the Yankees have not yet beaten us in the production of fat stock of the best quality, some of the rules of their fat-stock shows are in advance of our own. A most important feature is the encouragement given to produce animals that, when fattened, produce the best quality of flesh. Prizes are frequently awarded in our shows to cattle whose meat contains an ab normal, not to say disgusting, proportion of fat to lean, and in which the fat is distributed in huge masses totally sepa rated from the lean, instead of being properly mixed through out. The evil is increasing rather than diminishing, and the amount of fat on the animal constantly secures him the award without due consideration of the quality and value of his flesh for human consumption. The Smithfield and other clubs would do well to follow the Chicago society, and insti tute prizes for dressed carcasses, and also for animals whose age and weight show the earliest maturity and the greatest disposition to fatten. By so doing, the usefulness of our Christmas fat-cattle shows would be greatly increased, and the public interest in them would increase also, or at least remain unabated."

SWIMMING SNAKE RIVER.—W. P. Hall, foreman for M. Ryan, recently arrived at the Snake river bridge at Black foot with 1800 head of cattle. The herd was very wild, as it had been made up of four different bands. An unsuccessful attempt was made to get the cattle across the bridge. Some of them had entered the river, and it was decided to swim the whole herd. Hall rode his horse out into the deep water above the bridge, but got into an eddy. He then called to S. C. Van Deventer to throw him a rope. Van De venter responded, but the rope caught in his spur, and he was pulled from his horse, and with the animal floundered in fifteen feet of water. He managed to remount the horse, which struck out immediately for the cattle in the middle of the river. After a hard struggle, and several narrow es capes similar to the one described, he reached the shore a mile below the bridge. Some of the cattle were carried two miles down the stream, but only eleven head of worn out and lame animals were lost. Van Deventer could not swim, and his escape from drowning seems wonderful. It is said to be the first time a mounted horse ever swam Snake river.—Oregon Statesman.

ENGLISH AND AMERICAN CATTLE COMPARED.—Americans have done more for the rank and file of their common native breeds in the last five years than English farmers have done for their rank and file during the last twenty years. If any one doubts this let him go and look at a lot of imported American beasts, and then go to the fairs and markets of any part of this country—with the exception of certain breed ing districts—and draw his own conclusions. Of course, in the United States cattle we now receive are the best they have to send, quite the pick of their markets; but five years ago they had few, if any, as good to send. As things are going on now, the cattle of Colorado and Texas will be a long way ahead of our ordinary cattle in ten years' time. The horned stock to be found in summer in the new Forest, in Hampshire, would be a disgrace to Montana itself.—Mark Lane Express.

It is reported that A. A. Longley of Truckee Meadows has been offered $29 per head for 100 head of cows for slaughter. His price was $30 per head. While they begin killing off the cows we are in danger of a milk and butter famine. So great has been the demand for beef cattle from the East—reaching out through the Great West to this State—that cows will be about all now left in the bovine line.

Hampshire sheep are but little known in this country, their next door neighbors, the Southdowns, being preferred. They own the remotest origin of any of the black-faced sheep; in England they are accorded first place as early maturers, their fertileness is remarkable and their growth before becom ing a year old is rivaled by no contending breed.

The two-year-old Hereford bull, Sir Bartle Frere, second prize at the Reading show, England, has been sold for $3,000. The destination is America.

# YACHTING.

## Ocean Cruising.

Cruising outside has never been popular here. In fact are very few yachts here in the fleet adapted to it. ness with big inner centerboards belong inside, and generally stay there. Outside the harbor the sea is rough and the d strong, and there are no little harbors to run to in case f bad weather. Most of those who have done any ocean cruising here have given it up after a few trials, finding it unpleasant. Yachting on the broad ocean is only pleasant in good large vessel, properly fitted for the purpose. When amped in a small yacht there is not much enjoyment. here is a good deal of "bosh" talked about ocean cruising. ome people imagine that a man who goes yachting and does ot go to sea is a sort of parlor sailor. They think when one oes sailing for pleasure, he ought to go into rough water and ake himself generally uncomfortable.

Some one of these people has been writing about the cruise the New York Yacht Club, and raking over the members ecause they stuck to smooth water. This is the way the ew York *Spirit of the Times* answers the individual referred t, and its remarks are more sensible than conventional:

"I notice a weekly of your city is inclined to belittle the uise of this club, insisting that its destination should have een Bermuda instead of Marblehead, and that the ocean ould be a more fitting sailing place than the Sound. 'If the object was mere social enjoyment,' the writer says, 'the Sound would be well enough.' Why, that is exactly the object. It is a pleasure cruise, and as all know who have had any sea experience, there is no pleasure in ocean sailing. 'Those who go to sea for pleasure,' says Jack, 'should go to —— for pastime,' and there never was a truer saying. They can never learn to be sailors,' says this cheerful idiot, whose idea of sailors is gained from the pages of the dime novel, or from the conventional stage representation. Well, they don't want to learn to be sailors, and if they did they are too old to begin, even out on the ocean. But they don't. The guests on board these vessels are brokers, bankers, clergymen, lawyers, doctors, etc., taking their holidays and enjoying a breath of sea air, and enjoying the advantages of a daily sea bath. If they desired to go to sea to rough it, as this chap would have them do, the pilot boat or the mackerel schooner would be the place for them rather than the yacht, which is, as its name implies, a vessel for pleasure sailing. Even so reprehensible a matter as eating clams may be indulged in by these gentlemen if they choose to eat them, and I would respectfully represent to this chap that it is none of his concern, and remind him of Jimmey Shaw, of Gloucester, who was hung because he did not mind his own business.

"What does he suppose to be the object of the cruise if it be not social enjoyment? Shall all these gentlemen come home with blistered hands, as well as sun-burnt faces! Must they hitch up their trousers when they return to the bosom of their families and greet their wives with 'Shiver my tarry top-lights and top-gallant eyebrows, old gal, how are you, and how are all the kids?' or some other equally salt expressions.

"There are seamen on board these yachts, and some very good ones, and the yachts themselves are staunch and strong, and one object of the cruise is to test the speed of the vessels and the skill of those who sail them, even to the extent of getting them underway in crowded roadsteads, where there is scarcely room, as this chap admits, for them to turn round. Whenever it is thought desirable for the owner of one of these vessels to go to the West Indies or to Bermuda, or even across the ocean, he has always been carried safely to his destination, and it seems curious that he can't take a party of his friends out on a pleasure sail without being told that he should make tarry sailors of them before he permits them to return.

"The idea of a chap that would be sick during a trip to Rockaway on a steamer, sitting in his den and writing about 'the life, adventures, trials and experiences of a seafaring man,' or of the 'halcyon' enjoyment of a fleet close reefed, struggling with the gale,' is a little too utterly comical for anything. I have had a trifle of that 'halcyon struggling with gales' in my young days, but, alas, I did not enjoy it, and I have never found, outside the pages of a novel, anyone that did."

At Lake George the other day there was a grand review of 78 canoes under sail. A steam launch ran up to the island, and soon afterward started for Crosbyside, five miles down the lake, towing nearly fifty canoes. So novel a tow attracted much attention as it passed down the lake, and was saluted and cheered by the guests of the several hotels as it went by. Various accessions to the ranks were made from several points on the lake, until a fleet of seventy-five was collected at the head of the lake. These were marshaled in three divisions, and, sailing down the lake, passed in review before Judge Nicholas Longworth, Commander of the Association at Crosbyside. The first division, consisting of light paddling canoes, was commanded by Vice-Commander Edwards, A. C. C., of the Peterboro Club. In the second division were the light sailing canoes, under command of Rear-Admiral Brentano, A. C. A., of the Knickerbocker Club, and the third division, composed of the heavier sailing canoes, was led by Commodore C. B. Vaux of the New York Club. The breeze was fresh from the southward, and the dainty white-winged fleet, with all colors flying, flew past the reviewing stand, making the prettiest marine picture ever seen on Lake George. The grassy slopes in front of Crosby House were crowded with spectators.

THE LAUNCH OF THE BEDOUIN.—The cutter-yacht Bedouin, which has been on stocks since February last, was launched Thursday afternoon, August 19th, from the yard of Henry Piepgras, Greenpoint. This yacht has the heaviest keel of any pleasure craft that has been built, there being thirty-five tons of lead in the keel. Captain Archibald Rodgers, of Hyde Park, on the Hudson, the owner of the yacht, was present at the launch. The Odin is said to be the largest cutter yacht ever built in this country. She will carry sixteen tons of ballast, and a crew of seven men and a captain will be required to sail her. She has six state-rooms elaborately finished, and the saloon is roomy and handsome. She is 82 feet long over all, 59 feet 9 inches width of beam, and 12 feet 6 inches depth of hold. She will be completed in about 14 days, and will cost when finished $40,000.

The "Mosquito race" of the S. F. Y. C. which comes off on the 16th is attracting some considerable attention. Yachts under 22 feet only are admitted. We expect that at least 50 or 60 yachts will enter. Last year the regatta was a successful one. No entrance fee is required, and plenty of prizes are to be given in the different classes.

The Lolita is going up to the Suisun marshes on the 11th inst. to stay all winter.

---

THE NEW YACHT.—The new yacht which Captain Turner is building for the Spreckles boys is progressing rapidly. She is now being planked up. She is 85 feet over all and 82 feet beam. Her frames are of Port Alford cedar, six inches square and double. Her planking is 2½ inches and the ceiling is three inches from the flat of the floor up. The stem is made of a fine laurel crook, which is sided 12 inches. Between it and the frame are natural crooks of strong wood to help secure the heel which carries ten tons of lead outside. Large bars of lead are to fit down between the frames. There is no black iron being used, all fastenings being galvanized iron or composition. The dead rise of the yacht is 35 degrees and she has a good "drag" to her keel, drawing a good deal more aft than forward. She has a handsome sheer and has 6 feet archway, which is more than Captain Turner usually gives his yachts. Those interested in yacht construction ought to visit the shipyard down on Channel street near Sixth, and look at the yacht while she is being built. She is to be first class in every respect.

The Chiquita has had a new bowsprit put on to accommodate a larger jib.

The Berne is to be used at Sherman Island this winter on a 'shooting box.'

The Catamarans did nothing extra in sailing in the eastern yacht club cruises.

The San Francisco Yacht Club has passed over its annual regatta this year, the fixed date being the first Saturday in August.

During the cruise of the New York Yacht Club, by invitation of the sailing-master of the schooner Phantom, E. Y. C., the sailing master of the N. Y. Yacht Club fleet were given a drive to Nahant and a dinner at that place.

The Pacific Yacht Club regatta which comes off on the 9th will be the first regatta of the year. It is hoped there will be plenty to enter. Our yachting has been dull this year and something is needed to enliven the yachtmen.

The sea at Newport, during the New York Yacht cruise, proved conclusively the superiority of the Montauk among the schooners, and she beat the Halcyon fairly and squarely; she needs wind, however, and in very light weather does not go as well as some of the others. It is, however, admitted by all that she is the fastest schooner that we have, and the problem set before our builders at present is to turn out something that will beat her. The coming schooner is to be of iron or steel, and such a one will be built, probably next season, by Mr. Pusk, of the Mischief. As one of the results of the present extremely successful cruise, we may look forward, next season, for more new vessels than have been added to the fleet in one year for a very long time.

---

## Elmo.

DANVILLE, Cal., Aug. 27.

BREEDER AND SPORTSMAN, 508 Montgomery St. *Dear Editor:* I noticed in your last issue the cut of the celebrated stallion Elmo, and one of the notable horses of California; and his breeding is such that you are right in calling him a notable horse, and to do him justice it would take two pages of your valuable paper.

Elmo has never shown to the public yet his greatest speed and power; this I know myself, for I have been in the stable with him for six long years, and in this time have rubbed him and driven him. You say that a former owner, Mr. Van Giesen, informed you that he had timed him quarters in thirty seconds; this I do not doubt in the least. I once saw him and Rosalind work together; Elmo started four lengths behind, the mile was in 2:22; Elmo closed this gap in the last quarter and you could not decide which was ahead at the wire. Dan Mace was on the back stretch timing them; and as soon as possible Mace came around to Elmo's stall. The door was closed and Hickok and myself were in the stall. Dan Mace rapped at the door and Hickok let him in. Mace said: "Ortn, that is as fast a horse as I ever saw up to this time." Hickok said: "yes, Mace, he is, and when he is right he can beat Lucy."

Now, dear Editor, let me speak my little piece. When you see such stallions as Electioneer, Sultan, Echo, Santa Claus, Whipple's Hambletonian, Buccaneer, Piedmont, Cook's Hambletonian, or any good Hambletonian horse served to Elmo mares, seven out of ten will beat 2:30, and if some of his get was worked and the same attention paid them as others get on this coast, you would see some of them stay in a race from one o'clock until six in the evening, and no time give it up, and that is the kind to have in a race.

We have a large five-year-old mare on this farm that never had over two months' fast work in her life all together, and never we handled by a professional driver, and she has trotted a mile over a bad copy track in 2:32, and the last half in 1:14, and she would have gone on another mile faster. It was hard to pull her up at the quarter pole. This mare met with a slight accident when three years old, and she is so growthy that she requires age. I know that Elmo's dam is claimed to be by Six Richard. When I was in Paris, Ky., I met a man by the name of H. W. Buness, Bourbon House, that knew Elmo's dam, and said that she was owned at that time forty miles from Paris, and that she was by Grey Eagle. Your readers can see that the Mohawk family is coming fast in the 2:20 list. Overman's record of 2:20½, and Yellow Dock. by Clark's Mohawk Jr. he by Mohawk, the sire of Elmo. Yellow Dock's record 2:20½. I look upon Elmo mares bred to Hambletonian stallions as great breeders.

I notice that you mention Almont as being on this coast. We have on this farm a bay mare by Almont, dam by Mambrino Prince, a son of Mambrino Chief, second dam Cripple, a son of Modoc, third dam by American Eclipse. Yours truly,

SAMUEL GAMPLE.

---

## THE KENNEL.

### Buy your Dogs at Home.

As the shooting season approaches, the importance of that indispensable adjunct to a sportsman's pleasure—a capable well trained dog—becomes more and more apparent and to such as do not possess this essential the all-absorbing question is how to get one. A simple solution of that important question can be found to a limited extent in the advertising columns of this paper where the notice of sportsmen is called to some thoroughbred Llewellyn setters for sale on reasonable terms. Some local shooters seem to hold the belief that a good dog cannot be obtained except in the east and will pass over a dog raised near home and offered for a low rate to purchase an inferior animal from the east at an abominably high price.

---

Rather than trust their next door neighbor they will be duped by a lengthy pedigree of high sounding titles, backed up by columns of turgid prosaic and fictitious exploits in the eastern sporting journals. The writer has seen many dogs imported from the east having the best of blood in their veins, yet almost useless to a hard working hunter. The writer has seen a number of these dogs brought from widely advertised eastern kennels, and they all appeared to have the serious faults of softness and lack of courage. Perhaps both of these faults arise from too much breeding into a fashionable strain, but sure it is that, from some cause or other, the fact is as stated. Such dogs may make a decent showing at a field trial run on fairly even ground, but in the hills and gulches, under a hot sun and with but little water they cannot do the work demanded by a California sportsman, and beside such a dog as J. K. Orr's old Gordon bitch, which has found game and retrieved for himself and Bogardus, who at the end of the day had 125 quail to show for their work, would cut but a poor figure. For duck retrieving, such dogs are worse than useless. They cannot and will not stand the hard work and cold water, and really for such work, where but little intelligence is required, a coarse, ordinary kind of dog is better than a fine bred animal.

### Canadian Kennel Club.

Public notice has been given of the issuance of letters patent, bearing date July 24, 1882, incorporating the dominion of Canada Kennel Club (limited) with Mr. Lindsay Russel of Ottawa, as President; and Mr. B. H. G. Vicars, of Ottawa, as Secretary and Treasurer. The capital stock of the club is $4,000. The following is a list of the provisional Direct or of the club. Lindsay Russel, Ottawa; J. A. Leah, Toronto; Lieut.-Gov. Dewdney; A. O. F. Coleman, V. S., Ottawa; Dr. Nevin, London, Ont.; F. P. Austin, Ottawa; C. V. J. M. Temple, Quebec; John Gilmour, Ottawa; F. H. D. Veith, Halifax; W. A. Allen, Ottawa; E. F. Stephenson, Winnipeg; H. Bailey Harrison, Tilsonburg; Christopher Robinson, Q. C., Toronto; Alonzo Wright, M. P., Ironsides; Hon. A. P. Caron, Ottawa; D. C. Plumb, Niagara; B. H. V. Vicars, Ottawa, provincial Secretary and Treasurer.

The national objects of the club are to encourage, throughout the whole Dominion, the importation, sale, breeding, training and exchange of highly bred dogs of all classes; to compile and publish a national stud book, in which dogs of every breed whelped or owned in the Dominion can be registered; to endeavor to secure such legislation as will protect the game of the country, and assist in the enforcement of existing laws having that object in view; generally to assist in the conviction and punishment of persons guilty of cruelty to animals, more especially the dog, and the various kinds of game; to encourage public exhibitions of dogs, such as bench shows and field trials; to encourage legitimate sport generally. The first general meeting of the shareholders will be held in the Russel House, Ottawa, Sept. 11, 1882, at 7:30 P. M., for the election of directors, and the transaction of other business.

### A Fresh Importation.

By Monday's overland train via the southern route there arrived in this city, consigned to Charles N. Post, Deputy Supreme Court Clerk, two thoroughbred Llewellyn setter puppies from the well known kennel of Arnold Burgess, at Hillsdale, Michigan. The brace comprises a dog red bitch "Dandy Berwyn" and "Chispa", the latter to be forwarded to John B. Martin, San Francisco. It color they are snow-white with lemon ticks. These puppies were sired by Dashing Berwyn, out of Queen Dido, the former being by Dash II., for whom Mr. Llewellyn paid $1,650 (which is said to be the highest price ever paid for a setter) and out of Countess Bear, whom that gentleman sold to the Mountview Kennel Club, of Tennessee. When that club disorganized he bought her again for $890 and took her back to England. Dashing Berwyn has one litter brother and two litter sisters in England—Dashing Bondhu, which won the English all-aged stakes in 1881, when only fourteen months old, and one of whose sons, Sable Bondhu, won this year's Derby; Dashing Beauty, which won the Derby in 1881, and Dashing Bear, which won the first prize for English setter bitches at the Alexandria bench show in 1881. Queen Dido was sired by Druid, which dog has the best foreign field trial record of any dog now in America, and Mr. Burgess paid Mr. Llewellyn $500, and out of Nineon (little sister of Champion Queen Mab) which also cost Mr. Burgess $500 in England. These are the puppies alluded to by Mr. Burgess in the *American Field* of July 22d, wherein he stated that they would the point scent staunchly, although not three months old.—*Sacramento Bee.*

### Cattle by Thousands.

The Reno (Oregon) *Gazette* in speaking of the cattle interests of that State says: "R. B. Todhunter branded last spring over 9,000 calves, and has sent to market this season 8,000 beef cattle. These figures prove Mr. Todhunter to be the largest stockraiser in the country. There are others who send more cattle to the market, but they buy them instead of raising them. He has over 20,000 head of stock cattle and over 100,000 acres of patented land. He got patents last month for 35,000 acres of swamp land in one bunch. He has about 1,000 bulls and 300 saddle horses. He employs fifty men, and puts up 20,000 tons of hay to guard against hard winters. He keeps 100 work horses, and raises enough grain to feed all his saddle and work stock. Besides his cattle, he has 700 or 800 stock horses, four jacks and fifty stallions. His stock is divided among five ranches—one known as the White House Ranch, lying just inside the Oregon line, where 5,000 head are kept; one in Long Valley, in the northwestern corner of Nevada, lying alongside of Surprise, supports 4,000 head; the Pyramid Ranch, lying at the northeastern corner of the lake, has 1,500 head and a lot of horses; the Abbott Ranch, at Steen's Mountain, feeds about 5,000, and Harney Valley about 3,000 more. The home ranch is about 25 miles from h's neighbor.

EASTERN FOX HUNTERS.—The first meet of the fox-hunting season took place Friday afternoon, Aug. 11th, at Bryers, Near Newport, Rhode Island. Mr. F. Gray Griswold acted as master, and Peter Smith took the position of first whip. Among those who assembled at the meet may be mentioned Mr. August Belmont, Miss Lorillard, Mrs. Martin Vanburen, Mr. and Mrs. Cornelius Vanderbilt, Mrs. James B. Reston, Gen. McKeever, Col. G. H. Waring and others. A large field participated in the hunt, including such prominent names as Mr. Pierre Lorillard, Jr., Mr. N. G. Lorillard, Mr. Geo. Stevens, Mr. Charles Carroll, Miss Emily Harrymore, Mr. Center Hitchcock, Miss Norman, Mr. Lloyd S. Bryce, Miss Hewitt, Mr. R. Belmont, Mr. Foxhall Keene, Mr. F. R. Appleton, Mr. Geo. S. Brown, of Baltimore, and Mr. Waterbury. The run occupied sixty minutes, and was one of the fastest on record in the annals of the Queens County Hunt. Messrs.,

Belmont and Bryce sustained a fall each, but neither was seriously injured. Finally the fox was run into the open, and a fair number of riders were in at the death. The brush was awarded to Miss Havemeyer, while the pads were given to Master Baldwin, a young huntsman of rare promise, and Mr. W. C. Witherbee. The run was not only very fast, but exciting, and will be long remembered by those who participated.—*Turf, Field and Farm.*

### Points of the Scotch Terrier.

After much reflection and frequent consultation with leading breeders, Mr. Vero Shaw has formulated the following new scale of points for judging the hard-haired Scotch Terrier:

Skull—(value 5) proportionately long, slightly domed, and covered with short hard hair about three-fourths inch long, or less. It should not be quite flat, as there should be a sort of stop, or drop, between the eyes.

Muzzle—(5) very powerful, and gradually tapering toward the nose, which should always be black and of a good size. The jaws should be perfectly level and the teeth square, though the nose projects somewhat over the mouth, which gives the impression of the upper jaw being longer than the under one.

Eyes—(5) set wide apart, of a dark brown or hazel color; small, piercing, very bright, and rather sunken.

Ears—(10) very small, prick or half prick, (the former is preferable,) but never drop. They should also be sharp pointed, and the hair on them should not be long, but velvety, and they should not be cut. The ears should be free from any fringe at the top.

Neck—(5) short, thick and muscular; strongly set on sloping shoulders.

Chest—(5) broad in comparison to the size of the dog and proportionately deep.

Body—(10) of moderate length, not so long as a Skye's, and rather flat sided; but well ribbed up, and exceedingly strong in hindquarters.

Legs and Feet—(10), both fore and hind legs, should be short, and very heavy in bone, the former being straight, or slightly bent, and well set on under the body, as the Scotch terrier should not be out at elbow. The hocks should be bent and the thighs very muscular; and the feet strong, small, and thickly covered with short hair, the fore feet being larger than the hind ones, and well let down on the ground.

The tail—(2½) which is never cut, should be about seven inches long, carried with a slight bend, and often gaily.

The Coat—(20) should be rather short (about two inches), intensely hard and wiry in texture, and very dense all over the body.

Size (10)—about fourteen pounds. Eighteen pounds for a dog, thirteen pounds to seventeen pounds for a bitch.

Color (21) steel or iron grey, brindle, black, red, wheaten, and even yellow or mustard color. It may be observed that mustard, black and red are not usually so popular as the other colors. White markings are m[illegible] objectionable.

General Appearance—(10), the fa[illegible] should wear a very sharp, bright, and active expression, and the head should be carried up. The dog (owing to the shortness of his coat) should appear to be higher on the legs than he really is; but, at the same time, he should look compact, and possessed of great muscle in his hind quarters. In fact, a Scotch terrier, though essentially a terrier, cannot be too powerfully put together. He should be from about 9 inches to 12 inches in height, and should have the appearance of being higher on the hind legs than on the fore.

Mr. Shaw also specifies the following faults:

Muzzle—either under or over-hung.

Eyes—large or light-colored.

Ears—large, round at the points, or drop. It is also a fault if they are too heavily covered with hair.

Coat—Any silkiness, wave, or tendency to curl is a serious blemish, as is also an open coat.

Size—Specimens over eighteen pounds should not be encouraged.

---

As an evidence of the popular interest felt in the dog and his development among Englishmen, the number of dog shows held in Britain may be cited. During the last week in July no less than nine dog shows were held at various points in the British Islands, namely, at Darlington, Chesterfield, Barnsley, Stockton-on-Tees, Pickering, Newport, Frizington, Pembroke and Glasgow.

COURSING MATCH.—Mark Devlin's well known dog Chief of the Canyon and W. Bird's Blue Cloud ran a match at Newark last Thursday in the presence of quite a large gathering of spectators. Game was easily found and good runs were had resulting in favor of Mark Devlin's dog. The match was decided too late to give particulars in this issue.

CHAMPION SETTER FOR SALE.—It is understood that Calvert Meade is willing to dispose of his celebrated Irish setter dog Dick, who took the first prize for Irish setters at the last bench show, held in this city. Dick is a grand looking, well upstanding dog, without a noticeable fault, and is said to be as good a field dog as he is good looking.

NO DOG SHOW.—The season is now so near that it is almost certain that all intention to hold a bench show this year has been abandoned. With all the setters, pointers and greyhounds either in the field or in training there would be little material left with which to make a dog show.

WELL BRED PUPS.—Crittenden Robinson has a well bred Irish setter pup about eight months old and a Llewellyn setter pup about seven months old which he will work on quail as soon as the season opens. They are already broke to heel, draw, and charge.

GREYHOUND PUPS.—The greyhound pups belonging to Mr. Keating out of his fawn bitch by the well known black dog Fides are remarkably well advanced and promise to make things lively next spring.

---

John K. Orr, Harry Babcock, P. McShane, Henry L. Fox, Mat Fuller, C. P. Gordon, Howard Black, S. B. Wakefield and F. F. Butler, members of the "Gun Club" had a grand dinner at the Maison Dore last Saturday, after their shoot at Bird's Point. The affair was a very enjoyable one, and several important subjects were discussed in relation to the gunning and fishing interests of the coast.

Three Chinamen were convicted and fined $50 or 50 days in the county jail for trapping quail at Suisun, Napa county, this week.

The Alameda County Sportsman's Club hold their last shoot of the season to-day at Bird's Point.

The Pacific Club shoots to-morrow (Sunday) at Bird's Point, for the last time this season.

## FISH.

### A Novel Style of Fishing.

Excise Commissioner William P. Mitchell and a few friends with their families are together at Bath, L. I. Among the boarders in the house is a Japanese student. He is a neat, bright, good-natured young man, and appears anxious to learn the ways of Americans. Commissioner Mitchell and friends have been playing tricks on the Japanest student. Not long ago they got up a game of base-ball. They kept the "Jap," as they called him, at the bat, by refusing or purposely failing to catch him out, and he ran around the bases all the afternoon. Next day the muscles of his legs were so sore he had to remain in bed. When he reappeared he climbed up a tree to look at young owls in a nest and discovered rotten apples.

One morning lately "Jap," while out rowing, came across a multitude of fish of all sizes and varieties floundering in the water. They showed their fins and appeared to keep within a certain space. The "Jap" thought he had struck a fish bonanza, and he resolved to keep his "find" a secret.

That afternoon Commissioner Nichols and a number of the boarders were walking along the shore, talking about fishing. The "Jap" said it was cruel and unfair to catch fish with hook, line and bait. "In Japan we catch them with our hands," he exclaimed, in good English. All his hearers, with the exception of Alderman Strack, were astonished; the alderman said he had read about Japanese diving into the water and chasing and catching fish just as fish-hawks do. "I will show you," ejaculated the Jap, "how to catch fish without hooks," and he got into a boat and rowed out about two hundred yards. He pitched the anchor over and pulled off his coat, vest and shirt. He was next seen to lie down in the boat, while he peeped carefully over the sides. Every now and then he would plunge his right hand into the water and would haul up a fish. "Look at him," yelled Commissioner Mitchell, "he is catching fish with his hands, by thunder!" The "Jap" continued "yanking" up the fish for over half an hour, much to the amazement of the boarders on the shore. When he rowed in, the boat contained fifty fish of all kinds. "That's the way we catch fish in Japan," he remarked, as he pulled the boat on the sands. Commissioner Mitchell had nothing to say, and Alderman Strack said that the "Jap" must have mesmerized the fish as they swam by.

That evening the boarders were on the balcony of the house, listening to versions of the fishing exploit, when the path gate was violently swung open, and a big Irishman in a blue shirt swaggered up and wanted to know "Who in —— had been robbing his fish-pond? Do you suppose," he yelled, "that I catch fish and put thim in a pond to furnish this ere shebang with? If you New Yorkers want fresh fish, go and catch 'em, or else pay for 'em. Who robbed my pond, that's what I'm after knowin'?" The "Jap" was pointed out, and he paid for his spoils very meekly. "You see," explained Mitchell, "he didn't know the fish were yours—he thought he'd found a nest of them."—*New York World.*

---

John Brown, Queen Victoria's servant, has received from her the sole right of fishing on the river between Invercauld Bridge and Balmoral Bridge. One day he landed fourteen fine salmon for the royal table, but still an expensive luxury when it is stated that her majesty pays $1500 a year for the rental of this part of the stream. The Princess Louise is an expert at angling, but she will scarcely find on this coast the sport for which Scottish and Canadian rivers are so famous, as our salmon will rarely rise to the fly.

A fly casting tournament, open to the anglers of the United States and Canada, is to be held in New York city during September. The management of the contest will be in the hands of Mr. Frederick Mather, Assistant United States Fish Commissioner. As yet the arrangements are not complete, but the Park Commissioners will be applied to for permission to allow the competition to be held on one of the ponds in Central Park.

A fly casting tournament, open to the anglers of the United States and Canada is to be held in New York during September, The management of the contest wirl be in the hands of Mr. Frederick Mather, Assistant United States Fish Commissioner. As yet the arrangements are not complete. but the Park Commissioners will be applied to for permission to allow the competition to be held on one of the ponds

The average catch of salmon in the seine before the State added to the number by artificial hatching was five million pounds. Under the present law the fish have so increased that the annual catch has more than doubled. The law is often violated by many unscrupulous men, and it is not an easy matter to correct them.

The striped bass, which the Fish Commissioners tried to introduce here, is a valuable fish of the Atlantic Coast, that is very game and supplies a large amount of food to the people of the Eastern States.

For all that this is the close season, salmon have been served on the hotel tables at Petaluma during the week of the Fair. They are purchased of fishermen from Tomales and the Sacramento River.

## ATHLETIC.

GEORGE BREAKS OTHER RECORDS.—Among the notable things done at the London Midland Athletic Club's sports, held at Stamford Bridge Grounds, London, England, July 28, was W. G. George's wonderful two-mile run, which beats anything done by any amateur. The race which brought about this wonderful piece of running, was won by H W Cross (385 yards start). George started from scratch, finished second, 4 2-5s behind the winner. George's time for each quarter of a mile is:

| Miles | M. | S. | Miles | M. | S. | Miles | M. | S. |
|---|---|---|---|---|---|---|---|---|
| ¼ | 1 | 1 1-5 | 1 | 4 | 30 3-5 | †3,000 yds | 7 | 58 1-5 |
| ½ | 2 | 7 2-5 | 2,000 yds | 5 | 10 3-5 | †1¾ | 8 | 11 4-5 |
| ‡1,000 yds | 2 | 10 4-5 | †1¼ | 6 | 44 | †2 | 9 | 25 3-5 |
| ¾ | 3 | 15 3-5 | †1½ | 6 | 57 3-5 | | | |

† Denotes fastest amateur time on record. ‡ Fastest English time, Myers having run 1,000 yards in 2m 13s.

---

OLYMPIC CLUB REGULAR TICKET.—For President, J. H. Jennings; Vice President, Martin J. Flavin; Treasurer, H. B. Russ; Secretary, R. S. Polastri; Leader, H. B. Cook. For Directors: J. B. Stetson, C. W. Platt, Joseph Lyons, W. C. Brown, Wm. Levision, Ed. A. Girving. Members' Independent Ticket: for President, Jas. H. Jennings, Vice President, Samuel Foster; Treasurer, H. B. Russ; Secretary, R. S. Polastri; Leader, H. B. Russ. For Directors: J. B. Stetson, C. W. Platt, Chas. S. Neal, Wm. C. Brown, W. F. Bouton, Thomas Pennell. The election takes place on Monday, Sept. 4th. Polls open from 2 to 9 P.M.

### Market Report.

FLOUR—Is in good supply and rates are somewhat easier than those of last week. We quote Best City Extra, $5 37½ @$5 50; Superfine, $4 50@$4 75; Interior Extra, $4 75@ $5 25; Interior Superfine, $3 75@$4 ꝑ bbl.

WHEAT—Is quiet. Some few parcels of mixed No. 1 and 2 shipping are reported as having changed hands at $1 65@ $1 67½, the latter an extreme price. Yesterday opened the new year and if transactions are yet somewhat light, there is every appearance of a large business for the coming season

BARLEY—Operators were too busy in making August deliveries to give much heed to new business. Small sales of coast feed are reported at $1 28, though $1 30 is the general asking figure. On November account sales were made on the of 31st 200 tons No. 1 feed at $1 26½ and 300 do at $1 26½ ꝑ ctl.

OATS—No heavy orders on the market. Sales are affected in a quiet way in jobbing quantities at a range of $1 55@ $1 75 ꝑ ctl. Market weak and declining.

RYE—The best bid on Thursday for September delivery was $1 90 ꝑ ctl. Sellers would not name a price.

GROUND BARLEY—Fair trade. Quotable at $30@$31 ꝑ ton.

BUCKWHEAT—Nominally quotable at $1 40 to $1 50 ꝑ ctl.

CRACKED CORN—Business not urgent. Quotable at $38 ꝑ ton.

SHORTS—Sellers are asking $17@$18 ꝑ ton.

MIDDLINGS—Quotable at $26@$28 ꝑ ton for lots at mill.

OILCAKE MEAL—The oil works sell to the trade at $32 50 ꝑ ton, less usual discount.

HAY—We quote: Alfalfa, $11@$13 50. Wheat, $13@ $15 50; Wild Oat, $12@$15 50 ꝑ ton.

STRAW—Quotable at 55@60c ꝑ bale.

HOPS—Local operators are paying from 40c to 50c ꝑ ℔ for good to choice.

SEEDS—We quote; Mustard, $2 50@$2 62½ for brown and $1 90@$2 for yellow; Canary, 5@5½c; Hemp, 6c; Rape 2½@3; Timothy, 7@8c for native, and 9@10c for imported; Alfalfa, 10@12½c; Flax, 2½@2¾ ꝑ ℔.

CORNMEAL—Local millers quote feed at $34 to $36 ꝑ ton; fine kinds for the table in large and small packages, 3c ꝑ ℔.

POTATOES—Receipts are fairly liberal, but stocks are kept low by constant good custom. Wharf rates are as follows: Early Rose, in sacks, 60@85c; boxes 80c@$1; Garnet Chile, 90c@$1 per ctl; Sweet, $2 12½@ $2 37½ per ctl.

ONIONS—Slow of sale. Quotable 50@70c per ctl. for Silverskins and 30@40 per sack for Red.

BEANS—Market weak. We quote prices for job lots as follows: Bayos, $2 50@2 60; Butter, $3 50@$3 75 for small and $4 for large; Lima, $3 75@$4; Pea, $3 50@$3 75; Pink, $2 40@$2 45; Red, $2 40@$2 45; small White, $3 50 @3 75; large White, $3@$3 50 ꝑ ctl.

VEGETABLES—Low prices continue to rule. Tomatoes are being dumped daily. We quote job lots as follows: Marrowfat squash, $7@$10 ꝑ ton; Artichokes, 10c ꝑ dozen; Parsnips, 75c; Beets, 75c; Carrots, 75c; Turnips, 75c@$1 ꝑ ctl; Cauliflower, 60@65c ꝑ dozen; Cabbage, 50@75c ꝑ ctl; Garlic, 1@1½c ꝑ ℔; Cucumbers, 15@30c ꝑ box; Green Peas, 2@3c ꝑ ℔; Green Peppers, 50@75c ꝑ box; Tomatoes 15@30c ꝑ box; Spinach, 25c ꝑ sack; Celery, 50c ꝑ dozen; Summer Squash, 30 to 50c ꝑ box; String Beans, 3c ꝑ ℔; Green Corn 5@10c ꝑ dozen; Okra, 50@75c; Egg Plant, 50@75c ꝑ box.

FRUIT—Peaches are in good demand, and stocks kept well cleaned up. Grapes are also in favor. Apples 25@50c ꝑ basket and 50@$1 ꝑ box; Pears, 25@40c ꝑ basket and 40@60c ꝑ box; Bartlett do, 50@75c ꝑ basket and $1@$1 50 ꝑ box; Nectarines, 75c@$1 ꝑ box; Strawberries, $10@12; Raspberries, $10@$12 ꝑ chest; Peaches, 35c to $1 ꝑ box, and 30@60c ꝑ basket for common and 75c@$1 ꝑ basket for choice; Figs, 40@75c ꝑ box; Grapes, 35@50c for common, 50@75c for Black Hamburg, 50@75c for Rose of Peru, and 50@80c ꝑ box for Muscat; Plumbs, 25@75c ꝑ box; Blackberries, $4@$5 ꝑ chest; Watermelons, $3 50@$8 ꝑ hundred; Cantaloupes, 50c@$1 ꝑ crate; Lemons, $8@9 ꝑ box for Sicily and 50c@$1 for California; Limes, $10@$11 ꝑ box for Mexican; Tamarinds, 12@15c ꝑ ℔; Bananas, $2@$3 50 per bunch; Pine-apples, $6@$8 per dozen; Tahiti Oranges, $35@$45 per thousand.

WOOL—The market continues to present an easy tone. Humboldt and Mendocino, ꝑ ℔ 25@26½c. Sonoma, 14@26c. Siskiyou and Modoc, 20@25c. San Joaquin, free 27@18c. San Joaquin, defective 15@16½c. Southern Coast, burry and egon, poor 18@19c. Valley Oregon, fine $25@27. Valley Orseedy 15@17c. Eastern Oregon, choice 23 to 24c. Eastern Oregon, coarse 23@24c.

HIDES AND SKINS—Values well maintained. Dealers are paying the following cash rates for lots in order: Dry Hides, usual selection, 20@20½; culls one-third less, and Mexican hides 1c. ꝑ ℔ less, Dry Kip, 18@19c; Salted Kip, 25 to 30 ℔s, 10c to 10½c; Salted Calf, 11 to 12½c per ℔; Dairy Calf, 65c to 70c each; Sheep Skins, 20 to 25c for Shearlings, 25 to 50c for short, 60 to 80c for medium, and 75c to $1 apiece for long wool and wool skins. Butchertown Green Skins bring higher prices.

Following are rates for whole carcasses from slaughterers to dealers:

BEEF—Prime, 7½ to 8c; medium grades, 6½c to 7c; inferior, 5½ to 6c per ℔.

VEAL—Large Calves, 6½ to 7c; small ones, 8 to 10c per ℔.

MUTTON—Wethers are quotable at 4½ to 5c and Ewes at 4 to 4½c per ℔, according to quality.

LAMB—Quotable at 6 to 6½c per ℔.

PORK—Live Hogs, 7½ to 8c for hard and 7c to 7½c for soft; dressed do, 10¾ to 11c per ℔ for hard grain hogs.

CHEESE—There is no change in the situation. Market easy. We quote jobbing lots as follows: California, 12½@ 13½c for choice; 10@12c for fair to good; do, factory, in boxes, 15@16c; Eastern, 16@17c; Western, 11@13½c per ℔.

EGGS—Many holders have been asking 40c today, and some few box lots changed hands at this figure. Invoice parcels generally sell at our range: California, choice, 35@38½c; Interior, 30@34c; Western, 22½@27½c per dozen.

PROVISIONS—Market, firm: Eastern Hams, 17½@18½c; California Hams, 16@16½c for plain, 16½@17c for sugar cured canvassed; Eastern Breakfast Bacon, 17½@18c; California Smoked Bacon, 16½ to 16¾c for heavy and medium, and 17½ to 18c for light and extra light; Clear Sides, 16½ to 16¾c; Pork $21 50 to $22 for Extra Prime, $24 to $25 for Prime Mess, $25 to $25 50 for Mess, $27 for Clear and $28 to $28 50 for Extra Clear; Pigs' Feet, $16 to $18 per bbl; Mess Beef, $14 for bbls and $7 for hf bbls; Extra Mess Beef, $14 50 to $15; Family Beef, $16 to $16 50 per bbl; California Smoked Beef, 14½ to 14¾c per ℔; Beef Tongues, $9 50 to $10 per doz; Eastern Lard, 15½c for tierces and 16½ to 17c per ℔ for pails; California do, 10-℔ tins, 14 to 15c; 5-℔ tins, 15 to 15½c; pails, 16 to 16½c; kegs, 15 to 15½c; Royal do, 16½ to 16½c for 10-℔, 16¼ to 16¾ for 5-℔ and 16¾ to 17c per ℔ for 3-℔ pails.

## POULTRY.

### Fowls in Orchards.

Nothing is more reasonable to conclude than that fire allowour fowls the range of the orchard they will in a great measure, if not thoroughly destroy the worms and the injurious insects that infest the tree. Presuming that it is generally understood that hen manure is one of the most powerful of fertilizers, by following out our suggestions it will be readily conceived that two, if not three material advantages are to be realized. This whole subject is based upon the idea that there are no chicken thieves in the neighborhood, or if there are that there are good dogs and shot-guns within reasonable distance. Set four stakes in the ground three feet from the trees, nailing slats to them, beginning three feet from the ground, for the fowls to roost on. This is done in order that the droppings may be left close to thetrunk, for two reasons; first, that the roots may receive the benefit of the manure; second, the droppings are so strongthat it is offensive to all kinds of worms that crawl on the ground, and will tend to prevent their approaching the trees. It is in our opinion that during the spring, summer and fall months fowls are benefited by being allowed to roost in the open air, especially in this country, where we have but little rain from May to October.—*Resources of Oregon and Washington.*

## ROWING.

San Francisco, Aug. 30.

Editor Breeder and Sportsman: Please be obliging enough to publish this article in your next issue.

The first barge crew of the South End Boat Club intend to compete for The Breeder and Sportsman's trophy to be rowed for upon Thanksgiving Day. As this is a new crew it would please us to try our muscular and physical strength with the supposed champion four-oared barge crew of this coast, the "Golden Gate," so that we could take a little pride out of them.

If the "Golden Gat's" think they can take that trophy from the "South Ends" without perspiring pretty freely, they will be very badly mistaken on that Thanksgiving afternoon; and if they have not game enough to compete against us, it wil be plainly seen thatGriffin and Brown do not row for pleasure or the healthfulness derived from rowing, but for the love of money. Yours truly,

WILLIAM THOMAS,
Captain of "South End" crew.

### Cattle in Nevada.

It is estimated that 40,000 and perhaps 50-000 head of stock cattle will be taken out of Nevada this year. Ora Haley, fo Laramie, has bought the Ritchie & Barnum herd of about 2,000 head. He is shipping east now from Iron Point. Russel & Bradley have made one drive of over 3,000 head, and L. Filmore will ship from Wells and Winnemucca over 2,500 head McCormick & Keogh Bros. will send out about 3,000 head, from the south-eastern part of the State mostly. Lieutenant-Governor Adams is driving out everything but cows and calves to the number of probably 2,500 head. It is saidhis entire herd will be taken over inside of two years, and Nyecounty will know him no more. Sparks & Tennon will take 7,000 head from north of the Wells. Hammond of Cheyenne, and others from Wyoming are buying and all they can get will go to Wyoming, and eventually find their way to Chicago. This is beside the natural shipments of fat cattle which will go to San Francisco for beef. It is thought that Nevada is being depleted too much and that it will take several years to fill up again to the capacity of the feed. The late rains have filled the country with feed and the State loses wealth by not having cattle to eat it up. Cattle men say that Nevada is far superior to Wyoming as a breeding country, but Wyoming excels in fattening grasses. The climate here is milder butthe feed there is richer and better. Some think it would pay to breed in Nevada and ship Wyearling and two-year olds toyoming to fatten.

*REMOVAL.*

HENRY STEIL,
HENRY STEIL,
IMPORTING TAILOR,
IMPORTING TAILOR,
HAS REMOVED TO HIS
NEW STORES, 621 and 623
MARKET STREET, PALACE HOTEL.

*TURF EXCHANGE.*

FARRELLY & MITCHELL,
433 California Street.

Fine Wines, Liquors & Cigars.
"Red Clover."

NEEDHAM'S RED CLOVER BLOSSOMS AND extracts are the greatest blood-purifier in the world; also a sure cure for cancer, and rheum, catarrh, bronchitis, etc. I can refer to many letters and testimonials of those who have been cured—some of them very remarkable. I will send circulars and testimonials to those wishing them. Address W. C. NEEDHAM, Box 612, San Jose, Cal., Sole agents for Pacific Coast.

---

### J. O'KANE,
*MANUFACTURER AND IMPORTER OF HARNESS, SADDLES, BLANKETS, WHIPS, BOOTS, ETC.*

**767 Market Street, San Francisco.**

SPECIAL ATTENTION GIVEN TO THE MANufacture of "boots" of all kinds for horses. Can refer to all the principal trainers and horsemen on the Pacific Coast.
N. B.—My acknowledged superiority in this branch of business is largely due to careful observation and the Valuable suggestions of the most skilful trainers of the United States, the benefits of which accrue to the public in the shape of a GENUINE WELL-FITTING ARTICLE. Sole agent for Dr. A. H. Dixon's Condition Powders and for Maltister's patent "Eureka" and "Eclipse" Toe Weights. Repairing done with neatness and dispatch. Has always on hand the finest assortment of English ladies' and gentlemen's saddles, bridles, whips, spurs, bits and 2½-B-face saddles.

### MME. EXILDA LA CHAPELLE,
*SPORTSMEN'S HEADQUARTERS.*

Northeast Corner Post Street & Central Av.

REFRESHMENTS AND LADIES' SITTING ROOM.

### H. H. WILSON & SON,
IMPORTERS AND DEALERS IN GUNS, PISTOLS, CUTLERY, FISHING TACKLE, AMMUNITION, ETC.

**513 Clay Street. San Francisco.**

### DAVID L. LEVY,
*JEWELER, DESIGNER OF MEDALS AND TESTIMONIALS.*

**39 Third Street. San Francisco.**

REPAIRING NEATLY DONE.

### DAN McCARTHY,
*LIVERY, BOARDING & SALE STABLE,*

**605 Howard Street. Near Second.**

LARGEST STOCK OF FAST LIVERY TEAMS in the State. First-class boarding. Horses bought and sold. Cash advanced on horses, buggies, sulkies, harness or anything connected with this business.

### PAUL FRIEDHOFER,
*PATHOLOGICAL HORSE-SHOER.*

**105 Commercial Street.**

Practical in all its various branches.

### J. CONDON'S
☞ HAND BALL COURT,
**733 Howard St., bet. Third & Fourth.**

Match Game every Sunday. Fine Wines and Cigars.

### G. H. STRONG,
*BICYCLES AND TRICYCLES.*

**752 Market Street.**

Repairs to order.    Elevator, 12 Front street.

*NO PAY IN ADVANCE.*

The Great Electric Hair Tonic.

The only cure remedy that will restore the hair.
LABORATORY AND SALESROOM, 132 TYLER STREET.
For sale by all druggists.

### BALL COURT,
**846. HOWARD STREET 846.**
Fine Wines, Liquors and Cigars.
Wm. AIKINS, Proprietor.

*FOR A COOL, REFRESHING DRINK,*
### Sample's Headquarters,
**231 Kearny Street, bet. Bush and Sutter.**
S. S. SAMPLE.

### Fine Thoroughbreds.
#### FOR SALE.
### SACRAMENTO STATE FAIR,
—1882.—

The subscriber has a lot of thoroughbred horses which wiill be offered at

#### Auction Sale.

During the State Fair Week at Sacramento. The lot consists of

Brood Mares — four-years-old, three-year-olds, two-year-olds and yearlings.

Comprising some as finely bred and promising animals as there are on the Coast.

W. L. PRITCHARD.

### Sporting Goods.

BOXING GLOVES, FOILS, COMBAT SWORDS, MASKS, INDIAN CLUBS, Hunting Knives. our own Manufacture DOG COLLARS AND CHAINS, Finest assortment in the city.    WILL & FINCK.
Leading Cutlers.     769 Market Street.

SEND YOUR FAVORS TO THE
(LACOWSKI)
FLYING CLAY PIGEON
PIERCE & CO., OAKLAND, CAL.
AGENTS FOR THE PACIFIC COAST.

---

### P. DOYLE,

| HARNESS; | COLLAR; | SADDLE |
| HARNESS; | COLLAR; | SADDLE |
| HARNESS; | COLLAR; | SADDLE |

AND

*HORSE BOOT MANUFACTURER.*
*HORSE BOOT MANUFACTURER.*

**1011 Market Street. San Francisco.**

All Work made of the best Materials, by Hand,
AND WARRANTED.

☞ SEND FOR PRICES. ☜

### J. A. McKERRON,
*MANUFACTURER OF FINE HARNESS.*

**337 Sutter Street.**

Between Dupont and Stockton, San Francisco.

Repairing neatly and promptly executed.

### GOLDEN GATE FAIR.

The GENTLEMAN'S ROADSTER RACE, No. 21, on the Society's Speed Programme having failed to fill, the Managers, hereby offer a fine set of harness made by A. W. Pelonit, of Oakland, of the value of $125, for gentlemen's roadsters, best two in three, owners to Drive.

### ENTRANCE FREE.

Entrance to this race is open to any animal owned and bona fide property, for at least 60 days prior to closing. Entries to close with the Secretary at 10 A.M. on Thursday, Sept. 7th.
LOCK BOX 1283, Oakland.    L. WALKER, Secretary.

### TURKISH & RUSSIAN
STEAM BATHS.

No. 799 Montgomery Street, near Washington. San Francisco.

RUSSIAN baths cure rheumatism.
   Turkish baths cure heart disease.
Sulphur baths cure skin disease.
   GrisAdelia baths cure poison oak.
Steam baths cure indotercrance.
   Medicated vapor baths cure catarrh, nasal, throat and lung diseases.

THESE BATHS CURE CONSTIPATION, PILES, liver and kidney diseases, fever and ague and biliousness, acting as a perfect rejuvenator for all nervousness and debility, and to recuperate the system after a long-continued sickness. When all other medicine have failed. Connected with these establishment is a competent physician, who attends those who need every attention and home comfort, including pleasant rooms and hygienic board. Send for circulars giving full description of these baths and cost for a course of treatment.

DR. JUSTIN GATES,
late of Sacramento, proprietor of the Turkish and Russian baths, medical sanitarium and steam bath drug store, 733 Montgomery street, San Francisco.

---

# GORDAN BROS.,
*DRAPERS AND TAILORS,*
**202 KEARNY STREET,**
NORTHEAST CORNER SUTTER,
SAN FRANCISCO.

JUST RECEIVED, THE LARGEST AND AND of most complete assortment of

### Fall and Winter Goods.

The most choice qualities,
    Neatest patterns and
       The latest Styles.

### THE VICTORIAN TROTTING CLUB,
(L'd)
MELBOURNE, AUSTRALIA,
—OFFER—

The undersmentioned Prize, to be competed for on a day to be named early in January next, 1883.

### PRIZE OF 2,500 DOLLARS,

With Entrance Fees and Sweepstakes of $50 each from Starters added.
Mile heats: best three in five.
Open to all comers, bar geldings.
Winner to receive $2,500; second, two-thirds of Sweep and Entrance Fees, and third, one-third. Entrance $50 each.

Entries must be in the hands of Secretary at or before the 1st WEDNESDAY in December, 1882. The Victorian Trotting Club holds membership in the National Trotting Association of the United States, under which Rules the races will be governed.
Any further information desired can be obtained by addressing.    R. J. GURNEY, Secretary,
Kirk Bazaar, Melbourne.

### California's Exposition for 1882
Sacramento, California.

Opens Monday, September 11th

Closes Saturday, September 16th.

A Holiday Week of Recreation and Sport.

### $40,000 IN CASH

To be awarded in Premiums.

The premium List is full and complete, and is divided into seven departments. The Society's Gold Medal (valued at $100) will be awarded to the most meritorious display in each department. The exhibition of live stock promises to be large and fully up to the standard in each class. The latest and newest designs in agricultural implements will be on exhibition. The products of the soil representing California's greatest interest, will be fully shown. The Speed Programme (for seven races) offers unusual attractions, and awards inbibing wherein the produce of California's Breeding Establishments will be shown in their respective classes. Wing Shooting, Ladies' Equestrianism, and other sports will be held daily at the Park during the Fair.

The G. P., R. R. Co. will transport articles to and from the Fair free of charge. Wells, Fargo & Co. will deliver packages free on returning over 30 pounds. Application for space both at Pavil and Pavilion should be made at once to the Secretary. Season tickets, admitting self and family, $5. Single admission, 50c.
HUGH M. LARUE, President.
EDWIN F. SMITH, Secretary.

---

## SPECIMEN OF OUR ARTIST'S HUMOR.

THE FISHMONGER.

HUNDREDS OF DELIGHTED ONES SEE, FOR THE FIRST TIME IN THEIR LIVES

### The Japanese Artist and Embroiderers

*At work in their native costumes at*

# Ichi Ban, 22 & 24 Geary St.

*The BREEDER AND SPORTSMAN is printed with SHATTUCK & FLETCHER'S INK*

## SATURDAY, SEPT. 23D.

## SEVENTEENTH
# INDUSTRIAL EXHIBITION
OF
## The Mechanics' Institute
OPENED TO THE PUBLIC ON

### TUESDAY, AUGUST 15, 1882,

AT

## THE NEW PAVILION,
Larkin, Hayes, Polk and Grove Sts.

AND CONTINUES UNTIL SEPT. 16.

PREMIUMS OF GOLD, SILVER AND BRONZE

J. H. CULVER, Sec'y.    J. H. GILMORE, Sup't.

## SECOND
# ANNUAL EXHIBITION
OF THE
## SAN MATEO AND SANTA
## CLARA COUNTY
## AGRICULTURAL ASSOCIATION
# NO. 5,
TO BE HELD AT
# SAN JOSE, CAL.,
......FROM......
## Sept. 25th to 30th, '82, inclusive

### SPEED PROGRAMME.

**FIRST DAY—Monday, Sept. 25th, 1882**

**SECOND DAY—Tuesday, Sept. 26th.**

**REMARKS AND CONDITIONS.**

T. S. MONTGOMERY, Secretary.

**THIRD DAY—Wednesday, Sept. 27th.**

**FOURTH DAY—Thursday, Sept. 28th.**

**FIFTH DAY—Friday, Sept. 29th.**

**SIXTH DAY—Saturday, Sept. 30th.**

**REMARKS AND CONDITIONS.**

A. KING, President

### Third Annual Fair.

## AGRICULTURAL ASSOCIATION.
### SIXTH DISTRICT.

### SPEED PROGRAMME.

**FIRST DAY—Tuesday, Oct. 17, 1882**

**SECOND DAY—Wednesday, Oct. 18.**

**THIRD DAY—Thursday, Oct. 19.**
**Grand Stock Parade.**

**FOURTH DAY—Friday, Oct. 20.**

**FIFTH DAY—Saturday, Oct. 21.**

**REMARKS AND CONDITIONS.**

J. L. PHELPS, Secretary.    J. U. SHIPPEE, President.

# Golden Gate Fair.

## SPEED PROGRAMME FOR 1882

## $10,000

### IN

## Stakes and Prizes

**FIRST DAY**—Monday, Sept. 4, 1882.

**SECOND DAY**—Tuesday, Sept. 5.

**THIRD DAY**—Wednesday, Sept. 6.

**FOURTH DAY**—Thursday, Sept. 7.

**FIFTH DAY**—Friday, Sept. 8.

**SIXTH DAY**—Saturday, Sept. 9.

### CONDITIONS.

L. WALKER, Secretary.     A. C. DIETZ, President.

---

*GOLDEN GATE FAIR.*

## BICYCLE RACE!
## BICYCLE RACE!

### BICYCLE RACE!
### BICYCLE RACE!

ON SATURDAY, SEPTEMBER 9TH,
FREE FOR ALL.

A DASH OF A MILE, FOR A PURSE OF $40, of which two-thirds to first and one-third to the second rider.

**ENTRIES FREE**

Nominations to be made on Monday, Sept. 4, 1882, by 8 p. m. at the latest.

L. WALKER, Secretary.

---

### REMARKS and CONDITIONS.

All trotting and pacing races are the best three in five except in two year old race, (else-where specified.)

# BREEDER AND SPORTSMAN

NO. 508 MONTGOMERY STREET.    Vol. I. No. 11.    SAN FRANCISCO, SATURDAY, SEPTEMBER 9. 1882.    SUBSCRIPTION FIVE DOLLARS A YEAR.

## NOTABLE HORSES OF CALIFORNIA.

### ALEXANDER.

The origin of the tribe, clan, family, whatever distinctive appellation is used, to designate the Clays has been partially explained in the histories of horses which have been given in previous numbers. The fountain head proper in Henry Clay, a son of Andrew Jackson, a grandson of the imported Barb Grand Bashaw. A son of Henry Clay, Cassius M. Clay, got Geo. M. Patchen and from this horse have sprung all those which are known as Patchens. The founder of the family was one of the great trotters, and as nearly as can be predicated has the right to be classed with the best. At the time he was performing, the art of training trotters had not been brought to

the perfection of the present day, and his record of 2:23¼ made twenty-two years ago is equivalent to several seconds faster in this era of improved tracks, vehicles, manner of treatment, etc. He was one of the grandest trotters ever seen; large and commanding in appearance, his action nearly perfect and with endurance of the highest order. His type has descended with more than ordinary fidelity to the members of the family, and the horse which has been taken for the present illustration carries the inheritance in an eminent degree. The sire of Alexander was Geo. M. Patchen Jr., better known, however, as "California Patchen." He is also

the sire of Sam Purdy (2:20½), Starr King (2:22), San Bruno (2:24½), Susie (2:26½), Vanderlynn (2:27), and several others either in the 2:30 class or very close to it. He was a fine performer, this son of the original Geo. M. Patchen, having a record of 2:27 and showing a flight of speed in some of his private trials which was very nearly at the top notch. According to an advertisement published in 1862, the dam of California Patchen was by Bellfounder, and her dam by Messenger Eclipse. This in all probability is correct, and the dam of Alexander was a mare brought here by Samuel Krim in an early day,

(Concluded on Page 9.)

## The Original Morgan's Pedigree.

WOODSTOCK, VT., Aug. 26, 1882.

EDITOR BREEDER AND SPORTSMAN: The Morgan breed of horses originated or were first bred in Vermont, and the founder of the breed was taken by Justin Morgan when a two-year-old colt, from Springfield, Mass., to Randolph, Vt. The colt in time was called the Morgan horse, and after awhile was given Mr. Morgan's full name. Thus it was the Morgan name was given to this breed or blood of horses. Mr. Morgan, whose name is so intimately connected with the Morgan horse, was born at West Springfield, Mass., in 1747. His father was only able to give him a common education. His health was poor, inclining to consumption, and he was not able to do hard work after he was twenty. He was an excellent penman and a very fine singer, and supported himself mostly by teaching singing, writing and common district schools. At about 30 he was married and the fruits of this marriage were one son and four daughters. The son, named after his father, was born march 15, 1776. It is evident that he took quite an interest in the horse as he owned or kept "Sportsman, a gray horse by Lindsey Arabian, from 1779 to 1782." In 1783 he advertizes Dimond. As Dimond is given as the sire of the dam of the horse Justin Morgan the advertisement is of value, and is here given from the *Massachusetts Gazette* for April 26, 1783:

WILL COVER THIS SEASON AT THE STABLE OF MR. JUSTIN Morgan in West Springfield, the horse called Dimond, who springing from a good mare, and from the horse formerly owned by Mr. Clough of Springfield.' West Springfield, April 26, 1788.

In 1788, Mr. Morgan advertized True Briton, or Beautiful Bay. From the *Hampshire Herald* of May 3, 1875:

THE ELEGANT FULL-BLOODED HORSE BEAUTIFUL BAY WILL cover this season at Justin Morgan's stable in West Springfield at 30s. the season.

True Briton was advertised to stand at John Morgan Jr's. stable at West Springfield the season of 1788, as early as April 16, and to the season of 1789. The advertisement for 1788 states that "it is the same horse that was kept three seasons ago at West Springfield by Justin Morgan and got so many fine colts that, this and the neighboring towns." True Briton was advertised the season of 1791 at East Hartford, Conn. The advertisement is of value and is here given in full:

BEAUTIFUL BAY, WILL COVER AT MY STABLE (FOR THE benefit of the public) at 15s. the season, cash or grain best fall, and 1s. the leap, paid down. His sire was the imported horse Traveler, owned in New Jersey. His dam, Denbury's imported mare. His colts are offered for one of his colts at 4d. days old at Leonardburgh, and it is affirmed that he sired six colts in one day at Springfield. He is in his prime, in fine color, bright bay, 15 hands high, trots and canters very light; the price is low and so is the price of shipping horses, one thing objected to in proportion to another. ELEAR NORTON, East Hartford, April 26, 1791.

The above is from the Connecticut *Courant* for may 9, 16 and 23. The *Courant* for June 6, 1791, states: "Beautiful Bay will not cover at East Hartford this season." It must be understood from this, that True Briton made the balance of the season of 1791 at some other place than East Hartford, and as it is stated by AD as well at Springfield, he may have been taken there.

March 12, 1788, Mr. Morgan took his place at West Springfield, which consisted of a horse, barn and two-thirds of an acre of land, to Abner Morgan, for £33, 17 shillings and 6 pence, and removed to Randolph. The month that Mr. Morgan removed to Randolph is not given. It was stated that it was in the spring of 1788. It is claimed he moved on an ox sled. That was the way they mostly moved at that time in Vermont. Some moved on horseback, and some with a wheel-barrow and a hand-sled. The roads were poor and there were no wagons or horses. The horses were mostly used at that time in Vermont by riding them. They were ridden when visits and journeys had to be made, and to the village, the church and the mill. Winters they were harnessed to the sled. As Mr. Morgan's name is not on the tax-list of Randolph for 1788, if he arrived in Randolph on or before the 20th of June, he had no taxable property. At that time all stock excepting sheep and the like were clergymen and schoolmasters were exempt from paying a poll-tax, and a person to be taxed must be a resident of the place on the 20th of June. If Mr. Morgan arrived at Randolph after the 20th of June, 1788, his name would not be on the list for that year, if he had taxable property. His daughter Nancy was born at Randolph, Sept. 3, 1788. Mr. Morgan's list for 1789 was three pounds and fifteen shillings, with a deduction of one pound and sixteen shillings; this shows that he may have owned a yearling colt that year. He was chosen Lister this year, and Town Clerk from 1790 to 1798. March 20, 1791, Mr. Morgan's wife Martha died and there can be no doubt but it was in the summer of this year that he visited Springfield, and he made the journey on horseback. He made this visit to get money that was due him in Springfield, and his son says instead of getting money as he expected he had to take two colts, one a two-year-old stud colt, and the other a three-year-old gelding colt. His son said, too, that his father was very much opposed to taking the two-year-old colt, on account of its being so small and scrubby, and it was only after the intervention of the friends of the two parties that the consented to, and a lawsuit was prevented. This is one of the cases that often happen where one has to take against his wish what he don't want, and which turns out in the end a blessing in disguise. Mr. Morgan little thought at the time he did not want to take the little scrubby colt that the colt would be the founder of a breed of horses that would be given his name. The fact that Mr. Morgan owned and took the colt to Vermont is all that causes his name to be mentioned at the present time.

Mr. Morgan in taking the colt to Vermont saw so many good qualities in him that he was so taken with him that he informed his friends on arriving home that he was going to keep the colt for a stock horse. This his friends, many of them, advised him not to do on account of his inferior size. In 1791 a law was passed in Vermont that all stallions two years old and upwards should be set in the list for 20 pounds. This fact speaks well for the colt. Mr. Morgan, with his large experience with horses, would not have paid in his limited circumstances this large tax on a horse of low, obscure blood and origin.

In 1790, Mr. Morgan's list was 23 pounds, 13 pounds larger than in 1791. His wife's sickness and death and his going to Springfield must have lessened his property in 1791 several pounds, yet his list the next year, 13 pounds larger. The only reasonable explanation for it is that he was taxed for a stallion in 1792. The following is Mr. Morgan's advertisement for the Figure horse, from Spooner's *Vermont Journal*, April 15, 1793. The paper was printed at Windsor, Vt.:

WILL COVER THIS SEASON AT CAPTAIN ELIAS SIGNEL'S STABLE in Randolph, and at Captain Joseph Cleveland's stable in Lebanon the famous Figure horse, from Hartford, Connecticut, at 16s. for the season if paid down, or 18s. if paid in the fall, in cash or grain at cash price. Said horse's beauty, strength and activity the subscriber declares himself the equal as he will be best satisfied to come and see. Said horse will be in Lebanon the second Monday in May next, there to continue two weeks and then return to Randolph, so to continue as said Cleveland's and Randolph's two weeks all each place through the season. JUSTIN MORGAN. Randolph, April 8, 1793.

This year, 1793, Mr. Morgan sold all of his real estate at Randolph and broke up keeping house. His children were found homes at Randolph. His son's and daughter Emily's home was with Daniel Carpenter. In 1794 Mr. Morgan's list, and the last one he has at Randolph, is just 20 pounds, and there can be no doubt but this 20 pounds is for a stallion. His list for 1793 was 27 pounds, and 8 pounds for 1790. Mr. Morgan advertises the Figure horse again the season of 1794. The following is the advertisement from Spooner's *Vermont Journal* for April 28, 1792:

THE BEAUTIFUL HORSE, FIGURE, WILL COVER THIS SEASON at the moderate price of 1s the single leap, 3? the season, if paid down or by the first of Sept. paid; if not paid then it will be 14 s. Said horse will be at the stable of EZRA REEVES in Randolph and Lieut. Durkee, or E. Stevens in Royalton. He will be kept at Randolph till the second Monday of may, when he will be taken to Royalton, there to be kept every Monday, Tuesday and Wednesday, then return to Randolph where he will continue Thursday, Friday and Saturday. As for a subscriber during the season. The subscriber flatters himself that his horse's strength, beauty and activity will bear comparison by the curious. Gentlemen attention will be paid in each of the above places. JUSTIN MORGAN. Randolph, April 21, 1794.

Without knowing more, it is hard now to say what horse the Figure horse was. He may be a been the horse Justin Morgan, but we think not. It is claimed on good authority that the three-year-old gelding colt was a grey stud colt, and was the Figure horse, and was taken north from Randolph. Grey Figure was advertised to stand at Williamstown, Vt., in 1795. The advertisement states that he was six years old, 15½ hands high and sired by old Grey Figure, an imported horse owned by Col. Hart, of Pennsylvania. The Figure horse was in Lebanon the 20th of June, 1793, according to Mr. Morgan's advertisement and it must mean Lebanon, N. H. Mr. Morgan did not pay a tax on two stallions at the same time. The United States law that was passed in 1803 taxing stallions $10 was avoided by many by stating that they did not breed them. It looks more reasonable that the Figure horse was a horse that Mr. Morgan took to keep, the same as he did Dimond and True Briton.

Seventeen hundred and ninety-five is the year that Mr. Morgan Sen. gave in 1842 as the year his father took the original Morgan horse to Vermont. He gave the year 1795 from memory and it was at accepted without any investigation. It is nothing strange that he made a mistake in the year, as he had not care to refer to. He told his son, H. D. Morgan, now of Stockbridge, that he had found that he had made some wrong statements in regard to his father's horse. H. D. Morgan says he understood his father that the horse was taken to Randolph before his father broke up keeping house, and there can be no doubt that he was. Mr. Morgan's means were limited and he needed what he had at Randolph. He did not do the business he did at Randolph. He did not wait seven years before going after it. The grand lists of Randolph show that he owned no property there after 1794, or before June 30, 1795. Randolph must have been his place of residence after 1794, as it was the home of his children, and it will be shown that his residence was there at the time of his death.

Mr. Linsley states that Mr. Morgan supported himself after he broke up keeping house by teaching. This shows he would not have been encumbered with a stallion. His son said the horse was five years old the spring that his father died. Mr. Weir says that Mr. Morgan did not own the horse at the time of his death and there cannot be much doubt that it was the spring of 1795 that Mr. Morgan sold the horse, and he was five years old at that time. This is why Mr. Morgan's son made the mistake he did. He remembered that there was something done in 1795 in regard to the horse, and gave it that that was the year he was taken to Vermont, when it was the year that his father sold him.

The grand list of Randolph shows that Wm. Rice had a list at Randolph from 1792 to 1797. This shows that he removed to Woodstock in 1796 or 7. Mr. Morgan's son sold his father's horse passed into the possession of Mr. Rice. Mr. Morgan died March 23d, 1798. It is stated by some that he died at Woodstock at Wm. Rice's, but the records in the Probate office in regard to Mr. Morgan's estate rather show that he died at Randolph. Spooner's *Vermont Journal* for April 19, 1799, contains the notice for the settlement of Justin Morgan's estate. The first volume of the records at the Probate office for the district of Randolph contains the appraisal of Mr. Morgan's property by the Commissioner at the time of his death. It is stated that the deceased was a resident of Randolph at the time of his death. The amount of property appraised is $160 12. There is no horse or stock of any kind appraised. A saddle and bridle are appraised $7; a whip, 17 cents; Bible and Testament, 25 cents; "Scott's *Lessons*, 30cents; "Pope Essay on Man," 10 cents; his clothing $32.09. The different articles of property are stated. The expense of last sickness is given: Dr. Bissel's bill, $4.69; Aaron Stearns' bill for nursing, $1.02. Messrs. Bissel and Stearns were residing at Randolph. A dividend of 16 cents is paid the creditors Nov. 18, 1800.

Mr. Lindsley states that Mr. Rice let Robert Evans of Randolph have the horse in 1801 and that he let John Goss have him in 1804, and that Mr. Goss let his brother David at St. Johnsbury have him; that he was taken back to Randolph in 1811 and kept there and in the vicinity until his death. The following advertisement shows that the horse was kept at Randolph the season of 1807. It is from the *Weekly Wanderer* of May 4, 1807. The *Wanderer* was printed at Randolph:

THE MORGAN HORSE WILL STAND THIS SEASON AT THE STABLE of John Goss, in Randolph. May 1, 1807.

It is claimed that he stood part of the time this season at Claremont, N. H. A private letter states that he was shown at the fair at Randolph in 1817. He died at Chelsea in February, 1819, or was killed. The cause of his death was a kick he received from a mare hitched in the barn beside him, there being only a pole between them. This is a sad end of so remarkable a horse, who was the founder of a distinct family of horses.

After the Morgans had become popular, it was desired to know the origin and blood of their founder. It was claimed by many that he was taken from Canada, and was a French horse. The June number of the Albany *Cultivator* for 1842 contained the statement of John Mayer, then of Lima, N. Y., that he resided at Springfield, Mass., near Justin Morgan, previous to his removal to Vermont, and that the two-year-old stallion that he took with him to Vermont was sired by a horse called True Briton, or Beautiful Bay; that Justin Morgan kept True Briton at Springfield one season, and two years after he, John Morgan, kept him two seasons. In the January number of the *Cultivator* for 1846, is Frederick Weir's statement in regard to the origin of the Morgan horse: "From my correspondence with Justin and John Morgan and others I am able to state the pedigree on both sides of the Morgan horse. He was foaled in 1793 and was sired by True Briton or Beautiful Bay, then kept by John Morgan at West Springfield. The dam of the Justin Morgan horse at the time he was sired was owned by Justin Morgan himself at Springfield, where he then lived.

The dam is described by Mr. John Morgan, who knew her, as of the Wild-air breed, of middling size, heavy chest, very light bay color, bushy mane and tail, the hair on the legs rather long and a smooth, handsome traveler. Her sire was Diamond, a thick, heavy horse with a heavy mane and tail, hairy legs, and a handsome traveler. Dimond was kept by Justin Morgan at the time the dam of the Morgan horse was sired. His sire was the Wild-air known as the Church horse; his dam, the noted imported mare Wild-air, owned by Capt. Samuel Burt, of Springfield, Mass. The Church horse's sire was Wild-air which was taken back to England."

The advertisement of Dimond shows that Justin Morgan kept Dimond the season of 1783, and that his sire was the Church horse. So much of what Mr. Weir says Mr. John Morgan wrote him is proved true, but the advertisement of Dimond does not sustain the Wild-air crosses and they cannot be considered true. Mr. Weir claims that John Morgan gave these Wild-air crosses in the letters that he received from him dated Jan. 9, 1845, and Jan. 31, 1845. Mr. Weir declines to let any one read these letters, or to have them published in full; only extracts from them have been published. This leads to the belief that they do not give the Wild-air cross as given by Mr. Weir and that this is the reason Mr. Weir does not want them published. The May number of the Albany *Cultivator* contains a second letter from Justin Morgan of Stockbridge, Vt., in which he states what Mr. Weir had already stated, that John Morgan kept True Briton the season that his father's horse was begotten.

The statements of Messrs. Morgan and Weir satisfied the public in regard to the origin of the Morgan horse. Mr. Linsley published his "Morgan Horses" in 1857. He restated what had been stated. He thought he had discovered an error in the Weir statement that "the dam of the Justin Morgan horse at the time he was sired was owned by Justin Morgan himself at Springfield, Mass., where he then lived." It was said then that the horse was foaled in 1793, and taken to Vermont in 1795, and this was an error, as Mr. Morgan removed to Vermont in 1788. But call it as it was, that the horse was foaled in 1789 and taken to Vermont in 1791, Mr. Morgan could have bred him. His Dimond mare was four years old in 1788. True Briton's advertisements showed he was at Springfield as early as April 16, 1878. Mr. Morgan could have bred his mare to him and moved to Vermont on snow. There have been years when one could not do this on snow. There have been years when one could not do this as he states: "He certainly was the property of True Briton." He says, too that he has not been able to find any trace of evidence that Justin Morgan kept Dimond, thinks John Morgan got the names confused, and that Sportsman was the sire of the dam of Justin Morgan instead of Dimond.

In 1878 it was discovered that John Morgan removed from Springfield to Lima, N. Y., in March, 1791, and it is claimed that he could not have known in regard to a colt that Justin Morgan took to Vermont in 1795. In 1879 the advertisements of True Briton for the seasons of 1786, 1788 and 1789 were found. These proved that True Briton was not the sire of the Justin Morgan, as he was got in 1792. The True Briton colt that John Morgan knew of Justin Morgan's taking to Vermont was one taken to Vermont in 1795, when he removed there, and was got in 1785, the season that Justin Morgan kept True Briton, and the original Morgan horse was another colt that Justin Morgan took to Vermont in 1796, that John Morgan knew nothing about. They would not admit that Justin Morgan's son made a mistake in the year that his father took the horse or colt to Vermont. It was the year 1795 for a certainty. Mr. Wallace accepted this theory, says the sire of the Justin Morgan is not known, and talks as though his blood was Dutch, because Mr. Morgan's son said his father called him a Dutch horse. They seemed to have forgotten the statement of John Morgan, that he kept True Briton the season he sired the colt that he knew Justin Morgan took to Vermont. The advertisement of John Morgan for True Briton, the season of 1788-9, showed that the colt he meant was not taken to Vermont in 1785, as the colt he meant was not then born.

The grand lists of Justin Morgan are soon found, and it is learned that when John Morgan removed to Lima, N. Y., he left a son John, of a few years of age, at Springfield; that the son visited the father at Lima when nineteen years of age; that the father visited Springfield; that his son removed to Bellows Falls, Vt., in 1829, and to Windsor, Vt., in 1833; that he visited his father at Lima while living at Windsor, and his father must have learned from him in regard to the Morgan horses of Vermont, and it was how he was so well posted in regard to them.

Mr. Wallace published the third volume of the "Trotting Register" the last of the year 1879. He says nothing in it about the pedigree of the horse Justin Morgan. In 1882 Mr. Wallace publishes his fourth volume of the "Trotting Register." He is silent in it in regard to the pedigree of the horse Justin Morgan, Jr., b., by True Briton." The time he was foaled and taken to Vermont should be corrected, for if he was sired by True Briton the season John Morgan kept him, he was not foaled in 1789 and taken to Vermont in 1791, as claimed.

ALLEN W. THOMSON.

THE BREEDER AND SPORTSMAN is the name of a new weekly paper, conducted by Jos. Cairn Simpson, and published at San Francisco, Cal., at five dollars per annum. The first copy is at hand. For beauty of typography, extent and variety of matter, and general make up, it is unexcelled by its contemporaries. Mr. Simpson is author of a popular book, called "Horse Portraiture," and for more than a quarter of a century has been a popular writer on horse and sporting matters. He is admirably qualified to conduct such an enterprise, and the breeders of the Pacific Coast are to be congratulated upon having so able and gifted a champion of their interests.—*St. Louis Rural World.*

# TURF AND TRACK.

## Fixed Events.

Golden Gate Fair, to be held at Oakland, from September 4th to the 9th inclusive.

Butte District Fair at Chico, from September 5th to September 8th inclusive.

El Dorado District Fair at Placerville, from September 5th to September 8th inclusive.

California State Fair. Annual meeting at Sacramento, from Monday, September 11th to 16th inclusive.

The San Joaquin Valley Association Fair at Stockton, from September 19th to the 23d inclusive.

Oregon State Fair at Salem, from September 18th and during the week.

The San Mateo and Santa Clara County Agricultural Association Fair at San Jose, September 25th to the 30th inclusive.

Humboldt and Mendocino District Fair at Rhonerville, September 19th to September 22d inclusive.

Modoc, Plumas and Lassen District Fair at Greenville, from October 3d to October 5th inclusive.

Monterey District Fair at Salinas City, from October 2d to October 6th inclusive.

Nevada State Fair at Reno, from Monday, October 2d to the 7th inclusive.

Mount Shasta Agricultural Association Fair at Yreka, October 4th, 5th, 6th and 7th.

Eastern Oregon Fine Stock Association at Union, from October 9th to the 14th inclusive.

Los Angeles Agricultural Association, at Los Angeles, from October 17th to 21st inclusive.

FAIRS AT THE EAST.

Minnesota State Fair at Farmington, August 31st to September 6th inclusive.

Iowa State Fair at Fairfield, September 1st to the 5th inclusive.

Minnesota Agricultural Association, at Minneapolis, September 4th to the 9th inclusive.

Nebraska State Fair, at Omaha, September 11th to the 16th inclusive.

Rhode Island State Fair, at Providence, September 12th to the 15th inclusive.

Pennsylvania State Fair, at Pittsburg, September 7th to the 21st inclusive.

Wisconsin State Fair, at Fond du Lac, September 11th to the 16th inclusive.

On ario Provincial Fair, at Toronto, September 15th to the 23d inclusive.

Connecticut State Fair, at Meriden, September 18th to the 22d inclusive.

New Jersey State Fair, at Monroe, September 18th to the 22d inclusive.

West Virginia Central Fair, at Clarksburg, September 19th to the 21st inclusive.

Indiana State Fair, at Indianapolis, September 25th to the 30th inclusive.

Western Michigan Fair, at Grand Rapids, September 25th to the 30th inclusive.

Texas State Fair, at Austin, October 17th to the 21st inclusive.

## Clingstone's first Defeat.

The Grand Special race at Utica on August 18th will create a sensation throughout the country and will be memorable as the first defeat of Clingstone. It was over this same course a year ago that he lost his first heat, but in it he made a break; but, fortunately for his backers, they did not meet a Waterloo, as little betting was effected on the race. The public had become strongly impressed with the idea that Thorne might snatch a heat from him, but there was little hope of his winning the race, so after the first heat Clingstone was as great a favorite as ever. The Utica meeting was not productive of heavy speculation, and had this reverse been sustained at Cleveland, or Buffalo, it would have been a severe blow to the friends of Clingstone, for an old pool clerk, who keeps the run of the betting from year to year, told me that there was more money changed hands at the Circuit meetings previous to Utica, than during any year since the pool law of New York State was enacted.

Now that Edwin Thorne has plucked the laurels from his doughty rival, I made a few brief inquiries of noted horsemen as to what they thought of the race. One said: "Oh, the day is raw and cold, and Clingstone may not be at himself." "Well, he was not badly off for speed," I suggested, "for he forced Thorne to the half in 1:07¾ the second heat, and the day is not so bad after all, as Murphy jogged in with Cornelia in 2:21¼; some made it faster." "That's so" chimed in a second trainer, "but it was warmer then than now, and Thorne is growing better and stronger all the time. You know it was more a difference in endurance than in speed between the horses in their other races." A third said: "The little bay gelding will lose little reputation by the defeat. He is one of the kind who will come again and take more of a beating than he received to-day before he is conquered."

The only non-starter for the special purse of $2,000 was J. B. Thomas. A murmur of admiration was heard as Clingstone appeared for the preliminary warming up, and Edwin Thorne was greeted with similar applause, for they were regarded as the contending horses, with public opinion in favor of Clingstone's success by a large majority. I have heard it claimed that the little bay "demon" was not himself to-day; but excuses are not in order. The truth is that Thorne is a better horse than he has been, and the sharp contests through the circuit have keyed him up to put in his heats closer together. He has already verified my prediction, made after the Buffalo race, viz: "It is not by any means a forlorn hope to cherish that he will wrest a heat, or possibly a race, from Clingstone before they close their engagements through the circuit."

But I look for Clingstone to redeem his laurels and continue to win the best three out of five races, even from as good a horse as Edwin Thorne, notwithstanding the great son of Thornedale has a marked advantage in his breaks, which are sometimes a positive advantage to him, while if Clingstone leaves his feet it is almost fatal to his chances for a heat or race, as was clearly shown to-day.

First heat.—Pools: Clingstone, $100; field, $20 to $25. The horses scored unevenly a number of times, with Thorne at the pole, So-So second, and Clingstone third. When the word was given all was working level. So-so was not up in her place, and Clingstone immediately ranged alongside of Thorne. He kept his nose on the leader's wheel around the turn, but Thorne opened a little daylight to the quarter in the neighborhood of 34s., with So-so a good third, Kate Sprague fourth, and Pickard last. The leaders began to draw away from the others on the second quarter, and Clingstone seemed to shoot up for a few strides, as if about to collar Thorne, and then the big chestnut would let out a link and keep him at his distance, a length behind to the half in 1:08¼. These movements were continued around the upper turn, and as they approached the three-quarter pole, which was made in 1-45, Saunders drew the whip on Clingstone, and was on Thorne's wheel as they straightened into the stretch. The small-fry of betters who crowd the open space in front of the grand stand and are always ready to catch "suckers" were soliciting bets of from a dollar upward that Clingstone would win it. Down the stretch they came, each horse and driver doing his level best. Clingstone got to Thorne's saddle-girths at the distance and closed up a little more before the finish, but, although apparently doing his level best, the chestnut beat him out by a neck, in 2:18½.

Second heat.—The Clingstone party were as confident as before the start, and stood ready to back their favorite at $100, the field ranging from $24 to $36, according to the way Thorne showed up in the scoring. Everybody anticipated a good heat, but the opinion prevailed that Thorne would be beaten at the finish, as usual. Clingstone scored up with determination in every movement, and, no matter what fielder proved laggard, he was there, even with Thorne, every time. "They're off," and the Paris Mutual machines were closed. The chief contestants were even as they left the wire, but Thorne was first under full headway, though Clingstone was in close pursuit of him, clinging to his wheel around the turn, and on to the quarter-pole in 34½ seconds. Inch by inch the little grey gelding crept up to Thorne's body, and, gaining little by little, he seemed to have the leader within his grasp at the half in 1:07¾. This uncommonly fast clip left the fielders far in the rear, Kate Sprague being the boss of the rear division, with So-so already beaten. After passing the half and rounding the turn leading from the backstretch, Thorne began to draw away a little, and the friends of Clingstone were exclaiming: "Oh, that is only Thorne carrying him out. You will see how he will cut him down in the straight work." And their words appeared to be true, as Clingstone gained on him at the three-quarter pole in 1:45; but just as he was making the last turn, and everyone was looking for a magnificent struggle, the pride of the Forest City broke. Those who were not in a position to see the unfortunate occurrence thought that the shout: "Clingstone has broken up," was only a joke; but as they saw Thorne passing under the wire three or four open lengths, with the hitherto unconquerable horse merely able to beat the others for second place, they learned that the shout was true. Time, 2:20¼.

Third Heat—There is a first time in everything, and now Clingstone sold in the field at $10 against $24 for Thorne, and never did a field look stronger than until within a few yards of the finish of this heat. The word was quickly given, and, in an instant, Thorne and Clingstone drew out from the others, entering into a desperate struggle. Clingstone is not to be shaken off this time. He drew up almost even at the quarter in 35¼ seconds, and kept gaining little by little, until at the half, in 1:10, he was even with Thorne. Hope here lent wings to him, and he carried Thorne to a short break. "He's got him at last. Why don't he let out a little more and take the pole!" cried his too-anxious backers. But, before he could do so, Thorne had settled, and trotted even into his place; but midway of the third quarter he could not stand the pressure, and again the big chestnut left his feet, running about fifty yards and maintaining his position. When he settled he went at Clingstone with renewed vigor, and they came into the stretch on almost even terms, Clingstone swinging well out. Thorne came up on the inside. Whip and rein were busily at work on each, and within fifty yards of the wire, when Clingstone, was even with his competitor, Saunders, seeming to fear that he would be beaten out, and placing too much confidence in the steadiness of his horse, let go of his head for an instant, as he raised his hand to give him an extra cut. This movement and the severe blow were more than Clingstone could stand, and he left his feet when the heat was almost won, running out two lengths behind Thorne. Time, 2:21. Kate Sprague was trotting steadily close to the pole, but Murphy brought Pickard up with a rush, and beat her out for third place and third money.—*Special Cor. N. Y. Spirit of the Times.*

## Saratoga Races.

The Saratoga Association brought its racing season for the current year to a close August 26th, with good weather, an excellent track and a very large attendance, including numerous ladies, and perhaps a larger number of Saratogians than has been present on any previous day of the meeting—the last day having for years been, as the late John Morrissey used to say, "Saratoga's day." Of the meeting, it can only be described as an unqualified success. Since July 11 there have been no less than forty days of continuous racing, as against thirty-seven days last year, when, as has been the case this year, the weather continued so fine that the meeting was run through without a single day's postponement. As to the financial success of the meeting, it is scarcely possible that the total of receipts will reach as large a figure as on some previous years, a fact due as much as anything to the falling off in the betting, caused principally by the absence of some of the larger Eastern stables. But there has been no falling off in the amount of money raced for in the shape of purses and added money to the stakes, which foots up $86,000, and which has been so nicely divided up that a majority of the owners of horses racing here during the meeting, which covered nearly seven weeks, obtained some portion of it. The 161 races run were won as follows: Eighteen by the Dwyer Brothers, fourteen by Milton Young, thirteen by C. Reed, ten by W. L. Cassidy, nine by Mr. J. A. Grinstead, eight by A. Burnham, six by ex-Governor Bowie, five by Bowen & Co., five by C. Boyle, five by W. M. Conner, five by J. P. Dawes, five by E. Heffner, four by Davis & Hall, four by Preakness Stable, four by W. Kavil, three by Noah Armstrong, three by Morris & Patten, two each by J. J. Merrill, J. W. Loud, W. P. Burch; P. C. Fox, D. Colaizzi, Mr. Abingdon, P. H. Duffy and J. C. Forbes, and one each by Connolly & Co., Darden & Co., W. A. Dun, Carson & McBride, Watts & Co., W. L. Scott, J. T. Williams, Graham Brothers (a dead heat which they divided with Governor Bowie), C. L. Hunt, Dr. Craik, Stevens & Co., A. J. Scott, Sheppard Brothers, F. Gebhard, J. H. Harbeck, W. K. Bender, Riley & Co., R. Leary and O. C. Lefevre. One conspicuous feature of the meeting has been the number of horses that have been sold, Mr. Doswell having sold all of his and Mr. Grinstead all but one during the meeting.

In "Krik's" letter to the New York *Herald* he remarks that the second race on the cards, the Baden-Baden Handicap, was the race of the day, and no doubt attracted the large crowd present. It had five srarters, and as a race it was one of the best of the meeting. All five of the contestants ran in close order, with the old favorite Bushwhacker in the lead, and although many present were disappointed in not seeing the last year's winner of the same race, Mr. Reed's Thora, take the lead in the last mile, as they wished her to do attended by Checkmate, they were treated to a splendid race between the two mares Ella Warfield and Lida Stanhope. The latter was superbly ridden by Shauer, who journeyed up from New York specially for the occasion, he winning with comparative ease in the best time ever made for three miles. Although Lida's ability to run a good distance was shown by what she did as a three-year-old, only a select few knew her real form to-day, and although she sold well up in the pools they made a good winning. The defeat of Ella Warfield was a sore disappointment to the Maryland and West Virginia party, as they knew Ella was just about good enough to run the distance nearly in record time, which they supposed would be sufficient to beat Thora and Lida Stanhope. Of course, Thora's inability to run the distance effectually settles her chances for the four-mile races at Sheepshead and Baltimore, while as to Bushwhacker, he made such a gallant effort that not a few were sorry when it was seen that he could not possibly reach the leaders after they had once run into the lead. The starters were Checkmate, at 118 pounds; Thora, at 117 pounds; Bushwhacker, 101 pounds; Lida Staubope, 100 pounds, and Ella Warfield, 92 pounds. Notwithstanding Thora's "quitting" exhibition a few days ago she was made the favorite, with Ella Warfield and Lida Stanhope each well supported, particularly the latter, for which Shaner had specially been engaged to ride. When the flag was dropped Thora was in front, with Checkmate second, Lida Stanhope third, Bushwhacker fourth and Ella Warfield last. In an instant Bushwhacker took the lead and, going right away, opened a gap of three lengths, and, with Checkmate second and Thora third, they ran nearly the whole of the first mile, which was ended with Bushwhacker leading two lengths, Checkmate second, half a length in front of Ella Warfield, who was one in front of Thora, and the latter half a length in front of Lida Stanhope, both fillies under a hard pull. Half way round the west turn Thora again showed third, but with that exception there was no other change in the second mile, all five running up the stretch good and strong, with Bushwhacker leading two lengths, followed by Checkmate, a length in front of Thora, who was the same distance in front of Ella Warfield, and the latter the same in front of Lida Staubope. Half-way round the west turn those who backed Thora knew her fate, for instead of moving up she dropped back while those who backed Ella Warfield were delighted to see her take second place. In the meantime Bushwhacker was still running very strong, but as they reached the woods the secret of the race was shown, for with the greatest ease Lida Staubope took the lead, and as she was followed by Ella Warfield, they passed the half with Lida Stanhope leading by half a length, Ella Warfield second, nearly clear of Bushwhacker, with both Thora and Checkmate out of the race. When well into the west turn Thora raised some little hope for her supporters by taking third place, but as she was unable to reach Lida and Ella, the attention of all present was turned to them. From the 500-yard pole they ran a tremendous race, both under the whip, with Lida leading by half a length, which distance separated them until they reached the pool-stands, at which point Shaner brought Lida Stanhope away from Ella Warfield, and amid the enthusiastic shouts of nearly all in the stand Lida Stanhope won a great race by two lengths and a half, Ella Warfield second, four lengths in front of Bushwhacker, who was three in front of Thora and the latter five in front of Checkmate. Time 5:25, which just beats the record for the distance by a quarter of a second. On the return to the scales both Lida Stanhope and Ella Warfield were loudly applauded, as they fully deserved to be, for it will be seen that from the time they began racing the pace increased wonderfully. The following is the time by quarters as taken by the timers:

1st, 29½; 2d, 28, half-mile, 0,57½; 3d, 28½, three-quarters, 1:26; 4th, 27, mile, 1:53; 5th, 27½, mile and a quarter, 2:20½; 6th, 27, mile and a half, 2:47½; 7th, 27½, mile and three-quarters, 3:15; 8th, 25, two miles, 3:40; 9th, 27, two miles and a quarter, 4:07; 10th, 26, two miles and a half, 4:36; 11th, 26, two miles and three-quarters, 4:59; 12th, 26, three miles, 5.25.

## The Utica Winners.

| Name. | Des. | Sire | Am'nt Won. | Best Time. |
|---|---|---|---|---|
| Alleghaney Boy | rn s | Wood's Hamblesonian | $225 | ...... |
| Babara Patchen | b m | Peck's Idol | 375 | ...... |
| Barrett | b s | Chester Chief | 150 | ...... |
| Buffalo Girl | b m | Pocahontas Boy | 225 | 2:14½ |
| Captain Lewis | ch g | Spink | 750 | 2:24½ |
| Clingstone | b g | Rysdyk | 750 | ...... |
| Cornelia | blk m | Bonner | 750 | 2:21½ |
| Edwin Thorne | ch g | Thornedale | 1,800 | 2:18½ |
| Eva | b m | Gray Wilkes | 375 | ...... |
| Fanny Witherspoon | ch m | Almont | 500 | 2:20 |
| Flora Belle | blk m | Stucker Rainbow | 750 | 2:15½ |
| Fred Douglass | ch s | Green's Bashaw | 300 | ...... |
| Gem | b m | Tom Rolfe | 150 | 2:19½ |
| Golden Rule | b m | Golden Bow | 150 | ...... |
| Humboldt | b g | Stocking Chief | 200 | ...... |
| J. P. Morris | br g | R. R. Morris | 1,000 | 2:24½ |
| Kate Sprague | br m | Governor Sprague | 450 | ...... |
| King Wilkes | br s | George Wilkes | 150 | ...... |
| Lucrece | b m | Robert Whalley | 22[illegible] | ...... |
| Lucy | gr m | Ned | 375 | 2:16¾ |
| Mamie | b m | Blue Bull | 375 | ...... |
| Mattie | b m | Rysdyk's Hambletonian | 150 | ...... |
| May Thorne | b m | Thornedale | 150 | ...... |
| Onawa | blk s | Goodwin's Hambletonian | 225 | ...... |
| Pickard | b g | Abdallah Pilot | 300 | ...... |
| Rigolette | b m | Exchequer | 225 | ...... |
| R. P. | b g | Happy Medium | 375 | 2:22½ |
| St. Cloud | b s | Conklin's Star | 375 | ...... |
| Sweetness | b m | ...... | 225 | ...... |
| Topsy | b m | Walkill Chief | 225 | ...... |
| Unolala | b m | Volunteer | 750 | 2:22½ |
| Wilson | b g | George Wilkes | 1,500 | 2:21½ |
| Yellow Dock | ch m | Clark's Mohawk Jr. | 750 | 2:20¾ |

DEATH OF CATESBY.—Ex-Governor Bowie has had the misfortune to lose his well-known thoroughbred race horse and sire, Catesby, the son of imported Eclipse and Katie, having died on Sunday last at his owner's farm, Fairview, in Prince George's county, Maryland. Catesby was bred by Mr. Bowie in 1870 and raised on the farm where he died. His racing career was by no means a brilliant one, though it promised to be so, when, on his first appearance, Catesby won the valuable Saratoga Stakes in 1872, beating Long Branch and such good ones as Springbok, Fellowcraft and Count D'Orsay in the ten that followed him home. Catesby next ran in the Kentucky Stakes, and later in the Nursery Stakes at Jerome Park, being third on each occasion. Catesby then fell a victim to the prevailing epidemic, the epizootic, and he was a long time ere he recovered, so long indeed that his three-year-old career was a failure, only one small purse at Jerome Park being credited to him.. As a four-year-old he ran a dead heat with Grainger at the Baltimore spring meeting, won a selling purse at Saratoga, and then closed the year with the most creditable performance since his initial success. This was the defeating Wildidle, B. F. Carver and Ransom in the Maturity Stakes at Jerome Park. In 1875 Catesby ran once unsuccessfully at Saratoga and was then sent back to Fairwiew. He began his stud career in 1876, producing Cinderella from one of the two mares sent to him. In 1877 he sired Crickmore, Compensation, Sportsman and a bay colt now used as a saddle horse by Mr. Bowie. Cinderella was turning out so badly as a yearling that the following year Catesby's services were dispensed with and he was sent to Virginia, where he remained for three seasons. The excellent running of Crickmore and Compensation in 1880 induced Mr. Bowie to have Catesby brought back, and he has been used at Fairview for two seasons since then.—*N. Y. Herald.*

A strange mistake was made one day last week by a pool firm at Brighton Beach near New York which cost them $302 50. The name of the winning horse in a race is telegraphed in cipher from the track to the pool-rooms. In the case in point the man whose business it is to receive these dispatches and announce the winners shouted "Madrigal wins," and $802 50 was paid out before he looked at the dispatch a second time and found he had read Madrigal for Miss Woodford, who had really won the race. $500 of the amount was refunded, but the holders of the remainder refused to return the money they had received.

## The Petaluma Fair.

PETALUMA, Sept. 30, 1882.

EDITOR BREEDER AND SPORTSMAN: The fair and races at Petaluma have closed, after having the most brilliant and successful season they ever knew. Notwithstanding that the grand stand is capable of seating several thousands of people, the place was so thronged as to hardly leave standing room. The last two days' races were very exciting. On Friday the races commenced with a two-year-old colt race, trotting for a purse of $300, with the following entries: G. C. Fountain's blk f May Day, Whitney's ch c Ideal, John Pfau's b g Mike, P. J. Shafter's g m, S. S. Drake's b c Standard, and J. E. Foster s f Clara Patterson. Of these the only starters were May Day and Ideal, the latter being the favorite in the pools at $15 to $10 for May Day. After some scoring they got a good send off, trotting very evenly and close together the whole heat, the only skip made in the heat being a slight break by May Day coming down the stretch. The favorite took this heat in 3:3¼ by only a length.

After this heat Ideal sold at the pool box for $10 to $4 50 for May Day with but few takers, but again were the knowing ones upset in their calculations, for after a very close heat Ideal broke near the wire and gave up the heat to May Day in 3:2. The result of this heat so dampened the ardor of the favorite's friends that no one could guess who the winner would be and there were no pools sold. The third heat, like all the others, was a very close one, but the bay mare proved to be the best horse and won the heat in 2:59½ by only a length. May Day is by Eugene Casserly, her dam by Toronto Chief, and is a very promising filly.

As the Consolation purse did not fill there was a made-up race for a purse of $400. The entries for this purse were J. Hugh's Cairo, Valensin's Crown Point and Titus' Bullet. Before the first heat Crown Point was a favorite in the pools, selling for $30, while the other two in the field sold at from $10 to $37. After some considerable scoring the horses were tapped off evenly, with the favorite inside, Bullet Second and Cairo on the outside. Crown Point immediately took the lead, and although he made quite a bad break before reaching the first quarter, never lost his vantage to the end, but took the heat in 2:30½. Cairo acted very badly during the whole heat, making no less than six bad breaks, and but for running would have been distanced. Bullet trotted evenly and well, but hadn't speed enough to keep him to the front. After this heat Crown Point sold in the pools for $20, while Cairo and Bullet sold for $12 and $14 respectively. This time the horses got the send-off at the first attempt and a good one too. As in the former heat, Cairo acted badly, breaking and running frequently, and coming around the lower turn he ran clear around Crown Point, taking the pole from him, and Crown Point himself making a bad break in the home stretch was unable to pass him again and the heat was given to Cairo by a length, Bullet third; time, 2:26. For all Crown point had lost a heat, he still remained a favorite in the pools, bringing $20 to $10 for the field, with Bullet and Cairo in it. This time there was some scoring before the horses got a good send-off. From the start the little chestnut went for the big bay, taking him off his feet twice before reaching the first quarter, and would have passed him there but went up himself. As it was, the quarter was made in 25 secs. and the half in 1:14; from there the struggle was a hot one until inside the distance Crown Point again drove the big horse off his feet and took the heat right out of his teeth in 2:27½. Business in the pools now closed, as the most sanguine friends of the field gave up in despair. After the usual rest the horses were called for the final heat. At the first trial the horses were off at a good start, the favorite taking the lead, and though collared by Cairo at the half-mile he had no trouble taking the lead, especially as Cairo made several bad breaks before reaching the goal. Time, 2:30¾.

SUMMARIES.

Petaluma, September 1, 1882.—Purse of $300 for district two-year-olds, mile and repeat.

| | | | |
|---|---|---|---|
| G. C. Fountain enters blk f May Day | 2 | 1 | 1 |
| A. P. Whitney enters ch c Ideal | 1 | 2 | 2 |

Time—3:03, 3:02, 2:59.

Same day.—Purse $400. An agreed race for named horses.

| | | | | |
|---|---|---|---|---|
| G. Valensin names ch s Crown Point | 1 | 2 | 1 | 1 |
| J. Hughes names c h Cairo | 2 | 1 | 2 | 2 |
| L. H. Titus names b g Bullet | 3 | 3 | 3 | 3 |

Time—2:30½, 2:26, 2:27½, 2:30¾.

The fifth and last day of the fair started in fair and beautiful although quite warm. There were four races commencing with a ¾-mile dash between Quin Sabe and Stella Clark for a purse of $100 which was won easily by the former in 1:20½. The second race was a yearling trotting race, one mile out; the starters were P. C. Rierdon's Blue Gown, P. J. Shafter's Viking and Needham's Conemara, for a purse of $150 which was won by Blue Gown, Viking 2nd, Conemara 3d, Blue Gown winning the heat and money. After this the two most interesting races of the week came off, a pacing race for a purse of $500 and a trotting race for purse of $500. The starters in the pacing race were Johnny Wiegle, E. P. Dennison's ch m Lady Hayes and Valensin's br m Ouida, Lady Hayes being the favorite in the pools at $20 against $20 for the other two. With very little trouble they were tapped off to a good start with Ouida 1st, Wiegle 2nd, and Lady Hayes outside; before reaching the first quarter both Lady H. and Wiegle had passed Ouida, who seemed to lack in speed and soon was a long distance behind the other two, who were pacing swiftly along, Lady H. a little in advance, a position which she held until near the wire when she broke and Johnny, who was close up, passed her and took the heat by a length in 2:25½. After this heat Wiegle became a favorite, selling for $20 against $15 for the other two. After the usual breathing spell they again received a good send off, Wiegle at once taking the lead, Lady H. close up and Ouida trailing away behind; and thus in one, two, three order, Lady H. a good second, Ouida barely saving her distance. Time 2:28. Wiegle now became a greater favorite than ever, selling for $25 to the others $7, but alas for human calculation, in the third heat Ouida, who seemed to be as fresh as a daisy while the others were tired, passed Lady H. before reaching the first quarter and crawled up into Johnny's wheel where she stayed until near the wire when by a gallant spurt she passed him and took the heat in 2:26½. In spite of Wiegle having lost a heat he was still favorite, selling for $20 while he others brought $14, but the favorite had had his day and the brown mare took the lead at once and maintained it to the end, winning this the fourth heat in 2:30½. After this, pool selling was at a stand still for this race. The fifth and last heat was but a repetition of the preceding one, Ouida taking it easily in 2:32½, winning the race and first money, Wiegle 2nd and Lady H. 3d. During the races here and at Santa Rosa the knowing ones have had several severe attacks of dismay but this was perhaps the worst of all. The final race of the meeting was a trotting race for the 2:30 class for a purse of $500. The entries were A. Waldstein's b s Albert W., W. D. Hammond's g s Poscora Hayward, Goldsmith's br s Inca and Henry McConn's Blackmore. Albert W. was the favorite in the pools, selling for $25, Poscora $12 and the rest in the field for $8. There was a great deal of scoring before the horses got the word but finally they received a fair start with Albert at the pole, Blackmore second, Poscora third and Inca last. Albert W. at once took the lead and retained it although crowded close by Poscora, who took second place before arriving at the first quarter, but at third quarter Inca came up and took second place and in that order they came in, Albert W. first, Inca second, Poscora third, Blackmore behind. Time 2:27. After this heat, Albert W. brought $20 in the pools while all the rest sold in the field for $5. This time they got a good send-off with but little scoring. Immediately after the start Inca made a break and Poscora took second place and all the way around she made the favorite step very lively and he barely beat her in 2.26½, Inca third, Blackmore fourth. After this heat, as every one believed that Albert W. would win; there was no pool selling. The fourth heat it seemed as though they never would cease scoring but after more than a dozen trials they at last received the word. Before getting around the first turn Albert W. made a break and Poscora took the pole away from him and held it until near the end, and it seemed as though he would win the heat, but when near the end Albert W. pressed him so hard that he broke and ran under the wire and the heat was given to Albert W., Inca third, Blackmore last. Time 2:24¾. So ended a very exciting and interesting meeting.

SUMMARIES.

PETALUMA, Sept. 2d, 1882.—Pacing Race, purse $500 for following entries:

| | | | | | |
|---|---|---|---|---|---|
| G. Valensin enters br m Oneida | 3 | 3 | 1 | 1 | 1 |
| Walter Mead enter d g Johnny Wiegle | 1 | 1 | 2 | 2 | 2 |
| E. P. Dennison enters ch m Lady Hays | 2 | 2 | 3 | 3 | 3 |

Time: 2:25½, 2:28, 2:26½, 2:30½, 2:32½.

SAME DAY.—Trotting Race—Purse $500, with the following entries:

| | | | |
|---|---|---|---|
| A. Waldstein enters b s Albert W | 1 | 1 | 1 |
| W. D. Hammond enters gr s Poscora | 3 | 2 | 2 |
| J. A. Goldsmith enters br s Inca | 2 | 3 | 3 |
| Henry McConn enters gr g Blackmore | 4 | 4 | 4 |

Time: 2:27, 2:26½, 2:24¾.

The resume of the week's proceedings must indeed be most gratifying to the Directors of the association, and to all those who were interested in the exhibition and races. The fair was an unprecedented success, and the visitors and the citizens of Petaluma seemed to be mutually pleased at the fact. The full list of awards is prepared but the pressure in our space causes its publication to be postponed until our next issue. Many thanks are due to W. E. Cox, the efficient Secretary of the association, for information and favors granted to the attachees of the BREEDER AND SPORTSMAN during the fair.

## The Golden Gate Fair.

The fifth annual fair of the Golden Gate District Association, representing the counties of San Francisco, Alameda and Contra Costa commenced on Monday last under the most favorable auspices. The weather was delightful and the trip across the bay was most enjoyable, a light wind tempering the warm atmosphere, but not sufficiently strong to disturb the glass-like waters that reflected with beautiful precision the hull, masts and rigging of the countless merchantmen at anchor in the harbor. On arriving at the fair grounds it was evident that unusual interest was already maifested in the success of the fair, as the attendance was far in excess of that of the first day on previous years, lines of vehicles almost doubling on the quarter stretch, while a great many ladies and children were comfortably ensconsed in the grand stands where an excellent view could be obtained of the races, with a superb vista of mountain scenery in the Contra Costa Range, which forms such a pretty background to the Oakland track.

As is usually the case on the first day of the Fair, the interest was mainly centered in the races, as the exhibition of live stock and agricultural implements is seldom complete before the Wednesday, but there was no lack of interest on that account as this was a great gathering of some of the leading men of the State, and for the time being the fields of potatoes were vacated, and on all sides were heard hearty greetings and friendly discussions in regard to the relative performances of the chief representatives of the California turf.

Promptly at two o'clock the horses were called up for the first race, the Golden Gate stake, a dash of three-quarters of a mile for two-year-olds, $50 each, $15 forfeit with $150 added in which were originally five entries, but as Satinet and Panama were absentees, the issue of the first struggle was left to Satanella of the Palo Alto stable, May B, belonging to Mr. Put. Robson and Mr. Coutts's filley, Flou Flou. As shown at the spring meeting of the blood horse association, these horses all possess a fair amount of speed, but they cannot as yet aspire to first-class honors, and the betting, as the result showed, ought to have been about even, but there were so many rumors bruited around in regard to a private trial at which Satanella had given a most satisfactory answer that there was a rush to get in, and just previous to the start she brought $20 against $5 each for May B and Flou Flou. As usual there was some delay in getting the horses to the post, and in this and the succeeding races much valuable time was lost at the starting post, that necessitated the postponement of a part of the final race until the next day. After a slight break away the fillies were sent on their destination with Flou Flou the quickest on her feet, but she was soon joined by Satanella, who ran with her neck-and-neck down the home-stretch until within a hundred yards of the wire, when Flou Flou was beaten, and the rider of Satanella slightly easing, George Hanson, who had been trailing within reaching distance, came up with a rush and May B won by nearly half a length in 1:17, which was not particularly fast, as the track was in fine order. The backers of the favorite were rather blue, as they maintained that it was the best jockey and not the best horse that had won.

The next race was the Alameda stake, a dash of a mile and a half for three-year-olds, $75 entrance, $25 forfeit, with $175, in which of the five original entries there were only two that sported silk, they being the Duke of Monday and Precious, the absentees being Fostress, Forest King and Maria E, the latter having been sent to Chico to fill her engagement there. At first the betting was pretty even but again there were sundry rumors in regard to the great improvement shown in the running of the Palo Alto filly and she gradually rose in the betting until the odds of $30 to $20 were freely laid upon her chances. Once more a great deal of time was lost, and the Duke in refusing to face the starter spilled Patsey Duffy on the soft earth as he backed suddenly around. At last, after half an hour's delay, they were sent off together and from the start it was evident that Precious was to make the running, as she led for a mile by two lengths, when the Duke moved up, and thence home to the wire the race was of the most exciting character, the horses and whips and spurs being locked together to the last stride, when the Duke succeeded in winning by half a dozen inches, amid the greatest excitement. The time was 2:41½, the fastest first being made in 2:50.

The third race was the Pardee stake heats of a mile for all ages, the starters Red Boy and Night Hawk. The betting was slightly in favor of the horse, and had the speculating fraternity known how good the mare was the odds would have been large on the other side. A capital start was given them at the first time of scoring. The mare had the inside and she commenced the work at a rapid rate. The quarter was made in 25 seconds, the half mile in 50¼, the mare still leading. She was yet in the lead at the three-quarters in 1:16 and the heat looked as though it was a foregone conclusion that she must win. But Patsy was riding for dear life and he managed to bring the horse under the wire a few inches in advance of the mare in the fastest time ever made in California, 1:42½. The result of this heat changed the betting in favor of Red Boy, though it was conceded that should he fall off a trifle the mare would beat him. She made a good effort though the horse won in 1:45½. Then came the trotting for a purse of $600, 2:40 class; in which were Freestone, Edwin Forest, Manon, Louis D—, Marin, San Mateo Belle, Vanderlynn, Frank Moscow, and Big Lize. In the betting, Manon was soon installed as first choice owing to her private reputation for great speed, and she brought $80 against $18 for San Mateo Belle, and $10 for Edwin Forrest, and $60 for the others comprised in the field. The usual difficulty was experienced by the Judge in getting so large a field away from the score on something approaching even terms, but all were trotting equally except Venderlynn, whose rank behavior betrayed his experience. Manon made her way to the front at the outset and successfully withstood all assaults, Louis D contesting the last quarter in a grand speedy style but being obliged to content himself with second place, the field ranging after him with Big Lize third, Freestone fourth, San Mateo Belle fifth, Frank Moscow sixth, Marin seventh, Edwin Forrest eighth, and Vanderlynn ninth. Time 2:26.

Manon took a still higher place in the betting after the first heat. Some scoring followed the call in the second attempt, the drivers at one turn mistaking the signal of the judges and going to the ¼ pole before they pulled up. When they did get the word on a tolerable start Manon and Louis D. both rushed for the point and in the brush Louis D skipped and swerved, colliding with Manon and splitting a wheel in the latter's sulky, but fortunately not causing any serious accident. The mare got a clear track before her near the ½ and although there was a momentary bunch at the head of the stretch she came under the wire with a length of daylight behind her, Marin second, San Mateo Belle third, Edwin Forrest fifth, Big Lize sixth, Frank Moscow seventh, Louis D eighth, Freestone distanced. Time 2:27.

In the pools Manon was now barred. In this heat Wm. Donathan essayed the management of Vanderlynn without much better success than had attended the efforts of Mr. Farrel. At the start Big Lize made a disastrous break and dropped to a hopeless position. Louis D and San Mateo Belle went to the quarter at a rapid gait, yoked like a double team, the favorite being seemingly boxed and Vanderlynn supplying a wing accompaniment between the leading pair and the rear guard. Positions were not materially changed for the rest of the mile, Louis D winning the heat in an exciting finish by half a length, San Mateo Belle second, Vanderlynn third, Manon fourth, Moscow fifth, Edwin Forrest sixth, Marin sevent and Big Lize eighth. Time 2:27½. Mr. Donathan complained that some loose horses running in the inclosure caused his horse to act badly and that was probably the reason why Vanderlynn was not penalized for running. As the hour was late and the shadows of evening drawing in the judges declared the finish of the race postponed until Tuesday afternoon.

On the second day the weather was delightful in the extreme and as there was a full programme of unusual interest, the attendance was far in excess of that of the previous day, the number of ladies on the grand stands and in the many vehicles that lined the quarter stretch giving an animated appearance to the track. The horses of the 2:40 class were called up promptly, but Edwin Forrest was withdrawn on account of lameness. There appeared to be such an unanimity of opinion among the drivers of the horses to make it "hot" for the favorite, that they scored time and again without an appreciable effort at getting together, and it was but at the fourteenth attempt that they were tapped off, Manon being the favorite at $30 against $6 for Louis D. and $7 for the field. Manon broke a few yards from the start, which was a very fair one, considering the number of horses, and Vanderlynn at first appeared in the van, but as he left his feet at the quarter post Louis D. assumed the lead, and Manon was seen coming through the ruck and taking a commanding position at his wheel. Thus they trotted well around the upper turn when Manon closed up and they were head and head until half down the homestretch, when the mare drew away and won the heat and race in 2:24, Louis D. being second and taking second and San Mateo Belle the third money. Manon made a very favorable debut and Mr. Knox, the former owner of Nutwood, who was present on the track, was much pleased with her performance as when he sold her with other stock he prophesied that she alone would bring back more than the entire purchase money. She is grandly bred, her sire being three-quarters of the same blood as Maude S, while the sire of her dam is the first son of Rysdyk's Hambletonian ever brought to this coast. Her gait is almost perfect, throwing the fore feet so well to the front that she covers more ground than might be imagined with a casual glance at her stride. If she continues to improve as in the past year, she will be one of the most valuable mares of her class on the coast.

In the 2:30 purse that followed, the betting was $100 in favor of Sweetness, $45 for the field and $50 for Albert W., although it was generally known that the driver of the stallion had requested the permission to withdraw the horse, as he did not deem him to be in a condition to trot in such company, but the request was not granted. After six attempts they got off to a good even start save that Poscora Hayward, who appeared to be a little lame in her exercise was in the rabble and broke at the draw gate. Sweetness at once took the lead with Nellie R in close attendance, while Albert W trained, as they passed the half mile in 1:12½: it was evident that the heat lay between the two mares, and Nellie breaking at the distance Sweetness won by a length in the fast time of 2:22, Albert W cleverly saving his distance and Poscora Hayward having hopelessly broken down. The next heat was almost a repetition of the previous one as when Nellie was at the wheel of the favorite she broke and Sweetness jogged in, the time being 2.24½. In the third heat the same tactics were resorted to, the mares trotting fast and furiously for the lead, while the horse made a waiting race of it. Sweetness and Nellie were lapped all the way round and the latter, keeping well to her stride, won by a neck after an exciting finish in 2:23½. Sweetness was still by far the favorite as Nellie was tiring after her exertions, but in the next heat Albert W. was on his good behavior and closed up on Sweetness at the three quarter pole, where he made a break, then quickly regaining his stride he was soon at the mare's wheel, but another skip lost him the advantage, and yet within the distance he came with a rushing speed and beat Sweetness out by somewhat more than half a length in 2:26½. The backers of the favorite felt somewhat aggrieved at the decision, as the horse had made two breaks in the heat, but they should have remembered that in each instance Albert W. perceptibly lost ground so the general uninterested opinion coincided with that of the judges. There was now a good deal of lofty betting around the pool box, and as those who had pinned their faith on Sweetness were desirous of hedging, the result was to make Albert W. first choice at $100 against $40 each for the two mares. The horse made the pace to and back stretch when he went up and Nellie took the lead, while Sweetness was trailing far in the rear. On the home stretch Albert trotted very fast but broke and, although he was quickly caught and came again, he was beaten out after a desperate and close finish in 2:26½, with Sweetness distanced. Still heavier betting on even terms, and Nellie trying to outfoot her rival who, making a break at the upper turn, seemed to have lost his chance of the heat, but he had the speed of the mare and was soon again on even terms and then outfooted her at every stride and won easily in 2:25. The last heat was never in danger, as Albert W. trotted squarely in the lead all the way around and won the heat and race in 2:26½. This was, thus far, the most exceptional trot of the meeting. Then came the pacing race for a purse of $500 in which were Corette, Lady Hayes, Oakland Boy and Ouida, the first named fetching $60 in the pools against $25 for Ouida and $20 for the field. The race was a very one-sided affair for although Lady Hayes showed in front to the half mile in the first heat, Corette went to the front and was never headed again throughout the whole race, winning in three straight heats in 2:23½, 2:22½ and 2:24, Ouida taking second and Lady Hayes third money, while Oakland Boy was distanced in the first heat.

On the Wednesday there was again an increase in the attendance and the weather simply delightful. The first race on the card was a two-mile dash, $100 each, $25 forfeit with $200 added, in which was entered Precious, Mollie H, Fred Collier, Night Hawk and Red Boy, and there was every expectation to see a rattling good race, but the two last had probably had enough running for a time after their mile and repeat on the previous Monday, and as Fred Collier was also an absentee the race was reduced to a fizzle. Precious was sent along briskly with the odds of a $100 to $20 on her, and at the end of half a mile she had Mollie H in difficulties, and hence bore the only chance of her been beaten was in her falling down. Precious made the first mile in 1:45 and the entire distance in 3:36, a very creditable showing that demonstrated the fact that had she not made a waiting race of it she would have beaten the Duke of Monday in the Alameda stakes, also run on the previous Monday. Then came the races for the three-year-olds in which were Adrian, Olivette, Bonnie Wood and Fred Arnold, the former being a big favorite[?] $40 against $20 for all others combined. Antaeo, belonging to J. C. Simpson was also entered in this race, but he had to be withdrawn on account of an attack of epizooty. This was also an uninteresting race as the other horses were no match whatever for Adrian. When the gong sounded for the start in the first heat the driver of Olivette mistook it for the recall signal and the horses were well on their way before he discovered his error. Bonnie Wood was for a good while in the lead, but she broke and afterwards the result was a mere exhibition of fine speed for Adrian, who made the quarter in 43 seconds, the half 1:22½ and the mile in 2:24½, winning by ten lengths from Bonnie Wood, and Olivette being distanced. The second heat was a mere repetition, the time for the winner being 42½ seconds for the quarter, 1:21½ to the half and 2:37½ to the mile, the placing being the same as before. In the final heat, Adrian won as he liked with Bonnie Wood second, the first quarter being in 40½ seconds, the half mile in 1:17½ and the mile in 2:33½.

The stock parade on Thursday was a grand display of all that connoisseurs do most admire in the higher order of the lower animals. The attendance of visitors was large, and with the neighing of high-spirited horses, the lowing of cattle and the stately procession on the course, they were presented with a living, breathing panorama that indicted[?] their closest attention and elicited continual expressions of pleasureable surprise. In affairs of this kind the interest increases as time advances and culminates on the last day, but the inexorable necessity of going to press on time knows no su_h law as delay, and all reference to the incidents and exhibits of the fair must be hurried and incomplete at this time, and reserved for digestion and elaborate treatment in the future.

The race for the 2:27 class, which followed, was shorn of much of its attraction from the fact of the forced withdrawal of Romero and from the rumour that Belle Echo was not quite herself. Consequently Brigadier was a great favorite in the pools at $100 to $40. The first heat seemed to be trotted slowly by mutual consent, Brigadier assuming the lead of about two lengths and keeping it to the end, in 2:27. The second heat was very interesting, for although the mare broke at the first turn and lost four lengths, Belle Echo, showing some of her famous speed, got at Brigadier's wheel on entering the homestretch and beat him out by a head in 2:23½. This result brought the mare into a better position in the pools, which she could not maintain in the succeeding heat. To an excellent start, Brigadier at a rapid gate went to the front at the first turn and led by a length at the half mile in 1:12½, and thence home. The result appeared to be in doubt to the last moment, as the finish was very close, the stallion winning a well-fought contest in 2:22½, both showing in the last half mile first and square trotting. It was now evident that the mare was not equal to the task of beating Brigadier, as he led from start to finish in 2:24½, and took the race, but at some future day she will take her revenge when at her best form. Altogether it was a fair race, with some fine bursts of speed for the two given horses.

On the fourth day the attendance was much larger during the morning hours, and the stock attracted much attention, the prevailing opinion being that the parade was a great credit to the Golden Gate Fair. Towards the afternoon, when the San Francisco delegation had arrived, the grounds presented a very animated appearance, there being a large number of ladies present on horseback, in carriages, and in the grand stands. The first was a trot for two-year-olds, in which there were but two nominations, both from the same stable, Nebuska, belonging to L. J. Rose, and Ruby, owned by T. W. Mackey, they both being sired by Sultan. As it was understood that this would be a real trial of speed, a good deal of money was invested, Nebuska holding the best position in the betting. Nebuska made the pace and was leading at the quarter in 37½ sos. to two lengths, but at the half, in 1:13, the gap had been reduced by half their distance, and Ruby gradually moving up the race appeared to be very evenly and steadily contested until the finish, when it was seen that Nebuska had a few inches the advantage, passing the wire in 2:20½, the best time made in the two-year-old form in a race, Eva having trotted at the last Sacramento fair against time in 2:26, and the later performances of Wildflower

in 2:21, is not likely to be forgotten for years and years to come. The second heat was a repetition of the first, save that at the distance when on pretty even terms, Ruby stayed the longest and won handily in 2:24½, the quarter having been made in 36½, the half in 1:10½. In the final heat Nebuska was so tired that she was not persevered with and Ruby jogged in, the time being 2:40. Nebuska was beaten, but then it must be remembered that she was sick for a long time this last summer, and is yet weak from its effects, and it may be she will show better powers of endurance when she has fully regained her strength. Mr. John W. Mackey was present and received many hearty congratulations on the success of Ruby, who promises to be a great credit to the Sunny Slope Stud Farm.

Then came a special trot between Frank Moscow, Marin, Rowdy Boy and Vanderlynn, the latter being installed a great favorite, and as he was well driven and in prime condition the race was never in danger, he coming out first in every heat, but the third one was given to Rowdy Boy, as Vanderlynn had indulged in some running in which the judges were of the opinion that he had gained too much ground before he was brought to his gait. The time was 2:30, 2:27, 2:30½, 2:28½. The races were brought to a conclusion with a selling price of $250, a dash of a mile, in which Euchre, with $100 to $20 on his chances, fairly galloped away from Haddington and Inauguration in 1:43½, and although the winner was entered to be sold at $300, there was no bid made for over and above that amount.

### The Horses.

Of the thoroughbreds in the stallion class, the veteran Thad Stevens is present in fine form, also Wm. Boot's Nathan Coombs by Lodi and Ira J. Gift's Iller by Wildidle.

Thoroughbred stallions one year old : J. C. Simpson's Sir Thad by Thad Stevens, dam Lady Amanda; Ira J. Gift's Billy Foot by Norfolk, dam Kate Gift.

Colt under one year : J. C. Simpson's Cito, by Joe Hooker, dam Too Soon.

Thoroughbred mare three years old and upward : J. C. Simpson's Too Soon, by Norfolk, dam Lady Davis.

Mare two years old : Ira J. Gift's Miss Gift, by Wildidle, dam Kate Gift.

J. C. Simpson's Lady Viva, by Three Cheers, dam Lady Amanda.

Mares one year : John Leach's Miss Stevens, by Thad Stevens, dam Minnie.

Families : R. P. Clement's Thad Stevens and 5 colts.

Families other than thoroughbred : Antonio Bellina, Hayward's General Grant and five colts.

Stallions of all work three years old and over : A. A. Smiler, Plesoonton, Carl Carr.

R. C. Baldwin, Danville, Gold Hill.

Henry Pierce, San Francisco, Alonzo Hayward.

Antonio Bellina, Haywards, Gen. Grant.

Ira Munion, Dixon, Pedro Jr.

E. Barnes, San Jose, Don Pedro.

Chisholm & Sacksider, Oakland, Black Prince.

L. Hewlett, Oakland, George Washington.

Stallions two years : J. J. Shafter, Olema, Black Prince.

Antonio Bellina, Haywards, May Boy.

W. S. Brown, Petaluma, Monarch.

Stallions one year : Antonio Bellina, Haywards, Frank.

Mares three year old and over : L. Hewlett, Oakland, Brownie H.

Antonia Bellina, Haywards, Dolly.

Mares one year : R. P. Clement Alameda, Lugina.

Ben E. Harris, St. Francisco, Abbotine

Filly under one year : Chisholm & Sacksider, Oakland, Lill.

Roadster stallions four years and over : W. K. Robinson, Santa Ana, Odd Fellow.

J. J. Shafter, Olema, Rustic.

W. D. Hammond, Oakland, Grand Moor.

Henry Pierce, San Francisco, Alonzo Hayward;

E. Stone, San Leandro, James Lick.

Stallion three years : J. F. Houghton, Oakland, Belmont Chief.

Stallion two years : Chas. Duerr, Sunol, Meteor.

Geo. Copsey, Oakland, Redwood.

L. Hewlett, Oakland, Echo Jr.

J. M. Learned, Stockton, Harmony.

Yearlings : J. J. Shafter, Olema, Sir King.

J. A. Goldsmith, Oakland, Sidney.

J. A. Goldsmith, Oakland, Judge S.

Antonio Bellina, Haywards, Elijah Mitchell.

J. C. Simpson, Oakland, Antevolo.

Sucking colts : W. D. Hammond, Oakland, Tom Moore.

Same, Maid of the Oak.

Antonio Bellina, Haywards, Royal Boy.

B. C. Harris, San Francisco, Littleton.

Same, Style.

Mares or geldings, three years : W. K. Robinson, Santa Ana, Patriarch.

D. Derry, Oakland, Molly.

W. D. Hammond, Oakland, Lady Lightfoot.

Same, Hambletonian.

S. Sonestock, Oakland, Prince.

Two years old : L. J. Rose, Los Angeles, No Name.

Yearlings : Chas. Duerr, Sunol, Goblette.

B. E. Harris, San Francisco, Rose Abbott.

Sucking colt : W. D. Hammond, Oakland, Maid of the Oak.

B. E. Harris, San Francisco, Littleton.

Same, Style.

Roadster matched span : C. Younger, San Jose, Whisper and Mate.

S. W. Sawyer, Oakland, Prince and Bill.

Newland & Pumyea, Oakland, Jack and John.

Draft Stallions : A. J. Pierce, Point Reyes, Charlemagne.

W. S. Brown, Petaluma, Tornado.

Chisholm & Sackrider, Oakland, French Spy (imp).

Same, Paquain.

Same, French Spy 2d.

Two years old : F. Thalman, Pinole, Pinole Chief.

One year old : Chisholm & Sacksider, Decide.

Under one year old : Chisholm Sacksider, Spy Jr.

Mare three years old : Chisholm & Sacksider, Kate.

W. S. Brown, Petaluma, Charlotte.

Chisholm & Sacksider, Lizzie.

Mare, under one year : Chisholm & Sacksider, Puss.

Carriage Horses : Mrs. Rose Duffy, Oakland, Jack and George.

Saddle Horses : B. E. Harris, Mike Peer.

Same, Major Jacks.

Ira Munion, John Henry.

### Cattle—Jerseys.

Henry Pierce of San Francisco, who is an enthuseastic admirer of the Channel Island strains, exhibits 19 head of thoroughbred Jerseys, at the head of which stands imported Victor of Yerba Buena, nine years old, who arrived this season. The yearling bulls William of Scituate and Electra[?] stand next, followed by Como of unadulterated blood, one of which, Fancy of Yerba Buena, is a granddaughter of Coomassie,

so celebrated in the annals of the Jerseys. Four yearling heifers and two yearling bulls, and four heifer and two bull calves less than one year old, make up Mr. Peiroe's herd at the fair grounds.

### Guernseys.

Mr. Pierce also shows five head of Guernseys, the bull Champion of Guernsey and four cows, all imported.

### Ayrshires.

Geo. Bennet of Redwood is the only breeder of Ayrshires represented and his exhibit includes the bulls Archie, 3 years, Lindo, 2 years, Macbeth, 1 year, and bull calf Melcomb, with six cows, all sleek and shining in the snug and diminutive form characteristic of the race.

### Durhams.

Of these the delegates were numerous. Col. Younger of Forest Hooker Farm, San Jose, eighteen head, the patriarch of which is the second Duke of Alameda, 4 years old, third Duke of Alameda, Forest King, and fourth Duke of Forest House, each 1 year following in the order named. The Colonel shows five cows over 1 year, four heifers 1 year, two bulls and two heifer calves.

### Paige Bros.

Of Sonoma, show fourteen head of Durhams—the bull El Medico, 6 years, at the head, with Lord of Clover and Cherry Prince, each two years, following; four cows, over one year; four yearling heifers, two bull calves, and one heifer calf under one year, complete the list. As may be expected, the stalls occupied by Col. Younger and Paige Bros. are much frequented by visitors, the opportunities for comparison being the leading attraction; but if a line can be drawn between the two herds, it must be done by some technical expert, and even then it would probably be more a question of predisposition than judgment, so even is the balance and so perfect in detail do these different collections appear to be.

### Miscellaneous.

In addition to the fine displays made by the systematic, in one sense, professional breeders, there are some by private parties that are of a character that evince a pardonable pride on the part of the exhibitors in their family pets, J. S. Wall, Oakland, shows bull Medoc, 2 years; cows, Young Duchess, 4 years, and Bonita, 3 years, and heifer calf, 6 months—all blue-blood Jersey.

P. J. Shafter, Olema, Jersey cow, Mouse, 4 years.

J. S. Emory, Oakland, Jersey bull, Terry, 1 year.

Wm. Mahoney, Berkeley, Jersey bull, Young Glory, 1 year.

F. K. Shattuck, Berkeley, Jersey bull, St. Valentine, 19 months.

A. J. Snyder, Oakland, Jersey bull, James Hayward, and cows, Lizzie, 6 years, and Dot, 1 year.

Mrs. R. P. Clement, Alameda, Jersey cows, Jessie Weeks Second, 6 years, Alfalfa, 4 years, Nancy, 2 years; heifers, Vira, 20 months, and Bunny S., 15 months.

F. K. Shattuck, Berkeley, Alderney cow.

### Sheep.

Col. Younger exhibits Cotswold ram, Hancock, and five ewes.

George Bank, Redwood, Southdown ram "No name."

J. H. Strobridge, Haywards, Spanish Merino ram and a pair of fine ewes; also a pair of fine lambs.

Woolsey & Son, Sonoma county, ram and pair of fine ewes and pair of fine lambs.

### Swine.

In this department A. C. Dietz exhibits a pair of Berkshires, and T. McInnery a Berkshire boar.

## BICYCLING.

Moore, the winner of the one and twenty-five mile English amateur championships, is now in this country, and will no doubt shortly give American riders a chance to find out what their relative speed is.

Two or three entries are promised from the professional ranks to compete for the prizes offered by the management of the Golden Gate Fair, and there will also be some fancy trick riding. This part of the programme takes place Saturday, the 9th.

Notwithstanding the prediction of one of the daily papers of this city, the entries for the athletic meeting of the 23d promise to be sufficiently numerous to make a series of very interesting races, with a good prospect that the Pacific coast record will be broken.

It is to be hoped that when the home production commences, the makers will carefully study the abandoned experiments, as well as the popular styles of the numerous English makers, so that whatever they produce shall at least be equal to what has already been done.

The Eastern bicyclist is not happy. With the thermometer away up in the nineties, and the perspiration starting from every pore as the least prospect of exertion, he is much more inclined to lounge at the various beaches, bathe in the surf, or taking yacht excursions than to work his own passage upon the inland.

The demand for tricycles in this country is slowly but steadily increasing. While the the three-wheeler is not likely to supplant the bicycle, it will make it possible for a larger number to enjoy the pleasure of wheeling, and not the least of the enjoyment will be the rides upon the "sociable" or double machine, with a lady companion.

The American Star bicycle, having the small wheel in front, has been pretty thoroughly tested by the Louisville (Ky.) bicyclists. One of the number purchased a Star, which not being approved by his fellow wheelmen, they commenced a systematic endeavor to run it out. The result has been to win friends for the novel machine, which has proved itself about equal to the old one in climbing far ahead of it on a down grade, and is not quite up to it on a level.

A Buffalo (N. Y.) man is reported to have constructed a steam-engine-driven tricycle. The engine is placed between the seat and the forward wheel, to which it gives the upright pattern and the fuel is gasoline which is supplied by pipes from a tank beneath the seat; the engine is of one and one-half horse power, and it is said that a consumption of one gallon of gasoline per hour will drive the machine for nine hours at the rate of fifteen or twenty miles per hour. We prefer to see it tested before giving entire credence to this statement as this is not the first experiment of this sort which we have seen.

Miss Lillian T. Smith, a young lady only eleven years of age, gave an exhibition of her shooting with the Ballard rifle last Tuesday at Petaluma. Of 170 balls thrown up twenty feet, twenty feet distant, she only missed nineteen. She shot at the rate of ten shots in 48 seconds. Very good for a little one.

## THE GUN.

### The Shooting Season.

To the Editor of the Breeder and Sportsman: The commencement of another shooting season is almost with us again, and for some weeks past the note of preparation for its coming is to be heard on all sides. The various gun stores seem well patronized by sportsmen laying in their stock of ammunition, ordering cartridges to be loaded, having their breech-loaders overhauled and put in perfect order, while a few are purchasing new ones. The new hammerless gun seems to be working its way into public favor, and we might as well acknowledge the fact at once that it is likely to become "the gun of the future." To the sportsman who handles and examines one of these recent guns for the first time it strikes him as if there was something wanting about it, the absence of hammers being most noticeable, but I am informed by those who have used these guns at the trap and on the field that nothing would induce them to go back to the hammer gun. All the crack makers of London and Birmingham are now turning out these beautiful weapons by hundreds. On the streets and on roads leading from the city are now to be seen sportsmen leading dogs, giving them the exercise needful to get them into condition for the opening day of the quail, etc. It is a well known fact, however, that the majority of our city bred and raised dogs are notoriously unfit for the duties required of them at the beginning of the shooting season. A dog with four or five months' rest in the interval between the closing of one season and opening of another soon runs into fat, gets lazy from want of proper exercise, and unless his owner begins in good time to put his animal into proper condition for hard work, the result is a used-up and foot-sore animal at the end of the first day, and unless the sportsman has an extra dog or a pair to fall back upon his pleasure is seriously interfered with.

A sportsman should begin to work his dog or dogs into condition at least six weeks before the shooting season opens, add the writer knows of no better plan for a city man to exercise his animals than by a sharp drive with a horse and buggy, or a gallop after a saddle horse over the hills or by-roads leading from town, the dog following behind, or, if the time and occupation of the sportsman will not permit of the above course, then to get up in the morning an hour earlier than usual and give the dog a spin around the two or three blocks in the vicinity, or on any road convenient, winding up with if bath or swim in a pond near by, or in the bay if possible. A good bath freshens up a dog wonderfully after exercise and is beneficial to him otherwise. It may be necessary to give the dog a little opening or reducing medicine and I think before beginning a course of training is indispensable and renders the animal more fit to receive his exercise. As to the relative merits of the different gun bores, 10, 12 or 16, I think this is altogether a matter of fancy. Much has been written pro and con on this subject in the various sporting papers, notably in the *American Field*, but write us men may from their various standpoints as to what they may consider as the best thing to use, men of sense and discretion will use their own judgment in the selection of a gun and be governed more by the style of shooting they are likely to have. For the exclusive wild-fire shooter, there can be no question, I presume, upon the merits of the larger bores and heavier guns, where large charges of powder are necessary, and for the upland shooter, (meaning at quail, snipe, etc. etc.), the small bores and lighter guns will be preferred. If I may be permitted an opinion on these matters, my preference for an all-round gun, fit to stop anything that flies up to 50 yards if properly bored, loaded and held straight, is the 12-bore of from 8 to 8½ lbs. weight, but if my extra, over shall permit of my being the owner of a pair of guns, then one should be a 12 of above weight and one a 10-bore; the first for the trap (if a trap shooter), ducks, etc., and the second for the rugged and steep hillsides of our State for quail, of say 6¼ pounds weight, neither barrel of the gun to be choked in the slightest degree. For the 12 and heavier gun I should have the sight either a perfect cylinder or not choked more than five thousandths of an inch, the left barrel about a modified choke, or as it is known in England by the term "a gunmaker's parlance of "shooting choke." Both guns to have the same bend, cast-off and pull of triggers as nearly as possible, to be made by a skillful gunmaker. Judging from my own observation, and from reports made by reliable and truthful sportsmen who have been in various parts of the State, the prospects for quail shooting are excellent.

The breeding season has been a very open one, the late rains to destroy the eggs or chill the young birds to death, and vermin, particularly ground, is being cleaned out rapidly. Every year, as far as I have seen on my own beat and passing through a good stretch of country adjacent to it, the birds are very numerous and were advanced, in fact, two weeks ago. I saw quail in Marin county of this year as large as the parent birds, the difference being only observable in plumage. I think I can safely congratulate my brother triggers in a promise of a very successful quail season.

Of ducks it is almost too early to speculate on the prospects as to what showing we are likely to have, but if the reports from the various marshes are to be believed the name of the local bred birds is legion. I really hope it is so, to make up, in some measure, for the disappointments of last year, which, in duck hunter's language, was known as an "off" year.

One word or two more and this article, such as it is, closes. It is a little bit of advice, especially to quail shooters. Remember that, in a great measure, it is to the farmer and rancher the quail shooter is indebted for the majority of his pleasure in quest of this game little bird. We should endeavor to identify ourselves with the interests of the farmer, and not antagonize him, as many of our thoughtless sportsmen do by leaving his gates open, and tearing down his fences, permitting his cattle to stray hither and thither, much to his disgust and often at his expense, and in a variety of other ways annoy him. This is not the way, take my word for it, for the quail sportsman to do. Let us be friendly to the farmer. Close the gates after you, climb the fences instead of pulling them down; and, above all things, be careful of fire, the worst enemy the rancher has to encounter and the most difficult to control when once it gains headway.

It has been the experience of the writer within, the past twenty-five years that eighteen times out of twenty, by the sportsman going direct to the house of the farmer or rancher and asking for permission to shoot over his lands, it has been cheerfully and readily granted, and frequently I have found the farmer or one of his boys, if he has any, willing to "show where the birds are located, and very often followed by a kind invitation to join the family at dinner. Therefore I

'dvise, let us be the farmer's friends, and he will reciprocate 'n common. Human nature is pretty much the same all over the civilized world.

In conclusion, my best wishes go with the California sportsman for a pleasant and successful season.

ANGLO CALIFORNIAN.

---

### Alameda Club at Bird's Point.

Saturday last the Alameda County Sportsman's Club met at Bird's Point for their last shoot this season, but very few of the members put in an appearance, only seven shooting.

The match was for the first and second medals, ten birds, twenty-one yards rise, eighty yards boundary. The judges chosen were Fred Butler and George Downey; and T. R. Hart was referee. The first medal was won by H. Havens, with the only clean score, Mr. Crellin retaining the second with nine kills. The birds were the finest lot that ever came from the trap, which accounts for the poor score.

After the club shoot, several matches followed. The first was a five-bird match; with fourteen entries, $2.50 each, and was divided between Mr. Gordon, Mr. Havens and Mr. Gallindo, with five kills. The next was a freeze-out, with five entries, $2.50 each, and was won by Lambert after nine kills. The next was a match of the same kind, nine entries, and was won by Henry Basford with only two kills.

| W. Crellin | 1 0 1 1 1 1 1 1 1 1—9 |
| C. E. Hopkins | 1 0 1 0 0 1 1 1 1 0—6 |
| A. Havens | 1 1 1 1 1 1 1 1 1 1—10 |
| W. W. Haskell | 1 1 1 1 1 1 1 1 1 1—10 |
| H. Mahew | 0 1 1 1 1 1 0 0 1 0—5 |
| F. Norton | 1 1 0 1 1 0 1 1 1 1—8 |
| J. H. Frisch | 1 1 0 1 1 0 1 0 1 1—7 |
*Dead out of bounds.

---

### Wild Rice for Ducks.

BATTLE MOUNTAIN, Nev., Aug. 25.

Editors Bee: Agreeably to promise in my article of last week, I submit a few remarks on the subject of wild rice planting in the duck marshes. Very few so-called sportsmen, even in the Northern and Eastern States, are fully aware of the great benefits derived from the sowing of this peculiar water-fowl feed. The consequence is that the knowing ones keep quiet and sow it in their favorite lakes and rivers and afterwards boast of their large bags of game to the uninitiated. I will relate one instance which will answer for many which I could repeat, and that is in regard to Horseshoe Lake, some seventeen miles north of Omaha, Nebraska. This lake was never considered good duck ground previously, owing to its close proximity to the city, and also to the Missouri river. The Omaha Sportsman's Club got the hint of sowing wild rice in the above lake from the Chicago *Field*. The result is that now they have the very best of duck, goose and swan shooting near at home, something they never dreamed of previously. One celebrated bag of game was made at this lake by General Crook of Indian fighting fame, when he killed and bagged in four hours, over decoys, 276 ducks—an average of sixty-nine per hour, with a ten-bore gun, shooting all on the wing and nearly all single. This was in 1880; and again, in 1881, General Crook and John Petty (of the firm of Petty & Collins, Omaha), at the annual club hunt of the Omaha Sportsman's Club, in the Spring of 1881, killed 580 ducks, brants and swans, all told, in ten hours' shooting with No. 10 guns. This is an average of fifty-eight per hour, or twenty-nine per hour for each shooter for ten hours. Many bags, nearly equal, have been made since, but I know of none at this spot. This shows the great advantage derived from the planting of wild rice, and I could give similar instances where it has been used in barren lakes and rivers in Nebraska, Illinois, Indiana, Michigan, Ohio and many other States, where the results were the same. When once rooted, wild rice generally crowds all other weeds out, and when ripe in the fall looks like an immense grain field from a distance, the straw being very similar to that of oats, excepting it grows from 4 to 8 feet high. It is much easier to get through and better for ducks to work in than the weeds, being more easily broken. The water-fowls feed on it from the time it sprouts in the spring until it ripens, and when the seeds fall they gather it from the bottom by diving. All kinds of water-fowl, from swans to teals, feed on it the year round, and some never leave a rice patch to balk, preferring to remain the year through. Water-fowlers claim that the birds get fat and lazy from eating it and have not the energy or desire to leave. It spreads rapidly, and a few 'acres sown will be scattered by the birds in a few years, spreading it over an entire lake or marsh.

Wild rice should be sown in the fall when wild seeds ripen and drop. All that is necessary is to sow it in the water from one to six inches deep, and also some should be scattered on the ground that overflows just before the fall rains set in. Some of the seeds will catch the next spring, and water-fowls will begin to feed on the young grass as soon as it is up, thereby insuring their presence ever after in increasing numbers; for every bird that has once been there and raised young will return with her young in the fall, and the young in turn will bring their young in the future, so they constantly increase year by year, and I would advise your sportsmen who have leased grounds to try it this fall. The seed can be procured of the editor of the *American Field*, E. Eaton, of Chicago, W. H. Holsbird of Valparaiso, Ind., or Petty & Collins, Omaha. It costs in the neighborhood of $12 per barrel. We have ordered some to sow this fall from the latter firm, which we propose to sow in the upper Humboldt river, in Nevada, which will eventually spread to the sink of the Humboldt, and your sportsmen must look out on Nevada will hold your ducks away until the last hole is frozen over with ice. Try wild rice, brother sportsmen.—*Hoosier*, in *Sacramento Bee*.

---

### The Watsonville Pigeon Shooting.

The match that came off last Sunday at Camp Goodall Driving Park was not so successful in all its details as had been anticipated. Although the Gilroy delegation included some good representatives shots, the list of entries was not numerous, a fact that may be attributed to the lack of birds on the grounds. We take the following account of the match from the *Bajaronian*:

"The match commenced at 1 o'clock and lasted about two hours. A sharp breeze blew across the grounds, but as the contestants shot with the wind it did not interfere with them but harassed in-flying birds. Most of the birds were strong flyers, but pigeons were a few squabs who would not fly. The match was shot to California State Sportsmen's Association rules, at 10 birds to each man, 21 yards rise, birds sprung from plunge traps. But few of the contestants had ever shot at pigeons, and hence many of the scores can be considered good, notably those of White, Frutig, Fletcher and Eustace. In our opinion White and Frutig were a close match and the best trap shots on the ground. Eustace and Fletcher are reliable shots, men who will always make a good average. Rea, who is a young man, is a coming shot, and has won the club medal at Gilroy. Millikin was the quickest snap shot, and like

Colebower his score does not show what he can do. Short also had bad luck. He is the present wearer of the Gilroy club medal. Johnny Paine was happy when he killed enough birds for that "pie." Wright of Gilroy is a good shot. He had the bad luck to lose a bird out of bounds, as also did Eustace and White. White's fourth bird, scored as a miss, is said to have dropped dead out of bounds. Rittenhouse suffered from tight loads in his shells. The following is the score, those marked with an asterisk being birds that fell dead out of bounds and were scored as misses:

| J. Colebower | 0 0 0 0 1 1 1 1 1 0—5 |
| J. Paine | 1 1 0 1 1 1 1 1 1 1—9 |
| Geo. C. White | 1 1 0 1 1 1 1 1 1 0—8 |
| E. Wright | 1 0 1 1 0 1 1 —6 |
| Rea | 0 1 1 1 0 0 1 1 1 1—7 |
| B. Rittenhouse | 0 1 0 0 1 0 0 1 1 0—4 |
| J. Millikin | 1 0 1 0 1 0 0 0 1 0—4 |
| M. Fletcher | 1 1 0 1 1 0 1 1 0 1—7 |
| E. W. Short | 0 0 1 1 0 0 0 1 0 0—4 |
| W. Frutig | 1 0 1 1 1 1 1 1 1 1—9 |
| G. Eustace | 1 1 1 1 0 1 0 1 1 1—8 |

Referee—H. D. Bartlett, of Gilroy.
Judges—H. M. Stitige, Gilroy, and J. S. Menasco, Watsonville.

The best of feeling prevailed throughout the match, and as honors were divided between Gilroy and Watsonville (two of the latter, on eight being from each place, and jointly dividing the purse), we expect to soon hear of a return match at Gilroy, at which, if given, Watsonville should be well represented.

---

### Shooting Match at San Bruno.

Last Sunday the free-for-all shooting match took place at San Bruno, and quite a crowd was there to witness some of the finest shooting that ever took place in California or any other place. The shooters were not so numerous as many expected, as only eleven entered. The entrance was $25, State rules governing, twenty-one yards rise, eighty yards boundary. Several clubs in different parts of the State were represented, among them the Vacaville Sportsman's Club having three representatives in the two Basford brothers and H. J. Dobbins; F. N. Lastreto of Stockton and H. Hopper of Petaluma. The shooting of Mr. Dobbins was very good indeed, he missing only one bird in the twenty-five, and that a very easy one. The Basford brothers shot as well as any one but they were unfortunate in having nothing but the very hardest birds to shoot and making the longest shots of the day. Next time we hope they will be more fortunate. Mr. Hopper did some very good shooting, and would be a very hard man to beat on a side hill at quail. Lastreto is also a very fine shot and one that will be hard to beat some other time. Mr. Maskey's shooting was very fine, he killing every bird and seemingly without an effort, dropping them all within a few feet of the trap and never having the trouble to retrieve them; he and Robinson would be a pair hard to beat. Robinson would have made a clean score if he had not carelessly neglected putting shot in his gun at the 14th bird, and that was the only miss he made at any shooting at forty-six birds. We can beat that! And Maskey killed thirty-one without a miss. Lambert, who took third prize, is also a first-class shot, missing one bird and the other dead out of bounds. In fact it would be hard to find any ten or eleven men to beat them in this or any other State, for they are all first-class shots. Maskey took first money, 40 per cent., Mr. Robinson and Mr. Dobbins shooting at 3 pair for second, Mr. Robinson killing all and taking second money, 30 per cent., Dobbins missing one in the shoot-off for third, 20 per cent., and Lambert 10 per cent. Only thirty-two birds missed out of two hundred and seventy shot at.

| H. Basford | 1 1 1 1 1 1 1 0 1 1 1 1 1 1 1 1 1 1 1 0 1 1 1 1 1—23 |
| F. Lambert | 1 1 1 1 1 1 1 1 1 1 0 1 1 1 1 1 1 1 1 1 1 1 1 0 1—23 |
| G. W. W. Robbin | 1 1 1 1 1 1 1 0 1 1 1 1 1 1 1 1 1 1 1 0 1 1 1 1 1—22 |
| F. Schmelkes | 1 1 1 1 1 0 1 1 1 1 1 1 1 1 1 1 1 0 0 1 1 1 1 1 1—22 |
| E. J. Dobbins | 1 1 1 1 1 1 1 1 1 1 1 1 1 1 1 1 1 1 1 1 1 1 0 1 1—24 |
| H. J. Dobbins | 1 1 1 1 1 1 1 1 1 1 1 1 1 1 1 1 1 1 1 1 1 1 1 1 1—25 |
| J. Maskey | 1 1 1 1 1 1 1 1 1 1 1 1 1 1 1 1 1 1 1 1 1 1 1 1 1—25 |
| Frank Maskey | 1 1 1 1 1 1 1 1 1 1 1 1 1 1 1 1 1 1 1 1 1 1 1 1 1—25 |
*Dead out of Bounds.

The shoot-off at 3 pair of double birds for second money won by Robinson with clean score taking second money, Dobbins missing one and taking third money.

| C. Robinson | 1 1 1 1 1 1—6 |
| Dobbins | 1 1 1 1 1 0—5 |

The first match following the main one was at six single birds, $5 entrance, divided 50, 30 and 20 per cent., three making clean scores, the money was equally divided between Robinson, Maskey and Henry Basford.

| F. Basford | 1 1 1 1 1 1—6 |
| C. Robinson | 1 1 1 1 1 1—6 |
| E. J. Dobbins | 1 1 1 0 1 1—5 |
| J. Maskey | 1 1 1 1 1 1—6 |
| F. N. Lastreto | 0 1 1 0 1 1—4 |
| H. Hopper | 1 1 0 1 1 0—4 |
| H. Basford | Withdrew |
| G. W. W. Robbin | 1 1 1 1 1 0—5 |
| Lambert | 1 1 1 0 1—4 |
| F. Pearson | 0 1 1 1 1 0—4 |
| Hopkins | 1 1 1 0—3 |
| Ropper | 1 1 0 1 1—4 |
| Lastreto | 1 1 0 1 1—4 |
*Dead out of bounds.

Next followed match at ten birds between Brown and Liddle, won by Brown:

| Brown | 1 1 1 1 1 1 1 1 1 1—10 |
| Liddle | 1 1 1 1 1 1 1 0 1 1—9 |

The next at 3 pair double birds, $5 entrance, divided between Robinson, H. Basford and Dobbins, after shooting at 3 pair to decide ties.

| Robinson | 1 1 1 1 1 1—6 |
| Maskey | 1 1 1 1 0 1—5 |
| Lambert | 1 1 1 0 1 1—5 |
| F. Basford | 1 1 1 1 1 1—6 |
| H. Basford | 1 1 1 1 1 1—6 |
| Dobbins | 1 1 1 1 1 1—6 |
| Lastreto | 1 1 1 0 1 1—5 |
*dead out of bounds.

| Robinson | 1 1 1—3 |
| Basford | 1 1 1—3 |
| Dobbins | 1 1 1—3 |
| Lastreto | 1 0 0—1 |

F. D. Russ and brother, William Russ, both of San Francisco, were at the instance of the California State Sportsman's Association arrested Tuesday last and taken over to Marin County by Deputy Sheriff Hawkins to answer for the offense of killing spotted fawns. Complaints against these parties have frequently been made, but this is the first time the necessary legal evidence has been obtained. The association intends to give them the benefit of a vigorous prosecution. Conviction, ostracism and public disgrace should justly be the reward of game law violators. The two defendants named were released on giving bail in the sum of $100.

The run of orders from the country on gun and ammunition stores shows that there will be a grand slaughter of the innocents as soon as the game law is out, on the 15th of this month.

A Large Bear.—Norman Kingsley killed a brown bear Thursday, August 17th, in the mountains west of Taylor's ranch, that weighs 700 lbs. The bear had been killing Tyler's cattle for some time, and in order to get rid of him, Kingsley had set a trap for his bearship near an animal he had killed the night before. When he came to get a second meal he got one of his feet into the trap, which he pulled loose from its moorings, and dragged the trap and chain with him into the brush. Kingsley took the trail and followed it until he found old Bruin, and with a well directed shot laid the cattle destroyer dead at his feet. He was not very fat, but would have got so in a very short time if he had been allowed to kill all the cattle he had wanted.—*People's Cause.*

Dr. Hayes denies the charge made against him in the Breeder and Sportsman of some weeks since that he killed an innocent, unoffending billy-goat, mistaking it for a deer, while deer-hunting in Nevada County. But the proof is overwhelmingly against him, as in the Pearson hog-killing case.

On August 27th a pigeon shooting match took place at Stockton between L. F. Lastreto and A. E. Mayers, 25 birds each, at 21 yards, with boundries fixed at 10 yards. Lastreto won. score, 20 to 15.

# THE RIFLE.

## Composition of Gunpowder.

BY DR. E. H. PARDEE.

(*Continued from No. 7.*)

Gunpowper is a mechanical combination of niter (or saltpeter), charcoal and sulphur, and while it may be regarded that the niter is the most important of all the ingredients, chemistry has elucidated the fact that no one of the three component parts can be taken away and any other substituted in its place that will make the compound as perfect as the original given us by Roger Bacon. Therefore it is safe to say that gunpowder has not undergone any material change, as regards its component parts, for the last six hundred years, while the material used has been refined and improved in many ways, resulting in a superior article, and now fitted to the different calibers, in accordance with established laws of gunnery.

Niter is a compound of three parts each of oxygen, nitrogen and potassium; and by the chemical action of these parts on each other, and the attraction and repulsion of affinities existing between them at a high temperature, an immense effect is produced on gunpowder by the application of fire.

It is true that gunpowder is made without the use of sulphur, and it has been claimed by some that it is not an active agent in the propellant power, but both experience and theory have taught that the compound is more complete with the addition of sulphur. Without it gunpowder is not capable of producing so perfect a gas, less regular in its action, more porous and friable, possessing less firmness in its granules, consequently cannot bear transportation without crumbling into dust, and more easily affected by damp and rainy weather.

Says the Edinburgh Encyclopedia: "There is one good reason for the use of sulphur, although it does not contribute to the production of any elastic fluid. The carbonic acid which is generated would doubtless combine with the potash, if it were not for the presence of sulphur, and thus so much of the elastic fluid would be lost. That this is the case we know to be true, from the fact that carbonate of potash is always formed when niter is decomposed by charcoal alone, which fact I shall almost immediately show." This, I have no doubt, is a fact, which I have proved to my entire satisfaction from experiments made on this subject, and which are in accordance with chemical analyses also. The sulphur is engaged during the combustion of the gunpowder, and expels a portion of the oxygen from the potash, and unites with the potassium and forms a sulphuret of that metal.

Any observing sportsman has witnessed the fact that no sulphuretted hydrogen can be detected by the sense of smell, or in fact by any ordinary tests, coming from the residuum always left in the breech of the gun after firing; but as soon as he puts down the wet wiping rod, the decomposition by the moisture which the sulphuret of potassium draws from the atmosphere causes, by this decomposition and liberation, a gas that makes the sportsman clasp his nose to prevent the inhalation of feted sulphuretted hydrogen, generally potassa, or that substance better known as potassium.

Chemical science has taught us, in the manufacture of gunpowder, that an exact amount of each ingredient is necessary in order to make the article perfect.

The government of the United States has adopted the present formula, and it is almost the same as that of England and other European nations: S plus $C^3$ plus K O N $O^3$ =3 C $O^2$ plus N plus S.

Recognizing that gunpowder is made strictly after the above formula, it becomes absolutely necessary, in order to acquire their most perfect combination and to secure the largest possible amount of gas, that the ingredients should be reduced to an impalpable powder before their combination, as it is a law both in philosophy and chemistry that the closer particles are united the more readily will their affinities be influenced the one for the other. Thus oxygen and hydrogen can be united so as to form water, but no union or combination will take place, for the good reason that the particles of the two gases are not sufficiently close to each other for their chemical affinities to be brought into play. But the brilliant discoveries in chemistry tell us that to create great pressure and force these gases together, an immediate combination takes place, and the production of water is the result. Therefore in order to insure the most perfect combination of the ingredients of gunpowder, the same conditions are necessary, that is, that the minute particles of niter, charcoal and sulphur must come in close contact, or the explosive power of the combination will be trifling at best.

In [illegible] communication I stated that in some subsequent [illegible] I would give the capacity of gas generated from one hun[illegible] grains of American rifle powder. It is an estimated [illegible] that to ignite 100 grains of gunpowder in an ordinary temperature of the atmosphere, that is, in the open and unconfined air, the gas would occupy a space three hundred times as great as that of the bulk of the powder used; but taking into consideration the intense heat at the instant of the explosion, the gases occupy at least *one thousand five hundred* times the space occupied by the original gunpowder.

But I am not satisfied with this imperfect explanation, and will illustrate so that the reader will more easily grasp the idea. Take a rifle barrel, caliber fifty-hundreths, or one-half inch in diameter, and one hundred grains of powder would fill the barrel about two inches at the breech; ignite this two inches of gunpowder, and you will have generated a gas that will fill a barrel three thousand inches long of the same caliber as that in which the gunpowder exploded. With this immense powder generated, in the twinkling of an eye, almost instantaneously, behind the projectile, starting it from its quiet state of inertia, at its point of initial velocity or 1,600 per second, is it to be wondered at that the leaden bullet undergoes the process of upsetting, or changing its original shape and contour? Or that the hard metal shot should break into fragmentary parts, and fly off in tangents like the asteroids of a once glorious and magnificent planet.

I will in due time refer to this almost incomprehensible power of powder gas, a subject so many are familiar with in its practical workings, but possess so limited a knowledge of the fundamental principles of the laws which govern it. I find very few sportsmen that will admit that there is any difference between the terms *propellant* and *explosive*, but there is such a striking difference that a little explanation will make it apparent to the causal observer—the terms are not and should not be used as synonymous, as all must admit that a chemical compound may possess the *explosive* power in a much greater degree than the propellant; fulminating gold, silver and mercury, and nitro-glycerine are all of the high order of explosives. But neither of them possesses the same projectile force that gunpowder does. Nothing can resist the exceeding intensity of the action of fulminating powder. A charge of dynamite when ignited exerts an equal power in all directions, and if it is carelessly placed on the top of a rock or boulder and ignited, it will overcome the cohesive power of the rock, and cause it to break into fragmontry parts as much as though it had been carefully laid beneath the rock when ignited.

Therefore a shot fired by any of these fulminates cannot be projected as by gunpowder, but has a tendency to split into fragmentary parts by the velocity created by its instantansons explosion.

I remember a few years ago, I had an esteemed friend who used gun-cotton in one of Billinghurt's bookjack-stocked pistols; while he claimed quite as good shooting as with gunpowder, it was done with composition hard-pointed bullets, and with very small charges of cotton. Any one can manufacture it with little expense, but I should advise all not to toy with it. The usual manner of preparing it is by steeping cotton or wool for a short time in a mixture of sulphuric and nitric acid; then washing and drying at a gentle heat. Gun-cotton chemically contains the elements of gunpowder, viz: carbon, nitrogen and oxygen; while at the same time it possesses another highly elastic gas, hydrogen.

The curvure in the fibers of the wool presents to the action of the flame a considerable surface in a small space, terminating as near as possible to the instantaneous, causing from its rapid ignition a violent recoil of the gun, as sufficient time is not given to put heavy bodies that lie in a state of inertia in motion, and as a consequence it cannot be used with either safety or satisfaction as a propelling force. Again it is an exceedingly dangerous compound, as numerous accidents have happened from its exposure to the sun, and other various causes.

I intended, Mr. Editor, to have closed my remarks on gunpowder in this communication, but as a full understanding of this subject will have a great bearing on my future remarks upon the theory of trajectory and projectile I will be compelled to ask your indulgence for extended remarks on this subject.

[*To be continued.*]

## The International Rifle Match.

For the first time since they were elected the American team were all present at Creedmoore on the 26th of August. The weather was splendid, except that a wind from 2 to 6 o'clock bothered the riflemen somewhat. Only the 200, 500, 600 and 1,000 yards ranges were shot over regularly, but each man was allowed to fire one or two shots over the 800 and 900 yards ranges in order to get the proper elevation and sight for the longest distance. No record of the shots fired over the last named ranges was kept. The shooting over the short distances was in the main very good, but at 1,000 yards it was poor. John Smith, of the Ninth New Jersey Regiment, headed the list with 118 points, C. W. Hinman following with 117, J. M. Pollard and T. J. Dolan with 115 and D. H. Ogden with 113 coming next in their order. Pollard made a clean score of 35 points at the 500-yard range, D. R. Atkinson being only one point behind. The coaching was done by Colonel Bodine, his adjutant, Captain C. F. Robbins, Ransome Rathburne and Dr. S. T. G. Dudley, who wore the uniform of the team of '77. The team, with three exceptions, used their own weapons to practice with. The exceptions were Messrs. Atkinson and Hinman, who used the new Remington-Hepburn rifle, and J. L. Paulding, who shot with the Hotchkiss gun. The following is the score:

| Name. | Yards 200. | 500. | 600. | 1,000. | Aggregate. |
|---|---|---|---|---|---|
| M. D. Hinds | 29 | 28 | 26 | 13 | 95 |
| D. H. Ogden | 29 | 29 | 28 | 27 | 113 |
| T. W. Griffith | 31 | 32 | 22 | 26 | 117 |
| N. D. Ward | 26 | 27 | 30 | 14 | 97 |
| D. R. Atkinson | 30 | 34 | 31 | 21 | 116 |
| C. W. Hinman | 31 | 30 | 31 | 25 | 117 |
| J. Smith | 31 | 29 | 22 | 26 | 118 |
| E. O. Shakespeare | 28 | 30 | 27 | 23 | 108 |
| A. B. Van Heusen | 29 | 31 | 24 | 24 | 108 |
| J. L. Paulding | 31 | 30 | 26 | 24 | 111 |
| Colonel G. E. P. Howard | 29 | 33 | 27 | 18 | 107 |
| J. McNevin | 28 | 28 | 24 | 19 | 99 |
| J. M. Pollard | 30 | 35 | 28 | 22 | 115 |
| S. E. Irlam | 28 | 21 | 20 | 17 | 86 |
| T. J. Dolan | 30 | 29 | 30 | 26 | 115 |
| Fred Adler | 30 | 30 | 24 | 11 | 95 |

The date of the match has been changed to September 14th and 15th, and the subscriptions for the necessary expenses amount to upwards of $2,000.

The National against the Carson Guard.—A rifle match came off last Sunday between the National Guard, Company C., 1st Regiment, and the Carson Guard of Nevada. The National Guard shot at Shell Mound Park and the Carson Guard at their range at Carson. The teams consisted of ten men each, ten shots at two ranges, 200 and 500 yards. The scores made by the National Guard were, Merryweather 43 at 200, 44 at 500, total 87; Cummings, 42 and 36—78; Kelly, 44 and 40—84; Raye, 42 and 47—89; Snook, 45 and 41—86; Sime, 42 and 42—84; Perkins, 43 and 41—84; Klein, Julius, 41 and 41—82; Templeton, 41 and 40—81; Klein, J. E., 43 and 46—89. Grand total, 834. The scores telegraphed of the Carson Guard were: Thaxton, 44 and 45—89; King, 42 and 46—88; Little, 43 and 45—88; Haskins, 40 and 44—84; Saffue, 44 and 40—84; Parker, 38 and 44—82; Cheney, 42 and 39—81; Crawford, 42 and 38—80; Borges, 40 and 39—79; Chesley, 39 and 37—76. Grand total, 819. The Carson Guard's representative at Shell Mound was Lieut. Pierce of the Oakland Light Cavalry, Lieut. Galusha of the Emmet Guard of Virginia City representing the National Guard at Carson.

The San Francisco Schuetzen Verein held their regular shooting tournament at the Alameda range last Sunday. The winners of the first three prizes on the Company targets are Messrs. Boeckmann, Schwavecke and Ehrenpfort. The Company prizes will be distributed next Friday. The winners of the first three prizes at the public targets are Messrs. Stanton, Kuhls and Shrecke. The special prize for the first bullseye in the morning was won by F. Brandt; the special prize for the last bullseye at night was won by Mr. Fischer, Jr.

Sept. 1st a rifle match took place at Schuetzen Park, Alameda, between Philo Jacobe and Henry Plagemann, in which Jacobe gave Plagemann the odds of 100 rings. The following are the totals in ten shots: Jacobe, 194, 205, 198, 220, 207, total, 1,024; Plagemann, 178, 179, 184, 169, 161, and 100 rings (given by Jacobe), total 971. This shows Jacobe to be the winner with 53 to spare.

# ATHLETICS.

One Hundred Yards in 9¼ sec?—From Winnipeg, Manitoba, under date of Aug, 19, we received the following: "The great foot race, one hundred yards, between Charles McIvor and an unknown, for $2,500 a side and the championship of America, took place this afternoon at 3 o'clock at Dufferin Park, and was witnessed by at least two thousand people. Great excitement prevailed, and from $2,500 to $3,000 are said to have changed hands. The unknown is given as D. H. Madara, of Rochester, N. Y., and is backed by George B. Eldridge, of the same city. The race was the best two in three heats, and two straight heats were taken by McIvor in 9¾ and 9¼ seconds. Mr. Armstrong of Detroit won a large amount on McIvor. McIvor always got the start on his opponent, but the latter almost made up the loss before the finish of the race. The winner won the first heat by two feet and the second by three feet. Pools were sold, prevailing odds being 100 to 70 in favor of McIvor."

We have written to several reputable parties who witnessed the contest, for information regarding the correctnes of the time and the amount of money posted. Until we hear from them, we will refrain from criticism, merely questioning the 9¼ sec. and the $5,000 stake; 9¼ is much too fast for McIvor, and $2,500 a side on a 100-yard sprint, that took place in Manitoba—well, we don't behave it.—*Turf, Field and Farm.*

Disputed Recent English Amateur Performances.—The 50 1-5 sec. 440 yards run of Mr. H. B. Ball, amateur, reported to have been made July 29th, at Home Park, Windsor, over grass, is not accepted by the more discriminating of our English contemporaries. The same runner's 220 yard performance at the Aug. 5 games of the Moreley Harriers, as well as his time in the 300 yard event, at the same meeting, is also questioned. Regarding these performances, *Bell's Life* says: "It is necessary to draw the line somewhere, and we must certainly do so at this latest of the Midland records. According to the official timekeeper, our London flyer did six yards inside "evens" in the 220-yards handicap, the race being alleged to have occupied 21 1-5 sec., and Ball getting within two yards of the winner. If this form were true, Myers and Phillips would have to "take a back seat," as Ball should be able to give either of them ten yards and hold them pretty safe. Yet, we fancy long odds would be laid against the scratch man, and by those, too, who do not as a rule throw their money away. Ball's reputed time in the 300 yards race is also rather too warm. He won that event in a canter by seven yards, "looking round all down the straight," and the time was given as 31 4-5 seconds, or about four yards and a half worse than Hutchin's best, or three yards better than Myer's record. Most likely the old excuses as to the course and the direction of the wind will be urged. In that case it would be obviously unfair to men who have achieved their records without adventitious aids, that a runner who is favored either by a downhill course or a gale of wind behind him should have the credit of beating their time.

## Late Base Ball Notes.

It is said that the Reddington and Olympic clubs will play a match at Sacramento during the State Fair, but it would be far more interesting to the public if the Olympics could arrange a match with a team chosen from the leading players of the Capital's clubs.

The juniors of the University have organized a base-ball club. The nine is composed as follows: Wallace catcher and captain, Ramm pitcher, Bosse first, Beatty second, Mezes third, Huggins left field, Chase center field, Pond short stop.

The Reddingtons played a match last Sunday morning with the Underwriters' club at the Recreation grounds that was well contested, the Reddingtons winning by a score of eleven runs to ten.

The game to-morrow at the Recreation grounds will be between the Renos and the Haverly Theater nine.

Joseph White, of Bake Oven, Wasco county, Oregon, began as a sheep herder in that region without funds five years ago. He recently sold his band of sheep for $6,000. From his this year's shearing he sold from 678 ewes, $1,178 worth of wool and raised 478 lambs.

We have received the first number of the Breeder and Sportsman, published at San Francisco, and edited by Mr. J. C Simpson, and it presents a fine appearance. It is the kind of a paper which has long been needed on the Pacific Coast, and it is hoped that it will meet with generous support. Its discussion of breeding topics will rouse interest in that subject and add to the value of the products of breeding farms, and its treatment of the turf will swell the receipts of racing parks. The journal which is devoted to breeding and sport, and which is conducted with enterprise and ability, frequently puts more money into other people's pockets than its own, but we cannot believe that such will be the result of Mr. Simpson's venture. If the breeders and track managers of the Pacific Coast do not sustain him, they will not deserve to reap the benefits which will grow under the fostering care of a vigorous home organ.—*Turf, Field and Farm.*

We are in receipt of a new paper, The Breeder and Sportsman, Joseph Cairn Simpson, editor and proprietor. Its typographical appearance is excellent, and it is devoted to the interest of stock-raising, as well as to a variety of other matters interesting to sportsmen. It is edited with marked ability, published in San Francisco, and we commend it to breeders, sportsmen and others.—*Lower Lake Bulletin.*

# THE
# Breeder and Sportsman.

PUBLISHED WEEKLY BY THE

BREEDER AND SPORTSMAN PUBLISHING CO.

THE TURF AND SPORTING AUTHORITY OF THE
PACIFIC COAST.

OFFICE, 508 MONTGOMERY STREET
P. O. Box 1286.

*Five dollars a year; three dollars for six months; one dollar and a
half for three months. Strictly in advance.*

MAKE ALL CHECKS, MONEY ORDERS, ETC., PAYABLE TO ORDER OF
BREEDER AND SPORTSMAN PUBLISHING CO.

*Money should be sent by postal order, draft or by registered letter, ad-
dressed to the "Breeder and Sportsman Publishing Company, San Francisco, Cal."*

*Communications must be accompanied by the writer's name and address,
not necessarily for publication, but as a private guarantee of good faith.*

JOSEPH CAIRN SIMPSON, - - - EDITOR.

San Francisco, Saturday, Sept. 9 , 1882.

## THE GOLDEN GATE FAIR.

The present fair of the Golden Gate Association has
been one of the most successful ever held. In fact at
the time of writing there has not been a hitch or anything to mar the smooth running of all the departments.
The decisions have been satisfactory all through, and
every contest evidently "straight." There have been
several notable performances. . The running of Red Boy
in the fastest time ever made on the Pacific Coast was
something of a surprise to those who were only aware of
his losing three of the big $5,000 matches, and speaks
well for the change of climate from Salt Lake to Oakland. . He is a fine looking horse showing the Sovereign
conformation as well as that of his son. As he only
beat Night Hawk by a few inches the honors may be
considered easy, and when it was granted that the mare
was scarcely up to the mark her performance was still
more wonderful. The two-year-old race was a very fair
one considering that the first and second in it had each
a penalty of five pounds and that between the three-
year-olds was one of the close finishes which always
raise the enthusiasm of the spectators. The two mile
run of Precious was proof that a faster pace in the other
for the first mile might have turned the tables, though
the Duke of Monday has such a rare flight of speed that
any one which beats him will have to rate along at a
good clip from start to finish. Even with the ten pounds
allowance the running of Euchre in 1:43¾ was a very
good showing as he still carried 108 pounds, and for Inauguration to keep so close to him with the same weight
is not a bad mark for a three-year-old.

The trotters have shown very well. Manon, the
handsome daughter of Nutwood, is surely an animal of
fine promise. For a five-year-old in her first race to
make 2:24 after rather a bad start compelling her to trot
around the others, making a break soon after the start, is
a very good record. The Nutwoods are certainly coming to the fore and the full seasons he made in California
will be of immense benefit to the stock of the State. Although sweetness was unfortunate it cannot be said that
she was in reality disgraced. The "leg" is a troublesome
thing for her trainer to contend against, and if she
were entirely sound the work might be more in accordance with ensuring her coming up to the mark for a
bruising race. Albert W. is a great colt; he had been in
the clutches of the pinkeye, had fallen down in transitu
to the Bay District, which mishap entailed broken knees,
and trotted two very hard races up the country. In the
race he won the intuition was to draw him, and his trainer was only a few minutes late to get him out of the
race. The rules are somewhat inexorable and the appeal to the judges to prevent him being "scratched"
had to be decided against. His combination of Electioneer
and John Nelson blood will give him a value outside of
the tracks, and his place in the stud is already assured.
Adrian, the three-year-old, which won in straight heats,
is also a remarkably promising colt. He is of fine size,
capital form and action that is an augury of still better
doings. He is a grandson of Alexander, his sire being
Reliance, and there is scarcely a question of his taking a
place in the gallery of notables at some future day. The
description of Alexander which accompanies the illustration of necessity too brief to do justice to the
claims of the horse and his distinguished relations on
this coast. When the busy season is over there will be
more time to enter into details, and fortunately for the
scribe who does the pen portraiture there is abundant
material in California for many disquisitions on breeding. Vanderlynn, the winner of the special race, is of the
same blood as Alexander on the side of the sire and with
that he combines some of the stoutest strains in the
American Stud Book. Although rather on the
"in and out" order, as shown by his public
performances, he is a horse of fine speed, and
that he will stay is a merit which should follow the inheritance. Being his first season, without any great
deal of preparatory work before trotting in races, there
are strong probabilities that he will develop into a first-
class performer.

The two-year-olds made a display which can only be
seen in California. Though Neluska has been sick for
some time, ailing so that blisters had to be resorted to,
she gave evidence that the family inheritance of speed
has fallen to her lot as well as the others which have the
same dam. It would have been better, perhaps, not to
have trotted her, as the difference between the time of
the first heat and the third was so great that to those who
were not aware of the difficulty she labored under it
seemed as though she would have to take rank with the
impostors which dazzle to mislead. She trotted the first
heat easily in 2:30½, and the merit of this performance is
apt to be overlooked in California where so many of the
same age have beaten it. Nevertheless, it is faster than
has ever been made outside of this State and the fastest
time on record when two or more trotters were engaged.

The falling off in the second was not great, but the
third showed a gap which was very marked. People
are prone to ascribe to one strain in a pedigree whatever
shortcomings there are, and a few who had backed Neluska gave her dam the anathemas for the lack in stamina of the daughter. As the winner, Ruby, is by the
same sire, this gave a little color to the claim, and had it
not been for the lack of condition which the sickness entailed the reasoning would be good. Ruby showed the
the very reverse qualities and it is nearly certain that
she could have trotted the third heat as fast, probably
faster, than either of the others. As she was bred by
Mr. Mackay there is an additional satisfaction to him in
the victory, and there is not a particle of risk in making
the prediction that she will eventually develop into a
first-class mare.

Mr. Rose will share in the glory as she was not only
bred at Sunny Slope, but has been trained there, and
only taken from "the stable" when the rules compelled
the change. We cannot close without congratulating the
managers of the Golden Gate Fair on the complete success of the exhibition. Though this was well-deserved
from the efforts which all made even labor does not always meet the proper reward. President, directors, secretary, superintendent, committees, in fact, every one
connected with the fair have worked hard to make it
deserving of support.

## A DEMORALIZING PRACTICE.

The indecent prominence given to the doings of a certain class of pugilists, by the daily newspapers and
the flashier periodicals of the Eastern States is being emulated by the California press with one or two honorable
exceptions and we regret to say that this ill-advised
puffing of the class of people who bear such names as
Tug Wilson and Slugger Sullivan is working a positive
injury to the rising generation. To speak of the men
whose names figure alternately as prize-fighters and va-
grants in the newspaper reports of the day, as athletes
and sportsmen, does an injury to the standing of athletics, more especially on this coast, where they are in need
of fostering care and liable to be blighted by the chilling
wind of adverse criticism. We are not at a loss to understand how a great and otherwise respectable newspaper
will deliberately become the organ of a Sullivan or a
McCormack, publish their slightest movements, and act
as their mouth-pieces to throw out challenges or answer
those from other men of the same class. It is bad taste
and worse morality to do this, yet such papers as the
New York Herald and Sun and their imitators on this
Coast actually employ special men to write up the doings
of brawlers, law-breakers and disturbers of the peace
who, under the thin disguise of a pair of leather gloves,
set at naught and defy the laws of the land.

A Captains Williams or a Captain Douglass, both of
whom are doubtless well meaning, respectable men, in
their way, dare to stand by and see the law against prize
fighting broken because they know that the "great
dailies" which are supposed to voice popular sentiment
will sustain the prize fighters and sneer at those who try
to suppress them. They argue that so long as the papers
do not cry out against these vulgar shows the public
want them and will express their displeasure at any attempt to stop such exhibitions. The papers justify the
police, but it is as well to stop for one instant and ask
how they justify themselves. Any city editor or publisher would, if asked this question, simply reply that
their province was to give the news, and that any show
that attracted the public attention was a proper thing to
mention, and if very popular, to report in detail. They
would further say: "The people like to read of such
things and therefore we publish them." Now the instant
these excuses are looked into and weighed their shallow-
ness is painfully apparent, and reduced to plain language they simply mean that the publishers report such
affairs regardless of decency and morality, because their
publication pays. The excuse that "the people have to
read about prize fights," really means that the dregs of
the people will buy a paper if they know it contains such
a report. The people who do this are not regular newspaper subscribers, hence they have to make a special
purchase at single rates, and the extra sales in this way
will often put a hundred dollars or more into the pocket
of the publisher. We do not believe that any paper in
this city would lose a single subscriber if it ceased to
publish these obnoxious accounts of affairs which are not
sport but simply brutal exhibitions gotten up for the
purpose of making gate money.

In writing of this subject one naturally asks: "Where
is this sort of thing to stop?" Day by day the papers become more and more vulgar and vie with each
other in pandering to the coarser tastes of the people.
If it is proper to report prize-fights because it pays, is
it not equally proper to report the evidence of brutality
and bestiality with which our divorce courts teem? They
are not more corrupting than the vivid photographs of
fights, and are only a shade nastier to people of real culture and refined tastes. It is true the reports of which
we complain are not worse than contemporary publications in book form. Perhaps they are not as bad as the
degrading realisms of Zola and Ouida, but it must
be remembered that though it is possible to keep these
books from the young and pure, a daily newspaper is
ubiquitous and if the daughters and sons of the house
are not allowed to read them in the parlor they can find
them in the servants' hall. To us the present question
of importance is: "How do these reports injure the interests of athletics in California?" To us the answer is
self-evident. It is that by meretriciously exalting, as
sport, brutal and degrading exhibitions which are not
sport they injure the character and check the advance of
those athletic and manly exercises to which the youth of
this country, not forced to labor hard, must look for
physical perfection; nay, for the least claim to be considered physically men. They cause a gentleman who
has learned enough of boxing to be able to defend his
person from attack or punish a ruffian to be spoken of
with contempt as a shoulder-hitter, and so far have they
blunted the public sense of propriety that less than two
months ago one reputable paper actually conned over
the names of gentlemen, members of the Olympic club,
in search of some one to pit against the champion brawl-
er and ruffian of America.

A rough is exalted to the place of a hero, and not a
large paper in New York manly enough to pull the
plumes of victory from his unhandsome heart and paint
him ruffian as he is. We say that they injure reputable
sport by their unsavory association, the same as the
cheating tricks of the sharper years ago have made the
race-track shunned by certain persons to this very day.
If we are wrong we are open to correction but if we are
right we will be vindicated in time. We have not in the
past and will not in the future speak of their exhibitions
or report them in any tone or temper differing from
this writing, and from the support awarded to this paper
by the respectable public we shall draw our conclusions
as to the acceptability of the course which in the interest
of true sport we have adopted.

## THE STANFORD STAKES.

The third payment of $100 in the Stanford Stake
will be due the 21st inst. The race is to be trotted on
the third Saturday in October, the 21st, over the Bay
District course, and according to the conditions the last
payment has to be made thirty days previous to the
time set for trotting. Notice, accompanied with the
$100, on or before the time, to Jos. Cairn Simpson, Secre-
tary of Stanford Stake, or R. T. Smith, Treasurer,
Pacific Breeders' Association. This is the largest trotting
stake for three-year-old colts which has been gotten up,
and is likely to result in a very good race.

## EDITORIAL NOTES.

The two-year-old trotting races excite a great
deal of attention, and the performances of Ruby and Neluska
in their race at Oakland, show that we are not likely to forfeit the reputation California has acquired of being second to
no other State in the development of young trotters of high
degree. . The race at the State Fair on Tuesday next will be
still more interesting as Palo Alto is represented in the nominations by Flower Girl, an own sister to Wildflower, and by
Sallie Benton by General Benton, his dam Sontag Mohawk,
while Dr. Hicks has also entered his fine filly Pride by Buccaneer, dam by Flaxtail. With the exception of the last
named all the above figure in the race for the same class at
San Jose, and it will doubtless be one of the best attractions
on the card of the San Mateo and Santa Clara Association
that will induce a large number of San Franciscans to pay a
visit to San Jose to witness this contest, the more so as the
2:25 class comes off on the same day.

## THE STATE FAIR.

That the coming State Fair will be the finest exhibition ever held at Sacramento is beyond doubt. The entries in the speed purses, insure this most attractive feature of all being superior to any of former years, and from the number of stalls engaged, and the space in the pavilion applied for, everything in connection with it justifies the most sanguine predictions. There is also an appearance of the finest weather, if the isothermal sharps are not entirely off in their ratiocinations.

It is unnecessary to do more than call attention to the advertisements in the appropriate columns which give the entries in the various purses to show that the racing and trotting cannot be otherwise than first-class. People are so well aware of the fact that a large attendance from San Francisco is beyond doubt and we would advise those who have not already made arrangements to secure rooms by letter or telegram. Notwithstanding that the indications are that a larger concourse of people will visit Sacramento the coming week than ever before owing to the well-known hospitality of the citizens, there need be no fear of not obtaining rooms. At the State Fair especially the latch strings are never pulled in.

## THE KENNEL.

### The Gordon Setter.

The following interesting account of the origin of the Gordon setter is from an article by Harry Malcolm in the *American Field:*

"This favorite breed of setters was called Gordons after the late and last George, Duke of Gordon, because they were first brought out by his father and him when he was Marquis of Huntley, and lived at Huntley Lodge. From this place many noblemen and gentlemen obtained specimens of the breed, and their descendants retain the strain to this day; such as Lord Lovat, Lord Kintore, General Leith, Lord Panmure, Captain Barclay, of Urie, etc. Of course, all these crack shots and sportsmen mentioned have long passed away but they were of the right stuff, and knew well a good setter. At the time to which I have referred a Mr. Richie, an Englishman, was head-keeper of the Marquis at Huntley Lodge, and was considered in his day the best breaker of dogs in the kingdom. It was nothing uncommon for him to hunt three brace together, and he could handle them properly without any trouble. He was succeeded by Matthew Jubb, as head-keeper, who came from Innis House, and who is still alive.

"Matthew Jubb was the first man with the Duke who bred the black, white and tan, about which there was a controversy years ago in a London paper—some writers asserting that the black, white and tan were the original breed kept by his Grace, others holding to only two colors in the animal; and lately in the *Live Stock Journal* I have seen it boldly asserted by a writer (to whom I shall have to refer by-and-by) that the black, white and tan were the first favorites. Jubb is still alive, or was a year ago, and is still at Gordon Castle, and could possibly be asked for his opinion. He brought the dogs to London, where they were sold at Tattersalls on the death of the Duke, and I know a keeper with whom he lodged while on his journey, to whom he stated that two or three of the black, white and tans were his own property, and I believe he sold them to considerable advantage. A trusty authority and excellent writer on dogs, Idstone, I believe, purchased some of these dogs, and bred from them, vastly improving their shape and appearance. No one living has done more for this valuable breed of setters than Idstone, who deserves every credit. The imported Gordons, now at the Marquis of Huntley's seat, Aboyne Castle, were produced by Idstone, and not only there, but at many other places I could name. I have seen many grand Gordons in England, and feel thankful to my neighbors for showing such respect for the northern setter. I have already mentioned Idstone. Besides him we have the late Mr. Stokes, of Grindon Rectory, a most enthusiastic admirer of the breed. He was the owner of Shot (he was a grand dog) and the famous bitch Daisy. These two dogs used to sweep the boards of prizes at every show where they were exhibited. Another grand dog of which I am very fond is Grouse, which I am sure would make a first-class stud dog, and is a thorough Gordon. Mr. Allison's Reuben is also a very nice animal indeed, and others I could name, but I shall only mention one more—Young Lorn—the property of Mr. H. Gibbs, of Aberdeen, which has been very highly spoken of in the *Live Stock Journal* and other papers. This dog has a grand pedigree, and I know that not only at the stud, but in the field, he has proved himself as good as he is bonny. I may add another one, viz. Captain Fairquhar's of Lowndes Square. They are of Lord Lovat's strain, and are certainly very fine specimens. This breed is almost in every kennel in the north and west of Scotland, and all who have them or have seen them at work admire them. The cross of white was by an English dog, called at that time, and may be yet, the New Forest setter breed, which was a present to the Duke."

Strathbogie then describes what he thinks a Gordon setter should be: "His head should be long and high, square muzzle, muscle longish, back rather short, shoulders well sloped or oblique, forelegs straight and well feathered, with good hard pads, good bent sticles, which give one a notion of going. Tail short, compared with some breeds, and with a grand fringe. The tan on muzzle, legs, tail, etc., should be of a bright sienna color, and there should be no mixture of black hairs through the tan. The chest is deep, with well-arched ribs, giving plenty of bellows room. Altogether, taken from any point of view, the dog gives one the idea of great powers of going, and his finely feathered feet show he was made for much endurance. No one could look on his bonny face, with that rich hazel eye 'ever waiting, ever loving,' without noticing the great amount of intelligence and kindness this dog is gifted with. In short, he is not only 'the old man's dog' but he has been for many years also the young nobleman's and young chief's only favorite setter, and is likely to continue so. The inherited sagacity of the pure Gordon is distinguishable by his adapting himself instinctively to the fluctuating scenes, which, according to the soil and atmosphere, he shows or of depressed, carrying his head low in sultry weather and high in breeze, etc."

SPREAD THE NEWS.—Not the least important work that is being done by the BREEDER AND SPORTSMAN is the dissemination of correct information through the East in regard to California sport. In the last issue of the *Turf, Field and Farm* to hand we notice three items about California dogs, all founded upon articles which appeared in this column. We often copy freely from the *Turf* and always find its news reliable, and we are pleased to see that the *Turf* pays a similar compliment to the BREEDER. We want the people East to see the spirits of this State as they really exist, and to cease regarding California sportsmen as a cross between a poacher and a cowboy, and that is one of the reasons why in times past we have pointed out failings as freely as we have commanded excellence.

### The Coach Dog.

Perhaps the most beautiful of all the smooth haired breed of dogs is the Dalmatian, oftener called the carriage dog, and in England the Talbot from the family name of the first Earl of Shrewsbury, who was generally identified with the in troduction of the breed to Great Britain. The breed is really a small type of the great Danish dog commonly though incorrectly known in America as the Siberian bloodhound or Siberian mastiff or German boarhound, for they are all one and the same breed and possess the distinction of being the tallest and largest species of the canine race. These were the spotted dogs given by Pan to Diana, the goddess of hunting, and are generally supposed to be the dogs of Epicus. The great Danes are used in Europe for boar hunting and in Siberia for tracking criminals who have escaped. They are said to possess marvelous powers of scent though some splendid specimens of the breed in the possession of J. W. Ames, Warden of the State Prison at San Quentin, cannot be induced to take up a cold scent. Perhaps in this instance lack of practice for several generations may have caused the power of scent to deteriorate, for several instances are known in England where they have taken up a trail two days old. They are fleet and strong and belong to the class known to the ancients as *celeres et fragrans*, that is, dogs that could run fast, like the greyhound, and could also fight like the great dogs of Molossice, of whom Plum says: "They disdain to attack a bear or wild boar but could easily slay a lion or elephant. The breed of great Danes is becoming scarce. The Dalmatian or lesser Dane is so common on all our streets as to receive little notice, though on account of their great intelligence and faithfulness the breed is worthy of the greatest consideration. In England and America they are only used as ornaments to follow the carriage and suit themselves around the hallway, and so constantly are they associated with horses that it is often thought that they have little love for the companionship of man and are lacking in the qualities of affection and obedience.

No greater mistake than this was ever made, for in all the best qualities they rank second to no other breed. The French call them *le braque de Bengal*, and often use them in hunting and in fact it is generally claimed by French writers on this subject that they are a cross with the pointer and the greater Dane. As a proof that even so high an authority as Gouste was badly mistaken in stating that the breed lacks intelligence and affection it is not necessary to go outside the city of San Francisco. Captain Harris, the well known horseman, has a dog of this breed called King, which will perform more tricks and of a more intricate character than any poodle ever trained for a circus. Those who attended the first dog show ever held in this city, October, 1877, will probably remember the performance given by King on a platform in the center of the hall, and which included walking along a piece of 2x4 scantling raised 20 feet from the ground, standing on the back of a common chair, fetching different articles selected in accordance with the word of command and at infinite variety of tricks demanding the highest quality of obedience and canine reason. The writer has a dog of this breed which will select from a pile at his command either quail, robin, hare or dove. It is in the habit of bringing in the newspaper every morning and has learned to distinguish between a copy of the *Call* left for his owner and a copy of the *Chronicle* left for the next door neighbor. The papers generally lie close together. They are folded exactly the same, yet after a few lessons the dog invariably brings in the right one. He will also bring boots and slippers, hat or cane when ordered and do all the tricks usually taught to pet dogs. He has always been kept in the house and does not show the slightest desire for the company of horses. He has a great aversion to salt water, yet he is so obedient that by will jump into the bay for a stick when ordered though the struggle between duty and desire is a hard one. His only vice is a fondness for hunting chickens but a word will always cause him to desist from this offense against canine morality and neighborly courtesy. Another dog of this breed known to the writer has as good a nose as the ordinary pointer and will find game readily, though on account of his small size he is not of much value as a hunting dog. These examples are sufficient to show that the breed is inferior to none and if owners of such dogs would only take a little pains to teach them they would find the experiment well rewarded.

COURSING AT PETALUMA.—There are few places on the coast that afford better facilities to a city coursing man to give his dogs a good run than Petaluma. The Sunday sportsmen sue to this pleasant spot allow for six hours' sport, more than enough to tire both men and dogs. The fare is a mere trifle, and one can always be sure of finding half a dozen hares.

The BREEDER AND SPORTSMAN has been publishing some very fine illustrations of California horses, that of Abbotsford in the August 5 number being particularly noticeable. Mr. E. Wyttenbach is the artist to whom Mr. Simpson has had the good fortune to secure. Mr. Simpson seems to have made a great success with his paper.—*N. Y. Sportsman.*

### The Olympics at the Fair.

Next Wednesday evening, Sept. 13, the usual routine of the Mechanics' Fair will be varied by a gymnastic and athletic exhibition under the auspices of the Olympic Club. The club programme will be varied and entertaining as the accommodations in the pavilion will permit. The fair this season is unusually attractive, and is well patronized, but an evening set apart for the benefit of the Olympic Club (a club unrivaled in its combination of gymnastic, athletic and social features), should attract the largest audience of the season. The programme is as follows: Groupings, club swinging, gladiatorial groupings, perch bar, fencing, juveniles, boxing, horizontal bar, acrobatics and tug of war.

(Continued from page 1.)

and she was by a son of Brown's Bellfounder: who was by imported Bellfounder from Lady Allport by Mambrino. There has been a great deal of controversy over the Bellfounder blood in Hambletonian. Some have given it the preference over the Abdallah strain, but at all events the combination has been a happy nick beyond question. The back crosses of Alexander come from the 'old fashioned, hard-bottomed sort' which delighted in a distance of ground. But the best evidence of the value of a stallion is what the progeny has done, and for the small opportunity which Alexander has had in the stud there could scarcely be a better showing. There is Tommy Dodd with a record of 2.24, made when he was suffering from a 'leg' which would have stopped many horses from making an effort. Reliance, 2.25 at five years old and with a flight of speed that proved a capacity far inside of that mark, Nelly Patchen, 2.27, and the only California-bred trotter which is credited with a victory in England, and Alex. Button, a winner at three years old in 2.29, and at four in 2.26½. It is almost supererogatory to add a written description to the portrayal of our artist. The points are delineated with a fidelity which can scarcely be bettered, and anyone seeing the picture could select the original in a field of a thousand. Alexander is a very handsome shade of bay, is nearly sixteen hands in height, and one of the most symmetrically formed trotting horses ever seen. He shows a great deal of quality and yet, with immense muscular power. Altogether it is seldom that a finer specimen of the American trotter is seen in any country and even among the notabilities of California he is worthy of a high place. This is praise enough, for a horse which can occupy a front position on the Pacific Coast is worthy of the same rank in any country. The family connections on both sides of the continent represent the best on the brain, and we add him to the picture gallery of the BREEDER AND SPORTSMAN with the feeling that he is fully entitled to the place. In writing this brief sketch we nearly overlooked what he had done himself. Though it could scarcely be called training, he won a record of 2.31½, and Bud Doble drove him a trial in 2.26.

### The Chico Fair.

CHICO, Sept. 1, 1882.
EDITOR BREEDER AND SPORTSMAN:—Our District Fair opened on the 5th with a fair attendance. There was but one race on the cards, 2.30, free to all, best 3 in 5 to harness, for a purse of $350; first horse sixth-tenths, second three-tenths, third one-tenth that closed with the following entries: E. Downer names g g Chap Winston, C. Sherman names g g Carlisle by Plumas, Chas. Shear names blk g Slim Jim by Tyler's Blackhawk, and were allotted positions in order named: Carlisle, Winston, Slim Jim. After two false starts they got the word with Carlisle slightly in the lead but broke after going two hundred yards, slim Jim following suit immediately after, Winston leading to the quarter pole in 42½ seconds, at the half in 1.23 and the mile in 2.43, Carlisle second, Slim Jim distanced. After three ineffectual attempts they got the word with Carlisle slightly in the lead but Winston had too much speed and led at the quarter pole two lengths in 37½ seconds; Carlisle moved up to him on the back stretch but broke just before reaching the half in 1.13½. Winston kept up his lick trotting and Carlisle breaking, Winston winning the heat, race and money, Carlisle distanced for running; time, 2.27.

There was a marked improvement in the attendance on the second day, there being two running races on the card; the first a dash-of a mile for all three-year-olds, Dooley Stake, $25 entrance p. p. $125 added. George Hearst enters ch f Maria F.; J. Q. Anderson enters Minnie Bell, by Joe Daniels, dam by Norfolk; A. Miller names Lady Partisan, by Partisan, dam by Jewel. Betting on this race about 5 to 3, Maria F. being the favorite over the other two. After one false break they got sent off with Maria F. a length in the rear, but when they showed around the turn Maria was on even terms, and after leaving the quarter pole showed a length to the front which she increased to three at the half in 51 seconds, three-quarter pole 1.19, and finished an easy winner in 1.46½, Minnie Bell second. Then came Reavis Stake, 1¼ miles, free handicap, entrance $50, $25 forfeit, $10 to declare, $200 added, declaration to be made September 1st, weights published Aug. 29th, closed with the following nominations: Geo. Hearst enters ch s Slim Jim, Brown by Forster; Ab Ellis enters b g Shiner by Norfolk by Rifleman; Thos. Hazlet names ch g Jubilee by Norfolk by Lodi; F. M. Coltherp names Bob Ingersoll, pedigree not given; Shemler & Ayers enter b g Joe Howell by Bonnie Scotland; Etta Sheppard by im. Sovereign; George Hearst names Jim Brown by Forster; W. Hunter enters Fred Hunter b g, by Norfolk, by Lodi. There was a spirited competition in the pools, Brown selling for a few times favorite but they chopped on Howell at the same odds, $20 to $16½. The Hunter was drawn and left five starters; they got a passable send-off; Brown and Ingersoll came very near being left at the post, and I think if starters would adopt it as a rule when they warn a jockey twice to come up and he refuses, to send him off there would be less false breaks and better s starts. Jubilee rushed off in the lead with the three others bunched close up, Jim Brown seven lengths in the rear; when they passed the stand entering the backstretch Howell and Shiner moved up and Howell took the lead before they reached the half-mile pole, which he opened to a gap of six lengths at the three-quarter pole, when Shiner and Jim Brown come with a rush and they finished Howell first by two lengths in front of Brown with Shiner lapped on his hip, the others strung out.

OCCASIONALLY.

# HERD AND SWINE.

## Color in Jerseys.

A close attention to this valuable and beautiful breed of cattle has convinced me that "breeding for color," i. e., to the exclusion of white, has been carried out in many cases with a total disregard to milking qualities, and, as your article truly says, much injury has been done to the breed thereby. The fashion for "whole color" was, I believe, originally set by the Americans, but they, with their natural acuteness, have for some time back been aware of the error of "going for color" alone, and many of their most noted butter-making cows are now broken colored. It will scarcely be credited, although it is a fact, that there are gentlemen officiating at the present day as judges at shows who will not award a prize to an animal with white about it, because for that reason they do not consider it to be true bred. On the other hand, the late Mr. Jessett, of Mottesbone, Isle of Wight, who was a first-rate judge of a Jersey, would never have a cow without white about her, averring that, unless it had, the animal had some other than pure Jersey blood in her.

Of course, if an animal with all milking points perfect is at the same time whole colored, it is the more valuable, but it is the greatest absurdity to set color either of body or tongue before these essential qualifications, and either in judging or choosing a Jersey with regard to the great attribute of the breed, milk and butter indications should be the *sine qua non*, the color of the body and tongue being after-considerations.

Upon the same question the *Farmer's Gazette*, Dublin, upon color-judging and the crossing of Jerseys upon other breeds, has the following: "Jerseys, in their island home, are found of many colors, from the ever-fashionable silver gray—a color which was rarely found till within the last few years—down to the common red and white; some, but very few, are black, and it is generally considered that a cow of this color gives the richest milk of all. Whole, self, or solid colors, by which are understood cows of one color—that is, without any white—have of late years been the fashion in this country; but it is asserted by many, and with justice, that great injury has been done to the breed by this fancy, and fancy it may well be called, since on the island—their native home—no attention whatever is paid to the color, the greatest aim of the best breeders being a graceful form and grand milking qualities. Before a judge (says the *Frome Times*) enters upon his duties at an Island show, he has to make a solemn declaration that he will fairly and honorably judge according to the best of his ability, without favor or affection. If we had this rule at all our shows, less grumbling would be the result, neither should we hear the judges so often accused of partiality in their awards. It would be their safeguard.

Every breeder knows how difficult it is to breed for color, and when self-colors are bred for, and agreeably expected, from the sire and dam being self-colored, disappointment often results. Cattle will throw back, and thus we find calves with white; so often from a self-colored bull and a parti-colored cow, a white-colored calf is unexpectedly obtained. For beauty and appearance I prefer the cattle of one color, providing the milking qualities are not lost, but never discard a good milker for her color, as fashionable breeders have so often learned to their cost. My favorite color of all is a solid orange gray, with a white muzzle, and her ears tipped with a black fringe. The crossing of the Short-horn with the Jersey has often been tried, and has sometimes been attended with success; but as they are larger, and consequently larger consumers of food, nothing is obtained except size; for I have never known a cross-bred Jersey make more butter, although she will give more milk than a really good Island cow. Yet the cross-bred is nearly always superior to a Short-horn for milking properties alone. If Jerseys should be crossed at all, the South Ham Devon is the best, and I have seen one really good cow from this cross, and so like a Jersey that, with the exception of being a little large, one could hardly tell the difference.

The great thing in choosing a Jersey is to be sure that her udder is large and not fleshy, extending behind as nearly as possible to the vulva, and reaching in front nearly to the navel; so that as much milk may be obtained from her front quarters as from her hind ones. Her milk veins must also be sought for and examined; feel and see that they are large and swelling, especially noticing that the hole where the veins enter the body is so large that you can easily push the top of your second finger into them. She should also have a deep orange color inside her ears; the deeper the color is, the richer her milk.—*London Live Stock Journal.*

## Advice to Dairymen.

The fourteenth annual report of the Northwestern Association contains much valuable information taken from those having experience in this business. It is well known that milk speedily becomes tainted when brought more or less into contact with matter charged with odor, and the following remarks in the pamphlet are very pertinent to the matter:

"The water used to wash this butter must not be taken from a well that is any way influenced by the washings of the factory, nor drawn from a wooden cistern. We think that as much butter is spoiled from being washed in impure water as from any other one cause.

"It is of the greatest importance that we use good salt—that which is free from shells, scales and dirt; the finer the better, in our opinion. Fine salt dissolves quickly, and leaves no gritty taste. Our butter stands twenty hours after being salted, when it is re-worked and packed for the market. If it stands longer, it becomes set, and, after working, has the appearance of re-worked butter. As to package, we cannot always suit ourselves, as different markets want different packages.

"Absolute cleanliness in every department of the creamery is necessary. The accumulation of filth in drains, in corners, under stairs, or even in the immediate vicinity, outside of the building, soon develops bad odors, which are taken up by the cream, working sure destruction to the butter. We once lost $60 on two days' butter, by thoughtlessly having our butter-maker go out to the piggery and catch twenty pigs. Although, on returning to the factory, he washed his hands in the usual way, yet enough of the scent adhered to his hands and clothes to cause the above loss. At another time our butter was complained of, and remained for some time in a condition that brought criticism and a serious loss—we being compelled to take back much of the butter, or submit to a large reduction in the price. At last, the trouble was found, in the fact that the butter-maker was in the habit of cleaning his horse in the same clothes in which he worked the butter. As soon as this was corrected, we had no more trouble. We mention these causes, as they are out of the usual path where we are in the habit of looking."

The Manufacture of Condensed Milk.—Dr. Voelcker makes the startling statement in a recent report on condensed milk that it is manufactured mostly from skimmed milk or from milk naturally poor in fat. There are, on the average, 118 parts of casein to 100 of fat in unskimmed milk, but in skimmed milk, with 0·75 per cent. of the fat left in it, there are about 500 parts of casein to 100 parts of fat. In the case of more than 50 analyses of American, Italian, Swiss, German, Belgian and English condensed milk, made from 1870 to 1880, I found the highest proportion of casein to fat to be 173 to 100 in a Belgian sample; six others contain 150 or more of casein, and one sample has 132 of casein to 100 of fat; all the rest have from 130 down to less than 100 parts of casein to 100 of fat—more than ten of these better brands contain less casein than fat. If only skimmed milk were used, or if it were very largely used, in all or in most cases we should have from 300 to 500 parts of casein to 100 of fat. Either Dr. Voelcker has been misrepresented, or else a very decided change has taken place in the methods of this manufacture within the past two years.

An English Dairy Farm.—A number of gentlemen interested in agriculture recently visited the farms of the Short-horn Dairy Company, near Brentwood. The party was under the guidance of the Earl of Dunmore (Chairman of the Company), and Mr. Collinson Hall (Managing Director), and was shown the workings of the system under which the cattle (which are all Short-horns) are stall fed on the produce of the farms mixed with a proportion of foreign food, for the most part half malted. The cattle are housed in concrete-built sheds with mangers, always kept clean, above which flows a constant stream of pure water, so that the animals can drink whenever they wish from a clear stream. When the company acquired the business they took 470 head of cattle. The stock had increased in less than eighteen months to 1,120 head of cattle. The Company is now farming 2,200 acres of land, and has, besides the cattle, 500 Southdown sheep and 400 pigs. They send to London 160,000 quarts of milk weekly.

Kindness to Cattle.—A shipment of twenty-two car-loads of cattle left the Chicago stock-yards Aug. 30th on a special train for New York via the Grand Trunk and Erie roads. The cars used were those of the Montgomery Palace Stock-Car Company of New York, so arranged that the cattle can be fed and watered on the train without unloading. They are supplied with water at the same time the engine is taking water at the stations and their feed is let down while the train is moving from bins at the top of the car. It is expected the trip will be made in sixty hours instead of five days. It is thought that the animals can be put in compartments and loading effected in about the same time as upon ordinary stock cars. A Pullman coach attached to the train was occupied by Hon. Hylas Sabin, Railroad Commissioner of Ohio, Mr. Horn, representing the Illinois Humane Society, the officers of the car company and others.

Registering the Yield of Each Cow.—In a catalogue of sale in 1846 of Short-horns, with a few Alderneys, the property of Mr. Lakin, of Beauchamp's Court, four miles from Worcester, this statement was made by the auctioneers: "It has been a remarkable feature in Mr. Lakin's system of farming that he registered the yield of milk, showing the annual quantity given by each cow, enabling him thereby to select his rearing calves from the best milkers." Whereupon a correspondent of the English *Agricultural Gazette* asks: "Are these registers in existence?" Such documents gain in value by time, and it would be curious to learn, in the now increasing attention which is paid to dairying, if Mr. Lakin had better returns in 1846 than he can show at the present time.

A Hint For the Cattle Fairs.—Quite a sensation was caused at the Ayr Show, by the turning out of the prize-ring of three animals entered by the Duke of Buccleuch. The examiners said that the beasts had been "doctored"—that is their teats had been bound around with tape to give them a nicely rounded appearance, which scores so many points in a severe competition. Mr. Cranston, the Duke's representative, pleaded hard for the restoration of the animals to the ring, even if they were debarred from taking prizes, but the judges were firm, and declined to look at the beasts which had been condemned by the examiner as having been tampered with.

# BASE BALL.

## The Niantics vs. the Haverlys.

The match between these clubs that was played last Sunday at the Recreation Grounds was not distinguished by much brilliant fielding but this may in part be attributed to the heavy dust that was at times blown across the field. The Niantics led off with a heavy score of ten, and although the Haverlys played fairly an uphill game, they were beaten in the end by one innnings and three runs. Following is the score:

NIANTIC.

| | TB. | R. | B.H. | P.O. | A. | E. |
|---|---|---|---|---|---|---|
| Emerson, 3d b | 5 | 3 | 2 | 2 | 1 | 1 |
| Incell, r. f | 5 | 2 | 0 | 0 | 6 | 1 |
| Donahue, s. s | 5 | 1 | 1 | 1 | 3 | 0 |
| Egan, 1st b | 5 | 1 | 1 | 11 | 0 | 0 |
| Arnold, c. f | 5 | 2 | 1 | 0 | 0 | 1 |
| Finn, 3 | 5 | 1 | 1 | 13 | 4 | 0 |
| Sweeney, p | 5 | 2 | 1 | 0 | 8 | 0 |
| Robinson, l. f | 4 | 1 | 2 | 0 | 0 | 0 |
| Fogarty, 2d b | 4 | 1 | 1 | 0 | 2 | 1 |
| Totals | 43 | 14 | 10 | 27 | 24 | 4 |

HAVERLY.

| | TB. | R. | B.H. | P.O. | A. | E. |
|---|---|---|---|---|---|---|
| Meegan, 2d b. and s. s | 5 | 1 | 0 | 0 | 1 | 1 |
| Lawton, c. f. and 2d b | 5 | 1 | 1 | 6 | 1 | 1 |
| J. Carroll, p. and s. s | 5 | 2 | 2 | 2 | 4 | 1 |
| F. Carroll, c | 5 | 2 | 1 | 8 | 1 | 1 |
| Levy, l. f | 5 | 0 | 1 | 2 | 0 | 1 |
| McCord, s. s. and 3d b | 4 | 2 | 0 | 1 | 3 | 3 |
| Sharkey, r. f | 4 | 1 | 2 | 0 | 0 | 1 |
| Boyce, c. f. and 2d b | 4 | 1 | 1 | 2 | 0 | 2 |
| Pratt, 1st b | 4 | 1 | 0 | 3 | 0 | 2 |
| Totals | 41 | 11 | 8 | 24 | 10 | 13 |

| Innings | 1 | 2 | 3 | 4 | 5 | 6 | 7 | 8 | 9 | |
|---|---|---|---|---|---|---|---|---|---|---|
| Niantic | 10 | 1 | 2 | 1 | 0 | 0 | 0 | 0 | * | —14 |
| Haverly | 2 | 3 | 1 | 0 | 1 | 0 | 2 | 2 | 0 | —11 |

*Played but eight innings.

Earned runs—Niantic 1, Haverly 1. Home runs—J. Carroll 1, Emerson 1. Three-base hits—Sharkey 1, Finn 1. Two-base hits—Lawton. First on errors—Haverly 3, Niantic 10. Left on bases—Haverly 8, Niantic 3. Struck out—Haverly 9, Niantic 3. Base on balls—Haverly 4, Niantic 1. Double plays—McCord and Carroll, Lawton and Pratt. Passed balls—Finn 5, Lawton 1, F. Carroll 1. Wild pitch—Sweeney 2. Umpire—Start of the Renos.

# ROWING.

## The Saratoga Regatta.

The Subscription Regatta, conceived, managed and carried out by a committe of visitors at Saratoga, come off on August 25th with a success never before equaled by any professional or amateur regatta on Lake Saratoga. We take the following full account of the races from Krik's letter in the *New York World*:

"The contestants, both amateurs and professionals, made a fine exhibition, the professional race being one of the best ever seen in this country. Five amateurs and seven professionals responded to the call of the referee, and as both races were rowed and the results known to the crowd before 6 o'clock, Mr. Referee Stanford not only deserved the praise of all, but, as was suggested, he deserved to be used as the subject of Roger's next group of statuary, and to be represented standing on the bow of Mr. Durkee's yacht, hat, in hand, with the timers, Edgar M. Johnson and Phil Dwyer, immediately behind him, the group to be labeled: 'A referee who knew his rights and carried them out to the letter.' So punctually were the details carried out that at exactly 3:55 the 'get ready' gun was fired from Mr. Moon's boat, the Luna, to which five of the dozen entries for the amateur race responded.

"FIRST RACE.

"Saratoga Lake, N. Y., August 25th.—Amateur single-scull race, free to all, three miles, with a turn, for prizes given by a visitor's committee; to the first a piece of plate valued at $200, to the second a gold medal valued at $100 and to the third a silver medal valued at $50.

| | |
|---|---|
| P. Holmes, Pawtucket, R. I. | 1 |
| J. Kirby, Pawtucket, R. I. | 2 |
| J. Pilkington, Metropolitan B. C., New York | 3 |
| C. E. Bulger, Mutual B. C., Albany, N. Y. | 4 |
| P. A. Dempsey, Philadelphia, Pa. | disq |
| R. Larmon, Union Springs, R. C. | dr |
| H. E. O'Brien, Boston, Mass. | dr |
| J. J. Murphy, junior champion United States, Boston, Mass. | dr |
| J. I. Smith, Palisade Boat Club, Yonkers, N. Y. | dr |
| D. Lambert, Seaside Boat Club, Brooklyn, N. Y. | dr |
| J. O'Brien, Boston, Mass. | dr |
| O. P. Nolan, Seaside Boat Club, Brooklyn, N. Y. | dr |

Betting.—The field, $100; Mr. Homes, from $90 down to $75.

"At the start, which was a good one, Holmes from the extreme western stake took the lead, and with Kirby second and Bulger third they rowed nearly a quarter of a mile, when the last named failed to hold his position and was passed by both Pilkington and Dempsey. The two Rhode Islanders in the mean time had secured such a lead and were laying such a good course that at the mile post there were a dozen lengths between them and Pilkington and Dempsey. Holmes was first to reach the turning point, which he made in about 9m. 50s., followed by Kirby, Dempsey, Pilkington and so late by Bulger that the referee's boat could not wait. Once round Holmes laid a good course over towards the western shore, and although not in any way hurried he kept the pace good, and with his friend Kirby a few lengths away he rowed to the end, winning by about a dozen lengths, followed out by Kirby, about three lengths in front of Dempsey, who was two in front of Pilkington. As soon as he could reach the referee's boat Mr. Dempsey claimed a foul against Mr. Holmes, but to his own surprise he was informed that he himself was disqualified, having turned the stake-boat the wrong way, and that his complaint would not be entertained. With this the result of the race was announced: Holmes, first, time 21m. 16½s; Kirby, second, 21m. 48s.; and Pilkington, third, 21m. 56s., and with that announcement the gun was fired for the professionals to get ready.

"As the smoke of the gun drifted across the smooth surface of the lake all were interested to see who would be the starters of the nine entered. It was known that Plaisted would not and that Elliott, having found that he was in no condition for a hard race, had also decided not to row. In other words, the Englishman found out that he could not make a 'deal,' and so wisely refrained from showing how hollow his pretensions are now. Among those first to show were Lee, Hosmer, Sheldon and Ross. The last named attracted much attention and in his white-sleeved shirt and home-darned brown drawers he looked in fine condition. Ten Eyck was the next to show, followed a few minutes later by Riley, who, although somewhat under the weather, decided to row. Several minutes elapsed and there began to be a general inquiry for Courtney. Some expressed a belief that he would not start, and an offer was then made on the Luna to bet its owner $100 to $60 against Courtney. Mr. Moon said he would wait until he saw Charley in his boat, and not a few began to look as if they feared some new accident had happened. Finally, however, Courtney appeared. He looked well in his sleeveless white shirt, blue drawers and blue kerchief, and as he rowed to his station Mr. Moon took the $100 to $60 offered and in turn offered to do so again, which was declined. With a few more minutes delay, caused by the contestants putting on their colors, they finally took the several stations assigned them.

"SECOND RACE.

"Saratoga Lake, N. Y., August 25.—Professional single scull, free for all, three miles with a turn, for prizes given by a visitor's committee; to the first, $1,000; to the second, $200, and to the third, $100.

| | |
|---|---|
| G. W. Lee, Newark, N. J. | 1 |
| C. E. Courtney, Union Springs, N. Y. | 2 |
| Wallace Ross, St. John, N. B. | 3 |
| H. Sheldon, Saratoga, N. Y. | 4 |
| G. H. Hosmer, Boston, Mass. | 5 |
| J. A. Ten Eyck, Peekskill, N. Y. | * |
| J. H. Riley, Saratoga, N. Y. | * |
| W. Elliott, Newcastle, England | dr |
| F. A. Plaisted, Boston, Mass. | dr |

*Fouled.

Betting.—Ross, $375; Courtney, $200; field, $45.

"As the seven contestants waited at their several stakes they not only looked well, but promised to make a race of unequaled merit. With a few words of warning from Mr. Stanford, he gave them the word 'Go' to a splendid start. For a furlong no one seemed to have any advantage, but before they had rowed a quarter of a mile Lee from the extreme western station began to show in front, with Courtney and Ross pulling out on the eastern side, Hosmer and Riley being well up between Lee and the two cracks, while close up with them was Sheldon on the western side and Ten Eyck on the eastern, all rowing so closely together that it was difficult to say which of the four, Lee, Hosmer, Ross or Courtney, was actually in the lead, and they kept so not only for a mile, but right on down to the turning stake, which Lee reached first, but with the others so close up that all four were engaged in turning at the same time. Lee made a splendid turn, Courtney a bad one, as also did Ross. Hosmer had just got around when Riley ran into him, his boat passing over the stern of Hosmer's. For an instant both men seemed to be in danger of sinking, and both the referee and press boats steamed out of their course for a rescue, but as three or four row-boats were seen making for them they were left and the two steam-boats turned to follow the contestants, of whom there were really but three left, for not only were Hosmer and Riley out of the race, but Ten Eyck and Sheldon were so far behind Lee, Courtney and

Ross that neither the referee nor the press boat could wait for them. At the end of two miles Ross was also virtually out of the race, the interest in which from that point centered in the efforts of Lee and Courtney. The former was rowing a magnificent course, having somewhat unfairly the assistance of several of the amateurs that had rowed in the previous race, while Courtney had not only to row but to watch his course. He did both wonderfully well, but in Lee he found a stubborn antagonist, and notwithstanding all the encouragement that the crowd could give the ex-champion he could not pass the Newark man, who, rowing good and strong right to the end, was the first to pass the finishing point he winning by a couple of lengths from Courtney with Ross a bad third. The others were virtually nowhere.

"As soon as possible the referee and press boats came together, when it was announced that Lee was the winner in 20m. 45½s., Courtney second in 20m. 48½s. and Ross third in 21m. 31s., and with three cheers for the referee the crowd broke for home in every direction, convinced that with good management it is still possible to have honest professional sculling, that of the seven that started Lee was really the best man under the condition of the race, and that while both Courtney and Ross might beat him in a match, it would be only after a terrific struggle. The time would have been a little easier but for a northerly breeze which sprang up just at the turn and which was dead against the rowers all the way back.

"George W. Lee, the winner, was born at Newark and is twenty-four years of age. He is five feet ten inches tall and weighs 153 pounds. He began his career on the Passaic River as an amateur and was very successful. In 1878 he won the amateur championship of the United States, and the following year went to England. While there he was defeated by Moss at Henley. On his return he determined to enter the professional arena and was defeated in a match with John A. Kennedy, of Portland. Since then he has been a contestant at the numerous regattas throughout the country, meeting with some success. On July 4, 1882, he won the Boston race, defeating Conley, Ham, Hosmer, Riley and Plaisted. In his last race, about a month ago, he defeated Riley and Dempsey on Lake Keuka, N. Y. While practicing Thursday last Lee was swamped, smashing a new boat belonging to Riley and just barely escaping a watery grave."

DOUBTS OVER HONESTY.—Sampson, the editor of the London Referee, places no faith in the professions of the two leading oarsmen of the world. He says in the last number of the Referee which has come to hand:

According to American sporting papers, Hanlan and Ross are now exchanging vigorous defiances. Most likely there is a purpose to be, served by this portion of the programme which has not as yet made itself manifest to the outer world. For the last three or four years Hanlan and Ross have either been the closest friends or the bitterest enemies, and I shouldn't like to say which of these attitudes is the most dangerous to a confiding public. When Ross and Hanlan do row—providing Providence at last permits of this perennial engagement being brought to a conclusion—is likely enough, we shall be left more in the dark than we are now as to which is really the superior sculler. Both fit and well, and with a guarantee that the race was fair and square, it would be a good thing to lay odds on one, and that one not the Black Brunswicker. But that Hanlan and Ross ever will row a genuine match I do not believe, unless indeed the match that will probably be made soon becomes genuine by Hanlan "putting the double on." The merest novice must by this time be aware that Hanlan and Ross have something in their mind's eyes beyond the desire for discovering which is the better man. It is pitiable to think that the two fastest and best scullers that the world has yet produced should descend to this sort of work, but what can be expected of professional rowing men after recent experiences? Notwithstanding the horror or confession will create in the minds of such as do not dare to think that "men ever willingly row behind, I will admit that to me the chief cause for regret in all this negotiation is the clumsy way in which piratical design has been allowed to expose itself. Hanlan's much-advertised illness now turns out to have been merely a feint for the purpose of extricating himself from the Ross engagement. Malingering is a new form of professional device; when it is again adopted, the interesting individual should take care not to recover too quickly. I am in receipt of information upon which I can rely—which comes from various sources, all of them independent—to the effect that if Hanlan had been half as bad with typhoid fever as he was said to be, his recovery and return to robust health would have been a feat on record such as the medical profession never believed possible previously.

PROSPECTS OF A FINE RACE.—The Detroit correspondent of the Turf, Field and Farm writes that journal, under date of Aug. 19, as follows: John McEldowney, backed by a prominent and wealthy citizen, is endeavoring to get up a regatta on the island course here in October, in which there will be two great events: A four-oared race between the fastest fours in this country, and a professional sculling race participated in by Hanlan (if he will row), Ross, Plaisted, Hosmer, Riley, Lee and all the other first-class scullers in the United States and Canada. Since the Centennials so handsomely won the National and Northwestern championship in the regatta here, a great many rowing men and the public generally have expressed a desire to see them pitted against the Hilldales, with whom they would make a very interesting race. A number of the best oarsmen in the country, who attended the recent regattas, have also expressed great anxiety to meet the champions of last year and this year in a four-oared contest. Holmes and Appley, Kirby and Cattanach have organized themselves into a four-oared crew for that purpose, and those who saw the first two win the pair-oars race in the Northwestern, and saw the other two scull, will know that they would give any four in the world a hard race. O'Connell and Buckley, the Portland scullers, say they also have a four-oared crew "by the sad sea waves," which they will enter in the proposed regatta, and which they think can win. Yates, the two Muchanoros and another, constituting the Farragut four, of Chicago, are also eager for the contest, so that if the consent of the Hilldales to row on their return from England can be obtained the regatta will make one of the finest aquatic contests ever had in this country. It is proposed to give as prizes for the winning four gold watches and chains, worth $250 apiece; and for the professional sculling race $300 in money to first; $200 to second, and $100 to third. Correspondence has been opened with the Hilldales, to see if they will enter, before anything definite is decided upon.

GABRIEL DISPLAYS MOORE.—The state mile with a turn race for $1,000, between George Geisel, of this city, and J. H. Moore, of Westchester, was rowed on Little Neck Bay, Long Island Sound, August 23rd. Moore was the favorite but Geisel outrowed him, winning easily in 30 min. 11 sec.

## The Hilldales in England.

There has been a great deal of unmerited abuse heaped upon the heads of the amateur oarsmen of England by some of the sporting journals of this country, who do not understand the difficult position made for the different crews by the action of the English Rowing Association. It is with a view of dispelling some of the prejudices arising from an indiscriminate abuse against the English oarsman, that we take the following article from Land and Water, the most able and conservative journal of aquatic and field sports in England, giving a resume of the positions held by the Hilldales and the English crews:

In all branches of sport the present is an age of associations. Swimmers, runners, bicyclists, foot-ball players, have all their associations or unions. Now quite recently it has been discovered that there is in existence an association who have vested in themselves the sole and absolute control of all English amateur oarsmen, and all matters relating to amateur aquatic sport. It is somewhat strange that this autocratic body, self-elected and apparently irresponsible to any other authority, or even the will of the majority of its constituents, is able to completely paralyze the action of our oarsmen and keep them in the most abject subjection to its own commands and behests. It is no doubt a very useful thing for an association to possess this complete authority, but when that association uses this authority against the wishes of nearly the whole of the body it is supposed to represent, and does its best to bring the members into contempt and ridicule, the sooner the association is done away with the better. The Amateur Rowing Association (so-called) in the case of the Hilldale crew has undoubtedly brought English amateur rowing and oarsmen into a most humiliating and degrading position, and the sooner this type tree of the amateur crowing world is uprooted the better for sport and our English character for pluck and fair play.

The American Association of Amateur Oarsmen, with great enterprise and praiseworthy ambition, have sent over to this country their champion four-oared crew, to test the relative merits of the best American and English amateur talent in fours. It was no secret that they were coming, and that they were not going to enter at Henley, but at the other regattas in England; and, if possible, row matches against our best club fours. Other strangers have done this, been duly accepted as amateurs, rowed with our old crews, generally were beaten, without any objections being raised by an association, club, or committee. Special regulations were then made for foreign entries, so that there might be no hitch or question on the subject of the entry of a foreign crew or oarsmen. The Hilldale men were therefore perfectly justified in assuming that there would not be any further proofs required as to their status, especially when they came as the representative crew of the American Association. On their arrival here, they, however, found nothing but difficulties and impediments thrown in their way. First, they discovered that the Metropolitan Regatta entries were hedged around, as regards foreigners, with all the clauses of the Henley rules. As this was unknown to nearly everybody outside the London R. C. committee, it is not surprising the Hilldale men unprepared as to the entry date and the affidavits. Although the Marlow Regatta committee were English enough to take the strangers' entry, and the long-expected trial between the two styles was about to be tested, the English Association at once determined to put their authority to the test, and issued a ukase which virtually closed the door of every amateur regatta and club against our visitors. Since then the Association has dogged the unfortunate Hilldales' footsteps, and on every occasion when the strangers seemed likely to obtain a race or an entry at a regatta, its machinery of terrorism was put in motion, and the Boycotting process extended. More recently the Hilldales have openly challenged the Thames R. C. to row them a match, and although the members of their club almost to a man are anxious to accept the challenge, for the honor of their club and country, the association sternly refuses to allow the vetoed-for trial.

Here the matter at present rests. The Association is supposed to be making inquiries in America as to the bona fides of the Hilldales crew's declarations, and, then, if these inquiries are considered satisfactory, permission will be given to the club to row as desired. It is difficult to know which is the most astonishing fact, either the cowardice and want of self-reliance of the modern race of amateur oarsmen, or the daring impudence of the self-elected body which is able to obtain such implied obedience to its commands. They do not make the slightest explanation or defense of their conduct or procedure, which are both undefensible, untoward-handed and cowardly. The whole of the amateur rowing world is against the association's actions, and yet no club or body of oarsmen have sufficient pluck to shake themselves free from the trammels of such an organization. The American have a just grievance against English hospitality, fair play, pluck, and justice, and this present assumption of strict amateurism by the association is something very new in the annals of amateur rowing. At country regattas, and even at Henley itself, our best clubs and University crews have frequently met oarsmen of the mechanic, artisan, and laborer class, and have suffered very much by the contaminating influence of such antagonism. This makes the present rabid craze in the amateur interest all the more inexcusable when a foreigner is in the case.

HANLAN'S LATEST PROPOSITION TO ROSS.—Edward Hanlan has written the following letter to the Toronto Globe. In answer to Mr. Ross' challenge to me, I may say that I have thoroughly made up my mind not to row any race this year, and therefore cannot accommodate Mr. Ross, who seems to be eager to wrest the championship from me. But I hereby make him an offer. I will consent to row him four or five miles on any course between here and New York, next June, for $3,000 a side and the championship of the world. If Mr. Ross does not embrace this opportunity for making a match, there is every probability that I will not be able to accommodate him with a race even next year. I may be engaged in business which will prevent me making any matches unless I have long notice ahead. If he entertains this proposition he can send along articles of agreement.
TORONTO, Aug. 21.          EDWARD HANLAN.

A SWEEPING CHALLENGE.—Wallace Ross publishes a card stating that he has received no reply to his challenge from Hanlan, wherein Ross offered to row him for $1,000 a side and the championship of the world. Ross claims the championship. He refers to his inability for two years to get a race with Hanlan, but offers to accommodate him this year or next. Finally, Ross offers to defend the challenge against all comers, and will make a "match with "any one for from $1,000 to $5,000 a side, Hanlan preferred.

THE HILLSDALES' PROPOSITION.—The four-oared crew of the Thames Boat Club, which has accepted the Hilldales' challenge to a race, will make up as follows: H. B. Tween, bow; J. Bastie, No. 2; H. Rush, No. 3, and J. Canton, stroke. This race will be rowed early in September.

THE NATIONAL REGATTA.—The tenth annual regatta of amateur oarsmen was rowed August 8th and 9th at Detroit. The course was a mile and a half straight down stream, the current averaging about one mile and a half an hour. The course was staked at right angles with the Island Survey Stakes, instead of with the channel, the consequence being diagonal lines at start and finish, which, in one case, at least, caused much discussion; one crew claiming to have won by ten lengths, while in fact they had barely that number of feet lead, and they could not understand it. No regatta ever had finer accommodations for seeing races than those provided by the committee in the shape of a grand stand on the island, where every one of the three thousand occupants could see every stroke rowed, from start to finish, with a common glass, and the only pity is, that the stand was not built twice as large, for, in spite of the weather, it was filled each day, and during the Northwestern Regatta, which followed on the 10th and 11th, crowds were unable to get inside the grand stand inclosure. The weather was everything but good, and, during the whole two days, the course was not once smooth for a shell race. The officers postponed races from time to time until the water should smooth out or the rain stop; but got through the whole programme each day, and no races went over. The weather had been bad for a whole week. After the stand was half full Tuesday, the heavens opened and a tremendous thunderstorm came up and drenched the crowd, who had no escape, but it soon cleared up and the sun restored good humor. At the time set for the race the rain was coming down in torrents and the lightning was flashing beautifully. The crowd was given between two peals of thunder and the rain almost immediately laid the oarsmen from view.

The trial heats were rowed with the following on the second day the final heats were rowed with the following results:

Senior four, final heat, water good, wind light, up stream —Centennial B. C., 8m. 27s.; Wyandotte B. C., 8m. 34s.; Chatham B. C., 9m. 54½s. For nearly half a mile the crews pulled side by side, Chatham getting too far out into the stream. At the half, Centennial showed a slight lead, rowing 46 strokes per minute, while Chatham was doing 44 and Wyandotte 42, the Centennials rowing in much the best form of the three, and getting the most speed, gradually drew away. At the mile Wyandotte spurted desperately, but although their stroke went up to 48 they could not overhaul the little Centennials, who kept up their even 46, not seeming to think that there was the least danger of their being caught. As they neared the finish Chatham hit her up to 48 but could not reduce the distance, the Centennials finally crossing the line without a spurt, leading the Wyandottes by about two open lengths, Chatham last by several lengths.

The Centennial Club was organized in 1876, and for four years rowed just well enough to be beaten in every race they entered. Various changes have been made in their crew, and in 1880 they commenced going to regattas and picking up points on rowing which they applied, and progressed so successfully that they were the only crew who made the Hilldales row at the Northwestern regatta, and this year, with one entirely green man in their boat, they can probably outrow any amateur crew in America.

Senior single-sculls, final heat, water in very fine condition.—Holmes, 10m. 5s.; Laing, 10m. 9s.; Kirby, 10m. 14½s. Holmes got slightly the best of the send-off, but was closely followed by Laing who was lapped on to him, while Kirby in turn was lapped on to Laing, and so the three rowed to the half mile very close together. Here Holmes tried to shake off Laing but could do it. Kirby spurted and drew up alongside the Canadian, whom the other two now had in a pocket, and who spurted again and again, each time a foul being the result, and during the second half mile, a half dozen fouls were committed by one or the other. The pace all the way was a killing one, and at the mile Kirby and Laing dropped back. Holmes taking a good length lead and finally winning the race by a short length, Laing about that distance ahead of Kirby. All entered protests, but the referee decided promptly that the men had all been in the wrong at times, and placed them in the order of the finish. The Post and Tribune said: "Not even Holmes, who thus retained the championship he won in 1881 seemed satisfied, and the oarsmen rowed away to the boathouse together, scolding each other like a parcel of old women. Laing indeed had the worst of it in the race, which looked as if the Eastern men had conspired to beat him."

As the ex-champion amateur is receiving a good deal of advertising, he has been winning several races, one of which was a close brush with the coroner. Only the other day he was handled as having swallowed a few pounds of poisoned ice cream and then stimulated by that headache diet he threw himself into his scull and raced second to Lee scull in front of Ross on the 25th ult. at Saratoga Lake. He told all his friends that he was going to win the race and the non-sliding believers in his word got badly cinched. We next hear of Courtney defeating Lee at Canandaigua Lake in the extraordinary time of 19 min. 31½ sec. for the mile with a turn. All these remarkable achievements seem to indicate that it is in the programme for Courtney to row Ross for the championship of the world when the Brunswicker shall have grown tired of challenging Hanlan who will not row any one this year. Notwithstanding the eccentricity of his rowing career there are hosts of rowing men and admirers of the aquatic sport who still regard Courtney as the best oarsman in the world and would put their money on him to a match with Ross. It is not at all improbable that their judgment of Courtney's ability to defeat Ross may be correct, but the prudence of betting that he would do it would be quite a different matter.

CHANGE IN A CREW.—It is very likely that Louis White, captain of the Pioneer four, will not take part in the combat for the BREEDER AND SPORTSMAN cup on Thanksgiving day. Mr. White has been engaged in a new business which takes him out of the city two weeks in a month and it will be impossible for him to train properly for the match. An effort will be made to supply his place by either Al Tobin, who is one of the most reliable bowmen, or Wm. J. Burke, late of the Cork Rowing Club. Both of these gentlemen have not done much rowing during the past year and it is not easy to draw them into hard practice again. Mr. Burke is a famous stroke and if he should consent to take a seat in the Pioneer boat the positions of the crew would be changed and John Sullivan, who now pulls stroke, placed in the forward seat with Al Tobin in the crew; the four would be a strong one, as Mr. Tobin steers admirably. As there is plenty of time before the race will take place the necessary changes will be made and the crew made as strong as possible.

TRITON ENTERTAINMENT. — The Triton Swimming and Boating Club will give its first social party on Sept. 30, at Turner Hall, Turk street. Handsome cards of invitation have been issued to the various rowing clubs. The committee having charge of the entertainment are—Committee of arrangement: E. Kehrlein, C. Rudolph, B. Oliver, A. F. Schuppert, A. B. Tuckey. Reception Committee: A. Tuckey, J. Artigues, B. Kehrlein. J. Hanghy, W. Poehlmon. Floor Committee: V. Kehrlein, J. W. Heerdwick, A. L. Schuppert, J. Kehrlein, H. Tuckey.

THE PROBABLE PROGRAMME.—It looks very much as if Courtney is to be brought out again as champion of the world. The plans of these professional oarsmen are so complicated as the programmes of the professional politician, and when they seem to be making headway in one direction it is always prudent to keep a look-out on the opposite course. One can never tell where the wily gentry are going to turn on their tracks and elude the public eye. Last year Courtney rowed in the Toronto regatta and made a pretty fair showing, but the matches between Hanlan and Boyd and Trickett distracted attention from the ex-champion amateur and towards the end of the boating season he dropped out of sight. This year there is no one to row Ross a match race.

## YACHTING.

### Why Not Race?

A few weeks ago the BREEDER AND SPORTSMAN published some reasons why yachtsmen did not enter their boats for races more frequently, and why yacht racing was on the decline. These reasons are those shown by experience. They are not commonly recognized outside of yachting circles, but those who have ever had anything to do with getting up races or regattas know with what difficulty every one is brought up to the scratch. It will be thought that everything is going on swimmingly until all of a sudden one man will change his mind, whereupon half a dozen more will have fault to find and will draw out or want conditions which cannot be complied with. It is very hard to get a lot of yacht-owners to agree to enter their boats for a race, especially if one very fast yacht is likely to get the prize. During the New York Club contest recently a spirit of this kind was shown, as will be seen by the following statement by a correspondent:

"The schooner Montauk did not start in the race of last Monday. Various reasons are given for not starting. It was said that Mr. Piatt having that he had been styled a 'mug hunter,' decided to show that he was not by declining to start for this particular mug; but I judge the real reason to be that the Halcyon, which had come on from Vineyard Haven with the fleet, instead of coming into Marblehead with the fleet, went to Boston and was hauled out and had her bottom cleaned. Then she went to her owner's place at Nahant, where she was stripped for the fray, every superfluous article having been sent ashore; and Mr. Piatt, of the Montauk, or, more properly, Captain Joe Ellsworth, who was charged with the conduct of her racing, did not deem it advisable to race under unfair conditions, the Montauk being obliged to go in cruising trim, with anchors on the bow, tanks full of water, ice-house full, etc.

"As the result proved, the Montauk could have won had she started, for she went over the course with the Halcyon, starting behind her and finishing ahead. It was to be regretted that she did not start, as it permitted an Eastern schooner to again capture the prize. This has been done now for many years, and the Montauk was relied on this year to revenge the result. Last year the Tidal Wave, the only schooner of the fleet that could have captured the Eastern schooners, was barred out by the unjust p di of—not the club but—the fleet captain against the gentleman in whose charge she had been placed by her owner, and this year the New Yorkers have been prevented from capturing the schooner cup by a childish notion that a shrewd Yankee trick had been played on them. There was nothing reprehensible in the conduct of Mr. Payne, the owner of the Halcyon. It was his duty, representing, as he did, the Eastern Club, to put his vessel in as perfect a condition as possible for the race, and so long as he violated no rule he is not blameworthy. The Montauk should have started, and if beaten, then all this extra preparation of the Halcyon could have been alleged in excuse, and if she conquered, then her triumph would have been all the more.

"These petty jockeyings by boats with a reputation for speed, such as refusing to start when there is the least doubt of their winning, should be discountenanced by all means by a club such as the New York, which is an association of gentlemen, and not a sporting organization at all. While all should desire to win as a matter of course, they should enter their boats for the sake of the race, and not for the sake of the victory. It is this spirit that has made it well-nigh impossible to have a regatta.

"'I've got no chance,' says Mr. A., 'and why should I enter!'

"'My boat has got a reputation for speed,' says Mr. B., 'and why should I jeopardize it! If she should be beaten it would detract $2,000 from her value.

"'They call me a mug-hunter,' says Mr. C., 'and I'll show 'em I ain't one. I've got a boat faster than any that is entered, but I won't start her, though I could take the prize as easy as not if I chose.'

"Then others object to the score of canvas. They have no balloon sails, and others have, and so, as I have before this pointed out, the money spent for the regatta might as well be saved."

The Chispa now flies the owl flag.

The Clara will not sail in the race to-day. There are no other boats of her class to compete with and the schooners are all too large for her.

The little Whitewing has been made ready for the fray and hopes to clean the O'Connor and Fleur de Lis on Saturday; she is not, however, sure of the Nellie.

The Casco looks very handsome under sail, and last Sunday in the channel in the stormy breeze, just heeled over a little, she made a perfect picture of a fine yacht.

The Pacific Yacht Club regatta committee consists of W. H. Mastenstein, Con O'Connor and G. J. Denny. The judges are J. C. Kelly and C. O'Connor, John L. Eckley being referee.

The Bohemian Yacht Club is going to open its new club house on the 16th with suitable ceremonies. There are only five members of this club, each one being a yacht owner. The members are all of them also members of the San Francisco Yacht Club, using the wharf, etc., of that club as a landing place. Their new house is a little gem of a place, very neatly fitted up.

The yacht Turner is building for the Spreckels brothers is all planked up and they are waiting for deck plank to go ahead with that part of the work. Port Orford cedar ($50 per M.) is used for deck plank. The yacht will be completed in two months. The internal arrangements are not yet fully decided on. With an 85 foot yacht and no centerboard in the way there is plenty of room.

The small yacht race of the San Francisco Yacht Club will take place on the 16th inst. over the same course as last year. In addition to the usual plungers, sloops, etc., there will be 12 or 15 whitehall boats. City yawl boats and boats from Oakland will make up the fleet. The classes will be within five foot limits, and in each class will time allowance be given. There is a good deal of interest manifested among the runners of small yachts and the race will, no doubt, be a very interesting one.

The "fast and favorite" yacht Nellie is not going "for blood" in the race to-day apparently, for she has not been taken out of the water to be cleaned. She was last on the dry dock some time in July; moreover, her owner, Mr. Bowie, is going to sail her himself, the one who usually sails her, Captain Murphy, going on the Ariel with Turner. The crew that usually sails on the Nellie is also going on the Ariel, so the Nellie will not be in good shape for a race. She has enough glory, however, to let some other yacht have a show.

The schooner Ariel is sailing much better than she ever did before, since she has a new Bermudian mainsail, lead keel, etc. But she has not sailed in the past two weeks as she did at first when launched. Perhaps she is foul. At one time the Ariel almost beat the Nellie; now she cannot come so near it as Commodore McDonough's fine yacht Aggie, which now carries the prize flag of the Pacific Yacht Club, and is expected to take it again in the race on Saturday. However she has a team to work against. The Ariel, Nellie, Fleur de Lis, Annie, O'Connor and Whitewing are all "going for her scalp." She has a good deal of allowance to give these yachts and must keep running to beat them. The Ariel and Nellie in particular are going to be hard to beat. Turner is going to sail the Ariel and Hyde Bowie will sail the Nellie.

## FISH.

### Fishing in Oregon.

The fishing season is about ended, and the general cry is "no fish," unless you go away up the Mackensie or the headwaters of the Clackamas. Within forty miles of Portland, trout fishing is virtually at an end until such times as a riper civilization shall guarantee more stringent and arbitrary laws for the preservation of streams. If men would content themselves with one or two dozen good-sized trout and throw back all the little fingerlings, to give them a chance to grow, Oregon would continue to be a good trout-fishing State for many years. But the love of making a big count is set so deep in the breasts of some men that they will keep on catching them by hundreds, regardless of whether they can use them or not. So they bring back to town the surplus and distribute them among their friends, and the streams are furnishing food to men who never think of incurring the toil and labor required to catch them.

Then there are the dynamite fiends, who sink their encored cartridges in the streams and kill five fish where they actually catch one. This has been a pretty strong game about Seattle and Tacoma, which once boasted an abundance of the most beautiful and gamest of trout. Now it is almost impossible to catch a dozen trout in a day's fishing in any of those streams. There is a villainous offense and calls for the severest punishment. Those who practice it are generally low men, of coarse and brutal natures, whom a few months in jail would benefit on general principles.

The incoming legislature will be permitted to enact a general and stringent law that will discriminate between the words "game" and "meat," and teach these wretched poachers that they cannot wantonly destroy fish in our beautiful streams without incurring heavy fines and imprisonments. Then we may be able to give the fish a chance to grow and to breed, and expect these lazy vagabonds to go to work. Not an angler ever was known that destroys and exterminates as many fish in a week as these giant powder fiends are doing in a day. If they go on in this way for five years longer, split-bamboo rods will be worth about a dollar apiece.—The Oregonian.

BASS FISHING.—In Virginia they seem to think the carp is a good biter and puller, more particularly in the month of August. A gentleman gives his experience as follows: "We found these fish would not bite at worms, but would at bread, and that the best bread with which to bait the hook is the crust of a baker's loaf or roll, fastened on the hook with the crust side up. Our party, including some old and experienced anglers, were astonished to see how some of the fish bit in genuine black bass style. In bottom and wind the black bass does not compare with the carp. We tried this and among fish the carp is what an old-fashioned foxhound is among dogs—a little slow, but of long enduring power. This fish, we believe, fights as gamely for life when in water as a mountain trout. It does not pull so hard as a bass will for a little while, but long after a bass would throw up the sponge' this carp comes up smiling, and you cannot see that it has lost a particle of its power to repeat the same thing for many rounds. The truth is that of the carp we caught, though allowed to play a long time, not one of them said 'I give it up,' but continued to die last to fight hard. To any man of soul who knows what good sport is, we would say: Make a pond, get some (as many as you can) young carp and put them in said pond. Throw out some scraps of bread to these fish once a day, and in twelve months you can have such sport as would have electrified old Isaac Walton."

A MEAN TRICK.—The other day a well-known sportsman doing business on the south side of J. street, between Second and Third, went fishing. The first thing he did was to cast his expensive throw-line from the bow of the boat without first taking the precaution to fasten it. He got out other tackle, however, and set to work in a lively way, and soon began to drop perch, catfish, etc., into the bag suspended from the side of the boat. After he had taken a goodly number, he drew in his sack to start for home, when he made the disheartening discovery that some thoughtful friend had cut open the bottom of it before he left town. He is still on the warpath.—Sacramento Bee.

It is stated by one of the pilots that in the vicinity of the wreck of the steamer Escambia on the bar outside the Golden Gate, the fishing is very good. Since the wreck occurred it seems that large quantities of fish have gathered in the neighborhood. Why this is so is not known, unless they find food in the great quantities of wheat which have come out of the steamer's hold. Whatever the reason, there are plenty of fish there. It will not do, however, to go there in a skiff or a Whitehall boat, so the fish are likely to remain abundant unless they migrate to the neighborhood of the seawall where they can rejoice the hearts of many anglers by their presence.

A WASTE OF FINE SALMON.—The thousands of pounds of salmon that have gone to waste during the last few days have aroused the indignation of all true sportsmen. The fish that have been thrown into the bay would, judiciously caught, have supplied hundreds of people with substantial food. It is without doubt a fact that the salmon that spoiled on the wharves and steamers were caught before the season opened and it seems as if something might be done by our Fish Commissioners to punish the violators of the law, and were there such men as the late B. B. Redding at the head of fishing matters there would no doubt be some steps taken in the matter. There is a little satisfaction for us to know that these salmon catchers have had all their work and expense of shipping for nothing by the fish spoiling on their hands.

Many of the trout streams are pretty low now and afford no sport.

They have introduced the California trout into New Zealand.

Some of the yachtmen had very good sport in Vancouver Straits last Sunday.

A number of people were fishing on the shoal ground near Anita rock last Sunday.

Giant powder is used for fishing on the Hudson river, and sportsmen are trying to stop it.

The trout are all down at the lower end of the stream, our headwaters being no longer fashionable.

Last Sunday morning the Market Inspector condemned as unfit for food 21,000 pounds of salmon.

Wm. T. May with H. C. Neff caught 35 pounds of rock cod in one hour at Alcatraz Island on Friday, the 1st inst.

Before long the split bamboos will be in ordinary and the shotguns taken as the reigning favorite.

People who expect to go up to the Cloud river next season are very much disgusted to read of the killing and wasting of thousands of salmon in the bay.

On Sunday last there were a great many boats anchored all along the Sancileto shore, and inquiry among the occupants showed they were having fine sport.

On the Yuba and American rivers there is very fine Eastern and California trout fishing lately. The Eastern trout were placed in these rivers several years ago by the Fish Commissioners and now weigh from ½ to 1½ pounds each.

A large number of black bass are being put in Lake San Andreas not only for the purpose of stocking the lake, but also to exterminate a small fish called the stickleback which gets into the small pipes in the city, as San Andreas is one of the Spring Valley Water Co.'s reservoirs.

In measuring distance on the water for fly casting tournament the method adopted is to have a cord with buoys attached, weighted underneath, so that when the cord is stretched the buoys stand upright, and the numbers are easily read for some distance. Buoys placed five feet apart. The first buoy is marked 25; a knot is tied in the rope at zero, that is, drawn to the stake from which they cast, so that the buoys register correctly. The odd feet between the buoys are estimated, if the full distance is not reached, as it would take so many buoys to mark every foot.

It seems astonishing that people who will talk about fish and fishing by the hour will not write about the same subject for a minute. As a rule it is difficult to get much information from anglers for publication. They have their favorite streams, which they keep quiet about, and their favorite flies, which they keep secret. When one goes to them to find out about these things they will talk about them but will not give permission to publish the facts. Nor will they take up a pen to write a few points which will be of interest to their fellow sportsmen. Yet these same men will quickly find fault if there is not plenty of fresh news for them. This is not a "growl" but only a "hint."

The intention of the originators of fly casting contests was to encourage and instruct amateurs in fly-casting; but, by some means, of late years the judges have laid but little stress upon any of the points except distance, a ruling that some object to from the fact that while a man may be able to cast a long distance, he may at the same time do it in the most awkward manner, and in the nice points in handling a fly-rod for fishing, such as "dropping" (in being able to cast his fly direct to a certain spot), "delicacy" (in being able to drop his fly lightly upon the water), and "style" (being able to handle his rod easily and gracefully, using both hands equally well, in fact, a practical fly fisherman) be entirely deficient.

If any one catches a flounder in the bay with numerous teeth in a double row, on both jaws, irregular in size, with large hooked upcurved ones among the smaller upright teeth, he will know he has caught the rare hook-billed flounder. Sometimes they grow to eighteen inches in length. The fish in form is extremely slender, the greatest width scarcely extending one fourth of the total length, and tapering rapidly toward the extremities. The head enters about 4½ times in the total length, and is narrow, with an immense mouth, the upper jaw of which exceeds in length the one-half of that of the head. The eyes are almost even in front, the upper one placed almost across the top of the head. The scales of the fish are large and soft; the fish is sometimes caught in these waters, but not very often.

A ROYAL BATTUE IN GERMANY.—At Hohenwald is situated the royal game preserve of Germany—a large tract of woodland stocked with game birds and animals, the buck-wild or red deer being conspicuous. At various intervals in the forests are glades of considerable extent, and on each of these is a buck-site, or shooting-box, half hidden in foliage. In these structures the adventurous sportsmen ensconce themselves and wait the coming of the deer driven past them by bands of peasants who, stationed at intervals, advance, in beating the bushes and trees, thus drawing the deer from their retreats. The danger is not great, and to an American sportsman it would seem that the excitement of the chase must be entirely wanting; but it suits the convenience and ease of the nobility, and that is the chief end and aim among these doughty Nimrods.

WILD HORSES IN IDAHO.—It is stated by cowboys engaged on Snake River, Idaho, that a band of over 500 horses, mostly Indian ponies, are running in the Snake River bottoms without any claimants. The Indian ponies have been running loose in that section since the removal of the Bannock Indians from the reservation, having escaped at that time, and since then many horses owned by prospectors and others have been missed, and are, no doubt, with the wild ponies. Some of the Wood River boys propose organizing a party and striking out to capture the entire band.

## Trotting at the East.

By cable we learn that the Charter Oak Park races closed on September 1st. The 2:19-class race Minnie B won; Pickard second, William third, Driver fourth, Dumboldt ruled off. Time—2:21, 2:21½, 2:20½, 2:20, 2:21½, 2:23. The on-to-all race Santa Claus won; Fanny Witherspoon second. Time—2:17½, 2:19½, 2:21½. The three-minute class race Wilson won; Eva second, Sweetness third, Red Bird fourth. Time—2:25½, 2:22½, 2:23.

The Springfield (Mass.) meeting commenced the Hampden Park on September 5th. In the 2:29 class, Yellow Dock won; St. Cloud, alley Boy, George A, Independence, and rufus in the order named. Time—2:22½, 2:23, 2:25½. In the 2:23 class, Captain Lewis won; Florence Maid, Lucrece, and R P in the order named. Time—2:20½, 2:20½, 2:22½.

The fall meeting of the Cleveland Trotting lub opened on September 5th. In the 2:40 class, Fred Golddust won; Sam'l T. Tilden second, Kittie Patchen third, Colonel Banister fourth; best time, 2:27½. In the 2:29 class, wing won; Dot Junior second, Rigolette third, Polka Dot fourth; best time, 2:21½. he two mile running race between Miss Williams of Kansas and Miss Burke of Nebraska, was won by Miss Williams in straight eats; time, 3:46½, 3:55½.

Foxhall, Bookmaker, Romeo and Wallenstein have been accepted for the Cesarewitch stakes, October 10th at New Market, and Iroquois, Nereid, Sachem, Aranza, Foxhall, Don Lano, Bookmaker, Romeo and Wallenstein have been accepted for the Cambridgeshire stakes, October 24th. Both these important handicaps were won last year by Mr. Keene's one, Foxhall.

At Minneapolis on Sept. 7th, in the first ace for the 2:40 class, Prince Arthur won, own Wilkes second, Mollie B. third, Lady Corecco fourth; time, 2:27½, 2:27½, 2:29½. In a pacing race for a purse of $5,000, four 6als were made, when the race was postponed. The horses paced as follows: Gem, 2, 1, 1; Buffalo Girl, 2, 1, 5, 2; Mattie unter, 1, 4, 2, 3; Flora Bells, 3, 3, 3, 4; ncy, 4, 5, 5; time—2:19½, 2:19½, 2:17½, 2:17½.

At the Cleveland meeting was a four-in-hand team race, which trotted the second heat in 1:46½, beating the best previous record for our-in-hand teams 7½ seconds.

At the Hampden Park races on the 7th, Clingstone gave an exhibition of speed for a purse of $3,000, trotting three heats in 2:20, 2:19 and 2:18. In the 2:34-class race six heats were trotted. The result was: Louise N. 1, May Thorne, 2; Barrett, 3; Winchester Maid, 4; Time — 2:30, 2:26, 2:26, 2:26, 2:27½, 2:25½. In the 2:26 class Ona'wa was first Mannie second, John Hall third, Ethel Medium fourth. Time—2:21½, 2:23½, 2:22½, 2:22½.

## The Chico Fair.

It is pleasant to learn that the fair of the third District Agricultural Society, composed of the counties of Sutter, Yuba, Butte, Colusa, Tehama, Yolo and Sacramento, is proving in popularity every year, and that more sternous efforts have been made to insure its success. The track has been very much improved under the charge of Charles Sherman, dispite the fact that no races have taken place this season at the driving park. The fair opened on the 5th, but as is usually the case there was a great deal of delay in getting the exhibits into order, as the secretary, J. H. Krause, was busy all the day in regDating the entries, the same showing thus far a notable increase on those of the previous years. On the succeeding day the pavilion was in far better order, and the visitors were generally pleased with the result, although a few vacant spaces that were bespoken showed that some exhibitors were yet to retard at the races. There was the largest show of good stock ever seen at these fairs, and the racing gave general satisfaction to the large crowd of visitors who were present. On the opening day the first race was for a purse of $450, trotting, for the 2:30 class. The entries were: Winston, Slim Jim and Carlisle. The former won in three straight heats. Best time, 2:27. Slim Jim was distanced in the first heat, and Carlisle in the second heat. On the second day there was a large crowd at the track. The first race was running a mile dash, for $150. Maria F., Minnie Bell and Lady Partisan started. Maria F. won easily; Minnie Bell second and Lady Partisan third. Time 1:46½. The second race a free handicap, running, one and an eighth mile entrance $50, $25 forfeit, $200 added. Fred Hunter, Shiner, Jubilee, Jim Brown, Ingersoll and Howell started. Howell won. Time, 1:57½.

The first attraction on Thursday was the parade of horses and cattle. Next came the ladies' tournament. The entries were: Mrs. B. C. Tretry, Mrs. R. A. McCormick, Miss Horner and Miss Annie Clark. They gave a fine exhibition of equestrianism, and the large audience expressed great satisfaction. The judges will award the prizes to-morrow morning. Following the tournament was a race of a mile and a half, for three-year-olds. Sweepstakes and Maria F., Miller entered Lady Partisan, and Anderson entered Minnie Bell Maria F. won the race and money. Time—2:68½. The second race was running, one mile and repeat, for a purse of $250. Hunter, Shiner and Jubilee were entered. Jubilee won the first heat. Time—1:46; Shiner won the second heat. Time—1:46½; Jubilee won the next heat and race. Time—1:59½. The third race was trotting; $150, for three-year-olds; three in five. Monte, Telegraph and Zulu Chief entered. Monte won the first heat. Time—2:54½, and Telegraph the sec-

ond. Time—2:58. The race was postponed until the next day.

THE ENTRY FOR THE SARATOGA STAKES.—The entries for the great stakes of next year and of 1884 that were recently closed, show such a large increase in the number of subscribers that all fear that the "boom" of last year and of this year up to the present will not be sustained is at an end. Not only have the entries for the Saratoga events greatly swell, but those to be run at Jerome Park, Sheepshead Bay and Monmouth Park also show an increase. The number of entries for the Saratoga events as closed on the 15th, compared with those for the previous four years, are as follows:

| | 1882. | 1881. | 1880. | 1879. | 1878. |
|---|---|---|---|---|---|
| Saratoga Stake, 2 y o..... | 62 | 46 | 47 | 18 | 40 |
| Kentucky Stake, 3 y o..... | 67 | 97 | 90 | 92 | 21 |
| Travers Stake, 3 y o..... | 77 | 54 | 56 | 36 | 44 |
| Alabama Stake, 3 y o..... | 72 | 50 | 61 | 18 | 36 |
| Kenner Stake, 3 y o..... | 57 | 44 | 47 | 97 | 40 |

In addition to the stakes given above, the two new three-year-old stakes—the Iroquois and Foxhall—both received a large entry, the Iroquois 54 and the Foxhall 96. One reason, perhaps, for the large increase is that all the stakes have a small declaration clause—for the Saratoga and Kentucky $20 if declared on the 1st of next January, and for the three-year-olds $25 if declared out by January 1, 1884. Among the subscribers for both the two and three-year-old stakes appear the names of Mr. Kelso, N. W. Kittson, Oden Bowie, Churchill & Johnson, T. J. Megibben, R. W. Walden, Dwyer Brothers, W. M. Conner, C. Reed, Milton Young, W. A. Dun, Appleby & Johnson, W. L. Scott, the Suffolk and Preakness stables, and a dozen others; but the great eastern stables—the Lorillards, the Belmonts, Withers, and others—are apparently conspicuous by their absence.

AMERICAN HORSES FROM ENGLAND.—Mr. James B. Keene has weeded out his English stable, as four of his thoroughbreds have recently returned to New York. These are Bushman, b. c., 4 by Glenelg—Anna Bush; Seminole, ch. c., 4 by Australian—Alabama; General Scott, 3 by Glen Athol—Lotta, and Cromwell, br. c., 3, by King Alfonso—Quickstep. All four were bred in America, and have been sent back after various phases of lack of success on the English turf, three having started and none being bracketed as winners. The passage over was a long and tedious one, beset with waste prevailing during the best part of the journey, which occupied thirteen days. The horses are now quartered at the Sheepshead Bay track in charge of Warfield, a young colored man, who rode and won the Breeders' Stake at 1880. Although the horses have been in their present quarters two or three days they bear the marks of the voyage and perhaps lack of good treatment. In the stable are also Palmetto and Manhattan, both two-year-olds, which are expected to start at the Sheepshead Bay autumn meeting. Dan Sparling has been retired to Harrisburg, Va., where, under charge of P. A. Dangerfield, he will be put to the stud.

ELECTRIFIED HORSES.—A great-crowd collected recently in Nassau street, New York, to see the astonishing conduct of the horses at a certain point in the road. One horse no sooner reacheithe mysterious spot than it reared, pawed the air for a moment, and then started off at a speed that fairly took away the driver's breath. Other animals acted in a similarly inexplicable manner, to the astonishment of the spectators. It was at length discovered that a discharge of electricity underground was the cause of the trouble, the electricity communicating with the horses through their iron shoes. A policeman gave notification of the disturbance to the Edison Company, and the current was cut off. "You see," said Edison, "excavations are made from time to time for the laying of steam heating pipes, and this causes us no end of trouble. Our conductors become undermined and get pressed down upon the pipes, so that when a heavy truck passes along there is a jar, and an electric shock is the result."

THE LAWS OF THE TURF.—Donohue, the jockey, has brought an action for libel against James Kelly, the bookmaker, placing the damages at $10,000, and Kelly has furnished bail to the sum of $3,000. The action is based on a turf event which occurred at the Monmouth Park meeting. On July 30 Donohue was mounted on John H. Harbeck's horse, Marathon, who was backed heavily to win the race. Carrol Livingston's horse, Hospodar, came in ahead and it was charged on the course at the time that Hospodar won the race because Marathon was "pulled" by the jockey. Kelly was the principal accuser against Donohue. He said that Donohue while pretending to whip Marathon with his right hand was holding him back with his left hand, and that Donohue was bribed to do so by F. Theodore Walton, proprietor of the St. James Hotel.

THE PURSE OF $10,000 offered by W. F. Balch of Boston, and to be decided on September 14th at the Beacon Park, closed on August 31st, when the fourth payment was made together with the following nominations: Fanny Witherspoon, Black Cloud, Helena, Clingstone, Parana, Edwin Thorne, Humboldt and Santa Claus. There were thirteen entries paid up, so evidently there were some nominators who could not find horses of sufficient speed to contest with those who would probably be named. It promises to be the sensational trot of the season.

OLYMPIC CLUB ELECTION. — The Olympic Club election on Monday last resulted, after a close contest, in the victory of the following compromise ticket: President, Horace F. Fletcher; Vice-President, Martin J. Flavin; Treasurer, Henry B. Russ; Secretary, Richard I. Polaski; Leader, Hiram B. Cook. Directors—James B. Stetson, Charles W. Platt, James H. Jennings, Joseph Lyons, Wm. Levison, Wm. C. Brown.

The first conviction in Los Angeles county for shooting game out of season was obtained on Tuesday last. The prosecution was made by the Los Angeles Sportsmen's Club.

## Market Report.

FLOUR—Market fairly firm. We quote as follows: Best City Extra, $5 37½@$5 50; Superfine, $4 50@$4 75; Interior Extra, $4 75@$5 25; Interior Superfine $3 75@$4 00.

WHEAT—The situation is less favorable for the selling interest, and it any great pressure were made to realize, a bad break would probably be the result. The shipping figures are reported to be $1 97½. Such sales of good shipping in small parcels reported as low as $1 62 and No. 2 White, September delivery, at $1 52@1 85.

BARLEY—The deliveries of October and November show no end of the situation. Prices range, for No 1 Feed, October, from 93 87@90½ bid; do November, 92 85; August 93 87 to brewing, $1 20; coast Chevalier, $1 30; coast Feed, $1 17 @ $1 25.

OATS—The market is well supplied and the price unsteady. The range for good lots is from $1 88½ @1 40 @ ctl.

RYE—92 05 to bid and and $2 97½ asked for No 1, September.

BRAN—We quote: Alfalfa, $11 60@13 50; Wheat $13 50@16; Wild Oat, $12 50@15 50 @ ton.

STRAW—Quotable at 60@80 @ bale.

BEANS — quoted at: Bayos, $3 40@$3 60; Butter, $5 50@$5 50 for small and $3 60@85 for large; Limas, 90 @ 90@$5 75; Peas, $3 50; Pinks, $2 90@$3 25; Red, 92@92 25; small White, 90 for; large White, 92 50@ $2 40 @ ctl.

ONIONS—Silvermines sell for 50@75c @ ctl, and Red for 50@60c @ sack.

POTATOES—Small choice lots only sell at the express quotation. Wharf rates are as follows: Early Rose, 60@65c; Jersey Blue, $1 25@1 15 @ ctl; sweet, 90c @ lb.

DRIED FRUITS—We quote as follows: Live Currants, apricots, 16@21 c; do Sples, 12@21½c; Prunella, 22@25 for old and 24 @25c for young, 15@20c for Pears; 5@7c for quartered Apples; 4@5c for sliced; 6@8c for Peaches, 8@10 for apple; Plums, 15@20 @ ib.

GAME — We quote, Hare, $1 75@$2 25; Rabbits, 75c, $1@1½c; Dvc, $1 50@1 75 @ pair; Geese, $1@1 25@ pair; do Quail, $1 25@1 50 @ doz; Venison, 10@12½c @ lb.

PROVISIONS—Values steady. We quote: Eastern Hams, 17@18½@c; California Hams, 14@15½c for plain, 16@17c for sugar-cured; Eastern Breakfast bacon, 17@18½c; California Smoked Bacon, 15@16c for heavy and medium, and 17@18½c for light and extra light; Clear Sides, 14@16c; Pork, 22 50 for Extra, 20@21 for Prime Mess, $22 00@$22 50 for pair; Clorlings, $23 00 for Mess, $27 50 Clear, and $20 00@20 50 for extra Clear; Pigs' Feet, $14@15; Mess Beef, $14 for bbls and 87 for hf bbls; extra Mess Beef, 8 for halfbbls; Family Beef, $1@9@10 @ ctl for bbls.

HONEY—Comb, 14@17c; extracted, 7@8c @ lb.

EGGS—Eastern arrivals would break prices, as the inquiry at present can is said to be very limited. We quote prices: California choice, 40@45c; Interior, 35@40½c; Eastern, 30@32½c; Oregon, 38@37½c @ doz.

BUTTER—An absence of outside orders and close purchases on the part of local buyers give the market an easy drift. Fancy, etc, choice, 30@37½c; fair to good, 32@35c; ordinary lots from country choice, 25@32½c; pickled roll, 27@30½c; Eastern, 15@18c for ordinary; pickled roll, 20@22½c; Eastern, No 1 32½c for creamery.

CHEESE—Market easy, and quotations are. California, 12@16½c for choice; good, 10@12½c; do factory, in boxes, 16@17½c; Eastern Oregon, choice, 12@15c; Eastern Oregon, fair to good, 10@12½c; Young America, 16@18c; Valley Oregon, fine, 15@18c; Valley Oregon, fair, 10@15c @ lb.

HIDES AND SKINS—Fair business reported. Dealers are paying the following cash rates for hides in order; Dry hides, usual selection, 18@20c; cull, one-third less, and Mexican Hides 14 @ 16 less; Dry Kip, 18@20c; Dry Calf, 18@20c; Salted Steers over 50 lbs, 10 @ 9; Steers and Cows, medium, 10c; light Medium, 9c; cull one-third off; Salt Kip, 9c; Salt Calf, 11@12c; do light, 11@12c @ lb; Culls one-third off.

WOOL—The wool so far has not been productive of any notable result. Inquiry limited. We quote: Humboldt and Mendocino, 25@28c @ lb; choice, 24@25c; Stanford and Modoc, 20@25c; San Joaquin, free, 17@19½c; San Joaquin, defective, 9@12c; Southern Coast, heavy and feedy, 15@21c; Eastern Oregon, choice, 18@22c; Eastern Oregon fair, 14@17c; Northern Oregon, choice, 22@25c; Oregon, fair, 18@20c; Valley Oregon, choice, 20@27c @ lb.

FRUIT—Supplies are not coming forward quite so freely, and demand still active and some advance our quotations. We quote: Apples, 60@90c @ box; pears, $1 50@$2; Peaches, 50@75c @ box; Apricots, 75@$1 @ box; Cherries, 75@$1 @ box; Plums 50@75c @ box; Raspberries, $100@$1 50 chest; Strawberries, $7@$10 @ chest; Nectarines, 50@75c @ box; Grapes, 75c@$1 @ box; Tomatoes, 50@75c @ box; Cherry plums 50@75c @ box; Crabapples, 50@80c @ box; Green Corn, 10@15c @ doz; Figs, 25@35c @ box; Musk Melons, $1@$1 50 @ doz; Watermelons, $5@$15 @ hundred.

MEATS—Following are the rates for whole carcasses from slaughterers to dealers: BEEF—Prime, 7@8c; medium grade, 6@7c; inferior, 5@6c @ lb. VEAL—Large Calves, 6@7c; small ones, 8@10c @ lb. MUTTON—wethers are quotable at 4½@5½c and Ewes at 4@4½c @ lb, according to quality. LAMB—Quotable at 6@8½c @ lb. PORK—Live Hogs, 7@7½c for hard and 7@7½c for soft; dressed do, 10@10½c @ lb for hard grain hogs.

## TURF EXCHANGE.

## FARRELLY & MITCHELL,

**435 California Street.**

Fine Wines, Liquors & Cigars.

### SPECIMEN OF OUR ARTIST'S HUMOR.

THE FISHMONGER.

HUNDREDS OF DELIGHTED ONES SEE, FOR THE FIRST TIME IN THEIR LIVES

## The Japanese Artist and Embroiderers

*At work in their native costumes at*

# Ichi Ban, 22 & 24 Geary St.

*The BREEDER AND SPORTSMAN is printed with SHATTUCK & FLETCHER'S INK*

L. U. Shippee enters s h ——, by Nutwood; dam by Chieftain.

No. 2—PACIFIC COAST TROTTING—2:25 Class; purse $1,000, and $200 added if more than ten entries. Four moneys.

F. A. Raish enters b g Blackmith Boy, by Chieftain dam McCracken mare.
W. H. Henderson enters —, by Big Lize.
H. B. Cooper enters s b Frank Moscow, by Frank Moscow; dam unknown.
G. Bergard enters g r Allen Roy; pedigree unknown.
W. F. Price enters b m San Mateo Belle, by Speculation; dam, Young Lady Vernon.
John McIntyre enters ch g Edwin Forrest, by Blackbird; dam unknown.

Chas. H. Shear enters A. C. Bechtol's blk g Slim Jim, by Taylor horse; dam unknown.
James Garland enters g g Rowdy Boy, by Rustic; dam by Belmont.
C. Van Buren enters Peter Coutts' b m Manon, by Nutwood; dam, Addie.
L. R. Titus enters b s Echo, by Echo; dam by Belmont.
Patrick Farrell enters b g Vanderpool, by George M. Patchen; dam, a Joseph mare.
G. W. Trabern enters b h DeVolution, by Prince of Orange; dam by Rysdyk's Hambletonian.
Lewis Duncan enters s Louis D——.
H. W. Crandall enters Wm. Biller's b m Blanche, by Gray McClelland; dam by John Nelson.

**WEDNESDAY, SEPT. 20th.**

No. 4—DISTRICT RUNNING—For three-year-olds; purse $300. Closed with six entries. Dash 1 1-4 miles.
Colonel G. Denney enters b s Dave Devil, by Imp. Partizan; dam by Shannon.
G. W. Trabern enters b s Kate Carson, by Joe Daniels; dam, Belle Mohawk, by Norfolk.
W. L. Ashe enters b s Real Terry, by California; dam, Laura Barnes.

Colonel G. Denney enters b s Red Catcher, by Specier; dam, Pet, by Young Melbourne.
J. A. Shepherd enters g m Minnie Belle, by Joe Daniels; dam by Norfolk.
Charles McLaughlin enters ——, by Thad Stevens.

No. 5—PACIFIC COAST TROTTING—2:25 Class; purse $1,000, and $200 added if more than ten entries. Four moneys.
James M. Learned enters b s Reliance, by Alexander; dam, Maud, by Mambrino Rattler.
H. R. Covey enters Leland Stanford's b g Captain Smith, by Locomotive; dam, Maid of Clay, by Henry Clay.
G. Valensin enters s s Crown Point, by Speculation.

John Hughes enters b h Cairo, by Chieftain; dam by Odd Fellow.
John A. Goldsmith enters blk s Director, by Dictator; dam by Mambrino Chief.
Jackson Cochran enters ch g Ashley, by Plumas; dam by George.

L. U. Titus enters br m Rehora, by Echo; dam, the Young Mare.
F. M. Dodge enters ch M Honesty, by Prism; dam by Imp.
L. J. Rose enters blk s Del Sur, by The Moor; dam, Gretchen, by Mambrino Pilot.
G. W. Wiley enters ch g Starr King, by Geo. M. Patchen, Jr., dam Mary Wonder.

**THURSDAY, SEPT. 21st.**

No. 6—PACIFIC COAST RUNNING—Mile and repeat; purse $350, and if 1-10 is less, the horse making the low est record will receive $60 additional. Four moneys.
D. Appleby, for H. C. Judson, enters ——, in May D., by Wildidle; dam, Nettle Brown, by Hubbard.
George Howson enters ch g Jim Douglass, by Wildidle; dam, Norfolk Mare.

Wm. L. Pritchard enters s s Inauguration, by Wildidle; dam, Mingo.
George Bayard enters b s Duke of Monday, by Monday; dam Jennie.
L. H. Titus enters b s Fred, by Wildidle; dam, Frank.

No. 7—DISTRICT—TROTTING—For two-year-olds purse $300. Closed with ten entries.
D. Goldsmith enters b s Alpine, by Algona; dam as Ongena mare.

W. W. Traben enters blk f Baby Mine, by Nephew; dam by Harmon Blackhawk.
J. M. Learned enters b s Harmony, by Reliance; dam by Mambrino Rattler.
M. J. McCloud enters br s Judge Paterspo, by Nephew; dam, Dingo.
D. Valensin enters b f Magdalena, by Fearless; dam, unknown.

W. W. Traben enters b s Alphena, by Mambrino Wilkes dam Jenny Mason.
M. Rowe enters b s John O'Brien, by Mambrino Wilkes; dam by Tecumseh.
Fred Arnold enters br s Era Ha, by Nephew; dam by Speculation Hambletonian.
L. U. Shippee enters b f ——, by Echo; dam by Don Victor.
Wm. M. Murray enters b f Marcod Girl, by Nephew; dam by Morgan.

**FRIDAY, SEPT. 22D.**

No. 8—PACIFIC COAST RUNNING—Free for all; two miles and repeat; purse $800, and $200 added if more than ten entries. Four moneys.
P. Siegler enters b g Night Hawk, by Imported Hubbingdon; dam by Norfolk.
Jack Douglass enters ch b s Jack Douglass, by Wildidle; dam, Lady Clare, by Norfolk.
L. H. Titus enters Leland Stanford's b m Precious, by Leinster; dam, Frolic, by Thad Stevens.
William L. Appleby enters Ed. C. Judson's b s Patrol, by Wildidle; dam, Nettle Brown.
William Boots enters b s Hollis H., by Wildidle; dam by Norfolk.
J. F. Gilmer enters b s Red Boy, by War Dance; dam Nielson.

No. 9—DISTRICT—RUNNING—For three-year-olds and over; purse $800; heat two in three; 7 to enter, 4 to start. Four moneys.

Jack Douglass enters ch s Jack Douglass, by Wildidle; dam, Lady Clare, by Norfolk.
W. L. Ashe enters br s Real Terry, by California; dam, Laura Barnes.
Colonel G. Denney enters br s Bird Catcher, by Specier; dam, Pet, by Young Melbourne.
B. C. Holly enters b s Samuel, by Samuel Harrison, by Thad Stevens.
Wm. L. Pritchard enters s s Kate Carson, by Joe Daniels; dam by Norfolk.
John Miller enters b s Picnic, by Joe Daniels; dam by Norfolk.
J. A. Shepherd enters g m Minnie Belle, by Joe Daniels; dam by Norfolk.
Sell Patton enters b s George Bander, by ——; dam, Puss Fisher, by Lodi.
A. L. Randall enters s s Joe Daniels, Jr., by Joe Daniels; dam, Julia, by Bruce Eagle.
A. Miller enters b m Lady Partisan, by Partisan; dam, sister of Trumpf Charmaine.
H. E. Faggott enters br s Idler, by Wildidle; dam, Kate Gift.

No. 10—PACIFIC COAST TROTTING—For horses owned on the Pacific Coast, July 1st, 1882; 2:22 Class; purse $1,000, and $200 added if more than ten subscribers. The nominator may be required to name his horse, but should sign his cash $12.50, with his own track, August 1, 1882. He has then earned the right to start any horse eligible that he may fully control, providing the horse he starts is named to the Secretary, September 1, 1882. Four moneys.
Nominators—Charles W. Welby, G. Valensin, John A. Goldsmith, L. H. Titus, J. B. McDonald.

**SATURDAY, SEPT. 23D.**

No. 11—PACIFIC COAST TROTTING—2:26 Class; purse $1,000, and $200 added if more than ten entries. Four moneys.
M. McCarty enters b g Hancock.
H. R. Covey enters Leland Stanford's br g Captain Smith, by Locomotive; dam, Maid of Clay, by Henry Clay.
C. Bernard enters g g Allen Roy.
Ralph Dorsey enters Eugene Mare's ch g Trump Winston (formerly Kent), by Primus; dam, Lady Pipe.
G. W. Wiley enters ch g Starr King, by Electioneer; dam by John Nelson.
John A. Goldsmith enters blk s Director, by Dictator; dam by Mambrino Chief.
John A. Goldsmith enters b m Sweetness, by Volunteer; dam by Edward Everett.
E. Giddings enters b s John B. Pritch's ch m Nellie R., by General McClellan, Jr.; dam, Susie Williams.
J. B. McDonald names b s Brigadier, by General Benton; dam by Williamson's Belmont.
Harvey O'Neal enters Joseph Cairn Simpson's b g Billy Hayward; dam, Lady Hayward.
No. 12—PACIFIC COAST PACING—2:25 Class; purse $600, and $200 added if more than ten entries. Four moneys.

[Columns of extremely dense classified entries continue. Second column:]

T. L. Young enters g g Colonel Dicker.
G. Valensin enters b m Guida.
L. R. Titus enters b m Corotta, by Winthrop; dam by Owen Dale.
B. C. Holly enters s s Ladys Mare, by Hiram Cherry; dam, Belgian mare.
L. U. Shippee enters W M. Hammond's s s Oakland Boy, by Winthrop; dam, a Blackbird mare.

In addition to other premiums, H. T. Dorrance will offer a set of choice track harness. Valued at $60, for the horse owned in the District that makes the fastest trotting record at the Stockton Fair. He also offers a $30-jockey saddle to the horse that makes the fastest running mile record owned in the District at the Fair.

Bring a green owner of Mambrino Wilkes, offers a special premium at our Fair, a silver bowl and water, for the best two-year-old colt sired by the above horse. Also, for the second best colt, a silver water pitcher. The colts to be shown at the Stockton Fair.

**REMARKS AND CONDITIONS.**

All Trotting Races: best three in five, except numbers 7 and 9.

In all these Races (Pacific Coast Novelty Race excepted) five per cent of the purse, and five per cent of stakes, must accompany all nominations, and the remaining five per cent of purse when the entries close.

When there are eight or more to start in a Trotting Race, the races shall be 100 classed.

Rules of the National Trotting Association to govern trotting, except as specified; but the Board of Managers reserve the right to trot heats of any two classes alternately, or to start a special race between heats.

All two-year-olds, when running in their classes, shall carry 100 pounds, with the usual allowances for mares and colts.

All three-year-olds, when running in their classes, to carry 110 pounds, with the usual allowances as above; other-wise, old weights to govern.

For a walk-over in any race a horse shall only be entitled to his own entrance fee and one-quarter of the entrance received from the other entries for said purse; and a horse winning a race entitled to first money only, except when distancing the field, then entitled to first and third moneys only; a horse winning two heats out of three entitled to all but fourth money only.

Horses entered in purses can only be drawn by consent of the Judges.

The Board reserves the right to change the day and hour of any race, if they deem it necessary.

Rules of the Pacific Coast Blood Horse Association to govern Running Races, including additions to rules, except as specially provided.

In all Running Races colts to be worn by riders, and in all other races, any other particulars that will enable specta-tors to identify the horses in the race.

Races to commence each day at 1 o'clock P. M. sharp.

The track is first-class, having been improved; stables hay and straw free to competitors.

J. L. PHELPS, Secretary.

     L. U. SHIPPEE, President.

---

## $12,500

## In Purses and Stakes.

### CALIFORNIA

## STATE FAIR

### SPEED PROGRAMME

### FOR 1882.

**FIRST DAY—MONDAY, SEPT. 11.**

No. 1—RUNNING—INTRODUCTION STAKE.—For all ages; three-quarters of a mile dash; $50 entrance, $15 forfeit; $300 added; second to save stake.
No. 2—RUNNING—THE WINTERS STAKE.—For two-year-olds; $100 each, h f; $25 declaration; $300 added.
No. 3—TROTTING—2:27 Class; purse $800.
No. 4—RUNNING—FREE PURSE, $250.
No. 5—TROTTING—2:40 Class; purse $500.

**SECOND DAY—TUESDAY, SEPT. 12.**

No. 5—TROTTING— 2:25 class; purse, $1,000. Mile heats, 3 in 5.
No. 6—RUNNING—CALIFORNIA DERBY STAKE
No. 7—RUNNING—FREE PURSE, $250.

**THIRD DAY—WEDNESDAY, SEPT. 18.**

No. 8—RUNNING—FILLY STAKE FOR TWO YEAR OLD FILLIES.
No. 9—RUNNING—JENNIE D. STAKE.
No. 10—RUNNING—PROTECTIVE STAKE
No. 11—TROTTING—Purse, $500.

**FOURTH DAY—THURSDAY, SEPT. 41.**

No. 12—TROTTING—2:22 class; purse, $1,500. Mile heats, 3 in 5.
No. 13—RUNNING—

**FIFTH DAY—FRIDAY, SEPT. 15.**

No. 14—RUNNING—COLT AND FILLY STAKE

**SIXTH DAY—SATURDAY, SEPT. 16.**

No. 15—TROTTING—Purse, $600; for double teams of trotters.
No. 16—TROTTING—OCCIDENT STAKE FOR 1882, closed in 1881.
No. 17—SPECIAL TROT AGAINST TIME.—$250 to plate will be awarded to any stallion that beats the best trotting time (2:19.)
GENTLEMEN'S SADDLE HORSE RACE—Purse $100.

## REMARKS and CONDITIONS.

All trotting and pacing races are the best three in five except the two year old trot, unless otherwise specified; five to enter and three to start. Entrance ten per cent of purse. Moneys divided as follows: Purse divided at the rate of sixty per cent. to first horse, thirty to second, and ten per cent. to third.

National Association Rules to govern trotting; but the Board reserves the right to trot heats of any two classes alternately, if necessary to close on day, as to trot a special race between heats.

All two-year-olds, when running in their classes, shall carry one hundred pounds, with the usual allowance for mares and geldings.

All three-year-olds, when running at their classes, to carry one hundred and ten pounds, with the usual allowance as above.

Those who have nominated in the above purses may start any horse nominated and not yet paid, providing they comply with the requirements as to the Secretary, at Sacramento, on the Saturday preceding, not on the Monday previous; and on the second day following, and entry therein must be strictly adhered to.

No added money paid for a walk-over.

Horses entered in purses can only be drawn by consent of the Judges.

Rules of the Pacific Coast Blood Horse Association (old edition) to govern all running races, except when qualification named are otherwise specified.

EDWIN F. SMITH,     VALUE,     Secretary.     President.

# BREEDER AND SPORTSMAN

Vol. I, No. 11.
NO. 508 MONTGOMERY STREET.

SAN FRANCISCO, SATURDAY, SEPTEMBER 16, 1882.

SUBSCRIPTION
FIVE DOLLARS A YEAR.

EXILE--By Echo, his dam, Belle Mason, by Belmont.

Again is presented an illustration of a type, and in our estimation as nearly the model form for a trotter as can be found, when there is an admixture of other blood than that of the thoroughbred. That the "highest form" of the racehorse is also the most favorable for speed at the trot, has been our belief for many years, though, as is well known, there are other qualities that are of still more importance than high form, and in the fast trotter as well as in the fast racehorse there must be a capacity which is not indicated by the physical configuration. The fast trotter must also inherit an adaptability to acquire the fast-trotting step, and the combination of the Hambletonian, and other families of trotters, with the thoroughbred has given the inheritance, and the mingling of the blood of Echo and the old thoroughbreds of California has proved to be a successful admixture, well adapted for road and track. As was shown in the article accompanying the picture of Echo, he had a good share of thoroughbred blood, and according to the theory of some of the writers, his greatest success should have followed the coupling with mares of cold blood. But there is a progression in breeding trotters as in everything else, and now the most intelligent breeders are seeking for further infusions of thoroughbred blood. Maud S., Clingstone, Black Cloud, and many others have one grandparent thoroughbred, and with scarcely an exception the crack performers of the day are strongly combined with it in the near crosses. There is not room in this article, however, to present a list of the notabilities of the track which are bred in this way, but only the ultra-bigoted advocates of cold blood will deny that there is an increased finish in the animals possessing the "royal blood." The portraiture, as the others which have preceded it, is an admirable likeness of the animal. Exile is a very handsome horse as the representation shows; a bright bay with near hind foot white, a touch of white on the right fore foot with a diamond-shaped star in the forehead. His coat is "silky" and the hair in the mane and tail is fine. He is magnificently adorned in this respect, both mane and tail being long and very full. He is fifteen and a half hands high and as wiry in form as a four-miler. He was foaled in 1876, bred by F. M. Slaughter, who still owns his dam. She is by Belmont, thoroughbred, his dam Lucy Johnson by The Pony, a son of imported Leviathan, and her grandam Catalpa by Frank. The favorite dam of Exile was by John Richards,

one of the great horses of his day, a brother to Betsey Richards, one of those Col. R. W. Johnson intended to run against American Eclipse, but going wrong, Henry was substituted. With the American Star, Kentucky Whip and Shakespeare crosses in Echo, and the known thoroughbred blood in the sire of Echo, Ryedyk's Hambletonian, it is not surprising that Exile should show "a deal of quality." He has shown so much speed that before the sale to J. B. Haggin, Wm. Titus entered him through the circuit, and he was confident that he would have made a good record. His brother, Joe Hamilton, now owned by G. Valensin of Hicksville, Sacramento county, Cal., was one of the most prominent colts of his day, and when four years old was only beaten by a neck a third heat in 2:30; He was then troubled with "a leg" which interfered with his training, and incapacitated him so that he has not started since. That Echo has been remarkably successful as the progenitor of trotters few will deny, and besides Exile and his brother there is Belle Echo to prove the value of the combination of Echo and Belmont blood. It is rare, indeed, that excellence on the track is not followed by excellence in the stud, and hence we confidently predict that the subject of this sketch will excel in both spheres.

# CORRESPONDENCE.

## Pictures of Horses.

Under the above caption a correspondent sends in the following article, and the reasoning would hold good in a majority of cases.

Three of the series published in the BREEDER AND SPORTSMEN are from photographs, and, according to our view, those which the artist drew from life are superior. But it is not often that an artist can be obtained who has the talent for animal delineation such as Mr. Wyttenbach possesses. The talent is rare, as it requires a knowledge of the form of the horse as well as the skill to place it on paper or canvas. There is scarcely one photograph in ten which is anything near the faithful portrayal of the animal. To be perfect every portion of the body would have to be equally distant from the camera, and these without a motion to mar the shadow on the plate. We have scores of photographs which if copied exactly as they are would be hideous caricatures of the animals they are intended to represent, and the very best of them require corrections before publication.

We can assure our correspondent that every picture is a faithful representation of the animal; nearly every one of them admirable:

STOCKTON, Sept. 6, 1882.

EDITOR BREEDER AND SPORTSMAN, *Dear Sir:* The interest that attaches to pictures of horses or of human beings is much alike. If you cannot see the person in question, the next best thing is the picture of that person.

A picture is of value or not according to the fact whether the truthful or the fanciful about it predominates. All reliable sincere people seek the reality before the fictitious or imaginative.

When is a picture of the horse truthful? Not often is it correct when it depends upon the integrity and talent of the artist. The lack of ability to faithfully delineate an animal is so prevalent that any drawing of a horse is almost fated to be defective. I would not look with favor upon any picture of a horse made by an artist of less merit and fidelity than that which belonged to Rosa Bonheur. This rule would condemn the majority of the painted pictures of horses in this country.

With common sense and common honesty, or rather that which belongs to the high order of business integrity—a photograph exhibits a likeness that is correct. But even the photographer, through purpose or fashion, will distort and falsify the picture of a person, if the instrument and sitter are brought too near to each other. Therefore, the picture of a famous horse to me is of no value that is not made from a photograph.

Some years ago a paper on the Pacific Coast published a picture of Flora Temple. Some time thereafter the writer saw a picture of Flora Temple with her colt, made from a photograph and published as a frontispiece to a book which treated of the horse and his development. That likeness was strong and captivating. It was self-evident and harmonious throughout. It was beautiful and instructive without glamour. It was truthful as artistic. The other artificial picture of that renowned mare—I think in the *Spirit of the Times*—was no more like Flora Temple than she was like a greyhound. It was a mockery.

Why not let the pictures of horses, in your good paper, be photographic likenesses? Then we should feel that after seeing the image of the animal we shall not be disappointed at the actual view of the original. Respectfully yours,

A. S. H.

## Whipple's Hambletonian.

EDITOR BREEDER AND SPORTSMAN: There having been many inquiries about Whipple's Hambletonian I send you the following history: This grand old horse ranks well up among the celebrated trotting sires of America, and to-day holds the prestige on this coast. It was in the year 1863 that Mr. S. B. Whipple purchased in the State of New York the above named stallion, then a three-year-old, and brought him to California. The arrival of this horse laid the foundation for the successful breeding of trotters on the Pacific Coast. Whipple's Hambletonian, or as he is familiarly called the "old horse," is a rich chestnut, standing 15¾ hands high. His sire by Guy Miller, by Rysdyk's Hambletonian, dam Martha Washington, by Burr's Washington, her dam by Abdallah. He trotted but four races, and never failed to bring home first money; his record is 2:39, made in his five-year-old form (certainly a very fair record for a colt seventeen years ago), and without doubt he would have lowered it a peg or two previous to the accident that befell him (being hurt across the loins on the boat while going to Sacramento). He had pulled George Evans a half mile, to wagon, in 1:09. The accident referred to above compelled his owner to withdraw him from the turf, where he could not help but make his mark, and to place him in the stud, where all was uncertainty; but the son of Guy Miller proved equal to the emergency, as his get will show.

The old horse served seven mares during his first season (1864); all proved in foal; the most promising of the seven colts died when three years old. The remaining six were: Lady Blanchard, trotted but one season, won five races out of six and retired with a record of 2:26½; Westfield, record 2:26½, made when dead lame; Ajax, record 2:29, the winner of the $10,000 aside race with Alexander; Countess, who gave the charmed 2:30 list a tight rub for admittance, and though she more than once beat thirty in private trials, never accomplished more than 2:33 in public. Starr Queen, out of an American Starr mare, a fine large chestnut, was thought more of than her half sister, that wondrous little mare, Harvest Queen, but recieving an injury was used for a brood mare. The last of the six was the brown colt owned by Mr, Arguilla of Santa Clara, a very speedy horse.

Since his first season in the stud, which alone makes him stand parallel with the most illustrious sires of America, he has shown such celebrities as Graves, 2:19; Empress, 2:24; Lou Whipple, 2:26½; Alameda Maid, 2:27½; Maggie C, 2:27½; Rustic, 2:30; Whipple, 2:34; Medora, 2:33½, in a fifth heat, when three years old; Mayboy, four years old, dam Harvest Queen, has made his mile over a private course in 2:31. Whipple's Hambletonian is the grandsire of Volunteer, 2:27; Honesty, 2:25½ (four years old) and Rowdy Boy.

Whipple's Hambletonian, though twenty-two years old, is still in a good hardy condition, and bids fair to equal the ripe old age of his illustrious grandsire, Rysdyk's Hambletonian, and who will say that he is a degenerated grandson of that famous horse?

SAN MATEO.

MARYSVILLE, Sept. 8, 1882.

EDITOR BREEDER AND SPORTSMAN, *Dear Sir:* Noticing an inquiry for information regarding Billy McCracken I append the following:

"Billy McCracken, black stallion, foaled 1850, died August 1871, owned by D. E. Knight, Marysville, Yuba county, Cal. by Morgan Black Hawk, son of Hill's Black Hawk—dam a messenger mare by Hambletonian horse." I am quoting the words of the stud bill. Billy McCracken is half brother to Young Flora Temple, Black Swan of Wisconsin, and Paul Jones of Oregon. Billy McCracken took first premium at State Fair of Wisconsin when five years old. Billy McCracken has trotted five miles in 14 m. and 10s., and challenged any stallions for a race of five or ten miles without any takers. He was bought by J. G. McCracken when four months old, kept a number of years by him and then sold to D. E. Knighs, Marysville, Yuba county, Cal., who owned him sixteen years. The dam of Overman was afterwards bred by Mr. Mendenhall to Milton Medium (record 2:25½), son of Happy Medium. The dam of Susie Brown (2:42½), winner of *Spirit of Times* Stake at Sacramento, was by Billy McCracken, also dam of yearling trotter Chevalier, entered to trot at Sacramento. D. E. Knight has a yearling filly by Brigadier, dam by Billy McCracken, that trots quarters in 43 seconds and halves in 1:27. The McCrackens are a gamy up-headed tribe of horses, and will go the length of the road without whip or spur, remarkably docile and gentle in harness, with plenty of courage, a race of pleasant and cheerful drivers and the very acme of gentlemen's roadsters, I regard his fillies as the coming brood mares of this State as they seem to nick well to the stallions that have been bred to them. They put that race horse courage in their offspring which is such a valuable quality in the horse. Yours, etc.

FRANK GRANT.

# TURF AND TRACK.

## Fixed Events.

The San Joaquin Valley Association Fair at Stockton, from September 19th to the 23d inclusive.

Oregon State Fair at Salem, from September 18th and during the week.

The San Mateo and Santa Clara County Agricultural Association Fair at San Jose, September 25th to the 30th inclusive.

Humboldt and Mendocino District Fair at Rhonerville, September 19th to September 23d inclusive.

Modoc, Plumas and Lassen District Fair at Greenville, from October 2d to October 5th inclusive.

Monterey District Fair at Salinas City, from October 3d to October 6th inclusive.

Nevada State Fair at Reno, from Monday, October 2d to the 7th inclusive.

Mount Shasta Agricultural Association Fair at Yreka, October 4th, 5th, 6th and 7th.

Eastern Oregon Fine Stock Association at Union, from October 9th to the 14th inclusive.

Los Angeles Agricultural Association, at Los Angeles, from October 17th to 21st inclusive.

FAIRS AT THE EAST.

Pennsylvania State Fair, at Pittsburg, September 7th to the 21st inclusive.

Wisconsin State Fair, at Fond du Lac, September 11th to the 16th inclusive.

Ontario Provincial Fair, at Toronto, September 18th to the 23d inclusive.

Connecticut State Fair, at Meriden, September 18th to the 22d inclusive.

New Jersey State Fair, at Monroe, September 18th to the 22d inclusive.

West Virginia Central Fair, at Clarksburg, September 19th to the 21st inclusive.

Indiana State Fair, at Indianapolis, September 25th to the 30th inclusive.

Western Michigan Fair, at Grand Rapids, September 25th to the 30th inclusive.

Texas State Fair, at Austin, October 17th to the 21st inclusive.

## Winners at Poughkeepsie.

| Winner. | Sire. | Class. | Amt. won. | Best time. |
|---|---|---|---|---|
| Buffalo girl (pacer)...... | Pocahontas Boy... | Free for all | $375 | 2:15½ |
| Clemmie G.......... | Magic .......... | 2:21 | 500 | 2:22¼ |
| Cornelia .......... | Col. Bonner...... | 2:26 | 375 | 2:23 |
| Cora Belmont.......... | Belmont .......... | 2:23 | 500 | 2:24½ |
| Edwin Thorne.......... | Thornedale ....... | Grand Special | 750 | 2:18½ |
| Fanny Witherspoon... | Almont.......... | 2:19 | 1,000 | 2:18½ |
| Flora Belle (pacer).... | Stuker's Rainbow. | Free for all | 750 | 2:18½ |
| George M.......... | Westfield Boy.... | 2:23 | 300 | 2:25½ |
| Gladiator .......... | Blue Bull.......... | 2:38 | 500 | 2:25½ |
| Independence.......... | Young Hindoo.... | 2:29 | 375 | 2:23½ |
| J. P. Morris.......... | R. B. Morris...... | 2:21 | 1,000 | 2:21½ |
| Limber Jack (pacer)... | .................. | 2:25 | 500 | 2:19 |
| May Thorne.......... | Thornedale ....... | 2:33 | 500 | 2:26½ |
| Overman .......... | Elmo .......... | 2:29 | 750 | 22:1½ |
| Onawa .......... | Goodwin's H'tonian | 2:26 | 750 | 2:23½ |
| Phyllis.......... | Phil Sheridan..... | 2:26 | 225 | 2:21 |
| Santa Claus.......... | Strathmore........ | Grand Special | 1,500 | 2:20 |
| Sweetness.......... | Young Volunteer. | 3:00 | 500 | 2:30 |
| Topsy.......... | Walkill Chief..... | 2:38 | 250 | 2:21½ |
| Unolala.......... | Volunteer ........ | 2:23 | 1,000 | 2:24½ |

ON INSTRUCTIONS TO JOCKEYS.—Captain Hayes in his book "Riding in the Flat and Across Country" makes some pertinent remarks on this important subject: "With a young hand instruction may be necessary, but if the jockey be a fairly good one, the riding should be left to his discretion. It is impossible to forsee all possible circumstances, and decisions must be taken on the spur of the moment. As for starting, he calls attention to the necessity for "getting off" as quickly as possible—a matter in which, though it is obviously of paramount importance, some people would appear to be strangely indifferent. As he says: "Whatever distance is lost at the start must be made up when the horses are galloping, at which time the effort to regain the lost lengths may very possibly be equivalent to throwing away an advantage of as many pounds.

The St. Leger, the last great three-year-old sweepstake in England, comes off on the 13th inst., and is commencing to attract a good deal of attention. As things run, the two favorites are trained in the same stable and as the owners are averse to any trial, it is difficult to pick the winner. Lord Stamford's filly, Geheimness, the winner of the Oaks, and the Duke of Westminister's filly, Shotover, the winner of the Two Thousand Guineas and the Derby, are equal favorites at nine to four. These, with Quicklime and Sweatbread, are absolutely the only animals backed. The prestige of her Derby performance will probably cause Shotover to start the first favorite. There are half a dozen American horses in, but there is little chance of repeating our last year's victory with a second Iroquois.

When Edwin Thorne was taken back to his stall after his defeat of Clingstone at Utica a great crowd flocked around the victorious horse. "It makes a great difference," said Turner, "whether you win or lose. Heretofore we have had three men call upon us after a race, now we have three hundred."

G. W. Bowen & Co., Runnymede Farm, Paris, Ky., have sold to Messrs. Dwyer Bros. the bay colt Barnes, two years old, by Billet, out of Mercedes, Runnymede's dam, by Melbourne Jr., for $12,000.

Milton Young, Henderson, Ky., has purchased from the Dyer Bros., Brooklyn, N. Y., the chestnut colt Onondaga, three years old, by Leamington, out of Susan Bean, Sensation's dam, for $6,000. He is likely to prove very valuable at the stud.

## Disreputable Turf Practices.

As the legitimate racing season of 1882 is fast drawing to a close, the officers of the different clubs should take some action to get rid of a certain betting class that has sprung into existence and increased in number within the last few years. There is a growing and menacing danger to the turf, arising from the actions and methods of this class of men, more especially to the Eastern associations.

In noticing the charges recently preferred by Mr. Kelly against Mr. Walton, better known as the Great American Plunger, few of the papers that discussed the matter laid any stress upon the methods Mr. Walton pursues to obtain the information upon which he bets large sums of money. No one seems to look at the demoralization certain to result to the turf by the use Mr. Walton makes of money in the way of presents to trainers and jockeys. If traced out in all its connections and bearings it will be found a questionable scheme by which he fills his purse at the expense of owners and the public. If his methods are legitimate and proper, why is it that he never applies to the owners of horses. the proper and only source from which information should be sought or obtained, but it is sought and obtained by nocturnal visits to trainers and jockeys? In the last few years Mr. Walton has taken from owners, bookmakers and the public a vast sum of money in America and England, agreeable with his own reports. How was this money obtained? For what purpose has he given large sums to trainers and jockeys? Legitimate and honest turf transactions require no such heavy disbursements of money to trainers and jockeys as he has made. There is more in it than meets the eye. There is something behind all this more than information; it smells strongly of corruption and bribery. It is no excuse to say that others also have used money for the same purpose. If this is so, it is no defense of the practice, and is a still stronger argument why the turf authorities should squelch it. If Mr. Walton is allowed or others are allowed to use money where it is most effective in eliciting information which is alone the property of the owner, what hope can there be to maintain the purity of the turf?

If this system of Mr. Walton and his followers is not arrested it must lead to a loss of public confidence. This loss of public confidence will end in decay and the disintegration of the turf. The doings of these vampires are already a stench in the nostrils of honest patrons of the turf, and it is high time that the clubs of the country take the matter in hand and rid our race courses of such characters. The laws are sufficient, and if not, frame one to meet the case. Every one who runs a horse or visits a race course agrees when he enters the grounds to abide by the laws governing the club, and in accepting or purchasing a ticket assents to be controlled by its rules as long as he remains on the grounds. This is a plain statement of what ought to be an accepted truth. It is the principle of every honest and correct individual or turfman. But a class have sprung up who boldly assert the right of going upon our race courses, and by the free use of money obtaining information the exclusive property of owners from their trainers and jockeys, and surprising to say there are plenty of persons to be found who admire and praise this sort of dishonesty, and call it shrewdness. What right has any person to take the property of another without giving an equivalent?

The safety and welfare of the turf dominates all the rights and privileges of such as Walton and his followers, and nothing is so shameful and dangerous to the rights of owners and our courses as the methods brought into practice by these plungers on one side and trainers and jockeys on the other. No one can deny that the turf suffers great injury and discredit by reason of Mr. Walton's course, and it is plain to be seen that it will suffer greater damage if he is permitted to pursue his present methods. The officers of our clubs must take a bold and manly stand for the maintenance of the purity of the turf. There is no middle ground or room for compromise between the purity of the turf and corruption. There is no room on the turf for Mr. Walton's system and that of his followers. He and they have brought and will continue to bring discredit upon honest sport, and they have no right to stay and practice what is detrimental to fair and legitimate racing.—*National Live Stock Journal.*

HOW CLINGSTONE'S SPEED WAS DEVELOPED. — Mr. C. F. Predmore had charge of Mr. Pond's stable, and developed Clingstone. When the horse was three years old Mr. Predmore thought he would feel of him. He trotted a half mile in 1:32, and the next week covered the distance in 1:27. He was out of condition at Meriden, and trotted against Magnet and Jewell, and was beaten. He was taken home, where he trotted a mile in 2:53, and a week after that went around the track in 2:46. He was given a rest, and then showed 2:42. Mr. Pond had seen none of these trials, but some days later went to the track for the purpose of holding his watch on him. He trotted in 2:42, and with a brief rest repeated in 3:39¾. Late in the fall the three-year-old was given a trial with the stallion Thomas Jefferson for company, and he made his mile in 2:36½. He was not speeded again that year, but was jogged to sleigh during the winter. As a four-year-old his trials were 2:35, 2:31, 2:32, and a repeat in 2:26½. He had no engagements as a five-year-old, but late in the fall trotted a mile in 2:19. As a six-year-old he was given a trial previous to going to Fleetwood Park. The day was hot but the track was fast. The trials were 2:23, 2:24, 2:14 and 2:14½. The last quarter of the last mile was trotted in 31 seconds. Mr. Predmore says he always found the horse cheerful and ready to go, and he believes that he can beat 2:13.—*Turf, Field and Farm.*

The weights for the Cesarewitch and Cambridgeshire handicaps have been issued. The former at two miles, two furlongs and twenty-eight yards, will be run October 10, and the top weights are Mr. J. R. Keene's Foxhall, four years, and Mr. H. Bragg's Victor Emmanuel, five years, each 136 pounds; Mr. Pierre Lorillard's Iroquois, four years, 135 pounds; Duke of Hamilton's Fiddler, four years, 133 pounds, and Lord Ellesmere's Wallenstein, five years, 132 pounds. The Cambridgeshire, one mile and 240 yards, will be run October 24, for which Foxhall is weighted at 136 pounds, as also is Sir John D. Astley's six-year-old horse Peter. Iroquois has 132 pounds and Wallenstein 126 pounds.

ANOTHER PURCHASE BY VANDERBILT.—That fine young promising mare Early Rose has been purchased by W. H. Vanderbilt. During the late meeting at Buffalo, New York, Mr. Vanderbilt made a proposition to purchase the mare for $16,000 provided she could show 2:18. A trial was made but the fastest that could be shown was 2:19. Subsequently Mr. Vanderbilt reduced his offer $2,500, and it was accepted. Early Rose is a brown mare, by Almont, dam Jennie, by Flying Cloud. She began last season with a record of 2:36 and reduced it to 2:25½ and now she leaves the turf with a public record of 2:20½.

## The Golden Gate Fair.

ınother grand day was the unanimous verdict of all who ended the fair of the Golden Gate Association Friday, the inst. The encomiums of the weather became somewhat notonous, as a finer five days than from Monday until day night are rarely enjoyed. Those who went over on 1 P. M. boat from the city were aware that the largest at-dance of the week was assured. The boat was crowded, d nine-tenths of those on board sought the Berkeley train en the wharf was reached. The train was a long one, and was not surprising that many who were accustomed to vel by that route thought they had made a mistake and ; on the wrong cars. Large as the numbers were who came that train the arrivals by carriages, wagons and horse cars m Oakland were still larger, and when the horses were led for the Consolation purse the assemblage was far great-than on any preceding days, more people, probably, than d been on any two of the previous days, and whether this s owing to the attractions of the 2:25 class, or the ladies' nestrianism, was a mooted question, only to be settled by preferences of those who were called upon to arbitrate. made little difference to the exchequer of the association at the motive was which induced people to attend, and tainly those who made a part of the throng were eased that they had so much and so good company. The track was in the same condition as it has been before, d there was also the same hearty concurrence in the de-ion of the judges. As will be disclosed by reading the scription of the heats, the judges were in some doubt ether the distancing of Starr King was intentional or not, d the "in and out" work of the horses is certain to awaken spicion, whether merited or not. There were also adverse ticisms on the way that Dictator was driven in Santa Rosa d here, and, popular as his pilot is, it is sure that he will be ittle more careful if he escapes ostracism. It is also certain at the day of "helpers" is nearly played out in California, d a few well deserved penalties will prove a cure for both these evils. There is trouble for spectators to reconcile mpletely opposite doings, and though sickness, accidents other causes may work wonderful changes, the opposites usually laid to the drivers. Legitimate criticism is usually luable, and now, at the outset of the circuit, it will behoove knights of the whip and snaffle to be careful of their con-ct. There is nothing more certain than that punishment follow "proven" guilt and popularity or standing be of avail if "led astray." It is scarcely neccessary to add to e description of the heats. Reliance gave conclusive proof at his name is most clearly a misnomer. Winning in 2:22½ d then distanced the next heat some seconds less shows e nomenclature in his case is wrong, though Honesty indi-ted that his name was well chosen. Had Ashley kept out his way he would have been nearer at the finish, and it ght have been that in one of the games his nose might have en in front. The following is a description of the various ats: In the Consolation race the start was excellent, ghthawk in front as they passed the stand, a sition held to the finish, a savage application whip and steel by the rider of Inauguration in the t quarter making no appreciable change. Time, mile and quarter, 2:12: last mile 1:46½. Pools—Nighthawk $115, In-guration $108, and at the start Nighthawk $50, Inaugu-tion $20.

The ladies who were to compete for the prizes offered by e association for equestriennes came upon the course and xhibited their grace in the saddles and skill in the menage a a series of maneuvers on the stretch, during which time he judges took notes for the awards. Seven ladies appeared, nost of them unfortunate in not having horses sufficiently ducated to enable the riders to display their accomplish-nents to the best advantage, but the exhibition was very fine, nd elicited the closest attention from the large audience and requent applause as the fair contestants dashed past the tand. The decision was in favor of Miss Penniman of San ose, as entitled to the first prize, Miss Ellis of San Francisco econd, Miss Marchang of Alameda third, Miss Peters of akland fourth, Miss Long fifth, Mrs. A. E. Sessions sixth, nd Miss Chisholm seventh.

The event of the day from the pool-box standpoint was illed promptly, and the lottery for position placed Ashley at e pole, Del Sur second, Honesty third, Starr King urth, Director fifth, Cairo sixth and Reliance outside. here was some tedious scoring for a start, Starr King and el Sur being somewhat rank and indisposed. When they are sent away, in tolerable order, Reliance shot ahead and oon had the better of Ashley and Honesty, and was on even rms with the best of the field. At the turn Del Sur broke d fell back, Cairo following suit soon after. At the quarter ime 37½) Reliance was leading, Starr King pushing him close d Del Sur going third. Around the further turn Starr ing closed with the leader, and there were frequent offers of oney that he would win; but up the stretch, although he me fast and true, Reliance drew away and came to the ore winner by a length, Starr King second, Director third, ario fourth, Honesty fifth, Ashley sixth and Del Sur last. he judges decided to penalize Cairo for running in the first arter, and placed him seventh, thus changing the position Honesty to fourth, Ashley to fifth and Del Sur to sixth; me, 2:22½.

Second Heat.—The Director party had backed their favor-e heavily from the first and were more than pleased when eliance won a heat and helped to bring up the field in the ols. The betting before the start for the second heat was, irector $100, field 70. Director scored in the front rank hen they came up for the word, and at the first turn, where eliance and Starr King both made wild breaks, the favorite ade his first appearance as a leader, going past the quarter 36½ with a commanding lead, the others well bunched three ngths behind. In the straight work of the back stretch po-tions improved somewhat, but Director allowed nothing oser than on his wheel. Near the half Reliance and Starr ing both broke again badly, and when the rest of the field unded into the homestretch both the awkward ones were a stance behind. Honesty came forward in the trot home, t the son of Dictator was in his element, and reached the ire first by a length; Honesty second, Ashley third, Del ır fourth, Cairo fifth, Starr King and Reliance distanced. ime—2:24½. The judges deliberated long before making the nouncement the cause of the hesitation being an impres-on that Starr King had been handled in the heat with a pur-se to get him behind the flag, but finally concluded to allow m to retire. Complaint was also made that Ashley had in-rfered with the speed of Honesty, and Mr. Kennedy was monished to be more careful in the future.

Third Heat.—With the field reduced to five, a good start as soon effected, Director leading away at a spinning gait, ıt not at any time getting far from the field. The quarter s made in 36½, and the half in 1:12½. Both Honesty d Cairo were lapped on to Director, but not able to reach s collar. In the stretch the three had a lively set-to, but iro fell off before the distance was reached, and Honesty uld do no more than score a good second; Cairo third, Del Sur fourth and Ashley fifth. Time—2:24. Ashley crossed the line fourth, but was reduced to the last place for bad behavior.

Fourth Heat.—Further complaint of the conduct of Ashley's driver was made by the owner of Honesty, and in the interval the judges decided to remove the offending reinsman and appoint another in his stead. When the word was given the position was as good as could be desired, Director getting away handily with the lead after a few strides had been made. Honesty was close up at the quarter, and at the half Cairo and Del Sur both joined the company. Ashley was practically out of the race, and certainly interfered with no one more. In the stretch Honesty and Cairo repeated the performance of the previous heat with the same result; Director first, Honesty second, Cairo third, Del Sur fourth, Ashley fifth. Time—2:24½.

### The Close of the Fair.

If universal commendation is a recompense for months of hard work, the president, directors and secretary of the Golden Gate Fair Association have been amply remunerated. The encomiums came from all sides, and even the "chronic kickers" were subdued after a feeble attempt to raise a muss upon one occasion, heartily joining in the plaudits when the futility of the attempt became evident. It is extremely rare that a week's trotting and racing is got through without some disagreeable attending circumstances, and though in the 2:25 class there was room for aspersions on the conduct of the drivers, that was the only race which had a show of crookedness. It is difficult at times to determine the right and wrong, and circumstances may naturally arise which look like proofs of wrong-doing. That the managers did everything in their power to overcome all objections is cheerfully conceded, and hereafter the clan of this meeting will aid them.

The weather of Saturday was superb; that of the whole week was so good that the most captious of critics could not find fault with it. The track has been kept in admirable order, and the time made in nearly all the races is proof that that the contestants were far above the average in their respective classes. Although there is little necessity for adding to the detailed accounts of the heats, the combination race between the one trotter and three pacers is worthy of comment. The winner, Corette, appears to be destined to take a prominent place in the pacing fraternity, and "Old Gib" displayed powers which his most ardent admirers did not credit him with possessing. Corette is a very handsome mare, and as these two races are the only ones in which she has participated, there is a strong probability that a little longer training will develop still more speed. She never made a break in any of the heats, and although Gibraltar did his best in the first heat, was relieved in the second by Weigle, and again essayed in the third, the young mare was too much for the combination. There was fast work all through. In the second heat, when Weigle made his endeavor, the quarter was reached in 33½ secs., and the half-mile in 1:08. The first quarter on the Oakland track has always been considered slow, and if Weigle had been able to keep up the pace, the mile would have been still faster.

The race throughout was very satisfactory, and the mixing of the "lateral" and "diagonal" movements a good idea.

In the roadster race there was a queer finale. Emperor had the race when a hundred yards from home, being several lengths in the lead at that point, but his amateur driver took a pull; and before he could get him in motion again the mare won. The time shows that it was a very creditable performance for roadsters. The following is the account of the heats:

The opening turf event was a special trot against time, for yearlings, for a purse of $50. Five colts had been entered, but J. C. Simpson's Antevolo, by Electioneer, and P. J. Shafter's Viking, by Rustic, were the only two trotted. L. J. Rose had an unnamed entry, but the colt was quite lame, and the judges permitted him to be withdrawn. The purse was for the colt that made the best mile, three trials being allowed, if desired. Antevolo appeared first, and in his second trial scored his mile handily in 3:07, a highly creditable performance for a yearling without training and without shoes. Mr. Shafter's entry was also driven two trials, his best time being 3:16. The purse was awarded to Antevolo.

The last regular purse of the meeting was free for all trotters and pacers, and Corrette, Johnny Wiegle and Lady Hays, pacers, and Gibraltar, trotter, came to the wire as claimants for the money, subject to the usual contingency of winning it before taking it. Gibraltar had the call in the pools at the opening, but the betting gradually changed in favor of Corette, and before the start she was a decided favorite. Corette drew the pole, with Gibraltar second, Lady Hays third, and Johnny Wiegle outside. At the word Corette and Gibraltar got away together, the other two dropping astern, Lady Hays last. At the quarter Gibraltar was still lapped on to the handsome little mare, with Wiegle close up. Time—35½. Down to the half in 1:10 Corette began to open a gap, and at the head of the homestretch had a certain lead. Down the stretch Gibraltar thundered at a tremendous pace, but Corette skipped along without apparent effort, and crossed the line winner by two lengths; Gibraltar second, Wiegle third, Lady Hays fourth. Time, 2:20.

Second heat—Corette was not fixed in the estimation of the speculators, and $40 for the mare to $20 for the whole field against her was about the average of the pools. At the start Wiegle made a bold brush for the front, and went around the turn like the wind, Corette dropping in close behind him, and Gibraltar third. The pace was too hot for Lady Hays, and she broke badly before the quarter pole was reached. Wiegle showing his head there in 33½, and continued his triumphant career to the half in 1:08, where Corette and Gibraltar were close on to him. Around the turn and up the stretch Corette paced past Wiegle so smoothly that she scarcely seemed to touch the ground, and came to the wire a winner by three lengths; Wiegle second, Gibraltar third, Lady Hays distanced. Time, 2:19.

Third heat—The start was unexceptionable, but early in the fight Gibraltar made a wild break, running to the front and barely escaping a disastrous collision with Corette. He was pulled down reasonably soon, but not as quickly as some observers thought he should have been, but at the quarter in 36½ the little mare was again on even terms with him and began to show in front. Gibraltar struggled to keep in her company, and at the three-quarter mark in 1:46½ he was still on her wheel, but from there she drew away and won again by a safe margin; Gibraltar second, Weigle third. Time—2:21½.

The concluding piece was a race for a set of harness, open to roadsters driven to road wagons, the owners to drive. J. M. Learned's Allie Ray, W. S. Hewlett's Brownie H. and Mr. Sawyer's Emperor went for the prize. Allie and Emperor to carts and Brownie to wagon. There was some betting that Allie Ray would take the straps. At the start Brownie broke badly, and at the quarter pole Allie was leading, with Emperor second, but thence Brownie successively overtook and passed the others, winning the heat easily; Allie Ray second, Emperor third. Time—2:41.

Second Heat—At the turn Emperor and Brownie both broke up, Emperor getting his feet first and going to the front, Brownie following closely, and leaving Mr. Learned in the tail of the procession. Brownie closed with Emperor at the half, and was in a fair way to repeat the story of the first heat, when a bad break sent Mr. Hewlett to the rear, and gave the heat to Emperor; Allie second, Brownie third. Time—2:42.

Third Heat—Allie began the breaking in this heat. Brownie doing a share, and Emperor going for business without a skip. Brownie got to the quarter first, but was unsteady and made frequent breaks, that gave Emperor all the opportunity the most anxious seeker after a new harness could desire. At the head of the stretch Emperor was far ahead, and was let down to a jog, but Brownie got level again, and crept past the leader, apparently unnoticed, and won the heat and prize, greatly to the surprise of Mr. Sawyer and the amusement of the spectators. Time—2:46.

Mrs. J. Raynor of San Francisco and J. W. Coming of North Temescal had on exhibition three coops of chickens called the Langshan. These fowls are large, color black, average ten pounds in weight and are good egg producers.

The following is a complete list of the premiums awarded to exhibitors:

### Horses.

Thoroughbred stallions, three years old and over, first premium to Thad Stephens, owned by R. P. Clement; second premium to Nathan Coomb, owned by Wm. Boots.

Thoroughbred stallions, one year old first premium to Sir Thad, owned by J. C. Simpson; second premium to Billy Foote, owned by W. A. J. Gift.

Thoroughbred stallions, under one year, premium to Cito, owned by J. C. Simpson.

Thoroughbred mares, three years old and up, first premium to Too Soon, owned by J. C. Simpson.

Thoroughbred mares, two years old, first to Miss Gift, owned by W. A. J. Gift; second to Lady Viva, owned by J. C. Simpson.

Thoroughbred mares, one year, first to Legina, owned by R. P. Clement. The committee recommended a special diploma to Miss Stevens, owned by J. Leech.

Thoroughbred families, first to Thad Stephens and five colts, owned by R. P. Clement.

Families other than thoroughbred, first to General Grant and five colts, owned by Antonio Bellina.

Horses of all work, for stallions three years old and over, first to General Grant, owned by A. Bellina; second to Gold Hill, owned by R. O. Baldwin. For stallions two years old, first to May Boy, owned by A. Bellina; second to Black Prince, owned by P. J. Shafter. For stallions, one year old, first to Frank, owned by A. Bellina. Colt under one year, first to Little Prince, owned by Chisholm & Sackrider; second to "Butt Cutt," owned by A. Bellina.

Mares of all work, for three years and over, first to Brownie H., owned by H. Hewlett; second to Dollie, owned by A. Bellina. For one year and over, first to Abboteen, owned by Ben Harris. For filly under one year, to Lill, owned by Chisholm & Sackrider.

Roadsters, stallion, four years, first to Rustic, owned by P. J. Shafter; second to Odd Fellow, owned by W. K. Robinson. Stallion, three years, first to Belmont Chief, owned by J. F. Houghton; second to Anteeo, owned by J. C. Simpson. Stallion, two years old, first to Echo Sr., owned by L. Newlett; second to Redwood, owned by George Copsey. Yearlings, first to Sydney, second to Judge S., both owned by J. Goldsmith. Sucking colt, first to Tom Moore, owned by W. D. Hammond; second to Royal Bow, owned by A. Bellina.

Mares or geldings, four years—First, unknown, owned by Mark Rollins. Three years old—first to Patriarch, owned by W. K. Robinson; second Lady Lightfoot, owned by W. D. Hammond; two years old, to No Name, owned by J. L. Rose; one year old, to Rose Abbot, owned by B. E. Harris.

Matched span, first to Jack and John, owned by Newland & Pumyea; second to Prince and Bill, owned by S. W. Sawyer.

Draught horses, stallions, three years old, first to Tornado, owned by W. S. Brown; second, to French Spy, owned by Chisholm and Sackrider; two years old, to Penola Chief, owned by F. Toleman; one year old, to Deceda, owned by Chisholm & Sackrider; under one year, to French Spy Jr., same owners.

Mares, one year old, first to Gertrude, owned by W. S. Brown; second to Lizzie, owned by Chisholm and Sackrider; under one year, to Puss, same owner.

Carriage horses, first premium to Jack and George, owned by Mrs. R. Duffy.

Saddle horses, first premium to Mike Price, second to Major, both owned by Ben Harris.

Sweepstake stallions, any breed, first to Anteeo, owned by J. C. Simpson; second to Odd Fellow, owned by W. K. Robinson.

Sweepstake Mares, First to Lady Viva, owned by J. C. Simpson.

Jacks, first to John Henry, owned by W. A. Memyan.

### Durham Cattle.

Bulls, three years and over, first to Second Duke of Alameda, owned by Coleman Younger; second to El Medico, owned by Paige Bros. Two years old, first to Cherry Prince, second to Lord Clover, both owned by Paige Bros. One year old, first to Forest King, second to Fourth Duke of Forest Home, Coleman Younger. Bull calf under one year, first to Eighth Duke of Forest Home, Coleman Younger; second premium to Roscoe, same owner.

Cows, three years old, first to Jessie Maynard, second to Red Dolly Second, Coleman Younger. Two years old, first to Oxford Rose, Coleman Younger; second to Belle of Sonom, Paige Bros; one year, first to Belle Medico, Paige Bros.; heifer calf, under one year, to Red Dolly Fourteenth, Coleman Younger.

### Ayrshire Cattle.

Bulls, three years old, to Archie, George Bennett; two years old, Lindo, same owner; calf, to Malcolm, same owner.

Cows, three years old, first, to Stelita, G. Bennett; second, to Ethel Brown, same owner; two years old, to Stellanita, same owner; one year old, to Sultana, same owner; heifer calf, to Sybil, same owner.

### Sweepstakes—Durhams.

Bulls, first premium to Second Duke of Alameda; second to Third Duke of Alameda, Coleman Younger.

Cows, first to Jessie Maynard; second to Red Dolly Second, Colman Younger.

### Sweepstakes—Ayrshires, Jerseys or Alderneys.

Bulls, first premium to Archie (Ayrshire, owned by G. Bennett; second to Champion of Guernsey, Henry Pierce.

Cows, first premium to Rumor Second, (Jersey), Henry Pierce; second to Lane, (Ayrshire), owned by G. Bennett.

### Herds—Durhams.

Over two years old, one male and two females: First, to Second Duke of Alameda, with cows, Rose of Forest Home, Red Dolly Second, Jessie Maynard, Red Dolly Fifth, Coleman Younger.

Under one year, one male and five females; bull, Third Duke of Alameda; cows, Red Dolly Ninth, Red Dolly Eleventh, Lauraine Fifth, Rose of Forest Home Fourth, Rose of Forest Home Ninth, Coleman Younger.

### Herds—Jerseys and Alderneys.

Over two years, one male and four females, bull, Victor of Yerba Buena; cows, Bloomer Second, Oakland Maid, Mon Plaisir, Fairy of Yerba Buena, Henry Pierce.

Under two years, bull, William Scituate; cows, Eva Third of Yerba Buena, Coquette of Yerba Buena, Carrie of Yerba Buena, Flora Third of Yerba Buena, Henry Pierce.

### Herds—Guernseys.

One male and four females, bull, Champion; cows, Lizzie, Lassie, Lillie, Daisy, Henry Pierce.

### Best Jersey, Alderney or Guernsey in Class.

Bulls, three years and over, first to Victor, Yerba Buena, second, to Champion of Guernsey, Henry Pierce. Two years old, first premium to James Hayward, A. J. Snyder; second, to Modoc, Jessie Wall. One year old, first to William Scituate; second to Electric, Yerba Buena, Henry Pierce. Under one year, first to Shotover, Henry Pierce.

Cows 3 years and over, first to Bloomer Second; second to Fairy of Yerba Buena, Henry Pierce. Two-year-olds, first to Nancy, Mrs. R. P. Clement. One year old, first to Carrie of Yerba Buena; second to Eva Third of Yerba Buena. Best calf, first to Coommassie, Yerba Buena, second to Delta of Yerba Buena. Henry Pierce.

### Graded Cattle.

Best cow, three years and over, first to Betsy, F. Rosenstock. Two years old, First to Minnie, F. Rosenstock.

### Sheep.

Spanish Merino, ram, two years and over, to Sprightly, J. H. Trowbridge. One year old, first to Comet; second to Lightly; same owner. Pen of five ewes, two years and over, No. 2, J. H. Trowbridge. Pen of five ewes, one year and under two, same owner. Pen of five ewe lambs, same owner. Pen of one ram and five lambs, same owner.

Cotswold, first to ram Hancock, Coleman Younger.

Southdown, Premium to ram "No Name," G. Bement; pen of five ewes, Coleman Younger.

### Hogs.

Essex and Berkshire, best boar, first premium; best sow, first premium, owned by C. L. Dietz.

### Poultry.

Light Brahmas, first premium to E. Woolfeden.

Dark Brahmas, first premium to same owner.

Partridge Cochins, to W. Hubbard.

Buff Cochins, to E. Woolfeden; Plymouth Rocks, to J. N. Lund; brown Leghorns, to same owner; golden-spangled Polish, to A. J. Jackson, black-breasted game, to C. L. Dietz; blue game, to W. H. Hubbard, black breasted game bantams, to J. N. Lund; black African bantam, to C. L. Dietz; white pile game bantam, to C. L. Dietz.

Langshan, special premium for new breed, to Mrs. J. Raynor.

White-faced Black Spanish, to J. W. Cummings.

Pekin Duck, to C. L. Dietz.

For the largest collection of poultry, to J. N. Lund.

Pigeons, Jacobins, special premium to J. N. Lund; Carriers, premium to C. L. Dietz; Flying Pouters, to same owner.

## Summaries.

### RACING.

Golden Gate Fair, Oakland Trotting Park, Sept. 4, 1882.—Golden Gate stake.—For all two-year-olds; three-quarter mile dash; $50 entrance; $15 forfeit; $150 added; second colt to save stake; Winners 5 pounds extra.

P. Robson's May B., by Shannon, 112lbs ... 1
Leland Stanford's ch f Satanella, by Leveler—Frou-Frou by Asteroid, 112lbs ... 2
Peter Coutts' blk f Flou-Flou, by Monday—Jennie C., 107lbs ... 3
Leland Stanford's ch f Satinet, by Wildidle—Rose by Cheatham, paid forfeit.
Peter Coutts' Panama, by Shannon—Abbie W., paid forfeit.
Time—1:17.

Same Day.—Alameda stake for three-year-olds; one and one-half mile dash; $75 entrance; $25 forfeit; $175 added; second to save stake.

Geo. Hearst's b h Duke of Monday, by Monday—Demirep, 116lbs Duffy ... 1
Leland Stanford's b f Precious, by Lever—Frolic, 115lbs ... 2
Leland Stanford's ch f Fostress, by Foster—Planetia by Planet, paid forfeit.
Peter Coutts' b c Forest King, by Monday—Abbie W., paid forfeit.
George Hearst's ch f Marie F., by Leinster—Flush, paid forfeit.
Time—2:41½.

Same Day.—Pardee stake.—Free for all; one mile and repeat; $75 entrance; $25 forfeit; $200 added, second to save stake.

J. T. Gilmer's b h Red Boy, by War Dance—Neilson, 118lbs ... 1 1
P. J. Shafter's b m Night Hawk, by imp. Haddington—Norfolk, 115lbs Ross ... 2 2
Leland Stanford's b f Precious, by Lever—Frolic by Thunder, paid forfeit.
Leland Standford's ch f Fostress, by Foster—Planetia by Planet, paid forfeit.
Henry Schwartz's Sister to Lottery, by Monday—Virgina, paid forfeit.
Stemler & Ayers' ch g Fred Collier, by Joe Norfolk—Puss by Norfolk, paid forfeit.
Time—1:42½, 1:45½.

Sept. 6.—Free for all; two mile dash; $100 entrance; $25 forfeit; $250 added; second to save stake.

Leland Stanford's b f Precious, by Lever—Frolic by Thunder ... 1
Wm. Boots' b m Mollie H., by Wildidle—Mamie Hall by Norfolk ... 2
P. J. Shafter's b m Night Hawk, by imp. Haddington, dam by Norfolk, paid forfeit.
J. T. Gilmer's b h Red Boy, by War Dance—Neilson, paid forfeit.
Stemler & Ayers' ch g Fred Collier, by Joe Hooker—Puss by Norfolk, paid forfeit.
Time—3:36.

Sept. 7.—Selling Race.—Purse $250; $175 to first, $75 to second; one mile.

J. T. Gilmer's ch c Euchre, by Leinster—Flush, $500, 108lbs ... 1
Wm. Boots' ch c Inauguration, by Wildidle—Miami by Belmont, $1,000, 108lbs ... 2
P. J. Shafter's blk m Night Hawk, by imp. Haddington,—dam by Norfolk, $800, 114 lbs ... 3
H. Schwartz's Sister to Lottery, by Monday—Virginia ... drawn
Stemler & Ayres' b g Joe Howell, by imp. Bonnie Scotland—Eva Shepherd ... drawn
Time—1:43½.

Sept. 8.—Consolation Purse.—$250 for beaten horses; $175 to first; $75 to second; dash of one mile and a quarter.

P. J. Shafter's b m Night Hawk, by imp. Haddington, dam by Norfolk, 115lbs ... 1
Wm. Boots' ch c Inauguration, by Wildidle—Miami by Belmont 108lbs ... 2
Time—2:12.

### TROTTING AND PACING.

Sept. 4.—2:40 Class; purse, $600; $360 to first; $180 to second; $60 to third horse; mile heats 3 in 5.

| | | | | |
|---|---|---|---|---|
| Peter Coutts' b f Manon, by Nutwood | 1 | 1 | 4 | 1 |
| Louis Duncan's b g Louis D. | 2 | 8 | 1 | 2 |
| W. Z. Price's b m San Mateo Belle, by Speculation | 5 | 4 | 2 | 4 |
| B. F. Miller's b s Marin, by Geo M. Patchen Jr. | 7 | 2 | 7 | 3 |
| W. H. Henderson's b m Big Lize | 3 | 6 | 8 | 7 |
| A. B. Cooper's ch g Frank Moscow, by Frank Moscow | 6 | 7 | 5 | 6 |
| P. Farrell's s h Vanderlynn by Geo. M. Patchen | 9 | 5 | 3 | 5 |

| | | | | |
|---|---|---|---|---|
| Jno. McIntyre's ch g Edwin Forrest by Blackbird | 8 | 4 | 6 dr | |
| Mart Rollin's b g Freestone by Capt. Webster | 4 | dis | | |
| L. W. Titus' b s Exile by Echo | withdrawn | | | |
| Jas. Garland's gr g Rowdy Boy by Rustic | withdrawn | | | |
| G. Bernard's gr g Allen Boy | withdrawn | | | |

Time—2:26, 2:27, 2:27½, 2:24.

Sept. 5—2:30 class, purse $800, $480 to first, $240 to second, $80 to third horse, mile heats, three in five:

| | | | | | | | |
|---|---|---|---|---|---|---|---|
| A. Waldstein's b s Albert W. by Electioneer | 3 | 3 | 3 | 1 | 2 | 1 | 1 |
| S. Sperry's ch m Nellie R, by Gen. McClellan | 2 | 2 | 1 | 3 | 1 | 2 | 2 |
| J. A. Goldsmith's b m Sweetness, by Volunteer | 1 | 1 | 2 | 2 | dis | | |
| W. D. Hammond's gr Poscora Hayward, by Billy Hayward | dis | | | | | | |
| S. Crandall's b m Blanche, by Gray McClellan | withdrawn | | | | | | |

Time—2:22, 2:24½, 2:23½, 2:26½, 2:25½, 2:25, 2:26½.

Same day.—Pacing, free for all, purse $500, $300 to first, $150 to second, $50 to third horse (Washington and Johnny Wiegle to Wagon):

| | | | |
|---|---|---|---|
| L. E. Yates' b m Corette, by Winthrop | 1 | 1 | 1 |
| G. Valensin's br m Ouida, by Black Hawk | 2 | 3 | 3 |
| E. S. Denison's ch m Lady Hays, by Hiram Tracy | 3 | 3 | 2 |
| A. L. Hinds' ch s Oakland Boy, by Winthrop | dis | | |

Time—2:23½, 2:22½, 2:24.

Sept. 6—Trotting for all three-year-olds, purse $600, $360 to first, $180 to second, $60 to third horse, mile heats, three in five;

| | | | |
|---|---|---|---|
| J. M. Learned's Adrian, by Reliance | 1 | 1 | 1 |
| H. Meek's br f Bonnie Wood, by Nutwood | 2 | 2 | 2 |
| Irving Ayres', blk g Fred Arnold, by Nephew | 3 | 3 | 3 |
| A. C. Dietz' ch f Olivette, by Whipple's Hambleton | dis | | |
| J. C. Simpson's bc Anteeo, by Electioneer | dwn | | |
| J. B. Wyman's b c Commodore by Conductor | dwn | | |
| Babb's b f by Admiral | dwn | | |

Time—2:41½, 2:37½, 2:33½.

Same Day.—Trotting, 2:22 class, purse $800, $480 to first, $240 to second, $80 to third horse, mile heats, 3 in 5.

| | | | | |
|---|---|---|---|---|
| J. B. Macdonald's b s Brigadier, by Happy Medium | 1 | 2 | 1 | 1 |
| L. H. Titus' b m Belle Echo, by Echo | 2 | 1 | 2 | 2 |
| J. A. Goldsmith's gr s Romero, by A. W. Richmond | drawn | | | |

Time—2:27, 2:23½, 2:22½, 2:24½.

Sept. 7.—Trotting for two-year-olds. Purse $400, $168 to first, $67 20 to second, $44 80 to third horse, mile heats, two in three:

| | | | |
|---|---|---|---|
| S. Rosener's (J. W. Mackay's) b f Ruby by Sultan | 2 | 1 | 1 |
| L. J. Rose's b f Neluska, by Sultan | 1 | 2 | 2 |

Time—2:30½ 2:34½ 2:40.

Same day.—Trotting. Special purse of $600, $265 to first, $180 to second, $85 to third, $60 to fourth horse, mile heats, three in five.

| | | | | |
|---|---|---|---|---|
| P. Farrell's b h Vanderlynn, by Geo. M. Patchen | 1 | 1 | 2 | 1 |
| Jas. Garland's gr g Rowdy Boy, by Rustic | 4 | 2 | 1 | 3 |
| A. B. Cooper's ch g Frank Moscow, by Moscow | 3 | 3 | 3 | 2 |
| S. Crandall's b s Marin, by Geo. M. Patchen Jr. | 2 | 4 | 4 | 4 |

Time—2:30, 2:27½, 2:30½, 2:28½.

Sept. 8.—Trotting, 2:25 class. Purse $800, $480 to first, $240 to second, $80 to third horse, mile heats, three in 5:

| | | | | |
|---|---|---|---|---|
| J. A. Goldsmith's blk s Director, by Dictator | 3 | 1 | 1 | 1 |
| J. H. Dodge's ch s Honesty by Priam | 4 | 2 | 2 | 2 |
| Jno. Hughes' b g Cairo, by Chieftain | 7 | 5 | 3 | 3 |
| L. J. Rose's blk s Del Sur, by The Moor | 6 | 4 | 4 | 4 |
| J. Cochran's ch g Ashley, by Plumas | 5 | 3 | 5 | 5 |
| C. W. Welby's ch g Starr King, by Geo. M. Patchen | 2 | dis | | |
| J. M. Learned's b s Reliance, by Alexander | 1 | dis | | |
| L. H. Titus' b m Echora, by Echo | withdwn | | | |
| G Valensin's ch s Crown Point | withdwn | | | |

Time, 2:22½, 2:24½, 2:24, 2:24½.

Sept. 9.—Trotting, special against time for all yearlings for a purse of $50, one mile.

J. C. Simpson's Antevolo, by Electioneer ... 1
Time—3:07.
P. J. Shafter's gr c Viking, by Rustic ... 2
Time—3:16.
Geo. Bayless' ch f Dawn, by Nutwood ... withdrawn
J. A. McLeland's b c Mt. Vernon, by Nutwood ... "
J. J. Rose's c by Sultan ... "

## Chico Fair.

Chico, Sept. 7, 1882.

Mr. Editor: There was a large increase in the attendance at the park to-day. The first on the programme was ladies' tournament and prizes were awarded in the order named: Miss Lena Homer first, $30, Mrs. Frefoy second, $20, Miss Nellie McCormack third, $15, Miss Annie Clark fourth, $10.

Misses twelve years and under: Miss Nellie Sherman first, Lizzie Decker second, Miss Winnie Williams third, Matilda Gorre fourth, Miss Eva Clark fifth. The ladies and misses presented a very fine appearance and did some very fine feats of horsemanship.

The first race on the cards for the third day was the Chico Hotel Stakes, one and one-half mile dash, free for all three-year-olds, entrance $40, $25 forfeit, $300 added, second horse to save stake. Closed with following entries: Geo. Hearst names ch f Maria F., by Leinster, Flush—A. Miller, names b g Lady Partisan by Partisan, Jewell. J. Q. Anderson names g f Minnie Bell by Joe Daniels, by Norfolk; 115 pounds on each. Betting 6 to 2 on Maria F., and the result sustained the judgment of those betting the odds, as she won, Minnie Bell second, Partisan third. Time—quarter mile 32s., one-half 59, three-fourth 1:28, one 1:55, one and one-fourth 2:22½, one and one-half 2:48½.

Same day, second race, running, one mile and repeat, best 2 in 3. Closed with following entries: Ab Ellis names Shiner by Norfolk, by Lodi, 111 pounds. W. Hunter names b g Fred Hunter by Norfolk, by Rifleman, 111 pounds. Thos. Hazlet names ch g Jubilee by Norfolk, by Lodi, four years, 105 pounds.

Pools on this heat, Shiner $10, Jubilee $4, Hunter $2 and $3. Jubilee jumped off in the lead and led to the quarter pole in 27s., half in 53s., three-fourths 21s., mile 1:46½, Shiner second, Hunter distanced. Second heat, Shiner jumped off two lengths in the lead; as they entered the back stretch, Jubilee lapped him and they ran head and head until half way round far turn, where from some cause the chestnut was seen to toss his head in the air twice and commence to lose ground, Shiner winning the heat by one length, and now came a howl from the backers of Jubilee that he was being pulled. When they came out for the third heat the rider of Maria F. was placed on Jubilee and Johny Branan on Shiner. They made three false starts, when they got the word with Shiner a length the worst of it; he lapped him on the back stretch but was beaten by a length. Now I would like to know what benefit there is derived by simply dismounting a jockey for fraud as plain as this case was without attaching some punishment to the dismount.

SUMMARY.

Thomas Hazlet names ch g Jubilee, 4 yrs., 105 lbs ... 1 2 1
Ab Ellis names b g Shiner, aged, 111 lbs ... 2 1 2
W. Hunter names b g Fred Hunter, aged, 111 lbs ... Dist.

Same day, trotting race for three-year-olds to harness. The following horses started and were allotted positions in order named: Zulu Chief, Telegraph, Katy Almont. Telegraph was favorite over both the others, $10 to $6. After four ineffectual attempts they got the word to a very even start; the filly outfooted both around the turn in 41s. and came home a length better than Telegraph, he four in front of Zulu Chief.

The second heat they were sent away after four attempts, Telegraph in the lead, and was never headed. The race was postponed until next day, 1:30 P. M. sharp. A little larger crowd than yesterday, fully one thousand persons being present, the quarter stretch rails having teams hitched as thick as they could stand, a large proportion of spectators being ladies, and their handsome toilets lent an additional attraction to the scene.

SUMMARY.

E. Downer enters b g Telegraph by Tilton Almont ... 2 1 1 1
Billips enters blk f Katy Almont by Tilton Almont ... 1 2 2 2
J. L. Sullivan enters b g Zulu Chief by Tilton Almont ... 3 3 Dist.
Time—2:54, 2:58, 2:48, 2:54½.

Fourth day, running, mile and repeat, best 2 in 3, free for all, purse $400, entries closed Sept. 5th, 8 P. M., first horse to get six-tenths, second three-tenths, third one-tenth. Entries, Joe Howell by Bonnie Scotland, by imp. Sovereign, aged, 115 pounds. Maria F. by Leinster—Flush, 3 years, 105 pounds. Howell had the pole; time, first heat by quarters, first quarter 27½, one-half 53½, three-fourths, 1:20. Time—1:46½. Second heat, first quarter 29, one-half 54½, three-fourths, 1:21. Time—1:46½.

Official timers, J. T. McIntosh, Chico, Fred Shafer Esq., Wm. Harkey, Marysville. Same day, agreed trotting race, closed with the following entries, and were allotted positions in order named, Dutchman (rec 2:30½,) Bones, Roanone, blk s Challenge.

SUMMARY.

Chas. Sherman enters Roanoke ... 1 2 2 2
J. T. McIntosh enters Dutchman ... 2 1 1 1
Jas. Sullivan enters Bones ... 3 3 3 3
Challenge ... 4 4 Dist.
Time—2:45½, 2:39, 2:40½, 2:42½.

Fifth and last day. The attendance was as large as any previous day. The first race on the cards was a pacing race. C. D. Coward names b g Roden, Nelson McDonald names ro g Buz., Chas Shlutius names blk g Prince.

SUMMARY.

Roden ... 1 1 1
Buz. ... 2 2 2
Prince ... Dist
Time—2:48½, 2:48½, 2:47½.

Same day.—Agreed trotting race, 3 in 5 to harness, owners to drive.

Z. W. Burnham names b g Dutchman ... 1 2 1 1
Chas Sherman names b g Roanoke ... 2 1 2 2
Time—2:44, 2:38½, 1:46½, 2:37½.

The running race for mules did not fill.

I take this opportunity of returning thanks to the officers of the association for many favors granted.

The show of horses and cattle beats any fair ever held here. Every stall was occupied and some had to stable their horses in sheep-pens.

Premiums were awarded as follows:

### Horses.

Thoroughbred stallions, W. L. Sullivan, Sacramento, Jim Brown.

Thoroughbred mares, J. Q. Anderson, Stockton, Minnie Bell; A. J. Stemler, Sacramento, Lady Partisan.

Graded stallions, J. J. Reaves, Blackbird, 3 years; same. William B, 2 years; James Hasty, Chief, 1 year.

Graded Mares, Ben True, Nellie, 3 years and over; David Snyder, Lucy Toleman; J. J. Reaves, Belle Howard, 2 years; J. T. McIntosh, Sallie M., 1 year; J. J. Reaves, Lady Hilda Second, 1 year.

Stallions, T. Garrett, Chief, 3 years; John Grabley, Sir Tom; Alfred Cross, Cub, 2 years.

Mares, J. J. Reaves, Lancet, 3 years; Alfred Cross, Beckey Second; David Snyder, Nellie, 2 years.

J. C. Hess, Willows, Napoleon, 3 years; J. W. Hedge, Oroville, Black Tom, 2 years.

Roadsters, Chas. Sherman, Carlisle, 4 years; Shorty, Roanoke, 2 years.

Gelding roadsters, Carnell, Colusa, Telegraph.

Two years old, L. H. McIntosh, Colusa, Prince; L. D. Jenkin, Olimps, Rockwell.

Roadster stallion, J. T. McIntosh, Singleton, 3 years.

Roadster mares, James Hasty, Blue Bell, 3 years; D. M. Hooper, Rodie Ann, 3 years; Chas. Sherman, Belle Kimball, 2 years; J. T. McIntosh, Exact Second, 2 years.

Carriage horses, Allen Henry, Don and Joe.

Best single carriage horse, W. A. Titreau, Polly.

Roadster team, A. Bullard, Dave and Heitsick; Herman Bay, Cloud and Nig.

Saddle horse, Burke, Johnnie.

Colts, Jas. Hasty, Chico, yearling; J. W. Fritters, Orphan Boy, second best.

Sucking colts, J. T. McIntosh, Signate; Ben True, Ben T, second best.

Yearling mare colts, J. T. McIntosh, Sallie M; Chas. Sherman, Chevalier.

Sucking mare colts, J. J. Reaves, Chico Maid; J. T. McIntosh, Solitaire.

Sweepstakes, stallion, J. J. Reaves, Blackbird.

Mare, J. T. McIntosh, Exact.

### Jacks and Mules.

A. B. Collins, Prince, 2 years; J. J. Reaves, Humbolt, 2 years; A. B. Collins, Jack, 1 year.

### Cattle—Durhams.

Bulls, J. J. Reaves, Twilight, 3 years; M. Wicks, Oroville, Major Butler Second, 3 years; J. J. Reaves, Henry Clay, 1 year; M. Wicks, Oroville, Louan, 1 year; M. Wicks, Oroville, Dexter, bull calf; J. J. Reaves, Stonewall, second best.

Cows, M. Wicks, Oroville, Frantic Louan, 3 years; J. J. Reaves, Sallie Short, 3 years; J. J. Reaves, Queen Victoria, 2 years; M. Wick, Oroville, Frantic 24th, 2 years old; J. J. Reaves, Beauty; M. Wicks, Oroville, Matilda, heifer calf; J. J. Reaves, best herd.

### Devons.

Bulls, R. McEnespy, Ben Butler.

Cows, R. McEnespy, May Flower, 3 years; same, Queen Second, 3 years; same, Maud, 2 years; same, Spy, 1 year; same, Calf, Trixy.

### Jerseys.

Bull, A. B. Collins, Hawkins.

Cows, Geo. F. Hawkins, Roxana, 3 years; Geo. F. Hawkins, Dutchie, 3 years; A. B. Collins, Maud, 2 years; A. B. Collins, Blackey, 2 years; Geo. F. Hawkins, Bessie, 1 year.

### Graded (Jerseys.)

A. B. Collins, Nellie, 3 years old; A. B. Collins, Bridget Second, 3 years.

### Swine.

Best China boar, M. Wicks, Oroville, Gabriell.

Best China sow, M. Wicks, Oroville, Betty.

Finest and fattest hog, J. W. Paden, Silrina.

Best five pigs under six months, Chas. Sherman.

### Goats.

M. Wicks, Oroville, Jack; same, Jarad; same, Lizzie; same, Jennie; same, four kids.

### Poultry.

A. B. Collins, best five varieties; same, light Brahmas; same, trio black Cochins; same, best Game cock; Matilda J. Clark, Nelson, trio Selkies; same, Buff Cochins; same, white Cochins; same, Brahma cock under 1 year; Charley Henry, Nelson; China geese; B. F. Allen, Pekin ducks; Willie Reed, Nelson, Bronze turkey; Wm. Cleveland, Nelson, turkey gobbler.

### Machinery.

M. L. Mery, Farm and Feed Mill; J. M. Ormsby, Sewing Machines; Hubbard & Earll, Display Harvesting Tools; Hubbard & Earll, Best Well Pump; Hubbard & Earll, Best Gang Plow.

## The State Fair.

ever before in the history of the California State Agricul- l Society was there a more auspicious opening. From first there has been a good attendance, increasing as the k wore away, and the machinery running as smoothly as ld be desired. The stock exhibition has been very fine, he departments well filled, and when the conclusion es it is safe to assert that the returns will show to the sfaction of every one interested. The racing and trotting e been first class and with scarcely an exception every se a contest to the end of the last heat.

### The Races.

here could scarcely be a finer day for the races than the rnoon of Monday. There was no great degree of warmth, l yet there was caloric enough in the atmosphere to en- e the "sweating out" of the horses. There was a fine at- dance for the opening day and a good deal of speculation. e first on the list was a dash of three-quarters of a mile, entries and conditions will be found in the summary. In pool-selling before the start Premium and Jim Renwick rnated as favorites, the rate being $50 on each of them, ) on Atalanta and $40 on the others grouped in "the field." the starting point it was difficult to tell the different ses unless by those who were posted about the "colors;" ugh there was only a short delay at the post—one false rt—when the flag fell to a very good send-off excepting that and Premium were slow in getting under motion. The ding horses for a time were Atalanta, Jim Renwick and Douglas, and it looked as if the race was going to be con- ed to a struggle between the trio, but "t' auld mare" came ng with a rush, Ella Doane also improved her position, d though Jim Douglas essayed to get to the front it was not day, Premium winning by an open length from Ella, Jim air third. The following is the

SUMMARY.

GRICULTURAL PARK COURSE, SACRAMENTO, September 11.—Running, roduction stake for all ages; three-quarters of a mile dash; $50 en- nce, $15 forfeit, $200 added, second to save stake.

. Mulkey names ch m Premium (10), by Carter, dam Flying Cloud, 111 pounds........ 1
C. Judson names b m Ella Doane (aged), by Wildidle, dam Nettie Brown by Rifleman, 114 pounds........ 2
orge Howson names b s Jim Douglas (4), by Wildidle, dam by Norfolk, 106 pounds........ 3
Van Buren names P. Coutts' b c Forest King (3), by Monday, dam Abbie W., 95 pounds........ 0
W. Trahern names ch f Kate Carson (3), by Joe Daniels, dam by Norfolk, 92 pounds........ 0
n. Boots names b g Bob (3) by Bob Wooding, dam Gladiola by Norfolk, 92 pounds........ 0
eo. Winters names ch f Atalanta (3), by Norfolk, dam Lady Jane, 92 pounds........ 0
unler & Ayres name ch g Jim Renwick (4), by Joe Hooker, dam Big Gun, 105 pounds........ 0

Time—1:16.

The second race was the Breeders' stake for three-year-olds, dash of a mile and a half, that closed with nineteen entries $50 entrance, play or pay, with $300 added money. Of ese the only starters were John Windover's Captain Kidd, eorge Hearst's Maria F and Duke of Monday, and the Palo lto filly Precious. Mr. Hearst's pair were favorites in the ools, selling for $100 against $75 for Precious and $10 for aptain Kidd. The horses were promptly dispatched at the rst trial, Maria F. starting off in the lead to make the pace ot for Precious, while the Duke was evidently biding his ime. As they passed the wire for the first time Maria was eading by a length, with Captain Kidd third, and the Duke aking up his lost ground rather too quickly it seemed for he length of distance he had to travel. At the half-mile it as apparent that Maria F and Captain Kidd had to succumb, or they resigned the lead to the Duke and Precious, who egan a desperate brush that lasted to the drawgate, when he Duke, under the whip, swerved from the outside towards he inside rail, and the result was then never doubtful, as, lthough Duffy rallied the Duke, he was beaten by Precious n 2:38, Captain Kidd being a poor third and Maria F. last.

SUMMARY.

Same day.—Running, Breeder's stake, for foals of 1879, one and a half ile dash; $50 entrance, p. p., $300 added. Closed March 1st with ineteen nominations.

alo Alto Stock Farm names b f Precious, by Lever, dam Frolic, by Thunder, 107 pounds........ 1
eorge Hearst names b c Duke of Monday, dam Demirep, by Young Melbourne, 110 pounds........ 2
hn Windover names b c Captain Kidd, by Leinster, dam Tibbie Dunbar, 110 pounds........ 3
eorge Hearst names ch f Maria F, by Leinster, dam Flush, 107 pounds........ 4

Time—2:38.

The third race was for a selling purse of $300, heats of a ile for all ages, and there were nine entries, five of which ame to the post. These were Joe Howell, Euchre, Inaugu- ation, Patrol and Vila Randlett. Joe Howell was largely the avorite in the pools, selling for $100, Euchre bringing $50, 15 for the three others combined. Under the conditions oe Howell had six pounds from the old schedule of weights nder which the State Fair races were run. Inauguration nd Patrol had their weight up, Vila Randlett five pounds ff.

Owing to the refractoriness of Vila Randlett there was some rouble in getting them off, and when the flag fell she had a rifle the best of the start. Patrol soon joined her, and round the further turn all were in a bunch. It was a pretty ace home, but at the drawgate "Old Joe" came away and on with apparently something in hand in 1:44. Euchre as second, Inauguration third, Vila Randlett fourth and atrol last.

The pool selling was at an end. The few sold showed Joe Howell such a favorite as to bring $40 for $2 on all the others. The heat showed that the estimate of the old veteran was one too high, for although Inauguration led at the quarter nd a half, proving himself a good colt, Joe was first in the tretch and first under the wire. The positions will be found n the

SUMMARY.

Same day.—Running; selling race, purse $250, free for all, one mile nd repeat, second horse to receive $75, entrance five per cent. to third orse. Horses entered to be sold for $1,500 to carry entitled weight, ne pound off for each $100 under fixed valuation.

emler & Ayres name b g Joe Howell (10), $900, by Bonnie Scotland, dam Eva Shepherd, by Imported Sovereign, 105 pounds.... 1 1
Wm. Boots names ch c Inauguration (3), $1,500, by Wildidle, dam Miami, 95 pounds........ 3 2
. T. Gilmer names ch h Euchre (5), $600, by Leinster, dam Flush, 105 pounds........ 2 4
W. L. Pritchard names g m Vila Randlett (4) $1,000, by Waterford, dam Little Sophie, 100 pounds........ 4 3
I. C. Judson names b c Patrol (3), $1,500, by Wildidle, dam Nettie Brown, by Rifeman, 95 pounds........ 5 5

Time—1:44, 1:44.

The next race was the 2:40 trotting class, and of the eleven ntries, six came to the front, viz: Louis D, Manon, Van- derlynn, Rowdy Boy, Marin and Big Lize. Manon was argely the favorite in the pools before the start, bringing $68 to $11 for Vanderlynn and $12 for all the others. This was long odds for a five-year-old filly, at the outset of her career, and though the form she showed at Oakland appeared to justify the high estimate the result proved that there was misfortune to mar the scheme.

The first heat there was a good deal of scoring. The starting judge had to impose several fines, in one instance five of the six drivers being mulcted. The eighth score brought them near enough together to tap the bell, Big Lize slightly in the lead, but at the half mile pole Manon was first with Rowdy Boy on her wheel. The gray obtained the advantage and was first at the three-quarter-pole when he was passed by Manon, who won the heat in 2:25. The placing of the others will be found in the summary appended.

The second heat was startling to the backers of the fa- vorite. Manon led at the start but broke before rounding the turn, losing ground. At the half mile the field was strung out with Rowdy Boy in the lead though at the three- quarters Manon came up apparently the winner of the heat, but the judges penalized her for a run on the back-stretch and gave the heat to Louis D, Big Lize placed second. Time, 2:24¾.

The third heat Louis D took the lead with Rowdy Boy second at the half mile. Rounding the further turn there was a change of places, a general mixing, which made it al- most impossible to say what the positions were at this point, and the contest down the stretch was remarkably good. Louis D amazed the spectators by coming to the score first with Vanderlynn second and the others as given in the sum- mary. Time, 2:24¼.

The fourth and last heat was trotted when it was growing dusk, and patrols were appointed. Louis D. and Vanderlynn had a fight for precedence and before the quarter was reached Van's nose showed in front. At the half mile Louis D. had much the best of it, a straggling field behind him. There was a closing up when the straight work was reached but not enough to jeopardize the chances of Louis D., who won in 2:25¼ with Big Lize second. This gave huge Elizabeth the third money, Manon having made the second prize score in the first heat.

SUMMARY.

Same Day.—No. 4, Trotting, 2:40 class, purse, $1,000, mile heats, 3 in 5.

Louis Duncan names b g Louis D., by King William, son of Whipple's Hambletonian, dam unknown........ 4 1 1 1
W. H. Henderson names —— Big Lize, by ——........ 6 2 5 2
C. Van Buren names P Coutts' b m Manon, by Nutwood, dam Addie........ 1 3 3 3
B. T. Miller names b s Marin, by Patchen, dam unknown........ 3 4 4 6
P. Farrell names bh Vanderlynn, by Geo. M. Patchen, dam a Joseph mare........ 5 6 2 4
James Garland names g g Rowdy Boy, by Rustic, dam by Belmont........ 2 5 6 5

Time—2:25, 2:24¾, 2:24¼, 2:25¼.

There was an increased attendance at the track on Tues- day afternoon, the second day of the fair, and everything went along smoothly. The president insisted that the drivers should wear distinctive colors, and though there were a few recalcitrants all had to comply, and the consequence was that the races were far more satisfactory to the public and enabled the reporters to follow the horses with more accu- racy. This was a wise measure which should be followed by the other fairs.

The first race called was the 2:25 class for a purse of $1,- 200, and of the nine entries only Ashley was withdrawn.

Director, owing to the Oakland showing, was made first choice at $100 against $15 for Starr King, $12 for Crown Point and $25 for the field, composed of Capt. Smith, Hon- esty, Del Sur and Reliance, the latter proving himself exces- sively unreliable by getting distanced in the first heat. After ten false starts, they were sent off well together and Starr King, driven in an able and determined manner by Tim Kennedy, made for the lead and broke at the first turn and they almost all followed suit so that Goldsmith was balked in his efforts to get through the scampering steeds. When they settled down to their work Starr King was in the lead with Honesty and Capt. Smith in fair attendance, but at the upper turn Director was seen coming up, and he took the place of Honesty, who found the pace too hot for him, and so after a very close and exciting finish Starr King won by three-quarters of a length, Captain Smith being a poor third. This heat in no wise decreased the faith held by his backers in Director's speed and they backed him as fully as before. In the second heat Goldsmith was not caught nap- ping as he went at once to the front and leading at the half by ten lengths he won handily in 2:25¼ with Starr King second and Cairo a bad third. Crown Point was now withdrawn on account of lameness and Director with $100 to $20 on his chances cut out all the work in the two final heats and won as he liked, Starr King being second and Cairo next in the third heat, and Honesty second and Del Sur third in the final heat, the time being 2:24 and 2:25.

SUMMARY.

AGRICULTURAL PARK COURSE, SACRAMENTO, September 12.—Trotting, 2:25 class, purse, $1,200, mile heats, 3 in 5.

J. A. Goldsmith names blk s Director by Dictator, dam by Mambrino Chief........ 2 1 1 1
C. W. Welby names ch g Starr King by Geo. M. Patchen, dam Mary Wonder........ 1 2 2 6
John Hughes names b h Cairo by Chieftain, dam by Odd Fellow........ 7 3 3 4
J. H. Dodge names ch h Honesty by Priam, dam by Chieftain........ 4 4 6 2
Palo Alto Stock Farm names br g Capt. Smith by Locomotive dam Maid of Clay........ 3 6 4 5
L. J. Rose names blk s Del Sur by The Moor, dam Gretchen, by Mambrino Pilot........ 5 5 5 3
G. Valensin names ch s Crown Point by Speculation, dam Young Martha, by Patchen........ 6 7 dr
James M. Learned names b h Reliance by Alexander, dam Rattler mare........ dis

Time—2:23¼, 2:25¼, 2:24, 2:25.

The next after the 2:25 trot was a purse of $300, a dash of a mile, for yearlings, in which were entered Chevalier, by Charles Sherman, Mount Vernon, by M. E. Cloud, Rose Ab- bot, by Ben E. Harris, the Sultan—Gertrude colt by L. J. Rose, and the filly by Priam, the dam by Chieftain by W. H. Parker. The youngsters were all pretty unruly except Mr. Rose's colt who won by six lengths in 3:04¼, while the others timed it a second less, the quarter being made in 49¼ sec- onds, the half in 1:34¼ while the Priam filly came in second in 3:08 after making a very bad break when within reaching distance of home. It was a good performnace and Mr. Rose named the colt Edwin.

SUMMARY.

Same Day.—Trotting, purse, $300, for yearlings, dash one mile, to rule.

L. J. Rose names b c ——........ 1
Charles Sherman names b c Chevalier........ 2
Ben E. Harris names ch f Rose Abbott........ 3
J. A McCloud names b c Mt. Vernon........ 4
W. H. Parker names L. U. Shippee's c f ——........ 5

Time—3:04¼.

Then came up for discussion the purse of $500, mile and repeat, for two-year-olds, in which were entered Neluska, by Sultan from Gretchen, owned by L. J. Rose; Ruby, by Sultan, dam by Hambletonian, belonging to John W. Mac- kay and Pride, by Buccaneer, dam by Flaxtail, owned by M. W. Hicks. The little betting that took place was in favor of Ruby, and regrets were freely expressed that neither Flower Girl nor Sallie Benton belonging to the Palo Alto farm had put in an appearance to fill this engagement. There was an immense deal of scoring, as Dr. Hicks' filly was evidently out of condition through a long spell of epizooty and could not score with her stronger opponents. Ruby started out in the first heat and at the half-mile led Neluska by ten lengths and won as she liked in 3:33. In the second heat Ruby was not on her best behavior, making three or four bad breaks, of which Neluska took advantage to get a good lead, and al- though Goldsmith brought Ruby down the home stretch at a very fast gait, Neluska won by a head in 3:33. The final heat was very one sided, as Neluska was tired out and Pride for the nonce had lost her former speed, so Ruby won easily in 2:34½ with Pride second and Neluska last. For two-year- olds this was a great performance and caused much favorable comment.

SUMMARY.

Same Day.—Trotting, purse, $500, mile heats, for two-year-olds.

S. Rosener names J. W. Mackay's b f Ruby, by Sultan, dam by Hambletonian........ 1 2 1
L. J. Rose names br f Neluska, by Sultan, dam Gretchen........ 2 1 3
M. W. Hicks names b f Pride, by Buccaneer, dam by Flaxtail........ 3 3 2

Time—2:33, 2:33, 2:34½.

### The Third Day.

At the Park Wednesday morning, there being no parade of stock, the attendance was not so large as Tuesday, but the races drew as large a crowd as has been seen there for many a day. The feature of the exercises in the forenoon was a walking match for draft stallions for several prizes. The first prize was a farm wagon worth $150. The second prize, $25, was offered by the Society. The rules required the carrying a ton, which was of grain, on light four-wheeled wagons. Honest John, owned by T. W. Williamson of Sacramento; Monarch, owned by H. W. Wilson of Nicolaus, and Con- querer, owned by C. Porter of Marysville, were entered. Monarch won the first prize, making the mile in 12:40½; Con- querer took the second prize.

### The Races.

The third day again opened auspiciously; there was a fine attendance and though the afternoon was warm, so warm as to make the visitors from the Bay divest themselves of all warm clothing, replacing it with linen, the horses started out well and the racing was capital. Night Hawk astonished and pleased the spectators by making the fastest mile ever run on the Pacific Coast, and as will be seen by the report the race was a good one all through. Judge Shafter was warmly congratulated on having bred so good a mare, and the Haddington-Norfolk blood the happiest kind of nick.

P. A. Finigan was starter and succeeded admirably in the trying position.

The first race was the filly stake for two-year-olds, a dash of five-eighths of a mile, $50 each, $15 forfeit, with $200 added. There were originally eight subscribers but only two came to the post, George Howson's Augusta E selling at $60 against Mr. Coutts' Flou Flou at $20. There was seem- ingly no reason for this difference in the odds, because Flou Flou had shown great speed in her trials in the spring, but afterwards she went amiss and now has recovered somewhat of her old form. Flou Flou was out off to make the run- ning but Augusta E. closed up and made an excellent effort on the homestretch but she was beaten out by Flou Flou in 1:02½.

SUMMARY.

AGRICULTURAL PARK COURSE, SACRAMENTO, September 13.—No 8, run- ning, two-year-old fillies; five-eighths mile; $50 entrance, $15 forfeit, $200 added, second to receive $75, third $25.

C. Van Buren's blk f Flou Flou........ 1
George Howson's br f Augusta E........ 2

Time—1:02½.

The second race was the California Derby Stake for three- year-olds, a dash of a mile and a half, $100 entrance, $25 for- feit, with $250 added, $100 to the second and $50 to the third horse. For this there came up only three contestants, Maria F. and the Duke of Monday belonging to George Hearst, and Captain Kidd named by W. L. Pritchard. The betting was $100 to $45 on the Hearst stable, and when they were given the word Maria took up the running and passed the stand a length in advance of Captain Kidd whose Jockey was sawing the horse's head off in his attempt to keep him in reserve, but ineffectually, as the Captain was jumped out be- fore he had gone a mile. Thus left to themselves, the two came rattling down the stretch and finished well in 2:40, the Duke taking the victor's spoils. Judge McKinstry was en- tered also in this race but did not start.

SUMMARY.

Same day—No. 9, running, California Derby stake; three-year-olds, one and a half mile dash, $100 entrance, $25 forfeit, $250 added, second horse $100, third $50.

Hearst's b c Duke of Monday........ 1
Hearst's ch f Maria F........ 2
Pritchard's b c Kidd........ 3

Time—2:40.

Next on the programme was the Jennie B stake, a dash of a mile for all ages, $50 entrance, $15 forfeit with $200 added. In this there were Red Boy, a great favorite in the betting, Night Hawk, May D, Forest King and Frank Rhodes. On the fall of the flag both Red Boy and Night Hawk, who were on the outside position, made a rush for the pole and at too close proximity for safety, but luckily a collision was avoided and they both began to race at a clipping gait, Night Hawk always having slightly the advantage of Red Boy, and holding her position, she shook off Red Boy's desperate challenge at the draw gate and won in 1:42¼, the fastest time made on the Coast, and, as it beat Jennie B's record in this race, 1:42½, it will hereafter be named the Night Hawk Stake until her time is beaten.

SUMMARY.

Same day—Jennie B stake, running, for all ages, dash of one mile; $50 entrance, $15 forfeit, $200 added, second horse $75, third $25. Stake to be named after the winner if Jennie B.'s time, 1:42½, is beaten.

Night Hawk b m........ 1
Red Boy b h........ 2
May D. ch m........ 3
Forest King b c........ 4
Frank Rhoads, b a........ 5

Time—1:42¼.

The next race was the selling race, a dash of a mile and an eighth for a purse of $250, $100 to second horse and five per cent. of the purse to the third. Horses entered to be sold for $1,000 to carry usual weight and two pounds off for every $100 under that valuation. In this race there were only three entries, Joe Howell, aged, entered to be sold at $800, selling in the pools at $100 against $20 for Joe Daniels' Jim, aged, at $250, and Lady Partisan, three years old, for $1,000, both in the field. At the end of half a mile Joe Howell held them both safe and cantered home in 2:00¼, Joe Daniels taking second and Lady Partisan third money.

SUMMARY.

Same day—Running, one and one-eighth miles, selling race. Purse $250, second $100, entrance (5 per cent.) to third horse. Two pounds

(Concluded on page 185.)

## THE GUN.

### Deer—Not Darlings.

SAN FRANCISCO, September 9, 1892.

TO THE EDITORS OF THE BREEDER AND SPORTSMAN:—
Gun stocks, not corn stalks, were at a premium last week, when four popular amateurs in company with a dispenser of pills and paregoric shook off the tug of San Francisco's beautiful autumn do take a biennial perspiring peripatetic outing in the viticultural Sonoma valley, so as to be the better prepared for herculean efforts in the stock arena and for the nonce to satisfy their epicurean tastes and poodle-dog' desires. The party was composed of that celebrated fox-hound-hunter H. F., the genial "Clough," Marshal of San Francisco's most aspiring rival, C. D. L., the manipulator in quaint and unique designed tissue papers commonly called "stocks," A. M. K., the popular druggist, and T. J., the celebrated Nimrod agent of W. P. & Co., together with five 14 ℔. guns, 3 lame fox-hounds and 3 gallons of extra dry yet superior soothing syrup, landed in high spirit and with beating hearts in the town of Petaluma. There the high-toned livery establishment of that most classic burg were truly weighed in the balance, and the necessary contracts for the safe delivery of the party on the "Rancho Purdslits de Jesus Christo" signed and sworn to. The heretofore depreciated aspirations of L. as a shotgun-nist were so self-evident that even the member of the Oakland Gun Club became too modest to by conclusions and his much-bragged-of Dog George lost all sporting proclivities and so disgusted poor F. that he offered him at once for sale for 10 cents to every stranger he met.

The duty of providing the necessary provender for the supper devolved solely and undisputed upon the member with the Claybrough. He succeeded in dispatching between eighteen doves and five jacks to the rest of the party's one and one-half gallons of bug-poison, and after traveling nearly all day camp was struck and the team and prairie schooner, less one supernumerated mule (destined for pack purposes, returned to Petaluma. Night coming on the atmosphere and out-door exercise so exhilarated the nerves of the member of the Pharmaceutical Society and the Guardian of the Peace that the Zulu war-dance as executed by them would have resulted in an engagement for the terms of their "natural life" had the same been witnessed by a theatrical manager of experience. True, C, with his lame ankle, went through the different evolutions and gyrations with the gracefulness and agility of a wounded duck, but his performance as a whole proved truly astounding.

In the morning it was found that from the violent exercise of the night previous the Doctor's twenty-minutes pedal extremities were too much swollen to admit of ascending the twenty-degree incline, and he was left to see that the soothing syrup did not evaporate in the dry atmosphere. The remaining quartet walked, they claimed, between ninety-four miles, when suddenly the musical intonations of the fox hounds caused them to precipitate themselves prostrate upon the ground so as to permit sins free selected "bucks" to vault over them. Two of these were shot on the wing by the whole party, honors being easy; L., however; having again gained the palm of glory by throwing between forty-two shots of his Winchester in the four-foot space of a six-months-old buck at about 3,000 yards. The antiquated specimen of the jackass cross was then brought into requisition, causing J. to nearly break the Jewish commandments and his trousers, and C. to catechise in fourteen languages. By the aid of a derrick constructed out of poison oak the two deer were duly loaded in true mountaineer style and piloted to camp. The Doctor (who, by the way, is an expert horticulturist) was found to have planted all the loose pigars or "Teamsters Regalias stink adores Half Amass dammens" in true Egyptian war-map style, his crop promising a fair return to the first strolling crank who desires to relieve Sonomites of any landscape. The deer, being drawn and quartered in true barbarian style, were cooked by the doctor "Braises a la Mayonaise" and devoured by the famished quintet with great gusto.

The next day the Doctor rose at 9 A. M., and succeeded in walking one and one-half miles up hill in three hours; when just as he was trying to rest his weary limbs a bounding buck, flushed by the advance pickets, rushed headlong at the Doctor; the bullet from his self-discharged gun was heard by him to "pluck" the side of the deer, and throwing his horn useless article of warfare at the animal, he, with drawn Bowie knife, descended to the single combat. His tremendous movements precipitated him headlong into a friendly mesquite bush, money, watch and keys seeking different positions in the field. In this round, the deer escaped, and after selecting the most precious of his personal effects, the Doctor, disgusted, tired and worn out, sought the shades of a friendly tavern where for six hours he enjoyed the unbounded admiration of the natives, by his display of the "vernacular" and science in "Pedro for the drinks." He is said to have drank between two barrels of beer and to have won between nine hundred games. Next day F., C., J. and L. jointly killed the largest buck of the season, the same weighing 142 ℔. dressed; this being shipped to the city caused a serious decline in the price of venison (read Journal of Commerce that date) and that night the conductor of the down train as well as the passengers in the "smoker" found one more short deer hunting, fox hounds and Pedro than I possibly could have space to narrate here. The quintet propose at an early date to repeat their experiment and we sincerely trust they will, as our stock of jerked venison is getting low.

ONIX.

A NEW GUN FACTORY FOR THE PACIFIC COAST.—We learn from the Eureka Democratic Standard that the Finch gun is soon to be put upon the market. Parties arrived here recently from the East with whom Mr. Finch has made final arrangements for entering upon the manufacture of the gun in regular shape. The company has rented the upper story of Richardson's moulding mill and is now at work fitting up the various machines which will be required in the business. The factory is to have a capacity of twenty guns a day. It will take some two months before they will be in shape to go to work upon the first gun. We hope this will prove a successful industry.

Duck and snipe are very plentiful in Carson and Washoe valleys. Nevada hunters are bagging large numbers.

This season wild turkeys are more numerous than usual in the western parts of Texas and along the line of the railroads.

In Solano county last week a conviction was had in the case of three Chinaman that were arrested for trapping quail. They paid the fines of $60 each. It is a pity that a few white Chinese quail slayers could not be dealt with similarly.

## THE RIFLE.

### Snap Shooting.

EDITOR BREEDER AND SPORTSMAN, Dear sir: A few weeks ago I noticed an article in your paper on the subject of snap shooting with the rifle, and asking correspondence from those who had tried it.

I have been very fond of hunting for a great many years, and have always been out with the gun a dozen or more times every season, but never got to be what you would call a good shot.

I had a habit of getting flustered every time anything came in range, and instead of taking deliberate aim and firing I would pull the trigger without just knowing where my gun was pointing and trust to luck for a hit. I don't think I averaged one bird in five and when one did fall it was a surprise.

I knew just as well as I knew anything what the trouble was, and after every shot I would make up my mind that I would be deliberate next time and be sure I saw the game in the right place, over the gun, but just as often I would " slip up" on the result and blaze away by guess.

One day I ran across Col. Horace Fletcher's "A. B. C. Snap Shooting" book, and became interested in the method of practice he advocate.

I bought a 22 caliber Ballard rifle, a lot of cartridges and a kill-all and went over to the beach opposite the Presidio to try it—I got a boy to throw up the ball for me to shoot at, and began. I think I fired two hundred times before I made a hit, but when I did I saw just how I did it and felt sure I could do it again—and I did—hitting one out of about every five for the next hundred and gradually improving till I could average every other one. I think I shot away seven or eight hundred cartridges and when I got home I was all tired out but I had got better acquainted with a gun than I had ever been before in my whole experience—and I had never enjoyed myself so much with any sport. The next Sunday I went again, taking a couple of friends along to show them something—for I felt as if I could hit anything—but to my disgust I couldn't do as well as I had in the latter part of my practice the first day and I felt a little bit ashamed on account of my assumption, but after I had warmed up a little I got back my skill and did well.

I kept this practice up every Sunday for a couple of months, doing better sometimes than others but all the time improving and getting so that I handled the rifle scarcely knowing that I had anything in my hands because I became so used to the motion of holding it, and in the same way that a person uses a pen in writing without being conscious of holding one in his hand.

The next time I went out after birds I found that I had accomplished wonders; I didn't get at all excited as I used to but I knocked them over just as easy as possible, getting fully as many as I missed, and had accomplished something which all the shooting I could have had in ' the field would never have taught me.

I believe it to be the true way to learn to shoot, and I have no doubt but that any one can pick it up as quickly as I did and save a great deal of disappointment and cartridges which are wasted in the tules and brush.

G. A. GREEN.

### The International Rifle Team.

The first two practice shoots of the team selected to represent the National-Guard of America in the contest with the British Volunteers at Creedmoor, September 15 and 16, have proved very unsatisfactory in their results, as may be seen by a glance at the scores which appear in their proper department. American riflemen everywhere will feel disappointed when they find the team making poorer scores, when shooting as a team, than they did as individuals in the competitions for places. Then they were shooting against each other, now they are shooting to assist each other in every possible way under the rules. Their scores should, by all rules, be superior to those made in competing practice, but they are not; they are greatly inferior.

We have the greatest confidence in the ability of their captain, Col. Bodine, to organize the team in such shape as to overcome most of these troubles before the match take place, as his experience in such matters is great, but to make his efforts successful the members of the team must come harmoniously to his support, and engage in constant and transmitting practice.

The contest is more than a simple question of skill between English and American riflemen; it is a test of the skilled labor of both nations as applied to the production of a military rifle. When this match was entered into, our riflemen had given comparatively little attention to the military weapon, while English mechanics have for years been engaged in perfecting the rifle with special regard to military service. In view of the present outlook of continental affairs resulting from the condition of matters in Egypt, when a general European war may develop at any moment, this question assumes more than ordinary importance. In such event, the European governments would look to American arsenals and factories, as in times past, for the best military weapon, and the success of our team in the coming match would go largely toward sustaining the past reputation.

We regret to see the disposition shown in some quarters to find fault with the composition of the team on the ground of nationality. It is too late to raise such a question now. Every American will admit, that in a contest of this kind it were better that our team should consist entirely of those who have achieved their reputation on this side of the water; but every rifleman will agree with us, that the eve of the match is no time for making changes in the personnel of the team. They have been selected by open competition; their positions are supposed to be due to merit proven by actual performances; and to let any such feeling at this late date enter into the motives governing their selection can only lead to disintegration and certain failure. Let other matters than nationality enter into consideration at this late day.—The American Field.

A TEAM TROPHY.—It is proposed to present to the victorious team in the coming international military match an appropriate trophy commemorative of the event, the same to be held subject to the result of the match of the succeeding year. The design which has been submitted to the directors of the National Rifle Association, and is favored by them, is thus described: It consists of a vase modeled after those found in the Mississippi valley mounds, beautifully engraved with appropriate emblems, and having suitable inscriptions in rustic lettering. The vase stands on four American eagles. The cover is surmounted by an Indian hunter in the act of drawing his bow. The figure is remarkably graceful, and the whole effect of the piece is novel and strik-

ing. The proposed material is silver, and the estimated cost runs from $1,000 to $1,500. Of the required sum $300 is already secured. General Edward L. Molineux, president of the association, promises $100; J. Seabury, the secretary, subscribes a like amount, and Franklin Osgood also engages to give $100. With this beginning General Molineux has little doubt but he will secure the balance. He said that as soon as $1,000 was guaranteed the trophy would be ordered, but not sooner. His idea was that it should be offered as a gift of the United States to the military marksmen of England and America, and he said that if it were secured President Arthur would be invited to present it to the winning team; or if that were impossible, to allow it to be presented in his name.—New York Clipper.

A rifle match came off on the 7th inst. between N. Williams and S. I. Kellogg of Oakland and G. C. Thaxter and J. R. King of Carson, Nev. The Oakland team shot at Shell Mound Park and the Carson team at Carson. The match was fifty shots each at 200 and 500 yard ranges. Something invariably happens to N. Williams to prevent him doing his best shooting; this time, after a few shots, the breech was blown out of his gun, but on the whole the Oakland team did pretty good shooting as the score shows:

200 YARDS.

S. I. Kellogg—4 4 5 5 4 4 4 5 4 4 4 4 4 4 4 5 4 4 4 4 4 4 4 4 4
5 5 4 5 4 4 5 4 4 4 5 4 4 5 4 4 5 5 4 4 4—220.
Nick Williams—5 4 4 4 4 4 5 5 4 5 5 4 4 4 5 4 4 4 5 4 4 4 4 4 5
5 4 4 5 4 4 5 4 4 4 4 4 4 4 5 4 4 5—220.

500 YARDS.

S. I. Kellogg—4 5 5 4 5 4 5 4 4 4 5 4 4 5 4 4 4 5 4 4 5 5 4 4 4
4 5 4 4 4 4 4 4 4 5 4 4 5 4 4 4—224.
Nick Williams—4 4 4 4 5 4 4 4 4 5 4 4 4 4 4 4 5 4 4 4 4 4 4 4 5
4 4 4 4 4 4 4 4 4 5 4 4 4 4 4 5 3—219.

The next day the scores of the Carson team were telegraphed as follows:

200 YARDS.

J. R. King—4 4 4 5 5 4 4 4 4 4 4 4 5 4 4 4 4 4 4 4 5 4 4 4 4
4 4 4 4 4 5 4 4 4 4 4 4 4 4 4—219.
G. C. Thaxter—4 5 4 4 5 5 4 4 4 5 4 4 4 5 4 4 4 4 4 4 4 4
5 4 4 5 4 4 4 5 4 4 4 4 4 4—221.

500 YARDS.

J. R. King—5 5 5 4 4 5 5 5 4 4 4 4 4 5 5 4 5 4 4 4 4 5 4 5 5
5 5 5 5 5 4 4 4 4 4 4 4 4 4 5—231.
G. C. Thaxter—4 4 4 4 4 4 4 4 4 4 5 5 5 5 4 5 4 4 4 4 5 5 4 5
4 4 4 4 4 4 4 4 4 5 4 4 4 4 4—226.

Grand totals—Oakland Team, 883; Carson Team, 890.

The guns used by these men were the regular military rifles, open sights and triggers of a six pound pull. The figures show G. C. Thaxter with seventeen consecutive bull's-eyes on the 500-yard target. When one takes into consideration what the ordinary military rifle is, with open sights and heavy pull of trigger, he is almost ready to say that such shooting can't be done. Have the Carson gentlemen any recorded scores of former shooting that will stand a comparison with their last? There used to be a legend among the Indians that by incantation and an invocation of the spirit of the evil one, silver bullets could be cast that never miss the mark. Have King and Thaxter discovered the secret of the moulding? It is to be hoped that they did not shoot either the marker or scorer with any of their silver bullets.

## ROWING.

### The Records Beaten.

The race between Courtney and Lee on Candarago Lake, Sept. 1, was witnessed by an immense concourse of spectators. The New York Herald correspondent furnished a two-column telegraphic report of the race, from which graphic account the following particulars are obtained:

By half-past two o'clock the eligible points of observation on the western bank of the lake for a long way down the course were deeply fringed with spectators. Of course the greater numbers gathered in the neighborhood of the starting buoys, opposite the sloping grounds of Mr. Charles Chamberlain's farm, which, by the way, had been thrown open with characteristic liberality by their owner, who, though a farmer, admires all sport of an innocent nature. Carriages were massed solidly behind pedestrians, and the scene presented by the handsomely attired assemblage from the lake was most strikingly picturesque. On the Eastern shore was congregated another large crowd, though these people had only an indifferent view of the great contest. At twenty-three minutes past three the men were called out. Both had come from the village at noon and had been keeping quiet at the Lake House, on the Eastern shore, so upon the signal to come to the starting point a minute or so only elapsed ere they appeared in their shells, which had been in care of friends in the bowling alley, a hundred yards from the dock. Courtney was the first to pull out to his starting buoy, which was the one nearest the western shore. His appearance was hailed with rousing cheers, which were repeated when his athletic opponent followed three minutes later.

Charley wore a white shirt, dark blue knee breeches, and blue handkerchief around his head. George wore a similar shirt and knee breeches, with a red handkerchief about his head.

An anxious expression was observable upon the countenances of many of those on shore, who closely scrutinized the competitors as they left the dock at the Lake House in their dainty shells for the starting buoys, there to wait patiently for the signal which was to form the prelude to the victory of one and the downfall of the other.

In point of condition there was little to choose between the two men, for both were fairly trained and although Lee looked slightly bigger than when at Saratoga, there was no mistaking the fact that he was very missingly developed and was working in good form. Courtney had lost much of that frightened expression which he usually wears prior to a race; his eyes looked brighter, his skin looked ruddier and the muscles were little more prominent than a week ago. He was never better in his life; therefore his own party never looked for a victory for him. "Give us a fine day and smooth water and we shall win easily," they said, and they were certainly favored in this respect, for the afternoon proved gloriously fine and the lake was placid as a brook. In addition to this the weather remained clear, and a breeze that never happened again occurred to help the oarsmen, or soon as they turned the one mile and a half buoys the wind veered to the southward and back in the following wake in their southerly. It was as if the elements were bent to square themselves for their unseemly conduct of the previous twenty-four hours.

There was no delay whatever. The scullers had a previously burst and then dropped back to the starting buoys. At 3:28½ o'clock Referee Brandege gave the word which set the men on their journey. Courtney lost half a stroke at starting; his chronograph was so placed in his boat that he would note the pace he was making. From the tremendous use at which the boat went away it was patent that they made up his mind to do the greater part of his work at the beginning of the race, with a view of securing such a lead as would give him the command of his opponent to a certain extent, and by acting discouragingly upon the latter perhaps materially aid in gaining the day. It had been anticipated by Lee's friends, and thought possible by the backers of Courtney, that the former would immediately show in front. But for the starting of his chronograph Courtney would have got away evenly with the other, getting his work in at the rate of thirty to the minute. He quickly drew level with the Newark man, who was doing thirty-two strokes and pulling for dear life. The adherents of Lee, who had been willing to bet more than the other party cared to accept that their man would at least keep the lead from the start until rounding the half way buoys, were soon astonished to see Charley not only maintain his position, but gradually, inch by inch, rush his boat ahead.

Lee made desperate efforts to hold his powerful opponent and did so for a brief period, but then Courtney, wrenching his sculls through the placid water with an expenditure of power which sent his boat fairly flying down the lake, again commenced to edge ahead, and when nearly three-quarters of a mile from the start he was nearly a length the best of it.

Courtney was now working his sculls at the rate of twenty-nine a minute, while Lee was doing thirty, and pulling each stroke strong and clean. Approaching the turning buoys they had a very sharp tussle, being for a second on almost even terms, but as before muscle and skill carried the day. Going ahead again the brawny armed carpenter from Union Springs turned his mark buoy at the one mile and a half in just 9 minutes, 45 seconds, while Lee was 9 minutes, $45\frac{1}{2}$ seconds in getting around.

Such a close race had never been seen by any of the spectators or officials, and the interest was now coupled with intense excitement.

When straightened for the home work Courtney dropped his stroke to twenty-eight, and Lee almost passed him, rowing in good shape and with great strength. Charley subsequently explained that his right arm had troubled him for a day or two, and he desired to give it a rest, as he feared that the excitement might bring on lameness.

Lee's lead was for a brief period only, as Charley, at the two-mile point, had again reached the post of honor, and he was pulling so grandly it was dollars to farthings on his winning. At two miles and a half Charley was three-quarters of a length ahead, and holding his man beautifully. One-quarter of a mile further on, Courtney drew his sculls through the water more firmly than ever, and then led a length. As the last quarter was reached Charley dipped the old blades to the tune of thirty-one, and, as he drew further away from his plucky opponent, the cries of the spectators on shore were deafening.

A spurt of decided earnestness finished the great race, and when Professor George R. Smith dropped the blue flag, denoting Courtney's victory, his shell was one and a half lengths in front of Lee's.

The victory of Courtney seemed very satisfactory, and cheers and the waving of handkerchiefs were universal. He pulled up to the referee's boat as soon as practicable, and then Mr. Brandegee said:

"Mr. Courtney, I award you this race in the unprecedented time of 19m. $21\frac{1}{2}$s.

Lee's time was then given at 16m. $35\frac{1}{2}$s. This speed shows that winner and loser are extraordinary men.

The following particulars concerning the contestants and their boats are interesting:

Charles E. Courtney of Union Springs, N. Y., is thirty-four years old, six feet and one-half inch in hight, and weighs $167\frac{1}{2}$ pounds. He rowed a paper boat $30\frac{1}{2}$ feet long, $11\frac{1}{2}$ inches beam, $5\frac{1}{2}$ inches deep and weighing thirty pounds, built by Waters & Sons, of Troy, N. Y.

George W. Lee, of Newark, N. J., is twenty-six years old, five feet nine inches in hight and weighs 158 pounds. He rowed a cedar boat $30\frac{1}{2}$ feet long, $10\frac{3}{4}$ inches beam, $5\frac{1}{2}$ inches deep and weighing thirty-one pounds, built by William Wallace, of Newark, N. J.

A Defaulter's Stakeholder.—How much actual fact is there, I wonder, in a curious story that is going about concerning the Hanlan-Ross difference? For some little time now American papers which touch on sport have referred mysteriously to a loss of £200 by Ross. This, they insinuate, sometimes remotely, sometimes pointedly, should be shared equally by Hanlan, seeing that through him the loss was made. Not often is it that professional scullers in their designs upon an easy-going, not to say idiotic, public, are brought to grief by one of their own instruments. Therefore it may be as well to tell the story of Ross' ill-fortune as he himself tells it. Upon being interviewed two or three weeks back, he stated that the £200 which he put up for his match with Hanlan had never been returned him, the sporting editor of a paper in Toronto, with whom it was deposited, having gone away, and forgotten to leave either it or his address behind him. The stake-holding paper referred to contained a few weeks back a notice that this same sporting editor had departed, and that the proprietors were in no way responsible for his actions. If the story be as told by Ross, he has no reason to fear that his money is gone. The proprietors in question are legally responsible to him for money entrusted to their representative, if it was entruted to him as such. Their ignorance of this great truth need make no difference to Ross. *"Qui facit per alium facit per se"* is a legal maxim which obtains in all parts of her Majesty's dependencies, including Canada. Providing the paper is worth £200, the fact that this sum was entrusted to a servant of the proprietors, and not to the proprietors themselves, would be no bar whatever to Ross' recovering it. If my memory does not mislead me, this has been proved before now here in London. When deposits are made at the office of a sporting paper, the proprietor of such paper is responsible for them. The statement that clerk or cashier, sub-editor or reporter, has absconded with the money, would in no way hold him harmless.—*Pendragon, in the Referee.*

Still Another Challenge: The latest card from Wallace Ross has been telegraphed across the continent and runs as follows:

"I am prepared to defend the title of champion, which I now hold by reason of Hanlan's reported failure to accept any challenge against any sculler, whether from Toronto or any other part of the world, and am open to a match under the usual championship conditions as to distance and the amount of stakes, which Hanlan well knows, and £200 a side. I prefer to row Hanlan a race of this kind, and as an inducement shall give him the champion's right to name the course, and will allow a mutual agreement as to the condition of the water. The race must, however, be rowed five weeks from date."

Considering that Hanlan has published several cards announcing that he would row no one this year the defiant proclamation of the New Brunswicker is robbed of much of its value. It is high time for the telegraph agents to give these aspiring champions a rest and allow them to remain in obscurity until they have done something more meritorious than to sound their own praises through the columns of the newspapers.

## A Card from J. D. Griffin.

Editor Breeder and Sportsman, Sir: In the issue of your interesting paper of August 26th, L. C. White, Captain of the Pioneer crew, hits me and my club by saying we can row better on a sheet of paper than on water. Mr. White is well aware that the Golden Gates challenged his club several times and they would not accept. Is he also aware that his club had a standing challenge of $5,000, against any club-crew in this State? I accepted this standing challenge through a friend, Mr. Ellis, but that glorious challenge of the Pioneers fell through. "They were only rowing on paper". Mr. White must acknowledge that in his club house committees from my club and his were to meet and make arangements for a race, but the Pioneers failed to come to time. I said they would beat them, he said it looked like it. I will challenge Mr. White to show me an instance, when myself or my crew rowed first-class men against second-class men or second against juniors, but Mr. White has rowed a first-class crew out of his house against juniors for the Lumbermen's cup, but the juniors very gentlemanly drew out of the race after training hard for two weeks. I can hardly blame the Pioneers to steal a victory if they can, it is so long since they have won a square race. The Pioneers can keep in training from now until Thanksgiving Day. The Golden Gates will not go into training till two weeks before that day, and in their old lapstreak will give them the hardest race they ever had in their fine paper shell. I have got a son, a light weight, that will row Mr White or any man in his club a single shell race except Dan Leahy or Ned Nelson, for any reasonable amount, say $100 or $1000. This is what the tail of my literary kite can swing in or out of a row boat. As you are anxious for a race I will match you a crew outside of the Brown crew against any four men in your club, a lapstreak or barge race. I will be light with you, say a $40 prize.

As for the delay in complimenting Mr. Yale it was on account of two of the officers of one of the clubs being out of town.

In answer to Captain Thomas of the South End Club, he is well aware that the arangement before the Lumbermen's Picnic regatta was, that in the near future they would row for $100 a side, but the vain glorious South End crew won by a scratch through a foul. They raised the sum to $250 a side thinking they had a dead thing, but they were sadly mistaken. It is plain to be seen that the South Enders row for money and not for pleasure or health. The Golden Gates row, game and honest races and are not tools to any club in the 4th of July regattas.

J. D. Griffin,
Treas. G. Gate Rowing Club.

## Challenge.

To the Editor of the Breeder and Sportsman: We the undersigned members of the first crew of the Golden Gate do hereby challenge any crew in the South Ends, or in the Pioneers, for a purse of from $500 to $1,000, to be rowed in barge or lapstreak.

Signed,
James Brown, Bow.
P. Kaegan, Forward Waist.
J. Kaegan, Aft "
J. Walthour, Stroke.

If the South Ends or the Pioneers think we are rowing on paper let them put up the above sum of money and that will talk.

## Only a Gambler's "Squeal."

The men who were unfortunate in backing Ross in the Saratoga professional single-scull race are filling the papers with startling news. They aver that Ross was bought off, and that Courtney sold out to Lee. They seem to forget the fact that in 1877, over the same water, Courtney, who was then looked upon as invincible, rowed the three miles, with a turn, in 20:$47\frac{3}{4}$, while Lee's time in Friday's race was 20:$43\frac{1}{2}$, and Courtney's 20:48—only a quarter second slower than his '77 performance. Courtney's record, 20:$14\frac{1}{2}$, was not made at Saratoga, as has been erroneously reported, but at Owego, in October, 1877. Ross was in no condition to row such a hard race as Lee won over Courtney, and it is contemptible business, now that he is beaten, after having made a game struggle, for his friends and backers to cry "wolf."

In connection with this, we have received the following card from Mr. John H. Robbins, of the Associated Press, on of the managers of the late regatta:

Editors Turf, Field and Farm: I have been handed a slip containing some telegrams printed in a Philadelphia paper, which reflect on the late boat race at Saratoga Lake. The first telegram, a special from Auburn, pronounces the race a "skin;" the next attempts to show how the skin was put up; the third attempts to show how the pool-box was manipulated, and another how Riley was a participant in the alleged outrage. A paper that would print such malicious stuff is not worthy of being read by any lover of honest sport. The race in question was most assuredly rowed on its merits, and Courtney rowed to win, and had he not fouled the number attached to his stake he certainly would have won. He lost 22 seconds turning the buoy. This fact seems to have been lost sight of. Courtney was not paying attention to Lee. He was determined to beat Ross. When he turned around to look for Lee and saw him seven lengths in the lead after turning the stake, then he set himself to work and rowed as grand a stern race as ever a man saw, finishng a short length behind Lee, who never was in finer condition. Regarding the pool-box, $10,000 is all that Mr. Cathcart's books show were bet. Ross averaged as first choice, $325, Courtney as second choice averaged $195, while the field, with Lee in it, went begging throughout the entire selling. seldom bringing over $35. This fact alone tells the story and is the indicator that an honest race was rowed. The first to cry skin are the losers. Courtney's race defies the allegations of the mean, contemptible gamblers who are so loud in their denunciations. Mr. Roche, who bet three-fifths of the money lost on Ross, cannot speak in too high terms of Courtney. Why? Because he saw the race. Nine of the fields that were sold during the pooling were purchased by horse-racing men; some of them had never seen a boat race. Mr. Meeker, who lost heavily on Ross, expressed himself satisfied, and I could recount to you numerous facts that would knock this combination of gamblers' squeal and penny-a-liners' ambition into a cocked hat. As regards the statement that Jim Riley was employed to foul Hosmer, I do not hesitate to call the man who uttered the statement a liar. Yours truly,

John H. Robbins.
—*Turf, Field and Farm.*

The Course was Correct.—Lest there should be any question regarding the accuracy of the measurements of the course on Lake Candaraga, on which Courtney made his recent great record, the following affidavit is published:

"Otsego county, ss.: Jay L. Comstock, being duly sworn, deposes and says that he has been a practical surveyor for thirty or more years last past; that the buoys for the race between Charles E. Courtney of Union Springs, N. Y., and George W. Lee of Newark, N. J., were located and placed by me, and under my direction, near the west shore of Canadaraga Lake, on the 30th and 31st of August, 1882; that the said race was rowed by the said Courtney and Lee on the 1st day of September, 1882, as this deponent is informed and believes; that the distance between such buoys, as placed by me, was measured under my direction and computed by me, and is $1\frac{1}{2}$ miles and no less.

J. L. Comstock.

"Subscribed and sworn before me this 1st day of September, 1882.

A. C. Tennants,
"Notary Public in and for Otsego county, N. Y."

Three miles in 19:$31\frac{3}{4}$ is very fast going for a man who had so many mishaps. It is almost certain that this record will be accepted by the authorities. Dan Leahy made a more wonderful record over the Saucelito course in his five mile race with Hoyt, and the surveyor testified to the correctness of the course, but Dan gets in place this year in the accepted rowing records. Anything extraordinary of which California would like to boast is generally denounced as suspicious by Eastern authorities and not accepted until the performance has been repeated in the East.

Rowing at Long Bridge.—The Golden Gate club extended its hospitalities last Sunday to the visiting oarsmen of the Dolphin and Triton clubs of North Beach. The afternoon was enlivened by racing over the course to the rolling mills and back. The first contest was a scratch between the crews of the Golden Gate Club. H. Peterson, John Keegan, C. Smith and J. Griffin manned the Golden Gates' barge Gov. Perkins. P. Keegan, J. Lamb, J. Brown and D. Griffin manned the Dolphins' barge Dolphin. The superior qualities of the Gov. Perkins enabled the first named crew to get off quickest and at the mile buoy they had a commanding lead of several lengths. They increased the advantage on the run home going almost as they pleased. Both crews showed good form considering the circumstances under which the race was rowed. A race between the Dolphin and Triton crews followed on the same course. The Triton four were James Hughey, S. L. Schuppert, B. Kehrlein and J. Kehrlein. The Dolphin's four were S. Rathkoph, W. Whistler, G. Van Guelpen and T. Frazer. The Tritons had the best of the send-off and led to the rolling mills. In making the turn the bowman of the Dolphin lost the button of his oar and the boat came round so slowly that the Tritons gained a commanding lead and won easily. While the victory of the Tritons was not unexpected, the Dolphins' defeat is not by any means a disgrace, and another contest under different conditions would be interesting and agreeable to the lovers of rowing.

Draw it Mild.—Mr. Louis White, of the Pioneer Rowing Club, and Mr. J. D. Griffin, of the Golden Gate Club, are railing at each other through the papers. Mr. White insinuated that Mr. Griffin's club was better able to row on paper than in a boat, and Mr. Griffin retorts by sneers at the capabilities of Mr. White and his compeers of the Pioneer Club. If this kind of thing goes on the disinterested reader will begin to think that there is some ground for the implied charges made by both gentlemen. Instead of wasting time in writing challenges and manufacturing bad sarcasms, which have no particular interest for the public, it would be better for the rival oarsmen to keep their peace until they meet on the water, which they can soon do in a legitimate, manly and decorous manner. There is a time-honored proverb about boasting before one puts on his armor and after he has taken it off, that might be pondered over with much profit by the ardent competitors of the Golden Gate and Pioneer Clubs. We have more than once heard our great champions promise to eat their boots if they got beaten and though they did not win they are not visibly suffering from the indigestion that should follow if they had kept their bonds. Buckle down to your oars, gentlemen, and avoid printer's ink. It is not at all conducive to muscular vigor.

A Square Race.—The Boston *Herald* says: The absurd story that the Saratoga boat race was "dropped" to Lee is almost too ridiculous to comment on. The contestants did their best to win, and the time would have been much faster than it was if the struggle had not been so hard a one. Every man who has rowed a boat race knows that the excitement of competition is weakening, and lessens the power of each stroke long before the race is finished. A man starting for a trial on a three-mile course can often row the distance nearly a minute faster by judging his strength and lasting qualities, and using them accordingly, than if he engaged in a race with several others and was forced to do his best from the beginning. At Saratoga, Courtney had the task before him of rowing down Ross, Hosmer and Lee, each of whom fought him in turn and kept him spurting all the way. The time made in that race, under the circumstances, was remarkable.

A Fast Amateur.—The time announced for Holmes in the amateur race at Saratoga was several seconds slower than the distance was rowed in. The gentlemen who acted as time-keepers, not clearly understanding the rules, dropped the flag when the stern of Holmes' boat crossed the line, whereas they should have timed from the bow. The amateur champion stopped rowing just as his bow reached the line, and his shell moved slowly past the timekeepers. It is safe to say that Holmes rowed the three miles, under the rules of racing, in 21m. 10s., instead of 21m. $16\frac{1}{2}$s., as given. Lee's time was abaut 20m. 40s., so that the champion amateur's performance was a great one.

Rowing at Portland.—In the annual four-oared race for the Grant cup, which took place at Portland, Oregon, last Saturday, the Portland Rowing Association won, beating the Willamettes nearly one hundred yards. The course was three miles with a turn. Time, 19:20. The bow oar of the Willamettes was taken ill at the turn, but until then the race was close. The Portlands have won the cup in three races, and it now goes to their club permanently.

Courtney has not yet responded to Kennedy's offer to row him for $1,500 or $2,000 a side. Such a race would prepare Charley for a meeting with Ross, which now seems almost inevitable.

William Elliott, ex-champion sculler of England, intends returning to the old country in October, but he says he will come back to America in the spring. He will not be missed if he fails to keep his promise.

## THE
# Breeder and Sportsman.

PUBLISHED WEEKLY BY THE

BREEDER AND SPORTSMAN PUBLISHING CO.

THE TURF AND SPORTING AUTHORITY OF THE
PACIFIC COAST.

OFFICE, 508 MONTGOMERY STREET
P. O. Box 1838.

*Five dollars a year; three dollars for six months; one dollar and a
half for three months. Strictly in advance*

MAKE ALL CHECKS, MONEY ORDERS, ETC., PAYABLE TO ORDER OF
BREEDER AND SPORTSMAN PUBLISHING CO.

*Money should be sent by postal order, draft or by registered letter, ad
dressed to the "Breeder and Sportsman Publishing Company, San Fran
cisco, Cal."*

*Communications must be accompanied by the writer's name and address,
not necessarily for publication, but as a private guarantee of good faith.*

JOSEPH CAIRN SIMPSON, - - - EDITOR

San Francisco, Saturday, Sept. 16, 1882.

### THE ETHICS OF THE TRACK.

There must be an entire revision of the code of morals by which the drivers of track trotters are governed. Laws which are obeyed, not enforced, rules of conduct which are cheerfully submitted to from the consciousness of rectitude on the part of those who come under the control. There must be a higher sense of honor, a higher plane than smartness, a grander object than to manipulate races so as to make the most money out of them. In the old days of racing, a man who was found guilty of dishonest practices on the turf had to submit to social banishment. He was held to be unfit for the companionship of gentlemen and placed in the same standing as a petty thief, or trick-of-the-loop operator.

But the phase of the question which we shall consider now is a practice which does not meet with the reprobation it so justly deserves. This is a combination among the drivers to "play" the fastest horse. The manager of the horse which is conceded to be the superior enters into an agreement to divide the profits. This is with the express understanding that the contracting parties shall all work to the same end. There may be six horses in the race. D. is held to be the safest to put money upon. E. is speedy but unreliable. S. R. is badly handled, or still worse, roguishly handled. D. S. and H. are thought to have so little chance that they are left out of the combination as well as the uncertain R. But to guard against any contretemps A. is delegated a part which will prevent those who are not in the pool from upsetting the calculations. He is chosen as a helper to the prospective winner. Help at the right time is of incalculable service. A slight assistance at the critical moment may be an advantage which insures victory. It may be "carrying a contending horse out," it may be surrendering a position to the favored one. Under such an arrangement the driver of the favorite has a comparatively easy task to perform. For instance in making the second curve we will suppose that A. and H. are lapped, the former on the inside and leading a trifle. D. saves all the ground he can by keeping close to the inner rail behind A., and when the homestretch is reached A. carries H. out and gives D. the pole, so that in place of going around the two he has saved many yards, and wins a heat which he otherwise would lose. It may have been that there has been no infringement of the rules, according to a strict construction, and this one thing decides the race. If even it be found necessary for A. to do something which will subject him to punishment nine times in ten a fine is the penalty. The largest fine the judges can impose is a trifle in comparison with the pecuniary return from the sharp practice, and though it is paid with the greatest display of indignation there is an inward chuckle over the success of the scheme. Were every race a stubborn fight by everyone engaged in it there might be fully as much foul driving. We always sympathize with a driver who in the eagerness to win infringes, but when the guilty act is done to aid and abet in carrying out a nefarious combination, can see him punished to the full extent of the law. These combinations are the hardest things the judges have to meet. The only evidence, perhaps, is the betting, and that is oftentimes illusory. Men of sanguine temperament have an overweening confidence in their horses, and will back them when the calmer can see that there is no hope for them to win. There are races when the betting misleads those who are the most acute in "catching points," and if that were taken as a guide and verdicts based on it without corroborative testimony great injustice would follow. But how can these things be remedied? is a pertinent question, and what rules shall be framed to correct the evil? There may be amendments to the code which will assist, though our greatest hope are in the drivers themselves. There must be an endeavor to increase the standard of morality, and if a driver does not come up to the requirements get rid of

him. Owners are frequently more to blame than the persons they employ. They are careless in this respect, criminally careless. They will put horses in the hands of men who are notorious for a want of honesty, and laugh over the stories which brand the relators as the lowest kind of thieves.

There should be a determination on the part of owners and drivers to elevate the profession, among the latter there should be an esprit to make their business rank as highly as any other. To be a good driver—a good trainer especially, demands ability of a high order. There must be a level head, an inquiring mind, industry in study as well as to carry out the lessons which study gives. When this is combined with a high sense of honor, a resolution never to do anything that will jeopardize the standing, to frown on any schemes which are not based on the strictest honesty, then there will be little necessity for rigid rules. Let us hope that this day is not far off, and when it comes the only opposition to the fast trotter will be from those too bigoted to enjoy any of the good things of this world.

### THE FAIRS.

The fairs of the Sonoma and Marin and the Golden Gate Associations have passed, and now as we write that of the California State Agricultural Society draws to a close. To say that the Oakland and Petaluma exhibitions were satisfactory in every respect is only to reiterate what has been universally acknowledged. The new grounds of the former association have removed all cause of complaint, and it is conceded by all those who attended that it is hereafter destined to be one of the foremost of the California fairs. The great advantage is in ownership. There is not a member who will not take an interest in every tree and shrub that is planted, every adornment that is added. Even those who argued that the old park was good enough will acknowledge their shortsightedness, and heartily applaud the energy which carried the opposed projects to a successful termination.

There is no more beautiful location in the vicinity of San Francisco than the Oakland Trotting Park. Directly opposite Golden Gate, within the sound of the waves, it is so sheltered that rough breezes are of rare occurrence.

The plantation that skirts the shore is not the only protection. To the East is the Contra Costa range, an the eddy which flows back carries the trade winds above the level of the course. Nearer still there is a belt of timber. Along San Pablo Avenue, from the drive which leads to the park on the south, to the northern limits, are handsome residences, around them trees of such size that our Eastern visitors can scarcely credit the story that they are only of twenty years' growth. Between the natural coppice on the west and the partially artificial on the east, the park nestles, cozy as a " clearing" in the woods.

It only required a little aid from the architect, the builder and the landscape gardener to make it one of the handsomest places in the whole country, and which could not fail to attract a multitude of visitors at all seasons of the year. With these improvements the fair week would interest such assemblages of people as throng the park at St. Louis when the annual exposition is held. The ownership vested in an enterprising body of men who would make the necessary improvements, it is safe to predict that five years will return every dollar invested, with a valuable property left. This is all that is needed to place the Golden Gate Association on the right foundation, a guarantee that for many years there will be a park worthy of the two large cities to which it is contiguous. There is now a good prospect that the property will be purchased in time so that the desired changes can be made for the fair of 1883, and then the Golden Gate will be on the same footing as the sister societies.

We read and hear great things of the California State exhibition. This is the first time we have missed witnessing it since "living on the Coast," and we lament the "stern necessity" that compelled the lapse. In fact there is not one of the fairs of this State that has not attractions, and to a person of leisure who could spend the time there would be continual pleasure.

Sacramento is just the place for the State Fair. The capital of the State, it is meet that the exhibiton embracing the whole country should be held there. Apart from it being the location of the other branches of the State Government, there are advantages that cannot be overlooked. We have often adverted to them, and in a mere sketch of this kind there is no necessity for repetition. There is little question that the display of stock is as good as has ever been held there, and this promises a grand display indeed. Every department is reported equally well filled with articles on exhibition, and so far the races have been very satisfactory. We anticipated hearing encomiums regarding the manner in which everything has been conducted, as it would be difficult to find a more efficient set of officers.

### LETTER FROM MR. FINIGAN.

Below will be found the copy of a letter from Mr. Finigan in response to that which accompanied the medal presented Mr. F. by the Santa Clara Valley Agricultural Association, a description of which was given in the "Breeder and Sportsman."

In the first place it was a very graceful act on the part of Mr. Finigan when he helped the managers out of their dilemma at the time of the visit of General Grant to the San Jose Fair; in the second it was a graceful acknowledgment by the association, and the reply is equally felicitous. It is a great pleasure in these days, when so many owners of horses merely regard them as the means of making money, to find one imbued with the old-time spirit, one who has no mercenary motives in keeping a "stable," and who does so from a true love of sport without a sordid thought. It is true that to be able to do so a man must have the necessary means, that there are plenty of such who are as intent on emoluments as the poorest, and not a few of them who are more rigid in their exactions, than those who depend upon the race:

ALDERNEY FARM, Sept. 8, 1882.

TO THE BOARD OF DIRECTORS, SANTA CLARA VALLEY AGRICULTURAL SOCIETY, *Gentlemen:* Your highly esteemed favor came to hand in due time. How to thank your honorable board I know not. To say that I was surprised beyond language to express would only convey a small portion of my appreciation of your costly and highly-prized medal. It is so perfect in design, massive in form, pure and glittering, who could be so indifferent as so not to make it a life-long memento of the kind donors. I assure you, gentlemen, I will never tarnish it as long as I live, and the S. C. V. A. Society, will always shine bright in my remembrance. Were the inscription, design, and superb mechanical skill on the plainest of metal, in place of the choicest, it would be a present dear to me as long as I live, and at death I will bequeath it to the child most in favor with me, to the one of my children who I think will regard it the highest, and who after me will bear in loved remembrance the S. C. V. Society.

Before Santa Claus went East he trotted fourteen races, all of which he won, but I prize your medal more than all the rest of his winnings, though there was placed a large amount to the credit side of his account. The stamp on coin is the same. It is simply the government certificate of its value, and as they are issued from the mint there is no difference. There is only one medal such as you have sent me, and as I have stated before it is to me beyond price, as it bears the stamp of kind feelings embodied in the inscription, and recalls one of the pleasantest moments of my life.

The great pleasure of that occasion was in being able to assist you in entertaining your distinguished guest, and General Grant was doubly pleased, as up to that time he had never seen a trotter go so fast.

The five-year-old record of Santa Claus still stands at the head of the list. He repeated the 2:18 over your track on the occasion referred to, and that is the last time when a colt of his age showed so much. It yet leads a bold and defiant challenge, and I propose to accept the offer, and with a son of Santa Claus excel the time of the sire. I can assure you, gentlemen, that the ground I shall select for the trial will be that on which this was made, and I feel the utmost confidence in the result. Should the son equal or surpass the time of the sire on the same track, and in the presence of the kind friends to whom I am indebted beyond terms to express, it will be an additional source of gratification.

That Santa Claus has keep up his California reputation, and to-day stands at the head of the list of trotting stallions, is very gratifying to me, as my interest is still as great as when I was the owner; greater as the token of your goodwill has come since I parted with him, and this hightens the interest.

Again, gentlemen, permit me to thank you. I shall visit your coming fair, when I can return my heartfelt thanks in person. The medal I will bring, so that those of your members who have not seen it can have the opportunity.

With assurances of respect and esteem I am, gentlemen, very sincerely, your obedient servant,

P. A. FINIGAN.

### OUR HORSES IN THE EAST.

At last there is a crumb of satisfaction in the news from the Orient. On Tuesday last at Sheepshead Bay, Coney Island, N. Y., Luck B beat a strong field of two-year-olds, and Duchess of Norfolk won a sweepstakes for all ages. This is probably the turning point in the run of bad luck and from this time on we hope to record many victories. The California horses are named in nearly all the stakes at the fall meeting at Chicago, which opens October 3, and this will end in time for them to take part in the Pacific Coast races in November. The following is the telegraphic account:

In the fourth race, one mile, for two-year-olds, P. Lorillard's Breeze and Battledore sold for $540, Baron Feverot $300, Magenta $125, Empress $105, Vintage $90, Lucky B $60 and the held $70. After a little delay an even start was made, with all but Vintage, who was nearly left at the post. Breeze took the lead, but was passed by Bridesmaid on the turn, and the latter gave way to Baron Feverot as they neared the half. Turning into the stretch, Lucy B and Empress, ther of whom had been among the first five during the vious running, moved to the front. Lucky B won the race three lengths. The French pools paid $40 90 post odds of ht to one against the winner. In the first race, 1¼ miles all ages, handicap sweepstakes, Carley B sold at $575, lla $220, Duchess of Norfolk $110, Wedding Day $100, die Oreal $70 and the field $85. Carley B took the lead h Nettie second and Della third. At the stand Carley B i Nettie were on even terms. As they passed the half le Carley B led by a length with Duchess of Norfolk ond. As they made the turn into the stretch Carley B d Duchess of Norfolk were on even terms, the latter be- 'ng to draw away. The Duchess of Norfolk won by arly two lengths. The French pools paid $50 70 post ds; seven to one against the winner.

## "THE FIFTEENTH."

The opening of the shooting season, which dated from sterday, has been looked forward to for many weeks by e enthusiastic disciples of the gun. Breech-loaders ve been overhauled, cartridges loaded and shooting ps put in order. Yesterday hundreds left the city xious to have the first "whack" at the quail or duck. e ferry boats and cars have been overrun by men and gs all heading for the country.

To-day and to-morrow many hundreds who were un- le to be out on the 15th will make it lively for the as t unsuspecting birds. Up on the marshes the duck en will get their pick of young mallards, which have en raised there, and the season's quail everywhere will kept moving pretty lively.

The shooting season this year seems to have attracted en more than ordinary attention. Gunsmiths report greater demaud than usual for things in their line. his is their harvest time and the boys' money flies free- when getting ready for the fun.

The next few days both dogs and men will be hard orked. New dogs will develop then bad or good qual- ies, and there will be a great deal of powder burned and athers scattered. The first few day's sport only serves whet the demand of the ardent gunner to renewed ex- tion, and for many weeks to come the birds will be kept oving.

## HE SECRETARY OF THE STATE FAIR.

We hear that an effort has been made to have Edwin . Smith, the efficient Secretary of the California State Agricultural Society, removed, the animus of the attack being occasioned by Mr. Smith having written two articles for the "Breeder and Sportsman."

While we cannot believe that a single director will pay any attention to a charge based on such frivolous grouds t cannot be passed without comment. It is admitted by every one with whom we have conversed that Mr. Smith has performed the duties of his office in the most satisfactory manner, not only in regard to the office work, as all of those who have had business to transact with the society are well pleased and write in the highest commendation. Prompt, active, urbane, sys- tematic and untiring he unites the qualities which are so essential in the office he fills and without a word of dis- paragement intended for others who have preceded him in the position we hold that it would be a serious detriment to the society and every one outside of the association who is interested in any portion of the great exhibition to lose his services.

We have not the least fear that the Board of Directors of the California State Agricultural Society will lend themselves to a scheme so much below the dignity of themselves or the office they hold. They are gentlemen and this secures them from the obloquy of furthering the spite of any individual.

Furthermore we can hardly credit the report that a person of any standing should approach them with such an impudent request.

## LOS ANGELES FAIR.

The dates of the Los Angeles Fair are Oct. 6, 18, 19, 20 and 21. In the advertisement the first day is omitted from an error in the copy, and the correction was not received in time to be made in this number. The officers of the society are: F. J. Barretto, President; E. F. Spence, Treasurer; R. H. Hewitt, Secretary and Superintendent.

## PACIFIC BLOOD HORSE ASSOCIATION.

The fall meeting will commence with an "Introductory day," Saturday, November 15th, the regular days following on the 18th, 20th and 21st. The programme will appear in the next number.

The Mosquito Regatta of the San Francisco Yacht Club comes off over the short course on Saturday, the 23d inst.

The Bohemian Yacht Club opens its new club house to-day.

*Concluded from page 181,*

off for each $100 unber fixed valuation. Horses to be sold for $1,000 to carry entitled weight.

| | |
|---|---|
| Joe Howell b g | 1 |
| Joe Daniels Jr. ch g | 2 |
| Lady Partisan b f | 3 |

Time—2:00½.

The last race was for the 2:30 class, and as it had been fully shown that Sweetness was the fastest of all those entered, although it was doubted whether she could stay, she was eagerly sought after at $100, while Nellie R. brought $40, and the field $60, in which were Albert W., Manon and Tump Winston. Albert W. and Nellie both went to the front in this heat with Sweetness, but the former was rank and Nellie broke badly at the back-stretch, and as Sweetness appears to be steadiness itself, she won after a slashing finish with Albert W in 2:24, Nellie R being third and Winston last. As Albert W had shown so well in this heat and as Charley Marvin was given charge of Nellie R, the hopes of the fielders revived and against $90 for Sweetness, Albert W brought $45, Nellie R $35 and the field $20.

The next was a finely trotted heat, as when in the back stretch opposite the grand stand, Sweetness, hard pressed, was only a short length ahead of Nellie R, she leading Albert W by half that distance. They all three came down the homestretch in beautiful style, but close at the draw gate Nellie could not stand the strain and was off her feet and Sweetness outtrotted Albert W by a length amid a great deal of excitement and applause; the time being 2:21½.

The fielders kept up a brave mien and they wagered freely on even terms that Sweetness would not win the race, counting that if she could only be beaten one heat her chances would be at an end. Sweetness again cut out the pace and soon opened a gap of two lengths and although in the upper turn Albert W and Nellie R closed on her, she maintained her position to the end, winning by a length from her in 2:22½. Albert W took the second and Nellie the third money and this well contested race brought the day's proceedings to a close.

SUMMARY.

Same day—No. 12, trotting, 2:30 class, mile heats, 3 in 5, purse $1,200; first horse $720, second $360, third $120.

| | | | |
|---|---|---|---|
| Sweetness b m | 1 | 1 | 1 |
| Albert W b h | 2 | 2 | 4 |
| Manon b m | 4 | 3 | 3 |
| Nellie R ch m | 3 | 4 | 2 |
| Tump. Winston ch g | 5 | 5 | 5 |

Time—2:24, 2:21½, 2:22½.

### The Fourth Day.

One of the old-time rousing crowds were on hand to witness the races Thursday afternoon. The hot north wind was met by the breeze which had come through Golden Gate and following the valley northward routed the unwelcome visitor. There is great relief when the red-mouthed demon of the north is exorcised and his place taken by the sweet breath of the Pacific.

Notwithstanding the room on the stands they were densely packed, every seat occupied and the ground for carriages was completely filled. Hundreds were congregated between the stands and the quarter stretch, and altogether the concourse was probablv as large as has ever been seen at Agricultural Park. The management continues to give complete satisfaction, all the officers being complimented, and the secretary, who has been untiring in his efforts from the close of the last Fair until the present time, was heartily applauded for his zeal and official labor.

The first race on the programme was the 2:22, the entries, Brigadier, Romero and Belle Echo. With the knowledge that Romero had not recovered from a severe attack of pinkeye, which threw him out of training so far as giving him fast work went, and even if he had not been subjected to the weakening effect of the disease, the break in his work was sufficient to incapacitate him for making a bruising race, under the circumstances he made a fine performance, as 2:20 is the fastest heat trotted in California this year, and is the fastest time ever made by a California bred stallion.

The betting immediately before the start was $70 on Romero, $50 on Brigadier and $15 on Belle Echo.

For the first heat little time was wasted in scoring as at the third attempt a good start was given.

At the outset Romero took advantage of his position at the pole, and at the quarter he was well to the fore, leading Brigadier by four lengths, he being half that distance ahead of the mare. Shortly afterwards Brigadier made a bad break and lost so much ground that his driver probably thought he had no chance of winning the heat, so he reserved his horse for future operations. In the mean time Belle Echo had closed up toward the leader, who passed the half-mile post in 1:10½, and thence they came around the upper turn, but Belle Echo could never get within more than a length of Romero, and when at the drawgate she was driven to her utmost, she wobbled for a moment and then was off her feet, and Romero jogged past the wire in 2:22½, with Belle Echo second and Brigadier last.

The betting after this heat was $100 on Romero to $40 on the other two. The start for the second heat was not long delayed. Romero again started off in the lead, but Brigadier this time would not allow him to open up any gap, and moving up he reached Romero's flank; but the latter, under pressure, resumed the lead by a length, and so they traveled to the half mile post in 1:10, and all around the upper turn Brigadier seemed to improve his position inch by inch, and on entering the homestretch Brigadier was lapping the leader, and thence they came like a double team, until at the drawbridge Goldsmith was seen urging his horse to the utmost, and under the pressure he broke, and amid the wildest excitement the crowd congregated at that point breaking into the open course with yells of delight, Brigadier came away and won the heat in 2:23.

Previous to the fourth heat betting was very heavy, and indeed it was constantly chopping all through the race. After Romero's winning the first two heats, those who had backed Brigadier hedged their bets and now the Romero party were following suit, they paying $150 for Brigadier against $80 for Romero, and a great many backed Belle Echo up to $70, so as to stand even or suffer a small loss, the pool-box being probably the largest winner through its commissions. In this heat Brigadier went ahead, accompanied by Belle Echo, while Romero played a waiting game; but when on the upper turn the mare broke badly. Goldsmith brought up Romero at his utmost speed, but he could not reach the leader; he winning by four lengths in 2:28½.

The fifth heat was something of a surprise. The betting ruled $90 on Brigadier to $20 on the other two, and again a good start was given. At the half-mile post Brigadier was Just lapped by the two others, but Brigadier around the upper turn gradually drew away from them and seemed to be winning handily, when Mr. Titus brought Belle Echo up with a tremendous rush of speed, and secured a dead heat in 2:27½, with Romero last.

In the sixth heat Brigadier appeared to be the freshest and the odds were $50 to $20 in his favor. He set out at a brisker pace on the next heat and kept Belle Echo just at his wheel, and trotting evenly down the homestrech it looked almost like a second dead heat, when at the drawgate Belle lef her feet and Brigadier won the heat and race by four lengths in 2:25½ from Belle Echo, Romero following her at a like distance.

SUMMARY.

AGRICULTURAL PARK COURSE, SACRAMENTO, SEPTEMBER 14,—Trotting 2:22 class, purse $1,200, mile heats, 3 in 5.

| | | | | | | |
|---|---|---|---|---|---|---|
| J. B. McDonald's b s Brigadier | 3 | 2 | 1 | 1 | 0 | 1 |
| J. A. Goldsmith's g s Romero | 1 | 1 | 2 | 2 | 3 | 3 |
| L. H. Titus's b m Belle Echo | 2 | 3 | 3 | 3 | 0 | 2 |

Time—2:22½, 2:20, 2:23, 2:12½, 2 27½, 2:25½.

### The Pacing Race.

In the pacing race Corrette was largely the favorite with the betters, and though she took the first heat from being set back for a running break, the judges awarded the heat to Ouida. There was no change in the betting. The placing of each of the heats will be found in the annexed

SUMMARY.

Same day—Pacing, 2:25 class, purse $500, mile heats 3 in 5.

| | | | | |
|---|---|---|---|---|
| L. E. Yates' b m Corette | 4 | 1 | 1 | 1 |
| G. Valensin's br m Ouida | 1 | 4 | 3 | 2 |
| E. S. Dennison's ch m Lady Hays | 2 | 2 | 4 | 4 |
| A. L. Hinds' ch h Oakland Boy | 3 | 3 | 2 | 3 |

Time—2.24, 2.24, 2,25½, 2.27.

### The Two Mile Race.

Vanderlynn was greatly the favorite in the heat of two miles, San Mateo Belle and Slim Jim the only starters against him. The odds in his favor were $60 to $20, and he won very handily.

SUMMARY.

Same day—Trotting, two miles and repeat, 2:40 horses, purse $800.

| | | |
|---|---|---|
| P. Farrell's b h Vanderlynn | 1 | 1 |
| W. Z. Price's b m San Mateo Belle | 2 | 2 |
| C. H. Shearer's blk g Slim Jim | 3 | dist |

Time—5.03½, 5.07.

## EDITORIAL NOTES.

**The San Joaquin Valley Fair.**—Ho! for Stockton. Today will bring to an end the great Fair of the whole of the commonwealth; Tuesday next will bring the opening of the great Fair of the San Joaquin. In all of the States excepting California, the State Fairs so completely overshadow all the others that there is little chance for comparison. Here the District Fairs are also great exhibitions, and that which is held at the Capital of the rich valley has attractions sufficient to secure the attendance of a vast assemblage. The premium list is liberal in all its departments, the speed programme outranks any other in the State for the magnitude of the purses offared. This liberality has secured an entry list which assures the highest class of sport, and in addition to the amounts on which an entrance fee is charged, sums are added which will be a powerful incentive to the making of fast time. There is a glamour to the American people in witnessing previous records beaten. There isan enthusiasm following fast time which it is difficult for less mercurial folks to understand. When all the horses are likely to go fast there is a still greater desire to see them perform, as this is a guarantee of good races as well as fast time. It is unnecessary to reiterate that the horses in the classes at Stockton are so near together that the excitement in every race must continue from the start of the first heat to the finish of the last, as the record of the previous races proves it. Not a single trotting horse has won through. The most fortunate of them like Sweetness and Director have been beaten in their classes, and the warfare is sure to be a violent struggle all through. It is also unnecessary to acquaint those who have visited Stockton in previous years that there is a strict impartiality observed, and that the management is superior. This is well known and there are often inducements to make the trip exceedingly pleasant.

**Night Hawk.**—There cheers for the bonnie bay mare. She has cut down the California record to 1:42¼, and that is not a very big gap to close if even the fractions of seconds are troublesome when the time to equal is recorded as fast as 1:40½. That is Boardman's at Sheapshead Bay, but he was a four-year-old and only carried 91 pounds, whereas under the same schedule as Night Hawk ran under, it would have been 108 pounds. Ten Broeck's running against time does not come into competition, as there is a great difference between that and having a field of horses to contend against. One and three-quarters seconds is something of an undertaking, and yet we think there is a California bred colt which will be able when four years old and with 91 pounds up to make a mark in favor of the Occident.

**Gibraltar** scarcely ever in a race fails to show that he is a wonderful horse. In the race with Corette and Weigle last Saturday, at the Oakland Trotting Park, he forced Corette to 2:20, and was so close up that the race was apparently doubtful until the last moment. The most acute critic of the "looks of a trotter" could scarcely believe it possible for him to go the pace, and fewer still concede that "gameness" was his forte. The young pacing mare, too, gave evidence that she is certain to take a front rank in the grand army of side wheelers. This was her second race, and though in the second heat Weigle went at her from the score, took the track and went whirling to the half in 1:08, it did not disconcert her in the least. She drew up to him at will and won quite handily in 2:19. She had just recovered from an attack of the "pinkeye" and it seems reasonable to expect much from her in the future.

Fred S. Butler, the artistic member of the "Cordelia Shooting Club," has produced a very handsome picture of all the members of the club composed of the following members: Pres., E. T. Bent; Secy., Fred S. Butler; Commissary, C. W. Kellogg, Harry Babcock, T. C. Friedlander, Wm. S. Bradford, Ward McAllister, John K. Orr, W. McPherson, Hall McAllister. Their headquarters are on the Yacht Lolita, which is in charge of Chas. Chittenden at Teal Station. Some of the members left for the happy hunting grounds Thursday to be on hand for the opening day. Among them are Messrs. Bradford, Kellogg, Orr, Babcock and H. McAllister.

## HERD AND SWINE.

### Pure-Bred, Thoroughbred and Full-Bloods.

In answer to the questions as to the number of crosses it requires to produce a thoroughbred animal, and as to the difference between a full-bred and a thoroughbred, the *Prairie Farmer* gives us the following full and explicit replies:

"1. A pure bred animal is one that has descended from a pure original race without admixture of other blood. The Devons are a pure race of cattle. The wild cattle of Chillingham may be called a pure race. The true Arabian horse is a pure race. Wild animals are pure races.

"2. A thoroughbred is an animal originally of mixed lineage, but which has been interbred so long without recourse to foreign sources, that the progeny comes true or nearly true to the type established. The Shorthorns and Herefords among cattle, and the racers among horses arising from a mixed lineage, are thoroughbreds. That they have not yet ceased the endeavor to improve these breeds, through the careful selections of sires and dams, always carefully within the line of the oldest and well defined blood of the varieties from which they originally sprang, is proof that breeders do not believe that their ultimate excellence has been reached.

"3. The term full blood indicates neither purity of blood nor thorough breeding, except relatively. An animal of the common blood of a country may be bred indefinitely to a pure blood, and yet never reach purity. The first would be one-half blood; the third cross seven-eighths blood; the fourth cross, fifteen-sixteenths; the fifth thirty-three-thirty-fourth of the pure or the thoroughbred blood, if none other had been used in the cross. Yet the resulting progeny would always contain a fraction of the original or pure blood. Yet often seven-eighths, and especially three fifteen-sixteenths bred show the characteristics, to a great degree, that none but experts can distinguish from outward observation between the full blood or thoroughbred type. Hence seven-eighths and fifteen-sixteenths bred animals are by courtesy called full-bloods. A grade is an animal containing some pure or thoroughbred blood. A seven-eighths grade is sometimes called high grade."

### Green Feed for Pigs.

The writer is raising about fifty pigs, which he hopes to market about Christmas or New Years, especially if the remunerative prices still prevail, and they will. These pigs were farrowed in June, and have been kept growing from the start. They are a mixture of Berkshire, Poland-China and Jersey Red. They at the present and rising prices of corn, and with the prospect of not one-fourth of a crop, it seems quite a difficult thing to make pork. We are giving these youngsters and their mothers three barrels of soft feed per day, consisting of a mixture of milk (in moderate amount), a dash of ground oil-cake, bran, corn-meal and water—the proportion of the last article being very large. In addition to this, on a dry soon, inaccessible to the sows, the pigs are treated to a peck or more of shelled corn and, two or three pails of sweet milk per day. It is simply wonderful how quite young pigs will get away with the old corn—and how much good it will seem to do them. But the biggest and best element of food these porkers, old and young, are getting, is all the green oats and peas they can consume, in addition to the above. We sowed about an acre and a quarter with oats and peas, in proportions as nearly equal as possible. As soon as they had grown tall enough to make a swath we began mowing them for these sows and pigs, although it seemed scarcely economical to do so. The high price of corn, however, left no other alternative. We have still left enough of this green food to last a week or more, and after that the old ones will have jewelry put in their noses to prevent them from rooting, and the herd will be turned on an early mowed meadow, where the young clover will be eight or ten inches high. Very soon after the older pigs will be weaned. We have a field of sweet corn for the cows and pigs, from which we shall very soon begin to draw such supplies as they will need. Later, we intend to have as much green rye as our stock can eat.

Upon this regimen our breeding sows have kept "in good heart," not getting thin and weak, while the pigs have been growing without any sort of check or hindrance. There is not a runt or stunted pig in the entire lot. If we get any corn, to finish off with we expect them to weigh upon an average two hundred pounds each by the 1st of January. But if the corn crop fails, as it now seems there is immediate danger of its doing, our hogs will be fit for the cleaver before our green food gives out. And that is the way we raise our pigs this year; not expensively, for the green feed, which costs next to nothing at all, is, now, and has for several weeks been the main reliance—the sheet anchor, so to speak, of our this year's venture in swine. It would simply astonish those people who keep their pigs on corn and water in close pen, to see the satisfied way a quiet young pig will devour a large green pea vine, made still more succulent and refreshing by the morning dew! The way to make cheap and healthy pork is to provide such green food as we have mentioned, and then so feed the animals that their appetites are always kept sharp and exacting.—*Hon. Charles Aldrich, in the Iowa Homestead.*

SHEEP AND CATTLE IN OREGON.—A Cattle buyer reports to the Greenville (Plumas county) *Bulletin* that beef cattle in Oregon are very scarce and consequently high. Sometime a buyer can strike an Oregonian who will let beef cattle go at 4 cents a pound, on foot, but a well posted seller wants 7 cents. The dealer spoken of by the *Bulletin* says he left a buyer in Oregon who wanted to invest $10,000 in beef cattle, but had not found enough animals to make it an object to invest. The beef-steak will soon be only obtainable by a millionaire or by a newspaper man, which is about the same thing. On the other hand the *Eastern Oregonian* states that there are 300,000 head of sheep at present in the mountains, all owned in Umatilla county. These sheep are worth on an average $2 each, making a total of $600,000 for one of Umatilla's branches of business. There were driven out of the country this year nearly 100,000 sheep and there still remain in the country, it is said, 500,000 head of sheep. So if beef becomes scarce they can fall back from the juicy steak do the tender mutton chop.

By a gentleman just returned from an overland trip to San Luis Obispo, we are informed that a mysterious disease is making havoc among cattle in that county. The animals which are attacked by it die suddenly and swell within a few hours after death to an enormous bulk. Dissections of the carcasses reveal nothing as to the causes of the disease.—*Monterey Democrat.*

### A Safe Investment.

We count that the highest style of cattle rearing in which the farmer breeds, rears and fattens the cattle which he markets. In many cases we believe this course will give the best profit, but it is not adapted to the circumstances of all farmers. There are many for whom it is best to purchase the grown animal and fatten it. There are localities in which trial shows that animals can be bought for feeding to better advantage than they can be reared.

Just now many are hesitating whether to buy. It may be questionable whether much profit will result from fattening cattle this fall or winter, if they must be bought at full prices. But it seems to us, all the indications are that the purchase of young stock, of fair quality, at present prices, will prove a good investment to farmers who have a good supply of grass, and of "rough feed" for the winter. Making no attempt to predict prices, it seem certain that there can not be at over supply of good cattle ready for market next year. We may have as high-priced corn next year as we now have, but this is improbable; as next year's crop will probably be larger than that now growing. Compared with the price of good fat cattle, prices for young stock are low.

There is force in the saying that "young stock will grow up to their price, even if that be too high." A half cent or a cent per pound on a grown steer is an important matter; on a calf or yearling it is of much less consequence. Increase of weight is nowhere made so easily and so cheaply as on a good pasture. Yet we have known men, even with unstocked pastures, delay buying until the season was nearly over, paying for two or three hundred of pounds more than would have been necessary had the animal been bought in the spring.

Late in the season, delay is frequently advisable. Many farmers are so unfortunately situated that they are compelled to sell when the season of grazing is over. So that prices are often lower in November than in October. Again, the buyer in early winter often pays for less pounds than if he had bought from the grass, with the cattle full of "sap." Inexperienced breeders are sometimes sorely perplexed at the slight gain of their stock in the early winter. Shrewd buyers understand the reason and are often able to take advantage of it.

We repeat our belief that the purchase of young stock now is a safe investment, where there is a good supply of food for the autumn and winter.—*Eastern Exchange.*

### The Polled-Angus Craze.

The craze for the Polled-Angus cattle continues without signs of diminution. American buyers are purchasing everything that can be secured in Scotland, and the breeders of the Black hornless cattle are gradually putting up prices. The cattle thus far brought to this country are certainly worthy representatives of the polled breed, which has within the last two years come into such prominence. Within the last three or four months over three hundred polled cattle have been brought to American and Canadian ports and quarantined, and as fast as the rules of the quarantine can be complied with and the cattle pass the inspectors' examinations they have been forwarded to the farms of the breeders, who see in this breed of cattle the foundation of a class which will at least equal any of the best known families thus far introduced into America.

Several small herds have gone into Nebraska; Iowa breeders have not invested to any great extent, while Illinois and Indiana breeders seem to have thus far taken the lead in point of numbers exported. It is not probable that breeders can afford to raise the price of stock, as the country to be realized from their ownership coming, as a matter of course, from judicious crossing upon native stock. It will be several years before the cross will begin to show itself, and the result will be watched with great interest, particularly on the great western plains and ranches.—*Chicago Tribune.*

### Premiums Awarded at the Petaluma Fair.

**Class 8—Thoroughbred Cattle.**

J. B. Redmond, best Durham bull 4 years old or over, Little Pat, $20.

Page Bros., best Durham bull 2 years and under 3, Cherry Prince, $10

Sylvester Scott, best Durham bull 1 year and under 2, Royal Oxford, $8.

J. B. Redmond, best Durham bull calf, Orion, $5.

Page Bros., best Durham cow 4 years old or over, Belle Christmas, $15.

Page Bros., best Durham cow 3 years and under 4, Rosetta, $10.

Page Bros., best Durham heifer 2 years and under 3, Belle Sonoma, $8.

J. B. Redmond, best Durham heifer, 1 year and under 2, Queen XIII, $6.

J. B. Redmond, best Durham heifer calf, Nymph XII., $4.

J. R. Rose, best Devon bull, 2 years and under 3, Curly John, $10.

J. R. Rose, best Devon calf, Sonoma Boy, $5.

J. R. Rose, best Devon cow, 4 years old and over, Maud III, $15.

J. R. Rose, best Devon cow, 3 years and under 4, Ruby, $10.

J. R. Rose, best Devon heifer, 2 years old and under 3, Lolo, $8.

J. R. Rose, best Devon heifer, 1 year and under two, Buttercup, $5.

J. R. Rose, best Devon heifer calf, Winona, $4.

Jas. Biggins, best Ayrshire bull 4 years old or over, Duke, $20.

Geo. Bement, best Ayrshire bull 3 years and under 4, Archie, $15.

Geo. Bement, best Ayrshire bull 2 years and under 3, Aldo, $10.

Geo. Bement, best Ayrshire bull 1 year and under 2, Macbeth, $8.

Geo. Bement, best Ayrshire bull calf, Malcolm, $5.

Geo. Bement, best Ayrshire cow 4 years old and over, Ethel Brown, $15.

Geo. Bement, best Ayrshire cow 3 years and under 4, Elaine, $10.

Geo. Bement, best Ayrshire heifer 2 years and under 3, Stellinite, $8.

Geo. Bement, best Ayrshire heifer, 1 year and under 2, Sultana, $5.

Geo. Bement, best Ayrshire heifer calf, Sybil, $4.

P. J. Shafter, best Alderney bull 4 years old or over, Bismarck, $20.

Mrs. T. M. Chapman, best Alderney bull 3 years and under 4, Billy, $15.

D. S. Dickson, best Alderney bull 2 years and under 3, Gen. Grant $10.

Francis De Long, best Alderney cow 4 years and over, Fashion $15.

A. P. Whitney, best Alderney heifer 2 years and under 3, Olivia IV., $8.

**Sweepstakes.**

Page Bros., best thoroughbred Durham herd of not less than six animals, with one bull 2 years old or over, and not more than one 2-year-old and 1 yearling, owned by one person, Cherry Prince and five cows, $15.

J. R. Rose, best thoroughbred Devon herd of not less than six animals, with one bull 2 years old or over, and not more than one 2-year-old and one yearling, owned by one person, Curly John and five cows, $15.

Geo. Bement, best thoroughbred Ayrshire herd of not less than six animals, with one bull 2 years old and over, and not more than one 2-year-old and one yearling, owned by one person, Archie and five cows, $15.

**Class 9—Graded Stock.**

I. R. Jewell, best bull 4 years old or over, Duke, $10.

F. Starke, best bull 3 years and under 4, Valentine, $7

Fred Woodworth, best bull 1 year and under 2, El Medico, Jr., $4.

A. J. Pierce, best bull calf, Poney, $3.

Wm. Hill, best cow 4 years old or over, Beauty, $8.

Ralph Woodworth, best heifer 1 year and under 2, Pansy, 4.

A. J. Pierce, best heifer calf, Blossom, $3.

**Class 10—Thoroughbred Sheep.**

E. W. Woolsey, best Spanish ram, $8.

E. W. Woolsey, best five Spanish ewes, $8.

E. W. Woolsey, best five Spanish ram lambs, $2 50.

E. W. Woolsey, best five Spanish ewe lambs, $2 50.

R. H. Crane, Santa Rose, best Shropshire ram, $8.

B. H. Crane, best five Shropshire ewes, $8.

S. W. Kenyon, best Southdown ram, $8.

R. H. Crane, best five Southdown ewes, $8.

Robert Crane, best five Southdown ram lambs, $2 50.

R. H. Crane, best five Southdown ewe lambs, $2 50.

L. W. Walker, best Cotswold ram, $8.

**Class 11—Swine.**

P. J. Shafter, best Berkshire boar, $8.

F. Starke, best Berkshire sow, $6.

R. H. Crane, best China Poland boar, $8.

R. H. Crane, best China Poland sow, $6.

Fred Starke, best five pigs of any breed, $5.

**Class 1—Thoroughbred Horses.**

J. B. Chase, best stallion 4 years old or over, Wheatley, diploma and $20.

Wm. Bihler, best mare 4 years old or over, Jeanette, $15.

C. Underhill, best mare 3 years old or under 4, Nora, $12.

F. Carroll, best mare 2 years or under 3, Alice, $8.

C. Underhill, best mare 1 year and under 2, name, $6.

M. C. Fisher, best sucking horse colt, Duke, $7.

C. Underhill, best sucking mare colt, no name, $5.

C. Underhill, best stallion and six colts, Wheatley and family, $20.

**Class 2—Graded Horses.**

S. S. Drake, best stallion 4 years old or over, Admiral, diploma and $15.

Fred Kuhnle, best stallion, 2 years and under 3, Billy Wilson, 9.

Jos. Biggins, best stallion, 1 year and under 2, Comet, $6.

Jos. Biggins, best mare 4 years old and over, Katie Wat, $15.

S. S. Drake, best mare 3 years old and under four, Alada, $9.

Jos. Biggins, best mare 2 years old and under 3, Fanny Kuhnle, $7.

Fred. Kuhnle, best mare 1 year old and under 2, Lottie Wilson, $6.

S. S. Drake, best sucking horse colt, no name, $5.

Jos. Biggins, best sucking mare colt, Mollie K., $5.

S. S. Drake, best stallion and six colts, Admiral and family, $20.

**Class 3—Horses of All Work.**

Petaluma Horse Breeders' Association, best stallion 4 years old and over, Crown Prince, diploma and $15.

Pat Bennett, best stallion 3 years and under 4, Petaluma Prince, $12.

P. J. Shafter, best stallion 2 years and under 3, Black Prince, $8.

Russell, best stallion, 1 year and under 2, Lafayette, $6 John.

Willis Faught, best mare 4 years old and over, Dolly, $12.

J. R. Rose best mare 3 years and under 4, Topsy, $9.

Willis Faught, best mare 2 years and under 3, Peggy, $7.

V. Berri, best mare 1 year and under 2, Mary, $6.

J. R. Rose, best sucking horse colt, McPherson, $5.

V. Berri, best sucking mare colt, no name, $5.

Petaluma Horse Breeders' Association, best stallion and six colts, Crown Prince and family, $20.

**Class 4—Draft Horses.**

Wm. Skillman, best stallion 4 years or over (Duke De Chartres barred) Tornado, diploma and $15.

A. J. Pierce, best stallion three years old and under 4, Charlemagne, $12.

P. McAuliffe, best stallion 2 years and under 3, Pollock II, $8.

P. McAuliffe, best stallion 1 year and under 2, Young Duke, $6.

Wm. Bihler, best mare 4 years and over, Doll, $12.

Wm. Hill, best mare 2 years and under 3, Annie, $7.

Theo. Skillman, best mare 1 year and under 2, Gertrude, $6.

S. Gilmore, best sucking horse colt, Pride of the West, $5.

J. Danber best sucking mare colt, no name, $5.

Petaluma Horse Breeders' Association, best stallion and six colts, Duke De Chartres and family, $20.

**Class 5—Roadsters.**

Wm. Bihler, best stallion 4 years old or over, Grey Mc. Clellan, diploma and $15.

Wm. Bih , best stallion 3 years and under 4, Buck Foster, $12. ler

P. J. Shafter, best stallion 2 years and under 3, Grayson, $8.

P. J. Shafter, best mare 4 years old and over, Julia, $12.

P. J. Shafter, best mare 3 years and under 4, Deby Mott, $9.

Wm. Bihler, best mare 2 years and under 3, Sally, $7.

G. W. Savage, best colt 1 year and under 2, sired by a roadster stallion, Eureka, $6.

F. W. Loeber, best stallion and six colts, Whippleton and family, $20.

**Class 6—Standard Trotters.**

P. J. Shafter, best stallion 4 years old or over, Rustic, $15.

**Class 7—Carriage and Saddle Horses and Jacks.**

A. R. Frazer, best matched carriage team, sixteen hands or over, owned and used as such by one person, Dick and Aleck, $15.

F. W. Loeber, best single buggy horse, no name, $7.

J. Conway, best saddle horse, three distinct gaits, Bony Boy, $5.

Sylvester Scott, best jack, Monarch, $10.
Sylvester Scott, best jennet, Fanny $8.

**Class 12—Pure Bred Poultry.**

Morris Brothers, best exhibit not less than five varieties, 10; best pair light Brahma fowls, $2 50; best pair dark rahma fowls, $2 50; best pair Partridge Cochin fowls, 2 50; best pair black Cochin fowls, $2 50; best pair white cochin fowls, $2 50; best Plymouth Rock fowls, $2 50; best air white Leghorn fowls, $2 50; best pair white-faced lack Spanish, $2 50; best pair black and white crested olish, $2 50; best pair silver spangled Hamburg fowls, 2 50; best pair black Hamburg fowls, $2 50; best pair lack-breasted Game Bantam fowls, $2 50; best pair sea-right Bantam fowls, $2 50; best pair Bronze turkeys, $5; best pair wild turkeys, $5; best pair white Holland turkeys, $5; best pair Toulouse geese, $3; best pair Bremen geese, $3; best pair Poland geese, $3; best pair Guinea fowls, $2 50; best pair Peacocks, $3.

Mrs. Wm. Hill, best pair Buff Cochin fowls, $2 50; best pair black African Bantam fowls, $2 50.

L. C. Byce, best pair brown Leghorn fowls, $2 50.

W. D. Freeman, best pair gold spangled Polish fowls, $2 50; best pair golden spangled Hamburgs, $2 50; best pair Houdan fowls, $2 50.

T. B. Carey, best pair black-breasted Game fowls, $2 50; best pair brown-red Game fowls, $2 50; best pair blue Game fowls, $2 50.

G. W. Ward, best pair China geese, $3.

E. K. Evans, best pair Pekin ducks, $2 50.

J. K. Fix, best pair Muscovy ducks, $2 50.

**Class 3—Carriages, Buggies and Wagons.**

Wm. Zartman & Co, best exhibit carriages, buggies and wagons, $20.

B. Spotward & Co., second best exhibit, $12.

Wm. Zartman & Co., best family carriage, $10.

Wm. Zartman & Co., best buggy, $8.

D. W. C. Putnam, best breaking cart. $4.

E. Hopes, best spring wagon, $8.

H. Pimm, best carriage painting, $8.

Gwinn & Brainerd, best carriage trimming, $8.

**Class 3—Saddlery and Harness.**

Gwinn & Brainerd, best exhibit saddlery, diploma and $15.

Gwinn & Brainerd, best set double harness, $7.

Gwinn & Brainerd, best set single harness, $5.

Gwinn & Brainerd, best saddle, $4.

**Class 4—Agricultural Implements.**

E. J. Holly, best cultivator, $5.

Wm. H. Worth, best cheese press, (honorable mention for cheese press screw), $5.

## CRICKET.

### The Australians in England.

In the way of cricket the visit of the Australians to England has given an immense impetus to this healthy and inspiriting game. The colonists have played havoc with the county teams and other organized clubs of the second class. The great match of the players of England and the Australians the former won in one inning, with thirty-four runs to spare. Afterwards they took their revenge in vanquishing the gentlemen players also in one inning, with a run to spare, and strange to say, there was the same record in 1878, when the gentlemen beat the Australian team. They will return home through the United States, and will play two or three matches in New York and Philadelphia before leaving for San Francisco. At a rough estimate they have as yet captured some twenty-eight games, losing only three or four, and the Cambridge University team, of which we take the following account from the *Referee*, was one of the best contested of the entire series:

Remembering that the members of Cambridge university have on two occasions defeated formidable elevens emanating from Australia, it is no wonder that such a contest as the above caused considerable interest in the cricket world. The team selected on this occasion to represent the Light Blues was a very strong one, though it was not quite the same as advertised. Mr. J. E. K. Studd being unable to play on account of indisposition, Mr. C. H. Allcock, who has never gained the "blue," but has made a lot of runs in minor matches, figured in his place. On the side of the Australians Messrs. Palmer and Giffen were missing, and Murdoch kept wicket in place of Blackham. The United Service Recreation ground was very carefully prepared for the event, the wicket having been rolled and watered daily for some weeks past. Heavy rain fell here on Wednesday, however, and this made it rather slow and holding, but it played fairly well throughout the day. The Australian captain won the toss, but after a careful examination of the wicket he elected to put in his opponents. Whether this was good judgment is doubtful, as the Light Blues succeeded in obtaining 196 before they were dismissed. The wicket played none too well, especially towards the close of Thursday's play. The batting of Mr. Lucas was the feature of the combined team's innings; it was a piece of undoubtedly bad luck his being run out. Mr. Thornton hit freely, and with greater judgment than usual, and both Messrs. A. Lyttelton and C. T. Studd met the bowling in good style. On the conclusion of the first day's play the Light Blues had finished their innings for 196 runs, and the Australians had scored 27 for one wicket, Jones, who had played a ball into his wicket, after scoring four runs. When time was called, Blackham was not out sixteen, and Garrett six. On Friday the wicket had not quite recovered itself, and was still slow; there was, nevertheless, a capital day's cricket. The Australians did not do nearly as much as might have been expected, and the total of the innings only amounted to 141, or 55 behind their opponents' score. Blackham and Bannerman played capitally, but received little assistance. C. A. Smith, the young Brazen amateur, was put on late in the innings, and bowled remarkably well, taking four wickets for sixteen runs. Murdoch was bowled without making a run. In the second innings of Cambridge the Australians bowled admirably, and the score was increased with considerable difficulty. The Hon. Alfred Lyttelton, however, played splendid cricket, showing excellent defense, hitting out well whenever an opportunity presented it. He was still not out at the call of time, and had made 59. The contest was resumed to-day in dull weather and in the presence of a moderate company. Then the score stood—Cambridge, first innings, 196; second innings, 131 for six wickets. Australians, first innings, 141. At five minutes past twelve the brothers Lyttelton continued the Cambridge batting to the bowling of Boyle and Spofforth. Mr. Alfred Lyttelton was caught 'at mid-on by Boyle off Spofforth for 3. Mr. Allcock, played on from Spofforth for 7. Mr. Smith was bowled by Spofforth for 0, and the Cambridge second innings closed at 152 at 12.35. With 207 to get to win, the Australians sent

in Bannerman and Massie to open their second innings. Massie was bowled after making 6. Bonnor hit tremendously, and put an altogether different appearance on the game. He ought twice to have been caught at slip, but his play was wonderfully vigorous. Of course the Cantabs tried several bowling changes, but Bonnor held them in check for a long time, and it was not until he had compiled 66 that he was caught and bowled. His innings was made up of four 6's, six 4's, three 3's, a 2, and seven singles. Jones gave Jup trouble, but Murdoch and Bannerman played steadily and well, and took the score up to 153 before the latter was caught behind the wicket for a patiently-played 30. With six good wickets to fall, and sixty-five runs to get to win, it seemed certain that the Australians would gain a victory, but the game took an extraordinary turn in favor of the Cantabs, who bowled and fielded splendidly. Murdoch was caught at slip for an admirable 43, and then in quick succession Horan, Blackham, M'Donnell, Garrett and Boyle were dismissed, the innings closing for 187. Thus the Cantabs proved victorious by twenty runs, amidst a scene of the wildest excitement. Score:

CAMBRIDGE UNIVERSITY.

| | | | |
|---|---|---|---|
| Massie, A Littelton b Jones | 25 | c M'Donnel l b Boyle | 81 |
| C. I. Thornton b Spofforth | 40 | c M'Donnell b Boyle | 1 |
| A. P. Lucas run out | 42 | b Spofforth | 9 |
| C.T. Studd c Murdoch b Bannerman | 28 | c Bannerman b Boyle | 12 |
| G. B. Studd c Blackham b Boyle | 1 | c Boyle b Spofforth | 13 |
| G. B. Steele b Boyle | 18 | c Bannerman b Boyle | 10 |
| Hon. E. Lyttelton c Boyle b Spofforth | 16 | c Boyle b Spofforth | 8 |
| H. Whitfeld not out | 3 | c Spofforth b Boyle | 8 |
| C. H. Allcock c Spofforth b Boyle | 0 | b Spofforth | 7 |
| C. A. Smith b Spofforth | 2 | b Spofforth | 0 |
| P. H. Morton c Murdoch b Spofforth | 4 | not out | 5 |
| Extras | 13 | Extras | 15 |
| **Total** | **196** | **Total** | **152** |

AUSTRALIANS.

| | | | |
|---|---|---|---|
| Jones b Morton | 4 | b Morton | 0 |
| Blackham c G. B. Studd b C. T. Studd | 35 | c A. Lyttelton b Allcock | 2 |
| Gaffett c A. Lyttelton b C. T. Studd | 14 | c E. Lyttelton b Steel | 5 |
| Bannerman l b W. b Smith | 26 | c A. Lyttelton b Allcock | 30 |
| Murdoch b Morton | 0 | c Steele b Allcock | 43 |
| Homan c Steele b Smith | 18 | c and b Steel | 0 |
| Massie c and b Allcock | 1 | b Allcock | 6 |
| M'Donnell b Allcock | 11 | c Thornton b Steel | 5 |
| Bonnor not out | 15 | c and b Steel | 66 |
| Boyle b Smith | 14 | b Steel | 11 |
| Spofforth b Smith | 0 | not out | 1 |
| Extras | 8 | Extras | 9 |
| **Total** | **141** | **Total** | **187** |

The BREEDER AND SPORTSMAN is the title of an elegant sixteen-page weekly journal, published in San Francisco, the initial number of which has just made its appearance. The engraved heading of the BREEDER AND SPORTSMAN is the prettiest piece of work in that line that we have ever seen. The artist has won a genuine triumph, for he has not only incorporated in his beautiful design water and foliage, fruit and blossoms, fine horses, cattle and dogs, but all the emblems and symbols of sporting life. Joseph Cairn Simpson, the veteran turfman and accomplished gentleman, is the proprietor of this new venture in the field of journalism. Here supported by an able corps of writers, all of them well trained in the several departments over which they have been called to preside. The BREEDER AND SPORTSMAN deserves and will achieve success. Its field is large and remunerative. Each of the San Francisco and Sacramento dailies dishes up a weekly pot pourri of sporting news. There are the *California Spirit of the Times*, the *Pacific Life* and the *Olympian*—all specially devoted to the subject and making fortunes rapidly for their owners. The thirst of the California public for sporting intelligence, however, remains unappeased, and Mr. Simpson's splendid journal comes in to relieve the stress. An attractive feature of the new paper is the appearance each week of a drawing of some one or other of the "Notable Horses of California"—Mr. Winters' Duchess of Norfolk leading off in the first number. The Breeders of the Pacific Coast, from the Columbia to the Colorado, and from the Sierras to the sea, should now stand in with Joe Simpson and make this journal a financial success. He has done more than any other man in America to elevate the turf and advance the breeding interests of the Pacific Coast.—*Territorial Enterprise.*

TRICKETT'S TALK.—On his return to Australia Edward Trickett was received with open arms, and the commotion of reception got $2,000 in his vest pocket "just for luck." Trickett said it was impossible for him to express his thanks for the hearty reception he had received in coming home as a defeated man. He was so sanguine of success that, when beaten, it was a deathblow to him. He was assured they all felt it very much, but not worse than he did. He believed he could beat Hanlan, and tried him a second time, but had failed. In Canada he was treated thoroughly well, and had met with a hearty welcome in England. He did not succeed in meeting Hanlan in Canada, and had to return to England to suffer a second defeat. [Cheers.] It was a pleasure to find his old friends standing by him with all friendship, as though he were going away, and that they thought none the less of him on account of his defeat. Although he thought he could beat Hanlan in the first contest, he was worse beaten on the second. Trickett said that Hanlan was the greatest rower in the world, and superior to anything he had ever witnessed. When he defeated him (Trickett) he could not altogether understand how it was done, and undoubtedly he was the greatest man in the world. "I laughed," said the speaker, "at the idea of this little man beating me, but, by Jove, he did."

HOOTING THE JOCKEY.—The English have a rough and tumble style of showing their displeasure at a steal that is surprising to an American who is accustomed, under such circumstances, simply to talk about the matter in a manner more or less profane. Thus we find that recently at Egham racecourse (the Runnymede of Magna Charta fame) the three-year-old stakes caused a great sensation in consequence of the general body of the public being unaware of the fact that Mr. Evans, as part owner of Marden and sole owner of Refiner had declared to win with the former, who carried his colors, and had copious odds laid on him. The declaration came too late for everybody to know of it, and the uninformed not only hooted the jockeys of both Marden and Refiner as they returned to the place of weighing, but took serious liberties with Cranham, the jockey of Refiner.

THE BREEDER AND SPORTSMAN is the name of a new weekly paper, conducted by Jos. Cairn Simpson, and published at San Francisco, Cal., at five dollars per annum. The first copy is at hand. For beauty of typography, extent and variety of matter, and general make up, it is unexcelled by its contemporaries. Mr. Simpson is author of a popular book, called "Horse Portraiture," and for more than a quarter of a century has been a popular writer on horse and sporting matters. He is admirably qualified to conduct such an enterprise, and the breeders of the Pacific Coast are to be congratulated upon having so able and gifted a champion of their interests.—*St. Louis Rural World.*

## POULTRY.

### The Care of Poultry.

Many mistakes are made in the management of fowls. On most farms no person has especial charge of the fowls. Some one looks carefully after the wants of the horses, sheep, cows and pigs, but the fowls are often left to take care of themselves. Young chickens, ducks and geese demand constant care, or many of them will die from exposure and other causes. It is as necessary for success to have some one in charge of the poultry yard, as of the barn, stable and pig pen. A person too young or too old for hard work in the field or house can generally be found who can take care of fowls at small expense. Another mistake is in keeping birds until they are too old to be profitable. Chickens will generally bring a higher price when they are large enough for the gridiron than after they are more mature. By selling them when they are quite young many losses are prevented and much food saved. Male birds should in every instance be sold as soon as they get their growth. They should never be kept till after they are mature except for breeding purposes. Young hens, ducks and geese lay more eggs than old ones, and are consequently more desirable to keep for other purposes than for sitting on eggs and taking care of young. Another mistake is made in trying to keep fowls in the same building with farm animals. They should for a variety of reasons be kept in quarters by themselves. By adopting the practice of early marketing a great saving can be made in the matter of affording protection. Still another mistake is made in not furnishing a variety of food for fowls. They generally eat too much corn and not enough fish, meat, vegetables and small grain. There is generally more profit in feeding milk to fowls than to any kind of animals.

## YACHTING.

### Types of Models.

The old and long-continued discussion on the question of deep and shallow models for speed in yachts will probably never be concluded. The advocates of each type can see nothing in the other. The man with the deep yacht calls the other type a skimming dish and a wash bowl; the man with the center-board yacht calls the other one a "lead mine," "a plank on edge," etc. Whenever the deep cutter wins a race there is great rejoicing among the keel men; but this is quickly turned into mourning by the defeat which is sure to follow. Last season in eastern waters the Madge seemed to show that keels were in the ascendancy. This year the Maggie came over to tackle bigger boats, and, being confessed the best 15 tonner in England, it was thought she would clean out our centerboards without trouble. But this was found to be a mistake. She won once two races and then was beaten two days in succession. The race with the Viper was even in this particular but she was badly beaten; the cutter Oriva was also beaten by the centerboards. During the recent cruises of the New York and other clubs great interest was shown in this question of type. The time has come to see what a correspondent of the *Spirit of the Times* has to say in this direction, as he has been with the yachts and has had an opportunity to compare the vessels as they sailed:

In the race of Monday, the squadron race, the Maggie was beaten, not only by the New York sloop Vixen, which led her over twenty-four minutes, but by the Boston sloop Hera, which beat her over five minutes. What then! Shall I say that the larger cutter which Mr. Warren expects to bring over here next season will not beat the Fannie or the Gracie? By no means; but this I will say, that with strong breeze and smooth water I don't believe that there is a cutter afloat that can beat the Fanny or the Gracie. Should the race, however, take place in the fall with a reefing breeze and a jump of a sea, I think that the cutter would win.

This cruise of the New York Club has been an important one, as determining definitely the advantages of different types of models, and the conclusion is, as it has ever been, that for our ordinary cruising weather in our yachting months of June, July and August, the broad, shallow centerboard is the best. That she is the more comfortable has never been denied; that she is, on account of her light draughts, handier is evident, and the only reason that could by any possibility be offered why we should change our broad, comfortable and convenient centerboard boats for the narrow, uncomfortable and inconvenient deep and expensive keel boats, was that the latter were the faster. This cruise has demonstrated that they are not. That skimming-dish of the skimming-dishes, Fanny, defeats the Oriva; the Vixen beats the Maggie, and in the passage from New Bedford to Vineyard Haven, that skimming-dish the Madeleine, with only working canvas, and that gray with extreme old age, comes up with and passes through the lee of the new and deep schooner Montauk, equipped with racing canvas brand new; and the Halcyon, another skimming dish, wins the Marblehead regatta.

While sailing against second-class boats both the Montauk and the Maggie won races with ease, but the Montauk had never been matched against the Palmer, Madeleine or Columbia, nor three fastest schooners, and the Maggie had not been matched against the Vixen, Regina, Fanita, or Vālkyr, our four fastest sloops. Never since the first cutter was built in this country has this type of boat done as well in comparison with the centerboards as has the Oriva during this cruise, and I have been quick to note and comment on her success; but she was beaten by the Vixen in the New London race, when both were classed together, and was also beaten by the Vixen in the race of last Monday, when they were classed separately, the elapsed time of the Vixen being less than that of the Oriva. Here, then, is the result as clearly demonstrated as anything can be. In everything but weather, when our boats will hardly get steerage way, the cutter will go a little, and will beat them in a reefing breeze, and in a sea the cutter will beat a centerboard. In our ordinary cruising weather and water—and such as we have had during the late cruise is a fair sample—the beamy centerboard will beat the cutter. As I stated in my last, the result of the cruise will be the introduction of an improved model, which will be, as I stated some years ago, a deep centerboard boat of ample beam.

The idea that you can't combine beam and depth and secure speed has been exploded by the success of the Montauk, which stands to-day the queen of the fleet, and will retain the title unless challenged and beaten by the Madeleine or Columbia, and the idiots who have favored the introduction of the shortness of the British fleet, on the assumption that their narrowness gave them speed, quite overlooked the fact that in all cases the builders of these boats gave them all the beam possible and would gladly have given them more if the class had permitted.

I see by the papers that the cutter Bedouin, built by Piepgras for Mr. Rodgers, has been launched. I trust that an extreme racing rig has been put upon her, and that she may develop a speed superior to the Gracie or the Fancy. I fear, however, that the British idea of rig—correct enough there—will be found too limited for our weather and waters, and that for the first season, the Bedouin will be a failure.

## The Pacific Yacht Club Regatta.

The second annual regatta of the Pacific Yacht Club on Saturday last was in some respects the best ever held on this bay. The day was delightful and there was a good breeze all over the course, lighter however to leeward, as usual, than it was in the channel. There were five large schooners matched against each other, and there was one sloop and a yawl. The fleet looked very handsome indeed, as light sails were carried wherever possible. The only thing to mar the interest of the day was the confusion which resulted from most of the yachts being behind time at the start and the unfortunate misunderstanding which this occasioned in the end.

The gun fired promptly at 1 P. M. when the judges, Messrs. Eckley, Kelly and O'Connor, stood on Mission Rock wharf to see the yachts pass the line.

The first to make her appearance was the splendid big yacht Aggie, belonging to Vice-Commodore Macdonough, the largest one of the fleet. She went by under a cloud of canvas, carrying in addition to her working canvas both fore and main gaff-topsail, staysail, balloon jib and a watersail on her main-boom. The sloop Annie followed, with working sails, balloon jib and topsail. Then came the schooner Whitewing, with balloon jib, staysail and topsail. Commodore Floyd's schooner Ariel then came along, with balloon jib, watersail on main-boom, and a very large staysail. Following her came the Fleur de Lis, with a balloon jib, staysail and topsail. The Ella, with her new yawl-rig, went by next and the favorite Nellie brought up the rear. The Nellie had in addition to plain and a balloon jib and a very large staysail, which set very well and did its work finely.

The only yacht which went over the line at the proper time was the Aggie, as the rules of the race required that all which were not past the line within fifteen minutes after gunfire should have their time taken as if they had gone by fifteen minutes after. All the time therefore, after the fifteen minutes, was a dead loss to them.

The Aggie crossed at 1:09:13, so she was within limits. At the end of the fifteen minutes there was not a yacht in sight from the judges' position, all coming up behind Mission rock with a head tide and not too strong a breeze.

The judges were afraid the race would be spoiled, so it was informally agreed to take the time as they passed and ignore the fifteen minute rule. At all events the referee called out the time as they went by, the official timer called the time and the official time-keeper took it down, as the yachts actually passed. Everyone supposed therefore—until some time afterwards—that the fifteen minute limit rule was suspended or ignored. The Annie passed at 1:18:34; Whitewing, 1:19:37; Ariel, 1:20:55; Fleur de Lis, 1:21:08; Nellie, 1:24:30, and Ella, 1:23:13. The wind lightened along under the lee of the rolling mills and sugar refinery, and some were nearly becalmed. The Aggie, the largest, was far ahead, the rest being in a bunch. The breeze was steady and not strong, and all light sails were carried. From the start to Hunter's Point, the Ariel beat the Aggie 1:22, the Nellie 3:39, the Fleur de Lis 2:46 and the Whitewing 3:16. From Hunter's Point to Oakland was a pretty sight but there were no special features to notice except that the Ariel continued to gain, and from the start to Oakland beat the Aggie 3:16, the Nellie 2:46, Fleur de Lis 2:59, and Whitewing 4:12.

When the yachts got their sheets aft rounding the leeward stake boats they all stood along a short distance to get everything fairly set and then most of them made a short hitch on the starboard tack, the Annie, however, standing on direct for Goat Island. The Fleur de Lis, failing to pass the Whitewing, and being close on her weather quarter, also tacked and started after the Annie.

None of the yachts passed along the city front. They kept out in the ship channel and even to leeward in that. The Aggie, way ahead, led out unto the channel, standing out as far as Blossom Rock before tacking down towards the Fort.

The Ariel, Whitewing, Fleur de Lis and Annie all kept to leeward, weathering Goat Island by about a mile, and then standing out into the channel, heading on the port tack for Sheep Island. The wind gradually let them up, however, so they could point to windward of Angel Island while on the same tack.

The Ariel and Nellie stood on, the wind, letting them gradually head up until they pointed for Sancelito, all this time without making a tack. They stood on up until abreast of the bight of Richardson's bay before tacking to fetch the stake boat, which they did on the next leg. The Fleur de Lis, Whitewing and Annie kept down in the main channel to the southward of Alcatraz, following the Aggie. This yacht rounded the Fort Point boat first and the others followed in the order named in the accompanying table, all getting light sails as before were prompt and sails eased off. The time made in beating to windward was as follows:

| | hr. | min. | sec. | | hr. | min. | sec. |
|---|---|---|---|---|---|---|---|
| Aggie..... | 1 | 8 | 30 | Fleur de Lis.... | 1 | 18 | 50 |
| Nellie..... | 1 | 16 | 10 | Annie..... | 1 | 28 | 32 |
| Ariel..... | 1 | 17 | 20 | Whitewing... | 1 | 24 | 43 |

The Aggie here beat the Nellie on this stretch 7 minutes, 31 seconds.

The wind gradually lightened as they ran to leeward and it was much lighter off Goat Island. The Aggie ran into the light wind first and the others crept up to her. But she also ran into the stronger breeze beyond the stake boat first and again crept away from those yet in the light breeze. The strong wind she carried home as they all did when they struck it. The run to leeward was made in the following time:

| Boat | M.S | Boat | M.S. |
|---|---|---|---|
| Nellie..... | 54:07 | Fleur de Lis..... | 56:05 |
| Whitewing..... | 63:03 | Annie..... | 56:32 |
| Ariel..... | 60:40 | Aggie..... | 56:56 |

When abreast of Goat Island the Aggie met, as we have said, light winds, which accounts for her position on the list.

The Aggie passed over the line first, followed by the Ariel. Then the Nellie came along, the Annie, Fleur de Lis and Whitewing following in order named.

Some one in the crowd with the judges called out when the Nellie passed by that she had beaten the Aggie over two minutes, whereupon one of the judges announced that the Nellie had done no such thing as her time was to be taken at 1:15 instead of 1:04:30. As she had really started 9 minutes and 30 seconds behind this, it was just so much added to the time and gave the prize to the Aggie. This rule was

eventually enforced. Instead therefore of the Nellie winning first prize, Aggie second, and Annie third, the judges' ruling gave first prize to Aggie, second to Nellie, and third to Annie.

In our table, the "actual time" gives the figures of actual time as well as the real time of starting given in the first column. The "corrected time" shows the real result, the allowances being taken off. The judges' time shows the yachts as if they had all except the Aggie started at 1:15.

The following table shows the record of the race.

By reading the column "corrected time" the result of the race from actual sailing with usual allowances will be seen. By adding the judges' time it will show how prizes were awarded on the decision before alluded to.

As to this decision, it has given rise to great discussion. The original rule should have been adhered to, but it was not. Once broken, however, the judges had no right to turn to it again after the end of the race, thereby so deciding the result of the race that the first place in it would be changed. No fault whatever could have been found had the rule been adhered to, although in the paragraph of the printed rules, saying yachts must cross within 15 minutes of gun fire, there was no hour named for said gun fire.

Actually, the Nellie beat the Aggie 2m. 50s.; by the judges' time the Nellie was beaten 6m. 40s. by the Aggie, that is, the Nellie was timed as starting at 1:15 instead of 1:24.30 when she did start. It is interesting to note that the Aggie beat the Nellie to windward from the Oakland stake boat 7m. 31s., and the Nellie beat the Aggie to leeward between the same stake boats 4m. 49s. Over the course the Nellie beat the Fleur de Lis 11m. 59s.; beat the Aggie 2m. 50s., and beat the Ariel 8m. 18s. It is worthy of note also that not only did the Aggie and Nellie beat the Fleur de Lis, but the Ariel and Annie did so also. The Fleur de Lis best outsails that 7m. 31s., and the Nellie beat the Aggie to leeward between the same stake boats 4m. 49s. Over the course the Nellie beat the Fleur de Lis 11m. 59s.

The little Ella came out as a yawl with new sails; her driver set like a bag and was worse than useless. In fact in beating to windward it had to be furled. Nevertheless her owner, under these great disadvantages, with a new rig, poor sails, and being the smallest yacht, pluckily went around the course, staying way behind. But the judges did not even pay her the compliment of waiting to take her time at the finish, though she was rounding Hunter's at the Whitewing crossed the line, moreover, she got guyed and made fun of in the newspapers. Of course this will encourage him, and others who see the example, to put in small yachts to make up a show in the next regatta. This is one of the reasons why yacht racing has fallen off here as elsewhere, as we have taken occasion to explain in a previous article.

The Aggie was sailed by Dave Wheeler, Ariel by Captain Turner and Captain Murphy; Nellie by Hyde Bowie and Sam McDowell; Annie by Stewart Menzies; Fleur de Lis by Capt. Galloway and Mr. White; Whitewing by Pete Deming and Ella by Fulton Berry.

We understand that Mr. Bowie declines to receive the second prize, thinking himself entitled to the first. Whatever the disposition of the prizes, there is no question that with her legitimate allowance the Nellie beat all the other yachts. She was sailed by two amateurs and had not been cleaned or specially prepared for the race. The two largest competitors were prepared for the race and were sailed by professional sailors. The Turner model therefore showed itself superior in this race to those of Poillon and Fish of New York, Hall of Fort Ludlow and Stone and Nichols of San Francisco.

The Annie sailed very well. She too was handled by an amateur and had not been put in the way to be cleaned. Until the boat blown channel she did not show up well, but gradually came forward in going down along North Beach. It was her day exactly and with a good sloop man at the tiller, a clean and smooth bottom, good spinnaker and topsail she could have made it lively for others. Still it is hardly fair sailing her against much larger boats with such usual allowance.

The three-quarters of a minute time allowance on the water line is a relic of past ages anyhow and ought to be abolished.

## FISH.

### A Fishing Party.

Last Sunday morning at 1 o'clock the tug Hercules and the yacht Azalene with a party of forty persons cast off from Mission street wharf, bound for the fishing grounds near the Farallone Islands. The day opened to very pleasant and the party would have had a good time had it not been for a heavy ground swell which made all hands—or rather all stomachs —feel very uncomfortable. Seasickness, like death, leveled all, lawyers, bankers, coal merchants and the prosecuting

attorney, to the lowly bed of misery. A joke is told of Mr. Walter B. Lyon's fishing: Though the sickest of the sick, he was too plucky to return without casting a line; he cast and pulled a large rock cod to the surface of the water, but was too sick to draw it in and there they gazed at each other—both with their mouths open—until Mr. Lyon received help from others of the party. There were about seventy fine rock cod caught on the two boats. The fishers returned to the city at 6 o'clock. Messrs. Searles and Scott were the gentlemen who attended to the getting up of the expedition. Mr. Searles was the only one who did not get sick.

Senator W. W. Traylor has been appointed Fish Commissioner by the Governor, to fill the vacancy caused by the death of B. B. Redding. Mr. Traylor is an enthusiastic angler and it is to be hoped that his health will permit him to give that attention to the duties of his new position which is so much needed and to which his tastes so strongly incline.

## ATHLETICS.

Once again the Olympic Club has survived the agonies of the annual election of officers. For several weeks previous to and especially on the actual day of balloting; partisan feeling raged with unusual virulence, and no doubt the younger and more inexperienced members were agreeably surprised last Monday evening to observe the friendliness and good nature of the members present at the installation of the new board of officers. The enthusiasm with which each little extemporaneous speech was received should be an extinguisher of all the "late unpleasantness," and an assurance that every individual member has the welfare of the club at heart, and intends to support the new officers in their avowed intentions, individually and collectively, of raising the reputation of the club one peg higher. The old members are justly proud of its past reputation and stand ready to show about all future success. The new ones must get their share of credits. With Horace Fletcher at the helm, backed by a board of officers composed equally of old and experienced members and new and enthusiastic ones, the coming year promises to be a red letter in the history of the club. The finest rooms in the world, consisting of a fine gymnasium and running gallery, well supplied with the best paraphernalia known, superintended by unsurpassed instructors in gymnastics, sparring and fencing, a cosy and well-stocked reading-room, elegant parlor for ladies, the best private billiard and chess rooms on the Coast (and William to handicap uncertain games), every employe of the club anxious to make the club-rooms an agreeable place of resort to each individual member; outdoor grounds in Oakland with splendid accommodations for athletics and base ball, and a nine that has yet to acknowledge a single defeat, more attractions promised by the new Board of Directors—well, what more is wanted? The prospects for the coming year are unusually encouraging. As a gymnastic club the Olympic has always been the representative of California, San Francisco, and of the entire Pacific Coast. It now has a membership of fully seven hundred, and should take the lead in athletics, rowing and all other outdoor sports. The seasons on this Coast are so well defined, and the membership of the club so large, that there need be no difficulty in encouraging every department of indoor, and outside, gentlemanly sports, if the members will really take hold in earnest, with the honest intention of helping each other for the benefit of the club. The new board and the support of every individual member of the club, have already earnestly undertaken the duties of their positions. Help them out for the next year, and the club will receive the benefit.

Each individual member of the new board of officers in the Olympic Club is much exercised as to the modus operandi necessary to secure the gold medal in the officers' race next Saturday. The late secretary has already realized that his present colleagues would smile audibly at any attempt to repeat the little dodge of which he was an unsophisticated victim last May, and is fearful that his diabolical designs on various sections of a brother director's running apparatus will be of little avail against so wary an opponent. Our worthy President consoles himself with the reflection that his dignity will not permit his being roped in a second time by his best friends. He is perfectly willing to sacrifice business and pleasure for the benefit of the club, but no such little job as the last one in his in. Not much! Any suggestion, between now and next Saturday, that will secure the trophy for the coming year, will be thankfully received and properly rewarded by any one of several ambitious official sprinters.

Last Wednesday; evening the Mechanics' Pavilion was filled to overflowing by the friends of the Olympic Club, the largest audience of the season being present. During the progress of the exhibition the entire gallery, and every possible space on the main floor from which a view of the exercises could be had, were crowded by interested visitors. The accident to R. F. Stombs necessitated the omission of some of the best features of the programme. Most fortunately Mr. Stombs was not seriously injured although at present he is a sight to behold and is slightly bearish over his sore head. The club will probably repeat the performance next week, on which occasion he intends to "do the perch" or break something. Financially the affair was very successful.

The art of training is an ancient one, and in early days among the Greeks was quite simple. The regimen consisted chiefly of cheese and figs, and the body was hardened by exposure to all sorts of weather and by frequent plunges into cold water, while oil was daily rubbed over the joints to make them supple. The decadence of sports began with the Greeks, when through niceties in training, the chances of competition could not be taken by the people at large, and athletics rivalry became purely professional. Athletic sports lose their chief value when taken up in them is expected only from those who are paid for exhibiting it, while all others are made either idle lookers-on or foolish betters on the result.

In the 100 yards scratch run next Saturday, Masterson of the Lacrosse Club appears to have a walk-over for the gold medal. With Haley barred there is no amateur on the Coast at present that can compete with him from scratch, if he does as well in a race as he does in private trials. Several members of the Olympic Club think he will weaken when he toes the mark for the actual contest, and do not propose to be beaten by him in worse time than 10½ seconds. That's right; fight it out.

The Bodie champion weight-tosser, who is supposed to be capable of putting a sixteen-pound weight about forty-three feet, is expected to be on the Olympic Club grounds to-morrow. As he is anxious to back himself heavily to put any of the standard weights an extraordinary distance, we cannot hope to see him extend himself in an exhibition before a few amateurs, but still it will be considerable satisfaction to the athletically inclined members of the club to see him put the above mentioned weight close to forty feet.

R. S. Haley has been training faithfully for some time, with the avowed purpose of making a record for himself and beating club and Pacific Coast records, at two distinct sprint distances. He is still undecided as to whether he will try 100 and 220 yards or 220 and 440 yards. Judging from his recent trials, he will probably lower the present record at 220 yards (his own twenty-three seconds being the best on the coast). J. T. Belcher's fifty and three-fifths at 440 yards requires more strength than he has shown this year, and unless he improves very much in the last two weeks he will surely fail to beat or even equal it, and to do even time at 100 yards, with an exacting starter and prompt timer, he needs to be in the pink of condition. Haley has the natural gift of speed at any distance from 100 to 800 yards, but lacks strength. When he acquires the latter requisite he will be fit to represent the Olympic Club in the best of company.

As an inducement to the amateurs of the Coast, the Olympic club has decided to award gold medals in several events, next Saturday, in open events, to any one beating club or Pacific Coast records from scratch. Haley will probably secure one of them in the 220 yards, and perhaps another in the running wide jump, and will undoubtedly try for another at same standard sprint distance. Slater has long been anxious to distinguish himself at pole vaulting, but has been waiting to capture something more than an ordinary medal. Brown knows all about the running high jump, and wants the pegs raised to a respectable hight without any preliminary foolishness. In the other events members of the O. C.—well, they are not talking very loud.

# BICYCLE.

## The English Championship.

The English twenty-mile professional championship race took place on he 21st of August on the Belgrave Road Grounds, Leicester. We give below an account of the race:

Of the ten competitors who entered, Keen and Duncan were the only non-starters, and at a quarter to seven o'clock the following were sent on the journey: Howell, Wood, Derkinderen, Garrard, P. Kaye, Edlin, Waller and Warwick. Upon the signal being given Garrard rushed off with the lead, followed by Wood, the first lap of the eighty required to complete the distance occupying forty-five seconds. When a mile had been run in three minutes, one second, Garrard was still taking his opponents along at a good pace, and Edlin was first to be in difficulties. At two miles Garrard was at the head of affairs, Warwick bringing up the rear. In the succeeding laps, some capital spurting was witnessed, and at five miles the leading men were Derkinderen, Waller, Garrard and Wood, Kaye, Howell and Warwick lying close up, although the last named did not seem to relish the business. Derkinderen, Garrard, Wood and Howell in turn made the running up to the ten mile (32m. 31s.), but during the next two miles the Newcastle man had changed. At fourteen miles the local man spurted, and the fifteen miles were recorded in forty-nine minutes, thirty-one seconds. Wood still held the lead, closely followed Garrard, Derkinderen, Walter, Howell and Warwick, and three miles from the finish, these fairly settled down to their work, and the pace rapidly increased. Garrard now dashed to the front, but directly afterwards Warwick took the lead for the first time. Some grand spurting ensued, which resulted in Howell taking the lead, the excitement growing intense. Entering the nineteeth mile, Wood, Kaye, Edlin, and Warwick gave up, and a quarter of a lap from home Howell held the lead, with Garrard and Derkinderen close up. Rounding the bend for the post, Garrard, by a tremendous effort, got on even terms with Howell, and in the last few yards got his wheel in front, and won a splendid race by half a yaid, Derkinderen two yards in the rear. Time, 1h. 5m. 40s. Mr. F. G. Walker was referee and time-keeper.

The fall meeting of the Olympic Athletic Club which takes place upon Saturday, the 23d of September, promises to bring out some fine racing in the various bicycle contests. The programme of the wheelmen as announced embraces a half mile, one mile aud a two mile race, and a dash of one fifth of a mile, (once around the track). This latter to be ridden by each compititor singly and the time to be taken by the judges. It is the intention to make this the finest race meeting of the season and entries are being made for the various events.

Country roads at this season of the year are badly cut up and deep with dust, so that any extended bicycle trips are out of the question. The roads out of Oakland as far as San Leandro and San Lorenzo are, however, kept well watered and the Oakland riders may enjoy a twenty-five or thirty miles run at any time over good roads.

The Golden Gate Fair Association offered among other prizes one of fifty dollars for an open one mile bicycle race, thirty-five to the first and fifteen to the second. This brought out two compititors, F. F. Merrill, the professional trick rider, and W. S. Hull, one of his pupils. The time given was 3 min. 40 sec. for Merrill, who won the race, and 3 min. 54 sec. for Hull.

The Beacon Park track, Boston, Mass., has been at last repaired and put in excellent order under the immediate direction of John S. Prince, and is this week opened to practice. It is well provided with dressing-rooms and other facilities, and ought to become a popular resort of wheelmen for both racing and practice. We understand that J. S. Prince will at present have the management of the track, and will give his personal attention to training competitors and others.

There seems to be no limit to the speed of bicycles under favorable circumstances. Not only has Cortis done twenty miles within an hour, but one hundred and ninety-three and a half miles of road have been traversed in the short time of 18h. 55m. by W. T. Sutton of the London Scottish Bicycle Club.

The same gentlemen will attempt to do two hundred and thirty miles in twenty-four hours. Such traveling as this should forever silence the "croakers" one meets with occasionally, who still doubt the practicability of the bicycle.

The Oakland Bicycle Club held its regular monthly meeting on Saturday evening, September 8th, at 912 Broadway, transacting the usual routine business, electing several new members and making arrangements for future runs.

## Market Report.

FLOUR—We quote as follows: Best City Extra, $5 37½@$5 50; Superfine, $4 50@$4 75; Interior Extra, $4 75@$5 25; Interior Superfine $3 75@$4 ℔ bbl.

WHEAT—With lower freights and a stronger market in England holders are firm and offerings light and there has been a marked advance for all grades. We quote No. 1 November, at $1 71½; No. 2, September, $1 62½ and do. November at $1 65.

BARLEY—Heavy arrivals have forced the price down a few cents since last week, although there is a lively export demand, especially for Chevalier. We quote good feed, $1 30; common do $1 27½; new brewing, $1 35@$1 40 per cental.

OATS—The market is rather quiet and prices range from $1 50@$1 70.

RYE—There has been a lowering of holders' prices during the week, though but few sales. For No. 1 $2 25 may be counted as the outside price.

HAY—We quote: Alfalfa, $11@$13 50; Wheat $13@$15 50; Wild Oat, $12@$15 ℔ ton.

HOPS—Medium, 35@40c; good to choice, $45@50c pr lb.

STRAW—Quotable at 50@55c ℔ bale.

BEANS—quoted at: Bayos, $2 40@$2 50; Butter, $3 25@$3 50 for small and $3 60@$3 80 for large; Lima, $3 50@$3 75; Pea, $2 50; Pink, $2@$2 25; Red, $2@$2 25; small White, $2 50; large White, $2 30@$2 40 ℔ ctl.

ONIONS—Silverskins sell for 50@70c ℔ ctl, and Red for 30@40c ℔ sack.

POTATOES—Prices are lower. We quote wharf rates; Early Rose, 85c@$1; Garnet Chile, 95c@$1 05 ℔ ctl; Sweet, $1 50@$1 75 ℔ ctl.

GAME—We quote; Hare, $1 75@$2 25; Rabbits $1@$1 50; Doves, 50@75c ℔ dozen; Venison, 10@12c ℔ lb.

PROVISIONS—Values steady. We quote; Eastern Hams, 13½@19c; California Hams, 16½@16¾c for plain, 16½@17c for sugar-cured canvased; Eastern Breakfast Bacon, 17½@18c; California Smoked Bacon, 16½@16¾c for heavy and medium, and 17½@18c for light and extra light; Clear Sides, 16½@16¾c; Pork, $21 50@$22 for extra Prime, $24@$25 for Prime Mess, $25@$25 50 for Mess, $27 for Clear and $28@$28 50 for extra Clear; Pigs' Feet, $16@$18 ℔ bbl; Mess Beef, $14 for bbls and $7 for hf bbls; Extra Mess Beef, $14 50@$15; Family Beef, $16@$18 50 @ bbl.

POULTRY.—With a strong demand prices have gone up and there are indications that will be still higher before they are lower. Job lots quoted: Live Turkeys, gobblers, 18@20c; do Hens, 17@19c; Roosters, $3 50@$6 50 for old and $5@$7 for young Hens, $6@$8 50; Broilers, $3@$4 50 according to size; Ducks, $5@$7 ℔ doz; Geese, $1@$1 25 ℔ pair; Goslings, $1 50@$1 75 ℔ pair.

HONEY—Comb, 14@17c; extracted, 7@9c ℔ lb.

EGGS—There has been a marked decline since our last report. We quote prices; California choice, 35@41c; Interior, 32½@35c; Utah, 25@35c ℔ doz.

BUTTER—Prices remain practically unchanged. We quote; Fancy, 40c; choice, 35@37½c; fair to good, 26@32½c; interior lots from country stores, 23@25c; firkin, 29@31c for good to choice, and 25@27½c for ordinary; pickled roll, 30@32½c; Eastern, 20@25c ℔ lb.

CHEESE—With a quiet market we quote: California, 12½@13½c for choice; 10@12c from fair to good; do. factory, in boxes, 15@16c; Eastern, 16@17c; Western, 11@13½c ℔ lb.

HIDES AND SKINS—Dry hides, 20@20½c; culls one-third less, and Mexican Hides 1c ℔ lb less. Dry Kip, 18@19c; Dry Calf, 21@22c; Slated Steers, over 55 lbs, 11c ℔ lb; Steers and Cows, medium, 10c; light do, 7½c; Salted Kip, 15 to 30 lbs, 10@10½c; Salted Calf, 11@12½c ℔ lb; Dairy Calf, 65@70c each; Sheep Skins, 20@25c for Shearlings; 25@50c for short, 60@80c for medium, and 75c@1$ apeice for long wool and wool skins. Butchertown Green Skins bring higher prices.

TALLOW—Good demand, quotable at 8½@8¾c ℔ lb for rendered and 10½@11c for refined, both in shipping order.

WOOL—Sales are light and mostly confined to fall. We quote: Humboldt and Mendocino, 25@26½c ℔ lb; Sonoma, 24@26c; Siskiyou and Modoc, 20@25c; San Joaquin, free, 17@18c; Southern Coast, burry and seedy, 15@17c; Eastern Oregon, choice, 23@24c; Eastern Oregon fair, 20@22c; Eastern Oregon, poor, 18@19c; Valley Oregon, fine, 25@27c; valley Oregon, coarse, 23@24c.

FRUIT—Apples are more plentiful and consequently lower, while the supply of pears and raspberries is limited and prices are higher than last week. We quote; Apples, 75@$1 ℔ box for good; Pears, 25@40c ℔ bskt and 40@60c ℔ box; Bartlett do, $1 50@$2 ℔ basket and $1 50@$2 ℔ box; Strawberries, $8@$10 ℔ chest; Raspberries, $10@$12 ℔ chest; Peaches, 35c@$1 ℔ box and 30@60c ℔ bskt; Figs, 40@75c ℔ box; Grapes, 35@50c fo common, 60@75c for Black Hamburg, 60@75c for Rose of Peru, 50@75c ℔ box for Muscat and 75c@$1 ℔ box for Tokay; Plums, 25@75c ℔ box; Quinces, 75c@$1 ℔ box; Blackberries, $2@$6 ℔ chest; Watermelons, @$3 $7 ℔ hundred; Cantaloupes, 75c@$1 ℔ crate; Lemons, $8@$9 ℔ box for Sicily and $1@$1 50 for California; Limes, $14@$15 ℔ box for Mexican; Bananas, $2@$3 50 ℔ bunch; Pineapples, $6@$8 ℔ dozen; Tahiti Oranges, $35@$45 ℔ thousand.

VEGETABLES—We quote: Marrowfat Squash, $5@$8 ℔ ton; Carrots, 30@50c; Turnips, 75c@$1; Cauliflower, 60@65c ℔ dozen; Cabbage, 50@75c ℔ ctl; Garlic, 1@1½c ℔ lb; Cucumbers, 25@30c ℔ box; Green Peas, 4c ℔ lb; Green Peppers, 50@75c ℔ box; Tomatoes, 15@30c ℔ box; Celery, 50c ℔ doz; Summer Squash, 50c ℔ box; String Beans, 3@4c ℔ lb; Green Corn, 7@15c ℔ doz; Okra, 50@75c; Egg Plant, 50@75c ℔ box.

MEATS—Following are the rates for whole carcasses from slaughterers to dealers:

BEEF—Prime, 7½@8c; medium grade, 6½@7c; inferior, 5½@6c ℔ lb.

VEAL—Large Calves, 6½@7c; small ones, 8@10c ℔ lb.

MUTTON—Wethers are quotable at 4½@5c and Ewes at 4@4½c ℔ lb, according to quality.

LAMB—Quotable at 6@6½c ℔ lb.

PORK—Live Hogs, 7½@7¾c for hard and 7@7½c for soft; dressed do, 10½@10¾c ℔ lb for hard grain hogs.

| LEAVE FOR | DESTINATION | ARRIVE FROM |
|---|---|---|
| | Antioch and Martinez | |
| | Benicia | |
| | Calistoga and Napa | |
| | Deming, El Paso } Express | |
| | Knight's Landing | |
| | Los Angeles and Deming | |
| | Livermore and Pleasanton | |
| | Madera and Fresno | |
| | Marysville and Chico | |
| | Niles and Haywards | |
| | Ogden and } Express | |
| | Redding and Red Bluff | |
| | Sacramento } via Benicia | |
| | Sacramento River Steamers | |
| | San Jose | |
| | Vallejo | |
| | Virginia City | |
| | Willows and } | |

| LEAVE S.F. | DESTINATION | ARRIVE S.F. |
|---|---|---|
| | San Mateo, Redwood and Menlo Park | |
| | Santa Clara, San Jose, and Principal Way Stations | |
| | Gilroy, Pajaro, Castroville and Salinas | |
| | Hollister, and Tres Pinos | |
| | Monterey, Watsonville, Camp Goodall, Aptos, Camp San Jose, Soquel and Santa Cruz | |
| | Soledad and Way Stations | |

## $12,500

### In Purses and Stakes.

CALIFORNIA

# STATE FAIR

### SPEED PROGRAMME

FOR 1882.

FIRST DAY—Monday, Sept. 11.

No. 1—RUNNING—INTRODUCTION STAKE—For all ages; three-quarters of a mile dash; $50 entrance, $25 forfeit; $300 added; second to save stake.

No. 2—TROTTING—2:28 class; purse, $1,000. Mile heats, 3 in 5.

No. 3—RUNNING—BREEDER STAKE—For foals of 1879; one and a half mile dash; $50 entrance, p. p.; $300 added. Closed March 1st with nominations following:

No. 4—PACIFIC COAST RUNNING—Mile and repeat; purse $600; and if 1 dd it beaten, the horse making the lowest second will receive $300 additional. Four entries.

SATURDAY, SEPT. 23D.

REMARKS and CONDITIONS.

All Trotting Races best three in five, except numbers 1 and 2.

SECOND DAY—Tuesday, Sept. 12.

No. 5—RUNNING—FULLY STAKE FOR TWO YEAR OLD FILLIES—Five-eighths of a mile; $50 entrance; $15 forfeit; $300 added; second to receive $75; third, $25.

THIRD DAY—Wednesday, Sept. 13.

FOURTH DAY—Thursday, Sept. 41.

No. 12—TROTTING—2:22 class; purse, $1,000. Mile heats, 3 in 5.

FIFTH DAY—Friday, Sept. 15.

No. 16—RUNNING—COLT AND FILLY STAKE—$50; $300 added; second horse, $50; third, $25.

SIXTH DAY—Saturday, Sept. 16.

No. 1—TROTTING—Purse, $600; for double teams of 2:30 horses.

REMARKS and CONDITIONS.

EDWIN F. SMITH,　　　　HUGH M. LaRUE,
Secretary.　　　　President

# BREEDER AND SPORTSMAN

Vol. I. No. 13.
NO. 508 MONTGOMERY STREET.

SAN FRANCISCO, SATURDAY, SEPTEMBER 23, 1882.

SUBSCRIPTION
FIVE DOLLARS A YEAR.

## HORSE HISTORY.

### A Notable of War Times.

There is ofttimes a spice of romance in the history of horses, strange vicissitudes in their lives which are almost a parallel to the striking changes which sometimes occur in human life. The following sketch, cut from the *Call* of last Sunday, recalls the history of one animal which has had a checkered existence:

"Git Up, Chee-ka-go."

Fenton White, a special policeman in Hayes Valley, is an admirer of fast horses, and is of the opinion that he can tell a horse's gait by simply looking at him. Last Monday some of his acquaintances, wishing to test his judgment of trotting, took a horse, put old, worn and patched harness on his back, and hitched him to a dilapidated old wagon which they hired from a rag, bottle and glass man, and had the owner of the wagon drive out to a place in the valley where White is frequently to be found.

The acquaintances soon followed, and meeting White, engaged him in conversation on horses.

"Now," said one of them, "what do you think of that broncho?" pointing to the animal hitched to the rag, bottle and glass wagon.

"White smiled but made no reply.

"What do you think he'll make a mile in?" asked the speaker.

White examined the horse with the air of a connoisseur and then declared that he was satisfied that the animal could not make it inside of ten minutes.

"What's the time of that nag?" asked one of the party of the driver.

"I guess about four minutes."

"I'll bet that he'll trot inside of 3:30," said the one who had broached the subject, and after some parley White put up $25, which was covered by the one who had made the offer.

The animal was driven to the Bay District Park, harnessed to a sulky, and trotted at a slow gait once around the track. When the animal was taken under the string the man who drove him touched him up with the whip, hollowed "Git up! Chee-ka-go," and away went the horse and made the mile in 2:36. White admitted that he had lost, and he was then informed that the animal was Chicago, a once celebrated trotter with a record, but retired from the turf several years ago. White consoles himself now by saying: "Well, it was worth $25 to see the old horse warm up to his work."

To commence the history after the style of the old-time story book: On a bright spring morning in that part of Kentucky where the blue-grass is the sweetest, and the birds sing the most joyous notes, a brown foal was gamboling about his dam. It is twenty-three years and over since that gay youngster was performing his glad antics, and as he caracoled through all the paces of the manege, his owner felt satisfied that the object he had in view was accomplished. His aim was to breed a first-class saddle horse, and a favorite old mare by American Eclipse was coupled with Ole Bull, a son of the old pacer Pilot. He anticipated that the union of the blood of the horse which was the acknowledged champion of the turf, never having lost a race even when matched against the choice of the whole South, and that of the "Canuck" would "fill the bill," and as the colt had got the quality from his dam and the desired gait from the sire he felt that his wish was to be gratified. In this he was not disappointed. As he grew from colthood to maturity he improved, fell readily into all the saddle gaits, and at the same time was tractable and took kindly to harness. He did not show any trotting speed, however, ambling at the start, and if pressed for greater speed would singlefoot and pace, much as he did when carrying a rider.

During the year Harvey B. Ring made a contract to furnish "hard bread" to the army and his bakery was in the suburbs of Louisville. The owner of the colt loaned him to Mr. Ring to drive in his business and harnessed to a road wagon he would jog pleasantly to the bakery and back, and stand quietly without "hitching."

There were huge piles of empty barrels in front of the bakery, and one day while he was left standing at the door, he took a fancy to investigate. He did it carelessly, moving one and then another, until he caught one with his teeth and pulled it out. Down came the stack with a horrible uproar, the barrels rolling in all directions.; Never was a colt more demoralized, and away he went at a rate which would not have discredited his illustrious grandsire on the maternal side of the house. The racket brought all hands to the door but all that could be seen was casks still rolling, and a fleeing brown phantom with a black streak behind him. But there was a counter pull. The blood of the Canuck was putting a break on that of the high-mettled racer and the pace was too severe to last. He was too much frightened to think of the manege gait, too anxious to get away from the din and the crazy dance of the barrels to go slow, and the "black drop" forbade keeping up the speed at the gallop. He struck a square, open trot, with grand action, head high in the air, and kept up his stride until he reached his stable in the city. As was the case with old Topgallant, accident had developed unthought-of capacity. He was placed in training and in his first race christened "Hardbread." He performed so well that he was purchased by John Aiken, of Pittsburg, a hale, hearty old man who had a great fancy for the sports of the track, a straightforward, bluff old fellow, who carried his sixty-five years as lightly as though the years had been under two score, and his cheek was ruddy though his hair was streaked with gray. He placed Hardbread in the hands of a driver who years ago acquired notoriety on this coast, also a big, powerful looking man and somewhat given to swagger and "blow." They came to Chicago and Hardbread was engaged in the races. There was sharp practice and that night "Old John" met his driver in a livery stable kept by Edward Price. He asked him a question to which the driver gave an answer to that was palpably false.

"You are a liar and thief, Col. D——," replied the owner of Hardbread.

"If you were not an old man I would lick you," was the response.

"Take that, you ——," was the counter reply and the valiant Colonel was crying "murder," and "take him off," in less time than it requires to write the description.

"How much will you give for the horse, Mr. Price," was the next query, and the livery man named a sum much below his value. "He is yours; write a bill of sale," and Hardbread was transferred in due legal form to his new owner. At that time the famous driver, Jim Rockey, was working Mr. Price's horses, and the name was changed to that of the skillful whip. He trotted under that name many good races, and was then sold to Henry Graves, a man who has had as much to do with the old trotting days and up to the last few years of the present, as 'any man in the country. He was the owner of Lady Jane when she beat Jack Rossiter and other cracks of that time, and though he aided in moving the Indians from Chicago it is long odds that he was a delighted spectator at the last great meeting at the "City by the Lake."

After awhile there was a disagreement between him and the driver of the quondam Hardbread, and he was rechristened Chicago. In the summer of 1868 he was matched against the stallion Young Bashaw, then thought to be the fastest and best horse in the West, and capable of successfully coping with the flyers of the country. Young Bashaw was owned by A. F. Fawcett, who sold Dexter to Robert Bonner, and he firmly believed him to be the "king of the track." We were in New York when the matches came off, and now, writing entirely from memory, we do not attempt to give the particulars, but the remembrance is very distinct of the telegram which was brought up the long flight of stairs to the *Turf, Field and Farm* office that Chicago had won the first of the series, the time 2:24½. This was capital time fourteen years ago, and stamped Chicago as one of the good horses of any part of the country.

In 1871 he created still more of a sensation. There was a free-for-all purse at Chicago and it was well known that Goldsmith Maid and Lucy would be in it, and there was one a surprise when the entry box was opened and the name of Chicago was found. The purse was $5,000, $2,500 to the first, $1,500 to the second and $1,000 to the third. When the race came off there was still more surprise as at one time it looked as though he were going to win the third heat. He was some distance in the rear when the horses came into the stretch, but was rapidly overhauling the leaders, and such a shout went up as is rarely heard on a race course, and a man who now holds a high position in the National Trotting Association became so excited he fairly shrieked "Chicago will win," and for the only time in our long acquaintance with him accompanied the exclamation with the sharpest kind of an epithet which some might have thought profane. But it was too much to expect of even so good a horse as our hero was on that day, and he was forced to succumb to the reigning belles of the track.

To the best of our recollection it was in 1871 or 1872 that we received a letter from a friend in New York to buy Chicago for him. He was a liberal purchaser, very fond of the fast trotter, and owned several, some of which we had bought for him. In the whirligig of events he has become associated with the press and is now the editor of a New York paper as widely known as any journal in the United States. The price authorized was $13,000, and though we felt that it was in reality rather more than the horse was worth and that he ought to be obtained for less money, the letter was read to Mr. Graves. The answer was to the point. "Thirteen thousand dollars, why it would not buy the hairs in his tail" was the reply. "I have three horses the poorest of which it would take $20,000 to get and Chicago is not that one."

It is unnecessary to follow his career since he came to California, but enough has been shown to display the vicissitudes in equine life. From a valuation of a sum akin to a respectable fortune to being harnessed to an old wagon filled with rubbish, the driver shouting rags, sacks and bottles through the byways of the city is a sorrowful denouement. Poor old Hardbread. Perhaps as he stands with his head down while his owner is chaffering for the refuse he hauls he is recalling his early days, the green pasture fields of his old Kentucky home, the happy, happy days of colthood, the caracoling through the streets of Louisville gay and graceful, and the dream of the rolling, rattling barrels. He rises his head, and it may be that he again hears the cheers, the frantic shouts as he is pressing the Queens to do their best to reach the score first. Who can say that there is no gift of retrospection granted? Let us believe that there is, and that the pleasure of memory is some atonement for his hard lot.

Hanging on the wall of the editorial room of the BREEDER AND SPORTSMAN is a picture. It can scarcely be called a picture, more properly an unfinished sketch. In the background there are rounded, wooded hills, a stream winding through a meadow, between the hills, and the foreground representing an opening in an oak forest with a horse darting through on a fast trot. But there are blotches of white on the canvas and on the right the trees are incomplete. That, too, has a history, a history in part connected with the subject of this sketch. When Henry Graves was the owner of Chicago he employed the artist Scott to make paintings of his favorite horses. Queen of the West, a handsome grey mare by Pilot Jr., was the subject of one. She was of the fastest sort, had trotted half a mile in 1:03 in her training, but fully as unreliable as she was fast. The second was Bay Henry by Mambrino Chief, from a thoroughbred mare and also a remarkably fine looking horse, and the third was Chicago. A Mr. Loomis was then associated with Mr. Graves in the ownership of the horses, and he made some remark which Scott did not like. Besides the finished picture which showed Chicago harnessed to a sulky he had made a sketch of the horse in motion entirely untrammeled; not a strap upon him. The latter was the most lifelike, the most spirited of the two. He would not let the owners have the finis icture which he entrusted to our care. The sketch he presented us with.

Some time before the great fire in Chicago D. A. Gage, with whom we were then associated in a horse breeding establishment, was made acquainted with the necessities of a Norwegian artist, so poor that he was actually in want. There was none more liberal than Mr. Gage, and after presenting the artist with money enough to relieve him he gave him a commission to put Atwood Place, where we then lived, on canvas, and for which he paid him a large sum in advance. The house, a pretty cottage surrounded with large oaks, made a pretty picture, and admirably the artist succeeded in reproducing it. When finished it was hung in the rotunda of the Sherman House and elicited many encomiums. While working at that we suggested that he should take the sketch of Chicago and fill in a landscape, complete the coloring of the horse, have it chromoed, and under the title of "the frotter at play" it would be likely to meet with a sale which would remunerate him. He spent the week days at Atwood Place, the Sundays with his family in Chicago. Sunday night Chicago was a mass of flame, Monday it was a reeking ruin. From that time we never could get a trace of the artist; the picture which was finished was burned in the Sherman House, and the unfinished sketch on the walls is all that remains. The artist undoubtedly perished in the fire as Mr. Gage had obtained plenty of work for him in the future.

There are other sad remembrances connected with the horse. The man who drove him and gave him his first name, after making a fortune in oil speculations, moved to Denver, where he committed suicide. One of his former owners died from the effects of excess, and poor Jim Rockey, one of the best drivers that ever sat in a sulky, went completely to the bad and died when he should have been in the prime of his usefulness.

# TURF AND TRACK.

## Fixed Events.

## The Contra Costa Fair.

The 24th annual fair of the Contra Costa Agricultural Association commenced on Monday, the 11th, and ended last Saturday. The directors of the association labored hard and faithfully to make the fair a success and if it has not come up to their expectations it was no fault of theirs. The premiums offered for home and farm productions, and the purses offered as inducements for the sporting classes to bring out their fast horses, show the liberality and the lively interest they have for the welfare of the organization.

On the first, second and third days the attendance was very small, but as the week advanced the numbers increased and gave the fair grounds quite a lively appearance.

It was without doubt held too early in the season as the farmers had not finished their harvesting, and being held at the same time as the State Fair it did not turn out as successfully as in former years.

The fair grounds are situated between, and half a mile distant from, the towns of Concord and Pacheco. The pavilion is a large and commodious building and quite handy to the grand stand and the judges' stand. The numerous productions of the field speak well for Contra Costa farmers; the homes with their ample specimens of handiwork and the works of local artists deserved their share of praise. The stock sheds and stalls are well arranged and capable of accommodating quite large numbers of stock, but their capacity was not found this year to any great extent.

The race track is in rather bad order but a winter's rain will pack it down and in time it will be excelled by few others.

Many of the races on the programme were not filled and special purses were made up to take their places. Among the principal races was one for all yearlings in the county that came off on Monday. The babies trotted well and showed much promise of future greatness. Capt. Durham entered Oscar; J. E. Tennent, Don Carlos; J. B. Tennent, Pinole Jr.; R. H. Nason, F. McGuire and J. H. Nason's, McVey. The race was best three in five. R. H. Nason's F. McGuire won the first and second heats and first money, $35; Oscar second money, $10; McVey third $5. Don Carlos and Pinole Jr. were distanced in the first heat.

The second was a running race, free to all two-year-olds in the county, for a purse of $50; $35 for the first, $10 for the second, and $5 for the third, best three in five. Rosetta, Lady Emma, and Idler were the horses. Mr. Gehr's Idler won the race and first and third money, Lady Emma second. The trotting race of Tuesday was the most exciting race of all. The purse was $250, free to all horses owned in the county; first horse $165, second $60, and third $25. John Rogers entered Berney; H. G. Cox, Vengeance; J. E. Durham, Conductor; N. Gruber, Gipsy Huntington and R. H. Nason, Urania. The horses took their positions in the order above mentioned; Urania was the favorite. The first heat was trotted in 2:46, the horses coming in in the same order that they started. On the second heat Urania was let out and showed what she could do, going under the wire in 2:46 with Vengeance second, Gipsy Huntington third, Berney fourth and Conductor fifth. The third heat was made in 2:44, the horses all doing their best. Urania came in first, Berney second, Vengeance third, Conductor fourth and Gipsy Huntington fifth. Urania won the fourth heat and first money, $165;

Barney second money, $60; Vengeance third money, $25; Conductor fourth and Gipsy Huntington distanced; time 2:44.

The second race of Tuesday was for pacing, horses that could beat 2:50. R. H. Nason entered Doc; T. Downing Silvertail, and Capt. Downing Onward. Onward won the race and first money in one heat leaving Doc and Silvertail outside of distance. After this came a running race, free to all horses in the county. Purse $150. First horse $100; second horse $35; third horse $15. T. Padhoo entered Dick Ruby, W. A. J. Gift, Idler, and B. McKinny, Lady Emma. In the first heat Idler lost considerable on the start but crowded Dick Ruby on the homestretch. Dick Ruby won the heat, Idler second, Lady Emma distanced; time 1:49. Idler won the second heat in 1:52, the third heat in 2:01 and the fourth heat and first money in 1:57½, Dick Ruby winning the second money. On Thursday only one race on the programme was filled but several special purses were made up and competed for, one of which caused considerable excitement which was not down on the bills. The race was for a purse of $100, best 3 in 5. Capt. Durham entered Ned; H. G. Cox, Vengeance, and N. Gruber, Gipsy Huntington. The first heat was won by Gipsy Huntington, Vengeance second and Ned third. Time 2:58½. On the second heat Ned came in first, Vengeance second and Gipsy Huntington third; time 2:55½. Complaint was made against H. G. Cox, the driver of Vengeance, for foul driving and a marshal was ordered to escort Mr. Cox around the track; on the following heat, which was the third, the marshal reported that Cox was not driving to win. When Cox heard the report he drove toward the stalls but when he reached the gate he struck his horse with the whip, dashed through the gate and started for the county road. Both marshals started in pursuit of the horse and a lively race took place around a stubble field before the horse was captured and returned to the track. Cox's excuse for this singular conduct was that he "was afraid of violence from those who had bet on his horse; and also that his home was coming down with the pinkeye, and he wished to withdraw from the race." The only race of any note on Friday was for a purse of $150. Barney, Jim Lee, Chicago and Urania were entered. The best time was 2:42; the race and first money was won by Urania. There were no races on Saturday owing to a heavy rain. The award of prizes on stock will be published later.

## Fall Meeting P. C. B. H. A.

The programme of the Fall meeting of the Pacific Coast Blood Horse Association is as follows:

Introductory day, Saturday, November 11. No. 1, purse $300; free for all, $10 each; a dash of three-quarters of a mile.

No. 2, purse $300; free for all maidens, $10 each; one mile, entrance money to second horse.

No. 3, Handicap stake for all ages, free for all; $25 entrance and $10 if declared, $250 added; $50 to second horse; a dash of a mile and an eighth.

No. 4, selling purse, $300; a mile and a quarter for all ages; entrance free; $50 to second horse. The winner to be sold at auction; horses entered for $1,500 to carry regular weight, if for $1,000, five pounds allowed; if for $750, ten pounds; if for $500, seventeen pounds; and if for $300, twenty-two pounds. Any one can claim the winner, and the excess realized beyond the amount at which the horse is entered to be divided between the association and the owner of the second horse.

First day, regular meeting, November 15. No. 1, the Ladies' stake.

No. 2, purse of $250, free for all, three-quarters of a mile and repeat, entrance free; the winner of the dash of three-quarters on the first day to carry 10 pounds extra.

No. 3, the Vestal Stake.

No. 4, handicap purse of $250 for two-year-olds; $25 each and $10 if declared; $50 to the second horse, dash of a mile. Second day, regular meeting, November 18. No. 1, purse of $200, a dash of seven-eighths of a mile. $50 to the second horse; entrance free; the winner of the three-quarter dash to carry ten pounds extra.

No. 1, purse of $250; heats of a mile and an eighth, entrance free; $50 to second horse; maiden three-year-olds allowed seven pounds; four-year-olds twelve pounds, and maiden five-year-olds and over twenty pounds; the winner of the dash at this distance on the first day to carry five pounds extra.

No. 3, handicap purse of $250 for all three-year-olds. A dash of a mile and quarter; $25 each and $15 if declared; the second horse to receive $50.

No. 4, purse $250, a mile and repeat over four hurdles; $50 to second horse. Entrance free.

Third day regular meeting, November 23. No. 1, the Finnegan stake.

No. 2, the Pame stake.

No. 3, the Baldwin stake.

No. 4, Consolation purse of $200, of which $50 to the second horse; entrance free; a mile dash; horses beaten twice allowed ten pounds, and three times, fifteen pounds.

In the stakes already filled there are many nominations and in order to encourage this style of running it has been decided to give a second purse for a hurdle race, of which the particulars will be given in our next issue.

## The Colts That Have Gone East.

From the following note it will be seen that the Palo Alto colts are now well on their way to the scene of their engagements, and it also gives dates and places where they will trot. It appears like a short time to get them in readiness to trot in less than two weeks from the time of their arrival in New York, but if the weather is favorable we think it will be all right. The latter part of September is generally fine in that country, though in some years the equinoctial storms extend into October. The news will be eagerly awaited in California, and if there are no mishaps we have the utmost confidence that they will win through.

PALO ALTO, Sept. 18, 1882.

EDITOR BREEDER AND SPORTSMAN: The following is a list of the colts shipped East on Sunday last, and their engagements:

Wildflower, 3 yrs. Mall Stakes, Oct. 3, New York.
Mariet, 3 yrs. Mall Stakes, Oct. 3, New York.
Bertha, 3 yrs. Kentucky Stakes, Oct. 11, Lexington, Ky.
Hinda Rose, 2 yrs. Lexington Stakes, Oct. 10, Lexington, Ky.
Flower Girl, 2 yrs. Lexington Stakes, Oct. 10, Lexington.
Kentucky Stakes, 76 nominations, 36 declarations.
Lexington Stakes, 85 nominations, 96 declarations.

The above stock was shipped in charge of Chas. Marvin.

Yours truly,
FRANK COVEY.

## The State Fair.

The weather on the Friday was a very welcome contrast to the intense heat of the Tuesday and Wednesday, when every one, and especially those living on the Bay, suffered immensely from its effects. During the morning there was a great deal of talk indulged in concerning the race of the 2:22 class, and the general idea prevailed that if Romero, through his recent sickness, had not been short of work, the final result would have been different, and the many stories were amusing how hundreds and hundreds were at stake, that by careful and systematic hedging resulted in the gain or loss of only a few dollars. Through an error made in the transcribing of the race from the original notes, the principal heat was omitted from our report last week, and the following is another account of this very interesting race:

There was but little difficulty in getting them off on even terms, Goldsmith sending Romero at once to the fore and at the half, in the fairly good time of 1:10½, the gray led by three lengths, Brigadier, driven by his owner, having lost in a break, while Belle Echo, also piloted by her owner, was apparently being held in reserve. After the first half the pace became slower, Belle Echo getting off her feet, and although Brigadier closed up part of the distance, that separated him from the winner, Romero finished in a jog in 2:22½. The second heat was of a far more lively character and this time Brigadier was shaken up to his work and he was almost lapped with Romero when the latter reached the half mile in the fast time of 1:08, and Romero trotting very squarely finished the heat in 2:20 by three lengths from Brigadier, the mare making a poor third. The announcement of the time was received by the public with applause, but his backers were less confident about his being able to repeat in any such time.

Nevertheless there was as yet but little hedging as it was also thought that Romero could finish the race in the next heat, and $100 to $40 were still wagered freely on his chances. Romero to a fair start again tried to outspeed Brigadier, but the latter put in some pretty bursts of speed that kept him always within reaching distance and along the upper turn he gradually closed up, so that on swinging into the home stretch he was at Romero's wheel and although he was urged to his greatest speed, a bad skip ended his chances and Brigadier dashed under the wire the winner in 2:23, the half having been made in 1:10.

Now the boys began to be alarmed and there was a good deal of hedging on both sides that made up a very profitable race for the poolbox. Brigadier sold on an average at $150 against $80 for Romero while Belle Echo brought $75 on the strength of a report that she had been kept in reserve for a brilliant finish. This time it was Brigadier who assumed the initiative and Belle Echo was sometimes in pretty close attendance, but when the bell was reached in 1:14 and Brigadier was well in advance it appeared evident to the staunchest friends of Romero that he was not in condition to last through a race of split heats. But he still made a good effort in the homestretch and was only beaten out by Brigadier by four lengths in 2:23½.

Now there was a stampede to hedge the Romero tickets and Brigadier sold for $100 to $30 on the field. This time again the pace was of a leisurely description, Brigadier reaching the half mile in 1:15 with both the others on even terms just lapping him. Here the speed was increased and the three came down the stretch with Brigadier still well in the lead when within the last fifty yards Belle Echo was brought up with a masterly rush, and they went under the wire so closely locked that the judges decided it a dead heat in 2:27½. The final heat was altogether between Belle Echo and Brigadier, the odds being $30 to $20 in the latter's favor. The two horses trotted to the half lapped together in 1:13½, while Romero's movements were hampered by a bad break on the first turn. They trotted together admirably and it so even terms that it looked like a repetition of a dead heat when at the draw gate Belle left her feet and could never close the gap, Brigadier being pressed to the finish in 2:25½, and yet as before mentioned the original backers of Brigadier were not happy, as they had so carefully hedged their bets that they lost on their investments.

The card for the Friday was composed of four running races, the first of which was the colt and filly stake, a dash of a mile for two-year-olds, $50 entrance, $15 forfeit, with $300 added. There were ten original entries, but only three sported sill. May B running highest in the pools at $50 against $35 for Flou Flou and $5 for Certiorari. Among the principal absentees were Satanella of the Palo Alto stable, Lou Spencer, belonging to Mr. Winters, and Panama, owned by Mr. Coutts. It was an easy task for Mr. Finigan, who acted as starter, to get them off pretty well together, and May B at once shot to the front, with Flou Flou held readily within reaching distance, and thus they traveled well around the upper turn when Flou Flou gradually moved up and challenging May B at the distance won a beautifully contested race by a short head in 1:46½, Certiorari being a poor third.

SUMMARY.

AGRICULTURAL PARK, SACRAMENTO, September 15.—Colt and Filly Stake, for two-year-olds, dash of one mile, $50 entrance, $15 forfeit, $300 added; second horse, $50, third, $25. Ten entries, of which seven pay forfeit.

C. Von Doren names F. Coutts' blk f Flou Flou, by Monday, dam Jennie C. 67 pounds. . . . . . . . . . . . . . . . . . . . . . . . . . . . . . . . 1
Pot. Sctson names ch f May B, by Wildidle, dam Jessie B., 97 pounds. 2
G. W. Trahern names ch g Certiorari, by Joe Daniels, dam by Norfolk, 97 pounds. . . . . . . . . . . . . . . . . . . . . . . . . . . . . . . . 3
Time—1:46½.

The next was a selling race for all ages, a dash of a mile and a quarter, in which Ella Doane was privately announced as a sure thing and consequently she fetched the highest price at about $35 against $40 for the field in which were Haddington, Vila Rathleti, Enchre and Sister to Lottery. The race was entirely between Ella Doane and Haddington, both carrying nearly even weights. At the drop of the flag Haddington moved briskly to the front and at the end of half a mile was fully five lengths ahead of Ella, and going so easily that it looked as if the favorite was destined to be bowled over for the second time in the day, but down the back stretch and around the straight Ella, Enchre and Vila moved closer up and at the draw gate they were all whipping save Ella and she out-stayed them all, winning in a handy manner in 2:10½, Haddington a good second, and Vila Rathleti a fair third.

SUMMARY.

Same day.—Selling race, purse $300, for all ages; dash of one and a quarter miles; fixed valuation at $500 on which, horses to carry full weight; allowance of three pounds for each $100 below the fixed value down to $300, to which value horses are eligible; $50 to second horse; entrance free. Winner if beaten to be sold for $500.
H. C. Judson names b m Ella Doane, by Wildidle, dam Nettie brown, 107 lbs . . . . . . . . . . . . . . . . . . . . . . . . . . . . . . . . . . 1
P. J. Shafter names b h (?) Haddington ($1,000), by imported Buckden, dam by Norfolk, 118 lbs . . . . . . . . . . . . . . . . . . . . . . . 2
W. L. Pritchard names b f (?) Vila Rathleti ($1,000), by Wildidle, dam Lille brown, 105 lbs. . . . . . . . . . . . . . . . . . . . . . . . . 3
R. McGrath names b m Sister to Lottery ($500), by Monday, dam Urquide, 82 lbs. . . . . . . . . . . . . . . . . . . . . . . . . . . . . . . . . 0
J. P. Gilson names ch h (?) Enchre ($500), by Leinster, dam Flash, 107 lbs. . . . . . . . . . . . . . . . . . . . . . . . . . . . . . . . . . . 0
Time—2:10½.

the field became first choice at $50, but there was seemingly no desire among the backers of Honesty to hedge their investments, as he sold for $35 and Ashley for $8. In this heat Del Sur was left on a run and Ashley passed Cairo at the quarter as he was indulging in the same jumping, but Cairo soon resumed the advantage, and although Honesty this time made an effort to come up, Cairo beat him out by two lengths in 2:28¼, Ashley being a poor third and Tump Winston distanced. Now there was some lively betting, the field bringing $120, $40 for Honesty and $10 for Ashley, and when his backers were abandoning his chances Honesty took it into his head to make a rattling good heat, for although both Cairo and Ashley were ahead of him at the half mile, he was even with them on the homestretch and after a handsome tussle: Honesty won in 2:26½ by a short head from Cairo, Del Sur being third. Honesty was again installed first choice at $50 against $40 for the field, but this time Cairo gave a good proof of his endurance, for he waltzed away from his opponents and won in 2:27 by seven open lengths from Honesty, Del Sur being a poor third, and this brought the week's meeting to a rather tame conclusion.

SUMMARY.

Same Day—Purse, $600; for arranged entries, divided at the same rates as in all the other purses, sixty per cent. to the first, thirty per cent. to the second and ten per cent. to the third horse.

| | | | | | |
|---|---|---|---|---|---|
| John Hughes names ch h Cairo, by Cheiftain, dam unknown | 3 | 1 | 1 | 2 | 1 |
| J. H. Dodge names ch h Honesty, by Priam, dam by Cheiftain | 4 | 3 | 2 | 1 | 2 |
| L. J. Rose enters blk s Del Sur, by The Moor, dam Gretchen | 1 | 5 | 4 | 3 | 3 |
| Jackson Cochran names ch g Ashley, by Plumas, dam by George | 2 | 4 | 3 | 4 | 4 |
| Eugene Mara names ch g Tump Winston, by Primus, dam Lady Don | 5 | 2 | dist. | | |

Time—2:25¾, 2:26½, 2:28¼, 2:26½, 2:27.

### Stock Exhibits and Premiums.

The exhibits of blood stock, horses, cattle, sheep and swine at the State Fair which closed last Saturday were larger and more varied than have ever been before seen at Agricultural Park and indicated a healthy and increasing interest in the breeding of the noblest specimens of the bluest blood. The great increase in the number of exhibitors in these departments is a matter of congratulation and satisfaction to those who hope and desire to see California moving toward that place in the first rank to which she is entitled as the natural home of the equine and bovine nobility. Farmers recognize the value of book pedigrees as they never have before and the gentlemen of wealth who can find congenial employment for their money and tastes in a systematic effort to attain perfection in the lower animals are steadily growing in number. One of the notable features of the fair this year was the exhibit of Mr. J. B. Haggin, which included thoroughbred horses of the most unexceptionable strains, standard trotters, draft and coach horses. The collection was larger than that of any other single exhibition and of a character that elicited the unqualified admiration of the lookers-on, both the versed and unversed in horse lore. All branches of the horse family were represented among the different competitors for prizes and the specimens submitted were of the finest in their several classes. Of the cattle, Col. Younger was alone as an exhibitor of Shorthorns and deserved the many high encomiums his herd received. In the list of Jerseys, many breeders appeared, Henry Pierce of this city being the largest, with twenty-eight thoroughbreds. Major Robert Beck was at the fore and carried off the first prize with his handsome bulls. R. Noel of Grass Valley and Jas. Askew of Placerville also showed fine herds of Jerseys and divided the honors with the valley breeders. Ayrshires, Devons, and other less prominent herds were present in the highest types. Appended is a list of the exhibits, and the premiums awarded:

#### Entries in Horse Department.

Thoroughbred stallions, 4 years and over, Wm. M. Murray, Tulare, Saml. Stephenson, by Thad Stevens—by Rifleman.

Wm. Boots, Milpitas, Nathan Coombs, by Lodi—Miama.

Geo. Hearst, San Francisco, Jim Brown, by Foster—Flush.

Three-year-olds, W. M. Murray, Tulare, Bird Catcher (brother to Modoc).

Two-year-olds, W. L. Pritchard, Berrian, by Bazaar—Avail.

Thoroughbred mares, 4 years old and over, Wm. Boots, Milpitas, Mollie H, by Wildidle—Mamie Hall.

Three-year-olds, A. M. Ottenback, Routier Station, Sacramento county, Lillie S, by Leinster—by Breckenridge.

Two-year-olds J. B. Haggin, Young Flush, by Leinster—Flush; ditto, Irene by Leinster, ditto—Irene Harding.

Yearlings, J. B. Haggin, Rosebella, by King Alphonso—Miranda; ditto, Joy, by Lever—Alix; ditto, Mariposa, Monarchist—Heliotrope; ditto, Faustini, by imported Glenelg—Marmot; ditto, Lina, by King Alphonso—Titania; ditto, Mileta, by Lever—Malta; ditto, Ginlietta, by Monarchist—Alert; ditto, Hirondelle, by imported Glenelg—Susie Linwood; ditto, Sweetbriar, by Virgil—Impudence; ditto, Schoolgirl, by Pat Malloy—Gleniune; ditto, My Love, by Virgil—Lightfoot; ditto, La Favorita, by Glenelg—Edeny.

Families not thoroughbred, sire and not less than 5 colts, S. S. Drake, Vallejo, Admiral and 10 colts, by Volunteer—Lady Pierson.

Families not thoroughbred, dam and not less than 2 colts, Wm. Bandeen, Hicksville, Dollie and 2 colts, by Tecumseh—by St. Clair.

Class 2, horses of all work, stallions, 4 years and over, W. A. Munnion, Dixon, Pedro, Jr., by Pedro—Kentucky Whip Stock.

J. Bassett, Elk Grove, Charlie, by Charlie—Unknown; ditto, Byron, by Charlie, ditto—unknown; ditto, Bob, by Charlie unknown.

A. Bellina, Haywards, Gen. Grant Jr., by Gen. Grant—Morgan Mare.

W. R. Cummington, Nicolaus, Montreal Telegraph, by Champion—Blanche; ditto, Levy Slaggard, by Capt. Slaggard—Lucy.

E. Comstock, Sacramento, Prince, by Sir Wm. Wallace—Polly.

A. Martin, Davisville, Yolo county, Frank Murphy, by Tam O'Shanter—Norman.

J. W. Chiles, Davisville, Joe, Joe Daniels—Unknown.

T. Van Vechten, Brighton, Sacramento county, Combination, by Vibrator—Hambeltonian.

J. B. Haggin, San Francisco, Admiral, an imported French stallion, three years old.

Wm. McClellan, Madison, Prince, Clydesdale—unknown.

J. Rassett, Elk Grove, John, by Charlie—Unknown.

A. D. Miller, Brighton, Hamilton, by Cal. Star—Nelson.

Two-year-olds, J. Rassett, Elk Grove, Prince, by Charlie—unknown.

A. Bellina, Haywards, Mayboy, by Gen. Grant Jr.—by Belmont.

P. J. Shafter, Olema, Black Prince, by Crown Prince—Runk mare.

Yearlings, S. W. Horn, Sutter Creek, Major Nelson, by Chieftain—by Nelson.

A. Bellina, Haywards, Frank, by Gen. Grant Jr.—by Rattler; ditto, Elijah Belmont, by Gen. Grant—Belmont mare.

For the next race there were great expectations, it being a post stake, a dash of three miles, $100 entrance, with $500 added, weight 100 pounds save for three-year-olds, they to carry 90 pounds. There were six entries, namely: W. Boots, Palo Alto Stock Farm, W. L. Pritchard, George Hearst, J. T. Gilmer and Stemler & Ayres. Now from this list it appeared as if Precious, Jim Brown, Red Boy and Fred Collier would all be started for this valuable stake, but the lovers of a well contested race were doomed to disappointment, as when the nominations closed on the Wednesday evening it was found that there were only three, Wm. Boots naming Mollie H; W. L. Pritchard, Captain Kidd, and Stemler & Ayres, Fred Collier. This race seemed almost a walk-over for Fred Collier and odds were freely laid at $100 to $15 in his favor but as a miniature simoon broke over the track just before the horses were called to the post, the quotations became rapidly reduced and $20 to $25 could be obtained on the field against $80 for Fred. There were several reasons adduced for the change, one being that Fred Collier had not quite recovered from his sickness, and that he would find it hard to go the distance at any kind of a good pace. Then there were some dark hints thrown out that Captain Kidd was a far better horse than he was given credit for, and that if he could be controlled he would give a good account of himself, but this he disproved, immediately he arrived at the post, as at the first false start he broke away and galloped nearly half a mile before he was got under control. Again the wind came whirling the sand up in countless eddies, and in such masses that sad havoc was played with the costumes of the ladies and children who crowded the grand stand, and at times the clouds of dust were so dense that no view could be obtained of the track on the opposite and upper turns, a strong presage of an approaching heavy rain storm. The race requires but very little description. Captain Kidd, apparently overpowering his jockey, rushed off at a terrible pace, and when he finished the first mile in 1:45½ with Fred and Mollie respectively twenty and twenty-five lengths behind, it was evident he could not keep up the pace, as already he showed signs of distress. Shortly after passing the grand stand the Captain began falling back and on the mid back stretch Fred Collier assumed the lead amid great applause and at the completion of the second mile in 3:38 he led Kidd by thirty lengths and soon after the latter fell back to the rear division, but Mollie H had no chance whatever to close the gap between her and the leader, and Fred won in 5:40 by a couple of hundred yards with Captain Kidd beaten off.

SUMMARY.

Same day—Post Stake, dash of three miles, free for all, $100 entrance, $500 added, weight 100 pounds, three-year-olds 90 pounds, second horse to receive $150, third $100. Starters to be named to the Secretary Wednesday evening, at or before 8 o'clock P. M., the subscribers being Wm. Boots, Palo Alto Stock Farm, W. L. Pritchard, George Hearst, J. T. Gilmer, and Stemler & Ayres.

| | |
|---|---|
| Stemler & Ayres name ch g Fred Collier, 4 years, by Joe Hooker, dam Puss, by Norfolk | 1 |
| Wm. Boots names b m Mollie H, 5 years, by Wildidle, dam Mamie Hall, by Norfolk | 2 |
| W. L. Pritchard names b c Captain Kidd, 3 years, by Leinster, dam Tibbie Dunbar | 3 |

Time—5:40.

The fourth race was a Consolation purse of $250 for beaten horses, entrance free, a mile and repeat, in which were nominated Maria F, Atalanta, May D and Jim Douglas; the entries being made immediately before the running of the Post Stake. As the meeting was drawing to a close in a betting point of view there was a general scramble among the talent either to make up their losses or to increase their little hoard in this race and betting was consequently very heavy while the mutual pools were, as in all running races, totally inadequate to the demand. Curious to relate, May D was made first choice, probably on a favorable answer to some private trial; but public form was far from being ignored and Maria L and Atalanta both had enthusiastic supporters while the fine running of Jim Douglas last year was not forgotten.

It was now 4:30; the sky again grew dark, clouds of dust raised by contesting winds blowing from all quarters, apparently, swept up and down the track, and filled the air so that one could not see a distance of fifty yards. Hats were blown across the paddock, light wraps wafted aloft, parasols reversed, plumes disarranged, bonnets crushed in, horse nets torn off or turned over the animals' heads, the cards on the judges' bulletin board torn down, and all sorts of light damage done. The people enjoyed the scene immensely, and cheered loudly every unlucky pedestrian who went scudding after his fleeing hat. Presently thunder was heard, sheet and forked lightning flashes athwart the lowering sky, and just as the Consolation race was called, down came the rain. Then there was one of the liveliest and most amusing scenes witnessed that has been recorded. Twelve hundred people in the paddock and on the course broke for cover, while the 7,000 under shelter poked all sorts of fun at them, and gave them sonorous and gratuitous advice how to dodge between the drops and pick themselves out of the sloppy mud of the track that developed in ten seconds after the down-pour began. For the next half hour, between the laughter of one side, and the chagrin of the other, the storm, mud, thunder and lightning, the dripping jockeys and the drenched pedestrians, there was merriment and entertainment enough to satisfy the most laughter-loving mortal ever born. The race was sent off in the midst of the rain, and part of it was run in mud hoof deep. The jockeys came in so covered with mud, and their faces so plastered with mother earth, that it was difficult to recognize them, while their silk and satin uniforms were fairly ruined. It was their own desire to run the race, despite the storm, for at one time the Board of Judges were on the point of ordering the race postponed.

As may be supposed there was not so much trouble sending the horses off as there was to get the jockeys out from the eaves that gave them shelter from the drenching rain. At the first trial they were dispatched to a somewhat straggling start, Atalanta forcing the pace at a furious rate and at every stride bespattering May D and Maria F, who were striving to get up with her, but in vain as she finished first in 1:44½, two lengths ahead of May D, with Jim Douglas a fair third. This was considered very fast time by those who had not had experience on the Eastern race courses, where it is known that when the rain has not the time to soak into the second and hard coating, the track is not made much heavier by a strong rain storm, as the effects are felt much more on the succeeding day. Atalanta now became the best choice, but there were a great many who freely backed Maria F, as she had shown rough, but good honest form all through the season, while the other two met with only lukewarm support. In the second heat Jim Douglas at first made the running and at the half mile post he just led the three others all bunched, but he could no longer keep the pace and resigned the first position to May D, who, as they rattled down the homestretch, looked a winner, but Maria F gradually overhauled her and beat her out in 1:47, with Atalanta a good third. There was now a great deal of betting on the final heat, Maria F selling for $60 against $10 for May D, and $25 for the other two combined. A prettier finale was never seen on a race course, Atalanta running up to Maria F for the lead and never being able to get more than the shortest of necks ahead, and thus at the hight of their speed they went around locked together as a team and as they entered the homestretch Atalanta was seen to give way a little and an excited trainer offered $100 to $10 that she was beaten, that was quickly taken up by one of the directors of the Blood Horse Association, and it looked as if the long odds were lost, as Atalanta, with great gameness, came again, but amid yells and applause, whipping and spurring, Maria F headed the race in 1:47 by the shortest of heads, the general belief being that the two fillies were so evenly matched that if Maria F. had held the outside position the result would have been reversed.

SUMMARY.

Consolation Purse, $250 for beaten horses; one mile and repeat; entrance free; second horse to receive $50.

| | | | |
|---|---|---|---|
| George Hearst names ch f Maria F, by Leinster, dam Flush, 3 years, 92 pounds | 4 | 1 | 1 |
| Theodore Winter names ch f Atalanta, by Norfolk, dam Lady Jane, 92 pounds | 1 | 3 | 2 |
| H. C. Judson names ch m May D, 4 years, by Wildidle, dam Nettie Brown, by Rifleman, 105 pounds | 2 | 2 | 3 |
| George Howson names b s Jim Douglas, 4 years, by Wildidle, dam by Norfolk, 108 pounds | 3 | 4 | 4 |

Time, 1:44½, 1:47, 1:47.

### Saturday.

Through reasons over which the Society had no control, the final day of the meeting did not possess those attractions that in some years caused the receipts at the Park to equal if not to exceed those of any previous day of the meeting. The first on the card was a double team race for a purse of $800 for the 2:40, class which fell through by reason of ailments in one horse in each team. Then the purse for the 2:19 class failed to fill and to take its place the directors offered a purse for runner of $350 for a mile and repeat race; that was the first one on the card and included in the entries were Nighthawk, Howell and Frank Rhoades, Maria F being withdrawn after her punishing race of the previous day. To use a very common but expressive word, there seemed to be a little "shenanagin" going on in regard to the betting in this race. On the evening before, there was some rivalry for first position between Howell and Nighthawk, the former selling at last as first favorite at $50 to $40 with $5 to Frank Rhoades. In the morning there was a good deal of useless cackle indulged in as to a rider being got at to throw a heat and other nonsense that induced Mr. Shafter to give the mount on Nighthawk to Howson a resolution that in the way of results was lamentable indeed as the mare is very difficult to manage, and as she was already somewhat sore and ill tempered, it is not astonishing that she could not run anywhere up to her previous bright record and consequently was beaten. But nevertheless Nighthawk was made a great favorite in the pools, selling for $100 against $65 for Howell and $10 for Frank Rhoades. The mare was terribly fractious, greatly delaying the start, but when the flag was dropped Frank rushed for the lead and held it for nearly half a mile and at that point the three were all on even terms, but on the home stretch Howell came away and won handily in 1:43½, Nighthawk a fair second. In the second and final heat Howell was a great favorite and he had a slight advantage under a pull, all the way round, and although Nighthawk made a desperate finish under whip and spur, Howell took the race easily in 1:45.

SUMMARY.

AGRICULTURAL PARK, SACRAMENTO, September 16,—Purse of $350, the second horse to receive the entries, five per cent. of the purse and the third horse $50; a mile and repeat.

| | | |
|---|---|---|
| Stemler & Ayres name b g Joe Howell, aged, by Bonnie Scotland dam Eva Sheppard, by imported Sovereign, 111 pounds | 1 | 1 |
| P. J. Shafter names b m Nighthawk, five years, by imported Haddington, dam by Norfolk, 111 pounds | 2 | 1 |
| W. H. Pritchard names b s Frank Rhoades, four years, by Leinster, dam Addie A., 103 pounds | 3 | 3 |

Time—1:43½, 1:45.

The next race for decision was the famous Occident Stake, in which of all the original entries only five made their third payments, and as they have all suffered more or less from the epizooty, there was but one that made her appearance and that was Bertha of the Palo Alto stable, and she walked over for the stakes and piece of plate presented by the Association.

SUMMARY.

Same day—Occident Stake for 1882, closed in 1881, and the third payments have been made on the following:

| | |
|---|---|
| Leland Stanford names b f Bertha, by Electioneer, dam American Girl, by Toronto Sontag | w o. |
| James M. Learned names b c Adrian, by Reliance, Dam by Kentucky Hunter | pd ft. |
| J. C. Simpson names b c Anteeo, by Electioneer, dam Columbine, by A. W. Richmond | pd ft. |
| H. Waldstein names b f Nellie W, by Electioneer, dam full sister to Aurora, by John Nelson | pd ft. |
| Leland Stanford names b c Benedt, by Gen. Benton, dam Lucetta, by Rysdyk's Hambletonian | pd ft. |

Next on the card was a race for gentlemen's saddle horses in which professional riders were barred. The entries were Prince, Truant, Nellie Woods, John and a chestnut horse without a name. At the drop of the flag the running was made by the two latter, but before they reached the half mile they were both pumped out and John took the lead, while Truant was gently held in reserve, and when, while well in the homestretch, he was let loose, he won with something to spare in 1:55, with Prince second two lengths ahead of John and Nellie Woods pulling up far in the rear. The race was well ridden on the winning and second horses.

SUMMARY

Gentlemen's Saddle Horse Race; Purse $100; dash of one mile; weight not less than 140 pounds. Professional riders barred.

| | |
|---|---|
| O. C. Jackson names ch b Truant | 1 |
| Fred Bridge name ch h Prince | 2 |
| Henry Clemp names b h John | 3 |
| B. W. Cavanaugh names ch h —— | 4 |
| J. L. Zuver names ch m Nellie Woods | 5 |

Time—1:55.

It had been announced that Wildflower would trot against her record of 2:21, but she in turn was suffering from the prevailing complaint and she was merely shown in the track, where her fine and graceful form elicited many favorable comments.

The last was an arranged race for a purse of $600, in which Honesty was whooped up into the first position, and until the contest was at an end he was almost always the favorite and his sanguine backers realized that "Honesty is not always the best policy." He sold for $80 against $25 for Ashley and a like amount for the field, in which were Cairo, Del Sur and Tump Winston. Why Ashley should sell over Cairo as second favorite was a conundrum no one could understand, and before the race was over many regretted that they had not followed the British example and "taken Cairo." The first heat was all between Del Sur and Ashley, and the former beat the latter out by a length in 2:25¾, and at double that length came Cairo, and then the favorite, with Winston last. In the second heat Del Sur again made the pace but with a bad break he resigned the position to Ashley who in turn was lapped at the half mile and then passed by Cairo, who finished a pretty heat first in 2:26½, two lengths ahead of Tump Winston, with Honesty a fair third. At last

Under one year, A. Bellina, Haywards—Rowdy Boy, by Gen. Grant Jr. by—Belmont; ditto, Butt Out, by Gen. Grant —by Belmont.

Horses of all work, mares, four years and over, J. Bassett, Elk Grove, Lucy, by Charlie—unknown.

A. Bellina, Haywards, Dollie, unknown—unknown.

E. Comstock, Sacramento, Coalie, by Old John Nelson— Pollie.

S. S. Drake, Vallejo, Eva, by Admiral—unknown.

A. D. Miller, Brighton, Lucy Gray, by Senator—Hambletonian; ditto, Perch, by Idol—Black Hawk and Messenger.

Four years old and over with colt, M. Wick, Oroville, Fly and colt, Clydesdale—Potomac mare.

Two-year-olds, S. S. Drake, Vallejo, Mary, by Admiral —unknown.

Yearlings, B. E. Harris, San Francisco, Abbottine, by Abbotsford—Lena Bowles.

R. Brown, Brighton, Fanny, by Franklin—Messenger.

Sucking colt, E. Comstock, Sacramento, Lena, by Leinster —Cora.

Class 3, draft horses, stallions, four years and over, A. J. Ogden, Woodland, Tam O'Shanter, by T. O'Shanter—unknown J. Coonrod, Davisville, Norman, by imported Cupid— Young America; T. Skillman, Petaluma, Tornado, by imported St. Lawrence—imported Eureka; A. H. Thomassen, Routier Station, Highland Laddie, by Wm. Wallace—by Laboo; T. Williamson, Sacramento, Honest Tom, by Tom Thumb— Maud; C. Porter, Marysville, Conqueror, by Conqueror—St. Lawrence mare; H. H. Wilson, Nicolaus, St. Lawrence, by Champion Bell Eyre—St. Lawrence mare; J. B. Haggin, San Francisco, Black Prince, by imported Shire Horse.

Three-year-olds, R. J. Merkley Sacramento, Normandy II by Normandy—Nellie; A. J. Pierce, Petaluma, Charlemagne, by Duke de Chartres—Susie Ross; P. H. Murphy, Brighton, Grey Eagle, by Normandy—Black Maria.

Yearlings, R. J. Ourrey, Dixon, Nimbus, by Duke of Mayoss—Clydesdale mare; T. Skillman, Petaluma, Model, by Tornado—Lucy

Under one year old, R. J. Ourrey, Dixon, Chief, by Duke of Mayoss—Mag; E. Comstock, Sacramento, Maje, by Grey Eagle—Maud.

Draft horses, mares, four years and over, with colt, R. J. Ourrey, Dixon, Mag and colt, by Tam O'Shanter—unknown; R. J. Merkley, Sacramento, Nellie and colt, by Lafayette— English draft mare; E. Comstock, Sacramento, May and colt, by Sir Tom Wallace—Polly.

Four years and over without colt, C. Thodt, Dixon, Fanny, pedigree unknown; ditto, Daisy, by Norman—unknown; E. Comstock, Sacramento, Maud, by Sir Tom Wallace—Polly.

Three-year-olds, C. Thodt, Dixon, Lucy—pedigree unknown.

Two-year-olds, R. J. Merkley, Sacramento, Fanchon, by Normandy—Nellie.

Yearling, T. Skillman, Petaluma, Gertrude, by Tornado— unknown; A. H. Thomassen, Routier's Station, Lady St. Patrick, by Highland Laddie—unknown.

Sucking colt, R. J. Merkley, Sacramento, Juanita, by Sir Archer—Nellie; A. H. Thomassen, Routier's Station, Jennie, by Highland Laddie—unknown.

Roadsters, stallions four years and over, Jno. Denton, Grass Valley, Don Castor, by Elmo—Lady Emile; H. Webster, Sacramento, Jack Wilson, by Jno. Wilson, Flag of Truce, by Messenger; A. T. Hatch, Suisun, Admar, by Admiral—Bruna; J. Fitzgerald, Woodland, Killarney, by Black Ralph—Eclipse mare; F. J. Shafter, Olema, Rustic, by Whipple's Hambletonian—by Belmont; Wm. Rawson, Woodland, Victor, by Echo—by Woodburn; J. B. Haggin, San Francisco, Zulu Chief, by Mohawk Chief—Sallie Cone Up; W. E. Robinson, Santa Ana, Odd Fellow, by Echo—Theoria; M. W. Hicks, Florin, Sacramento county, Prompter, by Blue Bull— Prairie Bird.

Three-year-olds W. M. Murray, Tulare, Fresno Boy, by Monday—unknown; ditto, Sorrel Frank, by Fatchen—by Belmont; ditto, William W, by Washington—by Signal; M. W. Hicks, Florin, Starling by Egmont—by Flaxtail.

Two-year-olds, A. M. Otterbeck, Routier's Station, Rival, by Buccaneer—by Compromise; J. M. Learned, Stockton, Harmony, by Reliance—by Kentucky Hunter; Wm. Ingram, Lemoore, Tulare county, Almora, by Algonis—Oregon mare; S. S. Drake, Vallejo, Argenta, by Admiral—by Speculation; Standard, by Admiral—by Mohawk; J. A. McCloud, Stockton, Judge Fatchen by Nephew—by Chieftain; A. D. Miller, Brighton, Sacramento county, Young Dushaw, by Buccaneer—Tecumseoh; M. W. Hicks, Florin, Privateer, by Buccaneer—by Marion.

Yearlings, H. Webster, Sacramento, ch e, by Jack Wilson— unknown; ditto, Jack Wilson—unknown; J. C. Hasty, Chico, California Chief, by Buccaneer—Volcian; ditto, Chico by Buccaneer, by Reno; B. F. True, Chico, Ralph T, by Buccaneer— Harkaway; L. G. Ross, San Gabriel, br c, by Sultan—Gertrude; S. S. Drake, Vallejo, Aleck, by Admiral—by Ventura; A. J. Frost, Sacramento, Roscoe, by Brigadier—Flora F.

Sucking colts, B. F. True, Chico, Ben T, by Singleton— Harkaway; B. E. Harris, San Francisco, Style, by Del Sur—by Tenbrook; ditto, Littleton, by Arkburton—Smoothbriar; S. S. Drake, Vallejo, Amateur, by Admiral—Mary; R. H. Newton, Woodland, Del Sur Jr., by Del Sur—by Black Ralph.

Roadsters, mares, four years and over, G. W. Hancock, Sacramento, Jennie St. Clair, by old St. Clair—by Livingston; ditto, Lolo, Nelson, by Jno. Nelson—unknown; J. M. Learned, Stockton, Ollie Ray, by Reliance—by Signal; S. Tutt, Cottonwood, Yolo county, Katie, by Dietz' St. Clair—by Tom Moore; C. Younger, Forest Home, Fanny, by Black Eagle—Black Maria; P. Van Nechsen, Brighton, Nelly by Liberator—Morgan mare; W. J. O'Brien, Sacramento, Allie Ray, by Tecumseh— Messenger mare; M. W. Hicks, Florin, Pearl, by Blue Bull— by Flaxtail.

Three-year-olds, S. Tutt, Cottonwood, Yolo county, Susie, by Tortillote—Dietz' St. Clair; J. B. McDonald, Marysville, Hazel Kirke, by Brigadier—by Jim Brown; S. S. Drake, Vallejo, o, Sister, by Admiral—Black Flora.

Two-year-olds, J. B. McDonald, Marysville, Yuba Maid, by Brigadier—Reese River; J. B. Haggin, S. F., Lady Gray, by Algona—by Jack Hawkins.

Yearlings, B. E. Harris, S. F., Rose Abbott, by Abbotsford— Young Rosedale; S. S. Drake, Vallejo, Flora, by Admiral— Flora; M. Toomey, Brighton, Minnie Toomey, by Adonis— Lady Brighton; M. W. Hicks, Florin, Clara, by Buccaneer —by Wayland Forest; ditto, Cora, by Buccaneer—by Blue Bull.

Sucking colts, G. W. Hancock, Sacramento, Daisy, by Nutwood—Jennie St. Clair; ditto, Thela, by Nutwood—Lola Nelson; S. S. Drake, Vallejo, Peggie, by Admiral—unknown.

Class 5, carriage horses, matched span, B. Madden, Dixon, Peanut and Pop Corn, by Challenge, Young Nelson—unknown; W. R. S. Foye, Sacramento, Frank and Charles, by Challenge—Morgan mare.

Class 6, roadster teams, H. Stegall, Woodland, Ralph sis-

ters, by Black Ralph—dam unknown; A. H. Thomassen, Routier's Station, Jane, unknown—by Laboo; ditto, Lena T, Hambletonian—Morgan Blackhawk.

Class 7, standard trotters, stallions, four years old and over, J. B. Haggin, S. F., Alaska, by Electioneer—Lucy.

Yearlings, J. A. McCloud, Stockton, Mt. Vernon, by Nutwood—Chieftain.

Standard trotters, mares, E. E. Miller Jr., S. F., Adella, by Fred Low—Addie Lee; J. B. Haggin, S. F., Woodbine, by Electioneer—Woodbine.

Class 8, saddle horses, B. E. Harris, S. F., Mike Price, by Irvington—Min Price; Vanity, by Belmont—Big Lize; W. S. Enos, Davisville, Finto, by Dick Turpin—Nellie.

Class 9, sweepstakes horses, stallions, J. B. Haggin, S. F., Echo, by Rysdyk's Hambletonian—by Magnolia; Algona, by Almont—Emma Kincaid.

Sweepstakes horses, mares, R. J. Merkley, Sacramento, Nellie, by Lafayette—English draft mare; J. B. Haggin, S. F., Woodbine, by Electioneer—Woodbine.

Class 10, jacks, four years and over, W. A. Munnion, Dixon, Jno. Henry by imp. Mammoth; J. Coonrod, Davisville, Black Jack—pedigree unknown.

Three years old. L. U. Shippee, Stockton, Castilian, by Sure John—Carlisle.

Yearling, L. U. Shippee, Stockton, Duchess, by Royal Duke—Revelle; Beauty, by Goliah—by blk Warrior.

Mules, best span, W. Miner, Davisville, Collo and Jamie, by Merritt's Jack—dam unknown.

## Cattle

Durhams, E. Comstock, Sacramento, 3 head; P. H. Murphy, Brighton, 4 head; R. J. Merkley, Sacramento, 8 head; M. Wick, Sacramento, 13 head; C. Younger, Forest Home, 20 head.

Jerseys, Henry Pierce, San Francisco, 23 head; Robert Beck, San Francisco, 12 head; R. Noel, Grass Valley, 12 head; F. Stadtch, Sacramento, 9 head; Jas. Askew, Placerville, 6 head; J. Lyon, Placerville, 4 head; Wm. Hook, Sacramento, 2 head; M. W. Clitus, Jas Jose, 1 head; P. F. Lowell, Sacramento, 1 head; a. Landers, Sacramento, 1 head.

Devons, R. McEnespy, Chico, 7 head; C. M. Bryant, Chico, 1 head.

Ayrshires, George Bement, Redwood City, 10 head.

Guernseys, Henry Pierce, San Francisco, 6 head.

Herds, Durham old herds, C. Younger and M. Wick; young herds, C. Younger and M. Wick.

Jerseys, old herds, Henry Price and R. Noel; young herd, Henry Price.

Guernsey herd, Henry Price.

Devon herd, R. McEnespy.

Ayrshire herd, George Bement.

Sweepstakes, cattle, best bull, C. Younger and M. Wick.

Best bull and three of his calves, C. Younger and M. Wick.

Milch cows, George Bement and J. Askew.

Fat cattle, C. Younger and M. Wick.

## Sheep

French Merinos, J. R. Branton, Reno, Nev., 1 head.

Spanish Merinos, J. H. Strowbridge, Haywards, 13 head; F. Bullard, Woodland, 13 head.

Shropshires, J. B. Hoyt, Suisun, 12 head.

Cotswolds, C. Younger, Forest Home, 26 head.

Southdowns, Geo. Bement, Redwood City, 1 head.

Crossed sheep, J. B. Hoyt, Suisun, 10 head.

Sheep, sweepstakes, J. H. Strowbridge and F. Bullard.

## Swine

Berkshires, Thomas Waite, Brighton, 2 head; John Rider, Sacramento, 10 head; J. Kennedy, Sacramento, 1 head.

Poland China, E. Gallup, Hanford, 14 head; Jos. Melvin, Davisville, 5 head.

Swine, sweepstakes, best boar, John Rider; best sow, John Rider; best pen of six pigs, J. Melvin, Davisville; John Rider, Sacramento; M. Sprague, Sacramento.

Family of nine, John Rider and J. Melvin.

## Poultry

Chickens, T. Morris, Sonoma, 15 pairs; R. G. Head, Napa, 4 pairs; Thomas Waite, Brighton, 8 pairs; J. Coonrod, Davisville, 2 pairs; J. E. Roberts, Sacramento, 1 pair; F. S. George, Sacramento, 1 pair.

Turkeys, T. D. Morris, Sonoma, 1 pair; R. G. Head, Napa, 1 pair.

Ducks, Thomas Waite, Brighton, 1 pair; B. G. Cosby, Sacramento, 1 pair; R. G. Head, Napa, 1 pair.

Geese, T. D. Morris, Sonoma, 1 pair; T. D. Morris, Sonoma, 3 pairs.

## Premiums—Horses.

Class 1, Thoroughbred horses, stallions, best three-year-old, Jim Brown owned by George Hearst, $40. Second best, Nathan Coombs owned by William Boots, Milpitas, $20.

Mares, best four-year-old, Mollie H. owned by William Boots, Milpitas, $40.

Best two-year-old, Irena, owned by J. B. Haggin, $15; second best two-year-old, Young Flush owned by J. B. Haggin, $7 50.

Best yearling, School Girl, owned by J. B. Haggin, $10; second best yearling, old Hirondell, owned by J. B. Haggin, $5.

Animals not thoroughbred, stallion and five colts, Admiral and five colts, owned by S. S. Drake, Vallejo, $50; dam and two colts, owned by William Sandeen, Hicksville.

Class 2, horses of all work, stallions, best four-year-old, Admiral, owned by J. B. Haggin, $40.

Best two years old and over, General Grant Jr., owned by A. Bellina, Haywards, $30.

Best three-year-old, John, owned by J. Bassett, Elk Grove, $30.

Best two-year-old, Prince, owned by P. J. Shafter, Olema; second best two-year-old, Prince, owned by Wm. McClellan, Madison, Yolo county, $15.

Best yearling, Major Nelson, owned by G. W. Horn, Sutter Creek, $15; second best yearling, Frank, owned by A. Bellina, Haywards, $7 50.

Mares, best four years old and over, Coalie, owned by E. Comstock, Sacramento, $40; second best four years old and over, Eva, owned by S. S. Drake, Vallejo, $15;

Best two-years-old and over, Mary, owned by S. S. Drake, Vallejo, $15; best yearling, Abbottine, owned by B. E. Harris, San Francisco, $10; second best yearling, Fannie, owned by R. Brown, Brighton, $5.

Best sucking colt, Lena, owned by E. Comstock, Sacramento, $10.

Class 3, draft horses, stallions, best four years old and over, Tornado, owned by T. Skillman, Petaluma, $40. Second best two years old and over, Black Prince, owned by J. B. Haggin, $30.

Best three-year-old, Normandy 2, owned by R. J. Merklen, Sacramento, $30. Second best three-year-old, Charlemagne, owned by A. J. Price, Petaluma, $15.

Best two-year-old, Monarch, owned by T. Skillman, Petaluma, $20; second best two-year-old Billie, owned by E. Comstock, Sacramento, $10.

Best yearling, Nimbus, owned by R. J. Ourrey, Dixon, $15.

Best under one year, Grey Chief, owned by R. J. Curry, Dixon, $10; second best under one year old, Maje, owned by E. Comstock, Sacramento, $5.

Sweepstakes, best stallion, Al Gona, owned by J. B. Haggin, $100, or silver pitcher; best mare, Woodbine, owned by J. B. Haggin, $100, or silver pitcher.

Roadsters, stallions, best yearling and over, Rustic, owned by F. J Shafter, $40; second, Zulu Chief, owned by J. B. Haggin, $20.

Best three-year-old, Starling, owned by M. W; Hicks, $30.

Best yearling, Privateer, owned by M. W. Hicks, $20; second, Almora, owned by Wm. Ingram.

Best yearling, California Chief, owned by J. C. Hasty, $15; second, Roscoe, owned by A. J. Frost.

Best sucking colt, Del Sur Jr., owned by R. H. Newton, of Woodland, $10; second, Ben T, owned by B. F. True.

Mares, best four years old and over, Maggie A, owned by W. J. O'Brien, $40; second, Allie Ray, owned by J. M. Learned.

Best three-year-old, Hazel Kirke, owned by J. B. McDonald, $30; second, Tartilote, owned by S. Tutt.

Best two-year-old, Lady Gray, owned by J. B. Haggin, $20; second, Yuba Maid, J. B. McDonald.

Best yearling, Clara, M. W. Hicks, $10; second, Cora, M. W. Hicks.

Sucking colt, Daisy, George W. Hancock, $10; second, Theta, George W. Hancock.

Mares, best four years old and over, with colt, Nellie and colt, owned by R. J. Merkley, Sacramento, $40; second best four years old and over, with colt, May and colt, owned by E. Comstock, Sacramento, $15.

Best four years old and over, Fannie, owned by C. Thodt, Dixon; second best four years old and over, Maud, owned by E. Comstock, Sacramento, $15.

Best three-year-old, Lucy, owned by C. Thodt, Dixon, $30.

Best two-year-old, Fanchon, owned by R. J. Merkley, Sacramento, $15.

Best yearling, Gertrude, owned by T. Skillman, Petaluma, $10.

Best sucking colt, Juanita, owned by R. J. Merkley, $10; second best sucking colt, Jennie, owned by A. H. Thomassen, Routier Statror.

Class 5, best matched span carriage horses, owned and used as such by one person, Frank and Charley, owned by W. R. S. Foye, Sacramento, silver goblet or $40; second best ditto, Peanut and Popcorn, owned by B. Madden, Dixon, silver goblet or $20.

Class 6, Best double-team roadsters, owned and used as such by one person, Ralph Sisters, owned by H. Stegall, Woodland, silver goblet or $40. Second best ditto, Jane and Lena T, owned by A. A. Thomassen, Routier Station, silver goblet or $20.

Class 7, standard trotters, stallions, best four years old and over, Alaska, owned by J. B. Haggin, $40.

Best yearling, Mount Vernon, owned by J. A. McCloud, Stockton, $15.

Mares, Best four yearsold and over, Woodbine, owned by J. B. Haggin, $40; second best, Adalin, owned by E. H. Miller Jr., $25.

Class 8, saddle horses, best saddle horse, Vanity, owned by Benjamin E. Harris, $25; second best, Mike Price, owned by Benjamin E. Harris, $10.

Class 9, jacks, best four years old and over, John Henry, owned by W. A. Munnion, Dixon, $40; second best, Black Jack, owned by J. Conrad, Davis, $20.

Best three years old, Castilian, owned by L. U. Shippee, Stockton, $30.

Jennies, best four years old and over, Beauty, owned by L. U. Shippee, Stockton, $30; second best, owned by L. U. Shippee, Stockton, $15.

Mules, best span, Charlie and Jennie, owned by N. Miner, Davis, $35.

Walking match for draft stallions, St. Lawrence, owned by H. H. Wilson, Sacramento, second best, Conqueror, owned C. Porter, Marysville.

## Cattle

Devons, bulls, best three year old and over, Ben Butler, premium, R. McEnespy.

Cows, best three years old and over, Queen, owned by C. M. Bryant, first premium; Mayflower, second premium, owned by R. McEnespy.

Best two years old, Maud, premium, owned by R. McEnespy.

Best yearling, Spry, premium, owned by R. McEnespy.

Best heifer calf, Trixie, premium, R. McEnespy.

Ayrshires, bulls, best three years old and over, Archie, premium, George Bement.

Best two-year-old, Lindo, premium, George Bement.

Best yearling, Macbeth, premium, George Bement.

Best bull calf, Malcomb, premium, George Bement.

Cows, best three years over, Stella, first premium, George Bement; also Ethel Brown, second premium.

Best three-year-old, Stellitita, premium, George Bement.

Best yearling, Sultana, premium, George Bement.

Best heifer calf, Sybil, premium, George Bement.

Herds, Durham, best herd of Durham thoroughbreds over two years old, consisting of one male and four females, owned by one person, C. Younger, first premium; M. Wick, second prem.

Best herd of thoroughbred Durham cattle under two years, consisting of one male and four females, owned by one person, C. Younger, first premium; M. Wick, second.

Jerseys, best herd over two years old, consisting as above, and same conditions, first premium, Henry Pierce; second premium, R. Noell.

Best herd under two years old, same conditions, Henry Pierce first premium.

Guernsey cattle, best herd of any age, consisting of same conditions as to number and ownership, Henry Pierce, first premium.

Devous, best herd of any age, same conditions, R. McEnespy, premium.

Ayrshires, best herd, under same conditions, George Bement premium.

Alderney, Jerseys and Guernseys in one class, bulls, best three year olds and over, Buffalo Bill, Robert Beck owner, first premium; General Grant, J. Askew owner, second premium.

Best two-year-old, Commodore, first premium, R. Noell owner; Garfield, second premium, J. Lyon.

Best yearling William of Solitude, first premium, Henry Pierce owner; Fred Baker, second premium, owned by William Hook.

Best bull calf, Shotover, first premium, Henry Pierce owner; Buffalo Bill, second premium, Robert Beck owner.

Cows, best three years old and over, Daisy, first premium, Henry Pierce owner; Katie, second premium, R. Noell owner.

Best two-year-old, Miss Murdock, first premium, Robert Beck owner; Nellie, second premium, R. Noell, owner.

Best yearling, Carrie, first premium, Henry Pierce owner; First Duke of Eldorado, second premium, J. Askew owner.

Best heifer calf, Paragon, first premium, R. Noell owner; Olita, second premium, P, Stanton owner.

Cows, best three years old and over, Rose, premium, R. J. Mockley.

Best two-year-old, Chut, premium, E. Comstock.

Best yearling, Blossom, premium, P. J. Murphy.

Best heifer calf, Pink, premium, J. Lyon.

Sweepstakes, best bull of any age or breed, Second Duke of Alameda, first premium, C. Younger.

Best cow of any age or breed, Gem, first premium, M. Wick.

Best bull and three of his calves under one year old, second, Duke of Alameda, three calves, first premium.

**Swine.**

Swine, best boar, two years or over, prize $20, awarded to Prince, owned by J. Kennedy; second prize, $10, Jolly, owned by John Rider.

Berkshire best breeping sow, first prize, Maud Hamilton, owned by John Rider; second prize, Pacific Queen, owned by Thomas Waite.

Best pair of pigs under ten months, first prize, Nimbus and Laguna, owned by John Rider;

Poland-China boars, first premium, King of Bonnieview, owned by E. Galley.

Best six months old and under one year, first premium, John, entered by J. M. Davis; second prize, Black Boy, owned by E. Gallup.

Poland-China breeding sows, first prize, Cantilina, owned by E. Gallup; second prize, Daisy, owned by J. M. Davis.

Sweepstakes, best boar, first premium, John Rider.

Also for best sow.

Best pen of six pigs, M. Sprague, first premium.

**Poultry.**

Best pair of light brahmas, first premium, T. D. Morris and A. G. Head.

Best pair of dark brahmas, premium, T. D. Morris.

Cochin partridges, first premium, Thos. Waite.

Black cochins, first premium, T. D. Morris.

Silver Spangled Hamburgs, first premium, Thomas Waite.

White Leghorns, Thomas Waite.

White-faced, Beack Spanish, first premium, T. D. Morris.

Plymouth Rock, first premium, R. G. Head.

Houdans, premium, Thomas Waite.

Golden Seabrights, premium, Thomas Waite.

Bronze turkeys, premium, R. G. Head.

Pekin ducks, premium, R. G. Head.

Rouen ducks, R. G. Head.

Toulouse geese, premium, T. D. Morris.

Bremen geese, premium, T. D. Morris.

China geese, premium, T. D. Morris.

Langshans, premium, R, G. Head.

## The Stockton Fair.

The rain on Saturday last put the finishing touch on the track and it could scarcely have been in better condition to make fast time in the trotting contests. Too hard, perhaps for the gallopers, and rather too much so for working even the trotters upon, but yet the soaking had given it considerable elasticity, and still the surface was beautifully smooth. The time of the various contests proves, that the course was in the right order, and that the managers were anxious that the premiums offered for bettering the specified time should be awarded. The weather has been delightful and the chances for grumbling narrowed to a minimum. The crowds in attendance were as orderly, probably more so, than a convention of ministers, and everything gone off smoothly. From the following account it will be seen that there was little chance for complaint.

The first race on the card was "District Running," for three-year-olds and over, heats of a mile, for a purse of $500. Jack Douglas, Sam Stevenson, Bird Catcher, Joe Daniels Jr., Pic Nic, Minnie Belle and Lady Partisan came to the post. Pools, Jack Douglas $60, Sam Stevenson $20, Bird Catcher $12, field $38. After considerable maneuvering a tolerable start was effected and they were sent away for the first heat.

When the flag fell Stevenson showed a facility in starting not possessed, or at least exercised, by any other horse in the field. Almost before the flag had touched the ground he was a clear two lengths in advance and when the first turn came he had increased the advantage to four lengths. At this point Duffy took his horse in hand and he ran steadily down the back stretch, having a strong lead at the half with Bird-Catcher, Jack Douglas, Joe Davis Jr. and Pic Nic well together in the order named, Minnie Belle and Lady Partisan further back. In the farther turn Minnie Belle parted company with Lady Partisan and moved up to the second tier and at the three-quarter mark there was a general draw of whips on all but Stevenson. The gap was closed partially in the run home but Duffy merely slackened his pull a little and sitting in his saddle like a centaur landed the son of old Thad under the wire, winner by two lengths, Bird Catcher second, Jack Douglas third, Joe Daniels Jr. fourth, Pic Nic fifth, Minnie Belle sixth, Lady Partisan distanced. Time, 1:45. Pools, Stevenson $40, Jack Douglas $10, field $9. The Paris Mutuals ($2 50) paid first heat $7 70; second heat $4 40; Killip & Co.'s book not open.

At the start Stevenson went to the fore with the same readiness displayed in the preceding heat and the general outline of the running was much the same: Stevenson in hand, the field urged to their utmost. Result, Stevenson first, Jack Douglas second, Bird Catcher third, Minnie Belle fourth, Joe Daniels Jr. fifth, Pic Nic sixth. Time, 1:45½.

**SUMMARY.**

SAN JOAQUIN VALLEY FAIR, STOCKTON, Sept. 19.--District running, for three-year-olds, and 1 mile heats, purse $500, four moneys.

| | | |
|---|---|---|
| W. M. Murray names ch h Sam Stevenson, by Thad Stevens--dam by Rifleman, 5 years, 114 lbs, Duffy | 1 | 1 |
| Jack Douglas names ch h Jack Douglas, by Wildidle--Lady Clare, 5 years, 114 lbs, Ross | 3 | 2 |
| C. Dorsey names br c Bird Catcher, by Specter--Pet, 3 years, 95 lbs Howson | 2 | 3 |
| J. N. Randall names ch g Joe Daniels Jr., by Joe Daniels--Julia, 5 years, 111 lbs. Ross | 4 | 4 |
| J. A. Shepherd names g m Minnie Belle, by Joe Daniels--by Norfolk, 3 years, 92 lbs, White | 6 | 4 |
| John Miller names br m Pic Nic, by Joe Daniels--by Norfolk, 4 years, 105 lbs, Glade | 5 | 6 |
| A. Miller names b m Lady Partisan, by Partisan--Sister to Tommy Chandler, 3 years, 92 lbs, Whitcock | dis | |

Time--1:46, 1:45½.

W. L. Ashe's br g Reel Terry, by California—Laura Barnes; G. W. Trahern's ch m Kate Carson, by Joe Daniels—by Norfolk; Seth Peyton's b g Geo. Bender, by ———, dam Sugar Plum; W. E. Pigott's br c Idler, by Wildidle--Kate Gift; were named in the race but did not start.

The second event was the purse for trotters of the 2:36 class. This race closed with fourteen nominations but various causes had brought the field down to four actual starters. Prominent among these causes were the pinkeye and the superior prowess of Manon. But the race itself was another evidence that no man holds the world in his hand even though he does own a speedy trotter. Manon met with inglorious defeat and had figures marked upon the board that it was beyond her power to reach. After the first heat of Tuesday it seemed as though there was nothing in the race; Manon, Vanderlynn, Frank Moscow and Big Lize were to start, and sporting men took too much stock in the doctrine of accidents to lay dollars against cents on a three in five race. Later on the announcement that Mr. Goldsmith would drive Vanderlynn brought about a change. Mr. Goldsmith is fortunate in the possession of a circle of friends who repose the utmost confidence in his abilities and his honesty. No doubt he deserves it as many of those who thus regard him are gentlemen of discrimination and judgment. His success with Cairo at Sacramento last Saturday seemed to indicate that his fingers know just the touch for "bucking" trotters, and when it was settled that he would drive on Tuesday there was money ready to be laid on Vanderlynn. It was an untried experiment and the odds were long but there was quite an active business done in the pool rooms at the rate of $30 for Manon, $16 for Vanderlynn and $7 for the field. When the horses were called there was a little difficulty in getting off, caused by the bad behavior of Big Lize. When the bell did tap it was on a good start and the business began at once. Vanderlynn went to the front with a spurt and Manon left her feet almost at the same time. She did not lose by the break and at the quarter, which Vanderlynn touched in 36, Manon was close behind, Frank Moscow a good third and Big Lize in difficulty ten lengths in the rear. On the back stretch Big Lize went to pieces and lost her hope of saving distance. At the half in 1:11 Vanderlynn had two lengths the lead, and around the turn the little mare made a brush for him and broke at his wheel as they reached the three-quarter pole and Vanderlynn carried off the honors of the heat, Manon second, Frank Moscow third, Big Lize distanced. Time, 2:22.

In the pools Manon was put into the field and business opened with Vanderlynn $30, field $23, but gradually changed until when the names were called the prevailing rate was Vanderlynn $30, field $40. When the bell struck Manon left her feet and ran a full eighth of a mile before McCartney got her to a trot again. In the meantime Vanderlynn was going lively and passed the half in 37½, two lengths ahead of the mare; at the half in 1:13 there was no change, but on the turn Manon broke again and Moscow followed her example. Vanderlynn swung into the stretch with the heat already won and came to the score four lengths in advance of Manon, Moscow four lengths further back. Time—2:25½.

Vanderlynn stock had now taken a boom and the closing sales before the start were three to one in his favor. It was a heat of breaks. At the outset Manon broke badly and ran three hundred yards. Soon after passing the quarter Vanderlynn made a vicious break, going to the rear, and for the first time Moscow was in front. On the far turn Vanderlynn broke again and Manon and Moscow were left to fight it out in their own way. Manon settled and overhauled Moscow with a steady stride bringing her to the mile in 2:28, Moscow second, Vanderlynn third.

Vanderlynn's behavior in the third heat braced the field up somewhat, and the last sales were Vanderlynn $25, field $16. At the word Manon broke and made another long run gaining perceptibly and almost moving past Vaderlynn, who had got away first. After passing the quarter Vanderlynn made a break but soon settled and at the half the three went in a bunch, Manon showing her head in front. Around the turn Moscow fell to the rear, and at the three-quarter pole Manon and Vanderlynn were on even terms, but in the trot up the stretch the pace got hot and the mare broke, leaving Vanderlynn to win the heat and race as suited him. Manon second, Moscow third. Time, 2:26½. The Paris mutuals paid, first heat, $7:65; second heat, $4:35; fourth heart, $2:95.

**SUMMARY.**

Same Day.—Pacific Coast Trotting; 2:36 class. Purse $1,000 and $200 added if more than ten entries. Four moneys.

| | | | | |
|---|---|---|---|---|
| P. Farrell names b h Vanderlynn | 1 | 1 | 3 | 1 |
| P. Coutts names b m Manon | 2 | 2 | 1 | 2 |
| H. B. Cooper names b h Frank Moscow | 3 | 3 | 3 | 3 |
| W. H. Henderson names b m Big Lize | dis | | | |

Time—2:22, 2:25½, 2:28, 2:26½.

F. S. Hatch's Blacksmith Boy, G. Bernard's Allen Boy, W. Z. Price's San Mateo Belle, John McIntyres' Edwin Forest, C. H. Shears' Slim Jim, James Garlands' Rowdy Boy, L. H. Titus' Exile, G. W. Trahern's Revolution, Louis Duncans' Louis D, and S. Crandall's Blanche were drawn.

The third race was a mile trot for yearlings. No. 5 on the society's programme was called and decided between heats of the last race. Only two appeared, L. U. Shippee's ch f (sister to Honesty), by Priam and J. H. McCloud's b h Mt. Vernon, by Nutwood. They started off more after the manner of older horses and Mr. Shippee's filly was an easy winner. Time, 3:03. Mt. Vernon's time, 3:09.

**Second Day.**

On Wednesday the day was pleasanter if possible than on Tuesday and the attendance at the grand stand and carriage parks was large and extremely brilliant and fashionable. On account of the late arrival of some of the stock for exhibition and the difficulty in making room for it all in due season the first parade was postponed till Thursday. The interest centered on the races, of which there were three on the programme. The first number was a mile dash for two-year-olds owned in the district and it was a slow race for the speculators. G. W. Trahern's Certiorari, T. H. Williams Jr's Bryant W, D. S. Terry's, Lara and Jas. F. Mahon's Gracie Mahon started, the odds being so long on Certiorari as to preclude betting although a few outsiders who had noted his indifferent performance at Sacramento last week laid a little money against him. When the starters' flag fell the position was only tolerable. Bryant W cut out the running at once, the other three being willing he should do so to all appearances. At the quarter in 27 and the half in 52¼ Bryant W was first, Gracie Mahon second, Certiorari third, and Lara last, all running in a line. Around the turn they closed in a bunch and the favorite in a few strides placed himself in front. Turning the three-quarters Certiorari left them rapidly and galloped under the wire, winning by ten lengths, Lara second, Bryant W third, Gracie Mahon fourth. Time—1:48. Pools, Certiorari $25 to $20, Bryant, W $16 to 10, field $9 to $7. The Paris mutuals paid $5 90.

**SUMMARY.**

SAN JOAQUIN VALLEY FAIR, STOCKTON, Wednesday, September 20.--District running for two-year-olds; miledash; purse $400; four moneys.

| | |
|---|---|
| G. W. Traherne names ch g Certiorari by Joe Daniels--by Norfolk 97 lbs; Whitlock | 1 |
| D. S. Terry names ch g Lara by Joe Daniels--by Woodburn, 97 lbs, Hull | 2 |
| T. H. Williams Jr. names br c Bryant W by Monday--Bete, 100 lbs, Howson | 3 |
| J. F. Mahon name b g Gracie Mahon by Modoc--by Norfolk, 97 lbs, Ross | 4 |

Time--1:48.

The second event was trotting for a prize of $1,000, for the 2:25 class. Cairo, Starr King, Director, Echora and Honesty answered the call and were assigned positions in the order named. In the betting it was four to one in favor of Director and but little money was put in, but some pools were sold for second place, the odds varying with the fluctuations of the race.

First heat. When the word was given Director was not up in his place and he broke up within four lengths of the score. Starr King went around the two first, the others well together behind him, and he passed the quarter in 35½ with a clear advantage of three lengths. On the straight work to the half, Echora spurted to King's wheel and Cairo broke and fell to the rear. The time to the half was 1:10½ with King first, Echora second, Honesty third, Director fourth, and Cairo last, there being an interval of two lengths between Echora and Honesty and four lengths between Director and Cairo. As they rounded into the stretch Director came first for a few strides but his driver changed his mind and took him back, leaving King and Echora to settle the heat between them. The two finished up the stretch on almost even terms, the mare making a little skip in the first dash, but near the distance King made a bad break and all but Cairo gave him the go-by, Echora arriving at the wire first, Director second, Honesty third, Starr King fourth, Cairo fifth. Time 2:23½. Pools, Director $100, field $15, Starr King $12.

Director barred, Starr King $30, Echora $15, field $12.

Second heat. At the tap of the bell Echora broke and Starr King again went to the quarter first (time 35) with daylight between him and Echora, Director third. In the straight Director worked gradually past Echora and she left her feet in an effort to hold her ground. At the half in 1:10½. King was still leading, Director second, Echora last. In the last quarter Director trotted to King but allowed him to win the heat by a head, Director second, Honesty third, Echora (reduced by the judges for breaking) fourth, Cairo fifth. Time 2:22½. Pools, Director $100, Echora $16, Field $7.

Third heat. Director got away level this heat and took his usual place in front and from here to the end of the race the interest was in the struggle between Echora and Starr King for the second place. At the quarter Echora was a close second to Director (time, 36s.) and in the back stretch King made a wild break that increased her advantage. Around the turn Echora was three lengths ahead of King, but he closed the gap and the two had a lively set-to in the stretch, Echora beating him to the score by half a length, Cairo fourth, Honesty fifth. Time, 2:23½. Pools, Director $100. Starr King $24, field $14. Director barred, Starr King $30, field $20.

Fourth heat. At the outset Director broke and Starr King was pulled to the pole, suddenly causing Mr. Titus to check his mare and pull out. King was first to the quarter in thirty-six seconds, Director close behind and Echora third, but making frequent skips. Before the half was reached (1:11½), Director was in front and from there home it was a jog, Starr King second. Honesty third, Echora fourth, Cairo fifth. Time, 2:25½. Pools, Director $50, field $18. Director barred, Echora $30, field, $10.

Fifth heat. The last mile was devoid of interest as Echora had given up the fight. Director won as he pleased, King second, Honesty third, Echora fourth, and Cairo fifth. Time, 2:26½.

**SUMMARY.**

Same Day.—Trotting, 2:25 class. Purse, $1,000, and $200 added if more than ten entries. Four moneys.

| | | | | | |
|---|---|---|---|---|---|
| J. A. Goldsmith names blk s Director, by Dictator | 2 | 2 | 1 | 1 | 1 |
| C. W. Welby names ch g Starr King, by Geo. M. Patchen | 4 | 1 | 3 | 2 | 2 |
| L. H. Titus names br m Echora, by Echo | 1 | 4 | 2 | 4 | 4 |
| J. H. Dodge names ch h Honesty, by Priam | 3 | 3 | 5 | 3 | 3 |
| J. Hughes names b g Cairo, by Chieftain | 5 | 5 | 4 | 5 | 5 |

J. M. Learned's b s Reliance, by Alexander, H. R. Covey's b g Capt. Smith, by Locomotive, G. Valensin's ch s Crown Point, by Speculation, J. Cochran's ch g Ashley, by Plumas, and L. J. Rose's blk s Del Sur, by the Moor were drawn.

The third race was for district trotters. Patchen, Silver Threads and Mac appeared but while going for the wind Silver Threads and Mac collided and both ran away. The drivers were thrown out but not seriously injured, but Mac demolished the sulky and bruised himself so badly that he was drawn from the race. Silver Threads was caught and brought back and the remaining two were set off for the race. It was not an affair of much consequence. Silver Thread won the first heat by trotting in the lead from wire to wire. Time—2:45½. He was also given the second heat by the judges, who set Patchen back for running although he crossed the score first. Time—2:43 Patchen won the third in 2:46 and the finish was postponed till Thursday.

The attendance on Thursday was far above the most sanguine expectations of the directors, the grand stand being packed. In the unfinished contest of the preceding day Patchen won easily in 2:40½ and 2:40½. The first race was a mile and repeat which was won by May D in straight heats in 1:44 and 1:44¾, Jim Douglas second and Inauguration third. The second was a trot for district two-year-olds, mile and repeat, in which Mr. Vischer's Magdalene was first in 2:45 and 2:43, with J. W. Warren's Alpheus second, H. Robinson's Almore third, and G. W. Trahern's Baby Mine fourth. The third race was a special trot between Tump Winston, Ashley and Frank Moscow, which was won by the former, he taking the first, second and fourth heats, the third being given to Moscow, both the others being put back for running, Time—2:26¾, 2:27, 2:30¼, 2:30½. Of these races and of the ladies' tournament, a full account will be given in our next.

RACES AT GREENVILLE.—Owing to the rain the races set for the 18th inst. were postponed until the following day. The track was in good order. The first race was a trot, 2:35 class. Roanoke and Plough Boy were the only contestants. The former was the favorite at two to one. Roanoke took the lead easily from the start and won in three straight heats; best time, 2:46½. The second race was in the two-year-old class, in which there were but two entries, Mollie and June, which was won by the former at a very slow gait. The third race was in the three minute class. Mollie Barnes and Billy were entered. There was no contest. Mollie was first and Billy nowhere. He ran most of the way and was distanced the first heat. Time—3:20. The fourth race was running, mile heats. There were three entries—Redlight, Snuffbox and Overland Pat. Pat was the favorite and won the race; Snuffbox second, Redlight distanced. Best time—1:56½. The fifth race was a half-mile dash, for which there were five entries. Lillie, Rose Ballinger, Nellie Banta, Summit and Nellie G. Rose was the favorite and won in 53 seconds.

## The Great Boston Trotting Race.

The Blanchard $10,000 race for horses of the 2:17 class at Beacon Park, which had been looked forward to with great interest, took place on the 14th. The rain of the previous night and that afternoon served to make the track heavy, and deterred many townspeople from attending. The weather partially cleared before noon, and it was decided not to postpone the race. A light wind improved the condition of the track, and when the horses were called it was in fair shape. From eleven o'clock until the middle of the afternoon the thoroughfares leading to the park were lined with conveyances filled with people, while special trains frequently brought large numbers. There were fully 15,000 people on the grounds, and a most lively scene was presented, delegations being present from all parts of the country. Before the race, betting was about even on Edwin Thorne and Clingstone, Thorne being a slight favorite, with Santa Claus third choice. The judges were W. H. Wilson of Cynthiana, Kentucky, C. H. Keeler and B. F. Ricker of Boston. Keeler also acted as starter.

The horses were called at two o'clock promptly, but did not appear upon the track until half an hour later, when they drew positions as follows: Fanny Witherspoon first, Santa Claus second, Clingstone third; Parana fourth, Edwin Thorne fifth, Helene sixth, Humboldt seventh. All the horses appeared in good condition except Santa Claus. He was quite lame. Nevertheless he trotted throughout the race. In the first heat much time was lost in scoring, fifteen times the horses coming to the wire and as many times were they sent back. On the sixteenth attempt a fair start was made with Parana slightly in the lead. Thorne came to the front at the turn with Parana, Helene and Clingstone following in the order named, and thus they went to the half. Here Parana fell back into fourth place, Helene came up, and from here to the homestretch made a pretty race with Thorne. On the homestretch, however, Thorne pulled away from the mare and won by at least three lengths; Clingstone third, Fanny Witherspoon fourth, Santa Claus fifth, Parana sixth, Humboldt last, Edwin Thorne now sold for fifty dollars for the field.

For the second heat the horses were sent off well together on the fifth scoring. Again Edwin Thorne led after passing the quarter, Helene second, and Clingstone third. Here Clingstone overtook Helene, and gained second position. The other horses, except Parana and Humboldt, gradually closed up and coming into the homestretch were well bunched. Helene and Santa Claus here broke and fell back, but Thorne, Clingstone and Witherspoon kept together and trotted splendidly. Thorne however had a slight advantage, and was closely pressed by Clingstone. This order was maintained down the homestretch, where all the horses showed fine speed. Clingstone was out-traveled and could not overcome Thorne's advantage, and Thorne finished winner by a head, Clingstone second, Fanny Witherspoon third, Santa Claus fourth, Parana fifth, Helene sixth, Humboldt seventh. Thorne stock here boomed, and he sold for $50 against $21 for the field.

The celebrated stallion Smuggler, winner of the stallion race of 1874, and who has the best record of any stallion in the world, was now exhibited upon the track, and was greeted with great enthusiasm.

In the third heat Edwin Thorne, Santa Claus, Clingstone and Parana rounded the turn in the order named, and so continued to the backstretch. Here Santa Claus overtook Thorne, and the two went neck and neck to the three-quarter pole amid great excitement. Clingstone came up with Thorne and Santa Claus, and the three kept abreast till half way down the stretch, when Thorne pulled ahead. Clingstone, by a fine burst of speed, passed Santa Claus when within a few rods of the finish, and came under the wire less than half a length behind Thorne. The order of the finish was: Thorne 1, Clingstone 2, Santa Claus 3, Parana 4, Helene 5, Fanny Witherspoon 6, Humboldt 7. Edwin Thorne consequently took first money, Clingstone second, Helene third and Santa Claus fourth. Following is a

SUMMARY:

Special race, for horses of the 2:17 class. Purse, $10,000; divided.

| | | | |
|---|---|---|---|
| Edwin Thorne | 1 | 1 | 1 |
| Clingstone | 3 | 2 | 2 |
| Helene | 2 | 6 | 5 |
| Santa Claus | 5 | 4 | 3 |
| Fanny Witherspoon | 4 | 3 | 6 |
| Parana | 6 | 5 | 4 |
| Humboldt | 7 | 7 | 7 |

## Pertinent Remarks on "Fixed" Races.

The authorities at Saratoga a short time since ruled off two Canadian jockeys, McBride and Phair, for fraud. It appears that three horses, Turfman, Raven, and Bailey, were engaged in a handicap hurdle race, and it is claimed an arrangement had been entered into to pull Raven and Bailey and make a "sure" thing of it for Turfman. This intention was carried out, but the game was so clumsily played that McBride, the rider of Raven, and Phair, who had the mount on Bailey, were called by the judges to the stand, and, being unable to make any defense, were promptly ruled off the course. Now, so far so good, but we would ask the managers of the Saratoga Association if they think they have done their whole duty in the matter. They were satisfied that the jockeys they punished deliberately pulled their horses back and made no attempt to win or they would not have ruled them off, but they surely are not simple enough to imagine that the riders were the only guilty parties in the affair. Jockeys who go into such business ninety-nine times out of a hundred do it at the instigation of bigger rascals than themselves; theirs is not the head to plan the swindle, they are merely the tools with which the work is performed. It is as plain as noonday that somebody stood behind McBride and Phair and planned the trick, and who the wire-pullers were it is the bounden duty of the Saratoga authorities to ascertain. It is scarcely necessary to suggest to experienced turfmen how best to proceed, but there is little doubt in our minds that if the tools were given to understand that their reinstation depended upon their exposing their principals the truth would soon be ascertained. A prominent gentleman of this city who was present the day the race was run was steered by the owner of one of the three horses to the tune of a couple of hundred on Raven, and other Canadians present were treated in the same way, so that no preference was shown by those who worked the oracle. Phair, one of the expelled jockeys, has been in this city for a few days past, and we are informed on good authority has boasted that certain parties at Saratoga have told him to keep away for a few weeks, then come back, and the chances were that it would be made all right. If any such promise as this has been made, the why and wherefore it would be advisable to learn. Certainly no honorable turfman would desire to lend his influence to reinstate a dishonest jockey unless he had most positive proof that he had repented of his rascality; then who would exert himself in the matter? The answer seems plain enough that some person or persons at Saratoga who benefited by the work in question are interested in getting the judgment reversed. The sport of the turf has made marvelous strides upwards in the favor of the American people within the past ten years, but it behooves those who occupy the places of authority to see to it that it is kept as free from suspicion as possible. Fast as it rose, it will sink with greater rapidity if honest men who now walk the quarterstretch are liable to be pounced upon by sharpers and the selection of a winning horse is to be made dependent upon its position in the betting. McBride and Phair, if guilty of the charge they have been punished for, are the tools of others. Who these others are is the question asked of the Saratoga Association, and they owe it to their own reputation to make an effort to find out. Hundreds of dollars were taken from the turfmen of this city on this race we allude to, and it is little satisfaction to them that while the judge's action substantiated their own opinion that they had been swindled, no attempts were made to reach the real culprits. If an attempt is made by Phair and McBride to enter or ride a horse on a Canadian racecourse while under expulsion by the Saratoga Association we hope they may be firmly dealt with. The Ontario Jockey Club and the Province of Quebec Turf Club are the representative turf institutions of their respective provinces, and as they advertise to race under the rules of the American Jockey Club they must pay heed to the judgments of the chief American turf organization. The latter having done a part of their duty in this matter, we wait to see if they are willing to perform the balance which, as honest men, it is their duty to undertake, even though influence at Saratoga be brought to bear to stay proceedings. Make McBride and Phair tell the whole story.—*Canadian Sportsman.*

## Blair Athol.

The death of Blair Athol, which occurred in England a few days since, following close upon that of Adventurer, leaves a void in the ranks of the English stud fathers which cannot soon be filled, for whatever may be said of Blair Athol's career as a stallion, he was the darling of English breeders, who stuck to him through thick and thin. It is not a little curious but still a fact often remarked by observers of racing affairs, that the greatest successes have been obtained by turfmen with horses bred from their own strains, of which the cases of Lord Jersey, Sir Joseph Hawley, Lord Glasgow, Lord Falmouth and Mr. King are conspicuous examples. Queen Mary may truly be said to have laid the foundations of I'Anson fortunes, which Blink Bonny built upon, and her son, Blair Athol, "crowned the edifice."

Blair Athol was the first son and second foal of Blink Bonny, who was seven years old when she foaled him, Stockwell, his sire, being twelve. He was a chestnut, with a white face, and, as a colt, was so gross and loose-framed that it was deemed best not to run him as a two-year-old, and accordingly he did not make his bow to the public until he stripped for the Derby of 1864. His private reputation however was so great that he started favorite, and though he ran sluggish, his green jacket shot to the front at Tattenham Corner when Snowden called upon him. The Grand Prize of Paris was his next essay, but he could do no better than run second to Vermont. There was great excitement in England at the time, and it was darkly hinted that the late Napoleon had something to do with the result. Blair Athol re-crossed the channel, and the following week appeared at Ascot, where he met and defeated Ely, one of the best and handsomest horses in England. At the York August meeting The Miner beat him, but in the St. Leger he turned the tables upon his critics, and won in the grandest style.

He had now become the property of Mr. Jackson, the famous Yorkshire book-maker, and was retired from the post to the paddock as sound as bell-metal. In his first season he got a winner of the One Thousand Guineas in Scottish Queen, but, before this, failing health had caused Mr. Jackson to break up his stud, and at the auction sale Blair Athol fell to Mr. Blenkiron for 5,000 guineas, and was transferred to Middle Park, where he remained until 1872, when the death of Mr. Blenkiron caused the dispersal of that gigantic stud. In the meantime the fame of Blair Athol was at its flood-tide. Prince Charles had taken the field, and was enjoying the reputation of being the fleetest horse ever saddled at Newmarket; and, by his aid and that of his numerous progeny, Blair led the list of winning stallions. When he was offered for sale, with the rest of the Middle Park stock, commissions from Australia, Germany, France and Austria were sent to purchase him. A stock company was agitated in this city with a view to his purchase. England took the alarm. The press rang with calls for the formation of a stock company for the purpose of saving to England the mighty Blair and the cream of the brood mares.

The result was the formation of the Cobham Stud Company. The sale occupied three days, and was attended by thousands. When Blair Athol made his appearance in the ring he was received with thunders of applause. Mr. Tattersall made a speech, in which he told the assemblage that Blair "was the best horse in the world." Then the bidding began. The English, who loved the horse, watched the proceedings closely, and as the bidding rose by thousands, the most feverish anxiety was manifested, particularly when the French and Austrian commissioners clung tenaciously to the horse. But the spirit of patriotism would not allow Blair to be taken from England, and he was knocked down at the enormous figure of 12,500 guineas amid the wildest cheering. The breaking up of the Cobham Stud again sent him to the hammer in the autumn of 1879, when he was sold for 4,500 guineas, and last season he was resold for 1,950 guineas.

Probably no stallion since Stockwell has enjoyed such a monopoly of the best of English mares. His success in getting winners was great, but it can hardly be said that he got any number of real first-class performers. Prince Charlie, Craig Miller, and Silvio were his best colts, winning the Guineas, a Derby, and two St. Legers, and while his daughters failed to place the Oaks to his credit, his Scottish Queen and Cecilia won the One Thousand. His get have shown some tendency to softness, and did not train on, but their speed was of the highest order. Blair Athol's progeny have made quite an impression in this country, his son, Glen Athol, being the sire of Glenmore and Checkmate. Mr. Withers has a son of Blair's in Stonehenge, the sire of the Julietta colt and Buckstone. Blair's daughter, Highland Lassie, at Mr. Lorillard's, is the dam of Neva, Neriad, and Nimrod. Whatever may be said of the softness of his get in England, certain it is that in Glenmore and Checkmate he has given us through his son two of the best campaigners of the day. He has played his part in the world's affairs, and challenged its admiration, and his death will be sure to cause a pang of regret wherever the merits of a good horse are known and appreciated.—*N. Y. Spirit of the Times.*

A Valuable Brood Mare.—One of the most noted and valuable brood mares ever owned in New England was May Queen, a daughter of the famous trotting stallion Ethan Allen. Her dam was the noted pacing mare Pocahontas, one of the fastest of her kind upon the turf. It is stated upon apparently good authority that she was once driven a full mile by Adam Carpenter over the Union course, drawing a wagon weighing 135 pounds, in 2:10, which is 1¼ seconds faster than the best pacing heat on record. The estimated value of May Queen's produce before being trained was as follows: Prudence, by Daniel Lambert, $6,500; Dolly Varden, by Daniel Lambert, $10,000; May Flower, by Daniel Lambert, $4,000; May Morning, by Daniel Lambert, $2,500. May Morning is the dam of Revenue, formerly Pilgrim, by Smuggler, for which Com. Kittson paid last summer $13,000. May Queen's next was Driving Wind, by Mambrino Prince, $1,500; Hurricane, by Fearnaught, $5,000; Tempest, by Fearnaught, $1,000; Boston Boy, by Abraham, a son of Daniel Lambert, $1,000; a colt, by King Philip, son of Jay Gould, $1,000; Virginia Jefferson, by Thomas Jefferson, $2,000; Gypsy May, by Thomas Jefferson, $1,500; making a total of eleven valued at $33,000. It is noticeable that her produce by Daniel Lambert is estimated much higher on an average than the others, which, considering the fact that both May Queen and Daniel Lambert were the offspring of Ethan Allen, may be thought remarkable.—*American Cultivator.*

Care of the Buggy.—We lay it down as an axiom, says an exchange, that the farmer who cannot afford a cover for his implements and vehicles has no business with a buggy. A buggy is too frail and delicate to stand heat and storms. The buggy must be kept housed when not in use. When brought out of the house it should be dusted off with a feather duster. If it comes home muddy it should be cleaned before putting in the house. It may be inconvenient, but in the end it will pay. There is no need of taking it to a creek, and there attack it with the old scrub broom. Take a bucket or two of water and a sponge and gently wash the top, then the bed, and wring out a chamois and wipe so no water stands on the varnish. Whenever water dries on varnish it will lose its luster. A bucket and a sponge and chamois and feather duster are as necessary adjuncts to a farmer's buggy as a wrench. A careful man will have his buggy look neat and last three times as long as the class first named. The average farmer can ill afford to buy a buggy and harness for pleasure. And neither he nor any other farmer can afford to neglect and destroy them. Wastefulness treads on the heels of extravagance, and the model farmer will not tolerate either on his premises.

## The Hartford Winners.

| Name. | Des. | Sire. | Amt. Won. | Best Time. |
|---|---|---|---|---|
| Adele Gould | ch m | Jay Gould | $300 | .... |
| Aldine | br m | Almont | 1750 | 2:19½ |
| Barbara Patchen | b m | Aker's Idol | 150 | .... |
| Barrett | b s | Chester Chief | 250 | .... |
| Black Cloud | blk s | Ashland Chief | 1000 | 2:17¾ |
| Brandy Boy | b g | Admiral Patchen | 500 | .... |
| Buffalo Girl | b m | Pocahontas Boy | 750 | 2:16 |
| Captain Lewis | ch g | Spink | 500 | 2:23¾ |
| Clemmie G | ch m | Magic | 1000 | 2:21¼ |
| Clingstone | b g | Rysdyk | 1000 | 2:17 |
| Cora Belmont | gr m | Belmont | 200 | .... |
| Cornelia | blk m | Bonner | 225 | .... |
| Driver | b g | Volunteer | 200 | .... |
| Eva | b m | George Wilkes | 500 | .... |
| Edwin Thorne | ch g | Thornedale | 2000 | 2:17 |
| Fred Douglass | ch s | Green's Bashaw | 300 | .... |
| Forest Patchen | br g | King Patchen | 200 | .... |
| Flora Belle | blk m | Stucker Rainbow | 150 | .... |
| Flora F | b m | Clear Grit | 500 | .... |
| Fuller | b g | Clear Grit | 500 | 2:17½ |
| Fanny Witherspoon | ch m | Almont | 750 | .... |
| Gem | b m | Tom Rolfe | 375 | 2:15 |
| Gladiator | b g | Blue Bull | 500 | 2:23¾ |
| Independence | b s | Young Hindoo | 150 | .... |
| Lucy | gr m | Ned | 225 | 2:18¼ |
| Mattie Bond | b m | Tom Hal | 150 | .... |
| May Thorne | b m | Thornedale | 150 | .... |
| Minnie R | b m | J. C. Breckenridge | 1000 | 2:20 |
| Onawa | blk s | Goodwins Hambletonian | 150 | .... |
| Overman | ch g | Elmo | 750 | 2:21¼ |
| Pickard | b g | Abdallah Pilot | 500 | 2:20¾ |
| Phyllis | br m | Phil Sheridan | 375 | .... |
| Rigolette | b m | Exchequer | 225 | .... |
| R. P | b g | Happy Medium | 300 | .... |
| Red Bird | b g | Grey Eagle | 100 | .... |
| Sweetness | b m | Young Volunteer | 150 | .... |
| Santa Claus | b s | Strathmore | 1500 | 2:17½ |
| Von Arnim | b s | Sentinel | 500 | .... |
| Warrior | b g | Warrior | 250 | 2:26½ |
| Winchester Maid | blk m | Hamlet | 100 | .... |
| William H | b g | Young Wilkes | 300 | 2:21 |
| Yellow Dock | ch m | Clark's Mohawk Jr. | 375 | .... |

# FISH.

## The Fisheries in Oregon.

It is pleasant to remark that the *Oregonian* sounds a word of warning as to the future of the river fisheries in that prosperous State, but in the following extract from an article on that subject the journal is apparently oblivious of the fact that an export duty is against the laws of the Union, and that even if imposed it would place Oregon at a disadvantage in the marts of the world. The question arises if it be not more rightly a matter of joint State and Federal expenditure and supervision:

A State hatchery should be established for salmon and trout at some point so far inland that the young fish will not be able to reach the sea until they have attained sufficient size and strength to protect them from their natural enemies. This involves the expenditure of money, it is true, but it can easily be obtained by taxing the products of the canneries, say two cents on each case of salmon put up by them. The output of the Oregon side of the river is about 324,000 cases for 1882, which would give $6,500 as a revenue for maintaining the hatchery. This hatchery should be, in our belief, established at a point east of The Dalles, either in the Des Chutes, the Grand Ronde or the Imnaha, subject to the decision of the commissioners.

It will require $1,500 a year for the salary of a superintendent of the hatchery, and $1,000 more for the wages of his assistant. First class talent, (and in this juncture we can afford to employ none other) will demand first-class pay, and a man like Seth Green, or Livingston Stone, is worth at least $250 per month for the six months of the breeding season. The assistant superintendent does not require much greater qualifications than sobriety and fidelity. He will be required to remain at the hatchery during the entire year, to assist the superintendent during the season of propagation, and to keep the state's property clean and in good repair. The commissioners should not exceed three in number, and should receive about ten dollars per day for six days in each year, to hold semi-annual meetings of the board, paying their own traveling expenses out of their *per diem*, and reporting biennially to each session of the legislative assembly.

One of the board should act as president, and another as secretary. The state should issue stamps of the value of two cents each to be placed upon each case of canned salmon entered for export at the custom house of Portland or Astoria, on the sale of which some compensation should be allowed, say three per cent., to the secretary of the board. He would have all the work of the concern to perform, and this would give him $250 a year against $60 for each of the other two members. Failure to stamp each and every case according to the requirements of the act, should involve a fine of $60 for the first offense and $100 for each subsequent one, to be paid into the state treasury and set apart into the fishery fund, less say twenty per cent. for collection, to be paid to the court collecting it. This would, in our belief, afford ample revenue for re-stocking the Columbia river, and carry over a surplus in each and every year to provide against unforeseen accidents to the state's property.

In our belief the cause of failure in the Clackamas hatchery was its want of proper location. It was in charge of competent officers, and all its details were properly and regularly carried out, hence no fault can be found on that score. The next hatchery built should be further inland and, should that prove no better than the one on Clackamas, locations should be changed from time to time until the right place is found. The effects of pisciculture in California have already been felt in Oregon, for there has not been a day in July or August of the present year that shad have not been taken in the harbor of Astoria. None of these fish were ever planted here. True to their natural migratory habits, they wended their way northward from San Francisco, where they were hatched, and probably the same run of fish is now somewhere about the Fraser or the Skeena in British Columbia. These fish were two years old and were of delicate flavor.

In some places in Germany are trout ponds in which the trout are simply fattened, not raised. The dealers buy, often at great distances, young trout measuring five or six inches in length, which have been caught in brooks, and place them in the ponds. Here they are sorted according to years and fed with the worthless cyprinoids which are caught in large numbers in some of the rivers. In Heidelberg and Wurzberg these food-fish are generally placed in the ponds alive, but in Mayence they are only put in dead. The former method of feeding is more convenient and may be especially recommended in small ponds where the trout have not far to look for food. The method of feeding with dead fish is, however, better calculated to fatten the trout.

The most destructive element to fish in Nevada so far is the great quantity of sawdust annually discharged into the Carson and Truckee rivers. There being no effective law to prevent it, all attempts at remedy have proved futile, and until some strong reciprocal laws between California and Nevada can be adopted and enforced, no relief from this practice can be hoped for. The large amount of capital invested in the manufacture of lumber will hardly give way to the comparatively insignificant revenue or employment derived from the fish business, hence without kindly considerate protection by the lumber interest in the absence of needed laws we must expect instead of an increase a gradual diminution of fish in the rivers above named and their tributaries.

A sight that attracted general notice last Sunday afternoon on the seawall was the extraordinary run of young fish that was noticeable along the three last sections of the seawall, and at the time that the tide was going out millions apparently of small fishes, of two and three inches in length, wiggled past at a depth of one or two feet, their presence being shown by the countless flashes of their silver sides as they moved in a southerly direction for a considerable portion of an hour. This was probably owing to an organized attack of sturgeons, just as the menhaden in New York waters are pursued in so remorseless a manner that they throw themselves on the sands to be out of the way of the Bluefish that prey upon them.

"Uncle Sam," said a colored boy to black Samuel, a negro who used to bottom chairs for Colonel Sandy Faulkner, "whar yer gwine?" "Gwine fishin', chile; why ye ax me!" "Did yer know that Aunt Tildy is dead?" "Go on, chile! Is dat a fack? Yer doan mean ter say dat my wife is dead!" "Yes sah." "When she die?" "Dis mornin'." "Wall, I'se sorry I wan't dar! Tell 'em to go an' make 'rangements, dat I'll be back agin de funeral. I'se done dug worms for bait now. Wish I'd knowed it sooner."—Arkansas Traveler.

Before starting to spend any money in beginning a piscicultural establishment, a man ought to inform himself as accurately as possible regarding the water which will be at his command. He must know the average quantity of water; counting the dry season; he must know the temperature of the water during the greatest heat and the greatest cold. Although such kinds seem almost superfluous, they are nevertheless much needed.

Every season the chances of catching trout near this city are lessened. This does not make very much difference to professional anglers, as there is; but to persons who have only an occasional outing it means giving up fishing altogether. We know of several people who are fond of fishing who have not wet a line for a long time because they knew that it would be time wasted to go to the creeks where they were once accustomed to find good sport.

The sea fishing outside the heads is said to be very good just now and some fine catches have been made. The pilots who have an opportunity once in a while report that the fishing was never better. Strange to say, the tom-cod are plenty wherever there is a protected nook.

The anglers are hanging up their rods and taking down their guns. The fishing season is pretty well over. The creeks are low and the fish have been pretty well hunted. Lots of them are no longer green and a footstep is enough to send them to deep holes for half a day.

A beginner in pisciculture is generally mistaken as regards the quantity of the food required, thinking that it is sufficient to let a proper quantity of water flow through his ponds but forgetting that fish live in the water but not by the water.

The first number of the BREEDER AND SPORTSMAN, published in San Francisco, reached our eastern a few days ago. It is a very handsome journal, devoted to field sports and the turf. The illustration of Electioneer on the title page is an artistic effort far above those seen ordinarily in sporting papers. Joseph Cairn Simpson is the editor, and judging from his leading articles, he is the right man in the right place. We will always welcome the BREEDER AND SPORTSMAN with pleasure, and read the accounts of that wonderful country where it is published.—Southern Industries, Nashville, Tenn.

## BICYCLING.

### A Steam Tricycle.

A Buffalo man has perfected an important invention which is nothing less than a steam tricycle. It is expected that it is destined to revolutionize the modes of travel on the highway. It at first sight resembles a low, open buggy or buckboard. The seat is placed between the two principal wheels, the third wheel being in front, about five feet away from the other. It is smaller, and is used for guiding the vehicle. The two main wheels are the same as those used in bicycles. The motive power is applied to them by means of a small spur wheel and a few feet of belting or chain. The engine and boiler are located between the seat and the forward wheel. They take up very little space, and much of the machinery will be enclosed in a wooden case when the vehicle is completed. The engine is a one and a half horse power, and it rests on the bottom of the conveyance. The exhaust is underneath, and will be nearly noiseless and invisible. The cylinder is two by four inches. The generator is upright and stands directly over the neat little boiler. For fuel gasoline is used, and two gallons of this fluid, surrounded by water, will be carried in a reservoir under the seat. It will be conveyed to the furnace by means of tubes. It is claimed that one gallon will be sufficient to run the engine for nine hours at the rate of fifteen to twenty miles an hour. The tricycle as it now stands cost about $200, but can be duplicated for $150.

BICYCLE TOURNAMENT.—The Springfield (Mass.) Bicycle Club has perfected a grand meet and tournament, to be held on Wednesday afternoon and evening, Sept. 20. The programme consists of a twenty-mile professional race, for a purse of $500, by J. S. Prince of Boston, champion of the United States, against Thomas Harrison and James Mellen, who will alternate every five miles; a five-mile professional ladies' race, for a purse of $200; and the following amateur races, open to all amateurs: Five-mile race, three prizes, value $125; two-mile race, three prizes, value $125; one-mile race, three prizes, value $75; half-mile dash, three prizes, value $50; slow race, 100 yds., three prizes, value $25; one mile, without hands, three prizes, value $30; half-mile race for boys under 15 years of age, three prizes, value $30. The one and two mile races will be run in heats, best two in three. These races will take place on Hampden Park. A handsome gold and silver-plated bicycle bugle, value $30, will be presented to the club having the largest number of wheelmen in the parade. At the skating rink in the evening the following prizes will be contested for: Best-drilled club of not less than eight members, three prizes, value $100; best single fancy riding, three prizes, value $75; best double fancy riding, three prizes, value $75.—N. Y. Clipper.

On Wednesday, August 2nd, the Wanderers B. C. held their second running race meeting upon the Surbiton grounds, London, England. The important event was the twenty mile race between the present amateur champion, H. L. Cortis, and the Hon. Ion Keith Falconer, the race being also against time. The track was far inferior in surface to the Crystal Palace track upon which the record was made the previous week, and early in the evening there was a strong south-west wind blowing with sharp showers falling at intervals. Shortly after 7 the riders started, an outsider acting as pace-maker, Cortis leading and Keith Falconer bringing up the rear. The first mile was done in exactly three minutes. Nothing of importance occurred until the seventh mile, when Keith Falconer finding the pace too hot for him withdrew. From this time Cortis went on assisted by the different racing men, who relieved each other at intervals in keeping up the pace, until the last lap, when Cortis put on a tremendous burst and left his companion, completing the twenty miles in 59 m. 20 1-5 seconds.

WHY NOT TRY THE BICYCLE.—The English physicians are just at this moment differing as to the amount of physical exercise necessary to create or destroy health in the human system. One side of the disagreeing doctors claim that eight hours' exercise a day is absolutely essential, and advocate walking as the best form. The others hold that such an amount of exertion is injurious and long walks are positively deleterious to the system. They claim that the passive exercise of riding is much more wholesome than the active exertion of pedestrianism. There are other physicians who are solving the problem in favor of the bicycle, and now-a-days the village doctor often leaves his mount at the porch, instead of tying it up to the garden gate as in former days.

Another exciting finish took place at the Leicestershire Cricket Ground Saturday, Aug. 5th, being the occasion of the second twenty-five mile professional championship race. It will be remembered that the first race was run off May 27th, after two dead heats, by R. James, of Birmingham, and F. Wood, of Leicester. Both James and Wood met with accidents a short time previous to the present race, but Wood was able to start. The other contestants were R. Harwell, professional one mile champion, G. W. Waller, A. E. Derkinderin, C. R. Garrard and F. De Clury, the latter of Paris. The lead was taken by the riders alternately, although some of them seemed anxious to make the pace very fast. Five miles was done in 17:19, ten miles in 33:45, and twenty miles in 1 h., 7.59, which will give a chance for comparison with Cortis' twenty-mile time. The Frenchman gave up three laps from the finish, and Walter soon after, leaving the others to fight it out in the last lap, which they did with a tremendous rush, Harwell fairly lifting his machine through the tape, half a yard in front of Derkinderin, with Wood immediately in the rear. Time, 1 h. 24:15.

The following item, clipped from a daily paper, ought to cheer the hearts of the bicycler, as indicating that the public apathy respecting had kept highways is not universal: "Reading, Pa., August 21.—The fifty-five Councilmen of this city, and the Mayor, were arrested to-day by virtue of a bench warrant issued in pursuance of the indictments found against them last week for not keeping the streets in proper repair. They gave bail for their appearance at the November court." Here, as we have often urged, is proper work for the local wheelmen in all parts of the country. Throw your votes and influence for municipal officers, and especially for road commissioners, for men who are public-spirited, liberal, and regardful for the good name of their city or town, irrespective of party politics, which latter element ought never to enter into local elections.

We are glad to see that the excellent literary monthly, the Brooklyn Advance, has taken up the advocacy of bicycling. It not only indicates the wisdom of its managers, but evinces the general and growing recognition of the wheel as a factor in healthful physical development and recreation.—Ex.

An English bicycling paper, the Cyclist, has called attention lately to the practice in certain localities of offering money or plate, at option of winner, as prizes in events advertised for amateurs. This opens the interesting question whether the losers would be amateurs if plate is chosen, and professionals if the money went taken. At all events, it is clear that the practice is questionable, and I trust it will not find supporters in this country.

W. J. Morgan, the Canadian bicycle champion, offers to ride any man in America, John S. Prince preferred. A two mile race for from $200 to $500 a side; the race to take place in any city in the United States in four weeks from signing articles.

At Salt Lake City, July, 24 the Salt Lake Bicycle Club held one-mile and ten-mile events, the first race being won by William Jennings in 3m. 20s.; James Wood second in 3m. 36¼s. Jennings also won the ten-mile race in 40m.

San Francisco Bicycle Club men have been accorded partial riding privileges in Golden Gate Park, under limitations and at certain hours. This will do for a beginning, but the time must come when their full rights will be conceded.

W. J. Morgan is willing to race any bicycler in America except J. S. Prince, 50 miles, for $200 a side; or he will race Prince one hundred miles for the same amount.

The price of suspenders for holding up stockings has gone up, while the monkey wrench still holds its price at seventy-five cents.—Springfield (Ohio) News. Now, how do you apply the monkey wrench for the purpose?

Cortis not only got married the day after his great twenty-mile ride but spent his honeymoon on a social trip.

Factious youngster to party [of bicyclers passing along: "Why don't you keep step?"

## BASE BALL.

### The Renos and Niantics.

It was a red letter day last Sunday at the Recreation Grounds, the weather being delightful, the attendance large and well pleased, and the game between the Niantics and the Renos being stubbornly contested until the last inning, when the Renos could not secure one run to the their antagonists. The game was played well, but few faults being made on either side, and the spectators were warm in their demonstration of approval of a good play, as the game advanced to its final stages. Following is the score:

| NIANTICS. | | | | | | RENOS. | | | | | |
|---|---|---|---|---|---|---|---|---|---|---|---|
| | T.B. | R. | B.H. | P.O. | A. | E. | | T.B. | R. | B.H. | P.O. | A. | E. |
| Incell, c. f. | 5 | 0 | 0 | 0 | 0 | 0 | Barnes, 1b. | 4 | 1 | 2 | 10 | 1 | 0 |
| T. Sweeney, 3b. | 5 | 1 | 0 | 0 | 4 | Sweeney, p. | 1 | 3 | 2 | 1 | 0 |
| Donahue, s. s. | 5 | 1 | 0 | 0 | 1 | Riordan, 3b. | 4 | 1 | 0 | 2 | 1 | 1 |
| Egan, 1b. | 5 | 1 | 1 | 13 | 0 | Lake, 2b. | 4 | 1 | 1 | 0 | 0 | 0 |
| Finn, s. | 4 | 1 | 1 | 3 | 8 | Stark, c. f. | 4 | 0 | 0 | 1 | 1 |
| Sweeney, p. | 4 | 1 | 1 | 16 | Cadogan, c. f. | 4 | 0 | 0 | 1 | 2 |
| Sullivan, l. f. | 4 | 1 | 3 | 1 | Cowgan, c. | 4 | 0 | 0 | 10 | 0 |
| Fogarty, 2b. | 4 | 1 | 0 | 0 | 3 | McElroy, p. | 4 | 1 | 0 | 13 | 1 |
| F. Carroll, r. f. | 4 | 1 | 0 | 0 | 0 | Sheridan, 2b. | 4 | 0 | 0 | 1 | 0 |
| Totals | 40 | 6 | 9 | 27 | 34 | 9 | Totals | 26 | 5 | 4 | 27 | 19 | 7 |

Innings.............. 1 2 3 4 5 6 7 8 9
Niantics.............. 0 0 2 1 0 0 3 0 x—6
Renos................. 1 1 0 0 0 0 2 0 0—5

Earned runs—Niantics 1.
Home run—Sweeney.
Two-base hit—Sullivan.
Bases on balls—Niantics 2.
Double plays—Riordan and Sheridan.
Passed balls—Cowgan 1, Finn 4.
Wild pitches—McElroy 1.
Struck out—Niantics 7, Renos 7.
First base on errors—Niantics 4, Renos 6.
Left on bases—Niantics 6, Renos 8.
Umpire—Pete Meagan of the Californias.
Scorer—F. F. Hennesy.
Time of game—Two hours.

### The Howards and Olympics.

These clubs met at the Oakland Grounds on Sunday last and played a rather one-sided game, the Olympics starting off with a rattling score of four runs, and thenceforward they rested on their laurels and were badly beaten, as the following score shows:

| HOWARDS. | | | | | | OLYMPICS. | | | | | |
|---|---|---|---|---|---|---|---|---|---|---|---|
| | T.B. | R. | B.H. | P.O. | A. | E. | | T.B. | R. | B.H. | P.O. | A. | E. |
| Hardie, c. | 5 | 1 | 2 | 11 | 4 | 4 | Neal, p. | 3 | 1 | 1 | 3 | 1 | 3 |
| McCarthy, s. s. | 4 | 2 | 0 | 1 | 2 | Sheet, 3b. | 4 | 1 | 1 | 1 | 0 |
| Boyce, 3b. | 6 | 0 | 0 | 4 | 1 | Fitzgerald, s. s. | 4 | 1 | 0 | 2 | 1 |
| O'Rane, 2b. | 4 | 3 | 4 | 4 | Barton, 2b. | 4 | 1 | 0 | 3 | 3 |
| Dibble, p. | 4 | 1 | 1 | 0 | 8 | Van Dyke, l.f. | 4 | 0 | 0 | 1 | 0 |
| Kennedy, r. f. | 4 | 1 | 0 | 1 | Burt, 1b. | 4 | 0 | 4 | 6 | 0 |
| Van Court, l. f. | 4 | 0 | 0 | 1 | Kelly, c. f. | 4 | 0 | 0 | 1 | 1 |
| Young, s. | 4 | 1 | 0 | 0 | Hall, r. f. | 4 | 0 | 0 | 0 | 0 |
| Stose, s. | 4 | 1 | 0 | 0 | Brown, c. | 4 | 0 | 0 | 6 | 1 |
| Totals | 39 | 8 | 27 | 10 | Totals | 34 | 4 | 6 | 27 | 18 |

Innings................. 1 2 3 4 5 6 7 8 9
Olympics................. 0 0 0 0 0 0 0 0 0—4
Howards.................. 3 0 0 0 0 0 0 0 0—8

Time of game—One hour and forty-five minutes.
Scorer—Mr. Straus.
Umpire—J. Carroll of the Californias.

The Rural Home B. B. Club which was organized some months ago would like to meet some of the amateur clubs of San Francisco. Clubs desiring games will please notify E. Gunn, County Clerk's office, to that effect and they will be accommodated on any Saturday. The nine consists of the following players: J. Lowik, pitcher; Max Brockett, catcher; S. Hunter, 1st base; Cranz, 2nd base; A. Jenkins, s. s.; Coffee, 3d base; Gunn, left field; T. Jenkins, center field; Nat Page, right field.

THE BREEDER AND SPORTSMAN is the name of a new weekly paper, conducted by Jos. Cairn Simpson, and published at San Francisco, Cal., at five dollars per annum. The first copy is at hand. For beauty of typography, extent and variety of matter, and general make up, it is unexcelled by its contemporaries. Mr. Simpson is author of a popular book, entitled "Horse Portraiture," and for more than a quarter of a century has been a popular writer on sporting matters. He is admirably qualified to conduct such an enterprise, and the breeders of the Pacific Coast are to be congratulated upon having so able and gifted a champion of their interests.—St. Louis Rural World.

THE

# Breeder and Sportsman.

PUBLISHED WEEKLY BY THE

BREEDER AND SPORTSMAN PUBLISHING CO.

THE TURF AND SPORTING AUTHORITY OF THE
PACIFIC COAST.

**OFFICE, 508 MONTGOMERY STREET**

P. O. Box 1386.

*Five dollars a year; three dollars for six months; one dollar and a
half for three months. Strictly in advance*

MAKE ALL CHECKS, MONEY ORDERS, ETC., PAYABLE TO ORDER OF
BREEDER AND SPORTSMAN PUBLISHING CO.

*Money should be sent by postal order, draft or by registered letter, ad
dressed to the "Breeder and Sportsman Publishing Company, San Fran
cisco, Cal."*

*Communications must be accompanied by the writer's name and address,
not necessarily for publication, but as a private guarantee of good faith*

JOSEPH CAIRN SIMPSON,   -   -   -   EDITOR

San Francisco, Saturday, Sept. 23, 1882.

## "DECLARING TO WIN."

One of the most pernicious practices on the turf is the
following an English custom, always of doubtful propriety, many times the vehicle of unmitigated rascality.
That is when an owner had two or more horses in the
same race that he could select which he would win with
and if before the race he made the intention public, it
was held sufficient to absolve him from censure if even
the poorest were the winners. There is not a single argument that will justify such a course, but a hundred reasons why it should be abolished. It gives an opportunity to fleece the unwary betters; it disgusts the spectators,
when the palpably superior horse is made to give way
to an inferior. There is nothing in the rules which can
be twisted so as to sanction the practice, but, to the
contrary, a provision to punish those who are guilty.
The owner and trainer who gives the instructions, the
jockey who rides the horse which could have won, are
amenable, and in accordance with the law should be
expelled. It does not require a rigid construction to
punish under the circumstances but it is the imperative
duty of the judges to inflict the penalty. This, of
course, is a hard thing to do when there are so many
vicious precedents to sustain the action, but if the officers
of the association or judges of the race should notify
parties who have more than one horse engaged that they
must strive to win if even the contestants are both in
in the same stable no fault could be found with the punishment which would follow transgression. We would
like to see such a rule embodied in the code of the Pacific
Coast Blood Horse Association, not that it is required to
enable the proper steps for the correction of the evil, but
to place it beyond question. Either that or incorporating
the same restriction on starting as there is in heat races,
and only admitting one horse in the same interest to
start.

The latter plan might work injuriously to the nominator inasmuch as he would be deprived of a privilege
of testing as many colts as he chooses to pay the stakes
upon, and when there is a prize to the second as well as
to the first to be won. By insisting that there should be
a race, no injustice is done to the owner; the betters are
protected; though far beyond the welfare of those, who
speculate are the true interests of turf sports. This interest is sure to suffer when the general public have
cause for dissatisfaction. A large majority of those who
attend race meetings cannot see the points which the
betters are governed by, nor understand the logic that
gives any owner the right to perpetrate a fraud. A
fraud it certainly is when in place of a contest they have
been promised by witness one jockey "pulling the head
off his horse" to enable another to reach the winning
score first. Neither can it be reconciled to the common
understanding that an action which is met with the
severest punishment in one case should be considered an
innocent device in the other. A satisfactory explanation
cannot be given. The reasoning based on precedents will
not answer. Because Lord So-and-so declared to win
with A. when his horse B. was known to be superior, and
that this privilege is granted in a country four or five
thousand miles away, it would also follow that as Black
Donald "lifted" herds of cattle a couple of centuries ago
it was all right to steal a fat steer when the latter was
at a low ebb. The day of the empty platter with a pair
of spurs served for supper has passed, and if the sports of
the turf are brought to a standard that will insure the
support of the right-minded they must be based on a
higher plane. The argument that the betters are protected by the "stable" in place of the horse being sold in
the pools has not the weight of a feather in the balance.
There are other rights besides the settlements of wagers
to consider, more momentous questions at issue than
"protection" to those who invest in the pool-box. Even
this protection is denied when this course is sanctioned.
There may be those who do not buy pools who like to in-

tensify the interest of the race by a wager, perhaps
small, it may be large. The riders are mounted and A.
says to B. "I will take the horse with the colors scarlet
jacket and black cap against any you will name for $—."
"All right," responds B, "I will take the scarlet jacket
and yellow cap." Scarlet and black is pulled to a standstill and scarlet and yellow wins. It is a palpable fraud,
a self-evident piece of rascality, and the innocent speculators await the verdict. If there is a telegraph board
they are amazed to see that the positions are awarded as
they came in and preparations made for another race. The
whole thing is a roaring farce if robbery can be termed
fun, a caricature of the "royal sport," far beneath a
donkey race when the long-eared coursers are compelled
to do their best. Thousands join A. and B. in saying if
this be racing the less of it the better. Indignant, disgusted, disappointed in their expectation of seeing a race,
all the false reasoning in the world cannot reconcile them,
nor any number of titled delinquents to share the opprobrium cause them to acquiesce in considering it right.

We write plainly, feeling that more depends upon a
proper view being taken of the malpractice than many
realize who are equally as intent on bringing
the turf above reproach, but who have not given the
thought it demands to foresee the consequences. We
have advocated the abrogation of heat-racing on this
very ground, and because it gives a chance for combinations to defeat the better horse. In heats where one is
"laid up" in order to give him a better chance to win;
in a dash he is laid up to lose provided he has a stable
companion that suits "the book" better. In either case
there is an opportunity for faultfinding, and whatever is
inimical to the general appreciation we desire to see removed.

## BOOK-BETTING VS. POOLS.

There has been a good deal of discussion whether the
English system of "book-betting" or the American pools
should have the preference with the backers of horses.
In England and Australia where there is so much speculation on the turf, and many who desire to invest something before the races come off, the argument is in favor
of the English method. This is more especially the case
as from the greater certainty of "getting round" the
bookmaker is enabled to lay larger odds. In this country, however, there is no comparison between the two and
the auction and mutual pools combined are by far superior. An illustration came to our knowledge which will
be applicable. A person who wanted to invest a little
money on the races at Sacramento took the programme,
and out of the eleven nominations in race No. 1 he selected Jim Renwick and Jim Douglas, at the odds of
$30 to $10 against each. In No. 2, there were nineteen
nominations and his choice was Precious, against her
getting $40 to $10. In No. 3· there were nine entries
and Joe'Howell was booked at $30 to $10. In No. 8
Flou Flou was his choice at $30 to $10, there being eight
nominations, and in No. 9 he took Precious, six being
named in it. In No. 10 there was thirteen nominations
and Jim Douglas at $40 to $10 was the investment. In
No. 11, of the nine entries Belshar at $60 to $10 and Joe
Howell at $20 to $10 were booked, and in No. 16 Flou
Flou and Satanella were coupled, the former at $40 to
$10, the latter at $30 to $10, there being ten nominations.
In No. 17, of the twelve entries he selected Joe Howell at
$20 to $10. As a matter of explanation, he had no knowledge of what the odds would be, leaving the money with
a friend to give the bookmaker. It was certainly a poor
investment according to the calculation of the chances
from the numbers engaged. He had $120 at hazard and
the most he could win was $240 or the "short odds" of 2
to 1. But "all's well that ends well," as the following
account shows:

WINNING TICKETS.

| | |
|---|---:|
| No. 3, Precious | $ 80 |
| No. 7, Joe Howell | 40 |
| No. 8, Jim Flou | 40 |
| No. 11, Joe Howell | 20 |
| No. 16, Flou Flou | 30 |
| | $210 |

Thus he was $90 "ahead" but the most remarkable
feature was that with the exception of No. 1, in which
Jim Renwick and Jim Douglas were beaten, every race
that he had a starter in he won on. Four of the selections did not start, and in No. 11 and No. 16 he had a
loser coupled with a winner. It was a rare stroke of
good luck seldom witnessed, and without a parallel so
far as we are acquainted. But any one of the least knowledge of pools can see how much better the money could
have been invested. It is true that there was the advantage of being able to lay a little money without being
present, and also the opportunity to restrict the risk to a
definite sum. To offset this in pools the money would
have been returned for non-starters excepting when these
were in the field, and to the mutuals the amount can be
combined to advantage, and we hope to see the odds
in the books more in accordance with that which the
pools show.

## THE STATE FAIR.

Despite the "pinkeye," and the rain that deluged the
track on Friday, the State Fair was a grand success.
Successful from every point of view and in every department. The racing and trotting was in the main excellent and the decisions of the judges acquiesced in by a
large majority of the spectators. The rainstorm was an
innovation, and though unwelcome was, nevertheless,
heartily enjoyed, rather a paradoxical statement, though
the ludicrous feature made amends for the discomfort.
Californians were treated to a scene which is common in
the east. The heavy showers came after the riders were
weighed and mounted, the starter was on the ground,
and then there was such a downpour that the water was
inches deep on the track. Atalanta got off with the
lead, and those behind him were so mud-bespattered that
the colors were undistinguishable. Elsewhere there is
an account so that repetition is unnecessary. It is rare indeed, when an eastern meeting does not include just
such a spectacle, and a "good mud horse" wins over
fields that can easily beat him when the course is dry.
It will be some time before space enough can be given to
publish a proper review of what the horses have done at
the fairs. In order to have the material to do them
justice it will be necessary to await the close of the circuit. At one of them, perhaps, a horse was out of condition and did not come up to the form he afterwards
displayed, while the prevailing epizooty caught others
in its clutches and they fell short of the expectations of
owners and trainers. Notwithstanding the attending
drawbacks the horses have shown remarkably well, and
when the horse history of the year is compiled, California as usual will not be behind.

The managers of the fair are the recipients of eulogies
from all sides. There is usually a great deal of sore-
headedativeness, if one may be permitted to coin a word
to express the bickering of those who have been disappointed, but this season it is only the chronically captious who grumble. The President has labored assiduously and been ably supported by the members of the
board, while the secretary has been awarded golden
commendations for the thorough manner which has
characterized his management of the office. Not merely
during the fair, as from the close of the last exhibition
until the completion of this, he has labored with enthusiasm. The crowning thought in his mind was the success of the fair, and he went at the work with energy and
continued it with determination. During the whole of
the summer the track has been kept in first-rate order,
and in lieu of the usual complaints there have been warm
eulogies.

It is now understood that steps will be taken to remedy
the only defect in the course. As it now is the "first
turn" is very short, and the track narrows suddenly
from the starting point. With a large field of horses it
is almost impossible to avoid collision or losing of
places, and abrupt curvature makes it trying on the
horses' legs. The contemplated plan is to make the
semi-circle much easier by increasing the radius and carrying the backstretch a good deal further eastward.
The judges' stand will be moved so as to give more room
after the start, and we earnestly urge that it be placed
on the proper side of the track which, of course, is opposite from where it is at present. The whole track will
be carried further away from the grand stands so that
there will be a space available for a "quarter-stretch,"
and the sale of tickets to the quarter-stretch will be so
much larger than the present that the revenue from this
source will soon pay the cost of the improvements.
The State Fair of 1882 has come to an end, but the lesson it has given will have an influence for years. The
money value of the teachings, could it be figured, would
reach an enormous sum, though there are other influences of more actual value than dollars and cents. It
teaches a better system of rural life, and these teachings
end in happier homes, better people, better citizens.
That the fair of 1882 will be still superior is an insured
fact, as the experience of every year adds to the knowledge of the managers.

## TROTTING AT MELBOURNE, AUSTRALIA.

Heretofore we have noticed the $2,500 trotting purse
that has been advertised to be trotted over the Elsterne-
wick track, Melbourne, Australia. A double purpose
can be effected by making entries in it, as any good
horse which trots there can be sold for a round sum.
It would well repay the expense for the breeders here
to take measures that would insure several starters from
California, and by making a joint venture, so far as
sharing the expense, the outlay could be reduced to a
minimum sum. With these entries for this State and
the horses already in Australia, there will be a field that
will attract an attendance of at least twenty thousand
of the sport-loving inhabitants, and there will be plenty
other opportunities given for them to display their pow-

ers. It was a wise movement on the part of the club there to restrict t he entries to procreative animals, inducing the importation of the class which will be of the most benefit. After the fairs are over we hope to see arrangements made for shipping quite a number of the right sort of trotters, and above all other considerations the right sort of men to accompany them.

## OUR ILLUSTRATIONS.

There is the first break in the picture gallery of the "Breeder and Sportsman." Twelve illustrations have been given, ten of notables and two of types of what we regard as a good combination of blood to produce the fast trotter. One of these, Antevolo, since the picture was given trotted a mile at the Golden Gate Fair in 3:07, and that for a colt, not then sixteen months old, with scarcely any training, and "barefooted," proves that he has the gift naturally. The other has shown "lowdown in the twenties," so that it is reasonable to expect that he will be entitled to a place among "the notables" in the not very far-off future.

The break, however, is only temporary, and the illustrations will be resumed before long. As has been stated before, the series will comprise others than fast horses, or those of breeding which insure speed at the trot and gallop. The coach-horse, we learn, is represented in California by one of the finest specimens ever imported and we long his picture will grace the title page. In due course of time there will be cattle pictures, dogs, etc. One thing has followed the interregnum of the kings and queens of the turf and track, and that is the opportunity to see what a really handsome "heading" the artist has supplied us with. Joined to the fine pictures of the horses it is not so striking as when the letter-press takes up the most of the first page.

## THE FILLIES' YEAR.

Lord Falmouth's brown filly Dutch Oven first, Lord Stamford's brown filly Geheimniss second, the Duke of Westminster's Shotover third, is the placing in the great St. Leger of 1882. Of the fourteen starters four were fillies, and thus the old adage that September is the month for them to show to advantage is again proved to be true. There was not much interest taken in the race in America this year, as it was concluded that not one of "our colts" had shown form that would warrant even the most sanguine to look for victory. Sachem running into fourth place will be something of a surprise to many, and securing the next place to the fillies is further proof that the English three-year-old colts are an inferior lot. It was more of a surprise that Dutch Oven gained the first prize as after the race at York the odds were 100 to 1 against her, and but for the money which is always put on "Archer's mount" that would probably have been the rate at the start. As it was forty to one was laid and the backers of the popular jockey reaped a rich reward. J. R. Keene's Romeo, a brother to Monitor, made a poor showing.

## THE STOCKTON FAIR.

As we write, Friday morning, the Stockton Fair is in full swing. From our correspondent we learn that it is by far the most successful ever held. The stock on exhibition filled the stalls on the track and many of them had to be quartered outside. The animals in every department are superior, and as will be seen by the reports in another column the racing and trotting has been very satisfactory.

The attendance has been in excess of former years, every day showing an increase over former exhibitions and the management is pronounced to be of the best kind. One capital move was made in the suppression of gambling both on the fair grounds and in the city. The practice tolerated heretofore was the only point in the management of the San Joaquin Fair that could be found fault with, and we are much pleased to learn that it has been done away with.

The liberality displayed in "getting up" the programme was well worthy of a liberal return, and it is very gratifying to all concerned that it met with a liberal response.

## EDITORIAL NOTES.

**Horses For Sale.**—In the advertising column will be found notices of the auction sale of thoroughbreds belonging to W. L. Pritchard and a yearling trotting colt of rare breeding. Those which Mr. Pritchard offers are well worthy the attention of buyers. The breeding is very fine and the success which has followed the colts of the same strains is sufficient guarantee that there must be high excellence in those offered. Lena Dunbar, Jim Brown, Maria F, Enclure, Patsy Duffy and others are sufficient illustrations of the value of the blood, and as to good looks, that will be found satisfactory upon examination. The pressure of other business compels Mr. Pritchard to part with them, and there can scarcely be a

question that great bargains can be had at the sale. The present popularity of racing at the East has increased the number of meetings to such an extent that the value of blood stock has been greatly enhanced in the home-breeding regions, and it will not be long until California is drawn upon extensively to furnish animals. There cannot be a more auspicious time to engage in the breeding and rearing of thoroughbreds, and the sale which is to be held on Monday, the 16th of November, gives a capital opportunity to purchase. The yearling colt offered is an animal of the highest form, and his blood will be found of great service to cross with the Hambletonian and other strains. We brought his dam here when a yearling, and she was one of the most promising we ever saw. When three years old she trotted three-quarters of a mile in 1:55, a 2:34 gait, and she was only broken that spring. Owing to an injury she received in the stable she had to be thrown out of training. The combination of Belmont, Mambrino Chief, American Eclipse and Blackbird is sure to mingle harmoniously with the other trotting families.

**To Judge** by the number of challenges that have been flying around for the past week, the bay must be covered with ambitious oarsmen practicing for important contests. So far, however, not a match has been made. Nothing, has yet come of Jim Branne's defy to young Griffin, and the elder Griffin has not covered the deposit of $500, made with the BREEDER AND SPORTSMAN by representatives of the Pioneer club. Mr. Griffin offered in print to match his son against any man in the Pioneer club except Leahy and Nelson and his second crew against the Pioneers' best crew. The Pioneers have deposited $500 and offer to match a scull-or against the best sculler in the Golden Gate club, who is of course Peterson, and also to match a crew against Mr. Griffin's best crew for $1,000. On Tuesday Mr. Griffin complained that sufficient time to make the match had not been granted him, and the Pioneer men extended it several days and left their money in the BREEDER AND SPORTSMAN office. This looked like business. Peterson is a professional waterman who ought to be able to row any man in the world. Mr. Griffin, after several days to consider, offered to match a four-oar crew against the Pioneers; but as the Pioneers had expressly stipulated that the sculler's race and the four-oar race should take place after the offer was declined. On Friday afternoon, the specified time for making the match having expired, the Pioneer representatives withdrew their money.

**Krick's "Guide to the Turf."**—We are in receipt of the September edition of this extremely valuable work, and it is praise enough to say that it is fully up to the standard of former volumes. It is difficult to account for the absence of support which this work receives on the Pacific Coast. Fortunately the labor of the compiler is better appreciated in the East, or rather it is found so indispensable there that no one who has any fondness for racing can do without it. The growth of racing in the United States has been so great that the summaries, brief comments on the condition of the track, rates of betting, and the index of names of the horses which have run, occupy 343 pages of Nonpareil. The under gives the sire and dam and the pages where the races are to be found. When inclosed in brackets it means that the animal won, and from that practice has originated the term "bracketed," meaning a winner. Those who have had something to do with putting races in shape for the papers have a knowledge of how vast the labor of putting them in shape, and though turfmen, breeders, trainers, etc., if at all intelligent, can scarcely get along without it, yet the frequenters of the track get a benefit far beyond the cost. For this handsome volume the price is only fifty cents. Address H. G. Crickmore, *The New York World*, 31 and 32 Park Row, N. Y.

**Overman** has been matched against Helene for $2,500 a side, the race to be trotted on the Gentlemen's Driving Association track, N. Y. The day of the trot is to be named between the 1st and 15th of October. Helene has a record of 2:21, so that Overman has three-fourths of a second the best of it on that score. The match is attracting a great deal of attention in New York and more interest is taken in it than in any which has come off for some time. Overman is thought to have rather the best of it, though the mare is very fast. As Hickock drives Overman, and Murphy Helene, there is talent on both sides. and unquestionably the race will be one of the best of the season.

**Goldsmith** received universal commendations for the able manner he handled Cairo in the special race at Sacramento. That the enormiums were well-deserved there cannot be the least doubt, as every one we have heard speak of it joins in extolling the skill he displayed. Those who have seen Cairo in his previous races are aware that he was very unsteady, breaking, pulling and generally unmanageable. By a slight change in his harness, the removal of weights and skillful manipulations of the reins he only made one break during the race, and scored his first victory of the season.

**Old Joe Howell** has added another feather to his plume, or rather, like that of the Prince of Wales, there are three as a record of his time of victories at the State Fair. He is a wonderful old horse, and seems likely to emulate the doings of the "Cariale Gelding" of the olden time, which ran successfully until he was eighteen years old. We have been taken to task for giving his pedigree as being from Eva Shepherd, while it has been stated that his dam was Etta Shippen. The former is correct, as we were instrumental in C. C. Parks (who bred for Howell) buying her at the sale of D. A. Gaze, 1860, then being in foal to Bonnie Scotland, and that fall we sold him the horse. There is scarcely a proba-

bility that Etta Shippen ever was bred to Bonnie Scotland. Mr. Parks was starting his breeding farm at Glen Flora at that time, and when he purchased Eva Shepherd it was with the intention of using her in the trotting stud, but the purchaser of Bonnie Scotland changed his views. We sold him Maude, by imported Australian, and from her he bred "Papermaker."

**Lady Viva**, two years old, by Three Cheers, from Lady Amanda, by imported Hurrah, and Sir Thad, one year old, by Norfolk or Thad Stevens, from Lady Amanda, has gone into Mr. Winters' stable and will be trained by Dudley Allen. Lady Viva is in the two-year-old stakes of the Pacific Coast Blood Home Association, but as she never had a saddle on up to the time of reaching Sacramento Thursday last there is scant time to get her in any order.

**Duroc Swine.**—In another part of the paper will be found a capital article written by Col. F. D. Curtis for the *Breeders' Gazette* from which it was copied, and without giving that spirited journal credit. This came from the "form" going to press before we were aware of it, the intention being to precede it with some remarks in which the credit would have been awarded. There can scarcely be a doubt that this breed of hogs is well adapted to the California climate and will be found a valuable addition to the Berkshires, Essex, Magie's and other dark-colored swine.

## Helpers.

From the following, cut from the last number of the *Turf, Field and Farm*, it will be seen that there are others who agree with us that some plan should be adopted to stop the evil of helpers in trotting races. In fact the ideas are so similar that it appears as though our views were based upon those of our contemporary, though the article was in type before the *Turf, Field and Farm* reached here. If all of the papers were to take the same stand there is not a question that measures will be taken to correct this evil, and it is the duty of the journals that make the sports of the track a speciality to have the practice done away with. United effort will accomplish the purpose and that without other rules than are now in force. The helper must be punished so severely that one offense will be all that is necessary to get rid of him entirely. With support from the papers the "charity" of the judges will be replaced with an indisposition to do their part in counteracting the schemes, and a few combinations broken will have the effect to stop others being entered into:

There is a practice somewhat difficult to reach, and yet is doing harm to the turf, and that is of forming a combination to help this or that horse to win. When a driver is satisfied that he sits behind a horse which has not speed enough to show the way to the wire he makes an arrangement to help, for a consideration, what he regards as the most formidable contestant. The help consists in surrendering the pole to the animal of his choice, should he be fortunate enough to get it, or in giving up to him any place of advantage he may hold. It further consists in doing everything which can be done under a strained interpretation of the rules to block the way of a dangerous rival. For instance, the helper has speed, if used in bursts, to trot around the horse, to which he is opposed, and he does so without interference, but when he is fairly in front he takes his horse back and compels the other to shorten its stride, or to pull out and trot around him. Much of this would be deemed fair under the rules, were each driver using his art to get his own horse to the score first, but it is not fair when done in the interests of a combination. The difficulty of determining where an unlawful combination exists is the protection under which the practice spreads and grows. It is easy to suspect, but suspicion is not proof. The rules are broad enough to cover the case, but it is rare to find three men in the judges' stand who will agree to narrow the definition and to sternly impose the penalty. It is the usual desire to exercise charity, and to allow plenty of latitude to the drivers. There are drivers who will not abuse the generosity of the stand, but, unfortunately, they can be counted upon the fingers of the hand, and so do not form the common standard of action. The only remedy which suggests itself is for the judges to make up their minds that tolerance is working injury to the turf, and to stop looking at a race with charity in their eyes. This helping business has been carried too far. If efforts are not made to put an end to it, the grumbling of owners will be louder, and trickery every year will become more and more apparent.

## The Ladies' Tournament at the State Fair.

The equestrian display on Friday of the State Fair was the best ever seen on such occasions, both in regard to the number of entries as also to the skill, dash and grace shown by most of the young ladies who participated in the tournament. At the best of times it is a thankless task trying to adjudicate fairly on the proficiency shown on such occasions, and the president in making the award stated that the judges had studiously avoided taking the names of the ladies who contested, and that thereby their opinion was unbiased by the slightest form of favoritism, and the ladies were recognized only as bearers of certain numbers on their saddles. There was a great deal of trotting and galloping indulged in by the contestants one by one, both in the saddle and on the bare back, and one or two showed good trick riding, but owing to the horses not having been properly trained, or not being under the complete control of their riders, the evolutions in squads were very poorly managed. There was some divergence of opinion as to the relative merits of the young equestriennes and there was far from being unanimity in regard to the awards made by the judges, which were as follows: First prize, Mrs. Marchand; second, Miss Belle Ellis; third, Miss Nellie Ilyau; fourth, Mrs. Treffry; fifth, Miss Katie Londale; sixth, Miss Mabel Lusebach; seventh, Miss Carpenter; eighth, Mrs. Kate George; ninth, Alice Odbert; tenth, Edith Bradford; eleventh, Emma Londale. There were fourteen prizes awarded to the best bareback riders, as follows: First prize, Miss Carpenter, second, Miss Mabel Lusebach; third, Miss Nellie Ryan.

# ROWING.

THE HILLSDALES.—The telegraph announces that the Hillsdale four are coming back from England. The race with the Thames crew last week proved a most unfortunate affair for the Americans. Defeat under any circumstances is not pleasant, but in the case of the Hillsdales, after all the challenging and railing against the committees, the pill of misfortune must have been a very bitter one to swallow. The Hillsdales as previously remarked in these columns are not entitled to much sympathy. Had they acted in a sensible and business-like manner, made their arrangements properly and been sure before leaving America that they would be allowed to row in English regattas, their return would have been very different from what it is. They might have been beaten but they would not have been insulted as well as humiliated. Considering the rough and discouraging treatment that the Hillsdales met in England, they could not have been expected to do as well in a race as if they had been favorably received and allowed to proceed systematically with their training. The race has decided nothing. The question of the comparative merits of English and American champion fours is still unsettled. When the captain of the Hillsdale crew broke his slide his men were leading the Thames crew but there was still a long course before them and he would have been a wise man who could predict that the Englishmen would not get to the front before the finish. Many a good crew and sculler has been half a dozen-lengths behind midway in the Thames course and in the last two miles pulled up and won easily. Boat racing is very uncertain, and unless it is a Hanlan who is to the front early in the race, it is a poor speculation betting that he will keep there over a four or five mile course. While the Hillsdales are very fast over one and a half and two mile courses they have no record over longer stretches of water, and as they practice a new style of rowing it is not certain that they can go the championship distances at their best pace. It is to be regretted that the Thames men refused to give the Hillsdales another race and their refusal to do so may indicate that they had had enough of the Americans. The crew that rowed the American four is not regarded by English professional oarsmen as the strongest amateur four that could be got together on the Thames. The London Rowing Club could put forward a much stronger crew and it is likely that such would have been the programme if the Americans had won their first match.

COURTNEY'S GREAT PERFORMANCE.—The *Turf, Field and Farm* says: In the three-mile single-scull race at Saratoga, August 25, Courtney finished second to Lee, who won in the very good time of 20 minutes 43¼ seconds, and immediately after the race the opinion was advanced that Courtney would have been victorious had he not fouled the number attached to his stake. As the foul cost him 20 seconds, and as his time was about 5½ seconds slower than Lee's, the opinion was well founded. On Canadargo Lake, at Richfield Springs, September 1, Courtney rowed Lee a three-mile race and vanquished him in the wonderful time of 19 minutes 31¼ seconds. The time of Lee was considerably faster than that made in the Saratoga race. It was 19 minutes 35¼ seconds. As the course was carefully measured, and as the watches were held by men of experience and reputation, we must accept the returns as correct. Courtney appears to be gaining courage. He has his nervous system under better control. He has been like a sensitively organized colt, which raises the hopes of its owner by astonishing trials, but which gets frightened when at the post and is unable to perform in a way satisfactory to any one. The thought of the race and the sight of the crowd seem to have half paralyzed him, and he was met with defeat after defeat when victory was within his grasp. Now that he has stepped out of the timid, fawn-like state, and demonstrated to himself and the world that he is gifted with great skill and power at the sculls, it is to be hoped that confidence will not again desert him. He ought to be able to vanquish both Hanlan and Ross.

SOMNAMBULISTIC OARSMEN.—The latest reported eccentricity of Charles Courtney is somnambulism. Some of the sporting journals are poking a good deal of fun at the Saratoga sculler because of his alleged propensity for taking exercise in his sleep.

Although it is likely that the story of Courtney's sleep-walking originated in the lively imagination of some reporter, it is a fact that somnambulism effects some famous oarsmen. One of the bright and shining lights of the Pioneer Rowing club who some time ago dropped $500 on a three-mile race is accustomed to train for his matches by a regular night ramble in undress. A couple of nights before his last race he created a panic in his boarding house by using the dining room as a sprinting path. As he was making the tenth lap the landlady rushed in thinking that a Greenback convention had met in the dining room, and discovered the somnambulistic athlete flying around with as much contempt for superfluous clothing as the Long Bridge oarsmen show every Sunday when they go out to scare away all the sensitive females on shore.

AN ENTERPRISING CLUB.—The Ariel Rowing Club has probably less to say in the newspapers than any other club in San Francisco, but notwithstanding its silence it is always to the front when there is any rowing to be done. While some of the other clubs are blowing their horns and trying to startle the world with the praise of what they are going to do, the Ariels quietly keep on practicing and when Thanksgiving Day comes they will be found none the worse for their modest reticence. Last week they purchased the four-oar paper shell, formerly used with such determination but bad luck by the St. George Rowing Club. With some alterations in the rig of the boat she will be well suited to the Ariel four. Last Sunday they were practicing in the new craft, but the novelty had not worn off and their style could not have been considered a sample of what they will do in a few weeks.

COURTNEY'S LATEST VICTORY.—Until of late it was the regular thing to expect Courtney to get beaten in every race in which he entered. The burly carpenter seems determined to change the order of things, for he is begining to figure prominently as a winner. A dispatch from Alexandria Bay (N. Y.), dated September 18th, thus describes the race on Poplar Bay, St. Lawrence river, between Courtney, Ten Eyck and Dempsey:

"A mile and a quarter from the turn Courtney was leading Ten Eyck two lengths and rowing thirty-four strokes to the minute. He passed home an easy winner by the same lead. Time 20:59½. Dempsey was fully half a mile behind. The water was not good, but the men were willing to start. Courtney said it was the hardest race he ever rowed. Ten Eyck was quite exhausted."

AN ATHLETIC STATESMAN.—Thomas Murphy of the Potrero, Vice-president of the Pioneer Rowing Club and Champion wherry rower of the Pacific Coast, has been temporarily attracted from the aquatic arena by the prospective spoils of office. It was thought that Thomas would enliven Thanksgiving Day by a match on wherries with that tireless sculler R. C. Lyne of the Pioneer Rowing Club, but the glittering attractions of a statesman's career have interfered with the anticipated sport. Mr. Murphy is an announced candidate for the Legislature and the sentiment of the rowing clubs is strongly in his favor. A vote taken on Sunday at Long Bridge would send Thomas flying in a special train to Sacramento and make him Chairman of the Assembly.

A VETERAN HEARD FROM.—John Griffin's challenge on behalf of his son has drawn out the following defiant card from Jim Brannen, the veteran oarsman of the Pioneer club:

"In reply to J. D. Griffin's challenge to match his son against any member of the Pioneer Rowing Club, barring D. Leahy and E. Nelson, I will match P. J. Brennan for $1,000 a side, any distance from three to five miles, the race to be rowed in six weeks from signing articles. A forfeit of $250 awaits your pleasure. JAMES E. BRANNEN."

# YACHTING.

## The Mosquito-Regatta.

The following are the rules of the Mosquito regatta, which comes off to-day at 1:30, starting from Long Bridge. The regatta will be under the auspices of the San Francisco Yacht Club:

Class 1 includes Whitehall boats; class 2, yachts fifteen and under twenty feet, length on deck; class 3, yachts twenty and under twenty-five feet, length on deck; class 4, yachts twenty-five and under thirty feet, length on deck; class 5, yachts thirty and under thirty-five feet, length on deck.

A time allowance of one minute to the foot, difference in length over all, will be given. This allowance will only be given to the boats on each class separately. A twenty-four-foot boat will have to give two minutes to a twenty-two-foot boat, for instance, but has nothing to do with boats out of her class.

The course is as follows: Crossing a line from the end of Long Bridge to the southerly line of Mission Rock, thence to and around a stake boat (yacht Chispa) anchored about three yarters of a mile east of Mission Street wharf in mid channel, thence to and around stake-boat (yacht Aggie, about half-way between Mission Rock and Alameda wharf, and in line with these two points), thence to Mission Rock again, passing to southward of it, and crossing starting line.

All boats must take this course. Fourth and fifth-class boats must, however, continue on, passing to westward of Mission Rock, thence to leeward and around the Alameda stake-boat again and back to starting point, passing southward of Mission Rock, and crossing starting line to finish. In this second turn, it is to be understood that the stake-boat Chispa, off the city front is omitted.

The sails allowed are as follows: For plungers, mainsail; for sloops, jib and mainsail; for yawls, jib, mainsail and driver, and for schooners, jib, foresail and mainsail. No light sails allowed. All yachts must carry a number on the starboard side of mainsail, which will be furnished by the committee on the morning of the race. As to crews, class 1 and 2 may carry four men; class 3, five men; class 4, six men, and 5 class may carry seven men.

On the morning of the race, yachts will form in line according to classes:

Class 1 will anchor in line, south and east of Long Wharf; class 2 will anchor in line, east and abreast of class 1; class 3 will anchor in line south of class 1; class 4 will anchor in line south of class 2; class 5 will anchor in line south of class 4.

The Committee will be present when the lines are formed, and all are requested to endeavor to second their efforts by prompt compliance with directions.

The preparatory whistle will be blown from the judges' steamer at 1:30 P. M., when all yachts may set after-sails.

At 1:35 P. M., the second whistle will be blown, when class 1 will slip their moorings, and get under weigh.

At 1:38 P. M., the third whistle will be blown, when class 2 will get under weigh.

At 1:41 P. M., the fourth whistle will be blown, when class 3 will get under weigh.

At 1:44 P. M., the fifth whistle will be blown, when class 4 will get under weigh.

At 1:47 P. M., the sixth whistle will be blown, when class 5 will get under weigh.

Anchors may be slipped or weighed, as preferred.

The regular sailing rules of the San Francisco Yacht Club will govern this race.

Yachts fouling stake-boats, or competing yachts, will forfeit all claims to prizes.

The yacht nearest the stake-boat will be considered ahead, and if forced against the stake-boat, the one so forcing her will be barred out.

No shifting of ballast will be allowed during the race.

Yachts on port tack must give way to those on starboard tack.

Yachts running free must give way to yachts running by the wind.

Large yachts when passing, should go to leeward of smaller ones, and give smaller classes every chance.

The committee reserve the right to exclude any entries they may think proper, or to subdivide the classes; and also to decide all questions of any kind which may arise during the sailing of the regatta.

Two or three prizes will be given in each class, and will be distributed immediately after the race, at Mission Rock. All competitors are requested to come to judges' boat as soon as the race is over.

On Saturday last the Bohemian Yacht Club opened its new quarters at Saucelito. This new club is really a social one, all of its members being already members of the San Francisco Yacht Club. Her house is back of the San Francisco's and the landings have to be made at the S. F. Y. C. wharf and steps. There are only six members in the new club, J. C. Macdonough of the yacht Aggie, Jno. Rae Hamilton, yacht Clara, H. Tevis, yacht Whitewing, I Gutte, yacht Chispa and J. D. and A. B. Spreckels, whose new yacht is not yet launched. It is not the intention to admit any more members. There is an idea of opposition to the present clubs. The club house is neatly fitted up and when everything is in place will be quite elegant. On Saturday last a couple of hundred ladies and gentlemen went over to the inauguration of the club house. After an inspection of the premises all hands adjourned to the more spacious hall of the San Francisco Yacht Club where some literary exercises were held, presided over by George Bromley, Daniel O'Connell and others. Members of the Loring club furnished excellent vocal music. On the conclusion of the exercises the guests repaired to the tents, where table was spread and an old-

The Casco has been out a good deal lately.

The Gaviota lies at North Beach and is not used much.

The Flirt, Thetes and Spray are pretty evenly matched and ought to make a good race.

Commodore Harrison is around again in the Frolic, and keeps up her reputation for cruising.

The Consuelo and the Sweetheart will represent Lake Merrit in the Mosquito regatta to-day.

The Oakland boat Bessie which took the prize last year at the Mosquito race has been taken up river by some young men for a "shooting box."

The plunger Skipper, belonging to Capt. Ed. Munfrey of the Potrero, is a heeler in a breeze, and should the wind be pert to-day is expected to show her heels to some of the light weather crafts.

Lake Merrit is now the liveliest sailing place in the country. There are so many boats there that on Sundays there is great sport among those sailing them. It is not lonesome sailing, as it is on the bay.

The new yacht built by Turner for the Spreckels brothers will be launched in a few days. Those who want to see her on the ways will have to be quick about making their visit. The new yacht will be fitted up after she is in the water.

The Lolita has gone up to the Suisun marshes to stay for the winter as a "shooting box." She is moored where she was last year, in the Frankhorn slough, near the railway bridge at Teal station. A full outfit of hunting boats, traps, etc. has been taken up, and Captain Chittenden is prepared for a long siege upon the the ducks.

Commodore Macdonough and Mr. Gutte very peacefully permit their fine yachts to go as stake boats to encourage the "Mocquitos." It is but just to say that Mr. Bowie of the Nellie, Commodore Harrison of the Frolic, Mr. Hawkins of the Annie, and other gentlemen also volunteered their yachts and their services; all this is good for "the cause."

The 36 foot plungers, Restless Boss and Annie, were expected to go on the Mosquito race to-day, After a good deal of talk, however, and after a prize was provided, a race between them had to be given up. The Annie's sails were old and the owner did not want to sail except with new sails; the Boss was busy carrying oysters and couldn't be spared from trade long enough to be cleaned and put in readiness. This is the usual result in trying to put evenly matched boats to sail in a race on the bay.

fashioned clam bake had been prepared by Charley Dexter. After lunch music was provided for dancing but the guests seemed to prefer visiting the yachts. Small boats were in readiness at the float to take people on board the yachts which were moored near by, all decorated and decked out in gay bunting of all colors. The owners of the respective yachts were on hand to receive their guests and dispense hospitality. A special steamer was provided to take the visitors home though many returned in the ferry. All expressed themselves as having had a very good time.

# ATHLETICS.

## Another Amateur Sprinter.

At last another amateur sprinter has appeared that seems fit to compete with R. S. Haley from scratch. Masterson, of the Lacrosse Club, has very lately shown the ability to do 100 yards in 10 1-5 in a trial and at the rate he has been improving during the last two months, he is likely to do even time before the season is over. A match for a gold medal has been made between himself and Haley, the event to take place to-day, on the grounds of the O. A. A., and will be the most exciting contest on the programme of the fall meeting. It is well known that Haley can do 10 1-5, and that he invariably makes a game finish in all his races, and he will have hosts of friends on the grounds full of faith that he will be the first to breast the tape at the finish. And he has the additional encouragement of knowing that Masterson has never before shown himself, in an actual race, to be better than a fourth or fifth rate amateur. In the O. A. C. meeting last May, with 2½ yards in the 100 handicap, he failed to get a place in his trial. In the 440 handicap he won first, starting at the ten yards mark, but was completely run out in the slow time of 57¾ seconds. His excuse for his bad showings on that occasion was that he was sick and out of condition, but was fairly forced to compete by the taunts of outside individuals. Since that time he has improved wonderfully, and has demonstrated his ability to give six yards to some of his opponents in the spring meeting and jog by the side of them for the last 25 or 30 yards. He does it so easily and quietly that it is very aggravating to the doubters.

There seems to be a feeling among the members of the O. A. C. that he will quit in a hard contest, and also that he cannot run beyond 60 or 70 yards. In the 440 yards last May he struggled as gamely for the last 40 or 50 yards as any one could wish, and the amount of work he does on the grounds every Sunday morning is sufficient testimony as to his staying qualities. An hour of Lacrosse, running wide and high jumping, a try at the hurdles, perhaps a 220 yards dash, from one to two or three rounds of the track at different times with different members of his own club whom he is constantly coaching and encouraging, and after all that the strength and speed remaining to make an extraordinary showing in any of the impromptu 100 yards handicaps among the sprinters present, and a stride of 7 feet 2 inches in the last spurt—well, he will bear watching, and being a healthy man, of good physique, promises to be the leading athlete in all running and jumping events on the coast. Even if defeated in his match to-day with R. S. Haley, we still feel confident that he will in the near future demonstrate his ability to compete with any amateur at any distance below and including 440 yards, and attend to his own business for a living at the same time. He should become a member of the Olympic club and the club should see that he does.

AN INVITATION.—The Triton swimming and boating club hereby respectfully invites all rowing clubs to be present at their social gathering to be held at their boat house next Sunday, Sept. 24th, at 9 A. M. VAL KEHRLEIN JR.,
Sec. T. S. & B. C.

San Francisco, Sept. 21.

The bicycle races to take place to-day at the meeting of the Olympic Athletic Club promise to be well contested, and if we are not much at fault will show a material lowering of the Pacific Coast record at one mile.

# THE RIFLE.

## The International Rifle Match.

When the rival teams for international honors came down to daily practice, it was evident that the result of the match was a foregone conclusion, as at such distance the British team showed an average score that almost invariably showed a slight advance on that of the Americans, and that was bound to count heavily in the aggregate. It must be at once confessed that in making the match we labored under a great disadvantage, as among the British Volunteers it is a part of their yearly duty to go through a regular course of musketry drill and to fire a certain number of rounds in single, squad and skirmishing order, each shot being as carefully marked as in a prize match. Then there is not only a spirit of emulation but also the many valuable prizes offered for competition, that induce many to make a study of marksmanship and thus in organizing a team there is a far greater field to pick from in Great Britain and Ireland than there is in this country. It is pleasing to say that our men accepted their defeat with the feeling of gentlemen and in toasting the victors Colonel Bodine, the coach of our team, (congratulated the victors and expressed the hope that the Americans would be able to turn the tables on their opponents in the return match to be held at Wimbledon next year, a wish that we thoroughly indorse, and that was received by the British, on hospitable thoughts intent, with great applause. Annexed is an account of the targets, as also the score made at each distance:

There are three descriptions of targets in use at Creedmoor, styled first, second and third class. The first-class target is used at all distances over 600 yards. It is six feet high by twelve wide. The bull's-eye is thirty-six inches in diameter. It is surrounded by another circle known as the "center," fifty-four inches in diameter. Without this is a square known as the "inner," six feet by six feet. The remaining oblong, three feet by six feet, at each end of the target, is termed the "outer." The second-class target is six feet by six feet and is used at all distances over 300 and to 600 yards. The bull's-eye is twenty-two inches in diameter, the "center" is thirty-eight inches in diameter, and the "inner" fifty-four inches in diameter. The remainder of the target forms the "outer." The third-class target is six feet high by four feet wide and is used at all distances up to and including 300 yards. The bull's-eye is eight inches in diameter, the "center" twenty-six inches in diameter, the "inner" forty-six inches in diameter and the remainder of the target forms the "outer." On all the targets a shot on the bull's-eye scores five points, on the "center" four points, on the "inner," three points and on the "outer" two points. The targets are made of cast-iron and are placed along two long embankments at the north end of the range.

On the embankment on the left-hand side of the range are placed eleven targets of the third class. On the other embankment are twenty-one targets of the first and second classes; those of the first class being grouped on the right hand side, and those of the second class on the left. The third class targets have their bulls'-eyes about six feet above the level of the range, the bulls'-eye of the first and second-class targets the range being about ten feet above the level of the range. The embankment behind the mid-range and long-range targets—the targets of the first and second classes—is about twenty-five feet high; that behind the third class or short-range target being much lower. Each embankment is surmounted by a thick board fence as a still further protection against badly aimed bullets. Beneath each embankment and in front of the targets is a covered way or tunnel about six feet by four feet where the markers are stationed. Fronting each target is a skylight and a trap door. When the target is struck the marker looking through the skylight sees the mark left by the bullet. He pulls a lever which opens the trap-door and at the same time causes to be displayed a red-colored disc on the right hand-corner of the target which indicates that the target is not to be shot on until the disc is removed, which is done by closing the trap-door. Then through the open trap-door the marker raises a pole with a disc attached to it, which by its color, indicates to the scorer what part of the target has been struck. When the bull's-eye has been struck he raises a white disc; for a "center," a red disc; for an "inner," a white disc with a black cross, and for an "outer," a red disc. To the reverse side of each disc is attached a brush. These brushes are used to paint over the marks made on the target by the bullets, so that when the marker signals to the scorer the number of points made, he at the same time obliterates the impression left by the bullet. The target being thus kept clean the marker can see readily where each fresh bullet strikes.

At the 200-yard range the Americans made the following scores: Hinds 29, Dolan 25, Alder 27, Ogden 27, Atkinson 29, McNevin 22, Pollard 29, Shakspeare 25, Paulding 27, Smith 30. Total, 331. The British made: Parry 28, Heup 31, Goodyear 33, Boulter 26, Oliver 29, Pearse 25, Dods 31, McVittie 31, Goodsell 29, Humphrey 27, Bates 26, Caldwell 24, Hinman 30, Howard 31. Total, 342.

In the 500 yards the score of the Americans was: Hinds 29, Ogden 31, McNevin, 33, Atkinson 32, Howard 29, Shakspeare 29, Dolan 28, Alder 30, Pollard 31, Hinman 32, Smith 34, Paulding 31. Grand total, 369. British team: Parry 30, Goodyear 31, Caldwell 33, Dods 31, Bates 31, McVittie 34, Heup 34, Boulter 32. Pearse 32, Oliver 30, Humphrey 32, Goodsell 27. Grand total, 373. The result of the firing at the 500 yards added nine points to the lead the British secured at the 200-yard range, making a total lead in favor of the British of 16 points. The spectators now conceded a victory to the visitors. Their shooting was remarkably strong. McVittie and Heup made 34 out of possible 35. Humphrey, one of the best shots in the British team, was completely run off his feet.

After the finish at 500 yards the men were soon at work upon the 600 yards range. The wind by this time had fallen considerably. The following is the score at 600 yards: American total—Ogden 31, Hinman 28, Hinds 26, Alder 23, Dolan 24, Atkinson 27, McNevin 30, Pollard 33, Shakspeare 29, Howard 25, Paulding 24, Smith 31. Grand total, 343. British score—Goodyear 24, Pearse 27, Parry 27, Boulter 32, Heup 26, Dods 32, Caldwell 31, Goodsell 30, Oliver 29, McVittie 30, Humphrey 24, Bates 29. Grand total, 344.

The aggregate scores at the three ranges were: Americans, 1,043; British, 1,069. Of the British team, McVittie made the highest aggregate score at the three ranges, scoring 95. Of the American team, Smith made the highest aggregate score at the three ranges, scoring 93.

On the 15th at the 800-yard range the score of the Americans was, Hinds 19, Dolan 17, McNevin 17, Hinman 19, Smith 20, Paulding 20, Ogden 27, [Atkinson 23, Pollard 23,] Shakspeare 16, Howard 19. Total for Americans at 800 yards, 255. British—Heup 10, Boulter 31; Godsel 29, Humphrey 31, Caldwell 31, Pearse 29, Goods 29, Parry 25, Bates 24, McVittie 26, Oliver 21. Dodds 26. Total for British, 293.

The score at 900 yards was: American—Hinds 19, Ogden 17, McNevin 24, Atkinson 23, Howard 17, Shakspeare 25, Dolan 27, Alder 22, Pollard 28, Hinman 26, Smith 26, Paulding 20. Grand total, 271. British—Parry 24, Goodyear 26, Caldwell 26, Dods 26, Bates 28, McVittie 30, Heup 15, Goodsall 24. Grand total, 313.

The score at a 1000 yards was: Americans—Hinds 10; Ogden 20, McNevin 23, Atkinson 19, Howard 29, Shakspeare 21, Dolan 21, Alder 11, Pollard 18, Hinman, 23, Smith 21, Paulding 20. Grand total, 236. British—Parry 31, Goodyear 26, Caldwell 28, Dods 20, Bates 25, McVittie 25, Heup 24, Boulter 24; Pearse 27, Oliver 27, Humphrey 32, Goodsell 22. Grand total, 307.

Grand aggregate total of the two days' shooting—Americans, 1,805; British, 1,975.

## That Shooting at Carson.

CARSON CITY, NEVADA, September 19, 1882.

EDITOR BREEDER AND SPORTSMAN: In your issue of the 16th inst. I find the record of the rifle match of the 7th between Messrs. Williams, Kellogg, King and Thaxter, and I also notice your doubting and somewhat facetious remarks relative to the handsome score made by the latter gentlemen.

The Carson Guards, a regularly organized military company, is composed of honorable men and among them King and Thaxter; the practice of target shooting with this company is done for improvement and is not conducted to deceive anyone. I placed the target in position, saw every shot made, removed the target and had it photographed, a copy of which is herewith enclosed, and I confidently assert that it has not been tampered with, but that every shot was made as telegraphed and as they appear on the photograph, and would send you the 200-yard score had it not been made on an iron target.

These two gentlemen are not the only good shots in our company, as we have a team of twelve men that for money, most-agates, marbles, Indian legends, or photos of Kellogg and Williams' score, can beat the score of the American team in the International match.

This is intended as a challenge, and with malice prepense and aforethought, and knowing how words sound and what they mean, it is so written a challenge as open and broad as the universe is boundless.

If you harbor a thought that these two gentlemen cannot repeat the score, come up here, act as marker, and if they fail you can win money enough to make you to travel in foreign lands in Pullman palace cars during the rest of your days and make valuable presents to your multitude of friends, and the money you will win will tend to increase your friends, and also a present to your subscriber and to your servant, Rick B. Shay. Very Respectfully,
         HUDS O. PARKER,
         Captain Carson Guards.

Note by the editor of the BREEDER AND SPORTSMAN—It is pleasant to call attention to the remarkably fine score made by Messrs. King and Thaxter, and in order to promote a spirit of emulation among our own marksmen a fac simile of the target is hereto appended, taken from the photograph so courteously sent by Captain Parker, commanding the Carson Guard.

One hundred shots, 500 yards.

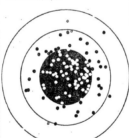

X / Sighting-shots.

THE SCHUETZEN CLUB.—The California Schuetzen Club held its monthly medal and bulls-eye shooting on Sunday last at Alameda Schuetzen Park. The shooting was made especially interesting by Mr. Freese, a member of the club, giving a beautiful silver goblet as first prize for the 'best center shot. The following is the result of the contest:—First prize for best center, O. Rapp, silver goblet; second prize, A. Strecker; third, F. Freese; fourth, Zecher; fifth, P. Jacoby; sixth, A. Rahwyler; seventh, Krahmann; eighth, H. C. Smith; ninth, C. C. Bhofle; tenth, K. Wertheimer; eleventh, Bertram; twelfth, Roschel; thirteenth, C. Adam; fourteenth, Rox; fifteenth, Langenheim; sixteenth, Eckmann; seventeenth, Maag; eighteenth, Greiner; nineteenth, L. Haake; twentieth, Thompson; twenty-first, Folkers Jr.; twenty-second, Nobmann. First-class medal, H. C. Smith, 403 rings; second-class, Krahmann, 376 rings; third-class, Hoz, 307 rings.

The club will hold its grand prize shooting at the same park on Sunday, Oct. 1st, at which both prizes and sweepstakes will be shot for. There are three styles of shooting, at bullseye targets, at man targets and at honorary targets. The shooting is open to all comers and promises to be the most successful reunion ever held by the club.

There ought to be a more systematic method of getting up rifle matches between teams of different companies of the National Guard than is now the case. With a proper spirit of emulation, and especially with practice and the proper study of winds and atmospheric changes, San Francisco ought to turn out a team chosen from the National Guard that could beat the score of the American team in the recent international match.

The Turner Sharpshooters held their monthly medal shooting last Sunday at Alameda Schuetzen Park with the following results: Champion medal D. Schoenfield, 407 rings; first-class medal O. Burmeister, 352 rings; second-class medal Charles Huber, 303 rings; third-class medal Charles Sagehorn, 277 rings.

## California Horses at the East.

NEW YORK, Sept. 13.

MY DEAR MR. SIMPSON:—I was at Sheepshead yesterday and had the pleasure of witnessing two grand racing events wherein Lucky B and the Duchess of Norfolk won their respective races of a mile and a half with comparative ease. The betting on each race was about the same, being ten to one against the winning, and consequently the Bookmakers were heavy losers.

Our friend Walton, the Plunger, backed the wrong ones and fell heavily. E. J. Baldwin, it is said, won about $15,000, O. P. Keys pocketed about $8,000, J. F. Hutchinson $5,000, and indeed all the Californians won handsomely.

The horses in Mr. Baldwin's stable have been sick and in miserably bad shape, especially so while at Monmouth Park, but their removal to Sheepshead Bay has proved highly beneficial. I hope, and now believe, that you will hear grand reports from this stable hereafter.

I have heard much of your new paper. I wish you would send to me the back numbers and consider me a regular subscriber from the start, and I will remit my subscription soon as I receive the papers.

Wishing you prosperity and many happy days, and with kind remembrance of yourself and family, I am,
         Sincerely your friend,
         W. J. WELCH.

THE FUTURE OF THE BEEF MARKET.—Owing to the easy exportation of fresh meat to Europe, the price of beef has gone up very rapidly in the last year, and the cause which sent it up will keep it at a good, round figure for many years. The offal of the Colusa county farms, now wasted, would feed a million dollars' worth of cattle. But not only will the price of beef keep up, but mutton and pork must follow. There is hardly any product so profitable as pork at five cents on foot, and we think the outlook promises that it will remain above that figure for some years to come. See how many hogs a little alfalfa patch will keep until the stubble is ready to fatten them. How many thousand acres of stubble went to waste this year in Colusa county? Stock, cattle and sheep will live on straw, and it costs less than a dollar a ton to stack straw so as that it will last for years. There is more money in attending to saving these things, than attempting to plant, in a wasteful manner, great areas of wheat. And besides, a system of stock-growing keeps the land from wearing out. Pasturing always improves land. These things are worth the earnest consideration of the farmers of the county.—Colusa Sun.

# THE GUN.

## Good Shooting.

DENVERTON, CAL., September 19, 1882.

EDITOR BREEDER AND SPORTSMAN, Dear Sir: Thinking that the following might be of interest I send it:

Ed. Stewart and myself, at the Harmon ponds, north of the Montezuma Slough, on the morning of the 15th, killed 22 mallards, 8 cinnamon teal and 6 grey geese. These geese were the first of the season, in fact were killed from the first flocks seen in this section this year. The prospects for a good duck and snipe crop are excellent. Yours, etc,
         JIM MACK.

Mr. O'Keif has returned from Jersey Landing and reports very good duck shooting in that vicinity.

Sam Hunter and Geo. Coffee with the aid of the two faithful young setters, Bess and Nell, succeeded in bagging 34 quail near Niles, on Sunday morning before 10 o'clock.

Fred Johnson went down to the Bouchard Brothers' ranch, near Pescadero, and bagged about twelve dozen quail in three days. He says that quail and rabbits are very plentiful in San Mateo county. Fred is a member of the Cosmopolitan Club and is a first-class huntsman.

A. F. Adams and Mr. Floyd spent a few hours last Saturday in the Morgan Valley, among the quail. The quail are as plentiful in this valley as elsewhere but the difficulty is in getting them when killed, as the brush is so thick that the dogs are unable to work well and so many are lost. Messrs. Adams and Floyd in two hours' shooting bagged fifty quail and several rabbits.

A party of five members of the Cordelia Club opened the season by a hunting trip to their preserve in the Suisun marshes. They went up Thursday evening and had good luck on Friday by bagging fifty-five birds, mallards, teal and a few sprig; most of the latter were young and in good condition. Beside their own boats and scows, the Cordelia Club has leased Capt. Chittenden's yacht "Lolita" for the season and has had Captain C. sworn in as deputy sheriff to protect the marshes.

While walking near the Oakland ferry the other evening we ran across a sportsman just returned from a day's hunt over the bay. On inquiring what success he had met with, he pointed to a well-filled game bag lying on the sidewalk. We wished to examine its contents but he remonstrated, as he couldn't stop just then. By insisting for a short time we carried the point and drew out six quail, two doves and a fine, young—rooster—the result of his day's hunt. As he had some good cigars to offer, there will be no names mentioned.

Messrs. C. Robinson, R. E. Wilson and T. Pearson, of the Sportsman's Club, opened the season with a hunt on Grass Valley farm in Alameda county. These three gentlemen bagged fifty quail. They say that quail are scarce in that section of the country. Aside from the game killed by the party Mr. Pearson had a little sport on his own hook. Soon after getting out he accidentally fired a charge of bird shot into the rear portion of the anatomy of his favorite hunting dog; and a little later he—by accident of course—fired into a flock of tame turkeys, killing four of the number. Mr. Pearson will please remember that the open season on turkeys does not begin till just before the holidays. We cannot find authority for the open season for dogs.

The morning of September 15th opened up one of the best seasons for quail that has been known for years. Every one who could get away from business shouldered his gun and began a second Waterloo on the beautiful tribe. Many left the city for the hunting grounds the day before, so as to be on hand for the first shot of the season at the earliest break of dawn on Friday morning. For several days following the battle raged. From nearly every ravine, woodland and marsh within a day's ride of San Francisco, could be heard the reports of fire-arms. The farmer, with his old-fashioned army musket; the market and pot-hunter with his double-bending shotgun, and the sportsman with his latest improved fowling piece, all joined in the slaughter of the innocents.

## Wing Shooting at the State Fair.

The wing and trap shooting under the management of the Forrester Club of the Capital city was one of the chief features of the State Fair and it is to be regretted that owing to our crowded columns we cannot devote the full space to the proceedings they so well deserve. The arrangements were very complete save that more commodious quarters could be furnished to the scorers and the press gang. The birds were very fair considering the difficulty there is in procuring on average assortment at rates that are not too high, and the trapping gave general satisfaction. The general attraction of the meeting was the opening match in which most of the gun clubs throughout the State were well represented. As there were some forty entries it was neccessary to divide them into four squads and as the following score will show there was some very effective shooting done, the conditions being twelve birds, twenty-one yards rise and eighty yards boundary.

THE FIRST SQUAD.

| | | |
|---|---|---|
| F. J. Bassford | 0 1 1 0 1 1 1 0 0 1 1 1 | 8 |
| A. J. Vermilya | 0 1 1 1 1 1 0 0 1 1 0 1 | 8 |
| F. Lastreto | 1 1 1 1 1 1 1 1 * 1 1 1 | 11 |
| F. Maskey | 1 1 0 1 * 1 1 1 0 1 0 1 | 8 |
| J. W. Todd | 0 0 1 1 1 1 1 1 1 1 1 1 | 10 |
| J. L. Zouver | 1 1 0 0 1 1 1 1 1 1 1 1 | 10 |
| Geo. Routier | 1 1 1 1 1 1 1 1 1 0 1 1 | 11 |
| J. T. McIntosh | 1 1 1 1 1 1 1 1 1 1 1 1 | 12 |
| J. H. Burnett | 1 1 1 1 1 1 1 1 0 1 0 1 | 10 |
| Chas. Reames | 0 1 1 0 1 1 * 0 1 0 1 1 | 7 |

*Died out of bounds.

THE SECOND SQUAD.

| | | |
|---|---|---|
| F. D. Weeks | 1 1 1 1 1 1 1 0 1 1 1 1 | 11 |
| H. Hopper | 1 1 1 0 1 0 1 1 1 1 1 1 | 10 |
| C. H. Pracht | 1 1 1 1 0 1 1 1 1 1 1 1 | 11 |
| F. Shepler | 1 1 1 1 1 1 1 0 1 1 1 1 | 11 |
| C. Honeschell | 1 1 1 1 1 1 1 0 1 1 1 1 | 11 |
| B. Hobenschell | 1 0 1 1 0 1 0 0 1 1 1 1 | 8 |
| W. Thomas | 1 1 1 1 1 1 1 1 1 1 1 1 | 12 |
| W. E. Pierson | 1 1 1 1 1 1 1 1 1 1 0 0 | 10 |
| F. Welden | 1 1 1 1 0 1 1 1 1 0 1 0 | 9 |
| K. Robbins | 1 0 1 1 1 0 1 1 1 1 1 1 | 10 |

THE THIRD SQUD.

| | | |
|---|---|---|
| J. M. Bassford | 1 1 1 1 1 0 1 1 1 0 1 1 | 10 |
| B. A. Bassford | 1 0 1 1 1 1 1 1 1 0 | withd'n |
| G. D. Adams | 1 0 0 1 1 1 1 0 1 1 0 0 | 7 |
| F. G. Sefler | 1 1 1 1 1 1 1 1 1 1 1 1 | 12 |
| J. F. White | 1 1 1 1 0 1 0 1 1 1 1 1 | 10 |
| A. Graves | 0 1 1 1 1 1 0 0 1 1 0 0 | 7 |
| C. C. Brown | 1 1 1 0 1 1 1 1 1 1 0 1 | 10 |
| H. Creed | 1 1 1 1 0 1 1 1 1 1 1 1 | 11 |
| C. E. Mack | 1 1 1 1 1 1 1 0 1 1 0 1 | 10 |
| N. B. Scott | 1 1 1 1 1 1 1 1 1 1 0 1 | 11 |

THE FOURTH SQUAD.

| | | |
|---|---|---|
| C. Menke | 1 1 1 1 1 1 1 0 0 1 1 1 | 10 |
| W. Shelden | 1 1 1 1 1 1 1 0 0 1 1 0 | 9 |
| F. Nesbit | 1 1 1 1 1 0 1 1 1 1 0 1 | 10 |
| B. Bassford | 0 1 0 1 1 1 1 1 1 1 1 1 | 10 |
| H. Gerber | 1 1 1 1 1 1 1 1 0 1 1 1 | 11 |
| T. Lopez | 1 1 1 1 1 1 1 1 1 1 1 1 | 12 |
| Otto Miller | 0 0 1 1 1 0 0 1 1 1 1 1 | 8 |
| A. Schnabel | 1 1 1 1 1 1 1 1 1 1 1 1 | 12 |
| J. Parrott | 1 1 1 1 1 1 1 1 1 1 1 1 | 12 |
| J. Gerber | 1 1 0 1 1 1 1 1 1 0 1 1 | 10 |
| F. Rubstaller | 1 1 1 1 1 0 1 1 1 1 1 1 | 11 |

TIES OF TWELVE.

Ties of twelve were then shot off at double birds, at eighteen yards rise, resulting in the following excellent scores:

| | | | |
|---|---|---|---|
| J. F. McIntosh | 1 1 | 1 0 | 1 0 |
| William Thomas | 1 0 | 1 1 | 1 1 |
| F. J. Lefler | 1 1 | 1 1 | 1 1 |
| J. Lopez | 1 1 | 1 1 | 1 0 |
| A. Schnabel | 1 1 | 1 0 | 1 1 |
| J. Parrott | 1 1 | 1 0 | 1 1 |

Lefler took the first prize. The tie on five birds—Wm. Thomas and A. Schnabel—divided the second prize.

On the second day the chief interest was centered in a fifteen bird tournament, $20 entrance, twenty-one yards rise, plunge trap by agreement to be designated and eighty yards boundary, in which there were twenty entries with the prizes thus arranged: First $120; second $100; third $80; fourth $60 and fifth $40. Again there were made some excellent scores, but some of those who made such a fine exhibit on the opening day could not maintain their record. Following is the score:

| | | |
|---|---|---|
| P. D. Weeks | 0 1 1 1 1 1 1 1 1 1 1 1 1 0 1 | 13 |
| J. Parrott | 1 0 1 1 1 1 1 1 * 0 w | |
| N. B. Scott | 1 1 1 1 1 1 1 1 1 1 0 1 1 1 0 | 13 |
| Geo. Routier | 0 1 1 1 1 1 1 1 1 1 1 1 1 1 1 | 14 |
| B. Bassford | 0 1 1 1 1 1 0 1 1 1 0 1 1 0 1 | 11 |
| J. H. Burnett | 1 1 1 1 1 1 1 1 1 1 1 1 1 1 * | 14 |
| H. Hopper | 1 0 1 1 1 1 1 1 1 1 1 1 1 0 1 | 13 |
| J. A. Warnock | 0 1 0 * 0 1 1 1 1 1 1 1 1 1 1 | 11 |
| W. Thomas | 1 1 0 0 0 0 w | |
| F. Lefler | 1 1 1 1 1 1 1 1 1 1 1 1 1 1 0 | 14 |
| F. Maskey | 1 1 0 1 1 1 1 1 1 * 1 1 1 0 0 | 11 |
| F. Lastreto | 1 1 0 0 1 1 1 1 * w | |
| C. Hohenschell | 1 1 1 0 1 1 1 1 1 1 1 1 1 1 1 | 14 |
| J. T. McIntosh | 1 0 1 1 1 1 0 1 1 1 1 1 1 1 1 | 13 |
| F. Pracht | 1 1 1 1 0 1 0 1 w | |
| F. Bassford | 0 1 0 1 1 1 1 0 0 1 1 1 0 0 1 | 9 |
| J. Lopez | 1 0 1 0 1 1 1 1 1 1 0 0 1 0 w | |
| F. Weldon | 1 1 1 0 1 1 1 1 1 1 1 1 1 1 0 | 13 |
| A. Schnabel | 1 1 1 1 1 0 1 0 1 1 1 1 1 1 1 | 13 |
| G. W. Locket | 1 1 0 * 1 1 1 0 0 0 1 0 1 0 0 | 7 |
| H. A. Bassford | 0 1 1 0 0 1 1 1 1 1 1 0 1 0 0 | 9 |

* Died out of bounds. w withdrawn.

Ties of fourteen were shot off in three pairs of doubles at eighteen yards rise with the annexed score.

| | | | |
|---|---|---|---|
| Routier | 1 1 | 1 0 | 1 1 |
| Burnett | 1 1 | 0 1 | 1 0 |
| Hohenschell | 1 1 | 1 1 | 1 0 |
| Lefler | 1 1 | 1 1 | 1 0 |

On the above the three with a score of five shot off the ties, resulting in the victory of Mr. Routier, who took the first prize, Messrs. Lefler and Hohenschell dividing the second and third prizes and Mr. Burnett taking the fourth money, and Weldon the remaining prize after shooting off the thirteen ties.

These were the principal events of the meeting, but there were several matches shot with varying results, and when the birds gave out there resort was had to the clay pigeons, which appeared to give general satisfaction. Altogether the meeting was a success, but it is to be regretted that all the crack shots were not gathered together on such an occasion as the State Fair wing tournament.

## Marsh Pheasants and Mud-larks.

San Francisco, Sept. 21.

To the Editor of the Breeder and Sportsman: The proverbial saying that "newspaper reporters won't lie" never was more forcibly illustrated than in the case of the local scribe of the Oakland *Peanut*, who met and interviewed the Homer F. hunting party on Sunday last at Alameda. This party, composed of C. D. L. and H. F., had hied themselves to the tule-covered pastoral regions near Alvarado, determined to kill a million or so of ducks, or ascertain the reason why. The shooting over the first ground prospected was in strong language remonstrated against by a gentleman tramp from the Emeral Isle, who, never having possession of two feet of arable land before, in a boisterous manner asserted that there "wuz to be no hunting on moi grounds." The query cleverly put by L. by "what in hades is there to hunt here?" nearly caused the son of Erin to forget that it was Sunday, and so affrighted the party that they missed the only spoonbill that just then rose some 500 yards distant.

A weary tramp of eight miles over a miserable and rough country brought them to a friendly tavern kept by mine most genial host, Dugan, who not only proved himself a clever caterer, but most expert pedro player. In the bout between F. and mine host, the former is said to have lost $19 worth of beer, which truly and forever settled that gentleman's heretofore unascertained capacity for that beverage. Whilst resting themselves the party were enlivened by the advent of a pure and unadulterated Dutchman who had been all morning trying to "shute mud-larks." Even the would-be member of the Academy of Sciences was unacquainted with this new ornithological specimen as he expressed it and upon investigating the foreigner's game-bag, it was ascertained to contain two chickens, one killdee and two meadow-larks. By the aid of an improvised interpreter the party ascertained that "mud-larks" were meant to be meadow larks and the chickens were duly declared and assured to the foreigner to be game-birds called in California "marsh-pheasants." This so elated the member from Germany that he nearly flooded the party with an unlimited supply of beer and Limburger cheese. It was found upon further investigation that when the German refugee shot his "marsh-pheasants" in the barn-yard a weary and unsophisticated yet very tippling tramp was enjoying his noon-day nap under the friendly shade of a willow. The report and shot whistling over him so scared him that he rushed forth declaring himself to be shot, a few drops of water having fallen by the concussion from the willow tree upon his bare arm, causing him to imagine that he was bleeding to death. A few drinks systematically administered soon restored his equipoise of mind and he left if not a wiser at least a fuller man. The afternoon was spent by F. and L. in hunting quail, which with their heavy duck-guns, No. 6 shot, gum boots and no dogs was by no means a light undertaking. They succeeded in getting fifty-four of these poor harmless birds into a bag which was duly tied and the party started homeward. On the train at Alameda they encountered the aforesaid reporter of the Oakland *Peanut*. The member from Germany also being on board his two chickens were duly exhibited by F. to the astonished gaze of the verdant follower of Bohemian proclivities and declared to be "marsh-pheasants" and by him fully believed to be such until some meddlesome busy body gave it all away to him. Verily, of such, few will enter the kingdom of heaven. Yours,

Onix.

Company C of the First Regiment has put up two prizes, $10 in gold and an amethyst gold ring, for the two men who will make the highest scores in the company team that is to shoot for the Andrews trophy of the California Rifle Association. There will be four competitions. In the first, that was held on the 17th of this month, Capt. Templeton led the list with 90 points; Lieut. J. E. Klein came in second with 85 points of a possible 100.

To encourage shooting the officers of the First Regiment, at their monthly meeting, gave $100 to be divided among the ten men of the regiment who should win a place in the Centennial match of the California Rifle Association. If the officers of the Second Regiment would do likewise they could produce a team of as good sharpshooters as those of the First.

Quail are very plentiful all over the country. The marshes and sloughs are well stocked with mallard, teal, and such water fowl as rear their young in California. The numbers of migratory birds that have come from the north have caused some comment among the hunters, as it is an unusual occurrence for them to appear before the first rains. These forerunners from the north are fat and plump, showing that there has been a good season at the northern feeding ground this year. With the first rains will come thousands of ducks of all kinds and the markets will be well supplied. Nearly all of the sportsmen's clubs have been making preparations for the season's shooting, and will, from time to time, as their business permits, go to their preserves to get the benefit of the money that they have laid out to keep the grounds in order and free from poachers.

## The Olympic Club Meeting.

Following is the programme of the fall meeting of the Olympic Club that comes off this afternoon at their grounds at Oakland. It is well arranged and the meeting ought to be patronized by all lovers of athletic sports:

No. 1, 100 yards handicap run, open, trial heats, first in each to win the final trial, First heat, W. R. Stewart scratch, W. D. O'Kane two yards, F. M. Day five yards. Second heat, W. C. Brown one yard, Eugene Van Court four yards, A. L. Harris four yards. Third heat, E. J. Emmons one yard, L. H. Slater four yards, C. L. Ebner five yards.

No 2, one mile scratch run, open, R. H. Hamell, V. C. Driffield, A. W. Brown, C. A. & L. C.

No. 3, one mile handicap bicycle race, open, H. C. Finkler scratch, Geo. L. King fifty yards

No. 4, 100 yards handicap run, final heat.

No. 5, 100 yards scratch run, match race between R. S. Haley and Jos. Masterson, C. A. and L. C.

No. 6, 100 yards handicap run, O. C. Juvenile Class, 17 H. Smith, 18 E. Jennings, 19 B. E. Haley, 20 W. B. Hearst, 21 S. Edward, 22 H. Mentz, 23 W. Van Bergen, 24 G. Van Bergen, 25 J. H. Rosseter, 26 T. R. Barney and 27 A. Kelleher.

No. 7, pole leaping, handicap, open, 8 C. H. Slater, 28 E. G. Rodolph five inches, 9 C. L. Ebner 8 inches.

No. 8, six mile handicap race, match race between 29 C. Burckhalter scratch, 30 J. H. Tompson, 140 yds.

No. 9, 100 yards scratch run, open, R. S. Haley barred. 4 W. C. Brown, 7 E. S. Emmons, 1 W. R. Stewart, 2 W. D. O'Kane, 16 Jos. Masterson, C. A. & L. C.

No. 10, running wide jump, open, 9 C. L. Ebner, 4 W. C. Brown, 15 R. S. Haley.

No. 11, 220 yards handicap run, O. C. juvenile class, 24 G. Van Bergen, 23 W. Van Bergen, 31 H. Audiffred.

No. 12, 220 yards handicap run, open, 1 W. R. Stewart scratch, 4 W. C. Brown 5 yards, 32 A. L. Harris 9 yards, 7 E. S. Emmons 4 yards, 3 W. D. O'Kane 8 yatds, 8 C. H. Slater 10 yards, 3 F. M. Day 10 yards.

No. 13, half mile handicap race, 33 George L. King scratch, 20 C. Burchhalter 35 yards, 34 R. F. Verrinder 70 yards.

No. 14, running high jump, open, 15 R. S. Haley, 8 C. H. Slater, 9 C. L. Ebner, 28 E. G. Rodolph.

No. 15, Officers' race, 100 yards scratch run.

No. 16, Putting 16-lb weight, open, 1 W. R. Stewart, 8 C. H. Slater 9 C. L. Ebner, 2 W. D. O'Kane.

No. 17, one-fifth mile bicycle race, each to ride separately, 33 George L. King, 13 H. C. Finckler.

No. 18, throwing base-ball, open, W. V. Watson, N. W Leonard, G. W. Ebner, C. J. Bosworth, W. F. Bouton, L. Hardie, F. S. Beck, H. C. Gilmer, J. J. Kelly.

No. 19, 220 yards hurdle race, scratch, open, 5 hurdles 3 ft. 6 in. high, 4 W. C. Brown, 7 E. S. Emmons, 9 C. L. Ebner, 28 E. G. Rodolph, 16 Jos. Masterson, 15 R. S. Haley.

Games called at 2 p. m., referee, W, M. Sime; judges C. R. Browne; ——— starter N. W. Leonard; timekeepers P. McIntyre, D. Eireman, H. B. Cook; clerk of course R. T. Stombs.

The Olympic night at the Fair, last Wednesday, showed conclusively that the club has the good wishes of all San Franciscans. Notwithstanding the fact that the date of the entertainment was announced but one day in advance the audience was too large to allow all a good view of the performance, and the occasional views obtained of the stage were only an aggravation to those in the back rows of the gallery. No accident happened to mar the pleasure of the entertainment, and each event on the programme was executed in a style that will help to maintain the past reputation of the club. The juvenile class is a new feature but already demonstrates the wisdom of its promoters, and promises to develop a large number of first-class amateur gymnasts. The club apparently has entered upon a new era of prosperity. The alteration of the rooms now in progress, will, if possible, make them more attractive than ever, and the indications are that the members generally, old and new, propose shortly to organize a large exercising class for the coming in-door season, with the purpose of giving several unique and attractive entertainments during the winter. The first will probably take place in the club rooms and be strictly invitation. The present management of the club will be successful without any doubt.

## Market Report.

FLOUR—In good demand. We quote as follows: Best City Extra $5 37½@$5 50; Superfine, $4 50@$4 75; Interior Extra, $4 75@$5 25; Interior Superfine $3 75@$4 ℔ bbl.

WHEAT—Shippers are in want of floating grain and will pay $1 67½ for suitable quality. For low grades there is but little demand. Choice White commands $1 70 for milling purposes. No. 1 White October $1 68½, do buyer 1882, $2 74; do No. 2, October $1 63 and $1 63½. The Liverpool market is said to be still weaker.

BARLEY—Considerable business has been done lately in feed in the speculative line. Spot business is not very active. Small sales in Coast Chevalier are reported at $1 30; Standard is worth $1 50; brewing is quoted at $1 35@$1 37½ per cental.

OATS—The market is well supplied and values irregular. The range of the market is $1 45@$1 65 ℔ ctl.

RYE—But little good quality offering. No. 1 is quoted at $2 25 ℔ ctl.

HAY—We quote: Alfalfa, $11@$13 50; Wheat $13@$15 50; Wild Oat, $12@$15 50 ℔ ton.

STRAW—Quotable at 50@60c ℔ bale.

BEANS—quoted at: Bayos, $2 40@$2 50; Butter, $3 25@$3 50 for small and $3 60@$3 80 for large; Lima, $3 50@$3 75; Pea, $3 50; Pink, $2@$2 25; Red, $2@$2 25; small White, $2 50; large White, $2 30@$2 40 ℔ ctl.

DRIED PEAS—Niles, $2; Blackeye, $2 25@$2 50 ℔ ctl.

ONIONS—The market still exhibits an easy tone. Quotable at 50@65c ℔ ctl.

POTATOES—No large stock on hand. We quote wharf rates: Early Rose, 65c@85c; Garnet Chile, $1@$1 10 Early Goodrich 85c@$1; Peerless, 60c@$1 ℔ ctl; Sweet, $1@$1 25 ℔ ctl.

GAME—Receipts small and quality bad, owing to warm weather. We quote; Quail, 50c@$1 ℔ dozen; Mallard ducks, $3@$3 50; Sprigs, $1 50@$1 75; Teal, $1 50@$1 75; Hare, $1 75@$2 25; Rabbits $1@$1 50; Doves, 50@75c ℔ dozen; Venison, 10@12c ℔ lb.

PROVISIONS—Market steady. We quote; Eastern Hams, 18½@19c; California Hams, 16½@16¾c for plain, 16½@17c for sugar-cured canvased; Eastern Breakfast Bacon, 17½@18c; California Smoked Bacon, 16½@16¾c for heavy and medium, and 17½@18c for light and extra light; Clear Sides, 16½@16¾c; Pork, $21 50@$22 for extra Prime, $24@$25 for Prime Mess, $25@$25 50 for Mess, $27 for Clear and $28@$28 50 for extra Clear; Pigs' Feet, $15@$18 ℔ bbl; Mess Beef, $14 for bbls and $7 for hf bbls; Extra Mess Beef, $14 50@$15; Family Beef, $16@$16 50 @ bbl; California Smoked Beef, 14½@14¾c ℔ lb.

POULTRY.—Firm at prices annexed. We quote: Live Turkeys, gobblers, 17@19c; do Hens, 16@18c; Roosters, $5 50@$6 50 for old and $6@$8 for young Hens $6@$8; Broilers, $3 50@$5 according to size; Ducks, $5@$6 50 ℔ doz; Geese, $1@$1 25 ℔ pair; Goslings, $1 50@$1 75 ℔ pair.

HONEY—Comb, 14@17c; extracted, 7@9c ℔ lb.

EGGS—The inquiry is mainly for choice parcels. California choice, 37½@40c; Interior, 32½@35c; Utah, 25@32½c ℔ doz.

BUTTER—Fancy brands are very scarce, and higher prices are asked. We quote: Fancy, 40@42½c; choice, 35@37½c; fair to good, 30@32½c; inferior lots from country stores, 23@25c; firkin, 29@31c for good to choice, and 25@27½c for ordinary; pickled roll, 30@32½c; Eastern, 20@25c ℔ lb.

CHEESE—Supply liberal. We quote prices for lots as follows: California, 12½@13½c for choice; 10@12c from fair to good; do, factory, in boxes, 13@16c; Eastern, 16@17c; Western, 11@13½c ℔ lb.

HIDES AND SKINS—The market is firm. Dealers are paying the following cash rates for lots in order: Dry hides, usual selection, 20@20½c; culls one-third less, and Mexican Hides 1c ℔ lb less. Dry Kip, 18@19c; Dry Calf, 21@22c; Salted Steers, over 55lbs, 11c ℔ lb; Steers and Cows, medium, 10c; light do, 9½c; Salted Kip, 15 to 30 lbs, 10@10½c; Salted Calf, 11@12½c ℔ lb; Dairy Calf, 65@70c each; Sheep Skins, 20@25c for Shearlings; 25@50c for short, 60@80c for medium, and 75c@$1 apiece for long wool and wool skins. Butchertown Green Skins bring higher prices.

TALLOW—Good demand, quotable at 8½c ℔ lb for rendered and 11½@12c for refined, both in shipping order.

WOOL—There is not as yet any renewal of business on Eastern account. We quote spring: Humboldt and Mendocino, 25@26½c ℔ lb; Sonoma, 23@25c; Siskiyou and Modoc, 22@24c; San Joaquin free, 17@18c; Southern Coast, burry and seedy, 15@17c; Eastern Oregon, choice, 23@24c; Eastern Oregon fair, 20@22c; Eastern Oregon, poor, 18@19c; Valley Oregon, fine, 25@27c; Valley Oregon, coarse, 23@20c. We quote fall: San Joaquin and coast, 10@12c; San Joaquin and coast Lamb, 12@14; Northern fall, free, 15@17c; Northern fall, defective, 13@14; Northern fall, Lamb, 16@17½c.

FRUIT—All kinds are meeting with tolerably good custom. We quote jobbing lots as follows: Apples, 30@50c for common and 75@$1 ℔ box for good; Pears, 40@60c ℔ box; Bartlett do, $1 50 to $2 ℔ box; Strawberries, $8@$10 ℔ chest; Raspberries, $10@$12 ℔ chest; Peaches, 35c@$1 ℔ box and 30@60c ℔ bskt; Figs, 40@75c ℔ box; Grapes, 35@50c for common, 50@75c for Black Hamburg, 50@75c for Rose of Peru, 50@75c ℔ box for Muscat and 75c@$1 ℔ box for Tokay; Plums, 25@75c ℔ box; Quinces, 75c@$1box; Blackberries, $2@$3 ℔ chest; Watermelons, $4@$9 ℔ hundred; Cantaloupes, 75c@$1 ℔ crate; Lemons, $8@$10 ℔ box for Sicily and $1@$1 50 for California; Limes, $14@$15 ℔ box for Mexican; Bananas, $2@$3 50 ℔ bunch; Pineapples, $6@$8 ℔ dozen; Tahiti Oranges, $35@$45 ℔ thousand. Casaba Melon, 12@15c apiece. Tahiti Oranges are offering at $30 ℔ thousand.

VEGETABLES—Buyers can about name their own figures for Tomatoes and Cucumbers. We quote jobbing lots as follows: Marrowfat Squash, $7@$10 ℔ ton; Carrots, 30@50c; Turnips, 75c@$1; Cauliflower, 60@65c ℔ dozen; Cabbage, 50@75c ℔ ctl; Garlic, 1@1½c ℔ lb; Cucumbers, 15@25c ℔ box; Green Peas, 3c ℔ lb; Green Peppers, 50@75c ℔ box; Tomatoes, 15@25c ℔ box; Celery, 50c ℔ doz; Summer Squash, 50@75c ℔ box; String Beans, 2½@3 ℔ lb; Green Corn, 7@15c ℔ doz; Okra, 50@75c; Egg Plant, 50@75c ℔ box.

MEATS—Following are the rates for whole carcasses from slaughterers to dealers:

BEEF—Prime, 7½@8c; medium grade, 6½@7c; inferior, 5½@6c ℔ lb.

VEAL—Large Calves, 8½@7c; small ones, 8@10c ℔ lb.

MUTTON—Wethers are quotable at 4½@5c and Ewes at 4@4½c ℔ lb, according to quality.

LAMB—Quotable at 6@6½c ℔ lb.

PORK—Live Hogs, 7½@7¾c for hard and 7@7¼c for soft; dressed do, 10½@10¾c ℔ lb for hard grain hogs.

## HERD AND SWINE.

### Jersey Reds, Durocs and Red Berkshires.

There has been some dust thrown in the eyes of the public by certain breeders of red hogs. It is foolish for any breeders of red hogs in New Jersey to claim that he has the only pure-bred red hogs, or Jersey Reds, as they are called in that State. One breeder in New Jersey, who claims to have the "pure breed," and that all others are mixed or spurious, I imagine would have hard work to give correct pedigrees more than a dozen years back. Less than a dozen years ago his father wrote me that he could not tell the origin of the red hogs of New Jersey, neither was any citizen of that State, in response to my inquiries, able to give their history. I also inserted notices in some of the leading agricultural journals asking for their history; but obtained no response. After a careful investigation I became satisfied that these hogs, as well as the other families of red hogs, were descended from the old Berkshires, and so reported to the National Swine Breeders' Convention. No one has ever disputed that statement. Since that time I have seen an old English work, printed nearly a hundred years ago, which confirms the impression; as, in the description of the old-fashioned Berkshires, the color and characteristics of the modern red hogs are accounted for. It is said that the Tamworths, the red hogs of England, are an off-shoot of the Berkshire. A few importations of these hogs have been made recently, for the purpose of crossing them upon the red hogs in America. This red blood has been so strong in America that it has preserved itself, although the crosses upon it have been innumerable. This is particularly the case in New Jersey and along the Atlantic coast where these hogs were quite extensively bred. I saw them twenty years ago in Maryland, as well as in New Jersey, and they were red-and-white, sometimes marked with black; but always long in the body, coarse in the bone, with heavy coats of hair and bristles. There was no attempt in those days at breeding them strictly pure, any more than others than was of the Duroc, another family of red hogs bred in Saratoga Co., N.Y. The Durocs seem to have been brought to this section from Connecticut, where red hogs have been bred and called Red Berkshires. The stock seems to have become run out in that State. The Durocs of Saratoga were descended from a pair of pigs brought into the vicinity by a Mr. Kelsey, who said they were imported; but whether he meant from Connecticut or Great Britain it is not known. This was about sixty years ago. Other pigs were afterwards brought from Connecticut to a different part of the county. The stock from these two different families has been bred in the county ever since. No particular system or purity in breeding seems to have been followed with the Durocs more than with the Jersey Reds, until within a few years, since they were brought into notice by the National Swine Breeder's Convention.

The original and the purest type of a Jersey Red is a coarser and larger hog than the Duroc, and of course they are superior to the latter, so much as greater size is an advantage. The Durocs are finer boned and will mature sooner an t fatten younger. Both families possess the general characteristics of strong constitutional vigor and hearty appetites, with strong digestion and prolificness most remarkable—the natural result of their characteristics. They are wonderfully hardy and possess an ability to take care of themselves which is quite gratifying. Several breeders met together a few years ago and determined to begin breeding the Durocs, as they were called—the name being a fancy of Mr. Kelsey's, after the noted stallion Duroc—by selecting the best blood to be obtained and the nearest like a good Berkshire type. They adopted a standard of characteristics which has been put on record, but which it would be well to repeat. They also determined to give these hogs their true name, Red Berkshire. The true Duroc or Red Berkshire, quoting from a former article in the *Rural New Yorker*, as now bred by those who are aiming to keep the breed intact and establish them as thoroughbred, should be long and quite deep-bodied; not round, but broad on the back and holding the width well out to the hips and hams. The head should be small compared with the body, with the cheek broad and full. The neck should be short and thick, and the legs slightly curved, with the nose rather longer than in the English breeds, the ear rather large and lopped over the eye. They are not fine-lined nor yet coarse, but medium; the legs medium in length and size, but set well under the body and well apart, and not cut up high in the flank or above the hose. The hams should be broad and full well down to the hook. There should be a good coat of hair of medium fineness, inclined to bristles at the top of the shoulders, the tail being hairy and not small; the hair usually straight, but in some cases a little wavy.

The color should be red, varying from dark glossy cherry red, and even brownish hairs, to light yellowish red, with occasionally a small fleck of black on the belly and legs. The darker shades of red are preferred by most breeders, and this is the type of color most desirable. In disposition they are remarkably mild and gentle, and are so docile that they are readily confined by low fences. They are kind and careful mothers and wonderfully prolific. They have a remarkable ability to digest food and make growth. This is owing to their hardy constitutions and perfection in the proportions of their bodies, and the strong blood which has made its mark so notably for more than half a century.

It is a common thing for Duroc pigs at six months of age to weigh 300 pounds, and at eight and ten months to turn the scales at 400 or 500 pounds. Hogs a year and a half old have weighed from 700 to 800 pounds. Pigs four weeks old will weigh from twenty to thirty pounds and measure over two feet in length and from six to eight inches across the shoulders. For rapid growth and ability to lay on flesh the Durocs are not excelled. The meat is not coarse-grained, but fine and tender. Their powers of assimilating food are so great that they readily eat coarse food more dainty breeds would not touch, and will even fatten on grass alone; and in winter will eat with avidity clover, hay and roots which other hogs will refuse. They are not subject to mange or liable to get sun-burnt, and are adapted to all climates.

MANAGEMENT OF SWINE.—In discussing the management of swine, Prof. Knapp of Iowa says: Perhaps the radical change should be less in the food than in the proportion it is fed. Corn is healthy enough when given in moderate quantities; when it is considered a healthy food, but hogs can be injured upon that as readily as upon corn. The hog has an appetite beyond his capacity to digest, and so long as that is the case, he must not be given full rations of concentrated food until within a few weeks of the pork barrel. There are two practical methods. First, in case the farmer has no roots nor pasture, he can grind his corn and mix with it wheat bran. Half bran and half corn meal by bulk make a good mixture for all kinds of stock. For pigs, add a little salt and oil meal; for pigs under 100 pounds, use some milk; older than this, water will do. Second, the purchase of large quantities of wheat bran is expensive for the general farmer; corn and clover are the profitable crops to be fed. In such cases the cheap food to go with the corn is sugar beets in the winter and clover in the summer. Roots could be raised on the farm that will answer a better purpose than sugar beets for the main dependence of store hogs during the winter, and with suitable machinery and some knowledge few crops can be produced at greater profit.

### Miscellaneous Awards at the Chico Fair.

**Household.**

Mrs. C. C. Goree, Best Stocking Yarn; Mrs. C. C. Schoonover, Best 10 yds Rag Carpet; Mrs. J. E. Walker, 2nd Best 10 yds Rag Carpet; Mrs. Windern, Best Hooked Rug; Mrs. Stumpf, Best Collection Rugs; Mrs. J. H. Guill, Best Knit Cotton Stockings; Mrs. C. C. Goree, Best Knit Wool Stockings; Mrs. C. C. Schoonover, Best Knit Wool Socks; P. Peters & Bros., Best Display Dry Goods; Mrs. G. F. Jones, Best Display Fancy Goods; Mrs. G. F. Jones, Knit Rug.

Mrs. Phillips, Ottoman Cover; Dora Chandler, Fancy Chair Cushion and Sack; Mrs. G. F. Jones, Crochet Shawl; Mrs. Eitel, Lamp Stand Mat; Mrs. C. F Jones, Silk Embroidery; Mrs. W. H. Earll, Ornamental Needlework; Mrs. J. F. Decker, Embroidered Sofa Cushion; Mrs. A. C. Broyles, Embroidered Handkerchief; Mrs. A. M. Barley, Chenille Work; Miss Carrie Burroughs, Lace Handkerchief; Mrs. J. M. Ormsby, Best Bead Embroidery; Mrs. Wm. Estee, Embroidered Pillow Shams.

Mrs. J Phillips, Worsted Quilt; Mrs. Eitel, Card Board Work; Miss Decker, Embroidery on Canvas; Mrs. E. A. Warren, Tufted Cushion; Sarah F. Swanson, Display Feather and Worsted Work; Mrs. Albert Jones, Best Feather-edge Braid, Velvet Bonnet; Velvet Hat, Display Feathers, Artificial Flowers; Mrs. A. C. Broyles, Variety Linen Embroidery; Mrs. F. A. S. Jones, Specimen Wax Flowers; Mrs. Mickey, Worsted and Linen Work; Mrs. Jones, Cane Work; Mrs. Jones, Leaf Work; Mrs. Jones, Shell Work; Mrs. J. H. Guill, Specimen Braid Work; Miss Gussie Jansen, Embroidered Picture; Mrs. S. J. Barkley Silk Quilt; Mrs. Reister, Patchwork Quilt; Mrs. Hooper, Afghan; Mrs. A. C. Broyles, Outline Embroidery; Mrs. A. C. Broyles, Best Embroidery; Mrs. A. M. Barley, Lambrequin; Miss Gussie Jansen, Fine Lace work.

Mr. J. S. Hill, Toilet Set Complete; Mrs. A. F. Estel, Wax Leaves; Mrs. J. J. Hassell, Hand-made Dress; Miss T. J. Decker, Sofa Cushion.

**Juvenile Department.**

Miss M. Goree, Best pr. Knit Wool Stockings; Miss Lorine Nelson, Charm String; Miss Alice Jones, Bracket Lambrequin.

**Manufactures.**

L. A. Reister, 2 Sets Double Harness; L. A. Reister, 4 Sets Single Harness; L. A. Reister, Display of Saddle Bridles.

Farrell & Co., Display of Tinware; Farrell & Co., Plumber's Goods; Farrell & Co., Exhibit of Wire Cloth; Hubbard & Sommers, Display of Silverware; Hubbard & Earll, Display of Gas Chandeliers; Hubbard & Earll, General Hardware; Hubbard & Earll, Display of Mechanic's Tools.

Farrell & Co., Oil Stove; Farrell & Co., Parlor Stove; Farrell & Co., Hollow Iron Ware; Farrell & Co., Gas and Water Pipes.

Farrell & Co., assortment of bathing tubs; Hubbard & Earll, Cooking stove for wood; same, cooking range.

De Toe & Riggs, San Francisco, display of musical instruments; same, best piano made in United States; same, best organ made in United States.

Farrell & Co., double barrel shotgun; same, sporting rifle; same, breach-loading shotgun.

Mrs. C. C. Goree, display of home made soap; Mrs. J. H. Guill, soft soap.

E. A. Warren, display of confectionaries.

J. T Newman, Stoneware and pipes; Wm. Proud, Oenological display.

**Grain, etc.**

John Bidwell, 1 bushel of any one kind of wheat; Fred Wakefield, 1 sack of barley; Hubbard & Shaw, 1 sack of corn; John Bidwell, best table vegetables; Mrs. J. Bidwell, collection of ornamental foliage.

J. H. Guill, best display of butter in pound rolls; David Reid, second best display of butter in pound rolls.

**Cooking.**

Miss Hattie Mandeville, best wheat bread; same, brown bread; same, raised biscuit; Mrs. J. E. Walker, best soda biscuit; Mrs. J. F. Fisher, best salt-rising bread; Mrs. A. F. Eitel, best corn bread; Mrs. A. T. Eitel, best yeast powder biscuit.

**Fruit**

Mr. Harris, Best display of apples; J. Bidwell; second best display of apples; J. H. Guill, best display of pears; J. Bidwell, second best display of pears; Mr. Harris, best three varieties pears; Mr. Harris, best display peaches; J. Bidwell, second best display peaches; J. H. Guill, best four varieties of plums; J. Bidwell, second best four varieties plums; M. Z. Moore, Best pomegranates; J. Bidwell, best figs; Mr. Harris, best oranges.

**Preserves. Jellies. Etc.**

E. B. Stucky, exhibit of honey; Mrs. J. E. Watson; best three jars currant jelly; Mrs. R. Diller, assorted jellies; same, display of fruit in glass; Mrs. J. M. Moore, raspberry jelly; same, blackberry jelly; Della Goodrich, best display of preserves; Mrs. Erza Booth, second best display of preserves; same, best display of pickles.

J. Bidwell, best display of apples; same, pears; same, peaches; same, plums; same, apricots; Chester Walker, best 10 pounds dried figs; J. Bidwell, best dried raisins, J. H. Guill, best dried berries; J. H. Guill, half peck soft shell almonds.

**Miscellaneous**

Mrs. F. A. S. Jones, profile picture; Miss Emma Crew, Landscape painting, same, California scenery, same, best oil painting on canvas.

J. F. Cole, exhibit of penmanship; Mrs. A. A. Hubbard, screen painting in oil or canvas; D. H. Wood, exhibit of photographs.

G. W. Crapo, 7 frames; same, 1 air castle; same, 1 card receiver.

J. W. Pettinger, Smith's patent churn.

E. M. Allen, picture frames, pocket knife work.

J. H. Guill, Barle, child's dress, 70 years old, made in Paris, France.

J. H. Guill, improved churn.

J. H. Guill, exhibition California hardwood.

Mrs. J. H. Guill, home made vinegar.

J. M. Denely, case velvet frames.

Mrs. S. T. Tuttle, 37 articles made with hand first saw.

Mrs. James Peal, fancy card basket.

A. L. Knowlton, geological display.

Chico Cannery, best display of fruit in cans.

## THE KENNEL.

**Fixtures.**

BENCH SHOWS.—Western Pennsylvania Society's English Setter Bench Show Derby, Pittsburgh, Pa., for English setter puppies whelped on or after March 1, 1882. Entries closed December 1, Dec. I. R. Elliston, Allegheny City, Pa., secretary.

Otter Rod and Gun Club's trials on quails, near Gilroy, California, October 18. Open to dogs owned in California, Oregon, Nevada and Arizona. E. Leavesley, secretary, Gilroy, California.

Eastern Field Trials Club's trials on quails, near High Point, N.C., November 17. Entries to Derby close July 1; to All-Age and Members' Stake, November 1. Fred. N. Hall, secretary, P.O. Box 84, New York.

National American Kennel Club's trials on quails, Grand Junction, Tenn., December 4. D. Bryson, Memphis, Tenn., secretary.

### American Fox Hunters.

Great Britain is the home of all that is best and noblest in field sports, and there is little cause for wonder that Americans who are mainly the descendants of Britons should often copy their sporting fashions from the old country. America has only originated three sports—trotting, baseball and lacrosse—and has imported three hundred. This is natural enough, yet whenever the editor or correspondent of a daily paper is short of ideas he turns his massive intellect to flying shafts of ridicule to be hurled against gentlemen in America who practice English games. The fox hunters of New Jersey and Newport may not be as bold riders, nor the foxes so fast a game as those of Galway or Milton, but that is no reason why the American fox hunters should be a butt for the ridicule of men who never get astride of any horse except a saw-horse, nor hunt for any game larger than the pestiferous fleas which infest their offices. The average Californian is a better, bolder rider than the average Englishman and will gallop his mustang where the Englishman's hunter could not keep his feet. The people of New York, like the people of all large cities, are not as a rule good riders simply because they have no place in which to practice, and their attempts to get practice by fox hunting at Newport, instead of deserving ridicule deserve praise. The writer has seen many a fox hunt in this State and has followed some of the best packs in England and is free to confess that the work is far harder here though the pace may be a little faster in England. It is no burlesque of sport to gallop over plains as closely furrowed with gopher holes as a small-pot patient's face is with pits; and what the sport lacks in danger here from stiff fences it makes up in the stake. Americans who are rich enough to follow as fast fleet of the ground, on which a fall means a week in bed. The sport is perhaps harder and rougher here than at Newport but it is dollars to cents that those who ridicule the Newport fox hunters could not stay with them five minutes.

SHEEP DOG TRIAL.—From the *Live Stock Journal and Fancier Gazette*, comes the news that the first trials of the East Lothian Sheep-dog Trial Club were in all respects successful. The entries numbered eighteen. Mr. J. Mack's Tuck was first; Mr. T. Gibson's Fly second; Mr. J. Bald's Reeve third; Mr. G. Dod's Yarrow fourth. The form of the trial was as follows: Three wild mountain sheep were let loose a large pen of sheep at one end of the course. Two poles, with two flags on the top, were erected in the center of the course, ten feet wide; a flag was placed at the extreme opposite end of the course. The dogs were required to drive these sheep through between these two poles to the flag at the extreme opposite end, where all the sheep were separated so the dogs were tried. This proved a most difficult piece of work, testing the dogs very hard. Only three were unable to accomplish this task, which were disqualified for the next part of the trial. After this had been accomplished, and all the sheep put in one lot, each man with his dog was required to cut off these sheep from the large flock, drive them along the course, where a small pen was placed in the open, into which they were required to pen their sheep. This proved a most difficult piece of work, the pen only being four feet wide at the entrance. They were afterwards removed to the large pen, where they were first let out. This enabled the judges to form a selection of the best dogs, six of which in point of merit it was difficult to decide between. A very scientific and meritorious competition was held to decide for the first and second places two of great merit, Gilholm's Fly and Mack's Tuck. The latter, however, securing first honor, excelling in being steadier and under better command, accountable by being a year older. This terminated a keen and good sheep-dog competition. The attendance was pretty large considering the unfavorable weather.

A TALL STORY.—Recently, when the Denver train was was coming in from the West, as it passed Kearney, a village forty-one miles west of Grand Island, a setter dog jumped on to the front of the postal car, next to the engine, and persisted in riding. Those who observed him tried to coax him off, but without success. They then pulled him off, but as soon as released he jumped on again, and persisted in having a first-class railroad ride. When he reached Grand Island another effort was made to get him off the cars, but he would not have it that way, and maintained his position on the front of the car while the engine was changed, never faltering when the new engine was backed down and coupled on. The trip was continued six miles further east, to a side track where the Denver train from the East passes the one from the West. Here he quietly leaped off, and as quickly jumped on the front of the postal car attached to the other train, and began to bark as though he had got home. In this car was his master, whom he had gone to meet. All this ride was taken in the middle of the night. The whole transaction seems marvelous, but the strangest part is that he should have kept the run of the trains and have calculated correctly the train that his master would arrive on. This story is vouched for by Mr. Alexander Stewart, who runs one of the passenger engines from North Platte to Grand Island.

DEATH OF CARLOWITZ.—The well known Laverack setter dog Carlowitz, by Pilkington's Dash out of Countess, died recently at the kennel of his owner, Mr. James E. Goodsell, from old age, being at the time of his death in his tenth year. He left quite a number of his progeny out of Laverack and other bitches, the most noted of which is, perhaps, Royal Duke out of True, Sister to Mr. Luther Adam's Drake.—*American Field.*

### National American Club Trials.

The first field trials of the National American Kennel Club on prairie chickens commenced near Fairmont, Minn., Monday morning, September 4th. The attendance of sportsmen was very large, representatives being present from the East, West and South. The weather on the opening day was clear but very warm; Tuesday was clear and pleasant. Owing to an accidental injury, Hon. B. E. Kennedy, of Omaha, Neb., one of the judges selected, was unable to attend, and Mr. B.

Waters, of Canterbury, Conn., was selected by the contestants to act as judge pro tem during the running on Monday. Mr. E. C. Sterling, of St. Louis, Mo., was selected to fill the place of the absent judge for the balance of the trial, taking the position Tuesday morning, as Mr. Waters had entries in the Free-for-All which follows the Derby. The birds were not as plenty as was expected. The running commenced with the American Field Derby, for which there were forty-five nominations, sixteen of which completed their entries. Pools were sold before the trial commenced, with Mr. Joseph E. Dew's American Dan favorite in the first pool, after which Mr. George C. Marsh's Gilderoy sold favorite in the balance. The following heats were run in the American Field Derby up to Tuesday evening, resulting as follows:

FIRST SERIES.

Else beat Prairie Mollie.
Gilderoy beat Josephine.
Pink B. beat Scott.
American Dan beat St. Elm IV.
Cavalier beat Count Dad.
Prince Noble beat Acme (withdrawn).
Prairie Wonder beat Frank (withdrawn).
Countess Mollie beat Countess May II.

SECOND SERIES.

Gilderoy beat Else.
Pink B. beat American Dan.

This concluded the running Tuesday night, with Cavalier and Prince Noble to go down in the morning.

The free-for-all closed with twenty-eight entries, which were drawn to run as follows:

| Messrs. P. H. and D. Bryson's Sue, by Druid—Ruby (setter). | Mr. W. H. Colnard's Countess Druid, by Druid—Princess Draco (setter). |
| Mr. H. M. Short's Frank H. (setter). | Mr. C. C. Calkins' Broker, by Druid—Clio (setter). |
| Mr. George Knowles' Klunick—Huck by Bed's Druid—Beeslie's Lee (setter). | Mr. Luther Adams' Bessie, by Dash III—Countess II (setter). |
| Mr. E. F. Stoddard's Rodine, by New Jersey (pointer). | Mr. W. B. Hughes' Maxim, by Garnet—Fili (pointer). |
| Dr. W. R. Daly's Jess, by Don—Flash (setter). | Mr. B. F. Vandervoort's Christmas Bill, by Luck of Eden Hall—Beauty Money (pointer). |
| Sportsman's Kennel's Prairie Ranger, by Charm—Pearl (setter). | Mr. Luther Adams' Shadow, by Lincoln—Daisy Dean (setter). |
| Mr. C. C. Sanborn's Count Noble, by Count Wind'em—Nora (setter). | Mr. H. B. Hartson's London, by Paris—Lili (setter). |
| Dr. D. C. Sanborn's Dashing Novice, by Dash II—Novel (setter). | Mr. W. Tallman's Foreman, by Dashing Monarch—Fairy II (setter). |
| Mr. W. B. Hughes' Meteor, by Garnet—Fili (pointer). | Sportsman's Kennel's Pride, by Charm—Fly (setter). |
| Mr. J. W. Orth's Gertrude, by Gladstone—Nellie (setter). | Mr. J. J. Snellenburg's May Laverack, by Thunder—Spot (setter). |
| Mr. L. Kunzler's Clementine D., by Dash III—Cornelia (setter). | Mr. J. B. McIntosh's Biz, by Dash—McIntosh's Fleet (setter). |
| Dr. M. McDonald's Rock, by Rex—Belle | Dr. S. Fleet Speir's Maida, by Doth—Clio (setter). |
| Mr. R. O'Brien's Dash, by Bob—Pet (setter). | Mr. J. Otto Donner's Bessie B. by Rangell II—Bella (setter). |
| Mr. R. B. Morgan's (Mr. C. E. Felton's) Prairie Punch, by Charm—Pearl (setter). | Mr. R. T. Vandervoort's Don Rango—Peg (pointer). |

Mr. Sterling having resigned, owing to the duties being so arduous, Mr. F. B. Wilson was selected to act in his place on Monday with Messrs. Morford and Bergundthal.

The following is the order in which the heats were run and won:

**American Field Derby.**

Else beat Prairie Mollie, Gilderoy beat Josephine, Pink B. beat Scott, American Dan beat St. Elmo IV., Cavalier beat Count Dad, Prince Noble beat Acme, (withdrawn); Countess Mollie beat Countess May II.

Second Series—Gilderoy beat Else, Pink B. beat American Dan, Prince Noble beat Cavalier, Prairie Wonder and Countess Mollie were taken up not to be put down again, and the judges reserved their decision.

Third Series—Pink beat Gilderoy, Prince Noble (a bye).

Fourth Series—Prince Noble beat Pink B., and won first money.

Fifth Series—Pink B. beat Cavalier (withdrawn) and won second money.

Sixth Series—American Dan beat Scott, Gilderoy (a bye).

Seventh Series—American Dan beat Gilderoy, and won third money.

Eighth Series—St. Elmo IV. was withdrawn, and Gilderoy and Scott divided fourth money.

**All Aged Stake.**

Sue beat Countess Druid, Frank H. beat Broker, Bessie (Adams') beat Klunickelnuck, Maxim beat Bodine (withdrawn). Prairie Ranger beat Shadow, Count Noble beat London, Dashing Novice beat Foreman, Meteor beat Pride, Gertrude beat May Laverack, Biz beat Clementine D., Rock beat Maida, Bessie (Donner's) beat Dash, Don beat Prairie Punch (withdrawn). Christmas Bill and Jess were taken up not to be put down again, and the judges reserved their decision.

Second series—Sue beat Bessie (Adams'), Frank H. beat Maxim, Count Noble beat Prairie Ranger, Gertrude beat Biz, Rock beat Bessie (Donner's), Don beat Dashing Novice, Meteor was withdrawn.

Third series—Sue beat Count Noble, Gertrude beat Frank H., Don beat Rock.

Fourth series—Sue beat Gertrude, Don (a bye).

Fifth series—Don beat Sue, and won first money.

The judges place the dogs for the remaining prizes as follows: Sue four-fifths, and Dashing Novice one-fifth of second money; Gertrude, Count Noble and Adams' Bessie equal third; Biz and Prairie Ranger equal fourth.

Don was awarded the Pennsylvania Cup for best dog in All Aged Stake, and the prize of $20 offered for the best pointer.

Count Dad was awarded the Pennsylvania cup in the Derby, and the prize of $50 offered for the best dog or bitch entered and run by the individual, club or association making the most entries in the Derby.

Gertrude and Rock divided prize, $50, for best pointer or setter, dog or bitch, in the All Aged Stake, which handler has not worked a dog in a previous trial.

Col. W. E. Hughes withdrew Meteor after he had won his first heat, for the reason that he was desirous of having some shooting, and feared that the conclusion of the trials would extend beyond the time he could absent himself from home. Having understood that the withdrawal of Meteor had been construed by some of the owners of setters to result from fear to have Meteor meet some of the setters, Mr. E. C. Sterling, for the St. Louis Kennel Club, handed the American Field on Saturday night a challenge to be made public at once, to the effect that if a setter should win the All Aged Stake, the St. Louis Kennel Club would run Meteor against

## Pacific Coast Coursers.

The coursing season will be formally opened in this State at the end of the coursing month. The Pacific Coast Coursing Club, president, Mark Devlin, will be first in the field, their match taking place at Merced on October 25th and 26th. The club leaves San Francisco October 24th.

Charles Fowler, Judge Pennie and T. Bradley have been selected as a committee on arrangements. The stud book of the club shows the following pups whelped within two years and eligible to competition in puppy or sapling stakes, as their ages may determine: Mark Devlin's litter of 6 2 dogs, 4 bitches, 2 blk, 2 w and bd, 1 bd, 1 brown. Ben Tomey—Pride of the Canyon, April 3d, 1881.

P. K. Jacoby, b and w b Cassie Maria; Paul Jones—Laura Wright, July 11th, 1881.

N. Petersen, w d Nick Black Jack, Lady Ross, May 28th, 1881; blk and w d Prince, f and w b, Lady Prince Black Jack—unknown, August 18th, 1881.

H. McGurty, blk d, bd b, b and w b, unknown, October 11th, 1881.

W. Halpin, f and w d, Toney f and w b Lady Place, blk and w b Nora Creona; Menlo Boy—Bird Sallie, March 7th, 1881.

C. O. K. Jeffcots, bd b Last Rose of Summer, Bummer—Restless, July 6th, 1882.

A. A. Funcke, blk and w d Burjo Black Jack—Juno, July 11th, 1881.

Christopher Johnson, be d and 2 be d, Speculation—Lady Amanda, March 22d, 1881.

J. Stadfelt, w b Cleopatra, Speculation—Sacramento Belle, May 27th, 1881.

F. Ryan bd d, be b, blk b, bd b, Ben Franklin—Maid of Gwin, July 16th, 1881.

J. Dregan's 6 pups by Ben Tomey—Sadie Henry, August 3d, 1882.

Mark Devlin's 7 pups by Foxall—Pride of the Canyon, August 7th, 1882.

B. Griffith's f and w b Dido, Tipperary boy—Dixie's Nellie, July, 1881.

Charles Fowler, b and w d by Captain, imported from Australia—Blue Bell b and w d by Captain—Blue Bell.

As usual the opening of the season brings a good deal of speculation as to probable winners, many of which are doubtless pretty near the mark. Among the most promising of the old dogs is Charles Fowler's blue bitch Delelrete, by Speculation—Lady Amanda. She is getting in good condition, and at Merced will be open to match any dog on the grounds for $50 a side, provided, of course, that no accident happens to her in training. Mark Devlin's Chief of the Canyon, is doing regular work and will be able to give a good account of himself. W. Bessie's Maid of San Francisco, by Towey—Pride of the Canyon, is also spoken of prominently. Chris Johnson will probably run his black dog, litter brother to Fowler's Delelrete.

It is said that Mr. Carroll's f and w d Paul Jones, by Gentleman Jones—Brunch, has been transferred to a member of the Pacific Coast Club and will run in their meeting this fall. If he gets in good condition, which is rather a difficult matter for him to do, he will be found a warm competitor for the first honors.

A DASTARDLY ACT. — On the 20th of July the pointer dog Ned Buntline, owned by Mr. J. M. Bowen, of Woodcliff, Rowayton, Conn., was shot in the heart while standing with his head erect and killed, and the charge is made that the shooting was done by a neighbor, Mr. Vincent Colyer, an artist. Mr. Bowen holds as sacred the property right in dogs, especially as a law is on the books in this State of Connecticut, requiring all owners to register, and charging a fee of $1.50 for registration. He has employed counsel, and brought in the Superior Court, sitting at Stamford, a suit of Colyer, laying his damages at $1,000, and the case will be called for trial the latter part of September. If it is proven that Mr. Colyer shot Ned Buntline without cause, it is to be hoped that he will be made to pay its full value of the dog. The pointer or setter, however, which is worth, outside of sentiment, $1,000, is not often met with. Mr. Bowen may have owned such a dog, but we apprehend that the jury will scale the damages down a little. Dog owners everywhere are interested in this case, and they should give Mr. Bowen their moral support.—Turf, Field and Farm.

RETRIEVER. The opening of the duck season has caused quite a demand for good hardy retrievers. The Irish water spaniel is generally preferred here, but it is hard to find a better and more serviceable dog than the curly or wavy-coated English retriever, a breed of dogs very scarce in this State. As several inquiries have been made for both these classes of dogs the kennel editor would be pleased to hear from persons having any such for disposal.

GERMAN FIELD TRIALS.—The field trials to be held in Germany this month promise to be a successful meeting. The trials will take place on the shooting grounds of Prince Albert Solms and the Darmstadt shooting club. No dog will be allowed to compete whose pedigree cannot be proved either by the English kennel club stud book, or the German stud book.

## Racing at Sheepshead Bay.

On September 14th the meeting was continued with the fullest success, and in the mile dash the California stable was represented but Grismer in the mile dash would not rival Lucky R and the Duchess of Norfolk in their victories, as he could only secure second honors.

In the first race, three-quarters of a mile, Little Phil was first, Gus Matthews second, Little Fred third. Time—1:56¼. In the second race, one mile, President Jennings was first, Pinafore second, Jennie third. Time—2:00. In the one mile dash Little Minch won, Grismer second, King Fan third. Time 1:45. In the mile and three furlongs Mirror won easily, Folio second, Bancroft third. Time—2:24¼. In the mile and furlong Follow won, Sweethome second, Saunterer third. Time—1:57. In the one mile, all ages, Girofle won, Barrett second, Bootjack third. Time—1:41½. In the steeplechase, inside course, Sweetbome won, Felix second, Ruby Clark third. Frank Short fell as the wall jump and Falconbridge walked home. Time—4:57½.

The World, speaking of the above race between Barrett, Bootjack and Girofle, at Coney Island says: Ever since it was announced, feeling has run high as to which would win, Barrett or Girofle. Betting was very heavy, in admirers of Barrett and Girofle literally throwing money into the boxes. The supporters of Barrett were specially confi-

dent but the climax was reached when Walton, the plunger, bet a well-known Anglo-American firm $10,000 against $14,000 that Girofle would beat Barrett, and in a few minutes afterwards but the same firm $10,000 even the same way, making a bet of $20,000 to $24,000. This, if not absolutely the largest transaction seen on the race track for some years, is certainly very nearly the largest. The race was easily won by Girofle in 1:41½.

On September 19th it appeared as if the Californians were to have another day's success as Gano was in the first race, and the Duchess of Norfolk in the third, at her favorite distance, a mile and a half, but unfortunately she was disqualified on account of a foul and the race was given to Herbert, the second horse. The first race was three-fourths of a mile.—Gano first, Lizzie Mc second, Felicia third. Time—1:16½. One mile—Breeze first, Little Fred second, Hickory Jim third. Time—1:42. Baby fell. One mile and a half—Duchess of Norfolk first, Herbert second, Frank B. third. Time 2:38½. Duchess was disqualified, owing to a foul, and Herbert was given the race. Blenheim Maid third. Two mile—Fair Count won easily, Bushwhacker second, Hole third. Time—3:32½. Seven furlongs—Bruno first, Bancroft second, Buccaneer third. Time—1:29½. The winner was bought by Torrence for $1,350. Steeple chase, inside course—Bernardine first; Lilly Moyson second, Frank Short third. Time—4:54. Belle of the North fell.

## How Well-known Philadelphians Take Care of their Stock.

[Philadelphia Correspondence.]

There are in the city of Philadelphia quite a number of very large stabling establishments, where horses are not only kept for ordinary hire, but where blooded fast runners owned by private gentlemen are boarded, and where they receive medical treatment when necessary. Some of these livery-boarding establishments are really large and beautiful buildings in external appearance, while the internal arrangements are simply perfection in every respect. Few first-class hotels provide for their guests better accommodations in every respect than those prominent stable proprietors provide for the horses committed to their care. The greater number of these first-rate stables are situated in the northern portion of the city, but there are some excellent ones in the southern section, or that part known as the "old District of Southwark." The writer happened to be "down town" recently, and looked in at two or three of these stables, and the first one visited was the large establishment of William S. Campbell & Son, Nos. 623, 625, 627 and 629 Wharton street. On entering the well-appointed office I was met by Mr. Campbell's son, who really runs the stable, his father having partially retired from active work, and, being seated, we had a pleasant "horse-talk." I learned from Mr. Campbell that he boards about forty horses, consisting of some of the best private stock down town. Mr. Campbell remarked: "We get $25 per head for boarding horses, and as that is the highest price paid, it follows we only have good stock. Many of our horses are well-known on the track, and among them are Fanny Price, a fine mare; L. Lane's team, who have a record of 2:40 together, and some fine trotters, owned by such citizens as Common Councilman J. J. Gallagher; Edward Cobb, Assistant Commissioner of Highways; John C. McMenamin, City Commissioner; Wm. Wilder, John H. Young, and others, including the Farrell Brothers."

The conversation then turned on the care and treatment of horses, and I asked Mr. Campbell if he had ever used St. Jacobs Oil for any of the horses under his charge when they required rubbing.

Mr. Campbell said: "Yes, we have used St. Jacobs Oil, and I think it is a capital thing for horses; I intend to keep on using it on every horse that requires a liniment."

I said: "Tell me on what horses you have used St. Jacobs Oil, and how the remedy operated."

Mr. Campbell then said: "My father owns a bay colt named Billy, a very fine animal, that we think a great deal of. We value Billy at $1,000, and are very careful of him. He is about five years old, and is well known in these parts. A short time since I noticed something was the matter with Billy; the muscles of one of his legs appeared to be contracted, and he was somewhat strained by fast traveling. I happened to have some St. Jacobs Oil on hand, that the family had been using for rheumatism, and I rubbed Billy well with it several times, and he recovered entirely in a very short time. I am satisfied St. Jacobs Oil cured him quicker than any other remedy would have done. We also owns a fine gray horse named Hopeful, who had what we call sweeney, or a drying-up of the shoulder. We tried St. Jacobs Oil in his case, and it was really remarkable how soon the liniment cured his complaint. To show you that the Oil did its work well, my father sold Hopeful recently for a good price, and before he was sold he underwent a careful examination, and it was found he was perfectly sound. If St. Jacobs Oil had not been used for his shoulder I don't believe we could have sold the horse so easily or for such a good price."

## BELMONT—MAMBRINO CHIEF—BLACK-BIRD. For Sale.

BAY YEARLING COLT, BY PILOT, GRANDSON OF WILLIAM-son's Belmont, his dam by Almanera (by Mambrino Chief, from Suwarrow by American Eclipse) grandam Grisle, by Simpson's Blackbird. Is now in Oakland at the stable of

JOS. CAIRN SIMPSON.

## Fine Thoroughbreds for Sale.

BY DIRECTION of Mr. W. L. PRITCHARD we will offer for sale at public auction at 12 m. at the grounds of the BAY DISTRICT ASSOCIATION, SAN FRANCISCO.

On Thursday, November 16th,

A choice lot of thoroughbred horses, comprising BROOD MARES, FOUR-YEAR-OLDS, THREE-YEAR-OLDS, TWO-YEAR-OLDS & YEARLINGS.

These animals are of the choicest blood and offered a rare opportunity of purchasing first-class stock. For other information or catalogues apply to W. L. PRITCHARD, Sacramento, or

KILLIP & CO., Auctioneers, SAN FRANCISCO.

**J. A. McKERRON,**

*MANUFACTURER OF FINE HARNESS.*

**227 Sutter Street,**

BETWEEN DUPONT AND STOCKTON, SAN FRANCISCO.

*Repairing neatly and promptly executed.*

---

**H. H. WILSON & SON,**

IMPORTERS OF AND DEALERS IN
GUNS, PISTOLS, CUTLERY, FISHING
TACKLE, AMMUNITION, ETC.

**513 Clay Street. San Francisco.**

---

**DAVID L. LEVY,**

*JEWELER, DESIGNER OF MEDALS
AND TESTIMONIALS,*

**39 Third Street, San Francisco.**

REPAIRING NEATLY DONE.

---

**DAN McCARTHY,**

*LIVERY, BOARDING & SALE STABLE,*

**608 Howard Street, Near Second.**

LARGEST STOCK OF FAST LIVERY TEAMS in the State. First-class boarding. Horses bought and sold. Cash advanced on horses, buggies, sulkies, harness or anything connected with the business.

---

**PAUL FRIEDHOFER,**

*PATHOLOGICAL HORSE-SHOER*

**105 Commercial Street.**

*Practical in all its various branches.*

---

### Third Annual Fair.

---

**AGRICULTURAL ASSOCIATION.**

SIXTH DISTRICT.

---

*AT THE CITY OF LOS ANGELES,*

**October 16th, 17th, 18th, 19th, 20th
and 21st.**

---

**SPEED PROGRAMME.**

---

**FIRST DAY**—MONDAY, Oct. 16, 1882

**SECOND DAY**—TUESDAY, Oct. 17, 1882.
No. 1. District, trotting, 3 minute class; purse, $200.
No. 2. District, trotting, 2:38 class; purse, $400.
No. 3. District, running, colt race, free for all 3-year-olds, half mile dash; purse, $300.

**THIRD DAY**—WEDNESDAY, Oct. 18.
No. 4. Trotting, free for all that never beat 2:30; purse $500.

SAME DAY.
No. 5. District, running, free for all, half mile and repeat; purse, $500.

SAME DAY.
No. 6. Running, free for all, mile and repeat; purse, $600.

**FOURTH DAY**—THURSDAY, Oct. 19.

Grand Stock Parade.
A liberal purse will be offered for a long distance riding match. Arrangements are being perfected.
No. 7. District, trotting, 3-year-olds and under; purse $400.

**FIFTH DAY**—FRIDAY, Oct. 20.
No. 8. District, trotting, 2:40 class; purse, $400.
No. 9. District, running, 2-year-old, three-quarter mile dash; purse, $300.

**SIXTH DAY**—SATURDAY, Oct. 21.
No. 10. Trotting, free for all; purse, $600.

SAME DAY.
No. 11. District, running, free for all, three-quarters of mile dash; purse $500.

SAME DAY.
No. 12. Running, free for all, 2 mile dash; purse, $700.

REMARKS AND CONDITIONS.
All trotting races are the three best in five, unless otherwise specified, three to enter and two to start; entrance fee, 10 per cent. on purse, to accompany nominations. Purses divided at the rate of 60 per cent. to first, 30 per cent. to second, and 10 per cent. to third.
All running purses to be divided, two-thirds to the first horse and one-third to the second horse; four to enter and two to start, except race No. 11, three to enter and two to start.
National Association Rules to govern trotting; but to Board reserves the right to trot heats of any two alternately, if necessary to finish any day's racing, or to trot a special race between heats.
To fill running races, four or more subscribers are required.
For two-year-olds, when running in their classes, all carry 89 pounds, with the usual allowance for sexual privileges.

[continued text columns]

---

---

**J. CONDON'S**

☞ *HAND BALL COURT,* ☜

**733 Howard St., bet. Third & Fourth.**

*Match Game every Sunday. Fine Wines and
Liquors.*

---

**G. H. STRONG,**

*BICYCLES AND TRICYCLES.*

**252 Market Street.**

Repairs to order.    Elevator, 12 Front street

---

**BALL COURT,**

**846.** *HOWARD STREET* **846.**

Fine Wines, Liquors and Cigars.

WM. AIKINS, Proprietor.

---

**MME. EXILDA LA CHAPELLE,**

*SPORTSMEN'S HEADQUARTERS.*

Northeast Corner Post Street & Central Av.

REFRESHMENTS AND LADIES' SITTING ROOM.

---

**T. G. PARKER & CO.,**

*THE AMERICAN TAILORING ESTAB-
LISHMENT,*

**237 Kearny Street, near Bush.**

Business Suits.........................$25 to $35
Dress Suits..............................$40 to $60

*No Chinese labor employed, nor shoddy trim-
mings used.*

---

**ENGLISH SETTER PUPPIES**

*FOR SALE.*

BY MR. THOMAS BENNETT'S REGENT, out of Waddington's Daisy; and Mr. Thomas Bennett's Regent, out of Leavesley's Juno. Both Daisy and Juno are field trial winners. Price $25 and $35. Apply to
E. LEAVESLEY, Gilroy.

---

**INTERESTING.**

THE SEMI-WEEKLY EAST OREGONIAN, published in Pendleton, Umatilla County, Oregon, the Pilot Rock and Interprise, of any address three months, $1; six months, $1.75; twelve months, $3. Sample copy of paper and picture, 10 cents. The best and truest description of Umatilla —the great Wheat and sheep country—Wet Weather. Address EAST OREGONIAN PUBLISHING COMPANY, Pendleton, Umatilla County, Oregon.

---

**SPEED PROGRAMME**
OF THE

Mount Shasta Agricultural
Association,

**TO BE HELD IN**

YREKA, SISKIYOU CO.,

Wednesday, - - October 4th, 1882.

For racing purposes their district shall comprise Siskiyou, Shasta, Trinity and Modoc Counties, Cal., and Jackson and Lake Counties, Oregon.
No bottle shall be eligible to any of the Siskiyou District Races unless owned in the District prior to October, 1881.

**FIRST DAY**—WEDNESDAY, Oct. 4.
No. 1—TROTTING—Free for all: 3 in 5; purse, $300 Fired horse receives $400 second horse, $100. Entrance 10 per cent. of purse; 3 to enter. 2 to start. Entries close September 1st.
No. 2—RUNNING—Dash of a mile and a half; free for all horses owned in the District; purse, $100; entrance 20.

**SECOND DAY**—THURSDAY, Oct. 5.
No. 3—TROTTING—Free for all sucked horses owned in the District; 3 in 5; purse, $75; entrance $5, added.
No. 4—RUNNING—Half mile and Repeat; free for all horses owned in the District; purse $75; entrance $5, added.
No. 5—TROTTING—Free for all three-year-olds and under owned in the District; best three of five; purse $75; entrance $5, added.

**THIRD DAY**—FRIDAY, Oct. 6.
(Grand parade of Stock)
No. 6—TROTTING—Free for all in the District; 3 in 5; purse, $300; entrance $5, added.
No. 7—FOOT RACE—75 yards and repeat; purse, $50; entrance $5.
No. 8—RUNNING—Free for all three-year-olds and under owned in the District; dash of three-quarters of a mile; purse, $75; entrance $5, added.

**FOURTH DAY**—SATURDAY, Oct. 7.
No. 9—RUNNING—Free for all; 3 in 5; purse $300. Fired horse receives $400 second horse, $100; entrance 5 per cent. of purse; 3 to enter, 2 to start. Entries close Sept. 1st.
No. 10—TROTTING—Free for all horses in the District that have never beaten three minutes; 3 in 5; purse, $300; entrance $5, added.

Rules and Regulations.
1st. The above purses will be given without discount.
2nd. In all District Races the second horse to save entrance fee.
3rd. Entries to be placed in the entry box, kept for that purpose at the Pavilion, prior to 9 o'clock P. M. on the day prior to the race.
4th. Entries must give name, pedigree, and description of horse entered as far as known.
5th. In all District Races two or more entries make a field.
6th. All trotting races must be to harness.
7th. National Trotting Association Rules to govern trotting.

8th. Free for all, in races 1 and 9, means just what it says, and all entries to those races must be made with the Secretary on or before September 1st.

J. SWAIN, President,
H. MAGOFFEY, Secretary.

---

**"Red Clover."**

NEEDHAM'S RED CLOVER BLOSSOMS AND extracts are the greatest blood-purifier in the world; also a sure cure for cancer, salt rheum, catarrh, etc., etc. I can refer to numbers of testimonials of those who have been benefited—some of them very remarkable. I will send circulars and testimonials to those wishing them. Address
W. L. NEEDHAM, Box 422, San Jose, Cal.,
Sole agent for Pacific Coast.   sfml

---

**TURF EXCHANGE.**

**FARRELLY & MITCHELL,**

**435 California Street.**

**Fine Wines, Liquors & Cigars.**

---

**THE VICTORIAN TROTTING CLUB**

(Ltd.)

MELBOURNE, AUSTRALIA,

—OFFER—

The unstream-lined Prize, to be competed for on a day to be named early in January next, 1883.

### PRIZE OF 2,500 DOLLARS,

With Entrance Fees and Sweepstakes of $80 each from the fifth added; Mile heats; best three in five. Open to all horses, no geldings. Winner to receive $2,000; second, two-thirds of Sweep and Entrance Fees, and third, one-third. Entrance 5 per cent.
Entries must be in the hands of Secretary on or before WEDNESDAY, 13th December, 1882.

The Victorian Trotting Club holds membership in the National Trotting Association of the United States. Races will be governed.
Any further information desired can be obtained by addressing R. J. CARNEY, Secretary,
Kirk Bazaar, Melbourne.

---

**SECOND
ANNUAL EXHIBITION**

OF THE

**SAN MATEO AND SANTA
CLARA COUNTY
AGRICULTURAL ASSOCIATION
NO. 5,**

TO BE HELD AT

**SAN JOSE, CAL.**

......FROM......

**Sept. 25th to 30th, '82' inclusive**

*SPEED PROGRAMME.*

FIRST DAY—Monday, Sept. 25, 1882.
No. 1. TROTTING—2:40 class. Purse, $600.
  C. Van Buren, of Mayfield, enters Peter Coulie's b m Manon, by Norwood, dam Adele.
[entries list continues]

SECOND DAY—Tuesday, Sept. 26th.

THIRD DAY—Wednesday, Sept. 27th.

FOURTH DAY—Thursday, Sept. 28th.

FIFTH DAY—Friday, Sept. 29th.

SIXTH DAY—Saturday, Sept. 30th.

REMARKS AND CONDITIONS.

T. S. MONTGOMERY, Secretary.

# HORSE HISTORY.

## Albert W.

:t is only a few years since George Wilkes trotted in 2:22, i that performance placed him first on the list of trotting llions. At that time Ericsson had the pride of place ong four-year-olds with 2:30 to his credit. Both of these re regarded as wonderful performances, and deservedly so, i now we have the pleasure of recording the same time as ıt of Wilkes for a California-bred four-year-old, and to emasize the feat the 2:22 was made in a third heat, repeatin a fourth, and the fifth only a half a second slower. is would have been a creditable performance for a stallion any age; when made by one of the age of Albert W, it kes rank with the very best and entitles him to a prominnt place among the "notables" of any country.

On the same day (Saturday last) there was a race for four-.ar-olds at Chicago, and the telegraph brings the intelliance that Jay Eye See won the first, third and fourth heats ı 2:22¼, 2:19, 2:19. There is an erroneous statement in the legram that the winner is a stallion, as unfortunately the eat colt is a eunuch. The great advantage which follows nasculation on the trotting tracks is too well known to reaire argument, and as is shown by the records there is only ıe instance where an entire horse leads, that being the re-year-old record of Santa Claus (2:18). Smuggler is five conds behind Maud S, four in the rear of St. Julien; Rarus, rinket, Goldsmith Maid, Clingstone and Hopeful also having tter records. From this it is not out of the way to estimate that e three seconds which Jay Eye See leads Albert W does not ve the gelding the preference. We do not wish to detract ı iota from the well-earned fame of the son of Dictator, nor ıve we the least desire to give Albert W greater prominence an he deserves. The gelding is entitled to the credit of trotıg the best race which has ever been made by colts of any s, and thb stallion by far the best of male performers before e "mouth was full."

'o breeders the most prominent features are the lines of blood hich have led to such an astonishing result, and both of them ve the same answer, viz: A combination of the Hambleaian with fresh infusion of thoroughbred blood. Jay Eye e is by Dictator, his dam (the dam of Dexter) by Seeley's nerican Star. The dam of Jay Eye See, Midnight, is by lot Jr., her dam, Twilight, by Lexington and thoroughbred. idnight is also the dam of Noontide, a mare with a record 2:20½, and as she is by Herald is nearly a sister in blood Jay Eye See. American Star was a highly bred horse, so at the racing blood predominates in the victor at Chicago. The dam of Albert W is a sister to Aurora, by John Nelson, d John Nelson was by imported Trustee, from the Redond mare, by Adallah. This pedigree has been questioned t only by those who have such a violent antipathy to the oroughbred that it warps their judgment and forbids a adid weighing of testimony. They are ready to believe s most absurd stories when these fall in with their notions, pugn the evidence of reliable men when it runs counter their views, and profess rather to believe the maunderings of me one overcome with the senility of over fourscore years, an proof which was accepted as correct at a contemporaous period. We have before us an advertisement of John lson, published in 1860, soon after the horse was brought re, and the following is a transcript:

The fine trotting stallion John Nelson will stand at Robert atty's "White House" during the season beginning March He is a rich, bright chestnut, with a star on the forehead, d two white hind feet and is fifteen hands high. Terms the season, $75.

John Nelson is by imported Trustee out of the Redmond re (who trotted in 3:35), by Abdallah, he by Mambrino and by imported Messenger. John Nelson is half brother to celebrated trotting gelding, Trustee, who trotted twenty les in the unprecedented time of 59:35½, and he bears the ne relationship to Fashion, Revenue and Reube Rynders, all splendid four-mile racers. His half brother, Revenue, now stands at Versailles, Ky., for $150 the season.

Mares left at the stables of Messrs. Porter & Flenner will receive prompt attention. Parties living at a distance, requiring the services of the horse, will please address them, or J. M. DANIELS,

134 Kearney Street, San Francisco.

Now this advertisement was published in the *California Spirit of the Times*, that exchanged with the papers of the time, and any man who had one-half of the experience of Mr. Daniels would know that a false pedigree would soon be detected. Like many others it was never questioned until it was supposed that years enough had elapsed to bring it in doubt. At all events the get of John Nelson show nnmistakeable signs of "blood," and many of them display the Abdallah characteristics. The double Abdallah cross is shown in many of the crack performers, and even when derived in double quantity through two strains of Rysdyk's Hambletonian. Goldsmith Maid is a notable example of the first, Clingstone of the second, and illustrations could be multiplied until tiresome of the "potency" of the dual progenitors.

John Nelson the last we heard of him was still alive, and the last time we saw him he was active as a colt, and showed scarcely any of the effects of the many years he has lived. As the sire of Nerea, Aurora, Governor Stanford and others he has gained a place among the "standard" sires, though from present indications the second generation will show still more speed, and Nelson mares be highly valued in the stud.

Of Electioneer, the sire of Albert W, there is little necessity of adding to what has already been published in this paper. He is, without doubt, the most remarkable trotting sire that has ever appeared. He was scarcely known outside of Stonyford when Governor Stanford purchased him and, in the short time since his home has been in California, his colts stand first on the list in the yearlings, the three fastest two-year-olds, and the fastest four-year-old stallion. The figures stand 2:36½ for Hinda Rose, yearling; 2:21 for Wildflower, 2:24½ for Bonita and 2:25½ for Fred Crocker, two-year-olds; 2:22, 2:22½, 2:24 for third, fourth and fifth heats of Albert W, the last won in a jog, and from all appearances the winner could have made it as fast as either of the others. But the public performances of the get of Electioneer, brilliant as they are, do not show the entirety of his merit as the progenitor of fast trotters. We have yet to see an Electioneer which does not give promise of making a fast trotter. Speed is not their only inheritance. Take them together and they are of the highest form found in the get of a trotting-bred horse, and very many of them show a degree of quality akin to the thoroughbred. Sound-headed, docile, with great power which will enable them to haul heavy weight and give them the front rank as road horses, stylish, symmetrical, handsome color, it would be difficult to name a valuable quality, essential for the road and track, that they do not possess. With all the "prepotency" which characterizes this son of Rysdyk's Hambeltonian and Green Mountain Maid it has been his good fortune in California to be mated with the right sort of mares. This gives the stock a value greater than could be derived from one parent, and assures the continuation of these valuable qualities. There is not a state in the Union that is better supplied with the material for fast trotters than California, and, in fact, with so great a variety of strains. We have the best of the Eastern blood with the addition of Belmont and St. Clair, and are fortunate, too, in the conjunction of Trustee and Abdallah in John Nelson. Albert W is about 15½, he may be a trifle over that hight, and is a shapely colt all over. He is a bright bay with black points, his coat very fine. He is one of the long order in the formation, and like a majority of the Electioneers somewhat higher over the croup than the withers; he has a splendid set of limbs, and his action is very fine. That he is an improving colt is shown by his races of last year and this. Every race he takes part in shows an improvement on those which came before, and though his three-year-old record of 2:32½ was not the measure of his speed when he trotted with Sweetheart at San Jose last Fall, it would be an exacting owner who was not satisfied with the ten and a half seconds of improvement from that figure in a little less than twelve months. In order to show in this place how good a colt he was last Saturday, the description of the race by "our special commissioner" is transferred from its place to finish this sketch. We were in hopes to accompany this sketch with a picture of the "crack four-year-old," but will have to defer the portraiture to another time:

The race closed with nine entries, but with some disqualified and some drawn the starters were reduced to three, Sweetness, Nellie R and Albert W. Sweetness was a great favorite in betting circles partly from the manner in which she had won her race at Sacramento and partly found the prestige that attaches to Goldsmith and Mr. Salisbury's stable in these later meetings of the circuit. Pools sold before the start ran: Sweetness $50, Nellie R $18, Albert W $12. In the lottery for positions Albert W drew the first prize with Sweetness second and Nellie R outside. Scoring for the word in the first heat was somewhat tedious through the rank behavior of Albert W, who acted as if there was lax discipline in the school where he studied. When the bell did tap they were all in good shape but the colt broke at the sound and commenced the service with a sharp run. Sweetness took the lead at once with Nellie R on her wheel and thus they went to the quarter in 36. At that point Nelile R broke up and Albert W took the second place, Sweetness in the meantime opening a gap of three lengths. Before the half was reached Albert W again left his feet and Nellie R sped around the turn after the leader, leaving the colt eight lengths in the rear. Nellie closed the gap rapidly and at the three-quarter pole was at Sweetness' wheel, Albert having also shortened the interval a couple of lengths. In the trot up the stretch, Nellie pushed Sweetness to a break and came to the wire first in a jog, Sweetness second, Albert W third. Time 2:22½. It appeared from this trial that Sweetness was not herself and the speculators who had backed her heavily in the pools made haste to secure themselves by putting in large sums on the big chestnut, an operation that proved to be a repetition of the old story of out of the frying-pan into the fire. The first pool sold was Nellie R $150, Sweetness $70, Albert W $27, and the last one before the start was Nellie R $40, Sweetness $16, Albert W $14.

Second heat. There was less difficulty in starting for this mile, Sweetness getting away first, but Nellie R showing such a measure of speed that she was taken back and brought to the work gradually. Albert had overcome his disposition to break and was trotting squarely close in the trail. At the quarter in 35½ Sweetness showed in front but at the half in 1:10 Nellie R was neck and neck with her, Albert five lenghts behind. Around the turn was without change and in the home work Goldsmith with whip and voice urged his mare to her utmost but Nellie was in her happiest mood and she came under the wire without hard driving, winner by half a length, Albert W third. Time 2:20. The rush to "get out" was greater than ever. The first pool sold was Nellie R $200, Sweetness $27, Albert $25, but as the selling progressed the excited speculators cooled somewhat and the last pool was Nellie R $110, Albert W $30, Sweetness $10.

Third heat. They got away together and at the quarter in 36 Nellie R was in front and Albert W behind but all lapped. In the backstretch the colt skipped and found himself the last member in the line by a length, Nellie R drawing away slightly from Sweetness. They reached the half in 1:10½. Around the turn they came in a string, but at the three-quarter mark Sweetness broke up and the colt began his chase after Nellie R. Sperry heard the long, steady stroke behind him and knew what was in the wind. He struck his mare two or three sharp blows with his whip but she was done. Her speed and heart had both left her and Albert W swept past at a pace he had not before shown in the race, passing the stand winner by three open lengths, Nellie R second, Sweetness third. Time 2:22.

There was another revolution in betting. Nothing could be plainer to the habitue of the tracks than that the col had the race cornered. In the pools it was three to one on Albert W against the field.

Fourth heat. Albert W. showed the way to the quarter in 36½ but in the straight work broke up and at the half in 1:11 there was a bunch with Sweetness first and Albert last. Around the turn he worked into second place and up the stretch beat Sweetness handily by three lengths, Nellie R third. Time 2:22.

Fifth heat. Albert W. went off first with Sweetness close up, Nellie R breaking badly at the first turn. At the quarter in 36½ and the half in 1:10½ the colt was leading with Sweetness on his wheel Nellie R ten lengths behind. From there home the colt came at a steady clip, being practically alone in the race. He won the heat by six lengths, Sweetness second Nellie R third. Time 2:24.

Saturday, September 22—Pacific Coast trotting; 2:22 Class; purse $1,000, and $200 added if made than ten entries. Four nonays.
A. Waldstein names b s Albert W, by Electioneer—by John Nelson........................ 1 1 1
S. Sperry names ch m Nellie R, by Gen McClellan Jr.... 1 1 2 3 3
J. A. Goldsmith names b m Sweetness, by Volunteer.... 3 3 2 2
D. McCarty's b g Haddock, R. R. Curly's b g Capt. Smith, G. Bernard's g Allen Roy, D. Mead's b g Tinny Winkle, J. A. Goldsmith's blk f Director and W. D. Hammond's Joaquin Haywards drawn.
Time—2:22, 2:2.0 2:22, 2:222, 2:24.

## TURF AND TRACK.

### Fixed Events.

Macon, Plumas and Lassen District Fair at Greenville, from October 2d to October 9th inclusive.
Northern District Fair at Susanville City, from October 2d to October 6th inclusive.
Nevada State Fair at Reno, from Monday, October 1d to the 7th inclusive.
Mount Shasta Agricultural Association Fair at Yreka, October 6th, 5th, 6th and 7th.
Eastern Oregon Fair Stock Association at Union, from October 8th to the 9th inclusive.
Los Angeles Agricultural Association, at Los Angeles, from October 17th to the 27th.
Fall meeting of the Pacific Coast Blood Horse Association, November 11th, 15th, 18th and 22d.

**FAIRS IN THE EAST.**

Texas State Fair, at Austin, October 17th to the 31st inclusive.

### Billy McCracken and His Sire.

EDITOR BREEDER AND SPORTSMAN: Dear Sir: In a recent issue of the BREEDER AND SPORTSMAN you solicited information regarding the stallion Billy McCracken, and I give you the following statement of facts regarding his history and that of his sire, McCracken's Black Hawk, or Morgan Black Hawk as he was sometimes called. For the truth of the statement I refer to O. C. McCracken, Esq., of San Francisco, from whom the same was obtained about two months since. Billy McCracken was bred by a Mr. Letts, then of Medina, New York, and was sired by McCracken's Black Hawk, his dam being the "Letts mare," then owned by Mr. Letts and said to be of Messenger blood. He was foaled in 1850 and was sold at ten months old for $90 to Mr. H. M. Beers of Medina, for Mr. O. C. McCracken. Mr. McCracken procured him kept at Medina for two years, when in 1853 he took him to Chicago where he then lived. Mr McCraken removed to Oshkosh, Wisconsin, the next year and took Billy with him, where he was kept till he was brought to Marysville, California, in 1861. He was used in the stud at Oshkosh while there, and afterwards at Marysville until he died. After making the season of 1861, he was sold to Mr. D. E. Knight of Marysville, in whose ownership he there after continued. He was handled for speed a few months by Otis Dimick, then of Milwaukee, Wisconsin, and in 1855 or 1856 trotted and won a race at an agricultural fair at that place against eight stallions; best time 2:49, the track being about ten seconds slow. The stock which he left in Wisconsin is said to have been held in much favor, so much so that there was an effort made by some of the leading horsemen of Winnebago county to get him back there. Mr. John De Mass of Detroit, Michigan, is said to have handled one of his get which showed 2:28 in his work and another is said to have shown a mile in 2:25 at Milwaukee, under the saddle, with Mr. O. A. Hickok holding the reins. Mr. McCracken was unable to give the names of either of these horses, but stated that Judge J. McM. Shafter probably could give the name of the one handled by De Mass, as De Mass at one time communicated with him about the horse. Your correspondent, Frank Grant, would do many of your readers a kindness by giving the time, place and circumstances under which Billy trotted five miles in 14m. and 10s.

McCracken's Blackhawk, the sire of Billy, was purchased in 1848 in Vermont, by Hon. Silas Burroughs, then of Medina, New York, and was soon after (being then two years old) sold to Andrew Ellicott of that place. Mr. Ellicott came to California soon after and died here, and the horse in 1850 was sold to J. O. McCracken, then of Medina. Mr. McCracken placed him in the stud at Lockport, New York, for one season, and one or two seasons afterwards he stood at or near Buffalo in charge of Mr. Samuel Twitchell. Mr. J. G. McCracken meantime moved to Kenosha, Wisconsin, and took the horse there about the year 1853, where he did service in the stud until 1860, when he was brought to California by McCracken. He remained the property of Mr. McCracken until his death. He made the most of his season at Stockton, in charge of Dr. C. Grattan (at whose ranch he died), occasionally standing for a time at the ranch of his owner at Georgetown, about fourteen miles from Sacramento. He died about 1871. Of the get of this horse little need be said for the information of your readers in this State. They are quite as well known here as the get of any horse ever brought to the State. No horse in the State has produced a better class of livery and road horses considering his opportunities in the stud. It is questionable if he ever was coupled with a mare in this State which could trot a mile in three minutes and yet he is standard by reason of his get.

### The San Jose Fair.

Of all the cities that form the racing circuit of the Pacific Coast the inhabitants of San Jose claim the foremost position both in regard to its site and its facilities for carrying out a well organized fair that will be a credit to the two lovely and flourishing counties, San Mateo and Santa Clara, of which the district is composed. The city is admirably laid out, the streets being broad and kept in almost perfect order, while its shady avenues forming pleasant drives into the country are perhaps unrivaled throughout the land. The city shows evident signs of prosperity and its commercial marts are not confined to one or two streets, but radiate in many directions from the fuel but lofty electric tower which may be considered the center of the town. The grounds of the Association are situated about a mile from this point on a bend of the Santa Clara avenue, and with the improvements already made, combined with those whose execution is projected, they will soon stand unrivaled within the State especially in the way of trees of which there are excellent specimens on every side with foliage that denotes a sturdy and luxuriant growth. San Jose, although situated within a district noted for its ranches rich with horses and cattle of the highest breeding, labors under one serious disadvantage in the arrangement of the fair, and especially so as regards the speed programme, as the entries close generally at the same time as the other meetings of the circuit and as it is the last one of the series, the fields are apt to be diminished in the different classes, owing to the enforced withdrawal of those horses who have succumbed to the trials of the campaign, or others that are not deemed sufficiently speedy to contest with the best of the class. The result of this almost unavoidable dilemma was seen in the races of the first day, when fields representing eleven and eight nominations respectively were reduced to three and four who trotted for the purses. This is acknowledged by the Directors of the association to be a grave matter of discussion in the future, as when there is an absence of excitement and of speculation, the races are not apt to draw such a large attendance as would otherwise be the case. It is true, as some of these gentlemen argue, that the past season has been very exceptional in its character, as the horses have more or less suffered from the prevailing epizooty, and that the number of race horses has been seriously diminished by the small but valuable draft that was sent to the East. Nevertheless there are others among those who have the interests of the Association at heart, who maintain that it would be better in the future to bar the winners of the 2:40, 2:35, 2:30 and 2:25 class at San Jose, and instead to offer two special purses to close at the expiration of the State and of the Stockton Fair. This in connection with a project to penalize the thoroughbred winners at the previous fairs, is a matter of debate that will be closely scrutinized during the winter months when more editorial space can be devoted to such an important change of base.

As regards the weather, the fair opened under the most advantageous circumstances, the sun shining brightly but tempered by cool zephyrs that scarcely moved the foliage, but that were very refreshing on the track. The grounds show signs of evident improvement. A judges' stand has also been built on the inside of the track, but the quarters for the timers and reporters beneath are far too restricted for a track of such pretensions. The track has been carefully prepared and perhaps was somewhat more favorable for fast time among the runners than the trotters, and all the arrangements had evidently received the careful supervision of the Secretary and of the Superintendent.

The pretty city put on its gala appearance on the opening day, and although the attendance at the races appeared to show a falling off, there was really an increase of $150 in the receipts of the same day over the previous year, which was accounted to be a good omen for the success of the meeting.

#### The Races.

As originally planned the programme of the first day was perhaps the strongest of the meeting, the two races being for the 2:40 class, in which there were eleven entries, and for the 2:25 class, in which there were eight nominations. In these two classes there was a fine field of horses, and the races taking place at the commencement of the circuit there would have been much excitement and heavy investments anent the result, but the experience gained in Oakland, Stockton, and at the State Fair was such as to greatly restrict operations and it was only on the respective merits of Vanderlyn and Manon that there appeared to exist a difference of opinion and even in that case the betting was not of a very exciting order.

Of the eleven entered in the $500 purse for the 2:40 class there were but four who finished up the circuit and probably two of these started merely with the idea of securing some of the minor money. Vanderlynn and Manon sold about even at $35 against $5 for the two others together, namely Frank Moscow and Big Lize. There was a great deal of useless scoring that delayed the opening of proceedings and a little more decision on the part of the judge who presided at the gong would have been pleasing to the drivers as they were often past the wire before they knew whether it was a send-off or not. Finally they getaway with Manon on the outside with decidedly the worst of the start while Moscow took advantage of his position at the pole to take a good lead, but when they had well rounded the first turn Manon was rapidly recovering her position, as both she and Vanderlynn passed him in succession and they made a good trot home, the race being handsomely her advantage to the finish by more than a length, Moscow being a fair third, with Big Lize fourth, and the time, 2:26½. After the even there was but a slight advance made on Manon's chances as Vanderlynn brought $40 to her $30 and the field $3, that being offered more on the faith of Big Lize's appearance than on Moscow's efforts. This true Manon made the pace lively to the quarter with Vanderlynn in close attendance and Big Lize on a big jump, but when she was gotten to her best she trotted at such a gait as made the fielders think they had found a bonanza, passing both the horses but failing to reach Manon who won by two lengths in 2:26. This settled the betting for the next heat, that also finished the race, for although Manon and Vanderlynn trotted fast and evenly all the way round and they were well lapped, at the wire it appeared as if the mare had always something in hand, and this reward the faith of her backers. The time was 2:25 and Big Lize was distanced through the effect of a disastrous break.

SUMMARY.
San Jose, September 25—Trotting purse of $500 for the 2:40 class.
C. Van Buren names P. Cottle's b m Manch, by McWood, dam Ashton..... 1 1 1
F. Farrell names b h Vanderlynn, by George M. Patchen, dam by Belmont........ 3 2 2
B. B. Cottle names a g Frank Moscow, by Frank Moscow, dam unknown............ 2 3 3
W. A. Hackman's Black b c Big Lize.................... dis
Louis D. Allen Roy, San Mateo Belle Manon, Freestone, Edwin Forrest and Rowdy Boy were entered but did not start.
Time—2:26½, 2:26, 2:25.

The second race was of a very one-sided description as regards speculation, although many fair judges were of the

opinion that a better showing might have been made both in regard to speed and to well contested heats. Of the eight entries only three came on the track and Director was installed first favorite at $50 to $10 for Cairo and Starr King combined. From the commencement to the finish there was not a ripple of excitement raised in regard to the issue, save perhaps among a few adepts who wagered on the point of second money between Cairo and Starr King. Cairo, aided by his position at the pole and seconded by a slight break on the part of Director at the first turn, assumed the lead, but at mid back stretch he was passed very leisurely by Director, who responding to his name, had it all his own way, winning the heat easily in 2:28½, with Cairo second and Starr King last, an announcement that was received with a few shouts of derision. In the next it was the turn of Starr King to effect a slight diversion on the part of the fielders, and he led Director at the quarter and was at his wheel as they turned into the third turn, but here he had seemingly enough, as Director came away with comparative ease and beat him out in 2:26. This was certainly a notch lower in the way of time, and a few trifling bets were made that the three horses that are about the best representatives of the 2:25 class would not beat the 2:25 record made previously in the 2:40 class. But it so happened that the third heat was the best of the three, for although Director's chances were never in danger, Cairo trotted him to a fairly close finish, the time being 2:24½.

SUMMARY.
Same day—Trotting Purse of $750 for 2:25 class.
J. A. Goldsmith names b s Director, by Dictator, dam by Mambrino Chief...................... 1 1 1
John Hughes names b g Cairo, by Chieftain, dam unknown..... 2 3 2
C. W. Welby names ch g Starr King, by George M. Patchen Jr., from Mary Wonder................. 3 2 3
Crown Point, Reform, Captain Smith, Del Sur and Ashley were also entered but did not start.
Time—2:26½, 2:26, 2:24½.

On the second day there was a decided improvement in the attendance, and there were many ladies and children present, either in the grand stand or in private vehicles adjoining the inclosure in the quarter stretch. The outlook was not very favorable for a good day's racing as there were but three running events on the card, and of these the first was a walk-over, though between two prominent stables, Mr. Coutts' and the Palo Alto ranch, were represented among the nominations.

SUMMARY.
San Jose, September 26—Running race, for two year olds, a dash of three-quarters of a mile, $50 entrance, $15 forfeit, $50 added, second to receive his entrance and one-third of the added money.
George Howson names b f Augusta E, by Monday, dam by Norfolk w o
Sahsalita, Bryant W., Panama and Flor Flora paid forfeit.

In the other races the principal horses were but fairly represented and the reason, as stated by a prominent trainer, was that the purses at San Jose are too small considering the expense of training and transportation, and that the Reno fair offers much more attractive premiums. For the Inglatory Stake for two-year-olds, a dash of three-quarters of a mile, George Howson walked over for the four forfeits, amounting in all to $90, the association reserving the $125 added money, and thus the entire amount offered for the day was only $925, and it was argued that a little more liberality on the part of the association would insure much larger returns.

The second race was a mile dash for all ages, in which May D had been in great demand on the previous evening, but rumors were prevalent that she was not in thorough condition and Nighthawk sold favorite in the pools at $40 just before the start, with $25 for May D and $6 for the field, in which were Jim Douglas and Bob, the latter a fast but very unreliable nag. Nighthawk appears to have been spoilt in her training as she is very vicious now every time she starts, and naturally so, when every slight hound she makes she gets heavy strokes across the face, a method not conducive to improve her temper. The start was delayed half an hour through the tricking and rearing of Bob and Nighthawk in the vain attempt to get them near the other horses, but at last Mr. Finigan got them on pretty even terms, save that Nighthawk on the extreme outside was a short length behind and her jockey instead of accepting the position and trying her to keep her place deliberately drew to the rails with the idea probably of riding a waiting race. So it was a mistaken policy as her chances were gone. Bob taking up the running at his wild pace to the half mile post when May D moved up and was shortly afterwards joined by Nighthawk and Jim Douglas, and in this order they galloped to the distance when Nighthawk was beaten and Douglas challenging May D passed her without an effort and won easily in 1:45½. Some complaints were made by the backers of Nighthawk about the start, but the opinion of the best judges, except those who were influenced in her favor, was that Douglas won with five pounds to spare. These complaints being reported to Mr. Finigan he instantly gave in his resignation as starter and W. Donathan took the position. It seems to be a pity that the English rules that prohibit any unfavorable remarks being made to the starter are not respected here, for no gentleman likes to lay himself open to bitter reproaches that he knows full well that he has never deserved and consequently it will be found extremely difficult to get a gentleman who is fully qualified to accept such an ungrateful office.

SUMMARY.
Same day—Running for all ages, a dash; $50 entrance, $15 forfeit, with $125 added; second horse to receive his entrance and one-third of added money.
George Howson names b h Jim Douglas, by Wildidle, dam by Norfolk, four years, 108 pounds........ 1
H. C. Judson names ch m May D, by Wildidle dam Nettie Brown, by Rifleman, four years, 108 pounds.... 2
P. J. Shafter names b m Nighthawk, by imported Haddington, dam by Norfolk, five years, 111 pounds.................. 3
Wm. Boots names b g Bob, by Bob Wooding, dam by Norfolk, three years, 90 pounds............. 4
Fred Collier, Joe Howell, Joe Daniels Jr., Forest King and Bed Boy were entered but did not start.
Time 1:45½.

The next race was a mile and repeat selling race in which Haddington and Belshaw were about equally in favor in the betting while Bender sold at an extreme outside price. Haddington had slightly the best of the send-off, but within a few yards Belshaw was up with him and at the half mile he had half a length the best, with Bender gradually taking the second place, and in that position the heat was galloped in the slow time of 1:47½. And now the quid-nuncs were on the qui-vive to know what it all meant, and at first Balshaw sold even at $30 against the two others, but when it became rumored about that Haddington had told up the heat and was sure to win, there was such a rush to get on that $40 was bid eagerly against $25 on Belshaw's chances. But it was a false alarm and even if Haddington had been reserved for the second heat, he was too of slight account as Belshaw raced him on even terms to the half mile and then gradually drew away, winning in a handy manner by two lengths in 1:43 with Bender distanced. The winner was entered to be sold at $400 and even at that price after such a fine display of there was no bid for Belshaw beyond that amount. At st he would be worth perhaps double the money.

SUMMARY.

e day—Running, selling race, purse $200, mile and repeat, sec- horse, $175, entrance 5 per cent. to third horse. Horses en- to be sold for $1,000 to carry entitled weight. Two pounds off for $100 under fixed valuation. Winner can be claimed by any one.

. Judson names b g Belshaw, 4 years, by Wildidle, dam by rcules, $400, 98 pounds.......... 1 1
Shafter names b h Haddington, by imp. Haddington, dam by rfolk, $800, 110 pounds.......... 3 2
yton names b g Geo. Bender, aged, dam Sugar Plum, sire un- own, $500, 110 pounds.......... 1 dist

:hre and Joe Howell were entered but did not start and Jack las' entry was void on account of the death of the nominator.

Time—1:47¼, 1:43.

ednesday is generally looked upon as the gala day e Fair and certainly on this occasion there were enough ctions offered to please the most fastidious taste. In the place the exhibition of stock was then complete, and al- gh lacking in numbers and varieties of stock was gener- considered as showing fair progress on that of previous . In the next place there was a pigeon match organized r the management of the San Jose Sportsmen's Club, an nization composed not only of good shots but of men are zealous in the preservation of our game and fishing ests. Between the races there was also a ladies' eques- tournament, in which some of the most skillful and ful horsewomen had entered their names. With such ctions and a close race between such noted trotters as tness and Nellie R for the sterner sex and the sporting , a great crowd of visitors was expected and the most uine expectations of the directors were more than amply ed. The charming enclosure presented a very bright rance with its number of equipages, many of which the heats were driven at a reckless rate from point to to gain a better view of the horses, but luckily not the est accident marred the pleasure of the day.

e principal race was a purse of $400 for the 2:30 class ich of the four original entries, only Sweetness and R put in an appearance. For days previous to the event had been a great deal of talk indulged in by our racing urs in regard to the respective merits of the two fleet , the general impression that Sweetness was lacking in g qualities having been somewhat modified by her per- nce at Stockton during the previous week. It was gen- y understood that it would be, as tersely said, "an up and race" but the result was certainly at variance with that position, if the wails and reproaches of the losers are to aken into consideration. Before a heat was trotted there e such fluctuations in the betting as foretold nasty weather hose who had not a chart of the rocks and eddies through ch they were steering, and even a few who by blind nce were in the tide of success were almost wrecked as went around in the third heat. For the first twenty ls the betting was quiet and but little changed at $25 Sweetness against $20 for Nellie, but suddenly there was dical variation and made so rapidly that the pools at once me doubled and tripled in amounts and such was the de- to invest in Nellie's chances that pools sold as fast as y could be booked at $50 for her against $25 for Sweet- s. The track was rather lumpy and unfavorable for very t time, and perhaps if there was any openly expressed inion as to the change in the betting it may have been at- uted to this fact, as Nellie was still considered the best yer of the two.

The horses were sent off at the second attempt and indeed through the race there was that lack of zeal to obtain a od position at the start which has generally been more lly displayed when a great deal of coin depended on the re- lt. The two mares trotted evenly around the first turn ien Nellie was off her feet to such a bad break that when e recovered her gait Sweetness was some ten lengths ahead d although Nellie rapidly closed the gap to within about o lengths, she was up again and Sweetness won by five ngths in 2:24.

Strange to say, after this exhibition of speed, Nellie s a greater favorite in the pools than ever, for if Sweet- ss was taken as first choice at $40 as much as $70 was in- antly bid for Nellie, and the betting was fast and furi- s, ending at $40 to $25 in Nellie's favor. From this time tward until the race was ended the interest was mainly ntered in the happenings between the heats, and e sporting elements which were gathered around e pool box in their investments eagerly scanned every ovement that would throw a light upon the ultimate re- lt, while the timid betters restricted their operations the French pools.

Again there was a very even start and they trotted like a am to the half-mile where Sweetness in the inside ap- eared to have a slight advantage, but Nellie had resumed r position for the home struggle when at the entrance to e stretch she was again in the air and Sweetness won by o lengths with something to spare in 2:24. Now there s some degree of hedging on both sides apparently among ool holders but generally the staunch and true stood to eir favorites with undaunted mien, the backers of Sweet- ss being confident that although Nellie might win the xt heat she could not be driven all to pieces as had been en on a previous occasion at Oakland. The betting on an erage was $40 to $20 in favor of Sweetness, and the follow- g trot was the prettiest contested of the race, for the mares re lapped all the way around and it was only within the st two furlongs that it was seen that Nellie had the foot of r antagonist, she winning in 2:23¾ by an open length, although eetness was pushed to the very top of her speed. There s apparently but little to choose in regard to their relative ances but betting was now languishing, perhaps on the ct that a great many had their money in the pool box and more to risk, while the general public held aloof and let he sports," as they termed them, fight it out on what line ey chose. Among the disinterested spectators the pre- iling impression was that Nellie would win easily the two xt heats, but the betting was only about $40 to $25 in r favor. Such was the ultimate result, as Sweetness peared to have lost all her speed, her dash and courage, and though in the fourth heat she was within a length of Nellie at e half-mile post, the latter drew away and won as she ted by half a dozen lengths in 2:29. The battle was now l over and Nellie, with $100 to $15 on her chances, rushed ay with the lead and although as in the previous heats eetness was severely urged with the whip, she gradually l back beaten, and Nellie R won the heat in a jog in 2:34. revious to the declaration of the result a noted professional iver protested to the judges that the race was not quite the square, but those gentlemen appeared to ignore Mr. rrell's experience in such matters and gave without hesi- tion the race to Nellie R.

SUMMARY.

San Jose, Sept. 27.—Trotting, purse $400, for the 2:30 class.

Perry names J. & W. S. Fritch's ch m Nellie R.......... 2 2 1 1 1
hn A. Goldsmith names b m Sweetness.......... 1 1 2 2 2

Pescora Hayward and Tump Winston were entered but did not rt.

Time—2:24, 2:24, 2:22¾, 2:29, 2:34

### The Ladies' Tournament.

The equestrian display at the San Jose fair was one of the chief attractions on Wednesday but the trotting race was so prolonged that many of the spectators went home before the ladies were called up to contest for the prizes offered by the Association. There were fine young equestriennes who took part in the proceedings, Miss N. M. Penniman, Miss Amanda Rogers, Miss Lottie Bose, Miss Lena Bose and Miss Kate Galbreath. There was a good display of grace and skill made on the occasion and it was difficult for the judges to distribute the prizes in a manner that should please the public and especially the participants in the tournament. Owing to the lateness of the hour the evolutions were of the simplest character and the decisions were finally made as follows: For graceful riding, Miss Amanda Rogers; Miss N. M. Penniman second and Miss Kate Galbreath third prize. For skillful riding; Miss Penniman, first prize, Miss Rogers second and Miss Galbreath third prize. The last feature was a dash of three-quarters of a mile in which Miss Penniman led from the start and took the first premium, with Miss Rogers second and Miss Lottie Bose third, with the two others in close pursuit. In these displays there is a great deal in the possession of a good horse, and it would be an excellent idea to arrange so that each lady should give an exhibition of grace and skill on the same horse that had been regularly broken in at a riding school, and that neither of the contestants had ever ridden before. As it is now the horses in most cases are not worthy of the occasion.

### Thursday.

The events of Thursday were interesting in their way, as will be gleaned from the following telegraphic summary. Full description from our representative will appear next week: The first race was running, for three-year-olds, a mile dash, between Judson's Patrol and Van Buren's Forest King. The former was the favorite by 25 to 16. The race was a very pretty one and was won by Forest King by a length. Time, 2:02. The next was a special trotting race for a purse of $300, between Brandon's Ashley and Pete Williams' Frank Moscow. The latter was the favorite, selling at $30 to $21 for Ashley. The first two heats were won by Ashley, time, 2:35½ and 2:33¾. The driver of Moscow was then changed and pools sold at close to $40 on Moscow to $17 for Ashley. The third and fourth heats were won by Moscow. Time, 2:33½ and 2:30½. The fifth heat caused great excitement, Ashley keeping ahead till the homestretch, when Moscow came alongside and when within forty feet of the string Moscow broke and, gaining a length ahead, came in first. Time, 2:34½. The judges awarded first money to Moscow over the protest of Ashley's driver and amid the excitement of the crowd. The general opinion seemed to be that Moscow lost the heat by breaking. After this came the pacing race between Corette and Johnny Weigle. No pools were sold, the belief being general that Corette would have a walk over, and so it proved. The first three heats were won by Corette. Time, 2:24, 2:26½, 2:34¼. The hurdle race postponed from yesterday had for contestants Miss Ida Johnson, J. W. Gannoz and J. Smith. It was won by Gannoz.

## Closed Stakes.

The following are the nominations in the stakes already closed to be run at the fall meeting of the Blood Horse Association:

Vestal Stake, for three-year-old fillies, one and one-quarter miles; $25 p.p.; $300 added, second to receive $100, third to save stake. Closed August 2d.

No. 1. Theo. Winters names ch f by Norfolk, dam Mattie A.
No. 2. " " names b f by Norfolk, dam Marion.
No. 3. " " names b f by Norfolk, dam Golden Gate.
No. 4. E. J. Baldwin names ch f Anita by Rutherford, dam Josie C.
No. 5. H. R. Covey names b f by Springfield, dam Boydana.
No. 6. " " b f by Longfellow, dam Miss Campbell.
No. 7. " " b f by Lever, dam Frolic.
No. 8. " " ch f by Longfellow, dam Robin Girl.
No. 9. James B. Chase, names f Lady Clare by Joe Daniels; dam by Owen Dale.
No. 10. James B. Chase names ch f Annie Lawrie by Hubbard, dam Mayflower.
No. 11. C. M. Chase names br f (sister to Raven) by Monday, dam Camilla Urso.
No. 12. Henry Schwartz names b f (sister to Lottery) by Monday; dam Virginia by Revenue.

Fame Stake, for three-year-olds; dash of two miles; $100 each, $25 forfeit; $500 added; second to have $150, third to save stake. Closed August 2d.

No. 1. Theo. Winters names b c "305" by Norfolk, dam Addie C.
No. 2. " " b c by Norfolk, dam Ballinette.
No. 3, " " ch f by Norfolk, dam Mattie A.
No. 4. " " b f by Norfolk, dam Marion.
No. 5. " " b f by Norfolk, dam Golden Gate.
No. 6. E. J. Baldwin names b c Albert C by Rutherford, dam Maggie Emerson.
No. 7. E. J, Baldwin names ch f Anita by Rutherford, dam Josie C.
No. 8. H. R. Covey names ch c by Lever, dam Cuba.
No. 9. H. R. Covey names ch c by Foster, dam Pienetia.
No. 10. H. R. Covey names ch f by Longfellow, dam Robin Girl.
No. 12. James Mee names b c Judge McKinstry by Thad Stevens or Grinstead, dam Katie Pease.
No. 12. James B. Chase names b. c. Rhoderick Dhu by Joe Daniels, dam Wild Rose.
No. 13. James B. Chase names ch f Annie Laurie by Hubbard, dam Mayflower.
No. 14. Peter Coutts names br c Forest King by Monday. dam Abbie W.
No 15. C. M. Chase names br f (sister to Raven) by Monday, dam Cammilla Urso.
No. 16. Frank DePeyster names b c by Monday, dam Lizzie Martin.
No. 17. Henry Schwartz names b c (sister to Lottery) by Monday, dam Virginia, by Revenue.
No. 18. W. H. Combs names br c by Bayswater, Dam Ruth Ryan, by Lodi.

Ladies' stake for two-year-old fillies; $50 entrance. $25 forfeit, $200 added; three-quarters of a mile; second to save entrance.

No. 1. Jos. Cairn Simpson names Lady Viva.
No. 2. Put Robson names Shannon and Jessie R filly.
No. 3. Peter Coutts names Flou-Flou.
No. 4. Thos. Atchison names California and Rosetland filly.
No. 5. Theo. Winters names Norfolk and Ballinette filly.
No. 6. Theo. Winters names Norfolk and Ballerina filly.
No. 7. Theo. Winters names Norfolk and Mattie A. filly.
No. 8. J. B. Chase names b f Marion by Hubbard, dam Electra.
No. 9. J. B. Chase names ch f Laura by Shannon, dam Folly.
No. 10. W. A. J. Gift names Miss Gift.
No. 11. Caleb Dorsey names b f by imported Partisan, dam Pet.
No. 12. Caleb Dorsey names ch f by imported Partisan, dam Lexingtona.
No. 13. Palo Alto Stable names Leveller and Frou-Frou filly.
No. 14. Palo Alto Stable names Hubbard and Tehama filly.
No. 15. Palo Alto Stable names Wildidle and Rose filly.
No. 16. Palo Alto Stable names br f by Shannon, dam Camilla Urso.
No. 17. J. B. Haggin names Nubia.
No. 18. J. D. Haggin names Irene.
No. 19. J. B. Haggin names Sophia.
No. 20. J. B. Haggin names Belle.

Finigan Stake, for two-year-olds; dash of a mile, $50 each; $25 forfeit; $250 added; second to save stake.

No. 1. Jos. Cairn Simpson names Lady Viva.
No. 2. Put. Robson names Shannon and Jessie R filly.
No. 3. Peter Coutts names Auriol.
No. 4. Peter Coutts names Panama.
No. 5. Peter Coutts names Flou-Flou.
No. 6. Thos. Atchison names California and Rosetland filly.
No. 7. Theo. Winters names Norfolk and Addie C colt.
No. 8. Theo. Winters names Norfolk and Maggie Dale colt.
No. 9. Theo. Winters names California and Puss colt.
No. 10. Theo. Winters names Norfolk and Ballinette filly.
No. 11. Theo. Winters names Norfolk and Ballerina filly.
No. 12. Theo. Winters names Norfolk and Mattie A filly.
No. 13. J. B. Chase names Marian.
No. 14. J. B. Chase names Laura.
No. 15. W. A. Gift names Miss Gift.
No. 16. E. J. Baldwin names Grisner.
No. 17. E. J. Baldwin names Lucky B.
No. 18. E. J. Baldwin names Gano.
No. 19. Palo Alto stable names Leveller and Frou Frou filly.
No. 20. Palo Alto Stable names Hubbard and Tehama filly.
No. 21. Palo Alto Stable names Shannon and Camilla Urso filly.
No. 22. Palo Alto Stable names Shannon and Emma Robson gelding.
No. 23. W. H. Coombs names Shannon dam Eva Ashton.
No. 24. Wm. Boots names Bob Wooding and Lizzie Marshal colt.
No. 25. J. B. Haggin names Nubia.
No. 26. J. B. Haggin names Belle.
No. 27. J. B. Haggin names Irene.
No. 28. J. B. Haggin names Sophia.
No. 29. J. B. Haggin names Del Paso.

## A Hat-Case Full of Money.

Mr. James Rice, in his "History of the British Turf," tells us that the victory of Ellington for the Derby of 1856 "was marked by a singular incident in connection with his trainer." The horse had been heavily backed for the Epsom race, but suffered a humiliating defeat when he ran for the Dee Stakes at Chester, so that all possibility of "hedging" was out of the question. "The result was," says Mr. Rice, "that against his will Mr. Thomas Dawson, the trainer of Ellington, won £25,000 by his horse's victory. On the Monday after the race Mr. Dawson went to Tattersall's to recive his money. The whole of it was paid to him in bank notes. After the settling he dined, and took the train for the North, having first packed his bank notes in an old leather hat-case without any lock, and tied simply with a piece of string. Mr. Dawson fell to sleep in the train, and when the guard, who knew him well, awoke him at Northampton, and told him that he must change carriages, Mr. Dawson got out of the train, leaving the old hat-case behind him. In those days telegraphy was not so simple and easy a matter as it is now, and Mr. Dawson did not recover his hat-case for a whole week, during which time it had traveled to Edinburgh, Aberdeen and various other places. Ultimately it came back to the rightful owner and with all the notes safe inside."

We need hardly add that, despite his characteristic and unmercenary indifference to money, the celebrated "Tom Dawson," than whom no more popular or large-hearted trainer ever plied his difficult and responsible craft, took care to display no solicitude about the missing hat-case, and abstained altogether from revealing the nature of its contents. He merely told the stationmaster at Leybourne that it was an article he had owned for a great number of years, and that as, in addition, there were some papers in it which were of no use to any one but himself, he should like to recover possession of it.

The Breeder and Sportsman is the title of an elegant sixteen-page weekly journal, published in San Francisco, the initial number of which has just made its appearance. The engraved heading of the Breeder and Sportsman is the prettiest piece of work in that line that we have ever seen. The artist has won a genuine triumph, for he has not only incorporated in his beautiful design water and foliage, fruit and blossoms, fine horses, cattle and dogs, but all the emblems and symbols of sporting life. Joseph Cairn Simpson, the veteran turfman and accomplished gentleman, is the proprietor of this new venture in the field of journalism. He is supported by an able corps of writers, all of them well trained in the several departments over which they have been called to preside. The Breeder and Sportsman deserves and will achieve success. Its field is large and remunerative. Each of the San Francisco and Sacramento dailies dishes up a weekly pot pourri of sporting news. There are the *California Spirit of the Times*, the *Pacific Life* and the *Olympian*—all specially devoted to the subject and making fortunes rapidly for their owners. The thirst of the California public for sporting intelligence, however, remains unappeased, and Mr. Simpson's splendid journal comes in to relieve the stress. An attractive feature of the new paper is the appearance each week of a drawing of some one or other of the "Notable Horses of California"—Mr. Winters' Duchess of Norfolk leading off in the first number. The Breeders of the Pacific Coast, from the Columbia to the Colorado, and from the Sierras to the sea, should now stand in with Joe Simpson and make this journal a financial success. He has done more than any other man in America to elevate the turf and advance the breeding interests of the Pacific Coast.—*Territorial Enterprise.*

Gov. Stanford's car-load of colts, in charge of Charles Marvin, arrived safely at Albany, New York, on Wednesday. They will remain there a few days before being taken to Fleetwood Park. They are all reported to be in excellent condition.

## The Stockton Fair.

Thursday was the great day of the week for gate money. The grand stand was packed to its utmost capacity and the carriages stretched away east and west from the judges' stand, five tiers deep. At 12:30 the unfinished race of the previous day was called up and soon disposed of, Patchen winning in a jog in 2:40½, 2:40¾.

SUMMARY.

September 20 and 21.—District trotting, purse, $500, four moneys.

John Williams (L. U. Shippee) names b c ———, by Inauguration........ 2 2 1 1 1
W. H. Parker names g s Silver Thread, by The Moor...... 1 1 2 2 2
John Patterson's b m Mollie P. by McClellan; J. A McCloud's br g ———, and Harris & Wolf's b g Mac, by McClellan were drawn.

Time—2:45½, 2:43, 2:46, 2:40½, 2:40¾.

The first event on the day's programme was a free-for-all running race, heats of a mile. May D, Jim Douglas and Inauguration started, May a strong favorite in the betting-pools going May D $40, field $21.

First heat. The start was not first class for a mile heat, there being a difference of a clear length between the horses, Jim Douglas, who had the inside, getting away first and the favorite, who was outside, last. They ran in this position to the quarter in 26½. In the straight work May D moved up to Douglas' saddle and the gap between Inauguration and the leaders began to widen. At the half, in 51, he was four lengths back. Around the turn they ran steadily, May D gradually gaining, and at the head of the stretch they were on even terms. In the run home May held the edge over Douglas and after a determined effort he was taken back at the distance and the mare came to the wire winner by three lengths, Douglas second, Inauguration third. Time 1:44. After this mile there was no doubt as to the final result, and pools went May D $30, field $5.

Second heat. The start was much the same as before except that May D having the pole got the advantage and Inauguration the disadvantage of being sent off in a line. May D was taken in hand at the turn and Douglas was first at the quarter in 26, but the mare resumed the lead in the back stretch where she and Douglas had a run for it, reaching the one-half in 50. In the lower turn Douglas surrendered and May galloped home an easy winner, Douglas second, Inauguration third. Time 1:44¾.

Paris Mutuals paid first heat $4 30, second heat $3 05.

SUMMARY.

Thursday, September 21.—Pacific Coast running, mile and repeat, purse $500, and if 1:43 is beaten the horse making the lowest record will receive $200 additional. Four monies.

W. L. Appleby (H. C. Judson) names ch m May D by Wildidle—Nettie Brown, 4 years, 100 lbs (Appleby)........ 1 1
George Densdale names b s Jim Douglas by Wildidle—Norfolk mare, 4 years, 108 lbs, (Howson)........ 2 2
Wm. Boots names ch c Inauguration, by Wildidle—Miami, 3 years, 100 lbs, (Kennedy)........ 3 3
George Hearst's b c Duke of Monday—Nemefret, drawn.

Time—1:44, 1:44¾.

As a substitute for a district trot which did not fill a special for Ashley, Tump Winston and Frank Moscow was offered and they were called up at the conclusion of the mile and repeat just described. On this race there was considerable business done in the pools before the start with Ashley for a favorite the average being Ashley $25, Winston $13, Moscow $5. Moscow drew the pole, Ashley second, Winston outside, and they got away level for the first heat. At the start Ashley broke badly and continued that skipping for which he has been so frequently anathematized throughout the mile. Moscow also left his feet at the quarter and Winston was the only one who showed any real disposition to trot. He showed in front at the head of the stretch and was an easy winner by five lengths, Ashley second, Moscow third. Time, 2:26¾.

Second Heat. Winston came to the front in the betting at long figures, for Ashley money must be hedged. The pools went Winston $160, Ashley $60, Moscow $16. When the word was given Ashley was running and they got to the quarter well in a bunch, Winston showing a head in advance. From there he was never headed, Ashley and Moscow rushing after him up the stretch with skips and bounds but failing to reach his throatlatch. Winston first, Ashley second, Moscow third. Time 2:27.

Third heat. Winston now brought three for one in the pools and they got a fair start for the third mile. On the first turn Winston made his first break and both Ashley and Moscow left him behind. Down the stretch and around the turn Ashley was leading and as they swung into the stretch Winston overhauled him but broke badly in the effort. They came to the were with Ashley first, and Winston second, but the judges lifted Moscow over their heads as a reward for having done some square work and placed him first, Winston second and Ashley third. Time 2:30½.

Fourth heat. On the first turn Winston and Ashley both broke and Moscow went to the quarter with a long lead, Ashley second. At the half they had closed the gap but Moscow held the front to the three-quarter pole, when he broke up and Winston went past him, coming home winne of the heat and race, Moscow second, Ashley third. Time 2:30½. There was a general feeling of relief when the affair was over.

SUMMARY.

Same day—Special trot for Tump Winston, Ashley and Frank Moscow. Purse $400.

E. Mara names ch g Tump Winston by Primus—Lady Don..1 1 2 1
A. B. Cooper names ch h Frank Moscow, by Frank Moscow....3 3 1 2
T. Kennedy names ch g Ashley, by Plumas........2 2 3 3

Time—2:26¾—2:27—2:30½—2:30½.

The third number was a trot for district two-year-olds. Eleven colts had been named, but the pinkeye kept out all but four and these started rather under protest as none of them were well and it was with great reluctance that the several owners consented to start. The colts entered were Baby Mine, Magdalene, Alpheus and Almoone, position being in this order. The race had but little interest as it was purely a matter of condition and no real test of the qualities of the colts. Magdalene had two to one the best of it and won in a jog in two heats:

SUMMARY.

Same Day—District trotting, for two-year-olds. Purse $800.

D. Vishoer names b f Magdalene, by Peerless........ 1 1
J. W. Warren names b s Alpheus, by Mambrino Wilkes........ 2 3
H. Robinson names ch c Almoone, by Algona........ 4 2
G. W. Trahern names blk f Baby Mine by Nephew........ 3 4

Time 2:45, 2:48.

E. Gidding's b c Alpha, by Algona; J. M. Learned's b c Harmony, by Reliance; J. A. McCloud's br c Judge Patterson, by Nephew; L. M. Morse's b c John O'Brien, by Mambrino Wilkes; Fred Arnold's br c Ha Ha, by Nephew; L. U. Shippee' b f by Echo and W. M. Murray's b f Merced Girl, by Nephew, drawn.

### The Lady Riders.

During the afternoon the ladies' equestrian tournament open to all the ladies in the State was called up and decided, and six ladies competed, all capital riders, but as is always the case some were but poorly mounted and it was more a question of horses than riders. Ladies should not feel disappointed if they fail of prizes when they appear mounted upon staid old family cobs who look and act as if they subsisted upon a diet of catechisms and who have no more gait or style than a sawhorse. Judges cannot imagine what accomplishments a lady may have as a horsewoman. They must see them displayed, and if it be true that some ladies of ability in this direction cannot command fit steeds for such an exhibition they will save themselves mortification by submitting to outrageous fortune and staying out of the ring. The judges after mature deliberation awarded the first prize, $40, to Miss Amanda Rogers of San Jose; second, $25, to Miss Belle Ellis of Sacramento; third, $15, to Mrs. B. C. Trefry of Tulare. This exhausted the association premiums, but the judges were so charmed with the riding of Miss Irene C. Bailey of Stockton, a petite little lady of thirteen summers, that they awarded her a fourth prize of $15, which they made up from their private purses.

### Fourth Day.

Friday was the great day for the sporting men for the principal events of the week were set for that afternoon, the two mile and repeat running race and the trot for the 2:22 class in which Romero and Brigadier were to try conclusions under circumstances somewhat more favorable for a test than had been previously offered this season. The running race was first and Judge Shafter came up on the morning train to see Nighthawk tried at a distance and in a race that tries the best. Nighthawk, Jack Douglas, Patrol and Mollie H were announced to start and a lively business was done in the pools for so long a figure as Nighthawk commanded, viz: $50 to $12 for the others in the field. The day was fine and the track a trifle safer for galloping than it had been in the preceding days of the meeting. The favorite stripped in fine condition and all the others were held to be quite satisfactory by their owners except Jack Douglas, who had a bad leg—too bad to be punished by such a run as two mile heats. Little time was spent in preliminaries and the horses were sent off with a fair start for the first heat. Nighthawk forced the pace at the start and had a strong lead when she was taken in hand in the first turn. To the quarter in 25 and the half in 51½, they were running in a line, Nighthawk first, Patrol second, Douglas third, and Mollie H last. In the stretch Patrol lapped the leader, both running steadily, and they passed the stand at the end of the first mile in this position. Time, 1:50½. There was no change to near the half when Douglas made a game run for a short distance, but failing to reach the front he fell back to third. In the stretch whips were drawn on all of them but Nighthawk came away so rapidly that she was soon taken back again and won the heat at a gallop with Patrol second, Jack Douglas third, Mollie H distanced, Time, 3:40½.

Second heat. Nighthawk made the pace as before, Patrol going second under a gentle pull, Douglas third. They went the first mile without change, time, quarter 27, half 54, the favorite passing the stand under a strong pull in 1:50½. At the same point as in the first heat Douglas made another run and succeeded in establishing himself in second place. Nighthawk came home at her own pace, Douglas arriving second by a length, Patrol another length behind. Time, 3:38½.

SUMMARY.

Friday, September 22 Pacific Coast running, free for all, two miles and repeat, purse $800 and $200 added if more than ten entries. Four moneys.

P. J. Shafter names b m Nighthawk, by imp. Haddington—by Norfolk, 5 years, 111 lbs, (Ross)........ 1 1
Jack Douglas names ch s Jack Douglas, by Wildidle—Lady Clare 5 yrs. 114 lbs (Howson)........ 3 2
H. C. Judson names b c Patrol, by Wildidle—Nettie Brown, 3 yrs, 95 lbs. (Whitlock)........ 2 3
W. Boots names b m Mollie H, by Wildidle—Mamie Hall, 5 yrs, 111 lbs, (Kennedy)........ dist.
J. T. Gilmer's b s Red Boy by War Dance, drawn.

Time—3:40½, 3:38½.

Next came a mile and repeat for district three-year-olds. Starters, Birdcatcher, Kate Carson, Minnie Belle and Reel Terry. Birdcatcher was a high favorite with the speculators and the result showed their confidence well bestowed. He had the race at his mercy in any and all stages of it, Minnie Belle having gameness enough but not the speed to bring the fight to a successful issue. The heats were not of special interest on account of the enveloping shadow of the favorite, who won as he willed in two heats, Minnie Belle second, Kate Carson third, Reel Terry distanced in the first heat.

SUMMARY.

Same Day.—District running, for three-year-olds, purse $800.

Col. C. Dorsey names b c Birdcatcher, by Specter—Pet, 95 lbs (Howson)........ 1 1
J. A. Shepherd names g m Minnie Belle, by Joe Daniels—by Norfolk, 92 lbs (Gaglenda)........ 2 2
G. W. Trahern names ch f Kate Carson, by Joe Daniels—Belle Mahone 92 lbs, (Ross)........ 3 3
W. L. Ashe names br g Reel Terry, by California—Laura Barnes, 92 lbs (Kennedy)........ dis

Time—1:46, 1:49½.

Next came the event of the day, the trot for the 2:22 class. It was known that Romero had improved greatly since the race at Sacramento. Although he still showed the presence of the prevailing epidemic in a slight discharge from the nostrils and a tucked-up appearance in his flanks, he had begun to resume his coltish airs when taken out for his exercise and it looked as though he would stand a good chance in a race not too long drawn out by splitting heats. This feeling was enough to make him a slight favorite in the pools. Brigadier sold close up, for the honest bay stallion had shown a mile in 2:19½ in his work on Tuesday and was a factor not to be disregarded in the calculations. The day and track suited Romero to perfection. A large amount of money was laid on him during the morning hours and when the horses were called every one was keyed up to the highest point, some of curiosity, some of hope and some of fear. Starr King drew the inside position, Brigadier second and Romero third. They got the word on a good start, all trotting squarely and braced for the work. Around the turn Brigadier showed his head in front and at the quarter in 35½ he was almost a length in the lead, King close in the wake next the pole. To the half in 1:09½ proved fast for King and he began to fall away and around the farther turn Romero was at Brigadier's saddle, and as they turned the three-quarter pole they were squarely yoked, King five lengths in the rear. McDonald drew his whip on Brigadier but the grey drew away so easily that he saw it was useless and drove his horse home without urging. Romero being also let down and crossing the score at an easy trot two lengths in the lead, Brigadier second, King a fair third. Time 2:20.

The doubters now began to lose their doubts and there was a movement towards the pool box to hedge the Brigadier moneys. The average sales were Romero $60, field $35.

Second heat. King broke at the start and the other two went around the course like a double team. The time to the quarter was 36 and to the half 1:10, and so smooth and quiet was the gait that it was not until the interested speculators noted that back quarter in 34 that they realized how fast the pace was getting. Positions were unchanged until the straight mile home was entered, when Romero drew away a length, apparently as he pleased, Brigadier surrendering at the distance. Romero first, Brigadier second, Starr King third. Time, 2:19½. Starr King was in a good position comparatively at the finish and must have trotted the mile better than 2:22. The betting was now 4 to 1 on Romero.

Third heat. While scoring for the word Brigadier pulled a plate and half an hour's delay occurred before he was ready to start. The accident of the lost plate was the reason of discovering that Brigadier's feet had been pared too thin for so hard a track, and he was becoming tender, if not decidedly lame. Mr. McDo a d prizes his horse too highly to inflict any unnecessary punishment, but under the circumstances he decided not to ask permission to draw him from the race although he ran no chance of winning. At the start Starr King fouled Romero and broke him up. There was a murmur ran through the crowd when the grey settled five lengths behind but from that time to the finish he gained steadily, working past the others in the stretch with ease and coming to the score winner of the heat and race, Brigadier second, Starr King third. Time, 2:22.

SUMMARY.

Same day—Pacific Coast trotting. For horses owned on the Pacific Coast July 1, 1882, 2:22 class; Purse $1,500, and $500 added if more than ten subscribers. The nominator not required to name his horse, but simply send his cash ($150) with his own name August 1, 1882. He has then earned the right to start any horse eligible that he may fully control, provided the horse he starts be named to the Secretary, September 1, 1882. Four moneys: closed with five subscribers.

J. A. Goldsmith names g s Romero, by A. W. Richmond........1 1 1
J. B. McDonald names b s Brigadier, by Happy Medium........2 2 2
C. W. Welby names b g Starr King, by Geo. M. Patchen........3 3 3
G. Valensin's, b s Gibraltar, by Echo; and L. H. Titus b m Belle Echo, by Echo, drawn.

Time—2:20—2:19½—2:22.

At ten o'clock on Monday, Ouida and Dickey finished the race, Oakland Boy being ruled out for not securing a heat in five. The brown mare was the better horse and won the sixth heat easily. Time 2:29½.

SUMMARY.

September 23 and 25—Pacific Coast Pacing, 2:25 class, purse $400. Four moneys:

G. Valensin names br m Ouida, by Blackhawk........ 3 1 1 2 0 1
T. J. Young names s g Col. Dickey........ 1 3 3 1 0 2
A. L. Hinds names ch s Oakland Boy, by Winthrop... 2 2 2 3 3 r o
E. S. Dennison names ch m Lady Hays, by Hiram Tracy........ dis
L. E. Yates names b m Corette, by Winthrop........ drawn.

Time—2:35, 2:29, 2:30½, 2:32, 2:31, 2:29½.

### Ladies of the District.

A turnament open only to ladies of the district was also included in the afternoon's exercises. Six ladies competed and the four prizes were distributed as follows: First $40, Mrs. Thompson; second $30, Mrs. B. C. Trefry; third $20, Mrs. Goff; fourth $10, Miss Bailey.

### Fifth Day.

Saturday, the fifth and last day was intended, by the managers to be a short one, as there was a general desire on the part of the visitors to get away for home on the evening boats and trains. The races fixed for the day were trotting for 2:28 class and pacing free for all. Our notes of the first event will be found on the first page as an appropriate part of a sketch of Albert W. Between the races Mr. Yates speeded Corette around the track for the delectation of the audience, and she paced the mile in 2:17, the fastest mile ever paced in the State and the fastest ever made by pacer or trotter over the Stockton course. Mr. Yates started with the intention of showing a figure under 20 and giving his mare her head allowed her to make the pace herself with the above result. In the interval a private match was also run between D. S. Terry's ch g Lara and T. H. Williams Jr's. b s Bryant W., three-quarter of a mile. They got away with an exact start, Bryant W showing a front at the half but in the run home, which was close and hard, Lara was clearly the best horse and went to the front when within reach of the wire. Time 1:19.

SUMMARY.

Saturday, September 23.—Private match for $200, three-fourths of a mile.

D. S. Terry names ch g Laura, by Joe Daniels—Woodburn, 2 years, (Whitlock)........ 1
T. H. Williams Jr. names br s Bryant W, by Monday—Bete, 2 years, (Ross)........ 2

Time—1:19.

The last act was free for all pacers. Corette was withdrawn and Ouida, Oakland Boy, Lady Hays ond Col. Dickey started. The race was more conspicuous for running than for pacing. The first heat was won by Dickey, Oakland Boy second, Ouida third, Lady Hays dancing herself out of the race on the backstretch. Time, 2:35. The second heat was recorded in Ouida's favor, Oakland Boy second, Dickey last. Time, 2:29. In the third heat the positions were the same. Time, 2:30½. The fourth mile was captured by Dickey, Ouida second, Oakland Boy third. Time, 2:32. Fifth heat dead heat between Ouida and Dickey, both running when they came to the wire, Oakland Boy third. Time 2:31. The finish of the race was then postponed till Monday on account of the darkness.

### The Stock Department.

In addition to the stock from the State at large, which had been shown at Oakland and Sacramento, we noted the following strictly district exhibits in the various classes:

#### Thoroughbreds.

Stallions, three years old and over, C. McLaughlin, Bantas, Pescadero, by Wildidle—Mamie Barnes.

H. S. Sargent, Stockton, Joe Daniels, by Australian—Dolly Carter.

Mares, one year old, J. N. Randall, Turlock, Alice B, by Joe Daniels—Sugar Plum.

#### Horses for all Purposes.

Stallions, three years old and over, Dr. C. Grattan, Stockton, Hambletonian King, by Gen. Dana—by American Boy.

T. E. B. Rice, Modesto, Honest George, by Lummix.

G. W. Trahern, Stockton, Nephew Jr., by Nephew—by Chieftain.

H. S. Sargent, Stockton, Village Boy, by Blackhawk.

J. A. McCloud, Stockton, Chieftain Jr., by Chieftain—by Planter.

Two-year-olds, W. G. Phelps, Stockton, Duroc, by Nephew—Sultana.

J. A. McCloud, Stockton, May Boy, by McCloud's Chieftain—by Henry Clay.

J. W. Whitney, Stockton, ———, by Priam—by Chieftain.

Sucking colts, Dr. C. Grattan, Stockton, Dandy, by Hambletonian King—by Blackhawk.

E. Stevens, Bantas, ———, by Stonewall Jackson.

Mares, three years old and over, Dr. C. Grattan, Stockton, Fannie, by Sherman's Blackhawk.

Noyes Bailey, Stockton, Kittie B, by Chieftain.

W. G. Phelps, Stockton, May, by Gen. Sherman—Sultana.

Two-year-olds, Wm. Thomas, Douglas Flat, Calaveras county, Mollie Miller, by John Miller—Clydesdale mare.

#### Roadsters.

Stallions, four years old and over, G. W. Trahern, Stockton, Nephew, by Mambrino—Sister to Pacing Abdallah.

W. S. Alexander, Stockton, Ben Allen, by Sportsman—by Belmont.

W. E. Morris, Stockton, Upright, by Whipple's Hambletonian—Gilroy Belle.

Smith Akers, Oakdale, Comet, by Old Comet—Morgan mare.

Three-year-olds, J. A. McCloud, Stockton, Judge Patterson, by Nephew—Daisy.

Yearlings, W. G. Phelps, Stockton, Estrella by Silver Threads—Lucinda, by McClellan.

Morris Bailey, Stockton, ch c, by Hawthorne—by Volscian.

G. Valenzin, Hicksville, blk colt by Buccaneer—by Volscian.

### Mares and Geldings.

Four-year-olds, Sargent Bros., Woodbridge, ch g San Joaquin, by Patchen—Blackhawk mare.

L. U. Shippee, Stockton, b m Daisy, by Chieftain.

Same owner, blk m, by McCracken's Blackhawk.

Same owner, ch m Phoebe Cary, by Chieftain—by Jim Crow.

W. B. Ledbetts, Stockton, b g Little Mac, by 'Gen. McClellan—Chieftain mare.

Three-year-olds, Morris Bailey, Stockton, b m, by McCloud's Chieftain—by Old Fellow.

Two-year-olds, W. G. Phelps, Stockton, b m Lucia, by Nephew—Lucinda.

W. E. Morris, Stockton, g f Cyclone, by Priam—Gilroy Belle.

Yearling fillies, Noyes Bailey, Stockton, b f Hattie B, by Nutwood—by Chieftain.

Roadsters, matched spans, L. M. Morse, Stockton, John O'Brien and mate, both by Mambrino Wilkes.

L. U. Shippee, Stockton, b g, by Geo. M. Patchen, and b g, by Chieftain.

Sucking colt, L. U. Shippee, Stockton, b c, by Abbottsford—by McCracken's Blackhawk.

### Draft Horses.

Stallions, three years old, E. Stevens, Bantas, Donald Dinnie, by Donald Dinnie Sr.—by Clydesdale.

C. McLaughlin, Bantas, Gen. Grant.

J. C. Gage, Stockton, Little Raven.

L. U. Shippee, Stockton, Prince Consort Jr.

Sucking colts, Uriah Martin, Stockton, b c, by Enterprise—Fannie.

Mares, three years and over, Uriah Martin, Stockton, Fannie, by Houston horse.

Carriage horses, span sixteen hands, owned by one person, O. Johnson, Modesto, b g, by Priam—Belmont mare; and a Hercules—same pedigree.

M. Freno, Adams, ch g, by Priam, and ch g by Chieftain.

S. P. Bailey, Stockton, George, by Cornice, and Prince, by Chieftain.

L. Gerisch, Stockton, pair chestnut geldings, by Yorktown.

Single buggy horses, O. Johnson, Modesto, Silvertail, by Priam—Belmont mare.

W. G. Phelps, Stockton, Flora, by David Hill—Sultana.

### Jacks.

Freeman and Shippee, Stockton, Castilian.

H. S. Sargent, Stockton, Golconda.

E. Stevens, Bantas, Henry Ward Beecher.

L. D. Shippee, Stockton, Bob Roy.

### Jennets.

Freeman and Shippee, Stockton, Duchess.

Same owners, Beauty.

### Mules.

Pairs—Hayes & Nicewonger, Stockton, King & Jack.

L. U. Shippee, Stockton, Pet & Susie.

Same owner, a pair without names.

### Cattle.

In this department the only district exhibitors were H. S. Sargent of Stockton, who showed a small herd of Jerseys, and E. Wood of Modesto, Jerseys in grades.

### Sheep.

Spanish Merinos by L. U. Shippee.

### Swine.

Berkshire, by L. U. Shippee.

Poland Chinas, by Dr. C. Grattan.

### The Prize Winners.

Thoroughbred horses, best stallion, three years old and over, to H. S. Sargent for Joe Daniels. Second to Wm. Boots for Mambrino Coombs.

Best mare, three years and over, to Wm. Boots for Mollie Hall.

Horses for all purposes, best stallion, three years and over, to G. W. Trahern for Nephew Jr. Two years old, to J. H. Whitney for ch s —— by Priam, second premium, recommended to W. G. Phelps for Duroc. Best sucking colt, to Dr. O. Grattan for Dandy.

Best mare, three years and over, to L. Hewlett, Oakland, for Brownie H. Two years old, to Wm. Thomas, Douglas Flat, for Mollie Miller.

Roadsters, best stallion, four years and over, to Walter Morris, Stockton, for Upright. Two years old, to L. Hewlett, Oakland, for Echo Jr. Yearling, to G. Valenzin, for blk s ——, by Buccaneer. Sucking colt, to L. U. Shippee, for b c ——, by Abbottsford.

Best mare or gelding, four years and over, to C. Younger, for br g Whisper. Three years old, to J. B. McDonald, Marysville, for Hazel Kirke. Two years old, to Walter Morris, Stockton, for Cyclone. Yearling, to Noyes Bailey, Stockton, for Hattie B. Sucking filly, to Noyes Bailey for b f ——, by Hawthorne.

Draft horses, best stallion, four years and over, to F. Skillman, Petaluma, for Tornado. Two years old, to F. Skillman for Monarch. Sucking colt, to Uriah Martin, Stockton, for Enterprise. Mare, three years and over, to Uriah Martin for Fannie. Yearling, to F. Skillman for Gertrude. Second premium for stallions three years and over recommended to L. U. Shippee, for Prince Consort Jr.

Carriage Horses, best span, 16 hands, to O. Johnson, Modesto, for Hercules and brother. Second, to L. Gerlach, Stockton, for pair chestnut geldings. Single buggy horse, to O. Johnson for Silvertail. Second recommended to W. G. Phelps for Flora. Jacks, best two years and over, to R. J. Greene, San Francisco, for Lippincott. Jennets, best to Freeman and Shippee for Duchess.

Mules, best pair, to L. U. Shippee for Pet and Susie.

### Cattle.

Durhams, best bull, three years and over, to C. Younger, for second Duke of Alameda. One year old, to same owner for Forest King. Bull calf, to same owner for Eighth Duke of Forest Home. Best cow, three years and over, to same owner for Jessie Maynard. Two years old to same owner for Oxford Rose Third. One year old, to same owner for Fifth Lenan of Forest Home. Heifer calf, to same owner for Tenth Rose of Forest Home.

Jerseys, best bull, three years old and over, to E. Woods, Modesto, for Pinafore. Two years old, to H. S. Sargent, Stockton, for Ezra Mameluke. Best cow, three years old and over, to H. S. Sargent for Daisy. Two years old, to same

---

owner, for Clark Beauty. One year old, to same owner for Queen.

Ayrshires, best bull, three years old and over, to Archie. Two years old to Lindo. One year old to Macbeth. Best cow, three years and over, to Stellita. One year old, to Stellita. Special premium recommended to bull calf Malcomb and heifer calf Sybil. All the cattle in this class were owned by Geo. Bement, Redwood City.

Graded cattle, best cow, three years old and over, to E. Woods, Modesto, for Mattie.

Herds, best herd over two and one-half years and best under two and one-half years, both to C. Younger. Special premium recommended to George Bement's herd of Ayrshires.

### Sheep.

Spanish Merinos, five premiums, to L. U. Shippee.

Cotswolds, three premiums to C. Younger.

Southdowns, premium to Geo. Bement.

### Swine.

Berkshire, best boar and best sow, to L. U. Shippee.

Poland China, best boar and sow, to Dr. C. Grattan.

### Poultry.

Premiums to Thos. Warte of Brighton Poultry yard, Sacramento county, for seven varieties, and premiums recommended for six other varieties. Mr. Warte exhibited Langshana, Plymouth Rocks, Partridge Cochins, Houdans, Brown Leghorns, Spangled Hamburgs, Golden Sea-bright Bantams and Pekin Ducks, all imported and of the purest strains, as well as Light Brahmas, White Brahmas, White Leghorns and Black Spanish, trios, and a pair of Tulous geese of his own breeding from imported stock. His display of pure bred poultry was probably the largest and most varied ever seen at a California fair.

---

## Contra Costa County Fair Premiums.

Below is the list of premiums for the live stock awarded at the Contra Costa County Fair, held at Pacheco. The stock was led past the judges' and the grand stands on several occasions and on the whole made a good display. Those who received prizes for their live stock were:

### Horses.

Thoroughbred horses, W. A. Gift, Martinez, best mare two years old, Miss Gift; no competition; premium recommended.

W. A. Gift, Martinez, best yearling, Billy Foot; no competition; premium recommended.

W. A. Gift, Martinez, best stallion, three years old; no competition; premium recommended.

Roadsters, C. T. McClellan, Pacheco, best sucking colt, Carrie.

J. B. Tennett, Pinole, two years old, Trinket; premium recommended; no competition.

S. Soto, Concord, second single carriage horse, three years old, Barney.

John Galindo, Concord, second best stallion, three years old, Romeo.

N. Graber, Walnut Creek, best mare five years old, Gipsey Huntington.

J. McDonald, Pacheco, best stallion, four years old, Adventure.

Chas. McClellan, Pacheco, second best mare, five years old, Frankie Eaton.

J. E. Durham, Pacheco, best chestnut colt, one year old, Oscar.

W. H. Wells, Walnut Creek, best single carriage horse, Billy.

J. E. Durham, Pacheco, best stallion, five years, Conductor; no competition; premium recommended.

A. A. Miller, Pleasanton, best two-year-old stallion, Meteor.

J. E. Durham, Pacheco, second best two-year-old stallion, Rocky.

A. Boss, Pacheco, best double carriage team, Mollie and Tray.

Mr. Tewksbury, second best carriage team.

H. M. Hallenbeck, Martinez, second best sucking colt, Nettie.

Draft horses, A. Boss, Pacheco, best draught mare, two years old, Emma.

S. Soto, Concord, best stallion, four years old, Paris Boy.

W. W. Beauchamp, Pacheco, mare three years old, Sheriff.

A. C. Samuels, Concord, best stallion, two years old, Patsion.

A. Boss, Pacheco, best sucking colt, Dick, no competition; premium recommended.

H. Stout, Alamo, second best mare, three years old, Hermoine.

W. W. Beauchamp, Pacheco, second best mare, three years old, Minnie.

Sweepstakes, W. Caven, Concord, best pair work horses, Dan and Jack; premium recommended.

A. A. Miller, Pleasanton, best stallion five years old, Carl Carr; no competition; premium recommended.

H. M. Hallenbeck, Martinez, best stallion, three years old, Glory.

T. G. Witten, Pacheco, best sucking colt, Sailor Boy.

T. W. Huckstrap, Pacheco, second best three-year-old stallion, Hector.

J. Nottingham, best mare, four years, Green.

T. G. Witten, Pacheco, second best four years mare, Belle.

J. B. Tennett, Pinole, second best yearling, Pinole Jr.

John Brady, Pacheco, second best sucking colt, yearling, Maud S Jr.

### Cattle.

Jersey cows, C. Dickenson, Concord, best Jersey bull, four years old, Hector.

B. Webb, Pacheco, second best cow, two years old, and calf, Beauty.

W. W. Beauchamp, Pacheco, best cow and calf, Madam Cotton.

W. W. Beauchamp, Pacheco, best cow and calf, bull, Dan Cook.

Graded cattle, cross breeds, T. C. Whitten, Pacheco, second best cow, four-year-old, Beauty.

C. Dickinson, Concord, best yearling heifer, Rose.

J. O'Boone, Danville, best cow, five years old, Jennie.

J. S. Williams, Concord, best cow, five years old, Lisa.

Thos. Downing, Concord, best cow, second best yearling heifer, Belle.

J. S. Williams, Concord, best two-year-old heifer, Rose. Considering the large number of competitors and the large number of awards that were made it will be seen that the directors of the association did all in their power to make the fair a success, and if it did not come up to their expectations it was surely no fault of theirs.

---

## The Great St. Leger.

Next to the Derby the Doncaster St. Leger holds rank among the turfmen of the world. The north country people think that it is entitled to the preference, and the crown which is awarded the Epsom victor is considered only a temporary sovereignty unless he places the double event to his credit.

Never before have the Derby and St. Leger been won in the same year by fillies, and the high excellence which the two that run first, second and third in the St. Leger have shown, warrants the rehearsal of the description of the battle. The account of the race was cabled to the New York *Herald*:

The race for the St. Leger Stakes for three-year-olds at the Doncaster September meeting to-day was won by Lord Falmouth's brown filly Dutch Oven. Mr. T. Cannon's brown filly Geheimniss, the favorite, came in second, and the Duke of Westminister's chestnut filly Shotover third. Dutch Oven won by a length and a half. There was a distance of two lengths between the second and third horses. Mr. Lovitland's Sachem was beaten three furlongs from home. The time of Dutch Oven was 3:16. Dutch Oven was first away, followed by Fenelon, Actress, Sachem and Marden for a quarter of a mile, when Actress took the lead. Baliol, Marden, Fenelon and Geheimniss were close up, with Shotover heading, the next lot. They maintained this order fairly in to the straight, when Geheimniss went to the front. Dutch Oven came through the horses at the distance. Sachem finished fourth.

The following is a complete list of the starters: Dutch Oven, Geheimniss, Shotover, Sweetbread, Quicklime, Fenelon, Sachem, Marden, Romeo, Laureate, Battlefield, the Hygeia colt, Baliol and Actress.

The latest betting was 11 to 8 on Geheimniss, 7 to 1 against Shotover, 15 to 1 against Sweetbread, 20 to 1 against Fenelon, 40 to 1 against Dutch Oven, 40 to 1 against Quicklime, 100 to 1 against Romeo, 100 to 1 against the Hygeia colt and 100 to 1 against Baliol.

### SUMMARY.

The St. Leger Stakes of 25 sovs. each, for three-year-old colts, 8 st. 10 lbs., and fillies 8 st. 5 lbs.; the winner of the second home to receive 300 sovs., and the third 150 sovs., out of the stakes. One mile, seven furlongs, about one mile, six furlongs and 132 yards; 201 subscribers.

Lord Falmouth's br f Dutch Oven, by Dutch Master, out of Cantiniere (Archer) .......................................... 1

Lord Stamford's br f Geheimniss, by Rosicrucian, out of Nameless (Cannon) .......................................... 2

The Duke of Westminster's ch f Shotover, by Hermit, out of Stray Shot (Rossiter) .......................................... 3

Mr. Gerard's b c Sweetbread, by Brown Bread, out of Pether (Fordham) .......................................... 0

Lord Bradford's b c Quicklime, by Wenlock, out of Duveneay (Wood) .......................................... 0

Baron R. Selliliere's ch c Fenelon, by Flageolet, out of Fashaise (Watts) .......................................... 0

Mr. P. Lorillard's ch c Sachem, by War Dance, out of Sly Boots (Webb) .......................................... 0

Mr. E. b Romeo b c Romeo, by Glencoe, out of Alice (Cannon) .......................................... 0

Mr. J. R. Keene's b c Marden, by Hermit, out of Barberina (Wyatt) .......................................... 0

Mrs. Craven's br c Laureate, by Rosicrucian, out of Laura, by Orlando (Goater) .......................................... 0

Lord Bradford's b c Battlefield, by Springfield, out of Quick Match (Snowden) .......................................... 0

Mr. R. Jardine's br c Hygeia, by Hygeia (Osborne) .......................................... 0

Mr. M. Dawson's ch c Baliol, by Blair Athol, out of Marigold (Woodburn) .......................................... 0

The Duke of Hamilton's br f Actress, by Barbillon, out of Music (Martin) .......................................... 0

The frequency with which fillies have won the St. Leger Stakes, as witness Jannette, Apology, Marie Stuart, Hannah, Formosa, Achievement, etc., has caused the month of September to be known as the mares' month. This year the fillies began early in the season to evince their superiority over the opposite sex and Shotover immortalized herself by winning both the two thousand guineas and the Derby. Geheimniss, trained in the same stable as Shotover, won the Oaks and was considered to be the better of the two, although as they were never tried together either in private or public this was somewhat of a surmise. Granting that Shotover was better than any of the colts and yet inferior to Geheimniss, it looked very much as if the fillies could make a stronger showing than usual at Doncaster. The pair received additional and unexpected reinforcement, and by means of Dutch Oven's wonderful return to her form of a year ago three fillies are recorded as first, second and third for the St. Leger, a state of affairs without a parallel in the records of the race, which extends as far back as 1776, although it was not regularly known as the St. Leger until two years later. This is the fourth winner of the race ridden by Archer, who was on Silvio in 1877, Jannette in 1878 and Iroquois last year. The former two were owned by Lord Falmouth, who yesterday won his third St. Leger.

Dutch Oven, like all the horses Lord Falmouth races, was bred by himself and is by Dutch Master, a new sire so far as Lord Falmouth is concerned, out of Cantiniere. She is therefore a half sister of Bal Gal, who was got by Adventurer and who succumbed to throat troubles, as it was feared Dutch Oven had done early this year. As a two-year-old the heroine of yesterday's race had a very successful career and with good health it was confidently expected she would win many of her important three-year-old engagements. The new year had hardly opened, however, before the hopes of those who had wagered on her winning the Derby, to which three-year-old race winter betting was entirely confined, were shattered. Newmarket touts noticed her absence from the string of horses that filed out from Matthew Dawson's vast training establishment for their morning exercise, and the rumor that she was on the sick list was soon verified and severe influenza stated to be the trouble. Bal Gal had been treated in the same manner and her brilliant career brought to a summary termination, and it was feared that her near relative, Dutch Oven, was but another instance of the bad policy of breeding from a dam with a tendency to perpetuate her own physical defects. Dutch Oven was absent from exercise for many weeks, and when she once more began galloping the horse-watchers reported that she "made a noise" so her Derby prospects were considered to be hopeless. A rearer may win over the comparatively flat Newmarket courses, as testified to by the successes of Prince Charlie and Lord Falmouth's Chairbent in the Two Thousand Guineas, but at Epsom the journey to kill at the start and again at the finish invariably stops a horse affected in his wind. Dutch Oven was so far recovered by April that her preparation for the Derby was proceeded with, and so well did she progress that her old followers rallied on her side and she started as fourth favorite at the short price of 10 to 1. In the race she never dangerous and finished a long way behind the front rank. As Goodwood she was one of a field of six to start for the Sussex Stakes, and even money was wagered on her, but she was a bad third to two such indifferent performers as Comte Alfred and Battlefield.

At York meeting, held last month, Dutch Oven ran two races. The first was the Yorkshire Oaks of a mile and a quarter, and with only Actress and Confusion to run against her the Oven won with the greatest ease. This faint indication of her being able to race again was not good enough to induce anyone to accept the offer of 1,000 to 45 against her made after the race. Two days later she was started for the Great Yorkshire Stakes of a mile and three-quarters and as the four against her were very poor, St. Marguerite having become a rogue, Dutch Oven was made a favorite at six to four against her. She ran well for a mile and a half, and when the real racing began dropped back, and finished third, four lengths behind the winner, a colt named Peppermint, owned and ridden by John Osborne. Before running in this race the wager of £1,000 to £30 had been accepted about Dutch Oven for the St. Leger, but after the race £1,000 to £10 was on offer, but no takers. It is no wonder therefore that for the St. Leger her chance should be considered a perfectly hopeless one. As she was ridden by Archer, who has a large following of speculators on his mounts, no matter what he is rid ng, her price of forty to one may be more strictly speaking recorded as the odds laid against the jockey than against the mare, who, if any other rider had been on her, would probably have been in the 100 to 1 division. In addition to the performances of Dutch Oven this year recited above she ran as follows last year:

Newmarket, July 5.—Third to Kermesse for July Stakes, T. Y. C.
Manchester, July 15.—Won the Great Lancashire Yearling Stakes, five furlongs.
Goodwood, July 26.—Won the Richmond Stakes, T. Y. C.
Goodwood, July 28.—Won Rous Memorial Stakes, T. Y. C.
York, August 24.—Second to Nellie for Prince of Wales Stakes, T. Y. C.
Derby, September 1.—Won the Champion Breeders' Foal Stakes, five furlongs.
Doncaster, September 13.—Second to Kermesse for the Champagne Stakes.
Newmarket, September 27.—Walked over for the Buckenham Stakes, T. Y. C.
Newmarket, September 19.—Won the Triennial Product Stakes, T. Y. C.
Newmarket, September 30.—Won the Rous Memorial Stakes, Rous course.
Newmarket, October 10.—Won the Clearwell Stakes, T. Y. C.

The Kingsclere fillies, who ran second and third, were thus spoken of in a recent issue of the London *Sportsman* in reviewing their prospects of success: "On the Doncaster St. Leger neither layers nor backers appear to have yet come to any decisive decision of importance as to whether Shotover or Geheimniss will turn out to be the more worthy of support. There is, however, one matter connected with these two fillies, one act that proves the thoroughly sportsmanlike and gentlemanly conduct on the part of the two noblemen who own them, and which speculators great and small on the turf will know how to appreciate. This is the declaration, that has undoubtedly emanated direct from the Kingsclere stable, to the effect that both the clippers of the season will run for the great race of the north quite independently of each other. We most of us know there was a general impression before the Derby that Geheimniss had beaten Shotover in a trial, but that story has been contradicted and reiterated with appparently such good grounds for the two opposite assertions that I am at a loss to say which is correct. Let this be as it may, it will be as well to remember that both Derby and Oaks winners take a lot of beating for the Doncaster St. Léger. Lord Clifden lost the Derby only by the hairs of his nose, and, with Macaroni out of the way, he took the St. Leger and beat Queen Bertha, winner of the Oaks, into second place. Then came Gladiateur, who had won the Derby and Two Thousand Guineas, and he beat Regalia, the heroine of the Oaks, into the same position. Achievement was second for the Oaks, and took the Doncaster event. Following this mare were Formosa, Hannah, Marie Stuart, Apology and Jannette, who all won the Oaks, and subsequently galloped in the footsteps of each other to victory on the Town Moor. It may be said that the Derby, as a rule, takes a lot more winning than the Oaks, but those mares I have named were exceptionally good animals, and the same remark applies to Shotover and Geheimniss. The latter was opposed by two fillies at Epsom that ranked in the first class as two-year-olds, and she beat them both very easily, St. Marguerite being two lengths in her rear and Nellie a bad third. It is, indeed, a very fine point between the pair of fillies at Kingsclere as to which will be the better of the two at Doncaster. As regards the style and symmetry of the two fillies there is a considerable difference. In fact, there is not another mare or horse in training made in a similar mould to Geheimniss—when taken as a whole. She is, however, remarkable for the excellence of the most essential points that are almost invariably seen in a race-horse of high class, while for size and length combined I do not think there is her superior in the whole of the entries. Her forelegs are certainly not perfection in shape, but they are strong in bone and sinew, and not only stood firm through her two-year-old career but carried her well in her preparation for the Oaks and down the hill with the tremendous impetus of her great speed and strain upon them in the descent from Tattenham Corner.

Shotover would be faultless in her formation if she had a little more power in her loins, but horsemen are well aware that this deficiency is more common with the feminine than the masculine gender in the equine race. Her action may be truthfully described as the "poetry of motion" and her symmetry, with the exception of the slight defect to which I have referred, is as true as if dame Nature had designed it as a prize model. Her legs and feet are strong and very well formed, while for blood-like style and general beauty of outline she has few equals and no superiors now in training. To see Tom Cannon ride Shotover in her races is both a treat and a study for a really practical horseman. How she was beaten by St. Marguerite for the One Thousand Guineas is, however, something of a mystery to me; particularly as the winner has performed in a moderate fashion on three other occasions, before and since the race—at the Craven, Epsom and Ascot meetings. Shotover was, however, defeated by only a neck for the One Thousand, and the probability is that, like others of the Newminster family, she requires more time to get fairly on her legs again than was allowed her after her severe race for the Two Thousand Guineas, and her effort against perfectly fresh opponents in the sister race, only forty-eight hours afterward, on Friday.

## The Racing of Two-Year-Olds.

That ably-conducted journal, the London *Field*, in its issue of August 19, has a leading editorial in which it gives currency to a rumor to the effect that Lord Falmouth has intimated an intention to run no more colts or fillies for two-year-old engagements, and proceeds to make this the text of a violent attack upon two-year-old racing. Were it not that the *Field* has for a long time past been an avowed opponent of the racing of two-year-olds, we would feel tempted to pass its latest effusion as one of those periodical aberrations into which sporting writers often fall, and in Cassandra-like tones announce that a black cloud is hanging over the turf, threatening its destruction. The evils of two-year-old racing have been preached for the last fifty years, and the arguments urged against the practice are familiar to all. Yet during the period no institution has attained greater growth. In England its increase has been remarkable, and here no less so. Fifteen years ago the two-year-old races in the United States could almost be counted on the fingers; at present they are part of each day's programme. Not this alone, but the entries to the stakes exclusively for two-year-olds outnumber any other; the fields are larger, and more speculation is indulged over these events than any other species of contest.

We are not among those who would allow the abuse of a practice to compel us to call for its abolition. We are free to confess that we believe the strain put upon two-year-olds is getting to be greater than the average colt or filly can bear, and that within the past few seasons more than one promising youngster has been lost to the turf from a greediness on the part of its owner to gather the fruit ere it was ripe. But to make these cases the basis of a crusade against the racing of two-year-olds would be to act against the best interests of the turf and the improvement of the qualities of the blood-horse to which the turf is supposed to owe its existence. The rumored intention of Lord Falmouth to abandon the racing of two-year-olds is characteristic of the extremist. The loudest-mouthed apostle of temperance is usually a reformed drunkard, and if there is one man who has, by the force of example, done more than another to encourage the racing of two-year-olds in England that man is Lord Falmouth. No one has less reason to complain of the results. His brilliant two-year-olds have usually trained on; the Derby, Oaks, the Guineas and St. Leger glories have been all his, and for a decade past his name has been in the front rank of the winning owners. The *Field* seems to labor under the belief that the racing of two-year-olds is prejudicial to a colt's chances for the Derby, and quotes the effete practice of the gouty Dukes of Grafton, who were gathered to their fathers fifty years ago, and further supports its theory by observing that, of the seven Derby winners trained by Robert Robson, not one had ever been stripped in public until three years old. This is all very well, but in opposition to this it may be remarked that, of the forty-two Derby winners since 1840, only four were non-performers at two years old. The story of Thormanby is often quoted, and may be again, as it is an all-powerful argument, showing what a race-horse is capable of doing.

He began as a two-year-old on the 30th of March, and ran fourteen races, winning nine; and not only won the Derby and many other races the following year, but was a better horse at four years old than he was at two, and was only beaten once, and then in the Goodwood Cup, in which he conceded 14 lbs to the winner, a six-year-old, and set the seal to his racing glory by winning the Gold Cup at Ascot. The famous Blink Bonny ran eleven times as a two-year-old; yet she won the Derby and Oaks at three, and lived to throw a Derby winner in Blair Athol, who did not run as a two-year-old, but whose stock had a sad tendency to softness. Blink Bonny's distinguished relative, Caller Ou, ran twelve times at two years old; yet she not only won the St. Ledger at three, but ran eighty-six races at three, four, five and six years old, all at long distances, most of them being Queen's Plates and Cups, at two, three and four miles. Indeed, it would be hard to name a half-dozen really first-class English horses which have appeared within the past forty years but which have raced in their two-year-old form. Voltigeur, The Flying Dutchman, Teddington, Kingston, Stockwell, West Australian, and Rataplan, of the great era between 1850 and 1855, all appeared as two-year-olds, and afterward gained the highest distinction as stayers, and are to this day the pride and boast of England. Of the later era, Thormanby, Gladiateur, Cremorne, Blue Gown, Fille de l'Air, Sterling, Petrarch, Isonomy, Bend Or, and Robert the Devil, all ran as two-year-olds, and their after career is too recent to recapitulate. Iroquois and Foxhall both ran at two years old, the former appearing twelve times. Fisherman did not start at two years old, because his conformation was so bad and his frame so loose that he could not be trained. Blair Athol did not, because he was too big; Favonius did not for reasons unknown. Doncaster was trained as a two-year-old, when he was known as All Heart and No Peel, and would certainly have raced, as Mr. Merry, his owner, was not sparing of his two-year-olds, but in the July of his two-year-old season he was so badly kicked as to compel his being stopped.

Although two-year-old racing is of comparatively recent growth on our turf, its history repeats that of England. Kentucky raced at two years old, so did Henry Bassett, Enquirer, Kingfisher, Aristides, Joe Daniels, Springbok, Ten Broeck and King Alfonso. So did Parole, who made a hard campaign at that age and was the best of the year, yet Parole, in his tenth year, is still upon the turf, beating some of the best. But then some of the wiseacres have refused to admit Parole to a place among the anointed, and deny that he was ever a first-class horse. For our part we consider that he was quite first-class in the ordinary acceptation of the term. He was the best horse in the country when he left it for England, in 1879, and carried his triumphal march into England. If he is not first-class, he has at least the credit of having beaten more first-class ones than any horse that has ever appeared upon the turf. Duke of Magenta, Bramble, Spendthrift, Monitor, Thora, Luke Blackburn, Hindoo, Glidelia, Bend Or, Crickmore, and Harold, all ran at two years old, and unless it be Eole and Glenmore, it will be difficult to name a horse of any note of the present day, in this country, but raced at that age.

For our part, we consider racing at two years old as a necessity to the development of higher powers in the race-horse. The experience of practical men has demonstrated to them that a colt untrained at that age is not only unmanageable after, but has a tendency to grow soft and never develop the speed of one handled early. Moreover, in the present day an economic spirit prevails. Racing is an expensive amusement, and the owner who chooses to let his two-year-olds remain idle eating their heads off will find little reward for his forbearance. Two-year-old racing is, no doubt, carried to excess, but to abolish it would be a serious blow to the turf, and an obstacle to the improvement of the blood-horse.—*N. Y. Spirit of the Times.*

## The Embryo.

EDITOR BREEDER AND SPORTSMAN: Again I am in receipt of your valuable paper. Again I look in vain for some information in regard to the Embryo Stakes to be trotted this year.

It would be a matter of great interest to nearly every trotting horseman and breeder in the State to know who have paid up, the day of the trot, and where the trot will take place.

As I understand it Messrs. Harris and Simpson are the managers or should be, for they are the parties that got up this stake, received entries, forfeits, etc., and they should now give us the information that all who have entered, at least, are anxious and have a right to expect. If this stake is to be a success it will require more than the first advertisement for entries. It will be necessary for those who have taken the first steps in the matter to see its full carrying out to the end and to see that the rules are complied with and that those who do not pay forfeits or declare out and pay are suspended until they do pay. Last year's Embryo is still unsettled. Some paid, some did not, and no one to look after it.

L. J. ROSE, Sunny Slope.

## Weights of the P. C. B. H. A.

Appended is the scale of weights adopted by the Pacific Coast Blood Horse Association, at the annual meeting in November, 1881. Until further notice these weights will be required in all races run under the direction of the Association except those stakes that closed before the date of their adoption. The scale is the same as that of the American jockey club:

TWO-YEAR-OLDS.

| Distances | May. | June. | July. | Aug. | Sept. | Oct. & Nov. |
|---|---|---|---|---|---|---|
| Half-mile | 80 | 82 | 86 | [illegible] | 92 | 95 |
| ¾ mile | 75 | 77 | 80 | 84 | 87 | 90 |
| One mile | .. | .. | 75 | 77 | 81 | 83 |
| Mile and a half | .. | .. | .. | .. | 75 | 78 |
| Two miles | .. | .. | .. | .. | .. | 75 |

THREE-YEAR-OLDS.

| Distances. | May. | June. | July. | Aug. | Sept. | Oct. & Nov. |
|---|---|---|---|---|---|---|
| Half-mile | 105 | 107 | 109 | 111 | 112 | 113 |
| ¾ of a mile | 106 | 107 | 109 | 111 | 112 | 113 |
| One mile | 102 | 103 | 105 | 107 | 108 | 109 |
| Mile and a half | 100 | 101 | 103 | 105 | 106 | 117 |
| Two miles | 98 | 99 | 101 | 103 | 104 | 106 |
| 2½ miles | 97 | 98 | 100 | 102 | 103 | 104 |
| Three miles | 96 | 97 | 99 | 101 | 102 | 103 |
| Four miles | 95 | 96 | 98 | 100 | 101 | 102 |

FOUR-YEAR-OLDS.

Four-year-olds, at all distances, from the beginning of the season in May, to close of November, carry 118 lbs.

FIVE-YEAR-OLDS.

| Distances. | May. | June. | July. | Aug. | Sept. | Oct. & Nov. |
|---|---|---|---|---|---|---|
| Half-mile | 120 | 120 | 118 | 118 | 118 | 118 |
| ¾ mile | 120 | 120 | 120 | 118 | 118 | 118 |
| One mile | 122 | 122 | 120 | 120 | 118 | 118 |
| Mile and a half | 123 | 122 | 121 | 120 | 120 | 120 |
| Two miles | 124 | 123 | 122 | 121 | 120 | 120 |
| 2½ miles | 125 | 124 | 123 | 122 | 121 | 120 |
| Three miles | 126 | 125 | 124 | 123 | 122 | 121 |
| Four miles | 127 | 126 | 125 | 124 | 124 | 122 |

SIX YEARS AND AGED.

| Distances. | May. | June. | July. | Aug. | Sept. | Oct. & Nov. |
|---|---|---|---|---|---|---|
| Half-mile | 120 | 120 | 118 | 118 | 118 | 118 |
| ¾ mile | 120 | 120 | 120 | 118 | 118 | 118 |
| One mile | 122 | 122 | 120 | 120 | 118 | 118 |
| Mile and a half | 124 | 123 | 122 | 121 | 120 | 120 |
| Two miles | 125 | 124 | 123 | 122 | 121 | 120 |
| 2½ miles | 126 | 125 | 124 | 123 | 122 | 121 |
| Three miles | 127 | 126 | 125 | 124 | 123 | 122 |
| Four miles | 128 | 127 | 126 | 125 | 124 | 123 |

In races of intermediate lengths the weights for the shorter distance are to be carried.

In races exclusively for three-year-olds or four-year-olds, the weight shall be 118 lbs; and in races exclusively for two-year-olds, the weight shall be 110 lbs.

Except in handicaps, and in races where the weights are fixed absolutely in the articles, fillies two years old and geldings of all ages shall be allowed 3 lbs., and mares three years old and upward, shall be allowed 5 lbs. before September 1, and three pounds afterwards.

Welter weights shall be 28 lbs. added to weight for age, and in the absence of conditions, shall be the weights for steeplechases and hurdle races.

No horse shall carry less than 75 lbs. in any purse or sweepstakes.

"Next to Ex-Governor Stanford of California, Governor Gosper of Prescott, Arizona, is the largest owner of horses on the Pacific Coast."

The above paragraph which is now going the rounds of the press, is probably incorrect. It undoubtedly means well-bred animals and without being informed of the number of Governor Gosper's horses, we are under the impression that J. B. Haggin's stud contains the most. At the Rancho Del Paso are over 200 horses, a large majority of them of fine breeding.

SPEED PREMIUMS.—At the Stockton fair last week H. T. Dorrance offered a special premium of a $25 saddle to the horse owned in the district who made the fastest running mile during the meeting, and a set of track harness valued at $65 to the district horse that made the fastest trotting record. The saddle was awarded to Sam Stevison, who won the first heat of the mile and repeat race of Tuesday in 1:45. The harness fell to L. U. Shippee's bay colt by Inauguration, who scored a fourth heat in 2:40¼.

MAMBRINO WILKES PRIZES.—Mr. Irving Ayres, owner of Maubrino Wilkes, offered two prizes at the Stockton fair for the best two-year-old colts sired by his horse. Eight competed the first prize, a handsome silver tea set, which was given C. F. Perkins for the bay gelding Josh Whitcomb, dam by to Chieftain; and the second, a silver pitcher, to J. W. Warren, for the brown stallion Alpheus, dam by Major Mono.

Dutch Oven, the St. Leger winner, scored another victory last Monday in the fourth Great Foal Stakes at Newmarket. Shrewsbury and Nellie ran a dead heat for second place. There were seven starters, including Gerald.

The first number of the BREEDER AND SPORTSMAN, published in San Francisco, reached our sanctum a few days ago. It is a very handsome journal, devoted to field sports in general. The illustration of Electioneer on the title page is an artistic effort far above those seen ordinarily in sporting papers. Joseph Cairn Simpson is the editor, and judging from his leading articles, he is the right man in the right place. We will always welcome the BREEDER AND SPORTSMAN with pleasure, and read the accounts of that wonderful country where it is published.—*Southern Industries, Nashville, Tenn.*

THE BREEDER AND SPORTSMAN is the name of a new weekl paper, conducted by Jos. Cairn Simpson, and published a San Francisco, Cal., at five dollars per annum. The first copy is at hand. For beauty of typography, extent and variety of matter, and general make up, it is unexcelled by its cony temporaries. Mr. Simpson is author of a popular book called "Horse Portraiture," and for more than a quarter of a century has been a popular writer on horse and sporting matters. He is admirably qualified to conduct such an enterprise, and the breeders of the Pacific Coast are to be congratulated upon having so able and gifted a champion of their interests.—*St. Louis Rural World.*

# ROWING.

## Mr. Brennan's Challenge.

Ed. Breeder and Sportsman: In answer to what appears to be a challenge from Jas. E. Brennan to match P. J. Brennan against my son for $1,000 a side I desire to say that I have twice waited upon Mr. Brennan in this matter without getting any satisfactory or definite answer and do not propose to waste further time or trouble with it. Mr. Brennan knows where I can be found and if he means business I invite him to call. My money is ready. J. D. Griffin,

239 Steuart street, City.

---

The Long Bridge Oarsmen.—There are three crews in training for the race on Thanksgiving Day for the cup offered by the Breeder and Sportsman. The Golden Gate Club has purchased a wooden shell from the defunct St. George Rowing Club of Oakland. On Sunday the practice of the Pioneer crew and the Golden Gate crew was watched with interest by a number of spectators on Long Bridge. The water was in good condition for the display of form. The Pioneer crew had at the stroke a newly-arrived English oarsman who is said by some to be John Largan, the Thames sculler. This, however, is hardly probable, as according to English exchanges Largan sailed from Liverpool for Australia some time ago, taking with him his boats and trainer, intending to take part in the Punch regatta at Sydney. The new arrival is a strapping fellow and rowed in good form, but his style did not amaze nor discourage the local oarsmen. The Golden Gate crew appeared upon the water soon after the Pioneer crew and made a very favorable impression. Although unused to their boat, the Golden Gate four showed a fine pace and pulled with a vigor that gave promise of their ability to stay a three-mile course after they have have had a few weeks' practice. On the showing made on Sunday the Golden Gate Club should win, unless their boat proves far inferior to the paper shells which the Pioneer and Ariel crews will row. It is not likely that the Golden Gate crew will be handicapped in that respect, however, for the St. George crew could always make better time in their old wooden shell than in their new paper boat. While practicing for the McKinley cup the St. Georges in their old boat rowed a two-mile trial faster by sixteen seconds than a trial in the paper boat under similar conditions of tide and weather.

---

Unfair Criticism.—There are few professional athletes who have been as roughly and unfairly treated by the sporting press as Hanlan. To judge by the cards and challenges and the criticisms aimed at the unfortunate Toronto oarsman one would think that he is a craven-hearted individual, who has to be forced by abuse into displaying his powers. Whenever he hesitates for a day to accept a challenge which possesses no pecuniary profit to him, the champion of the world hears on all sides denunciations of his lack of spirit if not of actual cowardice. Now the fact is that if ever there was an athlete who was entitled to the most courteous consideration that athlete is the Toronto oarsman. He has in rapid succession met the best men of the world and in some thirty-four or five match races rowed to win and never once lowered his colors. He has crossed the ocean several times to meet the champions of England and Australia, while he might dodge behind some good excuse and decline to risk his reputation by encountering such formidable adversaries. While well and unhampered by business cares, he has always been ready to row any man in the world, and it is therefore rather a small proceeding to denounce him at this late day as a weak-minded specimen because after rising from a sick bed he declines to match himself against some of the best men in the world. Taking advantage of Hanlan's sickness Ross has claimed the championship of the world, but there is no credit in the title acquired in such a way and its possession will be all the more unfortunate for Ross when he meets the real champion fit and well.

---

Kennedy Challenges Hanlan.—John A. Kenndy of Portland having failed to get a match with Courtney has published the following card in the *Boston Herald:*

"*To the Editor of the Herald:* Having seen the challenge of Edward Hanlan addressed to Courtney, Ross or Lee, to row a three-mile race for $2,500 a side on any course between Boston and Washington some time within two months, and the same having failed of acceptance, I hereby offer to row Edward Hanlan a race, under the conditions he has named, at Boston, Silver Lake, Greenwood Lake, Philadelphia or Washington, as mutually agreed upon. This proposition to remain open for ten days, and, in case of non-acceptance, to be open to any sculler in the world. As an earnest of intention I inclose draft for $1,000.

"I have until now refrained from addressing any challenge to Mr. Hanlan on account of his published statement that he would not row a race this season; but, as he has recently publicly offered to match himself to row this year, I offer him the opportunity others have declined.

"John A. Kennedy.

"Portland, Maine, Sept. 15."

Kennedy is regarded by several professional scullers who have practiced in the same course with him a very speedy oarsman. After Courtney had made his fast time with Lee at Richfield Springs, Kennedy challenged him to a three-mile race and deposited $1,000 to back the race. His challenge has gone unaccepted, and as Kennedy, as well as Davis, contemplates abandoning boat racing, he has determined to have, if possible, one good race with a first-class man before he retires from boating, and to show his friends what he is capable of accomplishing in a single-scull shell. He seek royal game, and enters the field of first-class oarsmen to row the man who won the championship of America, England and the world, and attained higher distinction than any other oarsman ever aspired to.

---

The Halifax Regatta.—Two days of very good racing took place on Belford Basin, September 6th and 7th. The first event of the day was the three-mile race for four-oared lapstreak gigs. The entries were: Griswold crew of Halifax, Riley-Ferguson crew of Halifax, Morash crew of Lunenburg, Ross-Foley crew of Halifax, West End crew of Boston, Williams crew of Halifax, and Enterprise crew of Salem, Mass. The Boston four showed a little gain at the start, and pulling strong and well, they soon showed a length in advance. The Boston boat made the turn first, two lengths ahead, and was followed by the Williams and the Griswold crews. On the homestretch the Boston men continued to gain, but there was a good race between the Williams and Griswold crews for second place. Williams' crew proved too much for the Griswolds and came in second, about four lengths in rear of the West End men, followed close by the Griswolds. The Williams crew protested against the West End crew receiving first place on the ground of turning the stake boat contrary to the rules. The time made by the leading boat was 20m. 18¼s., and that by the second 20m. 37s. The race in double sculls—Hamm and Conley, being the only competitors, went over the course alone and obtained the prize. The distance was three miles, and the time made 20m. 48¼s. On the row-off of the four-oared race the Boston crew again won. Time, 24m. 30s.

Three-mile race, single sculls—Entries: Hosmer of Boston, Lee of New York, Conley of Halifax, McInenery and Driscoll of Lowell, Mass., Hamm and Smith of Halifax, and Plaisted of Boston. Lee and Plaisted did not appear. Hamm almost immediately took the lead, and passed the first mile a length and a half ahead of Smith and Hosmer, who were close together. At the mile and a half Hosmer had gained on Smith, with Conley a good fourth, and the other two some distance behind. Turning the buoy one of Hamm's rowlocks got out of order, and he had to stop. The delay, though brief, enabled Hosmer to get a slight lead. Smith and Conley were following him, with Hamm fourth. Conley soon caught and passed Smith, and settled down to catch Hosmer, which he did before the end of the second mile. Hosmer put on a spurt, and a beautiful race between them took place, the Bostonian holding half a length's advantage. The lead was soon taken and maintained by Conley, while Smith by this time was considerably behind Hosmer. Conley finished first in 21m., 46s., four lengths ahead of Hosmer, who was followed close by Hamm, Smith fourth, Driscoll and McInenery far in the rear.

Consolation race—Driscoll 1, McInenery 2.

---

Boating at North Beach.—On Sunday last the Tritop Boat Club entertained a number of visitors. Several scratch races enlivened the afternoon. The first race was between two crews from the Triton Club in the barges Argonaut and Lady Washington, the prizes being a gold badge for each member of the crew. The Argonaut crew was composed of Val Kehrlein Jr., Charles Rudolph, B. Kehrlein, Jos. Kehrlein and A. R. Tuckey, and the Lady Washington was manned by E. Borremans, A. L. Schuppert, Harry Tuckey, James Haughy and B. Tuckey. The course chosen was from the Triton club-house to and around Alcatraz Island and back to the club house. The Argonaut crew led their opponents all the way round the course, finishing four lengths in the lead. Time, 28:56.

A wherry race between E. Borremans and Harry Tuckey from the Triton boat-house to Meiggs' wharf and return was won by Borremans.

A scratch race followed between the following named crews: J. D. Griffin, Otto Rudolph, James Haughy and Ed. Peterson rowing the Lady Washington, H. Dobbin, W. Dunn, B. Kehrlein and B. Tuckey rowing the Arion, Dan Griffin, Jos. Kehrlein, A. P. Rothkopf and F. Fraser in the Argonaut, and a crew in the barge Governor Perkins, consisting of J. Lamb, J. Flinn, Aug. Schuppert, H. Tuckey. The course was from the Triton boat house to a point of Meiggs' wharf, thence around a schooner anchored out in the stream and back to the club house. The race was won by the crew in the Lady Washington, Gov. Perkins second, Argonaut third, Arion fourth.

A scratch race then took place between the crews of the barges Argonaut, Gov. Perkins and Arion. The Argonaut crew was composed of Ad. Schuppert, J. Wilser, T. Watson, W. Smith; the Gov. Perkins' crew of A. R. Tuckey, C. Ru-Rudolph, P. G. McVeigh, E. Gerlach, and barge Arion, J. Clark, W. J. Farron, A. Klumpp, B. Kehrlein, and E. Borremans. The course was the same as in the preceding race, and the race was won by the Argonaut crew; Perkins crew second, Arion crew third.

The last event of the day was between the barges Argonaut and Perkins; the Perkins crew being J. D. Griffin, J. Lamb, B. Kehrlein, J. Haughy. The Argonaut crew was composed of Jim Brown, J. Keegan, P. Keegan and Ed. Peterson. The race was won by the Perkins crew.

---

Errors in Timing.—Nothing could be more unreliable than time as a test of the merits of oarsmen. Judging by the time made at Richfield Springs by Courtney, that sculler should be able to beat any man in the world, but there is strong proof that he cannot beat some men in the second class. The authorities have not yet accepted his wonderful record as correct. The Boston *Herald* of the 17th inst. has the following reference to it:

"The time for the three miles rowed at Lake Maranocoot last Wednesday when Riley and Kennedy rowed their race was incorrect. Kennedy reached the turning stake in 9 minutes and 40 seconds from the time of starting, and was 17 seconds ahead of Riley. He gained 3 seconds more on Riley going back, and made the entire distance in 20 m. 35s., Riley's time being 20m. 53½s. The timekeeper made a mistake of one minute in calculation, just as the timekeeper in the Courtney-Lee race at Richfield Springs is thought by many oarsmen to have done.

Laycock's Ambition.—Jack Largan, who some months ago beat Laycock and Pearce on the Thames, has written to some friends in this city that Laycock will come to commence next spring and try conclusions with the best oarsmen in this country. Largan states that the improvement in Laycock's style is wonderful. When Laycock first appeared on the Thames he rowed in the same bad form as Trickett. The art of the sliding reef was unknown to him and he used sculls that lapped about a foot. After seeing the rig of the American boats the burly Australian reconstructed his style of rowing and he now uses the regulation short sculls with wide blades and a slide twenty-six inches long. Largan thinks that the Australian's pace has improved wonderfully and that he ought to be able to give Hanlan a close rub and to beat Ross or Courtney.

---

The World's Championship.—Hanlan, Courtney and Kennedy met at Portland, Maine, on Tuesday last, and after a lengthy discussion decided to postpone their race till June, 1883. The stake money will be put up three weeks in advance of the races. The date of the races is to be named six weeks previous, and the date is to be mutually agreed upon. Three weeks must intervene between the race between Hanlan and Ross and that between Hanlan and Kennedy.

---

Sculling in England.—The race for the amateur championship of England and the Wingfield diamond sculls was rowed for over Putney Mortlake (River Thames) course on the 21st ult. The contestants were Willoughby Grove, of the London Rowing Club, and Alexander Payne, of the Mousley Boat Club. Payne won in 27m. 35s, Grove's time being 28m 1s.

---

Match at Shuffle Board.—A match game of shuffle board for $250 a side by Wm. Ryan and Arthur Quinn against John Farrelly and Samuel Costello takes place at Farrelly & Mitchell's saloon, 435 California street, between the hours of 12 and 4 o'clock p. m. Saturday.

# THE PADDOCK.

## The Dangu Sale.

Another thoroughbred from France is coming to America and according to all the "experts" he will be a valuable addition to the blood stock of the country. Still it is a singular location for a thoroughbred which has cost nearly $40,000 to be sent to Erie, Pennsylvania, though Mr. Scott may think that if Erdenhiem has been such a great success as a breeding farm, turning out Parole, Iroquois and many other top-sawyers in the southeastern portion of the State, the northwest may be equally as fortunate.

The cable of the 8th announces that W. L. Scott, of Erie, Pa., had purchased at the sale of the Dangu Stud, in France, the celebrated French race-horse Rayon D'Or. The reported price is $30,000, the sale being made by Mr. Easton, of the American Horse Exchange, and if breeding and performances are elements of success in a stallion, and we think they are, Mr. Scott has one which quite fills the bill. Rayon D'Or is a son of the French horse Flageolet, who won the Criterion Stakes and Goodwood Cup. Flageolet was a son of Plutus, who was by Trumpeter, and from a daughter of Planet (son of Bay Middleton and a sister to Plenipotentiary), grandam Alice Bray, by Venison, great grandam Darkness, by Glencoe. Flageolet's dam was La Favorite, by Monarque; second dam Constance, by Gladiator; third dam Lanterne, by Hercule. The dam of Rayon D'Or is Araucaria, by Ambrose (son of Touchstone and Annette, by Priam), from the famous Pocahontas, by Glencoe. It will be seen that Rayon D'Or has the double cross of Glencoe, which breeders now consider the keystone to success in this country, and as it is backed by foreign strains, breeders on this side of the water need not fear mating double Glencoe mares to him. He has also the double cross of Touchstone, through Trumpeter and Ambrose, and these, with his crosses of Venison, Priam, Monarque, and Gladiator, form a very happy combination of blood.

Rayon D'Or was bred at the Dangu Stud in 1876. As a two-year-old he ran eleven races, winning four of them, viz.: The Levant, a sweepstakes at Doncaster, in which he beat Charibert, the after winner of the Two Thousand, the Clearwell, and the Glasgow. As a three-year-old Rayon D'Or ran twelve times, winning seven. His victories were the St. James Palace Stakes, beating Charibert, Ruperra, The Scot and three others. At Goodwood he won the Sussex Stakes, at Doncaster the St. Leger, in which he defeated a field of sixteen. The French colt won by five lengths pulling double. So sound and true were his legs that he never wore bandages until a fortnight ago, and then after some grit had worked under his boot and slightly grazed one of his legs as observed by a commissioner of the *Sporting Life*, who says: "When Araucaria's son was stripped on Doncaster Moor, even those who looked him over at Goodwood, prior to his cutting down Ruperra and others for the Sussex Stakes, will be forcibly struck by the improvement which Tom Jennings has wrought in the big chestnut, who has grown out and developed in muscle to the most extraordinary degree; in fact, if he goes on furnishing thus until next summer, he will be noted a magnificent colt, even by his numerous decriers. * * * Rayon D'Or's change, for the better, is most marked; in fact, it would puzzle me to recall to mind any three-year-old who has trained on so well and so rapidly." The next day Rayon D'Or walked over for the Zetland Stakes. At Newmarket, in October, he won the Great Foal Stakes. At the same meeting he was beaten three-quarters of a length by Bay Archie, to whom he conceded seven pounds, for the Newmarket St. Leger. He then won the Select stakes, beating a field of seven, pulling double by six lengths, and followed it up, winning the Second Great Challenge stakes, in which he gave away three years to our Parole, but closed the season by being beaten by Out of Bounds, to whom he conceded sixteen pounds in a handicap.

At four years old Rayon D'Or started six times, winning the Prix du Cadrau (2½ miles), and the Prix Rainbow (3½ miles), at Paris. He then walked over for the Port Stakes, at Newmarket, and the Prince of Wales Stakes, same place. At Ascot he won the Rous Memorial, with 132 lbs. up, and was beaten for the Hardwicke Stakes by Exeter, to whom he conceded 10 lbs. He ran no more, but from the above it will be seen that his performances were of a high class. He carried the highest weights over long distances, and possessed the speed to do so successfully; thus he cannot be denied the lasting qualities which many of our old fogy turfmen are prone to deny to imported horses. There can be no mistaking that the French have never ceased to pay a proper attention to the development of stamina, and on his sire's side Rayon D'Or is French bred for upward of four generations, dating back to the earliest French ventures in blood stock.

At the time of his St. Leger victory, the English writers described him as a chestnut, standing 16 hands, and the longest horse that stripped for that race. His best points are said to be his immense length, superbly placed shoulders, wide hips, and good legs. His defects are stated to be a weak neck, narrow chest, and light flank. As a youngster he was also held to be wanting in muscular development of the quarters, but time has remedied that. As yet, it is not known when the horse will arrive here, but all students of the Stud-book and Racing Calendar cannot but feel that he is a valuable acquisition to our racing blood.—*New York Spirit of the Times.*

---

The Lorillard Stable in England.—Mr. P. Lorillard has engaged Barrett, formerly with the Michel Grove stables, to train his horses at Newmarket. The Manchester *Sporting Chronicle*, while negotiations were in progress for a new trainer, reported as follows: "There is a rumor that Tom Cannon will shortly take the responsibility of Mr. Lorillard's horses in training, Pincus having gone to America. It almost approaches a certainty that the popular jockey trainer has been asked to train them. There is nothing new in the fact that stables which in one year have carried all before should do little or no good the next, but Mr. Lorillard has certainly had bad times this season with Gerald and others. The greatest blow, however, must naturally arise from the fact that Wallenstein and Passaic—two cast-offs of the stable—have this year carried off so many valuable turf prizes, showing either a lack of judgment on the part of those interested, or giving another instance as to how much the vulgar commodity called luck influences the too-too-utterly fascinating pastime of racing.

---

Sold.—Gracie Mahon, the bay filly by Modoc, dam by Norfolk, who ran fourth for the purse for two-year-olds at Stockton on Wednesday of last week, was sold the same day by her owner, Jas. F. Mahon, to Edward Fay of this city. Price $250.

# The Breeder and Sportsman.

PUBLISHED WEEKLY BY THE

BREEDER AND SPORTSMAN PUBLISHING CO.

THE TURF AND SPORTING AUTHORITY OF THE
PACIFIC COAST.

**OFFICE, 508 MONTGOMERY STREET**
P. O. Box 1233.

*Five dollars a year; three dollars for six months; one dollar and a
half for three months. Strictly in advance*

MAKE ALL CHECKS, MONEY ORDERS, ETC., PAYABLE TO ORDER OF
BREEDER AND SPORTSMAN PUBLISHING CO.

*Money should be sent by postal-rder, draft or by registered letter, ad
dressed to the "Breeder and Sportsman Publishing Company, San Francisco, Cal."*

*Communications must be accompanied by the writer's name and address,
not necessarily for publication, but as a private guarantee of good faith*

JOSEPH CAIRN SIMPSON, - - - EDITOR

San Francisco, Saturday, Sept. 30, 1882.

## ENFORCE THE RULES.

We do not consider it necessary to offer apologies for repeating appeals to the judges of races to enforce the rules. As guardians of the sports of the turf and track, they must be inflexible in carrying out the provisions of the code, and punish with inexorable firmness the infractions which bring racing and trotting into discredit. The continued prosperity depends on the elimination of fraudulent practices, and the magnitude of the interests at stake demands the correction of evils which are now partially condoned. If owners, jockeys and drivers do not follow the proper course they must be compelled to, or be otherwise banished from all participation.

We learn of two things at the late Stockton Fair that deserve severe censure, and which, unfortunately, were not properly dealt with. The fault does not rest so much with the judges of the races in which the violations of the rules took place, as in a lax and prevailing habit of measuring the evil by the results which follow. This practice has emboldened drivers to take risks which they would have avoided if punishment was sure to follow whether the result of the heat or race was changed or not.

One of the wrongs alluded to was of a peculiar character, and it is claimed that it was done in order to give a chance for second money, and if so the object was effected. The history of the heat, as given to us, was that Starr King was in the lead, beating Director by a short head, without an effort being made by the driver of Director to win the heat. Echora won the first heat meritoriously, and hence any horse which beat her for second money, (unless she was distanced,) would have to win a heat.

Now the only valid excuse which a driver trying to win can offer for not trying to win a heat, is, when such a course increases his chances of victory. To favor another horse, to influence the betting, or, in fact, anything which lessens the chances to win, is contrary to, all sound principles of honor and honesty, as well as being contrary to trotting law. In a case where it is palpable that the object was to unduly favor any one of the contestants, the judges if leniently inclined ought to fine the erring driver to the full extent of the law; if they are guided by a consideration for the future welfare of the sport any fine they could impose would not be commensurate, and suspension or expulsion should be the award. There must be no dallying with crimes of this character, no waiting to see how the race will end before inflicting the penalty. The wrong done to the person who had fairly earned the second money was small in comparison with the example which was set. We all know the vicious effects of bad precedents, and the proneness of people to excuse misconduct on the plea that others had done so without rebuke.

The other violation of the rules reported was the foul driving of Starr King in order to try and defeat Romero, and for which he was fined $25. It should have been four times that amount if a fine was imposed, but fines will not prove a remedy for this kind of work when large amounts are at stake. And yet we consider the deliberately throwing away a heat a worse crime than when a man commits a foul in his anxiety to win. If the foul is done to "help" stops one else there is no excuse and condign punishment should invariably follow. If either is done by men who are prominent in the profession, the more necessity for strict ruling, and the justice which is invoked to lash the inferior while the upper goes scot free is a temporizing folly, to call it no worse name. The higher the position the greater the amenability to law, and the more beneficial the example.

## THE FAIR OF THE SAN JOAQUIN.

There are good reports from this popular exhibition, and all who attended speak in the highest terms of the general management and especially of the capital sport which was given. The only exceptions are in regard to the circumstances mentioned in another article and the greatest share of the blame rightfully falls on the offending drivers. There was a series of notable performances.

The yearling filly, sister to Honesty, by trotting in 3:03 takes the foremost rank for one of her age actually competing in a race with colts of her age. Her sire, Priam, will deservedly rank high as a getter of trotters, and as he is by Whipple's Hambletonian, his dam Revere by imported Glencoe, a thoroughbred mare, his breeding is of a kind that will warrant excellence in the stud. There is another colt by him from Gilroy Belle by Lodi which is highly spoken of, and though Honesty was rather out-classed in those he met in this year's circuit, he is a grand colt and sure to make his mark in the future. Elsewhere Albert W receive the commendation he is fully entitled to, and again we repeat that his race with the fast mare Nellie R and Sweetness is the best four-year-old performance ever recorded. We are informed that before the season of 1882 is ended there will be an effort to subtract the three seconds which Jay Eyre See leads him, and if he should it will be a feat well worthy of the foremost place. But it is a tremendous task which the wonderful gelding has given him, and it is asking too much for an entire colt to accomplish. It was a great pity that Brigadier met with the mishap, as there is no question from all we can learn that he was a better horse than ever before, and to beat him Romero would have knocked every heat low in the teens. A gentleman who informs us, and a close observer too, that the back quarter was trotted in 32 seconds, and that the blood was actually exuding through the sole of his feet. This paring and cutting down the sole of the foot to such a thinness is one of the worst things that can be done. As it was Romero displayed wonderful speed when he had scarcely been trained for sometime before he trotted at Sacramento and according to those who were cognizant of the situation he was in, not yet recovered from the pinkeye, it was certainly a wonderful performance. Should he completely recover from the epizooty there is little question that he can make a mark that will place him in the front rank of five-year-olds. Vanderlynn in trotting in 2:22 is worthily entitled to a good place, and so is Nellie R and the two-year-olds did well, so that there was scarcely a race which was not good. Corette has gained renown, and astonished nearly every one by her fast work after so little training. Her 2:17 was made so easily that it was evident she could have gone still faster if it had been necessary. If nothing happens her she will have to go East, as the side-wheelers of this coast are not capable of contending against her.

Taken together the San Joaquin fair has been the best that was ever held. The time of the various contests has been good and the exhibition classes were superior. The president, directors, and all of the officers of the association have labored intelligently and assiduously, and the result has been a success in every respect. We are much pleased to record the great event which took place, and very sorry that business compelled us to labor at home in place of attending the circuit.

## THE P. C. B. H. A. FALL MEETING.

In another column will be found the advertisement of the fall meeting of the above association, and in the "turf and track" department the nominations in the stakes that are to be decided at this meeting. There could not be a better showing for a successful meeting. In the Ladies' Stake for two-year-old fillies are twenty nominations, and in the Finigan Stake for all two-year-olds are twenty-nine. In the Vestal Stake for three-year-old fillies are twelve nominations, and in the Fame Stake for all three-year-olds are eighteen. In the Baldwin, a post stake for all ages, a dash of four miles, are six subscribers, and the programme which will close on the 10th of October completes the bill. The time fixed, November 11th, 18th and 23d, will give the horses plenty of time to recover from the running during the fairs, and also for the California colts in the East to recuperate from the effects of the journey. The stakes and purses which are yet open and will close on the 10th proximo are well arranged and soon after the closing the course will be selected where the races will be run, and all the other arrangements completed.

By referring to the nominations in the stakes that closed the 1st of August, 1880 and 1881, it will be seen that there is as nearly a certainty of good racing as can be, and those which are yet to close will have a large number of entries.

## THE EMBRYO OF 1879.

In another part of this paper will be found a letter from Mr. Rose concerning the Embryo stake of 1879 and 1880-81. We have been awaiting the close of the San Jose fair when we will meet Captain Harris and publish the names of those who have been "declared out" of the stakes of 1880 and 1881. In the stake of 1879 there is no provision for declaring out. The forfeit is $25, which has to be paid ten days before the time fixed for trotting, or the subscriber is held for the whole amount of the stake. The date of trotting has been fixed ever since the first advertisement, viz: the first Saturday in November. The track has not been selected yet. We will consult with A. P. Whitney and Captain Ben E. Harris, and hope to give all the particulars in the next number of this paper.

## THE NELLIE R—SWEETNESS RACE.

As will be learned by the report of our special commissioner the race between Nellie R and Sweetness at San Jose on Wednesday was the cause of a good many reproachful comments. The charge was made that Goldsmith had lost the race purposely, and certainly there were reasons for making it. We do not think, however, that the defeat of Sweetness was intentional on the part of her driver. From information obtained from a trustworthy source there cannot be a question that Goldsmith lost quite a large sum of money on his mare, and from the accounts there is nothing to prove that she could have won. She is notoriously "soft," and after one hard fight in a heat she is ready to succumb. This may be in part owing to the leg which precludes the right sort of training, though as far as we have seen she has neither the physical nor mental capacity to endure a severe trial. There must be a whole lot of cold crosses in her pedigree to nullify so many strains that are known to be of the right stamp. But for all this we do not like the way Goldsmith manages his horses, and this is the only thing which gives color to the charge. Director at Santa Rosa was either started, in a shape which should have kept him from taking part or for a wrong motive. Romero at Sacramento was given a "stent" that demanded the best of condition, and the conceding a heat to Starr King at Stockton cannot be reconciled with straightforward dealing. Mr. Goldsmith is a man of capacity. For one of his years he is entitled to high rank in the profession. He is industrious, of pleasing manners, intelligent and more than usually attentive to his business. It may be that there is an overpowering jealousy on the part of some of the drivers and the whole thing is viewed through jaundiced optics. Our commissioner may have been swayed by the clamor though there cannot be a shadow of aspersion on the straightforwardness of his motives, and to his reportorial instincts he made a faithful transcript of what was passing. These occurrences are peculiarly unfortunate, and every one who has the turf interests at heart must do their utmost to correct them.

## THE SHOOTING SEASON.

It did not require the intelligence conveyed in numerous newspapers to cause a traveler on the Oakland ferry boats to know that the "open season" had come. The evening of the 14th, there was a crowd of eager sportsmen on the way to the selected grounds, and again on the morning of the 15th. But Saturday, towards the latter part of the afternoon, the crowd had swelled into a multitude, and rather a mixed multitude at that. Never before did we see such a variety of dogs which were deemed worthy of taking the field. A few handsome setters of the fashionable line, now and then an old-fashioned pointer, spaniels, retrievers, but the great majority of such a mongrel class that it would have puzzled even our kennel editor to tell what combination had resulted in such queer representatives of the canine race. The accouterments in many cases were as queer as the dogs, but for all that, you could see anticipated pleasure beaming from the eye, and hope gave a roseate hue to the future. We could fully appreciate the feelings, especially of the neophyte "shootists." Although, a long time ago, how anxiously was awaited the first "good tracking snow," and the right sort of a day for deer hunting.

The snow must be deep enough so that the twigs would not crackle under foot, and if there was a high wind to relieve the boughs of the white drapery so much the better. If lucky enough to jump a deer reposing under the shelter of a low-branched hemlock it would not run far with an avalanche of snow falling from the branches, and then the wind made music among the twigs which muffled the sound of the footsteps. We have followed the track of a big buck from early in the morning until it was too dark to distinguish the footprints without a thought of weariness until the trail was forsaken, happy if now and then a glimpse of a white tail was caught as it flashed through the gaps in the underbrush, and eager to try again on the following morning.

The California sportsman is fortunate in being able to gratify his fondness for shooting without the discomfort which attended still-hunting in the woods of Northern

Pennsylvania in the winter time. Trailing through two or three feet of newly fallen snow with now and then a dab of it filling neck and ears, running or rather floundering through the mixture when the tracks showed that the deer had taken fright, perspiration streaming from every pore, and then cautiously creeping when the "signs" gave a token that the animal was not far in advance. What a contrast to the December days of this country and also what a contrast in the chances for the sports of the field. In those old-time sporting days we refer to the choice was restricted; excepting wild pigeons in the spring and autumn, and pheasants (ruffed grouse) and a staaggling wild duck there were no other birds. Foxes were numerous and afforded capital sport with hounds, though the country was so rough that a legitimate fox hunt would have been an impossibility. In the big woods were bears and panthers, and forty years ago plenty of deer. Here there is such a wide variety that the difficulty is to select the game, and from the tufted quail to the wild goose, and from the squirrel to the grizzly, there are opportunities for rare sport.

That many have had fine sport is shown by the famous "bags" reported, and as the season advances there will, doubtless, be still better returns.

## EDITORIAL NOTES.

**Erratum.**—With the hurry of late copy and the disadvantages under which printers labor who are yet unfamiliar with the destinctive language of the turf and the points where absolute precision is required several errors have crept into the BREEDER AND SPORTSMAN of late. Some of these are of importance as changing the status of horses in the record. The official summaries of the Sacramento meeting will be printed in these columns in the near future, entire. In the race won by Director at Stockton he was credited, through a typographical error, with figures that would bar him from the 2:23 class and to set him right we reproduce the summary of that race corrected to conform to the facts.

SUMMARY.

Same Day.—Trotting. 2:25 class. Purse, $1,000, and $200 added if more than ten entries. Four moneys.

| | | | | | |
|---|---|---|---|---|---|
| J. A. Goldsmith names blk s Director by Dictator | 2 | 2 | 1 | 1 | 1 |
| C. W. Welby names ch g Starr King, by Geo. M. Patchen | 4 | 1 | 3 | 2 | 2 |
| L. H. Titus names br m Echora, by Echo | 1 | 4 | 2 | 4 | 4 |
| J. H. Dodge names ch h Honesty, by Priam | 3 | 3 | 5 | 3 | 3 |
| J. Hughes names b g Cairo, by Chieftain | 5 | 5 | 4 | 5 | 5 |

Time—2:25½, 2:28½, 2:23½, 2:25½, 2:26½.

J. M. Learned's b s Reliance, by Alexander, H. R. Covey's b g Cap't. Smith, by Locomotive, G. Valensin's ch s Crown Point, by Speculation, J. Cochran's ch g Ashley, by Plumas, and L. J. Rose's blk s Del Sur, by The Moor were drawn.

**The Stallion Race** at Chicago was won by Monroe Chief in 2:20, 2:21½, 2:22; Black Cloud second. Romero trotted in Stockton in 2,20, 2:19½, 2:22 with Brigadier second. This is certainly a better showing than the Eastern contestants displayed, and when it is taken into consideration that Romero is only five years old the superiority is still more manifest. It is merely a question of a few years when California will take first place in all of the records as she now does in the yearling, two-year-old and four-year-old stallion calendar. It was very unfortunate that Brigadier had been lamed by the smith paring his feet too thin, or the time would have been faster. The general opinion was that the bay was a better horse than ever before, and with his feet right the teens should have been made in every heat.

**The Nutwood Colt** advertised for sale by George W. Hancock of Sacramento, should be a valuable acquisition to almost any stud farm. His dam being by John Nelson greatly enhances his value. We learn that he is a very fine looking colt.

The Hambletonian stallion also advertised is fashionably bred and is well worth the attention of purchasers.

**Tulare Valley Fair.**—John F. Uhlhorn, Secretary of the Tulare Valley Agricultural Association, writing under date of the 27th instant, says:

"The Second Annual Fair of the Tulare Agricultural Association will take place at Visalia, commencing October 11th and closing on the 14th. Many fine horses from Fresno, Kern and Tulare counties are here and training for the races to be held at the time. The fair promises to be one of the largest ever held in the way of exhibition of stock. We are in the midst of a stock-raising country, and some of the best in the State have been raised here.

## The Double Team Controversy.

"The trial" of Aldine and Early Rose at Hartford when they were timed in 2:16½, has solicited more than the usual amount of discussion and comment. As Mr. Vanderbilt will not wager money on his horses, a friend has secured the services of the fast team, and the following pronunciamento appears in the New York *Herald*:

TO THE EDITOR OF THE HERALD: Some of the papers of this city have several times within the last few days contained slurs and pretended doubts of the time made by Mr. Vanderbilt's team, Early Rose and Aldine, at Hartford, September 13. On that occasion there were four or five gentlemen entirely unknown to Mr. Vanderbilt and who were accustomed to timing horses present, who timed the horses in 2:16½ and at the driver's request made an affidavit of the fact. I wish here to ask, are these men not to be believed just as much as the individual friends of Mr. Work, who timed his horses at Fleetwood, July 13, and which time neither Mr. Vanderbilt or his friends have never disputed? Is it consistent for persons who were not at Hartford to deny these gentlemen's statements, carefully keeping their own names private? Why should not this team of mares beat Edward and Swiveller? I am only one of hundreds who think they can do it single or double every day in the week. Mr. Work has said publicly several times of late that he would trot his horses for fabulous amounts against Early Rose and Aldine next week (meaning this week) which conclusively shows that they are in condition. He has named large amounts, knowing that Mr. Vanderbilt never bets on his horses, and thinking that no one else would bet him the large sum named. Mr. Vanderbilt believes his team made 2:16½; and thinks that with the driver who drove them they can beat it, and so does the writer of this. In this belief and to stop all talk about the speed of these horses the writer has asked Mr. Vanderbilt for the loan of his team for a few days, and he has assented. I now offer to bet that the mare Aldine, owned by Mr. Vanderbilt, will beat either of Mr. Work's horses, best three in five, on Monday of next week, at Charter Oak Park track, Hartford, Conn.; $10,000 that Early Rose, the other of Mr. Vanderbilt's horses, will beat the other of Mr. Work's horses, best three in five, on Wednesday of next week, at the same track, and $10,000 that Early Rose and Aldine together will beat Edward and Swiveller, the horses referred to above, best three in five, in double harness, on Saturday of next week, Mr. Work to have the choice of which of his horses he will trot against Aldine on Monday; all these bets to be taken or none. The money to be deposited with the editor of the *New York Herald* and the races to be play or pay, these propositions to be accepted on Thursday morning, 21st instant, and the money to be deposited within twenty-four hours thereafter. If the days named should prove stormy the race to take place the first good day thereafter. Charter Oak track has been named because it is in the National Association and no one can object to it.

NEW YORK, Sept. 18, 1882, T. C. E.

## Californians at Sheepshead Bay

The following accounts of Gano's victory and the Duchess of Norfolk's unfortunate contretemps at Sheepshead Bay on September 19 are from the New York *World*:

Handicap Sweepstakes of $20 each, half forfeit, for two-year-olds, with $600 added; the second to receive $150 out of the stakes. Three-quarters of a mile.

E. J. Baldwin names b c Gano, by Grinstead, dam Santa Anita, 94 pounds.......(M. Donohue) 1
G. T. Johnson names ch f Lizzie Mc, by Alarm, dam Lady Motley, 80 pounds.......(Rayford) 2
Frederick Carter names b f Felicia, by Ill Used, dam Felucca, 92 pounds.......(Barnes) 3
P. H. Ryan names ch f Adalgisa, by Count d'Orsey, dam Adosinda, 92 pounds.......(Barrett) 4
James T. Williams names ch f Pearl Thorne, by Pat Malloy, dam Dolly Morgan, 87 pounds.......(Young) 5
Preakness Stables names b f Vintage, by Virgil, dam Madame Dudley, 80 pounds.......(J. Donohue) 6
G. L. Lorrillard names b c Magnate, by Glenelg, dam Minx, 88 pounds.......(Brennan) 7
John Kay names ch f Caramel, by Monarchist, dam Bon Bon, 80 pounds.......(Greenhouse) 8
J. R. Keene names b f Palmetto, by Virgil, dam Squeeze 'Em, 83 pounds.......(Cunningham) 9
J. Carter & Co. name b f Bridesmaid, by Bonnie Scotland, dam Miss Austine, 84 pounds.......(Harrington) 10
A. Burnham names ch g Baron Feverot, by Bonnie Scotland, dam Lady Lindora, 93 pounds.......(Higgs) dr

Time—1:16½.

Gano was the favorite, selling in the pools for $100; Felicia and Magnate, $80 each; Vintage, $60; Pearl Thorne, $40; the field, $120. In the betting there was 7 to 2 against Gano, 5 to 1 each against Vintage and Felicia, 6 to 1 against Magnate, 8 to 1 against Pearl Thorne and Adalgisa, 10 to 1 against Lizzie Mc, 12 to 1 against Palmetto, 20 to 1 against Caramel and 30 to 1 against Bridesmaid. The mutuals paid $17 70.

Vintage was the first away, Bridesmaid second, Palmetto third, Magnate fourth, Felicia fifth, Gano sixth, Adalgisa seventh, Pearl Thorne, Caramel and Lizzie Mc being far in the rear. Going down the back stretch to the three furlong pole Palmetto lead by a head, Vintage second, two lengths in front of Felicia, Bridesmaid fourth, Magnate fifth, the others following as best they could. At the half-mile pole Vintage led half a length, Palmetto second, a length in front of Felicia, third, she a length and a half in front of Magnate, Gano fifth, Bridesmaid sixth, Pearl Thorne seventh, Lizzie Mc eighth, Caramel ninth, Adalgisa tenth. A change of positions rapidly occurred on the lower turn, and as the youngsters passed the three-quarter pole Gano was leading a length, Felicia second, half a length in front of Magnate, Vintage fourth, Pearl Thorne fifth, the others close up. From that place to the stand Gano had nothing to do but gallop home an easy winner by two lengths, Lizzie Mc second, four lengths in front of Felicia, third, Adalgisa fourth, Pearl Thorne fifth, Vintage sixth, Magnate seventh, Caramel eighth, Palmetto ninth, Bridesmaid tenth. Baron Faverot did not start. Time, 1:16½.

A Handicap Sweepstake of $30 each, half forfeit, for three-year-olds, with $600 added; the second to receive $150 out of the stakes. One mile and a half.

P. Lorillard names ch c Herbert, by Glenelg, dam Kate Mattingly, 105 pounds.......(W. Donahue) 1
A. Burnham names b g Frankey B, by Monarchist, dam Alala, 105 pounds.......(Higgs) 2
Dwyer & Brother name b g Blenheim, by Billet, dam Keno, 90 pounds.......(Sheridan) 3
G. L. Lorillard names ch c Volusia, by Pat Malloy, dam Vandalia, 90 pounds.......(Brennan) 4
D. Colaizzi names b f Laura Glass, by Buckden, dam On Time, 98 pounds.......(O'Leary) 5
Theo. Winters names b f Duchess of Norfolk, by Norfolk, dam Marion, 82 pounds.......(M. Donahue) 6

Time—2:39½.

Duchess of Norfolk was the favorite, selling in the pools for $460; Herbert, $240; Frankey B, $80; Blenheim, $60; the field, $90. In the books there were six to five against Duchess of Norfolk, five to two against Herbert, seven to one against Laura Glass, eight to one each against Frank B and Blenheim, and ten to one against Volusia. The mutuals paid $15 70.

Duchess of Norfolk led to a scattering start, Frankey B. second, Volusia third, Laura Glass fourth, Blenheim fifth, Herbert sixth. When the horses passed the three-quarter pole Blenheim and Duchess of Norfolk were running head and head half a length in front of Frankey B third, half a head in front of Laura Glass fourth, Herbert fifth, Volusia sixth. When the horses passed the judges' stand Blenheim led by a head, Duchess of Norfolk second, one length in front of Frankey B, Laura Glass fourth, Herbert fifth, Volusia sixth. Duchess of Norfolk led around the upper turn by a neck and passed the quarter pole half a length in front of Blenheim, the latter three lengths in advance of Frankey B, he one length ahead of Herbert, fourth; the latter three lengths in advance of Laura Glass, she three lengths ahead of Volusia, who was indulging in his usual game of sulks. Duchess of Norfolk showed the way down the backstretch and led a length at the half-mile pole. Blenheim second, two lengths in front of Frankey B; Herbert fourth, Volusia fifth, Laura Glass, sixth. Going around the lower turn Duchess of Norfolk had half a length the best of it, Frankey B and Herbert side and side, second and third, the others following some distance away. Getting into the homestretch Herbert on the outside passed Duchess of Norfolk at the seven-furlong pole, and led a trifle at the foot of the grand stand, where the Duchess of Norfolk, being whipped, swerved in on Herbert, fouling him and knocking him out of his stride, and coming on she passed the judges' stand a length in front of Herbert. The judges were unanimous in giving the race to Herbert and placing Duchess of Norfolk last in the race. The judges placed Herbert first, Frankey B second, Blenheim third, Volnsia fourth, Laura Glass fifth and Duchess of Norfolk sixth. Time 2:39½.

## The Oregon Cup.

SUMMARY.

SALEM, Sept. 22.—The Oregon cup, of $1,000 value, for all ages, first horse $700, second $200, third $100. Two and a quarter miles.

Cy. Mulky names br c Billy Coombs, by Shannon, out of Ruth Ryan, by Lodi, 4 yrs. 108 lbs....... 1
Foster Bros. names ch h Connor, by Norfolk, 5 years, 114 lbs....... 2
Jerome Porters names ch m Trade Dollar, by Norfolk, 5 years, 114 lbs....... 3

The time by quarters was as follows:

| | |
|---|---|
| First quarter | :27 |
| Half mile | :55½ |
| Three quarters | 1:23 |
| One mile | 1:50½ |
| Mile and a quarter | 2:17 |
| Mile and a half | 2:45½ |
| Mile and three-quarters | 3:12½ |
| Two miles | 3:41 |
| Two and a quarter miles | 4:09 |

The horses walked to the saddling post and were stripped off to the view of a handful of admirers. The mellow Septemper sun fell upon their satin-like coats with a glow of impartial tenderness, as Trade Dollar pranced about in her gleam of golden chestnut, while Connor's rich bronze made a still further contrast with the rare rosewood tint of the Idaho colt. In the meantime ten thousand people were crowding into the grand stand and awaiting the signal for an event which would change the ownership of ten thousand dollars in less than five minutes.

William Bigham, of Spokane Falls, had been chosen as starter, and he got the horses in place just before 2 o'clock. Taking his flag in hand, he said, "move up now, boys," and the gallant steeds cantered up to the score. Seeing they were all under full headway, he threw down the flag with Coombs about twenty feet behind the other two. Trade Dollar took the lead at once, hotly pursued by Connor, while young Smith took his colt well in hand and prepared for a waiting race. As they came by the stand a volley of cheers went up from the crowd. "Trade Dollar forever," cried a Walla Walla man. "Look at the old cock with the specks, how he's hoofin' it," said a southern Oregon man. The real winner glided along behind them with strong but stealthy stride. The other two boys were laying back and pulling while Louis sat perfectly upright, but it was the great strong neck of the big colt that pulled him into this position. Connor's white nose began to show in front of the mare as they passed the quarter pole, and half a mile of the Journey was over. Still the daughter of Norfolk stubbornly contested every inch of the ground with him while the brown colt was fighting for the bit behind them. Louis had pulled in close to the fence and was running as short a race as possible. At the half-mile pole the old horse was still in front, yet Trade Dollar did not yield but kept on his shoulder with unflinching gameness. Just as they reached the three-quarter pole from which they had started, Connor let in a ray of daylight between them, but the mare moved up again and he was unable to take the track from her until half way down the stretch. A roar of enthusiasm went up as Connor ran by the stand a length ahead of the mare, while Coombs was now so close on her heels that he looked fit to cut her down. Away they go around the turn and Louis gives the colt his head. Now he leaps ahead amid loud cheers and laps Trade Dollar. She falls back badly cramped, and the colt now goes up to the old white-faced stud. Cooper calls on Connor and the old horse puts forth another effort although his game leg is beginning to pain him. As they go up the backstretch for the last time there is an effort to do or die. Coombs forges ahead, inch by inch, with his stealthy, insidious stride. He is at Connor's saddle, now on his neck at the half-mile pole, a mile and three-quarters gone, and now they are preparing to round the bend. Cooper is urging his horse quietly all the time while outside of him strides along the dark specter, ridden by the purple Jacket. They are out of the straight run and rounding the bend. Smith shakes up the big colt and quick as a flash he is in front far enough to take the track. As he hugs the fence closely he casts a glance over his shoulder and sees Connor in terrible distress. The game leg has gone by the board at last, and Trade Dollar, badly cramped, has rallied again for the final effort. Poor old Connor, game and true, staggers home like a drunken man, under the sharp lash of Cooper's whip, but the trick is done and the race is out and gone. Billy Coombs has won it in 4:09, having cantered home all through the last quarter. An analysis of the race by quarters, given below, will show that it was ridden with admirable judgment was one not remarkable for any great burst of speed. But the rating was superb and nicely calculated for a victory without distressing the horse. Coombs blew out finely and was fit to run again at the end of twenty minutes, while Trade Dollar was terribly distressed. Connor's tendons had sprung so as to preclude all hope of his ever participating in another contest.

Seldom has a race been run, in Oregon or anywhere else, where there was so much good feeling exhibited and so much of that genuine love of fair play which should animate every contest of this kind. Men must run to win reputation as well as money, and to accomplish that end the best horse must be allowed to win. That such was the result of Friday's race no sane man could doubt. True it is that Connor has a faster record than that of this race, but it was evident to the eye of the greatest novice in racing that Coombs won with plenty to spare and that, when occasion may require it, he will be able to beat the record of this race by a handsome margin. Praises from fair lips greeted the conquerer whose gaily dressed jockey rode him off in triumph, while a few of more tender nature lingered to gaze upon the great white-legged chestnut whose sun had set forever. He had fallen like Boabdil on his shield, never to rise again. Never again will the silken jacket gleam above his burnished hide; never again will the prick of steel make its mute appeal to his heart of oak; but future generations of high-mettled racers, foaled under the balmy skies of the far-off Modoc land, shall proudly own him as their sire and bear his owners' colors to fame and victory. The game old mare was taken with cramps about a mile and a quarter out in the race, and when she came out she was jumping straight up and down, as horses do in that condition. Buchanan handled her very carefully, after the race, and she was soon feeling a good deal better. This mare will probably be retired from the turf next spring, and bred to Glen Dudly or Old Lodi. The breeders of our State can now see what they lost when they let the sire of Billy Coombs go back to California, for he was offered for $800 at Salem. Gov. Stanford owns him now, and would not take five times that amount for him.—*Portland Oregonian.*

## YACHTING.

### The Mosquito Race.

The regatta last Saturday under the auspices of the San Francisco Yacht Club for the small yachts of the bay was in every respect successful. There were a goodly number of entries, the wind was steady enough, the water smooth, and the day fine. A more good-humored crowd never competed in a regatta. The start was not as good and even as it was last year, owing to the boats not having been formed in lines according to class, but they generally got off well together, except the Chiquita, Skipper and Three Brothers, each of which started behind her class somewhat.

The Whitehall boats went off first, in pretty good style. They were as follows: Faugh-a-Ballagh, Dreadnaught, Pride of the Bay, Rough and Ready, Captain Bennett, Frank Ellison, Walk-along-John, Thos. Kendall, Unknown and Standby. Then the second class followed three minutes later, and so on untill all five classes were sailing along, the rear being brought up by the Italian fisherman's boat. Pretty soon the whole fleet was off, and being joined by a lot of big yachts a very picturesque sight was presented. Among the other yachts out were the Casco, with a large Oakland party aboard; the Lillie, Emerald, Startled Fawn, Magic, Clara, Nellie, Ariel (schooner), and Frolic. The wind held steady all around the course and the boats generally were well sailed. The following table shows the results:

SECOND CLASS.

| Name. | Length. | Actual Time. | Corrected Time. |
|---|---|---|---|
| Lark............. | .19:5 | 1:48:13 | 1:27:34 |
| Con O'Connor......... | .16 | 1:08:57 | 1:37:27 |
| Squibob............ | .20 | 1:59:00 | 1:38:33 |
| Cora............... | .16 | 1:24:25 | 2:05:25 |
| Chiquita............ | .20 | 1:52:00 | 2:17:00 |
| Rooster............. | .17.6 | 2:05:10 | 2:07:53 |
| Triton............. | .19.8 | | |

THIRD CLASS.

| Name. | Length. | Actual Time. | Corrected Time. |
|---|---|---|---|
| Carrie.............. | .14 | | 1:12:06 |
| Fleetwing.......... | .14.11 | 1:22:05 | 1:12:06 |
| Blackbird........... | .13.9 | 1:27:08 | 1:13:52 |
| Belle.............. | .21.6 | 1:26:15 | 1:22:45 |
| Leslie Ethel........ | .20.64 | 1:27:42 | 1:44:12 |
| Skipper............ | .21.6 | 1:37:00 | 1:44:50 |
| Rush.............. | .20 | 2:12:00 | 2:12:30 |
| Shadow............ | .23.6 | | Withdrawn |

FOURTH CLASS.

| Name. | Length. | Actual Time. | Corrected Time. |
|---|---|---|---|
| Fawn.............. | .18.8 | 1:26:44 | 1:39:00 |
| "76"............... | .28.6 | 1:33:25 | 1:24:02 |
| Daisy............. | .17.8 | 1:42:36 | 1:22:40 |

FIFTH CLASS.

| Name. | Length. | Actual Time. | Corrected Time. |
|---|---|---|---|
| Thetis............ | .26.6 | 2:07:40 | 1:56:16 |
| Flirt............. | .22.2 | 2:09:03 | 2:07:33 |

SIXTH CLASS (FISHERMEN).

| Name. | Length. | Actual Time. | Corrected Time. |
|---|---|---|---|
| Shamrock.......... | .34.8 | | 1:36:43 |
| Three Brothers...... | .33.6 | 1:56:25 | 1:51:46 |
| John of Procida..... | .23.9 | 1:34:25 | 1:22:28 |
| Bottle Meyer....... | .23.8 | 1:34:30 | 1:22:16 |

FOR THE FLAG.

| Flag. | Length. | Actual Time. | Corrected Time. | Race. |
|---|---|---|---|---|
| Thetis............ | .26.6 | | 1:07:46 | 1 |
| Flirt............. | .22.2 | 1:59:12 | 1:11:12 | 2 |

The first race was composed of Whitehall boats. The first one in was the Captain Bennett, sailed by Mr. Fitzgerald. She started at 1:43 and got back at 3:07:55... This boat was built by O'Connell of North Beach. The second was Faugh-a-Ballagh, built by Twohig of South Beach and sailed by F. Fitzgerald, her owner. She came in at 3:11:35. The third was the John Kendall, sailed by Tommy Kendall. She started at 1:43 and got in at 3:15:45. Among the other boats in the race were a lot of New York built craft, but they were beaten by the home production.

The Lark won second class first prize, O'Connor second prize and Squibob third prize.

The Carrie won first honors in third class, Fleetwing second, Blackbird third, Belle fourth.

The Fawn took first prize in fourth class and the '76' took second.

The Thetis won the first prize in class five, and took the prize flag for fastest corrected time.

The Shamrock took first prize for fishermen's boats, Three Brothers second and John of Procida third.

Altogether the Mosquito race was a very successful one and will keep repeating.

AN INTERESTING CANOE.—Captain S. D. Kendall's canoe is a marvel in the matter of construction. He built the canoe himself, made the paddle, sails and oars, and has invented and constructed the best set of infolding outriggers that can be found in any light craft. The hull is constructed on the "up and down nailed carvel system." The smooth outside and inside, her shell being made of smooth streaks only one-half inch wide by one-fourth inch thick. These strips are nailed upon the light ribs, or timbers, and galvanized brads are driven perpendicularly through two strips and into the third streak below. These brads are three inches apart. The ribs are of red elm, set three inches apart. The deck, though only one-fourth of an inch in thickness, is, by this system of nailing, made so strong that a man weighing 175 pounds can stand and step about upon it. The keelson is ten inches wide and the inch in thickness, beveled from the keel to the thickness of the planking. Weight of canoe with oars, paddle, spars, sails, rudder and hatches, 100 pounds. This canoe is the last one of several built by this amateur canoeist, and there is an immense amount of work and thought represented in the details of a most interesting little craft which is appropriately named "Solid Comfort."

SMALL YACHTS HAVE RIGHTS.—The New York Forest and Stream says: The collision between the sloop Sagitta and the schooner Varema while working out of New Bedford harbor in company with the New York Y. C. fleet has not been correctly reported. Both were on starboard tack, the Sagitta leading and holding a closer wind. Varema overtook the sloop and finding that she could not weather, attempted to run her lee too late, poking her jibboom through Sagitta's mainsail, and causing other damage necessitating a vexatious delay for repairs. It is altogether too common for large vessels to ignore the rights of smaller yachts, in the belief that the latter will keep clear rather than risk collision. The rule of the road should be strictly observed as a matter of pride, to say nothing of the law. Too many skippers slightly assume the responsibility of disregarding the rules to save a little trouble. Ordinary considerations and courtesy should prompt large yachts to go through the lee of small ones, unless at undue risk or sacrifice to themselves.

The officers of the London, England, Cruising Club have decided to offer a prize to each member of the club as shall, in the opinion of the officers, have carried out the most enterprising, skillful and successful cruise of the season of 1892. In awarding the prize, regard will be had to the nature, size and accommodation of the yacht, boat or canoe, in which the cruise shall have been carried out, the method of camping or sleeping out, etc., so as to give an equal chance to the owners of small and large craft. Competitors must send in accounts of their cruises to the rear-commodore, signed with their names, before the 1st of November, 1882, and the winning cruise will be published as such in Hunt's Magazine.

Two gentlemen have left the Canoe Islands, Lake George, for an extended cruise bound for the Gulf of Mexico. They will haul over into Lake Champlain from Lake George, cruise to Whitehall, and follow the canal to Troy, on the Hudson River. Then they will cruise on the Erie canal westward to Buffalo on Lake Erie. The coast of Lake Erie will be worked as far as Cleveland, Ohio. From Cleveland the canoeists will proceed to Cincinnati, on the Ohio River. From Cincinnati they will descend the Ohio and Mississippi to New Orleans, and will cross that city to Lake Fontchartrain and the Gulf of Mexico. They will then continue along the coast eastward and southward until they have passed Cape Sable on the southwest end of Florida. If time permits the canoeists will push there explorations around the southern through Card's Sound and Biscay Bay to Cape Florida, and from that locality proceed northward on their homeward journey.

Hereshoff's high speed yacht Permalia seems to be doing pretty well. The Toronto Globe gives the following concerning a race with a fast lake steamer, Aug. 18. "The much-talked of race between the steamer City of Cleveland and the new yacht Permalia took place to-day. The run was made from the Star Island House to St. Clair, a distance of about twenty-seven miles, resulting in the Permalia beating the steamer nearly half a mile. The yacht is a grand success throughout, both in speed and comfort. There are prospects of another race next Thursday, on the down-trip of the Cleveland."

The first 40-ton cutter Annaeona may come to New York waters next season. She is 68 feet long, 11 feet 6 inches beam and 96 draught. Says Bell's Life: "The Annaeona, with a new bowsprit, took the Cowes Town Cup, and proved herself to be undoubtedly the best boat of her rig and size that ever answered the starting gun. Possibly Mr. Hedderwick may now put his last year's notion into shape, and take her to New York.

During the race the other day some of the big yachts were poorly handled. One very large yacht nearly ran over a small one. The small one, was in the race and the big one, not the small one was by the wind and the other one running free, and there was no excuse except very bad seamanship or extreme carelessness. The nearness of collision made the little fellow keep away and he lost nearly several minutes in the race.

An enterprising photographer took a set of instantaneous views of the mosquito race on Saturday. In addition to the small yachts, he obtained pictures of the Chispa, Clara and others all under way in a very good breeze. The picture shows 22 boats, all under sail at once and racing. The pictures of the fishermen's boats are particularly good.

Mr. Rogers' new cutter Bedouin is about complete, and will sail on a cruise next week. Without doubt, she is the finest yacht ever built in this country. It is probable, also, that she will be fast, as her rig is a very taunt one. The only drawback is her extreme draught, which will close to her many of our harbors.—Spirit of the Times.

The old steam yacht Hrisk, built for Ralston, has been overhauled, practically rebuilt, had new engines and boilers put in her, and now belongs to Captain Simpson. She has been tried and found to work well. She will go up the Coast before long.

## THE GUN.

### Game Preserves in the Marshes.

It is only within the past few years that such things as game preserves have been thought of in California, and even now they are mainly confined to the limited regions of the river marsh lands, and are few in number. The growth of the railroad system of the State and the improved facilities for sportsmen to get to hunting grounds has had the usual effect of increasing the number of hunters and decreasing the game. People fond of duck hunting find to their dismay when they reach a point where the railroad passes a good marsh that lots of people get off at the same station. On the marshes south of this city on both sides of the bay this remark is particularly applicable as any hunter knows.

The tule lands on the Sacramento and San Joaquin rivers, and the extensive marshes surrounding Suisun bay form the favorite resorts of our water fowl. Ducks of all varieties swarm there in the season, and some of them remain there to breed. Geese are abundant; in fact so much so as to be a nuisance. So many hunters from the city visit these marshes on Saturdays and Sundays as to scatter the game and frighten it off, or drive it over into the large bays.

A number of gentlemen fond of duck hunting have formed shooting clubs, leased tracts of land on these marshes or islands, and keep the ponds there for their own sport. They have a man in charge and ward off "pot hunters" and others who invade the premises.

As an illustration of how this sort of thing is done, when done in style, the example may be cited of the Teal Shooting Club, which is composed of a number of gentlemen of this city. This is our most wealthy club, has the best outfit and has the best ponds in the State.

Their preserve is in the Suisun marsh, where the railroad crosses Cordelia creek and the Frankhorn slough. They have what are known as the Frankhorn ponds. James Payne some years since leased this large tract and shot on it for the market. By and by it became so noted and so many people came there that he built and fitted up an ark and for a consideration gave hunters the privilege of shooting there. He furnished accommodations, "grub," boats and men, so the place soon became a favorite one to visit.

When the railroad was completed across the marsh from Benicia to Suisun a flag station called Teal was established for the accommodation of hunters. It is near by this station that the arks are kept.

The Teal Shooting Club bought from Payne his lease of these grounds for some $2,000, taking his ark, duck boats and outfit. The ark is 36x14 feet with three-foot guards around it. It has a dining-room, kitchen and storeroom, all neatly fitted up. They have had also a new ark built with a hull 36x16, with three-foot guards, and have fitted it up in fine style. In it there are eight staterooms, one for each member, with names on the doors, with wash-stands, hair mattresses, brussels carpets, etc. The commissary arrangements are all on the ark. They have also a third boat or ark, a scow about 36 feet long and 14 feet wide, which is occupied by the men.

James Payne manages the preserve and is paid $100 a month for his services. There are also two men to clean guns, take care of boats, row the gentlemen out to the blinds and do chores generally. They also have a Chinese cook and a Japanese steward. The table is set with silver and china as at home and everything is of the best. The club has invested some $5,000 in privileges, arks, boats, etc. It was organized August 30, 1882.—G. Frank Smith is president, W. F. Fuller commissary, W. F. Whittier treasurer and vice president, John Taylor secretary. The other members are W. S. Hopkins, H. C. Titcomb, W. W. Traylor and E. S. Floyd.

The marsh on which these yards are situated is a salt water one and has many fine ponds. It only takes about two hours to get to the shooting grounds from this city.

Thus far no very big strings of game have been taken in these marshes as it is too early, yet. The largest string by any one of this club in the opening of the season was 36. The ponds have been baited and when the rains come good sport is expected. It will be seen by what we have said that systematic preserving of hunting grounds is carried out here on a scale which insures good sport for those fortunate enough to belong to the clubs which maintain preserves.

### Costly Sport in Scotland.

An "intending offerer" must decide first on the rent he proposes to pay, next what kinds of games he wants to shoot, whether he desires to fish, and if so, salmon or trout or both; then as to the accommodation he will require at the lodge. Rents vary from £100 up to £5,000. Small places will afford plenty of amusement, and even if the bag is not large there are the pleasure and benefits of entire change of air, scene and mode of life. But nothing can be got under £400 if plenty of sport is desired, and to the rental must be added wages of keepers and gillies. If both deer and grouse are necessary, a rental of at least £1,000 will have to be paid. Black Mounts Forest, in Argyleshire, which is leased by Lord Dudley from Lord Breadalbane, extends over 80,000 acres and affords every description of shooting and excellent loch fishing. It is offered at £3,000. Balmaacan, Lord Seafield's forest in Inverness-shire, has been rented to Sir Henry Allsopp (who rented Black Mount last season) at £3,000. It extends over 33,000 acres, and 50 stags may be counted out. There is also fine cover and mixed shooting over 12,000 acres. Moy (Sir John Ramsden's), on the shore of Loch Laggan, is let at £400, with 5,000 acres of moor, last year's bag being about 180 brace of grouse; but the lodge here is exceptionally good, and the fishing is capital. Lord Middleton's forest of Applecross, in Rosshire, which extends over nearly 60,000 acres, is let at £2,500. The six great sporting counties of Scotland contain over 8,000,000 acres of shooting ground. The shooting rentals of Inverness and Perth are each larger than was paid for the whole county at the commencement of the present century. Sir John Ramsden receives nearly £8,000 for his Badenoch shootings, retaining the great forest Ardverikie in his own hands. Sir G. Macpherson Grant receives £5,800 for the three forests in the same district, and Lord Seafield's rental exceeds £12,000. The principal shootings in Forfar belong to Lords Dalhousie and Airlie; the sporting rental of the former £6,000, and he keeps a large extent of ground in his own hands. Perhaps the finest "all around" sport in the country is obtained on the island of Arran, which belongs to the Duke of Hamilton, and is a vast game preserve. Shootings are usually let for four months, from the middle of July, but sport in the grouse moors ceases, as a rule, early in September, and although the season lasts till December 10, it is rarely that a lodge is inhabited after the beginning of October.—London Pall Mall Gazette.

AN EXCITING CHASE.—Jack Campbell, of Hot Springs Hotel, about forty miles from Reno, had a wild adventure recently, which came near winding up with a Coroner's inquest. He was riding over a very rough country, when a huge buck sprang up in the trail ahead of him, and started off at a flying gait. Jack slapped the steel to his animal and went in pursuit of the flying venison. Up hill and down dale they went—through brush and across creeks—until they came to the edge of a very steep precipice, where the buck halted for a second, as if dismayed by the deep chasm before him. That lost second cost him his life, as Jack came upon him and flung a lasso over his horns. Before his horse could get his balance and brace himself, the buck jumped over the bluff and down into the ravine went the whole party. Stunned for an instant, they picked themselves up and the scene began. The infuriated buck charged upon Campbell, who was tied up in the lasso, but he managed to get a good hold of the animal's horns and protect himself from serious injury until he got out of the snarl, when he jumped upon his horse and dragged the deer to his feet. The well-trained vaquero-horse held the deer down while Jack cut his throat. Lon is Dean brought half of the animal to town, as evidence that Campbell told a straight story about the affair.—Sierra Tribune.

Every year from some section of the country or other we hear complaints from farmers of the carelessness of hunters. Gates are left open; poultry and cattle are shot—by intent as well as accident—worst of all is the carelessness with fire. Often a camp-fire is left burning, a strong wind arises and scatters the sparks, and in a short time acres of stubble, pasture or woodland are destroyed by the devouring elements. Every one knows how much damage to property and danger to life these fires are, and no true sportsman will abuse the privileges extended by the owners of property in the country. We hear complaint from Mr. R. R. Smith, who has a ranch on the Lower Sacramento road. For several years sportsmen have found good hunting grounds on Mr. Smith's property. Last year eight of his cows were shot, by hunters, and this year they have begun again by killing another. His stubble fields have been fired and he has been annoyed in many ways. Patience has at last ceased to be a virtue and Mr. Smith will prosecute any one found hunting on his premises without permission. There is game enough in the country and sport enough in hunting without damaging property or endangering life. We are confident that none of the members of any of the sporting clubs participate in this malicious mischief. We hope that there will be no more cause for complaints from the farmers in future.

The Butte Record has been informed by some of the crack hunters of Chico that game is not so plentiful around there this season, but sport is looked for further on. Some of the shooters went out the other day during the rain, but returned with very few ducks. With the quail hunters it was different. They got a reasonable number of quail, and also some doves. The hunters say it is too early in the season for duck shooting; that they have not come back to their winter resorts. The geese have been coming back slowly for the last few days; but they appear to be making their way to the great tules along the lower Sacramento.

## Trap Shooting in San Jose.

...embers of the San Jose Sportsmen's Club shot for the ...es offered by the Fair Association, last Wednesday morn...at the Fair grounds. The prizes were: first, gold medal; ...nd, silver medal; third; silver goblet. The shooting was ...ay pigeons; eighteen yards, rises to rule.

THE SCORE:

pluell..........................1 9 0 0 0 0 1 1 0 1 0 1 0 0 1 0 0 0 0—7
...............................1 9 1 1 1 1 0 0 0 1 1 0 1 1 0 0 1 0 0 0—11
...as...........................1 1 1 1 1 1 0 0 1 1 1 5 1 1 1 1 1 1 1—18
...ndall.........................1 1 1 0 0 1 1 0 0 1 1 1 1 1 1 1 1 1 1—16
...rdall.........................1 0 1 0 1 1 1 1 1 1 1 1 1 1 1 1 1 1—18
...os...........................1 1 6 1 * 1 1 1 6 1 0 1 0 1 0 1 1 0—13
...illes.........................1 1 1 1 * 1 1 1 1 1 0 0 1 1 1—16
...ale...........................1 1 1 1 0 1 1 1 1 1 1 1 1 1 1 1—17

*Foul cartridges.

...lles, Delmas and Coykendall shot off the tie of 18 at ten ...ds, picking the gun from the ground, with the following ...ult:

..............................1 1 0 1 1 1 1 1—9
...rkendall.....................0 1 1 1 0 0 1 1 1—7

Delmas was declared winner of the first prize and Coyken...l of the second.

For third prize Stern and Tisdale tied on 17, and they shot ...e birds, with the following result:

...rn.............................1 1 1 1—4
...dale..........................1 0 1 1 1—4

Stern was declared winner of the third prize.
Shipley, of Sacramento, and Coykendall also shot a match ...$10 a side, twenty clay pigeons, eighteen yards rise. ...ipley won with the following score:

...pley...........................1 1 1 1 1 1 1 1 1 1 1 1 1 1 1 1—20
...kendall........................1 1 1 1 1 1 1 1 1 0 1 1 1 1—19

S. J. Lank of Wells, Fargo & Co. and A. W. Davidson of ...kland left Alameda last week by team, for a hunting ex...rsion. They proceeded first to San Leandro and Haywards ...d then up the Castro Valley as far as Amador. At the lat-...place they found large numbers of quail and had their ...st shooting. From here the hunters went to Sunol and ...joyed some lively sport. The return was made by the ...n Jose Mission but there was but little game in sight in ...at vicinity. These gentlemen were out three days, of which ...e was occupied in traveling; in the other two days two ...undred quail were bagged and they were satisfied with their ...cursion.

A party composed of F. H. Putzman, J. Brovell, A. Hig-...ins, Mr. Stockpool, W. Golcher, J. J. O'Brien, R. Elion, ...r. Shorten and E. W. Blaney last week went out on a three ...ay's hunt near San Jose Mission. Like many others they ...und too little water but lots of game. The two ...tail are wild and stay in the gulches and heavy brush; the ...carcity of water, too, keeps the game back in the hills. As ...here has been no rain yet the weeds, especially tar weeds, ...re stiff and make it very hard for the dogs to work. For all ...the obstacles the party bagged 43 dozen quail.

A sportsman of considerable experience and observation ...ays: " I have always noticed before a rain storm that quail ...re very uneasy and hard to approach. They leave the low-...ands and open pastures and hide in the heaviest brush and ...imber; even in these retreats they are alarmed and fly on ...he approach of the hunter. They do not leave their hiding ...places until after the storm is past. I consider that, to one ...familiar) with game and their habits, quail are as good as ...a barometer, and attribute the poor bags made in the last few ...days to the presence of a rainstorm in the near future."

Mr. N. L. Kirk, who is superintending the construction ...of a new bridge in Butte county, has received a begu-...iful large pair of elk antlers to be used as an ornament for ...he bridge. These antlers are so large that, when placed on ...the floor, prongs down, an arch is formed almost large enough ...for a man to walk under. This is a new idea for ornament-...ng a bridge, but it is a good one.

Aside from game being very plentiful this year, we have ...cool and delightful weather which is very agreeable to hunt-...ing. The heavy dews that fall during the night leave the ...ground in good condition in the morning for the dogs to ...cent the game. The coolness of the weather permits of the ...transportation of game to the markets from distant parts of ...the country.

Several flocks of canvasbacks have made their appearance ...at the marshes along the rivers. This is something unusual ...as they seldom come in before the first rains. The early ap-...pearance of migratory birds seems, as many think, an indi-...cation of an early or else a very wet winter.

Deer, grouse and quail are very abundant at Lake Taho...e. The loggers at the logging camps feast to their hearts' con-...tent on grouse and quail, but so far no deer has been killed, ...although numbers of them have been seen. The trout are ...not biting well now, although a few are being caught.

A gentleman, Mr. Bender, was down near San Mateo last ...Sunday and bagged eighteen quail and several rabbits. ...Along the line of the S. F. R. R., within a day's ride of San ...Francisco, game is not so plentiful as it was expected it ...would be earlier in the season.

Last week Thomas Lawson, while hunting near Avon ...station, shot twelve mallard ducks and a pelican in two shots ...from his gun. In the pelican's crook was found twelve fish. ...This is the last "fish story."

The birds are not very plentiful yet up in the marshes. ...Although none have come in to light, a few geese have been ...seen. Most of the ducks are young ones bred in the marsh. ...They are mainly mallard and teal.

H. A. Wilson went to Millbrae last Sunday and had good ...luck. The day was very warm and the quail stayed in the ...shade so that it was hard to get many good shots.

A good many mosquitoes yet up in the marshes. More ...plentiful than ducks. They not so far away before next ...month, when the ducks will come.

A buck was shipped to this city from Cloverdale last Tues-...day that tipped the beam at 155 pounds. He was killed at ...the Fairbanks place near Anderson valley.

Sportsmen from Marysville report an abundance of ducks ...and geese in the Sacramento tules. The present cool weather ...is very favorable for shooting.

A California lion, measuring nine feet two inches from the ...end of his nose to the tip of his tail, was killed recently in ...San Luis Obispo county.

H. C. Golcher and D. Berdwick bagged thirty-six quail near ...San Mateo last Sunday. The shooting in that vicinity is not ...of the best.

---

Mr. R. Liddle was hunting near Saucelito last week and ...says there are too many hunters to allow very good bags being ...made.

There is a good deal of style up in the marshes now-a-days ...where the shooting clubs have their arks.

The Cordelia Shooting Club boys only got 12 to 20 birds ...apiece on the opening of the season.

Those fond of water fowl hunting are anxiously waiting for ...the first rains.

Hawking is once more becoming fashionable in England.

## THE RIFLE.

### Close of the Fall Meeting at Creedmoor.

There were three events contested at Creedmoor yesterday ...—the last of the list, and which were to close the fall meet-...ing. They were the Military Championship, the Continuous ...and the Consolation matches in their final stages. The two ...former included a large number of entries and the scores are so ...completely mixed that it will require at least two days to put ...them into such a shape as to determine the winners. They ...will be announced as soon as known. Great interest was ...centered in the Military Championship match, as it was ...known that two of the competitors, Mr. W. M. Farrow, of ...the Newport Artillery, and Col. E. B. Sanford, of the First ...Division, New York staff, were to use British rifles in the ...match, and test for themselves the superior qualities claimed ...for the weapons by the English. Mr. Farrow purchased his ...from R: McVittie, and Colonel Sanford's was the property of ...Sir Henry Halford. Both weapons were used in the inter-...national match. The result of the shooting yesterday justi-...fied the Englishmen, and left the question almost beyond ...doubt that the weapons are the best in present use for long-...distance shooting and superior to the American gun. Both ...gentlemen express satisfaction with them. Mr. Farrow won ...the match; making 84 out of a possible 105, with J. M. Pol-...lard of the American team second, and Colonel Sanford third. ...Under the conditions, it was open to the highest 60 in the ...first stage, the competitors to shoot seven rounds each over ...the 800, 900 and 1000 yards ranges, using any military ...weapon that has been adopted by any national or state gov-...ernment. There were only nine entries, although there were ...ten prizes. The tenth prize reverts to the National Rifle ...Association. The winner holds the title of Military Cham-...pion of the United States for one year, and besides becoming ...the owner of the $50 gold badge receives $25 in cash. The ...remaining prizes are in cash, the second being $20, the third, ...fourth and fifth $10, and the remainder $5 each.

SANTA ROSA, September 25, 1881.
EDITOR BREEDER AND SPORTSMAN: Your excellent paper ...comes regularly, but you do not afford in your account this ...week of the International Rifle Match, a most useful piece of ...information—viz., what sort of guns were used by the re-...spective teams. Every daily paper gives me a telegram to ...the effect that Sir Henry Halford asserted that the Americans ...lost, because their rifles were inferior to the British guns, but ...not one vouchsafes to tell us anything about the guns. The ...matter is of very great interest and even importance. The ...''Britishers'' have heretofore used a muzzle loading rifle ...made in Dublin—I think by Reilly—but as we have hither-...to beaten them it was supposed that the American breech-...loaders led the van. If our breech-loaders have lost their ...prestige or the British have invented better guns, riflemen ...in this country would like to know it. Can't you give the ...desired information in your next?

Very Respectfully, E. J. WHIPPLE.

In answer to the above questions we will say that the rifles ...used by both teams were admissible under the conditions de-...fining a military weapon, but in reality they were, as we are ...informed, the long range or small bore sporting barrels with ...only military stocks and mountings. The rifles used in the ...International match were a class of arms not in use by any ...organized military company. Ten members of the British ...team used the breech-loading Metford rifle, and two of the...short Webley's patent. They use a 540-grain bullet, having a ...charge of from 75 to 85 grains of powder. The Americans ...had nine Hepburn-Remington guns of .44 caliber among ...them, chambered for a .40 caliber shell, and two Sharps' ...Borchard's .45-caliber, with one Hotchkiss repeater. The ...English guns were of .45 caliber, the same as the Metford-...Henry, which is now the regulation weapon of the British ...service.

In regard to Sir Henry Halford attributing the victory to ...the superiority of weapons used by the English, he might ...justly have added that it was the superiority of the men as ...well. It is to be hoped that should the English and Ameri-...cans ever compete again, with the rifle, for honors or prizes, ...the Americans will send out their best arms and best ...trained men instead of their second-class. We have as good ...sharpshooters and as good rifles as any in the world and the ...last defeat of the American team will be a lesson not soon ...forgot.

THE RIFLE TEAMS AT WEST POINT.—The British and ...American rifle teams made an excursion to West Point last ...Monday, by invitation of the American Rifle Association, on ...the steamer Nelson T. Hopkins. A stay of three hours was ...made at West Point. At the wharf the riflemen were met by ...Lieut. Gilmore, and at the adjutant's office they were intro-...duced to the Commandant, General Merritt. After a stroll ...over the grounds the visitors witnessed a battalion drill by ...the cadets, which was followed by a dress parade. Colonel ...Walrond left the party at West Point, and will proceed to ...Winnipeg to engage in deer-hunting. He will sail for Europe ...October 26.

A farmer in the vicinity of Creedmoor was observed in the ...act of driving his sheep into the barn for safety last week, and ...when asked by a neighbor why he confined his flock at such ...an hour, replied significantly: " I hear that the American ...riflemen are going to practice this afternoon."

The Thirteenth Regiment, N. G. S. N. Y., gave a grand ...military review, followed by a festival and concert in honor ...of the British and American rifle teams, at Manhattan Beach, ...last Monday evening.

Sir Henry Halford and some of the members of the British ...military rifle team sailed last Tuesday from New York for ...England.

General Phil Sherman and party have returned home from ...a hunting trip in the Yellowstone country, and report a pleas-...ant and successful hunt.

---

## THE KENNEL.

### Gilroy Field Trials.

The date set for running the Gilroy field trials has been ...postponed until Monday, November 27th. This was done ...at the request of a number of gentlemen who have dogs en-...tered and who found that the extra time was needed to en-...able them to give the requisite training. We want to see the ...sportsmen of the State put their shoulders to the wheel and ...make these trials a grand success. To lend a helping hand ...will cost but a little trouble and that will be repaid ...by the pleasure of seeing the trials run and the satisfaction ...or knowing that one is helping along an exhibition that will ...eventually redound to the benefit of every sportsman in the ...State. There is no need to tell the experienced shooter the ...advantage of field trials but gentlemen who are just begin-...ning to shoot and own a dog might ask "of what benefit to ...me can these trials be?" The answer is that they will teach ...much that all sportsmen should know about the handling of ...dogs in the field and further by making the business of breed-...ing setters and pointers more profitable than it is at present ...they will add to the number of those who engage in it and ...make well broken dogs more easy to get than they are at ...present. They will also teach which is the breed and strain ...of dogs best adapted to quail hunting in this State, a ques-...tion that is by no means definitely settled as yet. The first ...and even the second year may not tell much but if a certain ...strain of dogs win at these trials several years in succession ...t will be a rational conclusion to arrive at that such strain is ...the best for California. Then again the trials will win over ...many a proselyte to the sportsman's creed. As well adver-...tised public exhibitions they will attract many persons who ...otherwise would never think of going to see how a brace of ...dogs work on game and these who are a first mere specta-...tors will, by degrees, come within the reach of that spell ...which all field sports throw around their votaries and once ...within that potent influence they may be numbered among ...the glorious ranks of sportsmen. A few selfish people may ...say that there are enough shooters already to kill all the ...game accessible to city folks, but, as every sportsman is also ...a game preserver, it is fair to conclude that the newaddi-...tions to the ranks will earn their game in advance by ...furthering the cause of game protection which is sadly ...in need of their help. Of the delights of attending a well ...managed field trial those who have been there never weary ; f ...telling. It is not given to every man who has the desire to ...own a good dog, but next to the enjoyment of seeing one's ...own dog work is the pleasure of seeing the skill of another's. ...What can be finer on a pleasant day, such as Gilroy always ...has in October, than to stand and watch a finely broken pair ...of pointers, quartering their ground. Their pace is almost ...as fast as a pair of racers till the keen scent warns one or ...the other the game is near. Then the attitude of a ''point'' ...finer than the grandest conception of artist or sculptor gives ...rare delight to the spectator. Every hair on the dog was ...rigid and every limb as motionless as though he was sud-...denly turned to stone. His companion backs him softly and ...there they stand, a sight for the gods to gaze on until, a mo-...tion from the handler orders the leading dog to move up to ...his game. How cautiously he works ahead and how wist-...fully the other looks if ordered to ''charge'' or remain still. ...Soon the bird is flushed and brought down by a skillful ...shot. The well-trained animal ''drops'' and crouches on the ...ground as though driven into the earth and awaits the ...command to ''go fetch.'' How joyfully this order is obeyed ...and how demurely his companion awaits its instructions to ...come to heel or go look for fresh game. The delights with ...which the dead or wounded bird is handled is a triumph of ...the trainer's art. Not a feather misplaced or crushed, not a ...mark to tell that the bird when laid in the shooters' hand ...has ever been between the cruel jaws of a dog. No pen can ...tell the delights of witnessing man's control of the lower ...animals and the animal's intelligence when well trained. ...To be felt it needs be seen and we advise all who can spare ...the time to put aside all other enjoyments and make it their ...business to be present at the Gilroy field trials.

### Pioneer Coursing Club.

For some time past the Pioneer Coursing Club of San ...Francisco has not held its regular monthly meetings and an ...impression has gone abroad that the club is defunct. This ...is not the case though it is true that the members are rather ...scattered at the present time and do not show as much en-...thusiasm in the sport as was their wont a few years ago. In ...all probability the club will hold a meeting this fall as has ...been the custom for many years past but owing to many dis-...couraging circumstances it will be necessary to make the ...match an open one. Of those who a few years ago made the ...club the leader in coursing in this State but few are left in ...San Francisco. Tom Tconstead is away as well as Wilson ...Davidson the energetic secretary and perhaps the best slip-...per that ever loosed a pair of dogs in America. P. Lynan ...has made his home in Sacramento where he is an authority ...on the sport and is organizing a club that will be a credit to ...the capital city. Poor old Captain Plaice, one of the great-...est lovers of the leash this State has ever seen, is dead though ...not forgotten, and pups that he reared, now grown up into ...old dogs, are making his name remembered wherever there ...is a coursing match held in this State. Sam Jones, of Stock-...ton, Matkew Jones, of Merced and Paul Jones, of San Fran-...cisco, were among the last litter the kindly old gentle-...man raised and all have done well in the field. Many of ...the past twelve months, Mat Curry is not breeding any ...dogs now though when the club comes together ...again he will doubtless be on hand to lend tone to ...the sport. James Adams has had no worthy representatives ...in the field since Ruler beat Milnethaha after the game little ...bitch had won three years in succession. He had to succumb ...next year to Dr. Mearns' Monarch, a splendid son of Frank-...lin's old blue dog, who would have won many more laurels ...for the doctor had not a sudden and violent death ended his ...career. Dr. Mearns has not been at a meeting since Mon-...arch's death though he has nearly always a dog or two ...entered in his name. Dr. Sharkey has cast in his dog with ...one of the younger clubs, and so has Judge Frazie and ...Franklin and W. Ryan and Douglas and Berry and Carroll ...and many more of the old guard whose names do not readily ...come to mind. Of those who are left of the old Pioneer ...club, J. Adams, Glen Dixon and N. Curry are the best known ...and whether they have enough energy left to bring back the ...club to its pristine vigor is a question which time alone can ...answer. For our part we rather think that with the infusion ...of a little fresh blood the old club will once again take its ...place as California Coursing Club No. 1.

There are dogs and dogs and no end of dogs but not all ...either useful, beautiful or desirable. A few days ago a firm ...of theatrical managers in New York advertised for a Ne...

poundland dog to appear in a new play, and the next morning Booth's Theater was besieged and the streets blockaded by a crowd of about five hundred persons with every description of dogs, from the microscopical black and tan to the gigantic mastiff.

## Eastern Field Trials.

The following description of the closing heat of the Western field trials run at Fairmont, September 12, is from the *New York Herald*. For a piece of concise descriptive writing it could hardly be excelled: "The first brace put down were Gertrude and Frank H to finish the undecided of Saturday. Frank ran wild and did not obey with any promptness, nor was his nose in good order, so that Gertrude who is superior in speed and quartering, had him beaten by two points, according to the judge's books, without retrieving which it seems she will not do. Five minutes, rest was given, and then Gertrude and Sue were put down together. They are evenly matched in size, but Gertrude outstyled Sue, who, however, has a trifle more speed and ranges better. There is not much choice between them in quartering, but when it came down to finding birds and pointing them, stanching without flushes, then Sue had it her own way and won easily. Gertrude made three bad flushes and only got one good point, while Sue got four.

Dan and Sue were then put down after a brief interval of fifteen minutes. Both went off with equal speed, but Dan almost instantly got down to business. Casting into a stubble field he struck a stylish point, turned, roaded some distance down wind and flushed three birds just as he straightened out stiff. He dropped to wing. Ranging on he came to a stanch point, and his handler approaching, he roaded steadily down wind for some sixty yards and found his bird, which was missed. This was very fine work. Getting into a stubble field both dogs quartered beautifully and ranged wide, doing the prettiest work of the day. Moving on to another stubble Sue made a very fine point and then flushed the covey; both dropped to wing. Dan then ranged ahead and got a long point at a covey away up wind which flushed wild as the wagon approached. Dan again pointed, going up a ridge side, but no bird was found, though an old cock flushed wild to the right. Dan and Sue, the former some ten yards to the rear, dropped instantaneously. Ordered on Dan began to road and Sue to quarter and this she did ahead of him as he roaded till she flushed the birds. Moving into long grass Sue flushed a single bird and Dan won. He is an imported liver and white pointer dog, by Price's Bang, out of Fern, a stoutly built tremendously muscled dog of fine nose and wonderful stanchness and perseverance. Every one is satisfied that the best dog won. Mr. Vandervoorts handles his dog as if he knew he had a good one and intended he should work out his own success."

# HERD AND SWINE.

## Fitting Cattle for Sale.

Breeders are in the habit of feeding their young bulls pretty heavy, making them fat, if they can, because few men are well enough versed in fine-bred cattle to enable them to judge of the merits of an animal, young or old, upon his record and points, unless the points are points of fat. A man who has learned cattle thoroughly can safely trust himself to buy an animal thin in flesh, provided he can learn of the ancestry, and has the pedigree before him. But the inexperienced buyer will take the fat bull or heifer with many faults covered, or at least obscured by fat, and leave the meritorious one standing in the stall, because not so fat and sleek as the other.

That excessive efforts have been made to fit animals for sale, to the detriment of their breeding qualities, we well know. But fitting within reasonable limits is warrantable, because buyers require animals to be attractive to the eye. The merchant places his goods in the most attractive shape, to insure a sale and in doing so merely carries out the common practice in all lines of business. The man having a lot of horses or mules to sell feeds them up to a state of fatness. Common custom grants this privilege, and no exceptions are taken. Therefore, if the novice is unable to judge of what he regards as merit, the beast being thin or in moderate flesh only, he had better secure the services of some one better informed than himself. He employs the shoemaker or tailor to make his boots and coat, simply because they are lines of business he acknowledges ignorance of, but he blunders ahead and buys animals that are in no wise suitable to be used as breeders. The coat and boots wear out, causing no waste, while the indiscreet purchase in the matter of the breeding animal may leave the impress of his imperfections upon every young thing of his kind on the farm. And the impress he leaves is very hard to overcome.

Tendency to grow into good shape is inherent in all animals that have been bred under proper rules, and this tendency shows itself to the practiced eye, no matter what the state of keeping. So in fitting for sale, whether public or private, the breeder it he fattens his animals does so to meet the demand of an average customer, who, as stated, will turn from the premises of the breeder that shows meritorious animals in moderate flesh to those of the man who fattens his inferior beast up to the point best calculated to captivate the novice.

Now if, under this rule of practice, the buyer gets encumbered with animals who fail to produce, he has no right to reflect upon anyone but himself, much less to bring the seller into court—we have mentioned a rule of law which contemplates that the buyer shall use due diligence, keeping his eyes open, and if there is any outward defect he is presumed to have discovered it.

Excessive and harmful fatness is a condition entirely apparent, and the man who is induced to buy on account of the animal being fat should clearly not turn his back upon the condition he has imposed, even though it entail a measure of disaster. There is a lesson to the progressive man in a shoddy coat. This lesson costs but a trifle compared to those which many a man has been called upon to encounter during a considerable portion of his early career as a breeder. The fruits of errors made in establishing a herd or flock do not wear out at the end of a year, but multiply and disappoint the owner.

It may be argued that we have no evidence that a given animal will fatten in a becoming manner until this evidence is seen through the accumulation of fat upon its back. Such an argument can have no force before accumulated facts, and the man who is governed by such a proposition unwittingly ignores an inflexible law—heredity—and pays, in many cases, a dollar a pound for flesh that has cost a twentieth part of this sum to put on, and is worth far less, practically, than a like number of pounds of flesh upon the steer intended for slaughter.—*National Live Stock Journal.*

---

## The Turf in Greeneville.

RENO, Sept. 25, 1882.

EDITOR BREEDER AND SPORTSMAN: You will see by this that I am some distance from home and as there was no correspondent of your paper in Greeneville I took the liberty of sending you the result of the fair. At the pavilion the last two days' attendance was very slim but increased so that the close was fully up to previous seasons. There were some very fine displays. Notably the ladies department which showed they took a lively interest in the success of the exhibition, the judges of the week were Messrs. Thomson, Hargraves and Flournoy. Track very heavy.

SUMMARIES.

GREENVILLE, CAL., September 19.—Postponed from 18th, on account of bad weather. Trotting, mile heats, three in five, 2:36 class, three or more to start; two or more to start.

Roanoke......................................................... 1 1 1

Time—2:46½, 2:46½, 2:47½.

Same day—Trotting, two-year-olds, heats of a mile.

G f Mollie.......................................................... 1 1
J f Jesse Bell........................................................ 2 2

Time—2:57, 2:58.

Same day—Free for all, three minute class, three in, five mile heats; purse $150.

Charles Sherman names b g Ray Scilly............................. 1 1
Mr. Kingsbury names b m Mollie Burns.............................dist

Time—2:38.

Same day—Running, three in five, mile heats, purse $200 of which $150 to first, $80 to second, $20 to third.

J. Dyson names Snuff Box.............................................. 2 2 1
D. D. Nieman names Overland Pat...................................... 1 1 2
J. Gray names Red Light............................................distanced.

Time last given.

Same day—Dash of half mile, purse $80, $40 to first $12 to second.

D. D. Nieman names Ross Bollinger................................... 2 2 1
W. C. Cole names ch m Nellie Burns................................... 1 1 2
Sam Gowen b f names blk m Lillie Odell............................... 3 3 3
D. D. Monroe names b m Nellie G....................................
J. Dyson names g g Summit............................................ 4

Time—50s.

September 20th, purse $300 a side, dash of half mile.

W. C. Cole names ch m Nellie Burns................................... 1 1
Sam Gowen b f names blk b g Headlight................................ 2 2

Time—52s.

Same day—Two-thirty class, mile heats, three in five, purse $250.

Charles Sherman names b g Carlisle.................................... 2 1 1
Mr. Kingsbury names b m Mollie Spencer.............................. 1 3 3

Time—2:50, 2:45½, 2:39½, 2:32½, 2:39.

Same day—Running, mile heat, two in three, purse $200.

W. C. Cole names ch m Nellie Burns................................... 1 1
D. D. Nieman names b m Ross Bollinger............................... 2 2
J. Dyson names b m Snuff Box......................................... 3 3

Time—52s.

Same day—Two mile dash, double teams, purse $250.

Charles Sherman names Moench and mate.............................. 1 1
Charles Lawrence names William Tell and mate...................... 2 2

Time—7:54.

September 21.—Trotting, mile heats, three in five, purse $150.

Charles Sherman names Roanoke....................................... 2 1 1 1
Charles Lawrence names Plow Boy...................................... 1 2 2 2
Mr. Kingsbury names Mollie Burns....................................dist

Time—2:35½, 2:40, 2:41, 2:45½.

Same day—Running, mile dash, purse $80.

Nellie Burns, 115lbs.................................................. 1
Snuff Box, 114lbs................................................... 2
Red Light, 111lbs.................................................. 3
Ross Bollinger, 111 lbs............................................

Time—1:52.

Same day—Running, dash one quarter mile, purse, $40, four starters, Nellie Burns.

Time—26½ seconds.

Same day—One mile and repeat, double teams for horses that have never been hitched, purse, $60, mile heats $20, second $15.

B. S. Gray names General Lee and mate............................... 1 1
T. Barham names Gray Billy and mate................................. 2 2

Time—3:40, 3:45½, 3:50.

Same day—Free for all, trotting, mile heats, three in five, purse, $250, first horse $150, second $75, third $25.

T. Sprouls names b g Carlisle......................................... 2 0 1 1
K. T. Spence names b m Nellie Spencer............................... 1 2 2 2
C. Lawrence names g f William Tell.................................drawn.

Time—2:38½, 2:40½, 2:45½, 2:39, 2:35, 2:33.

Same day—Running, two mile heats, purse, $200 of which $150 to first horse, $50 to second.

D. D. Nieman names Overland Pat, 112lbs............................ 1 1
Sam Gowen J f names Red Light, 107lbs.............................. 2 2
Sam Ryan names L. Clark, 104lbs....................................dis

No heat given.

September 23, mile run—Match, double teams for $100 a side.

Mr. Barham names Gray Billy and mate............................... 1 1
B. Gray names General Lee and mate.................................. 2 2

Time—3:45.

Same day—One-quarter mile dash, purse $60.

Joe Dyson names b m Die West Mare................................... 1
Sam Gowen J f, names b g Red Light................................. 2

Time—24 seconds.

Same day—Match foot race, dash of a mile, between Blake and Indian John Blake while he is a boy.

Time—5:45.

---

## Stock Entries at San Jose.

HORSES FOR ALL WORK—Four years old stallion, James Weatherhead, San Jose Chief.

Stallion four years old, A. T. Hatch, of Vallejo, Adimar.

Stallion four years old, Massey Thomas, of Gilroy, Pollock.

Stallion three years old, D. Hellyer, of Milpitas, Clifford.

Stallion two years old, S. S. Drake, of Vallejo, Lake.

Stallion two years old, same party, Hendricks.

Stallion one year old, Young St. Lawrence, is entered.

Mare two years old, T. Andrews, of San Jose, Minnie.

Mare one year old, same party, Louise.

Mare one year old, T. W. Barstow, Beauty.

Mare four years old and over, Wm. Boots, Milpitas, Mollie M.

Mares—Best three year old, A. Barras, San Jose, a mare.

FAMILIES OTHER THAN THOROUGHBREDS.

S. S. Drake, of Vallejo, Admiral and six colts.

HORSES of ALL WORK—Mares—Best four years old and over, S. S. Drake, Vallejo, Eva.

Mare four years old and over, S. S. Drake, Vallejo, Eva.

Stallion four years old, A. Barris, San Jose, Dom Pedro.

Mare two year old, C. H. Carey, San Jose, Emma Belle.

Stallion two year old, Louis Verdon, San Jose, John.

Stallion one year old, Geo. Kost, San Jose, Edwin Forest;

J. Weatherhead, San Jose, Young St. Lawrence.

Four years old and over, Young Comet, by B. F. Fish, of Santa Clara.

Two year old, Fleetwood, by E. S. Smith, San Jose.

DAIRY HORSES—Stallions—W. P. Philips, Hollister, California Chief; J. S. Gracia, Twelve-Mile House, Ottawa Chief.

SCORING COLT—S. H. Chase, San Jose, Paul Revere.

George Kost, Gilroy, Prince Albert.

DAIRY HORSES—Mares four years old and over, S. H. Chase, San Jose, Lute. Mares three years old, P. H. Doyle, Santa Clara, Lady Hercules; George Easton, Gilroy, Flora.

ROADSTERS—Stallions three years old, E. S. Smith, San Jose, Baywood.

Two year old, E. S. Smith, San Jose, Sweetwood.

Stallion four year old and over, Wm. Boots, Milpitas, Northern Combs, Kingston and Inauguration.

ROADSTERS—Mares four years old and over, E. Topham, Milpitas, Belle.

Three years old, S. S. Drake, Vallejo, Sister.

Two years old, E. Topham, Milpitas, Lady Nutwood.

Geldings—T. W. Barstow, San Jose, Frank.

FAMILIES—THOROUGHBREDS—Sire with not less than five colts, Judson, Wild Idle with five colts.

Thoroughbred dam with three colts, Judson, Nettle Brown.

Maggie and three colts, Napoleon, Fan and Bess, by Jas. Lendrum, of San Jose.

Bess, by James Lendrum, of San Jose.

THOROUGHBRED STALLIONS—Best four years old and over, H. C. Judson, Santa Clara, Wildidle.

Best three year old, Young Hercules, by Charles Clark, Milpitas.

Best two year old, Napoleon, James Lendrum, San Jose.

Best one year old, George, by Thomas Gallagher, San Jose.

THOROUGHBRED MARES—Best four year old and over, H. C. Judson, Santa Clara, Ella Doane.

Best two year old, O. Boutlier, Willows, Princess.

Best mare, four years old and over, Maggie, by James Lendrum, of San Jose.

Best one year old, Fan, by James Lendrum, of San Jose.

CATTLE—Ayrshire Bulls—Three years old and over, George Bement, Redwood City, Archie.

Two year old, George Bement, Lindo.

One year old, George Bement, Macbeth.

Bull calf, George Bement, Malcolm.

AYRSHIRE Cows—Cow and calf under one year, George Bement, Lady Merryton and calf, Selina and two calves.

Three years old and over, George Bement, Blaine, Ethel Brown and Stellita.

JERSEY BULLS—Two years old and over, C. B. Polhemus, Jersey Boy.

Three years old and over, General Grant, by B. F. Fish, Santa Clara.

One year old and over, J. T. Hoyt, San Mateo, Oscar Wilde, Don Juan and Banker.

One year old, Oscar Wilde and Don Juan, by C. B. Polhemus.

Same, Banker, by J. T. Hoyt, San Mateo.

Best bull calf, Tom and Jerry, by C. B. Polhemus.

JERSEYS Cows—Cow and calf, C. B. Polhemus, Cherry and calf, Matalia and calf.

Three year cow, C. B. Polhemus, Cherry, Fairy 2d, Pearl 3d.

Two year old, C. B. Polhemus, Matilla 2d, Pearl 3d.

One year old, C. B. Polhemus Gipsey 2d, Sun Flower.

BEST THOROUGHBRED HERD—C. B. Polhemus, Jersey Boy, Cherry, Matella, Pearl 2d, Fairy 2d.

Two years old, George Bement, Stellinita.

One year old, George Bement, Sultana.

Heifer calf, George Bement, Sibyl.

Herd Ayrshire Cattle—George Bement, Archie (bull), Lady Merryton, Stelzita, Ethel Brown and Elaine (cows).

BULL, DURHAM—Best three year old and over, let Duke of Alameda, Mrs. M. E. Bradley, San Jose.

Same, Duke of the Valley, by William Quinn, Santa Clara.

Same, 2d Duke of Alameda, by C. Younger, San Jose.

Best one year old, 6th Duke of Alameda, by Mrs. M. E. Bradley, San Jose; also by same, Centerville Duke.

Same, Forest King, by C. Younger.

Same by same, Duke of Forest King.

Cows—DURHAM—English Betsey, by P. H. Doyle, 3d and calf, by Mrs. M. E. Bradley.

Same, Fushia, by Wm. Quinn, Santa Clara.

Same, Second Rose of Forest Home and calf, by C. Younger.

Best three year old and over, Fushia 4th, Wm. Quinn; same, Lady May and Maid of Erin; same, Red Dolly 2d same, Jessie Maynard and 1st Golden Gate.

Best two year old, Leonora B, by Mrs. M. E. Bradley.

Same, 7th Rose of Forest Home, by C. Younger; by same Oxford Rose 3d.

Best one year old, Mabel Boyd, May Queen, by Mrs. M. E. Bradley.

Same, Innocence, by Wm. Quinn.

Same, Red Dolly 11th, by C. Younger; also 6th, Lou Ann of Forest Home and 5th Rose of Forest Home.

Best heifer calf, Peach Blossom, by Wm. Quinn, Santa Clara; also Lady Ann; also Woodland.

Same, Red Dolly 14th, by C. Younger.

SWINE—Best Berkshire Boar—Waldo, by Tyler Beach, San Jose.

Same, Bob Bidley, by Mrs. M. E. Bradley.

Best Berkshire sow—Lizzie 8, by Tyler Beach.

Same, Lizzie 1st, by Mrs. M. E. Bradley.

Finest and fattest hog, entry by Tyler Beach.

Best five pigs, entry by P. H. Doyle, Santa Clara.

Same, entry by Tyler Beach.

Same, entry by Mrs. M. E. Bradley.

Best Essex Sow—English Betsey, by P. H. Doyle, Santa Clara.

GOATS—Angora Buck—Billy, 3rd, by Emile Portal, San Jose.

C. Younger, San Jose, five.

HERDS OF BEEF CATTLE.—Wm. Quinn, Santa Clara, 'enters five.

C. Younger, San Jose, five.

SWEEPSTAKES BULL, ANY BREED.—Wm. Quinn enters Duke of the Valley.

C. Younger enters 2d Duke of Alameda; also Forest King; also 4th Duke of Forest Home.

SWEEPSTAKE COW, ANY BREED.—Wm. Quinn enters Fushia Fourth, Lady Mary.

C. Younger enters Jessie Maynard, Red Dolly 2d and Oxford Rose 3d.

SHEEP—MERINO—Best ram—A. Agnew, Santa Clara, Long Wool 2d.

Same, William Quinn, Santa Clara, Jim.

Same class—best ewe—A. Agnew, Jennie.

Same, Wm. Quinn, Hattie.

COTSWOLD—Best ram. Mr. King, Prince.

Same, C. Younger, Hancock No. 35.

Same—Best ewe, Wm. Quinn, Winnifaro.

Same, Solano Mack, by P. J. Beale.

Same, C. Younger, No Name and No Name 2d.

Same—Best pen ram lambs, C. Younger.

Same—Best pen, C. Younger, five ewe lambs.

Same, Wm. Quinn, five ewe lambs.

GRADED SHEEP—Rams, Wm. Quinn, Fred.

Same—Ewe, Wm. Quinn, Susie and Jane.

# BICYCLING.

## Olympic Bicycle Race.

Although the fall meeting of the Olympic Athletic Club on the 23d did not bring out as large a field of starters in the bicycling event as usual, there was some good racing, and better time was made than had previously been accomplished on this track.

The strong westerly winds which prevail during the summer in this vicinity are prejudicial to the highest speed as they meet the rider full in the face upon two sides, while he is not correspondingly benefited upon the other sides which are sheltered by the stands and dressing rooms.

The track on Saturday was in fair condition but the wind was strong.

The first race was a match between J. H. Thompson with 140 yards and C. Burkhalter scratch. At the start Thompson went off at a good rate and very nearly maintained his handicap, but in the second lap Burkhalter began to reduce it and gaining steadily the remainder of the distance, passed Thompson just after entering the home stretch for the last time, winning by a few yards in 3m. 56½s.

The second was a mile handicap with H. C. Finkler at scratch, George L. King 50 yards and George Strong 120 yards. A start being effected all but King got off well, and Finkler immediately set the pace, gaining rapidly upon King for the first lap and giving promise of cutting the Pacific Coast record, which his friends thought he would be able to do easily, but the wind, and possibly being a little amiss, soon told upon him, and he ceased to gain. After the second lap King drew away from him somewhat, at the same time decreasing the distance between himself and Strong, until in the last half of the last lap he was within a few yards of the latter, but he was not quite able to make up the remainder of the distance and was beaten out by about two yards; time 3m. 10 3-5s. Finkler about 60 yards away.

The third race was a half mile handicap, with George L. King at scratch, C. Burkhalter 35 yards, R. F. Verrinder 70 yards. Verrinder held his lead well, the others closing up slowly until the last half of the last lap, when they were pretty well bunched. Rounding the last turn a table cloth would have covered the three and at about half the distance down the stretch King drew a foot or two ahead of Verrinder who led Burkhalter by about the same distance. Time, 1m. 34 3-5s.

The final event was a single lap (one fifth of a mile) each rider to run singly and his time to be taken. The entries were King and Finkler, the first making the lap in 32 3-5s. and the latter in 35s.

## Fifty Mile Bicycle Race.

The interest in bicycling in this city is so great and a "boom" so very apparent that 68 persons, including spectators and officials were present on the grounds of the Manhattan Athletic Club to witness the interesting bicycle race. Promptly at 3:05 Referee Curtis started the following five competitors: W. J. Smith, of the Manhattan Athletic Club; A. R. Ives, Brooklyn Athletic Club; Lewis Hamilton of New Haven, V. C. Place, Greenville, Pa., and B. G. Sanford, Ixion Bicycle Club. Smith took the lead closely followed by Sanford and Place, and forced the pace, soon lapping Hamilton and Ives, and thus joined the five, forming a curious procession for over twenty miles, each one alternately leading. Sanford was mounted on a 50 in. Rudge, Place rode a 54 in. Harvard, three inches too small, Smith a rapid racer, 54 in., Ives, a 52 in. Challenger, while Hamilton towered above them all on his 60 in. Yale. Hamilton is the young man who won the two and five mile races at Springfield and has never won any long races, having merely entered to "learn something" which he probably did. Had he followed the leaders more closely, he would probably have had second place, his last ten miles showing some excellent riding. He rode in good form and held the pole closer than his competitors. Smith is the well-known rider who ran the League championship last year, but having been lately married was not in as good form as he might show. He is better adapted to short races.

Mr. Place is a new rider and but lately seen on the path. He recently made a mile in the fast time of 2m. 58s., and mounted on a 57 in. machine, his proper size, will prove a worthy competitor in the future. He seems strong and a good spurter, and experienced more difficulty in keeping his place in the line than in going ahead. Sanford was the only New York man in the race and was last man in the fifty-mile race at the Institute. Since that he has trained carefully and surprised himself and his friends by securing second. He rode in good form and with excellent judgment. Ives is a stranger and had he not been taken with cramps would probably have been near at hand at the finish. Place was the first to finish the ten miles in 41m. 2s,. but Smith led at the twenty miles in 1h. 2m. 41¾s. At the thirtieth mile Sanford was to the front, the watches showing 2h. 4m. 47s. for the distance. At this point Smith, who had indulged in occasional spurts in the hope of gaining a lap or two, was taken with cramps and dismounted to be rubbed. He remounted again and struggled along for a few laps a quarter of a mile in the rear, but was obliged to succumb to the inevitable and withdrew altogether. Lap after lap was reeled off until the fortieth mile was reached by Place in 2h. 46m. 38s., and Sanford followed three-quarters of a second later. At this point Ives also became cramped and withdrew, leaving Hamilton three laps behind Sanford and Place. The tall man then went to the front and surprised all by spurting finely, and was soon within a lap of Sanford. The long journey, however, told upon him and he was obliged to content himself with third place. Place appeared at this point in fine condition, and in the last mile spurted and ran easily in 3h. 29m. 11½s., Sanford second in 3h. 28. 45s., and Hamilton third in 3h. 29m. 28½s. All three men were ahead of the best American record for out-door track. The following are the times of the three leaders at every ten miles:

| Miles. | Place. H. M. S. | Sanford. H. M. S. | Smith. H. M. S. | Hamilton. H. M. S. |
|---|---|---|---|---|
| 10 | 41 2 | 41 2¼ | 41 2½ | ....... |
| 20 | 1 21 42 | 1 21 41½ | 1 21 41½ | ....... |
| 30 | 2 4 47½ | 2 4 47 | 2 4 48 | ....... |
| 40* | 2 46 38 | 2 46 38½ | withdrew | 2 48 3 |
| 50* | 3 27 11½ | 3 28 45 | ......... | 3 29 28½ |

*Best out-door record.

The race was well managed and all the rules were properly complied with. The following were the officers of the day: W. B. Curtis, referee; G. Thomas, Elliott Mason, F. Jenkins, judges; M. McEwen, C. J. Connell, timers; F. Abbott, F. G. Bourne, G. Brady, J. M. Young, J. McMahon, C. Suckow, timers; F. S. Graham, clerk of course; G. M. L. Sacks, marshal.—*The Wheel.*

## Holidays on the Bicycle.

He gets most out of his vacation who most thoroughly breaks away from the routine of the year's work, and most completely insulates himself from business. In the doing of this the bicycle has great advantages. It takes a man "far from the madding crowd." Americans go on a vacation as elephants go to water, in herds; a few great centers congest with a fevered mass of pleasure seekers. "The pursuit of happiness" is the "inalienable right" of every American citizen. The way of seeking it is as truly American as the object sought. Mountains swarm, seaside resorts are stuffed, springs are crowded with people in search of rest. The music changes, the dance goes on, the summer waltz is even more tiresome than the winter german. The wheel puts an end to this, throws a man upon himself for company, drops him at a farm house for the night, commands communion with nature, unfolds the beauties of hill and valley as a panorama, refuses to wear away the night in riot and excess, and, more vigorously than old Puritan laws, insist upon the night for rest. It cuts the telegraph wire that trails behind him like a spider's thread, always ready to call him back. It taboos the daily mail and paper, until, like Philip Nolan, one feels like "a man without a country." It leads one along labyrinthian by-ways, and calls a halt in the most obscure and out-of-the-way places. The bicycle insures insulation; without it, a vacation is a failure.

It forbids baggage. The impediments of the old army, the curse of vacation, are left behind. Light marching order is the condition of success. The Saratoga trunk, that deep pit through which so many modern Josephs go to prison, is closed, and even Mrs. Grundy is content when the wheel is the excuse for comfort instead of conformity.

The wheel demands exercise. Laziness can loll in drawing-room cars, and slothfulness sit on a steamer's deck, but the wheel, like the law of labor, demands sweat and toil as the price of bread, and like it, too, gives an appetite for the food earned.

The wheel is economical. The average vacation, like Pharao's lean kine, eats up the fat of the rest of the year. A can of oil feeds and doctors the steely steed. Like the beggar at the Barmacide feast, it eats nothing. There is no groom to fee, no waiter to tip.

Then, too, the rider must be sober. This horse cares for no stirrup cup; a clear head, a steady hand, or an early fall and a winter of discontent will surely follow.

"Turn, turn, my wheel! What is begun
At daybreak must at dark be done.
To-morrow will be another day.
Stop, stop, my wheel! Too soon, too soon
The noon will be the afternoon,
Too soon to-day be yesterday."

—*Ex.*

## The Worcester Races.

A large number of people assembled at the New England State Fair at Worcester, Sept. 4th, to witness the annual races under the auspices of Worcester and Aeolus Clubs, who organized and carried out an interesting programme. The half mile trotting track was in fair condition, but lack of rain had rendered the surface dusty and a trifle rough. The management was efficient and prompt, and everything went smoothly; in fact the starter gave Moore no rest, and ran the events in rapid succession. We protest against the growing custom of running long races in heats, and had a few handicaps been thrown in, there would have been more starters. The fact that Frank Moore, the English champion, had entered having been largely advertised, it kept back many who would have ridden. Moore started in every race and won all of them easily, thus reducing the result of the races to an almost certainty.

The first heat of the two-mile race was won by Moore in 6m. 51s. Geo. W. Hendee, of Springfield, finishing the distance in 6:53. Moore allowed his contestants to lead in turn, and spurted to the front about 300 yards from home. The second heat was a repetition of the first, the time being slower, Moore crossing the line in 7m. 20¾s, Hendee taking second place in 7:21.

The mile race was but a repetition of the first as regards result, Moore winning both heats in 3 m. 12¾s.,* and 3:24¼, with A. D. Claflin second in 3:21¾ and 3:24¾. W. R. Pitman was allowed to ride under protest and secured third place. Claflin is considered a fast rider, having made two miles in 6:21¾ at Boston, April 8th. The half-mile race was contested by four men out of a field of sixteen. Pitman took the lead and held it until the quarter, when Moore passed him, followed by J. W. Wattles, Jr. About one hundred yards from the finish Pitman spurted and closed the distance between Wattles and himself, but could not pass him, and secured third place. Moore's time was 1:35 for the first heat, and 1:34 for the second.

A number of wheelmen from Boston and vicinity were present, and about 190 participated in a parade previous to the races.

The visitors were handsomely entertained by the home clubs, and every arrangement was satisfactory; no accidents of any kind occurred to mar the pleasures of the day.—*Wheel.*

PRINCE AND MLLE. ARMAINDO.—About five hundred persons, many of them ladies, assembled at the Polo Grounds in New York August 26, to witness the 25-mile race between John S. Prince and Mlle. Louise Armaindo, the latter being allowed three miles start. Prince rode a 54-inch Yale, and Armaindo rode one of similar make with 51-inch wheel. The riders left the starting point at 5:16 o'clock. Prince took the lead and increased the distance from his opponent steadily, passing her lap after lap, until Armaindo crossed the line on the second lap of her third mile, when he crossed off one mile from his handicap. Prince kept increasing his speed, and passed Armaindo a second time, two miles ahead, on the second lap of the fourteenth mile. The lady rode very gracefully. The perspiration rolled off her face, and it was evident that she was too heavily clad for such arduous exercise at this season of the year. It was growing dark when Prince made the second lap of the third mile of his handicap. The excitement grew intense. The crowd cheered and the ladies waved their handkerchiefs. Armaindo worked her pedals like the cranks of a locomotive, but Prince was not idle, and he overtook and passed her on the second lap of the last mile, winning the race by 34 seconds. The New York *Times* gives the score as follows:

| Miles. | PRINCE. H. M. S. | ARMAINDO H. M. S. | Miles. | PRINCE. H. M. S. | ARMAINDO. H. M. S. |
|---|---|---|---|---|---|
| 1 | 0 3 30 | 0 3 50 | 14 | 0 51 29 | 1 0 32 |
| 2 | 0 6 58 | 0 7 55 | 15 | 0 55 41 | 1 5 6 |
| 3 | 0 10 28 | 0 12 5 | 16 | 0 59 49 | 1 9 53 |
| 4 | 0 14 3 | 0 16 22 | 17 | 1 3 59 | 1 14 42 |
| 5 | 0 17 39 | 0 20 32 | 18 | 1 7 43 | 1 19 35 |
| 6 | 0 21 14 | 0 24 51 | 19 | 1 11 48 | 1 24 28 |
| 7 | 0 24 48 | 0 29 13 | 20 | 1 15 57 | 1 29 17 |
| 8 | 0 28 26 | 0 33 25 | 21 | 1 20 23 | 1 34 10 |
| 9 | 0 32 5 | 0 38 10 | 22 | 1 25 6 | 1 38 50 |
| 10 | 0 35 44 | 0 42 20 | 23 | 1 29 38 | ...... |
| 11 | 0 39 37 | 0 47 7 | 24 | 1 34 12 | ...... |
| 12 | 0 43 25 | 0 51 33 | 25 | 1 38 15 | ...... |
| 13 | 0 47 24 | 0 56 18 | | | |

Previous to the principal contest, a bicycle race of ten miles was contested between Edwin Oliver of the Citizens' Bicycle Club of New York, A. R. Ives of the Brooklyn Athletic Club, and Frank Moore, the Champion of England. Ives rapidly fell behind from the start. Oliver kept ahead of the British champion until the last lap, and apparently thought he had an easy victory. On the final lap Moore "let himself out," and won the race in 0:39:41. Oliver was as much surprised at the result as any of the spectators.

The track was in a wretched condition, being soft and broken in many places, considering which, although Prince was at no time pushed and won easily, the time was very good. In the 50-mile contest with Armaindo in the Institute Building, his 25-mile time was 1h. 26m. 46s., and the lady's 22-mile was 1h. 29m. 30½s.

A Philadelphia paper, speaking of the result of opening Prospect Park to the wheelmen, says: "Bicycles, no longer banished, are on the increase. Here and there a family party who had come out by steamboat, horse cars, or park train, with prettily dressed children rolling about on the turf, or carrying luncheon to and fro, showing an unmistakable interest in a distant bicycler making fast time on the asphalt. Arriving under their particular poplar-tree, he would swing himself from his saddle, and stabling his "wheel" upon the grass, stand revealed as the *pater-familias*, instead of the boy of seventeen he had passed for on the road. Climbed upon by merry children, and prone on the grass when the music begins again, what a healthy, happy ending for a city man of the business day!"

The "Archer up" jockey cap is by far the neatest and jauntiest head-gear for racing we have seen. It is made of silk in the regular jockey cap shape, with a small silk knot at the top. An effort will be made to have them manufactured in this country, as at present they cannot be obtained here unless imported from England.

We in this country are being gradually educated up to the standard of medium weight roadsters, say about 40 lbs. for a 50-inch bicycle, and it is believed that all the imported makes so deservedly popular will show a decided tendency hereafter toward lightening their newer patterns, instead of making them heavier.

The third competition for the £50 challenge cup, presented by the Crystal Palace Company to be competed for annually under the rules of the Bicycle Union, was won on the Crystal Palace track, August 17, by C. D. Vesey of the Surrey Bicycle Club. Distance, 15 miles; time. 46m. 22 3-5s.

Although tobacco may be "a lone man's companion, a bachelor's friend, a hungry man's food, a sad man's cordial, a wakeful man's sleep, and a chilly man's fire," it should be discarded by all men in training, if they would arrive at the best results and have what is termed "good wind."

The holding of a social evening and the formal awarding of prizes after race meetings seems to be very common in England, and might well be copied here. The social element which exists to a large extent among club members is one of the pleasantest features of wheeling.

The distrust in light and medium weight machines is fast disappearing in England, owing probably to the vast improvement in construction which has taken place of late years, and which has proved that quantity of metal is by no means synonymous with strength.

# BASE BALL.

## The Howards vs. the Olympics.

For some time past there has been a question of forming a new club from among the members of the Olympic club, and this idea has been carried out, the new organization appearing last Sunday in a match with the Olympics, being the first of a series of the best three out of five games for the possession of the Howard trophy. As might be expected the new club was no match for its friendly rivals on the diamond field, but it is composed of excellent material, and with practice and experience the team will doubtless show great improvement, especially when the men get accustomed to their positions in the field and can bat with more freedom and effect. The game for to-morrow at the same grounds being a match between the Olympics and Redingtons, that promises to be a close and interesting contest. We append the score of last Sunday's game:

| HOWARDS. | T.B. | R. | B.H. | P.O. | A. | E. | OLYMPICS. | T.B. | R. | B.H. | P.O. | A. | E. |
|---|---|---|---|---|---|---|---|---|---|---|---|---|---|
| Johnson, c. | 5 | 0 | 1 | 2 | 1 | 1 | Neal, p. | 6 | 2 | 2 | 1 | 10 | 2 |
| Maxwell, 1b. | 4 | 0 | 0 | 4 | 2 | 2 | Van Bergen s.s. | 6 | 3 | 2 | 0 | 6 | 0 |
| Campbell, c. f. | 4 | 0 | 0 | 4 | 1 | 3 | Barton, 2b. | 6 | 3 | 1 | 0 | 1 | 1 |
| Kane 2b. | 4 | 0 | 0 | 3 | 2 | 1 | Ebner, 3b. | 6 | 4 | 2 | 2 | 1 | 0 |
| Hamilton, 3b. | 4 | 0 | 1 | 7 | 1 | 2 | Burt 1b. | 6 | 3 | 3 | 12 | 0 | 2 |
| Buckingham p | 4 | 0 | 1 | 0 | 4 | 0 | Fitzgerald, c. f. | 5 | 1 | 3 | 1 | 0 | 0 |
| Stone, s. s. | 4 | 1 | 0 | 4 | 2 | 3 | Sumner, c. | 6 | 1 | 3 | 9 | 3 | 0 |
| Dibble, r. f. | 4 | 1 | 1 | 0 | 6 | 3 | Van Dyke l. f. | 5 | 1 | 3 | 2 | 0 | 0 |
| Van Court, l. f. | 4 | 1 | 2 | 3 | 2 | 0 | Kelly, r. f. | 6 | 1 | 1 | 0 | 0 | 1 |
| Totals | 37 | 3 | 6 | 27 | 21 | 15 | Totals | 55 | 19 | 20 | 27 | 21 | 6 |

| Innings | 1 | 2 | 3 | 4 | 5 | 6 | 7 | 8 | 9 | |
|---|---|---|---|---|---|---|---|---|---|---|
| Olympics | 4 | 0 | 0 | 4 | 0 | 2 | 1 | 2 | 6 | 19 |
| Howards | 0 | 0 | 0 | 0 | 3 | 0 | 0 | 0 | 0 | 3 |

Earned runs—Olympics 3. Two base hits—Fitzgerald, Van Dyke and Buckingham. Wild pitches—Olympics 1, Howards 4. Time of game—Two hours. Umpire—Gus Pratt of Haverly's. Scorer—M. Straus.

## The Niantics vs the Haverlys.

These two clubs met at the Recreation Grounds last Sunday, and there were bright anticipations of a grand display of skill, but these were soon dispelled, as taken altogether the game was about the poorest exhibition ever yet given at these grounds by such organizations as the Niantics and the Haverlys, although it must be owned that the Niantics were laboring under the disadvantage of three of their best men being absent. The play needs no special mention, and it is to be hoped, for the sake of the reputation of the clubs, that we shall see no repetition of last Sunday's game. The following is the score:

| NIANTICS. | T. B. | R. | B.H. | P.O. | A. | E. | HAVERLYS. | T.B. | R. | B.H. | P.O. | A. | E. |
|---|---|---|---|---|---|---|---|---|---|---|---|---|---|
| Incell, p. | 6 | 0 | 0 | 1 | 10 | 1 | J. Carroll, p. | 7 | 1 | 2 | 9 | 9 | 2 |
| Emmerson, 3b. | 5 | 2 | 3 | 1 | 2 | 2 | Levy, c. f. | 6 | 4 | 4 | 1 | 0 | 0 |
| Donahue, s. s. | 5 | 0 | 2 | 1 | 5 | 1 | Meegan, s.s. | 6 | 2 | 2 | 1 | 3 | 3 |
| Egan, 1b. | 5 | 2 | 1 | 16 | 0 | 0 | McDonald, 3b. | 6 | 1 | 2 | 2 | 1 | 0 |
| Finn, 2b. | 5 | 3 | 2 | 5 | 3 | 1 | Sohr, l. f. | 6 | 3 | 2 | 0 | 0 | 0 |
| Arnold, c. f. | 5 | 0 | 1 | 0 | 0 | 0 | F. Carroll, c. | 6 | 5 | 4 | 8 | 0 | 2 |
| Robinson, c. | 5 | 1 | 2 | 2 | 2 | 2 | McCord, 1b. | 6 | 3 | 1 | 10 | 0 | 1 |
| Fogarty, l. f. | 5 | 0 | 0 | 0 | 0 | 3 | Pope, r. f. | 6 | 4 | 3 | 1 | 0 | 1 |
| Corbett, r. f. | 5 | 2 | 1 | 1 | 0 | 1 | Gagus, 3b. | 6 | 3 | 1 | 2 | 0 | 2 |
| Totals | 46 | 10 | 12 | 27 | 22 | 11 | Totals | 55 | 25 | 21 | 27 | 13 | 13 |

| Innings | 1 | 2 | 3 | 4 | 5 | 6 | 7 | 8 | 9 |
|---|---|---|---|---|---|---|---|---|---|
| Haverlys | 4 | 2 | 2 | 6 | 0 | 7 | 1 | 0 | [illegible] |
| Niantics | 0 | 1 | 3 | 0 | 4 | 0 | 0 | 1 | [illegible] |

For the past two months a large number of the members of the Olympic Club and other gentlemen interested in base ball matters have used all their endeavors to bring about a match between the Olympic Club nine and the Redington & Co. nine and it was not until last Tuesday that a game was finally arranged between these two nines. The Redingtons were organized at the beginning of the present season, and are under the management of Mr. Albert D. Dugan. They have played several games and generally come out victorious. They are in splendid practice and are handsomely uniformed and equipped. The Olympic nine is composed of members of the Olympic Club and is under the guidance of Mr. Chas. S. Neal and Wm. Bouton. This club was also organized this season and the members have been in constant practice. They have played a number of games and have only been defeated once, and that by the Redingtons, but in a second game with the same nine the Olympics were victorious, hence the interest in this match. The Olympics are all powerful men and heavy batters, while the Redingtons are rather slight and make up in their lively fielding what they lack in batting. The game will take place on Sunday next, Oct. 1st, at the Olympic Club grounds, Oakland. Game will be called at 11 A. M. Admission to the ground is free and a very large attendance is expected.

# ATHLETICS.

## Olympic Club, Fall Meeting.

The most interesting subject of conversation in athletic circles at present is the 100 yds. dash between Haley and Masterson last Saturday, at the Olympic Club Fall Meeting, on the Club grounds in Oakland. The match was made the Sunday previous, and on that day Masterson could have easily defeated Haly, as the latter was unable to repeat in better time than 10¼, but the few days intervening between that time and the actual race put him in first-class condition for a short dash, and he finished the last forty yards in grand style, winning by fully 4½ feet, and looked around for his opponent ten yards from the tape. As it was a match between the two, they both broke over the mark simultaneously four times without being penalized. The actual start was conceded by both competitors, the starter, and all of the spectators, to have been perfectly even; and the pistol was undoubtedly fired before they had gone over the mark. At sixty yards they were perfectly even, but at that point Haley settled down to business and began to draw away, and in a few more strides was safe to win. Masterson need not have been beaten more than three feet, but a few yards from home, realizing that a struggle was useless, began to ease up, and the verdict was a beating of from 1½ to 2 yds. Outside of a few prejudiced individuals it has been well known for the last two years that Haley was a first-class amateur sprinter, and, by the by, his most venemous enemies of the past are now the most anxious to convince the balance of the athletic world that he is entitled to the best amateur record for the distance. On this peninsula, as some of our eastern contemporaries are well aware, we are blessed with an extremely equitable temparature, and the extremes of other localities, even on the Pacific Coast, are very trying to residents of San Francisco, until they are thoroughly acclimated. A first-class San Francisco athlete is liable to be defeated any time during the warm season fifty miles from this city, by a second-class man, and if sent east during the summer would be too debilitated by the heat and change of climate to rate higher than third class. Athletics on this coast are still in their infancy, and it is almost useless to hope that another effort will be made for some time to come towards sending representatives East. However, we will bide our time, and when the general public learns to appreciate legitimate amateur athletics, the best athletics in the world will be rapidly developed, and California will brag of something besides climate and horses.

Haley is capable of competing in the best of company in any amateur event from 100 to 220 yards that may take place in this vicinity, and if any amateur from the East should happen out this way next season, Haley will be ready to prove what he can do, and Masterson bids fair to divide the honors with him. Another match between them is on the tapis for next Thanksgiving Day, and if Masterson is properly trained for the event, it will be hard to name the winner in advance. Brooks promises to come out here next year in condition for a race, and with Haley end Masterson as representatives we should be able to show the rest of the world that we are not so green as they think we are. The following is a summary of the events of the day:

One hundred yards handicap, open. First trial heat, W. R. Stewart, scratch, 1; F. M. Day, 5 yards, 2; W. D. O'Kane, 2 yards, 3; time 10 4-5 seconds. Second heat, A. L. Harris, 4 yards, 1; Wm. C. Brown, 1 yard, 2; Eugene Van Court, 4 yards, 3; time 10 3-4 seconds. Third heat, C. H. Slater, 4 yards, 1; E. S. Emmons, 1 yard, 2; time 10 3-5. Final heat, C. H. Slater, 1; A. L. Harris, 2; W. R. Stewart, 3; time 10½ seconds.

One mile scratch, A. W. Brown, C. A. and L. C., 1; P. H. Hamell, O. A. C., 2. Time 6 mins., one-fourth second (leather medals are in order).

One mile handicap bicycle race. C. Burckhalter, scratch, 1; J. H. Thompson, 140 yards, 2. Time 3:56½.

One hundred yards scratch run, R. S. Haley, O. A. C., 1; Jas. Masterson, C. A. and L. C., 2; time 9 4-5. The time as given by each individual timer was: H. B. Cook, 9¾; P. McIntyre, 9 4-5; W. R. Melville, 10 seconds.

One hundred yards handicap run, O. C. juvenile class, H. Smith, 1; E. Jennings, 2. Time 14½.

Pole leaping handicap, C. L. Ebner, 8 inches, 1, height, 8 ft., 5 in.; C. H. Slater, 2; E. G. Rodolph, 3.

One mile handicap bicycle race, Geo. H. Strong, 120 yards, 1, Geo. L. King, 50 yards, 2; H. C. Finkler, scratch, 3. Time 3:10 3-5.

One hundred yards scratch run, open, R. S. Haley barred. Jos. Masterson 1, W. R. Stewart 2, time, 10:15.

Running wide jump, R. S. Haley 1, (18 ft. 2½ in.), L. Ebner 2, Wm. D. O'Kane 3.

Two hundred and twenty yards handicap, O C Juvenile class, W. Van Bergen 1, H. Audifred 2; time, 25½.

Two hundred and twenty yards handicap run, C. H. Slater 10 yards, 1; A. L. Harris 9 yards, 2; E. S. Emmons 4 yards, 3; time, 23 2-5.

Eight hundred and eighty yards handicap bicycle race, George L. King scratch, 1; R. F. Verrinder 70 yards, 2; C. Burckhalter 35 yards, 3; time, 1:34 3-5.

Running high jump, C. L. Ebner 1, (5 ft. 2 in.), C. H. Slater 2, (5 ft. 1 in.), E. G. Rodolph 0, R. S. Haley 0.

Wm. C. Brown was the entry for the officers' one hundred yards run, and covered the distance in 11 seconds, coached by Masterson.

Putting 16 lb weight, Cornelius Donohoe 1, (32 ft. 3½ in.); C. H. Slater 2, (29 ft. 7 in.) O'Kane entered a protest against Donohoe. The committee allowed him to compete, and reserved their decision.

One-fifth mile bicycle race, each to ride separately against time. George L. King 1, time 32½, H. C. Finkler 2.

Throwing baseball, W. F. Bouton 1, (296 ft. 2 in.), N. W. Leonard 2, (277 ft. 5 in.)

Two hundred and twenty yards scratch hurdle race, 5 hurdles, 3 ft. 6 in.; C. H. Slater 1, E. G. Rodolph 2; time, 30¾. Brown balked at the third hurdle and stopped.

# FISH.

Fin Power of the Trout.—Some time ago the President of one of our national banks, and a lumberman of large experience in the North Woods, told me that on one occasion he saw trout surmounting a waterfall down which the water came vertically in one broad sheet. He said the trout would swim directly up in this sheet of water unless their fins, owing to the small volume of water, would extend beyond it, when they would fall back and try again. This was new to me and I would like to hear what others have to say on the subject. My informant was convinced that the force and direct downfall of water would not impede the passage of a trout, provided the sheet of water was thick enough for the fish to use his fins.—*A. N. C., in American Angler.*

An Outrage.—Young shad are being caught in large numbers in seines by the Italian fishermen at Saucelito. On Sunday last at least fifty of these fish were thus taken between old and new Saucelito, and, to make matters worse, bought for use of one of the yacht club houses in the neighborhood. The fish ran about half a pound in weight. We are informed that the purveyor in this case is a leading officer of the yacht club.

Puget Sound Salmon.—The silver salmon this season are very small, but the Chinook fish are correspondingly large. Near the mouth of Dunwanish river the bay is literally dotted with canoes and boats, the occupants of which are engaged in fishing. The ruling price now is five cents for good sized salmon, but as the season advances the price will decline.—*Post-Intelligencer.*

A most interesting method of fattening fish is that of Mr. Kuffer, superintendent of the royal fisheries at Munich. Partly in small stone troughs and partly in small ponds trout may be seen by the hundred weight, not only alongside of each other, but in a literal sense above each other. In some of the stone troughs there are certainly more trout than water; but not only trout, but the magnificent saibling of the Schiller Lake, large Salmon *hucho*, enormous numbers of splendid eels from Italy; and above everything else, hundreds of thousands of crawfish are here gathered within a narrow space and enjoy the most careful treatment.

Large piscicultural establishments have been started by men who possessed little or no theoretical knowledge. People will begin, not with 5,000 to 10,000 trout eggs, but with hundreds of thousands, yea, millions of eggs, in the hope that large profits will quickly be realized. If, as will generally be the case, these profits do not come; if, on the contrary, failure is succeeded by failure, the whole cause is condemned, and we often hear it said: "So-and so has also commenced to raise trout, but of course nothing came of it, pisculture is a delusion."

The reasons why most of our piscicultural establishments proper do not flourish are manifold. The chief cause, however, has been carelessness in the selection of a location. And where the location and the condition of the water were favorable, it is often impossible to procure suitable food in sufficient quantities, at any rate at a reasonable price.

Last Tuesday twenty pounds of salmon was caught in the Feather River, near the mouth of the Yuba. These are the first salmon caught in the Feather for many years. Their presence might not have been known had not one of the fish run on a sandbank and been caught.

The huchen (Salmon *hucho*), on account of its great voracity and because it never eats anything that is dead, is only suited for raising in ponds where there are large numbers of small and otherwise worthless fish.

The fish in the streams of Montana and Idaho in the vicinity of the railroad are being destroyed by wholesale, both whites and Chinese using giant powder to effect their destruction.

Good trout fishing can be had at the mouths of some of the creeks emptying into the bay. The fish are awaiting the first rains in order to run up to the breeding grounds.

The cannery at Benicia closed last Tuesday evening for th season, owing to the scarcity of salmon. The cannery at Martinez has also shut down.

Several parties of anglers went down to Moss Landing, Monterey Bay, Sunday, and had fine sport catching crabs and smelt. Mark Hudson, Stub Ben and party caught 175 smelt, Ed Card caught over fifty, and William Courtright caught eighty-five smelt and twenty-two crabs. These fish were caught with hook and line. The same day several large hauls were made at the Camp Goodall wharf. The bay seems to be full of smelt this year. The Chinese fishermen at Aptos and Soquel are making large hauls daily, and shipping the same to San Francisco.

An effort is being made to introduce more extensively the black bass into English waters. Some of the nobility who have angled for perch only object to the western fish as they think that bass are not gamey enough. In this idea they are wrong as the black bass is the pluckeist and hardest fighter that the fresh water can boast of.

C. H. Precht caught a string of fifty tom cods last Sunday at the sea wall. Many of the fish weighed one and a half pounds.

A note from a correspondent at Pescadero says that tront are now plentiful there and running large.

The trout fishing privilege expires by limitation to-day.

# POULTRY.

## Brief Suggestions.

Breeders of Plymouth Rocks declare that a mating of dark medium hens and light medium cocks produced the greatest number of good cockerels for breeding or for exhibition.

If you have one or two good breeds of fowls, it is better to spend time improving them than to be hankering after others, unless you have abundant means and plenty of room.

One of the best tonics for chickens, and probably one of the simplest, is to keep a handful of old rusty nails—the more rust on them the better—in each dish from which they drink. The rust is the oxide of iron sold by the druggists, and the home-made is as good as the sale article.

If chickens have sore eyes (though they ought not to do so, and won't if your management is correct from the beginning, before the eggs are laid) you can apply glycerine to good advantage, one small drop to each eye. This will soften the edges of the lids so that the bird can open them.

You can raise ducks and geese without an abundance of water. There is more fun, of course, in seeing them swim in brooks, rivers or ponds, yet if you give them enough pure water to drink, and allow them an occasional plunge bath, they will thrive first-rate with no water range.

The first eggs of the litter are always the best for hatching. After a hen has produced twenty or thirty eggs in perhaps as many consecutive days, the strain upon her strength is very great, and consequently the eggs become impaired in vitality and capacity to produce vigorous chickens.

Clear rye bran should never be fed to fowls, on account of its swelling and caking in masses in the crop, and proving fatal to chicken-life not unfrequently. It will thus, sodden and increase in bulk very rapidly before digesting, causing rupture of the crop, if any great quantity has been eaten.

"What is worth doing at all is worth doing well." This proverb will nowhere apply better than to the care of poultry. Without constant attention and thoroughness, success is not to be expected. Some kinds of business may be occasionally slighted without serious harm, but in this occupation one mishap may blast the hopes of a whole season.

Young chickens drink a great deal of water, but they, in common with all animals, know just how much they need. Mix your corn and dough very dry and crumbly, therefore, and let the fowls drink fresh, cool, clean water after they are through eating. If your mess is mixed too thin and sloppy you will force them to swallow more water then they need, in order to get at their feed.—*The American Poultry Yard.*

Lorrillard's Aranza won the Great Eastern Railway Handicap at Newmarket last Tuesday, and Lorillard's Sachem and Keene's Bookmaker are at the head in the betting on the Cambridgeshire Stakes, which will be run over the same course October 14th.

We Have Seen Such There.—Given a strong pair of lines with a spirited horse at one end and a fool at the other, and we have every requisite for an impressive scene. The driver now pulls a strong rein, then gives a jerk or two, anon measures the whip on the horse's flank and sides, and—well, scene number two is before us, in which appears a horse being treated with St. Jacobs Oil for his cuts and bruises, a foolish man, under the same treatment for the improvement of his battered anatomy, and the carriage builder with an account half a yard long for repairs to a once magnificent buggy. No use of talking, it takes brains and St. Jacobs Oil to drive a spirited horse successfully.—*N. Y. Spirit.*

ONLY $8.

OUR NEW AMERICAN LEVER WATCH!

After months of labor and experiment, we have at last brought to perfection A NEW WATCH. It is a Key Winding Watch with the celebrated Anchor Lever Movement, Expansion Balance, Fully Jeweled.

They are made of the best material, and in the very best manner, so as to insure good time-keeping qualities. The Cases are made of our Celebrated Composition metal known as Aluminum Gold. This metal has a sufficient amount of gold in the composition to give the watch a genuine gold appearance. Indeed it cannot be told from a genuine Gold Watch except by the best judges as the metal stands the acid test as well as pure gold. The cases are finely engraved or engine turned and are massive and strong and very handsome making it just the watch for Railroad men, Mechanics and all laboring men who require a good strong watch and an accurate time-keeper. For trading and speculative purposes, it is superior to any watch ever before offered. They can be sold readily for $15 and $20 each, and traded so as to realize double those amounts. Farmers as well as Agents can handle these watches to advantage, as they can be readily exchanged for stock or goods. We send the watch free by registered mail, on receipt of $8.00. Or we will send it C. O. D. on receipt of $1.00 on account; the balance can be paid at the express office. We also have very fine Aluminum Gold Chains at $1.00 each. Beautiful Medallion Charms 50 cents. We have hundreds of testimonials, but have room for only two.

Hot Springs, Ark., June 3d, 1882.

World Man'f'g Co. Gents:—The New American Aluminum Gold Watch I ordered of you some time ago was duly received, and I am so well pleased with it that I enclose Seven Dollars, P. O. order, on account, for which please forward by express C. O. D. for balance, three more of the same style with chains to match. Respectfully, Carleton Taylor.

Leavenworth, Kan., Aug. 7th, 1882.

World Man'f'g Co. Gents.—The Aluminum Gold American Lever Watch purchased from your firm has proved a good time-keeper, and gives perfect satisfaction. Enclosed find cash for two more, same style. Yours, G. P. [illegible]

Send all orders to WORLD MANUF'G CO., 122 Nassau Street, New York.

*It is seldom that we meet with an article that so fully corresponds with its advertised good qualities as does the New American Lever Watch. It has the advantage of being made of that precious metal Aluminum Gold; its works are of the best make, and the general style of the case rank it with the best Watches made anywhere. We recommend it to our readers as a Watch that will give entire satisfaction.*

## Market Report.

FLOUR—Good jobbing trade. We quote: Best City Extra, $6 87½@$6 50; Superfine, $4 50@$4 75; Interior Extra, $4 75@$5 25; Interior Superfine $3 75@$4 25 ℔ bbl.

WHEAT—The market is very dull at present with no immediate prospect for the better. The condition is no doubt owing to the inactivity of foreign markets. Small spot lots of No. 1 bring $1 86 and at these figures there is but little demand. The range of prices are October $1 80, and November $1 70.

BARLEY—Feed is strong with an upward tendency. Sales of October are $1 30, $1 31¼, and some as high as $1 32. November $1 33. Brewing and Chevalier receive but little notice.

OATS—Plenty of this grain are offered than they were last week. The range is from $1 47½@$1 67½ ℔ ctl.

RYE—Receipts are moderately free. There is a fair demand for No. 1 which is quoted at $2 25@$2 75 for No. 2 quality.

FEED—The selling rates for bran at the mills range from $18 50@$19 ℔ ton. Ground Barley, prices steady and quoted at $29@$31 ℔ ton. Cracked Corn, quoted at $38 ℔ ton. Shorts, selling rates $20 50 ℔ ton. Middlings, quotable at $29@$29 ℔ ton for job at mill. Oilcake meal, the oil works sell to the trade at $33 50 ℔ ton, less the usual discount.

HAY—We quote: Alfalfa, $11 20@$14 50. Wheat $13 @$15. Wild Oat, $13@$15 50 ℔ ton.

STRAW—Quotable at 60@80c ℔ bale.

BEANS—We quote for jobbing lots: Bayos $3 20@$3 25; Butter, $3 25@$3 25 for small and $3 40@$3 60 for large; Lima, $5 50@$5 75; Pea, $5 50@$5 75; Pink, $3@$3 25; Red, $3 25@$3 50; small White, $3 40; large White, $3 25@$3 50 ℔ ctl.

DRIED PEAS—Niles, 6c; Blackeye, $2 25@$2 50 ℔ ctl.

POTATOES—Wharf rates are as follows: Early Rose, 50@60c; Garnet Chili, 50@55c; Early Goodrich 70@75c; Peerless, 50@55c; Sweet, $1 50 ℔ ctl.

ONIONS—Prices continue easy. Supplies large. Quotable at 50@65c ℔ ctl.

GAME—Is very scarce for this time of the year. Good prices are paid as the following shows: Quail, $1 50@$2 75 ℔ dozen; Mallard Ducks, $3 50@$4 00; Sprig, $2@$3 50; Teal, $1 75@$2 25; Widgeon, $1 50@$1 75; Hare $1 75@$2 00; Rabbits, $1 50@$1 50; Doves, 50 @75c ℔ dozen; Venison, $5@12c ℔ lb.

POULTRY—The market is steady. We quote: Live Turkeys, gobblers, 17@19c; do Hens, 18@21c; Roosters, $5@$6 50 for old and $3@$3 50 for young; Hens $4@$6 50; Broilers, $3 50@$4 50 according to size; Ducks, $5 50@$7 50 doz; Geese, $1 25@$1 50 ℔ pair; Goslings, $1 50@$2 50 ℔ pair.

PROVISIONS—We quote lots as follows: Eastern Hams, 18@20½c; California Hams, 16@16½c; for plain, 16@21½c for sugar-cured canvassed; Eastern Breakfast Bacon, 17@21½c; California Smoked Bacon, 16@16½c for heavy and medium, and 17@18c for light and extra light; Clear Sides, 15@16½c Pork, $21 50@$22 for extra Prime, $26@$26 50 for Prime Mess, $23@$23 50 for Mess, $27 for Clear and $23@$23 50 for extra Clear; Pigs' Feet, $12@$12 50 ℔ bbl; Mess Beef, $14 for hds and $7 for ½ bbl Extra Mess Beef, $14 50@$15; Family Beef, $15@$16 50 ℔ bbl; California Smoked Beef, 14@16½c ℔ lb.

LARD—We quote in tierces, 13@14c ℔ lb.

BUTTER—We quote prices for jobbing lots as follows: Fancy, 47c choice, 43@45c; fair to good, 38@40c; inferior lots from country stores, 18@ 22c; firkin, 38@40c for good to choice, and 18@27c for ordinary; pickled roll, 32@33c; Eastern, 30@35c ℔ lb.

EGGS—In fair demand. We quote as follows: California choice, 37@40c; Interior, 33@35c; Utah, 32@35c ℔ doz.

CHEESE—We quote: California, 15@12½c for choice; 10@12½c for fair to good do. factory, 11@12½c; Eastern, 15@17c ℔ lb.

FRUIT—The several descriptions continue to be well represented. We quote prices as follows: Apples, 50@60c for common and 75@90c ℔ box for good; Pears, 40@60c ℔ box; Bartlett do, $1 50 to $2 ℔ box; Blackberries, $5@$6 50 ℔ chest; Raspberries, $10@$12½ ℔ chest; Peaches, 50@60c 25 ℔ box; Figs, 40@75c ℔ chest; Grapes, 30@60c for common, 40@60c for Black Hamburg, 50@75c for Rose of Peru, 40@50c for Muscat and 75@$1 for California; Plums, 50@75c ℔ box; Quinces, 50@60c box; Blackberries, 18@20c ℔ lb; Crabapples, 50@75c ℔ box; Cantaloupes, 75@$1 ℔ dozen; Lemons, 35@50 ℔ box for Sicily and $1 50 $5 for California; Oranges, $1 for Mexican, Bananas, $2 50 to $5 ℔ bunch; Pineapples, 30@35c ℔ dozen.

TROPICAL—Unchanged. We quote: Marrowfat Squash, 80@$1 ℔ ton; Carrots, 50@75c ℔ ctl; Cauliflower, 50@75c ℔ dozen; Cabbage, 50@75c ℔ ctl; Garlic, 12@14c ℔ lb; Cucumbers, 15@25c ℔ box; Green Peas, 3@5c ℔ lb; Green Peppers, 50@75c ℔ box; Tomatoes, 10@50c ℔ box; Celery, 60c ℔ dozen; Dried Okra, 30c ℔ lb.

HIDES AND SKINS—No material change. Dealers are paying the following cash rates for lots in order: Dry hides, butcher selection, 20c; culls one-third less, and Mexican Hides 1c ℔ lb less. Dry Kip, 18@19c; Dry Calf, 18@20c; Salted Steers, over 50lbs. 11c ℔ lb; Steers and Cows, medium, 10c; light do, 9c; Salted Kip, 11c; do No. 10@10½c; Salted Calf, 11@11½c ℔ lb; Dairy Calf, 6@9½c each; Sheep Skins, 30@75c for Shearlings; $1@$1 50 for medium; $1@$1 50 apiece for long Wool and Wool skins. Butchertown Green Skins bring higher prices.

WOOL—The inquiry is not very good at present. We quote spring: Humboldt and Mendocino, 20@24c ℔ lb; Sonoma, 18@20c; Siskiyou and Modoc, 14@18c; San Joaquin free 17@18c; Northern Coast, burry and seedy, 15@17c; Eastern Oregon choice, 20@22c; Valley Oregon free, 18@20c; Valley Oregon Coarse, 20@22c. We quote fall: San Joaquin and coast, 10@13c; Eastern Oregon choice, 18@20c; Northern fall, free, 10@11c; Northern fall, defective, 10@14c; Northern fall, Lamb, 16@21c; Fall medium grade, 6@8½c in terior, 5@6½c ℔ lb.

BEEF—Prime, 7@8½c; medium grade, 6@6½c; inferior, 5@6½c ℔ lb.

VEAL—Large Calves, 6@7c; small ones, 8@10c ℔ lb.

MUTTON—Wethers are quotable at 6@6½c and Ewes at 4@5c ℔ lb, according to quality.

LAMB—Quotable at 6@6½c ℔ lb.

PORK—Live Hogs, 7@7½c for hard and 6@6½c for soft; dressed do, 10@11½c ℔ lb for hard grain hogs.

## FOR SALE.

A VERY FINE HAMBLETONIAN STALLION, imported from Portland, N. Y., sired while old mahogany bay; sixteen hands high; perfectly sound; well broken; very stylish; (and over $1,500, property of a banker; full pedigree got by Hambletonian Prince, by Volunteer. Can be seen at STUD STABLES.

### Belmont—Mambrino Chief—Blackbird, for Sale.

BAY YEARLING COLT, BY PILOT, GRANDSON of Williamson's Belmont, his dam by Alhambra (by Mambrino Chief, from Susan, by American Eclipse) grandam Grisly, by Simpson's Blackbird. Is now in Oakland at the stable of

JOS. CAIRN SIMPSON.

### Fine Nutwood Horse Colt for Sale.

CHESTNUT COLT ONE YEAR OLD, BY NUTwood, out of one of the best road mares in the State; by John Nelson. The colt is 15½ hands high, finely and powerfully built and shows good action. Apply to
GEO. W. HANCOCK, Sacramento.

---

## Fall Race Meeting.

### PACIFIC COAST
## Blood Horse Association

**Introductory Day—Saturday, November 11th.**

No. 1—Purse $250; free for all; $10 each; a dash of three-quarters of a mile; entrance money to second horse.

No. 2—Purse $200; free for all maidens; $10 each; one mile; entrance money to second horse.

No. 3—Handicap Stake for all ages; free for all; $20 entrance, and $5 declared; $50 added; $60 to second horse; a dash of a mile and an eighth.

No. 4—Selling Purse, $300; a mile and a quarter; for all ages; entrance fee; $60 to the second horse; the winner to be sold at auction; horses entered for $1,000 to carry Regular weight; if for $1,000, five pounds allowed; if for $700, ten pounds; if for $500, seventeen pounds, and if for $300, twenty-two pounds. All who can claim the winner, and the surplus realized beyond the amount at which the horse is entered to be divided between the association and the owner of the second horse.

**First Day Regular Meeting—November 15th.**

No. 1—The Ladies' Stake. Closed.
No. 5—Purse $250; free for all; three-quarters of a mile and repeat; $50 to second horse; entrance free; the winner of the dash of three-quarters on the first day to carry ten pounds extra.
No. 6—The Vestal Stake. Closed.
No. 7—Handicap purse of $350 for two-year-olds; $30 each and $15 if declared; $60 to the second horse; dash of a mile.
No. 8—Purse $500; a mile and a quarter over five hundred; $50 to second horse; entrance free.

**Second, Day Regular Meeting—November 18th.**

No. 10—Purse of $300; a dash of seven-eighths of a mile; $60 to the second horse; entrance free; the winner of the three-quarter dash or three-quarters and repeat to carry ten pounds extra; winner of both events to carry fifteen pounds extra.
No. 11—Purse of $350; heats of a mile and an eighth; entrance free; $60 to second horse; maiden three-year-olds allowed seven pounds; four-year-olds twelve pounds; five-year-olds and over fifteen pounds; the winner of the dash at this distance on the first day to carry five pounds extra.
No. 12—Handicap purse of $200 for all three-year-olds. A dash of a mile and a quarter; $20 each, and $10 if declared; the second horse to receive $60.
No. 13—Purse $250; a mile and repeat over four hundred; $60 to second horse; entrance free.

**Third Day Regular Meeting—November 22d.**

No. 14—The Tijuan Stake. Closed.
No. 15—The Parole Stake. Closed.
No. 16—The Railway Stake. Closed.
No. 17—Consolation Purse of $300, of which $50 to the second horse; dash of one mile and a half; horses beaten once allowed five pounds, twice ten pounds and three times fifteen pounds.

Entries to stakes and purses not marked closed will close October 15, 1882.

Rules to close will be run under weights adopted at last annual meeting, which are the same as those of the American Jockey Club.

Non-payment will be placed on the same footing as members of the association in regard to the payment of purses and stakes. Entries and stakes liable to a deficiency the winners will receive a pro-rata division.

Parties making nominations will be required to record colors at time of making entries, and after proof will not be allowed to ride in other colors. This rule will be strictly enforced.

All nominations in stakes and entries in purses must be made on or before the first day of October next, and directed to C. M. CHASE, Assistant Secretary, Box 1881, P. O., San Francisco. To be valid they must be plainly postmarked on that-day, October 10th.

THEO. WINTERS, President.
JOS. CAIRN SIMPSON, Secy.
C. M. CHASE, Assistant Secretary.

## Fine Thoroughbreds
### FOR SALE.

BY DIRECTION OF MR. W. L. PRITCHARD We will offer for sale at public auction at 11 a. m. on the grounds of the

## Bay District Association
### SAN FRANCISCO,

ON THURSDAY, NOVEMBER 16, a choice lot of thoroughbred horses, comprising

**Brood Mares — four-year-olds, three-year-olds, two-year-olds and yearlings.**

These animals are of the choicest blood and afford a rare opportunity of purchasing first-class stock. For other information of catalogues apply to

W. L. PRITCHARD, San Francisco,
or KILLIP & CO., Auctioneers.

### "Red Clover."

NEEDHAM'S RED CLOVER BLOSSOMS AND extracts are the greatest blood-purifier in the world; also a sure cure for cancer, salt rheum, catarrh, bronchitis, etc. I can send to many letters and testimonials from all who have been cured—some of them very remarkable. I will send circulars and testimonials to those wishing them. Address
W. C. NEEDHAM, Box 422, San Jose, Cal.,
Sole agent for Pacific Coast.

### ENGLISH SETTER PUPPIES
#### FOR SALE.

BY MR. THOMAS BENNETT'S REGENT, OUT of Waddington's Judy; and Mr. Thomas Bennett's Regent, out of Leavesley's June. Both Daisy and June are field trial winners. Price $25 and $50. Apply to
H. C. LEAVESLEY, Gilroy.

### INTERESTING.

THE SEMI-WEEKLY EAST OREGONIAN With pictures of Pendleton, Centerville, Weston Umatilla City, Echo City, Pilot Rock and Prospect, to any address; 10½c, six months, $1 75; twelve months, $3 50; per year; postage paid; will publish a fine front head description of Umatilla the City of the West and Stock county—crops, stock, mines—of the season. Address EAST OREGONIAN PUBLISHING COMPANY, Pendleton, Umatilla county, Oregon.

J. A. McKERRON,
MANUFACTURER OF FINE HARNESS.
327 Sutter Street.
BETWEEN DUPONT AND STOCKTON, SAN FRANCISCO.
Repairing neatly and promptly executed.

---

---

## Third Annual Fair.

### AGRICULTURAL ASSOCIATION.
#### SIXTH DISTRICT.
### AT THE CITY OF LOS ANGELES,
**October 16th, 17th, 18th, 19th, 20th and 21st.**

### SPEED PROGRAMME.

**FIRST DAY—MONDAY, OCT. 16, 1882.**

**SECOND DAY—TUESDAY, OCT. 17, 1882.**
No. 1. District, trotting, 2 minute class; purse, $600.
No. 2. District, trotting, 2 26 class; purse, $400.
No. 3. District, running, colt race, free for all 3-year-olds, half mile dash; purse, $600.

**THIRD DAY—WEDNESDAY, OCT. 18.**
No. 4. Trotting, free for all that never beat 2 30; purse $600.

**SAME DAY.**
No. 5. District, running, free for all, half mile and repeat; purse, $350.

No. 6. Running, free for all, mile and repeat; purse, $500.

**FOURTH DAY—THURSDAY, OCT. 19.**
**Grand Stock Parade.**

Ladies' riding match, distance, ladies miles, distance 5 miles; purse $375, distance as follows: First money, $175; second money, $100.

No. 7. District, trotting, 3-year-olds and under; purse $500.

**FIFTH DAY—FRIDAY, OCT. 20.**
No. 8. District, trotting, 2 40 class; purse, $600.
No. 9. District, running, 3-year-olds, three-quarter mile dash; purse, $350.

**SIXTH DAY—SATURDAY, OCT. 21.**
No. 10. Trotting, free for all; purse, $800.

**SAME DAY.**
No. 11. District, running, free for all, three-quarters of a mile dash; purse $350.

No. 12. Running, free for all, 1 mile dash; purse, $500.

### REMARKS AND CONDITIONS.

All trotting races are the best in five, unless otherwise specified. Three to enter and two to start. Entrance fee, 10 per cent. on purse, to accompany nomination. Purses divided at 75 and 25 per cent of the purse, to second, and 10 per cent. to third.

In running races where three to enter, two to start, colts allowed one-third to third heats; four to enter three to start, with one-fourth of purse to second, and one-eighth to the second horse; four or two classes alternately, if necessary to finish any day's racing or to find a special race between heats.

To fill Purse Races, four or more substitutes are necessary.

All the two-year-olds, wide Running in their classes alternately, if necessary to finish any day's racing with the usual allowance for increased pedigree.

All three-year-old, wide Running in their classes, up to 100 pounds, with the District allowance as above. No added money for a Walk-over.

Horses entered in purses can only be drawn by consent of the Judges.

Rules of the Pacific Coast Blood Horse Association will govern to govern running races, except those conditioned upon this Programme.

National Association Rules to govern trotting; but the Board reserve the right to trot heats of any two classes alternately, if necessary to finish any day's racing, or to find a special race between heats.

All entries must be in writing, and signed, and give name of horse, also name and residence of owner, in running Purse, full colors to be worn by Rider; and the name of the stable and number and color of Stallion to be designated upon programme by the Rider's color.

Entries to all the above races to close with the Secretary on Saturday, Sept. 16, 1882.

Write "Entrance Blanks" as conditions of purse.

Note—"Rule" is barred from trotting Races 1, 7 and 10.
J. BARETTO, President.
R. N. HEWITT, Secretary.

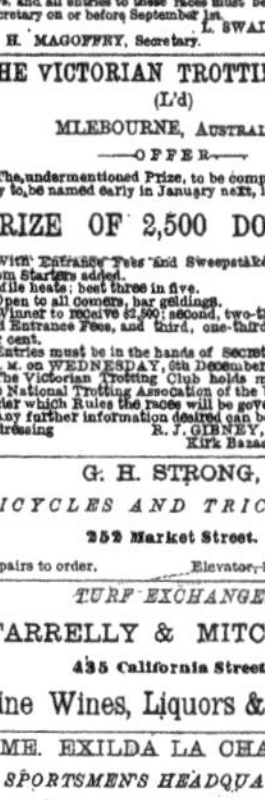

### DAVID L. LEVY,
JEWELER, DESIGNER OF MEDALS AND TESTIMONIALS.
29 Third-street, San Francisco.
REPAIRING NEATLY DONE.

### DAN McCARTHY,
LIVERY, BOARDING & SALE STABLE.
608 Howard Street, Near Second.
LARGEST STOCK OF FAST LIVERY TEAMS in the State. First-class boarding. Horses bought and sold. Cash advanced on horses, buggies, sulkies, harness or anything connected with the business.

### PAUL FRIEDHOFER,
PATHOLOGICAL HORSE-SHOER
105 Commercial Street.
Practical in all its various branches.

# BREEDER AND SPORTSMAN

Vol. I, No. 15.
NO. 508 MONTGOMERY STREET.

SAN FRANCISCO, SATURDAY, OCTOBER 7, 1882.

SUBSCRIPTION
FIVE DOLLARS A YEAR.

## THE CARRIAGE AND COACH HORSE.

ADMIRÁBLE. Owned by J. B. Haggin, Rancho Del Paso.

Sufficient size, harmony of proportion, style, high spirit, utility, proper action, good sense and a good color are among the qualities imperatively demanded in carriage rses. Although generally regarded as being synonymous are is quite a difference between the animal that has the sential requirements for a carriage horse, and those which s be rated as good "coachers." The former must be the user animal, handsome, more highly finished, with a greater gree of symmetry, more graceful in movement, and with a eater turn of trotting speed. Bulk and smoothness of outle, with a lofty carriage, and something of what may be rmed a lordly air, will cover many defects in the coach-horse. at is the technical coach-horse. The purpose being to use em to haul the cumbersome vehicle kept more for show an anything else and with heavy harness rendered still avier with massive ornamentation. The equipages of the gh functionaries and nobility of the old world were of a t1 which precluded anything like rapidity of motion, Not

only heavy but awkward, devoid of beauty, lumbering cars that necessitated ponderous animals to draw them. A very large proportion of the carriage of the United States are of a different pattern, and those that are denominated coaches are distinct as can be from the European type. The clumsy horse, however stately, is entirely out of place. There must be a greater degree of activity, there must be higher form, there must be beauty independent of gorgeous trappings, a fitness for the demands of a people who have a greater share of horse leatheticism, and who have a keener appreciation of suitability. The scarcity of fine carriage horses in the cities does not argue that this position is untenable, for that arises from the country not being able to supply the want. Since the mania for breeding fast trotters has overspread the whole country, the breeding of carriage horses has been sadly neglected. Speed was held to be the only quality that would repay, and in the blind race for phenomenal trotters there was a sacrifice of important points. This was more

peculiarly the case a few years ago, as at the present time many of the stallions which are the most successful as the progenitors of fast trotters have also the characteristics that are needed for the carriage. There are also breeders who are aiming to produce the proper type without anticipation of trotting speed in this class, and are giving attention to the breeding, form, action, size, style, color, etc., independent of anything else.

The illustration preceding this article is an accurate representation of an animal which has been selected for this purpose, and in our estimation he is so very nearly a model of what the carriage horse ought to be that a reference to the picture is all-sufficient to give the idea so far as outlines are concerned. There is scarcely a point that needs correction, and though some might be better pleased with a straighter hip we prefer that there should be slope enough to insure greater freedom in the action of the hind legs, which this form of quarter certainly gives, When the inominatum is nearly horizontal, and the buttocks full, it gives a round appearance which many fancy, but in that case the stifle is placed too high and there is a constraint that influences the action prejudicially. In the case before us the angle is not abrupt, but at a declination which does not mar the beauty of the quarter, while it gives a much better "set" to the limb. We allude to this as the only point in the configuration of Admirable which good judges of equine form would be likely to differ about, as it would be a captious critic, indeed, who was not willing to admit the correctness of form in every other respect.

Admirable was bred in France, as the following translation of the government certificate shows:

(Translation.)

**National Stud.**

| | |
|---|---|
| CERTIFICATE OF BIRTH.<br>Product of the National Stallion.<br>Subject to a tax of 12 cents.<br>Article 48 of Model Order No. 26 If it is a thoroughbred mare, mention will be made of the fact.<br>Government Stamp.<br>Description.<br>name Admirable<br>Color, redish or chestnut.<br>Head do.<br>Legs do,<br>Seal of the Depot of Stallions of St. Lo. (Manche). | I, the undersigned, Director of the Depot of Stallions of St. Lo, do hereby certify that it is proven by the certificate of covering, and of the declaration in proper form, which have been deposited in my hands, that the mare named Miss Coy (by Pretty Boy and Kapisat) one-half thoroughbred, born in 1873 in Normandy, height 156 centimeters, color bay, head —, legs —, and belonging to Mr. Milet who resides at St. Marcouf, Department of La Manche, was covered in 1877 by the National Stallion named Jackson (by Jackson's Quicksilver and Tamworth) No. 176—one-half thoroughbred, born in 1869 in England—height, 162 centimeters, color, dark brown, head — legs — and belonging to the Depot of Stallions of St. Lo. and from which was produced the foal herein described (in the margin) which foal was born at St. Marcouf on the 14th day of April, 1878.<br>In proof of which I have signed and delivered this certificate at St. Lo. on the 31st day of December, 1878. The Director,<br>A. PROUNVAUX. |

Admirable was selected by a son of the owner, B. A. Haggin of New York City, and this young gentleman must have a very correct eye for proportion and admirable judgment to chose the animal he has selected. The certificate requires explanation. The marginal notes refer to the colt, the body of the certificate to the parents. To extend the description, Admirable is a bright chestnut of the most beautiful shade. There are such a variety of shades of this color that it is almost impossible to describe the exact tinge with words, though it would be difficult to obtain a handsomer hue. The coat is silky, as fine, indeed, as that of the highest bred racehorse, and the hairs in the mane and tail are also fine. The shade is uniform, head, neck, body and legs alike, the only divergence being a small white spot on the coronet of the near hind foot, and a black spot about the size of half a dollar on the quarter. Looking at him as a whole he will impress the scrutinizer as exhibiting a deal of character.

And, by the way, the whole picture which a horse presents is the best manner of forming a correct estimate of his value. There must be a harmonious entirety, a complete figure filling the eye with justness of proportion, a comprehensive image on the retina, a fitness of parts only discoverable by the animal being in a position that enables the observer to gauge eveything at the same time. Thus we always like to take the first look at some distancefrom the animal and when Admirable was led out of the barn into the sunshine we never saw a horse that better "filled the eye" for the purpose he was purchased for. He would strike any person as something beyond the ordinary run of fine horses. The novice in horse affairs, no matter how stolid, could not withold his admiration; the critical judge of equine form might fancy that he was imposed upon by the *glamouirie* of style and color, and anticipate that analysis will show defects that would mar the finished picture, and be surprised to find so little to find fault with on a close inspection. We have always held that the most perfect type, the nearest model to a perfect horse would only be found in the thoroughbred. This we still believe, and yet for a carriage horse there are models which would not be proper for the racecourse. In giving the points of the subject of this sketch it may puzzle some to understand why this configuration is unsuitable for the course. There have been many good racehorses which did not show as high racing form, but as is well known there are other things beside form necessary. As, however, the consideration is entirely in another field than the racecourse, therefore the adaptability for carriage uses is the topic to be commented upon.

Admirable when he left France was 15¾ hands high. He was then only a trifle over four years old and now the standard shows him to have gained nearly half an inch in height, and when fully matured there is little doubt that he will exceed sixteen hands. He is a long horse for his height, and with an unusual development of muscle. He is wonderfully deep through the heart, giving him an immense girth, and the barrel is full and round. The quarters are very muscular, the second thigh powerful and the loin braced with strong fillets. The withers are high and the shoulder blades are long and wide, and with more obliquity than is usually seen even in horses which are considered excellent in this point. The neck is set on the body admirably, being deep and full at the base, tapering to the throttle. The head is small, with a good deal of width between the eyes, the muzzle fine, and eyes full. The ears are slim and pointed, the nostrils cleanly cut, in fact the head is about as handsome as can be conceived. The head, neck, shoulders and chest are a beau ideal of what they should be in a carriage horse, and though there is rather more space between the forelegs than would be proper in a racer, the breadth of the front part of the chest is an evidence of a strong constitution and the brisket could not be improved. The legs are capital. Arms and gaskins large, without a particle of cloddiness, hock and knees clean and truly formed, and from these joints to the ankles there is plenty of bone, and better yet plenty of tendon. The pasterns are "springy," having the proper angle, and the lower part filling the hoof. The feet are very good, the horn being dark and evidently of good quality. They are just the kind to stand pavements or macadamized roads, having a good width of heel and the foot nearly circular. The position of the limbs is faultless. Both the fore and the hind legs "come to the ground right," and support the body in a graceful way. From the shape of the shoulder and neck, and the setting on of the head, there must be "style" enough to suit the most fastidious, and this configuration also governs the action in a measure. From "both ends" having the proper "speed angles" we were prepared to see the right kind of action for the carriage, but we did not expect to witness such a display as he made when turned loose in the corral. When he finished his play at the gallop, and he was as active as a cat in his bounds, he struck off at such a bold, free gait as would delight the trotting enthusiast, and yet there was an elegance of movement that could not fail to attract attention on the drives of the park. That he will get fast trotters we have not the least doubt, and with the proper education make one himself. But he has a more important mission than the getting of trotters, and that is founding a family of carriage horses. There are too many ordinary trotters, a scarcity of carriage horses almost amounting to a dearth. With both in view the breeder will find surer remuneration. But still with all the advancement there has been the last ten years in improving the form of the trotter until many of the popular trotting sires are of a type that fits them for the carriage, the breeder who aims at a distinct animal will be the most successful. The horse intended for the family carriage should never be put through a course of the usual track training. There are few which do not acquire habits inimical for the uses, and as the main endeavor in the training of trotters is to develop speed, the teachings are not of the kind that are the best adapted for the future purpose.

There is not a shadow of doubt that a person who engages in the breeding of carriage horses, having the proper animals and conducting the business with any degree of intelligence, will find it remunerative.

The picture of Admirable will afford the idea of the proper form in the sire and the dams must be chosen with a similar formation.

As the certified pedigree shows there is a great deal of thoroughbred blood in Admirable. The English practice of calling all "one-half thoroughbred" or half-bred where there is any stain in the pedigree misleads American readers, as a horse which possesses thirty-one parts of thoroughbred blood in thirty-two would still have the br. b. put opposite his name in the stud book.

The other blood in Admirable must be of the finer type of the Norman, the smaller, more active breed which are used for rapid travel, and it is safe to assert that at least three-quarters are of the pure strain. There is scarcely a trace of any thing else in his appearance and only the slightest token of a different mixture. Owing to the universal custom in France, the dock has been shortened, though there is plenty of evidence that Nature had endowed him with plenty of hirsute adornment.

We are pleased to present this picture. It is a valuable addition to the gallery and will convey a better idea of what the carriage horse should be than pages of printed description.

# TURF AND TRACK.

**CLOSING OF ENTRIES.—Do not forget that the stakes and purses of the Fall meeting of the Pacific Coast Blood-Horse Association other than the "fixed events" close on Tuesday next, the 10th instant. See advertisements for particulars.**

## Fixed Events.

Eastern Oregon Fine Stock Association at Union, from October 9th to the 14th inclusive.

Los Angeles Agricultural Association, at Los Angeles, from October 17th to 21st inclusive.

Fall meeting of the Pacific Coast Blood Horse Association, November 11th, 16th, 18th and 23d.

FAIRS AT THE EAST.

Texas State Fair, at Austin, October 17th to the 21st inclusive.

THE PLUNGER'S PURCHASE.—Henry Newbold of Pleasure Bay has sold to Mr. F. Theodore Walton the Newbold farm for $10,000. Mr. Newbold says Mr. Walton has purchased the property for the purpose of placing upon it a stock farm for racing horses and utilizing the rest for a mile running track. The Newbold farm is a peninsula, three-quarters of a mile from the seashore. It is delightfully situated and almost entirely surrounded by the waters of Pleasure Bay. It has an area of a square mile. The purchase of Mr. Walton is received with much satisfaction by the summer hotel-keepers and residents of Long Branch. It is believed that a racing course in close proximity to the seashore would greatly benefit Long Branch, and it is said that Mr. Newbold has kept it reserved for that purpose, offering it at a most reasonable figure. Monmouth Park is over three miles from Long Branch, and the hotel-keepers say they receive no benefit from it. Before purchasing the Newbold property, it is said Mr. Walton endeavored to purchase a tract of land lying between the ocean and Pleasure Bay, but he could not secure enough of it upon which there was room for a mile running track. The Shrewsbury river is now navigable as far as Branchport, beyond the Newbold farm, and a steamer plies between it and New York. This would give greater facilities in carrying the horses than Monmouth Park has.

## Fastest Record.

OAKLAND, Cal., Sept. 28, 1882.

EDITOR BREEDER AND SPORTSMAN, *Dear Sir:* Will you kindly decide a wager, and inform me whether the fastest time has been made by a trotting or a pacing horse, and give me the record of each. I understand that Sleepy Tom paced a mile this summer in 2:06. By answering the above you will greatly oblige A SUBSCRIBER.

Answer.—Maud S, trotting, 2:10¼, Aug. 11, 1881; Little Brown Jug, pacing, 2:11¾, Aug 24, 1881. We have never heard of Sleepy Tom pacing so fast.

## Sensational Races at Coney Island.

The fall meeting of the Coney Island Jockey Club at Sheepshead Bay has proved to be most successful both in a racing and financial point of view. This is owing to the ever varying programmes that are framed so as to bring together the best horses in the country on even terms, and also to the fact that the association are most liberal in the way of premiums. One of the best arranged contests came off at the late meeting when Girofle, Bootjack and Barrett were brought together in a sweepstake of $500 play or pay, with $2,500 added, a dash of a mile, with weights ten pounds below the regular scale. We take the following account of the race from the *New York Sportsman*, merely adding that the fastest mile yet run on this course was made by Boardman, 1:40¼, on Sept. 20th, 1880, when carrying but 91 pounds as a four-year-old:

The great event of the day was now called and it was made the medium of some of the heaviest wagering ever recorded on horse-racing in this country. Walton, the bugbear of the bookmakers, wagered $15,000 to $21,000 on Girofle; $10,000 of this was betted with Haughton & Reed, and the remainder with D. Johnson. The mere fact of these bets having been accepted by the bookmakers shows that they have prospered this season, and calculated that to lose would not hurt them. When the horses went to the post it was a time for stilled heart-beats. Bootjack, with James McLaughlin up, had the inside, and was as eager to get off as if he really had a chance. Man and horse seemed to be so perfectly in accord as to warrant the opinion that the term "centaur" would be well applied in this instance. Girofle had the center, and was ridden by William Donohue. Needless to say that all the senses of this jockey were on the alert to-day, and his mount would not suffer by the start if he could help it. Barrett had the outside and was ridden by Lloyd Hughes, who had never before been on his back, if we recollect aright. He had good reason to know the horse's speed, however, for twice had his mount, Spinaway, gone down before this fellow at Mommouth Park in 1880. Feakes' wife was dead, and this, together with the severe sacrifice necessary to make the weight, debarred that artist from being on Barrett's back. Shaner, as stated elsewhere, was seriously ill and could not ride. In spite of all this, however, Barrett was the choice in pools and book-betting. Perhaps Mr. Lorillard's bad luck all day would turn, some said; and others thought to see Girofle beaten, because the pair were now at even weights. Barrett delayed the start a long time. Twice he was turned right, but if the conscientious and painstaking starter had dropped the flag then the race would have been over at once, for the brute each time whirled round again. Finally Barrett was placed between Bootjack and Girofle, and, a good opportunity serving, the flag fell with all three in good motion. For nearly half a furlong the "pole" horse, Bootjack, had speed enough to retain a slight lead. Then Barret's lightning stroke sent him to the front, and he soon had a lead of a length and a half, and going along the backstretch it was two. At the half it was reduced to a length and a half again, with Girofle a head in advance of Bootjack. In the next quarter of a mile the grand mare slowly but surely shut up the daylight and was lapping the big horse at the three-quarters. At the head of the stretch she was at his head; a furlong from home he was beaten, and could not or would not respond to Hughes' call, and Donohue, looking around, yet never relaxing his driving, shot his mare home a length and a half in front. Bootjack was of course pulled up when it was useless to persevere, but his owners have now a good line with which to try their youngsters and any other that they may buy. The time of the mile was 1:41¼—very fast indeed, and it is possible that it is a shade too fast for Barrett's capacity in his best day. Yet he gave this mare 10 pounds at Long Branch and was beaten only three-quarters of a length. Such a horse as Barrett would break a millionaire if he backed him in accordance with his latest form.

GRAND SWEEPSTAKES, ONE MILE.

SHEEPSHEAD BAY, September 14, 1882.—Grand sweepstakes of $500 each, play or pay, with $2,500 added by the association, of which $500 to the second; weights 10lbs. below the scale; 4 entries; one mile.

E. V. Snedeker & Co. name ch m Girofle, 5 years, by Leamington—Satan, by Lexington, 105 lbs. (W Donohue.)........ 1

P. Lorillard names b h Barrett, 4 years, by Bonnie Scotland—Sue Walton, 108 lbs. (Hughes.)........ 2

Dwyer Bros. name ch g Bootjack, 4 years, by Bonnie Scotland—Sparrowgrass, 105 lbs. (J. McLaughlin.)........ 3

Time—1:41¼.

Pools: Barrett $225, Girofle $175, Bootjack $65. Betting: Even agst Barrett, 6 to 5 agst Girofle, and 6 to 1 agst Bootjack. Mutuels paid $10 85.

On the 23d the meeting was brought to a close amid a regular old-fashioned rain storm, but the club resolved to let the racing go on, as the Directors wished to follow out the English system of running "shine or rain," and certainly that appears to be the more sportsmanlike way of conducting the proceedings, although the receipts must suffer in consequence. Considering the circumstances the attendance was good, and there was much interest attached to the four mile and repeat race that soon threatened to be counted among the glories of the past. Of this race and of the general results of the meeting we give the following extracts taken from the *New York World*:

The fourth race, the Great Long Island Stakes, at four-mile-heats, was the race of the day, and, in the estimation of many of the "old timers," it was the race of the meeting. To the majority of this class it is needless to say that, with meetings extended for weeks and with racing nearly every day, it is impossible to train and run horses at four mile heats, or even at four miles. It is a fact that such races are much more profitable to the associations than to owners, as the training of such horses for long races and for the cups at two miles and a quarter means to the latter the ruin of many of their best horses. Certainly the Dwyers found it so in the case of Hindoo. Years ago owners could afford to lay up horses through their two and partly through their three-year-old years with a view of slow and gradual development into cup and four-mile horses. But with the establishment of the valuable two-year-old and three-year-old stakes, owners now find it to their advantage to develop speed in preference to bottom, and in doing so, horses able to run four miles and repeat are now so rare that the Coney Island Jockey Club will next year reduce the Great Long Island Stakes to a dash of four miles. Of course such action is to be regretted, but as it can scarcely be avoided it is to be hoped that every year will yet show a few horses of the Glenmore-Bushwhacker-Lida Stanhope type, for, whether or not they compare with the great four-mile horses of a quarter of a century ago, they are certainly the best we have now. Of the three named, which were the only starters, Glenmore carried 114 pounds, with James McLaughlin in the saddle; Bushwhacker, 111 pounds, with Cyrus Holloway, and Lida Stanhope, 105 pounds, with Shaner "up." Glenmore was the favorite, with Lida Stanhope second choice. As the flag was dropped, Bushwhacker took the lead, and to the great delight of the "stable gang," he was never headed in the race. For the first mile he led Lida Stanhope by nearly four lengths, the latter running from a length to two lengths in front of Glenmore. There was but little change in the running of the second mile other than that in the first quarter Glenmore moved up to within half a length of Lida, but dropped again as they went down the backstretch, while on the Stable turn Lida Stanhope closed upon Bushwhacker as if to "feel" him. The three ended the two miles with Bushwhacker leading by four lengths and Lida Stanhope two in front of Glenmore. The third mile was nearly a repetition of the second, with the exception that both Lida and Glenmore closed up much of the gap, Lida especially, for at the end of the three miles she amid the shouts of her admirers showed a head in front of Bushwhacker, with Glenmore a length and a half away. Lida's lead was brief, for at the members' stand Bushwhacker again took the lead and at the quarter he was a length in front of the filly, she the same in front of Glenmore. Before they reached the grove Glenmore passed Lida and she rapidly dropped to the rear. McLaughlin at once made strong efforts to reach Bushwhacker, who not only responded to Holloway's call but from a lead of a length, which he held at the end of three miles and a half, he gradually drew away and finally amid some little cheering "old Bush" galloped past the judges the winner of the heat by eight lengths, with Glenmore second and Lida Stanhope just inside the distance. Time 8:01¼, which was nearly a minute faster than was generally thought it would be run in. As to the fractional time the rain came down so heavy that it was impossible to flag the quarters, but the first mile was run in 2:03¼ and the two miles in 4:05, after which the pace increased somewhat.

In the betting between the heats Bushwhacker, showing much the freshest, was made a strong favorite. All three appeared promptly at the call, Bushwhacker being received with some applause, as also was Lida Stanhope, but Glenmore was decidedly the favorite with the crowd. They got the flag with Glenmore a trifle in front, but he instantly gave place to Bushwhacker, who led by a length at the quarter and two lengths at the half, Lida Stanhope being so far back as to be virtually out of the race unless some accident should happen to the leaders. In the run round by the stables McLaughlin moved Glenmore up to within a length of Bushwhacker, but dropped back again in the stretch so that at the end of the mile Bushwhacker was leading by two lengths. There was but little change in the running of the second mile until just at the end, when McLaughlin again closed up and they finished the two miles just a length apart, with Lida 80 yards behind them. In running the third mile McLaughlin held Glenmore just a length behind Bushwhacker until they reached the half-mile pole, when he closed up and the two ran lapped—a scant half length apart—to the three-quarters, where they got on even terms. As they made the turn into the stretch, Glenmore showed in front and amid the greatest excitement he led by a length at the lower end of the stand and by two lengths at the end of the three miles. He kept on to the turn when, as Glenmore began to slacken up, many realized that McLaughlin evidently thought that he had gone four miles and that he had won the heat, but seeing that Holloway and Bushwhacker were keeping right on, they having passed him at the members' stand, he again began to ride Glenmore. But the chance was gone. Bushwhacker had a lead of three lengths at the quarter and he gradually increased it to eight lengths at the half and if he had kept right on he could have left Glenmore outside the distance, but Holloway eased up in the stretch and slowly galloped home the winner of the heat and race by forty yards, with Glenmore second, so far in front of Lida Stanhope that she was several lengths outside the flag. Time, 8:10. To say that the admirers of Bushwhacker were enthusiastic scarcely does them justice. They shouted, threw up their hats, and as a Glenmore man remarked, "acted like a lot of children out on a holiday who, the rain meanwhile pouring down in torrents, desired to do some silly thing that should completely put into the shade their foolish action in going to the races on such a day." But then they were winners, while the "growler" was a loser and an exception. Hundreds that had backed Glenmore were glad to see Bushwhacker the winner. Some had seen the little Tennessee "runt" run all his races from his first three-year-old effort at Baltimore, in May, 1877, when he ran unplaced to Lucifer, Clovertrook and Diamond. They had seen him win the two-mile heats at Baltimore in 1878, when he won the first heat in 3:36 and the third in 3:38½, Princeton beating him by a short head for the second heat in 36½. They had seen him two days after win the Bowie stakes at four mile heats, he taking the first heat in 7:31 and the third in 8:29, Princeton again beating him for the second heat by the shortest of heads in 7:36½. In fact there were some present that had seen him run in all his races, of which the above was his forty-third, while some remember having seen his dam, Annie Bush, win the Post Stakes at New Orleans in the spring of 1872, when she distanced the field, Nannie Douglas winning the first heat in 7:39 and Annie Bush the second and third heats in 7:38½ and 8:21, the race being run over the old Metarie Course.

Sheepshead Bay, September 23.—The Great Long Island Stakes, for all ages, at $250 each for starters, with $2,500 added, of which $500 to the second, and the Woodlawn Vase (presented to the club by the Dywer Brothers), to become the property of the subscriber winning the race for two years in succession; horses entered March 1 to pay $50 forfeit, by June 1 $100 forfeit, and by September 1 $150 forfeit; closed with seven subscribers of which three were made by March 1 and four by September 1; five-year-old and aged horses to carry 114 pounds, four-year-olds, 108 pounds, three-year-olds, 95 pounds; sex allowances. four-mile-heats. [Note.—W. Jennings won a claim to the Woodlawn Vase in 1881 with Glenmore].

G. B. Bryson names b g Bushwhacker, aged, by Bonnie Scotland, dam Annie Bush, 111lbs. (C. Holloway.)........ 1 1
W. Jennings names ch h Glenmore, aged, by Glen Athol, dam Lotta, 114 lbs. (J. McLaughlin.)........ 2 2
J. W. Loud names ch f Lida Stanhope, 4, by Waverly, dam Ada Cheatham, 105 lbs. (Shaner.)........ 3dis

Time—8:01¼, 8:10.

Pools.—Before: Glenmore, $300; Lida Stanhope, $235; Bushwhacker, $115. After first heat: Bushwhacker, $250; the field $15. Betting.—Even money against Glenmore, 8 to 5 against Lida Stanhope, and 3 to 1 against Bushwhacker. After first heat: 7 to 2 on Bushwhacker, 3 to 1 against Glenmore, and 50 to 1 against Lida Stanhope. Mutuals paid $23 and $6 40.

The meeting as ended above is in every respect the best yet given by the Coney Island Jockey Club, and although the last two days, the ninth and tenth of the meeting, were marred by bad weather, the attendance on the other days was so large that the meeting will be a decided success from a pecuniary point of view. During the meeting fifty-nine races were run, with a total of 414 starters, and to which the club contributed in purses and added money nearly $42,000, while so thoroughly was the money divided that the fifty-nine races were won by thirty-seven different owners or stables, among them being several from California, Utah, Missouri, Alabama, Ohio, Canada and other points nearer New York, viz: four each by Mr. Pierre Lorillard and W. C. Daly, three each by the Dwyer Brothers and E. Heffner, two each by Morris & Patten, W. L. Cassidy, Snedeker & Co., C. Reed, F. Robinson, E. J. Baldwin, M. J. Daly, E. Corrigan, J. Henry, E. J. McElmeel, J. McMahon and Davis and Hall and one each by G. B. Bryson, H. J. Woodford, J. McCullough, J. F. Caldwell, J. H. Harbeck, W. Lakeland, G. L. Lorillard, Ackerman & Co., D. D. Davis, C. D. Holmes, A. Burnham, F. Gebhard, C. Boyle, M. Kenney, T. Winters, C. Askey, Wm. Jennings, Wilson & Co., C. H. Pettingill, the Old Mill Stable, and the Pelham Stable. Another feature of the meeting has been the success of the stables known as Brighton Beach stables which won no less than thirty-eight out of fifty-nine races run. In distances the club also kept up the excellent standard set by the Monmouth Park and Saratoga associations of running a good average of long-distance races. The number of races at the several distances was as follows: 1 at five furlongs, 10 at three-quarters of a mile, 14 at a mile, 1 at a mile and half a furlong, 5 at a mile and a furlong, 3 at a mile and a quarter, 3 at a mile and three furlongs, 4 at a mile and a half, 1 at a mile and 5 furlongs, 2 at a mile and three-quarters, 1 at two miles, 1 at three miles, 1 at four-mile heats, 1 at heats of a mile and a furlong, 1 at mile heats and 10 steeplechases. The betting has been the heaviest of any meeting during the year, especially in the books and Mutuels.

**Bushwhacker.**

Perhaps of all horses that are or have been on the turf for the last ten years none lack the grace and beauty usually associated with the thoroughbred so much as Bushwhacker, the winner of the Long Island Stakes at Sheepshead Bay. Yet in breeding he is the peer of scores of vastly better looking horses. To begin with, his sire was the famous Bonnie Scotland, in whom the best blood of England was represented. His dam, Annie Bush, was by Lexington, out of Banner, she by imported Albion, out of Clara Howard, by imported Barefoot (winner of the St. Leger in 1823), and she out of the imported mare bred by Lord Grosvenor and imported by C. H. Hall, of New York, in 1824. As to Lexington's breeding and his standard as a sire nothing need be said, his honors, like those of Stockwell in England, being above praise. Annie Bush had a very successful turf career, for which she was trained by George Rice and owned by Jim McCormick, now of New York. She won over the Metarie track, at New Orleans, in April, 1872—a mile and a quarter in 2:14½—and at four-mile heats, nine days afterwards, in 7:39, 7:38½ and 8:21, Nannie Douglas winning the first heat. On April 20 of the same year, over the old Fair Grounds track, and at the inaugural meeting of the then new Louisiana Jockey Club, she again won at four-mile heats in 7:36 and 7:51½, when with 101 pounds she beat the five-year-olds Morlacchi and Tom Corbett, each carrying 107 pounds. Afterwards, in May, at Nashville she won at two-mile heats in 3:38 and 3:39 and two days later at three miles in 5:53, which may be said to have ended her career, for although she ran once in 1873 she had virtually broken down.

Annie Bush was then bred to Bonnie Scotland, the produce of which in 1874 was a bay colt which was subsequently called Bushwhacker. During the summer both Annie Bush and her colt were stolen and concealed in the woods, where for the want of proper food the growth of the colt was so "stunted" that at his first appearance on the turf at Baltimore in May, 1877, he was hailed with shouts of laughter and was called by some "Doswell's mule," and only last Saturday he was said to look like a well-fed canal horse. When a two-year-old he was sold or presented to Major T. W. Doswell, of Hanover, under whose colors he ran until he was sold to his present owner, Mr. G. B. Bryson, in 1881. Bushwhacker was never a great success on the turf. Ill-luck seems to have followed him, for on several occasions just as he had been got in prime condition some accident has happened, as in 1879, when he only ran twice, from which he recovered only to go amiss again in the spring of 1880, from which he did not recover until the spring of 1881. His full record is as follows:

| Year. | Age. | Times started. | Times first. | Times second. | Times third. | Gross earnings. |
|---|---|---|---|---|---|---|
| 1877........ | Three years old........ | 10 | — | 3 | 2 | $ 195 |
| 1878........ | Four years old........ | 13 | 4 | 7 | 1 | 5,350 |
| 1879........ | Five years old........ | 2 | — | 1 | 1 | 300 |
| 1881........ | Seven years old........ | 9 | 1 | 1 | 2 | 2,135 |
| 1882........ | Eight years old........ | 12 | 1 | 1 | 4 | 3,375 |
| Totals........ | | 46 | 6 | 13 | 10 | $11,355 |

Bushwhacker may possibly start for the Bowie Stakes at Baltimore in October, for although Mr. Bryson is not a subscriber, if Bushwhacker retains his form until the day before the race (October 20), one of the seven subscribers will no doubt be glad to transfer his subscription to Mr. Bryson, especially as the Pimlico track is the scene of "old Bush's" greatest triumphs, for it was over that track that in October, 1878, he won his two-mile heats and the Bowie Stakes at four-mile heats, the former in 3:36, 3:36½ and 3:38½ and the latter in 7:31, 7:36½ and 8:29, Princeton winning the second heats in both races by the shortest of heads.

The Vanderbilt Team.—At the recent trial at Hartford, W. B. Bair, who has charge of the horses, made the following remarks to "Veritas," the correspondent of the New York *Spirit of the Times:* "Receiving instructions from Mr. Vanderbilt, I had the track scraped, judges appointed, and drove them, as is well known, and accredited, a mile in 2:16½—going the first half in 1:08, by two accurate watches, one of them being the timer presented me by Mr. Vanderbilt. It stopped at 2:16 2-5 in the hands of Mr. Hyde, a wealthy and reliable gentleman of Hartford. I carried twelve pounds of dead weight, making 152 lbs. for the driver. As to the qualities of the team, I never saw or heard of a pair of horses that fall into each other's ways, and mate so quickly, as these mares do. They drive like one horse, on same kinds of bits—an ordinary gum bit. I think Rose is a little the fastest, but Aldine rates very steadily; they work evenly together, and have never made a break with me. I feel confident Mr. Vanderbilt can drive them to road wagon in 2:18, over Fleetwood Course. He has already sent them to the half in 1:08, and they would certainly come home in 1:10. I am willing to bet as much as a man in my circumstances ought that I can beat 2:16¾ with them over Fleetwood, and if they will give me odds [illegible] to beat 2:16,"

## The San Jose Fair.

The meeting on Thursday was again favored with beautiful weather, but there was a large falling off in the attendance, owing to the lack of exciting events in the programme. The first race on the card was a dash of a mile and one-eighth, $5 each, $15 forfeit, with $175 added, a stake that closed with seven entries but of these only two came to the post, H. C. Judson's Patrol and P. Coutts' Forest King. As in most of the races at this meeting there were some notable changes in the betting previous to the start, the odds at first being $25 to $20 in favor of the King, but veering afterwards to the same amount on the chances of Patrol. There was a great deal of jumping and cavorting around that delayed the start but at last Donathan dropped the flag to an excellent start and the horses passed the wire and around the back stretch like a team, but at the half mile post Forest King went ahead, stride by stride, and at the three-quarters he had his adversary beaten, and finished an easy winner by three lengths in 2:02.

In the 2:36 class for a purse of $400 there were originally nine entries, but such was the reputation gained by P. Coutts' fine mare Manon that all the others withdrew, not even contesting for the second and third moneys, and she walked over for the entries, amounting to $360, the association thus gaining $40 by the transaction. Here was another event that was originally looked for as an exciting race, but the effect was discounted at the previous meetings.

The chief event of the day was the special trot for a purse of $300, between Frank Moscow and Ashley, that in the absence of more exciting races was made the medium of some slight speculation, the betting being about $30 to $20 in favor of Moscow. To an outsider these odds seemed to be beyond the bounds of prudence but such was the desire to get on Moscow that even $50 to $25 was laid on him before the start. In the first heat, Ashley, driven by Pete Brandow with 26 pounds overweight, trotted squarely at a slow gait with a skip near the quarter, and won handily in 2:35½ by nearly two lengths, Moscow, probably, not being meant for this heat. This success did not change the ideas of those who were backing Moscow as the desire to invest became so strong that $30 to $8 was freely laid on his winning the race. The next heat was such as to give the spectators an idea that it was a real contest as the two horses were sent along at a little more lively gait, and they were lapped until well into the home stretch where Moscow broke and lost ground and Ashley won by half a length in 2:33¾. Notwithstanding this success, it was rumored freely that Frank could win at any and all times when called upon to do so, and so Moscow was still a greater favorite than before the first heat, selling at $40 to $25 as fast as the pools could be written off. This state of the betting may also be attributed to the fact that Goldsmith would take the reins over the favorite instead of Williams, and the as yet unknown factor was discussed as to what distance in a mile was represented by an overweight in the driver of some 25 pounds. The horses went off very evenly for the third heat, and in the mid back stretch Moscow indulged in one of his peculiar skips of some half dozen strides in which he generally gains a slight advantage, but nearing the half he was off his feet in a more serious manner and lost upwards of a length before he was brought to his gait; thence by square trotting he regained his position until, within fifty yards of the wire, he skipped again, and came under the wire by the shortest of heads in 2:33¼. The backers of Moscow feared that all their investments were lost, but after a short discussion the heat was given to Frank amid mingled cheers and hisses, and cries of "another job" that seemingly in no way disconcerted the judges. It was now $50 to $20 against Ashley, and that mainly through the hedging of some Moscow money under the belief that the race was not such a sure thing as it was cracked up to be. The two final heats were again well contested and Moscow at once took advantage of his position at the pole to make the gait a fast one, and he carried Ashley to a skip on the back stretch but the latter, recovering, came fast and was only beaten out at the finish by Moscow in 2:30½ by about three-quarters of a length. With $25 to $5 on him, Frank Moscow repeated his tactics of the preceding heat, but this time he himself made a skip near the half mile, repeated the clever movement half way between the three-quarter pole and the distance pole gaining about a third of a length, and then broke once more within a short distance of the wire, finishing on a run in 2:34½. This time there was no delay in rendering the decision, as before Brandow could call the attention of the judges to the runs indulged in by Moscow, the latter was declared the winner of the heat and race. Again was the decision received with hisses and even curses connected with the opprobrious term of "thieves," conduct that ought not to have been allowed for a moment, considering that beyond all cavil the gentlemen in the judges' stand were acting to the best of their knowledge and ability. A protest was entered by Pete Brandow in regard to the decision, but at a meeting of the Board of Directors held the same evening, the verdict of the judges was ratified in full and yet some old and experienced turfists maintain that in full justice Ashley was entitled to four heats out of the five that were trotted.

The next race was a purse of $300, free for all pacers, in which there were three starters out of the seven original entries, but no great interest was taken in the event, as it was deemed to be a mere walk-over for Corette, John Wiegle and Washington contesting merely for second honors. There was no betting and the race requires but a very slight description, Corette in each heat going off with the lead and holding it as easily as did Johnny Wiegle the second position, Mr. Yates' fleet mare taking the the three straight heats in 2:24, 2:26½ and 2:34½.

SUMMARIES.

San Jose, September 25.—Running; a dash of a mile and an eighth, $50 each, $15 forfeit, with $175 added; second horse to receive his entrance and one-third of added money.

C. Van Buren enters P. Coutts' b c Forest King, by Monday from Abbie W........ 1
H. C. Judson enters b c Patrol by Wildidle, dam Nettie Brown........ 2

Inauguration, Fostress, Reel Terry, Myra F., Red Boy, and the Duke of Monday were entered but did not start.

Time—2:02.

Same day—Purse $300, free for all pacers.

L. E. Yates names c m Corette by Winthrop, her dam by Ladd's Kentucky Hunter........ 1 1 1
Walter Mead names d g Johnny Wiegle........ 2 2 2
H. A. Van Arminge names blk s Washington........ 3 3 3

Oakland Boy and Lady Hayes were entered but did not start.

Time—2:24, 2:26½, 2:34½.

Same day—Purse $400 for the 2:36 class.

C. Van Buren names P. Coutts' c m Manon by Nutwood........ w o

Revolution, Louis D, Pauline, Eddie F, James Lick, Blanche, San Mateo Belle and Rowdy Boy paid forfeit.

Same day—Special purse of $300 of which $100 to the second horse.

H. B. Cooper names Frank Moscow by Frank Moscow........ 2 2 1 1 1
Jackson Cochran names ch g Ashley, by Plumas, dam by George........ 1 1 2 2 2

Time—2:35½, 2:33¾, 2:33¼, 2:30½, 2:34½.

On the Friday the weather was somewhat chilly in the morning, premonitory of the rain that on the succeeding [illegible] put an end to the races. Nevertheless, toward [illegible] the sun came out and the attendance was nearly up to the average. The proceedings were again delayed and it was fully three-quarters of an hour after the advertised time when the bell summoned the jockeys to the post for the first race, a dash of a mile and a half, $50 each, $15 forfeit, with $200 added. There was a good deal of speculation on this race, the pools selling on the previous evening at $60 on May D and Bender (who were supposed to start) as the field against $40 for Nighthawk, but on the track it was stated that Bender would pay forfeit, and the pools varied greatly in Nighthawk's favor, she bringing $30 against $15 for May D, but when they came on the course the appearance of the latter was considered so favorable that the odds were somewhat reduced in her favor. After a little jockeying for position, the pair were sent off on pretty even terms, Nighthawk at the pole having slightly the best of it, and she made the pace very lively, passing the stand with the advantage of almost a length, but then May D moved up very quietly and as the horses completed the mile, in 1:43, Nighthawk was being urged along and only had a neck and shoulders the best of it. Along the upper turn they ran closely locked together, and at the seven furlongs May D was a little to the fore, but Nighthawk again came bravely to the front and after a desperate finish was only beaten out by the shortest of heads.

The next was a race against time for the society's gold medal, to beat the best California record at a mile, 1:42¼, made by Nighthawk at Sacramento. The only one to make the essay was Belshaw, who on the previous Tuesday had made a mile in 1:43 with 93 pounds, and as he was allowed to go now at catch weight, it was generally thought that he would capture the medal, but even then he would by no means have equaled Nighthawk's performance, as on the occasion mentioned she carried 111 pounds as a five-year-old. Belshaw, ridden by a boy weighing perhaps sixty-five pounds, ran well around to the home stretch in good time, making the half in 50 seconds, but he suddenly slowed up, and although he was roused and sent along again at a lively pace he could only make the mile in 1:42¾.

The next race was made the event of the day and it was a small bonanza for the fielders, who picked up large pools with ridiculously small investments. It was a special race, three-quarters of a mile and repeat, in which George Howson's Jim Douglas with 108 pounds was made an immense favorite at $40 against $20 for the entire field, composed of Ella Doane, Forest King and Haddington, while in subsequent pools he brought $50 against $25 for Ella and $12 for the field.

Writing after the event is decided this seems to be very rash betting, as both Ella Doane and Forest King are known to have speed when at themselves, and Haddington can stay well, even if he is not a flyer of high degree. But these things are but little considered amid the excitement of pool selling and his adherents pointed to the fine form shown last year by Douglas; as also to the easy manner in which he had won his race on the previous Monday, and one enthusiast offered to bet that he would never be headed in any one heat. As usual in these short races there were a great many breakaways before the horses could be got anywhere near into line. When the flag was dropped Ella Doane was the quickest on her feet and she cut out the running with Forest King in close attendance and they were soon neck and neck, two lengths ahead of Douglas, while Haddington was evidently biding for a more favorable opportunity. Up to the last stretch the finish between the two leading horses was very exciting but finally Ella outstayed her opponent and won by the shortest of necks in 1:15½, only half a second beneath the best time ever made in the State. It was so evident that Douglas had made no pretensions for the heat and that he was in fine fettle, that he now became a better favorite than ever, selling at $30 against $10 for Ella and $5 for the field. It was now more difficult than ever to get the horses off on even terms and the delay caused by a long succession of false starts was tedious in the extreme, and at last when the word was given there was a somewhat straggling start at that. Again Ella showed prominently all through the heat, leading both Douglas and Forest King at the start, but Howson in trying to escape a pocket seemed to get dangerously near the leading mare, but at the half mile they were both in line with Forest King within good reaching distance. From this point to the wire it would be impossible to witness a closer contest for when well within the homestretch, the King joined conclusions with the leaders, and it looked like a dead heat, but Douglas in the center managed to better his position in the last few strides and won in 1:17, by a short head from Ella Doane, she leading Forest King by a like distance, while Haddington still reserved his forces. The rider of the mare made a complaint that Howson had cut him down, but the latter showed that Douglas had also been in a scrimmage, but luckily they were slight flesh wounds that had no influence on the ultimate result.

The betting that ensued showed great strength in an unexpected quarter, the backers of Haddington coming squarely to the front and showing for the first time the real Simon Pure of the day. Douglas was nevertheless still favorite at $20, the field bringing $15 and Ella Doane $7. After many a tedious false start, Haddington got away slightly in the lead, with the King lapping, and thus they ran until the drawgate where Haddington drew away and won, hands down, in 1:16¼, by three lengths from Forest King, while Douglas was a poor third. Forest King was sent to the stable under the rule of not having won a heat in three, and there was a good deal of squaring of accounts in the pools, they ranging at about $50 for Haddington, $25 for Doane, and $17 for Douglas. Ella Doane jumped off in the lead and tried to get clear of her opponents, but Haddington had been kept so in reserve that he had plenty of speed in him, and on the homestretch he came away and won in a handy manner in 1:18¼ by three lenghts from Ella Doane, with Douglas third by a like distance. Another proof of the axiom that the race is not always to the speediest horse.

SUMMARIES.

SAN JOSE, September 29.—Running, free for all, a dash of a mile and a half: $50 each, $15 forfeit, $200 added, the second horse to receive his entrance and one-third of the added money.

H. C. Judson names ch m May D, four years, by Wildidle—Nettie Brown........1
P. J. Shafter names b m Nighthawk, by imported Haddington—by Norfolk........2

Jack Douglas, George Bender, Mollie H, Precious, Red Boy, Myra and Fred Collier were entered but did not start.

Time—2:36.

Same day—Purse of $400, of which $100 to the second horse, three quarters of a mile and repeat.

P. J. Shafter names b s Haddington, five years, by imported Haddington—by Norfolk........4 4 1 1
H. C. Judson names b m Ella Doane, aged, by Wildidle—Mattie Brown........1 2 4
George Howson names b s Jim Douglas,—by Norfolk, four years........3 1 3 3
C. Van Buren names b c Forest King, three years, by Monday—Abbie W........2 3 2 ro

Time—1:15½, 1:17, 1:16¼, 1:18¼.

Sandwiched in between the two last heats of the running race, the horses were called up for the purse of $400 for the 2:27 class in which Cairo and Starr King were the only opponents, the three others engaged therein having been withdrawn. The race was looked on as a foregone conclusion for Starr King and no pools were sold on the result. There was but little scoring and immediately the gong was sounded, Starr King went leisurely to the front, but a bad break near the half-mile post set him back and a repetition on the home stretch led to the belief that Cairo might win the heat, but Starr King settled down to a square trot, came up very fast and beat Cairo by the shortest of heads in 2:27½.

As at the conclusion of the running race the sun had only just disappeared beneath the horizon, there was ample time for another heat, if not even to finish the race, but the judges announced a postponement and then it became known that the programme of the fourth day of the fair had been strengthened by the addition of a $750 purse for Abbottsford, Director and Gibraltar, which would certainly of itself have formed a strong and attractive card, and during the evening there was a good deal of wagering on the result. Unfortunately the morning had a very inauspicious look, and by the time the visitors were ready to go out to the grounds, it began to drizzle and soon it increased to a soaking rain that necessitated another postponement, but not until Starr King and Cairo had trotted another heat, which after a great deal of splashing and dashing in the muddy track was won by Cairo in 2:41½.

On Monday, when the horses were called up for the unfinished race, the track was found to be in a fair condition, but somewhat heavy near the inner rail. Starr King, despite the fact that he was suffering a little from lameness, was made the favorite at $20 to $10, as Cairo was also ailing from a swollen leg. In each heat Cairo got the advantage around the first turn, but at the quarter Starr King was in the lead, and finished first by from a length to a length and a half in each instance in 2:25½ and 2:25¾. The race was somewhat unique in its character, as it took three days to bring it to a conclusion. The next event was a purse of $500, two miles and repeat, for the 2:30 class, in which Bullet, Freestone and Tump Winston were withdrawn, leaving the contest to Albert W and Vanderlynn, the betting being $100 to $30 in favor of the former horse. Vanderlynn took the lead and held it well to the half-mile post, when he got off his feet and commenced a succession of breaks that destroyed his chances, as on each occasion when he was getting down to his gait and diminishing the gap between himself and the leader, he would get again on the run, and thus enabled Albert W to jog in an easy winner in 5:04¾.

In the second heat Vanderlynn was much steadier in his gait and he trotted the first mile without a skip in 2:24½, and passed the wire an open length ahead of Albert W, but on the first turn he made a break at the quarter. Albert W was in the lead, but near the half-mile post he was on the run and resigned his position to Vanderlynn, who, on the homestretch, trotting very squarely, looked like a winner, but Albert W came up with a fine burst of speed and carried Vanderlynn off his feet near the draw-gate, winning the heat and race in 4:51. This is another fine performance on the part of Albert W, and many good judges think that with a good track this promising son of Electioneer would lower the best record at the distance, namely that of Steve Maxwell, 4:48½, made at Rochester in August, 1880.

Miss Penniman then gave an exhibition of her talents as an equestrian both in the saddle and in bareback riding that elicited much applause and that was rewarded with the bestowal of the gold medal of the association.

The last race was a buggy race, a dash of two miles for horses owned in the district, to be driven by their owners. There were seven entries, and the following six started: Nettie H, (who was a favorite at even money against all the others,) Tom, No Name, Nig, Little Sam and Prince. As may be imagined, there was a great deal of scoring before an even start could be given, and when the gong was sounded, one horse after another got on the run, the favorite especially ruining the chances of her backers by her rank behavior. As the horses came around for the second time to the half-mile post, it looked as if Mr. Horace Hawes would be the winner, but unfortunately No Name went off his feet, and Tom secured the victory for Mr. Saunders in the fair time of 5:51.

This race brought the fair to a conclusion, that would have proved more satisfactory to the visitors and to the association had not the rain so seriously interfered with the races, and that on the day which generally shows the largest receipts of the meeting. Much of the success of the fair was due to the untiring energy of the able and efficient secretary of the association, T. S. Montgomery, to whom many thanks are due from the members of the press who were present, for his courteous attention. With a little more vim, enterprise and liberality among the members of the association, the San Jose Fair might be made the most attractive and prosperous of all the district meetings in the State, and it would be pleasant to see steps taken at once to place San Jose in that proud position.

SUMMARIES.

SAN JOSE, September 29, 30, and October 2.—Purse for the 2:27 class.

C. W. Welby names ch g Starr King, by George M. Patchen Jr., dam Mary Wonder........1 2 1 1
John Hughes names b g Cairo, by Chieftain, dam unknown..2 1 2 2

Prince Allen, Captain Smith and Director were entered but did not start.

Time—2:27, 2:41½, 2:25½, 2:37½.

Same day—Trotting for the 2:30 class, two miles and repeat, for a purse of $500.

A. Waldstein names b s Albert W, by Electioneer, dam by John Nelson........1 1
P. Farrell names b h Vanderlynn, by George M. Patchen, dam by Joseph........2 2

Bullet, Freestone and Tump Winston were entered but did not start.

Time—5:04¾, 4:51.

Same day—Buggy-horse race. Two mile dash, entrance, $10; first horse, $70, second horse, $30; third horse, silver pitcher. Horses entered into this race must have been owned in the district prior to July 1, and be driven by owner to buggy. No horse having a record will be allowed to start. Whisper barred.

Mr. Saunders names blk g Tom........1
Horace Hawes names b g No Name........2
F. L. Duncan names b g Little Sam........3
J. D. Roberts names blk g Nig........4
W. H. Hollenbeck names br m Nellie H........5
Martin & Carrick name d g Prince........6

Time—5:51.

Premiums were awarded as follows:

**Stallions.**

Best four years old and over, J. & H. C. Judson, Santa Clara, Wildidle, $15.
Second best, Wm. Boots, Milpitas, Kington, $10.
Best three-year-old, Wm. Boots, Inauguration, $10.

**Thoroughbred Mares.**

Best four years old and over, Wm. Boots, Molly H., $10.
Second best, J. & H. C. Judson, Ella Doane, $5.

**Thoroughbred Families.**

Best thoroughbred sire with not less than five colts, all thoroughbreds, J. H. C. Judson, Wididle and five colts, $25.
Best thoroughbred dam, with not less than three colts, all thoroughbreds, J. and H. C. Judson, Nettie Brown and colts, $20

**Horses For All Work.**

Best four years old and over, A. T. Hatch, Suisun, Admar, $10.
Second best, A. Barris, San Jose, Dom Pedro, $5.
Best three-year-old, D. Hellyer, San Jose, Clifford, $8.
Second best. S. S. Drake, Vallejo, Drake, $4.
Best two-year-old, Edward Moran, San Sose, Nutwood, $5.
Second best, J. Weatherford, San Jose, Young St. Lawrence, $3.

**Mares For All Work.**

Best four-year-old, S. S. Drake, Eve, $8.
Second best, John Wright, Polly, $4.
Best three-year-old, A. Barris, (no name) $6.
Best two-year-old, T. Andrews, Minnie, $5.
Best yearling, S. S. Drake, Lena, $4
Second best, T. W. Barstow, Beauty, $2.
The committee on the above were R. H. Newton, Geo. W. Wilson and J. W. Chapman.

**Draft Stallions.**

Best four years old and over, J. Garcia, Twelve-Mile House, Ottawa Chief, $10.
Best three-year-old, Charles Clark, Milpitas, Young Hercules, $8.
Second best, W. P. Phillips, California Chief, $4.
Best two-year-old, James Lendrum, Napoleon, $6.
Best yearling, Thomas Gallagher, George, $5.
Best sucking colt, S. H. Chase, Paul Revere, $3.
Second best, Geo. Easton, Gilroy, Prince Albert, $2.

**Mares.**

Best four years old and over, S. H. Chase, Date, $8.
Second best, Jas. Lendrum, Maggie, $5.
Best three-year-old, P. H. Doyle, Lady Hercules, $7.
Best yearling, James Lendrum, Fan, $4.
Best sucking colt, James Lendrum, Bess, $3.
The committee were John Bubb, P. Matthews and W. Jacklin.

**Roadster Stallions.**

Best three-year-old, E. S. Smith, Boy Wood, $8.
Best two-year-old, E. S. Smith, Fleet Wood, $7.

**Roadster Mares.**

Best four-year-old, E. Topham, Milpitas, Belle, $8.
Best three-year-old, I. S. Drake, Sister, $7.
Best two-year-old, E. Topham, Lady Nutwood, $5.

**Gelding Roadsters.**

Best four years old and over, Edward Younger, Whisper, $10.
Special premium recommended on T. W. Barstow's Frank.
The Committee on the above were G. W. Wilson, A. L. Chapman and C. E. Chapman.

**Jacks and Jennies.**

Best jack, four year old and over, R. J. Green, San Francisco, Lippencott, $8.
The Committee were John Matthews, P. Babb, and M. Jackson.

**Durham Bulls.**

Best threes year old and over, Mrs. E. Bradley, First Duke of Alemeda, $15.
Second best, Wm. Quinn, Santa Clara, Duke of the Valley, $10.
Best yearling, C. Younger, Forest King, $7.
Second best, Mrs. Bradley, Centerville Duke, $5.

**Best Durham Bull Calf.**

Mrs. M. E. Bradley, Royal Bengal, $5.
Second best, C. Younger, 8th Duke of Forest Home, $3.

**Cows—Durham.**

Best cow and calf, Mrs. Bradley, Fanny Third and calf, $15.
Second best, William Quinn, Fuschia Second and calf.
Best three years old and over, C. Younger, Oxford Rose Third, $12.
Second best, Seventh Rose of Forest, $6.
Best yearling, Col. Younger, Red Dolly Eleventh, $7.
Second best, Wm. Quinn, Innocence, $5.

**Best Durham Heifer Calf.**

Wm. Quinn, Peach Blossom, $5.
Second best, C. Younger, Red Dolly Fourteenth, $3.
The committee were John Kay, Dr. J. P. Dubley and Moses Shellenberger.

**Jersey Bulls.**

Best three years old and over, B. F. Fish, General Grant, $15.
Best two years old and over, C. B. Polhemus, Jersey Boy, $12.
Best yearling, C. B, Polhemus, Oscar Wilde, $7.
Second best yearling, J. T. Hoyt, San Mateo, Banker, $5.

**Best Jersey Bull Calf.**

C. B. Polhemus, Tom, $5.
Second best, C. B. Polhemus, Jersey, $3.

**Best Jersey Cow and Calf.**

C. B. Polhemus, Cherry and calf, $15.
Second best, Matella and calf, $10.
Best three years old and over, C. B. Polhemus, Fairy, $15.
Second best, C. B. Polhemus, Pearl, $10.
Best two-year-old, C. B. Polhemus, Matella, $12.
Best yearling, C. B. Polhemus, Gypsey, $7.
Second best, C. B. Polhemus, Pearl 3d, $6.
Second best, C. B. Polhemus, Sunflower, $5.

**Best Jersey Heifer Calf.**

C. B. Polhemus, Bessie 4th, $5.

**Best Thoroughbred Herd of Jerseys.**

C. B. Polhemus, Jersey Bay, Cherry, Matella, Pearl, $20.
Second best, C. B. Polhemus, Fairy 2d.
The committee were R. G. Sneath, Thomas Waite and C. Peebles.

**Ayershires—Bulls.**

Best three-year-old, George Bement, Redwood City, Archie, $15. Same, best yearling, Macbeth, $7. Same, best bull calf, Malcolm, $5.

**Ayrshires—Cows.**

Best three-year-old, George Bement, Elaine, $15. Same, second best. George Bement, Ethel Brown, $10. Same, best two-year-old, Stellinita, $12. Same, best yearling, Sultana, $7. Same, best heifer calf, Sybil, $5. Same, best cow and calf, Lady Merryton and calf, $15. Seme, second best, Stellinita and two calves, $10.

**Best Thoroughbred Herd.**

George Bement, bull Archie and cows Lady Merryton, Stellita, Ethel Brown and Elaine, $10.
The committee were H. Tillotson, A. Wylie and Tom Hildreth.

**Graded Cattle.**

Best cow, four years old, J. B. J. Porter, Belle 1st, $10.
Best yearling, G. P. Beal, Fawn, $5.
The committee were R. G. Sneath, Thos. Waite and C. Peebles.

**Sweepstakes.**

Best bull of any breed or age, C. Younger, second Duke of

umeda, $15 ; same, best cow, Jessie Maynard, $15 ; same, t bull and three calves, Eighth Duke of Alameda, $15. he committee were Paris Kilburn and Thos. Rea.

## Sheep and Goats.

est Merino ram, A. Agnew, Santa Clara, on Longwool, $10·
est Merino ewe, A. Agnew, on Jennie, $10.
est Southdown ram, George Bement, on Sonoma, $10.
est Southdown ewe, J. P. Bubb, Saratoga, on Queen, $10.
est Cotswold ram, Wm. Quinn, on Prince, $10.
est Cotswold ewe, C. Younger, on No Name, $10; same best three ram lambs, $5.
est pen five ewe lambs, Wm. Quinn, $5.
est graded ram, Wm. Quinn, on Fred, $5; same, best ewe, ne, $5.
The committee were W. A. Z. Edwards, John Selby and J. Carr.

## Swine.

Best Best Berkshire boar, Tyler Beach, Waldo, $5; same, st sow, Lizzie, $5.
Best Essex sow, F. H. Doyle, English Betsey, $5.
Best two pigs, any breed, Tyler Beach, $5.
Red Berkshire, Thos. H. Laine, recommended premium, as ere were none provided.
Finest and fattest hog, Tyler Beach, $5.

## Poultry.

Best trio Brahmas, T. J. Waite of Brighton, $2 50.
Best trio Cochins, same, $2 50.
Best trio, Hambargha, same, $2 50.
Best trio Leghorns, O. J. Albee, Santa Clara, $2 50.
Best trio Plymouth Rocks, T. J. Waite, $2 50.
Best trio Bantams, same, $2 50.
Premiums recommended to Mrs. S. Newhall and Mrs. Rayr on Langshans.
Best trio Houdans, premium recommended to T. J. Waite, o award in premium list.
Premium recommended to O. J. Albee on three American zabrights.
Best trio bronze turkeys, T. Miles, $5.
Best trio geese, Louis Verdon Jr., $3.
Best trio ducks, Mrs. S. Newhall, $5.

## Agricultural Machines.

Best display of agricultural machines and implements, armers' Union, $20.
Best horse hay rake, A. S. Babcock & Co., $3.
Best older mill, Farmers' Union, $2.
Best hay and straw cutter, A. S. Babcock & Co., $2.
Best hand corn-sheller, Farmers' Union, diploma.
Best lawn mower, Farmers' Union, $2.
Best header, Farmers' Union, $10.
Best grain sowing machine (broadcast), Farmers' Union $5.
Best self-raking and reaping machine, Farmers' Union, $5.
Best reaping machine, Farmers' Union, $5.
Best mowing machine, E. W. Mills, on Victor mowing machine, $5.
Best combined reaper and mower, Farmers' Union, diloma.
Best display of reaping and mowing machines, Farmers' nion, diploma.
Best self-binder and harvester, Farmers' Union, $5.
Best barrow, Farmers' Union, $5.
Best cultivator, A. S. Babcock & Co., $5.
Best horse hoe, Farmers' Union, diploma.
Best double shovel plow, Farmers' Union, diploma.
Best elevator for stacking grain, W. T. Adel, $5.
Best track cleaner for mower (not on premium list) Committee award premium to W. Prindle, Santa Clara.
Best fanning mill, Farmers' Union, diploma.
Best platform scale, Farmers' Union, diploma.
Best farm or road scraper, A. S. Babcock & Co., $5.
Best wind mill, George H. McDonald & Co., on Centennial wind mill and pump, $5 on each.
Best fruit dryer, Daniel Dempsey, of San Francisco.
Best gang plow, Farmers' Union, $5.
Best sulky plow, Farmers' Union, diploma.
Best double plow, Farmers' Union, diploma.
Best side hill plow, A. S. Babcock & Co., $5.
Best sod plow, Farmers' Union, $5.
Best one-horse plow, Farmers' Union, $5
Best plow, all purposes, Farmers' Union, diploma.
Best two-horse family carriage, F. Jung, San Jose, $10.
Best one-horse family carriage, A. S. Babcock & Co., $5.
Best top-buggy, A. S. Babcock & Co., $5.
Best open buggy, Haiman & Normandin, $5.
Best two-seated open carriage, same, $7 50.
Best farm wagon for general purposes, A. S. Babcock & Co., $10.
Best spring market wagon, H. Prindle, $5.
Best driving cart, W. T. Adel. $5.
Best ladies' phaeton, A. S. Babcock & Co., $10.
Best two-wheeled phaeton (not on premium list), F. Cambert.
Best exhibit of carriage painting, F. Jung, $7 50.

## American Horses in England.

The season thus far has been very unfortunate for our horses in England and if the Americans do not capture some of the important autumn handicaps, it is to be feared that the stable bids will show a woeful balance to the wrong side, and this fact is rendered still more unpleasant when we recall the brilliant victories gained by them in the preceding year. There seems to be something ominous in the absence of both Iroquois and Foxhall from their engagements, but it is to be hoped that they will make their reappearance in fine fettle before the racing campaign is brought to a conclusion. The three-year-olds in both stables seem to be of a very moderate order, Gerald and Sachem being only good enough to run into a third or fourth position, and unfortunately in the racing of the two-year-olds there has not yet been shown any such form as will better our chances for the great three-year-old sweepstakes of next year.

After such a long series of defeats it is cheering to hear of the success in Aranza at the Great Eastern Handicap at Newmarket last week. This fine four-year-old mare, by Bonnie Scotland, from Arizona, was purchased last year by Mr. P. Lorillard for the special purpose of entering her in the large and valuable handicaps in England, she having previously won such important three-year-old events as Maxwell House and the Tennessee Stallion Stakes at Nashville, the Tobacco Stakes at Louisville and the Hotel Stakes at St. Louis. As usual it was some time before she got over the effects of the change in climate, and she had only run three times this season with barren results until last week she scored her first victory on English soil. From the state of the odds we fear that she was not backed freely for the event, as so little was thought of her chances that 20 to 1 was freely offered against her just before the start. The race was run over the Brethy Stakes course (three-quarters of a mile) and Aranza won with the greatest ease by half a dozen lengths. Sir George Chetwynd's Hornpipe, with the odds at 7 to 4 against him, was

second, with Mr. T. Featherstonhaugh's War Horn, at 7 to 1, third. Lord Cadogan's Masurka, at 33 to 1, got away in the lead, followed by Aranza and War Horn. Martin on Aranza waited to "the bushes," where Aranza took the lead, and won, as stated, by six lengths. This sudden showing of form by Aranza, taken in connection with very favorable training reports about Mr. Keene's Bookmaker, a four-year-old, handicapped at 104 pounds for the Cambridgeshire, pushed him and Mr. Lorillard's three-year-old Sachem, at 99 pounds, to the top of the "lists" for that race, with 14 to 1 offered against each of them.

It is a notorious fact that in racing a great deal is ascribed to luck, and last year Fortune was lavish in her treatment of American horses, but this season the fickle goddess has changed the channel of her gifts, they almost all flowing to the remarkable three-year-old fillies that have carried off all the chief stakes of the year. Let us hope we shall have better luck next time.

## The Los Angeles Fair.

Following are the nominations made in the races of the Los Angeles Fair, that commence on October 16th, and lasts throughout the week:

No. 1. Purse of $300 for the three minute class. L. H. Titus, enters b m Hattie Johnson; L. J. Felton, br g Hunter; E. L. Mayberry, b m Lady Washington; L. J. Rose, Don Carlos.

No. 2. Purse of $400 for the 2:38 class. John Reynolds' b g Prentice Boy.

No. 3. Purse of $300, a half mile dash for all two-year runners has the following names: B. P. Hill, br f Augusta E; H. M. Johnston, s f Ela; Andres Machado, br f Ballona; J. W. Adams, b f Aunt Betsy; Hill & Gries, blk f Dotty Dimple.

No. 4. Purse of $500 for the 2:30 class, L. H. Titus, b g Bullett; John Reynolds, b g Prentice Boy; N. A. Covarrubias, s g Charlie D.

No. 5. District running, a purse of $245, half mile and repeat, g Covarrubias, blk g Otto K; H. M. Johnston, s f Ela; T. A. Pellett, b m Mollie Adams; F. Sepulveda, s g Fox; M. A. Forster, g m Minnie, and br m Fele; Hill & Gries b f Belle G.

No. 6. Purse of $290, a mile and repeat, running, E. S. Paddock, b br g Joe Dion; F. Estrdillo, br s Klipspringer; Cyrus Lyon, b m Mestiza; M. A. Forster, b m Fele; Hill & Gries b s Wildfile.

No. 7. Purse $350, district trotting, three-year-olds and under. Wm. Smith, b m Kate Render; F. M. Slaughter, b f Tempest; L. J. Rose, g g Centre.

No. 8. Purse $400, district trotting for the 2:45 class. L. H. Titus, b m Hattie Johnson; L. J Felton, br g Hunter; E. L. Mayberry, b m Lady Washington; L. J. Rose s g Don Carlos.

No. 9. Purse $300, running, district two-year-olds, a dash of three quarters of a mile. B. P. Hill, br f, Augusta E; H. M. Johnson, s f Ela; Andres Machado, b m Ballona, J. W. A. Adams, b f Aunt Betsey; Hill & Gries blk f Dotty Dimple.

No. 10. Purse $500, free for all, L. H. Titus, b m Belle Echo; N. A. Covarrubias, d g Charlie D; L. J. Rose, b s Del Sur.

No. 11. Purse $250, running, free for all district horses, a dash of three-quarters of a mile, T. A.' Pellett, b m Mollie Adams; N. A. Covarrubias, blk g Otto K; M. A. Forster, g m Minnie; Hill & Gries b f Belle G.

No. 12. Purse $350, free for all, a dash of two miles, E. S. Paddock br g Joe Dion; F. Estrdillo, br s Klipspringer; Cyrus Lyon, b m Mestiza; Hill & Gries b sWildfile.

## A World-Wide Evil.

In regard to the system of touting, now so prevalent, we find that in England racing laws prescribe heavy penalties upon any person watching a trial or gallop, unless with the consent of the owner. The result of this is that only the lowest grade of broken-down grooms and turf followers are thus employed; but still each gallop on public training-grounds like Newmarket and Epsom is watched, whilst private gallops like Middleham, Malton and Whitewall are also frequented by the class who, for a bribe, risk all pains and penalties in order to furnish information to their patrons. Clear streams do not generally flow from foul sources and the value of the information so gained, as well as the propriety of its application, is certainly doubtful.

In Australia, touting is not deprecated when fairly done. In the neighborhood of each of the chief cities public training-grounds are formed by the various racing clubs on, or in contiguity to, the race-courses under their control. In the season, gentlemen of position and education, pencil and note-book in hand, represent the various journals, and in their columns furnish full and exhaustive accounts of the work done by each animal, and note the fact of any horse's absence from work. These reports are eagerly read throughout the colonies, and certainly do much to promote and keep up the interest in the great racing events of the year. Naturally enough, a great many owners, and all trainers, dislike this; but that it is more to their ultimate benefit as a body than to their disadvantage is hardly to be doubted. One horse does a good gallop to-day; his work is published and read, and hundreds put a little on him. Next week or next day another pleases the scribes, and he in turn is also published. By the time that one recedes in favor; and so, for these months prior to the Melbourne Cup, continual changes take place, horse after horse is supported, and when any stable has satisfied itself, the books are enabled to lay as much money as is wanted against its chances. That owners, as well as trainers, can always guard against any real knowledge, beyond that of a horse looking well, being obtained upon the training-ground by merely watching work, is well known, and has been frequently shown by the prices obtainable on the short book about winners who, like Zulu, have done all their work subject to such inspection; but there is here, as well as in England, a class who, by suborning stable-boys and boy-jockeys, obtain stable secrets which are as much the property of the owner and trainer as is the money in their pockets or the clothes on their back.

Round the principal rendezvous of those who bet, the class in question congregate at night, and consist of trainers who, through interruption or foul play, have fallen into poverty; jockeys who, through dishonest conduct, have forfeited public trust; stable-lads who, from want of ability and from expiery, have never attained a higher rank; with a mixed host of card-sharpers and thieves. These profess to furnish reliable information, to the backer who is fool enough to trust them, and from him receive a slight fee for information supplied. Meanwhile the layer, by whom the tout in question is supported, meets the unwary one, and knowing the information he has received, and perhaps having heard a little as to lameness etc., lays the desired one a price about the defunct animal. That amongst the host of men in the ring some are found who act as we have described we know, whilst on the other hand the conduct of others is most

upright and manly; but that some more stringent regulation than now exist should be brought in to prevent the corruption of stable lads by the class we have above described is certainly most desirable. — The Federal Australian.

## Milton Young's Retirement.

The sale of Milton Young's racing stable to Mr. R. C. Fats, of St. Louis, for $25,000 is explained by Mr. Young's intention to retire from the "post to the paddock." Having purchased McGrathiana, the celebrated racing and stud farm of the late Price McGrath, he will hereafter devote his time to breeding, believing, as he said to a Courier-Journal reporter on Sunday, "that breeding is better as a permanent business than racing." Mr. Young said he had no reason to complain of any lack of success on the turf, for during the three years he had been racing he had won over $90,000 in purses and stakes. As a breeder Mr. Young begins with the three-year-old colt Onondaga and the five-year-old horse Duke of Montrose at the head of the establishment. Both are well bred and represent thoroughly well their two families. Onondaga is by Leamington, out of Susan Beane, by Lexington, and is a full brother to Mr. George L. Lorillard's young stallion Sensation, who was believed by many to have been the best two-year-old ever trained in this country, while Onondaga himself was the best of the Leamington two-year-olds last year, he winning four out of nine races, including the Juvenile, the July and the Kentucky Stakes. The Duke of Montrose is by Waverly, dam Kelpie, by Bonnie Scotland. He was a fairly good racehorse, with good speed and bottom, and, as Mr. Young says " he intends to keep up with the procession and breed that which is in most demand," his two stallions should in a few years become very popular. His list of mares at present is as follows:

Beatitude, 6, by Bonnie Scotland, dam Mariposa.
Bliss, 5, by Bonnie Scotland, dam Mariposa.
Beatrice, 3, by Bonnie Scotland, dam Mariposa.
Belle of Maywood, 4, by Hunter's Lexington, dam Julia Mattingly.
Black Maria, 3, by Bonnie Scotland, dam Planchette.
Fonwitch, 4, by King Alfonso, dam Weatherwitch.
Gladiola, 4, by Glengarry, dam Waltz.
Kelpie, (1866), by Bonnie Scotland, dam Sister of Euric.
Matagorda, 5, by Glengarry, dam Mattie Morgan.
Olivia, 3, by The Ill-Used, dam Olitipa.
Perhaps, 3, by Australian, dam Mishap.
Patti, 4, by Billet, dam Dora.
Soxodont, 3, by Longfellow, dam Sallie Morgan.
Square Dance, 3, by War Dance, dam Bee Dogherty.
Wildfire, 3, by Leamington, dam Madge.

Of this year's youngsters Mr. Young has two foals, one out of Beatitude, by King Alfonso, and the other out of Perhaps, by St. Martin. Of the mares bred this year Beatrice and Belle of Maywood are thought to be in foal to Glen Athol, Beatrice, Soxodont and Gladiola to Alfonso, Perhaps to Lisbon, Kelpie to imported Thunderstorm, Fonwitch to imported Blue Mantle, Black Maria to King Ban and Matagorda to Enquirer. Mr. Young took possession of McGrathiana on the first of the present month and he hopes to rival the breeding of such flyers as Tom Bowling, Aristides, Calvin, Chesapeake and many others that have made that Stud Farm so famous.

## The $10,000 Purse.

In spite of the unfavorable weather which prevailed until nearly noon of the 14th inst., some 12,000 people gathered at Beacon Park to witness the struggle for the $10,000 purse offered by Mr. D. H. Blanchard of this city, open to all horses which had not beaten 2:17 previous to the beginning of the present season. Nine of the original thirteen nominations fulfilled the requirements and were eligible to start, but Aldina, which had lately been sold to Commodore Vanderbilt, and the noted trotting stallion Black Cloud, named by Col. Russell, failed to put in an appearance, thus leaving seven starters, viz: Edwin Thorn, Clingstone, Helena, Santa Claus, Fanny Witherspoon, Parana and Humboldt. When the horses were brought out for their preparatory exercise, it was noticeable that Santa Claus was suffering from lameness so that many thought he would be drawn, yet others who saw him win the great Stallion Race at Boston last year, expressed the opinion that he was as lame then as now. Those who watched him closely, however, could not fail to notice that he was suffering at every step. Edwin Thorne and Clingstone appeared to be in excellent condition. Fanny Witherspoon, although in fair condition, did not appear quite fit to trot for a man's life, while Helena, Parana and Humboldt were thought to be in too fast company to stand any chance of winning their entrance money. Parana was by far the most beautiful animal of the lot, and although she did not win any part of the purse, she won the admiration of every one who appreciates a fine trotter.

The story of the race is soon told. After scoring a full hour, during which the horses came down eighteen times for the word, they were sent away. In two minutes and nineteen seconds from the time the word was given Edwin Thorne passed under the wire winner of the first heat, with Helene second, Clingstone third, Fanny Witherspoon fourth, Santa Claus fifth, Parana sixth and Humboldt in the rear, which position he maintained to the close of the race. The second heat was won by Thorne. Time, 2:19; Clingstone second, Witherspoon third, Santa Claus fourth, Parana fifth, Humboldt sixth. The third heat was intensely interesting, especially down the back stretch, where the plucky stallion, cripple as he was, worked his way up until his nose showed up in front of Thorne, who was leading the lot; but as they swung into the homestretch Thorne forged ahead with Santa Claus close upon his wheel; at the distance stand Clingstone showed that he had the speed of the lot, giving Santa Claus the good-by, made a rush for Thorne, upon which he was gaining rapidly as the chestnut went under the wire, with Clingstone upon his wheel. Time, 2:18½. Santa Claus third, Parana fourth, Helena fifth, Witherspoon sixth, Humboldt seventh. First money, $5,000, went to Edwin Thorne; second, $2,500, to Clingstone; third, $1,500, to Helene; and the fourth, $1,000, to Santa Claus. During the intervals between the second and third heats the king of the trotting stallions, Smuggler, with a record of 2:15½ and forty-four heats below 2:20 to his credit, was led upon the track where he was received with enthusiastic applause. The race was a success in every sense of the word, and must have netted the enterprising originator between $10,000 and $15,000 and the wish is freely expressed that such a race may become an annual event, but on some more suitable track than that of Beacon Park.

## As to Graves.

EDITOR BREEDER AND SPORTSMAN: What is Graves' best time, and when and where made? RECORD.

ANSWER.—2:19; made at Stockton, Sept. 20, 1874·

## HERD AND SWINE.

### Crossing for Beef Production.

It is useless to attempt to settle the question as to just how many crosses from a beef-making breed are best calculated for producing rapid fattening steers. The varying tendencies which occur in the practice of crossing are so great, depending upon anatomical formation, physiological peculiarities, quietness of temper, and vigor of digestion in both sire and dam, that it is a study worthy of careful attention from such breeders and farmers as are engaged in crossing up for meat production.

If we set out to breed for milk production, we are not liable to be left in any doubt as to our success, for the quart measure is a test that cannot be ignored. Twice a day this measurement makes its record of quantity, while the increase in the growth and fattening of a given steer is seldom taken upon the farm from calfhood to day of marketing.

His periods of gain, as a rule, come when warm weather and grass are in season, continuing while these last; and his periods of loss, as a rule, come when frost nips the grass and cold weather pinches the hide and flesh. When the dairy cow is overtaken by cold weather, the pail records the fact with unvarying certainty, and the promptness with which this is done is fully equal to its certainty. If we could have these daily reminder in the case of the growing or fattening steer, the lessons would be of value, and give us a key to the success of our plan of crossing up, which all experience goes to show we do not resort to the scales to obtain, either in the case of the animal, or the food he consumes.

So, from these premises—and these only partially cover the ground—we deduce that the real inwardness of crossing up for profitable meat production is very far from being mastered. Results are quite variable, even where the means used are, even in the opinion of the service, the same. Some very thin-fleshed cows, from certain bulls, produce progeny that grow rapidly; and when they are ready to feed off, the response from the food given is very prompt and satisfactory. In such cases there are anatomical and physiological reasons which, while they are not quite apparent to every one, nevertheless exist; and if not clearly discoverable in the make-up of the immediate progenitors, they rest upon a base not very remote. Cattle are in one regard like members of the human family, in that there are no two alike. It is true of shepherds and herdsmen that where they have long been familiar with a flock or herd, they know each animal under their care, though the numbers be large. For each purpose for which cattle are bred, the aim of the breeder is to have them all like that one. This feat has never yet been accomplished, nor ever will be. It is quite possible to breed and rear a lot of young cattle that will feed almost as near alike as pigs of a given litter. But nature has planted a safeguard against the utter confusion which would follow a too close resemblance among the members of the human family; and the same safeguard is thrown around the brute creation.

It is quite well established that the tendency of flesh-making may be made somewhat uniform in a herd, while it is certain that a oneness of feature never has been, and to any great extent never will be. Cattle and other animals, both wild and domestic, distinguish each other by sight, though massed together in large herds. In the case of Gypsies—and the same may be said of Jews—transmission having been confined within the circle of their own race—the peculiar features of each have been perpetuated. But in these cases we observe that likeness carries dissimilarity along with it. The same may be said of the cattle of the island of Jersey.

Intensely inbred for a long time, their peculiar features are very deeply planted; yet every individual animal is unlike every other one, upon the island or anywhere else, no matter how bred and reared. The peculiarities found in these cattle are the opposite of those that insure prompt taking on of flesh. But this very fact affords a lesson to the breeder of steers, for the rule as to transmittal of peculiarities works both ways with equal certainty. Hence, even for breeding steers, as men who are engaged in this industry have much at stake, the rules that govern a breeder of cattle of the highest type should hold good with them. Any breed of cattle, and we may say the same of cattle that are of no particular breed—mongrels—depend, for any fixed peculiarity they may possess, upon concentration of blood, and in looking for a male with a flock or herd, for the breeding steers for beef purpose, the mongrel intense flesh-making tendencies should be sought for, and none others accepted. That this be present in the individual to be used merely does not of itself afford a guarantee. Evidence of a long-fixed tendency to fatten in the progenitors should alone satisfy. In the ratio of the possession of this can the males selected for breeding steers be depended upon with any class of cows; yet, of course, the leaven of the cow goes into the calf, and her quality is by no means a matter of indifference.—National Live Stock Journal.

### Popularizing New Breeds.

Perhaps the most striking feature of the improved stock breeding interests in this country of recent years is the growth in favor of breeds which were almost unknown a few years ago; as a rule this has not been an indication of loss of favor by the old established breeds. These do not monopolize attention and interest as formerly, but they are, generally, being bred in increased numbers, and with an increasing number of admirers. Shorthorns and Jerseys are bred in larger numbers than ever; the one was almost alone as improved beef breed, and the other had no rival in the Guernsey. Hereford breeders have, as yet, suffered no injury because the Black Scots have suddenly shot almost or quite to the front. The increasing importation of English draft horses does not seem to discourage the importers and breeders of Clydesdales and French drafts. Our country is so large, the demand for good animals so great, and the variations of tastes and conditions so marked that there is still room for all.

The friends of the more-recently introduced breeds are properly anxious to increase their popularity. We will gladly help them to spread abroad a knowledge of their merits—we have done more in this line than any other periodical in like time. The friend and admirer of all 'worthy breeds, we may be permitted to urge that lessons be learned from the experience of those who have handled the old-time favorites.

Every popular breed has suffered from the indiscreet or extravagant claims of some of its admirers. It does no good, but does do harm, to loudly praise our favorite breed, or unjustly criticise other breeds; and it ought to be kept in mind that its special friend of one breed is almost certainly biased in its favor, and to some extent prejudiced against others. Such a man may safely imitate Holmes in his resolve not to write as funny things as he could, that is, he may safely make his claims a little less strong than he believes the facts will warrant. An intelligent, conscientious man who is handling rival breeds is in the best position, perhaps, to give justice to each. He rests, of course, under the temptation to make the most of the special merits of each breed—balancing the one against the other. We urge the breeders and admirers of each new candidate for public favor not to make the mistake of relying on extravagant claims, and to do as little as possible of fault-finding with rival breeds. As a rule, it is better to make praise positive rather than comparative.

Each new competitor for favor must prove itself worthy of that favor. Deserved reputation in other countries will not suffice for permanent reputation here. For instance, the polled Scotch breeds have long maintained a first-class reputation in their own country for the quality of their meat. Suppose American breeders should have been content to rely on this—these breeds would soon have lost favor in this country. The cattle must be shown at the fairs and fat-stock shows; fat bullocks must be put in markets here, if the highest reputation is to be preserved.

Public-spirited, broad-minded treatment of all questions relative to the breeds in question will ultimately prove the wiser policy. Anything which looks like a desire to keep the breed in a few hands, or which has the appearance of trying to have a "ring" or "clique" in control of its destinies, will work harm. The more widely the breed can be distributed in good hands—the larger the number of enterprising breeders interested in it—the better.

Above all things, let those most interested put down all attempts to create any standards other than those relative to practical excellence. Don't let shades of color, shape or size of horn, or ear, or tail, or like points, be brought forward as tests of fashionableness or price.—Breeder's Gazette.

### Fattening Cattle.

Most animals eat in proportion to their weight, under average conditions of age, temperature and fatness.

Give fattening cattle as much as they will eat and often—five times a day.

Never give rapid changes of food, but change often.

A good guide for a safe quantity of grain per day to mature an animal is one pound to each hundred of their weight; thus an animal weighing 1,000 pounds may receive ten pounds of grain.

Every stall feeding in the fall will make the winter's progress more certain by thirty per cent.

Give as much water and salt at all times as they will take.

In using roots, it is one guide to give just so much, in association with other things, so that the animal may not take any water.

In buildings have warmth with complete ventilation, with correct currents, but never under 40 nor over 70 degrees Fah.

A cold, damp, airy temperature will cause animals to consume more food without corresponding result in bone, muscle, flesh or fat, much being used to keep up warmth.

Stall feeding is better for fat making than box or yard management, irrespective of health.

The growing animal, intended for beef, requires a little exercise daily, to promote muscle and strength of constitution; when ripe, only so much as to be able to walk to market.

Currying daily is equal to seven per cent. of the increase.

Keep the temperature of the body about 100 deg., not under 95 nor over 145 deg., Fahrenheit.

Don't forget that one animal's meat may be another animal's poison.

It takes three days of good food to make up for one of bad food.

Get rid of every fattening cattle beast before it is three years old.

Every day an animal is kept, after being prime, there is loss exclusive of manure.

The external evidences of primeness are full rumps, flanks, twist, shoulder, purse, vein and eye.

A good cattle man means a difference of one-fourth. He should know the likes and dislikes of every animal.

It pays to keep one man in constant attendance on thirty head of fattening cattle.

Immediately when an animal begins to fret for food, immediately it begins to lose flesh; never check the fattening process.

Never begin fattening without a definite plan.

There is no loss in feeding a cattle beast well for the sake of the manure alone.

No cattle beast whatever will pay for the direct increase to the weight from the consumption of any kind or quantity of food—the manure must be properly valued.

On an average it costs, on charging every possible item, 12 cents for every additional pound added to the weight of a two or three-year-old fattening beast.

In this country the market value of store cattle can be increased 36 per cent. during six months of the fattening finish.

In order to secure a sure profit, no store cattle beast, of the right stamp and well done to, can be sold at less than 4½ cts. per pound, live weight.—From the advance Report of the Experimental Department of Ontario Agricult ural College.

### Pigs For Profit.

Col. F. D. Curtis, a veteran swine grower, gives the following condensed instructions in the American Agriculturist for September on raising pigs for profit:

The care of pigs in summer can be made less troublesome and more profitable than is usually the case. Unless confined in restricted quarters, pigs are liable to break out and do mischief. They are not adapted to be kept with other stock, so no animal likes to feed after pigs, and while this dislike is so marked that animals will not eat out of the same vessel from which pigs have been fed, or in which they have "messed," they may be forced from hunger to eat the grass in the pasture where they run, but it is not wise to compel them to do so. For these reasons, farmers generally keep pigs shut up in pens where they must be supplied with all the food they require. Sometimes this condition is improved upon by allowing them a small range upon the ground. This is better than close confinement in the pen, as it makes them more comfortable and healthy, but it does not lessen very much the amount of care they require, as the supply of food is soon exhausted. It is a better plan to have the inclosure so large that the pigs cannot readily consume all the grass and make it bare for any kind of vegetation. When pigs are not rung to prevent rooting, they will soon spoil a small inclosure and also damage a larger one. This injury to the pasture can only be prevented by inserting in their snouts two or three rings made of malleable wire. Care should be taken to have the ends of the wire straight so that they will not spill out. Every farm should contain a pasture for pigs, set apart for their exclusive use. It should be large enough to afford them ample space, so that while feeding off one portion the grass will grow on the rest of it, to afford continuous feed. The size of the pasture must be regulated by the number of pigs to be kept. An acre is sufficient for three or four hogs, especially if the ground has been seeded with orchard grass, which starts the quickest and furnishes more feed than most other grasses. The manure from the hogs will increase the growth. The fences should be of a substantial character, so that the pigs will not break out. An unruly hog is the hardest kind of an animal to confine, hence the importance of good fences, to prevent their becoming breechy; a board fence or a stone wall is the best.

### The Best Breed of Sheep.

Which is the best breed of sheep? Is it the Cotswolds, with their noble presence, great antiquity, thorough pedigree, their health, hardiness, longevity, and heavy fleeces and heavy carcasses, their prolificacy or good nursing qualities? Is it the Leicesters, with finer bone, greater refinement of carcass, fleece and points, aptitude to fat, good wool, neat outline, desirable fiber, length-of staple and profitable limbs? Is it the Southdowns, medium size, extreme hardiness, adaptation to hill pastures, grand symmetry, unequaled mutton, early maturity, tough constitution and productiveness in breeding coupled with surety of raising? Is it the Merino, with their swollen form, fine wool, hardihood, fine fleece, impervious, felt-like covering, their remarkable fecundity, and good motherhood? Is it any of these, or some fixed grade of these, or is it each and all? By fixed grades or crosses we mean such breeds as Oxfordshire, Hampshire, Lincolnshire downs, etc. Is it some one, or all of these? We contend that it is all. No one breed is best for all climates and conditions, no one breed is equally adapted to mountain pastures and to plains. Each is best where it thrives the best. Let the shepherd study the breeds, study his wants, study his pasturage, climate, and market, and then select with judgment derived from knowledge. Size of flock, surface, soil, exposure, all should be taken into account. These are questions all must study and determine for themselves and they are points that underlie all success in sheep husbandry. All are best where best adapted. All are worst where worse conditioned. We need each and all. We have diversity enough to accommodate all.—Farm and Garden.

Room For Both.—Mr. Samuel C. Kent, of West Grove, Pa., in his new catalogue of the Avon herd of Guernseys, compares them with the Jerseys in the following language:

"As to the merits of the Guernseys, we would state that previous to our visit to the Channel Islands, we were strictly Jersey; but after a few weeks' sojourn, first on one, then on the other, our prejudice, as it surely was, gave way to a deep admiration of the lovely, golde-skinned Guernsey cattle, and we concluded to at least divide our interests between the two breeds; and while we still love the Jerseys, and believe them indispensable, we can see many traits of excellence in the Guernseys not found in the Jerseys; and while the Jerseys will ever, we believe, retain their general favor, the Guernseys must stand first for their greater physical power over the Jerseys, and deeper-colored and richer milk and butter products over all breeds. They are said not to be so pretty and fancy-like; but they are not at all homely to us."

## BICYCLING.

### Beacon Park Races.

A ten mile amateur and a five mile professional race took place September 18th, at Beacon Park, Boston. The weather was exceptionally fine and some good riding was done by the English rider Moore although he was not pushed by his competitors. The event began about half past four o'clock with the amateur race, the distance being ten miles, and the starters were Frank Moore of Birmingham, England, J. S. Deane of Boston, E. D. Claflin of Newton, E. M. Bent of Framingham, and J. Hewitt of Boston. Moore gave his competitors each one minute start but made up the handicap in the third mile, all the others except Deane having retired previous to this time. Moore however went on to secure a record and completed the ten miles in 33:34. Deane finishing in 37:44.

The professional race was for five miles, J. S. Prince allowing his competitors, J. R. Mellin and Thomas Harrison, forty seconds start. Harrison led for three laps and took Mellin's place to the end of the two and a quarter miles, when Prince overtook him and began rapidly to catch up Mellin's allowance also, but as usual, when he came up with his adversary's rear wheel he held there until the last lap, and on the home stretch the two came down neck and neck, Mellin making a gallant effort to keep the front, but without avail. Prince crossing the line the winner in 17:1. Frank Moore, the English one and twenty-five mile champion, is said to have completed a practice mile upon the Beacon Park track recently in 2:56, which shows that the track at least is not at fault if fast times are not made by the American riders.

What 'cyclist has not been troubled with the discomforts of clothing wet with perspiration after a hard run, when the cold, clammy garments suggest chills and colds, with their attendant evils? To avoid these annoyances, the costume should be made of serge or flannel, with waistbands and pockets of thin flannel. A suit constructed in this way and worn with woolen underclothing, will be found comfortable and healthy. Linen or cotton is an abomination, and as such should be discarded by all engaged in athletic exercises. The jacket should fit snugly, an incident should all the clothing of the 'cyclist, as even if the underclothing is damp, the danger of catching cold is not so great, because the spaces left by loose fitting garments allow them to grow cold. The 'cyclist can easily carry a woolen Jersey to put on during stops, or in the evening when the air is cooler. When touring the clothing should be thoroughly dried and warmed each night, in order that it may be fit for wearing in the morning. Avoid all cheap clothing, as it is poor economy in the end, and a 'cyclist in cheap and ill-fitting garments is a sight well calculated to draw tears from a stone.—World.

The Sacramento riders of the wheel have finally effected an organization, having formed a club on the 24th of August with Douglas Lindley president, Russel P. Flint captain, and E. B. Carroll and H. A. Marvin lieutenants. R. H. Hawley secretary and treasurer, and A. Scheld bugler.

The ruins of the past few days have been sufficient to lay the dust, and as soon as the roads become smooth again there will be a fine opportunity for our wheelmen to try some extended country trips before the heavy winter rains finally set in.

The hundred-mile race between Prince and Morgan is to be run at the opening of the Casino in Boston in November. The championship point has been dropped and Morgan will receive a mile handicap. The stakes will be $500 a side.

# FISH.

## Fish Farming.

There are but few persons who realize how much can be made by "fish farming." A few acres of ground, an artesian well and a few good fish, and one has, in a short time, a business that he can rely on. When traveling in Contra Costa County, we made the acquaintance of Mr. C. Dickenson, who for several years has devoted his time and attention to raising fish. Mr. Dickenson has a small farm of about twenty acres, near the town of Concord. About four years ago he made up his mind to experiment a little with the raising of fish. The first step was to sink an artesian well, at no very great expense, and then to dig out and arrange flood-gates to two or three ponds. The next was to stock these ponds. The fish that he selected was the European or German Carp. As he could not obtain any of the species in this country at the time, that were fit for breeding purposes, he sent to Germany, and after much trouble and expense succeeded in introducing to the waters of his ponds about eight fish that averaged five inches in length. This was four years ago. Mr. D. has increased the size and number of his ponds; he now has five ponds that average 60 feet square and these five ponds contain about 6,000 carp that run from 4 to 15 pounds in weight. He has also stocked the two ponds on Kimbal's Island near Antioch; these small bodies of water contain about 3,000 fish. Mr. D. says that the cost of keeping these fish is very light; what a dog would eat will feed a large number of fish. The breeding ponds ought to be shallow—not more than 12 or 14 inches deep—with sloping banks and a mud bottom. Carp require a muddy bottom in order to do well, and many persons suppose that these fish are not fit to eat as they taste of the mud, but this objection is easily overcome by putting the fish into a small pond or tank with a gravel bottom and running water a few days before putting on the table. By this means the muddy or earthy flavor entirely disappears and a very fine flavored fish is had; the best size for table use is about 2½ pounds; those weighing 12 or 15 pounds, though good eating are rather coarse of grain.

Mr. Dickenson is not sending any to speak of to the market, as he has orders from gentlemen from many parts of the country, for fish to stock their private ponds. Several lots have been sent to the Sandwich Islands and are doing well there from last accounts. Aside from being an excellent food-fish, the carp takes the bait well and is a plucky fighter and will afford the angler any amount of sport. There are many other kinds of fish that could be raised both for profit and sport among the many varieties is the trout, which is receiving its share of attention as the following from the *Modoc Independent* shows :

"Mr. H. Woodson, who owns a ranch at Lake Annie, near Fort Bidwell, has been engaged in the business of trout-raising for the past three years, and has met with remarkable success. Three years ago Mr. Woodson procured a number of small trout from one of the streams which empty into Pit river, and although there was not at that time a fish of any kind in Lake Annie, the waters of the lake are now swarming with nice trout. Mr. W. states that in May last he caught fish from the lake that weighed 7 pounds—they having been in the lake just 31 months. A short time ago he caught twelve trout which were only one year old, and the aggregate weight of the 12 fish was 22 pounds. He sells fish in the Fort Bidwell market at 25 cents per pound, and finds the business very remunerative. Others in Surprise Valley are turning their attention to fish culture, and Mr. Woodson finds no difficulty in disposing of his young fish at $30 per thousand."

## On Fish Propagation.

The wonderful effect of artificial propagation is shown in the following extract from a letter from Seth Green, a man who stands pre-eminent in this most novel and useful science:

"Through the methods employed by the New York Fish Commissioners in shad propagation, methods which were discovered by me in the year 1867, the Hudson and other rivers have been made to produce as many shad as they ever before were known to produce. Under date of June 14, 1882, I am in receipt of a letter from Mr. P. A. M. Van Wyck, of New Hamburgh, N. Y., which says that about twelve years ago the shad had been so nearly caught out of the Hudson that the fishermen abandoned the river because they could not make it pay. The season of 1882, owing to the efforts of the New York Fish Commissioners, shad were more plentiful than ever known before. Within a distance of six miles, 30,830 full-grown shad were taken. Mr. Van Wyck has kindly given me the names and number of fish caught by each fisherman, and the list is now before me.

"There has been a great deal of newspaper talk about the propagation of striped bass, cod and Spanish mackerel, and some cod are claimed to have been hatched, but as yet no way has been discovered to any knowledge successfully to obtain the spawn and propagate these species. I believe it is the duty of the United States Fish Commission to keep on experimenting until some way is discovered to propagate successfully these fish, but no large outlay need be made until such plans are hit upon. It does not properly belong to State enterprise to stock the ocean, which is United States waters, and for which proper appropriations are made by the government.

"In conclusion, I will add that there is no simpler way to practice fish culture than on paper, and it requires but a slight movement of the pen to convert thousands into millions."

TOO BIG TO SWALLOW.—The Calhoun (Georgia) *Times*, with an air of modesty that disarms it of any how-is-that-for-high appearance, tells the following truth: "About two weeks ago Mr. Smith, living a few miles from Calhoun, Georgia, on the Oostanaula river, lost a yearling heifer, about three years old, and as it was fine stock, made diligent search, but could not find it. A few days ago a party of young men fishing in the river were attracted by the smell of a dead carcass, and upon examining the cause, lo, behold! they found a monster catfish, which had swallowed the calf, and the horns of the calf becoming entangled in the fish's gills had drowned the fish. The fish measured exactly twenty-three feet and one-quarter inches in length, and was five feet, eight and one-quarter inches across the head, and from the length of his whiskers supposed to be one hundred and seventeen years old."

The *Farmer's Journal* says that "At Elyria, Ohio, the other morning, nearly a peck of young salmon trout, six inches in length fell from the clouds into a single door yard." Is this the effect of the use of giant powder in California streams?

A Modesto Justice of the Peace this week fined one Miranda $50 for erecting a dam in the Tuolumne river over which the fish could not go.

---

## The International Fisheries Exhibition.

Professor Spencer F. Baird has recently prepared and published a valuable synopsis of the objects of the great International Exhibition of Fish and Fisheries to be held at London, in May, 1883, and the part to be taken therein by America. From this manual we take the following extracts:

"In the collective exhibit will be shown, in a systematic and synoptical manner, illustrations of our marine and freshwater animals of economic value, together with the apparatus and methods of their capture and utilization; and the commercial, scientific, social, historical, and legislative aspect of the fisheries. It will include the most striking features of similar exhibits made by the Fish Commission in the Philadelphia Exhibition of 1876, and the International Fishery Exhibition at Berlin, in 1880, together with many additional ones never previously attempted. The major part of this display will be borrowed from the collections of the National Museum in Washington, but it will be necessary to secure the right of placing in this department such of the private exhibits as can there be shown to the best advantage, it being the understanding that these are not to be excluded from competition.

"It is considered especially desirable that the department of competitive exhibits shall contain a very complete representation of the various food preparations of fish—canned, dried, pickled, smoked, etc.—there being a constantly increasing demand in England for goods of this description, shipments to that country amounting, in 1881, to more than $2,000,000, in addition to the very large exports to other parts of Europe and to the European colonies in the east. Manufacturers of boats and boat-fittings, angling apparatus and costumes, and other similar articles are also urged to contribute."

---

## A Fight of Sea Monsters.

General Spinner, the hero that used to sign the treasury notes, sends the following descriptive letter of a fight among sea monsters on the coast of Florida on South Beach, below Mayport. "Early yesterday morning, as I went to my canal surf bath, accompanied by my daughter, Mrs. Shumaker, we witnessed what has probably never before been seen. The ocean was unusually placid, but a strange commotion in the surf was noticed. On nearing the shore it was seen that a fierce battle was raging between two schools of fish. It was high tide and the water was shallow, so that the caudal and dorsal fins of both these kinds of sea monsters were constantly seen above water. The onslaught of each of the combatants, of which from sixteen to twenty were in view, was fierce and terrific. A disabled saw fish was stranded. I waded in to him and with a piece of floor board gave him the coup de grace. He measured nearly fifteen feet and carried a sword three and a half feet long with over fifty teeth on its margin. It was found that one of the sharks had bitten a piece out of his side equal to a foot square, through which his bowels protruded. At one time it looked as though another pair of the combatants would be stranded, for in their struggle they came so near the shore that they touched bottom all the time, but they managed to join their companions in deep water, and after fifteen minutes all the belligerents disappeared, to the great relief of those who cared more for sea bathing than seeing the terrific fights of sea monsters. My daughter will carry the saw of the captured fish to her home as a memento and trophy of the great conflict, and for an addition to her cabinet of ocean curiosities.—*Florida Dispatch*.

---

## A New Food Fish Discovered.

Captain Joseph W. Collins, of Gloucester, arrived home on September 29th, from an experimental trip in the smack Josie Reeves, of New York, to the edge of the Gulf stream in search of the fish in the interest of the United States Fish Commission. The smack fished for three days over the ground where the fish had been found in the greatest abundance for the past three years, making two sets of trawls a day, covering fifty miles of territory without taking a tile fish. The trip, however, resulted in the discovery of a new food fish, believed to be of great value, specimens of which were brought up on the trawls from a depth of about 120 fathoms in latitude 40 degrees 2 minutes, longitude 71 degrees 2 minutes west. The fish somewhat resemble sea bass, with upside differences, the under side being beautifully mottled with a delicate shade of pink on a cream colored ground. The back is of a mottled pink and reddish brown. The fish has thirteen spines in the dorsal fin and the pectoral fins are unusually large. The specimens taken were from one pound to four pounds in weight. When cooked the fish is white and delicious. Specimens were brought on ice and in alcohol, and have been sent to Washington for identification and a name.

SEEKING PLEASURE UNDER DIFFICULTIES.—Some Renoites went down to Pyramid lake last week to hunt and fish. They went out into the lake and boarded a "lone barren isle"—an island alive with rattlesnakes. While on the island they were caught by the late big storm, and having but a frail bit of a boat, were forced to remain there among the snakes two days and nights. On account of the many snakes they dare not seek shelter among the rocks. They were obliged to camp and sleep on the beach, where they were exposed to the full fury of the storm. Then we learn that at Donner creek the water is very low at present, and the trout in it can almost be caught with the hands. The only drawback to the sport of fishing in it, is the tendency the cattle along the creek have to chase the fisherman, and because gored pants are not fashionable.

SWARMING SALMON.—The Yale (B. C.) *Sentinel* says: "All along the edge of the river the water is black with salmon, while all the creeks for a long distance up are jammed with them. Millions are to be seen. As the water goes down in the creeks, thousands are left to die along the edge and where the water is shallow or dries up. Such sights are not in the recollection of the oldest inhabitant. On Monday Mr. Judkins, a photographer, proceeded to Gordon creek bridge and took a number of views of the salmon swarming along the edge and at the mouth of the creek."

SALMON IN THE YUBA.—On Tuesday last some of the men standing on the levee opposite the mouth of the Yuba river, noticed a floundering and splashing in the wet sand, which constitutes the principal element of that stream, and thinking that it was a beaver, secured a boat and crossed to the place, and captured the cause of the commotion, which proved to be not a beaver, but a large salmon weighing 32 pounds. The cessation of hydraulic mining on the Feather river has rendered that stream comparatively clear, and fish are in consequence making their way up its waters.—*Sutter County Farmer.*

---

IRELAND'S NEWEST GRIEVANCE.—The Fishery Commissioners give the most doleful accounts of the produce of her seas. Once Dublin Bay was famous for its herrings. In the autumn that little harbor of Dunleary, a well-known haunt of fishermen and smugglers, would be filled with the brown sails of the Cornish luggers. They will scarcely come over this year—at least, but if they read the reports of the Commissioners and believe in them. It seems that in 1878 there were nearly 130,000 meese of herrings captured, while last year the take did not amount to a third of that figure ; and what is more distressing is that this deficiency is gradual. From 1877 to 1882 year after year the falling-off has progressed. If there was a sudden failure it might be accounted for by a disease of the fish, but a gradual and continuous dwindling looks as if the herrings were following the example of the peasantry, and leaving the shores of the island.

Obstructing the salmon by an impassible rack really amounts to the same as confining them in pens, except that it is on a larger scale. As the rack prevents them from going up the river, and their irrepressible instinct to ascend the river keeps them from going down, they become confined on a large scale under the most favorable conditions possible. Their native river is their prison. All their surroundings are natural and healthful. They have the whole volume of the river for their water supply, and in every way it is the most desirable form of confinement possible. Nothing better could be wished. The great advantage of this method of confinement showed itself as soon as it was tried in a vastly improved condition of the salmon in the McCloud river. When before hundreds of the spawning salmon died in the artificial ponds and corrals in which they were placed, now none whatever die, or appear even to suffer, from the effects of their confinement.

Since the artificial hatching has been carried on at McCloud river the salmon in the Sacramento have immensely increased; so much so that, although the same time has increased, and the sea-lions and the fishermen also, the salmon have nevertheless, made a steady gain in numbers; or, to use the words of the late Hon. B. B. Redding, the secretary of the California fish commission, "the commission has, with the aid of the artificial hatching of salmon, beaten the sea-lions, the canneries, and the fishermen combined."

Parties returning from Pescadero say that salmon-trout are running in from the sea in large numbers. These fish weigh from four ounces to one and a half pounds. They take most any bait and are very gamy and fight to the last. It is more than likely that if our anglers would search they could find plenty of these fish in nearly all the lagoons and creeks along the coast that open into the ocean. As the brook and mountain trout season is over, it is to be hoped that the salmon trout will take their place.

Last Sunday Mr. Barbin chartered the schooner Eudora and took a party of forty persons out on a fishing excursion on the bay. The best grounds were found in the vicinity of Angel Island where the party stayed until it began to rain and they had to abandon their sport till a more favorable time. A great many other boats, containing enthusiastic fishers who ran the risk of a wetting, were out, but they, too, got wet and pulled for the shore.

Reports are current that large numbers of salmon trout have run into the creek near Mussel Rock, San Mateo county. This creek was formerly used by the Acclimating Society for the propagation of fish and found to be a very good place for those purposes.

A fish pond at Benton Park, St. Louis, was stocked last spring with twenty carp, and now there are three thousand of them. A carp should be two or three years old before it becomes food.

Good fishing was had last Sunday at the Anita Rocks near Harbor View. Two parties who were out caught forty-eight pounds of rock cod and might have got a great many more had they not been driven to shelter by the rain.

It is a well-known fact that salt water fish are very fond of wheat. No doubt some of our fishermen will find good fishing in the vicinity of the place where the wheat-laden barge Commerce turned over last Sunday.

During the past week large strings of tom cod have been caught from off the wharves.

The run of tom cod in the Columbia river is very large.

---

## California Horses in Australia.

That trotting enthusiast, Dr. Weir, has let no grass grow under his feet since leaving Melbourne—it seems only the other day—for he has already reached Sydney, and will soon be in Victoria with the nine nags he has specially selected in the States for our trotting turf. He arrived in the sister colony last Friday by the Zelandia, and the following is a list of the horses he has brought, with the authentic pedigrees, viz: Violetta, bay mare, five-year-old, by Echo, dam Nita, by Sawyer's Hambletonian, he by Whipple's Hambletonian, Echo by Rysdyk's Hambletonian. Daisy, chestnut mare, four-year-old, by Elmo, dam Bracelet, by David Hill's Clara, ch m, four-year-old, by Elmo, dam Bessie, Kickuk. Ella Chieftain, ch m, eight-year-old, by Chieftain, dam Susie, by Kentucky Hunter. Swamp Angel, bay m, aged, by David H I record 2:34½, at Marysville, Cal. Midnight, b g, four-year old, by Elmo, dam Maggie, by Whipple's Hambletonian. Richard, bay g, seven-year-old, by Gen. M. Patchen, dam Susie Simpson, by Owen Dale, he by Belmont—Owen Dale, dam Mary Downing, by American Eclipse. Oliver, bay g, eight-year-old, by imported Hercules, dam by Belmont, he by American Boy; record 2:37, at Sacramento, Cal., 1878.—*The Melbourne Sportsman.*

---

## The Crocodile in Florida.

Recent investigations have shown that the crocodile is to be found in the less frequented parts of Florida, where it has long been confounded with the alligator, and a single specimen is now among the collection of reptiles at the Smithsonian Institution. The great point of difference between crocodiles and alligators is that the former live in salt water, bayous or creeks near the sea, while the latter are to be found only in the fresh water streams. The crocodile, caynan, gavial and alligator are all types of one group, the crocodilia. In these reptiles the heart resembles that of birds more than that of any cold-blooded animals. The ventricle is completely divided by a septum into two chambers, the venous and arterial blood join outside of the heart, and the blood is birdlike. The muzzle of the alligator is in a straight line, but that of the crocodile is much narrower behind the nostrils. There are also other anatomical differences. The crocodile is known among the Indians as the "long-nosed alligator." The Florida crocodile is the crocodilus acutus of Cuvier, and is entirely identical with the Jamaica species, but is entirely different from the cayman of Guiana, South America.

# THE
# Breeder and Sportsman.
PUBLISHED WEEKLY BY THE
BREEDER AND SPORTSMAN PUBLISHING CO.
THE TURF AND SPORTING AUTHORITY OF THE PACIFIC COAST.

**OFFICE, 508 MONTGOMERY STREET**
P. O. Box 1338.

*Five dollars a year ; three dollars for six months ; one dollar and a half for three months. Strictly in advance.*

MAKE ALL CHECKS, MONEY ORDERS ETC., PAYABLE TO ORDER OF BREEDER AND SPORTSMAN PUBLISHING CO.

Money should be sent by postal order, draft or by registered letter, addressed to the "Breeder and Sportsman Publishing Company, San Francisco, Cal."

Communications must be accompanied by the writer's name and address, not necessarily for publication, but as a private guarantee of good faith.

JOSEPH CAIRN SIMPSON, - - - EDITOR

San Francisco, Saturday, October 7, 1882.

**CLOSING OF ENTRIES.**—Do not forget that the stakes and purses of the Fall meeting of the Pacific Coast Blood-Horse Association other than the "fixed events" close on Tuesday next, the 10th instant. See advertisements for particulars.

## A GOOD IDEA.

In a conversation with P. A. Finigan a few days ago he advanced an idea which struck us as being a capital plan of avoiding difficulties that have beset the judges at many of the points of the circuit. The proposition was that the presidents of the fairs should join in forming a committee from which the judges could be chosen, and enough of them attend the various meetings to have the requisite number in the stand during the races. Thus there would be a similarity of ruling at all of the main points, and the drivers understand just what they would be required to do. As it now stands there is a disposition to avoid giving offense, fearing that strict enforcement might militate against the entries in the future. There is also a serious trouble in obtaining men who are conversant with the rules, and who have the firmness to punish violations so effectually as to preclude a repetition. The only drawback we can see is that it might be difficult to induce the presidents to attend all of the fairs, and in lieu of that efficacious method the next best thing, perhaps, would be the selection of a man to assist the president of each association in discharging the duties. There would have to be a joint action of the societies in making the selection and a joint sharing of the expense. It would be necessary to make the remuneration so liberal that a proper man could be obtained, and there is scarcely a question that however liberal the salary the benefits would far exceed the cost. The drivers are so much interested as the associations in having the proper men in the stand. Far more so as they are more intimately concerned with the future well-doing of track sports, and if they had sense enough to see that there was a future there would be far less trouble to manage them. Unfortunately a large majority are influenced by what is immediately in sight, and a double eagle or two obscures their vision so that they cannot see the hundreds of dollars in the distance. Under the supervision of a man who was thoroughly versed, not only in the trotting rules but also up to all the tricks and devices they could employ; who they knew would inflict penalties for every infringement, and whom they could not "bamboozle" or mislead, they would be compelled to good behavior. They would also be aware that justness would mark the awards, and protection be given when others would attempt to wrong them. Such an aid in the stand would be invaluable. Every fair and meeting would add to his knowledge of the men and horses, and his whole business be the perfecting the knowledge necessary for the duties of his station. He could watch the horses at exercise and keep a lookout for the manipulations of the pool box. He would be the Argus of the tracks, and the knowledge that there was a keen eye noting every movement, and a stern judge to call to account, would have a potent effect in preventing the planning of wrong-doing. Under the present system the judges have the slightest possible knowledge of the horses. It may be that the only time they are seen is during the pendency of a race and in many instances we have known judges who could not distinguish the entries nor tell which was which until one or more heats had been trotted. The contemplated official could commence his duties before the fairs took place. A month might be advantageously employed in visiting the various training grounds and taking notes of the horses which were engaged in the circuit. He would become familiar with their peculiarities, and conversant with the drivers' tactics. When the meetings began his whole time, outside of the duties in the stand, could be given to observation and acquiring information that would be of the greatest value in arriving at correct conclusions. Between the heats he would be ready to make critical examinations, and detect "arrangements;" an "expert" capable of discovering at a glance things which would not strike a casual observer, and ready to take steps to counteract the mischief. The old adage that "an ounce of prevention is better than a pound of cure" is peculiarly applicable. When men are aware that the chances for them "getting away" with a piece of rascality are so slim that the odds are very long that there will be detection and punishment they are not apt to take the hazard. No one could find fault with this espionage. The honest man is pleased to have his honesty placed beyond question, and does not take exceptions to any watch which is placed over him. The rogue is only honest through compulsion and compulsory methods are the sole resort.

From a long experience in trotting affairs we are well aware that charges of dishonesty in the drivers are made in many cases where there is nothing to warrant the accusation. The "steals" are the exceptions, though candor compels the admission that occasionally there is robbery in comparison with which the highwayman has an honorable occupation. To adopt a course whereby the guilt or innocence is made apparent removes a great deal of the stigma which at present clouds the sports of the track, and a return of public confidence would be a grand boon to all of those who depend upon them for a livelihood. This confidence would naturally follow as the knowledge that such effectual guards had been raised must have that effect, and those who now suffer under the imputation of dishonest practices be relieved of the load of obloquy and restored to a correct position.

It may seem that it is too much power to intrust into one man's hands. It would certainly make it obligatory that due caution be observed in making the selection. With an adequate compensation we do not think there would be any difficulty in filling the office. A thousand dollars for two months' work would be money well spent, and that divided between six associations should not be considered burdensome. The honest drivers have everything to gain in an assurance that the rules will be impartially enforced, and that their rights are fully guaranteed by being placed under competent judges. The dishonest must be compelled to the right course and like children who, where entreaties fail, are forced to take medicine, must swallow the pill in spite of their grimaces. In their own slang they "must take the medicine without kicking."

## THE BAY DISTRICT PROGRAMME.

Quite a comprehensive programme is partially outlined for the Bay District course. The intention is to give a series of races during the Saturdays of this month, with a trotting meeting in November, probably after the close of the Pacific Coast Blood-Horse meeting. The classification will be such as to bring together the celebrities of the Coast, and there will also be premiums offered to excel the trotting records of the East from yearlings to four-year-olds.

The Stanford Stake for three-year-olds is to be trotted on Saturday, the 21st instant, and to make out the afternoon's sport it is probable that a stallion race will be arranged. The talk is now for heats of two miles between Director, Abbotsford and Albert W. and this is sure to result in a race which will be well worth witnessing. There is no question of the capacity of either of them to accomplish the distance, and their speed is very nearly equal. Each will have staunch supporters in the betting and, without doubt, there will be changes in the favoritism before the race is finished. The Stanford Stake is the rarest trotting colt stake which was ever gotten up, and there will be $3,000 for the youngsters to strive for. According to the division this will give $2,400 to the first, $800 to the second and $400 to the third. Palo Alto can elect between the get of Electioneer and General Benton to represent that great breeding farm, R. H. Miller Jr. has an Electioneer from Addie Lee, and Jos. Cairn Simpson has an Electioneer from Columbine by A. W. Richmond. Should Palo decide to start an Electioneer it will be one of the most remarkable of circumstances ever known in a stake race. There were originally twenty-one nominations, five of these were by Electioneer. As Palo Alto had two named only one could start. Mr. Walstein made the second payment on Nellie W., a sister to Albert W., and had it not been for a violent attack of pinkeye which compelled her being thrown entirely up, she would have started. As it is, unless something occurs in the next two weeks, there will be two, and as nearly as can be foretold at present a strong probability of a trio of Electioneers contending for the rich prizes. The premiums which are to be awarded for the lowering of the Eastern records should attract large assemblages to the Bay District course. It is something that should interest every inhabitant of California. What has already been done has brought California prominently before the world as a country which presents advantages for trotting-horse breeding beyond any other. For two years the two-year-olds have eclipsed all others, and in the last year, those which were a year younger left such a gap as to preclude the thoughts of successful competition. Ten seconds is the California advance in the two-year-olds, twenty and a quarter seconds the hiatus between the Occident and the Orient in the yearling class, and that, too, by taking an Eastern trial as the mark. The time which will be the objective point is for yearlings 2:36½, for two-year-olds 2:31, for three-year-olds 2:21, for four-year-olds 2.19, and for five-year-olds 2:18. We have strong faith in the prophesy that four of the five will be beaten, and were it not for the draft which has taken the crack three-year-olds away would look for a lowering of all. We know of an individual who will wager a hundred or two that a majority of them will be lowered, and odds will be given that the yearling and two-year-old is defeated.

The two years 1880 and 1881 show a galaxy of California youngsters, In these there have been five two-year-olds which have beaten the best of the East, the slowest with four and a half seconds to her credit, and two yearlings, twelve and a quarter seconds being the difference between the fastest of the East and the second here Both last year and this our four-year-old stallions have taken the lead, and though the five-year-old which is in the "top notch," was bred in the East, the speed was developed in California, and it was here where they scored the double victory. Now that the managers of the Bay District course have planned such a brilliant fall campaign, it will be singular indeed if the people of San Francisco do not support them by a liberal attendance. If they should fail to respond, there is small encouragement to keep open a park that would be the pride of any city on the other side of the "Rockies," and the gates might as well be closed. There is little danger however of there being such a calamitous winding up, and with good weather there is almost a certainty of full houses."

## THE EMBRYO STAKES.

On the Oakland Trotting Park Saturday, the 5th day of November next, will be decided three Embryo Stakes. These are the yearling trot for foals of 1881, a dash of a mile; the two-year-old trot, for foals of 1880, heats of a mile, and the three-year-old trot, for foals of 1879, heats of a mile, best 3 in 5. This will make a lively after noon, and keep the officials busy to get through with them. But as the rules fix on 1 p. m., as "the hour for starting, after the first of September, there will be no trouble should there be a punctual observance of the rules, and this is sure to be the case. The Embryo is a peculiar stake, there being nothing at all analogous to it in the trotting line. In some respects it is similar to the Produce Stakes on the turf, but differs from these, inasmuch as it gives the opportunity for naming in either the yearling, two-year-old, or three-year-old form, or if all three as the subscriber chooses.

The first one gotten up was in 1879, and in that there was no provision for declaring out, excepting the payment of forfeits ten days before the race was to be trotted. In that year the nominating fee was $10, the forfeit $25, the stake $100, each. Subsequently the fee accompanying the nominations was reduced to $5, and provision was made for " declaring out," on the first of September of each year, by the payment of $10. Thus far the three-year-old of this year, all colts that are alive are liable for a forfeit of $25, and if this is not paid on or before the 25th of October, they will be held for the whole amount of the stakes. Next week we will publish the names of those who have declared out of the yearling and two-year-old stakes, as we did not get the information in time for this number. There were originally named thirty-two in the yearling, forty-six in the two year-old, and forty-three in the three-year-old, provision was made for " declaring out," from which deaths reported to the Secretary are five in the yearling, nine in the two-year-old, and eleven in the three-year old. There are enough left in each of the stakes to give the assurance of three capital races, and we also hear that L. E. Yates will drive his fast pacing mare Corette on that day, his object being to show a fast mile. That she is capable of getting "low down in the teens," we proven at Stockton, and it is almost a certainty that she will reveal a degree of speed which has never bee equaled by a horse in their first season. With anything like good weather, the track will be put in such order as to give both her and the colts a good chance to distinguish themselves. The Oakland course is now one of the best in the State, being safe and fast. As it is reached in thirty-five minutes from the city, and without change of cars, it has also the merit of accessibility.

## WILDFLOWER.

We never felt the least misgiving that Wildflower would be beaten in the Mall stakes. If even the pink eye had made a clutch for her breathing apparatus before starting on the journey. From the telegraphic ac count the only effort was to win, and then was one Eastern colt good enough to force her to shut out the others. It is likely, however, that before her return she may give the Eastern folks a taste of her quality and return here in time to knock out the 2:21 of Phil Thompson. This singular form of episoety that by common consent has been dubbed pinkeye has wrought great havoc among the horses of the coast, and that without showing in a serious form excepting in rare instances. Horses would act well and apparently feel well, and at the same time be incapable of doing anything like as well as before the attack, and a relapse has alway proved to be more severe than the first inroad of the disease. The Palo Alto colts were greatly hindered, some of them like Bonita being completely used up, and scarcely one which did not suffer. Marlet will also do something before he comes home, and we shall be greatly disappointed if Hinda Rose and Flower Girl do not earn some bright garlands.

## A JUNCTION OF FORCES.

Palo Alto has absorbed Matadero, land, horses, Holsteins, Ayrshires, and a grand acquisition it is. It makes that magnificent training ground complete as it adds a course for the training of race horses, and now both divisions have separate quarters. This is an important feature, as even on private tracks there is trouble in "working" both together. The stabling at Matadero is as good as need be, in fact the boxes are roomy and substantially built, with every necessary convenience. The training track is a mile in circuit, the soil is better adapted for the training of race horses than at Palo Alto, there is plenty of pasture land, paddocks, etc., and without having an inkling of what Governor Stanford's intentions are, we take the liberty of guessing that henceforth Matadero will be the thoroughbred breeding farm, and of course the home of the cattle.

There are some very valuable acquisitions to the horse department. The thoroughbred stallion ranks very high as the getter of race horses, and there are mares of admitted excellence.

There are some very good trotting brood mares, and trotting-bred colts, a mare by Volunteer, a sister of Voltaire, others by Young Consternation, California Abdallah, Elmo, etc. The youngsters are by Electioneer, Nutwood and General Benton, and are a finely grown and shapely lot.

While we congratulate Governor Stanford on such a brilliant accession to the Palo Alto forces, the country can ill afford to lose Mr. Coutts from the list of breeders. Before being to Europe he assured us that if he sold Matadero he would purchase another farm in California. He did not consider that it was large enough to suit his purpose, viz: breeding stock on a larger scale than he had hitherto pursued. He furthermore said that his stay in Europe would be limited to sufficient time for the education of his children, and that he preferred California for a home to any other country. We shall expect to see him again engaged in horsebreeding, and if he carries out his former intentions, he will import some of the best thoroughbreds he can obtain in France and England. There will be a very general desire to see him again in the ranks.

## THE FALL RACE MEETING—CLOSING OF ENTRIES.

On Tuesday next the nominations in the extra stake and the entries to the purse, fall meeting of the Pacific Coast Blood-Horse Association will close.

By reference to the advertisement it will be seen that a very liberal bill is presented, and that four days of capital racing is nearly sure to follow. As far as we have learned the horses are doing well, and there is a likelihood of more exciting contests than has taken place during the year on this Coast. "The tourists" will be back in time to participate, though they will have a hard task before them to beat those which have not been compelled to endure the vicissitudes of the Eastern climate. The death of Flou-Flou has made a gap in the two-year-old rank which is a serious breach, and from what we learn the treatment was not up to the latest method of handling pneumonia. It is said that she was bled twice and the draughts on vitality copious in both instances. "Bleed till the animal reels" was the old-time advice in cases of violent inflammation, though the modern practice ignores the use of the lancet and phleam. She was a remarkably handsome filly, and gave evidence of possessing racing powers of a high class. The Duke of Monday, Precious, Maria F. etc. will not give the Duchess an easy victory, and the older horses that are now in training are a superior lot.

The track on which the races will be run will be selected soon after the closing of the entries, and whether the Bay District or the Oakland course be selected there is no question of everything being done to put it in the best order.

---

The early rain is an indication that November will be fine—so at least the weather sharps predict—and with good weather there will be a rousing attendance.

## EDITORIAL NOTES.

**Lady Washington.**—The Salt Lake horse, Ewing, that raised a sensation in Cleveland by trotting "very low down in the twenties," is California-bred. His sire was Primus and his dam, LadyWashington, now owned on the Rancho Del Pasos, was by American Boy Jr., the sire of the dam of Venture and of the pacer Dan Rice. She is a fine looking old mare with evidently more racing blood than what she gets through her sire. American Boy Jr. was by American Boy, the sire of Belmont, his dam by Shakespeare, granddam Cincinnatus. We write from memory and perhaps the Shakespeare and Cincinnatus cross should be transposed. At all events, the kindred cross to Belmont figures in Ewing, and has been of immense service in helping out the Primus, as Mambrino Rattler did in Magdallah.

**A very interesting** communication from our Sydney correspondent "Echo" came too late for insertion in this number, and also an article from a valued contributor indorsing the course taken by the BREEDER AND SPORTSMAN in relation to a better system of correcting the evils that are now the greatest drawback to the welfare of the turf and track, was a little behind. Both are of a kind that will keep without deterioration. We have taken measures to secure correspondents in the Australian colonies, and the turf news from that country will be duly attended to.

**The Bay District Association Races.**—From an announcement made in another column, it will be seen that there are two purses offered by the Bay District Association, the races to take place on the 14th and 28th insts. The first a purse of $500, is for the 2:23, horses and now that the best performers in the recent circuit are barred from this class, through the lowering of their record, we may see an excellent contest with such nominations as Ashley, Frank Moscow, Tump Winston, Inca, Captain Smith, Marin, Honesty, Cairo and other horses of the class. The race for the 28th inst., is a special purse of $500 for the following horses: Macon, Vanderlynn, Nellie R, Sweetness, Albert W, and Starr King. If these horses can be brought together, it will be one of the most exciting races of the season, as each one of these fine trotters has its adherents, and there will be a great amount of speculation in the result. It is to be hoped that these races will meet with a full and prompt response from owners, and that the attendance will be so large as to justify the managers of the association in arranging a Summer and Fall trotting season, on a permanent basis.

We sincerely hope that the owners of trotters will make entries in the purse advertised to be trotted in January next on the Elsternwick track, Melbourne, Australia. The winner will receive $2,500, the only fee being a stake of $50 each, and it is safe to say that a stallion that wins can be sold for a remunerative price. Honesty would be a capital horse to take, and there are half a dozen others which would do credit to California, though it would be more to our future interests if the selections were those which have been bred on this Coast. The fast trotting stallions bred in California are numerous, and with scarcely an exception are of good size and high form. Among the naives are Romero, 2:19½, Albert W. 2:22, Gibraltar, 2:22½, Honesty, 2:25½, Alex Button, 2:26½, Reliance 2:22½, etc. Albert W., Honesty and Alex Button made the records at four years old, and Romero at five. There are mares which could be included in the shipment and by sending a number the expenses would be reduced,

**The breeders of California** can well afford to share in the expense of a venture, and ship quite a number of colts and fillies of the proper breeding with the horses intended to take part in Australian trotting. If merchants saw the same opportunity for extending their trade they would at once take the necessary steps to introduce their wares, and that is all good policy in mercantile affairs is assuredly wise on the part of breeders. There is also a chance to make exchanges, and by securing some of the best strains of Australian thoroughbred blood, and when California is in a position to supply the East with race horses there is not a particle of doubt of the demand being fully as great as the supply. There must be an effort to find other than home markets or horses will be so largely in excess of the home wants that the breeding of them will have to be restricted. There is a surplus here now; in five years the trouble will be greater, though with well-directed efforts to show the kind we possess there will be purchasers in excess.

**CLOSING OF ENTRIES.**—Do not forget that the stakes and purses of the Fall meeting of the Pacific Coast Blood Horse Association other than the "fixed events" close on Tuesday next, the 10th instant. See advertisement for particulars.

**A new species of fish,** fit to be served at a Cabinet dinner, has just been discovered, it is said, off the coast of Massachusetts, in the ocean track over which President Arthur has just been sailing about in the Government yacht. The fish is described as having thirteen spines in its dorsal fin and as being mottled with a delicate shade of pink on a cream-colored ground—clearly a strong-backed and comley fish! The specimens taken have been sent to Washington for classification and a name. Perhaps this new visitor came this way to congratulate the President on his veto of the River and Harbor bill. But be that as it may, why not call it the "Arthur fish" in compliment to the most accomplished and devoted angler who ever filled the Presidential chair!—*N. Y. World.*

---

## Wildflower Wins.

A dispatch from New York yesterday morning gives the following account of the trot for the Malt stakes and other notes of an interesting day for breeders and others interested in trotting.

The second day of the Breeder's meeting was held yesterday afternoon at the Gentleman's Driving Park, Morrisania, and a very attractive programme was offered, the races being full of interest. Many others than breeders came especially to see the California youngsters, and during the morning a number of fast trots were shown. Among them, a mile in 2:27½ by Charley Rodgers, son of Schtyler Colfax, one of Tippoo, and a half-mile in 1:09 by the bay mare Isabella, by Dictator, dam by Dorsey's Gold Dust. She is a very speedy animal and is expected to show a fast mile on Saturday. St. Gothard was sent to beat 2:30 for a consideration, and trotted a mile in 2:29. A remarkably fine colt, Income, three years old, by Inheritor, dam by Cuyler, was shown. He is owned by W. J. Welsh of California.

The regular programme began punctually on time. The four events on the card were well contested, Rosewood winning the national trotting stallion stakes for three-year-olds in straight heats. The Sequel Stakes for 2:40 mares was won by Guess Not after a spirited contest with Solo, a good second in each heat.

The Malt Stakes, in which all present were specially interested, had five starters, including ex-Governor Stanford's California-bred filly Wildflower, with a record of 2:21, made in the last year. She had five competitors, Baker and Harigan's Meander, W. H. Taller's Senator Sprague, R. Steel's Ernest, Mall's Raven and L. Kirkpatrick's Lucy Waiter. It was generally admitted that Wildflower would win, but it was hoped she would be made to trot in a time something near her record, but such was not the case. She won the first heat fairly, in a good contest, in 2:32, with Meander second. The second heat was entirely between Wildflower and Meander, the former winning in 2:27½, with Meander second and others outside the flag.

## The Duchess of Norfolk.

There seems to exist a great difference of opinion as to the justness of the decision given recently at Sheepshead Bay, that disqualified the Duchess of Norfolk in an important race, through an alleged foul made by her in connection with Herbert, better known as Tom Plunket. It is very seldom that similar complaints are entertained by the judges, and it is indeed unfortunate that the California stable, in its ill luck, should be the sufferer in this instance. The following letter, from the *N. Y. Spirit of the Times*, explains the grievance:

"NEW YORK, September 26.

"Confirming 'Vigilant's' comments on the alleged foul claimed against the Duchess of Norfolk, at the instance of Herbert, I, Lorrillard, owner of Herbert, in the handicap sweepstakes for three-year-olds at Sheepshead Bay Course, 19th inst., viz.: 'There was a slight collision, perhaps; but no palpable foul,' etc. I beg to say, as a spectator of the race, and who takes a deep interest in the success of the Pacific slope stables, that I think the Duchess of Norfolk, her owners and friends were most unfairly treated. In point of fact, there was no apparent fouling or interference in any way with Herbert's winning the race if he was able. The judges of the day, therefore, exhibited the Duchess of Norfolk's number as winner, and pools were paid thereon until Herbert's jockey was sent to the stand. The rider of the Duchess, although a brother of the complaining jockey, gave him a point blank denial, but was not listened to by the judges. The California party feeling aggrieved, I am prepared to match the Duchess of Norfolk against Herbert for $5,000 or upward, a similar race, the track and judges to be mutually chosen.

"W. J. WELCH, 61 Broadway, New York City."

## Departure of the British Rifle Team.

Sir Henry Halford, with eleven members of the British team, sailed on the Arizona, of the Guion line, last week for Liverpool. General Wingate, Colonel Bodine, Colonel Schermerhorn, Major Morse, Captain Salinski, Mr. O. J. Seabury, Secretary of the National Rifle Association, and many of the members of the American team assembled at the pier to bid farewell to their friends and his successful opponents. No speeches were made, but mutual expressions of good-will were frequent and the prospect of renewing acquaintance at Wimbledon next year excited pleasant anticipations on both sides. The members of the British team expressed themselves much gratified with their treatment here. A few of them have been so favorably impressed with the country that they think it not improbable that they may return here some day to live permanently. The members of the British team who still remain in the country are Colonel Walrond, M. P., who is hunting deer at Winnipeg; Major Humphry, who with his wife has gone to Indiana to visit Colonel Fenton, a member of the British team of 1876, now residing in that State, and Lieutenant Heap, who desires to see more of New York.

From the San Jose *Mercury* we learn that Mr. Thos. Blake of Blake's ranch on the Almeda road, who went to England some months ago in the interest of his breeding stables, returned home last Saturday, bringing with him two of England's best productions in horse flesh, one being a beautiful black draft stallion, and the other a splendid black, for carriage purposes. The farmers and horsebreeders of that valley especially should congratulate Mr. Blake for this valuable addition to his already fine stable of horses.

In the double-team trot on Saturday at the Greenville race track, McBeth's team beat Dr. Gray's best two in three for a purse of $500. A half-mile match race for $100 a side came off on the same track on October 1st, between Overland Pat and Nellie Bante, resulting in a victory for Bante.

There is a project on foot to lay out a track in the neighborhood of Quincy. We should be pleased to see it carried into execution as in the American Valley there are large numbers of young horses that with a little training might realize good sums as fast roadsters or good trotters. Every race track adds greatly to the resources of the State.

SPORTSMEN OF THE FAR WEST.—Our valued contemporary, the California BREEDER AND SPORTSMAN, which we regard as pre-eminently the sporting journal of the Pacific coast, takes occasion in a recent issue to remark: We want the people East to see the sports of this State as they really exist, and to cease regarding California sportsmen as a cross between a poacher and a cowboy, and that is one of the reasons why, in times past, we have pointed out failings as freely as we have commended excellence.—*The Turf, Field and Farm.*

# THE GUN.

## The California State Sportsman's Association.

There is scarcely a State in the Union where sportsmen have not organized themselves into an association. The avowed objects of such are to unite in securing the enactment of wise and efficient laws for the protection of game and fish, and the observance and enforcement of such laws.

In many of the older States, such associations have been in existence for a long time. They have enlisted the aid and support of some of the ablest and best men in the country, and have become important and influential factors in the body politic. The preservation, protection, acclimatization and propagation of game and fish, are questions of greater importance than one would naturally suppose who had given no attention to the subject.

These questions are important because game and fish, (1) form a prominent food supply, (2) afford occupation and profit to a large element in every community and (3) afford sport to sportsmen. It is a well-known fact that as civilization advances, wild game disappears or becomes depleted by the natural instinct of timidity and by the ruthless and unmerciful slaughter of the hunter. Dams or other obstructions are placed in streams, so that large numbers of fish are deprived of their spawning grounds, and are forced to go elsewhere. The bays, rivers and lakes are continuously dragged by nets, and it is only a matter of a little time when the old fable is exemplified, the goose that lays the golden eggs is killed, and then there are no more eggs.

California is no exception to the rule. Although the State has been and even now may be considered as the sportsman's paradise, yet it is safe to say there is no member of the fraternity of sportsmen who has not recognized the immediate necessity for some time past of inaugurating measures for securing unity of action upon the important questions suggested.

Profiting by the examples set elsewhere a call was made upon sportsmen throughout the State to meet in convention at Stockton on the 27th of June, 1891, for the purpose of organizing a State Sportsman's Association. In response to the call a number of gentlemen met at the time and place appointed, and the result was the organization of what is known as the "California State Sportsman's Association." Officers were duly elected and a constitution and a code of by-laws were adopted. The objects of the association as designated by the constitution, stated generally, are:

1. To introduce and acclimatize suitable game and fish.
2. To secure the enactment of wise laws, and to urge the enforcement of the same.
3. To bring men of kindred tastes into more intimate connections and relations, in order that all proper rights, privileges and pleasures may be secured to those whose instincts make them lovers of the rod and gun.
4. To further the interests of sportsmen.

Membership was limited to clubs regularly organized for the protection of game and fish, each club being entitled to be represented at all meetings of the association by two delegates. The membership fee is only one dollar for each member of a club, and dues two dollars annually from each member.

On the 4th of May of the present year, (the first annual meeting was held at San Francisco. Thirteen out of the fourteen clubs belonging to the association were represented by delegates. There were three sessions of the convention before the labors were concluded. The work done can only be appreciated after reading a full report of the proceedings, which have been published in pamphlet form, and a copy of which any of your readers may obtain by application made to the Secretary. Stated generally, the time was mostly devoted to the reading of papers pertinent to subjects most interesting to sportsmen, and to the discussion of game and fish laws. The convention was composed of representative sportsmen from every section of the State, and of various callings and professions. Most perfect harmony prevailed throughout all of its deliberations as well as enthusiasm upon the success of the one year's work of the association. While great importance is to be attached to these annual meetings, it must be borne in mind that the real work of the association is done by its individual members and officers during the close season.

Violators of the game and fish laws are to be detected, prosecutions to be instituted, evidence to be secured, trials to be conducted, etc.

The association in the performance of its duties meets with many obstacles, the most serious of which is in the securing of convictions. As a rule the defendant demands a trial by jury. These juries are usually composed of a class of men who are not in sympathy with the objects of the association, and no matter how convincing the proof may be of the guilt of the accused they do not regard the violator of the game law as a criminal, and the result generally is either an acquittal or a disagreement. In the latter case a new trial is had which involves a great deal of additional labor and expense. On the other hand when a conviction is secured the defendant moves for a new trial and takes an appeal.

At the present writing the association is interested in two appeals where convictions have been secured and in one case where a jury has twice disagreed. The individual members who have charge of these cases are determined no matter what the expense or labor may be to follow them to their conclusion. Another serious obstacle in the way of carrying out the objects of the association is a want of means. It has no source of revenue other than that derived from the membership fee and dues herein above referred to. With its somewhat limited membership the aggregate of this revenue does not exceed five or six hundred dollars per annum. Considering the task undertaken it requires the severest economy on the part of its officers to make both ends meet at the close of the year, and necessarily limits the work of the association. At the last annual meeting above referred to an amendment to the by-laws was adopted by which individual membership is allowed. The object of this amendment was to enlist the support of a large class among sportsmen who are not members of clubs, and thereby increase the membership and revenue, and besides to lend dignity and importance to the body itself. Several names of this latter class have been proposed, and since the last meeting several clubs have joined. There is one other obstacle in the way of the association and that is an unjust and unfounded prejudice which exists among a certain class, based upon the idea that it is gotten up for the purpose of having a pigeon "slaughter" as the tournaments are called. That a deep-set prejudice against pigeon trap shooting does exist, and whether just or unjust, it is not the object of this article to defend or oppose, must be recognized, and the feelings of this class should not be ignored. It is true that at the time of the annual meeting a wing shooting tournament is held, but this is only an incident to the meeting, as the sequence will prove.

The Board of Directors of the association have general supervision of this tournament, and the details thereof in their discretion may also be managed by them, but the details thus far have been managed by the local clubs of the place when the convention is held.

The object of thus retaining the charge and control is to preserve the dignity of the association, and to prevent anything being done which might bring it into disrepute.

The by-laws provide that not a dollar of the funds of the association shall be used in these tournaments. The reason for providing for the holding of these wing shooting tournaments at the time of the annual meeting is that they are an absolute necessity. As before suggested, delegates to these meetings come from all sections of the State, from as far south as Los Angeles and from as far north as Mendocino and Butte counties. No provision is made for re-imbursing the delegates their expenses incident to attending these meetings, neither by the association nor by the respective clubs they represent. In order, therefore, to secure a fair representation of its members it is indispensable that some entertainment should be provided for them. By this means sportsmen have an opportunity to vie with each other in friendly tests of skill. There should, therefore, be no prejudice against the association on the score of pigeon shooting. It is safe to say that when the association shall have so far advanced towards the attainment of its objects that its members will alone be sufficient, or other means are adopted, to insure proper representation, then will the tournaments no longer overlap an incident. It would not be just in this article to anticipate the secretary's report of what has been done by the association during the season just closed, but it is enough to say that its labors and those of its members have not been in vain and that on the 15th day of September of this year not a quail or a duck could be found upon the bill of fare of any restaurant or in any stall of the markets in this city. If there is any credit in this to be given to any one, it belongs solely to the association. The purpose of this article is to make public the fact that there is a State Sportsman's association, to show what its objects are, how earnestly the statement of these objects are being prosecuted, to wipe out any unjust prejudice existing against it, and to enlist the countenance, aid and support of the public and particularly of all true sportsmen in the carrying on of the noble work. If any one of these purposes is accomplished, no matter in how slight a degree, the writer himself will feel amply rewarded for his trouble. WILSON E. ROMAN.

## Grizzly Bear Hunt.

A party consisting of Prof. Hicklin. Sam Waltz and G. G. Rigdon returned last week from an extended trip to the Wallowa valley, Chief Joseph's old home. They expressed different opinions about the valley, but agree in saying that it is good for stock, fish and game of various kinds. It abounds in deer, of which one of the party killed three. One day while on one of the mountain ranges they saw, within a few yards of them, four grizzly bears. Waltz dismounted and was about to open fire on them when the professor suggested that he had better be a little careful, for if one of them was wounded they would probably attack the whole party, and make mince meat of some or all of them, and their wives would never see them again in this world—perhaps not in the next. These words, being full of wisdom, caused Mr. W. to cease looking through the sights of his Winchester, and Mr. Rigdon to lower his needle gun. There was another fact which largely influenced them in adopting a pacific policy. That was that both the hunters had only two cartridges each, their main supply being some distance from them. They retreated, and went for ammunition; and when they returned the grizzlies were retreating in good shape to a thicket, but before they entered it Waltz fired and broke the leg of the largest one, and all four soon disappeared in the thicket. A dog was sent in, but he acted very queer; he would not go in, nor would he growl or bark, or even raise the hair on his back like "quills on the fretful porcupine." The grizzlies did not show any signs of fight, except to make a terrible noise in the thicket, and our hunters concluded that they had not lost any bear and then left them alone in their glory and solitude.—Baker City (Or.) Reville.

Hunters report quail as scarce and shy, the result of shooting out of season. We are informed that reputable dealers in this place shipped quail to San Francisco a week prior to the expiration of the close season. Where is our Sportsman's Club and what are they doing?—Santa Cruz Courier-Item.

The Sportsman's clubs have done all in their power to bring to justice all violators of the game law, but when we take into consideration the difficulty of obtaining conviction and punishment, even where it has been proved that the laws have been violated, we cannot lay the fault to the clubs but to the juries who have the trying of such cases. Many persons have been arrested and tried for taking or having fish and game in their possession out of season and the evidence that was given to prove them to be guilty, yet they went scot-free because they had the sympathy of the judge or the jury that tried them. No, the Sportsman's clubs are not to blame but public sentiment.

FIVE SCORE.—Such of our sportsmen as want good duck shooting will do well to go down to the sink of the Humboldt. The snowstorms in the upper country have driven millions of water fowl of all kinds down to the southward. All accounts are to the effect that game is unusually abundant at the sink. A Piute who was in town yesterday—with about four bushels of ducks—being asked about the outlook for game whence they came, said: "Down Stillwater many, O, many!" and he waved his hand as though skimming then, like flies; from a vast area of the lake.—Virginia Enterprise.

Sunday a number of huntsmen went over to Sancelito and the marshes and fields adjacent; many journeyed further north along the line of the N. P. R. R., but they most all returned with very little game and considerable water. The quail were really and hard to get near. During the rain, which lasted the best part of the day, the game on the marshes took to the cover of the weeds and grass, much to the discomfiture of those who had braved both sun and storm to have a day's shooting.

Pity the poor rail, mud-hen or other bird unfortunate enough to fly across the Alameda or Brooklyn marshes, especially on Sunday, as these places are so close to civilization there seem to be more hunters than birds. Happy may the man be who can bring home even a feather as a specimen of his marksmanship.

Mr. C. D. Ladd, with a small camping party, spent several days last week near Searsville. They found the game, especially quail, quite plentiful, and brought back some large bags. Mr. Ladd, more fortunate than the rest, shot a fine large buck which, when dressed, weighed one hundred and eighteen pounds.

General Erwin was up at Sherman Island last Sunday but did not have very good luck. Nearly all the ducks he saw were flying very high and towards the south; there are but few ducks on the island or marshes in that vicinity. Those that are there are mallard and teal and the birds that raise their young in California.

Aug. Herring exhibed to us on Tuesday last a white squirrel which his boys had killed on his ranch in this county. The little fellow's coat is the color of a very light iron-gray, and is the same throughout.—Sutter Farmer.

In a half-hour's shoot on the Roosevelt Club's lake, near the Union House, Charles C. Mack Jr. last Saturday evening killed 31 ducks, all mallards and teal. Others shooting near by got from five to a dozen each.—Sacramento Bee.

Those hunters who would like sport a little more exciting than shooting quail or ducks can have all they wish by a trip to the outskirts of Sacramento, where, it is reported, bears are quite plentiful.

We understand that the ducks shot in the vicinity of Sacramento are very poor, both in flesh and flavor. The water before the rains was very low in the lakes and sloughs and food scarce.

Wild ducks are plentiful but quail are scarce, says the Reno Gazette. Very few deer are being killed. Trout from the big lakes are easily got, but mountain fish are not to be had.

Good bags of quail have been made the past week across the San Mateo county line, although the shooting is reported not as good as it has been in previous seasons.

Mr. Precht is having a small boat built for his use among the marshes during the duck season.

Doves are said to be plentiful in the vicinity of Vacaville.

# THE RIFLE.

## The California Schuetzen Club Tournament.

Last Sunday, October 1st, the California Schuetzen Club gave a grand shooting tournament at Schuetzen Park, Alameda. This was the largest rifle event of the season on the Pacific coast, there being nearly $600 in money prizes competed for, besides $300 in jewelry, silverware and other valuables. There were three classes of targets used. On the bullseye targets there were thirty prizes given; on this target there were also fifteen prizes given for the most bullseyes made during the day.

As a word of explanation, the target used is the regular Creedmoor target with a small six-inch pasteboard bullseye, with one-inch rings set in the center of the large bullseye. As soon as the six-inch bullseye is hit a flag is raised, the pasteboard center is taken from the target and numbered and another one put up in the place. At the wave of the flag the number is put down also at the marker's stand, opposite the name of the shooter. The numbers on the bullseyes are then compared with the numbers on the book and the result of each shot is easily found by the use of an instrument that measures to a one-thousandth part of an inch. There can be no question regarding the fairness, as each bullseye is measured before the name of the owner is ascertained. On the man targets there were twenty-one prizes; these targets represented the upper part of a man and are thirty inches high and twenty inches broad at the bottom. There were fifty prizes given in valuables. The day opened up very cloudy with indications of rain before night. The shooting began at 9 o'clock in the morning and closed at 5 o'clock in the evening. Under the circumstances the attendance was very large and all entered into the sport with considerable enthusiasm. An intermission of one hour was given at noon. As a prize was given for the first bullseye made after dinner, as well as for the first in the forenoon, all the riflemen were on the stand for the word to shoot, when the word was given a perfect sheet of smoke and fire shot out from under the shade. Mr. A. Sticker made the lucky shot. From 1 to 3:30 o'clock the rain poured down in torrents, which made the shooting very bad, as the targets could hardly be seen. One gentleman said "there was water enough to float the bullets down to the targets." On Monday evening the prizes were distributed at Verein Eintracht Hall on Post street. Following is the list of prizes and the scores made by the riflemen:

Best center shots, J. Stanton, $50; F. Kuhnle, $40; A. Strecker, $30; W. Ehrenpfort, $25; Carr, $20; John Mengel, $17 50; F. Frandt, $15; A. Kahnweiler, $12 50; Captain Straight, $11; K. Wertheimer, $10; George Schmidt, $9; C. Adams, $8; Kuhls, $7 50; C. Ladd, $7; Rapp, $6 50; F. Jacoby, $6; W. Thompson, $5 50; Wollam, $5; Hatje, $4 50; J. Hugg $4; Boeckmann, $3 50; C. Saagehorn, $3 50; Rapp, $3 50; C. Rolfs, $3; E. C. Smitt, $3; T. Giantini, $2 50; Williams, $2 50; J. Horstmann, $2 50; Bert Lean, $2; Mayy, $1.

Bullseye shots during the day, Rahwyler, 78, $20; Strecker, 54, $15; Kuhls, 53, $10; Jacoby, 52, $8; Stanton, 50, $7; Kuhnle, 46, $6; Ehrenpfort, 35, $5; Smith, 32, $4; Rohlfs, 33, $3 50; Adams, 27, $3; Hatje, 27, $2 50; Ferken, 25, $2 50; Carr, 25, $2; Hug, 17, $1 50; Grantine, 16, $1; Horstmann, 16, $1; Straight, 13, $1; Boeckmann, 13, $1.

Man targets, Strecker, 75, $20; Perkins, 72, $15; Freese, 72, $12 50; Rahwyler, 71, $10; Mr. Carr, 71, $9; Boeckmann, 70, $8; Hug, 70, $7; Klann, 59, $6; Browning, 69, $6; Kuhnle, 68, $5; Stevens, 68, $5; Merryweather, 68, $4 50; Jacoby, 67, $4; Dr. Boyson, 67, $4; Johnston, 66, $3; Kuhls, 65, $2 50; Sime, 65, $2 50; Bruner, 65, $2; Mr. H. Smith, 65, $1 50; Beaver, 65, $1 50.

Honorary target, Ranfing 70, shotgun; Ehrenpfort 70, soup ladle; Jacoby 60, six silver forks; Strecker 66, carving set; Stanton 68, six tablespoons; Kuhls 66, six teaspoons; Rohlfs 66, silver goblet; Hug 66, six teaspoons; Boeckmann 66, six teaspoons; Carr 65, sleeve buttons; Mengel 65, six teaspoons; Kuhnle 65, silver set; Ladd 65, quartz studs; frau pitcher; Beaver 64, cameo ring; Brandt 64, case of whisky; Fischer 64, silver watch; Bartelson 64, rug; Hatje 64, cameo ring; Boyson 64, silver knife; Adams 63, quartz studs; Heisenberg 63, ring; Mauser 63, sleeve buttons; Bruner 63, opera glasses; Wertheimer 63, quartz buttons; Streeth 63, glove box; Fortmann 63, napkin ring; Zscher 63, pair of boots; Sagehorn 62, scarf pin; Rahwyler 62, case of wine; Schmitt 62, studs; Johnson 61, pistol; Hunke 61, watch chain; Lime 61, parlor pistol; Hatje 61, hat; Hadsfeldt 61, hat; Thompson 60, pistol; Crow 60, box of cigars; Honeyer 60, case of wine; Schmidt 60, box of cigars; Schmidt 59, box of cigars; Burmeister 58, case of wine; Heath 58, locket; Gempoll 58, goblet; Gumblo 58, goblet; Mortenson 58, powder flask; Utording 58, box of wine; Kramer 57, meerschaum pipe; Lügenfelser 57, belt; Hugenits 57, snuff box.

One dollar prizes were given to those who made the first and last bullseyes in the morning and those who made the first and last in the afternoon. The first was won by Geo.

edt, the second by Dr. Boyson, the third by A. Stucker
.he forth by Mr. Roschell. After the distribution of
irizes *Philo Jacoby* was presented by the members of
.lub with a beautiful gold medal. This was given as a
. of respect and an appreciation of the active interest
Mr. Jacoby has for the welfare of the organization, even
. sacrificing of his own interests.

## The California Rifle Association.

the 28th and 29th of this month the above named
iization will hold their fall meeting at Shell Mound
Berkeley. This shooting tournament promises to be
urgest held for several years on this coast. The value of
irizes offered will draw out a great many marksmen, not
of this State but from Oregon, Washington Territory and
sh Columbia. The following is the programme of the
has:

### Rifle Matches.

For the trophy presented by Governor Perkins. Open
il members of the association, the National Guard of Cal-
ornia, and officers and men of the army and navy. Dis-
e, 200 yards. Ten shots with any military rifle. Entries
mited, but regular turns must be taken if other competi-
are at the firing point. In the match there will be
a seven cash prizes, namely: $15, $10, $5, $4, $3, $2,
in addition to the medal, which is the first prize, to be-
e the property of the marksman who shall first win in
e times at regular meetings of the C. R. A. Captain J.
inson won it November 21, 1880; Sergeant N. Williams
it May 29, 1881; Sergeant F. Kuhnle won it October 16,

For the Gen. Barnes trophy. Same additional cash
ss, terms and conditions as in first match. To become
property of the marksman who shall first win it three
s at regular meetings of the C. R. A. Sergeant N. Wil-
s won it May 29, 1881, and October 16, 1881; Lieutenant
uhnle won it June 4, 1882.
Short range match. Open to all comers. Distance, 200
i, and five shots, with any military rifle, at a ring target.
es limited to five for each competitor; must be at least
y first entries before the match is opened. Entrance fee,
50 for first entry; $1 for each subsequent entry. Twenty-
cash prizes as follows: $20, $15, $12, $9, $8, $7, $6,
$4, $3, four of $2 50 each, two of $2 each, two of $1 50
h, and two $1 each.
Military match. Open to all comers. Distances, 200
500 yards; aggregate scores, ten shots at each distance.
s any military rifle; entries limited to five for each com-
tor, and no competitor can re-enter until finished the
ceding entry; must be at least thirty first entries before
match is opened; $2 50 for first entry, and $1 for each
isequent one. Ten cash prizes, as follows: $20, $17, $15,
$10, $7, $6, $3, $2, $1.
Andrew's silver challenge trophy match (military teams).
n to teams of six representatives from any company of
ntry, artillery, cavalry, and cadets, enrolled in the Na-
al Guard of California, Nevada, Oregon or Washington
tory, or any company of the U. S. army and navy.
s competitors must be certified by the commanding officers
their respective companies to be active members of said
anizations, and to have been such Sept. 30, 1882. They
t appear in full dress, or undress uniform of their regi-
nt, and under command of a commissioned officer. Dis-
ice, 200 and 500 yards for infantry and artillery teams,
d 200 and 400 yards for cavalry teams. Position, 200
rds, standing; 400 and 500 yards, any, without artificial
st. Rounds, ten at each distance, with two sighting shots
500 yards. Weapons, U. S. Springfield rifle for infantry
d artillery teams, and Springfield carbines for cavalry teams
with any military sight. Entrance fee, $10 for each team.
izes may be made on the ground. There will be given to
. four individual members of the competing teams who
de the highest score cash prizes as follows: $10, $6, $3.
To become the property of the company whose team
ill first win it three times at regular meetings of the C. R.
Co. E, First Infantry, N. G. C., won it May 29, 1881, by
core of 487; Co. E, First Infantry, won it Octo-
r 17, 1881, by a score of 515; Co. C, First Infantry, N.
C., won it June 4, 1882, by a score of 503.
3. Nevada State trophy match, for a silver cup. Open to
ams of ten representatives (instead of fifteen as the pro-
mme stated), from any company of infantry, artillery,
valry and cadets enrolled in the National Guard of Cali-
rnia, Nevada, Oregon, or Washington Territory, or any
mpany of the U. S. army or navy. The competitors must
certified by the commanding officers of their respective
mpanies to be active members of said organization, and to
ve been such on Sept. 30, 1882. Distance, 200 yards; ten
ands with any military rifle. Entrance fee, $10 for each
m. There will be given to the five individual members of
competing teams, who make the highest scores, cash
izes as follows: $5, $4, $3, $2, $1.
7. Short range trophy match, for a silver goblet. Same
ims, conditions and cash prizes as match, excepting
ims of six men from any company, regiment, or battalion.
trance fee, $10.

### Pacific $1,000 Rifle Match.

pen to teams of ten representatives from any State, Ter-
ory, Province, or department of the U. S. army or navy,
. competitors must be certified by the Adjutant-General of
eir respective commands. They must appear in full dress
undress uniform. Distances, 200 and 500 yards; position,
) yards, standing; 500 yards, any, without artificial rest.
. S.—Teams using Snider-Enfield rifle allowed same
sition at 200 yards as at 500 yards. Rounds, two sighting
500 yards, and ten scoring shots at each distance. Weapons,
s issued by State or Government. Entrance fee, $10 for
ch company.
Prizes, to the team making the highest aggregate score, at
two distances, a bronze challenge trophy. This trophy
be held for one year by the Adjutant-General of the com-
nd, upon the expiration of which he is to surrender it to
: C. R. A., to be again competed for, under the same con-
ions, at the place where the trophy is held, the team win-
g the trophy to hold it forever. There will be given to
. five individual members of the competing teams making
e highest scores, cash prizes, as follows: $10, $7 50, $5,
50, $1.
Won October 17, 1881, by California team, by a score of
, 50, $1.

### Centennial Trophy Match.

pen to teams of ten men from any regiment or battalion
infantry, artillery, cavalry, and cadets enrolled in the
tional Guard of California. The competitors must be
tified by the commanding officers of their respective regi-
nts. They must appear in the full dress or undress of
ir regiments. Distances, 200 and 500 yards; position,
stion,200 yards, standing; 500 yards, any, without artifi-
l rest; rounds, two sighting at 500 yards, and ten scoring
ats at each distance; weapon, U. S. Springfield Rifle; en-

---

trance, $10 for each regiment. Entries may be made on the
ground.
Prizes. To the regiment whose team makes the highest
aggregate score, at the two distances, a silver challenge trophy, presented by the City of San Francisco. This trophy
to be held by the commanding officer of the victorious regiment for one year, upon the expiration of which time he is
to surrender it to the C. R. A., to be again competed for under the same conditions. Cash to the winning team, $25.
This trophy has been won for the last six years successively by the First Infantry, N. G. C. The Association now
offers it as a prize to be retained by the team which shall
first win it five times at regular meetings of the C. R. A.
commencing with this meeting.

### Pistol Matches.

California Rifle Association pistol trophy (value, $100).
To become the property of the team which shall win it three
times at regular meetings. Open to teams of ten men from
any organized pistol club, company, or police force; there
may be two teams from each company of the San Francisco
Police. Distance, 30 yards, fifteen shots to each man,
with a Smith and Wesson 45 caliber revolver; entrance fee, $10
for each team. There will be given to the four individual
members of the competing teams who make the highest
scores, cash prizes, as follows: $10, $6, $3, $1.
Open to all comers. Distance, 30 yards; 10 shots with any
45 caliber revolver, at a ring target. Must be at least 30
first entries before the match is opened. Entrance fee, $2 50
for first entry; $1 each subsequent entry. Twenty- cash
prizes, as follows: $20, $15, $10, $7, four of $5 each, four
of $4 each, four of $2 each, four of $1 each.
There will be no third match for pistol teams as stated in
the programme.

### Honorary Matches.

1. Open to members of the Association, National Guard of
California, officers and men of the army and Navy. Distance 200 yards, and five shots with any military rifle, at a
ring target; limited to one entry each. Entrance fee $1.
Prizes to be announced on day of match, and successful
competitors to choose according to their scores.
2. Open to all members of the Association, of any organized
pistol club, company or police force. Distance 30 yards; five
shots each with any (45 cal.) revolver, at a ring target.
Entries limited to one each. Entrance fee $1. Prizes to be
announced on day of match, and successful competitors to
choose according to their scores.

### Pool Shooting.

1. Open to all comers. Distance, 200 yards. Entries unlimited; any military rifle. Entrance fee, 10 cents for each
shot. Sixty per cent. of the gross receipts to be divided
among holders of bullseye tickets.
2 Open to all comers. Distance, 100 feet. Entries unlimited, any (45 cal.) revolver. Entries, 10 cents for each shot.
Sixty per cent. of the gross receipts to be divided among
holders of bullseye tickets.

### Rules to Govern Above Matches.

1. All military rifles, and all revolvers, to have six pound
pull of trigger.
2. No sighting shots allowed unless so stated in conditions
of match.
3. Pistol team match, bullseye to be eight inches in diameter other pistol matches four inches.
4. No competitor shall receive more than one prize in one
match.
5. The V, VIII, IX and the I Pistol matches will be shot on
Saturday, the 28th. The VI and VII on the 29th. All other
matches on both days.
6. The Association reserves the right to pay the prizes or
return the entrance fee in those matches requiring a certain
number of entries before opening, provided the requisite
number of entries are not made, and will open the matches
on the 28th, and hold them open during the two days.
7. Creedmoor rules to govern in all other respects.
8. Weapons must not be loaded until at the firing point.
9. Tickets for the various matches must be procured of
the Secretary of the C. R. A., on the ground, and entries
made with him.
10. The President, or in his absence the Vice-President of
the C. R. A., will act as executive officer, and his decision
shall be final on any question arising, which he deems necessary to be decided at the time.
11. A member of the C. R. A. will be appointed by the executive officer to take charge and have the direction of each
match.

---

## ATHLETICS.

### The Olympic Club Meetings.

Our local athletes have not yet recovered from the excitement of the last Olympic club meeting, and the discussions
as to the relative merits of competitors in the different events
are, as usual, too heated and prejudiced to warrant the belief
that the conclusions drawn by the debaters are the legitimate
results of cool and dispassionate arguments based on past
performances of local athletes. In one event a sprinter is
credited with being able to beat another three yards in 100,
and the opposition stand ready to gamble on a scratch race.
In another case it is argued that one man is able to beat a
rival fully four yards, whereas it is a well-known fact that in
a scratch race between the two, if there were odds in the
betting it would most likely be just the other way. Again,
the decision is that eleven yards or more would be about the
right handicap between two of the competitors, and if the
eleven yards man should propose a match of that kind he
would be laughed at, and be asked if he did not want a nice
gold medal given him. The handicapping in every event will
stand comparison with those of any other part of the world.
It is very seldom that all are satisfied before the race, the rule
being that almost all but the winners are dissatisfied and
know all about it afterwards. Immediately after a meeting
there is usually a great deal said, and many opinions expressed that will not stand the test of cool argument and
figures, or a challenge for an expensive gold medal. The relative merits of different individuals can be easily decided
in special matches, and, if decided in that manner now,
would be a welcome substitute to arm-chair arguments, and
go far towards developing a lasting interest in athletics on
this Coast.
Our local athletes are longing to hear the opinion of Eastern authorities as to the credibility of Haley's 100 yards in
9 4-5. If an account of the performance was wired East the
next day, their verdict will be known here before this appears
in print. However, it is expected that the times of the event
will have to stand the lashing, as there can be no question
as to the fairness of the start. "People that live in glass
houses," etc. In order to give Myers 10 seconds they have
sometimes been compelled to crouch 10 men with 10½,
and at other times ignore the well-known fact that the

---

starter allowed Myers to start the pistol from two to three
yards over the mark. Or, if they believe that Myers can do
even time, and that Haley is a third-class amateur, let them
send Myers out here, and if their judgment is not at fault
they need not be so much afraid of the expense. From their
own newspapers we learn that they back Myers loyally, to the
tune of several thousand dollars, in any important event,
and we might as well acknowledge that, even if it should be
an amateur event, we don't propose to be bluffed by Eastern
records obtained by favorable starting. Haley defeated
Masterson fully 4½ feet, but for all that Masterson would
now find many friends and backers if matched to run
Myers 100 yards from scratch. It is only within the last
three or four weeks that Masterson has done anything to
warrant the suspicion that he could do better than 10¼
seconds, and, taking into consideration his occupation,
working ten hours a day, six days out of seven every week
in the year, barring holidays, and as a consequence having
few opportunities for training, it shows poor judgment to
decide that he has already found his level. The Olympic
Club has decided to hold another meeting next Thanksgiving
Day. Masterson proposes to have another try at Haley on
that occasion, and his club and friends announce the intention in advance of attending strictly to his preparation for the
event, and promise not to plead lack of condition on his part
if he is defeated. It will be a race that should be seen to be
appreciated. The University athletes also promise numerous entries. A game of base-ball between the Olympic nine
and the Redingtons will be the first event on the programme,
to be followed by several athletic competitions, and, weather
permitting, the day's entertainment should be the best of the
season.

SOME HIGH JUMPING.—A high jump of six feet, six inches
is not such an every day performance that one should pass it
by unnoticed when it is made. At the Irish athletic championship meeting P. Davin cleared this wonderful hight,
which is within three-quarters of an inch of the record of his
own making. Mr. J. Brooks, the Oxonian, it may be remembered, cleared six feet two and a half inches; but no other
athlete has ever got within half of six feet in a fair leap. To
most of us, although we may not be so bad as Leech's stout
gentleman, who found himself unequal to jumping over a
walking-stick laid upon the ground, such leaping almost approaches the superhuman. Five feet will probably be more
than the average acrobat can accomplish, with all his lifelong
training.—*London World.*

THE INTERNATIONAL CRICKET MATCH.—The committee appointed to select a team of eighteen players for the Philadel-
phia-Australia match, fixed to take place on October 11, 12
and 13, met recently and made the following selections: From
the Young American club, C. A., D. S. and E. S. Newhall, T.
H. Dixon and E. W. Clark Jr.; from the Germantown club,
W. Brockie, W. C. Morgan (No. 3) and George Bromhead;
from the Marions, Shaw, J. B. Thayer, C. E. Haines and W.
C. Lowery; from the Belmont club, J. I. Scott and A. M.
Weed; from the Girards, J. and H. Hargrave and from the
Oxfords, H. MacNutt. The Australians are to leave Liverpool on the Alaska on Sept. 30, and will play a New York
eighteen at the Hoboken grounds on October 9 and 10. Im-
mediately after the Philadelphia game they will leave for San
Francisco, from whence they will sail for Sidney on the 21st
of October.

William Edwards, the long distance champion walker of
Australia, has issued a challenge to walk Charles A. Harriman, or any walker in America, six days, fair heel-and-toe,
for $2,500 a side, giving $375 for expenses, the match to take
place in Australia.

AN UNKIND CUT.—A San Francisco amateur, and member
of the Olympic Club, is said to have been the author of the
comments on the Haley and Masterson race, in last week's
*News Letter.* Next wise man !

---

## BASE BALL.

### The Olympics vs. the Redingtons.

Had it not been for the threatening state of the weather,
there would have been a much larger attendance at the Oakland Grounds on Sunday last to witness the second game
between the Olympic and Redington clubs; as it was, there
was quite an appreciative crowd present, including a few
ladies in the grand stand who appeared to take a lively interest in the proceedings. It is pleasant to note the revival in
this attractive and healthy game that is now going on among
our young men who find pleasure after business hours in
adding to their skill and experience at the bat or in the field,
so that when their club enters into a friendly contest with
another organization, they feel that their play is worthy to
some degree of appreciation and even of outspoken praise.
Among the several strong amateur teams that have been
formed during the past season, the Redingtons have already
assumed a prominent position and should the members keep
up their practice, we shall soon see a keen rivalry as to the
possession of the pennant among the amateur players of the
coast. For this same revival in interest in the game, we must
give the Olympic club all due honor, and especially to its
athletes who have taken great pains in teaching the young
grounds and in keeping them in excellent order, and we
should like to see lawn tennis meetings held there under the
auspices of the club in which the ladies could take a prominent part.
The game was very closely contested and while a few of
the members were somewhat erratic in their fielding, both
sides played very well, and up to the last, when the rain
came pouring down and put an end to the game, there were
double on which side victory would perch. As it was, only
seven innings were played on either side and the score stood
four runs to two in favor of the Redingtons when the game
was closed. These clubs will meet again on the same grounds
on Thanksgiving day, and great interest will be evinced as
to the result. Following is the score:

| REDINGTONS. | | | | | | | OLYMPICS. | | | | | | |
|---|---|---|---|---|---|---|---|---|---|---|---|---|---|
| | T.B. | R. | B.H. | P.O. | A. | E. | | T.B. | R. | B.H. | P.O. | A. | E. |
| Ambuster, 1 f.... | 4 | 0 | 1 | 1 | 0 | 0 | Van Bergen, s.s.. | 4 | 0 | 1 | 1 | 2 | 0 |
| Pope, 2b......... | 4 | 2 | 1 | 1 | 1 | 2 | Neal, p.......... | 4 | 0 | 0 | 0 | 7 | 0 |
| Bennett, 3 and p. | 4 | 0 | 2 | 0 | 3 | 0 | Ebner, 3b........ | 2 | 0 | 0 | 2 | 2 | 3 |
| Lemon, 1b....... | 4 | 2 | 1 | 10 | 0 | 1 | Bouton, 2b....... | 3 | 0 | 1 | 3 | 2 | 1 |
| Evatt, p and Bb. | 4 | 0 | 0 | 0 | 7 | 0 | Port, 1b......... | 3 | 0 | 0 | 9 | 0 | 0 |
| Lewis, c........ | 4 | 0 | 1 | 4 | 1 | 1 | Fitzgerald, c.&cf | 3 | 0 | 0 | 4 | 1 | 0 |
| Morgan, s. s..... | 4 | 1 | 1 | 1 | 4 | 0 | Sumetrz, c and c.f | 3 | 1 | 1 | 2 | 0 | 0 |
| Dillon, c. f...... | 4 | 0 | 1 | 1 | 0 | 0 | Van Dyke, l. f... | 3 | 0 | 0 | 1 | 0 | 0 |
| Mullen, r. f..... | 3 | 1 | 1 | 3 | 0 | 0 | Kelly, r. f...... | 3 | 0 | 0 | 1 | 0 | 0 |
| Totals.......... | 34 | 4 | 10 | 21 | 16 | 4 | Totals.......... | 29 | 2 | 4 | 21 | 18 | 5 |

Innings...........................| 1 | 2 | 3 | 4 | 5 | 6 | 7 |
Redingtons........................| 1 | 0 | 0 | 2 | 0 | 1 | 0—4 |
Olympics..........................| 0 | 1 | 0 | 1 | 0 | 0 | 0—2 |

Two base hits—Lewis. Passed balls—Olympics 5, Redingtons 3.
Umpire—E. Van Court. Scorer—M. Shattuc.

## YACHTING.

### Fast Steam Yacht.

Following is a description of a new iron steam yacht being built by Muldoon at Killerlane, N. Y.: She is 75 feet long, 15 feet wide, 7 feet 6 inches depth of hold, and of 5 feet 6 inches draught of water. Her keel and stem is of bar iron, 4x1 inches, and her propeller post and forging, 5x1 inches. Her frames are of angle iron 2¼x2¼, 15 inches apart, and abreast of the engines and boiler will be strengthened with reverse angle irons of the same size. The skeleon is of a double angle iron 4x4. Her plating is of the best flange iron; garboard straks, 5-16 thick; the remainder 4-16. Her boiler will be of the horizontal return, flue and tubular variety, 10 feet 6 inches long, 6 feet 6 inches diameter, and shell ⅓ inch thick. Its working pressure will be 100 pounds to the square inch, and it will drive a single, vertical direct acting engine14x16, it is calculated about 200 revolutions per minute, and will turn a screw wheel of 5 feet 6 inches in diameter and 8 feet pitch—all giving an estimated speed of 17 knots. She will have a trunk cabin finished in the choicest of hard woods, with all modern improvements. This yacht was designed by J. Muldoon for Mr. Williams of Lake Champlain, and is building under the supervision of William J. Carmichael, the intention of both owners and builders being to produce a craft as fast as the fastest and of a sufficient strength to navigate either inland or "off-shore" waters. Her propelling wheel will doubtless be made of an elastic composite metal, as late experiments in Europe have established the fact that a certain degree of flexibility in the blades of a screw propellor wheel, when it is driven fast, increases its efficiency; and should the estimated speed of this yacht be obtained, in view of her great proportionate width, such result will excel any all previous attempts at naval steam engineering in any country.

### Catamarans.

These double-hulled boats have not been successful in this bay, the waters of which appear to be too rough for them. Several have been built and tried here. One capsized and another got partially wrecked off several occasions. A fine one was imported from the East, but it cost too much to keep her in order and she is now up Sonoma slough, we believe. It seems however as if these craft would be just the thing for the Sacramento and San Joaquin rivers where there is a great deal of current, but where the water is smooth. In working up against the current they would go with a very light breeze indeed, there being so little resistance. Here is a story of a catamaran which we take from an Eastern paper, and which shows how they sometimes get wrecked: "The catamaran Teaser, owned by Capt. A. W. Haines of the Seawahaka Yacht Club, was not lost at sea, as reported in Sunday's papers. Mr. Adolph Pannick and the captain of the catamaran were the only persons on board. Mr. Pannick said yesterday that the Teaser left Babylon at 1 p. m. last Tuesday. When five miles to the westward of Fire Island Inlet the riding bar, a stout piece of ash which connects the two hulls, broke, and in breaking it made a hole in the port hull, which began to fill. They took in the mainsail and ran under the jib for the inlet. The damaged hull filled and sank when within a few feet of the breakers. They put on life-preservers, launched a canoe, and reached the beach safely. The life-saving crew at Oakland Beach went out in a life-boat and bent a line on the floating hull, which had not become disengaged entirely from the submerged one, and towed the Teaser to the beach. She is slightly damaged in one hull, and the iron work is badly twisted and strained, but can easily be repaired. The Teaser is a Herreshoff catamaran, 32 feet in length.

"These swift and peculiar craft are becoming popular, and, though considered by some as dangerous, this is the first serious accident which has happened since 1877, when the Amaryllis was 'pitchpoled' in the bay. The Amaryllis was racing in a stiff breeze with the Gilpin. A flaw struck her, her bows went under, her stern went high in air, and she turned a complete somersault, sending Capt. Fred Hughes and his first mate, John Lahey, high through the air. Catamarans cannot capsize, and it is claimed that the improved ones cannot pitchpole. Capt. Hughes has one of the improved kind and, seated on his medicine chest, he laughs at the waves as he whirls along at the rate of twenty miles an hour, to the astonishment of coasters and fishermen."

A Corinthian race has been arranged between three schooner yachts of this bay. Mr. Gutte is to sail his yacht the Chispa; Mr. J. D. Spreckels, the Whitewing; Mr. Adolph Spreckels, the Fleur de Lis. No lightsails are to be carried, and only two men in addition to the helmsman are allowed on each yacht. Each of the Spreckels brothers thinks he is a decidedly better sailor than Mr. Gutte. Mr. Gutte bases his hopes of victory on the speed of his yacht and her well-known "balance." She is so evenly balanced that she will nearly steer herself. Not long since she was left by the wind for twenty-five minutes and the helm was not touched during that time. Yet she went straight on her course. The Whitewing has these same characteristics to some extent. The stake boats will be volunteers. Mr. Gutte has not sailed his own boat as much as Mr. J. D. Spreckels has his, but each of the gentlemen thinks he is a better helmsman than the other. This little brush will be an interesting one to see.

Lester Wallack has bought a steam yacht—the Skylark, and now the famous Columbia is for sale. With the great growth of the steam yachting interests, that of sailing yachts is likely to fall off. When people are absolutely sure of getting here or there and have none of the excitement of overcoming Nature's adversities of wind and tide, much of the pleasure of yachting is gone, as skill, endurance and knowledge are no longer requisite. Steam yachting seems more like a trip in the ferry boat. The only saving clause is that steam yachts are continually breaking down so there is some little uncertainty and excitement in this direction at least.

When Mr. Work was informed of the 2:16½ of Aldine and Early Rose, he is reported to have said : "I will bet a cotton apple; I will bet an old silver watch; I will bet $5,000, $10,000, $25,000, $50,000 that the Vanderbilt team cannot beat Dick Swiveller and Edward a mile to road wagon." Early

Rose is by Almont, out of Jennie, by Flying Cloud, and her record is 2:20½. Aldine is by Almont, out of Mother Hubbard, by Toronto, and her record is 2:19½.—*Turf, Field and Farm.*

The Royal Canadians have done doing things in the right way; but two or three years ago yachts intended to take part in their races were paid no attention to, their dinghays being refused even the privilege of landing at the club's dock. Now, members of other clubs are invited to attend, and owners of yachts are asked to assemble off the club house; the accommodation of which is proffered them, also the use of the club's steam yacht to convey them to and from the city. The change is a highly desirable one.

The sale of the schooner yacht Nellie to Mr. Merion Donohue and a couple of other young gentlemen is announced, and Mr. Bowie gives up his favorite racer. The Nellie has made a very good record for herself since Captain Turner launched her. She was built to order of Mr. Bowie, and he has owned her until now. It is stated that her new owners are to refurnish and refit the cabin and make some minor changes.

The hull, spars and iron work of the plunger Restless cost $1,900. She is thirty-six feet long, thirteen and a half feet beam and three and a half feet draught. The sail cost $90, and her ship chandler will have $130. These figures will give an idea of the cost of such a craft. The boat carried out a party of fifty-two one day last week.

The Spreckels brothers' new keel yacht, on the ways at Turners' yard, Channel street, is all ready for launching. Work is now being done on the inside. It will not be very long before the yacht will be put into service.

By the end of this month many of the yachts will be laid up for the winter. In the Eastern States already many of the fleet are in winter quarters.

The schooner-yacht Dauntless has sailed for Europe, having on board her owner, Mr. Caldwell H. Coit, and a party of his friends.

It is stated that Mr. Bowie and his brother and Frank Murphy are to build a keel schooner yacht, six feet longer than the Nellie.

The man on the Frolic got hurt last week with a boat hook.

### The War of the Millionaires.

And now Frank Work responds to the challenge of "T. C. E" by publishing the following in the *Herald* of the next morning. It is "a very pretty quarrel" on paper, which it is evident will be the only battle ground, and there is scarcely a chance that anything further will result from it. After all the controversies are beneficial to the breeder as the desire of wealthy men to obtain fast road-horses, has fully as much influence in keeping up the price of trotters as the investments for track purposes. The top prices have been paid by this class of man, and there is no question that Robert Bonner alone has been the means of an immense sum of money being paid to breeders:

NEW YORK, Sept. 19, 1882.

To THE EDITOR OF THE HERALD: In the HERALD of this date "T. C. E" makes a series of propositions for a test of the relative speed of Mr. W. H. Vanderbilt's team and the team Edward and Swiveller, owned by myself. Horsemen will understand why it is impossible for me to accept these propositions, but it may be necessary to give some information to others. Early Rose and Aldine are two mares which have been trotting all this season throughout the circuit and have been hardened by continued heat races, so that they are to-day in perfect condition. On the other hand, "T.C.E." knows that Edward and Swiveler have not undergone the preparation necessary to enable them to engage in the series of races which he proposes. It is well-known to him that the team has been kept, not at the track, but at my own stables continuously for two years past. They have been on the road and are in no condition to trot heat races. They are therefore in this respect placed at a disadvantage.

In order, however, to show my confidence in the superior speed of my team, I am willing to make a match with Edward and Swiveller against early Rose and Aldine to trot a competition mile for $10,000 a side, or I will trot my team against Mr. Vanderbilt's team a time race of one mile, owners to toss which team to go first, and the second team to trot within one-half hour after the first team has trotted the mile, and the team which trots the fastest mile to take the stakes. Of course I stipulate for a good day and good track, and that the match shall take place on the Fleetwood Course, both teams now being in this city. Further I will wager "T. C. E." $10,000 that the team of Mr. Vanderbilt cannot equal or surpass the record of Edward and Swiveler on the Fleetwood track, carrying the same weight to road wagon.

FRANK WORK.

This brought the following "answer in replication," from Mr. Eastman, which is the latest ebullition on the subject:

"NEW YORK, September 20.

"TO THE EDITOR OF THE HERALD: My article in the *Herald* of Tuesday was drawn exactly to meet the boasts of Mr. Work, made to myself and others on several occasions within the last few days, that he could beat either of Mr. Vanderbilt's horses, single or double, and would trot them for any amount. But now, when offered a chance to test the question, he has backed out, and that ends it. Mr. Work's proposal to test Mr. Vanderbilt's team at Fleetwood, where Mr. Work's horses have been used for the past three years, is all very well for that gentleman, but I believe Mr. Vanderbilt's team now has the call, they have trotted a mile on the Charter Oak track in 2:16⅓, of which fact I will bet $10,000. As to the record of which Mr. Work boasts, neither Mr. Work's nor Mr. Vanderbilt's teams have any record according to the rules of the National Trotting Association, Article 43, section 1, which says: 'A record can be made only in a public race.' This, however, does not deny that both teams have made the time given them, viz. : Mr. Work's team 2:16½, and Mr. Vanderbilt's 2:16½. The offers I made in Tuesday's *Herald* were simply accepting Mr. Work's proposal.

Yours,
T. C. EASTMAN.

P.s. Saturday sees a great exodus of gunners from this city. The ferries and trains carry a large proportion of sportsmen as their Saturday and Sunday passengers.

Capt. Chittenden, keeper of the Cordelia Sporting Club's preserves, in Suisun bay, was in town this week. The mosquitoes have left some of him, but not much.

## THE KENNEL.

### Gordon Setters' Standard.

The following letter to the Field will be found of interest to admirers of the Gordon setter:

"I would ask a small space in the columns of your valuable paper, in order to express my opinion of the Gordon setter, his merits in the field, and as a gentleman sportsman's dog, and as such I claim he has no equal. Although my experience in dog ology may not be as extensive as many others, yet for several years I have made my business the handling and breaking dogs. I have handled all kinds of setters and pointers, and I have no hesitancy in saying that I consider the Gordon setter, for all work (not wishing to over rate them) equal to any, if not superior.

In support of this, I would say: Naturally they are inclined, especially when young, to be a little timid, hence in breaking they require careful handling. It will not do to be harsh with them, but get their confidence and they will do your bidding with delight. I have broken them so that I never was compelled to strike a blow in order to prevent them from breaking shot or chasing birds.

Their fineness of nose is equal, if not superior to any dog I ever handled.

It is claimed by some that they are the* "old man's dog," pottirers, etc. This I claim is due in a great measure to their breaking. Severe treatment will cow them, especially at first, but give them range, let them chase if they want to, and after they become anxious to hunt and range bring them down moderately by degrees, and I guarantee you will have a good dog—one that it will be a pleasure and satisfaction to shoot over.

But I started to say something about the standard by which those noble dogs are judged at our bench shows. They have abandoned the Gordon standard and judge them as black and tans—to suit some breeder's idea perhaps, because he had a dog that was evenly marked, otherwise, possibly, he was inferior in many points, but he was nice black and tan. What an idea! Take the late Cleveland Bench Show, for instance. The rule or standard called for black and tans; every other quality was ignored; black and tan was called for, and they had to have it, and, actually, first in the open class was given to a dog that was half Irish and half Gordon. If he had been a bulldog it would have been the same. The judge did his duty. There was the rule laid down, and he could not vary from it. Again, at Pittsburg, I think in 1880, in the champion class, champion Bob and Rupert were shown together, and the prize given to Bob, when Rupert would score more points than Bob, according to Stonehenge. He was better built, or put together; and had better head, better ears, and was built for endurance; yet there was the inevitable—his tan was clouded, therefore he could not win. Is it not time we had a change? A change is demanded. I am not prepared to say what change, or what points are absolutely necessary to bring about that change, but will leave that to wiser heads than mine. Only I would suggest that color or markings count not over first. Then we can breed for field qualities, and not for color or markings; and by so doing we will bring our beautiful Gordon setters to the front where they rightly belong.

And again, I demand that they have an equal showing with other strains of sporting dogs. Give them for fifty or forty-five pounds, and for light weights, some prefer light or smaller dogs, while others prefer the larger size. But let them be Gordons, whether they are black and tan, or black and white, or coal black, and then judge them according to their true merits. The general build or make up of the dog for physical endurance should count largely in his favor. I would also advocate a native class, as there are many fine dogs through the country that cannot produce a straight pedigree, and such should not be ignored by any means. This is what I honestly think and know about Gordon setters; and if I have furnished any ideas, or shed any light on the subject that would be of any benefit to any one, or to the best style of dogs that ever pointed a quail or woodcock, I am satisfied.

I. HASKELL.

### Burgess Sat Upon.

Arnold Burgess whose savage attack on Mr. Leavesly will be long remembered is not quite so highly honored a prophet in his own country as he would have folks believe. The following rap at his knuckles is from a recent article in the American Field:

I shall not notice all Mr. Burgess has said about the color, for it would involve the gentleman in a labyrinth of inconsistencies that would afford no one any pleasure, and himself much discomfort. But for the benefit of the uninitiated I will say, that all the leading breakers of this country have long known the nose twisting process, but prefer to use the spike collar. If Mr. Burgess, with a very limited knowledge of dog breaking, is superior, in the matter of teaching dogs to retrieve to Messrs. Dew, Sanborn, Waters, Whitford, Waddington, Campbell and a host of other trainers with national reputations, besides a large majority of our leading amateur breakers, then knowledge IS not power, nor does experience avail anything, and it were uselessto offer any testimony in opposition to anything Mr. Burgess might choose to say.

I could not offer a stronger test of the value of the spike collar in retrieving that the indorsement of the best professional and amateur breakers in the land. I know there have been some dogs given up by breakers that may have afterward been broken by some other process, but there is nothing strange in this, as some breakers will not waste their time on a dog that's will cost perhaps, more than his full value to break; so that dogs being given up by one breaker and afterward broken by another does not prove that one breaker or his system is superior to the other. I can name a number of dogs that have been ruined by the nose-twisting plan, and can also name a number that have been ruined with the collar can name dogs in which the nose-twisting process failed and the spike collar plan succeeded, and I can also name a number of dogs that could by no possible means have been broken to retrieve except with a spike collar. These exceptions offer no proof one way or the other, as every rule has its exceptions. The best proof, I consider, is the fact that the spike collar is used by all the leading breakers, with marked success, in preference to the method Mr. Burgess seems to prefer. If the dogs these gentlemen run in public are perfect in retrieving beyond criticism, a novice, like Mr. Burgess, will find he has set himself a ridiculously difficult task to write down their methods.

## A Bold Challenge.

When the St. Louis Kennel Club withdrew their pointer entries from competition at Fairmont the setter men gave a loud hurrah and said that pointers had no chance. Their joy was short. First a pointer won the "free for all" and on Saturday night Mr. E. C. Sterling, the president of the St. Louis Kennel Club, handed to the *Field* the following challenge:

FAIRMONT, Minn., Sept. 9.

DR. N. ROWE, EDITOR AMERICAN FIELD, *Dear Sir:* We understand that the withdrawal of Maxim and Meteor, the pointers imported by this club for one of its members, from further competition in the Free for All Stake, has created in some quarters the impression that the cause of withdrawal was the belief that the dogs had not the ability to win, or that the party who entered them lacked confidence in the judges.

Neither was the case, and in proof of it, we propose, in case the winner of the first prize in the Free For All Stake is a setter, to run Meteor against him for $1,000 a side, on prairie chickens for three days, under the National American Kennel Club rules, and near Fairmont, Minnesota, beginning the morning after the trials close.

The dogs to be worked as in ordinary field shooting. The judges to go in wagon. The handlers to accompany them and to remain together and work, excepting that the dogs are to be kept down when either handler wishes it under the direction of the judges. All points to be shot over by the judges, and the birds to be retrieved by the dogs. The match to begin at sunrise and close at sunset each day, with three hours for rest and luncheon each day. The dogs to be down, at the option of either holder, during the hours allowed for the match.

Transportation, refreshments and accommodation for the night, to be furnished and the expense borne by the losing party.

The dogs to be hunted against the wind when practicable.

Each party to name a judge, the editor of the *American Field* to act as referee.

Please make this challenge public at the trials.

We enclose $500 as forfeit.

For the St. Louis Kennel Club.
E. C. STERLING, President.

So far this challenge has not been accepted, as the winner was a pointer, but it is open to any setter.

## California Coursing Club.

The members of this properous organization which, though one of the youngest coursing clubs in the State, is second to none in the size of its membership roll, the wealth of its treasury, the activity of its members and the speed and bottom of its dogs, held a meeting last Wednesday night at Eintracht hall, No. 519 California street. A goodly number of members answered to roll call and sat in deliberation under Chairman John Hughes. "Gentlemen," said the chair after the roll of delinquents had been called, "the business that calls us together to-night is the making of arrangements for what I hope will be the largest and best club coursing match ever held in California."

"I move to amend the chairman's remarks by inserting the words United States in the place of California," interposed Mr. Shankey.

Without noticing the interruption, save with a slight frown the chair proceeded: "Gentlemen, the most important of all the business devolving upon you in connection with this match is the securing of railroad accommodation for the conveyance of the club and its guests, and by way of parenthesis I may here add that all gentlemen who love the sport of coursing well enough to plank down $5 for a ticket to Merced are the guests of the club. I am aware that political subjects are not allowed to be touched upon in this club, but I must say that in its past dealings with the Southern Pacific this club has always found what is commonly represented to be a soulless corporation a most obliging and reasonable body, therefore I apprehend that the club will have no difficulty in securing all the cars it may need at such prices as will make our trip but a slight burden on the members of the club. To make a suitable contract with the railroad company and also print such bills and tickets as the club will need, I appoint as a special committee, with full power to act, Messrs. J. F. Carroll, J. J. Murphy and Dr. J. M. Sharkey, and now call upon the worthy treasurer to let the club know how much cash it has on hand."

Thus introduced Treasurer Murphy took the floor. Thi gentlemen has a happy knack of making statistics and figures interesting to the dullest mind and his vast experience with complicated accounts enables him to disclose the condition of the club at an instant's notice.

"Gentlemen," he said, "it is with great pleasure that I inform you that the club has a cash balance in its treasury free from all claims of $231 60.

"Move we donate the odd sixty cents to the Sportsman's Club to assist in prosecuting violators of the game laws," said a delegate in the rear of the hall, but he was promptly suppressed and his motion declared out of order.

The chair then called for an expression of opinion on the number of dogs likely to compete in the meeting at Merced on November 15th and 16th. On comparing notes it was found that the "Old Dog Stake" would probably have 32 starters and the "Puppy Stake" 16.

Under the head of memberships seven names were presented and as all their owners successfully passed the ordeal of a ballot that number was added to the roll of the club.

After the usual closing rites of good fellowship the club adjourned to the call of the chair.

AUSTRALIAN COURSING.—Here in California we are apt to fancy that twenty-four runs is a hard day's work in the coursing field. In Australia they do the work quicker, but then their game is not as staunch as ours. At the Australian club spring meeting, held August 26 on the Werribee, the local reporter says: "Hares were again most plentiful, and it remains to record the unprecedented fact that eleven courses were run from the Norfolk plantation in half an hour, and before the circumference of the dial was complete the eighteenth brace were in slips. During my experience only remember this to have been excelled once, viz: at Abergele in North Wales, where nineteen courses were run within the hour."

## Coursing in Australia.

The following extract from the Sydney Mail will be of interest to the many old Australian coursers now in this State. Mr. J. Weir is a resident of San Francisco:

A meeting of the committee of the New South Wales Coursing Club was held September 2, at Tattersall's Club. Present—Mr. G. Lee Lord (in the chair), Messrs. J. Weir, W. Cooper, A. L. Park, J. C. Low, G. Thornton Jun. and Dr. Belisario. Some discussion took place with regard to the improvements on New Plumpton, and it was ultimately resolved that a sub-committee, consisting of Messrs. G. Lee Lord, W. R. Hall, P. Lamb, and S. Burdekin, M. L. A., be appointed to supervise the necessary works. It was resolved that if the Victorian Coursing Club appoint Mr. Gaden as judge for next season, he receive a similar appointment from this club, Mr. W. Pitt having decided to retire. The chairman brought under the notice of the meeting the propriety of holding a meeting at Bathurst next season. It was pointed out that if the club consented to go to Bathurst next season it would bind itself to go always; that the meeting at the City of the Plains had always been a loss to the club from a pecuniary point of view, and that the people did not support the meetings. Mr. A. L. Park said that he thought the Bathurst coursing men were deserving of every consideration at the hands of the members of this club, especially when it was remembered that there would most probably have been no coursing at all in New South Wales at the present time if it had not been for the coursing men of Bathurst. Ultimately it was resolved "That, so far as this committee is concerned, it agrees to hold the first meeting of the season at Bathurst, provided that a Plumpton is being formed."

DOG SHARPERS.—Gentlemen who are thinking of sending East for dogs should pay heed to the lesson contained in the following note from Connecticut: "The notorious dog swindler, Fowler, alias Pollard, Hammond, Chester, etc., is now in jail at this place awaiting trial, and to give parties swindled by him a chance to come forward and testify against him. He has been carrying on his nefarious business here for several months, and I have been watching him for some time. I think he has been advertising in the *American Field*, under the name of C. E. Pollard. His right name is Frank Fowler, and he is a native of Moodus, Conn. If any of the victims whom he has swindled will come forward and testify against the arrant rascal, they will greatly oblige your humble servant. GEO. H. PARKINSON.

SALE OF GREYHOUNDS IN AUSTRALIA.—Mr. W. B. Rounsewell, a prominent sportsman of Australia, recently sold at auction his famous kennel of greyhounds, realizing prices far above the average. The attendance of coursing men from the various colonies was large and the bidding spirited. The saplings (i. e., the pups) were sold at very high figures, a litter of five selling at 322 guineas, and the first choice in one lot 91 guineas. Several were sold at 50 guineas, and the average price was 27 guineas each for the entire kennel of 58 greyhounds. This is believed to be the highest average realized at any sale of greyhounds in either England or Australia, and evinces the growing love for the noble sport of coursing which extends to most of the British possessions.

HE TOOK THE BISCUIT.—An Englishman who is described as having a pug nose and dogmatic manner lately arrived in the lone Star State and displayed a most remarkable familiarity with dogs and their points, in conversing with one of the natives. Finally he inquired, in a patronizing tone: "D'ye knaw who took the first prize at the London Bench show?" "Can't say that I do," responded the Texan. "Well, hit was myself, you know, that took the first prize at the dog show." The American cordially replied: "I don't doubt it; I might have guessed as much, to look at you." After deep reflection the immigrant has decided to lay the matter before the British Consul, for the purpose of learning whether the Texan's remarks were complimentary "or both-erwise."

COURSING AT BENICIA.—Last Sunday the light rain of the day before had put the ground in splendid order for coursing and quite a large number of gentlemen took advantage of the weather to give their dogs a little training, out on the Government reservation at Benicia, which is well stocked with hares. About 20 greyhounds were taken up on the early train, and the party enjoyed seventeen excellent runs, which resulted in as many "kills." Judge Mee was in ecstacies over the way in which his two saplings worked their game and Cautz's Pride of the Village also came in for a share of the general admiration.

Mr. Keating, Superintendent of the City and County Alms House, is an ardent lover of a good greyhound and a first-class hand for training one for a match. He has a couple of old dogs at his place coming into condition, to run with the California Club this fall. It will take a hard combination of ill luck to beat one, or both of them, out of a prize. Mr. Keating is one of the best losers in the State and never allows a frown to ruffle his features when he sees a race going against him. In this respect he will serve as a good model to several gentlemen who shall be nameless.

W. Duggan received a shipment of hares last week to help stock his coursing ground at Newark. They were turned loose in a large field which is closely fenced. A few died, but the remainder took kindly to their new home and in a short time will be in good order to furnish sport for the San Francisco greyhounds. Mr. Davis, President of the South Pacific Coast Railroad Company, is doing all in his power to make Duggan's enterprise a success and if money and intelligence can make the place go it will soon be no mean rival to Plumpton & Gosport.

DEATH OF A FAMOUS DOG.—Mr. David Snowcraft's well-known dog Let-me-Go, imported from England for running purposes, and winner of several important races, died recently in Philadelphia.

Eole's time, 5:26½, in the three-mile race for the Autumn Cup at Sheepshead Bay, is the best on record with the weight (120 lb) up, and, all things considered, was the most creditable performance ever accomplished at the distance, although Lida Stanhope (who ran second to him) has the fastest record, (5:25), made with 102 pounds up at Saratoga two weeks previously.

## Racing at Chicago.

The fall meeting of the Chicago Driving Park Association commenced on October 4, and among the numerous entries in the different races were our California horses that will probably be shipped homeward immediately after these engagements. We append the meager telegraphic dispatches giving an account of the races:

On the opening day the weather was cool and the track fast. The attendance was light. In the seventh-eighth-mile, Avalon won, Lord Lyon second, Dave Yandell third. Time, 1:29½. In the three-fourth-mile, Murmur won, Idle Pat second, Jack Galt third. Time 1:17½. In the one-and-a-half-mile, John Sullivan won, Ruth second, Ranger third. Time 2:42. In the mile heats, Harry Gilmore won; Dregan Bell second, J. W. Norton third. Time—1:43¾, 1:45, 1:46¾.

The weather on the second day was rainy and the track slow. The one-and-one-eighth-mile race, all ages, Boze Sedam won, Harry F. second, Topsy third. Time, 1:57. In the race for the Northwestern stakes, one mile and three quarters, all ages, two started. John Davis won, Bonnie Bird second. The five-eighths of a mile heats, all ages, Eva wo , Alfaretta second, Bell Boy third. Time—1:03, 1:05½. T e steeple chase, short course, Guy won, King Dutchman second, Eva A. third. Time, 4:12.

Last Thursday was known in Chicago as the Derby Day. The weather was warm, the track fast, and the attendance large. In the one-mile for two-year-olds, Azlee won; Lord Raglan second, Idle Pat third. Time, 1:45½. In the selling purse, one and a quarter miles, all ages, George Hakes won; Maniton second, Flanders third. Time, 2:11. In the mile heats for three-years-olds, John Sullivan won; Ruth second, Effie H third. Time, 1:44½, 1:45¾. In the handicap purse Dave Yandell won; Ella Rowett second. Time, 3:07.

## The El Dorado Association.

The El Dorado District Agricultural Association propose to hold their annual fair in 1883 at Grass Valley, and in 1884 at Nevada City. Nevada county is in the El Dorado District according to the statutes of this State. In a short while the Directors of this Association will visit Nevada county in order to see what arrangements can be made for holding the fair two years in this county. It is quite probable that Glenbrook Park can be had for race course purposes, and for the show for stock. That the park belongs to a public spirited gentleman is why we say it can be had for the purpose mentioned. The year of the fair at Grass Valley all the pavilion business, such as a display of productions of this district, machinery for agriculture and mining, cabinets of mineral specimens, etc., etc., would be at Grass Valley. The year for Nevada City all those things would be displayed at that place. There is no doubt but that successes can be made of these two proposed fairs, and we think all our people will give the business every possible help. Nevada county is rich in resources of almost every kind and it is to be hoped that she will not be wanting in energy to show such resources to all the world, now that an opportunity do so is promised. Such a fair will be no useless and expensive military encampment arrangement, but will bring out to public view the things of use that Nevada county so amply possesses.—*Grass Valley Tidings.*

## Racing at Jerome Park.

The fall meeting of the American Jockey Club, commenced last Tuesday and held on intervening days, will last until the end of next week. About this time New York society is on the return from Europe and from the American watering places and as the city is filled with strangers Jerome Park presents a very brilliant appearance, on the race days especially, when the handsome and picturesque grounds are lighted up with the full rays of the autumn sun. The track is unique in its way, the club house being built on the prominent knoll that projects right in to the track, thus making it somewhat of the shape of the letter B, with the lower loop very much smaller than the upper one. At the end of about a third of a mile the horses come sweeping around the bluff and pass within a few feet of the home stretch and the turn in and out again is so rapid that it is feared that some accident will occur there some day when there is a large field of horses engaged, and to this fact must be ascribed the difference of time shown by horses on this track compared with their own record on race courses laid out on the most approved plans.

The American Jockey Club is recognized as standing at the head of all similar organizations in the United States, and with lavish distribution of its rich revenues and receipts it has not only greatly encouraged the breeding of thoroughbreds, but has also stimulated the growth of racing, which has been so immeasurably increased throughout the country within the last few years.

We have as yet but the telegraphic account of the opening day, which is as follows: "The first race, 1¼ miles, Free Gold won; Della second, Hilarity third. Time, 2:16½. In the second race, 1¾ miles, Miss Lumley won; Amazon second, Elkhorn Lass third. Time, 3:20. In the third race, ¾ mile, Breeze won; Cyril second, Bella third. Time, 1:20. In the 1¼ miles, Parnell won; Springfield second, General Monroe third. Time 2:01½. In the 1 mile Rochester and Vagrant started, and the former won easily. Time 1:55. Day Dawn and Gimlet started in the hurdle race, 1 mile, and Gimlet won. In the steeplechase, full course, Ike Bonham won; Harry Gow second, Bernardine third. Time, 4:30."

On Thursday, October 5th, in the two and quarter mile the starters were Girofle, W. Donohue and Fair Count. Fair Count led for the first two miles by two lengths; Girofle then gradually took the lead in the stretch and won in a gallop by five lengths. Time, 4:11. In the mile and an eighth Kennesaw won; Duke of Montalaban second, Valparaiso third. Time, 2:01¾. In the steeplechase, short course, Post Guard won; Harry Gow second, Revenge third. Time, 3:33½. Bernadine fell at the first jump and died soon after. Nolan, the jockey, was slightly injured. Private betting was very extensive between b kmakers and customers well enough known to warrant redit business.

## ROWING.

### Aquatic Bluffers.

The bluffer is a type of athlete that just now appears to flourish along the water front. We cannot take up any daily newspaper that gives a column to sporting events without being surprised by a string of challenges to row for fabulous amounts. The uninitiated reader after a perusal of these cartels is generally impressed with the idea that the rowing clubs are full of embryo and full-fledged Haulans, who are ready to meet anything capable of pulling an oar, and are constantly giving exhibitions of their powers. The lamentable truth is that these vaunting athletes seldom does anything resolutely except the reporter to whom they convey their challenges and would as easily be led into the small-pox hospital during an epidemic as into a genuine match race. When congregated on the wharf and watching the practice of some oarsmen they are the bravest men born that ever pulled off a rowing shirt, but when the exigencies of a match call for the appearance of their hard coin they are generally as hard to find as a summer duck and less easy to approach. No amount of cajolery or intimidation can drag them to the center when they knew that getting there means they must "put up or shut up." For those unpleasant peculiarities the newspapers which print the aquatic 'bluffers' cards are largely to blame. It ought to be the rule with all sporting editors to ignore a challenge unless accompanied by a deposit to bind the match. Such a precaution would soon weed out the athlete frauds who have no more honesty or manly aspiration than to toot their horns and disappear as soon as the noise attracts any one who might be capable and anxious to take the conceit out of them. During the past month half a dozen challenges to important races have been published in San Francisco papers. Some of the authors of these challenges are very inferior oarsmen, but these cards read like the defiant proposition of a champion of the world who had honestly earned his title. Except in one case, that of Jack Hallinan, not a cent accompanied any of these challenges. Before Hallinan issued his card, John Griffin had claimed much space and attention for the alleged merits of certain men 'whom he desired to match. Mr. Griffin's challenges were sweeping but unfortunately they were not accompanied by coin. Mr. Hallinan listened patiently and respectfully to Mr. Griffin and then made the latter gentleman an offer which was bolder than Mr. Griffin had declared that he would accept. Mr. Griffin offered to match a second-class crew against a first-class crew of the Pioneer club, and a second-class sculler against the best man in the Pioneer house, Leahy excepted. Mr. Hallinan offered to match a Pioneer crew against Mr. Griffin's best crew and a Pioneer sculler against Mr. Griffin's very best man. Mr. Hallinan accompanied this challenge with a deposit of $250 that remained for nearly two weeks in the office of the BREEDER AND SPORTSMAN but nothing came of it. It was never covered. Contemporaneously with this fiasco James Brannan advertised that he would match his brother, Pat Brannan, against Dennis Griffin for $500 or $1,000 a side and announced that a deposit of $250 was awaiting Mr. Griffin's pleasure. This was not true. Not a cent was deposited and at this late day the match still hangs fire. Still Mr. Griffin and Mr. Brannan keep rowing industriously through the columns of the newspapers. Mr. Brannan insists that he is willing to make the match and Mr. Griffin advertises that he cannot persuade Mr. Brannan to visit his shop and sign articles. There is nothing more palpable than the fact that when two men are not afraid to make a match and desire to make it, they can readily find time and means to come together and put up the money. Equally palpable is the fact that where in the language of the poet "one's afraid and the other dar sent," no amount of time will enable them to find one another. Last Sunday Mr. Brannan was in the Pioneer boat house and Mr. Griffin in the Golden Gate house, fifty yards further down the wharf. Mr. Griffin in reply to his apparently earnest inquiries was assured of the whereabouts of Mr. Brannan and Mr. Brannan was kept equally well posted on the whereabouts of Mr. Griffin. There was no toll-gate between the boat houses and no galling gun or even bulldogs to keep the ambitious oarsmen apart but strange to state they did not meet. For several long hours they remained mutually conscious of the opportunity to get together and settle their little dispute but they did not settle it. No sooner had Mr. Brannan bethought himself out of sight on the blue waters of the bay than young Mr. Griffin eagerly sought the Pioneer boat house in quest of the absent oarsman and bespoke the anxiety of his sire to make the long-talked-of match. Meantime, however, the sire kept well out in the stream in a whitehall boat manned by two lusty oarsmen who were capable of placing a wide stretch of water between them and the shore at short notice. After satisfying himself that Mr. Brannan was not to be found Mr. Griffin rowed off victoriously and next morning the astonished world learned with mingled sorrow and indignation that the match still hung fire. Mr. Brannan, however, had assured the Call reporter that he was as eager as ever for the race and Mr. Griffin had pledged his word that the desire to arrange the match was the dearest wish of his intrepid soul. There is an excellent rule in some rowing clubs that a member who offers to row a race as a member of the club without obtaining the sanction of his club is liable to expulsion. There is also a rule that a man who issues a challenge and backs out of it forfeits his membership. It would be well for the credit of rowing in San Francisco if the clubs would draft these rules and these by-laws and thus put an embargo on the popular pastime of rowing races in printer's ink.

### The International Boat Race.

The weather on the 15th was everything that could be desired for an aquatic contest. Those heavy, leaden clouds which have of late overhung the metropolis had dispersed, and the sun shone out brilliantly, the atmosphere being warm and summer-like. Four steamers had been engaged to accompany the race—one on behalf of each of the crews, one to carry the umpire and one for the members of the press. All were fairly patronised. The Thames R. O. boat sported the Union Jack at the stern, while the steamer of the Hillsdales proudly "flew" the Stars and Stripes. There was a large attendance of spectators at Putney, especially in the vicinity of the boat houses, and extending away in the direction of the mile-mark. Again at Hammersmith a huge multitude had assembled. At about a quarter to three o'clock the steamers moved away to take up position. The statesboats were anchored about midway between the old "Bells" hostelry and the Star and Garter—a rival perhaps about eighty yards above the aqueduct. At precisely six minutes to three o'clock the Thames R. C. crew got afloat from their boat-house, and paddled off amidst hearty cheers. They were attired in white jerseys, each man wearing on his arm a ribbon of the "drab color"—stripes of red, white and black. They proceeded slowly down against ...

by the way, was running up smartly, and waited for their opponents. The latter crew was somewhat dilatory in manning their craft, and it was fully three o'clock ere they were discernable. They too were heartily applauded. They wore a dark blue jersey, and all affected dark-blue silk caps save the bow oar, who had a head covering of light blue. It shortly became apparent that some difficulty respecting the umpiring of the race had occurred. F. S. Gulston, London R. C., who had originally been selected, had telegraphed from Plymouth that he was unavoidably prevented being present, and this left the competitors in a temporary fix." Ultimately, however, J. G. Chambers was asked to act, and he at once consented. The Thames crew, having won the toss, selected the outside, or Surrey berth, which was as nearly as possible in mid-river. There was no wind worth mentioning, and this position placed him upon the very top of the tide. It should be observed that some speculation took place on the race, although it was of a curious character; 2 to 1 on the Thames crew had been laid in London during the morning, but at Putney 6 to 4 was accepted, and ultimately 5 to 4 on the Thames found no acceptor on the boats, though we understand 7 to 6 on shore was freely laid.

The Hillsdales experienced some difficulty in ranging up to their stakeboat, and once fouled the chain which moored the craft in getting to its place. Just, however, as they got into position, a steam-tug, the Rover, with a huge barge in tow, came through the aqueduct, creating a tremendous wash and hindering the start for some time. At length, at 2:5:46 exactly, Mr. Chambers gave the word "Go!" and immediately the race commenced. The Hillsdales, setting down to work on the instant, securing the best of the start, and striking at the tremendous rate of 49 per minute to their rivals' 42, quickly forged ahead. It must be confessed that there was something eminently more business-like about the Thames R. O. style of progressing than that of their antagonists, though they did not seem to get so much speed upon their boat. The Londoners utilised their slide well, and, though their time at the commencement was somewhat indifferent, they soon settled down to work in earnest. The Hillsdales, on the contrary, seemed all abroad for a few seconds. Their stroke was short and snatchy, and they did not seem to slide more than six inches, and to finish that short distance long ere they had completed their pull. Still they got their boat along at a rare rate, and at the Creek (time 1:00) were well to the fore. Ere this, however, they had commenced shooting over towards the Surrey shore, and people began, even while the boats were wide apart, to fear that a foul would occur. These anticipations were shortly unhappily verified. More and more the Hillsdales, who had slightly over a length's lead, bored the Thames to the southern bank, the Londoners generously giving way and apparently striving only to avoid the tremendous backwash they were receiving. At any moment they might, by straightening their boat, have occasioned a foul, which must inevitably have been given in their favor; but they seemed anxious to avert this catastrophe, and thus after time veered off. A crisis, however, was at hand. Right ahead lay a three-laden barge, which could not be missed, and the Thames men were compelled to head up river to avoid a collision. The moment they did so, pulling hard to straighten their boat, they ran right into the Hillsdales, and the two craft remained locked together for some seconds. Men in both boats held up their hands as claiming the foul, and then the American crew went away with a good lead through the Thames, having to drop round their stern and pass to nor'ard. The time to Craven Steps was 2:35. At the mile point the Hillsdales were well clear, their record being 4:23.

Both crews now began to steer very wildly, and further fouls might have occurred at any moment. The Hillsdales crossed the bows of the Thames, and the latter, after rowing for a short distance immediately astern of their opponents, went out Middlesex wards, and avoided the wash. The Hillsdales veered back; once more treated the Thames to a heavy "sea," and suddenly made as though about to land at the Crab Tree. In short they could not keep their boat straight, and their antagonists were in but slightly better trim. The time to the old-fashioned inn above named was 5:22, and to the Soap Works 5:49. From this point the rivals took a zigzag course, the Hillsdales being the more unfortunate of the pair, and there was exhibited a really deplorable bit of steering. At length, however, the Americans got straight, and, dashing their oars with tremendous energy, they went smartly away, and at Hammersmith Bridge (time, 7:53) were leading by eight seconds, or nearly three lengths and a half. Amidst roars of applause the Trans-atlantic visitors, keeping up their hard work, increased their advantage, until off the Old Mills the Thames spurted valiantly and drew up slightly. Both now once more steered all over the river, the Thames being especially wild. Just off the famous wood-pile—the spot where Tom Blackman came to grief when rowing Laycock—one of the Hillsdales as nearly as possible caught a crab and set the boat rocking violently. The men, however, steadied themselves, and progressed to Thorneycroft's, where, being about three lengths to the good, with the Thames coming up hand over hand, the Americans, to the intense surprise of all onlookers, stopped dead. For a few seconds they seemed in the utmost confusion, and then Mr. Terwilliger, the captain, rose and removed his sliding-seat, holding it up in the air, and then pitched it towards the shore. It was rendered perfectly evident that his slide had come to grief, and everyone expected that the Hillsdales would pause, never to resume. They, however, went to work again, the Thames being now four or five lengths ahead, and strove manfully; but all was in vain. Their boat rocked terribly, and they went literally all over the river. No further description is necessary. The Londoners slowed down and reached Barnes Bridge in 17:14 or 17:15 from their rivals, finishing in 20:40 to their rivals' 20:53. We believe no official appeal was made to the umpire, who, however, had no hesitation in awarding the race to the Thames crew.

Every true lover of rowing will agree that the race was characterised by most deplorable incidents. We should have been delighted had the contest been conducted throughout minus accidents, and we have no doubt whatever that all the members of the competing crews would have been similarly pleased. That unhappy foul, however, ere half a mile had been traversed, deprived the struggle of all interest. It was felt at once that the issue must be decided on that collision, and it was equally apparent that the Americans were to blame. They were guilty of an error of judgment—or, perhaps, in other words, they stood convicted of an inability to steer properly. No impartial person would accuse them of wilful misconduct. They never sought a collision, we are convinced. They had no reason to do so, for at the moment the catastrophe occurred they were going at a better pace than their opponents, and, had they only been able to keep straight, would probably soon have assumed a commanding lead. We do not like the Hillsdale's mode of execution. It is short and jerky. The men rely chiefly upon arm-work, and experience has shown this to be inefficient. Still it is a matter for marvel that the amateur champions of America should be

able to get such a pace on their boat. They are as phenomenal in this respect as was Mr. of Richmond, who, to the amazement of all beholders, won the Chinnery Junior prize last year. We really believe that, barring accidents, the Americans would have won yesterday. Had they maintained a good course they would, ere the Soap Works had been reached, have obtained such a commanding lead that they could have afforded to slow down and take a rest. As it was, a series of regrettable fiascos occurred, and it is really to be deplored that the umpire had no real ground for ordering the men to row again. His decision was perfectly just and fair, yet had it happened that another race could be requested we should probably have seen a result which would have been more satisfactory, whether the English crew had won or lost.—The London Sportsman.

THE PACIFIC COAST CHAMPIONSHIP.—As Thanksgiving Day approaches the interest in the proposed contest for a cup offered by the BREEDER AND SPORTSMAN increases among the oarsmen. The Golden Gate club has finally determined to compete for the trophy, so that a race between at least three first-class crews is announced. The Pioneers a few weeks ago seemed to have a very good chance of winning the championship but changes in their crew have spoiled their prospects and unless they can reorganize their champion four within the next few weeks the cup will hardly be added to the club's collection of trophies. Louis White who seems a better man at the sweeps than with the sculls has been compelled by business to withdraw from the crew, another valued member of the crew has left the State, and unfortunately the club can furnish no substitutes who are up to the champion form. The Arial club 'on the contrary has plenty of material for a first-class crew and with its new paper shell will stand an excellent chance of winning. The Golden Gate Club has a good boat and a very strong crew. So far the Golden Gate crew has been seldom seen on the water but in a few weeks will commence regular practice. The Pioneer crew took a spin last Sunday evening with Pat Brannan at stroke, Lyne and Crowly in the waist and John Sullivan at the bow. They seemed to row very evenly but their pace was slow. Mr. Long or Alt. Tobin will have to be substituted for Sullivan in the bow and the remainder of the boat reorganized before they can get down to anything like a good even pace.

KENNEDY'S HARNESS.—The Boston Herald of the 22d ult. says: "Hanlan was the lion of the hour at Point of Pines last Tuesday, and received the warmest praise. One incident occurred during the afternoon which is worthy of the space given it. An impression has long prevailed among some of the old people at the North end that Davis of Portland either has an "infernal machine" with which to propel his boat, or is favored by some other infernal means. Two old fellows who had taken a holiday to see the regatta at Chelsea Beach were smoking their pipes and discussing the abilities of oarsmen past and present, when one of the two, who seemed to be better informed than the other, as he was doing much of the talking, pointed Hanlan out to his friend. They both admired the Toronto sculler's graceful build, and, soon afterward, Kennedy passed them, and was pointed out as the man who had challenged Hanlan. "What!" exclaimed the now thoroughly aroused friend of the man who 'knew all about it,' "is that the little leprechaun that's to row Hanlan!" "Sh! Cwee," was the response, "wh! I tell you. He be with Davis; an' Davis have harness for him."

COURTNEY'S CONFECTIONS.—Lee and Hosmer were not dismayed by Courtney's wonderful record at .Richfield springs. The two oarsmen have deposited bail with the Boston Herald for three mile races with the Saratoga sculler. Hosmer in his challenge says that when Courtney thinks he can outrow any oarsman in America except Hanlan he shows that his estimate of the scullers of the day is incorrect. Both Lee and Hosmer are ready to make a match for $500 or $1,000 a side and row in any neutral water.

REFORMED POLICEMAN.—Dan Leahy the ex-champion oarsman of California has left the police force and returned to his honest trade. The monotony of pacing up and down Geary street grew intolerable to the noble oarsman and he formed the sensible resolution to hand in his resignation. That document is now before the Police Commissioners so that there is a prospect of a good man returning to the sport in which he was so successfully popular.

JERSEYS VS. GUERNSEYS.—In the Rural New Yorker, Richard Goodman Jr. replies with some warmth to a statement giving a preference to the Guernseys over Jerseys. He says: "The leading breeders of Guernseys, while claiming more beef, and a deeper color for the milk and its products, have never claimed a higher flavor, an equal quantity, nor an approach to the quality of the Jersey butter. As I understand it, the popularity of the Jerseys rests primarily on the firmness of the butter in dog days and its excellent grain the year round; and secondly, upon their great annual butter yield. The color of the butter is the only point we Jersey men yield to the breeders of Guernseys, and as compared with the flavor, texture and annual product, this matter of color is of least importance, especially as it is easily imitated by the harmless and agreeable annatto. As to the flavor of the butter of the Jerseys, I have never heard any experienced person suggest that that of any other breed equaled it. In texture it is not approached by the butter of any other breed. And the butter of the Guernseys is notoriously oily. As to the annual and weekly product, Jerseymen have not only taken the lead, but feel well satisfied that they will each year increase their distance. In fact the very claim of caress for the Guernseys would seem to be the strongest argument against their value as butter producers. Fat on caress and fat in the udder will not go together."

HINTS ON ROASTING WILD DUCK.—If the "wild flavor" of game, such as geese, ducks, etc., is disliked, they may be soaked over night in cold water, or pare a fresh lemon without breaking the thin, white inside skin, put inside the game for a day or two, renewing the lemon every twelve hours. This will absorb unpleasant flavors from almost all meat and game. Some lay slices of onion over the game while cooking and remove before serving. Young ducks should roast from 25 to 30 minutes; full-grown for an hour or more with frequent basting. Some prefer them underdone, served very hot; but thorough cooking will prove more generally palatable.

I have to acknowledge the receipt from San Francisco of the fourth and fifth numbers of the BREEDER AND SPORTSMAN and they more than keep up the promise of the opening copy. They also contain very finished portraits of the trotting sires, Echo and Electioneer.—The Rider.

... number of the BREEDER AND SPORTSMAN, ... Joseph Cairn Simpson, has been received. ... a fine appearance, and its general makeup ... fit to journalism. The out on the first ... noted New York horse Duchess, is a fine ... Mr. Simpson is aided in his editorial corps of well known journalists, among ... any Wilson, who has been long identified ... apers of the stump of the BREEDER AND SPORTSMAN. T. T. Williams has charge of all that ... kennel; Charles G. Tole is ranching editor; ... cussah, of athletics; George A. Strong, in ... The publication is devoted to other minor ... The turf has the first place, and is to receive attention. It is a worthy paper, devoted to ... cause, and we desire it all success possible. Single copies and be canvassed. Address ... DER AND SPORTSMAN, 608 Montgomery street, San Francisco.—Calavera Prospect.

... ny has been formed to publish in San Francisco chess journal devoted to sport and breeding. Joseph Cairn Simpson has been selected. The issue will be weekly, and the paper called the BREEDER AND SPORTSMAN. Particular attention will be paid to the breeding, raising and tion of horses. Mr. Simpson, as a writer, ... and a handler of horses, has been before ... for more than a quarter of a century, and ... qualified to take control of the journal. "... a Portraiture," first published in the Turf, ... Farm, is a standard work, and the only reliable author has not seen fit to prepare a ... frame for the press. The BREEDER AND SPORTSMAN will be a sixteen-page paper, and the first number will be published July 1st. The subscription price is five dollars per annum, and Mr. address is 608 Montgomery street, San Francisco.—Turf, Field and Farm.

## Market Report.

-Fair inquiry. We quote: Best City ..., 5c; Superfine, $6.50@$6.75 ...

... —There is but little activity in the wheat ... ing for $2.00 to the side while and recent ... vale of brings which has a remaining in ... operators. Shippers offer at ...; millers are paying $1.65 ... g bales, but few transactions are made every ..., The Liverpool market has made no change ... hts lately that would affect the local market.

... —Feed is in good demand and sales are heavy. Over $4.00 tons changed hands in one ... over $4.00 tons No. 1 Feed, November, $1.51 ... 4th; $2.00 do December, $1.25 ... ... $2.00 do No. 2 October, $2.90 old do; $1.25 ... No 1863. $1.25 ... Brewing meets with ... inquiry on call. Spot lots of good are ... 85 ... in good demand, quotable, according to ... 86@$1.00 per ctl.

... 1. In $2.00 No 2; $2.00 to first, second. ... quotable at $2.00 per ton. Ground Bar ... ton; Cracked Corn $2.00 ton. Shorts selling $30 @$36; $2.00 ton; Oilcake meal is as sell to the trade at $32.00 ton, less discount. Middlings, $2.50 ton for mill.

-s has has done considerable damage to the stock on the wharf. It is calculated that tons have suffered injury to the extent of per ton. Market testerday steady. We ... Halls, $18 @$18.50; White $18.50; ... $18.50 bale.

-Quotable at $5.00 bale. All kinds are firmly held. We quote ... 7c; Butter, ...; $2.50 for small ...; $2.50 for large; Lima, $2.50@$2.75;

... Peas, $2.50@$2.75; Pink, $2.50@$2.75; Red, $2.50@$2.75; small White, $2.90; large White, $2.90@$3.00 ctl.

POTATOES.—Prices keep fairly uniform. ... sales are as follows: Early River, 50c@60c; Garnet Chile, 60c@80c; Early Goodrich 75c@$1; Peerless, 60c@80c; Sweet, $2.75@$3.25 ctl.

ONIONS.—Market rather dull. Quotable at 60c@80c ctl.

PROVISIONS—Market firm. We quote: Eastern Hams, 15@16c; California Hams, 16@16½c for plain, 16@17½c for sugar-cured deviled. Eastern Breakfast Bacon, 17@18c; California Smoked Bacon, 10@15c for heavy and medium, and 17½c do for light and extra light; Clear Sides, 13@14½c; Pork, $21 500 $22 for extra Prime; Barreled Beef, $12 extra mess, $10 for mess. Prime Mess, $22 @$16.50 for Mess, $27 for Clear, ... $26 @$26.50 for extra Clear; Pigs' Feet, $14 ... $9 bbl; Mess Beef, $14 @$14.50 and $7 for ½ bbls Extra Mess Beef, $14 @$15; Family Beef, $14 @$16 ... ½ bbl; California Smoked Beef, 14@14½c ... ...

BUTTER—Trade is active, but fancy grades are scarce and above market. We quote Fancy, 45c; choice, 40@44c; fair to good, 36@40c; inferior, 30c. Roll, country stores, 30@35c; Firkin, 30@36c for good to choice, and 20@27c for ordinary; pickled roll, 35@38c; Eastern, 30@35c ℔.

EGGS—The market continues to improve. Sales are reported on an advance on last weeks' figures. We quote as follows: California choice, 40@45c; Eastern, choice; Utah, 35@36c ℔ dox.

CHEESE—is selling freely. We quote: California, 15@16½c for choice; Western, 8c ℔ dox. 10@11½ for fair to good; do, factory, in boxes, 15@16½c; Eastern, 15@16½c; Western, 11@15c per ℔.

HONEY—Comb 14@15c, extracted 7@10c ℔ ℔.

FRUIT—Only grade of choice quality bring full figures. Strawberries sold better to-day. We quote: Apples, 50@80c for common and $1.25 ℔ box for good; Pears, 40@50c ℔ box; Strawberries, 80@$1 ℔ chest; Peaches, 60@80c ℔ ℔ box; Figs, 40@75c ℔ box; Grapes, 30@50c for common, 50@80c for black Hamburg, 50@75c for Tokay and Port, 80@75c ℔ box for Muscat and 50@80c ℔ box for Tokay; Plums, 50@75c ℔ box; Quinces, 75@$1 box; Watermelons, $4@$8 ℔ hundred; Cantaloupes, 50@60c ℔ crate; Lemons, $7.50 for Sicily and $9 ℔ box for California; Limes, 25@$7 ℔ box for Mexican; Bananas, $2@$3.50 ℔ bunch; Tahiti Oranges, 25@$8 ℔ hundred.

VEGETABLES—No change. Marrowfat Squash, 85@80c ℔ box; Carrots, 50@60c; Turnips, 75@80c; Beets, 75@80c ℔ box; Garlic, 10@12c ℔ ℔; Cucumbers, 30@50c ℔ box; Green Peas, 2@3c ℔; Green Peppers, 10@12½c ℔ box; Tomatoes, 1@2½c ℔ box; Celery, 50c ℔ dox; Summer Squash, 80@75c ℔ box; String Beans, 1@2½c do; Lima Beans, 4@5c per ℔; Green Corn, 7½c @ 10c ℔ dox; Okra, 7@10c; Dry Peppers, 50@75c ℔ box; Dried Okra, 30c per ℔.

POULTRY—Steady. We quote: Live Turkeys, 20@25c; Hens, $6.50@$7 ℔ dozen; Roosters, $6@$6.50 for old and $3.50@$4.50 for young; Hens, $5@$7 ℔ dozen; Broilers according to size; Ducks, $6.50@$9 ℔ dox; Geese, 8@$9 ℔ pair; Goslings, $7.50@$9 ℔ pair.

GAME—Good prices are being paid as yet, but it is expected that they will last very soon. We quote: Quail, $1.75@$2; Hare, $2.50@$3; Mallard Ducks, ... $2.75@$3.50; Snipe, English 50c; Teal, $2.50@$3; Widgeon, $2.25@$2.75; Brant, $1.75@$2; Rabbits, $1.50@$1.75; Venison, 8@10c ℔ ℔.

WOOL—Sales at present are limited to local wants. We quote Spring: Humboldt and Mendocino, 20@25c ℔ ℔; Sonoma, 20@21c; San Joaquin free 20@19c; Mendocino free, 14@21c; Northern Coast, heavy and dusty, 10@17c; Eastern Oregon choice, 20@23c ℔; Eastern Oregon fair, 14@18c; Northern Oregon, free, 23@27c; Valley Oregon, choice, 18@25c; San Joaquin and Coast, 10@15c; San Joaquin and Coast Lamb, good, 12@14c; Northern, fall, free, 14@17c; Northern fall, defective, 11@14c; Northern fall, Lamb, 13@17c; Free Mountain, 13@18c.

HIDES AND SKINS—Prices have improved. Sales are paying the following rates for hide by order: Dry hides, selected, 18c ℔ ℔; Culls over-selected, 15c; Dry light hides, salted 8@9c; Dry Kip and Calf, 16c; Salted Steers, over extra, 11c ℔ ℔; Steers and Cows, medium, 10c; light do, 8c; Salted Kip, 10 to 30 lbs, 8c; Salted Calf, 14@16 ℔ ℔; Dairy Calf, 7@8@9c each; Sheep Skins, 50@75c for Shearlings; 90@$1 for short, 75c@$1 for medium, and $1.25@$1.50 apiece for long wool and over; Goats, 35c; Buckskin, Green Skins bring higher prices.

TALLOW—Quotable at 8@8½c ℔ ℔ for rendered and 11@12½c for refined, both in shipping order.

BEEF—Prime, 7½@8c; medium grade, 6@7c; inferior, 4@5c ℔ ℔.

VEAL—Large Calves, 7@8½c; small ones, 9@10c ℔ ℔.

MUTTON—Wethers are quotable at 8@9c and Ewes at 6@7c ℔ ℔, according to quality.

LAMB—Quotable at 8@9c ℔ ℔.

PORK—Live Hogs, 7@7½c for hard and 6@6½c for soft; dressed do, 10@10½c ℔ ℔ for hard grain hogs.

---

## Fall Race Meeting.

### PACIFIC COAST

# Blood Horse Association

**Introductory Day—Saturday, November 11th.**

No. 1—Purse $200 free for all; $10 each; a dash of three-quarters of a mile; entrance money to second horse.

No. 2—Purse $200; free for all maidens; $10 dash; one mile; $50 to the second horse.

No. 3—Handicap Stake for all Ages; free for all; $25 entrance, and $10 declared; $50 added; $50 to second horse; a dash of a mile and an eighth.

No. 4—Selling Purse, $200; a mile and a quarter; for all ages; entrance free; $90 to the second horse; the winner to be sold at auction; horses entered for $1,500 to carry fixture weight; if for $1,000, five pounds allowed; if for $700, ten pounds; if for $500, seventeen pounds, and if for $200, twenty-two pounds. Any one can claim the winner, and the owner realized before the race shall take place. Anything beaten in this race which the horse is entered to be divided between the association and the owner of the second horse.

### First Day Regular Meeting—November 15th.

No. 1—The Ladies' Stake. Closed.

No. 2—Purse $250; free for all; three-quarters of a mile and $9,000; $50 to second horse; entrance free; for the winner of all three quarters on the first day to carry ten pounds extra.

No. 3—The Vestal Stake. Closed.

No. 4—Handicap Purse of $250 for two-year-olds; $50 each and $10 if declared; $40 to the second horse; dash of a mile.

No. 5—Purse $300; a mile and a quarter over five hundred. $50 to second horse; entrance free.

### Second Day Regular Meeting—November 18th.

No. 1—Purse of $100; a dash of seven-eighths of a mile; $50 to the second horse; entrance free; the winner of the three-quarter dash on the first day to carry ten pounds extra; winner of both events to carry five pounds extra.

No. 2—The Purse of $350; mile heats; of a mile and three-eighths; maiden 2-year-olds; this day allowed; $50 each and $10 forfeit; closed; $50 to second horse; entrance free.

No. 3—Handicap Stake for all three-year-olds; $25 each and $10 if declared; the second horse to receive $50.

No. 4—Purse $300; a mile and repeat over four hundred; $50 to second horse; entrance free.

### Third Day Regular Meeting—November 23d.

No. 1—The Flying Stake. Closed.

No. 2—The Fame Stake. Closed.

No. 3—The Railway Stake. Closed.

No. 4—Consolation Purse $200; of which $50 to the second horse; entrance free; a mile dash; open to all horses beaten during the meeting, twice and not winning one race after the first day.

No. 5—Free Purse, $250; of which $50 to the second horse; mile heats; three in five; free for all.

Non-members will be placed on the same footing as members of the association in regard to the awards of purses and stakes. All entries must be named to the Secretary on or before the day of closing; to close on the 1st of October. Those must be made in accordance with the rules governing the association. All entries in purses must be made on or before the last day of October. This rule will be strictly enforced.

All purses and stakes and entries in purses must be made on or before the last day of October the 1st, 1882. THEO. WINTERS, President; JOS. CAIRN SIMPSON, Sec'y; C. M. CHASE, Assistant Secretary.

**THEO. WINTERS,** President.

JOS. CAIRN SIMPSON, Sec'y.
C. M. CHASE, Assistant Secretary.

---

## FOR SALE.

A VERY FINE HAMBLETONIAN STALLION, imported from Syracuse, N. Y.; nine years old; mahogany bay; sixteen hands high; perfectly sound and kind; very gentle; sired by Hambletonian, by Volunteer. Can be seen and can be had on ... at this office.

---

## Fine Nutwood Horse Colt for Sale.

CHESTNUT COLT ONE YEAR OLD AT NUT-WOOD, out of dam of Nellie by the stud ... by Jack Nelson. The colt is six hands high, heavy and powerfully built and shows good action. Apply to

GEO. W. HANCOCK.

---

## INTERESTING.

THE SEMI-WEEKLY EAST OREGONIAN, with subjects of Pendleton, Centerville, Weston, Umatilla City, Echo City, Pilot Rock and Heppner, to any address from readings, $3; six months, $1.75 ... ...; single subscription, 5c. Subscription of ... Stock Breeders and principal owners of the Wheat and Stock Raising county—over medium AGRICULTURAL OREGONIAN PUBLISHING COMPANY, Pendleton, Umatilla county, Oregon.

---

### J. A. McKERRON,

*MANUFACTURER OF FINE HARNESS.*

**227 Sutter Street.**

BETWEEN DUPONT AND STOCKTON, SAN FRANCISCO.

*Repairing neatly and promptly executed.*

---

### DAVID L. LEVY,

*JEWELER, DEALER OF MEDALS AND TESTIMONIALS,*

**39 Third Street, San Francisco.**

REPAIRING NEATLY DONE.

---

### DAN McCARTHY,

*LIVERY, BOARDING & SALE STABLE,*

**608 Howard Street. Near Second.**

LARGEST STOCK OF FAST LIVERY TEAMS in the state. First-class boarding. Horses bought and sold. Cash advanced on tables, buggies, stables, harness or anything connected with the business.

---

### G. H. STRONG,

*BICYCLES and TRICYCLES.*

**252 Market Street.**

Repairs to order.       Elevator, 12 Front street.

---

### MME. EXILDA LA CHAPELLE,

*SPORTSMEN'S HEADQUARTERS.*

**Northeast Corner Post Street & Central Av.**

REFRESHMENT ... ROOM.

---

# Third Annual Fair.

## AGRICULTURAL ASSOCIATION.

### SIXTH DISTRICT.

### AT THE CITY OF LOS ANGELES,

**October 16th, 17th, 18th, 19th, 20th and 21st.**

### SPEED PROGRAMME.

**FIRST DAY—MONDAY, OCT. 16, 1882.**

No. 1. District, trotting, 3 minute class; purse, $300.
No. 2. District, trotting, 2:35 class; purse, $400.
No. 3. District, running; dash, free for all 3-year-olds, half mile dash; purse, $200.

**SECOND DAY—TUESDAY, OCT. 17, 1882.**

No. 1. District, trotting, 2:30 class; purse, $500.
No. 2. District, running, 1 mile dash and repeat; purse, $300.

**THIRD DAY—WEDNESDAY, OCT. 18.**

No. 4. Trotting, free for all that never beat 2:30; purse $500.

SAME DAY.

No. 5. District running, free for all, half mile and repeat; purse, $300.

SAME DAY.

No. 6. Running, free for all, mile and repeat; purse, $400.

**FOURTH DAY—THURSDAY, OCT. 19.**

### Grand Stock Parade.

Ladies' riding match, distance half mile, entrance free; open, $7; divided as follows: First money, $175; second money, $100.

No. 7. District, trotting, 3-year-olds and under; purse $300.

**FIFTH DAY—FRIDAY, OCT. 20.**

No. 8. District, trotting, 2:40 class; purse $300.
No. 9. District, running, 3-year-old, three-quarter mile dash; purse, $300.

**SIXTH DAY—SATURDAY, OCT. 21.**

No. 10. Trotting, free for all; purse, $500.

SAME DAY.

No. 11. District running, free for all, three-quarters of a mile dash; purse $300.

SAME DAY.

No. 12. Running, free for all, 1 mile dash; purse, $500.

### REMARKS AND CONDITIONS.

All trotting races are the three best in five, unless otherwise specified, three to enter and two to start entrance fee, 10 per cent, on purse, in all cases when otherwise specified, unless otherwise indicated, all running purses to be divided, two-thirds to the first horse. In any case, in other conditions where not otherwise specified, except race No. 1, there will be no entrance fee for the district.

National Association Rules to govern trotting; but the Board reserves the right to trot heats of any two classes alternately should they think the day's racing or to trot a special race between heats. In the running events, four or more entries are required.

All the two-year-olds, when running in their classes, shall carry 110 pounds, with the usual allowance for ... ... ...

All three-year-olds, when running in their classes, to carry 115 pounds. When a horse is distanced in any of the ... races ... will be ... the association.

Horses entered in purses can only be drawn by ... entry.

Rules of the Pacific Coast Blood Horse Association will govern all running events, except where otherwise herein specified.

All entries must be in writing, giving name, age, color and marks of horses; also, name of sire and dam of each horse. Should more than the required number of horses start, they will be ... purse of entered closed to be closed the ... to the entry on that day. OCTOBER 9th.

Entries in all the above races to close with the Secretary on Monday, July 31, 1882.

W. L. FRITCHARD, President.
... EATON, Secretary ... ...

R. H. HEWITT, Secretary.

---

# Fine Thoroughbreds

FOR SALE.

BY DIRECTION OF MR. W. L. FRITCHARD we will offer for sale at public auction at Bay District Association

# Bay District Association

SAN FRANCISCO,

**ON THURSDAY, NOVEMBER 16.**

A choice lot of thoroughbred horses, consisting of

Brood Mares — four-year-olds, three-year-olds, two-year-olds and yearlings.

These animals are of the choicest blood and afford a rare opportunity of purchasing first-class stock. For other information or catalogue apply to

W. L. FRITCHARD,
Sacramento,
or KILLIP & CO., Auctioneers.

---

## LLEWELLYN SETTERS

FOR SALE.

For lack of room to keep them, the owner will sell two

Blue Belton Setter Pups.

From Belton and Belle, the son of Jessie—by "Dan—" by Belton out of Nellie. These pups are seven and one-half months old, ready to break, and will be sold for $12 each. For information apply at the office of BREEDER AND SPORTSMAN.

---

## ENGLISH SETTER PUPPIES

FOR SALE.

BY MR. THOMAS BENNETT'S REGENT, out of Washington's Daisy; and Mr. Thomas Bennett's Regent, out of Leaverley's Juno. Both Daisy and Juno are field trial winners. Price $25 and $10. Apply to
E. LEAVESLEY, Gilroy.

---

## Belmont—Mambrino Chief—Blackbird, for Sale.

BAY YEARLING COLT, BY PILOT, GRANDSON of Williamson's Belmont, his dam by Alhambra by Mambrino Chief; from Susan, by American Eclipse; grandam Oriole, by Simpson's Blackbird. Is now in Oakland at the stable of
JOS. CAIRN SIMPSON.

---

## ENGLISH SETTERS.

A BRACE OF THOROUGHBRED SETTERS, well broke, for sale. Apply to
E. LEAVESLEY, Gilroy.

SPECIMEN OF OUR ARTIST'S HUMOR

THE FISHMONGER.

HUNDREDS OF DELIGHTED ONES SEE, FOR THE FIRST TIME IN THEIR LIVES

The Japanese Artist and Embroiderers

At work in their native costumes at

**Ichi Ban, 22 & 24 Geary St.**

The BREEDER AND SPORTSMAN is printed with SHATTUCK & FLETCHER'S INK

Vol. I. No. 15.
NO. 508 MONTGOMERY STREET.

# BREEDER AND SPORTSMAN

SAN FRANCISCO, SATURDAY, OCTOBER 14, 1882.

SUBSCRIPTION
FIVE DOLLARS A YEAR.

## THE DRAFT HORSE.

### BLACK PRINCE. Owned By J. B. Haggin, Rancho Del Paso.

When, accompanied by Mr. Wyttenbach, we journeyed to the Rancho del Paso a couple of weeks ago, it was not with the expectation of seeing three such magnificent specimens of the equine race as the trio which the artist sketched. This week we give an accurate representation of the ponderous member of the triumvirate, and in doing so feel that he claims to be considered a notable if even he has not the gift of speed. Not exactly deficient in this respect, as at a square heel and toe he can over the ground rapidly for the progression that is confined to a walk, especially when the inertia of a heavily laden cart has to be overcome, and after

being started kept moving. There is an immense amount of bone and muscle in the elephantine proportions of Black Prince, and that, too, without the usual amount of coarseness which is seen in the draft horse. As an observer remarked the weight is behind the collar, as all in front of it is not overloaded. The head is not the huge parallelogram, or the neck, at the setting on of the head, like a section of a forty gallon cask, which oftentimes mars animals of the class, and notwithstanding the bulk there is a compactness which is an indication of being able to do a good proportion of work without being laid up. Many large horses are "soft."

Two or three day's work in a week is their limit, and when the tasks are at all severe they are done and must have time to recuperate.

The "Shire Horse" appears to be finding admirers whenever introduced. And though comparatively of recent date, or rather of recent importation into the United States, the popularity has created a large demand. The "Shire farmers" of England have been perfecting the breed for many years until at present the type is so well established that they are as distinct as the Clydesdale. It is claimed that they are hardier than any of the larger breeds, and this is a value quality, in fact, does away with the greatest objection to the breeding of them. Those who have used them for increasing the size of work horses also claim that the blood assimilates with the ordinary mares of the country, and while the offspring show more resemblance to the sire, there are no striking incongruities, but a general blending of both parents. It is oftentimes the case that when the parents are radically different the offspring are not homogeneous. There are, perhaps, the small limbs of one with the heavy body of the other, or these conditions are changed, and the large uncouth legs support a light body. With such symmetry of proportion as is witnessed in the] subject of this sketch there are not the same chances for the produce being a gross mixture of the sire and dam and there is a more perfect assimilation. There is little necessity for urging breeders to give more attention to size in horses which are bred for the purpose of moving heavy loads. "Weight in the collar" has a value when trucks and drays have to be hauled with tons of load upon them, and two horses of suitable size can draw a plow which four ordinary animals could not move.

According to our ideas Black Prince is nearly a model of the heavy draft horse, and his picture will corroborate this opinion. He is a handsome horse for one of this kind, a dappled black relieved by the white markings which are shown. He was selected in England by B. A. Haggin, a son of his owner, and as was stated last week this young gentleman must have a correct eye for horses of different strains Black Prince was foaled in 1876 and was bred by James Cropley, of Cambridgeshire, England. He is recorded in the English Cart-Horse Stud Book, that volume being constructed on the same plan as the Herd Books, giving each male a number, that of Black Prince being 176. His sire was Hercules, 1,024, and his dam was by Farmers' Friend. He took the first prize at Tring, England, being exhibited by W. R. Rowland of whom he was purchased by Mr. Haggin and imported last season. His colts in England have also been prize winners whenever shown. At the California State Agricultural Fair, in 1881, he was awarded the first premium.

We are well pleased to present to our subscribers so perfect a representation of the draft horse, assuring them that it is a capital likeness of the animal without a point being flattered in the drawing. His weight ranges from 1850 to 1950 pounds.

# TURF AND TRACK.

## Cause and Effect.

New York, is in a spasm of bigotory and a spirit of fanaticism not at all in keeping with the age we live in is engaged in a crusade against any and all manner of speculation in sports of the track. As a few well meaning friends of the turf in this State are anxious to try the experiment of abolishing betting we append the following from the *Herald's* account of the opening day at Jerome Park, as a hint to these gentlemen as to the effect of such a policy:

A large crowd gathered at Jerome Park yesterday to witness the races, but when they began to look about them for the bookmakers to back their choice on the first race, having made their selections on the cars on their way there from their racing cards, they were much surprised to find that inspector Dilke was ahead of them, and had giving notice to the managers of Jerome Park that no betting would be allowed to take place there during the meeting. Under and around the shed built expressly for the bookmakers at the upper end of the grand stand, were congregated a great crowd of people discussing the absurdity of the order for stopping book betting in this city, while it is allowed at every other race course in this State and in every State in the Union. A few men tried the experiment of making bets in opposition to the orders of Mr. Dilke, but were quickly arrested and taken out of the course to the station house in 132d street, where they were discharged by promising not to attempt bookmaking again at Jerome Park until the law gave them permission to do so. The racing was called on promptly at the hour named; but the usual interest in the running was not to be seen, and at the finish of the race the enthusiasm of the backers of winners was not heard, and although the struggles in the five contests that came off were just as exciting as ever before they were not hailed with the delight usually manifested on such occasions.

And again on the second day the *Herald* notes:

Jerome Park presented a dull appearance yesterday, the usual crowds on the grand stand and the lawn in front, the club house and the surrounding hills being conspicuous by their absence. Never before on a race day do we remember seeing so few people at Jerome Park. The programme of the racing to take place was assuredly a good one, and the only reason that could be given for the lack of attendance was the fact that the police were to be there, as they were on the first day of the meeting, to arrest any person who might be seen indulging in backing the horse he fancied in the races to come off. And no doubt this was the cause of the slim attendance, and it is feared this state of affairs will continue throughout the meeting unless some arrangements can be made.

## New South Wales Sporting.

SYDNEY, N. S. W., Sept. 7, 1882.

EDITOR BREEDER AND SPORTSMAN: The great spring racing carnival of the Antipodes in now in full swing. You will observe that we commence about the same month of the year that you do with your trotting, a sport which is in its mere infancy in the colonies, but promises with a little encouragement and with a few gentlemen like Dr. Jno. Weir at the head of affairs, to move along swimmingly. Our "spring" opened with two small meetings over Randwick course, held more for the purpose of bringing together owners and horses in and about the metropolis, the stakes not being of much value. At Hawksbury, a place situated about 35 miles from Sydney, two days' racing was held. The attendance was fair while the weather was threatening, and slight showers fell but in no manner interfered with the sport. Five events were set down for decision. The hurdle race of miles fell to Mr. H. Huberts' b g Basilisk, by Gulgory, carrying 136 lbs., Nigger (119 lbs) second, and Highflyer (132 lbs.) third. Won easily by six lengths. Time 4:2. Cedric won the Public Auction Stakes of one mile in 1:46¾, carrying 91 lbs.

Hawkesbury Guineas, of $55 each for starters only, with $1,050 added. For 3-year-olds; colts, 117 lbs., fillies, 112 lbs.; geldings at starting allowed 5 lbs., Second horse $130 from the prize. 1 mile.

Hon. J. White's br f Hecla, by Maribyrnong—Alpaca (J. Williamson)........ 1
Mr. P. J. M'Alister's b f Jessie (Gainsforth)........ 2
F. Wentworth's b f Vaucluse (W. Murphy)........ 3
A. Busby's br c Fandango (Colley)
Captain Osborne's ch c Trumpet Major
Mr. T. Brown's ch c Cetewayo (P. Pigott)
E. Chippendale's b f Piracy (James Roarty).
Betting: 2 to 1 against Hecla, 3 to 1 Fandango.
Won easily. Time—1:45 2-5.

PLACED HORSES FOR THE HAWKESBURY GUINEAS.

| Yr. | First. | Second. | Third. | Time |
|---|---|---|---|---|
| 1871 | Whalebone | Aveline | J.L. | 2:40 |
| 1872 | M'Callum Mohr | Silver Fox | Blue Peter | 2:51 |
| 1873 | Sterling | Speculation | Goldsbrough | 1:52 2-10 |
| 1874 | Kingsborough | Llama | Neredah | 1:48 6-10 |
| 1875 | Malta | Richmond | Sylvia Colt | 1:45 2-10 |
| 1876 | Tonal | The Cardinal | Queen's Head | 1:45 8-10 |
| 1877 | Woodlands | Black Eagle | Excelsior | 1:47 8-10 |
| 1878 | His Lordship | Emily | Lilian | 1:45 8-10 |
| 1879 | Falmouth | Gainsborough | Baronet | 1:49 |
| 1880 | Geraldine | Sapphire | Kamilaroi | 1:45 8:10 |
| 1881 | Monmouth | Marmora | The Gem | 1:47 2-10 |
| 1882 | Hecla | Jessie | Vaucluse | 1:45 4-10 |

In 1873 the name of the race was changed from "The Derby" to "The Guineas," and the distance made one mile instead of a mile and a quarter.

County Purse sweep of $15 each for starters only; for all horses; second horse $50 from the prize, was won by Messrs. Spence and Inhernys Hastings by Wilberforce, imported, by Oxford, carrying 92½ lbs. Brian Boru by John Bull, carrying 112 lbs., second, Mulatto, 124 lbs., third, the mile and a quarter occupying 2:13. This race made the chances of the second and third pretty "rosy" for the Hawkesbury Grand Handicap of 1½ miles where they each had 14 lbs. less to carry. Strong, with 126 lbs. on his back, ran in this race but never gained a position, having heavy "bar shoes" on. The day wound up by Eva (3 years 101 lbs.) a speedy little mare, by old Kelpit (a son of English Weatherbit), winning the Maiden Plate of $25 each for starters only, with $500 added; weight for age, 1¼ miles, Malta, (103 lbs.) second, Velontine, (121 lbs.) third. Time—2:15.

If weather and attendance have any tendency to make a meeting successful then the second day of Hawkesbury could lay claim to being in every sense a success. There was one matter, however, which made the termination rather unwholesome to honorable racing men, and that the winning of the big handicap by String, after starting, in the County Purse the first day, among inferior animals, and never getting a place. In the Hawkesbury handicap his shoes were removed, (we always run our horses here in their bare feet, when the owner intends to win, otherwise we know he is out for an "airing" and try to get off weight,) and he won the fastest recorded mile and a half run for in the Australian colonies. There was a general outcry among the public and it was thought that the stewards would have taken some action in the matter, but it appears that even in the antipodes, like other worlds, there is a "lair for the rich and the poor." If Mr. R. Rouse, the owner of String, intended to act squarely he should have publicly declared on the board his intention of simply sending his horse for a gallop, and not have misled the public, who made his horse at one tine first favorite, but the bookmaker who knew better kept on "laying" him. I do not think the owner had any ulterior motives, but to say the least of it, the matter was unsavory.

SUMMARY.

Mares' Produce Stakes, a sweepstakes of $25 each for starters only, with $500 added by the R. R. C., and $250 for the breeder of the winning horse. For three-year-olds; colts 117 lbs., fillies 112 lbs.; 1¼ mile.

Hon. J. White's br f Hecla, by Maribyrnong—Alpaca (J. Williamson)........ 1
Messrs. Spence and M'Inberny's b c Hastings (late Waterloo), by Wilberforce—Carlotta (Gainsforth)........ 2
Mr. C. T. Roberts' b or br f Eva, by Kelpie—Tiara (Mathews)........ 3
Messrs. A. and W. Busby's bl or br c Fandango, by Hawthornden—Espagnola (Colley).
Betting: 3 to 2 on Hecla, 4 to 1 against others.

PEDIGREE AND PERFORMANCES OF THE WINNER.

| | | | | | |
|---|---|---|---|---|---|
| HECLA. | Maribyrnong | Fisherman | Heron | Bustard | Castrel, Miss Hap |
| | | | | Daughter of | Orville, Rosanne |
| | | | Mainbrace | Sheet Anchor | Lottery, Morgiana |
| | | | | Daughter of | Bay Middleton, Nitocris |
| | | Rose de Florence | The Flying Dutchman | Bay Middleton | Sultan, Cobweb |
| | | | | Barbelle | Sandbeck, Darioletta |
| | | | Boarding School Miss | Plenepotentiary | Emilina, Harriet |
| | | | | Marpessa | Maley, Clare |
| | Alpaca | Kingston | Kingston | Venison | Partisan, Fawn |
| | | | | Queen Anne | Slane, Garcia |
| | | | England's Beauty | Birdcatcher | Sir Hercules, Guiccioli |
| | | | | Prairie Bird | Touchstone, Zilla |
| | | Lilla | New Chum | Camel | Camel, Miss Skim |
| | | | | Industry | St. John, Lady Jane |
| | | | Eva | Young Marquis | Little John, Beeswing |
| | | | | Daughter of | Toss, Mr. Walker's mare |

The winner first made her appearance as a two-year-old at the Victorian R. C. Autumn Meeting, in the Ascot Vale Stakes, three-quarter mile, when she was unplaced, Navigator being the winner. She was also unplaced in the Nursery Stakes, won by Solitude, at the same meeting. Coming to Hawkesbury a little later on she ran good second to Piracy in the Claret Stakes of five furlongs. Vaucluse then defeated her after a good finish in the Maiden Plate, which were the only races she appeared in during the meeting. At the Australian J. C. meeting following, Navigator beat her in the run home for the Champagne, Yeomans, who was piloting her, losing his whip; and in the Sire's Produce Stakes she again met with defeat from Jessie. On Thursday last, the opening day of the Hawkesbury Spring Meeting, she left the paddock first favorite for the Hawkesbury Guineas, which she won just as easily as the Mares' Produce Staks on Saturday.

SUMMARY.

Hawkesbury Grand Handicap, a sweepstake of $50 each for starters only, with $1,500 added, for all horses. The winner to receive 75 per cent. second horse 15 per cent. and third horse 10 per cent of the gross amount. 1½ mile.

Mr. R. Rouse's ch h Sting, by Grandmaster, by Gladiateur—Queen Bee, 4 yrs, 112 lbs. (M'Grade)........ 1
C. T. Robert's ch g Masquerade, aged, 86 lbs (Nicholson)........ 2
P. J. Cox's b g Britisher, 4 yrs, 98 lbs (Cracknell)........ 3
R. Howie's g h Suwarrow, 5 yrs, 114 lbs (Graham).
W. Forrester's bl h Gipsy Cooper, 6 yrs, 112 lbs (Huxley).
J. M'Grade's b h Mulatto, 5 yrs, 110 (O'Brien).
J. Abraham's ch h Saunterer, aged, 108 lbs (Gainsforth).
J. Tait's b h Strathearn, aged, 100 lbs. (Hales)
T. Brown's br g Brian Boru, 4 yrs, 98 lbs. (J. Williamson).
W. Kelso's br h Lord Orville, aged, 98 lbs. (Kelso).
Hon. J. Eales' b g Comet (late Manilla, 6 yrs, 98 lbs (Raynor).
Mr. N. T. Payton's br m Prima Donna, aged, 96 lbs. (Gorman).
R. J. Newland's b h Kingsworth, aged, 96 lbs (Nerriker).
W. and J. Lee's b m Harebell, 3 yrs.
W. Kite's b h Hesper, 4 yrs.
R. J. Roberts's br h Shadow.
F. Wentworth's b f Vanclaus, 3 yrs.
Hon. J. White's ch c Morpeth, 3 yrs.
Mr. W. Archer's b g Bryan O'Lynn.
Messrs. Hough and Powell's b f Rosemary, 3 yrs.
Betting: 4 to 1 against Kingsworth, 5 to 1 Masquerade, 3 to 1 Brian Born and Gipsey Cooper, 10 to 1 Strathearn and Mulatto, 12 to 1 Comet and Prima Donna, 10 to 5 others.

WINNERS OF THE HAWKESBURY GRAND HANDICAP.

| Yr. | Owner. | Winner. | Age | Wt. | | Time. | |
|---|---|---|---|---|---|---|---|
| 1871 | J. Iliffe | Aruma | a | 7 | 6 | 3 | 42 |
| 1872 | Bloomfield | Dagworth | 4 | 7 | 4 | 3 | 37 |
| 1873 | E. De Mestre | Dagworth | 5 | 6 | 10 | 3 | 40 4-10 |
| 1874 | J. Tait | Goldsbrough | 4 | 7 | 7 | 3 | 40 |
| 1875 | J. Wallis | Calumny | 6 | 8 | 4 | 3 | 25 |
| 1876 | A. Foweson | Sunlight | a | 7 | 8 | 3 | 34 |
| 1877 | J. Mayo* | Janitor | 5 | 8 | 7 | 3 | 14 |
| 1878 | A. Lodert† | The Dean | 4 | 7 | 3 | 2 | 5 |
| 1879 | J. Waters‡ | Kinsman | 5 | 6 | 4 | 2 | 41 3-10 |
| 1880 | J. Burton | Hesperian | 4 | 6 | 0 | 2 | 33 9-10 |
| 1881 | W. A. Long | Trump Yoss | 6 | 7 | 9 | 2 | 33 |
| 1882 | R. Rouse | Sting | 4 | 6 | 0 | 2 | 36¾ |

*This year the distance was altered from 2 miles to 1¾ miles.
†Woodlands 8st 1lb, finished first, but was disqualified for not drawing weight.
‡This year the distance was altered to 1½ miles.

| | | | | | |
|---|---|---|---|---|---|
| STING | Grand Master | Gladiateur | Monarque | The Baron, or Sting | The Emperor |
| | | | | Echidna | Economist, Miss Pratt |
| | | | Miss Gladiator | Gladiator | Partisan, Pauline |
| | | | | Taffrail | Sheet Anchor, The Warwick mare |
| | | Celerima | Stockwell | The Baron | Bird Catcher, Echidna |
| | | | | Pocahontas | Glencoe, Marpecca |
| | | | Slander | Pantaloon | Castree, Idalia |
| | | | | Pasquinade | Camel, Bantar |
| | Queen Bee | New Warrior | Phyrrhus I. | Epirus | Langor, Olympia |
| | | | | Fortress | Defence, Jewess |
| | | | Colocynth | Physician | Brutandorf, Primetto |
| | | | | Cameline | Whalebone, Maiden |
| | | Busy Bee | Magnus | Phyrrhus I. | Epirus, Fortress |
| | | | | Sleight of Hand or Doormouse | Young Phantom, Sister to Barefoot |
| | | | Industry | St. John | Sir Nicholas, Thunderboldt |
| | | | | Crazy Jane | Emigrant, Stella |

Sting is a good-looking chestnut horse and now four years old, and was bred by Mr. S. Blackman, near Mudgee, N. S. Wales. As a two-year-old he started at Mudgee, but we have no record of his performance. At the same age he ran second in the Maiden Plate at Coonamble, and with 8st was beaten by Kingsworth in the Flying Handicap at the same meeting. As a three-year-old he won the Town Plate, one and one-half miles, at Orange, carrying 7st 1 lb, in 2:49, Harebell being second. On the second day he won the Town Plate, two miles, 7st 3lb, in 3:41, Stella, 7st 7 lb, being second. Journeying to Mudgee he secured the one and one-half miles handicap, and then at Mudgee won the Turf Club handicap, one and one-half miles, 8st 5 lb, in 2:46 1-5, Fleetwing, 7st 3lb, being second. His last performance, up to the winning of the race under notice, was on Thursday in the County Purse, when he was not placed. All his performances are confined to N. S. Wales.

The two-year-old stakes, three furlongs for colts, 108 lbs., fillies 106 lbs., was won by W. Stewart's b c Kingslake by Maribyrnong, his sire imported Fisherman, dam Rosedale, Morceau second, Trisran third. Time 37½. For the members' handicap, 7 furlongs, Mr. J. Dugin's b filly Venice, 3 years, by Malta, carrying 96 pounds, passed the judges' box first, W. J. Brown's gr c Saconarn, 112 pounds, second, Mr. Gosper's b c Malta, 100 pounds, second. Time, 1:30½. The Prince of Wales Stakes, 6 furlongs, was won by Mr. J. Oneer's ch g Bob Sawyer, by Oliver Twist. Time, 1:17. The Turf Club handicap of $25 each for starters only, with $500 added, distance 1 mile, was won by Mr. R. J. Nowland's b h Kingsworth, aged, by Barbarian, 112 pounds; Mr. J. Abraham's b h Balthagan, 6 years, 102 pounds, second, Mr. James Maijos' gr m Hypatia, 6 years, 102 pounds, third. Time, 2:14½. This concluded a nice two days' racing and a week afterwards we are hurled into the midst of the great spring carnival of the Australian Jockey Club, a reunion which in point of racing interest is second to the great Melbourne Cup meeting held under the auspices of the Victoria Race Club. The opening day was greeted with delightful spring-like weather, the heat at times bordering almost on a summer's day, while the attendance was the largest ever known at the Roundwick Race Course. Proceedings opened with a hurdle race of 2½ miles, for which nine horses sported silk, the favorite, Sportsman, being badly beaten by Basilisk, carrying 138 pounds, Sportsman (154 pounds) second, Annie Laurie (147 pounds) third. Time 5m. The Trial Stakes brought out nine starters, eight of which were three-year-olds and was won by Mr. Thos. Brown's gr c Saconaro, 107 pounds, by Maribyrnong—Sappho, Mr. Fagin's b f Belle Bird (102 pounds) second, Mr. B. Osborne's br f Brunette, (102 pounds) third. Time, 2:15½.

The above three are each three-year-olds. The A. J. C. Derby Stakes now occupied all attention and four candidates out of an original entry of eighty-two subscribers faced the starter. The following are the conditions:

THE DERBY.

A sweepstake of $150 each, 5 ft. For three-year-old colts, 122 pounds, and fillies 117 pounds. If more than twenty subscribers the owner of the second horse to receive $300 out of the stake. The forfeit to be paid before 4 p. m. on the day preceding the race, or the nominator will be liable for the whole stake. One mile and a half.

Mr. E. DeMestre names br c Navigator, 3 years, (Hales)............. 1
Hon J. White names br c Segenhoe, 3 years, (Yeomans)............. 2
Captain Rossi names br c Lord Loftus, 3 years, (Thomas)............. †
Mr. E. De Mestre names br c Nicholas (Colley)............. †

Betting, 6 to 2 on Segenhoe; 5 to 2 against Navigator; 10 to 1 against others.

After one attempt the flag fell to a good start, Nicholas going at once to the front in the interest of Navigator. Nicholas led Lord Loftus eight lengths past the stand, then a length away came Navigator, with Segenhoe a length away last. No alteration till they reached the back of the course, where Nicholas's lead had been decreased to half a length, Segenhoe being still last. Over the hill they began to close up, Loftus joining Nicholas, and Segenhoe coming fast on the outside. Loftus was first into the straight, but at the distance post was passed by Navigator on the inside and Segenhoe on the outside. A great race home ensued in favor of the former by a length and a half, Nicholas and Lord Loftus running a dead heat for third place. Time, 2:48½.

WINNERS OF THE A. J. C. DERBY.

| Yr. | Owner. | Winner. | Sire. | Time |
|---|---|---|---|---|
| | | | | m. s. |
| 1865 | Cheeke | Clove | Magnus | 2:51 |
| 1866 | J. Tait | The Barb | Sir Hercules | 2:48½ |
| 1867 | J. Tait | Fireworks | Kelpie | 2:48 |
| 1868 | Thompson | The Duke | Kingston | 2:50 |
| 1869 | H. Fisher | Charon | Ferryman | 2:47½ |
| 1870 | J. Tait | Florence | Boiardo | 2:51 |
| 1871 | T. Lee | Javelin | Yattendon | 2:47 |
| 1872 | W. Winch | Loup Garou | Lord of Linne | 2:46½ |
| 1873 | T. J. Ryan | Benvolio | Peter Wilkins | 2:48½ |
| 1874 | Sir Hercules Robinson | Kingsborough | Kingston | 2:50 |
| 1875 | E. Jellet | Richmond | Maribyrnong | 2:45 |
| 1876 | C. B. Fisher | Robinson Crusoe | Angler | 2:43½ |
| 1877 | J. Silberberg | Woodlands | Maribyrnong | 2:49½ |
| 1878 | E. De Mestre | His Lordship | The Marquis | 2:55 |
| 1879 | E. Lee | Nellie | T. Whiffer (E) | 2:51½ |
| 1880 | J. S. Smith | Grand Flaneur | Yattendon | 2:45 1-5 |
| 1881 | Osborne | Wheatear | Epigram | 2:55 |
| 1882 | E. De Mestre | Navigator | Robinson Crusoe | 2:48½ |

The win of Mr. E. De Mestre was very popular and well received hythe public.

The Epsom handicap, one mile, one furlong, sweep of $25 each, with $1,000 added, was won by Mr. C. T. Roberts' ch g Masquerade, by The Drummer, imported, (106 lbs.) who was first favorite in the Hawesbury handicap, but making his effort in that race too soon tired down Brian Boru, (114 lbs.) second; Balthagan, (102 lbs.) third. Time, 1:57½. The Spring Stakes, weight for age, one and a half miles, a sweep of $25 each with $1,000 added, fell to Hecla, three years, 128 pounds, beating Barber, aged, 132 pounds, Drummer, four years, 126 pounds. Welter handicap, one and a quarter miles, was appropriated by the old one-eyed son of Bylong, Saunterer, who carried (134 pounds) beating Miss Whippler (112 pounds) and Hastings, (110 pounds) in 2:14½.

The second day or "metropolitan day," as it is called, opened equally as auspiciously as the first or Derby day by Mr. J. Dillon's b m Twilight, by The Drummer. Twilight opened the ball by winning The Shorts, a handicap of $500, three-quarter mile, carrying 122 pounds. Venice, three-year-old and Waxworks, four-year-old, ran a dead heat for second place, each carrying 115 pounds. In the Spring Marden Stakes Hecla gave us another taste of her quality of winning easy with leaving the paddock at 6 to 4 on her, and it clearly shows from her running what Mr. Farrell, the trainer of her and Segenhoe—the Derby favorite—made in scratching her for the blue ribbon of the N. S. Wales turf. Great interest is centered in her meeting the Derby winner to-day in the Mare's Produce Stakes, 1½ miles. The Great Metropolitan Stakes of $100 each, with $2,500 added, two miles, was appropiated by Masquerade, carrying eighty-six pounds, showing at once what a good thing her party had for the Hawkesbury event. Comet, another gelding by The Drummer, and Britisher, by John Bull, imported, each having an impost of ninety-six pounds, ran second and third respectively in one of the fastest run races known over Randwick, the winner having plenty left in her after passing the winning post. Appended is a table of winners and placed horses for the Metropolitan Stakes, showing the different times:

| Year. | First. | Second. | Third. | Time. | |
|---|---|---|---|---|---|
| 1866 | Bylong | Yattendon | Tim Whiffler | 3 42½ | |
| 1867 | Tim Whiffler | Rose of Australia | Birmingham | 3 38 | 6-10 |
| 1868 | The Barb | Tim Whiffler | Bylong | 3 37 | 3-10 |
| 1869 | Circassian | Grey Momus | Warrior | 3 44½ | |
| 1870 | Croydon | Tim Whiffler | Trump Card | 3 43 | |
| 1871 | Rosebud | The Pearl | Barbelle | 3 40½ | |
| 1872 | Dagworth | Clansman | The Quack | 3 33 | 8-10 |
| 1873 | Horatio | Myrtle | The Arrow | 3 42½ | |
| 1874 | Sterling | Goldsbrough | Maid of Avenal | 3 36½ | |
| 1875 | Goldsbrough | Kingsborough | Kingfisher | 3 32 | 1-5 |
| 1876 | Nemesis | Rataplan | Irish Stew | 3 33 | 8-10 |
| 1877 | Amendment | The Painter | Timothy | 3 35 | 3-10 |
| 1878 | Democrat | The Dean | Colima | 3 38 | |
| 1879 | Secundus | Lord Burghley | Strathearn | 3 36 | 8-10 |
| 1880 | The Pontiff | Hesperian | Lord Burghley | 3 31 | 6-10 |
| 1881 | Hesperian | Waxy | Wellington | 3 32 | 4-10 |
| 1882 | Masquerade | Comet | Britisher | 3 33 | |

The Selling Plate was won by Mr. H. C. Dongar's br f Preciosa, three years, Kanaka and Hopeful second and third. This was a bit of an upset to backers who fancied Rosinante and Kanka, the former getting fourth. In the Squatters' handicap, Brian Boru, carrying 118 pounds, started with the odds of six to four on him and won cleverly by a neck from Hypatia (119 po nd ), and Willeroo, (96 pounds).

The third daycommences to-day, Thursday, September 7, an account of which I cannot forward you owing to the 'Frisco mail closing at 3 o'clock and racing commencing at 1:15 p. m.

There is very little doing in the aquatics. Laycock has landed and is well, while E. Trickett is keeping a public house on Bridge street, Sydney. The coursing and football season are just over and attention is now turned to cricket.

The arrival of Dr. Jno. New with a string of trotters has a tendency to make the people talk about forming a track, but talk is cheap. I would like to see a company start and form a track now that the Doctor is present as he could give them good advice. We are not half so go-ahead as the Victorians but slow and sure. I do not despair of seeing trotting go ahead here; the people are only beginning to get a knowledge of the sport, through frequent importations of trotters, and making themselves more conversant with it through reading the different American papers which arrive here. Your very interesting sporting journal is widely circulated in this colony, and I believe also in Victoria. ECHO.

## Bootjack's Victories.

SACRAMENTO CITY, October 8, 1882.

Please inform me of the name of the running horse that has won the most races in America this year and oblige

Yours truly,
FRANK FERN.

This query would require a great deal of research to answer authoritatively. From a somewhat hurried look we are under the impression that Bootjack, by Bonnie Scotland, is at the head of the list, having won up to the 12th of October eleven races, and Brambaletta, by the same sire, won ten up to the time she met with the injury. When the year is up, thanks to "Krick," there will be no trouble to give a correct reply.

## Racing and Trotting in Washington Ter.

GOLDENDALE, W. T., Sept. 26, 1872. Trotting for three-year-olds, beats of a mile.

G. W. Waldron's ch f Maud Knox.............. 1 1
Stone & Washburn's blk s Black Prince.............. 2 2
Al Brown's b g Dan.............. dist.

Time, 3:17½, 3:21½.

Same day—Running, for two-year-olds, half mile dash.

Wm. Gilmores' Baby Belmont.............. 1
Stone & Washburns' Nellie Linden.............. 2
P. Fitzpatrick's Boots Filly.............. 3

Time, 56½.

Won by two lengths.

September 27.—Trotting for stallions, beats of a mile, three in five.

G. W. Waldron's Johnny Knox by General Knox.............. 1
J. W. Washburn's Dick Morgan.............. dist.

Time, 2:59.

Same day—Running, for three-year-olds, dash of a mile.

Stone & Washburn's Lucy Lindsay.............. 1
J. Harris' Murphy filly.............. 2
Wm. Gilmore's Pup.............. 3

Time, 1:59.

September 28.—Running for saddle horses, dash of half a mile.

John Martin's Beauty.............. 1
Stone & Washburn's Big Gun.............. 2
W. D. Gilmore's Happy Sal.............. 3
B. Johnson's Tony.............. 4
C. N. Smith's Tim.............. 5
H. Pustin's Eagle Bird.............. 6
T. Weed's Black Bird.............. 7
A. T. Bunnel's Hard Bargain..............

No time.

Sept. 29.—Trotting, mile heats, three in five.

Stone & Washburn's ch g Sleepy George.............. 1 1 1
Geo. Waldron's ch g Maud Knox.............. 2 2 2

Time, 2:29, —, —.

Same day—Running, dash of a mile.

H. Duston's b m Bunch Grass.............. 1
W. T. Mulvanill's b s Sam.............. 2
J. Harris' w s Lindsey Urvine.............. 3

Time, 1:49.

At the conclusion of the running race the brown stallion, Lindsey Urvine, was sold at auction for $355.

## The California Trotters.

The eight young trotters shipped from Sacramento by ex-Governor Leland Stanford of California took up their quarters at the Gentlemen's Driving Park yesterday morning, and are in the first row of stalls on the hill to the left of the entrance gates. Mr. Marvin is in charge of the stable and he will be remembered as the driver of Smuggler when the latter was the sensational horse of the trotting turf. The horses were exactly two weeks on the journey across the continent, though from this must be deducted a short stop at Ogden, then two days at Omaha and from Wednesday morning to Sunday at Island Park, Albany. A special car is run by Mr Stanford for the purpose of shipping his valuable trotters in, and it was in this equine palace car that the eight journeyed from California. Mr. Marvin said they had all fallen away very much in flesh since leaving home, and that while in the car not one of the eight would eat anything but hay. Notwithstanding this however, they are a grand lot as viewed in their boxes, and when exhibited on the track will doubtless be worthier yet of admiration. The eight are as follows:

Wildflower, 3 years, by Electioneer, dam Mayflower, by St. Clair. Has a two-year-old record of 2:21. Is a rich bay with black points. Shows great muscular development, with a blood-like head and clean cut limbs on which the veins stand out with great prominence.

Marlet, 3 years, by Electioneer, dam Martie, by Whipple's Hambletonian. This is a bay gelding, and is entered in the Mali Stakes with Wildflower. Is lengthy, with a speedy look about him, but lacks the symmetry of Wildflower.

Bertha, 3 years, by Electioneer, dam by Sontag by Mohawk out of Laura Keene. A remarkably large, bright bay mare, standing 16·1 hands, and notwithstanding her size, is well furnished and seems to have stood the journey better than several of the others. Is engaged in stakes at Lexington, Ky.

Stella, three years, by Electioneer, dam Lady Rose, by Gen. Taylor.

Unique, 3 years, by Electioneer, dam Barnes' Idol.

Ned Fay, 3 years, by Electioneer, dam Mary, by Fred Low. The latter three were sent on to be kept in New York. The first two are fillies and the latter a gelding.

Hinda Rose, 2 years, by Electioneer, dam Beautiful Bells, by the Moor. As a yearling this filly trotted in 2:36, and has every appearance of being able to do as remarkable a feat as a two-year-old. She is a brown in color, with a thoroughbred look about her head and legs. Her quarters have something approaching the droop, and the immense length from the point of the hip to the hock indicates great reach, behind which there is sufficient muscle to back up. Hinda Rose is engaged at Lexington.

Flower Girl, 2 years, is own sister to Wildflower, whom she resembles very much.—*N. Y. Herald.*

At Euston Hall, in 1799, was foaled the Duke of Grafton's first Derby winner, Tyrant by the curiously named Pot-8-os out of one of his Grace's own mares. Apropos of Pot-8-os the question is constantly being asked where he derived his singular name? and we may as well give the traditional story here. It was originally intended to have given the chestnut son of Eclipse, the name of Potatoes which it must be admitted was not itself a high-sounding appellation for a thoroughbred, and when Lord Abingdon who had bred him happened to mention his intention to his trainer in the stable, a small lad was so much struck with the absurdity of the name that he involuntarily burst into a hearty laugh. His Lordship good humoredly turned to him and saying, "So you don't like the name, my boy, eh?" picked up a piece of chalk and handing it to the lad added, "Nevertheless we shall have it, and if you can write it up over his corn bin I will give you this crown piece." The boy took the chalk and wrote "Pot-8-os" and His Lordship was so tickled with the lad's ingenuous version that he retained the spelling of the word.

The horsemen of Plumas county are talking over a proposition to build a track in American Valley.

## Turf Gossip.

"Vigilant," the genial and gossipy writer who presides over the "Turf and Track" department of the New York *Spirit of the Times*, invests the driest details with a halo of cheerfulness that indexes a happy soul. He always says something pleasant in the pleasantest sort of way and the following brochure is a fair sample of his weekly literary salad:

Louisville and Brighton Beach have monopolized attention the past week, but next week the autum meeting of the American Jockey Club will be in full blast at Jerome Park, which will soon be putting on its October tints, rendering its world-renowned beauty more marked than ever, and Chicago will open the ball on Tuesday.

The sensation of the week has been the sale by Mr. Milton Young, of Henderson, Ky., of his entire racing stable to Mr. R. C. Pate, of St. Louis, for $25,000, the transfer to be made at the close of the Louisville meeting. It has been understood for some time past that Mr. Young contemplated retiring from the turf and devoting himself to breeding, for which purpose he recently purchased the McGrathiana farm, paying nearly $47,000. Mr. Young had freely stated that his racing stable was for sale, and when the Louisville meeting opened Mr. Pate came on, and closed the bargain on Saturday night last, the 23d inst. He takes all the horses in training, with the exception of Square Dance and Patti, which Mr. Young desires to retain for the stud. The following is a full list of the stock sold:

Boatman, b g, three years, by imported Bonnie Scotland—Valerian.

Monogram, b g, three years, by imported Buckden—Monomanis.

Ascender, b g, two years, by imported Buckden—Ascension.

Bondholder, b c, two years, by imported Bonnie Scotland—Glentina.

Vera, b f, two years, by King Alfonso—Veritas.

Bacarat, br g, two years, by imported Bonnie Scotland—Robinet.

Tangent, ch g, two years, by imported Great Tom—Vanilla.

Yearlings.—Empire, gr g, by Enquirer—Alice Murphy.

Embargo, ch g, by Enquirer—Fannie Mattingly.

Endymion, b g, by Enquirer—Bergamot.

Envoy, ch g, by Enquirer—Satinet.

Rex, ch g, by King Alfonso—Queen Victoria.

Nannie D, b f, by Enquirer—Glentina (Bondholder's dam.)

Maria D, b f, by Lisbon—Crucifix.

Longway, b g, by Longfellow—Sallie Morgan.

Tattoo, ch f, by imported Great Tom—Sparrowgrass.

Trinket, b f, by imported Great Tom—Robinet.

Trophy, b f, by imported Great Tom—Bonnie Meade.

Mr. Plate, the purchaser, resides at St. Louis, where he has been long known in sporting circles, having been for some time identified with trotting interests, being the owner of Woodford Mambrino, Lucille, and Kate Middleton. Mr. Pate has signalized his entry on the turf with a master stroke of judgment, having engaged Ed. Brown ("Brown Dick"), who has always been Mr. Young's trainer. Thus, the horses will not change trainers, and there is less likelihood of their losing form, as is often the case when trainers are changed. The fillies included in the above list revert to Mr. Young upon their leaving the turf, Mr. Pate having their racing qualities only.

A *Courier-Journal* reporter gives the following account of his interview with Mr. Young, at Louisville:

"Yes," he replied, "I take possession of McGrathiana in October, and will immediately set to work to breeding the thoroughbred. My intentions have been all along to do this, and the opportunities presented themselves, and I would not let them slip, fearing that at some future time I might regret it."

"Yes," replied the reporter, "you're right; running the racer is risky business."

"Oh, I don't know that it is so risky," replied Mr. Young; "I think I could continue at it and make money; but what I want is some permanent, steady business."

"It costs a great deal for the running expenses of a stable, doesn't it?" asked the reporter.

"Yes, the expenses are very heavy," he replied. "For one like the one I have been running, it would require the horses to win $25,000 during the season to make any money. During the three years which I have been in the business my stables have won $91,000 in purses and stakes. Of course the winnings on the outside in the pools are not mentioned.

"You will commence right away to breeding?," asked the reporter.

"Yes: I guess I have as fine a lot of young brood mares as there is in the country, with the exception of Lorillard. I have watched my opportunity, and picked up the best that was to be had. My young stallion Onondago has not a peer anywhere for breeding. He is a brother to Sensation, the best two-year-old that ever appeared, and Susquehanna, too, was a fine performer at that age. The popular idea now is for short dashes and early development. Most all of the older turfmen still adhere to the old prejudices for four miles, but I intend to keep up with the procession and breed that which is in demand. Short dashes and speed are now wanted, and Onondago cames from a family of that character of performers."

"What stock have you now on hand for your establishment?" asked the reporter.

"Well, there is Onondago, three years, by Leamington—Susan Beane; Duke of Montrose, five years, by Waverley—Kelpey; Fonwich, four years, (sister to Fonso), and out of the grandam of Hindoo; Beatitude, six years, Bliss, five years, and Beatrice, three years, full sisters, by Bonnie Scotland—Mariposa; Black Maria, three years, full sister to Bancroft; Kelpie, fourteen years, the dam of Janet; Olivia, three years, by The Ill-Used—Olitipa; Wildfire, three years, by Leamington—Madge, by Australian; Perhaps, eight years, the dam of Perplex; Matagorda, six years, by Glengarry; Uena, three years, by Virgil, dam a full sister to Springbok; Sozodont, three years, by Longfellow; Belle of Maywood, four years, full sister to Belle of Nelson, by Hunter's Lexington; Gladiola, four years, by Glengarry—Waltz, the dam of Glidella; Patti, four years, by imp. Billet—Dora, by Pat Malloy; Square Dance, three years, by War Dance—Sue Dougherty, by Mickey Free. All of them, too," continued Mr. Young, "are from the best families of winners."

"You will hardly be prepared for a sale in the spring?" asked the reporter.

"No; I have but two foals now—one out of Beatitude, by King Alfonso; the other by St Martin—Perhaps. Nearly all of my mares are, however now in foal. There are Be[illegible]rice and Belle of Maywood, in foal to Glen Athol; Be[illegible] Sozodont and Glidela to King Alfonso; Perhaps to L[illegible] Kelpie to imported Thunderstorm (she got a good [illegible]

Janet by Lightning); Fonwich to imported Bluemantle, Keene's recent importation; Nina and Black Maria to King Ban, and Matagorda to Enquirer."

The Donohoe family are becoming as noted and as numerous on our turf as ever the Day family were in England when George IV said he could never tell which was "old John Day," and which was "young John Day." Of the Donohues, there is "Billy," the bright particular star of jockeydom; there is "Mike" fast developing into a rival of his elder brother; there is "J. Donohue," already one of the cleverest of the featherweights; and finally there is Old Joe. Now, for flat races. As an owner of steeplechasers, he has a national reputation, and is the most jolly, rollicking Irishman that ever hunted a fox over the Long Island plains, or the Jersey Palisades, and his adventures and escapades would fill a small volume. A cloud ruffled his massive brow, struggling for mastery, with a half-amused uncertain smile that played about his lips when we met him in the paddock, at Sheepshead Bay, last Thursday. Evidently something was wrong with old Joe, and, presuming upon old acquaintance, we ventured to ask what was the matter.

"Matther is it? An' shure phat d'ye suppose wud be t'matther wid a man whin an ould thafe ov an officer threatins to arrist 'im for nothin' at all!" was his indignant reply.

"Who was this?" we asked, with some surprise.

"One ov ould Bergh's men—one ov thim Cruelthy to Animals Society fellers."

"On what charge?"

"Fur whippin' an sphurrin' a horse, he sez, I rode in a race. Did ye ever hear t'loike o' that now?"

"No, I did not, but, I must confess, I don't exactly understand the affair."

"Who can understand t'loikes ov thim fellows, anyhow? I was standin' here a minute ago, Jimmy Jinnins an' meself, whin who shuld stip up but a feller as thall as t'house, wid a hat on his head loike a sea captin."

"'Is Doneyhue yer name?' sez he.

"'It is,' sez I.

"'So I'm towld,' sez he.

"'Thin phat did ye ax me for?' sez I.

"'Y're accused,' sez he, 'ov whippin' and half murtherin' a harse wid yer whip an sphurs. T' evening phaper has a long account ov it, an' calls t'attinshun ov t' Society ov t' Previnshin ov Cruelthy to Animals to 't. Y're loiable t' arrist,' sez he. 'T' Societhy don't want t' make any trouble wid ye, qut I warn ye not t' do t'loike o' that agin now. Ye'd ought to be ashamed, an auld hathin loike yorself batin' an' abusin' a poor divil ov a harse."

"'And phat sort of a man are you?" sez I.

"'I'll show ye,' sez he.

"'Phat t' divil's matther wid ye?' sez I.

"'Nothin,' sez he.

"'D'ye think I'm an Italian?' sez I.

"'I do not,' sez he.

"'Thin phat are ye graffin' about?' sez I.

"'Did'nt ye rhide t' harse till he was half kilt?' sez he.

"'Do I luk loike a man that wud be afther rhidin' a harse in a race?' sez I; 't' loike ov me, two hundred pounds weight; sure ye're a daft man."

"'Well,' sez he, 'the phaper sez it was J. Doneyhue, and ye acknowledge th' same is yer name.'

"'Me name is J. Doneyhue,' sez I, 'it might be Jim, it might be John, but it's Joe.'

"'That's all roight,' sez he 'but here's t' phaper; now see fur yerself,' and he sticks a sliph ov newsphaper foreninst me. The phaper sed that 'J. Donohue, the jockey, whipped and sphurred t' harse Ninus unmurciful.' Thin I begun t' understand. I tould 'im it was the boy that rides for Jeter Walden, and he went off. Av coorse, I don't care a toss of er copper, but it's t' mean consate ov t' thing, d'ye moind. T' loikes of fellers loike thim meddlin' wid things they don't know nuthin' about, an' taken t' loikes ov meself for a bit ov a jock that rides at 88lbs. Shure it's ruinashun t' counthry's goin' to.'"

Rica, the noted daughter of Kingfisher and Lady Mentmore, is expected to make her reappearance at Jerome Park. Last season Rica stamped herself quite the best of the two-year-old division, and it was thought Mr. Kelso had got a bargain when, in October, he purchased her of Mr. Belmont for $7,500, the three-year-old filly stakes being considered quite at her mercy. She, however, has been a great disappointment, being hardly up to the mark at any time, owing so sore withers, which, at Monmouth Park, threatened to become fistulous, and she was sent home. She began mending at once, and will reappear in the Huntor Stakes, with a good chance of winning.

Mr. Richard Roche, of St. Louis, has purchased of Messrs. Bowen & Co. the brown filly Miss Woodford, two years, by Billet—Fancy Jane, by Neil Robinson, second dam by Knight of St. George, third dam by Glencoe. Miss Woodford, as will be noticed by the above pedigree, is a full sister to Belle of Runnymede, and has, during the past season, proved herself one of the best two-year-olds of the year, winning the Ladies' Stakes at Chicago, and the Spinaway and Misses' Stakes at Saratoga. She will prove a valuable recruit to Mr. Roche's racing team, as she is engaged in all the great three-year-old filly stakes at Lexington, Louisville, Jerome Park, Coney Island, Monmouth and Saratoga.

The Dwyer Bros. always rise equal to the occasion. The breakdown of Runnymede and Onondaga left them practically unrepresented in the three-year-old stakes, but on Tuesday they purchased of Mr. A. Burnham the black gelding Carley B, by Virgil—Ladylike, by Leamington, who will carry their red jacket in the Jerome Stakes at Jerome Park. The price is said to be $6,000, but, as he is also engaged in the Breckenridge Stakes at Baltimore, and both events are very open, his success would return the Dwyers the purchase-money.

An amusing case of "diamond cut diamond" occurred at Sheepshead Bay on Saturday. Mr. Robinson's Little Fred won the selling race, and when, as is customary in selling races, the horse was offered at auction, the owner of Little Phil, who had run second, was found running the bidding up until Mr. Robinson had to bid $1,600 to save his horse. He thereupon availed himself of the clause in Rule 53, and entering the weighing-room claimed Little Phil, by paying the latter's selling price and the amount of the purse—$2,000.

King Alfred, the English stallion, was sold recently in England for $125. He is a son of King Tom and a mare by Bay Middleton, and in Baron Rothschild's colors ran second to Blue Gown for the Derby in 1868. Some ten years later the success of Phaeton and King Ernest attracted the attention of Americans toward the merits of the sons of King Tom as sires, and a prominent American breeder negotiated for the purchase and importation of King Alfred, but through some misunderstanding the bargain was never consummated.

The announcement is made of the sale of Florac, the brood mare, by Mr. Scully to Mr. T. Berry, of Lexington, Ky. Florac is a bay mare, bred by Major B. G. Thomas in 1864, and is a daughter of Mickey Free (imp.), from Dixie (dam of Herzog), by Sovereign; 2d dam St. Mary, by Hamlet; 3d dam Vamp (imp.), by Langar; 4th dam Wire, by Waxy. Florac is the dam of Warfield and Ella Warfield. With her Mr. Berry purchased her bay filly foal, by Thunderstorm (imp.).

Major B. G. Thomas has sold to W. Walker, the jockey, the bay colt Hassan. He is a two-year-old, by Lelaps, from Haz'em, by Australian; 2d dam Hira (the dam of Himyar), by Lexington. Hassan is a colt of a most racing-like cut, and won his first race at the present Louisville meeting, having the speed of the family.

Captain Cottrill has sold to Mr. V. L. Kirkham, of Nashville, Tenn., the chestnut gelding Mediator, 3 years, by Buckden—Meanness, by Brown Dick, after he had won the mile heat race at Louisville, on Tuesday, in 1:44¼—1:45. Price $2,500.

Charley Sait, the noted steeplechase rider, has accepted the position of whipper-in to the Meadow Brook Hunt. Charley, as a horse-man, has no superior, and his conquests on Deadhead and Derby are well remembered.

Messrs. J. N. Ackerman & Co. have purchased of Morris & Hatten the bay gelding Morgan Spy, 3 years, by John Morgan—Calomel, by Canwell; 2d dam Dora, by Australian. He is a fairish sort of horse, possessing a good turn of speed, but does not fancy a distance.

The English horse Roseberry, who was the first horse to win the Cesarewitch and Cambridgeshire in the same season (1876), was sold recently to Mr. Vyner for $2,000. He is a son of Speculum and Ladylike, by Newminster.

Mr. A. J. Cassatt has presented the chestnut filly Foxglove, 2 years, by Lever—Lady Way, by Eclipse; 2d dam Sp ig (Volturno's dam), by Lexington, to his trainer, Mr. R. [illegible] Pryor.

## Track Government.

Editor Breeder and Sportsman: I would like to assist you and all true friends of the turf in scoring the obnoxious and unprincipled few who unfortunately are to be seen on most of our tracks, and in devising some means if possible of ridding the sporting community of their disagreeable presence. Our State is yet young in her breeding and racing experience but is undoubtedly destined to take a leading place in the matter of thoroughbred horses and where the thoroughbred is once planted the trotter naturally follows. To insure first-class sport both runners and trotters should be in the hands of gentlemen. While I have not been identified with runners, I am free to admit that as a general thing they are in better hands than the trotters, and the gentlemen of the running turf are prompt to reform abuses whenever they appear. I think the trotting men will have to follow suit. Measures to do away with tricks and tricksters are what every lover of the turf should labor to promote. To my mind the dash plan of racing as adopted by the Jockey clubs is a great assistance as it does away with the possibility of "putting up jobs" between heats and the execrable "helper" loses his vocation in a great measure. That alone is a great point gained in the direction of reform as the helper is a noisome nettle among the flowers. If he cannot be weeded out, brand; brand conspicuously. Let the gentlemen of this State interested in trotting and pacing organize an association and let at least each county be represented at the meetings. One meeting a year with good attendance would be sufficient, and it should be he held at the conclusion of the last fall meeting. The presidents of the different associations could assist in bringing about such a mutual understanding as would be beneficial to all concerned. They would have the data fresh in their memories and all grievances, real or imaginary, could be properly adjusted and the pruning knife in skillful hands at this season would only leave the healthy plants for the next year. There is a great deal of loose accusation at all of our district fairs and race meetings, and there is a good chance for a smart manipulator, late from college, to run amuck at least for one year. He could hardly hope to succeed in repeating the business as a rule, but if rumor be credietd this is the second season that two students from an Eastern institute have, as the gamins say: "got away with the cake." There should be some duly authorized association or board to meet immediately after the fairs and investigate all charges while they are fresh, publicly, without fear or favor. If an accusation be found ru let the guilty party be promptly punished; if charges made are false let there be a public exoneration. It is true that many of these charges recklessly made have no foundation in fact and in such cases it is not only justice to the individual wrongfully accused that he have early hearing, but it is policy that cannot be gainsayed to dissipate as soon as possible a scandal that affects the integrity of the turf everywhere. In your columns last week you formulated an idea suggested by Mr. P. A. Finigan regarding judges. Mr. Editor, while I see nothing but excellence in that plan I go further. The judges are responsible to the public for the conduct of all persons on the grounds, the drivers and riders in particular. I would suggest that the different presidents, when they are competent to act, are the proper ones to judge the whole circuit, and there ought to be three to open and if possible close the small circuit in this State. With the same vigilant eye over every meeting, the manipulator would have to be cautious indeed, for it is seldom that tricks, be they ever so cleverly performed, do not become known soon after and generally in time to meet the trickster at the next town in the circuit. Three competent judges is what the circuit wants, or two beside the president of the one where the meeting is being held. I do not desire to trench on you patience or your space by elaborating the idea further at this time, but I have been brought to give the subject some thought by observing the spectacle of the smaller towns of a circuit at the mercy of a combination between conscienceless speculators and corrupt drivers.

County Town.

Nellie R and Her Admirers.—We have referred to this remarkable filly on several occasions, knowing that a great many of our readers feel an interest in her performance for several reasons, and among them: She is a Petaluma production, and is owned here; her sire and very many of her near relatives may be found in this county; and, lastly, from the time when she hauled a buggy, when three years old, in 3:00, without any training, this writer thought her to be the best filly in the State, and now, considering the limited amount of work and training she has received, he believes her to be the fastest living trotter! Certainly no other animal has trotted so fast with as little handling. All her training does not amount to as much as the Palo Alto colts receive by the time they are one year and a half old.—*Petaluma Argus.*

## Name Claimed.

Editor Breeder and Sportsman: Palo Alto claims the name Genaral McDowell, for bay colt, large star, foaled February 7, 1881, by Norfolk, dam Boydana, by imported Knight of St. George.

F. W. Covey.

## Jay Eye See's Great Performance.

In view of the admirable qualities shown by Albert W during the recent circuit we give the annexed account of the race won by his great rival Jay Eye See at the Chicago Driving Park on Sept. 23d.

The race was a special four-year-old stake race of $2,250, in which, of the several entries only Bronze appeared to compete. At the July meeting of the Chicago Driving Park a race of extraordinary interest occurred between Bronze and Jay Eye See, in which the latter was beaten in the seventh heat by a bad send-off, Bronze being the winner of the race. There has been much talk of a match between Bronze and the Case colt, but they have not met since then until to-day, when both appeared on the track at the Horse Fair to start for the four-year-old prize. Other colts had been entered, but only Bronze and Jay Eye See started. Jay Eye See took the first heat in 2:22½, winning without difficulty, but laid up in the second, which was won by bronze in 2:29½. In the third heat, however, it was determined to make a record. The Racine colt was in fine form, and the two preceding heats had only been preparatory work for him. The driver of Jay Eye See was told to cut loose, and did so, trotting the mile in 2:19, the colt going perfectly level up to within 50 feet of the wire, when he broke and was not again settled. It was so evident that he would have finished faster but for the break that the driver was told to make another trial. In the fourth heat the colt trotted without skip or hitch from wire to wire, and finished again in 2:19, again beating the record, the best four-year-old record of Trinket, 2:19¾. The pace was too hot for Bronze, who did little more than get inside the flag. Jay Eye See was sired by Dictator, a son of Rysdyk's Hambletonian, and his dam was Midnight, also the dam of Noontide, with a record of 2:20½, Midnight's sire being Pilot Jr. Mr. Case, the owner of Jay Eye See, is a wealthy man, and is able to indulge in the luxury of owning the fastest and gamest four-year-old trotter in the world.

## Jay Eye See and Bronze.

From an Eastern exchange we take the following rather "free color" sketch of the two famous four-year-olds of the eastern side of the mountains:

Jay Eye See was purchased in Kentucky, in April, 1880, from Col. Richard West, at Edge Hill farm, where he was bred, by Mr. J. I. Case of Racine, along with five other two-year-olds, all sired by Dictator, the full brother of the mighty Dexter. He was the last colt selected, as he was considered rather small. As before remarked, his sire was Dictator, dam by Pilot Jr. (Old Midnight) out of Twilight, by Lexington, out of Daylight, by Glencoe, out of a mare by Wagner, etc. Well, the thoroughbred lines come pretty direct here, certain. In Dictator we find the Hambletonian blood and the thoroughbred blood of American Star. To say the least, all the blood lines indicate speed. He is now 15¼ hands, black and (what a pity) gelded. In his conformation, he is level and even, about the same hight forward as behind. He has a clean cut, intelligent head, full eye, neatly-pointed nose, neck of fine proportions, a little longer than the average Hambletonian; his back straight, and smoothly coupled; a well-rounded barrel, slightly sloping rump, his quarters, stifles and gaskins, remarkably developed, give him a blocky appearance; in fact, when in road form, he is in the form of the handsome Ethan Allen Morgan Black Hawk. While he has powerful propelling powers, his almost brother in blood, Code, who is a much faster colt than he has shown, is rather of a light hamed horse.

Jay Eye See, in his jogs, has the nod of Maud S, Darby, Maze-Manie, and many other celebrities, but he is as sound as a dollar, with the best of legs and feet, his tendons and muscles are cat-gut and case-hardened steel; in his disposition he is docile and tractable, and has always becu a pet with Mr. Case and his family, as well as with his careful and painstaking driver, Mr. Bither. He wears no toe-weights, simply an eleven-ounce shoe forward and five-ounce behind, and has full free knee-action, Code differing here again as he carries a six-ounce toe-weight. Mr. Wallace may become interested in Jay Eye See, as he will here find a double cross to the pacing Pilots, a cross to the pacing Hambletonians. "Explain?" I will sometime; and he must admit a strong infusion of the thoroughbred, and yet no toe-weights to make him trot, no toe-weights to make him overcome the lack of knee-action, so claimed, for the thoroughbred.

Jay Eye See was taken to Wisconsin after his purchase, was hardly broken in the fall, being a two-yeaar-old, and run out until April, 1881; his breaking was then completed, and inside of six weeks he trotted half a mile in 1:18. Mr. Case, who has watched the development of this colt carefully, ordered him out to grass at once. "I am afraid you will hurt him," he would often remark to Mr. Bither. He was taken up Oct. 1; in the last of the month trotted a half mile in 1:14½, when Mr. Case requested "Ed" to stop his fast work and prepare him for his winter's jogging. He was jogged to the pole all winter beside Edwin B, went to the track May 23, and the first week in July trotted Mr. Case's half-mile track in 2:23, the last half in 1:06. No horse ever owned by Mr. Case, Gov. Sprague not excepted, had been able to equal this performance. We next find him here, and selling in pools: Bronze, $50; Waiting, $18; Jay Eye See, $15; field, $15. Of course those that knew did, and why not? And they would, but for the judges' stand. So you see they did not and I know how it is myself. Jay Eye See has been developed, and made a trotter by the careful watching and handling of Edward Bither, who has had excellent success in developing the colts of Mr. Case. "Ed" says, when he shows up Phallas, the five-year-old son of Dictator, and Betsy Trotwood, the people will begin to think that the Dictators are quite a trotting family. Phallus can beat 2:30 by several seconds at any time—has, in fact, recently. His favorites, however, are two colts by Gov. Sprague, that are "doing splendidly."

Dictator, who is so rapidly gaining the first place among the sons of Hambletonian, I saw in Kentucky last week. He is one of the highest finished and most blood-like sons of Hambletonian I ever saw. His full brother, Dexter, many of your readers have seen, and I can best describe him as being in the same perfect mould, only a size smaller. He has the pure, rapid, merry, easy gait of Dexter, which he has imparted to Jay Eye See, and most of his get. Dictator, Doble says, had as much speed as Dexter, but an accident compelled his retirement from the turf. The performance of Code and Jay Eye See will make him a greater favorite with breeders in Kentucky. Victoria, by Dictator, also owned by Mr. Case, with three weeks' handling on the track, trotted a slow half-mile track in 2:27, and 2:20 would have been no mark for her. She sprained her ankle, and was at once placed among the brood mares.

Well, I had better not enthuse over Bronze, for she is now the property of your Commissioner. For her I paid $7,500, and I think in a race with the crack four-year-olds of the country, she would sell "even up." In the fifth heat, trotted in 2:22½, she was beaten a neck only. She is a beautiful bronze bay, 15¾ hands high, very blood-like, and exquisitely formed. She is a Goldsmith Maid in type, only a size larger, and a little higher on the withers, giving a handsome finish. She went into this race sadly out of form, having lost a very easy race for her a week ago. Her gait is not high and showy, but she glides along with a well-measured pace, in a rapid, stealing manner that gets the best of a watch, instead of like too many high-actioned laboring horses that go so much slower than the watch. She has magnificent legs and feet, not a puff nor a pimple, and is of the improving sort. She wears a 12-ounce shoe forward, and 6-ounce behind. This will seem very remarkable when I state all I now know of her breeding. She was bred at the cross-roads town of Pleasant Valley, Switzerland county, Indiana, near the Ohio River, by a Mr. Hart, in August, 1881. When three she was ridden into North Vernon, and paced a half-mile to saddle in 1:17. Buck Dickerson then purchased her for $175. Shortly after she paced in a race in 2:37, and Geo. N. Dickerson purchased her from his brother. In the fall she seemed inclined to trot, and he trotted her to a road wagon at the fair in 2:47. She ran out all last winter, and in February was placed in the hands of Thomas Dickerson, another brother, to be handled. She took at once kindly to trotting, and in May, at Marysville, Ky., could have won her race, and, if necessary, trotted in 2:23; she did show in the race 2:27. From there she can be followed through her campaign to Chicago. She has not only been carefully trained by Thomas, but another brother, Scott, who acted as groom.

Her breeding? Well, she was by Morrison's Morgan Messenger Jr., he by Curtis' Morgan Messenger, he by Green Mountain Morgan. Her dam will, in time, be fully traced, as well as the blood-lines of sires. Her sire, now dead, was a fast pacer, record 2:27, and has left a speedy progeny behind him. Now we find here a mare by a pacing horse, her dam a trotting mare, a natural pacer for three years, changing her gait without any of the appliances now used, toe-weights, etc. In form she knocks all the anatomical structure theories into a "cocked hat," for she is as clean-cut and handsomely turned as any model race or trotting horse. She will be heard from hereafter.

## Eastern Colt Stake.

The Stake for three-year-olds trotted on the first day of the Breeders' meeting is thus described by the *Herald*:

With a good day and track the Trotting Horse Breeders' Association began their sixth annual meeting at the Gentleman's Driving Park yesterday. The attendance was good and among those present were General U. S. Grant, General F. B. Tracy, Mr. W. H. Vanderbilt, Captain Jake Vanderbilt, Joseph Harker, General W. T. Watkins, W. T. Mali, Edwin Thorne, Frank Work, T. C. Eastman, David and Robert Bonner, J. P. Wiser; J. W. Shaw, Charles Backman, Robert Steel, Alden Goldsmith, Shepherd Knapp, Phineas Jones, Colonel Fellows, H. M. Whitehead, Aden S. Swan, S. J. Morgan, H. C. McDowell and many other well known gentlemen. Although each of the three events which produced races were won in straight heats, they were all of great interest, as the horses were driven out for the purpose of obtaining as fast a record as possible. Alroy won the Nursery Stakes very easily and his record of 2:27½ is the best ever made by an Eastern bred colt. He is a bay with black points, of good apperance, with a fine, open gait, and is all over a trotter. Alroy was bred by General F. B. Tracy at Marshland Stud Farm, Owego, N. Y. and was broken and trained by Hendrickson, who drove him in the race. The judges were Mr. W. T. Mali, David Bonner and S. J. Morgan; Distance Judge, Jonathan Hawkins; Clerk of the Course, J. W. Gray, Secretary, L. D. Packer.

SUMMARY.

NATIONAL ASSOCIATION OF TROTTING HORSE BREEDERS, SIXTH ANNUAL MEETING, GENTLEMEN'S DRIVING PARK, MORISIANA, N. Y., October 3, 1882.—FIRST RACE.—The Annual Nursery Stakes for foals of 1879, to be trotted (when three years old) at the fall meeting of 1882; $20 entrance, payable as follows: $10 to accompany nomination, May 1, 1880; $15 additional July 1, 1882, and the remainder twenty days before the meeting, September 13, after which the whole becomes play or pay. Closed May 1, 1880, with 34 nominations, value $[illegible].

F. B. Tracy names b c Alroy, by Peacemaker—Mason Girl, by Arabian Chief (Hendrickson)........1 1

C. Stanford names br c Victor Clay, by Victor Mohawk—Lady Clay (Van Patten and Murphy)........2dis

TIME.

| | Quarter. | Half. | Three-Quarters. | Mile. |
|---|---|---|---|---|
| First heat | 41½ | 1:21 | 2:02 | 2:41½ |
| Second heat | 36½ | 1:12 | 1:50 | 2:27½ |

First heat. Thalia had made good her final dèposit but was withdrawn owing to lameness. Alroy had the pole and drew out a length from Victor Clay on the first turn and they trotted thus to the half-mile, where Victor Clay made a skip and lost another length. Alroy led by two lengths to the three-quarter pole, after which he was eased and Victor Clay lapped him out under the wire.

Second heat. As it was known that Alroy was to be driven out Murpby was put up behind Victor Clay to try and save the colt being distanced. It was of no use, however, as Alroy went right away from him and was over six lengths in front as soon as they swung clear around the turn. Without skip or break Alroy completed his mile in 2:27½ and Victor Clay was run home from the point of rocks to save distance, but wrs shut out.

## The Blood Horse Entries.

Entries to the open stakes and purses of the fall meeting of the Blood Horse Association closed last Tuesday. The nominations are as follows:

No. 1. Night Hawk, Garfield. Premium," Forest King, May D, Jim Douglas, Jim Renwick, Joe Howell, Atalanta.

No. 2. Judge McKinstry, Joe Dion, Lizzie Martin colt, Joe G, Bob, Patrol, Capt. Kidd, Hattie Ball.

No. 3. Maria F, Haddington, Forest King, Nathan Coombs, Ella Doane, Birdcatcher, Fred Collier, Joe Howell, Atalanta, Frank Rhoads.

No. 4. Haddington, Euchre, Geo. Bender, Jack, Belshaw, Joe Howell, Frank Rhoads.

No. 6. Night Hawk, Garfield, Premium, Forest King, May D, Ella Doane, Haddington, Jim Renwick, Fred Collier, Joe Howell, Frank Rhoads.

No. 8. May B, Camille Urso filly, Lou Spencer, Clara W.

No. 9. Joe G, Mollie H, Hattie B.

No. 10. Night Hawk, Garfield, Premium, Duke of Monday, Joe G, Forest King, Bob, May D, Ella Doane, Haddington, Jim Douglas, Jim Renwick, Fred Collier, Joe Howell, Atalanta, Lizzie P.

No. 11. Duke of Monday, Joe Dion, Lizzie Martin colt, Geo. Bender, Nathan Coombs, Belshaw, Precious, Fred Collier, Joe Howell, Capt. Kidd, Judge McKinstry.

No. 12. Garfield, Maria F, Forest King, Inauguration, Birdcatcher, Hattie B, Atalanta, Lizzie P.

No. 13. Joe G, Mollie H, Hattie B.

## John Nelson's Pedigree.

PORTLAND, Oregon, October 6, 1882.

EDITOR BREEDER AND SPORTSMAN: I see by your issue of the 30th ult that parties in your State are seeking to cast discredit upon the pedigree of the old sway-backed sorrel stud, John Nelson, the maternal grandsire of the wonderful trotting colt, Albert W. I should as soon think of questioning the pedigree of Norfolk or Lodi; not that Nelson was a thoroughbred horse like them, but because his pedigree was authenticated by affidavit made before the clerk of a court of record and duly attested.

John Nelson arrived from Panama some time in March, 1859, in company with a brown four-year-old called Blackleg, sired by Bigart's Rattler, of Sandy Hill, New York. The latter horse left no stock worthy of note, but Nelson bred well for the chance he had. He covered a few mares in 1859, at Star Ranch, a few miles out of Sacramento on the old Auburn road, where his owner, Edwin M. Pitcher, resided. Mr. Pitcher was a dairyman and ran milk wagons into Sacramento from 1852 to 1860. He died of pulmonary consumption along in May, 1860, and was mourned by a host of friends, for a kinder-hearted gentleman never breathed. If the old horse is alive he must be thirty-two years old, as I understood Mr. Pitcher to say he was nine years old at the time of his arrival in the State.

The advertisement over the signature of John M. Daniels I wrote myself at Mr. Daniels' own request, and Mr. Pitcher was present. It was the last time he ever was in San Francisco. He had the certified pedigree of the horse in his possession at the time and from it I condensed the substance of the advertisement. Daniel C. Muir, now a resident of Olympia, W. T., was Nelson's groom at that time. Pat Hunt, now dead, was working him at the Pioneer track and drove him a mile one morning in 2:36. But that was alone and Nelson was such an excitable horse that he could not trot in company. My own belief is that any good level-headed trotter that could close up three heats in 2:40 could beat him for this reason.

Just prior to the appearance of this advertisement Pat Hunt came into the *Spirit of the Times* office and inserted a challenge which I also wrote at his request, offering to trot Nelson two-mile heats against any stallion in the State within two weeks. Werner's Rattler was up to that time the acknowledged champion stallion, and his owners, Fred Werner and Ewing M. Skaggs, were very indignant about it for this reason. Their horse had been given no work during the winter, while Nelson was hard in flesh and able to trot very fast. On the other hand it would have taken eight weeks to get Rattler into fix, and here was a big season at hand with forty mares at $100 each. It certainly was taking snap judgment on them and they naturally felt angry at Hunt, as well as myself for writing out his banter.

On the day before the $10,000 match at four-mile heats between Ashland and Langford, won by the latter, I met Mr. Werner in front of the Empire Market. He talked over the matter in a very gentlemanly way, though it was plain he felt hurt about it. He then authorized us to write out a challenge to which he signed his name, offering to trot Rattler against John Nelson or any other horse in California, two miles and repeat, for from $2,500 to $10,000 a side, at the option of the acceptor, the race to take place at Sacramento during the month of October following the season. This met no acceptance and, as Mr. Pitcher died the following week, the parties concluded that "the least said, the soonest mended." If you can find files of the Sacramento *Union* for May 1860, you will find the counter-challenge signed by Mr. Werner.

The attempt to cast a stigma upon the pedigree of John Nelson, at this late day, I can only regard as disgracefully pitiable. His get—Aurora, Nerea and others of less note—have proven his prepotency as a sire; and when they seek to cast a cloud on his pedigree they also attempt to smirch the good name of a dead man who was the soul of honesty and liberal to a fault. Ned Pitcher was not the man to stoop to such a coarse offence as obtaining money under false pretenses; nor would John Daniels have advertised any horse whose lineage would not bear strict scrutiny at the hands of critical judges. I do not know the owner of Albert W, but think he has a good horse and that after winning laurels on the turf he should not be defrauded of honors in the stud by the slanders of meanly-disposed men whose sole cause of grievance is malicious jealousy. Yours truly,

THOS. B. MERRY.

Dugald J. Bannatyne, the well-known turfman, last week commenced a suit in the Chancery Court at Trenton, N. J., to restrain the officers and agents of the Monmouth Park Racing Association from holding races upon its track or betting upon the premises. The complainant has been running his horses on the track at Long Branch for a number of years. Last winter he was fined $100 by the Executive Committee for inducing a trainer to leave the service of J. B. Pryor, and paid the money under protest. He subsequently commenced suit to recover $1,000 damages from Secretary Coster, which case was dismissed, the Court deciding that it had no jurisdiction. So persistent became his annoyances that last August he was ruled off the track.

The love of the ancient but illegal pastime of cock-fighting does not seem to have expired in New South Wales, although it has died a forced death in Melbourne. Only last week there was to have been a large main fought near Sydney, the parties thereto having chartered a special steamer for the trysting ground, and taking with them some five dozen well-trained birds. Someone, however, had "split," and the bobbies, having followed on their track, spoiled the intended sport. Several of the backers of the gamecocks were known persons of social status.

Mexico Bill, the healthy and affable frontiersman, whose picturesque appearance attracts so much attention, last evening made a wager of $10 against $100 that "A man can not marry his widow's sister." When he found that a divorced wife is in law a widow, he drew his money.—*Stockton Herald*.

The longest bicycle club run on record was that recently made by five members of the Boston Bicycle Club. The party left Northboro, Mass., at 4:38 a. m. and passed through South Farmington, Natic, Dedham, Stoughton, Brocton, Quincey and Waltham and reached Boston at 9:30 p. m. The total time in running 102 miles was 14h. 34m.

## Thoroughbreds.

EDITOR BREEDER AND SPORTSMAN: Again a week has passed and again "ye merry amateurs" went forth to seek ye short winged quail. This time the locality selected was the Sartoris Rancho near Petaluma, and the party consisted of five, embracing as usual C. D. L. of San Francisco, T. J. the great express agent, F. F. the champion masher and for heavy weights S. St. J. and Henry S. of the Petaluma mercantile fraternity; as for dogs there were only twenty-seven of all sizes, styles and breeds accompanying the party. The munitions of war presented a most formidable appearance and an inventory of them would almost fill a column. The most noteworthy and dangerous however was an instrument resembling a mitrialeuse, one small sized barrel, strongly resembling that which usually contains — bug poison, four kegs of powder and a small dry goods box full of cartridges. The usual Sunday-go-to-meeting Jimmy-go-slow-style, of a team was procured or rather purchased for about nineteen dollars and ye merry procession moved. The appearance of "ye gang" was that of the ideal border ruffians, in Beadle's celebrated dime novel story of "Ye Tiger Slayers" or the Howling Borealis of the North; and the musical intonations of the would-be songsters of the Petaluma Loring Club strongly reminded your correspondent of the harmonious discord engendered by a first class Chinese dramatic company; this interspersed at incorrect intervals with the yelping and howling of the mongrel thoroughbreds, raised the enthusiasm of the Petaluma denizens who were unfortunate enough to witness the scene to such an unwonted degree that their solitary guardian of the peace went off and got sick on the strength of it. At least it is so conjectured.

The scene of their would-be exploits, located eight miles from Petaluma, was reached in six hours and thirty minutes, the enormous exertion of this unequal time causing one of the horses to blush, and the other, a would-be thoroughbred (for he was sired by a mule and damned by everybody) to lie down and die. This momentarily disconcerted the party, until it was explained by C. D. L. that he had given the horse about a teaspoonful of Petaluma whisky which at once satisfactorily explained the thoroughbred's untimely demise. The eulogy of "Quam whisky, damn, badum," being duly pronounced, the party proceeded to the fields for sport. Every bush and declivity for sixteen square miles was duly scoured, and the united result of these efforts proved to be four poor measly rabbits of the jackass species, one quail and four "mud-larks;" until St. J. arrived from the next ranch with sixteen poor and sickly looking quail that evidently had been trapped for over a month and looking as though they had been imported from St. Johnsbury, Vermont. This the gentleman stoutly and most positively denied, still the credulity of the party was but little strengthened by the advent of another hunter of the proverbial "Sunday-Dutchman-style." This Nimrod had a "dogg, und he vas a pinter, he vas shust peat any dogg vat never vas, und could reprieve efferyting." When placed on exhibition the thoroughbred (?) was pronounced a perfect specimen of the "Sooner" breed, and upon a small stick being thrown about ten feet by his owner, the "dogg" with well-drawn in tail, slunk between his master's legs, which so exasperated the exile from Germany that he grabbed the poor brute by the ears and tail and proceeded to annihilate him. This proceeding was promptly stopped by the spectators, for it was learned that the Dutchman was no other than a celebrated (?) dog trainer from the Mission. After the usual feast of reason, wit and whisky, the party returned with elevated spirits to Petaluma, where the customary pedro appendages were engaged in and continued on the train home, which was reached in the usual condition of tired, dusty and hungry. More anon. Yours,

ONIX.

## Making a Horse Win.

A reporter met a jockey of Rutherford while dining at the Winter Palace in St. Petersburg a short time after that huge sporting wrangle, and in the course of a conversation on turf matters the astute prodder of horse-flesh said with a child-like and ingenious smile:

"Would you like to know the dead inside facts as to how that race was won?"

"Why, you rode the best horse, didn't you?" we asked.

"Not a bit of it," replied the jockey, with a grin. The fact was that Rutherford was only about the fourth choice, and was not rated at more than eighth or ninth in the pools. True Blue, Katy Pease and Thad Stevens all had the call over Ruthy. But it happened that my horse was a 'bolter,' and to steady him and prevent his flying the track, I put blinders and goggles on him. You noticed them, I suppose."

"There were two horses rigged that way," we replied.

"Exactly. Stevens was a nervous critter, also, and as soon as his trainer saw how the goggles steadied my horse, he put 'em on Thad, too. The day before the race a big idea occurred to me. I got a couple of pairs of magnifying lenses and quietly put 'em in place of the plain glasses in the goggles of both horses. Catch on to the idea?"

"Well, partly."

"The only difference was that in Stevens' bridles I fastened the glasses with the bulge inside, so as to make them diminishing glasses. Dont you see?"

"Like looking through the wrong end of an opera-glass, eh?"

"Exactly. The result was that while Rutherford was encouraged all the way by the course seeming only 200 yards long, the quarter flags appeared ten miles apart to Stevens. You see a horse can be discouraged as well as a man."

"Great scheme, that."

"Well, I should smile. Ruthy thought he was in for a little quarter race, and it kept up his heart, so that when he had nearly done the last mile and swung into the home stretch, and I called on him to let out his last link, he thought the judges' stand was right under his nose, so he came home like an express train on a down grade; but Stevens, who thought he had about fifteen miles futher to go, went all to pieces, as you remember, and almost lay down on the track, he was so mentally caved in, as it were."

# HERD AND SWINE.

## Shorthorn Reform

"Whom the gods would destroy, they first make mad." I am unwilling to believe that "the gods" or any one else (unless, indeed, it be T. L. M.) have fully made up their minds to destroy the Shorthorn race of cattle. Nevertheless, as a breeder of Shorthorns and an admirer of them in their better forms, it is a source of constant misgiving to me to observe the prevalence of a mental epidemic which, in the opinion of many thoughtful men, threatens the future of the breed. Any system of breeding which annually turns out as many long-legged, light-fleshed, unthrifty cattle as may be found among the Shorthorns of the present day is radically defective. Any plan of breeding which yearly sends forth large numbers of such deficient cattle to our Western plains and scatters them broadcast all through our great agricultural regions needs to be thoroughly revolutionized and reformed, if the breed is to be saved from ultimate ruin. These libels upon the Shorthorn race are expected to maintain its high reputation and character as a beef-producing breed; but having been bred for fashion instead of beef, they fail to produce satisfactory results when placed alongside the more sensibly-bred Angus and Herefords. I cannot believe that a solitary man, among all those engaged in turning out these "pure" or "fancy-bred" cattle is willfully endeavoring to bring disgrace upon the Shorthorn name. On the contrary, every such person within the range of my acquaintance sincerely believes that he is battling for the purest (and therefore ( best) Shorthorns on top of earth. If such men actually believe they have the best and urge all breeders to head their herds with line-bred bulls, regardless of merit, for one I must say they certainly are mad—blind to the highest and best interests of the Shorthorn breed. They talk of "strong " breeding and prepotency, which is all well enough when it means the power to transmit a fine carcass of beef; but when it means its is too often the case) a certainty of transmitting light, airy, racehorse attributes, how can a man, who expects to face the steer beef breeds, put such a bull upon his herd? The prevailing habit of buying breeding bulls solely upon the alleged reputation of their gr. gr. gr. gr. grandsires and grandams, instead of examining the animal itself and its more immediate ancestors, is working the ruin of many of our noblest herds. I would not, by any means, condemn all that is of fashionable descent. Such a sire as the 4,500 guinea Duke of Connaught, owned by Lord Fitzhardinge, is fit to head any herd of cattle extant; but because this is so, it does not necessarily follow that every bull of the six Bates and various Bell-Bates tribes, in any way connected with the English Duke, is a proper bull to breed from. If the fashionably-bred relative is possessed of good beef points the case is of course altered.

We have too many "tribes" among our Shorthorns. The word "family" should be made to take a "back seat" in the Shorthorn vocabulary. It has stood out in bold, full-faced letters long enough; too long, in fact, for any one good. The same error is likely to be committed by the breeders of other cattle. The rage is running rampant through the Jersey camp; and Angus breeders are already talking glibly of their Prides, Ericas, etc., thus nurturing an aristocracy of blood rather than of pounds avoirdupois of profitable beef, which may some day, unless handled with care, react injuriously upon the breed.

The question of the future beef supply is one of almost boundless possibilities. The breed which at the fat-stock shows and shambles gives the best returns, is the breed of the future. There are some among those engaged in breeding Shorthorns who select their sires for the beef they carry, and for the beef known to have been possessed by their immediate ancestors. Such men have nothing to fear from any other breed known to cattle men. There is yet plenty of good material out of which to work the salvation of the Shorthorn, but it must be carefully husbanded, and kept free from cross likely to impair its future usefulness. Shorthorn herds in which heavy flesh (rather than fashion and fine style) has been the controlling principle, will in the near future become mines of wealth to their fortunate owners. Such herds have a great and important mission to perform—the rescuing of the noblest race of cattle that ever trod our pastures from utter annihilation. I believe a revolution is coming in the business of breeding Shorthorns. I can confidently there are many men of sufficient intelligence in the business to perceive it, and provide for its certain coming. This will consist in a return to first principles, and an adoption of the methods by which the Herefords and Angus have been raised to their present high position—the methods by which the Shorthorn originally attained its surpassing excellence.

The war of the races is certain to go on. Ignorance, superstition and prejudice are gradually being overcome by reason and intelligence, even unto the uttermost ends of the earth. The breeders of Shorthorns will ultimately realize that they are not exempt from the operation of the grand principle of "the survival of the fittest." If they so breed their cattle as to render them inferior to their powerful rivals, like Othello, they will soon find their occupation gone. Occasional show-yard triumphs will not save them. The ruin and file of the breed is where the improvement is most needed.—W. *In the Breeder's Gazette.*

## Cattle Breeding and Farming

The husbandman who follows mixed farming has more or less to do with cattle. It is a very profitable branch of agriculture where the farmer is prepared to attend to it, but like every other business, needs it. The farmer who takes hold of cattle for profit, should have

1. Good and early pastures.
2. Good water.
3. Comfortable stock barns, and should purchase no stock that travels under the euphonious names of "scrub," "knob gnat," etc. Blood will tell in nothing quicker nor to better profit than in cattle. High grade cattle, or at least those animals that show marks of some good blood, are the only ones I have reference to now. "Scrubs," no doubt, have their value and their charms, but it requires a man who has had more experience with them than I have had to point out where the profit comes in. That are hairy, but possess none of those points set down in the "scale of points for cattle" adopted by the Shorthorn and Jersey Clubs of the United States.

For the benefit of those who have had less experience than myself, I will mention a few points by which well-bred animals may be recognized:

1. A small head and broad, dish face.
2. Small horns and ears.
3. Straight back and wide across the hips.
4. Fine hair and small bone.
5. Nine times out of ten an animal having any pure blood in its veins will have a large, quiet eye, and will be gentle in disposition. A wild, vicious look out of the eye indicates a poor feeder the world over, just as it is conclusive evidence of mongrel blood.

Much has been written about the best breed of cattle for the farmer, and the verdict has been made in favor of the Shorthorn. They mature earlier, lay on fat faster and on less food, and, it is claimed, have less offal and waste to their weight than any other breed in our reach. If this is true—and there is no doubt of it—the Shorthorns should have a representative on every farm in the United States where cattle are to be found. Most of the Shorthorn families combine fine milking qualities with their other excellences. A Shorthorn male put upon a common cow will invariably produce a good feeder; no breed impresses its good points so unmistakably on the first cross as this one. For five years past I have had access to a high cast Shorthorn bull, and have tested the matter of superiority between his offspring and the offspring of another bull of good make, but common blood. The difference was so noted in favor of Shorthorn that steers of the same age brought one-third and sometimes one-half more when put on the market, after having been fed on the same feed in quality and quantity, and grazed in the same pastures.

Now for an item from my own experience to prove that good grade cattle are profitable even when loosely handled. Last fall I purchased thirteen calves at an average of $9 15. They were yearlings. The winter was mild, though provender was high. I sold my timothy hay, that I had intended to feed my calves, at $1 and $1 25 per hundred, and turned my calves into a fifty acre wheat field, housing them every night and every day that the weather was inclement or gave promise of being so. They ate during the time they were housed two-thirds of a stack of timothy, which was worth $65. That was all. In the spring I turned them to clover, and the middle of August sold them at $27 50 per head.

This is given as an example of what may be done in one branch of the business. Those desiring to raise Shorthorns or Jerseys for pleasure or profit should buy from none but reliable dealers of long standing, and no farmer should use any but a thoroughbred bull.—*The Farming World.*

## The Fat Stock Show

Of this annual exhibition which will open to the public at the Exposition building, Chicago, on the 16th of November, and the contest for supremacy between rival breeds of cattle, the Illinois correspondent of the *Country Gentleman* has this to say:

"The contest for the supremacy between the Shorthorn and the Hereford breeders, which has been a marked, if not always a pleasant phase of the four previous fat stock shows, is likely to be considerably intensified this year, both parties leaving the last meeting with a resolution of carrying all before them in 1882. Mr. Gillette, whose out-door fed grade Shorthorn steers have contributed much to the shows of former years, has become a competitor in the line of stall-feeding. His stall-fed animals are likely to produce as great a sensation as his rough steers four years ago. Then there is the question whether the prizes will be awarded to the fattest bullock, or whether to the one, regardless of weight and size, which will cut up into the largest quantities of butcher's meat. Last year there was a division on that question, one committee deciding one way and another the other. But it is likely that new competition will appear for the first time, among which are the Black Polled Angus cattle for which a demand has been developed within a year or two. For a year or two breeding specimens of the Black Angus cattle have been seen at most of the large western fairs, but no grade or full-blood steers, for the reason they were not in the country. But fair representations of what these steers may become at two or three years old are likely to be entered for competition at Chicago. There is no doubt that the day for extra fat and heavy steers has passed for some time to come, for even now 1,200 pound steers fetch better prices than those weighing 1,600 pounds, where both are of the same quality. Since the Polled Angus met the changed taste of the public, the desire to see fine specimens of them will be nearly universal.

BUTTER COWS.—The agricultural papers are teeming with reports of large yields of butter, chiefly from cows of Jersey blood, indicating the strong interest which the subject of improved stock of this kind has obtained upon the agricultural community. In breeding for useful qualities the claim that "blood tells" in cows as well as in other branches of breeding has recently received a forcible demonstration in the case of the young cow Bomba, 10,330, that last summer accomplished a two months' (62 days) test in which she gave for the first month 89 pounds 14 ounces and for the second 84 pounds 5 ounces of thoroughly worked butter, weighed before salting. She is less than four years old, has had two calves, and after being four months in milk is reported to be still making 2½ pounds of butter a day. As the yield exceeds any heretofore reported of so young a cow, her owner, Mr. A. B. Darling, has addressed a request to the Directors of the American Jersey Cattle Club for the appointment of a disinterested committee to inspect a special test of the cow. She is the result of a peculiarly strong combination of the blood of other great butter cows. Beginning back four generations with Colonel Hoe's Alpha, whose incomplete tests uniformly indicated over 20 pounds a week, her pedigree takes in Europa, that noted cow 16 pounds a week; Eurotas, that made 778 pounds in a year; imported Violet, whose partial tests were equivalent to nearly 20 pounds a week; and also derives the English Rioter blood, which was the crowning success of forty years' careful breeding from tested cows by Mr. Philip Dauncey, of Horwood, England, whose dairy for years supplied the Queen's table, and whose stock, descended from his bull Rioter, had brought by far the highest auction prices reached in England long before Eurotas and other great butter cows had demonstrated its value in this country. By such methods of breeding for a direct purpose as Bomba illustrates American breeders expect to gradually establish a fixed quality, confirmed by generations of special merit, that will transmit useful results, and raise Jersey from her average standing as a merely ornamental cow to one of unsurpassed value in her specialty.—*N. Y. World.*

An English authority states that, in the management and breeding of cattle of valuable pedigree, economy of rearing is not much studied, the object being to obtain a well-grown animal irrespective of cost. Ample box and yard accommodation is provided, and the calves run with their dams in the pastures in fine weather or are kept in boxes and turned with them for half an hour several times a day. The calves are early taught to eat linseed cake and bean meal with hay or grass and cut roots. They are weaned at from six to eight months old and in winter are kept in yards partially covered, and fed with hay or chopped grass and pulped or cut roots, with three or four pounds daily of linseed cake or her similar extra food. In the following summer they . . b on the pastures, shelter against sun and rain being ac-

## Tuberculosis in Cattle.

The extent to which this malignant malady prevails has not been fully recognized by live-stock men in different sections of the country, and owing to its insidious nature, as well as the length of time that an animal will often survive an attack, its ravages have ever been overlooked, or ascribed to other causes. But the rapid strides which it has made of late years, and the hold that it has gained, even on our pure-bred stock, renders it, says Professor Whalley, one of the most important questions affecting the well-being of the bovine species. In fact, it ranks among the few great scourges of the land, and though our losses, thus far, have been trifling as compared to other plagues, which sweep their victims off in a summary manner, yet the effects of this disease can only be realized, as he further observes, when we take into account the vast deterioration, the slow but certain declination of many of our best herds, the destruction of a large portion of our animal supplies, and the danger to human life, which can no longer be considered chimerical.

That neat stock have a strong tubercular diathesis, as shown by their ready tendency to take on this disease, no well-informed veterinarian will deny; and, accordingly, we find that cattle are far more frequently affected than any other domestic animals. The temperament and physical conformation undoubtedly contribute much in this direction; for animals of a phlegmatic type, with an attenuated form, long limbs, and narrow chest, are usually the first victims of the malady. Breeders should, therefore, strive to avoid the possibility of transmitting such diseased qualities. It is found less frequently in oxen than in cows, especially those that have been kept in dairies for any length of time; hence, lactation is supposed to be a predisposing cause.

The cold, damp sheds, the dark, underground stables, and other ill-ventilated abodes, as well as the character of the food, all conspire to rekindle those constitutional taints into morbid activity. If we inquire further into the cause of this increased susceptibility to the infection, as seen more especially in certain strains of pure-bred stock, we shall find that heredity and multiplied consanguinity play no subordinate part. Any physical weakness which the sire or dam may possess is liable to be transmitted to the immediate progeny; but if one generation escapes, the trouble may appear in the next, in accordance with the well established principle of atavism. In fact, diseased conditions are inherited, and we believe that there is no predisposing cause which exercises such a potent influence in the production of this malady as the pernicious system of in-and-in breeding. Thus, from parent to offspring, from one generation to another, we often see this fatal tendency transmitted in unbroken succession; and the more complicated the relationship becomes, the greater is the virulence of the resulting product. In spite, therefore, of the many palpable examples of this broken law, some breeders still pursue, year by year, the suicidal policy of clinging to one strain, regardless of the impending consequence.

This constitutional taint, according to Professor Cobnheim, has nothing to do with the facility for receiving the tubercular virus, but is a product of the existing malady. Animals, therefore, possessing this habit of body are not more disposed to take on the disease than others, for they are already infected. Consequently, all such individuals having a tubercular diathesis, have contracted the disease in early life, or have received the morbid germs by hereditary transmission.

The contagious nature of tuberculosis, as shown by recent experiments on animals, alluded to in the July number of the Journal can no longer be doubted; and it is now conceded by comparative pathologists that the bovine form of this disease is identical with that of man. Accordingly, there is great liability of its transmission, either by inoculation or ingestion. The extension of this malady, therefore, by inhalation, is always liable to occur when animals are so arranged that the sick and healthy ones can get their heads together, or feed from the same manger. The hay may thus become contaminated, and the infection take place through the digestive organs. Dr. Grad's observations on the spread of this disease by contaminated stalls, are very conclusive, as he had found that cows had become infected, and had died, one after another, from being confined in the same location, without the apartment having been sufficiently renovated and cleaned. Hence, farmers cannot be too careful in guarding against such exposures, which are always liable to occur in our large dairies.

The supposed air of one of these affected animals is not unfrequently so laden with virulent matter, especially in the advanced stages, that it is not safe for another creature to inhale it. This mode of transmission, by the lungs, which was first suggested by Dr. Moregagni, of Italy, more than a hundred years ago, and has found many advocates among physicians and veterinarians, has now been confirmed by the experiments of Dr. Tappeiner, of Meran, in causing animals to inhale the fine particles of tubercular matter from the air of a room in which the virus had been evaporated by a steam atomizer. This experiment was very successful, as nearly all of the animals showed well-marked miliary tubercles in both lungs or being killed, thus demonstrating, in a very satisfactory manner, that the disease is contagious by the breath.

The investigations that Dr. Koch, of Germany, has undertaken, are well calculated to arouse public attention, and possibly throw a new light on the subject. But it is not opportune on this occasion to discuss the merits of his alleged discoveries, which have already been widely published; and therefore suffice it to say, that we shall hail with pleasure any advancement of science in this direction.

The nature of this widespread and destructive malady has now been sufficiently set forth, in all of its pathological bearings, to awaken the desired interest among live-stock men that the subject demands. In fact, this disease is already a national calamity; but in the absence of statistics it will be impossible to estimate, with any degree of accuracy, the enormous extent to which it prevails among our dairy stock. If our calculations, however, even be based upon the inspectors' reports of Italy, Bavaria, and other German States, we must conclude that five per cent, at least, are affected, and with every facility for rapid increase. In certain districts, as we are assured by able veterinarians, thirty per cent. of the cattle suffer from tuberculosis, and with many high-priced herds this scourge yearly claims its victims.

The experience of this affection, in a sanitary point of view, will call for the therefore mature deliberation of the *savans* of the profession to devise some measures in behalf of the

bile welfare that will protect our tables, control this in its eas-
y traffic in consumptive beef, and eventually eradicate this
sease, like pleuro-pnemonia, from the land.—*National Live
ock Journal.*

### The Duchesses.

The tradition that the Duchesses descend from stock kept
the possession of the Duke of Northumberland's family for
ro hundred years, may be for the present put aside. I
ive not seen any late refutation of the late Mr. Storer's ar-
ment against it. The existence of such a tradition, how-
er, may be taken for what it is worth, as suggestive of a
obability that antecedent to the pedigree beginning with
unes Brown's Red Bull, the ancestors of the Duchesses
ere for many years select and superior cattle.

James Brown's Red Bull (or Old Bull) 97 in the Herd-
ook, has no date of birth recorded in his entry. He was
red by Mr. John Thompson, of Girlington Hall, and his
re was Mr. William Barker's bull 51, his dam not mentioned.
arker's bull, of the early Shorthorn yellow-red and white
lor, was by Lakeland's son of the Studley Bull 626; so that
imes Brown's Old Red Bull, the first recorded sire of the
uchesses, was a great-grandson of the Studley Bull, the
rliest Shorthorn sire on record of which we read. Allen's
History," page 28, tells us: "He was calved in 1737, and of
e Barningham (Milbank) stock, which came from Studley
Yorkshire, where they had existed for many years. He
described by one who often saw him as having possessed
onderful girth, and depth of fore-quarters, very short legs,
neat frame, and light offal." The Herd-book only says:
Red-and-white, bred by Mr. Sharter, of Chilton." None of
ie dams of these early bulls are named, so that we can trace
ie pedigree only in the male line direct. Whatever we may
ink in these days, it is evident that the old breeders thought
uch of the sire, and, when George Coates went about collecting materials for the first volume of the Herd-book, they
could more readily supply to him particulars of the male
than of the female lines of breeding.

Mr. Charles Colling is said to have obtained his first
Duchess cow, known as the "Stanwick Duchess," or "Stanwick Cow," by James Brown's Red Bull, in 1784. Assuming
the correctness of the dates given, and assuming also that no
generation has slipped out of notice, we must be struck by
the length of time between the birth of the Studley Bull and
Mr. Colling's purchase of the Stanwick cow—the Studley
Bull's great-great-grand-daughter—47 years. This is quite
possible, and, if correct, shows that the early Shorthorns
lived and bred to good old age. Allowing the odd seven years
for the age (which I do not remember to have seen stated)
of the Stanwick Duchess when Mr. Charles Colling bought
her, we have an average of ten years between parent and offspring, all through.

The Stanwick Duchess was mated with Hubback 319, who
had exactly the same length of descent from the Studley Bull,
in male line, direct, as the Stanwick Duchess had by her sire,
They were both fourth in descent from the Studley Bull.
The excellence of her offspring by Hubback attracted the notice of Mr. Bates, who, in or about 1804, purchased from Mr.
Charles Colling her grand-daughter, Duchess by Daisy Bull
186, dam by Favorite 252. In this cow there was a compound of the strains of Mr. Charles Colling's Old Daisy and
Mr. Maynard's now Favorite or Lady Maynard (of whom the
bull Favorite was an inbred descendant) with the Hubback
blood, which indeed was included in that of the Daisy and
Favorite families.

Duchess by Daisy Bull did not leave any female offspring
in Mr. Bates' herd (which at that time was at Halton Castle,
not at Kirklevington), but before Mr. Bates bought her she
had produced a heifer in the Ketton herd, and this daughter,
breeding to Comet 155 (the son of the bull Favorite, out of
the same bull Favorite's own daughter, who was, moreover,
out of the same Favorite's mother), gave birth to the heifer
purchased by Mr. Bates at Mr. Charles Colling's sale in 1810,
then named Young Duchess, afterwards Duchess 1st, from
whom the "Duchesses" are lineally descended.—*Wm. Hous-
man, in English Live-Stock Journal.*

### Fancy Prices of Breeders.

What are high prices for breeding animals? The question
is one which will bear some consideration, since a misunderstanding of this point may, and certainly has, cost breeders
much money, care and labor. There were to-day hundreds
of cattle in the market for which three cents per pound on
foot was the best price which could be coaxed from the buyers, and the stock was clear at that figure. There were at the
same time sales of cattle at six and one-half cents; and there
was less difficulty about getting the last mentioned figures
than in securing the lower price for the inferior stock. Yet
it is safe to assert, that up to the time the cattle were placed
in the market there was not near fifty per cent. difference
between the cost of the two classes of stock. The scrubs had
eaten more than one-half as much as had the well-bred ones;
they had required as many months of shelter and labor; they
had occupied as many stalls, or stalls, or as much space at
the feed trough; and they had had the interest of the capital
invested in them at least as long as had the better bred animals. The cost of marketing the scrubs exceeded that of
selling the better stock; for the commission, feed bills, and
yard charges were based upon the number sold, and
not upon the sum received by the consignor—in short, all
the expenses attending the marketing of a scrub worth $25
are, excepting the single item of freight, as great as those
necessary to the marketing of a bullock worth $125; and
even in the matter of freight the difference in cost is but
slight.

We cannot honestly claim that all this difference is due to
a difference in the breeding of the stock, for there can be no
doubt that much has come from the different treatment given
by those who owned them, but it would probably be true in
this as in most other cases, that "the bull was half the herd."
The fact is too generally admitted to need reassertion here,
that the cattle got by a pure-bred sire, of one of the approved
beef breeds, will make more and better beef in two years than
the scrub native will make in four years, with like care and
fully double the quantity of food. In the production of milk
the influence of good blood is even more necessary than in
growing beeves, for a poor milk producer is a constant drain
upon the purse of her owner. A cow which will yield two
hundred pounds of butter per year is worth more than twice
as much each year as the one which can give but half that
quantity, since the cost of feeding a good cow is no more
than that of feeding an inferior scrub. The
scrub will require as much space, care, food and attention, as
the best cow in the herd. The calf of a pure-bred animal will
bring as much money as can be got for four or five calves
from scrubs. If we multiply this difference in value of individuals by the number of the progeny they may reasonably
be expected to produce, and in the case of cows by the number of years they will probably be in service, we will arrive

at something near their real value; and this will be
found to exceed what are termed "fancy prices. The influence
of good blood, under proper management, grows and spreads
so rapidly and widely that its value is almost incalculable.—
*The Breeder's Gazette.*

## THE PADDOCK.

### The Profits on Fine Draft Horses.

David Stuart, of Lakeville, ascertained at an early day
that it would pay to raise large horses and acted upon that
information. He was among the first to breed to the Duke
de Chartres and has sold his colts while young for more than
he could get for aged horses of the common herd. Prince
Charlie, however, was his ideal of a draft colt, and he resolved to keep him till he could tell what kind of a horse he
would make. He brought Charlie to the Petaluma Fair last
year and exhibited him as a three-year-old. He was surprised that Charlie got left; so in order to find out whether
the colt really had merit—or whether he was blinded
by his love for Charlie—he concluded that the judges of
horses in other places should pass upon him. So Charlie was
taken to the State Fair, to the Oakland Fair, the Stockton
Fair and to the Fair at San Jose, where the colt was exhibited
in the three-year-old draft class and walked away with the
first premium at each of these fairs. His owner felt better
and was more than ever determined to keep him. But
others wanted Charlie and they bid up on him till day before yesterday, when an offer of $1,800, cash, was more than
Mr. Stuart could refuse. Well, Charlie will leave us, but
Mr. Stuart has more young Dukes and will soon have another four-year-old to sell for $1,800. The demand for
these big Normans is increasing, and it is every day becoming better known that Petaluma is the place to find them.
At two and three years of age a Duke colt will bring $250 to
$300. It will cost just as much to raise a three-year-old
steer, or plug horse, which will only bring $50 to $75. It
will be seen at a glance that the profits on the big Norman are
out of all proportion with the profits on the plug.—*Petaluma
Argus.*

### Management of the Stallion after the Season.

The condition of the stallion for the next season's business
will depend largely upon the manner in which he he is kept
from the close of the present one until the next season commences. In most cases the period from the first of October
to the first of March is one in which the stallion is not called
upon to do duty in the stud, and usually but little is done
after July 1st. It is a period of rest, of recuperation from
the drain upon the functions of the sexual organs which service in the stud has required, but it should not be a season
of pampered and overfed indolence, as is too often the case.
When it is convenient to do so, the very best thing to do is
to work him right along, as though you intended that he
should earn his living. This we are satisfied from experience
is the best treatment for stallions of any breed, and will result not only in bringing the horse to the beginning of the
next season in better condition than any other, but the
probabilities are that horses so treated will get more and
better foals than one that is not worked during this period.

But in very many cases, and especially in large breeding
establishments, and with thoroughbred stallions, the course
recommended above is practically out of the question. The
next best thing, then, if the horse must perforce remain in
comparative idleness during the period mentioned, is to pro-
v de him with a large pad dock—the larger the better alway
—and let him have the run of it at all times, during pleasant
weather, stabling him regularly; the utmost attention must
be paid to his bowels lest he should become constipated—a
condition that can usually be prevented, or remedied, should
it occur, by the use of an occasional bran mash.

The necessity for this change in diet from grain to coarse
and bulky food, like hay or corn fodder, is increased in proportion to the confinement to which the horse must be subjected. There is nothing that will so soon destroy the health
and vigor of the horse, and especially of his genital organs, as
close confinement and high feeding; and the man who expects
to keep his horse in show condition the year around will find
that he has undertaken a difficult job. It will work in some
cases for a year or two; but, like constant indulgence in intoxicating liquors in man, it will, in the end, sap the strongest
constitution.—*Breeder's Gazette.*

### Stalls for Harness Horses.

The soundness and suppleness of the harness horse depends very largely upon his stall treatment and accommodations. Casual thought would conclude that the abuse of the
horse consists in over work, undue exposure, and insufficient
food. But equally destructive with either one of the agencies
is his stall mismanagement.

Prominent among these abuses is the excessive inclination
of the stall. In order to have rapid drainage, the grade of
the stall is made so steep that frequently the horse is made
very tired, by practically thus standing up-hill, while he
should under more favorable circumstances be resting. The
weight of the carcass is thereby thrown largely upon the hind
quarters, and the result is sometimes weakness, if not soreness
over the loins, and probably with equal frequency, stiff
wind galls, enlarged flexors, swollen ankles, or incipient occult curbs and spavins. This is a very unnatural standing
position of the horse in a state of freedom. Whether protecting himself from the storm, or standing still after being satisfied with grazing, he invariably either chooses level ground or
a position slightly descending, in which the forehanded portion of the carcass is appreciably lower than the hips. The
physiological reason of this position is manifest upon careful
examination. The office of the front feet and limbs while in
motion is largely to sustain the body, to prevent it falling
headlong, while the hind limbs and feet propel it forward.
In a state of rest, therefore, it follows that the burden of the
weight can be more comfortably sustained by the front limbs
and feet. When the body is pinched at the reverse inclination by the steep grade of the stall, the horse frequently shifts
the weight from one hind limb to the other, in s ch a manner as to indicate his discomfort. If he must stand in a narrow stall, it should be made more nearly level, and the activity of the groom be aroused to keep it scrupulously clean.
The twin cruelty of its steep grade is its narrow dimensions. In many instances it is so confined that the horse
cannot lie down without striking the caps of his hips in the
act of lying down. Even if he escape the sides of the stall,
and shows no bare spots on his hips, the stall is so cramped
that he can never stretch out his limbs in restful comfort,
but is compelled to draw them up under his body. The
luxury of a full length extension of the limbs is not the
only comfort thereby prevented. The horse is not only
robbed of this very restful position, but his legs are constantly

cramped, frequently disfigured with arm boils, caused by the
pressure of the heel calkins against the posterior portion of
the fore-arm, and the body has not the requisite space to
bear its weight upon the ample cushion of the muscles, which
in the dumb brute creation, as in man, is Nature's method of
satisfactory repose. Even when standing up, the frequency
with which he protests against the narrow confines of his imprisonment by violently kicking against the sides
of the stall and the equal frequency with
which he becomes a crib-biter show the positive injuries of narrow stalls. Nearly akin to these tortures of the
narrow stall is the necessity of keeping the horse tied short
by the head. This barbarity in livery stables to
such an extent that, quite often, the horse is not able to rest
even his head at length upon the floor. It is so unusual
sight to see horses in crowded stables reclining at night with
the poll of the head on the floor, while the mouth and lower
portion of the face are raised by the short halter strap several
inches above the ground. Many observers have wondered at
the wakefulness of such horses at all hours of the night.
But when the tortures to which they are thus subjected are
humanely considered, the surprise is greater that they manage
so well to sleep, and measurably to preserve their health and
strength.—*Live Stock Journal.*

### Competition Between Draft Horses.

An English writer thus discourses in the Chicago *Live
Stock Journal* on draft horses and the modes of selection:

I notice that the different breeds of heavy draft horses are
placed in competition at many of the fairs in the United
States. With us, here in England, such a competition would
be simply useless, for more than one reason. The established breeds have have fitted into their places like round and
square pegs into round and square holes, and the only actual
rivalry existing here is in respect of the Shire-bred and
Clydesdale breeds in town. So far as the show yard is concerned, it would be worse than useless to pit breed against
breed, for the judges are all partisans, and so, to a great extent, are the users. In the United States neither of the three
British breeds of draft horses are established, and what they
will have to do is, to displace the French horses on the score
of actual merit. I am presuming that heavy European horses
are as yet practically unknown in American cities, where the
French horses have hitherto been the only animals of the
kind in general use. There should be some sort of actual
trial provided. The old sand bag arrangement died out in
Suffolk before my time. For my own part I believe staunchness to be as hereditable as sidebones, and yet nobody now
thinks of stipulating that a stallion should be a "good drawer,"
as in the good old times. Good and fast walking is another
all-important point in connection with the usefulness of a
town draft horse. These practical matters are more likely to
be brought to the front in the United States than they are
here, where things run in one groove for generations, and all
"innovations" are resisted as radical notions, tending to undermine the constitution of the country. Why should not
an entire horse be put to a trial of strength, courage and endurance? Are not these qualities which are to be desired in
his offspring? And would not a horse possessing such qualities be likely to transmit them to his stock?

With regard to a competition between different breeds of
horses, I do not quite see why a satisfactory award can be
given, unless there is some actual trial work going on. It
would be possible to pick out the horse which has the greatest number of good points; for example : A model of form
may have had feet; a three-cornered, clumsy-looking animal
may have the best of feet and legs; whilst a third animal,
the aggregate of whose points does not amount to much,
may charm the judges directly he begins to move, with clean
walking action. I should be decided, first of all, what constitutes hereditary unsoundness, and a couple of duly qualified veterinary surgeons be appointed to cast out all horses
possessing such unsoundness, before the judges commence
their work. Then, I should imagine the horse with the best
feet and legs, the greatest power and best action will win.
But it is possible that this horse might be bad-tempered or
false; what then! I notice that trotting stallions are not
spoken of by their appearance, but by their "record"; and
I cannot help thinking that a draft stallion should be estimated very much by the dead weight he has been known to
move—three fair pulls by one ; at best. It will be said that these
horses have not been used to such work, and, as a matter of
fact, some of them have never done anything at all worthy
the name of work. That, however, is no reason why the
element of actual trial should not be introduced into all
horse competitions. Suppose, for example, some one from
the Western States wished to import a Scotch Collie dog.
Would he prefer one that had taken chief honors at a dog
show—say; at Birmingham, or at the Crystal Palace—for perfection of hair, color, and "doggy" points, or one that had
beaten all the field, penning sheep at a competitive trial?
I know which Collie I would rather breed from if I wanted
his progeny for use as Shepherd's dogs. And I would rather
breed from a stallion that would go down on his knees half-
a-dozen times in succession, pulling at a dead weight, than
from one that could only prance around a show ring on two
legs at a time. "No feet, no horse," is true enough, because
if a horse has good feet, he can be made to use them, whatever else is bad; but a horse with good feet and legs, powerfully made, and with a good heart, is the horse for me.

### Horseback Riding.

There is nothing so good for the youthful blood as "pure
and sparkling water" and riding on horseback. The habit
should be cultivated by all of our young people, especially
young ladies. An early morning's ride gives vigor and health
to mind and body and makes the female face glow with health
which is beauty. Horseback riding develops the muscles,
promotes digestion and makes one become happy and contented, and always a useful art. A number of Grass Valley and
Nevada City young ladies may be seen almost any evening,
seated upon dashing steeds, galloping away at full speed
toward health and happiness. These girls are always rosy
cheeked of face and lithe of form and are consequently good
natured and apt to marry good men. There is nothing prettier than to see the female form divine seated upon a gallant horse; old women look at them with envy and bearded
men do a good deal of gnashing as the fair equestrienne dashes
by. Ride horseback every time you get an opportunity and
you may live to enjoy a ripe old age and, if you don't fall off
and if your mind is particularly active and sound, you may
become the editor of a newspaper.—*Grass Valley Daily
Tidings.*

The display of stock at the Lake county Fair was the largest ever witnessed in that county.

## THE
# Breeder and Sportsman.

PUBLISHED WEEKLY BY THE

BREEDER AND SPORTSMAN PUBLISHING CO.

THE TURF AND SPORTING AUTHORITY OF THE
PACIFIC COAST.

### OFFICE, 508 MONTGOMERY STREET
P. O. Box 1838.

*Five dollars a year; three dollars for six months; one dollar and a
half for three months. Strictly in advance.*

MAKE ALL CHECKS, MONEY ORDERS, ETC., PAYABLE TO ORDER OF
BREEDER AND SPORTSMAN PUBLISHING CO.

*Money should be sent by postal order, draft or by registered letter, ad-
dressed to the "Breeder and Sportsman Publishing Company, San Francisco, Cal."*

*Communications must be accompanied by the writer's name and address,
not necessarily for publication, but as a private guarantee of good faith*

JOSEPH CAIRN SIMPSON, - - - EDITOR

ADVERTISING RATES.—Displayed $1 50 per inch each insertion or pro
rata for less space. Reading Notices, set in brevier type and having no
foot matter to crowd per line each insertion. Lines will average ten
words. A discount of 10 per cent. will be allowed on 3 months; 20 per cent.
on 6 months and 30 per cent. on 12 months Contracts. No extra rate
charged for cuts or cutting of Column Rules. No Reading notice take for
less than 50 cents each insertion.

San Francisco, Saturday, October 14, 1882.

## WHAT OTHERS THINK.

In the leading article last week we strayed from the idea of a committee of the presidents of the fairs, acting as judges in the races of the circuit, to an individual selected by the various associations whose duty it would be to aid in the troublesome business. This arose from the evident difficulty there would be in securing the attendance of enough of the presidents for the functions, and this consideration led to adopting some other method that did not present the same difficulty.

From conversations with men well qualified to judge, the idea meets with favor, and encourages further elucidation. The only objection that is really of much weight is that it places a great deal of power in the hands of one man; as, to make his aid effective, it will be necessary that his associates depend a great deal on his judgment in arriving at conclusions. Still they would exercise a potent effect in guarding against a wrong use of his position, and it would be a bold as well as a bad man who would take the risk of lending himself to any scheme that was not correct. As was stated in the article of last week the salary should be liberal in order to secure the right kind of an officer. This would be an additional incentive to a careful performance of the trust, for when found to be a valuable adjunct in the government of races, there would be a certainty of retaining the office "during good behavior." When the Bay District course was first opened a permanent judge was employed. We thought well of the plan, and the outcry against it was prompted, in the main, by those whose interests ran counter to fair decisions. Still the objections to a permanent judge, employed by and paid by one association, do not hold good where there is totally a different status.

There is a wide difference which will be apparent when the subject is given proper attention. The servant of one body, it might be claimed that he favored the interests of that association, but when his services are secured for the general good the only inducement would be to perform the duties in accordance with the requirements of the office. An impartial judge, uninfluenced by favoritism, or unbiased by a desire to give any one the advantage, he would secure the hearty support of all those who are intent on building up the trotting interest. Owners, trainers, drivers who only desire to have the rules enforced, who do not seek an unfair advantage or that which will require an unjust construction of the rules would be suited under the guardianship of a man thoroughly posted in the code of the National Trotting Association and in whose integrity they would have the fullest confidence. An officer of the contemplated stamp could not fail to be a safeguard to those who only desire to be guided by the rules and protected by the rules, and it is nearly unnecessary to state that oftentimes this protection is denied, not from any intention to do wrong as, in a large majority of cases, when errors are made in the stand, they arise from a lack of knowledge or an anxiety to harmonize. Not unfrequently a driver who has the control of one or more trotters of celebrity is granted favors which are withheld from those who are not so fortunate in this respect. He is petted and flattered, his wrongdoings condoned, fearing that in the future he will use his influence to decrease the entries. He grandiloquently states than he will never again trot a horse on the track that has awakened his ire when he does not own a dollar's interest in the animal he drives. He arrogantly usurps the duties of ownership and threatens with all the autocratism of a Bashaw of over so many tails what he will accomplish. His vaporings have an effect on those who have a pecuniary interest in the meeting, and as a matter of policy they restrain their indignation and permit him to do as he pleases. Sup-

ported by a man who had nothing to gain from the drivers, knowing that there was a combined effort to correct the abuses, and that there would be a uniformity of rulings, the big little man would be compelled to stand on the same platform as those who had not the backing of track celebrities, and equal justice prevail.

From every point of view there are manifestly advantages to be gained, with the one exception, perhaps, of the difficulty of finding a suitable man. We know of several that would "fill the bill," and we are under the impression that one gentleman of our acquaintance might be prevailed upon to accept who would be exactly the "right man in the right place." This is the merest surmise, however, as we are entirely in the dark regarding what his views are, and it may be that he will not agree in the propriety of the measure. While it would be so much the better to have a man who has had experience in trotting affairs these requirements would not be an absolute necessity. With honesty, good, sound judgment, firmness of character, and a fair knowledge of trotting horses it would not take very long to 'perfect himself in the details. The man whom we refer to could soon instruct another in the duties appertaining to the office. He is one of the very best judges we ever saw occupy the stand, and is more than usually adroit in detecting anything like unfair practice. He has a great fondness for sports of the track, and no one would labor harder to rid them of objectionable features. For the good of the cause it might be that he could be induced to serve for one season, and in the mean time take an apprentice to raise to a higher degree. Possessing large means it is not likely that any pecuniary consideration would influence him to accept the burden, but in order to give the project a fair trial it may be possible that he will lend a hand. Should the various associations conclude to try the scheme we will use all our powers of persuasion to prevail on him to give it a "good send-off," confident that will be sufficient to make it effective, consequently popular.

## NOTABLE RACES AT SAN JOSE.

There have been many notable races since the California circuit commenced at Santa Rosa. Horses have distinguished themselves by performances exceedingly creditable, and these not restricted to one class or place. Some of them have been reviewed in the "Breeder and Sportsman," not so fully though as they will when the time comes for the consideration of the breeding questions. As the days grow short in duration of sunshine, and the evenings long, there is more of an inclination to give heed to the problems that breeders are the most interested in.

The last number of this paper contained the reports of two races that are eminently worthy of editorial comment, and which are entitled to rank with the best of the year. The first was a mile and a half dash between May D and Night Hawk, the second a trotting race of heats of two miles in which Albert W and Vanderlynn were the contestants. Both were brilliant efforts. In the mile and a half race it was a run from start to finish, a hot contest for nearly every yard of the distance. Night Hawk on the inside made the running and at the half mile had a length the best of it. The mile was run in 1:43 and then there was only half a length between them. The finish gave May D the race by a short head so that the record is fairly shared by both, though inasmuch as May D had the outside she had actually run some fifteen or twenty feet the furthest. One mile and a half in 2:36 has only been beaten three times. Luke Blackburn ran at Monmouth Park in 2:34. Tom Bowling at Lexington, Kentucky, in 2:34½ and Checkmate in 2:35½. Hindoo ran in 2:36, and this as a three-year-old with 118 lbs up. Checkmate, six years old, carried 119 lbs, Tom Bowling, four years, 104 lbs and Luke Blackburn, three years, 102 lbs. May D, four years old had 105 lbs. and Night Hawk five, 111 lbs. The fastest California time previously made is to the credit of Jim Brown, at the State Fair last fall, when he ran in 2:36½. It will be readily granted that both of these animals are worthy of a good place, and as May D is by Wildidle from Nettie Brown, by Rifleman, there is a double Glencoe cross. Night Hawk is by imported Haddington from a Norfolk mare so that both of them share in the blood of Lexington, and each with Glencoe blood. May D has the outcross of Australian, and 'Night Hawk of Kingston, the sire of Haddington. Both Australian and Kingston are among the top-sawyers of the English turf, and it is gratifying to find their descendant keeping up the renown of their ancestors. To run so close to the fastest is a merit which is easily understood for though many are given to underrate the time standard as a means of comparing the merits of horses, in this country, where the tracks are so nearly uniform, the reports of the watch have a great bearing in making a correct estimate. To reduce the California record three-quarters of a second is something of which the owners should feel

proud, and when also that is so very near the best of the East there are additional causes for congratulation.

The time of the second heat of the Albert W, and Vanderlynn race, is the third in the Calendar. Steve Maxwell at Rochester, August 11th, 1880, trotted in 4:48½ and for twenty-one years before that of Flora Temple, 4:50½, retained the of pride place. A second heat in 4:51, and that accomplished by a four-year-old stallion, can be placed alongside of the others, without losing by comparison. There had been rain, soaking the track until the races had to be postponed, and, when the heats of two miles were trotted, it was still far from being in the best order. The first heat in 5:04½ was not bad under the circumstances, and then the reduction from that time of 13½ seconds stamped both horses as capable of going the route in very fast time. There is scarcely a question that Vanderlynn can equal the time of Sten Maxwell and Albert W. excel it.

## THE HAMMOND SALE.

In the advertising columns will be found a notice of the sale by Killip & Co., of the Stock of N. D. Hammond. Some very valuable animals are offered. Pocora Hayward demonstrated capacity which gives him a good position in the ranks of trotting stallions, and had it not been for the drawback of lameness, precluding him from filling his engagements in the circuit, he would have reduced his record of 2:25 materially. His colts are showing very well, and there is a report from Sacramento, that his yearling from A. Rose is showing a flight of speed that marks him for a wonder. The Grand Moor was bred at Sunny Slope, and is a fine looking, big horse, that should prove a famous foal-getter. His half brother, Sultan, has already acquired a world wide reputation, and another of the same relationship, Del Sur, is also making his mark. The three are by The Moor, and though the practice has been to call only those from the same mare half brothers, there is more of technicality than sense in the distinction. As will be seen some desirable mares and colts are offered, and the sale takes place on Wednesday, the 26th inst, at the Dexter Stables, Oakland.

## LOS ANGELES FAIR.

There is a grand prospect for the fair at Los Angeles, which commences next Monday. Never before has there been so much interest taken by the people of the lower country, and we hear that there will be large delegations from all of the towns to the southward.

There is little doubt that in the course of a few years the sixth district will occupy a prominent position among the California agricultural exhibitions. It is not only the great wine and orange section of the State, but it is equally as famous as a horse-breeding section. Sunny Slope, Santa Anita, Dew Drop and Elk breeding farm have turned out some of the best, and these have made their mark in the East as well as at home.

It is a grand place to visit at this season of the year, and those from the upper country who can afford the time could not put in a more pleasant week than that on which the fair is held. There are many interesting points to visit, and the mornings of October are so lovely in that climate that there is an actual and intense enjoyment in existence. Now that the trip has been shortened to a few hours, the time in transition is not burdensome, and there is a promise of grand sport on the track as is shown by the entries published last week.

## THE PEDIGREE OF JOHN NELSON.

We are very much obliged to our friend Thomas B. Merry for his letter in relation to the pedigree of John Nelson. It was not in this country where the question of the authenticity of the breeding was raised, but by some of those rabid, crazy, mendacious, thoroughbred-hating scribes of the East. The whole animus was to gratify a disposition to discredit trotting pedigrees with thoroughbred strains, but the game is so nearly played out that few comparatively are misled by the attacks. Mr. Merry has, probably, a more intimate knowledge of the old-time horses of the Pacific Coast than any other person, and he will place us under additional obligations by sending an occasional screed to the "Breeder and Sportsman."

## THE VICTORY OF WILDFLOWER.

The mail accounts of the race for the Mali Stakes won by Wildflower, do not add much to the telegram received here at the time. The N. Y. Herald credits the stopping of her work for three weeks and the long journey had affected her prejudicially. It is stated that she went short in scoring for the first heat, and that must have been occasioned by a lack of form. When she trotted her great race against time last fall and also ıen she made the quarter in 32 seconds her action wa ːmarkably good. She was not long-strided but oved with the greatest ease and covered ground ɩough. The "let up" in her work had probably more ı do with loss of speed than the effects of the journey, ı the Electioneers need a good deal of exercise to develop ıeir speed. The first race which Wildflower trotted as far beneath the rate which she showed afterwards, ıd every time she was brought out she went faster. hen the pinkeye seized her so that she could not be exbited at the State Fair, and another "let up" was the ːonsequence. We have the greatest faith in Governor ßtanford's assertion that the most disastrous results ollow compulsory breaks in training, and especially with colts. Should Wildflower be granted the opportunity of trotting a few races before the season closes, she will convince the Eastern people that her action is all right, and that she can handily lower the records. The following is a

SUMMARY.

GENTLEMEN'S DRIVING PARK, N. Y., October 5, 1882.—The Mali Stakes, for foals of 1879; $250 entrance, with $500 added by Mr. H. W. T. Mali; closed July 2, 1881, with thirty-four nominations, in which the second payment of $50 forfeit was due May 1, 1882, and the final payment of $150 forfeit due September 13, 1882; value, $4,500.

| | | |
|---|---|---|
| Palo Alto Stock Farm names b f Wildflower, by Electioneer—Mayflower, by St. Clair. (Marvin) | 1 | 1 |
| Baker & Harrigan name br c Meander, by Belmont—Minerva, by Pilot Jr. (Murphy) | 2 | 2 |
| W. H. Tailor names b g Senater Sprague—Mils C, by Blue Bull. (Hurd) | 3 | dis |
| T. Kilpatrick names b f Lucy Walter, by Sir Walter—Semonita, by Sentinel. (Webber) | 5 | dis |
| R. Steel names b c Earnest Maltravers, by Happy Medium—Priceless, by Volunteer. (Irwin) | 4 | dr. |

TIME.

| | Quarter. | Half. | Three-quarters. | Mile. |
|---|---|---|---|---|
| First heat | .37¼ | 1:14 | 1:52¼ | 2:32 |
| Second heat | .36¾ | 1:12 | 1:49¾ | 2:27½ |

## THE COMING RACE MEETING.

The list of entries published elsewhere is a conclusive testimony that the approaching fall meeting of the Pacific Coast Blood-Horse Association is sure to be successful and a very exciting one. This estimate is not only predicated on the number but has the better base of those engaged being so nearly together, that the contests are certain to be the hottest kind of battles. Thus far there are nine in purse, No. 1, a dash of three-quarters of a mile, in No. 2, one mile for maidens, there are eight, in No. 3, 1¼ miles handicap, there are ten, and in No. 4, which is a selling race 1¼ miles, there are seven entries. These races come off on the first day, Saturday, November 11th and there cannot fail to be fine sport. On the second day of the meeting, first regular day, fine races are on the bill. The Ladies' and Vestal Stakes are among the "fixed events," the nominations in which were published two weeks ago. The extra races are heats of three-quarters of a mile, eleven entries, a handicap dash of a mile for two-year-olds, three in it, and a hurdle race of 1¼ miles, over five hurdles with three jumpers engaged.

November 18 are four races, with sixteen, nine, nine and three, the latter being a hurdle race, and on the closing day, November 23, there are the Finigan Stake, with twenty-nine nominations, the Fame Stake with six subscribers. The Finigan is a dash of a mile for two-year-olds, the Fame Stake a dash of two miles for three-year-olds, and the Baldwin is a post-stake of four miles.

The usual Consolation Purse closes the meeting, and any one who will take the trouble to look over the list of entries and nominations will agree with us that there cannot be a failure and that the racing will be of the best description.

## EDITORIAL NOTES.

**The trotting stock** of W. D. Hammond of Oakland will be sold at auction by Killip & Co., on the 26th inst. at the Dexter Stables, Oakland. The catalogue includes the stallions Poscora Hayward and Grand Moor, the brood mares, Lady Lightfoot and Hambletonia, and some colts that will attract the attention of horsemen. An announcement of the sale will be found in the advertising columns of the BREEDER AND SPORTSMAN this week.

**In Last Weeks Breeder and Sportsman** in the note regarding the record of Graves by a typographical error the year was given as 1874. Graves' fastest heat, 2:19, was made at Stockton, September 20, 1879.

**The three Embryo Stakes** that are to be decided on the Oakland Trotting Park Saturday, the 4th of November, will be the first time in the history of the track when yearlings, two-year-olds and three-year-olds will be brought together in important stakes in the same afternoon, and there is already a mild interest manifested. A table was prepared by the Secretary for publication in this number of the BREEDER AND SPORTSMAN, but as it was found necessary to write to a subscriber to clear up a little ambiguity in the declarations, the publication had to be postponed until next week.

**Metropolitan** by Echo from Black Swan by Ten Broeck, and, consequently, a brother to Annie Laurie, T. B. Merry informs us won a second heat at Walla Walla on the 5th inst. in 2:36. It was a very close thing between him and Adelaide by Alwood and altogether the best two-year-old race ever trotted in the North Pacific Coast. Metropolitan was sold by J. B. Haggin to Charles Russell of Walla Walla, and Dr. Mack is the owner of Adelaide, and also his sire Alwood.

**The Stanford Stakes** are to be decided next Saturday the 21st inst. on the Bay District course, and there is a likelihood of another race being gotten up to make out the sport of the afternoon. As has been previously stated, this is the largest trotting-colt stake ever gotten up, and the amount now at issue is $3,500. We must acknowledge that the stake has an absorbing interest to us, having a colt engaged in it, and what with the pinkeye and the rain interfering with his work, we are somewhatt "tribulated." We anticipated giving him ever so many heats to-day, and Thursday being so beautiful and every one predicting a cessation of the downfall for some time, that all we did was to "fag him out" a little. Friday morning there was a gentle rain, but coming so easily and methodically that it was evident it was more than a passing shower. Inasmuch as there was no provision for "good day and good track" there can be no postponement and those which have such a wet weather track as there is at Palo Alto or the sandy streets of Oakland to work upon, have a great advantage over the macadam or adobe we are confined to.

**Ho! for Australia.**—In our next we will be able to give the names of the horses that are to be sent to Australia to trot at the meeting of the Victoria Club. There is now the likelihood of quite a delegation being sent, and those of the right stamp, with which we are well pleased.

**Hurrah for Hinds.**—Again the California banner flies from the ramparts, and this time over the hitherto invincible stronghold of the Kentucky Breeders. The race took place on the 11th, and the only intelligence is the following meager telegram which was received by Governor Stanford:

LEXINGTON (Ky.), Oct. 11.—Hinda Rose won the race today in the two-year old class. Lost first heat, time 2:36; won second heat, time 2:31½; won third heat, time 2:32; lots to spare. Eight started.

Next week we will give a full account of the race.

# BICYCLING.

## Annual Twenty-mile Championship Race of the Boston Bicycle Club.

The third annual twenty-mile contest for the gold medal and championship of the Boston Bicycle Club was held at Beacon Park, Boston, Sept. 9, and proved both interesting and successful.

The track was in good condition, but a very strong wind was blowing, at times almost a gale, which rendered very fast time impossible. There were eight entries, but Messrs. J. S. Dean and W. B. Everett withdrew, and the following faced the starter: W. H. Edmands, F. H. Childs, F. Morris, C. L. Clark, B. L. Knapp, L. T. Frye. This was the first appearance of Mr. Frye upon the race path since his serious road accident last May, and he was welcomed cordially, and his riding was watched with much interest. At the sound of the pistol all got off well, Clark taking the lead, and completed the lap in the following order: Clark, Edmands, Frye, Knapp, Childs, Morris. Then Frye took the lead and maintained the position throughout the race, riding in his usual fine form and continually increasing his lead. On the third lap Clark fell back to third place, and Morris, who now began to show his mettle, was rapidly overhauling all those between himself and Frye, and on the completion of the second mile ranked second, with Edmands, Clark, Childs and Knapp following in that order, which remained unchanged to the end, except that Clark withdrew at three miles and a quarter, Knapp at thirteen miles and Childs at fourteen and three quarters. Meanwhile the other three stuck to the path despite the discouraging effect of the high wind, each desiring to beat the club record or at least win a standard medal. The timers knew already that Frye would beat Stall's time if he met with no mishap, and Morris also was showing wonderful endurance and constantly increasing his lead on Edmands. The riders were now being urged and encouraged by the spectators, and Capt. A. D. Claflin of the Newton Club went on the pace for Frye, assisting him materially, while Clark of the Bostons again took took the track to help Edmands, whose chances for securing a medal began to look slim; Morris, however, being now not only sure of his medal, but also sure to beat Stall's time. Frye completed his race a mile and a quarter ahead of Morris, and the latter came in about the same distance ahead of Edmands, who also won a medal by four and a half seconds inside of the standard time. The times taken were as follows:

| | 5 miles | 10 miles | 15 miles | 20 miles. |
|---|---|---|---|---|
| Frye | 18:28 | 37:41 | 56:56¼ | 1:15:34½ |
| Morris | | 40:19¼ | 1:00:15¾ | 1:21:12½ |
| Edmands | | ...... | ...... | 1:24:55½ |

The championship medal must be won three times to become the permanent property of the winner. The machines ridden by the winners were: Frye, a 58-inch Yale racing machine; Morris, a 52-inch Yale roadster; Edmands, a 56-inch British Challenge. Frye and Morris both beat the best outdoor time, although the record is much lower, C. D. Vesey of Surrey, England, making it at the American Institute Rink in New York in 1h. 15m. 4s.—*World.*

## The Bicycle Tournament.

The bicycling tournament which took place September 20th under the auspices of the Springfield (Mass.) Club was the most successful event of the kind which has yet taken place in this country.

It was extensively advertised, circulars were sent out, and preparations made on a large scale. The prizes for the races were valuable, amounting to some $475 for the amateur races and $500 for the professional race, besides $200 for the ladies' race.

Many wheelmen came on the previous day, and on the morning of the event a large number of others arrived so that when the hour for the parade arrived there were some two hundred to join in the procession, representing twenty-five or thirty clubs, from different States. The procession was formed in two columns each preceded by a brass band of twenty pieces, and after, the parade dismounted at the fair grounds for the races. Everybody who could get away seemed to have gone, and the crowd at the Park was estimated at from twelve to thirteen thousand persons. The day was pleasant, no sun or wind, and the track which is of clay was in fine condition.

Nine men started in the mile race, getting off well together, but Hendee of Springfield and Moore the English mile champion of this year soon drew out from the rest, Moore following close upon Hendee's wheel until in the home stretch he passed the latter and crossed the line in 2:54¾. Hendee, 2:55, Norton of Natick, 3:14. The second heat was a repetition of the first, the times being 2:57¼ for Moore, 2:57¾ for Hendee, and 3:07½ for Norton.

Seven started in the two mile race, V. C. Place of Greenville, Penn., leading until the home stretch was entered forth for the last time, when after a gallant struggle Moore passed him, winning the heat in 6:14 Place 6:14¼. The second heat was a repetition of the first, Moore's time, being 6:21½, Place 6:23½. The half mile dash brought out seven starters, the winner being Hendee in 1:24¾ Hatch of Northboro second in 1:29¾

The five mile race had six starters, but the judges insisted upon the Englishman giving the other competitors a start of thirty seconds. Place soon gained a good lead, and was followed by Claflin of Newton. As soon as Moore was allowed to start, he began to gain at once and soon overtook the majority of the riders, but Place and Claflin maintained their lead until the commenement of the fourth mile, when the positions were: Place, Moore and Claflin, Moore soon overtook Place, and followed him until in the home stretch he put on a spurt, which was answered by the Pennsylvanian, and the two came down the stretch side by side, but Moore made a tremendous final effort and passed under the wire two seconds ahead of Place; time from commencement being 16:17¾. Deducting Moore's handicap of thirty seconds, his actual time was 15:47¾.

Louise Armaindo having no female competitors, her manager rode with her in the five mile race, receiving a start of half a mile. Louise soon overtook him and completed the five miles in 20:55½. In the twenty mile professional race, G. S. Prince allowed G. E. Mellin and Thos. Harrison to ride five miles each at a time, winning finally in 1:8:10½ The one, two and five mile records were all lowered at this meeting.

The recent road race in England had fourteen contestants. The winner made the first fifty miles in 3:47:40, something over thirteen miles an hour up hill and down. This shows that the tricycle is by no means as slow as some may think.

The Philadelphians are preparing for a meeting of bicyclists on the occasion of the bi-centennial celebration, and expect to have a large attendance and a good time.

The English five mile professional race at the Ayleston grounds, September 9, was won by F. Wood, who beat R. Howell, the one mile champion, in 14:42 2-5, this being the best on record.

At Exetef, September 2, one mile was done upon a bicycle in 3:31 2-5 and three miles in 12:28 1-5.

## Sea Gull.

SACRAMENTO, October 12, 1882.

EDITOR BREEDER AND SPORTSMEN: I find the sire of "American Boy" (sire of "Belmont"), to be "Sea Gull." There are several Sea Gulls. I believe however that the sire of "American Boy" was by imported "Expedition." Am I correct in my inference? WILBER F. SMITH.

Answer.—You are correct, Sea Gull the sire of American Boy was by imported Expedition, dam by imported Sourcrout.

# POULTRY.

## Poultry Raising.

An English contemporary gives the following facts concerning the methods of poultry raising in Sussex, England: The usual food for fattening consists of ground oats, suet and milk—skimmed or unskimmed—to which sometimes a little linseed oil is added, especially in winter. At first chickens have to be fed carefully, if not charily. Allowing them three weeks, they are as a rule kept on oatmeal (made into gruel) one week; then suet is added, and the last week they are crammed. Milk is highly valued as an addition to the ordinary diet, and one poultry breeder has used as much as $50 worth a week. Cramming is done with a machine, and the chickens have their crops filled twice a day. This process is continued for about a week, supposing a preparatory course to have been gone through. After about a fortnight the food ceases to take effect; but so long as they are not kept beyond the proper period, it is surprising how few deaths occur in their ranks.

Fowls or chickens are fattened up to any weight, two pounds, or five, or eight, or more. Mr. Oliver produced one weighing thirteen pounds. There are farmers who lay themselves out for this as a specialty, fattening all the year round, and keeping their coops full. Among this class Mr. Joseph Oliver takes the lead, keeping about 200 dozen always in hand, and killing forty dozen at a time in the busy season, even 6 times a week. He uses nearly 700 sacks of oats a quarter, $800 worth of milk, and 9800 pounds of suet. He keeps six men constantly employed, and about twenty women. It is estimated that no less than $350,000 per year is realized by the sale of chickens in the small district bordering on Brighton, the queen of the English watering places.

BLACKLEG.—The Dallas *Times Mountaineer* says: "It appears that this disease is making ravages among the cattle in the southern portion of this country, and several have already died from that cause. The Prineville paper learns from the boys who have just returned from the round-up at Bear creek that it is raging among the cattle of that section. It is not known to what extent the disease has spread, but many calves have died from its effects. It is chiefly confined to calves and yearlings, causing death in a few hours after its appearance. Under the circumstances, situated as the cattle men are, and having such large numbers to care for, it is impossible to apply any remedy, and the contagion must take its course, with what disastrous results we are unable to foresee."

J. Jacobs, M. R. Chamblin, R. Black, Ed. Schnafel, F. C. Bethell, F. Struvel, Frank Staples and J. R. Hall have been elected members of the San Jose Sportsmens' Club.

G. Valensin's brown pacing mare Ouida died on the ranch of her owner near Hicksville, Sacramento county, after the close of the Stockton fair.

## THE GUN.

### The Ladies to the Front.

Des Moines, Iowa.

Editor American Field: About the last days of August, my daughter, who lives in Pueblo, Col., was on her way home from this place, over the C. B. and Q. R. R. via Denver, and she writes me as follows:

"We met a young woman on the cars, going prairie chicken shooting, with her own gun and dog. She had a lovely brown velvet hunting suit on, and seemed a real lady in every way."

I would be glad if those ladies than do would go hunting, and if more of them could handle a double gun well, and shoot on the wing. With lady companions, some of us would carry a better moral bearing into the field, have more genuine pleasure and sport, and drink less whisky and beer. It is true that with these lady companions we might kill less game than we now do, but it is time we should slack up on this wholesale slaughtering business. Game is getting too scarce for this, and we should not go hunting solely to kill, but for recreation and enjoyment. Our hunting parties should be genuine pleasure parties, and for this our wives, sisters and daughters would be no detraction to the true gentleman.

Furthermore, our shooting tournaments might properly be attended and participated in by ladies. Ladies are the soul of archery circles, and they could properly and well be of good clubs. Archery practice is but tame sport compared with that of the double gun, and ladies' tastes are not dull. They would appreciate the change to the gun with delight, as soon as it became popular. The traps, distances and clay birds and glass balls could be arranged to equalize the ten and twelve gauge of the gentlemen with the sixteens and twenties of the ladies, and where is there a true gentleman or sportsman who would not enjoy a clay bird or glass ball tournament on a beautiful lawn, in which ladies would be his competitors and his equals in the matches?

Eland.

You are right, Eland; we, too, would be glad to have the ladies more expert in the use of the double gun. If there is anything the ladies are afraid of it is a gun—or a mouse. Archery practice is good in the main, but it has its bad as well as good points. You say our moral bearing would be improved. Now what will make a man swear quicker, when he is just ready to shoot, than a gentle female voice calling : "Oh, George! do come and help me over the fence," or "what shall I do! I've got a blackberry stickin' in my stocking." Away goes the game and a man's moral bearing is elevated—perhaps.

Yes, it would be very romantic to go hunting with a nice young lady and you are quite right in your remark that there would be less game killed; in fact we doubt if there would be any killed.

No doubt game would like the new idea. All one would have to look out for would be to see that he did not get shot himself. You say that our hunting parties would be genuine pleasure parties; true, it would be very much like a Dutch picnic where one takes "his sisters and his cousins and his aunts." Eland, we are afraid your theory will take too great a hold on our hunters, as they will all be taking their mother-in-laws out hunting. Though we would not joke on such matters, the idea is very suggestive and we are afraid that the joke would fall on the mother-in-law. No, these lady hunters will never do; no married man who has his life insured would feel safe for a moment while in the field as he would be, asleep or awake, continually haunted by a night-mare of glass balls, clay pigeons, mangled hunting dogs, accidents and many other things equally horrible.

### Prairie Hens.

The prairie hen, or pinnated grouse, is a peculiar form of the grouse family restricted to the United States, and found chiefly on comparatively open plains and prairies. It is found in great numbers on the plains of the Western States, and forms a favorite object of sport. They are a bold, almost an unapproachable bird, especially in fat countries like the prairies. They are very wary and have good eyes and quick ears. If the sportsman descends upon them from an eminence they are sure to spy him and hide or fly off to a distance. This species, once common in the Atlantic States, is now mostly confined to the West. The old name in New York was heath hen.

It has a tail of eighteen feathers, short, truncate, and much graduated, and a tuft of long, lanceolate feathers on each side of the neck, covering a bare space capable of considerable inflation. The plumage is covered with transverse bands of white on a brown ground, the latter nearly black, and the former with a rufous tinge above; long feathers of the throat black, though different specimens vary much in color. The length is about seventeen inches, with an extent of wings of twenty-eight inches, and an average weight of three pounds. The species is at once recognizable by the extension of feathers to the lower end of the tarsus, the alb-blackers, and the long and lanceolate feathers of the sides of the neck and the short subtruncate tail.

This species feeds chiefly upon acorns, buds, leaves, berries and grains. In some places it encroaches considerably upon the domains of the farmer. These birds do not migrate, but remain all the year in their favorite and barren grounds. In the spring the males are in the habit of meeting at break of day in what we call "scratching places," where they revel and strut with great pomp and engage in fierce contests, uttering a peculiar sound rendered more intense by the large inflated sacs on the sides of the neck. Their flesh, though rather dry is excellent food, and during the cool season immense numbers are forwarded from the West to our Eastern markets.—American Cultivator.

Ducks, since the rain of last week and the fore part of this, are becoming more plentiful, and our local sportsmen get very fair bags when they go out now. One young gentleman bagged thirty—mallards and sprigs—on Tuesday last, and nearly all report the same average of "luck."—Solano Republican.

The Supervisors of Santa Clara county have enacted an ordinance for the protection of female deer, which includes all the provisions of the code lately in existence for the same purpose.

### Eastern Game Laws.

In New York a reference to the game laws shows that. the wild fowl shooting on Long Island begins on October 1 and may be carried on until the first of next May. Already the restrictions have been removed as regards the killing of ruffed grouse (partridges) and woodcock, and both these choice birds can be shot until the beginning of the new year, while deer can be hunted until the 1st of December. But the law also goes on to say that neither quail nor rabbits can be killed until the 1st of November, and at all times no game can be legally exported from the State. Over in New Jersey the second season of the year for shooting woodcock opens Oct. 1st and continues until Nov. 16.

The law also provides that the pinnated grouse (prairie chicken) may be shot on the 15th inst. by all those who happen to meet one in their travels, and between that date and the first day of winter; but, as in New York, all persons are forbidden to shoot or have in possession until November 1st any quail, ruffed grouse (partridge) or rabbit, when they may be killed until January 1st. But discriminations against non-residents obtain in New Jersey, and all who go afield must be armed with a license. The New Jersey Fish and Game Protective Society has jurisdiction over the entire State, of which Mr. W. L. Force, of Plainfield, N. J., is secretary, and those who wish to shoot or fish in Camden, Gloucester, Atlantic, Salem, Cumberland and Cape May counties must obtain a membership certificate of the West Jersey Game Protective Society, Mr. W. T. Miller, secretary, Camden, N. J.

In Connecticut, however, the law is more uniform in its opening day than in that in the above named States, and the season for woodcock, ruffed grouse and quail shooting is ushered in October 1, and remains intact until January 1. Wild fowl shooting is also in season at this time, as it opened on September 1 and will continue to May 1, but those who follow it are restricted to shooting none but shoulder guns, and the selling for fowl and the employment of sink boxes on the feeding-grounds is expressly forbidden. Rail also may be shot until the 1st of January next.

In Pennsylvania, to where a large constituency of city sportsmen wend their way, ruffed grouse shooting opens October 1 and does not close until January 1. The same dates also govern the killing of pinnated grouse in those sections where recently these prairie hanuting birds have been introduced. Deer can also be shot from October 1 until December 1, and quail and wild turkeys from the 15th inst. until January 1; but rabbits are not legal prey till November 1, and after that date may be killed on to January 1; Woodcock, however, are in season from July 4 to January 1; squirrels from September 1 to the end of the year, and wild fowl from September 1 to the 15th of next May. The law which regulates the shooting in Pike county differs slightly from the general law and reads as follows: "Deer may be shot from October 1 to December 1, but in no event shall they be killed in the water. Wood ducks from October 1 to January 1, rabbits from October 15 to December 15, squirrels from September 1 to December 15, woodcock until December 15, quail from October 15 to December 1, and ruffed grouse from September 15 to December 15." The penalty for infringement of these laws ranges from $5 to $25 for each bird or species of ground game shot out of season.

### Imperfect Game Protection.

Game protection as it stands to-day is a by-word and a reproach to all those outside of a lunatic asylum. There is not one man out of ten thousand who deliberately or ignorantly infringes the game laws that he brought up with a round turn and made to pay the penalty for his selfish misconduct. Gallons of ink are wasted every year in discussing the subject, but until country squires are bred with thicker blood in their veins and stiffer spines the great majority of appeals to them will end in a farce. Cringing in face of their duty, from either an idiotic fear of having their barns and hay ricks burned down, their stock "pissoed," or not "likin' to go agin a neighbor," they listen in owlish solemnity to indisputable charges. For show's sake they appeal to their better halves "to find out them law books" which have been mislaid. After a tedious delay, during which the law-breaker avails himself of the opportunity of decamping for parts unknown, the bound statutes are forthcoming, only to be thumbed and stared at and finally closed. The fiat then goes forth "that it ain't no case." That settles it.

Or else the local constable (generally the boss poacher of the place) is hunted up and employed to arrest "them gunners who has been shootin'them birds that oughtano." They are oity men the chances of a capture within the State lines is extremely remote, while should the law-breakers be to the manner born : they are let off, or, should the charges be forced to trial, they have the pleasure of being tried by twelve of their peers who knock off business for the day for what they generally see fit to call a "picnic," and after the aquittal of the wrong-doer the till of the village barroom reaps a harvest of dimes and the informing sportsman is execrated, and, if wise, "takes out." All this in the face of great inconvenience and some expense is apt to dishearten the most resolute or Quixotic game protectionist, and it is no wonder that an experience in county law is his first and last, and for the rest of his sporting life he creepeth not out of his shell.

### Baited Ponds.

In those places in the marshes and tule lands where game preserves are kept by shooting clubs, it is now the custom to bait the ponds. To do this wheat is scattered about on the surface and sinks in the shoal water where the ducks find it. At the early part of the season a yacht which was sent up with the boats, traps, etc., of a shooting club, took a ton and a half of wheat for this purpose. Periodically, wheat is scattered about on the ponds for the purpose indicated and it serves to keep the ponds attractive to the wild game. The birds will flock on to these baited ponds when they neglect those which have not been so prepared, so it pays to carry out the practice. The gamekeepers find it advisable also to cut ditches in the summer to let the water into the ponds so as to be sure of the natural feel in the ponds being renewed. Some seasons in a large section of swamp land the natural feed does not seem to grow and the ducks will desert such places for localities where there is more feed. But hunters who care to take the trouble can always prevent their ponds being barren by seeing that the water is allowed to flood them at the proper season.

All such things are now attended to by the keepers in the various game preserves, so that the sportsmen who belong to the clubs are assured of good sport, by enticing to their ponds, by means of abundance of food, flocks of game which might otherwise scatter about.

With the advent of the ducks and the rain comes the demand for rubber boots. The perfect rubber covering for hunting purposes is yet to be invented.

A Hunting Party.—Mr. C. W. Kellogg, W. R. Bashford, Wm. Anderson and Geo. Schareig went out on a hunting and camping expedition last week. They camped on the Ralston ranch near San Gregorio, San Mateo county, where quail were found to be plentiful. In two days' shooting the party bagged seven dozen quail beside other game. The birds were very shy and hard to approach when on open ground, flying quickly to the brush on the least sound of the footfall of the hunter. There are a few deer on the Ralston ranch and other ranches in the vicinity but as the farmers allow only their friends to hunt on these farms the animals are seldom disturbed. The tent was pitched near the Corte Madera creek and the campers had some very good sport with their fishing tackle as the trout in that stream are of good size and take the bait in a manner that makes the sport interesting. One very large trout was caught that weighed over four pounds. As this fish was caught different from any of the others that had been caught it is supposed that it is one that was put in the McCloud river some time ago. Wherever it came from it is a perfect beauty. The party returned last Saturday having been out four days.

Since the rains ducks have put in their appearance in many localities. So far this year there has not been more than five canvas backs killed, although several large flocks have been seen but like most of the migratory birds seen this season, they are traveling towards the south. Sprig have been shipped to this market from the northland are quite as plentiful as any other wild fowl. Most all of the quail come from the lower counties; Bakersfield supplies San Francisco with the most, but a great many, too, come from Los Angeles. Up to the present time game of all kinds has been very scarce in this market and consequently the prices very high. The market hunters have been in full glory as they set their own figures for their game; two hunters in one of the northern counties have sent, since the opening of the season, over $800 worth of game, mostly ducks, to San Francisco; they have made hay while the sun shone, but since the wet weather the prospect is that there will be more hunters, more game and lower prices.

A gentleman of considerable experience and observation says that "many persons are mistaken in the idea that rain is all that is necessary to bring ducks and wild fowl from the north. We have had plenty rain but the birds have not come in very plentifully yet; who ever heard of ducks that were afraid of water! What does start the birds from the north is the cold weather, as they can generally find good feeding grounds until the frosts come and freeze the marshes or form a coat of ice on the lakes and ponds; then the wild fowl migrate to warm climes. We have had earlier rains this year but the hunting this season is far behind that of last, as last year though the rains were much later, the frosts were much earlier and the ducks more plentiful."

Game of all kinds is very plentiful in the vicinity of Webber and Independence lakes. Those who would like large game can have all they want as there are a great many deer and bear; the latter make sad havoc among the live stock, especially the sheep. Grouse are also found here in large numbers. These birds are in good condition, of fine flavor and average about one half size larger than quail. The snow that frequently falls at this time of the year makes the hunting very interesting as the game can be easily tracked.

The rains have brought the ducks down into the lower bays, and over on the flats on the opposite side of the bays several large flocks have been seen. They are mainly coarse ducks, not generally considered edible, but the good ones come with them. It will not be long now before we see large flocks in the bays. Then the "flights" will begin—the regular "flights" morning and evening when so many hundreds of ducks are bagged by hunters.

The first canvasback of the season was killed at Knight's Landing and sent to Chas. Kaeding, of the firm of Liddle & Kaeding. It was not in good condition, but Mr. K. says that the old bird brought along the flavor, and he feels flattered with eating the first bird of the season.

Several hunting parties left for the tules and Contra Costa county hills in search of game Saturday. Those who went across the straits, report having met with pretty good luck, some getting two dozen quail each. The report from the duck hunters was not very favorable.

The trustees of the cemetery at Yreka have been annoyed by some hunters that are too lazy to scout the hills and have taken to shooting quail within the limits of the "city of the dead." Notice has been given prohibiting any more hunting in the cemetery.

We hear one of the shooting clubs is talking of a steam launch to be used for hunting purposes. In going about among the sloughs a steam launch is sometimes handy; but not very much slough hunting is done.

The shooting on the Tule Bell Club grounds, we hear is still poor, but the members expect that in the last storms, will bring the duck down. Last year they had the best shooting in the marshes for over three months.

Messrs. Liddle and Brown were out hunting last Sunday and bagged over one hundred quail, and say there is excellent shooting in that neighborhood, but will not say where that place is.

Messrs. Colby and Smith, on Monday and Tuesday, at their ponds at Courtland, killed nearly five hundred sprigtail, widgeon, teal and mallard ; these men are hunting for the market.

Last week Mr. Lambert bagged, in one day's shooting near Courtland, two hundred fine widgeon. Courtland is an unhealthy place for wild fowl.

In Mendocino county panthers, wild-cats and "varmints" are very numerous in the woods near the coast, having been driven there by the recent fires.

A Mr. Williams residing near Cloverdale killed a buck last week which he claims is the largest of the season. He weighed 200 pounds.

During a three days' deer hunt in the southern portion of Monterey county recently twenty-seven deer were slaughtered.

Messrs. Davis and Bennett killed some three dozen quail in the vicinity of Sancelito, last Sunday.

A buck weighing 161 pounds was killed in an alfalfa patch near Amador last week.

Quail are reported plentiful in the Pacheco hills between Gilroy and Los Banos.

Game is reported plenty in the Sonoma marsh below the embarcadero.

A few English snipe have been found in the neighborhood of Alviso.

# THE RIFLE.

## Next Year's Contest at Wimbledon.

Now that the International Rifle Match of 1882 is over there is no harm in saying that a large number of thoughtful riflemen in this country, whenever they could overcome the promptings of pride, were almost inclined to hope that it would end in a victory for the visitors. No lack of patriotic spirit gave rise to this feeling, but a genuine and earnest interest in the progress of marksmanship, and a fixed opinion that defeat would do more than success to forward it in the ranks of the American National Guard. The process of reasoning is very simple. Unfailing victory has led to overconfidence, that to apathy, and apathy to decadence. The public have lost interest to a great extent in the sport, regarding the result of every foreign contest as a foregone conclusion; the military, from whose ranks the shooting men should naturally be recruited, had ceased to recognize the need for constant and conscientious work, imagining for the most part that all they had to do was pick up their guns and "lick creation." A good whipping, it was argued, under these circumstances, was likely to have about the same effect on the rifle world that it might on a spoiled child. An awakening to the great truth that labor is the price of success was looked for, and a consequent renewal of hard work. The rifle manufacturers and ammunition companies, too, might, it was thought, be stirred up to provide a gun for the American soldier that might in some degree be fit to match the splendid English weapon.

There is great reason to believe that all the best effects that were anticipated from defeat will be realized. The directors of the National Rifle Association are thoroughly alive to the requirements of the hour. The body of riflemen so far from being downcast by their defeat, are already looking forward to the possibility of victory at Wimbledon next summer. Whether the manufacturers of arms and ammunition can be induced to do anything of their own accord is doubtful, but independent experiments are already in progress looking to improvement in both, and there are hopes that when the next match is shot the American team will not be so miserably handicapped as it was this time.

The Board of Directors of the National Rifle Association will meet to-day, and then the whole subject will come up for discussion. Under the first shock of defeat a few persons advocated asking a delay of the British. "There is no hope of our winning next year," was the cry, "let us have the return match put off to 1884, and we will work hard to win a match." A strong feeling has now grown up against this policy as both dishonorable and impolitic. "We entered into a definite contract as could be to go to Wimbledon next year," said a rifleman of high standing, speaking of this proposal. "If we had not done so the English would never have come here. They said so plainly. They have done their part; now let us do ours. If we do not we lay ourselves open to strictures that would be more bitter to us than a dozen defeats. See how teams from one part or another of the United Kingdom came here several successive years in the face of repeated failure. How would we look in contrast with them if our first reverse should make us supplicate for delay? Oh! no, we've got to go through with it, no matter what the result, or else confess ourselves very weak spirited indeed." These comments may be taken as the expression of the general opinion, but, nevertheless, it is probable that the subject will be broached at the meeting of the Board. The opposition will be very strong, however, and it is likely to be voted down—perhaps unanimously. Another concession will probably be asked of the British. It has already been spoken of to Sir Henry Halford, Colonel Walrond and Major Humphry, who are members of the Council of the Rifle Association of Great Britain, and they showed a disposition to grant it. According to the present conditions every member of either team must, at the time of the contest, have been one year a member in good standing of a volunteer or national guard organization. As the next match will take place in June or July this makes it impossible for crack shots, who might enlist after the result of the last match was known, to take part in the next one. This would be a serious disadvantage to the American side, though but little to the British. To cite cases in point: J. H. Brown, one of the best known long range shots in the country, has very lately joined the Twelfth Regiment; W. W. De Forest, a young rifleman of very great skill, has become a member of the Seventh. Several other good men are quite willing to join the militia if by doing so they can qualify for places on the next team. It is, of course, understood that these, enlistments are bona fide. The men go in prepared to perform active service throughout a full term of enlistment, and it is to be hoped that on obtaining guarantees to that effect the British Council will admit them to the match. The National Rifle Association will not, however, be entirely dependent upon such cases for new material.

Many men already enrolled are coming forward, promising to train for the contest. A prominent member of the Amateur Rifle Club, who holds a commission on General Shaler's staff, has signified his intention of being a competitor for a place on the team. There are hopes that Colonel Bodine and several other old-time team men may go into practice; Mr. Farrow, who now holds the military championship, intends to practice military shooting all the fall and next spring and several members of the Seventh regiment, well-known and tried shots, propose to take the field for places on the team. Altogether it is pretty certain that twelve men, much stronger as a body than the beaten team of 1882, can be got together. Now comes the question: "How shall they be chosen?" This is one of the points that will have to be most carefully considered by the National Rifle Association. There is a growing disgust against the system of competitions which has always prevailed heretofore. The best men, it is held, are never really the most successful in them; some of the best men are prevented by circumstances from even entering them. Nothing more is really known of a rifleman at the end of such a test than at the beginning, it is argued. The man who goes through with flying colors may break down under the great pressure of the final event. The really reliable man may be travel, or a little out of practice, and so may fall behind. It is pointed out that the man who headed the list in the August competitions this year did not ultimately get on the team. The opinion is freely expressed by some that the competitive system is neither more nor less than a refuge for those in authority from the responsibility of picking a team from the whole body of riflemen on the basis of known records, and a shield to them from the criticisms of the disappointed. English teams are always selected in this way. The famous "English twenties," are selected in this manner year after year by the executive officer of the National Association, and all teams for important events are made up from men of proven skill, without any preliminary trials, while the strictness of British military discipline stifles every murmur on the part of the rejected. The team that came here this year was picked in the same fashion by Sir Henry Halford, Colonel Walrond and Major Humphrey. It is true competitive scores were shot, but they were really of no avail, for the committee did not bring to America at all the men who made the highest average, because they considered him unreliable. It is quite probable that the American team of 1883 will be chosen in just this manner by a committee of the National Rifle Association—at least, a strong agitation in that direction will, it is expected, be made in the Board. A majority of members are also in favor of appointing the captain of the team instead of allowing the team to elect him. An elected team captain has never the same influence with his men that an appointed one exercises. The authority of this officer is supposed to be full, final and unquestionable. How can any one exercise such power over men, whose creature, in a certain sense, he is? One reason for proceeding in the manner indicated as regards the choice of both teams and captains is the very short time available before the next match comes on. To make the most of this short period a series of practice matches will be begun next month. They will be shot weekly, at 600, 800, 900 and 1,000 yards, which are the ranges at which careful training is most needed, and will be in all respects similar in conditions to the international event. They are to be open to all comers and suitable prizes will be offered.

But supposing the team chosen and supposing it to consist of the best possible men, a serious difficulty would still exist in the lack of proper weapons and ammunition for them. Sir Henry Halford said several times before he sailed that in his opinion the defeat of his opponents was more due to the guns than the men. All parties are now agreed upon this point. Several of the Englishmen's guns have been purchased, and experiment shows them to be far superior to the home article. A member of the American team who secured an English gun has had a wax impression taken of the chamber and the part of the barrel adjacent to it. He speaks with the greatest admiration of the admirable finish. He finds that the barrel is widened out the least bit at its rear end, so that the bullet never encounters a sharp edge which could damage the patch, but is launched as it were through a funnel direct into the rifling of the barrel. The deep, sharp groove of the American guns is also conceded now to have been a mistake. It damaged the bullets, interfering with their flight, and besides, caused "leading" in the bore. The shallow rifling of the English gun is recognized as far preferable for a match wherein cleaning is not allowed. Colonel Bodine and others are carefully studying the whole matter now, and it is thought very likely that they will be able in a month or two to give points to the gunsmiths which during the winter may fructify into a serviceable weapon. Then there is the ammunition question. The members of the British team used seventy-five and eighty grains of powder, while the Americans used 90 to 103. Of course the soiling and consequent inaccuracy of the guns of the latter was much the greater of the two. But it appears that from superiority of manufacture the seventy-five grains of British powder was equal or superior in force to the American ninety, and the best men in this country say they cannot do with a smaller charge than this at low ranges. Some are in favor of adopting an English powder at once, but there is still some hope that a better grade may be procured here before the date of the match comes around.—N. Y. Herald, Oct. 3.

## Shooting at Creedmoor.

Last week the Qualification and Champion Marksman's matches were shot for at Creedmoor. In the Qualification match at 100 and 300 yards, five shots at each distance, about 100 men competed, the entries numbering 272. The leading scores were as follows:

| Name | 100 yds. | 300 yds. | Total. |
|---|---|---|---|
| I. L. Price, 7th Reg | 24 | 24 | 48 |
| W. J. Underwood Jr. 7th Reg | 24 | 24 | 48 |
| N. T. Lockwood, 7th Reg | 24 | 24 | 48 |
| C. J. Dehm, 18th Reg | 23 | 24 | 47 |
| G. W. Munson, 7th Reg | 24 | 23 | 47 |
| J. R. Shepherd, 23d Reg | 21 | 24 | 45 |
| J. James | 22 | 23 | 45 |
| E. Lyons, 23d Reg | 21 | 24 | 45 |
| J. Schallern, 14th Reg | 21 | 23 | 44 |

The first five won cash prizes of about $13 each.

The Champion Marksman's Badge match had about 200 competitors out of 479 entries. Five shots at each of the distances of 200 and 500 yards were allowed, and all members of the New York National Guard making twenty-five out of the possible fifty points qualified for and won a State Marksman's badge. In addition to this inducement (and besides the gold badge offered as first prize) ten silver medals were presented by the association to as many marksmen, the names and scores of the winners being shown above, those marked " being winners at former competitions, and consequently ineligible at this:

| Name. | 200 yds. | 500 yds. | Aggre- gate. |
|---|---|---|---|
| Private *T. Lockwood, *7th Reg | 22 | 24 | 46 |
| Private W. J. Underwood Jr.,* 7th Reg | 22 | 22 | 44 |
| Captain John Kerr, * 69th Reg | 22 | 22 | 44 |
| Sergeant J. McNevin, * 12th Reg | 20 | 23 | 43 |
| Private F. Schubarth, 14th Reg | 20 | 22 | 42 |
| Lieutenant E. Farrelly, 69th Reg | 19 | 23 | 42 |
| Private T. Barton, 7th Reg | 21 | 20 | 41 |
| Private W. P. Picket, 23d Reg | 20 | 21 | 41 |
| Sergeant J. S. Shepherd, * 23d Reg | 19 | 22 | 41 |
| Private G. De Bouillier, 7th Reg | 21 | 19 | 40 |
| Lieutenant J. B. Dewson, 7th Reg | 21 | 19 | 40 |
| Private H. V. D. Black, 7th Reg | 20 | 19 | 39 |
| Private J. M. Schuyler, 7th Reg | 18 | 21 | 39 |
| Private W. J. Fitzsimmons, 7th Reg | 18 | 20 | 38 |
| Private G. A. Jones, 13th Reg | 21 | 17 | 38 |

At Alameda Schuetzen Park, Sunday last, the California Schuetzen Club held their regular monthly medal shooting with the following results. The first class medal was won by H. Zecher, 385 rings; second class, J. H. Fisher Jr., 390 rings; third class, H. Holtz, 327. Next Sunday there will be a prize bullseye shooting among the members of this club. The interest they take in shooting is manifested by the continuous practice of the members of the organization.

The English Rifle Team, after visiting Niagara Falls, and other points of interest in and about New York, sailed for England, on Tuesday, Sept. 26, in the Guion steamer Arizona. Previous to their departure a farewell reception was tendered them at the rooms of the New York Rifle Club, where informal and heartfelt expressions of good-will were given, and the visitors bidden bon voyage.

A BALL-ROOM car is the greatest novelty introduced on the Chicago, Milwaukee and St. Paul road, and recently a merry party of St. Louis belles and beaux made an excursion over the road and danced the "racquet" with the train moving, at forty miles an hour.

# YACHTING.

## What Yachting Costs.

"That nice little show on Decoration day," said an experienced yachtman of New York, to a reporter for the Mail, "costs the yacht owners of the city not less than $20,000. It takes money, I tell you, to put a yacht in condition for such a sail even when she is in commission and everything seems to be ready. It was something nice to see the sails of my 'sloop flipping in the wind as we rounded the Southwest Spit. Well, every flap costs me about $50, that's all." This gentleman who has, perhaps, built, bought and sailed more sloop and schooner yachts than any other man in America, was in excellent position to tell something about the expenses of yachting. He had been opening his pockets very liberally for a dozen years or so, paying sailors and sailmakers, cooks, stewards, captains and painters, and he seemed inclined to tell his experience. He said that his first yacht, a sloop, cost him $15,000. "When she was all ready," he continued, "the furniture in, the crew on board, and the pantry and wine closets stocked', I anchored her off Tompkinsville and invited a party of friends to go out and take a sail. Before the mainmast was hoisted for the first trip, that sloop cost me $16,500. The season's sport, as I thought it then, or work, as I am inclined now to think was, stood me in $8,000 more, or so close to $25,000, all told, it would make your head swim." "What are some of the expenses of keeping up a good-sized yacht?" Exactly the same as keeping up a good-sized house, that is to say, just what the owner will stand. If he has $20,000 to spare, and is easy in money matters and fond of company, a season of yachting will cost him $20,00. If he is close, does things on a small scale and has little company, he may squeeze through on $3,000. You can get a sailing master like a watch, for any price. I pay some $2,500 a year, and consider him cheap. I have had one steward for four years at $100 a month for the season. Champagne is pre-eminently the yachtman's weakness, and champagne costs money—good champagne. A man can drink twice as much without feeling any bad effects when he is on the salt water as when he is ashore. Then, besides these bills, you have your regular salary list, payable monthly. This varies in price with the size and character of the yacht. My list averages over $500 a month. Some are more and some are less. I need not mention the trifling matter of cigars. They must be the best always, and cost nearly as much as the food "

## Why Yachting is Expensive.

We have spoken of the subject several times and the following from the New York Herald corroborates our views: "One point to be touched upon is the inferior manner in which many of the new yachts are rigged. There can be seen masts with almost no shrouds on, no runners, light gear in every part, flying jibbooms that cannot be housed, sails that cannot be made to stand on account of the miserable gear, long foretopmasts that will not bear any strain because they are too long for their diameters and would buckle up if the sail was carried on them. There is one new boat, however, that would be half if she were decently rigged. Perhaps she will be rigged within a year or two by putting on better rigging, as part after part is carried away. This is the common method, and there is more money in the plan for all concerned except the owners. The constant alterations is what makes yachting so expensive and vexatious. The late lamentable failures in some large and medium sized boats are due to this very thing. After a season of humiliation some change is made, and so it goes on, until at last the stately vessel remains at anchor, too bashful to go out in company with other fast boats. Why this vexation? In many cases it comes of simply imitating sailing masters, to whom everything is referred. The fastest boats are those really run by their owners. Let no one for a moment imagine that there is any antagonism to sailing masters—a most worthy and deserving class of men. Their thoughts are properly taken up with care and management of their boats and how to get the most out of them, and this they will generally accomplish if let's alone. The reasons, however, for a vessel's performance are entirely out of their line, and never should be left to them. When owners learn that the manning, fitting and rigging of boats should be done by men who make a business of that sort of work, and that the sailing should be done by some one else, then they will face smaller bills to pay, sail their boats for better prices, win more cups and go through the valley of humiliation less frequently."

WOOD OR IRON FASTENING FOR YACHTS.—In speaking of the subject of fastening for yachts, Dana Kirby, the well-known New York yacht builder, says in Forest and Stream:

I wish to reply first to your strictures on the construction of our large sloops. You say that "all these large sloops are structurally weak;" that "Julia leaked like a basket;" that "Gracie followed suit." All this may be true, but you go on to say that last fall the "new Pocahontas suffered the same complaint," which is at variance with the facts in the case. The new Pocahontas did not leak last fall. Her pumps were not touched during her trials nor after her return. If all vessels were built as solid and fastened as well as Pocahontas, there would be no leakage from straining in carrying sail. She was purposely built strong enough to go to sea, to Europe, or anywhere else desired. You speak of through fastening, to which I do not object, if it is the right kind and put in in a proper manner. Grant, I am told, is through fastened—that is, treenailed, which I suppose is what you mean, and no doubt Julia is fastened in the same way; yet, according to report, they wring and leak. Why? You say for want of through fastening. But as they are through fastened, that cannot be the trouble. In my judgment, treenail or wood fastening is evidently defective, particularly in light frames, and is not near as good as long spike, with iron butt bolts, well ceiled up inside. This is the way Pocahontas is fastened, and she does not and will not wring or leak from carrying sail. The defects of treenail fastening are: First. That the plank in many places do not touch the frame. When a vessel is to be treenailed, planks are not just spike enough in the plank to hold on. Of course it does not touch the frame in many places, as I treenails will not draw it up, for they have no head. In fact, treenails make no effort to get the plank "to," for they do not know whether it is "to" or not, for surely if treenailed be seen. Spikes will draw the plank close against the frames, because they have heads, and if long enough they cannot be drawn out, hence you get a more solid job. An inch wooden pin is not as strong as a 1 7/16 or 1 inch square iron spike. Another defect in treenailing is in the boring the frame and plank for the treenails.

Now the thinnest of these larger sloops are probably not sided more than four inches. Pocahontas is four and one-half inches, and doubled, of course. Now a treenail, to [b] good for anything, should not be less than an inch. Then, if two treenails to the frame, you cut out two inches of the frame, and wide plank would need three of four; there you would have but four, five or six inches of wood left in the frame. Boring the frame and plank in that manner cannot but weaken the frame and plank. Fastening the plank on with wood is but a clumsy old-fashioned way at the best. More through fastening would be necessary if a light frame is used, but then fasten with iron, not wood.

THE ANNASONA.—The forty ton cutter Annasona is the one which is expected to come over here from England next season to try for the America cup. Here is what *Bell's Life* says of her:

"The latest performances of this marvel have certainly been something astounding. Who would have thought that a 40-tonner could beat boats more than double her size in a strong breeze and sea, and that, too, without time allowance? Yet such was the *fact*, the Annasona handsomely defeating the Lorna, Mr. Morley's yawl, by five minutes clear. This supports what Dennan, who sailed the little Madge in America, said, that the boat to go across to New York for the America Cup would be a good clever 40-tonner. Mr. Hedderwick meant to go last year, and no doubt would go right off now with his vessel, but the American conditions make it 100 to one in their favor. There can be no doubt whatever now as to the Annasona being the boat, and there can be as little doubt as to O'Neill's being the man, holding, as he does, a mate's deep-sea certificate."

NEW CUTTER.—We take the following from the Boston *Herald:* "The new cutter building by Lawley & Son, at their yard in South Boston, for Rear Commodore Charles A. Welch, Boston Y. C., is 38½-6in, overall 51ft. load line, 10ft. beam, 7ft. draught, flush deck, with 6ft. under the car lines. The cabin will be 8ft. 4in. long, with modern improvements. The forecastle will be 12ft. long, and will be provided with accomodations for the crew. The frame is of best live oak, two inches square, doubled, space 12in. between centers. The planking is one and a half inches, best selected Michigan hard pine, four inches wide and runs the entire length without butts. On the keel there is an iron shoe, weighing six and a half tons, firmly secured by iron floors on the inside. The deck will be laid with clear white pine, one and a half inches square. The masts will be 30ft. long above deck, eight and a half inches at partners; housing topmast, 24ft. long; bowsprit outboard, 19ft; gaff, 23ft. 3in.; boom, 31ft. 6in.; hoist of sail, 20ft."

The Spreckels Brothers' new yacht is to have sliding topmasts. She will not be launched until the joiner work is all completed, which will not be for several weeks yet. Her inside finish will be quite elaborate.

This is the time of year to go up river cruising as the nights are cool, the mosquitoes gone, the winds variable and light, and there is some game to be had.

We hear of no big yachts being contracted for this fall, though there has been some talk about one this summer.

The San Francisco Yacht Club will give a "closing day" dance at the club-house, Sancelito, this month.

Very few cruises took place this season. In fact, the yachting season has been a dull one.

The Aggie is on the dry dock being cleaned. She will soon be laid up for the season.

The Chispa is going for a cruise up Montezuma Creek before being laid up.

The Clara is going off for an up river trip of a week or so.

The Emerald takes out quite a large party to-day.

The Chispa will be taken up into fresh water this winter.

Dr. Tucker has been out cruising in the Frolic.

### Growth of Sportsmanship in America.

The versatile writer and classical scholar, Col. Thomas Picton, in a recent biographical sketch of Frank Forester, alludes to the lasting influence of the sporting author as follows: When he lived and wrote, the term sportsman, in this country, was associated with card-playing and similar diversions. He aimed to give the word higher, broader meaning. He believed that if our American men could be drawn from their offices and counting-rooms to forest and field, to breathe pure air and commune with nature, they would be benefited, physically, morally and mentally, and come to enjoy a larger existence. He expressed this belief in his conversations and inoculated it in his writings. The revolution in public sentiment has gone rapidly forward. To be a sportsman now means to be skilled in the use of rod and gun, fond of the wholesome, exhilarating excitements which bring rest to mind and recuperation to body—and professional and business men are not averse to having the term applied to them. Ministers compose the majority membership of many fishing clubs. Game preserves are established, and game laws are enacted and enforced. Nation and State make ample provision for restocking rivers and streams. Refuges built at public expense afford recreation for private citizens, whose practiced aim has made a world-wide reputation for American riflemen, as valuable for us in moral effect as a small standing army. Young men of means are abandoning fashional watering places for Adirondack lakes, Maine forests and western game regions."

THE YAK.—The yak is found in a wild as well as in a do mesticated state. Formerly very little was known of the wild variety. Nothing can be made dissimilar than the two varieties. The wild one inhabits the loftiest peaks, seldom venturing below the perpetual snows, except during unusually severe weather. It is a fierce brute, and has been known to exceed sixteen hands in height. Hue records crossing a stream in which a wild herd of yak had been imbedded in the ice and frozen to death, their forms being perfectly distinguishable through the ice. To the Tartars it is a most useful animal, being employed not only as food but as a beast of burden, and its sure-footedness renders it invaluable for mountain travelling. Hue describes whole droves with their loads on their backs sliding down the frozen sides of steep mountains.

## ROWING.

### More about the Hillsdales.

Sampson of the London *Referee,* who is the most unsparing of English sporting critics, says of the race between the Thames four and the American amateurs:

"The Amateur Rowing Association is likely to survive the cruel handling it received for refusing to recognize the Hillsdale four. It is with deep regret I have to make the statement, but it has to be made, that worse business was never done in an amateur boat-race than that done by Hillsdale at Putney on Friday. Directly after the start they came over into the Thames men's water, and commenced to bore them right across the river. Thames, who had the Surrey station, gave away and though a foul seemed bound to follow every stroke it was avoided for a time by the home crew going close, and closer in-shore until both boats were a good sixty yards out of their proper courses. Just before reaching Craven Steps the long impending collision took place, but still the Hillsdales, though singularly enough one of them put up his hand to claim the foul, continued their boring tactics. They went off with a lead of a clear length, and seemed so determined to keep to the Surrey side that Hastie passed under their stern, and took the Middlesex station. Whatever may have been the cause of it, such a piece of business as this has, I think, never before been seen on the London river. Certainly no professionals would have dared do such a thing, even in the bad old days before the present boat-racing laws were framed. So unknownd a beginning naturally disconcerted the Englishmen who were rowing; as for their friends on board the accompanying steamers, they groaned and hooted as though possessed by the celebrated seven devils. By and by, spectators calmed down again, and though for a long while it looked as if Thames must lose, a dignified silence followed the fast noisy demonstration of disgust and anger.

If there was any advantage at the start, it was obtained by Thames, but the Hillsdales, striking twenty-six strokes in the first half minute, drew up at once, and ran rapidly in front. In the next half they struck twenty-three, total forty-nine or the first minute! They threw the water up in shoals, and their boat ran upon anything but an even keel, but the pace was tremendous. The Creek was reached in 1:10 Hillsdale leading by nearly their own length. It was, I imagine, to a foolish and ill-advised endeavor to take Thames' water that the unhappy business already described was due. Let this be as it may, no more deliberate and injurious piece of boring can be imagined. Thames' who rowed at forty-nine in the first half-minute and twenty in the second, were going to handsome style until thrown out of gear by the extraordinary action of their opponents. After the foul they might have comfortably flustered, and as the Yankees continued to cross and cross in front of them, giving them their backwash in regular professional style, it is not surprising that the Thames men should be somewhat abroad, and that their boat should have rowed considerably. Hastie could not make out what to do. Every time he tried to go up, the Hillsdales barred his progress, and no one could tell for the life of him which side would, in the course of the next minute or so, be selected by the leading steersman. At the so-called mile-post—thus, 4:26—the Hillsdales were two clear lengths in front, first time since they had left their stakeboats. At the top of the Eyot, the Thames men, who were nearing for the Middlesex side, were only their own length behind. At Thorneycroft's they overlapped, when, all of a sudden, the Americans stopped rowing and the race was over.

When this occurred, the men had been rowing 12min 36 sec. No. 2 in the stopping boat held up a piece of bow's sliding seat so as to show that an accident had happened. After a cessation of less than ten seconds they went on again; but by now Thames were a long way ahead, and past all hope of catching. So far as form went, the Hillsdales rowed just as well after the accident as they rowed before it. They had never slid more than a handsbreadth—indeed, I have seen men slide further and fresh seats—and so the loss to bow was of the smallest importance. Thames had a blow or two and then went on again, coming out at the railway bridge so as to pass under the center arch. Here 14 sec divided the boats—17:15 and17:29. Between here and home Hillsdale gained a trifle,;the times as taken opposite the judge's boat being—Thames, 20:40 Hilsdale, 20:53. No appeal was made to the umpire. None was necessary, seeing that the men who suffered so severely from the foul, managed to get home in front despite it.

THE CHALLENGE CUP.—A meeting of representatives of the three clubs which intend to take part in the contest for the Challenge Cup offered by the BREEDER AND SPORTSMAN was held on Tuesday evening. Mr. Doblin, president of the Golden Gate club, represented that organization. The Pioneer club was represented by L. C. White and Thomas Flynn, and the Ariel club by Leander Stevenson and the Branch brothers. The Ariel men produced a decided preference for a course on Richardson's Bay which is not subject to the changes of tide and wind that make Long Bridge course so unfair. The representatives of the other clubs were opposed to crossing the Bay to find a course and thought the possible advantages of smooth water and a fair tide would not compensate for the trouble and expense of the trip. It was finally agreed to have the race on the Long Bridge, three-mile course which is much fairer than the two-mile course. The three-mile course gives a stretch of a quarter of a mile of good water at the start and is therefore not so objectionable as the two-mile course where the boat having the outside station is nearly always handicapped out of the race. The Pioneer representatives were anxious for a two-mile race but the others thought that anything less than three miles should not be rowed and were disposed to make it longer. Unless the crews do a little more training than is customary with Long Bridge oarsmen, they will find the three-mile course long enough. The meeting was most harmonious and the majority rule being cheerfully recognized there was no trouble in settling the conditions of the contest.

RETURN OF THE HILLSDALES.—Among the passengers on the steamship Indiana, which arrived at Philadelphia on the last from Liverpool, were the four members of the Hillsdale Rowing Club who competed last month on the Thames with a crew of the Thames Rowing Club. They were met at the wharf by a committee of the Schuylkill Navy and escorted to the Colonade Hotel. The committee tendered them a banquet on behalf of the Schuylkill Navy on Tuesday evening, but the Hillsdale oarsmen were compelled to decline on account of private engagements at home.

## ATHLETICS.

### The Great Contest.

The entries for the great six-day pedestrian contest at Madison Square Garden comprise the most remarkable array of men ever gathered together in a race of the kind. Of the eight men entered for the race seven have beaten 555 miles and all of them have records better than 555 miles. The list comprises George Hazael, Charles Rowell, Patrick J. Fitzgerald, John Hughes, George D. Noremac, Frank Hart, Daniel J. Herty and Robert J. Vint. The winner will have no easy task, for to carry away the palm from all these giants requires a struggle compared to which former tests of endurance upon the track are insignificant. Hazael with his recent championship to defend; Rowell with his defeat of last spring to efface; Fitzgerald with his grand record of 586 miles to encourage him, and the large stake at issue, all tend to call forth superhuman efforts, and there is little doubt the October race will carry the record beyond even its present marvelous figures.

Rowell, who has returned to the city, expresses the utmost confidence in his ability to win, and feels assured he will not be affected by a return of the unfortunate sickness that cost ed ed his defeat last spring. Hazael, who is training on Long Island, is under the care of Harry Vaughan, and is also in excellent health and condition. He is confident that he will make it warm work for any one to take the championship away from him. Fitzgerald, who may be said to have been in constant training all summer, is now in better condition than when he made his big record. Hughes, Noremac, Hart, Vint and Herty are all doing finely, and the same admirable spirits and confidence mark the utterance of each. The supposed arrangements for the race are in every respect excellent, and there is little doubt but that the attendance will be very large, an indication of which is had in the offer already received of $6,500 for the bar privilege alone. The race will commence at midnight of Sunday, October 22.—*Herald.*

### Human Endurance in the Water.

Man and animals are able to sustain themselves for long distances in the water, and would do so oftener were they not incapacitated, in regard to the former at least, by sheer terror, as well as complete ignorance of their real powers. Webb's wonderful endurance will never be forgotten. But there are other instances only less remarkable. Some years since, the second mate of a ship fell overboard while in the act of hoisting a sail. It was blowing fresh; the time was night, and the place some miles out on the stormy German ocean. The hardy fellow, nevertheless, managed to gain the English coast. Brook, with a dozen other pilots, was plying for fares by Yarmouth; and as the main sheet was belayed, a sudden gust of wind upset the boat, when presently all perished except Brook himself, who from four in the afternoon of an October evening to one the next morning, swam thirteen miles before he was able to hail a vessel at anchor in the offing. Animals themselves are capable of swimming immense distances, although unable to rest by the way. A dog recently swam thirty miles in America to rejoin his master. A mule and a dog, washed overboard in the Bay of Biscay; have been known to make their way to shore. A dog swam ashore at the Cape of Good Hope with a letter in its mouth. The crew of the ship to which the dog belonged all perished, which they need not have done had they only ventured to tread water as the dog did. As a certain ship was laboring heavily in the trough of the sea, it was found useful, in order to lighten the vessel, to throw some troop horses overboard. The poor things, say informant, a staff-surgeon, told me, when they found themselves abandoned, raced round and swam for miles after the vessel.

### The University Field Day.

Next Saturday the University athletes, weather permitting, will give their closing meeting for the season, on the new grounds near the University. Their lady friends have taken a deep interest in athletics, and have undertaken the task of erecting a Grand Stand on the grounds. Feminine friendship is a grand incentive for all athletes, amateur and professional, (we say, the Olympics propose to go right over there and wear out the new cinder path (the only one, by the way) this side of the Rockies.) The Olympic Club athletes think they never have had a fair show at their University rivals, but hope for a change this time. If this meeting does not demonstrate the superiority of one or the other, the University athletes should send a large number of competitors to the O. A. C. games next Thanksgiving Day. The various handicaps of the two meetings will at least give the handicappers a fair idea of the relative merits of the members of each club, and insure close and interesting competitions in all future events.

### The Record is Safe.

"Our Correspondent" in the New York *Clipper* has settled the matter satisfactorily. "Being known as one of the most accurate timers on the Pacific Coast, " and "having timed Hsley in 10 sec, on several occasions, " the times with which he was credited in his 100 yds race with Masterson we un doubtedly correct. The fact that "Our Correspondent" was not on the grounds the day of the race is a matter of no small moment to be noticed. That so he young man ould nested with the News Letter, throw a few figures at him. P. S. The *Clipper* itself remarks that it has written for further information." Can we believe that it doubts its accredited "athletic" correspondent?

The Hilsdale men are all in good health, and Captain Terwilliger said that while he regretted the misfortune surrounding their English visit he was well satisfied that the masses in England were disposed to fair play and to show them every consideration. He said that they were barred from the races for which they were entered by the efforts of a few individuals who seemed determined to make their stay as unpleasant as possible. He expressed the firm belief that the race with the Thames crew could have been won by his men if the accident to the seat of their boat had not occurred, and he denied that the crew was in any way distressed at the time of the casualty. He confirmed this remark by producing the record of the race, which showed that after his men had stopped and allowed the English four to pass the Hilsdale boat gained several lengths on the Englishmen before the finish. He also said that the Englishmen had acknowledged that the Hilsdale four was the fastest crew they ever encountered. Two days before the race the crew rode over the course in practice in 20:17. A new race was asked for, but the Thames men declined to row on the day appointed, although they did appear next day in their club regatta.

### A Wise Reporter.

the News Letter account of the 100 yards race between
' and Masterson, the reporter has figured a little beyond
pth. Melville's time was 10 seconds. Cook's 9⅔ and
tyre's 9 4-5. The News Letter says: '' If Cook was cor-
Haley and Masterson had gone 7 feet 6 inches before
ille started his watch. If McIntyre was correct, they
raxeled 2 yards before Melville had started. his watch,
'c versa.'' It is our opinion that the Latin quotation
I be more aptly applied by an expert mathematician.

## FISH.

### An Angler's Tournament.

e following description of the preparations for the forth-
ng fly-casting tournament is from the New York Herald
e 5th inst.:

e preparations already made for the Anglers' Tourna-
t, to be held on the borders of the Harlem Lake in Cen-
Park, indicate that the occasion will bring together a fine
pany of fly-casters and expert handlers of the rod. There
be eight distinct contests, covering casting the fly as for
on and trout, together with bait-casting for striped bass
racticed at the seashore. The tournament is open to all
ers, without restriction. From letters already received
he committee of arrangements it is likely that there will
ver fifty entries for the several valuable prizes donated.
tournament will be entirely an anglers' one, without
nection with any other sport. It will be a novelty, as it
be the first display of the sort ever given in this city,
being held in Central Park, it can be witnessed by the
lic without charge. The contests, which will be held on
ober 19 and succeeding days, will be under the control of
mmittee of well known anglers and lovers of fishing
t as follows: Francis Endicott, president Richmond
nty (N. Y.) Game and Fish Protective Association, chair-
; James Benkard, president South Side Sportsmans'Club
ong Island; Walter M. Brackett, vice-president Massa-
setts Fish and Protective Society, Boston; Eugene G
ckford, New York Fish Commissioner; S. M. Blatchford,
ibsockst chib, New York; Martin B. Brown, Wawayanda
, New York; Henry F. Crosby, Willowemoc club, New
k; Dr. A. Ferber, New York; James Geddes, Onandaga
ling club, Syracuse; Dr. J. A. Henshall, Cynthiana, Ken-
cy; Fred Mather, Forest and Stream, New York; Profes-
Alfred M. Mayer, Stevens Institute of Technology, Ho-
en, N. J.; Barnet Phillips, secretary American Fish
tural Association, New York; George W. Van Siclen,
lowemoc club, New York; James L. Vallotin, president
que Island chib.

esterday afternoon the committee met at the office of the
rest and Stream, No. 39 Park Row, and discussed the ar-
gements. A set of rules to govern the competitions were
pted and at a meeting to be held during the coming week
ale of points will be adopted and the list of judges agreed
n. The rules read as follows:

ingle Hand Casting.—1. No rod shall exceed eleven
d a half feet in length and it shall be used with a single
nd.

2. Any style of reel or line may be used, but a leader or
sting line of single gut of not less than eight feet in length,
which three flies, one stretcher and two droppers shall be
ached.

3. No allowance of distance shall be made for difference
length of rod.

4. Persons entering these contests shall draw lots to de-
mine the order in which they shall cast and shall be ready
cast when called by the judges.

5. Each contestant shall be allowed five minutes to cast
r distance and will then stand aside until called in his turn
cast for delicacy and accuracy, for which he will also be
owed five minutes.

6. The distance shall be measured by a line with marked
oys stretched on the water, said line to be measured and
rifled by the judges, at least once, each day of the casting.
mark shall be made on the ground from which the buoy
e shall measure and the caster may stand with his toe
nching this mark, but must not advance beyond it. Should
step back of it, unless so directed by the judges, the loss
distance shall be his.

7. The stretcher fly must remain at the end of the casting
ie in all casts. The others are not deemed so important.
contestant may claim time for repairs, which shall be al-
wed by the judges, or the judges may call the next in turn
cast while repairs are making.

Salmon Fly Casting.—The foregoing rules shall govern
cept that the rods shall not exceed twenty feet in length
d may be used with both hands, and that only one fly will
required.

Heavy Bass Casting.—Rods shall not exceed ten feet in
ngth, any reel may be used, but the line shall be of linen
t less than twelve threads. The cast shall be made with
kers weighing two and one-half ounces. (These will be
rnished by the committee.) The casts shall be made in
e formed by the buoy line and a line parallel to it and dis-
ot twenty feet. Each contestant shall be allowed five
sts. His casts within the lines shall be measured, added
d divided by five, and the result shall constitute his score.
Light Bass Casting.—The heavy bass rules shall govern ex-
pt that the sinker shall be one ounce, and there shall be
restriction on lines.

### The Pleasures of Fishing.

The author of that entertaining and instructive work, en-
led ''By Fell and Fjord,'' thus alludes to the pleasure of
gling, and displays a keen appreciation of the art, with a
ility for describing it which is seldom surpassed by any
so wield the rod and pen :

'' It is hard to say why it should be so enjoyable. Perhaps
is because no out-door pursuit lets the spirit of nature so
bre and saturate the mind as the gentle craft. Gardening,
mpared to it, is too active in its continuous work ; sketch-
g is a struggle ; the scene is too rapidly changed in travel ;
ook, of course, brings its own thoughts, and doing noth-
g brings a kind of rusty retribution ; but while lingering
side still or rushing waters, occupied but not absorbed,
e whole power of the scene and the season seems to sink
to our very heart. Thus, though the angler may enjoy
od sport, we find he or she is generally content to do with-
t it ; the spaces when nothing happens are so distant and
at a rush of fish becomes sometimes even rather a trouble,
d were it continuous would spoil the delicate flavor of the
ort. We are of the opinion that fishing from a bank is
ich pleasanter than from a boat, though, of course, a lady,
she does not wade, is more likely to take a large fish from
oat. But there is a touch of monotony in rowing to and
over much the same sort of water, perhaps getting chilled,
d having little to do but look out for a rise; while wandering by the river-side from pool to shallow, from shallow
to run, is most fascinating, even it it infers wet feet, possible
falls, and more trouble in securing the fish. But why do I
speak of fish when so often it is rather

The Waist-apttles are singing
Theif melodies unto me

while loitering on a sweet June day by one of those beautiful streams, whose ripple flows through one's summer dreams
like delicate music? Yes, believe me, you people who glance
with incredulous contempt at the literature of the gentle
craft, the sweetest fancies haunt the still or running waters,
the fairest imaginings people the solitude. Let it be a solitude—angling is no social sport. You may have a friend
within call—probably you will forget whether you have or
not ; but a friend beside you is likely to be a disturbance or
a rival.''—Turf, Field and Farm.

PACIFIC COAST FISHERIES.—The denizens of the Pacific
Coast are pre-eminently a fish-eating people, to which fact,
perhaps, may be attributed the great brain force which is so
characteristic of all who are so fortunate as to reside in this
part of the world. Oregon catches 20,000 tons, California
12,000 tons, Alaska 53,000 tons and Washington Territory
2,800 tons. The salmon catch alone weighs 26,000 tons. The
catch of shrimps and crabs amounts to 1,250 tons, and of abalones, oysters and mussels, 4,000 tons. The value of the
annual catch (including the enhancement in price by canning
salmon) is $9,246,000. The fresh fish are valued at $3,640,-
000; the crabs, shrimps, etc., at $66,000; the oysters, mussels,
abalones, etc., at $703,000. The annual products of the
fisheries of British Columbia are worth about $1,400,000, and
those of Pacific Mexico about $400,000—making the total
value of the annual fish catch of our coast almost $11,000,000.

A FAMOUS ROGUE ELEPHANT SHOT.—Albert G. R. Theobald
of the Forest Department has succeeded in shooting the famous elephant of the Poonay Hills, in the Kollegal Taluk.
Mr. Theobald was twice charged by the brute, which was a
huge tusker, measuring eleven feet in height, and which
kept the villagers in terror for a long time. This elephant
was a few years back driven into the Kollegal Keddah, at Al-
lambady, but he resisted every effort to capture him, and being such a large tusker, no pains were spared to secure him,
though it was all in vain. Out of the 26 elephants captured
with him, he killed no less than 19, and finally broke through
the keddah gate in spite of the shots fired at him andthe fires
kept burning. After his escape he is known to have killed
three, two women and a man, and many others had narrow
escapes from his furious headlong charges. Besides human
beings, he has killed several cattle, and destroyed great
quantities of standing crops, causing immense loss to the
ryots...

There is no more interesting fact in connection with the
propagation of fishes than that of their return to the original
spawning ground at the expiration of a given time. The
young fish also hatched out at any point, will in their turn
seek the same place for the purpose of reproduction. Numerous instances of this fact are on record; thus, Mr. Wilmot,
who for several years past has been engaged in hatching out
salmon at Newcastle, on the north shore of Lake Ontario, has
presented to the United States Fish Commission the stuffed
specimen of a female fish, from which he had taken eggs for
three successive years, as were indicated by his marks,
which were apparent on the skin. At the United States salmon hatching station on the Penobscot, Mr. Charles G. Atkins has been in the habit of tagging and numbering the fish
which he captures for his purpose and which are released in
Penobscot Bay when he has finished operations with them.
Of those quite an appreciable number have been taken in
subsequent years, identified by their labels. A still further
instance of this is shown in regard to the California salmon.
Mr. R. D. Hume of Oregon marked a hundred fish, letting
them go, and the next year he is' said to have retaken ten of
the number.

In comparison with the impurities brought to the river-
bottom by the sawdust, and the consequent destruction of
the fish eggs, its other injurious influences on the fisheries
are hardly to be taken into account, although in themselves
they are by no means inconsiderable. Thus, there can be
hardly a doubt that when the water rises and causes the
masses of sawdust which have gathered in the river to move,
a large number of young fish are carried away with it and
are gradually buried in the newly formed piles of sawdust.
This is particularly the case during the spring, when the
young fish are as yet very weak and cannot swim far. It is
also highly probable that the sawdust floating about in the
water kills a large number of young fish in the act of breathing, because they can hardly avoid swallowing particles of it
which stick fast in the gills and thus eventually cause their
death.

The sea eel grows twice as long as our river eel (specimens
measuring six feet in length are by no means uncommon),
and outwardly differs from the latter by the different formation of the jaws and dorsal fins. In the sea eel the latter begins immediately back of the pectoral fins, while in the river
eel it is placed farther back. In the sea eel the upper jaw
protrudes over the lower jaw ; in the river eel the reverse is
the case. The position and formation of the internal, especially the sexual organs, is very similar in both. But while the
river eel grows up in the rivers and only goes into the sea to
spawn, the sea eel never leaves the sea. The sea eel stands
imprisonment very well, and grows rapidly.

The fisherman who go to Sancelito have, for the last four
weeks, had exceptionally good sport off Lime Point, the fish
running from one to three pounds in weight and a catch of
sixty or seventy-five pounds is no unusual day's sport.
It is said that bum-cod and smelt are biting along the Sancelito shores and a good day's fishing can be had at a very
small expense.

A gentleman has just returned from a three weeks' trip to
Webber Lake and says there is excellent fishing there.
Thirty five trout that average one and a quarter pounds is
considered an easy day's catch. These trout take either
spoon or fly quite readily and are very gamy. During a snow
storm that occurred a few weeks ago the sport was simply
''immense.''

At some of the county, fairs in the North Pacific country, in
addition to a programme of races and a ladies' riding tournament, the managers provide a department for babies with
appropriate prizes for the handsomest. All fashions move in
cycles and this return to ancient custom is very popular
with the provincials.

Trout are bought on the shores of Independence Lake fo:
twenty-five cents a pound and shipped to Virginia City where
they find a ready market at a good profit to the shipper.
Over $900 worth of trout were sold from this lake last season.

The St. Augustine (Fla.) Weekly says: ''On Tuesday after
noon the fishermen reported that they have never seen for
years past such an immense shoal of mullet near the North
beach as on that day. The fish lined the shore as far as the
eye could reach down the coast, and were of very large size.
Although there were so many fish, it was impossible to catch
any number of them, in consequence of the great number of
sharks among the fish. If one did not cover a shark in the
cast of his net, he would tackle the fish in the net as it was
dragged ashore, and tear it to pieces. The quantity of mullet and sharks was a sight rarely seen.''

That the menhaden have not all disappeared, is proved by
the statement of Professor Baird, who, while on a recent
trip in the steamer Fishhawk, when ten miles southwest of
No Man's Island, passed through an immense school of them.
The steamer was moving at the rate of nine miles an hour,
and it was an hour and three-quarters passing through the
school. The number of fish must have been almost beyond
computation.

Dr. Gunther says there are seven thousand species of fish
now known to men of science. When a man sits on the river
banks half a day watching a cork idly floating on the stream,
and comes home with a sun-burned nose and not a single
specimen of these seven thousand species, he is inclined to
think that Dr. Gunther is a patent-medicine advertisement.—
Norristown Herald.

Some Scotch doctors in the Highlands use carrier pigeons
to send prescriptions to their surgeries, and to bring them
tidings of a patient's condition. The tricycle has become exceedingly popular with these gentlemen, and one of them
boasts that he has ridden five thousand miles on his in a hilly
country.

President Arthur and party have recently been on a fishing
excursion to Eel Bay. Among the catch, which was a very
large one, was a fine muscalonge captured by the President's
hook, on which they dined al fresco.

Two weeks ago Chas. Kaeding received thirteen Eastern
speckled trout, (Salmo .Tontinalis) that were raised in the
neighborhood of Washoe. The fish weighed over one-half
pound each.

On the west side of Man Island, flounders are being
caught in large numbers. There is some dispute among
fishermen as to whether it is really the flounder or plaice.

Thousands of fish are destroyed in the vicinity of Zeopus
Island, up the Hudson River, by the use of torpedoes.

The bay at Monterey was literally alive last Sunday with
amateur and professional mackerel fishermen.

W. A. J. Gift has sold his two-year-old filly ''Miss Gift.''
to Leland Stanford for the sum of $2,000.

The fishing around the bay last Sunday was very poor, although a few good catches were made.

### A Family of Monkeys.

Hindoos do not hurry themselves in anything they
do, but the monkeys have lots of time to spare and
plenty of patience, and in the real affair of the crow has
stolen a little, and the dog had its morsel, and the children are all satisfied, the poor fragments of the meal are
thrown out on the ground for the blunder-logue, the
monkey people ; and it is soon discussed—the mother
feeding the baby before she eats herself. When every
house thus, in turn, has been visited, and no chance of
further '' out-door' relief '' remains, the monkeys go off
to the well. The women are all here again, drawing
the water for the day, and the monkeys sit and wait, the
old ones in the front, sententious and serious, and the
youngsters rolling about in the dust behind them, till at
last some girls see the creatures waiting, and—in the
name of rain,'' spill a loth full of water in a hollow of
the ground, and the monkeys come round it in a circle
and stoop down and drink, with their tails all curled up
over their backs like notes of interrogation. There is no
contention or jostling. A forward child gets a box over
the ear, perhaps, but each one, as it has satisfied its
thirst, steps quietly out of the circle and wipes its
mouth. The day thus fairly commenced, they go off to
see what luck may bring them. The grain-keeper's shop
tempts them to loiter, but the experience of previous attempts makes theft hopeless; for the baunya, with all
his spare, is very nimble on his legs and an astonishing
good shot with a pipkin. So the monkeys make their
salaams to him and pass on to the fields. If the corn is
ripe they can soon eat enough for the day ; but if not,
they go wandering about picking up morsels here and insect and there a berry, till the sun gets too hot, and th m
they creep up in the dark shade of the mango tops and
snooze through the afternoon. In the evening they are
back in the village again to share its comforts and entertainments. They assist at the convocation of the elders
and the roups of the children, looking on when the
faquir comes up to collect his little dues of salt, corn
and oil, and from him in their turn exacting a pious toll.
They listen gravely to the village musician till they get
sleepy, and then one by one they clamber up into the
peepul. And we miss sitting round the fire with their
pipes can see, if they look up, the whole colony of the
blunder-logue asleep in rows in the tree above them.
—Under the Sun—Phil Robinson.

### A Strange Bird.

Mr. Benjamin Farley, who resides on Mr. Boss's place a
few miles from town, says a strange bird appeared in his
neighborhood about two months ago, and seems to have taken
up his residence there. He is a beautiful songster,and sings
in that section. The bird is about one-third larger than a
pigeon, and has a hook bill. His color is—breast, a bright
pink; neck, head and beak a perfect white; back, a sort of
dull blue. The bird is quite tame when in a tree or brush. It
is evidently a species of parrot—perhaps an escape from some
private cage. Mr. Farley is anxious to have the bird classified.—San Jose Mercury.

The first number of the BREEDER and SPORTSMAN is hand
edited by Joseph Cairn Simpson and his talented associates.
Some of the young men around town who delight to shoot
and come home with a true chickens from the brush, bears
from the bramble or any other ambitions sport away from
home, should subscribe for it. Call around to this office.
take a seat and peruse a specimen copy.—East Oregonian.
July 14.

# THE KENNEL.

## The Setter in a New Light.

The popular idea of this dog is usually in accord with the style of dog most in vogue in the district. This is but natural, but it has given rise to a multitude of misconceptions about canine characteristics. Among sportsmen who disdain the ownership and companionship of any but well-trained, highly-intelligent animals the dog is looked upon as but little inferior to a good man, and not a few enthusiasts will tell you that the average dog is better than the average human. That is because they either are unacquainted with the average dog or are wont to associate with a mighty mean class of men. My observation of dogs leads me to say that they are a very mixed lot, and I agree with Phil Robinson that in the world of English literature good dogs have had the field all to themselves and have been put forward as the true type of the canine species when really to be correct writers should have taken their types for the purpose of generalization from among the mean dogs. Before the advent of Idstone, Foster, Shaw, Youatt, Stonehenge and Hutchins the lore of dogs was unwritten. These men started in on a virgin field. The public mind was in a clean state on the dog question and consequently in a good condition to receive impressions. All the writers named took a high moral ground about dogs. They put the dog on a pedestal and deified him so that now-a-days no man dare say a word against his character, as a class. The character of the average dog as portrayed by all previous writers is a fraud, and the world owes a debt of gratitude to Phil Robinson for his breezy exposure of that fraud. written without malice to the dog or fear of the dog's defenders. I love a dog well but I love my race better and I am about tired of having a dog's virtues put up for men to pattern by when all the virtue a dog possesses he gets from contact with man. The dog that gave his life to save his master's child and the dog that died while chasing a hare are held up as models of fidelity. They are nothing of the kind. The one was defending his own life also and got into all the trouble from his meddlesome interference with something that did not concern him, and the other died because he was fool enough to run at great speed on a hot day with a full stomach. He was so anxious to kill a poor, inoffensive hare that, like many a greedy man, he overmatched himself, and his own greed proved his downfall. About half the men you meet are cowards, but all the dogs are cowards at heart. A few men are thieves but I have yet to see the dog that would not steal when he became hungry and nine-tenths of them will steal for the pure lust of larceny. Dogs are lazy, thriftless, improvident, cowardly, truckling, impudent, affectionate (when it pays), fawning, sycophantic, bullying, hypocritical, shiftless, aimless, dependent, irritable, presumptuous, assuming, vain to a degree, faithless, and forgetful. With this array of bad qualities against them what good qualities have they as an offset. They will do man's work, minister to his pleasure, guard his house, though for that matter a savory meal will debauch the best of them, and the dog never lived that would not let his master's house, herds and family go to the deuce if he sniffed a chance for an amour with one of the opposite sex. When young they are good natured with the small and weak because they like fun, but when they arrive at the age of discretion they are not to be trusted and can better be ruled by fear than by affection. Take the setter for an instance. He is often called the king of the canine race though for my part I fancy that the dog world is a republic and not a monarchy. There are aristocratic dogs and the setter is one of them, but their pretensions are not allowed by their brethren and they may be fairly classed along with the snobs in this great Republic who, having more impudence and more cash than their fellow men; pretend to belong to a different tribe. As with the snob so it is with the setter. He is only arrogant when prosperous. Give a setter a good home, plenty to eat, care and attention, and not too much work in the field he is an overbearing, impudent, pretentious snob to the less fortunate members of his race. His dainty strut and upturned nose when he comes across a street cur are a study and can be compared to nothing human except the sneer of a well-fed menial who has got a place at his former companion who is out of pocket, out of elbows and out of place. With good health, a full belly, fine features full distended, well-combed hair, cleaned ears and carefully tended feet your well-bred setter is a thing of beauty. He towers above his fellows socially as does the British bank clerk when airing his short coat and dogskin gloves at a Saucelito picnic. Full contentment is in his every look, self-satisfaction beams from his eye. He strides like a holiday-making servant girl in Sunday's best arrayed. His arrogant mien would shame a city supervisor and put to the blush the presenter of an address to a visiting magnate in a country village. He is handsome and he knows it, respected and he knows it, and a miserable fraud and he does not know it. Let him out without a tag, throw the hoodlum who runs the pound wagon across his path, let the lasso whirl around his neck, throw him into the pound pen, and what an abject self-confessed fraud he is. He mopes and sulks and squirms while your genuine out and out currish pariah, the tool and sport of ill-conditioned circumstances is as happy and chipper in the pound as anywhere else, your high bred setter in adversity has not pluck enough to snap when kicked, nor courage enough to growl when he finds his stomach protesting against its unwonted lack of food. He has no natural courage, no self-reliance and no hope, reversing the celebrated saying of Isaac Kalloch, "he is the solemnest thing in all animated nature except a Baptist minister caught in the wrong stall." At home in the midst of prosperity he is turbulent in the kitchen and around the stables, and truckling when by chance he is allowed in the parlor. He might bite a scullion or snap at a Chinese vegetable peddler but how the hypocrite fawns when his master in a fit of ill-humor gives him a rib-bursting kick. He knows he is a slave and a dog and does not resist the brutality. The much despised and oft slandered cat would not do that. Rub her fur the wrong way and she will hiss and spit. Pull her ears and she will bite and scratch, kick her and she will either fly at you or leave the room in as well expressed a passion of rage as though she were a servant girl who had slammed the door after her when reprimanded for having put too much salt in the soup. The more your setter is beaten the more he will crawl on his belly and fawn and slobber over the hand that dealt the cruel and generally unnecessary blow.

A dog, a woman and a walnut tree,
The more you whip them the better they be.

Thus runs the old rhyme and, gentle reader, the old writers were closer observers of dog nature and human nature than are the scribblers of to-day. The only fixed quality in the setter is his sense of fear. Once he gets afraid of any one or anything, all the world cannot remove his terror. Did you ever try to cure a gun-shy setter? If you did, you know something of a setter's cowardice? If you never tried it, my advice like Twain's to persons about to get married is "don't." The terror, cross stupidity and ignorance he will display will disenchant you of dogs once and forever. You don't believe it? Well, ask any dog trainer what means he uses to break a dog. His answer will surely be "fear." He may talk some rot about the law of kindness, moral suasion and patience, but press him closely as to his methods and he will tell you of his whip and his spike collar and his cruel throat check and his force system and ball full of tacks until you are convinced that about the only chord in the dog's nature he finds it pays to work on is fear. Next to fear the largest part of the setter's make-up is cunning and that he inherits from his ancestor the wolf. Sometimes he puts most of his cunning to good use in the field, but often he displays the most marked ability in larcenies, evasion of his share of any duty, naughty mischief and elfish acts generally. He will road a quail to the admiration of all, but will display more skill and zest in worrying a pet cat or perchance an industrious hen. Beat him for a fault and he is not cured but simply gives you twice as much trouble to catch him in its perpetration next time. When doubtful as to whether he was caught, the rogue will put on a look so demure that having seen him doing wrong you almost doubt the evidence of your senses. When he has done wrong and knows that you know it how he will fawn and crawl, and sneak and drag his tail between his legs until he looks as if he had no tail at all. How he will grovel and debase himself and wait for the expectant blow and when beaten he professes to be twice as fond of you as ever. I don't believe him. He makes up his mind to a dire revenge then and there but is too much of a coward to put it into effect. He intends to run away and leave you for ever, but the remembrance of the flesh pots and the warm kennel are stronger than his sense of injured dignity. The fellow is a natural lackey. Feed him and house him and he will serve you though your livery be a disgrace and your service a cruel one. A bone is a salve for a blow and a meal will make amends to him for the most brutal lashing that ever animal received. The next most prominent trait in his character is his inordinate, stupendous and unsurpassable vanity and self conceit. See how he struts around after the order has been obeyed and how promptly he comes to heel to hear the words "good dog" that tickles his vanity. Call him fool, blockhead and knave and show by tone and gesture that the words are meant and he will cringe and cry worse than though you had broken a ramrod across his loins or lodged a dose of shot in his hide for flushing his birds. Caress another dog while he is around, the jealous fellow will sulk and vent his splenetic anger more openly than for any other cause. Call him "good dog" before a stranger and he goes crazy with self satisfied vanity. Rebuke him in public and he will neither forget nor forgive the insult for months. He hunts according to orders not because he loves the sport, for his natural instinct is to rush into every bird he sees but because in the first place he is afraid to disobey, in the second he wants his vanity tickled by a few words of praise when the bird is retrieved, and he wants to show off just as a boy will show off his skill at play when strangers are around. The pointer's character has more good traits than the setter's but contains so much of evil that he is entitled to second on the list of bad dogs. EDWIN.

## Will Herzberg Explain?

That little band of mutual admirers who run the *American Field* and who evince a desire to run also the balance of the country must feel rather chagrined to find published in the *Turf, Field and Farm* the following extract from an English publication called *Land and Water:*

There is now on foot in America a subscription for carrying out the suggestion of E. Armstrong to erect a monument to the memory of the late Mr. E. Laverack, and at the instance of the editor of the *American Field* (Chicago) Mr. E. A. Herzberg is energetically acting in gathering subscriptions, and undoubtedly he is well qualified to act in that capacity, for of all the Laverack supporters he has proved to demonstration that it is possible to reproduce the Laverack setter on its original lines with all its original surroundings. He has been able to resurrect even the very rocks and rushes upon which the original dogs—or, at least, one of them—stood when their portraits were taken. I had thought that the original type of setter, as bred by Mr. Laverack, was a thing of the past. This, by the instance now before me, is, however, quite a mistaken idea. The instance I refer to has, by publication of the animal's portrait in the *Chicago Field* for Jan. 1, 1881, become public property, and therefore it is permissible to comment upon it. The portrait is "a portrait of the pure Laverack setter dog Aldershot, owned by Mr. E. A. Herzberg of Brooklyn, New York, imported by him June 29, last year, (1880). Aldershot is a lemon belton, and was whelped September 11, 1878. He was bred by Mr. J. R. Robinson, of Sunderland, England, and is by Emperor Fred. Emperor Fred is by Blue Prince (Pride of the Border—Nellie), and out of Daisy (Blue Prince—Corse)." The above is a quotation from the *Chicago Field*, in the same number as that in which the portrait of Aldershot appeared. Now, here is where the remarkable coincidence appears. In Laverack's book there is a portrait of Fred IV. The picture is a moderate production of the chromo-lithograph order, and has many faults in drawing. The print of Aldershot is very much the same picture in drawing and surroundings, only the position of the dog is exactly reversed. I was so struck by the resemblance of the two portraits that I took a pair of compasses and measured all the limbs, the body, the head, and every other part of the two animals. The only difference I found was in the length of the stern, and I attribute this to the fact that the space at command of the newspaper printer would not allow of the extra thirty-second of an inch. America must be a grand country to admit of a breed being as true to original type as this, and to produce such men as Mr. Herzberg, who has (out of reverence for the memory of Laverack probably) even imported the rocks, stones and rushes upon which Fred IV stood when his portrait was taken. I am grieved to find, though, that his Yankee enterprise and the rest of it was not sufficient to devise a means of carrying off the English landscape in the background of the picture. Probably he could not get a ship big enough; but these are details which, like the remainder of the circumstances above narrated, seem to admit of considerable explanation from Mr. E. A. Herzberg.

PETALUMA COURSING CLUB.—The Petaluma Coursing Clu will hold the first meeting of the season on Mecham's Ranch about 6 miles from Petaluma, on Tuesday, October 24. An old dog and puppy stake will be run. Entries free to all dogs in the State. The grounds are said to be well able to afford fine sport and game is plentiful.

## Fixed Events.

Coursing match—Petaluma Coursing Club—Open—Old dog and puppy stake, October 24th, at Mechanic's Ranch, Petaluma.

Coursing match—Pacific Coast Coursing Club—Private—Old dog and puppy stake, October 25th and 26th, at Merced. Entries close Oct. 21st. J. Bryan, Secretary.

Coursing match—California Coursing Club's—Private—Old dog and puppy stake, November 15th and 16th, at Merced. Entries close Nov. 11th. J. J. Murphy, Secretary.

A VALUABLE WORK.—We have to acknowledge the receipt from the author of a copy of General Hutchinson's valuable work on the most easy and expeditious methods of breaking dogs for the field. The work is one of the most valuable ever published and has reached its seventh edition already. No sportsman's or trainer's library is complete without a copy. The publisher is John Murray, Albermarle Street, London, and the price of the work in England is seven shillings and sixpence. The work contains a large number of illustrations and is beautifully printed and bound. The General's sketches of hunting at home and abroad are graphically written and will well repay perusal even by those who do not specially care for dogs, whether broken or unbroken.

## Shipping Mules.

The correspondent of the London *Daily News* who went to the Egyptain war describes the common occurrence of shipping mules and horses in the following outburst of hyperbole:

"Sing, O Muse! the wrath of Pegasus, be-strapped in mundane canvas and leather, who struck deadly panic into the souls of Moslem syces and stretched Seedee Arabs with aching limbs upon their untimely couch! Pegasus had just seen a mule go up and knew what was coming; but he suffered himself to be half led, half dragged to the spot above which an iron chain, ending in a big thick hook, dangled, like the chain of Father Zeus, from heaven. Gora-wallahs, (native grooms) approached Pegasus soothingly, and patted and stroked his arched neck and inquiring nose. Pegasus appeared to be reassured; so did the four Gora-wallahs, watched by a dumb and curious multitude. Two of the four, one on either side, next passed something like a tarpaulin beneath the body of Pegasus; they did it tentatively, tenderly—with all the tenderness of fond mamma applying the first mustard poultice to her adored child. But Pegasus? a thought darted through his brain—a saddle not on his back, but on his stomach; horrid reversal of the constitution and course of nature—a spark from Tartarus flashed in the eye of Pegasus, upreared the strong neck, out flew the bright shod heels, and round went Pegasus at a mad gallop, enlarging, so to speak, the circle of his acquaintances, pitching syces and gora-wallahs head over heels, damaging bags of grain and pots of "ghee" and shivering an empty cask into lucifer matches. Only the syce with the head-rope held his ground, or more correctly the horse held him—in nautical phrase, Pegasus dragged his anchor. After a while Pegasus was brought to, but only to treat the Port Trust and the Transport authorities to the same performance. Act one—to wit, the patting and the coaxing—always came off without a hitch; but act two as regularly began and ended in disaster. At the first touch of the canvas jacket on his stomach off Pegasus would spring, as if he were the long lost "Mexican Plate," improved by possessing all the fiends of Gadar.

But at last—at last—the canvas was passed round and the iron hook, above the Pegasean spine, fastened with a click in less than a twinkling of the Pegasean ear; and in less than another twinkling a small boy—a real, not a figurative Cockney Arab—with light hydraulic touch sent Pegasus flying forty feet up and away into the empty air. How completely Pegasus lost all self-control, all sense of dignity! No classic repose about him in that singular crisis of his fate. One would grieve to think that Aurora's steeds could ever have behaved as indecorously as their nineteenth-century relative, when they shook 'the darkness from their manes and beat the twilight into flakes of fire.' He, too, our Pegasus, beat the air, he kicked it, he spurned it, and with such vigor that he looked as if he had sixteen legs instead of four; he wiggled in his canvas belt, he snorted, yelled, screamed, screeched most demoniacally. And now, O, Jupiter! the change from the Zenith to the Nadir of the ridiculous. As Pegasus hung poised for a moment forty feet over the yawning hole into which he was to be deposited, he became mute; his legs slowly lengthened downwards, hardening, splaywise, into the rigidity of iron; his ears pointed, searchingly, outwards and downwards, seemingly, I am loth to say, more elongated than they really were; and from side to side, and upwards and downwards, surveying earth and sky, and the smoking chimney and the taper masts, and the 'Blue Peter' and the cook's cuddy, and the signal halyards of the good ship Morton Hall, Pegasus continued turning his slow head in a confusion of astonishment and fright. And then—oh, that I should write it!—Pegasus was lowered into the hold like a limp dishcloth. I have met writers of slow growth who, with half-absent, half-introspective gaze, have given me another version of Pegasus in harness, but I never believed them. I have seen many a cart-horse or useful cob fulfilling his natural destiny 'in harness,' but Pegasus never, except at this memorable hour at the Prince's Dock, Bombay. To tell the whole story, I should have to repeat the above description 167 times, for 160 mules and 7 horses were lifted on board."

## Pin Pool.

SACRAMENTO, September 18, 1882.

TO THE EDITOR OF THE BREEDER AND SPORTSMAN. Inclosed I send a diagram of the position of a pin, after a stroke in a game of pin pool. You will perceive that the pin is supported in position by one ball, and touches another, but it is still on the spot. Phelan claims the pin not to be down, while the rules, according to Brunswick & Balke Co. claim it to be down. Please decide which is right and you will oblige the pool players of California. JOE BOWERS.

Answer.—After submitting the question to all the acknowledged experts in this city, including J. W. Brunswick & Balke Co., the decision has been unanimous that the pin is up. In this we concur, as we fail to see how it could be held otherwise under any rule or practice now in vogue.

One day a week for loading shells for Sunday's sport is laid out by a good many hunting men for the whole duck season.

A man who does not belong to a shooting club now-a-days does not get the cream of the shooting.

## THE TURF.

### ...ething About Brighton Beach.

... reporter of this journal lately met with James McGowan, the Secretary for the ...hton Beach Racing Association, and ...ed a number of things new to him riding the turf. Mr. McGowan is an old-...sportsman, and a man who has been a ...er of sporting events for a long time. He ...be remembered as being for a long time ...ciated with the late Mr. John Morrissey at ...toga, and is will be remembered also that ... great success attending the races at that ...ous watering place was, in a great meas-...if not altogether, due to the wise manage-...t and knowledge of Mr. McGowan, the reporter was informed of the ins and ...s of horse racing, and the careful training ...tender handling necessary to the full de-...pment of the "crack trotter," the hot ...l, and the blanketings and rubbings, etc. ...on a crack receives before and after the ...e, all this was explained to him; how the ...ses are cared for when they are in good ...dition, and how they are doctored when ...y are not, all that was duly considered too. ...e would judge from the manner in which McGowan speaks that St. Jacobs Oil, the ...at German Remedy, is as much and as ...cessfully used on horses as on men. Mr. ...owan said:

Since St. Jacobs Oil has been introduced ... remedy it has supplanted almost all other ...licines, and it is not to be wondered at when ... consider the vast amount of good perform-...gy that wonderful remedy. St. Jacobs Oil proved itself in my hands an infallible ...edy. I have used it both at home and in ...stables. At home it has cured both my-...f and my folks on a number of occasions. ...m all I can gather I actually believe it is ... al in most of the training stables in the ...tled States. The stables in which St. ...obs Oil cannot be found are few and far ...ween, and I know that some of the very ...est stock on the track last season owe their ...ccess to a plentiful use, by their grooms, of ...Jacobs Oil. To refer again to personal ... of it, I would say that I applied the oil ... a case of rheumatism, and found in it all ...ould ask. My wife used it also, and it ...red her; in short, it may be said to have no ...al, whether for the human family or the ...mb creation. A visit to Brighton Beach ...ce Track, through the coming season at any ...e, will convince the most skeptical of that, ...he or they will find St. Jacobs Oil in use ...ong the gatherers there, both for them-...ves and their horses.—*Brooklyn Eagle*.

A new paper from the PACIFIC Coast makes the ap-...aarance here, the SAN FRANCISCO BREEDER AND ...PORTSMAN, the first number of which was issued ...ly 1st. It is well got up and printed, and, although ...king general notes of sporting matters, is devoted ...gely to breeding and trotting interests. The To-...nto correspondent of the BREEDER is Mr. James ...ng, who is well qualified to attend to its interests. Toronto Mail.

### Market Report.

FLOUR—In demand at full figures. We quote: Best ...ily Extra, $5 87½@$6 50; Superfine, $4 50@$4 75; ...terior Extra, $4 75@$5 25; Interior Superfine $3 75 ...@$4 50.

WHEAT—Holders are not anxious about selling; ...ippers cannot get much as they would like at $1 60. ...ported saleshave small in amount, and indicate no ...ange in values. Sales were recently made of No. ... November at $1 60.

BARLEY—The market is not very active and Values ...nly sustained. Sales recently made were at the ...llowing figures: No. 1 Feed, October, $1 33⅓ ...$1 44⅓; 90 toes December, $1 20; 160 do No. ...November, $1 30; 100 do seller 1882, 61 39 ⅓ @1 ...rewing in quotable at $1 26@2.1 27⅔ @ c1. 600 do ...steunary, $1 34 ⅓ c1.

OATS—Fired good inquiry, and holders have no fear ... being able to dispose of all stock. The range of ... market continues steady at $1 50 to $1 65, though ...reased rates are paid for fancy milling parcels.

RYE—Quotable at $1 60@$1 1½ for No. 1 and $1 55 ...@1 75 per c1 for No 2 grade.

FEED—Quotable at $19@$19, per ton. Ground Bar-...y $23@$27 pr ton: Cracked Corn$26 @ ton. Short-...ders are asking $20 50@$21 @ ton: Oilcake ton ...al c1 worth sell to the trade at $32 50 @ ton, less ... usual discount. Middlings, $23@$29 @ ton for ...ts of the mill.

HAY—Alfalfa, $15 50@$14; Wheat $16@$16; Wild ...at, $14@$16; Stable, $14@$16 ½ @ ton.

STRAW—Quotable at 75c @ bale.

BEANS—Bayos $3 85@4; Butter, $3 35@$3 50 for ...mall and $8 50@$3 75 for large; Lima, $4 40@ ...$ 4½ Pea, $5 50@$5 35; Pink, $2 85@$6l; Red, ... $3@$3 50; small White, $4 @ c; large White, ... $5@@$ 2 c1.

POTATOES—Red, 65@$1 10; Early Rose, $1@$1 20; ...arnet Chile, 90@$1 20 ; Early Goodrich $5c@$1 15; ...erivee, 85@$1 30 ; Sweet, $1 35 @ c1.

ONIONS—Good qualities will not bring over 50c as ... extreme. Sales of poor were made yesterday at ...w as 35c @ c1.

PROVISIONS—Eastern Hams, 16@18⅓c; California, ...ams, 16@16⅛c for plain, 16⅓ @17c for engg-...ared canvased; Eastern Breakfast Bacon, 17⅓@ ...c; California Smoked Bacon 16⅓@16⅓c for heavy ...nd medium, and 17⅓@18c for light and extra light; ...lear Sides, 16@16⅛c; Pork, 65⅓ 50⅓;15 for extra ...rime, 65@@$20 for Prime Mess, $15@$ 50 for ...tess, $27 50? Clear and 60 50@$20 for extra Clear; ...igs' Feet, $10@@$15 @ bbl; Mess Beef, $14 for kbls ...nd 67 for bl bbls; Extra Mess Beef, $14 50@$15; ...amily Beef, $16@$16 50 @ bbl; California Smoked ...eet, 14½@4½ @ lb.

BUTTER—We quote jobbing lots: Fancy, 47; ...hoice, 42⅓@45c; fair to good, 36@40c; inferior to ...rime cookery stores, 3 2@25c; firkin, 38@40⅓c for ...cod to choice, and 30@32c for ordinary; pickled ...ll, 30@ 40c; Eastern, $4 @ c for @ lb.

EGGS—California fresh, 45c; interior, 39@42½c; ...lah, 37½@37½c; Western, 40c @ doz.

CHEESE—California, 13@13⅓c for choice; 10@11 ...c fair to good; 6c factory; in boxes, 81@9⅓; Eastern, ...9@17c; Western, 8⅓;15c per lb.

POULTRY—Live Turkeys, gobblers, 18@19c; do ...ens, 18@17c ; Roosters, $9 50@$6 50 for old; young, ... $6 25@$6 50, according to size; Ducks, $4 50@$7 @ ...dozen; Geese, $9 5@$1 35 @ pair; Goslings, $1 50@ ... $ 7 @ pair.

GAME—All consignments to meet sell readily ; ...uail, $1 50@$2 dozen; Mallard Ducks, $4 60@$60 50; ...prig, $2 50@$3; Teal, $2@$2 50; Widgeon, $3 to ... 3 50 ; Hare $4@$4 25; Rabbits, $1 25@$1 75; Veni-...on, 6@8c @ lb.

---

WOOL—Sales at present are limited to local wants ...We quote spring: Humboldt and Mendocino, 26@ ...30c @ lb; Sonoma, 22@25c; San Joaquin free 17@ ...18c; San Joaquin defective, 14@15c; Southern Coast, ...burry and seedy, 13@17c; Eastern Oregon choice, ...23@24c; Eastern Oregon fair, 20@22c; Eastern Ore-...gon poor, 16@18c; Valley Oregon, fine, 20@22c; ...Valley Oregon, coarse, 23@25c. We quote fall: San ...Joaquin and coast, 10@12c; San Joaquin and coast ...Lamb, good, 13@14c; Northern fall, free, 14@15c; ...Northern fall, defective, 11@12; Northern fall, ...Lamb, 12@17⅓; Free Mountain, 17@18c @ lb.

HIDES AND SKINS—Dry hides, usual selection. ...19@⅓ 20c @ lb; culls one-third less, and Mexi-...can Hides 1c @ lb less. Dry Kip, 18c; Dry Calf, ...22@23c; Salted Steers, over 55lbs,11c @ lb; Steers ...and Cows, medium, 10c; light do, 9c; Salted Kip, 15 to ...25 lbs, 11c; Salted Calf, 14@15c @ lb; Dairy Calf 12@ ...25c each; Sheep Skins, 25@50c for Shearlings; 50@75c ...for short, 90@@1 for medium, and $1 @ $1 50 apiece ...or long wool and wool skins. Butcherdown Green ...Skins bring higher prices.

TALLOW—Quotable at 8@9c @ lb for rendered ...and 11⅓@1⅓c for refined, both in shipping order.

MEATS—Following are rates for whole carcasses ...from slaughterers to dealers:

BEEF—Prime, 7@8⅓c; medium grade, 6⅓@7c; in-...terior, 5⅓@6c @ lb.

VEAL—Large Calves, 7½@8⅓; small ones, 8@9⅓c ... @ lb.

MUTTON—Wethers are quotable at 6⅓@6c and Ewes ...at 5⅓@6c @ lb, according to quality.

LAMB—Quotable at 6½@8c @ lb.

PORK—Live Hogs, 6⅓@7⅓c for hard and 6½@6½c for ...soft; dressed do, 10@10½c @ lb for hard grain hogs.

---

## KILLIP & CO.,

LIVE STOCK & GENERAL AUCTIONEERS,

N. E. Cor. Kearny and Sutter Sts.

### THURSDAY, OCT. 26TH, 1882,

at 12 o'clock, noon.

BY ORDER OF MR. W. D. HAMMOND we will sell his fine trotting stock, comprising, among others, the noted stallions :

### POSCORA HAYWARD

(record 2:24), by Billy Hayward, dam Poscora Maid, by Leamark's Fueces, he by Old Fucecs, g. d. by Ro-...nel's Black Hawk. Billy Hayward by Geo. M. Patchen Jr., dam Old Peanuts.

### GRAND MOOR

by The Moor, dam Vashti, by Mambrino Patchen, g. ...Kate Taber, by the Drakin horse. Mambrino Patchen ...by Mambrino Chief, dam by Gano, by American ...Eclipse, g. d. by Sir William, a grandson of Sir Archy. ...Mambrino Chief by Mambrino Paymaster, by Mam-...brino, by imported Messenger.

Brood mares :

### LADY LIGHTFOOT,

by Fault's Abdallah, dam by Lightning, g. d. by Bel-...mont. Abdallah by Ryadyk's Hambletonian, dam ...Kitty Darling by Kty Darling. g. d. by son of Mambri-...no, by imported Messenger.

### HAMBLETONIA.

Sorrel mare, nine years old. By Whipple's Hamble-...nian. Dam the Ralston mare, thoroughbred.

Colts:

Weanling, by GRAND MOOR, from LADY LIGHT-...FOOT.

Weanling by GRAND MOOR, from HAMBLETO-...NIA.

Filly two years old, by Baby, dam Hambletonia, by ...Whipple's Hambletonian. Baby by Speculation, dam ...Martha, by Joseph; g. d. Young Dixie, by Easton's ...David Hill, g. d. f. Diana, by Vermout Hambletonian.

*Farming Implements, Wagons, Sulkies, etc.*

☞ For catalogue and other information apply to ...KILLIP & CO., northeast corner Kearny and Sutter ...streets.

---

## OAKLAND TROTTING PARK.

FOR FOALS OF 1878, 1880 AND 1881. YEARLING ...race, dash of a mile. Two-year-old race, heats of a ...mile. Three-year-old race, heats three in five.

### SATURDAY, NOVEMBER 4TH, 1882

JOS. CAIRN SIMPSON, Chairman.

J. P. WHITNEY, Treasurer.

B. E. HARRIS, Secretary.

---

## J. A. McKERRON,

MANUFACTURER OF FINE HARNESS.

327 Sutter Street.

BETWEEN DUPONT AND STOCKTON, SAN FRANCISCO

HORSE BOOTS A SPECIALTY.

*Repairing neatly and promptly executed.*

---

## DAVID L. LEVY,

JEWELER, DESIGNER OF MEDALS

AND TESTIMONIALS,

39 Third Street. San Francisco.

REPAIRING NEATLY DONE.

---

## DAN McCARTHY,

LIVERY, BOARDING & SALE STABLE,

608 Howard Street, Near Second.

LARGEST STOCK OF FAST LIVERY TRAMS in the State. First-class boarding. Horses bought ...and sold. Cash advanced on horses, buggies, sulkies, ...harness or any thing connected with the business.

---

## G. H. STRONG,

BICYCLES AND TRICYCLES,

252 Market Street.

Repairs to order.      Elevator, 12 Front street

Belmont—Mambrino Chief—Black-

bird, for Sale.

BAY YEARLING COLT, By PILOT, GRANDSON ...of Williamson's Belmont, his dam by Alhambra, ...by Mambrino Chief, from Reeca, by American Eclipse; ...grandam Cricket, by Simpson's Blackbird. Is now in ...Oakland at the stable of

JOS. CAIRN SIMPSON.

ENGLISH SETTERS.

A BRACE OF THOROUGHBRED SETTERS, ...well broke, for sale. Address

E. LEAVESLEY, Gilroy.

---

---

**SPECIMEN OF OUR ARTIST'S HUMOR**

THE FISHMONGER.

HUNDREDS OF DELIGHTED ONES SEE, FOR THE FIRST TIME IN THEIR LIVES

**The Japanese Artist and Embroiderers**

*At work in their native costumes at*

**Ichi Ban, 22 & 24 Geary St.**

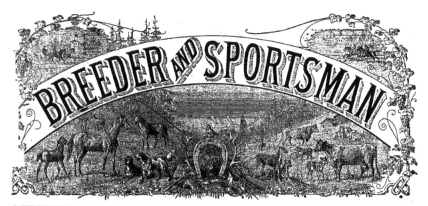

# BREEDER AND SPORTSMAN

Vol. 1. No. 17.
NO. 508 MONTGOMERY STREET.

SAN FRANCISCO, SATURDAY, OCTOBER 21, 1882.

FIVE DOLLARS A YEAR.

**ALGONA.** By Almont—Emma Kinkead, by Conscript. Owned by J. B. Haggin, Rancho Del Paso.

Of all the celebrated race-horse breeders of Kentucky thirty years ago and over, none were better known than "Uncle Ned." Blackburn, as every one termed him, and it was just as generally acknowledged that he was without a peer in presenting the points of a favorite horse. The parson in Bracebridge Hall, immortalized by Washington Irving for his fervid eulogy on the brown gelding, would have fallen far short if attempting to equal one of Uncle Ned's fervent and graphic descriptions.

There was a dinner party at Equoria at which were congregated the talent, beauty and wealth of the old Commonwealth, as Uncle Ned was as famous for his hospitality as his knowledge of equine points, and Mrs. Blackburn was equally as celebrated for directing the culinary affairs in a proper way. And, by the way, the old-fashioned Kentucky cookery was the perfection of gastronomic art, and to our taste, at least, could give odds to the most celebrated of the French professors. Among the guests was Henry Clay, and after the cloth was removed and the viands replaced with the decanters, he addressed the host: "Uncle Ned, there are several of us who are anxious to hear how you are going to overcome the obstacles in the way regarding Boston who,

we learn you have lately secured. Heretofore you have exhausted the English language in your panegyrics, and the trouble for you will be to find adjectives not already worn threadbare."

"Whip was the finest horse that ever trod the green pasture fields of Kentucky. American Eclipse was the only race-horse the world ever held. His son, Grey Medoc, was, if anything, his superior, and the speech you made from the hurricane deck of the steamer which bore him from Louisiana was thought worthy of the foremost papers of the Continent: Then there was Camden combining the Eclipse and

Sir Archy strains of America, with a daughter of the immortal Whisker for his maternal parent, and a host of others which have graced your stables. Now how about Boston?"

"Fill your glasses gentlemen, and I will tell you," was the response of Uncle Ned.

"Boston among horses, as Henry Clay among men, first, foremost, the best, no matter what the company they fall in."

This was a happy reply, and though for the time the great orator could not overcome his feelings so as to make a fitting answer, the hearty cheers which rang again and again from the assembly were proof of how apropos it was considered. In Kentucky especially. There might be other countries whete the "first, foremost and best" might not have been granted; in the "race-horse region" it would have been considered the rankest heresy to question.

We are in somewhat the same predicament that was supposed to entangle Uncle Ned without the same chance to escape. Every illustration that has appeared in the BREEDER AND SPORTSMAN is of a horse that has the strongest claims for eulogistic description. Though some of them cannot be claimed to have achieved fame either in their own person or that of their descendants, they are admirable types of the classes to which they belong. So far a large majority have been trotters, and without wishing to give this peculiarly American class an undue preference, they come before the public more prominently than any others, and are also of the track horses more numerous. Again they have been within easier reach of our artist, and his business is such as to preclude the making of long trips at this season of the year. But with the single exception of the picture of the yearling, Antevolo, there is not a single one which is not well worthy of a place in our picture gallery, and even the baby serves to show that the combination of Hambletonian and thoroughbred blood results in offspring that can lay claim to "high quality."

To return, however, to the task of accompanying the admirable representation of Mr. Wyttenbach with a written description, we will have to reiterate what we have previously stated. When the portrait of Piedmont was given, we considered him very nearly the best specimen of the trotting horse we had seen, that is, his form was nearer to our ideal of the speed formation than any horse which had not more thoroughbred blood. And now, we are in doubt whether he or Algona is entitled to the preference. There is a strong resemblance in these two sons of Almont, and still there is a difference which would require careful study before authoritatively awarding the certificate.

Algona is a bright chestnut, 16½ hands high. The shade could scarcely be improved, rather lighter than Piedmont and with equally as fine a coat. His chest is deep and the shoulders well-placed. The barrel is full with the back ribs long. From the loin to the nostrils he is almost a model, and his quarters are also good. Not quite so powerful as Piedmont displays, and this is a point in favor of the son of May Ferguson, though Algona is now highly finished, and with lighter action and more taking style. The limbs all through are first rate, and capital feet. It is unnecessary to extend the description further, especially when we would have to rehearse the terms used before, although it may be as well to say that he is a remarkably "even-balanced" horse, and that there is not a weak point in his configuration. His pedigree will bear the most exacting scrutiny. His sire has gained such a high and emphatically well-deserved reputation that it is only necessary to refer to it to a large majority of our readers, though the whole of the Pacific Coast is so much interested in the get of Almont that we transfer from General Wither's catalogue his account of the famous stallion:

Almont, dark red bay, black points, the black extending above knees and hock; fifteen hands two and one-fourth inches high; foaled in 1864. Weight, 1,150 pounds, by Alexander Abdallah.

First dam Sally Anderson, by Mambrino Chief.

Second dam Kate, by Alexander Pilot Sr.

Third dam a fine mare owned by the late W. H. Pope of Louisville, Ky., said to be and no doubt thoroughbred.

Almont made his first season in the stud in 1869, and the first of his produce started in 1873 at two and three years old. Four of his get started and all were winners. In 1874 five of his get started and four of them won, among them the four-year-old Allie West, who made a record of 2:29½, the fastest ever made by a four-year-old to that date. In 1875 eleven started and six were winners, among them Piedmont, who made a four-year-old record of 2:30¼ in third heat, the fastest ever made to that date by a four-year-old in third heat; and Allie West after a full season in the stud reduced his record to 2:25. Up to and including 1876, Almont had thirteen winners. That year they started in twenty-four races; won first money in eight, second money in eight, and third money in two, winning money in over two-thirds of the races in which they started. In 1877 four new winners came out, among them Katie Jackson, four-year-old record of 2:25¾ in third heat, and Alice West, four-year-old record of 2:29¼ in fourth heat. 1878 brought out nine new winners, among them Aldine, with five-year-old record of 2:28¾ in seventh heat. Easter Maid this year reduced her record to 2:29, and Alice West reduced hers to 2:27. In 1879 fourteen new winners came out. Ella Earl made a record of 2:25; Fanny Witherspoon (five years old), 2:26; Musette, 2:30, and Clermont, 2:30, and Alice West reduced her record to 2:26. In 1880 thirteen new winners were added to the list, and four new ones entered the 2:30 class, viz.: Piedmont, record 2:21¼ (public trial of 2:18½); Alta (six years old), 2:25½, in sixth heath; Sannie G., 2:27, and Una, 2:29 in third heat. Musette reduced her previous record of 2:30 to 2:29¼, in third heat, winning the second, third and seventh heats. Fanny Witherspoon reduced her record to 2:25 in sixth heat, winning fifth, sixth and seventh heats.

The results of the trotting season of 1881 added more to the reputation of the Almonts than any previous year. A number of his production won. Two new ones made records of 2:26 or better, and two others made records below 2:26. Early Rose made a record of 2:25½ in third heat, winning fourth heat and race in 2:26½. Hamlin's Almont Jr. made a record of 2:26 in second heat, winning the third heat and race in 2:27¾. Piedmont reduced his record to 2:17¼, made in fourth heat, the fastest record ever made by any stallion in second, third or fourth heat, and only excelled by Smuggler's 2:15¼, which was made in the first heat of a race which he lost, being beaten by Goldsmith Maid in 2:17¼ in fourth heat. Piedmont won his race, making a record of 2:19½ in fifth heat and 2:21 in sixth heat. Fanny Witherspoon made a record of 2:19¾ in third heat and won the fourth heat in 2:20. Aldine won a six heat race, reducing her record to 2:26¼ in third heat, and winning sixth heat in 2:27¼. King Almont won a six heat race, making a record of 2:30½ in fifth heat, and Una made a two-mile record of 4:54¼.

Almont now has to his credit about sixty winners of contested races, a larger number than ever sired by any trotting stallion of his age. Attention is called to the fact that one-fourth of all his winners of races have records of 2:30 and better, and that most of them have made their fastest records in the third and subsequent heats; thus showing gameness and endurance, as well as speed.

A critical examination of Almont's pedigree will in part explain why he has been so successful as a trotting sire. While an illustrious ancestry is indispensable to a successful sire, and no breeder should use in the stud any but a well bred stallion, there are other important requisites to be considered in the selection of a trotting sire. These will be noticed in the conclusion.

Almont was sired by Alexander Abdallah, who, as a trotting sire, was the greatest and most prepotent son of Rysdyk's Hambletonian. The Hambletonian family of trotters stand, by the record, far in advance of any other trotting family in the production of fast trotters. More than one-third of all the trotters that have ever made a record of 2:30 or better are descendants Rysdyk's Hambletonian in the direct male line. He himself sired thirty-five such trotters, the greatest number ever sired by any stallion, and fifty-six of his sons have already become the sires of 2:30 trotters, a number not approached by the sons of any other stallion. There are only eighty-five horses that have made records of 2:20 or better, and thirty-three of these are descendants of Rysdyk's Hambletonian in the direct male line. Of the 9,357 heats trotted in 2:30 and better, the descendants of Hambletonian have won 3,638, being largely over one-third of the whole number. Only sixty-nine have records below 2:20, and twenty-seven of these are descendant of Hambletonian, winning about half of all the heats ever trotted below 2:20. Maud S, with a record 2:10½, and St. Julien 2:11¼, were sired by sons of Hambletonian.

The dam of Almont was by Mambrino Chief, who by the record stands second to Rysdyk's Hambletonian as a progenitor of 2:20 and better trotters; and had he lived as long, and enjoyed the same opportunities in the stud, would most probably have equaled, if not excelled him as a progenitor of fast trotters. Mambrino, though he only had a comparatively brief career in the stud, as he died in March, 1862, after having only made seven seasons in Kentucky, sired nine sons and daughters that made public records below 2:30; and seventy-four trotters with records of 2:30 or better have descended from him in the direct male line, winning 719 heats. Eight trotters with records of 2:20 or better have descended from him, a larger number than are to the credit of any other contemporaneous sire except Rysdyk's Hambletonian. Among these was the celebrated Lady Thorne, who beat all her competitors, including the noted Goldsmith Maid, in numerous races, and but for an injury received while being loaded on the cars, bid fair to trot close to, if not below, 2:10 if her driver's statement is to be credited.

The attention of breeders is directed to the important fact that the daughters of Mambrino Chief have produced more trotters with records below 2:30 than the daughters of Rysdyk's Hambletonian, though there are probably twenty times as many of Hambletonian's daughters in use as brood mares. Twenty-six trotters with records of 2:30 or better have been produced by granddaughters of Hambletonian, twenty-three of them having records below 2:30; only one of them, however, has entered the 2:20 class. Twenty-four trotters with records below 2:30 have been produced by granddaughters of Mambrino Chief, five of them with records of 2:20 or better, or just five times as many 2:20 or better trotters as the granddaughters of Hambletonian have produced. This showing is greatly to the credit of the Mambrino Chief family, as there are probably ten times as many mares sired by sons of Hambletonian as by the sons of Mambrino Chief. This clearly demonstrates the great value of the Mambrino blood, and tends strongly to prove that with equal chances in the stud Mambrino Chief would have been a formidable competitor of Hambletonian for the first position as a trotting sire.

Almont's grandam was by Alexander's Pilot Jr., a trotter himself and one of the most impressive sires that ever lived. It is to his blood that the breeders of fast trotters should resort for the double purpose of an outcross for the Hambletonian, Mambrino Chief, Clay and Morgan families, as well as for utilizing the valuable qualities of the thoroughbred. Experience has demonstrated that the Pilot blood fuses more readily with other strains than any other known to the breeder. There is nothing refractory about it. It seems to mingle readily with other trotting strains, and while it exercises a marked influence, does not, as is often the case with outcrosses, antagonize and neutralize the valuable qualities of the other families, but usually acts in harmony with and adds to them. For overcoming the tendency of the thoroughbred to gallop, and utilizing at the trotting gait their high nervous energies and great capacity for speed, no cross has proven so efficient. This is no mere theory, but has its foundation in well authenticated facts. Pilot Jr., out of the thoroughbred running mare Tell-Tale, by Telamon, produced Tattler, who at five years old made a record of 2:26, the fastest to that date. Tattler sired Voltaire, with record of 2:20¼, and Indianapolis, with record of 2:21.

Out of the mare Croppy, by the thoroughbred horse Medoc, and her dam and grandam, both by thoroughbred running horses, and her third dam claimed to be thoroughbred, Pilot Jr. sired the fast trotter John Morgan, who in 1860 made a two-mile record of 5:00½, and in 1864 made a record of 2:24.

Bred to the thoroughbred mare Sally Russell, by Boston, the produce was Miss Russell, and Miss Russell produced Maud S, record 2:10¼, the fastest ever made, and Nutwood, 2:18¾, to the cover of different stallions.

Pilot Jr. sired the mare Waterwitch, and she produced to Mambrino Pilot (by Mambrino Chief, out of Juliet, by Pilot Jr., second dam by Webster, thoroughbred son of Medoc; third dam by thoroughbred Blackburn's Whip), the great trotter Mambrino Gift, who made a record of 2:20, being the fastest stallion record up to that date.

Waterwitch also produced Scotland, with a record of 2:22½, sired by the thoroughbred running stallion Bonnie Scotland, imported.

These instances, selected from many others that could be cited, should convince breeders of the superlative value of the Pilot blood, either for an outcross on other trotting families, or to introduce and utilize the blood of the thoroughbred running horse in breeding trotters.

Pilot Jr. was a purely gaited and fast trotter himself, and seven of his sons and daughters made records of from 2:24 to 2:30. Many who never saw him and were not acquainted with his history suppose he was a pacer. He was no pacer, but was as square a trotter as there was in Kentucky, and his produce had much less disposition to pace than did the produce of Rysdyk's Hambletonian. He was a horse of fine style and high finish, making a fine appearance in harness, and moving with remarkable vim and resolution.

Kate, the grandam of Almont, resembled her sire, Pilot Jr., in color, finish and gait. Capt. R. C. Anderson, who owned Kate, in a letter speaks of her thus: "Her speed and steadiness at the trot in the pasture were so remarkable, that the wonderful and seemingly fabulous stories told of swift pacers and trotters on the plains with flying manes and flashing eyes, and head erect—great leaders of the herd, and rivaling the winds in their fleetness—seemed no longer improbable. I thought then, and I think still, that she was the greatest untrained and undeveloped trotter I ever saw at three years old. I say this in the face of the prodigious and almost incredible feats of precocious trotters since that day, and after witnessing the performances of that truly wonderful colt Crittenden at the same age."

The third dam of Almont was the Pope mare, claimed to be thoroughbred. Capt. Anderson, speaking of her in the same letter quoted from, says: "She was doubtless thoroughbred. Everything about her history and appearance served to confirm this belief. I remember her distinctly—a dark brown mare, without white, so gentle and sensible, so sweet tempered, and yet so handsome and spirited, that she might have been in the mind of the genial Washington Irving when he drew the pleasant picture of the country preacher, who, from his earnestness and zeal, seemed to be expounding the law and the prophets, but who, upon a near approach, proved to be expatiating eloquently on the merits of a dark brown horse.

"She was about 15½ hands high, with every mark of blood, even to the gait of the runner, in slow or rapid motion. She was taken by a friend from the blue grass region and sold to my uncle, Mr. Pope, as a thoroughbred, with the promise, upon his return from the South, to send the pedigree in full, and properly authenticated; but as people are proverbially negligent of such promises, and my uncle was indifferent, the matter was neglected, and when my investigations began the former owner had died, and the pedigree could never be obtained. She was bred once to Old Wagner, and the colt, a handsome chestnut, was sold to Indiana and lost sight of before my return to the farm. She went to Wagner at the request of Colonel Campbell, who admired the mare and insisted on giving my uncle a season to his horse."

Since the publication of the catalogue the Almonts have largely increased their renown. The famous mares Aldine and Early Rose, are now one of the sensations of the day, and the wonderful performance at Hartford, while not perhaps "technical" as some have claimed, appears to be well enough authenticated as to do away with reasonable doubts of the correctness of the report.

On the side of the dam Algona has strong support.

His first dam Emma Kinkead, by Conscript (son of Cassius M. Clay Jr., and brother to American Clay.)

Second dam, Effey Dean, by Mambrino Chief.

Third dam, by Powell's Bertrand, son of Bertrand, by Sir Archy, and his grandam by imported Mambrino.

Thus it will be seen that Algona has a double cross of Mambrino Chief and only one remove further off than Piedmont, and has also the backing of the thoroughbred.

Algona was foaled May 12, 1876, bred by General W. T. Withers, sold by him to John H. Danielson of California, of whom he was purchased by Mr. Haggin last spring.

That he is destined to be a successful stock-getter is beyond question. His form and pedigree would give ample token of that, and his only colt that has started in a race was Almoone at Stockton, when, though suffering from the prevailing epidemic, he was second in the last heat, in 2:43. For two-year-olds this was not a bad showing, though when all right he can show a much faster gait. Almoone resembles his sire very much, another strong point in a sire, and a few weeks ago he was purchased of Mr. Danielson at a large figure.

## Deciding a Bet.

The suit of Dan McCarthy, the horse dealer, against C. P. Tinkham, to recover $100 balance due on a bet, in which the defendant acted as stakeholder, was on trial before Judge Edmonds yesterday. It appeared from the testimony of McCarthy that he had bet $100 with Drury Melone that one of a pair of horses that the latter was offering for sale was fourteen years of age, while Melone bet $100 that the animal was under eight years. Tinkham, a book-keeper for R. B. Woodward & Co., was made stakeholder, and McCarthy agreed to leave the decision of the bet to Melone. A few days after the bet was made Melone tendered McCarthy $100, and placed it on the seat of his buggy, claiming that the bet had been decided by veterinary surgeons as against McCarthy, out he (Melone) would let him off for old acquaintance sake. McCarthy refused to accept the money except as in part payment of the bet, and said he should hold Tinkham responsible for the other $100. McCarthy claimed that the horse was so old that his age could not be proved except by the certificate of his breeder, and this Melone failed to produce, although he knew the breeder.

Mr. Melone testified to having had the horse examined by several veterinary surgeons, and that they had all stated that he was under eight years of age, but that owing to an injury of his mouth, sustained while a colt, he might be taken for an old horse.

The Court rendered a decision for defendant, on the ground that any time prior to the decision of a bet the parties to the wager had a right to withdraw their bets, and that the $100 paid McCarthy was his interest in the bet.

McCarthy left the court-room declaring that the only way to get even on Melone was to bet him $100 that the horse was thirteen years of age, which he could prove, but Melone declined to accept the proposition.—*Call.*

The races expected to come off over the Boise City, Idaho, course were indefinitely postponed on account of continued rains. The Park association announce that the meeting will be held at the earliest day which the weather and condition of the track will allow.

# TURF AND TRACK.

## Oregon Turf Notes.

here is no more racing in this part of the country until next r, and our reports of the doings of Walla Walla and Baker are somewhat meager. Patsy Duffy being out of train-and Red Boy having left the country, naturally detracts n the usual interest felt at those places, especially when we ember that Wreath and Frankie Devine, either of which deemed able to beat Ordnance over a distance of ground, e broken down and been put to breeding. Frankie De-s is in foal to Chesapeake, Ross Mansfield has been bred Patsy Duffy, and Wreath to Marmaduke. Out of these ons will come some rapid horses.

he North-western District Society should go to work and n stakes for running and trotting colts foaled in 1881, and e them on the 1st of May, next. The entrance in each ke should be fifty dollars, payable in five installments of dollars each, open to all colts bred in Oregon, Washing-and Idaho. The running stake should be three-quarters mile and the first a mile and repeat. The produce of such ros as Trifle, Georgia A, Annie Laurie, Pirouette, Tidal ve and Jewel, should make a good field, to say nothing of at might come from the Grand Ronde country. And as the trotting state, we are confident that there would be at it fifteen entries from east of the mountains. There's re they raise the horses, but Portland is where the money and to Portland they must look for their market.

illy Coombs, the handsome four-year-old who won the gon cup at Salem in such a hollow style, left here last nday morning for Baker City. There was a purse of $500 he run for at that place yesterday, in which Billy would obably meet Ordnance, the flying daughter of War Dance. e has not been doing very well this season and it would t surprise us to hear that Billy had beaten her in spite of short time allotted to him for his journey to that place. t if she has regained her form of last year by this time, she ll make it very tropical for the brown stallion, as the race mile heats, three in five, a distance better suited to her an to him, judging by his running at Salem. If all the runs that ever ran on the Oregon tracks could be put to-ther in a four-mile dash, and DesChutes' rider instructed "make the track and keep it," the race would lie between lly Coombs, Fred Collier, Council Bluffs and Foster; and all s others would be beaten off, Red Boy included.

From the Walla Walla fair comes the astonishing intelli-nce that Charles Russell's two-year-old colt Metropolitan, Echo, won the stake at that place beating Dr. Mack's filly lelaide, by Alwood out of Bon Bon by Belltounder, in the pital time of 0:45, 2:26½. While this is not equal to the rformances of Wildflower and Marlet, it is certainly very st trotting, as the best three-year-old time at Salem was col-le of 2:55. And the most remarkable feature is that Dr. ack's filly was close up in each heat. Russell's colt was ed in California and was bought at a high price, while the otor's filly is "native and to the manor born." All horse-en are well aware that the mild California winters admit of lts being worked from November till April, while here the eather is so severe that they must be kept up and fed. It therefore no wild guess to conjecture that for every day's ork Adelaide has received on the track, Mr. Russell's colt as received two. A California three-year-old, worked as hey worked the youngsters at Palo Alto and Sunny Slope, is a far advanced in training as an Oregon or Walla Walla colt of five years. Hence, all things considered, we don't think Dr. Mack has any real cause to feel bad over it; for Metropol-tan would not have acquired a record that would have shut him out of the 2:40 class for next year had not the beautiful aughter of Alwood forced him to that figure. We believe hat in Adelaide the doctor has a second Faustina and that he logic of future events will prove it. No other sire in Oregon or Washington Ter. has produced, in a single season, hree such colts as Au Revoir, America and Adelaide. And when Sonny Mack's tidy bay filly, Souvenir, comes on the rack next year we suppose it will be the doctor's turn to re-mind folks of that homely old adage about "the proof of the udding." It is true that Alwood has had the daughters of belltounder as a foundation for the popularity which, we be-lieve, awaits him as a trotting sire; but other sires have had he same chance and have not improved by it. Major Ma-one, of Grant county has purchased the gray stallion, Hanni-al, by Reed's Hambletonian out of Kitty Lawn, by Silver uke. Silver Duke (2:26½), died last week at Waukegan, Ill. The colt was sold for $300 to W. G. Boughey, at Mr. Reed's ale; and he has parted with him on private terms to Mr. Ma-or, who takes him up into the wilderness as a successor to hampion Knox, who left many fine fillies in that neighbor-ood. Hannibal has a fine gait and, when he gets his growth, e will be heard from as a game and resolute horse.—T. B. *Merry in the Oregonian.*

## Dissatisfaction over the St. Leger.

The recent winning of the English St. Leger by Dutch Oven has given rise to all sorts of ugly rumors and talk re-garding the manner in which Lord Falmouth's famous filly ass been handled this season, and some of the comments upon her recent performances are anything but kindly in tone. The London *Sporting and Dramatic News*, which is generally very conservative regarding matters in which the good name of a trainer or owner of race-horses is involved, speaks out very plainly. Dutch Oven, it says, has won the St. Leger, hough men who have watched the filly's career carefully this eason may well have hesitated to believe their eyes when hey saw the finish of the race, or read the announcements n the newspapers. After this the turf analyst may well give up his studies; public form is certainly no guide. How many pounds did Shotover give Battlefield at Ascot? thirteen pounds we think it was, and she won in a canter by four lengths—Shotover, bear in mind, who is much inferior to Bereximine. At Goodwood, Battlefield (9 st. 1 lb.) beats Dutch Oven (6 st. 10 lbs.) with the greatest of ease, and this puts Dutch Oven a long way behind Battlefield, who is a long way behind Shotover—21 lbs. at least. How far this running makes Geheimniss superior to Dutch Oven the reader may alculate for himself—about 2 st. 10 lbs. we should say; and ret Dutch Oven wins quite comfortably. Truly, had the mare belonged to some owners very ugly things would be aid !

## Answers to Correspondents.

James Mack, Stillwater, Nevada.—April Fool, b m, foaled 1868, bred by Sprague & Akers, Kansas, by Waterloo.
First dam Fanny Dally, by Blackbonse.
Second dam Amo Harper, by imported Sagbrough.
Third dam Ellen Puckett, by Sir Richard.
Fourth dam by Stockholder.
Fifth dam by Old Conqueror.
Sixth dam by Brinkley's Peacock.
Bruce's American Stud Book, vol. 1st, page 410.

## Last Day at Jerome Park.

The non-appearance of the California stables at Chicago is accounted for in the following reports of racing at Jerome Park where it appears they had engagements. The track was heavy from recent rains but was regarded by local chroniclers as "safe," a modern expression for "unfit for fast work." Clara D scored a win at one mile and an eighth, Gano ran second in a three-quarter mile dash in 1:19, Duchess of Norfolk third in a mile and three-quarters and Grismer was placed last in a field of six at three-quarters of a mile.

FIRST RACE.

Purse $500, for all ages.  Three-quarters of a mile.
Dwyer Brothers name c b g Bootjack, by Bonnie Scotland, dam Spur-now grass, 4 years old, 118 lbs.? McLaughlin ..................... 1
E. J. Baldwin names Gano, by Grinstead, dam Santa Anita, 3 years old, 90 lbs. (Williams? ......................... 2
W. L. Cassidy names c h Saunterer, by Leamington, dam Lemonade. 4 years old, 118 lbs (Barbee) ......................... 3
J. E. Kelly names c b f Bella, by Fiddlesticks, dam Bernice, 3 years old, 87 lbs (Sheridan) .......................... 4
W. Donahue name b c Strathspey, by Glenelg, dam La Polka, 4 years old, 118 lbs, W. Donahue .......................... 5
F. Robinson names b c Little Phil, by Enquirer, dam Nancy Mc-Nairy, 4 years old, 118 lbs.Murphy? ..................... 6
Time—1:19.

Bootjack was a great favorite over the field. After a half a dozen breakaways the flag fell to a capital start, with, Saunt-erer leading. Bootjack second, Strathspey third, the others nearly parallel. When the horses came to the foot of the bluff Bootjack had his head in front of Bella, Saunterer third, Strathspey fourth, Little Phil fifth, Gano sixth—all lapped one on the other. Going around the hill at the half-mile pole Bella was leading by a neck, Saunterer second, a head in front of Bootjack, he about the same distance in advance of Strathspey, Little Phil fifth, Gano sixth. When the horses came in view on the lower turn Bella was leading by three-quarters of a length, Saunterer second, one length in front of Bootjack, he half a length in front of Strathspey, Gano fifth, Little Phil sixth. As the horses passed the three-quarter pole Bella led by a head, Saunterer second, half a length in front of Bootjack and Strathspey, the latter pair nearly parallel, Gano fifth, Little Phil sixth. Getting into the homestretch an exciting struggle was indulged in by all the contestants, which terminated at the judges' stand by Bootjack winning the race by three-quarters of a length, Gano second, a head in advance of Saunterer, he half a length in front of Bella, Strathspey fifth, Little Phil sixth. Time, 1:19.

SECOND RACE.

Handicap sweepstakes, for two-year-olds, $25 each, and only $5 if de-clared out, with $300 added; the second to receive $125 out of the stakes. Three-quarters of a mile.
L. A. Ehlers names c b c Ciltonelan, by Alarm, dam Atalanisist, 93 lbs (Riley?) ............................. 1
Dwyer Brothers name c b g Wandering, by Wanderer, dam Ringlet, 98 lbs (Sheridan) ........................ 2
P. H. Ryan names c b f Adalgisa, by Count D'Orsay, dam Adacinda, 95 lbs ................................. 3
D. D. Withers name b c Buckstone, by Stonehenge, dam Mary Stone? lbs. 103 lbs (Evans) ...................... 4
J. E. Kelly names b c Carlyle, by Ill Used, dam Circassian, 95 lbs (Brennan) ........................ 5
E. J. Baldwin name c b c Grismer, by Grinstead, dam Jennie D, 95 lbs (M. Donahue) ...................... 6
Time—1:20½.

Buckstone was the favorite. The youngsters had a capital start after a few break-aways, Carlyle leading, Circassian sec-ond, Wandering third, Adalgisa fourth, Grismer fifth, Buck-stone sixth. When they came to the foot of the bluff Wan-dering led by a head, Carlyle second, Circassian third, Adal-gisa fourth, Grismer fifth, Buckstone sixth. Wandering led out of eight around the hill by a head, Carlyle second, a length in front of Circassian, Adalgisa fourth, Buckstone fifth, Grismer sixth, all lapped one on the other. When the youngsters came in view on the lower turn Wandering was leading by a length, Buckstone second, a head in advance of Carlyle, Adalgisa fourth, Circassian fifth, Grismer sixth. When they passed the three-quarter pole Wandering and Buckstone were parallel, Circassian third, Adalgisa fourth, Carlyle fifth, Grismer sixth. A fine run up the homestretch and Circassian won the race by a length, Wandering second, half a length in fro t of Adalgisa, Buckstone fourth, Carlyle fifth, Grismer sixth. Time, 1:20½.

THIRD RACE.

Handicap sweepstakes of $25 each, and only $5 if declared out, with $300 added; the second to receive $125 out of the stakes. One mile and an eighth.
E. J Baldwin names b m Clara D, by Glenelg, dam The Nun, aged, 99 lbs. (M. Donahue) ......................... 1
Pierson s Stable names b g Duke of Montalban, by King Alfonso, dam Magenta, 4 years old, 98 lbs (Riley) ............ 2
C. Boyle names b c Springfield, by Bonnie Scotland, dam Botzquet, 4 years old, 108 lbs. (Blaylock) ................ 3
Graham Brothers name c b Brunswick, by Barney Williams, dam Maud Lynn, 8 years old, 104 lbs. (Evans) ............ 4
Dwyer Brothers name b b g Carley B, by Virgil, dam Ladylike, 3 years old, 110 lbs. (J. McLaughlin) ................. 5
Appleby & Johnson name b c Jack of Hearts, by Ill Used, dam Nel-lie James, 4 years old, 114 lbs. (Evans) ............... 6
F. Robinson names b g Little Fred, by Reform, dam Yorkshire Lass, 4 years old, 103 lbs. (Barbee) ................. 7
D. D. Withers name c b g Duplex, by King Ernest, or Macaroon, dam Echo, 3 years old, 94 lbs. (Sheridan) ............... 8
Rockaway Stable names b g Rochester, by Vauxhall, dam Heather-bell, 6 years old, 90 lbs. (Purcell) ............... 9
Time—2:01.

Carley B was the favorite, Jack of Hearts second choice. Duplex was first away, Brunswick second, Carley B third, the others close up. When the horses passed the judges' stand Clara D was leading by a head, Brunswick second, Du-plex third, Carley B fourth, Little Fred fifth, Springfield sixth, Jack of Hearts seventh, Duke of Montalban eighth, Rochester ninth. Clara D drew clear of the others on the upper turn, and at the quarter pole she led a length and a half, Brunswick second, a length and a half in front of Car-ley B, he half a length in advance of Duke of Montalban, Little Fred fifth, Springfield sixth, Jack of Hearts seventh, Rochester eighth, Duplex ninth. Clara D came down to the foot of the bluff leading two lengths, Brunswick second, two lengths in front of Duke of Montalban, Carley B fourth, Little Fred fifth, Jack of Hearts sixth, the others as before noted. Clara D led around the hill out of eight by two lengths, and when she came in view on the lower turn she still had that advantage, with Brunswick second, Little Fred third, Carley B fourth, Springfield fifth, the others close up in a bunch. Clara D led a length at the three-quarter pole, Brunswick second, Little Fred third, the others still bunched. A fine run up the homestretch and Clara D won the race by a length, Duke of Montalban second, a head in front of Springfield third, the latter a neck in advance of Brunswick, Carley B fifth, Jack of Hearts sixth, Little Fred seventh, Rochester eighth, Duplex ninth. Time 2:01.

FIFTH RACE.

Handicap sweepstakes of $50 each, and only $10 if declared, with $300 added; the second to receive $300 out of the stakes. One mile and three-quarters.
E. J. McKinnelI name b c Genelel Monroe, by Tom Bowling, dam Minnie T. Morgan, 4 years old, 112 lbs. (Blaylock) ............ 1
F. Gebbard names b c Eole, by Eolus, dam War Song, 4 years old, 126 lbs. (Barbee) ......................... 2

T. Winter names b f Duchess of Norfolk, by Norfolk, dam Marian, 3 years old, 100 lbs. (M. Donahue) ...................... 3
F. Morris names b c Priam, by Prophet, dam Repartime, 4 years old, 108 lbs. (Evans) ....................... 4
O. B. Bryson names b g Bushwhacker, by Bonnie Scotland, dam Annie Bush, aged, 108 lbs. (J. McLaughlin) ................... 5
R. Roche names b c Hilarity, by Bonnie Scotland, dam Belliah, 3 years old, 85 lbs. (Sheridan) ...................... 6
M. S. Berger names c b f Elkhorn Lass, by Glenelg, dam Flaxwork, 3 years old, 90 lbs. (Riley) ...................... 7
Time—3:15.

Eole was the favorite. The horses had a capital start, Hi-larity leading a trifle, Eole second, Duchess of Norfolk third, Priam fourth, the others close up. When they reached the foot of the bluff Priam had his head in front, Hilarity sec-ond, Eole third, Duchess of Norfolk fourth, Bushwhacker fifth, General Monroe sixth, Elkhorn Lass seventh. Going out of sight around the hill Hilarity was leading, Priam sec-ond, General Monroe third, Bushwhacker fourth, Duchess of Norfolk fifth, Eole sixth, Bushwhacker seventh. When the horses appeared in view on the lower turn Bushwhacker was in the lead, Priam second, Eole third, Elkhorn Lass fourth—these four very close together. Bushwhacker was first at the three-quarter pole, led up the quarter stretch and passed the judges' stand a head in front of Priam second, Eole third, Duchess of Norfolk fourth, Hilarity fifth, Gen-eral Monroe sixth, Elkhorn Lass seventh, all in a bunch. Going around the upper turn Priam passed Bushwhacker and led by a head at the quarter pole, Eole second, Duchess of Norfolk third, General Monroe fourth, Bushwhacker fifth, the others struggling on close up. Coming down the hill, as they passed the foot of the bluff Priam led one length, Gen-eral Monroe second, a length ahead of Eole, he a length in front of Duchess of Norfolk, Bushwhacker fifth, Hilarity sixth, Elkhorn Lass seventh. Priam, General Monroe, Eole and Duchess of Norfolk passed out of sight around the hill half a length apart in the order given, with the others some-what spread out. When the horses appeared in view on the lower turn General Monroe had a neck the best of it, with Priam second, the latter a length in front of Duchess of Nor-folk, she a head in advance of Eole, fourth, Bushwhacker fifth, Hilarity sixth, Elkhorn Lass seventh. As the horses passed the three-quarter pole General Monroe was leading, Eole second, Priam third, Duchess of Norfolk fourth, the others beaten and falling back. Getting into the home stretch the race was highly exciting. General Monroe came on in front of Eole, and finished a winner by three-quarters of a length, Eole four lengths ahead of Duchess of Norfolk, third, she four lengths ahead of Priam, Bushwhacker fifth, Hilar-ity sixth, Elkhorn Lass seventh. Time, 3:15.

## Lady Thorne's Mysterious Mile.

We presume our readers have all heard of that very pri-vate trial in the year 1870, when Mace drove Lady Thorne a ghostly mile in the gray of the morning, and only two others, John L. Doty and Wm. H. Saunders, timed the mare. In regard to this trial her driver said: "I never saw Lady Thorne trot a full mile at her best but once, and there are two other men living beside myself who can tell how fast that was. But I shall never tell, and it is probable that they will not. It was so fast that it would not be credited by the pub-lic, and so we agreed that we would never mention the time. But I will say this much: it was a faster gait for the whole mile than I ever saw kept up by any other horse for a single quarter." For a round dozen of years did Dan Mace main-tain his determination to "never tell," but in an unguarded moment, a short time ago, out popped the secret. On the occasion to which we refer Dan had become much interested in conversation with a gentleman about that year, 1870, when Lady Thorne was to meet Goldsmith Maid at Buffalo. She had beaten the Maid whenever they had contended on East-ern tracks that year, and it is probable the bay mare was quite confident of a victory at Buffalo. Dan, after the trial referred to, felt abundant confidence himself, and he related on this recent occasion how he met Mr. Smith, the owner of the Maid, and told him he would beat her.
"But," said Mr. Smith, "we can trot three heats better than 2:20."
"So can I," said Dan.
"We can trot three heats better than 2:18. "
"So can I," said Dan.
"We can trot three heats better than 2:16. "
"So can I," said Dan.
The gentleman to whom Mace related the foregoing con-versation casually asked: "Why, Dan, how fast did you ever drive Thorne?"
Dan impulsively replied: "I drove her a mile just as fast as a mile was ever trotted in public, and the last half in 1:05. "
The secret of a decade was now more fully out. Lady Thorne trotted a trial in 1870 in 2:09, last half in 1:05, timed by two of the most experienced men on the turf, both still in the flesh, and driven by a man who now lacks only two years of his threescore.—*Wilkes' Spirit of the Times.*

## The Boy With a Nag That Can Trot.

"So, Christopher, you have bought a horse," observed Mr. Gandy, as he pleasantly surveyed his son. "That business are you going into? "
"Business—er—o—business; well, my dear sir, the fact is, I have been tumbling on to something that can trot."
"You shouldn't have done it, Christopher," said the old gentleman kindly; "you are not young enough; your bones are set, and you are too fat. You can never be an emperor of the arena, Christopher. Do not tumble or engage in any gymnastics on the animal again."
"Of course, I only meant that I have been lucky enough to discover something with speed, and have picked it up for a mere song."
"A colt?"
"Well, no, emphatically; but her pedigree is a poem—dam Mme. Spavin, sire Signor Botts; own sister to Blind Staggers and Sougrease."
"You will soon do it," mused the old gentleman, as a soft light played about his eyes; "you will soon be there, Christopher. There are a great many of you scattered through the country; you blossom at every rural crossing, my boy. You will soon pose on a contrivance like a hay rake with the teeth out you will round your shoulders to give an artistic outline to a spotted shirt with baggy sleeves nd a balloony back, and as you sit on your vehicle by a pump you will look pensively out from under a cap peak built like the bill of a sugar scoop, and as you tilt your cigar ash to the level of your right eye, and keep silently fanning the tail of your animal with a two foot whip, you will lose yourself in the enchantment of turf reverie. The by standers may never know that you cannot distinguish the points of a mare from those of a mermaid, Christopher, just as long as you are oblivious to this knowledge, I see no rea-son why you should not enjoy your soothing reflections.—*Rochester Express.*

## Exhibition of Trotting by Mr. Work's Team.

There has been so much gossip of late at Delmonico's and the clubs about the great performance which was to be expected of Mr. Work's double team in a display of speed at the Fleetwood track on Thursday afternoon that many amateurs were induced to visit the place yesterday with high expectations. Fortunately the day and the track were fine for a fast performance. Everything was in favor of the horses, as is shown by the wonderful speed made by Governor Stanford's three-year-old of 2:27½. At 4 o'clock, the appointed time, Mr. Mace was on the ground in apple-pie order with Mr. Work's team, Edward and Swiveller, attended by a runner to spur them to their utmost. Mr. Work and his friends were loud in their talk of the great things that were to be done, and his men felt sure that they were to witch the world with the noblest trotting performance ever achieved. Mr. W. H. Vanderbilt was there, looking on no doubt in great anxiety and alarm as to the event. But the upshot showed that nothing more is to be expected of horses or of men than the best they can do. Driven by Mace, the greatest double-team driver alive, Edward and Swiveller trotted their mile, according to the judges, in 2:20½. Mr. Work's friends were sadly disappointed. The horses and their driver did their utmost, but they were asked to beat a record of 2.16½, which good judges before the experiment was made had pronounced to be beyond their capacity. There was a large attendance and the colts all made a fine show.—*World.*

## Foxhall's Yearling Sister.

"Rapier," in the *Illustrated Sporting and Dramatic News*, says of Foxhall's sister: "One of the handsomest yearlings in training—not one of the biggest, but one of the best shaped—is certainly the yearling sister to Foxhall. 'Handsome is, etc.' The gallant little filly has, of course, had no opportunity of showing her powers of speed as yet and the only capacity she has exhibited is as a mouser! Her distinguished brother, as I reported after a visit some time since to Mr. William Day's, had adopted—or had been adopted by—a couple of kittens. His little sister kills her own mice, and rats as well. Two of the latter were recently found slain in her manger, and the little cannibal is reported to have killed and eaten a mouse! This is very singular, and a glance at her kind and intelligent head does not support the idea of her being ignorant of the fact that fillies are not carnivorous. If make and shape go for anything, anyhow, Foxhall's sister will be distinguished as a racer and not as a slayer of rats and mice, and such small deer."

## Gate Money Race Courses in England.

Quite a number of gate money race courses have been and are being constructed in England, and many there be who are very strongly opposed to the invention. Their greatest objection appears to be that the number of race-horses is even now insufficient to provide good fields at the present meetings and that if additional ones are brought forward something else than thoroughbreds will have to be pressed into service. The Jockey Club is called upon to interfere and the prophecy is made that the day is not far distant when it will have to take decided steps on the gate money question. A very wise man once observed that it took a quarter of a century to make the British public understand the merits of any discussion going on, so that according to very high English turf authority it will be necessary for a move to be made long before the general public have made up their minds on the subject.

EQUESTRIENNES.—The equestrienne match came off at the Agricultural Park, Salinas, last Tuesday forenoon, seven ladies contesting for the prizes, which were awarded as follows:

First Prize—Miss Emma Connelly, a silver water pitcher and cup.
Second Prize—Miss Jessie Sherwood, silver cake basket.
Third Prize—Miss Mary Woolridge, silver jewel case.
Fourth Prize—Miss Rosa Sherwood, silver butter dish.
Fifth Prize—Miss M. Gilkey, silver card receiver.
Sixth Prize—Miss R. C. Ayers, pair silver napkin rings.
Miss Jennie Williams was awarded a special prize of $10.

John Hibberd of Bethnal Green, London, attempted the feat of walking twenty-one miles in three hours at the Prince of Wales Grounds, Bow, on September 18. The weather was all that could be desired for a task of the kind, as there was scarcely a breath of wind stirring and, fortunately for the pedestrian, kept so during the match. On getting the signal to go he started at a fair pace, and covered the first couple of miles in 15:23, four miles in 31:12, six miles in 47:35, and seven miles and a half, less fifty yards, in the first hour. Even money was now offered on the man. Eight miles occupied 1:4:18; ten miles, 1:21:23; twelve miles, 1:38:22; fourteen miles, 1:55:44, and at the expiration of the second hour had traversed fourteen miles and a half, less fifty-five yards, going in the fairest possible manner, G. Tag, of Haggerstone, occasionally relieving Gregory for a lap or two in taking him along. Odds were now offered on the pedestrian, but no one seemed inclined to bet on the result. Sixteen miles were completed in 2:13:14, eighteen miles in 2:31:32, twenty miles in 2:50:11, and the full distance, twenty-one miles, in 2:59:20, Hibberd thus winning by forty seconds.

The race for the Great Eastern Railway Handicap, won by Mr. Lorillard's Aranza, 91 lbs., was a run away affair. After the start had been delayed some minutes by the vagaries of Adrastus, who broke away and galloped the entire course, Aranza, on the left, made the running from War Horn and Mazurka, most prominent of the others being Hornpipe, Dunmore, Atalanta and Reputation. They ran thus until half-way down Bushes Hill, when Hornpipe took second place, but she could never get on terms with Aranza, who won easily by half a dozen lengths; War Horn was a bad third. Mazurka was fourth, Dunmore, Atalanta and Fetterless next, and Adrastus last throughout. Value of the stakes £502. Aranza was ridden by E. Martin, who last year won on John Ridd. Rain fell heavily while the race was being run, and Loates, who rode War Horn, was two pounds over weight when he returned to the scale, but as such a contingency is provided for by Rule 31, the horse retained third place.

The brown pacing mare Ouida, whose death was noted last week, was for several years on the turf and had a record of 2:25½. She was engaged in the last race at the Stockton meeting, which she won, and at its finish was retired to the brood farm of her owner, Mr. Valensin. She died three days afterward. She had been bred to Buccaneer, and a post mortem revealed that she was in foal with a horse colt.

Mr. Goldsmith is driving Romero and Director together on the road and says they go like one horse. Romero has entirely recovered from the epizootic and the reports are that he shows a wonderful flight of speed when allowed to have his head.

## Races at Yreka.

The horsemen congregated at the Yreka track became a little impatient at the repeated postponements made necessary by incessant rains, and amused themselves by getting up some independent races which are epitomized in the following summaries:

Oct. 7.—Running dash of half a mile for citizen's purse of $50, entrance $5 added, first horse to obtain three-fourths of money, and second horse one-fourth.

| | |
|---|---|
| G. W. Rucker's Snip | 1 |
| Jas. Muse's Hancock | 2 |
| S. S. Ford's Ida Hammond | 3 |
| E. Flitner's sorrel Jim | 4 |

Time 53.

Track very heavy.

Oct. 9.—Society's purse of $80, for running race, entrance $5 added. First horse to first quarter, $10; first horse to second quarter, $15; first horse to third quarter, $20; first horse out a mile, $30.

| | |
|---|---|
| Jas. Muse's Hancock | 1 |
| S. S. Ford's Ida Hammond | 2 |
| G. W. Rucker's Brick Pomeroy | 3 |
| E. Flitner's Nellie Mack | 4 |
| C. Tolman's Dick | 5 |

Time 1:53½.

Hancock won at all quarters.

On Monday the fair was inaugurated, and the storm having cleared away and a general sunshine put the tracks in good condition, the *Journal* notes that there were more horses quartered at the fair grounds than had been seen at any previous fair, and had not the continued storms and repeated postponements of the exhibition had a tendency to discourage the attendance, 1882 would have been the most successful fair ever seen in the Northern tier. As it was it compared favorably with any of the preceding. The turf events up to the time of our going to press were as follows:

Oct. 16, 1882.—Trotting, free for all; 3 in 5; purse $500. First horse receives $400; second horse, $100. Entrance 10 per cent. of purse; 5 to enter, 3 to start.

| | | | |
|---|---|---|---|
| Jay Beach's b s Altamont by Almont | 1 | 1 | 1 |
| Jas. Sutherland's b m Nellie | 2 | 2 | 2 |
| Geo. Stephenson's ch g Professor | dist. | | |

Time—2:40½, 2:40½, 2:37½.

Same day—Running, dash of a mile and a half, free for all horses owned in the district; purse $100; entrance, $5 added.

| | |
|---|---|
| Jas. Muse's Hancock | 1 |

Harry B, Ida Hammond, Brick Pomeroy and Wilson also ran.

Time—2:48½

Oct. 17.—Trotting, free for all untried horses owned in the District; 2 in 3; purse, $75; entrance, $5, added.

| | |
|---|---|
| Wm. Eckheart's b s Curtis | 1 |
| Jay Beach's Favorite | dist. |
| J. Tierney's May D. | dist. |
| Ned O'Niel's Ned | dist. |

Time—3:26½

Same day—Running, half mile and repeat; free for all horses owned in the District; purse; $75; entrance, $5, added.

| | | |
|---|---|---|
| Jas. Muse's b g Up and Up | 1 | 1 |
| Geo. Rucker's Snip | 2 | 2 |
| —— Blaine's Harry B | 3 | 3 |

Time—52½, 52½.

Same day—Trotting, free for all three-year-olds and under, owned in the District; 2 in 3; purse, $75, entrance, $5, added.

| | | |
|---|---|---|
| J. Beach's Xylophone | 1 | 1 |
| J. McDonald's Sleepy Kate | 2 | dist. |

Time—3:19½, 2:57.

Oct. 18.—Trotting, free for all in the District; 3 in 5; purse $100, and entrance, $5, added.

| | | | | |
|---|---|---|---|---|
| J. Beach's b f Maggie Arnold by Almont—Alice Drake | 2 | 1 | 1 | 1 |
| Jas. Sutherland's b m Nellie | 1 | 2 | 2 | 2 |

Time—2:46½, 2:36½, 2:35, 2:37½.

Same day—Running, dash of three-quarters of a mile.

| | |
|---|---|
| A. D. Richard's Fred Wickine | 1 |
| Jas. Muse's b g Flying Gelding | 2 |
| S. Wilson's Jennie H. | 3 |

Time—1:20½.

Oct. 19.—Running, free for all mile heats.

| | | | |
|---|---|---|---|
| H. Blains Barry B. | 2 | 1 | 1 |
| Jas. Muse's Hancock | 1 | 2 | d. |
| Jas. Greggs Charlie | dist. | | |

Time—1:50½.

Same day—Trotting free for all horses that have never beaten three minutes.

| | |
|---|---|
| J. Tiernans Tyler | 1 |
| Jas. Sutherland Sorrel Dick | dist. |

Time—2:57.

## Trotting at Melbourne.

We take the subjoined account of trotting on the new course of the Victoria Trotting Club from the *Australasian:*

With only a small programme before the public it could hardly be expected that there would be a large attendance at Elsternwick park on Saturday. However, some 400 or 500 persons found their way to the newly-formed track, which was very heavy from recent rains, and consequently slow time was prophesied. There was a fair sprinkling of ladies in the grand stand, and though the sport was pronounced slow, the fair sex appeared to enjoy the outing on so fine a day. A start was made with the Maiden Trot, which attracted seven to the post, Leithamstead being most fancied, and though he did not occupy a prominent position for the first part of the journey, he came through in the last quarter and won cleverly, and repeating the performance in the next heat, he won the stake. The winner is by Panic's son Alarm, who is said to be sire of several promising trotters. Seven numbers went up for the three-minute class trot, and as Contractor was in capital form he was installed first favorite. The American quickly showed his superiority by drawing away from his opponents, and though he broke badly between the half-mile and three-quarter post, he soon settled down into a beautiful swinging gait, and distanced every thing but Native Cat, who was some sixty yards off. The time for the heat was 2:48½, and considering that the track must have been some 10 or 12 seconds slow, this was a very meritorious performance. Of course as all but Native Cat had been distanced by Contractor, only the two started for the second heat, which was an easy thing for the American, who bowled along in fine style and without a skip or a jump trotted the mile in 2:54, only jogging home from the three-quarter pole. Repeating the performance in the third heat Contractor won the purse. As this brought the card to a very early close, it was decided to give a purse of 10 sovs. for the beaten lot, and for this three started. Yendon showed most speed for the first half mile, but he broke badly when Conquering Hero got on terms with him, and then the latter accomplished an easy victory. Mulholland, who drove Yendon in the three-minute class, was fined £5 for shouting loudly as the horses were on the back stretch, and the owner of Prince was fined £2 for not scratching in time. The following are the results:

MAIDEN TROT

Of 40 sovs. Mile heats. Best two in three.

| | | |
|---|---|---|
| Mr. Jas. Scoble names g g Leithamstead, 6 years, by Alarm. (Upjohn) | 1 | 1 |
| Mr. F. English names br g Neptune, aged, (P. J. Brady) | 2 | 2 |

Time—3:20, 3:16½.

THREE-MINUTE CLASS.

Purse of 70 sovs. Mile heats. Best three in five.

| | | | |
|---|---|---|---|
| Mr. J. J. Miller names b h Contractor, aged, by Ajax. (H. L. Shepherd) | 1 | 1 | 1 |
| Mr. F. C. Goyder names g g Native Cat, aged. (D. Collins) | 2 | 2 | 2 |
| Mr. J. A. Roberts names b g Yendon, aged. (Mulholland) | dist. | | |
| Mr. J. Munday names b g Conquering Hero, aged. (Brady) | dist. | | |
| Mr. P. J. Boddy names bl m Black Diamond, aged. (E. Giles) | dist. | | |
| Mr. J. J. Miller names b m Fright, 5 years. (M. Griffen) | dist. | | |

Time—2:48½, 2:54, 2:55½.

TWO-MILE FLUTTER

Of 10 sovs. For maidens and distanced horses.

| | |
|---|---|
| Mr. J. Munday names b g Conquering Hero, aged, by Daniel Boone. (Brady) | 1 |
| Mr. J. A. Roberts names b h Yendon, aged. (Mulholland) | |
| Mr. J. J. Miller names b m Fright, 5 years. (Shepherd) | |

Time—5:55½.

## Monterey District Fair.

The fair of the Monterey District Association closed at Salinas last Tuesday, having commenced on the preceding Thursday. The weather was unfavorable throughout and the races and other exercises were held, as it were, between showers. Under such climatic conditions the attendance was of course, comparatively small. The number of horses on exhibition was unusual and showed very decided progress in that direction; of cattle, sheep and hogs the exhibition was small but the quality and breeding of the animals shown were of a superior order.

RESUME OF THE RACING.

MONTEREY DISTRICT FAIR, SALINAS, October 5th, 1882.—Running novelty race of one mile and a quarter, purse $300, horse first to first quarter, $50; first half, $50; first three-quarter, $50; first mile, $50, mile and a quarter, $100.

| | |
|---|---|
| P. J. Shafter names b h Haddington | 1 |

C. H. Waters' Laliah Cooler, Duncan's Quien Sabe, Innes' Stumbling Dick, C. H. Waters' Bay Charley and J. Handley's Brown Lucy also ran. Laliah Cooler won the first quarter in 25½, Haddington winning all other quarters and the race.

Time—2:16½.

Same day—Trotting, free for all horses owned in the district.

| | | | | |
|---|---|---|---|---|
| S. K. Trefry names b g Bay Frank | 1 | 2 | 1 | 1 |
| D. W. Evans names b g Pajaro Chief | 5 | 1 | 2 | 2 |

Wm. Pack's b g Leland Stanford, Z. Hebert's g m Maggie Vorhees and L. Anzer's g m Ella P also trotted but their placing is not given.

Time—3:04, 2:54½, 2:57½, 2:49½, —.

October 6th—Trotting for all horses owned in the district, purse $300 three monies

| | | | |
|---|---|---|---|
| James Delaney names b g Gabilan Joe | 1 | 1 | 1 |
| R. D. Brown's names s g Sorrel Frank | 2 | 2 | 2 |
| E. J. Swift names blk m Nell Briody | 3 | 3 | 3 |
| J. D. Carr names b s Gen. Lee | 4 | dist. | |

Time—2:40½, 2:39½, 2:40½.

Same day—Running, free for all, half a mile.

| | |
|---|---|
| J. Handley names b m Brown Lucy | 1 |
| C. H. Waters names b g Bay Charley | 2 |
| W. Cavanaugh names ch m Fanny | 3 |
| Alf Innes names g g Trouble | 4 |
| R. B. Cockrill names b s Bob | 5 |

Time 52½.

October 9th—Trotting free for all three-year olds owned in the district.

| | | | | | |
|---|---|---|---|---|---|
| G. Fancher names b g Eddy | 2 | 2 | 1 | 1 | 1 |
| H. Tracy names g m Maggie | 1 | 1 | 2 | 2 | 2 |

C. Rodriguez's ch m Queen Bee, Z. Hebert's b m Flora Carr and H. Falkenburg's ch g Bluster also trotted but their placing was not reported.

Time—3:26, 3:16, 3:09, 3:12½.

Same day—Trotting, free for all stallions owned in the district.

| | |
|---|---|
| J. G. Sanchez names b s Billy Matthews | 1 |
| H. Tracy names Carr's Mambrino | dist. |
| J. D. Carr names b s Gen. Lee | dr. |

Time—2:57½.

Same day—Trotting, for all two-year-olds owned in the district.

| | | |
|---|---|---|
| J. A. Heard names b s Billy Donathan | 1 | 1 |
| Z. Hebert names b g Tommy | 2 | 2 |

No time given.

On the 10th there was a race for District double teams which was trotted in the rain. As our report contains neither the placing of the teams nor the time of the heats it is useless for either the purposes of record or information and we omit it.

**Stock Exhibits and Premiums.**

Roadsters, best stallions 4 years old and over, J. D. Carr enters Carr's Mambrino, P. E. G. Anzar enters Splann. Premium to Carr's Mambrino, $20.

Best mare 4 years old and over, P. E. G. Anzar enters Tilla T, which receives premium, $10.

Best mare 4 years old, J. D. Carr enters Sweetness. Premium awarded, $5.

Horses for all purposes, stallions 4 years old and over, M. Wolters enters Luceonia, J. D. Carr enters Gen, Lee, Jas. Delaney enters Tom Vernon, Chas. Luce enters Alisal Chief. R. Corey enters Vermont, Jr., Chrisman & Franks enter Patchen George. Vermont Jr., takes the premium, $20.

Best stallion 3 years old, Jno, Brown enters Commodore, J. R. Hebbron enters St. George, R. Corey enters Billy. Premium to St. George, $15.

Best stallion 2 years old, Hiram Corey enters Clarence King, P. E. G. Anzer enters Billy Donathan. Premium to Clarence King, $10.

Best stallion 1 year old, J. D. Carr enters Busted, C. Luce enters Star of the West, Premium to Busted, $7.50.

Best sucking colts, J. D. Carr enters one colt, John Sexton enters Billy, J. B. Iverson enters Starr, H. Corey enters one colt, E. W. Cox enters one colt. Premium to Iverson's colt, $5.

Best gelding 3 years and over, J. D. Carr enters Trouble and Gen. Johnson, D. A. Evans enters Pajaro Chief. Premium to Gen. Johnson, $15

Best mare 4 years old and over, George McIntyre enters Nell, J. B. Iverson enters Lizzie, J. D. Carr enters Clara. Premium to Clara, $15,

Best mare 2 years old, J. D. Carr enters Mamie, Premium, $7 50

Best mare 1 year old, Jno. Sexton enters Belle. Premium, $5.

Best mare 4 years old and over, with colt, J. D. Carr enters Lady Merrill and colt, same enters Lady Grey Eagle and colt, Jno. Sexton enters Lucy and colt, same enters Julia and colt, Robt. Garside enters Mollie and colt, same enters Julia and colt, H. Corey enters Belle and colt, John Brown enters Jenny and colt. Premium to Jenny, $10.

Best mare 3 years old J. D. Carr enters Clara.

Draft horses, best stallion 3 years old and over, P. Conroy enters Frank the Plow Boy, Wm. Robson enters Prince Charlie, D. Hargens enters Prince. Premium to Prince Charlie.

Best stallion 2 years old, L. B. Wilmouth enters Pride. Premium, $10.

Best mare 3 years old, H. Corey enters Rosa. Premium, $10.

Best sucking colt, John Brown enters Favorite, John Sexton enters Billy, Robt. Garside enters Frank and John. Premium to Favorite, $5.

Carriage horses, used and owned by one man, J. D. Carr enters Mac and Joe, J. B. Iverson enters Orphan Boy and Frank. Premium to Mac and Joe, $10.

Best span of buggy horses, J. D. Carr enters Jackson and Lee, J. P. Sargent enters Lady May and Lady Washington, Wm. Gift enters Fly and Skip, T. F. Faw enters Jessie and Dick, Greg Sanchez enters Kate and Nellie. Premum to kson and Lee, $7 50.

est single buggy horse, J. D. Carr enters Jerry, P. Kil-n enters Sarpedon. Premium to Sarpedon, $5.

weepstakes, Best stallion with 4 or more of his colts, M. lters enters Lucionia and 4 of his colts, J. D. Carr enters nbrino with 4 colts, Chas. Luce enters Alisal Chief and lts. Premium to Lucionia, $20.

est mare with 4 or more colts, J. D. Carr enters Lady rrill and 5 colts. Premium, $20.

Best stallion of any age or breed, J. D. Carr enters Carr's mbrimo, same enters Gen. Lee, P. Conroy enters Frank Plow Boy, D. Hargens enters Prince, H. Corey enters rmont Jr. and Billy, P. E. G. Anzer enters Billy Dona-an, J. R. Hebbron enters St. George, H. Corey enters arence King. First premium to St. George, $15, second emium to Vermont Jr., $10.

Best mare of any age or breed, J. D. Carr enters Sweet-ss and Clara, H. Corey enters Belle, J. L. Kestar enters n Luis Maid. First premium to San Luis Maid, $15, cond premium to Clara, $10.

Best gelding of any age or breed, J. D. Carr enters Trouble, Kilburn enters Sarpedon, J. D. Carr enters Gen. Jackson, W. Evans enters Pajaro Chief. Premium to Pajaro ief, $10.

Best colt of any age or breed, R. Garside enters one colt, B. Iverson enters Star, Chas. Luce enters Star of the est. Premium to Star.

Cattle, best Jersey Bull, George Pomeroy enters Captain ck. Premium, $5.

Best grade bull, B. Hitchcock enters Jack, Phil Collins en-rs George Graves. Premium to Jack, $10.

Best graded cow 3 years old and over, Phil Collins enters dy Escolle, G. McIntyre enters Pet and Rose, Jas. Delaney ters Belle. Premium to Lady Escolle, $10.

Sheep, to all these sheep premiums were awarded. Merino, st ram, J. D. Carr enters Monarch, Jim and Chief.

Best ewe, J. D. Carr enters Beauty and Daisy.

Best 3 lamb rams, J. E. Carr enters three.

Best pen of not less than 5 lambs, J. D. Carr enters five,

Best family, of 2 rams, 2 ewes and lambs, J D. Carr enters mily.

Southdowns, J. D. Carr enters 1 ram, 1 ewe, 3 ram lambs, en of 5 ewe lambs.

Best ram for all purposes, J. D. Carr enters Monarch.

Best ewe for all purposes, J. D. Carr enters Daisy.

Swine, Parker's Duroc pigs took the premiums.

Best boar of any breed, Wm. M. R. Parker enters Jack, J. Hebbron enters Black Sam.

Best sow of any breed, W. M. R. Parker enters Sally.

Best pair of pigs under 6 months, W. M. R. Parker enters pair pigs.

Poultry, H. C. Tuttle exhibits 1 pair Black Spanish fowls, pair of Light Brahmas, 1 pair of Houdans, 1 pair of Brown eghorns, 1 pair of Plymouth Rocks, 1 pair of Toulouse eese, George Pomeroy exhibits 1 pair of White Leghorns, P. Nance exhibits 1 pair Plymouth Rocks, each of the bove received a premium.

### Hinda Rose in Kentucky.

We are indebted to the Lexington, Ky., *Live Stock Record* or the following account of the trot for the Lexington Stakes n the first day of the Kentucky Breeders' meeting, the 11th inst:

The heavy rain that fell on Thursday necessitated a post-ponement of the trots until Wednesday. A heavy rain fell again that night and to-day the track had dried sufficiently to make the going safe but not fast. The Lexington Stakes for two-year-olds brought seven to the post, with the California filly, Hinda Rose a big favorite. She lost the first heat by getting away badly, but won the second and third in good style.

First heat—Early Dawn in the lead, Fugue second, Lexington Wilkes third, followed by Stuart, Wilkes Boy, Lizzie Wilkes and Hinda Rose, the later pacing. Fugue took the lead on the turn, was never headed, and won easily by four lengths; Hinda Rose who got squared before reaching the quarter and trotted fast was second, Wilkes Boy third, Early Dawn fourth, Lizzie Wilkes fifth, Stuart and Lexington Wilkes distanced. Quarter 40½, half 1:16¾, three-quarters, 1:55¼, heat 2:36¾.

Second heat—Fugue in the lead, Hinda Rose second, Early Dawn third, Wilkes Boy fourth, Lizzie Wilkes fifth. Fugue broke at the quarter, Hinda Rose taking the lead, Fugue second, they trotted in this order to the three-quarter where Fugue broke and again within the distance, Hinda Rose winning the heat by six lengths, Fugue second, two lengths in front of Wilkes Boy, third, Lizzie Wilkes fourth, Early Dawn fifth; the three latter were afterwards declared distanced for running. Quarter 38¾, half 1:15½, three-quarters 1:52¾, mile 2:32.

Third heat, Hinda Rose in the lead, was never headed, Fugue lay at her wheel to well within the distance when she broke, Hinda Rose winning by six lengths, Fugue second. Quarter 39, half 1:16, three quarters 1:54½, heat 2:32.

SUMMARY.

Kentucky Trotting Horse Breeders' Association. First day, October 11, 1882—First trot, Lexington Stakes for two-year-olds, $50 each, half forfeit, and $10 declaration if made on or before June 1, 1882; $100 added; two-thirds of the whole stake to the first horse; two-thirds of the remainder to second; the balance to the third. Mile heats. Eighty-five nominations, thirty-six of whom have declared. Value, $1,835.

| | | | |
|---|---|---|---|
| Palo Alto Stud names br f Hinda Rose, by Electioneer, dam Beautiful Bells, by The Moor | 2 | 1 | 1 |
| H. O. McDowell names b f Fugue, by King Rede, dam Fuga, by Geo. Wilkes | 1 | 2 | 2 |
| T. Anglin names br c Wilkes' Boy, by Geo. Wilkes, dam Mambrino Patchen | 3 | dis | |
| L. E. Simmon names b f Early Dawn, by George Wilkes, dam by Mambrino Star | 4 | dis | |
| J. T. Shackleford names b f Lizzie Wilkes, by George Wilkes, dam Laura, by Joe Hooker | 5 | dis | |
| Dr. S. Pierce names b c Lexington Wilkes, by George Wilkes, dam Jennie Anderson, by American Clay | dis | | |
| J. T. McMillan names b c Stuart, by Strathmore, dam by Almont | dis | | |

Time—2:36¾, 2:32, 2:32.

Betting, Hinda Rose, $70; Fugue, $45; field, $12.
Second heat, Hinda Rose, $50; field, $40.
Third heat, no betting.

### The Fair at Los Angeles.

The Los Angeles fair opened last Tuesday under favorable conditions notwithstanding the frequent rains and vexatious delays caused thereby. The details of the exhibition will receive extended notice next week. The number of horses and cattle at the grounds is largely in excess of any previous fair and the whole is a pronounced success. Through the non-receipt of our own report we clip the following account of the first day's races from the Los Angeles *Herald* of Wednesday:

The first race was for the three-minute class, best three in five; purse $300. In the pools and on the ground Lady Washington was a prime favorite, selling at two to one against Don Carlos, and finally two to one against the field. The first heat was started at half-past two, all four going out well together, with Lady Washington in the lead; Don Carlos, Hunter and Hattie Johnson in the order named. Lady Washington won the heat easily in 2:36½; Don Carlos a good second, Hunter third, and Hattie Johnson a bad fourth.

The second heat was neither as interesting nor as exciting as the first. Lady Washington won this heat in 2:39, followed closely by Don Carlos; Hattie Johnson third, Hunter fourth. For a time it looked as though Rose's Don Carlos was going to win the heat, as at the three-quarter pole the sorrel colt was at the heels of the pretty bay mare. She, however, made the string a couple of lengths ahead of Don Carlos.

The third heat was decidedly the most exciting of the day. The bell called back the horses twice on a false start, caused by Hattie Johnson's breaking, but they got off well in a bunch on the third trial, with Hunter leading, Lady Washington, Don Carlos and Hattie Johnson following. Before the quarter stretch had been passed the favorite took the head of the procession, with Hunter coming up behind her, Don Carlos and Hattie Johnson in the rear. After the half-mile had been made, however, Don Carlos shot past Hunter and made for Lady Washington, but the little bay would have none of it, and came in under the wire in beautiful style in 2:37½, with Don Carlos a short length behind, Hunter third, Hattie Johnson last. Don Carlos won second money and Hunter the $30 awarded to the third horse.

SUMMARY.

Los Angeles, Cal, Oct. 17th, 1882.—Trotting, for the three minute class.

| | | | |
|---|---|---|---|
| E. L. Mayberry's b m Lady Washington | 1 | 1 | 1 |
| L. J. Roses' Don Carlos | 2 | 2 | 2 |
| L. J. Felton's br g Hunter | 3 | 4 | 3 |
| L. H. Titus' b m Hattie Johnson | 4 | 3 | 4 |

Time—2:36½, 2:39; 2:37½.

The second race was running, dash of half a mile, open for all two-year-olds. Five entries had bern booked, but on the call ouly three starters put in an appearance. These were: Dottie Dimple, Ballona Girl and Aunt Betsy. Aunt Betsy sold high first choice, the pools going twenty to eight for her against the field. From the jump it was plain to see that neither of her competitors could touch her, and she came in under a light pull in 48¾ several lengths in the lead. The race was a beautiful one, as both Dottie Dimple and Ballona did their best to catch the fleet bay filly, but could not do it.

SUMMARY.

Same day—Running, half-mile dash for all two-year-olds.

| | |
|---|---|
| J. W. Adams' b f Aunt Betsy | 1 |
| Hill & Gries' blk f Dottie Dimple | 2 |
| A. Machador's br f Ballona Girl | 3 |

Time—48¾.

# BICYCLING.

Ladies' Costume.—Lady tricyclists should *look* as nearly as possible as though no alteration had been made in their ordinary dress; but for health and comfort's sake the stereotyped underclothing must be radically altered. The linen usually worn next the skin is fatal to health, slight perspiration making it so damp as to strike cold to the chest, back, and in fact every part of the body in contact with it. Male tricyclists and bycyclists have long found out that flannel must be worn next the skin at all seasons. Let the linen, then, be altogether banished from the tricyclist's wardrobe, the chemise being replaced by a soft, smooth flannel vest, and the nether limbs encased in flannel, cut exactly like a man's riding breeches, without any superfluous fullness to crease up. In really hot weather, for brisk riding, nothing else is required save the orthodox skirt, as described by "Dot," which can be weighted round the edge, as ladies' riding habits are, to secure immunity from the wind blowing the kilting about the ankles; but when the weather is cooler, or only gentle riding is being indulged in, the divided skirt can be added, under the outer skirt, and an extra flannel or wool vest if desired. The wool "jerseys" which were so fashionable are very handy things to carry in the luggage bag on a long ride, in case the weather becoming cooler towards evening should make an extra garment desirable; and when a mid-day stoppage is to be made a change of dry flannel in the bag will also be appreciated.—*Tricyclist.*

The *Cyclist* editor, who has been riding a tricycle for several months past in admiration of its comforts and capacities, and in the *Cyclist* has devoted more space to the eulogizing of the three-wheeler than of the bicycle, recently, just for a change, took out his forsaken 54-inch tandem, and now writes ecstatically of the pleasure and exhilaration derived from the higher speed obtained and advantages utilized, and many minor gains of biking over triking, and expresses the hope that he shall long continue faithful to his first love.

Will Rose writes from Central City, Neb., 25. September: "You may tell the boys of the wheel that I have reached this point on my journey from Danville, Ill., to San Francisco, Cal., and am in good health and spirits. Have found considerable sand in this part of the state, and lots of sand bars. I start from here to-day on across Nebraska. Expect to reach Cheyenne City, Wyoming, by next Saturday night. It is getting thinly populated in this part of the country, and lonesome work for one wheelman.

With the advent of pleasant weather again enthusiastic riders are making preparations for country tours. This calculation will be somewhat interfered with, however, by the action of the country road makers who have taken advantage of the time to give many of the roads a new coating of gravel, which will render them unridable for at least a month.

Quite a number of the riders of the Oakland and San Francisco clubs have taken to amateur photographing and may often be seen out with all the paraphenalia of the wandering artist perpetuating in tangible form many of the beautiful views to be met with on a day's run.

Roads and weather permitting, the Oakland Bicycle Club will take a run to San Leandre and vicinity on the 22d.

A gentleman from Sebastopol, Sonoma county, has captured a great curiosity in the shape of a quadruple fish with four heads and four tails, the body being grown together after the Siamese twin style. The fish is about seven inches long and four inches square, and belongs to the perch family. It is a voracious feeder.

It is calculated that about one hundred and fifty pounds of rabbits and quail are shipped daily from Santa Ana to Los Angeles, which is the largest game shipping port of the southern counties.

# POULTRY.

## Table Poultry.

The chicken question, says the *Home Farm*, presents an anomalous condition in this country. Wherever we go, north or south or anywhere, we find farmers, merchants, mechanics and sometimes even sailors breeding poultry, contending at fairs, advertising through the papers and raising a general hue and cry in behalf their pets, and on account of nothing on earth but the feathers. One would think from all the fuss that those people were breeding ostriches instead of chickens; that feathers were of more value in the market than flesh; that the American people preferred to wear feathers on their bodies rather than put flesh in their bodies. Nothing finds favor with these chicken fanciers except the so-called blooded or thoroughbred fowls that are simply bred to the feather. The size of the Brahma is sacrificed to the correctness of the tail and hackle markings. The Dorking has lost his breast in the struggle to preserve the flesh color of the legs and the uniformity of the feather markings. How far this craze has gone in England we are not informed, but we know some of the best table fowls known to the trade were originated there.

In France not only are breeds of fine table fowls originated, but according to all reports they are still bred with an eye singly to table qualities; and not only this, but methods of feeding to the end of quick maturity, economy of flesh production and perfection of flesh quality are closely practiced and experimented with. The French seem to understand this question as a practical one, and go at it in a way to make fowls not only a pleasure to breed, but a profit to handle. Chicken food that is wasted by the ton in this country, as dead horses, stale bread, etc., is carefully husbanded and turned to the finest kind of chicken flesh in France. Our people are so fearfully squeamish about such things, that, while they can stand and see the hen eat worms and carrion at her own sweet will and chop her head off the next hour to put her in the pot, they will not hear of such a thing as feeding her carrion as a business. The lady who eats the oyster raw from the shell is horrified at the Italian who does the same with the snail.

It is a wonder to many people why Americans can succeed so well with fancy fowls, and yet meet with repeated and unvarying failure when they attempt to raise fowls for market. In one they succeed, with the other there seems to be no profit. It looks as though the American character was built upon too large a scale to make a profit with fowls unless he can get from $3 to $10 apiece for his cocks and hens. No one seems to be able to reduce this thing to a purely business basis. It has been our pleasure to examine the equipments of many farms where it was intended to raise poultry on a grand scale, and, generally, from the elaborate and costly fixtures, one would think the purpose was to raise children rather than chickens. It is very doubtful if a large establishment can ever be made a success from the start. Just as large oaks from little acorns grow, a large establishment must grow out of a small beginning that has developed a capacity in the owner for conducting a large business. We hope some day to see this, but not until the craze about color markings has somewhat subsided.

## Value of Pure Bred Fowls.

The editor of the *Poultry Monthly* says:

Our experience compels us to say there is no stock as productive as our thoroughbred; because they have been bred in accordance with a system, and with the object in view of producing qualities of great excellence. It matters not what branch of the poultry trade you begin with, whether you breed the fancy varieties for sale or exhibition, the heavier kind for the food market, or the medium size for their eggs alone.

Under the very best management, our pure bred invariably give better satisfaction and prove more remunerative than fowls not bred to any degree of excellence. But it is with this as with all kinds of stock, or engaging in enterprise or occupation, the interest and pleasure that is awakened by the first step in the right direction goes a great way to gain in much shorter time the experience necessary to success, which only could be gained through years of arduous labor and attention, if the wrong course were pursued in the beginning.

Poultry keeping can be made an auxiliary to other pursuits without infringing upon the time of the keeper, and will bring a quick and handsome return for the food and care given them. It costs no more to feed and keep a flock of improved fowls than it does the common sorts. It is a waste of time and money to breed from poor stock, and it is the poorest economy to buy poor trash, though represented to be as good as the best. Those who have turned their attention to breeding and keeping up the character and excellence of their fowl stock have satisfied themselves of the importance of keeping good birds, and know the higher the quality the better the results, and that they never will be, in our generation at least, a drug in the poultry market.

Poultry breeders do not seem to appreciate the great value of bones for their fowls, and but a limited few ever make use of them for this purpose. No matter whether the birds are confined or not, they are sure to be benefited by a moderate quantity of bones, though those which are kept in close confinement need them most. Nearly every family of any size have refuse bones enough from the kitchen to afford the poultry quite a treat from time to time, and when this is not the case, or when the supply runs short, enough can be procured each week from the nearest butcher at a very small price, many butchers being glad to give them away to get rid of them. These can be crushed by using a large stone and a heavy hammer, though there is now a very good and cheap mill made for the purpose—costing but $5 without legs and $7 with legs—which pays for itself several times over during the season, where large flocks of fowls are kept, as it not only grinds and crushes bones, but also oyster shells, corn, etc. The bones crush best when dry, and should be reduced to about the size of a small pea. They are put in small troughs or boxes, under cover, where the fowls can eat what they want and to suit their pleasure.—*Poultryman.*

## Answers to Correspondents.

Subscriber, San Francisco.—1. Lady Amanda beat Electra on two occasions. At Sacramento Sept. 25th, 1875, in a dash of a mile for all ages and at the Bay District course, San Francisco, Oct. 23d, 1875, in the Coleman handicap, mile heats.

2. Joe Hooker never had a career on the turf to describe. His temper was spoiled when he was a two-year-old and he never started in a race but once, the California Spirit of the Times Stake for three-year-olds at Sacramento Sept. 15th, 1875. In that race he was second in the first heat and distanced in the second. He was not trained afterward.

## HERD AND SWINE.

### Sanborn's Experience in Feeding.

The published details of the experiments of J. W. Sanborn, Superintendent of the College Farm at Hanover, N. H., now of the Agricultural College at Columbia, Missouri, contain interesting results, some of which we give our readers in condensed form on the present occasion.

The experiments in feeding calves present some facts which may be of some value to meat raisers. Two calves were taken, four and a half weeks old, both together weighing 283 pounds, and were fed twenty quarts of skimmed milk daily late in November. They gained in eighteen days thirty-nine pounds. Over eight quarts of milk were required for one pound in growth. For the next fourteen days a pound of mixed meal was added to the milk each day, and they gained sixty-three pounds, at a cost of 2.2 cents per pound. For the next fourteen days they had two pounds of meal and 4 pounds of hay added to the milk each day, and they gained fifty-nine pounds at a cost of 3 cents a pound. For the next fourteen days they had nearly the same feed, and gained seventy-one pounds at a cost 2.7 cents a pound. During the next fourteen days they gained sixty pounds on the same food, with some addition of hay, at a cost of 3.5 cents. Fourteen days later they had gained sixty-three pounds, with added meal and hay, at a cost per pound of 3.9 cents. The lesson taught by these results was that the older the meat, the more costly; but through the whole, although in winter, there was an actual profit, rating the meal at 1.4 cents a pound, the milk at four mills, and the hay $10 per ton. This was a single limited experience, but it shows the importance to farmers of knowing at what age of animals it is most profitable to feed or dispose of them. We reserve to the details of the above experiment that there was a slight increase in the amount of food given when the weight of animals had largely increased.

Other experiments were made, with those averaging 425 pounds each, to determine the probable amount of food animals would consume. They were found to require 3½ per cent. of their live weight daily in hay, the small amount of grain being estimated in hay. Ten pounds of hay were required for one pound of growth. Additional trials were made with two year steers, weighing from 1,000 to 1,100 pounds. An average of eight experiments, extending from 28 to 90 days, gave a consumption of 2.16 per cent. of their live weight daily, with an average gain of 0.85 of a pound. The important fact was determined that the older and larger the animal grows, the more food it requires to make a pound of growth.

Some valuable experiments were also made with roots as food. For growing cattle, carrots brought nothing, but they proved very much better for milk and butter than swedes or mangolds. The latter was found more than useless for milk cows, as compared with other food, while for growing animals they brought one dollar and seventy-five cents a ton, rating hay at ten dollars a ton. Prof. Sanborn allude to the old analytic methods of determining the value of foods, and these applied to carrots would show 1.36 of albuminoids. By the present method it is cut down to only 0.26. This fact bears rather hard on the infallibility of abstract scientific teaching.

Extended experiments were made with potatoes. The general conclusions reached indicated the great superiority of the products in quantity from large whole potatoes as seed. The average yield per acre for four seasons was, for large whole potatoes, 280 bushels per acre; for small whole potatoes, 182 bushels; from one eye to a hill, 66 bushels; two eyes to a hill, 134 bushels; three eyes, 154 bushels. The "seed ends" gave 152 bushels; stem ends, 132 bushels. The ground was evidently well adapted to potatoes, as the products show; but one essential part is not stated, namely, the dry or moist condition of the soil, or early or late planting. In the experiments which we have made with large and small seed, the difference in the size of the potatoes yielded was imperceptible, and it was only by weighing that a slight difference was found in favor of the large seed. But the soil was deep, moist and mellow. When planted late, and in a dry soil, the small potatoes scarcely grew at all. The large potatoes weighed from a fourth to half a pound; the small ones not half an ounce.

The results of the feeding of early and late cut hay to steers indicated the superior quality of that cut ten days after bloom to earlier cuttings. In 1879 timothy was cut at three different periods—before, during and after bloom—the later cut proving more abundant in growth and more efficacious as food for both steers and milch cows. In 1880 extended trials were made in feeding hay cut at two different periods. The early was cut two or three days before bloom; the late three weeks afterwards, or when the seeds were formed but not ripe—a difference of twenty-three days between. Cows fed upon the early hay ate about six per cent. more of it, and gave about six per cent. more of milk. But those fed on the early hay did not gain any, while those on the late hay gained in weight for the last two weeks twenty-seven pounds. There was a slight falling off in the milk of the late hay, but it gave the richest cream, and the animals ate less and gained in weight. These experiments on the whole do not appear to sustain the common opinion that hay cut very early is decidedly better than if cut while the seed is forming. There is another strong reason afforded by Prof. Sanborn's experiments against cutting very early, or when one-fourth of the heads were in bloom. Ten days later-cut hay weighed one-fifth more per acre in one experiment, and about one-fourth more in another instance, hay cut eight days before blooming weighed only two-thirds as much per acre as when cut while the seeds were formed, but yet small. These results, which were nearly the same at each repetition of the experiment, show a greater difference than those reported by Prof. Jordan, cited on page 566 of the current volume; but this difference would be increased by the weighing of the hay in Prof. Sanborn's experiment being deferred till the following spring, when all would be thoroughly cured.

Experiments of the character above mentioned must of course be repeated many times, to remove the chances for various temporary influences; but so far as these abundant trials made by Prof. S. go, they are a valuable contribution to well-defined agricultural knowledge, for which he should receive the thanks of the farming community.

Mrs. M. R. Pleasants offers as a special premium a pair of Angora kids. Value $50. To any lady in the State who makes the best exhibit of 20 pounds of extracted and 10 pounds of comb honey at the agricultural fair in Los Angeles.

The Sierra Bonita ranch in Graham county, Arizona, comprises 500 square miles. It is stocked with 8,000 head of cattle and 500 horses.

Analysis of green rye shows it to be nearly equal to clover for fodder, and better than grass in blossom.

### Notable Sale of Jerseys.

The oft-made prediction that the fancy for Jersey cattle will speedily decline seems further off than ever with each sale of animals of good pedigree. On the 4th instant Mr. T. S. Cooper, of Coopersburg, Pa., disposed of a grand lot of his imported cattle. The sale was held at the American Horse Exchange, New York, and Mr. Easton, the manager, who officiated as the auctioneer, succeeded in realizing for the owner the highest average ever obtained for so large a number of lots. Seventy-five head were brought to the hammer, and the total of $46,685 was reached, an average of $622 each. The highest price paid was $3,100 for the famous Coomassie bull, "Sir George," three years old, which is also the highest figure ever reached for a Jersey in this or any other country, and Colonel Henry S. Russell, of Milton, Mass., may well feel gratified in possessing so noble an animal. Cicero, two years old, another bull of the Coomassie strain, was the admiration of all present and could be have shown heifers as old as Sir George's he would no doubt have also gone above $5,000. He was purchased by Mr. W. H. Wilkinson, of Holyoke, Mass., for $3,100. The highest priced female was Mabel 2d, six years, also of the Coomassie strain, and Colonel Russell was again the fortunate purchaser at $2,000; her two year daughter went to Mr. W. K. Vanderbilt for $1,200 and her five weeks heifer calf realized $625. Mabel 5th, seven months old, a sister to Mabel 2d, by Sir George, was also secured by Colonel Russell for $1,350. As will be seen by the list below the cattle were well scattered over the different States.

| | |
|---|---|
| Emmy Holmes, 4 years; C. A. Morgan, Wethersfield, Mass. | $800 |
| Joliet of Linden, 4 years; F. W. Tripler, West Stockbridge, Mass. | 450 |
| Mlle. Potter, 4 years; W. S. Vanderbilt, New York | 600 |
| Jane of Linden, 1 year; W. H. Wilkinson, Greenwich, Conn. | 250 |
| Browney of Linden, 1 year; N. Wilkinson, Greenwich, Conn. | 225 |
| Imperatrice, 3 years; F. Holbrook, Stockbridge, Mass. | 550 |
| Goodrich, 3 years; C. C. Wheelwright, Boston, Mass. | 550 |
| Byron, 3 years; W. K. Vanderbilt | 800 |
| Griselle, 3 years; F. Erickson, New York | 350 |
| Princess Alexandra, 3 years; F. Hoffman | 410 |
| Marguis Operation (bull), 1 year; D. Cragg, Clossena | 80 |
| Cicero (bull) 2 years; W. H. Wilkinson | 3,100 |
| Fleur de l'Air 2d, 4 months; G. Blanchard, Portland, Me. | 210 |
| Lady Young 2d, 2 years; F. Erickson | 275 |
| Young Coomo (bull), 5 months; D. A. Given, Cynicana, Ky. | 325 |
| Lady Young, 6 months; F. W. Tripler | 375 |
| Beady, 1 year; A. T. Howe, Boston, Mass. | 225 |
| Valedine of Linden, 3 years; N. Wilkinson | 300 |
| Ostewayo's Valentine, 3 months; S. M. Noe, Shelbyville, Ky. | 225 |
| Token 2d, 1 year; W. K. Vanderbilt | 375 |
| Carlo's Daisy, 1 year; A. Barber, New York | 250 |
| Lady Coomassie, 5 months; H. S. Russell, Milton, Mass. | 1,100 |
| LightBoot, 7 months; W. K. Vanderbilt | 310 |
| Mabel 3d, 7 months; W. K. Vanderbilt | 425 |
| Tenant, 5 months; C. H. Morgan, Worcester, Mass. | 410 |
| Coomo's Fanny, 3 months; Colonel Russell | 420 |
| Fenier 2d, 1 year; L. A. Mills, Middlefield, Conn. | 400 |
| Violette, 1 year; S. S. Ayres, Red Bank, N. J. | 210 |
| Isabella, 2d, 7 months; Noe & Carroll, Fredericksburg, Va. | 325 |
| Sylvie of Linden, 1 year; W. W. Burgess, Bayonne, N. J. | 300 |
| Sylvie 2d, 4 years; Colonel Russell | 300 |
| Valentine 2d, 4 years; D. M. Lovell, Tioga, Pa. | 325 |
| Livery of Linden, 3 years; F. E. Hale, Groveland, Mass. | 425 |
| Tilly of Linden, 1 year; A. E. Barber | 450 |
| Agate of Linden, 2 years; H. Prince, South Center Bay, L. I. | 400 |
| Engima 2d, 1 year; W. N. Neltnan, Lime Rock, Conn. | 400 |
| Millie 2d, 4 years; Colonel Russell, Milton, Mass. | 3,200 |
| Medusie, 3 years; W. K. Vanderbilt | 575 |
| Medusie, 2d, 6 months; D. E. Knight, Philadelphia, Pa. | 225 |
| Imelle 2d, 1 year; Colonel Russell | 3,100 |
| Sir George (bull), 3 years; Colonel Russell | 3,100 |
| Pertonette, 1 year; W. K. Vanderbilt | 350 |
| Philine of Linden, 3 years; Colonel Russell | 375 |
| Agate 2d, 4 months; George Blanchard, Portland, Me. | 275 |
| Redlow's Perfection, 3 years; Colonel Russell | 400 |
| Linden 2d, 2 years; C. Shipley, Stockbridge, Pa. | 400 |
| Lisbeth, 4 years; C. L. Pumells, Bristol, Conn. | 375 |
| Liberty 2d, 5 months; J. L. Stadtman, Louisville, Ky. | 375 |
| Julio Gray, 3 years; C. W. Barnum, Lime Rock, Conn. | 300 |
| Coomo Juno, 2 months; B. F. Appleton, New York | 400 |
| Njuore, 1 year; Thomas Allen, Princeton, Mass. | 730 |
| Bianco Flower's 2d, 3 years; W. K. Vanderbilt | 760 |
| Fair Linden, 1 year; R. A. Russell, Barrington, Mass. | 320 |
| Sachen 2d, 3 years; W. B. Dickerman, New York | 375 |
| Empress, 3 years; C. H. Crosby, Bridgeport, Conn. | 425 |
| Agate 2d, 3 years; E. E. Knight, Philadelphia, Pa. | 300 |
| Faytlan, 3 years; Colonel Russell | 500 |
| Maturity of Linden, 3 years; Holmes & Crary, New Britain, Conn. | 425 |
| Mulberry of Linden, 2d, 1 year; J. E. Vaitse, Worcester, Mass. | 350 |
| Rainbow, 3 years; Moulton Brothers, West Randolph, Vt. | 350 |
| City Cento (bull), 7 months; D. A. Given | 225 |
| Bobby's Surprise, 1 year; W. A. Vanderbilt | 1,100 |
| Bobby's Pride, 2 years; Colonel Russell | 500 |
| Bobby's Prize, Francis W. Ward, New York | 1,000 |
| Daisy of Linden, 3 years; D. P. Appleton | 415 |
| Daisy Boy's Name, 3 years; D. M. Morgan | 500 |
| Linden Jay, 1 year; F. W. Tripler | 450 |
| Penhall, 3 years; W. H. Wilkinson | 240 |
| Mendota 3d, 3 years; J. L. Stadtman, Louisville, Ky. | 240 |
| Circle 2d, 1 year; F. Erickson | 450 |
| Ostewayo's Joliet, 1 year; M. B. Rowe, Fredericksburg, Va. | 400 |
| Circeo's Alderney, 4 years; W. K. Vanderbilt | 600 |
| **Total** | **$46,685** |

### Wool and Mutton Farming.

It is to be very much regretted that notwithstanding the pretty general diffusion of good ideas throughout the country, we see the short-sighted policy adopted by many sheep owners of using either ram lambs or inferior old ones, because thereby they are enabled to save a few dollars. Although the price for wool is at present low, mutton is bringing a good figure, and holders of inferior bred sheep are obtaining more money from their sheep than they ever thought of getting, and hence they are satisfied; but we wonder if such people ever contrast their prices with those which other people get for well-bred, well-cared-for animals. The system of keeping inferior animals where good ones could be equally well kept, and of course with a better profit, is very reprehensible, especially so when we remember the many facilities for getting good ewes and rams. To possess a fairly good flock of ewes, and a ram of good dimensions and good wool, and of so chance breeding, is to have the first thing needed, but this in itself will not be sufficient, if the necessary amount of forethought, energy and intelligence is not forthcoming, and it is often owing to the want of these latter qualifications that so many failures in sheep farming take place.

On farms that are not naturally sheep farms, but where cattle are kept, we think it a profitable venture to run some sheep; that is, if the requisite time and attention can be given to them; but in such cases all that should be that sheep ought not to be bolted with cattle, but should be made to follow the heavier stock, as they are moved from field to field. We are aware that many good agriculturalists are opposed to the mixture system of feeding sheep and cattle, but we believe that practical experience in the matter has long since proved that it is beneficial to the land, as well as profitable to the owner. We have often seen fields in dry summer time so parched, that although they were intended for cattle, no cattle could live on them, while sheep would not only have found subsistence but would have fatten on it; this we hold was a loss to the farmer. In like manner, many a farm has fields attached to it on which, during the autumn months, cattle could not be kept, but on which sheep could have ample subsistence and thrive well. There are other uses also

### to be claimed for running sheep on the farm with cattle;

they clear off all the grass left by the heavier stock, and this, as well as by their droppings, produce a close, even growth for them when they are again put on the pasture.

Sheep are also very useful in clearing pastures of many of the weed pests that sometimes infest them; in fact, some of the most pernicious of these are greedily eaten by them when in a young state—the repeated eating down of these weeds ultimately destroys them and thoroughly rids the pastures of their presence. With prices as they now stand, and as they are likely to continue, holders of sheep need not hesitate to use artificial food in their feeding. In using rich food for the feeding of sheep, folding on the poor pasture, if convenient, ought to be selected, as the enriching power of sheep manure when thus fed is very considerable. It is in fact well known to sheep farmers that lands worn out and of little value have been permanently benefited by the folding and grazing of sheep on them when fed with oil cake or other rich foods; and in calculating farm profits, the farmer should always take into account the improvements the lands have received, owing to this class of feeding. This is a point which most of our stock owners seldom take into consideration when casting up their profits, but if looked into it must be seen that it is a matter that should never be lost sight of. There cannot be a doubt that sheep farming, either in breeding, feeding or fattening, is paying and sure to pay; but by a much more extended and better system of selecting at least well-bred rams the addition to the sheep profit of this country might be increased by at least one-fourth.—Rural World.

### The Dorset Sheep.

This is a horned sheep, indigenous to a small district in the South of England, and has been long bred there, chiefly from its habit of yeaning lambs so early that they can be marketed from Christmas to the middle of January. As there are no others to compete with them at this season, they bring an extravagant price, which, although they are quite small in size at the time, pays their breeders a fair profit.

Like most other southern sheep in England, during some years past, their breeders have been improving them in form and increasing their size. In the case of the Dorsets, this has been done mainly by careful selections, with now and then a single cross of the Down rams on their ewes, and then going back again to Dorset rams, on this half-breed produce. The sheep are naturally quite hardy, and it is said they are not made less so by this cross; nor has their fecundity been diminished, they still continuing to bring twins in most instances. Those yeaning early in October sometimes breed again in April; but this double production annually is not generally approved of, as it weakens the ewes, and they cannot bring forth so hardy and thrifty an offspring after this.—National Live-Stock Journal, Chicago.

### Effect of Odors on Milk.

Upon this question Professor Arnold, in the work "American Dairying," says: The London Milk Journal cites instances where milk that has stood a short time in the presence of persons sick with typhoid fever, or been handled by parties before fully recovering from the small-pox, has spread these diseases as effectually as if the persons themselves had been present. Scarlatina, measles and other contagious diseases have been spread in the same way. The peculiar smell of a cellar is indelibly impressed upon all the butter made from milk still standing in it. A few puffs from a pipe or a cigar will scent all the milk in the room, and a smoking lamp will soon do the same. A pail of milk standing ten minutes where it will be tainted by the scent of a strong-smelling stable, or any other offensive odor, will imbibe a taint that will never leave it. A maker of gilt-edged butter objects to cooling warm milk in the room where his milk stands for the cream to rise, because he says the odor escaping from the new milk while cooling is taken in by the other milk and retained to the injury of his butter. This may seem like descending to little things, but it must be remembered that it is the sum of such little things that determines whether the products of the dairy are to be sold at cost or below, or as a high-priced luxury. If milk is to be converted into an article of the latter class, it must be handled and kept in clean and sweet vessels, and must stand in pure fresh air, such as would be desirable and healthy for people to breathe.

### History of Alfalfa.

Alfalfa—or, more properly, lucerne—has a history enveloped in the mists of antiquity. It was known as a valuable fodder plant in ancient Media, 500 years before the Christian era. From Media it found its way to Greece, thence to the Roman Empire. Prof. McBryde tells us that lucerne was among the cultivated leguminous plants in the days of Cato, Virgil, and Varro; while Columella, with other Roman writers on husbandry, gave full directions for its cultivation, it bring then held valuable not only as a forage plant, but as a rotation crop for wheat and other cereals. From Rome it passed to France and Spain, when it received the name it is now generally known by in North America, where for centuries it grew wild on the plains of Buenos Ayres, and was supposed to be a plant of native growth. In Mexico it was the staple crop of the country at the time of the conquest. It was introduced into California from Chili, where it passed under the name of Chili Clover, and the seed is still imported from that country to supply the needs of the farmers of the Pacific Slope.

### Texas Fever.

The first sign of anything wrong in a cow is its failing in milk, a refusal to feed, standing apart from other cattle in the field; the faces becomes hard and dry, emaciation follows, the animal passes bloody urine, and in a few days death ensues. By post mortem we find enlarged spleen and liver, with clots and abscesses frequently, and the liver having a peculiar yellow or brownish appearance. In a number of cattle that we examined we found the same appearance generally. The flesh takes on a black, yellowish appearance, caused by an excess of the coloring matter of the gall, and in every case becoming putrid in a short time as the result of congestion. This is Texas fever.

### Weight of Live Cattle.

Measure in inches the girth around the breast just behind the shoulder blade, and the length of the back from the tail to the shoulder blade. Multiply girth by length and divide by 114. If the girth is less than three feet, multiply the quotient by 11; if between three and five, by 16; between five and seven, by 23; between seven and nine, by 31. If the animal is lean, deduct one-twentieth from the result; or take girth and length in feet, multiply square of girth by length, and multiply the product by 3.36. Live weight multiplied by 1.06 gives net weight—nearly.—New York Tribune.

Iowa has nearly 1,000,000 cows, valued at $27 per head, or a total of $27,000,000.

Cattle are dying from disease in parts of San Benito county.

## Judging Sheep—Points of Excellence.

The Indiana State Wool Growers' Association has devoted much time to the preparation of a scale of points of excellence for the assistance of the breeders of the different classes of sheep, as well as for the judges of sheep at the fairs.

In bringing the matter before the association, the committee having it in charge said:

In presenting this knowledge to the Wool Growers' Association of the State of Indiana, your committee has been to a great deal of trouble and bother in summing up what we consider to be the greatest benefit to the Association.

The scale of points to be taken into consideration in the breeding of all the different breeds of sheep, is the blood of the sire and the dam. This must be ascertained before we commence to breed oursheep up to a standard, or otherwise we had better not try to breed to any given point, for without pure blood being infused into our flocks, it would be useless to make the trial.

Scale of 100 points for Cotswold sheep:

Blood—Thoroughbred, purely bred from one or more importations of Cotswold sheep of some reputable breeder from England. Seven points.

Head—Not too fine; moderately small and broad between the eyes and nostrils, but without a short, thick appearance, and in young animals, covered on crown with long lustrous wool. Seven points.

Face—Either white or slightly mixed with grey, or white dappled with brown. Four points.

Nostril—Wide and expanded, bone dark. One point.

Eyes—Prominent but mild looking. Two points.

Ears—Broad, long, moderately thin and covered with short wool. Four points.

Collar—Full from breast, and shoulders tapering gradually all the way to where the head and neck joins. The neck of rams should be short, thick and strong, indicating constitutional vigor. The neck of ewes should be fine and graceful, and free from coarse and loose skin. (Collar five points with ewe.) Six points.

Shoulders—Broad and full, and at the same time join so gracefully to the collar forward, and the chin backward, as not to leave the least hollow in either place. Seven points.

Fore Legs—The mutton on the arm or fore thigh should come quite to the knee—leg upright with heavy bone, being clear from superfluous skin with wool to fetlocks, and may be mixed with grey. Four points.

Breast—Broad and well formed, keeping the legs wide apart. Girth on chest full and deep. Eight points.

Fore Flank—Quite full, not showing hollow behind the shoulder. (Four points with ewe.) Five points.

Back and Loin—Broad, flat and straight, from which the ribs must spring with a fine, circular arch, and covering of rams well covered with wool. Ten points.

Belly—Straight on underline. (Five points with ewe.) Three points.

Quarters—Long and full with mutton quite down to the hock. Eight points.

Hock—Should neither stand in or out. Two points.

Twist—Or junction inside the thighs should be deep, wide, and full; which with a broad breast, will keep the legs open and upright. Four points.

Fleece—The whole body should be covered with long, lustrous wool. Eighteen points.

One hundred points of excellence for Merino sheep:

Blood—Thoroughbred—i. e., purely bred from one or more of the direct importations of Merino sheep from Spain, prior to the year 1812, without admixture of any other blood. One point.

Constitution—Indicated by form of body; deep, large breast cavity, broad back, heavy quarters, with muscular development forming capacious abdomen. Skin thick, but soft, of fine texture, and pink color; expansive nostril, brilliant eyes, healthful countenance, and good size, age considered. Fifteen points.

Size—In fair condition, with fleece of twelve months' growth; full grown rams should weigh not less than 150 pounds, and ewes not less than 110 pounds. Seven points.

General appearance—Good carriage, bold style, elastic movement, showing in particular parts, as well as general outline symmetry of form. Three points.

Body—Throughout, heavy bones, well proportioned in length, smooth joints, ribs starting horizontally from backbone and well rounded to the breastbone, which should be wide, strong and prominent in front; strong backbone, straight and well proportioned as to length. Heavy, muscular quarters, deep through and squarly formed behind and before, with shoulders well set on, neither projecting sharply above the backbone, nor standing so wide and flat as to increase unevenness at the hip and shoulder. Folds on the ram should be larger than on the ewes. Large and pendulous folds from the chin or jaws succeeding each other down the neck to the brisket, ending with a large fold or "apron," and extending up the sides of the neck, but lighter if at all extending over top of neck, also behind the fore-leg or shoulder, one on front of hind leg, hanging well down across the flank, also on rear of hind legs or quarters, extending upward toward the tail, with one or two on and around the tail, giving the animal a square appearance on the hind quarters, and straight down as may be from end of tail to hock joints and hind feet. Eighteen points.

Head—Wide between the ears, and between the eyes and across the nose; short from top of head to tip of nose, face straight; eyes clear and prominent; ears thick, medium size, and, together with face, nose and lips, white and covered with soft fur or downy wool. Ewes should have no appearance of horns; while upon rams the horns should be clear in color, symmetrically curved, without tendency to press upon the sides of the head or to extreme expansion. Six points.

Neck—Medium length, good bone and muscular developments; and especially with the ram, heavier toward the shoulders, well set high up, and rising from that point to the back of the head. Five points.

Legs and feet—Legs medium or short in length, straight and set well apart forward and back, heavy bone, smooth joints, with large muscular development of the forearm; thick, heavy thighs, wide down to hock joints, and from knee joints downward covered with short wool, or the soft furry covering peculiar to the ears and face; hoofs well shaped and of clear color. Five points.

Covering—Tendency to hair and gare upon any part of the sheep is to be avoided. Evenness of fleece in length, quality, density, luster, crimp, trueness, strength and elasticity, covering the entire body, belly and legs to the knees; head well covered forward, squarely to a line in front of the eyes; well filled between the eyes and ears of horns, and well upon the cheeks; muzzle clear, with small opening up to and around the eyes. Scrotum of rams covered with wool free from tendency to hair. Fifteen points.

Quality—Medium, but such as are known in our markets as fine delaine and fine clothing wool, distinctly better in quality, luster, crimp, and elasticity than the wools of same length grown upon the common grade sheep. Five points.

Density—Shown by the compactness of the fleece throughout, which should open free but close, showing very little of the skin at any point, even at the extremities. Ten points.

Length—At one year's growth not less than two and one-half inches, and as near as may be uniform in length to the extremities of the fleece. Five points.

Oil—Evenly distributed; soft and flowing freely from skin to surface medium in quality, and of a light color. Five points.

One hundred points of excellency for the Down sheep:

Blood—Purely bred from one or more of direct importation from Great Britain. Ten points.

Constitution—Constitution and quality indicated by the form of body; deep and large in breast and through the heart, back, straight and well covered with lean meat or muscle; wide and full in the thigh, deep in flank, but soft and of a saffron color; prominent, brilliant eyes and healthful countenance. Twenty-five points.

Size—In fair condition when fully matured, rams should weigh not less than one hundred pounds, and ewes not less than one hundred and seventy-five pounds. Ten points.

General appearance—General appearance and character, good carriage; head well up, elastic movement, showing great symmetry of form and uniformity of character throughout. Ten points.

Body—Well proportioned, small bones, great scale and length, well finished hind quarters, thick back and loins, standing with legs well placed outside, breast wide and prominent in front, brisket wide and extending well forward. Ten points.

Head—Head short and broad; wide between the ears and between the eyes; short from top of head to tip of nose, ears short, of medium size and covered with downy wool; head should be well covered with wool to a point even with eyes, without any appearance of horns, color dark brown in some families and fawn color in others without speck or spot; light muzzle not objectionable. Ten points.

Neck—Short and heavy, especially towards shoulders. Five points.

Legs and feet—Broad and short and well set apart, color same as head and wooled to the hoof, which must be well shaped. Five points.

Covering—Body, belly, head, and legs well covered with fleece of even length and quality. Scrotum of rams well covered. Ten points.

Quality of wool—Medium such as is known in our markets as "medium delaine" and "half-combed wool," strong, fine, lustrous fiber, without tendency to mat or felt together, and at one year's growth not less than three and one-half inches in length. Five points.

## How Breeds are Formed.

An inquirer writing to the *Breeders' Gazette*, says: I would like to know how to get a thoroughbred, or in other words, a distinct breed, and that paper after some preliminary remarks replies as follows:

If a common mare be bred to a strictly thoroughbred horse, the produce is half blood. By continuing this process, breeding the female produce to a thoroughbred, until you reach five crosses, under the American rule, the produce would be entitled to a registry as a thoroughbred, and would be entitled to compete for premiums offered for thoroughbred horses. But in England a horse is not regarded as a thoroughbred, and is not accorded a place in the stud book, unless his lineage can be traced in unbroken succession, and without admixture, to Oriental blood.

With cattle in the United States the usage is not so uniform. No amount of crossing with pure blood will entitle an animal to entry in the Jersey Herd Registry. It must be a purely-bred animal, imported direct from the Isle of Jersey, under certain restriction, or descended, on both sides, from imported and recorded sire and dam, without any admixture whatever of alien or unrecorded blood, or it is not recognized as a thoroughbred Jersey. With Shorthorns the regulations are somewhat different in the two herd books. The American Herd Book is conducted under the rule adopted by the American Association of Shorthorn Breeders at Indianapolis several years ago, which is as follows:

"Resolved, That the ancestry of the animals should be traced on both sides to imported animals (Shorthorns) or to those heretofore recorded in the American Herd Book, with pedigrees not false or spurious, before they can be entitled to registry."

This rule was amended a few years later by the same association, by the adoption of a vague and obscurely worded resolution, which, being interpreted, means, if it means anything, about as follows: If the animals that were not eligible under the above rule have, by accident or oversight, been once recorded in the American Herd Book, no matter how far short they may have come of filling the required standard, the descendants of animals wrongfully recorded may be admitted, provided five crosses of recorded or recordable blood can be shown in the case of females, and six such crosses for bulls. Subsequently, however, this association rescinded all of its rules, leaving the whole matter in the hands of the publishers of the herd books; and the publishers of the American Herd Book have announced that they will be governed in the future by the rule as amended above.

Under this rule as amended, our correspondent may commence with a thoroughbred bull and a common cow, and he may use nothing but thoroughbred bulls on the produce for twenty generations, and it would still not be entitled to an entry in an American Shorthorn Herd book unless the common cow with which he commences has, by some accident, been accorded a place in the record; but as this Herd Book, established many years prior to the adoption of the Indianapolis rule, contains many animals that would not have been entitled to registry under this rule, the effect of the foregoing regulation is to authorize the recording of the descendants of such animals, without regard to the eligibility of their ancestors.

The rule adopted by the Shorthorn Record is still more rigorous. Nothing is admitted to this record that cannot trace, in unbroken succession, without admixture, to imported sire and dam.

The English Shorthorn Herd Book, which is controlled by an association of Shorthorn breeders, is conducted upon a different basis. Cows showing four crosses of approved Shorthorn blood, and bulls with five such crosses, are admitted to registry and are classed as thoroughbred Shorthorns. The Canadian Shorthorn Herd Book has been conducted under the same rule as the English, but recently a more strict constriction has been adopted.

We think our correspondent will find the foregoing a full answer to his question. It will be seen that the simple fact that an animal is registered does not make it a thoroughbred; but it is perhaps safe to assume that, if an animal is entered in a given register, the editor has investigated the alleged pedigree, and that it is eligible under the rule adopted for his government; and, in proportion as the editor is known to be careful, accurate and strict in the enforcement of this rule, is the recorded pedigree to be relied upon as coming up to the required standard. But it should be borne in mind that the stud books and the herd books are used only as convenient places for recording pedigrees, and the breeder must look to the pedigree itself, and trace it through all of its collateral lines before he can decide as to its value.

## Shall we Ring the Hogs?

Experience teaches that the ringing of hogs when properly done, and done at the right time, is an advisable measure. The assertion sometimes made that hogs if habitually allowed to run at large will not injure meadows or pastures by rooting when turned upon them cannot be relied on. They may, for awhile, behave themselves very well, and roam a pasture for weeks, scarcely turning a sod. Seeing this, the owner is satisfied in his own mind that rings may be dispensed with, when soon after, having ceased to watch them, the rascals from some unaccountable reason begin rooting and in a short time will have done more damage, times over, than it would have cost to ring them. Such experience as this leads to the conclusion that the safest way is to use the rings whenever hogs are allowed to range where their rooting would be an injury.

The continuous use of rings the year round or their use on swine of all ages and sizes is not advisable. In the spring of the year they are generally the most needed. If hogs that were treated to rings in the spring are still on hand in the fall, it is usually best to remove the rings, particularly if the hogs are turned on the mast or are expected to follow cattle in feed lots or stalk fields.

It sometimes happens that a valuable brood sow acquires such bad habits as lifting gates or breaking fences. A couple of rings in the nose of such an animal will put her on good behavior the most effectually of anything ever tried. So also a sow that is vicious or cross to other hogs; a good ring in her nose will prove to be a wonderful tamer. A stock boar, if inclined to be unruly, should be treated the same way.

Of the different kinds of patented hog rings before the public, it may be said that they are all good enough, some, perhaps, being more easily applied and lasting longer than others. Of those not patented a horse-shoe nail or a piece of common No. 12 wire makes a very good and cheap ring, and one readily used with the help of a double-edged awl or common punch for making the holes in the rim of the snout and a pair of small pinchers for closing the rings after being inserted.

## Sure Death to Lice.

Take a bar of common soap, place in a pan containing a little water, then heat until melted down, then add carbolic acid crystals (carbolic acid crystals can be had of any druggist in one-pound bottles at seventy-five cents each), at least one ounce of acid to each pound of soap used; there is no danger if used stronger. To reduce the crystals to a fluid state remove the cork from the bottle, place in water and heat the water, when it may be easily poured out and mixed with soap. When cool, a strong soap suds made with this soap will be sure death to all insects that live on domestic animals. It will cure mange, barn itch, and all cutaneous diseases, and make a cheap and effective sheep dip. When cattle are hide bound, or the hair does not appear healthy, a wash of the suds will prove a benefit, as it cleanses and heals in cases of sores. It is a good and sure disinfectant, safe and effectual, and will be found useful for a great variety of purposes.—*Pennsylvania Farmer.*

Milking a heifer for the first time requires patience for they will almost invariably kick. In such a case, pen a broad strap around their body just in front of the udder, and buckle it up moderately tight, and as soon as she gets quiet (for she may dance around a little at first, take your pail, sit down and go to milking, for she is as harmless as a kitten. Do not attempt to use a rope instead of a strap, for it will not answer. This is a much better method than tying the legs, etc., as it does not hurt the animal in the least. A few applications of the strap, with plenty of patience and kindness, will cure the most obstinate case.

Alfalfa has proven to the Colorado ranchman that more sheep can be kept on a given area of land than was ever dreamed of by the most enthusiastic ranchman of the plains.

Ezra Fleming, of Wyoming, sheared 80,000 pounds of wool from 5,000 sheep last spring. An average of 12 pounds is pretty good for a flock of 5,000 head.

There are, in the state of Ohio, over 800 flocks of thoroughbred Merino sheep.

The total valuation of Colorado cattle is $14,450,000.

## Olive Culture.

Ellwood Cooper of Santa Barbara, the leading olive grower of California, says he has three eighty years old that have produced two thousand gallons of olives to the acre. This would be equivalent to 250 gallons of oil to the acre, and oil finds a ready market at $6 a gallon. The yield of one acre would thus be $1,250, which for a hundred-acre ranch would be a pretty fair income. But these figures are not represented to apply to any except the very choicest trees and an uncommonly good year. Yet even computing the profits of olive culture at as low a figure as one-tenth, a twenty-acre ranch would support a family very comfortably after six or seven years of waiting. One of the great advantages of olive culture is the fact that irrigation is not needed. In a climate where there is a scarcity of rain, as in California, this is a matter of much importance. The olive tree also grows very old. There are trees in Asia Minor that are known to be over 1,200 years old, and are still in full bearing.—*Ventura Signal.*

## The Sweepstakes Lie.

Arizona can boast of a good many talented liars, but judging from the following, from a Colorado exchange, the centennial State can justly lay claim to the boss: "Bill Nuckells, a prospector, fell down a prospect shaft forty feet deep, right into a nest of black snakes. Most men would have died of fright, but Nuckells was not that sort of a man. He tied several snakes together and started them up the side of the shaft, tying on a fresh snake as fast as the rear went up. Pretty soon the head of the snakes got over the edge and started down hill. Nuckells kept tying on fresh reptiles until he had used up a couple of hundred—every snake that was in the shaft. By this time the crowd of snakes was strong enough to pull him out of the shaft, and he soon reached Mad's ranch, safe and sound."—*Tombstone Epitaph.*

THE

# Breeder and Sportsman.

PUBLISHED WEEKLY BY THE

BREEDER AND SPORTSMAN PUBLISHING CO.

THE TURF AND SPORTING AUTHORITY OF THE
PACIFIC COAST.

**OFFICE, 508 MONTGOMERY STREET**
P. O. Box 1886.

*Five dollars a year ; three dollars for six months ; one dollar and a
half for three months. Strictly in advance.*

MAKE ALL ORDERS, MONEY ORDERS, ETC., PAYABLE TO ORDER OF
BREEDER AND SPORTSMAN PUBLISHING CO.

*Money should be sent by postal order, draft or by registered letter, ad-
dressed to the "Breeder and Sportsman Publishing Company, San Francisco, Cal."*

*Communications must be accompanied by the writer's name and address,
not necessarily for publication, but as a private guarantee of good faith*

JOSEPH CAIRN SIMPSON, - - - Editor

San Francisco, Saturday, October 21, 1882.

## "YOURS IN WRATH."

Early Saturday afternoon we received a postal card
from our old friend, Judge S————, calling attention to
the biggest kind of a blunder made in the streship of
Haddington. It was a blunder for which there may be
explanation but without excuse. It cannot be laid on
typesetters, proof reader or anyone save the editor, and
all squirming and wriggling will be of no avail in removing the stigma. The offense was in giving Kingston
as the sire of Haddington when King of Trumps stands
credited with the paternity, and that without question
or cavil.

Had we be*an* misled by the Judge's chirography, an
apology might be offered, as it would require a Philadelphia lawyer, or the decipherer of the hieroglyphics on
the obelisk, to determine which of the two names was
meant.

Not in this instance, however, as the postal had King
of Trumps printed upon it so neatly that it is evident
the Judge is aware of his regular handwriting being
somewhat obscure, and has practiced lettering until he
can take rank among the accomplished knights of the
pen in forming letters that cannot mislead. There was
no mistaking the curt valedictory, which we have transferred to the head of this article, if even it was in Italian
characters, and we are not sure that an action would not
lie for a breach of the postal laws regarding the sending
of cards through the mail. There is little question that
a jury would think the provocation sufficient and on
mature consideration in place of calling the Judge to
account, manfully acknowledge the error, and promise to
be more circumspect in the future. Some way we got
Hercules and Haddington decidedly mixed, and it is
something congratulatory that we did not get the Bay
Middleton cross in as well as the Kingston. The truth is
that the notice of the first mares was written at home
after the morning visit to the barn when we found
Anteeo's jaws all swollen, and the space which should
have been immediately behind them filled, so as to give
him the look of a chipmunk, with his chops full of corn.
In ten days the Stanford was to be trotted and the black
devil had again got him in his clutches.

We wrote of the great doings at San Jose, all the time
busily thinking of the Stanford, and our chances in it,
tinged with the deepest kind of ultramarine. Fortunately a trotting cross was not interpolated, as in that
case in place of a postal we should have expected two
hundred and sixty pounds of "wrath" lying in wait for
us at the foot of the stairs, and though possessing a fair
share of the editorial courage, we should certainly have
shown more " foot than game." " A guilty conscience,"
the old adage says, "makes cowards of us all," and though
there had been an Electioneer strain smuggled in through
the sire, an Almont in the dam, and a whole gallery of
celebrated ancestors of trotting proclivities figuring in
the genealogical table, we never would have delayed to
explain to the irate Judge the honor we had done him.
Nevertheless, we did inadvertently give Night Hawk a
distinguished sire, while the swollen neck was a
haunting torment, and the expectant dollars were being
transformed into leather medals. It was bad enough to
surrender the cool hundred in the Occident Cup without
a struggle, and now to see three times as much
squandered, to say nothing of the great expectations, bringing on a sort of forlorn hope
at the best, vanishing like a dream of finding
no end of money and sinking in a futile search for a
pocket in the nightshirt to put it in. But yet there may
be a crumb of comfort to us, and, perhaps, a trifle of
information to others, caught in the same fix, by recount-
ing the present standing of the case and the means taken

to remedy the trouble. That was Friday morning when
the discovery was made and that night it was thoroughly
rubbed with a mixture of sweet oil and turpentine. The
next morning there was a visible decrease and this,
Sunday evening, it has got so nearly to its proper shape
that he has been "pointed " for work to-morrow. Should
he return a favorable answer to the questions asked,
"cool out" all right and not cough during or after the
exercise, the oil and turpentine shall have due praise.
By the way, one of the most celebrated of the English
trainers of half a century ago considered turpentine and
cream, mixed in equal parts, the very best thing for
throat ailments, and also used it for injuries to the pipe.
It may prove very valuable to contract the swellings
that have been one of the peculiarities of pinkeye, and
also be of service in checking the attending cough.

## THE COURSING SEASON.

Once more the lovers of the leash may rejoice that the
hours of idleness have passed and the busy time of the
coursing season is at hand. Again the note of preparation is sounded through the kennels in the land and busy
trainers are day by day engaged in the pleasant task of
conditioning the long tails. Men and dogs alike look
forward eagerly to the day when on the vast plains of
the San Joaquin the fleet animals will be loosed to try
conclusions with each other and the flying jack rabbit.
Talk of the excitement and sport of any other kind of
hunting! Why, it is nonsense to compare any sport in
the field with the pleasure of coursing. How eagerly
one watches for the expected game and how critically
one surveys the motions of the active slipper who with a
pair of dogs wildly tugging at the slips is compelled to
keep his wits about him and see that they hold the game
in view until he is straight ahead and both are going
even. How the blood tingles through one's veins when
a favorite dog flies from slips like bolt from bow and by
superior speed opens a gap in the run up, takes the first
turn and insures itself a victory unless some untoward
accident occurs. How the mercurial spirits, raised to the
highest pitch of excitement by a favorite's speed, fall
when an awkward turn throws him out and gives a
big advantage to his closer working opponent. And
then how they rise again when after getting straightened out the favorite's speed again tells and he shows in
the lead. A " go bye," a " go bye,", is shouted from all
parts of the field until the warning voices of the stewards
giving orders for quiet bring the shooters down to earth
again from the boundless realms of pleasure into which
success and the bracing open air had taken them.

A kill at last cleverly made is the signal for one and
all to sink back in their seats except the two owners who
are riding furiously over the plain to pick up their dogs
before the starting up of another hare shall send them
off again, for this abundance and wide scattering of the
game is the one drawback that coursing has in this State.
How then anxiously all wait until the verdict of the judge
lets loose the tongue of criticism, for your true courser
never attempts to give a decision of a run until the judge
is heard from. Pleasantly enough this losers take their
defeat and gleefully the winners herald their success,
bets are quickly paid, the next pair are put in slips and
all is made ready to repeat the stirring scene. Search
one wide world over and one will fail to find any sport
so free, fair, manly and untrammeled by any taint of
cruelty as our California coursing. Unlike England and
Australia, the hares are not beaten out of plantations nor
let out of preserves. They are given all the advantages.
They are on their own domain consecrated to them by
its utter uselessness for any other purpose, for where we
course in California a dozen of sheep could not find sustenance on a hundred acres. Every inch of the land
they know, for every day they traverse it in search of
food or to avoid their enemies, the rattlesnakes and the
coyotes and the big squirrel hawks. They are fleet as
the wind and staunch as a thoroughbred horse and can
laugh to scorn the puny efforts of a brace of freshly imported English greyhounds whose wind' and' bottom are
not the best.

Our native dogs have more endurance than their English ancestors with perhaps a trifle less speed, but we
have seen a hare run a pair of them to a standstill after
a four-mile chase at a pace that made it impossible for
the best horse in the State to keep the judge in sight.
Twenty or forty miles they can run without sighting a
fence or meeting any natural obstacle before them except
the glacial mounds over which they bound at a pace that
puts a horse to shame and makes the judge tremble for
his own and his horse's life. It is no child's play following a course. We have been there, and in our own person, impressed upon us by falls from treacherous squirrel
holes, can attest the spice of danger there lies in the
sport for those who take a horse and go to the front.
We have seen as good riders as ever bestrode a horse
pitched twenty feet over their steeds' heads, when the
poor animals, going at full speed, were brought to a sud-

den halt by plunging both fore feet in a squirrel hole.
We have seen an eager dog on hare intent, meet a similar
fate and go whirling head over heels like a street gamin
turning a wheel. For those who love a life of ease a
buggy makes a good substitute for a horse.

We want to see this noble sport become the sport of
this State, as it is the greatest English winter sport.
We want to see kennels and coursing clubs throughout
the length and breadth of the land, and above all, we
hope that as in the past' the sport will always be kept
pure and clean and free from reproach. We go to press
before the entries for the Pacific Coast Club match which
close to-night are made, but next Wednesday morning
we will be one of the first to leave the El Capitan Hotel,
and our readers may rely upon it that our columns will
contain all that is worth knowing about the first fall
match of the season of 1882.

## THE STANFORD STAKE.

To-day on the Bay District course this stake of 1882
will be decided provided the day and track are in accordance with the conditions. We were led into error last
week by only referring to the original advertisement, and
overlooked the addenda made by the managers previous
to the second payment. In order that our readers may
understand the exact position of the Stanford Stake we
republish the conditions governing it from the outset.
There were twenty-one nominations:

PACIFIC BREEDERS' ASSOCIATION—THE STANFORD STAKE—
   a sweepstakes for trotting colts and fillies, foals of 1879, $500 each,
$100 payable on the first of January, 1881, at which time the stake will
close, $100 on the first day of January, 1882, and $100 thirty days before
the day fixed for trotting. Whatever amount up to be completed forfeit,
and the neglect to pay at the specified time incurring forfeit of previous payments. The race to be heats of a mile, best 3 in 5, in harness.
First to receive six-tenths of the whole sum, the second two-tenths,
the third one-tenth. In addition to the stakes and forfeits, the proprietor of the gate money, proof on pool sales, and all other sources of
enrollment will constitute the gross amount to be divided in the foregoing proportions. Or in lieu of these, the association will add a sum
not less than $1,000. Five or more subscribers $1,000. The race to be
trotted in 1882, not sooner than the latter part of August. The exact
date to be fixed and announced on the 1st of January, 1882, or sooner.
Race to be governed by the rules of the Pacific Association controlled by
the duly elected officers, and subjected to its rules. Nominations to
be made to Jos. Cairn Simpson, "California Spirit of the Times," on or
before the first day of January, 1881. The colts must be named, the
names and pedigree, so far as known, given.

Second advertisement.

STANFORD STAKES, 1882—THE STANFORD STAKES FOR THE
   foals of 1879, which closed the first of January, 1881, with twenty-one
nominations, and in which $100 is to be paid on or before the first of
January, 1882, has been fixed for decision on the third Saturday in October—good day and track—to come off on the Bay District Course, San
Francisco, if the day and track are not good, on the Saturday following
that date when the track and day are good, excepting the third Saturday
in November, when the Embryo Stake is to be trotted. Those having
nominations must send the second installment of $100 to N. T. Smith,
Treasurer, corner of Fourth and Townsend streets, San Francisco, on
or before the first of January, 1882, or the previous payments will be forfeited. JAS. McM. SHAFTER, President; A. P.
WHITNEY, Vice-President; N. T. Smith, Treasurer; Jos. Cairn Simpson, Secretary pro tem.

Executive Committee—Leland Stanford, Jas. B. Haggin, L. J. Rose,
A. P. Whitney, R. H. Miller, Jr., H. W. Seale, N. T. Smith, F. A. Finigan,
John Boggs, William Corbitt, J. McM. Shafter.

## TWO-YEAR-OLD TROTTING AT WALLA WALLA.

Although the "Oregonian" corroborates the intelligence
sent us by T. B. Merry that Metropolitan beat Adelaide
in 2:45, 2:36½, we think there must be some mistake in
the figures. Mr. Haggin informs us that the colt was
foaled in May, 1881, so that he is only a yearling, and the
probable solution is that the time of the last heat should
be 2:36½. That would imply that he had been named
in a race for two-years-olds or under, and should that
prove to be the case it is one of the greatest performances on record. The account copied from the "Oregonian"
was also written by Mr. Merry and the presumption is
he has been misled by the telegram being at fault. He
is also mistaken in the amount of work Metropolitan has
had, as before the sale to Mr. Russell, little had been
done with him. The price paid, $500, was certainly very
low for a colt of his breeding and the reason he was disposed of for so small an amount was that the yearling by
Poscora Hay ward from A. Rose was more highly thought
of. If frequently happens that the most acute judges err
in choosing between youngsters, and whichever way
this turns out it is sure that this son of Echo and
Black Swan is a rare jewel. We shall await the confirmation of the report with some anxiety, for should it
prove that the figures are correct (there cannot be a mistake about the age) it will take the first place in the
yearling record.

## ANNUAL MEETING P. C. B. H. A.

The annual meeting of the P. C. Blood Horse Association
will take place on Nov. 7th, and inasmuch as that is
election day it may be that it will be necessary to ad-
journ to a later date. There should be a meeting of the
Trustees to fix on the track to hold the fall meeting and
other business that is pressing, and probably a quorum
could be got the first of the coming week. Three weeks
from to-day the race meeting will commence, and there
is scant time to make the preparations. It may be that
the president will notify us in time for the call to appear
in this number of the paper,

## HONESTY FOR AUSTRALIA.

n the Steamer City of New York which sails from port, bound for Australia, to-morrow, this very prom-g trotting stallion will be a passenger.

his will not only make a prominent entry in the 00 purse given by the Victorian Trotting Club, but be a valuable addition to the breeding farms of that try. We scarcely know of a stallion that will be of service, his breeding being of the best kind, and his will certainly please, as the Australians are capital es of equine proportions. His size is a great point favor, and his action is very fine. Then he is one he most honest trotters ever seen on the track, and keep "putting in his heats" as long as the race s. This quality could scarcely be lacking from his ding, as he has any amount of stout strains in his ralogical tree. In direct descent from Rysdyk's nbletonian on the side of the sire, two crosses of Ab-ah Hiatoga, and then Glencoe, Harkforward, Ameri-Eclipse, etc. to give finish and backing to the whole. Victorian Club are well repaid for the outlay of ad-ising in the "Breeder and Sportsman" if the only were the entry of Honesty, and, consequently, xportation. But this is likely to be only the fore-er of other animals of great promise, and by her year there will be several to follow. California lers realise the importance of sending the best ani-, and though, of course, there may be speculators ge on the track for the only purpose of making in-liate profit from their ventures, our neighbors in the dle of the Pacific are to acute to be easily imposed m. The breeder has an enduring stake, and the effect-one sale is only a small thing in comparison with future outlook. That there will be mutual advan-e in the interchange of the stock of the country is ured. California can supply every want of the onies, so far as furnishing procreative animals for the tting stud, and in return this state will be greatly efited by the introduction of some of the best racing od of the Antipodes.

We sincerely trust that Honesty will make a pleasant yage. Having been instrumental in sending him ere is an anxiety that he should do well. We are well tisfied that he is the right kind of a horse to make a vora ble impression on the Australians, and with a fair are of good luck he will make his mark.

Mr. Harry Whiting will accompany Honesty and look ter him during the voyage and in the preparation for e race.

---

### P. C. B. H. A.

By a communication from the President we are quested to give notice that there will be a meeting of a Board of Trustees of the Pacific Coast Blood Horse sociation at the office of the "Breeder and Sportsman" xt Monday, the 23d inst. at 2 o'clock p. m. A full at-ndance is desired as business of importance will come fore the meeting.

---

### EDITORIAL NOTES.

**High Prices for Jerseys.**—We reproduce from an stern authority an account of a recent sale of Jersey cattle New York at which seventy-five head, fifteen being calves, re disposed of at an average price of $625 per head. The rsey boom seems to continue with increased volume. At the le above mentioned the highest price reached was $5,100 r the bull Sir George, and this is said to be the highest gure ever paid for either bull or cow in this or any other ountry. Sir George was one-eighth Coomassie, and apropos this fact Mr. Henry Pierce of this city has in his Yerba uena herd two heifers one-eighth bred and one one-fourth this fashionable and highly prized strain. Mr. Pierce is rw on a visit to his old home in East Baldwin, Maine, here the home farm is stocked with Jerseys of the Coomas-a, Stoke, Farmers' [Glory, Fansey and Rex strains, the rd being valued at $75,000. Mr. Pierce proposes to nd out some Coomassies, Scituates and Farmers' Glorys to rengthen the Yerba Buena herd with fresh and fashionable ood.

**Embryo Stake.**—Those who have not already de-ired out of the Embryo Stake for the year 1882, should member that their last chance to pay the forfeit of $25 will pire on the 25th in st. All unpaid declarations having been ade in due time must be paid on or before that date or ey will become responsible for $100, the full amount of e stake. And all forfeits occurring on that date must then paid or the subscriber will also be responsible for the full ount of the stake, $100 for each nomination. Notice ould be sent to Capt. B. E. Harris, 1609 Washington reet, San Francisco, and payment made by the time ecified.

---

### H. R. Covey—In Memoriam.

Harris R. Covey is no more. A brave and generous art lies silent in death. This announcement will send sorrowing pang through the bosom of many a warm d trusting friend. Few were so widely and favorably nown. Born, to use his own favorite phrase "in the

---

Western part of York State," a farmer's son, he inher-ited and innate love for the horse. Among the early emigrants to California he settled in Sacramento and through his strong will, active brain and great energy, at once became one of the leading citizens, in that, even at that early date, important town. Connecting himself with the old California Stage Company, a monstrous corporation well known to old Californians he amassed a rapid fortune. In 1853 he visited his old home. Upon his return he found the Stage Company affairs in an un-satisfactory condition and a settlement reduced his ample fortune to a pittance. Undaunted he engaged in the Livery business with his old personal friend Geo. H. Thomas, now of Walla Walla W. T. In this connection he became one of the best known men in Northern Cali-fornia. Some years later he removed to San Francisco, associating himself with the late Richard Gough and afterward became proprietor of the noted Fashion Stable on Sutter street, the firm being Porter & Covey.

H. R. Covey was no ordinary man. Of great organiz-ing power, his fertile brain and strong will greatly im-pressed every organization and business enterprise with which he became connected. A charter member of the California State Agricultural Society, he was for years one of its leading spirits. He was a prominent member of the Bay View Park Association. In conjunction with the late John M. Duncan and other prominent citizens he organized the old Bay District Agricultural Associa-tion, and in his brain originated the plan which gave to San Francisco, the magnificent Racing Park, known as the Bay District Fair Grounds. In all these enterprises, he assumed a commanding position, and his clear views and practical ideas were generally accepted without question.

But it was at the famous Palo Alto stock farm that he ac-quired an almost national reputation. Gov. Stanford's great sagacity coupled with an intimate knowledge of and high per-sonal regard for the man, led him to select him as the proper person to assist him in carrying out his great project; a most happy choice! He brought to the position a ripe experience which was invaluable to the master mind. The most perfect harmony existed between them and the result has astonished the world. To him was entrusted the delicate and important task of making the Eastern purchases of stock, and how well he succeeded the famous reputation of California's young trotters will attest. All his energies were devoted to his task and his great hope was to be able to produce an animal "na-tive to the soil" that would "lower the record."

To the writer he was greatly endeared, a close business connection extending through several years, and a warm personal friendship, existing with, scarcely a _ippp_ for a quarter of a century gave a glimpse into the inner life of the man. With the brain and strength of a giant and the heart of an ox, he was gentle and yielding as a child. With no re-gard for self, his friends and family occupied his entire thoughts. Few were so ready to give, none more willing to serve a friend. His devotion to his life time friend and pat-ron Leland Stanford was most touching. He died literally at his post, with the harness on, serving him whose friend-ship he valued above life. Of devoted friends he had a legion. Some have preceded him into the dark valley, others are now sincere and humble mourners over his lifeless clay. He has gone! In the very sight of the magnificent enter-prise which will serve as his monument, he will lie quietly until summoned by the great Redeemer at the final awaken-ing.

"Good friend! Brave heart! Hail and farewell."

C. M. C.

---

# THE PADDOCK.

### Kentucky Mules in Egypt.

The N. Y. Times, speaking of the purchase and shipment of mules from the United States to the British army in Egypt, makes the following proposition as to the manner of their use :

The British General is an intelligent and well-read man, and he would never dream of employing Kentucky mules in connection with batteries. The experiment was tried during our civil war and with the most disastrous results. In the rare cases where a battery drawn by mules lasted long enough to reach a position assigned to it on the battlefield it never proved to be of any service. The mules, the moment they were detached from the gun, invariably began an assault on the entire battery. Time after time the spirits of the Con-federates were raised by seeing what they imagined to be the explosion of a magazine in the Federal lines. They saw the air filled with guns, broken wheels and artillerymen, and it was not until they noticed the absence of smoke and noise that they could be persuaded that the phenomenon was the result of mules. Experience taught us that sixteen mules could kick a four-gun battery, including artillerymen and ammunition, into small fragments in six minutes by the watch, and after seven or eight batteries had been thus de-stroyed an order was issued forbidding the use of mules in the artillery service. The fact seems to be that the Kentucky mule has a peculiar hatred of guns. It was a Kentucky mule that, while being led through a siege battery at Peters-burg, kicked a 300-pound Parrott gun into the shape of a stovepipe elbow with a single kick, and the two mules that kicked through the twelve-inch armor of the Amicken-waupsiammonutae's turret, while that famous monitor was lying at the Williamsburg wharf, were Kentucky mules in-spired by hatred of the two sixteen-inch turret guns which, as the Captain of the monitor sadly remembers, they finally kicked overboard. To suppose that Sir Garnet is ignorant of these facts is nonsense and he would have been little else than a madman had he intended to place his artillery at the mercy of Kentucky mules. His object in importing them and timing their arrival so that they should land in Egypt ten days after the cessation of hostilities was therefore some-thing very different from what the public had imagined it to be.

The landing of the mules at Alexandria will unquestion-ably strike terror to the Egyptians. The former animals have brooded over the wrongs they have endured during their confinement on shipboard, and they will land in a more than usually gloomy and vindictive frame of mind. The Arab donkey boys will crowd around them, regarding them as a new style of donkey, and the mules will improve the occa-sion. The four thousand donkey boys will sail simultane-ously through the air, and the mules, whose appetite will have merely been whetted by the trifling exercise of kicking ten donkey boys each, will roam through the city ready to take a hand—or rather a heel—whenever an opportunity of kicking an Egyptian presents itself.

---

### Rheumatism.

When a horse falls lame at uncertain and irregular inter-vals, and suddenly recovers and as suddenly falls lame again, it indicates that the cause is rheumatism. Rheumatism is a form of inflammation arising from a disordered and usually acid state of the blood, and attacks the fibrous structures, the muscles and tendons of the body. It is frequently constitu-tional and hereditary, and shifts from place to place without warning and very suddenly, and it may as rapidly disappear by warmth, the heat of the sun, or a change of weather, rainy, warm weather being favorable. Indigestion will cause it to appear, or a cold, or even exposure to a slight change of temperature.

Distemper is an indefinite term used by horsemen generally for all diseases of a catarrhal nature. The equine family when suffering from any disease of the respiratory organs, from a severe cold to an attack of the lungs, is said to have the dis-temper. All horses are liable to have common catarrh, in-fluenza, strangles, bronchitis, pneumonia, pleurisy, etc., etc., and the symptoms which accompany each of these diseases require very different treatment. Hence, to classify all of these maladies under one head is not only wrong but liable to lead to serious errors in treatment. That form of horse dis-temper known as "strangles" is of very common occurrence, especially among young horses, the treatment of which, (un-less it should become complicated) is very simple. This dis-ease usually commences with the common appearance of mild catarrh or as popularly expressed of slight colds. The horse is somewhat dull, has often cough, some soreness of throat, a slight disinclination for food, but still more for water. The under part of the throat (in the intermaxillar space) swells, it is hot and tender, sometimes the swelling extends so as to include the whole space between the lower jaws, on the sec-ond of third day a discharge takes place from the nose of a muco-purulent character, in more severe cases a mucus secre-tion mixed with saliva flows from the mouth in large quanti-ties. Treatment: place the animal in a well-ventilated box stall, and apply a blister over the tumor, between the jaws, over which a poultice of flax-seed and bran may be constantly kept; when the tumor is sufficiently matured it should be freely lanced. It is of special good idea to steam the nose once or twice a day by allowing the patient to inhale the vapor from hot water and bran.—Farmers' Review.

The Marysville Appeal says that an epidemic is reducing the number of horses and mules in that section. The dis-ease is characterized by a cough and fever. Its manifesta-tions are confined to the head. There is a discharge from the nose, and the disease in some other respects seems to be of the nature of glanders. Every case of it is said to have proved fatal. It has existed in that section for some months. J. Tom's has lost several animals from its attacks, and on Wed-nesday Mr. Nash, at the request of the owner, shot two of Justus Greely's horses suffering from the disease:

---

### A Peculiarly Complicated Case.

(Millersburg (Pa.) Herald.)

It is not often that we are called upon to chronicle a case so persistent in its nature and inimical in its influence as the following one, communicated under the signature of Mr. Bonsall himself, the interested party, and detailing an ex-perience which, though painful and harassing in its nature and continuity, has had, so it appears, a most desirable and happy outcome. We give it in Mr. Bonsall's own words :

"LIVERPOOL, Pa., Feb. 28, 1882.

'This is to certify that I, J. E. Bonsall, postmaster at Liver-pool, Perry county, Pa., do voluntarily tender the subjoined statement : I was attacked with inflammatory rheumatism and suffered with it twenty-five weeks; the greater part of the time I was not able to move a limb, and had to be lifted around like a child. I was attended by two of the best physicians that could be had in this section at that time, who attended me twice a day as long as there was any hope for me, but finally gave me up, declaring that it was impossible for me to get well. From the stupefied long rest I partially lost the use of my right arm, which be-came stiff at the elbow joint. After the physicians ceased attendingme, and my friends commenced to use some domes-tic remedies, I began to recover slowly, and in about two months more was able to walk supported by a cane. I finally recovered my health pretty well but was subject to rheumatism whenever there would be a change in the weather, or when I would get my feet the least damp. I began to engage in light employment, taught school and then engaged in clerking in a mercantile business. I was here subject to frequent attacks of the disease which would last for a day or two, when I would be around again. In the spring of 1865 I went away to superintend a mer-cantile enterprise and I got along very well until the sum-mer of 1866, when I overheated myself working in a damp cellar, and was attacked immediately with rheumatism and fever. The doctor worked nearly all night with me, the first night I was sick, to keep it from going to my heart. For three weeks I was very ill; I then commenced to recover slowly until I was able to walk around with a cane. Then came a relapse and for two weeks longer I was very sick; however, I finally recovered so that I could attend to business part of the time, but was hardly ever free from the trouble. About this time I was completely discouraged; I spent hundreds of dollars, trying every new doctor and new medicine that I could hear of; I gradually grew worse, so that I was incapacitated for any business. I finally con-cluded to come back to my native home, but I found no re-lief. I tried everything without receiving any good. The winter of 1879 and 1880 I was so used up with rheuma-tism that I could scarcely walk from my house to my office and back again, and had to take morphine powders to get any rest at all. About that time I saw the magical medi-cine, St. Jacobs Oil, advertised in a Western paper, and read the wonderful cures that had been effected by its use. I purchased one-half dozen bottles and used it freely, rub-bing it inthoroughly by the warm stove, and then wrap-ping the painful parts in flannel cloths saturated with it. I was nearly blistered but kept at it until it made a cure. It is now over two years and I have never felt anything of rheumatism since. It is almost miraculous the effect it has had on me. Change ofweather, damp or cold does not affect me a particle. I am perfectly free from the terrible disease, after being afflicted with it for thirty-four years.

The above is a true statement of my case and not in the least exaggerated; I was really worse than I have stated above. Respectfully, "J. E. BONSALL, P. M.

---

J. Russ Kinyon of Fort Jones and A. D. (Dick) Richards of Yreka have been recommended to the Governor for ap-pointment as directors of the Mt. Shasta Agricultural Dis-trict Association. These are both excellent selections and their appointment will undoubtedly follow without delay.

# THE GUN.

## Rail Shooting.

While the recent invasion of the watery element is accredited with doing an unaccountable amount of damage the storm of the last few days, on the principle that "it is an ill wind that blows nobody good," was an unexpected boon to the shooting fraternity of this vicinity. It was heralded, as is usual on occasions of violent atmospheric changes, at this season, by a flight of aquatic birds as unprecedented in quantity in late years as was the violence and persistency of the storm. Along the coast vast battalions of golden plover, generaled by their usual leaders, the short bill curlew, were observed to pass on the afternoon of Wednesday of last week. At almost every propitious halting place the army gave out large detachments, and those that cared to be by the down-pour on Thursday and Friday reaped, in addition to a thorough soaking, a golden, feathery harvest. Even the inland meadows and pastures remote from the seaboard, on which there has been a dearth of shootable birds this season, were for a day or two supplied with an abundance of game, and had the storm abated before the lowlands were submerged, the visitors, no doubt, would have tarried until their ranks were sadly thinned by the discharges of our ever watchful sportsmen. It, however, turned out for once there was such a thing as "a drop too much," and the birds, unable to find a haven of rest, again collected and braved the storm for a less watery climate. But during their short sojourn the bags of curlew, plover, yellow legs and even of teal were sufficiently large to remind the oldest inhabitants of the glory of past such past encounters of many years ago.

But notwithstanding this exodus followed so closely on the heels of the advent, the flood which now rests upon the marsh land secures good sport for the next six weeks to come. Until it recedes, the surface will be covered with the early varieties of wild fowl, and when the waters go out they will leave the meadows a tempting paradise for the English snipe on their return from their love bowers at the North. There will be no excuse for the woodcock not to resort forbidden to the freshened covers where waits such a dainty bill of fare; hence there is something more substantial than shadows on which to reckon a good season of sport ahead. It will be several weeks, however, before we can expect to see the upland bottoms in a proper condition to receive game, and in the meanwhile those who are never satisfied unless shooting at something, must fill up the gap with excursions in quest of that most delightful sport, rail shooting.

This sport, which comes at a season sandwiched between the summer and autumn campaigns of the sportsman, is a great favorite with many who live adjacent to the proper grounds. It is pursued in a manner so unlike any other variety of shooting, that its novelty has gained a large following; besides, it is a sport that requires but a fragment of a day, and in its pursuit but little exertion. Of all the different kinds of shooting in the sportsman's calendar rail shooting as carried on on the Hackensack, near by, and the Delaware, but three hours sway, is the most luxurious. No special dress is required by its disciples, as the shooter stands in a clean boat, which is propelled through the reeds at high tide by a "pole man " or " pusher," and, barring the chances of taking a header overboard, the rail can be keeled over on a "swallow tail" as readily as out of the most orthodox shooting jacket. In this sport both old and young can participate on an equal footing, while the fat man can teeter at the bow without becoming unpleasantly moist, and the thin one will not run the risk of disappearing in the mud as if hit by a spile driver. There is no walking to do, and those accustomed to watch the performance of the bareback riders soon acquit themselves of the necessary knack of balancing and remaining upright in the boat. Added to all this, as the best time occurs in the afternoon, there is no necessity for the sportsman to sit up all night to get an early start in the morning, and last, but not least, dogs are not required for this sport, so that the shooting man without one, temporarily ceases to be a bore and a bugbear to his friends.

From the immemorial rail shooting has been synonymous with fine sport, just as rail and reed birds on toast are indicative of good living; and as the native birds of the upland grow more scarce so is the situation of the shooting fraternity directed to migratory visitants.

In this immediate vicinity, no bird is better known than the little rail. Although scarce on Long Island, the broad and extensive marshes which lie adjacent to the Hackensack and Passaic, and more especially the low meadow lands traversed by the estuaries of the last named river, are usually abundantly supplied at this season of the year with several varieties of the skulking water fowl. They are commonly known as the sora, Virginia and king rail, distinct from their brother, the clapper rail or mud hen, which makes his abode only on salt marshes. The king rail is but seldom met with, but the first two named birds are found in the early autumn by those in quest of English snipe, and as the rail emit a watery game scent they are frequently trailed and pointed by the dogs of the sportsman; indeed some carriers of the gun go afield expressly to shoot these delicious little birds, and large bags are oftentimes made when the water covers the meadows about half knee deep. But this method of pursuit is extremely laborious, nor are the bags by any means as large as made by "boating" for them.

It was not long since that the vicinity of the quaint old town of Hackensack, N. J., enjoyed the reputation of being a first-class rail ground, but the shooting there of past years has been chiefly confined to the barrooms, where the pushers congregated to watch for their lawful prey. At Milford, Conn., on Long Island Sound and about the mouth of the Housatonic there are always good days during the season, but the paradise for rail shooters in these times is along the Delaware river, on the tidewater of the James, and on the eastern branch of the Potomac. As the last named places are too remote, the sportsman of this city and Philadelphia center on the first named river. There for miles—in fact, from Trenton to the Delaware capes—the reedy shores attract numbers of rail as well as rice and reed birds. There these birds resort to feed on the seeds of the several aquatic plants, of which they are immoderately fond. These seeds, which appear to be the zizania paniculata effasa of Linnaeus and the zizania clavulosa of Willinden, grow up from the soft, muddy shores of the tidewater, which are alternately dry and covered with four or five feet of water. They grow to a height of ten feet, and enclose together that except at or near highwater a boat can with difficulty make its way through them.

The plan adopted in this section of the country is to select a day when strong easterly winds prevail, which back up the waters of Delaware bay and cause high tides, for the success of good sport depends entirely on the height of the tide and the afternoon flood tides are known to rise several inches higher than those which occur in the morning, they are generally selected. At the approach of high water,

the sportsman gets into the gunning boat and is rowed to the grounds by his "pusher." On entering the reeds he takes his stand just forward of the center of the boat; the pusher then proceeds to propel the skiff through the tops of the reeds by means of a long pole, by which he also steers his course. The rail, which take refuge as the tide advances in the matted reeds and floating drift stuff, take wing as the boat comes plowing through their skulking places. Their flight is generally slow, and with their legs dangling down, they therefore afford an easy object of aim. No sooner do they rise than the pusher calls "Mark." It is then that the gunner commences his work, and until the falling of the tide obliges the boat to leave the marsh, he shoots at each rise, while the pusher marks the birds that fall and gathers them as he travels on his way. The proficiency with which many of the Delaware pushers mark down the dead birds and retrieve them is absolutely wonderful. Frequently there are as many as a dozen birds lying about the boat, but although there is a general sameness in the reeds they seldom lose a "killed" rail. At the most the sport does not last longer than three hours, but in that time the marsh is traversed by hundreds of boats, many of whom on a good tide "boat" over a hundred birds. As high as two hundred and twenty-eight were shot by a well-known Philadelphian in a single tide one day last season; but no great bags have been made previous to the storm this year. Indeed, the shooting as yet has been unusually light, and the boats have not averaged over twenty birds. Although the sport is generally prolific of large results it is attended with danger, as often the boats congregate at some favorite spot, and their close proximity, hidden as they are from each other by the high cat-tails and wild oats, is apt to wind up in the shooting of some of their occupants. Of the two, the gun and the pusher, the latter stands in the most danger, as his raised position, on the stern board of the boat exposes him far more than the gunner who stands on the keel boards. The smallest sizes of shot are used, however, and it is said the pushers get used to the peppering, just as the proverbial eel does to the skinning. This is borne out by an incident which occurred last week. A well-known lawyer of Philadelphia was tempting his luck on the marshes below that city, when he saw what he took for a rail tangled in the reeds. On firing at the object point blank he was startled by seeing a gigantic negro leap into the air and with a rail shriek out: "Shoot again." He did not wait for results, but returned to Chester forthwith, but on the way over his pusher quietly remarked that he "guessed there was nothin' de matter wid de gun dis time," a remark that the law is rather apt to give vent to after a series of easy misses.—N. Y. Herald.

## The English Poacher.

There is no parish in England without its poacher, and in some two, three, or more may be found. I do not speak of occasional transgressors of the game laws, as idle fellows out on Sundays or holidays, who spend them in the capture of game partly for the pot, but as much by way of pastime. These are poachers too, punishable and punished all the same; but they are not accounted in the category of the regular, or as he is often styled, "professional," poacher. This, he does not style himself so, only by his trade having earned the designation; instead, he generally pretends to have some trade or other industry; and ostensibly practices it during the day. When night comes on, down go his trade tools, and in their place arming himself with nets, wire-snare, gins and guns, he is off to the game preserves. But there is also the poacher pur sang, who disdains all such subterfuge, regardless of reputation as of law, who for his livelihood depends solely on the sale of the game he may capture. Not such a poor dependence is it, either, considering that hares sell for a dollar each, pheasants the same, partridges a dollar and a half the brace, and woodcocks two dollars the couple. True, these are the retail prices; but the licensed game-dealer himself—he must be licensed—has to give figures close up to them, whether he purchases from the owners of preserves or otherwise. He is not supposed to negotiate with the poacher at all, though he often undoubtedly does, and as the traffic is illegal, with as much danger to the buyer as to the seller, the restriction in price is not so great as might be supposed. In any case, the poacher receives a fair remuneration; and the more when his dealings are direct with the consumer, as they generally are. He can almost always dispose of hare or pheasant, sub rosa, to the semi-gentility residing in villas, and the shopkeepers of the towns; besides there is never wanting in any neighborhood a publican who makes surreptitious game-dealing a specialty, and is ready to act as his "fence" and receiver. It will thus be seen that he has no difficulty in finding a market for his commodities; and, supposing him to take only a single hare or pheasant in the night, greater are his gains than those of the poor laborer who toils all day for a scant two-shilling wage. From a night's poaching, however, there will frequently accrue many heads of game; hence the temptation to follow it as a profession.

In the pursuit of his unlawful calling, the regular poacher displays remarkable skill, having an intimate acquaintance with all the ways of the game birds and animals, and the modes of capturing them. He will find the tree on which pheasants roost at night by the accumulation of their droppings underneath; the hare he catches in wire snares set in the breaks or "gaps" of hedges, where "puss" is in the habit of passing through; while the partridge he takes in the stubble, by means of long nets; or confers or two assist him to extend them. Sometimes a whole covey will be captured at a single draw. Passing through a district of country where game is zealously preserved, one often sees a stubble-field with branches of hawthorn sticking up here and there over it; the object being to obstruct night-netting by poachers. True, these might pluck the thorns up and clear them out of the way; but in doing so the birds would be flushed and cleared off soon. In most neighborhoods the rabbit is the poacher's best source of supply and emolument, its capture paying him better than even that of the nobler sort of game. And of late, more than ever, the price of rabbits having risen to a remarkable degree. But a few years ago, the indigenous wild species could have been purchased in any part of England for sixpence or twelve cents; now it is three times as much. This is partly due to the increased scale of prices for butcher's meat, the use of rabbit's flesh being found an economy. But there is also a greater appreciation of it in modern days as a delicacy, many people relaxing it so, and when properly cooked it is. Of course the poacher does not get eightenpence for a rabbit; but he has no difficulty in obtaining tenpence or a shilling. He had needs, however, be cautious in his dealings with this as with other game; they are equally under protection of the game statutes as property. A reason not so remote but related the law relating to them, as also to hares, giving tenant farmers a limited leave to kill them on their own land. Agricultural depression, with the outcry raised at the damage done to crops by the "ground game," as these are called, led to the passing of this act, which, however, has no beneficial bearing on the poor

man, against whom game and sport are alike tabooed. As to the poacher, it affects him for the worse, making every farmer a zealous watcher and aid to the gamekeeper; still poaching is not put down, but goes on as ever.

A gang of three or four poachers, working together, will capture two or three score rabbits in a night's excursion. They take them in various ways; one of which is by wire snares, set as for hares in the hedge-breaks or on the beaten "runs," when the rabbits are abroad feeding; then the poacher's dog, trained to do his part, chases the animal into them. Sometimes the snares are left set over day, to be revisited on the following night; but this is rather risky, leaving traces that may be discovered and utilized by the keeper and his watchers. When the warren itself is attacked, the poacher goes about his work in a different way, calling the ferret to his aid. The mode of procedure is to fix nets over the mouths of the burrows, then send the ferrets in, when the rabbits bolting out are enmeshed and got their necks instantly broken by a wrench from the poacher's wrist. There is no poacher without a pair or more of these trained and well-trained weasels, the most efficient assistants; and for a reason—imparted to me in confidence by one of the fraternity—the white, pink-eyed variety is preferred to the brown or "fitchet ferret;" the former from its color being easier seen in the darkness and so better for poaching, mostly done by night. In addition to his ferrets, the poacher keeps a dog, and sometimes two, in which case one will be a half-breed greyhound or lurch for "coursing" hares, when the opportunity offers at early morn or in a moonlight night. He carries a gun, too, though not always; and even when thus armed uses it sparingly, dreading betrayal by its report. The gun itself is peculiar and known as a "poacher's gun," being short-barrelled and easily taken to pieces for deposit in the inside pockets of his coat. These are ample, in fact the whole skirt is a pocket round and round, capable of containing quite a hamper full of hares and pheasants.

In the personal appearance of the out-and-out poacher there is an idiosyncrasy, both as to dress and general bearing. His garb is very much like that of a gamekeeper, only not so neat and new, and would better compare with a suit the gamekeeper had cast off. The coat is of a brown but faded velveteen, with four outside flap pockets besides the great inner one; vest of the same material; kneebreeches and gaiters of fustian or corduroy; and stout, heavy-soled half-boots, hobnailed and laced. Add a soft felt hat worn slouchingly, with a necktie loosely knotted, usually a red cotton kerchief, and you have the English poacher in the costume he most commonly affects. Not less characteristic is the expression of his features, which, though they may be naturally sinister, still have a cast about them telling of prison experience. No wonder they should; for rare is the poacher who has not spent a portion of his life inside the walls of a jail on being locked up repeatedly for spells longer or shorter. An outlaw by his own seeking and bringing about, he is often deserving of outlawry in its worst form—a very wretch and ruffian. But it would be untruthful to say that all poachers are so, or even the majority of them. Many show traits of character more commendable than condemnable; among these a proud independence of spirit, which possibly has much to do in making them what they are. For it can not be denied that in the mind of the English poor man there is an instinctive idea of resistance to law seeming oppressive—no more can it in questioned its too often having reason for it. One good quality the poacher possesses in a high degree—courage; and the very fact of his being a poacher is good proof of it. But there is other and better evidence, though bad for him, produced at almost every Petty Sessions, and certainly at every Assizes; often proof of too much courage, getting him sentenced to penal servitude for life, it not actually sent to the scaffold. "Affrays," as they are termed, between parties of poachers and game-keepers are of frequent occurrence; fierce encounters, with firearms used on both sides, as in a battle, often resulting in fatal wounds or death itself upon the spot. When beset upon such desperate resistance the poachers generally go disguised and with masked or blackened faces, though not always.

The penalty for poaching varies with the nature of the offense; the season of the year, the hours of the day or night, even religion affecting it. As, for instance, taking game on a Sunday or Christmas Day subjects the taker to a fine of £5, and for killing game birds during the close season the fine is £1 per head of those killed. These penalties, however, are not special to poachers, the owners of the game being liable to them. The laws that more affect the poacher come under the head of "Trespass," and he is termed a "trespasser in pursuit of game." When caught so trespassing in the day (which is defined as "from the beginning of the last hour before sunrise and concluding with the expiration of the first hour after sunset") the penalty is £5 and costs. If the trespass be by night it is punished not by fine but imprisonment, and the term is accumulative; for a first offense three months, with sureties required at its expiration; for a second, six months, with double the amount in money securities not to offend again; and in case of a third or further trespass it is treated as "misdemeanor." And if the trespasser refuse to give his name to those who have the right to demand it of him, offer resistance to them, or use violence, the punishment assumes a still more serious phase, especially if he be a known poacher; and above all, where there are several acting together and armed.

As may be supposed, gamekeepers and policemen are empowered to make summary arrest of those they may suspect of being poachers, and were this power confined to its legitimate purpose there would be no great harm in it. Unfortunately, however, it is not thus restricted, but too often stretched and abused, especially by the policeman. Exulting in the possession of this almost irresponsible authority, he also glories in making a display or it; the consequence being that many a poor laborer, returning wearied from his day's work, with no more thought of game-stealing than the man in the moon, is brought up by bail as of a highwayman to "stand and deliver."—Captain Mayne Reid, in the N. Y. Tribune.

A gentleman living at Cloverdale went over the district burned over by the recent fire that raged in the woods west of Cloverdale for several days, and informed us that he ran across the charred bodies of four deer in one place, two in another and six in another, that must have been surrounded by the flames and dashing to and fro in great puzzledom. He says the flames traveled with lightning rapidity, leaping gorges, jumping gaps and barren places and, where the wild oats were thickest, running like a horse. He thinks a large number of animals, wild and otherwise, must have perished.—Lakeport Bee-Democrat.

THEORY OF THE GROUSE DISEASE.—A sportsman in Scotland advances as a reason for the grouse disease on the moors the fact that countless pellets of lead are scattered broadcast over the grounds during the shooting season, and that many of these are unwarily picked up by these birds, causing inflammation and often death.

**MR. WALTER SCOTT AS A SPORTSMAN.**—It is well known that Walter Scott was passionately fond of shooting, fishing, the chase—a propensity which gained for him, among certain admirers, the sobriquet of the "sportsman-bard," a former housekeeper of the great novelist and poet is now living in the Empire State, at the advanced age of 89 years. Referring to Scott's love of field sports in a recent interview, the aged domestic said: "We often used to wonder when Sir Walter found time to write his books. He was with his dogs at noon and never came back till night, George Thompson often hunted with him. Sir Walter had dogs, and we always saw them at night, before he came night, frisking together. He had two long staghounds, a pointer and three Scotch terriers. We found, after we had on a long time with Sir Walter, that he rose early in the morning and worked hard at his books before anybody was up."—*Turf, Field and Farm.*

**BIG GAME.**—A favorite sport in Brazil and the West Indies consists in hunting humming-birds. The natives arm themselves with blow-guns made of reeds, perhaps only thirteen or fifteen inches long, and take pellets of cotton wool; with these they aim and so stun the little creatures that they fall an easy prey to their pursuers, and the beautiful image is uninjured. Travelers in countries where the humming-bird abounds form themselves into parties for this sport, and use common table salt as shot. Penetrating the skin, it has not yet spoiling the plumage, such a charge kills the bird, and great numbers are secured in this manner.

**THE GUN CLUBS OF BROOKLYN.**—It may be said that Brooklyn is not only a city of churches but a city of sportsmen, as indicated by the fact that there are some fifteen gun clubs, with a membership ranging from twenty-five to two hundred each. That Brooklyn should take rank as one of the first, if not the foremost city in the land, as regards a sportsman's clubs, is not surprising when we reflect that the most eminent clergymen—Henry Ward Beecher and T. De-Witt Talmage—warmly advocate the sports of the field.

**GOAT-SUCKERS.**—The other day, Hubert Naughton Jr., of this city, shot a bird which was new to all who examined it. It had very fine, silky feathers; had wings somewhat like a small chicken hawk; head rather owlish in appearance, but did not have the talons of a carnivorous bird. For the size of the bird, its mouth was extremely large, and was surrounded with feelers or bristles like those on a cat's nose. A careful examination of the beak convinced us that it was what it was what is known in Europe as a goat-sucker, on the popular belief that it sucks the cow's and goat's milk, infecting the animals with a deadly disease.—*Petaluma Argus.*

A **NEW CLUB.**—A sportsman's club is being organized in this county and will unite and co-operate with the California State Sportsman's Association in protecting game and fish and in the prosecution of all violators of the game laws. The members and gentlemen of the highest standing who begin to realize the importance of preserving the game of California. The name of the club has not been decided upon yet. We wish the sportsmen success with their new club.

The Greenville *Bulletin* says: On a ride around the valley last week we were surprised at the quantity of game in the shape of quail, grouse and squirrels. Just before starting, Will Murray came in with five dozen quail he had shot in about two hours in the timber near town. Both birds and squirrels are now quite fat, having been running in the grain all summer and fall. The quail can be heard on the road all the way around, but they are most plentiful on the north side near the Boyden and Banta ranches, where they are continually heard. The grouse are not as plentiful as the quail, and keep higher up in the mountains. There are very few ducks in the valley. Gray squirrels are numerous; when near the Blood ranch we saw a large hawk flying with something in his talons and on crying out he dropped it and it proved to be a very large squirrel which he had just captured.

There is a flutter among scientific men over the arrival in New York of the body of a male gorilla. The specimen was forwarded by Professor Cope and has had a trip of something like 8,000 miles. The animal was at one time the terror of a certain African jungle, 400 miles from the Gaboon. He was chased to a settlement called Kangwe on the Ogové River and there killed by a bullet in the left eye. Some missionaries residing there saw by the gorilla's appearance that he was an old fellow of no mean pretensions and being confident that such a large animal would be prized by American scientists they bartered some beads for his carcass and shipped it to Philadelphia. The animal is over five feet eight inches high. His arms are four feet six inches long and he is supposed to be twenty-five or thirty years old.—*N. Y. World.*

Some Los Angeles county boys were deer hunting in the mountains, and while stealing their way along a narrow ravine, were suddenly startled by hearing a loud cracking in the brush on the bank of the ravine. They beheld an immense bear emerge from the bushes directly in front of them, dropped their rifles in astonishment and turned to run, but brush was too quick for them. With a ferocious growl he sprang after them and struck the hindmost urchin a blow which relieved him of most of his clothing, but he escaped without further injury.

As usual, during the past week the Teal Shooting Club have had good shooting at their ponds on the Chamberlain tract ; many fine bags have been made by the members. The reason of their success while others have failed is that their ponds are all shallow and baited and are frequented by ducks that feed in shallow water mostly.

Good quail shooting is said to be had in the neighborhood of Niles. As soon as this fact becomes generally known outside of the sportsman's clubs, there will be more hunters than birds, and, like the Indian's winter stores, "they will last pretty quick."

Many persons went quail hunting in the vicinity of Millbrae last Sunday. The birds were wilder and more scarce than ever, and when the hunters returned, their game bags run from fifteen to zero. Isn't it about time to give Millbrae a rest?

Deer are reported thick in the neighborhood of Sierra Madre Valley, Los Angeles, coming down into the fields in broad daylight and eating pumpkins.

In the vicinity of Watsonville ducks are becoming plentiful on the lakes and sloughs, also snipe are appearing in goodly numbers.

A party of careless hunters near Galt last week shot and killed a fine yearling colt of John Blair's.

## Game Protection.

Nevada county ought to abound in game of all kinds above any region known. In the close season the Sportsmen's Club look out that the game law is not violated, and in the open season when the rains come no one goes hunting. The law protects the game for part of the year and the laziness of our sporting gentlemen does the same protecting the balance of the time. It is said that there has not been, this season, a single quail in the Grass Valley market.

The good rifle shots of Grass Valley are also protectors of the deer tribe. These good shots all have excellent guns of the latest and most approved make and patent. They have the very best ammunition in the world and they spare no pains to fit themselves out for a successful hunt. Their guns are globe sighted or telescopic sighted and are greased with watchmaker's oil, and all the modern improvements have our good rifle shots. They go to the forests, but bring home no deer.

There is a tow-headed youth down in the lower part of Grass Valley township who hunts deer. This youth is powerful awkward. He grew up so rapidly that he is water-jointed. He cannot help being awkward. He has an old rifle that his grandfather brought from Missouri in the early days. This old gun has an octagonal barrel, and the stock runs out to the end of the barrel. An old wire has reinforced the handle part of the stock. The lock is partly held in place by a twine string. The gun, it is said, did duty at the battle of New Orleans, and she has, since that battle, been changed from a flint and steel to a percussion. That is all the modern improvements the tow-headed youth's gun has ever had. The youth moulds his own bullets, measures his powder in the palm of his hand, greases the "patching" around his bullet with tallow held in a hole in the stock of his gun, and yet with all that he kills deer. This tow-headed youth, with his awkwardness, watery joints and primitive gun, brings venison to market.

It will soon be time to quit killing deer. That Supervisor's law which extended the open season in Nevada county is not a law at all, but is an illegal enactment. The mating season for deer is almost here and they should not be slaughtered.—*Grass Valley Tidings.*

**THE BIGGEST YET.**—R. H. Lee, the surveyor, Tom Shaw and Major Collins, while at Sawtooth last week, heard that good sport could be had at the slaughter-pen any night, in killing bear. They therefore provided themselves with Winchester rifles and struck out one evening, and were smoking cigars and considering the advisability of climbing upon the scaffolding, when a creaking of underbrush startled them. They got ready to fire all together at the word "three." A bear approached, and when a few yards off all fired at once and the bear, rising upon his hind legs, fell over and rolled into the creek. The bold huntsmen approached and poured a second volley into Mr. Bear, when they saw it was surely dead. An examination proved that the first volley had been fatal, as two bullets struck upon its forehead and the other entered one of its eyes. Fifteen men with a sled took the bear to town, where it was weighed, and it tipped the beam at 1,400 pounds. It was of the bald-faced species, and one of the largest yet killed. Its paws were sixteen inches long, and its jaws resembled a Blake ore-crusher's. This is the largest bear killed this season.—*Wood River (Idaho) Times.*

**JUDICIAL DEER STORY.**—Judge Pressley relates an incident that happened to a friend of his while hunting near the head of Santa Rosa creek. It was some thing in this way: His friend shot at a deer, and at the crack of the gun the animal fell, as if dead in its tracks. The hunter ran up to it to cut its throat, and while in the act of doing so, the deer jumped up, and then a tussle began, and it was some time before he succeeded in killing it. Upon investigation to find where the bullet struck, the place could not be found; and when about to "give it up" as a mysterious shot, he discovered that the ball had hit the deer on the tip end of one of the horns, the blow of which had stunned and knocked it down. And thus venison was obtained without the ball ever touching the flesh. This is a pretty good "deer story," but as we have heard others far more "mysterious" than this, and as it came from his honor, Judge Pressley, we have no cause to doubt its truthfulness.—*Santa Barbara Republican.*

A **GOOD SHOT.**—An expert took a trip out to Deer Creek, yesterday, to secure some ore for assaying from the bottom of a 30-foot shaft which Sam Connor was having sunk on the ledge. Laying down his gun and lunch, he swung down the windlass rope to the first platform, and then descended again to the bottom. While picking for ore-samples the light was obscured from above, and looking up he saw a monstrous stag eating his lunch at the collar of the shaft. It was but the impulse of a second, and he drew his revolver and fired. The stag reared and plunged and landed across the shaft where it lodged just long enough to permit the miner to scramble up one set of timbers under the platform—and not an instant too soon, as the stag came and over and to the bottom, and is lying there yet. The hero of this adventure threatens vengeance if his name is stated, as he fears that the Police Gazette will illustrate him.—*Wood River Times.*

A young man of rather a German accent and appearance strolled into one of the gun stores last Monday morning and remarked to the proprietor: "Mr. L——, I vos von tam fool; Saturday I makes mine mind up to gatches some fishes on de next lay. Sunday, I goes to Lagunitas mit all my vishing tackle, but ven I got there I finds dot I left mine vish hooks at home, by Chove! I stays there all tay und svares mit all my might, pecause I couldn't porrow some hooks or go home dill six o'clock. By tam!"

Game still continues to be scarce in the markets. Sprig are the most plentiful. Half a dozen canvasbacks were brought in on last Monday and they sold quickly at one dollar a pair. There are a great many quail in the market that look as if they had been shot with a trap instead of a gun, as there are no shot marks on them.

Mr. Berwick of San Francisco and Mr. Burns of San Mateo were on a joint hunt at the latter place. The result of the day's hunt was thirty-five quail. They found the birds quite plentiful but rather wild and the sport very lively as quick shooting was required in order to get any game.

Messrs. Precht and Hart were down near Belmont last Sunday and returned with the best filled bags of the day. Most of the game were rail and curlew. There was quite a large number of sportsmen down there but the game was rather scarce.

All those who contemplate going deer hunting this year should hurry up as the close season begins on the first of November.

**GAME BECOMING DOCILE.**—The last storm was so severe that the elk and deer were all driven from the mountains to the foothills and gulches, and men working at various mines along Wood River state that scarcely any morning passes that from a dozen to a hundred deer are not counted upon the hillsides. They add that they are becoming very docile.—*Wood River (Idaho) Times.*

**DEER.**—Wm. Wilbourn has killed some half a dozen deer within the past two weeks. Last week he killed a buck which dressed 175 pounds. The animal had a magnificent pair of horns which Mr. W. intends to mount as a hat rack.—*Downieville Messenger.*

Mr. A. S. Jordan killed a large male deer two miles from Summerville, on the Turnback creek. Mr. Jordan was quail hunting with a very small gun and using No. 5 shot. After shooting the deer through the kidneys, he ran about 300 yards and lay down, and submitted to having his throat cut. Four other large deer have been seen in that vicinity, and it is said to be better hunting thereabouts than much higher up in the hills.—*Mokelumne Independent.*

In Marin County, Mr. G. W. W. Roche killed a large buck, awful swamped, that weighed one hundred and fifty pound, but from the quality of the meat that he furnished a sporting friend, there is a grave suspicion that it was a spotted fawn.

The duck shooting at Sherman Island still continues to be very good. Bouldin Island, where there is usually such good shooting, is not any better.

F. Masky and T. Pierson were near Belmont last Sunday and bagged two dozen quail between them.

In different localities a few English snipe have been killed but as a rule they are very scarce.

Bear and cougars are killing calves, hogs and sheep in upper Placer county.

# THE RIFLE.

## The Shooting Tournament.

Two rifle teams will be down from Nevada to participate in the fall tournament of the California Rifle Association, one from Carson, the other from Virginia City. They will arrive on Monday by a special excursion train and will take part in all the matches that they can, but they would like best to take home with them the Pacific Slope and the Andrews trophies, as the California riflemen would have to cross the mountains in order to win them back again.

Company C, First Regiment, will enter three teams to compete for the several prizes. The team selected to shoot for the Andrews trophy, distance 300 and 500 yards, is composed of Messrs. T. T. Kelly, R. G. Perkins, H. T. Sims, J. E. Kein, F. Cummings and E. N. Snook. Company C also enters teams of six and ten men for matches 6 and 7 at 200 yards.

Company D, Second Artillery Regiment, will enter teams for the Andrews trophy and match No. 6.

Company E, First Regiment, will also enter teams for the Andrews trophy and match No. 6.

The men of the First Regiment selected to shoot for the Centennial trophy are T. T. Kelly, H. T. Sims, L. G. Perkins, Thomas Carson, Mr. Leaman, T. Murphy, F. Cummings, Mr. Fredricks, J. E. Kein and Louis Barnes.

The Second Regiment have not selected their teams but as they always send out first class marksmen there is no fear but what they will come in for their share of the prizes.

Company F First Regiment, will enter teams for the short range matches.

Many other teams will be entered in the different matches which we will mention later.

It is understood that the Carson and Virginia pistol teams who were to take part in this shooting have come to the conclusion that it is almost too far to go for a little sport. We hear that Captain Short's men are making some fine scores. The Citizens team is not behindhand this time. Captain Douglas' two teams are practicing and will take their places among the best marksmen.

Sharpshooters are taking a livelier interest in shooting matches than they ever have before and this tournament promises to be the largest ever held on this coast.

## Ball-Breaking at Bellville, Nev.

A large and enthusiastic crowd gathered at Bellville on Sunday morning last to witness the second glass-ball shooting match. There was a fair representation from this place and the sport opened at 12 o'clock with eleven entries, each of whom paid $5 for the privilege of exhibiting his marksmanship, and the chance of winning either the first or second prize, the pool money being so divided. Aside from the prize money there was much coin displayed, not a shot being made except some one wanted to bet something on the shooter breaking or missing the ball. At noon the vicinity of the shooter's position partook of a scene in the stock exchange at the hour of a lively session. The Bellville boys are a plucky lot, and enjoy betting at any kind of a game. J. M. Bell distinguished himself at this match, missing but one of the fifteen balls, and would probably have got that had not the trap thrown it so that it was between him and the sun. He, of course, took first money and Billy Craddock second, as will be seen by the appended scores:

| | | | | | | | | | | | | | | | | |
|---|---|---|---|---|---|---|---|---|---|---|---|---|---|---|---|---|
| C. R. Edwards | 0 | 0 | 0 | 0 | 0 | 1 | 1 | 0 | 0 | 0 | 0 | 0 | 0 | — | 2 |
| F. D. Gilbert | 1 | 1 | 0 | 1 | 1 | 1 | 0 | 1 | 1 | 1 | 1 | 0 | 1 | — | 10 |
| J. M. Bell | 1 | 1 | 1 | 1 | 0 | 1 | 1 | 1 | 1 | 1 | 1 | 1 | 1 | — | 14 |
| W. Craddock | 0 | 1 | 1 | 1 | 1 | 1 | 1 | 1 | 1 | 0 | 1 | 1 | 1 | — | 12 |
| E. B. Cushman | 0 | 0 | 0 | 0 | 0 | 0 | 0 | 0 | 0 | 0 | 1 | 0 | 0 | — | 1 |
| J. Smith | 0 | 0 | 0 | 0 | 1 | 0 | 0 | 0 | 0 | 0 | 0 | 0 | 0 | — | 1 |
| J. Moore | 0 | 1 | 1 | 1 | 0 | 0 | 1 | 1 | 1 | 1 | 1 | 1 | 0 | — | 10 |
| H. Taylor | 0 | 1 | 0 | 0 | 1 | 0 | 1 | 0 | 0 | 1 | 0 | 0 | 0 | — | 4 |
| L. McCleary | 0 | 0 | 0 | 0 | 0 | 0 | 0 | 0 | 0 | 0 | 0 | 0 | 0 | — | 0 |
| J. F. Johnson | 1 | 0 | 0 | 0 | 1 | 0 | 0 | 0 | 0 | 1 | 0 | 0 | 1 | — | 4 |
| L. Smith | 1 | 1 | 1 | 0 | 0 | 1 | 0 | 1 | 1 | 0 | 1 | 1 | 1 | — | 11 |

The day was a beautiful one for sport, and caused an eagerness for more of the sort. There will be allowed all who can and wish to shoot to-morrow. No one who has ever shot at balls can take part in to-morrow's match, and the fun is for those who have never tried it.

anticipation will be immense. There are eighteen entries already, which number will probably swell to twenty or more, as several parties here are discussing the idea of attending.—*Candelaria (Nev.) True Fissure.*

At Shell Mound.—Last Sunday at Shell Mound three members of the San Francisco Fusileers met in a friendly shooting match. The rifles used were the military Springfield; distance 200 yards. The following are the results.

| | | |
|---|---|---|
| Fred Kuhls | 3 4 4 5 4 5 4 4 4 4—41<br>5 4 5 4 3 4 4 4 4 4—41 | 82 |
| Louis Haake | 4 4 3 5 4 3 4 4 4 4—39<br>3 3 5 5 4 4 5 4 5 4—42 | 81 |
| H. J. Mangels | 4 4 4 4 4 4 4 4 5 4—41<br>4 4 5 4 4 4 4 4 5 4—42 | 83 |

Previous to the shooting there had been some dispute as to which of the three was the best marksman but the scores above settle the question.

Good Shooting.—Riflemen mustered in force at Walnut-hill Range, Mass., Oct. 4, when the surroundings were all favorable and excellent marksmanship was shown, as witness the following score for the long-range competition, each contestant firing fifteen shots at each of the three ranges—800, 900, and 1,000 yards: W. Gerrish, 72, 72, 70—214; W. H. Jackson, 75, 71, 68—214; F. W. Simpson, 72 68, 67—207; F. J. Rabbeth, 70, 63, 68—201; D. Webster, 73, 64, 63—200.

The *Turf, Field and Farm* says: When the report of the English riflemen's recent victory at Creedmoor reached the other side of the Atlantic, an arrogant Briton rose to the occasion with the remark that England was first in everything. "Why, if we declared war against the blarsted Americans, we'd whip them out of their boots," said he. "What, agin?" cooly queried a Yankee who had been listening to the harangue.

# ATHLETICS.

## Sprint Running in the North Country.

Pendleton, Oregon, had an event of great interest to the local sports on the 7th inst., which is described by the *East Oregonian*:

Saturday afternoon last was a lively day in Pendleton. People were in town with plenty of money from all parts of the county. The hour for the foot race arrived and the principal actors were in readiness when time was called. The first race was between Geo. W. Bishop of Pendleton and J. W. Barber of Birch Creek, for $500 a side. The race was won by Bishop easily; time 11¼ seconds; distance, 100 yards. The second race was between J. W. Barber and a supposed sheep herder by the name of Rivers, for $250 a side. This race was easily won by Rivers in 11 seconds. It is very plain now to the backers of Barber that Rivers is a professional and can beat any man in the State. He was brought up here with the intention to win a "big pile" by running against the winner. His backers believing Barber would win the first race, made the race between Barber and Rivers, but as Bishop won the race it placed things in such a light that the "pile" was not quite as big as was expected. The most friendly feeling prevailed between all parties and not a disturbance arose of any kind. Bishop's friends were wild and congratulated their hero fervently. An immense amount was up on this race and it is supposed that at least $4,000 changed hands on the first race and about $1,000 on the second. Barber acknowledged his defeat with a good grace and made many friends by his quiet, gentlemanly ways. To the victor belongs the spoils, Mr. Bishop receiving about $300 for his share of the victory.

Last Sunday, on the O. A. C. grounds, Masterson, without making any apparent effort, cleared 20 ft. 2¼ inches in a running wide jump. The measurement was the actual jump from toe to heel, without regard to the scratch start, and of course is not to be compared to a jump made in a *bona fide* contest governed by the rule for such events. Very few athletes are capable of clearing that distance under the most favorable circumstances, and with the best of preparation. Masterson jumped offhand, very carelessly, three times, clearing 19 feet the first effort and landing almost in an upright position, 19 ft 7 inches the second time, and 20 feet 2¼ inches at the third attempt. The footing on the grounds is bad for jumping, being very loose and sandy and the run to the take off a very perceptible up grade. Masterson has been slightly overworked and stale for the last two months. Since his race with Haley he has stopped training, gained five pounds in weight, and also regained the vim and energy necessary for jumping or a sprint race. Haley's best jump from toe to heel is exactly the same distance, and neither one ever had any special practice or training for a running wide jump. Haley's reputation as a sprinter is so well known that he need not fear newspaper criticisms. The O. A. C. athletes are anxious to see Masterson enrolled as one of their members, and if any two rival athletes would like to compete against Haley and Masterson they can be accommodated in five events viz: 100, 150 and 220 yards running high and standing wide jumps. Only the best need apply.

Masterson has indirectly challenged Haley for another 100 yard dash for a $20 gold medal, the match to be decided at O. A. C. meeting next Thanksgiving day. Haley refuses to run for a medal that he might have to pay for himself. He says that if his Club will hang up the trophy he will run. The last race between the two men was for an Olympic Club medal, and Haley represented his Club in a style that will not soon be forgotten by any one that saw the race, and did the best 100 yard performance that has ever been seen on the Pacific Coast. If Masterson's Club is not satisfied with the result and wants another try at Haley, it is their turn to hang up the medal.

In the weight putting, at the last O. A. C. Games, Wm. D. O'Kane entered a protest against Donohue, alleging that he was a professional. The committee reserved their decision and allowed Donohue to compete. Since that time the Committee has sent him a written notice of the protest which he has failed to answer. They therefore sustain the protest, and will award the gold medal to Slater.

University games postponed to Nov. 4th.

A. L. Balmer, a well-known member of the Caledonian Club of this city, is Noremac's trainer for the coming six-day contest in New York.

# THE KENNEL.

## The Coursing Match.

To-night, at 539 California street, the Pacific Coast Coursing Club will meet to accept entries and hold the drawing for their coursing match which will take place at Merced on Wednesday and Thursday next. Any person who takes an interest in the sport will be welcomed at the drawing and it behooves all who have dogs to run and are members of the club to be on hand to elect men to fill the important positions of judges, slipper and field stewards. A large list of entries is looked for—at least thirty-two in the "old dog stake" and sixteen in the "puppy stake." It costs only $5 for a ticket in the club's special car for Merced and as the weather is fine and the sport promises to be excellent, the club's hospitality will likely be tested to its fullest capacity.

## The Pointer in a New Light.

The pointer is a far manlier dog than the setter and I conceive that to be a high compliment to the pointer, having become convinced that the only admirable qualities modern dogs possess are those which they have learned from contact with man. It is the popular disbelief of this phase in dog character that necessitates a thorough education of the masses on the dog question. Congress might do much worse than appoint a committee of able naturalists to look into the matter, prepare a report and distribute pamphlets containing complete and well considered information on all the points of canine character. As a race we get our erroneous conception of the character of dogs in our earliest childhood. Around the wall of the very room in which I was born—and mature research has convinced me that ninety per cent. of all white children are born under similar conditions—were hung engravings representing the better and manlier side of dog character. There was Landseer's celebrated picture of an alleged Newfoundland, which by the way was a mongrel, performing his great act of rescuing a little child from a wreck. On the opposite side of the room hung the companion picture representing the same mongrel lying at ease and decorated with a medal setting forth that the brute in question was "a distinguished member of the Royal Humane Society." Another of my earliest recollections is of a picture of a noble looking St. Bernard spaniel carrying food and wine to a snow bound traveler in the Alps. And still another was the picture of an enormous Danish boarhound engaged in deadly combat with a wolf. A little child sleeping in a cradle near by was intended to give the impression that the civilized wolf was defending his master's child from the attack of the uncivilized wolf. But the artist had been a trifle too true to nature and the look on the hound's face showed plainly that he had only raised hades, so to speak, because the intruder had shown signs of carrying off a tender morsel of meat he had designs on for his own dinner. So long as the hound was well fed the child might be safe, but forget to feed him for a couple of days and the chances are that he would take a notion to sample baby meat.

These later reflections on the character of that boarhound are very different from my early impressions. Reared in an atmosphere of love and respect for dogs and their many virtues and taught that the highest type of man could well afford to pattern by the meanest type of dog, there is little wonder that like a majority of people I grew up with a firm belief that a dog was the noblest and purest of all animals, man not excepted. The influence of the pictures and early teachings quieted all doubts which arose and it was not until I had owned and trained a few dozen dogs of all kinds that I dared to become a heretic and a doubter of dog belief. So highly is an escape from the thralldom of dog superstition to be valued that one can never too highly value the labors of the pioneers and apostles of the new belief or heresy that a good man is the superior of a good dog and a bad man the equal of the best dog that ever lived. It is no easy task to shake off the old creed and adopt the new. So many of the old artists and writers were enthusiastic preachers of the old creed, that the amount of evidence in its favor is enormous. A great poet and author sung the praises of Gelert, the faithful hound. Lawrence Sterne painted beautiful word pictures having for a subject "The Dog's Fidelity." Landseer's pictures prove him a priest of the old creed. His follower Ansdell, an artist of rare ability, took up his master's theme. And even so keen and correct an observer as Charles Dickens fell into the common error or was afraid to shake off the old yoke when he portrayed his wonderful picture of Bill Syke's bull pup. It is due to the modern American humorists to say that their writings have done much to pave the way for a universal escape from the old bondage. The yellow dog of Mark Twain was probably the first animal held up to ridicule and it is not hard to believe that the lack of dog belief is broken as soon as folks generally gain strength enough to put aside so much of the old superstition as will enable them to laugh at any member of the species. The next dog held up to public contempt was the inevitable pantaloon-bosem-sampling yard-dog of Bob Burdette and the Chicago *Tribune* novelist. With that breaker up of quiet flirtatious before their eyes, the young men of America are gradually beginning to look upon the dog in his true light. They laugh at the sorrows of Gwendolin Mahafferty and Reginald De Courcy O'Brien but take care to make a good dog of their best girl's old man's yard-protector before they start out for a front gate flirtation, by a careful administration of phosphorous or strychnine. This is a cheering advance in the new belief, but I would rather see the creed grow from the enlightenment of the masses than from such ignoble feelings as scorn or hate for personal wrongs and bosem-bereft pants.

New ideas are generally promulgated in America by means of societies and it would be no bad plan to organize a "society for the presentation of dog character in its true light." The society could meet and hear papers and issue campaign documents. As a frontispiece for its works it could use to good advantage a drawing of the horrible scene enacted by a couple of dogs who recently were caught devouring the body of their dead mistress. All of this is a digression from the subject of pointers in the concrete but pertinent, in that pointers being dogs partake largely of those characteristics common to all dogs. The pointer is not a pure breed of dog, nor was one ever met any more pure in heart or temper than in blood. He is a cross between the fox-hound and the spaniel, preserving all the mean qualities of both breeds. To the cunning of the spaniel he adds the ferocity and blood-thirsty nature of the hound. He knows more about game and its habits than any dog that lives and has the keenest scent of any dog that hunts mutely, Arnold Burgess to the contrary notwithstanding. He is not such a miserable, fawning, hypocritical wretch as the setter but makes up for the lack of those qualities by the possession of an amount of deviltry hard to gauge. He never forgives a blow and frequently has pluck enough to avenge an insult, which is more than can be said of the setter. He is a hard dog to break of chasing hares and sheep, but his incomparable power of scent on a hot, dry day makes up for this weakness. The meanest kind of pointer is the Russian dog, and the poorest the double-nosed pointer. The fellow's principal vice is his slyness and sullen disposition. "He is sly, devilish sly," and nothing delights him so much as playing tricks on his master. He is a natural Arab among dogs. A spiteful, cunning, larcenous, law-breaking, irritating brute with no redeeming qualities except his occasional display of courage and his exquisite sense of smell.

Listen to what General Hutchinson says on this subject in his invaluable work on dog breaking: "I once possessed a pointer who behaved admirably while under my eye, but who, if he could cunningly contrive to get on the other side of rising ground, would invariably, instead of pointing, make a rush at any game he came across, determined, as my Irish friend used to say, 'to take his diversion,' and it was most curious to remark how immediately his pace would slacken, and how promptly he would resume a cautious carriage the moment he preceived I again had the power of observing him. His proceedings displayed so much sagacity that though I was extremely vexed, I could hardly find it in my heart to punish him as he deserved."

This is from a man whose knowledge of dogs is unequaled and who believed in the law of kindness and a good whip as the best rules for training all kinds of dogs.

The Spanish pointer is a heavier dog than the common pointer and possesses a proportionately greater amount of meanness and ill nature. It was a dog of this breed which when offended by being called to heel while other dogs were "quartering" a field, took a novel revenge on his master. The instant he was released he rushed ahead and scared every bird in the field out of range, determined that if he could not hunt himself no other dogs should. Doubtless he was a lineal descendant of the original "dog in the manger," who, I really believe, was the ancestor of all living dogs and succeeded in transmitting his special vice to all his offspring. Your pointer seldom makes friends with any man or any other dog. He is a natural bully and will fight (a smaller dog) at the drop of a hat or sooner. On that account he is generally awarded about the same amount and kind of homage among dogs as is the prize fighter or bully among men. His face is a good indication of his cruel nature. Broad between the eyes, heavy jaws, cunning eyes, and pugnacious nose are the most marked features. It makes me disgusted to see such an animal put up as a type for men to pattern by. Why, he has only got one sense that amounts to anything, the sense of smell. He only knows his master by his smell and by his scent alone gauges his estimate of nearly everything. Cut or injure his olfactory nerves and he could not pick his best friend out of a crowd of three. The smell of his master is associated with a whip and feeding time. It is true he can be taught to obey nearly every kind of signal bnt he has to be taught first to obey by means of coercion or bribes. He will hunt game he is not allowed to eat because he loves the smell of a bird. Refuse to allow him to nose the birds when killed and it is ten to one he will bolt home in disgust at pursuing a work that affords him no pleasure. He does not hunt to oblige or please his master, for he will do as much for a stranger and equally well, provided he is watched. Let him out of your sight and the brute will obey his natural instinct and rush in to get a smell at every bird that comes under range of his powerful scent, but a lifetime of bribes and abuse will scarce suffice to make him give up his natural preference for fur and stick to feather. All the good qualities in his nature he has gained by the careful teaching of man and that he can perform seemingly wonderful feats is but little in praise of the dog for, a hawk, a hunting leopard, a monkey, a flea or a sparrow are equally susceptible to careful instruction. The greyhound comes next in the scale of canine badness and is a far manlier dog than either setter or pointer.

Edwin.

## Fox-Hunting out of Season.

A lover of the chase in a recent communication to one of the leading daily journals takes occasion to make the following suggestions in regard to midsummer fox-hunting. His remarks are practical, and we commend them to the attention of our readers:

I have read with pleasure the article in to-day's issue regarding the popular pastime of fox-hunting. There is no doubt it is a pleasure that should be encouraged in this country; but there certainly should not be any hunting out of the hunting season. It is, to my mind, the most injurious thing to legitimate hunting to continue it as they have for several seasons at Newport. Who on earth ever heard of hunting in August, especially under such suns as we have, excelled for heat scarcely anywhere on earth? Fancy the discomfort and cruelty to man and beast. How it was possible for Frank Griswold, Elliott Zabriskie, the Sandford boys, young Pierre Lorillard and other sensible young men to encourage this sport out of season I cannot for the life of me imagine. No wonder the farmers growled and objected to hunting before the oats or corn were gathered. There is no hunting country in the wide, wide world that would have tolerated such wanton wickedness for a day. August weather—just think of it! weather that tries the souls of men and the hearts of horses—to call upon them for this sort of work! Fie! fire! out upon such trifling as this! By all means go on with hunting. That our country is all over ill adapted to it, being nearly all post and rail or too small patches of land with stone walls, is true. Still, we must put up with what we have and make the best of it, for our horses, with the little experimental hunting done in the States, have shown an amount of adaptability to the work that would appear almost incredible to the fox-hunting expert of the Old World. Under normal conditions by all means, then, let hunting be encouraged. It is, by all odds, the father of sports—far ahead of any health-giving pleasure ever devised; but for the sake of the noble art of 'cross country work give up the circus performances and brass band—the midsummer hunting season at Newport.

Thoroughbred.

The Moodus Dog Swindler.—The notorious dog swindler of Moodus, Conn., who has defrauded so many sportsmen through his tempting advertisements in various journals, under the names of Pollard, Chester, Fowler, Hammond, etc., has at last come to grief, and is in jail at Middletown, Conn,

An English contemporary records the
ving remarkable accident in the hunting field, as having
red to Mr. T. Dawson, huntsman of the West Kent
ounds: The pack were out cub-hunting on the estate of
Jeorge Wood, at West Court, Southfleet, when Dawson's
: suddenly disappeared from under him, having fallen
draw-well some five-and-twenty feet deep. Fortunate-
rider saved himself by hanging on to the boughs of a
The first whip, Will Percy, was lowered into the pit,
ound the horse on his back, with the saddle smashed to
s, and the animal was very savage at first and bit at Per-
It took a little more than two hours to get the horse up,
it was found he was not in the least hurt, though of
very stiff. A couple of fox-hounds and a fox-terrier
ell with the horse, the former being uninjured, but the
r, having broken his leg, was destroyed. There are, it
, two more similar pits in this wood, and they should
ut delay be railed around, as being covered up with
wood, it is impossible to see where they are, and next
any one falls into them the result may prove more dis-
s.

re will be a coursing match, free for all dogs in the
at Corcoran's ranch on the Mokelumne Hill road, to-
w, 22d.

# ROWING.

## English Amateurism.

he London *Field* expresses delight at the unpleasant re-
s of the race on the Thames, between the Hillsdale and
umes crews. The *Field* explains in a decidedly plain man-
why the visits of American amateur oarsmen to England
not desired. The *Field* is an exponent of the ideas of the
sses of Englishmen whose pride it is to keep the cuentch-
of amateurism pure and undefiled by contact with base
lians whose prowess would be likely to paralyze aristo-
ic muscle. This eminently critical and respectable Eng-
journal trusts that in the "ill-advised match" between the
sdale and Thames crews it "has seen the last of the vis-
to England of these pseudo amateurs from across the At-
ic." The *Field* shows how utterly impossible it is to rec-
le the fastidious authorities of English amateurism to
competition of representatives of the aquatic ability of
erican tradesmen and mechanics. Did any hope exist
the standard of American amateurism might be raised
*Field* could regard with some degree of complacency the
spect of another international race. But unfortunately
the *Field's* peace of mind the degradation of American
ateurism is hopeless. Our fastidious English contempo-
y thus bewails the mournful disrespectability of American
as which tolerate the competition of ordinary mechanics
th hardly and blue-blooded bank clerks and fifteen-dollar
ok-keepers in insurance offices:

We have little room to be sanguine that the American row-
g world will ever be induced to make its definition of ama-
ur status to once more approximate to our own standard,
ad for this reason, that the classes in society from which in
ngland amateurs chiefly spring do not in America take
indly to rowing as a pastime; they look down on it, and,
nless as their universities, the young men of good family
ould as soon be seen by their parents in a casino as in the
unks of a rowing club. And it is equally unfortunate that
ie universities in America are themselves socially so mixed
class that many a man who by calling and mode of life
ould be an artisan and hence belong to the professional
ses obtains a seat in a college crew. Even in dealing, there-
re, with crews from American universities we must care-
ully divest ourselves of the notion that membership of a
ollege is synonymous with amateur status, according to our
nglish requirements. We have from the first deprecated
ie late match in every shape, still more the tacit recognition,
s a corollary, by the English club, of the claims of the Hills-
ale crew to be amateurs, and equally the deduction, by a
arge portion of the press and the public, that the match was
n international one in the sense of the Thames crew being
ccredited representatives of British amateur oarsmanship.
Jevertheless, if this match, and the expose which it has pro-
uced of the character and characteristics of so-called Ameri-
an amateurs, should have the effect of inducing English au-
iorities in future to abstain from accepting American cre-
entials on *ex parte* statements; and if, also, the "National
Association of Amateur Oarsmen," U. S. A., will kindly keep
> the restriction of which we published a copy in our issue
f last week, and insist on being recognized *ex-officio*, or not
t all, in England, we shall gladly admit that for once out of
vil cometh good.

American oarsmen ought to feel deeply grateful to the
'eld for its candid statement of the reasons which made the
isit of American amateurs to England about as welcome as
ie small-pox. In plain words the *Field's* long article means
nat if American oarsmen go to England as professed profes-
onals they will be cheerfully welcomed and carefully com-
nended to the company of a social fellowship of the publicans
round Putney or the jolly young watermen of Blackfriars who
ave to hire some one to sign their names to articles of agree-
ients when they make a match. But if American amateurs
ross the Atlantic expecting social recognition from the aristo-
natic bank clerks who maintain the dignity of their high stand-
ng as members of the London Rowing Club on $100 a year,
ien the American amateurs greatly miscalculate the English
entiment towards them and should be speedily brought
n a sense of their inferiority and disreputability as inter-
opers, and "cads."

THE CHAMPIONSHIP.—The Pioneer crew began to train reg-
larly this week for the Thanksgiving Day race for the
BREEDER AND SPORTSMAN's cup, the possession of which will
arry with it the championship of the Pacific Coast. The
ompeting oarsmen are all satisfied with the arrangements
iade by the three interested clubs, with regard to length and
osition of the course. As some doubts exist of the correct-
ess of the Long Bridge three-mile course it will be accu-
ately surveyed before Thanksgiving Day so as to make the
me record of some value. It would be as well when a sur-
ey is being made to test the accuracy of the alleged two

miles usually rowed. Dan Leahy has made some wonderful
trials over the two-mile course and has frequently expressed
the belief that it was short, but the scullers who have been
falling outside the 15 minute mark in their trial think differently. It is not yet definitely settled who shall represent the
Pioneer Club in the Thanksgiving Day race. Mike Long the
veteran oarsman has been rowing in the bow of the Pioneer
boat during the past week but it is not certain that he will consent to take part in the contest. Both the Ariel and the Golden
Gate Clubs have finally decided on their crews. The Golden
Gate crew is a very strong one but it seems to us that the
Ariel four might easily be strengthened. The four men who
will row own the boat, however, and think that their financial
interest is paramount to that of the club. The wisdom of
their opinion will be shown on Thanksgiving Day.

THE PIONEER CLUB.—The annual meeting of the Pioneer
Rowing Club was held last Sunday. The reports of the Secretary, Trustees and Treasurer showed that the condition of
the Club's affairs was most satisfactory. Officers were elected
as follows: President, T. E. Flynn; Vice-President, L. C.
White; Treasurer, John Sullivan; Captain, P. J. Brennan;
Lieutenant, Henry Price; Trustees, T. H. Murphy, R. C.
Lyne, J. P. Brennan. During the year the Pioneer Club has
built an addition to the boat-house and added to its stock of
boats. It has now a flourishing membership and more boats
than any other club on the Coast.

HOSMER'S VICTORY.—At the Lake Massabesic regatta, at
Manchester, N. H., October 2, George H. Hosmer, George W.
Lee, James Riley, Daniel Driscol, P. McInerney and J.
Carey competed for the professional single scull pull over a 2½
mile with a turn course. Hosmer won, Lee second, McIner-
ney third; time, 18:07. The four-oared race was won by the
West End crew. Courtney gave an exhibition pull and beat
the time made in the single scull race.

THE TIME TOO FAST.—Hanlan is evidently of the same
opinion as Ross, Kennedy and thousands of others regarding the three-mile time of George W. Lee and Charles Courtney. In Boston recently he was asked if he could row faster
than the above-named scullers are said to have done at Richfield Springs. He said that although he didn't think he
could row so fast he could defeat them on that or any other
course.

GEO. GAISEL has posted $100 with W. B. Curtis to bind a
challenge issued by William Elliott for another three-mile
race, on Greenwood Lake, Saratoga Lake, the Passaic river
at Newark, or any fair course except Flushing Bay.

# YACHTING.

## Launching a Cutter.

From the New York *Spirit of the Times* we take the following:

Mr. James Stillman's fine cutter Wenonah was successfully
launched on the 21st inst. from the yard of Henry Piepgras,
her builder, at Pottery Beach, Brooklyn, E. D. The weather
was most unpropitious, it having been the first day of the
equinoctial storm, and a chill northeast wind and dull leaden
sky made the occasion rather a gloomy one. Scarce any
publicity had been given to the event, and the attendance was
small. Mr. M. Roosevelt Schuyler attended on behalf of
Mr. Stillman, and performed the christening ceremony. The
only others of any note that were present were Mr. John
Harvey, the designer of the yacht, Commodore C. S. Lee, of
the Seawanhaka Yacht Club, and Mr. J. Frederick Tams, of
the same club. Mr. Stillman, it is said, has been deterred,
by sickness in his family, from making an intended cruise in
the Wenonah this fall, and, therefore, has not hastened her
completion in any way, and as a result of this he will probably have a more perfect vessel.

The completion of this vessel and the Bedouin should put
an end to all controversy as to superiority of type. We have
now these two cutters, in addition to the Oriva, Maggie and
Muriel, besides a score or so vessels of the cutter type in
Eastern waters. And the cutters may now be left to improve
themselves if they can. An cause of expense is worth a
pound of theory, and if these vessels are superior to the
beamy centerboard sloop, the American yachtmen will quickly find it out, and they will replace the centerboard.

We have never thought that they were superior, and don't
think so now, but we dont pretend to be the embodiment of
all the yachting wisdom of the world, and it may be that we
are mistaken. One very serious objection to them is their
great cost. For what the Wenonah cost three centerboard
sloops of the same length could be built, and the cost, therefore, is a serious objection to the cutter. But it is not a fatal
one, and we have plenty of rich men who can stand the cost
without inconvenience. Moreover, it is not absolutely essential that the cutter shall be as expensively built as the Wenonah, Bedouin, and Oriva have been, and the same model
may be had at far less cost. A more serious objection is the
at present apparent necessity of English canvas, and an
English skipper and crew. But this necessity is more apparent than real, and if this type of boat shall become common, the Yankee skipper will soon learn how to handle them
quite as well as the imported captain can. The great draught
of water is another objection, closing, as it does, to them
many harbors; but then it may be urged that, with this type
of boat, there is not the same necessity of making a harbor as
in the case of the centerboard, and if Long Island Sound be
barred to them they can have ample room out on the ocean.
So, then, we are disposed to give them a fair show, and, so far
as this particular boat is concerned, we wish her every success.

The outerlooked very handsome as she rested on the ways
previous to the launch. Her topmast was on end, and her
spars, except the main boom, were in place. From her main
truck floated an American ensign, this being the only attempt
at ornamentation. From each haws-pipe a stout rope led
with slack enough to allow for the yacht to clear her ways;
turns being then taken around two heavy timbers anchored
in the ground, at which were stationed two of the most trusty
of her crew to see that her way was checked ere she reached
the bulkhead forming the outer line of the basin in front of
the shipyard. Owing to her peculiar shape, the yacht had to
be hung in chains for her whole length, no part of her bottom
being flat enough to rest directly on the ways. The work of
wedging up began at 3:15 and consisted merely of tightening
the chains. Ten minutes sufficed for this, and then beginning aft, one after the other the blocks, on which her keel
had rested since it was laid, were knocked out with a heavy
battering ram, and the keel rested in the bight of the chains,
the ends of which were fast to the standard affixed to her
bilges, the lower ends of which rested on the well-greased

ways. At 3:45 the woodlocks, which bound the sliding to the
fixed ways, were knocked out, and the yacht was free to go.
She did not, however, start, and for the moment it was feared
that the great heat of the previous day had melted the grease,
and that the boat would stick on the ways. Half a dozen
blows of a ram, however, on the end of, the ways started
them all away the cutter went down the incline, taking the
water beautifully and floating clear of the ways; she shot
across the basin, the head lines checking her way just before
she reached the outer bulkhead.

The Wenonah belongs to the New York Eastern, Seawanhaka, Larchmont, and St. Augustine Yacht Clubs. Her
owner, who formerly owned the schooner Wanderer, and
later the cutter Muriel, the sloop Regina and steam yacht
Lurline, is one of the most prominent yachtsmen in this
country. Not being able to obtain an American register for a
cutter built in England, he has, in order to test the comparative merits of the two types of boats—British and American
—as fairly as possible, had the Wenonah built from plans of
Messrs. Harvey and Pryor, of London, and her sails made by
Lapthorne, the most approved of British sailmakers. She
has been rigged, and will be sailed by Captain Harlow and a
picked British crew, brought here from England for this purpose. Except, therefore, that she has been built here, the
Wenonah is to all intents and purposes a British yacht. Her
dimensions are: Length over all, 72 ft.; on water line, 60 ft.;
extreme beam, 14 ft.; depth of hold, 10 ft. 6 in.; draught of
water, 10 ft. 6 in. She is ballasted entirely with lead,
twenty-four tons of it being cast in one piece, on her keel,
and about as much more into the inside, moulded to fit her
frames. Her spars are much more taunt than is customary
in British yachts, the yachting weather here being much
lighter than in the channels. Her mast is 66 ft. 6 in. extreme length. From deck to mast-head it is 55 ft.; the topmast is 40 ft.; boom, 58 ft.; gaff, 38 ft.; bowsprit, out-board,
28 ft. The latter is round and fitted to house or reef. Her
cost will be, when complete, about $30,000.

CLOSING DAY.—The following sailing orders have been
issued by Commodore Harrison of the San Francisco Yacht
Club for Closing Day:

Yachts will assemble off the Club House at Sancelito, and
anchor as most convenient, previous to 1 o'clock p. m. on
Saturday, October 25th, 1882.

At 2 p. m., the fleet will "dress ship."

At 3:00 p. m., the "preparatory gun" will fire, and five
minutes later, the "starting gun," when the fleet will get
under way, and proceed to Mare Island, anchoring on the
Vallejo shore, and well north of the ferry landing.

On Sunday, October 29th, at 12 o'clock, noon, the "preparatory gun" will fire, and five minutes later the "starting
gun," when the fleet will get under way, but not cross the
line of the Georgia Street wharf until the flag-ship hauls down
her ensign and fires another gun, which will be when the
yachts are well together, and then will "try rate of sailing"
to San Francisco, passing to the west of Blossom Rock buoy.

Yachts will observe the gun for "colors" as 8 a. m.

Yachts shall set no canvas before the "preparatory gun"
and shall not hoist head-sails, or back ground until after the
firing of the "starting gun."

An interesting race will come off to-day over the S. F. Y. C.
course between the Chispa and Whitewing. It is a Corinthian race and a test of the skill of Messrs. I. Gutte and John
D. Spreckels. The latter will sail the Whitewing; the former
the Chispa. No light sails will be used. Only four men are
allowed aboard. The judges are Capt. Cummings, Fulton
Berry and Charley Hale. Each of the two gentlemen who are
to sail the yachts thinks he is the most skillful helmsman,
and this test is to decide the mooted point. The Chispa is
acknowledged the faster yacht, but Mr. Spreckels has had
more experience in sailing than his opponent.

The San Francisco Yacht Club will "close the season" on
October 28 in the usual manner by a dance at the club-house
at Sancelito and a moonlight sail to Vallejo. There will be
dancing from 3 to 6 p. m., and guests will return at 6:30 p. m.
The yachts will leave for their cruise before the guests depart,
so the start can be seen. This is the last yachting event of
the season of 1882. It has not been a very brilliant one
from any point of view.

Dr. Merritt has laid the Casco up for the winter at her old
berth alongside the Webster St. bridge in Oakland harbor.
She has a canvas awning over her fore and aft. Her sides
have been covered with old carpets and canvas so she shall
not dry out. Her spars have been oiled. The Casco has
done little outside cruising this season.

The Anita has had a redwood house built over her cabin
which will remain while she is up in the marshes. It serves
the purpose of enlarging her accommodations very materially.
In fact it makes a two-story yacht of her.

The Canadian sloop yacht Atlanta, which raced for the
America's Cup as the champion of the Bay of Quinte Yacht
Club, has been seized by the United States Marshal for an un-
paid ship-chandler's bill.

Captain Mintrey's skipper is on the beach in Oakland
Creek alongside Farmer's boat-shop, being overhauled. She
is to have an eight-foot gaff instead of the little short one she
has been carrying.

The Emerald got becalmed on Saturday evening and had
to stay out all night with a good-sized party aboard.

The Flirt has been laid up in Oakland Creek for the winter. She is alongside the old St. George boat house.

The yawl Ariel has been put on the beach to find a leak.
She wanted cleaning too.

The new owners of the Nellie seem to be enjoying their
purchase.

The Aggie has been on the dry dock and been cleaned.

The Violet is laid up in Oakland Creek for the winter.

The Lively is laid up in Oakland Creek.

The Chispa was on the ways last week.

Now is the time for up-river cruising.

Dutch Oven's winnings from her first race up to and concluding the Thirty-fourth Triennial Stakes at Newmarket on
September 27 amount to £16,900 10s.

# CRICKET.

## Cricket at East Portland.

Moral—When the wicket man turneth away from his wicketness he shall save his bacon. And don't you forget it.
—*Dr. Watts.*

P. S.—Not with the old eleven of malice and wickedness, but with the eleven that are bred up to sincerity and truth.
—*From a Grog-orion Chant.*

The cricket-playing tars from the vessels in port met on the East Portland Cricket grounds on Saturday afternoon, as arranged, but after waiting for their opponents till half-past three, and only one member of the club turning up, they resolved to have a friendly match among themselves, Mr. Warren and Captain Mearns kindly consenting to act as umpires.

The weather was everything that could be desired, just sufficient rain falling to lay the dust.

The result of the match was as follows:

**CAPT. FOWLER'S SIDE.**

| | |
|---|---|
| Fenton, run out b. Murray | 10 |
| Emory bowled Reid | 5 |
| Gipps, run out b. Reid | 2 |
| Chevers, not out | 1 |
| Fennig, caught out b. Murray | 6 |
| Bennett, bowled Reid | 5 |
| Mack, bowled Murray | 3 |
| West, caught Bennett, bowled Reid | 2 |
| Capt. Fowler, caught Hale, b. Reid | 7 |

| | |
|---|---|
| Wickets | 6 |
| Extras | 0 |
| Wides | 9 |

**CAPT. MILNE'S SIDE.**

| | |
|---|---|
| Cook, run out | 12 |
| Hale, caught West, bowled Emory | 4 |
| Hutchinson, caught Penny, b. Fenton | 3 |
| Murray, run out | 3 |
| Kennedy, b. Emory | 14 |
| Watt, b. Fenton | 4 |
| Nelson, b. Fenton | 4 |
| Reid, b. Emory | 3 |
| Capt. Milne, stumped Fenton, b. Emory | 5 |
| Becket, not out | 6 |

| | |
|---|---|
| Wickets | 100 |
| Bye | 4 |

| | |
|---|---|
| Total | 111 |

As the tits tars will shortly be leaving port they wish before sailing to tender their sincere thanks, through the *Oregonian*, to the president and members of the P. C. C. for their kindness in giving them the use of their grounds and cricket gear, which has afforded them so much pleasure during their stay in Portland, and they wish that every success may attend them in their future career.—*Oregonian.*

## Australian Cricketers in New York.

The Australian cricketers now in the East seem to have nothing but walk-overs this season. The following review of the games played last week is from the *World:*

The Australian cricketers first visited New York in October, 1878, and in the first week of that month played against an eighteen of St. George, Staten Island and Manhattan clubs. In that match the Australian eleven—which included Messrs. Spofforth, Boole, Garrett, Murdoch, Horan, Blackham and Bannerman of the present visiting team—found some trouble in defeating the New York eighteen by a score of 70 and 92 (162) to 63 and 98 (161), the Australians having five wickets to fall when they exceeded the local team's score. Yesterday the world's champion team of cricketers—for that is what this present Australian team is—played against an eighteen of the St. George, Staten Island, Manhattan, Newark and other clubs on the same field at Hoboken, and this time the visitors without any special effort disposed of the eighteen for twenty-five runs off the bat. In fact the Australians, who are noted for their field skill, made rather an inferior exhibition in the support of the bowling, catch after catch being missed in a manner rather surprising to the spectators. But the contrast between the batting of the two eighteens of 1878 and 1882 was rendered more striking by the fact that the weak batting was followed by still worse fielding. In fact it was made painfully evident that since the last visit of the Australians cricket has degenerated mainly here. There was but one redeeming feature of yesterday's cricket on the part of the eighteen, and that was some remarkably effective bowling, notably in the case of Lane and McColl. In 1878 the eighteen's fielding and bowling was the best ever shown by a local team in an international match. This time, while the bowling was up to the mark, the fielding, as a whole, was simply wretched. Had the eighteen's bowling been well backed up in the field the Australians would not have scored 70 runs. As it was, they ran up only 110 for the loss of nine wickets—quite a small score for such an eleven. Of this number Murdoch contributed an unearned score of fifty, he giving two easy chances for catches after scoring a dozen. Giffen added thirty-six, all of which, save the last run, were well earned by good all-round hitting, combined with a steady defense. All the others failed to contribute even average figures. The wicket was a bowler's wicket and it exactly suited Spofforth, who took ten wickets for twelve runs. Lane, on the other side, took five wickets for twenty-three runs, a fine record against the bats opposed to him. McColl took two wickets for three runs and proved himself a damaging bowler to the visitors after the fifth wicket fell. Bannister was terribly punished with a score of thirty-seven runs off twenty-four balls. Blackham and Spofforth are the two Australian not-outs and they will resume their positions at the wickets to-day, and the chances are that the eighteen will have to go in to get nearly a hundred runs to escape a defeat in one inning, and unless a surprising improvement is shown in their play this is something they are not likely to do. The attendance was larger than expected, and the number of veteran cricketers present was noteworthy. The champion oarsman of the world, Hanlan, was a guest of the Australians at the club-house Monday. The score of Monday's play is as follows:

**NEW YORK.**

| | |
|---|---|
| Wilson, c. Giffen, b. Boyle | 3 |
| Bannister, b. Spofforth | 6 |
| Brooks, b. Spofforth | 1 |
| Lane, b. Spofforth | 0 |
| Mart, c. Murdoch, b. Boyle | 1 |
| Bally, b. Spofforth | 0 |
| Davey, c. Blackham, b. Boyle | 0 |
| McLachlan, b. Spofforth | 4 |
| Capt. White, l. b. w. b. Spofforth | 0 |
| Lambken, l.b.w icket, b. Boyle | 0 |
| Bannerman, b. Spofforth | 1 |
| McColl, c. Jones, b. Boyle | 1 |
| Middclinson, b. Boyle | 0 |
| Mearns, c. Massie, b. Spofforth | 0 |
| S. Moore, st. Blackham, b. Spofforth | 0 |
| Hill, b. Spofforth | 0 |
| Cleverly, not out | 0 |
| Armstrong, b. Spofforth | 0 |
| Bye | 7 |

| | |
|---|---|
| Totals | 37 |

| | |
|---|---|
| FALL OF WICKETS | |

New York—5, 3, 3, 9, 10, 11, 12, 15, 18, 19, 19, 21, 26, 26, 27, 27, 27.

**AUSTRALIANS.**

| | |
|---|---|
| Massie, b. Lane | 0 |
| Bannerman, b. Mart | 6 |
| Murdoch, c. Hutchinson, b. Lane | 50 |
| Horan, b. Lane | 6 |
| Bonnor, b. Cleverly | 6 |
| Giffen, l. b. w. b. McColl | 36 |
| Jones, b. McColl | 0 |
| Garrett, b. Lane | 0 |
| Boyle, c. Hutchinson, b. Lane | 2 |
| Spofforth, not out | 0 |
| Bye | 4 |

| | |
|---|---|
| Total | 110 |

| | |
|---|---|
| FALL OF WICKETS | |

Australians—6, 8, 29, 82, 106, 106, 107, 110, 110—110.
Umpires—Messrs. Allworth and Midwinter. Time of game—Four hours and twenty minutes.

**Second Day.**

The cricket match between the New York eighteen and the Australians was continued yesterday at Hoboken and was won by the champions with seven wickets to spare. The day was all that could be asked, both for players and spectators, and those present enjoyed a very pleasant afternoon's outing. When the stumps were drawn on Monday Blackham and Spofforth were the "not outs." The latter was disposed of yesterday for 2, having been handsomely bowled by Lane, which left Blackham to carry his bat out for 6, with a total of 116 runs for the inning. The "eighteen" then began their second inning, and as Spofforth and Boyle were not put on to bowl it was quickly seen that the Australian captain had decided to give the eighteen a chance, and it was fair, all-round cricket until Lane was called, after which the play was made much sharper, the crack bowlers going in again, but the eighteen continued to do well and it was not until they had scored 102 runs that they were all disposed of, which, with the 37 scored in the first inning, made a grand total of 139 against the Australians' 116 in their first inning, which compelled them again to go to the bat. They found the bowling so good, however, that three wickets fell for 11, the feature of the playing being the handsome throwing out of Spofforth by Cleverly. The few remaining necessary runs were, however, quickly scored, leaving the total of the game as follows:

**AUSTRALIANS.**

| First Inning. | | Second Inning. |
|---|---|---|
| Massie, b. Lane | 6 | |
| Bannerman, b. Mart | 9 | |
| Murdoch, b. Hutchinson, b. Lane | 54 | not out |
| Lane | 34 | not out |
| Horan, b. Lane | 6 | |
| Bonnor, b. Cleverly | 6 | not out |
| Giffen, l. b. w. b. McColl | 36 | |
| Blackham, not out | 6 | |
| Jones, b. McColl | 0 | b. Lane |
| Garrett, b. Lane | 0 | b. McColl |
| Boyle, c. Hutchinson | 2 | thrown out, Cleverly |
| Spofforth, b. Lane | 2 | |
| Bye | 4 | Bye |

| | |
|---|---|
| Total | 116 |
| Total | 14 |

First Inning—6, 8, 29, 82, 106, 106, 107, 110, 110, 116—116.
Second Inning—6, 7, 10, 14—14.

**THE EIGHTEEN.**

| First Inning. | | Second Inning. |
|---|---|---|
| Wilson, c. Giffen, b. Boyle | 3 | c. Bannerman, b. Boyle |
| Bannister, b. Spofforth | 1 | c. sub. b. Murdoch |
| Brooks, b. Spofforth | 1 | b. Giffen |
| Lane, b. Spofforth | 0 | c. Massie, b. Murdoch |
| Mart, c. Murdoch, b. Boyle | 1 | b. Spofforth |
| Bally, b. Spofforth | 0 | c. Massie, b. Boyle |
| Davey, st. Blackham, b. Boyle | 0 | b. Boyle |
| McLachlan, b. Spofforth | 4 | b. Spofforth |
| Capt. White, l. b. w., b. Spofforth | 0 | |
| Lamb in, hit wicket, b. Boyle | 0 | st. Blackham, b. Boyle |
| Salngder, c. Bannerman, b. Boyle | 0 | c. Boyle, b. Spofforth |
| Lane | 1 | c. Murdoch, b. Boyle |
| McColl, c. Jones, b. Boyle | 1 | b. Spofforth |
| Hutchinson, b. Boyle | 0 | c. Giffen, b. Boyle |
| Mearns, c. Massie, b. Spofforth | 0 | b. Spofforth |
| J. S. Moore, st. Blackham | 0 | |
| Hill, b. Spofforth | 0 | b. Blackham, b. Spofforth |
| Cleverly not out | 0 | st. Blackham, b. Murdoch |
| Armstrong, b. Spofforth | 0 | b. Spofforth |
| Bye | 7 | |

| | |
|---|---|
| Totals | 37 |
| Totals | 102 |

First Inning—3, 3, 3, 9, 10, 11, 12, 15, 18, 19, 19, 21, 26, 26, 27, 27, 27—37.
Second Inning—6, 29, 45, 56, 70, 72, 74, 75, 76, 86, 86, 86, 87, 87, 96, 96, 102—102.
Grand Total, 129.
Umpires—Messrs. Allworth and Midwinter.

# FISH.

## Habits of Black Bass.

Seth Green, in a note to the New York *Herald* regarding the efforts to stock English waters with American black bass, gives the following items of interest on fish culture:

I notice in your issue of October 3 an article entitled "Black Bass in England," and making the announcement that Mr. W. T. Silk, of Burghly Park, Stamford, is now in this country for the purpose of procuring another supply of black bass for English waters. I observe in the article that Mr. Silk is to obtain for transportation the small black bass three and four inches long, and I would suggest that he take the large or mature black bass, from three-quarters of a pound up, instead of the smaller ones. One pair of mature black bass would produce at least 2,000 or 3,000 young the first year, undoubtedly a greater quantity than will be transported.

The black bass, unlike the salmon family, protect their young until they are old enough to take care of themselves. If 200 mature black bass could be deposited in English waters suitable for them, fifty each in four different bodies of water, their increase would stock all Great Britain in a few years. The great food for black bass is the fresh water lobster or crawfish, and if the English waters do not contain them I would advise transporting a large quantity. The success in stocking all waters is as much dependent upon the food supply as on the depositing of the fish themselves.

## Black Bass in English Waters.

We have before alluded to the success attending the efforts of English anglers and fish culturists in the introduction of black bass on the other side of the Atlantic, and the growing appreciation of its game qualities abroad. Englishmen are proverbially fond of all manly field sports, and many of them make occasional visits to America for the purpose of enjoying a greater variety of shooting and fishing than can

be obtained elsewhere. The game qualities of the black bass attracted the attention and admiration of certain anglers from Britain, and the glowing reports given to the fraternity in Merrie England through the *Field* and the *Fishing Gazette* awakened a general desire to know more of the fish. In 1878 a lot, consisting of about 150 black bass from the upper Delaware, were placed in Whitewater Lake, a preserve owned by the Marquis of Exeter, and the year after nearly a thousand of the same species were transferred to the lake, where they thrived and grew to maturity. The success of this experiment was such that W. T. Silk, one of the most practical fish culturists of England, who superintended the transplanting of the first and second lots, has recently returned for a larger supply, to be taken from Greenwood Lake and the Delaware. Mr. Silk proposes to secure about 2,000 of the small-mouthed variety, and these will be distributed in different parts of England, a portion being intended for the Norfolk Acclimatization Society, and others for the Westminster Aquarium, the public reservoir at Wakefield, in Yorkshire, and also for the preserves of the Duke of Manchester, and Mr. R. B. Marston, editor of the English *Fishing Gazette.* Many well-known lovers of the angle throughout Great Britain are enthusiastic over the acquisition of such a game fish as the black bass, which is now recognized as second only to the trout by those best qualified to judge.—*Turf, Field and Farm.*

## Smelt in Fresh Water.

The delicate texture and delicious flavor of the smelt give it rank with the most delectable of the sea fishes. People whose homes are near the coast and where it abounds, appreciate it as a luxury; and if it would bear transportation as well as the oyster, the demand for it, at great distances in the interior, would be much above the present sources of supply.

Were it generally known that this fish is adapted to fresh water, and may be successfully planted in most of our large, clear lakes, there would be a great call for it for stocking purposes. A few smelt put in Lake Champlain several years ago have led to their permanent establishment in that water; and those who have eaten them pronounce them fully equal in quality to those of salt water growth. In 1880, some furnished by Mr. Blackford were put into Otsego Lake, which seemed one of the best adapted to test them. Circumstances not favorable to a successful plant may have prevented success in this case, as none of the product have been seen in the lake. But the experiment is worth continuing.—*From the Forthcoming Report of the New York Fish Commission.*

## How an Alligator Dines.

—An alligator's throat is an animated sewer. Everything which lodges in its mouth goes down. He is a lazy dog, and instead of hunting for something to eat he lets his victims hunt for him. That is, he lies with his great mouth open, apparently dead, like the 'possum. Soon a bug crawls into it, then a fly, then several gnats and a colony of mosquitos. The alligator doesn't close his mouth yet. He is waiting for a whole drove of things. He does his eating by wholesale. A little later a lizard will cool himself under the shade of his upper jaw. Then a few frogs will hop up to catch the mosquitos. Then more mosquitos and gnats will light on the frogs. Finally a whole village of insects and reptiles settle down for an afternoon picnic. Then all at once there is an earthquake. The big jaw falls, the alligator blinks one eye, gulps down the whole menagerie, and opens his great front door again for more.

## Stocking Ohio Waters with Eels.

—During the past season Sandusky Bay and the rivers at Port Clinton, Huron and Vermillion have been liberally stocked with eels by the Fish Commissioners.

The U. S. Fish Commission for several years past has been sending eggs of the California salmon (*S. quinnat*) to Germany, Holland and France. From some cause or other these attempts to plant our salmon in European waters have met with more or less failure, owing principally to the agents sent in charge being unable to secure the necessary accommodation for the eggs on shipboard, the parts of the vessel assigned to them being generally too warm, the supply of ice limited, etc.

The Clackamas river is one of the great natural spawning grounds of the Chinook salmon (*salmo quinnat*). Probably no tributary of the Columbia has abounded so profusely with salmon in past years as this river. A high natural fall on the Willamette at Oregon City, just above the mouth of the Clackamas, forces all the salmon of the Willamette up the Clackamas, and vast herds of them have consequently been in the habit of crowding into that river to spawn.

The fishing around the bay last Sunday was exceptionally good. At Sausolito the catches were large and well assorted; often a tomcod and smelt or smelt and rockcod were pulled in at the same time on the line. A great many persons were fishing along the Sausolito shore and they all returned satisfied.

In transporting the eggs of salmon and trout it is of the utmost importance that the center of eggs should not be allowed to have too high a temperature. This is destruction to salmon eggs in transit no matter how they are packed.

The Antioch *Ledger* states that a salmon caught near that place recently is found to be branded "U. S. F. Co." The brand had evidently been put there by some member of the United States Fish Commission.

The Truckee *Republican* says this season of the year is the pleasantest time to visit the various lakes in that vicinity. The weather is delightful and game is plentiful and fishing fair.

Salmon have put in an appearance in Eel river, and the fishermen are now all ready for the season's work.

Salmon in the Shasta river are abundant.

## Cost of Big Guns.

The enormous power of modern great guns is well indicated in the statement that the largest on board of the vessels of the British fleet now in Alexandria harbor is capable of throwing a projectile weighing 1,700 lbs. at a velocity of over a mile in four seconds—equal to a weight of 27,215 tons of metal, falling a distance of one foot on an object. It takes 370 pounds of powder to fire this shot at this velocity, so anyone versed in the prices of steel and saltpeter can calculate the cost of every shot that these guns will throw. It will be found that every report will cost not very far from $1,000.

In Ohio a dog is property. In Georgia he is a proprietor. To come down to round figures, seven bob-tailed curs in Georgia are worth more than all the sheep in the State put together.—*Atlanta Constitution.*

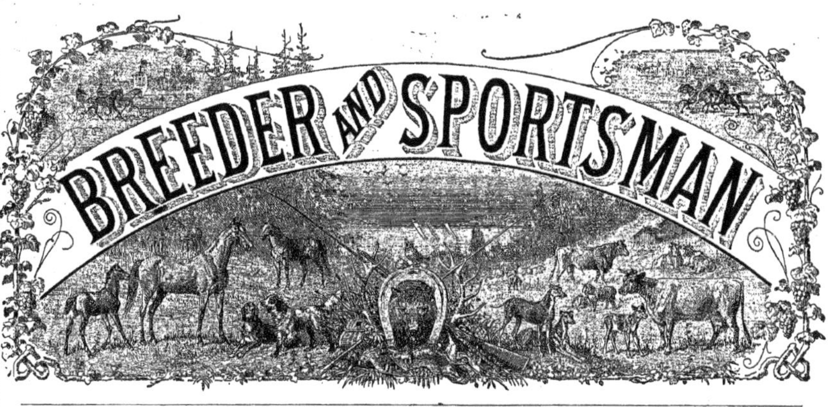


Vol. I. No. 18.
NO. 508 MONTGOMERY STREET. SAN FRANCISCO, SATURDAY, OCTOBER 28, 1882. SUBSCRIPTION FIVE DOLLARS A YEAR.

# TURF AND TRACK.

## The Cook Stock Farm Stallions.

DANVILLE, Oct. 24, 1882.

EDITOR BREEDER AND SPORTSMAN: I have received some half a dozen letters in the last month, asking me what stallions we intended to keep on the farm and if we could serve mares. I will answer through your valuable paper and give the breeding of them, but as for whether they will be kept on the farm for service or sold, I cannot now answer, since Mr. Cook's death, but will let you know later.

Cook's Hambletonian, bay colt, foaled in 1881, by Egbert; first dam by Woodford Mambrino; second dam by Alexander's Abdallah; third dam by Robert Bruce, he by Clinton, a son of Sir Archy; fourth dam by Muckle John; fifth dam by Trumpator; sixth dam by Stramboni. Egbert by Rysdyk's Hambletonian; first dam by Messenger Duroc, son of Rysdyk's Hambletonian; second dam by Holbert colt, (a pacer) son of Rysdyk's Hambletonian; third dam by the Utter horse, a son of Hoyt's Comet; fourth dam, sister to the dam of Messenger Duroc, by Roe Abdallah Chief. Woodford Mambrino by Mambrino Chief, with record of 2:21¼, and the sire of Convoy (2:22); Mambrino Dudley (2:22), Abbotsford (2:21½); Princeps, the sire of Trinket, record 2:14; Alexander's Abdallah the sire of Goldsmith Maid (2:14); Roselind (2:21); the sire of the dam of Princeps the sire of Trinket (2:14); the sire of Almont the sire of Piedmont (2:17); Early Rose (2:18); Aldine (2:19); Messenger Duroc the sire of Prospero (2:20); Elaine (2:20); Dame Trout (2:22); Charles Champlip (2:21½).

Your readers can see that this colt represents some of the best on the turf, and with so many crosses to imported Messenger, imported Diomed, Abdallah and Rysdyk's Hambletonian, he cannot fail to become a great sire of trotters.

Steinway, bay horse two white heels, by Strathmore. First dam Abbess, record 2:34, and the dam of Solo, five-year-old record 2:28, by Albion, the sire of Vanity Fair, record 2:24; second dam by Hathaway's Halcorn a pacer, he by Halcorn, he by Virginian, son of Sir Archy; third dam by Crowell, he by Bertrand, a son of Sir Archy; fourth dam by Marshal Ney, he by imported Emancipation; fifth dam by Bertrand, son of Sir Archy. Strathmore, by Rysdyk's Hambletonian. First dam Lady Waltermire, which was a fast mare in her day. The late Hiram Woodruff drove her to wagon a trial in 2:28. Her dam by North American, he by Sir Walter, dam a pacing mare. Sir Walter by Hickory, son of imported Diomed. Second dam by Harris Hambletonian, he by Bishop's Hambletonian, a son of imported Messenger.

Strathmore is the sire of Santa Claus, record 2:17½; Chestnut Hill (2:22); Allice Stoner (five-year-old fifth heat 2:24); Steinway, two-year-old record third heat 2:31¼, last half 1:10¾; three-year-old record 2:25¼, fourth heat, last half 1:10. This is the fastest for a stallion at that age two and three years old. Solo, full sister to Steinway, five-year-old record 2:28, and private trial 2:22. Monitor, four-year-old record fifth heat 2:29. North American, the sire of White Hall, he the sire of Rhode Island, he the sire of Gov. Sprague the sire of Kate Sprague, with record 2:18.

Clois, brown colt, foaled 1882, tan flanks, no white, by Sultan, the sire of Sweetheart, three-year-old record 2:22½; Eva, two-year-old record 2:26, and others that can beat 2:30. First dam by Thorndale the sire of Edward Thorne, record 2:16; Daisy Dale (2:19); May Thorne (2:26). Second dam by Rysdyk's Hambletonian. Third dam by Mambrino Paymaster. Thorndale, record 2:22, by Alexander's Abdallah, the sire Goldsmith Maid (2:14). First dam Dolly, the dam of Director, record 2:23¾, and Onward, record 2:25, by Mambrino Chief the sire of Lady Thorn, record 2:18¼. This colt ought to be a great sire of trotters and he is already a trotter for a youngster. Your readers can see that he is nicely bred and represents some of the best trotting strains on the turf.

Pax, bay colt, star, off hind pastern white, foaled 1882, by Steinway, record, three-year-old, 2:25¼. First dam Priceless, sister to Driver, record 2:19, by Volunteer the sire of St. Julian (2:11¼), Allia (2:19), Gloster (2:17¼). Second dam by Silvertail, he by American Star. Third dam by Aron's Gray Messenger, he by Imported Messenger. This is a fine and game looking colt and is already a trotter for a young one. He cannot fail to be a great sire of trotters and one that can go the route, as he has so many speedy crosses and so much hot blood in his veins.

Cresco, bay colt, hind ankles white, by Strathmore, the sire of Santa Claus (2:27½), Chestnut Hill (2:22½), Steinway (2:25¼) Alice Stoner, (2:24) Monitor (2:29). First dam Alla, (trial three years old 2:27), by Almont the sire of Piedmont (2:17¼). Early Rose (2:18), Aldine (2:29), and the two last in double harness 2:16½; second dam by Mambrino Prince, record 2:29, he by Mambrino Chief the sire of Lady Thorn (2:18¼); third dam by Cripple, a son of Medoc; fourth dam by American Eclipse.

Almont by Alexander's Abdallah, sire of Goldsmith Maid (2:14.) First dam, Sally Anderson, by Mambrino Chief; second dam, Old Kate, by Pilot Jr.; Third dam a thoroughbred.

Mambrino Prince, by Mambrino Chief. First dam, Sally Woodford, Wedgwood's dam, record 2:19, by Woodford; second dam by Hunt's Commodore. This colt ought to make a trotter and a sire of trotters.

Crisis, chestnut colt, foaled 1882, white face, two white fore legs, by Alexander, son of California Patchen. Alexander the sire of Tommy Dodd (2:24), Alex Button, (four-year-old record 2:56), Reliance (2:22), and others below 2:30. First dam by imported Mango, second dam by imported Sovereign, third dam by imported Albion, fourth dam by Whisker. This colt will make a great out-cross with Hambletonian, Mambrino Chief, Pilot Jr. or Clay blood and will be reserved as a stallion for that purpose.

Belnor, bay, star, black points, by Strathmore, a son of Rysdyk's Hambletonian. First dam Coster, record 2:26; second dam Calypso, by Mambrino Chief; third dam by Senator, a thoroughbred; fourth dam by Woodpecker, the sire of the renowned Gray Eagle.

Coster, by Caliban, record 2:34.. First dam by Davy Crocket, a pacer. Caliban by Mambrino Pilot, saddle record 2:27½, and the sire of Harris (2:17¾), Mambrino Gift (2:20), by Cassis M. Clay Jr. This colt your readers can see has a combination of all the best trotting blood, one cross Hambletonian, one White Hall, two Mambrino Chief, one Pilot, one of the Clay, and two crosses of thoroughbred. This colt has a half brother on the farm now by Steinway, foaled this year. Yours,

SAM'L GAMBLE,
Superintendent Dan'l Cook Stock Farm.

## A Turf Recollection.

The following from the Chicago *Breeders' Gazette* will recall to old turfmen a tragic incident which created a marked sensation at the time of its occurrence:

Not many days ago there died, on a farm near this city, a horse with whose earlier days was connected the most tragic incident in the history of the trotting turf. This horse was Cooley; and to the older generation of those who are interested in turf sports the name will be a familiar one, while there are but few of the younger generation, especially in Chicago and vicinity, who have not often heard it mentioned.

Sixteen years ago the twenty-second of last month, the old Chicago Driving Park, situated at the corner of State and Thirty-second streets, in this city, was the scene of a race which ended in a bloody tragedy, and which for ten years afterwards made trotting in Chicago almost disreputable. The contending horses in that race were Cooley, at that time capable of beating anything in the West, and Gen. Butler, a celebrated Eastern trotter. It was announced as a match for $5,000 a side, and as both horses had made a national reputation by their performances, there were at least 7,000 people at the track on the day of the race. Cooley, as before stated, was a Chicago horse, being owned by Hiram Hastings of this city, while Gen. Butler was the property of Charles Revere, a well-known butcher of New York city. Gen. Butler was brought to Chicago by Wm. McKeever, a young man well-known in turf circles, although not a professional driver, his owner not accompanying the horse. Sam Crooks, then as now a driver, with headquarters in this city, had driven Butler in several of his races, and was selected by McKeever to pilot the horse in his great contest with Cooley. Bill Riley, a driver who had recently come from Detroit to Chicago, was behind Cooley. The story of the race is soon told. Cooley won the first two heats in slow time, and then the backers of Gen. Butler demanded that a new driver be put behind him. The change was made, McKeever winning the third and fourth heats with Gen. Butler in much faster time than the preceding ones had been trotted in. When the horses came out for the fifth and deciding heat it was nearly dark, the only light being from the moon, which had just risen. Just before the start was made, McKeever went into the bar and called for a drink of brandy, saying to Billy Boyle, who was in charge of the place, that he would pay for it as soon as the heat was over. He had his coat buttoned tightly around his throat, his gloves on, and whip in hand; in fact he was ready to step into the sulky. These are the last words McKeever is known to have spoken. He mounted the sulky, and after a few scorings, was sent away for the final journey of the race, and of his life.

Along side the backstretch of the track was a wooden building, used for the exhibiton of machinery during the fair which had just been held. When the horses disappeared dehind this structure in the fifth heat they were on nearly even terms, Butler having the pole and being a trifle ahead. The next thing that the crowd saw was Butler coming down the home stretch at a fearful rate of speed. It was so dark that not even the gait of the horse could be plainly distinguished, and as he went flying under the wire the watch of the timing judge was stopped at 2:10¼. There was a white blanket strapped to the seat of Butler's sulky, and as the black horse dashed past the stand it was flapping in the darkness, drawing some into the belief that McKeever had lost his coat during the heat and was driving in his shirt sleeves. It was soon seen, however, that there was no one in the sulky, and suspicions of foul play were at once aroused, as Riley, the driver of Cooley, had been heard to utter threats while the scoring for the heat was in progress. In a short time Butler came thundering down the home stretch again, all efforts to stop him being unavailing. In the meantime Cooley had reached the wire, Riley saying that McKeever had fallen out on the back stretch and been hurt. When Butler had completed three circuits of the track he ran to the gate leading to the stables, and was stopped by his rubber, Mike Ward (who died two years ago last winter in New York) and John Crocker, afterward well known as the driver of Grey Salem.

The crowd rushed around to the place where the killing occurred, and there, just north of the half-mile pole, poor McKeever was found lying on his back unconscious, his skull having been split from the right temple to a point near the base of the brain. The cause of his injury was soon made clear. A piece of the guard-board that formed a portion of the inside fence of the track was lying near him, and on one end of it were clots of blood and hair. It was evident that the board had been held out by some murderous rascal who was determined that Butler should lose the race, even if a human life was sacrificed to attain that end. McKeever was alive; although unconscious, when picked up, but died the following day. The question of who killed him was never solved. The judges of the race declared all bets off, and expelled Riley, the driver of Cooley, from all tracks in the United States. There was no National Association at that time, but the action of the Chicago track was honored by all others. Riley was locked up on the evening of the race, on suspicion of knowing more than he told about the murder; but the coroner's jury could find no evidence on which to hold him. A couple of brothers named Hickey were also arrested; but nothing was done with them. Of the persons who were actively interested in the race, and those whose names have been mentioned in this article, many are still alive. Riley, Cooley's driver, was, at last accounts, in Detroit, being in the employ of the Hon. Wm. H. Duncan, of that city. Sam Crook, who drove Butler the first two heats of the race, is still a resident of Chicago, but seldom appears in the sulky. Revere, the owner of Butler, died some three years ago in New York. The Hickey boys are dead; and Billy Boyle, the last man to wnom McKeever spoke, is the proprietor of a restaurant in this city.

Cooley trotted but few races after the one in which McKeever met his death; but his fastest record, 2:26, was obtained at Ottawa, Ill., Nov. 2, 1866. After that season he did little or no trotting; and for fifteeu years has lived a life of idleness on the Hastings farm, near Riverside, where he died the other day from old age—nearly twenty-eight years old. Gen. Butler, who was foaled two years before Cooley is still alive, and doing service as a road horse in New York. He will soon have reached his 30th birthday; and with his death, which cannot be far distant, will end the history of the race that set the country agog in 1866.

The Lambert stock seems destined to become as popular in Vermont as that of his famous grandsire Black Hawk was in his palmiest days. At the recent State fair at Montpelier, Vt., Ben Franklin was awarded the gold medal for four best colts, some of which we learn were sold at high figures. Ben Franklin is a chestnut horse, standing about 15¾ hands high, foaled in 1873, bred and owned by Mr. H. T. Cutts, Orwell, Vt., and got by Daniel Lambert. His dam, Black Kate, was a daughter of Addison, he by Vermont Black Hawk, from which it will be seen that he possesses a double strain of Black Hawk blood. He has a record of 2:29, made at Providence, R. I., Sept. 24, 1877, but can trot much faster. His full brother Addison Lambert, foaled in 1872, has a record of 2:27. The breeding of the above horses is very similar to that of Jubilee Lambert, now owned in Kentucky, whose record is 2:25. The latter is a son of Daniel Lambert, and his dam like that of Ben Franklin, is also a granddaughter of old Black Hawk.

## A Bilious Opponent.

The following communication, upon a subject that has been heretofore treated at some length in these columns, has been sent us by a correspondent who takes an active inerest in turf matters generally and the State Agricultural Society particularly. Many of the statements are, to say the least, strange, and indicate a dyspeptic and fault-finding condition which claims for the writer some considerations of sympathy for his mental ill-health. We feel sure that under any other circumstances he would not be so reckless with the facts. And even in that view we are prone to think that he has not revised his letter and that it is an illustration of how a well intending writer may, in his anxiety to use strong language, say a great deal more than he means.

SACRAMENTO, Oct. 16, 1882.

TO THE EDITOR OF THE BREEDER AND SPORTSMAN, Dear Sir: Your article "What Others Think" on one man power in the judges' stand, leads me to enter my protest against the adoption of any such "rule." First, it has been tried in this State and inside of a month the gambling fraternity run and trotted every race in the circuit. Secondly, when the gamblers were not interested the parties that named the Judge were, and run him (the judge) in their interest, or to get even with some person or horseman they did not like. Now, sir, we have the largest assemblage of horsemen (both runners and trotters) in the State, and we get along well with them. Why? Because the riders and drivers know that if there is anything wrong and any of them are caught they will surely be punished. And if the presidents of agricultural societies would have horses and riders do what is right and fair, they must enforce the rules and not cater to any driver, as no man wants to keep his horses in the stables doing nothing when money is to be won by trotting or running for it. You say you have a man in your mind that is wealthy and could not be bought; now, sir, there are many ways a gentleman may be influenced besides by giving money. I have known friendship to overstep the "rules" and to warp the judgment of good men in the judges stand. For my part, I want three judge's to judge a race, and those selected by the President of the Society. Then you have only one man to blame for a bad decision or for the selection of incompetent judges. How long is it since the Blood Horse Association got free of one man power? It has taken the combined efforts of nearly all the breeders to get clear of it, and then the State Society had to alter weights, and are in receipt of many communications to give more heat races, as the public are tired of dashes; they don't give a farmer an opportunity to judge of the staying qualities of the horse in case he wishes to breed to, or purchase. Respectfully, TURF.

## The Los Angeles Fair.

EDITOR BREEDER AND SPORTSMAN: The Los Angeles fair has been a very successful one and the attendance reminded one of the days gone by when everybody attended the fair and races. This infuses new life in the public and it may be taken as a certainty that the future is full of promises for the Sixth District Association. Already new improvements are discussed in the ornamenting and improving the grounds. One of the most urgent of these is the improvement of the track, for as it is it is unsafe and slow for trotters. It requires plowing and covering with soil which will give better footing to the trotter. It is now very sandy, almost sand, which is heavy everywhere, and all cut up into ruts and chuck holes, making it very slow and unsafe. This can be easily seen by you from the race between Del Sur and Belle Echo; the speed of both are known to you and both were probably in the best condition of any time this year, yet 2:28 was the fastest mile trotted. It was the race of the meeting, for it was a contest and uncertain until the last heat was trotted, and it created much excitement and large sums were bet on the result. The handsome daughter of Echo was a strong favorite, for even when the heats were even, it was thought that Del Sur would quit, but in this they were deceived, for the black son of The Moor trotted as game a race as ever was trotted by a horse, winning the second, fourth and fifth, the summary of the time being 2:30, 2:28, 2:30, 2:29, 2:29. The trouble with Del Sur has been that he never had a fair chance, for as a two-year-old he began stud service and by the 1st of July his training would begin to trot in August, and generally being a little over-matched. This has kept him on a continued strain, this year he has had more work and it is now late in the season, giving him time to get hardened. Then, too, he has more age, being six years old, and I prophecy that there will be no more talk about his quitting. We had some remarkable performances and we will continue to have, for there is no superior climate, no more fertile soil to produce nutricious grasses nor grain, or purer water in the world.

Don Carlos, a two-year-old by Del Sur out of a Moor mare, was the contestant in the 3 minute and 2:45 classes, with four entries of aged horses. He took his chances with them, scored with them and drove out Lady Washington twice in 2:36½, and one of these a last heat on this slow track, being second in all the six heats and never over a length behind at the finish in any of the heats. This was a wonderful performance for a two-year-old and Los Angeles may claim that this was the first time a two-year-old ever trotted with aged horses and yet, too, being the contesting horse. It, too, is a card for those who believe in inbreeding, for his dam as well as his sire are by The Moor, g d thoroughbred. This colt is as sound to-day as when he was foaled and not a blemish or pimple can be found on him. He was up with Rose's stable at Oakland and no doubt you may remember him—a sorrel colt, four white feet and blaze and a perfect type of the thoroughbred in conformation.

We had, too, another sensation in a two-year-old filly by Hardwood, out of Peggy Ringold who ran a half mile, 100 lbs up, with very great ease in 48½. She is a bay filly of good size and good form and much substance. If nothing happens to her she will add luster to Los Angeles county. That this county has been the nursery of some of the fastest native horses has always been true and this was shown, too, in the 50 mile race which was won by Machados with horses all of his own breeding and largly California native stock, and it was entirely owing to the superiority of the horses that he won, for the American contestant was much the quickest in his mounts and best rider. It was a race of intense interest and excitement for it was a contest from the word go. The American would, as a rule, come in 20 feet behind, yet would get mounted and 20 yards away, but the Californian would pass him before a quarter was run. In the 48th mile the American had the lead by, say, 100 yards and it looked almost a sure thing for him, but in making his mount for the 49th mile, the attendant pulled the blanket from the horse's head before he got a hold of the pummel of the saddle. The horse being only half-broke and wild tore away and knocked the rider over. Before he could be caught and mounted the Californian was 200 yards away and although he gained some in his 50th mount, yet the gap was too long for him to overcome.

This is, I believe, the best race at the distance by about ten minutes ever run, it having been run in 1 hour and 52 minutes. LOS ANGELES.

## Ringing Reminiscences.

In the fall the unsucessful horseman's fancy lightly turns to thoughts of securing a dilapidated trotter with a fast record, and by trotting him at three-minute races at county fairs gaining for himself the wherewithal to purchase oats during the winter months. But, although the evil of "ringing" is still a serious one to the trotting turf, there exists at present but little chance for the promoters of such iniquity to obtain any great amount of money by their machinations. But in the days gone by the condition of affairs was different, and many are the interesting stories told of how horses with records low in the twenties were carried about the country for purposes of fraud. One of the best of these is in relation to the notorious Small Hopes, now the property of Mr. Vanderbilt, that in the fall of 1875 made the famous campaign of outlawry which resulted in the expulsion from National Association tracks of the horse, and all who were connected with the affair. Charley Perkins, a resident of Rochester, N. Y., and a well-known sporting character, was general manager of the expedition, the other parties interested in the scheme being Deyo, a Michigan horseman, who owned Small Hopes, and Billy McGuigan, the driver. After a successful career in the West, where Small Hopes trotted as Lothair, Lapland, etc., a jump was made to a town in Massachusetts, for the purpose of giving the horse a rest. While there the entries for a fall meeting to be held at Boston were about to close, and on the night when it was necessary to make the nomination Perkins and McGuigan were seated in the reading-room of the hotel where they were stopping. McGuigan secured pen and paper, and was ready to write out the entry.

"What classes shall we put him in?" he asked Perkins.

"The 3:00 and 2:40," was the reply.

"All right. What shall we call him this time?"

Perkins hesitated a for moment but could think of nothing suitable. Finally McGuigan's eye was attracted by the heading, in big black letters, of a newspaper article which lay on the table. "The Westbrook Tragedy," read McGuigan aloud, "what's that?"

"That's it," said Perkins, "call him Westbrook," and so the entry of Westbrook was duly forwarded.

"When the day of the race arrived," said McGuigan, telling the story not long ago to a party of acquaintances, "the little horse could go like a shot. The 3:00 class was the first called, and there were nine starters. Perkins and I had canvassed the situation, and concluded to lay Small Hopes up the first heat in order to make the betting good. So when the word was given I took him in hand and finished last, a grey mare winning the heat in 2:29, and being evidently the best one in the lot. As Small Hopes could trot in about 2:16 we felt easy, and bought every pool on our horse. When a start for the second heat was made I gave Small Hopes his head, and the little fellow went around the first time like a ghost. Just before reaching the quarter pole I noticed that two other horses were alongside of me, and so when we struck into the back stretch I clucked to my horse, and as he at once struck a 2:20 gait I concluded that the other pair would soon be far in the rear. I went to the half-mile pole at a fearful clip, and soon after passing that point happened to look around over my right shoulder; there were the other two horses lying on my wheel as unconcerned as if we were only out for a jog. I was considerably surprised, but supposed that in some accountable manner Small Hopes must have lost his speed, as otherwise I could not imagine how the others had kept so close to me. I drove along, and soon saw that my horse could beat them, although he had to keep hustling to do it. Down the home stretch we came neck-and-neck, but just at the finish I let loose of Small Hopes a little, and he won the heat by a nose.

"Pretty soon the time was announced—2:21¼, and then the secret was out. There were two other ringers besides Small Hopes in the race, and each man had laid up his horse in the first heat to get good betting. We got it, but it didn't do us any good, for the judges declared race, pools, and everything else off, and we considered ourselves lucky to get out of the town alive."

## A Sermon Against the Race-Horse.

A fault-finding preacher at Port Hope, talking on a subject he knows nothing about, has been saying hard things about the, to him, monstrous iniquity of racing horses. But, strange to say, the same gentleman can imagine no harm in aquatic contests. It is to him quite natural that people should like to see boat races, and we therefore respectfully ask of this reverend censor why the people do like to witness such sport? The answer is plain to the ordinary worldly mind, but perhaps to spiritual clay the meaning is not so clear. The attraction about boat-racing, as of any other sport, is a desire to see a struggle for supremacy, a hard-fought persistent effort by one man to prove his superiority over his opponents, and he who proves himself the best performer is for the time being the idol of the populace. It is the crucial test of competition that has made apparent the victors' superiority, just as it is the racecourse that proves the superior speed and staying qualities of one horse over another. If the sports of the turf in England had not for a century been the favorite pastime of kings, nobles, and people, the perfect thoroughbred of to-day would have been an unknown animal. The American trotter is also an outgrowth of the racecourse. It not only offered large money prizes to spur the energy and skill of breeders but it popularized trotting with the people, bred a taste in the minds of wealthy men for speedy roadsters and thus opened up a mine of untold wealth to those who breed such stock. The old story "blood will tell" is true as gospel; even among the preachers who keep horses very man of them to our knowledge prefer to own one that has some "go" in him and lots of them are by no means backward on the road in accepting a challenge for a brush. Millions of dollars are now invested in the breeding of running and trotting horses, and the prizes of the turf are not only valued by owners of stock for their pecuniary worth, but as the one unfailing agency that stamps the value of their possessions. A two-year-old colt in his paddock may not show himself possessed of any wonderful points but let him run a mile in 1:41 and he is, worth thousands where before hundreds would have gauged his figure. The great turf performer is the popular sire, and to-day in Canada the reason that we have a better class of horses than we had twenty years ago is owing to the fact that such race horses as Jack the Barber, Sir Archibald, Ruric, Extra, King Tom, Helmbold, Thunder, Judge Curtis and others of the same stamp were brought here. A race-meeting under popular management is just as orderly a gathering as a camp meeting, and so long as the Anglo-Saxon race people this continent it will be just as popular a resort, even though all the preachers in the country were to thunder forth their denunciations. Clericals in England of much greater importance than the Port Hope Rev. have bred and raced horses, and we doubt not were just as highly regarded as though they had rolled their eyes skywards and piled on the agony about the villainies of the quarter stretch.—*Canadian Sportsman.*

## Winthrop Morrill.

In the death of Winthrop Morrill, Maine loses a grand old horse, one of the most successful of all the Morgan family, and in fact the only real Morgan in this State. I claim him to have more of the original Morgan blood than any other stallion now living. Thinking that a review of his past history would be of interest to the readers of your paper, I give a few facts in connection with his career.

Winthrop Morrill was foaled in Barre, Vt., in 1855, and was the property of Rodney Bradford of that place. He was sired by young Morrill, by old Morrill. His dam was sired by the Huckins horse, a son of Royal Morgan, called also Morgan Rattler. His next dam by Morgan Eagle and his next by Bulrush Morgan. He had two crosses of Messenger blood and one of Duroc. The one line to the Vance horse, through Old Morrill and the dam of Morgan Eagle, being by Callender, son of American Eclipse, and the result of this breeding in Winthrop Morrill produced a trotting sire of remarkable success. Winthrop Morrill was a dark bay horse, with black points, with a star in his forehead; off hind ankle white, about 15½ hands high and weighed 1050 lbs. His head was clean and intelligent; neck long and blood-like and carried in splendid style; shoulders sloping and strong, chest deep, back strong and beautiful in contour from withers to haunches, barrel round and well ribbed back; tail large, firmly set on and well carried; limbs good and well muscled, hind pastern straight, upper bone of forearm let down low at the knee, cannon bone short, feet blue, tough and excellent, ears tapering and lively, eyes bright and very prominent.

He was placed in training when from three to four years old, and developed wonderful speed at trotting, striding from 20 to 22 feet, with a great deal of hock and knee action, very open-gaited behind and very true forward. Too severe work while young caused him to shift from a trot to a pace. Repeated attempts to break him of the habit failed, as toe-weights and heavy shoes were unheard of at that time. After getting this habit of pacing he was traded to Ashur Savage, then of Waterville. After trying to break him of pacing, without success, Mr. Savage traded him to Ira Doolittle of Waterville; this was in the spring of 1862. After keeping him a few days, he traded him to Amos Garland of Skowhegan, and he, in turn, to a Mr. Kenddall of the same place and he traded him to Mr. Weymouth of Sangersville, Me., and after a few days he disposed of him to Joseph Skillings of Ripley, costing Mr. Skillings $60. I purchased him in company with Samuel Skillings and brought him to Winthrop in October, 1862, paying the small price of $100. While in my possession he paced a carefully measured mile on Lake Maranocook, without any fitting in 2:33; the last quarter in 32 seconds, at the rate of a mile in 2:8, two men to a sleigh, and was not up to his speed until the first half mile was passed, on account of shelly ice. I have no doubt that on a good snow track he could have paced easily in 2:20. He was used for general farm work, plowing and harrowing a great deal during the spring of 1863. Working him seemed to square him out and he began trotting with the same shoes that he wore pacing, (I have one now in my possession that weighs three-fourths of a pound,) and trotted quarters in 35 and 37 seconds, to a wagon. I sold him to the late Charles G. Jackson in June, 1863, for $600. He was used by him exclusively in the stud. He was sold to the late T. B. Williams of Boston in the fall of '72 for the sum of $8,500. After the death of Mr. Williams he was purchased by John F. Mills of Boston and sent to my stable in the spring of 1878. After keeping him three years in the stud, I sold a half interest for Mr. Mills to B. F. Fairbanks of Winthrop, Mr. Mills still owning one-half interest, and at the time of his death he was owned by Mills and Fairbanks.

He was first named by Mr. Jackson, Morrill Eclipse. After one season his name was changed to Winthrop Boy, and finally, again, changed to Winthrop Morrill. While living, Mr. Jackson was much attached to him, and just before his death requested that the old horse should be harnessed into the hearse and draw him to his last resting place, a desire which was literally fulfilled.

As a sire of trotters he ranked with the best. In 1877 he stood five on the list, as but four, living or dead, had more in the 2:30 lists. He has eight in the 2:30 list, besides several that could beat 2:30, kept for family use, prominent among whom are Honest Harry (record 2:22¼; a quarter in 30 seconds, and fifty heats belows 2:30). Ben Morrill (2:27 and a four-year old record of half a mile in 1:13, mile 2:32½. The fastest four-year old record of any Maine colt.) Ed Getchell, (2:27;) Glen Gary, (2:27;) Sam Curtis, (2:28, the seventh heat in a race;) Fleetwood, (2:29;) J. G. Morrill, (2:29, and a three-year old record of 2:50, which has never been beaten in Maine;) Baby Boy, (2:30;) Sweet Briar, (2:32½;) sold with mate to Senator Jones of Nevada for $15,000; Charlie Morrill, (2:33, could beat 2:30;) Modoc, (2:33½;) Bell Morrill, (2:34;) Yellow Dog, (2:35;) Watch Maker, (2:35;) Purity, (2:37;) and many other fast ones, including W. Morrill, (2:37½;) Lady Morrill, Little Fraud, Young Winthrop Morrill, Rowe Horse, Lady Mansfield, Knox Morrill. He was also sire of dam of Dr. Franklin, (record, 2:31,) and many others. His career in the stud, all other things considered, has been wonderful. He rests under a beautiful maple tree in a field on a nice ridge of land on my farm, two miles from Winthrop village. His name and age will be cut on the maple tree at the head of his grave, and the grounds will be well cared for. GEORGE C. GOODALE.

Mr Pierre Lorillard has sold to parties in England the thee-year-old colt Gerald, by Saxon, dam Girl of the Period, for $2,500. Gerald was sent across the water last year but has not run successfully, being afflicted with so bad a temper that his speed is thereby rendered useless.

Ned Stokes, proprietor of the "handsomest bar-room in the world," has never been seen drinking there. The prices are so high he has to go outside.

## Betting at Race Meetings.

The very marked falling off in the attendance at Jerome Park during the late fall meeting of the American Jockey Club is plainly suggestive of the fact that if the betting element is eliminated from the race tracks our first-class racing associations must go to the wall. There is no use in disguising the truth. Sooner or later it must have made itself apparent to all lovers of turf sports, for the meeting in question proved that those who were loudest in their denunciation of betting on the course were notably conspicuous for their absence. So far as the *morale* is concerned, therefore, the inquisitorial action of the police authorities, instead of having a tendency to attract large numbers of these straight-laced moralists, with one exception there was scarcely a corporal's guard in attendance on any day of the meeting. There is something more in this spasmodic crusade against betting than at first glance appears upon the surface. Taking for granted the fact that it will ultimately lead to the total suppression of racing, it inevitably follows that it will also lead to the extinction of one of the largest and most profitable industries in the country—the breeding and rearing of thoroughbred horses. Without racing, this industry, involving millions of dollars, must naturally die out. Admitting all the uses to which the thoroughbred horse can be applied, without racing, the demand would be insufficient to make the business longer profitable. Thousands have been spent by breeders for particular selections of the thoroughbred horse in order to build up and preserve the purity of their blood-stock. Science has been brought to bear to perfect the animal in his conformation, with a view to unite grace with speed, courage with endurance. All this has been achieved, and the result is a marvelous type of commingled beauty, strength and usefulness. In war the thoroughbred is sought for to equip the cavalry service. For the private carriage and for the saddle he is equally in demand as a cross with other varieties in producing a desired type. The trotter and roadster are nothing without a liberal infusion of his blood. The farmer has found his native stock greatly improved by the admixture with the thoroughbred; and not a single instance is recorded where this strain of blood has been crossed with any other that it has not built up and improved it. Now, we would like to inquire of those who are opposed to racing, on principle, whether they have ever inquired how this perfected state of the noblest animal on the face of the earth is produced? If they are uninformed it is time they should know. The thoroughbred, the most perfect type of the horse, is created by selections of the most perfect specimens of animals, racing in a direct line, to Eastern origin, weeding them to the best families of similar strains, and in raining them from infancy to endure the ordeal necessary to fit them for the turf, thus uniting speed with stamina and endurance. Without racing this training process will be discontinued, and rapid deterioration of the thoroughbred will surely follow. But it will not do to anticipate any such amenable finale. Public sentiment has not yet reached that fancied status which is to consign the "sport of kings" to an ignominious end. Nor will the average public be content to see pass away a pastime which has proved a never-ending, never-tiring source of pleasure.

For over two centuries horse racing has lived and thrived, despite occasional fanatical crusades waged against it. As we have before had occasion to remark, there are times when irregularities and abuses find their way upon the turf; but whenever they have been made apparent on the course controlled by respectable associations they have been summarily rooted out. Bookmaking in connection with horse-racing has never been considered an evil. The better class of jockeys simply desire to have it hidden from the public eye and kept away from the rising youth of our populous cities. I men desire to back their opinions in a quiet way, they should be allowed to do so, unawed by any police regulations. The racing associations are for the most part corporations, owning or leasing the land upon which their courses and heir club-houses and stands are built. As corporate institutions, therefore, they should be allowed the exercise of certain rights. Under their auspices visitors, in speculating on turf event, do not infringe the statute pertaining to gambling any more than members of the stock board in speculating in stocks. Speculation in some shape underlies every department of human life; even the church is not free from it. All resolves itself into the doctrine of chances—risking a certain amount to attain a prospective advance. Let betting, therefore, with certain restrictions and under the auspices of the clubs, be legalized by legislative enactment. This will ultimately do away with pool-selling in the cities and other methods of surreptitiously evading the existing statute.—*Turf, Field and Farm.*

## High Priced Boots.

The editor of the London *Sporting and Dramatic News*, which paper may be considered as the leading one of its class in England, is evidently not a person gifted with the retentive powers of memory which are an essential attribute of a successful American journalist, and, like many another Englishman, he is sadly at sea when discussing matters relative to American customs. Not long ago he had a chat with Mr. Chas. Bathgate, who has been managing Mr. J. R. Keene's stable of American race-horses in England, and the conversation turned upon the American trotter, and, according to the London editor, some very extraordinary statements regarding the style in which that useful animal is equipped or his races were made. "The weights," he says, "differing a weight, are only one of many things to be considered. The trotters are often shod with a shoe of a different weight each foot, and some of these boots—not of the sort similar to us, but casings of leather extending from the fetlock joint right up the animal's body! The manufacture of such boots as these, which strengthen without impeding the horse, is, of course, a fine art, and sometimes a man pays as much as £100 for a carefully-made pair. All this is somewhat strange to English notions, but in the face of results attained it must be admitted that those who have the management of American trotters know what they are about."

One hundred pounds, or five hundred dollars, for a carefully-made pair of boots "extending from the fetlock joint right up the animal's body," would be deemed a rather exorbitant price, even by the most ardent advocate of those useful appliances, and as a matter of fact a man might buy every known kind and variety of boot used on a trotting horse without expending one-fifth of the sum mentioned by the London editor as "sometimes paid for a carefully-made pair."

Gen. Abe Buford of Kentucky, whose joining of the church at long ago was made the subject of so much newspaper comment, has not entirely lost his love for the turf. He cted as one of the judges during the recent running meeting at Louisville.

The prices paid for yearlings in England this season are very high. A yearling by Hampton, out of Loch Garry, for 1,850 guineas. A yearling by Strathconan brought 1,100 guineas, while one by Rosicrucian fetched 800 guineas.

## Gate Money at Newmarket.

The Newmarket stewards appear to have become suddenly aware that cabs and carriages are used as movable stands, and that they have for long been a source of loss to the Newmarket revenue. Over and above the opportunity which it gives for betting, the ring at Newmarket offers no attractions to the racegoer—it is hardly likely to be said that it offers the attraction of seclusion—and so gentlemen who engage a vehicle for the day feel themselves much better off in it than they would feel in any of the enclosures, and have until now saved their money into the bargain. So far as betting goes, one of the party can take a ticket and execute whatever commissions are entrusted to him, or the pass-out checks can be exchanged, and each one have a turn inside as agreement permits or occasion requires. Speaking in all sincerity, I don't know that there is any reason why the Jockey Club should be abused all over again for levying a toll of one sovereign per week—in addition to the already existent top-of-the-town impost—upon all cabs and carriages that pass on to the heath. Once started on the money making road, it is only natural that those who control the races at Newmarket shall pursue it thoroughly. In no other direction have we found men starting in the gate-money business ready or willing to give up any of its minor advantages. The appetite for gate money, as is well known, grows by what it feeds on. All we have now to do is to wonder whether any fresh design can be engineered by the Jockey Club with a view to gathering in still further profits, short of the one long and final step which will cause a charge to be made to foot passengers before they are permitted to venture upon the classic heath, salute the ditch, back the winners or the losers, and do any of the other things which are so essential to the existence of all true and noble sportsmen. That this departure can be postponed for many years after the way in which the Jockey Club has shown itself inclined towards gate-money in every other possible and probable way, I for one do not believe. Nor, unpleasant as the aspect of gate-money always was and always must be if brought into immediate contact with the dogma that racing is conducted for sport's sake and for sport's sake only, and that all who have anything to do with the culling of its wires would die rather than make a penny by doing so, there will not be much reason to regret the alteration. When it comes, the old precept must be swept away with what is left of the old practice—which, goodness knows, is little enough now—and race-arranging being then a thorough-going commercial pursuit, will have to be conducted on a thorough-going commercial principle.—*Pendragon in the Referee.*

Mike Murphy, the well-known trainer, died at Louisville Hospital, Sept. 19. Murphy was a native of Nova Scotia, and was for some time in the stable of the late Major Bacon. Subsequently he began riding steeplechasers, and achieved considerable reputation through Duffy, Labelle, Mikesian, and Trouble. He trained for Mr. Bannatyne, Mr. Thompson and others. In 1880 he trained for Barton & West, and upon the purchase of Gabriel by Apple-gate Bros. went with Gabriel into their service. As a steeplechase rider, Mike had no superior in his time, and as a trainer, he was quite successful. Like the English jockey, Bill Scott, his estimate of a horse was quite correct, and generally made up at a glance. He had, indeed, that peculiar gift of forming a correct and sweeping opinion of a horse at first sight, which is accorded to few men in the profession. We have known him for many years, and often enjoyed his reminiscences of the turf, which were useful to us in compiling the series of "Between the Flags," written by us some two years ago. His memory was wonderful, and his stories of men and horses delivered with humor, that showed him as possessing a keen appreciation of the funny side of human nature. He was generous to a fault, and there is scarcely one of his acquaintances but has a story to tell of "poor Mike." Illustrative of his better qualities. The immediate cause of his death was dropsy.—*New York Spirit of the Times.*

## Vanderbilt Beaten.

The great fight between Wm. H. Vanderbilt and Frank Work grows stronger every day. When a man worth $200,-000,000 and another worth $30,000,000 see fit to engage in a furious quarrel it is the province of citizens worth less than those vast amounts to stand respectfully by and view the war. However, the citizens, no matter how lowly they may be, cannot be restrained from taking an interest in the war of these financial leviathans. They do take an interest, and such a boiling one that the before-mentioned quarrel is actually and undeniably the talk of the city. It is all about horses. Mr. Work owns what he and many other turfites believe to be the fastest team that ever trotted on mother earth. His team, Dick Swiveller and Edward, trotted a mile in 2:16½ to a road wagon a few months ago, and the people of New York howled with delight. New York is now a great racing center, and no city in America has more enthusiastic turfmen. Well, Mr. Vanderbilt always believed he possessed the fastest team on earth in Small Hopes and Lady Mack, but he changed his mind when Mr. Work passed him with ease. Then Mr. Vanderbilt procured the team that he averred emphatically would make the complacent owner of Swiveller and Edward eat his dust. This team was Leander and Lysander; but alas! the great two-hundred-millionaire was again lost in a cloud of dust. He took William H, a particularly fast and even trotter, from his stable and harnessed him up with the peerless mare, Maud S. "Now," said Mr. V., "bring forth Mr. Work and his alleged fast team." Mr. Work came out and was seen plainly by Mr. Vanderbilt, who followed him about and had an excellent view from the rear throughout. This last defeat was a severe blow to the great railroad magnate. He became despondent of ever beating the astounding time of Mr. Work's team, 2:16½, and did less driving than before for some weeks, when he suddenly began to talk in the most mysterious and portentous manner of a team of his. No details could be wrung out of him by his friends, and he smiled with an air of superiority on the public. Then came the news over the wires from Hartford, Conn., that Mr. Vanderbilt's new team, Aldine and Early Rose, had done a mile without a break in 2:16½—a quarter of a second better than Frank Work's best time. Nobody believed it until a number of eye-witnesses testified to its accuracy, and then there was a great cry for a race between the two crack teams. Nothing was easier, said Mr. Vanderbilt and Mr. Work, and they went at it at once and got things so thoroughly complicated in two days that the muddle now looks as though it would never be righted. Each gentleman sent the other elaborate and intricate challenges two or three times a day, and each insisted that the own particular challenge should be answered first. They are at it yet, sending challenges and accusing each other of every crime, while the public howls for a race.—*New York Letter.*

Mr. R. H. Nason, of Concord, is about to construct a private race track.

## Answers to Correspondents.

SALEM, Or., October 7, 1885.

EDITOR BREEDER AND SPORTSMAN: Will you please answer through the columns of your valuable paper: 1st. What is the breeding of the colt that won the District Trotting Purse trotted at Stockton on September 20th and 21st? In your paper you state that he is by Inauguration. As we have a stallion here of the same name, I wish to know if he is by him. He came from Stockton, Cal., in February, 1880, and was by Alexander. 2nd. What is the age of the colt? Is he a stallion? 3rd. What is his best time to harness? By answering you will greatly oblige a subscriber. C. W. J.

Answer.—1. Bay Gelding by Inauguration, (he by Alexander) dam by Morgan Rattler. Owned by L. U. Shippee, Stockton.

2. Six years old, broken this year. Record, 2:40½. Can trot in 2:35.

The identity of the stallion now in Oregon our correspondent must settle for himself, as we have no positive information, although we have no doubt it is the same horse. A prominent horseman of the San Joaquin has this to say of him:

Inauguration, by Alexander, was a brown stallion about fifteen and a half hands, and very even in his make-up. He stood one season and made a light business. What colts did come have proved as saleable as any stallion that ever had a chance here. They all averaged sixteen hands, kind, good color, good bone, even, well gaited and natural trotters. Many of our people remark that Inauguration proved he was a paying stock horse, and he never should have been allowed to leave here. He is one of a few stallions that out-breeds himself for size, color and bone.

SACRAMENTO, October 23, 1882.

EDITOR BREEDER AND SPORTSMAN: Please answer the following questions and oblige an old subscriber to decide a wager. A bets that the horse named Abe Edginton (grey horse) has a record as good as 2:20; B bets that he has no such fast record. Please decide in your next, and what time did he make in Stockton, if any. Please give his best record. J. P. E.

Answer.—B wins. Abe Edginton's best record is 2:23½, made at San Jose, October 1st, 1878. He did not win a heat at Stockton and consequently did not make any record there. He started in a race that was won by Graves in straight heats, Doty being naked second and Edginton third.

PENRYN, Oct. 22.

EDITOR BREEDER AND SPORTSMAN: Please give me the names of some breeders of the Duroc and Jersey Red hogs, and oblige E. G. N.

Answer.—Address "The Laurellas Ranch," Monterey, Cal.

MICHIGAN BAR, Nov. 19, '82.

EDITOR BREEDER AND SPORTSMAN:—Please explain through the columns of your paper the meaning of a "selling race"—that is the rules and laws governing that class of races. SUBSCRIBER.

Answer.—A selling race is one where the horses are entered to be sold for a certain sum named in the entry. The system is perhaps best illustrated by the following published conditions taken from the advertisement of the forthcoming fall meeting of the Pacific Coast Blood Horse Association:

Selling Purse, $200; a mile and a quarter; for all ages; entrance free; $50 to second horse; the winner to be sold at auction; horses entered for $1,500 to carry regular weight; if for $1,000, five pounds allowed; if for $750, ten pounds; if for $500, seventeen pounds, and if for $300, twenty-one pounds. Any one can claim the winner, and the excess realized beyond the amount at which the horse is entered to be divided between the association and the owner of the second horse.

The rules bearing on the subject are as follows:

Rule 63—When it is made a condition of any race that the winner shall be sold for any given sum, the owner of the second horse being first entitled, etc., no other person than one who ran a horse in the race shall be entitled to claim. The claim must be made to the judges or clerk of the course within a quarter of an hour after the race. The horse claimed shall not be delivered unless the amount is paid by ten o'clock at night on the day of the race, otherwise the party claiming shall not be entitled to demand the horse at any future period; but nevertheless, the owner of the horse may insist upon the claimant taking and paying for the horse claimed.

Rule 64—When it is a condition of a selling race that the winner shall be put up at auction after the race the half of any surplus which may thereby be obtained over and above the price for which the horse was entered to be sold, shall be paid to the owner of the second horse, and this shall not invalidate the privilege of the second horse as to the price claim of any beaten horse, under rule 63.

Rule 65—Any horse running for a selling race is liable to be claimed by the owner of any other horse in the race for the price for which he is entered to be sold and the amount of the stake; the owner of the horse entered to be first entitled to the claim, and the others in the order in which their horses are placed, and the winner to have the last claim.

Rule 66—No person can claim more than one horse in the same race, and if two or more persons equally entitled wish to claim, they shall draw lots for the priority.

Rule 67—Any person who refuses to deliver or fails to pay for a horse purchased or claimed in a selling race shall be ruled off the course.

MAGDALENE.—D. C. Horton of Tulare has purchased of D. Visscher of Stockton the two-year-old bay filly Magdalene, the price paid being $1,500. Magdalene was broken last January and was put into training in June, speeding her first mile in 2:57. In the purse for two-year-olds at the Stockton fair this fall she won at a jog in 2:43. Three colts started against her but all were more or less enervated by the pink-eye and she was not called upon to make an effort in the race. Magdalene was sired by Peerless, he by Green's Winthrop. The pedigree of her dam was never traced. The filly will be continued in training and if no accident befalls her will make her mark.

### Racing Reminiscences.

It was well along in the fall of 1852 when I reached Lexington, Ky., and saw for the first time a race "run for blood." Five horses started, the favorite being Mr. John Clay's bay colt, Star Davis, by Glencoe, out of Margaret Woods, by Priam. He was a good bay about 15 hands 3 inches high, and the heaviest horse for his height that I ever saw. The race was mile heats 3 in 5, and the Star won in three straight heats. He was always the last horse off and the last horse at the half mile pole by about twenty yards. Around the turn he would move up so as to get within about two lengths of the head of the stretch, when his rider, Ned Tompson, would shake the bit through his mouth and he would come away from his horses with ease. He banged in all three heats below 1:46, and could have run any one of them in 1:43 had he been sent for it. In the same stable with Star Davis was a beautiful chestnut filly, likewise a three-year-old, that has since become famous through a grandson, I allude to Madeleine, grand dam of Iroquois, the only American horse that ever won the English Derby. She won a two mile stake for colts and fillies at the same meeting with most ridiculous ease, and two years later, after I had started for California, she was sold to some men up in Michigan. There she remained in obscurity for years, until after Planet had gained a fame that was as wide as the continent; and then people wanted Boston mares to breed to Revenue. After months of diligent search Col. S. D. Bruce, then a comparatively poor man, but now enjoying a princely income as publisher of the "Turf, Field and Farm," purchased her for a small figure and brought her back to "the dark and bloody ground." There she produced the bay filly Income, by Revenue, since the dam of Income- mode, that ran a mile in 1:44 with 140 pounds up; and Maggie B. B, the dam of the noted Derby horse, Iro- quois. Trade Dollar always reminds me of Madelaine, save that the daughter of Boston and Magnolia had a lower and prettier way of going and did not shuffle so in her gait. These two colts of Clay's were foaled just about thirty years too soon, in my belief. Were they now on the turf in their three-year-old form, they would win a princely fortune every time they started. A purse of $500 was a big thing in those days, while now every steeple chase run at Long Branch, Baltimore or Sara- toga, is worth many times that sum. Star Davis would have filled the place of Luke Blackburn, and Madelaine would have stood in Thora's shoes, winning all the lon- ger events; and Clay, instead of retiring from the turf in disgust and devoting himself to religious observances, would have been far ahead of the Lorillards and the Dwyers. He was unquestionably the best amateur trainer in America, and bothered the professionals sorely on several occasions. One time he had a chestnut colt called Princeton, that the "touts" were watching very closely, and a gray horse called Blue Ruin, that had never run better than a bang-up second. Clay knew the notorious Charley Reilly was watching his horses, so he got some mosquito bar stuff and encased Princeton in it till he looked like a gray horse in the dark- ness. He then got a sorrel colt off his ranch and put up Princeton's rider on the green 'un. He sent them two miles at their best gait while the real Princeton lay asleep in his stable, for it was three o'clock in the morning. Char- ley Reilly went down to Louisville and reported to his crowd of blackleg employers that Princeton could not go a bit, and Blue Ruin could beat him anywhere after they had gone a mile. Clay wrote to his friends to bet all they could that Princeton won the two mile post stakes. He then engaged Gilpatrick to ride the race. Their calculations came near coming to grief, for in the second mile of the second heat Gil broke a stirrup strap, but hung on like grim death and got over the line ahead of Die Clapperton. Gilpatrick is still living though he has not ridden in many years, his last mount of note being on Lodi against Norfolk at San Francisco. Another noted Jockey of that era, now dead, was the notorious Jack Ford. He was a consummate rascal but evaded punishment by often doing things not provided for in the racing rules. Among these was his celebrated ruse to close out his adversaries in a four mile race, run at Smithland, at the mouth of the Cumberland river, nearly forty years ago. Ford was riding Denmark, by Hedgeford, out of Betsy Harrison, by Aratus. The other entries were Jerry Lancaster, ridden by John Dunn, who died in California, and Mary Waller, ridden by Steve Welch, who rode Gray Eagle in the great race with Wagner. The race was four miles and repeat, and Mary Waller had won the first heat, Denmark dropping well within his distance. In the second heat Jerry Lancaster took the lead going into the second mile, hotly pursued by Denmark. In this position they ran through the third mile, and on the fourth Denmark was at Jerry's throttle going up the back stretch, John Dunn looked around at Ford, who said:

"Well, I'll keep you a playing that clip, next mile I'll beat you."

"Next mile!" cried Dunn, "why, this is the fourth mile."

"Not much," said the old rascal Ford, "it's only the third."

So after they passed the stand they ran another mile and Lancaster was completely pumped out.

Major Shrover was very angry, at John, Dunn for having run a mile that, like Rip Van Winkle's dram, "didn't count," and Dunn tried to throw the blame on Ford. Shrover appealed to the judges, who de- cided that Dunn was not there to take anybody's else word—he should have known for himself. The conse- quence was that Ford won the third heat on Denmark, beating Jerry Lancaster and distancing Mary Waller, and in the fourth heat, making sixteen miles in all, Denmark galloped home a winner of the race. It is from this old brown horse, Denmark, that the famous stock of saddle horses, for which Central Kentucky is so noted, is descended. Ford wanted to go to England with Richard Ten Broeck, when that gentleman took over Lecompte, Prior and Prioress, but he did not go. Three years later Mr. Ten Broeck sent over Starke, Op-

timist, Umpire and Satellite, and Ford went with them. Jack said he wanted to see one Derby and then die. He saw one, too, won by Thormanby, with Dundee on three legs at his throat latch, and the American colt, Umpire, by Lecompte, out of Alice Carneal, beaten away off yonder. Ford's money was all on Dundee, and he stood to win about $1,400 with $1 50 had Dundee won. Several days before the Derby was won there had been a very late session of Parliament and several mem- bers went over from London to the downs in a drag to see the flyers take their morning exercise. They were all of the lardy-dah sort, and on reaching the heath they saw Starke and Umpire taking a slow center Fordaus was on the colt and Jack Ford on the old horse. Now the American seat—standing in the stirrups, virtually, looks odd to the average Britisher, and one of the haw- haws asked a stable boy who stood near:

"Aw, Bob, what 'orse is that big red chestnut?"

"That's Starke, sir, favorite for the Goodwood."

"Aw, and I say," 'cos that a top of 'im?"

"That's Ford, sir, a celebrated American jockey."

"Aw, the beggar—you know—he cawn't ride in a cart with the sideboards hup; you know," said my lord with ineffable disgust. But nevertheless Starke won the Goodwood Stakes of 1859 and the cup of the following year, and was finally sold to go to Russia for the imperial stud. There was another horse that should never have been allowed to leave America, nor his half brother Lecompte. These horses were invaluable to the breeding interests of America and worth comparatively nothing in Europe. There was no horse in America as fit for the Lexington races as Starke. His great sire and blood- like appearance made him look like a king among horses. Gilpatrick was the neatest dressed rider of all the era and used to have all his suits made by Aronez of New York. He was a good rider in an era that boasted of fields of three or four horses ; but in the great mob of twelve or fourteen that are running now, he would scarcely ride inside of it. The best rider I saw while I was back East in 1862 was a boy named Billy Burgoyne, whose left arm was paralyzed so he could not whip severely with it; and he used to get a terrible lot of speed out of a tired horse without punishing him to death. Another great rider of that era was a slave negro belonging to Col. D. F. Kenner of Louisiana. Abe looked more like a monkey than any human being I ever saw, not even excepting McIntosh of the Callender minstrels. But how he could ride, and what a sight it was to see him on top of grand old Paris, the last of the Glencoes, coming down the homestretch of the Me- tairie with five thousand hats swinging in the air and two thousand tiny gloved hands applauding the prize of Louisiana. After the war, the old darkey went to the north and rode Idlewild in the four mile race won by Kentucky on the inauguration of Jerome Park. I shall never forget his ear-to-ear grin when he won, or his pa- thetic stutter when he lost. He rode Eagle in the race for the Jersey Derby won by Norfolk, when the favorite Kentucky came in fourth. Abe looked at Norfolk as he dismounted and told Col. Philo Bush:

"Fore de Lord, kernel, a ghost o-c-could't get a-h-h- head of dat white-legged colt."

Tom Patterson of Alabama, was the greatest of all the old-time trainers, and the first man to work his horses naked. Prior to that time, it was the fashion to keep horses blanketed all the while, whether at exercise or in the stable. "Old Pat" got the idea that it made horses delicate and therefore abandoned it, except in severely cold weather. One day somebody asked him why he didn't wear more blankets on his horses.

"Bekase I think if ther Lord had wanted blankets on a hoss, he'd a put 'em thar hisself. Ef a hoss wasn't de- signed to do no better nor that, he'd a long hair, like a buffer, don't you understand?"

Pat had an awful race once at Mobile with his old mare Charmer (the grand dam of the Duchess of Nor- folk), against the flying terror, Wade Hampton. Wade won the first heat through mud ankle deep, and the old mare came within a couple of feet of getting the flag in her face. "Old Pat" went up into the judges' stand and begged of Judge Neil Robinson to be allowed to with- draw his mare, but Judge Robinson refused in a firm but courteous manner. "Forty to five on Wade," was the cry all over the stretch.

"Bring in your horses," cried the judge.

"Please, judges, kaint I draw my mar," pleaded Patter- son, "she kaint win one end of this yer race."

"Is your mare lame? If so, you can withdraw her," replied Judge Robinson.

"No, she ain't lame, but I don't see no good of running her to death for nuthin'" said Pat.

"You should have thought of that before," replied Judge Robinson.

"Old Pat" went down stairs, sorrowfully enough and saddled his mare. As they turned loose, a shower of rain came down as if it had been shaken out of a sheet, and after running a mile, Hampton showed signs of temper. Finally he came down to a walk and could not be urged out of it. Honest old Charmer went along and won the race, distancing Wade by over half a mile. It was very much like getting struck by lightning, at least Patterson thought so. Another famous trainer of those days was James Benson Pryor of Natches, commonly called Ben for short. He had a dairy near that city and supplied most of the citizens with milk, save in the win- ter and spring months, when his son ran the business and he went to New Orleans to train Mr. Ten Broeck's horses. He trained Lexington in every race he ran under that famous name, though it must be told that the most noteable of all American horses ran two races under the name of "Darby," while owned by Dr. War- field of Lexington. The doctor was the handsomest and most courtly of men, and it was his son's wife who wrote the finest of all American novels. "The House, hold of Bouverie." Well, when Ten Broeck went to England on his second voyage he took old man Pryor over to train Starke for the Goodwood cup. He also trained Umpire for the Derby and as the colt had won

all his two-year-old stakes, he became a hot favorite the blue ribbon of the English turf. But as the train season progressed it was plainly to be seen that the r was too long (a mile and a half), for the son of Al And old man Pryor would groan: "Oh, Mr. Ten Bro of we only had old Rex hesh in place of Umpire would be jest like stealin' this yere race."

The old man thought Dundee could win the race so but he broke down in the mighty struggle and Thorm by carried off the glittering prize. Next year Pr came back to Mississippi and the civil war broke him completely. The troops killed off his cows and burnt his buildings, and he was forced to go north for a liv hood in his old age. He is living near Holmdel, N. on a little farm, and rides over occasionally to the L Branch races. For an illiterate man, he was a wonde sagacity and honor, and in a career of forty odd years the turf, his name was never coupled with one disrepu ble transaction. The last horse of any note that trained was St. Martin, the property of James A. G stead, of Kentucky. A tough customer was a horse cal London that Pryor trained for Mr. Ten Broeck, whil England. He could kick higher and faster, than horse in the United Kingdom. One day while old I was saddling him for a race, along came a son of Emerald Isle, with a new plug hat on. London las out with both heels and knocked the Patlander's caub into a total wreck. The Irishmann ran up to Mr. Broeck, saying: "Plaze, boss, is that your horse ?"

"Yes, my name is Ten Broeck."

"I don't care if your name is Eleven Brooks, I w my hat," said Paddy.

"I don't know anything about your hat," replied Kentuckian.

"Sure, yer horse kicked it off me head entirely."

"Suppose he did. You ought to know enough not go near him. That's London."

"Faix, I don't care a dom if his name was Doob Ye'll be afther payin' me for me hat."

"Mr. Ten Broeck gave him five crowns, and I settled it. Gilpatrick used to tell the story with g gusto.

"Won in a walk," is a favorite English way of say a that a horse won so easily as to afford no idea of a str gle. Some years ago a Washington County horse nar Hiram Abiff, was taken over to Victoria and sold to of the tribe of Jonbool. The next fall they had races Beacon hill, and the only starters in the mile dash Hiram Abiff and a bald-faced bay horse from Nanai called Smiling Tom. The coal mines being shut down the Nanaimo miners were at the races and betting mo like water. The race was run from end to end," as late John Harper would have expressed it, and after most vigorous whipping, spurring and rolling, the l horse won by about three feet through sheer gamen Some fellows who had been up the stretch ran down a the crowd and closed in behind the horse and and as his chum:

"Baw'n, who won t' race!"

"Dang it, mon, auld Tom won in a walk," retorted tyke proudly.—[T. B. M., in Portland "Oregonirn."

---

### Running and Trotting at Los Angeles.

Oct. 18—Purse, $650, Trotting, 2:30 class.
N. A. Covarrubias names b g Charley D............. 3  1  1
L. H. Titus names b g Buld............................. 1  2  2
Jno. Reynolds names b g Prentice Boy................. 2  3  3
    Time—2:35, 2:38, 2:36, 2:36.

Same day—Purse $245. Running, half mile and repeat.
A. Covarrubias names blk g Otto E......................
J. Sepulveda names g Fox................................
Hill & Gries name b f Belle O............................
M. A. Foster names g m Mamie...........................
    Time—50, 49.

Oct. 19—Purse $260. Running, one mile and repeat.
Hill & Gries name b s Wildidler..........................
Cyrus Lyons names b m Mestiza..........................
    Time—1:46½, —.

Same day—Purse $260. District trotting three-year-olds and un
L. J. Rose named g g Centre..............................
Wm. Smith name b m Katie Bender......................
F. M. Slaughter names b t Chappel......................
    Time—2:50, 2:50, 2:56½.

Same day—Special trot for horses not entered in other races
have never trotted for money.
S. L. Mayberry names g m Mary Jane...................
L. G. Root names bik m Debonnaire....................
Dr. Cooper names g g Draper.............................
    Time—2:47, 2:49, 2:48.

October 20.—Purse, $200, district trotting, 2:40 class.
A. L. Mayberry name b m lady Washington.............
L. J. Rose names a b bay Nettie..........................
J. J. Fallon names br g Prince............................
L. H. Titus names b m Belln Johnson....................
    Time—2:44½, 2:40, 2:36½.

Same day—purse, $300, running for district two-year-olds, d
three-quarters of a mile.
J. W. Adams names b f Annt Betsey.....................
Hill & Gries names blk f Dottie Dimple................
M. M. Johnson names c f Els..............................
    Time—1:26§.

October 21.—Purse, $650, trotting free for all.
L. J. Rose names blk t Del Sur............................ 2  1  1
L. H. Titus names b g Belle Bitte......................... 1  2  2
    Time—2:30, 2:26, 2:30, 2:29.

Same day—purse, $300, running free for all district horses, d
three-quarters of a mile.
N. A. Covarrubias names blk g Otto E...................
Hill & Gries name b f Belle O............................
    Time—1:18½.

Same day—purse, $350, running free for all, dash of two and a
ter miles.
Hill & Gries names b s Wildidler.........................
F. Estudillo names br s Klipperlanger...................
Cyrus Lyons names b s Mestiza...........................
    Time—4:19.

A new journal is to be established in San Francisco dev to the interests of stock-breeding and out-door sports course the breeding of horses, and especially race horses trotting and running, will receive most attention, but val information will be given on the breeding of all kinds of s A paper of this kind could be made of great value to all br ers and stockmen, and if the proposed journal shall prov be ably managed, it will be very likely to gain a liberal port among them. The first number of the paper w issued on the first of next month, and will contain at pages of reading matter. It will be called the Breeder Sportsman. The paper will be issued weekly and will five dollars per year.—Greenville Bulletin, June 21st.

## FISH.

### Stocking Notes.

Brook trout, put into mild, still water are thrown away; Jack bass, placed in a pond with mud or grass bottom will not thrive. They must have rock or gravel, where crayfish, their favorite food, abound. Oswego bass, in the water first rated, will increase, multiply, and make glad the heart of the fisherman. Salmon trout will not remain in running streams, no matter how pure the water, and the lordly salmon himself is no particular about the temperature of the water he inhabits that human investigation has hardly yet been able to tell just what it should be. We can judge best by leaving him to choose for himself.

Of all fish that have come under the observation of the commission, none have done as well, according to the cost, as the black bass—usually styled, in contradistinction to others of this general family, the "small-mouthed bass." This fish does its own hatching and attends to its own nursery duties. Of vigorous, yet clean appetite, he grows apace, and where the location suits him, takes a lease for life, with a contingent interest for his posterity. A good black bass lake or stream will bear more fishing to the acre than any other fish water. The Oswego bass and the perch pike are also cheaply secured, readily kept, and are profitable for both food and sport.

Discoveries made lately touching the breeding habits of striped bass, Spanish mackerel, and other choice sea fish, point to the facility with which these may be artificially reared. It has been established by sufficient trial that the striped bass, when deposited of proper age, will thrive in salt water. We have record of one put into a pond in Connecticut, that was taken out a few years subsequently, weighing twelve pounds. A number of good specimens have been found, also, in Lake Ontario, where a small plant was made a few years ago by this Commission.

When it is considered that these fish grow rapidly and to a vast size, and their gamey qualities are such as to call for the angler's best skill, and that as a table fish, few, of other rich or fresh water habit, excel them, the policy of extending their production must be universally admitted.—*Report of the N. Y. Fish Commission.*

### Bay Fishing.

Last Sunday a larger number of persons went out fishing on the bay than have been out for a long time; not only on the wharves and along the sea wall but every boat that could be hired was out and filled with anglers. From Sancelito south to Point Diablo, there were about sixty boats strung along, most of which contained amateur fishermen. From Point Diablo along by the Anita rocks to Raccoon straits were about one hundred and fifty more boats. Although the day was pleasant, fishing was as a rule quite poor. The average fish was five pounds, though many caught much more. From the bonus rockcod, blue rockfish and sea trout were the principal fish caught, while at the wharves tomcod bit the best. The best fishing ground heard of was the waters near Arch and Bird rocks, in which vicinity boats were lying all day. At the wharves the best strings of fish caught were those of three boys who pulled in 305 tomcod between a house of 9 and 3 o'clock.

Fishing at the railroad wharves, Oakland, was very good, most of the catches being tomcod and a few sole.

On Saturday last ex-School Director Van Schaick and party are out fishing near Angel Island and Raccoon straits. They made a catch of 185 fine rockcod.

The Hard-Head or black salmon is really an exceedingly rare trout and reaches a weight from fourteen to eighteen pounds. It inhabits the mouths of large rivers, such as the Columbia, Skeena, Fraser, and is occasionally found in Puget sound. It appears to spawn in spring somewhat earlier than the salmon, and occurs upon the coast at the same time as the latter. In some regions it is liked as a food fish, but in the Columbia the flesh is very white and it is considered useless. The body is less deep than that of the salmon, and the tail much heavier.

The unknown food fish discovered a few weeks ago by Capt. Collins while searching for the fish proves to be a close relation of a Norway haddock. It is found in great abundance in the waters of the Madeiras. The fact that it has signaled to American waters will be a stimulus to the fish commission to gather specimens for cultivation here under the improved processes which have been attended with such marketable success.

Last Sunday Messrs. Wm. Lockart, Frank Denning and W. T. Bogart were out at Point Diablo on a fishing expedition. They had unusually good luck, catching all they could carry home. Cabezonnas, or bullheads as they are sometimes called, sea trout and black rockcod comprised the fish; the weight ran from one and a half to three pounds each. Good fishing can always be had in this vicinity.

The surf-smelt, which is not found south of Monterey bay, very abundant in Puget sound, where it spawns in the surf in its spring. It reaches nearly a foot in length and is held in high esteem as a pan fish. In the markets of San Francisco it is tolerably common but seldom exceeds eight inches in length.

The Oregon trout or *Salmo Clarki* is very abundant in all the lakes and rivers north of Mount Shasta but is not found south of that locality. It is abundant in the salt water of Puget Sound, where it is taken in seines in great numbers. It reaches a weight of two or three pounds and is reckoned an excellent food-fish.

From the investigations of naturalists it would appear that a trout lives to a green old age. An instance is given of a trout domesticated in an English well, having attained the age of nearly forty years, though its weight never exceeded two pounds.

South of the Ventura river there are no streams on our coast which run freely into the sea, as the rivulets terminate in lagoons separated from the ocean by sand bars. In fact, this is a characteristic of most of the small rivers of this coast.

The salmon fisheries of the Pacific Coast have increased more than twenty-fold within ten years, and last year's product was nearly 1,000,000 cases, worth $5,000,000.

A Texas paper describes an 8,000 acre ranch in that state entirely devoted to the breeding of ponies for children. The feeding stock consists of seven Shetland stallions and forty-two mares, all thoroughbred, and two hundred small spotted pony mares. These little ponies range over the prairies like sheep, and are described as very gentle.

## BICYCLING.

### The Bicycle in Carson.

On any warm, pleasant afternoon the bicyclists of Carson gather in force on the Capitol square, and as soon as they begin their interesting and astonishing feats with the winged wheel, a crowd of spectators almost immediately collects. The riders in this city are Hume Yerington and Ernest Hall. Mr. Yerington is considered as the leading exponent of the science in Carson, and is looked upon by the rest (Mr. Hall) with a sort of reverence. The latter is a pupil of the former. Yerington makes a strong and rapid rider, his immense limb reach giving him a decided advantage over his short legged pupil. The latter makes up in nerve, however, what he lacks in science and covers technical deficiencies with dash and daring. Yesterday afternoon at 2 o'clock Mr. Yerington rolled into the Capitol square by way of the northwest postern gate, and at precisely a few minutes later Mr. Hall enters the other diagonal corner. The intervening Capitol building was all that prevented their seeing each other.

From a bicycling standpoint "a meet" is a term intended to designate a collection of bicycles at one place, and is a short way of speaking of a tournament. Two bicycles in one place might, we think, come within the meaning of the term. The meet took place in front of the Capitol steps; Yerington's bicycle threw its hind wheel under the fore quarters of Hall's and then by a dexterous movement caught the big wheel under the ice and getting the grapevine lock the two wrestled a spell, and then like a flash Hall sent his left wheel into Yerington's stomach and executed a double twist with his outer rim. This settled the round and Yerington's machine went down, but skillfully managed to take the other with it. An expert bicyclist may sometimes be thrown but he can always manage to bring down his adversary with him. By this time fifty Washoe Indians and over a hundred whites had gathered to see the sport. The referee declared the meet a draw and both men saved their bacon.

After the machines had been separated Yerington mounted and took a run about the walks and executed some of his daring and original feats. The flip is a figure of his own invention and commands itself to amateur riders as easy of accomplishment and sufficiently showy to be depended upon to win the applause of a crowd. Riding down toward the corner of the walk he caught the curb stone at the turn and shooting over the fore wheel landed on his hands, while the bicycle, turning a graceful handspring, went clean over the man, the small wheel describing the segment of the Arctic circle in the air. The expert endeavored to come up on the side and climb over on to the machine again, but was not rapid enough to catch the small wheel. The little wheel seemed to have the start somehow, and won the heat. The figure as far as executed by Yerington was novel and instructive and well received by the spectators.

The flying leap was next introduced by Hall. Coming down the walk at a 4:02 pace he made straight for a post inscribed: "Keep off the grass!" and so splendid was his aim that he knocked it down at the first attempt. This swerved him to the left end, flushed with success he shot to the fence, hitting an iron post with singular accuracy directly in the center. He then left the bicycle temporarily and came over the fence into the crowd and knocked a Piute Indian senseless. He thinks if he had secured a better start he might have scored two Indians. The feat was loudly applauded.

The *carie de fo* grae is an offspring of the flying leap, only in a more modified form. The object is to swing the hind wheel around a post so that the body will be thrown forward and the rider, dexterously catching his feet on the handles, grabs up handfuls of gravel in front. It is considered bad form for the feet to slip off the handles or get back on the pedals.

The lock is a pretty figure if well executed. Two riders ride together like knights in a tourney, and as they are just abreast each man swerves his hind wheel to the right and the two lock together. Then the machines spin round like a top, and if the dishes of the riders are of different colors a beautiful variegated effect is produced and the spectators can keep right along distinguishing the man they are betting on. The one that falls nearest the center scores a point.

The exchange is a neat coup d'état invented by Mr. Hall. Two riders meet at a speed of twenty-five miles an hour, and when the wheels clash each man turns a somersault in the air and comes down on the other man's bicycle. If the machines themselves combine in the somersaults and make a sort of fusion business out of it, it is called the "double exchange." After this act the machines are sent to the nearest watchmaker for rest and repairs. Next week the Bicycle Club will give an exhibition of some new and startling combinations—*Carson Appeal.*

TRICYCLES AND MOUNTED POLICEMEN.—Several gentlemen who were summonsed on Saturday for furious riding on a tricycle have discovered, at the cost of 42s., that that vehicle cannot outrun the constable—or rather outtricycle the mounted policeman. Whether the one who has had sixteen years of experience of bicycles and tricycles can ever be seriously believed that a mounted constable cannot gallop eight miles an hour it seems useless to discuss. But it must have been a sight suggestive of John Gilpin or Dick Turpin to have seen this figurative tricyclist hotly pursued for a quarter of an hour by a mounted policeman. Another's excuse was that having performed sixty miles he was incapable of fourteen miles an hour. The inhabitants of Kensington seem to have laid down a playground for all the cyclists of London in this long stretch of wood reaching to Hammersmith. It seems rather hard that they should have vehicles that go fourteen miles an hour careering up and down it as at present; so far as speed goes they might as well have railway trains, for some scarcely exceed that pace.—*Pall Mall Gazette, Sept 25.*

A Massachusetts bicyclist, taking his machine with him on an excursion to Prince Edward's Island, was obliged to deposit sixty dollars as a guarantee that the machine would not be left upon the island. This was refunded upon his leaving for home, but when he arrived in Boston he was obliged to pay the usual import duty of thirty-five per cent before the revenue officers would give him the machine, although it had once paid its duty when originally imported.

The new American monthly magazine, *The Wheelman*, makes its first appearance in October. It is by far the most pretentious publication which has yet appeared in connection with bicycling, and has some of the best writers upon the subject as regular contributors. The design of the cover is attractive and the typographical work is excellent.

The president of a Kentucky turnpike has announced in a published advertisement that he will "prosecute as public nuisances" all parties riding on bicycles on his turnpike, because they "endanger the lives of those traveling in vehicles on said road." And the bicyclers are laughing at him and his threats.

Quite a number of Eastern clubs have shown an ambition to undertake long rides, with a view to completing as many miles in one day as possible. The Boston Club led off with 102 miles and were followed by the Massachusetts Club with 118 miles, and, lastly the Ascham Club, of Worcester, with 135 miles. Single riders have exceeded this in many instances. The riding time has, thus far, in this country been confined usually to the hours of daylight. In England, however, twenty-four hour trips have been made and a distance of 212 miles covered.

It was the intention of some members of the local clubs to make a long tour to the southward with an aim to the rolling up of a good record of miles for one day's travel, if the weather should permit it this month, but the roads are not in the best condition and it has been decided to postpone the run until it can be accomplished with more comfort and there is a likelihood of making a better record.

It is said that a medal will be given to the bicyclist who succeeds in beating the Pacific Coast record for one mile, at the Thanksgiving Day meeting of the Olympic Club. Weather permitting, and track in good condition, we think we can name one and perhaps two who can do it.

The Sacramento Club has obtained the privilege of the Pavilion for winter riding, which to those who know Sacramento in the rainy season, would seem to be the only chance the riders of that city would have for their favorite exercise.

In a recent twenty-four hours trial of the "Facile" safety machines upon the London and Bath roads, England, twenty-six riders started. The runners completed 214½ miles in the twenty-four hours.

"How shall I pronounce," asked an "anxious inquirer."
"The Wheel bicycle, of which I'm an admirer."
"Well," said the editor, "I'll swear by St. Michael
The way to pronounce it is simply bicycle."

## LATEST OF ALL SORTS.

### The New York Walking Match.

At 2 p. m. on the 23d the score in the six-days walking-match at New York stood: Hughes, 116; Hazel, 106; Rowell, 99; Hart, 96; Noremac, 91; Herty, 90; Panchot, 99; Vint, 79.

At 11 p. m. the score stood: Hughes, 148, Rowell, 135; Hazael, 135, Hart, 131; Noremac, 123; Panchot, 120; Herty, 116; Fitzgerald, 114; Vint, 95.

At 1 the next morning it was: Hughes, 150; Hart, 139; Hazel, 137; Rowell, 135; Noremac, 125; Fitzgerald, 122; Panchot, 120; Herty, 120; Vint, 101.

The showing at 10 p. m. on the 24th was: Hughes, 244; miles, Rowell, 239; Hazael, 235; Hart, 228; Fitzgerald, 222; Noremac, 221; Herty, 213; Panchot, 200; Vint, 179.

At 1 a. m. on the 25th Hughes had made 252 miles, Hazael 244, Rowell 240, Hart 232, Fitzgerald 226, Noremac 224, Herty 210, Panchot 200, Vint 190.

Hazel forged ahead after this and at 1 a. m. Thursday morning, 26th, he was in the lead, the score standing: Hazael 343, Hughes 342, Rowell 341, Fitzgerald 334, Noremac 330, Hart 325, Herty 309, Vint 285. At this date Panchot had withdrawn, with a score of 220.

By 3 o'clock p. m. Fitzgerald had attained the lead and Hazael was again behind Hughes. The score stood: Fitzgerald, 400 miles; Hughes, 399; Hazael, 393; Noremac, 391; Rowell, 377; Hart, 372; Herty, 363; Vint, 336.

At 5:23 p. m. Rowell retired to his tent, and all sorts of rumors concerning his condition were in circulation. A 7 o'clock it was generally known that he had given up the race, and at 8 o'clock the ex-champion quitted the race with a score of 384 miles and three laps. Rowell's stop was due to the irregular action of his heart. He was found after withdrawal, lying on his cot with his feet propped up. He was anxious to continue the race, expressing confidence in his ability to win, but his trainers and backers, recognizing the seriousness of the case, refused to allow him to do so.

At 1 a. m. yesterday (Friday) the score stood: Fitzgerald, 431; Noremac, 422; Hughes, 420; Hart, 408; Herty, 402; Vint, 374. Hazael retired when his score was 414 miles and one lap. His knees had given out. Noremac was the favorite in the betting at that time.

The third annual district firemen's tournament for Santa Clara, Santa Cruz, Monterey and San Benito counties took place at Hollister last Tuesday. The races were for volunteer hose and hook and ladder companies. Teams were entered from each of the counties. The Eagles of San Juan won the hook and ladder first prize, running three hundred yards, putting up a thirty-five foot ladder perpendicularly in the street with a man to ascend to the top in fifty-four seconds. The Pioneers of Hollister won the second prize. The Eurekas of Hollister won the first prize for juvenile hook and ladder companies. The first prize for hose companies was won by the Fajaros of Watsonville, who ran four hundred yards, connected with the hydrant at the three-hundred yard post, broke the coupling and got on water in 1:16½, also winning the Watsonville diamond belt. The second prize was a tie between the Pilots of Santa Cruz and the Hopes of Santa. Clara. The third prize was won by the Alerts of Santa Cruz in 1:30. The fourth prize, a handsome stopwatch, was presented to C. W. Waldron, President of the State Firemen's Association. The next tournament will take place at Gilroy, May 2, 1883.

King Kalakaua of the Sandwich Islands, is the owner of a bay stallion, three years old, by Almont, out of Violet, by Ryedyk's Hambletonian; second dam Sallie Fearles (dam of Peacemaker) by Smith's Clay. He was selected by the King in person one year ago, and will be shipped from Fairlawn, where he now is, in December next. He is 16 hands, has plenty of bone and substance, and is very finely gaited. His breeding and his size will make him valuable for stock purposes in the Sandwich Islands.

Last evening the captains of the several teams that take part in to-day's shooting tournament at Shell Mound, met at the armory of Company C, on Post street, to decide on what targets their respective teams should use, beside the many preliminaries always attending such occasions.

THE BREEDER AND SPORTSMAN made its appearance Saturday last, and presents a healthy appearance. Its editorial ability is of the best, while typographically speaking it is unique. Its various departments are well arranged, and the journal is destined to win popular favor among all classes. *Galt Gazette, July 15.*

# HERD AND SWINE.

## Angus and Galloway—The Difference.

A correspondent of that paper writes the *Breeders' Gazette* that he has repeatedly read in its columns that there is a difference between the Angus and Galloway polled cattle of Scotland, and asks for enlightenment on the subject at the hands of that journal, whereupon it proceeds to say, that, "in the first place, both breeds are alike in being hornless, and in being usually alike in color, and from their general make-up we should suppose them to have been, at no very remote time, one and the same breed. But as bred for several years past the Angus are finer-boned, finer-haired animals, and apparently earlier in maturing than their long-haired, coarser, and we really think hardier cousins, the Galloways. The Galloways are almost as shaggy coated as the West Highlanders; the bone of 'the tail is thick and strong, as are all of their bones—in short, hardiness and good ' wrestling ' qualities are written all over their general make-up, and we doubt, after all, whether there is any breed of cattle, save the native Texan, that can compare with them in adaptation to the conditions of life that prevail on our western plains. Whether the finer-boned, earlier maturing Angus or Aberdeen polled cattle are, all things considered, to be preferred over the Galloways for our great cattle ranches, remains to be tested. So far as tried both are well liked, but we do not consider the question of superiority by any means yet settled."

## Vast Winter Range.

The stockmen of Eastern and Southern Oregon are now making preparations to abandon the summer ranges and drive their stock to the Oregon desert, in Grant and Wascoe counties, a vast territory of grazing land, erroneously called a desert, upon which snow seldom falls to any considerable depth, and where cattle and sheep find an abundance of feed from November until May. The very rigorous weather and deep snows in the region of the summer ranges of that country render it impossible to winter stock upon them, no matter how judicious the preparation made, without very serious loss. A subterranean river has been discovered some distance out in the plains of this desert, at a point where the surface concealing it has been broken through. It is a distance of but a few feet to the water from the surface and it is thought that the discovery will result in great good for the stock raisers, as, for instance, during an unusually dry winter much of their stock can be saved, when, without access to other sources of water supply, many cattle perish from thirst. This, however, seldom occurs, as the dew on the grass and herbage in the morning is generally ample for watering purposes.—*North Pacific Rural Spirit.*

## Artichokes for Stock.

Some weeks ago the *Gazette* started a paragraph about the value of artichokes as food for stock, including cattle. It has brought out the following from Charles E. Allen, Manhattan, Kan., as to culture, habits, yield and destruction of these valuable roots: "How the ground very early in the spring; cut the tubers to one eye in each piece; plant three and a half by one and a half feet apart, and cultivate the same as early potatoes; the richer the ground the better. They will yield from 600 to 1,000 bushels per acre in rich soil with good cultivation. The tops can be gathered and cured same as corn fodder. Stock will eat them as readily as hay or corn fodder. Should you wish to clean your ground of them let them grow twelve or fourteen inches in the spring, then turn your stock on them; they are as easily destroyed as potatoes. After the tubers grow, if the tops are eaten off, it will kill them. Cattle, horses, hogs, sheep and all stock eat them greedily. The 'Jerusalem' is the best kind; on rich soil the stalks will grow from six to twelve feet high, branching out with from twenty to fifty blossoms."

## Where Jersey Cows Come From.

Jersey Island, the place from where we obtain the favorite Jersey cow, is a small spot of land. If squared, it is six and three-quarters miles each way. Yet this little island has a population of 600,000 human beings, and has over 12,000 cattle, and had that amount for the last twenty years, for the census of 1861 gives Jersey Island 12,037. And they export annually on the average 2,000 head. Roughly speaking, they manage to support one head of kine to every acre, while in England there is only one head to every ten acres, therefore, in proportion to its size Jersey exports as many cattle every year as England contains. If England should export cattle at the same rate, her whole stock would be swept away in a single year. A good Jersey cow will yield half her own weight in butter a year—she rarely exceeds eight hundred pounds, and her average weight at home is about seven hundred pounds. What little spot on earth can make a better showing?

## CHEESE-MAKING IN WASHOE.—The *Reno Gazette* says:

Theodore Winters owns the grounds at Ophir, twenty miles south of Reno, where the old ruins stand that once were the mill and reduction works, the first cost of which was over $1,000,000. Mr. Winters will cover the old walls with roofs and make a vast cheese factory of them. He is now milking seventy cows on his ranch, one mile away, and the number will be increased to 100. In addition 150 cows will be kept on the Ophir ranch. He is now making butter, which sells readily at Virginia City, but butter-making will cease and all the milk will be hauled to Ophir as soon as the vats are ready for cheese-making. If any of his neighbors have milk to spare the dairy will buy it or make cheese on shares. Three buildings will be covered in to store cheese and contain vats heated by steam, where all the milk will stand until it thickens.

## LINCOLN SHEEP.

—These are the heaviest sheep in existence. A sheep of this breed at forty months old has weighed 96½ pounds a quarter, a two-year-old 91 pounds a quarter, and a yearling 71 pounds. The wool is long and lustrous, measuring nine inches or more, the fleeces usually weighing from 9 to 10 pounds, and there is one instance where a fleece weighed 26½ pounds. These sheep require heavy feeding of grass, hay and roots; hence in England they are chiefly found in rich alluvial districts. It is yet questionable whether these sheep will pay in this country or not.

All loose hairs and dirt removed from the bodies of animals by brushwork, as well as old bedding, should be collected in a heap and burned. The presence of vermin on live stock can never be successfully combated by simply applying a certain remedy to the bodies of the animals, and not, at the same time, attending to the general cleanliness of these, as well as of their surroundings.

## Silos and Ensilage.

Last June the Commissioners of Agriculture addressed a letter to upwards of 100 farmers and dairymen in different sections of the country, asking the results of their experience and observations in the matter of silos and ensilage. The following is a summary showing the general drift of practice and opinion on the several points enumerated in the schedule of questions, of those who have responded to the inquiries of the department. It is intended here to give a comprehensive view of the whole subject in the combined light of the statements which appear separately in the appendix.

Location of silo—A few have been built at a distance from the stables, but generally the silos are located with reference to convenience in feeding, in, under, or adjacent to the feeding-room. Local considerations will determine whether the silo should be below the surface, or above, or partly below and partly above. This is not essential. Where the stables are in the basement of a bank barn, the bottom of the silo may be on the same level, or a few feet below, and the top even with the upper floor. This arrangement combines the greatest facilities for filling, weighing, and feeding.

Form of silo—With rare exceptions the silos described show a rectangular, horizontal section; a few have the " corners cut off, " and one is octagonal. (The cylindrical form, of which there is no instance in the accompanying statements, seems to have obvious advantages. If under ground, a cylindrical wall is self-supporting against outside pressure, and may be much lighter than would be safe in any other form. If of wood and above ground, the walls may be stayed with iron bands. In any case, for a given capacity, the cylindrical form requires the least possible amount of wall.) A given weight of ensilage in a deep silo requires less extraneous pressure, and exposes less surface to the air, than it would in a shallow silo. For these reasons depth is important. If too deep there is danger of expressing juice from the ensilage at the bottom. Where the ensilage is cut down in a vertical section for feeding, a narrow silo has the advantage of exposing little surface to the air.

Capacity of silo—The silos reported vary in capacity from 384 to 19,500 cubic feet. If entirely full of compressed ensilage the smallest would hold 9.1 and the largest 480 tons, estimating fifty pounds to the cubic foot. Practically, the capacity of a silo is less to the extent that the ensilage settles under pressure. This should not exceed one-fourth, though in shallow silos, or those filled rapidly and with little treading, it is likely to be much more. A temporary curb is sometimes added to the silo proper, so that the latter may be full when the settling ceases.

Walls of silo—For walls underground, stone, brick and concrete are used. The choice in any case may safely depend on the cost. In firm soils that do not become saturated with water, walls are not essential to the preservation of ensilage. Above ground, two thicknesses of inch boards, with sheathing paper between (the latter said by some to be unnecessary) seem to be sufficient, if supported against lateral pressure from the ensilage.

Cover—A layer of straw or hay will serve in some measure to exclude air, but is not necessary. Generally boards or planks are placed directly on the ensilage. The cover is sometimes made in sections two feet or more wide; oftener each plank is separate. The cover is generally put on these weights, having in view the uncovering of a part of the silo while the weight remains on the rest. Rough boards, with no attempt at matching, have been used successfully. A little space should be allowed between the walls and cover, that there may be no interference as the settling progresses.

Weight—Any heavy material may be used. The amount required depends on various conditions. It will be noticed that practices and opinions differ widely. The object is always to make the ensilage compact, and thereby leave little room for air, on which depend fermentation and decay. In a deep silo the greater part is sufficiently compressed by a few feet of ensilage at the top, so that there is small percentage of waste, even when no weight is applied above the ensilage. Screws are used by some instead of weights. The objection to them is that they are not self-acting, like gravity.

Cost—The cost of silos, per ton of capacity, varies from $4 to $5, for walls of heavy masonry and superstructures of elaborate finish, and fifty cents or less for the simplest wooden silos. Earth silos, without wall, can be excavated with plow and scraper, when other work is not pressing, at a trifling cost.

Crops for ensilage—Corn takes the lead of ensilage crops. Rye is grown by many in connection with corn, to make the ground producing a crop of each in a season. Oats, sorghum, Hungarian grass, field peas, clover, in fact, almost every crop used for soiling has been stored in silos and taken out in condition. There are indications that some materials have their value enhanced by the fermentation of the silo, while in others there is loss. The relative values for ensilage of the different soiling crops, can only be determined through careful tests, often repeated, by practical men. All thoughtful farmers would be glad to get more value from the bulky fodder of their corn crops than is found in any of the common methods. There are accounts of plucking the ears when the kernels were well glazed, and putting the fodder into the silo. The value of such ensilage, and the loss, if any, to the grain are not sufficiently ascertained to warrant positive statements.

Planting and cultivation—Thorough preparation before planting is essential. Corn, sorghum, and similar crops should be planted in rows. The quantity of seed corn varies from eight quarts to a bushel and a half for an acre. A smoothing harrow does the work of cultivating perfectly, and with little expense, while the corn is small.

When crops are at their best for ensilage—The common practice is to put crops into the silo when their full growth has been reached, and before ripening begins. Manifestly, one rule will not answer all purposes. The stock to be fed and the object in feeding must be considered in determining when the crop should be cut. On this point most depends much of the value of the ensilage.

Yield of ensilage crops—Corn produces more fodder per acre than any other crop mentioned. The average for corn is not far from twenty tons—which speaks well for land and culture. The largest yield from a single acre was fifty-eight tons; the average of a large area on the farm was only twelve and a half tons.

Kind of corn best for ensilage—The largest is generally preferred; hence seed grown in a warmer climate is in demand. It is conceded by many that the fodder of sweet corn is worth more, pound for pound, than that of larger kinds, for soiling. Some hold that the same superiority is retained in the ensilage, while others think that the advantage after fermentation is on the other side. The sweet varieties do not yield large crops.

Preparing fodder for the silo—The mowing machine is sometimes used for cutting corn in the field—often the work is done by hand. Various cutters, having carriers attached for elevated silos, are in use and are generally driven by

horses, steam or water power. Fine cutting—a half inch less—is in favor. It packs closer, and for this reason is likely to keep better than coarse ensilage. Fodder of any kind may be put in whole, and, if as closely compressed as fodder, will keep as well, if not better, but it requires much greater pressure.

Filling the silo—During the process of filling the ensilage should be kept level and well trodden. A horse may be used very effectively for the latter. Some attach much importance to rapid filling, while others make it more a matter of convenience. With the packing equally thorough rapid filling is probably best. The cost, from field to silo, is variously reported, from thirty-five cents—and in a single instance ten or twelve cents—for labor alone, to $2 and upwards per ton; though the higher amounts include the entire cost of the crop, not the harvesting alone. There is a general expectation that experience will bring a considerable reduction in the cost of filling. It is probable that, with more general adoption of ensilage, the best machinery will be provided by men who will make a business of filling silos. This could hardly fail to lessen the cost and bring the benefit of the improvements within the reach of many who otherwise would not begin. The ensilage should remain under pressure at least until cool, and be uncovered after that when wanted. Condition of ensilage when opened—In nearly all cases the loss by decay was very slight, and confined to the top and sides where there was more or less exposure to the air. Generally the ensilage has kept perfectly for several months, showing the deterioration while any remained in the silo, excepting where exposed for a considerable time. It is best to uncover a whole silo or compartment of a silo, at once, and thus expose a new surface each day, that no cut down is continued...

Value of ensilage for milch cows—Ensilage has been fed to milch cows more generally than to any other class of stock, and no unfavorable results are reported. There can be little doubt that its greatest value will always be found in this connection. Several feeders consider it equal in value to one third of its weight of the best hay, and some rate it higher. There is a marked increase in quantity and improvement in quality of milk and butter after changing from dry feed to ensilage, corresponding with the effects of a similar change to fresh pasture. A few seeming exceptions are noted, which will probably find explanations in defects easily remedied rather than in such as are inherent.

Value for other stock—Ensilage has been fed to all classes of farm stock, including swine and poultry, with results most uniformly favorable. Exceptions are noted in the statements of Messrs. Coe Brothers and C. B. Henderson, who it appears that horses were injuriously affected. It should be borne in mind in this connection that ensilage is simply wilted fodder, and may vary as much in quality as hay. The ensilage that is best for a milch cow may be injurious to a horse, and that on which a horse would thrive might render a poor return to the milk pail. Cows give milk are fed fifty to sixty pounds with some dry fodder and grain.

Method of feeding—Experiments are made in feeding ensilage exclusively, and results have varied with the quality of ensilage and the stock fed. It is certain that ensilage of corn will wilte in blossom, or earlier, is not alone sufficient for milch cows. It is best to feed hay once a day, and some grain or other rich food, unless the latter is supplied in the ensilage as it is when corn has reached or passed the roasting ear stage before coming. Ensilage, as it is commonly understood, is a substitute for hay and coarse fodder generally, and does take the place of grain. The condition of stock fed on ensilage, both as to health and gain in weight, has been uniformly favorable.

As to the profitableness of ensilage—There is hardly a doubt expressed on this point—certainly not a dissenting opinion.

Remarks—The general use of ensilage must depend largely on its cheapness. Costly silos and expensive machinery must always be an insurmountable obstacle to a majority of farmers. For this reason, experience tending to show that it essential to the preservation of fodder in silos, is of the first importance. Especial attention is invited to the earth silo mentioned in the statement of Francis Morris, Esq., of Oakland Manor, Md. Mr. Morris is a pioneer in ensilage in America, his first silo having been built and filled in 1876. These were in the basement of his barn, walls of masonry. The next year he made a trench in sloping ground so that a cart could be backed in at the lower end for conveying the silage to the feeding room. The sides are sloping and the average depth does not exceed six feet. The cost is simply the cost of digging a ditch of similar dimensions. This trench was filled in 1877 and regularly since, and has kept fodder in some kind in different places for convenience in filling. He used a large cutter driven by a windmill, and packs in the ensilage by treading with horses. The filling is carried several feet above the surface of the ground, and rounded up at the center, the excavated earth serving to confine the ensilage, covering it first roofing-felt, and then earth for weight. Mr. Morris has put in whole fodder and it has kept perfectly. He cuts it fine, mainly for convenience in handling and feeding. Whole fodder should be laid across, rather than lengthwise in the trench, so that it can be taken out easily. In order that the extent of Mr. Morris's operations may be understood, it is proper to add that his estate of Oakland Manor comprises about 1,700 acres. His wheat crop this year, 1882, is 5,000 bushels, and his corn is expected to reach the same amount. The meadows yield upwards of 200 tons annually. The stock consists of fifty horses and mules, 100 cattle, 100 sheep, and fifty hogs. And as the whole is managed on business principles, Mr. Morris very justly esteems his earth silo of primary importance.—*Boston Cultivator.*

The cattle belonging to Mr. Goodwin, of Watsonville, poisoned on Mr. John Bennett's ranch, in the Comstock district are affected with a peculiar but fatal disease. In scantiness like the bloody murrain. The cattle are first attacked with severe trembling and in a few minutes they are dead. An investigation developed the fact that the flesh beneath the skin, around the neck, breast and shoulders are stunted, that the appearance of being beaten by a club, and the blood is congealed and mushy. Quite a number have already died. The cattle in Priest valley are also dying from a disease which causes them to bleed at the nose. There appears to be indications forestalling the sickness, but the blood runs from the nose, causing the death of the animal.—*Hollister Democrat.*

The French Minister of Agriculture has placed at M. Pasteur's disposal a butcher shop in Paris, in which he can continue his investigations into the nature, cause and prevention of contagious diseases among animals.

We are informed that the firm of Riley & Harden, cattle dealers residing in this county, have cleared so far this year over $70,000 in their business. Last year they cleared over $50,000.—*Petaluma Courier.*

## Good and Bad Milkers.

few poor cows are quite apt, in one way or another, to k into a dairy, and by their diminutive yield barely pay heir keeping, and perhaps not even that, but cause an al loss. A dairyman of our acquaintance, having forty s, found by measuring the milk that he had five in his d that did not give milk enough in the whole season to for their keeping by twenty-five dollars apiece. He had others that paid their keeping and twenty-five dollars a d more. The profit and loss on these cows just balanced h other; he kept the ten cows a year for nothing, losing whole of his time and labor in caring for them and their k, besides the depreciation of stock and the interest on cost, which was not taken into the reckoning. When I collecting cows for the first dairy I set up, an aged and erving dairyman said to me: "Look out for good cows; re is a great deal of money made in this country by dairy-, but it is all made from the good cows." The difference ween a good cow and a poor one is not generally appre-d. Oftener than otherwise the price at which cows are ght and sold is made to accord with the amount of milk r will give. But this is not a sound way of estimating r value. Beef cattle may be estimated by the pounds of f they will make. A bullock that will make 500 pounds eef may be worth half as much as one that will make 0 pounds; but the cow that produces only 100 pounds of ter a year is not worth half as much as one that will make pounds in the same time. As it will take the former cow years to make as much butter as the latter will in one, will cost the owner a year's keeping more than the other will to get the same amount. The butter from the poor r costs double what it does from the good one, and is pro-ced at a ruinous rate to the farmer. Such a cow will not r the cost of keeping, and is only fit for the shambles. s ought certainly never to occupy a place in the dairy t the loss sustained by a small yield of milk is not all occa-ned by a bad selection of cows. Many cows which other-se might be classed as profitable milkers are made unprofit-e by the treatment they receive at the hands of the dairy-n. Careless milking, harsh treatment, worrying, and ex-ure to severe storms and to extremes of heat and cold, te the flow of milk and occasion much needless loss. enty-five per cent. variation in the annual product is dily made by kindness and severity. Comfort and a satis-i quietude are very efficient in promoting a liberal flow milk. Full feeding is equally important, as the want of it perhaps, the most prolific cause of abatement in the re-es of the dairy. In a large percentage of dairies the yield milk is annually made to dwindle down to the limit of difable production, and sometimes below it, from the defi-ncy and irregularity in the food supply. Very few dairy-n give their cows as much as they need to eat, except for hort time in the season. In the spring and early summer, en the ground is moist and warm, a vigorous growth of ss is produced, and a flush of food supplies the cows for a e with all they can appropriate, and crowded bags and ring pails attest their full supply. But presently, in the , hot and dry days of August, the ground becomes ched, and the grass stops growing and dries up. If the s can fill themselves during the day they are commonly wed to run without any additional food. As grass fails quantity and quality, and more labor is required to get it, is consumed, and the milk diminishes.—*Irish Farmer.*

QUALITY RATHER THAN QUANTITY.—An over production of ly given article of trade or commerce usually causes a re-action in price. Hence those who count their wealth by e quantity standard are not infrequently sadly disappoint-l when at the final reckoning of the profits for the season ey find them much less than they had expected. It is well erefore that all who would keep on the safe side for success ould bear in mind that although the demand for quantity ay be more than supplied, that for quality is seldom if ever lly met. As a rule the better grades of manufactured articles, s well as live stock, always meet with a ready sale. To roduce the best animals for the purpose they are designed, ould be the aim of every true breeder. He who succeeds this will scarcely fail of a two-fold reward—the satisfaction seeing improved stock about him, and of receiving good rices for what he may have to sell.—*Swine Breeders' Manual.*

Johnny Love, residing near this place, owns twenty-one eep, from which about 200 pounds of wool was sheared st long since, or an average of nearly ten pounds per head. he fleece of one of the wethers weighed fifteen pounds. hese sheep are part Merino; but the secret of this handsome ield is the good treatment they received.—*Jacksonville, Or-on, Times.*

A fine sample of clover, which had been in ensilage for y. was exhibited on the New York Produce Exchange the her day. When taken out the clover was found to be in od and wholesome condition. The trial took place at nterton, N. Y. Mr. H. B. Brown of that place is the ntleman who has made the successful experiment.

One of the curious industries of New York City is gather-g the stale bread from hotels and restaurants, and grinding up into food for poultry and pigs. The Astor House sells stale bread for $800 annually. The contractor has 100,000 invested in the business, and keeps nine teams at ork.

A leading dealer in dairy products in New York informs e *Dairyman* that the introduction of oleomargarine has creased the sale of good butter. It has also increased the uantity of good butter by driving the inferior qualities out the markets.

New York has 1,437,855 milch cows, or upwards of eleven er cent. of the total number in the whole country, 12,443,-3. Illinois has 863,913 cows, Iowa 854,187, Pennsylvania 4,166 and Ohio 767,043.

Ohio produces upwards of 25,000,000 pounds of wool, or arly one-sixth of the whole product of the United States. alifornia follows next, with 16,738,036 pounds, and Michi-n third 11,888,497 pounds.

A small, early maturing hog is much more valuable than a rge one, as no more food will be required to raise two quick owing ones than will for a large but slow all-fat hog.

A cow on the ranch of E. A. Sawyer, at San Felipe, gave th this week to triplets. The three little calves are all of od size and all healthy, hearty and frisky.

Never feed decayed roots of any kind to cows giving milk as decayed turnip fed to one cow will affect the milk of the whole entire herd.

At the Kansas City cattle sale on the 12th instant, sixty-ne head of polled Angus and Galloway cattle were sold. he sale aggregated $28,720.

## Creameries.

After a fair, patient trial of both methods, our creamery men are generally well satisfied that the best results are ob-tained when the milk is delivered at the creamery. Butter thus made commands a higher price in the market.

Our creamery men pay their patrons on the fifteenth of every month for the milk furnished the previous month.

The price paid for milk is and must be variable. Our creameries are now paying sixty cents per hundred weight. In the winter season they have paid as high as $1.25.

The foreman of a creamery here gets $40 per month, and ordinary laborers $1 per day.

Ice is not needed for the milk if you have cold well water, but in order to keep your butter in a No. 1 condition while getting ready for shipping, you need ice for a refrigerator to keep your butter in.

For an ordinary sized creamery a good horse-power is suf-ficient and better, (all things being considered) than an engine although many of the creameries have the engine.

While you cannot be sure that your patrons will supply you with milk or cream regularly through all kinds of weather you can be sure that they will work for their own interests, and our farmers find that it pays better to take their milk to the creamery and bring home sour milk and buttermilk for their hogs than to attempt to make it up at home. I have never heard any word of complaint on that score. Our creamery men here in Monticello make about 2,000 pounds of butter every day, part of it being from cream-eries outside of Monticello that they contract.

They ship an immense amount of butter to Europe, being put up in two-pound cans, soldered airtight. I have some-times thought that the creamery business might be overdone, but there is always a demand for a good first-class article, and creamery butter cannot be bought here to-day for less than twenty-five cents per pound. The farmers of our vicinity are making money rapidly from the sale of milk, and the creamery men seem to be getting rich also. For setting the milk deep tin pails are now used. 8½ inches in diameter by 24 inches deep.—*J. R. Stillman, Monticello, Iowa.*

A dairyman should study the peculiarities of each cow. Some cows will appropriate all the extra food they can digest to the secretion of milk, and even deplete their own systems to keep up the flow of milk. Such cows should be especially well provided for—their generosity should be reciprocated. These are the cows that pay for feeding. They pay back the principal with a large percentage of interest on all the extra food given them. They are only good cows that will pay for extra feeding—in fact, they are only good cows that will pay for feeding at all. And a dairyman may rest assured that a cow that will not respond to liberal feeding by an equal increase of milk is not worth keeping, and instead of adding to his income, runs him in debt every year.

The cheapest and one of the best means of ridding stock of lice consists in the free application of ordinary wood ashes, frequent brushing, removal of old and dirty bedding, occa-sional application of boiling hot water to the wood work of stalls, sheds and sties or limestone washing of the same.

Those who have fed their surplus fruit to hogs say that their stock are in excellent and healthy condition. Fruit makes fine sweet pork.

Mr. Edward Atkinson of Brooklyn is keeping three cows on what he raises from one-half an acre of land. The sys-tem of ensilage does it.

## POULTRY.

### Fowls, Capons and Turkeys.

In selecting fowls to be fattened for the market, choose only those with a yellow flesh; and the larger breeds will be found most profitable. The Brahmas and Cochins are very large fowls, and with good feeding become plump and bring high prices, either in the early fall or winter. The Ply-mouth Rock, thoroughly fattened, is one of the best for boil-ing and broiling. White flesh fowls are in less demand and never command the price which is paid for the others. Hence the Black Spanish, White Dorking and other breeds of that sort are of less value for the table. Several of the French breeds look well when dressed, especially the Houdans, which are delicately fleshed and have a form well adapted to fat, which they take on rapidly. Many of the farmers in Maine, New Hampshire and Vermont still cling to the old-fashioned breed of "dung-hill" fowls. These are, as a rule, all white-meated, and when they reach the market sell at comparatively small prices. It does not pay to raise this kind of stock, for it costs as much to keep such fowls as it does any others. Those who desire to realize the highest profits from poultry raising should dispose of the dung-hills and substitute some of the large breeds.

It should be borne in mind that size is not the only thing necessary for the realization of good prices. Large framed chickens often run to bone, and are without fat or meat. A large, plump chicken is what is wanted, but size should never be sacrificed to plumpness.

As with almost all other articles of food, efforts more or less successful are made to adulterate or sell for capons fowls which are not. Extra large fat chickens, known as "slips," are often sent in to be sold under the name of capons. The dealers, however, readily distinguish them, and, unless with their connivance, which cannot usually be obtained, the fraud fails. Genuine capons are very fine, brilliant plumage, and when sent to the market have only the feathers plucked from the body—wing, tail, leg and neck feathers being left on. At the time when capons begin to arrive all other kinds of fowl are sold at a low price, and the capons bring ten cents per pound more. Those who have succeeded in raising them have found the business a profitable one, and it is very likely that if the business were carefully conducted it might be made quite profitable on a large scale.

In France, in the markets, capons are a favorite article of food, and are of large size and great weight. They may be nearly always purchased and fetch much better prices than common fowls, their flesh remaining tender up to the age of two years, whereas a fowl of that age is only eatable boiled, steamed or else cooked in some similar way. In France they manage their poultry very much better than is done in the United States. Peasants and farmers alike contrive to make a handsome profit out of poultry and there are very few agri-culturists among them who do not keep some feathered fowls. They, however, do not farm as we do, and this is one of the great mistakes we make—that poultry farming to be a profit-able business must be conducted on a large scale. In France there are very few, if any, really large poultry farms, but yet poultry keeping is a general industry. Care, even on the largest farms, is bestowed on the young birds, and a general supervision is extended over both young and old stock. The peasants, of course, keep only a few fowls, but then they all keep poultry, and all look forward to their chickens and eggs

bringing a little grist to the mill; and the result to the country at large is that it is famed for its poultry produce, and sup-plies other countries out of its abundance.

Fowls should, of course, be killed in the most merciful way, and our dealers believe it can be best done by cutting the jugular vein in the neck. This is not only an expeditious method of causing death, but the fowl bleeds freely and leaves the flesh perfectly white. As soon as death ensues, pluck at once while the bird is warm, as the process can then be accomplished much more rapidly than if the bird is al-lowed to hang until cold. Never scald a fowl if it can be helped, for wet-picked poultry is not wanted in this market and only sells for low prices. As soon as the fowl is picked take off the head at the throat, strip the blood out of the neck, peel back the skin a little, remove a portion of the neck-bone, then, just before packing, draw the skin over the end and tie and trim neatly.

Even after the best method, of selecting, fattening and killing poultry have been practiced, there will still be a poor result unless the fowls are properly packed for the market, appearance here counting very largely on the price to be ob-tained. In the first place all kinds of poultry must be en-tirely cold before being packed. All the animal heat must be driven out, yet the meat should not be frozen, for if this is not done it will almost surely spoil. Then it should be sorted carefully into No. 1 and No. 2 lots, all old stock being put in the latter. Boxes make the best packages, and these must be perfectly dry and clean. Line the boxes with brown paper and never use straw, nor wrap each fowl separately. Pack as closely as possible, backs upwards, legs staight out, and see that the boxes are full, so that when the covers are nailed on there can be no possibility of the contents shifting about. Boxes should contain from 100 to 200 pounds, larger ones being inconvenient to handle and more liable to get injured.

The business of selling poultry is largely done by commis-sion merchants, who, as a rule, in this city have a high repu-tation. After the producer has selected his merchant or firm with whom he desires to deal, and has prepared and packed his stock for shipment as nicely as he can, let him make his contract for transportation as cheaply as may be and mark the packages plainly, giving the street and number, or stall in market. It would also be well to mark on the cover of the box the grade of the contents, as well as the gross weight and correct tare. Then send full advices and invoices by mail, immediately after the goods are shipped, and all con-fusion and trouble will be avoided.—*American Cultivator.*

### Poultry Hints.

Feed the young fowl stock generously for two months be-fore marketing. A full feed in the morning, of boiled pota-toes or other vegetables mashed up with bran and shorts, and all the corn they will eat at night, will, if they have a free range, be sufficient. During the last two weeks before market-ing mix the boiled vegetables with corn meal instead of the bran and shorts.

Look out for the old fowls when they are moulting. I don't mean that you are to dose and mess the fowls with a little of this and a good deal of that to enable them to "pass through this critical period with safety." I don't believe in any nonsense of that kind. Moulting is a natural process, and all that good healthy fowls need is plenty of good food. Feed cooked vegetables, wheat, bran and shorts, oats, corn, wheat or wheat screening, and an occasional meal of sun-flower seeds with lots of milk to drink and your fowls will come through all right. Moulting fowls that cannot pull through on this bill of fare had better die and have done with it. When the fowls are moulting separate the cocks from the hens.

The wise poultry raiser will at some convenient time be-fore wet weather comes lay in a supply of fine dry road dust for use in the fowl house the coming winter. Likewise he will see that the poultry house is cleaned up and whitewashed, and if repairs are needed to make the building comfortable, he will attend to that in due season.

Don't attempt to keep over more fowls than you have room for. It is folly to attempt to winter 50 fowls in the space that 20 should occupy; bear that in mind when you fix up your fowls for market.

"Little things !" Yes, but it is these little things well looked after that change the balance from the debit to the credit side of the poultry account.—*Writer in Prairie Far-mer.*

H. T. Sandford sold 42½ dozen eggs from a flock of about 40 hens, from Sept. 4th to Oct. 10th, realizing $13 55 from the sales. The food for the fowls did not cost over $3 50 during that time; is there no profit in poultry raising ?—*Healdsburg Flag.*

The destruction of trees and shrubs and consequent bare, bleak, dry, unproductive and unhealthy present condition of the islands and districts of Greece and the regions around, once famous for their charms of shade, verdure, fertility and populousness, is charged to the browsing of goats. The government of Cyprus is considering how these animals can best be reduced or confined. Goats were introduced into an-other English island—Saint Helena—within a century, and the trees and shrubbery suddenly and rapidly died off so soon as they began to be numerous. The same obstacle in a dif-ferent and less degree is a rock of stumbling in our attempts at forestry. A chief item of expense in many situations is that of fencing in the ground planted, until the trees attain a size unattackable by cattle. For best results, close planting and entire exclusion of animals are preferable. On most farms pasture is at times an utmost necessity. Every rod of ground that will yield any at all must be utilized. If there is no grass the foliage and even the stems of trees must serve. Hence, with the best of intentions for conservation, some unlucky day or pinching season occurs, when the hitherto well nursed plantation is browsed, broken and greatly injur-ed, if not ruined.

RIFLE LOTTERY.—A correspondent of the *American Field* says: Having been an attendant at Creedmoor during the late fall meeting, and participated in some of the matches, I desire to call your attention, and that of riflemen at large, to the novel method the New York Rifle Association have of de-ciding the first prizes in their rifle matches. Likewise he will see that it is a lottery marksmen tie for first place, the association (not in the pres-ence of the shooters) "draw lots" for the prizes. This is hardly a proper test of skill with the rifle. If it is a lottery they are conducting, why not give all a chance for the first prize ? I will mention another matter which will interest riflemen. The five-hundred-yards continuous match was laid out for the New York militia. They were allowed to make fifty-two t10 ten shots; but western guardsmen were al-lowed but fifty points for the same number of bull's-eyes. This might be termed a sort of "skinning the outsiders" as no respectable rifle club will allow any shooter more than five points for a bull's-eye.

# Breeder and Sportsman.

PUBLISHED WEEKLY BY THE

BREEDER AND SPORTSMAN PUBLISHING CO.

THE TURF AND SPORTING AUTHORITY OF THE PACIFIC COAST.

OFFICE, 508 MONTGOMERY STREET

P. O. Box 1338.

*Five dollars a year; three dollars for six months; one dollar and a half for three months. Strictly in advance.*

MAKE ALL CHECKS, MONEY ORDERS, ETC., PAYABLE TO ORDER OF BREEDER AND SPORTSMAN PUBLISHING CO.

*Money should be sent by postal order, draft or by registered letter, addressed to the "Breeder and Sportsman Publishing Company, San Francisco, Cal."*

*Communications must be accompanied by the writer's name and address, not necessarily for publication, but as a private guarantee of good faith*

JOSEPH CAIRN SIMPSON,   -   -   -   EDITOR

ADVERTISING RATES.—Displayed $1.50 per inch each insertion or pro rata for less space. Reading Notices, set in brevier type and having the foot marks, 30 CENTS per line each insertion. Lines will average ten words. A discount of 10 per cent. will be allowed on 3 months, 30 per cent. on 6 months and 60 per cent. on 12 months contracts. No extra rate charged for cuts or cutting of column rules. No reading notice take for less than 50 cents each insertion.

San Francisco, Saturday, October 28, 1882.

## CLOSE OF THE YACHTING SEASON.

The yachting season of 1882 will be formally closed to-day by the San Francisco Yacht Club, which gives a dance at its club house and afterwards takes its last cruise to Vallejo. Already some of the yachts have gone into winter quarters, where they will remain until the breezes begin again in the spring. It is not to be inferred from this that all yachting is given up for some month's for some of the yachts are kept in commission all winter. In fact there are those who prefer the winter sailing. But winter sailing takes time. The winds are light and it sometimes takes as long to go five miles in the winter as it does to go fifty in the summer when the trade winds are blowing. For those who have time the winter sailing has many charms.

This season has not been a very successful one from any point of view. The fleet has not increased at all; in fact it has decreased, as some have gone into trade that were yachts, and only one or two new ones have been built. Then as to races there have been no startling events. The San Francisco Yacht Club omitted its annual regatta this year through lack of enthusiasm of its members. Enough racing yachts could not be got together. The Pacific Club got up a race which was a very pretty spectacle but owing to an unfortunate misunderstanding the results were not satisfactory. The Mosquito regatta arranged by the S. F. Y. C. went off very well but even that did not, in numbers, come up to the event of the year previous. The cruises in squadron have not been successful this season and have not been numerous.

Though individual owners seem to have a good time there seems to be a painful lack of harmony which is keeping the sport of yachting behind its proper position. It is to be hoped this will be remedied before another season, or club influences will wane still further and we shall have a lot of free lances.

During the off months, the yachtsmen go somewhat into the literature of yachting. They now have time to go into discussions and take up such things as they will not attend to during the busy part of the season. Time allowance, measurement, rigging, construction, etc., will come in for a share of attention. The S. F. Y. C. some years ago inaugurated a series of lectures on nautical subjects and they appeared to be very successful. These could be again commenced. There is no better way to get at the opinions of the members than to get up lectures and discussions during the winter months.

From now on the yachts must be kept in snug quarters as the gales may come at any time and the ordinary anchorages are not safe enough since they are not sheltered from the southeast winds. The reason most of the yachts are laid up in winter is not, as many suppose, because of the gales but because there is no wind that can be counted on as a surety and what there is is usually very light, unless there is a gale. The trip through San Pablo Bay which is sometimes a rough one in summer is now as smooth a one as a general thing as could be experienced. But it may take two days to get there from Vallejo. The club houses of the clubs remain open all winter and the yachtsmen can congregate there more or less on Sundays and "fight their battles o'er again."

The "Breeder and Sportsman" has done its share in encouraging the sport during the season and will give more or less of interest during the winter. Our yachting column always contains what fresh matter there is going and served up in a practical way that we are sure our yachting readers appreciate.

We hear that Harry Babcock of the Cordelia club shot fifty-six birds the other day at the preserve of the club.

## METROPOLITAN'S PERFORMANCE.

Efforts to get full light on the colt trot at Walla Walla where the yearling Metropolitan was reported to have scored a mile in 2:36½ have not been entirely successful. A letter of inquiry addressed to T. B. Merry elicited the following response, which, while it adds no facts to the case, does confirm the first report that the colt trotted a remarkable race and showed himself to be a great prize for his owner. "All I know about the colt race is that on the 5th inst., at Walla Walla, in a purse given for two-year-olds, the colt sold by Mr. Haggin to Charles Russel was started by consent of the parties owning the other two entries. Dr. Mack's filly Adelaide by Alwood had been given what you might really call work for about six weeks. She is an open gaited mare, fully 15:2½ high, and moves very much like Ned Parker's old mare California Damsel. In my belief nothing yet foaled in this part of the world is her equal. She can beat any three-year-old in the Willamette valley with as little exertion as Metropolitan beat her. I was busy at home and could not go up to attend the Walla Walla fair. Levi Knott, who went up on business, wired me the result of the colt trot that night and I knew nothing of the Echo colt being a yearling until after Mr. Knott's return to this city. He came into my office in his rough off hand way, and I began to question him in regard to the trot. I tell it about in his own words: "Why," said he, "that colt can't begin to run as fast as he can trot. He cut away from that mare like she had been anchored with a ton of ballast, and she is the best thing ever foaled around here. He went patterin' along like a p'inter dog and I didn't realize what he was a doin' till he was past the half mile stake at better than a 40 clip. He took the whip like an old stager, an' while she could never get by him she made him trot the last half the fastest. He went loafin' along as if he hadn't any business of his own in the world. He didn't appear to be trottin' a bit."

From this homely but lucid description we feel sure that there was an error in the time report. Metropolitan beyond a doubt trotted leisurely in the race and it is hardly possible that a yearling could jog in 2:36½ without showing some evidence of phenomenal speed before the race. A mile in 2:36½, accepting that as the correct time, is a great performance for a yearling with so short a season of training and the importance of the feat is augmented by the fact that it was done without severe effort or any attempt at a full display of his powers.

## THE STANFORD STAKE.

There has been quite an excitement about the Stanford Stake. The largest colt stake ever trotted for, and consequently, more enthusiasm. The twenty-one nominations originally made were a token of a good race, and though this dwindled to three starters there was still a stubborn contest between two of the colts. Inasmuch as we were disappointed in obtaining the out of the winner we will have to defer the history until next week. Adair won handsomely, Clay getting the second heat. In the next issue will be a portrait of the winner and a full description of the race.

## EDITORIAL NOTES.

**Game Preserves.**—The organization of shooting-clubs and the securing of game preserves goes on all over the coast and there is a prospect that the threatened decimation of game will be checked. We give place elsewhere to a communication in defense of pot hunters. From our correspondent's standpoint this much anathematized class are engaged only in a fight for bread. A simple effort for existence is certainly no crime moral or legal if not made by questionable methods and the pot hunter as pictured by "Agricola" might look the rest of the world in the face with good grace, but such is not the pot hunter of reality. It is not the reasonable killing for market that is making barren our game ranges but the merciless slaughter, the "after me the deluge" style of market hunting. The night shooting, swivel guns, traps, nets and kindred contrivances that not only destroy game in quantities but drive away the survivors from their accustomed haunts and keep them away until they become acclimated in some more retired and inaccessible locality where they are not troubled by the enemy. This style of hunting has gone on without interruption for years in California and the effect on the game supply has not only been marked but threatens its total annihilation. The preserve is the only system that will call a halt in this destructive business. Let individuals or associations secure control of the favorable localities and by a well enforced code of regulations restrict the killing of game to reasonable limits. People who have been accustomed to unrestricted license will say that the preserve is aristocratic and un-American, but it is not true for all that. It is a reasonable, sensible and judicious method of protecting and increasing the game that is fast disappearing from land and water, and is in fact an absolute necessity. Legislatures make laws for the protection of game but they are ineffectual for the purpose because of the difficulty in finding officers who will enforce or even assist in enforcing

them. The rights that attach to private ownership cannot be ignored by courts or constables and it is only by putting the plains and marshes in that category that the objects aimed at by game laws can be attained.

A Complete List of the members of the Blood Horse Association will be given in these columns next week. Correspondents who have made requests for such publication will please observe.

## Handicap Weights.

In the handicaps to be run during the fall meeting of the Blood Horse Association, the following weights have been fixed by the official handicapper, C. M. Chase:

| Name of Horses. | Age. | Entitled to carry. | Weight to be carried. |
|---|---|---|---|
| 1¼ MILES, SATURDAY, NOV. 11. | | | |
| Marta F | 3 | 106 | 106 |
| Haddington | 5 | 118 | 108 |
| Forrest King | 5 | 109 | 100 |
| Nathan Coombs | aged | 118 | 100 |
| Rita Doane | 3 | 112 | 108 |
| Birdcatcher | 3 | 109 | 97 |
| Atalanta | 3 | 100 | 100 |
| Frank Rhoades | 4 | 118 | 108 |
| Fred Collier | 3 | 118 | 118 |
| Joe Howard | aged | 118 | 118 |
| Nellie | 3 | 109 | 110 |
| TWO-YEAR-OLD—ONE MILE. WEDNESDAY, NOV. 15. | | | |
| May B | 2 | 107 | 107 |
| Camille Urso filly | 2 | 107 | 100 |
| Lou Spencer | 2 | 107 | 102 |
| Clara W | 2 | 107 | 100 |
| 1¼ MILES, SATURDAY, NOV. 18. | | | |
| Garfield | 3 | 106 | 100 |
| Marta F | 3 | 106 | 106 |
| Forrest King | 5 | 109 | 100 |
| Inauguration | 3 | 100 | 100 |
| Birdcatcher | 3 | 109 | 95 |
| Battle D | 3 | 106 | 95 |
| Atalanta | 3 | 100 | 100 |
| Lizzie P | 3 | 109 | 85 |
| Jocko | 3 | 109 | 100 |

## Seth Green on Carp Ponds.

ROCHESTER, N. Y., Oct. 10, 1882.

There are many artesian wells scattered all over the Western country, and most of them are many miles from any lakes or streams or fish markets. It is my opinion that nearly every flowing well would furnish enough surplus water to supply a pond which will keep a family in fish. A very small stream will furnish enough water for some fish. I would recommend carp as being the fish most likely to be a success, as they require less care than any other kind. I do not consider them the very best fish there is, because of the years I have been used to eating the best kinds our country affords. But I remember when my mother cooked the suckers and shiners I caught with a pin-hook, they were the best fish there was. It would undoubtedly be the same with families raised on carp.

My opinion has often been asked how a carp pond should be constructed for family use. The pond can be made in any shape to suit the locality, but I would prefer egg shape, if the locality was just as suitable for it. The pond would breed flies of a great many kinds, one of the kinds being mosquitoes. The larva of all flies is the best food for young fish. I have bred them by the bushel, but some of the mosquitoes would be apt to take wing before the pond got well stocked with young fish, and to protect the family in a measure I would advise building the pond to the leeward of the house in the prevailing wind of the locality. If, for instance, the prevailing wind was from the west, the pond should be built to the east, northeast or southeast of the house. I would prefer the pond to the southeast, because if placed directly to the east the house would make a lee under which the mosquitoes could easily reach it. The mosquitoes can beat any sailing craft before the wind, but on the other hand so is where its the rece, as they have no keel. The whole human family should be thankful to the Creator for not putting a keel on them, and if their bowsprit had not been quite so sharp, they might not receive so many backhandled salutes from the verandas of the Long Island hotels, but would be just as useful and ornamental.

The pond can be built with plow and scraper. It should have a deep place in the center, and be shallow on the edges. If you have square sides the young fish will have no protection from the old ones. When scraping is commenced, carry the dirt as far back as you intend making the lower outside of your embankment, and keep scraping until the pond is four to six feet deep in the center. If the locality is such that the ice freezes very thick the ponds should be made deeper and holes kept open through the ice during the winter to keep the fish from suffocating. If the embankment is raised three feet and pounded down and sodded or sown to grass, the water could be raised so that ten three feet in the center would have to be excavated in order to have a pond six feet deep. The whole pond should be sown with some kind of grass or water plant, with the exception of about fifty or seventy-five feet square in the center. The grass and water-plants make the spawning grounds, breed, food and protect the young. The pond should not contain any other kind of fish, and if the grass gets too thick it can be raked out.

SETH GREEN.

We are glad to announce that the Royce Bros., near Columbus, Wis., have been very successful in breeding trotting colts from a cross of trotting stallions upon thoroughbred mares. In fact, no one but the Royces has attempted this practice to any extent, saving Ex-Governor Stanford in California. The Royces have something like fifty colts from which they hope to make the test. Their stallions are Aster, by Almont, out of a mare by Brown Chief, son of Mambrino Chief; Executor by Administrator, son of Hambletonian, out of Valley Rose by Peck's Idol, son of Mambrino Chief; Tuckahoe by Mambrino Patchen, son of Mambrino Chief, dam by Carlisle's Tuckahoe, etc. All these stallions are over 16 hands high, all of them strong and boney horses, and all three of them have fine trotting action. The mares have been chosen from among thoroughbred families known to possess good trotting action and plenty of bone. Hence we shall look for good results from these experiments. The Royces have, besides these thoroughbred mares, a large lot of Mambrino Chief, Hambletonian, Morgan and other well-bred mares, the colts from which number fully 100. All of their horses are large, size being one of the objects aimed at. *Dunton's Spirit.*

The army rifle shooting contest at Leavenworth, Kas., Oct. 25th and 26th, resulted in a victory for the Division of the Atlantic over the Division of the Pacific by twelve points, with the Division of the Missouri away behind,

## YACHTING.

### Ocean Yachting.

Ocean yachting with San Francisco yachtmen has never been much followed. In the first place the Pacific is so big it takes a long time to get anywhere, then our bar is very rough, and worst of all there are few harbors on the coast. The coast line is rugged and rocky, with bars at the mouths of rivers, and fogs prevail for many months. The Casco, owned by Dr. Merritt, has been on some very long voyages, but none of the other yachts have gone further than Monterey or Santa Cruz. As for ocean racing we found out long since there was "nothing in it." With a rough bar at the outset it is discouraging for even the largest boats to start. Not that the yachts are not fit for it, for some of them are. But there is little sport bucking around in a heavy sea fit only for pilot boat work. To show that almost the same feeling exists East we quote the following from last week's New York *Spirit*:

There has been quite a persistent effort, since the return of the vessels of the New York Yacht Club from their cruise to the eastward, on the part of some few of the club members, to get up an ocean race for either the Brenton's Reef or the Cape May Challenge Cups, but so far as can be learned, this has met with but slight encouragement from the yacht-owners, and it is hardly probable that either of these races will be sailed. The fact is, yacht-owners don't care to go to sea, and the more experience they have of ocean yachting, the less they like it. It is not that there is the least distrust of their vessels, for there are few of them but what could safely cross the ocean if such a trip were required of them, but there is neither pleasure nor sport in ocean yachting in any month, and certainly but little can be expected in the month of October. The previous races for these cups have proved nothing as regards the sailing qualities of the boats which started, and have been determined largely by luck.

The week, for instance, between the Dreadnaught and Palmer, some years ago, for the Cape May Cup, was won by the Dreadnaught, although the Palmer was the fastest boat. That between the Atlanta and Idler on a subsequent occasion was won by the Atlanta purely by a "fluke." The Idler beat the Atlanta seven minutes in the beat from Bay Ridge to the Sandy Hook Lightship, and then, after the start, the Idler got becalmed close in shore, and the Atlanta, a mile or so further off, kept a light air and fanned ahead, and got a lead of four or five miles to the lightship on the Five Fathom Bank, turning it just as a fresh southwest wind sprang up, and with a northerly tide just making. By the time that the Idler reached the mark, the Atlanta was hull down on her way to New York.

We remember the names of the Idler, Dreadnaught, Vesta and Rambler; of the Resolute, Vesta, and another, of the Dauntless and Resolute, etc., all around this Cape May mark, although not all for the challenge cup, but in every instance, except, perhaps, that of the Dauntless and Resolute, the boat which won did not do so on her merit, but her success was largely due to luck.

And as with the Cape May races so with those around the Brenton's reef lightship, the most notable of which were between the Madeleine and Rambler, before the Rambler was lengthened. Both of these were won by the Rambler, but there can be no doubt but that the Madeleine was the fastest yacht. If these cups are to be sailed for, the races ought not to be fixed later than September 15, and the latter part of August would be a still better time.

It would be a good thing, we think, to fix a day for each at the beginning of every season, just as the date is fixed for the annual cruise or for the June regatta, then the owners could arrange beforehand, and we think each match would fill. The nonsense talked and written about the desirability of ocean yachting, is, in every instance, from men who know nothing about it. Certainly no sailor would advocate it; but a couple of such races might, we think, be sailed each year, if for no other purpose than to show how infinitely superior the Sound is for pleasure sailing to the ocean. Next season then, at the meeting when the date is fixed for the annual regatta, let the dates be fixed for these cup races.

Of course, after they shall have been made, the yachts winning them will hold down until challenged, and as they are the seeds, so to speak, out of which grow other cups, their acquisition is not to be despised. Formerly they were of the nature of elephants, and the winner had to hold his yacht ready to race at all times, with the cheerful chance of loosing, but no counter chance of winning. All this, however, has been altered, and now the challenger must deposit with the Regatta Committee a certain sum of money, which, in the event of his not winning the race, is invested in a cup which becomes the bona fide property of the challenged. The owner, therefore, of a smart schooner may extensively ornament his sideboard by reason of successfully holding one of these cups.

The model yachts have not been heard of much lately. At one time there was quite an enthusiastic crowd of model sailors and many handsome little craft were built. Now that one of the Oakland creek boathouses has come into the possession of one of the model yacht men and the boats can be kept there, it is a pity that the sport is not resumed. If we recollect aright there were forty-odd models in the second race which took place in Oakland creek. If some one were to start up the amusement again others would follow.

The yacht built for the Spreckels brothers by Capt. Turner was launched on Wednesday last from the yard on Channel street. The boat is not finished yet and none of her rigging has yet been put in place. Capt. Cummings, the most skillful rigger in the country and who knows more about fancy work on rigging, etc., than any one around these parts, has charge of the spar. He is superintending the work in the loft. When this yacht is finished her pillow work will excel that of any in our waters.

This has not been a very brilliant yachting season when we take into consideration the fact that there are two clubs here and a good many yachts. It wants a good strong pull all together to keep things lively, and this year there has been a good deal of pulling the wrong way. Until all the petty differences are overcome the yachting fraternity need not expect any great revival of the sport.

It is not any longer safe to leave yachts in Mission bay or other unprotected places, as a southeaster may come at any time. Unless there is some one aboard to look out for things there is danger of accident. Even with good ground tackle it is not all right, for some one else may not have good tackle and drag them foul.

The sharpie Daisy is lying alongside of the Casco but is not used much.

The Golden Gate Yacht Club accompanied by their lady and gentlemen friends will hold their last sail this season on Sunday next, October 29th. The yacht Lillie, sailed by Wm. Schwerin, will carry the party to the Sancelito Club House, where the usual lunch will be served.

The race which came off last Saturday was not finished, owing to the lack of wind. The Whitewing and Chispa tried to give or the course, but at half past four they had only got as far as the ferry slip on the way to the fort and there had to give it up. It is not probable that any more races will take place this season.

There will be a trip to Vallejo by the San Francisco to-day after the dance at the club-house at Saucelito. Many of the yachts are laid up so there is not expected to be a large attendance on the cruise. The dances of the club are good, however, and there is always a first-class crowd present.

Commodore Macdonough has laid up the Aggie for the season in the Brooklyn basin at the upper end of Oakland Creek. She will probably be kept there all winter as the winds are now so light that it is hardly worth while to keep so large a yacht in commission.

The calm weather has played havoc with the yachting in this bay of late. Yachts have been caught out late and some of them have had to stay out all night.

The Mist has been laid up for the season in Oakland Creek. She has been covered all up with canvas and some other stuff to keep her from drying up in the sun.

The Elia is going up with the fleet to-day. Mr. Berry is one of our most enthusiastic yachtmen, and keeps his little craft moving as much as possible.

The Spreckels yacht will probably be used some this winter and will be all in good trim by the opening of the season.

Some of the Eastern yacht clubs have social gatherings in the winter. The South Boston is one of these.

The Startled Fawn has been hauled out of water for the season on the ways over on the Potrero.

The Violet is lying below bridges in Oakland creek. She has not been used much this season.

The Emerald has been on the ways this week being cleaned for the Vallejo cruise.

The little Ariel has been leaking badly but it has now been stopped.

## ROWING.

The Boston *Herald* says of the regatta at Lake Massabesic, N. H., October 3: The main race was between George W. Lee, of Newark, George H. Hosmer, of Boston, and James E. Riley, of Saratoga. The Saratogian was not rated very highly in the pools, but his more favored competitors were aware that he had good days and bad ones, and that he was just as liable to appear at the float strong, fast and with good staying power, as he was any other way, and hence looked upon him with respect and distrust. "Jim," said Lee, just before the race was called, while Hosmer, Lee and Riley were resting under a wide-spreading tree near the lake, "George and I will put in $25 each, and you put in $25 more, and go and beat Driscoll. You can do it to-day." Whether Riley was suspicious of the offer, or thought he was a good enough man to be a winner, it was impossible to divine, but he rejected the offer, and in the race paid more attention to Lee and Hosmer than he did to Driscoll. Indeed, they paid the greatest attention to him, for, on the way to the upper stake, he gave them both a great lead, and rowed as well as he has at any time this season. Lee and Hosmer made a desperate and successful effort to get a lead on him, and when they had done so they flanked him in much a way that he was badly pocketed, and could only get out of his predicament at their own sweet wills. He made a game race, however, and was well up with them when the stakes were reached. Hosmer turned first, Lee closely following him, and Riley third. The race was then over. Indeed, the only race witnessed was in the early part of the race, when Hosmer and Lee strove to get Riley in the pocket. Lee made no further effort to get to the front. Near the finish he put on a spurt, as also did Hosmer, and the crowd cheered lustily, but, as the result was controlled by the money in the pool box, and the race had been arranged for Lee to lose, in the interest of honesty between those who were dishonest, it became necessary to carry out the agreement. Riley made a grand struggle at the finish, and gained rapidly on the leaders, and it was thought by many that he finished first, but he completed the course outside the line of floats, and was disqualified. Driscoll who came in fourth, made the same mistake, and was also disqualified, the third prize going to "Big Pat." First and second moneys, whatever they may be, were awarded respectively to Hosmer and Lee. The time was not officially taken, but was reported to be about 18:3. Of course there was a wrangle following the announcement; hard things were said and severe reflections made, but "the decision of the referee was final and without appeal."

FLOCKING TO CALIFORNIA.—John A. Kennedy, who is matched to row Hanlan next summer, will probably winter in California and train on San Francisco Bay so as to be ready for the opening of the boating season in the spring. F. Davis, brother of M. A. Davis, the noted Portland oarsman, is now in the city and last Sunday watched the practice of the three crews that are to take part in the race for the BREEDER AND SPORTSMAN cup. Mr. Davis was amazed by the climate of California at this season of the year with its warm days that can only be equaled by the early September weather of the East. Mr. Davis thinks that Kennedy will be here soon. It is likely that in a few weeks Jack Largan, the famous English sculler who beat Laycock and Pearce on the Thames last summer, will arrive from Australia with Fearn, the champion English swimmer. Largan will stay in California while awaiting the opening of the boating season in the East, where he intends to try conclusions with Hosmer, Riley, and if successful with the second class men to fly at higher game. Fleming, the California champion, will have an opportunity to test his speed and endurance with Fearn when that celebrity shall have arrived.

THE CHALLENGE CUP.—The Pioneer Club has at last decided on its crew for the race on Thanksgiving Day for the BREEDER AND SPORTSMAN'S cup. John Sullivan will be stroke, R. C. Lyns will pull No. 3, or R. Crowley will puW No. 2 and

Mike Long, the veteran bowman of the Pioneer Club, will occupy the first seat. The crew is a strong one and pulls in much better form than any other crew that has been got together by the Pioneer Club. Whether they have the necessary pace is a question that can only be decided on Thanksgiving Day. The Ariel four consisting of Corcoran, stroke, the Branch brothers in the waist and Leander Stevenson at the bow oar are practicing regularly, but they do not appear to make the headway necessary to carry off the trophy. Last week a scratch four in an old wooden boat took three lengths from them over the mile and beat them out, but whether the racing four were extended all the way is not certain. If they were they will have to mend their pace a great deal to get the cup. The Golden Gate four show form and are regarded by the Long Bridge men as sure winners. They had a brush last Sunday with the Pioneer crew but to a close observer it looked as if each crew was waiting for the other.

### Hanlan's New Boat.

A number of prominent oarsmen met yesterday morning in the shop of "Bill" Olliver, at Harlem, to witness the laying of the keel of a new shell boat for the champion rower of the world, Edward Hanlan. On Sunday last Hanlan, while rowing on the Harlem, asked if there was any builder that understood the fitting of Clasper's patent "fin," a device for the steadying of the boat in windy weather. The person whom he asked replied: "Oh, yes; Bill Olliver used to be Clasper's right-hand man." Hanlan forthwith made the acquaintance of Olliver, to whom he stated just what he wanted, adding: "You can take your own time about the building of her. I wont need her before the spring." The boat ordered by Hanlan will be of Spanish cedar, thirty-one feet six inches long, eleven inches wide, and will weigh when finished twenty-eight pounds, row-locks included. She will be fitted with three water-tight compartments, the bulkheads being at either end of the cock pit, so that in case the boat should ship a sea the water would remain in the cock-pit, the strongest part of the boat, as well as being the most convenient place in the boat for weight-carrying. The patent "fin" is an arrangement similar to the centerboard of a sailing vessel. It is of steel, one thirty-second of an inch in thickness, twelve inches in length and three inches deep. It is placed about four feet from the stern-post in a water-tight brass well and is fitted with notches and can be lowered and raised at will, according to the state of the weather. This boat, when finished, will be the first ever built in America fitted with the "fin."

Hanlan said to a *World* reporter that he had seen the watermen on the Thames and Tyne use the contrivance with good effect, and first used it himself in his race with Trickett, when he rowed for the *Sportsman* Challenge Cup. He was so well pleased with it that he bought a half dozen of the fins. He had found the fin much more efficacious than the "windsail," which is an American patent, and that a rower using the fin had no one-hand rowing. The fin, if down, of course militates against the rounding of a stake-boat in a race rowed with a turn, but this difficulty could be in a great measure obviated by raising the fin one or two notches, while that part of it which was down, though small, indeed, would be of more service than the windsail. In a race rowed before the wind its use could be dispensed with, and though made of steel, the weight was not more than that of the wooden windsail.

Elliot, the ex-champion of England, who was defeated by Hanlan for the Sportsman Challenge Trophy for the first time on June 16, 1879, and rowed the course from "Mansion House to Scotswood Bridge" in 21:01, the fastest time on record, was present and told the *World* reporter that he was in fine condition for his race on Monday with James Riley, and was confident of winning. He also said that he had made another match with George Gaisel, whom he recently defeated, the race to be for $1,000, to take place on the Paxie River, Newark, on Monday, the 23d inst., the distance to be three miles—one and one-half mile with a turn. He was so confident of winning both of these races that he had forwarded to the "Old Country" a challenge to row any man in England for the championship and from £100 to £500 a side. He would in all probability return to England immediately after his race with Gaisel, provided nothing of importance occured to detain him in this country.—*World, October 15.*

PROPOSED SCULLERS' RACE.—A sweepstake race on Thanksgiving Day over the Long Bridge two-mile course is proposed. Pat Brannan has signified his readiness to enter and hopes to meet Denis Griffin who has been loud in his newspaper declarations of a desire to row. Mr. Griffin does not come to the center and cover Mr. Brennan's deposit for a race for large stakes but he may have no objection to the sweepstake arrangement where a fair payee can be won by a small outlay. The proposition is to make the entrance fee $20 and let the winner take the purse. The Pioneer Club will give three entries including Pat Brennan, who desires to show that he can lower Griffin's colors. He means business and the Golden Gate sculler can hardly afford to let an opportunity for a race pass.

The Harvard scratch races, discontinued for some years, were revived this fall and some exciting sport was seen on the Charles river in front of the Harvard boat-houses. Three races were announced for Senior eights, Freshmen eights and single working boats, but the second event on the programme was given up. The course was a short one, beginning at the Western avenue bridge and finishing at Stickney's lumber wharf above the boat-house. There were four entries for the Senior eights. Just before reaching the finish No. 2 and No. 3 crews fouled badly and by direction of the judges all but No. 4 were directed to row over the course again. In the second trial Capt. Burch's crew dropped out at the boat house and Capt. Hammond's crew won by three-quarters of a length in 53s. The time in the first trial for the two leading boats was 58½s. For single-scull working boats there were three starters, who took positions as follows: T. R. Agassiz, J. Lawrence and Fearnes. The first named won in 1:35. Penrose was second.

If you are a farmer be a good one. Farm well. Have a good orchard, good garden, good stock, and an intelligent family. Be intelligent yourself, and thus secure the respect of all who know you.

For Sale—The target used by the American rifle team. It is slightly injured by exposure to the weather, but otherwise it is as good as new.—*Chicago Tribune.*

It will not be long now before the birds will begin to come in plentifully and we shall soon begin to record big bags from all quarters.

## THE GUN.

### He Thought They were Geese.

For some little time the farmers along the various lines of railroad in this State have noticed a strange and unaccountable mortality among their sheep. Every month or so they would find from six to a dozen ewes or bucks wrapped in the cold embrace of death and without any apparent cause. Long the shepherds wondered and long the farmers murmured. Men were discharged and replaced by others whose character was so good that it could withstand the most suspicious appearances. Dogs who labored under the slightest suspicion of being sheep biters were instantly suspended from duty and by the neck; a double lookout was kept for snakes and cayotes but all was in vain, and day by day the wall of the sheep men was heard in the land as they sorrowed for mutton that had flown and lambs that would gambol no more. Rewards were offered for any clue to the nature of the disease and the Academy of Sciences and the different agricultural societies were requested to lend their brains to the task of solving the riddle. They all failed ignominiously. Now we do not for one instant pretend to possess more sense than the aggregate of all those learned men, but we rather flatter ourselves that we tumbled to the racket, so to speak, just as soon as we heard of a little incident last week. One of the clerks in charge of the railroad pay car is a rubiginous, albeit a pleasant youth of athletic proclivities and sporting aspirations. On the running path and on the diamond field for ball he has shone like a brilliant meteor.

As an oarsman he has pulled races without fear (of a ducking) or reproach (of having beaten a smaller man than himself.) As a boxer he was thought to be the only local champion worthy to pit against the heroic Sullivan, the great Bostonian bruiser. Elated with all these athletic triumphs he recently purchased a gun and commenced to "banger." As the car in which he traveled on his various errands would be whirled along the great San Joaquin plains, he would have his fellow clerks to watch inside while he would group himself upon the platform and bang away at every animate thing that came within 100 yards of the track.

A few days since his fellow clerks noticed him firing point blank into a flock of sheep. One of them went out and asked him what he meant by such improper conduct.

"Why, there is no harm in that," said the shooter, "any man can shoot wild geese in this part of the State."

"Great God, man, you don't mean to say you mistook them for geese? why, they are sheep."

Upon receipt of the startling intelligence the shooter, who is nearsighted, procured a glass and looked long and earnestly at the startled flock, while the boys waited around anxious to hear what he would say. At last he laid the glass down and quietly remarked: "Well, they are sheep but all I can say is that I have been shooting sheep like that for geese for the past three months."

He has put his gun away and vows he will never shoot again, but it is more than a waiter's life is worth to ask him at the table whether he prefers wild geese or mutton.

### Domesticating the Ruffed Grouse.

It has been a matter of general belief that the ruffed grouse, more familiarly, though erroneously, known as partridge, could not be domesticated. Several instances that have been made public during the last few years in regard to tame birds of this species seem to disprove this theory. One of our exchanges, the Catskill Examiner, thus describes an occurrence of this kind:

"We believe that the partridge can be domesticated. An attempt was made some years ago on Long Island, which was partially successful. In severe winters at the West, during heavy snow falls, they have been known to approach granaries and barns, and to feed in common with poultry. We had, several years past, a somewhat singular experience with a single specimen of this shy bird, which may be worth relating, as it is a strong proof of the possibility of their domestication. One evening we found a full grown partridge under some currant bushes. It was a strong, fine bird, and did not seem afraid, although after the habit of its kind, it was quite watchful. He walked towards us and caged it, but in efforts to release itself were so severe that we resolved to give it its liberty. Strange to say, it seemed grateful, and allowed quiet handling. We had several broods of young chickens, and at feeding time it regularly appeared among them for its portion of food. At night it made its home on a low grape trellis, and on occasions of any one passing beneath it would make a slight noise and would permit a touch of the hand. A bit of red color in a dress or in any other shape always seemed to excite it, and it would chase the children up and down the garden walk as long as the offensive color was displayed. As cold weather approached the bird sought warmer shelter, and found a roosting place in the chicken house very near the fowls. He had remained with us nearly the entire summer and suddenly disappeared, the probability being that he was stolen."—Turf, Field and Farm.

DEATH OF CON ZINGO.—Con Zingg, the well-known gunsmith, and fancy rifle-marksman, died Thursday morning, after many months' illness from pulmonary troubles. For the last few years he has devoted much of his time to the shooting-gallery business, having had galleries at Sacramento, Stockton, Santa Cruz, Salinas, and at other points. He recently reopened a gallery in this city, in the Hensley House Block, in charge of Billy King, who has been his head man for many years. Mr. Zingg was a kindhearted gentleman, well liked by a host of friends. He was a most skillful and ingenious worker in iron or brass, having made a remarkable contrivance known as "The Soldier's Dream," with moving images, etc., as an attraction for his galleries. It is a masterpiece of mechanical skill. He was on the streets only a few days ago, and held out bravely and patiently till the last.— San Jose Mercury.

HUNTING IN MARYLAND.—In ye olden days, before the "little unpleasantness," the vales of Maryland used to echo to the deep baying of the hounds and the cheery music of the huntsman's horn; but of late years the noble pastime has been little patronized. It is therefore pleasant to read that the old fire has been rekindled, and the reawakened enthusiasm is likely once again to make popular a day with the hounds in Maryland. Several packs of good dogs are now owned there, and the farmers are taking quite an interest in the sport.

There are plenty of ducks near Alvarado but they are wild and fly high,

---

### Wild Fowl Shooting.

Bring out the trusty beech-loader and let us hear the click of the lock once again. "They shall be sweet music to our ears," as Charles XII said at Putolwa, as the screaming shot and shrapnel were flying over his head. For the next five months we shall hear the scream of the wild fowl on the crisp, wintry air as they wing their southward flight back from the vast fens of Alaska and the lonely glens of Ouinaca. Listen to the clang of the strong-winged phalanx above us.

Hawak, ap-hawak! and for'ard
From the frozen land in the far east
They go to their goodly cone.
Whoo they goose can ing,
What a struggling gander flag,
As they come from the frozen zone?
With opening throat and cheery,
O'er clouds they leap thro' the vasty deep.
The vaulted dome along.

No other land has such wild fowl shooting as Oregon. She boasts of the fine ducks of the northern waters, canvas-back and pin-tail particularly, and all those of the New England shores, except the great black duck, which is as black as a mallard and fully equal to it in flavor. The mallard breeds with us and so does the toothsome little teal, and therefore it is right that these varieties should be protected by law; but it is a grave doubt whether there ever was a canvas-back or pin-tail hatched in the State of Oregon. And certain beyond the shadow of doubt is it that the widgeon is an Arctic bird in its incubation and the rearing of its young. In the bright summer days when the parent mallard is croaking in the slushy fens of the Swinomish or the broad lagoons of the Pen O'Orille, then the widgeon is nestling her infant brood in the wilds of Alaska where the white man's gun is never heard. Hence legislation in favor of these birds is needless, as a means of increasing their numbers.

Down in California the widgeon is about as abundant as all the other varieties of the south tribe put together. The flesh has a salty taste, as compared with that of the mallard, and is vastly inferior to the pin-tail and canvas-back. Wherever mallards are worth one dollar per pair you should be able to get pin-tails for $1 25, canvas-backs for $1 50, and widgeons for seventy-five cents. That is about the way our markets run, and you will be surprised to learn that in New York the canvas-back is never sold for less than $2 a pair and from that to $3. The Baltimoreans claim that they have the best oysters in the world, which we are willing to concede. They also boast of the best canvas-backs in America, which we deny. The Oregon bird is just as delicate in flavor, and uniformly fatter. The wild celery of the Potomac is the boast of the Baltimore epicures, but we have seen nothing yet to make us "go back" on the wapato or water-artichoke of Oregon.

Daniel Webster and Henry Clay, both noted for their bout gout, used to quarrel like grizzlies over the relative merits of the canvas-back and pin-tail ducks, Mr. Clay espousing the cause of the brick-topped gentleman while Mr. Webster was equally enthusiastic in his advocacy of the duck with the long pennants flying from his guard as he scudded through the chill and cheerless winter air. And as they were the best of friends it was always a mooted point between them. But they were very much edified once by a practical joke played upon a congressman named Ben Turrell, from one of the western New York districts, by Gilbert Davidson, of Albany, a business partner of Erastus Corning. Davidson had dined at a club in Washington at the time that the discussion on the duck question was at its very height between the two great Whig leaders. Among the guests at the club was Ben Turrell and he made the duck case the subject of conversation during dinner. Gil Davidson conceived the idea of a practical joke at the expense of the rural congressman. He arranged for a great dinner party on the following evening, and had invited the "mighty man of Marshfield" on the strength of an old personal acquaintance. He was not acquainted with Mr. Clay but knew Arnold Harris, who introduced him to the "Great Commoner." There were twelve covers laid, with raw oysters and Chablis to open the feast, followed by that genuine southern dish of terrapin and hominy. Then came the roast ducks—a pair of pin-tails and a pair of canvas backs. Mr. Webster had been posted and just as the first cork popped he was asked which kind of a duck he preferred.

"Pin-tail, Mr. Davidson, by all means," was his reply.

Gilbert then turned to Mr. Clay and asked what he would be helped to.

"Canvas-back, my dear sir," answered the sage of Ashland.

When it came Turrell's turn he also took canvas-back and said he never ate pin-tail.

"Can you tell the difference?" asked Davidson.

"Tell the difference," with a sneer of contempt, "of course I can tell it. A blind man could tell it easily."

It was then agreed that Mr. Turrell should be blindfolded and a piece from each duck placed upon his plate. While the bandage was being arranged, Mr. Davidson adroitly cut off a piece of canvas-back and slipped it over on the dish, with the pin-tails. This done, the handkerchief was removed from Mr. Turrell's eyes and he was handed a plate containing two slices of roast duck. He cut off a bit of one, and chewed it with a complacent smile. "Ah, my dear little canvas-back, you're the jockey for me."

Mr. Davidson began to look serious, but Turrell took up a bit of the other duck and barely nibbled at it, saying:

"That confounded pin-tail. I would as soon eat sole-leather."

A roar of laughter greeted this remark and Ben Turrell looked askance at the company. He was reassured by Mr. Webster, who said, in his quiet way: "Mr. Turrell, both of those slices were cut from the same duck and for the sake of northern pride I regret to say that duck was a canvas-back."

A volley of laughter arose at this and Turrell got very red in the face. He never forgave Gil Davidson for playing this joke.

Canvas-backs should be roasted over a quick fire and never stuffed, like mallards or pin-tails, except in one way. If you can procure fresh mushrooms, not the canned trash for sale in our stores, then you will have something fit to stuff canvas-backs. Take two parts of mushrooms and salt them an hour before using them; then add one part each of stale bread and mashed potatoes. Mix them well together and cook the ducks ten minutes longer than you would if they were not stuffed. For canvas-backs there is but one gravy, composed of whatever comes from the birds while cooking, to which add a tumbler of port wine, a teaspoonful of salt and a saltspoonful each of cayenne and mustard. This is the recipe of Col. Jack Gambill, one of the greatest gourmands on the Pacific Coast, and the prince of jovial companions. Many's the good hunt we have had together in the tall redwoods of Mendocino, and many's the good dinner old Jack has cooked for me at the camp-fire, seasoned with that best of all condiments—a good appetite. What nights we have slept together in the woods, with such genial companions as Ned Cohen, Ward and Ira Eaton, Tom Battelle, Gen.

---

Jack Addison, Dr. Aylette and Jim Biddle. Old Jack marched along with his big ten-gauge gun, looking like Agamemnon born anew to conquer another Troy. Of all that party old Jack and I are the only ones alive. He is 73 years old and, for all that, the most erect figure and flashing presence that walks the streets of San Francisco. He has often promised me to come up and spend a week at the Swinomish flats, which lie between Puget Sound and Bellingham bay, but not a sign have I seen of Jack.

But speaking of duck shooting, I do hope to see the time when a sporting car will form a part of the trains out of Portland, for there is wildfowl shooting all along the 'Northern Pacific line, after you pass Walhila. As for the lower Columbia, the cheapest way is for a dozen companionable fellows to charter some little boat like the Toledo or Manzanita and go down to the Willamette slough or on those sloughs back of Martin's Island. The sport of shooting then is all that now enters into the consideration, for game is so cheap in our city markets that it will be found cheaper to buy mallards and canvas-backs than to shoot them. Some of the lands about Portland have assumed high values during the past two years, just because of duck ponds filled with wapatos on those lands. Last year a new experiment was made by George L. Curry of this city, in planting the wooms which grows in the southern Oregon lakes and is said to be the mallard's favorite food. The mallard is not a fish-eating duck under any circumstances, though he is notorious for devouring young frogs during the spring months. The widgeon is a grass-eating duck and the craw will show contents similar to those of the gray goose in seven cases out of ten. During the cold days when the ponds and sloughs along the Columbia are frozen over, the canvas-back takes himself to Shoalwater bay or Tillamook harbor, where he lives on young oysters; but whenever he feels the weather moderating, he will plume his wings for an inland flight and seek his favorite feeding-grounds in the Columbia bottoms where grows the succulent wapato.

No such devastation to wild geese prevails in Oregon as in California, and why I cannot well see. The geese have to fly across Oregon in autumn, and how they fail to visit her wheat fields and pull up the growing grain like they do in our sister state, utterly passes my comprehension. They gather in vast flocks in the counties of Butte and Colusa so that the farmers hire a patrol to shoot them and furnish ammunition and board to the hunters. From October to the last of February any good shot can earn sixty dollars per month in slaughtering geese on those large ranches. Strange to say, this great butchery of geese, so systematically practiced from year to year, does not seem to diminish their numbers. The only way I can account for the lack of like occurrences here is that the geese fly across here at night, but the most part. Now a big flock of honkers, if going before the wind, will easily travel fifty miles per hour; and three hours of steady flight would take them up into the "coast fork" country, where there are but few cultivated farms. There they can alight for rest and food, and then resume flight next day. It is calculated that two days' flight will bring them into the head of the Sacramento valley, where they go as they do on the Swinomish flats, scurrying hither and thither and alighting wherever they see no gunmen. The flight of the mallard and canvas-back is very rapid and that of the teal swifter than either. Audubon computes it at nine miles per hour. All geese and ducks fly in a triangle, except the pin-tails, which fly in a sort of semi-circle. In all their triangular flights, the ducks and geese are led by a male bird who immediately towers aloft at the first sign of danger and the others follow him. Wild geese in Colusa sell at three bits a piece for "honkers" and two bits for white ones and brant. Two years ago a farmer of our acquaintance, who had put in 1300 acres of grain near Princeton, furnished ammunition and board to two brothers to kill geese, with the understanding that they were not to leave the grounds during daylight or while there was a goose in sight. These two young fellows were therefore obliged to hire a neighbor's lad to haul their geese to Princeton and Colusa, and peddle the birds out of the wagon. At the end of the season they had something to show for it, as they plucked all the geese shot late in the day, cut out the breasts which they pickled and smoked, and melted the fat off the rest of the carcass. Their assets footed up as follows:

| | |
|---|---|
| Geese peddled | $842 50 |
| Feathers sold, 150 lbs. at 30 cts. | 54 00 |
| Six barrels of smoked breasts | 160 00 |
| Forty pounds goose grease, at 25 cts. | 10 00 |
| | $666 50 |

There never was any way by which those men would have made as good wages at hard labor on a ranch; but shooting geese day after day, in fair weather and foul, ceases to be sport. It is like eating boiled quail for breakfast every morning for a month. Nobody has ever began to shoot geese in Oregon on a scale large enough to warrant the smoking of geese breasts, but they are for sale at several of our principal family groceries after January and, for a change, they are very toothsome. But in some parts of Lane and Linn counties, from January to April, the farmers are greatly annoyed by mallards and widgeons, which destroy the young grain. In England the use of fyke nets has been carried on for sixty odd years, especially in the fens of Lincolnshire, where thousands of these ducks are caught annually and shipped to the markets of London and Liverpool. The nets are never set in the day time, and the silly ducks never see them. Just at sundown they are placed in the little narrow sloughs and the fowler goes home for the night. Before daylight he is out with lantern in hand to empty his nets in which he finds many of his birds strangled to death. Before its good daylight his nets are washed and hung up to dry, and he is picking his birds for market. Nets similar to these can be procured in New York at $60 each, and I know of no better investment for a farmer who does not shoot. Speaking from the standpoint of a man who loves a good hand day's hunt as well as any man between the two oceans, I should not like to see nets introduced into Oregon; but if farmers want to be cheaply rid of wild fowl in their grain, that is the way to go about it. It remains a business. But my idea is that the best fun is to choose up sides, as they do at Albany, and have one party kill the ducks and geese, the losing side to pay for a champagne supper. This generally gives a good day's sport at a trifling cost and winds up in a social reunion where mirth and jollity prevail, till the clock hands, clasped together, warn you that it is time for sweet repose. One thing I hope will be kept in sight. That is, that no true sportsman will ever be guilty of such low sport as those whose grounds he may shoot; and every careful sportsman will look, before firing, to see that he does not hit some farmer's cattle or horses. Mr. Dupen, of Wasco, has introduced a bill to amend the Trespass Act, and it provides very severe penalties. But an acquaintance of five years with the gentleman leads me to believe that he never would have originated such a proposition had not his fences been broken down and his live stock injured by a lot of conscienceless tramps whose motto is "devil take the hindmost." Every good man feels inter-seated in seeing such fellows severely punished and especially when they make no effort to repair the damage they have done. But I must close for I hear the Larline's whistle and in two hours I shall be standing before the decoys. Dine with me on widgeon to-morrow at 5 p. m.—*T. B. Merry in the Oregonian.*

## Gilroy Rod and Gun Club.

Through the kindness of Mr. Henry Miller of the firm of Miller & Lux, the Gilroy Club has leased, at a nominal rent, the "Soap Lake" and its surrounding sloughs, with permission to put up a boat house and necessary buildings for the convenience of the club. Soap Lake, as it is named, was in early days a great resort for native Californians to obtain an alkali for making soap. It is much frequented by ducks and geese, also snipe, and a few years ago they might be counted by the millions, but market hunters and promiscuous night shooting—that deadly practice of driving off game—have almost ruined the lake for hunting purposes. It is the intention of the club to protect and preserve the game in the lake, and while they have no idea of denying to any honorable sportsman a day's enjoyment in hunting, they are determined to put a stop to wholesale pot hunting and nightshooting. They also intend to stock the lake with carp and catfish, for which the water is fortunately adapted.

Mr. Miller, who, as well as his untiring energy in business, inherits the love of sport natural to his countrymen, offers to assist the enterprise in a pecuniary as well as personal sense. He speaks feelingly of the time when he first entered upon his ranch, how he could ride on the hills and see deer running round and flocks of quail in all directions, where now it is a blank as far as game is concerned. He intends to re-stock the ranch, import Bob Whites from the East and make it what it used to be, a sportsman's paradise.

## A Plea for the "Pot Hunters."

Los Gatos, Oct. 23, 1882.

Editor Breeder and Sportsman: I frequently observe sneering allusions to "pot hunters" in the newspapers, and I have observed that the Breeder and Sportsman is no exception. I would like to ask a few questions of these superior beings, the lordly professional sportsmen, who look down with so much contempt upon those who use the gun to win the daily bread for themselves, their wives and their little ones: Is it any disgrace to hunt deer or quail or other game with the object of making an honest living instead of merely as an idle pastime? Is it a disgrace here in America to be obliged to labor for one's bread? Are the game laws of this country made exclusively for the benefit of an aristocracy of "professionals" who occasionally leave the counters and desks of things San Francisco offices to enjoy a day's sport in the hills, or are they, as I had supposed, passed principally with the object of preserving and fostering an important source of food supply?

I observed the other day, in the "Rowing" column of the Breeder and Sportsman, an able article on the treatment received by the Hilladales in England, wherein some English writer was quoted as having sneered at American alleged amateurs because, instead of being made up of professional men, they were composed in part of artisans and mechanics, whom English gentlemen could not afford to associate with as equals. I was pleased to see the position taken that the mechanic in America was just as good as the lawyer or the bank clerk, if not better. Will not the same idea as properly apply in the "Gun" department of your paper as in the "Rowing" department, or are we to have one code of heraldry for rowers and another for gunners?

For my own part I fail to see the justice of game laws passed by the State if they are passed exclusively for the benefit of professional sports. If the "pot hunter" is without the pale of the law, or if, obeying the law, he is to be looked down upon as something akin to a sneak thief, and regarded with contempt by a class who ape the manners of the aristocracy of the old world, I fail to see the justice of either such law or such practice. During the close season the farmer morning after morning looks with rueful face at his desolated melon-patches and girdled fruit-trees, destroyed by deer against which he cannot fence and which he is not allowed to shoot. His ripening grapes are devoured by the same by quail. Yet he submits, and we hear no protests against the law, because he regards it as one of those instances where one does must suffer for the general good, and while the crops for which he has toiled are ruined he considers that it is for the preservation of one of the important food resources of the country. If he is here in error, and if the principal object of the law is to afford a pastime for the clerks and barkeepers of the cities, while "pot hunting" is to be frowned down, I think the patience of the farmers is expended in the wrong direction.

Agricola.

W. Golcher, Jerry Browell Jr., Al. Higgins and Dr. Kane braved last Sunday's heat and went to the quail grounds near Mission San Jose. Mr. Golcher bagged eight quail which was all that was killed that day. As the San Jose farmers are now taking the precaution to pen up their poultry from Saturday evening to Monday morning—to prevent accidents —so the hunters returned without anything to show for the trip.

At Alvarado near where the best sugar refinery is situated is a favorite feeding ground for English snipe; these birds seem to be quite fond of picking over the refuse from the refinery. Mr. Pierman and Mr. Hoffling were down last Sunday and bagged forty-five snipe.

Messrs. Haskell and Adams were on the Brooklyn marshes last Sunday forenoon and had good luck, taking into consideration how many hunters there were shooting on these marshes. Twenty-two birds were bagged between the two.

There are a great many ducks in the marshes near Melrose but they only stay during the night, and on the report of the first gun in the morning they take wing in a body and fly out into the bay where they remain till nightfall.

F. Butler and W. Richards were at the Cordelia Club's preserve last Sunday and say they bagged 100 ducks. These gentlemen are pretty good shots or else the birds came in livelier than usual.

It is now the fashion in France for the ladies to go out shooting with their husbands and brothers. France takes the lead when it comes to starting new fashions, or reviving old ones.

The early appearance of wild fowl in the vicinity of New Orleans presages an equally premature winter according to the theory of "weather-wise" gunners in that region.

## The Shooting Season.

So far this year this season has been a failure, as far as hunting is concerned, though not too far has the season advanced yet but that it may be interesting before the close. Just before the opening most encouraging reports came from all parts of the country—quail on the hills and in the valleys, ducks plentiful in the marshes and innumerable deer in the mountains. As far as deer hunting is concerned, many have been killed and it is well that there were no more of the beautiful animals slaughtered. On the first day of the season a perfect tornado of flying lead burst upon the unsuspecting game. For a day or two large bags were secured; then the quail gathered together their thinned ranks and flew to the brush and woodlands, since when but few large bags have been made.

With the water fowl it has been nearly the same; only those birds that raise their young in the marshes have been killed. There have been but few flocks of migratory birds in yet and every stray incoming flock has been looked upon by the hunter as the forerunner of large numbers to follow. The season in the far north has been exceptionally mild and the feeding grounds are still good. Anxiously are our sportsmen waiting for heavy frosts and chilly winds to freeze the lakes and rivers of the north and drive the feathered wanderers to our warmer and pleasanter clime. Well can be applied the words of Bryant:

Vainly the fowler's eye
Hath marked thy distant flight to do thee wrong,
As darkly seen against the crimson sky
Thy figure floats along.

To the individual with gun and dog who has lain in his hunting boat or behind the "blind" so long, in vain, watching the western sky for a flock of canvasbacks or honkers on which to show his ability as a hunter. From all indications there will be a change in the weather soon and the waiting of ambitious sports will be of short duration.

Nothing makes an old hand madder than to find himself on the marsh near some green land who begins whacking away right and left before it is light enough to see to shoot properly in the morning. Some men think that when they hear the rattle of wings near their blinds it is incumbent on them to shoot on general principles. It is not only a waste of powder and shot but a positive damage. The ducks are much more frightened at the flashes of the guns than they are at the sound of the discharge. When therefore careless men blaze away so early the ducks are frightened off the marshes into the bays. No one should ever fire before the dawn is sufficiently advanced to prevent the fire of the guns from being plainly seen. Most old hunters understand this but many new men have not had it explained to them.

Mr. Precht was up last Sunday near Novato and had some good shooting. All kinds of game are plentiful. In a few hours he bagged seventeen English snipe, nineteen quail and twenty-one ducks; most of the latter were quail and they were fat and in fine order. There are a great many deer in the hills but they are hunted most mercilessly by a party of Frenchmen from San Francisco, who repair to the hills every Sunday with their hounds and chase, as we understand, everything that starts up. One market hunter has killed over forty bucks this season in this vicinity.

A warm discussion is going on in the New York papers as to the alleged cruelty of fox-hunting. One of the writers tells the story that the late Thomas Ashton Smith, an Englishman, on being reproached by a clergyman for being so cruel as to hunt foxes; made answer: "My friend, the man likes it, the ladies like it, the dogs like it and the horses like it, and who the devil ever heard a fox say he didn't like it? So why should we stop it?"

During the past week the markets have been better supplied with game of all kinds than they have been before this year. Nearly all the ducks come from the San Joaquin and Sacramento rivers, and they are mostly small birds, teal, widgeon and sprig. When the street hawkers begin their cry of "Wild game!" as they have already, the boys can begin to put on their rubber boots and start for the marshes.

There are quite a number of deer in the hills back of Congress Springs. One individual—a market hunter, by the way—who sports the sobriquet of "Buckskin Joe" killed as high as eight deer in one week a short time ago. This was a fair week's work for him and the question naturally arises: "Does he kill bucks only?"

Mr. Jas. B. Brown and party have been over near Monticello and have had good luck in deer hunting. They have been out a week or ten days and have killed seven deer. Mr. W. J. Shrieve who has the gun store on Montgomery street was the recipient of one-half a buck, the nicest piece of venison he has ever tasted.

At the Alameda County Sportsman's Club's preserves at Mallard Station there has, of late, been some very good shooting; hunters have brought from twelve to twenty ducks a day. The club has recently formed a new constitution and code of by-laws.

Messrs. Misner, Hammell and Fine saw a California lion while hunting near Novato one day last week. Novato is a fine hunting resort, as all kinds of game are plentiful in that neighborhood.

In a two days' shoot last week, near Petaluma, Messrs. John Andrews and H. A. Foster of Petaluma killed twelve dozen quail and forty-three hare—and it wasn't a very good day either.

At Los Gatos there are but few quail, though at the opening of the season they were quite numerous. The market hunters made it so lively for them that those that are left are very wild.

The Cloverdale *Reveille* says that F. W. Merritt and Wm. Larrison killed twenty-five deer this season while going to and from their work near the Geyser toll road.

A deer milk white in color was recently sent from Maine to one of the dealers in Quincy market, Boston. It is said to be the first albino ever seen in that city.

Dick Brooks and Chas. Dall were at Sherman Island last Sunday and bagged sixty duck between them.

Mr. John Pollock was up at Union Island last Sunday and killed twenty-one ducks and one honker.

Mr. F. Bender was down at Alvarado last Sunday and came home with twenty-four ducks.

A few flocks of geese have been seen in the marshes in the vicinity of Petaluma.

The Teal Shooting Club at its hunting preserve on the Suisun marshes killed in one month 1,007 birds—this from Sept. 15 to Oct. 15. At this rate the shooting has not been at all bad for it is yet early in the season and the best shooting has not commenced. The grounds of this club are amongst the best in the State. We recently gave a description of the preserve and the outfit of the club.

Sprig, teal and widgeon are plentiful for this time in the season up in the marshes, but the canvas backs have not begun to show up yet. All the shooters are waiting for the favorite "cans." Without a few "cans" a day's sport is not complete.

# THE RIFLE.

## Riflemen.

The greatest shooting tournament ever held on the Pacific Coast takes place to-day and will be continued till to-morrow evening. This, as we all know, is given by the California Rifle Association, an organization worthy of receiving the patronage of all riflemen and sharpshooters on the coast. The association was incorporated June 7, 1875, and, like any other organization that has existed seven years, it has seen its hard times. The first president was Col. H. G. Shaw. Under the management of this gentleman and the Board of Directors the association prospered for three or four years, when a change was noticed as riflemen took less interest in the tournaments and only a few of our military companies took part in the shooting. By examining old records the conclusions arrived at are that the old Board of Directors were a little too cautious in the matter of offering prizes and other inducements to get rifle teams into competition. Since the election of the last Board of Directors and with Col. J. Dickinson as President a new and livelier interest has been taken in shooting. The cash prizes, trophies and medals offered have brought to the front all the old teams and many other teams from distant parts of the country. A rifle team from Victoria, B. C., and another one from Washington Territory were intending to participate in to-day's shooting but both for some cause or other have been disappointed. Though the northern sharpshooters could not come down, the California riflemen have the pleasure of contesting with equally as good shots from across the mountains. The Carson guards of Carson City and the Emmet Guards of Virginia City, Nevada, have sent representatives from their respective companies, to carry off, if they can, some of the prizes.

The visitors from Carson City are: Captain Crawford, Mr. Thaxter, Captain Parker, Mr. King, Sargent Saffell, Mr. Little, Mr. Slocum, Mr. Haskins, Mr. Cowing and others. From Virginia City come Captain Gallagher, Lieut. Galusha, H. H. Burk and J. C. Kane. It is to be regretted that business prevented two or three more of the best shots from coming down.

In our next issue we will give a full account of the California Rifle Association's fall tournament.

## Company D.

Last Sunday the sixteenth annual target excursion of Company D, Second Artillery Regiment—N. G. C., took place at Shell Mound Park. The Company's medals and prizes were shot for but will not be distributed till one week from to-morrow. The rifles used were the U. S. Springfield. The winners of cash prizes and their scores on the public target were:

| | | |
|---|---|---|
| Y. C. Erbin | .12 12–24 | $20 00 |
| J. Kahl | .11 12–23 | 12 00 |
| F. Erbin | .6 15–21 | 10 00 |
| J. C. Lohmeyer | .10 10–20 | 7 00 |
| L. Haake | .10 10–20 | 6 00 |
| M. Fortman | .9 10–19 | 3 00 |
| G. Schnee | .12 6–18 | 2 00 |
| H. Stell | .7 12–19 | 1 00 |

## The S. F. Fusilers.

Last Sunday the San Francisco Fusileers, Company C., Second Artillery Regiment, N. G. C., held their last quarterly shooting for this year at the Shell Mound shooting range. The following are the scores of the riflemen in their respective classes:

FIRST CLASS.

| | |
|---|---|
| 1st, Sargeant Otto Lemke | .4 5 4 4 4 5 5 5 4—45 |
| 2d, Corporal E. J. Mangels | .5 4 5 4 4 5 5 4 4—43 |
| 3d, Private C. Schreiber | .4 4 5 4 4 3 5 4 4—39 |
| 4th, Private F. Kuhls | .3 4 4 4 4 4 4 4 3—39 |
| 5th, Private E. Petri | .4 4 4 4 5 2 4 4 4—39 |

SECOND CLASS.

| | |
|---|---|
| 1st, L. Haake | .4 4 4 3 5 4 4 5 4—42 |
| 2d, Sargeant D. Wurthern | .5 4 5 4 4 4 3 4 4—41 |
| 3d, Sergeant F. R. Will | .3 3 2 4 4 4 5 4 4—39 |
| 4th, Sergeant A. Huber | .4 4 4 3 4 3 4 4 4—38 |
| 5th, Private Grimm | .3 4 4 4 3 4 4 4 4—38 |

THIRD CLASS.

| | |
|---|---|
| 1st, Henry W. Frank | .4 3 3 5 4 5 3 4 4—36 |
| 2d, Joseph Schmitz | .3 4 4 4 3 4 4 0 5—31 |
| 3d, Corporal H. Schmeasser | .4 4 4 4 4 3 0 3 3—29 |
| 4th, Private J. C. Schmann | .3 2 4 3 4 0 3 2 3—24 |
| 5th, Private Schuelkan | .4 0 3 0 2 0 3 2 4—18 |

Col. Bodine's Report.—Col. Bodine, who has been selected to act as Captain of the American Rifle Team in the International match of 1883, has recently given "an account of his stewardship" in the shape of a voluminous report, stating his views as to the cause of the recent defeat at Creedmoor, and making a number of suggestions for consideration by the Board of Directors of the National Rifle Association. He frankly admits that the American defeat was due as much to ineffective arms as to inexperience, and makes the admonishing contention that he merely acted as a figurehead, or "went through the motions"—as he expressed it—in coaching the team. The series of experiments by our riflemen, at a time when all should have settled down to careful practice, he condemns as unwise, but this foresight was not sufficient to prevent it.

California Schuetzen Club.—October 15th this club held a prize shooting in Alameda Schuetzen Park for best center shots. All members fired at thirty-six-inch targets, distance 200 yards. Those shots striking the six-inch bullseye were measured and prizes awarded accordingly. 1st Prize Halwyler; 2nd Bertelsen; 3rd Zecher; 4th Baerwald; 5th Jacoby; 6th Bremer Jr.; 7th Wertheimer; 8th Rapp; 9th Eckmann; 10th Bremer Sr.; 11th Roscheli; 12th Strecker; 13th Boeckmann; 14th Hatje; 15th Kvahman; 16th Bremer Jr. 17th Hotr; 18th Adams; 19th Lingenfelsen; 20th Thompson; 21st Fischer; 22nd Hauser; 23rd Schurer; 24th Meehl; 25th Utchig; 26th Saegehorn; 27th Hosveyer.

## THE KENNEL.

### Pacific Coast Coursing Club.

Last Saturday night the members of the Pacific Coast Coursing Club held their drawing of dogs to run at the fall match. The list of entries was not quite up to the expectations of the sanguine ones but it was fairly good considering the fact that the match was a club match and entries were confined to dogs actually owned by members of the club. The dogs were drawn as follows:

Old Dog Stake—First prize, $70; second, $40; third, $30; fourth, $20. C. Fowler's be b Delebute against W. Halpin's b and w b Culverin.

C. O. K. Jeffcott's bd and w b Lady Bird against Mark Devlin's w and bd d Chief of the Canyon.

C. O. K. Jeffcott's be and w d Spa Boy against W. Shay's w b Theresa.

J. Egan's bd and w b Lady Franklin against J. C. Pennie's f d Duke.

T. Cronin's b and w b Minnie against M. Devlin's be b Tampete.

W. W. Sessions' b b Maid of San Francisco against F. Brady's w and bd d Paul Jones.

J. Dugan's bd and w d Foxhall against W. Halpin's be and w d Blue Cloud.

J. Dugan's bd and w b Sally Henry against J. C. Pennie's f and w d Cherokee.

D. L. Levy's f and w b Lady Plaice against C. Fowler's b d Corrooburry.

J. C. Pennie's bd d Longfellow against T. Cronin's f and w d Farnell.

Puppy Stake—First prize, $40; second prize, $20. T. Brady's bd d Lady Costello against W. W. Sessions' b and w b Bingo of San Francisco.

F. K. Jacoby's b and w b Cassa Maria against T. Brady's b and w d Connaught Ranger.

D. L. Levy's b d Bingo against T. Cronin's b and w b Lily of Killarney.

J. C. Pennie's b d Master Joe against M. Devlin's b and w d Michael Davitt.

When the time came to select officers to carry on the match the first named for judge was Sheriff A. J. Meany of Merced, whose kindness to coursing men visiting Merced is so well known as to be taken as a matter of course (this is not a joke). Under the rules of this club three judges are required and to look after Meany, J. Dillon and Chris Johnson were selected. Joe Stadfelt was selected for slipper, Mark Devlin President, Judge J. C. Pennie Vice-President, Charles Fowler Treasurer, J. J. Bryan Secretary, and for the important offices of field stewards M. Galvin, J. Brady and Charles Fowler were pressed into service. The members of the club and guests left San Francisco at 4 p. m. last Tuesday. The crowd numbered seventy-six, including a round dozen of ladies, and for their accommodation and that of the dogs two special cars were hitched on to the Southern Pacific local train. This was one car more than the railroad officials expected to be called on to furnish and though the train was delayed some time there was no grumbling and everything was done to make the jovial excursionists comfortable. Seventy-six ordinary people could ride from San Francisco to New York without raising their voices louder than that tone which gentlemen generally use to enliven the movements of a sleeping car porter, but with coursing men it is somewhat different.

As soon as the train started Mark Delvin and Judge Pennie who, under ordinary circumstances, are quite demure folks, engineered all the ladies and old fogies into one car and put the boys in the other. Then the fun commenced. An aggressive youth in paternurally loud cheek suit boxed with black braid, and who so persistently murdered what he was pleased to call his "aches" produced two instruments of torture, sometimes called concertinas from a value and proceeded to inflict on the crowd a new version of "Sadie Ray," set to slow time. He was waited upon by a committee who offered him the choice of throwing his concertinas out the window or being thrown out himself. He refused both, and what happened then is best not told for fear some estimable citizen might be compromised. Suffice it to say, neither he nor the concertinas have been heard of since, unless the body picked up near Long Wharf yesterday should turn out to be his corpse. When he was gone a well-known member of the bar sang: "Wearing of the Green," while the boys chipped in with the chorus of "Marching through Georgia." The other passengers on the train said they would willingly dispense with the serenade but when the conductor told them he had no power to interfere they either resigned themselves to their fate or got off at the next station to wait for Wednesday's train. By the time Lathrop and supper were reached the boys were so hoarse that peace was assured for the rest of the trip and a holy calm settled on the car, only broken when a dog chanced to howl or one of the jokers of the crowd smashed in the hat of a misguided man who thought he had a right to sleep. About 10.30 p. m. Merced was reached; but a description of Merced is so important a matter that it is necessary to commence a fresh paragraph.

The chief point of interest about Merced is the El Capitan Hotel, kept by a bloated aristocrat named Bloss, who has been the autocrat of Yosemite excursionists, so long that one naturally takes off his hat and bows to the ground before daring to ask for a bed. The man does not live brave enough to slap Bloss on the back and say: "Blossom, old boy, just fire this value into No. 12 and tell that cursed cook of yours to fix me a rare steak."

Bloss is a stylish man in his dress; not quite so nifty as Ed Fay, the toney gimslinger of the Palace Hotel, but able to give points to Bank Commissioner J. M. Litchfield or Postmaster Backus. In fact, Bloss is so stylish and his bashery so vast that one scarce knows which is Merced and which is Bloss and the El Capitan Hotel. Since the southern overland road has opened and Bloss has a chance to bankrupt two sets of passengers a day instead of only one as before, he has grown so much in girth that it is hard to tell at times whether one is asking Bloss to give him a room in the hotel or asking

the hotel to furnish a nice room with a bay window in Bloss.

Merced also possesses a fine courthouse and schoolhouse, besides a few stores and the finest lot of saloons to be found outside of San Francisco. The saloon business is the chief industry in Merced. When a sheepherder or a thresher hand has amassed $100 he instantly opens a saloon in Merced and keeps it open until the Sheriff comes along and closes it. The duller the season the more saloons in Merced. So this year as the wheat crop is a half failure the saloon crop is booming. When Merced was the headquarters of the Yosemite travel and could not half a dozen tourists every day the people got high-toned and put on airs about such small places as Modesto and Stockton. But now that Yosemite passengers start from Madera it is possible to find a Merced man who will admit that his town is not much bigger than London and New York combined. Fandango houses are a time-honored institution in Merced. What coin the saloons let slip they absorb. They are said to be very lively places, but your correspondent has no personal knowledge of them and has so far failed to find any San Francisco visitors who have paid them a visit.

The arrivals included over seventy members of the Pacific Coast Coursing Club, besides many visitors. On Wednesday morning these, with a very large addition from the population of Merced, repaired to the coursing grounds. The ground was in splendid condition for travel, the weather left nothing to be desired, and a finer day's sport is seldom enjoyed. The results of the day's racing were as follows:

Old Dog Stake, first ties—W. Halpin's Culverine beat C. Fowler's Delebute.

Mark Devlin's Chief of the Canyon beat C. O. K. Jeffcott's Ladybird.

C. O. K. Jeffcott's Spa Boy beat J. Shay's Theresa.

J. Shay's Lady Franklin beat J. C. Pennie's Duke.

M. Devlin's Tampete beat T. Cronin's Minnie, after an undecided course.

T. Brady's Paul Jones beat W. Sessions' Maid of San Francisco.

M. Halpin's Blue Cloud beat J. Dugan's Foxhall.

J. Dugan's Sally Henry beat J. C. Pennie's Cherokee.

D. L. Levy's Lady Plaice beat C. Fowler's Corroraway.

T. Cronin's Farnell ran a bye in the absence of J. C. Pennie's Longfellow.

Second ties—Chief of the Canyon beat Culverine.

Lady Franklin beat Spa Boy.

Tampete beat Paul Jones.

Sally Henry beat Blue Cloud.

Lady Plaice beat Farnell.

Third ties—Chief of the Canyon beat Lady Franklin.

Tampete beat Sally Henry, after an undecided course.

Lady Plaice ran a bye.

This concluded the day's out-door sport, but to write the history of the evening's doings, from the time that the grand attack was made by the tired and hungry mob on Bloss' larder to the time of the retirement of the last of the boys, would require more time and space than we are able to devote to it this week. Suffice it to say that the dog fanciers slept that night as only men can sleep who have ridden all day at break-neck speed over the rough plain prepared by Nature in California, and improved by squirrels and gophers, for the breaking of unwary horses' legs and riders' necks.

On Thursday morning the sport was renewed with the following results:

Old Dog Stakes, Final ties—Mark Devlin's Chief of the Canyon beat Lady Plaice.

Tampete and Chief of the Canyon being both owned by Mark Devlin did not run off, but divided first and second prizes.

D. L. Levy's Lady Plaice won third prize and J. Egan's Lady Franklin fourth prize.

Puppy Stakes, First ties—T. Brady's Lady Costello beat W. Sessions' Chief of San Francisco.

T. Brady's Connaught Ranger beat Jacoby's Cassa Maria.

T. Cronin's Lily of Killarney beat M. Galvin's Bingo.

M. Devlin's Michael Davitt beat J. C. Pennie's Master Joe.

Second ties—Connaught Ranger beat Lady Costello.

Lily of Killarney beat Michael Davitt.

In the final race T. Cronin's Lily of Killarney won the first prize, Connaught Ranger second.

The Consolation race was won by W. Halpin's Culverine, J. C. Pennie's Cherokee second, W. Halpin's Blue Cloud third.

C. Fowler's Delebute beat Maid of San Francisco in a private match for a heavy stake.

This closed the meeting and on Friday the special train brought home two car-loads of well-satisfied and thoroughly tired admirers of the noble canis.

### Nice Points in Dog Law.

That extreme good fellow, the dog, has become rather an expensive companion to keep, and, indeed, when the "Friend of Man" costs 7s. 6d. a year, payable to the authorities of the Inland Revenue on the first of every January, the man, especially if he be a poor one, may have to acknowledge with a sigh that a four-footed friend is not one "for the likes of him," and surrender to richer folks the privilege of keeping dogs at all. At Worship Street Police Court last Saturday the valuable time of the magistrate was taken up with the hearing of over twenty summonses taken out by the Inland Revenue against persons who had failed to satisfy the authorities with respect to the payment of their dog-licenses. In one case the defendant pleaded that he was not the owner of the animal in question, but that it had belonged to his former landlord, and that the dog had "stuck to the premises." But the magistrate told this defendant that the person who is the occupier of the premises on which a dog is found taxable under the act to pay for a license, even though the premises should be only a portion of a house, and the occupier only a lodger. The defendant could not deny that he had fed the dog, although he added that he had tried to "stray it" and the magistrate, holding the fact of feeding to be a constructive "harboring" of the dog, fined the "coupler" five shillings. If the animal who "sticks to the premises," and who declines to be "strayed," be a dog of anything like right feeling, he will at once return to his right owner, and refrain from "sticking" to a place where his presence is obviously unwelcome.

Some of the defendants urged that they had taken out licenses late that year and that they thought the payment cleared them for twelve months; but it was explained that all licenses, even if taken out at Christmas, expired on the 31st of December. One defendant, however, triumphed over the tax-gatherer. This was a lady who stated that the dog in respect to which she had been summoned was not her property, but belonged to a lodger who was in her debt, and that she only held the dog as a security. The magistrate decided

that, under the circumstances, she was not liable, and the summons was withdrawn.—London Telegraph.

### Gilroy Field Trials.

Mr. W. F. Whittier of the firm of Whittier, Fuller & Co. has presented to the Executive Committee of the Gilroy Field Trials a silver cup, value $25, for the best brace of puppies run at the trials, the property of any member of the Gilroy Rod and Gun Club. This is a good beginning on the part of Mr. Whittier, who is a good judge of dogs and has had for some years the finest breed on this coast. The example should be followed by other wealthy sportsmen, as the only way to purify our breed of dogs is to let us see them perform in public, and by a union of judgment decide which are the best. Field trials are only in their infancy here and require the patronage and help of all good sportsmen to make them what they will be in a few years, a self-sustaining institution. No one can read the carefully reported account of the trials on prairie chickens at Fairmount, Minnesota, without being amazed at the vast improvement of a few years in the sporting dogs of this country, and we have no hesitation in saying that we can shortly throw down the gauntlet to England herself and challenge her with pointers and setters as successfully as we do with our high-flying racers that so completely astonished the aristocratic breeders at Epsom and Newmarket. We would suggest to our wealthy sportsmen—to whom the value of the thing is absolutely nothing—that they offer a prize for the best broke dog at the trials irrespective of natural qualities, and also one for the dog with the best natural qualities, irrespective of breaking. There are many dogs whose natural qualities are of the grandest description that from some cause or other will not break well for a public trial, and require more time than this is usually allowed for a trial run off their superfluous energy and show their real merits. Take the great Countess for example, who in one of her early trials scampered over two or three thousand acres of grain, before Mr. Burkele, the best trainer in England, could whistle her in. Then again, take the Irish setter, he is generally so full of spirit and life that the time is up and he is put out of the race before he has really got a clear understanding of what he is doing, when, give him the whole day, and he will probably discount his antagonist. The trials are fixed for Monday, Nov. 27th, and we hope to see a good showing of dogs from this city; otherwise we shall be outdone by Portland, Oregon, which has already four entered.

### Llewellin's Setter.

The following letter to the Turf, Field and Farm will be of interest to many persons in this State; though open to considerable criticism:

You will oblige me if you can insert the following statements, which I desire to address to those American sportsmen who are interested in the strain of setters which bears my name:

I brought forward a protest before the committee of the Kennel Club, proving the impurity of Pride of the Border.

I also denounced the probability that my old Countess was sister to Pride of the Border.

The definition of a Llewellin setter is, and always has been, the blood of Duke and Rhœbe (or of Duke or Rhœbe) with the Laverack.

I have proved, by the evidence I laid before the Kennel Club, that Pride of the Border was not bred as Laverack stated in his pedigree tables. Since the date when I laid that evidence before the committee fresh information and come to hand from Sir F. Graham and Ed Armstrong, and has been let out by the Laverack defenders themselves, which shows that the rest of the ancestors of Pride of the Border are bred in the same way as Pride himself, and that consequently all the descendants of these dogs have those same crosses in them.

Sir F. Graham states that Mr. Laverack bought his original setter bitch from Mr. Cornell, banker of Carlisle, for £8 8s. and crossing her with his (Sir F. Graham's) strain, formed his breed.

Ed Armstrong states that Sir F. Graham is perfectly right in the above statement, and that the bitch alluded to was bought on his father's recommendation, and that Laverack made frequent crosses to his knowledge, from the late Sir James Graham's kennels, and from that of the present baronet (Sir F. Graham.)

The evidence laid by me before the Kennel Club proved a very recent cross of red Irish blood to have been made by Laverack in his breed, and to this fact I wish to call particular attention.

The decision of the Kennel Club on my protest has given to these various crosses the right to the appellation, "pure Laverack."

The definition of Llewellin setter was given and accepted several years previous to the date when the Kennel Club gave their definition of "pure Laverack."

It has frequently been pointed out by myself and friends, in American papers, that the red setters going under the name of "pure Laverack," are not such.

I hereby give notice that no dog that inherits this red blood however much he may be crossed with any breed has a right to the name of "Llewellin setter," for under that protest from me.

The dogs so-called pure Laveracks having this red blood, and whose descendants are thus barred, are Laverack's Mystery, Ned, Hollin's Tory.

The reason for the above action I shall be ready and desirous to explain to anyone interested in Llewellin setters, but I am determined to avoid empty discussion and abusive personalities, such as have been admitted into certain of your contemporaries. I will, therefore, produce to any meeting of gentlemen interested in Llewellin setters, or forward to any person who shall have a suitable introduction, a copy of the proofs in support of my action.

The cross with red Irish blood, which was made at a recent date by Mr. Laverack, caused to his breed a loss both in show and field qualities at once striking and disastrous. The dogs of Laverack's breed which did great things, and caused his name to be known, were all of a date prior to his introduction of Irish blood, viz., Countess, Nellie and Daisy.

I also experimented with Irish blood on Laverack's breed at about the same date as he did, and the result was the same, viz., loss in high qualities. I, however, succeeded better in my experiments with Irish blood than Laverack did, for while he failed in producing one single animal of that cross of either show or field merit. I produced Flame, a [champion] winner at our largest shows, and the dam of the winners, Mr. Duncan's Rival and Thetis, and Shorthose's (late Mr. Duncan's) Roval, also the field winer Sampson.

Still, although I could produce better results when crossing with Irish blood than Laverack, that cross was far inferior to my other cross, viz., that with the Duke and Rhœbe blood, which has done so well. I therefore had enough of crosses with Irish blood, and made a complete clearance of all dogs so bred from my kennel.

The dogs of Laverack's breed of a date prior to his crossing with Irish blood were superior animals, and it is that Laverack blood, and that alone, that my breed possesses. The Laverack blood which flows in the veins of the Llewellin setter is wholly and entirely Laverack's blood prior to his infusion of red Irish, and no Laverack setter possessing in the slightest degree that recent cross has been bred from by me. Laveracks of a date many years previous to the Irish crosses alone have been used in the formation of what is known as the Llewellin setter.

The evidence of Sir F. Graham, etc., goes to show that the composition of the early Laveracks (prior to the Irish cross) was of blood very similar to that of Duke, through that of Sir Vincent Corbet's kennel, etc., and that therefore those old Laveracks possessed blood resembling that of the strain termed the "Llewellin setter."

I have shown that after Mr. Laverack spoiled those old Laveracks by crossing with Irish blood, they lost completely in all high qualities, and that the only dogs of his breed which made his name famous were those old Laveracks before the unlucky Irish cross, and the composition of which old Laveracks Sir F. Graham has pointed out.

The similarity in blood between the Laveracks of that early date and the Llewellin setter, and the superiority of both those old Laveracks and of the Llewellin setter to the recent Irish crosses, explains the reason of the success of those old Laveracks. Yours truly, R. Ll. Purcell Llewellin.

Forse House, Lybster, Caithness, Scotland, Sept. 24, 1882.

## ATHLETICS.

### The Usual Result.

On the 12th inst there was a wrestling match at Irving Hall, New York, between chosen members of the New York and Boston police. A. Quigley represented the New York police force and Walter E. Brown the Boston force. The men were called on to wrestle an hour each at Greco-Roman and collar and elbow, and the man getting the most falls to be declared the winner of the style and he who got a majority of falls on both styles to be declared the winner of the match, to bear the title of champion of the police forces of Boston and New York and to receive a gold medal worth $100. Shortly after 8 o'clock the men appeared on the stage. Brown was dressed in a white sleeveless shirt, drawers of the same color, and trunks of black velvet trimmed with gold lace. Quigley was clad in red drawers, white shirt and blue trunks. F. J. Griffen, of Boston, was umpire to Brown, and Quigley had as his umpire a Captain James Daley. Harry Hill was referee. Brown won the toss for choice of styles, and selected to wrestle, collar and elbow. At first both were wary. Brown was soon on his back by a "trip and twitch and back heel," amid great cheers for the New Yorker. Time of bout was six minutes. At 8:31 the men after five minutes' rest, jumped on the mattress for a second bout. They had been wrestling 2:15, when, amid great excitement Quigley caught a right "finger" on Brown and threw him in the air. Brown, however, was not to be caught so soon, and, by a quick movement, made a beautiful bridge, thus saving a fall. They were then separated and started afresh and kept up a continual series of tugs and taps for the remainder of the hour, without a fall being gained by either man, and the bout ended with a point in favor of Quigley. At 9:37 o'clock time was called for the Greco-Roman contest, the men for this bout appearing minus their shirts. No time was spent in useless maneuvering, but work, and good work, too, was immediately begun. After struggling three minutes Quigley caught Brown and held him between the stage and the ceiling and threw him to the ground. Brown made a bridge but the referee gave the fall to Quigley. This evoked a deal of discussion, Brown claiming that it was no fall, while Quigley on the contrary maintained that he threw Brown fairly. Brown then signified his willingness to at any time wrestle Quigley, but that he must refuse to proceed with the present contest, as he thought he had been unfairly dealt with. Every person in the hall then attempted to clamber upon the stage, but were prevented from so doing by the police. Harry Hill presented the medal to Quigley.

### Myers and George Matched.

Upon the arrival of W. G. George, of Worcester, England, the celebrated amateur athlete, and his friend, W. H. Caldicott, on Saturday last, and of which mention was made in the _World_ of last Sunday, he at once began negotiations for a series of races with L. E. Myers, the amateur champion of the world. These for a time were unsuccessful, owing to the obstinacy of both men in maintaining their claims to run their favorite distances first, Myers wishing to run a half mile and George nominating as his choice a mile. No matters stood until George, who had made the journey at an expense of time and money, with no hope of pecuniary reward, despaired of closing the negotiations. On Friday night, before Myers left for Philadelphia, where he ran yesterday, a meeting was called in the parlors of Gus L. M. Sacha, at the Windsor Hotel, and at which George, Caldicott, Myers, W. B. Curtis, G. W. Carr and George H. Thomas were present. Mr. Curtis explained the way in which George was induced to visit this country. It seems that when Myers was in England, in 1881 he challenged George, but the latter being ill, nothing was done. Upon the return of Myers to this country he received word that George was willing and even anxious to run him any distance over half a mile. Myers was then led down to business and could not again cross the Atlantic. Learning this, Mr. Wm. B. Curtis, on the part of the New York Athletic Club, extended to George an invitation to visit this country and run a series of races at one-half of a mile, three-quarters of a mile and a mile, to be the guest of the club. This was accepted by the Mosely Harrier Club, to which Mr. George belongs.

These points were considered by the meeting and it was decided to toss to see who would have the privilege of naming the distance to be first run. This was won by Myers, who chose the half mile. George then nominated to have the mile as the second event. This left the three-quarter mile to be the last to be decided. The dates were arranged as follows: Half-mile race, Saturday, November 4; one-mile race, Saturday, November 11; three-quarter-mile-race, Saturday, November 18. In addition to these, the Manhattan Athletic Club propose to give a ten-mile handicap run, in which George will be placed on scratch and a number of the best runners for the distance will be given start varying from half a mile to a mile.—_World._

George in New York.—Among the pa ng on the steamer City of Rome, which arrived at the p rn Satur-

d ay, Oct. 7, was the English amateur champion runner W. G George, who came to this country for the purpose of testing his powers against those of the American champion, L.E.Myers, in a series of match races at half a mile, three-quarters of a mile and one mile. To those who take interest in athletic matters the performances of George are almost as familiar as those of Myers, and as we gave a very full sketch of his career before the public in our issue of April 15 last, it will suffice to say here that his time for each mile from one (4:19 2-5) up to ten (57:55½) is the best on record by an amateur, as is also his time for three-quarters of a mile (3:8 2-5). Myers has the record for all the regulation and some other distances up to and including a half mile (1:55 3-5) and 1,000 yards (2:13), while his time for three-quarters of a mile is 3:13½, made more than two years ago: Since then he has improved at middle-distance running, and is thought to be capable, when fit, of showing considerably faster time. The only race of the three now arranged which is considered to be really in doubt is the six-furlong dash, the latter being generally conceded to the American, while it is believed that George can scarcely lose at a mile. The stranger was met at the pier by a number of well-known athletes, who drove his arrival have been making it as pleasant as possible for him, and he has already seen considerable of the inside and outside of New York. George is twenty-four years of age, stand 5 feet, 11½ inches, in height, in condition weighs 147 pounds, and is a modest gentleman of pleasant manners, well calculated to win friends among strangers. He is the guest of the New York Athletic Club, on whose track at Mott Haven he will prepare for the coming races, making his home at the Knickerbocker hotel hard by. All that is now wanted is for the weather to hold good during the work of preparation, so that both men may appear at the mark in the best of condition.—_New York Clipper._

The _Turf, Field and Farm_ and the _New York Spirit of the Times,_ in their comments on Haley's 9 4-5 performance, quote from the prominent San Francisco papers, including this journal. We beg leave to state that we are not in the fight for the 100 yards time record, and reference to our files will fail to convict us of any such weakness. All intelligent amateur or professional athletes are well aware of the chances for errors in timing or starting a race of 100 yards, and it takes more than one performance to convince them of the genuineness of any ten-second record. Our remarks in regard to the effect of warm weather on a native of San Francisco are mockingly quoted by the _Turf, Field and Farm,_ and editorially it reminds us that our representative athletes were East in September. We would remind our brother scribe that all the Eastern newspapers last September, both daily and weekly (and if we are not very much mistaken the _Turf, Field and Farm_ was one of them), were teeming with accounts of the unprecedented heat of that particular month, and were loud in their lamentations for the sufferings of President Garfield, which, as they openly stated, were on account of the extreme and unusual heat. Pacific Coast athletes are now well aware that the warm weather did not seriously affect Sime or Hawes, the handicapping and their performances being the same as in San Francisco. Haley, as is well known both here and there, did not train enough to show how the weather would affect him. Brown, when he left here, was undoubtedly the best amateur that had ever been seen on the Pacific Coast at any distance from 120 yards up to and including 440 yards. He was burdened with a superabundance of soft flesh, and needed plenty of time, but easy work, to prepare him for any race beyond 100 yards. Unfortunately he was the one that was prostrated by the heat of that particular September, and California was badly left in the championship and other meetings. This year Haley can give Belcher more than one yard in a dash of 100, with Belcher at his best. Perhaps Haley cannot do even time. We don't propose to argue that point, but if Myers can come out here and beat him (or Masterson) 100 yards, with a p n at start, his friends can rest assured that they will win more than they lost on the Brooks-Myers race. The remarks about the college days of the _Pacific Life_ reporter were probably intended to be sarcastic, and the 10½ seconds was undoubtedly a typographical error of at least one small second.

The usual small audience witnessed the shoulder and elbow wrestling match, last Monday evening at Turn Verein Hall, between McMillan, the Bodie champion, and Homer Lane. One individual mournfully remarked that a Democratic meeting had captured a majority of the lovers of a square wrestle, and consequently the money received at the door would be correspondingly small. He was right. The average San Francisco sport well knows the difference between an honest contest and a job match. As one intelligent party in the audience sententiously remarked, when bantered for a bet. "I don't bet on what no man can do—unless I have a hand in it myself." Early in the evening bets were made of $4 50 to $2 50 in favor of McMillan. The programme opened with the customary song, a recitation, and, for the inevitable encore, "one of my own composition." Next came two glove contests that were really earnest but friendly affairs, unlike the usual hoodrum shams seen at such entertainments. There was some difficulty in selecting a referee for the wrestling match, but about 9:30 everything was arranged satisfactorily and the principals appeared on the stage. Homer Lane showed the most science, his opponent making very little play, seemingly depending almost entirely on his weight and strength. The Bodie man very soon threw the ex-champion, but the decision of the referee was "no fall." When time was again called Lane quickly and most unaccountably treated McMillan to a square back fall to the immense delight of the sporting fraternity present, who, however, failed to take the bets that were freely offered by McMillan's friends that he would win the match. In the next two rounds Lane was entirely on the defensive, but McMillan won both too easily to make it interesting for the audience. He had backed himself with his own money.

The following is a verbatim copy of a challenge posted on the Olympic Club bulletin board:

Challenge—The California Athletic and Lacrosse Club will match Jos. Masterson against any one amateur on this Coast, R. S. Haley preferred, in a series of events to take place on any day, for a medal valued at from twenty to fifty dollars and the Coast championship. Starter to be mutually agreed upon, each man to select one judge, who shall appoint a third, and National Amateur Association rules to govern. An answer to this will receive prompt attention by addressing

A. H. Groom,
Pres. C. A. and L. C. 229 Leavenworth street.

Addenda—The competition shall comprise nine events, each club to name four and toss for the odd.

### Field Day Open Events.

The open events at the University meeting next Saturday will be 100 and 220-yard handicaps, 190 and 440-yard and one-mile scratch, and running high jump. Games will be called promptly at 2 p. m.

## CRICKET.

The Australian Cricketers arrived on the overland train last Friday morning and as the steamer did not sail until Sunday it was expected that they would give an exhibition of their play on Saturday. They were most likely tired of hippodroming for only four of them were present at the Recreation Grounds, where a game was arranged between a picked team and the Occident side. The Australians divided, two on each side, and the result was as follows:

PICKED NINE.

| | |
|---|---|
| Sloan b. Watson | 7 |
| McArthur c. Aikin b. Waterman | 0 |
| Fairfel b. Benjamin | 0 |
| Purdy b. Waterman | 9 |
| Fowler ran out. | 0 |
| Massey b. Moran | 11 |
| Brown b. Waterman | 0 |
| Riemer b. Moran | 0 |
| Foulks b. Moran | 0 |
| G. Theobald b. Waterman | 0 |
| Cameron b. Waterman | 0 |
| William b. Waterman | 1 |
| McDonnell stumped Callahan b. Horan | 1 |
| Aspinwall b. Waterman | 0 |
| Reddick b. Waterman | 1 |
| J. Theobald not out. | 0 |
| Gray b. Watson | 0 |
| Adams stumped Callahan b. Horan | 0 |
| Bye 13, leg bye 2, wides 0, balls 0. | 15 |
| Total | 47 |

OCCIDENT.

| | |
|---|---|
| Callahan b. Purdy. | 9 |
| Aikin c. Massey b. Massey | 1 |
| Jaffa b. Purdy | 13 |
| Horan c. Massey b. Purdy | 17 |
| Sanderson c. Massey b. Purdy. | 2 |
| Benjamin b. Purdy. | 3 |
| Leisey b. Massey. | 4 |
| Waterman b. Massey | 1 |
| Armitage c Brown b. Purdy. | 4 |
| Mathers b. Massey | 0 |
| Havens b. Purdy. | 0 |
| Moran not out. | 0 |
| Mathies c. Massey. | 0 |
| Bye 15, leg bye 0, wides 4 | 19 |
| Total | 72 |

## BASE BALL.

### Olympics vs. Redingtons.

Last Sunday at the Oakland Ball grounds the second game between the Olympic and Redington nines was played and resulted in the following score:

| REDINGTONS. | T.B. | R. | B.H. | P.O. | A. | E. | OLYMPIC. | T.B. | R. | B.H. | P.O. | A. | E. |
|---|---|---|---|---|---|---|---|---|---|---|---|---|---|
| Ambuster, M & ss. | 5 | 1 | 1 | 0 | 2 | 1 | Neal, p r f. | 4 | 0 | 1 | 3 | 0 | 0 |
| Arnold, 2b. | 5 | 2 | 1 | 2 | 0 | 1 | Van Bergen, l f | 4 | 0 | 1 | 2 | 3 | 0 |
| Bennell, 3b. | 4 | 1 | 0 | 3 | 0 | 2 | Conn, s s, p. | 4 | 0 | 0 | 1 | 0 | 0 |
| Lomas, 1b. | 4 | 0 | 1 | 6 | 0 | 0 | Engel, 3b. | 4 | 0 | 0 | 1 | 0 | 2 |
| Evett, p. | 4 | 2 | 3 | 0 | 5 | 0 | Borden, 2b. | 4 | 0 | 0 | 1 | 1 | 0 |
| Lewis, c and l f | 4 | 1 | 0 | 6 | 1 | 1 | Beck, 1b. | 4 | 1 | 1 | 7 | 0 | 0 |
| Moran, s s and c. | 4 | 1 | 0 | 3 | 7 | 0 | Fitzgerald, c. | 4 | 1 | 1 | 0 | 0 | 2 |
| Dillon, c f. | 4 | 0 | 0 | 1 | 0 | 0 | Sumner, c f. | 4 | 1 | 1 | 0 | 0 | 0 |
| Mullen, r f. | 4 | 0 | 0 | 0 | 0 | 0 | Kelly, r f, ss. | 4 | 2 | 1 | 1 | 2 | 0 |
| Totals | 39 | 9 | 7 | 19 | 27 | 16 | Totals | 44 | 5 | 6 | 12 | 24 | 16 |

Innings | 1 2 3 4 5 6 7 8 9
Redingtons | 0 1 3 0 0 2 1 2 0
Olympics | 2 0 0 0 0 3 0 0 0

Two-base hit—Beck. Three-base hit—Fitzgerald. Double plays—Borden and Conn, and Borden, Van Bergen and Beck. Passed balls—Lewis 3, Fitzgerald 1. Umpire—E. Van Court of the Howards. Time of game—Two hours and a half.

### Haverlys vs. Renos.

At the Recreation Grounds on the same afternoon an indifferent game was played between the Haverlys and Renos. The score tells the story.

| HAVERLYS. | T.B. | R. | B.H. | P.O. | A. | E. | RENOS. | T.B. | R. | B.H. | P.O. | A. | E. |
|---|---|---|---|---|---|---|---|---|---|---|---|---|---|
| J. Carroll, 1b. | 6 | 4 | 1 | 1 | 0 | 0 | Barnes, 1b. | 4 | 3 | 1 | 10 | 0 | 1 |
| Levy, r f. | 5 | 4 | 1 | 6 | 0 | 0 | Swanton, r, f. | 4 | 0 | 0 | 0 | 1 | 3 |
| Sohr, 3b. | 5 | 2 | 1 | 0 | 0 | 0 | Riordan, p, 3b. | 4 | 1 | 1 | 1 | 4 | 1 |
| Meegan, l f. | 5 | 1 | 2 | 1 | 0 | 0 | Lake, c. | 4 | 1 | 1 | 3 | 0 | 2 |
| McVey, c f. | 5 | 1 | 3 | 3 | 1 | 1 | Start, s s. | 4 | 0 | 0 | 0 | 0 | 1 |
| Lawton, 2b. | 5 | 2 | 1 | 8 | 0 | 1 | Callopue, c f. | 4 | 0 | 0 | 1 | 1 | 0 |
| Gagan, s s. | 5 | 2 | 2 | 3 | 1 | 1 | Sheridan, 2b. | 4 | 1 | 0 | 3 | 1 | 2 |
| Pratt, p. | 5 | 1 | 0 | 0 | 0 | 0 | Creegan, c. | 3 | 0 | 0 | 10 | 4 | 3 |
| | | | | | | | McElroy, p. | 3 | 1 | 0 | 0 | 1 | 0 |
| Totals | 46 | 22 | 12 | 17 | 14 | 5 | Totals | 34 | 6 | 4 | 28 | 14 | 13 |

Innings | 1 2 3 4 5 6 7 8 9
Haverlys | ... |
Renos | ... |

Earned Runs—Renos 1. Home Runs—J. Carroll, McVey. Three base hit—Riordan. Two base hit—Lawton. Bases on called balls—Haverlys 4. Struck out—Haverlys 3, Renos 4. First base on errors—Haverlys 7, Renos 5. Passed balls—Creegan 3, Sheridan 1, Callopue 2. Wild pitches—Meegan 1, McElroy 2. Left on base—Renos 3. Umpire—M. E. Fine of Muldics. Scorer—John P. Kennedy. Time—Three Hours.

### Sporting Churchmen.

A minister entered his horse at a county fair up in Wisconsin, and got into the sulky and drove. When one of the drivers ran his horse and passed the parson on the backstretch, the minister went into the judges' stand and made as grand a "kick" as an editor. Another man who drove in one of the races was a Methodist, and when the drivers tried to crowd him to the fence he made their spokes rattle like the strokes of an enraged parent on the seat of the youthful pantaloons. And so when the professional walked into the judges' stand to make his complaint against the man of God, there stood the Methodist with his whip raised over his head, ready to chastise the artist if he dared to utter a falsehood. It is needless to say the case went by default, as the professional dare not make the false complaint. The next week the two Christians were hauled up before the church committee appointed to try them, and both were condemned and excommunicated. The church became divided in consequence and the parson was installed by friends of the horse in a dilapidated hall to proclaim the church and the turf until a $100,000 house can be built for him where the right to visit the racecourse or drive a trotting horse will be incorporated into the church code.—_Dunton's Spi —_.

## A Terrapin Farm.

Leaving the beach and the sand mounds upon which Atlantic City rests, the eye meets the great salt marshes of the Jersey coast, which stretch back until the level coarse sedgy grass meets the horizon's edge. Dank and dark the slimy morass, home of the crawling reptiles and succeeding billions of mosquitoes, which have remained undisturbed through countless ages of time, until lo! lonah! Some wide awake Jerseymen have laid the hand of industry upon the muddy waste, and a so-called "terrapin farm" is the result. While it has been proved by actual experiment that terrapin can be raised on a small scale, it remains for the future to disclose whether the Jersey farms will be able to furnish the great cities with this most delectable dish as pronounced by the highest order of epicurean talent. For many years terrapin have been found in abundance in this locality, but the increasing demand of the New York and Philadelphia markets has drained the resources of the whole Jersey coast, and it is only a question of time near at hand when terrapin in its native wilds will become nearly if not quite extinct. To overcome this fearful famine a limited number of Jerseymen have made this delicious reptile a study, and the knowledge secured resulted in the farm, which bids fair to rank among Atlantic City's rarest attractions. So far not much beauty has been evolved, but Cape May has been beaten, and this alone is sufficient to bring a profitable return for the outlay. When State Senator Gardiner began his searching explorations into terrapin lore he found that scientists had sadly neglected to concern themselves about the domestic life of the Jersey "diamond back." Prof. Baird, of the Smithsonian sepulture at Washington, was approached on the subject, but he proudly pointed to his fossil remains of the "diamond back" of the saurian age, and proved that the turtles of that day were abundantly able to grub along without the aid of prying Jerseymen. In order to overcome the lack of scientific information a small family of terrapins was collected a few years ago, and it has proved a most interesting study to learn the taste, inclinations, length of life, as well as the time it takes to reach its greatest perfection. The "diamond back" terrapin never leaves its home by the sea, while nearly every moment of its life is spent burrowing in the salt water mud, where it lies torpid more than six months of the year, losing nothing, however, but apparently drawing sustenance from the mud where it is buried. As thousands of dollars have been already invested in this new industry, the importance of the subject is readily brought to mind. After five years of existence a well-behaved terrapin leaves the bottom of the muddy salt pond, crawls to the edge of the adjoining warm sand in the balmy month of June, and deposits from fourteen to twenty eggs, which she carefully conceals in the warm sand. After this performance Mme. Terrapin goes back to her bed or bed of mud with all the calm indifference of modern motherhood. But a foe of the most relentless kind is at hand in the shape of a bird called the crow, which speedily unearths the terrapin eggs, and they are dispatched at one solitary banquet. Senator Gardiner believes that the crow has more to do with the extinction of the terrapin than the hunter who makes it his business to furnish the markets. It is known that the young terrapin sleeps during the first year of existence, never leaving the spot where it is deposited, freezing and thawing within the bosom of mother Earth and growing like the roots that surround it. It is believed by some of the investigating Jerseymen that two years of terrapin life are spent in this torpid state, without movement or scarce any change. From its second to its fifth year the terrapin leads a kind of a vagrant life and is let alone because of no market value. In this safety from voracious crabs and fish, because it is continually burrows in the soft mud, never venturing any distance out to sea. Hence its name "terra," which means earth, and "pin" because it sticks so close to it. Sometimes the little reptile burrows three feet down in the soft mud. During this period of youthful growth it feeds on the refuse of clam, oyster and other little shell-like creations with which salt water so abundantly abounds, but when permitted to choose its food, as it is allowed to do when undergoing education at the hands of a Jerseyman, it is known to pass by all the old sea food and feast on dried beef—in other words, when Senator Gardiner placed a bill of fare before his terrapin, oyster, clam and other delicacies were rejected, while dried beef was found to be exactly what was wanted. The experiment was tried so often there can be no mistake about a terrapin's taste. When the reptile is five years old it measures nearly six inches across its diamond armor. It is now ready for the market, though it has not reached perfect maturity. When it has attained its seventh year in romantic flavor assumes its highest perfection, and a morsel has been found fit for the palate of the gods. Senator Gardiner's terrapin farm begins within a few feet of his garden and only a little way from the rear cottage door. Let the reader imagine a strip of dry earth joining the great salt marsh which stretches to the "inlet" covering some in extent, To the right a large shallow pond has been excavated, which is filled afresh twice a day by the salt water pushed in by the tides. Winding here and there through the sedgy plain are the narrow canals which lead to the pond and terminate at the inlet, and only the wind-mills are necessary to complete a Holland landscape. At intervals a rude construction of timber is noticed, which is placed to govern the inflowing waters as well as to ward off the deleterious encroachment of frost and ice. A fence surrounds the pond, which has been sunk three feet in the mud, as this depth has been found necessary to keep the terrapin from crawling away. A brilliant panorama appears before the vision of Atlantic City's "terrapin farmer." In his declining years he sits in his cottage by the sea. At his feet spread out his financial possessions which he has wrested from the savage morass. Beyond lie the placid waters of the ocean dotted with the fishing yachts which carry his diamond-back treasures beyond the seas.—*Philadelphia Times.*

## Defying Death.

The Philadelphia *Times* gives the following detailed description of the dangerous and daring act of Signor Leonati, who is daily running the risk of breaking his neck in making a series of ascensions and descensions on an elevated spiral roadway with an ordinary Columbia bicycle. According to the *Times'* description of the novel and dangerous performance: "The track is just twelve inches in diameter, without a railing or safeguard of any kind. It rises ten inches in thirty-six and describes a circle of only twelve feet in diameter. The distance he has to travel from the ground to the top of the canvas is some 250 feet. This act is certainly the most wonderful and dangerous performance ever accomplished, and Leonati was the first to attempt it and the only one ever able to accomplish it. Only a few days ago a daring gymnast attempted to imitate it in the city of Boston, and before he had reached one-quarter of the way up the spiral he fell and broke his neck, despite the arrangements he had made to save himself by means of a guard rope, a thing Leonati does not use. He rides on a spider

bicycle, with a 40-inch wheel and a 15-inch trail wheel. In going around the constant curve of one spiral the wheels are spread apart six inches, so that he has only three inches on either side to ride upon. That is, if either wheel should go to one side or the other but three inches it would leave the track and the daring rider would be dashed to the ground beneath and could only be saved from serious injury or death by a miracle, and it is safe to assume that the day of miracles has passed. Any one, then, who has seen a person ride upon a frail, unsteady, wiggling bicycle can appreciate, perhaps, the hazardous nature of the performance, even if it were done on an elevated straight track, with but three inches of room on either side of the wheels; but when it comes to a track that is not only a small circle, but ascends to a ratio of ten to thirty inches, it passes the comprehension of possibility. Still more marvelous than the ascent is the descent. First of all is the start. All bicycle riders know the difficulty of mounting a bicycle and retaining equilibrium without having given it an impetus; that it is next to impossible to mount a bicycle while it is standing still and start off. Well, this is just what Leonati has to do. At the top of the spiral the track is level about the length of the machine and widened about a foot. Arriving at the top, he lifts his machine around. The wheels stand facing—nothing—empty air, with nothing below it but the ground, some sixty feet below. When he mounts his bicycle he starts it from a dead stand still, and instantly turns the wheel to the left. There is no chance to remedy a mistake or to start over again. The start has to be accurate itself or it is the last of Signor Leonati, and once started, the same supreme control of nerve and muscle must be maintained throughout the perilous journey. It is, indeed, the most sensational performance before the public."

## City Farmers.

The direct interest taken in agriculture by many residents of cities we count a fortunate thing. In many ways men who have spent the greater part of their lives in cities have done much for American agriculture. Such men often came from the farm as boys or young men, and, when wealth has been accumulated, are glad to gratify the taste for farming which has all along clung to them. Sometimes they engage in farming chiefly or mainly for pleasure or recreation; sometimes engaging in it on an extensive scale with the expectation of making money by it.

Occasionally we find "practical men" speaking of this class with ill-disguised jealousy, or even with contempt; but we are glad to believe this is becoming more rare than it once was. Our country is broad enough so that there is no need for jealousy, especially of a class whose influence, as a whole, is decidedly for good.

That the "city farmers" often make mistakes, must be admitted. Sometimes these mistakes are serious. That they sometimes start out in the business with over confidence in their untried plans, we must also admit. But in almost every line of farming, and perhaps most of all in the encouragement of improved stock, they have done good. It would be invidious to name a list, but every intelligent reader can readily name men who are, or have been, among the most efficient friends of some valuable breed of stock, and who belong to the class of which we write.

It seems to us every well commendable, when a gentleman who seeks change from the cares of business or professional duties, attempts to secure this by purchasing, improving, and perhaps living on a farm. Oftentimes he adds greatly to his own pleasure, as well as being of much service to others. If he make his pleasure a source of profit, so much the better; but if not, the attempt has not necessarily been a failure. To build a costly mansion in the city and fill it with works of art, is not necessarily an objectionable mode of spending money. Neither is it to buy a farm, improve it, and stock it with well-bred animals, even though no direct profit result in either case.

It is not necessary that all who have a taste for country life should imitate those who have purchased large estates and made expenditures on a large scale. There is a temptation to over-do in this direction. In both large and small cities are many men who could well afford to become the owners of comparatively small farms, and who would find them a source of pleasure and of fair profit. There is room for real enjoyment in the care of a good farm; in seeing it improve; and especially in seeing the crops, or plants; or animals, becoming better year by year.—*Breeder's Gazette.*

## A Beautiful Experiment.

A curious and little-known experiment, showing the resistance of the air in guns, is described by Professor Daniel Colladon, of Geneva. He was in the habit of showing it to his classes. It resembles a feat that was sometimes performed by soldiers with the old Swiss carbines. M. Colladon fully charged with compressed air the hollow iron breech of an air gun, serving as a reservoir. Having screwed up the gun he introduced a round lead ball, running freely but nearly filling the bore; then placing the gun vertical, he seized the upper end and pressed his thumb vigorously on the mouth. The gun was then "fired" by an assistant; the thumb remained in position, and the ball was heard to fall back in the bore. Thereupon, after recharging the breech with the same ball, he shot the latter at a pine board about four inches thick, or a pane of glass, and it passed through. The experiment, M. Colladon says, is without danger, if the operator is sure of the strength of his thumb, if the gun is more than 32 inches long, and if the ball is spherical and nearly fills the gun (in which it must act like a piston). The least uncertainty in the very vigorous pressure of the thumb and the hermetic closure of the gun may entail serious injury to the thumb. While M. Colladon has performed the experiment twenty or thirty times without the least inconvenience either from shock or heat, a trial of it is perhaps hardly to be recommended.

## California "Blue Laws."

We have discovered a new issue upon which the next campaign can be fought by the two political parties. The repeal or non-repeal of the present Sunday law is the great dividing question at present. But how about the following relic of the "Blue Laws"?

"Sec. 396. Every person driving any conveyance drawn by horses, upon any public road, or way, who causes or suffers his horse to run, with intent to pass another conveyance, or to prevent such other from passing his own, is guilty of a misdemeanor."

We call the attention of our zealous conservators of the laws to this statute. No more will the gentle racer be urged to the top of his speed in the vain hope of passing some rival's Goldsmith Maid. Here is a brilliant opportunity for our constables: every time a farmer suffers his team to attempt to pass some sluggish neighbor who is jaunting slowly home, he is guilty of a misdemeanor. No matter how much dust the traveler receives from some mule team which hap-

pens to be ahead of him on the highway, if he runs his horses to get ahead of the plodding mules he becomes a criminal, and is liable to spend three months under the gentle wings of our amiable Sheriff. We call the attention of our friends to this statute so that in the future when coming to town they will gently walk their horses, or if they want to make haste they must hitch up a pair of goats or cows to their wagon.—*Modesto Journal.*

## Straw Lumber.

There can be no question that straw lumber is admirably adapted to many kinds of finishing work, barrels, table, and counter tops, fine doors and ornamental work; and we are assured that it can be produced and sold in competition with wide walnut at about one-half the price of the latter. The standard manufacture is in widths of thirty-two inches, a length of twelve feet, and a thickness corresponding to that of surfaced boards. These dimensions may be varied to suit such orders as may be given, and embrace any width, length or thickness. Unlike lumber, however, narrower widths are the most costly. The straw lumber may be ripped with the hand saw or the buzz saw, may be run through the sticker for the manufacture of moldings, and takes a nail or screw about as well as oak. It may be finished with varnish or with paint, and is susceptible of a high polish. It is practically water and fire proof, being manufactured under 500 degrees of heat, and we are assured has been boiled for some hours without any apparent change of structure. Its tensile strength is greater than that of walnut or oak, and its weight about one-fifth greater than the former when dry. It is made from any kind of straw, including hemp and flat fiber—in fact, from any material that will make pulp—and a ton of straw will produce 1,000 feet of boards. The pulp is rolled into thin sheets, a number of which, corresponding with the thickness of the lumber desired, are placed together with a peculiar cement, which is claimed to be waterproof, and are then rolled under a pressure sufficient to amalgamate them into a solid mass, which may be worked with a plane if desired.

When it is remembered that it takes 100 years to grow a tree to maturity, suiting it to commercial purposes—and a tree producing 32-inch lumber will require fully twice that time—while 20,000 feet per acre is a large yield under the most favorable circumstances, it will at once be realized that where 3,000 feet can be taken from an acre of ground for an indefinite number of years, the process which enables such a result to be accomplished, and which will yield a really valuable lumber, is one of real importance. We look for valuable results in the future in the manufacture of lumber from what is practically waste material, but which will be produced in endless quantities so long as the United States maintains its character as a grain-producing country.

## How to Swim.

—There is really no mystery in learning to swim—an accomplishment which is possessed in perfection by the most stupid of frogs. More than once I have explained how any one can teach themselves. The trunk less the limbs is heavier than water; with the arms, it is lighter; all, therefore, that a person has to do is to acquire the habit of drawing in the breath when he is preparing to make a stroke. Let any one do this and keep calm, and he will find that he can swim. But, perhaps it is better to acquire confidence by a preliminary course of floating. To do this it is only necessary to lie flat on the water, stretch out the arms with the palms of the hands downward, throw back the head, and whenever the body sinks low, slowly fill the lungs with air.—*London Truth.*

The Purity of Field Sports.—Young Californians take to the rod and the gun and the yacht—that is, a good many of them—and their example has a salutary effect upon the others who prefer the attraction of the billiard and bar-room. We do not mean that young men should allow their taste for field sports to interfere with the serious business of life, and it rarely does; but there is no man uglier than the sun who does not feel the better, mentally and physically, for a day among the quails or ducks, or on the foaming brook with the electric shock of a two pounder thrilling him from his finger-ends clear down to his toes. There is no guile in the fields; no sin, no temptation. There is no wrangling of men, no pot, but pure and safe, and the delight of space and absence of confined streets, and stifling odors.—*S. F. Exchange.*

Turtle Secrecy.—The mother turtles lay three times a year depositing sometimes as many as 100 eggs as a laying, and carefully covering them up with sand, so that it requires an experienced searcher to detect them. The Indians of the Orinoco and the Amazon obtain from these eggs a kind of clear sweet oil, which they use instead of butter. About 5,000 eggs are required to fill one of their jars with oil, yet so abundantly are they deposited that about 5,000 jars are put up yearly at the mouth one of the rivers. The harvest is estimated by the acre.

The largest sale of hops ever made in California took place on Monday at Sacramento. The hops were raised by H. Whittenbrock, and consisted of 700 bales. The amount involved was nearly $85,000. The negotiations were conducted on the part of the buyers by Newbourg & Lage, for Paul J. Crowley, of San Francisco. The hops will be shipped to England.

## Market Report.

FLOUR.— We quote: Best City Extra, $5 37½@$5 50; Superfine, $4 25@$4 75; Interior Extra, $4 75@$5 25; Interior Superfine $4 75@$5 12½.

WHEAT—The market at present is not very active. There are more sellers than buyers. The Liverpool market has changed for the worse and it is to be supposed better local markets would be affected by the change. A sale of 100 tons No. 1 quality recently made at $1 55 and also another of No. 1 October at $1 54 2½ ctl.

BARLEY—There is less activity in the market than there has been for a long time. Spot lots of feed are quoted at $1 37½@$1 60½; Brewing $1 66@$1 75.

OATS—The better grades are in good demand. The best quotations: feed $1 60@$1 75; Good to choice $1 70@$1 85; Surprise $1 80@$2.

RYE—Quotable at $1 00@$1 12½ for No. 1, and $1 00@$1 75 per ctl for No. 2 grade.

FEED—Ground Barley, $28@$30 per ton; Middlings, $26@$28 per ton; Bran, $17½@$20 per ton; Hay, $14@$18 per ton; Straw, 45@60 cts. per bale.

MIDDLINGS—$26@$28 $0 ton for lots at the mill.

PROVISIONS—Eastern Hams, 13@15c per lb; California Smoked Bacon, 10½@11½c per lb; Clear Sides, 10½@11c; Lard, 10@11½c per lb for tierces, and 12½c in tins.

ONIONS—Common are quoted at 75@90c per ctl; Silverskin, $1 25@$1 50.

POTATOES—Red, $1@$1 10; Early Rose, 75@90c; Garnet Chile, 60@75c.

## FALL RACE MEETING.
## FALL RACE MEETING

# Pacific Coast Blood Horse Association.
## 1882.

### Introductory Day—Saturday, November 11th.

No. 1—Purse $250; free for all; but each; a dash of three-quarters of a mile; $50 to second money to second horse.

NIGHT HAWK.
GARFIELD.
PREMIUM.
FOREST KING.
MAY D.
JIM DOUGLAS.
JIM RENWICK.
JOE HOWELL.
ATALANTA.

No. 2—Purse $250; free for all maidens; $10 each; one entrance; $50 to second horse.

JUDGE McKINSTRY.
JOE DION.
LIZZIE MARTIN COLT.
JOE G.
BOB.
PATROL.
CAPT. KIDD.
MATTIE BALL.

No. 3—Handicap dash for all ages; $250 for all; $25 entrance, and $10 if declared; $50 added; $50 to second horse; a dash of a mile and an eighth.

MARIA F.
HADDINGTON.
FOREST KING.
NATHAN COOMBS.
ELLA DOANE.
BIRDCATCHER.
JOE HOWELL.
FRANK RHOADS.
BOLIS.

No. 4—Selling purse, $250; a mile and a quarter; for all ages; entrance free; $50 to the second horse; the winner to be sold at auction; horses entered for $1,500 to carry regular weight; if for $1,000, five pounds allowed; if for $750, ten pounds; if for $500, seventeen pounds, and if for $250, twenty-two pounds. Any one can claim the winner, and the excess realized beyond the amount at which the horse is entered to be divided between the association and the owner of the second horse.

HADDINGTON.
EUCHRE.
GEO. BENDER.
JACK.
BELSHAW.
JOE HOWELL.
FRANK RHOADS.

### First day Regular Meeting—November 15th.

No. 5—The Ladies' Stake.

LADY VIVA.
SHANNON AND JESSIE R FILLY.
FLOU-FLOU.
CALIFORNIA AND ROSTLAND FILLY.
NORFOLK AND BALLINETTE FILLY.
NORFOLK AND BALLERINA FILLY.
NORFOLK AND MATTIE A FILLY.
MARION.
LAURA.
MISS GIFT.
PARTISAN AND PET FILLY.
PARTISAN AND LEXINGTONA FILLY.
LEVELLER AND FROU-FROU FILLY.
HUBBARD AND TEHAMA FILLY.
WILDIDLE AND ROSE FILLY.
SHANNON AND CAMILLA URSO FILLY.
NUBIA.
IRENE.
SOPHIA.
BELLE.

No. 6—Purse $250; free for all; three-quarters of a mile and repeat; $50 to second horse; entrance free; the winner of the dash of three-quarters on the first day to carry ten pounds extra.

NIGHT HAWK.
GARFIELD.
PREMIUM.
FOREST KING.
MAY D.
ELLA DOANE.
HADDINGTON.
JIM RENWICK.
FRED COLLIER.
JOE HOWELL.
FRANK RHOADS.

No. 7—The Vestal Stake.

NORFOLK AND MATTIE A FILLY.
NORFOLK AND MARION FILLY.
NORFOLK AND GOLDEN GATE FILLY.
ANITA.
SPRINGFIELD AND BOYDANA FILLY.
LONGFELLOW AND Miss CAMPBELL FILLY.
LEVER AND FROLIC FILLY.
LONGFELLOW AND ROBIN GIRL FILLY.
LADY CLARE.
ANNIE LAWRIE.
MONDAY AND CAMILLA URSO FILLY.
MONDAY AND VIRGINIA FILLY.

No. 8—Handicap purse of $250 for two-year-olds; $25 each and $10 if declared; $50 to the second horse; dash of a mile.

MAY D.
CAMILLA URSO FILLY.
LUC SPENCER.
CLARA W.

No. 9—Purse $250; a mile and a quarter over five hurdles; $50 to second horse; entrance free.

JOE G.

### Second Day Regular Meeting—November 18th.

No. 10—Purse of $250; a dash of seven-eighths of a mile; $50 to the second horse; entrance free; the winner of the three-quarter dash or eighth-quarter and repeat to carry ten pounds extra; winner of both events to carry fifteen pounds extra.

NIGHT HAWK.
GARFIELD.
PREMIUM.
DUKE OF MONDAY.
JOE G.
FOREST KING.
BOB.
MAY D.
ELLA DOANE.
HADDINGTON.
JIM RENWICK.
JIM DOUGLAS.
FRED COLLIER.
JOE HOWELL.
ATALANTA.
LIZZIE P.

No. 11—Purse of $250; heats of a mile and an eighth; entrance free; $50 to second horse; maiden three-year-olds allowed seven pounds; four-year-olds twelve pounds; maidens five years old and over twenty pounds; the winner of the dash at this distance on the first day to carry five pounds extra.

DUKE OF MONDAY.
JOE DION.
LIZZIE MARTIN COLT.
GEO. BENDER.
NATHAN COOMBS.
PRECIOUS.
FRED COLLIER.
JOE HOWELL.
CAPT. KIDD.
JUDGE McKINSTRY.

No. 12—Handicap purse of $250 for all three-year-olds; a dash of a mile and a quarter; $25 each and $10 if declared; the second horse to receive $50.

GARFIELD.
MARIA F.
FOREST KING.
INAUGURATION.
BIRDCATCHER.
MATTIE B.
ATALANTA.
LIZZIE P.
JOCKO.

No. 13—Purse $250; a mile and repeat over four hurdles; $50 to second horse; entrance free.

JOE G.
MOLLIE H.
HATTIE B.

### Third Day Regular Meeting—November 23d.

No. 14—The Finigan Stake.

LADY VIVA.
SHANNON AND JESSIE R FILLY.
AURIOL.
FLOU-FLOU.
CALIFORNIA AND ROSTLAND FILLY.
NORFOLK AND ADDIE C COLT.
NORFOLK AND MAGGIE DALE COLT.
CALIFORNIA AND FOSS COLT.
NORFOLK AND BALLINETTE FILLY.
NORFOLK AND BALLERINA FILLY.
NORFOLK AND MATTIE A FILLY.
MARIAN.
LAURA.
MISS GIFT.
GRINER.
LUCKY B.
GANG.
LEVELLER AND FROU-FROU FILLY.
HUBBARD AND TEHAMA FILLY.
SHANNON AND CAMILLA URSO FILLY.
SHANNON AND EMMA ROBSON GELDING.
SHANNON.
BOB WOODING AND LIZZIE MARSHAL COLT.
NUBIA.
BELLE.
IRENE.
SOPHIA.
DEL PASO.

No. 15—The Fame Stake.

"250."

NORFOLK AND BELLINETTE COLT.
NORFOLK AND MATTIE A FILLY.
NORFOLK AND MARION FILLY.
NORFOLK AND GOLDEN GATE FILLY.
ANITA.
LEVER AND CUBA COLT.
FOSTER AND PLANETIA COLT.
LONGFELLOW AND ROBIN GIRL FILLY.
JUDGE McKINSTRY.
RHODERICK DHU.
ANNIE LAURIE.
FOREST KING.
MONDAY AND CAMILLA URSO FILLY.
MONDAY AND LIZZIE MARTIN COLT.
MONDAY AND VIRGINIA COLT.
BAYSWATER AND BONNY RYAN COLT.

No. 16—The Baldwin Stake, with $ subscribers.

No. 17—Consolation purse of $250, of which $50 to the second horse; entrance free; a mile dash; horses beaten once allowed five pounds, twice ten pounds and three times fifteen pounds.

THEO. WINTERS,
JOS. CAIRN SIMPSON, Sec'y.    President.
C. M. CHASE, Assistant Secretary.

SPECIMEN OF OUR ARTIST'S HUMOR

THE FISHMONGER.

HUNDREDS OF DELIGHTED 'ONES [SEE,] FOR THE FIRST TIME IN THEIR LIVES

The Japanese Artist and Embroiderers

*At work in their native costumes at*

**Ichi Ban, 22 & 24 Geary St.**

*THE BREEDER AND SPORTSMAN is printed with SHATTUCK & FLETCHER'S INK*

NO. 508 MONTGOMERY STREET.  Vol. I. No. 18  SAN FRANCISCO, SATURDAY, NOVEMBER 4, 1882.  SUBSCRIPTION FIVE DOLLARS A YEAR.

## THE STANFORD STAKE.

### ADAIR—By Electioneer.

Again it becomes necessary to eulogize the work of our artist, and, in presenting the picture of the winner of the first Stanford Stake, claim that as a likeness it would be difficult to improve upon it. It is an admirable representation of the colt, and there are few who will not agree with us that he has the formation of a fast trotter. He is a "rangy" blood-like animal of fine size and plenty of substance.

There is a good deal of resemblance to the "King of the Track," St. Julien, and there is much of the same easy method of covering the ground. Little exuberance of action, a sort of "stealing gait," that is more effective than the more showy bending of knee and hock. This appears to be a family characteristic of the Electioneers, and scarcely one of them that does not exhibit the graceful, gliding action that is now more thought of than the sharp-bending of the knee in old times thought to be so essential to trotting speed. He is fully fifteen and three-quarters hands high, and is of the "lengthy" order in his build.

It is almost supererogatory to add written description to that of the artist further than to state that he is a very handsome shade of bay, without any white markings. The most striking thing in his configuration is the capacious chest and good middle piece, and what some regard as defective, rather a "slack loin." As very many of the best race horses and trotters we have known have this formation we are inclined to think that there has been an erroneous impression concerning the shape of this part of the body, and when there is width enough it matters little if there is a droop in front of

the coupling. So many of the descendants of imported Bedford show the peculiarity that it has been designated as the "Bedford hump," and the prominence of the spinous processes at this point certainly gives a better chance for the attachment of the muscles.

Without going into a minute description of Adair it will be sufficient to say that he is a "taking colt" in his whole appearance, and will attract attention from the critical as well as those who are not so well posted on the form of the horse. It is only necessary to refer to his sire, Electioneer, as he stands without question as the most wonderful trotting sire of the day. In the Stanford stake of the twenty-one nominations six were the get of Electioneer and the three starters were

Concluded on page 297.

## N. S. WALES SPORTING ITEMS.

### Our Regular Letter from the Antipodes—Racing, Rowing, Etc.

SYDNEY, N. S. W., Oct. 5, 1882

EDITOR BREEDER AND SPORTSMAN: In my last and first Sydney letter to the BREEDER AND SPORTSMAN I was unfortunately, I mean for your readers' sake, taken at a slight disadvantage, inasmuch as our great spring racing carnival was at its zenith, and Thursday, the day on which I penned most of my notes, our publishing day, so that you can guess of the amount of worry and anxiety there was in my mind at the time. Our Australian Jockey Club spring meeting extends over four days, two of which I sent you, and wherein I stated that many admirers of the Hon. James White's stable were fully expectant to witness the downfall of the A. J. C. Derby winner, Navigator by Hecla, in the same stable as Segenhoe, who had held the position of favorite. Those who expected Mr. E. De Mestre's handsome and symmetrical colt unable to pace alongside of Hecla over one mile and a quarter were doomed to disappointment as will be learned anon. Thursday (Sept. 7) opened with charming weather; indeed the weather throughout the reunion has been all that could be desired and much too so for the good of the country. In the suburban handicap of seven furlongs a great surprise was in store for backers. Twenty-two runners faced the flag; Stockdale was considered very good goods at four to one. It seems rather strange that the favorite belonged to Tom Brown's stable and the winner, Rupert, was an "offcast" from the same stable. Rupert is a hollow-backed animal with a very light "middle piece" but as nice a "fore hand" as you would see on any racehorse. He is sired by the well-known stallion King of the Ring, his dam Musidora, she also the dam of the Derby and Oaks winners Miss Jessie and Briesie, the filly who won V. R. C. Derby, Oaks and Cup, so that you will perceive what a long and illustrious line of ancestors Rupert hails from. The Grand Stand Plate of $750 for three-year-olds and upwards, one mile and a quarter, was won by Tom Brown's brown gelding Brian Boru (108 pounds), Hopeful (105 pounds) second, and Balthazar (105 pounds) third. Time, 2:16. The winner was afterwards submitted to auction and realized $1,350, the club benefiting through the sale to the amount of $600, the gelding having been entered for sale at $750. The next race was eagerly looked forward to as several of the "cracks" met over a mile and a quarter journey at weight-for-age. Here again Sting justified the confidence of his party by winning from Sweet William and Saionara. The latter, a three-year-old, carried 107 pounds while the former pair (4 years) carried 126 pounds. A field of eleven came to the post. The time was 2:13 and considered very good. All attention was now turned to the four candidates for the A. J. C. Mares' Produce Stakes, one and a quarter miles, colts 122 pounds, fillies 117 pounds. The betting was 5 to 4 on Hecla and even money against Navigator. Nicholas, a stable companion of Navigator, made all running for half the journey, when Hecla, at the four furlong post, went to the front. At the turn into the home stretch Navigator went up to Hecla and at the distance came away and won comfortably by two lengths, the mare not appearing to finish very kindly. The withdrawal of Segenhoe from this race was a great disappointment to his backers, but owing to a bruised heel which he received his trainer thought it advisable to scratch him rather than injure his chance for the V. R. C. Derby, which is run for on the 28th of October, for which event Navigator is first favorite and Segenhoe next, despite the easy defeat he met with at Randwick course (New South Wales). Guesswork from South Australia, and winner of the blue ribbon there, is greatly fancied, and Frying-pan from Saucepan, the dam of Haricot, the Melbourne Cup winner, and Irish Stew, a good handicap animal, have come into great favor during the past week. The day terminated by Mr. Fitz Wentworth's brown horse Sardonyx, by Fireworks, from Onyx, carrying 106 pounds, beating Proctor (122 pounds), Balmoral (112 pounds) and twenty others for the Sydney Handicap. Value, $1,000; distance, 1½ miles. Time, 2:39¾. In this race four horses fell through, one, Harebell, catching her fore feet in the heels of Comet and falling. Several of the riders received ugly bruises, but none of them are seriously injured, unless Williamson with a fractured shoulder blade.

The fourth and concluding day was ushered in with the same characteristic weather of the meeting, and the attendance—about 25,000—the largest ever seen on Randwick course.

Proceedings opened with the hurdle race, for which event four started, and was won by Dr. W. R. Cortiss' Nigger (by the way, the racing disciple of Esculapius is a brother to the celebrated bicycle rider, who is about to find his way back once more to the antipodes). The members' Handicap, a sweep of $25 each, $1 forfeit, with $500 added, one miles and a furlong, was won by a very handsome chestnut filly belonging to Mr. E. De Mestre, named Malmaison, by Robinson Crusoe (Derby winner, and the only survivor of the number of horses who went out in the ill-fated City of Melbourne in 1876) from Rose d'Amour, one of the best and gamest little mares of her day that ever graced a racecourse, and was very successful while trained by Mr. Jno. Tait, of "Barb" celebrity. Boscawen (104 pounds), second; Belvibere (107 pounds), third. Eight others started. Time, 1:59½. A good deal of speculation ensued over the Randwick Plate, of $1,500, for three-year-olds and upwards; second horse $500 from the prize; weight for age; three miles. Six started. Betting, two to one against Sting, three to one against Proctor, four and six to one against any other. Lord Burghley (135 pounds), made the pace for the first two miles then "died away" and Proctor almost immediately assumed command, but only for a couple of furlongs, as The Drummer and Sweet William, both full of running closed on him and Sting coming very fast on the outside of his field was nearly on even terms with them as they swung round the "home turn" into the "stretch." At the distance Sting challenged Drummer and Sweet William, a great race ensued for supremacy between the trio, ending in favor of Sting, passing the judges' box by a clear length from The Drummer, a head separating the latter from Sweet William. Time, 5:50—rather slow, which is accounted for by the fact of the race being made too much a "waiting one." Great excitement prevailed over the next event when the popular "yellow and black" and all "black and yellow cap" of "honest Jno. Tait" were seen to the front for the Waverly Handicap, a sweep of $25 each, $1 forfeit, with $1,000 added. One and three-quarters miles. The winner, Strathearn, is an aged brown horse, by The Barb, dam Mavourneen, a highly prized brood mare belonging to Jno. Tait. Strathearn carried 103 pounds; Harebell, (94 pounds), second; Balmoral (122 pounds), third; besides eleven others started. Time, 3:06, which is very fast. Old Jno. Tait's colors have not been seen passing the judges' box first for many a long day, and the spectators were quite beside themselves with excitement. He left the saddling paddock at the odds of twenty to one against him, while four to one was the best offer against Harebell.

The Steeplechase was of a similar monetary condition to the abovementioned handicap; distance three miles, and resulted in an easy victory for Hotspur, an animal nearly twenty years old, the favorite, Kanaka, getting second honors.

The gathering was successfully wound up by Mr. W. Forrester's black horse Gypsy Cooper (aged, 120 lbs), beating Hon. John Earle's Comet (122 lbs), Prima Donna (104 lbs) and twelve others for the Free Handicap of $500 with a sweep of $5 each to go to the second horse; one mile and a quarter; time, 2:12.

The above-named spring meeting of the Australian Jockey Club is characterized as one of the best ever held on Randwick racecourse since its commencement, the club making nearly $8,000 clear profit. A great number of alterations are now going on at the course and when next summer's meeting is held quite a change for the better will have come over the scene in the Leger stand. Several minor meetings, such as Orange and Dubbo spring meetings, have taken place since, but not of sufficient importance for me to chronicle.

The all-absorbing question now is who shall win the Caulfield Guineas and cup, run for in Victoria on the 7th and 16th of October. Then follows the greatest spring event of the year, the Melbourne cup, for which event Sweet William rules first favorite at 100 to 12, and Connamulla at 100 to 10. About any other 100 to 8 down to 2 is obtainable. The first-mentioned meeting will throw considerable light on the form of a few of the principal horses. Navigator is firm for the V. R. C. Derby and Segenhoe is coming into more favor.

The cricket season is now in full swing and each ground is full every Saturday, busy at practice. So far no matches of any great importance have taken place. The Hon. Ivo Bligh's English cricketers are expected shortly to arrive, following the Australian eleven.

There is very little new in the trotting world unless a small meeting held at Elsternwick park in connection with the Victoria Trotting Club be deemed worthy of mention. The first event was a maiden trot of $200 and sweep of $10; mile heats, best two in three. It was won by Mr. C. Colbath's. g. m. Bella Campbell, aged, who won the first and third heats; Mr. P. G. Dixon's Maid of Mona, by Merryhawk, winning the second. Time, 2:52, 2:55¾, 2:50¾.

Three-minute class, $350 and sweep of $15; two-mile heats, best two in three. The first heat was won by Mr. J. J. Miller's b. m. Fright, by Alarm. Time, 5:46½. Mr. D. Collins' g. g. Leithamstead, by Alarm (ridden to saddle), won the next two heats straight away in 5:40¾ and 5:41.

Dr. J. Weir has diposed of his lot and is now busying himself about home cares.

#### Aquatics.

The p i ip feature in the aquatic world has been the farewell dinner given to the well-known barrister Mr. J. H. Want, the popular commodore of the Prince Alfred Yacht Club, by the Vice Commodore, Dr. Milford. Mr. J. H. Want, who is suffering slightly from over-exertion in his profession, has resolved to recover his health by traveling round the world. He will visit Colombo, India, China, Japan, San Francisco and through America. His loss will be greatly felt in the aquatic circles of New South Wales, such an interest has he taken in yachting. Besides, he is one of the best of jovial good fellows. It is his intention, should he see a nice craft of about forty tons, to buy her and bring her out to the colonies.

Another event that is creating some speculation in the Parramatta River is the result of the Francis Punch trophy of $1,500 to be competed for by all comers pulling a pair of sculls in wager boats on a straightaway course on the Parramatta River. Mr. Punch also agreed to increase the amount to £500 provided in the event of two rowers from America and two from England coming to compete. However this last did not eventuate, and the race has been entirely left to colonial scullers, in fact, to New South Welshmen, for Bob Edwards, of Melbourne, thinking the company "too hot" for him, declined to row. Largan, of England, entered, and sent out his boats and trainer, but he himself has never shown up, and, it is believed, is looking for a long lost brother in America. Perkins, a young English professional, said to be a speedy man for a mile, and with an elegant finish in his rowing, entered, and came out to the colony, but thought there was "not sufficient in it" for him to show his powers, declined to row, after being placed in a division, but will be heard of shortly in a match that will be arranged. The trophy was therefore left in the hands of Trickett, Laycock, Rush, Beach, M'Donald and Pearce, and on Wednesday, the 4th of October, those divisions pulled the first heat. Appended are the results:

FIRST HEAT, FIRST DIVISION.

Course: From Bathing-house, Charity Point, to Gladesville Wharf.
E. C. Laycock, Sydney, 12st 8lb........1
D. M'Donnell, Clarence, 10st 2lb........2

Immediately on the arrival of the umpire's boat at the starting point both men paddled over to the bathing-house, and not an instant was lost in getting the men away. Elias Laycock appeared as fit as a fiddle and greatly pleased his supporters. M'Donnell also looked well, but was, of course, entirely overmatched. At Uhr's Point Laycock led by four lengths, pulling 30 strokes per minute to M'Donnell's 28. Laycock continued leisurely on, frequently allowing his opponent to gain on him. At Putney something appeared to have gone wrong with M'Donnell's slide, for he suddenly stopped, but again went on, and made frequent efforts to catch Laycock, without avail, as he came in winner easily by a dozen lengths. Time, 17:42.

SECOND DIVISION.

Course: From Gladesville Wharf to Bathing-house, Charity Point.
Michael Rush, Clarence, 12st 4lb........1
H. Pearce, Sydney, 13st........2

Rush looked exceedingly well and strong, but Pearce appeared to have too much flesh on him to pull well. Both men were sent away without delay, Rush having a slight lead, and Pearce making for the southern shore. At Hen and Chickens Wharf both men were level, pulling 38 against the tide. At Putney Rush, pulling easily, was leading by three lengths. After passing Putney, Pearce put on a spurt, but Rush increased his lead to six lengths off Blaxland's Point, Pearce apparently laboring a good deal. Off Gascoine's Rush took a rest for a few seconds, and allowed Pearce to come up to him, but he was then off and away again; and notwithstanding Pearce's efforts, beat him on the fall of the flag by half a length. Time, 18:32.

THIRD DIVISION.

Course; same as No. 1.
E. Trickett, Sydney, 12 st. 6 lb........1
W. Beach, Dapto, 11 st 10 lb........2

The appearance of Edward Trickett once more on the river was the signal for a burst of applause from the company on the steamers, and he paddled past to the starting point. He certainly looked the pink of perfection, and those who fancied him out of sorts, must have been much at fault, for it was universally agreed amongst his numerous friends that they had never seen him look in better condition. Beach looked exceedingly well, and the power, manner, and style in which he rowed, showed him to be wonderfully improved; although he may not gain a place on this occasion, it is quite vident that he is the coming man amongst Australian sailors. Both men got away together, and rowing a strong steady stroke, Trickett obtained a lead of half a length, and for some distance both men rowed stroke for stroke, Beach watching his opponent carefully. It was soon quite evident that Beach was not so easily shaken off, both men rowing in earnest, Trickett's style magnificent, and off Blaxland's Point Beach had gained and got a half a length lead from Trickett. The first mile was done in 6:20., Beach leading at the beacon by half a length and clearing a foul with his right scull, which gave a chance to Trickett to close up, but Beach again took a short lead, pulling strongly and eliciting much favorable comment. At Putney a foul occurred, but the men quickly extricated themselves and got away, Trickett first, and soon got a lead of a length and a half, which he then increased to four lengths, and afterwarts to sixth lengths; but, before reaching Gladesville, it was reduced to three, by which distance Trickett first passed the flagboat. Both men were heartily cheered. Time; 17:27.

Second heats—The second heats will be rowed this Oct., 5th afternoon, in which there will be two divisions.

First division, Beach, Pearce, Trickett.

Second division, M'Donald, Rush, Laycock.

The following is a letter published by Perkins in the Sydney newspapers, on which I will not comment.

"TO THE EDITOR OF THE EVENING NEWS, *Sir*: As, in my opinion, the public is entitled to some explanation for my sudden withdrawal from this contest, I beg herewith to give, through the medium of your columns, my reason. In the first place, I have to complain of the marked discourtsey with which I have been treated by the committee. Notwithstanding the terms of Mr. Punch's prospectus, in which it was stated that the boats of competitors would be brought out free, and an arrangement had been made with the P. and O. and Orient lines for a reduction in the passage money, I had not only to pay full freight for my boat, but the entire rate of passage as well. On going up the river to train, I addressed a polite letter to the committee, asking them, if they felt disposed, to grant me something towards my training expenses, I being the only competitor who had traveled 16,000 miles at his own expense to compete with Australian oarsmen. To this letter I received no reply. Under these circumstances, acting under the advice of my friends, I have resolved to withdraw from the contest. I may also add, to use a popular term, that there is very little "in it" as a monetary speculation for a young sculler, inasmuch as Mr. Punch has secured all the steamers, and there has been no talk, so far as I can gather, of any consolation stakes for the unsuccessful competitors. Yours, etc., G. J. PERKINS.

"Harbor View Hotel, Dawes Point, October 3."

## BICYCLING.

### Six Days' Bicycling.

A six days' go-as-you-please for the professional championship of Australia and a money prize, supplemented by a cup, presented by the proprietors of the Melbourne *Sportsman*, was commenced at Melbourne on Sept. 18, at 11 o'clock. Seven competitors started, comprising: J. Rolfe (champion), 56-inch machine; W. J. Press (champion, S. A.), 56-inch machine; J. Thomas (Victoria Club), 58-inch machine; J. Hoskins (Victoria Club), 54-inch machine; Hourigan (Victoria Club), 54-inch machine; Mitchell (unattached), 54-inch machine, and Maddigan (Seymour), 54-inch machine. With the exception of Maddigan, all the competitors kept on the track until time was called at eleven p. m. The score board registered as follows:

MONDAY.

| | Miles. | Yards. |
|---|---|---|
| Press | 166 | 416 |
| Thomas | 164 | 344 |
| J. Rolfe | 163 | 810 |
| J. Hoskins | 148 | 1390 |
| Houirgan | 136 | 842 |
| Mitchell | 128 | 486 |
| Maddigan | 60 | 518 |

TUESDAY.

| | Miles. | Yards. |
|---|---|---|
| Press | 323 | 772 |
| Rolfe | 320 | 1582 |
| Thomas | 316 | 330 |
| Hoskins | 288 | 312 |
| Mitchell | 272 | 1276 |
| Hourigan | 212 | 924 |
| Maddigan | 60 | 796 |

WEDNESDAY.

| | Miles. | Yards. |
|---|---|---|
| Press | 474 | 175 |
| Rolfe | 470 | 230 |
| Thomas | 456 | 83 |
| Mitchell | 410 | 86 |
| Hoskins | 387 | 1080 |

THURSDAY.

| | Miles. | Yards. |
|---|---|---|
| Press | 593 | 1650 |
| Rolfe | 592 | 220 |
| Thomas | 576 | 884 |
| Mitchell | 536 | 70 |
| Hoskins | 466 | 1600 |

FRIDAY.

| | Miles. | Yards. |
|---|---|---|
| Press | 723 | 346 |
| Rolfe | 722 | 710 |
| Thomas | 695 | 780 |
| Mitchell | 655 | 300 |
| Hoskins | 513 | 900 |

SATURDAY.

| | Miles. | Yards. |
|---|---|---|
| Press | 854 | 960 |
| Rolfe | 852 | 1570 |
| Thomas | 793 | 540 |
| Mitchell | 751 | 480 |
| Hoskins | 541 | 170 |
| Hourigan | 268 | |
| Madigan | 80 | 496 |

The result was a victory for W. J. Press, the champion of South Australia. Press kept the strong lead he held of Rolfe till Friday night, when the latter reduced it to about a mile, both men finishing up fresh at 10:45, with Thomas second, 695 miles, 780 yards, and Mitchell fourth, 655 miles, 300 yards. On Saturday morning the men resumed the track at a fair pace, and continued steadily all the afternoon to the evening, when the pace became much faster, Rolfe spurting frequently to reduce the distance between him and Press. The latter, however, kept on in fine style, and when the pistol was fired had won by almost a mile and a half. Thomas, who had retired after scoring 793 miles, 540 yards, secured third prize, Mirchell fourth, and Hoskins fifth. The machines ridden by Press, Rolfe and Thomas were each a 52-inch Singer, and that by Mitchell a 50-inch Club.

# TURF AND TRACK.

## "Old Bush."

ushwhacker, Bonnie Scotland's ill-used son, won the wie stakes at Pimlico October 21st, although he did not meet enmore as was hoped. The following description is from New York *World's* report:

At the fall of the flag Hartford was in front, but he quickly re place to Bushwhacker, who led at the quarter by three igths, with Hartford second, five lengths in front of Ella arfield. There was no change in placing and but little in distances apart for the first three miles, where Bush- acker only led by a length and a half, with Hartford but ree lengths in front of Warfield. In the run round the ru on the last mile the distances were equalized by two igths each, which was gradually reduced as they went down backstretch, first by Ella Warfield passing Hartford and sing up on Bushwhacker, until at the half mile, amid the outs of a majority present, Ella Warfield showed at Bush- acker's saddle skirts, and as she headed him in the next lf dozen strides the enthusiasm was redoubled. In the n around the turn Ella increased her lead to a length and a lf, and as Hartford continued to drop back it was plain at he would be distanced. As they ran past the three- arters and round the turn Murphy made a slight effort to ad Bushwhacker along, but as the old veteran did not re- ond with any great show of speed he took a steady pull d Ella Warfield galloped home an easy winner of the heat half a dozen lengths in 7:35½, with Hartford away outside e distance. The instant both horses were unsaddled they ere quickly led away, Ella Warfield to be cared for by Bill rd, assisted by her owners and other Maryland experts, hile Bushwhacker had the attentions of his regular trainer, cCabe, assisted by Jim Williams. At first the mare seemed have the most friends, but before the forty minutes expired e followers of Bushwhacker rallied and considerable money as bet at "evens." In fact was public opinion so evenly di- ded that, while in the closing pools Bushwhacker was a tri- the favorite, Ella Warfield had the call all along the line bookmakers.

In response to the call, Bushwhacker was the first on the ack, but Ella Warfield was the first mounted, both being re- eived with some applause. They promptly took their posi- ons and without any delay galloped up for the flag, which hey got, Bushwhacker taking the lead and opening a gap f four lengths, which advantage he held for the whole of the rst mile. At the beginning of the second mile Ella Warfield ropped back a trifle, which allowed Bushwhacker to lead by ully six lengths for the whole of that mile. But as they be- an the third mile Shauer somewhat unexpectedly cut loose nd in the first quarter closed up within two lengths, and eeping right along he reached Bushwhacker just before the alf. For nearly a quarter of a mile the two men ran on as ven terms as they could, with the admirers of both horses honting all they could. Among those best informed as to he old-time system of racing it was freely said that Shauer ad made his run fully a mile too early, and as Bushwhacker ed by nearly half a length at the end of a third mile, not a ew said that the filly would never again head him, which roved to be true, for at the club-house Bushwhacker began gradually to draw away, leading by two lengths at the quarter and four at the half, after which Murphy eased up and slow- ly galloped up the stretch, the winner of the heat by a dozen lengths in the fairly good time of 7:46. Again both horses were promptly taken in hand and Ella Warfield given a slow gallop up the home stretch under heavy blankets. As usual there were plenty of rumors but no betting. Those that had backed Buckwhacker before the race were contented to remain where they were. In fact, the only offers made were 7 to 1 against Ella Warfield. During the forty minutes' interval every rumor possible was floated and it was affirmed that "Bushwhacker had broken down," that "the race would be postponed until Monday" and that "Ella Warfield was lame." In the meantime it grew so dark that the moon began to make shadows and the crowd to grow impatient. About 5:45 the horses were called and they promptly appeared, and were as fresh as horses could be that had already run eight miles. They took the flag together and Bushwhacker at once took the lead. Galloping out into the gloaming the two ran down the backstretch like shadows. But at the end of the first three miles the white face of old Bushwhacker was the first to catch the eye of the crowd and to be saluted with ringing cheers. At the end of the third mile Ella Warfield was only three lengths behind Bushwhacker, and as she reduced it to two lengths at the quarter and got up even with him at the half an unparalleled scene of enthusiasm followed. The two ran so even round the far turn that in the little light left they looked like one horse, but the last quarter was too much for the mare. She dropped back on the turn and was finally beaten for the heat and race by two lengths in 9:00½ and with that announcement the crowd broke for home, satisfied that if they had not seen the fastest Bowie on record they had seen Bushwhacker win. He is the only horse that has suc- ceeded in doing so twice, and he has run twelve miles each time to do so. In fact, as an old admirer said: "'Old Bush' never won a dollar that he did not have to work for."

---

The American entries for the Doncaster St. Leger of 1884 are as follows: Mr. H. Keene's bay filly, by The Ill-Used out of Lady Mentmore. Mr. J. R. Keene's chestnut colt, by King Alfonso out of Hester; bay colt, by Monarchist out of Return; bay colt, by Virgil out of Boniform; bay filly (sister of Foxhall), by King Alfonso out of Jamaica; Mr. P. Lorillard's Pontiac, De Soto, Choctaw, Emperor, Nitocris, Vixtrix, bay colt by Duke of Magenta out of Hortense; bay colt by Duke of Magenta out of The Squaw. For the Park Hill Stakes, Mr. J. R. Keene enters the sister to Foxhall and Mr. Lorillard enters Nitocris, Newana and Vixtrix. For the Kempton Park July Meeting of 1883, Mr. J. R. Keene makes the same entries in the International Two-year-old Plate, which he names for the St. Leger, and they are also entered in the Kempton Park Grand Prize, to be run at the May meeting of 1884. In the Great International Breeders' Foal Stakes, to be run at Kempton Park August meeting, 1885, the entry appears of Mr. J. R. Keene's bay colt, by Cremorne out of Rustic Queen. Mr. Keene also repeats his St. Leger entries in the Great Sapling Stakes, to be run for at Sandown Park Autumn Meeting, 1883, and enters the Boniform and Return colts in the Hurstbourne Stakes, Stockbridge, 1883, and the Rustic Queen colt in the Stockbridge Foal Stakes of 1884.

---

There was a tremendous race at Lexington, Ky., October 16, between Budd Doble's brown stallion Monroe Chief and W. F. Anderson's bay mare Rosa Wilkes. The stallion won the first heat by a head, in 2:19½; the mare won the second in 2:19½, and the third in 2:19¾; the fourth heat was dead, in 2:20, and the stallion won the fifth and sixth, time of each heat, 2:21¾.

# THE FRENCH DERBY.

## A Vivacious Description of the Great Prix du Jockey Club.

The "Derby" is a great Parisian event, a "sporting solemnity" that no one of any consequence in boulevard and boudoir dares to miss. The real name of the race is the Prix du Jockey Club; but the French imitate the English in turf matters (just as we do in America) and call it the Derby! It is run for on a Sunday, always in the same week as the great Epsom event, and over the beautiful course at royal Chantilly. I hurried to the Gare du Nord at an early hour, there to find a score or more of "horsey" fellows, each and every one of whom was for giving me a "tip" which might surely be depended on. I am always getting tips, and yet I never win anything. The tip which my coachman came near giving me as he turned the corner of the Rue Lafayette was the nearest to a success that I remember to have ever had.

The sky is blue, the heat overpowering, the crowd is great, and Chantilly is far away. We take our seats in the car and en route study the programme. Two bookmakers opposite me look mysteriously solemn, but depend on't they won't find me among the many who are seduced into betting by their eloquent offers to lay this and that odds against the Quick-as-Lightning, the Rent Day (because it comes round so soon) or the Ghost-of-Lexington of my imagination. Ah! here is Chantilly station, and yonder is the forest, with its tender green, its pretty lanes, and its paths carpeted with moss and wild flowers. There is a fine collection of antique carriages, which have come in from all the surrounding country, seedy and disconsolate looking affairs, springs worn out, sad, funereal-looking concerns, into which we mount and move on. The sun continues to burn hot, the long lanes disappear in distant thickets, far away in the horizon "a cloud no bigger than a man's hand" shows itself, slowly climbs the sky and grows greater as it grows older. All the whips are cracking, the carriages creaking, and the "old stock in harness" raising great clouds of dust, through which hundreds and thousands of "sporting" mortals, not millionaires like myself, slowly plod their weary way. Out yonder, at the feet of ancient oaks, parties are breakfasting on a cold bite and a bottle of red wine. Further on are lines on lines of betting men, standing on chairs and stools crying the figures which, after much mathematical calculation, they imagine will prevent their taking a tumble. Already the favorite, Comte Alfred, for whom the renowned Archer has been brought over, begins to go behind in the betting, but those who have confidence in the Chamant Stables shrug their shoulders and proudly walk up and down the lawn wearing the stable colors at their button-holes. So, too, promenade the supporters of Legrange, of Ephrussi, of de Castries, of Lupin; of Delmarre, of all of them.

The crowd becomes enormous. The cloud has crept on apace until now the sky is overcast, but it is not time yet for the rain to come down. There are two or three hundred *petits creves* over by the buffet, all with the same hat, the same trousers, the same eyeglass in one eye, the same pink ticket dangling on the same riding-coat; they all have the same thought, which is to "pose" until people look at them, and that makes them very happy. It is a magnificent sight that we are overlooking. In front, the handsome chateau and private grounds of that popular Orleans prince known as Duc D'Aumale; then the prim houses of this little town; and then, in the foreground, the thousands upon thousands in the free fields of Chantilly. The private stand of the Orleans family is crowded. Monseigneur the Duke has given a breakfast party to fifty-two invited guests, all of whom have gone over the course; and I recognize among the number the Count de Paris and his son, the Duc D'Orleans; his two brothers, the Duc de Chartres and the Duc D'Aumale; his uncle, the Duc de Nemours; also, the Duc de Nevars, the Prince Czartoryski, the Duc D'Audiffret-Pasquier, Alexandre Dumas, Meissonier, Gerome, the Count von Moltke, Minister from Denmark, and a host of others, including many ladies of the *vrai monde*, and children of all ages. The Orleanists are as prolific as Hibernians, most of whom are also descendants of kings, to hear them tell it. The grand stand is filled with people of both sexes, and the sun shines down upon the many-colored throng. The orange, the blue, the red, the maroon, the yellow, the this, the that, and the other color worn by well-dressed jockeys stand out in picturesque contrast to the gray-green foliage of nature and the works of art which women of elegance and beauty have donned for the day. Decidedly checkered patterns are prominent, and there are exquisite satins and silks, and laces and diamonds, with hats that look like inverted fruit-baskets—those kind that came into Paris holding cherries and strawberries; also Rembrandt hats, loaded with feathers; the eyes, the lips, and the complexion all painted with great care, and every mother's child of them "too lovely for anything."

But suddenly a majestic thunder-clap rolls along, then comes down the hurried rain. A while ago what a lovely *coup d'oeil*; now what a spattering. The crowd rushes for the stand, the *couloises* are jammed, there is no standing room in the buffet, men put on their rubber coats, women their waterproofs and dusters; fine feathers and flowers are covered with satin skirts and starched peticoats; little heels sink into the mud; umbrellas are up, and so are the jockeys for the first race. As I dashed out through the dismal wet to see the finish, I pass a *belle petite*, who is swearing away like a Chicago hotel-keeper because in the crowd some unfortunate person has happened to let some drops of champagne fall on her lovely dress of resida silk, the skirt of which is fluted like the pipes of a church organ. The rain lasts but a short time, but meanwhile bets are being made on the Derby. The quotations on Comte-Alfred still keep going down, and these of Dandin keep going up. The names of Hottot and Vigilant are whispered about, but the despised Saint James has but few to do him reverence. At last, however, the cloud passes; the thunder ceases, the rain stops, and the *pelouse* resumes its animation. Delicious perfumes come from the dampened woods, diamond drops sparkle in all the tree-tops and on "blades o' grass," eyes brighten, and women's lips take on that same eternal smile.

But the riders are up and the horses are paraded past us in single file, seventeen of the best three-year-old colts that France can boast of. There are three false starts, and when the good one comes, poor Rovey, who has his horse where he shouldn't have been, is left far in the rear. It is easy to see that Archer will not win; and the new favorite is making a capital pace of it, leading all the way round. In the last 350 yards Saint James and Jasmin lap Dandin, and all three run to the post in close order. An immense shout goes up. Some cry this name and some cry that; there is a clatter of hoofs, a flash of red, of blue, and of violet, and it is over. One of our well-beloved cousins from the other side of the channel cries out: "A dead 'eat, by Jove!" and so it is, with Jasmin only a throat-latch behind the winning couple. The owners, Count Legrange and Michael Ephrussi decide to divide the stakes, 109,800 francs, and all the world fall to growling because the race is not decided as it should be. I heard a good deal said about the excellence of Goater's jockeyship, and, being of a curious disposition, I ventured to ask one gentleman, who is particularly loud in his praise of that individual's riding, the reason for the faith that is within him.

"Why, man, didn't you see the finish? Didn't you see how Goster lifted Dandin along at the post, and so escaped defeat. Didn't you see it?"

Of course I saw it, and confessed it; but I also told him that I saw Hopkins' riding, and that if it hadn't been for the way he handled himself and Saint James, Goater would have won beyond peradventure. I added further that it was all very well to hurrah for Goater, who is a "fashionable jock," but that, in common fancies, the youngster who had the mount of one of the far-away fielders—so far, in fact, that on Saturday they were laying 50 to 1, and yesterday, at the post 30 to 1 against his winning—should come in for his share of praise also, and having expressed myself freely and fully to the effect that Hopkins had done better than Goater, because, if handicapped, Dandin would have had to give Saint James at least fourteen pounds, I hurried off to ask the Orleans princes and their illustrious guests what they thought about it.

With his usual courtesy, the Duc d'Aumale expressed his perfect willingness to be interviewed. I asked him if he would be willing to tell me something about the origin of racing at Chantilly. "While cantering one afternoon in front of the chateau," said he, "in company with a dozen or so of gentlemen, it suddenly occurred to me that the sod was very elastic, and that it was quite the equal of the turf at Newmarket. So we arranged for a race. We made up a pool and M. de Normade, one of the best gentlemen riders we have ever had in France, was the winner. That was in 1833."

"Tell me something about the French Derby."

"Well, the young gentlemen of our house took these races held on our estate under their patronage. In 1835, the Duc d'Orleans and the Duc de Nemours arranged for a race which they called the Derby, in imitation of that of Epsom; and they devoted themselves from that time to making Chantilly the rendezvous of fashion and of high life that would rival the famous meetings at royal Ascot. The first Derby was run in 1836, with a modest 5,000 francs of added money, which, as you know, has grown by degrees to the large sum of 50,000. But here is Madame the Vicomtesse de Greffulte; I will ask her to tell you something of the past history of the Derby."

His royal highness presented your correspondent "in due form" to the noble lady, who, although quite sixty years of age, has all the charms and elegances of a young woman of thirty. She smiled very sweetly, and said:

"I remember perfectly the fetes of 1841, for that was the year the good Queen Victoria gave to the world his royal highness the Prince of Wales, whom we all love very much. The races lasted from Thursday, May 13, to Sunday, 16th, inclusive. The Orleans princes had issued their invitations, but the space was so limited that a great many noble ladies and gentlemen were obliged to look on the fetes from a distance. The honors were done by the Prince Royal, with that gracious affability that won him the hearts of all. He was assisted by the Duchesse d'Orleans, the Duchesse de Nemours, whose husband was fighting in Africa, and by the Prince de Joinville, whom you afterwards saw on General McClellan's staff in America, by Madame Meuche de Loisnes, by la Baronne Liadieres, and by Madam Firmin Rogier—the one as brown as an olive, the other as fair as an ear of wheat—and by Madame Baignieres, sister of Charles Laffitte. They were all rivals in beauty and fashion, all equal in social position. Nothing was spared to make those four days one continuous and brilliant fete. On Thursday, after the races, there was a reception and grand ball, at the Chantilly Chateau. On Friday the artistes of the Comedie Francaise came out to give performances. On Saturday there were no races, but, instead, we had a grand stag hunt in the forest; and in the evening there was a *curee froid* by torchlight in the great courtyard of the chateau. Then, on Sunday, came the Derby, and, later on, there was a *fete de nuit* in the park. The groves were filled with musicians, the trees with lanterns, and the thickets with bengal flames and fire-works, that lit up the lakes and streams, on which floated boat-loads of fair and brave ones from home and afar.

"In the town everything was at fever heat. There was a coming and a going, of which no description of mine can give you any idea. The place was crowded to its very attic. The hotels and houses were taken by storm, and the residents exacted the most exorbitant prices for all that was occupied. Gentlemen had to pay as high as 50 francs for a basin of water in which to wash their hands, and 50 more for the corner of a table on which to eat the cold victuals that their valets had brought from Paris. Along with the invited guests at the Chateau, there were also a more bourgeoise society. It was made up of the wealthier financiers of the Chausse d'Autin, and of rich merchants. All these people had arranged for a life of four days in the country. The ladies displayed the most extravagant toilets, and gave themselves up to competition in the way of hats and head dress. The latest innovations of Palmyra—the Worth of 1841—hats discovered by Herbault in his learned studies; collars and sleeves, in which Colliot displayed his great genius, made their first appearance at Chantilly. The ladies betted among themseves, with their husbands, or with their lovers, and the stakes were left to the discretion of the losers.

"There was, also, another monde which came to Chantilly, filling it with its noise and follies. Many of the gentlemen, not satisfied with bringing out supplies of food and changes of linen, also gave places in their carriages to the gay demoiselles. The town was overrun with the fair but fast ones of the Capital. Their fetes rivaled the royal ones in number and in elegance. The Rue de Paris became a branch of the Boulevard de Gand. The *lions* and the *lorettes* danced, gambled and supped without intermission. It was a bacchanalian revel of four days and as many nights, and into which our husbands made altogether too many excursions. And, in the camps, in all the mondes, the upper, the lower, and the middle, the whole of this merry crowd shouted, that Sunday afternoon, the name of Poetess, winner of the great event, and hurrahed for her owner, Lord Henry Seymour!" —*J. H. Hayne in New York Spirit.*

---

Some fine Arab horses were sold at auction a few weeks ago in London, England. About two hundred persons were present at the sale, among them Lord Bradford, Lord Rosslyn, Lord Hardings and Mr. Percy Wyndham. Eleven horses were offered, and the total proceeds were $7,750. Pharaoh, a pure Arab stallion, brought $2,625 from Count Potoki, who takes him to Poland. Brood mares avaraged $600 each, and a two-year-old filly went for $750.

---

Kensington Park, at Melbourne, Australia, containing 190 acres, including the racecourse, has been sold for sub-division purposes, for £48,000.

## Racing and Religion.

The *London Sportsman* makes the case of Abe Buford a peg on which to hand the following sensible homily on the comparative "depravity" of the turf:

Col. Abe Buford of the United States of America, ex-militaire, ex-owner of racehorses, and present active and conscientious "member of the church," has recently adopted a course of action from which many courageous men would shrink. As a preliminary he has frankly owned to an error of judgment. It is not every one who would do this publicly. But more important still, he has had the courage to avow that the pursuit of racing is not necessarily sinful and provocative of duplicity and dishonesty, and he has boldly proclaimed that he thinks he can run racehorses without detriment to his professions of religion. We are sorry indeed to say that therein Col. Abe Buford will forfeit the respect and esteem of many pious, but narrow-minded people, both in his own country and in this. Perhaps the valiant soldier has made up his mind to bear with equinimity all the opposition and odium which his latest protestations may entail. If so, all honor to him for so doing. And we say again that his courage is admirable in the extreme, and may profitably be imitated by those who, perhaps, are "halting between two opinions"—fear of what "the world" so-called might say, and inclination to do that which innate conviction deems proper and right. When some years ago Col. Abe Buford joined "the church" he promptly sold all his racehorses, and relinquished his connection with the turf. He owns that at the time he deemed this the only course left open to him under the circumstances—or, in other words, that the pursuit of racing was not compatible with a profession of piety. The possibility is that he was thereupon welcomed as "a brand snatched from the burning," and some of the "unco guid" rejoiced that he had been led to turn from the error of his ways. What they will say now that the Colonel has decided to again evince interest and take an active part in sport we cannot divine. But, as we have suggested, many may regard hm as a renegade, and treat him accordingly. And this consideration leads us to glance at the absurd prejudices and miserable bigotry entertained by certain classes in England. We have already accused detractors of racing of "narrow-mindedness," and we are prepared to prove that they may properly and justly be so denominated. As was the case with the Pharisees of old, they "strain at a gnat and swallow a camel." Take the instance of a person who sometimes speculates on races. The pious accuse him of endeavoring to wrongfully deprive his neighbor of his substance. They overlook the fact that the "neighbour" now and again has what racing men term a "look in" and wins. In such case, may it be asked, is he equally culpable? But if speculators on races are to be branded with infamy, is it not strange that the gamblers in stocks and shares should escape soot free? They are thorough-going adherents of the "doctrine of chances," and yet they are never treated to opprobrium. Quite as justly, we think, might a provision dealer be accused of iniquity, when, being possessed of capital, he purchases largely in a falling market with the idea of hoarding up his stock until affairs shall take a turn for the better. Who would adjudge such a person to be guilty of defrauding the public? Speaking plainly, the spirit of speculation pervades all classes of society, and very usefully so. Let us take an extreme illustration, as some people might designate it, though such instances are by no means rare. Now and again persons hear that railway extensions have been determined upon in certain localities of crowded cities, and they thereupon buy up all the premises on the projected route. Perhaps the sellers of the property know of the railway scheme. Therefore, can it be said that they are defrauded? Again, the purchaser doubtless reckons upon striking an uncommonly good bargain with the enterprising railway company when they shall need his newly-acquired possessions. To adopt the epithet applied in racing matters, the man who buys such property is a double-dyed scoundrel. But no—his mode of procedure is characterized by the conveniently harmless term "enterprise." And the same word is supposed to adequately describe stock exchange operations. The truth of the matter is, an immensity of sentimental humbug prevails with regard to the turf. Now and again dishonest persons venture more than they are capable of paying. This is deplorable. But in other speculative projects people are continually doing the same. The only difference seems to be—adopting, of course, the popular view—that as far as regards racing the defaulter is a downright scamp and villian, whereas in respect of commercial transactions he has simply been "unwise" or "unfortunate." We certainly feel that a debt of gratitude is owing to Colonel Abe Buford for having pluckily assumed a stand against vulgar prejudice. The owner of racehorses may be as just and equitable in his dealings with all mankind as the common trader. But stupidly sentimental notions have stigmatized him, and it will be long ere silly and unjust ideas are dispelled. Colonel Abe Buford has taken a step in the right direction. May others speedily imitate him.

---

SOME KENTUCKY TWO-YEAR-OLDS.—Cardinal McCloskey, by Ten Broeck, out of Waterwitch (Fonso's dam), by Weatherbit. This promises to make a real, clinking, good three-year-old, barring his size. He has both speed and bottom, the two great requisites of a first-class race-horse. Leonatus, a large bay, by Longfellow, dam Semper Felix, by imported Phæton, is a grand colt, with great speed, and is sure to make his mark; indeed we have seen few better looking ones in years, or one that has a finer turn of speed. He got off badly in the Maiden Stakes at Louisville, won by Cardinal McCloskey, in a deep track, in 1:22. He was ridden very badly by the little boy West, who ran him next to the rails in the deepest part of the track, and finished second. Queen Ban, a splendid daughter of the young rising sire, King Ban, out of War Reel, by War Dance, barring accidents, promises to be one of the best fillies seen on the turf in years. She has size, great quality, uniting both speed and bottom, and won the Blue Grass Stake in 1:16 quite handily, beating Bellona, Miss Woodford and others. The other two-year-old is Lord Raglan, by Ten Broeck, dam Catina, who won the Welter race, in 1:46¾, with 113 pounds up. He is a large colt, and, barring his curby-looking hocks, is a grand big youngster. Ten Broeck and imported King Ban added much to their reputations as sires by the performances of their two-year-olds at Louisville. The Kentucky Derby, next year, with Lord Raglan, Barnes, Ascendor, Cardinal McCloskey (late Tenwitch), Queen Ban, Punster, Violator, Pike's Pride, Hassan, Bondholder, etc., all of whom are engaged, will make it one of the best races of the year.—*Live Stock Record.*

---

There was a running race at Stewart's Point, Sonoma county, last Saturday, between three horses entered by Dan Stump, Jas. McClellan and Wm. Norton. The race was a quarter of a mile, best two in three, for a saddle and bridle. Stump's bay raked in the trappings.

## Trotting in Australia.

The Melbourne *Federal Australian* recounts a trotting meeting at Elsternwick course:

The Victorian Trotting Club held another meeting Sept. 21st on the new track at Elsternwick, in the presence of a moderate number of visitors. The weather was beautifully fine; but, although the fields were large, some of the finishes were very uninteresting. The course was in tolerably good order, although slightly cut up. The first event on the card was the Maiden trot, for which eight horses sported silk. Maid of Mona was installed first favorite, five to two on her being freely offered at the start. Bella Campbell, however, who got well away at the start, fairly did what she pleased with her opponents, and won easily from Maid of Mona, who just saved being distanced.

In the second heat Bella Campbell broke when she seemed to be winning easily, and taking a long while to settle down was defeated; but in the third heat she retrieved her honors, winning cleverly. The American system of pool selling was introduced, Mr. Goyder acting as auctioneer, the winner receiving the whole money in the pool less 5 per cent. commission to that official. Thus a buyer gave £7 for first pick and selected Maid of Mona, the total amount in the pool being £12 whilst the winner went for ten shillings. Of course the first buyer makes the price and protects himself by running the other buyers up; thus, in a subsequent heat, a well-known sweep-promoter gave £5 for first pick of two starters and chose the non-favorite, and then bid up for the other to £5, when it was knocked down to him. He thus received his own money less ten shillings commission. Native Cat was made hot favorite for the three minute class; but he broke badly and the race lay between Leithamstead and Fright, both by Mr. Cripp's horse Alarm. Had Fright's driver displayed more patience she might have won the last two heats, as she did the first; but he bustled her, and she broke badly, and was defeated. Below are details:

MAIDEN TROT

of 40 sovs. Mile heats. Best two in three.

| | | | |
|---|---|---|---|
| M. C. Colbath names g m Bella Campbell, aged. (Milson) | 1 | 2 | 1 |
| Mr. P. G. Dixon names br m Maid of Mona, aged. (Giles) | 2 | 1 | 2 |
| Mr. J. Male names ch m Jessie, aged. (Childs) | dis | | |
| Mr. J. Cleeland names br m Darebin Maid, aged. (Cleeland) | dis | | |
| Mr. W. Wood names b g Whiskey, aged. (Fisher) | dis | | |
| Mr. L. Leonard names blk m Eleanor, aged. (Grimwood) | dis | | |
| Mr. T. N. Curnow names br m Victoria B, aged. (Sheppard) | dis | | |

Time—2:52, 2:55½, 2:50¾.

Betting: Five to 2 on Maid of Mona, 3 to 1 against Whiskey, 5 to 1 the others.

At the start Maid of Mona rushed to the front, but was immediately passed by Bella Campbell, who forged ahead and soon placed a long lead to her credit. The first quarter post was reached in 42, the half-mile post in 1:25, the three-quarter-mile post in 2:5½, and the winning post in 2:52. Bella Campbell was never caught and won easily, Maid of Mona being nearly distanced. Time, 2:52.

There was very little betting on the second heat, 3 to 1 being offered on Bella Campbell, without takers.

A good start was effected, of which Maid of Mona had slightly the best. Bella Campbell, however, soon assumed lead, and maintained it until within half a mile from home, when she broke badly, and allowed the Maid to get on terms. The pair then raced up the straight, but Bella Campbell breaking again, Maid of Mona won easily.

In the third heat the quarter-mile post was reached in 42, the half-mile in 1:25, the three-quarter post in 2:4, and the winning post in 2:55½.

Betting: Even on Maid of Mona.

Bella Campbell went to the front soon after starting, reaching the quarter post in 41½, the half-mile in 1:22½, the three-quarter post in 2:3, and the mile in 2:50¾.

THREE MINUTE CLASS,

Of sixty sovs. Two-mile heats. Best two in three.

| | | | |
|---|---|---|---|
| Mr. J. Collins names g g Leithamstead, 5 years, by Alarm, Bragy | 2 | 1 | 1 |
| Mr. J. J. Miller names b m Fright, 5 years, Sheppard | 1 | 2 | 2 |
| Mr. F. Robin names g g Native Cat, aged, Collins | 3 | 0 | 6 |
| Mr. F. Robin names b g Captain Darborn, Owner | dist. | | |

Betting: Even on Native Cat, three to two Leithamstead, seven to four Fright, five to one Captain Darborn.

The lot were dispatched to a moderate start. Native Cat took the lead, closely followed by Fright, with Captain Darborn last. The latter, however, soon made up his ground and headed the Cat, who was in turn passed by Leithamstead. They continued in this order until the first round had been nearly traversed, when Fright took command and led to the finish, followed by Leithamstead, who secured second place, with Native Cat third. In this heat the first quarter-mile post was reached in 42s., the half-mile in 1:12; three-quarters in 2:12; the mile in 2:54; the one and a quarter mile post in 3:37; the mile and a half in 4:20; and the mile and three-quarter post in 5:2; and the two miles in 5:46½.

In the second heat the betting was two to one on Fright, four to one against the others. Fright got the best of the start followed by Native Cat, with Leithamstead last. They proceeded in the order above named until nearly home, when Fright broke. Leithamstead passed Native Cat and overhauled Fright. The latter struggled on gamely up the straight, but she broke again, and the grey horse won easily. Time, first quarter post, 42s; one-half mile, 1:28; three-quarter mile, 2:9; one mile, 2:53; one and a quarter miles, 3:35; one and a half miles, 4:17; one and three-quarter miles, 4:58; two miles, 5:40¾.

The betting was even in the third heat. Fright led to the half-mile post, where she left her feet, but repassed the grey. Approaching the three-quarter post she again broke, and the grey trotting steadily beat her by six lengths in 5:41½.

---

From accounts Hinda Rose's performance electrified the Kentucky breeders. They all with one accord said she was a wonder, and took their defeat quietly, making no excuses. Gov. Stanford has reason to feel proud of the victory. It was a hazardous undertaking to take a two-year-old filly from California to New York, and then south, and expect to beat a field of Kentucky colts, on their native soil. The judges were Col. R. West, James Miller, and T. J. Megibben. Timers, Dr. Herr. Geo. Linderberger, and B. G. Bruce.

The six-days' go-as-you-please walking match in New York ended at 10 o'clock last Saturday, the score standing: Fitzgerald, 577 miles, 2 laps; Noremac, 567 miles, 4 laps; Herty, 541 miles, 1 lap, Hughes 525 miles. The gross receipts, including the bar and all other privileges, amount to $26,373; rent, $10,000. The other expenses, including 15 per cent. to Peter Duryea, will reduce the net receipts to almost nothing.

Mason Chief, by Mambrino Patchen, dam by Alexander's Abdallah, a stallion imported from Kentucky by G. W. Peck of Aumsville, Marion county, Oregon, has arrived safely at Portland. Mason Chief is described as dark brown without a white hair on him, five years old and is 16 hands high, a finely formed horse, and to the eye a true type of the American trotter.

## Gano at Pimlico.

The Eclectic stakes at Pimlico, run on Saturday, October 21st, were handsomely won by E. J. Baldwin's Gano. The following description of the running is kindly furnished us by Mr. H. G. Crickmore of the New York *World* and "Krik's Guide to the Turf."

The Eclectic Stakes, for two-year-olds, at $200 each, half forfeit, with $700 added by the association and $600 by Messrs. A. H. Cridge & Co., of which $400 to the second; the third to save its stake; colts to carry 110 lbs.; fillies and geldings, 107 lbs.; subscribers allowed to name and start more than one horse upon paying a separate subscription for each starter; closed with eleven subscribers; one mile.

| | |
|---|---|
| C. Reed names E. J. Baldwin's b c Gano, by Grinstead, dam Santa Anita, 110 lbs. (Halloway) | 1 |
| C. Bowie names br f Empress, by Narragansett, dam Mandina, 107 lbs. (W. Donohue) | 2 |
| P. Lorillard names b f Breeze, by Alarm, dam Blairgowrie, 107 lbs. (Shauer) | 3 |
| D. Pulsifer names E. J. Baldwin's Lucky B, 110 lbs. (Blaylock) | d |
| J. E. Kelly names ch f Bella, 107 lbs. (Hughes) | d |
| F. Gebhard names ch c Eolist, 110 lbs. (Barbee) | d |
| G. Bowie names ch f Fairview, 107 lbs. (Huston) | d |
| Dwyer Bros. name ch g Wandering, 107 lbs. (J. McLaughlin) | d |

Time—1:45¾.

Pools.—Breeze, $100; Baldwin's pair, $100; Bella and Wandering, each $40, Eolist, $25; Bowie's pair, $25. Betting.—Nine to 5 against Breeze, 3 to 1 against Gano, 6 to 1 against Wandering, 7 to 1 against Bella, 8 to 1 against Eolist and 10 to 1 against Lucky B, Fairview and Empress. Mutuels paid $18 70.

After nearly forty minutes' delay during which the antics and temper shown by Wandering, Lucky B and Bella nearly exhausted not only the patience of the starter but of very many of the crowd, the flag was dropped to an even start with Eolist, Bella and Wandering in the lead followed closely by Empress, Fairview and Gano with Lucky B last. In the round by the club house Eolist secured a lead of nearly two lengths, but as Fairview got out of the crowd she raced up to Eolist so that at the quarter he led by only a length with Fairview and Wandering together followed by Bella and Breeze with Gano, Lucky B and Empress bringing up in the rear. The race down the backstretch to the stables was very fast, and as they were running well out Shauer got through, with Breeze taking second place. She was only a length behind Eolist at the half-mile, with Fairview at her saddle skirts and Bella alongside of Fairview, closely followed by Gano and Empress. Before they reached the turn Breeze passed Eolist, and opposite the tree she was leading by nearly two lengths amidst the enthusiastic shouts of her backers, "Breeze wins." At the bend of the track in the three-quarters both Fairview and Bella dropped back, as also did Wandering, their places being taken by Empress and Gano, both of whom closed up quickly on Breeze, so that at the three-quarters the favorite only led by a head, with Empress second, half a length in front of Gano, he half a length in front of Bella, with Eolist and Lucky B in immediate attendance. Breeze retained her lead until well into the stretch, when Gano under whip closed up and the two reached the seven furlongs nearly together. Half way up to the pickets Billy Donohue closed up with Empress, and challenging Breeze and Gano, the favorite almost instantly dropped back. Gano, however, drew away, and amidst the greatest excitement crossed the line the winner by a length in front of Breeze. Close up was lucky B, followed by Bella and Eolist with Fairview and Wandering bringing up the rear. The success of the Californian was received with some applause which was almost instantly hushed as the rumor ran through the crowd like wildfire that Governor Bowie had made an objection to Gano on the ground that he was a three-year-old. The judges took the matter under consideration, and as Mr. Baldwin, who was present, quickly furnished satisfactory evidence that the question of Gano's age had been settled in California before he left that State last June, the judges promptly hung out the numbers of the horses as they finished, Gano first; Empress second and Breeze third.

---

Racing appears to be overdone in England as well as in some other countries at times. An English paper says: The failure of the Liverpool meeting was complete and ignominious. About £3,000 was added to the various events, and the average of the fields was under four. It would be in vain to search the volumes of "Races Past" for an example of a handicap to which £500 is added attracting but four starters. After this collapse, surely the managers will recognize the propriety of their forthwith abolishing this "fixture," and they will do well to do their best to improve the character of the sport at the spring and autumn meetings, which of late has left much to be desired.

## The Turf in Oregon.

UNION, Oregon, Oct 12, 1882.—Novelty race for two-year-olds; purse $150; first at half $50, at three-quarters $50, at end of mile $50.

| | |
|---|---|
| Wm. Claypool's Mazourka | 1 |
| A. Labuff's Cheater | 2 |
| F. T. Glisan's Cap Wilson | 3 |

Time—2:04.

Same day—Trot for two-year-olds; mile heats, two in three; Purse $100, $75, $25.

| | | | |
|---|---|---|---|
| J. Cavinees' Laura C | 1 | 2 | 1 |
| S. Crowell's Au Revoir | 2 | 1 | 2 |
| F. T. Glisan's Henry | 3 | 3 | 3 |

Time—3:27, 3:28, 3:28.

Track heavy from recent rains.

CITY VIEW DRIVING TRACK, PORTLAND, Oct. 21, 1882.—Trotting race, for foals of 1880, mile heats, two in three; entrance $60 each, payable $20 April 1st, $20 June 1st and $20 day before the race; total amount $480; first horse six-tenths, second three-tenths and third the remainder.

| | | |
|---|---|---|
| John Harkins, East Portland, names r f Flora H, by Kisber, dam by Pathfinder | 1 | 1 |
| John Pender, Vancouver, W. T., names s c Young Kisber, by Kisber, dam by Milliman's Bellfounder | 2 | 2 |
| Lou Godard, Portland, names b c Ben, by Kisber, dam Minnie | 3 | 3 |

Time—3:37, 3:26½.

Same day—Purse $250; three-fourths of a mile.

| | |
|---|---|
| R. E. Bybee's b f Neyella (2), by California—Laura Barnes, 99 lbs | 1 |
| W. G. Scoggin's br h Jim Merritt (5), by Langford—Sweetwater, 120 lbs | 2 |

Time—1:19½.

The track was heavy and the horses ran twenty feet from the pole. Jim Merritt was the favorite at $10 to $6 and had the inside to an even start. They ran head and head for the first hundred yards, when the filly showed a neck ahead. Merritt immediately closed the gap and they ran deadlocked until they entered the homestretch, when the weight told on the horse: Neyella won by three-quarters of a length.

---

The fall races at Prineville, Waso county, Oregon, will commence Nov. 30th and continue three days. The races are to be under the management of J. B. Lafolette, A. B. Webdell, John L. Luckey and John E. Harris; races to be governed by the rules of the Oregon State Agricultural Society; three to enter and two to start; no horses eligible except Wasco county raised horses; Cotton Nose and Lula Biggs barred.

During the Yreka fair Jay Beach sold to Dr. J. W. Robertson of Yreka a pair of high bred two-year-old colts, which the doctor will convert into a spanking road team.

## Pro and Con.

Down in Australia, where they have very stringent laws ainst gambling, the Paris Mutual plan of pool betting has en legalized, although not without some misgivings as to e effect upon public morals. For the purpose of determining the latter point a commissioner was appointed by the vernment to watch the workings of the machine and report s impressions, which he does in the following language: "As jards the working of the totalizator it is difficult to state thoritatively whether it has been beneficial or otherwise ring the short time it has been legalized. Presuming that tting is a vice, it is impossible to say whether the money ked through the totalizator would be greater or less than e money that would have been staked had it not been in istence. I will, however, point out some of what appear me to be the main advantages and disadvantages of the talizator, by which its benefit or otherwise may be some at tested. Its advantages are: It gives fairer odds in ost cases, as the public can use their own knowledge and dgment, and act accordingly, without being misled or in ced to stake their money by misrepresentations. It affords s inducement to dishonest running on the part of owners persons having the control of horses, and of dishonest ting on the part of the jockeys, inasmuch as what may be rmed ' individual ' betting is greatly lessened. It lessens credit 'betting, and the effect of this would, I think, lessen e temptation that would exist for people without means to n into debt, or commit crime in order to meet the losses hich are brought about by betting. A man who has no sans would probably not commit a crime, or even run into bt, for the purpose of obtaining money to put into the talizator. The crime of embezzlement by young men to y racing bets has very much decreased since its introduc on. It materially lessens the bookmakers' occupation, the set of which is that most of the money which passes ough it remains in the colony. This was not so formerly, the bookmakers were mostly men from the other colonies, o came here about the time of a race meeting, and who, ourse, carried their earnings away with them, as much as 9,000 having been thus taken away on one occasion. It s away with 'welshers,'a class of men who frequent e meetings, and who have either no means to pay or the inclination to pay what they have lost. The foregoing ap r to be the advantages of the totalizator. The disadvan es are: It increases the number of bettors on the course, many a man puts some money into the totalizator who ould never think of making a bet with a bookmaker. It is t to promote over-racing. I mean that the probable ofits to the proprietors are apt to induce them to have re race meetings than they otherwise would. This is, of urse, an evil that might be remedied by limiting the number t times at which it might be used. "

## Racing at Boise City, Idaho.

MONDAY, Oct. 22, 1882.—Purse, $100, free for all two-year-olds, dash half a mile.
N. Nellis names Hattie Harris .......................... 1
J. Fenner names Bob Ingersoll ......................... 2
J. Thurman names Sarah ................................ 3
Time—54.

Same day—Purse, $100; handicap for all ages, three-quarters of a le.
ne. Early names b g Dundrum, by Melbourne Jr.—Parquette...... 1
J. Thurman names Screwdriver ........................... 2
M. Hellis names ch h Portland ........................... 3
Time—1:22, 1:24.

Same day Sat.—Purse, $100, for three-year-olds and under, Idaho bred and raised, half-mile heats.
M. Nellis names Hattie Harris .......................... 1
J. Thurman names Billy Baywood ....................... 2
A. O. Miller names Whalebone ......................... 3
Time—54, 54.

Same day—Purse, $200 for named horses running, mile heats.
M. Fenner names Tim Brainard......................... 2 1 1
M. Nellis names Portland.............................. 1 2 2
A. O. Miller names Idaho Chief........................ 3 3 3
Time—1:54, 1:56, 3:10.

WEDNESDAY, Oct. 25—Purse, $100; handicap for all ages; half mile heats.
J. Thurman names Screwdriver.......................... 1 1
M. Fenner names Tim Brainard......................... 2 2
John Early names Dundrum............................. 3 3
Time—52, 54.

Same day—Purse $100, for three year-olds and under, beats of a mile.
J. Thurman names Billy Baywood........................ 1 1
M. Fenner names Bob Ingersoll......................... 2 2
A. O. Miller names Idaho Chief......................... 3 3
Time—1:56, 2:10.

THURSDAY, Oct. 26—Purse $125, for two-year-olds, three quarters of a mile.
M. Nellis names Hattie Harris.......................... 1
M. Fenner, names Bob Ingersoll......................... 2
J. Thurman names Sarah............................... 3
No time.

Same day—Purse $150; handicap for all ages, heats of a mile.
M. Fenner names Tim Brainard......................... 1 1
M. Nellis names Portland.............................. 2 2
J. Thurman names Screwdriver.......................... 3 3
Time—1:52, 1:55, 2:00.

TROTTING.

BOISE CITY, Idaho, Oct. 26, 1882—Trotting for three-minute class.
N. O. Smith names Eastman's Pet....................... 1 1
Orlando Robbins names Lady Lightfoot.................. 2 2
Dow Vincent names Owyhee Jim......................... dis
Eugene Goffe names Billy Bliss......................... dis
Time—3:22½, 3:18½.

MR. LORILLARD'S NEW TRAINER.—Tom Cannon, Mr.Pierre Lorillard's new trainer, was in grand form at the Newmarket Second October meeting, when he divided the riding honors with Charles Wood, each riding nine winners to four by Archer and three by Fordham. In five of the nine races won by Cannon he wore Lord Rosebery's 'primrose and rose,'viz: on Kermesse in the "dead heat" with Mr. Leopold de Roth schild's Nellie for the Select Stakes, on Prudhomme for the Cambridgeshire Welter Stakes, on Kermesse for the Newmar ket Oaks, on Roysterer for the Third Welter Handicap and on Bonnie Jean for the Prendergast Stakes. Lord Rosebery also won the Ditch Mile Nursery Handicap for two-year-olds at a mile, the winner being ridden by Lemair at 113 pounds. The other races won by Cannon include one each for Lord Stam ford, Lord Ellesmere, Mr. H. E. Beddington and Mr. Pierre Lorillard—for the last named he won the Bedford Stakes with Tonch-Me-Not. Seven of the nine races won by Woods were with the 'all azarie"of Mr. W. S. Crawford, viz: the October Produce and the Middle Park Plate with Macheath, the Ce sarewich Trial Handicap with Edelweiss, the Royal Stakes with Bonnie Lass, the Cesarewich with Corrie Boy, the Ashley Stakes, for which Keir "walked over," and a "head heat" for the Champion with Thebais. Woods also won a race for Sir John D. Astley, and one for Mr. Girard. Archer's four vic tories were one each for Mr. Girard, Mr. Lefevre, Lord Fal mouth and Mr. A. Cooper, while, Fordham's three were the Clearwell Stakes and the Second October Nursery for Mr. Lefevre and the "dead heat" for the Select Stakes on Nellis for Mr. Leopold de Rothschild,  -

## The Cambridgeshire.

The forty-fourth renewal of the Cambridgeshire Stakes, a handicap for three-year-olds and upwards, at £25 each, £15 forfeit, only £5 if de clared on or before Sept. 5, with £300 added, the second to receive £100 out of the stakes, the third to save his stake; entrance £3; the winner of the Doncaster St. Leger to carry 7 lb. ; winners of a handicap of the value of £300, after the publication of the weights (August 31), to carry 10 lb., or of any other handicap £5 extra; the winner of the Cesarewich to carry 14 lb extra, but if also the winner of the St. Leger, to carry only 4lb extra ; closed with 137 subscribers, of which 93 declared: Cambridge shire course, 1 mile and 240 yards.

Mr. R. Peck's b f Hackness, 4, by Albert Victor, dam Cicely Hackett, 86 lb ................................................ 1
Mr. Jardine's br'g Shrewbury, 3, by Brown Bread, dam Vengeance, 94 lb ................................................ 2
Lord Colthorpe's b c Vennets, 3, by Playfair, dam Wild Duchess, 93 lb ................................................ 3
Twenty-eight others ran, including Mr. F. Lorillard's Sachem, 3, 89 lb. Mr. J. R. Keene's Don Fulano, 4, 112 lb., and Bookmaker, 4, 100 lb., and Lord Ellesmere's Wallenstein, 3, 126 lb.

Hackness the winner of Cambridgeshire, was rescued, as it were, from the hunting field. She did not run as a three-year-old nor as a four-year-old until she started for the Cam bridgeshire. At one time she was fancied for the Cesarewich but, as the party controlling her could not get their money on at odds to suit them, they scratched her. Hackness was bred by Mr. Deighton and was sold a yearling at Cobham on Saturday, July 14, 1879, by Mr. Rymill to a Mr. Foy for 500 guineas, As a two-year-old, in 1880, she ran in seven races, carrying the colors of Mr. Foy in five of them. She won the Kempton Park March two-year-old plate and a selling sweep stakes over the Rous course at the Newmarket first October meeting, after which she was sold to Mr. T. Brown for 500 guineas. The next time she was seen she ran as the property of Mr. R. Stuart, under whose colors she was beaten twice. Since then she has never once shown in a race, but she did so well in the hunting field that she was laid up for a handi cap, and getting into the Cambridge at 85 pounds (being the lightest weighted four-year-old in the race) she won probably with a stone in hand and landed a large pot of money for those who own her, the odds at last mail advices being 100 to 6 against her, at which date Bell's Life said : "Hopper has three under his charge in Peregrine, Blue Ribbon and Hack ness. It strikes me the first two are not likely to see the post. If Hopper wins, it will be with Hackness. With a start her prospects of success are very seductive, after what was seen of her in the gallop with her stable companions, Blue Rib bon and Fortissimo, just previous to the Doncaster meeting, and more recently with her owner's purchase at that meeting, Ballot, who was in good form at the time."

## The Final Course.

Years ago, at a race at Ascot, the famous horse Tiberius broke his leg by bounding against one of the posts of the bar rier just after the start. His owner, Lord Millbank, lost heavily in bets, besides the value of the horse, the law of the course being that accidents should not be taken into ac count as relieving a horse in case of defeat. Three days after wards Lord Millbank gave a sumptuous dinner, to which the most distinguished of the English peerage had been invited, and at which they were present. The conviviality ran high. Toward the close, and at a late hour, after numerous toasts had been drunk, the noble host arose at the head of the table, and proposed that they should drink to the memory of the departed Tiberius. It was clamorously received. The mas ter of the feast remained standing, with a brimming glass in his hand. "We drink to Tiberius," he said, "the most beau tiful, the most enduring, the most courageous, and the most spirited courser that ever trod the British turf." Shouts of applause shook the walls. "You know," continued his lord ship, "the achievements of the horse." His deeds belong to history. Fame has taken charge of his glory. But it re mained for me—for you, my lords and gentlemen—to do honor to the mortal remains. I wished that this noble courser should have a burial worthy of his deservings. He has had it. My cook had fifty prepared him for the memory of the departed Tiberius. Ah, my lords and gentlemen, the meat which you have relished so keenly, and the rich flavor and delicacy of which have awakened so much inquiry, was Tiberius. My grand courser hath found a fitting sepulture. May your digestion be light!" For a brief space the enthu siasm of the company received a check; but the meat had been good nevertheless, and with another burst of applause, the idea took the turn of a sublimity, and more bumpers were drunk to the memory of the strangely entombed Tiberius.

The weak points of a horse can be better discovered while standing than while moving. If he is sound he will stand firmly and squarely on his limbs without moving any of them, the feet planting flatly upon the ground, with legs plump and naturally poised. If one foot is thrown forward with the toe pointing to the ground and the heel raised, or if the foot is lifted from the ground and the weight taken from it, disease may be suspected, or at least tenderness, which is a precursor of disease. If the horse stands with his feet spread apart, or straddles with the hind legs, there is weakness in the loins and the kidneys are disordered. Heavy pulling bends the knees. British or milky cast eyes in horses indicate moon blindness, or something else. A bad tempered horse keeps his ears thrown back. A kicking horse is apt to have scarred legs. A stumbling horse has blemished knees. When the skin is rough and harsh, and does not move easily and smoothly to the touch, the horse is a heavy eater and his digestion is bad. Never buy a horse whose respiratory organs are at all impaired. Place your ear at the side of the heart, and if a wheezing sound is heard, it is an indication of trouble—let him go.

SALE OF TROTTING STOCK.—A large sale of trotting stock the consignment of Mr. Charles Backman, proprietor of Stony ford Stock Farm, tok place in New York Oct. 24th. The sale attracted a large gathering of horsemen, among them Messrs. Robert, David and Ally Bonner, George B. Alley, H. W. T. Mall, W. H. Wilson, C. S. Moulton, Shepard F. Knapp and Jonathan Hawkins. The prices obtained were low, the bidding not being at all spirited. A number of excellent ani mals went for almost nothing, the gray stallion Exchange, by Rysdyk's Hambletonian, a perfectly sound horse, selling for $115. The highest amount obtained for any one animal was $500, for a four-year-old filly, by Messenger Duroc, out of Rosetta, by Rysdyk's Hambletonian. Mr. Robert Bonner was the purchaser. The next highest price was $475, for the five-year-old mare Ellie, by Messenger Duroc, out of Mary Sanford, by the Plunkett horse, that went to Mr. Ally Bon ner. Fifty-one head of stock were sold, the sale in the ag gregate amounting to $12,175, an average of not quite $239 per head.

May Queen (record 2:20) by Alexander's Norman, out of Jennie by Crockett's Arabian, has been purchased from Dr. Gulick of Crockett by Gov. Stanford to add to his breeding estab lishment at Palo Alto.

## Pooling.

Our Australian cousins are taking kindly to many of the American sporting notions and no doubt will find them all useful and convenient in their way. Since the advent in the colonies of the trotting horse and the consequent interest in trotting events the adoption of the timing system is ex tending to the running races, which will be found an excellent idea. The Paris mutual pool system has also been intro duced and is on trial, meeting, of course, with some ob jection from people who have not yet become familiar with its workings. From the following extract from the Mel bourne Sportsman it appears that the auction pool plan is also to be tried, and if properly conducted, we prophesy that the turfmen and speculators will adopt it on every course in the colonies:

A novelty in the way of post speculation is about to be introduced to Australia by the Victoria Trotting Club, it being notified by the secretary that "pool betting"—i. e. the putting up to public competition all starting horses in the same way as in Calcutta sweeps—will be carried out at El sternwick next Saturday. This style of investment, how ever, will be strictly confined to members of the Victoria Sport ing Club, and the fee for joining "the happy band" till the end of the present year is only one guinea, which also in cludes the privileges of admission for a gentleman and two ladies to the commodious stand. Applicants must send in their names, when they will be duly balloted for.

TROTTERS IN THE COLONIES.—Four of the American trot ting mares, and one of the geldings, imported by Dr. Weir, have been sold at satisfactory prices, through Mr. T. S. Clib born, of Sydney. Daisy has become the property of Mr. J. Miller, Ella Chieftain of Mr. Jennings, and Richard of Mr. Stevens, whilst Mr. Andrew Town bought Clara and Violetta for breeding purposes. The pedigree and the personal quali ties of these horses have already been referred to in these columns, and the purchasers and the seller are alike to be congratulated on their bargains. In addition to the two trot ting mares mentioned above, the celebrated American bred trotting stallion, Childs Harold, has just arrived to his order from England, where he has been making himself a grand reputation, as also in France, where he has been giving the Mounseers a turn. On the Alexandra Park track he did the fastest time ever made in the old country—to wit, a mile in 2:34 with ease, and half a mile in 1:13. Childs Harold was got by the same sire as the world-famed Maud S., so this speed is not to be wondered at. An entire called Blackwood Abdallah, imported to New Zealand from California, had al ready been secured by Mr. Town, who evidently "means business."—Melbourne Sportsman.

# ATHLETICS.

## University Field Day.

The University games take place to-day on their new grounds in Berkley. The programme includes nineteen events, and the meeting will probably be the best they have yet given. The following is a list of the events of the day:

1. Throwing base ball.
2. Putting weight.
3. Mile walk.
4. (a) 100 yards scratch (seniors). (b) 100 yards scratch (juniors). (c) 100 yards scratch (sophomores). (d) 100 yards scratch (freshmen).
5. Standing broad jump.
6. 100 yards handicap open.
7. 100 yards scratch run, match race.
8. 440 yards scratch open.
9. 100 yards scratch winners of No. 4.
10. Standing high jump.
11. 220 yards handicap open.
12. Running high jump.
13. Running wide jump.
14. Running hop, step and jump.
15. One mile scratch open.
16. Running high jump.
17. 440 yards run open.
18. 120 yards hurdle race.
19. Tug of War.

For the open events the following entries were made in the list posted in the Olympic Club which closed at 12 o'clock last Wednesday: 100, yards handicap, open—Wm. C. Brown, C. H. Slater, C. L. Ebner, W. R. Stewart and S. S. Emmons of the Olympic Athletic Club; Jos. Masterson, Cal. Athletic and Lacrosse Club; Jas. Thornton, Andrew Loeber and Thos. McGovern, Golden Gate Athletic Club; J. M. Bonner and A. L. Harris.

Two hundred and twenty yards handicap, open—C. H. Slater, E. S. Emmons and W. R. Stewart, O. A. C.; Jos. Mas terson, C. A. and L. C.; Thos. McGovern, G. G. A. C.; J. M. Bonner and A. L. Harris.

Four hundred and forty yards scratch, open—Jos. Master son, C. A. and L. C.; W. R. Stewart, O. A. C.

One mile scratch, open—D. Eiseman and Eugene Van Court, O. A. C.; Thos. McGovern, Howard Vernon and Ed. Lond, G. G. A. C.

Running high jump, open—C. H. Slater and C. L. Ebner, O. A. C.

One hundred and twenty yards scratch, open—W. R. Stew art, Wm. C. Brown, C. H. Slater, O. A. C.; and A. L. Harris. Games will be called at 2 p. m.

NOTE.—Since the above was set in type it has been decided to postpone the University Field day to Nov. 11.

INTERNATIONAL ATHLETICS.—The programme has been an nounced for the Athletic meetings at which Mr. W. G. George of the Moseley Harriers, Birmingham, England, and Mr. E. Myers, of the Manhattan Athletic Club, run their match races. For the first day, Nov. 4, on which occasion the cracks decide the half mile match, the following events will be decided, open to all comers:m 150 yards, one mile and a three miles bicycle race, all handicaps. On Nov. 11, the day of the mile race, the three outside events are handicape at 220 yards, half a mile, and a one mile bicycle race. For the last day, Nov. 18, the handicaps are 100 yards, 440 yards and one mile walk. On that day the match is at three-quarters of a mile. The entries for each meeting close on the preceding Monday, and silver cups will be given to first and second. Mr. George is getting along well in his training and those who know most about what he has been doing state that record time will be beaten in each of the three races if the winner is run out.

The New York Athletic Club will hold a meeting on their Mott Haven ground on election day. There will be two open handicaps, one at 300 yards and the other at 1,000 yards, and at the latter W. G. George will be at scratch. The valuable Travers medal and the new Osiricha medal will be competed for by the club members.—Herald.

## THE PADDOCK.

### Breeding Horses.

The farmer who proposes to breed horses should have a well-defined object in view. The breeding of draft horses is profitable business, if properly conducted. The breeding of the Clyde, the Percheron and the English draft can be made to pay on large, productive farms, and it is better to adhere to one breed than to cross breed. Large, common mares can be bought and their produce by stallions of the above named breeds would sell at good prices. The brood mares and colts should be well fed so as to give good size and early maturity. The demand in the lumber regions and in our large cities for large, strong horses is considerable, and good prices are paid.

The general purpose horse is another good kind to breed. They should not be so large as the draft, should have size, say sixteen hands, and be well proportioned, and have good style, good solid color, good action and there should be as much similarity as possible in the general form, color and make up of those that are raised. This breeding to one stallion one year, and to another quite different one another year, is not quite the thing. Get a good idea in the mind of what you want to breed, and try to approach it as near as possible from year to year. The best way to do it is to get a stallion that is the ideal of what you want to raise in size, style and carriage, and then get mares as near what you would like to raise as possible, and success is almost certain if proper care is taken of the brood mares and their produce, for like begets like.

There is a wide demand for the general purpose horse, for he answers for the buggy, carriage and business of all kinds. He is in general demand for any kind of farm work. Of course the finer and better those that are raised, the better prices they will command. If in addition to good size, style, form and color, there is good trotting action, so much the better—for speed adds to the value. There are plenty of high bred trotting stallions and mares having all the qualities desired, such as size, form, color, etc., that could be selected and used for breeding purposes for the general purpose horse with the best results. Such horses as would be produced from such selected stock would find ready sale at large prices in any market. If the investment would be too great to get such brood mares, select the best within your reach as a means, for the high bred stallion does much to imprint his form and action on his progeny. Of course if trotting speed was one of the main objects aimed at, a different course should be pursued in the selection of brood mares. They should have good trotting action and should have speed at that gait, for speed in both sire and dam is quite essential to insure speed in the progeny.

There are many earnest, intelligent breeders of horses in the country, and they should aid in encouraging a better system of breeding by writing for the public press. We need almost have line upon line and precept upon precept to effect a change.—*Rural World.*

### The Tandem.

The driver of a tandem must not only be an accomplished horseman, thoroughly able to master his team, but he must give his undivided attention to his horses. Old drivers say that it is easier to manage six horses before a coach than two horses in a tandem. A four-horse tandem may be "set up" for a trifle over $4,000, and a two-horse one for something less than $2,000. For the more elaborate equippage the figures are: for the coach, about $2,500; for the four horses, $1,000; for a plain road harness, $500, and servants' liveries, $250. For the two-horse turn out, the tandem-cart costs only about $800, the two horses $500, the harness $350, and the groom's livery $175. These are very low figures compared with the cost of setting up and maintaining a four-in-hand coach. Col. Kane has made public his memorandum of a season's expenses with the Tally-ho, reaching consider-ably over $6,000 of which $1,850 was for the keeping of six teen horses seven months, at $15 a month each; five grooms for seven months, at $40 a month each; showing sixteen horses, $7 a month each, $224; guard's salary, $1,000; depreciation in coach, $500; new set wheels, var-nishing and general repairs, $250; depreciation and repairs to harness, etc., $400, and rent of city stable, $800. This, it will be seen, makes no account of the original cost of the equippage, but only of the running expenses. In driving a tandem a gentleman may use a two-wheel dog-cart, a gig, a Tilbury, a White-chapel, or Surrey cart, or even a brougham. The gentleman usually wears a loose-fitting drab or gray overcoat, with wide sleeves and a low-crowned hat. The groom wears narrow breeches, and top boots, a close-fitting coat, and a tall hat.—*Dunton's Spirit of the Turf.*

### Feeding Young Colts.

A correspondent who has just lost a brood mare, leaving a colt five days old, asks for advice as to the best method of feeding the little orphan, to which the *Breeders' Gazette* answers:

The best possible substitute for the milk of the dam is cow's milk. It should be sweetened at first, as the milk of the mare is sweeter than that of the cow. A little patient effort will soon result in teaching the colt to drink milk readily, but be careful not to give him too much at a time. A half pint is quite sufficient for a colt of the age mentioned; but the ration should be repeated often, not less than six times a day, the idea being to really give the colt all it will need, but to feed so often that it will not require much at a time. As that colt grows older, the ration should be increased, and grass, with oats, should be added as soon as the colt is old enough to eat. No ration is better for a colt than cow's milk with these adjuncts. After the colt is two months old, skim milk should be substituted for the fresh cow's milk. Should there be any trouble from constipation it will be well to add one pint of oil meal per day to the ration; in fact, we would recommend the use of oil meal in all cases, as it furnishes a large proportion of muscle and bone forming food. If the oil meal is not obtainable, flaxseed may be used. A half pint of flaxseed boiled with two quarts of bran will make two good feeds for a colt, and this ration may profitably be alternated with other food.

---

### The Brood Mare.

The object we have in view in horse breeding should be an annual improvement. The investment is remunerative when applied to good shape, soundness, and vigorous action, com-bined with the stoutest and most fashionable blood in the several classes. Horse breeding can only pay by the breed-ing of the very best, for which the demand exceeds supply, which phase of the case has ruled strong for two years with-out alteration; the difficulty is to get horses good enough for the best London trade.

It is important to regard constitution in the parentage, apart from the essential consideration of size, freedom from hereditary blemish or defect, good, sound legs and feet, a symmetrical body, wind, eye-sight. Action is contributed by the mare in regard to force, by the sire with regard to di-rection. These are influenced by the deep shoulder, the moderate arm, length and muscularity of the forearm, a well defined trapezium at the back of the knee, and well de-fined sesamoid bones at the upper posterior portion of the fetlock, shortness from the knee down, length in all bones, capability of mobility in the super structure. Good shoulders are deep and well laid back in a good horses. Quality in the hindquarters is determined by proportion of parts—loins, thighs, gaskins, hocks—strong loins, muscular thighs and gaskins, clean, bold hocks, the point of the hock in all cases well defined. We thus have considered the bases of speed, action, endurance. Beauty of proportion and style of move-ment are features so harness, lack or hunter breeder can af-ford to despise; and the same holds good in regard to heavy draft horse stock for export.

Leading breeders have always a high standard as a fixed aim; in some cases their efforts excel, in others fall short of their ideal. When the latter is the case the mare is in-variably at fault. An upstanding roomy mare—that is, one with a lofty fore-hand, a long barrel, well-coupled up or ribbed home, wide across the hips, deep at fore and back rib, evincing genfesbility, but no droop in the quarter, on short, flat, clean legs—this would be the brood mare of our choice to recoup outlay.

Mares with their first foals require the greatest attention. The mare should be served nine days after foaling, and again tried at the end of a fortnight. If the mare then re-fuses, it is conclusive; but should she stand, she must be tried on the termination of another fourteen days' interval. Mares have a strong aversion to smells—viz: tar, carrion, vegetable putrefaction. The leaves of the willow and sorb are equally obnoxious. Pine varnish in the material that should be used, rather than tar, for palings. All excitement should be avoided—the neighing of entires, etc.

For foaling a roomy, sheltered, and well-ventilated box is a desideratum; No draught; nicely littered down, level and soft in surface, not too deep. The mare must be watered three times a day. Mares at this season are liable to gorge themselves with clean litter, and they frequently exhibit a morbid appetite, which must be restrained. Therefore dry, used litter, taken from under other horses, is the best for present use. Register the time when the mare should foal down. Ten days before she is likely to foal make the neces-sary preparations and frequently examine her at least twice or three times a day without disturbing her, and the event, means a nocturnal visit or two must be paid. A roomy mare, naturally fed, neither too gross nor too poor, seldom require external aid. A waxy substance on the teat, a sink-ing and expansion of the pelvis, rendering the act of parturi-tion hazy, are unmistakable signs. After delivery the mare will lick her foal—leave her to it, but watch the placenta or afterbirth that it does not recede; and when it has come away remove it. Give the mare a nice pailful of warm linseed gruel, succeeded by a bran mash. Get the foal to suck as soon as you conveniently can. In any case of difficulty or doubt, do not delay to call in your professional friend and ad-viser, the qualified veterinary surgeon.

Most of the treatments relative to the brood mare accept the cardinal features of first-rate management applicable to neat stock—quiet, cleanliness, supervision.—*R. H. Hill-house*, in *English Agricultural Gazette.*

### Persistent Pinkeye.

A correspondent of the *New York Spirit* has been talking with the Kentucky breeders about the pinkeye and relates their experience and observations:

The pinkeye has been prevalent in Kentucky since last spring. The stock of all the breeders have suffered more or less from it, some of them losing as many as fourteen head. Dr. Herr says he has not had any fatal cases as yet, although some of his stock have been attacked twice. The Doctor is of the opinion that it is only contagious by reason of remo-val to certain localities. For instance, if a horse is removed from this State to a distant part of the country, or vice versa, he would be apt to contract the disease, if it was prevalent at his new home; but, take a horse from home who is suffering from it to another section where it is not epidemic, it would not be contagious.' He thinks it is in the air, and it is epi-demical in the same sense as yellow fever or cholera visits the human family. It is now assuming a milder form in Ken-tucky. Some of the animals show a lingering constitutional weakness, and any horse that has had it severely in the spring, has not been in fit condition to trot a good race since. Some horses are predisposed to a certain class of diseases, and those who are predisposed to pinkeye have more difficulty in recovering from it. The Doctor adds that he has known horses to have apparently recovered, and another attack would develop itself in a milder form—he lets mild cases run out in the open air, but if severe, he gives them consti-tutional treatment.

B. S. Stroder relates his experience as follows: Our stock has been ailing all season, owing to pinkeye. We cannot get them into marketable shape; business was very good with us in the spring, but we have had forty head under treatment during summer, and eight of them died. It often leaves con-stitutional troubles, such as rheumatism, muscular prostra-tion, and occasionally affects the wind. It is a very deceptive and baffling disease, for when they are to all appearances over it, and you begin working them, they seem to have lost their strength. It requires patience and good care to await their recuperation. Col. Stone has a brood mare that con-tracted it three times. I learn they have lost 14 head from pinkeye at Alexander's Woodburn Farm, and Gen. Withers has had a hard stage of it with his stock.

Cribbing in Horses: I see an inquiry asking for a cure. I will give you a cure generally successful in a young horse, and sometimes for old ones. Get some cayenne pepper (red pepper pods will do), and make a strong pepper tea. Wash the salt manger and feed-box thoroughly with the tea boiled down very strong. Also wash the hack-yoke, and wagon or sleigh-tongue, if driving the horse daily. Do this once a week for several weeks, and if it is a young horse it will most likely cure him. A good many old ones have also been cured.—*Cor, Ex.*

---

### The Care of Farm Horses.

Very much is said, in a general way, regarding the care and feeding of the farm horse, to fit him for the labor he has to perform without injury to his health, and that the greatest amount of labor may be obtained at the smallest cost. The constitution of horses vary in their requirements as much as the constitutions of men, rendering it impossible to give minute directions for their care, as in each case a knowledge of these requirements is necessary to form an opinion. Personal obser-vation alone will be necessary to designate this treatment, as the same feed that profits with one will destroy with another. The nervous, active race horse, whose entire usefulness is exhausted in the shortest possible time, is treated upon prin-ciples that ages of experience has taught as the best calcu-lated to attain that object. The careful groom will observe the languid movement, which indicates a loss of vitality, and if from his observation he is satisfied that his horse is suffering from fever or other derangement, he should lose no time in applying the proper remedies and at once change his food, even if necessary to change the labor he is performing, to give him time and opportunity to recuperate his vitality and overcome the effects of his climatic change. Self-inter-est demands that he be protected from the cruelties or ill-temper those having him in charge so often expose him to, as well, also, as the pain and suffering which avarice inflicts through the neglect to furnish him with proper food and gen-eral attention, and that those alone be retained in his care and management that have given voice that "the merciful man is merciful to his horse."—*Rural Messenger.*

### The Walking Horse.

The English have a saying: "A riding horse is not worth its corn if it cannot walk well." We condense some excel-lent "walking talk" from an English contemporary:

The walk is one of the principal paces of a town hack, one of the greatest luxuries of a hard-worked man, be he a law-yer, doctor, artist, judge, politician, or city financier. A horse may be a very good hunter, yet a bad walker, but then he is fit only for the stable of a rich man. A hunter that can walk safely and fast home is a luxurious treasure.

The walk is the pace that may be vastly improved without the rider having any of the natural and acquired talents of the professional horse breaker. But he must have patience. "To make a horse walk well," says the author of "The Book of the Horses," "there is nothing more stupid than ill tem-per, the use of the whip, and the abuse of the spurs."

A hack, to make a first-class walker, must have the courageous temperament that never shies, when once settled down from early morn freshness, and also the natural form and action that makes him carry his head in the right place and step out of the ground.

Four miles an hour at a stretch, done in harmonious ca-dence at the first asking, without tumbling, dropping, shuf-fling, or breaking, is very good work. To do five miles an hour in good form is a very rare performance.

We are told that there are some horses that can walk six miles an hour with a light load, but have never seen any-thing like this. We were once riding a nearly thoroughbred horse, over sixteen hands high, with the wild stag hounds, and left off nine miles from the horse's stable. He did the distance, and brought us back in time to dress for dinner, in an hour and twenty minutes. That is about five miles and one-third in an hour.

To improve the walk the first step is to sit down on the horse and ride at a sharp pace until he is settled, without fatiguing him. Then, if he is young, be content with the slowest pace of walking, as long as he does not break and jog. At every break he must be stopped firmly, collected, and made to begin again. This is the best practice in return-ing home to your hack's stable and corn. Of course, it is no use to waste time over an aged hack whose habits are fixed, or a horse foaled to stumble all his life.

The young one must be firmly and sensibly held, so that he will be compelled to move each and alternately and prop-er-ly put on his heels; and thus induce him to bring his hind legs under him in regular time, in support of his fore legs. While the reins restrain him, the spurs, gently used, urge him, and the corn invites him to step out his best. By these means, patiently practiced day after day, a really clever hack will get into the habit of walking at his best pace as soon as the rider mounts and indicates by the pressure of his legs that such is his pleasure.

Young horses and thoroughbreds drafted from the turf in-to hack or hunter stables should be often ridden across the deep furrows of plowed clay fields, both at the walk and trot. Riding across turnips set on the ridge will improve the action of four-year-olds to that the walk and trot, if their forelimbs are so made as to be capable of high, true action. Finally, with time and patience, most young horses' style and pace in walking can be greatly improved.

TAX BEST DRAFT HORSES.—The *Mark Lane Express* of London, having circulated questions respecting draft horses among a number of great firms, etc., employing them, has obtained much information in reply. To the question: "Is there any breed of heavy draft horses which, more than any other, is especially adapted to heavy work in paved towns?" the Southampton Dock Company replies: "With twenty-five years' experience we find that Belgian and English mixed-breed horses are best adapted for heavy work on paved and rough roads. Geldings are always preferred and roans are the favorite color." Messrs. Courage, great London brewers, object to heavy flesh-legged horses for work on the stones. As to heavy-legged horses opinions are divided. Mr. Wallis, of Dublin, who houses the express wagons of several leading Irish railroads, says that the English and Scotch horses are much more easily managed than the Irish. One authority pronounces in favor of the mixed Belgian and English horses so far as price, power and durability are concerned, but most are decidedly in favor of the breeds of the United Kingdom. The best of foreign breeds will not, they say, stand the stones.

A late number of a London live stock paper says: Over-big horses for any purpose are a mistake; so the corporation have found out. When they started to do their own scavengering, instead of contracting for it, they selected all the giants they could get—17 hands was preferred. The mistake has been found out; 16 hands is now the favored height. These do more work, are less subject to roaring, and are altogether more healthy.

F. F. Burt has on his ranch in Tehama county a Clydes-dale stallion of two years, that weighs 1,110 pounds. He con-siders him to be the largest animal of his age in the state of that breed.

## How Horses are Made Stylish.

The New York *Times* "gives away" some of the secrets of aining subjects for horses, and shows how jockeys manage transform an ordinary roadster into a high-stepping carriage horse, with a thoroughbred air about him. To a reporter of the *Times*, a veterinary surgeon said:

"The great thing is to make a horse look like a thoroughbred. I don't suppose you know what a thoroughbred is. He is a horse with a pedigree, with blue blood in his veins, r many generations. Any judge of horses can tell one in a inute. I will tell you some of his characteristics. His ack, to begin with, is beautiful curved. He holds his ead up, with his chin drawn in towards his breast when in arness. He has delicate legs and feet almost like a deer. He is a succession of lines of beauty. His neck is not set ito his body, as if a carpenter put it there, but joins it gently and gracefully with a long sweep. His body, immediately ebind the fore legs, comes down almost to a point. After a light curve in the fore part of his back, his back is almost traight all the way to the tail. He lifts his feet high when e walks. His tail falls with a graceful arch, and hangs like festoon at the back. Look at one of the fine thoroughbreds ou see on the race tracks. Just in front of the hind legs ou can span him with your arms. But measure that horse round the body, just behind the fore legs, and you will find e is as big around as an elephantine dray horse. Here lies is strength and staying power. His heart and lungs are arge and work with great power. When he comes in from a ong race his lungs work like a mill. This is not because he is xhausted—it is a sign of health, strength, vitality. His nukles re hardly bigger than your wrist, but take a section of bone at of the ankle of a thoroughbred, and a section of the same ength out of the ankle of a cart horse; although the latter ay be twice as large in circumference, the piece out of the xoroughbred will weigh the heavier. The thoroughbred's ones are solid, compact and heavy, while the bones of the common horse are spongy and weak. It is on the same principle that some gentlemen with wrists like a woman's are stronger than gigantic laborers. This is the perfect horse. He is found in his best estate in Arabia. The Anglo Arabian horses rank next. All our finest thoroughbreds are Anglo Arabians.

"Now, what the horse dealers have to do," the surgeon continued, "is to take a common horse and make him look as much like a thoroughbred as possible. The plebian horse stretches out his neck. He drags his feet along; his tail hangs straight down. His back, instead of being a straight line, sags down toward the tail. He is a succession of unsightly angles. If he is sound and hearty, he is worth, perhaps $200 in his natural state. The dealer takes him in hand, spends perhaps $50 on him, and makes him worth $500. A good part of the work is legitimate training. Some of it, perhaps, is cruel. I will describe it to you and you may draw your own conclusions. I do not do this because it does not pay me in my business, but I am well posted on the way it is done.

"We will say," continued the doctor, "that I am a horse dealer engaged in the business of improving horses. A country horse comes in and I buy him. He is awkward, gawky, and countrified. He is, in short, compared with city horses, just what an awkward backwoodsman is compared with a polished gentleman. First of all I fatten him up, give him good feed and have him carefully groomed twice a day to make him smooth. It is a new experience for him, and he likes it. It is like a boarder in a Water street boarding house going to a first-class hotel to live. It makes him good natured and happy. No matter how sleek and fat he may be no gentleman would have him in front of his carriage as long as he carries his nose out in the air and his neck is straight like a piece of board. He must be made to arch his neck and to pull in his chin. I put a 'mouthing iron' on him. This is a solid iron bar, like a heavy bit, with rings on the ends. At the middle of it there have y tassels are fastened so they will rest on top of the tongue. This weight of iron makes him lower his chin and draw it in toward his breast. I put a surcingle on him, put straps through the rings in the ends of the mouth-iron, fasten the other ends of the straps to the surcingle, and brace them up tight. This makes the horse arch his neck. He must do it whether he wants to or not. Two or three weeks of this treatment will get him in the habit of holding his head properly. It is painful to the horse, of course. Sometimes they make a fuss, and I have known them to faint with the weight of iron on their tongue. But they generally stand it very well. The mouthing-iron is removed only when the horses are feeding, and the feed box is so arranged in a short stall that the horse has to keep his chin drawn back to reach the oats. You can always tell a horse that has been treated in this way, for it drives up the glands on the side of the head, toward the ears, and swell. They remain somewhat distorted permanently.

"This makes the head and neck question all right. But the horse still drags his feet along the ground like a man in loose slippers. I send a ton or less of straw to a clean part of the stable-yard and have it spread loosely over the yard till it is perhaps two feet deep, not too close. While the mouthing-iron is still in the horse's mouth, I have one of the grooms take him out into this straw and walk him about for three or four hours every day. This soon gets him into the habit of stepping high, for lifts his feet well up to get clear of the straw. While one groom leads the horse another goes behind and turns the straw up with a pitchfork to prevent it from packing. This process, singularly enough, has the same effect upon the groom in a limited degree, that it has upon the horse.' It teaches him to step high, and does him no harm. If the owner of the horse should see him after he had gone through two or three weeks of this training he would not recognize him.

"The front end of the horse by this time is all right. Now for the other end. What looks more ungraceful than to see a horse with his tail held down close against his flanks like a cow or mule? He must be taught to hold his tail out and give it a graceful curve. Formerly this was done by nicking the tail on the under side, so that it became sore, and the horse then held it up because it pained him whenever it touched his body. But Mr. Bergh considered this cruel, as it undoubtedly was, and put a stop to it in this city. As soon as the head and neck are right the horse is fastened in a stall with a pulley in the ceiling immediately over his tail, a cord is put through this pulley, with a weight of ten or fifteen pounds on one end. The other end is fastened to the upper part of the horse's tail. The weight keeps the tail elevated, and gives it a pretty curve. It does not answer ' to do' this while the mouthing-iron is at work, for the unusual sensation at the mouth and tail at the same time would fret him too much, and, perhaps, injure his health. There is some little risk in the tail improvement. The horse will fight hard to which his tail out of the fastening; and if he tries to be stripped pretty tight. If he pulls too hard on it the strap may rut and the sore become irritated. I have known horses to die of lockjaw from the process.

"These are the principal methods employed," the surgeon concluded, "to turn country boobies into city swells. Thous-

ands of horses are so trained every year. There are many other devices—so many, indeed, that it would take me all day and half the night to describe them. It is an easy matter to give the horse a shiny appearance. Take any horse, trained or untrained, thoroughbred or common stock, feed him well, groom him well and often, and you may use his sleek side for a mirror. Look out for that gray mare, she's a little ugly. Good morning."

## An Oft Told Tale.

If you want to test and bring to the surface the meanest trait in man's composition—if you would know whether he has a heart as big as a bullock's or small enough to rattle in a mustard seed and mean enough to steal acorns from a blind sow—just let him have your horse to work for his feed, and in ninety-nine cases out of a hundred, five dollars to a green persimmon is a safe bet that he returns you a lame skeleton without shoes. This is a sad commentary upon the intelligence and humanity of the majority of men, but as true as gospel, and we need not go outside of this city to find a number of instances in proof of the assertion. Within the present hour we have seen two such cases, and although we are generally disposed to be lenient toward evil doers, it would afford us the greatest pleasure to see the gates of the penitentiary closed behind a man who would starve and abuse a dumb brute—indeed we would find no fault with the death penalty to see such a man step from the scaffold to eternity, for we sincerely believe if there is such a thing as an unpardonable sin, cruelty to dumb animals is that sin. Liverymen can preach a more intelligent sermon on human depravity than the wisest minister who has had no experience in their line, and they would make excellent detectives for if a crime were committed by an unknown, they would have no trouble in tracing it to some unprincipled individual who had at one time or another abused a hired horse. We have known men who would drive a hired horse as long as he could go, and abuse and starve him nearly to death, but would take good care of him if he were their own individual property, not because of any kindly feeling toward the poor dumb servant, but because their money was at stake, and ill treatment would cause him to depreciate in value. Then there are others, not only men, but women, who, through ignorance or moral depravity, seem to think a horse should be able to go as long and as fast as the vehicle can run, and without any further care or consideration than either wagon or harness require. But if we could have the making of law and the control of judges the plea of ignorance would not save them from punishment—and a light fine or a few days jail, either, but we would class them with wife-beaters, re-establish the pillory and whipping post, and deal out justice in doses that the vilest criminal would deserve. If their crime is the result of ignorance it is of a kind that can only be enlightened by the whipping post, and if prompted by pure meanness, unadulterated depravity, the severest punishment short of death should be applied and repeated till a cure is affected, or the fiend placed beyond the power to torture his superiors in all that is good and noble on earth.—*Western Sportsmen.*

## A Mule Story of Mexico.

A *Standard* reporter dropped in at the rooms of the Saserac Lying Club yesterday as one of the new members was relating the following yarn. It is a true "tail," and a fair sample of the capabilities of the members of the club: While at Gustemala recently I was traveling from Esquintla to the capital city over one of the most rugged and villainous roads to be found probably the wide world over. On nearing the summit of a high range of hills, where a turn of the road revealed an immense ravine or chasm some 500 feet deep, I overtook a Mexican riding a mule with a string of five more attached to the leader. The custom of leading mules in that country is as follows: Their tails are tied in knots with a bunch of grass or cornstalk leaves, fastened to each as a tail. A strip of cowhide is firmly tied from the tail of the leading mule around the neck of the one following, and so on to the last. The rider mounts the leader and urges him on by a vigorous application of whip and spur, the belated tails enticing the rest to follow. The leading mule stumbling over a boulder, the rider commenced to yell, whip and spur. This unlooked for indignity made the mule lash out, reaching the head of No. 2 with a terrific whack. He aroused and insulted, did likewise, with like result to No. 3, who followed suit on to No. 4. Ditto from 4 to 5, and 5 to 6, who, being last, had to kick at vacancy. Here then were six mules all kicking behind, as mules never kicked before. The Mexican swore, spurred and whipped to his utmost. It was soon evident they were backing down the hill with the sheer force of kicking. It was the most indecorous sight I ever saw. I expected every moment something would give way, but rider, mules, tails and cowhide held together. At last the edge of the precipice was reached by the hind mule, who tumbled over, dragging the next after him—still kicking. He pulled the one preceding over, still kicking, and so on until the first was reached—all kicking. Looking down a ravine, I could dimly discern the whole mass of mularity all in a heap, still kicking, and for aught I know are still kicking there to this day, as a Gustemala mule never, no never, tires of kicking.—*Portland (Or.) Standard.*

A colored blacksmith of Vienna, Georgia, was shoeing a mule not long ago, when the animal disengaged itself and drove one of its hind feet against the negro's head with the force of a battering ram. A few days later some one asked the owner if the blacksmith sustained severe injuries. "I can't say that he did," responded the man, dejectedly, "but the mule goes on three legs."

# HERD AND SWINE.

## Sheep Raising in Dakota.

The Yankton *Press* has the following in relation to the sheep interests of that Territory:

Sheep farming in Dakota has been demonstrated by practical men to be a profitable enterprise. Sheep have had experience in, and understand the business, to be a safe and profitable enterprise. The dryness of the atmosphere in winter time, and its purity and healthfulness at all seasons, the abundance and nutritiousness of the native grasses, and other favorable conditions, insure the health and good condition of the flocks at all seasons. These facts are becoming known to and are being taken advantage of by practical wool-growers, and a number of them have recently located in our territory and engaged in the business. Among the number is C. B. Bagley, who owns a range about fifteen miles from Yankton, in the northwestern part of Clay county. He owns a fine flock of Spanish Merino bucks and Cotswold sheep, in fine condition and health and returning a handsome profit on the capital invested. Mr. Bagley called

on us a few mornings since and showed us a fleece weighing twenty and one-half pounds, and it is the finest and best quality, worth in the market at present prices from thirty-two to thirty-five cents per pound. Mr. Bagley was formerly engaged in sheep raising in Vermont—a state which produces the finest sheep in the world, and may be said to be the world's market for the best and purest blood—and is, therefore, thoroughly posted in the business. He is confident that Dakota possesses as good, if not superior, natural advantages as Vermont for successful and profitable sheep farming, and founds his faith upon his personal experience in our territory.

## Dairy Notes.

As soon as I find an animal in distress from bloat, from eating wet grass or clover. I wet it along on the back with cold water, and I also place a large cloth or blanket of several thicknesses over the paunch; after being saturated with all the cold water that it will absorb, add over that a dry blanket. If the cold is properly applied, one will not have long to wait for a cure.—*J. R. Finley, Breckenridge, Mo.*

The Society of Public Analysis of Great Britain has adopted a standard for the poorest milk at 9 per cent. of solids and 2.5 per cent. of fats. Professor Cameron states that examinations of the milk of forty-two Shorthorn cows during the winter of 1880, gave 9.70 per cent. of solids and 4.20 per cent. of fats in the poorest milk, the cows being housed and well-fed. The average yield per day was 11½ quarts per cow. In every instance more milk was given in the morning than in the evening. The quality of the milk improved in each case as the time for calving drew near. The older cows were found to give both more and better milk than the younger ones.

It takes longer to churn the cream from a cow when farrow than when she is fresh. It is not a good practice, therefore, to mix the milk of a farrow cow with that of a cow recently in milk, if it is to be made into butter, as the cream will be so much the longer in churning that most of it will be left with the buttermilk. When the milking season is well advanced the difference in churning is less, and the farrow cow's milk can be mixed with better advantage.—*L. B. Arnold.*

The value of the butter product of the country is about five times that of cheese, but only 3 per cent. of it is as yet shipped aboard, while 30 per cent. of the cheese goes there. American dairymen have unquestionably succeeded remarkably in pleasing the palates of the English with their cheese, and even in continental countries, even in noted dairy districts like Holland and Belgium, American cheese is offered to the traveler. No packing of butter has as yet been able to bring the American maker into really serious competition with the French and other continental makers. The English like fresh butter. The shipments from New York, mainly to ports in Great Britain, from July 1, 1882, to January 11, 1882, were 16,898,482 pounds to 23,907,206 for the corresponding period last year.

On the Elgin, Ill., board of trade last year there were 287, 664 boxes of cheese sold, weighing 11,827,526 pounds. The highest price paid for cheese at Utica was 13½ cents; at Little Falls, 13 cents; at Elgin 13 cents. In all cases the cheese was full cream. The lowest price paid at Utica was 8½c, at Little Falls, 7c., at Elgin, 6c., the last being closely skimmed cheese. The Elgin board, therefore, reports more boxes of cheese sold than the Utica or Little Falls boards, though the weight is less. These figures are: 340,476 boxes, 14,444,750 pounds, for Utica; and 283,025 boxes, 15,181,500 pounds, for Little Falls. The Elgin board has transactions the year round and sold more cheese in December than any other month, January being the second.

The enormous quantity of cheese manufactured in this country, for export, as well as home consumption, leads us to ask why we should be under the necessity of importing milk sugar. Those who may be engaged in making the latter, or intending to embark therein, will be interested to learn of the latest improvement in that line. In the evaporation of whey, from which the cheese has been removed, a considerable portion of the sugar of milk is lost through conversion into uncrystallizable lactose by the action of the acid in the whey. Engling, therefore, recommends the neutralization of the acid with free chalk, and then after evaporating it to one-half, he allows it to settle. The clear liquid is afterwards decanted or drawn off from the precipitate, which consists of albumen and phosphate of lime, and evaporated until further. The sugar separates from the purified solution in different scales and crusts; upon further evaporation of the mother liquid, a second crop of crystals is obtained. The thick liquid that remains can be dialyzed, and more sugar obtained. From 100 quarts of summer whey eight pounds of refined milk sugar can be obtained.

## A Small Breed of Pigs.

An English contemporary speaking of a breed of pigmy porkers, three sows and a boar from Nepaul, on exhibition at the Zoological Gardens, London, says:

This species is so rare that since Hodson described these animals, fifty years ago, there has not been a single specimen attainable in Europe, and even the museums have been unable to get more than a single skin. They are very small in size, scarcely bigger than a large wild rabbit; or probably a better idea of their size may be formed by giving their weight at seven or eight pounds each. They are very active on their legs, running very swiftly, and they are very shy. Their skins are well covered with short, reddish-brown hair, or rather bristles; they are very clean feeders, and also very cleanly in their habits. Their flesh is esteemed very good for eating; and thus these interesting little porcines are naturally the subjects of other contemplations than their zoological reality. If they can be bred in the Gardens, the Society will reap profitable results repay the price given for them, by disposing of the first offspring to other menageries; and the acclimatization of the subsequent progeny would seem to be well worthy of attempt, as they might be kept seemingly without offensiveness in the yards and gardens of domestic houses, and be fed upon potato parings, vegetables and debris of food. They are very fond of rice, and will eat small portions of meat; but they will not touch the wash of greasy matters commonly given to ordinary pigs.

The Sierra *Leader* says: The recent storm caused havoc among the herds of the dairymen in the mountains. Stock has been scattered far and wide, many perishing from hunger and exposure. Every one was caught unawares, and had no time to collect their cattle and provide a shelter.

The trade in Angora goats is increasing wonderfully in Wyoming, Utah and Colorado, and during the past two years Mr. Bailey of Lander county, Nev., has disposed of over $30,000 worth of these goats.

THE

# Breeder and Sportsman.

PUBLISHED WEEKLY BY THE

BREEDER AND SPORTSMAN PUBLISHING CO.

THE TURF AND SPORTING AUTHORITY OF THE PACIFIC COAST.

OFFICE, 508 MONTGOMERY STREET

P. O. Box 1338.

*Five dollars a year; three dollars for six months; one dollar and a half for three months. Strictly in advance.*

MAKE ALL CHECKS, MONEY ORDERS, ETC., PAYABLE TO ORDER OF BREEDER AND SPORTSMAN PUBLISHING CO.

*Money should be sent by postal order, draft or by registered letter, addressed to the "Breeder and Sportsman Publishing Company, San Francisco, Cal."*

*Communications must be accompanied by the writer's name and address, not necessarily for publication, but as a private guarantee of good faith*

JOSEPH CAIRN SIMPSON, - - - EDITOR

ADVERTISING RATES.—Displayed $1 50 per inch each insertion or pro rata for less pace. Reading Notices, set in brevier type and having no foot marks, 20 cents per line each insertion. Lines will average ten words. A discount of 10 per cent. will be allowed on 3 months, 20 per cent. on 6 months and 30 per cent. on 12 months contracts. No extra rate charged for cuts or cutting of column rules. No reading notice take for less than 50 cents each insertion.

San Francisco, Saturday, November 4, 1882.

## THE EMBRYO STAKE.

The free rains this week have necessitated a postponement of the Embryo Stakes which were to have been trotted at Oakland Park to-day. The conditions require that in case of postponement the race shall be trotted on the first good day and track after the day first set. The unsettled weather makes it impossible to say now when the matter will be decided, but probably next Wednesday will be appointed. The three races which the stake requires should for the number and quality of the colts named be all good ones. In the yearling dash of a mile opinion seems to favor A. P. Whitney's Dawn by Nutwood, although Antevolo, full brother to Anteeo, Mr. Simpson's entry, is doing well and is much admired. Possibly one factor is omitted from the calculation, for a juvenile from Palo Alto, Albon by General Benton, will be among the starters and may prove to be a dark horse in the race. He has the advantage of being entirely sub rosa as far as what he is doing and can do is concerned, while the performances and progress of the others are well known to most people who feel any interest in them. Seven colts have paid stakes in the yearling class and it is probable that some more than the those above named will start—possibly the winner is yet in the shadow. Of the two-year-olds nine have paid stakes but the proportion of these that will show up when the race is called is at present unknown. It is assured that Mr. Rose's Neluska, Dr. Hick's Pride, and John Howe's filly will be among the starters and that will insure a good race shouid none of the remaining six appear—a contingency not probable. Of the three-year-olds fourteen have not declared out and the last will be the great race of the day. Anteeo, Fred Arnold, Bonnie and Nutwood Maid will be among the starters and the result cannot be prophesied. The three races of the stake will make a great day's sport and the behavior of the colts as a premonition of future stars of the turf will be watched with interest akin to anxiety.

## COURSING.

The California Coursing Club have decided to give a handsome gold cup for competition at the club coursing matches which take place in the fall of each year. We consider that this is one of the best ideas that conld have been advanced for the popularizing of this noble sport. One valuable cup, which must be won three times before it becomes the property of the nominator, is a far greater incentive to breed and train fine dogs than is the custom of giving three or four cups at each meeting. Cups and mugs won at coursing matches in this State have become rather common and cease to carry with them any distinctive honor, but the possession of such a cup as this club proposes to get up will be recognized as the highest honor to be obtained in this State in coursing competitions. A handsome parlor ornament, it would be with pride that the holder would show it to his friends and say: "This is the champion cup of the California Coursing Club. I won it at such a time with such a dog." It will also be productive of good fellowship, for the man who wins it will, of course, take many an occasion to fill it to the brim with sparkling wine in which to pledge the health of the good dog whose gallant speed and dauntless pluck put it in his possession. Its existence will always be a real tangible something to hold the club together, a sort of trust fund for the maintenance of coursing, and we predict that from the day it is first run for at Merced until the time when it shall have become necessary for the club to purchase another emblem the fortunes of the California Coursing Club will steadily increase.

## EDITORIAL NOTES.

**Californians** have a habit, a sort of second nature it is, of doing things in a whole-souled way; that is to say of throwing their whole energies into anything and everything they undertake. It is a peculiarity that makes an agreeable impression upon the stranger when he first sets foot on these shores and one that goes far to explain how a growth of thirty years shows such wonderful results in the western slope. Just now California is in the throes of an election and every other interest is secondary to the one of parties and candidates. It is a trifle awkward for one whose endeavor is to keep alive and promote matters that can by no manner of construction be made to take on a political character. If he approaches a man for information as to the history or lineage of a horse he is answered with the pedigree of a candidate. A query as to what may be the chances of a coming race, will in most cases elicit the reply that Brown will be elected beyond a doubt. Any attempt to discover anything new in the sporting world at this time is sure to be met with a disquisition on the management of "fights"—the favorite term for a political campaign. Politics are a necessary evil in this government and it is a healthy sign when all classes and all citizens take an active interest therein but it will be a relief when the ballots have been counted and the names of the successful ones been decided so that the city can settle back into its normal condition. We hope the political ardor will have cooled out before the inauguration of the Blood Horse meeting, that the good people of San Francisco may be in a condition to enjoy the sports of the turf and appreciate the efforts to amuse them. Politics have become a trifle tiresome to non-political journalism and it is with no little self congratulation that we view the near approach of election day.

**The Blood Horse Meeting.**—The committee of the Blood Horse Association to whom the business arrangements for the fall meeting were confided have decided upon the Bay District as the course over which the races will be run. The fields are very strong both in numbers and quality and the outlook is that this meeting will eclipse any former gatherings of the kind held on this Coast. The heavy rains this week ought to be succeeded by a season of our delightful fall weather if there is any logic in judging one season by another, and with a cool, bracing atmosphere, fine roads, and the complete and elegant appointments of the track to supplement the racing the meeting ought to attract a large attendance and be productive of good sport.

**Overman**—The match between Overman and J. P. Morris went off by the owner of Morris paying forfeit but the race with Helene after being postponed on account of unfavorable weather was trotted at Fleetwood Park, New York, last Wednesday. It was announced as a match for $2,000 a side and was won easily by Overman, who took the second, third and fourth heats in 2:21, 2:26½ 2:23½. These matches have caused Mr. Hickok's horse to be much discussed among horsemen and the turf editor of the *Herald* notes the report that some one says (perhaps the public) that Overman is a second St. Julien and can be sold for more money than any horse ever brought out if the owner wishes to sell.

**The death of H. R. Covey** and the purchase of the Coutts farm have brought about some minor changes at Gov. Stanford's establishment. The thoroughbreds will be as heretofore in charge of Henry Walsh but headquarters of that grand division will be at Matadero. The stock at Palo Alto will be in charge of C. Van Buren pending the return of Charles Marvin, who will then assume command of the trotters. Both divisions will be under the general superintendence of Major J. L. Rathbone, who will represent Gov. Stanford during the Governor's absence in the East.

**Rowdy Boy**, the well-known gray gelding by Rustic will be offered at auction on the Bay District course on the 16th inst. Rowdy Boy is one of the promising colts of the State. He is four years old and has a record of 2:31½ but was timed at the late State fair at 2:25 in a race where he was outclassed and could not win. He is stabled at Mr. Randlett's near the Oakland Trotting Park and can be seen at any time previous to the sale by applying to James Garland at Randlett's hotel.

**The chestnut trotting gelding Ashley** will be sold at auction by Killip & Co. at the Bay District track on Thursday, the 16th instant. Ashley has a record of 2:24½ and would make a capital roadster, being of good size and a steady goer at road paces. He drives single or double and would hold an easy edge over most of the road horses that go through the park, his turf training having been very thorough. It will be a rare opportunity to secure a fast one.

**J. A. Roberts** of Melbourne, Australia, the owner of Boccaccio has offered a purse for two-year-olds, the get of his stallion, to be trotted in the spring of 1883. The race will be a stake of $15 each, $150 added by Mr. Roberts. As Boccaccio did a fair business in the stud it is likely that a number of colts will be named in this stake, and the race will give some indication of the quality of the mares and the fitness of the climate for breeding and raising trotters.

**The peculiar fall weather** is regarded as very favorable for stock raisers, the warm rains bringing up the grass with such rapidity that cattle find an abundance of new feed already. The expected clear skies that were to follow the unusually early rains have not yet appeared and it looks as though the rainy season was to be strung along over five or six months. This will be good for grazing lands but augurs poorly for grain crops.

**Mike.**—J. A. Cardwell of Jacksonville, Oregon, has sold his stallion Mike to James Sutherland of Scott Valley, Siskiyou county. Mike is a son of old Vermont and has been kept at Scott Valley for several years, where he is very popular as a stock horse. He has sired several fair trotters but has had no opportunity to mate with mares that had speed or any of the requisites. He is a better horse than his colts so far show.

## POULTRY.

At the February meeting of the North American Poultry Association the subject of incubation was thoroughly discussed, and the following facts substantially established: That the only way to raise chickens with certainty for early market is by the use of incubators; that a good incubator will hatch from seventy to eighty per cent. of the eggs put in it; that people living in cities, who have not room to keep hens, can use incubators successfully, getting eggs from grocers and farmers near by; that with special care two hundred chickens may be raised to market size in a room fifteen feet square; that the business of raising poultry is particularly adapted to ladies and infirm people both in city and in country; that live chickens from eight to twelve weeks old will sell in the East in April, May, June and July at from 40 to 75 cents a pound, or from $1 to $1 50 each, according to variety and condition. [This is a mistake. They bring about 75 cents each at retail there in April.—Ed.] As the mass of the people are ignorant of the profits of poultry raising, cannot afford to buy expensive incubators, and do not know that they can make a good, cheap incubator themselves, with which to hatch both early and late chickens, the following resolution was adopted: Resolved, That the Secretary of the North American Poultry Association be authorized to inform the people, through a leading newspaper in each State, that plain directions and diagrams for making a good incubator, that they can make at home at a cost of less than $5, and that will hold 250 eggs, can be obtained by addressing our secretary.—*J. M. Bain, New Concord, Ohio.*

Americans can justly be proud of their achievements in the improvements of live stock, and in poultry especially, the justly famous Plymouth Rock breed of fowls being an enduring monument of pains-taking experience. There are various breeds of poultry which, for single and special purposes, may exceed the Plymouth Rocks, yet as a general purpose fowl where profit is desired, there is no better, nor is there likely to be. The farmer and fancier alike are loud in their praise, for they seem to "fill the bill" exactly. They are from medium to large in size, have plump, well-rounded bodies, and fit for table use at almost any age. They are hardy, good layers of large eggs, and the eggs are uniformly fertile. They make good, careful mothers, and are as free from disease as any other breed known. One feature which makes them especially desirable for southern breeders and farmers is that they feather up so quickly, when very young, and are thus secure against the fierce rays of the sun at this stage of their growth. The Asiatics (the Brahmas and Cochins) remain so long almost or entirely naked many of them become "scalded," causing them to droop or die, or else stunt them so badly that they seldom, if ever, get entirely over it, even when they are fully grown and matured.

In using eggs as food there is a danger of forgetting how useful they are. It is safe to say that more than one-half of all the millions of eggs which are consumed every year in this country are used in cakes, puddings, custards, cream, and confections. How much real good do these do? Dr. Holbrook says: "About one-third of the weight of an egg is solid nutriment. This is more than can be said of meat. There are no bones and tough pieces that must be laid aside. Practically an egg is animal food, and yet there is none of the disagreeable work of the butcher necessary to obtain it." This is where we find the true value of eggs. The mechanic opens his lunch basket and finds boiled eggs, containing more nutriment than meat. The labor of the afternoon is performed by their staying qualities, for an egg is animal food. There is a place for everything, and who shall say that the place for the egg is not on the tables as a substitute for meat?

## BASE BALL.

Following is the score of last Sunday's game between the Renos and the Niantics:

| RENOS. | T.B. | B.B. | H. | P.O. | A. | E. | NIANTICS. | T.R. | B.H. | H. | A. | P.O. | E. |
|---|---|---|---|---|---|---|---|---|---|---|---|---|---|
| Barnes, 1b | 5 | 2 | 1 | 13 | 0 | 0 | Donahue, b c | 4 | 1 | 1 | 0 | 1 | 0 |
| Swanton, r f | 5 | 1 | 0 | 0 | 1 | 3 | Arnold, s s | 5 | 1 | 0 | 0 | 0 | 2 |
| Riordan, 3b | 5 | 2 | 1 | 0 | 2 | 1 | Sullivan, l f | 5 | 1 | 1 | 0 | 0 | 0 |
| Lake, l f | 5 | 4 | 0 | 0 | 0 | 0 | Egan, 1b | 5 | 0 | 1 | 15 | 0 | 3 |
| Start, s s | 5 | 2 | 0 | 1 | 0 | 4 | Finn, 2b, p | 5 | 2 | 2 | 1 | 6 | 1 |
| Cadogan, c f | 5 | 0 | 0 | 0 | 0 | 0 | Sweeney, p, 2b | 5 | 2 | 2 | 1 | 10 | 3 |
| Sheridan, 2b | 5 | 1 | 1 | 6 | 0 | 3 | Hickey, 3b, c | 4 | 1 | 1 | 5 | 2 | 1 |
| Creegan, c | 4 | 0 | 0 | 7 | 4 | 2 | Incell, r f | 4 | 3 | 2 | 0 | 0 | 1 |
| McElroy, p | 4 | 2 | 1 | 0 | 12 | 2 | Carroll, c, 3b | 4 | 0 | 0 | 5 | 3 | 2 |
| Total | 43 | 14 | 4 | 27 | 19 | 14 | Total | 41 | 11 | 10 | 27 | 22 | 13 |

| Innings | 1 | 2 | 3 | 4 | 5 | 6 | 7 | 8 | 9 | |
|---|---|---|---|---|---|---|---|---|---|---|
| Renos | 0 | 1 | 2 | 9 | 0 | 1 | 0 | 0 | 1 | 14 |
| Niantics | 1 | 2 | 1 | 0 | 0 | 3 | 1 | 1 | 2 | 11 |

Mr. Robert Hall, butter inspector in Ohio, says: "When butter is properly churned, both as to time and temperature, it becomes firm with very little working, and it is tenacious; but its most desirable state is waxy, when it can be moulded into any shape, and may be drawn out a considerable length without breaking. It is then styled gilt-edged. It is only in this state that butter possesses that rich, nutty flavor and smell, and shows up a rich, golden-yellow color, which imparts so high a degree of pleasure in eating it, and which increases its value manifold. It is not always necessary, when it smells sweet, to taste butter in judging it. The smooth, unctuous feeling, in rubbing a little between the finger and thumb, expresses at once its rich quality; the nutty smell and rich aroma indicate a similar taste; and the bright golden, glistening, cream-colored surface shows its height of cleanliness. It may be necessary, at times, to use the trier, or even use it until you become an expert in testing by taste, smell and rubbing.

There is a shooting match to come off next Sunday at Shell Mound between teams of fifty each, men from the First and Second Artillery Regiments. The match is only a friendly competition.

*Concluded from page 289.*

all his sons. For the following notes concerning the dam of Adair we are under obligations to his owner, E. H. Miller Jr:

Addie Lee was bred by E. J. Winegar, Esq., of Fort Jones, Siskiyou county, Cal. Her sire was Culver's Blackhawk, Culver's Blackhawk was said to be by Dave Hill of Vermont out of a thoroughbred mare.

Addie's dam was Nancy, pedigree unknown, but was a trotting mare and one of other trotters than Addie.

In September, 1872, Addie got a record on a San Francisco half-mile track of 2:36½. [She was then in foal by California Blackbird, and dropped a colt, Berlin, April 11, 1873.

In 1874 I had her trained; she showed a mile in 2:27, on Oakland track, but she went lame from a splint. In 1875 I bred her to Fred Low and she dropped a colt, Adelia, April 21, '76- She was bred in '76 and '77 to Fred Low and dropped a colt to him each year, to wit: in 1877 and 1878; she was then bred to Electioneer and on May 2, 1879, dropped Adair and has been bred each year since (and dropped a colt every year) to Electioneer.

Berlin, her colt by California Blackbird, has a record of 2:29¼, got in a race at Sacramento (which he won) June 3, 1880, being at the time dead lame in both fore feet.

Adelia by Fred Low, has a record of 2:33 obtained last spring (in June) at Sacramento races, where she won both the 3 m. and 2:40 races.

Adair you know of—I have by Electioneer out of Addie, Adelia two-year-old, Adina, yearling, and a sucking colt, all as promising as Adair was at same ages.

## Stanford Stake, 1882. List of Nominations.

No. 1. Jos. Cairn Simpson, Oakland, names bay colt Anteeo, by Electioneer, his dam Columbine by A. W. Richmond, grandam Columbia by imp. Bonnie Scotland. Anteeo was foaled May 5, 1879; is dark bay, black points, save that the near hind foot is white and a small white spot on right hip.

No. 2. Palo Alto Stock Farm, H. R. Covey, Superintendent, names b f Bonnie, by General Benton, her dam America by Ryedyk's Hambletonian, grandam Fanny Star by Sealy's American Star. Bonnie was foaled March 14, 1879; is brown, star in forehead, white hind ankles.

No. 3. Palo Alto Stock Farm names ch f Isnia, by General Benton, her dam Irene by Mohawk Chief; Grandam Laura Keene by Ryedyk's Hambletonian. Isnia was foaled June 10, 1879, chestnut, star, white hind ankles.

No. 4. Palo Alto Stock Farm names b f Hattie C., by Electioneer, her dam Melinche by St. Clair. Hattie C., foaled April 1, 1879; is brown, hind feet white.

No. 5. Palo Alto Stock Farm names b f Benefit, by General Benton, his dam Lucetta by Ryedyk's Hambletonian, grandam Lucy Almack by Young Engineer. Benefit was foaled April 10, 1879, is bay, white blaze in face, white spot on near hip, and white spot on side.

No. 6. N. T. Smith, San Francisco, names br c Clay, by Electioneer, his dam Maid of Clay by Henry Clay, grandam by Buliface Consol, son of imp. Consol. Foaled Feb. 22, 1879.

No. 7. E. H. Miller Jr., San Francisco, names b c Adair by Electioneer, his dam Addie Lee by Culver's Blackhawk.

No. 8. C. A. Spreckels, San Francisco, names b c Gus S., by Speculation, his dam Jennie, a pacing mare, pedigree unknown. Gus S. is bay, star in forehead, both hind ankles white.

No. 9. C. A. Spreckels, San Francisco, names ch f Kevstone, by Speculation, her dam Lady Aptos by Lodi, grandam Keystone by imp. Lapidist. Keystone 'is chestnut, star in face, white spot on off knee, near hind leg white.

No. 10. Clara Spreckels, S. F., names b c Speculator, by Speculation, his dam Patsy, by Alexander, grandam Molly, bred in Ohio, from a Bacchus horse. Spectator is bay, star, four white feet.

No. 11. J. D. Spreckels, S. F. names b c I. N. Pool, by Speculation, his dam by Skaggs' Rattler. I. N. Pool is bay, small white spot in forehead, near fore foot and off hind ankle white.

No. 12. John Mangels, San Francisco, names ch c Settler, by Speculation, his dam Ceta by Alexander, grandam Nora by Glencoe. Settler is chestnut, white stripe in forehead, a little white on off hind ankle.

No. 13. A. Waldstein, San Francisco, names b f Nellie W, by Electioneer, her dam sister to Aurora, by John Nelson. Nellie is bay, three white feet.

No. 14. H. W. Seale, Mayfield, names ch f Hattie Weir, by Elmo, her dam, Ella, by Chieftain.

No. 15. H. W. Seale, Mayfield, names ch g Longfellow, by Primero, son of Elmo, pedigree of dam unknown.

No. 16. James Garland, San Francisco, names dark bay filly Fanny Wickham, by Irvington, her dam, Fanny Wickham, by Niagara, grandam Fanny Wickham, by Herald. Fanny Wickham was foaled May 24, 1879, bay, star, white hind foot.

No. 17. William Corbitt, San Francisco, names ch c Arthurton Jr., by Arthurton, brother to Irvington, his dam Castille. Arthurton Jr. was foaled March 28, 1879, chestnut, small star, white hind ankles, white fore foot.

No. 18. J. B. McDonald, Marysville, Cal., names g c Brigade, by Brigadier, his dam American Maid.

No. 19. L. J. Rose, Sunny Slope, Los Angeles county, Cal., names J. W. Mackey's b f Eva (sister to Sweetheart), by Sultan, her dam Minnehaha. Eva is bay, one white hind foot.

No. 20. L. J. Rose names blk f Oro, by Del Sur, her dam by The Moor. Oro is black, has two hind legs white up to the hooks, one fore foot the same, the other a little white on the coronet, blaze face, white on lower jaw, and center of tail white.

No. 21. M. Saulsbury, San Francisco, names br c Jack Gilmer, by Gibraltar, son of Echo, his dam Kitty Gavin, by Field's Royal George. Jack Gilmer is brown, with star in forehead.

## The Race.

Weather so lovely as to make the most extravagant praise of it seem but a poor effort to reach out for the unattainable, track in perfect order and all the concomitants that go to make it the ideal race meeting, had only induced a small number of devoted trotmen to be present when the great stake was trotted. But what an appreciative and truly critical crowd it was. Scarce a man among them but knew the points and performances of the horses as well as the men who had trained them and could gauge their speed almost to a second as they brushed around the track. Decently and in order the usual preliminaries were disposed of and then the work for which much labor and preparation had been spent commenced. In the sulky behind Adair sat Wilbur Smith, the man who had trained him. Calmly conscious of victory he handled his horse as though about to take him round the stretch for an exercise trot. Hank McGregory, of whom the

boys say that he can drive a horse without a watch and tell within two seconds how fast he is going, drove Clay while Joseph Cairn Simpson took the destinies of Anteeo into his hands. Two scores and away the trio went, Clay leading his sulky's length as he passed the stand with Adair and Anteeo as even as a double team. Where the track turns sharp at the top Clay left his feet and Smith, who had kept Adair well in hand, allowed him to go up to first place. Simpson seeing Clay was in trouble pushed Anteeo along, but at the quarter he broke badly and made no further effort in the heat. Adair made the quarter in 40 seconds and though five lengths ahead of Clay did not slacken speed but rather improved it making the second quarter in 38 or the half in 1:18. Clay was nearly four lengths behind at the three-quarter pole, reached in 1:58, but McGregory had hopes of winning the heat and shook him up for all he was worth. Smith evidently knew that he had a bit in hand with Adair for he made no responsive effort and trotting the heat out easily, won with three lengths to spare; Anteeo a poor third. Time, 2:36½. This was the fastest heat that Adair had ever trotted but the ease which he did the work and the evenness of his stride showed that on a pinch he could cut off nearly all the odd seconds, and made the betting men very eager to get a slice of the pie that was awaiting his backers.

The start of the second heat was very unsatisfactory to the friends of Anteeo, though later events showed that he was not well enough to win in any heat. After one false start they were tapped off. Anteeo was breaking before he reached the wire and his driver, not expecting a send-off, was caught napping. As before, Clay had the lead, which he lost at the top turn by a break. He caught soon and at the quarter was two lengths in advance of Adair. In this order they went to the half-mile where Clay broke again and Adair ranged alongside but did not seem able to pass. Clay caught his gait very quickly and behaving well drew away from Adair as they rounded the lower turn where Smith drove rather wide. Exactly at the bottom of the track Adair misbehaved for the first time in the race, making a most demoralizing break. When he caught, his stride was short and he seemed nervous. A few yards more and he broke again, allowing Anteeo, who had fallen away badly, to come up to his wheel. This inspired Adair with ambition and the balance of the heat he trotted beautifully but had lost so much ground that Clay had lengths to spare at the finish. Anteeo was a poor third. Time, 2:36½.

Backers looked dubious and in their anxiety to hedge sent Adair down to $9 in the pools against $20 for the field.

The third heat was the slowest of the race owing to the number of breaks made by the leading horse. Adair commenced by breaking as soon as the bell tapped and behaved so badly that when Clay and Anteeo were going on even terms at the quarter he seemed to be virtually out of the race. But when he turned into the straight stretch at the back of the track Adair began to recover from his troubles and trotted faster than ever before in his life. Anteeo had fallen away behind Clay and past him Adair went as though he belonged to another class. Before the half was reached McGregory was startled out of his contemplation of a clear course ahead of him, by seeing Adair push first his head alongside of his wheel and then introduce his entire body to the front place. When McGregory got over his surprise at the appearance of Adair, whom he had fondly imagined was yards in the rear, he gave Clay a shaking up; but in spite of all his efforts Clay could not shake the big bay colt off. He got discouraged in trying and broke at the bottom of the track. Adair was leading two lengths when they straightened out into the home stretch and had an easy race, but repeating his galloping performances, he fell away two lengths behind Clay. This was less than 200 yards from home and though Adair when he caught trotted fast his task seemed hopeless and second place would have been the limit of his success had not Clay most fortunately tired and left his feet a few yards from the wire. Adair went up with a rush and won the heat by a bare neck, Anteeo a poor third. Time 2:40.

The fourth heat was not very fast but it was the best contested and most exciting one of the whole race. The horses were rather fractious at the score and three false starts were made before they got away. Anteeo had no occasion to complain of the start this time, for he was a full length ahead when the wire was passed. Clay did not do at all as well and when the quarter pole was reached was a good distance behind the leaders who were going like a double team. The pace was too hot for Anteeo and Adair had 'only to keep moving to open a gap of two lengths before the half mile was made. Clay by this time had got down to work and passing Anteeo challenged Adair for the lead. From the last turn to the stables Adair and Clay were neck and neck. Anteeo, who seemed to improve always at the end of the mile was coming up very fast. It was any one's race at about twenty yards from home when Clay left his feet and Adair won by about a length and a half; less than half a length separated Anteeo from Clay. Time 2:38.

Adair's victory was very popular, and long and loud were the cheers that greeted him and his driver, Wilbur Smith, as they turned to come back to the start to weigh. The spectators were heartily pleased with the race all through, and were satisfied that at least for once in their lives they had seen three horses in a race all fully extended from end to end. The race deserves to rank high among those which conduce to the honor and popularity of the track. There is no other State in the Union that could produce three such starters in a stake race, and though the time was not as fast as some expected to see it is certain that any one of the three entries could have trotted as fast as thirty but for the ravages of pinkeye and its attendant loss of work.

## How to Make Fine Butter.

The process of making butter is an important one, for the best butter may be spoiled and poor butter improved in the working. When the butter is churned it is taken from the churn and placed on a smooth maple, birch or chestnut table or other butter worker, or put into a bowl. If the churn will admit of it the buttermilk may be drawn off and clear, cold water poured into it and the butter washed in that way in separate waters until it runs off quite clear and the butter is quite free and clear. This is indispensable if the butter is expected to keep well. It is then salted at the rate of one ounce to the pound of butter. The butter is pressed out with the ladle, and never to be worked by the hands under any circumstances, and the salt is spread over it; it is then doubled and spread out again and cut and gashed with the ladle, but never rubbed or plastered, but only squeezed and pressed, until the salt is pretty evenly mixed; it is then put away in a cool place for twenty-four hours or less, as may be convenient. It will then appear streaky and patchy, and is worked over in the same way as before until it becomes free from the streakiness and even in color, by thorough mixture of the salt. This is done by squeezing it with the ladle, a small piece at a time, and pressing it out into a flat sheet, doubling it, and again squeezing it out, so as to get all the salt and moisture in it evenly through the mass. The color is then alike all over.

No more working is then required. The first working requires ten minutes for twenty or twenty-five pounds, the second about fifteen minutes. It should then break with a coarse, uneven fracture, much like that of a piece of beeswax, and should appear when cut of a granular texture and quite free from greasiness, and fine drops of brine should follow the knife as it cuts. It is not well to try to get all the moisture out of the butter, as this improves its texture and flavor. If the cream has been well kept and the butter well made and churned, it should have a very sweet and fragrant scent, quite free from acidity or pungency. It is a peculiar scent, and belongs only to the best butter, and when this odor is absent the right flavor is wanting, because the scent and aroma, and the flavor as well are all attributes of pure fresh butter. The butter should be packed as soon as it is worked the last time; no butter needs a second working, the packing should be quite free from all disagreeable scent or impurity; white oak, spruce, or white ash, are the best materials for the tubs or pails. White oak has an agreeable scent when fresh and stands first for butter packages. The package should first be scalded, then rinsed in cold water, and then rubbed with a little salt, then rinsed with a little water, just enough to wash off the salt but not to freshen the wood, and the butter is packed in the damp pail at once, being pressed down solid so that no air holes are left. The pail is filled completely full, and may be covered with a piece of muslin dipped in brine, or with paraffine paper, and close up at once tightly and put away in a cool place or sold, which is the best plan.—*Chicago Weekly Herald.*

## Insects on the Surface of Oranges.

When a dish of oranges is seen on the table for dessert the fact is hardly realized that in all probability their surface is the habitat of an insect of the cocus family. This tiny creature is found on the orange skin in every state of transformation, from the egg to the perfect insect during the winter months, instead of remaining dormant in the cold weather as is the case with most of the insect tribe. It would hardly be possible to find a St. Michael's or Tangerine orange that had not hundreds of these little creatures in various stages of development on its surface. Lemons, too, are frequently covered. Upon inspection, the skin of an orange will be found to be dotted over with brownish scarlet spots of various sizes. These specks can be easily removed with a needle; and when placed under a microscope an interesting scene is presented, consisting of a large number of eggs which are oval while bodies standing on end, like little bags of flour, some of the inhabitants of which may very probably be seen in process of emerging from the open end of the egg. The female insect, upon leaving the egg, has six legs, two long hair-like appendages, and no wings; it thrusts a sucker into the orange in order to obtain nourishment, and never moves again, passing through the various stages of development until it lays its eggs and dies. In the case of the male, which is larger, the chrysalis after a short period opens, and the insect flies off. The male is supplied with wings twice the length of its body, and each of the legs has a hook-like projection. It has four eyes and two antennæ, and is so tiny that it cannot be seen when flying. From some parts of Spain oranges come to us having their surface covered with a cocus of quite a different type. The surface of oranges, indeed, affords the possessor of a microscope an infinite amount of interest and amusement.—*Chambers' Journal*

## Clean Stables.

There is possibly no more repulsive sight than a filthy cow-stable, and one in which dairy cattle are housed is especially offensive. It has been demonstrated that cows who are neglected in this respect fail to yield a perfect flow of milk, and it is reasonable to suppose such is the case. The richest of food may be given them, but if their condition in the stall is anything but thrifty there it is. The foul odom of a filthy barn must necessarily permeate not only the animal's hide, but it has been proved that the meat of stall-fed steers, who have been fattened under these circumstances, will, when put upon the block and cut up, taste of the stable impurities. It would seem, therefore, that owners should appreciate the force of the old adage that "cleanliness is next to godliness," and beyond the fact that they are enabled to receive additional profits by closely watching their stock and providing clean quarters for them, advance even one step higher, and from the stand-point of the humanitarian at least treat their stock with common decency. City consumers often detect to a greater or less extent the presence of the barn-yard odor in their milk. Barns for the accommodation of dairy cows should receive the same care as those devoted to the average horse. Their health depends largely on their surroundings, and rocking piles of manure with the foul air which essentially arises therefrom are not conducive to health, nor is it possible under these circumstances to furnish good, pure, wholesome milk.

Jay Beach is negotiating for a ranch in Rogue river valley probably in search of a better place to winter his trotters than he has at Linkville. Cascade farm is a healthy place and the pure air and substantial grasses insure hardy and vigorous horses, but the snow precludes that all-the-year round education which Mr. Beach's more southern neighbors are able to give their colts, and we suspect that he does not propose to allow these climatic disadvantages to continue.

The Walla Walla *Statesman* says that there is not a six months' supply of beef cattle in that section of the territory.

# THE RIFLE.

## SHOOTING AT BERKELEY.

### The California Rifle Association's Tournament at Shell Mound Park.

Last Saturday and Sunday the above named Association held their fall shooting at Shell Mound, Berkeley. The day was pleasant and quite calm for this time of the year; the attendance was large and composed of sharpshooters who took a keen interest in every shot that was fired.

The shooting for the first day began for the

#### Andrews Trophy.

This trophy was given to the Association by Col. A. A. Andrews of the Diamond Palace, to be competed for by military company teams. It was shot for first in May, 1881, and won by Company E, First Artillery Regiment; it was won at the fall shooting of that year by the same company. Last spring Company C, First Regiment, won it, and again last Saturday on a score of 519 which is the best score on record in the United States. The following are the individual scores:

COMPANY E, FIRST INFANTRY.

| | | |
|---|---|---|
| T. C. Carson | | 80 |
| W. F. Lohman | | 73 |
| M. N. Laufenberg | | 76 |
| J. Stewart | | 80 |
| T. Murphy | | 81 |
| L. Barrow | | 84 |
| **Total** | | **479** |

COMPANY C, FIRST INFANTRY.

| | | |
|---|---|---|
| B. T. Sims | | 86 |
| T. F. Kelly | | 84 |
| F. Cummings | | 84 |
| L. G. Perkins | | 87 |
| R. N. Scott | | 88 |
| S. E. Klein | | 82 |
| **Total** | | **519** |

#### Pacific Slope Match

was for a beautiful bronze figure of a horseman. This trophy was put up for the competition of all military teams of the Pacific Coast. It was shot for and won the first time in the fall meeting in 1881, by the California team. This time it was won by the Nevada team, whose score of 866 deserves special notice. The trophy will have to be shot for in Nevada the next time it is competed for.

NEVADA TEAM.

| | | |
|---|---|---|
| W. H. Burke | | 86 |
| G. C. Thaxter | | 91 |
| C. H. Galcaba | | 90 |
| W. M. Little | | 87 |
| Mr. Crawford | | 86 |
| Mr. Safell | | 88 |
| J. R. King | | 81 |
| Geo. Cowing | | 84 |
| H. G. Parker | | 88 |
| G. Gallagher | | 82 |
| **Total** | | **866** |

CALIFORNIA TEAM.

| | | |
|---|---|---|
| T. F. Kelly | | 88 |
| F. Kuhle | | 88 |
| S. I. Kellogg | | 85 |
| T. Carson | | 82 |
| C. B. Fennell | | 83 |
| L. Barrow | | 80 |
| L. G. Perkins | | 81 |
| William Wright | | 80 |
| J. Warren | | 78 |
| W. F. Leaman | | 84 |
| **Total** | | **817** |

#### The Centennial Trophy

was given by the City of San Francisco in 1876 for the competition of regimental teams of the National Guards of California. It has been won for seven years by the First Regiment. The original intention was to have the trophy shot for, for one hundred years, but on after consideration the time has been reduced to five years. The First Regiment have again laid their claim to the trophy by winning it the first time on the five year stretch.

FIRST REGIMENT INFANTRY, N. G. C.

| | | |
|---|---|---|
| J. E. Klein | | 90 |
| L. G. Perkins | | 88 |
| F. Cummings | | 86 |
| Corporal L. Barrow | | 87 |
| Sergeant T. Carson | | 84 |
| B. T. Sims | | 86 |
| Corporal Fredericks | | 88 |
| Private T. F. Kelly | | 85 |
| Private T. Murphy | | 82 |
| Private W. T. Leaman | | 81 |
| **Total** | | **860** |

SECOND ARTILLERY REGIMENT, N. G. C.

| | | |
|---|---|---|
| Corp. Fred Kuhle | | 87 |
| Lieut. E. G. Sprowl | | 88 |

PRIVATE COLUMN (continued)

| | | |
|---|---|---|
| Private W. Wright | | 86 |
| Lieut. J. F. Warren | | 84 |
| C. L. Leds | | 80 |
| Lieut. Wm. Shaunnessy | | 78 |
| Private C. B. Fennell | | 77 |
| Corp. H. J. Mangels | | 74 |
| Private G. S. Palmer | | 70 |
| Private Taylor | | 62 |
| **Total** | | **790** |

#### The Association Pistol Trophy.

In order to encourage pistol practice and pistol sharpshooters the association offered a silver cup of elegant design to the team that should win it three times. It was won the first time last spring by Capt. Douglas' team No. 1; Capt. S. F. Police; this fall by Captain Douglas' team, No. 1; Capt. Short's team, S. F. Police, and the Citizens' teams tied in points but the latter made the better score according to Creedmoor.

CO. A., S. F. POLICE—CAPT. DOUGLAS' TEAM, NO. 1.

| | | |
|---|---|---|
| S. Whitworth | | 73 |
| N. T. Fields | | 73 |
| M. Berges | | 73 |
| D. D. Linville | | 73 |
| W. D. Scott | | 71 |
| D. A. Peckinpah | | 70 |
| J. Clark | | 70 |
| F. Holland | | 70 |
| R. Cook | | 70 |
| J. C. Lane | | 70 |
| **Total (90 per cent.)** | | **705** |

CO. A., S. F. POLICE—CAPT. DOUGLAS' TEAM, NO. 2.

| | | |
|---|---|---|
| A. T. Field | | 73 |
| M. J. Onslop | | 72 |
| Jas. Gillin | | 72 |
| G. R. Purdy | | 72 |
| H. A. Patterson | | 72 |
| Thos. Flanders | | 71 |
| G. L. Case | | 70 |
| W. M. Briggs | | 70 |
| J. F. McCarthy | | 70 |
| G. G. Simons | | 70 |
| **Total (93 per cent.)** | | **693** |

CO. S. F. POLICE—CAPT. SHORT'S TEAM.

| | | |
|---|---|---|
| Langtree | | 73 |
| Oates | | 72 |
| Reynolds | | 71 |
| Cockrill | | 71 |
| Thompson | | 70 |
| Shear | | 70 |
| Boyd | | 70 |
| Smith | | 69 |
| Whalen | | 69 |
| Paddock | | 68 |
| **Total** | | **866** |

CITIZENS' TEAM.

| | | |
|---|---|---|
| John Olsen | | 73 |
| S. I. Kellogg | | 72 |
| T. R. Jones | | 70 |
| J. E. Klein | | 70 |
| G. E. Beaver | | 69 |
| H. D. Merriwether | | 68 |
| F. Kuhle | | 68 |
| Charlie Carr | | 68 |
| O. N. Thompson | | 68 |
| **Total** | | **693** |

### The Second Day.

The day was quite as pleasant as the day before; the attendance was just as large. Two days could not have been taken together that would have proved more satisfactory to the riflemen than those selected. There was just enough wind on both days to blow off the heated air or mirage that rises from the ground on warm days, and not enough to interfere with the shooting. The shooting of the second day began with the

#### Governor Perkins' Trophy.

This trophy was presented to the association by Governor Perkins in 1876. It was won the first time by F. Kuhnle, twice by Sergt. N. Williams of the Oakland Light Cavalry, and the last time by F. Kuhnle again. It has to be won three times by one person before it becomes his property. In connection with the trophy were seven cash prizes ranging from $15 to $1. The following are the competition and their scores:

PRIZE WINNERS.

| | | |
|---|---|---|
| Lieut. F. Kuhnle | | 48 |
| S. I. Kellogg | | 48 |
| T. F. Kelly | | 48 |
| R. N. Beaver | | 48 |
| H. D. Merryweather | | 48 |
| H. T. Sims | | 48 |
| F. Kuhle | | 48 |
| E. Williams | 49 J. E. Klein | 46 |
| M. Burke | 49 M. Laufenburg | 44 |
| M. Haake | 46 P. Jacoby | 44 |
| Geo. C. Haskins | 46 R. McMillingIN | 46 |

#### General Barnes' Trophy.

In 1876 Gen. Barnes gave a beautiful medal that goes under the above name. It has been won twice by Sergt. N. Williams, once by F. Kuhnle' and the last time by S. I. Kellogg. It has to be won three times by one person. The following are the competitors:

| | | |
|---|---|---|
| S. I. Kellogg | | 47 |
| T. F. Kelly | | 46 |
| F. Cummings | | 46 |
| F. Kuhnle | | 46 |
| J. E. Klein | | 46 |

#### Short Range Match.

was for $108, that was divided into twenty-one cash prizes. The shooting was done on a ring target. The following riflemen drew prizes:

| | | | | | | |
|---|---|---|---|---|---|---|
| B. T. Sims | | 9 | 10 | 11 | 12 | 12—66 |
| Thomas Gallagher | | 12 | 11 | 12 | 12 | 4—61 |
| R. N. Beaver | | 9 | 11 | 10 | 10 | 10—59 |
| L. G. Perkins | | 11 | 11 | 9 | 7 | 10—58 |
| H. G. Parker | | 9 | 11 | 11 | 10 | 7—57 |
| F. Kuhle | | 9 | 8 | 11 | 11 | 7—56 |
| G. S. Palmer | | 8 | 11 | 12 | 9 | 6—56 |
| L. Barrow | | 11 | 10 | 8 | 9 | 8—55 |
| Jul. Klein | | 11 | 11 | 10 | 9 | 4—55 |
| J. E. Klein | | 7 | 10 | 7 | 10 | 9—54 |
| M. N. Laufenburg | | 9 | 10 | 11 | 6 | 9—54 |
| T. Carson | | 10 | 9 | 7 | 8 | 8—53 |
| C. Cummings | | 10 | 7 | 8 | 10 | 8—53 |
| T. H. McMinnigay | | 5 | 8 | 11 | 9 | 9—53 |
| L. Haake | | 9 | 7 | 4 | 9 | 10—52 |
| J. E. Shwalt | | 8 | 9 | 10 | 7 | 9—52 |

#### Military Match.

This was a new match with all cash prizes. The distance was 200 and 500 yards, Creedmoor targets. We would call

attention to the first three scores, as they are the highest ever made with a military rifle.

PRIZE WINNERS.

| | | |
|---|---|---|
| G. C. Thaxter | | 95 |
| F. Kuhnle | | 94 |
| H. D. Merriwether | | 93 |
| F. Cumming | | 92 |
| S. I. Kellogg | | 92 |
| J. R. King | | 91 |
| F. Kuhle | | 91 |
| L. Barrow | | 90 |
| J. E. Klein | | 90 |
| Charlie Galcaba | | 90 |

#### The Nevada State Trophy.

This trophy is a silver cup, presented by General Batterman of Nevada. This is the first time it has been shot for, and only won by one point, by the team of Company C, First Regiment, over the Nevada Team.

COMPANY C, FIRST INFANTRY.

| | | |
|---|---|---|
| Sims | | 45 |
| Perkins | | 44 |
| Baye | | 44 |
| Cummings | | 44 |
| Kelly | | 44 |
| Templeton | | 40 |
| Scott | | 40 |
| Merriwether | | 40 |
| Klein | | 40 |
| Allen | | 40 |
| **Total** | | **433** |

NEVADA TEAM.

| | | |
|---|---|---|
| Thaxter | | 45 |
| Safell | | 44 |
| Slocum | | 44 |
| Crawford | | 43 |
| Gildrest | | 43 |
| Cowing | | 43 |
| Little | | 43 |
| King | | 43 |
| Haskins | | 41 |
| Parker | | 41 |
| **Total** | | **422** |

COMPANY C, SECOND ARTILLERY.

| | | |
|---|---|---|
| Lieut. Schoenfeld | | 44 |
| L. Haake | | 44 |
| G. Spencer | | 44 |
| H. J. Mangels | | 44 |
| F. Kuhle | | 43 |
| E. Louis | | 42 |
| M. Warckett | | 40 |
| A. Huber | | 40 |
| J. Plagemah | | 40 |
| P. H. Will | | 40 |
| **Total** | | **404** |

#### Short Range Trophy.

This trophy is a fine silver cup and it is the first time shot for. Six teams entered; again the Nevada team No. 1 and Company C. First Artillery came into very close contest, the latter again winning by only one point.

COMPANY C, FIRST INFANTRY.

| | | |
|---|---|---|
| H. D. Merriwether | | 42 |
| J. E. Klein | | 42 |
| T. F. Kelly | | 42 |
| T. Sims | | 42 |
| F. Cummings | | 42 |
| L. G. Perkins | | 42 |
| **Total** | | **360** |

NEVADA TEAM, NO. 1.

| | | |
|---|---|---|
| Galcaba | | 42 |
| Burke | | 42 |
| King | | 42 |
| Gildarist | | 42 |
| Slocum | | 42 |
| Thaxter | | 42 |
| **Total** | | **359** |

NEVADA TEAM, NO. 2.

| | | |
|---|---|---|
| Gallagher | | 42 |
| Safell | | 42 |
| Crawford | | 42 |
| Kane | | 42 |
| Cowing | | 42 |
| Little | | 42 |
| **Total** | | **350** |

COMPANY E, FIRST INFANTRY.

| | | |
|---|---|---|
| Carson | | 42 |
| Murphy | | 42 |
| Stewart | | 42 |
| Lohman | | 42 |
| Barrow | | 42 |
| Laufenberg | | 42 |
| **Total** | | **345** |

COMPANY B SECOND ARTILLERY.

| | | |
|---|---|---|
| Lieut. Schoenfeld | | 41 |
| L. Haake | | 41 |
| G. Spencer | | 41 |
| H. J. Mangels | | 41 |
| F. Kuhle | | 41 |
| O. Louis | | 41 |
| **Total** | | **340** |

RIFLE INFANTRY TEAM.

| | | |
|---|---|---|
| Lieut. Kuhnle | | 44 |
| Lieut. Green | | 44 |
| Sergt. Wilkinson | | 44 |
| Sergt. Mann | | 44 |
| Corp. Crawford | | 44 |
| Private Haight | | 44 |

#### Second Pistol Match.

Twenty cash prizes were offered and though the thirty entries were not all made the prizes have been paid. The distance shot was thirty yards at ring targets.

| | | | | | | | | | | | | |
|---|---|---|---|---|---|---|---|---|---|---|---|---|
| N. T. Fields | | 11 | 11 | 12 | 12 | 11 | 12 | 11 | 6 | 12 | 12—112 |
| G. E. Beaver | | 10 | 10 | 11 | 11 | 12 | 11 | 6 | 10 | 10—104 |
| D. A. Peckinpah | | 12 | 10 | 11 | 10 | 11 | 9 | 7 | 10 | 12—104 |
| B. Cockrill | | 10 | 11 | 9 | 11 | 11 | 9 | 11 | 11—104 |
| Harry Root | | 10 | 10 | 10 | 9 | 11 | 9 | 11 | 11—102 |
| J. E. Klein | | 10 | 10 | 9 | 11 | 11 | 9 | 10 | 10—100 |
| F. D. Linville | | 9 | 11 | 11 | 9 | 9 | 9 | 12—100 |
| Philo Jacoby | | 10 | 11 | 9 | 10 | 11 | 9 | 9—100 |
| O. N. Thompson | | 10 | 7 | 10 | 11 | 9 | 9 | 8—100 |
| L. Whitworth | | 8 | 10 | 11 | 11 | 11 | 11—99 |
| W. D. Scott | | 9 | 9 | 10 | 9 | 11 | 10—98 |
| John Olsen | | 8 | 11 | 10 | 12 | 10 | 9—98 |
| M. Berges | | 9 | 10 | 10 | 10 | 9 | 9—97 |
| J. Clark | | 10 | 9 | 9 | 10 | 11 | 7—97 |
| W. S. Coles | | 11 | 11 | 10 | 10 | 10 | 9—96 |
| F. Holland | | 9 | 10 | 8 | 10 | 11 | 7—95 |
| M. M. Purdy | | 9 | 12 | 11 | 11 | 9 | 7—94 |
| A. Sharp | | 11 | 10 | 11 | 9 | 11—92 |
| J. F. McCarthy | | 10 | 9 | 9 | 9 | 8—79 |

There never was a larger tournament held on this coast nor one that attracted the attention of the sharpshooter more. As the above scores show every victorious team or individual

or rather no points to spare. Two instances can be
one where the Nevada State Trophy hung on the
of one point and the other when the Short Range
was won on a similar circumstance. In the first
the Nevada team had made their score of 422 points,
y C's team had all shot but one man, Lieut. J. E.
is getting or not getting five bullseyes in his last
ould decide the match. Both teams stood in breath-
spense while Mr. Ellen was shooting, and on his
his fifth bullseye both teams gave him a rousing
In the Short Range match the circumstances stood
ly the same and Company C's man, Mr. F. Cummings,
loudly cheered when he made his final and deciding
Well might they be cheered, for the men from Nevada
ey shot against, were "foemen worthy of their steel,"
d it not been that one of the Nevada shots, Mr. Thax-
been sick for several months and was in poor shoot-
dition, the match might have terminated otherwise.
Nevada teams used the Sharps military rifle while the
uld teams used the Springfield military rifle. There are
ersons in the East who are partial to the Sharps rifle
inkthat a Springfield ought to be compared to the old-
ned musket for shooting qualities, but the above scores
that the Springfield rifle is got to be laughed at.
Tuesday evening the victorious teams assembled at the
ry head-quarters on New Montgomery street to receive
izes. After the trophies and medals had been distrib-
the cash prizes were given out; many of the smaller
prizes were donated to the Association by the more
minded. After the distribution was finished, Com-
C invited all the sharpshooters, military and private, to
armory on Post street, where they were entertained
usic speeches pertinent to the occasion, and recita-
Refreshments were served at 10 o'clock, after which
A. Andrews, in behalf of the members of Company
pped to the front and, with a well-worded speech, pre-
Col. J. H. Dickinson with a beautifully framed certifi-
f life membership in the company, as a token of the
t with which all the members hold their commander.
Association's cash receipts of this year amount to
0. The money paid out for cash prizes amounts to $1,900,
edals and trophies $300 and the other $100 or less has
paid for necessary expenses. There is some talk of the
lation getting a range of its own. This is a very good
and if a move is made in this direction it should receive
upport of all who are interested in rifle matters.

## The Next International Rifle Match.

e National Rifle Association held a meeting yesterday at
William street. Mr. Seabury read a draft of a letter
h the Committee on the Return International Match ask
empowered by the Executive Committee of the National
Association to address to the National Rifle Association
real Britain. The necessary authority was granted.
letter requests that the National Rifle Association of
t Britain will consent to such modifications of the con-
ns under which the last match was shot as will permit
a return match the use of the wind gauge on the rear
; the improved barley-corn sight, which is a straight
cal projection instead of being cone-shaped, as were the
ghts of the British team in the late match, and concede the
ility of National Guardsmen for places on the American
who may enlist on or between January 1, 1883. In-
eral terms it urges the advisability of rendering the con-
ons of this and subsequent international matches capable
uch changes as will admit the use of American improve-
ts may be made from time to time applicable to military
pons. The terms of the last match required that all mem-
of the American team should previously have been
mbers of the National Guard for one year. It is desired
hange this clause that there may be a large field from
ch to select the American team. The Executive Commit-
was also asked to authorize the purchase in England of
Mitford rifles, such as were used by the British team, the
set being to have on hand serviceable weapons in case
erican manufacturers should fail to produce in time a gun
al to the British. This was laid on the table on represen-
ons from Colonel Bodine and Colonel Litchfield that guns
american manufacture would soon be ready which would
fler such foreign purchases unnecessary; Colonel Bodine
lready testing a new gun.—N. Y. World, Oct. 20.

HONOLULU RIFLEMEN.—A rifle match took place about the
idle of last month between a team composed of officers of
United States steamer Alaska and a team selected from
Honolulu Rifle Association. His majesty, who is Presi-
t of the Association, did the honors of the occasion. The
ge selected was 200 yards, and resulted in favor of the
ska team by forty-one points.

t is commonly known that owls have two or three sets of
ing in the course of a season; but as far as I can make
, after sitting upon the first egg, or pair of eggs, and
ching the birds, no further effort in that direction is made.
ecely after the owlets are out of the shell, the hen-bird
s one or two more beautiful white eggs, but does not sit,
eting herself to feeding the insatiable little monsters she
started into life, and the warmth of their bodies hatches
next owlet. This one hatched, another egg is laid with
same result, that is rivelled by the young ones' warmth.
apes from the shell, and once more an egg or two occupy
nest, so that in the same corner in a shallow spot may be
n an owlet three-parts grown, another half grown, another
v hours old, and a couple of eggs—four stages in all;
t, if inspected by day, the three youngsters will be seen
ddled together in very good fellowship, one and all fast
ep, and the eggs in the coldest place outside. The sight
not pleasing, as may be supposed from the description of
young owls; but if the eye is offended, what is to be said
the nose? Take something in a bad state of putrefaction
t arithmetically square it; the result will be an approach
the foul odor of a nest of owls in hot weather. The
son is not far to seek, when it is borne in mind that the
t is a bird of prey; but all the same I have visited the nest
lier in the season, and found the place quite scentless,
t that, too, at a time when ranged in a semicircle about
young were no less than twenty-two young rats and full-
vn mice, so fresh that they must have been caught during
preceding night. the larder being supplemented by a
ple of young rabbits. It, then, a pair of owls provide so
any specimens of mischievous vermin in a night, they
tainly earn the title of friends of man. When hunting for
d, the owl glides along on silent wing beside some barn or
ck, and woe betide the cowering mouse or ratling that is
sy on the grain! As an owl passes over, down goes one
, and four sharp claws have snatched the little quadruped
m the ground, the four points seeming to slope toward a
mmon center, so that escape is impossible. Every seizure
performed with claws; the beak being reserved for dividing
r animal when too large.—London Graphic.

# THE GUN.

### Decoying Snipe.

The fondness which a large class of shooting men have
for what is known as "bay snipe shooting" cannot be
overestimated. Indeed, it is a sport which fills a gap in
the sportsman's year, as it occurs at a season when all
game birds save the woodcock are directed by law not to
be shot at or had in possession. They vary many persons
who are averse to taking the field during the heated
term prefer the pleasure of shooting at birds that come to
them rather than expose themselves to the discomforts
of toiling after the woodcock in its almost impenetrable
swamps. The pleasures of bay snipe shooting are many,
as it affords an endless variety of shots and requires but
little or no exertion to follow successfully, as the guns
is concealed in blinds and the birds are attracted within
shot by means of decoys or stools and by the whistled
imitation of their calls.

The practice of shooting fowl over decoys dates back to
a very early period, and for a long time only live birds
were employed by the sportsman. Then, in wild fowl
shooting, it was the customary practice to use wild ducks
and geese, tame birds resembling the wild ones in color
sometimes being selected by way of a makeshift, but the
wild birds that had been crippled and then tamed were
always preferred. These birds were readily taught to
invite their brethren to destruction, and the most clamorous were considered the most valuable. But in Italy
a revolving practice was in vogue, that of burning out
the eyes of the decoy fowl with a red hot needle. This
would make them very noisy, and the fowlers upheld
their cruelty by saying: "These are the happiest birds in
the world because they are always singing." Later on,
however, it was discovered that, except in geese and black
duck shooting, it was impracticable to collect live decoys,
so our handy bayman turned his attention to making a
wooden counterfeit, which was found to answer as an
economical and excellent substitute. Indeed, the custom
of manufacturing their own decoys has grown to be so
prevalent among the coast gunners that during the long
winter evenings it is a common thing to see the bayman
busily engaged in whittling away at a duck's head or a
set of snipe stools before his cheery cabin fire.

The snipe family, much less wary than their webfooted
cousins, were for a long time so plentiful that a sufficient
bag could be made by simply stationing one's self on the
meadows where they resorted to feed. But no sooner
was the flint and steel supplanted by the detonating system than they, too, had to be lured by the modernized
wooden stool. At first the counterfeits were clumsily
contrived, and even now in remote localities of our coast
triangular blocks, daubed with one color, with a ten-
penny nail stuck in one point for a bill, will be found
perched about on the mud flats during the season. But
the educated and methodic snipe of the fashionable gunning stations now demands a correctly modeled and artistically colored decoy, else he will say, "Not for foe."
while he quickly ascends to realms of bliss. But no
painted bird can be compared to the dead one, and most
of our most experienced gunners utilize the birds they
shoot by running the point of a reed or slight stick under the skin of the neck and set them up in natural
positions on the mud flats or sand bars. The best decoys, however, are the wing-tipped birds. They are
"pegged out"—that is, a string about a foot in length is
tied to one of their legs and the other end is secured to a
stick which is driven into the sand. No sooner does a
flock of birds come in sight than the cripples begin to
flutter in vain to join their traveling friends. This attracts the attention of the passers, and, after a few
repeated answers to each other's call, the flock circles
over the cripples, and often lights on the sand beside
them.

There is another way practiced by the gunners of
Southern New Jersey and Virginia which is the most
killing device known to the shooting. On the large,
bald marshes there the "Sickle bill" and "Jack" select
places to roost. Should the gunner be fortunate enough
to wing one of these birds he secretes himself in a bunch
of high grass. When the curlew return towards evening from their feeding grounds they lower their flight
and come whistling over the marsh. The gunner, who
holds the cripple by both legs, begins bobbing it up and
down and by pinching the back of its neck obliges it to
cry out. The moment the flock spy the fluttering bird
and hear its cry they wheel in their course and swoop
down upon it. Nor does the rattling of the shout into
their ranks appear to hinder their kindly intention to
succor an unfortunate brother; for they return again
and again to their aerial charge, until, dismayed and
alarmed at last by the incessant firing, the depleted flock
call together their scattered forces and bear away for a
safer retreat, leaving behind the ground covered with
the dead and wounded. In this way many birds are
killed, but in all by bird shooting a large number of
cripples are not recovered.

There is still another mode carried on for alluring the
bay snipe, which applies more strictly to the shooting of
the marlin willet, ornithologically called the semi-pal-
mated tatler. In the egging season these birds congregate in vast numbers on the low sandy beaches of Eastern
Virginia. There the gunner goes, taking with him a
sample of the orthodox "yaller dog." The little cur
has been trained to run within ten yards, or instantly return to his master at the sound of his whistle. No sooner
has the dog been let loose among the tribe of little
mothers than the utmost consternation prevails, the birds
leave the sand and fill the air with their plaintive and
terrified cries. Darting backward and forward at first,
and circling over the intruder, their fear soon gives way
to rage. At this they go, swooping down and almost
striking him with their bills and wings. Watching these
maneuvres from a distance stands the gunner. When
he sees that the birds have centered their whole attention upon the dog he gives a low whistle, and at straight
as an arrow the dog comes running to his master's feet,
while the infuriated birds follow him up, into the jaws
of death. Thus are the affectionate instincts of the mother

made use of by man to bring about her destruction.
Hundreds of willets are by this means toled up to the
gunner in one day, and the bags are often immense and
the profits correspondingly great. As a mode of butchery it is a success, but those who follow it deserve the
contempt of every gunner in the land. The dividing
line between killing cruelly and shooting for sport is
plainly defined, and the torturing of crippled birds as
described above does not belong to the true sportsman.

The shooting at bay snipe is either carried on from
blinds or boxes. The former are constructed on the bars
and high shoals and on the marshes, beside the ponds
where the tide does not reach. They are made of cedar
boughs and salt water bushes, grass, reeds, etc., and
often contain a bench for the accommodation of the
shooter. The boxes, however, are only used on the shoals
during ebb tide, or on the bald marshes where the wary
curlew makes his home. They are made of light material, so as to be easily handled, and in size resemble a
coffin somewhat. The box is taken to the shoals and
sunk in the sand, and as it is made watertight the shooter
can sit on his back without fear of a ducking. Whenever it is practicable the stools should be placed to the
windward of the blind, and at all times the decoys should
be set face to the wind. This arrangement will afford
much better flock shots, as the birds need the resistance
of the wind before alighting, and while circling to secure this advantage the flock is apt to double and "lap,"
and as the birds hustle together the best chances are
given for a raking shot.

The birds fly best during a stiff southwesterly wind.
their flights being conducted early in the morning and
late in the afternoon. In the middle of the day, except in cloudy or rainy weather, the last of the an
causes them to rest in their aerial voyage. But when a
"flight is on" there are always enough scattering flocks
passing during the midday to keep the eye of the shooter
on the constant lookout and his hand in practice. Seated in his place of concealment he watches the quarter
from where the birds are sure to come. Soon a small
cloud is seen approaching, which, as it nears, proves to be
a flock of snipe. Long before their shrill whistle is
borne down upon the wind the ever alert bayman has
sent out his call of welcome. Herein really lies his art,
and nothing but long practice will enable him to distinguish at the great distance the variety of birds coming
towards him; for out of the twenty or more different
kinds of bay snipe each variety has its own peculiar cry.
With rare skill can most bayman imitate each call, from
the prolonged, shrill quivering whistle of the jack curlew
and the plaintive treble notes of the black-breast plover
to the whispering chirp of the tiny oxeye. It is the tyro
alone who overdoes the matter and pays dear for his
whistle by seeing the birds swing away after having
headed for the stools and give his blind a wide berth.
—New York Herald.

### Bear vs. Panther.

Peter Stewart was once hunting in Rockland when he saw
some deer bones lying at the mouth of a crevice in some
rocks. He knew that it was a panther's den, and that the
bones were the remnant of a feast the companions had made
on a deer they had captured. Stewart hid himself behind a
tree and waited developments. Imagine his surprise when he
saw a big bear come out of the cave, carrying under his arm
a panther kitten, which was squalling and kicking with all its
might. The bear rose on its haunches and gave the kitten a
box or two on the ears with its fore paw, squeezed it to death
and threw it on the ground. The bear then returned to the
cave, and in a short time came out with another kitten under
its arm. This was treated as its companion had been. What
the future intentions of the bear were Stewart never found
out, for the second kitten had barely been stifled when the
mother panther appeared on the scene. This seemed to take
the bear by surprise. The old panther saw her kittens lying
on the ground. She bounded first to one and then to the
other, smelling and licking them, and uttering plaintive cries.
Then she turned to the bear, which remained in the erect position it had assumed when squeezing the second kitten to
death. With a yell that almost froze the blood of the hunter,
used as he was to the fury of panthers, she sprang upon the
bear, and fastened her claws in the shaggy coat and her fangs
in its throat. The bear hurled its antagonist ten feet away
with its powerful paws, and then attempted to escape a second attack by flight. But the panther was upon it in an instant,and a terrible conflict ensued. The bear endeavored to
catch the panther in its hug, but the latter was too agile, and
with every spring upon its huge enemy the panther inflicted
terrible wounds with its sharp claws. The blood poured
from a dozen great gashes in the bear's body, and at last the
panther leaped on the bear as it stood facing her, and fastening her teeth in its throat, thrust the long, sharp nails of her
hind feet into its vitals. The bear fell to the ground dead.
As the panther was returning to her dead kittens Stewart shot
her through the heart.

BAD LUCK.—Two young hunters got aboard the last train
from Alviso, last Sunday, and hastily pushing their game
bags under the seat sat down; their faces wore an expression
that resembled in length the resolutions of a temperance
meeting at the beginning of a political campaign. They said
but little and would not let anyone see the contents of the
bags. One of their friends, however, pulled the bag out from
under the back seat and found five ducks. The two hunters
finally let it out that they had lost their way in the fog
on the marshes and could not find the blinds till nearly 10
o'clock. This accounts for their bad luck and Mr. H. Gotcher
and T. Pearson may be congratulated in escaping the scandal of obliquity of vision over the gun barrel for it is not
charged by anyone that they scored any dogs, pigs or men or
turkeys on this trip.

CATCHING A BEAR WITH SALT.—Recently two teamsters,
coming to Hailey from Vienna, camped near the timber
above Boulder, one going out for game while the other remained to make bread. As he got out a sack of salt, a cinnamon bear approached, and the teamster, knowing about
catching bears with salt, held a handful out, which the bear
immediately licked clean—then asked for more. The third
handful was being approached when the other man returned,
and immediately took the trace-chains and some rope and
bound the bear tightly. His bearship stood the tying with
good humor, and was placed in the wagon and brought to
Hailey,

## Pheasant Shooting.

"I tell you what it be, sir, it ain't been no poachers at all, but you can't have both foxes and pheasants." The speaker was a burly Yorkshireman, clad in velveteens, a keeper on a northern estate, and the individual whom he addressed was his master, the landlord, the time 4 o'clock in the afternoon of a day in October. The gentleman in question had asked, as usual, a large party down to shoot his covers, and he was rather disgusted to find that the game on the property was less by half than they had found last year. Sit or seven years before there was no better stocked preserve in the whole country, but after a lapse of twenty years fox hunting had been reintroduced, and every lord, keen shots or otherwise, had been asked to support the M. F. H., who maintained the pack at his own expense. Foxes had been brought in and laid down in large numbers, and after a few years there was one to about every five acres of gorse or woodland. Game, of course, began to get very difficult to preserve, and each season saw a slight diminution in the death-rate at the close of the day's sport; but so long as the hedge-rows were full of rabbits, pheasants remained unmolested. Reynard will always prefer fur to feather if he can get it, but the moment fur begins to fail he will make a meal of anything. Indeed, I recollect seeing one on a cold winter day, when snow was on the ground, take, after much effort, the body of a dead cock off a pole in a field of young wheat. It is then that, in spite of all the precautions of "velveteens," pheasants begin to disappear, the old hen is lifted off her nest, or the whereabouts made known of the young brood by the evening crow of the old cock, and used one by one for breakfast or supper as required. Of course, the keeper is blamed for not watching better for poachers, but in a country where foxes abound poachers well know that the pheasants are not likely to repay them for their risk and trouble. Yet the keepers in such positions find themselves most awkwardly placed. The covers are drawn blank twice running, and then every hard-riding young squire openly giveth a verdict of "unjustifiable vulpecide." Not unfrequently the landlord of the estate, if a keen shot, gives his keeper orders not to kill foxes, but in such a way as to lead the man to shoot them when he gets a quiet chance, and there is nobody looking, and put them out of sight. Notwithstanding all that it is impossible to rear pheasants in the old-fashioned way in a fox-preserving country, and so we have during the past few years introduced the barn-door system with its most ungovernmentlike attendant, the battue. In the good old days of dumbers, pheasant shooting was a sport for princes, as nothing could be finer than the sensation experienced in knocking down a grand old cock as he came sailing majestically over the tree tops, straight in his flight as an arrow. Hens were spared in those days, and the birds reared were, in every sense of the word, wild, save that as the boxes in the woods they received their daily feed of Indian corn. Now we have pheasant farming carried out on an extensive scale, and in a year or two we shall no doubt see birds raised under steam incubators, and fed, as poultry is at present for market, by artificial processes. When that comes we shall no longer be able to class a pheasant as a wild bird, and we shall, indeed, have to take it out of the game list altogether. To describe the modern system of battue shooting is to describe that which is literally nothing else than pheasant slaughter—there is no sport in it. The birds are quite as tame as ordinary barn-door fowls, and, if the sportsman cared, would run to be fed from his hand, as they have done for weeks to the keepers. Possibly they have been made wild by noise, throwing of stones, and firing of guns a few days before the sportsman arrive, in order that they may take wing on the approach of the beaters, and, poor things, afford the sportsman(?), who, gloved and perfumed, waits, cigar in mouth, at the end of the wood to bowl them over as he would do a drop-kick at foot-ball—better shots. "Bouquets" or flights of a dozen or so, coming close enough to allow of eight or nine shots at once, are considered special little tid bits, but grand old "rocketers" come so rarely that when they do they are invariably missed. Some ignorant writers on such matters confound grouse driving with this unsportsmanlike system, but it is almost needless to state that such men have never fired at a driven grouse in all their lives. Nothing is more difficult to kill than the latter, which goes at such a rate of speed that the sportsman invariably misses it in rear, and the very best shots of Huntingham have been chagrined to find that, smart as they were over traps, they were no use at that sort of work at all.

Perhaps the most enjoyable of all pheasant shooting is to be found in the West Highlands of Scotland, where foxes are looked upon as vermin, and treated accordingly. There, on a nice morning in October, men on the lodge by the look side, are the keepers and the beaters, the latter mostly shepherds from off the hill. The dogs are a mixed lot, and comprise Clumbers and Sussex spaniels, retrievers, and occasionally rough-haired Scotch terriers, most useful for working out rabbits from braoken and gorse. The cover consists of the natural Scotch copsewood, of hazel, alder and birch or oak sapling, running along the fresh water or inland sea lough for miles, with here and there an isolated button standing in the middle of some corn fields. The game likely to be found will be black game, brown hares, woodcock (native), and pheasants, which have known no more domestication than an occasional handful of beans. The "rides" are roughly cut, and the ground the beaters have to pass over rough in the extreme. Sometimes, scrambling through thickets which one would think impenetrable, they will startle the woods with the cry of "Roe-deer away on the right," and the sportsman on the right hand side of the beat will feel his heart throb as a nice young roe steals out twenty yards in front of him, and gives a bound in the air as he sends the contents of his barrel to behind its foreleg. A minute more and the call is "Mark, woodcock," and sure enough over comes "Master Longbill," zig-zagging in his old way, skimming the trees. you are on his line in a moment, and down he goes. A brown hare steals out at your feet and is rolled over, but as yet you have come across no pheasants, though told that that part of the wood is full of them. Do not be afraid; they are only running on ahead, and won't rise till they come to the first break in the wood. You had better move on, however, and take up your place where you are likely to get a good chance at them. "Mark!" comes the call early again, and "What," you say, "is this coming along?" hard as a pheasant, but without the whirring noise which the latter makes with its wings—an old black cock going sixty miles an hour. Now be steady and let him cross above you, for he requires all the shot you can give him, and well driven home. He staggers under your right and you give him the left just as he is recovering. He reels, swings first to the left and then to the right, and comes down with a distinct thud. Be quick to load, however, for the beaters are fast closing up. You have just re-cocked, when "Mark!" is heard, followed by that well-known noise, "hoho!" Down he comes, a grand old fellow, who has had to make his living as best he could about the hedge rows, a beautiful wild bird, who would scorn to associate with his steam-hatched brethren of the South. He

---

is making his point for some outlying bottom, and will cross you on your right. He is going like a steam-engine, stately and straight, so get on his line and be well-forward." You think all this in one second if you are a sportsman and a shot—your right finger knows its business from long practice, there is a clear bang, and the bird that was sailing grandly and proudly through the air but a minute before, is falling dead head-long to the ground. "Mark!" again, and wheel to the left to hear the keeper, however, call out "Ware hen!" for the hens must be spared to breed. "Mark cock!" is followed, however, by another whirring of wings, and you swing in to him in the good old style, with an equally good result. After that there is some work on the left side, though nothing like the blazing that takes place at a hot corner in the south, and you shift to fresh ground. At the bottom some capital shots are made, the old cocks rising in grand style, and going away with that sailing flight which you only get in rough, untrimmed cover, unout by rides, and through which you have to scramble, require to be very manful and cleverly taken, otherwise you may lodge your shot in the trunk of some tree ten yards in front of you. When hens are to be protected—and we always try to see a return to the good old sportsmanlike system—the practice is difficult, as amongst the trees you are apt to pull on anything that rises. It is possibly no use, however, to write about pheasant shooting, except in what might be called the war correspondence style, as in our illustrated papers we see pictures which, with a few dead horses and men might pass for Tel-el-Kebir. It is a case of blaze! blaze! blaze! blood! blood! blood! with as much sport about it as an average London butcher can get any day at the public shambles.—Bell's Life.

STOLEN.—Last week the Cordelia Club had five duck boats with the appurtenances and four and one-half dozen decoys stolen from the ditch near the house where several of the members were sleeping. This theft was no doubt made out of sheer cussedness or spite by some of those hunters who are opposed to preserves and clubs. The boats could not have been taken very far from the marshes as the thieves would have been discovered before they could get away with the plunder, which is probably hidden in the tules on the river.

Rabbits have become such a pest in Golden Gate Park, destroying young trees as fast as they are set out and doing other mischief, that for over two months boys have been, with the sanction of the authorities, hunting them with dogs. All this being of no avail to reduce the number of these depredators, poison is to be scattered about to whest, and it will be unsafe for hunters to take rabbits or other wild game in the Park.

A pretty good score was made last Sunday by Billy Richards while shooting at the Cordelia Club preserve. He bagged (which means he brought in) ninety-two ducks for his day's shoot. When it is stated that this work was done with a No. 16 gauge Scott's hammerless gun, it shows good shooting and good-grounds. This is the biggest bag of the season.

Judge Belden, of San Jose, has crossed the mountain quail with the valley quail and the product is a beautiful bird, nearly as large as the mountain quail. Judge Belden is now experimenting by mating the male with the female of this cross, and, if successful, the product will be a distinct variety.

It is reported that the fall race meeting given by the Idaho Park Association was a failure. Upon this subject the Baker County Reveille says: It seems that a general depression came over all the race meetings in Eastern Oregon and Idaho this year—a fact which is greatly to be regretted.

Mr. C. Kellogg, Mr. Bradford and Mr. A. C. Tubbs of the Cordelia Club were up, last week, at the String of Ponds on the Club's preserve. In two days' shooting seventy-two ducks were bagged, most of which were widgeon; there were several sprig and teal but only four mallard.

We wish to rectify a mistake made in last week's issue; Mr. Harry Babcock of the Cordelia Club, bagged, week before last on the club's ponds, eighty-six instead of fifty-six ducks; this is the largest bag made this year, for one day's shooting on this preserve.

Messrs. Whittier, Fuller, Smith, Traylor and Titcomb—members of the Teal Shooting Club—were at their preserve at the Teal Station, last week, and bagged 181 ducks in one day's shooting.

Last week a party of three persons at Sherman Island killed fifty-five ducks in one forenoon. The bags were as follows: C i d Robinson 25, H. S. King 20, and Ramon Wilson 10, r t ten. en

Mr. Wilson and George Elliot were down last Sunday at Millbrae and bagged twenty-six quail. Mr. J. Kenegan was down there also and came home with seventeen quail.

English snipe are quite plentiful but very wild at Alvarado. Last Sunday a good many hunters made good bags of snipe and also of ducks.

The Suisun marsh is thought to be the best in the State for duck hunting. Certain parts, however, are preserved by shooting clubs.

Mr. Richards, Mr. Willard and Dr. Toland were last Sunday up on the doctor's preserve and bagged 180 ducks in the forenoon.

The quail range around Warm Springs has been shot over so much that twelve birds is now considered to be a large bag.

Coons are quite plentiful in the tules on the Suisun marshes. What a splendid place for a chicken ranch!

A pigeon shoot and a coursing match are being arranged for at Dixon to come of on the 29th and 30th inst.

Fred Butler brought in sixty-three birds last week while after ducks at the Cordelia Club preserve.

The lower bays are filled with coot since the rains. The ducks will soon be going in abundance.

A large buck was killed just back of the Mission San Jose, last week, by a gentleman of this city.

Some miscreant has been destroying fish in the Stanislaus river by the use of giant powder.

Mr. H. Spencer and Mr. Hofeling killed forty-seven ducks last Sunday at Alviso.

Mr. T. Bennet does not like hammerless guns. What is the matter?

Last Sunday George Muller bagged thirty-nine ducks a Alviso.

---

The Teal Shooting Club upon Suisun marsh quite frequently bag sixty birds a day to the man.

One evening recently 75 ducks were killed after 4 o'clock at Farm Station, Santa Clara county.

Mr. Whittier of the Teal Shooting Club bagged seventy-nine birds the other day.

Carson hunters are greatly disgusted with the scarcity of game this year.

The Cordelia Club has had good shooting lately.

## FISH:

### Habits of the Carp.

In central Europe, where the water of carp ponds becomes very cold, the fish will, at the beginning of the cold season, seek deeper water, making holes in the mud, where they pass the winter in a kind of sleep. They make a cavity in the muddy ground called a "kettle." In this they pass the time until spring, huddled together in concentric circles, with their heads together, the posterior part of the body raised and held immovable, scarcely lifting the gills for the process of breathing; and without taking a particle of food. It is a most striking fact that the carp, though it does not take any food during this winter sleep, yet does not diminish in weight. In the warm climate of Southern Europe, Italy, Spain, Dalmatia, etc., the fish become lively as a much earlier season in the spring, and it is doubtful if in these climates it ever goes into a lethargic state, or ceases to feed during the winter. When the spring is early or the water has become warmed by the sun, in Central Europe, it is ready to spawn by May and continues spawning at intervals for a month or two. Days and weeks may pass before it will have left the last egg to the care of nature. In Sicily, and in Algeria, which have climates not dissimilar to the interior of California, it commences to spawn in April. The female carp yields an immense number of eggs. One of five pounds, weight has produced half a million. The eggs are adhesive, and are, when extruded, attached to aquatic plants, brush or stones. The male fish follows the female among the growing water grass and weeds, and impregnates the eggs after they are extruded. If the weather is warm the young fish are hatched in about two weeks. Cold water delays the hatching of the eggs for about three weeks. Ponds of water with a rock bottom are not favorable to the growth of this fish. If the water is warm, and the pond has a muddy bottom, the young fish should, at the end of the third summer, weigh an average of three pounds. If the pond contains large quantities of food, the fish may weigh as much as five pounds at the close of the third year. The fish is said to live to a great age, and is also said to increase in weight up to about thirty years. Ponds for carp, in California, need not be over three feet in depth.

White sea bass are very abundant in spring and summer from San Francisco southward. This fish feeds on crustacea, anchovies, etc. The young are sold as sea trout, and are often considered by fishermen a distinct species. This is one of the most valuable food fishes of the coast, having firm, white flesh. Examples of from fifty to sixty pounds, weight are not rare in our markets.

Messrs. King, Roman, F. Deming and Bogart were fishing at Goat Island last Sunday. They found the fishing to be the best east of the Island. The fish bit as fast as the line was thrown over. Hundreds of eighty pounds of good fish were caught. Tomcod bit best on the flood tide and rockcod on the slack high water. The fishing in the vicinity promises to be very good during the winter.

Sunday last several parties were fishing at Ross' creek, just back of San Quentin, on the tide water. Owing to the extremely high tide but few salmon trout were taken, though many were seen during the preceding week. The best way to reach the fishing grounds is by Sancelito to Tamalpais station, from which a walk of a mile will bring one to the creek.

Last Sunday was good fishing in Oakland creek at Brooklyn; most of the fish caught were flounders. These same fish are said to be quite plentiful in Lake Merritt, but as the waters of the lake are confined and receive the sewerage of the city the fish have both a disgusting look and taste.

It has been reported that Throckmorton's Lagoon, about six miles back of Sancelito on the ocean side, is now open to the tide water and that a great many salmon trout have been seen in the lagoon.

The trout season closed on Tuesday last but fine sport can now be had with large fish at the mouths of all creeks running into the bay.

Ducks are now plentiful at Lake Merced; they have been coming in in large flocks for several days past.

On Oakland wharf large numbers of red-tail perch have been taken with hook and line during the past week.

## THE KENNEL.

### California Coursing Club.

Last Wednesday night the members of the California Coursing Club held a business and social meeting at 530 California street. The subject before the club for discussion was the best way to improve the breed of greyhounds belonging to the members of the club and all dogs throughout the State. Many valuable suggestions were offered and at last it was decided to procure a magnificent gold cup for competition among the club members, to belong forever to the nominator who wins it three times. The Treasurer reported between $300 and $400 cash on hand and no outstanding bills. Several members offered subscriptions toward the purchase of the cup and it was arranged to leave the matter in the hands of John F. Carroll, John Hughes and A. Jackson, who were appointed a committee to procure designs and estimates for the cup to be submitted to the club at its next meeting. After some debate it was decided that no dogs could compete at the coming fall meeting except those actually owned by members of the club. In addition to the cup the regular money prizes will be given at the coursing match. On Saturday night, November 11, the club will meet to receive entries, draw dogs, and appoint officers for the match, which will take place at Merced Wednesday and Thursday, November 15th and 16th. The time of departure and other matters will be found in our advertising columns.

## PACIFIC COAST CLUB MEETING.

### A Detailed Report of the Annual Coursing Match at Merced.

In giving a bare outline of the coursing match at Merced last week in our last issue we doubtless disappointed several people who expected to get a complete account earlier but the fact that under present sarangements it was not possible to get news in San Francisco from Merced after the match was over before this paper goes to press is the only reason we can offer. The match was one of the pleasantest affairs we have seen for many a day and we hope to assist at many such meetings in the future. It has been asserted in the past that one of the regulation episodes of a coursing match is a big kick from the losers. We are neither prepared to accept nor deny this theory, but we can say that the losers in the late match possessed such angelic tempers that they accepted the diots of the judges in the best possible spirit. Some complaint has been made about the lack of public spirit on the part of the Merced people who, though they make some profit out of these coursing matches, have not decency enough to provide rideable horses for the judges.

If the eternal fitness of things is any criterion by which one can judge of the reason for their existence it is safe to assume that Merced was created expressly as a coursing ground for San Francisco sportsmen. The country swarms with game of all kinds, from the agile rattlesnake to the lordly antelope, but it is of all places in the world the home and haunt of the hare, vulgarly called the jack rabbit. A Merced hare is meaner, smaller, can live on less, go faster and keep up his gait longer than the hare of any other country. There is a tradition in Merced that one old stub tailed hare has been chased by every coursing club that ever struck the town since 1856 and is good for ten years to come. He was on hand last Wednesday, and after leading a brace of dogs a fine chase of about three miles he finally made up his mind to run, which he did, at such a gait that both of the dogs sat down and cried with shame and grief. Merced stable keepers have a holy horror of San Francisco equestrians and keep in reserve for the judges at coursing matches a breed of animals said to be horses but which are slower than any animal previously discovered on this continent, and less fitted to carry a grown man at a decent gallop after a pair of dogs than a Mission goat would be to pack Chang, the Chinese giant. Apart from their slowness and weakness these wierd animals are to be condemned for having originated half a dozen gaits, each of which is a more exerculating instrument of torture than the other. One could forgive their trick of suddenly halting stock still when in the nearest approach to a gallop they ever reach, but their trick of rolling over whenever reminded by whip or spur that life is too short to waste at a three-miles-an-hour gait cannot be too severely deprecated. The secret of their existence leaked out the other day when a too frank stablesman incautiously admitted that they had been bought up from a batch of played-out Yosemite saddle horses. Merced may possess other features of interest than those enumerated but they are not obvious to the San Francisco visitor.

By 10 o'clock Wednesday morning the San Francisco contingent and a host of local celebrities were out on the coursing ground which is a level stretch of country about 10 miles west of the city. As soon as the wagons and buggies which took the visitors out to the grounds were formed in line President Devlin called for the first pair of dogs, and Charles Fowler's Delebute and W. Halpin's Culverin were handed-over to P. K. Jacoby who was chosen to act as slipper in the absence of Joe Stadfeldt. Meany was called away on business and after some persuasion T. T. Williams was induced to accept the saddle of torture along with J. Sillery and Chas. Johnson, the other judges. The three samples of crow-bait were bad even for Merced and after glancing at the squirrel holes that dotted the plain the three martyrs bade a tearful adieu to their wives and friends and prepared for the worst. A hare was soon started and away went the dogs, Delebute in the lead and the judges a good distance in the rear. Delebute made the first turn but came to grief in some safe ground where her lack of condition gave Culverin a chance to "go bye" and save herself and win a meritorious hill.

The next pair, Devlin's Chief of the Canyon and C. O. K. Jeffcott's Lady Bird, had the luck to pick up a Merced hare that evidently had a business appointment in San Francisco and was in a hurry not to keep the other fellow waiting. Chief led from slips and won a very hollow victory showing very marked superiority both of speed and work. The hare changed his mind when he had gone a mile or so and popped into a squirrel hole instead of putting the dogs to any further trouble.

C. O. K. Jeffcott's Spa Boy and J. Shay's Theresa were the next pair slipped. They struck a fast hare that went sailing away in a straight line almost disdaining to notice his pursuers until Theresa ran up and turned him on to some plowed land. Spa Boy took his work leisurely and allowed the bitch to serve herself before he went to work to reduce the value of the hare's life insurance policy. When he did start in he went to work with such earnestness that the hare headed for a place of safety in a patch of weeds half a mile ahead. Twice before he got there Spa Boy turned him and twice he "went bye" Theresa as if she was moored. When he reached the weeds the bitch was played out and so were the judges' horses. The finish will ever remain a mystery, unless Spa Boy can be taught to talk, but he fairly won the course from the work that was seen.

J. Ryan's Lady Franklin and J. C. Pennie's Duke wasted no time in nonsense when they sighted their game. The hare favored Duke at the start but Lady Franklin had the most bottom and won the course handily.

Tampete and Minnie were unfortunate in getting unsighted before they had made a point and had to be taken up for another course which was decided in favor of Tampete. The next race, between W. W. Sessions' Maid of San Francisco

and T. Brady's Paul Jones, was one of the best of the day. Paul led and made the first turn, but when they got straightened out, much to the surprise of all, Maid of San Francisco made a neat "go bye," the hare favoring her slightly in turning. Paul looked utterly disgusted and set to work to make up for lost time with such a hearty good will that Maid had but little further interest in the match. After a hard chase in rough, rolling ground, the hare was killed just as he was about to seek safety in a gopher hole.

W. Halpin's Blue Cloud beat J. Dugan's Foxhall with but little to spare. In the first of the race Foxhall led in points handsomely but tired away at the finish.

J. Dugan's Sally Henry and J. C. Pennie's Cherokee were a very even match. Cherokee had the most speed and made the first three and a half points, but when Sally got in she kept the hare to herself and after serving herself twice she guarded the hare in beautiful style and made one of the neatest kills that was seen during the match.

D. L. Levy's Lady Plaice beat Corronoway without allowing him to make more than one point in a long straggling course.

J. C. Pennie's Longfellow was too sick to run and T. Cronin's Parnell ran a "bye."

This finished the first ties and the party adjourned to lunch and to rest their bones. It was noticed that the judges took their lunch standing and though it wrung their hearts they most positively refused to join a party of ladies who had spread a nice repast on the green turf. Some one suggested that they change horses with each other after lunch, but as was instantly frowned down by the trio who preferred the beasts they knew to the ills they had no means of gauging.

After lunch the second ties were run off. As before, hares were plentiful and all that could be desired in the matter of speed and endurance.

Chief of the Canyon came against Culverin and had about all he could do to win the match. The hare chose a course over some ground so rough that one of the judges was afflicted with a complaint akin to sea-sickness from riding over the mounds.

Spa Boy and Lady Franklin were next paired. Lady Franklin led from the slips and never let her opponent in. It is but just to the hare to say that he beat both the dogs out of sight.

Tampete and Paul Jones gave the spectators a beautiful course. Paul Jones took the lead and twice worked the hare. He looked like a sure winner when he unfortunately stumbled in a hole and hurt his leg. This gave Tampete a chance to get in. She is a close working bitch and guarded the hare in splendid style, taking point after point without assistance for some time, until Jones came up and assisted her to make a kill which gave her the race.

Sally Henry beat Blue Cloud in a most hollow manner.

Lady Plaice and Parnell ran a smart course which was easily won by Lady Plaice.

This ended the second ties and Chief of the Canyon and Lady Franklin were put in slips for the third time over. Chief led from the slips and seemed to forget that there was another dog in the race for he and the hare had a little picnic all to themselves which ended when they had gone about a mile and a half.

The next pair slipped were Sally Henry and Tampete. Tampete opened a gap from the start and made a turn before Sally got up. The merit of the next turn lay with the hare, who swerved over to Sally. Sally took the hare all to herself and made three points before it ran into a hole. The points being even the judges gave it an undecided course and after the legal rest the pair were slipped again. Tampete took the lead and had things pretty much her own way. One of the judges by dint of beating and spurring him managed to surprise his horse into a gallop. When the mule recovered from his surprise he resented the affront by incontinently pitching head over heels in a gopher hole, landing his rider ten feet ahead and on his nose. Fortunately no more harm was done than a barked proboscis and a bruised shoulder. The judge remounted and saw the race out. Tampete won bravely.

Lady Plaice, being an odd dog on the card, ran a bye and finished up the day's sport.

After a bath and dinner the San Francisco visitors strolled out to take in the sights of Merced City. A political meeting in full blast at one end of town and a fight between two sheepherders at the other, were about all the sport that could be found, and the boys were at their wits' end when some genius suggested a dance. It took about three minutes to procure a band, which consisted of a guitar and a fiddle, a large saloon served for a hall, and then the fun commenced. There were not enough of the female sex to go around, so more than half of the sets were stag affairs, but the music ground away steadily and the boys kept up the fun until it was absolutely necessary to get a wash and brush up in time for breakfast.

On Thursday the party was early at the coursing grounds. The number present was larger than on the first day, many gentlemen living in the neighborhood having come out for a day's sport. Dr. Gale, U. S. N., was out with his wife and family, and young Mr. Ashe who owns a ranch near by and many others. The weather was perfect, just warm enough for buggy riding with not a spot of dust to cause discomfort. The final ties were called and Mark Devlin's Chief of the Canyon and Lady Plaice were put in slips. The three crow-baits that had tired the judges' patience the day before were again brought out and not another hare could be procured for love or money. "It had been a bad year," they said, "around Merced and horses were scarce." Resigning themselves to their perdices fate the judges mounted and the crowd moved ahead to beat up a hare. Puss was ready about 100 yards ahead and Jacoby stealing up on her with great caution gave the dogs an excellent send-off.

A Merced hare never commences to run real fast until the dogs take first turn out of her. Then when it is apparent that business is meant back go the long ears and away goes the hare, taking jumps of twenty-five feet at a bound. This particular hare had evidently been chased by a cur dog before and had a great contempt of the canine race. It just gamboled ahead until Chief of the Canyon, who had opened a wide gap between himself and Lady Plaice, reached for it with more than wide open. To see that hare turn again and then start off at a gait which would make a steam engine burst its boiler with envy and shame made the boys cheer, and made Chief of the Canyon feel as though the dog that despised the speed of the hare he is chasing lacks good sound sense. But Chief is a dog of nerve and he soon commenced to get over his disgust and pegged away in good style, utterly ignoring the fact that there was such a dog as Lady Plaice living. After he had twice turned Lady Plaice got in and took a hand in the game but Chief soon went by her. He named the hare and she made a good kill with his assistance. The course was awarded to Chief of the Canyon.

This left but two dogs in the match, Mark Devlin's Chief of the Canyon and a bitch bitch called Tampete, entered by the same gentleman. Tampete was imported two years ago

from the celebrated Trevor Kennel in England, b Mr. H. Tevis, and had run at Merced three times before without making a favorable record except for great speed out of slips. But on this occasion she had shown bottom as well as speed, and it looked as if when it came to the final course she would be the winner. Chief had cut the pad of his foot and lost a toenail. Considerable money was bet on the result and the spectators were rather surprised when Mark Devlin announced that as both the dogs belonged to him he would not run the final course off but would divide first and second honors between the dogs, as he had a perfect right to do under the rules of the club. Of course under these circumstances all bets on the result were drawn. But some of those who had bet against Chief of the Canyon for first place refused to divide the stakes and intend to send East for a decision on the subject.

Next came the Puppy Stakes and T. Brady's Lady Costello and W. W. Sessions' Chief of San Francisco were put in slips. Lady Costello led from slips, but the hare taking over a stretch of soft sand with some weeds blinked the dogs and threw both out before a point was made. When the dogs had passed puss came out again and the dogs, chancing to see her, gave chase once more. Lady Costello proved to be the best of the pair and won the race. They did not kill and were so unfortunate as to start up a fresh hare before they were caught which ruined Lady Costello's chance of a prize.

T. Brady's Connaght Ranger and P. K. Jacoby's Cassa Maria made a nice race. They worked the hare very closely and killed in good shape. Connaught Ranger showed the most speed and dash but was rather badly thrown out at the turns. In spite of this, however, he won handily.

T. Cronin's Lily of Killarney had an easy victory over M. Galvin's Bingo. After the first turn Bingo seemed to tire away and Lily had to do nearly all the work.

Mark Devlin's Michael Davitt beat J. C. Pennie's Master Joe with points to spare, though the result might have been different had the loser been put in proper shape for the race.

Second ties—Connaught Ranger and Lady Costello came together and made one of the best matches in the Puppy Stake. Ranger made the first turn and from that four points were evenly divided until the dogs got out of sight for an instant behind a patch of rolling ground. When they came in view Ranger was leading and from that out held the advantages of speed and work until puss holed.

Lily of Killarney beat Michael Davitt with points to spare, but owed some of the success to the fact that the hare threw Davitt out by doubling round a mound.

The final race between Lily of Killarney and Connaught Ranger was run on a level plateau of land in full view of all the spectators. Connaught Ranger led from the slips and made first turn and from that time to the kill the hare was never 30 feet from the dogs. They were beaten away a couple of times when Lily went by with a fine burst of speed and tripped the hare, who whirled around towards the Ranger. He turned back and away went hare and dogs like smoke. A meritorious kill finished the course and gave the first prize to Lily of Killarney, Connaught Ranger taking second honors.

A consolation race for beaten dogs, $5 entrance and $5 added by Moran of the Cosmopolitan hotel, was gotten up to finish the day's sport.

Sheriff Meany, of Merced, was unanimously elected- judge and P. K. Jacoby slipper. Six good courses ensued and first prize was handsomely won by W. Halpin's Culverine, J. C. Pennie's Cherokee second and P. Halpin's Blue Cloud third.

A match race was then made between Charles Fowler's Delebute and W. Sessions' Maid of San Francisco. The stake was $50. Delebute proved to be much the best dog and won with ease.

In concluding the report of this match a few words of praise must be said for P. K. Jacoby, the honorary slipper of the meeting. He performed his work well and fairly. Not a single dog got out of the slips and only one "no course" was run through dogs being unsighted at the start, no cause had for a slipper over such rough ground as the hares ran over last week. Sheriff Meany did all in his power to help the visitors enjoy themselves and even was so obliging as to loan his horse to the judges when the miserable animals hired by them threatened to die on their hands. Merced county is to be congratulated on having an official who can so generously and gracefully do the honors to visiting clubs and we hope to have the pleasure of meeting him at many a coursing match to come.

---

**FINE SETTER FOR SALE.**—In our advertising columns will be found a notice of a fine Gordon setter for sale. His owner is parting with him only because ill health makes it impossible for him to hunt. Dorr is a dog that has made a grand reputation East as a field trial dog, and his pedigree is unexceptionable. His owner refers by permission to the members of the Massachusetts Kennel Club and does not desire to sell until prospective buyers are well satisfied of the truth of all he claims for his dog. The following extract from the *Forest and Stream* shows in what repute Dorr is held where he has been seen working: "Dorr is a large sized dog with fine style, carrying his head well up, ranging and quartering in good style, showing superior nose, and considered by the judges and many others as the most stylish dog on point and back of any that ran. This I thought fully his equal in all except in staunchness and backing. Dorr stands either at point or back with his head and tail high, often taking his positional either; he does not seem to move a muscle of his body. I never saw one so staunch. Flint's style, both on point and back, is a low, crouching attitude, with head and tail on a line. Both retrieved well, pointed and backed, etc. This heat was given to Dorr, but, like the case between St. Elmo and Lizzie Lee, it was very close. In the closing decision of the judges, Lizzie Lee won first prize, St. Elmo second, Dorr third." Such a chance is seldom presented to Californians and we hope the dog will not be allowed to leave the State. It would be well for Mr. Taft to enter Dorr in the Gilroy Field Trials which will be run on November 27.

---

**A BIG DOG STAKE.**—The English coursing world is taking vast strides. It is contemplated getting up a monster stake to be run for at Plumpton, on 1st January 1883, and competed for by dog and bitch puppies born since the first day of January, 1881. The winner to receive the magnificent sum of £1,000 and a valuable cup, second dog £300, the next four dogs to receive £100, and the winners of two nail three courses £3 each. Thus if the stake is well filled the whole amount to be divided will amount to something like £1,060, being a much larger stake than the one competed for by Hugh Gosforth the latter end of last season, when Mr. Alexander's champion dog Alec Halliday proved victor in the Gold Cup Stakes.

A match trial of hounds will take place on Sunday between Silk's Fly, of San Jose, and Phillips' Prince, of Fairview. It will come of next week, on the San Benito river bed, near town, where hares are numerous.—*Hollister Advance.*

## YACHTING.

### An Electric Propeller.

The following article from the London "Times" will be of interest here as an indication of the introduction in the near future of a new agent for the propulsion of vessels, and one which has for many years been vainly sought. The experiment noted proves that, on a small scale, it has been made a success :

"Great Western Hotel, Paddington, Sept 28.—At half-past three this afternoon I found myself on board the little vessel Electricity, lying at her mooring off the wharf of the works of the Electrical Power Storage Company at Millwall. Save for the absence of steam and steam machinery, the little craft would have been appropriately called a steam launch. She is 28ft. in length and about 5ft. in the beam, drawing about 3ft. of water, and fitted with a 22-inch propeller screw. On board were stored away, under the flooring and seats, fore and aft, forty-five mysterious boxes, each a cube of about 10in. in dimensions. These boxes were nothing else than electric accumulators, of the latest type as devised by Messrs. Sellen and Volokmar, being a modification of the well-known Planté accumulator. Fully charged with electricity by wires leading from the dynamos or generators in the works, they were calculated to supply power for six hours, at the rate of four-horse power. These storage cells were placed in electrical connection with two Siemens' dynamos of the size known as D 3, furnished with proper reversing-gear and regulators, to serve as engines to drive the screw propeller. Either or both of these could be 'switched' into circuit at will.

"After a few minutes' run down the river, and a trial of the powers of the boat to go forward, slacken, or go astern at will, her head was turned city wards, and we sped silently along the southern shore, running a boat eight knots an hour against the tide. At thirty-seven minutes past four London Bridge was reached, when the head of the launch was put about. Slipping down the tide, the wharf at Millwall was gained at one minute past five, thus in twenty-four minutes terminating the trial trip of the Electricity.

"Calculations show that the expenditure of electric energy was at the rate of 3-11 horse power.

"It is now forty-three years since the Russian Jacobi first propelled a boat on the waters of the Neva by aid of a large but primitive electro-magnetic engine, worked by galvanic batteries of the old type, wherein zinc plates were dissolved in acid. Two years ago a little model boat was shown in Paris by M. Trouve, actuated by accumulators of the Faure-Planté type. The present is, however, not only the first electric boat that has been constructed in this country, but the very first in which the electric propulsion of a boat has been undertaken on a commercial scale. Looking at this first practical success, who shall say to what proportions this latest application may not attain in the next decade?  Yours,
"SILVANUS P. THOMPSON."

### The Seawanhaka Matches.

With the mosquito races of the present and the Seawanhaka races of the coming week the yachting season of 1882 will close. In regard to the latter, it does not seem, at the present writing, that the enterprise and liberality of the Seawanhaka Club will meet with the encouragement deserved from American yachtsmen. So far as now appears, the only typical American sloop that is to start will be the Gracie, and the races will prove nothing as to superiority of type. If the Gracie shall beat the cutters it will be said that no other result could have been expected from a yacht of her superior bulk, and if the cutters beat the Gracie the advocates of the sloop model will claim that she could not be expected to beat a cutter in a strong October breeze and sea, and so, after all, we must wait until the next season to determine the vexed question of superiority of model from actual experiment.

If the deep and narrow vessel is to become popular with American yachtsmen it must prove its superiority in the months of June, July and August, and on the placid waters of that "paltry sheet," Long Island sound. Doubtless our yachtowmen ought to cruise to the West Indies, or the Azores, but hitherto they have obstinately refused to do so, and there is too much reason to fear that for some years to come they will still obstinately refuse, and will prefer to sail in pleasant weather and quiet waters. It is here, then, that the cutters must compete for supremacy, and by Sept. 1 next an intelligent verdict may be given. The reason now about ending will be known as the cutter season, enough of these boats having been built to admit of fair comparison between the two types of model during the next season. The gentlemen of the Seawanhaka Club hoped to have had the Valkyr, Vixen, Fanita, Maggie, and a few of the fastest of the Eastern sloops, and there may be yet a larger number of starters than now appears probable, but it is not likely that this will be the case, for the reason that the season is too far advanced, and owners of sloops, even if they could spare the time necessary for these races, do not regard it as 'fair that they should match their boats against cutters at this season of the year when strong breezes and rough water are to be expected as a rule. Nevertheless, the Seawanhaka Club is to be commended for its effort to give a brilliant finish to an exceptionally successful yachting season, and if it shall turn out a fiasco the club will not be anywise to blame.—N. Y. Spirit.

Ex-Commodore L. A. Fish, of the Atlantic Yacht Club, has contracted with the Pollions for a centerboard schooner yacht of the following dimension: Length over all, 91 feet 6 inches; length on water line, 81 feet 6 inches; breadth of beam, 23 feet; depth of hold, 8 feet; draught of water, 6 feet 3 inches. Her design is by Mr. Philip Elsworth and the lines in character have more resemblance to those of the schooner yacht Comet than to those of the schooner Montauk, both of which are by the same designer.

---

The Albany Towing Company have three very fast tug boats, and the superintendent thinks them the best in the world. He will match them against any steam yachts for a distance of two hundred miles or more, and he said that he would wager $500 that any one of the three would come to Newburg from New York in 3 hours and 40 minutes. This would be at the rate of sixteen miles an hour, which is not only wonderful fast for tugboats, but is a good speed for a sidewheel steamer.

Forest and Stream hears that probably three small single-hand cutter yachts will be built by Stephens this winter, on lines similar to those published this week, and that a new 5-tonner is also in prospect. It has also been proposed to organize a special club in the interest of small yachts of this class. The model of the lines published can be seen at Mr. Stephens' shops, West Brighton, S. I., and is certain to be found very taking in type and appearance.

The cruise of the S. F. Y. C. to Vallejo was pleasant as far as weather was concerned, but it was a drift. Some of the yachts did not get up at all, there was so little wind. Those that went up, however, had a pleasant sail down. It is a little late in the season for cruises unless the yachtmen have plenty of time. But when they have to go to Vallejo and return 30 miles each way, in 24 hours, with light prevailing wind, there is apt to be some work about it.

The new boat building by Farmer has her deck on, and work will soon begin on the cabin. Her cock-pit floor is unusually high, the deck forming the seats.

The celebrated open sloop Sophia Emma has been sold to Mr. Charles Rorf, of the New Jersey Yacht Club, who proposes to take her to New Orleans.

The Seawanhaka club is doing a graceful thing in affording the British cutter Maggie another chance against the Vixen under circumstances more favorable for the cutter than the ones were at Marblehead.

It will not be worth while to look for much local yachting news hereafter as most of the boats will be laid up.

The Anna is going for a week's cruise up river after election day. The boys will try Montezuma Slough.

There was quite a little fleet went with the S. F. Y. C. to Vallejo and the closing trip was a success.

The Emerald only got as far as San Quentin Saturday night, and gave up going to Vallejo.

Spreckels, part has her spars all on. She will not be finished for some time yet.

The Emerald is going off on a duck hunting cruise next week.

The Lively has been dismantled and hauled out for the winter.

The little yawl Ariel has got back from a cruise up river.

The Azalea came over on this side on Wednesday.

The Mist has been taken into Oakland Creek.

The Clara did first rate on the trip to Vallejo.

The Chiquita is laid up at Oakland Creek.

## ROWING.

### The Challenge Cup—The Season Closing.

The race for the BREEDER AND SPORTSMAN'S cup on Thanksgiving Day (Nov. 30) will close the boating season on this coast. The season has not been productive of many sensational events despite the lively manner in which it opened with the establishment of several new clubs and a shower of challenges. The new club races that exused belged for decision the interest in rowing instead of to revive it, for the beaten club seemed to retire permanently from competition and have since been seen but little on the water. The clubs which have announced their intention to take part in the competition for the challenge cup are composed of strong material however than the willing organizations that have been almost snuffed out by mild defeat. Each of the three clubs that will compete for the BREEDER AND SPORTSMAN'S cup has enjoyed the chagrin of defeat as well as the gratification of victory without losing interest in aquatic sport. The three clubs go into the competition for the championship with the utmost confidence and whoever may win, it will be an assured fact that the trophy will fall to the most deserving crew. The weather has been unexpectedly unfavorable for practice so far. In other years at this season it was usually most advantageous but this year the rains have been remarkably early. A few weeks of good weather before Thanksgiving Day will enable the crews to make up for the indifferent practices which so far they have been able to take. The Pioneer crew rows together on an average three times a week and the members take in addition considerable exercise in sculling. The Ariels are out whenever they can get good weather. Golden Gate crew is equally industrious.

### English Opinion.

Pendragon in the London Referee prints the following comments on Kennedy, who is coming to California to winter and train for the match with Hanlan.

While Ross and Hanlan were conducting negotiations for their new match in the vain belief that between them lay the title of champion, another pro rushed suddenly forward and somewhat rudely altered the aspect of affairs. When Hanlan issued his challenge to the world for Ross, Courtney and Lee to represent the most prominent scullers in it. Ross' claims on first-class position we all know; Lee's victory at Saratoga, and Courtney's subsequent performance at Canadarago gave them—temporarily maybe, but still gave them—claim on that rank. As neither Lee nor Courtney cared to take up the challenge it seemed as if the question as to who is the absolutely best professional sculler in the world would have to be fought out between Ross and Hanlan, until a person named Kennedy appeared on the scene to dispute the claim with either or both of them. Kennedy's challenge as issued only matches Hanlan, but it is stated in papers that professes to know all about him that he is not particular. "Perhaps a recruit might chance to shoot great General Bonaparte." So ran the recruiting song early in the century; and on the same principle perhaps Kennedy might chance to take down Hanlan's number. Still it must be conceded that Kennedy's is a somewhat sudden development. Previously he has exhibited no desire to compete in "single-scull" matches with opponents of rank, though he and Davis have repeatedly dared the world to meet them in double harness. Readers may remember that when Ross and Hanlan, who were then

---

friendly, issued a challenge to double-scull any other couple, Trickett and Laycock being the men in their minds, the offer was accepted by Davis and Kennedy. After a good deal of paper war the affair fell through, owing, as was at the time stated, to the belief that Hanlan's partner rather too well inclined to the interests of Davis and Kennedy. That there was ground for this suspicion was shown soon after by their offering to match Ross against Hanlan. Those who supposed that Davis and Kennedy would stand any chance—in a straight race—with their more celebrated opponents, based their belief on the fact that Davis and Kennedy rowed so beautifully together, and got such way upon their boat directly a start was made, that they would be sure to baffle a couple more powerful than themselves, and perhaps far better individually, but not able to row so evenly or with such mechanical accuracy. According to all accounts, both Davis and Kennedy are lightweights somewhat about the size of little Cheaper, certainly a good deal smaller than Spencer. Without in any way believing that size is everything in sculling, it is bound to have its effect, everything else being equal. I for one certainly do not believe that anyone so very much smaller than Hanlan could make any impression on him after the first quarter of a mile, no matter how speedy at starting, and no matter how ready and anxious he may be for a match—in the columns of the local newspaper. That is, of course, without Hanlan's permission.

HANLAN'S CONDITION.—The Turf, Field and Farm states that Edward Hanlan is in New York for a few weeks. He looks well and hearty and takes an occasional pull over the Harlem river. In reply to a question as to whether he would row Courtney again he said : "It is not my place to challenge him, as I have beaten him twice ; but I will say this much, I will give him $500 if he will row me for $2,500 a side next year."

**Market Report.**

FLOUR—We quote : Best City Extra, $5 37@$5 50 ; Superfine, $4 30@ $4 75 ; Interior Extra, $4 75@$5 25 ; Interior Superfine $3 75@$4 ⅌ bbl.

WHEAT—The market still continues to be very quiet. The range of price for shipping parcels is from $1 60 to $1 65. The accepted figure for milling lots is $1 67½. Recent quotations are No. 2 November $1 61, do March $1 84 per ctl.

[The remainder of the Market Report consists of dense commodity price listings for BARLEY, OATS, BUCKWHEAT, RYE, FEED, HAY, PROVISIONS, FRUIT, VEGETABLES, POTATOES, ONIONS, BUTTER, CHEESE, POULTRY, GAME, HIDES AND SKINS, TALLOW, BEANS, MEATS, BEEF, VEAL, MUTTON, LARD, PORK, etc.]

## SPECIMEN OF OUR ARTIST'S HUMOR

THE FISHMONGER.

HUNDREDS OF DELIGHTED [ONES] SEE, FOR THE FIRST TIME IN THEIR LIVES

### The Japanese Artist and Embroiderers

At work in their native costumes at

## Ichi Ban, 22 & 24 Geary St.

The BREEDER AND SPORTSMAN is printed with SHATTUCK & FLETCHER'S INK.

## BODINE.

### eminiscences of an Old-Time Fast One—Campaigning in the Eastern Circuits.

When I took him in May, 1873, Bodine had a record of 30½, was not a pure-gaited horse, hitching very badly be-nd, and was a puller. I tried at first to improve his gait by king him back, hoping that by this means he would go ¡uarely, but it did no good. Finally I became disgusted ith him, and one day while working him on the Dexter ırk track, let go of him, and hit him a severe blow with the nip. He started of on the squarest kind of trot imaginable, ıd from that day never hitched a step. The first race in hich I drove Bodine was at Dexter Park, Chicago, July 1, 73, his opponents being Fred Hooper, Ripon Boy, Ella right, Byron, and some others. I won the second heat in :25½, but Fred Hooper captured the race, Bodine getting econd money. This race was trotted in the mud, and the ıext day Bodine went lame behind so badly that I was obliged o let him up until the following September, when I took iіm to Aurora, Ill., and trotted against Red Cloud, Brother Jonathan and Lady Mac, Bodine winning the race without owering his record. The following week we were at South Bend, Ind., where Mambrino Gift beat Bodine, my horse vinning two heats; and had Gift not had the assistance of Mollie Morris as a "helper," Bodine would certainly ıave captured the race. From South Bend I went to La Porte, where Bodine won a race in straight heats from Col. Barnes and Mollie Morris, the time of the fastest heat being !:27. The next week at Elgin, Ill., he defeated Ella Wright ınd Lady Fox, that race closing his trotting career for 1873. He had trotted his fastest heat (2:25½) in his first race, and I ıad never driven him a mile at greater speed, either in races r his work.

It was in 1874 that Bodine began to show what a really fast horse he was. I took him to Freeport, Ill., in May of hat year for preliminary work, and his first race of the sea-on was trotted there about the 1st of June, the other starters eing Pilot Temple and a chestnut horse called Dan, that ame from the West. Bodine beat them easily enough vithout lowering his record, and then we went into Grand Rapids where he had to trot against a large field—the best ne that he had ever met. For some reason, my horse was ll out of form and had so completely lost his speed that Red Cloud, Fred Hooper, St. James and Huntress all beat him in he race, the first-named winning. At Jackson, the following veek, about the same lot started, Fred Hooper being the fa-vorite, but Bodine had rounded-to in the meantime, and vent to the front easily in straight heats, Thomas L. Young etting second money and Hooper third. Dixon, Ill., was he next place at which we started, and here we struck Pilot Temple again, being entered against him in two races. The irst turn on this track was a very sharp one, and when we vent away in the first heat of the race, I sent my horse along o fast that when we made the turn the sulky capsized. The udges allowed me to start in the second heat, however, and won it. The third heat also fell to Bodine, and then the ace was postponed until the following morning. When we ame out to trot, I was surprised to have the judges announce hat they had decided to distance Bodine for the mishap of he previous day; but there was no appeal and the medicine ıad to go down. Two days later, Bodine and Pilot Temple ame together again, and had a hot race. I was very careful ıot to take any chances of being distanced, and after each ıorse had won two heats, and Bodine cooled out well for the ifth, I felt quite confident of winning. I beat Pilot Temple ıut a length or more, and supposed of course that the race vas ours. The driver of Pilot went to the judges, however, ınd charged me with foul driving, showing a place on his ıorse's foot where the hair had been knocked off and saying hat my sulky-wheel had done the damage. William Dickson, vho had driven Pilot the previous year, happened to be present, and told the judges that the scar was there when he had the horse; but it was no use, Bodine was set back to last place and the race given to Pilot Temple.

Cleveland was the place of our next race, and in it Bodine won the first heat in 2:22¼, that being the first time he had beaten his record of 2:25½, obtained early the previous season. He was beaten for the race however, Lula being victorions, and trotting the second heat in 2:20. At Buffalo, the following week, Bodine astonished the people by winning the race in sensational time. He lost his first two heats to Castle Boy, being a hot second each time, and then won the next three in 2:21¼, 2:21½, 2:21¼—the last heat being the fastest fifth heat ever trotted up to that time. Bodine was now in fine trim, and at Utica beat the same field, with the addition of Lula, in straight heats, without reducing his record. Then came a race at Hartford, the result of which caused considerable bad feeling at the time and created a good deal of comment. Bodine was entered in a race with Gloster, Sensation and others, and as Gloster had obtained a record of 2:17 at Rochester only two weeks previous, the race was considered a certainty for him, and nearly all the betting was between Bodine and Sensation for second place. Bodine won the first heat in 2:21, his fastest mile up to that time, but in the second heat made a break when half-way down the homestretch, and was beaten by Gloster. In the third heat I found that my horse could out-trot Gloster easily. I took the pole, and then waited for him so come up to me. When he did I carried him to a break, and then waited for him. I didn't want Bodine to beat 2:21 if it could be helped, and my idea was that this was the best way to accomplish that object. When we came to the finish of the mile I drove so as to just beat Gloster, and supposed that I had done so. But the judges gave the heat to the other horse, and then some of the New York crowd went to the judges and complained that I was pulling Bodine. They talked so eloquently that I was taken from behind Bodine before the fourth heat and Charley Green put up in my place. He didn't ask me how the horse was driven, but in scoring for the fourth heat used his whip very freely, and when the word was given Bodine made such a bad break that he never seemed to fully recover from it during the mile, and was away behind the distance flag when Gloster went under the wire. Probably the New York men who were so afraid I would pull Bodine felt easier after this performance. Of course by being distanced Bodine lost all claims to any part of the purse, and as he could not have failed to win first money, which was $2,000, the change of drivers was a rather serious misfortune to his owner, Mr. Goodrich. That gentleman vowed he would never again trot a horse over the Hartford track unless the matter was settled, and the following spring the Hartford Association paid him $1,000 to compromise the matter. This was the first time that a stranger ever held the lines over Bodine during the four years he was in my charge, and it was also the last. From Hartford he went to Mystic Park, Boston, and beat Lula, Hopeful, Castle Boy and George in a five-heat race without lowering Bodine's record, Lula winning the second heat in 2:18¼, and Hopeful the third in 2:23, Bodine being first or second every heat of the five. At Beacon Park, the following week, he defeated the same field and lowered his record to 2:19½, Hopeful being the contending horse. A race at Saginaw, Mich., where Cozette and Lady Turpin were beaten, closed the season.

By this time Bodine was recognized as a star trotter. I wintered him carefully in Chicago, and in the early part of June, 1876, went to Grand Haven, Mich., to trot the free-for-all there. On reaching the place I found that the only entries in the race were Bodine and Rarns, the latter horse having at that time a record of 2:20¾, and being in the care of James Page. As the race did not fill, the association offered a purse for Bodine to trot against 2:25, and although the track was a good one it was about all the horse could do to win it in 2:24¼. Going from Grand Haven to Grand Rapids, Bodine won a race, and then traveled on to Jackson, where he met American Girl for the first time. She sold about even against the field in the pools, the other starters being Bodine, Bella and Fred Hooper, but after winning the first heat was obliged to give way to Bodine, who took the next three, trotting one of them in 2:24, which was the fastest mile that had been trotted over the Jackson track at that time. At Saginaw, the following week Bodine trotted against Judge Fullerton and American Girl. He won the first heat in 2:19¼, which is his best record, but came as near losing it as a horse ever did and win. Soon after the word was given Judge Fullerton made a break, and knowing what a bad actor he was I supposed him out of the race for that heat at least. American Girl was ahead, and knowing my horse could beat her whenever I wanted him to, I stayed behind the mare until past the three-quarter pole. When Kelly, who was driving the Girl, swung into the homestretch, he went pretty well to the middle of the track, and as I was on the outside of him, it left room enough between American Girl and the pole for a horse to come through. When we were about half way down the homestretch, and had the Girl beaten, I happened to glance over my left shoulder and saw Fullerton clattering along on the inside of both of us. I started Bodine up, and from there to the wire it was about the hottest race a man ever saw. Fullerton being beaten a nose only in 2:19¼.

After this race Bodine showed lame in one of his forward logs, and as a splint soon developed itself he was turned out, not being taken up until January, 1876, when Dr. Paaron operated on him and the horse went sound. About the 1st of May I took Bodine to Kalamazoo, Mich., and began jogging him, the first race in which be started being at Jackson. The track was very muddy on the day of his race, and Bodine was the fourth horse at the finish, Frank Reeves winning. At Saginaw the next week Kansas Chief beat him, Bodine being sore from the Jackson race, but at Detroit he was a good horse, beating Kansas Chief, Gen. Garfield and Cozette. At Chicago, which was his next starting place, he defeated Mollie Morris, Gen. Garfield and Badger Girl, and then started through the central circuit in the free-for-all race against Goldsmith Maid, Smuggler, Lula, Lucille, Golddust and Judge Fullerton. In this series of races, which lasted seven weeks, Bodine was the only horse of the lot that trotted in every race, and in only one of them did he fail to win a part of the purse. That was at Cleveland, where Smuggler beat the Maid. At Buffalo Bodine met the same horses, and got third money, Goldsmith Maid winning. She did not start at Rochester, and here Bodine was fourth. At Utica he was third, and at Poughkeepsie second. In this race Smuggler, Lula and Judge Fullerton all broke soon after the word was given in the first heat, and Bodine forced the Maid out in 2:16¼, all the rest being distanced. The Hartford race was one of six heats, in each of which Bodine was fourth. Before starting in this race Mr. Alden Goldsmith suggested to me that if a heavier shoe was put on Bodine he would be steadier and go faster. Up to this time he had been wearing sixteen-ounce shoes, and, acting on Mr. Goldsmith's idea, I had him shod with nineteen ounces, but found that he did not go so fast nor so far. The next week, at Springfield, I put the light shoes on Bodine again, and he was second in the race to Goldsmith Maid, beating Smuggler and Judge Fullerton, neither of whom was distanced.

Bodine was then shipped back to Chicago. While at Hartford, Mr. Goodrich met Mr. Alley Bonner, and in the course of a conversation with him learned that his father, Mr. Robert Bonner, would pay a large price for any horse that could equal Dexter's feat of pulling a man and wagon weighing 319 pounds a mile in 2:21¼. On reaching Chicago, Mr. Goodrich decided to make a trial of this kind with Bodine, believing him capable of accomplishing the task. The horse was very thin from the hard races he had trotted, and I did not think it advisable to attempt the task, but Mr. Goodrich was anxious for the trial, and so we made it one afternoon at the Central Park track. I drove Bodine two heats to a skeleton wagon, the extra weight being made up by a bag of sand. The best the horse could do was 2:28, 2:27. That trial settled Bodine for the balance of the season. He had bled a little at the nose before that, but after the trial was over he bled very badly, and at no time that fall was he able to go a quarter in thirty-six seconds. We went to Cincinnati to trot against Rarns, Silversides, Cozette and Elsie Good. Rarus had shown a mile la 2:21¼ in his work, and his party were very anxious to have me send my horse a mile, but I knew he couldn't go fast enough to scare anybody, and so declined. Rarus won the race easily in 2:24, 2:25¼, 2:25¼, Silversides being second and Bodine third. That was the last race I ever drove Bodine, and a month or so later Mr. Goodrich gave the horse to Budd Doble, who took him to California, where he trotted several excellent races. In the spring of 1877 Bodine returned from California, and started in a race against Little Fred, at Dexter Park, being defeated; and with this race his turf career ended, he falling lame behind the day after the race, and never being started again.

In some respects Bodine was a peculiar horse to train. One feature of his disposition was that he never needed a "repeat," but in place of this it was necessary to move him up freely sharply for a quarter or a half mile every day, or else he would lose his speed. Another point was his jogging. He never wanted much of it, and after he had gone a mile and a half or two miles at a jogging pace he would want to speed. If you objected to his he would pull, and act mean in every way, acting as sulkily as a spoiled child. In fact he liked to have his own way about everything, and it was just as well to humor him. Road work he despised, and a very little of it would make him lose his speed. He was a very clean going horse, never needing boots of any kind, although I drove him with shin boots behind, having put them on originally because of a swelling on one of his ankles. I always drove him with a side-check and a snaffle bit. He would fight an overhead check, and if driven with a bar bit would drive on one line entirely. In disposition Bodine was very vicious, and was a really dangerous horse in the barn, unless constantly watched. He never wanted to make friends with man or beast, and was constantly on the lookout for some one to kick or bite. The various boys who took care of him knew this, and were careful in consequence, but all of them felt his teeth at some time. Going into his stall one day I incautiously picked up one of his front feet without first tying up his head, and the minute I stooped over he grabbed me by the back and shook me as a dog would a rat. At Buffalo, in 1874, I went into the stable after trotting a heat, and the boy incautiously turned Bodine around the wrong way, bringing me behind the horse. He at once began kicking in the most savage manner, knocking me down, and then hammering away at the walls of the stall while I crawled under him. A favorite trick of his, while stabled at Dexter Park, was to watch the stable door while being led by them in his walking exercise in the afternoon, and kick over anybody who might be sitting there. He didn't seem to know the difference between a chair and a man, for he would kick an empty chair left in the door just as savagely as though it were his worst enemy. But other horses, or the boys leading them, he would not molest, seeming to know that they were entitled to exemption from his anger. During the four years that I drove Bodine he won about $33,000 in purses, his cost price to Mr. Goodrich having been $10,000. He was sold about three years ago to a man named Reynolds, who lives near Springfield, Mass., and is now being driven on the road. —*P. V. Johnson, in Chicago Breeders' Gazette.*

### Three Barrels of Dead Rats.

One of the most remarkable occurrences of which we have ever heard took place in the northwest part of Talbot county on Tuesday last, in the shape of a huge rat slaughter. For some time past Mr. John Carlisle, a well-to-do farmer of this county, has been troubled with rats. There stands on his place, in one of his most fertile fields, a tenant log cabin, which for several years has been occupied and of late has been used by the proprietor as a general storage house, about 200 bushels of peas in the hull being the best article it contained. In the early spring Mr. C. planted the field on one side of his cabin in corn and when the corn grew up to half leg high, something began to cut it down, and by close watching he found that the rats were playing sad havoc with his corn, and he positively states that they cut down two acres of the cereal for him. On the other side of the house he planted cotton, and with equal emphasis he says the little varmints absolutely dug the cotton seeds from the rows and ate them up, doing this to such an extent that he had to plant over about two or three acres. So bad did they become at this time that he determined to try poison; so he bought of Dr. Bagwell a lot of "rough on rats," and put it out, and he says it killed so many of them that the vultures came and feasted on their carcasses. This had the effect to stop their depredations for a while; at least until the cotton began to open, when Mr. Carlisle soon had trouble with his rats again. They absolutely riddled his cotton as fast as it opened by picking it from the bolls and eating the seed and scattering it all over the field.

He tried rat poison again, but he found it no good, as the rats seemed to have learned better and refused to eat it. He next examined his peas that he had stored in the house, when he discovered that the rats had eaten all but about fifty bushels, and he put to the house two hundred bushels. Upon this discovery, Mr. Carlisle determined to make a new and different war upon the rats; so last Thursday he summoned his forces and went to battle. He is the possessor of two fine bulldogs, one of them being the finest we ever saw, and with these and five colored men he began to tear down the dirty chimney to the house. The house being located in an open field, the rats had no means of escape from the dogs and men, and, as the chimney was torn down, the rats poured down by hundreds, and were killed as fast as they came. This was kept up without intermission until the chimney was torn down to its foundation, when it was discovered that the rats had tunneled into the ground and had a tunnel from the chimney about twenty yards to an old hollow stump. This tunnel was about twelve inches in width, and was round and smooth with a large bed about two feet where the young were raised, and Mr. Carlisle says that the hole was jammed full of rats from the chimney to the stump. This rat tunnel was dug out and destroyed by inches by Mr. C. and his assistants, and he says that the rats were killed as they came to them, the dogs taking an active part all the way through and enjoying the fun hugely. Some of the rats were so large that the dogs had a regular battle with them; and the rats would grab the dog by the nose and bring a yell from him every time. It certainly must have been great sport to the participants.

The work lasted a half day, and when ended Mr. Carlisle had an empty four barrel brought and had the dead rats measured, as there were too many to count. He says that there were more than three barrels of rats piled on as long as the barrel would hold, and he estimates the number at more than three thousand. Many men discredit this rat story, but Mr. Carlisle says he can prove it to the satisfaction of any man; he solemnly declares it to be the truth. Now, then, who can beat it? —*Talbotton (Ga.) New Era.*

On our desk lies the BAZAAR AND SPORTSMAN, published by Joseph Cairn Simpson, 508 Montgomery St., San Francisco. It is a perfect typographical gem, and bears the impress of an excellent publication. Mr. Simpson is doubtless the best posted man in matters pertaining to turf and field sports, and will certainly make his journal a success. We welcome it to our exchange list.—*Sutler Co. Farmer.*

---

### TURF AND TRACK.

#### Two-Mile Performances.

We find, by reference to the compilation in Hiram Woodruff's book, that as long ago as 1842 Ripon trotted two miles, in harness, at Philadelphia, in 5:07. Prior to that notable performance had been under saddle, and Lady Suffolk had a record of 4:59 at that way of going. In 1849, at Union Course, L. I., Lady Moscow went to the head of the list, gaining a harness two-mile record of 5:04. At the Eclipse Course, June 23, 1859, Princess chipped two seconds from this record, but August 16, 1859, over the same track, Flora Temple cast all previous performances fairly into the shade by trotting two miles, in harness, in 4:50½. Perhaps it was on account of the apparent impossibility of surpassing this achievement that her two-mile heats went out of vogue. The years of the war followed, and very soon after its close the prevailing system of mile heats, best three in five, was inaugurated, and has since flourished well nigh to the exclusion of other ways of going. Certain it is that the 4:50½ of "the little bob-tailed mare" was almost old enough to vote before it was displaced from the head of the records. The old queen had her last unequalled distinction taken from her by the gray gelding Steve Maxwell, at Rochester, New York, August 16, 1880, he trotting two miles, in harness, in 4:48½, beating the feat of Flora Temple by plump two seconds. An analysis of this performance, which remained unequaled until last Saturday, will be of interest in comparison with the performance which surpassed it. In his first heat Steve Maxwell went to the quarter pole in 36½ seconds, a 4:52 gait; to the half in 1:12, a 4:48 gait; to the three-quarter pole in 1:45½, trotting the third quarter at a 2:14 gait to the mile, and finishing the first mile in 2:21, last quarter in 35½ seconds. He passed the fifth quarter in 2:56, at a 2:30 clip, trotting the full mile from that point to that point again in 2:19½, and passed the half, on the second round, in 3:22, trotting the mile measured from that post in 2:20. The speed for the first three-quarters of the distance, maintained to the finish, would have resulted in the heat being trotted a little better than 4:43, and as Steve Maxwell jogged in in 4:48½, it is probable that only merciful considerations prevented him from being driven out in 4:46, or thereabouts.

It will be noticed that this great performance of Steve Maxwell was very uneven in the rate of speed for different portions of the heat, one mile being trotted at a pace that would have finished the heat in 4:39, and a quarter of a mile at a rate that would have finished the heat, were it possible to have kept it up throughout, in 4:28. In this respect his feat strongly contrasts with that of last Saturday, of which we now inform our readers. As here was the brown stallion Monroe Chief, by Jim Monroe, dam by Bay Chief. In the early part of the week his grand finishes, in his severe race with Bess Wilkes, had attracted much attention, and resulted in his caging as a two-miler being canvassed among the horsemen of Lexington, Ky., where he was, and a wager was made that he could not beat the 4:48½ of Steve Maxwell, the Kentucky Horse Breeders' Association offering a silver cup, in addition, should the record be eclipsed. The day for the trial, Saturday, Oct. 21, was not altogether favorable, the track being heavy from recent rains, but Budd Doble brought out his stallion in grand condition. The timers in the stand were Dr. L. Herr, Col. R. S. Strader and Mr. B. J. Treacy. Doble set a rating pace for his horse, going to the quarter in 37½; the half in 1:13, the three-quarters in 1:48½, and trotting the first mile in 2:23. Here he was two seconds behind Steve Maxwell's time at the same point, but the sequel showed that Doble was regulating his horse to a speed that he could sustain throughout the heat. He went to the fifth quarter in 2:58, two seconds behind Maxwell, to the half on the second round, in 3:33, only one second behind Maxwell, and finished, full of trot, in 4:46, beating all previous records for two miles in harness, by two and a half seconds. While Maxwell trotted the first mile in 2:21, he dropped back in the second to 2:27½, but Monroe Chief trotted both its precisely the same time. This performance is one in which the judicious driver fairly shares the honors with the game and speedy horse.

The great achievement will stimulate discussion as to the possibilities of trotters at this distance, and while we do not expect that two-mile races will again become fashionable, there is no doubt that, from time to time, attempts will be made to acquire distinction in this direction. And there is also no doubt, fast as the performance of Monroe Chief is, that it is destined to be beaten and considerably beaten. Maud S., like Monroe Chief, is a very strong finisher of a mile heat, and at a much faster rate than the stallion has ever shown that he can go. When in good form, she can trot a mile in 2:15 or better, and last quarter the heat of the heat, and cross the score full of go. It is perfectly reasonable to believe that after trotting a mile in 2:20, a mere exercising gait for her, she could do another in 2:15, making the two miles in 4:35. Perhaps the Maud S. of the present will never make such trial, although she is to be trained with a view to being tracked next year, and may do so; but some Maud S. of the future is very certain at some time to place the two-mile mark several seconds further below that of Monroe Chief than he has suppressed the record of Steve Maxwell, or even of Flora Temple. And while experience has taught us that races of two-mile heats, between horses casually brought together in a class, are rather sorry exhibitions in these days, because animals are not trained with a view of going such a distance at a high rate of speed, and because they furnish too easy opportunities for trickery; yet we do favor these occasional supreme tests by our fastest trotters as proofs of the endurance begot by judicious breeding.—*New York Spirit.*

FIVE HORSES.—Capt. Ewing, of Shelby county, Mo., arrived at Fresno this week with a lot of the finest draft horses ever seen in this section. The imported horse Prince Napoleon has especially attracted much attention and been greatly admired by stock men who have seen him. There are also two Clydesdale horses in the lot. These fine horses will be a great advantage to the stock raisers of this section, and we hope that none of them will be sold outside of the county. They can be seen at Fleming's stables.—*Fresno Republican.*

There were three unimportant races at the track on Thursday, and not a large attendance. Too much election at present for Ventura to take much interest in races. The first race, a mile dash, was won by Wildifler over Peanuts. The second race was a trotting race, and was taken by Coronado, "bloc'" took skin horse over Jack Hill's bay in 3 minutes. The third and last was between Belle G., Doty Dimple and Sappe. At the three-quarter pole Seppe stumbled, fell and threw his rider. Belle G. came in ahead closely followed by Doty Dimple. As we go to press on Friday, the races are again in progress.—*Signal.*

---

### Answers to Correspondents.

LOUISVILLE, Ky., Oct. 3, 1882.
EDITOR BREEDER AND SPORTSMAN:—Will you please in your paper give the age and breeding of the filly Manon (by Nutwood) that recently made a record of 2:24?   J. W. D.

Answer—Manon, b f, foaled 1877, by Nutwood.
First dam Addie, by Hambletonian Chief.
Second dam by Harry Clay.

SAN FRANCISCO, Nov. 8, 1882.
EDITOR BREEDER AND SPORTSMAN: Please give in your columns the pedigree of Chieftain and oblige   B.

Answer—Chieftain, b h, foaled 1856, by Histogs (Old Togue) son of Rice's Histogs; dam by Trimble's Eclipse, son of American Eclipse.

#### The Starter.

Now that racing has been so firmly established in the South and West, a just criticism of the different official positions intimately connected with the racing itself must be of interest to all concerned. The owner or breeder is peculiarly interested in a very great degree when he brings his horse to the post, and every faculty known should be used by associations to enable the contests to be on equal terms. The starter, therefore, for the time being, is the one official on whose honesty and fairness all can safely count. Partiality or incompetency destroys the best of superiority in speed and bottom, for the demonstration of which the races were instituted. Of equal, if not more consequence, are the judges to whom all must bow, and from which there is no appeal. We can, therefore, presume that the starter and judges should be, like Cæsar's wife, above suspicion, possessing the confidence and trust of those so dependent on their honest administration of their duties. The rule on the subject reads as follows:

"No one interested in the result of a race, either because of ownership of any other horse, bets, or otherwise, shall act as judge or starter therein."

All racing law, therefore, recognizes the fact that to start or judge a race impartially precludes the idea of any interests by bets, or otherwise. There are large money transactions dependent on the result, and age and experience has taught that to be unbiased, we should have no interest in what we are to judge. Should not this same rule apply to the critics of the press? What right has the prophet of races, to be run, with pockets stuffed with pool tickets, his mind and judgment biased in every way, to undertake to criticise a start and race where his talent is used to excuse the error of his prophecy or to devise ways and means to palliate his want of judgment? The reporter or critic should be placed on the same category as the starter and judges. Then he could calmly judge of the requirements of the one, the fidelity of the other.

The honest efforts of a gentleman who, though he may err sometimes, are more acceptable to the public, to the uneasiness, and can front any, from recent experiences justly entertained, occasioned by those professional gentlemen who are known to be interested in the result of the races.

At New Orleans, Nashville, Louisville, and Lexington, the presidents of the associations start the horses, and during the recent meeting, which embraced sixty races, the average was the best seen for many a day.

Louisville, in the spring, is the great racing point where most of the young horses commence operations; hence, the number of green horses is greater, the fields larger, and the starting more difficult than elsewhere in America. Horses and jockeys in the fall are less troublesome in starting than in the spring on this account. Of course, this only applies when both are meant to aid the starter, and not to delay him in his efforts.

The public little appreciates the many arduous difficulties surrounding the position of starter. The great breeders of this country are those who keep up the racing interests, and to their petition the clubs above named have responded by nominating the official possessing in the greatest degree the confidence of the public and owners. Whatever redounds to the fairness of treatment of the breeders certainly can not be detrimental to the other owners of race horses.

On every large course there are always a certain class of privileged people who, under the guise of a friendly interest in the success of the club, advise the appointment of this or that friend for the most responsible position. The professional starters this season have given far less satisfaction to the owners of horses and the general public than the efforts of the non-professional gentlemen who head the different clubs already enumerated. Starting requires a control over the jockeys, engendered rather by respect for the honesty of intention and appreciation of a fixed desire on the part of the starter to give fair starts, rather than a tyrannical power to rule off, suspend, or fine the boys. Any familiarity between the jockey and the starter destroys at once the functions of the latter. Jockeys soon ascertain whether or not they can trifle with the starter, but to their credit it is said, that frequently, as in two-year-old short dashes, the colts themselves become hot and unmanageable, and many of the delays are thus but instances of the patient desire of the starter to do justice to all concerned, a fact not often considered by the public at large.—*Turf, Rod and Gun.*

Of the one hundred and eighty horses that have lowered their records in the 2:30 list this year, fifty-four of the number began their turf career in 1882, or at least had no record this year on field; seventeen of the horses without record in 1881, trotted this year in 2:25 or better; one hundred and nineteen are new to the 2:30 list; and forty-one of the one hundred and eighty are stallions, and have no average record of 2:26. Twenty-one of these forty-one are direct descendants in the paternal line of Rysdyk's Hambletonian. Moreover, of the one hundred and eighty horses, seventy-nine of that number are descendants of Hambletonian. It will be seen from the foregoing that Hambletonian blood is rapidly coming to the front—indeed, is there already. Not from any desire to push a horse or any number of them to the front do we give the above facts, but that those who have no time to investigate for themselves may see that it is a profitable study to note the families from which the dams of the 2:30 horses of 1882 have descended. Maurbrion Chief, 16; Henry Clay, 13; Morgan, 12; Rysdyk's Hambletonian, 9; thoroughbred, 8; American Star, 5, Champion, 4, and Pilot Jr., 4. It will thus be seen that while Hambletonian has contributed very much the largest number of the 2:30 list paternally, that maternally Maurbrion Chief, Henry Clay, and Justin Morgan all lead him largely.—*Dunton's Spirit.*

## orses that have Dropped into the Standard Class During 1882.

reat 2:30 list of trotters has been increased this season occasion of 141 new members. The entire list as it o date numbers nearly fifteen hundred horses that tted their mile in 2:30 or better. The 2:20 list, which st of lists, now has ninety-eight members, fourteen of ntered this season—a greater number than have an y previous year, with the exception of 1880. The ils trotted this season up to 2:14 by Clingstone, a yadyk, out of Gretchen, by Chosroes. The young ne unusually strong—two three-year-olds, five four- s and eight five-year-olds having made their marks. Of members sixty-five lowered their records, five improv- elr five-year-old form. The season developed several ena, among them the chestnut gelding Captain Lewis, rated as a green horse and never was defaeted. ve below a list of the new horses and also all horses re lowered their records up to date:

**New Horses For 1882.**

*[A long tabular list of horse entries with names, locations, dates, and times follows. The text is too small and faded to transcribe reliably.]*

---

## Patrons of the Turf.

During the reign of Henry VIII a bill for the improvement of the breed of horses was passed by Parliament. The preamble set forth the facts that as the generation and breed of good and strong horses within the realm extended not only to the great help and defense of the realm, but also a great commodity and profit to the inhabitants which is endangered by reason of small horses, etc. The bill authorized the destruction by the authorities of all stallions under fifteen hands high and mares under thirteen hands high found on the heaths, downs or pastures within the realm, etc. So Henry VIII may be claimed as the most prominent patron of the turf and the defender of the horse. Queen Elizabeth was a grand horse-woman and did much to improve the breed of horses, and to promote the interests of the turf. James I was a turf-man. He owned and ran successfully many horses during his reign. The Earl of Derby, whose wife was a Beaufort, founded the English Derby in the year 1780. The first English Derby was won by Diomed, who was imported to the United States, and from whom many of the horses of the present day have descended. The Derby is a race of one and one-half mile, and run by three-year-olds over the Epsom Downs, in May annually, where also is run the "Oaks," a race for fillies, same age and distance, and named after the country seat of Gen. Burgoyne. The St. Leger was founded in 1776, and is run in Doncaster, one and three-quarters mile. There are a number of other grand races in England, all of which are patronized by the first people of the realm. William IV established the Hampton Court Stud, and his daughter Queen Victoria has kept up the reputation of the stud in every possible way. Many thousand dollars are appropriated annually for the support of the English turf, and to have a Queen's Plate to be run for in every prominent city in the realm. Parliament adjourns as well as all conventions, both of State and of Church, to witness the running of the Derby. So you may truthfully say that all England is a patron of the turf, and that the grooms are truthful from the public treasury. Millions of people witness the Derby, and should a minister rise in his pulpit and cry out as they do in this country against the members of his church witnessing the race, he would simply be removed from the ministry. The Rev. Mr. King, who at one time was a member of Parliament of England, owned a stud of thoroughbred horses all his life, and he lived to be eighty years old. He trained and ran these successfully. He won the Oaks and St. Leger with Apology, and several Queen's plates with Holy Zion. Apology was lame just before running the Oaks and her trainer wished to scratch her. Mr. King said no, his friends had bet on his name and they should be protected if she was lame, and have a chance for their money. So she ran and won. The church at one time attempted to arraign the reverend turfman, but he defended his position so successfully that he was allowed to pursue the even tenor of his way. The ladies of Chicago have, as they have all over the country, adopted the race-horse fashion of bobbing the hair, and so why cannot the churchman follow the example of the Bishop of Canterbury and many other ministers in patronizing the turf. Washington, the father of our country, as pure a christian and patriot as ever breathed the breath of life, was a patron of the turf, and on many occasions had his friends gathered around him at Mount Vernon to engage in a fox chase with his hounds and horses, of which he was exceedingly fond. Henry Clay, the master spirit of Kentucky in his day, whose towering monument stands more conspicuous than all others in the heart of the Blue Grass country, was a patron of the turf, and a Christian who owned and bred at Ashland many grand horses, among whom were Yorkshire, Magnolia and others.

Gen. Grant's fondness and good judgment of the horse is proverbial. I know him pick the winner at St. Louis out of a large field, not knowing a single horse in the lot. I will be safe in stating that the Congress of the United States are patrons of the turf, if I am to judge by the number of the members that attended the Ten Broeck and Parole race at Baltimore two years since. I know Senators Bayard and Beck cannot stay away from a race when in reach. Their judgment is good, and they often back it. In fact, the enlightened Christian of England and New England are patrons of the turf. This current of liberality in church matters is moving west, and will soon be upon us with all its force. We have a club of Christian gentlemen at Jerome Park, headed by such men as Belmont, Jerome and others, where racing can with truth be compared to Cesar's wife—without suspicion—and when a sportsman or jockey is ruled off he may make his final bow to the turf, as his chances for reinstatement are slim indeed. Such I regret is not the case in the West.

We then have as patrons of the turf at the present day, the Queen of England, her son Prince Albert, Count Lagrave, Duke of Beaufort, Earl of Derby, and a host of lords and earls, all of whom are members of the church. In America we have the State of New York, Belmont Withers, Stanford, and a host of others. In Illinois you have Singleton, Bowett, Ayers, Dow, and many others, who, if not members of the church, ought to be. In Tennessee, Gen. Harding, Jackson, Cheatham, and Cockrill. In Kentucky, Alexander, Clay, Brodhead, Swigert, etc. In Maryland, Gov. Bowie and Hall. In Missouri, Gov. Crittenden, Hunt, Haney, and a host of others, all belonging to the church. So we may well say that both in England and in America the turf is strongly patronized by the church, although in order to keep up the traditional feeling against the turf, you will find some preachers to say that there is no sympathy between the church and the turf.

By introducing in the charters granted to the various jockey clubs a feature organizing the clubs as a banking institution, and making it a penal offense for any officer or agent of the club to be guilty of fraud, by punishing this fraud with five or more years in the penitentiary, there would be a strong tendency to lessen these evils. These evils are all charged against the horse. He has the size of the world to pack. He has not only the burdens of the world to bear, of the man who makes his bread by the sweat of his brow, but also the sins of the man who violates both the law of God and man. It is not altogether fair that all gambling should be charged to the horse; some of it should be charged to the soldiers. During the recent contest for prizes offered for the best drilled military company at Indianapolis, where many of the best organized bodies of men entered the arena, and where many thousand of people witnessed this grand display of military skill—on this contest many pools were sold, and much betting done. There was heavy gambling on the result, and dare you tell me that in consequence of this gambling it becomes the duty of a Christian to discourage the development of the military spirit of the youth of our country? That it is his duty to abandon the military organizations of the government through which we defend the nation in war? That we must throw away our arms, and give up everything on account of this gambling, and thus surrender at discretion to the great powers of his Satanic majesty? This giving up of everything would endanger the salvation of our souls far greater than a little betting where there was no fraud practiced. The Master does not love a coward, and an indolent Christian is his abhorrence. He has laid down certain duties for us to perform, and when we fail to perform these duties he will fail to fulfill his promises to us. He does not tell us to give up anything and serve him alone, nor did he tell us to stay away from the racecourse. Quite to the contrary, as St. Paul says: "Run that ye may obtain." God, to accomplish his great purpose of suppressing sin, sent forth his apostles over the world, two and two, armed and equipped with his divine powers and with orders to engage the enemy wherever found, and notwithstanding the aid of their great commander on high, the majority forfeited their lives in the war waged for the suppression of sin. And you tell me that I shall not follow their example. Yea, to elevate the turf I would, as the apostle did, be willing to forfeit my all, but as long as I do live I hope no one will attempt to fetter my conscience or force my opinions. "The right of private judgment and the liberty of conscience is the privilege and duty of all," so say the doctrinal views of my church. So this question of Church and Turf rests alone with me and my God, and man has no right to interfere so long as my Christian conduct and vital piety are safe. The liberality of the Christian Church, in thus placing this question where it legitimately belongs, is what won my allegiance, although by some it is styled an anti-turf church; still, when this question comes to be fairly discussed and properly understood, this impression will be dispelled.—*Church and Turf, by Gen. Abe Buford.*

---

## Vanderbilt's Stable.

As the dwellings of modern Americans of wealth have developed into palaces, so the stables of rich owners of horses have become buildings fitted up in a manner that surpasses in costliness and elegance the houses of a majority of the people. Pressed brick, brown stone and marble, costly woods and plate-glass combine to make the millionaire's stable a place of luxury and even splendor. Maud S and the other trotting wonders in which Wm. H. Vanderbilt takes pride are housed in a manner befitting the pets of the richest man in America.

A *Tribune* reporter visited Mr. Vanderbilt's stable at Fifty-second street and Madison avenue recently, and was shown through the building. Entering from the office the visitor found himself in a spacious room. It was just after dark, and numerous gas jets were burning around the walls, the light streaming through porcelain globes, each ornamented with a broad band in the center of which was a horse's head. Walls, floor and ceiling were all of polished wood, cherry, ash and black walnut being arranged in strips and panels in a way that brought out the beauties of each to the best advantage. In one place a long mirror reflected the line of somber and stately coaches opposite, and in another a case of nickel-plated bits, on a background of black, velvet, being glittering on the wall. A set of Fox's English hunting scenes, and oil portraits of Maud S and Fullerton, in heavy gilt frames, relieved the bareness of the east walls. In the corner, on a platform of cement a substeam was washing a light wagon which had been whirled over the road that afternoon behind Aldine and Early Rose. The stable implements which lay around him flashed in the gaslight with their heavy mountings of polished brass, and the pail in which he dipped his sponge was decorated with a thin coat of white and pale gloss. Only the man at work on the wagon in the corner and the long line of coaches against the wall gave the large, well-proportioned and highly elegant apartment any appearance of connection with a stable. There is no loose noise, no confusion and no dirt in this big hall at any time. Even when some famous trotter comes into the stable, fresh from some new exploit on the road, or the stout coach horses come in champing their bits and rattling their harness heavy with silver, the wheels of the light wagon or the heavy coach roll on a broad strip of carpet stretched diagonally across the floor, and there is no din or tumult.

Looking into the harness-room, large cases with fronts of plate glass extending on all sides were seen. The walls of the room above the cases were of plate glass, and the light from the courtyard streamed through in a flood upon the shining black and the gleaming silver of the harnesses. Here were all sorts of harnesses, from the plain affair whose only ornament was the monogram of Mr. Vanderbilt, to those in which the leather was almost hidden by a profusion of heavy silver decorations. At the command of Mr. Phelps, the superintendent of the stables, two grooms rolled back two immense sliding doors, and a dim-lit apartment, roofed by a dome of glass, was entered. Up and down the center, on the hard cement floor were ranged a row of light vehicles and around them extended a tanbark track. This is called the "walking track," and here the horses are exercised. The red pressed brick walls of this place were hung with pictures of hunting scenes and celebrated horses which, with their bits of color showing in the semi-obscurity, produced a pleasant and striking effect.

The most interesting part of the stable, however, was that devoted to its horses. Here the light from numerous gas-jets showed long lines of box-stalls of light and polished wood, trimmed with black walnut. Beyond was a line of open stalls where stood the powerful carriage horses. Even here there was no unpleasant odor, nothing but the smell of the clean straw with which the horses had been bedded down for the night. Up and down the passageway between the stalls moved the sturdy grooms, carrying feed for the animals and giving the last finishing touches to the bedding. The shadows cast by the walls, the deep panels of the roof and the dark forms of the coach horses produced a striking combination of light and shade. The picture was relieved and supplied with color by the bright blue checked skirts of the grooms and the matting of plaited straw and red tape behind the stalls of the coach horses, and the effect was still further heightened by the glitter of polished brass which adorned all the stable utensils and shone in the gaslight. Opening the door of a large box stall at the end of the room, the reporter entered it. The stall was lit only by the light that came over the top and was in a state of half darkness. In one corner, up to the fetlocks in straw, stood Maud S quietly eating her well-earned oats. Maud did not quite like the idea of being disturbed at her supper but, like a well-bred creature of gentle blood, gave very little indication of her annoyance. The blanket covering her was removed and her fleet-limbed symmetry was brought out to the fullest advantage by the background of light wood and straw. She submitted to being patted and caressed with the utmost unconcern when she saw that the intruder was Mr. Phelps, and paid strict attention to her supper.

Looking into the other stalls the other racers were seen quietly crunching away on their suppers in the twilight. Bay Dick looked up inquiringly at Mr. Phelps and the reporter entered his stall. After regarding his visitors intently for a moment he gave a contemptuous sniff and returned to his feed. When Aldine's stall was reached her blanket was removed and her good points commended upon. Aldine submitted gracefully—in fact, seemed rather to like it, and to be proud of the praise that was lavished upon her. Near the door leading into the courtyard was that apparently to be a box stall, but which, upon the door being opened, was seen to be a bedroom. Here every night sleeps one of the host lers, in order to be on hand if anything goes wrong with the horses. In the partition dividing the room from the main apartment burned a bright light, encased in glass. It was half in the sleeping-room and half outside, the light filtering into the sleeping-room through a green baize curtain, when the other lights are turned out this one is kept burning.

Mr. Vanderbilt's stable was begun in 1879 and finished in October of the following year. It cost $60,000 without the land, which is said to be worth at least as much more. The materials of which it is constructed are pressed brick and brownstone. It has a frontage of 75 feet in Fifty-second street and 100 feet in Madison avenue. All the rooms are spacious and the appointments of the finest. The box stall occupied by Maud S is 20x24 feet, and the others, though not so large, are still of good size.

There are at present in Mr. Vanderbilt's stable, Maud S, Aldine, Early Rose, Leander, Lysander, Bay Dick, Small Hopes, Charles Dickens and four coach horses, eight light wagons and two sulkies. Six men are employed as grooms and hostlers.—*New York Tribune.*

## Racing at Boise City, Idaho.

The fall meeting at Idaho Park, Boise City, was brought to a close on Oct. 28. The saddle race failed to fill and only one event was left on the card, but that was rendered some-what notable by the performance of the winning horse. The weather was fine and the tracking good condition.

SUMMARY.

Boise City, Idaho, Oct. 28, 1882—Purse $125, free for all, dash of one mile and a quarter.

| | |
|---|---|
| T. Smith names Hattie Harris | 1 |
| B. B. Badman names Warwick | 2 |
| H. Clark names Tim Brainard | 3 |
| John Earley names Dundrum | 4 |
| A. O. Miller names Idaho Chief | 5 |

Time—2:16½.

After several trials they got a good start and came down the stretch well in a bunch, but Warwick and Brainard soon drew ahead and as they went around the turn Hattie Harris was last. At the half mile pole she ran by Chief and Dundrum and as they entered the last quarter she was well back from the leaders but she came up the stretch with a terrific rush, passing the lead a length ahead of Brainard, who was half a length in front of Warwick. The filly carried fifteen pounds overweight.

This winner, a phenomenal two-year-old, is thus described by the Boise City *Statesman*:

Hattie Harris—This celebrated filly, owned by Tom Smith, of Koamtawville, has made so good a record at our races that we feel bound to give her a special notice, not that we would detract or say a word against any other horse in the race, for there were several that did well and made good time and won money, but it will be conceded on all sides that Hattie, although considerable was expected of her for an untrained colt, did not in any case disappoint her owner or the public. She was bred and raised in Idaho, and for that reason is a favorite. Of course she is a thoroughbred, having been sired by Matmadtike, dam Pierquette. Tom Smith, her owner, brought both dam and sire from Kentucky five years ago. The only race Hattie ever ran before her performance here last week was at star ranch, in September, when she ran a three-fourths mile dash with two other two-year-olds beating them easily, but we are not able to give us time. She ran four races last week on Idaho Park track near this

city, winning every race, two of them against aged horses. The first race was a half-mile dash, against horses of her own age, Monarch and Ingersoll, Hattie winning in 56 sec. The second race was half-mile heats against three-year-olds, Whalebone and Baywood; Hattie won the first heat in 54½, and the second heat in 54. Her third race was a three-quarter-mile dash against two-year-olds, Ingersoll and Monarch; Hattie carried seven pounds and won in 1:24. Her fourth or last race was a free for all, one and a quarter mile dash, against Brainard, Warwick, Chief and Dundrum, all aged horses; Hattie carried fifteen pounds overweight, not however as a penalty, but on account of her rider, and won this race in 2:16½. Smith was offered $1,000 for Hattie as soon as she made her last performance, and refused it.

## ATHLETICS.

### George and Myers.

The following regarding the rival athletes we take from the New York *Herald* of the 1st instant:

Sporting matters are somewhat dull at present. The racing season is past and the campaign trotters have left the track for the gentle exercise on the road; the baseball enthusiast let his ardor cool with the decision of the League championship, and the oarsmen, as their wont, are talking matches now that there is no possibility of rowing. All attention is therefore concentrated on the three great running matches which are to be decided on the Polo Ground track on Saturday next and the two succeeding Saturdays. The matches are between the two undoubted best men of the present day —and, for that matter, the best amateurs who have ever run —W. G. George of England, and L. E. Myers of New York. Mr. George unfortunately was not in good health while Myers was in England last year, and so he was anxious to meet the American, and had besides improved very much within the past year, he accepted an offer made for a series of three matches—one to be a half mile, which was presumed to be Myers' best distance; one a mile, at which distance George had eclipsed all amateur records when he ran it in 4:19 3-5, and third a compromise affair at the intermediate three-quarters of a mile.

Mr. George arrived here on the City of Rome on October 7, and on the following Monday took up his residence at Mott Haven, so as to be near the New York Athletic club grounds, where he would do his training. He was accompanied by a Mr. Caldicott, and they had a rough experience on board ship, so that Mr. George was pulled down when he arrived here. A *Herald* reporter visited the track yesterday morning to see Mr. George practice, and shortly before eleven o'clock the athlete prepared for his morning run, which consisted of one lap at a strong pace, followed after a brief interval by a fast run of two laps, and when he had got over that he had a steady striding run of four laps, the track being of five laps to the mile. No time was taken, and it was only by the eye that the pace could be judged. Mr. George differs completely in style from any amateur we have here, and displays strength to a marked degree at every stride, striking the ground hard and bounding off his toes with marked muscular effort. His stride is long and well sustained, the tape showing within a fraction of an inch of seven feet between the spike marks on the second lap of his two-lap run. His every movement and the way in which he carries his body betoken power, and Myers has in George a competitor worthy of his best effort. Speaking of his condition Mr. George said: "I was never better in my life. They told me at home I would never be able to run so fast here, but I think the other way, and believe I will run faster than I have ever done before. I am a ton heavier than when I began training. See, here is my daily weight stripped since I began work. You see I started as low as 142 pounds —that was the voyage did that—then I gradually got heavier until I reached 149 four days ago, since that I have lost half a pound a day, then am up to 147 again to-day, and I will run at that weight."

"What work do you want, Mr. George?"

"It depends on circumstances. In these distance races we vary work a good deal, but on an average it is about as follows: In the morning, about ten or eleven o'clock, two fast laps then a steady run of three-quarters to a mile and a quarter. In the afternoon I do a bit of sprinting, then a fast lap or two, and I might say, amuse myself about the track without doing a great deal of work."

"If it's a fair question what do you think of your chances?"

"Well, I think Myers ought to win the half, but he will have to run fast to do it—faster, I think, than he has yet shown; at least I hope so. In the mile we do not know what Myers can do; all we can say is, that he ought to run a best mile. I have shown there are no ifs in my case, and without wanting to express myself as being too confident, I expect to win the mile. The three-quarters I think we can leave till we have seen how the others turn out.

As Mr. George is a complete stranger to all but a very few the following particulars of his career will be of interest: He was born on September 9, 1858, at Calne, in Wiltshire, and started his athletic career in 1877 as a walker, and from that time to the present has been constantly at work, first walking, then bicycling, running, football and cross country running—in fact, all kinds of athletic sports. He did nothing very brilliant during his first year on the cinder-path. He ran in fifteen races, of which he won nine, was second three times and third once. On May 16, 1879, he won a 600 yards challenge cup at Birmingham cricket and football sports, and on the same day was first in a mile handicap from scratch, running through a field of fifty-two starters in 4:29. Prior to that, however, he had won the Midland cross country championship and later on took the mile championship in 4:36, and the four miles in 20:51. The years work resulted in eighteen wins, four times second and twice third, while he was unplaced but five times. In 1880 he retained the mile and four mile championships in 4:28 and 20:46, and on August 16, at London he won a mile handicap from scratch, in 4:23 1-5; and on September 6, at the same grounds, won a four mile handicap, from scratch, time 19:49 3-5, which is the fastest on record. During the year he took part in twelve races—won nine, second twice, unplaced once. In 1881 he won a great number of races, but did nothing in particular, his record being twenty-seven firsts, eight seconds, five thirds, unplaced thirteen times. On February 11, 1882, he won the Midland cross country championship, distance about ten miles; ran run to a half George won by a quarter of a mile, and this year's country champion-ship of England, distance 11¼ miles; 107 ran and he won by four hundred yards. On May 1 he won the Mosley Harriers Ten Mile Challenge Cup in 52:56 2-5—which is record time. On March 25, at Stamford Bridge, he won a seven mile handicap, from scratch, in 35:55 1-5—which is also record time. At Lillie Bridge, on June 3, he won a mile handicap from scratch, making the marvelous time of 4:19 3-5. On July 29,

at Stamford Bridge, he won a two mile handicap from scratch time 9:25 3-5, and during the year he has run in fifty-two races, of which he won thirty-four, was second six times third three times and unplaced nine times.

Mr. George holds the English best on record at 1,000 yards —2:16 1-5—and in addition to that the following best on records, which amply prove his marvelous speed as staying powers:

| Miles. | Min. | Sec. | | Miles. | Min. | S. |
|---|---|---|---|---|---|---|
| 1 | | 08 3-4 | | 4½ | | 22 59 |
| 2 | | 19 3-5 | | 4¾ | | 22 47 |
| 2,000 yards. | 5 | 10 3-5 | | 5 | | 26 54 |
| Miles. | | | | 5½ | | 29 31 |
| 3 | | 5 | 44 | 6 | | 32 40 |
| 4 | | 6 | 67 3-5 | 6½ | | 32 00 |
| 5 | | 8 | 13 4-5 | 7 | | 35 39 |
| 6 | | 9 | 26 5-5 | 7½ | | 38 38 |
| 7 | | 10 | 56 | 8 | | 42 11 |
| 8 | | 12 | 17 | 8½ | | 44 27 |
| 9 | | 13 | 36 | 9 | | 47 32 |
| 10 | | 14 | 42 4-5 | 9½ | | 50 30 |
| 11 | | 16 | 06 | 10 | | 52 56 2 |
| | | 17 | 29 | | | |
| | | 18 | 43 | | | |
| | | 20 | 49 3-5 | | | |
| | | 21 | 30 | | | |

The American champion, Lawrence E. Myers, has been before the public for a number of years, and his appearance as well as his records are well known to all who take any interest in athletics. The only athlete to approach him is his present antagonist, the two standing unrivaled and holding or capable of holding, every record from 100 yards upward. In one or two of the short distance races Myers does not hold the record, but it is more the lack of opportunity than ability that prevents his name figuring on the list. He will run a 115 pounds, and as he stands five feet seven and a half inches in height, which is four inches less than George, there will be a marked contrast in their appearance. For these races Myers has trained most carefully, and the effect of his steady application to his work and the rules of training are plainly visible. His running is done at the Manhattan track, and was there he was seen on Monday afternoon. He has muscled out in a really remarkable manner, and has the healthy look of a well trained athlete. In reply to a remark about his looking so well, he said: "Yes, I know I am; I was never in better health, and if I can't win it won't be because I am not well." His good health he attributes to the great care he has taken of himself. "I was determined as soon as George arrived to leave nothing undone, so I have left business alone entirely for three weeks now, exercising regular morning and afternoon, and keep good hours, and that's pretty hard to me to do, you know," he laughingly added. The routine of his daily work Myers detailed as follows: "In the morning run from a quarter to half a mile hard and do a lot of stretch. I have gone as far as two miles, and I don't find it hard to go a distance now. Then I sprint for a while before being rubbed down. I don't do so much in the afternoon after eating a big dinner I am lazy, so I take it easy. A fast lap, an easy half and a little fun with any of the boys who are practicing is about the regular afternoon's work." Myers' opinion as to the result of the three races is pretty nearly the same as that held by George; he expects to win the half-mile and be make to run fast for it; the mile he fancies George may have to beat the record to win, and the three-quarters' race is that-case will be a severe and close affair.

At the championship meeting Myers weighed 111 pounds and the additional four pounds have been put on in the right places. After the half-mile race on Saturday Myers will take longer work for the mile race of the next week. At present he only surmises what he may be able to do. He has made no trials and does not intend to. "If I can't win a trial won't help me to do it, and I am likelier to win without one any way."

In our last week's list of entries for the University Field Games, which take place to-day, the name of James Gosewell in the mile scratch, was inadvertently omitted. His only well known performance at that distance was in the Olympic Club games at the Mechanics' Pavilion, June 24, 1881. At the meeting he won the mile very easily. Myers ran about five minutes, and could have done better if pushed. If he as good a man now as he was then, the Olympic Club representatives cannot beat him, and it is not very likely that these races among the University athletes that can do five minutes.

The reports are that Haley says that he will not run Masterson again until next spring, and the latter is training for half-mile race. If they meet next season, both in proper condition, there will be some grand races between them, at various distances, as Masterson can run a good race at any distance up to a half-mile, if he is given the opportunity to train correctly. The worst trouble for him is that he works ten hours every day, and is overworked and stale when he toes the scratch for a race. He may be better situated next spring.

Duncan McMillan of Bodie is anxious for a match with the Stockton champion. He will compete with him for the best two out of three events, the events to be, putting the weight, throwing the hammer, and hitch and kick.

The University Field day has been postponed to Saturday, the 18th.

### Fruit For Fowls.

Fowls like a variety of food, and if long confined to any one kind, no matter how good it may be, will, ere long, become sickly and diseased, and cease to either improve or profitable.

Those birds which must be kept in confinement, either prevent the different breeds from mixing, during the breeding season, or on account of not having but little available space in which to keep the fowls, or to prevent them from tres-passing on gardens or lawns, set apart for other purposes, must have some green food, something to keep them thriving and healthy while they are kept on corn, wheat, and other grain food principally, and fruit comes in nicely to fill the bill. On nearly every place where poultry is reared there is much fruit of different kinds raised, and there is necessarily much which is not fit for sale or for family use; this when ripe enough, makes most excellent food for confined poultry.

There are also many peach and apple parings from the houses, which the fowls can and will make good use of; in fact, they will turn it into much more profit than will the pigs, which usually get these "pickings" which the poultry should have. When fruit is not raised on the place, at the nearest grocery store can be bought, for a few cents, a basket or two of soft and unsalable apples, pears or peaches, which the fowls will be very glad to get. Fruit has the beneficial influence on the health of fowls that it has on that of human beings.—*Poultry Monthly.*

# THE PADDOCK.

## Surgical Operations on Horses.

most every parish is a worthy individual called by the a horse doctor, but without any official qualification t office. At the same time hundreds of men have ery highly respected in their self-imposed calling, and wright practical knowledge a great many of them hardly be excelled. Many now living have had fifty dally experience among all sorts of cases, and, perhaps mpered than they might ha e been by medical rules, ve worked out the causes of diseases and found cures same by actual practice. The necessities of the times d a special education for veterinary surgeons, and it is hose who have worked hard for the science an injury r uneducated men to share the fruits of study and intion. A man possessing but a very moderate amount k learning forty years ago might well occupy a difference from one owning to such deficiencies et the t day.

nother generation none but qualified practitioners, g diploma in the same way as in the higher branch of dical profession, will be allowed to practice at all. No n complaint of this new order of things, as it must raise the veterinary profession to a higher standard ortance, and it will serve also to sweep away a great abuses that are still continued by the worst classes of horse doctors, and by some of those possessing great ence, but too old to benefit by what they would call ngled ideas and experiments. At a future day none ose who have been enlightened by a due course of and college training will be qualified to doctor and prefor our horses. It becomes, therefore, of more importce than ever to draw attention to those abuses which l be swept away before the new school gets fairly settheir work. Education must have a tendency to soften art towards the animal patient in this respect, and a well d mind must see that an animal which cannot tell us of : pains and ailments, and cannot assist himself towards very from any malady, demands even more thought t is absolutely necessary to bestow on the human sub- Ignorance or the absence of those special thoughts and probably does, ruin a great number of horses year, and it has often struck me that ill-shapen horses, bling goers, and the victims of palpable disease owe the of their misfortunes to some stupidly devised opera-

Firing, serving, the removing of tumors, and more s operations often enough inflict as much injury on a by the way in which they are performed, as if his ailwere allowed to remain unattended. The old-fashionle at a farm of calling the laborers together to coat the tunate patient on a straw bed, or often on a field, with he turf as a break, and with ropes fixed for the throw, ow pull together to bring the horse down with a crash, hud, sufficient to shake his limbs out of joint, is so very ent from the hospital bed, or table, with pillows and hands for support, and the power of speech to say if r that position hurts more or less. Do horses always ver these tremendous throws! and then the lengthened they are often held down, and all for reasons for which nimal has no guidance. Half the horse power of the atry at least, goes through this sort of thing, as required he necessity of castration, and it strikes me very forcibly a lot of horses are spoilt by that operation. We are es going weak from the hind quarter, or with no growth nuscles in the thighs, and there is altogether an appear-that at some time or other a wasting process must have a place which has altered the natural gait and formation he animal in many points. To those who observe as sly as we are always doing, this view of a horse must been by no means unfrequent, and these horses that to be the commonest bred are those that are chiefly nothe for the deficiencies I am alluding to. Thoroughbred es are usually performed upon by skilled veterinary sures and so are valuable hunting colts, but the ordinary ary colts very frequently fall under the hands of those still follow the old-fashioned plans of our forefathers. wretched colt is not prepared at all for the operation, the arrival of the horse doctor is the precursor of his g brought up from the field, and the farm hands are ight together to assist in casting the colt. There is a lot ones and bother about adjusting the rope; Jack or Tom s not do it right, and the doctor sings out to them, that in the meantime being half frightened to death, and dat his plunges and efforts to get away, and with his foredrawn up to his hind, a pull, a long pull, and a pull toer gives the poor young brute the biggest fall he has ever in his life. Then the operation is performed, not over tily, and somewhat roughly, according to the ideas of sci-ific veterinaries.

have seen the operation performed in the rough-and-tumway and in a very scientific way. In the latter case the e was thrown with the greatest care, and the operator previously very closely examined the bed, and instructed helpers, two of them being the two men, his straps being of his own contrivance. A horse operated upon by this lful hand I have seen driven in a gig nine days afterde, but one roughly performed upon I have seen no quar-sly stiff at the end of three weeks as to be scarcely able nove, and with that crippled appearance of hind quarter t denotes a probability to my eye of never recovering. will get right according to ordinary notions, but his walk l all his paces will be cramped, or he will go wide from ind, or he what some people call split up, and years after he these defections will be counted against his make and pe. According to my ideas a great deal depends upon this operation is performed, and I consider that owners olts, for the sake of their own pockets, besides every per idea of humanity, should consider this subject very ply before selecting an operator. I have heard that the st skilful hand ever seen in this country was an American ev years ago I know the operator I allude to performed n several colts that belonged to a friend of mine, and I s told that it was perfectly marvelous how he managed it as he never cast his patients, required very little assist-s and applied something that kept down all swelling l inflammation. Most of our modern veterinary surgeons , no doubt, skilful operators, and in this department of profession I feel sure that science has gained many steps on the old school of horse-doctors, however practical the ner may have been in the discovery and treatment of ordi-y diseases. The greatest improvement that I have no-d, however, has been the gradual adoption of chloroform several of the veterinary surgeons of my acquaintance in sty all the operations they are called upon to perform. I told by an excellent judge that a colt castrated under loroform is convalescent five times as quickly as one per-med upon in the ordinary way, no matter how skilful the erator may be, and that, in upwards of twenty cases, there s not been the smallest trace of mal-effect upon the ani-

mals. In such cases I am told that it is not necessary to throw the colts, nor to let them know that you are handling them at all, the colt being previously taught to come in a halter and stand still when required. By such a method nearly all shock to the system is avoided, and this is the danger that I maintain is so great in being likely to permanently injure a horse. Do away with the rough handling and keep the animal from the knowledge that something very hurtful has been done to him by his worst enemy, man, and there can be nothing to fear as to his deteriorating in his natural shape and make. Then why should not the use of chloroform become general for all the operations it may be found necessary to perform upon horses? There can be no objection urged against the expediency of using chloroform on the same plea to be advanced in the case of the human subject, that the administration may be dangerous to life, as, taking the exactly proportions of such accidents in the hands of the faculty, estimated at not one in five hundred, the loss of a horse against the greatly increased value of the many accounted for would be of the smallest consideration. At the same time, I do not believe that there would be any danger at all as regards horses, as the evidence of medical men would show that patients unfitted for the use of chloroform are those having an unusually weak action of the heart. Now, considering the enormous efforts of which horses are capable, it would appear very evident that the action of the heart was more powerful in the horse than in almost any other living creature, and that for that reason he should be the best subject of all for chloroform.

I am told by experienced veterinary surgeons that it is much easier to peform upon a horse under chloroform than when he is under the influence of fright and suffering, and the operation mentioned was serving, which could be done with the greatest nicety in the interval of insensibility. I bring forward the suggestion as regards horses mediocre I think thousands will be more fitted for general use by the adoption of such an assistant in necessary operations, and I plead on the score of humanity for animals that cannot speak to us to tell us how they suffer for our service, and do not understand that the treatment to which we put them may be for their ultimate benefit.—*Bell's Life.*

## Predilection for Glossy Coats.

Glossiness of coat and sleekness have their special attractions. The owner is (says Mr. W. Day) satisfied, and the gazing eye of the wondering multitude pleased. The trainer, who indulges in the practice, is pleased to see his horse, if not "the gloss of fashion and the mould of form," at least "the observed of all observers;" whilst the stable boy is half frantic with delight to observe the cunningly devised work of his own unaided hands.

Now I, for one, do not say for a moment that a horse is any the worse for trifling and tawdry embellishments, if legitimately achieved; just as I would not admit that he would be any better were he burnished like gold, striped like a zebra, and his attendant fancifully dressed like a zany. But there is too much inclination in this direction. Some, perhaps, would wish to plait or shave the tail and crimp or hog the mane to complete the picture.

I protest against the practice, because I ever looks are no test of condition. Bounteous nature has provided for the comfort and well-being of the animal kingdom warm covering of various sorts. To the horse has been given long hair, suitable to his nature, for his protection against the inclemency of winter. We all know that wild animals have a warmer covering in winter than in summer. It scarcely requires a naturalist to confirm what every observant person must be familiar with. We see that birds moult in autumn, that the feathers may be well grown, thick and long, against the approaching winter. Button, in his natural history, from which I take a few extracts bearing on the point, in speaking of the beaver: "It is winter they are chiefly sought, because their fur is not perfectly sound in any other season." Again, alluding to the sable, he says: "and yet this (winter) is the best season for hunting them, because their fur is better and more beautiful than in summer."

The same principle applies, almost in its entirety, to the horse. His coat, like theirs, is naturally longest in winter; although it can hardly be said to be then more beautiful, nor is it desirable that it should be so. Deprive him of this before summer, and you do him an incalculable, irreparable harm. Yet, for a fanciful purpose, he is subjected to all kinds of anomalies; kept improperly warm in the stables; made to take a daily condition-ball—and all for the removal of his greatest possible comfort, and the substitution for it of his summer coat in the depth of winter! Who shall say how many horses are annually lost in this way! And yet, with many, nothing but time and bitter experience will alter the practice. One thing may be safely predicated of it, a fact indeed that has not escaped even superficial observers—the home with the most glossy coat is least seen in public; that with the roughest most often.

But when the love of popularity, in whatever form, takes hold of the senses, folly is apt to oust reason. It is difficult to say to what lengths this may not be carried to secure the object of the ambition of the hour, or, it may be, lifetime. When its idol is the appearance of the horses, the stable becomes a hot-house, its inmates, sudatory creatures, whose stomachs are made the receptacle of the contents of a chemist's shop. This is hardly an exaggeration; for it is not possible to tell the ingredients of the condition-ball, or their possibly deadly effect. We know full well that beauty a man who has the charge of his master's hack or carriage horse has been detected administering the harmful ball, or even assent to in a crude form, to give the coat the desirable glossy appearance in winter as well as summer; with the result inevitable result—the death of the unfortunate animal and the punishment of the man; the latter richly deserved, it must be admitted.

Gentlemen are too willing to judge the appearance of their horses from the appearance of their coat. Were they to ask the desired information from the trainer, whose pleasure, duty and interest is to supply it, it would be more satisfactory to both. And though the result might not agree with the preconceived views of owners, they should still be content in the knowledge: first, that no one is so qualified to advise in such a matter as the trainer; secondly, no one has so sterling a motive to advise rightly. If this were the general practice, we should see horses looking better in summer, as they would be healthier, as well as in winter.—*Fancier.*

## Where is the Lameness Located?

It may also be asked: Can we detect the seat of the disease by the nature of the lameness? Generally speaking, we certainly can not, thought it will often materially assist our diagnosis. In shoulder lameness, we can generally ascertain the seat of mischief by the slow and labored extension of the limb, which is more evident in going down a

declivity, and likewise in the walk, than any other place, the horse having, in slow motion, more time to move the limb with the care that he wishes. In severe lameness from splints, there is often an unwillingness to bend the knee, this, however, is also shown in cases of slight strains of the sinews just under the knee. With these exceptions, the seat of disease, whether of the foot, pasterns or the fetlock, cannot be ascertained by the nature of the horse's action.

In examining a case of lameness, we should, if possible, have the horse in the stable, and without disturbing him observe whether he points a foot, and in what particular manner he so favors it. We should then have him led from the stable and trotted gently in hand on a hard road or pavement, giving him his head at the time. Having thus ascertained what leg he is lame in, we should proceed to discover the actual seat of the mischief. For this purpose, the finger and thumb should be carefully passed down the leg from the knee to the foot, to ascertain if there be any undue heat, or enlargement, or tenderness from pressure; we should also feel carefully the front and sides of the pasterns, as well as round the coronet. If a splint be the cause of lameness, the horse will evince considerable pain when it is pressed, and so likewise will he in lesions of the sinews.

Supposing that we have found no sufficient cause of lameness above, we must now direct our attention to the feet. In nearly every case, unless the mischief should be very clearly exhibited elsewhere, it will be advisable to remove the shoe; the foot should then be pared out, to ascertain if there be any wound or bruise in it. The nail holes should be carefully examined and pressed with the pincers, or gently struck with a hammer, to discover any symptoms of tenderness; the heels of the sole should be pared down, and the parts struck gently with a hammer; this is preferable to pressing the bar and crust with the pincers, as is usually done, for this often produces pain in some feet, when there is no disease, and often fails in causing pain in others, when there is a deep seated corn.

After paring awhile, the smith will very probably say there is no corn; but we must not be as satisfied until we have pared almost to the quick. If the horse be very lame from a corn he will almost always favor the foot; but in so doing he will not, however, extend his limb out straight to its full length, but will elevate the heel without extending the foot very far, which will give a knuckling appearance to the limb. Should none of these symptoms be exhibited, we must consider the disease to be deep-seated, and then it is all-important to ascertain if the animal points his foot; for, if such is the case, in all probability the cause of lameness exists in the navicular joint, supposing it was a fore foot we were examining.

It will seldom be necessary to go through these various manipulations seriatim; we may sometimes pounce upon the seat of lameness at once, and very often detect it after a moderate examination; but there are cases that will demand our utmost attention and experience, and will often put to a severe test the professional talents and tact of even the most skilled veterinarist.

Horses sometimes exhibit a slight lameness immediately after being shod, though quite sound before. Such cases may arise from the shoe being nailed on too tight, and are often relieved by removing the shoe and re-applying it more gently, this lameness most frequently occurs in horses with very thin horn, and is ascertained by the manner in which it comes on, and the absence of any other visible causes. The shoe in such a case may also have an improper bearing, pressing severely on weak spots, or on the sole or heels; or the heels or sole may have been pared too much, or unevenly.

Persons unaccustomed to horses will more frequently pronounce the wrong limb than the right in cases of slight lameness. The cause of their blunders may be thus easily explained. They perceive that a horse drops the moment one foot comes to the ground, and they immediately conclude that that must be the lame one, fancying that he drops from the pain received when it meets the ground; whereas the fact is, he rests in ease on the lame foot, and beats his whole weight on the sound one.

## The World's Great Catastrophes.

There have been solar, lunar, stellar catastrophes innumerable. But our world has especially suffered—plagues, epidemics, cyclones, eclipses, earthquakes. At one toss of the earth in Tamboro out of a city of 12,000 only 26 people escaped. On the 1st of November, 1775, at Lisbon, 60,000 perished in five minutes, and 200,000 before the earth stopped rocking. Many centuries have not been able to resurrect this Pompeii and Herculaneum which Vesuvius in a few hours buried. Rossberg mountain, in Switzerland, falls crushing the village of Goldau. One mountain in Italy destroys 200,-000 people while sound asleep in the night. By convulsion Japan was broken off from China, and the Caribean islands from the American coast. Near the mouth of the Ganges three islands had 340,000 inhabitants. In one night the sea swept over, leaving 315,000 dead. It has been lately demonstrated that a whole continent, reaching from Europe to America, has sunk; a continent that allowed people to cross from Spain to South America, and they did cross, some of the inhabitants of the sunken continent going to Europe and some going through the valley of the Mississippi and crossing out into Mexico, remains of their cities and graves found in Ohio and Colorado, and on the white oaks of, as various parts of our land; a whole contingent gone down between Europe and America—a continent once densely populated. The Azores that we see off the coast of Spain is the top of one of the great mountains of the sunken continent. Plato wrote of that continent, its glories and its ruin, and men thought it a romance. But a fleet of German, British, and American ships—the Gazelle, the Dolphin, and the Challenger—have revealed by deep sea soundings the entire contour of the sunken continent. The Australian archipelago is only the top of the mountains of a continent that once extended from India to America. The most of the earth is now water; once it was land. Scenes of trouble on rock and sky and sea, in earth's fauna and flora, geological trouble, oceanic trouble, political trouble, social trouble, domestic trouble. Standing in the presence of so many stupendous devastations, I tell you that the great need of the ages is divine sympathy and omnipotent comfort and they are to be found, not in the Brahma of the Hindoo nor the Allah of the Mohammedan, but in Jesus Christ, and to Him shall the gathering of the nations be.—*Extract from Dr. Talmage's Sermon, Sunday, Sept. 3d.*

**Mr. R. W. Kohler,** of Kohler's wax works brings to this State, from Sydney, Australia, the celebrated red greyhound dog Peasant Boy, by Mark Twain—Old Bet out of Bab at the Bowster, runner up to Lord Lurgan's Master Mc-Grath in the Waterloo Cup stakes of 1867. Peasant Boy is said to be a model dog and has taken many bench show prizes in the colonies. When over the effects of his sea voyage we should like to see him tried with some of the get of Speculation or other local sires.

## HERD AND SWINE.

### Splenic Apoplexy.

An alarming disease among cattle has been and is still prevalent in many parts of the country. About Lexington several cases have occurred. The disease is of a charbonne or septic character, attacking chiefly cattle two years old and older. Cows are more liable to it than others. It is analogous in character to the disease called black-leg or black-quarter in calves a year old and under, developed by the same causes, but affecting different organs.

The cause to which the disease is to be ascribed is undoubtedly the rank vegetation of this year. Grass has seldom been so luxuriant; cattle that have been changed from one part of the country to another—from poor pastures to where there is abundance of grass—cows that have undergone the same changes or have likewise been turned dry, lay on flesh rapidly, blood accumulates in the system and becomes loaded with effete matter, rendering it unfit for proper nutrition and causing a putrefactive condition. This altered condition of the blood causes it to accumulate in the soft structures of the body, in the areolar tissues producing black-quarter, and in the spleen, the uncous membranes of the intestine, etc. etc., producing splenic fever or apoplexy.

In some cases death is very sudden, in others the disease will progress gradually, the animal will be dull and feverish for some days—one day better, another worse—the pulse quickens, the breathing becomes hurried and painful, the bowels costive, the urine colored, in some cases black—these symptoms will continue for some days until death ensues. In a few cases the disease assumes a milder form, when the animal will, after a few days' sickness, recover its usual health.

Examination after death shows the spleen three or four times its normal size and weight, and gorged with blood, the uncous membrane of the bowels covered with petechial spots and patches of extravasated blood, the liver and the urinary organs exhibiting the same appearances.

The treatment of the disease is very unsatisfactory; when an animal is first taken the bowels, if costive, should be relieved by a dose of oil or by injections—two-drachm doses of chlorate of potash given three times a day, and if there is much fever an occasional dose of nitrous ether and belladonna will lessen it.

When the disease once appears in a herd—considering the cause to be a too abundant supply of nutritious food, producing this diseased condition of the blood, it will be necessary in order to effect a change in, or prevent that condition, to remove the stock to an old or bare pasture; good hay may be fed daily but by all means discontinue the run of an over-nutritious diet.—Live Stock Record.

### The Pig in Agriculture.

The pig has recently been spoken of in contempt when compared with our domestic animals. But if we examine his good qualities at all critically, we must award him a high place in agriculture. He is found to produce a pound of product from less feed than either cattle or sheep, and is, therefore, the most economical machine to manufacture our great corn crop into marketable meat. Our peoples are becoming wiser every year, and exporting less, proportionately, of the raw material and more of condensed product. If it takes seven pounds of corn on the average to make a pound of pork, as is no doubt the case, the farmer begins to see the economy of exporting one pound of pork, bacon or ham, instead of seven pounds of corn. The difference in cost of freight makes a fine profit of itself; besides, the pound of meat is usually worth more than seven pounds of corn in the foreign market. The production of pork should be encouraged on the further consideration that it carries off less of the valuable constituents of the soil than beef. The fat pig contains only three-fourths as much mineral matter per cwt. as the fat steer, and only two-fifths as much nitrogen per cwt.; and therefore the production of a ton of pork on the farm will carry off only a little more than half the fertility carried off by a ton of beef. Besides, a ton of beef will require nearly 50 per cent. more to produce it. This gives in round numbers 124 comparative effect of producing pork and beef. It is thus evident that the pig should have a high place in our agriculture; should be fostered in every way; his capabilities studied and pushed; his diseases carefully noted and prevented, for he is the most profitable meat-producing animal on the farm. The pig is an excellent adjunct to the dairy, turning all refuse milk and even whey into cash. As he is king of our meat exports, so let us treat him with great consideration.—Rural New Yorker.

Cooking Food for Hogs.—An extensive breeder, after feeding for eight or ten years, goes upon record in favor of cooking, and expresses the belief that one-fourth of the grain is saved thereby. The following experiment is given in his case: Two sows of the same litter, and the same every way, except in weight, were selected. No. 1 weighed 292 pounds and No. 2 280 pounds. No. 1 was fed for sixteen days on cooked unground corn, and from the consumption of two bushels and twenty-one quarts, gained thirty-six pounds. No. 2 was fed for the same time on raw whole corn, of which she consumed three bushels and three quarts and gain thirty pounds. Another instance is given in which shoats were fed on raw and cooked corn for six weeks, the result being that while those fed on raw corn gained two pounds to the bushel, those fed on cooked corn gained fifteen pounds to the bushel—results which are certainly worth the candid attention of breeders.

A Canadian Enterprise.—A special dispatch from London, England, to the Toronto Globe, says: "Another Canadian enterprise has been launched upon the market here. To-day the Canadian French Meat Importation Company issued its prospectus. The company has been formed for the purpose of placing cheap and wholesome meat at the command of all classes. It will import only the first quality of fresh meats of all kinds from Canada into the United Kingdom. The capital stock of the company is £50,000, in shares of £1 each. The Directors also draw attention in their prospectus to the well-known superiority of Canadian cattle over those from the United States. The company will be their own importers, and sell direct to the consumer from their own depot. The average cost of meat delivered in England is 5d per pound. A contract has been made with a responsible party in Canada to supply the meat.

The Auditor of Ohio reports 714,555 horses 1,318,755 cattle, 4,504,509 sheep and 1,924,077 hogs in the State and subject to taxation.

### Cattle on the Plains.

There may be said to be three great cattle belts in the country, to be designated respectively as the north; the northwest and the south belts. The first takes in Montana and Dakota, and is tributary to the Northern Pacific road; the second includes the western half of Nebraska and the territory of Wyoming, and is tributary to the Union Pacific road; and the third consists of vast portions of Texas and the Indian territory, and seeks an outlet through the Iron Mountain, the St. Louis and San Francisco, and other roads leading to St. Louis. Of the three the northwest belt is at present the most important, but that to the north of it is growing the most rapidly, and with the completion of the Northern Pacific Railroad will gain and retain the supremacy. I realized this fact from the manner in which the stockmen laughed at me when I inquired it was possible for cattle to go through the hard winters of that section unfed and unsheltered. "Why, way up in Dakota" was the reply, "the cattle come through the winters better than they do in Texas." I may here remark that anything like housing or feeding cattle in the winter is utterly impossible in any of the great belts. There is not timber enough in the territory of Wyoming to make sheds for the cattle owned here. And it is quite as unnecessary as it is impossible.

The cattle ranges of Nebraska begins about 200 miles west of Omaha. There is no line to mark where agriculture leaves off and grazing begins, but at about the point named timber and water become too scarce for profitable agriculture, and the ranchmen take up what the plowmen can't use. The land is owned in equal parts by the rancher and the Government, but is enjoyed free of rent by the cattle men. The ranchers vary according to the size of the herd and the run of the watercourse. The first essential in laying out a ranch is water. As for grass, there is always plenty of that, summer and winter. A moderate estimate is said to be two miles of water front, running twenty miles back, for each 1,000 head of cattle. So that a man with 20,000 head of cattle—which is about the largest number owned by any man and more than twice the average of all—would require forty miles of water front, running back twenty miles. It is not always an easy thing to find this. When found and occupied however, the rights of the finder and occupants respected, by his brother stockmen to the extent that he is allowed to remain in unmolested possession. It is a maxim among them that stockmen respect each other's rights. There are persons called jumpers, however, who looks pon the stockmen as having no rights which they are bound. to respect, and who make it a business to pick out there best land in a range and settle down upon it under the homestead or pre-emption laws, remaining just long enough to be bought out, when they move to another range to play the same part. The stockmen complain grievously about this as an annoyance from which they should be protected by law. They cannot buy the land from the Government in quantities to suit them, and they think Congress should pass a law allowing them to lease it [or a term of years, so as to allow them to improve it and to give them a fixed tenure. One of the gentlemen with whom I conversed on this subject told me of a queer mistake he had made by a failure to understand the nature of the United States land laws. A couple of years ago he commenced buying up land warrants, thinking that these documents gave the owner to a right to occupy and possess public lands for their face value. He bought $5,000 worth at an average of $1.25 per acre, and supposed he had nothing to do but find 4,000 unoccupied acres suitable to his purpose and call them his own." Imagine his astonishment when he discovered that although he held the title, as he supposed, to 4,000 acres, he could occupy for his own use but 160, that being the only amount which could be entered by land warrant by any one person, no matter how many land warrants he held! So his $5,000 investment was still on his hands.

It is undoubtedly true that Congress should regulate this matter for the benefit of the cattle men, but it is also true that in doing so Congress should carefully guard against rings and monopolies by restricting the amount of land to be leased to each person, and by giving as fair as possible, an equal chance to all who desire to invest in the business. The cattle men have their own association and their own regulations, which seem to be intended not only for the benefit of those who are in, but for the exclusion of those who are out. No cattle man has ever been known to encourage an outsider to embark in a cattle-raising business.

After a good deal of cross-questioning and figuring I arrived at some conclusions as to the profits of cattle raising as a business. I met one man, for instance, who had just returned from Chicago, where he had sold 1,000 head of cattle at an average of $40. They were a little over three years old and had been on the ranch two years. He bought them in 1880 for $8 a head. Counting interest, care taking, loss by death, and all other items of expense, they stood him, when put on the cars $11 50 each. Add to this an average of $5 each for transportation from Ogallala, Neb., to Chicago—$100 per car, the actual cost, and an average of twenty head to the car—and the animals on the market have cost him $16 50 each, leaving a net profit of $23,500 on the herd. This was simply one—and not a large one—of the many transactions made in the course of a year by the same stockman. Indeed, it was in the nature of an outside transaction, because the rule is to raise the cattle from birth instead of buying them at a year old.

This gentleman has already sold 16,500 head of cattle this year, and now has on his ranch 13,500 head, of which he expects to send about 5,000 head to market before the close of the season. It is very safe to say that a man starting with 2,500 head of cattle can, after the second year, keep up his herd and sell $25,000 worth of cattle every year. This is to say, he can net that amount after paying every dollar of expense. But 2,500 is considered a small ranch. The average is more than twice that number. Of possible and actual losses to the business there are really none to speak of. Two per cent. will cover all the losses by death for a good year, winter and summer, and, strange to say, the losses are greater in the summer than in the winter. In a very bad year, though, the losses is prevalent, the losses never exceed five per cent.

The stockman's year begins in May with what is called the "round up." At the end of the season, in early winter, the cattle are turned loose without herdsmen, and allowed to roam through the whole of western Nebraska and Wyoming, finding food and shelter as they can. When the spring opens a small army of cowboys is employed—each stockman contributing to the force in proportion to his interest—to range the whole plains, gather up the cattle, and drive them to certain stations or places previously agreed upon at a meeting of stockmen held at Cheyenne. From these immense gatherings each owner selects the cattle bearing his brand, and forms them into a herd to be driven to his ranch; he also brands the yearlings of his herd who have, up to this time, run with their mothers. After this grand division the cattle are put in charge of the cowboys for the summer.

The grass is fine and they improve rapidly, and are ready for the market in June or July. For the largest ranch the expense up to this time is not over $600. The cowboys get about $30 each for the "round up," but no stockman is allowed to furnish less than twelve, no matter how small his herd may be. Some are taxed as high as 2,000 cowboys. The master is all arranged at a meeting of the stockmen, held under the auspices of the Stockmen's Association. When the cattle are all gathered in and branded for the summer, the only help needed for the rest of the year is a sufficient number of cowboys to watch the herds, which is generally done by sleeping in the grass under some friendly shade. Three cowboys will take care of 5,000 cattle, keep them all together, and drive to the railroad station such as are to be sent to market.

### Grinding Cheese Curds.

The following question has been sent to us by a subscriber for information: "Do the factories of central New York grind all their curds, and what is the process?"

Yes, nearly all of our best factories grind their curds. Here and there is one which does not grind, but they are all gradually coming into the practice. We recall one of the very best which has not until this year ground the curd, but is now doing so, and will continue to do it.

The process is as follows: The milk is treated in the usual way until the whey is drawn. Then it is packed until the acid is developed sufficiently for the iron to draw threads of one-quarter to one-half inch long, and until the whey is well drained out of it. It is then run through the curd mill, some removing it to a curd sink for that purpose, and others grinding it over the vat. Most of the makers do not salt until after grinding, as it is thought that they can salt more evenly in the ground state. We do not see that it makes much difference, as factories which use either method sell here at the top of the market.

After grinding there is no hurry to put the curd to press. In hot weather particularly it will be all the better for the cheese, if the curd is allowed to lie from three-quarters to an hour before going to press. Thorough separation is more necessary for curd from poor milk than for the very best. If a lot of curd is particularly rebellious, it is put through the mill a second time, although this is only done occasionally on account of the extra work. In ordinary weather and with good milk, the curd is ground but once, and is put to press about half an hour afterward. Of course it is properly stirred after grinding, in order to facilitate the aeration and to prevent the particles from cohering together again.

It is much more convenient to use a curd mill in a factory that has steam power than in one without it. The labor of turning the mill, although not of long duration, requires quite an expenditure of muscular power, and in hot weather is really hard work. But where steam can be brought into use, it does the work easily and evenly, and all our large factories are supplied with this power. In fact, it may be said that as a general rule our fancy factories do grind their curds, and that the process is believed to be a very beneficial one in the months of June, July, August and September.—Utica Herald.

### Milking Qualities.

A copious flow of milk, sustained through many months, is a quality which has been produced by art in domestication. Wild cattle rarely provide more than enough milk to rear their offspring, and the flow of it is of a comparative short duration. Small in volume, the milk is rich in quality, but the lacteal organs soon dry off again. This, of course, is in harmony with the requirements of the young animals in a wild state, and is a correlation of the roving life and the hap-hazard feeding of the dams. More milk than the calf requires under such conditions would be a waste of material energy which nature does not encourage. It would, moreover, be an encumbrance to the mother. Wild cattle are neither good milkers nor good fatteners, and in parts of England where calves are allowed to run with their domesticated dams generation after generation, the breed of such animals is not favorable to milk-giving. Like the teat of the mare and ewe, the milk is smaller in quality and of short duration. The desultory and irregular sucking of a calf or foal or lamb is not conducive to the development of a large flow of milk, and it distinctly tends to shorten the flow. Hand-milking of a similar character has the same effect. Young people are allowed to learn how to milk on cows which are pulling dry for calving, not on those which are still in full flow. New beginners soon dry up a cow's milk, and bad milkers do the same. Heavy milking properties, then, are artificial, in the sense that they have been developed under domestication, and by careful breeding for a given end; yet, like many other qualities which are little more than perms in nature, they become hereditary by long usage. Few sorts of animals, if any, are more susceptible than cattle of being moulded into what we want no physical quality is so easily trained and developed as that of giving milk. It is a function which, constantly varying itself, can be dwarfed or extended at will. By means of intelligent training, kind treatment, and intelligent breeding, it can be developed and made hereditary; an opposite system keeps it in a state of nature. The habits of a cow and the food she receives have a good deal to do with her milking powers; quick and silent hand-milking does the rest. The practice of hand-milking cows has all along tended greatly to the development of the lacteal glands, and this development has become hereditary in our best milking breeds. The ewes of the Larzac breed of sheep, from whose milk the famous Roquefort cheese is made in France, have been hand-milked for generations, so that their milking qualities are now considerable and inherited. By repeatedly exciting the teats it is even possible to cause an animal that had never borne offspring to yield a small quantity of milk, and a cow sometimes remains barren several years after having had a calf, giving a profitable quantity of milk all the while.—London Live Stock Journal.

### Sheep and Goat Skins.

Few who have not especially investigated the facts have anything approaching an adequate conception of the magnitude of the trade in sheep and goat skins. The product from these skins goes into the multifarious manufactures of which morocco, kid, etc., form the basis, though by far the greater proportion is employed in the manufacture of women's and children's shoes. For most of these skins for shoemaking the United States, of course, depends upon the far East. For this there are two reasons. Very few goats are raised here; and the skins from American-bred sheep are not so close-grained and leathery as those from animals less highly bred, and reared under a more primitive system of husbandry.

Hindostan, the principal source of supply, has a yearly product of skins estimated at 40,000,000, pretty equally

ed between those from the sheep and those from the
The sheep alluded to is a poorly-covered animal—
n to the skin trade as hair sheep, and described as pre
ng an appearance midway between that of the sheep and
oat. Of these 40,000,000, nearly all the sheep skins are
ed in India, and a majority of the goat skins. The an-
number of these skins brought to the United States—
d upon the average for the past three years—is about
00 bales of 500 skins each—in round numbers 9,000,000
s. It will not be far from correct to divide this importa-
into three classes, say 5,000 bales—2,000,000 tanned
p skins, and 12,000 bales of goat skins, of which one-
are tanned and the remainder "raw." Thus the Indian
uct may be accounted for, viz:

| | |
|---|---|
| goat skins shipped to the United States | 3,000,000 |
| ed goat skins shipped to the United States | 3,000,000 |
| ed sheep skins shipped to the United States | 3,000,000 |
| ped to Europe and absorbed in India | 31,000,000 |
| | 40,000,000 |

e skins brought to the United States are sold to the
s at an average price of about fifty cents, and will supply
per" material for three to four pair of shoes each. When
bove figures are considered in connection with the sup-
d sheep skins obtained in this country, and the large
bers imported with the wool on from Madras, Bombay,
utta, Cape of Good Hope and South America, some esti-
may be had of the extent of consumption—reaching in-
very avenue of commerce and ramifying every line of
ry or necessity known to the household.

## A Dairy Phenomenon Explained.

n inquiring friend asks why the last part of a milking is
er than the first; accompanying the inquiry was the re-
k, that he has several times made the inquiry of parties
m he thought ought to know, but the answers have not
n either convincing or satisfactory. We may not succeed
better than those personally interrogated, in satisfying
inquisitiveness of our friend, but we will nevertheless
our version of the same.

he answer most commonly made to such an inquiry is,
the cream rises to the top of the milk in the udder, just
f would if standing in an open vessel. This answer, just
heavier part of the milk, naturally settling towards the
er part, or teats, is supposed to be drawn out first, and
lighter part, or cream, being in the highest part of the
er, would follow down as the milk from below was with-
wn, and would consequently be the last to be extracted.
s reasoning is generally accepted, and regarded as a satis-
explanation, but involves inconsistencies which, perhaps,
s been discovered by our friend, and give rise to his re-
ted inquiries. An answer like the above implies that the
der, or at least each quarter of it, is an unobstructed and
tinuous sack, like a bladder, with nothing in it to pre-
t the liquid contents from flowing up or down, or in any
ection, as gravity might lead them to move. If the mam-
ry gland was provided with a reservoir of the character
lied, in which the milk is contained was free to move, we
old expect, when the milk was drawn from a human
mmary gland, that the rule of richness would be the re-
rse of that with the cow—the last part of the milk drawn
could be the poorest, because the heavier and poorer por-
n of it would be expected to settle into the lower part of
e breast, below the nipple, and be the last to leave when
e gland was emptied; but it is not so. The same rule ap-
ies to both cow and woman, and involves an inconsistency
the explanation:

The interior of the mammary gland of a cow, and of other
imals as well, is not a continuous sack, like a bladder.
ere is no resemblance between the two organs. The udder
sembles a sponge than a bladder. It is exceedingly vas-
lar, and is made up of an immense number of small cavi-
s, varying in size from hay-seed to peas, which serve as
serveirs for holding milk, and which are separated from
ch other by membranes and tissue of variable thickness.
ese little reservoirs are all connected by a system of tubes
ich resemble blood-vessels; and which anastomose and
mify like blood-vessels. The cavities, or reservoirs, are
e else than globular enlargements of the tubes, more or
s distant from each other. As all the different branches
d divisions of veins in the system finally come together into
single vein at the heart, so all the tubes in each quarter of
e udder come together and end in a single tube in the teat.
ese tubes resemble blood-vessels in another respect. Both
tins and arteries are provided through their whole length
th valves, at varying distances, which allow the blood to
ss through them in only one direction. Through the ar-
ries the blood can only move away from the heart. In the
tns it can only move towards the heart. So the milk tubes,
werever they connect with their enlargements or reservoirs,
e provided with strictures, which can be opened or closed,
d which serve to prevent the milk from passing in more
an one direction. Milk can only move through them
wards the teat; never away from it. In one respect milk
bes differ from blood-vessels, which they so much resemble
many others. The ramifications or the branches of both
teries and veins terminate in a still more minute passage,
lled a capillary, at one end of which an artery ends, and at
e other a vein begins. The fine branches of the milk tubes,
stead of ending, like the blood-vessels, in a hair-like pas-
ge, terminate abruptly with an enlargement, or swell,
hich virtually caps the extremity of every division with a
inute globular sack or cavity, technically called a "follicle."
these follicles or cavities milk and cream originate and
owd out into the tubes connected with them, and thence
ward toward the teat. the tubes and reservoirs growing
rger as the distance to the teats shortens, while their con-
nts are increased by additions from intersecting branches.
nalogous to the progress of blood from the veins. In such
arrangement of reservoirs and tubes as this with the milk
ways moving forward, and barred from a backward move-
ent at the outlet of every little reservoir through which it
ast passes its devious way to the teat, it must be evident
at it would be impossible for the cream to get to the top of
e milk. If a sponge was filled with milk, the cream would
and a better chance of rising than it would of getting to the
pper part of the udder, through such a network of tubes
d stoppages. One might as well expect the red globules of
a blood could all rise to the top of his head, against the
rrent and valves in his veins.

There is a plainer and more natural way of accounting for
e accumulation of cream in the last part of a milking.
hile in the number and arrangement of the cavities a
orage somewhat resembles the interior of the udder, in one
spect it is quite different. The walls of the cavities in the
onge are always distended, whether filled or not, and, if
impressed, at once spring back on being released from the
essure. The walls of the milk tubes and reservoirs, and
e follicles or sacks at the extremities of their branches, are
wt collapsed and in contact, except when kept apart by
ving milk in them. With the constant inclination in their

walls to be in contact, it must be evident that a liquid would
ork its way through them more easily than a solid. Milk,
it must be remembered, is a mixture of liquid and solid matter, as much so as a mixture of brine and meal would be.
The serum or liquid part of milk is water, holding sugar and
cheesy matter in solution, just as the water in brine holds
salt in solution, and the cream globules are particles of fat in
a solid condition, and sustain the same relation to the liquid
part of milk as a meal does to brine, especially when mixed
with a brine just strong enough to incline the meal to float.

If it was attempted to pass either of these mixtures of
liquid and solid through the milk tubes, beginning at the
follicles, the liquids in either case would work along through
more readily than the solids. The meal in one case and the
fat globules in the other, would meet with impediment from
friction with the collapsing walls of the slender tubes, and
would fall behind in the journey, and be dripping out in the
last milking of the liquid, and this is just what happens in
the udder to make the last part of a milking richer in cream
than the first. The larger the globules of cream, the more
friction they meet with in moving along the tubes, and the
more gets left behind. It is for this reason that in milk having very large globules, like that of the Channel Island cows,
the difference between the first and last of a milking is greater than when they are small, as in the milk of the famous
Dutch cows.—Live Stock Journal.

## Stock Raising on Small Farms.

The owners of small farms, or farmers engaged in a system of mixed husbandry, often over-estimate the advantages
for stock raising possessed by those with large farms and who
make this a specialty. The latter do possess important advantages, but there are some compensations for the stockman
on a small scale.

The man with a thousand acres, a herd of hundreds, etc.,
can have men employed who will give their whole attention
to one branch of the work, and learn to do this better than
the average laborer. The large farmer has advantages in
selling. He can make up one to a dozen carloads of stock
ready for the market; can sort them to make them sell to the
best advantage; can have buyers come to his place, or can
ship as he chooses. Full use ofhome is foundforone or more
stallions, bulls, etc., and the cost of keeping them counts as
a little matter. But the small farmer—he with one hundred
acres, for instance—has also his advantages. He can rear
and feed a few colts, steers, pigs or lambs with almost no
outlay for extra labor and very little perceptible cost in good.
He needs horses for his farm work. Often brood mares
serve his purpose equally well, and the one, two or three
colts dropped each year cost comparatively little to rear.
Cows for a home supply of milk and butter, of course, will be
kept, and often there is abundance of grass in the pasture
for a few "young things," and in the winter the stalk-fields,
the straw stacks, the soft corn, etc., can be eaten by these,
when it might otherwise be mainly wasted. When feed fails
the large stock grower must have men whose main business
it is to feed-and care for the stock. The small farmer can
add the little additional work as a part of the necessary
"chores" and scarcely notice the extra time or
labor. Of two farmers of the class we are speaking of, the
one "with a little extra stock" will usually do as much and
as good work during the summer in the fields as his neighbor who "only keeps a cow or two, and enough hogs for his
own meat."

The small farmer has another advantage. It seems to be
a law of animal life that the fewer of any sort of animals that
are kept within a given area, the more healthy they are. We
once asked a large and very successful swine breeder this
question: "What is the greatest number of hogs that can be
kept together with the highest percentage of profit on each?"
To this he promptly answered: "One. The profit on each
hog decreases in proportion as you increase the number."
His idea was that the health and thrift of the herd decreased
in proportion as the numbers were augmented. The greater
economy of feeding and management possibly more than
for feeder may practice may possibly more than compensate
for this loss of health and thrift, but the illustration serves
to show that the advantages are not all on one side.

It is not necessary to money making and deserved success in the stock breeding that there should be a large herd
of stock. The late Mr. Sharpless, whose Jerseys had a reputation all over the country, is said to have rarely kept more
than a half-dozen cows; and on the Channel Islands nearly
all the herds are quite small. In horse breeding, there is no
reason why the man with three or four mares may not take a
high rank as a breeder.

Even for a "renter," if he can secure a lease or the land
for three or five years, a fair degree of attention to stock
growing will be much better than the exclusive grain growing, which is so often the rule with this class. We have
known instances in which two renters each seemed "to just
about make a living;" but at the end of five years one would
have a lot of live stock worth a few hundreds of dollars; the
other have less than when he commenced.

## The Theory of Generation.

The power of animals to propagate their own likeness
is hereditary, and transmitted from one generation to
another. The principle upon which the theory of generation
is founded reaches from the inception of the colt in embryo
to the delivery. The breeder, to be successful, must investigate causes that produce certain changes after the union
between the sexes, as well as the effect resulting from the influence of each parent over their offspring. The sire and
dam have their respective shares in propagating the form
and substance of their issue. They co-operate together in
generating the vital and physical powers of their produce;
and the breeder must understand the influence of each
partner, in order to mate progenitors so as to make congenial
hits. The food of the embryo is furnished entirely by the
mother. It is held by some physiologists that the health
and robust constitution of the colt will depend more upon
the health and physical power of the dam at the time of conception, than upon the condition of the sire. But this maternal influence is modified by other causes, such as long-
line breeding, coming down from an unbroken chain of powerful generators, and possessing the prepotent faculty of
entailing their breeding on an illustrious line of succession
in blood. The influence of sire and dam over their colts will
depend very much upon their blood, and the constitutional
superiority of one over the other. The strongest and best
bred animal will have the predominating influence over their
produce. The more prepotent, in consequence of the
the inbreeding—avoiding incest—the more certain the inheritance will be entailed, unaltered, on their colts.

Acquired qualities become hereditary from long-estab-
lished acquisition. The breeders of fast trotters find bred,
and possessed of the strongest physical powers. He is generally credited with the most influence in breeding.

If the mare runs back through a superior line of progeni.
tors, and has a more perfect inheritance than the sire, she
will entail the leading characteristics on her colts, and shape
the destinies of her issue. The rule is, that the parent which
has the most constitutional vigor, inherited from the most powerful progenitors, with fixed characteristics established in the
breed, will transmit that link-bred inheritance, and have the
most influence in breeding.

The influence that the sire has upon the dam on her first
impregnation, which appears to extend to her subsequent
colts, is a difficult problem to solve. There are several examples preserved in the Museum of the College of Surgeons
in England, where a quagga had been bred to an English
mare, and her colts ever afterwards, by English stallions, put
on the marks and color of the quagga—at least for three generations.

It is important that a stallion be selected to breed with a
young mare, for the first time, that is pure and unadulterated,
if it has such an impression on the nervous system that she
will entail the likeness of her first partner on the third generation of her colts. It has been held, upon this theory,
that if you breed a young thoroughbred mare to a cold-
blooded horse, her produce will be ever afterwards adulterated
with common blood, from the nervous effect upon the dam
from this first embrace. These experiments have been confined to the hog and the horse, and are too few and far between
to establish it as a general rule that will apply to other domestic
animals.

If the sire and dam have material points exactly alike, they will
transmit those points to their colts with so much force that they
will perpetuate them to another generation. The sire and
dam should be alike to breed well together. There will be a
uniformity in their stock that could never be realized from
dissimilar kinds. When the sire and dam are matched in size,
substance, speed, and stamina, they will have the same extra force in generation that a matched pair would have over a
single horse for service. The nearer the parents are alike,
the more certain they will be to transmit their likeness to
their young scions. The inbred progenitors are more alike
than those crossed out to strangers, and will have as hereditary force of character that those crossed out do not possess.
If the sire and dam come down from a very speedy race, and
both should be bred through the same fast line, they would
be likely to perpetuate speed to their issue, because they come
down from a common origin; and have got speed as a fixed
inheritance, established in the breed.

The Devon cattle are uniformly red; you can get no other
color, because red is a line-bred inheritance established in
the breed from time immemorial. If the sire and dam both
have fixed characteristics, they will transmit them to their
colts as sure as the Devon bull entails his color on his get.

In sheep husbandry, when the breeder gets possession of a
ram that is a superior stock getter, he places great value on
him. As soon as he is proved, his stock brings largely increased prices. They find a ready market, and prove a source
of revenue. It is indeed of some celebrated English breeders
of sheep that in their early experience they rented out their
rams for two or three dollars for the season. After they had
modeled them over into their own approved type, and raised
them up to a standard to meet the public approval, they could
rent out their best rams for several thousand dollars annually,
and there was great competition to get them at that.

This shows that skillful breeding will accomplish. It discovers the causes that produce the changes in the union of
sexes, and selects congenial partners. It imitates all imperfect animals from the breeding stable, and leaves nothing but
perfect parents to produce their kind.—National Live Stock
Journal.

## Dogs, the Farmer's Pest.

It is surprising that intelligent farmers will permit the existence of the droves of worthless curs which infest the country. Shepherd dogs, hounds, and well-bred field dogs are
all very well, because they are useful, and when carefully
bred, a source of revenue to the breeder. Of what amount,
however, is that large class of curs, mongrels, and half-starved
creatures, which are met at every turn in the country? They
must live, and to do that, they are compelled to become the
enemy even of the owner. The amount of property destroyed
by them in sheep alone, is annually very large, besides their
destruction of poultry and game. It is to be hoped that the
mania for keeping these worthless creatures will soon run its
course, though the speediest mode of bringing about the desired change, is the introduction of the already named varieties. The Legislature of this State once enacted a law taxing
dogs, but the law was so unpopular that it was subsequently
repealed. Was there ever such an evidence of ignorance?
If a man of common sense would only compute the cost of
feeding one of these worthless beasts, he would find it equal
to the support of at least a dozen sheep, or hogs, and as an
offset, nothing gained.

Shepherd dogs make useful and excellent watch dogs, and
no doubt if trained to do so would hunt rabbits and possums
as well as any other breeds. Their very keen scent
Thoroughbred hounds never kill sheep, therefore they are
harmless, and afford great sport to those who have as ear for
canine music. Field dogs have a weakness for sheep and
poultry, though if properly fed, and held in restraint, no
harm can come from them, while their produce are in great
demand, particularly when their pedigrees are above suspicion. Therefore, we conclude that the common dog should
be declared a nuisance, and at once exterminated. Let the
shepherd dog supplant the cur.—Southern Industries.

A New Mexican Volcano.—Near the town of Vallecitos,
N. M., situated about 12 miles southwest of Jemez Hot Springs,
and about three miles southwest of Vallecitos, is a volcano
that is now giving the inhabitants of that town much uneasiness. This volcano is burning more or less all the time, and
the fresh appearance of the lava around it shows clearly that
no great period of time has elapsed since the last eruption.
The people there say that this is the first time in their experience that the volcano has behaved in such an unruly manner. Frequent shocks of earthquake are felt, and loud rum-
blings, accompanied by puffs of smoke, issue from the crater.
It is the firm belief of everyone in the neighborhood that a
fearful eruption is about to take place, and many of the inhabitants of the town are moving up to Valtes for safety.

Dwarfed Kangaroos on the Staked Plains.—There is
said to be a kind of dwarfed kangaroo in the Staked Plains of
Northwestern Texas. Its body is about eight inches long; its
forelegs are not more than one and one-half or two inches in
length, while its hind legs are all of six inches. It has a
tail about eight inches long, completely bare except a tuft of
long hairs at the end and a ridge of short hairs on the upper
part. The animal is also a marsupial, the pouch being well
developed. It is of a soft blue color. Its only mode of loco-
motion is by jumping, precisely like the kangaroo. It jump-
eight or ten feet.—New Orleans Picayune.

## THE
# Breeder and Sportsman.

PUBLISHED WEEKLY BY THE

BREEDER AND SPORTSMAN PUBLISHING CO.

THE TURF AND SPORTING AUTHORITY OF THE
PACIFIC COAST.

OFFICE, 508 MONTGOMERY STREET
P. O. Box 2358.

*Five dollars a year; three dollars for six months; one dollar and a
half for three months. Strictly in advance.*

MAKE ALL CHECKS, MONEY ORDERS, ETC., PAYABLE TO ORDER OF
BREEDER AND SPORTSMAN PUBLISHING CO.

*Money should be sent by postal order, draft or by registered letter, ad
dressed to the "Breeder and Sportsman Publishing Company, San Fran
cisco, Cal."*

*Communications must be accompanied by the writer's name and address,
not necessarily for publication, but as a private guarantee of good faith*

JOSEPH CAIRN SIMPSON, - - - EDITOR

ADVERTISING RATES.—Displayed $1 50 per inch each insertion or pro
rata for less space. Reading Notices, set in brevier type and having no
foot marks, 30 cents per line each insertion. Lines will average ten
Words. A discount of 25 per cent. will be allowed on 3 months, 50 per cent.
on 6 months and 60 per cent. on 12 months contracts. No extra rate
charged for cuts or cutting of column rules. No reading notice taken for
less than 50 cents each insertion.

San Francisco, Saturday, November 11, 1882.

Mr. M. J. Henely is a duly authorized traveling agent
and correspondent for the "Breeder and Sportsman."

## P. C. B. H. A.

### The Fall Race Meeting—Bay District Course.

As has often been stated in this paper the fall meeting
of the Pacific Coast Blood Horse Association commences
to-day. For the particulars of the races, so far as the
stakes, purses and entries go; the advertisement will give
ample information, and to those who are conversant with
the horses nothing more is necessary to acquaint them
that that part of the programme is first rate. There are
others though not so "well posted," and many racing enthusiasts are looking for a different class of information
than the nominations and entries afford.

Well conducted racing meets with almost universal approbation. The only opposition comes from those who
have no knowledge of the sport, the austere, the bigoted,
the fanatic, and those who consider themselves too good
to look with favor on sports of any description. Some
have a stronger liking than others, but it must be conceded that there is no outdoor pastime which has such a
wide range in the civilised world. That the races which
have been held under the management of the Pacific
Coast Blood Horse Association have been eminently satisfactory is admitted by every one who has attended the
meetings and who is candid enough to acknowledge his
views. There has been such a well-grounded knowledge
that transgression would meet with condign punishment
that those who were not kept straight by a sense of
honor were compelled to honesty. Fortunately this
class of owners, trainers and jockeys is now so rare in
California that the rogues are the exception, and a large
majority of those engaged in the pursuit would scorn the
petty larceny proceedings which at one time prevailed.
Of the great number of races now under the auspices of
this society there was only one that had the semblance
of crookedness, and punishment followed immediately.
There are other duties pertaining to a Jockey Club, and
these, too, have been well done. The past is always accepted as an augury of the future, and the confidence of
the public so gained it is not likely will be lost. Punc-
tuality has been a prominent feature in the management,
and the assemblages have been as decorous as the most
fastidious could desire. There is then the most complete
guarantee, an assurance that the coming meeting will be
perfect as the preceding have been, and this first and essential point firmly established.

That the racing will be first-class we predict without a
shadow of doubt. This prophecy is grounded on what
the horses have done, and on the breeding and form of
the debutantes which will aid the third division in making every contest a fierce struggle for supremacy.

We cannot understand how any one can witness a good
race without feeling a pleasure it is almost impossible to
describe. There are few things in this life which will
compare with it. It may be that there is an excitement
in the battlefield more intense to one who has not the intensity of delight marred by craven fear. We have always imagined that to the brave a cavalry charge was
the acme of enjoyment, and that the few minutes were
crowded with emotions that years of ordinary life could
not furnish. But fortunately the "glorious panoply of
war" is a rare play, and there are horrors and devastations following in its wake.

Though the fields of turf battles in this country are
not verdant lawns, " mosses green or beds of roses where
you dream the rest," the brown ovals are the scene of
life and animation. The "warming up" is a pleasing
overture, and as the sheeted and hooded animals glide

by so gracefully, every motion is eagerly scanned by
those who have a monetary interest in the coming fight.
There are many changes wrought by the "preliminary
gallops," and a short, constrained stride dethrones the
favorite, while the sweeping easy action installs another
in the place. But when the clothing is stripped and the
graceful forms displayed there is interest to all. The
tiny manikins in silks and satins appear to be a part of
the animals, with coats almost as lustrous, and equally
as eager for the fray. Under the rules of this association there cannot be long delays at the post, and the vexatious waiting for a start is of rare occurrence. The red
flags fall and they are off. A compact body at first, but
soon there is a blending of colors, and then changes rapid and perplexing. Red is in the lead, and then the purple and gold, and then the yellow, and the green, and
all the colors of the rainbow, in various combinations,
have a prominent place. Past the stand for the first
time, and it is only the practised eye that can catch the
positions, as they flit past, drumming music from the
course, and there is silence and expectation. Around the
turn those on the outside are pulling back to save
ground, and two or three who have the advantage of the
inner part of the circle are opening a gap. The straight
running on the backstretch is almost sure to develop an
exciting interlude. There is a shortening of the gap,
and your favorite, perhaps, has joined the leaders. It is
too soon yet to predict the issue, and again the course
gives the advantage to those favored with the inside.
Some are already out of the race, but enough are left to
make the run home the grand finale of the contest.
There is little pulling now. One, maybe, with a trifle
the best of it at the seven-furlong mark, is braced a bit,
though the others are too close to cry much relief, and
a hundred yards from home every muscle and nerve of
horse and rider is strained to the utmost. There is a
roar of voices, a grand chorus of cheers and that one
race is over.

The cards for the opening day (to-day) show four contests, likely to prove as close and exciting as can be.
It is needless to give them in detail, in this place, as by
turning a few leaves, all the conditions and entries will
be found. As has been stated before, horsemen, generally, are cognizant of the merit of those engaged, and
this opinion is nearly unanimous that there will be arduous struggles in all of the four. This is an "extra day,"
being an addition to the regular programme, and a very
good one it is. The first "regular" day of the meeting
is next Wednesday, the 15th inst., and again a reference
to the advertisement will show that it will be a "gala
day" to those who attend. There are features which
"the ad. does not show. The first race is the Ladies'
Stake for two-year-old fillies, in which are twenty nominations; the distance three-quarters of a mile. In addition to the fillies that have shown so well in previous
races are others that promise well and this can scarcely
fail to be a merry spin.

The second race is heats of three-quarters of a mile,
and in this are eleven of the flyers of the coast. The
Vestal Stake is the third on the list, and in that is the
Duchess of Norfolk, Precious, sister to Lottery, and
several others of high breeding, and which report speaks
of as being very fast. The Vestal is a dash of one and
and a quarter miles, and now that the Duchess has returned from the Eastern tour, the interest in it will be
greatly enhanced. After the shaking up in the railroad
accident, to say nothing about the long trip from Baltimore, she will have a hard task to beat those which have
stayed at home. The fourth is a handicap for two-year-
olds, and then comes the hurdle race. This is one and a
quarter miles over five hurdles, and the three named in
it are said to be famous jumpers. A race "over the
sticks" is always popular, and when horses are up to the
business and the riders proficient it is a pleasing addition to those where there are no obstacles to overcome.

As there will be another issue of this paper before
the second and third "regular days," viz : the 18th and
23d inst., there will be a better opportunity to present
the attractions. It is sufficient at present to say that
there will be no flagging in the interest, and we were
not surprised to hear a man relating the difficulty he had
in selecting the days he would attend. By agreement
with his partner each were to have a couple of days at
the races, and the toss-up gave him the choice. After
patient study of the programme he was still at a loss,
and solicited our advice. We also "gave it up," further
than that he should include "The Baldwin," so that was
a dash of four miles, in which there was more than a
probability of six starters.

We have not written anything about the course, etc.,
and it would be a grave omission to have neglected that.
There is little necessity for extolling the Bay District
Course, as it is recognized to be one of the best in America. It is admirable from every point of view. The
track is safe and fast, the stands are commodious, and
from them and the balconies of the club house and hotel

every motion of the horse can be seen. The course and
appointments being all that can be desired, accessibility
is the next point to be considered. Again, it would be
difficult to improve on that. The cable road and the
steam dummy land passengers within a short distance of
the entrance, and the cars run in such close order that
they are rarely overcrowded for any length of time. As
the fare is only five cents and the time half an hour, it is
a cheap and expeditious method of "going to the races."
But to those who own horses, or who have the spare means
to hire, the drive is very enjoyable. Lately we crossed
the bay very early in the morning and drove to the
course. Leisurely we forced the horse to jog through the
park, and had it not been that we were restricted in time,
the sauntering jog would have been changed to a "pot-
tering" walk. Never before did it appear so beautiful.
There was dew on the grass and the air was full of
fragrance. Another day we returned when the sun was
dropping into the Pacific. The gloaming had beauties
as well as the morning, and at this time of the year mid-
day is also lovely. There are no rough winds now as in
summer time, and the sun sends warmer, cheerier rays.
We cannot see that there is anything in the way to
prevent the fall meeting, 1882, of the Pacific Coast Blood
Horse Association from being a complete success. The
purses are well arranged, the entry list is full, the contestants are worthy of each other. The horses which
have garnered honors by the Atlantic, on the "Eastern
shore," in the "city by the lake," are here to participate.
Thousands have cheered them to victory in that far-off
country, and it can scarcely be possible that there will
be any lack of numbers to give them a rousing welcome
home. There should be still heartier plaudits from the
shores of the Pacific, and this we confidently anticipate.

## THE STANFORD STAKE AND THE ELEC-
TIONEERS.

An error was made in the Adair article last week by
stating that six of the get of Electioneer, were nominated, whereas five were all. We consider that not, even the
very fast trotting of Wildflower, Bonita, Fred Crocker,
Hinda Rose and Albert W is better proof of the "potan-
cy" of Electioneer than the fact that of the twenty-one
nominations three of these five were the only starters in
the Stanford stake. This is something unparalleled in
the history of the turf or track, for though all the get of
one stallion have been starters in some of the running
stakes and purses the circumstances were entirely different. Here was a large stake with sixteen of the get of
other stallions of known merit. It closed at a time
when the Electioneers had not been tested, and another
singular and note-worthy circumstance was that in the
selections from Palo Alto, those which proved to be the
fastest were not named. Those of the right age were
Wildflower, Bonita, Marlet and Bertha, either one of
which it is fair to assume could have won it. People
are prone to give too much credit to an isolated case of
speed, and should a sire be lucky enough to get one
phenomenal performer, in their minds it outranks scores;
which are only slightly inferior. One lucky hit has
vast influence in forming their estimate, and the one example sufficient for them to base their views upon.
But when the offspring of a sire shows brilliant speed,
and this in many cases, and also a large number which
inherit a good share of it, that is the highest position obtainable in the stud.

Only a few years ago the time made by Adair and
Clay Jr. would have given them world-wide celebrity.
The trotting of Startle in 2:36 told him for $20,400, and
it is comparatively a short time ago when a three-year-
old beat 2:30, so that the 2:36½ of Clay Jr. and the 2:34½
of Adair give them a very respectable place in the calendar. The other contestant, Anteeo, made a very fine
showing for a colt that had attack after attack of pinkeye for months, and the week previous to the race his
throat was swollen so badly that the whole space between the jaw bones was filled.

There is another valuable quality which was demonstrated in the Stanford Stake, and that is the capacity
to stand training without injury. When so many of
the get of a horse, particularly all of the same age, are
trotting in races it is good proof that they are hardy as
well as fast.

## "TROUBLE, BUBBLE."

Now that the trouble is over, that the bubble has
"busted," let all hands turn out to the races.

The jubilant victors will be in the right mood to enjoy the sport, the defeated, despondant from unlooked-
for reverses, will have their spirits cheered by, the excitement of the races.

The loudest cheers, at first, will come from those who
were on the winning side. After a race or two the
blues will vanish, and the losers will vie with the con-
querors in giving the vivas as reasonably as a thousand

of men can voice. Neither party can afford to miss the opening day, and after that there will be no desire to neglect the others. Here is neutral ground for all parties to occupy. More interest will be felt in the winning of their favorites than those who have completed the political race. By the way, there is a good deal of similarity in the turf battles and the fights political, and, saying that the former is more honest, a straighter run, the resemblance is more than a sameness of outline. In both are handicaps, selling races, and jumping matches, and weighs to burden the good, and a remission of them to aid the inferior.

There is little necessity to expatiate on this as the analogy will strike every one who can make a comparison.

In the meantime let all attend, and our word for it, you politicians—at least those on the losing side—will leave the course in a more contented mood than when you went.

### ADHERE TO THE LAWS.

The only safeguard the sports of the turf and track can depend upon is a rigorous adherence to the laws that are framed for the government. There may appear to be a temporary gain by violation; there may seem to be substantial benefit in going contrary to the mandates, but time will prove that every trespass brings serious injury. We have heard people argue that there should be broad interpretations, that technicalities should be ignored, and that there should be latitude in construction, if even it had to be admitted that the looseness was directly opposite to the spirit and also the "letter of the law."

We are writing now more particularly in regard to the rules that govern entries and eligibility to participate in races.

Very wisely, indeed, they have been made strict, very properly framed so that there can be no deviation without infraction.

It may appear very hard that whereas a person has been forgetful or negligent, twenty-four hours' delay should entail a rejection of an entry, but if any time is given it may as well be a week as the seventh part of that time. The trotting rules were amended at the last Congress of the National Trotting Association, so that they are now the same as the racing. That is, a letter containing the entry, plainly postmarked on the date the entry closed, the entry is valid. Preceding that time it was necessary that there should be notice by telegram, registered letter, or the entry reach the person appointed to receive it by the specified time. We will not argue at present which we regard as the best plan, but urge that whichever is in force must be obeyed.

There is another rule equally as emphatic that requires absolute compliance, although there are cases that call loudly for its abrogation. That is the one entailing disqualification of the horse on the death of the owner. While it disqualifies it also relieves from engagements. It may be that large expense has been incurred in the rearing and training, and the expected return should be an asset of the estate as well as when a crop has been planted, and that the heirs be permitted to reap the benefit. But there the law is, however, plain, precise in language, no ambiguity or chance for different construction. Where the rules are plain there is only one course to pursue, and that is, to adhere to them rigidly, technically. A great deal is said about technicalities by those who advocate an easy, slipshod way of conducting races. It is generally thought to be a term of reproach and the technical man held worthy of reprobation. But whenever the close observance of the laws is lost sight of, be it called technical, there is sure to follow disaster at some time, and the only safety is to keep to the laws as closely as possible.

### WINTER SHOOTING GROUNDS.

While there is little change to be expected in the character of the shooting grounds along the bay shore south of this city, being as they are within the influence of the tides, there is more or less change among the tule islands where most of the shooting is done. At one time the water will be too deep, and another time there will be no ponds, or no feed. Then again the birds mysteriously migrate to or from particular islands from no obvious cause. Where there will be good shooting this year there will be none next.

It may interest many of our readers to know, in general terms, how the shooting is among the islands up river. In the Suisun marshes, where the Cordelia and Teal clubs have their preserves, and along on what are known as the "Hard Lands," the shooting has been good. The feed is good and the birds are plenty. Some very good bags have been made and the boys are all having good sport.

On the lower end of Sherman Island, which is usually looked upon as good shooting ground, there has been fair shooting this year, but it is very unsteady. There are

wide sheets of water there, interspersed with clumps of tule, making this a first rate place to shoot. But after a little rain the ducks leave the ponds and go off on to the high lands. After two days' rain they string out to the hills, where they stay three or four days and then move back. What ducks have been shot on Sherman are mainly small ones. The Tule Belle club have their preserve near Clark's Slough on this island.

On Brannan Island the water is very deep, averaging eight feet, and the hunters do their work sculling, which is hard work even for the professional. There are half a dozen professionals on this island.

On Andrews Island there is no cover, the country being very open. It is hard to find a blind on the island.

On Grand Island there is plenty of good feed but they are not killing very many ducks. What are killed, however, are good ones.

The well known Jersey tract on the right hand or mainland side of the San Joaquin, some distance above Antioch, there is now nothing, though it used to be a favorite hunting ground. The tract is dry as a bone. The heavy rains even did not put any water there, for what fall was absorbed as a sponge would take it up. If the rains are heavy again, now the ground is partly filled, some water will stand, but it will have to rain eight or ten days to do this. Last year there were more ducks killed on the Jersey tract than anywhere up river. They relieved it however, and mended the break in the levee, and the water was let out by floodgates. Some of the ponds last year were four feet deep so they would not drain off, but the dry weather of the summer dried them up.

Bouldin Island is all leveed and farmed now so there is no hunting.

Staten Island is pretty dry too; potatoes were raised all around the edge of the island last year, and there is only a little water on the middle.

The Sacramento river is turning out more game this year than the San Joaquin. On Monday evening there were only 20 sacks of game from the whole San Joaquin came to this city. More than half of these were geese.

One piece of ground up near Sacramento is doing very well now and is the choicest piece on the river. It has been leased by market hunters.

The lower end of Union Island is one solid swarm of geese. They fly in immense flocks and by their constant noise keep the ducks away. The ducks do not like to be near them so there are very few ducks on the island. At the head of the island at Naglee's there has been some good shooting lately, but the late rains drove the birds off to the high grounds.

The Alviso marshes ought to have plenty of ducks now after the rains. All along the shore on both sides of the bay there is more or less shooting if people can only get to places comparatively isolated. The Petaluma and Sonoma marshes are very little frequented by hunters from this city because there are no good and ready means of communication. Petaluma marshes used to be the best duck shooting station to be found.

### THE EMBRYOS.

Very unfortunate was the rainfall to the Embryos. Had the downpour of last week been postponed a few days there would have been three capital races last Saturday, and now there is no telling what the effect of this let up will be. It not only necessitated the postponement but it also stopped the work of the colts, so that for the best part of two weeks the exercise has been confined to jogging on the road. With one exception, Election day the track was in condition that work could be given, though it was so soft that it did not give much opportunity for speed unless to those whose gait was suitable. There are "experts" who predict that benefit will follow this enforced idleness, and that faster time will result. This is not our belief as a majority of fast trotters require fast work once in a while to key them up to the proper pitch. Nevertheless there is a good prospect for fine sport, and it is certain that the races for yearlings, two-year-olds and three-year-olds, on the same afternoon, is a novelty in the sports of the track. It is also certain that the youngsters that remain in are a good lot, and without anticipating anything sensational, we do not hesitate to hazard the prophesy that faster time will be made in two of these races than ever has been scored by the same class previously. That is in actual races when colts met in a real engagement.

At this time of writing the probability is that Monday will be the day. From present appearances it is not likely that the track will be in condition any longer, though good enough perhaps to "fog out" the day previous. Notwithstanding that postponed races usually do not awaken the original interest, in this case there appears to be a growing desire to witness the performances of the colts, and those who attend will be well repaid for the journey to the track. In another place we have descanted on the pleasure of a trip to the Bay District

course and the description falls far short of the reality. Equally enjoyable is the journey to the Oakland Trotting Park, and to those who live in San Francisco, the enjoyment is heightened by the contrast. The sail across the bay at this season of the year is a rare treat, and although for nearly nine years we have been making (with occasional breaks) daily trips, it is always a source of pleasure so much so that we sympathize with those who live on the wrong side, and feel surprised that Oakland has not, at least, one hundred thousand inhabitants. Since the Berkeley road was extended to the wharf, so that there is no change of cars, Shell Mound station, within a short distance of the gate of the Park, is so easily reached as Broadway, and the time is less, only thirty-five minutes from the foot of Market street. Should the matter be favorable so that the Embryos can be trotted on Monday, it will give the opportunity to those who visit and the trip alone will compensate them for the trouble the city to see the running to put in another "extra day," and outlay. But even the most ardent admirer of the "high-mettled racer" will find satisfaction in witnessing the contests of the highly-bred colts. There is a good outlook for a large attendance and with a reasonable expectation of a good entertainment.

### HOME AGAIN.

The California Stable has returned from the Eastern trip, and we are pleased to learn that they have come home in good shape so far as getting back sound is concerned. We have been so busy that it was out of the question to spend the time to visit them, and again we were unfortunate in being away from the office when Mr. L. R. Martin called or we might have obtained information from him that would be of interest to our readers. The matter is only deferred, however, and we feel satisfied that a history of the tour will be good reading at any time. There are surmises that need confirmation before appearing in type, and it is useless to speculate when facts can be obtained. It adds greatly to the interest of the race meeting that they will participate.

### THE THANKSGIVING DAY TROT.

Those who have horses that have a fair show to compete with the ones that are named should not fail to enter in the $1,000 trotting purse advertised in this paper. It is a liberal purse, especially for this season, of the year, and should meet with a liberal response. There being three "moneys" it gives an opportunity to others beside the winner, and there is another feature. If owners do not support the track by making entries, they cannot expect that tracks will be kept open at a loss, and any diminution in the number of courses near San Francisco will be a serious drawback to their interests.

### EDITORIAL NOTES.

A New Star seems to have arisen in the turf firmament of Idaho in the two-year-old filly Hattie Harris. At the late meeting of the Idaho Fork Club at Boise City Hattie Harris made her entree with considerable eclat. During the week she ran and won four races, one a dash of half a mile for two-year-olds in which three started, one of half-mile heats for three-year-olds and under, and a three-quarters dash for two-year-olds, and the last and best performance was on the closing day of the meeting when with fifteen pounds extra weight up she beat a field of aged horses a dash of one mile and a quarter. Hattie Harris was bred and raised in Idaho and will make her mark in the world of runners if that last effort has not sent her to the paddock permanently. She is by Marmaduke from Pironette, Marmaduke by Enquirer, dam Catina by imported Australian; Pironette by Harvey Villain, dam Farfaletta by imported Australian.

Next Thursday on the Bay District course Killip & Co. will offer at auction sale a consignment from the stud of W. L. Pritchard which is well worthy of the attention of purchasers of thoroughbreds. There is little question that the breeding of thoroughbreds is sure to be remunerative in California, and the day is not distant when there will be a demand greater than the breeders can supply. Notwithstanding the misfortunes that befel our horses in the East this season they made a good showing, and excellence once established is certain to bring buyers. Mr. Pritchard has many very finely bred animals and the success of the colts of his breeding is a guarantee of future well-doing. That bargains will be obtained is beyond doubt, as it is seldom the opportunity offers to obtain such high strains at "public outcry."

Killip & Co., on the same day as the Pritchard sale, will offer the trotters Rowdy Boy and Ashley. The former is one of the most promising four-year-olds on the Coast, and Ashley is too well known to require more than a notice. Rowdy Boy is by Rustic, and his dam was Louise by Belmont from Silver Cup. As the dam of Rustic was also by Belmont, there is a double influence of this valuable strain which insures him "going the route," and as he has shown 2:35 in his exercise, he has the gift of speed as well. Ashley in addition to his known track qualities is said to be a capital road horse, and with the speed he has it will take a top-notcher to beat for a brush or stay with him the "the length of the road."

## THE GUN.

### Deer Protection.

Wednesday the close season for deer in this State began according to law, and from then until July 1st of next year it will be unlawful for any person to kill that kind of game or to have it in his possession. The law is very strict, and under it a person can readily be convicted of caught transgressing its provisions. In some counties, however, the law is avoided by a class of hunters who have been given some semi-lawful permission by Supervisors to kill deer 'bout of season. The fact that nobody has as yet seen fit to bring these lawless shooters and equally lawless officers into court gives no justification to their acts. In Nevada county, wherein the Supervisors have taken it upon themselves to set the State law aside, there are, we believe one or more sportsman's clubs which belong to the State Sportsmen's Association, or have declared their intention of joining that body. The latter has a standing offer of reward for information that will lead to the detection of parties guilty of infractions of the law; and therefore we shall expect to hear of arrests being made in case deer should be openly killed in Nevada county after this date. The excuse offered by the Supervisors for their action (for it is only an excuse) is a very thin one, and does no credit to their intelligence as citizens nor their integrity as officials sworn to obey the laws. They were too ready to act upon the advice of lawyers who are not competent to construe the statutes, and the sooner they repeal their ordinances giving permission to kill deer out of season the sooner will they win the good opinion of all intelligent persons. Game protection is regarded too lightly altogether by those whose sworn duty it is to uphold the laws of the State. Even public opinion has not yet been fully aroused to its importance, and we only fear that the subject will be fully understood when it will be too late. Year by year the deer of California are killed by thousands out of pure wantonness (misnamed "sport") and for the value of their skins. Some men think it a great thing to boast of that they succeeded in killing a score of deer during the season, not one-fourth of which were eaten. They are simply killing he geese that lay the golden eggs, and we believe the child is already born in California who will live to see the day that deer will be entirely exterminated within her borders. This should not be and would not be if people would only give the subject the consideration which its importance merits. We only hope that our prediction may not be realized—that the sportsmen of California will yet rise in their might and drive the poachers, hide-hunters and big-score men from the field by securing the enactment of laws that will deal effectively with them. No class should have a monopoly of the wild game of the State. It should be protected for the use of all—those who are to come after us should have a chance as well as ourselves.—*Sacramento Bee.*

### Goose Herding.

The last issue of Frank Leslie's *Illustrated Weekly* contained on the first page a large illustration of a California goose-herding scene. The subject of the drawing was taken from an article which went the rounds of the California press last spring, describing the manner of killing wild geese on the Glenn ranch. The picture represents the air filled with geese, which are being fired upon by two men, attired in beads and buckskins and mounted upon spirited horses. How little these artists know about California goose-hunters! The goose-herder is generally mounted upon an old mule too lazy to move any faster than at a snail's pace, and we have even known some goose-hunters to be sent out on oxen. As a general thing the fellow who goes out to drive the geese away from growing grain is given an old Harper's Ferry gun that kicks harder than a Queen Anne musket. He moulds his own bullets, and naturally is a little careful about shooting many of them away. Goose-herding is considered the laziest job on a ranch, and one who follows it is generally looked upon with scorn. Now, while writing of goose-herding we don't mind telling of a two months' experience at that kind of work. Before coming to the Golden State, the writer of this had read of the magnificent sport to be had upon the ranches at shooting geese. In fact we had formed the same kind of an idea about it that the artist in Leslie has drawn. Being naturally fond of out-door sports, upon arriving at California we went immediately to an uncle's ranch, and there accepted a position as chief herder over the broad acres. The horse given us was a little old broken-down Indian pony, and the weapon with which we were to exterminate the feathered pests had done duty in the Revolutionary War. The first day in the field was cold and foggy, and riding around over a large field, fording sloughs and going hungry, was not a very delightful turn of the bright days we had anticipated. Days ranged into weeks and not a single goose had been killed, although huge quantities of powder and ball had been wasted. At about the close of the second month we put a dose of cold lead into the pony's head—accidentally—and the hard-hearted uncle didn't need us any longer. Goose-herding is not a joy to be "hankered arter"—it is far from being a spirited sport. To a person unacquainted with the occupation it might appear as being one grand, big hunt, but it isn't.—*Chico Record.*

HUNTING BY MOONLIGHT.—Commissioner Giroux, A. C. McAlpin, J. K. Hopkins and G. A. Kreakle went on a hunting excursion to the Sink of Humboldt two or three days ago. J. L. Guthrie, who returned from Lovelock yesterday, says the hunters went to Emmons' lower ranch, at the head of the lake, and camped. At night the air resounded with the gabbling of geese and the squawking of ducks, and the hunters, who had gone to bed early so as to be in good trim for the morrow, decided to get up and commence the slaughter of ducks and geese by moonlight. They dressed in a hurry and commenced firing at the fowls which were continually flying at low range over their heads and kept on until they had exhausted their ammunition, and the worst of it all was that they had to eat bacon for breakfast next morning, as they had killed neither duck nor goose.—*Silver State, Winnemucca, Nev.*

It is reported that in some places the new grass has attracted flocks of wild ducks and geese, which may in a measure account for the scarcity of water fowl in the marshes. Geese, both white and gray, are said to be plentiful at Union Island. There are not many of the sportsmen that kill these birds as they are quite heavy to carry away, and some lately arrived from the north have a fishy flavor.

Mr. Haskell was down at Mallard Station last Sunday and bagged twenty-eight ducks. Sprig at this place are the most plentiful, and are in good condition. Duck have been so numerous at this, the Alameda sportsman's preserve, as at any, and with every prospect of its good shooting holding out during the balance of the year.

### Moose Hunting in Nova Scotia.

The hunting season for moose in Nova Scotia commences on the 15th of September, when calling may be carried on with success. Calling is the art of imitating the bellowing of the cow moose during the running season, and thereby attracting the bulls to within range of the hunter's rifle; this acquirement is one which necessitates a deal of practice and skill, as a false note uttered would suffice to put an end to all hope of a bull's appearance. The Mic Mac Indians are the best callers though it is only a very small proportion of them who are really proficient in the art. The noise uttered by the cow moose is imitated through a birch bark horn some fourteen inches in length.

Though an exciting sport, calling has been condemned for reason of the alarming decrease of bulls which has taken place from the practice. In all parts of Nova Scotia, the number of cows predominate to such and extent over that of the bulls that only a proportion of the former can, during the running season, ever receive the attentions of their lords; it is therefore hoped that calling may, for a time, if not permanently, be stopped, as it bids fair, as at present carried on, to do more toward accomplishing the extinction of moose in the province, than any of the other many dangers the animal has to avoid.

Creeping or still hunting commences with the first snow and lasts till the end of January; it is on this epoch that I now propose to write a few lines. The ground selected for moose hunting must be one where the settler has not yet intruded, where the stillness of the forest is not disturbed by the strokes of the lumberer's ax, where the gold prospectors have not yet ventured. To reach a spot thus secluded and undisturbed many a weary mile along broken roads, over frozen lakes and through the pathless woods has to be tramped, and this too with the burden of a pack on one's shoulders containing provisions and requirements for the time intended by the hunters to be spent in the woods.

Camps exist throughout the country and it is in one of these the moose hunter makes his home—these abodes are generally wigwams, sometimes deserted lumberers' camps and often only lean-to's built against one of the large granite boulders which abound throughout many parts of the province. Let us then, reader, in the refuge release ourselves from our burdens and against this rock build our fire and commence by collecting sprigs of fir which for the next three weeks will represent our downy couches, while old Matthio, the hunter, unpacks the grub and foe, the cook, gets water from the lake and puts life in the old camp once more. No furniture is needed to make our home comfortable—no repairs to make our house habitable—nature in her bounty provides the wherewithal to meet the wants of the hunter, and demands nothing from him but to collect and make use of her supply. But of camp and camping doubtless my readers possess experience which renders further dilation concerning them unnecessary from me; let us then turn in for the night, sleep soundly, and dream of our success for the morrow.

"What sort of day, Matthio?" is the first question which issues from what might have been mistaken for a pile of blankets.

"Fine day, to-day."

Though the wind whistles thro' the pine trees and angry clouds are drifting apace overhead and though fully two feet of snow lies on the ground 'tis a fine day withal—so up out of that blanket, wash down those slices of salt pork with a dish full of tea, fasten on your snowshoes and take Matthio for your guide.

"How many rounds shall I take, Matthio?"

"Six plenty."

Away then across the frozen lake, through the grove of hackmatacks which skirts yonder hardwood ridge, plunge maple trees now carefully noting the wind Matthio strikes off in a direction which to most of us, my dear reader, would appear to be exactly opposite to the direction in which our game was heading. Follow him, however, put your snowshoes in the tracks of his and keep as close to your hunter as you're able.

"Look, Matthio, there's another track."

"Dat same; you load your gun all right."

Though confident of having come to the back of your opening the breech to assure yourself is at this time excusable. So blunder on again in the footprints of your Indian, who you see is once again off the track.

"My, don't you do dat, moose scare like any ting."

No, sir, you really must select some more fitting time for tumbling over windfalls and breaking sticks than when on a hot track, so withdraw your gun from the perpendicular position out of that snow heap, pick up your cap, clear your barrel of snow and along. Another curve is described, and the hunter again closes on the track, and there a few yards further on is the bed in which our noble game reposed last night; another curve, and yet another is described, each curve getting smaller, and the tracks each time they are reached getting fresher.

Stealthily now creeps the Indian, picking an easy path through the maze of trees, his ears and eyes are strained to catch sound or sight of the animal whose keen senses demand the display of the hunter's utmost craft.

Now, crouching, he passes under the splaying branches of the spruce trees; now noiselessly he bends and steps over a low bough which impedes his way; now he makes a detour to avoid a thick mass of fallen timber, through which it would be impossible to creep without noise—he stops and looks—and you, my dear sir, must really keep closer behind him. No; he uses all his brawn earth on the roots of a fallen tree; a little further and the Indian commences a fresh curve, but this time back in the direction of our advance. The limit of this curve is to within sight of our former footprints, and then wheeling about we proceed in a direction parallel to our last movement. This maneuver means that our hunter has overshot his mark and is now working down toward his game; an injudicious step at this critical period, the breaking of a twig or other clumsy trifle, would probably end our chance of sport for the day.

"I say, Matthio, look at that poro—"

"Moose!"

"Where?"

"Where! See! see! my soul! there."

"That black thing!"—bang—

"Fire again, quick!"—bang—and a severed branch of spruce falls to the ground.

"You hit him, sure 'nuff, first time," says the Indian, as he hurries to the spot where the beast stood. "Blood thar; we smoke pipe; he lie down."

So, after a bowl of tobacco, we leisurely proceed on the tracks. "He tumble 'gainst that tree; he lie down thar;" and there indeed is the blood-stained imprint of his huge form. A little further on, and there lies the noble animal himself, straining every muscle to rise to his forelegs, which are thrown out in front of him, his eyes staring in terror at his dreaded foes. Once more the woods ring out with the crack of a rifle, and our game lies lifeless in the snow.

By the foregoing sketch of a very ordinary moose hunt it will be seen that little else than a constitution capable of enduring fatigue and hard work is required from any one desirous of killing a moose, the Indian piloting you through the woods, tracking and pointing out your game, which when found generally presents a stationary mark at a distance of from twenty to sixty yards.

The Mic Mac Indians as moose hunters are unsurpassed. In disposition they are civil and obliging to the last degree; anxious always to make their employer's life in the woods as comfortable as surrounding circumstances will admit of. By nature they are inclined to shyness in the presence of white people, and it is a matter of great difficulty to extract information from them regarding their method of hunting or the means they adopt for finding their way through the intricacies of their forest home. The following item of conversation I once noted down—it being typical of an Indian's manner in answering questions:

"All these lakes run north and south, don't they Louis !"

Ind.: "Yes, some."

"Which way do those round the camp lie?"

Ind.: "North and south, guess."

"Then the head of this lake points north!"

Ind.: "Yes, dis lake runt east and west."

In conclusion, I may say a few words on the prospect of moose becoming extinct in the province of Nova Scotia. This prophecy is one which for years has been made by those who are always inclined to consider the present uncomparable with the past. Thinned out as moose have undoubtedly been through the use of traps and dogs for their destruction, and through the laws relative to their preservation being badly administered, there are still many localities in the province where moose are abundant, and it will be gratifying to sportsmen to learn that the game society is annually becoming more active in increasing its efforts in a proper direction, which, if continued in, will result in moose long continuing to roam and multiply throughout the vast domain of woodland which covers the province of Nova Scotia.—*American Field.*

### Great Fun Bison-Hunting—for the Bison.

Lieutenant Neville Chamberlain sends to the London *Field* a vivid account of his adventure with a bison when out shooting in the woods of the Maharajah of Mysore. He says: "I had no companion, so took with me one of the local shikaris, named Kampa, and another man to carry my spare rifle. My battery consisted of a D. B. 8-bore rifle and a D. B. 12-bore rifle. I took the 8-bore myself, and, giving Kampa my 12-bore, crawled up to the herd through the grass. Out of some high grass just in front of me rose a splendid old bull. He was only about twenty yards off, and was just moving behind a clump of bamboos, when I fired at the point of his shoulder with the 8-bore. A great stampede took place. The smoke hung in the long grass—which as I knelt was nearly up to my neck—and I could not see to give him the second barrel. I ran forward, but could see nothing; so, still running, I opened the breech of the rifle; threw out the empty cartridge, and was in the act of pushing a fresh cartridge home, when from behind a small, thick clump of bamboos, some five yards off, me and about thirty yards from where I had started. I heard a loud snort. Kampa gasped out, 'Kartli' (bison) and vanished; and at once the bull came charging down at me. I only had time, as he hurled himself at me, to spring behind a small tree on my left. He whizzed past like a battering-ram, cutting a large slab of bark out with one of his horns, and, turning almost in his own length, was round at me again. This occurred four or five times, but my attention was so fully taken up in dodging him that I could not get the rifle ready for use. To make a long story short, it ended by my catching my foot in a creeper. I fell over backwards, and as I rose he ran in and tossed me. One horn—I suppose his left one—fortunately went clean through my breeches and flannel shirt, tearing them to ribbons, and, as far as I can remember, I seemed to sit on his head, while the other horn passed under my right arm. He threw me a long way and I fell on my back under some bamboos, the rifle dropping out of my hand from the shock of being tossed. I was a good deal shaken and out of breath, but I think my first thought was that now he would leave me if I kept still; but he ran up again and stood over my body, shaking his huge head over my chest. I thought then that it was hopeless. I could think of nothing better to do to protect myself, so sat up and struck him four or five times with my hand, on the eye, which I could just reach when his head was down. He shook his head and pushed me back with his nose. I managed then to plant several severe kicks on his muzzle with my heavy hobnailed boots, and he commenced sparring at my legs with his horns. I did my best to keep them out of the way, but got a few bruises on the shins. This began to get monotonous, and I knew another toss would not find a friendly part of pants. He was still stamping over me when I got in a good volley of hobnails on his nose, shouted at him and sat up to hit him again; then, to my intense relief, he gave a bellow, left me and went crashing off down the hill. I never saw that bull again."

NOT A HUNTER'S PARADISE.—A lot of Reno "ramrods" a day or two since boarded a Nevada and Oregon train, and went out to the present terminus, 'Oneida Station. They struck out to the nearest timber, some eight miles distant, but found not even so much as a quail. That particular section was recently described as being filled with deer, grouse, sage hen, quail and all kinds of game. Now the settlers say that the storm has driven all the game up into the mountains. Storms are usually supposed to have the contrary effect. The hunting at Oneida is somewhat like the fishing at Reno. If you go there to fish when the water is low they tell you that you cannot wait till the river is up, if you wish to catch any fish; go when the water is high, and they tell you that any fool knows that fish never bite except when the river is low.—*Virginia (Nev.) Enterprise.*

Hunting parties at Millbrae have been having, during the last two weeks, quite a variety of luck, as the bags of quail have run from two dozen to nothing, and poor hunters having fair luck, where good shots had bad.

**A STRUGGLE WITH A BEAR.**—While Harry Tucker and Wellington Sprague, conductors of the Maine Central Railroad, together with Orville A. Robinson and A. Q. Leach of Portland, were on a hunting expedition at the forks of the Kennebeck a few days ago, they suddenly encountered a monstrous bear, which gave a savage snarl, and then started for them. The young men had no heavy ammunition, but they made quick use of what they had, pouring hot shot into bruin's body. Quickly reloading, they all fired again. This second round enraged the bear and she howled fiercely. Finally the fighting came to close quarters, and the hunters attacked the infuriated beast with the butts of their rifles. Tucker broke the stock of his rifle short off at the first blow, and reminded him of a monster pocket-knife which he had purchased at Bingham. Taking that out, he ordered his companions to come more hold the attention of the bear while he crawled behind her. The bear now stood erect on her haunches, and the three men were engaging her attention as well as they dared to do. Tucker rushed up behind her and plunged the knife deep into her side twice, his companions in the mean time rushed for her with their guns. The moment she felt Tucker behind her she turned and made a stab for his shoulder, just catching his coat and heavy shirt near her teeth. Before she could do more the stabs in her side ad done their work, and she fell dead with Tucker's clothing still in her teeth.—*Boston Journal.*

Many hunters who have been up along the narrow gauge railroad this week have had very good luck. Last Tuesday one young man left the city at 5 o'clock and returned at 5, with twelve quail, eight rabbits and other small game as the result of his day's sport.

Mr. Golcher was up last Sunday at Union Island and had other luck than any one on the island that day, bagging fifty ducks before 10 o'clock in the morning.

The sportsmen of Washington Territory are trying the experiment of stocking with the Bob White quail.

## THE RIFLE.

### The First and Second Regiments.

The spirit of friendly rivalry and competition seems at last to have taken hold of some of our riflemen. There is a stick of some sort or other every week and the scores made by the marksmen are second best to none of the East. If the military companies were to take hold of target shooting more, private teams and marksmen would take more interest in the use of the rifle. The California Rifle Association's last shooting tournament revived the interest considerably, as was manifested by the Second regiment sending a challenge to the First Regiment to shoot a match of fifty men, fine shots at the 200-yard target, Col. J. H. Dickinson of the First immediately accepted the challenge and last Sunday the match took place at Shell Mound. L. G. Perkins of the First Regiment made the best score that we can remember, and made the best score of the day. By the First Regiment the following scores were made:

| | | | |
|---|---|---|---|
| G. Fredericks............ | 21 | Burmester............ | 21 |
| B. F. Moss............... | 21 | H. M. Taylor......... | 20 |
| J. C. Dunn.............. | 18 | Corp. L. R. Townsend | 22 |
| C. T. Smith............. | 19 | Pritchard............ | 21 |
| J. Stockwell............ | 20 | Sergt. S. B. Burdick | 17 |
| J. H. Redberry......... | 18 | Cummings............ | 20 |
| Capt. J. E. McMenomY | 18 | Sergt. J. Klein...... | 20 |
| F. Hanson.............. | 17 | Corp. Hampton....... | 19 |
| G. F. Kelly............. | 20 | Herman.............. | 18 |
| M. Adams............... | 17 | Md. Duffy............ | 20 |
| B. McKnight........... | 16 | Lieut. E. T. Sime.... | 22 |
| C. Thompson........... | 20 | Capt. E. S. Templeton | 21 |
| S. F. Merry............ | 21 | Lieut. J. E. Klein.... | 21 |
| L. G. Perkins.......... | 24 | Ranie................ | 18 |
| H. H. Elder............ | 21 | Sergt. Poori......... | 19 |
| Sergt. Thos. Carson.... | 21 | Sergt. Gasser........ | 18 |
| A. P. Rapp.............. | 21 | Brown............... | 21 |
| Terman................ | 16 | Sergt. Thompson..... | 18 |
| Corp. L. Barrere....... | 20 | Rosch................ | 19 |
| Corp. L. W. Knowlton.. | 14 | Lieut. Geo. H. Strong | 19 |
| Peising................ | 19 | Hammond............ | 20 |
| Sergt. Beilley.......... | 19 | Col. J. H. Dickinson. | 21 |
| F. Allen................ | 18 | Sergt. Wilson........ | 20 |
| Sergt. Sauck........... | 22 | Corp. Leutschrug.... | 21 |
| Sergt. Geo. Perry...... | 20 | Sergt. Kneass........ | 12 |

Total (786 per cent.)...................................948

The scores of the Second Regiment were:

| | | | |
|---|---|---|---|
| Lieut. G. C. Peck........ | 19 | C. E. Fussell........ | 18 |
| Sergt. Wm. Kettleman.. | 19 | G. E. Clark.......... | 18 |
| Sergt. J. C. Summers... | 20 | J. P. Mulligan....... | 18 |
| Sergt. H. J. Wagner.... | 18 | Lieut. J. F. Wand.... | 19 |
| Wm. Shutes............ | 18 | Corp. Wm. Wright.... | 21 |
| George Prescott......... | 19 | Lotz................. | 16 |
| Corp. J. Wagner........ | 18 | Lieut. Stansbery..... | 20 |
| Corp. F. Smith......... | 18 | Thos. Casey.......... | 20 |
| J. O'Donnell........... | 18 | B. Strothers......... | 20 |
| D. Schnable............ | 21 | Taylor............... | 18 |
| M. Weif................ | 21 | F. Kelly............. | 19 |
| Lieut. J. K. Becker.... | 22 | E. Williams.......... | 19 |
| Sergt. G. Loughran..... | 21 | J. Beinfield.......... | 15 |
| L. Haake............... | 20 | V. Stumpf........... | 18 |
| F. Kalsh............... | 21 | G. L. Palmer......... | 19 |
| F. Pietre............... | 21 | Sergt. P. H. Will.... | 20 |
| M. J. Mangels.......... | 20 | Dobbears............ | 18 |
| D. Walburn............ | 21 | C. Repasa............ | 19 |
| J. Bruer............... | 20 | H. Schnamerr........ | 14 |
| J. C. Plagemann........ | 21 | W. Fisher........... | 21 |
| S. Wankin.............. | 21 | Capt. E. T. Webber.. | 18 |
| C. Wagner.............. | 18 | Capt. H. Frank...... | 20 |
| A. Huber............... | 20 | Lieut. E. G. Sprowl.. | 20 |
| G. Geos................ | 21 | Capt. W. Clark....... | 20 |
| O. F. Hoffman.......... | 19 | J. N. Flint.......... | 21 |

Total (787 per cent.)...................................923

The Second Regiment would have made a higher score if it had not been that eight of their best marksmen were absent. No doubt now that the ball is in motion, but we will see a great many more rifle matches take place in the vicinity of San Francisco than there ever have been before on the Pacific coast.

### Pistol Practice.

There never has until the last year been any interest taken in pistol practice. At the time that the California Rifle Association offered prizes to pistol teams Col. Beaver was almost the only enthusiast in this city. By the Colonel's unaided efforts he collected together and made up a team of pistol sharps and then sent a challenge to shoot a match with a team from the San Francisco police. The challenge was accepted and the match shot and won by the police. Since the first match many others for medals and trophies have been shot, beside many friendly contests. The police have as good shots as can be found but it is a rare or almost unheard-of thing for them to issue a challenge, although they always have accepted any from the Citizens' Team which in really the only one outside of the Police Teams. The Police, though they have considerable practice, compared to the Citizens, rarely have boyhaunless among themselves nor do they challenge anyone on the outside. They have a good range which is easy of access and as good Creedmoor targets as can be found anywhere: many friendly matches and contests might be held among themselves as teams or individual sharpshooters, or with the Citizens.

Had it not been for Col. Beaver, who is one of the best pistol shots on the coast, the Citizens' Team would to-day make a very poor showing and were it not for the Citizens Team it is doubtful whether the Police Team would exist, for like Alexander the Great of olden times, they would pine away for lack of exercise. The Citizens' Team has always been the challenging party and on account of the lack of practice they have many times been defeated; but they deserve praise for the interest they try to arouse in the shooting line and admiration for the pluck with which they meet better practiced men and get defeated; for it is only the lack of practice that has prevented them from carrying off the laurels on several occasions lately.

Matches could easily be arranged with teams in other parts of the country, and even in distant states, by both shooting on their respective ranges and sending the results to the other by mail or telegraph. It is to be hoped that the "you move first" principle will soon be dropped and that pistol practice will be raised and take its proper place among other amusements and tests of skill.

### Pistol Shooting.

Although it is as a rule deemed unfair to make public the scores made by individuals or teams in private practice for a match, the following performance of Captain Douglass' team of the San Francisco police is given as an exhibit of what can be done with the pistol in skillful hands. The preparation was for the California Rifle Association trophy, shot for on the 28th of October at Shell Mound Park. The score made by the team in the match is also given for comparison. The distance was 33½ yards, target regulation Creedmoor; but the practice score was made at 30 shots and a possible 150 while the match was at 15 shots and a possible 75, which different conditions must of course be taken into account in comparing the performances.

| | Private, Recorded. Oct. 28. | Oct. 25. |
|---|---|---|
| Briggs................ | 143 | 69 |
| Purdy................ | 141 | 71 |
| Wells................ | 141 | 71 |
| McCarthy............ | 144 | 67 |
| Holland.............. | 144 | 66 |
| Fragances............ | 145 | 71 |
| Lann................. | 148 | 66 |
| Scott................ | 146 | 71 |
| Clark................ | 148 | 70 |
| Sergent.............. | 143 | 72 |
| Field, A............. | 141 | 73 |
| Whitworth........... | 148 | 73 |

AT ALAMEDA.—Last Sunday the California Schuetzen Club at Schuetzen Park Alameda, held their monthly medal shooting. The class medals were won by the following riflemen:
First class, F. Kuhls, 416 rings.
Second class, C. Rapp, 318 rings.
Third class, C. Sageborn, 334 rings.

## FISH.

### "Never Knowed the Scientific Name Afore."

Why is it that certain men who are ordinarily decent and temperate will get drunk on the Fourth of July? Why is it that certain men who are ordinarily truthful and reliable will lie without stint when they strike the topic of their exploits with rod and reel? I doubt all fish stories. I have never read but one that bore upon its face an indication of truthfulness, or that a candid man might say was not the mere hallucination of the story-teller's brain, or the base fabrication of a depraved mind. I refer to that graphic and vivid-ious account of the desperate struggle Chauncie Dudley Warner had with the brook trout.

It was the close of a hot August day. Now I am not going to annoy you with a fish story. I am only going to premise that it had been a hot August day; that with my favorite green-heart rod, I had walked zealously all day long, and had captured but one bass; that the bass did not run off fifty yards of line at one fell swoop, making the reel to sing and smoke; that he did not tear madly through the water, leaving the usual foaming, boiling wake behind him; that he did not leap high into the air, and shaking the silver drops from his bronze armor, regard me with implacable looks of rage and hate. I am only going to premise that he was the sole result of my day's sport; that he weighed five pounds two ounces to a dot; that I had experienced no tremendous strain upon my system in landing him; that I had not even burst a suspender; and that on the porch of the village inn, at the close of the hot August day, the oldest inhabitant had contemptuously examined my rod, and had inquired with no little disdain if I caught fish "with that gad?"

The oldest inhabitant settled himself into his accustomed seat on the porch of the village inn. He tilted back his ruined hat, and turned the broad soles of his brogans towards the rising moon. And then as the sultry evening wore away, he rolled off an interminable yarn of how he had taken "a forty-pounder, by blank, sir," in Crooked Lake. Shall I tell you that fish story? I guess not. When the accusing angel finished his evening's labor with his string of lies; but she swung high in heaven, and the ink slumbered, a burnished sheet of silver under her beams, when the story was ended and the forty-pounder brought to shore. The doctor looked long and earnestly at the oldest inhabitant, and quietly remarked:

"That's the most mendacious piscatorial prevarication ever heard of!" and the old man, taking a fresh chew of tobacco, replied in his innocent way:

"You bet your life he was, but I never knowed the scientific name afore. Round here we always call him the musky-lunge."—*Cor. Angler.*

Salmon trout fishing near Tamalpius Station has been very poor during the past two weeks.

### Bay Fishing.

Bay fishing during the past week has been very poor. Many parties have been out but the catches were all small, and the fish are below the average in size. It is hardly to be expected that it would be otherwise as all experienced fishermen agree that on the last half or quarter of the moon that this is always the case. Many laugh at the idea that the moon affects the fishing, but the Portuguese and Italians, who are the best of fishermen, never count on making much profit from their pursuit during this part of the moon, at which time they say that nearly all the finny tribe stay close around their favorite hiding places. Along the Sancelito shores during this unfavorable time what few fish are out are caught either early in the morning or in the evening and even at these hours they do not stay in one locality but seem to be rushing by. But when the light of a new moon dances on the water it affects the fish as well as the tides and they come forth from the dark, unexplored caverns of the deep and make glad the heart of the fisherman by taking the hook on which temptingly dangles the sardine or shrimp. Occasionally one is fortunate enough, during this poor fishing time, to find the home or haunts where the fish are congregated, and they are usually assembled in large numbers and they bite quite lively. One of these places mentioned is on the east and north sides of Goat Island. There is good fishing at this place when there is none at all elsewhere. Many of the most experienced fisherman think that there will be some fine fishing during the winter months around the bay, and they have formed their opinions by the promises of the almanac, as showed by the almanac.

The average catch of salmon in the rivers, before the State added to the numbers by artificial hatching, was five million pounds. This, to persons not controlled by narrow personal interest or cupidity, would be convincing evidence of the wisdom of the State laws for the promotion and increase of this industry. Yet, strange as it may seem, it is the history of the fish industry of every State in the Union, and of all other countries, that when public moneys are used to add to the numbers of fish to be caught, not only the fishermen, but the owners of large capital invested in the business are remitting and persistent in their applications for the repeal of all that place any restriction upon unlimited fishing. The perpetuation of the salmon industry is absolutely dependent upon the fact that some of the fish must be allowed to pass the nets and reach the spawning grounds at the head waters. It is only at the sources of streams, and under the conditions there found, that the eggs will naturally develop into fish. It is only when the fish reach their spawning grounds that their eggs have become sufficiently matured so that they may be taken for artificial propagation. These facts are well known and undisputed, yet the Legislature is blessfully besieged to repeal the law, or to so change it that practically there should be no limit to fishing while there is a fish to be found in the rivers.

A NATIONAL ASSOCIATION—We learn that an effort is being made to organize a national association of anglers, under the name of "The National Rod and Reel Association. We also learn that the object of this organization shall be: First—the preservation of game fish by every possible means for those whose delight it is to take them by rod and reel. Second—The holding of an annual tournament to cultivate and compare excellence of rod and reel. The cultivation of that fraternal feeling which always exists among the lovers of the gentle art. We do not doubt that such an organization, if free from all entangling business alliances, will result in benefit to the angling interests of the Craft. We will "bide a wee"—for further knowledge of the matter—before we enthuse over it.—*Angler.*

When President Arthur was on his way from Alexandria bay to New York two little girls, aged 10 and 13 years, nieces of General Butterfield, were presented to him, they being passengers on the same car. When they told him that they, too, had been boating and fishing, he described to them the glorious sport he had on the St. Lawrence, and asked: "How would you like to catch a fifty-pound fish or fight and like yours, with a tip almost as slender as a rye straw? That beats bass-fishing. You have to play with the fish an hour or two sometimes, and be careful not to allow him to escape or break your rod." "Why," said Miss Thirteen-year-old, "a little girl up to Carlton caught a four-pound bass and broke the pole right off!" "Ah," replied the President, "when she gets older she will soon learn to play a larger fish than that on a light rod, and land him, too."

Anglers in the Adirondacks report the discovery of a new species of fish known as the "trout pickerel," which are found at the mouth of the Au Sable River. The new fish resembles the English pike. Its color is a light bronze, and the odor of the pickerel is not perceptible. It is very palatable.

The *American Angler* says, command us to our English brethren for the melody of their common names of fishes, viz.—the dab, the rough dab, the smear dab, the fluke, the carter, the lemon sole, the merry sole. All of which means "flounder."

Tuesday Horace D. Dunn and party were out fishing on the Sancelito shore. Most of the fishing was done in Horseshoe Bend. The catch was rather small but several of good size were taken; blue rockfish and sea trout were the most plentiful.

Capt. Douglass, warehouseman, caught several large brown rockcod while fishing near Sugar Loaf Cove near the rock. This was the best catch of Tuesday as some of them weighed three and a half pounds.

Several parties fishing in Racoon Straits recently have had very bad luck; many returning without even having a bite—except from the lunch basket.

A young gentleman who at one time aspired to be champion amateur sculler of the coast, and who was captain of the Columbia Rowing Club, made his first attempt as a yachtsman last Sunday, thinking he would like sailing. He sailed on to a mud flat first thing and having remained there three hours with nothing to eat, drink, or smoke, was rescued by a relief party which shored a skiff over the mud, then by means of planks the yachtsman was brought to the edge of the water and ferried across the creek. But he abandoned his yacht until high water when some one else took her to her moorings.

It is said that wild ducks have abandoned the meadow near Boynton and Steamboat Sloughs. An unsuccessful effort was made to sow wild rice there last spring.

## THE KENNEL.

### The Greyhound.

The greyhound is a long, lean animal, the giraffe of the canine race. He always seems to be in a contemplative humor; probably he is thinking of the past glories of his race. His breed has a history such as falls to the lot of no other dog and few animals except the monkey folks who fought with the gods gone by. Ovid's description of the greyhound counting a hare in his "Metamorph," book l, told in rhyme better than has ever been told since in prose the story of the fleet footed ones:

As when the impatient greyhound, slipped from far,
Bounds o'er the glade to course the fearful hare,
She in her speed does all her safety lay
And he with double speed pursues the prey,
O'erruns her at the sitting turn, but licks
His chaps in vain, yet blows upon the fix chair,
She seeks the shelter which the neighboring covert gives
And, painting it, she doubts if she yet lives.

The greyhound gave rare sport to the ancient Greeks, but their dogs were not a match in point of speed for the hound of the present day as ours are no match for them in point of size, strength and pluck. In spite of the slowness of their dogs the Greeks had good sport though horses, nets and as many as a dozen dogs were often used to capture one single hare. The ancients made rules for their sport not vastly dissimilar from those in vogue at the present time. Xenophen the younger ordered that a steward be appointed over the sport—to match the dogs, give orders to the field and direct when and how the competitors shall be slipped. The old Greeks were a jolly, easy-going lot. They never coursed a bagged hare nor beat a plantation for one but went out just as we do at Merced, scared up a hare and then loosed the dogs. From the sides of the mountains spectators watched the sport on adjacent plains. When Elfore was king of Mercia the greyhound graced the royal kennels. In the time of Canute he was reckoned the highest in rank of all the dogs and no one but freeholders were allowed to keep them. Henry II, Queen Bess, Edward I and Charles I were all devoted admirers of the greyhound. The owner of Gelert who slew the wolf to secure Llewellyn's heir lived early in the 13th century. From all that can be learned the greyhound proper is of Celtic origin and until Rome and Greece imported the pure breed from ancient British, their dogs were but poor animals. The first dog ever used for sport, the only one ever made a gentleman by law, the friend of $k_{1.3}$, and to-day the proudest beast of earls and dukes, is it any wonder that the greyhound holds himself aloof from other dogs and contemptuously pursues the tenor of his way without fear, love, affection or obeisance to any man. With pedigree going back before the time when Christ was crucified. When the Druids performed their mystic rites in British woods; before Roman, Saxon, Dane or Norman had set afilling foot on British soil; long ere the time when Phœnicians wrought for tin on Cornish Coast the greyhound was an occupant of British soil. He probably gamboled around when Adam and Eve made love in Eden, and was promptly on hand when Noah first started out in the moral circus business. He certainly tended flocks when Tubal Cain lodst among the bulrushes and made pipes that prefaced the invention of instrumental music. He helped lick the sores of Lazarus and his ancestors helped the Hebrews eat their manna when they were jogging around the wilderness trying to strike the main road for Jordan. The most prominent trait in the character of the greyhound is larceny. He is a thief from his earliest years and only Bves that he may learn roguery. Instead of the dog being a wolf in domesticated state there is good reason to believe that the wolf is simply a greyhound in a wild state. Both are surly, both are bloodthirsty, both are thieves and both can outrun and outlast any other animal although a false system of training has made the modern greyhound more fitted for a burst of speed than for a long enduring effort. But you will say the greyhound has no sense of smell. Has he not? I have one who will scent a quail or a robin as quickly almost and at as great a distance as any setter in the country and Bird's old Summer would not only scent a quail but would come to a staunch and dead point. He is accused of lacking sense when the fact is that he is about the deverest of all dogs only he will insist upon putting his skill to the one end and aim of his life—larceny; no ordinary lout, bolt or bar can keep him out when he wants to steal. He has been known to upset the pot on the hearth and steal the meat as soon as it was cool enough to mouth. The highest shelf in the cupboard, the topmost hook in the larder and the flitch that hangs from the rafters all fall an easy prey to his desire to steal. He can give points to Bates and the "Artful Dodger" is a mere tyro compared to an old greyhound. As soon as he gets over his youthful escapades for the chase he commences to show his cunning and becomes a worthless lurcher and it is only by keeping him away from hares for long spells that he can be stopped from that improper habit. There is one good thing about the greyhound. He is no cur and no sycophant. He never fawns and slavers over his master and never wags his tail in compliment of praise. He carries his independence far into the region of violence, and is a quarrelsome, dictatorial, faithless and irritable beast at best.

EDWIN.

### That Wretched Cut.

A short time since we had occasion to severely criticise a cut of the pug dog George, published in the American Field. John R. Sherlock of Southport, England, wrote to the editor of the Field a letter on the same subject intimating that if the cut was accurate the judges erred badly in giving George a prize. The editor of the Field replied as follows:

We consider it unjust to criticize George from the cut which appeared in the American Field, as it failed to do him justice. The original drawing of the dog was made, as all of Mr. Tracy's drawings are, correct, but while in the hands of the engraver some changes were made which deranged the features that have been the most severely criticized, features not possessed by the original, and for the appearance of which the engraver, and not Mr. Tracy, is responsible.

### Eastern Field Trials.

The judges for the Eastern Field Trials of 1882 will consist of Col. James Gordon of Pontotoc, Miss., Jos. J. Snellenburgh of New Brighton, Penn.; Jos. H. Dew, Columbia, Tenn., and Jno. M. Kinney, Staunton, Va. The old system of three judges will be adhered to as in previous years, each

stake being judged from end to end by the same judges. For entry blanks, running rules and particulars, all communications must be addressed to Washington A. Coster, treasurer and secretary, Flatbush, L. I. All dogs entered and in training for the trials at High Point, N. C., will be carried free when attended by owners or trainers, on presentation of a pass signed by the secretary. Dog passes furnished on application. State number of dogs and name of owner or trainer. Through the courtesy of the Pennsylvania R. R., Seaboard Air Line R. R. and associated railways of Virginia and the Carolinas, their baggage-masters have been instructed from headquarters to pass all dogs free when accompanied by owner or trainer, on presentation of a pass signed by the secretary of the Eastern Field Trials Club.

A SOCIABLE DOG.—An unheard of feat by a dog, which would seem incredible if not vouched for by several witnesses, occurred yesterday morning at 2520 Pacific street. Arthur W. Moore, the occupant of the premises, is having the house painted, and for the purpose of gaining access to the roof a ladder twenty-four feet in length was placed against the side of the dwelling. Mr. Moore is also the owner of a dog, of which he is now extremely proud. The painters had ascended the ladder yesterday, when the animal, who is of a sociable disposition, determined to seek their society. There was no way of carrying this project into execution except by taking to the ladder, which the dog at once proceeded to do. Those who witnessed the undertaking say that he dragged himself up the perilous passage by hanging on the rounds with the joints of his fore legs, supporting his weight with his hind legs against the lower rungs. Once the roof attained, the animal made his way up the steep incline to the peak, where he made his presence known by licking an unconscious painter, who was so frightened that he nearly lost his balance, and was in imminent danger of falling to the ground beneath. When the painter regained his balance of body and equanimity of mind he at once clutched the friendly brute and descended with him to the ground, where the ladder-climbing quadruped was received with spontaneous expressions of admiration.—Chronicle, Nov 1.

A singular and fatal accident happened to a dog on lower Mill street a day or two ago. He was on the porch of his owner's residence, which stood back from the street, when another dog passed along on the sidewalk, which seemed to irritate the residing dog and caused him to run along the porch and bark at the outsider. He was so intent upon this that he made a misstep over the side of the porch and fell to the ground, striking upon his nose and breaking his neck, and died almost instantly.—Grass Valley Union.

## ROWING.

### Peculiarities of Small Boats.

It is a curious circumstance that scarce any two localities in the world have the same description of either row or sail boats. One would be apt to suppose that a particular type of boat would be found by experience to be superior, and that in all localities where similar conditions of weather and water obtained, this style of boat would be adopted. It is not so, however. The ordinary Whitehall boat, which certainly seems as near perfection as can be imagined, will be found in very few places except our rivers. And where, except in Massachusetts, is the dory naturalized? Connecticut is the home of the sharpie, and this style does not flourish elsewhere to any appreciable extent.

Then look at the beautiful fishing boats of the St. Lawrence, evidently the outgrowth of the Indian's birch-bark canoe, the shape of which is still pretty faithfully preserved. All the tourists who have visited the Thousand Islands have seen, and probably sailed in, these beautiful craft, and a week ago President Arthur fished from one of them. They are about twenty-one feet long, three and a half feet wide at the broadest part, and fourteen inches deep. They row very easily, and their peculiar shape enables them to ride in safety over the highest waves of the broad river, and during the continuance of a northeast gale these are very formidable. They are built of Norway pine, with trimmings of cedar, and, as a rule, are left bright inside and out, the wood when oiled being very handsome. The most singular thing about them, however, is that, although without either centerboard or keel, and with a small split-sail, the mast for which is stepped well forward, these boats are sailed and worked to windward without the use of either oar or rudder, or anything which might be called a substitute for either.

In the summer time, as thousands of tourists can testify, races are gotten up, the course being to leeward and to windward, and the contestants are not allowed to carry either oar, paddle or rudder. The boatman steers his boat entirely by the sheet and by shifting his own weight forward or aft, according as he desires her to luff or bear away. When he desires to tack he hauls the sheet flat aft and goes forward, and his boat goes about. If he wishes to keep off, he goes aft and gives her sheet, and off she goes. We don't think these boats can be paralleled anywhere.

A PROFESSIONAL ASSOCIATION.—The Boston Herald publishes the following, which we heartily indorse, and commend to every gentlemanly professional oarsman: "It is very evident that, if professional rowing is ever again to become popular, it must be through some radical revolution of methods and practices. The professionals themselves realize this fact, and profess to be willing to take any steps necessary to regain public confidence. Nearly a year ago Mr. M. F. Davis of Portland suggested a professional rowing association, governed by responsible and respectable gentlemen, with rules of the strictest kind, providing for the expulsion of any oarsman or oarsmen found guilty of disreputable practices. This year the subject has been revived by Lee, Riley, Hosmer and others, all of whom desire immediate action. The suggestion is made that all professional scullers of the first, second and third class be invited to meet at Boston, and that some well-known gentlemen, patrons of aquatics, be invited to take part in the meeting, assist in organizing the association, and offer suggestions as to rules defining the object of the association and legislation protecting the general body of oarsmen from the reproach a few men may bring upon them.

LEE AND COURTNEY.—Geo. W. Lee made it thoroughly understood that he is not afraid to row Charles Courtney. Lee said: "I had money in the office of the Boston Herald for three weeks to back a challenge to Courtney, but he failed to meet me. He puts up no money with his challenge, and hence I shall pay no attention to it. At any time I am ready to accept a challenge from him if he will deposit money in New York to back it."

AN UNSATISFACTORY EXPERIMENT.—Hamm and Conley, having finished their engagement with the Halifax Rowing Association, will not row again under its auspices, or with partners, unless challenged. The association has been under heavy expense keeping two men and a trainer for some years, and the result has been highly unsatisfactory. Its men have been unchallenged, and their challenges have not been accepted. It feels that aquatic people abroad will have nothing to do with its men in match races, and regattas with short courses are not satisfactory. A prominent citizen of Halifax, who has faith in Hamm and Conley, and feels it would be a shame to have these retire permanently from aquatics thus early in their career, proposes that a big sweepstakes match be gotten up early next season, on some suitable waters where a four or five mile course can be had. He suggests that Hanlan, Ross, Kennedy, Courtney, Riley and Conley each deposit $1,000 or $500, to be divided into first and second prizes, and the third man to save his deposit. A match of this kind ought to be satisfactory to all concerned, and, if the oarsmen mentioned or others wish to go into the scheme, Hamm and Conley are ready, and the citizen referred to will back them.

ELLIOTT BEATEN.—Some time ago Elliott, the ex-champion of England beat Gaisel of New York very easily in a three-mile sculling race on Flushing Bay. Gaisel then claimed that he had been beaten by having his stake boat anchored so far out that he lost a hundred yards at the turn. A return match for $500 a side took place on the 22nd ult., at Newark, N. J. A more perfect walk-over never took place on this course before. Either party could have claimed the race, by fouling, had they so desired. An even start was effected, but Gaisel, pulling a long graceful stroke, soon forged ahead of his more jerky opponent. Elliott spurting up at the Eureka House, soon obtained a slight lead, and being out of his water, could easily have been fouled by Gaisel, if he so chose. Both men rowed well to the stake boat, when Elliott made a poor turn, Gaisel getting away in good form. From here home it was purely an exhibition race, Gaisel winning as he liked. No official time was taken, but a private timer marking it at 20.50.

THE BLUFFERS CRITICISED.—Some time ago the BREEDER AND SPORTSMAN called attention to the reprehensible practice of issuing challenges without any serious intention of rowing races. The New York Turf, Field and Farm has taken up the subject and comments as follows on the men to whom we called disrespectful attention:

"The humbugging practices of some amateur rowers are laid bare with an unsparing hand. The practice of issuing challenges when there is no intention to row a race or to try conclusions, is vigorously denounced. It seems that there are 'bluffers' not only among politicians, but also among amateur sportsmen, who endeavor to gain recognition and notoriety by challenging brother amateurs for large amounts of money, but who never intend that such challenges should be accepted. There is certainly a great difference between the number of challenges issued and the number of races rowed."

ATTRACTING ATTENTION.—The proposed race on Thanksgiving Day over the Long Bridge course for the BREEDER AND SPORTSMAN'S cup has attracted attention in New York. The Turf, Field and Farm says of the event:

"Great interest is manifested by the scullers of the Pacific slope in the four-oared race, to be rowed on Thanksgiving Day, for a valuable cup offered by the BREEDER AND SPORTSMAN. Crews from the Pioneer, Ariel and Golden Gate clubs are practicing for the event. At present the Pioneers have the call, but the other crews are working hard for success."

## YACHTING.

The sloop yacht Wave, S. Y. C., ower Commodore Barron, has gone into winter quarters at the Seawanhaka Basin, Edgewater, Staten Island. The Wave will be rerigged and given a new set of sails before the opening of the next season. She may get another chance at the Madge next season and if she does she will win this time.

The Larchmont Yacht Club seriously contemplates the building of a new club house. Fleming Point, a short distance from its present quarters, is said to be the site of the proposed new structure. The marvelous growth of the Larchmont during the year just passed, both in the matter of members and boats, has brought it to a foremost position in the yachting world.

The Casco is well laid up. Her sides and covered with carpets and canvas, her bowsprit and gibboom are covered and a large awning extends fore and aft. She is well protected from the weather, but the first southeaster will walk off with the awning.

The lines of the new schooner yacht for ex-Commodore L. A. Fish, of the Atlantic Yacht Club, are being laid down by Messrs. Poillon. The model was furnished by Mr. Philip Ellsworth.

There will be one yachtsman in the Legislature, Mr. James V. Coleman, one of the owners of the Annie, having been elected to the Assembly from San Mateo.

It is reported in yachting circles that Mr. Astor, owner of the schooner yacht Ambassadress, has given orders for a large steam yacht.

Though the Nellie got on to the Southampton shoal the other day no harm was done to her.

There is talk of a new yacht seventy feet long, with lead keel and all modern improvements.

Work is progressing slowly on the new yacht of the Spreckels Brothers.

Farmer is working away on his new yacht and the deck is now laid.

The Annie is going up river on a duck hunt next week.

The Chispa is to be kept in commission all winter.

The Pacifics close the season on the 18th.

Very light winds for sailing now-a-days.

The Emerald will be laid up next week.

Very little yachting going on now-a-days.

The Rambler has been laid up.

The Frolic has not been laid up yet.

The Tulare Valley fair was a pronounced success. The gate money received left a handsome net dividend in the treasury of the society, which is as it should be. It is claimed that there were 2,500 people present on the last day.

## BICYCLING.

### merican Wheelmen's League—Fall Meeting.

The fall meeting of the League of American Wheelmen took ace Oct. 20th at Beacon Park near Boston in the presence of a small number of spectators.

The entries for the one-mile championship were Lewis T. rye of Marlboro', Mass., the holder of the medal and title, eorge M. Hendee of Springfield, Mass., and V. C. Place of reenville, Pa. The men all looked and were in prime condition, and took their places in the following order: Frye at ole, Hendee second, Place third. At the sound of the pistol ll got off in good form, Frye taking the lead, his intention vidently being to keep the lea... and force the pace for the thers. These, however, showed their ability to take his pace nd followed him in close order during the first lap, and on he second Hendee let himself out, and made a pace for himelf which Frye, despite a gallant struggle, was unable to qual, and had to fall to second position, and the third quarer was entered in the following order: Hendee, Frye, Place.

Frye however was not to be easily beaten off and entered he last quarter well up with Hendee, but the latter increased is pace to such purpose that he soon left the other two a ong distance behind and coming down the home stretch with good burst of speed crossed the line the winner in 2.57. his is the gentleman who ran a close second to the English hampion Moore in less than 2.55 at the recent Springfield eeting, and he promises still further improvement next eason.

The next and final event was a five-mile amateur open race or two silver cups, first and second prizes, respectively. The starters were V. C. Place of Greenville, Pa., J. Wattie, Canton, Mass., and John Tacy, Lawrence, Mass.

A good start was effected, Place taking the lead, Tacy second, Wattie last, and this order was maintained throughout. Place's time was 17.30; Tacy's, 17.45½; Wattie's, 19.20. The track was in fair-condition, but the wind was quite strong, considering which the time was better than was expected.

Much discussion has arisen relative to the various so-called safety bicycles in which the tendency to "headers" is more or less averted by setting the saddle farther back and making the treadle connection with the crank by means of levers or in some similar manner. The results summed up appear to be that while these machines are somewhat slower and harder to drive than those of the ordinary forms, they are well adapted for elderly or timid riders, and make night riding comparatively safe for any one. The principal safety machine news before the public are the "Xtraordinary," in which the front fork has a considerable rake, the saddle being set correspondingly back, and the cranks are connected with side levers which extend back so as to bring the treadles beneath the rider; and the "Facile," in which a similar arrangement of side levers is applied: with a small wheel and vertical front forks. Upon this latter machine a distance of 214 miles was recently made in twenty-four hours upon the road from London to Bath.

Messrs. C. J. Holland and W. L. Jackson, of Medford, members of the Tremont Bicycle Club of Boston, made a run of one hundred and fifty-four miles Oct. 22. The start was made from Medford Center at 12:18 a. m., and the finish at 11:49 p. m. The route was to South Framingham, via Cambridge, Chestnut Hill, Newton Lower Falls, Wellesley, and Natick, returning by same road; then to Gloucester, via Malden, Saugus, Lynn, Salem, and Beverly, returning to Medford by same road, and again to South Framingham, and return to Medford as before, making a total distance of one hundred and fifty-four miles. Running time 20:30·0; time used for meals and rest, 3:1·0. The above is the longest run made in one day by any bicycle club in America.—World.

The second race for the English 20-mile professional championship was run on the Belgrave road ground, Leicester, Oct. 7, the competitors being J. Keen, London; R. Howell, Coventry; F. Wood, Leicester; R. James, Birmingham; C. B. Garrard, Coventry; B. Keen, London;F. Lees, Sheffield, and Warwick, Birmingham. The race was splendidly contested, J. Keen, James, Wood, Garrard, Lees, B. Keen and Howell leading at various times, and was finally won by Howell in 1:12:55, which beat the professional record made by Wood in July.

W. M. Woodside won the 50-mile bicycle championship of Ireland, Oct. 7, at Phoenix Park, Dublin. Time, 4:14·20. Raining, and track bad in consequence.

## BASE BALL.

### Olympics vs. Howards.

On Saturday last at the Olympic Grounds, Oakland, the third and final game for the Howard Trophy—a silver ball and the Olympic Club Championship for 1882—resulted in a victory for the Olympics by the following score:

| OLYMPICS. | T. R. | B. | N. | P. O. | A. | E. | | HOWARDS. | T. R. | B. | N. | P. O. | A. | E. |
|---|---|---|---|---|---|---|---|---|---|---|---|---|---|---|
| Neal, r f..... | 5 | 1 | 1 | 0 | 1 | 0 | |Jacobus,l.f.,of| 4 | 0 | 1 | 3 | 0 | 1 |
| Fitzgerald, c. | 5 | 4 | 3 | 12 | 3 | 1 | |McCord,s. s.. | 4 | 2 | 0 | 0 | 4 | 4 |
| Burt,1 b..... | 6 | 2 | 3 | 9 | 1 | 0 | |Buckingham, | | | | | | |
| Ebner, 3b..... | 5 | 1 | 1 | 2 | 0 | 1 | |2b......... | 4 | 0 | 0 | 2 | 2 | 1 |
| Hardie, 1 f.... | 5 | 1 | 1 | 0 | 0 | 0 | |Hardie, c.f.. | 4 | 0 | 0 | 1 | 0 | 0 |
| Redmond, p.. | 5 | 1 | 0 | 0 | 13 | 0 | |Kane, 1 f.,of 3 | 0 | 0 | 0 | 0 | 0 |
| Kelly, .l f.... | 4 | 1 | 0 | 2 | 0 | 0 | |Hamilton, 3b. | 3 | 0 | 1 | 4 | 1 | 1 |
| Sumner, c f.. | 4 | 0 | 0 | 1 | 0 | 0 | |Ruggles, 1b. | 3 | 0 | 0 | 8 | 0 | 3 |
| VanBergen,ss. | 5 | 0 | 0 | 2 | 0 | 0 | |Dibble, p.... | 3 | 0 | 1 | 0 | 5 | 1 |
| | | | | | | | |Van Court, r.f | 1 | 1 | 0 | 1 | 1 | 0 |
| Totals.....| 44 | 10 | 9 | 27 | 10 | 10 | |Totals......| 31 | 3 | 4 | 24 | 16 | 13 |

| Innings............................ | 1 | 2 | 3 | 4 | 5 | 6 | 7 | 8 | 9 | |
|---|---|---|---|---|---|---|---|---|---|---|
| Olympics.............................. | 1 | 1 | 3 | 3 | 0 | 1 | 0 | 2 | — | 10 |
| Howards.............................. | 0 | 0 | 0 | 0 | 0 | 0 | 2 | — | 3 |

Two-base hits—Fitzgerald, Burt, Jacobus. Hardie. First base on errors—Olympics 8, Howards 1. Struck out—Olympics 6, Howards 10. Wild pitches—Dibble 1. Passed balls—Fitzgerald 1, Hardie 8. Balls called—On Redmond 100, Dibble 42. Strikes called—Off Dibble 21, Redmond 90. Struck at and missed—Olympics 18, Howards 92. Game time—two hours. Umpire—Jerry Denny of the Providence Club. Soccer M. Strauss.

### Havelys vs. Niantics.

At the Recreation grounds last Saturday the above nines played eight innings with the following result, the game being brought to a close by the darkness:

Haverlys—J. Carroll, r. f., ran home 1 tall, 1 f.; b. Levy, c. f.; b. Morgan, p., 1; Fred Carroll, c., 2; McVey, 1st b.; Lawton, 3d b., 1; Morgan, l. f.; Gaine, 3d b., 1. Total. 39.
Niantics—Arnold, 3d b., 1 run; Incull, r. f., 0; Robinson, 1. f., 0; Egan, 1st b., 0; Hickle, c., 1; Sweeney, p., 1; Frank Carroll, c. f., 0; Manley, 3d b., 1. Total, 4.
Left on bases—Haverlys, 3; Niantics, 1. Bases on errors—Haverlys, 1.

## CRICKET.

### Occidents vs. Merions.

A cricket match was played Saturday afternoon on the Recreation Grounds between the Occident and Merion teams. The Occidents won by the following score:

**OCCIDENTS.**

| | |
|---|---|
| Cross, b. Theobold.................................. | 10 |
| Davenport, b. Webster............................... | 0 |
| J. Sanderson, b. Webster............................ | 0 |
| Waterman, l. b. Webster............................. | 0 |
| Turpey, b. Mathien Jr............................... | 0 |
| McGovern, c. Armatage.............................. | 0 |
| Clady, l. b. Mathien................................ | 2 |
| Stewart Sr. c. f. Mathien, b. Mathien Jr............ | 2 |
| Atken, b. & c. Benjamin............................. | 1 |
| Stewart, Jr., c. & b. Benjamin...................... | 2 |
| Sanderson Jr., not out.............................. | 2 |
| | |
| Runs............................................... | 43 |
| Byes............................................... | 9 |
| No balls........................................... | 2 |
| Wides.............................................. | 0 |
| | |
| Total innings...................................... | 54 |

**MARION.**

| | |
|---|---|
| Hill, run out, b. Waterman.......................... | 0 |
| Theobold, b. Waterman.............................. | 0 |
| Mict, b. Waterman.................................. | 0 |
| B. & Benjamin, b Stewart Jr......................... | 9 |
| E. J. Mathien, b. Stewart Jr........................ | 2 |
| Armatage, b. Waterman.............................. | 1 |
| F. Mathien, c. Turner, b. Waterman.................. | 2 |
| Burpett, b, Stewart Jr.............................. | 0 |
| B. Benjamin, b Stewart Jr........................... | 0 |
| Thompson, not out.................................. | 0 |
| Webster, b. Waterman............................... | 0 |
| | |
| Runs............................................... | 0 |
| Byes............................................... | 2 |
| No balls........................................... | 1 |
| | |
| Total innings...................................... | 21 |

Hippodrome cricket playing pays, as it is reported by the English papers that the Australian eleven, that left this city for home on the last steamer, netted $7,500 from one match they played in the old country and $5,500 in another.

## POULTRY.

### Little Chicks.

As soon as chickens are strong enough to follow the hen easily, I like to give them as much freedom as possible. Coops soon become filthy prisons, and the hen so longs for freedom, and can do so much in finding suitable food for her flock, that it seems cruel to confine her in a. coop. On the other hand, she can't always be allowed to roam at will, and so I usually compromise the matter by putting the hen into a good-sized yard, with a lath fence, through which the chickens can go in and out as they please, and the hen kept in partial confinement. She has then plenty of room for scratching without wearing out her feathers against the sides of the coop, and she is not half as liable to hurt the chickens. She and they can generally get some grass, and if the yard is planted with currant bushes or shrubbery close sort, there is a chance to gather insects and enjoy the shade on hot days. It is tolerably safe also against hawks and crows. These marauders don't like to venture into a yard for their prey, as it cramps their movements. Sometimes they will snap them up on the outside, but on the whole those who will try a yard for chickens will find them much more satisfactory than coops. The fence costs but little, and being put up in panels, which are wired to stakes driven in with an ax, it can easily be moved. The yard can, also, if not planted to trees or shrubbery, be spaded, and grain sown for the chickens to scratch out.

Some hens are murderously cross to other flocks of chickens, and it is a good plan to avoid this if possible. The Brahmas are generally very good in this matter, and can be more safely trusted than the smaller breeds; but to avoid this danger a little care is advisable. When a hen is sitting no young broods should have access to her, but just as she is hatching is the time to overcome her evil propensity. If there are older chickens about into whose company she may be thrown, it is well to put some of them under her at night. Of course, they must not be very large, nor is it best for her to see them when placed under her, or she may "make a fuss" about it. But she can be made amiable to the chickens then if ever, and if the chickens themselves are quiet, and do not go yelping about as soon as daylight comes, the operation may be a success. The young-bred fowls are generally uniform in color and marking, and when a hen is acquainted with one or two of a brood, it answers for all. The union of flocks is so often necessary that some attention to this matter is really important. Some flocks are deserted by the mother at too early an age, others may be reduced to a very few, so that a union is desirable, and if the owner is a little watchful, he can avoid much trouble by getting his hens to treat all chickens with civility.

It is not well to be in a great hurry to get small chickens to go to roost on poles or trees, or the regular flock roosting place. The breast bone is soft until a certain age is attained—say about three months—and a chicken forced into roosting as soon as the hen leaves the flock, will be pretty certain to have a crooked breast-bone. It may not, possibly, affect growth, but it will certainly affect sales, if noticed, and it not unlikely affects development. Until about three months old they had better sleep on the ground, or on a floor. After that the bones are so hard as not to be endangered.

Feeding, after the first week, may be of a very miscella neous order. There is not much danger of over-feeding, but there is great danger of waste unless care is observed. Rather frequent feeding is important—say four or five times a day if they do not run at large—but the amount should be only what they will eat clean. If some attempt is not made to estimate or note their capacities, a great deal will be wasted. There is no economy about a chicken, and so much is thrown for one to devour. If five times as much grain is thrown down as can be eaten, the surplus will be treated as indifferently as so much dirt. When it is defiled starvation even will not force a chicken to eat it. Dry grains are not so readily wasted as the mushy food often given, or milk. Into the latter they will get with their feet, if possible, and if any is left when their appetites are cloyed it, will not go far toward a second meal. For these reasons one had better feed too little than too much until he learns about how much is needed.

As an aid in the care of fowls, it is of considerable impor... tance that they shall not be afraid of the owner or his assist... ants. To this end "handle with care" from the first. One of the first steps to winning their confidence is to get them to eat from your hand. Though all are shy at first, the shy... ness can easily be overcome with either chickens or turkeys. Call them, and lay down your hand full of grain on the ground or floor. They will be timid at first, and the hen will perhaps give numerous warnings, but if you are persistent and gentle, and they are hungry, they will soon surrender, walk over your hand with the utmost familiarity, and even up your arm to your shoulder if there is any inducement. I have even had chickens and hens to take grain from between my teeth. But to gain and keep their confidence one must never be rough with them. "Shooing" them in angry tones, throwing sticks or stones, driving them about with brooms, or chasing with dogs, are all modes of making them wild and intractable. They are easily excited and alarmed, and the feeling is contagious, and when once they fear you confidence in harder to restore than to win at first. If they get into mischief it is very natural to make a great outcry about it, to throw clubs, brooms, or other missiles, or call the dog: but it is better, after all, to go about repairing damages very quietly. The damage generally is not enough to make it pay to make the flock afraid of you, and look upon you as an object of terror. The f, if set upon them, will often do more damage in three minutes than the fowls in three days. It is instinct which teaches them to eat what they like when they find it, and dogs, clubs, or other projectiles will never drive instinct from them. Let it remain, and use more gentle defensive means for saving the "garden sass."

Old hens are somewhat lawless in a garden or truck-patch, but small chickens are often of service there as insect hunt... ers and consumers. They go from plant to plant and leaf to leaf in search of insects, look on both sides, and pick off the parasite with less disregard of his feelings—if he has any—than we do of the chicken when we behead him for a pot-pie or a fricassee.

The best place I know of for a coop is in the garden when insects are plenty. There it will be of some service. The chicks will travel off quite long distances in search of game, but are pretty sure to get back when there is an imperative necessity, and their services an "bug" hunters are often of considerable value.—Breeders' Gazette.

---

Jay Beach has sold the three-year-old colt Zilophone, by Altamont, to Colonel W. S. Stone of Yreka for $1,000. Zilophone has a record of 2.57 but has trotted much faster, and Mr. Beach hoped to show low figures with him this year, but an almost fatal attack of pinkeye prevented his being trained. It is understood that Louis Huseman of Yreka, and W. J. Evans of Little Shasta are interested with Colonel Stone in this purchase and that the colt will be kept in Siskiyou county for stud service. Mr. Beach has also sold several roadsters this season for good prices, the horses being the get of Altamont from common mares. The stock at Cascade farm has been afflicted with virulent pinkeye this fall and several valuable animals have died from the disease. We trust that Mr. Beach's change of base to the Rogue river valley will prove a judicious one.

Sotoyome is the name claimed for a bay colt foaled 1881, by Pilot, his dam Avola, by Alhambra, grandam Oriole by Simpson's Blackbird, his third dam a "stray mare" taken up on the Masquteze bottom, Jackson county, Iowa, and which had the appearance of being well bred. Pilot by a son of Belmont, Alhambra by Mambrino Chief, his dam Susan (thoroughbred) by American Eclipse.

To-night the California Coursing Club will meet for the purpose of entering and drawing dogs, electing officers, etc., for the match that will take place on the Merced plains next Wednesday and Thursday. We hope to meet Mr. Meany up there at the match and congratulate him on his recent success. Several imported dogs that have been kept dark will run at this match.

The Chinamen in the Upper San Joaquin are taking large quantities of fish by set nets, contrary to law. If the local officials are indisposed to do their duty in the premises there ought to be citizens public spirited enough to compel them to.

A SPIDER CAPTURES A SNAKE.—Recently a young cowsucker snake about a foot long got into Justice Robinson's office, in the basement of Masonic Temple, Eureka, Md., and located itself under an old sofa in the back of the office, where an old spider had his headquarters. When the spider discovered his visitor he threw a web around the snake's neck and fastened it to the bottom of the sofa above the snake. He then proceeded to add another web, and another, and another, and another, until the combined webs made a strong cord, that completely fastened the snake so that it could not extricate itself. If it attempted to go forward the cord raised its head higher and higher, until his snakeship would be half off the floor. If it attempted to go backward, it ended in the same way. Such was the condition of the snake when it was found a few days afterward. In the mean time the spider was secure in his new abode, looking down upon the snake and awaiting results. Doubtless to the great disappointment of the spider, Mr. Robinson extricated the snake from its hanging position, killed it, and threw it out of the office.—Easton (Md.) Star.

William Borst, who died in Boston, last week, was in his earlier days a driver and trainer of trotters, having received his early lessons in the art from Hiram Woodruff many years ago. About the last honors of any prominence with which Borst's name was connected was Geo. Butler, his greatest success previous to assuming charge of "the Contraband" having been with Ethan Allen and running mate. Borst always took a great pride in Butler, and it was a sight never to be forgotten when the old horse and his driver came upon the track for a race. Butler's name and foretop would be decorated with gayly-colored ribbons, whilst Borst, attired in a velvet suit, and wearing a new pair of kid gloves, sat in a sulky that had been washed and polished until every part of it shone like a looking glass. In those days drivers of trotters were not, as a class, particular regarding their dress, and "the fashion plate," as Borst was called, never failed to attract attention. Of late years the deceased took no active interest in turf sports, being engaged in business in Boston.

## Claws for Breakfast.

I put it to an old practitioner, who before his conversion must have had frequent opportunities for discussing such matters with his companions, what was the punishment most dreaded by them, and he unhesitatingly replied: "Flogging." "You would recommend it as a means for putting a stop to the many desperate burglaries that have taken place lately?" "I didn't say I'd recommend it," he replied, with an earnest shake of his head and a twitching of the muscles about his mouth as though the subject involved certain experiences he could not recall without wincing. "If anything would put a stop to it it is flogging. But no man with feelings for his fellow-creatures, no matter how bad they might be, could recommend flogging—leastways, not if he knew anything about it himself. I hardly liked to put to him the delicate question, had he ever had his back scored with the knotted thongs?—now was it needful that I should do so. He screwed his mouth again and shrugged his shoulders shiveringly, and presently continued: "No one, except he has been through with it, can have any idea what the sufferings are. I have been through with it, and I've got the scars to prove, and I tell you this, sir, if I was so unfortunate as to slide back again to my wicked old ways and the judge was to put it to me, 'Will you have three years' penal and twenty-five lashes, or five years without 'em?' I'd take the five years and think it a light let off." It was evident to me from his manner of speaking he quite meant what he said, and that the opinion he had expressed was not hastily arrived at. I was not the less incredible, however. "How long a time does it take to give a man twenty-five lashes?" I asked him. "Well, they don't hurry over it," he replied, with another wince at the rueful reminiscence. "They lay it on pretty well as regular as clockwork, and you can tell to a tick when the next stinger is coming. I should think twenty-five might take as many 'arf minits." "And rather than bear twelve minutes and a half of sharp pain you would serve two-years' imprisonment?" "You don't know what you're talking about," he replied, and with an offended impatience that contrasted strangely with his hitherto meek and mild demeanor. "You speak as if a fellow as soon as he got his sentence was taken out of the dock straight and got his dose of the cat, and there was an end of it." "It can't much matter as to that," said I. "He has twenty-five lashes to receive, and they will cause him no more pain to-morrow or next week than if he was punished immediately." "Hah! that's where you're wrong," returned the convicted burglar, with an energetic shake of his head; "that's where everybody is wrong who argues a thing without knowing. It is bad enough when it comes; there's no mistake about that. But waiting for it is the worst part. No day or hour is mentioned for it at the time at which a man receives his sentence when he is to have 'claws for breakfast' as it is called. It may be to-morrow, or it may be a fortnight or three weeks hence. It didn't so much matter when old Calcraft had the handling of the cat; he hadn't got strength enough to lay it on so as to hurt very much, but it's an other matter when one of those blessed six-foot Millbank warders sets about you. They cut bits out, that's what they do, so well I know and could prove to this very day it was necessary. It must be a horrible sort of punishment or they wouldn't think it necessary to physic a man and get his body in order before they give it him. You know what, certain as death, is coming one day or other, and you go to bed every night and lay in a sweat for fear when the warder comes round at 6 next morning he'll say: 'You needn't put your shirt on this morning.' And if over-night the doctor should order you a couple of pills or a draught, you can't get a wink of sleep for thinking about it, and it very likely nothing comes of it that time, and you're kept three or four weeks at the same kind of torture. And at last you get it!" He closed the subject abruptly with these last words, but the shiver and the sudden close-setting of his teeth that accompanied the utterance of them told plainer than speech of the tenacity with which 'claws for breakfast' sticks in a man's memory.—London Telegraph.

## Brutal "Sport."

For over two hours yesterday the Boston bull-dogs, Pilot and Ned, fought each other. The encounter took place at a well-known sporting hostelry on the boulevard which leads to Coney Island, for $2,000. Ten times the amount was wagered on the result. Both canines are champions, and are the heroes of many hard-fought battles in the pit. They were as nearly matched in point of weight as could be desired, both turning the scale at twenty-seven pounds eight ounces. Pilot is a pure brindle, with one or two white spots on his body, one of these being over the lower jaw. Ned is nearly pure white, one or two liver-colored spots marking his side. The pit was situated near the roof of the building, and around it was ranged seats which rose one above the other and formed a regular amphitheatre, but they were much too light for the crowd that poured into the room. By actual count there were 450 faces around the pit, but this count did not take in a hundred or more who clamored for a sight at the conflict, and as soon as the dogs got together they clambered up the supports, which being very frail, gave way, and down tumbled the toy tier. The extra weight broke down the lower seats, and in an instant there was a struggling mass of humanity in the pit in the midst of the fighting dogs. Such crowding and elbowing is seldom seen. Finally, something like order was restored, and the discomforted ones found fresh roosting places; these in turn gave way, and there was nothing left but to literally take up a fresh standpoint with front row of spectators as supports. Everything was taken in the utmost good humor, and hundred dollar bills were handed across the pit in the most reckless manner; but the host of sporting men from Boston, Hartford, New Haven, Bridgeport, New York, Philadelphia and Baltimore, knew each other thoroughly, and the simple nod of the head was sufficient to register a bet of $500.

Everything went on swimmingly until the selection of a referee was attempted. The choosing of this functionary took up half an hour, but finally a well-known horse-racing man agreed to stand, and then the dogs were brought in for the washing and tasting process. Pilot was the first to get his bath, and after five minutes' manipulation he was pronounced presentable. Then Ned was brought out and washed in the most approved style. This took three minutes only, and the combatants were taken to their corners, Pilot in the northern end of the pit and Ned opposite. Time was called at 3:50 p. m., and no sooner had the word been given than Ned flew at Pilot's throat and turned him on his back, and the chewing and twisting process began. To equalise matters Pilot took Ned's fore leg in his mouth, and the fun began in earnest. Then it was nip for nip and gash for gash. Ned was the better wrestler and gave Pilot some ugly tosses, but he seemed to fight much better when he was under, and invariably secured a firm hold of Ned's jaw or leg as he went to the floor. After eight minutes' fighting both were covered with blood, and several times Ned howled as though he did not like the fangs that were constantly

---

being buried in his throat and sides; but he did not let up in the least, keeping up the gnawing process until the bones of Pilot's nose and jaw cracked loudly. There was twenty-minutes of hard work before either dog showed any inclination to take a rest, and then the cessation of hostilities was involuntary. Occasionally they would snap at each other, but the punishment administered was very light. After fighting twenty-eight minutes a claim was made that Pilot was fanged, and in his endeavors to take the tooth out of the lower lip Pilot's handler had his thumb bitten through. Soon after this the latter made a turn, and the animals were taken to their corners. The betting, which had been 8 to 4 on Pilot, now veered round to 6 to 4 on Ned.

After a fifteen seconds' breathing spell the canines went at it again. Ned forcing his antagonist all over the pit and fighting him to a standstill. Two or three turns were made in the hope that Pilot would not be able to come to the scratch, but he came bravely forward every time he was sent out, only to be fought down. Frequently he fell in the middle of the pit as though about to give up, but would make an effort to get at Ned's legs; but although he held him, no punishment was given by Pilot. Ned, on the contrary, kept on chewing at his antagonist's nose, and the minutes ran into hours. Now and then one or the other would turn, but both scratched every time they were sent out. When two hours had expired several backers of Pilot made a suggestion that it would be a good thing to take Pilot away before he died in the pit. His attendant, realizing that he stood in a good way to not only lose the fight but also his dog, accepted a proposition to take $25 and give up the fight, and in two hours' and two minutes Ned was declared victor. He was very sore in the forelegs, but was not badly punished elsewhere. Pilot, on the contrary, was terribly lacerated about the head and body, and will very probably die from his injuries.—New York Star.

## The Position of the Hop Crop.

As estimated by Bradstreet's, the domestic and foreign deficiency in hops is about 55,000,000 pounds, the consumption of the world being over 170,000,000 pounds. This view of the situation goes far to explain the necessity for the materially augmented prices asked during the past two months. In 1877 the quantity of hops carried over in the hop-growing countries of the world aggregated about 70,000,000 pounds, which is reflected in the quotations current at that time in the United States, three to eight cents per pound. In 1880 the world's demand was met by an even supply, in which was included stocks previously carried over. That year hops in this country averaged eighteen to twenty-five cents per pound. In 1881 it became necessary to glean carefully to avoid a squeeze in the hop market, as the falling off in the supply, as compared with the world's requirements, was about eight per cent. This year, however, the shortage unexpectedly became more pronounced, and is believed to be 33½ per cent. less than what is demanded.

Growers having any of the crop in hand are holding out for seventy and seventy-eight cents, and firm at that. Large holders in cities do not care to sell. The opinion is common that prices 1882 hops will touch $1 per Jan. 1, thus rivaling the record prominent cry for "dollar oil" with one for "dollar hops." The largest brewers in the United States have certain supplies of hops in store, which, except in a few instances, are limited. They appear to have faith, however, that a reaction must take place in the foreign market and effect the rates here, which will continue moderate. Additional supplies at more favorable terms than it is now possible for them to do. They are fortunate, as a rule, in having stored an unusually large quantity of beer and ale, and the recent advance of from fifty cents to $1 per barrel will, of course, react favorably upon the heavy stocks in vault, and in a large degree mitigate any loss in their season's business, owing to necessary increased outlay for hops.

The English hop crop has been characterized by various journals and by investors in American hops as "total failure." Late reports in competent agricultural publications do not bear out this assertion. The most conservative estimates of the requirements in England place the total for 1882–83 at 60,000,000 pounds and the English crop at 14,000,000 pounds. The latter total would hardly justify the appellation "a total failure," although admittedly a scant production. The English lookout for imports of hops is for about 6,000,000 pounds from the United States, about 9,500,000 pounds from Germany, 2,000,000 from Holland and Belgium, a total of 16,-000,000 pounds. This, with the English production, will aggregate 30,500,000 pounds, against the 60,000,000 pounds required. Such a shortage in the English market of course means high prices. The "first pocket" of the season sold for $2 45 per pound, which was, of course, a fancy figure, and by no means necessarily indicative of the range of prices for the season. Bulls in hops in London, however, fully expect to get eighty-five and ninety cents for their holdings, and there is little doubt that they will. In Belgium, as in England, the hops suffered severely from the aphides, mould and unfavorable weather. In France the crop is expected to be nearly the average, both in quantity and quality.

A SINGULAR LETTER.—"Was Ephraim Blaine a Catholic?" "No, indeed; all the Blaines were Protestants, but all the Gillespies were strong Catholics. That's why Eph was buried beside his wife in the Catholic graveyard. No, Eph Blaine did'nt belong to any church; he was too fond of his fun. I remember that when he was running for prothonotary of this county his opponents charged him with being a Catholic so as to arouse the Protestant element against him. There was a Catholic priest living here then by the name of Father McGuire. He and Eph Blaine were the best of friends, but he didn't go much on Eph's piety. To him Blaine applied for a certificate that he was not a member of his church. The priest, who was somewhat of a wag, but withal a splendid man, gave him a paper which read: 'This is to certify that Ephraim L. Blaine is not now nor never has been a member of the Catholic Church, and furthermore, in my opinion, he is not fit to be a member of any church.' This document pleased Blaine very much, and he often showed it to his friends years after it had the desired effect in his campaign for the county office. When Eph was elected prothonotary he left here and moved to Washington. I think James G. was then a good-sized boy."—Philadelphia Press.

On Oct. 13, at Newmarket, Walton, the "Plunger," won £8,000 on the victory of W. S. Crawford's two-year-old colt Energy, in the Great Challenge Stakes, and in the very next race of the day, the Newmarket Derby, landed £3,000 additional by Shrewsbury's success over Dutch Oven, the St. Leger veteran being a hot favorite, the result of the race at once establishing Mr. Jardine's colt at very short odds for the Cambridgeshire. Walton's efforts on the two races therefore netted $55,000.

**y District Association**   Races.

---

---

**FALL RACE MEETING.**

# Pacific Coast Blood Horse Association.

## 1882.

**BAY DISTRICT COURSE.**

Introductory Day—Saturday, November 11th.

No. 1—Purse $250; free for all; $10 each; a dash of three-quarters of a mile; entrance money to second horse.

NIGHT HAWK.
GARFIELD.
PREMIUM.
FOREST KING.
MAY D.
JIM DOUGLAS.
JIM RENWICK.
JOE HOWELL.
ATALANTA.

No. 2—Purse $250; free for all maidens; $10 each; one mile; entrance money to second horse.

JUDGE McKINSTRY.
JOE DION.
LIZZIE MARTIN COLT.
JOE G.
BOB.
PATROL.
CAPT. KIDD.
HATTIE BALL.

No. 3—Handicap stake for all ages; free for all; $25 each each, and $10 if declared; $50 added; $50 to second horse; a dash of a mile and an eighth.

MARIA F.
HADDINGTON.
FOREST KING.
NATHAN COOMBS.
ELLA DOANE.
BIRDCATCHER.
FRED COLLIER.
JOE HOWELL.
BOLIS.

No. 4—Selling purse, $300; a mile and a quarter; for all ages; entrance free; $50 to the second horse; the winner to be sold at auction; horses entered for $1,500 to carry regular weight; if for $1,200, five pounds allowed; if for $900, ten pounds; if for $600, twenty-five pounds; twenty-two pounds, $30 pounds who can claim the winner, and the excess realized beyond the amount at which the horse is entered to be divided between the association and the owner of the second horse.

HADDINGTON.
EUCHRE.
GEO. BENDER.
JACK.
BELSHAW.
JOE HOWELL.
FRANK RHOADS.

First day Regular Meeting—November 15th.

No. 5—The Ladies' Stake.

LADY VIVA.
MAY B.
FLOU-FLOU.
CALIFORNIA AND ROSETLAND FILLY.
CLARA W.
LOU SPENCER.
NORFOLK AND MATTIE A FILLY.
MARION.
LAURA.
MISS GIFT.
PARTISAN AND PET FILLY.
PARTISAN AND LEXINGTON FILLY.
SATANELLA.
HUBBARD AND TEHAMA FILLY.
WILDIDLE AND ROSE FILLY.
SHANNON AND CAMILLA URSO FILLY.
NUBIA.
IRENE.
SOPHIA.
BELLE.

No. 6—Purse $200; free for all; three-quarters of a mile and repeat; $50 to second horse; entrance free; the winner of the dash of three-quarters on the first day to carry ten pounds extra.

NIGHT HAWK.
GARFIELD.
PREMIUM.
FOREST KING.
MAY D.
ELLA DOANE.
HADDINGTON.
JIM RENWICK.
FRED COLLIER.
JOE HOWELL.
FRANK RHOADS.

No. 7—The Vestal Stake.

NORFOLK AND MATTIE A FILLY.
DUCHESS OF NORFOLK.
NORFOLK AND GOLDEN GATE FILLY.
ANITA.
SPRINGBOK AND BOYDANA FILLY.
LONGFELLOW AND MISS CAMPBELL FILLY.
PRECIOUS.
LONGFELLOW AND ROBIN GIRL FILLY.
LADY CLARE.
ANNIE LAWRIE.
MONDAY AND CAMILLA URSO FILLY.
MONDAY AND VIRGINIA FILLY.

No. 8—Handicap purse of $250 for two-year-olds; $25 each and $10 if declared; $50 to the second horse; dash of a mile.

MAY B.
CAMILLA URSO FILLY.
LOU SPENCER.
CLARA W.

No. 9—Purse $250; a mile and a quarter over five hurdles; $50 to second horse; entrance free.

JOE G.

---

MOLLIE H.
HATTIE B.

Second Day Regular Meeting—November 18th.

No. 10—Purse $250; a dash of seven-eighths of a mile; $50 to the second horse; entrance free; the winner of the three-quarter dash of three-quarters and repeat to carry ten pounds extra; winner of both events to carry fifteen pounds extra.

NIGHT HAWK.
GARFIELD.
PREMIUM.
DUKE OF MONDAY.
JOE G.
FOREST KING.
BOB.
MAY D.
ELLA DOANE.
HADDINGTON.
JIM DOUGLAS.
JIM RENWICK.
FRED COLLIER.
JOE HOWELL.
ATALANTA.
LIZZIE F.

No. 11—Purse of $300; heats of a mile and an eighth; entrance free; $50 to second horse; maiden three-year-olds allowed seven pounds; four-year-olds twelve pounds; maidens five years old and over twenty pounds; the winner of the dash at this distance on the first day to carry five pounds extra.

DUKE OF MONDAY.
JOE DION.
LIZZIE MARTIN COLT.
GEO. BENDER.
NATHAN COOMBS.
BELSHAW.
PRECIOUS.
FRED COLLIER.
JOE HOWELL.
CAPT. KIDD.
JUDGE McKINSTRY.

No. 12—Handicap purse of $250 for all three-year-olds; a dash of a mile and a quarter; $25 each and $10 if declared; the second horse to receive $50.

GARFIELD.
MARIA F.
FOREST KING.
INAUGURATION.
BIRDCATCHER.
HATTIE B.
ATALANTA.
LIZZIE F.
JOKO.

No. 13—Purse $250; a mile and repeat over four hurdles; $50 to second horse; entrance free.

JOE G.
MOLLIE H.
HATTIE B.

Third Day Regular Meeting—November 23d.

No. 14—The Finigan Stake.

LADY VIVA.
MAY B.
AURIOL.
PANAMA.
FLOU-FLOU.
CALIFORNIA AND ROSETLAND FILLY.
NORFOLK AND ADDIE C COLT.
NORFOLK AND MAGGIE DALE COLT.
CALIFORNIA AND FUBS COLT.
CLARA W.
LOU SPENCER.
NORFOLK AND MATTIE A FILLY.
MARION.
LAURA.
MISS GIFT.
GRISNER.
LUCKY B.
GANO.
SATANELLA.
HUBBARD AND TEHAMA FILLY.
SHANNON AND CAMILLA URSO FILLY.
SHANNON AND EMMA ROBSON GELDING.
SHANNON AND EVA ASHTON FILLY.
BOB WOODING AND LIZZIE MARSHAL COLT.
NUBIA.
BELLE.
IRENE.
SOPHIA.
DEL PASO.

No. 15—The Fame Stake.

NORFOLK AND BALLINETTE COLT.
NORFOLK AND MATTIE A FILLY.
DUCHESS OF NORFOLK.
NORFOLK AND GOLDEN GATE FILLY.
ANITA.
LEVER AND LOLA COLT.
FOSTER AND PLANXTIA COLT.
LONGFELLOW AND ROBIN GIRL FILLY.
JUDGE McKINSTRY.
RHODICILE No. 2.
ANNIE LAWRIE.
MONDAY AND CAMILLA URSO FILLY.
MONDAY AND LIZZIE MARTIN COLT.
MONDAY AND VIRGINIA COLT.
BAYSWATER AND RUTH RYAN COLT.

No. 16—The Baldwin Stake.

No. 17—Consolation purse of $250, of which $50 to the second horse; entrance free; a mile dash; horses beaten once allowed five pounds, twice ten pounds and three times fifteen pounds.

THEO. WINTERS, Sec'y.
C. M. CHASE, Assistant Secretary.

SPECIMEN OF OUR ARTIST'S HUMOR

THE FISHMONGER.

HUNDREDS OF DELIGHTED ONES SEE, FOR THE FIRST TIME IN THEIR LIVES

The Japanese Artist and Embroiderers

*At work in their native costumes at*

# Ichi Ban, 22 & 24 Geary St.

*The BREEDER AND SPORTSMAN is printed with SHATTUCK & FLETCHER'S INK*

NO. VOL. No. 2 MONTGOMERY STREET. SAN FRANCISCO, SATURDAY, NOVEMBER 18, 1882. SUBSCRIPTION FIVE DOLLARS A YEAR.

# TURF AND TRACK.

## P. C. B. H. A.

### Fall Meeting at the Bay District Course—Favorable Weather and Fine Racing.

**First Day.**

There was rime on the sidewalks last Saturday morning, though it was not long before the rays of the sun melted the hoar frost, and there was every indication that the day would be favorable for the opening of the fall meeting of the Pacific Coast Blood Horse Association. But at noontime the sky was overcast and there was a chilly wind from the north. The track was in much better condition than was anticipated, as it was thoroughly soaked from the rains of Wednesday, and on Thursday the horses were wallowing through the mud in the exercising which the trainers thought imperatively necessary to be given. Work must be done with gallopers, especially those which have not run for a while, and, wet or dry, the trainer is compelled to send them along. While the track was in fair condition, it was, probably, a trifle slow. Some rated it to be two seconds to the mile behind when in the best order, and others a second from what it will be when a few days more sunshine have reduced the moisture.

This course is peculiar in many respects. When just in the right shape it is doubtful if there is a "faster track" anywhere, and whenever it is in order to run upon it is a "safe" one. The only time when it could be regarded otherwise is when it is slippery on the surface or when it is so soft that the horses' feet sink to an undue depth. The substratum of sand permits the water which does not run off, to drain through, and at the same time retains the moisture so that there is elasticity with a firm foothold above. The turns are very easy, the first being some over a quarter of a mile, the curve gradually merging into the backstretch so that the horses adapt themselves to the change gradually.

The course and appointments are first-class, and it is a great pity that the citizens of San Francisco do not show a more hearty appreciation of it and the fine racing which has always been a feature of the meetings of this association by a large attendance. We sincerely wish that we could write conscientiously that the balconies of the club house and hotel and the seats of the grand stand were crowded to the fullest, and that standing room was at a premium, but we are sorry to say that though there was a fair concourse for the opening day in this city there is scarcely a city in the United States, of one quarter the size, where the numbers would not have been quadrupled.

It was a fair crowd, however, and well satisfied with the sport as was evidenced by the hearty cheers that greeted the winners, and better yet, without a whisper of dissatisfaction at the decision of the judges, or a question as to the honesty of the racing. The P. C. B. H. A. has effected a grand change in racing in California. The highwaymen of the course have been brought under control, or it will be better to write, the majority of them banished, so that in the many races run under the auspices only one had a taint, and in that the party was summarily punished. Then the sport has been systematized and brought in accordance with modern ideas. The old and barbarous custom of heats at long distances has been superseded by dashes, and in lieu of the dragging along of wearied limbs there are life, spirit and animation. All that is necessary to make the racing here equally as enjoyable as that at the East is to see twenty thousand people on the course every day of the meeting, and twice that number of thousands when the winding-up day comes. The time is not distant when such will be the case and in the not far-off future the association will be rewarded for its labors by an attendance commensurate with its deserving.

The first race was a dash of three-quarters, for a purse of $200; the entrée fee of $10 each going to the second in the race. There were nine entries; three of which were drawn, leaving Premium, ridden by Patsy Duffy; Jim Douglas, with Geo. Howson up; Jim Renwick, Estabrook the jockey; Forest King, with Charlie Ross for pilot, May D, Billy Appleby having the mount, and Garfield—a late importation from the Sandwich Islands, though bred in California—under the charge of Fred Carillo. They were awarded places in the order their names are written, and in the pool sales Premium was the favorite at the odds of $25 on her to $30 on all the others. The six presented a fine appearance when marshaled at the starting place, the quarter pole, and though there was some trouble in getting them together, it was not long until a very good start was affected. Garfield at once sprang off with the lead, with Premium in close order, the others not far behind, and the first quarter of a mile was run in twenty-four seconds, Garfield having half a length the advantage of Premium, the others in a bunch two or three lengths behind. It was evident that this fast pace could not be kept, though the next quarter was made in twenty-five seconds, the half-mile in forty-nine seconds, Garfield still leading; Premium second, May D and Jim Douglas closing the gap perceptibly. It was certain from their positions that there would be a lively race home, and before a hundred yards of the homestretch was made Garfield dropped back, beaten, leaving Premium in the lead. Jim Douglas was coming fast, however; and May D was determined to take an active part in the struggle. At the drawgate Douglas and Premium were on even terms, but from thence on Douglas had it all his own way, winning with something to spare, a length in front of Premium, the same distance between her and May D the distance accomplished in the fast time of 1:15. The others came in in straggling order, the riders pulling up when they found that a place was beyond their reach. The time is as fast as three-quarters of a mile has ever been run in California, and within one second of the best on record. Considering that the weights were according to the new schedule and the admitted slowness of the course it must be regarded as an extra good effort and gives Jim Douglas high rank among the flyers of the coast. He is a fine looking, strapping big horse, and as he made a season in the stud he is entitled to still more credit. He has a double cross of Lexington and also of Glencoe so that this great combination has lost none of its potency.

**SUMMARY.**

PACIFIC COAST BLOOD HORSE ASSOCIATION, FALL MEETING, BAY DISTRICT COURSE, SAN FRANCISCO Nov. 11, 1882.—Purse $200, free to all, $10 each. Entrance to second horse: dash of three-quarters of a mile.
Geo. Howson's b h Jim Douglas, by Wildidle—by Norfolk, 4 years 118 lbs. (Howson).................................................. 1
J. B. Haggin's ch m Premium, by Castor—by St. Louis, aged, 116 lbs. (Duffy)........................................................ 2
..and R. C. Judson's ch m May D, by Wildidle—Nettie Brown, 4 years 115 lbs. (Appleby)........................................... 3
H. H. Green's g c Garfield, by California—Queen, 3 years, 118 lbs. (Carillo)........................................................ 0
L. Stanford's br c Forest King, by Monday—Abbie W, 3 years 118 lbs. (Ross)........................................................ 0
Hinman & Ayers' ch g Jim Renwick, by Joe Hooker—Big Gun, 4 years. 115 lbs. Estabrook............................................ 0
Time 1:15.

The second race was a purse of $300, for "maidens"; i. e., horses that had never won a race, the $10 entrance fee going to the second horse; a dash of a mile. Of the eight entries four came to the front, viz., Joe Dion, George Howson, rider; Patrol, Billy Appleby; Judge McKinstry, Patsy Duffy; and Bob Wooding. —— Kennedy. The placing was as above, and the start was delayed by the fractiousness of Bob Wooding. He was a crazy horse, bounding into the air, notwithstanding there was a stalwart man hanging to his bridle, the jockey being unable to do anything with him, and in his mad efforts he broke the bridle. Replaced by another, with a safety cord on his lower jaw, even then it was almost impossible to arrange him, though after a short time a very fair start was given. Two of the horses had crossed the score when the flag fell with Crazy Bob two or three lengths behind it; though in fifty yards he had the field, and at the quarter pole he had opened a gap of many lengths, the others bunched so that it was difficult to tell which was second, though the favorite, Judge McKinstry, was in the rear. Bob keeping up his mad flight ran down the backstretch in twenty-five seconds, and Judge McKinstry pegging away that much in the rear of them. He had been so great a favorite that at the opening of the pool sales he brought $50 to $10 on all the others, and his supporters were despondent as his chances appeared to be of the slenderest sort. There was little change rounding the further turn until nearing the three-quarter pole, when Joe and Patrol closed on Bob, and the Judge mended his position a trifle. If he could not run fast he gave evidence of being able to keep up his lick, and at the seven furlong mark he was also past Bob, and a hundred yards further on he was even with Patrol. From there he had it all his own way and won by two lengths, Patrol second, Bob Wooding third and Joe Dion last. Time—1:46.

There was a difference of opinion in the judges, stand regarding the start in this race, one of the judges holding that as a portion of the horses were beyond the wire when the flag fell the race was void. Inasmuch as this question is considered on the editorial page it is only necessary to refer to it here.

The winner of this race is a remarkably handsome colt and though a little under size is likely to develop into a fine racehorse. He labors under the disadvantage of, not having been trained when a two-year old, and was unfortunate in the commencement of two seasons. Being very "high" when put in training his legs were buckskinned and for a time he was thrown out of training. He has a fine turn of speed which he did not show in any portion of the race so that when this gift returns he will be a dangerous competitor in future races. Whichever side of the paternal branch he belongs to, he has a valuable inheritance as "Old Thad" and Grinstead were "sure enough" racehorses, and his dam—well it is sufficient to say he is a son of Katie Pease.

**SUMMARY.**

Same day—Purse $300; free for all maidens; $10 each: entrance to second horse; dash of a mile.
Jas. Moe names b c Judge McKinstry, by Thad Stevens or Grinstead —Katie Pease, 3 yrs., 109 lbs. (Duffy)........................ 1
J. and H. C. Judson names b c Patrol, by Wildidle—Nettie Brown, 3 yrs., 109 lbs. (Appleby).................................... 2
Wm. Boots names b g Bob Wooding, by Bob Wooding—Gladiola, 3 yrs. 106 lbs. (Kennedy)........................................... 3
E. S. Paddock names b g Joe Dion, by Norfolk—Nevada, 4 yrs., 112 lbs. (Howson)................................................ 0
Time—1:46.

The third race was a handicap stake of $25 each, $250 added, a dash of one and one-eighth miles. The starters were Nathan Coombs, 100 pounds; Frank Rhoads, 105 pounds; Joe Howell, 120 pounds; Haddington, 106 pounds; Forest King, 105 pounds; Atalanta, 106 pounds, and Ella Doane, 108 pounds. At the start of the pool-selling Joe Howell was the favorite, when the speculators taking into consideration the heavy weight the old veteran was laden with, threw him up for Frank Rhoads, and just previous to the start he was only bringing $20 to $100-pools. Again there was a good start, and this time Haddington cut out the work. He was leading when the stand was passed for the first time, and at the quarter-pole, forty seconds from the start, he had opened a wide gap on all the others, which were running in a bunch. He was nearly as far in front at the half, the five furlongs run in 1:06½, and he still led around the turn. Ella Doane was coming on him however, and half-way from the three-quarter pole home she had him beaten, and it looked as though she had won the victory. Old Joe was also coming on the very outside of the track, having emerged from the ruck, nobody knew how, and with a rush that could not be stayed won a gallant fight—Ella Doane second, Haddington third—in 1:58. There had been cheers over the others as they crossed the score; in this there was a tumult of applause repeated when the riders returned to weigh in.

When there is more leisure time we will endeavor to give the history of this horse, and if it be found to be one of the most romantic in equine annals. Notwithstanding his ten years and scores upon scores of hard-run races he is as sound as when first put in training and a horse of very high form.

**SUMMARY.**

Same day—Haddington stake for all ages; $25 entrance and $10 if declared; $250 added; $50 to second horse; dash of a mile and one-eighth.
Hinman & Ayers names b g Joe Howell, by Bonnie Scotland—Eva Shephard, 120 lbs................................................... 1
J. and R. C. Judson name b m Ella Doane, by Wildidle—Nettie Brown, 108 lbs........................................................ 2
P. J. Shafter names b h Haddington, by imported Haddington—Prairie Flower, 106 lbs.............................................. 3
L. Stanford names br c Forest King, by Monday—Abbie W, 105 lbs.. 0
W. Boots names br h Nathan Coombs, by Leví—Miami, 100 lbs....... 0
Theo. Winters names ch f Atalanta, by Norfolk—Lady Jane, 106 lbs. 0
W. L. Pritchard names br c Frank Rhoads, by Leinster—Ada A, 108 lbs......................................................... 0
Time—1:58.

The concluding game was a selling race, Belshaw carrying ninety-eight pounds, Euchre 101 pounds and Frank Rhoads 113 pounds. These weights were adjusted by the prices they were entered to be sold for. Belshaw was the favorite in the pools, Euchre being the second choice. The purse was $300, with $50 to the second, the distance one and a quarter mile.

This brought the starting point at the three-quarter pole, and from the stand it could not be told which had the advantage when the flag fell. Belshaw led under the wire at the completion of the quarter, and when a half had been run Euchre was at his hip. Passing the half-mile pole, Belshaw had only a neck the best of it, and making the northern semi-circle it was head and head. Coming home at one time it looked as though Euchre had his opponent beaten, but Belshaw came again and won a fine race by half a length, Rhoads two lengths behind Euchre. Time, 2:14. It is seldom that four better races are seen in one afternoon, and these won encomiums on all sides.

Thus two of the get of Wildidle won races on the first day, and though Belshaw is not so well formed as the Wildidles usually are he is very speedy, especially with light weight, and as he grows older may increase in substance.

SUMMARY.

Same day—Selling Purse, $200; a mile and a quarter; entrance free; $50 to the second horse; the winner to be sold at auction; horses entered for $1,500 to carry regular weight; if for $1,000, five pounds allowed; if for $750, ten pounds; if for $500, seventeen pounds, and if for $300, twenty-two pounds. Any one can claim the winner, and the excess realized beyond the amount at which the horse is entered to be divided between the association and the owner of the second horse.

J. & H. C. Judson name b g Belshaw, by Wildidle, — by Hercules, 4 years, $500, 98 lbs........ 1
J. T. Gilmer names ch h Euchre, by Leinster — Flush, 5 years, $500, 101 lbs........ 2
W. L. Pritchard names b c Frank Rhoads, by Leinster, — Ada A, 4 years, $1,000, 119 lbs........ 3

Time—2:14.

The beaten horses are worthy of more than a passing notice. The second in the first race, Premium, has run her share of races, and many of them over hard tracks, without showing any indication of weakness in any place. Had it not been for the great pace which Garfield set for the first half-mile the result might have been different, at least so far that it would have been a neck and neck affair between her and the winner. Garfield has immense speed, and as it was claimed he was not in condition; that essential factor in his favor he will be troublesome to the best. Writing, however, on the eve of the second day of the meeting, it will be extremely hazardous to venture predictions which the morrow may upset, and the safest course will be to await the "current of events.

**Second Day.**

At noon on Wednesday the air was as balmy as that of a June evening in the Vale of Cashmere. A ride on the outside of the Geary street dummy was enjoyable if clad in the ordinary habiliments of summer, and all were offering congratulations at the grand prospect for the racing. There could not be a better time for horses to display their powers of speed and bottom, and prognostications were rife that at least one of the contests would show remarkable time. With all of this feeling it would have been an ultra sanguine man who would have ventured a prediction that there was to be a "smashing" of the record. At this time of the year it is hardly to be expected that horses, drilled to death with the races of the whole season, could excel previous efforts, and, notwithstanding the fine day, make the crowning effort of their career. The mellifluous atmosphere was a great point in their favor; that the course would be in the best possible condition was assured, and this opinion was corroborated on arrival. The track was as fast as it is possible to be, unless some inventive genius constructs one of gutta percha with a substratum of steel springs. There was just loose dirt enough to fill the hollow of the foot, and there was no "cupping," or giving way to retard the horses in their stride. The attendance was fair. Not so numerous as there should be when such a bill was offered, although there was the usual surging crowd on the slope between the hotel and the inner fence, and on the balcony of the Club house there was more than the usual quota of ladies and their escorts. A novel feature at a race meeting was a group of the "almond-eyed" picturesquely appareled Mongolians, and from the interest with which they watched the proceedings, doubtless they shared in the enjoyment of race day.

The first race to be decided was the Ladies' stake, a dash of three-quarters of a mile for two-year-old fillies. The stake for $50 each, $25 forfeit, and of the twenty nominations five came to the post. There were Marion, by Hubbard; Lou Spencer, by Norfolk; Laura, by Shannon; Satanella, by Leveller, and May B, by Shannon. The positions at the start were in the same order their names are written, and in the betting the Palo Alto filly Satanella was a great favorite, though she carried 4½ pounds over weight. The youngsters behaved very well, and after a few break aways; the flag was dropped. Lou Spencer had rather the best of the send-off, and she took advantage of it by going away at a great pace; and when the half-mile pole was passed, she had a lead which appeared enough to win the race. Satanella was running easily, however, and when fairly straightened into the home run she collared the leader, and from that point she had it all her own way, and won very handily in 1:16½; Lou Spencer second, Laura third, Marion fourth, and May B, who was not driven after it was evident she could not win, last.

SUMMARY.

Nov. 15—The Ladies' Stake, for two-year-old fillie, at $50 each, half forfeit; $200 added; second to save stake; three-quarters of a mile.

Palo Alto names ch f Satanella, by Leveler—Frou Frou (Fallon)........ 1
Theo. Winters names ch f Lou Spencer, by Norfolk—Ballerina, (Carter)........ 2
J. B. Chase names b f Laura, by Shannon—Folly, (Kelly)........ 3
J. B. Chase names b g Marion, by Hubbard—Electra, (Estabrook)........ 0
P. Robson names ch f May B, by Shannon—Jessie R, (Kennedy)........ 0

Time—1:16½.

The second race was heats of three-quarters of a mile and it is no exaggeration to state that it was the best field of horses that ever started in a race of this kind on the Pacific Coast. The result proved that it was as good as ever started on this continent, as the race takes precedence of all others, and the time for the three heats is the best on record. It is also the best for first and second heats, and the fastest time made by "aged" horses. There were eleven entries and seven starters. In the placing Night Hawk had the first position, and she was ridden by Fred Ross; Howell was second, with George Howson in the saddle; the third was Frank Rhoads: Ed Fallon the jockey; in the fourth place came Forest King, with Charley Ross to guide him; Premium fifth, Patsy Duffy the pilot; Garfield sixth, Fred Carillo holding the reins, and on the outskirts was May D with Billy Appleby in charge. It was not only a good field of horses, as there was an array of talent in the saddle, every one of the jockeys having the benefit of years of experience, some of them men of families, and their visages bearded and showing the lines which "wasting" is sure to produce. Shrewd, keen-looking little men, with determination in the eye, and a wiriness of frame which the tight-fitting breeches brought out in full relief. The schedule of weights adopted at the last annual meeting, being the same time as those of the American Jockey Club, Saratoga, Long Branch and Coney Island Jockey Club, permits men being employed in place of boys, and thus the horses have the benefit of experience, as well as the comparison being equal. Had this race been run with light weight the merit would have been overlooked and the fast time accredited to the difference. As it is, California can add another figure to the best, for though the winner was bred in Illinois, the "glorious climate" was necessary to give him the highest place in the record. With this array of craft and talent in the saddle it was not surprising that the starter had some difficulty in getting them off. In so short a race the start was everything, and these old watchful riders were thoroughly alive to the importance of getting the best of it. There was amusement to those at the starting point in getting the tactics, but to the other spectators the delay was irksome, and when the flag fell, there was a feeling of relief that the tiresome overture had come to an end. Premium had a trifle the best of it, and away she went at a tremendous pace. Howell, who had been largely the favorite in the pools, was second as they passed the quarter pole in twenty-five seconds, though at this early stage it was evident that it was not intended he should fight for this heat, and as the others drew up he was pulled back to an easy stride. Around the turn they whirled, Premium still leading, the others a neck behind. Nearing the three-quarter pole Forest King drew up, and from there all the way home he made a gallant run to reach the flying mare. She had it all her own way and won the heat with apparently something to spare in the very fast time of 1:14½. Forest King was on her hip, Frank Rhoads was close to him, Howell was cantering along fourth. May D was fifth, Night Hawk was sixth, and Garfield, who did not show any of the speed he exhibited in his former race, distanced. Joe Howell was still a prime favorite, and the result of the heat did not stagger the faith of his backers a particle. The money was rushed into the pool box as fast as the clerks could receive it, and for all Premium had shown such a wonderful flight of speed, the old veteran had supporters who claimed that he must be invincible. Fifty dollars on him, $26 on the field, $20 on Premium and $17 on Night Hawk, were the rates, and the only ones oblivious of the delay that again occurred at the start were the excited throng which surrounded the pool-sellers. Premium would rush off with one or two in company, and viciously switch her tail and refuse to come back to the starting point. Night Hawk would plunge into the air, and attempt to dance a hornpipe, while the others were cavorting around in a milder way. When the flag fell Premium was in motion first, and, as before, Joe Howell was keeping her company. But this time there was no pulling back, though Forest King was on her haunches as they rushed past the half-mile post in 24½ seconds. This place he surrendered to Howell on going around the turn, and then came the exciting part of the race. It was head and ears at the seven furlongs, but Howell had his ears pricked, while the mare was in trouble, and from the drawgate in he had it all his own way, crossing the score a length in advance of Premium, Frank Rhoads third, Night Hawk fourth, May D fifth, and Forest King last, the time the same as before, 1:14½.

The two fastest heats ever recorded, it was not surprising that Howell brought $25 to $7 on all the others, and there were more to invest on the favorite than those who were willing to take the short side, and yet there were some sanguine enough to think that Night Hawk had a show, and others who pinned their faith on May D. There was the same tiresome delay in getting them off for the third heat, and this time without the excitement of the betting to relieve the monotony. This time Night Hawk led soon after the word was given, and she had opened quite a gap at the half-mile, but rounding the turn all were in close order, though when nearly at the three-quarters, the cherry and pink on Howell was moving to the front. There was a light jacket in the throng, and when the run home was commenced it was gaining on Howell. This was borne by May D and the game filly made a grand effort to pluck the garland of victory. It was useless, however, as the favorite came under the wire a good length before her, with Night Hawk third, Premium fourth, Frank Rhoads fifth and Forest King sixth. The time was 1:15, and thus ended the best and fastest race ever run at the distance. Excepting Garfield, every horse in the race was worthy of a high place, and the gray from the dominions of King Kalakaua was evidently not at himself.

SUMMARY.

Same day—Purse $250, free for all; $50 to second horse; entrance free; three-quarters of a mile and repeat. Winner of dash of three-quarters in first day ten pounds extra.

Stemler & Ayres name b g Joe Howell, by Bonnie Scotland—Eva Sheppard, aged, 115 lbs, (Howson)........ 4 1 1
J. B. Haggin names ch m Premium, by Castor—by St. Louis, aged, 115 lbs, (Duffy)........ 1 2 4
J. and H. C. Judson name ch m May D, by Wildidle—Nettie Brown, 4 years, 115 lbs, (Appleby)........ 5 5 2
L. Stanford names br c Forest King, by Monday—Abbie W, 3 years, 113 lbs, (C. Ross)........ 2 6 6
W. L. Pritchard names b c Frank Rhoads, by Leinster—Ada A, 4 years, 118 lbs, (Fallon)........ 3 3 5
P. J. Shafter names b m Night Hawk, by imported Haddington—Napa Queen, 5 years, 125 lbs, (F. Ross)........ 6 4 3
R. J. Green names gr c Garfield, by California—Queen, 3 years, 113 lbs, (Courtney)........ dis.

Time—1:14½, 1:14½, 1:15.

The third race was the Vestal Stake for three-year-old fillies, a dash of one and one-fourth miles, and of the twelve nominations three were all that appeared. These were Precious, Duchess of Norfolk and Sister to Lottery. Howson was on the first, J. Courtney had the mount on the Duchess, and Fred Ross was on the Sister to Lottery. Precious was the favorite, as it was evident that Duchess of Norfolk was not within twenty-eight pounds of her old form, and when stripped she was deficient in muscle and had a jaded look which told of the effects of the long journey after the still longer Eastern campaign. Precious went away with the lead, running the first half-mile in 53 seconds, three-quarters in 1:20, the mile in 1:46½, and the race in 2:12½. The Duchess has evidently lost the fine turn of speed which she showed at the spring meeting, and appeared unable to extend herself on any portion of the ground. The Sister to Lottery was outpaced, giving Precious an easy thing of it from start to finish.

SUMMARY.

Same day—Vestal stakes; for three-year-old fillies; $25 each p. p.; $300 added; second to receive $100; third to save stake; dash of one and one-quarter miles.

Palo Alto names b f Precious, by Lever—Frolic, (Howson)........ 1
H. Schwartz names b f Sister to Lottery, by Monday—Virginia, (F. Ross)........ 2
Theo. Winters names b f Duchess of Norfolk, by Norfolk—Marion, (Courtney)........ 3

Time—2:12½.

The fourth race was a handicap for three-year-old fillies, the distance one mile, and the starters May B, 107 pounds, Lou Spencer, 102 pounds, and the Palo Alto Shannon-Camilla Urso filly, 100 pounds. It was dusk when the bell rang to summon the contestants, and when they were running only an occasional glimpse could be caught of the bright colors of the jockeys, and a shadowy outline of the flying steeds against the high fence of the track. It was a dreamy race—flying phantoms, indistinct as the misty steeds of Ossian—and not until they were within a furlong of home was it apparent which was the leader. Under the wire there was no difficulty, as May B had the lead by several lengths; Lou Spencer second, the other quite a distance in the rear. Time, 1:45.

SUMMARY.

Same day—Handicap purse; for two-year-olds; $25 each and $10 if declared; $250 added; second to receive $50; dash of a mile.

P. Robson names ch f May B, by Shannon—Jessie R, 107 lbs........ 1
Theo. Winters names b f Lou Spencer, by Norfolk—Ballerina, 102 lbs........ 2
Palo Alto names br f, by Shannon—Camillio Urso, 100 lbs........ 3

Time—1:45.

The hurdle race was postponed until Saturday.

## Spotting Ringers.

The crop of ringers has been very large in the more remote circuits east of the Rockies this year and they are reported everywhere from Maine to Salt Lake. The following story of a successful tour among the guileless turfmen of Iowa is told by the Chicago *Breeders' Gazette*:

"About the sickest job in that line that I ever knew to be done," remarked one of the party, "was by the crowd that had old Silversides out in Iowa this season and were trotting him in three-minute races under the name of Honest Tom."

"What! not the old grey horse that got a record of 2:22 at Columbus four years ago, and was broken down so badly across the back that it used to take four men a quarter of an hour to get him on his feet in the morning?" queried another of the party.

"That's the identical horse," responded the first individual, "and the curious part of it is that the old fellow has changed so that is oldest friends would be puzzled to know him. The story of his career this season is a pretty good one. Last spring a couple of men, named Carr and Robinson, who live in Norwalk, Nebraska, concluded they would buy a trotter, and went to Ohio for that purpose. Now I don't pretend to say whether they were after a 'ringer' or not, but anyhow they secured old Silversides, and entered him all through the 'Big Six' circuit as Honest Tom. At Cedar Rapids, the first place they were engaged, people began to tell them that Honest Tom was Silversides, but the Nebraska men wouldn't have it that way at all, because half the horsemen were just as certain that Tom wasn't Silversides as the other half were that he was. Peter Johnson was at the meeting, and after looking the horse over carefully said that he could not be Silversides, because that horse used to have a couple of shoe-boils, no traces of which were to be seen. Silversides also had bad legs, while Honest Tom's underpinning was in tip-top shape. But one morning Johnson stood a long while in front of the old horse, and finally noticed the white eye that all who have seen Silversides will remember. Then he joined the Silversides party.

"When the day for Honest Tom's race arrived, the officers of the association told Robinson that his horse had been entered in a class to which he was not eligible, and under a false name. Mr. Robinson was either pretty scared, or else made an elegant bluff at being so.

"'My God! gentlemen,' he said, 'don't talk that way; I am no swindler, but an honest farmer. I went down to Ohio and bought this horse from a banker. I am now satisfied that he is Silversides, and that I have been grossly imposed upon. You are perfectly welcome to my entrance money (Honest Tom was entered in three slow classes), but, for the sake of my reputation at home, don't expel me.'

"Of course," continued the narrator of the story, "the judges let the matter drop, as the horse had not started in a race; but Robinson was disgusted with trotting horses, and resolved to abandon the business at once. So he sold the horse, sulky, and two suits of horse clothing for $200, the purchasers being a couple of smart men from Cedar county, Ia. They knew more about trotters than Robinson did, and struck out on a new trail at once. Keeping for the old horse the name that Robinson had given him, they began a very successful career, trotting Silversides nine races in Iowa, and winning every one of them. Monticello, Maquoketa, Vinton, De Witt, Carthage, Tipton and Anamosa were among the places at which the grey performed, and at the last mentioned town he won a heat in 2:26½. The track was in the hands of men who were inclined to temper the record to the shorn trotter, and they volunteered the information to Honest Tom's driver that they would announce the time as 2:30½, in order to keep him in the 2:30 class. The driver thanked them profusely for their kindness, and then he went to the stable and laughed until the tears ran down his cheeks at the idea of keeping old Silversides in the 2:30 class. At Anamosa, Honest Tom struck Sucker Maid, Parkis' Abdallah, and a horse called Bay Henry, that some Iowa men bought in Chicago last winter, and have been trotting successfully. In this race Honest Tom trotted a half mile in 1:09½, showing that he had all of his old-time speed, and you can bet he has. He will be nineteen years old next spring, and, barring his weak back, is just as good as ever, as the suckers who were trotting against him last summer found out to their sorrow. When they learn that Honest Tom, the three-minute horse, was none other than Silversides, with a record of 2:22, there will be some tall swearing in Iowa, and don't you forget it."

## Large Colts.

EDITOR BREEDER AND SPORTSMAN: In your issue of the 4th inst. I notice the mention of a Clydesdale stallion of two years weighing 1,110 pounds, owned by F. F. Burt of Tehama county, who thinks him the largest animal of his age and breed in the State; weight per month, 46¼ pounds. I admit the above to be a good showing, but here are some figures: On the ranch of Moses Hopkins, Esq., two horses, when two years old, weighed respectively 1,418 and 1,437 pounds, making 2,855 pounds, or about 54¼ pounds each per month of age. One filly fifteen months old weighed 1,015 pounds, or 67⅔ pounds per month; also three others same age, equally large, not weighed. Mr. Hopkins raised and sold from the same sire a stallion that weighed 1,050 pounds at twelve months old, being 87½ pounds per month. These are all from the imported French horse "Idol" and are all fine style and free movers. I give them as samples of large horses raised in Sutter county. SUBSCRIBER.

ARRIVAL OF THOROUGHBREDS.—The steamship Erin, which conveyed on its last voyage home Mr. Lorillard's latest addition to his English racing establishment, brought back for that gentleman the colt by Scottish Chief, out of Seduision (the dam of Hermit), and Nereid, by Saxon, out of Highland Lassie. There were also three brood mares on board, and the five were taken to Mr. Stoddart's stables, Greenwich street, near Houston. Mr. Bishop, who had charge of the horses, stated to Mr. Stoddart that the reports in the English papers respecting the condition of those he had taken over to Tom Cannon's stable were gross exaggerations. They were landed in as good shape as any of the many shipments he had had charge of. At Liverpool they were met by Tom Cannon's head lad, who took them on to Stockbridge.

## Overman and Helene.

The following is the New York *Spirit's* account of the race between Overman and Helene:

In this age, when the trotting turf is accused of so many "sins of omission and commission," it is pleasant to us to record a race so fairly made and honorably carried out as the match between Mr. I. Cohnfield's chestnut mare Helene and Capt. Wm. Kohl's chestnut gelding Overman, and we should like to witness more matches of a similar character.

This event excited the greatest interest, and the race was well worth going a long journey to see. It was made to take place on Saturday last, a good day and track being stipulated; but as the track was then soft from recent rains, and would not suit Overman, it was postponed until yesterday. Leadeu skies and London fogs visited us in the interim, and so it was carried over until to-day. Fortunately, the morning opened with charming weather, the fog rolled away, the atmosphere was as mild as early autumn, and there was not sufficient breeze stirring to scatter the dying leaves. The patience of those who were anxious to be present at the race was severely tried as many returned home Saturday disappointed, and were not sure that it would be decided to-day until the announcement appeared on the tape at the different stations.

At the hour appointed there was a large muster of gentlemen interested in the sport, including Messrs. Wm. H. Vanderbilt, Frank Work, T. C. Eastman, Col. L. Kip Jr., Foster Dewey, Lawrence Jerome, Wm. Turnbull, W. H. Harbeck, A. J. Dam, Alex. Taylor Jr., J. S. Ferguson, George B. Alley, Edwin Thorne, J. C. De La Vergne, A. A. Bonner, W. F. Kidder, W. J. Welsh, C. S. Benham, Jason Miller, Capt. Lee Bumfreville, Frank Ferguson, I. I. Stillings, Chas. Backman, L. Lorillard, J. W. Shaw, Scott Leighton, the artist, and L. C. Chase of Boston, and hosts of others, with such old-timers as John Crooks, John Sherwood, Jake Somerindyke, John Rogers and a few others, who were "Fathers in Israel" when Flora was in her prime.

The judges selected were Messrs. David Bonner, Charles H. Raymond and W. H. Humphreys. The track was a trifle damp in places, but was put in smooth order by the Griffin road machine. The drivers thought it was about two seconds slow; but, from the speed shown by the horses, and appearance of the footing, we judge it was not more than a second slower than usual.

First heat—Helene drew the pole and Mr. Bonner dispatched them on first trial to an excellent start. The mare rushed off with the lead, and, being too anxious, trotted over herself on approaching the first turn and also at the lower entrance to the track, but her breaks were unimportant, and she led Overman a length to the quarter, in 35 seconds, gradually increasing the space to two lengths at the half, in 1:09. Hickok now began to call on Overman and he responded courageously, trotting the third quarter at a twenty gait. He reached the leader's wheel at the three-quarter pole in 1:46, but she gallantly held her own from this point. Both came down the stretch, driving with great determination, Overman's nose at the mare's quarters, and so they finished. Time, 2:23.

Second Heat—Opinions were about evenly divided, and Overman's friends asked no odds, feeling confident that the evidence he had given in the Grand Circuit of capability to fight the latter end of a heat and race would fully counterbalance Helene's terrific speed. On the other hand, the Helene division had noticed Overman on his tip toes in the homestretch, and felt assured that he could not make a break and beat her. So this heat was regarded as the turning point of the race. Helene set the pace too fast on the first score. Overman broke badly on second attempt, but on the third trial he was level and they received the word, the mare having a little the best of it which she was not slow to improve, trotting steadily to the quarter in 34½ seconds, two open lengths in advance of her formidable competitor, which distance she maintained to the half in 1:08. Hickok pursued the same tactics as in the first heat, and slowly but surely closed with her up the hill and past the point of rocks, where she made two short breaks, and he succeeded in collaring her within fifty yards of the three-quarter pole amid cries of "He's got her," but no, Murphy roused the mare and she carried him to a break and passed the three-quarter pole two lengths ahead, but Overman had now settled to his work and drew up so fast that he was on her wheel as they straightened into the homestretch; and again a desperate brush ensued, but the California gelding beat her cleverly by a neck and shoulders, and in a style that satisfied the spectators Helene had tackled the very best horse in the 2:21 class. Time 2:21.

Third Heat—Both horses promptly answered the summons of the bell, and the Overman party talked and offered to bet as if they were satisfied the race was his, bar accidents, but he had not won it yet by any means, as the sequel shows. They scored a few times, and were given an excellent send-off. Helene made the pace so hot around the first turn that Overman began to change feet, and finally went into the air; she broke simultaneously, but quickly settled. He ran half way to the quarter pole, and when he struck his gait, the mare had opened three lengths of daylight, which advantage she held to the quarter pole in 35 seconds, and to the half in 1:09. Again Overman began the closing process, making his effort to reach her on the third quarter, and looked dangerous at the three-quarter pole in 1:46½. From this point he stuck to her as close as wax, and neither had any advantage in the homestretch, until within fifty yards of the wire, the gelding made a game and gallant struggle, beating her half a length. Attention was called to his long run, but the judges thought he was entitled to the heat. Time, 2:22¼.

Fourth Heat—They came up level on first trial, Helene leading lightly. Hickok nodded for the word, which was given, and the mare's wonderful speed enabled her to take the pole on first turn. She showed in front, as usual, at the quarter, in 36 seconds, and drew away a little farther to the half in 1:10½, but Overman made up a little of the difference at this point, and charged the hill two lengths behind the leader. "Now they're even," cried an excited backer of Overman, as they drew under the shadow of the point of rocks, but he was mistaken; Helene held the lead by a length. With rare patience, Hickok waited, seeming to know that the last quarter would tell its tale, and Overman with ears pricked, came down the stretch strong as a lion. Murphy did not give it up, however; he disputed every inch of the road to the wire. They were side by side at the distance stand. Overman increased the pace, and the mare received a cut of the whip, for it was do or die. She broke, and made two or three jumps, but was neatly caught by Murphy, who rallied her again, and landed her, as it seemed to us, even with Overman; but, after brief deliberation, the announcement was: "Overman wins the heat and race. Time, 2:23¼."

SUMMARY.

MORRISANIA. Nov. 1.—Match, $8,000.

| | | | | |
|---|---|---|---|---|
| O. A. Hickok's ch g Overman, by Elmo | 2 | 1 | 1 | 1 |
| J. Murphy's ch m Helene, by Hambeltonian Prince | 1 | 2 | 2 | 2 |

Time, 2:23, 2:21, 2:22¼, 2:23¼.

## Trotting with Running Mate.

The record for this way of going was lowered on the second and third inst. at Narragansett Park, Providence, R. I., in a race between Barnaby & Co.'s Billy D and mate, and Alexander Brothers Yellow Dock and mate. The match was made for the second, but owing to various delays only two heats were trotted that day, both of which were won by the Alexander team. The time of the first heat was 2:16¾, of which the quarter was trotted in 0:34 and the half in 1:09. The second heat was trotted in 2:18, the quarter in 0:34 and the half in 1:09½.

The match was continued on the 3d, and resulted in the success of Yellow Dock in the best time ever made by a horse with running mate, viz: 2:11. The best previous time is that made by Billy D and mate at Boston last October, 2:14½. In the pool rooms heavy odds were offered on Yellow Dock but they found no takers. The weather was favorable for fast time, although a keen northwest wind prevailed. The teams responded very promptly to the call and were exercised for some ten or fifteen minutes on the track prior to the send-off. Tommy Foster, who trained Mr. Barnaby's pair for the race, relieved Dan Mace and was placed behind Billy D and mate. It was confidently expected that the Barnaby team would force the battle more closely in the hands of their trainer; yet it was known among a few that Murphy intended to speed his pair to some remarkably low time. At the send-off the Barnaby pair had a lead of a clear length, but as they reached the quarter turn Yellow Dock and mate drew up to the fore and at this moment Billy D lost his feet, was pulled down and then made a disastrous double break. Yellow Dock and mate swept along at a rapid gait, completing the quarter in 0:32½. Murphy then let them out with careful urging, and without a skip the half was completed in 1:04¾. For the three-quarters the time was given at 1:38½. Murphy gave close attention to his charge and sent them to the wire without any pulling, determined upon breaking the record. As they neared the finish, Mr. Alexander, the owner of Yellow Dock, ran up the track and swung his hat to Murphy to speed them faster. The mare responded to the urging, and amid the greatest enthusiasm she won the heat and race in 2:11, breaking the record of 2:14½ made by Billy D and mate at Beacon Park a year ago, by 3½ seconds. The time was promptly placed upon the slate, and the spectators greeted Murphy and the team with prolonged applause. The judges upon examination of their watches found that one recorded 2:10¾ while the others agreed upon 2:11. When the wire was reached by the Yellow Dock pair Foster had not reached the three-quarter pole, and he did not complete the mile but drove his pair to the stable via the backstretch. Murphy was 4½ pounds over weight.

SUMMARY.

NARRAGANSETT PARK, CRANSTON, R. I. November 2 and 3, 1882.—Match trot with running mate for $2,000; mile heats, best three in five, in harness.

| | | | |
|---|---|---|---|
| Alexander Brothers' ch m Yellow Dock and mate, Gabe Case (Murphy) | 1 | 1 | 1 |
| J. B. Barnaby's ch g Billy D and mate, Rival (D. Mace and Foster) | 2 | 2 | 2 |

TIME.

| | Quarter. | Half. | Three-quarters. | Mile. |
|---|---|---|---|---|
| First heat | 34 | 1:09 | 1:41½ | 2:16¾ |
| Second heat | 34 | 1:09½ | 1:49 | 2:18 |
| Third heat | 32½ | 1:04¾ | 1:38½ | 2:11 |

Yellow Dock, the winner, made her record of 2:20¾ at Utica last August, winning the 2:29 purse in three straight heats. She was brought out last fall under the name of Mohawk Maid and trotted in the slow classes at the Ohio fairs held at Columbus, Cleveland and Toledo. She never failed to get a share of the purse, and finally won two races, gaining a record of 2:29½ at Cleveland. She was then owned and driven by Mr. Wm. Yeazell, who also owned the Mohawk mare Fashion, (2:23½.) Yellow Dock was got by Clark's Mohawk Jr., out of a mare of Copperbottom blood, pedigree not traced. She stands 15¾ hands, a bright chestnut, of good proportions, with a slashing, open gait, and a fine turn of speed. She sometimes bucks and acts badly in starting, and requires a little holding together in getting away, but if she begins right, goes true and level for the mile. If pinched she cuts up a little soft at the finish, but comes again the next heat.

## The California Race-Horses.

On Tuesday of the present week the racing stables of E. J. Baldwin and Theodore Winters passed through Chicago en route for California. The lot included the Duchess of Norfolk, Clara D, Lucky B, Gano and Sunday, and were in charge of Mr. Lou Martin, their trainer. When this lot of horses left California last spring high hopes were entertained by Pacific Slope sportsmen that those representatives of the far West would return in the fall crowned with the laurels of victory, but these hopes were not realized. Before leaving California Duchess of Norfolk and Gano had run some very creditable races indeed, the colt winning at three-quarters of a mile in 1:15, while the filly showed both speed and staying powers by running over a cup course, two miles and a quarter, in 4:56¾. Clara D. had made the journey once before, having accompanied the wonderful mare Mollie McCarthy when she came to Chicago three summers ago, and won the Garden City Cup so easily from the largest and best field that ever started in this city for any race; while Lucky B and Sunday were known to be able to race a bit. When the stable reached Chicago last June, it was considered almost a certainty that Duchess of Norfolk would win the Illinois Derby at the meeting here, and as to Clara D's being beaten for the Cup, the Californians would hear of no argument. But wet weather and a heavy track were too much for the Duchess in her race, the prediction of Secretary Hall, of the Driving Park, that no filly would win the Derby, being amply verified by Gunnar and Stanton running first and second in that event; while John Davis led Clara D such a merry chase in the Cup that she was never able to get to him after the drum tapped. Going from here to Saratoga the stable fared but little better, defeat coming when the prospects of success seemed brightest; and when, at the close of the Baltimore meeting, a start was made for home, the result of the season's work was not encouraging. It is to be hoped, however, that the ill-luck of 1882 will not prevent Messrs. Baldwin & Winters from trying the venture again. They are both thorough sportsmen, taking the defeat philosophically, and wasting no time in idle regrets over what might have been, and will always receive a hearty and genuine welcome from all true lovers of sport.—*Breeders' Gazette*.

On the first day of the Newmarket Houghton meeting Mr. "Plunger" Walton's four-year-old colt Eliacin won the All-Aged Selling Plate and was sold after the race to Mr. Robert Peck for 570 guineas. The betting before the race was 11 to 8 on Eliacin.

It is said that Ed Stokes won $10.000 on the Overman-Helene match at Fleetwood Park.

## Judge Shafter's Questionable Position.

SAN FRANCISCO, Nov. 16, 1882.

EDITOR BREEDER AND SPORTSMAN: The position taken by Judge J. McM. Shafter on the questions that came up at the races for the Embryo Stakes last Monday has provoked a great deal of comment, universally adverse to the rulings. One point in the case seems to have escaped notice, and that is the fact that members of the Board of Appeals are not allowed the privilege even of the judges' stand. (See Sec. 18, By Laws National Association). Now Mr. Shafter certainly was ignorant of this fact, or willfully transgressed. I must conclude the former, for I am unwilling to credit the latter. Aside from his erroneous ruling in the case, his failure to apply the penalty provided in Rule 48 of the National Association, he made an egregious error in this and other instances, in presenting himself in the judges' stand to decide on what he might be called hereafter to review or adjudicate upon. In other words, as a member of the Pacific Coast Board of Appeals, to decide as to whether his judgment was correct as a presiding judge.

If it is asserted that Mr. Shafter as President of the Pacific Breeders' Association was excusable (for I am certain no one will contend for it as a right) for presenting himself in the judges' stand as Presiding Judge or Judge of any capacity, I respectfully submit that, as a member of the Board of Appeals, he outranked his position as president of any society, and if he had determined to act contrary to Sec. 187 of the By Laws of the National Association, it would have been a graceful act first to have announced his resignation as a member of the Board of Appeals.

The course of the Judge and his decisions has led to severe comments, and the tender situation of turf interests in our city has received another set-back to mar the prosperity so earnestly labored for and desired by many prominent breeders and turf patrons.

LEX.

## Trotting Stock for California.

Mr. Wm. Corbitt of San Mateo, who is now in the East, has made some important additions to his stock by purchases in Kentucky and elsewhere. He has bought from Col. R. P. Pepper, South Elkhorn Stock Farm, Frankfort, Ky., the black mare Alice Clay, by Almont, out of Rosa Clay (dam of Capoul, record 2:28) by American Clay, her dam by Downing's Bay Messenger, out of a mare by Cripple, in foal to Onward, and Woodford Queen, bay mare seven years old, by Almont, out of Virginia (dam of Woodford Chief, record 2:22½ at five years old and Confederate Chief, etc.), by Billy Townes, son of imported Fylde, in foal to Onward. From B. J. Treacy, Ashland Park Stock Farm, Lexington, Ky., the bay mare Maggie, eight years old, by Almont, dam by John Dillard, grandam by Park's Highlander, out of a mare by Grey Eagle. Maggie trotted a full mile in 2:39, and a half in 1:16 at three years old and was sold to a Chicago party as a roadster. She is in foal to George Wilkes. From Wm. Dunn, Cincinnati, Ohio, the four-year-old bay colt, by George Wilkes, dam by Mambrino Patchen out of Joe Bunker's dam by American Star. This is said to be one of the finest youngsters ever sired by the noted stallion George Wilkes, and Mr. Corbitt intends to use him for stud purposes.

Jim Rockey, one of the best trotting horse drivers of the day, worked for a man who had quite a number of trotters, and, as was usually the case with the knight of the whip and snaffle, he had anticipated his earnings and at the close of the season was several hundred dollars in debt to his employer. This was his invariable fix in the fall, but the request to square by giving a note for the amount was a new thing, as in former years, those he had been behind-hand with had known him well enough not to waste paper and ink in recording an asset of less value than the blank sheet. He readily acceded to sign the paper and while the clerk was writing it he looked through the plate glass window into Lake street. The snow was falling rapidly, and the sidewalks were coated to the depth of several inches. "What time," was the inquiry, "when shall I make this note payable?" Rockey did not hesitate for an instant, but with a flourish of his cap as though he was saluting cheers from the grand stand, he replied, "First good day and good track."

The following notices of motions have been published to be presented at the next meeting of the Jockey Club in England: There shall be not less than two races per day of a mile or upwards, nor more than three races per day confined to two-year-olds * * * * An amendment reads: That under no circumstances shall there be more than two five-furlong races for three-year-olds and upwards advertised for each day's racing. * * * * Mr. C. Alexander moves that no jockey be allowed to run a horse in which he has any interest, except in his own name, and that should it be brought to the notice of the Stewards that such rule had in any way been abused, his license should be immediately suspended. * * * * Mr. Craven will move as an amendment: That the Stewards are requested to exercise in future their discretionary power of withholding licenses from all jockeys who are owners or part owners of horses, or who notoriously bet on horse races.

The breeding of trotting horses is getting to be a large industry in this country. Millions of dollars are invested in the business. The California breeders have been outdoing the breeders of other sections, especially in early development of speed in their younglings. But we doubt whether they will be allowed to retain the supremacy. The Kentucky blood has been pretty well stirred up by the wonderful achievements of the Pacific Coast colts and fillies, and Kentuckians are dead game in a fight of any kind, and will not allow the well-earned laurels they had achieved to be so ruthlessly torn from their brows. They now mean business, and are preparing to contest for the laurels won by Californians. —*Rural World*.

The London *Sportsman* of the 24th ult. says in reference to the report that Mr. Keene was not satisfied with the management of his stable and that there would be a change: "In connection with William Day's charge I may note, on the authority of the veteran, that he has not heard a single word in reference to Mr. Keene's horses being taken from his care, while Mr. Bathgate, who has the control of Mr. Keene's stud of racers, is equally ignorant of any contemplated move; so we may take it for granted that Mr. Keene does not intend to desert Mr. Day, who has done so well for the American sportsman."

Of Mr. Keene's Bolero, (the brother of Captain W. M. Conner's Glidelia) which made his debut in the race for the Criterion Stakes, the *Sportsman* says: "If good looks go for anything the colt Bolero, by Bonnie Scotland, out of Waltz, should make a name for himself and do well in the interests of the American sportsman, Mr. Keene."

## The Embryo Stakes.

Four years ago the editor of this paper had a favorite young mare which, through the kindness of Governor Stanford, was in foal to Electioneer. She was by A. W. Richmond, her dam Columbia by imported Bonnie Scotland, grandam Young Fashion by imported Monarch, and the next dam the great Fashion by imported Trustee. This kind of breeding coupled with the Hambletonian and Clay in Electioneer and that "backed" by a fine "open gait" and a fair share of speed for the amount of training, gave us confidence to think that the expected foal would be good enough to warrant a challenge which was duly published. That challenge was a proffer to trot any colt of the same age as yearlings, two-year-olds and three-year-olds. The first race to be heats of a mile, the second and the third to be mile heats, best three in five.

Captain Ben. E Harris accepted with a Brigadier-Lena Bowles colt, and L. J. Rose suggested that it should be changed into a stake with the distances reduced to a mile dash for yearlings, heats of a mile for two-year-olds, and heats of a mile best three in five when they were three years old. The suggestion was adopted and Captain Harris named it the Embryo, as at the time of closing many of the colts were still in that state. We have not time to write more than the outline at present, and will have to be contented with this meager sketch. The challenger came into the world a shapely colt but as he grew in months he developed the characteristics of his maternal grandsire Bonnie Scotland, and was obstinate to a degree rarely witnessed in a young colt. "Mr. Druid" writes that Bonnie Scotland was the most obdurately lazy horse ever trained in England and it was difficult work for his rider to get him to move. His records show, however, that he was a great race horse and as the progenitor of race horses there is scarcely a course from the Atlantic to the Pacific that will not give proof. The descendant was fortunate enough to win the yearling and two-year-old events, and gave indications before the pinkeye got hold of him, that he would make a good showing in the three-year-old.

Seeing what an advantage it would be to breeders the Embryo was kept up, and this year for the first time the three stakes were to be decided in one afternoon.

A finer November afternoon than that of last Saturday can hardly be imagined. The sun shone brightly and there was scarcely any breeze to retard the horses. The track was in capital condition, saving that it was somewhat rough on the backstretch from the hoof-prints of the horses driven when it was soft, making slight inequalities. The attendance was rather slim partly owing to its being "steamer day," when men are more intent on collecting and paying bills than on taking their pleasure at the races.

The first called was for foals of 1881—yearlings—and three responded to the signal. There were Dawn, by Nutwood, Antevolo, by Electioneer and Sister to Honesty, by Priam. A protest was entered against Dawn starting on account of the nomination being defective, and certainly all the evidence confirmed the claim. After that protests were filed against the others on the most frivolous grounds, and this gave the opportunity for the judges to include all in their ban.

It is seldom that three finer colts are ever seen on a track. Dawn is furnished like a four-year-old, a muscular youngster and of very high form. Sister to Honesty is a big strapping filly, "lengthy" as well as high, and there cannot be a doubt that some day she will be well worthy of her relationship to her illustrious brother. Antevolo has as yet more of the baby appearance, and is much the youngest of the trio, having been foaled May 12th, though he has a highly bred look, and in contradistinction to his brother Anteeo, alluded to in the first part of this article, his temper could not be improved. He is free and resolute without being a particle flighty, and has also the valuable quality of "level-headedness." He has never worn a shoe or tip, and the only protections needed are light scalping boots. The lottery for positions gave Dawn the inside, Sister to Honesty second and Antevolo third, and after a couple of scores a very good start was effected. Dawn made a skip soon after though he caught like an old trotter, but before the first turn was half made the filly left her feet and the mishap was disastrous. Dawn swiftly sped along, Antevolo honestly striving to overhaul him, but the leader had too much speed, and though he again broke on the further turn owing to the Berkeley train passing at the time, there was nothing lost and he won an easy victory in 2:59, the fastest time ever made by a yearling in an actual race. Antevolo made the mile in 3:02, which was also faster than the previous record in a race, the filly third.

SUMMARY.

Oakland Trotting Park, Monday, Nov. 13, 1882.—Embryo stakes, for foals of 1881; $100 each; $25 forfeit; $10 declaration; dash of a mile; thirty-two nominations.

| | |
|---|---|
| A. P. Whitney's ch c Dawn, by Nutwood, his dam Countess | 1 |
| Jos. Cairn Simpson's br c Antevolo, by Electioneer, his dam Columbine | 2 |
| L. U. Shippee's ch f Sister to Honesty by Priam, her dam by Chieftain | 3 |

Time—2:59.

The second race brought out the two-year-olds, the starters Pride, by Buccaneer, Neluska by Sultan and Lillie Nutwood, by Nutwood. Neluska, and Pride are acknowledged to be two as promising fillies of their age as there are in the whole country, and there was much interest taken in the meeting. By agreement the distance was waived, and this gave a queer complexion to the race though it does not leave much room for detailed description.

In the first heat Neluska broke badly, continuing to break so that she was three hundred yards behind when Pride crossed the score in 2:43½ and Lillie Nutwood at least one hundred yards in front of her also. Without the interpolated condition the race would have been ended, and in the second heat there was a reversal. Neluska behaving better, outtrotted Pride around the first turn, and opened quite a gap, owing to a break of her opponent at the quarter pole. From there Pride steadily decreased the gap though unable to quite reach Neluska, who won in 2:35¾.

The third heat was an easy one for Pride. Trotting fast and steadily she left Neluska—who pulled up lame after the first heat—and had she kept up the rate to the winning post there is scarcely a question that the race record for two-year-olds would have been beaten. She was jogged the greater portion of the way from the seven furlong pole home, finishing in 2:33¼. The record which Neluska made at the Oakland Fair of 2:30½ is the fastest in the calendar for that age, when the contest was colt against colt, and the odd seconds could easily have been subtracted with a strong probability that twenties would have been reached if her owner had kept her going to the end.

SUMMARY.

Same day.—Embryo stakes for two-year-olds; $100 each $25 forfeit; $10 declaration; 46 nominations; heats of a mile; distance waived by agreement of the starters.

| | | | |
|---|---|---|---|
| Dr. M. W. Hicks' b f Pride, by Buccaneer, her dam by Flaxtail | 1 | 2 | 1 |
| L. J. Rose's br f Neluska by Sultan; her dam Gretchen, by Mambrino Pilot | 3 | 1 | 2 |
| Cy Arnold's bl f Lillie Nutwood, by Nutwood, her dam Lady Grant | 2 | 3 | 3 |

Time—2:43½, 2:35¾, 2:33¼.

The third race was that for three-year-olds, heats of a mile, best three in five, and of the forty-three original nominations only three appeared. The death of nominator or horse had made a serious breach in the number as thirteen were disqualified from that cause, sixteen had signified that they paid forfeit—there was no declaration in this stake—and the contestants were Bonnie, by General Benton, her dam Americus by Rysdyk's Hambletonian, Fred Arnold, by Nephew, his dam Fanny Fern by Jack Hawkins, and Anteeo, by Electioneer, his dam Columbine by A. W. Richmond. It would be a stickler, indeed, who did not admit that there was good breeding in this trio, and it is not often that three finer looking youngsters are seen on a course. Bonnie was largely the favorite in the pools as she had shown very fast quarters in her work at Palo Alto, report crediting her with a flight of speed far better than a twenty gait. Fred Arnold had trotted a fast and game race over the mountains, and though Anteeo had also displayed capacity in his exercise, the Bonnie Scotland characteristics alluded to before rendered it very doubtful if he could be depended upon when the most needed. Then the rains had sadly interfered with the workings of Fred Arnold and Anteeo, and to crown the bad luck which had followed the latter this summer the pinkeye culminated by an abscess forming between the lower jaw-bones which broke and suppurated the day before the race.

The placing gave Anteeo the pole, Fred Arnold second, Bonnie on the outside, and when the signal was given for the first heat Anteeo was in a tangling break which completely nullified the advantages of the inside position. Bonnie bettered hers with a rapidity that endorsed the reports of her speed, and not contented widened the gap the whole of the way around the oval. In no part of the heat was there a contest, and when she went under the wire in 2:34½ there was a long gap between her and Fred Arnold with a still larger space marking the distance that Anteeo was behind.

The second heat showed better. As before Bonnie took the lead though the colt kept closer to her, and as the quarter pole was passed she was only two lengths in front of Fred Arnold, with Anteeo at his wheel. She increased the gap on the backstretch, and the other two were head and head at the water-tank, where Fred broke, and Anteeo led. Around the turn it was 'nip and tuck' between them, Bonnie ten lengths in front at the three-quarter pole, but from there both gained on her. At the distance stand Fred broke again, and Anteeo showed a burst of speed and was rapidly overhauling the mare, when the effort was too great and he broke a few lengths from the score. Bonnie finished with his nose on her wheel in 2:37.

The third heat was a memorable one, as the rehearsal will show. Very foolishly, as it proved, "rattles" were put on Anteeo, thinking that they might accelerate his pace in getting away from the score, and with that and a "good start," his second position might enable him to take the pole. Though it was evident that this was a mistake, there was no chance to remedy the blunder as the word was given on the second score Bonnie behind but coming with such a rush that she went past Anteeo before fifty yards were accomplished and Fred also gave him the go by and took second place. About midway of the turn Bonnie broke, a disastrous break as Fred left her as though she had come to a standstill and notwithstanding Anteeo had caught the rattles twice with his hind foot and nearly fell he also passed her. Fred opened a gap, Anteeo tripping and blundering down the backstretch and Bonnie still at a lumbering gallop. Near the water tank she regained her trot passing Anteeo before he got to the half mile, Fred from sixty to eighty yards in front trotting steadily and fast. Bonnie flew around the turn and it was evident that Fred had slackened his rate, his driver evidently thinking he had the heat safe. He was near the inside of the track Bonnie well towards the outer rail, still trotting fast. At the distance stand the spectators were shouting to the driver of Fred Arnold to go along, and he responded with the remark: "I have got her," at the same time urging his horse to renewed efforts, and crossed the score half a length in front of her, with Anteeo a few lengths inside the distance flag, the time 2:40½. Fred Arnold had trotted the mile without a skip, no one claimed that she was nearer to him than half a length, and everyone wondering what delayed the judges in awarding him the heat. If they were surprised at the delay they were astonished when the announcement was made that Bonnie had won the race, Fred Arnold second and second money, Anteeo third and third money. This was received with a storm of denunciation, and the driver of Fred Arnold, aggravated so that he lost all his self-control, was fierce and vindictive in his accusations. It was assuredly enough to raise his ire, and if there ever was an excuse for this kind of language he used he had it. But it is unfortunate that he should have given away to the ebullition of temper, and sought redress in a quiet way, and thus ended a race which was about as vexatious as any that has taken place in a long time.

One noteworthy circumstance was the fact that Fred Arnold and Anteeo are the only two of the forty-three nominations which have taken part in the yearling two-year-old and three-year-old Embryos.

SUMMARY.

Same day—Embryo stakes for three-year-olds, foals of 1881, heats of a mile, best 3 in 5, in harness, $100 each, $25 forfeit, 43 nominations.

| | | | |
|---|---|---|---|
| Palo Alto b f Bonnie, by General Benton, her dam Americus by Rysdyk's Hambletonian | 1 | 1 | 1 |
| Wm. Johnson's bl c Fred Arnold, by Nephew, his dam Fanny Fern by Jack Hawkins | 2 | 3 | 2 |
| Jos. Cairn Simpson's b c Anteeo, by Electioneer, his dam Columbine by A. W. Richmond | 3 | 2 | 3 |

Time—2:34½, 2:37, 2:40½.

---

For seventy-six years the judge's box at Epsom has been in the family of John Francis Clark. For thirty years he has announced the winners of the Derby and Oaks, as his father and grandfather did before him, and as his son is likely to do in the future.

## Castration.

In some animals there will be a deal of local inflammation after the operation. It is, perhaps, more often seen in those colts that have been difficult to halter, and which got very heated prior to its performance. There is a swelling of the parts which, commencing about the second day, will extend all about the region of the wounds, rendering the skin here shining and tense, and proceeds in a direction forwards, involving the sheath and under surface of the belly. The colt will walk very stiffly, or be disinclined to move, and in some instances is more or less feverish. Cases like these require special attention, and every care should be taken to keep the wounds well open. Fomentations of warm water will tend to soothe pain and promote a healthy discharge; frequent gentle walking exercise should be given, and if the swelling becomes at all excessive, scarifications are of extreme benefit. The diet should be succulent and cooling.

It sometimes happens that a few hours after castration a colt that has apparently done very well will suddenly commence bleeding from the divided cords. There is, perhaps, nothing more likely to frighten a farmer than the sight of blood in cases of this sort. The hemorrhage may either be unavoidable, or it may be due to some mismanagement or carelessness in the performance of the operation; if owing to the latter, it occurs almost directly afterwards, and is, as a rule, only very partial, one of the vessels not having properly contracted within its sheath, or been wholly sealed up. Originated either from this cause or any other, there is but comparatively little reason to be alarmed or to take any desperate measures. One does not hear of horses bleeding to death after castration; there may be a few instances, it is true, but such are very rare. The blood, as a rule, flows but from one of the divided arteries, and if allowed to go on without any means whatever being taken to prevent it, would not proceed to any dangerous length. If professional aid is not forthcoming, it is best to dash cold water upon the sheath and scrotum. If it can be applied by means of a hose, so much the better, but this contrivance rarely exists on farms. Should these measures after a fair trial fail to arrest the hemorrhage, I have known the old-fashioned remedy of applying cobwebs to be most successful, causing the formation of a coagulum or clot in a very few minutes, and very soon get rid of the bleeding. Pouring cold water in addition over the loins is frequently advocated. In the most severe instances, where the above measures prove of no avail whatever, the animal must be recast, and the wounds in the scrotum plugged with fine tow or cotton wool, the plug being maintained in position by means of stitches.

Very few men who castrate horses will perform the operation without making proper examination of the parts for rupture or hernia. Should such exist, there is the special covered operation required, on which it is not now necessary to dwell, but many breeders will rather let the colt remain entire than run any risk with him. Occasionally it has happened that the hernia has been so slight, no knowledge of its existence being obtained previously, that it has gone unperceived during the operation, only becoming declared by the bowels descending through the rupture and wounds in the scotum a few hours afterwards. Whenever instances of this unfortunately do happen, I must advise the farmer or breeder to call in professional aid without delay; and beyond recasting the animal and putting him completely on his back, so as, if possible, to prevent further exit of the bowels, nothtng can be done till his arrival.

Peritonitis or inflammation of the external membrane of the bowels is one of the most serious consequences of castration, and there are but few colts which die from the results of the operation except from this cause. It is mainly brought on by the animal catching cold, or being operated on during cold, damp weather, or turned into a wet pasture; protected or aggravated inflammation in the scrotal wounds may, too, produce it, or the colt may have bruised himself severely whilst trying to escape from being caught. The patient will stand in one corner of the field or yard looking tucked up, dull and dejected; he is off his appetite, breathing with a certain amount of difficulty. Pressure to the abdomen will feel it very tense and hard, the bowels are constipated, and after a little time other symptoms, but suppressed, of abdominal pain will be present. Get him at once into a good warm loose box, and waste no time in getting proper aid to attend to the case.—*Cor. London Stockkeeper.*

---

Henry Jackson, a notorious Chicago horse sharp, whose game was to sell horses with bogus trotting pedigrees, has finally come to grief, having been convicted at Cleveland, Ohio, for obtaining money under false pretenses, and a term of imprisonment will probably follow.

The scratching of Abbotsford (late Mr. P. Lorillard's Mistake) for the Cambridgeshire after he had virtually been made second favorite was caused by lameness. It was said that he hit one of his legs in a gallop on Saturday morning, the 21st ult. Abbotsford was much fancied by the Newmarket people for the race.

---

People who want to see what a crowd there is that likes duck shooting want to go to the ferries on Saturday afternoon and see the crowd. There are some very funny costumes worn by the newly fledged hunters which excite the laughter of the "old hands."

Most of the ducks which are coming into the market just now come from down Merced way. That part of the country is so far off that city hunters will not be able to get much of the shooting.

Mayberry slough on Sherman Island and a little way above Antioch used to be a good place for shooters. A party has gone up there this week to try the luck at the old place.

The teal feed on what some people call teal grass which has a very fine seed and which is just now getting ripe. The birds are feeding on it heavy and are getting very fat.

There are considerable teal ducks out on Bouldin Island just now. They are pretty wild though the "scullers" and the hawks keep them moving pretty lively.

Billy Broden got ten cans, two mallards, twelve red-head, and twenty-six blue-bill up on Bouldin Island the other day. He tried the teal but they are pretty shy.

The Cordelia boys are having fine sport at their reserves, the birds staying there in a very satisfactory manner.

Several big flocks of swans have been seen up in the marshes of late. The "foreign birds" are coming in.

# ATHLETICS.

## Myers and George.

The first of the series of matches between the champions was decided on the 5th inst, and is thus described by the *Herald:*

Fully two thousand people visited the Polo Grounds yesterday afternoon for the purpose of witnessing the first race between the English champion, W. G. George, and the American champion, L. E. Myers. There was a poor representation of the fair sex so far as numbers were concerned, but that can easily be accounted for by the chilly weather, the northerly wind being anything but pleasant to face in the grand stands at the Polo Grounds. In order to entertain the visitors three additional athletic events were placed on the programme, but the 150 yards handicap was the only one to produce anything like racing. It was won by W. T. Stoddard, of the Manhattan Athletic Club, who had two yards start of Stafford and Derickson, the scratch men. Time, 15 3-4 seconds. W. Halpin of the American Athletic Club, with ten yards start, was second, and S. Derickson, of the Manhattan, third. The mile race was poorly contested, T. E. Delavey winning easily in the slow time of 4:53 4-5.

The next event was the center piece of the meeting, and the anxiety of the crowd was tested to its utmost by the arranging of the necessary preliminaries for the proper recording of the race. When all the timers had been stationed at their respective posts the rival athletes were called out. George was the first to appear from the old club house at the southwest corner of the grounds, and accompanied by his friend Mr. Caldicott went round to the starting point without coming near the stands. Myers was slow in getting ready, and George was kept several minutes waiting for the American champion. As Myers approached the starting point George came forward, and the pair shook hands cordially. A few moments later and they stood on the mark ready for the signal. The track being an exact third of a mile the start was made at the far corner from the grand stand, where the men had to finish. Myers was conspicuous in his all white costume, while George wore a black jersey and running trunks, the latter being tastefully embroidered with leaves in yellow silk. George had the inside position, next the curb, and, without any delay, the two stepped forward, toed the line and bent for the crack of the pistol. Mr. A. H. Curtis at once seized an opportunity, and as the men bounded from the mark a roar of "They're off!" rang out from the grand stands. Myers had no intention of running faster than he was obliged to do, hence he made a waiting race of it and allowed the Englishman to take a lead of two yards. On they sped around the lower turn and then up the straight. As they approached the stands the entire audience rose and cheered as if it were already the termination instead of only the first third of the struggle. Myers had now got within a yard of George, but going around the next turn he dropped back two yards behind again and remained content with that position till the first lap had been completed. Gradually and without any effort Myers began closing up the gap. Half-way around the lower turn he was within a yard; at 700 yards the yard had been diminished to a foot, and then a few strides further on the pair were level for the first time since they had left the starting line. It was then evident that Myers would win, and although George struggled on with indomitable gameness, he was no match at this distance for the light stepping American, who went to the front 100 yards from the finish and won with great ease by two yards and a half. Time for Myers, 1:56 3-5; for George, 1:57. Myers was one second behind his best record, while George beat his best previous performance by one and a fifth seconds. The fractional times were as follows: George, 220 yards, 26¾ seconds; one-sixth of a mile, 33 seconds; quarter of a mile, 55 1-5 seconds; one-third of a mile, 1:16 4-5; 660 yards, 1:26¼; 700 yards, 1:31 2-5 and 800 yards, Myers, 1:45; George, 1:45¼. As soon as the men had passed the crowd rushed into the enclosure, and Myers' admirers attempted to shoulder the winner, but it was a poor attempt, and Myers, slipping down quietly; retired to his dressing room, while George walked back to the club-house. Myers was perfectly fresh, and George showed no sign of weakness at the finish, but simply failed in pace.

The second event, the mile race, took place last Saturday, the 11th, and was won easily by George, who had sixteen yards to spare at the finish. The winner's time was 4:25; Meyers, 4:27¾. Betting even. The third race will be run today at the middle distance, three-quarters of a mile.

---

Next Saturday, Nov. 25th, at San Jose, a professional match will be decided between Harmon, the well-known sprint runner. and Gibson, a new arrival. Distance 135 yards. Harmon is known to be very fast up to 150 yards. Gibson came out here with the avowed intention of matching himself against F. E. Davis at 440 yards. As Davis is now in England running under the name of F. E. Cameron, the match fell through. If he is really able to compete with Davis at that distance he is a pretty good man, and Harmon is also hard to beat, at 135 yards, in a square match, if we can trust the Eastern papers. As the latter has never ran what can be called a race on this coast we know very little about him. He is supposed to be able to do 100 yards in even time. Perhaps he can, but there are very few admirers of a sprint race in this city, that will travel as far as San Jose and take the chances of seeing a good race. Perhaps there is more money in it there than there would be in the only city on the coast.

---

On election day the New York Athletic Club held their annual fall meeting, one of the events of which was a 1,000 yards handicap race with W. C. George, the English champion at scratch. When the pistol was fired George darted off like a flash, but Murphy, on the 45-yard mark, and Stonebridge, 110 yards, were just as fast, and started at a great pace that worried George somewhat. The wind, which blew from the north, militated against fast running. George caught Murphy about 220 yards from home, and though the latter responded bravely, the Englishman finally beat him three yards, never having caught Stonebridge, who finished ten yards to the fore. Stonebridge's time was 2:14⅗, George's time being 2:17¾.

---

At the date of this writing it is positively announced that the University Field games will take place Saturday, Nov. 18th, the date of this issue of our journal, on the Olympic Club grounds, corner Fourteenth and Center streets, Oakland. Unfavorable weather has necessitated two postponements of the events, and the weather indications at present lead us to fear that another postponement will be necessary. However, we will hope for the best. The outside entries are numerous, and if the handicaps are very close the open handicap events will be very interesting. It is mysteriously and wisely hinted that there is a dark horse in the scratch mile. We hope he will be able to beat 5 minutes. R. S. Haley is sick and has not entered any of the events.

The Atlantic and Columbia Athletic clubs held a joint handicap meeting at the grounds of the Manhattan Athletic Club, New York, on election day. There was a large attendance of spectators, and fifty or sixty ladies of the hundred or so present remained until the last event on the lengthy programme was decided. An open dash of 100 yards introduced the sports. Five trial heats were run, which qualified for the final heat W. T. Stoddart, Manhattan A. C., scratch; F. S. Roumage, Columbia A. C., eight yards; H. J. Duecla, New York city, eight yards; F. G. Abbott, Manhattan A. C., three yards. Smith won the final by one yard, Stoddart second and Abbott third, the struggle being very spirited. Time, 10¼ seconds. A walk of one mile for members of the Atlantic Club was won by G. H. Davidson, from scratch, in 8:22¼; W. J. Seidenberg was second with twenty seconds start. Four started in a run of half a mile for members of the Columbia club, E. A. Richard, from scratch, winning easily in 2:24¼. F. Gwynn, twenty yards, was second. Five members of the Columbia club started in a 220 yards hurdle race. G. Morrison, twelve yards, won easily. F. Gwynn, twelve yards, being second. C. Proctor, scratch, fell at the first hurdle and stumbled at the third. Time, 32½ seconds. Four Atlantic members started in a run of one mile from scratch and C. B. Davidson won in 5:45. Eleven went to their marks in an open run of three-quarters of a mile. T. F. Delaney, Gramercy A. C., scratch, beat E. A. Thompson, Manhattan A. C., by twenty yards, with J. Moorcraft, Gramercy A. C., 65 yards, third. Time, 3:27¼. A run of 100 yards for members of the Atlantic Club brought together in the final heat D. H. Babcock, scratch; C. W. Culver, 2 yards; C. H. Alliger won by a foot in 11¼ seconds, Davidson second and Babcock third. J. F. MacDonald New York Walking Club, 25 seconds start, won a walk of two miles in 16:04¾, actual time; G. D. Baird, New York city, was second. E. A. Thompson, Manhattan A. C., was the winner in an open two-mile bicycle race in 8:55¾. A half mile run, open to Atlantic members only, was won by C. D. Morrison from scratch in 2:36½. Six started in an open 300 yards run. H. L. Jacquelin, American A. C., won from scratch, in 36 1-5; C. L. Jacquelin, Manhattan A. C., was second, and H. M. Stone, Manhattan A. C., third. An Atlantic Club 220 yards run sent six to their marks. It was a good race throughout, C. W. Culver, 2 yards, winning on the tape, with G. Morrison, 5 yards, second, a foot in front of C. H. Alliger, 9 yards. A tug of war between teams of four wound up the sport. G. Richards, J. Lyons, A. Field and W. Hunter made up the winning team.

---

The following programme has been arranged to take place on Thanksgiving Day at Recreation Park, corner of Twenty-Fifth and Folsom streets: One-quarter-mile race, pedestrian; one-half-mile race, pedestrian; one-mile race, pedestrian; donkey race of one mile and repeat; in this race there will be four donkeys on the grounds, the riders will draw for choice of donkeys, and the race will be go-as-you-please; this race will be very interesting. Also a hound race between five hounds, best two out of three heats. Sport to commence at 1 p. m. sharp.

In the notice of the University field day last week an error occurs in the name of one of the participants. It was given as James Gorevan whereas it should have been Joseph T. Gorevan.

The Stockton champion declines a match with Duncan McMillan, of Bodie.

# BICYCLING.

## Influence of Bicycling on Road Laws.

There are manifest signs that the invention of the bicycle will also produce important and permanent effects upon the legislation of the country, particularly upon the laws for the creation and regulation of common highways. That their influence upon legislation will tend to promote the general welfare is apparent.

Of all modern inventions the bicycle may most justly be styled the perfect road tester. From no other vehicle does the rider descend with so much suddenness and *aplomb*, and with such serious emotion, to investigate a defect in the surface of the highway. It is the most sensitive of all vehicles to the slightest imperfections of any sort in the construction and condition of a road surface; and it communicates its discoveries to its rider directly, and in a manner which it is impossible to either ignore or forget. One who lolls in his carriage does not appreciate the effect upon his horses of a trifle of sand over the surface of a road, an unnecessarily steep grade, the roughness of a pavement which ought to be smooth, mud, stones, ruts, dim lights, wet paving blocks, slippery clay, icy streets, and other such evils. The jars, tremors, shocks, sudden strains, abrupt jerks and pushes, which worry the spirits and exhaust the strength, and speed of his team and wear out his vehicle do not affect his own person much. He knows them only through observation. The bicycle-rider, on the contrary, experiences all these evils in his own muscular and nervous system. He feels them himself, just as the horse does; and, if horses could talk, their expressions upon this subject would probably agree with those of the bicycle-rider, and form a concensus of equine and human opinions which would revolutionize legislation in a single campaign.

In many parts of the West thirty miles a day is considered good average speed for a week's journey by a first-rate horse or a span of horses, with a light traveling buggy or wagon, or 182 miles a week. With loads, a team will do well to average eighteen or twenty miles a day. With first-class macadam or gravel roads nearly double these distances may be traveled with more than double loads, and with less fatigue and wear and tear. There is no other p i improvement which pays farmers, rural villages, and all country towns and dwellers so large a percentage of profit as first-class roads.—*The Wheelman*.

---

A writer in the *Wheel* objects to any such thing as flying starts, in bicycle races, as suggested by some. This is what he says: Suppose six men in a line ride towards the scratch. One holds back; but, on nearing the line, spurts and crosses it with the others, and having the advantage of considerable more momentum, is well under way before the others are off. Would that be fair? You could not say he crossed the line ahead of the others, as he did not; but that such a rider would have a decided advantage over his competitors is plainly to be seen. The object of a standing start is to place competitors on an equitable basis. Again, to compare our records with foreign ones, we have adopted the foreign standard of track measurement, and certainly we ought to adopt the same rules in regard to the start. A flying start may look very pretty: but records made under such circumstances are not allowed to stand.

Harvard.—The second regular hare and hound chase of the club took place yesterday afternoon despite the high wind that was blowing, and was in all respects a thorough success. The hares—Messrs. Norton, '85, and Claflin, '86—left the steps of Matthews at precisely 3:19¼ o'clock. A dozen or more hounds who had assembled started seven minutes later, and from then on the race was an exciting one. The course lay through Brighton by indirect route to Watertown, thence to West Newton, on to the junction of Beacon and Washington streets, very near Newtonville. Here the hounds were encouraged by learning from the relay that joined them that the hares were hardly five minutes ahead of them. The road thence through Newton Center to Chestnut Hill Reservoir was perfect in all respects, and good riding was done by the hounds, that of Messrs. White and Maverick being especially good. At the reservoir the scent was lost, and fully three minutes were consumed before it was found again. Once more before reaching the finish the whole body of hounds were misled, and took a circuitous route before regaining the regular trail. Mr. Moffat was the first of the hounds to reach the finish, closely followed by Mr. Hemenway. The trial distance ridden was nearly nineteen miles, and the riding time of the hares was 1 hour, 26½ minutes, being remarkably good considering the high west wind that blew against them all the outward course. The riding time of the first hound was 1 hour, 28 minutes, 3 seconds. The hares chose good roads and so great was the success of the run that the management of the club felt encouraged to announce another for next Thursday afternoon. All riders connected with the University are invited to participate, whether they be members of the club or not.—*Wheel.*

---

Races were held upon the half mile track at the Driving Park commencing with a club drill by the Capital Bicycle club. After this there was a mile race which was won by E. A. Thompson in 3:09¼, W. R. Pitman second by nine inches. The second event was a mile dash for novices, which was won by C. H. Chickering, upon an American Star machine, in 3:20. The the third event was a two mile handicap, won by V. C. Place, from scratch, in 6:50. The five mile handicap was also won by Place, in 16:58¼. The half-mile race was won by Place in 1:30, and a consolation mile race was won by B. G. Sanford in 3:31. Exhibitions of fancy riding were then given by Rex Smith of the Capital Club upon an ordinary bicycle; Burt Pressey upon an American Star, and Edwin Dubois, a fourteen-year-old boy, upon an old fashioned velocipede. The prizes were gold and silver medals. The races were witnessed by about 3,000 people.

The recent Centennial celebration at Philadelphia gave the bicyclists of that city the opportunity for a celebration, of which they were not slow to avail themselve. The meet took place Oct. 26 at Fairmount Park. The run covered about ten miles up one side of the river, crossing at the falls and down upon the west side to the Belmont mansion. Four hundred and eighty-three riders were in line, the march occupying about an hour. After its completion, dinner was served, and in the evening an excursion was made by about 100 to Bryn Manor, a distance of eight miles, the lamps carried by nearly all making it a line sight.

In the matter of class handicaps, it might answer if the entries were very numerous; but our largest race meetings have rarely more than ten starters. We rather favor time handicaps, as then all competitors ride the full distance, and it permits all to make a record; besides it aids in forming a basis for future starts. What the league needs is an official handicapper, whose duty it shall be to keep a record of every race and every racing man. Such a thing is done in athletic circles, and why not in bicycling, which promises to outdo the highest point athletics has ever reached?

The next grand meeting of bicyclists will take place in Washington, Nov. 29, on the occasion of the National exposition in aid of the Garfield monument fund. A parade over the splendid asphalt streets, a review by the President, Generals, and foreign dignitaries, fancy riding and racing, will form a part of the features of the day.

A mile bicycle handicap is upon the programme of the Olympic Athletic Club sports at their grounds in Oakland, on Thanksgiving Day. The best riders will participate and the mile record may be lowered if the day and track are fine.

The latest long distance performance by a club was that of the Lawrence (Mass) B. C., on Friday, Oct. 27. Three members started at 12:30 a. m. and finished at 11:45 p. m., doing 169 miles in a running time of 17:15, rests; 6:03.

## Herbert Spencer's Views.

Herbert Spencer was tendered a complimentary dinner by over 200 gentlemen at Delmonico's on the 9th. William M. Evarts presided, and among the guests were William H. Hurlbut, Charles A. Dana and Henry Ward Beecher. Mr. Spencer, after giving thanks for his cordial reception, said; "It seems to me that in one respect Americans have diverged too widely from the savages. I do not mean to say that they are in general unduly civilized. Especially out in the West, men's dealings do not yet betray much of the sweetness and light which we are told distinguish the cultured man from the barbarians. You know that the primitive man, spurred by hunger, danger, revenge, can exert himself energetically for a time, but his energy is spasmodic, and monotonous daily toil is impossible to him. It is otherwise with the more developed man, when the discipline of social life gradually increased his aptitude for persistent industry, until, among us and still more among you, work has become with many a pastime. This contrast of nature has another aspect. The savage thinks only of present satisfactions and leaves future satisfactions uncared for. Contrariwise the American, eagerly pursuing future good, almost ignores what good the passing day offers him, and when future good is gained he neglects that while striving for some remoter good. What I have seen and heard during my stay among you has forced on me the belief that this slow change from habitual inertness to persistent activity has reached the extreme, from which there must be a counter-change, a reaction. Everywhere I have been struck with the number of faces which told in strong lines of the burdens that had to be borne. I have been struck with the large proportion of gray-haired men, and inquiries have brought out the fact that with you hair commonly begins to turn some ten years earlier than with us. Moreover, in every circle I have met men who had themselves suffered from nervous diseases, due to stress of business, or named friends who had either killed themselves by overwork or had been permanently incapacitated, or had wasted long periods in endeavors to recover health. I do but echo the opinions of all observing persons. I have spoken of the immense injury that is being done by this high-pressure life, as the physique is berng undermined."

---

The boys go up pretty regularly to the Teal station these days.

# HERD AND SWINE.

## Wheat Straw.

The feeding value of straw has been a matter of special experiment, inquiry with me for several years, the results of which have been so satisfactory that although located in an economic state of the economic East, I gave unusual care to its preservation and feeding, assuming it to have a higher value than most farmers attached to it. I have fed it with the same care that I would feed hay, using none of it for bedding, excepting 10 to 15 per cent. that would be left uneaten. Often I have succeeded in getting it all eaten. In my remarks thus far I refer mostly to oat and barley straw, either of which I assume to be worth more than wheat straw, yet the little wheat straw I have had to feed convinces me that it has a feeding value of no mean importance.

If we should look into the chemistry of wheat straw, as compared with oat and barley straw, and all of these as compared to timothy hay (Phleum Pratese), we should find that their theoretic value is quite high, if in the meanwhile we allow to carbohydrates a higher importance than German physiologists have allowed, as we undoubtedly should. Excepting a few samples of oat straw, analyzed for personal feeding trials at the New Hampshire Agricultural College, only one other of this straw, one of rye and one of buckwheat had been made two or three years ago straw. Dr. Ameeby made a compilation of American analyses of agricultural products. Therefore I shall have to use German results to show the comparative chemical composition of straws.

"Winter wheat straw: Ash, 4.6 per cent.; albuminoids, 3.0; crude fiber, 44; carbonate hydrates, 32.6; fats, 1.5; digestible, albuminoids, 0.8; digestible carbonate hydrates, 31.9; digestible fats, 0.4."

"Summer barley straw: Ash, 4.1 per cent.; albuminoids, 4.0; crude fibre, 40; carbonate hydrates, 36.2; fats, 1.4; digestible albuminoids, 1.4; digestible carbonate hydrates, 36.9; digestible fats, 0.4."

"Oat straw: Ash, 4.0 per cent.; albuminoids, 3.5; crude fiber, 43; carbonate hydrates, 34.2; fats, 1.2; digestible albuminoids, 1.3; digestible carbonate hydrates, 27.4; digestible fats, 0.6."

"Timothy hay: Ash, 4.5; albuminoids, 9.7; crude fiber, 29.7; carbonate hydrates, 45.8; fats, 40; digestible albuminoids, 5.8; digestible carbonate hydrates, 43.4; digestible fats, 1.4."

I do not present this table as a basis upon which to found the practical value of foods. I refrain also from adding the feeding tables of animal physiologists, because I hold that the attempt thus far to fix the value of foods in nutrition has failed because of false reasoning upon premises also false, being founded upon theoretical deductions rather than ascertained facts. So far as chemistry as yet divides for its feeder the nutrients of foods, the essential distinctions between wheat straw and the other straws named and between straws and timothy lies in less content of albuminoids and a greater proportion of fiber. I should also add in inferior digestibility. In a ration of twenty pounds each of wheat straw or timothy the albuminoids of the straw could be made equal to that of the hay ration in digestible amounts and would exceed it in total amount and largely fill the balance of digestible materials lacking in the straw as a whole. As regarding the fiber it must be remembered that it is nearly as digestible as the carbohydrates, so called; in fact fibre is a carbohydrate and performs the same office in nutrition.

This hasty glance of the table is only taken to show that the chemical make-up of straws is not incompatible with nutritive value. In practice I have unmistakably found that unpalatableness, rather than prominent nutritive, poverty lies at the root of the cause of the ill-name of straw. A steer that will consume twenty-five pounds of timothy per day will scarcely eat one-half the amount of straw. This I do not lay down as a mere proposition but as a fact ascertained by thousands of weighing. The force of this fact will be better impressed by another result noticed, I find that a 1,000-pound steer will consume 18 pounds of hay daily as food of support. In other words it requires 18 pounds of hay daily to maintain existence without growth. The steer consuming 25 pounds of hay is using seven pounds of excess food for growth. The straw fed steer takes less than the food of support and often falls off in weight. If this condition of things must exist, then straw will have no practical value, whatever the theoretical value may be; and this is what farmers often believe. Can straw be handled so as to covert its nutrition into cash value? I believe so. From homage to brevity I will return to the answer at a future date if it please the editor.—J. W. Sanborn in Rural World.

There is a salient feature in the Norwegian character which ought, I think, to be recorded, viz: kindness to domestic animals, which in that country are treated as the friends rather than the slaves of man. As a result, vicious horses are unknown; foals follow their dams at work in the fields or on the road as soon as they have sufficient strength and thus gently accustom themselves to harness. I heard of a foal trying to force its head into a collar in imitation of its mother. Horses are trained to obey the voice rather than the hand, bearing-reins are not used, and the whip, if carried at all, is hardly ever made use of. Great care is taken not to overload cattle, especially in the case of young horses, and consequently a broken knee is rarely seen, and the animals continue fat, in good condition and capable of work till the advanced age of twenty-five or thirty. So tame are the Norwegian horses and cows that they will allow casual passers-by to caress them without fear. Even domestic cattle will approach a boy with confidence, knowing that no chasing or worrying awaits them. One very hot summer's day I met a woman holding up an umbrella to carefully screen what I supposed was a little child at her side from the scorching rays of the mid-day sun, while her own head was covered only by a handkerchief. In driving by I tried to gain a glimpse of her charge and found, to my great surprise, that the object of her care was a fat, black pig. The question of humane methods of slaughtering animals has lately been prominently brought forward in England. In this the Norwegians show us a good example: they never use the knife without first stunning the animal. In the above remarks I am alluding to the country districts of Norway; in the towns the national characteristics become modified, even though under these conditions kindness to animals is still remarkable.—A. G. B. K. in London Times.

The latest cow story is the following from the Mercury of Saundersville, Georgia. Mr. M. H. Boyer, of our city, has a Jersey cow that gives butter and milk both. She gives such rich milk that in milking it into the bucket it churns it. Mr. B. tells us that he gives her no extra feed, only puts her to a good pasture. This is the kind of a cow to have. We examined the milk and butter after the cow was milked, and found large particles of butter in the milk.

## Swine Notes.

The Swine Breeders' Journal gives us some short and good points in its October number; a few of which we give our readers.

Warmth, cleanliness, and regularity in feeding a little good food, are the main secrets in rearing young pigs.

An occasional application of a mixture of equal parts of kerosene, vinegar and fish oil will eradicate lice from swine. Of the desirable qualities in a pig, a vigorous appetite is of the first importance, the next in importance is quietness in disposition.

A writer says: "Give your hogs a rubbing post, in some accessible part of their inclosure; it facilitates their keeping clean, and seems to afford them much satisfaction."

The hog cholera is prevailing in Pennsylvania and other states, as well as over the ocean in foreign lands. Owners will do well to keep a lookout for this terrible disease.

In feeding sweet milk to pigs, trials made at the Wisconsin experiment farm showed that on an average four pounds of corn meal were equal to twenty pounds of sweet skim milk, if fed separately.

Oil cake and cotton-seed meal is valuable feed for horses, cows, sheep and hogs, giving a healthy tone to the animal, fattening the lean ones and keeping them strong, healthy and vigorous. Fed with roots, the effect on animal life is astonishing.

The hog is naturally a gleaner and an economizer of the refuse and offal on the farm. Of all farm animals he is the only one that craves a variety of things. See that he gets what he wants, and the year's cash balance will foot up very satisfactory.

It is a good plan to feed store hogs regularly, but not too heavily, three times a day; give them abundance of raw material to work up into muscle, and have on hand a constant supply of charcoal or wood ashes. A mixture of the latter materials, experience has proven to be excellent in correcting acidity and improving digestion in swine.

Of the 30,000,000 to 40,000,000 hogs in the United States, three-fifths are raised in ten strictly Mississippi Valley States, namely, Illinois, Iowa, Missouri, Indiana, Ohio, Kentucky, Tennessee, Kansas, Nebraska and Wisconsin. These States produce annually nearly three-fourths of the entire corn crop of the country.

A Nebraska man says hay is good for hogs. Cut the hay short and mix with bran, shorts or middlings, and feed as other food. Hogs soon learn to like it, and if soaked in swill, or sloppfood, is it highly relished by them. In winter, use for hogs the same hay that you feed to your horses, and you will find that it will save bran, shorts or other food; it puts on flesh as rapidly as anything that can be given them.

Epilepsy in pigs is generally due to irritation of the digestive organs, from improper food, worms; etc. For pigs under three months old, give a teaspoonful of flour of sulphur. It may be given two or three times daily during a week, in a little thin gruel, which the pigs do not object to consume voluntarily. Change of food and comfortable quarters are essential; also plenty of sour milk, ample range of liberty, and pure water.

## No More Lard.

The South is to have a new industry, the manufacture of cotton seed oil. The Southern Cultivator says: "Refined cotton seed oil is everything that can be desired as a substitute for lard or other fats for culinary operations. For frying fish, for shortening bread, cakes or crusts, for making gravies, and so on, it is even superior to lard, imparting no unpleasant flavor or odor whatever; in a word, bringing no unsatisfactory results, dietary or otherwise; but on the other hand, making lighter and better bread, cakes and crusts than could be made with lard, and proved decidedly more digestible, to say nothing of being considerable cheaper. A pound of cotton seed oil, costing the consumer not more than twelve cents under the most unfavorable circumstances, will go fully as far in the culinary way as a pound and a half of lard. When a pan of steak has been fried with it, the oil not absorbed by the steak may be poured back into the dish and used again at another time, being just as clean and pure as it was before it was put over the fire. There is something about it which prevents a union with animal impurities. As a consequence of all this it is coming into rapid use, and the sooner it gets fully into use the better for the people, undoubtedly." A popular Southern writer treating on the same subject says: "When it has gone into general use, which is only a question of time, there will no longer exist an excuse for writing as an epitaph over the grave of departed Southern virgo: 'Died game—of the frying-pan.'"

And the strange story of cotton seed, the coming wonder, cannot be permitted to stop even here. The chemist has recently converted cotton seed oil into a substitute for butter; an article far superior to the best oleomargarine ever made, or gleage. It fills all the offices of butter, both for culinary and table use, and is coming rapidly into general favor, as it seems to give entire satisfaction wherever tested.

## Shipping Cattle.

Cattle are taken on and under deck in stalls measuring two feet eight inches on vessels sailing from New York, and two feet six inches on those from all other ports of the United States. These stalls are built under the supervision of an insurance inspector. During the summer shippers prefer to ship on deck, as the cattle get more air and come out fresher at the end of the voyage. On deck the steamships carry between 160 and 175 animals, the under deck about 225 head. Drinking-water is condensed by steam process on board for that use, one cannot itself proving a never-failing source of supply. The cattle are generally put on the steamer in the stream, after it has left the dock, an old ferry-boat usually being used for the purpose. The number of cattle to be taken is regulated by the insurance inspector, and cattle exporters must pay the entire freight, according to his report, even if they do not ship the entire number. Sheep and pigs are stowed away in stalls on deck where there is not enough room for the cattle. Sometimes in the early spring, when the sea is liable to disturbance, some of the cattle get overboard, and then a very lively time ensues in getting them out. The cattle are hoisted on board usually and lowered, two at a time, by a winch, into the hold. The allowance permitted from six to ten gallons a day to each bullock. The amount of fodder averages one ton to each animal. The rates of insurance apparently vary. Some shippers give it at 3 per cent. in summer to 10 per cent. in winter. There is some risk to cattle from perils of the sea in the latter season, as a heavy storm may make it necessary to lighten the ship by throwing the entire deckload of cattle overboard. The carrying capacity of the vessels, of course, varies, but the average, as given by an old shipper, may be put safely at 200 head at the shipment, taking large and small vessels into account. On some of the large steamers the number has reached 500, and one Boston steamer has carried as many as 841 head. The largest shipment from New York by one steamer was 650 head.—Pittsburgh Stockman.

## Easy Mode of Improving Cattle Stock.

An easy mode, and one reasonably inexpensive, at the same time, is what many farmers wait a good many years for and to many it never comes. It fails to come, in their case because of an excessively-cultivated cautiousness. It would seem that, after marketing scrub calves for a score of years or more, at less than half the price of well-bred ones, or furnishing grass and grain till they have reached an age to sell as third or fourth-grade stock in market, any man of reasonably fair discernment would have made up his mind that this was not profitable.

To a farmer who has all his active life been a grower of grain, because he has no taste for stockgrowing and, inferentially, no faith in it, as a business, it is quite likely better for him not to attempt the avocation of a breeder, as his practices would not be in keeping with the needs of young growing stock, neither of that more advanced, ready to be finished off. But we have a word to say to such as are fairly attentive to whatever they turn their hands to, and are willing to be guided by the signs of the times, indicated, in a measure, by articles published in recent numbers of the Journal, regarding the growing demand for meats. Nothing has occurred to weaken the arguments then used. On the other hand, the events of each day confirm them.

Turning off cattle younger than has heretofore been the custom will materially curtail the supply, because the practice strikes at the fountain head, taking to market what, under former years, would be called immature stock. Those who furnish the cattle for slaughter at a year and a half to three will find that the public demand is insatiable and annoyingly exacting as to quality. Scrubs will not fatten at the ages required, and it is quite generally dawning upon the minds of all observing farmers that a scrub steer, at three years old, has eaten all of value there is in him. He is not wanted then, is not salable, and is held and fed to maturity at a loss. At any rate, this will hold good upon any farm world, say $15 an acre, and in a locality where corn, taking one year with another, is worth more than twenty cents a bushel, and hay brings a price corresponding with this.

Therefore, it is of vital importance to every farmer to get out of this rut gradually, at least, discard the animals that have encumbered his acres, and replace them with such as meet the demands of the times, and command top prices from willing buyers. We read of a farmer, of very moderate means, who bought an in-calf heifer and a young bull at a moderate figure for reputable purely bred stock. The price for the two may have been $300; it may have been less than this. At any rate, by careful breeding for a period of ten years, he had reared eighty descendants of the heifer upon the farm. Twelve of these were cows, four heifers, and ten heifer calves. One grown bull and one bull calf made up the full number. It is reasonable to infer, that he had at least made sales of quite a number of males. On such a basis as this, always having a purely bred bull for use upon common cows, no prudent man can do otherwise than better his condition by doing as this man did.

A comparison made between the grades upon this man's farm, and another where a scrub bull had been kept during a period of ten years, would, of course, show a very marked contrast. So great would this be, in the matter of general appearance, as well as furnishing a basis for profitable feeding, that the original investment, conceding it to have been three hundred dollars, would be found to have been entirely warranted, estimating the improvements wrought upon the common cattle upon the farm alone. The reader hardly need be reminded that the consumption of food would be about alike in the case of the grade and the scrub; the taxes would scarcely vary. Interest upon stock and farm, taxes upon the latter, and general wear and tear would be the same with one class as with the other, while the gain in early maturity, thus enabling the owner to turn his money quickly, added to the gain in growth from a given amount of feed, and the selling contrast between having the stock anxiously sought after, at six or seven cents a pound, and having to hunt unwilling buyers at half the figures given, should enable any man, not wilfully blinded, to readily see that an expenditure in the direction indicated cannot well be otherwise than profitable.

As will readily be seen, there is quite a difference between deferring the purchase of improved cattle to a future day, say ten years ahead, that you may then have a cash balance to your credit and sufficient to enable you to buy a herd of fair dimensions at the start, and commencing as did the farmer referred to above, with a pair only, finding himself the possessor, at the end of ten years, of a herd of his own breeding, that, if bought at a single purchase, would cost several thousands. What is true of cattle in the direction named is equally true of other farm stock. A beginning in this can, with entire propriety, be like the commencement in other lines of business. The pioneer, on a new timbered farm, does not wait a decade for trees to rot, but clears a small space, commencing in a small way. Some very large manufacturers commenced with a single forge or bench, at the cross-roads. They did not wait to accumulate a large surplus of capital, but planned to make a given line grow from a small beginning, to be self-sustaining, eventually furnishing its own capital. If a man has not means to enable him to plant ten acres to potatoes, he can certainly plant a single eye of a potato, and from this his ability to plant ten acres from corps of his own growing is only a question of time. So, the single cow system will, with reasonably discreet management, insure to the owner a respectable herd without undue waiting. A cow bought for the boy of ten years, will, when the boy has attained his majority, furnish him a fair working capital to begin his business with.—Live Stock Journal.

## Scotch Shorthorns.

Scotch Shorthorns are attracting much attention in this country of late. As Scottish breeders have been careful to breed more for beef than for book, and have never hesitated to kill animals not up to a high standard as breeders, they have succeeded in producing what very many excellent judges in America as well as in the old country consider the very best families of Shorthorns known. The severe climate, exposure, and the system of breeding and feeding which have given to Scotch polled breeds their rugged character and unsurpassed capacity for making the best possible beef, and enduring the worst possible weather, have also given to the Cruickshank and other Scotch Shorthorns similar characteristics. Like the polled cattle and the Herefords, these Shorthorns are short in leg, full and fine in flesh, roomy in the barrel, as all good grazers must be, and carry a large amount of the most valuable beef. Maturing early, and with constitutions unharmed by severe breeding, they give a very satisfactory return for the care and money invested in them.

## The White Breeds of Swine.

All improvements in swine undoubtedly came from the domestic hog of China upon the native breeds of England. The hog of Europe, Asia, and Africa undoubtedly had a common origin, since they are fertile together, and the offspring are completely so from generation to generation. Thus the hog of all these countries has, without doubt, contributed to the improvement of our improved breeds, the hog of China and Siam probably having had a greater influence than all others whatsoever.

China has a civilization of greater antiquity than any other nation on earth. Its civilization dates back far beyond that of Egypt, for upon the monuments of ancient Egypt are Chinese inscriptions, showing that civilization probably came from the direction of China. Since when the hog came carefully to be bred is not known, but that the Chinese hog has been bred with care and attention in China from time immemorial there is no doubt, and this with special reference to early maturity and strong fattening propensities. In China, from its early civilization and the care bestowed upon the cultivation of the earth, we early find it occupied with a dense population. It still holds this pre-eminence of density of population. Thus everything there must conform itself to those conditions that will best subserve a struggle for life. They cannot afford to feed the larger animals, nor, indeed, any animal to a great size. Their systems are all artificial. Hence, we find the Chinese hog; hence, the prepotency of his blood; and for the reason that it had once attained a breed that answered the wants of the community, no further attempts were made in experimenting, but the dominant breed was kept intact.

They are a compact, rather small, chunky, white hog, of good constitution, active feeders, and with plenty of bone. It is the infusion of this blood that long since converted the semi-wild, raw-boned, strong-snouted, long-legged, bristly and hard-feeding hog of England, into the tolerably compact, deep-bodied, broad-backed and short-snouted hog of seventy years ago in England, and that by careful breeding has since given us the many admirable breeds of white swine that have successfully held the public taste. So improvement from careful breeding has from time to time appeared, and which from fineness of bone and aptitude for fattening in the smaller breeds, and for great bulk and substance, to-day are nowhere excelled, outside the mother country and America.

The wild hog is not indigenous to America. In its place appears, however, an allied animal, the peccary of the subtropical and tropical regions. These are two species, and were named *Dictyles*, double naveled, from a glandular opening in the back. One species (*D. torquatus*) is the collared peccary; the other (*D. labiatus*) is the white-lipped variety, and both inhabited originally the countries of the Atlantic from Guiana and Paraguay north to the Red river. They are smaller than the common hog of the Eastern hemisphere (*sus scrofa*), and covered with stiff bristles on the back, which, like the hair of all savage animals, are erected when angry or alarmed; but, unlike the hog, they are nearly destitute of a tail.

The original of the domestic hog of Great Britain was undoubtedly white or sandy. They were of two general classes; the smaller being dusky in color, with erect or partially erect ears, arched back, half wild, and generally found in the highlands and islands of Scotland. The second class were larger, with pendulous ears, generally white, but sometimes tawny or spotted with black. They were coarse, large-haired, arch-backed, long-legged and huge-snouted, and would not fatten until two or three years old; in fact, pretty much such a hog as used to be found wild in the Southern forests half a century ago.

Of the old modernized breeds of England we have accounts of the Hampshire hog—large, long in the neck and body, mostly white in color, but sometimes spotted black, showing industone probably both of China and Siam blood. They were said to fatten to a great weight when mature, and to have been celebrated for the goodness of their hams and bacon.

The Shropshire is another of the old English breeds, white, sometimes brindled with black on a sandy color. They were deep, but flat-sided hogs, wiry-haired, large-eared, long-nosed and long-legged. They were, however, not delicate in what they ate, garbage and distillers' mash all being thankfully taken, and fattened to 600 pounds and upwards.

The Ragawick breed seems to have been the giant breed of England. They were considered as among the most hardy and prolific of English breeds. Their ordinary weight is given at 600 to 900 pounds, and a hog of this breed is recorded to have reached the weight of 182 stone of eight pounds each, or 1,456 pounds. The old Yorkshire is recorded to have been one of the worst of English breeds, long-legged, weak-loined, not good in constitution, and, of course, bad winter feeders, or, as the old chroniclers expressed it, "bad sty pigs in winter." They, however, are said to have had the merit of being earlier fatteners than some of the so-called superior (larger) breeds. The first improvement is said to have been from the old Berkshire cross; they were still considered inferior to the then breeds of Northwestern English stock.

The old Wiltshire breed was a low, long-bodied, hollow-backed, high-rumped hog, round-boned, light-colored, and with rather large pointed ears.

The Northamptonshire old breed seems to have been a superior hog for that day. They are said to have been a handsome, small-eared, white, deep-sided hog, of medium bone, quick feeders, and good in their "proof."

The Lincolnshire breed was originally medium-sized white, or light-colored, and resembled the Northamptonshire swine, but inclining to curled or wooly hair.

The old Gloucestershire hog was a tall, long, white inferior hog, and was distinguished by its double wattle hanging down from the throat.

The Leicestershire breed, in its original form, was a large, deep, but flat-sided and light-spotted hog, with a rather good head and ear. It is the breed upon which Bakewell worked in his improvement of swine. This would seem to establish the fact that it was one of the best existing breeds of his day.

The Norfolks were small, short-bodied, erect-eared, thin-skinned, but easily fattened. They are reported to have been of various colors, generally white, inclining, however, to blueish, and sometimes streaked or scored with thin lines.

The Chinese hog, as originally known in England, is recorded to have been thin in hair, or almost bare as to the upper parts. The color was grey rather than white; the legs so short that the belly almost, or quite, swept the ground; short-snouted; short-tailed; the ears fine and falling over the eyes. Culley subsequently divided them into seven distinct races; but this is regarded as having been more fanciful than real.

The Berkshire originally was a tawny white, or reddish color, spotted here and there with black; the ears were large and drooped over the eyes; the body thick and close, and well made for that day; short-legged, fine-boned, kind feeders, and the flesh even then accounted as most excellent.

---

Even so late as forty years ago, as we knew the best of them, they inclined to be tawny colored and spotted.

A swing-tailed breed is also mentioned as being a useful, hardy, small hog, weighing well in proportion to its size. The Highland breeds were hogs ranging in the highlands of Scotland and the Hebrides, and have been thought to have been the original breed of the country. They were small, uniformly grey in color, shaggy-haired and with long bristles. They ran perfectly wild winter and summer, subsisting by grazing and rooting, and in the autumn became fat on mast.

In the Orkney Islands were found hogs of a dark red or brown, long-haired and bristled, with wooly hair beneath.

The old Irish hog is described as having been a long-legged, thin-sided, lank, unprofitable brute; probably, however, not more so than others of the semi-wild breeds, it being well known that the general improvement of swine was not attempted in Ireland until improvement had made considerable headway in England.

The Suffolks can scarcely be classed as among the older breeds of Great Britain. They are described as being white in color, small, delicate, short-haired, with pendant bellies and dish-faced. Evidently a modified white China hog.

The Essex, now the best of our small black hogs, was originally a long, flat-side, roach-backed, long-legged hog, with prick ears, and long head and hose. The bone was rather small and the color was white or black-and-white. They had little hair, were unquiet and great feeders, but fattened quickly. Undoubtedly they were a modified Siamese, their eminent modern qualities being due to Neapolitan blood and careful selection and breeding.—*Breeders' Gazette.*

## The Demand for Mohair.

During a recent walk through the largest woolen mill in the neighborhood of Philadelphia, the writer was surprised to find a large pile of bales filled with mohair. Upon inquiry the fact was elicited that already considerable machinery is running on fabrics composed of mohair, the majority of which is imported. This fact is especially interesting to those who have heard the absence of a market for mohair quoted as an argument against the profitable culture of Angora goats in the United States. This hair, though going into several other fabrics, is principally employed in the manufacture of plushes, for covering the seats of railroad cars—an industry just now attempted in this country. The proprietor of the mill above referred to admitted the superiority of the American mohair, and emphasized his conclusions by comparing samples of foreign and domestic product. With a fair market for their fleece—as reliable as that of wool—within ready reach, there seems no reason why the culture of Angora goats should not take its place beside that of the hitherto more popular and profitable farm animals. In fact, in many localities goats can be handled without at all interfering with other stock—as they prefer those hilly and arid localities inaccessible to most other animals. The time for sneering at efforts in the direction of introducing the Angora goat into the United States seems to have gone by forever.—*Breeders' Gazette.*

QUARANTINE STATIONS FOR IMPORTED CATTLE.—The Treasury Department is informed that arrangements are nearly completed at Baltimore, Boston and Portland for providing shelter and other accommodations for imported cattle. The station for the Maine district is at Deering, Cumberland county; that for the Boston district is at Waltham, on the Fitchburg Railroad, about ten miles from Boston, and the Baltimore station will probably be on the lands of the Baltimore and Ohio Railroad at its junction with the Baltimore and Potomac. The Government will furnish shelter and water and the owners will have provide for the feeding and care of the cattle. Heretofore importers have been compelled to quarantine cattle at their own expense, and as the Canadian Government provided free accommodations, cattle which otherwise would have come directly to the United States have gone to Canada. Already, however, importers are making arrangements to bring cattle into Boston and Baltimore. There are eighty-five head of polled Angus cattle from Scotland quarantined in the Maine district. Sites for the New York and Philadelphia districts have not yet been selected.

STOCK PROSPECTS IN ARIZONA.—The Happy Valley ranch, owned by Charles Paige and the Meadow Valley ranch, owned by Don Sanford, have passed into the hands of other parties. The consideration for the first was $30,000 and for the latter $80,000. Messrs. Paige and Sanford are both well known in Tombstone, and many of our citizens are familiar with the properties sold. The transfers were made through Judge Silent, who, together with his associates, is the purchaser of the Sanford ranch. The Happy Valley ranch was bought for Walter Vail, who proposes to use it for the breeding of fine blooded stock. It is situated north of Pantano and lies between mountains in the shape of an ellipse the hills converging to within a quarter of a mile of each other at one end, furnishing the only egress. The water supply is centrally located and is abundant. The Sanford ranch is well known the country over and occupies the whole of the intervening country between the Empire ranch and Tully & Ochoa's ranch at Pantano. Both are to be heavily stocked, the one with pure bloods and the other with improved cattle.—*Epitaph.*

WHAT GRADE JERSEY COWS WILL DO.—Mr. J. H. Vannuys, Johnson County, Indiana, has a herd of ten grade Jersey cows, which yielded him the following gross receipts from milk, cream and butter during the months named for 1881: January, $63 45; February, $70 07; March, $89 38; April, $60 07; May, $66 38; June, $58 93; July, $61 00; August, $82 35; September, $63 99; October, $65 34; November, $93 96; December, $73 17. Total, $813 84; an average of $81 38 per cow per year, besides the calves and milk. With another cow added, his receipts for the first four months of this year have averaged $87 95 per month, from eleven cows. Grade Jersey cows thus pay splendidly in the dairy business.—*Indiana Farmer, Indianapolis.*

AN exchange says: Missoula, M. T. has a cow that has seen a good deal of country. Raised in Wisconsin, she emigrated to Illinois, and after a year or so returned again to her native stable, thence following her owner's fortunes through Wisconsin, Iowa and Minnesota, along the line of the Northern Pacific as it was built west to Bismarck, through Dakota to Miles City and Billings, M. T. Then leaving the starting locomotive behind she followed her owner's wagon on to Bozeman, Helena and Missoula. She is called Trampoline, and valued by her owner much higher than the $250 price named for her.

At a recent sale of black Polled Angus cattle, held at the Home Bazaar, Aberdeen, Scotland, American buyers secured nearly all the best things. The average price paid was about $250.

---

## Parturient Apoplexy.

Parturient apoplexy, more familiarly known as puerperal, or milk fever, is a very frequent, and usually fatal disease among dairy stock. The losses which annually occur from the ravages of this malady is a great set-back to the enterprising young farmer whose means are somewhat limited, and who cannot afford to lose a valuable cow. It is therefore of the greatest importance to study this disease in its various phases, in order to be prepared to grapple with it in its incipient or primary stage, or, what appears still more sensible, to take the necessary precautions to prevent, if possible, the frequency of those attacks. The usual victims of puerperal fever, or those who are most susceptible to the disease, are dairy cows in which the elements of milk is abundant. High feeding, want of sufficient exercise, and neglect in proper ventilation and cleanliness, are the prolific causes which facts are suggestive of the propriety of giving such than ordinary attention to the care and management of in calf stock during the period of gestation, and especially at the time of approaching parturition. The period of life at which the disease is most likely to occur, is at the time of the birth of the third calf, and the season of the year when the disease is most prevalent is during the months of July, August, and September. Especially is this the case with cows which have been running all summer on luxuriant pasture. The sudden change in the system of the cow at the time when the blood is well charged with the elements of nutrition, from her dangerous plethoric condition, is more than nature can endure. The blood, which a short time before was directed to the womb, for the growth of the fœtus in utero, is now directed to the udder for the sustenance of the young-born calf; and if at this important time the skin and udder should perchance fail to perform their important functions, we should not be surprised if a determination of blood to the brain should be the result, and either congestion of the blood-vessels or rupture of their coats, causing extravasation of blood in the brain, thus producing coma and its fatal consequences. We now come to that part of the subject which is so important to all husbandmen, especially stock raisers. We refer to the best means of preventing the disease. We should first endeavor not to encourage the secretion of milk by feeding a rich, succulent diet. Cows which have been running on rich pasture, and are in full condition, should be removed three or four weeks before calving to some barren pasture, and fed on dry food. This will have a tendency to diminish the secretion of milk at or about the time of calving, which is of great importance. If the change from wet to dry food has a tendency to constipate the bowels, a mild aperient may be given. In no case should the cow be milked before calving, unless it becomes an absolute necessity, as by premature milking the secretion of the mammary glands is unduly excited, and a more copious supply of milk encouraged, which should be carefully avoided. It is a well-known fact, that cows which calve with comparative ease, and clean promptly, are the usual victims. Cattle owners should therefore be very watchful of those particular subjects.

After the cow has calved, the flow of milk should be encouraged by frequent milking. If the cow is full-fat condition, a cathartic should be administered, and nothing but a mild laxative diet should be fed. Care should also be taken not to expose her to any sudden change of temperature, or to any undue excitement, until all danger has passed by.

The treatment of a case of parturient apoplexy will very much depend on the stage of the disease in which the animal may be found. In the early or primary stage, bleeding from the jugular vein is recommended. However, our chief aim should be to equalize the circulation, and use every means to divert the blood from the brain to some remote organs, by restoring the action of the skin, bowels, kidneys, mammary glands, etc. Ice may be applied to the head, if necessary; clothing may be used to restore the action of the skin. If the legs are cold they should be rubbed with some stimulant and bandaged with red flannel. A cathartic should be administered as early as possible: 1 lb. of Epsom salts, with ½ oz. each of gentian and ginger, dissolved in 1 pint of hot water, may be given at one dose; and half the quantity may be repeated every four hours until the bowels are freely evacuated. The action of the cathartic may be promoted by the frequent administration of soap-suds injections. In extreme cases, turpentine enemas have an excellent effect. The flow of milk should be encouraged by frequent manipulation of the udder. Mustard blisters may also be applied along the whole course of the spine—say every four hours. Stimulants may be given as soon as practicable—brandy, whisky, and the carbonate of ammonia, in small and frequent doses, have a very desirable effect. It is also very necessary that the patient should be well nursed. A well ventilated stall, with plenty of good bedding, is essential. It will be a good idea to bolster up the head to prevent her from injuring her horns, and at the same time facilitate the flow of blood from the brain.—*Live Stock Journal.*

MANAGEMENT OF HEIFERS.—Pregnant animals should be fed and watered regularly; they should have the best of food and purest of water; snow water, as well as stagnant water, and also icy water, should be entirely avoided. The care in this stable, as well as out of doors, should have particular attention. Thus a too narrow stall, slippery floor, narrow standing doors, improper ventilation, and drafts of cold air, should be avoided or guarded against. As to the quantity of food, so much should be given that both the organism of the mother can be sustained sufficiently to insure the healthy development of the fœtus, and also allow a surplus for the production of milk. A too large quantity of nutritive food should not be given; nor, as a general rule, but even will produce lean and weak calves. Musty, rusty and dusty hay, brewer's grain, swill, and much oil cake, turnips and beets should be avoided. The heifer, when nearing her time, may be placed in a roomy box-stall, well littered, and so arranged that the view of her companions is not entirely obscured; and when about to calve she should be watched, but not unnecessarily interfered with. When the afterbirth is dropped it should be removed immediately and buried.

Sheep need protecting from rain. A fleece of wool after it has become saturated with water is a cold blanket for the animal to wear, and it takes a long time to dry it. An amount of food which would be sufficient to keep a sheep with a dry fleece in a thrifty condition would scarcely be sufficient to enable one with wet fleece to "hold its own." Besides, the sheep with a wet fleece is liable to take cold. It does not pay to allow sheep to become wet.

Fattening hogs—Do not forget to give charcoal liberally. Pigs are apt to suffer from a disordered stomach, which is relieved by charcoal. An occasional handful of wood ashes and sulphur will also be found beneficial.

THE

# Breeder and Sportsman.

PUBLISHED WEEKLY BY THE

BREEDER AND SPORTSMAN PUBLISHING CO.

THE TURF AND SPORTING AUTHORITY OF THE
PACIFIC COAST.

OFFICE, 508 MONTGOMERY STREET

P. O. Box 1236.

*Five dollars a year ; three dollars for six months ; one dollar and a
half for three months. Strictly in advance.*

MAKE ALL CHECKS, MONEY ORDERS, ETC., PAYABLE TO ORDER OF
BREEDER AND SPORTSMAN PUBLISHING CO.

*Money should be sent by postal order, draft or by registered letter, ad
dressed to the "Breeder and Sportsman Publishing Company, San Fran
cisco, Cal."*

*Communications must be accompanied by the writer's name and address,
not necessarily for publication, but as a private guarantee of good faith*

JOSEPH CAIRN SIMPSON, - - - - EDITOR

ADVERTISING RATES.—Displayed 50 per inch each insertion 30 per
rata for less space. Reading Notices set in brevier type and having 50
cent marks, 50 cents per line each insertion. Lines will average ten
words. A discount of 25 per cent. will be allowed on 3 months, 30 per cent.
on 6 months and 36 per cent. on 12 months contracts. No extra rate
charged for cuts or setting of columns prose. No reading notice take for
less than 50 cents each insertion.

San Francisco, Saturday, November 18, 1882.

Mr. M. J. Henley is a duly authorized traveling agent
and correspondent for the "Breeder and Sportsman."

## FALL RACE MEETING.

The Pacific Coast Blood-Horse Association, as hereto
fore, is successful in giving satisfaction with the two days
races which have taken place. In all our acquaintance
with turf sports we never knew so many meetings to be
held, and, so many races run with so little carping and
fault-finding as has been the case. To assist in this the
Association have had the valuable aid of owners, trainers
and jockeys. We know of only one instance where there
has been a deviation from a straightforward course.
This has been mainly due to a high sense of honor
among those who have the horse in charge, and those
who are not guided by the only true principle are well
aware that transgression will be followed by exemplary
punishment. While every officer and every member of
the association had labored assiduously for the welfare of
the association, the President is entitled to the highest
praise for his exertions. He has been extremely liberal
in a pecuniary sense, he has been more than liberal in
leaving his business at any time and traveling long dis
tances to attend the meetings. From the locality of
Messrs. Finigan and Schwartz, of the Board of Trustees,
these gentlemen have been called upon to perform a great
deal of hard work, and this has been done so thoroughly
and cheerfully, that it may be that some do not appre
ciate the services rendered. The assistant Secretary has
done all the work of the office from the time he took pos
session, and previously was always ready and willing to
lend a helping hand. As it now stands there is a bright
prospect for the association, and it only requires the
spirit which has prevailed in the past to render it all that
the most sanguine could desire in the near future.

There is little necessity for writing much, in addition
to the full reports of the races decided.

There is not a dissenting voice among those who at
tended in pronouncing eulogies and there has been praise
from every tongue.

The races at all distances have been good, with few ex
ceptions, that on Wednesday last at heats of three-quar
ters of a mile is by far the best ever run in the United
States. Previous to that race the best on record was
that of Knight Templar at Louisville, May 24th, 1880,
when, with 92 pounds, he being three years old, ran
in 1:15, 1:17. The only approach in an aged horse is
when Egypt ran at the same place, carrying 118 pounds
in 1:16, 1:17. Even among the dashes there is nothing
that will take any great precedence, as there has been no
animal over three years which has run faster than 1:15,
and 1:14 is the "top notch." The two-year-old Bar
rett, by the same horse as Joe Howell, occupies the first
place inasmuch as he ran in 1:14 with 110 pounds up,
and Knight Templar who shares the honor of the same
figures, only carried 77 pounds though a year older.
The race which will afford the best comparison is that
run by Governor at Sheepshead Bay, Sept. 25th, 1880.
He was two years old and carried 98 pounds. He ran a
dead heat with Ada in 1:14½, and in the "run off" second
1:14½. But in accordance with the rules a dead heat in
a dash gives an interval of rest, all the races for the May
being interpolated, so that makes quite a difference. We
do not intend, however, to write about the horses until
the racing is finished, as there may be changes startling
enough to upset previous calculations. A race run may
be all that was needed to perfect the condition, and the
colt which was inferior in the races past be an entirely
different animal in those to come.

There is a grand bill for to-day, and with many indi
cations that the weather will be all that can be desired.

In the first place the hurdle race, postponed from last
Wednesday will probably take the place of the one set for
to-day, and that carried over until the last day.

The first race is for a purse of $100 ; a dash of seven-eighths
of a mile, $50 to the second horse ; entrance free ; the winner
of the three-quarter dash or three-quarters and repeat to carry
ten pounds extra ; winner of both events to carry fifteen
pounds extra.

Night Hawk, Garfield, Premium, Duke of Monday, Joe G,
Forest King, Bob, May D, Ella Doane, Haddington, Jim
Douglas, Jim Renwick, Fred Collier, Joe Howell, Atlanta,
Lizzie P.

Here is a problem for the acute to solve, a "nut to
crack" that will take strong jaws to crack and shell and
get at the meat. The fanatics must be considered and
then look at the list of names, but have not the least de
sire to venture a prediction.

The second is a purse of $250 ; heats of a mile, and an
eighth ; entrance free ; $50 to second horse ; maiden three-
year-olds allowed seven pounds ; four-year-olds twelve pounds ;
maidens five years old and over twenty pounds ; the winner
of the dash at this distance on the first day to carry five
pounds extra. Duke of Monday, Joe Dion, Lizzie Martin
Colt, Geo. Bender, Nathan Coombs, Belshaw, Precious, Fred
Collier, Joe Howell, Capt. Kidd, Judge McKinstry.

Here again is a puzzle, the allowances coming into
the calculation, and the race that follows.

Handicap purse of $250 for all three-year-olds ; a dash of a
mile and a quarter ; $25 each and $15 if declared ; the second
horse to receive $50. Garfield, Maria F, Forest King, In
auguration, Birdcatcher, Hattie B, Atalanta, Lizzie F, Jocko.

As will be seen all of these races are departures from
the regular schedule of weights and this always compli
cates matters, adding to the "glorious uncertainty" and
increasing the interest. As there is only one heat race to
take up the time, there is no question that there being plenty
of daylight for the hurdle race, in which there are named
claimed by those who have seen them exercise to be the
best jumpers on the coast.

There is some probability of the four-mile race being
postponed from Thursday until Saturday. To do this
it is necessary to obtain the consent of all the parties
interested. Should this be done due notice will be given
in the daily papers, and it will also afford us the oppor
tunity to discuss it in a manner commensurate with the
programme.

The advertisement in this paper, however, is sufficient
to convince the most exacting that it will be a great day,
though for that matter every day has been good, and as
the races progress there has been an improvement on the
preceding and this is sure to continue to the end.

No one who has the least friendship for the "royal
sport" can afford to miss one day.

## DECISIONS IN THE EMBRYO STAKES.

It is always an unpleasant task to us to write words
of condemnation, though there are cases where it be
comes a duty that cannot be avoided. There is no phase
of journalism which makes that duty so irksome as a
turf paper presents, and those who are in a position so
onerous, and at the same time so important, are called
upon to castigate when they fain would applaud.

The turf and track have many enemies. Bitter foes,
who eagerly seize every opportunity to denounce, and
who pluck over anything which brings the sport into
discredit. But an editor who seeks to apologize for
wrong-doing is out of place. He must be fearless as
the surgeon who cuts deeply to remove the cause of
disease, and with courage enough to probe the wound to
the bottom. No matter whether the offender is in high
station or low, punishment must follow. When there is
a deviation from that course he loses the respect of men
whose good opinion is beyond price. Though "thrift
may follow fawning" there will be manifest disdain for the
menial who self-encircles his neck with the collar of ser
vility, after having inscribed it with a mark which de
notes his thralldom.

We have promised our readers that this journal would
be a faithful guardian of the interests it represents.
That so far as we have the ability we would do all in our
power to elevate the sports which are the main feature,
and believing that great injustice was done in the de
cision rendered in the third heat of the three-year-old
race by the judges we cannot pass it without recording
our opinion, sincerely trusting that it may be a warning
to those who occupy the station in the future. As we
are directly and personally interested in the decision
which permitted Dawn to start in the yearling race, we
will not take that into consideration at present, the ar
gument coming more appropriately hereafter. There
was, however, a legitimate subject of criticism in the pro
ceedings after the filing of the protest, and that was the
shyster trick of seeking to counteract the protest founded
on a substantial basis with others which had not even a
shadow to build upon. The announcement from the
stand that there were protests against all of the starters
in the race was the flimsiest sort of a veil to convey a
wrong impression to those in attendance that all were in
error, and yet as despicable as it was false.

There is another point in this part of the proceedings.
Hon. J. McM. Shafter was the presiding judge. When

the evidence, or rather before the evidence was presented,
in place of hearing it, he at once became an advocate
for Dawn starting, and showed that as an attorney he
had studied the case and was fortified in his position by
previous councils. More than that, he upbraided us
with "being a great stickler for rules, and yet violated the
rules more than anyone." On being asked to instance one
violation he referred to the concurrence of opinion with
his associate judges in the case of the starting in the
"Maiden race," which is treated in another place, that
opinion having been solicited as to the meaning and
intent of the rule.

From having a colt in each of the races under discus
sion this personal matter forces itself into consideration,
and we wish our readers to distinctly understand that in
the yearling race the sustaining of the protest will give
us first and third money ; in the three-year-old there was
the slightest show to better, the position awarded if the
ruling had been otherwise.

A full and complete description of the race will be
included in the appropriate place so that there is no neces
sity for a recapitulation. The reason given for taking
the heat away from Fred Arnold was that his driver
shouted. That the rules do not grant the judges the
power to make such a decision can be shown so plainly
as to be easily comprehended by those who are the least
conversant with them, though that there was any breach
of this kind the driver emphatically denies, and this de
nial is supported by our own knowledge. Rule 47 reads :—

Rule 47—Loud Shouting—Sec. 1. Any rider or driver
guilty of loud shouting, or making other improper noise, or
of making improper use of the whip during the pendency of
a heat, shall be punished by a fine not to exceed $25, or by
suspension during the meeting. [See also Rule 48.]

In collating and publishing the rules the secretary of
the National Trotting Association saw fit to add refer
ences in brackets to the other rules which, in his opinion,
had a bearing on the subject and rule 48 is as follows :

Rule 48—"Fouls"—Sec. 1. If any act or thing shall be
done by any owner, rider, driver, or their horse or horses,
during any race or in connection therewith, which does rules
define or warrant the judges in deciding to be fraudulent or
foul, and if no special provision is made in these rules to
meet the case, the judges shall have power to punish the of
fender by fine not to exceed $100, or by suspension or expul
sion. And in any case of foul riding or driving they shall
distance the offending horse, unless they believe such a de
cision will favor a fraud.

Sec. 2. The penalty imposed herein for "fouls" shall ap
ply to any act of a fraudulent nature, and to any unprin
cipled conduct such as tends to debase the character of the
trotting turf in the estimation of the public. [See Rule 39,
Sections 4 and 5 ; Rule 39, Section 11 ; See also Rules 39, 46
and 47.]

While these references might mislead a person not
familiar with construing written language, a lawyer
trained to the business could scarcely miscomprehend the
connection. Rule 47 is explicit, defining the penalty of
loud shouting to be a fine not to exceed $25, or by
suspension during the meeting. Rule 48 distinctly
states "and if no special provision is made in these rules
to meet the case, the judges shall have the power to pun
ish, etc." Here is a special provision so definite that it
cannot be misunderstood by any one that has sense
enough to read.

We must apologize for offering other arguments that a
transcript of the rules, as it appears like underrating the
intelligence of our readers to do more. The references in
brackets at the close of Section 2, Rule 48, have reference
to rules in which there is not a clause bearing on this
point and it is useless waste of space to copy any part
of them.

By referring to the account of the heat it will be seen
that Fred Arnold got the lead before two hundred yards
had been trotted, that he rapidly drew away from the
other horses so that when Bonnie passed the half-mile
he was sixty yards, or more, in the lead ; that at the
time the shouting is stated to have occurred the filly was
gaining on him, and that she did not break or even "wab
ble" after she entered the homestretch. There was a
wide space between them, and any notice that the driver
of Fred Arnold made could not interfere with her. It
was claimed that in the second heat in the close contest
between Anteeo and Fred Arnold down the stretch
Hinds shouted fully as loud as in the third heat. In this
case we have the fullest knowledge and know
that the only "shouting" was words of encour
agement to his colt in tones that could not
come within the meaning of the rule, or be twisted
into a violation. We have been in many races and never
saw one where we thought the drivers drove more fairly.
There was no getting in each other's way, and when
Bonnie made the break Hinds at once pulled away so as
to give her driver every opportunity to get her back to
her trot. He did not "take the track" until he was
many lengths in the lead, and when he was so far in ad
vance that even "loud shouting" could work no injury,
he kept up the same words of encouragement to his colt,
proving that his only object was to accelerate his move
ment. But this is also a superfluous statement, as taking
it for granted that he did shout loudly the rules expressly

stipulate what the penalty shall be, and no amount of erratic quibbling can give any other construction. The mandatè is clear. A fine, not exceeding $25; or suspension during the meeting, awaits the offender. That Judge Shafter is not capable of rightly construing such plain language will scarcely be conceded by those who know him. We understand that one of his associates, Hon. A. P. Whitney, did not agree with him; we have ample testimony to that effect. To get a majority it was necessery that one should coincide, and Dr. Tisdale, a resident of the Sandwich Islands, was that one. As he was selected by Judge Shafter himself it may be that the choice was made for the purpose of having a coadjutor, inasmuch as he was overruled by being in a minority in the case that arose on the Bay District course last Saturday. Apart from the direct effect on the race in question, there are reasons to fear that it will be seriously detrimental in the future. A palpable wrong committed in the stand is far worse than the misdoings of the drivers. It takes away the confidence of owners and drivers, and thoroughly disgusts the spectators. In this case there was universal condemnation, and the winners as well as the losers joined in fervid denunciations of the verdict. There is not the slightest question but that the Board of Review would set the verdict aside. We mention the Board of Review as in this district Judge Shafter is a member of the Board of Appeals in which there is a vacancy so that it could not be decided. As we understand that measures have been taken to fill the vacancy this state of affairs will soon be remedied, and the questions can be adjudicated, virtually barred at present.

## BEEF AND STOCK CATTLE.

In the first issues of this paper we referred in several articles to the prospects of the cattle business and also invited correspondence from the different stockmen on the coast regarding prices, increase, and condition of their herds. We did this in order to give the various cattle men a general idea of the prices ruling over the coast. We invite you again. It is for your benefit and we will be happy to receive whatever information you can send us. Prices as a rule this fall have been very good. On a general average they are from fifty to sixty per cent. better than they were last season and at the present time beef of any description commands extra prices while A 1 is hard to be had at prices above our quotations. The weather has been most favorable for grass in some localities, but we do not look for any fat cattle from the southern coast before the middle of March. In the meantime Nevada must be our source of supply, and from the firmness which the cattle are held by the parties who are feeding, beef must be still higher before spring and we are greatly mistaken if next year will not be a most profitable one for stockmen. All over the country to-day the eyes of capitalists are looking with envy upon the business which during the last three or four years. upon a small capital has paid such large profits, and all who are fortunate enough to still hold their herds from the grasp of the large corporations, which during the last year have been buying all that were purchasable, have reason to be thankful, for the outlook to-day is most encouraging. Our next issue will contain a few of the large sales that have been made this fall, and also of the movements of certain large buyers.

## WHEN HEAT IS VOID.

Rule 50—If the start takes place on the wrong side of the starting post, or if no person officially appointed occupies the Judges' stand, the heat or race is void and must be run again—in twenty minutes, if the distance to be run is two miles or less, and in thirty minutes, if over two miles.

In the "Maiden Race" last Saturday were four starters. One of them, Bob Wooding, was extremely fractious, and it was rare good fortune that he did not injure the man who was managing him or the jockey, and also good luck to get as good a start as was effected. The horses were turned the proper distance back of the starting post. The starter shouted go before either was at the score, but owing to his anxiety in watching Bob he was slow in dropping the flag. When that fell two of the horses might have been past the line, the third behind, the fourth two or three lengths in the rear. With such a horse as Bob in, it was one of the best starts we ever saw. The meaning of the rule is too plain to waste time in argument, and again we will not imply that our readers have so little common sense as to require further elucidation, than to say that the distance was run, and that the start did not "take place on the wrong side of the starrting point."

## EDITORIAL NOTES.

**Another Richmond.**—Nick Covarrubias of Los Angeles sold another Richmond colt a few days since, the purchaser being Raymundo Olivas of Ventura county. The colt is a three-year-old of the true Richmond shade of iron grey and was transferred for a consideration of $1,000. He took the first premium in the roadster class at the Los Angeles fair. Since the performances of Romero have given an inkling of the qualities of Richmond as a sire there is a great desire among breeders to get an infusion of the blood.

**The Supreme Court** has been kind enough to give its august affirmation to the old principle that a horse is not a mare but a mare may be a horse. This great question was presented to the court for determination in the case of the People vs Pico, on appeal from the Superior Court of Santa Clara County. The defendant was convicted of stealing a horse and his counsel asked that the judgement of guilty be set aside because the animal was a mare. The Court declined to take that view of the matter and held that the term "horse" applied to the whole equine race without regard to sex. So that question is settled. Whether a man who surreptitiously abstracts a mule may be properly called a horse-thief is yet to be judicially determined.

**The late importations** by Gov. Stanford to the Palo Alto breeding farm includes Lula, b m, record 2:15, 18 years old, by Alexander's Norman, dam Kate Crockett by imported Hooton; brown yearling filly by Governor Sprague, dam Lula; weanling black filly by George Wilkes, dam Lula; Brunette, br m, 23 years old, by Rysdyk's Hambletonian, dam Kate by Bellair; May Queen, record 2:20, b m, 14 years old, by Alexander's Norman, dam Jennie by Crockett's Arabian; Gazellé, record 2:21, b m, 17 years old, by Rysdyk's Hambletonian, dam Hattie Wood by Sayre's Harry Clay; bay filly, 4 years old, by Hambletonian Prince, dam Gazelle, and a brown yearling filly by Gov. Sprague, dam Gazelle.

**Another chance for the colts** to trot before the year 1882 comes to a close is contemplated. It is proposed to open a stake for three-year-olds, heats of two miles, $250 each, and a stake or purse for two-year-olds. The owner of Anteeo has signified his acceptance, and should the stake fail in getting three nominations, he will match him against any three-year-old for the same amount. Dr. Hicks will engage Pride, and it certainly seems that both should meet the approval of the owners.

**Orrin Hickok** is on his way west with St. Julian and Overman and report says he will challenge Romero for a match with Overman, Probably he will be accommodated and if such a match is made it will result in a hot and exciting contest. There has been no race on this coast for years that will attract such general public attention and we hope the report of Hickok's intention is true,

**The chestnut gelding Ashley**, record 2:25½ was sold at auction by Killip & Co. at the Bay District track last Thursday. R. F. Morrow was the purchaser at $1500. At the same sale the gray stallion Silverthreape by the Moor was disposed of to Henry White for $335. Ten head of brood mares and colts from the Coutts farm were sold for fair prices to various buyers.

**L. U. Shippee** of Stockton has purchased in the East a car load of Daniel Lambert mares and they are now on the way here. They will be taken to Mr. Shippee's ranch in the San Joaquin valley and California will thus keep pace with the fashion, for Daniel Lambert mares are in active demand with the eastern breeders nowadays.

**The brown stallion Buccaneer**, by Iowa Chief, now the property or Mr. G. Valensin, is quartered at the Bay District track where he has been placed in charge of J. A. Goldsmith to be trained. Buccaneer has shown a trial in 2:19½, and if he can escape a recurrence of an unfortunate lameness will speedily take rank with the fast trotters.

**In the report** of the race of three quarter-mile heats at the Blood Horse meeting, which appears on the second page, by a typographical error Night Hawk is given as carrying 125 pounds. It should read 115 pounds. The forms containing that portion of the paper were printed before the mistake was discovered.

**We are informed** by a private letter from New York that the mare Yellow Dock which made a mile with running mate at Providence, R. I., last week in 2:11 will probably be wintered in California and will be in the field for matches with Overman, Romero, and others of that class.

**Charlie D.**—John Hope of Santa Barbara has become the owner of the trotter Charlie D, having purchased him of N. A. Covarrubias of Los Angeles last week for $1,250. Charlie D has a record of 2:36 and won the race for the 2:30 class at the Los Angeles fair this fall.

**The Auction Sale** of thoroughbred stock belonging to W. L. Pritchard announced for last Thursday was postponed on account of the sickness of Mr. Pritchard. It will take place next Tuesday, the 21st inst., in frout of the Club Stables, Taylor street near Geary.

**Sale of a Richmond Colt.**—N. A. Covarrubias of Los Angeles has sold to T. B. More of Santa Barbara a grey gelding two years old, sired by A. W. Richmond and giving promise of making a fine horse. The price paid was $600.

THE BREEDER AND SPORTSMAN.—We have received in exchange the new California sporting paper with the above title. It is a handsome paper ably edited and will doubtless prove very popular. It is edited by Joseph Cairn Simpson, and is issued weekly from 508 Montgomery St., San Francisco, at $5.00 per anum.—*Maine Horse Breeders' Monthly.*

The largest combined butter aud cheese factory in the world, it is said, is located at Tremont, Nebraska.

## Merino Sheep.

This variety of sheep were imported originally into France and Spain. They were placed upon the government farm at Rambouillet, where every care was given them, and the greatest attention paid to increasing their produce of fleece. After years of experimenting, the animals were increased in size and weight nearly one hundred per cent., and the wool from twenty to twent-five. The fiber did not improve as was desired, but the attempt to combine in the same animal meat qualities as well as wool-bearing ones was assigned as the reason. During these experiments the sheep grew very large, were enormous feeders, but they lost those characteristics of wool bearers, and they were no longer as robust. Subsequent breeding has, however, not only restored them to their original excellence, but improved their wool growth on the ram about seventy-five per cent., and the ewes sixty-six. It required good management and about ninety years to accomplish this feat. The French were the first to produce a Merino combing wool, though subsequently they found rivals in America, Germany and Australia. The only difference between the breeds in the several countries is that the French ones still have larger carcasses.

*D. C.* Collins of Connecticut was the pioneer importer of Merino sheep in America. Stock breeders eagerly sought the new variety, hoping to improve their flocks, but were in most cases disappointed on account of the imported stocks being selected from those flocks which had been bred to increase their weight and carcass, and not those where that policy had not been followed. Later importations disproved any prejudice that the first one might have created against the breed. Numbers of them have found their way to California, where their success has been unparalleled. A Mr. Robert Blackerd of Calaveras county clipped from one of his a sixteen-months fleece which weighed fifty-one and a half pounds; the same animal clipped a forty-six-pound fleece at two years old. It is only just to say, however, in this connection that the climate of California being so dry, the wool retains a greater amount of oil than in other countries where the rainfall is large.

Mr. J. B. Ray, in an address to the New York Merino Sheep Breeders' Association, had the following to say on the points of Merino sheep:

"But few persons would prefer a staple of more than two and one-half inches for a ram, while many would be contented with a two-inch staple of highly crimped wool, provided the maximum density of fleece had been reached. Comparative evenness of fleece with as little glare as possible is an important point reached by our western breeders. Experience has fully demonstrated that great weight of fleece can be combined with the highest physical development, constitutional vigor and other points of perfection as indicated above. As to the point of oil, or yolk, the greatest amount that can be secreted without impairing the vitality of the animal is admissible in a ram. Most breeders prefer a coloring bordering on a buff, while thin, sticky oil of a greenish cast is highly objectionable. As to folds or wrinkles, which is a distinctive feature of the American Merino type, there might be a diversity of opinion as to size, location and number. Still it would be difficult to find a ram of such heavy pendulous neck, tail and flank as would disqualify him as a stock animal in any flock, while many would prefer that with the above he should have a large fold extending across the point of the shoulder, a considerable number on the sides extending in massive preportions well under and nearly across the belly, yet diminishing well in size and lost to view in full fleece before reaching the back, with numerous large folds lengthwise across the hips and stifles."

Those who fancy the delaine type are aiming in the main to secure the same points of American Merinos, while at the same time securing a longer staple of high quality of wool. As to folds or wrinkles, a good neck, tail and flanks are about all that is desirable, with little or none on the body. Thus we have before us a pen sketch of our ideal rams of the American and delaine Merino types.

ELECTRIC LIGHT IN THE CARS.—Persons in the rear car of a local train leaving Jersey City at 7:38 o'clock p. m. recently, on the Pennsylvania Railroad, were surprised at the ease with which they read their evening papers, and discovered with manifest pleasure that it was lighted by electricity. In the car were several guests, invited by Colonel J. R. Hosmer of the Light and Force Company of this city to inspect the new light, a trip being made to Newark. The car was lighted by seven incandescent lamps of the Edison make, fed from thirty Faure accumulators, which were placed in two boxes underneath the car, one on each side. The cells were a part of the number brought over from Europe on the steamship Labrador, and which were fully described in the *Times* of May 13, 1882, together with the method of their working. Each cell is 11½ inches in length and 5¼ inches in breadth, and 11 inches in depth. They are connected in a series, the main circuit to the lamps leaving the battery at the extreme ends. The boxes in which they were placed are seven feet six inches in length and sixteen inches wide. From a switch in the closet of the cars the lights can be turned on or extinguished, while each lamp is provided with a switch socket, so that it can be used independently of the other lamps. The wires pass from the batteries along the sides of the cars crossing over to each other where the lamps are placed.

The lamps in the cars give a steady, powerful light of twelve-candle power, and when the train was going at full speed did not flicker in the least. When half the lights were turned out there was no appreciable difference in the total light of the car, except that it was softer and more pleasant to read by. The heat from the lamps was about one-fifth the amount produced by gas. The electricity stored in the accumulators under the car is sufficient to keep all the lights running for sixteen hours without recharging. The car on the Pennsylvania road is the first that has been lighted in this country, and the light has been in use but two weeks, and has proved satisfactory. It is lighted on the same principle as the London limited express between London and Brighton, England, where it has been in use for several months.—*New York Times.*

The story of F. F. Burt's two-year-old Clydesdale, that weighs 1,110 pounds, is quite eclipsed by a correspondent in another column, who tells of some lusty youngsters bred and raised on the ranch of Moses Hopkins in Sutter county. Of these, two, aged two years and three months, weighed respectively, 1,418 and 1,437 pounds, or at the rate of 54¼ pounds per month; a third, a filly at fifteen months, tipped the beam at 1,015 pounds, or 67¾ pounds per month, and a stallion twelve months old weighed 1,050 pounds, or 87½ pounds per month. These colts were Percherons, and up to date are the greatest specimens of their kind on record here.

Dr. Voelcker reports that sixty-five Shorthorn cows averaged a milk yield of 642 gallons or 2568 quarts per annum, the food being grass and hay, with roots and straw in winter.

## THE GUN.

### "Did You Meet an Injun?"

Such is frequently the phrase used by certain persons on the Pacific Slope when they see an acquaintance returning to town laden down with grouse and other game birds, or "toting" a deer on his shoulders. To sensitive sportsmen it sounds so exceedingly sarcastic that they resent it by saying: "No; but I've just met a fool who belongs to an Old Maid's Club and asks silly questions," whilst others take it good naturedly and answer promptly in the affirmative, adding at the same time, that they had to kill the Siwash to get the birds.

The phrase has really a reason for existence, aside from its sarcasm, as the following incident will show: Two temporary residents of Olympia, W. T., one of whom was an author, and the other a public singer, decided one day to supply the Tacoma Hotel, at which they were stopping, with all the grouse the guests would need for a month. With this laudable object in view they engaged an Indian for the sum of one dollar to paddle them two miles down Puget Sound, and land them on a wooded promontory which was said to be "chock full" of grouse.

On stepping ashore they made preparations for an immediate slaughter of the feathered denizens of the forest, but as the day was very hot the birds had sought refuge in the highest trees, where it was almost impossible to see them, owing to the harmony of hue existing between their plumage and the foliage of the huge conifers. After tramping about for an hour and failing to find anything worth shooting, except a squirrel, the singer, who was no other than the comedian, Charles Vivian, now dead, suggested that they separate and work toward the town, to see if they would have any better luck.

The author, suspecting his motive in making the suggestion, assented to it immediately, so each took his own route homeward. Vivian made tracks for town as fast as his legs cared to carry him, while the author strolled about in the dense shrubbery, carefully peering into every clump for the sign of a grouse or a deer. Finding his efforts unavailing, he walked slowly homewards until he reached the long bridge that crosses Puget Sound opposite the town, and there he entered an Indian village to study its home life of the savage.

While he was looking around a smoke-filled wigwam of mats, he saw a large string of grouse lying on a bear robe in a corner.

Knowing that his companion would buy birds from any Indian he met rather than return with an empty bag, the author decided to play the same game, so he asked the wizened hag who was smoking a pipe in the middle of the hut how much she wanted for the lot. "Laketolik," was the answer, "Closh," exclaimed the author as he handed her the money; then shouldered three braces of birds and hurriedly started out into the fresh air. He looked very important and he trudged through the main street of the town, and to all persons who asked: "Did you meet an Injun?" he smilingly responded: "You bet, and a good one too."

On approaching the hotel he met an Indian who had often seen him and Vivian together, and who therefore presumed to ask him if the comedian was good pay. "What is the matter?" asked the addressed, in a very suspicious tone, the Siwash then told him that Vivian had bought a string of grouse from him, but had not paid for them, he being short of change. He had told him, however, to call at the hotel for his money. "You'll get it beyond doubt," observed the author, as his face beamed with the anticipated fun he would have in exposing his companion's nefarious mode of securing birds, and thus deceiving his innocent friends and acquaintances.

"Come along with me," said he to the Indian in classic Chinook, as he led the way to the hotel. He entered it through the back door, gave his birds to the cook, and told him to keep them concealed until they were wanted. He then requested the Indian to go to the front of the house, and wait there until called for. Leaving the savage to obey orders, the plotter walked into the bar-room and there saw the comedian, surrounded by a group of admiring loungers, who were listening with apparently intense interest to his description of how he had shot every bird of the nine brace of grouse that lay on the counter. The cause of this interest in his tale was soon made evident by his asking them to "pizen" themselves, an invitation which was promptly accepted by all.

After "pizening" themselves, which they did with great relish and the sensuous lip smacking of veteran "pizeners," Vivian resumed a description of his shooting exploits, telling how he had knocked those grouse down with a "right and left," and bagged two on the top of a fir tree at least two hundred feet high. Exclamations of wonder and delight greeted this statement, and increased as he, with a seriousness peculiarly his own, told of his doughty deeds. The author, who stood close beside him, although his presence was not known, asked him, after all the wonderful shots had been described, what he had killed the birds with.

The unexpected question, and from such a source, disconcerted him very much for a few moments, but he soon recovered his wits, and promptly answered: "With powder and shot."

"How many cartridges did you take out?" asked the pen driver.

"Thirty," was the answer.

"Then, allowing that you killed the nine brace in ten shots, you have twenty shells left.

"I've only got fifteen left."

Seeing his cartridge-box lying on the table, the author requested one of the loungers to see what number it contained, and by that means decide how many shots it required to kill the birds. The comedian objected strongly to this, but the crowd, seeing a chance for more drinks in the matter, overruled his objections, and one of them counted the cartridges in a most deliberate manner. When he finished he announced that there were twenty-nine shells left, and, therefore that Mr. Vivian had either killed eighteen birds with one shot, which was simply pot-hunting, and, ergo, a crime against true sport; or that he had stolen them, which was a crime against morality; or that he had bought them from a Siwash, which was a crime against all the statutes of the Territory, because such conduct was liable to deceive innocent whites; and, finally, that his celebrated shots were fibs, so that he was a criminal in any case. He then asked what ought to be done to such a man.

"Fine him the drinks," exclaimed half a dozen simultaneously. The comedian objected to this summary fine unless they could prove their charges.

"Can any one bring direct proof against him?" asked the self-appointed judge.

The author said he could, and, stepping outside the door, he led the red vendor of grouse before the court. On seeing the comedian he extended his hand, and, with a scowl on his face said: "Nika tickey moxt tolla" ("I want three dollars").

This elicited roars of laughter from the crowd, and without even waiting to be invited they waltzed up to the counter and asked for what fluids they wanted. The comedian paid the Indian in a hurry, threw down five dollars for the fluids, and balanced out of the house as rapidly as if he had been fired from a catapult. His guests cheered him as he disappeared, then blandly informed the landlord that they would "use up" that five dollars on "tarantula juice," before they left the place.

They then congratulated the author on the able manner in which he had exposed the nefarious plot of his companion and invited him to share in their refreshments.—Turf, Field and Farm.

### A Challenge.

The Sacramento Bee has the following to say of the challenge recently sent to the Forester Gun Club of that city: The O'Neill Gun Club of San Joaquin county has challenged the Forester Club of this city to a $500 pigeon match. We understand that the challenging club has recently been organized by consolidation with the Stockton Gun Club, and if so the members cannot reasonably expect the Foresters to accept the challenge. Both the O'Neills and Stocktons had a number of first-class trap-shots, and by consolidating they are enabled to select a team of fifteen fit to shoot against any team of a like number in the United States. They are all in practice, also, while the Foresters are not. The latter club is not, we understand, averse to shooting a match with either of the old clubs, but do not think it quite an even thing when the latter join forces. They should at least allow the challenged team to select a team from the county, as they have done. It is not an easy matter for a club with a membership of twenty-five or thirty to put a team of fifteen good trap-shooters in the field. The Foresters might select a team of six or eight men who could hold their own in any company, but unless allowed to recruit from another club they would not be wise in accepting the challenge sent them. Besides the stakes are too high. Five hundred dollars is too much money to be involved in the result of a match which ought to be of the most friendly character. It smacks too much of gambling. At most the sum should not exceed $100 or $150, or say enough to cover the expenses of the affair and provide a banquet for all concerned. If our Stockton friends will modify the terms of their challenge, we have no doubt the Foresters would take the chances of a match.

DUCKS.—We are occasionally led into wondering why more ducks are not bred and marketed among our poultry breeders in America. We have now in this country three or four varieties of imported ducks, at the head of which the Pekins stand to-day, without question, for size, early maturity, hardness and thrift. The Aylesbury (pure white, like the Pekin), and the Cayuga (black), are notable and of good quality. Each of these varieties, within our knowledge, has been successfully bred in New England, upon a country place where there was neither pond nor rivulet for their amusement on the farm. The ducklings were hatched under hens, and the ducks were raised with the other poultry, and fowls on the estate, with similar feed and care, the owner claiming that for marketing purposes ducks can be reared, like any other fowls, upon dry land, and he has found no perceptible difference in their proportionate thrift during the season, though in his experiments in the last two years his ducks never had access to any body of water. A pleasanter kind of poultry to keep we do not know of.—American Poultry Yard.

Archery is again being revived in this city and vicinity. For a long time the bow and arrows have remained unused and unstrung, but on next Thanksgiving Day there will be a match shot in which five or six teams will participate and where the superiority of marksmanship of the eastern or western bowmen will be decided. There will be at least two teams of California shots, four men to each team. The California teams are from the Pacific Archery Club and the Oakland Bow Club; there may be another team entered but it is not a fact as yet. The above mentioned archers are to shoot against the Highland Park Club and the Northside Archers of Chicago, weather permitting. The last is an important proviso. In the terms of the match as the weather in the east is very unreliable about Thanksgiving Day. The match is simply a friendly contest. The scores will be forwarded by mail or telegraph to each club and compared to decide who is the winner.

BIG SHOT.—Wednesday of last week four of the Davis crowd of hunters fired a volley into a flock of geese they caught in the act of rising from a pond. They only fired one shot each. As a result they gathered sixty-three dead birds and lost eight that were slightly wounded. That would be a good squad to hunt "moonshiners."—Gridley Herald.

At Johnstown, in Burlington county, New Jersey, lie the extensive game preserves of Mr. Pierre Lorillard, the famous turfman, who finds the sports of the field as attractive as the performances of his thoroughbreds. The preserves cover an area of several hundred acres, and a number of ponds, well stocked with game fish, are interspersed. The varieties of game are numerous, and include several foreign species, notably English pheasants. The pinnated grouse or prairie chicken, not, perhaps, to be found elsewhere in the Eastern States, lives and thrives on the large preserve. Quail, ruffed grouse and wild fowl are abundant. As a model game preserve the place compares favorably with some of the finest in Great Britain.

It may be well for sportsmen and others to know that the seemingly senseless phrase ending with "the goose hangs high," is a corruption of an old phrase, viz: "The goose honks high," and has reference to the sounding clangor of the wild goose squadrons winging their way northward in serene springtime, or southward in the autumn, when "everything is lovely."

Mr. F. Ladd at Alviso bagged fifteen ducks last Sunday. Two gentlemen in the same locality got thirty-one English snipe. At the same place and time Fred Johnson and a friend bagged seventy-five ducks. Though a good many hunters were at Alviso the shooting was exceptionally good, fifteen birds being the average of ducks killed.

At the regular meeting of the Gilroy Rod and Gun Club on the 8th the following gentlemen were proposed and unanimously elected members: Messrs. Sam Rea, Henry Reeves, Louis Loupe, T. B. Thomas, A. D. Tyson, Jas. F. Dunne, G. E. Henssey, P. B. Wilmarth and Charles Eisley.

Geese are very plentiful in the vicinity of Denverton, and upon the plains of Suisun.

### The Gun.

No longer have our hunters any cause for complaining. If they go out hunting now and return without any game it is because they don't know how to shoot and have left their purses at home. The rains that fell on the hills at the first of the month drew thousands of ducks from the marshes and coast away to feed on the young grass that sprung up on the hillsides, leaving the would-be sportsman with plenty of cartridges and no game. But during the last week or ten days the severe frosts have made it so uncomfortable as to drive the feathered wanderers from hills back to the marshes and bay. Since the cold snap the hunting has been better by far than it has been before this season. More game has been brought into the market this week than there has been before this year; between 350 and 400 sacks of ducks, averaging 40 birds to the sack, have been received by the commission merchants.

Last Sunday every early boat or train was loaded with hunters bound for the different hunting grounds that lay within a few hours' ride of the city; a great many started out the evening before, Saturday, in order to be on the grounds the first thing in the morning. Nearly all met with good success and the return trains and boats brought back satisfied crowds of hunters, dirty guns, quarrelling dogs and well-filled bags. The stories told by the hunters on the trains of their day's exploits would make one think "truth is stranger than fiction"—at least, that is, a stranger to the narrators. The reports from all parts of the country are the most encouraging, and at the present it promises to continue so to be during the remainder of the season.

### Up the River.

Fourteen members of the Union Island Club were at their preserve at Union Island last Sunday. The ducks are quite plentiful but they fly rather high. Canvasbacks are just beginning to come in in earnest. Ramon Wilson bagged four. Captain Goodall and Howard Black bagged one hundred and ten small ducks between them besides several mallards. The party, fourteen in number, bagged over three hundred ducks; the birds are all in the very best condition. The feed on the marshes and around the ponds is, excellent, and the cold weather promises to drive the ducks from the hills back again to the marshes.

One rather amusing occurrence took place, which, though at another's discomfiture, caused a general laugh. Mr. C. Kaeding was shooting from a very small boat. Maybe the boat was too small for Mr. Kaeding or else Mr. Kaeding was too large for the boat; at any rate Mr. Kaeding arose to get a shot at a pair of widgeon that were flying overhead, when in his excitement he lost his equilibrium, and after performing a war dance on the seats of the rocking cockle-shell, grasping wildly at nothing with one hand and flourishing his gun like a disabled windmill, he and the boat parted company. The boat shot backward like a race shell, while the gunner did a grand summersault and plunge act into the water which was a decided infringement on Dr. Boynton's original high water bag. For all this mishap Mr. Kaeding had the satisfaction of killing more snipe than any others of the party.

The marshes at Petaluma every Sunday are covered with hunters from San Francisco as well as from the adjoining country town. There is excellent hunting ducks of all kinds are flying all the time and good bags made by all who have the least idea of how a gun should be handled.

Capt. Stackpool, M. Wright and Mr. Putman last Sunday were over at Warm Springs and bagged 66 quail. The shooting is very good in this vicinity as hunters have not been over the hunting grounds as much recently as they did on the opening of the season.

Last Tuesday evening 295 sacks of game, most of which were ducks from the Sacramento and San Joaquin rivers. This is the largest day's receipts of this year or in fact of many years.

There were at least one hundred hunters at the wharf at Bird's point last Sunday, all of whom got a few ducks as a remuneration for the amount of ammunition wasted.

One gentleman at Mallard Station recently bagged four dozen English snipe. There is better hunting at this preserve than there has been at any time this year.

The snipe shooting at Alvarado last Sunday was very good. Mr. Gillette, president of the California Club, returned with the largest bag of the day.

Geese are said to be plentiful on Point Reyes, and canvasback ducks are coming in good numbers to the mouth of Salmon creek, near Olema.

There is good shooting to be had at San Pablo. Mr. Wilson and friend returned with twelve ducks, the result of a few hours' hunting.

Mr. A. Adams on the Brooklyn marshes last Sunday bagged fifteen ducks and several canvasbacks, all over-flying birds.

Mr. E. T. Bent and Mr. Stickney last Sunday were at the Cordelia Club's preserve and killed 55 ducks.

Reports from Ventura county are to the effect that game of all kinds is very abundant.

English snipe are plentiful in the Sonoma marsh below the Stage depot.

Last Sunday Mr. W. Golcher was at Alviso and killed thirty ducks.

PIGURS AFFECTED BY BLACKLEG.—The Dayton, Nev., Times says: "The cattle disease, blackleg, is caused by a cane-shaped parasite which enters the blood usually through the digestive organs. This animalcule was not at first supposed dangerous to man; but it is of a very low order and changes its habits of life readily. A few cases have occurred in the East, where men become victims of the disease, either through eating the meat of diseased animals or by accidental contact. The disease has been prevalent among the cattle in the eastern part of the State, and a number of Indians in the agricultural valleys are suffering from something which greatly resembles it. The anthrax parasite was discovered in the blood of a man who died with symptoms similar to blackleg, and there is scarcely a doubt that what is now affecting the Indians is the same malady, as they have been eating freely of the meat of cattle which were infected."

The ammonia exhaled from stables tends to make harness brittle. A little glycerine added to the grease with which harness is oiled will keep the leather soft and pliable,

# THE RIFLE.

## The International Rifle Match, 1883.

The Sub-Committee on the return International Rifle Match, and the Executive Committee of the National Rifle Association of America, at the joint meeting of Oct. 17, decided to request the British Rifle Association to so modify the terms of the International rifle contest that an American team would have some slight chance of winning the contest at Wimbledon in July, 1883. The following is the text of this letter, which was forwarded to the British N. N. A. on Wednesday, Nov. 1:

New York, Oct. 21, 1882.

To the Council of the National Rifle Association of Great Britain. *Gentlemen:* In accepting the original condition of your association in order to make the International match possible, especially the pledging of a return match by us, which you were unwilling to undertake, it is needless to disguise the fact that concessions were made by the National Rifle Association of America that were at variance and incompatible with American conceptions of progress in military arms; but in order to infuse new life into rifle practice, and a stimulus into the proposed competition, a large majority of the Board of Directors of our association surrendered what they considered valuable modern mechanical appliances, which are calculated to ensure greater accuracy in military rifles.

The first stage of the match has been completed by your achieving a splendid victory at Creedmoor—every condition in the contest was assuredly to your advantage. This uneven match has a dual object: First—that of creating a friendly rivalry between two great nations. Second—The bringing to a greater degree of perfection modern breech-loading military weapons. On the latter important subject please refer to enclosed copy of a paper read by Col. Bodine.

Our victories in former competitions of an international character were achieved with fine sporting or small bore match rifles, with quite perfect front and rear sights; with these special weapons we have invariably been successful, and, indeed, thoroughly believe that it would be a difficult undertaking for any nation to wrest from us our honorably-won laurels.

Military weapons with primitive open sights have not, with us, received the same attention from scientific or expert gunmakers as our fine match rifles; your own special military breech-loader is unquestionably superior to any military rifle in our country at present; the same observation refers to ammunition. Our defeat will undoubtedly lead to the production of an excellent weapon in the course of time. It we failed in this it would certainly be the first instance in our national history that we acknowledged ourselves unequal to a fair task in mechanics. At all events what we now ask is, that the return match be shot under more equal terms. By adopting the wind-gauge your team are accorded equal privileges. We are co-partners in any change of terms. We require the enlistments to be extended to Jan. 1, 1883, which rule is as much your property as ours. We ask for a modified barley-corn front sight because we know that it is an improvement on your own sight (and you have practically admitted this by notifying us that it will not be allowed at Wimbledon). Therefore, it must be apparent to you that what you demand in the return match is essentially an advance on the terms of the preliminary competition; besides, taking the suggestions as an entirety, they represent improvements in military rifles.

The most powerful reasons, however, for this change are also summed up in the statement that you have some three thousand (3,000) marksmen from which to select a team of twelve or fourteen, whilst we (who are in our infancy at the longest range, where we never had practice before with military guns until a few months before the actual match took place) have no more than one hundred (100) who could possibly use a military weapon at all the distances enumerated.

Therefore, we reiterate, in order to pledge ourselves to a return match, we made concessions that were disadvantageous to our marksmen, and in return we now urgently and respectfully request that you, in the interest of rifle practice, improved weapons, and future contests, grant us the following modifications and alterations as a recompense for our unqualified defeat:

First—The use of the wind-gauge.

Second—The use of the barley-corn sight, of practical design, with at the base, as approved by the War Department in 1879, in use in the United States Army, and as approved by the National Guard of various States.

Third—Enlistments on or before Jan. 1, 1883, to make National Guardsmen eligible.

An early reply will be appreciated, as our time is limited. Yours, George J. Seabury, Sec'y.

## The Rifle.

This week our local riflemen have been very quiet. Last Sunday some of the boys of the Second Regiment were at Shell Mound practicing but no matches of any consequence were shot.

Quite a number of men of Companies A, C, D, and E of the Second Regiment are practicing at the 500-yard targets. The inspector of Rifle Practice on the first Sunday of every month will have one or two targets open to anyone of the Second Regiment who is anxious to improve as a marksman.

It is understood that a friendly shooting match is to come off at a near day between Corporal Townsend of Company B and Lieut. McElhinney. The Corporal's good score at the last regimental shoot gives him high hopes of victory. Lieut. McElhinney is not a bad shot either.

In the First and Second Regiments a move is being made to create an interest in shooting among the younger members and those who do not belong to the teams. It is proposed that the riflemen be divided into two or three classes, and the men in order to remain in their respective classes must make a certain per cent. Those making the required per cent. will wear a medal or badge during the time that they make the required scores. As soon as one loses his interest and drops below the standard his medal or badge is taken away from him and given to one who will make the per cent. Some of the companies of the Second Regiment propose to give a medal to the person who shall hold the highest score for a certain length of time. The plan of wearing an ornamented button or red, white and blue badge will be sufficient to bring to the front a large number of men who, though at present ignorant of the handling of the rifle, may nevertheless, in time, develop into first-class riflemen. Probably from now on the sand hills at Shell Mound will be plowed with flying lead of embryo sharpshooters guns, but then it is practice that is the making of the boys. For a week or two the First Regiment will take hold of this matter in earnest.

---

The members of the California Rifle Association are still agitating the idea of getting a range of their own. It is proposed that a stock company be formed and shares sold to obtain sufficient capital to carry out the project. This important matter should receive the attention and co-operation of riflemen and teams. In fact it will succeed, for anything that Colonel Dickinson undertakes never turns out to be a failure.

Army Rifle Contest.—The army rifle-contest at Fort Leavenworth, Kansas, closed Oct. 27, the Atlantic Division taking the first medal. Generals Sherman and Sheridan, Senator and Mrs. Logan, and Major-General Pope were present. The following is the total score for the three days: Sergeant Barrett, Atlantic, 257; Sergeant Clark, Pacific, 256; Sergeant Daly, Atlantic, 248; Private Harrington, Pacific, 240; Lieut. Homer, Atlantic, 238; Sergeant James, Missouri, 236; Sergeant Stanton, Maine, 236; Sergeant Ship, Missouri, 234; Lieut. Meriam, Missouri, 229; Sergeant Bentley, Missouri, 229; Private Westgraff, Missouri, 228; Private O'Keeffe, Pacific, 222. The medals were presented to the winners by General Sherman on the parade ground before all the troops in the garrison.

The Pacific Coast Trophy won by the Nevada team at the California Rifle Association's last tournament is on exhibition in Carson City. It is admired by all, and there is considerable local pride felt in the team that won it.

## Ostrich Farming.

The New York *World* has discovered a man who is about to try the experiment of ostrich farming in the United States. In its issue of the 7th inst. it reports an interview with him:

Twenty-two ostriches, ten male and twelve female, were taken to Central Park yesterday by Dr. Prothre, who will keep them there until he has selected a suitable place for an ostrich farm in America. The price of ostrich feathers—all of which are imported and pay 30 per cent. duty—is very high, and in order to supply the trade a farm was started about four years ago at Hoboken by Mr. Charles Reiche. There were only six birds on the farm and for awhile they thrived very well, but suddenly the birds began to fall sick and in a short time all of them were dead. They were diseased and it was found that they had gained fat rapidly but not strength.

Dr. Prothre was found yesterday aboard the steamship Horpom, now lying in the East River, and was asked by the reporter about his birds. "We arrived from Buenos Ayres Wednesday," said Dr. Prothre, "having the twenty-two ostriches on board. These birds are part of a large cargo recently shipped by me from the southern part of Africa to Buenos Ayres. They are all about eight years old. Some of them have bred and the others are now ready to breed, but the cold weather will stop them from doing so. You probably want to know why I have brought the birds to this country. I will tell you. I have a large farm in Buenos Ayres and have been extensively exporting ostrich feathers from there. The birds there are all brought from Africa. The idea now is to start a similar farm here in the United States. I will shortly go through the Southern States and select a place for a farm. The birds can live here in any place where the temperature does not fall five degrees below the freezing point. Feathers are now sent from Africa and after 30 per cent. tariff is paid there is still a good profit, so you can see what a profit there will be if we can raise birds here. I think, too, that the birds will multiply faster here than in South Africa, for there a drought frequently kills three-quarters of one's stock. I have known years there when not one drop of rain has fallen during the entire twelve months. Food is also very scarce in South Africa. Mr. Baker, the United States Consul at Buenos Ayres, was the first person who gave me the idea of starting an American ostrich farm. If I am successful I will start extensive farms and will guarantee cheaper prices and much more elegant feathers than are now seen on ladies' hats on Broadway."

"What is one of your ostriches worth?" asked the reporter.

"I value them at $1,400 each. They are very dear, but their feathers are of a much finer kind than any in New York. Feathers in general are here taken from Barbary birds, in the northern part of Africa."

"How often do you pluck the bird's feathers?"

"Every seven months we cut the feathers and allow the quills to grow for about a month longer. White feathers are worth $175 a pound."

"What do you feed the birds on?"

"Generally we give them grain and grass. If the weather is not too cold I see no reason why farms should not be started here. All the birds want is a place to run in and some horses, small stones and grass to feed on. The cost of keeping them is little or nothing."

Dr Prothre further said that he would start a farm in New York State, but that he expected in a few years there would be many farms in the South, and that on account of the high prices of rent here he would be unable to compete with them.

An Expert Wanted.—There is one important industry in Detroit which, in the general sweep of protection, has yet remained unprotected. The subject agitating the official breast is the classification of frogs. The demand for them has increased, and the "pauper frogs" of Canada are impudent enough to attempt to compete with our own American marsh poultry. Under the treaty of Washington fish are admitted free, and the Canadians insist that frogs are fish. But the patriotic custom-house officer is not so easily deceived. He is a diligent student of natural history, has been to Barnum's great moral show, and knows that fish have no legs. The tadpole might possibly sneak in as a fish, and cheat the American Government out of its revenue by cunningly and knavishly growing into a frog after he had eluded the vigilance of the authorities; but a frog of full growth and sound mind is entitled to no such exemption. The Canadians ask, What is he then? He certainly cannot come under the head of cattle, even if he has four legs; he is not a bird; he swims and lives in the water, coming out only for purposes of recreation and for attending the dinners and suppers of his admirers. Secretary Folger, for fear of alienating the French voter at this election, declines giving an opinion. The frog, who will like him know, is a very delicate subject.—*Detroit Free Press.*

Bay and Cattle.—The scarcity of cattle in the East and the subsequent rise in the price of beef has aroused the cattle dealers to activity, and all the cattle are being fed that hay can be found for. There are more feeding at present in Honey Lake Valley than has ever been known before. There was an unusually large crop of hay raised there this year and it is now all sold, going readily at the fimt for five dollars and fifty cents and soon increasing to six dollars per ton. Over 4,000 head of beef cattle are being fattened in the Tule district alone.—*Greenville Bulletin.*

# THE PADDOCK.

## How to Improve the Horse's Pace.

We will take, to begin with, a horse of the slowest walking pace, say about three miles per hour. To improve this, put him alongside of a horse, either led or in harness, whose walk is about three and a half miles per hour, and when the three-miler has come to this, then put him alongside of a four-miler, and so go on increasing until he has reached the utmost limits of pace it is possible to get out of him. After this, in riding or driving, keep him steadily up to his best pace, and in process of time it may become almost natural and easy to him.

The reason (says an American contemporary) it is best to begin with the attempt to only increase his pace half a mile per hour is, if we tried at first to do it faster than this the horse would be constantly breaking into a trot, to keep up with his companion, and in consequence this walk could not be improved. The object is to keep him steadily to walk, and not permit him to break in. Trotting horses are improved in the same manner; they are kept as strictly to this pace as possible whenever exercised or used, and not allowed to gallop. If they break into a gallop any time, on being urged to do their utmost on the trot, they are instantly checked and brought back to a trot. But if a horse is naturally a slow walker, it will require considerable time and no little patience to much increase his speed at this gait.

A reliable fast walker must be born so, and the best, quickest, and in fact the cheapest way to get at this is to breed him. For this purpose select the fastest walking stallion to be found, and breed him to the fastest walking mare obtainable. As a general rule, these will drop fast-walking colts. The fastest of these when grown should be selected for breeding, and so go on rearing and selecting till the breed is as well established for fast walking as those of fast trotters or racers now are.

Some may think that special breeding to obtain fast walkers is not necessary, and that any sort of a horse can be trained to it. Such doubters have only to carefully compare the anatomy of a fast walking horse alongside that of a slow walker, to be convinced of the necessity of breeding for this special purpose, for the difference between the two in various nice points will be found considerable in bone, muscle, tendon, cord, and, to sum up, in general structure. Place a heavy farm or cart horse alongside of a fast trotter or racer, and see how very different they are in makeup; and how impossible it would be to increase the pace of the former, either in a trot or run, to that of the two latter. The thing is out of the question—all the teaching and training of the world would not do it. Now, as a general rule, like begets like; and if you want fast walkers, in order to obtain them of a natural, easy, reliable gait, they must be bred from fast walking parents.—*London Live Stock Journal.*

## Arrival of Rayon d'Or.

The steamship Queen from London, with the French-bred stallion Rayon d'Or and a dozen or more brood mares on board, arrived at New York, on Saturday, the 4th. Rayon d'Or, who won the St. Leger in 1879, was purchased at the recent sale of Count Lagrange's stud in France, through the American Horse Exchange of this city, at a cost of $30,000, for Mr. W. L. Scott, of Erie, Pa. Of the lot shipped it is understood that those belonging to Mr. Scott are in perfect condition, especially Rayon d'Or. Of three mares shipped by Mr. Tattersall to the Exchange two died. One of them was unfortunately a mare by Stockwell, 44 to the trip. Mr. Bishop, who came over in charge of Mr. Scott's lot, said that he has rarely seen worse weather than that experienced during the first half of the trip and it was during that period Mr. Tattersall's two mares received such injuries that they died. In connection with the storm, it may be said that the insurance company in which Mr. Scott's horses were insured cabled Mr. Easton in the matter of extra risk, which was not at all surprising considering that the weather was so bad three days after their departure from London that the captain of the Cambridgeshire Handicap at Newmarket had to be postponed, something almost unparalleled in the history of the English turf.

Stonewall Jackson's army horse, called "Little Sorrel," is twenty-six years of age and is still kindly cared for by General Jackson's father-in-law, Dr. Morrison, of Lincoln county, N. C. It is the horse on which General Jackson received his death wound.

Horses slobber from eating clover. This is annoying, especially in the driving horse, but the remedy is very simple and easy at hand, consisting of a head of cabbage fed to the horse just before using him for work or driving. It is cheap and effective.

# CRICKET.

## Merions vs. Occidents.

Following is the score of the match game played by the Merion and Occident elevens at the Recreation Grounds last Sunday:

MERIONS.

| | |
|---|---|
| Mell, a b Waterman | 12 |
| Hill, l b b Stewart | 8 |
| Burnett, b Waterman | 1 |
| Benjamin, c Stewart Sr., b Stewart Jr. | 9 |
| J. Mathieu, b y b Stewart | 7 |
| J. Mathieu, b Stewart | 3 |
| Theobold, c Sanderson, b Waterman | 4 |
| Benjamin Jr., b Stewart | 1 |
| Finlayson, b Waterman | 0 |
| Webster, not out | 1 |
| Harper, c Kennedy, b Waterman | 0 |
| Byes | 3 |
| Leg bye | 1 |
| **Total innings** | **44** |

OCCIDENTS.

| | |
|---|---|
| Aiken, b Theobold | 7 |
| Stewart Jr., b F. Mathieu | 2 |
| Ormsbee, c a b Webster | 1 |
| Sanderson Sr., c Burnett, b Benjamin Sr. | 4 |
| Waterman, run out | 8 |
| Washington, not out | 13 |
| Sanderson Jr., a b Theobold | 0 |
| Stewart Sr., b Theobold | 1 |
| Kennedy, not out | 0 |
| McKee, not out | 2 |
| Byes | 4 |
| Bye | 1 |
| Wide balls | 1 |
| Wide balls | 2 |
| **Total innings** | **46** |

## THE KENNEL.

### HOUNDS AND HARES.

**Meeting of the California Coursing club at Merced.**

Last Saturday night the California Coursing Club met and completed arrangements for their fall meeting. Twenty-four old dogs and eight puppies were entered and drawn as follows:

Ojd dogs—J. Ferrigo's f and bd d Longfellow against J. C. Murphy's b d Chinchilla.

J. C. Murphy's bound w b Lady Don against J. Franklin's be and w b Lady Franklin.

J. F. Carroll's bd and w d Paul Jones against W. Ryan's w b Lady Warwick.

H. Hart's b d Whipple against A Jackson's be d Stonewall Jackson.

A. Jackson's b b Australian Maid against J. M. Keating's b d Fides.

J. Ferrigo's r g Cherokee against M. Meredito's be d Limerick Boy.

J. Franklin's w d Dakota against E. Rodgers' w and bd b Lady Douglas.

A. Jackson's b and w d Orphan Boy against J. F. Carroll's w d Monarch.

J. Franklin's w and bd b Belfast Maid against M. Meredite's bd d Modoc.

S. Brinkerhoff's be and w d Blue Jacket against J. Franklin's be d Speranza.

Puppy stake—J. F. Carroll's bd and w d Connaught Ranger against A. Jackson's b b Zealandia.

John O'Donnell's bd d American Boy against J. J. Murphy's w and bd d Simcoe.

M. Meredite's be b Irish Girl against E. Rodgers' b d Sullivan.

J. L. Meares' b d Modoc against Dr. J. M. Sharkey's bd b Bunch.

For officers of the match, R. Warwick was chosen judge, W. Lane Slipper, J. Farrelly of San Francisco and J. O'Donnell and P. Harrington of Merced Field Stewards. The members of the club and friends to the number of forty-five left town Tuesday at 4 p. m., and after a cold, though pleasant ride arrived in Merced about 10:30 p. m. to find frost on the ground and snow on the mountain tops which, though miles away from the city, look to be only a few hundred yards distant, so rare and clear is the atmosphere. About 9 a. m. Wednesday all hands were on the plains where the match was to be run off. The weather was slightly thinly but so exhilarating it made one's blood literally surge through his veins and sent the spirit up to fever pitch. A finer lot of dogs than were assembled never appeared on the Merced plains and better promise of a pleasant, successful match was never given, but like many another promise, it was never fulfilled and all day long the sport was marred by vexatious accidents which finally culminated in a downright unpleasantness.

The chapter of accidents commenced as soon as J. C. Murphy's Chinchilla and J. Ferrigo's Longfellow were slipped. The miserable disgrace to the equine race miscalled a horse upon which Warwick had been mounted by a sore-eyed stable keeper was utterly unable to keep up with the dogs. Warwick never saw a point in the race and the course had to be given as undecided, entailing enough extra work upon the dog that eventually won, to put his chances of a prize at a very low figure. As soon as the dogs were caught they were slipped again and a good course ensued. Chinchilla was badly thrown out at the turns and proved a poor walker. Longfellow won with points to spare.

J. C. Murphy's Lady Don and J. F. Franklin's Lady Franklin gave the spectators an excellent view of a rather one-sided race. Franklin led from the slips and after Don had made a turn put in a go bye on the outer circle turned and served herself. Another "go bye" showed the boys that Lady Franklin had few superiors in this State in point of speed and the way in which she guarded a hare—proved her to be fully as good a worker. She won the course with many points in her favor.

J. F. Carroll's Paul Jones and W. Ryan's Lady Warwick made a pretty race for a few turns but the latter soon tired away and Jones had to finish almost alone. P. Riley's Whipple and A. Jackson's Stonewall Jackson had a long tiring course in which Jackson made more than two points to his opponent's one after the first turn, which he took in good style.

A. Jackson's imported Australian Maid and J. M. Keating's Fides were then handed over to the slipper. In some way Fides managed to get loose and after running a few yards started a hare. There was no other dog to assist him, the hare was fast and cunning, and poor Fides had to go fully two miles before he finally killed. All this was useless work and ruined his chance for a prize which up to that accident had been very good. After an interval the pair were slipped again. Fides showed great speed from the slips, made the first turn and killed, but the race was given a "no course." Before Australian Maid was taken up she found a fresh hare and equalized matters by taking a long course all alone. After taking a short rest this unfortunate pair of dogs were again slipped and ran a rattling course over a small piece of ground. Again their owners were doomed to disappointment. When the race was over it was found that the field steward had ordered the dogs to be slipped in the absence of the judge. Few men had ridden after the dogs and were competent to decide the match but Mr. Jackson insisted on his right to have the course decided by the regular judge and the work went for nothing. This was especially unfortunate for Fides, who had done far more work than the other dog. After lunch they were slipped again. Fides showed speed but soon tired and Australian Maid won by work at the end of a moderately long course. The victory was valueless for the amount of useless work done made it impossible for her to win another race. Hart's Black Cloud and Lady Mary prov-

ed to be a rather poor pair. The bitch was sick and could not run. Black Cloud opened a wide gap but never once "turned" before the hare reached cover, His lead entitled him to the race.

Dakota and Lady Douglas were both withdrawn.

J. Franklin's Belfast Maid and Mr. Meredite's Parnell were no even match. Parnell has a good turn of speed but is a very awkward dog at the turns. The Maid is a close worker and would score two points right along before he got straightened out. She also had the most bottom and won easily.

J. Franklin's Speculation Jr. and S. Brinkerhoff's Blue Jacket made an even race for some distance but either through an accident or by lack of bottom Blue Jacket went lame and was of no assistance to Speculation in the end of the race, which the latter won.

W. Lane's Pride of the Village gave J. Franklin's Speranza a handsome beating, making "go bye" after "go bye" and doing all the work in the match.

The second tie were run off after lunch without trouble or accident.

Longfellow who had run two courses was completely outmatched by Lady Franklin at every point.

Paul Jones and Stonewall Jackson had a hard, close race. The hare favored Jackson a trifle at the start. He scored a point for speed and another for the first turn. Then Paul took the hare, made a turn and a wrench and let Jackson in. The balance of the work was even up to the finish, where Paul Jones won the course by a handy kill.

Australian Maid, who was worn out by her bad luck in the first ties, was handily beaten by Black Cloud.

Monarch and Cherokee had a long race, the latter stopping before the finish. He did good work at the start and while in sight of the spectators but turned back before the race was over. Belfast Maid and Speculation coming together and both being the bona fide property of J. Franklin, that gentleman claimed the rule to guard and the Maid was matched against Pride of the Village, who broke her leg in the race before three points had been scored.

Speculation being an odd dog on the card ran a bye.

Paul Jones and Lady Franklin were then paired-for the third tie. Lady Franklin took the hare from the start and many of the spectators thought that "she had won but the judge decided otherwise.

Under the rule that dogs owned by the same member shall be guarded right through the match Black Cloud, which came naturally against Monarch, should have been matched against Franklin's Belfast Maid and Monarch should have been paired with Franklin's Speculation. President Sharkey had ordered Black Cloud and Monarch to align but his attention was called to the rule by Mr. Carroll, the owner of Monarch. He then ordered the mistake to be rectified at once. The slipper was told to stop but by some misunderstanding he let the dogs loose after a hare which jumped up at that moment. The race was won by Monarch. A claim was at once made by Franklin that this race was not for nothing and that the two dogs being improperly paired could neither win nor lose. By rule Franklin was, undoubtedly, right, but the President ordered the decision of the course to stand and gave the race to Monarch. After some discussion Franklin withdrew his dogs Belfast Maid and Speculation from the field. The President awarded first and second prizes to Paul Jones and Monarch, and put the third prize at Franklin's disposal.

On Thursday the Puppy Stake was run off as follows:

J. Jackson's Zealandia beat J. F. Carroll's Connaught Ranger.

J. J. Murphy's Simcoe beat John O'Donnell's American Boy.

M. Rodgers' Sullivan beat M. Meredith's Irish Girl.

After an undecided course J. M. Sharkey's Bunch ran a bye, in the absence of Dr. Meares' Modoc.

In the second ties Simcoe beat Zealandia and Sullivan beat Bunch.

Rodgers' Sullivan won the first prize by beating Simcoe in the final race.

A consolation race for beaten dogs closed the day's sport. J. C. Murphy's Chinchilla and J. Franklin's Speculation each won all their respective matches.

On account of darkness they did not run off the last race. Murphy and Franklin divided the first and second prizes.

### The Coming Field Trials.

GILROY, Nov. 14.

EDITOR BREEDER AND SPORTSMAN: At the last meeting of the Rod and Gun Club, preliminary steps were taken in the coming field trials. Committees were appointed to secure the prizes for the different classes of entries; also to secure the grounds and locate the hares which will claim special attention on the days set apart for the trials. It is but fair to state here that ground will be secured which has not been hunted upon this season by anyone, and those men who have allowed themselves to even think that our dogs will be acquainted with the ground by being trained or hunted upon it, and thereby be better able to contend for the prizes, will be happily disappointed, for such is not the case. Everything looks favorable for a successful field trial, as many entries are promised and many will conclude to enter yet as there are two weeks more. With fair weather; a few good flocks of quail, and a goodly number of entries of good and well trained dogs, our next trials will be of noteworthy interest and importance. Our friends Leavesly, Farmer and Bartlett, are doing manfully, and all interested in the sports and the breeding of fine dogs in this State should step forward and reward them for their diligent labor and study by putting their dogs in the field.

D. M. P.

### Mammitis.

Mammitis or inflammation of the milk gland is by no means an uncommon complaint in canine practice.

Causes—External injury, as blows, bruises, or wounds, exposure to cold and damp, retention of milk, etc.

Symptoms—The part affected is red, hot, somewhat hard, and excessively tender; the lacteal secretion is changed in character; at first the milk has a curdled appearance; subsequently it is mingled with blood, and ultimately pus, the natural secretion becoming then totally arrested. Matter having formed, may gradually approach the surface of the gland, point to a particular spot, and there be discharged, the whole gland being involved. Considerable febrile disturbance is present throughout.

In the early stage leeches may be applied to the part, and hot fomentations; a saline aperient should be administered, and perfect quietude on a soft bed enjoined. If the complaint results from retention of milk, owing to the removal or death of whelps, the sooner milking is allowed the better; whether the secretion be altered or not, even to pus, its direction to the channel of the teat and evacuation is strongly advisable, and much preferable to permitting abscesses to form, and point at the surface, and thus destroy a considerable portion of the gland.

When matter has formed, and is approaching the surface,

the sooner it is evacuated the better; otherwise, sinuses are liable to form, and render the case tedious and difficult.

Chronic mammitis is denoted by an indurated and enlarged condition of the gland; and may be the result of lingering subacute inflammation, or proceed from the acute form. It is attended with but little pain or constitutional disturbance; but unless early measures are taken for its removal, it becomes a permanent induration, and may ultimately, if existent, assume a scirrhous condition.

The daily application of iodine ointment, or the tincture, to the affected parts, and the iodine of potassium in one or two scruples daily internally, are the most effectual agents in this complaint. Repeated friction with the hand, is also of service, and where the enlargement is considerable and weighty, it may be conveniently and with benefit suspended, by means of a handkerchief tied over the back, or a net made for the purpose and fastened on the same way with tapes.

Lacteal tumors—The milk ducts are liable to become obstructed when not sufficiently drained of their contents, or from some malformation. Any such obstruction to the outflow of milk is calculated to produce much mischief. Lacteal tumors, perhaps the least hurtful that can arise, are thus frequently caused.

Symptoms—The mammary gland so affected is knotty, the irregularities being even, movable and painless. In the early stages these bodies have a fluctuating feel, which disappears as their period of existence lengthens.

Inflammatory action may be excited in them by injury, and suppuration result.

If the bitch is still in milk, the daily withdrawal of the secretion should be observed—by natural means if possible.

Milk is frequently secreted, independent of the animal parturiating, more especially if connection has taken place. Its removal, if abundant, is advisable, which may be done with the fingers. A smart dose of aperient medicine, and for a few days short commons, is also of service in dispersing it.

Where the animal is comparatively, or quite dry, and we have the tumors only to deal with, it becomes a question whether, so far as their direct treatment is concerned, we shall rely on external application or a surgical operation. If the tumors are of recent date and thoroughly, they may be punctured with some amount of success; if hardened and of long existence, their removal with the knife can be adopted with safety and success.

Individually, I should give the iodine a fair chance before resorting to either.—Stock Keeper.

GILROY ROD AND GUN CLUB.—At the regular meeting on the 8th, a communication from Senator W. W. Traylow was read offering a special prize to be contested for at the trials, which was thankfully accepted. We hope to have to record more of them and that every encouragement will be given by our wealthy and leading sportsmen to this annual dal trial of the Gilroy Club. Nine new members were proposed and elected, consisting of some of the largest land owners in the county, and other prominent and wealthy citizens. The trials will commence on Nov. 27.

## YACHTING.

Work is going steadily on with the Spreckels yacht and it will not be very long now before she will be in order to be tried. This will give us a chance to see what the keel boats will do with the centerboards. So far we have had no very startling results from keel boats in this bay. They thought that the old Cousins was going to beat all the other yachts but she did not do it. The Casco has never been tried in a race and we do not know exactly what she will do with the light draft vessels.

The main interest to yachting men just now is the recent race in New York to test sloops and cutters. The races were arranged by the Seawanhaka yacht club and there was a great deal of interest in them. Several good boats were brought but not so many as was expected. The schoon stand in as winning four times and the cutter twice. In the first class the sloop won twice and cutter once. In the second two different sloops each won a race, and the cutter one.

They have taken the Emerald over to Stone's to be laid up for the winter. She will be hauled out on the ways, which is always the best way to do when it is possible, for the yacht is then out of all harm. The sails, etc., will be stored ashore.

A lot of jolly yachtmen went to work shooting the other day in the preserve of the Teal shooting club, but the keeper, Jim Payne, soon showed them that they were in the wrong part of the country.

The Elia is going up river in a few days on a duck hunting expedition. She went up Sulpun Creek last winter and had pretty good luck. If they do not get much game they always have a good time on the Elia.

The New York Yacht Club is at last to have a clubhouse beside the water. The club is the largest in the United States but has now only rooms in the city, having no proper clubhouse.

The Rambler has had her sails unbent and has been moored off South San Francisco. It does not look like a very good place in a norther.

Farmer has sold his sailing skiff which has shown so much speed to the frequenters of Oakland creek to a boatman. He will build another soon.

The Azalene has gone up river with quite a party of people on a duck hunting expedition. She is gone to try the luck up about Antioch.

The Seawanhaka yacht club is going to build a clubhouse at the water's edge, where they should have had one long ago.

There is very little yachting news of a local nature these days as so many of the boats are laid up.

We do not hear of any small yachts being built here at present or of any planned.

The Annie is off on a duck cruise up river with quite a party. She went yesterday.

The Lively and Chiquita are lying side by side on the beach in Oakland.

The Virgin and Mist are lying near each other in Oakland Creek.

The Pacific yacht club close the season formally to-day.

Stonewall soon start work on a big schooner.

There has been pretty heavy shooting on Grand Island of late so the boys must be having good sport.

# FISH.

### Sport in an Emptied Pond.

A description in the *London Graphic* says: By this time the ditch through the middle was extending fast, water pouring off and the landing-net at work stopping fish like shoals of sprats from going toward the wire-protected drain, and these were scooped out, placed in buckets, and from thence carried to the tribe. The men worked furiously, evidently as delighted with the task as so many schoolboys, though extremely careful about getting in the mud. But we soon changed all that, for the water was now low enough for the great carp to be reached, and the smaller fry of roach and bream were left for the present, while the men laid down planks upon the mud, and approached the holes beneath the willows where it was known that the carp now lay. "Take care! Don't hurt them! Scoop 'em out wi' the trug. " Order after order, as the wooden buckets were handled; one was plunged in and shovelled out a great carp with a quarter of a painful of liquid mud. No calm sedateness now. The monarchs of the pond had felt their latent majesty touched and there was a tremendous splashing and plunging; the man who had scooped out the great fish was splattered with mud from head to foot; there was a plunge and the carp was gone. The mud was forgotten now in the excitement, as fresh efforts were made; the carp were scooped out and held down by main force as they gave displays of their tremendous muscular power, and were passed up the side—great golden fellows, thick, short, and fat, clothed in a scale armor that seemed to be composed of well-worn half-sovereigns, and panting and gaping with surprise as they were safely landed. Shouts and laughter greeted each of the great fellows, only one of which was as small as two pounds weight, the others running from three to five, and exhibiting a power that was marvelous in creatures of their size. Sometimes a great fellow eluded capture again and again, gliding between the hands, leaping out of the basket and making furious efforts to escape, but only to be caught again till the last was secured, and attention turned to the eels. This proved a task, indeed. The mud was entirely forgotten now, and as the big landing-net was brought into use, and the great fellows that glided over the mud like serpents were chased, they showed that they could travel tail first as fast as head first, and with the greatest ease. The landing net was held before them, and efforts made to drive them in; but generally without result, or if they were driven in, it was only for them to glide out more quickly. Hands were useless, shovels impotent, and the chase grew exciting in the extreme, as the men plunged in their bare arms to the shoulder, and drew from the mud again, looking as if they had gone in like Mr. Boffin, for fashion, and were wearing twenty-four button gloves of a gloomy hue. But lithe and strong as they were, the eels had to succumb, great two and three pound fellows, and were safely thrown out on the grass; the last of the small fish was secured, the whole of the water drained off, and nothing remained but three feet of mud. Nothing? Nothing but the eels that had dived in like worms. These were now attacked. The mud was stirred with poles or shovels till the lurking-place of one was found, when after a long fight, he would be secured, twisting, twining, and fighting for liberty; heeding delicate handling too, for these monsters of the pond bite hard and sharp. Deep down in the mud some forced themselves, but many were dug out and thrown or driven into places where they could be secured, and at last wet, muddy, and weary, the owner cried: "Quantum mell," beer for the second time was handed round, and the empty pond was left in peace till daybreak next morning, when the remaining eels were found to have come to the surface and were caught in the pools, where a little water had drained.

### Fishermen's Superstitions.

The "Fishermen's Own Book" contains an interesting chapter on the above subject, from the pen of Captain J. W. Collins, who says that the fact that fishermen seem to be more dependent upon luck than any other class of men, and that they are constantly meeting with events calculated to excite superstition, may account to some extent for their being credulous. Among the fisherman's superstitions of which he treats are a belief in lucky and unlucky sailing days; a belief in Fundie; the superstitions concerning dropping a hatch in the hold, breaking a looking-glass, driving a nail on Sunday, etc.; and instances are cited where such superstitions seem to have been well founded, and others in which they are shown to be without any foundation. Mr. Scudder, in his interesting report on the Greenland halibut fishery, treats briefly on the same subject. "The only difference between Sunday and any other day of the week," he says, "was that no nail must be driven on that day, for they said that would 'nail the trip.' Their superstitions are a little curious. The fold notion that any enterprise commenced on Friday would be unlucky has, in a great measure, disappeared on account of the fisherman having read in the papers a long list of great events that had happened on Friday. The objection to hammering on Sunday was so strong that the captain delayed fixing a part of the rigging from Sunday to Monday on this account. There is one superstition about which they are exceedingly particular. They will never leave a hatch upside down. I was in the cabin fixing the fire, and had taken up the hatch in the floor to get at the coal, which was kept in the bottom of the vessel, beneath the cabin floor. The hatch I had placed in such a manner against the side of the cabin that, if it had fallen down, it would have been bottom side up. One of the fishermen whom I had always regarded as very sensible, seeing the hatch in that position, said to me: 'Mr. Scudder, don't leave the hatch that way,' and when I asked him why, he explained that it it should slip down it would be upside down which should bring ill-luck upon the whole trip. I replied: 'Let's try it,' and knocked the hatch down on the floor bottom up. I do not remember of ever having been more surprised than I was to see him jump and turn the hatch over. He then said: 'I don't know what the captain would say if he saw that.' One of the fishermen told of a captain he was with who swore terribly at him because he pushed a dory off from the vessel with the dory toward the tide. I found, however, some difficulty in getting the men to acknowledge their belief in many superstitions, and I should not have found out those I have mentioned, had not the incident spoken of called them into action. I think as a whole, they were, for sea-going men, remarkably free from superstition."

A great many boats were fishing off the Sancelito shores last Sunday but the catches were very slim. Many did not get a nibble, while two or three was considered remarkably good luck.

A party of sixteen persons last Sunday were fishing in the tide waters near Tamalpais, averaging one-half of a fish each.

---

The fishing in Lake Tahoe last summer was better than ever before, and probably never has the wanton destruction of fish been so great. In June and July many visitors caught one hundred and two hundred and fifty fish a day. Many of them kept up the sport—if sport it can be called—during all of a long summer day, until then had caught from two hundred to two hundred and fifty fish. Of course no skill was really called for in this sort of fishing, as in salmon fly fishing. A large line and solid hook are used and baited, and when a trout is hooked, he is hauled in hand over hand, without skill or delay. In this way the destruction of fish was simply enormous. The proprietor of the stage line between Truckee and Tahoe City informed me that the down stage last summer frequently carried one thousand pounds of fish. That weight represented at least an equal number of fish, for the average weight is not, I judge, over a pound. Those who thus wantonly slaughtered such hecatombs of trout senselessly, if not brutally, specially recorded their names and exploits on the hotel registers. I fail to see any thing to boast of, but much to be ashamed of in such fishing. The good fishing will not, I suppose, last long, if such slaughter is kept up. The same is true of deer hunting. Professional game-law breakers now organize in June from Georgetown and other places, and go out and kill deer by the dozen, for their hides alone, three months before the deer shooting season opens. Two men thus fitted out at Georgetown killed seventy-five deer for their hides in last June, July and August. Another man had a special platform fitted over a deer lick where he could slaughter them unerringly and steadily with buckshot. Some of these deer murderers are as low and filthy a set of fellows in their appearance and habits as one could possibly meet anywhere. They are in painful contrast with the beautiful animals they slaughter, and the impressive mountain surroundings in which they carry on their destructive work.—*Bulletin.*

ANGLING AS A MEDICINE.—In his charming book, entitled "Pleasures of Angling," Mr. George Dawson very aptly remarks: I concur with those who speak of the pastime of angling as a medicine, not only from my own experience, although that may count for something, but from the great number of strong men with whom I have been brought in intimate contact during my more than thirty years of outdoor life, and who, from their youth up, have found nothing so invigorating as the pure air of the mountains; nothing so soothing, after the toil and worry and fret of business, as the silence of the woods; nothing so pervading in its mellowing influence upon nerve and brain and spirit as the pleasant murmur of the flowing river; nothing so health-giving as the aroma of nature's grand forest laboratory; and nothing so exhilarating as the rise and swirl and rush of trout or salmon. Those whom I have thus known, with scarcely an exception, have preserved the vigor of lusty youth longer and more uniformly than their contemporaries, who have sought other enjoyment from which I infer that but those who are blest with robust constitutions ever acquire a passion for angling, or that the pastime itself creates the healthful vitality which ensures a vigorous old age. But whether the pastime is merely preservative, or but actually creative, in its medicinal effects, it is certainly beneficent, and deserves the high place it holds in the affections of its happy, healthy and enthusiastic votaries.

THE FISHING SEASON.—The fish law shut out the anglers on Wednesday, and the trout will have a rest till the 1st day of April, 1883. The law is entirely wrong as far as Plumas is concerned, and a move should be made to have the time changed. As it now stands the open season commences just about the time the fish are spawning, and just when they should be protected. There is no reason for stopping the catching of fish in Plumas until the 1st of January, or even February, and then the close season should last until the 1st of June. April and May are the spawning months, varying a little, of course, in different seasons. If the fishermen would make the effort this change in the law, as regards our county, could be easily affected.—*Plumas National.*

LARGE CATFISH.—The Gridley *Herald* reports that John Thompson, a ranch hand working on a place near Shaeffer's Point, about twelve miles northwest of Gridley, Butte Co., while fishing in the Sacramento river, Sunday, landed a catfish weighing sixty-nine pounds, nine ounces. He killed it by hitting it in the head with an ax. This is the largest fish of the species we have heard of being caught in the State. Parties who ate of it tell us the meat was as palatable as that of the smaller cattle so plentiful in Butte creek.

The past week has been a very poor one for those who delight in taking the finny tribe in natural element. Angling in the tide waters for salmon trout has been very poor; several parties who have been out have returned without having had a bite. Around the bay, owing to the unfavorable condition of the tides, there have been no catches to speak of, and fishermen have come back with pretty much the same luck as their brothers of the limber rod. Yesterday and the day before owing to the unusually high tides were days favorable for good fishing, but very few took advantage of the tides, so the denizens of the deep suffered but a small loss. The next two weeks promise good fishing in the bay and those who find pleasure in holding a line over the side of a boat, or can sit all day with their legs dangling over the edge of a wharf grasping a bamboo pole, will no doubt be rewarded for their patience by good strings of fish.

In April, 1881, German carp about two inches long were placed in water at the Kansas Agricultural College farm. Just one year after ten of them were seined out, each of which measured thirteen inches and weighed one and one-half pounds, upon which fourteen months the college paper remarks: "In view of the facts that these fishes have lived in a square hole filled with water, the 'hole' being more like a house-cellar without the wall than a 'fish pond,' and have been fed only once a week, and oftener once a month, we are disposed to consider these carp the most profitable 'yard fowls' that have yet been introduced into this country.

The codfish, when at home rambling through the submarine forests, does not wear his vest unbuttoned, as he does while loading around the grocery stores of the United States.—*Bill Nye.*

About 1,500,000 shad have been placed in the waters of Arkansas and Texas during the past season by the Fish Commissioners.

In Arizona the penalty for using giant powder to kill fish is three or three hundred dollars or three months' imprisonment.

Mexican oysters and fish are now shipped into Arizona by rail direct from Guaymas.

---

## BASE BALL.

### Haverlys vs. Renos.

The game at the Recreation Grounds last Sunday occupied two hours. Denny and Irwin of the Providence nine played with the Renos. The score was as follows:

| HAVERLYS. | T.B. | R. | B.H. | P.O. | A. | E. | RENOS. | T.B. | R. | B.H. | P.O. | A. | E. |
|---|---|---|---|---|---|---|---|---|---|---|---|---|---|
| J. Carroll, s s. | 5 | 2 | 1 | 1 | 2 | 0 | Barnes, 1b.... | 5 | 1 | 0 | 11 | 0 | 3 |
| Levy, l f... | 5 | 2 | 1 | 0 | 0 | 0 | Denny, 3b.... | 5 | 1 | 1 | 3 | 3 | 0 |
| Meegan, p.... | 5 | 2 | 0 | 1 | 7 | 0 | Sturdan, p.... | 4 | 1 | 2 | 1 | 6 | 1 |
| McDonald, 3b... | 4 | 1 | 1 | 3 | 4 | 1 | Irwin, s s.... | 4 | 0 | 1 | 7 | 2 | 0 |
| F. Carroll, c.... | 4 | 1 | 1 | 4 | 5 | 2 | Lake, l f.... | 4 | 1 | 1 | 0 | 0 | 0 |
| McVey, 1b.... | 4 | 1 | 0 | 14 | 0 | 0 | Swanton, r f... | 4 | 0 | 0 | 2 | 0 | 0 |
| Sweeney, c f... | 4 | 0 | 1 | 2 | 0 | 0 | Hart, c f.... | 4 | 1 | 1 | 2 | 0 | 3 |
| Lawton, r f... | 4 | 0 | 0 | 1 | 0 | 0 | Sheridan, 2b... | 4 | 1 | 1 | 2 | 2 | 2 |
| Gagus, 2b.... | 4 | 2 | 1 | 1 | 1 | 0 | Creegan, c f... | 4 | 1 | 0 | 6 | 1 | 0 |
| **Totals**.... | 39 | 10 | 1 | 27 | 19 | 6 | **Totals**.... | 38 | 7 | 2 | 27 | 16 | 8 |

Innings..........................................1 2 3 4 5 6 7 8 9
Haverlys......................................1 0 1 0 2 0 6 1　5—16
Renos..........................................1 1 0 2 1 0 0 1　1—7

Earned runs—Haverlys 2, Renos 2. Three-base hits—J. Carroll, Swanton, Sheridan. Two-base hits—McDonald, Gagus, Denny. Bases on called balls—Haverlys 5, Renos 2. Passed ball—Irwin. Double play—Carroll and McVey. Wild pitches—Meegan 1.

The base ball match at Recreation Park to-morrow (Sunday), Denny and Irwin of the Providence Club, Taylor of the Atlantics of New York, and T. Brown of the Baltimore Club, will play with the Niantic and Reno clubs of this city; on this occasion the diamond will be changed back to the old position.

## Reproduction of the Dam in the Produce.

It is wonderful how minutely, in nervous temperament the produce is apt to be a reproduction of the dam. The most trivial eccentricity is apt to be inherited. For instance: The writer owned a road mare that had a peculiar habit of brushing the flies from her front limbs in summer-time, by crossing them and rubbing them together with almost human intelligence. No other horse in the pasture practiced the same effective plan till her colt, which was full-grown, imitated her to a dot. She used the same means to rid herself of the same annoyance.

Another instance is a fine illustration in point: Quite a celebrated road mare had a habit of working with the bit over the paved streets of the city on her way to the driving avenues in the suburbs. She would straighten out her head and neck; she would pull and haul and snatch at the reins till she would almost drag the driver over the dash-board, or suddenly snatch the lines from his hands. On the road in the pasture this was a pleasant driver; but on the streets this practice made her an exceedingly provoking and difficult animal to handle. After she was retired from harness for several years, she foaled a handsome colt, that in no portion of its outward formation resembled her. But when it was broken, and taught to speed in harness, it developed precisely the same nervous, eager hunching upon the bit that made her dam so disagreeable in a walk or jog on the pavements. The temperament of the dam, therefore, should be a matter of special inquiry. In a majority of instances, a dull, sluggish, nerveless mare, without ambition for speed, will produce a colt that demands the inspiration of the lash to develop his speed. The more cheerful and courageous the dam—provided it is not carried to the verge of unsteadiness, flightiness or hysterics, the more certain will the produce have game and courage and spirit to excel.—*Live-Stock Journal.*

## Observation of Stock.

Treatises upon stock breeding and management may be written—and even read—lectures given and attended, rules and directions laid down with the most restrict exactness, and committed to memory with the most determined perseverance, but success, after all, will depend much upon just this one condition—the use of the eyes. Has the master or manager of the stock ever cultivated his precious eyesight and does he make use of it? There are men who, having eyes, see not, and there are men whose quick sight nothing can escape. The latter may be, for former never can become (by their own inassisted endeavors), successful in their specdial business.

One way in which imperfect trained or untrained eyesight is often to be detected, is in the owner's want of knowledge of his animals. This affects the chances of success as a breeder rather than as a manager. He may be, to a certain extent, a good judge, that is to say, able to pick out good from bad or indifferent animals, but the preceptive faculty is evidently defective. He cannot appreciate the finer differences between animals, and so fails to acquire much that a keener and more comprehensive sight alone can give; unless, indeed, the fault be in what may be termed "sight-memory." Some persons can see and distinguish between, but cannot remember the objects of sight. The object is clear upon the mind, as upon the organs of vision, but the mind has no power of retention. The brain receives no lasting impression, yet the memory may, in general, be good. Persons who forget the distinguishing peculiarities, if not the very forms and colors of animals, almost as quickly as the animals pass out of sight, and fail to recognize to-day the cow or horse seen and particularly noticed only yesterday, may have good memories for dates, numbers, names and lots of other things their knowledge of which is not specially connected with the sense of sight; and, on the other hand, persons who can vividly recall whatever they have seen, may have the worst of memories for other matters. One may know an animal's pedigree by rote, and not know the animal when he repeatedly sees it; another, who would know the animal, once seen, if he met it at the antipodes, might not be able, by the strongest effort, to recollect its pedigree. A good memory in both lines of knowledge is of great service to the breeder, and should be cultivated by all present or intending breeders whose faculties are young enough to admit of improvement.—*National Live Stock Journal, Chicago.*

A DAIRY OF BLUE CHINA.—At the left wing of Sir Henry Peek's nearly completed house at Rousdon, Devon, is situated the dairy, which for beauty, solidity and originality of design has never been surpassed, and cannot be matched in all England. The floors and shelves and central tables are all formed of slabs of the purest marble, and in the center there is an immense china, the spray of which lends a delightful coolness to the air and Arcadian beauty to the scene. There is depicted on this china tiles, arranged in a continuous chain all round the apartment, scenes from every phase of rural life. There is also a magnificent marble fountain in the large yard beyond.—*London Live Stock Journal.*

## Starting Tree Seeds.

In these days of timber culture, when so much interest is being taken in the subject by many owners of treeless tracts of land, it becomes an important question to decide how to treat the seeds as well as seedlings. Only nurse them through the first two or three years, and but little care will be necessary in the future. Some species of seed-tree, as the oaks and maples, grow too readily, and occasionally the little radical or fruit root in these may, during moist weather, be noticed peeping out of the seed before dropping from the parent tree. Then again such seeds as the holly, juniper and yew will generally lie dormant in the ground for two and even three years. The proper treatment for the first is to dry them very slightly before committing them to their winter quarters; and for the latter class, place them in damp sand as quickly as possible after removal from the tree.

It is an excellent plan to wash off all the fleshy covering from pulpy seeds, as this acts more as a preservative than as an incentive to germination. A proper care of the tender young seedlings justifies us in protecting them from the direct rays of the sun and from the trying effect of high winds. This may be best effected by making frames of common, cheap boards, so as to form beds, say about six feet wide and of any height necessary. These are covered with lath racks or "shelters," four or six feet in size, with ordinary plastering lath tacked across them, leaving three-quarters of an inch between. Here may be started all seeds of difficult germination, as well as the rare species that we desire especially to grow. Many kinds, depending greatly on the size of the seed, must be covered very slightly with sand; in fact, merely hiding them from sight would be desirable. Others again of larger size require more soil over them, and those of larger dimensions, as the walnut, must be placed beneath the surface for three or four inches.

An excellent plan to observe, however, is to cover too little rather than too much, as seeds during germination decay very easily. Sharp, gritty sand or light sandy soil are about the best for covering seeds, although when peat and leaf-mold are readily procured, they will be found very serviceable for the purpose. When the young seedlings are two years old they must be transplanted, or if very close in the beds, they may be pricked out into other beds at one year old. Pinch off the tips of all long taproots and dip in thin mud before dibbling in their new homes. Again, cover the lath shades and mulch with moss if very valuable. Should dry weather set in, water thoroughly with a coarse hose or sprinkler, but toward autumn take off the racks to hasten the ripening process by means of the sun's rays.—*Josiah Hoopes.*

## The Rise in India Rubber.

The price of india rubber has taken another rocky jump upward, and fine Para grades are now held at $1 17, against 95@97½c a month ago, 82@84c in October, 1881, and 48@50c in 1878. The advance within the past ten days has been 19 @12c per pound, and has taken nearly everybody by surprise. Some of the largest manufacturers freely admit that they recently refused to buy rubber for delivery this month at 85c, and that they cannot purchase the same grade to-day below $1 15. This last advance has not been accompanied by large transactions, but is principally due to the sanguine anticipations of speculative holders.

That there has been an enormous increase in the consumption of this material not only for boots and shoes but for clothing and other goods during the past few years is now well known. The use of gossamer cloaks by ladies has become very general and the highest grade of rubber is invariably employed in their manufacture. Figures previously published in the *Bulletin* showed that the total consumption of rubber in the United States and Canada in each of the following years was as follows:

| | Pounds | | Pounds |
|---|---|---|---|
| 1881 | 19,380,000 | 1877 | 23,340,000 |
| 1880 | 16,086,000 | 1876 | 9,963,000 |
| 1879 | 17,694,000 | 1875 | 10,106,000 |
| 1878 | 13,160,000 | 1874 | 13,341,000 |

It will be seen that the years 1877, 1879 and 1881 each witnessed a marked increase in the rubber manufacturing facilities of the country. In 1881, with a consumption of 19,-380,000 pounds, the net receipts of rubber in the United States and Canada were but 18,047,000 pounds, and hence our supplies were reduced 1,333,000 pounds! That rubber should have gone up to $1 15 last spring, therefore, is now considered to have been very natural.

But since that time the production of india rubber in all quarters of the world has increased. The "bulls" in rubber always theorize that the native of Brazil is only inclined to cure as much rubber as will enable him to secure a bare existence, and that he consequently only produces half as much when the price goes up to $1 per pound as he would have produced at 50 cents. This theory is true in a measure, but the population of the rubber producing regions of South America is increasing pretty rapidly, and while each individual inhabitant may limit his earnings according to his daily wants, yet the number of producers is being augmented so such an extent that the actual receipts of rubber from Para are twice as large now as they were in 1870. There has been an average annual increase of 10 per cent. per annum in the receipts of Para rubber, and this year the increase is believed to have been fully 20 per cent. In Central America and Africa there has been a still greater enhancement of production. There are said to be fully 2,000,000 pounds of African rubber on the English market at the present time, and perhaps some American manufacturers may find that they can work in more or less African rubber where they have heretofore used the Para.

With all this increase in production which has occurred in these various quarters of the world, we find that the receipts of India rubber and guta percha in the United States a ton from January 1 to August 1, 1882, were 15,162,189 pounds, against 10,902,489 pounds during the corresponding seven months of 1881. This is an increase of nearly 50 per cent. If all the material has been absorbed, and consumption is being maintained at a rate sufficient to put this year's enhanced crop of rubber up to $1 17 a pound, then the manufacture of rubber goods in the United States during the past year must have increased beyond all knowledge and belief.—*Boston Commercial Bulletin.*

The London *World* says: "I have been much amused this week by reading that 'Marulon,' after possessing for years an unblemished reputation, has been discovered to be an immoral production. The funny part of the business is that the discovery has been made in the United States, the pure home of, &c." Certainly. Toronto is in Canada, which is not a British colony, but part of the United States—in fact, one of the counties of Chicago, a State destined, as the London *Times* lately said, to be 'one of the greatest grain-growing States of the Union.'"

## A Javanese Rampoken.

Yesterday took place the announced clearance among the tigers belonging to His Highness the Sultan, in order to make room for a fresh supply when the new tiger-pens will be built. At about 10 a. m. the Sultan, the Resident Military Commander, Assistant Resident and other spectators appeared behind the Kraton and seated themselves in a grand stand constructed for the purpose. Thousands of Javanese flocked to the spot to see the combats. Soon a fight between a royal tiger and a buffalo together in a pen was commenced. The tiger was several times tossed into the air and then gored to death by the buffalo, which had been made as furious as possible by peppered water, burning nettles and red-hot iron bars. This combat lasted fully two hours. Afterwards began the rampoken or tiger fight. On the plain alongside the Kraton stood Javanese armed with short spears fifteen to eighteen feet long, drawn up in rows, one behind the other, forming altogether an extraordinarily large square. The two foremost rows lay kneeling, the two hindmost stood erect. In the center of this open space were thirteen straw-roofed wooden pens, in each of which was a tiger. At a given signal a musical instrument called the gamelan begins playing a martial air to slow measure. Three tiger-keepers then step out of the ranks and approach the cage. Two of them bear each a burning torch, with which they set fire to the straw. The tiger, frightened by the shower of sparks, is then forced out into the open space, but knows not whither to turn. It rounds round and seeks whether it can find an outlet, until it endeavors either by a desperate spring to get away over the human wall which keeps it enclosed or tries to creep through underneath. But it falls pierced by the many spears which have struck it. It utters a savage cry, which is drowned by the applause and shouts of the multitude. In silent agony it strikes around furiously with its mighty paws. The shafts of the spears often break like glass. In such cases a single blow might cost the life of any unfortunate within reach of its claws. It is afterwards killed in due form. This scene took place in the same way thirteen times successively with as many tigers, the festivity closing at 3 p. m. Only a few accidents occurred. One soldier by ill-luck received a spear thrust while combating with a tiger and was severely wounded in the leg. A native received a bite when one of the tigers broke through the square and was killed outside it, after causing great commotion among the spectators.—*Java Bode.*

## The Story of a Steamer.

"Speaking about fast-running steamboats," said Thomas Hartshorn, recently, rolling his quid into his larboard jaw, and giving his Tuckapaw trousers a hitch (Mr. H. served on the ram Queen of the West), I suppose you never heard of the old Elephant that used to run between Cincinnati and New Orleans. She was a beauty. I suppose that when she was tied to the bank with a stern-line and bow-line she was one of the fastest boats on the rivers. She made one celebrated trip from New Orleans I think in '49. Her time was made a matter of record. It was seven days, six hours and three weeks. Coming up from New Orleans once the Captain was sitting at a table, and he noticed several big miles of fellows serving as cabin boys. He called the steward to him, and says he: 'Don't you think it would look better to have boys waiting on the table? I don't like to see men filling the place of cabin boys. Let 'em go and get some young chaps.' 'Why, blast it, Captain,' said the steward, 'them fellows were boys when we left New Orleans.'"

"The Elephant," continued Mr. Hartshorn, clinging to his nautical reminiscences, "was pulling out from Memphis one day, on a down trip, and somehow she got mixed up with a raft of saw logs. She broke one of the logs loose, and it floated out into the stream. The Elephant backed down the river and finally got alongside the log. Then commenced one of the nicest races you ever saw. There was a good stage of water, and the log boomed along right lively. For about a week they held together purty well, but the Elephant had to land at the mouth of the White river, and the log beat her into New Orleans about 90 minutes. There was something wrong about the Elephant's boilers, and she couldn't make steam properly. That's what the captain said. She was a nice boat to ship green fruit on.—*Memphis Avalanche.*

## The Lucky Horse-Shoe.

—The superstitious notions concerning the good luck attending the horse-shoe that have been handed down to us by tradition undoubtedly originated when horse-shoeing was in its infancy. History informs us that the veluonian art was practiced by priests and ancient times. The sacred smith not only fashioned the weapons, but shod the horses of heroes. The Druid priests are said to have been skillful workers in iron, and practiced the vulcanian art in great secrecy. The Anglo-Saxon monks are said to have been skillful workers in iron. The smith's art was so highly prized in the days of King Edgar that he enacted that the priests should learn and practice it. St. Dustin, who acquired great fame for being a cunning worker in iron, lived in the tenth century, and gave himself up to a solitary existence, practicing the art in secret. The mystery connected with this saint caused the simple people of his day to venerate him. St. Eloy was Bishop of Noyon, France, in the seventh century, and as a worker in metal (for he was a great goldsmith), became saint of horse-shoers and metal workers in nearly every country in Europe.

## An Iowa Boy's Heroism.

—Necessity often proves the value of a man, but we never read or better nerve than that displayed by the little night operator at Melrose, Ia., who was injured by the cars at that place. His name is Engler, and we are told his age is not much beyond 15. The wreck day night he got on No. 16 to ride down the road a short distance to close a switch. Just how or where it was we do not know, but the boy, while hanging on the car, was struck against a post, by which he had a thigh broken. The blow threw the boy between the cars and in falling he caught his arms around the draw-bars and in that position he was dragged some distance. He finally recovered himself sufficiently, climbed up on the draw-bars, then by the side ladder on top of the car, where he remained till the train reached Melrose. There, with his limb broken and bleeding, he was discovered by the trainmen. He never whimpered in the least and only remarked: "Boys, I believe I have had one of my legs broken; I wish you would help me down."—*Ottumwa Courier.*

## Keeping Apples.

—The essential requisites may be summed up thus: Pick without bruising; store without heating; winter without frosting; use one or more thermometers; preserve an unchanged temperature; guard against air currents; give needed ventilation; remove ripe specimens before decay; separate the fruit room from all other apartments. With these precautions and care, such apples as the Baldwin, Red Canada, Swaar, Fameuse and Northern Spy may be kept fresh into June and July, as we have had an opportunity for testing.—*Country Gentleman.*

## The Cat.

The cat is frankly, undisguisedly selfish; there is no denying that. It lives for self, and compasses its end without scruple, patient to wait, skillful to feign and scheme, and utterly pitiless and unrelenting. But should sportsmen be very severe on the creature that evidently enjoys with a gusto keen as their own pursuits of the helpless prey which it hunts and toys with, often as much for diversion as for hunger? One hopes, for the sake of the sportive birds and heedless mice, which it fascinates with its basilisk eyes and captures with its cruel paws, that there may be some occult provision of nature to disarm their fate of its terror. Perhaps the theory propounded by Dr. Livingstone when he records his feelings while in the lion's clutch—that the sensations of the prey are rather pleasing than otherwise—may be true. We hope so, but it must be confessed that appearances are not in favor. In early youth cat nature appears at its best. Once having emerged from the purring, sightless stage of its first nine days, the kitten becomes a winsome and attractive creature. "Cat-like" is a reproachable epithet aptly applied to women of the Becky Sharp type; but it is not considered derogatory to the most fascinating girl to be credited with kitten-like ways—for the kitten is the embodiment of playfulness and grace. The cruel instincts of its tribe are not, however, slow to assert themselves, and it is comical to hear the mimic growl of puny thunder with which the tiny creature gloats over its first mouse. In the pages of fable, puss has ever figured largely, but rarely after a flattering manner. His guile and subtilty form the salient points in the representations, and his character is painted akin to that of Master Reynard, the master of the craft. He is depicted as a demure hypocrite, a false hermit, a deceitful counselor, the murderer of the unwary, and the ally of witches and wizards. Rats in council debate how to baffle him. It is hopeless, they find, to dream of "belling the cat." Noiseless himself on his gloved feet, his keen ear is not to be caught napping.

## Sikh Horsemanship.

—The Anglo-Indian cavalry went into the Tel-el-Kebir fight with nothing on but a turban and a piece of cloth around the loins. The Arabs were greatly astonished at the apparition, and still more astonished to find their concentrate masters in the use of cold steel. The Sikh horsemen (who, it is well known, worship their swords, according to the teachings of their scripture, the Ad-Granth) refused to reload their revolvers. A French eye-witness of the scene says that the sabering was peculiarly terrible. These Eastern swordsmen never thrust, and seldom strike save at the arms and head, in almost every instance inflicting fatal wounds. Since the Indian mutiny, the English are careful to keep only a small number of these dangerous mercenaries under arms. They use no reins, guiding their horses only by a pressure of the knee, like the South American gauchos.

In the pinewoods of Mississippi, Georgia, and Alabama, when hogs are compelled to labor hard and root deep for a scanty living, the best breeds will degenerate into the long-nose, spindle-leg, razor-back beasts that are found there.

## Market Report.

FLOUR—We quote: Best City Extra, $5 60@6 00; Superfine, $4 50@5 00; Interior Extra, $4 75@5 25; Interior Superfine, $3 50@4 25.

WHEAT—For poorer classes there is but little demand while there is a good inquiry for good shipping grade. Millers ask for nothing but the best qualities and are willing to give $1 72½@1 75 for desirable lots.

BARLEY—During the past week the market has been very lively. Sales of December have been received at $1 55. Recent sales are No. 1 1 45; November, 1 45. There is little demand for No. 2 description, quoted at 40@42 c. Brewing $1 00@1 05.

OATS—Fair demand. Fair Feed, $1 70@1 75; Good, $1 75@1 80; Choice, $1 80@1 90 ¢ ctl.

RYE—Quotable at $1 72½@1 75 for No. 1, and $1 72½@1 75 for No. 2 grade.

FEED—Ground Barley, $22@25 ⅌ ton; Cracked Corn, $35 ⅌ ton. Bran, Middlings are asking $21 ⅌ ton. Oilcake is the article and the Oils are $21 50 ⅌ ton. Oilcake meal the universal demand. Middlings, $27@32 ⅌ ton per ton at the mill.

HAY—Alfalfa, $12@13 50; Wheat $13@16 50; Wild Oat, $15 50@16 50; Mixed, $14@16.

PROVISIONS—Eastern Hams, 15@17c; California Hams, 14@15c for plain; Eastern picnic or smoked cured, Eastern Breakfast Bacon, 15@16c; California Smoked Bacon, 13@14c for heavy and medium, and 15½@16c for light and extra light; Clear Sides, $12@12½; Pork, old, $21@22; for extra Prime, $19@20 for Prime Mess, $22@23 for Mess; New $23@24 for old Mess, $25@25½ for old Extra Prime Pork. Lard in the Kegs and tins, 12½@13½ ⅌ lb; California Smoked Beef, 14@15c ⅌ lb.

FRUIT—We quote: apples, 50@80c for common and 75@85 ⅌ box for good; Pears, 50@$1 25 ⅌ box; Strawberries, 35@40 ⅌ lb; Figs, 35@40c ⅌ box; Grapes, 50@75c ⅌ box for common; Lemons, $5 50@8 50 ⅌ box for Sicily, and $9 ⅌ box for California; Limes, $10@11 ⅌ box for Mexican; Bananas, $1@3 50 ⅌ bunch; Oranges, $4@4 50 ⅌ box for Mexican and $6@6 50 ⅌ box for California; Pineapples, $4@6 ⅌ doz; Tomatoes, 40@50c ⅌ box.

POTATOES—Early Goodrich 50@65c; Garnet Chili, 60@65 ⅌ ctl; Sweet $1 10@1 25; Peachblows, 65@90c; Tomales and Petaluma, 60@70c ⅌ ctl.

ONIONS—Quotable at 50@70c for good and 35@40 ⅌ sack for poor.

BEANS—Bayos $4 75@5; Butter, $4 75@5; Pea, $4 50@5; Pink, $4 50@5 ⅌ ctl; Red, $5@5 50; Lima, $4 75@5 50; Castor, 75c; Pink, $4 50@5.

EGGS—Ranch 40@42c; Eastern, 30@32 ⅌ doz; large White, 40@42 ⅌ doz.

BUTTER—We quote choice lots: Fancy, 37c; choice, 32@33c; fair, 27@28c; inferior lots from ordinary districts, 20@25c; Eastern, 30@35c ⅌ lb.

CHEESE—California choice, 14@15c; Interior, 10@13c; Eastern, 15@16 ⅌ lb; Young America, 16@18c ⅌ lb.

POULTRY—Live Turkeys, gobblers, 19@21c; do Hens, 16@18c; Roosters, $6 50@8 50 ⅌ doz; do Fryers, $4@5 ⅌ doz; Young, $3@4 ⅌ doz; Ducks, according to size, Geese, $2 50@3 ⅌ doz; Hares, 75c@$1 ⅌ pr; Rabbits, $1 50@2 ⅌ doz; Quail, $1 25@1 50 ⅌ doz.

GAME—Market well supplied this week. Mallard Ducks, $4@5 50 ⅌ doz; Sprig, 1 50@2 50; Canvasback Ducks, $5 50@6 50; Widgeon, $1 50@2 ⅌ doz; Teal, $1 25@1 75 ⅌ doz; Brandt, $1 50@2 50; Venison, $5@6 ⅌ ⅌ doz; Snipe, English, $2 50@3 ⅌ doz; Rabbits, $1 50@2 ⅌ doz.

WOOL—The limited business being transacted formed no index for quotations, which are wholly nominal.

HIDES AND SKINS—Dry hides, salted selections, 20@21c ⅌ lb; culls one-third less, and Murrain Hides in ⅌ ⅌ less. Dry Kip, 18@20c; Dry Calf, 25@27c; Salted Steers, over 55lbs, 10@11c; Steers and Cows, medium, 100 light do 9c; Salted Kip, 10 to 30 lbs, Salted Calf, 11@12c; Dairy Calf skins, 9c ⅌ lb; Sheep, Shearlings, 30@50c; Sheepskins, 75@$1 each, according to wool.

TALLOW—Quotable at 5@6½c ⅌ lb for rendered and 11@12½c for refined, both in shipping order.

MEAT—Following are the quotations for whole carcasses from slaughterers to dealers:

BEEF—First quality, 6@7c; medium grade, 5@6c; inferior, 5@5½c ⅌ lb.

VEAL—Large Calves, 7@8c; small ones, 8@9c ⅌ lb.

MUTTON—Wethers are quotable at 6@6½c and Ewes at 5½@6½c ⅌ lb, according to quality.

LAMB—Quotable at 8@9c ⅌ lb.

PORK—Live Hogs, 6@6½c for hard and 6@6½c for soft; dressed do 10@10½c ⅌ lb for hard grain hogs.

## THE CHARLES A. VOGELER CO.

### The New Partnership in the House of A. Vogeler & Co.

A most important change in one of the largest enterprises of the city took place yesterday, and inquiry was busy in gathering the facts.

Immediately following the death of Charles A. Vogeler the surviving partners of the house, of which he had been the moving spirit, issued a circular to the trade and press, which appeared in the columns of this paper. It made public an arrangement which in the exigencies of the moment was deemed necessary, and announced that it was the desire of all concerned to continue its affairs as they had been previously conducted.

It was learned, late last evening, that certain changes affecting the permanent establishment of the business has been resolved upon, and a circular to the Herald was dispatched to Colonel Charles Marshall, attorney for the estate of the late Charles A. Vogeler, where it was ascertained that negotiations had been concluded, as follows:

That the interests of the surviving partners had been purchased by Mr. Christian Devries, a member of the old and substantial house of William Davries & Co., and President of the National Bank of Baltimore, and that a new firm was about to be formed under the firm name of The Charles A. Vogeler Co., this name being in honor and perpetuation of the memory of the late Charles A. Vogeler. It was further ascertained that the new firm will be composed of the widow of the late Mr. Vogeler, the retaining her late husband's full interest; Mr. Christian Devries, as executive partner and financial head, and Mr. H. D. Umbstaetter, who, from the first step in the initial venture of the house of A. Vogeler & Co., was the manager of the advertising department and confidential adviser of Mr. Chas. A. Vogeler.

By this arrangement it has been fully determined that all the plans and business purposes of the late Charles A. Vogeler, the founder and executive manager of the late firm, shall be developed to their full fruition, and that the popular preparations of the house, prominent among which are St. Jacob's Oil and Dr. August Koenig's Hamburg Family Medicines, shall hold their high rank under new auspices and the new management.

There is one feature of this commercial episode which appeals strongly to the kindest feeling and points a touching moral. Mrs. Vogeler holds her relation in the firm with a wisely courage. Her whole future is centered in the resolve that the fruits of so valuable a life as that of her husband's, which was freely sacrificed in his zeal for the welfare of his native city, and that the aims and projects he pursued, shall not be permitted to languish,

but shall be revived and strengthened to its credit and to its honor and fame, and that she will strive to build for him an enduring monument in the enterprise of his own founding.
*Baltimore Herald, Oct. 14.*

# IMPROVED HORSE CLOTHING.

**Secured by Letters Patent** ISSUED MAY 27, 1879, REISSUED MAR. 29, 1881.

The above cut represents the body-piece, the patent also covering the improvements in the hood. The following are the claims granted:

1. An improved blanket or covering, consisting of the body-piece A, flap G, and the extension B, for front or united together, so as to cover the body and legs of the animal, all substantially as herein described.

2. The blanket or covering A, having the flap G, and the extensions B, to fit the fore and hind legs of the animal, the front fastenings F G, and the permanent straps or bands E, substantially as and for the purpose herein described.

3. The blanket or covering A, with its extensions B, permanent securing-bands E, and the front fastenings F G, in combination with the elastic neck-extension H, substantially as and for the purpose herein described.

4. The blanket A and hood J, in combination with the elastic connecting-strip I, substantially as described, and for the purpose set forth.

5. The close-fitting hood J, having the elastic band L beneath the jaws, so that they may be allowed to move without disturbing the fit, and adapted to be secured to the cover by means of straps, substantially as herein described.

6. The improvement in covering-blankets for animals, consisting of the blanket A, having the flap G, and permanent straps or bands E and B, to secure it around the body, whereby the loss of more surcingles is avoided, substantially as herein described.

The right to make clothing in the United States will be sold on a royalty. Apply to the patentee,

**JOS. CAIRN SIMPSON,**

SAN FRANCISCO, CAL.

---

## SPECIMEN OF OUR ARTIST'S HUMOR

THE FISHMONGER.

HUNDREDS OF DELIGHTED ONES SEE, FOR THE FIRST TIME IN THEIR LIVES

### The Japanese Artist and Embroiderers

*At work in their native costume at*

# Ichi Ban, 22 & 24 Geary St.

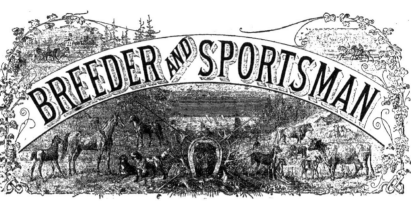

# BREEDER AND SPORTSMAN

Vol. I, No. 21.
NO. 508 MONTGOMERY STREET.　　SAN FRANCISCO, SATURDAY, NOVEMBER 25, 1882.　　SUBSCRIPTION
FIVE DOLLARS A YEAR.

## THE PADDOCK.

### An Equine Epizooty.

A disease of the nature of pinkeye is prevalent among the horses in the northern and southern parts of the county. John McNeill, a farmer on Old River near Tracy, has lost two valuable animals within a week, and he has three others that will not recover. Another farmer in the northern part of the county lost five and had to kill the sixth a few days ago. The horses refuse to eat, and stand around growing thinner and thinner until they die. The animals live less than a week from the time the symptoms first appear. It is said that while they become emaciated in body, their legs swell to a great size. As yet no remedy has been discovered that will cure the disease.—*Daily Evening Herald, Stockton.*

There is scarcely a question that the above is an aggravated type of the disease that has prevailed for the past season. Though it has been popularly termed "pinkeye," it is very different from that which was so named forty years ago, and the only analogy is the injection of the membrane lining the eyelids and nostrils.

It has been a baffling disease to us, and very different from anything we have previously known.

Of eight horses in our stable, only one escaped, viz.: Too Soon, a mare fifteen years old. The next oldest, X X, ten years old, had it quite severely, and has not yet entirely recovered after a duration of five months. Anteeo, three years old, attacked at the same time as X X, has been very peculiarly afflicted. For a long time he appeared to feel well, and never refused a feed until a few days before the race for the Stanford Stake, but he "lost his speed," and a brush of a quarter of a mile would tire him more than two miles at the same rate before he was attacked. His limbs would swell, perhaps a kind leg one morning, the next a fore. Though his testes are naturally small, with the power of drawing them up when in motion, at times they were swollen to an immense size, and the faculty of contraction lost. There would be sudden swelling of the neck at the junction with the head, and the fever before the Embryo Stakes were trotted, an abscess between the jaws became ripe and broke. There was not much of a discharge of pus at first, though by the latter part of the week the suppuration was free, and at this time of writing the opening is beginning to heal by granulation. The discharge from the nostrils was always slight, a sort of white mucus, though at times the coughing was so severe that there seemed to be danger of strangulation.

A two-year-old, Lady Viva, had it in a modified form, and when apparently entirely recovered she was sent to Sacramento to be trained in Mr. Winter's stable. She had been broken to harness and driven during the summer but never had a saddle on until she was sent to Sacramento the latter part of September. She had a relapse, more severe than at first, as she went off her feed, and had to be thrown out of training.

There were three yearlings, every one of them showing entirely different phases of disease. Antevolo, a brother to Anteeo, had been broken to harness and driven a short time before he was attacked. There was only a slight cough, and he never lost his spirits, and ate well with the exception of a day or two. One morning we found him with a swelling between the forelegs, and so sore and stiff that he had to be threatened with punishment to make him walk. So rapidly the swelling increased that it could almost be seen to progress, until it reached his sheath and enveloped the whole of his abdomen.

This state only lasted a short time, however, and though he was not harnessed for two or three weeks, in a week's time he had apparently recovered, and has been hearty and well ever since.

Sotoyome, a remarkably strongly-built colt, came from Mendocino county in August and had been taken with the disease during the journey. There was a distinct change in

his case. Though his legs swelled, and there was a slight running at the nose, the peculiarity was in his eyes. At first the charge of thick pus was from the left eye, and was so copious and acrid that it removed the hair from his cheek. Thinking that there might be some foreign substance in the eye, perhaps like a wild cat, a careful examination was made, but nothing could be discovered, and to prove that it came from the disease, after a lapse of several weeks, the other eye discharged the same kind of matter though much decreased in volume. While in this state he was broken to harness, and was somewhat dull; now that he has recovered he is as free and sprightly as can be desired. Sir Thad was similarly affected too, accompanied Lady Viva to Sacramento, and as in her case had a relapse.

Clito, the suckling, was the first in the stable to show the disease. He ran in a small lot with his mother and as the horses were driven on the abutting street, he would rush across for an interview. He ran freely at the nose, coughed some, but kept growing and doing as well as a colt could. Of course, he and his dam were liberally fed with hay and oats, twelve quarts of oats a day, which he ate his full share of. He was foaled the 6th of April and permitted to suck until the 14th inst., when we expected he might fall away. Such has not been the case, and, with the exception of Prince of Norfolk, we never saw a weanling that can compare with him for muscular development.

We instance these cases as showing what the pinkeye has been in our personal experience, and must conclude by saying that it is a mystery beyond our power to explain. In all probability the disease that is playing such havoc in San Joaquin is the same disease aggravated by the climatic change which have taken place in the last six weeks. It may be that the horses have been exposed to rain or cold drafts, or that a change has been made from idleness to severe labor or the reverse. We will be greatly obliged to our correspondents if they will favor us with their views, and those of them who had horses attacked, their method of treatment and results. All that we did was to give Dixon's condition powders, and in the case of Clito nothing was done.

### Rayon D'Or.

The following capital description of this celebrated horse is taken from the New York *Spirit of the Times*, and is so complete that there is no necessity for adding anything further. All of the New York papers join in eulogies and write in high praise of his form. The whole country will benefit by his importation, and in a few years, should there be no mishaps, his blood will be disseminated all over the whole country. It is supererogatory to descant on the value of the blood of the "late importations," as there are few indeed who will not concede the advantages.

There can scarcely be a question that the subject of the sketch will prove of the very highest class as a progenitor! The celebrated French race-horse and stallion Rayon d'Or arrived at this port on the steamer Queen of the National Line, on Saturday evening last, the 4th inst., after a passage of nearly fifteen days, having left Liverpool on the 21st ult. As is well known, Rayon d'Or was purchased on behalf of Mr. W. L. Scott of Erie, Pa., by Mr. William Easton, of the American Horse Exchange, at the sale at Dangu Stud in France, which took place early in September, the price paid being $30,000, which is the highest figure ever paid for an imported horse. Rayon d'Or was not brought from the vessel until Monday morning, and when he entered the Exchange Building, heavily blanketed, about half-past twelve, as Mr. Easton was selling the Lorillard lot, the crowd recognized him by his commanding presence, and there was a rush to get a look. He was walked straight to the box prepared for him, and at the conclusion of the sale was led out for inspection by Mr. John Davis, who brought him over, and deserves the most unstinted praise for the blooming condition

in which he landed him. There was some applause when the St. Leger winner was led into the ring looking like silk, and when he halted a murmur of admiration ran through the assemblage, and such expressions, as : "What a grand horse!" and "Such splendid shoulders!" and "What wonderful length!" were frequent. He was led about the ring for some time being posed in several attitudes, and was then returned to his box, where we afterwards visited him in company with Mr. Stull.

Rayon d'Or was bred by Mr. C. J. Lefevre, at the Chamant Stud, in France, in 1876. In color he is dark red chestnut of an exceeding rich hue, his flanks reflecting a golden sheen in the sunlight (hence his name, which, translated, means a ray of gold), and, beyond a roan star in his forehead, he has no marks. He is probably the tallest thoroughbred in America, standing 16½ß. His head is rather small, but shapely, and somewhat dished in the face; the eye is not particularly large, but placed high. His nostrils are large, but he is none too wide between the jaws for a horse of his undeniable clear wind. His cheeks are high, and the neck, at its setting on to the head, is deep. He has great reach in the neck, which is rather owed than crested, and though, horsemen as wont to dilate upon the beauty of the crested neck, it may be worth while calling their attention to the fact that the ewe-neck has been one of the characteristics of some of the greatest stayers. He does not mount up at the withers like his country-man, Mortemer, but his shoulders are the most superb imaginable, lying low and oblique, and of great length, and he has the "lean shoulder," over which old-time English critics rave. More beautifully placed shoulders we have never seen, and, added to this, he has great depth through the heart and girth. His whole forehand indicates great length of bridle, with his legs well under him, the arm of the swell being large and beautifully developed. His back is a model, being very short and broad over the loin, and the croup prominent. Behind the croup he cuts away somewhat, and the tail, which is set on rather high, has a curious rise at the root. His barrel is very round, with broad forearms, which arch in their curve from the spine making him more leggy in appearance than if his ribs were less curved and deeper. He couples well, and, though he might have more depth of quarters, nothing can exceed his enormous breadth and stifle power, and his gaskin or second thigh is massive. Rayon d'Or is what would be termed a "cat-hammed" horse, but there is a great sweep from the hip bone to the hocks, which are ever so slightly capped, but are models of size and bony formation, and well let down, while his legs are broad and flat. He fills in nicely behind the elbows, and, while he is a very short-backed horse, he covers a prodigious amount of ground. His feet are of good size, high and concave, but his pasterns are rather short and not clearly defined. This and an inclination to be rather flat-sided just at the flank are his principal defects, though we should rather have him a little less narrow in the chest. Otherwise, he is the most glorious horse the sun ever shone upon. His proportions are of the heroic mould, and he has by far greater length than any of the native strains to which our eye has become accustomed. His disposition is perfect, which speaks well for his handling, there being none of that wild-eyed viciousness seen in many of our stallions. As we stroked him in his box, Monday, his eye was as mild as a summer's morning, and he made no effort to resent the familiarity. We never saw a horse stand a voyage so well. The stalwart son of Flageolet was as blooming in his coat, which shone like satin, as Mr. Davis stripped him, and which in itself speaks volumes for the care bestowed upon horses imported through the agency of the American Horse Exchange, which has in its employ a corps of horsemen who would serve as models in many of our racing establishments.

### Hinda Rose Does a Fast Half-Mile.

New York, Nov. 23, 1882.

The *Herald* says: Governor Stanford's California filly, Hinda Rose, two years old, trotted half a mile over the track of the Gentlemen's Driving Park yesterday afternoon in 1:10½. The track was just quite fast, owing to a frost in the morning and the sun of the afternoon. She was timed by John Murphy and others and was driven by Marvin.

This is a wonderful performance though to many California trainers there is a phase of it which they will not understand. That is the effect of the frost. The surface freezes, solid perhaps, to a depth of two or more inches. The sun comes out and thaws a portion of it and that is as slippery as so much ice. Should it be warm enough to penetrate further the foot sinks through, and in either case it is a "slow track." It is very different from when the mud arises from rain and far more detrimental to speed.

# TURF AND TRACK.

## The Plunger and Jockey.

Walton is a godsend to the English knights of the equine reportorial pencil. There is scarcely a number of the turf papers of that country that has not something to relate about him as long as he is in that country; one of them relates the following anecdotes:

It is the pleasing habit of Luke the jockey (pleasing to backers of horses he does not ride, that is to say) to look round when he gets near the judge, divert his attention from his own horse and the winning post and take a friendly interest in the efforts of the other competitors. The result usually is that in a very few seconds he can see one or two of them without giving himself the trouble of turning his head just as the box is passed. Luke rode Sachem in the Cambridgeshire, and, as is known, the "American Plunger" backed the colt to win him some £50,000 or £70,000—in his calculations £10,000 more or less goes for nothing, though I confidently expect to see the day when Mr. Walton will consider such a wretched little sum as £10,000 of some importance. Knowing Luke's habit, therefore, Mr. Keene's master of the horse, Mr. Bathgate, a shrewd judge of riding and a keen observer, gave Mr. Walton a valuable tip before the race. "You go to Luke," he said, "and tell him that if he wins the race without looking round you'll give him £500." I do not know whether Mr. Walton knows much about racing, but he knows enough to be aware 'that a jockey is less likely to win if he turns round when he ought to be finishing and critically examines the rest of the field, and the Plunger went to Luke and promised him the money on the conditions named. As Luke was never far enough forward to look behind him for the probable winners he did not earn his reward.

And talking of "plungers" there have been others in America before the advent of Walton.- During the war there lived in St. Louis a man who made a great deal of money in government contracts. He was one of the best judges and handlers of mules in the country and was fortunate enough to be in with "the ring" that then controlled that business for the whole Northwest. As his bank account grew in size and assumed proportions in accordance with his desires he developed a fondness for turf and track sports, and in addition to owning racehorses and trotters he acquired wide-spread notoriety for the magnitude of his wagers. Though a liberal investor in the pools he was more partial toward "out-of-hand" betting as that attracted more attention and drew the eyes of the assemblage to his doings. He was a large, fine-looking man with a swarthy complexion and stentorian voice, and he had also a great fondness for showing off in the presence of the fair occupants of the ladies' stand. There was a trotting race in which he had a horse engaged, and in which was one belonging to Jim ———. The plunger had taken a prominent seat in the club stand, boasting of his horse and the money he would wager on him winning the victory, when it was at least ten to one the other way.

Somé Mary or Margaret managed to "carry the news" to Jim, and he was not long in taking a position in front of it.

"Mr. G———," he said, "I understand that your offer to bet $5,000 that your horse will be better than mine in this race."

"I do," was the prompt reply..

"Done," responds Jim, "I will make it again."

"All right, $10,000 that Billy beats Quaker," came 'from the plunger.

Penciling the bets in a memorandum book, Jim walked a few steps away and turning on his heel remarked: "We may as well go another $5,000, it is not much money for us you know." This was coming a little too hot for the big speculator, as there was a good prospect that Jim would keep badgering him as long as he had the advantage, and his tawny visage grew purple at the mortification of having to "back down" in the presence of hundreds of the belles of St. Louis.

"Hold on a minute," he exclaimed, and in a semitone lord enough for those in the vicinity to hear, continued: "I will bet him a $100,000," made his way to the quarter stretch. When he met Jim there was a change, and in a subdued voice he then accosted him:

"It is all right Jim, though you took me at an advantage and I will let the first $5,000 go, but you must let me off for the other."

"Very well," said Jim, "only be a little more careful how you shoot your mouth off again."

On another occasion there was a big race meeting in St. Louis and one of the big events was a purse of $5,000, heats of a mile, best three in five. Among the starters was Sue Lewis, a sister to Asteroid, and one of the first of the get of Lexington to show what a wonderful progenitor he was to become. She was owned by Joe Harper, and "send to send" running was his favorite instructions to his jockeys. She was ridden by "Old Abe," the most celebrated of the negro riders, who was just the one to get out the last link of the great speed which the mare was known to possess.

John M. Clay had Shedaddle in, Gil Patrick up, and there was another Yorkshire mare called Ann Travis with John Ford in the saddle. Writing entirely from recollection we are not positive about the other starters though as nearly as we can remember, Ed Thompson, George Cadwallader, and Tom Clark had mounts. The first heat Sue Lewis won quite handily but in the second these crafty old jocks got her pocketed, and held her back while Gil Patrick on Shedaddle opened a "fearful gap." The Abbey track had been a half mile and the only chance to extend it to a mile was to carry the same width which made the stretches over six hundred yards. They were forced to let her out at the head of the homestretch, though Shedaddle was so far in the lead that it appeared impossible for any horse to overtake her.

But Abe pulled her to the outside in order to obtain the firmer footing of the "walking path" and she came at a pace which would have tried the mettle of the fastest of the short horses to equal. It 'was a flash of chestnut with a black demon in the saddle, fairly writhing in contortions to increase the already marvelous speed,. A maniac rider, eyes flashing in excitement, and the foam seething through the clenched teeth, and the working of the muscles plainly visible under the light silken jacket. . He was gaining at every stride, and at the four-mile distance—one hundred and twenty yards in those days—there was only an open length between them. A quick, nervous touch of the spurs, a rapid and wicked out of the whip, some spasmodic movements of the reins and the chestnut mare and ebony rider are at the score a good length in front.

In company with R. A. Alexander we witnessed the race from the four-mile-distance stand. We never saw him nearly so much excited when his own horses were running, and when it became evident that Sue would win, he exclaimed:

"I have seen all the best jockeys of England ride, and not one of them is the peer of that old darky." It could not be gainsaid that it was a wonderful victory, but it was also as evident that after such superequine exertion it could not be expected that it would be repeated within the short time the rules gave between heats.

"Old John" left the mare in the "cooling out," tempting her to pick a few blades of grass he held in his hand. She scarcely nibbled at them, however, and the distended nostril, quivering limbs and heaving flanks; with the long shuddering inhalations 'told what a fearful struggle it had been. There were globules of blood on the white breeches of Abe and the pair leather tops of his boots, and the long shanks of the spurs were crimson.- His white teeth were yet firmly clenched, and his intensely black eye-still shone with the fierce excitement of the run home.

To any one who possessed a modicum of racing knowledge it was apparent that her chances for another heat were slim, indeed, but G——— was vociferating long odds that she would gain the victory.

"Five thousand to one," he shouted, "ten thousand to two thousand that Sue Lewis wins the race."

"Make it fifteen thousand to two and I will take 'it," responded a quiet looking man who spoke with an Irish accent.

"Thirteen to two," was the reply, flourishing a handful of greenbacks of large denominations in his hand.

"I'll take it;" the money was counted, placed in the stakeholder's hands and the wager consummated. .

It is almost needless to state that the "short end" won and the profits of a few carloads of mules were transferred to the British dominions.

It may not be out of place to "point 'a moral," with this short, unadorned tale, and that is the manifest injustice of this kind of racing. Singly, Sue Lewis could have easily beaten every one of her competitors, and even, without being caught in the pocket, she would, in all probability, have gained the victory. Not only unjust in causing her to lose that particular race, as it was a strain she never fully recovered from, and that fearful run after the exertion of the previous heat such a severe ordeal as to be a tax on her future career.

### Temper in American Horses in England.

There are comparatively few American bred horses in English training stables, and it is strange to note, says Rapier in the *Illustrated Sporting and Dramatic News*, how many of these have bad tempers. Foxhall and Iroquois are exceptions. The former has a tendency to shirk at visitors; and the unwary who went too near him carelessly might mistake the act for biting it he had a bit of their arm; but this is done with perfect good temper, and Iroquois is likewise amicable. Romeo, however, passed the first month of his residence in Wiltshire, I am told, almost on his hind legs, and with the best hands in the country on his mouth, he played the fool at the start for the Leger. Seminola, in one of his few essays, bolted at Kempton last year, jumped the rails and came near to killing his jockey. Comanche, in the first October Meeting at Newmarket, ran viciously against the palings of the enclosures and bolted Webb, saddle and all, off his back. Woodland showed temper and bolted twice when at the post at the same meeting. Golden Gate, in the Beaufort Handicap at Stockbridge, conducted himself vilely and had to be led to the post. General Scott emulated his misdeeds. Passaic, Wallenstein and Abbotsford wear the rogue's hood. Lord Murphy, one of Mr. Keene's, became as savage as a dog, and Gerald long since earned for himself at Newmarket the title of the mad horse. The question is whether the fault lies in the blood or the breeding. It is difficult to see how horses bred from some of our best strains of blood could be affected by the fact of being born in America, and the evil probably springs from the scant care bestowed on the breaking of the young ones. Two of the horses named above, however—Romeo and Golden Gate—were broken at Newmarket, though I do not know by whom or in what proportions the *sauviter in modo* and the *fortiter in re* were applied.

We have always been under the impression that a large proportion of vicious and unruly horses was caused by improper treatment, though there are strains of blood which are prone to become unmanageable. That so many of the American exportations have acquired the bad habits noted above can hardly be explained on this hypothesis, and it is difficult to account for the prevalence. Bad actions at the starting post are occasioned by several things. "Soreness" will give a colt a violent dislike to the course, though it often arises from severe punishment when running in a race. More races have been lost by an unmerciful use of the whip and spurs than have been won, and the severe flagellations that some jockeys give have an extremely pernicious effect. Public opinion is in a measure to blame for this unwarrantable treatment. If the rider does not thrash and spur the charge is made that he is "throwing" the race. In self-defense he inflicts punishment that he knows is wrong, and the animal has intelligence enough to know that it is unmerited, and fears a repetition when he is brought to face the starter. Very few horses require more than a touch of the spur or a sharp out of the whip, and where they are fully extended even this punishment may work injury. A slight motion of the bit, a cheering word, is oftentimes more potent, and at all times far better than a torrent of blows.

### MALI AND STANFORD STAKES.

#### The National Association of Trotting Horse Breeders.

NEW YORK, Nov. 4, 1882.

EDITOR BREEDER AND SPORTSMAN: You have several times lately referred to the "Stanford Stakes" as "the largest colt stakes ever trotted for." Permit me to say that this I believe is a mistake.

The Mali Stakes for foals of 1879, opened by this association and trotted for at its late annual meeting, amounted to $4,150, and was won by, the California-bred filly Wildflower.

I would in this connection call your attention among the other events of this association yet to be trotted for to the "Wilson Stakes," for foals of 1880, (to be trotted as four-year-olds) which with the subscription of the sires named and the sixty-three of their get originally nominated, on fifty of which second payments have already been made, now amount to $10,000 cash paid in, which with $50 each yet due from starters, it is reasonable to suppose will at maturity be increased to about $12,000.

This stake will probably be renewed the coming season upon conditions which will probably render it even more popular than before. L. D. PACKER, Secty.

Mr. Packer misunderstood us, as the claim was that for the number of colts engaged the Stanford was the largest trotting-colt stake ever decided.

Some years ago there was a stake for three-year-olds trotted on Shell Park, San Mateo county, that aggregated more money, as well as the Mali Stakes, but both of those had a larger number of nominations, with a greater number to start. We are pleased to hear that the Eastern Stakes for trotting colts are to be kept up, as there is not a State in the Union more interested in their perpetuation than California. There has been a grand beginning by Wildflower and Hinda Rose, and this will stimulate our wealthy breeders to make nominations. None of them can object to naming in the "Wilson Stakes," and every stallion of note on this coast should be represented. The position which we took long ago that trotting colt stakes were henceforth to be the events is becoming rapidly verified. Racing would lose the greater part of the interest if the contests were restricted to the old campaigners, and though the time classification obviates some of the difficulties, that has objectionable features which are a great drawback. We are much obliged to Mr. Packer for the letter and trust that he will keep us fully versed in regard to the doings of the association.

### English Racing.

LONDON, November 14, 1882.

The Shrewsbury November meeting began to-day, the principal race being the Great Shropshire Handicap over the New Mile. It had eleven starters and was won by Mr. Jardine's Experiment by fully six lengths, with the odds at 16 to 1 against her. The favorite was Lord Ellesmere's Lowland Chief with the odds at 4 to 1, but he failed to get a place, Mr. R. S. Evans' Falkirk running second and Mr. P. H. Cooper's George Mansfield third. The conditions were as follows:

SUMMARY.

The Great Shropshire Handicap, for three-year-olds and upwards, at £25 each, £10 forfeit, with £200 added, the second to save his stake; £6 each, the only liability if forfeit is declared by Tuesday, October 31; winners after the declaration of the weights selling this excepted, to carry 4 lbs. extra; twice, or once of £200, 16 lbs. extra; closed with 71 subscribers, of which 43 declared forfeit; New Straight Mile.

Mr. R. Jardine named b m Experiment, 5, by Friponnier, dam Wild Aggie, 102 lbs. ... 1
Mr. R. S. Evans named b c Falkirk, 4, by Scottish 'Chief, dam Little Jessima, 92 lbs. ... 2
Mr. P. H. Cooper named b or r c George Mansfield, 4, by George Frederick, dam Agnes de Mansfield, 88 lbs. ... 3

Eight others ran, including the four-year-old colt Lowland Chief, at 124 lbs.

The result of the Shropshire Handicap as above is a full proof of what has been repeatedly said, that the "back-end" handicaps in England are but little better than gambling affairs between a lot of "broken-down-no-account" horses and an occasional good one saved for certain races, for not one of eleven starts, including the Great Northern Leger of Stockton and the Park Hill Stakes at Doncaster. As a four-year-old he seemed to have gone to pieces. He ran eight times, of which he won only the Heaton Park Welter Cup Handicap at the Manchester autumn meeting, carrying 126 pounds. He subsequently ran fourth for the Lancashire Cup at the Manchester November meeting, which was his last appearance until the Western meeting at Ayr (Scotland) last September, when under Mr. Jardine's "blue and silver" he was third for the Ayr Gold Cup, which was probably his only race this year until the Shropshire Handicap, as above.—*New York World.*

Burt Scully, the well-known trainer of thoroughbred horses residing near Paris, Ky., was shot and instantly killed on the evening of the 31st ult., by Hooker Stivers, in Paris. The parties live on adjoining farms and the women of the two families quarreled about some turkeys. Sherman Stivers, aged seventeen years, a brother of Hooker, shot the turkeys which were claimed by Scully's housekeeper. Scully returned from the Memphis races soon after, and hearing of the case, and meeting young Stivers in a spring wagon, he took him out and boxed his ears. When Hooker Stivers heard of this, he placed a shot-gun in his buggy and drove to town to meet Scully. Upon seeing Scully, he called out to him and Scully started toward him, but when he got within a few feet of Stivers the latter deliberately shot him dead. Scully, according to the testimony of his nephew, was unarmed. Scully has been identified with the turf since he was eight years old, and has trained several winners. He was not regarded as a quarrelsome person.

Brighton Beach is to have an opposition. The Rockaway Jockey Club of Rockaway Beach, with a capital of $300,000, has obtained articles of incorporation. It understood that the club will build a race-track at Rockaway and by offering large purses endeavor to secure some of the patronage now bestowed on Brighton Beach.

# THE TROTTING COLTS OF 1882.

## The Strains United in the Youngsters who have Achieved Prominence.

The following from the *Turf, Field and Farm* of Nov. 11th is a very interesting description of the doings of the trotting colts in that section of the country. There is little to add at this time as when the year comes to an end we will have something to say about the California colts. There have been so many startling performances on this slope that the Eastern folks are prone to give attention only to those of that character, and when under the standard of the "top notch," underrate the effort. The colts here have done well, and Adrian, Adair, Clay Jr., and Bonnie among the three-year-olds, Pride, Ruby and Neluska in the two-year-old division, and Dawn, Mockingbird, Bedouin and Antevolo in the baby class merit more than a passing word.

Albert W, with all due regard for the champion four-year-old, Jay-eye-see, has claims for the first place, as we cannot agree that 2:22 in a last heat is his best performance, holding that a second heat of two miles on a soggy track compelling a wide detour on the turns, on account of the softness, in 4:51½ is the superior. It may be that he will be trotted to beat the 2:19 of the great son of Dictator, and with a fair prospect of accomplishing the task. The value of the thoroughbred blood in the trotter is becoming so apparent that only the obstinately stubborn now dispute it. The allusion in the closing paragraph is very happy:

When the leaves fall before the frosts and winds of November the trotting season is about over, especially here in the North, and we can learn something from a glance at the records. The prominent two-year-olds are Fugue and Hinda Rose, one Kentucky and the other California bred. The meeting of these two was looked forward to with much interest at Lexington in October. Hinda Rose had gained great renown by trotting in 2:36½ as a yearling, but it was argued that the long journey from the Pacific to the Atlantic coast, and from New York to Kentucky, would place her at a disadvantage with Fugue. Unfortunately Fugue had been weakened by epizootic, and ten days prior to the day appointed for the race at Lexington, Oct. 11, her driver had become fatally ill, and she was short of work. At the last moment Brassfield was secured to pilot her. The track was heavy but the day was fine. Hinda Rose had never appeared in company before, and she was nervous. She got off in a pace, and Fugue showed the way around the first turn and went under the wire in the lead in 2:36¾, distancing two of the field. In the second heat Hinda Rose acted as well as Marvin could ask, and she won in 2:32, with three in the field behind the flag. In the third heat the pace was too fast for Fugue, and Hinda Rose won in 2:32. Had the track been firm and elastic, 2:30 would have been beaten. Hinda Rose was got by Electioneer, out of Beautiful Bells, by The Moor, son of Clay Pilot; second dam Minnehaha (dam of Sweetheart and Eva), by Bald Chief, and third dam Nettie Clay, by C. M. Clay Jr. The dam of Green Mountain Maid; the dam of Electioneer, was a mare, judging from her form, three-quarters thoroughbred; but the stallion has produced colts with pure trotting action out of all kinds of dams—pacing, trotting and running. Clay Pilot was a son of Neaves' C. M. Clay Jr., and his dam was by Pilot Jr., son of a pacing and trotting horse and of a mare nearly thoroughbred. Bald Chief was a combination of trotting and running blood. His sire, Bay Chief, was a son of Mambrino Chief and a running bred mare, and his dam was by Hunt's Commodore, running stock. The first dam of C. M. Clay Jr. was by Abdallah, and the second dam by Lawrence's Eclipse. In Hinda Rose we find the trotting crosses on top, backed in every instance by thoroughbred strains. Her breeding, according to the judgment of some critics, is perfection. Fugue was got by King Rene, out of Fuga, by George Wilkes; second dam Betsy Trotwood by Clark Chief; third dam by Ericsson, and fourth dam by Sir William. Clark Chief was by Mambrino Chief, out of Little Nora, by Downing's Bay Messenger, and he met with great success in the stud, being the sire among others of Croxie and Woodford Chief. King Rene is by Belmont out of Blandina, a great brood mare by Mambrino Chief; second dam the Burch mare (dam of Rosalind), by Brown Pilot, the third dam said to be thoroughbred. Fugue is equally as well bred as Hinda Rose; the trotting crosses are on top supported by pacing and running strains; and many incline to the opinion that she will defeat in her three-year-old form the California bred filly.

The commanding three-year-olds of 1882 are Algath, Alroy, Wildflower, Code, Eva, Endymion and Butterfly. Algath, bred at Glenview, won a race at Louisville and then went to Chicago and reduced her record to 2:25½. She is rapid and has a level head, and it is claimed that she would have beaten 2:25 had the day been favorable. In the race she had to fight a raw, chilling wind. Her sire, Cuyler, was got by Rysdyk's Hambletonian out of Gray Rose, by Harris' Hambletonian, and her dam, Haroldine, was by Harold, out of Missouri, by Mambrino Chief, and she out of a mare by Woodford, thoroughbred son of Kosciusko. Woodbine, the dam of Woodford Mambino and Wedgewood, as is generally known, was a daughter of the same thoroughbred Woodford. In Algath we find a welding of Hambletonian, Mambrino Chief and running strains. In the middle of October her owners were ready and willing to ship her from Louisville to New York and trot her against the pick of the three-year-olds of the country. Alroy was bred at Marshland in Tioga county, New York, and he trotted three races at the meeting of the National Association of Trotting-Horse Breeders, held at the Gentlemen's Driving Park in September and October, and won all with ease. In the second heat of the Nursery Stakes he made a record of 2:27½, which is the best ever placed to the credit of an Eastern-bred colt. Peacemaker, the sire of Alroy, was got by Ryskyk's Hambletonian, out of Sallie Feagles, by Smith's Clay, and she was out of a mare by Hickory. Mason Girl, the dam of Alroy, is a daughter of Arabian Chief and Lady Mason, by Seely's American Star, grandam by Commodore; and Arabian Chief was by Toronto Chief, out of a mare highly bred and represented as having come from Arabia. Lady Mason was one of the gamest mares ever driven on the roads of Brooklyn, and her sire was largely running bred, as also was her dam. The Peacemaker blood is flashy, but the breeder of Alroy wisely backed it up with plastic running crosses, and thus gave us the fastest three-year-old ever foaled East of the Alleghanies. Butterfly was defeated in the three-year-old race at Chicago, but she had shown her owner 2:25 at Lexington before she was shipped North. Young Jim, the sire of Butterfly, was got by George Wilkes out of dam of Jim Irving, a mare by Lear's Sir William, a running-bred horse. The dam of Butterfly was by George Wilkes, but the filly has inherited the finish and nervous temperament of Young Jim. Eva is the sister of Sweetheart. Her sire was Sultan, a son of The Moor, and her dam Minnehaha. She was beaten in the three-year-old purse at Chicago by Code, having been demoralized by a collision with Butterfly; but in October she showed a mile in 2:26, and was anxious for a race with Wildflower, Algath and Alroy. Although not in the best of form, Code won the three-year-old purse at Chicago in July in 2:31¾, 2:33, 2:31. In September, at Maysville, he trotted against time and made a record of 2:30, and at the Fall Meeting of the Kentucky Trotting-Horse Breeders' Association, Oct. 12, he won the Kentucky stakes after a contest of five heats with Endymion and Jeptha D. He lost the first and second heats in 2:33½, 2:33½, but won the third, fourth and fifth heats in 2:31½, 2:30¾, 2:31. Code is a young horse of great resolution. His sire, Dictator, brother of Dexter, was got by Rysdyk's Hambletonian, out of Clara, by Seely's American Star, and his dam, Crop (dam of Blanch Amory), was by Pilot Jr. Seely's American Star was three-quarters running bred, and his blood gave fire and repeating capacity to Dexter. Pilot Jr. was by old pacing and trotting Pilot, out of Nancy Hope, by thoroughbred Havoc, and she out of Nancy Taylor, by Craig's Alfred, son of imported Medley. The running crosses are close up to the trotting crosses in Code, and it would be difficult to find a steadier performer in harness. Endymion, a black colt, won the Stallion Produce stakes at Lexington, Sept. 2, and made a record of 2:39½, and he won two heats, although out of form, from Code, in October, as stated above. He is by Dictator, out of Annie, by Morgan Rattler, and she out of a mare by Mambrino Chief. He has a great deal of the snap of Dexter. Wildflower trotted in 2:21 as a two-year-old, and after a long journey from California defeated, in her three-year-old form, at Gentlemen's Driving Park, in October, Meander, Senator Sprague, Lucy Walter and Earnest Maltravers. Her time was 2:32, 2:27½. She had no other engagement this side of the Rocky Mountains, although she was shipped from New York to Kentucky and back. She was bred at Palo Alto, and she was got by Electioneer, out of Mayflower, by St. Clair. At Sacramento, May 7, 1872, Mayflower made a record in a third heat of 2:30½, wearing shoes weighing two pounds each on her fore feet, in addition to a roll around each pastern filled with two pounds of shot. Her performance, rigged in this way, was simply wonderful. She is a mare of small stature, but is lengthy. The blood of St. Clair is not known, but all the circumstances lead to the belief that it was a mixture of pacing and thoroughbred strains.

The four-year-olds next invite attention. In the fore part of the season it was thought that Phil Thompson would have no rival. He had trotted in 2:21 as a three-year-old, had shown a trial in June of 2:21 on a track four seconds slow, and his owner challenged in vain for a match. He was taken to Chicago in July, where he got off, went to Buffalo and was placed in the hospital, where he came near dying, and now is in winter quarters at the Gentlemen's Driving Park, New York. Red Wilkes, the sire of Phil Thompson, was got by George Wilkes, out of Queen Dido, by Mambrino Chief; second dam by Red Jacket, and third dam believed to be thoroughbred. The dam of Phil Thompson was got by John Dillard, out of a mare by Gill's Vermont, and she was out of a mare by Herr's Bellfounder Jr. John Dillard was by Indian Chief, out of Lady Jackson, by Mack, by Hampton's Whip, py Blackburn's Whip; and Indian Chief was by imported Chief, out of a mare by Kirkland. Gill's Vermont was by Downing's Vermont, and Herr's Bellfounder Jr. was by Brown's Bellfounder, out of a mare by Shakespeare. All the bottom crosses of Phil Thompson's dam, a mare of great stamina, are thoroughbred. Farce showed a mile at Woodlake in 2:23, but she got off and did not start. She is by Princeps, out of Roma, by Golddust, and she out of a mare by Pilot Jr. Princeps is a son of Woodford Mambrino, son of Mambrino Chief and Woodbine, daughter of thoroughbred Woodford. Jay-eye-see stands out conspicuously as the great four-year-old trotter of 1882. At Chicago, in July, he trotted a great race in the four-year-old class. No special effort was made to win with him until in the fifth heat, which he captured in the fast time of 2:22¾. He also won the sixth heat in 2:23½. In the seventh heat he was sent away in a tangle, and Doble lost his temper and did not succeed in settling him until he was virtually out of the race. The heat was won by Waiting in the slow time of 2:30. Great as this performance was it was thrown into the shade by the four-year-old race at Chicago in September. Jay-eye-see lost the first heat to Bronze in 2:22¼, but won the second, third and fourth heats in 2:29½, 2:19, 2:19. He was shipped to Lexington in October, where he trotted a trial in 2:18¾ before he fell lame from bad shoeing, and was turned out. The feet of the Dictators have the Star defects, and they require scientific treatment in the blacksmith shop. Jay-eye-see is the fastest horse of his age and inches ever foaled. He is under 15 hands, and yet he has the speed of the whirlwind. He was got by Dictator, out of Midnight, by Pilot Jr., and she out of Twilight, thoroughbred daughter of Lexington. He is bred very much like Maud S, and the blood of the running horse predominates in him. Bronze was got by Morgan Messenger, a pacing horse, and her dam was a mare of fine breeding. In California, Saturday, Sept. 23, the bay stallion Albert W, four years old, won the 2:22 class, trotting the third heat in 2:22, the fourth in 2:22½, and the fifth heat in 2:24. He has trotted in several other races, but this is his best performance. Albert W was got by Electioneer, out of the sister of Aurora, by John Nelson, and John Nelson was by imported Trustee, out of the Redmond mare, by Abdallah. The great California four-year-old, like Jay-eye-see, has plenty of running blood in his veins, and the crosses are close up.

The lesson to be drawn from the story so briefly told is this: The man who sets up the dogma that a mixture of trotting and running strains will destroy the fast and light harness horse, mouths words in the face of facts. A judicious blending of plastic thoroughblood with cold trotting blood gives us finish, an outline in harmony with speed and the will or nerve force to strive to be first at the winning post. If we are wise we will draw our conclusions from the results of the great battles on the track, and not from theories born of prejudice in the unhealthy air of a garret, and which fly in the face of demonstrated truths.

## Racing Reminiscences.

We see in the last number of Mr. J. C. Simpson's paper, the Breeder and Sportsman, of Oct. 28th, an article with the above caption copied from a communication of T. B. M. in the Portland *Oregonian*. As a usual thing we do not notice the erroneous statements in the papers not specially devoted to turf matters, because if we did we would have no time or space to devote to anything else, but T. B. M.'s errors in turf matters are so glaring and some of his reflections so unjust on the living and dead that in deference to the truth of history we notice them. Certainly T. B. M. must have a fertile imagination, for he states many things in the wrong year, and some that never did happen. We will take up some of his statements and show their unreliability. He says: "It was well along in the fall of 1852 when I reached Lexington, Ky., and saw for the first time a race 'run for blood.' Five horses started, the favorite being Mr. John Clay's Star Davis. The race was mile heats, three in five, and the Star won in three straight heats. He banged in all heats below 1:46, and could have run any one of them in 1:43 had he been sent for it. In the same stable with Star Davis was a beautiful chestnut filly, likewise a three-year-old. I allude to Madeline, grandam of Iroquois. She won a two-mile stake for colts and fillies, at the same meeting, with most ridiculous ease.

Now the truth is Star Davis did not run at Lexington, Ky., the fall of 1852. He won the Association Stakes, mile heats, May 24th, 1852, beating four others in 1:47, 1:46½. So it will be seen that T. B. M.s report is a myth, as well as the time. Madeline did not run at the fall meeting, but ran May 27th, 1852, for a $150 purse, for all ages, mile heats, best three in five, which was won by Mr. Webb Ross' b c, 4 years, by Boston, dam Blinkey, 5 2 4 2 1 1; Big Indian, 4 years, 4 3 1 3 1 ds. Big Indian came in first for sixth heat, but was distanced for foul riding. Madeline, 3 years, 1 1 3 4 dr; Hexamiter, 4 years, 3 4 2 2 ds; Gulnare, 2 ds. Time—2:05½, 2:00½, 2:03½, 1:59, 1:59, 1:59. So this is incorrect also. Madeline was not brought back to Kentucky by Col, S. D. Bruce as T. B. M. says but was bought by the late Hon. James B. Clay of Gen. E. N. Wilcox of Detroit, Mich.

In the same connection he gives a mythical statement about Princeton and a horse called Blue Ruin. Mr. Clay never owned a horse called Blue Ruin, nor was ever Princeton entered in, or won a post stake, two mile heats. He won a sweepstakes for three-year-olds, two-mile heats, at Lexington, Ky., in 1855, beating a bay filly by Yorkshire, dam Dick Doty's dam, a ch c by Yorkshire, dam Minstrel, in 4:01, 3:43½, and the statement of T. B. M. about beating Die Clapperton in the second heat is untrue for the two never met in a race.

He gives a description of the celebrated John Ford and describes a race of four-mile heats that he says took place at Smithfield, Ky., between Denmark, Jerry, Lancaster and Mary Waller, of sixteen miles, won by Denmark. No such race ever took place. He also speaks of John Ford saying he wanted to see one Derby and then die. "He saw one, too, won by Thormanby with Dundee on three legs at his throatlatch, Umpire by Lecompte beaten away off yonder. Ford's money was all on Dundee, and he stood to win about $1,400 with $1.50 had Dundee won." Thormanby won the Derby in 1860, with the Wizard second, Horror third, Dangu fourth, Umpire finished seventh. Thirty horses started and the writer witnessed the race; Dundee was a two-year-old in 1860 and ran for the Derby in 1861, won by Kettledrum, Dundee beaten a length, second. So this statement is incorrect. Starke as he says won the Goodwood Stakes in 1859, but he did not win the Goodwood Cup the following year, 1860, but in 1861. He introduces the late Mr. Thos. Patterson into the article and represents him as speaking more ungrammically than a cornfield negro. While Mr. Patterson was not a man of much education, he used good language. He gives a race at Mobile, Ala., between Charmer and Wade Hampton; the latter won the first heat and Patterson wanted to draw Charmer, but the judges would not permit it. Wade Hampton sulked in the second heat and was distanced. No such race ever took place. These two met at Mobile in 1853, and Wade Hampton beat Charmer in straight heats in 3:50, 3:49. They met again the same week at the same place, three-mile heats, and Charmer distanced him the first heat. We think that T. B. M. has got mixed a race between Wade Hampton and Didie or Maid of Orleans, two-mile heats, that was run at New Orleans in 1854. Wade Hampton won the first heat, sulked in the second and was distanced.

He also introduces Mr. J. B. Pryor, and makes him, a very intelligent gentleman, talk in negro gibberish. Mr. Pryor went to England to train for Mr. Ten Broeck in 1860, and did not return to America the next year as stated by T. B. M., but trained for Mr. Ten Broeck until he gave up his stable in 1867; then Mr. Pryor trained for Baron Schickler in France until he came to train for Hon. A. Belmont in 1872. He tells a very amusing anecdote of a horse he says once owned by Mr. Ten Broeck, called London, who kicked off an Irishman's hat. It is a pity to destroy so good a story, but the truth must be told. Mr. Ten Broeck never owned a horse by the name of London.

T. B. M. has written a very amusing and readable article, and it seems a pity to destroy it. As a conglomeration of erroneous turf statements we have never seen its equal.—*Kentucky Live Stock Record.*

We publish the above in order that the errors may be corrected, though in justice to T. B. M. it is proper to state that the article in which the blunders were made was written where the author was without references, and writing entirely from memory they worked their way in. Again if it had been written for a turf paper more care would have been taken in the "reminiscences" and his memory stimulated to return the correct answer. We all know what a treacherous thing memory is after the lapse of so many years, especially to those who have witnessed a great deal of racing. Occurrences become blended and races "consumedly" mixed. The only safety for a turf writer is to go to the records whenever it is necessary to give dates, etc., and, not having these, and the object being to write a "readable" article for the Sunday edition of a daily paper, the lapses came in. Paradoxical as it may appear, men who have the faculty of a good memory are the most likely to fall in error. Depending upon that they are prone to avoid the labor of hunting up the proofs and this confidence is almost sure to lead to mistakes.

Had T. B. M. forseen that his article would meet the eye of so competent a critic as the editor of the Kentucky *Live Stock Record* more pains would have been taken. Written in the far-off (from Kentucky) Northwest, and for readers who could not otherwise than be pleased with the story, it effected its purpose. Captivated by the style our assistant copied it so that we did not see it until the paper came out or we would have corrected some of the mistakes. From having owned a daughter of Charmer we are somewhat familiar with the races run by her illustrious dam, and we are thus well aware that Mr. Pryor and Tom Patterson were placed in a false light. The allusion to John Ford probably arose from a statement made by him previous to his trip to England. Ford at one time trained for us, and the first work given the horses was on a private course on "Bird Farm" in Iowa. John would rehearse the scenes he witnessed and took part in in England with great gusto, and his stories had snap enough to interest his auditors, no matter how slight their inclination was horsewards. By the way, taking all things into consideration we regarded Ford as occupying the topmost round as a jockey, and, though at times somewhat erratic, a first-class trainer. We will not be positive, and if wrong Mr. Bruce will please correct; he was the only American jockey who won for Ten Broeck in England. Gil Patrick made such a blunder with Princess that he was sent home, though, perhaps, there were others who were successful.

## P. C. BLOOD HORSE ASSOCIATION.

### The Fall Meeting at the Bay District Course —Third Day.

The third day of the fall meeting of the Pacific Coast Blood Horse Association, was brought to a close on Saturday last. It ranks as second on the programme, though the racing on the "extra day" which marked the opening was too good to be ignored, and hence we number from that. It was a beautiful afternoon, for though there was "an eager and nipping air" as the sun drew near the horizon, and it became actually cold when old Sol became wrapped in the shining blanket of the Pacific, that was probably owing to the streets being somewhat damp and the absence of an electrical warming-pan to make them more comfortable. Those who went early enough, especially those who drove through the park, were well repaid for their promptness. There was scarcely the semblance of a breeze and the shrubbery and flowers were bright in the noonday sun. There were groups of happy people sauntering about, and the benches by the music stand were filled with occupants. A trio of cats were sunning themselves on the warm side of a pine tree, but the rustle of a bevy of quails awoke them into animation, and the grimalkins aroused from their languid position, and in an instant the sweet repose was transformed into activity. Crouching, gliding along, each took a different direction in order to surround the clump from which came the twittering of the birds, and halting to see what the result of the well-executed movement would be there was gratification that it was futile. A whirr of the wings, a rapid flight to another shelter, and three disappointed felines, showing plainly in their downcast looks and dejected demeanor their feelings of dejection, were the upshot. They will try again, however, and like a game horse coming againg and again persevere until they have made a quail supper, though the accessories of toast may be wanting, and there will be a lack of brimming "beakers" of champagne to wash it down. If they would confine themselves to a raid on the gophers which are rearing the dark mounds on the lawns and stand guard against the squirrels obtaining an entrance it will be all right, but we must acknowledge that we would rather see the handsome birds among the copses than pretentious ornamentation of another character.

The course was in the best possible condition. Some pronounced it too hard, but as the three days' racing has taken place without a single horse, so far as we know, "pulling up lame" that criticism is not deserved.

The attendance was much larger than on the previous days, and though the racing was well worthy of a far larger crowd, it was not bad for San Francisco. The great drawback is the opportunity which the racing ground in the park gives for a free sight, and more aggravating than that are the beer-houses on the corner. These have balconies almost abutting on the track fence, and these were crowded as close as they could be packed with a dense mass of people. Between the races they could sit at their ease and drink beer and when the horses were running as fine a view can be obtained as from any portion of the grounds, excepting when there is a close finish. Some plan will have to be hit upon to prevent these "deadheads" from occupying such an advantageous position, and though the view from the balconies of the beer-houses can be obstructed the spectators in the park will be able to see until the trees and shrubbery are dense enough to furnish a natural veil.

The first race was a dash of seven-eighths of a mile, with seventeen entries, seven of which came to the post. These were Jim Douglas, Joe Howell, Premium, Ella Doane, May D, Bolis, and Bob. At the first opening of the pool sales on the ground, Jim Douglas was a great favorite, selling for $50, Joe Howell $25, and the others grouped as the field, $20. There were changes before the start for the race, Jim Douglas, Joe Howell and "the field" selling for the same amounts. Bob was as crazy as in the race of a week ago. He did his best to unseat his rider, and after a false start, in which he ran 200 yards, it took some time to get him back to the score. It was a very difficult lot to handle, and the official who held the flag was unable to bring them into subjection. They danced for some time, and when the signal was given it was to about as bad a send-off as is ever seen. The two favorites were left away behind, so that there was a long gap between them and the leaders, and the race was virtually ended so far as they were concerned. At the outset, Premium was away with the first division, and she increased the lead to quite a gap as they passed the half-mile pole. When she went by the three-quarter mark Bolis and May D were the nearest, and Jim Douglas had closed a large portion of the immense gap, but he was still too far behind to have any hopes of victory. From that point home Premium had comparatively an easy task, winning with something to spare; May D was second, Jim Douglas, nothwithstanding the ground he had lost on the start, third. The rider of Howell wisely did not make a run for a victory, which was as nearly impossible as could be beyond his reach, and Bob, the horse which had made most of the trouble, reached the post last. There was no official time, though outsiders made it 1:29.

SUMMARY.

BAY DISTRICT COURSE, Saturday, November 18, 1882.—Purse $200, $50 to second; dash of seven-eighths of a mile; winners of three-mile dash or heats of three-quarters of a mile—on previous days—to carry ten pounds extra; of both events fifteen pounds extra.

J. B. Haggin's ch m Premium, aged, by Castro—by St. Louis (Patsy Duffy)........ 1
J. & H. C. Judson's ch m May D, 4 years, by Wildidle—Nettie Brown (Billy Appleby)........ 2
Geo. Howson's br c Jim Douglas, 4 years, by Wildidle—by Norfolk (10 lbs penalty) (H. Howson)........ 3
Joe Howell, Ella Doan, Bolis and Bob ran unplaced. No time.

The second race was heats of 1⅛ miles, the starters Fred Collier, Jo Dion, Nathan Coombs and Belshaw. Collier was a big favorite, bringing $60, while all the others were rated at $20, and the result of the race fully warranted this estimate. Though the favorite was pulled back to the last position when first passing the stand, and never made a run until fairly into the stretch, he led the others at the finish without having felt the tickling of whip or touch of spur. The heats were won so easily that there is no necessity for further description than to say that the first was made in 1:58¾, the second in 1:59½.

SUMMARY.

Same Day—Purse $250; second horse to receive $50; entrance free; heats of a mile and an eighth; maiden three-year-olds allowed seven pounds; four-year-olds, twelve pounds; and maidens five years old and over, twenty pounds; the winner of the dash at this distance on first day to carry five pounds extra.

Stemler & Ayers name ch c Fred Collier, 4 years, by Joe Hooker—Puss, by Norfolk (Patsy Duffy)........ 1 1
J. & H. C. Judson name b g Belshaw, 4 years, by Wildidle—by Hercules (Billy Appleby)........ 2 2
Wm. Boots names br h Nathan Coombs, aged, by Lodi—Miami, (carried three pounds over) (Fred Carillo)........ 3 3
E. S. Paddock names b g Joe Dion, 4 years, by Norfolk—Nevada (George Howson)........ 4 4

Time—1:58¾, 1:59½.

The next race proved to be lively in more ways than one. The betting was brisk, and though at the opening Forest King was a great favorite, just before the start, the field brought nearly as much money, and Maria F had admirers who rushed their money in at short odds. In the first race there were many pools sold, Douglas being a strong favorite at the opening, though a short time before the start it was even betting all around, Jim Douglas, Joe Howell and the field being the manner they were sold and the prices the same. It was so generally conceded that Fred Collier must win that in his race he was held at $60 to $20 against all the others before the first heat, and after winning that, the odds were so long that there were neither layers or takers. While Forest King kept the first place the men from the mountains stuck pertinaciously to the home-bred colt and their faith, as the sequel will show, ended in fruition.

It was a handicap for three-year-olds, and there were six starters, viz., Maria F., 106 pounds; Garfield, Forest King, Atalanta and Jocko, each with 100 pounds, and Lizzie P, 9 pounds. The distance was one and a quarter miles, and a better start was never given that number of horses. There was scarcely half a length difference when the flag fell and all were moving finely. It was a beautiful race. The six were in a bunch when they passed the stand, saving that Forest King had a lead of a length, though soon after he was pulled back and Lizzie P was first at the quarter-pole, the half-mile having been run in fifty-four seconds. She still led when the half-mile mark was reached, and at that point Jocko was second, the others so close together that it was difficult to separate them. About midway up the upper turn Jocko came up, and on entering the homestretch it was evident that there would be a merry run home. Garfield was on the outer side of the course, Jocko in the center, and behind them Forest King was coming, and the three had an exciting tussle as to which would reach the wire first. Neither of the others, however, could get to the Montana-bred colt, and he finished first, Forest King second, Garfield third, with the others not far behind; the time, 2:11.

The winner was bred in Helena, Montana, and is assuredly a very promising colt. He is by Carriboo, his dam Reply by Enquirer, and she from Colleen Bawn by Endorser, one of the late H. P. McGrath's favorite mares. Carriboo was by Lexington, his dam Alice Jones by imported Hedgeford, and she one of the "old blue hen's" chickens, being a daughter of Blue Bonnet by imported Hedgeford. This is a rare pedigree, Lexington on the sides of sire and dam, and that backed by a glorious galaxy of notable performers. Gano is a grand-daughter of Alice Jones, who was a sister to the dam of Sue Lewis and Asteroid, and from Blue Bonnet came Thunder, Lightning, Loadstone, Lancaster, etc. Carriboo gained distinction on the flat and over hurdles and at nearly all the distances. The following is the

SUMMARY.

J. P. Woolman names gr c Jocko, 109 lbs. (John Williams)........ 1
L. Stanford names br c Forest King, 109 lbs. (Ed. Fallon)........ 2
R. J. Green names gr c Garfield, 109 lbs. (Geo. Howson)........ 3
Geo. Hearst names ch f Maria F, 106 lbs........ 0
Theo. Winters names ch f Atalanta, 106 lbs........ 0
W. L. Pritchard names b f Lizzie P, 106 lbs........ 0

Time—2:11.

The hurdle race brought out two starters, Hattie B, by Norfolk, and Mollie H, by Wildidle. The race was one and one-quarter miles, over five hurdles, Hattie B the favorite. The first jockey who essayed to ride Mollie H, cantering her by the stretch, endeavored to make her jump the hurdle, when she tripped and he rolled off and for some time lay as though he were insensible. He was not hurt, and another being substituted they were soon off. Again Mollie H caught the first hurdle and turned it over, leaving almost a clear space for Hattie. Mollie was a long way in the lead when she passed the stand, and the second hurdle, a little further on, was handsomely accomplished. Hattie B also made a clean jump, though her competitor was at least fifty yards in front, and the third obstacle was handsomely overcome by both. Hattie B was only a few lengths behind at the fourth hurdle, near the half-mile pole, and as Mollie knocked it down in the leap the other did not have to waste her strength in vaulting. She took the lead before reaching the starting point. The first hurdle, according to the laws governing this kind of sport, could not be replaced, and from there it was a test of speed, which it fell to the lot of the favorite to place to her credit, Hattie B winning in 2:43.

And thus ended the sport of the afternoon, the only thing to mar the harmony being one of those unfortunate circumstances that once in a while occur. With such a horse as Bob there is always a liability, and, as the rule gives the power, the only course for the starter to pursue is to place such an animal in the rear of all the others, and at a distance that will not interfere.

#### Thursday.

The first race was the Frash Stakes, a sweepstake of $25, each, p. p., with $250 added, $75 to second horse, dash of half a mile. A very speedy field came to the post, and in the pool sales there was a lively competition, and in a majority of them only a trifle of difference. The average rate was $20 on Premium, $20 on Jim Douglas, $20 on the field, containing Garfield, Lou Spencer and Jim Renwick. These were the starters, the positions being as follows: Garfield had the pole, Jim Douglas second, Premium third, Lou Spencer fourth and Jim Renwick on the outside. After a few breakaways a very good start was obtained, though from the mud being the deepest on the inside, the favorite position was on the extreme outside. They ran fast around the turn, Premium in the lead, with Lou Spencer second and close on the haunches of the leader, the others in a bunch and not far behind. There was little change until about half way down the homestretch, where all were so close that it was difficult to separate them, though the orange jacket and cap, which were carried by Douglas, were rapidly coming to the front. Whips were whistling over all of them at the seven furlongs, but at the drawgate Douglas came along quite handily, and won with comparative ease in the very fast time, for the state of the track, of 50¼ seconds. Garfield and Jim Renwick were two lengths behind the leader, and were so close together that only those who had a position to look over the wire could decide which won. The judges awarded the place to Renwick, Premium fourth and Lou Spencer, who was not persevered with, fifth.

SUMMARY.

BAY DISTRICT COURSE, Monday, November 23, 1882.—Flash stake, $25 p.p.; 150 added; $75 to second horse; free for all; dash of half a mile.

Geo. Howson names b h Jim Douglas, 4 years, by Wildidle—by Norfolk (Howson)........ 1
Stemler & Ayres names g Jim Remwick, 4 years, by Joe Hooker—Puss (Appleby)........ 2
R. J. Green names gr c Garfield, 3 years, by California—Queen (Leigh)........ 3
J. B. Haggin names s m Premium, aged, by Castor—by St. Louis (Duffy)........ 0
Theo. Winters names b f Lou Spencer, 3 years, by Norfolk—Ballerina (Carter)........ 0

Time—50¼.

The second race was the Finigan stakes, for two-year-olds, and of the twenty-nine nominations four only appeared. These were E. J. Baldwin's Gano and Lucky B, Palo Alto's Satanella and J. B. Chase's Marian. The distance was a dash of a mile, and the Baldwin colts having shown such high form in the East were largely the favorites, especially as the muddy course was held to be greatly to the disadvantage of Satanella. The rates were $60 on the "Baldwin stable" to $33 on the others, and there was a deal of speculation on the race. A better start was never witnessed. The quartet passed under the wire so nearly parallel that the eye failed to detect the difference, though soon after Lucky B shot to the front, with Satanella second, Marian third, and Gano jogging along at his leisure in the rear. In this order they passed the quarter pole, and on the backstretch Satanella closed the gap, so at the half-mile she was only a neck behind, and at the three-quarters it was a head-and-head affair between the two. Coming home the rider gave Gano his head, and he rushed past the others so easily that the truth of the Eastern panegyrics was verified, and he came to the wire an easy winner, with his stable companion, Lucky B, half a length in front of Satanella, Marian some distance behind, the time 1:47½. This was a duplicate of the race here at the spring meeting, when the same colts ran first and second in the Connor stakes, which changed the title to that of Gano, as he beat the time made by Connor in his famous race at Carson.

SUMMARY.

Same day—Finigan Stake, $50 each, $25 forfeit, $250 added; second to save stake; for two-year-olds. Dash of a mile, twenty-nine nominations.

E. J. Baldwin names b c Gano, by Grinstead—Santa Anita (Williams). 1
E. J. Baldwin names b c Lucy B, by Rutherfurd—Maggie Emerson (Estabrook)........ 2
Palo Alto names ch f Satanella, by Leveller—Frou Frou (Carter)........ 3
J. B. Chase names b f Marian, by Hubbard—Electra (Kelly)........ 0

Time—1:47½.

The third race was the Fame stake, a dash of two miles for three-year-olds. The stakes were $100 each, $25 forfeit, $500 added, and there were eighteen nominations. Three of these paid up the full amount, viz: Fostress from Palo Alto, Judge McKinstry and Forest King. Fostress was the favorite with the betters, and just before the start the pools showed $130 on her, $60 on Judge McKinstry and $20 on Forest King. Again there was a good start, and when the flag fell Forest King cut out the work. The Judge was going short and stumpy, as though he were sore, and the pace was slow, as it took the leader 31½ seconds to reach the quarter. The favorite was galloping along easily in the rear, a position which was evidently in accordance with instructions, and at the half mile in 1:01, there was little change. At the finish of the first mile, 2:01, Judge McKinstry was in the lead, with Fortress in close attendance, and then the two contestants had as close a race as is generally seen, Forest King out of it entirely. They were right together as they passed the quarter pole for the second time in 2:29, and until half way down the stretch there was no perceptible advantage to either. Then Fostress showed a head in front, at the half-mile it was a neck, and there were still hopes for the colt. But, rounding the turn, he "gave it up," and from from thence the Palo Alto had it all her own way, galloping in six lengths in the lead of the judge in 3:51, Forest King a long way behind.

Owing to the state of the track, which would have made the hurdle race extremely perilous, it was postponed until next Saturday.

SUMMARY.

Same day—Fame Stake, $100 each, $25 forfeit, $500 added; second to receive $150; third to save stake. For three-year-olds. Dash of two miles, eighteen nominations.

Palo Alto names ch f Fostress, by Foster—Planetia (Fallon)........ 1
James Mee names b c Judge McKinstry, by Thad Stevens or Grinstead—Katie Pease (Howson)........ 2
Peter Coutts names b c Forest King, by Monday—Abbie W (White)........ 3

Time—3:57.

### A Mistake Corrected.

SAN FRANCISCO, Nov. 21, 1881.

EDITOR BREEDER AND SPORTSMAN: I desire a little space in which to do justice to two very worthy and popular horsemen, Messrs. Stemler and Ayers, of Oregon. Through an unfortunate misapprehension these gentlemen were reported to the National Trotting Association for the non-payment of entrance on Joe Howell in the selling race run at the Golden Gate Fair, September last.

Mr. Ayers called on me as Secretary, before leaving, and promptly settled his indebtedness to the association, with the exception of this entrance, and this was left open for inquiry at my request. He called again the same day, but being very busy and still being in doubt on the matter, he left, requesting me to notify him at Sacramento if he should be found indebted in any further sum. I subsequently wrote such a letter which Mr. Ayers says he failed to receive, and by reason of my report he was not allowed to start at Reno until the amount was paid. I am more than ready to say that Mr. Ayers is not, as appears from the above, a delinquent, and the reported suspension places him in a false light, which I very sincerely regret.

I am not surprised that Mr. Ayers should have felt surprised and indignant, and disposed to protest until the necessary explanations and apologies were made, when they were at once accepted in the spirit in which they were offered. It is too important that there should be a good understanding between all honorable horsemen, and the various associations, to let pass in silence these little sources of friction and causes of misunderstanding, which if let alone might grow into a large rupture, hence this statement is cheerfully made in the interest of harmony and good will as well as exact justice. Yours truly,

L. WALKER,
Secretary Golden Gate Fair Association.

## THE EMBRYO DISCUSSED.

### Letter from J. McM. Shafter on the Criticisms Published Last Week.

EDITOR BREEDER AND SPORTSMAN: The result of a few minutes' conversation with you this morning has induced me to destroy an article I had written in answer to your attack last week. This I do as proper under a proposed retraction hereafter adverted to. You further informed me that you intend to refer the matters connected with your article to the District Board of the National Trotting Association. As I am a member of that Board I shall confine this to matters merely personal.

It is impossible to conceal that after the retraction there still remains enough in your article to constitute a direct attack upon me, and attributing to me dishonorable conduct. I do not know what has been said to you about what transpired in the stand and you will as to all disputable points learn nothing from me. The general exclusion of the public from the stand is for the purpose of securing to the judges entire independence in the expression of their views, and in no material question, whether it does or does not relieve me from personal responsibility, will the rule of secrecy be violated by me on any material question. If others so violate it, I may defend myself. This, of course, relates to the position of judge alone.

As you assume to be the "faithful guardian of racing interests upon this coast," "I have to request that where you find it necessary to allude to me, you will do so by direct statement, and not by insinuations which suggest what you know is not true.

You not only insinuate but directly imply that I went into the stand on the Embryo race and called it Dr. Tisdale for the purpose of assisting Mr. Whitney, the treasurer of your association, in the perpetration of a fraud, and that I acted as the attorney to carry out this fraud in accordance to the conclusions of previous "counsels" held with him.

You must have known if you stopped to reflect a moment that this charge was destitute of even the color of probability. As to the appointment of the judges, I had not the slightest idea of being one until you said to me "you must go into the stand." I asked you to point out some two gentlemen who would act with me. You replied that Mr. Howes would act in the first race, Mr. Whitney being excluded by having a colt in it, but would take Mr. Howes' place in the succeeding races. You not naming another and not returning to me, and finding no one I knew that I could properly appoint, I called Dr. Tisdale, to whom I had been introduced that morning and who seemed conversant with the rules, to go into the stand.

I had never seen or known Dr. Tisdale until that morning. He seemed, and I believe is, an intelligent, honorable gentleman. I had never had a word of communication with Mr. Whitney as to his colt nor did I have any intimation from any human being, that there was any question about the eligibility of the colt to start. When about ready to start, Mr. Whitney having paid up his $100, you interposed an objection to Mr. Whitney's driver. Your objection was found to be unfounded, and you then abandoned it. You then objected to Mr. Whitney's entry on the ground that by the books of the Secretary it appeared that the colt Daven was entered only for the race of 1884. Surprised that Mr. Whitney should present a colt for a race two years too soon, I called for the original entry. It was found, and by all the judges considered sufficient. During the discussion it was asked why you had not informed Mr. Whitney of the alleged mistake and of your intended protest. This you did not answer, but insisted the book must govern in the decision, although you at the same time claimed that the entry itself was defective. At this point, you insist that my state of preparation was demonstrative of previous study, and fraudulent collusion, and that my expressions justify the belief you express. Not considering your failure to have given Mr. Whitney full information of your point, in season for him to save the expense of preparing his colt, and enabling him to keep his $100 in his pocket, as proper in a "faithful guardian" of honorable racing. I doubtless expressed my disapprobation in terms which I am pleased to know have not been misunderstood. It would certainly have been very singular if after forty-two years at the bar I had been ignorant of the multitudes of legal decisions which hold that when a man has done all he is required to do in order to obtain a privilege or right he cannot be deprived of it by any merely clerical mistake of a public officer. If Mr. Whitney's entry was valid originally no statement of the Secretary or his book could invalidate it; if bad it could not vitalize it. The book and the entry was all the evidence exhibited to which you allude, and was stated before I had anything to say regarding the validity of the entry. Your further say that the announcement from the stand that all the horses were protested but would be allowed to start, "was despicable as it was false." Your language, of course, signifies that the "announcement" was false.

This you withdraw, saying that you referred to the protest against your horse. I think upon reflection you will withdraw that also. Mr. Whitney acted upon direct information that you had never filed with the Secretary any written entry. The lodgee of papers in the hands of the Secretary did not contain your entry. I do not say but you made a proper entry, but Mr. Whitney acted upon a positive statement that you had not. Under such circumstances, you will hardly be willing to apply the words "despicable and false" to Mr. Whitney's action.

As to the decision in the third trot I propose to report it as well as other matters to the District Board. If any mistake occurred as to that race, I shall be as ready to correct it as though I had not been in the stand. A communication signed Lex, which I suppose was by some legal gentleman, requires reply. As to the general propriety of a member of the District Board going into the stand, from manifest considerations I agree with Lex.

He however makes the point that I am excluded from the stand under Art. 41, Sec. 18, by which members of the "Board of Appeals" are after February, 1880, excluded from the judges' stand. Lex mistakes the terms he uses. Sec. 4 of the same article defines the Board of Appeals. The District Board is not such Board of Appeals. While appeals are allowed to a District Board they are nowhere called Board of Appeals. Secs. 15, 16, 17, 18, Art. 41, speak of these several boards by their special name, and the term "Board of Appeals" is confined to the Board of Appeals, not exceeding fifteen in number, mentioned in Sec. 4. Art. 41, Sec. 20, by directing the appointment of supervisors and giving members of the Board of Appeals the right to supervise races, must by any fair construction give the right of presence in the stand. Sec. 8 makes the District

Board one of original as well as appellate jurisdiction. Practically the question is of very little consequence.

I am glad you have taken the occasion to refer to the decision at the Blood Horse meeting. In giving your opinion upon that matter you admit that the "starting post" is the "score" or the wire. That matter is then fixed. Your conclusion, I think, is incorrect, whether it is an imputation of want of "common sense" or not. You treat the start as being complete when the flag is dropped. The cry of "go" of the starter is in no way permissible. You seem to consider the dropping of the starter's flag as the start and undertake to raise the position of the horses at that time. This is directly in conflict with two rules.

Sec. 8 of the duties of officers says the assistant starter "shall hold his flag in plain sight" where he can be distinctly seen by the jockeys. The lowering the flag of the assistant starter "is the final signal that the horses have been started." Rule 43 says: "The horses shall be started by a flag (not by a 'go') unless otherwise ordered by the judges; and there shall be no start until, and no recall after, the assistant starter drops the flag in response to the signal from his chief." Now in this race according to my observation two horses were over the score, one at least two lengths, the third in the act of crossing, the others little behind, when the starter's flag dropped, and all of them over in full flight when the assistant starter's flag fell. If this was not a "start on the wrong side of the starting post" will you tell one who is wanting in what you call common sense, what is. If this is not a void start and heat will you tell us in a field of, say ten, how many may be over the score, and how far and how far off may the rest be down the quarter stretch, to make it "one of the best starts you ever saw." No one doubts the integrity of the starter. The refractory horse Bob occasioned just such a start at San Jose, Night Hawk was left, her head down the stretch, and was full fifty yards behind and beaten out a short length. All so that Bob could get a fair start. The same error occurred in the races in question and another still worse on Saturday last. I beg to suggest that this rule be changed and that the start be fixed when the BOB of the field is ready to go.

Look at the question of time. False time is severely punished. In a field one or two horses are two or three lengths over the score; the flag drops and the leading horse comes in. The timers stop the minute his nose touches the wire. The time is from a half to a whole second too short. Is this true or false time? The horse has actually run say 317 or 18 rods, instead of a full mile. Is this anything else but palming off a short track, and false time? Take the Jennie B stake race at Sacramento. Night Hawk and Red Boy were on the outside and behind the score when started. Supposing they had been on the inside with a couple of lengths advantage, with a full start I think that heat would have been as low as 1:41½. Supposing Night Hawk had got thirty feet over the score before the start was given, she would have come through in about 1:41½; if she had twenty feet the advantage she would have won, notwithstanding it actually took her 1:43 to run the mile, and would have obtained, not won, $200 extra—the name of the stake—and put up her mark nearly a second too high.

If these considerations do not convince your readers of common sense that horses must be approaching, or at the starting post, and not over it when the start is given, then I am for releasing gentlemen from the unpleasant task of starter, and turning it over to BOB.

Thirty minutes are now allowed in which to start horses. Where there is a refractory animal, if the time was shortened to twenty minutes, with a discretion in the starter as to the last ten minutes, the rule would be much improved; as it is the rule is inflexible and ought to be observed. I dissented from the decision alluded to, because it substituted the nerves or discretion of the starter for the rule. I am not and do not assume to be so "distinguished" as to be free from just criticism, nor do I feel the slightest reluctance in receding from an erroneous position, but I desire that criticism should be soberly conducted and that truth and not malice should dictate attack.

I have only here to say that I shall report the races in question to the District Board for its action. The president and myself have been endeavoring for nearly six months to get the vacancy filled in that board. When that is done you and others will have a fair hearing and just decision, without any regard to the judges from whom appeals are taken.

    J. McM. SHAFTER.

---

### A Russian River Home.

A five-acre apple orchard, twenty years old, at John N. Bailhache's ranch, southeast of town, yielded this year one thousand dollar's worth of shipping fruit, ordinary varieties. Mr. Bailhache has an elegant home place. The residence is no doubt the finest in Northern Sonoma, built on the bank of Russian River, near the base of Mt. Sotoyome, at the site of the first house constructed in the valley, by the founder of the Sotoyome grant in 1844. The adobe walls of the original building are still part of the new residence built by Mr. Bailhache a few years ago, and make the rooms cool in summer and warm in winter. Here Mr. Bailhache was married in 1856 to the eldest daughter of the proprietor of the grant, Mr. Henry D. Fitch, and here he now lives, surrounded by a large and interesting family.

The ranch consists of about 500 acres, of which five, as we have stated above, are occupied by a twenty-year-old apple orchard; five more by a three-year-old orchard of peaches and plums which will yield, when five years old, at present prices, $300 an acre, and from which he this year reaped a large corn crop from between the rows, fifteen acres in alfalfa, one of the best paying crops in the valley; sixty-five are in foreign vines two years old next spring, and which will yield when five years old at present prices full $150 an acre, and more as they grow older, and from which he has reaped large crops of corn and beans from between the rows. There is some hay land and four hundred acres of pasture on which roam 300 head of graded sheep, besides sundry head of horses and cows. The sheep never require feeding, and pay about $2 net per head per annum. Nearly all the work of this place this year was done by Mr. Bailhache and three of his sons.—Russian River Flag.

The following peculiar case is told the Chico Record by a gentleman just from the mountains of Modoc county: "A stockman had a stack of hay containing nearly two hundred tons, which was cut a little green. Shortly after it had been smoked a heavy rain fell upon it and a few days afterwards the hay commenced issuing smoke. It attracted considerable attention, and people traveled many miles to see the strange transactions. Sparks and smoke would belch out the top of the stack as though it was a volcano in an active state of eruption. Fire and smoke continued to issue from the stack for over ten days, when the whole thing suddenly burst out in flames one day and was quickly consumed."

---

### Why a Kerosene Lamp Bursts.

Girls, as well as boys, need to understand about kerosene explosions. A great many fatal accidents occur from trying to pour a little kerosene on the fire to make it kindle better, also by pouring oil into a lamp while it is lighted. Most persons suppose that it is the kerosene itself which explodes, and that if they are very careful to keep the oil itself from being touched by the fire or the light there will be no danger. But this is not so. If a can or a lamp is left almost half full of kerosene oil the oil will dry up—that is, "evaporate"—a little and will form, by mingling with the air in the upper part, a very explosive gas. You cannot see this gas any more than you can see air. But if it is disturbed and driven out, and a blaze reaches it, there will be a terrible explosion, although the blaze did not touch the oil. There are several other liquids used in houses and work-shops which will produce an explosive vapor in this way. Benzine is one; burning fluid is another, and naptha, alcohol, ether, chloroform may do the same thing.

In a New York workshop lately, there was a can of benzine or gasoline on the floor. A boy sixteen years old lighted a cigarette and threw the burning match on the floor close to the can. He did not dream there was any danger because the liquid was corked up in the can. But there was a great explosion and he was badly hurt. This seems very mysterious. The probability is that the can had been standing there a good while and a good deal of vapor had formed, some of which had leaked out around the stopper and was hanging in a sort of invisible cloud over and around the can; and this cloud, when the match struck it, exploded.

Suppose a girl tries to fill a kerosene lamp without first blowing it out. Of course the lamp is nearly empty or she would not care to fill it. This empty space is filled with a cloud of explosive vapor arising from the oil in the lamp. When she pushes the nozzle of the can into the lamp at the top, and begins to pour, the oil, running into the lamp, fills the empty space and pushes the cloud of explosive vapor up; the vapor is obliged to pour out over the edges of the lamp, at the top, into the room outside. Of course it strikes against the blazing wick which the girl is holding down by one side. The blaze of the wick sets the invisible cloud of vapor a-fire, and there is an explosion which ignites the oil and scatters it over her clothes and over the furniture of the room. This is the way in which a kerosene lamp bursts. The same thing may happen when a girl pours the oil over the fire in the range or stove, if there is a cloud of explosive vapor in the upper part of the can, or if the stove is hot enough to vaporize quickly some of the oil as it falls. Remember that it is not the oil but the invisible vapor which explodes. Taking care of the oil will not protect you. There is no safety except in the rule: Never pour oil on a lighted fire or into a lighted lamp.—Christian Union.

A CURIOUS FACT IN EVOLUTION.—All animal life is not subject to death, according to the American Journal of Science. Examining through a microscope one of those minute single-cell creatures known as a protozoon, the Journal remarks that we see it expanding into an ellipsoidal figure, which becomes for a time longer and longer. It then begins to contract about what we may, for the sake of popular intelligibility, call its equator. It assumes the form of two nearly globular bodies, connected, dumb-bell-like, by a narrow neck. This neck becomes narrower, and at last the two globes are set free, and appear as two individuals in place of one. What are the relations of these two beings to the antecedent form and to each other? We examine them with care; they are equal in size, alike in complexity, or rather simplicity, of structure. We cannot say that either of them is more mature or more rudimentary than the other. We can find in their separation from each other no analogy to the separation of the young animal or the egg from its mother, or to the liberation of a seed from a plant. Neither of them is parent, and neither offspring. Neither of them is older or younger than the other. The process of reproduction, or rather of multiplication, most, so far as we can see, be repeated in the same manner forever. Accidents excepted, there are immortal, and frequent as such accidents must be, the individuals whom they strike might, or rather would, like the rest of their community, have gone on living and splitting themselves up forever. It is strange, when examining certain infusoria under the microscope, to consider that these frail and tiny beings were living, not potentially in their ancestors, but really in their own person, perhaps in the Laurentian epoch.

A Michigan lumbering company are making sheet barrels by cutting a log into barrel lengths, softening them by a steaming process and then shaving each piece into a long sheet, unrolled like a carpet. Each sheet is then crosscut into such a length that when the two ends are brought together it is given the size and form of a barrel, without heads, the whole being done by machinery. This has proved a great improvement over the slave barrel in the cost of manufacturing as well as in the merits for use. The only drawback is that clear timber is required, all the knotty timber being rejected.

OF POLLED CATTLE.—An exchange published at Edinburg, Scotland, publishes the following two items in reference to Polled animals: The Earl of Southesk has purchased at a high price from Mr. Taylor of Rothieanay a very promising red calf, full brother to Lord Chancellor (1782), which won for Mr. Reid of Clisterly first prize at the recent Highland Society's show, and was sold at £600 to Mr. Hume, Barrelwell, for exportation. We are glad to learn that among the herds of Polled cattle which will date from 1882 is a herd just started by Mr. Farquhar, auctioneer and farmer, Old Echt, Aberdeenshire. He has purchased several handsome pedigreed cows ranging from $270 to $500.

At the sale of thoroughbreds of W. L. Pritchard at the Bay District Course Thursday, there were few buyers, and consequently low prices. Irene Harding, an old-time celebrity and capital brood mare, was bought by Theodore Winters for $135—less than one-half her value. Frank Rhoads was struck off to Wm. Ayres for $310. Captain Kidd, a brother to Lena Dunbar, sold for $255; a bay filly by Sumpter, $180; a thoroughbred saddlehorse, $125, and a daughter of Jenny Hull, $80.

## HERD AND SWINE.

### The Future Meat Supply.

Just where the future meat supply for this section of country is coming from is not apparent. Heretofore, Washington Territory has been the market to which buyers came, who supplied the shops in eastern markets. To-day, it begins to look as though we shall have to go out of the territory for our own meat supply for another season. From the Palouse region comes the report "the calves are dying of the diphtheria by the hundreds." From the Crab creek and Big Bend region comes word that "our section is a vast slaughter pen; the grass plains are strewn with carcasses of calves." The diseases have penetrated to the Spokane country, and the meat supply of one and two seasons hence is dying of blackleg or diphtheria. The same report comes from many of our farmers in our immediate vicinity, and really the matter begins to look rather serious, especially to those whose purses are not at all weighty except on Saturday evenings about six o'clock, and then only for a couple of hours. Beef will be very scarce in this region before many more months, and the price will certainly advance. Writing of the question of fat beef cattle, and the necessities that must naturally arise, an exchange says:

"The cities of the near future will demand better beef than those of any other pasture can furnish through the winter and spring, and how to provide good, marketable meats, for a fastidious market, is an important question. Of course, beef cattle must be stall-fed. The time has come when we must resort to all the best methods of older states in these respects. How to keep cattle thriving at least expense, and so make them profitable, is no light question to answer. Here again, ensilage comes in as a specific, for those who have experimented at the East, during the past winter, unanimously agree that ensilage furnishes the best and cheapest fodder for dairy use, or to make winter beef, and it has further been established that silos, or pits to preserve this fodder in, can be constructed at a very small cost, and that ensilage can be put up, cut in half-inch lengths, and then tramped down by stock, and afterward weighed with stone, at not to exceed $1 per ton, and three tons of it is said to equal one ton of dry hay. At the east, where both corn and sorghum thrive, and are used to fill silos, capable men assert that rye, wheat, oats, clover or orchard grass can be grown and put up as cheaply as corn, and answer much better; so that we have here the means to put up as good ensilage as can be made in the world, and therefore can as easily adopt the new system as they can at the East.—Walla Walla Statesman.

### Anthrax or Blackleg in Cattle.

This disease threatens the destruction of a large proportion of the cattle in this section of country, and we take it that any intelligent description of it and remedies proposed will be of interest and importance to our readers, especially to the farming community. Professor Law has made a full investigation of the disease and says:

There are two varieties of the disease, both depending on the presence of minute vegetable organisms (bacteria) which have acquired the dangerous faculty of living and increasing in the blood and tissues of the animal body. One form of the malady is the malignant anthrax proper—the malignant pustule of man—caused by an organism which exists in the blood and vital fluids in the form of microscopic staff-shaped bodies, as well as spherical ones. This type is readily communicable to all species of warm blooded animals unless they have already been rendered insusceptible by an earlier attack. The second form is associated with a microscopic organism which is found in the spherical form only in the blood and animal fluids, and which has not been found to attack readily other animals than cattle.

Both are equally dangerous to cattle; the first to cattle as dangerous to man and other warm-blooded animals. Whether the germs in both diseases are but varieties of the same organism remains to be seen; what is more immediately to the point is that both appear to follow the same law of development and to depend upon the same general conditions for the maintenance of their virulence. This is most inveterate if excluded from air, but is gradually lost in the presence of fresh air and moisture. To check the progress of the malady, therefore, and prevent new attacks, the exposed cattle should at once be moved to soil which is thoroughly drained and pervious to moisture.

The carcasses of the dead and all the products of the sick should be burned, or if buried it should be in a dry, porous soil with a covering of quick lime to favor speedy decomposition, and securely fenced in so that no other cattle can approach the place, nor eat the grass upon it for several years. If damp or impervious soil only is attainable for burial, then burning the carcasses is far to be preferred. When a pasture has once had an outbreak of blackleg, it cannot be considered safe for several years to come. The purification of such pastures may be expedited by placing them under a rotation of crops and allowing the soil to frequently be ploughed.

Then for the remedies which will check the development of any germs that may be present on the mouth, throat, stomach or bowels. For this purpose, one drachm carbolic acid and three drachms sulphate of iron may be dissolved daily to the drinking water of each adult animal, or sprinkled on its food. One drachm of potassium and one ounce chlorate of potassium may be used in the same way. Glauber salts should be used where there is a tendency to constipation. Young animals should be kept apart from the other cattle. Feed well and do not allow young cattle to get into a low condition of flesh.

DAIRYMAN'S PROTECTIVE ASSOCIATION.—A society of this name has been formed in this county, composed of our leading dairymen, who are aroused to the harm that will be caused to the butter market by the unscrupulous manipulations of oleomargarine, or what is vulgarly known as "bull butter." At their last meeting they passed a resolution pledging themselves not to consign any butter or cheese to firms that deal in oleomargarine. They also have issued a call to all the dairy counties in this State to meet on the 23th inst. to elect three delegates to meet in San Francisco on Dec. 12th, 1882, for the purpose of organizing a State association.—Santa Cruz Courier-Item.

It is stated by English papers that the "Short-horn Dairy Company," for the supply of milk to London, which is under the presidency of the Earl of Dunmore, now sends 160,000 quarts of milk to London each week, having 1,120 head of cattle, 500 sheep, with pigs and poultry, and using 140 horses in distributing the milk. The farms occupied by the company aggregate 2,200 acres. The stables seem to be arranged with reference to convenience rather than low cost of construction. The managers are confident of a good profit.

### Sale of Polled Cattle.

The enterprising breeders and ranchmen of the United States are evidently intent on having the best breeding stock to be had in any part of the world, and having once determined on that do not allow the matter of a few paltry hundreds of dollars to balk them in carrying out their purpose. Whilst therefore a very fine Shorthorn bull may be had at from one to three hundred dollars, we find men ready and willing to pay from five hundred to a thousand dollars for something else so long as it has the novelty of newness.

Witness the following from the Live Stock Indicator, of Kansas City, in reference to a sale of Polled cattle.

"On Thursday last was afforded the first opportunity to test at public sale the measure of favor with which the Scotch Polled cattle are regarded by the beef-producers of the new West. Here on that day Mr. Matthews offered for their inspection and bids a larger number of "blackskins" than had ever before been brought together on any similar occasion on this continent, and many thoughtful men were in much doubt as to how the experiment—and it was an experiment—would result. They queried among themselves if a considerable number of men would come here and pay prices as large or larger for these strange foreigners than would be necessary to procure the most approved and desirable Shorthorns or Herefords, whose qualities, characteristics and values have in our own climate been demonstrated beyond question. . . .

How these queries were answered, and that too by men who understand the worth and power of a dollar as thoroughly as any others living, is shown by our detailed report of the sale.

The Indicator regards the sale as a good one; fairly good for the seller, and very good on the whole for the buyers. The cattle did not sell so low as to deter the importation and offering of others, nor did they sell so high as to discourage the dissemination of them among men of even moderate means; that they went low enough is evidenced by the probable fact that as a lot they could not be duplicated in quality for the same money at the present time by any importer. Further proof of this may be found in the fact that at the recent sale in Scotland of Lord Airlie's herd, four Angus females of the Erica family, one a calf, one a yearling, one a four-year-old, and one eleven years old, brought an average of 500 guineas, or about $2,500 each, while at Mr. Matthew's sale seven head from the same family and probably just as well bred, and as good individually, viz: Fanny Fair, Young Maid of Tillygamont, Bonnet, Knight of Aberdeen, Cemble, Black Watch and Sir Loloc, sold for an average of $801.42 per head. We believe, as stated last week, that the dispersion of this collection of Polls marks a new era in the cattle breeding of the West; three years hence, Polled black steers that are now regarded as curiosities will come to our markets every day, and here, as on the range, in pasture or feed-lot, they will occupy a front rank. While by no means prepared to say they are better than any other breeds, we think there is good in them, and that there is ample room for all the Angus and Galloways to be had, especially when nine-tenths of the cattle of the country are the veriest scrubs. One notable feature of this sale is that a large proportion of the animals disposed of were bought by parties who will use them as crosses on the more common stock rather than to found or increase herds of thoroughbreds; they will at once be used for beef-raising purposes rather than speculation.

### England's Embargo on American Cattle.

England is without doubt a free trade country and her policy in that regard is not only fixed but apparently unalterably so. She has, however, a very clever way of taking care of her own industries whensoever the occasion calls for it, and of making a very thin excuse for her conduct. From the time that the shipment of beef cattle to that country became a fixed fact by the indomitable energy of American enterprise, the English government has not hesitated to do what it could to throw every obstacle in its way that, under semblance of law, could be conceived of; . . .

Under the rules now in force every beef from the United States must be slaughtered within a few hours after landing. This compels the owner to sell without regard to the condition of the market, and frequently brings heavy losses where, by a delay of a few days, a fair profit might be made. Those best acquainted with the business say that the loss on each beef animal from this cause is fully $15. This is as absolutely lost to the American producer and the British consumers as it would be if thrown into the Atlantic.

This is in effect the same as a direct tax levied upon those who breed and who feed the class of cattle wanted for the English market.

This it must be understood is pretentiously done for the purpose of preventing the introduction of pleuro-pneumonia from the United States and this, notwithstanding the fact that that country is the very hot-bed of the disease.

It is reported that since the year 1842 England, with all her efforts to guard against this insidious foe, has lost over $10,000,000 annually by means of it. Professor Law, of the United States Treasury Cattle Commission, says: "England, with her 6,000,000 cattle, has lost in deaths alone from lung fever in the course of forty years over $500,000,000.

But who ever heard of such a disease among the herds of the large breeding ranches in this country? Nor are there any two sides to this question as some would have us believe, for there is no possibility of our Western cattle carrying such a disease whilst yet it does not exist. It is a clear case of protection on the part of "Johnny Bull," and that aged sinner ought to be ashamed of it.

It illustrates, however, the facility a free trade government has of protecting its own where occasion requires it; hence, should the United States ever seek to retaliate it would be the easiest matter in the world for our own government to exact the same for all cattle landed on our shores from the pleuro-pneumonia infested "Tight Little Isle."—Colman's Rural World.

Hereford cattle are a distinct and pure breed of great antiquity. Their early history is uncertain, but it is generally allowed in England that there has been a breed of cattle, red and mostly with white face and markings, for at least 200 years in the county of Hereford and the neighboring counties. It is asserted that Lord Scudamore, who died in 1671, introduced some of the red with white-faced breed from Flanders. There was also a breed of cattle known in Herefordshire that were white with red ears, and so far back as the tenth century it is recorded that there was a herd of compensation to be paid for injury done by one prince to another at 100 white cows with red ears and a bull of the same color. It is fairly proved that the Herefords to-day have sprung directly from the old breeds of the district, the old gray Hereford coming from the white cattle with red ears, an occasional white Hereford cropping up as an additional proof of this statement.

### Among the Jerseys.

Respecting the large butter yields of Jersey and some other cattle an exchange has this to say:

"My great objection to the average Jersey record is based on the fact that men of good character put forward figures wholly upon the evidence of the herdsman, and the temptation to make a large showing is extraordinary. He adds that upon periodicals should rest somewhat the responsibility of presenting to the public only such records as are well substantiated by disinterested eye-witnesses."

And this is probably the idea entertained by the world at large because the temptation is great and apparent—discovery impossible. That some Jersey cows have made twenty-own pounds of butter a week we have no doubt; nay, we will go further, we will place on record our conviction that this can be easily established in several cases. Of this we think there is not a shadow of a doubt, for the owners are men of character, and of such character as they would not peril for all the Jerseys in America. We have met the breeders at home in very many of the breeding States, have talked with the herdsmen, seen their mode of operation and of keeping accounts, but have yet to see cause to question the accuracy of their reports. Of course such animals are rare and found only here and there, and then perhaps only in the hands of those who know how best to develop their qualities. But Jersey cows, Holstein cows and even Shorthorns can be found in comparative abundance that will make from seven to fourteen pounds of butter per week, and why not the Jersey, with whom butter is a speciality, make it exceptional cases 50 per cent. better? This questioning every man's veracity lest one's one savors of the old Stoic philosophy of always treating a friend in such a way as that should he ever become your enemy he could do you no harm, and your enemy in like manner that he might at any time become your friend; or in other words have confidence in nobody but yourself. It will not do—is not possible! Other men are as honest as we are and oftentimes doubtless much more so.—Colman's Rural World.

### Too Much Tallow.

Sensible people of course know that great masses of fat and tallow do not fill the requirements of first-class butcher's stock, and it would seem as though the great feeders of the country would discontinue a practice that not only ruins their stock, but actually detracts from their value upon the block. The intrinsic merit of a beef animal must be measured and determined solely upon the basis of the greatest proportion of good, choice meat, to gross weight, and the lessons of the fat stock show will be learned in vain unless the standard of excellence is finally placed upon that basis, as between the exhibitors of beef cattle. Animals fattened until they cannot get about without the greatest effort, and when once down in their stalls, can with the utmost difficulty regain their feet, are not the cattle sought by the meat cutter, who calculates upon a reasonable profit. It is all well enough to class cattle of this character as "Christmas beef," but the fact remains that their gigantic proportions really render them unprofitable to the average butcher. Many shrewd feeders have long been of the opinion that the premium list of the show should not include anything that would induce exhibitors to continue the evils of overfeeding, but as the Smithfield cattle club of London, at their annual shows, keep up and indorse the practice, there will probably be no cessation on this side of the water.

Many of the animals exhibited at fairs are simply overfed specimens of the bovine race, and the quality of the beef killed every year clearly shows that there is no profit in this method of feeding.

The subject is a very important one to the cattle interests of the entire country, and deserves the thoughtful attention of all breeders and feeders.—Prairie Farmer.

### Shorthorns vs. Other Breeds.

The English cling tenaciously to their dearly-loved Shorthorn cattle; and with good reason, as they have had better success with that breed than with any other. In the Agricultural Gazette's report of the dairy show at Islington, the Shorthorns, Jerseys, Ayrshires, and Kerries, all native cattle, are claimed to be much superior to foreign breeds. It says:

No better evidence of this country having got an enormous start of every other in the breeding of dairy cattle can be had than the opportunity to contrast the dairymen's Shorthorns with either the Dutch cattle, which have got such a footing in English sheds, or the Swiss, which are now recommended as a possible improvement. These Shorthorns and the Channel islands cattle of Mr. C. Simpson, Mr. J. Cantus, or Mr. J. James, or the Ayrshires of Messrs. Drew and Ferns, or the Kerries of Mr. B. Good are not only unsurpassed, but unsurpassable. Even the Dutch, good milkers as they are, will not bear comparison with the unpedigreed Shorthorns, which have as good udders and far finer carcasses; whilst the Swiss, for size at age, will not bear comparison with the English cross-breeds between the Jersey and Shorthorns which are not at all likely to be behind in quantity or quality of milk. These Swiss heifers are a good illustration of the way in which a man's recollections play him false. We see what we admire, mainly perhaps because the circumstances under which we see are favorable. The novelty makes us disparage older favorites. Nor shall we have cause to be put side with the old, it takes more than mere enthusiasm and the wish to be the pioneer of something fresh, to enable us to withstand the evidence of our senses. Neither eye nor hand could ascertain any point in which Swiss cows are likely to surpass what we have already; nor suggest any reason why we should give up our own breeds and go in for Swiss.

CLASSIFYING WOOLS.—A wool growers' convention was held at Sedalia, Mo., recently, and among the papers read was one by Mr. Henry Brown on the classification of wools. Classification, as he remarked, consists in sorting the fleeces as they come from the sacks into their proper classes. This has become a necessity, and is a benefit both to the seller and buyer. Different mills require different wools, and a mill using fine wools cannot use coarse wools. The direction of public requirements for goods is shown by the fact that a New England mill, which has been equipped only for the using of coarse wools, had its stock worth three times its par value a few years back; now that same stock is below par. The prosperity of the country demands fine clothes, and it takes fine wool to make them. Mr. Brown is a wool expert. He gave the different classes into which wool is divided, illustrating his words by several samples of wool. He urged the breeding of pure sheep, especially of fine wool rams, saying that fine wool was more profitable than coarse.—Prairie Farmer.

## The Beef Market.

Last July we gave our readers the best views then obtainable as to the future of the beef market. There were some who at that time claimed that we overrated and held our views entirely too high, but the price at which beef is held to-day fully verifies our statements, and once more proves that knowledge of the supply is most necessary in order to make statements months in advance; this in a measure we have from a pretty fair source, and hope that in the future our correspondents will keep us fully posted as regards their localities and in return we will give them all the information obtainable from other districts. This week, beef of all descriptions is held at a considerable advance over last, extra prime being held from 10 to 11 cts. and other grades range from 6¼ to 9.

The only large purchase of which we have information during the week was the sale of the well-known Santa Margarita ranch in San Diego county—one of the first ranches on the Pacific coast, both farming and grazing, and owned by the heirs of the late Don Juan Foster—the purchaser being the head man of the Nevada Bank and the price $450,000. The intention we believe is to stock it with improved cattle.

Quite good fishing is to be had off Bay View; the catches are principally rockcod and bluefish.

## POULTRY.

### Game Fowl as Food.

In an editorial article full of advice to a person who wishes to breed poultry, based on his personal experience as a hen-farmer, the editor of the "Sun" yesterday said that "game fowls have little flesh on their slender and steely bones." This remark would cause a casual observer to imagine that the game-cock and pullet must be little else than useless as an article of diet. That this is exactly the reverse of the fact is attested by the statements of several persons who, as epicures and sportsmen, were interviewed on the subject yesterday by the reporter of the "World." Vigilant, a well-known writer for the "Spirit of the Times," whose poem "Cockiana" has often been read with deep interest by those who delight in contests between game-cocks, was asked by a reporter of the "World": "Is the game chicken good eating?"

"Why, of course it is. Who says it is not?"

He was told that the editor of the "Sun" had said that while the fowl was good eating there was not much of it to be eaten.

"Well!" said he, "In England the game-chicken is bred as much for its edible as its fighting qualities, and Druid, in his 'Saddle and Sirloin,' tells how, away back when Dr. Syntax was famous on the Chester course, Dr. Bulliss was accustomed to entertain the racing celebrities of the day at a game-chicken dinner, and how, once when he was dining with Lord Derby, the grandfather of the present Earl, Lord Sefton, Mr. Leigh of Lyme, and other famous gentlemen, at the close of the Chester meeting in, I think, 1830, he exclaimed as a well-done cock of a breed famous for its fighting qualities that had been the especial pride of his father's was served up: 'My Lord, if my father knew that the cock had met such a fate he would be wild.' As for myself, I don't know what I would sooner have for dinner to-day than a broiled game pullet that had been hatched in March. I have many 'weeds' in my flock of game chickens that I use for eating purposes; by 'weeds' I mean cocks who have not the size to win a battle, and I am not the only one who pursues such a course. I can name many men well-known as statesmen and epicures to whom the gamy flavor of a well-turned pullet or cock is hailed as a toothsome viand second to none.

"But if you want undoubted authorities to contradict the inferences of the article in question, why just quote Wright's Illustrated Book of Poultry,' or Tegetmeier's work on game fowls. They will tell you as I do that the game cock, from its pure blood, gets white, delicate flesh, which when properly done makes the mouth of even a well-fed man water. Next to the game fowl in edible qualities are the Dorking and the Houdan in the order named. The latter breed is a cross between the Dorking and Poland and has a deep black flecked with white, with a large top-not, those having white legs being most in demand with poulterers. Any of those that I have mentioned are far in advance of the Plymouth Rocks or Brahmas, which the editor of the 'Sun' advised the proposed raiser of fowls to invest in. But I tell you who will give you much information about the good qualities of the game chicken, and that is Dr. John M. Carnochan."

Dr. Carnochan was called upon at his residence, No. 14 East Sixteenth street, and was asked whether the "Sun" was right in denying that the game chicken was good eating.

"Well! I do declare," said the doctor, "that's the first time I ever heard of such a thing. I keep game fowls at my place in the country because their eggs are so much better than those of the chickens usually known as barnyard fowls. And their flesh is so much better, too. Why, it stands to reason that if their blood and flesh were not improved by the breeding of them in a scientific manner, the trouble of the breeder would go for nothing, a fact that is not substantiated by the difference in prices between birds of good breeding and those whose pedigree are not known. Of course they get to be a little tough after they get to be a year old, but so do those of any breed, and therein is the secret why the person who respects his stomach insists upon being served with spring chicken. Game fowls are of a finer temperament their fibers are more closely knit. I suppose the editor of the 'Sun' thought it must naturally follow that they get tough on that account. But for my part I must have game-chicken broth, game-chicken pot-pie, game-chicken broil, roast, and in fact in every style in which a chicken can be served."

"But, Doctor, do you consider that the flesh of the game fowl, besides being more toothsome than the under-bred fowl, is more nutritious?"

"Yes; is there any one whose soul is so dead as not to recognize the fact? Why, the cock-fighters of Kentucky and New York and elsewhere when they have a bird maimed in battle take him home, fatten him up and eat him, and, though he is not a spring chicken, he is more toothsome than a Brahma, Cochin or Plymouth Rock of the same age or even younger. There are many of our best citizens, whose names I could give you, who breed and raise game chickens, not for their fighting qualities, but because they are sufficiently intelligent to recognize the fact that the game-cock, despite his bad name, is a most pleasing subject of discussion when trimmed with all the 'fixings.'" An authority on poultry-growing in New York city who was asked for information on the subject said in substance: "The article about poultry in yesterday's 'Sun' contained some excellent advice, but it lacked, in my opinion, the true ring. It read to me like the theoretical letters of gentlemen farmers who indulge in agricultural luxuries not dreamed about even by our practical men, and estimate their products at figures to correspond with the cost incurred in producing the same rather than at standard prices. Chickens that in the uncertain backward movements of a devoted but awkward mother. My own experience leads me to say that while Brahmas are not very first preference, both light and dark varieties produce not only exemplary mothers but pullets that with judicious care and feeding from thirty to forty eggs before they seek to hatch—a trait the value of which experienced poultry-growers understand and appreciate.

"The charge brought against the egg-bearing Leghorns, that these fowls do not lay their eggs when most needed, is, it appears to me, unjust to the fowl and derogatory to the knowledge of the writer. Leghorns are not only proverbially hardy but real marvels in the matter of egg-production, averaging sometimes 200 eggs per annum. With fowls of such capacity intelligent farmers regulate, almost at will, by proper care, shelter and food, the seasons at which this golden fruit shall drop, verifying the saying that the same intellectual gifts which make a man a great statesman or a great poet will also make him a great poultry-breeder.

"As regards the Plymouth Rock advised by the writer, I am free to admit the advice is safe. If one may believe all Mr. F. H. Corbin, of Newington, Conn., had to say, especially with reference to the improved strain, there is no better breed for either home consumption or market purposes, yet we must never place too much dependence on what fanciers claim for the fowl they are most interested in. Fortunately for the popularity of the Plymouth Rocks, however, the general verdict is in their favor, and there is, perhaps, no better fowl for those who desire both eggs and chickens. One standing in the position of a guide to confiding but ignorant seekers of the shortest road to greatest prosperity in the chicken business cannot give a trustworthy directions without other knowledge of the prospective poulterers' desires than the bald statement of wanting money. Let each honest inquirer state, first—Is his aim for eggs or for chicks, or for both; for a fancy market or a general one? Let him also give the locality of the market. There are fashions in poultry as well as in women's bonnets, and the fancier must provide birds of a feather to suit the caprices of his patrons.

"The paragraph devoted to the feeding of poultry is an important one and contains several important truths, among which appears the following: 'The main thing in a gallinaceous diet is undoubtedly grain.' Now, to insure a wise dispensation of this grain the adviser ought to have added—feed ground or soft food in the morning or whole grain at night. Amateurs always express surprise when told that fowls eat meat, while in point of fact there is no relish they enjoy more than a scrap of pork unless it be a leaf of lettuce or a crisp stalk of celery. Apples are also exceedingly fond of onions and have been known to eat hay when there was not a supply of fresh grass.

"Do I believe in glass houses for domestic fowls? Certainly. I advise, then, for all who have time and money at their command to experiment with fan__ breeds of handsome plumage and delicate constitutions, and do not care whether the eggs they break in their plates at breakfast cost twenty-five cents per dozen or $5. These experiments do a world of good; they teach men too poor to experiment in these directions for themselves the needlessness of elaborate houses and the unprofitableness of any but standard breeds for ordinary farm and marketing purposes. A thoroughly good house for birds to roost and lay in means to the wide-awake farmer who coins money out of his poultry yard a shelter from __sun and from wind—only this and nothing more. _With clean, well-ventilated water-proof houses, suitable runs, hardy breeds and judicious care,_ there is no reason why any man or woman who desires it should not obtain in the poultry business a fair interest on their money and pay for services rendered if there is a market within a reasonable distance."—New York World.

## The Bronze Turkey.

The American Cultivator has a very handsome sketch of a pair of bronze turkeys, and the following article in relation to the advantages they offer the poultry breeder. To an eastern farmer there appears to be a strange lack here in neglecting this part of rural husbandry. In such a climate as this with eggs at sixty cents a dozen and poultry at the present prices, it is not surprising that new comers should be astonished. The trouble is that the rearing of poultry for the market is ignored by many farmers, and the "chicken or duck ranchers" have the business in their hands. Large flocks cannot be kept so healthy as where the numbers are limited, and hence what will bring a profit as an incidental fails when it is the whole business.

The bronze turkey is perhaps no larger than the Narragansett or some other sorts from Rhode Island and eastern Connecticut, the section that largely supplies the Boston market, but for fine carriage and beauty of plumage it has no rival. Flocks carefully bred and well fed from the nest to the block, at Christmas, will dress, cocks eighteen to twenty pounds, and hens twelve to fourteen pounds. Yearling gobblers have been known to weigh fairly to thirty-two pounds and the hens fourteen to eighteen pounds, live weight. Adult birds sometimes reach forty pounds and upwards for the cocks, and twenty pounds and upwards for the hens, though such birds are rare specimens, and can only be had by breeding persistently from large stock and from mature birds, and by full feeding through the whole period of growth.

The common practice of breeding only from second-brood turkeys, and those that are not fit to kill at New Year's, is a very short-sighted policy. In nothing will a good selection pay better than in breeding this noble bird. In the wild state where "the survival of the fittest" is the rule, gobblers weighing forty pounds are not infrequent, and some are upon record weighing even fifty pounds. The prevailing custom of breeding from the smallest and cheapest keeps our markets full of birds that do not weigh more than eight or ten pounds dressed. The birds that are known to the Boston and Providence markets as Rhode Island turkeys run at least one-third larger, and lots of dressed gobblers averaging twenty pounds can be furnished by the dealers at New Year's or later, on very short notice. We know of one breeder and dealer who killed four adult gobblers one year that weighed, dressed, 196 pounds, or thirty-one and one-half pounds each.

In all the districts from which these supplies are drawn, the farmers have found that it pays to take extra pains with the turkey crop. There has been a steady gain in the average weight of the flocks sent to market at the three great festivals for the last twenty years, and the limit of perfection with this bird has by no means been reached. A large bronze gobbler, the offspring of a pair weighing sixty-two pounds, took the premium at the New York State Poultry Show, was brought into eastern Connecticut ten years ago. Three large flocks were raised from him, and nearly all of them were sold for breeding stock. The unanimous testimony of breeders, even in that district where large turkeys are common, is that their flocks have been greatly increased in size by this stock. Suppose there is only a gain of two pounds in the average size of a flock of one hundred birds, it makes a difference of 200 pounds, worth $40 at the average price of poultry in the Eastern markets. This is nearly all profit, for the turkeys get the most of their growth in the pastures and woods, and are only fed freely six weeks before marketing. Why, then, do not farmers generally buy better stock? The chief reason, probably, is the cost of such birds. It seems a large price to pay $5, $10 or $20 for a gobbler of extra weight, or for a hen weighing fifteen to twenty pounds, though such a pair of birds would leave their mark upon the broods of a whole neighborhood, and add hundreds of dollars to the value of annual sales for years to come.

The breeder of fine stock graduates the price of his birds, principally, according to their rapid development and weight. They will vary in weight considerably, even in the purest bred flocks. Gobblers weighing eighteen to nineteen pounds in December are common a quarter of the flock may reach twenty to twenty-one pounds, and a few may add a pound or two to these figures. The extra price asked for the bird which carries the last two or three pounds seems unreasonable to a novice in breeding, yet it is the cheapest part of the bird, for it is this which allows his superior constitution and aptness to take on flesh and fatten. It is the same principle, applied to poultry, which has given such wonderful results in the breeding of Shorthorn cattle. The large, well-shaped gobbler, beautifully marked and bred to beset of similar quality, will produce birds of good, strong constitution, and which will develop rapidly, and make the most flesh of a given amount of food. A seven months' bird of these of four pounds extra weight is quite sure to make a thirty-pound yearling, and such a yearling gobbler is worth a large price in any intelligent breeder's flock. There is no bird among all our fowls more susceptible of improvement than the turkey.

## Sex in Eggs.

A correspondent of the London Journal of Horticulture says in reference to this subject: "Last winter an old poultry-keeper told me he could distinguish the sex in eggs. I laughed at him and was none the less skeptical when he told me the following secret: Eggs with the air bladder in the center of the egg will produce cockerels; those with the bladder on one side will produce pullets. The old man was so confident that I decided to make experiments upon it this year. I have done so, carefully registering the egg-bladder vertically or bladder on the side, rejecting every one that was not absolutely one or the other, as in some cases very slightly out of the center. The following is the result: Fifty-eight chickens are hatched; three are dead and eleven are too young to decide upon the sex; of the remaining forty-four every one has turned out true to the old man's theory. This of course may be an accidental coincidence, but I shall certainly try the experiment again."

The above is valuable information, and the truth of it so easily tested that the experiments of one season will either verify or disprove it. To have the knowledge of governing sexes and be able to tell what the progeny will be, or even to forecast with reasonable probability, will be valuable indeed. That there may be some chance to determine what the sex will be while in embryo in eggs appears plausible, and as it is easily tested those interested can try the experiment.

THE

# Breeder and Sportsman.

PUBLISHED WEEKLY BY THE
BREEDER AND SPORTSMAN PUBLISHING CO.

THE TURF AND SPORTING AUTHORITY OF THE PACIFIC COAST.

OFFICE, 508 MONTGOMERY STREET
P. O. Box 1888.

*Five dollars a year; three dollars for six months; one dollar and a half for three months. Strictly in advance.*

MAKE ALL CHECKS, MONEY ORDERS, ETC., PAYABLE TO ORDER OF BREEDER AND SPORTSMAN PUBLISHING CO.

*Money should be sent by postal order, draft or by registered letter, addressed to the "Breeder and Sportsman Publishing Company, San Francisco, Cal."*

*Communications must be accompanied by the writer's name and address, not necessarily for publication, but as a private guarantee of good faith*

JOSEPH CAIRN SIMPSON, - - - EDITOR

ADVERTISING RATES.—Displayed $1 50 per inch each insertion or pro rata for less pace. Reading Notices set in brevier type and having no foot marks, 30 cents per line each insertion. Lines will average ten words. A discount of 10 per Cent. will be allowed on 3 months, 20 per cent. on 6 months and 30 per Cent. on 12 months contracts. No extra rate charged for cuts or cutting of column rules. No reading notice take for less than 60 Cents each insertion.

San Francisco, Saturday, November 25, 1882.

Mr. M. J. Henley is a duly authorized traveling agent and correspondent for the "Breeder and Sportsman."

## WELCOME HOME.

Something over three years ago the trotting world was startled with the intelligence that a mile had been made in $2.12\frac{3}{4}$ on a California track. The wires that transported the news were scarcely cold and the clicking of the instrument had hardly ceased until measures were taken to discredit the statement. For the second time in the history of trotting California had taken the first place in the calendar, and after a lapse of seven years had again rushed to the front. The length of the course, the "timing," the money consideration were all called in question, and a "newspaper war" inaugurated at times fierce and bitter. To a quiet looker-on the situation was inexplicable. A man unacquainted with the trotting arena would have been led to believe that something of great moment had occurred, and that such a turmoil over the fraction of a second was both absurd and ludicrous. To the initiated the meaning was palpable. It was the dethroning of a king, the hurling of one monarch from the throne, the crowning of a rival. The scepter was torn from the grasp of the Oriental to be transferred to the champion of the Setting Sun, and the hurrahs on the shore of the Pacific reverberated in a grand sonorous pæan, to the western boundary of the Atlantic.

It was a glorious triumph. The great chieftain with the plaudits of the whole world still ringing in his ears was a delighted spectator. Eagerly watching the flying steed, and closely scanning the delicate line which was marking the flight of time on the dial, he signified his approbation by joining in the chorus of cheers when the time was announced. Although the detractors were silenced by the overwhelming proof of the correctness of everything pertaining to the feat, it was the silence of sullenness, and there were inuendoes and whispers, and gesticulations and doubts. The king went East and lowered his California performance by subtracting one and a half seconds therefrom.

But he who so valiantly struggled on the shores of the bay, and still more swiftly sped where the graceful elms have given a name to a city, was doomed to defeat, and the diadem gallantly won, was worn by a queen. An empress, for assuredly the higher title was well deserved when the character of the contest is taken into consideration.

Home again, and it was thought that a winter time passed on the Golden Coast would so strengthen our champion that the odd second and something more would be taken off and that the interregnum would be of short duration. A short time before he started on the second crusade we saw him exercise on the tree-protected course at San Mateo. He went with the rush of a racehorse and although we had seen him trot a quarter at the Oakland track in thirty and one-quarter seconds, that flight of speed was surely excelled.

The second trip was disastrous. Potent as the spell with which Armida chained Rinaldo, there must have been some sorceress in league with the Empress to protect her crown. Maud S unquestioned held the sway, $2{:}10\frac{1}{4}$ emblazoned on her victorious banners which flaunted in the breeze, proudly defiant.

Anno Domini 1881 became a history of the past, 1882 it was trusted would tell a different tale. With that came unfulfilled hopes, and St. Julien was doomed to a whole season of inactivity. Epizooty had held him in thralldom before and he had to succumb to its enervating and baneful influence. This time it was an injury to his hock, and though he was never lame there was a protuberance that warned againt the perils of violent exercise The enlargement was at the lower part of the joint where the cuboides and upper part of the metatarsals join. Not exactly where the curb appear but a little inside. He was placed in the hand of Dr. Ormond of Milwaukee, as skilfull a veterinarian as there is in the country, and following his advice he was turned out, though still remaining in the doctor's care. That this advice was sound there is the proof of a leg as clean as the day he was first harnessed, without a trace of enlargement left.

We saw him Saturday evening at the Fashion stable, and if he had worn a short sweat-hood could not have believed that it was St. Julien. A big lusty horse, but apparently not within two inches as high as the quondam king, with immense quarters, shoulders covered with muscle, and a "middle piece" rivaling a hogshead in size. If Hickok had not been there we might have imagined that the head and neck of St. Julien had been put on a coach horse. This is the first real "let up" he has had since he has been in training, and should there be no further mishaps there is a good chance for him to regain his former place.

There came with St. Julien two "native Californians," one of them having achieved greatness since his departure, the other already celebrated before she left this coast. The big chestnut is Overman, a son of Elmo, and a more taking horse to the eye of a fancier is seldom seen.

A grand, majestic horse is Overman, and notwithstanding his large size is highly finished and with all "speed angles" which the late Dr. Weldon so highly extolled. That he is a trotter, his races the past summer have fully demonstrated, and that he is of the hardy, enduring sort is evident from his appearance. The races he has trotted and the long journey home have had no visibly injurious effect, as he has a good coating of flesh, and his legs are without puff or blemish. He has an immense turn of speed when fairly settled in his gait, and in the races at Buffalo came from the half-mile pole, in two heats, in $1{:}07\frac{1}{4}$ and 1:07. When he acquires the knack of "getting away from the score" as readily as he "comes home," it will take a top-sawyer to beat him.

There is some talk of a match between him and Romero, and should it be consummated it will be the great trotting event of the California year. There are those who think that Romero can come very near scoring the fastest time in the stallion record, and it is nearly certain that he will beat the best for a five-year-old. Overman is just the fellow to make him show his capacity, as it will never do for the grey to wait for the brush home, and it will take a great flight of speed to "stall him off" when he makes his final rush. With a continuance of good weather a match between these two noted flyers will draw an immense concourse to witness it, and we trust that not many days will elapse before it is announced. We did not see Eva and had only a glance at two of the importations of Mr. Corbitt which accompanied the celebrities across the continent. Intending to visit Mr. Corbitt's breeding farm in a short time we will defer remarks until the opportunity offers for closer examination.

## THE RIFLE.

Now that the turmoil of the election is over, and elation and regrets replaced by more equable feelings, Doctor Pardee favors us with the contenuation of his admirable treatise. It is the purpose of the doctor to make it a full and exhaustive essay, and certain it is that there is no one more competent.

We have always held that a man must be an "enthusiast," more or less, to properly handle any of the departments of sport. There must be a fondness, approaching to a passion, to enter into the spirit of it with zest, and the "Breeder and Sportsman" is fortunate in its correspondents being strongly imbued with this feeling, while the members of the regular staff have such strong predilections for their specialities that they cannot listen to discussions of other topics with any equanimity.

The "dog man" will be fidgetting in his chair when the "horse talk" is prolonged, and in order to get even with some one who has been expatiating on a marvelous performance of his favorite horse, break in with the history of a bull terrier killing ever so many barrels of rats. The yachting chief, oblivious to horses, dogs or rats, will be poring over the exchanges, searching for items of interest on the wave, and he who handles the rowing is in a deep study in the attempt to figure out the winners of the "Breeder and Sportsman" Cup. In stalks the bicycle man, stalwart and "Strong," the floor trembling as he brings his feet down with a vigor which the huge development of muscle on thigh and calf gives, and at every stride the feet come down as though propelling a "fifty-four inch" at racehorse pace. The athletic quill-driver is his antitheton. Small, wiry and nervous he is "drawn as fine" as a racehorse "pointed" for a hard contest, and there is scarcely a pound of adipose tissue in his whole frame.

It is safe to assert that Dr. Pardee has as full knowledge of all pertaining to the rifle as any man that lives, and as it is his intention to make the treatise an exhaustive exposition of the art, it will be of immense benefit to our readers.

## THE REPLY OF HON. J. McM. SHAFTER.

Elsewhere will be found the reply of Hon. J. McM. Shafter to the strictures of last week, and to which we call the attention of our readers. In the first place we must say that Judge Shafter read to us the communication, and either we did not comprehend it entirely from hearing it, or else some of the paragraphs escaped his eye so that a perusal gives different impressions than we obtained auricularly. Probably the former, and in one respect we are gratified, inasmuch as it gives the opportunity for explanations and counter charges which will afford a better understanding of the disputed points.

The only retraction we spoke of making was in regard to the construction of one sentence, in which the actual meaning was that the "announcement was despicable and false," when the intentou was to carry the idea that the protest against Antevolo was "despicable and false." That is the only retraction or change we thought of, or will admit until different evidence is offered from any we have yet seen or heard. That the entry of Antevolo was made in proper shape and in accordance with the trotting rules and the conditions of the advertisement we will be prepared to prove before the District Board on Monday next. That the entry of Dawn was not we will show so clearly that every doubt will be removed.

As the question is to be decided in so short a time there is no necessity for anticipating, and we pass it by. The only "insinuation" is in regard to the selection of Dr. Tisdale as an associate judge being made with a view to Mr. Shafter having a coadjutor, and subsequent events would have justified a direct statement in place of "may be." A "coadjutor" can be obtained without a direct understanding and a few minute's conversation determine what would be the result. But Judge Shafter does not state correctly the facts about the selection of the judge. We met him some little time before the race was to be called. He inquired if he was to go in the stand and our reply was: "Certainly." "Who else?" he responded, looking around at the few people present. All who had any knowledge of trotting rules being men who are in the practice of betting, we inquired if he did not know of some one. Then he mentioned the Doctor from the Sandwich Islands; he did not give his name, and then we informed him that after the first race, Mr. Whitney would act. Subsequent to this conversation we saw Mr. Howes and a good deal of solicitation prevailed upon him to fill the place, during the pendency of the yearling trot.

The charge against Steven Crandall, Mr. Whitney's driver, was entirely different from what Judge Shafter makes it appear. Mr. Crandall was suspended for non-payment of entrance money, and no notice had been given of the suspension having been removed. We did not make the charge but told Captain Harris, the secretary, and that holding membership in the National Trotting Association, we must enforce the rules. Mr. Whitney on being informed made the statement that he, Mr. Whitney, had settled the indebtedness, sent the penalty to the National Association, which of course, was held sufficient. The charge therefore though never made was not "unfounded."

The occurrences in the stand are misrepresented throughout. Until we went to the track shortly after 12 m., and for some time after, we were not aware that Dawn had put in an appearance. Driving Antevolo from the house only in time to "warm him up" before the race, which we did before alighting from the sulky, it was half past twelve ere we learned of his arrival an hour or so previous. No one at the Oakland Trotting Park had the slightest knowledge that he had left Petaluma and there was a general surprise. Had we been aware of it in time a much stronger case would have been presented, and now we will have to hark back to give a clear account. Some time in July, the date we are not sure of but it was since this office was occupied by us, we met Mr. Whitney, who asked whether the published statement or the books would govern an entry? Supposing he meant a newspaper publication the answer was promptly given, the book. A short time before the race was to come off Mr. Culver assisted us in looking over the lists in the endeavor to form some estimate what the sums would amount to. The first examined was the "Spirit of the Times" of March 5th, 1881, in which was a published list of the nominations received, 98, and the 94th was a colt, then foaled, by Nutwood from Countess, and a blank left in lieu of the stakes he was named in. Searching further on we found an "official list of nominations in the Embryo Trotting Stakes for foals of 1881" with Ben E. Harris' name attached as Secretary. Number ninety-four in this was Mr. Whitney's colt and in place of "in stakes of ——" appeared "in stake 1884." As there was a receipt appended bearing the date of March 11th, 1881, it must have been after this date the list was published. In the first publication the nominations of P. A. Finigan and E. H. Pardee were left blank in the same way; in the "official" they were filled in "in stakes of 1882, 1883, 1884."

On seeing this we at once said to Culver: "Whitney's colt is not in," as we had him marked in the computation, and that amount was stricken out of the calculation. Mr. Rose being in town was desirous that the stakes should be trotted on election day. He was in the office Saturday, and on the following Monday we saw Mr. Whitney in front of his store on California street. There was only a few moments for conversation, being desirous to cross on the 12 o'clock boat. On speaking to Mr. Whitney in regard to Mr. Rose's proposition, he said that it would be short notice to get his colt down. We answered: "You are not in the stake," and he said that he was and that the books would show it. We replied that in the situation the original entry would be necessary, when he said that if it was going to cause trouble he would leave the colt at home. Our reply was, that if he was entitled to start, he had the right to, and in that case to bring him.

The colt not making his appearance, and no one even having any knowledge that he was any where in the neighborhood until an hour and a half before the time for starting, we had not the least idea but that Mr. Whitney had found that he was not in the race. We were in a quandary what to do. It was a state of affairs which we sincerely regretted, and had come to the conclusion to let it go. Jogging up and down the stretch, John Williams, the driver of the sister to Honesty, inquired if Dawn had a right to start. On being answered in the negative, he stopped in front of the judges' stand and entered a verbal protest. Our course was hanging in the stand, and while seated in the sulky we told the judges that they would find the official list in a pocket-book in the breast pocket.

As there were other papers in it we concluded it would expedite matters if we aided in the search, and went into the stand. The official list was produced and Judge Shafter, without deigning to look at it, immediately commenced a tirade of arbitrary talk. We asked Harris for the books and the original entry, which he had entrusted to another man to bring from home. After a short time he returned, and a paper was submitted as the original. That this was faulty was evident at a glance, but satisfied that it would be decided as it was, a written protest was prepared and left in the hands of the Secretary to be filed if the decision was adverse and we left the stand.

Soon after that Judge Shafter summoned Mr. Whitney and after waiting a long time, the announcement was made that there were protests against all three. Judging from the hostile demeanor of the presiding judge, we at once came to the conclusion that he had suggested this course and it was a "shyster trick," "dispicable and mean." The question was never asked why we had not acquainted Mr. Whitney before, so there was no opportunity to answer. Again, Mr. Shafter implies that had their decision been otherwise, Mr. Whitney would have lost his $100. Even forty-two years of legal practice has failed to afford the proper education to construe racing and trotting rules, as had it been decided that Dawn was ineligible, the stake money would have been returned.

We are very much pleased to learn that Judge Shafter denies previous consultation, and also that Mr. Whitney was misled by a false statement when he entered the protest. In that case there was nothing wrong in entering the protest, and with the assurance, when I have not the least reason to dispute.

Judge Shafter does not quote correctly in writing: "faithful guardian of racing interests on this coast," as the words used were slightly different, and in his request that "when we find it necessary to allude to him we shall do it by direct statement," as he repeats the phrase it seems to have had a disturbing effect. Though it may appear to be an assumption which we are not entitled to, nevertheless we shall certainly do the best in our power to elevate the sports of the turf. If we have failed in the duty heretofore it has been on the side of leniency, and hereafter we will endeavor to profit by past experience. We agree with Mr. Shafter in the matter pertaining to a member of the Board being in the Judges' stand. His views are undoubtedly correct and those of "Lex" that the rules ought to be in place of what they are. That part of the communication which has reference to the starting in a running race we will discuss hereafter. It may be as well to state that the trotting and running rules have been conglomerated to furnish an argument and that the paragraph that treats of "false time" is based on the former.

With all due respect to the legal profession, we have long been impressed with the idea that the training necessary to constitute a good lawyer is inimical to "judging a horse race." Even "forty-two years at the bar" may intensify a proneness to look at only one side of the question, and the practice of turning every legal point, perhaps quibble, in the interests of a client interfere with a candid view of all phases of the question. Praiseworthy in a legal practitioner, when underhand advantages are not resorted to, it is out of place on the turf, and in lieu of a "faithful guardian" there is an advocate of the side to which his feelings lean.

### THE FOUR-MILE RACE TO-DAY.

This is bound to be a "grand gala day," as the best bill is offered that has been given in many years in California. Besides the hurdle race, a handicap of one and a quarter miles, and the Consolation purse, a dash of a mile, there is the Baldwin stake to be decided. This is a post stake of $250 each, pay or play, with $1,000 added, four miles. There are six subscribers which will give six starters. Although the horses were not in time to publish there is little question that the following will start: E. J. Baldwin's Clara D, Stemler & Ayres' Fred Collier, Wm. Boots' Nathan Coombs. Palo Alto has secured the subscription of George Hearst, and will run either Precious or Fostress, probably Precious. The subscription of J. T. Gilmore will be filled by Jocko, and Stemler & Ayres having secured the subscription of W. L. Pritchard, Joe Howell will fill that vacancy.

It is doubtful if a superior lot has ever started in a race at this distance since Wildidle, Grinstead and Rutherford ran in the same kind of a stake, and for the first time in the history of racing on this coast two three-year-olds will participate in a race at this distance. There are good reasons to warrant the prediction that the youngsters will make a good showing, if even they have the worst of it in the opinion of those who consider that more maturity is requisite to give the necessary stamina. Many of that age have distinguished themselves at the distance, and the breeding of the Palo Alto fillies and Jocko is of the real true blue sort. Precious is by Lever from Frolic by Lightning, and Fostress by Foster from Planetico by Planet. Lever and Foster are both by Lexington, and Lightning was also by Lexington. Planet, Lightning and Foster were all great performers over a distance of ground, and the blood on all sides is noted for endurance as well as speed. Jocko can show fully as good a "set of papers." His sire, Carriboo, was by Lexington, his dam Alice Jones by imported Glencoe, and her dam the noted Blue Bonnet by imported Hedgeford, the dam of Lightning, Loadstone, Lancaster, Thunder, etc. Then the dam of Jocko was Reply by Enquirer, from Colleen Bawn by Endorser, and her dam the noted Roxana. On the score of breeding it would be hard to excel, as those who are posted can testify, and the old adage that "an ounce of blood is worth more than a pound of bone," is peculiarly applicable when long distances are to be compassed.

Still there is a great lot to meet. Clara D, one of the best mares ever saddled for all kinds of races, with a fast three miles to her credit; and there is Fred Collier, the gallant white-legged son of Joe Hooker, who has also shown capacity for a distance; and the old veteran, Nathan Coombs, who won the cup at Sacramento, two and a quarter miles in 4:00½; and also that equine enigma, Joe Howell, which, like good wine, improves with age, and which seems likely to emulate the fame of some of the old-time worthies by running on until the teens come very nearly merging into the twenties.

There is every prospect that the track will be in the best order. The splattering through it yesterday will facilitate the drying, and so soon as the harrow can be used the superfluous moisture will rapidly evaporate. It will be in condition to harrow by noon to-day, and not a moment will be lost which can profitably be employed toward perfecting it for the grand contest. This will be the first four-mile race for many years, and from the great interest taken the course will be crowded with people. Some estimate the probable attendance at twenty thousand, and from such a brilliant prospect there should be a multitude of lookers-on.

### MEETING OF THE DISTRICT BOARD.

As will be learned from the following letter of the Chairman of the District Board, Pacific Division, a meeting has been called to adjust the difficulties which arose in the Embryo stake.

It is extremely gratifying to us to record this prompt action, and will give satisfaction to all interested. Much credit is due the chairman for the course taken.

SAN FRANCISCO, Nov. 21, 1882.

MR. JOS. CAIRN SIMPSON, EDITOR BREEDER AND SPORTSMAN, Dear Sir: Dissatisfaction having been expressed as to the decisions in the Embryo Stake trotted at Oakland on Monday, Nov. 14, if the parties complaining will bring the matter before the District Board the matter will be investigated.

For this purpose any and all parties interested are hereby invited and expected to appear before the board on Monday, Nov. 27, at 11 o'clock a. m., at the office of the BREEDER AND SPORTSMAN, 508 Montgomery street, and show cause against said decisions. Respectfully,
N. T. SMITH,
Chairman of Pacific District Board.

### FALL RACE MEETING.

To-day will bring to a close the fall meeting of the Pacific Coast Blood Horse Association. So far the meeting has been very successful and the promise for to-day is such that there cannot be a question that there will be a brilliant finish. Until the races of to-day are run it

would be premature to write a review, which will be more appropriate for next week.

It is not out of place, however, to state that the Association has lost none of its prestige, and those officers who have taken an active part in the management receive warm encomiums from all.

### Patagonian Horses.

Commander Musters, one of the royal navy, one of the family of famous Nottinghamshire squires of that name, wrote into "Travels in Patagonia," and although he lived with the natives, and apparently made a matrimonial alliance with a she savage, he never describes the horses that form so essential a part of Patagonian life. Lady Florence Dixie is the sister of the Marquis of Queensberry, well known in the boxing and steeplechase world. She is only 25 years of age; five years married to a Leicestershire baronet; and without phrase, as the French say, one of the hardest, if not the hardest huntress in the pasture counties round Leicester.

Having apparently found civilisation dull, a party was made up to hunt guanacos, (the wild llama) and ostriches in Patagonia, consisting of Lady Florence, her husband, her two brothers, the Marquis of Queensberry and Lord James Douglas—who out such an unpleasant figure in a dispute with a fisherman on the Thames—and their friend, the author of "Wanderings in Patagonia," the book that was the origin of this expedition.

The result is "Across Patagonia," in which, looking at the ordinary dull or flimsy character of "Travels of Ladies of Quality," one is agreeably surprised by its brightness and simplicity. There are only 250 pages, with a dozen illustrations, and only incidentally is there any description of the Patagonia horse.

The Indians, who have been represented as giants, were found by Alexander Dixie, "who stands six feet two inches high," to not exceed six feet. The first one seen on horseback, was a "very unprepossessing object—an unfavorable specimen; his burly body enveloped in a greasy guanaco cape, his feet bare, one of his heels armed with a curious and ingeniously made wooden spur." It turned out that he was looking for some horses. "He galloped away, and we admired the easy grace with which he sat on his well-bred little horse, which seemed able to do him good service, although considerably below his weight."

Lady Florence evidently wore breeches and boots, and rode like a man, although she never says so or refers to her dress at all, but she speaks of the horse she "bestrides," of "putting spurs," not spur, to her horse, and when she finds the lost horses of the whole party grazing quietly after hours of anxiety, she coaxes one until it allows her to put a scarf round its neck and mounts it bareback, without bridle and of course astride, and drives the troop back to the camp. In one of the illustrations a faint sketch of a young person riding like a boy must be meant for Lady Florence, who leaps on and off her horse as easily, apparently, as a whipper-in, or her brother the little marquis.

"Looking up the valley, we saw a dark mass moving slowly towards us. Presently it came nearer, and Gregoria cried out excitedly: 'That's not Indians, but a herd of wild horses; if we don't mind we shall lose our own.' Our anxhials were moving to and fro in a state of great excitement. One of the wild horses detached itself from the main troop, and galloped at full speed toward our horses. 'Quick! quick! your rifles, or we shall lose our tropilla,' said Gregoria. 'The wild stallion if not stopped will drive away our troop.'

"But the stallion flew like the wind. Bang went our three rifles, but he sped on unscathed, and was within twenty yards of our terrified animals, all huddled together in a corner of the valley far in front of us. 'We are lost,' cried the guides, filled with dismay at the thought of being without some 300 miles from our port.

"At this moment, Gregoria's big bay stallion, the master of our troop, rushed out to meet the enemy, both halting when they met. Then the two enemies, after pawing the air for a second or two, made a dash and engaged in fierce combat, chiefly with their teeth, but occasionally rearing and striking with their fore feet. Our sane horses were frightened, not daring to stir, while the wild horses trotted close up to the scene of battle looking on apparently much interested."

At the critical moment it was found that the party had no ammunition.

"The wild stallion was much the larger of the two. The tame one was beaten. The victor, with vicious bites and kicks, began to drive the tame troop of mares away."

Thus it is seen that wild animals are much larger than the Indian ponies of Texas and Mexico.

"We strained every nerve to get between the two troops. Our efforts would have been defeated had not our stallion suddenly re-appeared to fight for his wives. The combat was fiercer than the last. We got up to our horses, drove them towards the camp; but before we could reach it the wild stallion, having proved victor, again came swooping down, neighing proudly. We shouted, waved our hands as he approached. Within forty yards he stopped, circled round us, stamped, pawed, neighed angrily. We shouted to Asis. He brought us ammunition. At the disaster the stallion fled so rapidly that two or three bangs we had at him missed him. He made straight for his own troop. The moment he reached them they all started off at a gallop. They disappeared like lightning over the brow of a deep ravine, to emerge again in our view after a couple of seconds, scampering like goats up its opposite side, which rose almost perpendicularly six or seven hundred feet. In a twinkling they reached its crest at full gallop, and disappeared, leaving us marveling at their wonderful agility."

"I have been told," said Mr. Dubious, watching the great steam hammer in the rolling mill, "that a good hammerman can break the crystal of a watch with that thirty-ton hammer." "Yes, sir," said the hammerman, "it can be done." "I should like to see it," said Mr. Dubious, eagerly, feeling in his watch pocket. "I can do it, sir," replied the man. "And will you?" replied Mr. Dubious, drawing out his watch. "Come, I am anxious to see it tried." He laid his watch on the great anvil plate. The hammer rose up to its full height, and the next instant all its ponderous weight, with a crushing force that shook the ground for an acre round, came down on the watch. "There, sir," said the hammerman quietly, "if you don't believe that crystal is broken, just stoop down and you can see it sticking to the hammer." Mr. Dubious swallowed a whole procession of lumps and gasps before he could speak. "But I forgot to say," he exclaimed, "that it was to break the crystal without injuring the watch." "Oh, yes," said the hammerman, "yes, I know; I have heard that rubbish myself, but it's all gammon. I don't believe it can be done. But you can break the crystal every time.—Burlington Hawkeye.

## THE GUN.

ALONG THE NARROW GAUGE.—Every Sunday morning the 4.30 freight boat that connects with the narrow gauge railroad is actually packed with hunters bound for the marshes of Alviso, Alvarado and other way stations. Last Sunday morning the boat and train was so filled with hunters and dogs that only standing room could be had by many. A great many stopped at the bridge and wharf at Pacific avenue, Birds Point; at this place there were, during the day, over one hundred and fifty hunters. The ducks and shot began flying as soon as the first streak of daylight came over the eastern hills through the heavy fog-laden atmosphere. The birds continued to fly and the hunters to shoot till it was too dark to see. As the game flew very high there were not many large bags made but all got something for their ammunition.' Those who went to the Alvarado and Alviso marshes had better luck, many bringing home forty to sixty birds, though twenty was considered to be the average number. Of course those who went down the day before and shot by moonlight had better success.

LAW BREAKING.—We understand that the snow has driven the deer from the mountains of El Dorado county, down to the foothills, and, although this is the close season and it is a crime to shoot deer before the first of July, the people are slaughtering these beautiful animals most mercilessly. It is not to be wondered at that this kind of game is growing scarcer and scarcer every year. These animals come down to the valley to avoid starving to death or dying from the cold snap; they come, not as intruders but as sufferers seeking protection. It is a much-to-be-regretted fact that the county officials have taken no steps to prevent this massacre of the deer family. Should the Sportsman's Association take hold of the matter and endeavor to punish any offenders they will receive little or no aid from the officers of justice, judging from the way in which an El Dorado paper speaks of the matter.

A pistol team is being organized by the members of the California Schuetzen Club. It is to be composed of members of the club only and promises to be one of the crack teams of the coast, as those who are taking the [matter in hand are men who do not stop short of being among the best. This team expects to enter for the California Rifle Association Pistol trophy at the meeting next spring. The police may now get themselves into practice, as the new team put in a bid for the laurels.

If shotguns have been in active service this season so far, it is nothing to what they will be during the holidays. A great many persons who do not take the gun from off the deer-horns during the whole year are making preparations for grand hunting excursions on Thanksgiving Day. Several parties heard from are going off on hunting trips of two or three weeks.

A great many hunters were disappointed last Sunday. Those who were at Union and Sherman Island expected to have a fine day's shooting but at 6 o'clock in the morning the fog came in so thick and heavy that they could not see over twenty yards ahead. Ducks are quite plentiful and shooting generally is fine.

The Turner Sharpshooters held their monthly shooting tournament last Sunday at Schuetzen Park, Alameda. The champion medal was won by D. Schoenfeld with 371 rings. First-class medal by O. Burmeister, 339 rings; second-class, by R. Lorick, 280 rings; third-class by Chas. Sagehorn, 275 rings.

Mr. Abbey of San Jose has recently had a monster shotgun made to order. It weighs 20 pounds, 6 ounces, is a 10 bore and when stood up in out comes above the shoulder of an average-size man. It is intended for market hunting and promises to be rough on the game.

Next Thursday, Thanksgiving Day at Bird's Point, Alameda, there will be a pigeon shooting. Conditions are: entrance $5, 12 birds each, 21 yards rise. The prizes will be 30, 30 and 20 per cent. A lively time is anticipated.

At Alviso the shooting was very good; all who went down on Sunday last returned with something to show for their pains. Fred Johnson and brother got 54 ducks, Morris Sachborn 38 birds and an M. D., came away 28 better.

At Bear Valley it is reported that California lions and grizzlies are becoming quite a nuisance to stock men. Mr. Rodgers has recently had a fine horse killed by them.

Liddle & Kaeding have just received a stock of the New Improved Parker shotgun with the extension rib. These are the first guns of this kind brought to this city.

Few English snipe have been killed during the past week. Mr. Kaeding recently brought home one and one-half dozen as the result of a few hours' shooting.

Col. Beaver and Mr. McElhinney have joined the California Schuetzen Club. Both gentlemen are good shots with both pistol and rifle.

Next Sunday there is to be a turkey shooting among the members of the California Schuetzen Club at their range at Alameda.

Geo. Crocker and a party have gone South for a few weeks on a hunting excursion. Snipe and quail are going to suffer.

W. Winters and H. Hceth were at Mount Eden near Alviso and brought home 37 ducks and one gray goose.

Mr. Maynard and son killed 44 ducks before breakfast at the San Mateo marshes last Monday morning.

Messrs Stackpool, Wright and Putzman last Sunday were down at Warm Springs and bagged 75 quail.

On a moonlight night last week Mr. James L. Flood killed fifty-three ducks on his ponds at Menlo.

An elk was killed not very far from Gilroy last week, a most remarkable occurrence.

Messrs. Barrothlet, Borel and Richoir last week killed and brought home 127 ducks.

Many members of the Tule Bell Club report good shooting on Sherman Island.

In the vicinity of San Leandro cottontail rabbits are very numerous.

Good shooting is to be had at Alviso.

## "NUTMEGGERS" ON THE OTTAWA.

### Experience in the Lumber Regions of Canada—An Antidote for Dyspepsia.

Our home camp is now (Sept. 27) located on Lake Travers, Pittewawa river, Ontario, thirty miles back from the Ottawa river. Could you but fly over this section of country as the crow flies, from Little Mattawaska to the Ottawa, it would be a mystery of mysteries to you how we ever got here; but the little tell-tale blisters adorning each toe and heel unravel the whole thing. But never mind the blisters, we are here as snug as can be in an old lumberman's log cabin, thirty miles from the last settler. Our cabin is already adorned with strings of black duck, wood duck, teal, partridge and black bass, awaiting our all-increasing, all-devouring appetites.

By the way, speaking of black bass, you never saw such sport as we have with them. All the trouble is, we haven't any hooks and lines strong enough to hold them. With our lines doubled we are able to land some beauties. We caught one day before yesterday, fully three feet long, but could not land him, and had to let him break away, taking with him one of our largest trolling-spoons. Since that little circumstance we take the precaution to station a man in the stern of the boat with a rifle, and he puts a ball through the big ones before an attempt is made to land them. We captured one very successfully in that way this morning. They always come out of the water and take a look at our crew just before reaching the boat. They seem displeased at some member of the party, and always go below with a fright, taking the line and everything with them.

We have just taken our dinner of black bass, duck, partridge, cranberry and blueberry sauce, baked beans, biscuit and tea, all prepared with our little folding tin oven, bean-kettle, pail and frying-pan. Cooking utensils are not plenty, but we venture to assert that no dinner at Delmonico's was ever taken with a better relish. The amount of food we eat is something wonderful, and not one of the party feels any ill effects from it. We believe that the worst case of dyspepsia can be cured or permanently benefited by the judicious intermingling of the necessary hardships, deprivations, pleasures and labors of a camp located in a healthy wilderness like this. A person situated as we are to-day, one thousand miles from home and friends and thirty miles from the nearest settler, must feel that he is to rely principally upon his own exertions, and that he must hunt and fish or starve. Most subjects will at least try the former first, though I could name an occasional one who would almost cheerfully choose the latter were he obliged to decide between the two. I am not preaching to that kind of a man. He is past help. The only thing left for him to do is to marry and die young; but the active, go-ahead man, who, by reason of dyspepsia and its attendant ills, has lost his usual energy and ambition, and is almost incapacitated for business and comfort—I believe this to be just the place for him. I believe it will do what medicine and years of care and restrictive diet will not do. There are hardships connected with it, which, when they are past, are invariably looked back to with pleasure. A man feels a certain pride in knowing that he has been placed entirely upon his own resources, and that he had the strength and the will to overcome and conquer. I believe in going back so far from civilization that only its absolute necessities can be carried. Make the comforts as you go along. Too many seek to regain health and lost energies at fashionable watering-places, where every luxury can be supplied and every whim gratified. Look at the Canadian lumberman; he never had a sick day in his life, and he owns a stomach that will digest an iron wedge if you only sandwich it between two slices of fat pork.

I know from experience that a slice of plain bread, without butter, meat or sauce of any kind, tastes better in the woods than a boiled spring chicken at the best hotel in New York City. My theory is that it is not entirely the woods that bring this excellent appetite, but the hardships of getting into the woods, establishing your camp, with no stock of cooked provisions ahead, and not knowing where the next meal is to come from. Body and mind are both brought to a point where, if you have been reared in luxury and indulgence, they were perhaps never thought before. By the time you have got your camp prepared, banks toughed down, etc., you are getting hungry. You cannot step into the Astor House restaurant and order a beef-steak, and you have nothing but plain-bread and butter in the cabin. You feel a little above that, so you shoulder your rifle and go out, expecting to knock over a deer or a bear in a few minutes; but you don't find them and come back empty handed. You have something and so you must out again. After tramping around five or six hours, not finding so much as a crow, you are ready to lie down and die, but you finally come into camp with a chip squirrel and a partridge. By this time you are so hungry and faint you can hardly wait to have them dressed. When cooked they are eaten with such a relish as your fine dinners for the last six months have not been, and so is every meal after that while in camp. I can't believe a dyspeptic would be benefited in camp were he to drive in with his horse and carriage each day. But place him twenty-five miles back, where fish and game abound, with but one day's ration ahead, and he will certainly eat, laugh and grow fat. But, "hold on, hold on," I think I hear two or three individuals remark, "what kind of a side show is this? We though you were reporting for the party at Travers Lake, and we are not ready to buy our tickets for a course of lectures yet." True, true, but we are all apt to wander from the text. I have known a minister to preach a sermon on the subject of love, and before he was half way through, the congregation were mad enough to kick him out of doors.

The evening at Peter's camp was principally spent in listening to the quaint, funny and original sayings of Patsy, a relation of his life experience, etc. He fell in a hilarious mood, and we had a first-class evening's entertainment with an appreciative and attentive audience. There being a large number of wolves about the mountains this fall, we found that they had ruined our sport by driving the deer to the eastern shore of the lake, where we dare not put out on dog for fear of losing him, and the underbrush is so close that we cannot still-hunt with any success.

We heard wolves racing a deer around the mountain in the night. There is something exhilarating and exciting in listening to the baying of hounds on trail of a deer, but when wolves take the place of hounds the result makes it seem terrible. Patsy says that a large pack of them came yelling down the night before, and just as the poor deer was entering the lake and probable safety they caught him, and in an instant almost the howling, yelling pack had tore him in shreds. We put out the dog on the west side next morning but found no deer. The lake not being a great fish lake we decided to carry no longer. "Ah," says Patsy, "I knew that wud be the nixt thing if yo didn't bring in a deer. I've seen yo Americans mis........the dhune' adshu' slooo.. hure vot brekfas' down. ..  ll bee... l only had poor Bose here ......... needn't be talkin. ..  . . . . .  the Ottawa are his

places. Ye wudn't be aither laving ould Patsy so soon. I'd put ye in a deer afore ye could burn that stump of a segar in in yer teeth, but it's no use; poor Bosey's gone, he's gone. In the many years I've lived in that ould cabin, me an' me ould woman hev bro't up a family of ten childer, an' we niver had a death amongst us, an' I don't know how to bear one, an' still I used to kick an' thrash the devil out o' that dog whin he was wid me, but I take ivery blamed kick back to mesilf now."

We left Patsy's cabin and hospitality that afternoon, drove to Renfrew and ticketed up the road, traveled nearly all night, and Friday noon brought us to Bissell's Creek on the Ottawa River. Some half a dozen settlers have established homes here. We stayed over night expecting to find a team in the morning to take our flour, canoe and heavy luggage, and a guide to guide us back to the cabin we are now in at Travers Lake. We failed to get either, so we took two days' rations and our sleeping bags and rifles and started. Thirty miles seemed like a long tramp through the woods and swamps, and we expected to make a two days' journey of it; but we found an old lumberman's portage road which was quite passable most of the way. At noon and 5 p. m. we stopped, built a fire and made tea. No one voted to make a halt for the night, so we trudged along, and at 7.30 we hove in sight of Travers Lake. Here was a dilemma; our camp was on the opposite shore and our birch canoe thirty miles back; but a few rods down the shore of the lake we found a little tent belonging to some lumbermen, who are just establishing a camp a few miles further on up the little Mattawaska. We raised it, and soon had a rousing camp fire and a steaming supper.

We were tired and footsore, I assure you, but we slept nevertheless until daylight. Sunday morning was ushered in by Miner rousing us to hear a pack of wolves on a slope of the mountain to the left. Just then Brady discovered a deer swimming up the lake toward our camp. I wish you could have witnessed the rapidity with which our men sprung from their bunks, formed in a line and prepared for action. Guns were unlimbered, cartridges drives home, and before a raw recruit could have drawn on one stocking, Brady and Dorsey were charging down through the brush and fallen timber, with underclothing and rifles in position, colors flying and one breeches leg at half mast. Miner and Rardell, hatless, coatless and shoeless, made a gallant stand in the deep mud on the right flank of the enemy. 'Twas just at dawn

When cannons boomed from shore to shore, '
And small arms made a rattle;
Since war began I'm sure no man
Ere saw so strange a battle.

Well, after all, the deer turned out to be an otter, and that wasn't the worst turn out either, for it turned out that we lost him, but you must remember that it was Sunday morning. When we made the charge we supposed that we actually needed him, but we found that we could get along without him until Monday, and so killed no game, for at any rate he went. We knocked over partridge enough for a good Sunday dinner, and took a Sunday afternoon stroll and viewed the country about us. We found bear tracks very plenty all about us, and occasionally a moose track, but no deer (we had been told that we would fish nothing now on this side of the Pittewawa). We find black dusk nearly as large as geese in great numbers all around the lake.

This is just the season when lumber camps are being established away up the river. Two bateaux' loads of men went up yesterday, all soaked through and through. They had been three days reaching Travers Lake, and had a tour of five days ahead of them before they would reach their camp. The Pittewawa is very rapid, and in many places the men have to jump into the water up to their waists or shoulders, shoving the boat ahead of them or roping it over the rapids. All their luggage, consisting of trunks, cooking utensils, and sometimes barrels of pork and flour, must be carried around. Portages on the Pittewawa vary from ten rods to half a mile. A Canadian lumberman will take a barrel of pork on his back, with what they call a "tump line" across his forehead, and carry it through the brush and over the rocks of a quarter-mile portage without a grunt. This operation must be repeated again and again until bateaux (which of itself weighs about 1,200 pounds) and luggage is all over. The next quarter-mile perhaps must be journeyed over by the men wading waist-deep in the cold water; they do not pretend to keep dry. All they eat is bread and fat pork. Such is life to a Canadian lumberman. Their every-day life, each fall and spring, recalled one of the sad record of Lieutenant De Long's retreat over the ice floes from the lost steamer Jeannette.—B. G. A., in Forest and Stream.

Charles Dickens had a very good story about the early days of a renowned mourning establishment. The went therefore day about some morning and was ushered into a room where sat a shopman and attendant in woe-stricken habiliments who groaned out: "A father, a mother, perhaps a wife?" "Oh, no," said Dickens, "only a distant relative." "Oh, sir," said the funeral one, "you have made a mistake; this is the chamber of agonizing woe. John toll the bell and show the gentleman into the light affliction department."

The Russian horse is of small stature, hardy and muscular, capable of great endurance, inured by exposure to the cold and privations of a vigorous climate and the privations of an innutritious and scanty fare.

## THE RIFLE.

### A Rifle Match At Berkley.

A friendly rifle contest took place last Sunday at Shell Mound Park between Lient. E. G. Sprowl and P. H. McElhinney resulting in the latter winning by two points. The distance was 200 yards, 100 shots with Springfield Rifles, the scores made are:

| MCELHINNEY. | MR. SPROWL. |
|---|---|
| 4 3 5 4 4 | 4 5 5 4 4 |
| 4 3 4 4 4 | 4 4 5 4 4 |
| 4 4 5 4 4 | 4 4 5 4 5 |
| 4 5 4 5 4 | 4 4 5 4 4 |
| 4 5 4 4 4 | 4 4 5 4 4 |
| 4 4 5 4 4 | 4 4 5 4 4 |
| 4 4 4 5 4 | 4 4 5 4 4 |
| 5 4 4 5 4 | 4 4 4 4 4 |
| Total.............422 | Total.............420 |

At the time of the shooting the atmosphere was clear and no wind, so that the gentlemen had all in their favor for good shooting. Mr. McElhinney is going to shoot against Mr Townsend before long.

## ANCIENT AND MODERN ARMS.

### Propellant and Explosive Force—A Testing Machine that Tests Nothing.

BY DR. E. H. PARDEE.

(Continued from page 108.)

Common sense is a good commodity for one to possess, and when applied to the ordinary surroundings of life, will act as a safeguard in tracing the hidden mysteries of theory, from cause to effect.

A little engineering skill will prove to any one who will give the matter the attention it deserves that according to the density and weight of matter to be projected for a certain distance, the nature and power of the propellant force must be taken in consideration. The accumulative force must be gradual until the body at rest is put in motion, and then the accelerative until it has imparted to it its greatest point of velocity that it is capable of imparting, while, on the other hand, if it fails to do this, science has failed in taking from it the full horse power it possesses; which demonstrates that important fact, that we are using a superabundance of force, and making unnecessary wear and tear on our machinery and an inferior pressure on the other. The human mind is capable, by a little study, of applying properly the distribution of the forces, so that the safety and durability of the gun is insured and a great percentage of projectile force obtained from an equal quantity of powder, taking into consideration, of course, the granulation of the powder and the strength to the caliber and area of the gun.

Those who have given the subject any considerable thought must admit, that the use of granulated powder to meet the requirements of the caliber and length of the barrel will obviate the sharp recoil that must necessarily follow the use of fine, quick powder; and as steadiness of weapon is a fixed principle in the accuracy of range, the subject of granulation of gunpowder is an important factor for the sportsman to take into consideration. The advocates of fine grain powder will say: "Oh! it shoots stronger and as close as the coarse, for long distances," to which I reply that neither theory nor science will support their proposition, and my deductions are arrived at from the simple fact that the fine powder is more of a propulsive, and the large grain, as I have in some previous demonstration stated, is an expellant; this is maintained by a simple fact in philosophy, that in accordance with the law of resistance in aeriform fluids, the one is sooner reduced to medium velocity than the other which exerts its action more steadily and evenly. And then again the coarse grain is more safe; and to more fully illustrate my position I will state: Take a rifle-barrel thirty-four inches long, and half-inch caliber, and charge it with one hundred grains of fine gunpowder, and the ignition takes place so rapidly that the whole force of the gas takes place in the breech end of the gun, while coarse powder ignition takes place more slowly and distributes the force on the whole length of the gun barrel. Now, supposing this force to be five thousand pounds in the gun barrel when the powder is all burned, the fine ignites so rapidly that the whole five thousand pounds is exerted on the first half of the barrel, and that of the coarse, igniting more slowly, distributes its force of five thousand pounds on the whole length of the barrel; and as a consequence the danger of fracture or bursting the gun is only one-half as great with the use of the slow powder. Time must be given for every particle of matter to be put in motion from a state of rest, for it is impossible that the whole mass be exerted instantaneously, for instantly means one and the same time. To illustrate my position I will take a piece of wool as large as my arm, and lay it upon a block and have an axe-man sever it at one blow; now in the general acceptation of the term "instantly" one would say that the division of the piece of wood was instantaneous. But such is not the case, the ax falling by the vigor and force of the man's arm, in first came in contact with the first grain of wood, and one by one was severed, until the last one was separated. Now it follows that there was a considerable length of time between the division of the first and the last grain of wood severed by the ax. And again, there is a law in natural philosophy that forbids one substance occupying more than one space at the same time, making it impossible for the edge of the ax in the above illustration to be on the top and the bottom of the piece of wood at the same time.

Thus it is that the perfection of projectile science is to make the projectile take on its greatest velocity at the instant of leaving the muzzle of the gun; and I can only see one way to accomplish this important point, viz., to fit the granulation of the gun powder so that it will correspond to the length and caliber of the gun. And in order to more fully establish my position, I will take one hundred grains of Hazard's Sea Shooting powder, and load a rifle of fifty-one-hundredths caliber and the barrel being thirty-four inches long; I will now place upon this charge of powder a cylindro-conical bullet weighing 500 grains and will fire the gun, and by a certain process of reasoning I find the powder to be all ignited just as the bullet leaves the muzzle; therefore, my deductions are, that the bullet has taken its greatest initial velocity at the most opportune time.

Now I will load the same rifle with one-half of the same kind (50 grains) of powder and it must necessarily follow, with the same parity of reasoning, that the last grains of powder will be ignited when the bullet has traversed one-half the length of the barrel, and as a natural consequence, then and there acquires its greatest initial velocity. Then if my position be true, and from years of experiments I know it is, it follows that the bullet must travel the latter half of the barrel at a diminished velocity, and its velocity must continue to diminish, from the inability to the very muzzle of the barrel; for the following good reasons:—First—The column of air in front of the bullet is more condensed, as particle is more condensed, rendering continually an increased resistance to the passage of the bullet.

Secondly—The velocity is continually diminished by the increased friction against the barrel.

Thirdly, then, the perfection of projectile science is to make the projectile to acquire its greatest velocity at the very instant of its leaving the muzzle; and if by increasing the size of the grain of gunpowder, we can diminish the rapidity of its explosion, thus causing it to burn, and generate fresh gas up to the very muzzle of the gun, the projectile will then acquire the greatest velocity, and leave the gun with the satisfaction that the manipulation has been well done. The construction of the gun being perfect the vital question is, can the expellant force from gunpowder be made to conform to the condition of the gun, and approximate an equal perfection? From an experience of a quarter of a century, I contend that it can be done; and in some future article, relating to the rifle, I will endeavor to prove, from a series of demonstrations, how to do it.

When attending the National Exhibition at Philadelphia in 1876, a Canadian had on exhibition an instrument, gotten up for the purpose of testing to a dot the strength of different kinds of gunpowder. The inventor claimed much for it, and

---

to those unacquainted with the theory of propellant force took in much that the fellow got off in his flippant and gassy way, but after a little I found I began to chafe the man who had the machine in charge, and was told that he was not the inventor, but only a kind of supernumerary, and pleasantly invited me to call the next day, when the inventor would be present, and would be glad to answer all questions. During the night time this powder testing machine preyed like a nightmare upon my mind; and the following morning I found myself winding my way, through the vast multitude of people, to this (to me) wonderful machine. It was located near the spot where Krupp's wonderful and monster cannon was located, which, by the way, attracted more of my attention than all else on exhibition. I will first give an explanation of the machine and then my opinion regarding its merits. It consisted of a chamber closed by a spring, and loaded and fired like any common pistol. When the powder is ignited the spring moves forward, and moves a pointer or index round a graduated circle, resting in the simple fact, the quicker the powder the greater the force, as it was more of the explosive, then the propellant. And to me it was wholly unsatisfactory, and before I left my quondam friend, my questions had so pressed him for satisfactory answers that he declared there was no difference between the terms explosive and propellant forces.

As a matter of fact the thing was not meritorious, and was not worth the paper on which this article is written.

Much credit is due Dr. Hutson, an English mathematician, who died about one hundred years ago, for his scholastic achievements in sweeping away the mysterious cobwebs that overhung and left a dark shadow on the science and laws of gunnery. And to him is due by the elucidation, by a systematic course of deductions that now govern our present and modern system of gunnery.

"When in a state of explosion, the volume," says Dr. Hutton, "is at least increased eight times, and hence its immense force. The pressure exerted, if in a state of confinement, will depend on the dimensions of the vessel containing it; so that it would be no difficult undertaking to obtain any pressure above that of the atmosphere up, we may fearlessly say, to the enormously amount of four thousand pounds to the inch." In concluding this article, Mr. Editor, I will state that the fixed ammunition prepared with great care by the manufacturers of our recent breech-loading guns has sent a flag of truce upon this important subject; although I find a great defect in the fitting of ammunition to the condition of some of our best breech-loading long range target rifles, of which I will have occasion to speak in some future communication when dealing with American muzzle and breech loading target guns.

---

# FISH.

### Fishing in 1796.

From time immemorial the world has been flooded and swept with tidal waves of fish stories and it ever will be as long as humanity can make the elements of fact and fancy amalgamate, so no doubt they always can, and form a third piece of composition called a "fish story." From the time that a few small fishes supplied a hungry multitude or Jonah swallowed the whale, or vice versa, suffering humanity has been obliged to swallow fish stories—heads, tails, fins and hooks. Being afraid to draw on our own imagination for a fish yarn, for fear that it might be too large a one for our readers to absorb at one time, we take an extract from the memoirs of an old German gentleman who lived and was a young man in the time of our first president, George Washington. The year in which the following anecdote took place was 1796. The principal actor and narrator was Frier Adolph Grotjan, a young, well educated German, and a pioneer to our infant republic; he was at the time inconstant on his first voyage across the Atlantic to the United States. In his own language he tells the following story of his experience fishing in the mid-Atlantic:

During a continued and tiresome calm, whilst conversing with Captain Johnson on deck, I observed him, from time to time, attentively looking westward. Suddenly he called for his spy-glass, with which he seemed carefully to regard some object for a considerable time. At length he ordered the mate and steward to bring all the fishing-tackle on deck, observing with a smile, "There is great sport ahead." During all this time I saw nothing but sky and smooth water. However, after a while it became apparent that some object was floating in the water, around which for a considerable distance there appeared to be a strong ripple or roughening of the surface. The sight was still several miles ahead of us; and whilst we were very slowly approaching it, and all our fishing lines, hooks, gimps and harpoons were getting made ready for use, Captain Johnson explained to me that some piece of old wreck or mast was floating in the sea, and that the large rippling circle we perceived was caused by thousands of dolphins and other fish sporting and gamboling about it. The nearer we approached, the more astonishing and remarkable became the scene; and when we reached the object, which was an old mast of a ship covered with barnacles and shells, which we fastened to the side of our vessel, we could see became the center of this truly astonishing sport. Picture to yourself the sea as smooth as a mirror, our ship lying almost as still as if at anchor in a pond, surrounded on every side by many thousands of fishes of various sizes and shapes, more than a third of them being dolphins, sporting and leaping on the surface of the water. Picture, too, nearly thirty persons intoxicated by this sight, and eager to catch the precious prizes, employed on every part of the deck. Some of them had probably never fished, at least not at sea, and their awkward efforts proved not very dangerous to the finny tribe. Such, however, was the rapacity of the fish, that he who could well fasten a piece of pork to a hook would instantly get a bite, and it was owing to his own want of skill if he did not secure his prize. I was using for my bait the tafrail railing, and over the cabin windows, and had already secured two middle-sized dolphins, when one of the largest I ever saw, more than six feet long, swallowed my hook and ran with inconceivable swiftness. Captain Johnson halloed: "Play him, Grotjan, play him!" And play him I did, until the skin was nearly chafed from my hands by the friction of the line. I did not, however, let go altogether, but when my dolphin got tired I would gently haul him in, until a new freak would make him take another rapid start. In this manner I amused him until, at length, I got him close under the cabin window, where the captain had stationed himself, gimp in hand, and now struck him through the body, and had him hoisted into the cabin window. We never could have got that fish in any other manner, as my dolphin line was not near strong enough to have supported his weight. Our sport lasted for several hours, and the result of it was twenty-seven dolphins of various sizes, besides a large quantity of smaller fish.

Large flounders are being caught from the Oakland Creek. The best bait to use for these fish is shrimp.

---

### The California Trout.

There are several varieties which go by the name of the California trout. The differences between them are not radical, and arise, probably, from the influences of locality rather than from natural variation. The fish of highest development are found in the McCloud river, from which they take their distinctive name. They are the true rainbow trout, having a band of bright red, like the iris, along the whole extent of the lateral line. The mountain trout have the same marking but in fainter tint. In some specimens it is hardly perceptible. It has been noticed that in wild waters this tint is much more strongly brought out than in fish confined to artificial ponds. Occasionally, fish escape from the Caledonia pond to the open stream below. The influence of the wider range and of the change to natural food, largely crustaceous, is observed not only in the brighter colors, but in the greater vigor and more rapid development of the fish.

In producing and raising from helpless infancy some of the fish tribe, art may surpass nature, but only by a return to the ways of nature at the period when helplessness succeeds helplessness can the best development come.

The early history of our stock of California trout was given in the commissioner's last report; but the circumstances are of such interest that the story will bear reproduction and continuation.

In 1876 the commissioners received from a friendly correspondent 500 eggs of the California mountain trout. In due time these produced 300 fry. They lived and grew to be spawners.

At the age of three years, and when they had reached the average of a pound weight, they cast their first spawn. The product was 54,000 eggs. The usual percentage of these hatched, and with the exception of 17,000, kept for breeders were distributed throughout the State. In the spring of 1879 there were still living of the original stock 390 fish. Having increased in age and size, they gave a larger yield of spawn than in the year previous. Their production in the last named year was 94,000. Three thousand four hundred of these were retained in the hatchery. The remainder went out for distribution in orders. Our stock of breeding fish of this variety is now 3,000,000 to 4,000,000, all of which are already covered by orders, and the cry is still for more.

The spawning season commences about the first of March and continues till June. They, therefore, afford what the brook trout does not, good autumn fishing.

The California trout is, in its structure, pretty much the counterpart of our brook trout. It has not the carmine spots which distinguish its latter, yet it has the same dorsal mark, a slightly more forked tail, and the same color and texture of flesh. The general external color is a silvery green or olive, mottled with irregular spots of a black or darkish color. Along the lateral line is, as has been already stated, a marking of red of varying distinctness according to habit and habitat.

The fish is one of remarkable vigor and hardiness. It will thrive in water which to salmon and brook trout would be certain death. It will bear rough handling with comparative impunity, and bruises on its skin which in other fish would be followed by fungus and death make apparently no harmful impression. It is as active fish, and though it will thrive in either lake or river, loves best a swift running stream, and the most thoroughly aired water. It is a voracious feeder but its tastes are as delicate as others of the trout family. It loves best to take its food alive, and cannot resist the temptation of a struggling grasshopper or miller, no matter how full its maw may be already. No fish known is so certain as this to be attracted by the artificial fly. It does not matter much what the form or color may be, so that a motion is given to resemble life. In its greed for insect food it takes no account of seasons, and will rise as readily in January to a red fly when it is hardly possible for a natural fly to exist, as in July when the surface of the water swarms with insect life. It grows with nearly double the rapidity of the brook trout in the same water, and is, of all fish whose habitat is exclusively in fresh water, the most suitable for the large streams of the State of New York, like the upper Hudson, the Genessee, Mohawk, the East and West Canada creeks, the Moose, Black and Beaver rivers, and all other streams which over-much fishing, dams, saw-mills and other destructive agencies of human contriving have spoiled for good trout-fishing. Whether it can endure the poison of tanneries has not been yet tested. If it shall be found to stand this last desperate test, to which all others of the trout family have succumbed, it will deserve to take rank with the immortals.

The only unfavorable criticism which has been made on this fish is that they are not good keepers; that they rapidly soften after killing, and do not bear transportation well. This may be a disadvantage or an advantage, according to the standpoint from which it is considered. The residents in the neighborhood of trout streams do not care to have all the stock shipped to market; they want some for their own use; and if California trout will not bear transportation, there will be all the more to eat at home. No fish anywhere or at any time is as good as when fresh caught. The complaint of softness, we think, does not apply to all California trout, but to such as are caught out of season or in very mild waters. The quality of all trout is very much affected by the character of the water in which they live and by what they feed on. Speckled trout caught within a few weeks of spawning time, and after spawning, till they recover vigor, will be slimy and soft and tend quickly to putrefaction, and those that live in shallow water with muddy bottom, and feed on leeches and lizards, are never good keepers. Everyone who has done much trout fishing will have observed that fish caught in a running stream, especially if the stream be one much subject to rainfalls, soften much more quickly than those taken in lakes. Even on a good spring stream the angler will sometimes observe the ribs of the first trout protruding before the last has been put in the basket. On the other hand, the whole day's fishing on the lake will be firm and hard. California trout, in this respect, will not differ materially from any other trout.—Report of New York Fish Commission.

---

Sunday last there was excellent fishing on the Saucelito shore. Mr. W. T. Bopard, Mr. W. Lockhardt and F. Denning caught 70 pounds of black rock cod, many of which weighed two pounds apiece. The same party, with the addition of Mr. J. H. W. Riley, were at Goat Island the Friday before and caught all the fish, rock cod and tom cod, that they could carry home.

Mr. Jos. E. Shain on last Sunday had fine luck fishing along the Saucelito shore to Point Diablo. He fished in twenty-five or thirty feet of water and with a short rod and reel and caught a great many sea trout and rockcod.

Last Sunday Mr. Scott Tidball and party were fishing in the tide waters at Tamalpais creek. Mr. T. got four fine salmon trout that measured twenty inches. Others of the party had less luck.

# THE KENNEL.

## Rabies and Epilepsy.

The dog is a very susceptible and irritable animal. Various diseases, difficult teething, distemper, sudden exertion, over-joy, fright, so hasten or retard or derange the circulation of the blood through the brain, that there is a temporary loss of sensation and consciousness, and a violent spasmodic action of certain of the voluntary muscles. Suppose a dog to be ranging in the field, employed in the busy pursuit of game, or occasionally imagine him to be quiet at home. All at once he starts up, and barks violently, he scampers over the ground, or he dashes around the room; he runs against everything in his way, he turns about, and barks and snaps at it, he takes some kind of circular course until at length he is exhausted, and he falls. Sometimes the limbs are stretched out with tetanic rigidity, at other times they are moving with the utmost velocity, the head dashes again and again on the ground with frightful force, the eyes rolling out in their sockets, the teeth gnashed together, the foam thrown from the mouth, and all this time the dog is utterly insensible. This continues a quarter or half an hour, and sometimes for several hours, until at length, perfectly exhausted, the spasms cease, and he lies quiet or asleep for a while, and then slowly regains his consciousness, or awake only to experience a renewed epileptic attack, or awakes not at all.

It was only the other day I witnessed a poor animal attacked with these symptoms, while standing at the door of a shooting forge on Madison street. This one, now fresh in my mind, suggested the advisability of writing this article. The poor brute was knocked on the head with a hammer as being mad. This is the epilepsy to which the dog, from his superior intellectual development or general irritability, is subject to a greater degree than other domesticated animals, and they who know nothing about the matter, who mistake loss of sensation and consciousness for increased mental excitement, cry out that the dog is mad, and they follow him with every weapon of offense, and destroy him if they possibly can, or abandon themselves to unfounded but most distressing terror; if perchance they have been bitten by him during the fit.

There is nothing in this that ought to be for one moment confounded with rabies. Epilepsy and rabies are as plainly distinct as any two external affections can possibly be. The one is a perversion, the other a suspension of intellectual power. The one is an unconscious abandonment of muscular action to irresistible instinctive influence; there is method in the madness of the other, and the mind is actively employed in accomplishing its perverted fearful object. I cannot do better than to quote the language of the first scientific observer of this disease: "There is," says Dr. Blaine, V. S., "no rabid symptom whatever that at all resembles a fit, whether in the irritable or in the dumb variety. An epileptic fit is sudden; it completely bewilders the dog, and, after a determinate period, leaves him perfectly sensible and not at all irritable. In rabies there is no fit, no loss of recollection, no tumbling about wildly in convulsion; neither is there any marked break in the natural irritability attendant on rabies. If a dog in an epileptic fit should be so convulsed as to attempt to bite, it is evidently done without design—his attack is spasmodic—he snaps at anything, and it is quite as likely to be himself as anything beside. The irritability and mischievous attempts of the rabid dog have always method with them, and they evidently result from a mental purpose to do evil. The mad dog has usually a disposition to rove—the distempered one, never."

Further Cautions.—Enteritis and spasmodic colic have occasionally somewhat closely simulated rabies, and I confess that more than once I have for a while been unable satisfactorily to distinguish between them. There has been the same restlessness, scraping together of the bed, general irritability, intensely anxious look, and the howl has not been very dissimilar. The distinguishing symptoms of each are not, however, slow in developing themselves. If there is much restlessness and alteration, it is evidently with a design to inflict pain, and not from mere fidgetiness or ill-temper, displayed in the attempt to tear the bed to pieces rather than to smooth it. If there is irritability and ill-temper, it is exhibited only when the dog is annoyed and disturbed; there is no systematic plan to effect mischief. If there is the intensely anxious look, it is expressive more of pain than anger, it is a depressed, supplicating gaze, rather than a fiery, ferocious one; and if there is the howl once—what resembling the rabid one, it is preceded by a whine and a moan never heard in the rabid dog; it has not the prior characteristic bark of irritability or defiance, it is a howl, and not a mingled bark and howl. You may mistake or be undecided for a little while, but twelve hours will not pass without the different course of the two diseases removing all doubt about the nature of it.—A. E. Euard in American Field.

## A Smart Pup.

"A correspondent of the Forest and Stream, who writes from San Antonio, Texas, thus describes a young collie. — "I have seen him, at a word from the shepherd, round up and put between 1,600 or 1,700 sheep in a pen (many of them wild Mexicans), and not chase nor crowd any of them. The little chap would mass this large flock of scattered sheep and direct them toward the pen in half the time that several men could do it. When penning the sheep he had to work them down a long hill that sloped to a flat that the pen was built upon. When close in on any portion of the flock he could not see over them, and would scamper back up the hill and locate the position of the pen, and then flank his sheep according to his bearing. When the last sheep and frisky lamb was inside, he would lie down at the gate and slap the dust with his tail until the shepherd commenced putting up the poles that formed the gate, and I have seen him attempt to assist in that work by trying to drag the poles to the gate. At night he would keep the sheep in the pen, which consisted of brush, or if they broke out would promptly put them back I have herded those sheep myself, and slept in a small tent a few yards from the pen. In case of the movie rising full the sheep appeared to take it for sunrise and would break out. The first time it occurred during Dick's administration Dick put his paws upon my breast and licked my face and awoke me. I said 'Go for 'em, Dick!' and he did it and put the last sheep back in the pen, and then came back and tried to tell me that all was right. After that night he needed no further hints, but took the business into his own hands, of course. He had but little tuition, but he guarded that sheep pen as well as though he was five years of age instead of five months. If he had been guilty of any misbehavior for which he deserved punishment, he would rush off and round up his flock of sheep as though he wished to show work to atone for his misconduct. He had a nose like a blood-hound, and could follow a person's footsteps as well. I have left him asleep on the prairie more than once, stolen away

and hidden myself, and watched him follow my footsteps! He would trace every step until he found me, and then would quiver for joy.

## Gilroy Field Trials.

On Monday, November 27th, the field trials held under the management of the Gilroy Rod and Gun Club will be run off on some excellent quail grounds near Gilroy. The sportsmanlike spirit of a number of Oregon, San Francisco and Gilroy gentlemen has put these trials in a position to command success. The push, energy and perseverance of Mr. R. Leavesley, the Secretary of the club, upon whose shoulders most if not all of the detail work has fallen, cannot be too highly appreciated by those who hope to see these trials as popular in California as they are in the East. Entries for the trials close at 1 p. m. November the 26th, so at this time of writing (Thursday night) it is not possible to give anything like a complete list though all entered up to last Tuesday will be found below. The omission of pedigrees will be remedied in the future:

By Mr. Frank G. Abell, Portland, Oregon, Gordon setter Scott.
By Mr. Frank G. Abell, Portland, Oregon, Irish setter Bess.
By Mr. R. E. Bybee, Portland, Oregon, Irish setter Sandy.
By Mr. F. M. Spencer, Portland, Oregon, Llewellin setter Gem.
By Wm. Hedeman, San Francisco, Gordon setter Jim.
By M. F. Whittier, San Francisco, Llewellin setter Rock.
By Ed M. Moor, San Francisco, Llewellin setter Linnie.
By M. H. Briggs, Gilroy, Llewellin setter Count Warwick.
By M. H. Briggs, Gilroy, Irish setter Fern.
By Dan Leddy, San Jose, field trial setter Sport.
By Chas. Doerner, San Jose, field trial setter Blitz.
By E. Leavesley, Gilroy, field trial setter Don.
By E. Leavesley, Gilroy, field trial setter Juno.
By E. Leavesley, Gilroy, field trial setter Duke.
By E. Leavesley, Gilroy, English setter Mollie.
By J. L. Nickel, San Francisco, field trial setter King.
By H. D. Bartlett, San Francisco, field trial setter Rob Roy.
By D. M. Pyle, San Francisco, Llewellin setter Daisy.

SALE OF BELLE AND ROCK.—Mr. Lewis G. Clark, of New York, has purchased of Mr. Edmund Orgill the well-known pointers Rock (champion Rush ex Swayne's Nan) and Belle. Mr. Orgill has also sold, to Mr. Brewster, of Boston, a promising dog pup, by Champion ex Swayne's Nan.

DOMINION KENNEL CLUB.—The Dominion of Canada Kennel Club will soon increase the capital stock from $5,000 to $10,000, and inducements are to be held out, in the shape of important prizes, for the first annual bench show in March next, which will induce a large number of entries from England and the United States.—Turf, Field and Farm.

NEW KENNEL OF COCKER SPANIELS.—A new breeding kennel of Cocker spaniels has been recently established at Delhi, N. Y., by Chas. E. Hitt, who has 'christened it the Fleetwood Kennel.

# ATHLETICS.

## George Beats Myers.

The attendance at the Polo Grounds, New York, on the 11th inst., to witness the second race between W. G. George of the Moseley Harriers, of Birmingham, England, and E. C. Myers, of the Manhattan Athletic Club, proved that an athletic event worth seeing still has attractions for the public. Over three thousand persons were present, the ticket sellers being kept busy long after the preliminary races had been commenced, and a large number of ladies were in the grand stand. There was little fault to find with the weather, which was mild and pleasant, though as much time was wasted in preparations for the great race the evening chill was beginning to be perceptible. What wind there was did not hinder the runners, the homestretch being well sheltered, while it was in their favor on the opposite side of the grounds. Two good handicaps and a very tame bicycle race formed the extra programme and they were all decided before the champions made their appearance. The bicycle race was run in heats, best two in three, and was won by F. W. Hunter, Columbia Athletic Club, who, with twenty seconds start, was not caught in either of the first two heats. Time, 3.37, and 3.39 2-5. F. E. Davidson, Lenox Bicycle Club, was second on each occasion. The other starter, F. Jenkins, Manhattan Bycicle Club, was third in the first heat and only rode two laps in the second. A 240 yards handicap produced some interesting racing. B. Derickson, Manhattan Athletic Club, won the first heat from scratch by a foot from B. A. Stafford, of the American Athletic Club, 2 yards start, who beat J. I. Smith, Palisade Bicycle Club, 10 yards start, by the same distance. Time 26 2-5 seconds. The second heat was won by T. W. Stoddart, 2 yards start. E. C. Schuyler, 5 yards start, being beaten by a foot in 26 3-5 seconds. Both members of the Manhattan Club. G. H. Wood, of the Shamrock Lacrosse Club, started from scratch in the final heat, but one of his shoe-strings gave way and he had to stop to fasten it, so he could not finish the second heat. The final heat was taken by Stoddart, Derickson being a yard and a half behind him and a foot in front of Schuyler. Time 26 1-5 seconds. The half-mile handicap produced another close race between T. J. Murphy, Park A. C., the scratch man, and B. Stoll, American A. C., ten yards start. There were six other runners with longer starts, but the two named were in front at the head of the straight. Murphy was then leading, but he was getting very slow as he got opposite the old grand stand, seeing which Stoll made a determined effort and three yards from the tape was beaten. Murphy was now completely run out, and pitching forward, fell over the finish line as Stoll carried away the tape. Time. 2-2 2-5.

As soon as the half-mile race was over Jack Goulding brought out the horse-roller to give a finishing touch to the track, which he had got into very good shape indeed, though Friday's rain had made it dead. The day was rapidly drawing to a close, and as both Myers and George were anxious to get the race off they were ready before the signal to come out was given. George had again taken up his quarters at the old Polo Club house, from the far-staff of which the Union Jack of old England floated on the breeze, and as the tall Englishman walked up the track he was greeted in a manner which showed he had plenty of friends. Myers did not keep him waiting a moment, but at once came out of the room he occupied below the grand stand. It had been rumored during the afternoon that Myers was not well and was suffering from a cold, and he certainly did not look as bright as when he went to the scratch the previous Saturday. There

was a darkness under the eye and a pallor on the cheek which indicated anything but the condition he was expected to be in for a race at his opponent's best distance. Still his friends had confidence in his ability and there was a good deal of betting at even money, the Englishman being supported by a few bookmakers, with whose dealings it is only fair to say he had no connection whatever.

The work of removing their coats and wraps was but the work of a few seconds, and Mr. A. H. Curtis, as soon as they were ready, fired the pistol. George again had the inside position, and he at once began making the pace strong. Before he had gone 100 yards George was two yards in front of Myers, and this he increased to three yards on the back stretch. Rounding around the lower turn George added another yard to his advantage, and at the quarter mile, reached in 1:01½, he was leading by four yards. Coming down the homestretch Myers closed up slightly, and as George completed the first lap in 1:23 Myers was little more than two yards behind. A word from the latter's trainer, Jack Fraser, brought him back to his old place, four yards behind the Englishman, who, it was known, would run quite fast enough for Myers' weakened condition. At the half mile George was leading by five yards and his time was 2:05½. Again did Myers reduce the gap as he came to the stand and at the completion of the second lap, in 2:32 1-5, George was only three yards in front. As soon as the leader entered upon the last quarter of a mile he knew he must make an effort to shake off his fleet opponent and kill his speed if possible, so he dashed away at a great pace, and had way down the backstretch had a good six yards lead. He jumped away so suddenly that the advantage was gained before Myers was aware of it, but the latter in turn increased his pace, and was holding George all the way to the 220 yards mark. As soon as he got there Myers began pacing, and the cry was raised that he now was coming, and come he certainly did for another hundred yards, but then he was run out and commenced to get unsteady. George was doing his very utmost, for he knew by the shouts that Myers was making his expected effort, and bravely the Englishman struggled on tired and leg weary, but still in good shape. Fifty yards from the tape Myers was rolling about, and it looked as if he would fall, but he managed to keep on his legs, and as George breasted the tape Myers was fully twenty yards behind. The respective times for the full distance were—George, 4:27 3-5; Myers, 4:27 3-5. The crowd could not be restrained when the men were getting near the finish, but broke into the enclosure from all sides. They had good sense enough, however, to keep a clear course and allow the officials to have plenty of room. Cheer after cheer was given for the winner, who was too much exhausted, however, to realize much more than that he had won a hard race.

The timekeepers were distributed at distances of one-twelfth of a mile, and the following were the times returned for each twelfth:

| 1 | 0:12 | 5 | 1:45 | 9 | 3:24 |
| 2 | 0:24½ | 6 | 2:05½ | 10 | 3:43 1-5 |
| 3 | 0:37 | 7 | 2:20 | 11 | 3:59½ |
| 4 | 1:01½ | 8 | 2:32 | 12 | 4:22 3-5 |

The fractional times when George ran his great race on June 3, at Little Bridge grounds, London, were as follows: One-third, 1:17½; half mile, 2:04½; three-quarters, 3:03 3-5; one mile, 4:19 3-5.

After the race Myers was found in his room lying on a camp bedstead. When asked if he had anything to say respecting his defeat he stated that he was sorry he was not able to make a better fight of it. He had caught cold on Wednesday and had been poorly ever since. "I have lost four pounds and have been doing no work to reduce myself, so you may know that I am not in the shape I ought to be for a mile race with such a man as we all know George to be. I was not hopeful of winning, and yet I have run so well at times when I have felt poorly that I thought I might after all come somewhere near my expectations."

Mr. George was just pulling on his coat when the reporter arrived at his quarters at the other end of the grounds. He said: "Well, I tell you, although I beat Myers to-day there is very little between us. We are much nearer together than to-day's race would make us out to be, and the difference is more that of condition than anything else."

On Saturday next the third race of the series will be run, the distance being three-quarters of a mile, and as Myers won the half and George the mile the splitting-the-difference race to decide who is to have the trophy to be given to the winner of two out of three races.

The University Field games last Saturday were held on their own grounds in Berkeley. Their track is oval-shaped, 300 yards in circumference, and instead of being a cinder path, is composed entirely of the native soil. The grounds are quite sloping, and on the upper side the track is over two feet below the surface, and is correspondingly elevated on the lower side. It is too loose, heavy and uneven for fast time, and the 100 yards finish appeared higher than the starting point. The entire track needs a great deal of scraping and rolling. The grounds for jumping were miserable. The games were conducted in a very quiet and gentlemanly manner, marked by the entire absence of jealousy or ill-feeling in any contest, but dragged so much that several events were omitted on account of darkness. Col. George C. Edwards, of the University, and C. H. Slater and W. B. Melville of the Olympic Club, officiated as timers, and Wm. M. Sims of the O. C. as starter and handicapper in all the running events. The time was poor in every one, but the track is very much slower than the Olympic Club track. We were unable to obtain a detailed account of the events. The best time for 100 yards was 11 seconds. The only open events won by strangers were the 220 yards and one mile, W. L. Stewart, of the O. A. C., winning the first named, and Jas. Gorevan, of the Golden Gate Athletic Club, winning the mile easily in the slow time of 5:32.

The Olympic Club will give another out-door meeting Thanksgiving Day, on their grounds in Oakland. The first event will be a base ball game between the Olympics and Badington nines, to be followed by a handicap and bicycle races of one mile; 100 yards scratch run, open, R. S. Haley and Jas. Masterson barred; a 220 yards handicap, open, and 880 yards handicap, open. Besides these is already entered for the bicycle race, and King is expected to. They should both stop talking and start from scratch. Masterson is training specially for the 880 yards. W. R. Stewart is the only one in training that is supposed to be able to compete with him from scratch. Time will be called for the base ball game at 11 a. m.

All who wish to take part in the one-mile, one-half-mile, and one-quarter-mile foot races, also those who desire to enter their bounds in the hound race, which events are to come off at Recreation Park on Thanksgiving Day, will send their names or call at the Grounds before next Tuesday.

# ROWING.

## The Breeder and Sportsman Cup.

re are four San Francisco crews now in active training
t cup offered by the BREEDER AND SPORTSMAN and
by mutual consent will be regarded as emblematic of
hampionship of the Pacific coast. Last week there
but three crews in practice for the race but on Monday
new competitor appeared in the guise of the Golden
Rowing Club of which the officers are: Wm. F. Brown,
ient; H. J. Daly, vice president; T. J. Kaus, secretary;
Johnson, treasurer and Jas. B. Brown, captain. This
lub has entered as its crew in the race for the cup:
s Keegan, stroke; Patrick Keegan, after waist; Wm.
n, forward waist; Jas. Brown, bow. The crew is a
g one but is handicapped in its boat, as the only craft it
btain in time for the race is a lapstreak. It ought to
possible for the new crew in such a craft to keep coun-
over three miles with men boated as well as the Pio-
and Ariel crews will be. There was a flutter among
Pioneer men last Sunday on receipt of a letter from John
ivan, the stroke of the crew, announcing that he was
g to the country and desired the crew to find a substi-
t. It is not an easy matter within ten days of a race to
a substitute for the stroke-oar of the best crew of a club
Mr. Sullivan's proceeding received anything but compli-
tary notice. The club did the best it could, how-
and proceeded to reorganize the crew, though the
pects of winning the cup grew very dim. On Monday
Sullivan reconsidered his decision and wisely resumed
seat in the boat and has during the week kept steadily
aining. As now organized the Pioneer Crew is certainly
strongest and should have the race in hand at the stake
, but boating is a very uncertain sport and until a crew
come to the post well and fit it is unsafe to wager what
will do. The Ariel crew went into training under many
dvantages and at the time seemed a sure loser, but,
srtheless, kept on with admirable pluck and is now in ex-
nt form. The Golden Gate crew which was regarded by
Long Bridge men as the best four on the bay, has left the
and will be replaced by a "four" that is considered
uly inferior and has certainly had insufficient practice.
race will, however, be one of the best ever rowed on San
neisco Bay and will be contested to the full capacity of
of the competitors. The rivalry is almost fierce and the
who win will have to row from pistol shot to finish.
as the intention of the BREEDER AND SPORTSMAN to pub-
an engraving of the championship cup which has been
designed by Vanderslice & Co. and is of very hand-
e design. A delay of the engraving has delayed the pub-
tion of the picture but it will be given to the public sim-
neously with the report of the race.
he cup is supported by crossed oars and has on one side
ield for the names of the victors and on the other side
ngraving of a four-oar crew. The trophy will have to be
t twice by one club before it shall become the property of
club. To take charge of arrangements a committee con-
ting of Charles G. Yale, M. C. Conroy and James Esty, of
e Call has been appointed. All three are gentlemen who
e a great interest in aquatic sports and will exert them-
ves to make the race for the championship a credit to the
men of San Francisco. It may not be irrelevant here to
nark that it rests with the oarsmen themselves to make the
orts of the committee thoroughly successful. As the com-
ttion will doubtless be witnessed by a large number of
ectators, it behooves the competitors to conduct them-
ves with dignity and take success or defeat like men and
t accept either with the indiscreet elation of school boys or
affective ill-nature of an old fish-woman.
Rowing at Long Bridge has suffered more than once in
pular estimation by the inability of defeated oarsmen to
cept their loss with the composure becoming gentlemen.
n next important competition should be one to be remem-
red with pleasure, and as it will receive much attention the
son in it will not be soon forgotten. The committee of ar-
gements will select a referee and will if possible induce a
pular and fair-minded gentleman from the other side of
bay to officiate. The course will be properly measured
that the performance of the winning crew will constitute
first actual record ever made over the Long Bridge
urse.

Rose AND HIS RACES.—A dispatch from St. John, N. B.,
tes that Wallace Ross, who some weeks ago claimed the
natic championship of the world, will winter at home.
ting such exercise as will keep him in good trim for an
ly opening next year. There is no money on deposit to
d his match with Hanlan, but he says when they meet his
posit will be ready, and he and Hanlan will have the "sky"
one another that many boating men in the States and Can-
a have longed to see. It is not known where Ross will
in for his race with Hanlan, but it is a question whether
will again take his practice in Portland harbor under Ken-
ly's watchful eye, as he has done for two years past. The
partnership existing between Ross and Kennedy early this
ar has been dissolved, and, as Kennedy has as much on
handle as he can comfortably attend to, it is doubtful
Ross will row from the Dirigo clubhouse next season.
ny people here cannot understand why Ross wanted a
e for $6,000 with Hanlan, and refused to make a match
h Conley of the Halifax aquatic combination. It is known
d the Nova Scotians were very desirous of getting one race
h Ross before cold weather froze up the lakes and rivers,
I it is also known that of representative of the Halifax
wing association came to St. John and used his best en-
vors to get Wallace to row. The first proposition was for
ace on Bedford basin. This Ross peremptorily declined.
en the Halifax gentleman proposed a home-and-home
tch, one race to be rowed on Bedford basin and the other
the Kennebecassis river at St. John. This Ross also deed to consider. Further conversation developed the
t that Ross did not want to row in any event, but as he
de a proposition for one race on the Kennebecassis, he
uld row that race if he was forced into it. Thereupon, as
appeared that he was an unwilling party, negotiations
ased. To beat Hanlan next June Ross must be in far bet-
condition than he has shown this fall.

AKING LITTLE OF COURTNEY.—Edward Hanlan says that
will row Courtney next summer any race he chooses to
ke, not under three miles, for $2,500 a side, and he will
w Courtney $500 to make the race. He will row on any
er that Courtney names. He also says that he will bet
500 that he will beat any record that Courtney will make
t summer, he to row over the same course within an hour
r Courtney has pulled over it.

## A Proposed Sweepstake.

The Boston Herald furnishes the following: Mr. Spellman, manager of the Halifax Rowing Association's oarsmen,
spent a few days in this city recently, and, in conversation
on aquatic topics, said that one of the best means of renewing interest in professional sculling would be a regatta which
should bring all the best oarsmen in the world together,
and in which the contestants should row for their own
money.
"What is your proposition?" he was asked.
"Well," said Mr. Spellman, "I have given the subject
some consideration, and I think that a sweepstakes race of
$1,000 each ought to bring out at least six good men now on
this side of the Atlantic. I think that Hanlan, Courtney,
Ross, Kennedy and Lee would enter, and I am pretty sure
that Hamm and Conley would be among the first to send
their entrance money. I don't say that either of the Halifax
men can beat Hanlan or win first money. We don't know
until we have given them a trial, you know; but one or the
other of them ought to be able to win second or third money,
and, in that case, the association would not lose heavily, and
we would have the satisfaction of knowing just how good our
men were."
"What conditions would you frame for such a race?" he
was asked.
"In the first place," was the reply, "I would have a lake
or river selected by vote of the competitors, on which there
would be ample room for staking out a number of courses.
That is, I would have lines of flags, from start to turning
stake, to indicate the water which each contestant must keep
throughout the race, and I would have any man leaving his
own water disqualified. That would prevent fouling, unless
an oarsman intended to be deliberately intentional in doing
wrong. We would enter our Halifax men only in a race of
five miles—two and a half miles and return. If six scullers
started, there would be a sweepstake of $6,000. This I would
have divided so that the winner should get $3,500, the second
man $1,500 and the third man $1,000. Of course, wherever
a race of this kind is rowed, there will be gratuities or purses,
and any moneys from such sources I would have divided
among the three leading men in the same proportion as the
stakes are divided. A race such as I suggest would be the
greatest rowing event of the generation, and the public would
know that it was rowed on its merits, because I know two
men among those I have named who could not be drawn into
anything "queer," and would row, from start to finish, for
the first prize. Consequently there could be no corrupt combinations which would include these men. I hope to see
such a race between the men I have named."

HANLAN'S FUTURE.—Hanlan has been looking all over New
York for an opening, and it is very probable that he will decide to locate there if the inducements warrant it. The great
sculler realizes how easily he could have made a fortune had
he begun his career in New York, and thinks that even now
there ought to be a good opportunity for him to do well.
There are not enough admirers of good rowing in Toronto to
make it a desirable place for a champion to remain in, and,
consequently, Hanlan thinks of bidding adieu to his old
home and seeking a new one. A gentleman prominent in
aquatic sports in Halifax was here a few pays ago, and, in
course of conversation with Hanlan, suggested a double scull
race between Dominion oarsmen, Hanlan and Ross to make
one crew and Hamm and Conley the other; the race to take
place next season. Hanlan did not take kindly to the proposition, and, in fact, said that, if he should ever decide to row
in a double scull boat against the Halifax oarsmen, he would
select some one other than Ross to be his mate. The impression among boating men is that a match is ready for
Hanlan, no matter who he might select, as the Haligonians
are believed to be the fastest double in the world. Hanlan
has thought of spending the greater part of the winter season
in the South, giving exhibitions and keeping himself in good
condition for his races next season.

WHAT DOES IT MEAN.—The Boston Herald thinks that Wallace Ross says and writes many queer things. The oarsman's
latest is a letter written to "Pegasus," a writer on aquatics in
the London News of the World. Pegasus writes: "I have
received a letter from Wallace Ross, dated Oct. 14, and the
New Brunswick sculler denies the statement that has appeared
in the American papers to the effect that he is matched with
Hanlan. Ross still appears very anxious to measure blades
with Hanlan, and expresses a wish to row him during the
winter season on the Thames for the Sportsman cup and £200
a side, or anyone else that aspires to championship honors.
To arrive at this conclusion, Largan is the first person to be
challenged, but I hear that the levanting young Irishman has
no wish or inclination to defend his title to the cup so gra-
ciously conceded to him by Laycock. Largan did not go to
Australia (as I explained six weeks ago), but settled down in
San Francisco, where he is now engaged at his trade (house
building), and when he has succeeded in putting up one or
two for himself, he may return Mr. Deverenx the money due
to him." This must mean that the agreement "on honor"
between Ross and Hanlan for a race next June was either
made for the sake of appearances or that Ross intends to ignore his engagement with Hanlan. Perhaps Wallace can
satisfactorily explain his letter to Pegasus.

WARREN SMITH'S DECLINE.—A correspondent writing from
Halifax says: Warren Smith will not, in all probability,
row another race. Warren has been in bad hands since he
separated from the rowing association. He felt mortified and
angered because his old friends and employers of the association retired him, and for a long time he did not realize that
he had been going backward instead of improving in sculling. One of Smith's pastimes was wild-fowl shooting along
the shore in the winter season. He would lie prone on a
cake of ice for hours at a time waiting for birds to pass him.
In this way he contracted a succession of severe colds, and
when, a few months prior to the Hop Bitters regatta in
England, it was found that Smith was not as good a man as
formerly, his participation in the English race was opposed
by many members of the association. Warren's defeat
abroad demonstrated that he had lost his staying powers.
At one time in his association career he gave great promise
of being the premier sculler of the world, and all his old
friends and admirers to this day state that he was capable of
rowing two or three miles faster than any one ever rowed the
distance, but never was a good man for five miles.

Edward Hanlan, the champion oarsman, who for some time
past has been shopping in New York, has returned to Toronto
by way of Boston to settle up his business affairs there, after
which he will return to New York, where he will take up a
permanent residence. His racing programme for next season
has not yet been made up, but it is stated on good authority
that he will row "double" with George W. Lee, the Newark

sculler. This action is in all probability the result of a conversation that Hanlan lately had with Mr. Freeman of Halifax, in which the latter stated his willingness to match Hanlan and Connolly against Kennedy and Davis or any other
scullers "under one flag." Hanlan has therefore agreed to
become a citizen of the United States to overcome that stipulation, and it may therefore be considered a certainty that
the quartet named will compete in a pair-oared or double-
scull race next year.

Edward Hanlan was a visitor in this city last week, and
spent several days here. He says that John A. Kennedy will
give him a harder race than he has ever been obliged to row,
and adds: "But I will get there all the same."—Boston Herald.

# YACHTING.

As big keel boats seem to be all the fashion just now, here
is an account of the interior arrangements of one being built
on designs by A. Cary Smith, by Poillon Bros, for Vice Com.
modore Hovey of the Eastern Yacht Club. The dimensions
of the yacht are as follows: "Length on water line, 95
feet; length over all, 100 feet; breadth of beam, 22 feet 8
inches, depth, 13 feet; draught of water, 12 feet. The outside ballast, of lead, is about 11 tons. The main saloon will
be entered by a companionway 19 feet 6 inches abaft the
mainmast. On each side of the companionway a stateroom 8 feet long will be built. Aft of these staterooms, and
extending fully across the boat, will be the owner's room, 10
feet in length. Aft the owner's room will be bath and retiring rooms. Forward of the staterooms, on each side of the
companionway, is the main saloon, 13 feet 10 inches long by
21 feet wide. The mainmast comes down just abaft the forward bulkhead of the main saloon, on one side of which
there will be a tiled fireplace and on the other side a mahogany bookcase, designed so as to harmonize with the fire-
place. On the port side, forward of the main saloon, will be
a stateroom 7 feet 10 inches long, opening into a bathroom
forward. On the starboard side, opposite this stateroom, the
pantry will be placed. The captain's room will be forward of
the pantry, and on the same side of the boat. Still further forward are the rooms for the mate and steward. Between and forward of these rooms will be the galley, with a mess length
of 12 feet. Forward of the galley are the quarters for the
crew, which will be very roomy and well ventilated. The
main pumps will be placed just forward of the mainmast,
where they will be over the fastest part of the boat, thus
avoiding long and easily injured lead pipes. The skylights
over the owner's room and the galley will be made spacious, so
that the tops may be turned around to act as windsails.

In New York Mr. A. Cary Smith is building a large schooner yacht. He is also engaged in making designs for three
sloop yachts. The first will be 75 feet on water line, the second 66 feet on water line and the third 50 feet on water line.
These boats will be put in hand as soon as the drawings are
ready. Other boats are in contemplation, and without doubt
will be definitely decided upon at an early date. The vessels
already taking shape will aggregate in cost very close to
$100,000. Mr. Smith will have sole charge of the new boats
from the time of laying their keels to their trial trips. He
will furnish drawings in detail for all the boats, and also
for the gigs, cutters and other necessary small boats.

Mr. Harry Tevis has made arrangements, to have a large
fine keel yacht built. Mr. Hall, the builder of the Aggie, has
made the design, and she has been draughted, no model
having been made. Wm. Stone, the builder of the Stanley
Fawn, Magic, Peerless, Rambler, Lolita, Whitewing and
other yachts, will build the yacht. The yacht will be about
the size of that being built by Capt. Turner for the Spreckels
brothers, and while smaller than the Casco, will be larger
than the Chispa or Nellie. No pains will be spared to make
this the finest and fastest yacht in these waters.

The interior of the new yacht for the Spreckels brothers is
to be very handsome. The ceiling of the cabin is being ornamented with carved wood. The state-rooms are forward
and the main cabin aft, though it was at one time stated that
the cabin would be forward like the dining saloon of the
Casco.

There is talk of Henry White, who used to own an interest
in the Fleur de Lis, having a new 50-foot boat in the spring.
She will be a keel boat and will be schooner rigged. Keel
boats seem to be coming into favor out here just now.

Jack Purvis is making arrangements to launch the yacht
which he has been so long building in his yard in Oakland.
He has built a house down on the beach and will finish the
yacht there after she is in the water.

The Pacific Yacht Club closed the season formally on Saturday. The occasion was a social affair, no yachting feature
being connected with it. The prizes won at the September
regatta were presented.

George Farmer is building a new plunger for Lake Merritt.
She will be owned by Alexander Smith who now has the fastest boats on that sheet of water. Farmer is building this
boat to carry sail well.

A new sharpie has been built in Oakland which is to be
taken to Sonoma Creek. She is 26 feet long and will be sloop
rigged.

For the next two months there will be very little done by
the yachtsmen, the short days interfering with the sport.

The Annie went up river last week on a duck hunting expedition having quite a party on board.

The sharpie Daisy was out sailing last Sunday and as the
day was light she did very well.

The Ariel is lying in the channel in front of Turner's ship
yard, Mission bay.

The Elin has been off up river on a duck hunt, but has returned.

The Magic has been off on a duck hunt but has returned.

The Emerald has been hauled out of water for the winter.

The Fleur de Lis has gone up river on a trip after ducks.

The Lolita is still up in the marshes.

Articles incorporating the Umatilla Land and Sheep Company have been filed. Incorporators are Messrs. John Mc-
Craken, Charles Hodge, J. S. Cochran, W. R. Cunningham
and F. V. Andrews; capital stock, $50,000; principal office,
Portland. The chief objects of the company are to purchase
land near Heppner, Umatilla county, to grow wheat, to buy
and operate the Heppner flouring mill, and to raise sheep
and hogs. The company have secured nearly 4,000 acres of
land, well watered with living springs, and fronting on a
creek for three miles.—Weekly Statesman.

## THE MARYLAND KITCHEN.

### How to Cook the Oyster, Terrapin, and Canvasback of the Chesapeake Bay.

*Cooks, Connoisseurs, and Catchers—Baltimore Beauties and Baltimore Enterprise.*

[Special Correspondence of the BREEDER AND SPORTSMAN.]

BALTIMORE, (Md.) Nov. 8, 1882.

In a former letter I promised to give your readers an account, so far as limited space will permit, of the cooking of three famed delicacies for which Baltimore claims, I think very justly, to lead the world. I refer to the oyster, the canvasback, and the terrapin of the Chesapeake and its tributaries.

Before discussing the subject, however, I beg to quote the following item from the Baltimore *American* of the 27th ult., relating to some of the Arabian horses referred to in my description recently of Mr. John W. Garrett's beautiful farm Montebello:

"The skeleton of the celebrated Arabian mare Saieds, which died at Montebello during the past autumn, and which has been in the hands of Prof. Joseph Palmer, of the Smithsonian Institute, Washington, for mounting, was last week transferred to the Museum of Natural History at Druid Hill Park. Mr. John W. Garrett having presented it to the commissioners as an object of permanent interest. The work of Prof. Palmer has been skilfully and scientifically performed, and visitors to the park will be greatly interested as well as instructed by the opportunity thus afforded to study the distinctive and remarkable points of strength and beauty of the pure Arabian type. Saieds and Eanes, her mate, were purchased for eight thousand dollars in gold in Damascus in 1852, and imported by the late Wm. McDonald. They were considered so valuable that the Arab grooms who attended them in Syria accompanied them to this country. The immediate living descendants of Saieds now at Montebello are Adniack, sired by Burlington, son of George M. Patchen, record 2:23½; Sultana, sired by Bashaw Jr., record 2:24¾, and Gulnare, by Saladin, son of Daniel the Prophet. Mr. Garrett has also at Montebello numerous young animals of great style and beauty descended from Saieds. The skeleton of Eanes, the companion of Saieds, which was prepared under the direction of Prof. O. C. March, of Yale College, is now in the Peabody Museum, at New Haven, where it attracts great attention."

Now to the kitchen. There is an arbitrary sort of tradition which prevails here among cooks and connoisseurs, that the oyster is not fit to eat in any month from which there is absent the alphabetical letter "r." Be this as it may, to the sensitive taste of such, I have eaten them at riverside homes fresh from their native beds, fat and throbbing, and as sweet as a nut. No doubt the chill to the water from the frost without is as strengthening to the bivalve in his shell as to a mortal in his overcoat and he comes up to the surface smiling—as it were—on a cold December day in his best condition. There are so many and varied ways of placing the luscions morsel on the table that it has become an inflexible taste that in any form it is equally good to take. It is *en regle*, however, at luncheon, to appetize upon a half dozen uncooked and on the shell, as an earnest of the larger appetite that is thus revived for a banquet. The condition precedent is that such a snack must be highly fresh, seasoned only with a drop of lemon juice, and to help along it is the thing to munch a cracker. Liquid accompaniment should be a brewed beverage, as it has been found that spirituous drink renders the tender oyster tough and indigestible. You have heard of the restaurateur who coupled his name with the initials, "F. R. S." and being taken for a Fellow of the Royal Society expained that this addendum meant only "fried, roasted and stewed." This was business, and these are the favorite dishes with the crowd, but the private repast favors the escaloped or the broil, and in these forms, from some old Maryland kitchen, are the most sumptuous. An overdone oyster is a blunder worse than a crime, hence in stew or soup the liquor is first well cooked and savored, and the oyster is only introduced therein, to give it a swim in the boiling mixture. In a minute or two it "plumps," and retains all its form and flavor. One minute too long in the pot, it shrinks out of shape and loses all its luscious qualities. It has taken the experience of a life to render up a first-class fog. Not more than half a dozen Baltimore cooks have ever reached the exalted plane of knowing how to do it, and it is a secret of large profit to get one up on short notice. For be it known that out of this same experience the out-late husband who has been "detained down town on business" has found the sovereign solace for his spouse's ill humor at home in a charmimg box of fried. So it has become a fashion of long standing for these belated men of the town to take with them these mutual comforts, to assuage the harshness of a wifely greeting, and to ameliorate the conventionalities of a midnight reception. Take a good-sized oyster, plump it, then roll it with care in the best cracker dust, then dip in boiling butter or lard as one would a doughnut, and you have the idea; the exact turn, however, must remain hidden in the brain of the expert.

A roast on a coal fire is talent wasted and a good dish of spoiled. The thing to be cooked by this means is altogether too intimate with the fire and is corrupted by an evil communication with the gaseous influence of the coal. An old-fashioned fire-place is the domain of an oyster roast; a bed of live embers, the resting place of the pride of the epicure, for we can imagine its degree of heat to be just of the right intensity to open the shell almost by a touch, and that is enough to furnish a feast. The broil requires a miniature gridiron, made for the purpose, and I doubt if any is yet invented that will cook without scorching. Until some happy accident brings forth the perfected arrangement it is hardly worth our while to dwell upon this feature of the cuisine.

The escaloped is something dainty. It takes its name from a former mode of preparation, when the patty was covered with a fine crust, edged like a baker's pie. Now-a-days, we take a vegetable dish kept hot on the stove, place at the bottom of it a layer of dry toast, and this is the foundation. Cover this with oysters stewed and very little liquor, and so on with alternate layers until the dish is filled, the last top layer of oysters sprinkled with cracker dust and the whole is ready for a very brief basting, in the oven. The stew properly flavored with a pinch of some aromatic and watched with care in baking to brown merely, and the toast not permitted to become sodden, you would have an entree done up to the Queen's taste.

As we rise in the scale of the high-liver's delights let us take up next what to the epicure would probably rank first and which *sui generis* has no compeer as it is exclusively and peculiarly a product of the bay shore rivers of Maryland. It is true that the terrapin has been transplanted, and attempts have been made to cultivate and improve, by a system of culture, but the native haunts of the genuine diamond-back are the shoals and inland river-flats adjacent to the Chesapeake. The season is just now near at hand, and there are very few catchers for so large a market, the first for sale bringing prices which the rich alone can afford. Ranging as high as $50 per dozen in times of scarcity, and running down to twenty-four, or less, when plentiful, you can measure the expense of the far-famed stew with all the etceteras thrown in. Here let us halt; I am on the brink of the fathomless abyss of science, and fear to advance. Imagine all you may of the choicest compound of edibles, the rarest bird, the tenderest fowl, the most delicate fish, all commingling with spiciest condiments and a smack of royal Burgundy withal, and you can form some conception of the most tasteful viand of a Baltimore table.

There was a vender once, one of those quaint oddities which one will meet in the many strange vocations of a big city, who amassed a small fortune in the calling of the terrapin catcher. He was a portly, good-humored darkey who, beside his ordinary rude habiliments, wore heavy wooden clogs and yarn stockings to the knees, whose wonderful dexterity in always having the best and plenty of them was a marvel to the rest of his tribe. He took his orders from the homes of the well-to-do, disappeared suddenly, and suddenly reappeared with his rickety old wagon and forlorn looking "hoss." But alive and kicking under the hay which lined his shattered vehicle, were to be found scores of the rarest and richest terrapins. He was reticent and crafty, and wonder turned to fear at the celerity of his movements and the unvarying good luck of his catch. Darkies shook their heads and shunned him as in league with Satan—just as if the devil knew something about a terrapin stew—others fancied that the clogs and woolens had a special relevance to his strange pursuit. Howbeit, he was watched, tracked, run-down, in short, found out, and his monopoly of the diamond-shields became the spoil of invaders. He has gone out of the business in disgust, and the tramp of his heavy shoes, the creak of his shaky drag, are things of the past.

The next is a duck of a dish, but you who shoot whole flocks in the sport of a day cannot very well comprehend the difficulties and dangers in the hunt of the famous canvasback. Every kind of device has been resorted to, to get within easy shot of the wary fowl for a chance mark on the wing. But the cooking of it when brought down is more in the vein of this letter. Here comes up another of those hidden mysteries, wherein he who holds the key is as exclusive as a Knight Templar. Nevertheless, a young canvasback on the spit must be done to an exact turn, or turned over to the dogs. This nicety is an absolute neccessity of the art, for you must know that all the peculiar virtue of the bird's meat lies in the aroma which impregnates the flesh from the food it fattens on. This being of the tenderest roots, and the wild marsh celery, the racy flavor imparted is at once destroyed by bad cooking. I only know when well cooked it comes on a chestnut brown, simmering in the drippings of country butter, and is a feast for the gods. In quantity it is a little different from the Englishman's turkey which was too much for one meal but not quite enough for two, and two ducks for a hearty man is not much to smack one's chops at.

As to the hunt, the mid-winter cold on a dismal swamp where hunter often wades knee-deep is a sore provocation to rheumatism and kindred ills, but as your readers already know we have for every shooting bag the sovereign pain-curing antidote in the Great German Remedy, St. Jacobs Oil. As this has become the unexampled sensation of Southern enterprise known for its miraculous pain-curing properties, the difficulties of duck shooting are easily overcome. Like fame bearing the banner with a strange device, its career is onward and upward, and the new firm—a combination of great strength and wide business influence—has added increased vitality to its more than wonderful success. Mr. Christian Devries, now the leading partner of the house, himself a restored invalid from the use of the unequaled remedy, is a member of the firm of Wm. Devries & Co., one of the oldest and most substantial mercantile establishments of the country. President of the national bank of Baltimore, one of the oldest and soundest financial institutions of the city, and a director of the Western Maryland Railroad. Mr. H. D. Umbstaetter, the former advertising manager of the old firm, has been advanced to a partnership, and will continue his supervision of the most complete and perfect bureau of its kind in the world, handling as it does thousands and thousands of newspapers, with a corps of short-hand and type-writers, the most expert in the business.

But the point of good fortune taken from the sudden turn in the wheel lies in the fact that the widow of the late Mr. Vogeler should so happily arrange for the continuance of the business in his name in the magnificent structure which becomes a monument to perpetuate his great zeal and industry. She steps into her late husband's place as a partner in the concern.

And speaking of the bravery of women, one cannot do better than to turn to its most graceful adjunct, their beauty. There is something exceedingly attractive in that which gives fame to the pretty faces of the maidens of this place. I have studied it with some care, and have often paused to admire, but while I am free to praise the soft creme complexion and the swimming dark eye, I am just as free to say that the pink and white bloom on the cheek of a Pacific slope girl is a far more delicate type of loveliness. But so as not to invite attack, nor to endanger my peace of mind or personal safety on grounds where angels fear to tread, this is perhaps a good pause in which to close.

HIRAM HAPPY.

As early as 1810 Charles Colling of England sold his Short-horn bull, Comet, for $5,000.

## BASE BALL.

### Niantics vs. Renos.

The game at the Recreation Grounds Sunday resulted in the following score:

| NIANTICS. | T.B. | R. | B.H. | P. | A. | E. | RENOS. | T.B. | R. | B.B. | P.O. | A. | E. |
|---|---|---|---|---|---|---|---|---|---|---|---|---|---|
| Brown, r f | 6 | 1 | 1 | 1 | 2 | 2 | Barnes, 1b | 5 | 1 | 0 | 12 | 0 | 1 |
| Donohue, s s | 6 | 4 | 2 | 0 | 1 | 1 | Swanton, c f | 5 | 1 | 0 | 2 | 0 | 1 |
| Irwin, c & 3b | 6 | 1 | 1 | 6 | 3 | 1 | Denny, 3b | 5 | 3 | 2 | 2 | 3 | 2 |
| Robinson, c f | 6 | 1 | 2 | 0 | 0 | 0 | Riordan, 2b | 5 | 1 | 2 | 2 | 4 | 2 |
| Finn, 3b & c | 6 | 2 | 2 | 6 | 0 | 2 | Lake, l f | 5 | 1 | 1 | 0 | 0 | 1 |
| Sweeny, p | 5 | 1 | 2 | 2 | 17 | 0 | Sheridan, r f | 5 | 0 | 0 | 0 | 0 | 0 |
| Egan, 1b | 5 | 0 | 0 | 13 | 0 | 1 | Start, s s | 5 | 1 | 0 | 0 | 0 | 0 |
| Incell, l f | 5 | 1 | 0 | 0 | 0 | 0 | Creegan, c | 4 | 1 | 1 | 9 | 0 | 3 |
| Arnold, 2b | 5 | 1 | 1 | 3 | 1 | 7 | McElroy, p | 4 | 1 | 2 | 2 | 14 | 1 |
| Totals | 50 | 12 | 11 | 30 | 24 | 14 | Totals | 43 | 10 | 8 | 30 | 21 | 11 |

| Innings | 1 | 2 | 3 | 4 | 5 | 6 | 7 | 8 | 9 | 10 | |
|---|---|---|---|---|---|---|---|---|---|---|---|
| Niantics | 1 | 0 | 2 | 1 | 0 | 0 | 0 | 3 | 3 | 2 | 12 |
| Renos | 1 | 0 | 1 | 0 | 1 | 3 | 3 | 1 | 0 | 0 | 10 |

Earned runs—Niantics 2, Renos 1. Bases on balls—Niantics 5, Renos 1. Struck out—Renos 8, Niantics 4. Wild pitches—McElroy 1. Passed balls—Irwin 2, Finn 5, Creegan 3. Two-base hits—Riordan. Three-base hits—Finn, Sweeny. Home run—Denny. Double play—Sweeny. First base on errors—Renos 9, Niantics 5. Umpire—J. Taylor, Atlantics.

## Market Report.

FLOUR—We quote: Best City Extra, $5 37½@$5 50; Superfine, $4 50@$4 75; Interior Extra, $4 75@$5 25; Interior Superfine $3 55@$4 ⅌ bbl.

WHEAT—No demand for any but No. 1 grade which is strong at $1 70@$1 71¼. Good Coast Wheat sells as low as $1 40 ⅌ ctl. On call at Produce Exchange recently, sales were recorded as follows: No. 1 White November $1 74¼; do December $1 73@$1 75 ⅌ ctl.

BARLEY—Market steady. Recent sales No. 1 Feed December, $1 48@$1 48½; do January $1 50@$1 51. Brewing at wharf offered $1 48¾, no customers. Spot Feed, $1 46 and $1 47 asked.

OATS—Market steady. Fair Feed, $1 70@$1 75; Good, $1 75@$1 80; Choice, $1 80@$1 90 ⅌ ctl.

RYE—Quotable at $2 12½@$2 25 for No. 1, and $1 75@$1 90 per ctl for No. 2 grade.

FEED—Ground Barley, $32@$33 ⅌ ton; Cracked Corn, $38 ⅌ ton. Short, $20 ⅌ ton. Oilcake meal the oilworks sell to the trade at $32 50 ⅌ ton, less the usual discount. Middlings, $27@$28 ⅌ ton for lots at the mill.

HAY—Alfalfa, $11@$13; Wheat $16@$17; Wild Oat, $15@$17; Mixed $12@$14 ⅌ ton.

PROVISIONS—Eastern Hams, 19½@21c; California Hams, 16½@16¾c for plain, 16½@17c for sugar-cured canvased; Eastern Breakfast Bacon, 17½@18c; California Smoked Bacon 16½@16¾c for heavy and medium, and 17½@18c for light and extra light; Clear Sides, 16@16½c; Pork, $21 50@$22 for Extra Prime, $24@$25 for Prime Mess, $25@$26 50 for Mess, $27 for clear and $28@$28 50 for extra Clear; Pigs' Feet, $16@$18 ⅌ bbl; Mess beef, $17 for bbls and $8 for hf bbls; Extra Mess Beef, $16 for bbls and $8 50 for half bbls; Family Beef, $17@$17 50 ⅌ bbl; California Smoked Beef, 14@14½c ⅌ lb.

FRUIT—We quote: Apples, 30@50c for common and 75c@$1 ⅌ box for good; Pears, 50c@$1 25 ⅌ bx; Wine Grapes $20@$30 per ton. Figs, 50@$1 ⅌ box; Grapes, 75c@1 per box; Lemons, $6 50@$7 50 ⅌ box for Sicily and $3 ⅌ box for California; Limes, $3 50@$6 per box for Mexican; Bananas, $2@$3 50 ⅌ bunch; Mexican Oranges $20@$25 ⅌ thousand; California $2 25@$2 75 ⅌ box; New crop Western Cranberries are offering at $15@$17 ⅌ bbl.

VEGETABLES—We quote: Marrowfat Squash, $8@$10 ⅌ ton; Carrots, 30@35c; Turnips, 75c@$1; Cauliflower, 75c@$1 ⅌ dozen; Cabbage, 50@75c ⅌ ctl; Garlic, 4c ⅌ lb; Green Peas, 2½@3c ⅌ lb; Green Peppers, 50c@$1 ⅌ box; Tomatoes, 75@90c ⅌ box; Celery, 50c ⅌ doz; String Beans, 6@7c; Lima Beans, 5c ⅌ lb; Green Corn, 75c@$1 ⅌ box; Okra, 75c@$1; Egg Plant, 75c@$1 ⅌ box; Dried Okra, 18@20c; Dry Peppers, 15@18c ⅌ lb.

POTATOES—River Red, 60@75c; Early Rose, 75c@$1; Garnet Chile, $1@$1 10; Humboldt, 90c@$1; Tomales and Petaluma, 87½c@$1; Peerless $1@$1 10.

ONIONS—Quotable at 50@75c for good and 25@40 ⅌ sack for poor.

BEANS—Bayos $3 75@$4; Butter, $3@$3 10 for small and $3 20@$3 30 for large; Lima, $3 75@$4; Pea, $3@$3 25; Pink, $2 75@$3; Red, $2 75@$3; small White, $3@$3 25; large White, $2 75@$3 ⅌ ctl.

BUTTER—We quote jobbing lots: Fancy, 37½c; choice, 32½@35; fair to good, 27½@30c; inferior lots from country stores, 22@25c; firkin, 27@28c for good to choice, and 25@26c for ordinary; pickled roll, 26@28; Eastern, 18@22c ⅌ lb.

CHEESE—Prices steady. California, 13@14c for choice; 10@12½ for fair to good; do, factory, in boxes, $15@16; Eastern, 16@17c; Western, 8@12½c per lb.

EGGS—California choice, 50@53½c; Eastern, 37½@45c per doz.

POULTRY—Live Turkeys, gobblers, 10@13c; do Hens, 10@13c; do dressed, 12½@15c; Roosters, $5 50@$6 50 for old and $5 50@$6 for young; Hens $5 50@$6 50; Broilers, $4@$5, according to size; Ducks, $5 50@$8 ⅌ dozen; Geese, 1@$1 25 ⅌ pair; Goslings, $1 50@$2 ⅌ pair.

GAME—Market well supplied this week. Quail, 75c@$1 ⅌ dozen; Maliard Ducks, $2@$3 50; Sprigs, 1 25@$1 75; Canvasback, $2@$2 50; Brandt, $1@$1 12½; Gray Geese $2@$2 50; White Geese, $1 25@$1 50; Honkers, $3 75@$4; Snipe, $1 25@$1 50 for English and 50@75c for common; Teal, $1@$1 12½; Widgeon, $1@$1 12½; Hare, $1 75@$2 25; Rabbits, $1 25@$1 75.

WOOL—Light trade. No change in the prices. We quote: Choice Fall, 15@17c; Fair do, 13@14c; Defective Fall, 9@11c; Spring (free), 20@24c; Spring (defective), 15@18c ⅌ lb.

HIDES AND SKINS—Dry hides, usual selection, 20@21c ⅌ lb; culls one third less, and Mexican Hides 1c ⅌ lb less. Dry Kip, 18c@20c; Dry Calf, 21@22c; Salted Steers, over 55 lbs, 11c ⅌ lb; Steers and Cows, medium, 10c; light do, 9c; Salted Kip, 15 to 30 lbs, 11c; Salted Calf, 14@15c ⅌ lb; Dairy Calf 70@80c each; Sheep Skins, 25@30c for Shearlings; 30@50c for Short, 60@$1 for medium, and $1@$1 50 apiece for long wool and wool skins. Butchertown Green Skins bring higher prices.

TALLOW—Quotable at 9c@9½c ⅌ lb for rendered and 11½@12½c for refined, both in shipping order.

MEATS—Following are rates for whole carcasses from slaughterers to dealers:

BEEF—Prime, 9@10c; medium grade, 7½@8½c; inferior, 6@7c ⅌ lb.

VEAL—Large Calves, 7½@8½c; small ones, 9@10c ⅌ lb.

MUTTON—Wethers are quotable at 4@4½c and Ewes at 3½@4c ⅌ lb, according to quality.

LAMB—Quotable at 6@6½c ⅌ lb.

PORK—Live Hogs, 7½@7¾c for hard and 6¼c@6¾c for soft; dressed do 10@10½c ⅌ lb for hard grain hogs.

# "Tips and Toe-Weights."

A NATURAL AND PLAIN METHOD OF HORSE-SHOEING:

WITH

*AN APPENDIX TREATING OF THE ACTION OF THE RACE-HORSE AND TROTTER AS SHOWN BY INSTANTANEOUS PHOTOGRAPHY.*

TOE AND SIDE-WEIGHTS.

BY

JOSEPH CAIRN SIMPSON,

(AUTHOR OF "HORSE PORTRAITURE.")

"Round-hoofed, short-jointed, fetlocks shag and long."—*Shakespeare.*

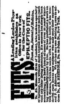

In Press, and will be Published about the first of January, 1883.

FITS. A Leading London Physician establishes an Office in New York for the Cure of EPILEPTIC FITS. *From Am. Journal of Medicine.*

VOL. 1. NO. 22.
NO. 508 MONTGOMERY STREET.
SAN FRANCISCO, SATURDAY, DECEMBER 2, 1882.
SUBSCRIPTION
FIVE DOLLARS A YEAR.

## THE BREEDER AND SPORTSMAN CUP (REDUCED ONE-HALF).

### The Race for the Cup.

The race for the cup offered by the BREEDER AND SPORTSMAN took place yesterday and like the majority of honestly contested boat races proved a complete surprise. The popular interest in the race was evinced by the immense number of people that assembled to witness the contest. Long Bridge was crowded with spectators and the rigging of the ships in Mission Bay was black with adventurous admirers of aquatic sport. The race was set for the forenoon but the delay in clearing the course of obstructions and in fixing stake-boats so as not to drag in the flood tide caused the event to be deided in the afternoon. The crowd looked on patiently at the preparations and when the competitors appeared, testified their interest by cheering. The Pioneer crew took a spin over the course an hour before the race, and then returned to their boat house. The Ariels were the first to show up in racing rig and carried on their boat—a precaution

which proved unnecessary as the air was still and the bay as smooth as a mirror. The Ariel four were Leander Stevenson bow, Oscar and Alf Branch in the waist and Jas. Corcoran stroke. The Golden City crew consisting of the Brown and Keegan brothers was next to appear. They rowed the Ariels old lapstreak boat and were looked upon as entirely out of the race. Their craft weighed at least twice as much as the boats used by the Pioneers and Ariels. The avowed object of the Golden Citys was to prove that handicapped as they were they could make a good showing with the Golden Gate crew. In this they were disappointed by the withdrawal of the Golden Gate crew at the very last moment. Waldhner the stroke of the Golden Gates, exhibited his bruised hand to the judges and declared his inability to row. The other members of the crew had been attending the club ball on the previous night and were even less fit and inclined to row than the stroke, and their entry was accordingly scratched from the list of starters. At noon the Pioneers,

Golden Citys and Ariels were afloat and the work of sending them off began.

The flood tide was running in with vigor and it was no easy task to get the boats in line. After several ineffectual attempts to get off on even terms a further delay was caused by the Pioneers breaking the steering wire of their rudder. Half an hour was spent in repairing the damage, and it was nearly 1 o'clock before George Strong, who acted as referee, could send the crews off. While the men were waiting at the line there was a good opportunity to compare them. The Ariel seemed much the lightest crew, and the Golden Citys the strongest. The Golden City four looked a very powerful lot and if well handled would have stood more than an even chance to win. The Ariels had the inside station; the Golden Citys next and the Pioneers outside. The start was fair. The Pioneers were the first to catch the water, but they had hardly pulled twenty strokes when the Ariels began to lead.

CONTINUED ON PAGE 362.

# THE STABLE.

## "Tips and Toe-Weights."

The editor of the BREEDER AND SPORTSMAN has a work in press which bears the caption of this article. The work consists of a series of papers, the first of which was published in April, 1876, and which were the result of experiments in shoeing conducted by the author extending from the fall of 1875 to the present date. The first article was written in April, 1876, and as the trials were made others followed. - - -

The work will contain an account of the various experiments and the lessons they gave.

The only horses which were available were those we owned and hence the field was narrowed and the trials prolonged. As there has been much discussion of late regarding the use of tips, several of our subscribers being anxious to learn what had been the result in the case of Anteeo, the colt which had elicited the discussion we resolved to anticipate the publication by giving the history of him and his brother Antevolo which has a direct bearing on the question.

In the cases of others experimented with there had been a chance for comparison as different patterns of shoes and tips had been tried, and every change carefully noted. But when Anteeo was broken we had become so thoroughly convinced of the superiority of the system which we now follow, that Anteeo has never worn a shoe on his front feet. A great majority of the trainers are of the opinion that he would trot a great deal faster if shod in the ordinary manner, though that idea is, of course, purely conjectural, not a single one of them having the knowledge that will warrant the authoritative statements promulgated.

When the work appears, those who read it will have an opportunity to form an estimate, as in all the cases cited there was an improvement of speed when tips were worn.

The extract published in this number of the paper was written the 4th of last March, when Anteeo was thirty-four months old, and the next issue will continue the history to the present day. It is also necessary to explain that in a preceding chapter there is an account of the partial conversion of a friend who saw the tips removed, the foot pared, and the tips reset on X X. Before that no argument could convince him that a horse could be driven daily on the streets of Oakland without further protection than a tip afforded, and not go lame. Argument was met with counter-argument and until he saw the practical results he obstinately adhered to his previous belief.

The chapter is under the title of

### "A Perfect Foot"

It may appear somewhat egotistical for the writer to illustrate the lessons on shoeing with histories of his own horses, but owing to the absence of other stock, that course is forced upon him, and without entering into minute, and perhaps, in some cases, tedious descriptions, the explanations would not be clear. The few which were available for experiments have necessarily extended the time to a long period, and it is now six years since the departure was made. In every case, excepting the one which will be the subject of this chapter, the animals experimented with had worn full shoes, and though this gave the opportunity of contrasting the systems, it is evident that others were needed to show the benefits which would follow from the functions of the foot never having been interfered with. The colt, Anteeo, gave this opportunity, and so far as can be determined by a trial, extending from the time he was nearly fourteen months old until now, when thirty-four lunar revolutions have elapsed since the date of his birth. The history of these twenty months of childhood had to be quite full in order to give, with clearness, the state of the case, and in order to show our friend the actual every-day life without the trouble of going over the pages of the journal, the information was condensed into the following synopsis:

"Anteeo was foaled on the 5th day of May, 1879. This being rather a "late colt" for California, we determined not to breed the mare, and permitted him to suck as long as it was deemed beneficial, though after he was six months old, it would have been as well to wean him, and the two months more were of little benefit. Before he was weaned he was led a few times by the side of his mother, showing fine action when trotting. The day he was eleven months old; led him by the side of X X, and occasionally afterwards; and on the 26th of April, timed him a quarter of a mile in 1:10. This was certainly a bit beginning, and on the 29th he made 1.07. Nothing more was done with him until June 3d, when led by the side of X X, he trotted a quarter in 1.05; and on the 5th and 7th, in 1:04. On June 12th he was harnessed and driven by the side of X X—the horse in the shafts of a breaking cart, the colt on the off side, his traces hitched to a whiffle-tree which was fastened to a bar tied to the shafts, and projecting far enough for the purpose. He had been driven previously with the harness on to accustom him to being reined, etc., and drove very quietly. On the 22d of June, he was shod with tips, weighing about four ounces each. His exercise was confined to leading him by the side of X X, and on the 29th of June he trotted the "back-quarter" in 58 seconds and the homestretch in 56 seconds. This was a manifest improvement, which was ascribed to the tips favoring his action; and on the 14th of July, he was limbed for a breaking cart, and he went quietly. On the 20th of July he was harnessed to a light sulky, but he could not trot within 15 seconds to the quarter as fast in that as when led. This was thought to be caused by striking his hind foot when going under the front, and rolls on his hind pasterns improved him, but not enough to show the speed when he was led. To test the effects of the toe-weights, on the 6th of August tips, with a "spur" welded to them, were put on, spur and tip weighing seven and one-half ounces, and on the following day he was driven with them and toe-weights of three and one-half ounces. He trotted better, but pulled up quite lame, which we thought was occasioned by paring the foot. The boy who held him at the shop ascribed it to a twitch the blacksmith gave his leg. He had driven the nails and taken the foot forward to clinch them, when the colt tried to get his foot away. The smith had a grasp with his left hand immediately below the knee, and the foot in his right, and when the colt struggled he snatched it violently upwards. The diagnosis of the boy proved correct, as ultimately there was swelling just below the trapezium. Think-

ing it more trivial than it afterwards proved, on the 9th a pair of hind shoes were put on, in order to hold a sculping boot, but the swelling and lameness continuing, notwithstanding fomentations and "cooling appliances, the shoes were pulled off, a light blister applied, and he was allowed to run for a small lot during the day. October 3d he was taken up and driven barefooted a quarter in 58 seconds, and on the 10th in 54 seconds. Previous to this we had given up all expectations of trotting him in the Embryo Stake of 1880, though the move was so satisfactory that it was concluded to give him another trial. On the 13th of October he was shod with tips in front, weighing six ounces each, and shoes behind, so as to attach sculping-boots. On that day he was weighed, and for a colt of seventeen months old he showed plenty of bulk, as the record was 810 pounds, and 14½ hands high. The 23d of October he was a trifle lame, and his work was limited to a jogging, with an occasional spurt of speed. On the 28th the tips were reset and lighter blind shoes put on. The tips had been worn some, and were filed down to 4½ ounces each, including the nails, and the shoes the same weight. He was driven the following day in 3:46, and we were satisfied that he could trot the mile better than 3:20. This view proved to be correct, as on Nov. 5th he won the stake in 3:17½, the last half in 1.37½, and evidently could have gone considerably faster. He was worked slow, and on Nov. 10th the tips were reset, and three-quarter shoes, covering the toe and outside wall of the hind feet, put on. The use of the three-quarter shoes has been partially explained in other articles, but later experiments have shaken the old belief, and the effects are so different from what was formerly anticipated that it is likely there will be a complete change. It will require one or more chapters to present the features, and as this is mainly to show the result of the use of tips, the consideration will be postponed. On the 12th of November he was driven in 46 seconds, and this was the fastest gait, he made in his yearling form. He was driven a few times on the road, and ran in a small lot during the winter, when the days were suitable. On the 4th of April, 1881, his feet were trimmed, and he was led to the track. On the 15th he was hitched to a breaking-cart, driven a few times, and again turned out.

In explanation of the erratic manner he was exercised during the summer of 1881 a brief statement is required. A colored boy who accompanied us from Chicago was the only help kept. He broke the colt and worked him and drove him in the race. From a fall, when holding hay into the barn, supplemented with a cold taken when on a duck-hunting expedition, his lungs were affected, and we did not feel that he ought to be permitted to risk the labor attending working and taking care of a colt none the easiest to manage. He was extremely sensitive about any one else taking care of him or others to drive, and we were too much occupied with work which had to be done to give him personal attention. Thus on the 8th of May he was driven to a breaking cart and turned in a small lot as before until June 1st, when he was driven slow in breaking cart until the 9th. On that date put on tips, weighing four ounces each, the day before he was shod behind with shoes covering the toe and outside, leaving the inner bare. After putting on the tips he was driven to a sulky for the first time since November, and moved fast. He was driven occasionally until June 29th, when having to attend the races at Sacramento he was turned in lot. The 11th of July put on tips weighing five and one-half ounces each, and he wore them until August 8th when they were replaced with others of seven and one-half ounces each. While wearing these he trotted a quarter in 43 seconds, and on the 29th of August they were taken off and others put on of three and three-fourths ounces. With the light ones he handled himself more satisfactorily, though having to attend the fairs of the Golden Gate and State Agricultural Society he was turned out, the tips being always left on when the time was expected to be short. He ran in the small lot during the day from the first to the 28th of September. On Oct. 6th put on weights weighing five and one-half ounces each, and on the 14th drove him a mile in 2.54½, the last half in 1.04, and keeping him all the time well within his rate. On the 18th he trotted a quarter in 40 seconds, and we felt assured that he could show a "thirty gait" if called upon. We drove him in the summer's work, though as is evident, it was of too desultory a character to be called training. Still it was a fair test of the tips both as to the effect on the feet and to improvement in trotting. We were led up part of the time, confined to our room from the 24th of October, and from then to the race he was in the hands of another colored boy who came from the East with us.

He won the second Embryo with him making the third heat in 2.62, when again he was turned out. On January 2nd of this year tips were put on, the same which he wore in the race, and from that time until the 28th he was allowed to run in the lot or exercise by leading when he was harnessed to the breaking cart. He was driven on the streets of Oakland, daily, generally long drive, and at these fast, the tips having been reset on February 7th, but merely paring enough so that the old nail holes could be used, and on the 23d, of February was the day fixed for our friend to witness the operation, and see the condition of the foot. The tips were semicircles with a diameter of five inches, and this brought the posterior portion about three-quarters of an inch in the rear of the point of the frog. They weighed seven ounces each and were three-eighths of an inch in thickness at the end, being a trifle thicker at the toe, the width at the toe seven-eighths of an inch and at the ends five-eighths. They were made of tool steel, the nail holes countersunk on the ground surface, in place of being "creased," the countersinking deep enough to imbed the head of the nail. From so little horn having been cut away when the tips were reset there was a superabundance of horn, and the shoulder for the end to rest against was cut deeper than was required to imbed the tip. The rasp was used to lower the outside of the wall, beveling it to the gauge mark on the outside, and back as far as the shoulder. He then called the attention of our friend to the heels of the foot, and width and elasticity of the frogs. There had not been wear enough to reduce the wall to the level of the sole and bars, and at was prominent and without a break. From the shoulder for the tip to rest against to the junction of the wall and bars was a little over two inches, and it would be impossible to improve on the general contour of the foot. This our friend admitted and when the knife was used to cut away the superfluous horn, back of the rasping, there was only a slight discoloration which the first shaving entirely removed. The enamel having been cut with the rasp, it was an easy thing to cut the other portion with the keen, thin hoof-knife, though the thinnest shavings were so tough as the best quality of whalebone. It was a work of time to get a smooth, perfect bearing for the tip to rest upon, and when a fine rasp and file was brought into play to perfect the fit it cut slowly. There were three nail holes on each side of the tip, and our friend thought two would be sufficient. The explanation for using three nails in place of two was that we desired a guard against any chance for motion between the end of the tip and the foot, and that where so long a tip was

used the rear nail was at the end. But we are now satisfied that a semicircle extends too far back, and that one-third will be ample protection. We have found that in a great majority of instances the rear nail, on one side or other, was broken, and this was caused by the expansion of the foot and reaching so far forward as the nailing. The nails used being next to the smallest size, the constant pressure from giving the foot an opportunity for free expansion broke the nail, whereas if limited to one-third of the circle, that would not be the case. That this would be ample protection we have not the least doubt and then three nails, one at the toe and one at each end, would hold it firmly in place. At all events when the foot is in a shape which will permit a trial we shall make the experiment. Our friend was also pleased with the system of nailing, viz: Driving the nail from the inside of the wall through it in place of splitting the enamel, and also at the use of a small gouge to remove only enough of the horn to receive the "clench," in place of cutting the enamel from one nail to the other, as when the file is used. The two exhibitions removed all doubts and he was lavish in his praises of a plan which had left a natural and perfect foot.

# CORRESPONDENCE.

## Cleora And Col. Dickey.

TISKILWA, Ills., Nov. 22, 1882.

EDITOR BREEDER AND SPORTSMAN, Dear Sir: As Cleora and myself are natives of the same county; i. e., Bureau, I claim the right of singing her praise, criticizing her actions or recording such incidents of her short but brilliant career, as came under my observation. The handsome easy-going black mare, that now makes a mate for the grey horse Independence, was first seen by myself at our agricultural fair of 1880, when she contested in the 3:20 class, winning over the then promising mare Clara M, of Ottawa, Ills. The action of the judges in that race had the effect of prejudicing my feelings against Cleora. Though the black mare trotted so squarely then as now, did not indulge in any running exploits, it was a great effort when she trotted in 2:50 and I have always considered that mare as the figure of her speed that season. In 1882 nothing was heard of Cleora and not until July 4th, 1882, did thoughts regarding her speed come to my mind. On the date mentioned she trotted in a matinee at Mendota, when her mile in 2:39 surprised all of her friends and every last one of them insisted that Cleora must be saved for the fall meeting at Chicago, when all those possessed with a pointer would make themselves rich. We all know how well the secret was kept, for when the first pool was sold Cleora was a great favorite and yet no one had at let the cat out of the bag.

At the La Salle meeting Mr. Harris drew his mare, fearing that she would have to obtain too fast a record, in order to win, and to his credit be it told, that the breeder of Cleora never allows a horse of his to be pulled.

Two weeks later I attended the Davenport meeting where I saw Cleora trot for the first time in a good field of horses, and this same 2:34 race came nearly proving a first class performance, heavy rains causing its final postponement after three heats had been trotted. Owen Farley, Maxie Cobb, Legal R, Milo G, Countryman and Judge Curtis were Cleora's contestants. Owen Farley was supposably the only horse that could make the black mare trot and when the horses were called and it was seen that Farley showed up lame every one posted looked to see a hollow race. Had the track been sand and dry the affair would have been a work of interest; as it was, however, the rain of the day and night previous made the track fully ten seconds slow and a tight race over it meant serious business for green horses.

Cleora gained the lead shortly after the word was given in the first heat and could have distanced every horse in the party had her driver not jogged the mare home.

Owen Farley was now drawn, Milo G had caught the flag and only five horses faced the starter for the second heat. Legal R and Maxie Cobb began to show up some this heat and the black mare was not allowed to come home as easily as upon the first occasion.

The third heat proved that Mr. Moris' fears were well grounded, when he remarked that his mare had received but little fast work, besides being very high in flesh, all of which led him to entertain grave doubts as to whether Cleora could stand another heat in the wind. Legal R was driven by W. H. Homer, in the third heat, in as heroic a manner as I ever saw a horse handled; his skill was rewarded by the manner in which the brown gelding clung to the raven-like mare; twice around that terribly heavy track, shake him off she could not; the heat showed clear grit and hard work, no time for brilliant bursts of speed, for the mare was tired, and when Grey discovered that Homer was likely to get home first he changed his position on the stretch in such a manner that Legal R was brought into dangerous proximity with Cleora's wheel, which fact caused the gelding to swerve and lose his stride. Homer was compelled to take him back, and finding the wire too near at hand to obtain the lost ground he consented himself by claiming a foul, which was willingly and promptly granted, thereby giving the heat to Legal R in 2.33. This was the first race that Grey had ever driven over a national track and his foul on the track was not committed with any malicious intent; he acted on the impulse of the moment, doing exactly, as he had dozens of times upon the country roads when some neighbor had endeavored to pass him and he drove them into the ditch or fence to keep them from it. Darkness compelled the postponement of the race, and when Friday morning came daylight showed a flooded track, and the rain which had fallen all night still continued to come down so easily that one could not get angry at dame Nature. After dinner, the officers of the society concluded to bring the meeting to a close and called the owners of the 2:34 horses together for settlement. Col. Dickey, whom many on the Pacific know, none to their sorrow, controlled the saddon Countryman, a son of Volunteer. While this sorrel horse is well bred and quite speedy, yet his long residence at Salt Lake and among the mountains of Colorado, wholly unfitted him for trotting in low latitudes and in this race he had to labor hard to save his distance.

The society proposed to settle; allow Cleora first money, Legal R second, Maxie Cobb third and Judge Curtis fourth, but in order to settle an undisturbed account, as is necessary to obtain the consent of all interested in the finish. When the adjustors came to speak to Col. Dickey regarding the matter, he blandly says : "Well, gentlemen, what you going to do for Countryman ?"

"For Countryman? do you suppose he had a show in that field of horses ?"

"Most certainly he had, until the race was finished and the summary proved to the contrary. I believe him to be the best wet weather horse that ever stepped from under a blanket, and I for one think this race will yet be an interesting one." "Now see here, Col.," testily remarked one of the adjusters, "we do not propose to have this race trotted the owner of Cleora is not willing to trot so valuable a mare in the rain and mud, and the best thing for you to do is to allow the race to go by default." "I am not acquainted with the owner of Cleora; I am only here to look after the best interests of Countryman. If Mr. Norris wishes to become acquainted with me, let him come around and introduce himself, I think he will find me a pleasant man to do business with. What am I to do? Trot it out of course. You haven't an idea that I am here for my health? I am not, and if you will pay me my entrance fee of $40, Countryman can stand in the stable and eat hay, otherwise, I am here to trot for the purse. Finding that the Colonel was determined, the owners of the four remaining horses decided to pay the $40 out of their earnings. When the amount was turned over to the manipulator of Countryman, that worthy thanked the givers most cordially, adding that it was a good thing to remember that it required a very cold day for Col. Dickey to get left on. Cleora recovered from this race very quickly and three weeks later obtained a record of 2:18½ at Chicago, after which she was sold for $15,000. Legal K did not round to so quickly as he had another severe race at St. Joe, Mo., the week following; however, this horse is a promising one in his class, (2:20) and I think another season will find him such. Mazie Cobb was sold the very day that Cleora was, to Col. A. H. Swan of Cheyenne, Wyoming, for $10,000, having shown a trial in 2:23 and obtaining a record of 2:30. This young horse is one of Happy Medium's handsomest sons and as a sire he should prove a success, while in the hands of James Page, the driver who brought out Earus, Mazie Cobb will undoubted drop close to 2:20. At Cheyenne Mr. Page has the brown stallion Envoy (2:29), whom he is wintering for the owner, Ben Hershey of Muscatine, Iowa. Envoy has not recovered from a severe attack of the pinkeye and Mr. Hershey thinks a year spent in that high country will restore his formerly splendid lung power. Countryman was shipped direct from Davenport to Salt Lake and we think his first and last race was trotted that Thursday in the mud, in places of low altitude.

Judge Curtis is being used by his owner, Isaac Waixel of Chicago, as a pole horse. Milo G retired to Cheyenne, along with Clay and Teaser, where they will eat prairie hay and expand their lungs with the rarified air of that locality.

COLUMBUS.

### Honolulu Letter.

HONOLULU, Nov. 13, 1882.

EDITOR BREEDER AND SPORTSMAN: The writer is frequently interrogated by correspondents in California regarding the game found in the Hawaiian islands. As the majority of visitors here come from San Francisco, perhaps a few words in your journal in relation thereto would not be amiss.

The only four-footed game indigenous to the islands are hogs, of which great numbers were found in all parts of the group when first discovered by white men. They are still quite numerous in the mountains. Cattle and goats were introduced into the islands by Vancouver in the early part of the present century, and their descendants, reinforced by the offspring of more recent importations, are to be met with in a wild state—the cattle are principally on the islands of Hawaii, Oahu and Maui, and the goats in all parts of the archipelago. They are often hunted and are the only game that affords any excitement.

Among the fowl, indigenous to the islands are Hawaiian geese—encountered in no other part of the world and in no other group of islands—and a species of duck, both very good eating. Three or four varieties of ducks visit the islands in the fall and winter, leaving for the North again in the spring. They are commonly known as "nor'west ducks." Curlews and plover also visit the islands at the same season, and are found frequenting the same localities as in other countries. Mud-hens exist in the marshes of all the islands but are not hunted. The principal game birds are the common barn-yard chickens and turkeys which have become wild, and are met with in the mountains of Oahu and other of the larger islands. Pheasants and stock-doves, both importations, are now also reckoned among the game birds, as are the California quails, which are multiplying quite rapidly in the islands of Oahu, Maui and Molokai. Pigeons are quite numerous in the vicinity of Honolulu and are frequently shot by the pot hunter. The mynah, a bird introduced from India, and much resembling the American magpie, is eaten by some, though not generally reckoned among the game birds of the islands.

Imported and insectivorous birds are protected by game laws, and in the district of Kona, Oahu, which comprises the district in which Honolulu is situated, persons wishing to shoot game must pay an annual license of $5. No license is required in any other part of the group. These laws, however, are openly violated every day, and prosecutions rarely, if ever, take place under them.

GEO. W. STEWART.

### From Denverton.

DENVERTON, Cal., Nov. 27, 1882.

EDITOR BREEDER AND SPORTSMAN, Dear Sir: Yesterday beheld the advent in our midst of a sportsman all the way from the bay—quite an event in this part of the country. I refer to Mr., Liddle of the firm of Liddle & Keeding. May his shadow never grow less. 'Tis rather small now but yesterday twenty-two snipe, thirteen ducks and a couple of geese found it much too large for them. There were four of us in the party. Joe Bassford bagged nineteen snipe and eleven ducks. Johnny Anderson, our deputy sheriff, got away with seventeen snipe, eight ducks and four bottles of St. Louis beer. Your humble servant by several scratch shots managed to pick up fifteen snipe and thirteen ducks, besides which the party killed three or four cocktails apiece. The cocktail is a bird which never flies but will run.

By the way just allow me to say a few words about this section's game resources: On the plains north and west of here a person shooting over goose decoys can easily kill a wagon load a day (small wagon).

In the tules south and west of the town ducks are very plentiful and on the marshy places where the tules have been led off by cattle, a man can kill on a good day a good bag of snipe. I know of two persons in four hours killing sixty-six, and on Nov. 24th two of us killed eighty-six ducks and one hundred hare got the papers to show for it.

Still, for all that, the town's in nine miles from the nearest railroad station and no hotel or other accommodations after you get here, so brother sportsman take a friend's advice and keep away. Yours etc.,

JIM MACK.

### THE EMBRYO STAKES.

**J. McM. Shafter's Letter Published Last Week and the Editor's Erroneous Decision.**

EDITOR BREEDER AND SPORTSMAN: The reference to the Embryo Stake at this time is more particularly made to bring to the notice of readers the subject of controversy, than to discuss the decision of the judges in that race, as the District Board of Appeals will probably promulgate their official action on that decision in the BREEDER AND SPORTSMAN of to-day.

But I desire while this matter is fresh to have determined the legality or illegality of a member of the Board of Appeals acting as a judge in any race. I use the term, "Board of Appeals" because right here will be the strength of my reply to Mr. Shafter, and my criticism of the concurrence in Mr. Shafter's views by the editor of this paper. And I must confess that it is with great timidity that I venture to confront two gentlemen, one a most thorough and accomplished lawyer, and the other the best informed and most reliable authority on all questions pertaining to turf matters, rules, laws and customs particularly.

It sometimes happens, however, that even the best learned and most enlightened men fall into error, or jump at conclusions. Premising that this may be the case in the present difference between Mr. Shafter and myself, in the views taken by me in an article of last week over the signature of Lex, I propose to consider whether I was mistaken in the term used, as alleged by Mr. Shafter, when I claimed he was a member of the Board of Appeals, or whether the editor was correct in his concurrence as to my error.

First. Judge Shafter says Section 4 of. the by-laws defines what constitutes the "Board of Appeals. This is true; and Sec. 4 says: "it shall not consist of more than fifteen members, to be chosen as hereinafter provided." Just so. Now to make this board, fifteen persons were chosen from five different districts in the United States, three in each of the districts, and the first named of each three was to be understood as the chairman of that portion of the "Board of Appeals," or "District Board of Appeals," as they are termed and known.

There is not, there never has been, and it was never intended there should be, any other body constituting a Board of Appeals. The action of a District Board of Appeals is conclusive in the decision, unless appeal is taken to the board of review, which is constituted of the five several chairmen of the District Board of Appeals, with the addition of the ex-officio members, the President and Vice-Presidents of the National Trotting association. The District Board, if it were not an integral of the Board of Appeals, would unquestionably have its decisions reviewed by such board if any existed, but there being no such creation or existence, the course followed is as in law to the next highest court, which is a Board of Review. I call upon Hon. J. McM. Shafter to point at a law or rule appointing or creating any other Board of Appeals than I have named above, and I ask him as a direct matter of fact and law, whether it is possible to escape the conviction that the Board of Appeals is apportioned to such district, with full power only to be reviewed by the Board of Review. Secs. 15, 16 and 17, of Art. 7 do not conflict with this stand. Sec. 18 of the same article very properly refers to the rejection of members of the Board of Appeals from the judges' stand at races, and this was introduced because it has been the custom of members of the Board of Appeals to assert this right, and in the stand, presuming upon their official position, to interfere with the rulings and decision of judges. There were weak men, weak men, and men learned of modesty and disregardful of propriety, that were accustomed to present themselves, claim admission by right, and evince overbearing insolence and officiousness toward judges in a race. They were wisely and properly excluded by the amendment of Sec. 18, Art. 7, quoted by Judge McM. Shafter.

So notorious and constant was the demand made, particularly at the last, by these gentlemen of the District Board of Appeals, and so offensive and disgusting did their presence and exercise of authority become, to patrons of the turf, and to officers of racing associations, that the National association was petitioned for redress, which they gave in the amendment of Sec. 18, Art. 7.

To argue as to the propriety of this amendment, as to its requirement, or as to its justice, there is no occasion. Judge McShafter says there can be but one opinion on this point, and the editor of the BREEDER AND SPORTSMAN states if "The law does not read so, it should." Judge Shafter says: "the District Board is not the Board of Appeals." If it is not, what is it, Judge? An appeal from a District Board if it were not the District Board of Appeals, I apprehend, would have to be taken to the Board of Appeals, as in regular order and from them to the Board of Review.

By every rule of common guidance, through sources of reason, and from every rule of legal rotation, I fail to see in the appointment of the fifteen gentlemen named in the by-laws of the National Association, and apportioned in five different districts, any other formation than a Board of Appeals in each district, call them District Boards or what you will. If they are not, then I ask Judge McShafter to point out who and what constitute the Board of Appeals.

Sec. 2 of Art. 52 of Rule and Regulations National association, says: "all decisions and rulings of the judges of any race, and of the several associations and proprietors belonging to the National Trotting Association, may be appealed to the "Board of Review" or to a "District Board."

Now here is the point drawn down to an end. There is no intermediate board named or recognized. It is simply the District Board of Appeals and the final decision of the court of last resort, the Board of Review. I refer Judge McShafter to Art. 7 of the by-law of the National Association. Secs. 6, 7, 8 and 9, which states that the Board of Review shall possess the authority conferred upon the Board of Appeals and shall hear all appeals from the District Board, etc., also to Sec. 4, Rule 51 of the by-laws, confirmatory of appeal from District Board to Board of Review, and to Rule 52, Sec. 2, as to appeals from an association to a District Board or to the Board of Review. In other words, to the lower court, the Board of Appeals, or to the court of last resort, the Board of Review.

I entered into this controversy with timidity as stated in the beginning of this communication, but I felt even though I was sadly at fault in my arguments and conclusions, and should be routed by Judge McShafter, and his superior ability, yet withal there was a gratification in differing with

an old and esteemed friend as I regard the gentleman, and I should be benefited at any rate by his superior wisdom and knowledge, and if I felt so toward this honorable gentleman I am quite sure the feelings were akin in undertaking any reply to the editor of this journal, but I must express surprise that the face of the rules and laws governing the Board of Appeals and his knowledge of how it was made up and for what purpose, and that the line of appeals was from judges to District Board of Appeals and thence to the Board of Reviews that he should hold that Lex was only correct as the rules "ought to be, not what they are." One word more and I have done. Judge Shafter has been pleased to allude to me as a legal gentleman. In this he might have intended sarcasm, or he may have been ignorant that I am simply a "hewer of wood and a drawer of water," but having in days gone by indulged somewhat in the ownership of trotters, and having a love of turf sports, I naturally have an interest in all races and decisions of any merit, and a relish for the observance of strict rule and propriety in all contests. LEX.

# THE PADDOCK.

### Big Colts.

The Vinalia Delta says: In September we mentioned that Mr. O. A. Norse, living near Antioch, had a two-year-old colt that weighed 1,419 pounds on the 16th of that month. On Wednesday of last week the animal was again weighed on the Government scales at the distillery, and tipped the beam at 1,530 pounds. Can any of our exchanges find a heavier animal?

From an exchange we learn that there is a colt at Elmira two years old and weighs 1,590 pounds. The animal was foaled on the 17th of May, is the property of M. D. Cooper and is a Norman and Clydesdale.

Both of these are of the heavy draft breeds, and now comes the information from the breeder of Goldust and Fred Arnold that he has a trotting-bred colt that is a "whapper" sure for one of the light harness division. The following is Mr. Johnson's letter:

My colt was foaled April 20, 1880, and weighed August 27, 1882, 1,140 pounds, in common growing order, fed on hay; only his height at the same time was 16 hands and one-half inch. He is by Nephew, his dam by Chieftain, grand-dam by Young Chloroform, great granddam by Peacock, he by Gray Eagle. Young Chloroform's dam by Boston, his sire Oddfellow. Taking his breeding into consideration I think he gets away with the draft colts and if he was put in the same order I think he will outweigh them; as he is a very large framed, heavy boned colt he would carry a good load of fat. I think he will weigh over 1,300 now; he is growing very fast. He is a mahogany bay, one hind foot white, with bone and muscle enough to satisfy anybody and I think he is the making of the fastest horse I ever raised.

W. JOHNSON.

Accompanying the letter was a certificate of A. C. Taylor, weigher, Gridley hay scales, verifying the weight.

OLD NOTIONS.—The old superstition that horseshoeing was an occult art, and the legend of St. Dustin, may have something to do in making people so obstinate in their adherence to the traditions of the forge, and there is little question that the many days of St. Dunstin, ten centuries ago, fabricated the same kind of shoes which smiths take delight in fashioning at the present day.

### That "Euqine Epizootic."

STOCKTON, Nov. 28, 1882.

TO THE EDITOR OF THE BREEDER AND SPORTSMAN, Dear Sir: I read in your publication of last week an article headed, "an equine epizootic," in which you informed your readers that according to a Stockton newspaper a bad disease is playing fearful havoc among the horses of San Joaquin county. At the same time you requested of your correspondents to favor you with their views of this disastrous disease, their methods of treatment and results.

Now I, for one of your readers, will satisfy you with a little information about that terrible disease. I am a veterinarian, practicing in Stockton for the last thirteen months, and say that I never found the horses of San Joaquin county so healthy as they have been for the last three or four weeks. It is true, the first few cold nights caused a few cases of pneumonia, and of a blood disease having a typhoid character, of which none turned out fatally; but it seems that now they are accustomed to the cold nights and can stand the weather and work admirably well.

As to those horses of John McNeill, mentioned in your paper, I must say that no regular veterinary surgeon has ever seen or examined them, and that, therefore, the real nature of that disease can be questioned. Most likely it was an aggravated case of influenza or pinkeye, and as this last named disease has been raging several months ago in Stanislaus county with a lenient character, and as only a few horses died out of so many affected, it can reasonably be supposed that the horses of J. McNeill would have recovered if the proper treatment had been applied at the proper time. There is no reason whatever for the Stockton newspaper to injure the trade in horses in our county and to publish all over California that as yet no remedy has been discovered that will cure that disease, except what they know from hearsay. In all probability these horses have died through improper treatment, bad care and sheer neglect on the part of the proprietor to call for the assistance of a competent adviser. That is the whole truth about this terrible disease. We find occasionally during the year similar cases, but they are isolated and of a purely sporadic type. Yours very respectfully, J. P. KLENCH.

The Napa Register says: "Malaga makes about 2,500,000 boxes annually, but there is abundant room in California for the culture of raisins to expand without coming in conflict with the foreign crop. Twenty-pound boxes of raisins bring at wholesale about ten to twelve cents per pound. The crop of last year raised in Yolo, Fresno and Los Angeles counties, including some small productions in Butte, Yuba and some of the foothill counties, is figured up at 150,000 boxes, which does not include the stock in the vicinity of production. An approximation of the crop for this year gives 139,200 boxes, although it is believed that the early raisins not set in the total would have reached 200,000 boxes, the entire output $400,000 to $500,000. The shipment East last year was 70,000 boxes. From these facts it is evident raisin production is becoming a settled industry in this form."

## About Fires.

If a careless hunter fires your woods, and, much to his consternation, the flames spread to your fields, and run along the fences to your barn, he is responsible for the whole loss, although he did his best to stay its progress. A man who wrongfully sets in operation a dangerous instrument, must take all the consequences directly caused thereby (21 Pick., 378; 43 Cal., 437; 2 Harr., 343). But as any farmer has a legal right to burn the brush, old stumps, etc., on his own land, if he does so at the proper times and in a proper manner, he is not responsible, if, by a sudden rise of wind or other cause, without negligence on his part, the fire is accidently communicated to a neighbor's premises, and causes him serious injury. The gist of his liability in such cases is some carelessness either in the time of setting the fire, or the manner of doing so, or in watching it afterward; and the man who suffers is bound to make it clear that the other was to blame; (54 Me., 259; 22 Barb., 619; 44 Barb., 424; 18 Me., 32; 11 Met., 460). But even your negligence will not always render you liable for the spread of a fire, unless it was originally kindled by you intentionally. Therefore, if your barn takes fire through your carelessness with the lantern, or that of your man with his pipe, and thereby your neighbor's property is also consumed, you are not bound to pay for it; the law seems to consider that you have suffered enough for your conduct in the loss of your own property; (1 Bl., Com. 431 ;37 Barb., 15; 35 N. Y., 210; 62 Penn. St., 353).

Still less would you be responsible if the fire originated from causes beyond your control. If your barn is struck by lightning, or your hay stack ignites by spontaneous combustion, without any fault on your part, and the flames spread to the adjoining owner's property, it would be hard indeed if you had not only to lose your own, but to pay for his also; (8 Johns, 422; 11 Q. B., 347). And I suppose, even if you were careless in not promptly and energetically putting it out when you could have done so, and it spreads beyond your control, this would not render you liable, as perhaps it might have done had you purposely set fire to your brush heap or stubble.

As to railroad fires the law is somewhat different from that relating to individuals. Formerly, and antecedently to any statutes, railroad companies were not liable for fires caused by locomotives, without proof of some negligence, either in the construction or mode of running the engine by which the fire was caused, or otherwise (5 H. & N., 694; 18 Barb., 80; 30 Iowa, 420; 15 Conn., 124; 37 Me., 93) but as the liabitity to such fires was so great, and the amount of damage so caused was very extensive, it became necessary to enlarge their liability; and now in Mass., by Gen. Stat., chap. 63, § 101, railroad corporations are liable for all damages to the buildings or personal property of the land owners along their route, arising from fire communicated by their locomotives, and without any proof of negligence or carelessness either in the company or any of its employes.

And this statute has a very liberal construction, extending not only to buildings immediately adjoining the railroad, and which are fired directly by sparks from the locomotives, but also to buildings a long distance from the road, and which are set on fire by sparks flying through the air from some building nearer by, which had first taken fire from the engines (13 Met., 90; 98 Mass., 414; 103 Mass., 586).

# TURF AND TRACK.

## Thanksgiving Day Races at Oakland Track.

"Spring-time, the last day of November," was the remark of an Eastern tourist at the Oakland Trotting Park yesterday afternoon. "The telegraph says fine sleighing in New York on Thanksgiving, and here are pasture fields with the grass above the horses' hoofs," was the response of his companion. The hills on the Contra Costa range even showed a green tinge, and there were watery-looking clouds with patches of blue sky, and at times the sun shone brightly. The temperature was in accordance with the other spring-like features, and the track was in good order; not quite so "fast" perhaps, as when in the best condition, though safe and only a trifle slow. The attendance was fair when the counter attractions of the day are considered, and there were a good many speculators investing in the pools. The first race was a dash of three-quarters of a mile for two-year-olds, the starters Marian, Dairymaid and May B. At first Dairymaid was the favorite, bringing $20 to $11 on Marian and $5 on May B. Then Marian took the lead, and the rate changed to $22 on her, $18 on Dairymaid, and $10 on May B. A capitol start was given the fillies, and when they passed the quarter pole there was not half a length between them, though May B making the pace rapid from the outset, established a lead of a length when half way down the backstretch. The others closed on her, and by the time they were half way around the further turn all were "lapped." From the three-quarters Marian had the race safe, and, although the others kept close to her until within one hundred yards of home, came away a couple of lengths in front of Dairymaid, who was then some distance in front of May B. Time, 1:16½.

The next race proved a windfall to the betters who took the "short end." It was a dash of 1⅛ miles, the starters Jim Renwick and Euchre. Even at the long odds of $20 to $6, it was difficult to obtain backers for Renwick. Those who had bought the big, blazed-faced chestnut had little hopes of winning, and many of them sold their tickets at a discount. Again there was a good start, the horses being exactly parallel when the flag fell. Jim Renwick had the inside position, which he surrendered to Euchre, the evident intention being to make a waiting race of it. Euchre led at the stand, the furlong being made in twelve seconds, and at the quarter pole, in twenty-nine seconds, Euchre was leading by six lengths. Euchre increased the speed, and at the half mile the watches marked 1:07. Renwick closed the gap somewhat when rounding the turn, and when fairly straightened into the homestretch, he made his run. Coming with a long sweeping stride, he rapidly overhauled Euchre. He was in the lead at the trotting distance, and though for a short time it appeared that Euchre would win, Renwick had another link in reserve, and he swept past the stand a length in front of his competitor. Time, 1:58½. The winner was admirably driven by Billy Appleby, and showed a better capacity for a distance than anyone gave him credit for. He is not thoroughbred, as his dam, Big Gun, was of Oregon short stock. His sire, Joe Hooker, is one of the most promising of the young sires of California, and is a very highly formed horse of the most fashionable breeding, being by Monday from Mayflower, by imported Eclipse, and his grandam Hennie Farrow.

The next race was a dash of one and one-quarter miles, the starters Jocko and Frank Rhoads. Jocko was the favorite in the pools, steadily increasing in favor from the opening until a start was effected. This was still a greater fall for the buyers than in the preceding race, inasmuch as there were plenty of supporters for Frank Rhoads at odds averaging $40 on him to $80 on Jocko. The race was unexpectedly one-sided. Rhoads took the lead from the start at a fast pace. The first quarter was run in 25 seconds, the half mile in 50½, three-quarters in 1:16½, the mile in 1:43, and though the official timers reported 2:11, the divergence from others in a better position to see, and who made it 2:09½, was doubtless owing to the white flag of the starter being held against the whitewashed fence. Though Jocko made several efforts he could not get nearer than two lengths of Rhoads, who won by twice that distance. For so few starters it was a fine afternoon's sport, and every one excepting the losers was well satisfied. The race came to a close in time for those who attended to come back to the city on the train leaving Shell Mound at 4:30, and the sail across the bay in the twilight of a spring evening was very enjoyable. There was a rush for seats on the deck of the steamer, and never in the glorious merry month of May was a seat in the open air more welcome. Ladies carried bouquets of gay flowers, and the perfume of mignonette and violets made the illusion complete. The excitement of the racing and trip combined gave zest for the Thanksgiving dinner, and the evening festivities were better relished.

SUMMARIES.

Oakland Trotting Park, Thursday, November 30.—Juvenile Stake; dash of three-quarters of a mile, for two-year-olds.

I. B. Chase names b f Marian ........ 1
C. Pacheco name b f Dairyman ........ 2
P. Robson names ch f May B ........ 3

Time—1:16½.

Hard Luck Stake; dash of one and an eighth miles.

Stemler & Ayres name s g Renwick ........ 1
M. M. Allen names ch h Euchre ........ 2
J. P. Woolman names b m Bolis ........ p'd forfeit

Time—1:58½.

Handicap; dash of one and a quarter miles.

W. L. Pritchard names b c F. Rhoades, 103 lbs ........ 1
J. P. Woolman names b c Jocko, 130 lbs ........ 2
Stemler & Ayres name b g Joe Howell ........ declared out

Official time—2:11. Outside, and probably correct, 2:09½.

## Morgan Blackhawk, Lancet and David Hill Jr

Morgan Black Hawk was sired by Hill's celebrated trotting horse, Black Hawk, and he by Sherman Morgan, and he by Justin Morgan, and he by True Briton, who was imported from England and used by General De Lancy as a charger while commanding the British forces on Long Island in 1777; True Briton was a thoroughbred horse of great speed and beauty. Black Hawk's dam, bred in New Brunswick, was three-fourths thoroughblood and distinguished for fast trotting. Morgan Black Hawk's dam was got by Liberty, and he by Duroc, grandam by Sir Charles; Sir Charles was got by Sir Archy, and he by imported Diomede (see stud-book); Sir Charles' dam was got by Plato, and he by imported Messenger—his grandam by Brutus, out of imported Brutus. Morgan Black Hawk was bred by Mr. Howard, of Addison, Vermont, and sold to Solomon Jewett, Esq., of Weybridge, Vermont, when two days old, and was afterwards sold by Mr. Jewett to Gen. Silas M. Borroughs of Medina, Orleans county, New York, when five months old. Old Liberty was bred by Col. Allen Smith of Addison, Vermont. Col. Smith rode Liberty from Troy, N. Y., to Boston, and then to Addison, Vermont, in four consecutive days, 360 miles; stayed in Boston one night, and returned to Boston again next day, when he set out with a drove of cattle, and was offered on his arrival $600 (which was equal to $6,000 now) for the horse. He was then about eighteen years old. Liberty served mares when he was twenty-seven years old, and died at twenty-nine years.

Morgan Black Hawk is sire of more fast trotting stock than any other horse of his age in America, some of which are enumerated, as follows: Young Flora Temple; Black Swan, of Wisconsin; Billy McCraken, that took the first premium at the State Fair of Wisconsin, when five years old, beating stallions of all blood and ages; Clifford, (two years old,) that took the first premium at the International Fair at Buffalo, N. Y., in 1859, the fifth time he was harnessed, distancing colt by Toronto Chief, and colt by State of Maine, distance three-quarters of a mile, time, 2:47; Grey Eagle, Young Tib Hinman, Young Daniel Webster, Billy Pratt; Niagara, now in Tennessee; Paul Jones of Oregon; and Lancet, now in Sacramento, who took the first premium at Racine, Wisconsin, in 1859, in 2:48, drawing man and sulky, weighing 300 pounds.

Said Black Hawk is half-brother to Paul Clifford, Black Ralph, (who has trotted in 2:27 at Saratoga Springs,) Belle of Saratoga, (who trotted in 2:28,) gelding Lancet, (who has trotted in 2:27,) Black Hawk Maid, Ethan Allen, (the fastest stallion in America,) Washtenaw Chief, and Stockbridge Chief of Ohio.

Lancet was sired by J. C. McCracken's Old Black Hawk; he by Sherman Morgan; he by Justin Morgan; he by True Briton, who was imported from England and used by General DeLancy as a charger while commanding the British forces on Long Island, in 1777. True Briton was a thoroughbred horse, of great speed and beauty.

Lancet's dam was the Adams filly; was a fast trotter; was sired by Emigrant, and imported from England.

Lancet is half-brother to Brown Mac, Billy McCracken, Dutchman, Lady Dooly, and numorous other trotters.

David Hill Jr., was sired by J. G. McCracken's celebrated horse, David Hill; he by Black Lyon; he by David Hill's famous trotting stallion Black Hawk; he by Sherman Morgan; he by Justice Morgan; he by True Briton, a thoroughbred horse of great speed and beauty, who was imported from England in 1777. David Hill's dam was got by Hambletonian; he by Abdallah; he by old Membrino; and he by imported Messenger. The dam of Hambletonian was the Charles Kent Mare by imported Bellfounder; Black Lyon's dam was by Liberty; he by Duroc; Grandam by Sir Charles; he by Sir Archey; and he by imported Diomede—see stud book—Sir Charles' dam was got by Plato, and he by imported Messenger; his grandam by Brutus, out of imported Brutus.

David Hill Jr.'s dam was sired by the original St. Lawrence, a thoroughbred Norman horse, and the fastest stallion in the world of his day; grand dam, Old Champlain, one of the best four mile thoroughbred Messenger horses in the United States.

David Hill Jr. is the sire of A. F. Smith's colt, George Treat, the fastest colt of his age in the United States. Also, F. M. Chapman's colt; also, a two-year-old filly which could show a three-minute gait, which J. L. Eoff paid $1,000 for one-half of her; also half brother to Dutchman, Sorrel Ned, Mountain Boy, and St. Lawrence, they all being out of the same mare by the original St. Lawrence. I have several others just as promising.

David Hill Jr. is a beautiful bay, with flowing mane and tail, is now nine years old, and weighs 1,180 lbs. and though he has never been trained is a very fast trotter. He was awarded first premium at the State Fair when one year old, also, at two years old. At three years old he was not on exhibition; at four years old, he took first premium, where there were twenty-six competitors, his father being one o them.

## FROM THE ANTIPODES.

### Turf Notes and Anticipations—A Visit to the Cripps' Stud Farm—Etc.

The Wollongong Turf Club to-day conclude their races, and the Burrowa Jockey Club commence their spring meeting, so our friends in New South Wales have choice of diversion; and in Tasmania the Southern Hunt Club meeting eventuates. To-morrow the Burrowa meeting will end, and the New Zealanders will be racing at Cromwell.

On Saturday the weights for the Berrima Handicaps will appear in New South Wales and in Victoria the Victoria Amateur Turf Club hold high festival at Caulfield when the Guineas and Great Foal Stakes will be run for, and one of the grandest days' racing yet seen south of the line may be anticipated. Since last meeting wonderful improvements have been carried out in paddock and stand by Mr. Bond, the energertic secretary, and his staunch henchman Mr. Broadbridge. The course never looked so well, and a gala day may be anticipated. Of probabilities I descant in another column; suffice it to say that, besides two big events above alluded to, a selling race, a handicap hurdle race, the Victoria Amateur Challenge Cup, and the Toorak Handicap furnish such attractions that all who have the slightest love of sport or pretentions to fashion should attend.

On Tuesday, the 10th inst., the weights for the minor handicaps of the second days' racing of the V. A. T. C. will be declared. In New Zealand the Hawkes Bay Club hold their gathering. In New South Wales non-acceptances must be declared, and general entries made, for the Berrima meeting.

In that colony, also, it is holiday time at Tamworth on Wednesday, the 11th, and Thursday, the 12th, the annual races being held on those dates, and from the character of the entries the sport should be good. Also, on Thursday, the 12th, non-acceptors must declare in the Caulfield Cup, or they will be considered acceptors, and held liable for the whole of the stake.

From Adelaide I learn that great dissatisfaction has been caused by the disqualification of Hotspur for the Hunters' Stakes at Morphettville, on the ground that the horse was not running for the entire benefit of his nominator, Mr. Birckford. The totalisator dividend has been paid, and, as it appears by the steward's decision that Hotspur was unqualified, and therefore not in the race, those who backed him had no chance to win, so ought to get their money back. I sincerely wish they may get it. His backers with the books refuse to part.

Among those defeated by Bandalbion at Mauritius were Trout, Greyhound, and Valentine. The first-named pair were for some time in Griffin's charge at Brighton.

The Adelaide division of the ring caught it very hot over Rory O'More in the Hunt Club Cup, the horse having been backed to win £2,000 by his party.

I have to acknowledge the receipt from the secretary, Mr. N. R. D. Bond, of the balance-sheet of receipts and expenditure of the Victoria Amateur Turf Club, for the year ending August 31, 1882, showing the income to be £2,412 for the past year, leaving £1,548 profit on the six meetings already held. So whilst a very heavy amount has been expended the club has lessened its liabilities by £591 19s. 11d. since last year. Every credit is due both to committee and secretary for this result.

I was rather lucky in my Dubbo and Muswellbrook fancies, Hesitation, Norman, Hypatia, and Wheel of Fortune, all proving winners. They had a repetition of the Navigator and Solitude business at Dubbo, as the owner of Kettledrum declared to win with Norman—but the rider of the former horse beat his stable companion by a neck after a punishing finish, having misunderstood orders.

Segenhoe and Hecla have improved greatly.

The Burrowa weights are out and appear herewith. Willeroo and Faith look best on paper for the Ballyryan Handicap. Juggler should win the hurdle race, and Willeroo and Mollie M'Carthy should fill the places in the Spring Handicap.

The Parramatta Jockey Club will celebrate the Prince of Wales' Birthday with a pleasant programme of five events, with added money amounting to 330 sovs. whilst on Saturday, the 11th of November, they add 300 sovs., to five races.

The Adelaide *Licensed Victuallers' Gazette* has the following pertinent remarks on "pleasing the public": "No one who has not had actual experience of the position can possibly realize the difficulties that beset the owner of a popular favorite for an important race, and the various ways—whether reasonable or unreasonable makes no difference—in which he is called upon to please the public. It is a fortunate thing for the turf in this colony that its most prominent patron is a gentleman who, like Lord Falmouth, 'never bets,' and to whom the amount of money spent in connection with his training stud is no object whatever. Sir Thomas Elder spares no expense in furthering his ambition to participate in sport of the highest class for itself alone, apart from any consideration of profit, and yet he cannot succeed in pleasing every section of our racing community at one and the same time. After Bassanio was beaten in the Derby, grumblers sprang up like mushrooms, and his defeat was charitably attributed to every cause but the right one. Had the horse been withdrawn from the race prior to the start, the ranks of the growlers would have been increased fourfold, and if the owner had made a public declaration in favor of the chestnut it would have been viewed with suspicion by a class who are ever ready to ascribe improper motives to any movement that conflicts with their own interests, Not one of those who lost money over Bassanio last Saturday can say that they were induced to do so by any representations emanating from either owner or trainer, and if they had only taken the trouble to make proper inquiry before investing their money on a forlorn hope, they would have learned how little chance they possessed of their realizing profit. Such a sensible course, however, was to them quite unnecessary; it was enough that Bassanio was bound to beat Guesswork on public form without harassing themselves by any thought of the relative condition of the pair at the present time, and so they assume the garb of injured innocence when called upon to pay the penalty of their neglect, and indulge in vituperation because the result of the race does not accord with their preconceived opinions. It is a monstrous doctrine that an owner shall be compelled to run his horses to please the public—or rather the sharps who have backed them—but we have no anticipation of ever seeing it enforced. If the poor public will persist in burning their fingers by meddling with other people's property, they must be content to pay the penalty, or reserve their investments for the totalisator, when they can make sure of having a race for their money."

The very handsome gold vase given to the Victoria Amateur Turf Club by Messrs. Wilson and Quirk, as the chief prize in the V. A. T. C. Challenge Cup, is on view at Messrs Brush and Drummond's, Collins street. Of chaste Etruscan design, its outlines are most graceful, and standing on a beautifully worked silver pediment, it shows to great advantage. The handles are ornamented with vine leaves of solid gold, and a horse's head springing from a circle of leaves surmounts the cover. The body of the vase has a spirited representation of the finish of a race above and below while it is handsomely chased with scroll and leaf work. This handsome prize will doubtless be daringly won, and highly prized by its fortunate recipient.

From New Zealand I learn that at the South Canterbury Hunt Club steeplechase, Mr. Armitage's Don won the cup, ridden by Mr. J. E. R. King, Leap Year and Warlock filling the places. The race was a severe one and only won by a length. Ten ran. The Ladies' Purse fell to Mr. H. Ford's Nutmeg, ridden by Mr. R. Ford, Gentle Annie being second, and Wild Rose third. The Don fell and struck Mr. King on the head, rendering him insensible. The Consolation was won by Warlock, piloted by Mr. J. R. Brown, and was won by a neck from Gentle Annie.

Mr. Pearson having resigned his position on the committee of the Victorian rooms, Mr. C. D. O'Halloran has been elected in his stead, whilst as chairman Mr. A. F. Sullivan succeeds him.

We are sorry to hear that Mr. Hassall's recent purchase for Western Australia, Orient, was, through rough weather, killed on the voyage thither. Although insured by Mr. Faille for £350, the loss of this horse is a very great one, as he was one of the best sons Fireworks left behind him.

The South Australian horses will arrive safely and most of the Sydney division are here, but Lord Burghley knocked himself about a good deal in transit.

Richmond has been sold to Mr. Blackler at a satisfactory price.

I have been requested by the trainer of Verdure, and by the gentlemen connected with the stable, to give a flat contradiction to a statement which has appeared in one or two of our contemporaries alleging that O'Brien was weighed out for, or was put on, Scandal in order to deceive the public in the Hamilton Flat Race, and afterwards was changed to Verdure. O'Brien weighed out for Verdure only, saddled the mare himself, and got on no other horse up to the time of the mischandling.

The A. J. C. have decided to follow the V. R. C.'s lead, and register bookmakers on payment of a fee.

That well known trainer, Mr. R. Howie, has commenced an action for £2,000 damages against the Ballarat Courier in respect of a paragraph in that paper having asserted that this well known trainer had been placed under restraint in a Sydney Lunatic Asylum. It is stated that Howie has suffered material loss by consequent removal of his patron's horses from his charge.

The Hon. James White and W. J. Clark are expected to arrive from England in time for the V. R. C. Spring Meeting.

In another column appears the advertisement of the popular Williamstown Racing Club's meeting, and the 9th of November, the Prince of Wales' Birthday, is the date chosen for the gathering, and thus direct opposition to the rampant V. A. T. C. is avoided. The programme is most racing-like, consisting of a handicap hurdle race of 50 sovs., two miles; Tregenis Stakes handicap of 75 sovs., five furlongs; Telegraph Stakes of 75 sovs., half a mile (a selling event); Galloway handicap of 40 sovs., five furlongs; Laverton Steeplechase of 50 sovs., two miles; and Williamstown Handicap of 100 sovs., one mile and a quarter, whilst in each event nominations are only 1 sov.

The second volume of the Australian Stud Book has made its appearance. From a hasty glance it appears a vast improvement even on the predecessor, and the compiler and publishers have done everything to make the book a necessity and an ornament. In our next issue I will deal more fully with this important subject.

In another column appears the advertisement of the Racing Result Telegraph Agency, under the conduct of the very enterprising firm of E. Byron Moore and Macleod, of the Exchange, Melbourne. This will meet a long felt want, as now the payment of a very trifling fee will allow any one in the most distant parts of Australia, in any country town, to be immediately apprised of the result of any race in which he may be interested. Messrs. Moore & Co. have secured a concession from the Telegraph Department, by which the rendering of this information will be wonderfully facilitated.

I paid a visit to the stables and stud farm of the Broken Cripps, at Flemington, yesterday, and, finding them at home, was received with every courtesy, and at once shown the sires and the training stables. During my stay the celebrated racing-galloway, Elsa May, arrived on a visit to Motea, whose strains of Melbourne, Touchstone, and Pantaloon blood should harmonize well with the Orlando, Stockwell, and Kingston blood she derives from Proto-Martyr and Ariel. The first horse shown me was Motea; and the chestnut brother to Darebin is even of greater substance than the celebrated Derby winner. His temper seems perfection, and although an immense horse, he is on such short legs and so well-proportioned that his size is hardly apparent, whilst his liberty of action is very noticeable. This young sire if properly mated cannot fail to achieve distinction. Alarm was next visited. A very lengthy brown horse, full of the characteristics of his sire Panic, a beautiful mover, and with enormously lengthy quarters. As a sire of trotters he has already gained celebrity, but in appearance he is all over a racehorse, and should get racehorses if a chance is afforded him. I next interviewed the galloway sire, Van Tromp; for a steeplechaser or hurdle-racer it would be hard to find his equal. Barely 14.2 in height, with clean, flat bones, he has the quality of the racehorse, and substance to carry 14 stone. A rich chestnut in colour, his head is of the true Stockwell type, whilst the speed he possesses has been evinced by repeated victories on the flat. His blood is a combination of that of Ace of Clubs, Touchstone, and the Premier. He should be well patronized by those desiring stylish pairs. The paddocks, which are situated at Essendon, comprise 160 acres of splendid grazing land. I now made a move for the training stables, and Expert, a lengthy chestnut colt by Sunlight, out of Express, was the first shown me. A white blaze and white hind foot give him a good deal of character, but he is rather narrow looking as yet, although, I should fancy, speedy. Squireen, who is hardly over his Maryborough greeding, occupied the opposite box, whilst next the colt Mistake, by Dante, out of Stockdove, is located, and very fresh and full of life this speedy colt looks, and wonderfully improved since I saw him at Adelaide. His pace as a two-year-old was marvelous, and his back now looks like carrying a bit of weight. Opposite the Derby candidate was Drumstick, a light bay three-year-old by The Drummer, marked with the running blaze and white hind foot so often seen in that horse's stock. This horse has grown, and improved greatly since he last appeared in public. Bismarck is a very nice little bay horse by Glorious, out of Regina, and is thickening up greatly, and next to him is Hector, a powerful son of Little Fish, whom I once saw win a steeplechase in the far West. He has also improved greatly since coming into his present quarters. Mariner, a

hardy-looking bay jumper by Troubadour out of Daisy, will yet win a name over sticks, and Andover is another in the same category; whilst that clever hunter, Pulex, is also located here. Coyotte, an old acquaintance, was next visited, but the black mare evidently needs time, and Miss Panic, who will also visit Motea, and the British Lion, who like most of the John Bull's looks light, were the remaining tenants of the boxes.

I regret to learn that the well-known trainer, F. Leng, whilst in a state of intoxication, attacked Van Tromp, without the owner's consent, and on being brought before the stewards was so incapable of realizing his position that he was suspended for six months; this sentence is endorsed by the V. R. C., and is likely to be by the V. A. T. C. committee. He being one of our best trainers, it is to be hoped that, in punishing him, care will be taken to conserve the interest of the innocent owners who have horses in his charge, as change of stable, and treatment so near to important engagements may seriously imperil their chances.

The weights for the Pindon Harriers gold vases appear herewith, and seem to have been most carefully adjusted. Although Ajax is top weight, he relatively meets all the horses which finished in front of him on Saturday on much better terms, and a most interesting contest should result. Several horses have been declared ineligible for the stake, and it is possible that among those which have been handicapped there are others who do not fulfil the conditions. Variable, Brownlock and Paddy Crutch, Fish and Murrambong, with the top weights, sadly Ben Accord look most dangerous, but the task of picking a winner here is beyond me.

I am sorry to hear that that truly sporting metallician, Mr. S. G. Cook, had really bad luck with his fine colt, George Rignold, by King Cole from Gonfalon, by the Hermit, purchased by him as a yearling at Messrs. Finlay's sale. In the race for the Flying Stakes on Saturday, the colt slipped and strained his back badly, but ran the race right out. On Saturday night he showed signs of severe internal injuries, and on Monday he had to be destroyed.—Federal Australian, Oct. 5th.

## What the Season has Demonstrated.

The fastest record made during the season of 1882 was by Clingstone in the great race with Edwin Thorne, So-So and J. B. Thomas at Cleveland, July 28. In the first heat every inch of the ground was contested, and Clingstone beat Edwin Thorne to the score by half a length in 2.14. In the second heat the quarter was trotted in 33¾ seconds, and the half-mile completed in 1.05. Here Edwin Thorne weakened through lack of condition, and Clingstone was left to finish the heat at his ease in 2.14¼. This practically ended the race. The time of the third heat was 2.22. At Buffalo the following week Clingstone and Edwin Thorne trotted the first heat side by side, and finished almost nose and nose in 2.14½. The judges decided in favor of Clingstone, who went on and won the race. At Rochester, Clingstone again won victorious, but at Utica, Hartford and Boston he lost with defeat. His legs are none of the best, and the severe campaign told upon him. He is of light blood, and has the drooping hip usually associated with the pacer. His sire, Rysdyk, was got by Rysdyk's Hambletonian, out of Lady Duke, thoroughbred daughter of Lexington, and his dam Gretchen, was by Chosroes, out of Sady Fallis, by Seely's American Star. It is bred to Hambletonian, and has a double infusion of running blood. His trotting action is smooth, almost perfect, and yet his blood lines are not in harmony with the theories of the little school which holds that every drop of thoroughbred is detrimental to trotting disposition and structure. The time of Edwin Thorne in the race at Cleveland was 2.14¼. He trotted on the outside of Clingstone the entire mile, and so he traveled the greater distance. At Buffalo he was beaten not over four inches in 2.14½, and at Utica, on a cold, raw day, he turned the tables on Clingstone, winning in 2.18½, 2.20½, 2.21. The track was slow. At Poughkeepsie he was defeated by Santa Claus, but at Hartford he was successful in 2.17, 2.22½, 2.21, after losing the first heat to Clingstone in 2.17. At Boston Park, Boston, a track not adapted to fast time, he won, Sept. 14, the Blanchard $10,000 purse, beating in straight heats Clingstone, Hulene, Santa Claus, Fanny Witherspoon, Parana and Humboldt, in 2.19, 2.19, 2.18½. Then he went into winter quarters. He is a horse of great substance, with sound legs, and does not wear out or weaken under the heavy work of a long campaign. His sire, Thorndale, was got by Alexander's Abdallah, out of Dolly, by Mambrino Chief, she out of a mare by a son of thoroughbred Potomac, and her dam by thoroughbred Saxe Weimar. Lady Lightfoot, the dam of Edwin Thorne, was got by Ashland, out of a mare by Eureka, and Ashland was by Mambrino Chief, out of Utilla, thoroughbred daughter of imported Margrave. The great chestnut, who vanquished the thought-to-be invincible Clingstone is intend to Mambrino Chief, and he has a double infusion of the stout racing blood. He is pure gaited, but has a nervous temperament. Minnie R. now a member of the powerful Kittson stable, defeated at Chicago, in the 2.23 class, Unolais, Buzz Medium and Tariff, reducing her record to 2.19. At Buffalo, in the special race, she started against Clingstone, Edwin Thorne, Kate Sprague and J. B. Thomas. In the first heat, which was trotted in 2.14½, she was a good third, and in the next heat she came down. McCarthy, who was behind her, took desperate chances to get through a narrow gap, but failed, and the mare tripped and fell when she looked very dangerous. At first it was thought she was dead, but she pulled herself together, and her injuries were found to be slight. Had she been able to get through and win the heat, the chances are that she would have captured the race, because she is a mare of superior bottom. At Poughkeepsie she was unsteady, and finished behind Santa Claus and Edwin Thorne, but at Hartford, on a track made heavy by rain, she won the 2.19 class, after losing the first heat to William H. in 2.21, and the second and third heats to Pickard in 2.21½, 2.20½. The time of the heats which she won was 2.20, 2.21½, 2.23. She is a courageous mare, with wonderful flashes of speed. She was bred in Lyon County, Kentucky, and she was got by a son of John C. Breckenridge, out of a blind mare of untraced blood, but having the form and characteristics of a thoroughbred. Her sire was advertised and patronized as a thoroughbred horse. She wears a 14-ounce shoe and a 4-ounce toe-weight. Rosa Wilkes made a great name on the trotting turf this season. The challenger attention at Chicago in the 2.25 class, beating with ease Lady Rose, Forrest Patchen and Joe Bunker, in 2.20½, 2.18½, 2.20½. At Cleveland she cut down a powerful field, composed of J. P. Morris, Fanny Witherspoon, William H. Early Rose, Angle W. Driver, Forrest Patchen and Calmar, and won in 2.18½, 2.18½, 2.48¼. After this her face was turned to the setting sun, and her next great race was at Lexington, in October, where she surrendered to Monroe Chief. Her toes were too long at the time for severe work, and Dobie, who drove the stallion, outgeneraled Cook, who was behind the mare. It was the hard-

est fought race of the year. Monroe Chief won the first in 2.19½, Ross Wilkes the second and third in 2.19½, 2.19½, the fourth was dead in 2.20, and the fifth and sixth heats were taken by the Chief in 2.20½, 2.21½. Had the driving been equal the mare, even with the neglected feet, would have proved victorious. The sire of Ross Wilkes was George Wilkes, and her dam was by Mambrino Patchen, son of Mambrino Chief, and a mare by Gano, by American Eclipse. In her we have a welding of Hambletonian, Mambrino Chief and thoroughbred strains.

In the 2.19 class at Chicago Fanny Witherspoon was the strongest competitor of Clingstone. She trotted four lengths farther in the first heat than any other horse, and she was upon Clingstone's wheel at the wire in 2.17, and she was second to him in the second and third heats in 2.18, 2.20. At Cleveland she was beaten by Rosa Wilkes; at Buffalo she was beaten by Adele Gould, after winning the second heat in 2.19; and the third heat in 2.19; at Utica she captured second money; at Poughkeepsie she showed her heels to Driver, Picard, Humboldt, William H and Capt. Emmons in 2.19, 2.18½, 2.19; and at Hartford, on a heavy track, she made the backers of Santa Claus look uneasy. The stallion won in 2.17½, 2.19½ 2.21½ but the mare came down the homestretch in each heat like uncorked lightning. She trotted the last half of the third mile in 1.06. At Boston she was unsteady and met with defeat in the Blanchard Purse. The trouble with her is that she is a slow scorer; she gets off badly on that account. She also is a big strider and does not like sharp turns. She was not driven with the greatest skill last summer and consequently does not stand as well in the summary as she otherwise would do. We heard Hickok rate her, just before he started for California, as a faster trotter than Clingstone. Her sire was Almont, and her dam was by Gough's Wagner, son of the great four-mile racehorse. She is level-headed and pure-gaited, and trots without weight in light plates. She got her harness action from Almont, and her high form and length of stride from her running-bred ancestors. The horse which have bought the six others horses of the turf, and which have borne the colors of their owners to the front, are not descended from soft and plebian families. In them we discover that trotting blood is warmly and stoutly supported by the blood of the horse whose form is of the highest type, a type identified with the greatest speed, that of the thoroughbred; and with the facts before him the wise man can draw his own conclusions.—Turf, Field and Farm.

## The Grey Trotter Joe Bunker.

It appears very probable to us that Joe Bunker is one of the very best horses ever got by the renowned George Wilkes. The breeder and owner of this young horse stood with him in the old stand on the far-side of the Fashion course and saw "The Brown Stallion" defeat Ethan Allen in his first great race. That was twenty years ago. Mr. Dunn then owned a beautiful blood-like gray mare, afterward called Lady, and she, in her old age, brought him Joe Bunker to the cover of George Wilkes. This gray mare Lady was an excellent roadster, fast, game and more intelligent than many men. She ambled off at the start just as another famous gray mare, Mr. Bonner's Peerless, used to do. They were both by American Star. The dam of Lady was the famous gray mare of the Messenger blood, owned and driven by the gentleman who built the high bridge over the Harlem river when the Croton water well brought into New York. She was called after him, and no trotter was ever more justly renowned in the vicinity of New York for speed, ability to pull weight, capacity to trot all day, and the next day too, and invincible, game and courage. Lady inherited these qualities from this mare and also from the valiant and unflinching horse American Star, her sire. They appear to have descended to her son Joe Bunker, as well be seen by the list of his performances below. He is seven years old, we not hurried in his early days, and is a steadily improving, fast, and stout young horse.

Joe Bunker started as a five-year-old at St. Louis, Mo., Sept. 30, 1880, in the 2.40 class, and was beaten by Alta, winning the first heat and the third heat in 2.28½. We next find him at Louisville, Ky., Oct. 6, where he won his maiden victory in a five-heat race, beating Largesse, Big Julia, Hardie, Lillian, Bill Bodifer and Annie Snyder, in 2.27½, 2.27½, 2.28. He wound up at Cincinnati, Oct. 9, winning a good five-heat race from Alta, Largesse, Effie G and Belle G. Time –2.31½, 2.33, 2.32½. Chester Park is a half-mile track, and was slow on this occasion. These three performances of Joe Bunker for the year 1880 were enough to show that he was cut out for a campaigner, and fit for good company.

In 1881 he laid up, starting but once, at Cincinnati, in the latter part of the season, and was beaten by his half-brother, Lumps, without getting a place of the purse. This season he started at Chicago, July 18, and was beaten by Rosa Wilkes and four others, being placed last in the first heat and distanced in the second. He next trotted at Cleveland, July 27, and was beaten by Aldine, getting fourth money. At La Salle, Ill., Aug. 16, he won a good five-heat race, beating Lucy, Big Soph Solon and Emma Earl, all old hands, in 2.29, 2.25½, 2.27½, 2.23. He was demonstrated that he had not lost his speed nor failed in his staying powers. At Cleveland, Sept. 7, he repeated the performance, defeating Dr. Norman —a very fast five-year-old—Ewing, Joe Ross, Hardwood, Gladstone, Abdallah Boy, E. M. Strong, Lady Thorne, and Harry Valor, in 2.21½, 2.24, 2.25½. He was at Toledo Sept. 12, where he won handsomely in a four-heat race, beating Harry Valor, Gift Jr., Abdallah Boy, Wild Senham and Gladiator, in 2.24½, 2.26, 2.27. His next contest was at Chicago, Sept. 16, where he won in straight heats, Ewing, Gladiator and George K being defeated in 2.25, 2.21, 2.22. His last appearance for the season was at Lexington, Ky., Oct. 11. Joe Ross, Lillian, Alice Stoner, and Judge Hawes lowered their flags to him in a four-heat race. The first heat he won was trotted in 2.20½—his best record—the remaining two in 2.23½ and 2.26. He has nineteen heats in 2.30 or better to his credit, an heat with the exception of his race at Chester Park in 1880, being slower than 2.29. The performances summer stated above are no indication of Joe Bunker's abilities. He is a very speedy horse, and game as they make them. Joe Bunker is by right of inheritance a trotting horse. His sire, George Wilkes, was himself a great trotter and a sire of trotters, nineteen of his get holding places in the great 2.30 list, seven of which entered this year. This is the greatest number contributed in one season by any trotting sire, with the exception of Blue Bull, who has an equal number for 1882. Through Joe's veins courses the stout and lasting Hambletonian blood, commingled with the speedy Clay and game American Star strains. The sire of Hambletonian Cross is one of the best on the American trotting turf; witness Darby, 2.17½; Nettie, 2.18, Driver, 2.19½; Orange Girl, 2.25; Honoraria, 2.26½; Powers, 2.21; Robert McGregor, 2.18; and Jay Gould, 2.21¼. George Wilkes' great daughter, Rosa Wilkes, is one of the sensational performers of the year, and there is no reason to behave Joe Bunker will not prove equally as great.—New York Sportsman.

## RACING REMINISCENCES.

### Trotters I Have Driven—Piedmont and the Races He Won for Me.

I now come to the stallion Piedmont, one of the fastest horses that I ever pulled a line over. He became a member of my stable in the spring of 1880, being at that time nine years old. Five years previous he had won the *Spirit of the Times* stake for four-year-olds, getting a record of 2:30½, which he had never lowered, although trotting some each year, and in addition had acquired the reputation of being a quitter. The first race I started him in was at Adrian, Mich., where he lost the first heat to Katie Barium, but won the next three easily, the time of the second heat being 2:29½—a reduction of his previous record of a full second. At Detroit the next week there was a large field, Black Cloud, who has since gained a record of 2:17¼, being a hot favorite, but I beat him with Piedmont in three heats without a struggle, the time being 2:24, 2:24¼, 2:24¼, my horse again reducing his record—this time five and a half seconds. We were to have trotted at Pontiac the following week, but the track was such a bad one we concluded not to start, and so Piedmont's next race was at Columbus, Ohio, where he met a large field of good horses. Abdallah Boy had won a good race at Toledo the week before, and was well backed, the pool-selling being lively, but Piedmont won handily in straight heats, the fastest one being in 2:25. This was the first time that Mr. S. J. Morgan, who owned the horse, had seen him trot. The first half-mile on this Columbus track is up hill, and the first turn a very short one. Piedmont could never trot a short turn fast, and in getting away for the last heat I sent him along too fast at this place, and he broke. When he caught I did not dare to go too fast up the hill for fear of pumping him out, as he had quit in all his western races, previous to this season, and I had not driven him long enough to know just what he was capable of doing. So I trailed along easily, and at the half-mile pole was fifth or sixth horse, but once on top of the hill Piedmont was set going, and at the three-quarter pole was in the lead. After the heat was over Mr. Morgan said he saw Piedmont break and fall behind. Just then he turned round to speak to a friend, and when he looked at the horses again Piedmont was in the lead. This was Morgan's version of it, but I told him he was so afraid the horse would be beaten that he could not bear to look at him, and shut his eyes. From Columbus we went to Fort Wayne, and there Piedmont was beaten in straight heats by Kitty Bates, who went the first mile in 2:23½—a merry clip over a half-mile track in the early part of the season. Piedmont could never trot a half-mile track fast, nor a mile track that cupped out, as he always wanted good footing, and the smoother and harder it was the better he liked it.

Then we came to Chicago, where Piedmont was engaged in two races: the stake for stallions that had never beaten 2:30, and the regular 2:30 race. In the first race the field of starters was a large one, including Piedmont, Black Cloud, Amber, Hambletonian Bashaw, and other good ones. Amber had been trotting good races down East, and was first choice in the pools, being backed very heavily by the Rochester party that came here with him. In the first heat Amber got off with the lead and passed the quarter pole first, but as soon as we straightened into the back stretch I sent Piedmont after him, and before we reached the three-quarter pole was in the lead and easing my horse back to him. Feek made several brushes at me with Amber going down the home stretch, but Piedmont won easily in 2:21¼, which was his fastest record up to that time. He also took the second and third heats, Hambletonian Bashaw being second in each of them. We did not start in the 2:30 race at this meeting.

After this race we thought it best to give Piedmont a rest during the hot summer months, and he was not trotted again until September, when he went to Minneapolis to trot against Hambletonian Bashaw and Bonesetter. Bashaw won the first heat in 2:27, and that was the first time that any stallion had beaten Piedmont a heat. I had always been afraid to drive him more than was absolutely necessary in order to keep the lead, and in this heat was pursuing the usual tactics. When about half-way down the home stretch Crawford set Hambletonian Bashaw to going; and as he was a horse of wonderful speed for a little ways, beat me for the heat in spite of all I could do. Bashaw was a horse that, if allowed to go the first three-quarters of a mile at moderate speed, would trot the last one very fast; and knowing this fact I resolved to drive the second heat differently. When we got the word I set the pace pretty strong, and Bashaw never got near me, Piedmont winning in 2:22, and also taking the next two heats. At Chicago, the following week, he had an easy race, Voltaire and Lida Bassett being the only other starters. Crawford had an idea that when Voltaire was just right he had a chance to beat Piedmont, and drove me out one heat in 2:21½.

Then came the race at St. Louis with France's Alexander. Both stallions had started out at the beginning of the season with records exactly alike, and Mr. France had made so much talk about his horse beating Piedmont that I was very glad to meet him right in his own town. In the draw for positions Alexander secured the pole, and Piedmont the outside, which reminded me of a meeting in Iowa that I once attended, where drivers knew several days in advance just what positions their horses were going to draw. When we got the word for the first heat Alexander had a little the best of the start, and led around the turn into the back stretch. Once into the straight work I let Piedmont step along some, and by the time the half-mile pole was reached he was leading Alexander. Half-way between the half and three-quarter poles Piedmont had trotted past Alexander, taken the pole from him, and I had taken my horse back and was watching the other horse. The first quarter of this mile was trotted in 35 seconds, and the half in 1:08, making 33 seconds for the second quarter; and as Piedmont was behind at the quarter pole and ahead at the half he must have been going some. That kind of work took all the trot out of Alexander, and just before reaching the three-quarter pole he made a break, and as he was not one of the kind that could catch and come again I won the heat in the slow time of 2:22½. The next two heats Piedmont won easily in slow time, one fast half-mile being all the medicine that Alexander wanted that day.

The next place at which Piedmont trotted was at Louisville, the other starters being Von Arnim and Voltaire, and at no time were they able to extend my horse. At the Lexington meeting we did not start Piedmont, but I drove him a mile one morning in his work in 2:18, and the next week showed him at Cynthiana, Ky., where he trotted an exhibition mile in 2:18¼, that being the last race of the season.

In the spring of 1881 I took charge of Piedmont again, and thought by the way he moved up in his work when asked to extend himself that he had more speed than ever, although I did not drive him a fast half or quarter before going to Michigan with my other horses. When I came back to Chicago, having been gone two weeks, with the intention of giving the horse a "repeat," Mr. Morgan said he was out of form, but could not tell why. The horse, he said, did not seem to have his speed, and seemed unwilling to do what he could. However, I "repeated" him, and the result only confirmed what Mr. Morgan had told me, as I had to work pretty hard to get a mile in 2:26 out of him. This, from a horse that had trotted quarters for me better than 33 seconds the previous season, was not very encouraging, especially as the first race in which we were to start him was the $5,000 stallion purse at Chicago in July, and as the time for that event was rapidly approaching, the prospect for winning any part of the money seemed slim, as against such competitors as Santa Claus, Robert McGregor, Wedgewood and Hannis, it was evident that none but a first-class horse, in first-class trim, stood any show. After this mile in 2:26 I went to Michigan again, but returned at the end of a week to see how the stallion was getting along. I gave him a slow mile, cooled out, and then sent him for the best he could do, the time being 2:23. This was an improvement of three seconds in seven days; but the time before the race was so short that it did not seem possible for a horse to improve sufficiently to put in three or four heats better than 2:20, as we knew must be done by the winner of the stallion purse. Piedmont was also entered in the 2:21 race at the Chicago meeting, and in it would meet France's Alexander, the horse he had beaten so easily at St. Louis the previous season, but that had since won the $10,000 stallion race at Rochester, N. Y., on the Fourth of July. Piedmont had not been entered in the Rochester race, and as Alexander had stayed out of the stallion race at Chicago they would have their first meeting in the 2:21 race. On the Sunday before the Chicago meeting I gave Piedmont his last fast work previous to the stallion race, which was to be trotted Tuesday. As before, I gave him one slow mile, and then drove him right up to his speed. The time was 2:19½; but I noticed that in the last part of the mile he seemed to have his old-time speed, and then, for the first time, it seemed to me that he ought to get a place in the stallion race, and win in the 2:21 class, for I knew the first race would do him good.

When the day of the stallion race came everybody knew that Piedmont had been out of form for a month, and in consequence he sold for about $10 in pools of $100 and over. My ideas on the subject were so strong that I did not back the horse, having only four pools on him, for which I paid $32, and taking those more as a matter of form than anything else. When we drew for positions Piedmont got the pole, and it occurred to me if I could win the first heat it would give me a good place in the race, and so when the word was given I drove for it. Robert McGregor and Santa Claus were my principal opponents in this mile, all being well together from the quarter pole, and in the homestretch it was a neck-and-neck struggle for supremacy. No one could pick the winner a hundred feet from the wire, but right at the finish McGregor came along with a burst of speed and won the heat by a head in 2:18, Santa Claus being second and Piedmont third; and persons who did not see this heat may know how close the finish was when I state that although Piedmont was the third horse his nose was not over three feet behind that of Santa Claus when the latter went under the wire. Hannis was fourth in this heat, Wedgewood fifth and Monroe Chief last. As my calculations in regard to this heat had gone so far amiss I concluded to lay my horse up in the second heat, thinking that perhaps such action would enable him to go the third mile better than he had the first. Consequently I was not particular in going away from the stand to hold my position, but after we had trotted three-quarters of a mile, it seemed to me that Piedmont could win. So I cut him loose, Santa Claus being the contending horse, but he beat me out a head in 2:17½ after one of the prettiest finishes ever seen.

There was now a great revolution in the betting, and as Piedmont was a Chicago horse, and had fought so well for every heat, his success was a popular one, especially as the time was, with the exception of Smuggler's 2:15¼, the fastest that had ever been made by a stallion. The other drivers had all been backing their own horses—the pool selling showed that—and seeing that matters were beginning to look squally, a caucus was held in regard to how the next heat was to be driven. It was finally decided to have Wedgewood sent after Piedmont single-handed. This arrangement suited me exactly, as I knew Piedmont could beat Wedgewood and have an easy heat himself. The result was in accordance with my views, as Piedmont won by four or five lengths in 2:19¼, never being headed in the mile.

Wedgewood, Hannis and Monroe Chief now went to the barn, not having won one heat in five, and only Piedmont, Santa Claus and McGregor started for the sixth heat, which Piedmont won easily by several lengths in 2:21, thus ending the fastest stallion race ever trotted, and one of the best six-heat races on record.

This race was trotted July 19th, and on the 26th Piedmont started in the 2:21 class against France's Alexander and Lucy. This was quite a betting race, as the Alexander party were confident that no stallion could defeat their horse, arguing that his seven-heat race at Rochester was better than the one trotted and won by Piedmont at Chicago, although if some of them had known more about that race perhaps they would not have been so sure of beating the chestnut. At all events they put up their money freely, and, as the Chicago boys did likewise, the pool-selling the evening before the race and the next day was of the liveliest description, even money being the rate at which the bets were made. All this time it seemed to me like a sure thing for Piedmont to beat Alexander; for the previous season he had trotted right around him over the St. Louis track, when Alexander had all his speed; and Piedmont's performance in the stallion race had demonstrated that he could stay. When we came to trot the race my expectations were fulfilled to the letter. Not having, apparently, profited by his experience the previous season, Gus. Wilson, who drove Alexander, attempted to take the pole from Piedmont as soon as the word for the first heat was given, but when he came down to the inside he found a horse there that could not only hold his own, but go faster than Alexander ever could. Wilson kept trying to get ahead of me, however, and when Alexander had reached the top of his speed, he naturally went into the air, and that was the last I saw of him in the heat, which Piedmont won easily in 2:18. In the second heat Wilson attempted to repeat the tactics of the first, and the result of this was that Alexander was distanced in 2:19¾, leaving only Lucy to be beaten the third heat, which Piedmont won in 2:19.

Then I concluded not to try for the next heat, and let the other horses go away ahead of me. McGregor got away with the lead, and when Splan came up with Wedgwood I let him go right past me, but when John got alongside of McGregor he asked Crawford, who was driving that horse, to let him have the heat. I thought Crawford said he would do so, and then I knew it would be necessary for me to go along with Piedmont in order to prevent Wedgewood's winning. I succeeded in doing this, but in going for McGregor Splan made me trot so wide on the turn that Turner slipped up on the inside with Hannis and beat me out for second place, McGregor winning the heat in 2:18½. But although my calculations regarding this heat had been upset, I was now more confident than ever, and began, for the first time, to think that Piedmont would win the race. McGregor, I could see, was tired, and as Mr. Morgan and myself walked to the stable I told him what I thought, and said that in the next heat I should drive for it from the time the word was given. When the horses came out Piedmont felt as gay as a lark, and in scoring for the send-off I could see that all his speed had returned. When the word was given I sent him along at a merry clip, had taken the pole before the first turn was reached, and was never headed in the mile, winning the heat easily in 2:17¼, the fastest one of the race. Santa Claus was second, but a long way off, and the rest strung out.

Then came Piedmont's races through the Central Circuit in the 2:21 class, winning at Buffalo in 2:20½, 2:22, 2:22; at Rochester in 2:20½, 2:19¼, 2:17¾; and at Utica in 2:21, 2:23¼, 2:19½. In neither of these races did he lose a heat, but at Hartford he struck Edwin Thorne for the first time, and was beaten in straight heats, the time being 2:17½, 2:18¼, 2:18¼, which was a good enough race to beat most horses. Our next engagement with Piedmont was in the $10,000 stallion race to be trotted at Boston, September 15th, and as the Hartford race took place August 25th, I had nearly three weeks' idle time on my hands. I kept my horse at Hartford until three or four days before the Boston race, and about a week previous to that event gave him five heats over the Hartford track in 2:27, 2:20½, 2:16¼, 2:17¼, 2:27. On the day the Boston race was trotted the Beacon Park track was rather soft, and the day a chilly one. Santa Claus won this race easily enough, the time of the fastest heat being 2:17¾. A great many people have asked me if Piedmont was not "off" that day. I don't think he was. The day was cold, and the track soft and cuppy, being exactly the condition of affairs which Piedmont did not like, a hot day and hard track being always necessary for him when his best performance was to be expected.

The turns on the Beacon Park track are very short, the same as on a half-mile track, and this was against Piedmont, as he never could trot that style of track while I had him. This was the only race that Piedmont ever lost to a stallion, and in turn he has beaten nearly all the prominent stallions in this country, the list of those who have succumbed to him including Monroe Chief Black Cloud, Von Arnim, Kentucky Wilkes, Robert McGregor, Wedgwood, Hannis, Bonesetter, Hambletonian Bashaw, Amber, Abdallah Boy, Santa Claus, France's Alexander and Voltaire. Piedmont was a horse that required a great deal of work to get him into condition for a race, and if he did not receive it he would lose his speed and be dull and sluggish. He was a hearty feeder. One peculiarity of his was that between the heats of a race he would puff and blow in a style that would make anyone think he was tired; but it was only a habit of his—he would make as much fuss after trotting a heat in 2:30 as if it had been 2:20. In the winter of 1881–82 Piedmont was sold to ex-Gov. Stanford, of California, for $27,500, and is now in the stud at the Palo Alto farm.—*Peter V. Johnson in the Breeders' Gazette.*

### Close of the Fall Race Meeting.

The fall meeting of the Pacific Coast Blood-Horse Association came to a close on Saturday last, and now it can be ranked as one of the successes of the season. The man who does the horse for a morning paper thus descants on the weather, and as he has come nearly describing it as it was, it comes in appropriately in this place.

"Dreary November." So say the English turf scribes when recording the races at the close of the season. In California the reverse is more generally the case, and more lovely weather it would be difficult to imagine than that which prevails for a good portion of the month. Yesterday there was an exception. Dreary, almost dismal, when compared with that of the preceding race day. There were clouds and fogs in the morning. At noon the sun, it was thought, would break the veil of vapor, and for a few minutes it was visible. Not bright and effulgent, however, but more like the broadside of a skimmed milk cheese suspended from the rafters of a smoky cabin. The clouds again closed, ominous, a warning of a downfall. The mists climbed the hills and hung in the ravines, and seemed to be ready on short notice to take the more palpable form of rain. The barometers in the windows of the shops gave forebodings of a change, and many who consulted them countermanded the order to get the carriage ready, and concluded that the promise of sport was too indefinite to warrant the journey. Notwithstanding the signs and omens, there was a very good attendance, more than was expected under the untoward circumstances, and somewhat relieved the somberness of the surroundings. The course was in bad condition. There had been clouds and vapor hanging over it since the rains of Wednesday night, and it was heavy, sticky, slow and altogether bad—slower than when the horses splashed through it on Thursday, the light mud having dried so that it was the consistence of thick mortar, and increasing the labor of getting through it, while the foothold was still more insecure.

Though the metaphor comparing the sun to a "skimmed milk cheese" is on the Hudibrastic order, he was a lucky scribe to get a glimpse of the great luminary at all. At the course the veil was too dense to show the least token that the sun had not set and at times the heavy fog would come in streamers of vapor, partially obscuring part of the track. It is safe to assert that it was the "slowest track" for horses to run a long race upon that had ever been known here. That is when racehorses actually ran, and the "old-timers" could not understand why the horses were called. The general idea was that there was likely to be a postponement, and this notion was so prevalent in the city that a very large majority of those who intended to go countermanded the order for teams and stayed at home.

A better idea of the slowness of the track can be obtained from the other races than the data furnished by the time of the four miles. Seven minutes, forty-five and a half seconds is not bad on a fair track and to arrive at a just estimate it will be better to consider the time of the other races.

Joe Howell carrying 124 pounds beat Frank Rhoads the shortest of short heads in 2:17. Frank Rhoads had a concession of 15 pounds, and Atalanta, who was a good third, carried 90 pounds. The time of 2:17 is at least six seconds slower than either of the horses could make the distance on a good track, and even this difference of nearly five seconds to a mile is not enough when the effect on a four-mile race is to be calculated. Twenty seconds off is

too much, and there can scarcely be a question that on
d day and a good track 7.25 would be beaten by the
er.

The weather was as great a drawback to theattendance as it
as to the horses, though we were glad to see one at least
ho was determined that all the discomforts should not
op him from enjoying the "four-mile-day." Colonel W.
. Barnes turned out in a very handsome drag—four-in-hand
ith everything requisite for the enjoyment of family and
iends. There were hampers of wine, and a luncheon which
ortsum and Mason could not surpass, and the colored man
ho had charge of the commissary gave proof that it was not
a new job to him. Under the sheds were a goodly number
of road horses, the rawness and dampness of the air precluding the field disp'lay of carriages.

While the great interest centered in the four-mile race, that
which preceded it evoked a good share of attention. It was
a handicap stake of $25 each, with $250 added; one and a
quarter miles. The starters were Joe Howell, 124 pounds;
Bolis, 105 pounds; Frank Rhoads, 103 pounds; Atalanta, 90
pounds and Garfield, 85 pounds. 'Patsy Duffy had the mount
on Joe Howell, Williams on Bolis, Howson, Rhoads; Luke
rode Atalanta and Sam Carter Garfield. At the opening of
the pool sales Howell was the favorite, bringing $50 to $30 on
Garfield, and $26 on the field, which embraced the other
three. The field appreciated before the start, and quite a
large amount was bet. There was a capital start, and that
without much delay, and as they swept past the stand Howell
was in the lead with Garfield second, but on the first turn
Rhoads passed both, and at the quarter-pole had established
himself first, the half-mile being made in 54 seconds. At the
half-mile mark, in 1.22, he was still leading, Howell second,
the others together, and there was not much change until the
horses were within a short distance of the stretch. Then Atalanta came with a rush, closing on the leaders, and the run
home was very exciting. Howell passed Frank Rhoads, and
at the drawgate it appeared as though he would win, "hands
down." Rhoads was not beaten yet, however, and though
half a length behind when within one hundred feet of the
score he came again gamely, and was only beaten by a "short
head." The weight was telling on the old veteran, though
bravely he carried it, and the crowd heartily cheered him as
he came back for his rider to weigh. Atalanta was third,
Garfield fourth and Bolis fifth. Time, 2:17.

SUMMARY.

BAY DISTRICT COURSE, Saturday, Nov. 25 1882.—FIRST RACE; handicap, $25 each; $50 if declared; $300 added; $75 Second horse. Free for
all. Dash of a mile and a quarter.
Shoaler a 4-year' b g Joe Howell, aged, by Bonnie Scotland—Eva Shep-
   pard, 124 lbs. (Duffy)...........................................1
W. L. Pritchard's b c Frank Rhoads, 4 years, by Leinster—Ada A., 103
   lbs. (Howson)...................................................2
Theo. Winters' ch m Atalanta, 3 years, by Norfolk—Lady Jane, 90 lbs.
   (Carter).......................................................3
J. T. Woolman's b m Bolis, 6 years, by imported Buckden—An-
   nie H. 105 lbs.................................................0
R. J. Green's g c Garfield, 3 years, by California—Queen, 85 lbs.........0
   Jonko and Mattie B paid forfeit.
                                 Time—2:17.

The betting was heavy on the four-mile race. A great deal
of money went into the box the night previous, and those
who had held aloof until they could get some line to guide
them, rushed their money in with a will. There were only
slight variations in the odds. The Palo Alto filly Precious
was the favorite from the first. She held that position all
through, and her supporters never wavered in their faith, nor
lost confidence in the handsome filly. A fair average of all
was: Precious, $100; the field, Clara D, and Nathan
Coombs, $60; Fred Collier, $50. A dense crowd surrounded
the auctioneer, and it was lively times for the clerks to receive the money and make out the tickets. When the horses
appeared the eye was eagerly scanned, and cognoscenti were
on the qui vive for some sign or token to guide them in their
choice. Clara D did quite a strong gallop down the stretch,
and though she evidently had picked up a good deal since
her return from the East, she still showed a lack of flesh for
a race of four miles on such a heavy track. Fred Collier took
it more leisurely, and when he was disrobed he appeared to
the eye to be in good condition. Precious was "blooming."
The covering removed, and her coat glistened even under the
lowering clouds, and if there had been bright sunshine it
would have been like the shield of Fingal that shone through
the fogs of the North. Nathan Coombs looked robust in
flesh, but his legs were palpably affected, and there
were prognostications of a breakdown, which proved to be
well-founded.

The drawing for positions gave Precious the pole, Clara D
second, Nathan Coombs third, Fred Collier on the outside.
Precious was ridden by Ed Fallon, Clara D by Fred Carillo,
Nathan Coombs by Fred Ross and Fred Collier by Patsy
Duffy. There was little time wasted after the riders were
mounted, and no trial of patience to the spectators. At the
second attempt the horses received a very good start, and as
they rounded the turn Clara-D led, Precious second, Fred
Collier third and Nathan Coombs fourth. At the quarter
pole Clara D was three lengths ahead of Precious, Fred Collier
being third and Nathan Coombs fourth. Time, 28½. Down
the backstretch there was but little change in their respective
positions, but Clara D. had a little wider gap between her and
Precious. Time at the half mile, 1.01. Rounding the further turn Clara D led Precious by six lengths, with seven or
eight lengths between her and Fred Collier, Nathan Coombs
two lengths in the rear of the latter, last of all. At the
three-quarter pole the time was 1.29, Clara D still leading,
with about the same advantage. In the run down the homestretch the leaders closed upon each other, but the others
were the same as before. Precious was within three lengths
of the leader. First mile, 1.59, Clara D leading.

She still led on, making the first turn the second time, with
Precious close up, Fred Collier third and Nathan Coombs
away in the rear. The time for the mile and a quarter was
2.26, Clara D two lengths ahead of Precious, who was several
lengths ahead of Fred Collier, third, Nathan Coombs being
last. Clara D was running easily, and the filly still more so.
Time at the mile and a half, 2.58½, Clara D still leading.
Rounding the further turn there was a very long gap between the two leaders and Fred Collier and Nathan Coombs.
Time for a mile and three-quarters, 3.29. Again those in the
rear closed up some on the gap, Clara D running strong and
fresh, and Precious very easily. The time for the two miles
was 3.66, Clara D three lengths ahead, Precious a length in
advance of Coombs, Collier fourth. This time around the
turn there was little change, only Clara D opened more of a
gap between her and Precious, she being at least fifty yards
in front of Coombs and Collier, who were running side by
side. Time for the two miles and a quarter, 2.47, Clara D
leading at a good pace, Precious pulling hard. When they
went down the backstretch for the third mile Collier took the
lead of Coombs and moved up a little closer. At the half-

mile pole Clara D led Precious about twelve yards, Fred Collier being third and Nathan Coombs falling back. Time,
4.56. Around the northern turn Clara D still led, with the
horses strung out behind, Fred Collier closing the gap at the
three-quarters, so that it was perceptibly reduced between
him and Precious as the three-quarter pole was passed in
5.25. In the run down the homestretch Collier closed still
more of the gap that marked the difference, and when Clara
D went under the wire for the third time in 5.53 he was
almost as near Precious as she was to the leader. But the
filly had not run hard yet, having pulled so hard that the
saddle slipped at the close of the first mile, and the rider was
almost on her withers, and when the tension on the reins was
removed she darted forward at a rate of speed that rapidly
diminished the distance between her and Clara D. Collier
fell back beaten, and Nathan, who had given way in his ailing leg on the previous mile, was far in the rear. The nose
of Precious was parallel with the hip of Clara before reaching
the quarter pole, and it was evident that the race from there
was to be a hot contest for the supremacy.

At every stride Precious was gaining, but at the half-mile
there was no perceptible difference, Collier at least forty yards
behind. It was also evident that whichever got the best of
the brush was almost sure to be the winner, and eagerly,
anxiously, excitedly the battle was watched. The man who
was taking the time of the fractions became so much interested that he forgot to touch the spring of the "split," and at
the quarter and half no time was recorded. A little beyond
the half-mile the nose of Precious was seen in front, a few
strides and there was a head to bar advantage, a little further and the neck was seen. The gallant old mare made a
heroic effort, reducing for a moment or two the lead by a few
inches. Bravely done, it was the last expiring throb. Heart,
lungs, muscles were overdone, and the gain came from the
nerve force, which was all that carried her along. The race
was ended. Precious keeping up her easy stride, widened
the gap, and though the other was lengths behind, she never
faltered or slackened, going under the wire with her " ears
pricked" and her action still showing vigor, Clara D some
twelve lengths in the rear, Collier a long way behind, and
Nathan Coombs, who had given away in a hind leg as well as
the front, hobbling midway of the stretch. The time of the
four miles was 7.49½, which was very fast for the state of the
track and the weight carried. The winner, Precious, as a
three-year-old filly, carried ninety-nine pounds; Fred Collier,
four years old, 115 pounds; Clara D, "aged," 100 pounds,
and Nathan Coombs, also aged, 123 pounds.

The winner is one of the most promising three-year-olds
for a distance that has ever appeared on the Pacific Coast.
She is quite a handsome filly, and of the best breeding. Her
sire is Lever, a son of Lexington, and her dam was by another son, Thunder, from an imported mare.

SUMMARY.

Same day—Second race; Baldwin Stake; $300 each, p p, $1,000 added;
   second to receive $400; third to save stake. Dash of four miles.
George Hearst's (Palo Alto) b m Precious (Ed. Fallon).................1
E. J. Baldwin's b m Clara D. (Fred Carillo)...........................2
Stemler & Ayres' s g Fred Collier (Patsy Duffy).......................3
W. Boots' br h Nathan Coombs (Fred Ross)..............................0
                                     Time—7.49½.

No starters for the subscriptions of W. L. Pritchard and J. T. Gilmore.

The Consolation Purse was the next on the cards. This
was a dash of a mile for a purse of $200, the weights being
governed by the number of times the entries had been beaten.
The starters were Haddington, 113 pounds; Frank Rhoads,
103 pounds; Forest King, 94 pounds, and Los Spencer, 92
pounds. At the first Haddington was the favorite, bringing
$70, Forest King $47½, and the other two $52½. Before the
start the field, containing Frank Rhoads, was the first choice,
and this proved to be the correct estimate. At the fall of the
starter's flag Frank Rhoads took the lead, and though Los
Spencer ran on the extreme outside of the track, she was only
a short distance behind him at the quarter. The run down
the backstretch was very pretty, Rhoads and Los having the
fun all to themselves. His kept close to him on the turn,
but was never able to reach him, though she finished a very
fair second, her jockey "Luke" worked bravely to secure the
victory, till the last moment. Forest King was a poor third a
half length in front of Haddington. Time, 1.49.

SUMMARY.

Same day—Third race; Consolation Purse; $200. entrance free;
second horse to receive $50. Dash of a mile. Weights were calcu-
lated five points; Dash of a mile. Weights were calculated five points,
Entries to be made at Judges' Stand immediately after the running of
preceding race.
W. L. Pritchard names Frank Rhoads 4 years, 103 pounds...............1
Theo. Alto names Los Spencer, 3 year, 92 pounds......................2
Palo Alto names Forest King, 3 years, 94 pounds......................3
J. McM Shafter names Haddington, 4 years, 108 pounds.................0
                                     Time—1.49.

The hurdle race proved to be a very good one. The starters were the same mares that ran a week ago, viz.: Hattie B,
and Mollie H. The former was a "tremendous favorite,"
and a great deal of money was put on her at the rate of $100
to $47. The now favorite had greatly improved in the tele-
rium, and had also the advantage of a better jockey. She
was ridden by a young man who had just returned from a
cruise in the Arctic, and the perils of the North had seasoned
him so that surmounting such trifling obstacles as a three-
foot-six hurdle was lightly thought. It was one of the
closest contests of the kind ever witnessed. Many of the
jumps were taken side by side, and Mollie H on this occasion
made the cleverest work. The first heat was nearly as close
as that between Howell and Rhoads, being won by Mollie H
by a short neck, and for the heavy, sticky track, the time
was fast—1.56½. In the second heat Hattie B took the lead,
and making cleaner jumps than before, she was first until
the last hurdle was cleared. Again the run home was close,
but this time Mollie B won by a length in 1.59. This closed
the fall meeting of the Pacific Coast Blood Horse Association,
which, notwithstanding the bad weather of the last two racing
days, has been a success from every point of view.

SUMMARY.

Same day—Fourth race; Purse, $250; entrance free; $50 to second
horse.  Heats of a mile over four hurdles.
W. Boots' b m Mollie H, 5 years, by Wildidle—Mamie Hall...........1  1
Theo. Winters' ch f Hattie B, 3 years, by Norfolk—Maggie Dale.......2  2
                                     Time—1.56½, 1.59.

## Yellow Dock.

NEW YORK, Nov. 22, 1882.

J. C. SIMPSON ESQ., Dear Sir: It was at first expected that
the owners of Yellow Dock were to send her to California
this winter but they have concluded not to do so.

Yours truly, W. J. WELCH.

We are sorry to hear that the owners of this celebrated
mare have given up the idea of wintering her on this coast.
Although Overman has beaten her, the great knack she displayed in getting over the ground with running mate is so
angury that she may have acquired a better method of keeping up her clip than when she got the worst of it. Elmo, Romero, Overman, Yellow Dock and others here would be an
attraction which would bring thousands to see them.

## ATHLETICS.

### George's Offer to Myers.

The New York World says: The unpleasant episode in the
series of international races between Messrs. George and
Myers, caused by the sickness of the latter, and the refusal of
the Committee of Games to agree to a postponement of the
three-quarters of a mile race, which was to be the deciding
event of the series, has been counterbalanced by the graceful
manner in which George, after reflection, has waived his
point and accepted the proposition of the Manhattan Athletic
Club to run Myers three-quarters of a mile on Thanksgiving
day on the grounds of the club. In a conversation with a reporter of the World yesterday George said: "The reports
printed in many of the newspapers are unjust to me; they attribute motives to me that I never entertained. They endeavor to make me appear as a runner seeking only empty
honors and gate money. I will run Myers three-quarters of
a mile on Thanksgiving Day. I want nothing to do with the
management of the committee, and should they withdraw it then the public will see that I am not at fault and am not the pot-hunter
that I have been represented to be. I like Myers very much
and I know that he is willing to run me at any time, and
would have run me to-day but for the pressure brought to
bear on him. It is a pity that he has not the management of
his own affairs."

Myers was found at the grounds of his club, Fifty-sixth
street and Eighth avenue. He said: "I am better to-day,
but not by any means well. I think it mean that George
should accuse me of shamming sickness to escape defeat. I
gave him the race last Saturday, and I did not think it fair to
sacrifice my friends by giving him another to-day. I was sick,
as my father and doctor can testify. The proposal of George
that we should race, and the fact that I was ill was not to be
made public until after my defeat, shows that he was after
the share of the gate money, which goes to his club."

Mr. Wm. B. Curtis, the referee of the two contests that have
taken place between George and Myers, was found at his office in Chambers street. He said: "The letter that was published over George's name in which he says that I was not
his financial agent left no other course open to me but to resign the position to which I was appointed by Mr. Jackson,
the President of the Moseley Harriers Club, of which George
is a member. He has behaved in a very unreasonable manner all through this affair. When I told him that the only
thing I could do would be to postpone the race, run three-
quarters of a mile against time or a handicap of the same distance, he would not listen to me and I left disgusted with the
whole affair."

Mr. George W. Thomas said: "I believe George is willing
to run, but he was obliged to come to to forfeit in order to
win bets. It is a well known fact that he was around the
Brower House all the evening previous to the last race, and
that it was through him that a large percentage in person in
such large numbers on that occasion. Why, he knew to a
penny what all the gamblers won—how much Arthur Chambers won, how much Lovell won, and so on, and still he has
the courage to say that we are the people who are more than
fond of betting."

In answer to this, Mr. Wm. H. Caldicott, George's friend
and club mate, said: "Of course, we were around the Brower
House. We claim the same right to bet a few pounds on the
race as the men of Myers' crowd had to bet the thousands of
dollars that they lost."

The following letter has been issued by George:

TO THE EDITOR OF THE WORLD, Sir: I have read in several papers of this morning, with mingled feelings of regret
and surprise, many things untrue and others only partially
so—altogether heaps which, if only half correct, would be a
disgrace to both English and American athletic sport. I
therefore beg to state that I will run Mr. L. E. Myers on
Thanksgiving Day (Nov. 30) certain. Every arrangement I
leave to the Manhattan Club. I deny that my object in visiting this country was otherwise than in the interests of amateur athletic sport, and remain yours truly,
                                            W. G. GEORGE.
Knickerbocker Hotel, Mott Haven, N. Y., Nov. 18.

### Meyers' Condition—Bets.

The New York World publishes the following communication, replying to the second that backers of George are winners:

In reading the World of this morning I see in your
published account of the Myers-George trouble that Mr.
George said that he never saw a man in finer condition than
Myers, and he thought that Myers would beat the record.
Now, on Sunday morning after that race Mr. Myers' father
told me that his son had been coughing throughout the
night and that he was evidently suffering from a severe cold.
During the week following Myers did little running, and
that at a slow pace, and he was still very ill when he went
into the mile race. Notwithstanding this, he beat his last
previous record at the distance, and at that walked in the
past thirty yards, which proves, to my mind at least, that
Myers was not overtrained, as I cannot see how a man could
be too fine and yet run up to his form.     JOHN FRASER.

Cannot you manage to give in your paper an explicit statement as to the bets on the George-Myers match go—
especially the point of those made in which George was
backed to win two out of three events?     E.

In the Examiner of last week Peter McIntyre is accused of
running a job race of 440 yards with the well-known professional F. R. Davis. McIntyre has never been known to run
an unfair race, and never countenanced a fraud in any match
in which he was interested. More than that, the reports of
all the daily papers, as well as the weekly sporting journals,
of that date will prove that G. Guerrero, with 25 yards handicap, was Davis' opponent in the race named by the Examiner,
and will also show that at the time McIntyre was 3,000 miles
away, in the East. No doubt the Examiner will gladly correct the error.

The Honolulu Athletic Association, organized some months
ago, and which has a large membership, is now erecting a
building for their gymnasium. This they will add to from
time to time as funds permit. The Y. M. C. A. of Honolulu
have a fine large brick building in process of construction in
the central part of the city, a portion of which will also be
devoted to a gymnasium.

The 135 yards match between Harmon and Gibson for
$250 a side was won easily by the former, in San Jose last
Saturday. The time taken was all the way from 13½ to 14
seconds. Gibson was beaten fully four yards.

# THE
# Breeder and Sportsman.

PUBLISHED WEEKLY BY THE
BREEDER AND SPORTSMAN PUBLISHING CO.

THE TURF AND SPORTING AUTHORITY OF THE
PACIFIC COAST.

### OFFICE, 508 MONTGOMERY STREET
P. O. Box 1838.

*Five dollars a year; three dollars for six months; one dollar and a half for three months. Strictly in advance.*

MAKE ALL CHECKS, MONEY ORDERS, ETC., PAYABLE TO ORDER OF
BREEDER AND SPORTSMAN PUBLISHING CO.

*Money should be sent by postal order, draft or by registered letter, addressed to the "Breeder and Sportsman Publishing Company, San Francisco, Cal."*

*Communications must be accompanied by the writer's name and address, not necessarily for publication, but as a private guarantee of good faith.*

JOSEPH CAIRN SIMPSON, - - - EDITOR

ADVERTISING RATES.—Displayed $1.50 per inch each insertion, or pro rate for less space. Reading Notices set in brevier type and having no food marks, 50 cents per line each insertion. Lines will average ten words. A discount of 10 per cent. will be allowed on 3 months, 20 per cent. on 6 months and 30 per cent. on 12 months contracts. No extra rate charged for cuts or cutting of column rules. No Trading notice taken for less than 50 cents each insertion.

San Francisco, Saturday, December 2, 1882.

Mr. M. J. Henley is a duly authorized traveling agent and correspondent for the "Breeder and Sportsman."

## DISTRICT BOARD NO. 5 AND THE HON. JAMES McM. SHAFTER.

We feel that the time has come when duty compels us to enter a vigorous protest against the manner in which a member of the board, James McM. Shafter, works against the interests of trotting on this Coast.

We shall do so plainly, emphatically, giving the reasons why we consider him unfit for the position he occupies, and that his present conduct and his antecedents are in direct opposition to the welfare and popularization of the sports of the track. There is an immense money of interest depending. There are graver questions at issue than dollars and cents.

While we are so situated as to have a direct personal interest, that has only a slight bearing in comparison with thta of the people who look for us to defend the cause of truth, honesty, fair dealing in whatever concerns the "turf and track," and as we have stated before, we will not prove recreant to the trust. In the first place we will present the objections to his present line of conduct, and then refer to the past, which is still further back, for the reasons why we have undertaken the unpleasant task, and why we demand that he shall be ousted from a position he does not fill as the incumbent of the place should.

In previous articles the manner in which he performed the duties of presiding judge has been duly commented upon. An appeal was taken from a decision given by him, and another decision so palpably wrong that the Chairman of the Board, N. T. Smith, felt it to be his duty to review it, and without a direct appeal called a session of the board to take testimony and pass upon them. This was done under the authority which the rules give, and this prompt action met with unanimous, and hearty approbation from every one, and the meeting was held last Monday.

A man in the same situation as Mr. Shafter, and who was at all sensitive about placing himself above just criticism, would have declined to act when former decisions were impugned and appeals taken.

The by-laws of the National Trotting Association expressly forbid a person who has sat and taken part in a District Board from voting when it comes before the Board of Review, and it certainly is as bad when a man makes a decision in the judges' stand and then takes part in a court, as one of the court, when it is acted upon for concurrence or reversal. Mr. Shafter not only did that but he took upon himself to be both judge and counsel, arbitrator and advocate, and availing himself of the license of a retained barrister, argued from the standpoint of clientage. And when rebuked in the latter character sought shelter beneath the ermine of judicial functions.

It was provoking though ludicrous, and the double part he was playing a source of surprise to those who attended. It was a repetition of "the form" he displayed in the stand, his evident aim being to guard one of the cases that was postponed until next Monday. Arbitrary, dogmatic, consequential, he sought to shape things to his own views, and asked question after question in relation to matters that had not the least bearing on the subject at issue. It was only necessary to contrast the behavior of the associate members of the board to obtain a striking exemplification of the difference between a judge who desires to obtain evidence bearing on both sides and one who is still more determined to twist and quibble.

The report of the Board, which will be found on the opposite page, came to this office Tuesday between 11 a.

m. and 12 m. It was in the writing of Mr. Shafter, sent for publication and signed by both members of the Board. The decision in the case of Antevolo was not correctly reported. That decision 'was that the protest was not sustained while the writing stated that "the decision of the judges in the case of Antevolo was affirmed." The decision of the judges was that all were protested, and all should start," leaving the settlement of the dispute to a future time, and to a higher court. Noticing this discrepancy we called upon Mr. Smith at his office and he made the interlineation which is in accordance with the facts. There could only be one purpose in using that language, and that to influence the cases undetermined. The next point on trial was the awarding of the third heat to Bonnie, when Fred Arnold came to the score first, the only charge being loud shouting. That of Dawn would have been given priority, but Mr. Whitney solicited time to obtain affidavits, and that morning having received a letter from L. U. Shippee requesting us to look after his interests, we asked that if time were given to Mr. Whitney the other should be postponed also. The only thing necessary in the case of the "Sister to Honesty" was an affidavit from her breeder, that the filly that trotted was the daughter of "Priam by Whipple's Hambletonian and Western Girl by Chieftain." The other clause in the protest had nothing to do with the case at all.

In the case of the three-year-old Embyro the ruling is correctly given and was all that could be done under the circumstances. The only power which the District Board has to correct it used, but the injustice of the judges could only be partially remedied. That Bonnie could win one heat easily is beyond question. That she won another, not quite so easily, was also apparent. The third heat she lost and there was a probability that the fourth on the same afternoon would go against her. Continued until the next day there might be "sorceress," or from her characteristics she might be "sour" and not disposed to trot. After an interval of four weeks she has only a first heat to win. That Mr. Shafter concurred in the reversal of his own decision is absolute proof of his unfitness for a place where his decision can work so much injustice. This is not the first instance of his obstinately "sticking" to a wrong ruling. At Petaluma three years ago he decided that Santa Claus was not entitled to a part of the entrance money for a "walk-over," adhered to it during the fair, and when on the boat coming home acknowledged in presence of Mr. Finigan and another that he was wrong. The agreeing with his associates may be offered to prove his candor in acknowledging his error when convinced. Should this view be accepted there must be an admission of imbecility, a lack of intelligence entirely at variance with the functions of a judge. There is little satisfaction in the admission of a wrong when the injury is beyond repair, though there may be cases in which confession will bring absolution. But after such an atonement, it can scarcely be expected that the parties who have suffered will put themselves in the way of injury from the same quarter. If a boy handles a gun so carelessly that he is unmitiment danger to others he is deprived of the arm. Should his incompetency result in wounding another there will be a closer surveillance.

There is a mass of verbiage in the report which may mislead those who merely glance at the rulings. That there was a proper appeal taken from the decision of the judges in the case of Dawn is beyond question. Mr. Williams made a verbal protest, and we wrote another and left it in the hands of the secretary to file should the decision be that Dawn could start. This Mr. Harris testified to, and as further proof that an appeal had been properly taken, a demand was made for the fee of $10, and the money accepted. But there is no necessity for occupying time as any person who will take the trouble to read Rule 16 will see. Rule 16 is quoted to sustain the queer decision that "the protestant should follow up an adverse decision by appeal." The word appeal is not found in Rule 16, protest being the term, and in this case synonymous. The "protest," written, was left in the hands of the secretary to file in case of an adverse decision to the verbal protest entered by John Williams; the secretary swore that such were his instructions, and that he followed them. No one questioned the right of the Board "to proceed as of original jurisdiction to inquire into any decision," and under this the three-year-old race was adjudicated. No appeal was taken in that case, Mr. Hinds declining to do so, thinking that it would require a long time to bring it to trial, and that the colt might be out of his hands long before a decision was reached. The promptness with which the chairman acted was not foreseen, and Mr. Hinds, being under the impression that it would have to go before the Board of Review, owing to the vacancy in the District Board, felt that he could not lie out of the money for, perhaps, a year or two.

The last paragraph commencing "we find as fact" has not a single fact to sustain it, and we feel confident that

Captain Smith did not understand that paragraph when he affixed his signature.

The Embryo Stakes have always had an organization behind them. In those for foals of 1879 and 1880 the organization was Joseph Cairn Simpson Chairman, A. P. Whitney Treasurer; and Ben E. Harris Secretary.

The only one turned over to the Pacific Breeders' Association (not the "Breeder Association") was that for foals of 1881, of which Jas. McM. Shafter was President, and A. P. Whitney Vice-President, and N. T. Smith Treasurer. The license was taken in the name of the Embryo Stakes in order to cover all three of the races, and the judges were the same all through excepting that A. P. Whitney took John Howes' place after the yearling race was decided. There is not one-half of the members of the National Association having a better organization, neither is an organization necessary to obtain membership, and the question of jurisdiction was a quibble raised by the "learned counsel" to embarrass the proceedings. We stated then that not one of the parties interested could afford to avail themselves of such a quibble, and no one did, even after the "member" of District Board No. 5 suggested the idea. The license granted by the National Association embraced all the Embryo Stakes to be decided this year, and all come under its protection.

Now if we understand the money part right—and we think we do—nominating fees, declarations, forfeits and stakes have been collected by the secretary, Ben E. Harris, and turned over to the treasurer, N. T. Smith, in the yearling race. That belonging to the two and three-year-old Mr. Whitney was the custodian of, and neither the funds nor the control of these races could be transferred to any one else. We have not the least doubt that such funds have been placed in the custody of Mr. Whitney, and no one will question the integrity or responsibility of either of the treasurers.

This is as far as there is the least necessity for arguments at present, so far as relates to the report. That report is presented as nearly in accordance with the copy as compositors and proofreader could accomplish. It is a literal transcript, and though there may be an excess of periods, the instructions were to follow the MS. as closely as possible.

Having occupied more space than can well be given at this time, other facts bearing on the incompatibility of Mr. Shafter are withheld. We sincerely hope that it will be unnecessary to give them more publicity than already is warranted. Yet we feel that as the editor of a paper established to protect the interests threatened it is an imperative duty, and one we cannot shirk, to demand for this good of the breeding, turf and track interests of the Pacific coast that the position Mr. Shafter occupies be filled by another, trusting that he will be convinced from nearly unanimous and overwhelming public opinion that he is not the "right man in the right place," and resign his membership in District Board No. 5. His peculiar temperament unfits him for that, or to be placed in the judges' stand, regardless of other and weightier considerations, and this is the verdict of every one who have heard speak in relation to the subject.

Prone to favor those from whom he expects favors, perverse to the verge of malignity to those he dislikes; arrogant, domineering, insulting to those who differ with Him in opinion, he has brought trouble into every association he has been connected with, and these palpable and universally accredited characteristics cannot be overcome by either social, financial or "political" standing, and this handicap to the trotting interests of the coast imposes a burden which cannot be borne.

## CHRISTMAS NUMBER SPIRIT OF THE NEW YORK TIMES.

Our spirited and enterprising contemporary under the above title is following its annual custom of publishing a Christmas number that will excel even its former efforts in that line. Acting on the principle that there must be an occasional relief from the usual themes and topics that are its distinguishing features, the best talent is employed in distinct branches of the literary professions, and a story by the great Wilkie Collins, an essay by Edmund Yates are among the offerings. The ranks of the old nobility are drawn upon, and Lady Violet Greville contributes the history of "Lord Carlton's Debt," while Dion Boucicault, George R. Sims, and others of great celebrity, complete the force. Any person who has the least taste for literary work "cannot afford" to miss purchasing the Christmas number of the "Spirit."

## HADDINGTON FOR SALE.

This well-bred horse is offered for sale and from his form and performances it is reasonable to expect that he will be successful in the stud. We have always regarded his sire, imported Haddington, as one of the finest bred horses ever brought here from England, and some of his blood will be an addition to any stud. The Norfolk strain gives additional value, and there is also a combination which has proved good on the trotting tracks.

## THE OCCIDENT CUP AND STANFORD STAKES.

The advertisement for the Occident Stake will be und in the appropriate column, and we feel confident hat it will receive a hearty support from the breeders of he Pacific Coast.

The importance of keeping up trotting colt stakes is ecoming more apparent every season, and there is not question that before many years they will be the rowning glory of the tracks. That there should be occasional failures is to be expected, but for all that, the aces in some instances do not come up to previous anicipations; the failures will decrease as the years roll round. There is a grand outlook for the youngsters of he sunny slope. There is not a State in the Union that n present such an array of trotting sires, not one of ie older commonwealths which can display a superiory in trotting dams. Outside of Palo Alto, with lectioneer, Whipple's Hambletonian, General Benton d Piedmont in the boxes, and the fields and paddocks utaining hundreds of the highest bred mares and foals the world, there are other large establishments at ell stocked, excepting in numbers, and scores of small eeders who are not afraid to meet the "big guns''; in tual warfare. Look at the array: Echo, Elmo, A. . Richmond, Buccaneer, Sultan, Brigadier, Abbotsford, Algona, Nephew, Arthurton, Steinway, Priam, Del Sur, Gibraltar, Albert W, Romero and Director, the get of Nutwood, Santa Claus, and many others which could be added the list. Is there anything "rash" in the prediction that in future years there will be an abundance of nominations, plenty of starters.

These two stakes are gotten up on the correct principle, and we hope that after this year all will follow the plan. In racing the practice has been to give the nominator or subscriber until the time the race took place, or at a previous date, named in the conditions, the right to enter without the payment of any sum. Followed in trotting stakes it has led to confusion and misunderstanding. The complicated conditions of the Embryo has been peculiarly prolific of entanglements. People engaged in racing are acquainted with what is required, the comparatively recent adoption of trotting stakes has prevented a complete understanding and numerous disagreeable features have sprung from the lack of knowledge. Thus a man who paid his forfeits in the two-year-old Embryo of last year considered that the payment absolved him from future engagements, notwithstanding that he had also entered for the three-year-old. It would take pages of this paper to describe the misunderstandings which have arisen, but in both the Occident and Stanford there is no chance for disagreement. In the former, $25 must accompany the nomination, in the latter $100. In the Occident if another $25 is not posted on the first of January the first payment is forfeited, and in the Stanford $100 has to go up on the same date to secure a continuation of the chances to contend. Ninety days before the time fixed for the race $50 more in the Occident, $100 in the Stanford, and at that time it can be definitely stated just how much money will be the reward of first, second and third. The Occident is under the control of the State Agricultural Society, and when the advertisement of the Stanford is published there will be a full account of the conditions. In this connection it may be as well to state that the second payment in the Stanford Stake, which closed on the first of January last, will be due and must be paid on or before the first of January, 1883, to N. T. Smith, Treasurer.

Next week we will publish a list of the nominations in that Stake so that the subscribers can be prepared. The second payment in the Occident is also due at the same date, Edwin F. Smith, Secretary of the State Agricultural Society, being the party to address. We have strayed away from the subject, though the digression was applicable, and return to the Stakes which close this year. Notwithstanding the phenomenal performances which were the great feature of 1881, we are of the opinion that the yearlings of 1882 are superior as a lot. There are very many which are well worthy of being named in the Stakes, and engagement will double their value.

We confidently anticipate a long list of names in both of these stakes.

## CLOSE OF THE FALL RACE MEETING.

The Fall Meeting of the Pacific Coast Blood Horse Association came to a conclusion Saturday. That it was successful is conceded by every one who attended, and another bright chapter can be added to those that have preceded it. We have witnessed many race meetings and can safely say that in the whole range of twenty-five years experience those of this association have given the most satisfaction to the public. The confidence now so firmly established will sustain the future, and with the advent of "better times" the financial success will be such as to warrant more money in purses, larger additions to stakes.

The whole object of this association is the advancement of the breeding and racing interests, and every dollar beyond expenses will be expended to further these interests. The only salary is to be to the person who performs the duties of Secretary, and that is only a reasonable compensation for the work done.

We have alluded before to the labor performed by the President, Theo. Winters, but desire to emphasize it more directly. He has added a large amount of money to stakes, though the loss of time and the traveling expenses would aggregate a much larger sum. If necessary he would leave his business, however urgent, and come from his home in Carson Valley to attend the meeting of the Board of Trustees, and at the race meetings none were more active, and his judgment never at fault regarding the best course to pursue. It is rare good fortune to the association that owing to the excitement of election day, the annual meeting was allowed to lapse, so that his services are secured for another year. Had an election been held he would have insisted on being released and no matter how good a man was chosen, in the present state of affairs it would have been detrimental to the interest of the society.

Again we must repeat the encomiums heretofore given to Messrs. P. A. Finigan and Henry Schwartz. Their locality necessarily throws a great deal of work on them, and this was performed so thoroughly, freely, unselfishly that the labor was underrated by those who are not versed in the amount of work a race meeting necessitates. We have been so very busy that it was out of the question to do any part of the work, and the duties of Trustee were also neglected. The gentleman, O. M. Chase, who has filled the place has done so in an eminently satisfactory manner, and not a solitary grumbler has found fault although the working members of the P. C. B. H. A. are worthy of high praise.

## PRECIOUS.

We feel sure that another bright luminary has surmounted the horizon, and that the filly which won the Baldwin Stake, no mishaps befalling, will figure conspicuously in the annals of the sport. She has the "right to be a good one." By Lever by Lexington, his dam Levity by imported Trustee, grandam the dam of Vandal by imported Tranby, and running into the same family maternally as Lexington, what could be better? Then her dam was a daughter of Thunder, a son of Lexington and Blue Bonnet, and the next dam was imported Siskin by Muscovite, and her dam Little Finch by Hornsea, and then comes Hinda by Sultan. Muscovite was by Hetman Platoff from a Camel mare, and her dam Lady Elizabeth by Lottery.

The pedigree is a "cracker" and accounts for the manner in which Precious ran through the heavy mud, and came to the finish with ears "pricked." While admitting the high excellence of the game little mare we must not lose sight of the part her trainer, Henry Walsh, played in the fight. That he has not a superior in the profession has long been our belief, and when a distance of ground has to be measured we doubt if he has an equal, although there are others of recognized ability, and of as high rank as those in the East.

To successfully prepare a horse for a four-mile race requires a blending of the old and new schools, and those which commenced their education in the old and completed in the new are the most likely to excel. Matt Allen, Piggott, De Feyster, Albert and several others are well worthy of more than a passing notice.

## OUR SANDWICH ISLAND CORRESPONDENT.

We are much gratified to number among our corps of correspondents George W. Stewart, who will, our readers, duly portend on what is going on in the sporting line in the "islands." Mr. Stewart is a thorough journalist, and his communications will be read with great attention.

## LEX ON THE BOARD OF APPEALS.

The argument of our esteemed correspondent Lex, regarding the Status of the Board of Appeals, is beyond question correct. We never disagreed with him on this point, and in the curt indorsement our intention was not to take opposite grounds to Lex on that point. The application of the clause he mentions is the only difference between us, and the meaning of the clause (after February 1860 this provision will not include the privilege of the judges' stand) is the only point at issue. This we construe that members of the Board of Appeals cannot claim the right, formerly granted, to occupy the stand in company with the elected judges, but when a member has been selected to fill the position of Judge the rules do not forbid him doing so. There is a manifest impropriety, in doing so, especially if the member is in his own district, and if he acts as such no fairminded man would afterwards take part in the District Board when appeals were taken from his decisions as judge of a race. The prohibition by a definite rule will be a wise provision, and when the next biennial meeting is held we will endeavor to have it adopted.

Upon hearing of objections to the rulings and decision of the judges of the race for the Embryo Stakes trotted at Oakland, Nov. 13th 1882, and testimony relative thereto, the said Board have arrived at the following conclusions:

The decision of said judges. as to the protest against Antevolo affirmed [to wit the protest against Antevolo is not sustained.]

The decision made in the three year old race. that Bonnie won the third heat and race is reversed. the said heat assigned to Frank Arnold, Bonnie second. Anteo third, and said Race is ordered to be concluded, on Saturday December 9th.

We think further that judges in said race should have fined both the drivers of Arnold and Anteo for improper noise but this duty having been neglected this Board does not in this instance inflict the penalty.

All other questions are adjourned until Monday Dec 4— 1882.

The judges as to the reversed ruling seem to have proceeded upon the ground that shouting and improper noise, constitutes foul driving within rule 46. We think by bring the case within the principle of the rules that the offence should have been one which affected some other horse which in this case did not occur.

Rules 47. 8. relate principally to the punishment of the driver. but the closing paragraph relates to the placing of the horse The judges seem to have affixed a mitigated penalty instead of the second one of distancing, for foul driving. We think still further that there are no appeals in either of these cases. a protest is simply to prevent an act to be done. an objection which the objector is at liberty to follow up or abandon at pleasure subject to rule 16. The protestant should follow up an adverse decision by appeal.

We likewise are of opinion that this Board has the right to proceed as of original jurisdiction to enquire into any declation at any race made under the rule of the National Association upon any information properly influencing their discretion. and have in these cases assumed such jurisdiction.

We find as fact. that the so called Embryo Stakes. has a very imperfect if any organization and that after many subscriptions had been obtained. said subscriptions were turned over to the Breeder association. to take further subscriptions and collect stakes and that it was this last association under which said races were held. The only license under which such races were trotted. was to the Embryo Association. We regret that our jurisdiction should be put in doubt. by this uncertainty as to whether we are acting pursuant to the authority of the National Association. The remaining questions will be disposed of as above indicated.

N. T. SMITH, President.
J.McM SHAFTER Member*

* The words inclosed in the brackets were interlined by Mr. Smith after Judge Shafter had written and signed the foregoing report.—ED. BREEDER AND SPORTSMAN.

# THE KENNEL.

The Dominion of Canada Kennel Club are making arrangements for a bench show, to be held at Ottawa this coming winter during the session of the Canadian Parliament. They have secured the services of Mr. Charles Lincoln, whose success in managing the details of bench shows is too well known to need further mention. Arrangements are being made to secure a large entry of dogs from England. One of the board of directors, a gentleman who is thoroughly conversant among the sportsmen of Great Britain, will attend all the leading shows in that country in the interests of the club. In addition to the exhibit of dogs, the club desire to make a full exibit of all kinds of sportsman's materials, and to that end will shortly issue a circular addressed to the manufacturers of such goods in the United States. They propose to attend to the customs duties upon all goods shipped them, place them in charge of competent men to exibit and sell, if possible, making returns free of commission, and shipping back unsold goods in good order. As the residents of the Dominion depend largely upon American firms for their supply of guns and other material, and as they have no firms engaged in that branch of business, this scheme should meet with favor from our manufacturers. It will also tend to promote the harmony that already exists between the sportsmen of the two countries. The club will offer between $1,500 and $2,000 in premiums, and confidently expect a fine exhibit of dogs, and a large attendance of representative men from all parts of the Dominion. Some of our California coursing men should exhibit greyhounds. They would surely be prize winners.

ENGLISH COURSING.—The South Lancashire Open Meeting for coursing was held October 17, and opened with the South Lancashire Derby, for dog puppies of 1881, with thirty-five starters. The stake was divided between Mr. T. D. Hornsby's Hesketh Bank (Meols Boy—Helen Stanley). Mr. J. Blackburn's Boundaway (Achilles—Bounceaway) and Mr. G. Foxcroft's Joykin (Banker—Miss Hawtins). The South Lancashire Oaks, for bitch puppies of 1881, had thirty-one starters, and was won by Mr. A. Myers' Mendicant (Hardy—Minx). The Scarisbrick Cup, for all ages, had thirty-two starters, and was divided between Mr. F. Skinner's Sheffield Steel (Master Sam—Thropham) and Mr. J. Smith's Stormer (Blusher—Gaudy Mary). The Crossens Stakes, for all ages, had thirty-two starters, and was won by Mr. R. V. Mather's Meols Diamond (King of Diamonds—Sal o' the Mill). The Coniculation Stakes, limited to eight dogs of all ages, was divided between Mr. R. B. Walker's Wright (Master Banrigh—Kennel-ale) and Mr. T. Graham's Glenakiri (Misterton—Annie McPiernon). At the Tamworth Open Meeting, held October 18 and 19, the Drayton Manor Stakes, for fifteen dogs of all ages, was won by Mr. R. P. Heatley's Rylan Prince (Highlander—Grace Cup); the Tweedale Stakes, for five dog puppies, was won by Mr. J. Bonnett's Benedict (Hylactor—Lady Annie); the Tamworth Stakes, for seven bitch puppies, was won by Mr. Byrne's Why! Dark Laura (Misterton—Helena); and the Bonehill Paddock Stakes, for eleven dogs of all ages, was divided between Mr. J. Parker's Worcester (Sir Arthur—) and Mr. G. Ainge's Bagman (Recorder—Pulborough I.

# HERD AND SWINE.

## Holstein Milk Records.

Notwithstanding the fact that we, as well as other breeders of the Holstein cattle, have frequently published the yearly milk record of our entire milking herd, yet we almost daily get inquiries in substance as follows: What amount of milk can a choice, well-selected, nice-bred herd of Holstein-cows be expected to average, etc.? This is not an easy question to answer definitely, as Holsteins, like all other breeds, vary more or less according to selection, breeding, family, etc. Certain families are more uniformly deep milkers and hold out better. Blood will tell in the dairy cow as well as in the race horse. This fact does not seem to be fully appreciated by dairymen generally. When this fact is more fully appreciated by dairymen in making selections, they will meet with more uniformly good success. We have in our herd this season nine three-year-old heifers (which include all the milking heifers of that age in our herd) which were all (except one which we bred) selected by us in Holland from dams with deep records and of the best breeding. The result we think fully justifies our belief that breeding is fully as essential in dairy cows as in any other class of stock. Most of them were imported in the fall as yearlings and dropped their first calves soon after coming out of quarantine, before some of them were two years old. As two-year-olds, although not acclimated, they milked remarkably, the highest record reaching 10,600 lbs. 13 oz. within the year. They all dropped their second calves during the last part of the past winter and spring, when nearly half of them were not yet three years old. The highest daily yield for the respective animals varies from 49 lbs. 4 oz. to 60 lbs., the highest daily average being 54 lbs. 12½ oz. The best month's record for each varied from 1,307 lbs. 11 oz. (one that was out of condition) to 1,733 lbs. 10 oz. Over half the number exceeded 1,500 lbs. in a month, the highest average being 1,561 lbs. 3 oz. Two of the number have not quite completed a six months' record, but the smallest milker for that time will go a little over 6,600 lbs., and the largest has made 8,703 lbs. 7 oz.; and the average will be, for the whole number, for the six months, a little over 7,500 lbs. Seven of these heifers we tested for butter late in the winter and early spring, on winter feed (the other counting in after our creamery was in full coo admit of trial of single animals). The lightest yield per week was 11 lbs. 8 oz. and the highest 14 lbs. 11½ oz., the average for the lot being 12 lbs. 12 oz. The butter was weighed after thorough working and before salting. These heifers were given only one trial of a week each, and two only one churning of four days; but we give the exact rate per week. Had we been able to give repeated tests, and had we fed for better instead of milk, we think some of these butter records might have been increased. It should be borne in mind that these butter records were all made on winter feed, also that the above milk records include every milking three-year-old in our herd. Three of the lot are of the Netherland family.—*Smith & Powell in the Breeders Gazette.*

## Changing Breeds.

It is not always good policy for the novice to start with too many breeds in the beginning. One may keep sitters and non sitters at the same time but will he becomes thoroughly posted in the cultivation of pure bred poultry two breeds at one time are enough. Too often we see young fanciers indulge in the habit of changing the breeds of their first choice for others before they have fairly tasted their qualities and quit them for something else no better, perhaps not so valuable, with nothing to guide or prompt them except the words of interested breeders who claim for their fowls transcendent merits, if they are to be believed.

Now, whatever may be said or written about pure bred fowls the majority of amateurs will have a first choice either in contemplation or in the beginning as they start out. Some will choose fowls of a certain color of plumage, because it suits their fancy or taste; others will have nothing but pure white or black plumaged birds, and many prefer variegated colors or tints in preference to all others.

We frequently see those whose tastes run to size or distinctiveness, and others to grotesque appearance or oddities. Taste is capricious with some, and in others it is permanent and unyielding. We are not willing to blame poultrymen for diversity of taste, when the example is set us by Dame Nature, who gives us such diversified beauty in the objects of the feathery creation. But the object of our suggestion as we set out is to advise young poultrymen to avoid the see-saw habit of changing breeds for some trivial reason, and to urge them not to keep a half-dozen or more varieties about them at the same time until they have thoroughly mastered the necessary knowledge and experience of keeping poultry in separate flocks.—*Poultry Monthly.*

## The Traveling Dairy.

It is refreshing to read of the journeys and lectures of a traveling educational dairy through parts of Ireland, inculcating districts from which we have had horrifying accounts of boycotting and butchery. The staff consisted of a lecturer (an Englishman) an Irish dairyman, John, in neat white jacket, and his wife, Ellen, in a dainty holland dress, both well girted with brogue and bright in looks. They were aided at times by "pretty Maggie Doyle," a deft handler of the pats of butter, which were made large or small in proportion to the demand and sold at the rate of two shillings per pound. The churn and other utensils were, of course, of the most approved pattern, and each day about sixteen gallons of cream were worked to morning and evening, the lecturer explaining the reasons for each step, and especially for the divergencies from old customs. Cleanliness and system were the foundation rules. A very interesting part of the proceedings everywhere was the conversation allowed after the lecture, and curious were many of the questions asked. The explanations and practical illustrations seemed to be well appreciated and observed with intelligent interest. The dairy was invited to many different places by some of the large landlords.—*New York Tribune.*

In the last fourteen years the number of sheep in Iowa has shrunk from 1,354,600 to 435,500 a loss of 67 per cent. Lack of proper shelter and food in winter, of fences to enable farmers to keep small flocks, and the ravages of the wolf and his congeners, the ubiquitous dog, are the chief causes of the decline of the most important branches of farming.

The Shorthorn herd owned and lately sold by Earl Beauchamp, Madresfield Court, Malvern, were noteworthy dairy stock. At a show a pair of cows gave twenty-three quarts before the judges. At the sale ninety-six animals averaged $168, which was considered very satisfactory.

In fat animals seventy-five to eighty-five per cent. of the total ash constituents are found in the bones.

## The Meat Supply.

The alarming discovery that the meat supply of the Pacific coast is failing, so much so that at least one San Francisco slaughtering firm is about importing cattle by the car-load from Chicago, is attracting attention to the subject of improvement in the breeds of cattle. The rapid appropriation for grain-growing of the vast ranges which have been devoted to cattle-raising on this coast, together with the natural and steady increase of manufactures and the consequent demand for food for operatives, may be set down as the principal causes for this shortage in meat. The shortage is not owing to any season of drouth, nor to any disease having swept off our stock, but to the above causes, and therefore cannot be treated as a temporary affair likely to disappear in a year or two. We may as well look the fact in the face that the meat shortage is a condition of affairs that has come to stay. As a result prices of meat will be higher; following this there will be a reduction in the per cent. of meat to vegetable foods consumed. The food of this coast has hitherto been more largely animal than of any other part of the Union. Probably one-third more beef and mutton per head of population is eaten in California than in Massachusetts. The tendency of density of population is toward vegetarianism in diet. And in proportion as meat becomes less a principal article of diet and more a semi-luxury, the demand for the best quality increases. *The North Pacific Rural Spirit* says:

There is not a civilized country under the sun that is not manifesting a deep interest in the question of meat supply. This is not unnatural, but on the other hand is in perfect keeping with a wise and comprehensive view of domestic economy. The progress of civilization is much more rapid than the unthinking people imagine. The progress, too, is in more ways than one, and each line of advancement, it may be said, tends to effect the same thing, and so effecting, necessarily tends to produce the same results. The world is fast being peopled and in consequence of this the public domain is rapidly becoming occupied. This lessens cheap supply, because as the public domain becomes settled, lands are enhanced in value. This cuts off the cheap herd system of live stock production. Lands that have for many years produced but one common beef animal to each four or five acres, are now worth $10 an acre to grow wheat and other productions upon. As a consequence the cheap meat supply is curtailed, and so supply the demand is better word, however, is necessity), meat must be grown that costs much more, and so much more that the general consumer is becoming alarmed, while, as a consequence, the wise producers are inquiring how they can best grow the supply. Civilization, however, is changing from a lower to a higher grade. The ways and customs of our forefathers are things of the past. A better article is required, and this applies as much to establish as wearing apparel, or vehicles or implements or to the houses that we live in, or to the furniture that fits them up. The scrub, grass-fed animals may be used for a while yet, but no longer than the demand lasts for canned meats for the poorer classes. The butcher's block cannot be supplied with meat that presents the trade mark of domestic feeding. The writer of this article becomes more than ordinarily interested when discussing this subject, for he is a witness as to what was but a few years ago thought to be an everlasting range [here in the West. Two-thirds of the Willamette valley was covered with the best natural grass ever looked upon, while from the Missouri river to the Cascade range of mountains was one great and grand pasture. It is either fenced up now and the land producing wheat or it is grazed off to the extent that we must admit that the range will last but a few years longer. The story is not half told. Greely's words "go West" are about to be fulfilled. This country is to be peopled not with pioneers from the West, but from the older countries and states, where for years they have been accustomed to beef that was produced by a wise system of feeding in place of beef taken from the range and slaughtered whether fat or lean. With these facts before us we do not admit that the question is one of very great importance. By another year the cattle men, not the present kind of cattle men exactly, but butchers, will be coming into Idaho and Eastern Oregon by the way of the Short Line Railroad, while the same cattle will be coming into Western Montana, Eastern Washington and Oregon by way of the Northern Pacific Railroad. These men will want beef cattle; beef that will do well for the Eastern cities without having first to be taken East and stall-fed. But then we must bear in mind that with these buyers will come immigration that will want breeding stock, and the people will want improved breeds and no others; if we have them, they will buy it but not, they will import them. At this point we would ask our breeders to stick a peg, for this state of affairs is calculated to operate to advantage if we have the quality of stock, for in this case the new comers can be supplied with breeding stock, while we will be prepared to furnish such beef as will suit the demand of those that will eat but the best. But suppose we have no breeding stock to sell to the new comers, and they are compelled to import breeding stock, they will, before our breeders can change off the scrubs for a better class, become the suppliers to the markets that many here are now expecting to supply. We are almost ashamed to urge the adoption of a course that is so plain. There are but three ways of improving stock, namely: by breeding the best, feeding and care. The improvement of meat animals is not so much of an undertaking as the improvement of homes. Good blooded males in the line of cattle, sheep and hogs can be purchased cheaper than stallions, and they are used for propagation in earlier ages. These advantages make their introduction cheaper than the introduction of homes. Then, again, the care of stallions is much more than is required of other breeding males.

**Overfed Pigs.**—The *Irish Farmers' Gazette* says: When young pigs are sick it may be pretty certainly understood that they have been overfed. The general treatment of pigs seems to be based upon the idea that they are naturally greedy and gluttonous animals, and that this habit should be encouraged as much as possible. Hence all the diseases which so frequently affect pigs. When a young pig is a tender animal, his stomach is not much larger than that of a human infant about as old, and yet people will cram the little creature with sour slop, grease, milk and corn meal until it can swallow no more. And when the pig is sick one wonders what is the matter. We do not feed lambs or calves, or colts, in that fashion, hence these are rarely diseased. Cough and difficulty of breathing is caused by indigestion, and the common disease of which partial paralysis of the hind parts is the chief symptom, and which is cerebrospinal meningitis, is caused by indigestion and mal nutrition, which cause disturbance of the circulation and congestion of the brain and spinal marrow, with loss of nervous power. The treatment is to give a dose of salts and one scruple of saltpeter daily afterwards, and feed very sparingly.

A tax of five shillings per head of cattle is imposed on the stockmen in Melbourne, Australia. They naturally seek the repeal of the oppressive law.

## Why the Difference.

"Well, Mr. Smith, I am out this morning to see if I can find a few fine beef steers. I heard you had some that you desired to dispose of."

"Yes, sir; I have ten or twelve, and they are what I call much above the average. They are three, four and five-year-olds in good condition, and I believe they will pull down 1,000 pounds each."

"Mr. Smith, what would you think if I were to tell you that I had just bought and paid for ten head of nice yearlings and two-year-olds that average 1,200 pounds?"

"Well, sir, I would travel some distance to see such a lot."

"Well, come along with me, it will not take us over an hour and a half to reach the spot."

"Are you in earnest? Have you cattle that will average 1,200 pounds, they being yearlings and two-year-old?"

"Certainly I have. Here are the weights":

| | lbs |
|---|---|
| 4 yearling steers | 4,800 lbs |
| 4 two-year-old steers | 4,000 lbs |
| 4 two-year-old steers | 4,000 lbs |
| | |
| Total | 11,600 lbs |

"What kind of cattle are they, my friend?"

"They are three-quarter Durhams."

"Well, what are such cattle worth?"

"I paid $7 50 per hundred for them."

"Do you want to see mine?"

"Yes, I will look at them. What breed are they, Mr. Smith?"

"I don't know sir. They are from cattle we have had in the family ever since I can remember."

"Good morning, Mr. Smith."

"Don't you want to buy them?"

"At what price?"

"Why, $7 50 of course; that's what you said you pay?"

"Mr. Smith, look here. I have the latest—the very latest—Chicago prices current, which reads, 'Choice to fancy, $8 25.' That is the kind I have bought. Your stock comes under the head of 'Lower quality or common steers,' and you see they are quoted at '$3 70@$4 00.'"

The above is one way of presenting a reality. Any breeder of stock who will take pains to read the Eastern market reports will see that there is just the difference between inferior to common steers and choice steers as cited above; and yet hundreds of people go right on raising the common stock.—*Exchange.*

## Berkshire Standard of Excellence.

In a note to the *Breeders' Gazette* "J. L. H." says: "To settle a dispute please publish a scale of points by which to judge Berkshire hogs—how many points, where located on the hog, and how to proceed to judge by points. What form should a hog have to be a perfect Berkshire? I contend there is a standard scale."

In reply that paper prints the following:

In Vol. II of the "American Berkshire Record" will be found the following standard of excellence and scale of points adopted by the American Berkshire Association:

| | |
|---|---|
| Color—Black, with white feet, face, tip of tail, and an occasional splash on the arms | 4 |
| Face and snout—Short; the former fine and well dished, and broad between the eyes | 5 |
| Eye—Very clear, rather large, dark hazel or grey | 4 |
| Ear—Generally almost erect, but sometimes inclined forward with a sharp point; small; thin, soft and fine and soft | 4 |
| Jowl—Full and heavy, running well back on the neck | 4 |
| Neck—Short, and broad on top | 4 |
| Hair—Fine and not soft, medium thickness | 5 |
| Skin—Smooth and pliable | 4 |
| Shoulder—Thick and even, broad on top, and thick through the back | 6 |
| Back—Broad, short and straight; ribs well sprung, coupling close up | 8 |
| Side—Deep, and well let down; straight on bottom line | 5 |
| Ham—Well back, and low down on leg, making nearly a straight line with the lower part of side | 8 |
| Loin—Full and wide | 5 |
| Hams—Deep and thick, extending well up on the back, and holding thickness well down to the hock | 10 |
| Legs—Short, straight and strong, set wide apart, with bone, and flesh well proportioned throughout; and broad, coupling close | 6 |
| Symmetry—Proportions throughout good, adapting largely on condition | 6 |
| Condition—In a good healthy growing state, but over-fed | 5 |
| Style—Attractive, spirited, indicative of thorough breeding and constitutional vigor | 5 |
| | 100 |

## Imported Cattle.

The steamship Greece of the National line, which arrived on Saturday evening brought a large consignment of thoroughbred stock, the property of Mr. T. S. Cooper of Coopersburg, Pa., consisting of ninety-eight head of Jersey cattle, thirty-six Oxfordshire down sheep and some Berkshire pigs. Considering the rough passage the stock arrived in excellent condition and there was not a single casualty to report. Mr. Cooper is well known in connection with the Jersey favor, and at the sale of his stock held at the Amazon Horse Exchange on the 4th of last month the bull Sir George was sold for $5,100, while thirty-five of the prized Coomassie strain averaged $910 each. The present consignment of cattle was purchased prior to the news of that sale having reached the Channel Islands, but yet so great has been the demand for choice stock that Mr. Cooper had to give large sums for the more valuable animals. One of the cows, Khedive's Primrose, two years old, is stated in the London *Live Stock Journal* to have cost $5,000, which is the largest sum ever paid on the island. The herdsmen was unable to give a full list of the Jerseys, but stated that nine were sired by Khedive and three by Vercunnus, both sons of Coomassie; nine by Guy Fawkes, two by Royalist and a number by Sir George, Cicero and other noted bulls. All of these belong to the three principal strains of the Coomassie family. The Jerseys will be taken to Coopersburg and there quarantined for the usual ninety days. The Oxfordshire downs were a fine lot of sheep—two rams and thirty-four ewes—and were from the noted flocks of Messrs. John Treadwell and Street. They go on to-day.

The composition of cow's milk is affected by various circumstances; under extreme conditions it may contain from ten to fifteen per cent. of dry matter. The milk is poorer when the quantity produced is large, or the diet insufficient, and richer when these conditions are reversed. A cow is generally in full milk from the second to the seventh week after calving; after this period the milk gradually diminishes in quantity, but increases in richness. A separation of cream takes place in the udder; the milk first drawn is poor in fat, the richness increasing as milking proceeds, the last drawn milk containing two or three times as much fat as the first drawn. The milk of old cows is commonly poorer than that of young ones.

## Creamery. Outfits.

Where it is only intended to handle the cream from a certain quantity of milk for butter making, the lists below will found to comprise all the articles absolutely required, with exception of the boiler required for making steam to warm cream-tempering vats in cold weather.

To handle the cream from milk of 50 cows for butter-making alone: One 100-gallon cream tempering vat; one 150-gallon revolving box churn, to run with hand or power, as desired; one factory size hand butter worker; two butter ladles; one 240-lb. Union counter scale with platform and tin scoop; one 14-quart iron clad pails; one 1-gallon dipper.

To make butter from cream of 100 cows: One 150-gallon cream tempering vat; one 200-gallon revolving box churn, to run with hand or power; one factory size hand butter worker; two butter ladles; one 240-lb. Union counter scale with platform and tin scoop; two 14-quart iron clad pails; one 1-gallon dipper.

From cream of 150 cows: One 200-gallon cream tempering vat; one 250-gallon revolving box churn; one factory size and butter worker; two butter ladles; one 240-lb. Union counter scale with platform and tin scoop; two 14-quart iron clad pails; one 1-gallon dipper.

From cream of 200 cows: Two 150-gallon cream tempering vats; one 300-gallon revolving box churn; one factory size and butter worker; two butter ladles; one 240-lb. Union counter scale with platform and tin scoop; two 14-quart iron clad tin pails; one 1-gallon dipper.

From cream of 400 cows: Two 300-gallon cream tempering vats; one 300-gallon revolving box churn, to run by power; one power butter worker; two butter ladles; one 240-lb. Union counter scale with platform and tin scoop; two 14-quart iron clad tin pails; one 1-gallon dipper.

From cream of 600 cows: Two 300-gallon cream tempering vats; two 300-gallon revolving box churns, for power; one power butter worker; two butter ladles; one 240-lb. Union counter scale, with platform and tin scoop; two 14-quart iron clad dairy pails; one 1-gallon dipper.

Cream tempering vats are made of all sizes. They are also complete cheese vats and may be used for cheese making if ever needed for that purpose. They are so constructed that cold water can be run around the tin vat in summer to cool the cream, and steam run on in cold weather to warm the cream, thus tempering it evenly and ripening it for churning as quickly as desired. It is a well established fact that cream should not be churned until slightly sour to obtain best results.—*Prairie Farmer.*

## Judging Fat Cattle.

Three classes may be supposed to have a direct interest in fat cattle—breeders and feeders, butchers and the consumers of beef. These will not have exactly the same standard. The feeder naturally prefers the animal which will make the largest return for the food eaten and the labor expended. The butcher desires the animal which will have the least waste—the greatest percentage of salable product. The consumer cares little so that he can get good beef, without an excess or deficiency of fat. The butcher may give his preference to an animal which has not been so profitable to the feeder as a somewhat coarser steer, with more offal. Admitting this difference in standard of judgment, it is still true that that there are common sense principles governing the selection of best animals. We name a few for those new in the business. We look for an animal which has made good use of a large quantity of food—consequently it mainly into good salable product. We can not dispense with head, feet, legs, tail, etc., but we want these as small as is consistent with their serving their proper purposes. Coarseness in these is also indicative of coarseness in all bones. We look for the most meat in the best places. The top half of a beef animal is worth more than the bottom; the back than the front. Heavy necks, excessive development of paunch or brisket, shoulders heavy and hind quarters light—these we all count undesirable points.

The old statement that the side view of the body of a fat steer, excluding head, neck and legs, should be as nearly as possible a parallelogram is a good one. Length is desirable, but usually the failure will be in depth rather than in length. Behind and before we should also have a near approach to a parallelogram, especially as seen from behind or at hips. It is more important that the top line should be straight than that the bottom line should be so. A well-filled flank is desirable but not so important as thickness of meat over the loins and back of the shoulders.

We may help our judgment by carefully considering the general appearance of the animal. A compact, symmetrical form, with smooth neck, short legs, well placed, good length from hip to rump, fully developed "round;" in general, broad, low, deep, well rounded body is every way preferable to the opposite qualities. Yet we may have too much of a good thing. "Pony bull" steers are not always the best. An inch or two extra length of leg may be easily counterbalanced by some more important quality.

The quality of the beef can not be certainly told while the animal is living. "Handling" quality will help us to form a correct estimate. Give a bright, healthful look, an abundant coat of soft, bright-looking hair, we want an animal with flesh evenly laid on, free from all patches or lumps of fat; a hide of medium thickness and softness, and flesh free from hardness and harshness on the one hand and from a soft, yielding, blubber-like feeling on the other.

The degree of fatness can not always be told by simply looking at the body. The rump bones well covered with fat, the scrotum broad and full, the neck well filled out, so that it is difficult to point out its line of union with the body, are indicative of a heavy coat of fat.

There are many nice points difficult to explain. Good judges may be decided in their preference for different animals. There are minor distinctions in judging males and females. There are special breed characteristics which assume undue importance to the admirers of each breed. But oftentimes the first good "all around look" at a lot of animals will enable one to give a correct judgment as to their relative merit. In acquiring this art, as in most others, long-continued practice—better if under guidance of a good teacher—is the surest means of becoming proficient. For this purpose, the Fat-Stock Show is the best school in America.—*The Breeders' Gazette.*

C. W. Garrett, Enfield, N. C., writes the Department of Agriculture that his experience with ensilage has been of a general nature. He has used pea vines chiefly, because in his early experiments he found his stock preferred them to any other material, and they were easily and cheaply produced. With the system of ensilage he claims to be feeding his stock at much less cost and trouble than ever before. His cattle perform their work and keep in much better condition than when fed on hay and fodder.

HIGH PRICED JERSEYS.—The creme-de-la-creme of imported Jersey cattle were sold as we have already announced in New York a week or two ago. It was reported by one of the papers as follows:

At the late sale of Mr. T. S. Cooper at New York city, 78 head of cattle brought an average of $634, the highest average ever attained for so many Jerseys at a public sale. Col. H. S. Russel, Home Farm, Milton, Mass., secured the bull, Sir George, winner of first prize over the Island in 1880 and 1881, at $5,100, the highest price ever made by a Jersey at public or private sale; Mabel 2d by Coffee, son of Coomassie, sold for $2,200, and goes to Home Farm. Cicero, winner of first prize on the Island in April last as a two-year-old, was sold to W. H. Wilkinson of Holyoke, Mass., for $3,100.

In animals that will sell for such prices there certainly must be some outcome, high though the prices are.—*Live Stock Journal.*

SALE OF CHOICE CATTLE.—A draft from the Hereford and Polled Angus herds of M. H. Cochran of Hillhurst, Quebec, Canada, was sold at auction at Dexter Park, Chicago, Nov. 22, and thirty-one Hereford and thirty-eight Angus were disposed of for a total of $32,960. The Herefords averaged $375, and the Angus, females $854, males $407. The Polled cattle were just out of quarantine after importation.

To ascertain the weight of cattle the following general rule will be of service to stockmen: Measure in inches the girt around the breast just behind the shoulder blade, and the length of the back from the tail to the shoulder blade. Multiply girt by length and divide by 114. If the girt is less than three feet, multiply the quotient by 11; if between three and five by 16; between five and seven by 23; between seven and nine by 31. If the animal is lean, deduct one-twentieth from the result, or take girt and length in feet, multiply square of girt by length, and multiply the product by 3.36. *Live Stock Journal.*

There is a real basis for the high prices of pedigree stock, whether sheep, cows or horses. It may seem absurd to pay $200 for a ram that weighs little more than 100 pounds; but if the progeny of this ram will shear eight to ten pounds of wool while common sheep average from five to six pounds, with the same cost of keeping, the use of the pedigree sheep as a breeder will pay heavy interest on much more than his increased price. It is not every farmer who can breed fancy stock with profit, but there is none who cannot improve his herds by the use of the best male parentage.—*Chicago Tribune.*

Stock-raising and feeding in the Northwest Territory has proved a success. In the spring of 1881 Wyld & Rourke wintered seventy-five cattle from the United States on the north side of the Saskatchewan. They were pleased with the results, and will carry as many more cattle through next winter.

# POULTRY.

## Chicken Chat.

We have been so busy getting ready for winter that we have had no time to attend to other people's business, but now that our chickens are all snug we feel like looking around and telling other people what they ought to do; so here we are again, ready to talk about poultry, answer your conundrums and make ourselves useful generally.

Let me see, Mr. Editor, didn't you say something about "seasonable suggestions?" Well, if you can find anything just now that is more seasonable than getting ready for cold weather, we would like to have you mention it. We have had a lovely, lingering fall, and the fowls have evidently appreciated it, for the early pullets have been laying this two months, the old hens have kept pretty steadily at work, and the late hatched chicks have been growing like weeds. But this pleasant weather will not last forever; one of these days, just when you get ready to quote the "oldest inhabitant," an "Arctic wave" will come along and freeze everything right up solid. So we advise the poultry keepers, who have not already prepared for cold weather, to set about the work without delay. Go right to work and make the hen house as comfortable as possible. There's no use talking—a comfortable house goes a long ways towards inducing hens to perform their duties in the egg line. You may have the finest lot of early pullets in the State, but if you compel them to roost out of doors, or in a shed where the wind, rain, snow and cold can get in without going round to the door, they won't lay one bit better than the scraggiest old hen on the premises. Mend the leaky roofs; no decent hen likes to sleep under a miniature shower bath. Mend the broken glass in the windows; and while you are about it, it would be a good plan to wash those windows—hens like to see daylight once in a while. Fasten the cracks and line the inside of the house with building paper. Air is a good thing, but no hen who has any regard for her health want to roost in front of a crack big enough to let in a small hurricane. And if the house is so situated that the wind can blow underneath, bank it up—the house, not the wind—it will add vastly to the comfort of the fowls.

Examine the perches, roosts, and likewise the fowls, and if you find lice, have a general clearing up before that Arctic wave gets along.

When your house is ready get the young fowl-stock out of the trees and put them under cover. Don't go out with a pole and beat about the trees and yell enough to raise the neighbors two miles away; but wait until it is quite dark, then take a ladder and an assistant, go quietly into the tree, secure the fowls and carry them to their quarters. If you happen to lose one don't chase it all over creation and frighten it out of a month's growth, just let it go and try again the next night. Keep the fowls in the hen house for several days, and the first time you let them out open the doors only an hour or so before sunset; in most cases every last chicken will return to the house to roost.

Look out for those late hatched chickens; if well fed and provided with a comfortable place to live in, they will grow right along, and the pullets will be ready to lay next spring, just when your early pullets are taking a rest; while the males will make first class market birds in March.

If you intend to buy any fowls to "improve" your present stock, buy now; you can buy cheaper than in the spring, and besides it is a wise plan to have the fowls together long enough to get acquainted, before the breeding season begins.

When you sell off the turkeys don't sell all the largest and keep only the small, late-hatched broods. Before you sell or kill a single turkey, select the very best for the next season's breeding stock. Sometimes it is good policy to keep the late turkeys through the winter and send them to market in March. They will grow right through the winter, and turkeys, good ones, always command a good price during the latter part of February and in March.—*Fanny Field in Prairie Farmer.*

## The Inspection of Eggs.

Many a housewife in this vicinity has expressed her surprise when purchasing fresh eggs from the market, and being in total ignorance whence they came, that they were so uniformly perfect and gave no signs of decay. The old joke of "spring chickens" in the eggs at boarding houses and hotels has also gone out of date and people now buy and eat of this favorite food with perfect confidence that it is fresh and wholesome. This state of affairs has been brought about by the custom, which has been universally adopted, of inspecting each egg separately by the dealers, and rejecting all that show the least sign of not being perfectly fresh.

There are few articles of farm produce which are so easily affected as eggs by a damp, foul atmosphere, and the extremes of heat and cold. The shell of an egg is exceedingly porous, and when the place of storage is too warm and dry the albumen evaporates, and when too cold and damp the egg seems to lose its vitality and rapidly becomes stale. The porous shell also admits of absorption, and a single rotten egg will contaminate whole dozens of eggs in the same package. The almost universal custom now is to ship eggs in cases expressly prepared for the purpose. This system of egg carriage, which was designed simply to prevent breakage, has done a great deal to improve the market quality of eggs. They do not come in contact with each other, and after they are once packed no amount of knocking about will addle them.

The system of inspection is called "candling" and the method may be described as follows: A dark room is provided, or a corner is curtained off from the store, in which no ray of sunlight is allowed to intrude. Within the enclosure a single candle, oil lamp or gas jet is provided so that the "candler" may face it conveniently and have the light on a level with his face. If the lot of eggs which he is to inspect is known to be a good one, that is, having come only a short distance, and from a person who has a good reputation, the operator greases three eggs in each hand from a case at his side and quickly passes each egg between the light and his eye. Those which are good have a clear transparent shell and a vividly rosy light shows through them. An egg which is perfectly fresh seems to carry its freshness with it and appeals to the favor of the sight at once.

A rotten or addled egg is perfectly opaque, black in color and is detected at once. Not so with those which are a "little old" or, having remained on one side for a considerable length of time, begin to show signs of decay. In these cases a small, sometimes a very faint black spot is seen and to the quick glance of the inspector this is enough to condemn it and consign it to a lot which is to be eaten at once, probably by the customers of cheap restaurants and boarding houses. In no case where the least sign of decay or age is visible, is the egg placed in the receptacle set apart for those of the first quality and known as "fresh." Should the consignment be found to "run bad," or come from a long distance, the inspector goes about his work in a much more deliberate fashion, for experience has taught him to be conscientious, and his work is much more difficult. In this case he only handles two eggs at a time, one in each hand, and the process is necessarily slower, more careful sorting being necessary.

With the best packing and the utmost care some eggs in every case or package are sure to crack. These the candler places on one side, generally with those that are slightly damaged or old, and all are sold together. In making his returns for the consignment the rule is for the dealer to allow one-half price for these, and this rule is found to work quite satisfactorily. In Chicago and some other markets "egg candling" is followed as a regular business by men who have become experts at the trade, for trade it really is. These men charge a regular price of ten cents per case of thirty-six dozen, and when they are at work are enabled to earn as much as $3 per day, or even more. In Boston the inspection is done by some one in the employ of the seller or by the seller himself, and no charge is made for the work. It may be safely said that our dealers as a rule are conscientious and furnish their customers with only fresh or first-class eggs. There are some, however, who do not pretend to be honest and only seem to care for the immediate profit. These men are soon well known and should be avoided, not only by the consumer, but also by the shipper. A shipper's reputation is quickly known by all the dealers in the market. They exchange notes and compare, one with the other, their observations on the quality, style of package and general qualities of merit or demerit of the different shippers, and will take nothing which comes from a man who is not considered by them first-class.—*Cultivator.*

## Pure Bred Fowls.

The editor of the *Poultry Monthly* says:

Our experience compels us to say there is no stock as productive as our thoroughbred, because they have been bred in accordance with a system, and with the object in view of producing qualities of great excellence. It matters not what branch of the poultry trade you breed, the fancy variety for sale or exhibition, the heavier kinds for the food market, or the medium size for their egg alone.

Under the very best management, our pure bred invariably give better satisfaction and prove more remunerative than fowls not bred to any degree of excellence. But it is with this as with all kinds of stock, or engaging in any enterprise or occupation, the interest and pleasure that is awakened by the first step in the right direction goes a great way to gain in much shorter time the experience necessary to success, which only could be gained through years of arduous labor and attention, if the wrong course were pursued in the beginning.

Poultry keeping can be made an auxiliary to other pursuits without infringing on the time of the keeper, and will bring in a quick and handsome return for the food and care given them. It costs no more to feed and keep a flock of improved fowls than it does the common sorts. It is a waste of time and money to breed from poor stock, and it is the poorest economy to buy poor trash, though represented to us as good as the best. Those who have turned their attention to breeding and keeping up the character and excellence of their fowl stock, have satisfied themselves of the importance of keeping good birds, and know that the higher the quality the better the results, and that they never will be, in our generation at least, a drug in the poultry market.—*Live Stock Journal.*

The brown Leghorns I find to be the best layers; and of all varieties there are none at the present day receiving more attention than the brown Leghorn. In color they have a decided advantage over their white brothers, who always look as though they were afraid of soiling their white coats, and look pale and sickly. The brown Leghorns have a dark, rich colored plumage, which makes them very attractive and perfect beauties. I would never exchange mine for the white.—*Journal of Agriculture.*

## THE GUN.

### The Pike County Coon-Hunters.

"I tell you I miss Uncle Billy C. Jaggar of Delaware township," said the Sheriff. "Poor Uncle Billy! He's a good ways now from Pike county—and especially from Delaware township."

"Yes," assented the County Clerk, "You're right, Sheriff, for if Billy C. ain't in heaven I won't give much for the chances of some other folks I know."

Uncle Billy C. Jaggar was a Pike county character—an honest, sharp-featured little man; one of the numerous and easy going family that lived down 'back o' Dingman's.' Uncle Billy had a shrill piping voice and a most comical way when he talked of emphasizing and punctuating his words and sentences. Added to this, he prefaced and interluded his remarks in a high falsetto hum which seemed to come clear from the top of his head. He had a good wife whom he called mother, and a runaway horse named Betsy Baker. He was known from one end of the county to the other, for he had followed his side-splitting little red nose into every corner of it. He had been either a witness, a juryman, or a litigant at every term of Pike county court for forty years, and when he died a few months ago, one of the old land-marks went down.

"I can see him the way he used to come in here court weeks," continued the Sheriff, "and I can hear him now. No toning fork that ever gave the pitch in a singing school could get within four inches of the key Uncle Billy hummed on. 'Hum, hum, hum, h-t-u-u-m, hum,' he'd sing, and 'Whell, gen-til-men,' he'd say, 'Whill-yum C. Jaggar, of Dellywar township, is hotched, on the jocey. Hum, hum, h-u-u-m hum. He's hotched on the jocees, gen-til-men, he'll try a leetle Boong'n. Hum, hum, hum, h-u-u-u-m, hum.' A leetle Boong'n an' the best you have, sir. Hjum, hum, hum, h-u-u-u-m, hum."

Uncle Billy used to say, 'some folks is partial to rye, but give me the good old Boong'n.'

"If anybody has a lively recollection of Uncle Billy," said the ex-District Attorney, "You know why, for I guess you all heard how he and I captured the coon down by the Hyman Westbrook place, a few years ago. You know I was on my way to Stroudsburg to meet the judge and some of the biggest lawyers there were in the district, on some law business, and I was topped out in the best suit of clothes that three years in the District Attorney's office could produce, including a new high hat. I had got down just this side of Hyman Westbrook's, where a big chestnut tree stands in a field near the road, and I saw Uncle Billy C. standing in under the tree and looking up among the branches. Betsy Baker and the hum-ber box wagon stood in the road. Now it was a peculiarity of Betsy Baker's that at one time you might fire a cannon off in under her and she'd never move, while at another time if a rooster should crow a hundred yards away she'd string things from Dan to Beersheba.

"Well, I stopped my horse opposite Uncle Billy. He never took his eyes from the trees, and I could hear him humming.

"'Hallo! Uncle Billy?' said I. 'What is it? What's up the tree?'

"'Hum, hum, hum; h-u-t-u-m, hum,' said Uncle Billy, without looking around.' 'Whell,' said he, 'it may be a catty-mount. Hum, hum, hum, h-t-u-u-m, hum, and maybe it's a bear. Hum, hum, hum, h-u-u-u-m, hum. But my belief, is sir, that it's a coon, sir. A great fine coon. Hum, hum, hum, h-u-u-u-m, hum.'

"'Well, Uncle Billy,' said I, on my tape in a minute, for you know if there is any one thing I do like it's hunting a coon;'if there's a coon in the tree,' said I, 'we must try to get it out.' So I jumped from my carriage and stood by the old man's side, and peered up into the tree. Sure enough, half way up the tree, to plait sight on a branch lay a big coon, looking as fat and sassy as a bigger baby playing with the griddle greaser. I had a small revolver, and I whipped it out in a minute. Uncle Billy had never lowered his eyes once, nor moved his head a lttle. 'At took aim he piped :

"'W-h-o-o-d, Betsy Baker! Hum, hum, hum, h-u-t-u-m, hum.'

"I fired. Betsy Baker never moved, and Uncle Billy never turned round to see whether she did or did not. The coon climbed higher up the tree. I fired again, and the coon got up still higher.

"'Hum, hum, hum, h-t-u-u-m, hum, hum,' sang Uncle Billy. 'Whell,' said he. 'Tis my impresshing, sir, that yore batter's does not carry guns enough, sir, to bring down the coon. Hum, hum, hum, h-u-u-u-m, hum. I have heard, that coons cand be shook out, of trees clint-ing the tree, sir, and kicking, on the limb. Hum, hum, hum, h-u-u-u-m, hum. Kicking hard, on the limb.'

"I was full of the excitement of the chase by this time, and Uncle Billy's hint was no sooner made than I was shinning up that chestnut tree like a bear after a bee's nest. I forgot all about the Stroudsburg judge and lawyers, my good clothes and my new high hat. I was reminded of the hat as I drew myself up on the bottom limb of the tree, for it was caught plumb on the top by a branch above me, as I rose to my feet, and shoved down over my eyes in less time than a steak of lightning could split a rooster. I pulled it off. It looked as if a yoke of oxen had rolled over it, and I dropped it to the ground. It was a hard job to crawl up through the branches, and when I got within reach of the coon I was sweating like the bottom skarjack on the plaster, and I felt as if I had been toyed with by a mad bull all over a ten-acre lot. I fired the rest of my cartridges at the coon, but it just laid there on the limb and grinned at me. That made me mad, so I crawled out, and, at the risk of dropping fifty feet to the ground, I gave the coon a kick longside the jaw that lifted it clear off the limb. It lifted me clear, too, and we both left the branch together. I flung one arm around the limb as I went down, and saved myself. I hung suspended in the air. As the coon went down he made a grab at me, and set his teeth deep enough in the calf of my leg to save himself. And there we hung. I on the tree and the coon on my leg. As I kicked and wriggled I could see Uncle Billy C. standing below, just as immovable, cool and deliberate as ever. You should have heard him give directions.

"'Hum, hum, hum; h-u-u-u-m, hum,' said he, 'Whell, sir, you, have him, now ! If I was, you, sir, I'd raise my other foot, and lift him a good 'un, on, the snoot. Hum, hum, hum, h-u-u-u-m, hum. A stiff 'un, on, the snoot, sir.'

"And I did give him a stiff un on the snoot. The coon had to drop, but he took a mouthful of my leg with him. The full broke his neck and killed him. As I struggled to draw myself on the limb Uncle Billy picked up the coon.

"'Hum, hum, hum, h-u-u-u-m, hum,' he sang. 'Whell, sir, he is a fine one. Hum, hum, hum; h-u-u-u-m, hum. A fine one, sir, as I ever see. He will weigh not less than sixteen pounds, sir. Hum, hum, hum; h-u-u-u-u-m, hum. Not an ounce less, sir.'

"And Uncle Billy deliberately carried the coon out to his wagon, chucked it in, climbed up to his sheepskin seat, and drove off without another word, leaving me sweating, bleeding and tattered in the top of the chestnut tree. When he had gone about a hundred yards I saw him hold the coon up by the tail, as if satisfying himself as to its heft once more. Then I shouted:

"'Uncle B-i-l-l-e-e!'

"Just then Betsy Baker took it into her head to runaway, and down the road she went, licky-ty-brindle, and I saw Uncle Billy no more. Well, there was hardly clothes enough left on me to wipe out a shotgun with, and I believe a tin-peddler refused to give my wife a 3-cent tin cup for the whole suit some time afterward. I had to drive back home thirteen miles and put on other clothes before I could go on.

"About a week afterward Uncle Billy came into my office, deliberate and very angry.

"'Whell, sir,' said he. 'Hum, hum, hum; h-u-u-u-m, hum. By shooting at Betsy Baker from the chestnut tree, sir, you caused her to run away. Hum, hum, hum, h-u-u-u-m, hum. She broke a thill, sir, to my best wagon, and now, sir, you must pay me $1 63, sir, or I will lay you on the shelf, sir, in the next election in Dellywar township!'

"I settled with Uncle Billy for three Boong'ns, and 'that's the way he and I captured the coon.'"—Cor. New York Sun.

A GOOD EXAMPLE.—We are glad to note the fact that the supervisors of Yolo county are taking an interest in the preservation of game. Like many counties Yolo has been overrun by a lot of men who make a practice of slaughtering deer in and out of season without regard to the laws of man or nature. The supervisors of the above mentioned county have passed more stringent laws and now offer rewards for information and the conviction of the lawbreakers; thus working in conjunction with the Sportsman's Association the deer hunters will find the soil of Yolo county too hot for them to follow their unlawful pursuit. What is the next county to be heard from.

On Thursday and Friday of last week Mr. C. W. Kellogg and Mr. Wm. Anderson were at Teal station preserve and had very good shooting. In the two days' shooting 116 birds were killed of which 34 were "cans," the rest mostly sprig and teal, and all the birds were in the very best condition. Mr. Kellogg had the good luck to bring down three large swans at two shots, hitting one with the left hand barrel and two as they came in line with the right. He used only No. 6 shot; these are the first swans killed though many have been shot at this year on this preserve.

Last Sunday Mr. Ramón Wilson and Mr. Crittenden Robinson were at Sherman Island and between them bagged 80 ducks, a great many of which were canvasbacks. During the day Mr. Wilson getting ready to get out of his boat did not select a very good place to alight without soiling his boots. The place he selected was in the middle of the pond in quite deep water. It is just as well to say that he alit without premeditation and got slightly moistened by coming in contact with the aqueous fluid. Folks will not know then that he got a "ducking."

There is fine bag shooting on the edge of the Suisun marsh. When a good position is secured early in the morning and the decoys anchored out, one can have all the shooting desired. A great many "cans" have been killed in this way.

Quite a large party were at Warm Springs last Sunday. The whole party bagged about 90 quail. The best bags were made by Messrs. Putnam, 23, Rondeau, 23, and Stackpool, 17. Quail are very scarce in this vicinity.

There is a rumor afoot to the effect, that several parties are about to lease a tract of 700 or 800 acres of the marsh land at Alvarado. It is expected that this will be made into another game preserve.

Hunters at Sherman Island had rather poor luck on Sunday last. The same may be said of the Teal station preserve; several were up but indifferent success they met with.

Mr. Chas Kaeding was over at Point Reyes this week shooting'quail and snipe and had very good luck; he reports hunting in that vicinity generally good.

G. T. Precht was at Badan station last Sunday shooting on private grounds and brought home 24 as fine English snipe as have been shot this year.

Thanksgiving Day many members of the Teal Shooting Club were at their preserve. We have not heard what success they met with.

The shooting up the rivers generally speaking is poor. The last small showers seem to have scattered ducks over the hills again.

Last Sunday Frank and Fred Walton found pretty good shooting on the Suisun marshes; they bagged 48 snipe and 36 ducks.

Messrs Brooks and O'Farrel were recently hunting on the San Joaquin River and returned with 28 ducks.

Fred Maskey says that quail shooting on Walnut Creek is about played out.

In a strong article in favor of the system of ensilage, the National Live Stock Journal says: "In best condition, in best condition, is very similar in chemical composition and food value, per ton, to turnips; and the meadow grasses, in their excellent condition, have a value nearly twice that of turnips, per weight. If, then, green corn and green grasses may be preserved, in all their succulence, for use when green feed fails, these may fully take the place of turnips and other roots in the growing as well as fattening ration. These grasses, thus preserved, must have even greater significance in our future system of feeding than turnips in that of England. The grasses, preserved in their green and succulent condition, are far superior to turnips, in the fact that they furnish a complete ration, and cattle may be properly fed on these without the use of grain. Grain or concentrated food, however, in moderate quantity, may often be properly fed upon good pasture, when the most rapid progress is desired, the animal being able to digest some concentrated food in addition to all the grass its stomach can utilize."

Several of the cattle of a herd attacked at the Jackson and the Grand Rapids, Mich., fairs last month have since died. A competent veterinarian has since been ordered by the United States Sanitary Cattle Commission to investigate the matter.

Anderson & Findlay, Lake Forest, Ill., have sent to Scotland to get twenty or twenty-five of the best Angus cattle money will buy from the highest-bred herds there. They have now one of the best herds in America.

## THE RIFLE.

### National Rifle Association.

The regular meeting of the Board of Directors of the National Rifle Association, was held on Tuesday, Nov. 14, General Molineux in the chair.

Colonel Bodine, from the Committee on International Military Match; reported that the committee. was in a fair way to obtain a good and satisfactory prize, but that examination was, as yet, imperfect. They were still experimenting on shells and bullets. The Colonel then asked that the Board empower the special committee to purchase a sufficient number of guns from the Messrs. Remington & Sons, stating that even if the order was given at this time, it would be close upon three months before the rifles would be ready for delivery, and that when the season opened the association ought to be ready to put a perfect gun in the hands of the selected team. Colonel Litchfield, from same committee, reported that there were several private parties at work perfecting new rifles, one of which would prove an excellent weapon. He said the committee were not yet through with the gun-makers, and he thought that more than one company would yet come to the front. Colonel Bodine at once denied that he specially favored any particular gun, the committee desired a good one, and that his great anxiety was to place a rifle in the hands of the men at the earliest possible day, so that sufficient practice could be had. The matter of, the purchase of the rifles was finally laid over until the next meeting of the board. Colonel Story, from the Range Committee, reported progress on the erection of buildings at the firing points, to enable the men to practice during the winter.

Some discussion was had on the manner in which the team of 1885 would be selected, Secretary Seabury denying the statement that the Board intended to select the team of 1886 without regard to competitions. Colonel Bodine stated that the old methods were, in this case, not available, as there would not be sufficient time for necessary competitions for places as last year. The team, however, would be selected from men who had made satisfactory scores. He suggested that commanders of organizations in the National Guard be authorized to detail members of their command to compete for places, that the records made in such competitions be attested and the men selected be provided with the necessary certificate from the Adjutant-General of their States, and then that competitions be held at Creedmoor in May next. General Molineux stated that the Board was anxiously awaiting a report from the committee, with all the necessary recommendations for the selection and government of the teams, and trusted that such a report would be ready at an early day.

The last defeat of the American team, humiliating though it was, for the Americans always have been at the head of all that has been undertaken, has had the effect of stirring up those at the head of rifle matches, and, at the band in 1885, it is to be hoped that those who have the affairs in hand will put ammunition, guns, and men into the field who will be at least the equals of those that are made across the water. Judging from the manner in which the association is going to work there is every chance that the next contest will be nearer equal. Col. Bodine's idea of selecting those men of the different organizations of the National Guard who have made the best scores is a good one as all those who aspire to rifle shooting honors will have a chance to decorate their brows with the laurels. We have as good sharpshooters on this side of the Rockies as can be found anywhere and it is to be hoped that the Pacific coast will send representatives to the next great contest.

### Rifle at Reno.

Last Sunday the Reno Guard held their shooting for the Regimental Medal. With the medal quite a number of company prizes were given. The following are the scores made:

| B. Smith.................. | 4 | 4 | 4 | 4 | 4 | 4 | 5—44 |
| C. L. Stoddard............ | 4 | 4 | 4 | 4 | 4 | 4 | 5—41 |
| O. Toealand............... | 4 | 4 | 4 | 4 | 4 | 4 | 4—40 |
| G. Toealand............... | 4 | 4 | 4 | 4 | 4 | 3 | 4—38 |
| Williams................. | 4 | 4 | 4 | 4 | 4 | 4 | 4—37 |
| E. Wheeler................ | 4 | 4 | 4 | 4 | 4 | 4 | 4—37 |
| B. Myers................. | 4 | 4 | 4 | 4 | 4 | 4 | 4—37 |
| L. Davis................. | 4 | 4 | 4 | 4 | 4 | 4 | 4—36 |
| D. Harrington............ | 4 | 4 | 4 | 4 | 4 | 4 | 4—35 |
| R. Remley................. | 4 | 4 | 4 | 4 | 4 | 4 | 4—33 |
| B. Frandsen.............. | 4 | 4 | 4 | 4 | 4 | 4 | 3—32 |
| D. Obertrick............. | 4 | 4 | 4 | 4 | 4 | 4 | 4—32 |
| L. Toealand.............. | 4 | 4 | 4 | 4 | 4 | 4 | 3—31 |
| G. W. Gosling............ | 4 | 4 | 4 | 4 | 4 | 4 | 4—30 |
| A. Moger................. | 4 | 4 | 4 | 4 | 4 | 4 | 4—30 |
| E. L. Bridges............ | 4 | 4 | 4 | 4 | 4 | 4 | 4—30 |
| F. Provis................ | 4 | 4 | 4 | 4 | 4 | 4 | 4—29 |
| J. F. Alexander.......... | 4 | 4 | 4 | 4 | 4 | 4 | 4—27 |
| A. C. Bragg.............. | 0 | 0 | 4 | 4 | 3 | 4 | 2—20 |
| O. Neumann............... | 0 | 0 | 0 | 4 | 4 | 2 | 4—18 |
| Total.................... | | | | | | | ...444 |

A Reno paper takes the occasion of the shooting to haul some of the poorer marksmen over the coals in a very unhandsome manner. Now, this is not the way to deal with unfortunate shots. Quite frequently a man may not be feeling well, which is sufficient excuse for a bad score. Our rifleman should be encouraged and not ridiculed, for it is not an unheard-of case where a poor beginner takes away the highest honors with a little practice. The next time that the Reno have a shooting the poor shots of the last will show better scores.

Company C of the First Regiment have their monthly company shooting to-morrow at Shell Mound Park. The companies of the First Regiment will not take any active figure in rifle matters until after their grand masquerade ball which comes off on the evening of December 8, after which several rifle matches will be put on the carpet.

A friendly rifle match comes off to-morrow at Shell Mound Park. F. Kuhnle and S. L. Kellogg will shoot against N. Williams and Col. Beaver; the conditions are 100 shots at 200 yards.

T. W. Harvey, Chicago, is about to lease a catalogue of his herd of Angus cattle, which includes a number of representatives of prize-winning herds of Scotland. Mr. Harvey's herd is near Syracuse, Neb.

English farmers are rejoicing because the movement of meats from America is decreasing. It is not said that other classes in England find cause for gladness in this falling off in the supplies of food.

Breeders of Shropshire sheep in England are forming a society for the publication of a flock-book and doing such other work as may be deemed for the good of the breeders.

## YACHTING.

### Cutter vs. Sloop.

s a general summing up of the results of the recent sloop cutter races in New York we can do no better than to te the following very fair article from the *Times:*

he yacht races sailed recently under the management of the wanhaka Corinthian Yacht Club showed plainly enough the American type of yacht is not inferior for racing oses to the cutter or English type. It is claimed by the ter advocates that the cutter can sail closer to the wind a, or, to phrase it nautically, "out point," the shallow broad beam American yacht, and can sail faster in gh water. The races of the week before last clearly dis-ted both claims. Two superior yachts of each type were obed in each of the two classes that sailed. In the first er) class were the sloop Gracie, so well known to New-kers, and the cutter Bedouin, a new yacht built according esigns obtained from England, equipped after the best glish manner, and manned by an English skipper and w. These two yachts are very nearly of the same size, the Gracie is slightly the larger, and has to give a corre-nding allowance of time. In the second class were the ter Oriva, which has proved herself to be an exceptionally t boat, and the sloop Fanita, which is one of the best ats of like size to be found anywhere. The Oriva had the vantage over the Fanita of being vastly better equipped th sails. The first day's race was not a satisfactory test, the Gracie, which had gained steadily on the Bedouin in nning before the wind, and with a free-sheet, broke her ering gear in rounding the Sandy Hook Light-ship just en the windward work was about to begin. That mishap d her easy victory for the Bedouin. The race in this class, wever, established the fact that the Bedouin is an exceed-gly fast sailer, and it may well be doubted if a better speci-en of the cutter could be found to represent that type sinst our sloops. A boat that can sail from ort Wadsworth by way of Buoy No. 16 to the Sandy Hook ight-ship, fully eighteen miles, in one hour and a alf, in a moderate wind, is beyond question a very fast sail-. The Bedouin did this, but the Gracie, notwithstanding a onsiderable deviation from her course in going to the south-ard of Buoy No. 8½, which amounted to fully a minute's loss f time, sailed the same distance in one hour and twenty-ight minutes. The race in the second class was an equally nsatisfactory test. The Fanita was badly handled, and verely thrown out of the race, but the Oriva was beaten by ie Valkyr, a sloop built on the compromise of the two types. the second and third days' races, however, over ocean ourses, which, if one claim of the cutter advocates is valid, ught to be the most favorable to that type of boat, the racie outsailed the Bedouin worse beating against the wind han she did going before it. Almost invariably during both aces, when the club's steamer was in position to afford an op-ortunity of judging, it was observable that the Gracie was closing closer to the wind than the Bedouin. But this was of all; in these ocean races, whenever the boats ran before the wind and the greatest spread of canvas was the most im-portant factor in the race, the Oriva gained visibly on the Fanita, but whenever they came to windward work and sails were shortened, the Fanita gained more than corre-spondingly on the Oriva. These facts effectually dispose of the theory that the cutter sails faster to the windward than the sloop. The other claim that the cutters make better headway than the sloops in rough water was shown to be equally unfounded. It was frequently observed that while the cutters were ducking their bowsprits at every plunge, and thereby losing their headway, the sloops were riding over the seas and going right ahead. But if the English cannot teach us how to build yachts, they unquestionably can show us how to make sails. The sails of the Bedouin and the Oriva, which were imported from England specially for those yachts, are simply superb, and as far superior to yacht sails obtain-able hereas to those of a Hudson River trading sloop. It is said that at one time American yacht sails excited the ad-miration of all Englishmen; now the tables are turned.

SEA GOING CATAMARAN.—People in the vicinity of the foot of Calvert street were considerably excited yesterday afternoon by the appearance of a strange craft, which made fast to an oyster dredger preparing for a cruise. The Cap-tain and two hands stepped ashore, and were busy answer-ing questions from a crowd of persons who had been at-tracted by the peculiar-looking visitor. The craft is known as a catamaran, and is called the Jessie. She is the property of Commodore Fred Hughes, of Yonkers, N. Y., and let's that place under his command on Monday last for an extended tour through the Southern waters. The speed which has al-ready been attained by the Jessie has exceeded 25 miles per hour, and the impossibility of its upsetting, and the fact that it can be used at sea as readily as in the smoother waters of the bay have had to revolutionize the style of fast-sailing crafts to be hereafter used in our regattas. The Jessie is the first catamaran which has ever boasted a cabin attachment. It was projected by Mr. Thomas Farren, of Yonkers, and Commodore Hughes expresses himself as highly pleased with his experience in it. The Jessie will remain here until Monday next. Mr. Stewart Latrobe is well known to be interested in this species of vessels, and will probably investigate the visitor to-day.—*Baltimore American.*

JAY GOULD NOT TO BE LAUNCHED AT.—A Washington dis-patch says : Cramp, who is building Jay Gould's yacht, has been, in consultation with the Naval Advisory Board, and says this contract with Gould is not to give him any definite number of knots, but to do the best that can be done with a vessel 217 feet long, with a fixed breadth of beam. He says that Jay Gould cannot bear to be tantalized, and that a New York dry goods dealer named Jarrett, who lives above Gould on the Hudson, has a yacht 142 feet long, which habitually passes Gould's yacht on the river. Jarrett, it seems, has a vicious way of coming down and firing a gun when he passes Gould's landing. Then, when he passes him on the river, he is bound to hit for a shocking and dreadful way from the deck of his yacht. Gould has no idea of going around the world, but does intend to stop this impertinence.

It is not often that we hear of an ocean race in this quar-ter of the world but one has been arranged for that will, when the time approaches, attract great attention. That is a yacht race of several thousand miles. Two yachts of this port will next season race down to the Sandwich Islands and back. The new yacht of the Spreckels brothers which has just been launched but not yet tried is one of the competitors. The other will be the yacht of Mr. Harry Tevis the keel of which has just been laid. The two yachts are nearly of equal size; in fact are just the same size, on water, line, 73 feet. The

Spreckels yacht is the widest; both draw 9 feet of water. The yachts will race down and remain at the islands a few weeks when they will start together for a beat back to San Francisco. This will be the greatest yachting event we have ever had here. The owners will go in their own yachts.

King Kalakaua's birthday, Nov. 16, was observed in Hono-lulu by yacht, boat, canoe, tug and swimming races; the pro-gramme embraced the whole day from 9 a. m. to 5 p. m. It was the most interesting day's sport of the kind ever en-joyed in the islands.

King Kalakaua has just had built at Honolulu a sloop-rigged yacht measuring thirty-one feet, six inches in length over all and about ten tons register. Her frame is of Amer-ican oak and native woods and her planking of pine.

The Frolic has not been laid up yet and ill probably now be kept in commission all winter. . .wl

The Chispa has not been laid up yet and it is not likely that she will be.

The light winds of late have made it bad for the few yachts in commission.

Farmer is at work on his new yacht and is putting on the deck.

Mo,,t of the yachts have been put in winter-quarters.

The Clara is being kept in commission this winter.

Purvis has his new yacht ready for launching.

## BICYCLING.

Tricyclists no doubt conjured up some very pleasant visions when they heard the other day that a successful experiment had been made with an electric tricycle. But a legal corre-spondent of the *Electrician* puts rather a damper on its pros-pects. "What is the use of an electric tricycle?" he asks. It appears that the new machine would fail under the rules of the Roads Act, which demands that every locomotive pro-pelled by any other than animal power on a turnpike road or public highway must have three persons to conduct it. One of these three, according to the Act, must precede the loco-motive on foot by not less than sixty yards, and must carry a red flag "constantly displayed." Riders and owners of horses he must warn, and perform other similar duties on behalf of the public safety. The speed, too, is regulated—in the streets of a town at two miles and on a highway at four miles an hour. Professor Ayrton will, however, probably find less difficulty in driving his electric tricycle through this Act of Parliament than O'Connell experienced with his coach-and-four.—*Pall Mall Gazette.*

A bicycle race for the five-mile championship of England took place recently upon the Crystal Palace track. The first heat of the third round brought together C. E. Liles and N. J. Saunders, winner of the recent fifteen-mile road champion-ship. The riding was so good that previous records for three four and five miles were beaten, the full time being 17.21 2-5. The final heat was run between Liles and H. W. Gaskell, resulting in a win for the former. He is a well-known bicyclist and promises well for the championship in this branch of the sport next season if he trains and runs for it seriously.

The Æolus club of Worcester, Mass., claims the long dis-tance championship for a single day's club run, by reason of two men starting and one man completing 179 miles within twenty-four hours. The distance was all made between the towns in the immediate vicinity of Boston, most of the road being ridden over two or three times, so that the rider might avail himself of the notably smooth roads of that neighbor-hood. While the ride was very creditable, it is not so much so as an equal distance between two places, the full distance, or half the distance and return, would have been.

Eight members of the Oakland Bicycle Club enjoyed a pleas-ant trip to San Leandro one day last week. After lunch a short stroll up the road toward Lake Chabat and return, and a leisurely ride home in the afternoon, not forgetting a call at Gives', made one of the pleasantest short trips of the sea-son.

The best long distance record yet made in this country is believed to have been accomplished by Mr. H. C. Eggers of the San Francisco Bicycling Club, who rode upon an eight-lap track in this city over two hundred miles in one day, and five hundred and forty three miles in three days.

### Roup.

The following remarks about this troublesome disease are taken from Diehl's *Poultry Doctor:*

Cause—This is considered one of the most dreaded and contagious diseases of poultry. It is caused principally by a neglect or want of attention to minor diseases of the air pas-sages produced by colds; if the breeder will attend to the above in time he will not only save himself a great amount of unpleasant doctoring, but the lives of many birds.

Symptoms are the same as in almost all other diseases produced by exposure to cold, wet and damp atmosphere, only it is of a more aggravated form; the discharge from the nose and eyes becomes thick, opaque and very offensive, the nostrils become filled up and closed by the discharge, the eyelids become swollen and stick together, and often the eyeball is quite concealed, and in severe cases the whole face would have been everlasting swelled by the diseased secretion, and the poor bird, being unable to feed itself, rapidly sinks away. The disease is highly contagious, it being communicated by the effluvia arising from the discharge as well as by the con-tamination of the drinking water by the sick bird's beak while drinking. Diseased birds as soon as noticed should be immediately removed from their well companions.

Remedy—The first thing towards a cure is to place the diseased bird in warm, dry quarters, give soft food, bathe the head with Castile soap and warm water, until the nos-trils are opened and the eyes relieved. The disease soon runs its course. In about a week the bird will be either al-most well, or so nearly that it had better be killed and deposited two feet under ground to prevent contagion.

The first number of the BREEDER AND SPORTSMAN, pub-lished in San Francisco, reached our sanctum a few days ago. It is a very handsome journal, devoted to field sports in general. The illustration of Electioneer on the title page is an artistic effort far above those seen ordinarily in sporting papers. Joseph Cairn Simpson is the editor, and judging from his leading articles, he is the right man in the right place. We will always welcome the BREEDER AND SPORTS-MAN with pleasure, and read the accounts of that wonderful country where it is published.—*Southern Industries, Nash-ville, Tenn.*

(CONCLUDED FROM PAGE 253)

The Golden Citys made a game struggle in their heavy lap-streak, until they come in collision with the Chispa buoy and broke two outriggers. This unfortunate accident in the first quarter mile of the race left the struggle between the Ariels and Pioneers. The contest was of short duration. The Ariels rowed in fine form, drew away from their op-ponents until at the three-quarters of a mile they were lead-ing them by three lengths. At the mile the race was over, barring accident, for the Pioneers were four lengths behind and plowing along with a jerky stroke that showed how the pace was telling on them. Approaching the stake-boats at the mile and a half, the Ariels steered badly and by going in shore lost several lengths but regained their advantage by an excellent turn. The Pioneers turned in a flurry and by pulling too soon made a wide detour that carried them into the tide and threw them further behind. They worked hard coming home but fell off at every stage of the journey and finished exactly a minute behind, the time for the winners being 20:17.

As the course had not been properly measured it is impos-sible to decide whether the time is fast or slow. The chances are favorable to its being slow, as the winners were not pushed and could have done much better and the Pioneers rowed so poorly that the fact of their being beaten does not make the performance remarkable. The Pioneers in their race showed all the bad effects of insufficient training. In practice pulls such fairtie do not appear but when the tension of a race begins to tell on them, the bad form that results from lack of training becomes conspicuous. With the exception of Robert Crowley there was no man in the Pioneer boat who was really in fair condition for a race. John Sullivan, the stroke, looked dead out of fix. R. C. Lyne did not possess the appearance of a man fit and well and Long the bowman had stepped back into a boat after years of absence and trained in a dozen easy rows. The performance of the Ariels on the contrary showed the benefits of careful and earnest preparation. Every man in the boat was fit to row the course out. Corcoran set them a telling stroke and as long as necessary they kept it. Their performance is de-serving of much praise, as they commenced training under discouraging circumstances and with the poorest chance of success. As the cup offered by the BREEDER AND SPORTSMAN carried with it the championship of the Pacific coast the Ariel crew now hold that title and the four who will at-tempt to wrest it from them will have to row a much faster race than that of yesterday if the victors only continue to-gether and follow the intelligent, determined course which they observed in preparing for their first contest.

## BASE BALL

### Olympics vs. Redingtons.

The match at the Olympic Athletic Club's grounds at Oak land on Thursday resulted in the following score:

| REDINGTONS. | T.B.R. | R. | P.O.A. E. | OLYMPICS. | T.B.R. | R. | P.O.A. E. |
|---|---|---|---|---|---|---|---|
| Jack Arnold, 2b.6 | 3 | 2 | 1 0 1 | Ed. Conn, s s.8 | 2 | 1 | 0 0 1 |
| J. Carroll, s s. | 2 | 2 | 0 1 1 | S.F. E. Beck, 1b.5 | 1 | 2 | 7 1 1 |
| Ed. Moran, c. | 3 | 3 | 3 11 | J.H. Van Bergen 1 f. | 1 | 2 | 1 2 0 |
| Ed. Bennett, p. | 2 | 3 | 0 0 | Gus Miner, 2b. | 4 | 5 | 3 1 0 |
| S.F. Ewart, 8b. | 1 | 1 | 3 | Sd. J. Fitzgerald c s | 3 | 2 | 0 0 1 |
| J. Lewis, l f. | 5 | 0 | 0 | W. F. Boston, 3b.4 | 1 | 0 | 0 1 |
| R. Leamon, 1b. | 5 | 9 | 1 12 | 1b. B. Redmond p.4 | 1 | 2 | 3 0 4 |
| D. Andrade, c f. | 3 | 1 | 3 | E. M. Bes, cf. | 4 | 0 | 1 1 1 |
| J. W. Mullen, r f.6 | 3 | 1 | 0 | 1J. J. Kelly, r l..4 | 1 | 0 | 1 1 0 |
| Totals.......6f 16 | 9 | 27 20 9 | | Totals.......33 | 6 | 4 | 24 17 |

Innings................................1 2 3 4 5 6 7 8 9
Olympics............................0 0 0 0 3 2 1 0 0
Redingtons..........................0 0 0 0 0 5 0 0 0—5

Two base hits—Bes, Redman and Carroll. Earned run—Arnold. First base on errors—Olympics 9, Redingtons 4. First base on called balls—Olympics 3, Redingtons 4. Left on bases—Olympics 6, Redingtons 7. Passed balls—Fitzgerald 3, Moran 4. Wild pitches—Redman 3, Conn 1. Scorer for the Redingtons, Walter Wallace; for the Olympics, W. Scho-field. Umpire—Eugene Van Court of the Howards.

## Great Mount St. Bernard Dog Show.

Says the *Sporting Life:* The St. Bernard Club's first grand show of St. Bernard dogs (under club rules), extending over three days, commenced on the 1st inst., the show taking place at the Duke of Wellington's Riding School, Knightsbridge. To collect under one roof no less than 252 specimens of the Mount St. Bernard breed must have proved a task of no ordinary difficulty, which few but the promoters of this most interesting exhibition could have surrounded. Unfortunately the space at our command will hardly allow us to do full the justice to the show, or go into comparative merits of all the noble animals on view, whose sagacity so closely approaches reason—the most devoted friends of man, and that, too, in the hour of his greatest need. When a man saves a single life at the risk of his own the deed invariably commands ad-miration—sometimes honor and reward—but many of the an-cestors of the docile monsters of the Alps exhibited have rescued dozens of human beings from beneath a thick carpet of snow, which, but for the poor dog's untiring exertions, would have been an everlasting funeral pall. One magnificent fellow is credited with saving twenty-two lives, ending his glorious career in a vain attempt to rescue another snowed-up traveler, and probably many of the exhibits would at a moment's notice willingly undertake a similar humane and disinterested errand. In a show of this magnitude it would be idle to expect to meet with every specimen absolutely pure, or taking the eye as representative animals. At the same time, the majority in all classes are worth a long jour-ney to witness, the prize-takers possessing all the grand points which have assisted to make the breed famous. With twenty classes, embracing 252 specimens, the task of judging was far from light, and extended into a very late hour, but was successfully accomplished by Rev. J. Cumming Macdona, whose decisions gave general satisfaction. The prices ranged from ten guineas to ten thousand—the latter, of course, pro-hibitive—but some at intermediate prices changed owners.

# FISH.

## Waterproofing Fish Lines.

In the winter of 1875-6, I was much interested in this subject of preparing fish-lines, and thought it would be a pleasant thing to do on stormy days, and that there would be such a satisfaction in showing nicely dressed lines to my friends, proudly saying: "I did it." Well, I treated several hundred pards of braided silk and linen, but I have never exhibited the result to any one but brother Hallock, and he will testify that I was not the least proud of my work.

I satisfied myself that boiled linseed oil was the proper agent to use, because it was recommended by those in authority on the tackle question. I bought one dozen braided lines, the greater part of them one hundred yards in length, but a few, fortunately, as it proved, only fifty yards. The material was silk in some, in others linen, but both were to be treated alike.

I went into a drug store to buy the boiled oil, and while talking to the druggist about what I proposed to do, a doctor who was present volunteered the information that I should use raw linseed oil. I listened to him as he talked very scientifically of the properties of the oils, raw and boiled, and their effect upon silk and linen, and was converted to his belief, wondering that I ever thought of using boiled oil, and why English and American anglers had made the mistake of recommending the wrong oil.

I bought the raw and put my lines into it in a body, and thereafter, for weeks, the attic looked as though there was a huge net stretched in it. I rubbed and dipped and rubbed again, and at last took the lines down finished, as I thought. I was mistaken, but there was oil enough in them to finish them, and it did, effectually.

I was so much in love with my work at the time, I thought I would prepare one more line for trolling, making it a perfect color for such fishing. I bought one hundred yards of braided silk, put it into my oil tank and then into a box of mahogany dust, afterward.

Having a fair stock of lines dressed in the orthodox manner, I could afford to experiment a little. So buying another silk line, I treated it to a coat of paraffine. I think the subsequent rubbing took all the paraffine off, and out of the line, but I am not sure.

I then tried another line in pure rubber dissolved in chloroform. I passed the line through the solution I was to coat it with, and the evaporation of the chloroform was to leave a thin coating of pure rubber on the line. This was perfect in theory, and in theory only. There may have been a touch of rubber here and there on the line when I finished, but it was very slight and very irregular. The cloroform did its duty nobly, too much. so, as it evaporated before the time put down on the programme.

My next attempt was with a linen line, thoroughly soaked in a solution of sugar of lead and alum, equal parts, powdered and dissolved in rain water.

When the fishing season opened I found all my nicely oiled lines were ruined and worthless, every-one, silk and linen. The two lines treated with rubber and paraffine I used, but dried them as though they had never cost me anything for waterproofing. The linen line which I had soaked in sugar of lead, alum and rain water, was absent from roll call before I satisfied myself as to its waterproof qualities, and has never been "accounted for."

After contemplating the wreck of oiled lines I did what I should have done at first, found some one who had made a success of waterproofing his own lines; and I am indebted to Mr. Walter M. Brackett, the Boston artist, and successful salmon angler, for raising me out of the quicksand of errors in which I found myself on the waterproofing question. I quote from one of his letters:

"Years ago I exhausted the subject of waterproofing fish lines by a series of experiments, and the result is that any lines composed of vegetable fibre are rendered useless by being treated with linseed oil. They may do for one season, but beyond that they are so weak as to be worthless. I have never found any ingredient that would meet all the requirements necessary, viz: to make them waterproof and flexible, and still retain their strength. There is, however, no difficulty in preparing silk lines. It should be done with properly boiled linseed oil, and not raw. The latter has more or less gluten in it, which has a tendency to render the lines stiff. I know of but one man, a scientific varnish maker, who understands preparing the oil, but any scientific varnish maker should boil you oil for the purpose, if you tell him what is required. I inclose you four samples of lines prepared with boiled oil. Nos. 1 and 2 have been used eight years and were always allowed to dry on the reel. In fact no care was ever taken to prevent their rotting. Nos. 3 and 4 have deen used three years, but were not prepared as successfully as Nos. 1 and 2. I always leave my lines two weeks before re-coating, which I do three times, always rubbing down with a piece of black silk."

I never saw finer samples of waterproofed lines, and I enclose them for your inspection, and that of others interested in the subject. As a general thing it is better to buy one's lines already dressed at the shops, as the tackle makers have all the appliances for doing the work thoroughly and well, but some anglers like to dress their own lines during the close season when they cannot fish. It is not fishing, but it is preparing for it, and there is a heap of pleasure in preparing.—*Cor. Angler*.

## Fishing for Rats.

A novel mode of catching rats is thus described in the *American Angler*. The writer says that a person having the patience of most fishermen can have much sport in hooking the vermin:

The warehouse adjoining his place of business is infested by these "filetails," and our friend may be seen in the early spring and late fall, on an occasional evening, just after dark, seated at the back window of his counting-room (overlooking the yard of the warehouse) with an ordinary rod in hand, strong linen line, and a spring hook, commonly called a "sockdolager," baited with a lump of fresh beef, patiently waiting for a bite. It does not tarry long, nor does it consume itself in nibbles, but with a hungry snap the bait is seized and the hooks of the sockdolager impale the rat, when the excitement commences.

A lusty rat is no mean antagonist at the end of a pliant pole and ten feet of line, and his plunges, twistings and straight-away dashes are more perplexing to the angler than the leaps, surges and sulkings of the gamy trout or bass. The rat is generally landed, after seasonable sport, and killed by a blow from a bludgeon.

In this connection we may state that thousands of small hooks are bought by sugar refiners for ratting purposes. The hooks are baited with small pieces of beef on each, and then distributed about the building. The rats swallow beef and hook—the first is digested, the latter is not—death of course results. The remedy is said to be infallible.

Those who are troubled with those pestilential rodents will have little sympathy for them under any circumstance that will lead to their capture. Still there is a taint of barbarism in catching them in the manner described. The water hides the struggle of the fish impaled on the hook, and the disciple of the "gentle art" is spared the exhibition of suffering which is shown in the air. It is not so bad as a steel trap, however, and still better than to depend on the hook, when swallowed, and a lingering death. Rats, gophers and the ground squirrel of California do an immense amount of damage, and any plan which will ead to their extermination will be gladly followed.

---

The Reno *Gazette* is responsible for the following fish story: A Chinaman fishing in the Truckee yesterday caught a thing that astonishes all who see it. It has wings, fins and legs, and flies, swims or walks with equal facility. It is entirely unlike anything ever seen before, and is really a wonderful curiosity. The wings are like those of a flying-fish; otherwise it resembles a lizard, except that the head is more pointed. It is about ten inches long, and will weigh two pounds or so.

---

CALIFORNIA HOPS.—While the hop crop is short almost everywhere this year, it is good in California, and our own hop-growers are among the fortunate. But this is not the most important feature or circumstance growing out of the shortage of the hop crop. California hops will now go all over the world, and consumers everywhere will have a first-rate opportunity to test them and learn their superior merits. The California hops are really superior to the best German hops, and, in fact, to hops grown in any other part of the world, and the present condition of the hop markets will give California an opportunity to secure this verdict, and will secure it wherever they are used. Already English buyers are among us with their orders for thousands of bales, and already they are confessing that our hops are superior to all others. These experts have not only given in their verdict to this effect, but they agree, also, that Sacramento hops have the advantage in some important respects over hops raised in any other locality in the State.—*Mendocino Dispatch*.

There is a craze at present in regard to hop culture, the high prices stimulating the efforts to increase the production.

The superiority of California grown hops is established, and there cannot be a question that the demand will always make the growing of them remunerative.

## The Whirligig of Time.

An old friend at Arcata sends the *Telephone* a clipping from *Porter's* (New York) *Spirit of the Times* which was published more than thirty years ago. It consists of a "Letter from the Pacific" and is dated "Steamship California, Pacific ocean, May 20, 1849." The value of the little slip of paper is enhanced by the age which it has attained, but to us it is for the time being more valuable for the remarkably wild statements which it contains. A sample extract will be evidence on that point:

"There are no good horses or stock of any kind in California, and though writers in your own, as well as in other journals, have praised its soil, I tell you that California, under any circumstances, can never be an agricultural country. We now have on board some of the boys returning home, satisfied that California is a humbug in all save its gold mines."

We almost hope that the author of that letter still lives, and that the following facts in refutation of the opinions above expressed may meet his eye. It might be a wonder to him to read that the lowest estimates made of the wheat yield in California for the year 1882 place it at 500,000 tons; that the total acreage of vineyards for the year is given at 100,000, and that last year's vintage produced 9,000,000 gallons. It might be a satisfaction to him to learn that at the end of thirty-three years California as a fruit-growing State is in the lead of any other—that she furnishes the markets of the Union, even to the Eastern seaboard, with the first fresh fruits of the year. He might be pleased to learn that the same statement will apply to California as a beef-producing State, and that her ranges are at this time being drained to supply the markets of States and Territories east of the Rocky Mountains. And to close this chapter it is only necessary to remind him that the census statistics show that in 1880 the State produced 304,795,000 feet of lumber, 242,400,000 laths, 138,718,000 shingles, 2,063,000 staves and 1,203,000 sets of barrel headings. —*Eureka Telephone*.

---

A company has been formed to publish in San Francisco a first-class journal devoted to sport and breeding, and Mr. Joseph Cairn Simpson has been selected to edit it. The issue will be weekly, and the paper will be called the BREEDER AND SPORTSMAN. Particular attention will be paid to the breeding, raising and education of horses. Mr. Simpson, as a writer, a student and a handler of horses, has been before the public for more than a quarter of a century, and he is well qualified to take control of the journal. His "Horse Portraiture," first published in the Turf, Field and Farm, is a standard work, and the only regret is that the author has not seen fit to prepare a second volume for the press. The BREEDER AND SPORTSMAN will be a sixteen-page paper, and the first number will be published July 1st. The subscription price is five dollars per annum, and Mr. Simpson's address is 508 Montgomery street, San Francisco.—Turf, Field and Farm.

## Market Report.

FLOUR—We quote: Best City Extra, $5 37½@$5 50; Superfine, $4 50@$4 75; Interior Extra, $4 75@$5 25; Interior Superfine $3 65@$4 ℔ bbl.

WHEAT—The market is fairly active and prices steady; $1 71¼@$1 71½ is considered as a fair quotation for No. 1 Standard, White. Recent sales choice milling lots of No. 1 White were made at $1 74@$1 74¼.

BARLEY—Market of rather a weak tone. We quote recent sales of No. 1 Feed December, $1 42½@$1 42¾; do. January, $1 42½@$1 42¾, do, February $1 43½, No. 2 December, $1 36 ℔ ctl; No. 1 Brewing $1 50 ℔ ctl.

OATS—Market steady. Fair Feed, $1 70@$1 75; Good, $1 75@$1 80; Choice, $1 85@$1 90 ℔ ctl. Milling $1 95@$2 ℔ ctl.

RYE—Quotable at $2 12½@$2 25 for No. 1, and $1 75 @$1 90 per ctl for No. 2 grade.

FEED—Ground Barley, $32@$33 ℔ ton; Cracked Corn, $38 ℔ ton. Shorts, $20 ℔ ton. Oilcake meal the oilworks sell to the trade at $32 50 ℔ ton, less the usual discount. Middlings, $27@$28 ℔ ton for lots at the mill.

HAY—Alfalfa, $11@$13; Wheat $16@$17; wild Oat, $15@$17; Mixed $12@$14 ℔ ton.

PROVISIONS—Eastern Hams, 19½@21c; California Hams, 16½@16¾c for plain, 16½@17c for sugar-cured canvased; Eastern Breakfast Bacon, 17½@18c; California Smoked Bacon 16½@16¾c for heavy and medium, and 16½@16¾c for light and extra light; Clear Sides, 16@16½c; Pork, $21 50@$22 for Extra Prime, $24 @25 for Prime Mess, $25@25 50 for Mess, $27 for clear and $28@28 50 for extra Clear; Pigs' Feet, $16@$18 ℔ bbl; Mess beef, $16, for bbls and $9,50 for hf bbls; Extra Mess Beef, $17 for bbls and $8 for half bbls; Family Beef, $18@18 50 ℔ bbl; California Smoked Beef, 14@14½c ℔ lb.

FRUIT—We quote: Apples, 30@50c for common and 75c@$1 ℔ box for good; Pears, 50c@1 25 ℔ bx; Wine Grapes $20@$30 per ton. Figs, 60c@$1 ℔ box; Grapes, 75c@1 per box; Lemons, $6@$7 ℔ box for Sicily and $5 50@$6 for Malaga; Limes, $3 50@$5 per box for Mexican; Bananas, $2@$3 50 ℔ bunch; Mexican Oranges $17@$20 ℔ thousand; California $2 25@$2 75 ℔ box; New Crop Western Cranberries are offering at $15@$17 ℔ bbl.

VEGETABLES—We quote: Marrowfat Squash, $8 @$10 ℔ ton; Carrots, 30@35c; Turnips, 75c@$1; Cauliflower, 75c@$1 ℔ dozen; Cabbage, 50@75c ℔ ctl; Garlic, 4c ℔ lb; Green Peas, 7@8c ℔ lb; Green Peppers, 50c@$1 ℔ box; Tomatoes, 75c ℔ box; Celery, 60c ℔ doz; String Beans, 10c; Lima Beans, 5c ℔ lb; Green Corn, 75c@$1 ℔ box; Okra, 75c@$1; Egg Plant, 75c@$1 ℔ box; Dried Okra, 18@20c; Dry Peppers, 15@18c ℔ lb.

POTATOES—River Red, 50@55c; Early Rose, 75c @$1; Garnet Chile, $1@$1 10; Humboldt, 90c@$1; Tomales and Petaluma, 87½c@$1; Peerless $1@$1 10.

ONIONS—Quotable at 60@70c for good and 25@40 ℔ sack for poor.

BEANS—Bayos $3 75@$4; Butter, $3@$3 10 for small and $3 20@$3 30 for large; Lima, $3 75@$4; Pea, $3@$3 25; Pink, $2 75@$3; Red, $2 75@$3; Small White, $3@$3 25; large White, $2 75@$3 ℔ ctl.

BUTTER—We quote jobbing lots: Fancy, 35c; choice, 32@34; fair to good, 27½@30c; inferior lots from country stores, 22@25c; firkin, 27@28c for good to choice, and 25@26c for ordinary; pickled roll, 26@28; Eastern, 18@22c ℔ lb.

CHEESE—Prices steady. California, 13@14c for choice; 10@12½ for fair to good; do, factory, in boxes, $15@16; Eastern, 16@17c; Western, 8@12½c per lb.

EGGS—California choice, 50c; Eastern, 35½@42½c per doz.

POULTRY—Live Turkeys, gobblers, 15@16c; do Hens, 15@16c; do dressed, 16@21c; Roosters, $5 50 @$5 50 for old and $5 50@6 for young; Hens $5.50@$6 50; Broilers, $4@$5, according to size; Ducks $6 50@$8 ℔ dozen; Geese, 1 50@$1 75 ℔ pair.

GAME—In good demand. Quail, $1@$1 12½ ℔ dozen; Mallard Ducks, $3 50@$4; Sprigs, $2 25@$2 50; Canvasback, $3 50@$4; Brandt, $1 50@$2; Gray Geese $2@$2 50; White Geese, $1 25@$1 50; Honkers, $5@$6; Snipe, $1 25@$1 50 for English and 50@75c for common; Teal, $1 25@$1 35; Widgeon, $1 25@$1 35; Hare, $1 75@$2 25; Rabbits, $1 25@$1 75.

WOOL—Light trade. No change in the prices. We quote: Choice Fall, 15@17c; Fair do, 13@14c; Defective Fall, 9@11c; Spring (free), 20@24c; Spring (defective), 15@18c ℔ lb.

HIDES AND SKINS—Dry hides, usual selection, 19@21c ℔ lb; culls one third less, and Mexican Hides 1c ℔ lb less. Dry Kip, 18c@20c; Dry Calf, 21@22c; Salted Steers, over 55 lbs, 11c ℔ lb; Steers and Cows, medium, 10c; light do, 9c; Salted Kip, 15 to 30 lbs. 11c; Salted Calf, 14@15c ℔ lb; Dairy Calf 70 @80c each; Sheep Skins, 25@30c for Shearlings; 30 @50c for Short, 50@$1 for medium, and $1@$1 50 apeice for long wool and wool skins. Butchertown Green Skins bring higher prices.

TALLOW—Quotable at 9c@9½c ℔ lb for rendered and 11½@12½c for refined, both in shipping order.

MEATS—Following are rates for whole carcasses from slaughterers to dealers:

BEEF—Prime, 8½@9c; medium grade, 7½@8c; inferior, 6@7c ℔ lb.

VEAL—Large Calves, 7½@8½c; small ones, 9@10c ℔ lb.

MUTTON—Wethers are quotable at 4@4½c and Ewes at 3½@4c ℔ lb, according to quality.

LAMB—Quotable at 6@6½c ℔ lb.

PORK—Live Hogs, 7½@7¾c for hard and 6¼c@6½c for soft; dressed do 10@10½c ℔ lb for hard grain hogs.

SPECIMEN OF OUR ARTIST'S HUMOR

THE FISHMONGER.

HUNDREDS OF DELIGHTED ONES SEE, FOR THE FIRST TIME IN THEIR LIVES

The Japanese Artist and Embroiderers

At work in their native costumes at

**Ichi Ban, 22 & 24 Geary St.**

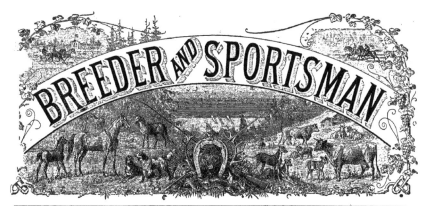

# BREEDER AND SPORTSMAN

Vol. I, No. 24.
NO. 508 MONTGOMERY STREET.

SAN FRANCISCO, SATURDAY, DECEMBER 9, 1882.

SUBSCRIPTION
FIVE DOLLARS A YEAR.

BUCCANEER.   Owned by G. Valensin, Arno Farm, Sacramento Co., Cal.

The two great trotting strains of the world have distinct origins. Mambrino, the thoroughbred son of imported Messenger, is the patriarch in one of them; Young Bashaw, the son of the imported Barb Grand Bashaw, the other. We give the pride of place to the sons, as, in the case of Mambrino, Hambletonians and Mambrino Chiefs originate from him, and the son of the Barb has the merit of being the head of the Bashaws, Clays, and other branches of the family which trace their lineage to this source. There are other branches of the Messengers that have gained distinction, though these are so completely overshadowed by the get of Mambrino that

a comparison can scarcely be made. While any candid man, who has the requisite knowledge, will readily concede that a majority of the great trotters have sprung from Mambrino, no one can deny that the others have occupied so prominent a position as to warrant placing them in the second position, and that position only slightly inferior. We have always claimed that there were good ones in all the prominent families, and that it would scarcely be fair to award the highest rank to one sept. The combinations of blood have resulted in the greatest successes, and the union of various lines give evidence of their importance to the breeder. St. Julien

brings the two together, and so does George Wilkes and Electioneer and others of high repute. But it is needless to go into a long argument as even those who are wedded to one family will acknowledge the merits, even though on rare occasions some one will be found who is prone to underrate those he has an antipathy to, that antipathy arising from an extreme jealousy that considers praise of another derogatory to those he fancies.

The illustration in this number is a capital specimen of the family to which he belongs. Size, color, gait, form, are characteristics, for though Grand Bashaw, and his son Yo-

Bashaw, were grey, black or dark brown has been the shade of a majority. As is well known, the grey is apt to change into black in the progeny, and then may come bays and chestnuts and other shades, marking after some ancestor or other far back in the genealogical tree. Grand Bashaw was imported from Tripoli by Commodore Morgan. He was called an Arabian though the weight of testimony is in favor of the Barb origin, and he was claimed at the time of importation to be the equal of any horse in the country in "point of beauty, action and speed." Bred to Pearl by First Consul, her dam Fancy by imported Messenger, and the next dam by imported Rockingham—the sire of the dam of Sir Archy—the produce was Young Bashaw. From Young Bashaw came Andrew Jackson, one of the great trotters of his day, and according to William T. Porter—a capital judge—a very blood-like animal. Long Island Black Hawk is the next name in the pedigree, and in this horse was united the two great families, Bashaw and Mambrino. The Messenger came in in the first remove, and as the history progresses it will be seen that there were still further additions of Mambrino blood. Long Island Black Hawk was emphatically one of the great trotters of his era, capable of pulling any reasonable weight and pulling it fast, too. He begot Vernol's Black Hawk from a mare by Webber's Kentucky Whip, and her dam was by Shakespeare, a son of Duroc. Vernol's Black Hawk was a very handsome horse, of the same color as his sire, black, and one of the noted road horses of New York. From Vernol's Black Hawk came Green's Bashaw, the dam of which was by Tom Thumb, and her dam was the dam of Rysdyk's Hambletonian. This horse we were well acquainted with. He was brought to Iowa when young, and we saw him trot nearly all of his races. He was a very handsome horse, and one of the "speediest" of his day. Far faster than his races showed as in that country and at that day the training of trotters was not so well understood, and the "ordering" him for races took away his speed. We have seen him trot a half mile in 1:08 and do it so easily that 2:20 would appear within his limit. He was very true in his action, and as eleven of his get are in the 2:30 list no further proof is required that he could perpetuate his qualities.

We well remember a very pretty bay horse which a Mr. Wetherbee brought from the East, and stood in Illinois and Iowa. This was Prophet, a son of Vermont Black Hawk, and a daughter of his was bred to Green's Bashaw, and the progeny was Iowa Chief. Corisande was a daughter of Iowa Chief and he trotted in 2:24½.

Buccaneer is also a son, and his dam was Tinsley Maid, by Tinsley's Flaxtail, and the second dam Fanny Fern, by Irwin's Tuckahoe. The pedigree of Flaxtail is not established though the weight of evidence points that her sire was Wilson's Blue Bull, and one thing is certain, that he was a horse of phenomenal speed as a pacer. Fanny Fern showed a public trial in 2:26, and her dam was by Leffler's Consul. The pedigree of Buccaneer shows a mixture of fashionable strains that betokens a trotting inheritance, and that his colts are destined to play a prominent part is well assured from what they have already done. When Doctor Hicks brought Pride to the Oakland Trotting Park, soon after she was a year old, no one would have supposed that before the season was over she would score such a performance as to give her celebrity wherever the fast trotter was known.

She had wintered poorly, was small and thin in flesh, and to one who was not acquainted with the beneficial effects of training it would have looked like cruelty to impose the task of hauling a sulky with a man in it. Even with the best of care it required months to give her a start, and there is little question that the "start" was equivalent to a loss of several months. When she did "round to" it was astonishing how rapidly she fell into a handy way of going. She was a "horned trotter," as the Kentucky darkies say, and developed a rate of speed that surprised everyone who saw her at work. It is scarcely necessary to do more than refer to her mile, in yearling form, in 2:44½, to show how rarely she was gifted, and her improvement since then has been commensurate with her early promise. Not only improvement in speed, as the fragile looking filly has developed into a muscular, highly-formed two-year-old, and in the race for the Embryo Stakes there is scarcely a doubt that in the third heat she could have excelled the previous records for colts of that age in an actual race, as she almost walked in 2:33¾.

But the trotting gift is not confined to this remarkable filly, as all of the get of Buccaneer, that had any work, show that they possess the knack.

Flight when a two-year-old showed a trial in 2:44, and got a record of 2:52. The following year although she did not appear to be quite "at herself" she won a heat in Stockton in 2:35, and as she was trotting against Albert W, it was something to deprive that good colt of one game in the rubber. She also won a heat from him at Sacramento the week before the trot at Stockton in 2:42½, getting second money in both races.

Privateer trotted in 3:05½ when a yearling, after being a very short time in training, and there has never been one of the get of Buccaneer trained which did not show a fine turn of speed. This is not the only merit, as they are highly formed, of good size, rugged and strong constitutions, and in the show ring at Sacramento State Fair, five got first premiums, and a yearling was also successful in getting first wherever shown.

Buccaneer was bred by Dr. M. W. Hicks, then living at Keokuk, Iowa, and foaled in 1874. While the picture is a capital representation of him, there are, of course, points that cannot be shown. A color is that of a dark brown, verging into black in places, with slashings of wine or tan color. He is a handsome horse from every point of view. Nearly sixteen hands in height, with fine length and his muscular development, especially in the quarters, immense. He has about 2:24 in his work, and a rate of speed in brushes much faster.

## THE STABLE.

### A Natural Foot.

A natural foot may not be perfect, and then there may be advantages in artificial appliances. But in a large majority of animals the feet are nearly right, if Nature has not been tampered with in the effort to make them so. If permitted to exercise on the same kind of ground which could be chosen in a natural range, it would be rare, indeed, when there was much divergence from the true form. By a natural range, we mean that part of a country which would be selected by horses which could follow what is called instinct, but which is so nearly allied to reason, that we never could see where the difference was. With the herbage equal, there will be a general resort to the highest ground; and if it is necessary to leave it to find water, as soon as thirst is assuaged, the band will return. Left to themselves, the firm ground is invariably chosen, and though they may be driven to seek refuge from the by standing immersed as much as possible, there is a disinclination to wet their feet and legs. The whole system of soaking the feet, stuffing with clay, cow-dung and hoof-pads is entirely contrary to nature; and the use of hoof-ointments of any description a departure which will end in injury. Even the washing of the legs is carried to an extent which does damage, and, as a rule, water should never be applied to the horn. It may require more work to cleanse the feet of the dirt which has been gathered in a drive through the mud, and to wash them and the legs with water is a labor-saving contrivance for the groom, but is a positive injury to the feet, and has also a tendency to crack the heels. There is trouble enough from the liability of the skin to crack between the foot and pastern without aggravating a tendency which is unavoidable at times, with the best of care. Cracked heels are one of the most pestering things which the trainer has to contend against in the category of minor troubles, and frequently they are of major importance. Not alone from the pain which causes the animal to shorten its stride, but in aggravated cases, the inflammatory action extends to the tendons, and the breaking down which results, if the work is continued, is due, perhaps, to the use of water. The erroneous impression which is so prevalent that moisture is beneficial to the foot has done great injury.

This has arisen from the palliation of the injuries which resulted from improper shoeing, and from the mutilations of the foot, which it is thought that it is the imperative duty of the blacksmith to accomplish. This renders the horn brittle, and temporary elasticity is gained by the artificial moisture. The natural foot has none of its functions impaired. The secretory vessels are allowed full play, strengthened by action, and the deposit, consequently, is of the right character. The thousands of minute tubes are filled with healthy fluid, and these are not marred by knife or nail. When worn away by the attrition between the foot and the ground there is the same safeguard against depletion as follows the searing of an artery, and the lower portion is glazed with the friction, which also accomplishes another beneficial duty, viz.: the prevention of absorption of moisture. Anyone who will take the trouble to examine the natural foot of the horse will find that ample provision has been made to exclude water. The horn is coated with an enamel which is as impervious to the entrance of moisture as a plate of glass, and the sole in a natural state will also exclude it. This phase of the foot question was forcibly presented from a conversation with a gentleman a few days ago. He had formerly been a blacksmith, but for the past number of years has been engaged in driving cattle, formerly from Texas and later from the mountain ranges. We obtained much valuable information from him, which will be briefly, and only in small part, alluded to now, as we hope to have a longer interview, and which we will endeavor to make a more satisfactory record of. He has had an experience which falls to the lot of few, and possessing keen powers of observation, he has been benefited by the experience in an unusual degree. With 250 saddle-horses in his employment, engaged in an arduous duties to try the feet and legs as could be imagined, we were prepared to hear him staunch in his advocacy of a natural foot, though we expected that more of the antiquated notions of the shoeing forge would be exhibited. One remark he made will be the limit in this article. "Give him," he said, "a horse with bad feet, no matter how bad, so long as the natural functions have not been entirely destroyed, and by the time there is growth enough to remove the brittleness from the nail holes down the cure in most cases will be accomplished." His treatment was to turn him barefooted on a proper range, and in place of this being the marshy ground which is usually recommended it was hilly rolling land. This he further illustrated by experience with a large band of cattle which he bought. They had become so foot-sore that they could not be driven, and were then feeding on the low ground. After the purchase he transferred them to the hills, and in a short time they were able to travel. The brittleness below the nail-holes is doubtless caused by cutting the tubes. The perforations which are made by the nails cut off the supply from above, and the cutting to prepare the horn for the reception of the shoe empties the lower part of the tubes of the fluid which gives vitality. We have had a capital illustration of this in Lady Viva, a filly which was two years old on the 3d inst. Nearly a year ago she suddenly exhibited lameness and most careful examination failed to discover the cause of it. Feeling that it was probably in the foot, every method was followed which promised amelioration, but without avail. It was several months before the cause of the trouble was manifest. She had a habit of climbing on the fence, resting her feet on the bar to which the boards were nailed, in order to look over, and doubtless, got a redwood sliver in her toe, at the junction of the sole and wall, which broke off so far into the horn as to escape the search. This came through at the coronet, leaving a crevice of three-quarters of an inch. This of course caused a separation of the horn, and though after there was growth enough to relieve the pain, the lameness vanished, it had been of such long standing as to interfere with the proportion of the foot. The one affected is still a trifle smaller than the other, and with higher heels. This came from the inflammatory action while the foreign substance was in the foot, and by keeping that part cut down so that the frog was brought into play, it has spread to nearly the natural proportion.

The crack in the horn was nearly three-quarters of an inch above the ground surface of the toe. When we began to drive her on the road, and not very long afterwards the toe broke away, leaving a gap the width of the crack. This compelled putting a tip on that foot, and in order that there should be no disparity, a tip was also put on the other. The tip weighed nearly four ounces each, and were put on the 13th of February. The driving commenced on the 26th, and she was driven entirely on the macadamized streets of Oakland, the others being too muddy to exercise her upon. The wall foot was slightly worn at the toe, though it did not require any "protection," and the intention was not to use even the tips for some time, if at all. On the 7th of March,

she lost the tip from the broken foot, and returned from the drive with the toe broken for half an inch or more on each side of the gap. That this break came from the brittleness caused by the separation of the tube is evident, for the hind feet which have not been protected, have not broken a particle, and are in capital condition. On the following day a tip was put on, and in order to set it properly, the horn had to be cut sufficiently to reach that which had been deposited since the break at the coronet. There was a palpable difference between that and the brittle portion, the former being much the toughest. The junction of the wall and sole gave evidence of the injury, there being an entirely different appearance at the point of contact from that of the well foot. If the examination had been thorough enough at the time of the injury to discover the sliver, the extraction of it would have saved the foot; and though the cutting necessary might have resulted in more acute lameness, it would have been for a brief period. We were much disappointed in not being able to try the experiment of using a natural foot without protection of any kind, but in this case will have to confine the tests to the hind feet. There is more of a sliding motion behind than in front, and as a general rule, the hind shoes have to be replaced while those in front are comparatively unworn. Some of the fast trotters will wear a hind shoe entirely out in two weeks, the front having only a slight bevel at the toe.—*Advance Sheets "Tips and Toe-Weights."*

## CORRESPONDENCE.

### New York Letter.

New York, Nov. 23, 1882.

Editor Breeder and Sportsman: Yesterday formally closed the racing season in this vicinity, for while that prerogative has generally been claimed by our American Jockey club's extra day in election week, this year the Brighton Beach Racing Association, having in its favor very exceptionally fine, mild weather for the season and plenty of horses, concluded to prolong its November meeting throughout the month if possible, and it actually reached the unprecedented number of 100 days' racing since May last, yesterday's "centennial" bringing up the total amount of money given to the winning stables during this period to over $105,000 ! Truly an unexampled and unequaled showing by any racing association in this country, or any other, for that matter. A notable feature also of the close of the third year's existence of Mr. Eugenean's much abused and much maligned track was the perfect harmony and absence of all strife of any nature which characterized yesterday's finale, something which could hardly be said of the last days of '80 and '81: when the racing was wound up, not exactly "in a blaze of glory," as on the present occasion, but in a much less satisfactory and brilliant style, considerable dissatisfaction (merited and unmerited) being then felt and openly expressed by not a few of the patrons of the racecourse by the sea. But 1882's good work will doubtless serve to soothe many a (Brighton Beach) turfman's troubled breast and prevent the resurrection of any dry bones or old scores of the former troublous days. The track has before it, with continued good management, a great future, for the next few years is likely to greatly increase its patronage, the great projected course of 1883 at Rockaway to the contrary notwithstanding. This latter project was thought at first glimpse to be the nucleus of a very formidable rival to both the C. I. J. C. and the B. B. R. A., but sober second thought has dissipated any such probability, and if the new enterprise on the beach at Rockaway ekes out a bare existence, it will be more than most turfmen hereabouts give it credit for.

A much more likely to be profitable venture just now, is the projected lease of the grounds of the Louisiana Jockey club at New Orleans, the old far-famed Metairie racecourse, by the proprietor of the aforesaid successful track at Brighton, W. A. Eugenean Esq., and if anyone can make continuous winter racing at the Crescent City popular, it will be this same "beach-comber" and his co-adjutors, who are just now in the very front rank as popular caterers to the taste of the racing public, and their number in these parts is legion.

Two of our most celebrated thoroughbreds have left these parts for "fairer fields and pastures new." What is our loss, however, is Kentucky's gain, for in Hindoo and Falsetto the blue grass region has two stallions with prospects second to none as probable sires of first-class turf performers, the former being without doubt the best horse on the American turf since Lexington's time, and the latter the champion three-year-old of 1879, the conqueror of the equally-famous Spendthrift. Hindoo goes to the home of imported Billet, the now widely-known Runnymede farm of Messrs. G. W. Bowen & Co. at Medway, Ky., while Falsetto now treads the aristocratic precincts of Alexander's turf-nursery at Woodburn. The exact figures at which the great son of Virgil and Florence changed owners have not yet been made public, Messrs. Bowen & Co. purchasing at the same time from the Dwyers two Leamington brood mares, and tendering in part payment the famous two-year-old filly Miss Woodford, by Billet, but the price of the horse was probably in the neighborhood of $12,500, and the exchange price of Miss Woodford something like $7,000.

Falsetto was sold by Mr. Lorillard to the Alexanders for $7,500 and he should be well worth over the money, though the number of stud sires now at Woodburn is rather out of proportion to the faculty of stud patrons. Mr. Morehead will, however, see to that, or if any way destitute brood mares for sale they know where to find a market for them. But at this present writing, what with the purchase of Miss Scott Young, Edinburgh and others, anything above the grade of mediocrity is quickly snapped up and it looks as if horse flesh will not be a drug in the market for some time to come.

Probably the finest looking, as he certainly is the highest prized specimen of the high type thoroughbred horse that ever reached these shores from away "over the briny" is the recent $25,000 importation of Mr. W. L. Scott of Pennsylvania railroad fame, the mighty Frenchman Rayon D'Or (red-gold).

Landing at the pier after an exceptionally rough and tempestuous ocean voyage in all the fire of virile health, he clearly showed to every bystander the possession of a wonderful reserve power and stamina by the kingly style in which he trod the shores of his new home, causing observers wonder in amazement at such great vitality and nervous rce, when is taken into consideration his recent arduous perience of the buffetings of old ocean, an experience hich proved so fatal to his illustrious predecessor, the ill-ted Blue Gown. In fact, two of Rayon D'Or's companions the voyage in question succumbed to their trials and und a grave in the mighty deep, and in a horse of such a aracter, the Erie stock farm and the country at large has und a prize indeed.

Since the son of Flageolet has been domiciled at the Ameri-n Horse Exchange in this city, he has been the cynosure all eyes and the throng has been so great as to cause the re-riction of the constant showing of the horse, as, like most obility, too much attention made him fretful and uneasy. he future stud career of this magnificent animal will be atched with great interest by all interested in breeding, r here is a horse of unusual power and size (16¾ hands), a rst-class racer himself, of unsurpassed lineage, embracing e most illustrious names in the French and British stud ooks, and if he fails (with proper advantages) to beget his ke, why then breeding is more or less of the lottery that any claim it to be. Hon. Leland Stanford's young trot-rs that are now sojourning with us at our Gentlemen's riving Park are in great fettle just now. Marion, the old pilot f the great Smuggler, is handling them with rare skill, and esterday Hinda Rose trotted a half-mile in 1:10¾ and Wild-ower the same distance in 1:08. The track was rough and rosty and both performances are great, when the very tender ge of the youngsters is remembered. The Governor was resent at the trials and unless a match is made for Wild-flower in the next two or three weeks, the whole stable will return to their home on the Pacific slope. Their popular owner will remain here and spend the winter with us.

Another shipment of fine stock that will soon be made to your State is now under waiting orders. They do not come under the head of quadrupeds but are of the biped persuasion. I refer to the herd of twenty-three ostriches now in our Central Park, where they are recuperating prior to shipment to California. Ostrich farming is rather a novelty in these parts, and the great birds have been the recipients of great attention, but on the sunny slopes and ranches of the golden State there is no reason why they should not thrive and multiply with as great success as on their own native pampas.

Your fellow townsman Jno. McCullough is still creating, under W. M. Conner's able management, his furore of old. Genial John says his old parts draw well enough. When they outlive their usefulness he will then think of new ones.

Yours,

PACIFIC.

## The Petaluma Colt Stakes.

EDITOR BREEDER AND SPORTSMAN: The prospectus of the Sonoma and Marin Agricultural Association for three colt stakes, to be given annually at the time of holding their agricultural exhibition at Petaluma, will probably be found elsewhere in this paper. That races for colts are now becoming the principal and most interesting events of the turf, there is no longer any question, and that the enterprising managers and directors of "Old Sonoma" and Marin are awake to this fact, their prospectus most fully demonstrates. The races named are for the respective ages of one, two and three years old, and beyond a doubt (if carried out) the result will be to promote a greater improvement in stock breeding than any open stake that has ever been offered since the organization of any agricultural association in the State. One of the most encouraging features is the low rate of percentage charged as an entrance fee on the amount of stakes and purses to be trotted for. The estimate shows that each main stake will not fall below $2,500, for which each nomination will be required to pay, in all, $50, and even this small sum is required in three quarterly installments of $10 each; with a final fee of $20, on the day of trotting for positions.

Hence the entrance on the whole amount of money to be trotted for in each stake will not exceed two per cent., and each entry thus paid will have a chance to win one of eight prizes, four of which will be found in the first, and four in the second class, whereas, heretofore, an entrance fee of ten per cent. has been invariably charged on all purses throughout the circuit of the fairs, with a chance at only the three divisions of the purse, or stake. Beside the advantage herein accruing directly to the stock breeders, the plan of dividing each main stake into two classes will greatly benefit the exhibition, as the programme will show that from the three main stakes there will be derived not less than eighteen interesting contests for the twenty-four prizes contained in the three stakes. This calculation is, of course, based upon the theory that in each stake there will be at least twenty starters for positions. This will give four classes of five in each, to trot under separate timers for starting positions in one of the classes. Then the six starters in each class will add two more events to the four already named, making six actual contests in each main stake, none of the entries being required to trot, but for positions, and for the money, should they get a place.

That this will prove one of the most popular schemes to encourage the breeding of fine horses, and to develop the merits of our best strains of trotting blood, I most freely predict.

RAMBLER.

SADDLEBACK, EAST BALDWIN, Maine, Nov. 27, 1882.

EDITOR BREEDER AND SPORTSMAN, *Dear Sir:* Your paper comes regularly to me, and I find much of interest in it, although I am so far from the seat of action. Having a large correspondence, taking the prominent stock papers of the United States, I being familiar with their merits, I know of none East which equals your paper. I wish you were located here (East) or that some of our old fogies would pattern after you. As a stock breeder I would quickly add my mite to your aid by advertising.

Let me also say, the recent illustrations of horses were unusually fine; our best do not equal them. I notice the quality of your paper stock, which may account in a measure for the freshness of the picture.

I take the liberty to send what is considered in New York one of the best wood-cuts yet printed. You will see it is not so fine as yours. I also add some photographs of my stock, etc. Very truly yours,

ONESTES PIERCE.

## NEW SOUTH WALES SPORTING.

### Our Regular Letter—An Exodus of Turfmen Drawn by Melbourne Attractions.

SYDNEY, Nov. 1, 1882.

Sporting matters in New South Wales are very stagnant and Sydney at the present time of writing is drained of every individual who has any pretension to follow racing. During the past ten weeks it is wonderful to note the lengthy list of overland passengers to Melbourne bent on paying a pilgrimage to the shrine of Flemington where the great Victoria racing club spring reunion is drawing to a close. Before narrating on the V. R. C. events it would be just as well for me to tell of the results at the Victoria Amateur Turf Club meeting held at Caulfield, 7th and 14th of October. This meeting under the able secretaryship of Mr. N. R. D. Bond, late sporting editor of the Melbourne *Leader*, promises to be second only to the V. R. C. spring meeting judging from the great attendance, large fields of horses and general excellence in management. I shall not weary your readers with any lengthy sermon anent the different events but give them in brief. Fine weather (a grand essential towards the success of a meeting) prevailed both days, but perhaps a trifle dirty. The ball was opened by a remarkably well bred two-year-old named Malparinka, by Proto Martyr from Sybil, winning the selling race of $500. His sire is by St. Albans (English), sire of Stockwell, from Laura G. by Orlando, while his dam Sybil is by English Tim Whiffler, got by Van Galen, son of Van Tromp. The hurdle race fell to Sportsman, carrying 156 pounds, and was ridden by the crack cross country rider, Tommy Corrigan, the two miles occupying 4:7½. St. Lawrence, by Glorious (imported) from Perfection, appropriated the Great Foal Stakes of $1,000 for two-year-olds. The Caulfield Guineas, the race of the day, and for three-year-olds, colts, 117 pounds, fillies, 112 pounds, was won by the Hon. Wm. Pearson's br c Fryingpan, by Bethnal Green (imported) from Saucepan; Boolka, by Glorious, second, and Guesswork, by Gang Forward (imported), third. The distance, one mile, occupied 1:47. The Amateur Challenge Cup steeplechase for gentleman riders was won by Mr. E. Miller's grey gelding Marquis, carrying 163 pounds, Glowlight, 175 pounds, second. Verdure, by Bethnal Green, wound up the day by winning the Toorak Handicap, carrying 107 pounds and running the mile in 1:46. On the second day the weather was fine but rather dusty and in the last race the riders could hardly see one another so great were the clouds of dust. Proceedings commenced by Lord of Clyde, 133 pounds, an animal fresh to jumping fame, winning the second handicap hurdle race, Merrymaid, 135 pounds, second, and Sportsman, 165 pounds, third. In the Nursery Handicap for two-year-olds Delusion, a filly by The Englishman (since dead), a son of English Edminster and Gebride Lady, won; fifteen others also ran. The *piece de resistance* of the gathering now came on for decision in the shape of the Caulfield Cup, a sweep of $50 each with $2,500 added in addition to a gold trophy, value $1,000, the gift of Mr. A. R. Blackwood, the second horse to receive $500, and the third $250; distance one and one-half miles. Assyrian was first favorite in the betting, and after being backed to win an immense sum of money, starting at 1,000 to 40, went to the post at 1,000 to 200 offered, 60 to 10 Fryingpan and Verdure, 200 to 10 Dougalson, 100 to 7 Little Jack, 100 to 6 each Gipsey Cooper, Gudary and Darebin. A field of 32 horses faced the starter and after a little delay Mr. Geo. Watson despatched the lot on very even terms, Dougalson being the first to get on his feet but was quickly passed by Verdure who took up the running at a great pace and led her field into the homestretch followed by Fryingpan, Little Jack, Gipsy Cooper and Assyrian. At the half distance Verdure looked all over a winner but going wide from the rails allowed Little Jack, who came with a great run, to come up on the inside, and just manage to beat the mare by half a length, Gipsey Cooper third two lengths away, then came the favorite, who had been interfered with in the race through colliding with Darebin and thereby throwing him out of his stride. The winner was not backed by the stable, they fancying in Mistaken they had a better colt. Joe Thompson the leviathan penciler never wrote his name in his book. Little Jack is sired by imported King Cole, by King Tom, by Harkaway, his dam Charade by Panic, by Alarm, by Venison. The Fridon Harriers' Gold Vase (gentleman riders) was won by Mr. Phillips' Blackthorn, 166 pounds; Alhambra, 172 pounds, second; Highflyer, 184 pounds, third. The above race is about two and a half miles over good stiff fences of over four feet high. Sailer (late Red Rover) won the open steeplechase. The meeting was successfully terminated by the Hon. W. B. Rounsevell's bay colt Prometheus, by Tubal Cain from Lurline, winning the Windsor Handicap of six furlongs, beating Saionara and twelve others. The betting was 60 to 40 on Prometheus.

All the attention of turfites is now centered in the great V. R. C. spring race carnival. The first day, 28th October, opened auspiciously, meeting with fine weather, large fields and good racing. Ten horses faced the flag for the Melbourne Stake, 1½ miles, weight for age, which was won by Darebin, 4 years old, 126 lbs., the Derby winner of last year; Belmont, 3 years, 112 lbs., second, Larpent, 6 years, 120 lbs., third. Time, 2:13. The Hotham Handicap, 1½ miles, and a distance was appropriated by Odd Trick, aged, by King of Clubs, a grandson of Stockwell's, carrying 104 lbs., Sardonyx, 4 years, 117 lbs., second, Commotion, 3 years, 131 lbs., third. One of the richest prizes given during the year is the Maribyrnong Plate (the Middle Park Plate of the Antipodes), a sweep of $150 cash with $2,500 added; two-year-old colts 8 st., 10 lbs., fillies 8 st., 5 lbs., distance 5 furlongs. New South Wales seems to have a mortgage on the annual event, and has won it six times out of the past seven years. This year there was a field of 26 starters and it fell to the Hon. E. K. Cox of Fernhill stud, one of our largest breeders, and perhaps one of the most successful. The winner, Narevia, is a racing-like black filly, by Gattendon (since dead), from Atholme, the dam of Geraldine (Hawkesbury Guineds winner); her dam was got by Blair Athol out of Habena by Irish Birdcatcher and her sire, Sir Hercules Kingsdale, was second and is by Maribyrnong from Rosedale (imported), her sire Tynedale, dam Thrift by Stockwell, consequently a close relation to Tristram. The South Australian filly Lady Jervois, by Emulation from Talkative, was third. Time, 1:4½, a trifle slower than last year. Another great event of the day was the Victorian Derby but in my own mind there could be little doubt about the result and it seems ridiculous how some people would persistently back Segenhoe after the bad beating he received from Navigator in the Sydny Derby; still the fact remains that many backed the former. When the horses were stripped in the paddock for inspection the general verdict was, as Mr. E. De Mestre's black colt, Navigator, stood quietly and as calm as if there was nothing the matter, that he had undergone an excellent preparation. His skin shone like satin, while his ribs were clean and his shoulders and thighs exposed great bosses of muscle, his head and throttle as clean as could be desired. Segenhoe looked lighter than at Randwick, but as "mean as a fish" behind; he seemes to have grown all in front with nothing left to propel him. Calma is a remarkably nice colt; so are Guesswork and Fryingpan, but the latter is a fractious brute; in fact the whole family were the same. Boolka I rather liked in condition, but he stands a trifle "in the leg" and appears more suited over a mile journey. A good start was effected, Guesswork going to the front and making most of the running. Racing along the even stretch Segenhoe slipped and lost several lengths. At the back of the course Guesswork and Transferred were leading two lengths. Approaching the scraping sheds and about half a mile from home Segenhoe and Navigator began to draw up to the leader. Swinging around the turn into the homestretch the order was Guesswork a length, Transferred and Segenhoe together, half a length off Navigator and Fryingpan, then Boolka and Standard Bearer. On reaching the distance post Guesswork hung out signals of distress and Segenhoe and Fryingpan commenced the battle of supremacy, and either looked a winner for the instant when Hales (on Navigator) called on the favorite and answering the summons was landed a winner by a clean length, Fryingpan second after beating Segenhoe on the post by a head. Cheers rent the air at the favorite's win as the public were large investors and the ring was now getting badly treated; the double Narevia and Navigator was backed for a "ton of money." Navigator hails from New South Wales and is sired by Robinson Crusoe, the only surviving animal that went out in the City of Adelaide steamer when so many good racehorses met with a watery grave. His sire, Angler, is a son of the old Heron horse Fisherman, dam Cocoanut, (imported) by Nalbourne from Miss Vivian. The mile and a half occupied 2:41½, which we reckon good time for a Derby. The Essenden Stakes, weight for age, 2 miles, was won by M. E. De Mestre's Sylvanus, 3 years, by Robinson Crusoe, carrying 104 lbs., and the day was brought to a close by M. J. Patterson's Wizard, 3 years, 101 lbs., winning the Coburg Stakes. The last three winners were ridden by our crack horseman, Tom Hale, the "Australian Fred Archer."

The weather on the 31st October (Tuesday), which promised to be fine in the early morning, completely altered, and when the horses returned to scale for the first race the rain came on, consequently the umbrella display was very large, considering there must been have nearly 75,000 people on the ground thus early in the day. The ladies were present in great numbers, their costumes being most magnificent. There was not accommodation in the grand stand for half of them, and, what with the dust and wet, their dresses must have suffered somewhat by the time the Cup was run. The attendance was one of the largest ever seen at Flemington. Belmont and Calma were right away from the others at the finish for the Maiden Plate, the former winning by a length. The winner is rather a nice looking colt by King of the Ring from Idalia, an own sister to Breiseis. In the Railway Stakes, Boolka, by Glorious, at last repaid his admirers a trifle of what he is indebted to them for past failures, in appropriating the above mile and a quarter race in 2:13½, which was fair going. The South Australian filly Lady Jervois maintained a superiority of pace over Halifax, hailing from Sydney, and Off Color, landing the Kensington Stakes in good style. The greatest surprise was now in store for backers, and as the rain began to descend in torrents the hopes of some backers dropped below zero, while to others it was highly acceptable, but in the end it suited few, the bookmakers as usual being immense winners, and may be said to have "skinned the lamb." When the 25 came to the post for the Cup, the usual breathless anxiety was noticeable among the onlookers until the flag fell and effected a good start. The early portion of the running was made by Flying Jib until nearing the stand, where Stockwell took up the running and carried it along at a merry pace as the field swept along the river stretch, Lord Burghley and Sting bringing up the rear. Assyrian, Gudarz, Little Jack, Darebin, Brunette, and Mistaken were in close attendance on the leaders, and when racing past the abattoirs Stockwell held a clear length and a half advantage of Gudarz and Little Jack, then Mistaken, getting into a more forward position. At the scraping sheds the field began to look spreadeagled. Stockwell swung round the home turn with a clear lead, next to him being Gudarz, half a length The Assyrian and Darebin, two lengths Sweet William and Lord Lisgar, then came Segenhoe and King of the Vale, Mistaken beaten off. A splendid race ensued at the distance, ending in Assyrian just beating Stockwell by a length, while an exciting tussle between Gudarz and Darebin resulted in the latter being defeated by a head for third place. Then came Sweet William, Mistaken, Segenhoe, Cunnamulla, Little Jack, the remainder coming in at length intervals, Sting, Savanaka, and Jessie being last. Time, 3:40. The winner is a very handsome horse, and full of quality, and was perhaps the fittest animal at Flemington. He was trained by Mr. Savill, of South Australia, and is owned by Messrs. Thos. Barnfield and J. Allison, well-known residents of Adelaide, and by this win they will have landed a nice stake. Assyrian, it will be remembered, started a very warm favorite for the Caulfield Cup, but was interfered with in the race, having collided with Darebin, which effectually spoilt any chance he may have possessed of winning. The winner is by the defunct Countryman, a son of English Stockwell, from the New South Wales mare Tinfinder, bred by Mr. Baldwin, and got by New Warrior from Deceptive, by Yelverton. Had Stockwell, the Tasmanian horse, won, it would no doubt have been a popular win, while Gudarz would have given the ring a "jar." It will be seen from the above that Victoria was not placed in the great V. R. C. Spring handicap of 1882. The St. Albans stable appear to have been in pretty good form, as they won the Darling Stakes with Essex, easily defeating Tamworth and Sinking Fund. In the Van Yean Stakes, Bagot scored a win for Tasmania, and this in a manner will compensate Mr. T. Reibey for his defeat of Stockwell in the Cup. It is worthy of note that all our principal winners so far are descended from Stockwell mares, a fact which our breeders are not slow to perceive. There is nothing of any moment transpiring in the trotting world.

#### Aquatics.

The yachting season has just opened and the harbor presents quite a flotilla of craft of all dimensions, but the weather has sadly interfered with the opening regattas, several having to put up with postponement through the inclement weather. In my last I mentioned the Francis Punch Trophy which was rowed for on the Parramatta river, and the less said about the result the better. Mud at any time will not stand stirring, and the above race was "very muddy." A good, honest, straightforward sculler won the race in Michael Rush, the Clarence river man, and a man of almost independent means, but an immense enthusiast of rowing. Beach, who was second, is comparatively unknown to aquatic fame, while Laycock rowed third. To show what the intentions of Laycock were, he offered, at the paying over of the prizes, to row the winner for $1,000, but Mr. Rush quietly refused to meet him, an action which meets with general approval here.

J. C. Laycock, a brother of Elias, won a race on the Parramatta river last Saturday for $75 a side against Sam Edwards. It was a hollow affair. Edwards protested on the grounds that Laygock had not pulled in an equal boat to his opponent.

The wet weather during the past two weeks has stopped cricket and nothing in the "big match" line has occurred. Great preparations are being made to recieve the Australian cricketers, who will be banqueted on their arrival in Sydney.

# TURF AND TRACK.

## Turf Reform.

The easy victories of Larpent and Ab dallah in their respective races at the Melbourne Hunt Club Meeting afford the most recent example of the little effect weight has upon a really good animal when well, and an other argument in favor of a fixed lowest top-weight in all races, varying with the distance to be traversed, but beneath which the handicapper may not begin his allotment of burdens. That the farther the above named horses had to go, so much the farther they would have beaten the fields on Saturday last, was plain to every spectator, and a three-year-old, with 7st. 2lb., and an aged mare with, 7st. 7lb., were, out of Larpent's thirteen opponents, the only ones that were capable of the semblance of a struggle with the big son of Cœur de Lion in the last part of the journey. That he had the race won at the turn home was palpable. As soon as the weights appeared, it was expected to be run in 1:45, and thus practically all but half a dozen were denied a chance.

That this is no individual instance of the inability of moderate horses to compete with really good ones when the latter have a racing weight is shown by manifold instances, Darebin's Adelaide Cup being a recent example, and of horses who ran at home, and whose descendants we have here, Fisherman, Rataplan, Chandos and Vespasian won under all burdens from two-year-olds up, and yet left the turf sound. Chandos, imported by Mr. E. K. Cox, won under 14st. 5lb., and ran thirty times; Rataplan, sire of the Drummer, won under 10st. 4lb., and ran seventy-one races, winning thirty. Vepasian, also imported by Mr. Cox, carried 10st. 4lb. and won the Chesterfield Cup. Fisherman, Mr. Fisher's old favorite, ran one hundred and thirty-six races, of which he won ninety-six, often carrying over ten stone, over three and four-mile courses. Thus the fear of crushing a good horse may evidently be set aside. The fact remains that horses are far more likely to receive injury in the hands of light-weight boys, who have not the strength to hold them together, than in the hands of men who have thoroughly learnt their business.

That horses do their work as well under heavy weights as under lighter burdens was shown by contrasting the race for the Melbourne Hunt Club Cup with that for the Open Steeplechase. A dozen started in the first-named event, ridden by amateurs, and at the turn home the whole field were well together, none having fallen in the race, the weights varying from 13st. 4 lb. to 10st. 7lb. In the Open Steeplechase, with nine runners in professional hands, with weights ranging from 11st. 6lb. to 9. st., only four got round without mishap, the top-weight winning.

Although we fear that we may perhaps weary our readers by continuously harping on this theme, the importance of the subject dealt with is our excuse, for only by persistence can reforms be effected. About two thousand horses ran in the Australian colonies last year, and of these only two hundred and twelve horses are credited as having won one hundred pounds or over. Only forty-two have won five hundred pounds or over, and only thirteen have appropriated prizes of or exceeding one thousand pounds.

We thus see the immense proportion of animals which, despite high breeding and high prices paid for them, belong to the moderate and the bad division. We advocate fair handicapping, so that any horse who, under the lightest burden that can be legally assigned him, can exhibit ordinary racing qualifications shall have a chance; but we are most decidedly opposed to any reduction of the present minimum weights in handicaps, as we consider those now in vogue barely heavy enough, and should much prefer seeing 6st. 7lb. the minimum at distances exceeding a mile, and 7st. and under that distance.

Already owners who have purchased horses at large prices, which have since turned out to be but moderate, are after a couple of years of expense therewith obliged to throw them, though sound, out of training, as unless a horse can run a mile and a half in 2:43 at Caulfield, or 2:38 at Flemington, he is denied a chance in any handicap; and suggestions are made of following the American trotter system, and establishing class races for horses that have never beaten 2:47 for a mile and a half, or 3:40 for two miles, so that some chance of earning their oats may be afforded the third rate division.

Whilst we utterly condemn this suggestion as only opening a door to fraud in causing good horses to be run byes and waited with, it shows how tightly the shoe pinches, and until it is impressed on our officials by the chief club that no horse's chance is to be absolutely annihilated, we can hardly hope to see horses properly brought together.

We have before this urged on the chief club the propriety of appointing a second handicapper, of taking the whole handicapping of clubs racing under its rules into the hands of its officers, and of having one of these officers present at every country meeting and at all the principal meetings of the sister colonies, each officer comparing with the other, but each making his own handicaps; the labor being thus divided, whilst each would avail himself of the knowledge of the other. The fees the chief club would derive from the various country clubs would go far to pay its handicappers' traveling expenses to the various meetings; and the position of the club and its prospects fully warrant the payment of much larger salaries than the one now paid.

Then, when handicapping is by the club's stern direction made a reality instead of a farce, means should be taken to prevent the handicappers' labors being neutralized by the inability af the starter. In Melbourne we are fortunate in securing the services of a gentleman who has no rival; but at country meetings, the infinite variety of bad starts is amazing. Flying starts are strictly forbidden by the V.R.C. rules, yet at every meeting they are witnessed, whilst at the principal meetings away from the metropolis horses are started inside the posts, thus rendering the race null and void, without even eliciting comment, and in nearly every instance the press chronicles a bad start. It might also be well if horses that do not want a good start, of which some are noticeable at every meeting, were quietly reported by the starter for the handicapper's information.—*Federal Australian.*

## RACING REMINISCENCES.

### J. B. Thomas and his Best Races—Chicago, Grand Rapids, Battle Creek, etc.

In the spring of 1881 Mr. L. P. Thompson of Clarence, Ia., placed in my charge the bay stallion J. B. Thomas, by Sterling, dam by Defiance. When the horse came to me, which was about the 1st of June, he had a record of 2:34¼, acquired the previous season, and my first experiences with him were of so unsatisfactory a nature that it did not seem probable he would lower those figures materially. In driving him at speed he hitched badly, and was generally so unsatisfactory in gait that I knew at once that a radical change was necessary. I had put sixteen-ounce shoes on his forward feet, and after driving him a few times without any noticeable improvement, concluded that more weight was what he needed. So a six-ounce toe weight was added, and the result was that Thomas at once struck a square, open trot, the extra weight being just the balance he wanted. After working him in the usual manner for a couple of weeks I drove him a mile at speed one morning, and he went the distance in 2:31½ with such ease to himself that I was satisfied he would be a good one before the season was over. Not long after this there was a matinee at the Chicago Driving park, one Saturday afternoon, and I started Thomas in a race against the bay gelding Resolution, by Swigert, whose record was 2:27. The race was a mile and repeat, and Thomas won it in 2:31½, 2:26¾, being sent for all he was worth the last heat. A few days after this I sent him a mile in 2:25, so that it will be seen he was coming to his speed all the time. The week following this 2:25 trial I went over to Central Park track determined to learn just how well the stallion could go three heats, for I had never yet sent him three miles at his best clip. The day and track were good, and the time of the trial was, 2:25½, 2:23¾, 2:24, which pleased me greatly, as I could see the horse was going a trifle within himself all the time, and had a steady, rating pace that was sure to make him dangerous in any race where he was not greatly out-classed in point of speed.

This trial took place on June 15th, and a few days later I shipped Thomas to Grand Rapids, Mich., where he was entered to trot in the 2:34 class, June 23d. The other starters were Jerome Eddy, Hermes, Grand Sentinel, Nigger Doctor and Toledo, and as the track was a half-mile one nobody expected that fast time would be made. Jerome Eddy, Thomas, Grand Sentinel and Hermes were all stallions, and the friends of Eddy were very confident that he could win, the horse having shown them some fast miles. They made him a great favorite in the pools, and when he had won the first heat from Thomas in 2:30½ the crowd seemed to think the race was over. But I had noticed, in working Thomas, that he had never wanted to go the first mile well, and was not disappointed at the result, although before the race was over Jerome Eddy turned out to be a better horse than I had rated him. In the second heat Eddy and Thomas got off together, and went the whole mile like a double team. Right at the finish, however, Thomas, had a little the most speed left, and was first under the wire by a neck or so in 2:27½. Having secured the pole, which is quite an advantage on a half-mile track, by winning this heat, I thought Thomas would win rather easily, but in the third heat Eddy hung to me all the way, and every inch of the mile was contested, Thomas winning by only a nose in 2:24. The fourth heat was much the same, and though Thomas got home first in 2:25, it was all he could do.

This was a remarkably good race for two young stallions to trot so early in the season, one of them reducing his record ten and a quarter seconds, and winning the heat by only a few inches; and it also showed me that Jerome Eddy was a hard horse to beat. But the most curious feature of the affair was that everybody except myself thought that Thomas was winning easily, when the truth is that I never worked harder in my life to get a horse home in front of another. So when the two horses met again at Iona the following week I expected another lightning race. As before, Thomas would not go well the first heat, which Jerome Eddy won in 2:28, but in the second mile my horse was ready to trot, and I beat Eddy out a neck in 2:24½, after a hard struggle; and whenever horses in the 2:34 class beat 2:25 on a half-mile track there is not much room for argument about their having plenty of speed. The third and fourth heats were won easily by Thomas in 2:27¾, 2:27¾. At Battle Creek, the following week, Jerome Eddy did not start, and Thomas won easily in 2:31¾, 2:31½, 2:33¾. On the same day that this race was trotted I saw the black gelding Troubadour beat Helene, big John, Clover, Ethel Medium, Elsie Groff and two others very easily in 2:26¾, 2:26¼, 2:27, and as J. B. Thomas was to meet him in the 2:30 class at the Chicago meeting, I watched him pretty carefully, and concluded that he would prove a hard one to beat. After the Battle Creek meeting both Thomas and Troubadour came to Chicago, and we had nearly two weeks of a rest before the meeting here began. I had a chance to see what the other horses in my race were doing. From all I could learn Troubadour was the only one I feared, and so on the night before the race I went into the Sherman House, where the pool selling was being done, and bought one ticket on Troubadour, paying $8 in $58 for it. My idea was that before the race was over Troubadour would be selling at much higher figures, and the public had made Thomas such a favorite, he selling over the entire field, that I did not deem it safe to put my money on him.

The race was begun on the first day of the meeting, Saturday, July 25th, being called rather late in the afterhoon. The purse was $1,500, with $500 extra to the winner of the fastest heat, if trotted better than 2:21. In all his Michigan races Thomas had not trotted the first heat well, but this time he went away rather better than usual, and although Troubadour led me a length to the three-quarter pole, I closed the gap coming down the homestretch, and was only beaten a neck in 2:20½. Then the race was postponed until the following Monday. Thomas had gone the first heat so well that I thought he would repeat the performance on Monday, and so did not give him a fast mile Sunday, although it was afterwards clear to me that this was a mistake. When he came out Monday afternoon to continue the race Thomas began acting badly, and when the word was given he made two breaks before reaching the quarter pole. This put him so far behind that I saw there was no chance of winning the heat, and laid my horse up. Annie W, who was in the race, had been well supported in the pools, and as there had been a great deal of talk about her great speed I supposed she would give Troubadour a hot fight for the heat. But, instead of this, she never got near him in the mile, he winning handily in 2:25, which was a very easy heat for him.

In the third heat Thomas acted like himself again, and I knew that the horse that beat him would have to go a lively mile. Troubadour was the quickest to get away from the wire, and led me a length at the quarter pole, but by the time half the mile had been trotted we were on pretty nearly even terms. Around the third turn Troubadour got away from me a little again, Thomas being on the outside. Coming down the homestretch I went at Thomas pretty strongly, but in spite of all my efforts Troubadour had a length th best of it at the distance stand, and seemed to be out-trotting my horse. He made a break at that point, however, and ran all the way to the wire, so that the judges gave the heat to Thomas in 2:18¾, which was the fastest mile he ever trotted, and also entitled him to the $500 extra money, unless the time of this heat should be beaten by some other horse, which I did not think was very probable.

The race had been a great betting one, and the men who had backed Troubadour for the money were well posted on trotting. I have been told that Budd Doble, who was interested in the success of the black horse, held a consultation with Dustin, who was driving him, after this heat had been won by Thomas, and that a change of programme was decided upon, it being agreed that in the fourth heat Troubadour should trail Thomas until well into the homestretch, and make his race from that point to the wire. This plan was carried out, Thomas leading for more than seven-eighths of a mile, when Troubadour came along and beat him in 2:23½. It was a peculiarity of Thomas that he would never do anything like his best when in front of the other horses in a race. He would not go up against the bit, and had to be driven all the time; but when head-and-head with another horse, or a little behind, he would be as steady as a clock and do his very best. My better plan in driving this heat would have been to have stayed behind Troubadour, although there is no certainty that this would have altered the result. As it was, my horse got $875 out of the race to Troubadour's $750, the extra $500 for trotting the fastest heat making the difference.

My next race with Thomas was at Buffalo, where Edwin Thorne, Kate Sprague, Pilot R and Jewett were the other starters. I won the first heat with Thomas in 2:22, and in the second made a dead heat with Thorne in 2:20½. The third heat I won in 2:21, but then Thorne went on and captured the race in 2:21, 2:23½, 2:21, 2:19¾. At Rochester, the following week, the same field, with the exception of Jewett, started. Thomas won the first heat in 2:20½; Kate Sprague the second and third in 2:18, 2:23½, and then Edwin Thorne came along and took the next three in 2:20, 2:19½, 2:25. In this race Thomas was first or second in every heat but one, and at its close I gave up the horse.—*Peter V. Johnson in the Breeder's Gazette.*

## Prospectus Petaluma Colt Stakes.

The directors of the Sonoma and Marin Agricultural Association are contemplating the inauguration of a series of trotting colt stakes on a grand scale.

The proposition is to make the races open to all colts and fillies of one, two, and three years old in the United States, to be given annually at Petaluma during the week of their fair with an entrance fee of $10 in each stake.

Nominations to be made with the Secretary of the Association and closed annually on the first day of January preceding each fair. An installment fee of $10 to be paid on the 15th of April thereafter, one of $10 on the 1st of July following, and one of $20 on the day of the race, before starting. Any subscriber who shall fail to pay his installments, when due, forfeits all previous payments. To the three stakes the association propose adding $1,000 each, which, together with all sums received (as forfeits and fees) in each stake, is to be divided into two main parts, or classes, of 4-5 in the first class, and 1-5 in the second. The money in the first class is to be so distributed that the four winning horses will receive respectively 8-20ths, 5-20ths, 4-20ths, 3-20ths, of their stake, according to positions at the finish of the race. The second class of winners to receive 4-10ths 3-10ths, 2-10ths and 1-10th of their stake respectively as they may stand at the conclusion of their race. Thus it may be seen, that if each main stake should amount to $2,500 (which is claimed to be a low estimate) the first class would get $2,000, of which the first horse in that class would receive $800, second, $500, third, $400, and the fourth $300. In the second class of the same stake, the first horse would receive $200, second $150, third $100, and the fourth $50, virtually making eight graded prizes in each main stake. The first class of starters in each to be composed of the six fastest foals, and the second class to consist of the six next fastest of the same age, thus making two independent final contests in each stake. The yearlings to trot a dash of one mile. Two-year-olds, heats of a mile, two in three. Three-year-olds to trot mile heats, three in five. The classification, and trials for positions in the different stakes, to be determined and governed by authority of the Sonoma and Marin Agricultural Association. All else, (not otherwise provided) to be governed by rules of the National Turf Association.

## The Track in Australia.

The Victoria Trotting Club will "hold high holiday" on Wednesday afternoon, on their beautiful Elsternwick track, and a large portion of the many thousands of horsey visitors now in Melbourne, as well as of our own metropolitan sports, are sure to put in an appearance. The programme provided is well diversified, and possesses considerable interest, there being a purse at one-mile heats, best three in five, and another at two mile heats, best two in three, besides a four miles match for £200, between those well-known public performers, Wanderer and Brown Hawk. For the club events, although the number of starters is limited, this does not so much matter in trotting as in galloping; nor, indeed, is it often—even in the home of this particular race, the United States—that a larger field faces the scratch than the number of entries promises on the present occasion. Moreover, in the "Free for All" Purse, those who may never have had an opportunity of witnessing the speed gait of American trotters. will now get a chance to see the already proved Commodore and Startle meet the just arrived Oliver and the unknown Red Star; and as all of these will be driven true Yankee style, in skeleton sulkies, and by skilled handlers of the reins; the contrast of the contest with that of the previous day's Melbourne's Cup will prove most marked. There will be plenty of trains, at the cheapest of fares, from the Hobson's Bay station, and the exceedingly well arranged course is only a step from the Elsternwick platform. If to-morrow does not result in being "a red-letter day" for the V. T. C., then will merit not receive its due reward.—*The Sportsman, Melbourne, Oct. 30th.*

NATIONAL TROTTING ASSOCIATION, DISTRICT BOARD No. 5, December 4, A. D. 1882.—The meeting of this Board called upon the written request of J. McM. Shafter adjourned from November 27th, A. D. 1882, to this day. The protest of Joseph Cairn Simpson to the colt Dawn, and the protest to the filly Mocking Bird, are severally overruled, and the decisions of the judges of the race as to said protests are in all respects affirmed. N. T. SMITH, President, and
J. McM. SHAFTER, Member said Board.

## Queer Laws.

The following which is copied from the *Referee* (London, England) of Nov. 12th shows what singular fancies the average legislator indulges in regard to betting. Some fanatic—it may be a fool—obtains a position where he has a voice in making laws. He is sure to run into some crotchet or other, and with others to support him, not so foolish or fanatical perhaps, but having a dread of running counter to the opinions of the "unco gude" laws as absurd as can be are placed upon the statute book. We have little faith in legislation when that is directed to compelling men to take the narrow grooves the bigots desire. So long as a man is a good citizen, in the generally accepted meaning of the term, we are willing that he should follow his own bent. As Jefferson so well expressed it "any man who is a good citizen, a good neighbor, good in his family relations, upright and honest in his dealings, he cannot have a bad religion." That view is gaining ground all over the civilized world, and as that becomes established, the spirit that led to the adoption of the "blue laws" will grow weaker :

The betting prosecution at Manchester, from which so much was expected one way or another, ended in a direct compromise. Mr. C. Russell, Q. C., M. P., who is popularly supposed to be the only member of the inner bar who knows anything about sport, was secured by the racecourse company, which undertook not only the defense of itself, but that of the incriminated bookmakers; and Mr. C. Russell, Q. C., M. P., suggested a course which received the full concurrence of the Salford bench of magistrates. The difference between tweedledum and tweedledee, even in matters of law, was never shown to greater advantage, or disadvantage, than by means of Mr. Russell's suggestion. Several times since the Act of 1853 was passed, it has been decided that the use of a stool, a hutch, or a box, the carrying of an umbrella, or the doing of anything which attracted special public attention to the user, carrier, or doer, constituted "a place" within the meaning of the Act; and that, therefore, the delinquent was punishable under its covenants and clauses. But where men who have not thus attracted public attention have betted, no matter whether they betted more or betted less than the users of stools, hutches, or boxes, or the carriers of umbrellas, they have been ruled outside the Act, and have escaped fine and imprisonment. His explanation of affairs formed the keystone of Mr. Russell's operations. He suggested that the Manchester Racecourse Company should admit the error of the men who rigged up stands in the course, or brought them there ready-made; throw themselves on the mercy of the Court, and crave forgiveness. But with regard to men who simply stood upon permanent steps not intended for purposes of betting, Mr. Russell submitted that their case was entirely different. The steps were constructed as steps, and as steps only, and not as a betting resort or "place," and their temporary use by betting men did not bring them within the purview of Sir Alexander Cockburn's Act. Therefore, those who simply betted upon the steps and did not use artificial means to attract observation were as innocent as babies. The prosecution having fallen in with this view, and the bench having concurred, nominal fines were inflicted upon two of the admittedly guilty wretches, and there the case ended, as the representatives of the Watch Committee said, for the present, at all events. The Watch Committee is doubtless satisfied; it has certainly proved its possession of power. Besides what it has done, the committee remains complete master of the field, as the summonses against the betting men who stood upon the steps were not withdrawn or dismissed, but simply adjourned sine die, so that in the event of any other annoyance on their part, proceedings can go on without having to be begun at the beginning.

Thus it will be seen that, in accordance with the administration of the Act of 1853 and its amendations and additions, minor sinners are once more the victims. Fortunately for them, they do not suffer in pocket this time as they have suffered before, owing to the generosity of the racecourse company; but the principle remains the same nevertheless. They will be allowed to go on committing the identical offense for which they have been convicted—so long as they commit it in a slightly different manner. It is fair to presume that when the law against ready-money betting was first established, the intention was to put down ready-money betting of all kinds and descriptions. Even then the law would have been sufficiently iniquitous, seeing that special exemption was made for a kind of betting which is infinitely more immoral and destructive than ready-money betting. But such moderation was found unpalatable jo those who make our laws and those who interpret them; and now we find one man allowed to bet as much as he likes, and stake the money beforehand, while another cannot even talk about such a hideous crime without being at once hauled before the magistrates.

As idea is prevalent among people who do not frequent racecourses, and yet who take an interest in what happens upon them, that all betting done inside the ring is done upon the Tattersall's, or credit principle. They hear of betting men being convicted for betting outside, and outside betting means in their minds ready-money betting; while inside betting is to them betting "on the nod," which is entirely above the ken of the bi'ry-eyed policeman, or whatsoever other person may be selected to mark down delinquents. As a matter of fact, the betting inside the rings is, as a rule, ready-money betting. For one who is sufficiently good, and known to be good, to obtain credit, there are always twenty who are almost unknown to the bookmakers, and who therefore deposit their money before the race, and, if successful, receive their winnings directly afterwards. Often enough, gentlemen who only bet from five to ten pounds at a time, and who could receive credit if they so desired it, prefer to pay as they go; sometimes because of the belief that if they were to bet "on the nod" they might lose hundreds where tens now satisfy them; sometimes because they like each race to stand by itself, and because they have no idea of making betting anything other than a mere passing amusement. Not only in this the case inside the ring; also inside it you may find men at every important meeting who do not use stools or hutches by Parliament and the judges, but who manage to dress themselves up so as to attract observation, and with observation increased caution.

What I can't understand is, that if it is wrong for a man to stand upon a piece of wood which raises him six inches above the ground, or to carry a gaudy umbrella, how can it be right for him to get himself up in a costume of most extraordinary character—of such a character as causes him to be looked at twenty times as much as he would be looked at if dressed in ordinary garb and standing on the tallest pedestal or carrying the largest and gaudiest umbrella obtainable ? The whole business is a muddle, and sorely requires reformation

At Newmarket, the headquarters of the turf, which is protected and cherished by a body of noblemen and gentlemen who hold absolute sway over racing and all that belongs to it, who are of the class which first caused the exemption of credit betting, an arrangement has been made by means of which ready-money betting is permitted, providing the layers pay the regulation fees for the ring, and do not attempt to defraud the proprietors of their dues and imposts. This in itself shows the current belief among people who know nothing of racing but what they read in the papers, that within the ring credit betting rules supreme, is nonsensical. That ready-money betting is against the law no man would attempt to deny; still, for nearly thirty years men have been convicted or have escaped conviction, not because they have or have not betted with ready money, but because it has been decided that they have or have not made "a place" within the meaning of the Act for the purpose of betting.

AGRICULTURAL PARK, SACRAMENTO, NOV. 30.
SUMMARY.

Match race. $200 a side; quarter mile.
Fred Bridge names s g Frank .......................................... 1
Joe Zuver names ch m Kitty Woods ................................ 2
    Time—0:24½.

Same day.
Purse and added stakes, $250; mile heats, three in five; for pacers.
J. W. Wilson names b g Roden .......................... 1  1  1
F. Sheplar names sp g Randy Andy .................. 2  3  2
C. H. Schluin names b g Shaker ....................... 3  2  3
    Time—2:36, 2:32, 2:32.

## Answers to Correspondents.

SACRAMENTO, Dec. 3, 1882.
EDITOR BREEDER AND SPORTSMAN, *Dear Sir:* Will there be a renewal of the Stanford Stakes this year for foals of 1881 to trot as three-year-olds in 1884 ? If so when does it close and how much is the first installment ? Yours truly,
                                                        INQUIRER.

Answer—Advertisements will soon appear giving all of the particulars.

Mc L. and H., Home Shoe Bend, Boise county, I. T.:
Wild Wood, b. c., foaled 1875, bred by John Hall, Alvarado, California, by Woodburn.
First dam Peggy Ringgold, by Ringgold.
Second dam Little Peggy, by Cripple.
Third dam Peggy Stewart, by Cook's Whip.
Fourth dam Mary Bedford, by Duke of Bedford.
Fifth dam by imported Speculator.
Sixth dam by Alexander's Dare Devil mare, by imported Dare Devil.
Seventh dam imported Trumpetta, by Trumpator.
Imported Trumpetta runs back through six generations to Daffodil's dam.
Woodburn, by Lexington, from Heads-I-Say, by imported Glencoe, grandam imported Heads-or-Tails, by Lottery.

A. M. E., Red Bluff.—Although there are diversities o opinion in regard to the question you propose, as to the propriety of "breeding a promising filly at three years of age, and whether it will retard the development?" We are under the impression that no ill results will follow. In some cases there appears to have been a decided advantage. At an early day we will make your query the subject of an article in which will be embodied the results of actual trials. There are instances enough to warrant the conclusion that an early exercise of maternal functions has been an advantage.

## LATEST OF ALL SORTS.

### Base Ball.

Ward, Welch and O'Neil have been engaged for the next season to pitch for the New York League nine. Ewing and Clapp will catch. The other players will be Reilly first base, Troy second, Hankinson third, Caskins short stop, Dorgan left field. Ward who is well-known in this city was with the Providence club during the season just closed. Sweeny, the pitcher of the Niantics, takes a favorite and a good attendance is expected. The game will be between two picked nines, including the best players of the Reno, Niantic and Haverly clubs.

There is likely to be two or three new amateur clubs in this city next season, and instead of the Oakland Grounds being monopolized by the Olympics, Redingtons and Howlands next year, we have few clubs will claim the same privileges on the grounds which have been accorded by the Olympic Athletic Club to the Redingtons. There is a likelihood that the Olympic Athletic Club will offer a handsome trophy for competition next season and permit all amateur clubs to enter into the contest for it.

Last Thanksgiving Day Messrs. Bogert, Turner and Stewart found a place on the Sancilito shore between Yellow Bluff and the Tide station where they caught 50 pounds of fine tomcod. On Saturday Mr. Denning and Bogert were over the east side of Goat Island and got 75 pounds of rockcod and tomcod. There will be good fishing during the coming week on the east side of Goat Island.

Dr. Pretheroe blind-folded with long stockings the twenty-two outriders at Central Park last Monday and shipped them to the certain farm to be established in California. The farm consists of 800 acres in San Bernardino county, and the cost of taking the ostriches thither from New York is $2,000.

Mr. W. S. Ruddick and Mr. J. M. Heinold, on the 25th of last month, killed 51 ducks, mostly mallards. This fine bag was made in the evening by moonlight near the artesian well at Mount Eden.

The man who loves his poultry stock will generally take good care of them and good care will make them valuable and productive.

The natural traits of the game fowl, their beautiful plumage, proud and majestic carriage, and the proverbial courage are qualities that are much admired.

## HERD AND SWINE.

### Blood Tells.

If farmers who have not yet imbibed ideas leading towards improvement in their meat producing animals could visit any one of the leading markets, in this or any other country, and witness the close discrimination practiced by buyers, no other evidence would be required to show the utter folly of attempting to force money from customers who are seeking a first rate article, by placing before them stock of low grade. The man who hauls shrunken wheat to market, knows what his reward will be, because close grading and no latitude is the rule with wheat. The same careful discrimination is placed upon all other products of the farm—fruit, vegetables, poultry, wools—and especially in dairy products are the lines drawn very closely.

There is a sharp, well defined meaning in the lesson to be gleaned from prices on butter, when the quotations show the unwarrantable range from thirty-three down to eight cents. The lesson is equally sharp and well defined when the quotations on steers vary from seven down to two and a quarter cents. The spectacle of a two and a quarter cent steer eating the grass off of land worth $50 an acre, and corn worth, in the crib, fifty cents a bushel, affords a sad commentary on the judgment of the farmer who tolerates such a practice. Yet, an approximation to this is the rules on many farms. For every car load that commands six to seven cents, there are twenty car loads, no one of which will go above five cents, a large proportion going below this figure.

After looking the contents of the pen carefully over, we invite a look among the quarters hung up in any wholesale slaughtering establishment, where several different grades of steers are killed and kept for sale to retail butchers. On two quarters hanging side by side, which, to a novice, may seem of equal value, there is often a difference of from three to four cents a pound. Follow these two grades of meat to the retail butchers, and you will find that certain shops always buy the cheaper, and others the higher grades; some, a very few, buy of two grades. Taking Chicago retail shops as examples, if you follow these quarters to the block, you will find the best steaks and roasts from the better grade, are sold at 18 to 20 cents a pound, while similar cuts from the lower grade are sold at 12 to 14.

Consumers, though not one in a thousand of them know that the quality hinges mainly upon the extent to which the lean proportion—in other words, the muscles—have fat distributed through and between their fibers, marbling the meat, have learned that the twenty-or-st meat has qualities which the twelve-cent never possessed; hence, those who can afford to pay the larger prices cheerfully permit the butcher to fill their orders at the top prices. Taking the main, while the channel through which one steer finds a ready buyer at seven cents, while another can only be put off at half the figure. If threecent butter would prove as palatable on the table as the thirty-five-cent butter, the butter priced would control the price of the other, and the two would come nearer together. For a like reason, if cuts from the low-priced steer would prove as savory on the table as those from the higher priced, then the disparity in price would be obliterated. Consumers are becoming, every year, better acquainted with these differences, while the great mass of them, through liberal wages received in manufacturing and mechanical pursuits generally, are better able to buy meat than formerly. It is not generally known that improvement in the quality of our meat producing animals received the first strong incentive through the demand which sprang up when so large a portion of the English population became operatives in manufactories, a century ago.—*National Live Stock Journal.*

### Butter-Making a Science.

There are very many things in the way of farming which any common greener can do. And just because men are able to dig a hole in the ground with a hoe, drop seed into it and cover the seed, and are able to raise what they are satisfied to call a crop, they think they are farmers. So it is in the dairy business. The cows are driven up and milked, the milk is put away, then skimmed; then comes the churning of the cream, which is followed by the salting and working. The breeding or blood of the cow is not studied; the food she is not regarded; the temperature of the milk-house is not looked after; the churn has no thermometer attached, and when the butter is to be worked no thought is given to the probable size of the butter globules or grain, because, as stated, the breeding of the cow is not known, and the butter is worked with about as much care and understanding as the brickmaker would observe in preparing mortar for brick. Many things are necessary to know in butter-making. Milk is a powerful absorbent, and will, therefore, absorb much impurity if uncleanliness should be found to exist. The quick accuracy of impurities such as belong in milk, as well as those absorbed by it, if allowed to remain in the butter, to become rancid should be well studied. If the cows are all about of the same blood, the butter globules will be about the same size, and when placed in a milk-house where the temperature is about 70 degrees above zero, the cream will rise about the same. After so many hours skim and churn in a churn having as little friction as possible, at a temperature of, say, 62 degrees; the butter will be all right if up to this time the premises have been kept clean. The milk must now be washed out—not worked out, because the very moment the working process is introduced the butter globules are liable to become broken, and a mixture of the oil and the milky portion takes place. Then there is no such thing as separating the objectionable portions from the butter. Salt should never be put into the butter until it is set aside. This is reasonable. Any one will admit in a moment that if salt be thrown into butter and worked before it is dissolved, it being hard as well as sharp edged, it will tend to break the globules or grain of the butter; hence the butter becomes greasy, and in place of a knife slipping through it like passing through a ripe apple, it pulls through and has the appearance of having been used in cutting lard.—*Rural Spirit.*

The "American Shorthorn Herd Book," the "American Record," and the "Ohio Shorthorn Record" have been consolidated as the "Shorthorn Breeders' Herd Book," under control of the American Association of Shorthorn Breeders, and there is peace in the Shorthorn camp.

The highest price ever paid for an animal on the Island of Jersey is reported to have been given a few days since by Mr. T. S. Cooper, for the cow Khedives Primrose. The rumor is that Mr. C. has bought the cow from Mr. Dorey for $5,000.

Quite a number of counties have selected delegates to the anti-bull butter convention, which will evidently be largely attended.

## When Doctors Disagree.

Like the scientific breeding of stock other than equine, veterinary science is yet in its infancy, though the rapid strides now being made in that line, especially by the aid of the microscope and other modern appliances, indicate that in a short time the treatment of diseases of animals will be reduced to an exact a science as medical men claim to have achieved in the treatment of human ailments. The scientific investigation into the causes, treatment and effects of diseases of domestic animals is being carried on more systematically and with more satisfactory results in France than in any other country, and the government of that country appropriates a large sum every year for the carrying on of such investigations. Vivisection, however revolting the very idea of it may at first be to those of a refined and sympathetic nature, has resulted in much good, and the pain deliberately imposed on a few animals by experimenters has resulted in the prevention or relieving of pain in many. So much are we indebted to the investigations carried on under the patronage of the French Government that one rarely sees any scientific treatise on any disease of animals without frequent allusions to the investigations of M. Pasteur. But yet, as we have intimated, the science is in its infancy, and "doctors disagree" at every turn. We publish this week an apparently well-digested paper read before the Ontario Veterinary College, in which anthrax, splenic fever, and beack quarter are expressly ascribed to the *Bacillus Anthracis*. In another column we reprint a scholarly article from the *Breeder's Gazette*, written by D. E. Salmon, D. M. V., the object of which is to convince the public that the *Bacillus Anthracis* is entirely absent in Texas fever. As the writer speaks from his own personal experience and investigation his assertions are worthy of consideration, and, in the absence of any further light, the general verdict will be that the Texas fever is distinct from anthrax. His assertions regarding splenic fever are not so pronounced. The subject is well worthy of careful study, especially as the anthrax proper is liable to attack humans as well as brutes. It is but a short time since the Indians of Carson valley were reported to be dying off of this disease, having contracted it by eating the carcasses of cattle which had died of blackleg, as the affection was called in that instance.

## The Supply of Hogs.

We think that neither the bulls nor the bears, with all their agencies or guesses, can deceive the public as to the great deficiency in the supply of hogs for the fall and winter market. The great scarcity and high price of corn in the corn belt for twelve months has caused farmers and feeders to hurry to market all hogs which could be passed off. And there has been a great reduction of the number of hogs kept for breeding. This has been the case in nearly all of the hog-producing regions of the United States, so the deficiency will be at least thirty per cent. below last or three previous years. This will make a material difference in the supply and demand. If all the packers do not combine and establish prices, the farmers may expect at least to decline in prices from the present. Corn last week, owing to the reliable reports of the crops, advanced largely in spite of all the bears could do. And there is scarcely a possibility that the deficiency in hogs can be made up in the next sixteen months. The breeding hogs and corn to feed are not in the country and farmers can rely on good prices for the next fall's hogs, if the business of the country is not controlled by an unholy combination. And with the facts so apparent it does not seem possible that any perversion of facts can possibly deceive anyone. And if all the packers meet as they usually do, and determine on low figures, it seems there ought to be an appeal to Cæsar with all of the vim which has heretofore had for self-defense.

The above from the *Iowa State Register* is undoubtedly the condition of the supply of hogs and corn. We are entirely at the mercy of the packers. If they see fit to meet and fix prices as they undoubtedly have done, there is no redress only for farmers to unite in slaughter their own hogs and await the time for further advances. We have in the larger cities a set of the most unprincipled swindlers and gamblers that ever infested civilized society. They are the curse of the age in which we live. The laws of supply and demand have nothing to do in fixing prices. It is all governed by a set of men whose only aim is to take advantage of the necessities of the people. It seems as if combinations now control most of our products; wheat is forced way up and down without cause. The lumber trade is governed by a combination of lumbermen and no one can now get a carload without paying the regular dealer at home his commission. In fact almost everything now is controlled by combinations. How long will our people submit, is the leading question now to be solved.—*Clipper*.

DRY MURRAIN, SO CALLED.—Impaction of the manifold or third stomach of cattle, generally due to excessive feeding on dry, coarse and fibrous food and insufficient drinking water, frequently proves fatal; if not energetically treated on the appearance of the first symptoms of disease. Dissolve an ounce each of common soda and Barbadoes aloes in half a pint of hot water, and add to this solution an ounce of oil of turpentine; also dissolve one pound of Glauber's salts in half a gallon of hot water; then mix these solutions together, and give it in one dose to cattle over a year and a half old; half such a dose to cattle from eight months to a year and a half, and a third of the quantity named to younger ones. Repeat the doses named every six hours, and at every intervening hour give half a gallon of flaxseed tea with an ounce of ground ginger; or, instead of the flaxseed tea, give a pint of raw linseed oil or molasses every intervening hour. Inject, as often, blood-warm soap-suds or salt water per rectum. Give walking exercise. After recovery give steamed, cooked or ground feed, among which, during a few days, mix a handful of ground willow bark.—*Breeder's Gazette*.

Goats' milk is sold in London at thirty-seven to fifty cents per quart. It is preferred by many for the food of very young children. English and Welsh cottagers find the keeping of goats for their milk a profitable business at the prices paid. The yield is generally very small; but a goat picks its own living with less expense to its owner than any other animal.

Cattle-raising, as well as manufacturing, is looking up in the South. The Agricultural College of Mississippi has lately had its large herd among the Galloway herds of Michigan looking for some breeding cattle.

California has one-tenth of the sheep in the United States.

## ANTHRAX IN CATTLE.

### Paper Read by H. B. Adair in the Ontario Veterinary College, Toronto.

Anthrax is one of the oldest known diseases, as well as the most virulent, no portion of the globe appearing to be exempt from it in one or more of its manifold forms, though warm countries and those where there is much marshy land, or the soil is tenacious of moisture, are the most subject to its ravages; its fatality has materially diminished where proper drainage and cultivation of the land have been adopted.

All animals are liable to become affected with this disease, man as well as beast; birds and fish are only subject to it under certain conditions. It is in herbivorous animals, however, that it appears to have a predisposition to develop chiefly, though others are equally susceptible when placed under suitable conditions for the reception of the poison. Whether the disease is manifested by the formation of a pustule or not, there are certain characteristics by which it is recognized; such as special alterations in the blood, which has a tendency to exude through the vessels, a very dark color, the formation of a feeble clot, a peculiar smell, and the presence in it of certain organisms termed bacteria, the germs of the disease; tumors in the spleen or a discolored and disorganized state of this organ are constant symptoms; so also is the sudden development of tumors, leading on to abscesses or gangrene.

Anthrax manifests itself in many different forms and is known by as many different names such as Charbon, etc., in the horse; Red-water, Splenic fever, Texas fever, Black Quarter, Gloss Anthrax, etc., in cattle.

In the horse I have never seen a case, but understand that it has prevailed to some extent in the Southern States in a sporadic form. The symptoms manifested are sudden sickness, and the noses of the disease is marked by a well developed febrile condition. The animal affected becomes comatose; there is great prostration, and the animal has a staggering gait. Respiration becomes accelerated, and the pulse, first full, rapidly becomes small and irregular, the motions of the heart strong and bounding, temperature high at first but soon falls, cost dull, hairs of mane tail easily pulled out, mucous membranes assume a yellow or red color, and are often covered with brown or black petechiæ, urine brown or reddish color. In animal evinces colicky pains, bowels constipated, fæces covered with bloody mucus, and discharge from the nose of an offensive odor. The morbid process continuing, all the symptoms increase, and the anal seal soon dies. Sometimes he falls and expires immediately, before any symptoms are noticed, or there may be external manifestations or tumory form, as in Black Quarter in cattle.

Red-water in cattle—This form takes its name from the color of the urine; it has prevailed to some extent in central Kentucky the past season, where I saw some cases. The symptoms were dullness, loss of appetite, dry muzzle, redness of conjunctiva, dullness of eye, black petechial spots on mucous membrane of nostril, respiration somewhat quickened, weakness in hind quarters, twitching of the muscles, in some cases diarrhea but generally constipation, with the passage with bloody mucus, urine of a cherry red color generally. In some exceptional cases it is black, temperature invariably high in first stages, from 103° deg. to 107° deg. F., pulse very much quickened, 70 to 95 per minute, and very distinct in fever stages. In milch cows secretion ceases entirely, the animal separate from the herd, become comatose and dies in from one hour to a week after being first noticed.

Black quarter—This form usually occurs in young animals from six months to two years old, especially those in the most thriving condition; what I have seen of this form was either sporadic or enzootic; the first thing that draws the attention of the herdsman is the death of one of his finest calves, which is followed by a second and sometimes even the whole lot will die in a single day; those that are subject to this form thrive with rapidity until they attain a high state of plethora, when some of them perhaps become lame, a swelling commences in some part of the body, generally about the hock; this is very hot and painful and is often mistaken for an injury, it rapidly extends up the limb, causing considerable tumefaction, first painful, afterward it becomes insensible, and gangrenous, cold, and crepitates on pressure, in consequence of accumulation of gases in the subcutaneous areolar tissue as a result of decomposition; when cut into it is found to be produced also by accumulation of putrid, sanious, and yellow gelatinous material underneath the skin and between the muscles of the part, also patches of black pulpy substance may be observed in various parts of the tumor; constitutional symptoms run high at this stage, the animal rapidly loses strength, maintains the recumbent position, becomes tympanitic and comatose; death may even take place in a few hours after the first manifestations of lameness or the patient may rally, the tumors slough and possibly recover. In splenic fever or Texas fever, commonly known by the latter name because of its ravages when Texas cattle come north, the germs, I think, never leave the Texas steer, and when under suitable causes they become active and produce the disease in an acute form death is the result.

Symptoms—Nervous excitement, muzzle dry and hot, membrane first congested, afterward becomes pale, temperature elevated, urine of high color and voided often, weakness of hind parts, shivering and either stupor or great excitement, the ears and legs become cold, tongue discolored, grinding of the teeth, foaming at the mouth, diarrhea with abdominal pain and finally convulsions and death by asthenia.

Lesions—One of the most noticeable is a tendency to rapid decomposition; early distention of the body with gas, rectum everted and of a deep red color; fetid discharges from the natural openings are very common. The blood is of a very dark color, does not coagulate, or if so, the clot has a peculiar sickening smell, it is usual to find bloody mucus in different parts of the body. The respiratory organs are generally normal. Spleen is invariably altered. The intestines are more or less congested, the liver enlarged, and the presence in the blood and other fluids of bacteria, the specific germ of this disease in whatever form it may manifest itself. If the disease has been of any duration the membranes will present a blanched, or bloody appearance.

Causes have been variously disputed until late investigation has brought the matter to an issue; it has been advanced, and the microscope was brought in to assist the researches of observers the influence of pastures and forage affected with parasitic organisms was recognized. Their minuteness, however, and the difficulty of determining the exact agents and their modes of introduction into the animal economy, left the whole matter in a state of doubt and speculation. Until recently it was thought that these diseases arose from too rich a diet, by which means the blood was so charged with nutritive matter that the digestive functions became impaired, and a septic action set up in that fluid. It

is now known, however, that these changes are entirely due to the presence in the blood of a parasitic organism termed the *Bacillus Anthracis*, which, acting upon the organic constituents of the blood, impairs and destroys its vitality.

These parasites are either minute "rods or filaments, or spheroid bodies," which are found in the blood of animals which have died of anthrax. They break up or resolve themselves into roundish bodies termed "spores," which retain their vitality for long periods outside the body, but are rapidly and indefinitely multiplied while in the system.

When an animal dies, and the fluid and excrements are left on the ground, the spores either sink into it and remain there or become washed away or removed to other places by the rain or other natural causes; thus we can account for the prevalence of this disease in low-lying places. When animals are buried the earth worms bring up the germs in their casts, and as they cling to the roots and stems of the grass and other plants, they are taken into the system in that way, which accounts for its outbreaks in places that have been grazed over for years without disease of any kind being known.

Dry and cold weather prevents the development of the parasites. Wet and warm weather favors their development, and dry and warm weather favors the vitality of the disease. They are introduced into the system through the mediums of the grass, water, etc. There can be no doubt that multitudes of these germs are destroyed by natural agencies, and that western prairie fires have this one redeeming point of aiding in their destruction. The way in which these parasites are distributed and conveyed into the system of animals has been determined by the researches of Professors Pasteur and Toussaint, who have not only proven that they are the sole cause of these diseases, but have succeeded in modifying their virulence, so as to be able to produce anthrax in a mild form, thus conferring immunity on animals exposed to contagion.

The treatment of anthrax has been very unsatisfactory, as there is a great tendency to putrefaction. I would advise antiseptics, alteratives and tonics. Isolate all sick animals, change those that are not yet affected to a high pasture away from stagnant water, and give the sick, morning and evening:

Chlorate of Potassa—2 ii.
Sulphite of Soda—z iv.
Carbolic Acid—z iss.

To be dissolved in water and mixed in soft food. Those that are not yet affected should have a constant supply of salt and pure water. All dead animals should be buried in their skins, and the yards disinfected with chloride of lime or carbolic acid, and barns with sulphurous fumes, as well as washing with carbolic acid solution.

## Origin of Red Hogs.

In a former article I spoke of the assumptions of breeders who claim that only their hogs are pure-bred, as absurd. I illustrated the idea by referring to the Poland-China hogs as an example, showing that there were different families of these hogs, of different breeding and crossing; but that when bred to a certain fixed standard of characteristics, and uniform in their breeding, they might be classed as thoroughbred. Suppose that one of the breeders of Poland-China should assume that his family of hogs were the only ones pure bred, and all others were not genuine, would he not occupy a position to invite criticism, if not of distrust? I have before me a catalogue of Mr. Clark Pettit, of New Jersey, which says: "The genuine 'improved Jersey Red swine' are descended from stock imported into Salem Co., N. J., from Europe at least forty years ago." Among the characteristics mentioned are "the red hair and fine symmetrical legs." One thing at a time; first, the origin. This much this young man knew all about the origin of Jersey Reds, when David Pettit, of Salem, N. J., a gentleman advanced in years, and one of the most intelligent farmers in the state (Clark's father, I believe), wrote me in 1872 that he could not give the origin of the Red hogs in New Jersey, but he had known of them for thirty years. D. M. Brown, of Windsor, N. J., wrote me at the same time that he had known of them for nearly fifty years, but he did not know how or where they originated. He described them as very long in the body, strong bone, coarse hair and growing to an enormous size. Other persons living in New Jersey, with whom I conversed at this time, gave the same testimony as Mr. Brown. Mr. Clark Pettit endeavors to convey the impression that his Jersey Reds are descended in a direct lineage from imported Jersey Reds from Europe, and that this lineage or descent can be traced for forty years. I have no objection to Mr. Pettit claiming that his Jersey Reds are better than any other; but I do object to his boastful claims of special purity of blood, except only as he may have or shall establish it by breeding; because I insist that older and perhaps wiser men than he, in his own State, who were disinterested, owned that they did not know the origin of these hogs. I do not know the origin, but I believe they are an offshoot of the old-fashioned Berkshires; or, in other language, they are descended from the early importations of Berkshires. Authentic history establishes the fact that red was a common color in Berkshires, and it still came up in the purest and best-bred families of the breed.

A few years ago, Wm. Crozier, a celebrated breeder at Northport, Long Island, N. Y., imported a number of Berkshires, and at the New York State Fair he generously gave me the choice of a boar pig out of a litter of nine, which were farrowed by one of his imported sows. I got A. B. Allen, the best authority on Berkshires in this country, to select the boar; and he picked out a rich plum-colored pig as his choice, remarking that "this indicated purity of blood." Why? Because it proved a direct lineage with the foundation stock in the shire or county of Berk. Mr. Pettit does not give the name of the breed imported, but leaves it to be understood that the hogs imported were Jersey Reds. Neither does he tell us the country. "From Europe" is rather indefinite.

The truth is, the Jersey reds are only one of the various families of red hogs in this country. They had been crossed for years with other hogs, but latterly with Chester Whites, and these cross-bred hogs, usualy red-and-white, but often all red, were really famous for growth and size. I never heard of the name Jersey Reds until I heard it by the late J. E. Lyman, formerly agricultural editor of the New York Tribune. Mr. Lyman, who lived in New Jersey at the time, was unable to obtain the origin. I do not know when the name was first given to this family of hogs, but I do know that it was first introduced into agricultural literature through my report on these meats in 1872 to the National Swine Breeders' Convention. Mr. Lippincott, of New Jersey, was the first man to advertise these under this name, in the *County Gentleman*, if I mistake not; and he was followed soon after by a Mr. Collins. These gentlemen made no pretensions to an imported lineage.

I think my report alluded to is nearest the truth, when I say "the positive origin of this family of swine is unknown."

It further says, under the head of characteristics, "a good specimen of a Jersey Red should be red in color, with a snout of moderate length, large lop ears, small head in proportion to the length and size of the body. They should be long in the body, standing high and rangy on their legs. Bone coarse, hairy tail and neck, and hair long, inclining to bristles on the back. They are valuable on account of their size and strong constitutions and especially for growth. They are not subject to mange." In my next article I will endeavor to give the history of the other families of red hogs, as far as it is known, and a description of them. The name Jersey Red is simply a local one, and Maryland Reds would have been just as appropriate, as the same kind of hogs were bred in that State. I recollect seeing a' sow, a good specimen of the red family of hogs, with a large litter of pigs, some of them red and others red-and-white, in war time feeding along Pennsylvania avenue. These hogs were quite common at that time, 1862 and 1863, about Washington. They undoubtedly had the same origin as the hogs in Jersey, viz., from the early importations of Berkshire, which they resembled in form and characteristics.—*Col. Curtis in the Breeder's Gazette.*

## Fattening Hogs in Large Numbers.

The attempt to fatten hogs in large numbers under one management is not so frequently made now as formerly. The general belief seems to be that they cannot be made to thrive when many are kept and fed together.

Wholesome feed, and that in variety, with good air and cleanliness, are well shown to be prime essentials to success in the handling of hogs. How to secure these with large herds, and at a cost which will leave a fair margin of profit, is a matter of interest to every one concerned in supplying the ever ready demand for fat hogs and pork products. At present prices the temptation to engage extensively in rearing and feeding hogs would with most farmers be irresistible could they but feel insured against the heavy losses from disease and death which almost invariably occur in large herds.

The practical experience of Messrs. Day Bros. of Sangamon county, Ill., on this subject may be worth relating.

During the past summer and early fall they bought up hundreds of hogs and shoats from within a circuit of twenty miles or less of their farm near Springfield. The most of their purchase were thin in flesh; in fact, many were what are usually termed mere shadows. Since the latter part of August they have been putting the feed into these hogs with a view to fattening them for the Chicago market. They have made a number of shipments to the present time, and now have on hand about 870 head, ranging in weight from 180 to 300 pounds each. These are all allowed to run together in a lot of about four acres, once covered with timber but now mostly cut off, leaving out trees enough for shade, etc., and yet sufficiently open to admit sunshine and a free circulation of air. They are fed on the ground with ear corn, sometimes old—that is, of last year—and sometimes new, jerked from the field with half the husks still on. Many of these husks are afterwards collected by the hogs at different places, usually under the trees, and used by them for bedding. To prevent these beds becoming foul, a one-horse rake is driven through the ground every day to collect the cobs and husks, and these are then burned on the bedding places with the husks gathered there by the hogs. The smoke and ashes, as well as the charred cobs made by these burnings, are believed to be conducive to the health of the lusty porkers. They certainly tend to prevent the accumulation of vermin and to promote cleanliness.

Besides the corn fed to the hogs they have access at all times to well-supplied swill troughs. The lines of goers and comers to and from these are kept up almost constantly. Even during the night they are visited by many that are too shy to come by day. The swill is made of rye-meal chiefly. To about 1,500 weight of rye-meal is added 100 weight of oil-meal, and the whole made into swill, in large tanks, with cold water, and allowed to become slightly sour before being fed. Arrangements are now in progress for using hot water instead of cold water. This, it is thought, will be an improvement as cold weather comes on.

The troughs from which the swill is fed are arranged with slats on each side, the lower ends being nailed to the upper edge of the trough and the upper ends to a long strip running the length of the trough, about fourteen inches above and directly over the middle. These slats are not placed opposite to each other, but are made to alternate. In this way no two hogs can face each other when feeding from opposite sides. This arrangement of the slats seems to completely prevent the hogs from getting into the troughs with their feet, and also to afford each a fair chance to feed without being crowded by his neighbor.

In addition to the corn and swill given them these hogs are turned into a meadow of about 100 acres early every morning, where they are allowed to remain until about 10 a. m. Here they get another change of feed, and such exercise as seems needful for them.

A more healthy and well-doing lot of hogs than these one seldom sees. They are picked over from time to time, and such taken out for shipment as are deemed at their best. They usually average, when shipped, about 236 pounds each, in car-load lots. As ripe hogs are taken out others are being put in. When new ones are bought they are kept in a separate inclosure for about two weeks before being turned in with the large herd. This is done as a precaution against the introduction of disease from outside herds.

Most of the hogs here are black, or nearly so. The proprietors are very decided in their preference for Berkshires and their crosses. They find them to fatten and round up more evenly than any others. Essex, they say, are too small, and Poland-Chinas are too coarse. White hogs they disparage altogether, although a few—perhaps two per cent.—may be found among those being fed.

The management here described seems to supply all the needed conditions to success. It is practicable, and apparently as economical as any that could be devised. The remarkably fine weather for the past two months has rendered needless all expense for shelter. Besides the saving in this respect, the excellent health and thrift of the hogs has, no doubt, been largely due to their freedom from the restraints and evils almost unavoidable when they are housed in bad weather.—*Phil. Thriftion.*

Australia has 80,000,000 sheep, against 36,000,000 in this country. The wool yield of Australian sheep has been very light; but the improvements made by importing American breeding stock are rapidly bringing it up. Some fine wool breeders have shipped rams to Australia at $100 to $500 per head, and the crosses from these fully double the original wool clip per sheep.

The blood of animals of an herbivorous nature that have been acclimatized in elevated regions has been found by M. P. Bert to be richer in oxygen than the blood of the similar animals inhabiting lands near the level of the sea.

## Texas Fever and Anthrax.

The gentleman who is giving the readers of the New York *Times* some lessons concerning Texas fever, and who hides his identity under a double asterisk, is not altogether satisfied with our criticisms in a recent number of the *Gazette.* "The statement in the *Times,*" says this writer, "is not only absolutely true, as can be proved by the statements of Dr. Salmon himself, but, moreover, it was calculated and intended to exert the very effect of preventing the encroachment of this dreaded disease upon new territory, by putting farmers on their guard against it."

When I made the "sweeping and serious charge" that newspapers and veterinarians were working together to deceive, I did not add that they were engaged in any conspiracy, or that they were intentionally doing this great injury to our country. My criticism were not aimed against the intentions, but against the actual results of teachings which directed farmers to take precautions that could have but little if any effect, while their attention was drawn away from the measures which could alone give relief. I would also like to say in this place that the veterinarians referred to are simply individuals who represent the profession only in their own imaginations: there can be no criticism aimed at the profession as a whole, which is as anxious for sound opinions on this question as any of us are.

The writer in the *Times* says: "Texan fever is a delusive misnomer, for the disease prevails all along the Gulf coast, from Florida to Texas, and occasionally occurs in the North from natural causes. It is known in Europe and England, and as splenic fever is included among the so-called anthrax diseases. Anthrax is not a specific name, nor one that in itself indicates any specific disease. It is the Greek word for coal or charcoal, and is used because the distinguishing feature of anthrax diseases is a carbonizing of the blood and the appearance of black or gangrenous lesions upon or in certain tissues or organs. The most pronounced of the anthrax diseases is 'black quarter,' the *Chabon* of the French; and this disease is marked not only by the black disorganized tissue under the skin on the shoulder or flank in many cases, but also by the enlarged, disorganized and black spleen. This latter is the most marked effect of splenic fever, the so-called Texan fever."

[S]plenic fever is a name applied to our Southern cattle fever by Prof. Gamgee, "for the reason that the disease is readily distinguished, as a rule, by the enlargement of the spleen." The study of this disease, he goes on to say, "has revealed characteristics hitherto unknown or undescribed in relation to any disease of man or animals." But to leave no doubt as to his opinion on this subject, he adds: "However warm the weather may be, cattle affected with splenic fever have not developed in their systems any poison like the anthrax poison; and the flesh, blood and other tissues of animals are incapable of inducing any disease in man or animals."

Prof. Gamgee is a European veterinarian of excellent reputation, perfectly familiar with the different forms of anthrax which occur in Europe, and, of course, with their form of splenic fever; and yet he tells us that the characteristics of Texas fever were hitherto undescribed in relation to any disease of man or animals, and that our cattle developed no poison like anthrax poison, and that their flesh and blood were incapable of transmitting the disease to either men or animals. Prof. Gamgee, it is not to be forgotten, is one of his very veterinarians who have made a careful study of Texas fever.

The only other veterinarian besides myself who has made anything like a scientific investigation of this disease is Prof. Law. You have only to turn to that excellent little compendium of his, "The Farmer's Veterinary Adviser," to see how widely he separates these two diseases. It is true that a century or two ago anthrax was not a specific name, and did not include any specific disease, but it is a great mistake to suppose that to be the case to-day. When a man speaks of anthrax or charbon he is understood the world over as referring to a specific disease—that caused by the *bacillus anthracis*; for though black quarter may etymologically be the type of the anthrax diseases, it has been separated from them within a few years, and while still spoken of in France as *charbon externe* or *symptomatique*, according to the classification of Chabert, it is well known to be a perfectly distinct disease.

When we speak of anthrax, charbon or the splenic fever of Europe, therefore, we can only refer to the disease caused by the *bacillus anthracis*, and of which the presence of this micro-organism in the blood is the *sine qua non* essential distinguishing feature. There is no possible chance for anyone at this day to dodge the fact that the splenic fever of England and of Europe is characterized by this parasite, and that it is a disease communicable to other animals beside the ox, and to man. Very well; has the *bacillus anthracis* ever been found in Texas fever? Has Texas fever, notwithstanding its enormous ravages in this country, ever been communicated to a man, or a sheep, or a hog? No; in the whole history of this disease there is not one authentic case of its affecting any except bovine animals; and in all the microscopic investigations of Prof. Gamgee, of Dr. Stiles, and of Billings and Curtis, the *bacillus anthracis* was never discovered. And after a longer series of investigations than was made by any of these gentlemen, and with, as I suspect, better facilities for exact scientific work, I am prepared to say that this parasite is not present in Texas fever, and that Prof. Gamgee was right in calling it a distinct and hitherto undescribed disease.

Grounds once infected with anthrax remain infected for years, while, without exception, when Texas fever is carried a considerable distance beyond the permanently infected district all signs of it disappear with the first freezing weather and it never reappears without a fresh importation.

Texas fever has become so serious a matter in this country that those who are interested in the continued success of our live stock industry can no longer allow teachings so full of danger and harm to go uncontested, and it is for this reason that, after devoting more time to a study of this disease than has been given to it by any other veterinarian, I have assumed the responsibility of saying that some things which have been considered true of it were entirely false, while other things were true which had not heretofore been suspected. My conclusions are susceptible of demonstration, and when those who contest them have sufficient reputation to justify the proceeding it will be an easy matter for us to meet before a committee of impartial scientific men and make such experiments as will leave no doubt in regard to the truth or falsity of our assertions.—*D. E. Salmon, D. M. V., in Breeder's Gazette.*

Recent purchases for export in Scotland include the five-year-old cow Novice 4191, a daughter of Juryman, bred at Cortachy; the three-year-old cow Fancy of Kelly 4486; the five-year-old Martha 6th 4483, and the two-year-old Arthetie 10th 4771—the three last all bred at Mains of Kelly—were bought for Mr. James J. Hill, president of the St. Paul, Minneapolis, and Manitoba Railway, St. Paul. Along with the cows comes the yearling bull Lord Chancellor 1782, bred at Rothiemay, which won first prize this year at the Royal Northern and Highland Society's shows.

## Goat Farming in England.

A unique agricultural experiment is being conducted on the Surrey Hills, says the London *Times.* About seven miles from Dorking, seven miles from Leatherhead, and the same distance from Guildford, has been started a goat dairy farm, devoted exclusively to the supply of goat's milk in large quantities, with subsidiary products of goat's milk, butter and cheese, skins for the butcher, and goat and kid skins for the glove maker and the boot maker. The spot selected is a holding of 310 acres on the surf of Lovelace's property, not far distant from the rabbit farm on the same estate. The soil is a gravely loam, naturally dry from being recumbent upon the chalk; and the altitude of nearly nine hundred feet above the sea level secures, under the moderate rainfall of Surrey, a climate well suited to the natural habits of these animals of the uplands. It is well known for herds of goats, vast tracts of poor mountain land in Italy and other continental countries would remain entirely unproductive, and although Surrey is so wealthy a residential province, it offers many thousands of acres of common or poorly cultivated land with light sandy soil which might be utilized with advantage for dairy farming by the aid of goats. It is not unlikely that the good work of the Baroness Burdett Coutts, the duke of Wellington, Mr. Holmes S. Pegler, and other members of the British Goat Society, may open a new departure in agriculture. At any rate, here is the first example in a practical shape, begun on a sufficient scale and based upon strictly commercial principles.

Lately visiting the farm in question, we found a herd of 120 milch goats, which is being increased to a proposed stock of 300. A couple of spacious, airy, well-ventilated barns, with sapbelted floors, and fitted with continuous feeding-troughs and racks round all sides, form comfortable quarters for the flock at night. Here the goats eat their allowances of hay and their feeds of oats and corn, having access always to lumps rock salt. They lie upon clean bedding of straw, which is renewed dry and clean with scrupulous care, and there is to trace at all of the unsavory odor popularly attributed to goats. In fact, it is only the male goat, which is ever offensive in this way; and the two kept at the farm are tethered and housed in places by themselves. The goats, young and old, appear clean and perfectly healthy; their bright, hairy coats are subjected to curry-combing; no troublesome foot disease demands attention, as in the case of sheep, and any internal ailments are promptly and successfully dealt with by homeopathic medicines, of which the manager, Mr. Farrer, speaks with the greatest confidence and satisfaction. In these houses the goats are milked twice daily, and three times a day for a period after kidding. The goat does not set her feet to be milked from one side, like a cow, but she is fastened by a leather collar round her neck attached to a chain, the milk-man, with his head resting on her tail, drawing her full, two-teated udder from behind.

By day the flock is ranging the fields of clover seeds and old pasture, but constantly tended, and kept herded round and out of reach of the quick-set fences, trees and plantations, by two attendants, who, though armed with whips, have seldom occasion to employ these weapons of alarm rather than of punishment. One of the men is a Welsh mountaineer, whose call the goats instantly obey, following in orderly fashion wherever the shepherd leads.

It does not appear that any special difficulty presents itself in the general management. Breeding is arranged so that the greater proportion of the goats drop kids twice in the year, being, moreover, timed to maintain a fixed number in full profit during every month, winter and summer. The yield of milk from each goat may average about two to three pints per day for seven or eight months in the year, and she gives three or four kids, in two kiddings, to be killed at three or six weeks old, as delicate, choice meat, superior to lamb. At present we believe kid meat, equal to fawn, is regularly supplied by only a single butcher at the west end, where it is duly appreciated, and realizes a high price accordingly. The cropping of the farm is planned to supply constant succession of grass for depasturing, straw for litter, and hay and roots for winter keep. What the expense and profit may be remains for experience to prove, but calculation of returns from the milk sold at 1 shilling 6 pence per quart, above the margin enough for a satisfactory commercial result to the undertaking. If successful, as expected, this example will doubtless be followed in many suitable highland situations within easy transport distance of large towns, where only an available supply of goats' milk is needed to call forth a plentiful demand.

A goat farm has been started by the Express Dairy company (limited) of Bloomsbury mansions, for the purpose of furnishing the London public with a valuable article of nursing and restorative diet, which medical men of the highest eminence are every day recommending for infants and invalid patients, but which is nowhere readily procurable or obtainable at any time for a reasonable price. Next to asses' milk (most difficult to find, except at a very high price, and then extremely limited in the supply) goats' milk approaches in composition most closely to mothers' milk, and its remarkable nutrient and invigorating properties, especially for saving weakly infants and restoring strength to consumptives, are understood in many countries in Europe. Yet, while in many continental cities herds of goats are daily driven through the street, serving fresh milk from house to house, in London goats' milk is to be had only in small and fitful supply, and the price charged is from 6 shillings 6 pence up to 4 shillings a quart. Besides, it has been lately observed by M. Parrot of the Hospital des Enfants Assistes of Paris, that kept in the city, the goat suffers from a diet lacking variety, and that its milk under the circumstances is not so valuable as when the animal is grazed in the country, and hence the importance of a supply of milk from a proper farm instead of from a city yard or mews. The Express Dairy company reckon that a price of 1 shilling 6 pence per quart is sufficient to enable them to supply the milk in bottles of a quart, pint or half pint each, the bottles, of a novel construction, being sealed at the farm, as a guarantee against the possibility of admixture with any milk from cows. Scientific elucidation of the properties of goats' milk points to the eireumstance of the cream globules being smaller and more numerous than in cows' milk as accounting for its being more easily digested by young children, and it is to be expected that dyspeptics and others will at least patronize the simple natural product to as large an extent as they now resort to manufactured or imported substitutes.

A Western cattle breeder reports that the greatest profit is made in the first year of an animal's growth. This is increased, but in less proportion, the second year. It kept a year longer not only is there no profit, but all the dear gain of the second year is wasted. This is a striking commentary on the advantage of early maturity.

Four Hereford calves are reported to have been lately sold from the herd of Benj. Hershey, of Muscatine, Ia., for $3,000.

THE

# Breeder and Sportsman.

PUBLISHED WEEKLY BY THE
BREEDER AND SPORTSMAN PUBLISHING CO.

THE TURF AND SPORTING AUTHORITY OF THE PACIFIC COAST.

OFFICE, 508 MONTGOMERY STREET
P. O. Box 1338.

*Five dollars a year; three dollars for six months; one dollar and a half for three months. Strictly in advance.*

MAKE ALL CHECKS, MONEY ORDERS, ETC., PAYABLE TO ORDER OF BREEDER AND SPORTSMAN PUBLISHING CO.

*Money should be sent by postal order, draft or by registered letter, addressed to the "Breeder and Sportsman Publishing Company, San Francisco, Cal."*

*Communications must be accompanied by the writer's name and address, not necessarily for publication, but as a private guarantee of good faith*

JOSEPH CAIRN SIMPSON, - - - EDITOR

ADVERTISING RATES.—Displayed $1 50 per inch each insertion or pro rata for less pace. Reading Notices set in brevier type and having no foot marks, 20 cents per line each insertion. Lines will average ten words. A discount of 10 per cent. will be allowed on 3 months, 20 per cent. on 6 months and 30 per cent. on 12 months contracts. No extra rate charged for cuts or cutting of column rules. No reading notice take for less than 50 cents each insertion.

San Francisco, Saturday, December 9, 1882.

Mr. M. J. Henley is a duly authorized traveling agent and correspondent for the "Breeder and Sportsman."

## LOS ANGELES COUNTY FOR HORSE-BREEDING.

To authoritatively give a preference to one county in California over all the others for breeding fine horses is something which we are not yet inclined to do.

There is such a wide range of country in this State so well adapted for the production of the highest type of racehorses and trotters that to those who are acquainted with one of these favored sections it can hardly seem possible that there should be any locality more advantageous.

With the knowledge obtained from nearly nine years' residence in California we are satisfied that no part of the State has superior advantages to those which are found in Los Angeles County for the production of the very highest grade of fine stock. With a climate which is unsurpassable, a soil which cannot be excelled, the purest water and herbage peculiarly well adapted for the dams and offspring, it is manifest that Nature has done her part. That man has accomplished his part, is also evident, and the records of the turf and track will show that for so short a time as horse-breeding has been pursued in that section, the success has been most flattering.

L. J. Rose of Sunny Slope may be termed the pioneer in breeding trotters, although about the same time his neighbor, L. H. Titus, commenced. Hancock M. Johnston, Captain Hutchinson, F. M. Slaughter and others followed, and now there are quite a number engaged in the pursuit. If we are not mistaken it was 1870, when Mr. Rose visited Atwood Place, on his return from Kentucky where he had bought some fillies to place in his Stud. Among them was Gretchen, the dam of Romero, Inca, Sable and Del Sur; Minnehaha, the dam of Beautiful Bells, Mabel, Phaceola, Sweetheart and Eva. Sultana the dam of Sultan, and Barbara, the dam of Len Rose. We cannot recall an instance where so few mares, and in so short a time, have made such a showing. The oldest of them, Gretchen, when purchased by Mr. Rose was only four years old, Minnehaha was two, Sultana a suckling, and the Sire, The Moor, which was to be placed at the head of the stud, three years old.

Mr. Titus brought with him Echo, a son of Rysdyk's Hambletonian, so that in the stables not more than a few hundred yards apart were representatives of the two great trotting families, Hambletonian and Bashaw. We are not informed whether Mr. Titus brought any brood mares with Echo, but we do know that he has been a great success on those of Califordia breeding. Joe Hamilton, Echora, Gibraltar, Belle Echo, Annie Laurie, Exile and many others well worthy of notice came from the mingling of the blood of the East and the West. It can scarcely be more than eleven years since these two stallions went into the stud, as Gibraltar and Echora are only ten years, and our recollection is that those were the first of his get in this state.

In 1874 we brought A. W. Richmond here, and in 1876 H. M. Johnson bought him and placed him in the stud. His oldest colts of Los Angeles birth are thus five years old and in the short time he has done enough to take rank with the duo of notables mentioned. But good as The Moor proved to be, his son Sultan has done better. Foaled in 1875 he has two daughters that showed 2:26½ and 2:26 when two years old, and one of them which scored 2:22½ when a three-year-old. He has still another daughter, Neluska, which has the fastest record, 2:30½, in an actual race for two-year-olds, and a son that has phenomenal speed though so unfortunate as to be debarred from exhibiting it in public. When there is an improvement over both parents it can justly be claimed that there must be climatic advantages as well as skillful breeding and training, and then when the result of ten years is so marked as to show a galaxy like the following there is the strongest proof of all the conditions being favorable. The horses bred in Los Angeles county stand:

| | |
|---|---|
| Romero—by A. W. Richmond | 2:19½ |
| Sweetheart, by Sultan (3 years) | 2:22½ |
| Gibraltar, by Echo | 2:22½ |
| Echora, by Echo | 2:23½ |
| Belle Echo, by Echo (4 years) | 2:23½ |
| Del Sur, by The Moor | 2:24 |
| Tommy Gates, by The Moor | 22:4 |
| Eva, by Sultan (2 years) | 2:26 |
| Inca, by Woodford Mambrino | 2:27 |
| Sir Guy, by The Moor | 2:28½ |
| Beautiful Bells, by The Moor | 2:29½ |
| Annie Laurie, by Echo (3 years) | 2:30 |

This list is not given as complete, and in fact it would be difficult to make it so without the assistance of those who are more familiar with the stock of that county. It would be a captious critic, however, who did not acknowledge the merit which is shown in that list, and an ultra hypercritical questioner who refused to accord praise to the county that gave them birth, and to those who bred and reared them.

The breeding of racehorses to any extent is of still later date than the production of trotters. Mr. Rose had a few thoroughbred mares, though we believe that Irene Harding is the only one he bought on his Eastern trip. H. M. Johnson has also bred a few, but the first to engage in the business on a scale commensurate with the production of trotters were E. J. Baldwin and Captain Hutchinson. The former gentleman is the only one who has bred and trained the progeny, and the few years that have elapsed since the Santa Anita stud was inaugurated have demonstrated that before long the position on the "legitimate," will be as high as the other. Albert C and Lucky B are above the average, and there is no question that Gano ranks with the best of the year, and is entitled to a high place with the cracks of any era.

Seven years ago we visited Los Angeles county and the impression then received that it could not be excelled as a horsebreeding district has never been given up. We copy from a description of the trip a few paragraphs in relation to Sunny Slope, and though it may appear that the colors are rather too bright it will only be to those who have never visited that section of the country.

There are, doubtless, great changes in that length of time, but the pasture fields, with the exception of the fences, were the same as in the days of the padres, and are perfect in natural beauty:

In the early gloaming, when the mountains were still glowing in the bright rays of the setting sun, we strolled with Mr. Rose to the fields in the rear of the cultivated part of the farm. Through the orange trees, by a smaller vineyard, where the choicest varieties of foreign grapes were gathered, up by the stream, walking on top of the old dam, the "centennial" of which has passed, into a field, where the brood mares were running.

Grass up to the ankles. Can it be possible that this is the last day of "gloomy November," when the most favored districts of the East are in slush and snow, and from whence already comes the account of frost twenty degrees below zero; piercing gales and vessels blockaded by ice. The mares are sleek as they nibble the juicy herbage; their coats are fine and their eyes lustrous, and they caper in glee as we approach to take a closer view. No need of barns or close stables here. They can breathe the warm air the whole of the year, and the rain is like an emollient bath.

They career over the field which is perennial in its greenness, for unlike almost any other place in California, springs break from the upper slope and spreading gently over the surface flow the whole of the year, natural irrigation giving life to the plants. We are anxious to get a close look at some of those we so highly admired a few days ago and we follow them to the eastern boundary of the field. We have become accustomed to surprises but here was the most surprising of any we had yet seen.

Beyond was another pasture field, a large field of several hundred acres, the one from which the weanlings were driven up the day of our first visit. From the elevation we could overlook it, and the most famous of the woodland pastures of Kentucky which we ever saw does not equal it in beauty. The thick growth of alfilerilla, burr clover and wild oats felt like a thick sod under the foot, a soft carpet which takes away the jar of the gallop as the colts rush past. Dotted over with trees, the symmetrical live oak with rounded top, in the foreground—back, tall sycamores and others of still higher growth. Meadow larks were twittering from the fence rails, robins, blackbirds and the California mocking-bird making melody from among the green branches. Immediately back from this field rises the slope which extends to the base of the mountain, and thousands of feet still higher are the jagged peaks. Every fissure, every rock, every gulch is brought out clear in the radiance of the sunlight which now is only shining about a third of the way from the summit, and we can see the shadows moving up, up and enveloping the former bright projection with a neutral tint, a purplish gray something like the early dawn of the morning.

The vesper of bells from the old Mission church, rings the closing of the day, the notes modulated by the distance until the chimes sound like fairy music, as the harmony is faintly echoed from cliff and crag. Had we waited a little longer until the moon's pale crescent was the only light, we are not sure but some of the "wee folks" might have appeared for an elfin dance on the green carpet under the live oaks, nearly as fairy-like a ball-room as that under the hawthorn on the banks of the Scottish brooklet, where we saw them so many, many long years ago. The recollection is rather indistinct, and shadowy, and it might have been the falling of the white blossoms in the moonlight, but we certainly thought we saw them at the time, and if there, why not here?

Perhaps even the older days of California, however dramatic like and shadowey, do not go far enough back to insure the "good people" making it their home, and they might be frightened at the frowning mountain apparently so near. But the green dell in the pasture field would surely be to their taste, and they would make a boat of the thick enameled deep green leaves of the orange and float down the stream when the leaves are in bloom, and the perfume of the blossoms fills the air with incense.

It was almost dark when we retraced our steps. The next morning was as beautiful as it was possible to imagine. The sun came up over the mountain, shining brightly; the grass was sparkling with dewdrops, appearing as though a shower of diamonds had fallen and attached themselves to every blade, and the birds' songs were more cheerful than in the evening before; another glance down the avenue bordered with the double row of orange trees, another walk to the barn to look at the colts, and we start for the train which will soon thunder by the old, thick-walled church. Little did its founders think that a hundred years would bring such changes. The next century can scarcely equal them.

## SPRING MEETING P. C. B. H. A.

It is time now that the Pacific Coast Blood Horse Association should be arranging the progrmme for the spring meeting of 1883. Though it may appear premature to commence the preparation for another meeting so soon after the close of that which is just past, it is none too early. Beside the fixed events to be decided at the spring meeting there must be additional stakes, and purses arranged to fill the gap. If we are to have hurdle races there must be a guarantee that there will be enough of them to warrant the training of horses for this kind of work. That there is the proper material in horses and riders is beyond dispute, and that they are attractive features to the public there can be no question. Recognized as a part of every day's sport by the Association the Fairs will incorporate them in the "speed programmes" and then there will be plenty of work for jumpers. Outside of those who are particularly interested in flat-racing the predilections are strongly in favor of hurdle-racing and the steeple chase. The education which is necessary for the first will be primary to that which will perfec the course for the other. With educated rider and horses trained to jump there is little danger, and yet remains the excitement to the spectators. Then by arranging the full programme and giving it publicity people can make preparations and train in accordance with the knowledge.

The great trouble with clubs and owners is to make the training of the other classes of horses than those in the front rank pay the expense incurred. Where there is a great deal of racing this is avoided. Handicaps, selling races, those in which winners are penalized and non-winners granted indulgences, are frequent, and so far as this practice can be incorporated in the racing on this coast so much the better it will be. There will be larger fields of starters and more interest taken. It is very seldom that there is a season when there is an equality among the performers. Usually there are a few which show such a decided superiority to the majority that there are no hopes of a contest; then the great equalizer comes in and a difference in the weight carried brings the crack on a level with the inferior. There is not a particle of sense in the outcry of "rewarding mediocrity." There is no sport in witnessing one horse galloping away from another. The great element of uncertainty must be a part of the contest to give it a zest. There must be a chance to lose as well as to win to set the blood bounding through veins and arteries. We offer these suggestions without a desire to regulate the action of the Association. The programmes so far have been very satisfactory, and there is little question that those in the future will not be of the same cast. The main thing is to come to a conclusion as soon as possible, and give owners and trainers a chance to get ready.

## THE LAST DECISION IN THE EMBRYO.

Elsewhere we publish the last decision in the Embryo stakes. It is in keeping with those given last week. We must give the "member" the credit for being a persistent misrepresenter. Still we are sorry to see him drag the "chairman" into the mistake.

The parties interested in the yearling race settled the misunderstanding, and on a basis which was satisfactory to all. District Board, No. 5 met on the day fixed at the previous meeting. There was no one to prosecute the appeal, none to defend. The decision of the judges was not "affirmed." As all will testify who were present the ruling from the stand was that all three of the colts started under protest. The only case tried was the protest against Antevolo. The decision was that the protest was not sustained. The "Board" also intimated that it was without jurisdiction. As a meeting of the Board cannot be held without two members being present it was idle to think of the postponed cases being tried before that tribunal. If it had jurisdiction Jas. McM. Shafter was incapacitated. We certainly should object to him passing on a case he had already decided. After two trials a third would be a greater blunder than we are in the habit of making.

Hereafter, in all probability, we will be compelled to write on this subject. For the present nothing more is necessary.

## THE CLOSE OF THE SEASON.

There are three weeks yet before 1882 comes to a close. California the "season" connot be said to have ended til the requiem is chanted for the old, anthems sung for a new. For the past two weeks there has been springne. The grass is green in the fields, there are flowers the gardens. The sun has set with a brilliancy akin that of June in less favored localities, and though the ys came obliquely there was a summer warmth in the ame. The golden weather has engendered regrets. grets that so many dear friends have to endure the gors of frost and snow, sleet and tempests. There is a mpensation, for the martyrs, the bliss of igrance, and the comforts of indoor life and bright, cheery es. It is too early yet to summarize what has been ne on the California turf and tracks, too soon to say hat positions our horses occupy in the calendar of the ar. There may be something startling yet to record. here is talk of a meeting which will bring some new rformers to the front, and though the task may appear forlorn hope, it may be that even the great scores of 81 may be bettered. There are rumors, and whispergs of great capacity, and the sequel will not be known til the pug log is glowing and the mistletoe hangs om the rafters.

And now after the above was written comes the intelgence that a "cold wave" has swept over the "West." ight degrees below zero at Chicago, fourteen below at eoria, and in Nebraska twenty-one degrees below the int marked by a cipher. A mixture of snow and salt as thought to be the initial from which to measure, nd this is warm in comparison to the mark so early hown. We have little patience to listen to the complaints when there is a fog in the morning, and almost a certainty that it will rise before 10 a. m., while at the same time there is a warmth in the air which does away with the necessity of an overcoat, and men in garments appropriate to summer in this locality are comfortable.

## P. V. JOHNSON'S RECOLLECTIONS.

We are sure that our readers will agree that the reminiscences of P. V. Johnson which we copy from the "Breeder's Gazette" are interesting reading. Peter writes a very pleasant story of the horses he has had in charge, and there is instruction as well as pleasure in the perusal. He is always ready to acknowledge what he has made a mistake in driving a race, and also gives his reasons for thinking that the preliminary work had not been proper. Better than that he is not prone to insinuate that the horse was not "given his head," and is better pleased to accept the conclusion that he had erred in some point than to plead "fear of a record."

In the case of J. B. Thomas, copied this week, he ascribes a great deal of the improvement to supplementing the shoe of sixteen ounces with a six-ounce toe-weight. This question of toe-weights is still a puzzling problem, and before a fair understanding is reached there will be necessary a great many experiments. The experiments of one will not be sufficient and there is an urgency for a " comparison of notes" among trainers to perfect the knowledge.

Just such histories as those we have copied will have a direct bearing, and if all the drivers follow the example, there will be a general acquirement of knowledge and the advantages shared by every one interested in the development of the trotter.

## Trotting on the Bay District Course.—On Saturday last a trotting race was commenced on the Bay District course. According to the advertised conditions the race was to be between "gentlemen's roadsters," and as frequently happens in this kind of races, there was some dissatisfaction. There were four engaged, Stranger," Proctor, Roan Tom and Fisher. At the opening of the pool sales, Stranger was largely the favorite, bringing $50 to $20 on Roan Tom. $6 on Fisher and $2 on Proctor. As Stranger won the first heat easily, the rates were $40 on him to $10 on all the others. The second heat Fisher won in improved time, and the pools marked $22 on Stranger, $20 on Fisher and $4 for the field. The Fisher stock appreciated before the start for the third heat and he was the favorite. This was also won by him in still faster time, which the summary will show, and that too after a contretemps on the first turn caused by Stranger taking the pole too quickly. There being a heavy fog the finish of the race was postponed until Monday. There was an evident intention on the part of all the others to work against Fisher, and this was carried to a point that was very near an infraction of the rules. Fisher won, however, showing a remarkably fine burst of speed in the last half mile, trotting the last quarter inside of 2:30. Mr. Scott, who entered and drove Fisher, was warmly congratulated. Strictly an amateur, and to win over such drivers as Donathan, Killip and Tim Kennedy, enhanced the pleasures of victory.

SUMMARY.

Bay District Course, Saturday and Monday Dec. 2. and 4—Trotting race; mile heats, three in five, to road wagons; purse and stake $100; entry per cent. to first horse, 25 to second and 15 per cent. to third.
T. A. Scott named s g Fisher.................................3 1 1 1
J. W. Killip named b g Stranger.............................1 2 2 2
Marks named b g Proctor..........................................2 4 3 3
J. B. Brown named r g Roan Tom..............................4 3 4 4
Time, 2:32, 2:45, 2:49, 2:40½

# POULTRY.

## Regulating the Sale of Poultry.

The ordinance passed by the Common Council of New York city last spring, to the effect that the crops of all fowls offered for sale in that city shall be free from food or other substances, and shrunken close to the body, is said to be working well. It is said to have been brought about by the practice of stuffing the crops after the fowls were killed, and even the throats. A similar ordinance would not be a bad one in Chicago. It would equalize the thing, so that honest shippers and dealers would have a fair show, and buyers would not have to pay turkey prices for musty corn and gravel.—Breeder's Gazette, Chicago.

Like the Massachusetts law requiring the sale of eggs by weight instead of by count, the New York law referred to above cannot fail in time to become general, though whether to legislative enactment or to common consent it will owe its adoption remains to be seen. The fixing by law of the weight of a dozen of eggs is just as legitimate and needful as the establishment of the legal weight of a bushel of grain. Laws vary in this regard, 32 pounds of oats being a legal bushel in some localities and 34 in others. Of course the California custom of selling grain and vegetables by the cental is an improvement on the Eastern system of a bushel which means 32, 34, 45, 56 or 60 pounds, according to the commodity and the place. But the selling of eggs by weight will some day be adopted here, as will the empty-crop ordinance of New York.

A correspondent of the " Poultry Yard" thus describes his new remedy for chicken cholera: " While our neighbors for several miles around us have lost nearly all their chickens from the so-called cholera, ours are in fine condition. They were attacked with the premonitory symptoms of the disease, which seemed to be epidemic here, but we cured them and have no trouble with them since having accidently found a cure. Out up onions with food, and administer once a day for several days, afterward once a week until cured. Also mix a little ground ginger with their meal, once every day or two. We also give them a little salt every two or three weeks, which we deem highly necessary, and above all things, keep watermelons, muskmelons and cucumbers away from them. The tops of celery cut up with their food will be found beneficial, and they appear to like it very well. Do not get these statements mixed up. The onions and ginger for the cholera, the remainder constant attention. Too much whole corn we have found injurious; we give meal, of this only once in three or four days. Raw onions and a very little ginger against the world for curing cholera, if the disease has not been allowed to run too far." We indorse, heartily the raw onions and ginger, but have never found melons injurious. Last summer we raised, in an amateur way, three hundred chickens and turkeys. Bushels of melon rinds and imperfect melons were thrown to them daily and eaten eagerly. Over ripe cucumbers were likewise devoured. We had no losses from any disease.—[Rural World.

"Do we derive a greater profit from the sitter than from the non-sitter," is as yet an unsettled question. The best of the non-sitters do not average over 180 eggs during the year, but the sitter is equally as sure for 132 or more. There is a difference of four dozen eggs, and as the non-sitters lay more eggs in the summer season than in winter, the monetary value will not exceed 75 cents as the measure of difference. Using the Leghorn as a sample of the non-sitting breeds, and the Brahma to represent the sitters, it cannot be denied the latter, being better winter layers, are nearly if not quite equal to the Leghorns in monetary product, even if the number of eggs laid is smaller, owing to the enhanced price of eggs during the cold term. But the young chicks, should be taken into the account, and on a average of only five to the brood after deducting loss and the low price of 20 cents per pound at two pounds each, the amount will be two dollars. Estimating yet lower in the price, making it 12½c per pound, we still have an advantage in favor of the sitter. The expense will correspond with the ratio of sale, and the same cannot be offset. The Leghorn matures earlier than the Brahma, and gains time in that respect. They take resting spells, however, from laying, and if they are not at work bringing forth chicks the time is lost. With all that may be said in favor of the non-sitter, it must be remembered that young chicks count in value as well as eggs.—[Farm and Garden.

Mating self-colored fowls, as the White Leghorn, Black Spanish, White Dorkings, etc., little difficulty is experienced, as the principal object in uniting the sexes is to blend the good qualities of the sire and dam, and make sure that we have clean and purely-bred stock with which to operate, of either of these kinds. In mating Colored Dorkings, Dark Brahmas, Partridge Cochins and other parti-colored fowls for the same purpose the matter becomes more difficult to manage successfully because it is necessary that the same even hue in plumage, pencillings and markings that is possessed by the chosen sires and dams should be secured in the offspring.

Always have good and fat poultry where possible ; in the country you may command it. About three weeks before you want to use them, six or twelve fowls, according to your consumption, should be put into the coop, and as you kill one or more replace them, to keep up the stock ; for the first week feed them alternate days with boiled rice and soaked bread and milk. The remainder of the time mix Indian meal with the skimmings of your stock pot and a teaspoon of moist sugar. The windows of your poultry-house must be darkened. Fowls should be carefully drawn, so that the gall bladder is uninjured.

Introduce new blood into your flock every year or so by either buying a cockerel or sittings of eggs from some reliable breeder.

Poor shelter, care and feed will in a few generations make scrubs of the finest stock.

## Food for Fattening.

We receive so many inquiries about this time every year as to the best methods and food to give poultry that is selected to fatten, we wish to give some general advice on the subject to those who may be ignorant on this particular business, which will engage the attention of a large share of our patrons during this and next month. November and December cover the winter early holidays, and Thanksgiving and Christmas will shortly come round again, when the turkeys and chickens, the geese and ducks will be in active demand for the palates of myriads who at this season of the year, especially, find it " a part of their common education " to luxuriate more or less on good fat poultry.

No green food is now desirable. All you are aiming for is to put additional flesh upon these fowls, and to do this in the shortest possible time. So long as they eat well they will gain in weight, up to a certain period, treated in this manner, and two or three weeks will bring them to their best. If they become cloyed, and lose their appetite at an earlier date, after thus being cooped up, kill them off at once. They have reached the most profitable day of their existence, and will no longer improve in the desired direction. In this simple way we have fattened many previously well-kept fowls in three weeks' time satisfactorily, and we have known many hundreds thus fattened that have dressed handsomely in some days less time, the mode thus briefly recommended being economical, as well as expeditio us, cleanly, and very convenient. A greater amount of flesh can be produced in proportion to the grain fed, when confinement is resorted to, and, if the prisoners are well attended, and the term of incarceration does not last too long, there is not much danger of disease.

We have not mentioned two prerequisites towards fattening fowls successfully and speedily, but we take it for granted that it will be understood that your birds, when cooped up for this purpose, shall be free from vermin, and during their confinement that they must be kept so. No greater drawback to the growth and improvement of domestic fowls exists than the presence of this pest upon their bodies, or in the pens to which they are limited. We therefore suggest that to fatten fowls profitably they must be kept from this annoyance during the process. Most depends on keeping the subjects in a condition free from worrying and distracting circumstances. Stick a pin here, you who are new to the business.—Poultry Yard.

The custom still in vogue in some parts of this country, of wringing the necks of fowls, seems a relic of barbarism. It is not only cruel, but is unsanitary. When killed in this way, instead of cutting the head off, the blood all remains in the body, rendering the flesh unwholesome, as it would be in the case of an ox. The blood is very putrefactive, as all may know by allowing some to remain in the sun half an hour in warm weather, emitting a bad odor in a very short time. When we remember that about one-half of the blood is composed of the waste and worn-out portions of the body, semi-poisonous, and that this particularly, with the pure portion, soon putrefies while remaining just where they are in life, it is evident that all of the flesh will become more or less affected by the putrescent mass. Instead of this barbarous wringing of the neck, it is advisable to cut the head off at a single blow with a sharp instrument, that the blood may freely flow with all of the waste matter. That this may be done effectually, it is well to hang by the legs as soon as possible that the blood may flow while still warm.

## Worms in Hogs.

Last fall Isom Vaughn, of Moralia, Oregon, lost fourteen head of hogs. He examined the last that died and found the entrails full of worms, varying in length from three to ten inches. No other hogs in the neighborhood were then known to be afflicted with them, but now others are losing hogs from the same cause. It seems to be more fatal among pigs than grown hogs.

Judging from the length of the worms, they are evidently of the Eustrogylus Gigas species. They almost invariably prove more fatal to pigs than to grown hogs. In severe attacks of this parasite the symptoms somewhat resemble cholera, and have been frequently confounded with that disease.

Treatment oftentimes proves unsuccessful. First, separate the diseased ones from the apparently healthy ones, and feed them pretty liberally with nutritious feed. Give a teaspoonful of the following mixture to the sick ones twice daily to the others of the same herd once daily : Powdered sulphate of iron, cinchona, gentian, ginger, and fenugreek, of each 2 oz.; powdered nux vomica and capsicum, of each 2 drs. Mix all the ingredients together thoroughly.—Cor. Rural Spirit

It seems as though such a dose as that ought to kill the worms, and the hogs too, and if that is the only treatment known we do not wonder " that treatment often proves unsuccessful. "

Some people are in the habit, when first sitting down to milk, of drawing a little milk to wet their hands and the teats of the cow. Such a practice is anything but cleanly, and should always be avoided. I have seen milkers with a reeking compound of milk, hairs and manure oozing from between their fingers and dropping into the pail. In this way some of the milk in our dairies receives a taint, the cause of which seems unaccountable to the dairyman, and which is imparted to the cream and butter. Cows do not milk any better with wet hands than with dry. In the summer, when the cows are in the pasture, the udder will usually be clean, except in wet weather ; still, if there is no occasion to wash the bag, it is always well to wipe it thoroughly with cloth, before milking, to remove loose hairs and dust.—New England Farmer.

The Breeder and Sportsman.—We have received in exchange the new California sporting paper with the above title. It is a handsome paper ably edited and will doubtless prove very popular. It is edited by Joseph Cairn Simpson, and is issued weekly from 508 Montgomery St., San Francisco, at $5.00 per annum.—Maine Horse Breeders' Monthly.

## THE GUN.

### Sport (?)

The Grass Valley *Tidings*, in speaking of killing deer out of season, lays the matter before its readers in a very forcible manner:

"Killing deer at this season must have great pleasure in it. The beasts are attending to their domestic affairs, and are so intent on obeying the command which tells them to study the multiplication table, that they heed not the hunter. Therefore they fall an easy prey to the gun of the man who sneaks up to them. The "antlered monarch" while waving his gentle-eyed sweetheart has no attention for the sportsman (?) who creeps through the brush for the purpose of firing a murderous shot into the bower of love. Hence, it is fun now, or sport, to kill the deer. The killer gets much meat without having to tire himself out with long walks, and without having to annoy himself with the exercise of skill and patience. The meat he gets, in these days, is very fine. Perhaps the flesh of a "settin' hen," after she has been attending to her incubation affairs on two sets of eggs, is about the only flesh that surpasses that of the swell-necked buck of the deer tribe at this season of the year. The timid doe is now an invalid, as Michelet would say, and her flesh is not fit for human food. At such times as these that are now prevailing among deer, even the wolf will not kill female or fawn of the deer, unless compelled so to do by the most pressing hunger. But the wolf is not a sportsman."

RAILROADING DEER.—The further from civilization that the deer tribe retreat the more eager seem the hunters to exterminate these beautiful animals. From across the mountains comes a paragraph from an exchange under the above heading: The stage messenger who runs on the N. &C. Co. of G. W. Meyleri killed a deer last Saturday just beyond Rock Springs. A passenger on the train saw seven or eight fine bucks and does standing on a bluff about 200 yards west of the track watching the train. The locomotive was stopped when the messenger jumped off and shot a nice fat doe. The rest of the band stood watching the wounded animal for several minutes after the shot was fired. The train then saw they see deer nearly every trip they make. Many of Reno's deer hunters are going out for a hunt in a day or two.

UP THE RIVER.—Hunting up the river is very poor—that is, the hunting is good enough, but the finding and killing is poor. Only a few good bags have been made. The ducks go on to the marshes and stay during the night but on the first report of the gun in the morning they are up and away and do not return till the evening. Ducks are seen by the thousands laying out in Suisun and San Pablo Bays but they are safe from the anxious hunters. Nothing disgusts the up river hunters more than to wait all day behind their blinds and just at dusk when they are returning to the city see large flocks of canvasbacks, widgeon and teal flying, to the very places where they have been all day. Ducks are getting cunning; they will not fly and they are unapproachable.

GEESE.—Wild geese are a great nuisance to the farmers of California, and killing and scaring them away forms one of the greatest items of expense to wheat growers. We understand that Dr. Glenn purchased twenty-five guns at one time a few days ago, for the purpose of killing or frightening the geese from his grain fields. He had, of course, a number of guns before this, so that it is fair to presume that he will have in the neighborhood of fifty men at this work. Several hundred men are required in this county for the work of "herding geese." When the wheat first comes up is the worst time.—*Colusa Sun.*

A CHANGE.—The Supervisors of Plumas county have changed the close season for deer and fish, so it is now lawful to shoot deer at any time between the 1st of July and the 1st of January; anglers may pursue their sport from May 1st to February 1st. The supervisors claim that the change that they have made in the law protects the deer and fish in Plumas county to better effect than the old laws did, but all the sportsmen think that they are overstepping their authority in meddling with laws passed by the Legislature.

THE PLACE FOR HUNTERS.—The sagebrush between Pete Flynn's and Cane Springs, on the Idaho Road, is said to be literally alive with sagehens and prairie chickens. The stage drivers say these game birds fly up all around the stage every day and a good hunter could bag a sack full of them in a very short time. The prairie chickens, though about the size of the birds of that name in the Western States, are somewhat lighter in color, and are known in some parts of the countryas "willow grouse."—*Silver State.*

Messrs. Hall, Ladd and Hardy shooting at Alviso last Sunday bagged seventy-five ducks, most of which they disposed of on the Oakland boat on their way home to less-fortunate hunters. All the hunters on that boat had something in the game line to exhibit to their friends by which to show their ability as good shots. Oh, deception ! Thy name is Nimrod.

At the head of the South Fork of Crooked river there is a lake where thousands of ducks rear their young, and at this time of the year, and in fact all winter, there are great numbers of swan, geese and ducks, that have never been hunted, and are very tame. The surrounding country is delightful, and for the hunter who is fond of wing shooting, this is a perfect paradise.—*Ex.*

A farmer near Gilroy has a trained cow to aid in hunting wild geese that are destroying his grain fields. The cow walks towards the flock of feeding destroyers very slowly and the hunter by the side opposite and at the word she will lie down while he discharges both barrels into the flock who up to the time of the report of the gun are unaware of the hunter's presence.

The vicinity of Bouldin Island is looming up a little in the direction of duck shooting. Some very good shoots have been made up there lately, 80 ducks being the biggest bag. They were principally teal. They are quite plentiful there at present and find good feed in the tthe grass. The ducks are all in their glory.

Duck-hunting near Watsonville is fine at present. An exchange says that every man that owns a gun or can buy, beg or borrow a gun is out with the attacking party and also that the ammunition dealers are the ones most benefited as the ducks don't seem to be worried by the presence of guns or hunters.

Has the hog that was shot, through sheer cussedness, at Sherman Island been paid for yet ?

## TIGER-SHOOTING ON THE HILLS.

### An Ambush by the Water—Attacking a Tiger in Her Mountain Lair.

It was about mid-day of the 29th March, 18—, that news was brought me of a large tiger at the Maharajpore waterfall called "Mothie Jharna." Almost about the same time a friend (a great sportsman) came from Maidah to my camp at Rajmahl with a view of accompanying me in any of my shooting excursions, as he knew I was always going somewhere for sport. I was indeed very glad to see him, and especially on account of the *bagh ka subber* just brought.

"Well, Whin," said my friend Erst, "now have you been pulling along these twenty days which I believe is about the time since I last saw you ?" "Very well, thanks," I rejoined, "but I hear poor Joe is still suffering from fever." "Yes, by-the-by he is, but what a strange thing is March and fever. Well, the more we live the more we learn !" "I say," I asked, "do you remember our last haunt at Feerpointee ? What a scratch, upon my word. The tiger well nigh took you !" "Ah ! yes, the beast, but hang that, have you any news to give ?"

"Well, perhaps I have, what then ? Do you suppose I am going to gratify your wish, nay lad nay, not yet." "Ah ! let us hear anything good !" "No, not yet; come, there is luncheon on table, and the rest by and by." "So saying I drew ur my chair, my friend followed suit, and we had a hearty tiff, washing it down with a bottle of good Burgundy, then offering my friend a cheroot, and taking one myself, walked leisurely into the sitting room and betaking ourselves to two easy chairs we sat puffing and chatting away until two, when I rose and told my companion it was high time to get ready, for our friend Mr. Stripes would come and miss us if we came later; and the acquaintanceship to be formed between us would have to be deferred to our disappointment. At half past two o'clock we left the camp, followed by some half a dozen followers. The sun was scorching hot, and the distance was not short, so putting spurs to our steeds, we galloped off, never as much on our way exchanging a word with each other. We reached in good time, and met the Soubhdars who had brought me *khubber*, sitting at the foot of the hills, where I had directed them to await me.

Here we dismounted, and, leaving the horses with some of the men, made straight for the basin where the tiger used to come to drink. Now the question arose where we were to take up our position, so as to be hidden from Stripes' observation, and still command a look of the entire basin. "A ledge of overhanging rock," remarked Erst, "is about the best, but where to find that." "Let us ascend a little to our left and I think we shall find some suitable place." "Yes, I think so;" we climbed a "little higher and got a place that suited us to "till." The arrangements completed, we took up our posts, and sat quietly watching. One, two, three hours passed, and nothing appeared, although once we heard a rustle, but it turned out to be a boar. Night had now fairly set in, and were it not for the moon who favored us with her light, we would have been wrapped in total darkness. However, that night saw not to be a blank in our sporting diary, and an hour or so after the old tusker's appearance we saw before us a beautiful Royal Bengal, of which even a Rajah need be proud. From where or how he came was matter for conjecture, as none of us (although we kept an unremitting watch) saw or heard his approach. But there he was, as large as life, and none could doubt his presence. We would fain have looked on, but our visitor seemed uneasy and was suspiciously eyeing every cover, as if he saw there was danger lurking about him. I do not know what made him suspicious, but that he had become so was beyond doubt. His head was turning from side to side, his grim orbs flashing like balls of fire, and he appeared as if doubtful what to do. Once he looked up in our direction, and we thought we were discovered; then, advancing quickly a few paces, he halted, steadfastly gazing at some object at our right. Then, as if to draw a motion from what he suspected, he crouched; finding however everything still and nothingless he rose and walked deliberately towards the water, reaching which he stooped and looked to quench his thirst. And well might he have looked, for just then were poised at him two deadly weapons by hand which were leveled; and the next moment leapt forth two burning streams, amidst two deafening reports that made the hills reverberate.

And buried wild nature's beauty from the rock he stood.
To a depth unknown, and from whence no sound we heard.
Save that of the wounded creature in his dying throes.

Oh the dull moan—that moan so full of significance and rare delight to a practised ear—and all was still. The work of blood was done. We did not have our places, but determined to stay here till the morning, as nothing could be more dangerous than finding our way out of the jungles at that late hour of the night. Nothing, however, occurred worth notice and the time passed rather heavily.

The grey tinge of morning appeared; the wild notes of the jay could be heard; the chirping of some thousands of sparrows, along with flocks of minas, showed that daybreak was at hand. Rising and telling my companion, who was half asleep, that it was time we should be gone, I ordered the men (four in number) who were to follow us to follow. We moved on; but instead of a retrograde march down bill, I was walking in a southerly direction which would take us to the summit. My friend observing this inquired whither I was going, and on my telling him that I proposed going to the top to see if we could not spy some game which would add to our bag, my friend seemed pleased, and added that it was just like me, to make the most of it which I could. A half hour's ascent brought us to the summit, and from here we looked about; and though I gave a deer once, it was too far to shoot. My friend also took, but for the same reason it not fire. "Come, let us go to the other hill yonder," I said to Erst, "and see if we cannot meet with better luck." "All right," he rejoined, and we were soon on its brow, trying to catch a glimpse at some unfortunate stag who might happen to be close by. But in this we were disappointed, seeing them descend by herds of ten and twelve toward the plain. While we were still gazing on our intended victims, and chewing, as one may well imagine, the cud of vexation, we heard the men half out; "Sahib," "sahib," and on looking round saw them standing near a large cave, and beckoning us to come. We went up directly, and they told us that there was some animal inside, as they heard something like a sneeze; and on going close distinctly recognized the breathing of some large beast. "What do you think it is, Erst?" "Why it may be a tiger, who can say." "That is just what I fancy it is." "Well, how do you propose to get him out?" "Get him out, that is beyond our power; we may bawl and shout as much as we like, but we shall never get him to budge an inch, you may rest assured. Had we a complete works, we need not have despaired, but as we are situated, we had better not meddle with him." "Oh! blow the rockets, I will not stir from here unless I get him out, or shoot him in his den." "Don't be foolish, Whin." "Foolish! ha-ha-ha, you

will see presently, Erst, or I be hanged," saying which I walked straight for the cave. My friend divining my intention ran and laid hold of me, remonstrating the while; but it was no use, my mind was made, and nothing could shake or alter my determination. Erst knowing this, let me go, only making me promise not to endanger my life by any act of imprudence.

I strode on to the mouth of the den, then stopping commenced a series of fearful yells in the hope of getting the monster out; but finding this fall I adopted another and much bolder expedient—that of peeping into the cave. True, my rifle was brought to my shoulder in so doing, but this availed me nothing. The moment I raised my head, with what intention is already known, the tiger, for such it was, sprang out; whether at me or simply to run away I cared not to know, but this much is certain that he sent me head over heels, and were it not for my bearer Ramkissen, who caught me when I fell, I should have been buried in the foot of the hill, and smashed to jelly. But the tiger did not go scot free; although dealt with so suddenly, I did not let him escape so easily, for the moment I saw his body above me (though in mid-air) I fired, shooting him through his intestines, (as we afterward found), and getting myself knocked on the head, by one of his hind paws coming in contact with my solah topee. While I fell pell-mell Erst did not stand an idle spectator, but watching the tiger as he descended, sent a ball after him, hitting him on the shoulder, which sent him rolling to the bottom of the (if I may be allowed to call it) valley. Here we met the brute trying to drag himself away, when I gave him the *coup de grace*. And thus we bagged two tigers —the first measuring 9 feet 8 inches, and the second 9 feet 3 inches, from tip of nose to insertion of tail.—*Whincop in the Asian.*

### Sportsmen's Tournament.

The sportsmen's tournament was very well attended yesterday by the crack shots from various parts of the county. There were twenty-two entries for the prizes. The day was fine for shooting. The following are the scores $m_4 d_4$:

| | | | | | | | | | | | | | | |
|---|---|---|---|---|---|---|---|---|---|---|---|---|---|---|
| J. P. Leonard | 0 | 1 | 1 | 0 | 0 | 0 | 0 | 0 | 0 | 0 | | —5 |
| ........... | 1 | 0 | 1 | 1 | 0 | 1 | 1 | 0 | 1 | 1 | | —9 |
| Wm. J. Morgan | 1 | 1 | 1 | 1 | 1 | 1 | 1 | 1 | 1 | 1 | | —10 |
| Spurgeon | 1 | 1 | 1 | 1 | 1 | 1 | 1 | 1 | 1 | 1 | | —10 |
| ..... | 1 | 1 | 0 | 1 | 1 | 1 | 1 | 1 | 1 | 1 | | —10 |
| O. B. Reading | 0 | 1 | 1 | 1 | 0 | 1 | 1 | 1 | 1 | 1 | | —9 |
| Lon Rose | 1 | 0 | 1 | 1 | 1 | 1 | 1 | 1 | 0 | 1 | | —8 |
| Thomas | 1 | 1 | 0 | 1 | 1 | 0 | 1 | 1 | 0 | 1 | | —7 |
| Leon D. Freer | 1 | 0 | 1 | 1 | 1 | 1 | 1 | 1 | 0 | 1 | | —9 |
| A. J. Jones | 0 | 1 | 1 | 0 | 1 | 0 | 1 | 0 | 0 | 0 | | —5 |
| Waldron | 0 | 1 | 1 | 0 | 0 | 1 | 1 | 0 | 1 | 1 | | —6 |
| Robt. W. Neable | 0 | 1 | 0 | 1 | 1 | 1 | 0 | 0 | 0 | 0 | | —6 |
| E. C. Quinby | 1 | 0 | 1 | 1 | 1 | 1 | 0 | 1 | 1 | 0 | | —9 |
| Henderson | 1 | 1 | 1 | 1 | 1 | 1 | 1 | 1 | 1 | 1 | | —10 |
| George Stevens | 1 | 1 | 0 | 0 | 0 | 1 | 1 | 0 | 0 | 0 | | —4 |
| George Trevor | 1 | 0 | 1 | 1 | 0 | 0 | 0 | 0 | 0 | 0 | | —4 |
| W. C. Halley | 0 | 0 | 0 | 1 | 0 | 1 | 0 | 1 | 1 | 0 | | —4 |
| P. O. Hundley | 1 | 0 | 1 | 1 | 1 | 1 | 0 | 1 | 1 | 1 | | —8 |
| Coburn | 0 | 0 | 0 | 0 | 1 | 1 | 1 | 1 | 0 | 0 | | —4 |
| Thos | 1 | 0 | 1 | 1 | 1 | 0 | 1 | 0 | 1 | 1 | | —7 |
| Brown | 1 | 1 | 0 | 1 | 0 | 1 | 0 | 0 | 1 | 1 | | —6 |

Mr. Spurgeon was awarded the first money and in shooting off the ties Mr. Rose won the second money; Mr. Henderson, the third; Mr. Reading, the fourth, and Mr. Scott the fifth.—*Oroville Mercury, Dec. 5th.*

A correspondent of the BREEDER AND SPORTSMAN up at Bouldin Island has been having a goose hunt. He started out a few mornings ago when the weather was foggy and went ahead before daylight guided by the noise of the geese. They were found on floating bogs, from six to fifty in number on each bog—as many as could stand or sit on them. Our friend made up his mind after one or two failures to blaze away at anything he saw white and he followed this rule until he had eleven. It was then good daylight and foggy as could be. He then got into a heavy bunch of tule where they had been feeding on young flag and staked out his dead geese. They made quite a fair flock and as our hunter was a good "caller" he had some fair sport, killing thirty-five white geese and four grey. The fog let up and so did the geese. These were killed with No. 7 chilled shot. Last season this same hunter killed 118 with No. 7 shot and this is his standard size for general duck-shooting and he makes a living out of shooting too. He uses four and a half drams of Hazard powder and an 8-pound No. 10 gun with case and an eighth ounce of shot to a load. Still he thinks a heavier gun would be better as it would not recoil so much.

The Chatham (N.B.) *World* makes affidavit to the following: On Tuesday evening last when George Trevors, who had been working in the steamship Coban, then lying at Mr. Sergeant's mill wharf, was done day's work, he had occasion to go up to the store of Daniel Baldwin to purchase a few articles. It was then dark, and when he started for his home in the Douglasfield, he took the short cut across the woods. He had gone about a mile and a half when he was attacked by a very large bear. Being unarmed and having no other weapon than a bottle of paraffine, he struck the bear and broke the bottle of oil over him. The bear sprang on him and commenced hugging him, when George had the presence of mind to light a match and set fire to him, and in three minutes she was all consumed but the head and shoulders. George then commenced to carry water in his hat to quench the fire to save the snout so as to get the bounty.

Mr. Rowell, the gunsmith, has on exhibition a rare species of the hen quail, recently killed at Kincaid's Flat. The distinguishing mark from others is the very light dove color and shining appearance of its feathers about the ... the under part of the wings being white—so that the bird on the wing has the resemblance of a white quail.—*Butte Record.*

Messrs. St. John and Fairbanks killed four dozen quail near Petaluma last Sunday. Savage Bros. slaughtered thirty-two ducks the same day, and T. D. Jacobs and Chas. Kelley bagged twenty ducks in a couple of hours' evening shooting.

A large bag of 172 ducks was brought from the Alviso marshes last Sunday. The good shots were Messrs. Johnson, Higgins, Lachman and Burrel. Jake Johnson made the highest score, killing sixty birds.

Mr. F. Butler was up the Suisun Creek last Sunday and killed 20 ducks. He says that one has to work hard and shoot very accurate to have any satisfaction hunting for a boat in the creek.

There is good hunting at Alviso and Alvarado marshes. Most all who go down have fair luck. Though the ducks all fly high they fly very lively so it makes it very interesting for the good shots.

Gun-making is one of the foremost industries in Syracuse, N.Y. The number of guns manufactured there during the past year are said to have been $200,000, based on a capital of only $95,000.

F. Adams in one day's shooting last week at Alvarado bagged twenty-six teal. A few evenings later he shot eight ducks in one hour on the Brooklyn marshes.

# THE RIFLE.

## An International Matter.

n the 21st of October a letter was sent by the Executive ommittee of the National Rifle Association to the tish National Rifle Association asking that body modify the conditions of the International contest for 1883. e requests made were:

First, the use of the wind-gauge.

Second, the use of barley-corn sights of practical strength; n at the base, as approved by the War Department in 1879, use by the U. S. army and approved by the National uard of various states.

Third, Enlistments on or before Jan. 1, 1883, to make National Guardsmen eligible.

The following letter from a special correspondent to the *irit of the Times* shows how the propositions were looked by the British N. R. A.:

LONDON, Nov. 2, 1882.

"SPIRIT OF THE TIMES, NEW YORK CITY: The Council ational Rifle Association met yesterday, and, in deference the wishes of the Directors of your N. R. A., agreed to ncede for the next match the use of the wind-gauge, similar those on some of your service rifles; also that efficient series in your National Guard and our Volunteers, dating from t of January in the year in which a match shall be shot, all make a man eligible to shoot in either team.

The British N. R. A., however, cannot admit the slim foreght as used by some of your men, nor its being dovetailed to the block, as a serviceable foresight for military purses, because they believe that it would not be strong ough for service, as a fall would be likely to break it off. either can they admit the pistol grip, on account of expense manufacture. The matter of cost, even to the amount of few pence per gun, has to be considered in a military arm hen they have to be made by the half million.

The rules which govern this match, and which they trust ll always govern it, are that it should be fought with arely military rifles. One of the rules of this late British team ad a slighter stock than they think advisable, allowing of a heavier barrel, and the council will hereafter endeavor to stop errors in this direction. Otherwise the rifles used by their team are pronounced by them in the strictest sense military, and are fit to put into the hands of troops in the field.

## At Shell Mound.

Last Sunday the friendly rifle contest among Messrs. Beaver, Kellogg, Kuhnle and Williams took place at Shell Mound Park. The day was fine and atmosphere clear, but a little wind, light as it was, was very unsteady; often the flag could point to the lower points of the compass between five or six shots. Col. Beaver was not in the best shooting condition but we think the scores as they stand will compare favorably with any that are made by Eastern sharpshooters. The conditions of the match were 100 shots at 200 yards offhand with a regular army musket, trigger of a six-pound pull. The following scores speak their own minds.

| COL. S. I. KELLOGG. | | | | | | | LIEUT. F. KUEHNLE. | | | | | | |
|---|---|---|---|---|---|---|---|---|---|---|---|---|---|
| 5 | 5 | 4 | 4 | 4 | 4 | 5..47 | 4 | 4 | 5 | 4 | 4 | 4 | 4..47 |
| 4 | 5 | 4 | 4 | 5 | 5 | 5..46 | 4 | 5 | 4 | 4 | 4 | 5 | 5..45 |
| 4 | 4 | 5 | 4 | 5 | 4 | 4..44 | 4 | 4 | 4 | 5 | 4 | 5 | 4..45 |
| 4 | 4 | 4 | 5 | 4 | 4 | 5..45 | 4 | 5 | 4 | 4 | 4 | 4 | 5..45 |
| 4 | 5 | 5 | 4 | 4 | 4 | 4..45 | 4 | 4 | 4 | 5 | 4 | 4 | 4..43 |
| 4 | 4 | 4 | 4 | 4 | 4 | 5..44 | 4 | 4 | 5 | 4 | 4 | 4 | 4..43 |

| Total............450 | Total............445 |

| COL. S. H. BEAVER. | | | | | | | SERG'T. W. WILLIAMS. | | | | | | |
|---|---|---|---|---|---|---|---|---|---|---|---|---|---|
| 4 | 4 | 4 | 4 | 4 | 4 | 4..41 | 4 | 4 | 4 | 4 | 4 | 4 | 5..45 |
| 4 | 4 | 4 | 5 | 5 | 4 | 4..44 | 5 | 4 | 4 | 4 | 4 | 4 | 4..44 |
| 4 | 5 | 5 | 4 | 4 | 4 | 4..45 | 4 | 5 | 4 | 4 | 5 | 4 | 4..44 |
| 4 | 4 | 4 | 4 | 4 | 4 | 4..42 | 4 | 4 | 4 | 4 | 4 | 4 | 4..42 |
| 4 | 4 | 4 | 4 | 4 | 5 | 4..43 | 4 | 4 | 5 | 4 | 4 | 4 | 4..43 |

| Total............ | Total............448 |

SAN FRANCISCO, Dec. 8, 1882.

EDITOR BREEDER AND SPORTSMAN: Being a constant reader of your weekly paper I feel constrained to write you a note asking you to urge on the C. R. A. to establish over the bay at or near Berkeley, Sancelito, San Rafael or somewhere near San Francisco a proper rifle range and ground for marksmen, and for amateurs in and out of the State National Guard. It should be for 200, 300, 500, 1,000, and 1,100 yard ranges, be of easy access, and cheap fare to and from the city, proper butts put up and buildings for members on the style of Creedmore in New York. Have a team and the markers there always on hand; assess each company say $7 per month for the right to practice at all times, week days and Sundays. There are fifteen companies here and in Oakland, which would be about $100 per month for the range to be kept up, or a joint-stock company could be formed to put the range in shape and have pigeon and all kinds of shooting with a race-course for foot, hurdles, and for base ball grounds, and all kinds of sports in connection with the range, all in one. I believe a big joint stock company could be formed and have it succeed. I won't take ten shares at $2.50 per share.

I wish you would write a good article and lay out the general features. I have a man in my eye (mind's eye) who would, I have no doubt, if he was engaged get in the interest of it, that is Wm. T. Colman. He has a lot of land near San Rafael and would help the association, making a long lease and taking stock also. Yours, with wishes for your success.

MARKSMAN, N. G. C.

COL. BODINE RESIGNS.—On Friday, Nov. 17, the Executive Committee of the National Rifle Association held a meeting and the following letter of resignation was received from Col. John Bodine, Captain of the American Team for 1883:

GENTLEMEN: For reasons which are satisfactory to myself I deem it expedient to most respectfully tender my resignation as Captain of the American Military Team of 1883. On severing my official connection with the team I beg to thank you most heartily for the courteous treatment received at your hands and for your efficient support in my efforts to promote the efficiency of the late team as well as to organize a representative military team for 1883, which it was to have been my honor to command. I beg you to accept my earnest thanks for the great favor conferred in appointing me to the responsible position which I now reluctantly resign, and assure you that I still retain the keenest interest in the match, and will spare no effort to promote its success. Very respectfully yours, JOHN BODINE.

The Colonel has always been an enthusiastic rifleman and as he is quite capable of filling the responsible position of captain of the American Team, his resignation was very reluctantly accepted by the Committee.

---

## ANCIENT AND MODERN ARMS.

### Gaspard Zoller's Experiment and Koster's Accidental Discovery.

BY DR. E. H. PARDEE.

*(Continued from page 347.)*

The treatment and discussion of a subject purely military in its character by one who has only made himself acquainted for the mere love of investigating the hidden mysteries pertaining to the laws and science of gunnery may seem to the reading public to demand an apology from me, for I am free to admit that to pronounce upon the most proper method of applying any fresh discoveries affecting the science of projectiles would come more properly within the purview of competent military men.

And if an apology be necessary for placing the result of my deductions and experiments with the rifle for the last quarter of a century before the readers of the BREEDER AND SPORTSMAN I will say that if the opinions expressed do not meet the entire concurrence of those who are better informed upon this subject than myself, the publication of my communications may at least induce other and probably abler advocates to come forward and assist in the development of this interesting but difficult question.

Very few persons, Mr. Editor, know how much scientific research, as well as practical experience, is necessary for the acquirement of a knowledge of the laws respecting rifle projectiles, and for correctly ascertaining their capabilities. Indeed, I am inclined to believe that it is difficult to find a subject more comprehensive in its nature and character than that pertaining to the manufacture and manipulation of the rifle. And let it be understood that whatever contributes to the perfection of small arms renders a corresponding improvement in cannon, as it is quite evident to all who attentively study the subject that the same precision and relative efficiency which characterize the ordinary rifle can be so certainly obtained with cannon.

The rifle has become so common that it is looked upon at the present time as a permanent fixture of the best regulated families. Men look upon it as a companion and speak of its capabilities with a feeling of pride and admiration. And a spirit of kindness is always seen, with a feeling of emulation, among gentlemen when in competition in testing the qualities of the gun and steadiness of the nerve on the target ground. What a feeling of self-reliance the marksman has when he takes his position and levels his piece for the bulleye! his organ of hope is "way up," and the look of satisfaction depicted on the smiling countenance if the white disk indicates the bullseye tells that the love he has for that rifle is far beyond description. That gun never lies to him; it is the best gun that the manufacturer ever made; it is true blue. But, Mr. Editor, let's ask the gentleman while wiping her for another shot wherein his rifle differs from any other gun. He will tell you it is a Sharp, and that rifle over there is a Ballard. "Yes, I know; but then where is the difference of mechanical ingenuity displayed that makes yours the better weapon? The Ballard looks like a good gun." "Well, yes; but then that fellow Sharp makes a darnation good gun, and he's hard to beat, bet yer life, and no feller has got a license to beat this gun a hundred successive shots for coarse gaid; she's a good one, I tell you; she chumps her balls all in the bulleye, and mighty near the center of the bulleye at that." Ask him if it has a uniform twist and the answer is quickly given: "Don't know." Inquire for the temper of his bullet and the response is: "Don't know." Ask for the turn of the rifling and the answer is the same: "Don't know." And so it goes with ninety-nine out of every hundred, that, automaton-like, they have learned to manipulate the rifle in about the same way that the poll-parrot learns to talk.

And so it is with the most of our gun-makers; they work as they were learned to work, by scribe rule, and not understanding the most simple principles of the laws of gunnery. A few years ago I remember listening to a gunmaker of San Francisco as he explained to a listener the reason of the grooves in a rifle being crooked. And the answer was given with so much intelligence that I shall never forget it, and the credulity of the customer took it all in with a smile of apparent satisfaction on his face, as transparent as though he had spoken the words: "I thought so." The answer from the worker of metal was as follows: "The riflings are crooked in order to make the ball go straight." A graphic answer, I must confess, and as truthful as graphic, and if he had carried his answer a little further by an illustration of the smoothbore, or by explaining that putting riffing in straight would make a ball go crooked, he would have closed the door behind him and left nothing more to be said on the subject.

And now, Mr. Editor, I am going to tell you, as near as historical facts will permit me, who it was that first rifled a gun-barrel, though it is by no means certain that I am correct, as different authors give the credit to different parties.

Gaspard Zoller, a gunmaker of Vienna, Austria, at about the end of the fifteenth century, sawed straight parallel grooves, in the shape of a letter V, in a gun-barrel. It was done ostensibly for two objects: First to prepare a place for the residuum always produced from the ignition of powder in a gun. Second, to lessen the friction of the bullet, as only a very small portion of the circumferences of the ball would come in contact with the points of the V-shaped riflings in its passage. And it was found an improvement over the old smoothbore, and much credit was due and given to this old Austrian Jew for so apparently small a favor. And upon his laurels he was content to live and see completed and perfected, by accident, that which he began upon a basis of both logic and reason. For good fellow! Peace to his ashes! Little did he think that what he had done was the beginning of a new era in the management of projectiles. Little did he think that the sixteen straight grooves he put in the first smoothbore gun were the inauguration of so great and stupendous a result. Though the name of Gaspard Zoller is not classed with that of Aerston, Morse, Harvey, Franklin or Field, it is simply an omission of the historian to "render unto Cæsar the things that are Cæsar's."

About a score of years after the improvement of the smoothbore by Zoller a gunsmith by the name of Koster, of Nuremburg, attempted the imitation of Zoller by putting in straight grooves, but by some mistake he got them inclined instead of straight, and as the grooves were all parallel to each other the idea struck him that he would test the shooting qualities of the barrel before he threw it away, as the grooves left the barrel too thin for reutting. And right there he found, though by mistake, that the steadiness of the flight of the bullets far surpassed anything that had ever been achieved in the expulsion of leaden bullets. Another milestone passed on the road to projectile science.

But the mystery was not solved, as no one could make clear the difficult problem why a bullet propelled from a gun-barrel with inclined grooves should bear toward a common center more evenly than a bullet from a gun with straight grooves, or without grooves at all. And for long years the theory seemed so absurd that it was with great difficulty that it found many followers. But the cold, frozen facts were there, and when placed on exhibition the result was always both convincing and satisfactory. The riflings, as I have already stated, were unlike our grooves at the present day, about one-half grooves and one-half lands, but like the letter V, and as a matter of reference I will make a pen sketch showing the muzzle end of one of these antiquated guns.

Now other difficulties began. to appear in fitting the bullet on these pointed riflings so as to prevent windage, and it was no small obstacle to overcome, as the reader will readily see. The grooves being deep, it was almost impossible to wash a leaden ball to their bottom, and yet it had to be done to prevent the escape of gas through the bottom of the grooves, thereby lessening the projectile force.

### Archery.

It was expected that two or three of our local archery clubs would put forth their best men on Thanksgiving Day and shoot against the scores made by Eastern clubs. Only one team from the Pacific Archery Club came to the Park. The shooting was done at the Golden Gate Park range. The distance was 60 yards, and 96 arrows each were shot. The following scores were made:

| J. P. ALLEN. | | GEO. W. KENNEY. | |
|---|---|---|---|
| Hits. | Points. | Hits. | Points. |
| 32... | ...120 | 16... | ...80 |
| 19... | ...89 | 18... | ...88 |
| 28... | ...106 | 19... | ...92 |
| 34... | ...179 | 20... | ...92 |
| Total.....494 | | Total......352 | |

| R. P. MURRAY. | | A. J. STERLING. | |
|---|---|---|---|
| Hits. | Points. | Hits. | Points. |
| 23... | ...63 | 11... | ...53 |
| 18... | ...56 | 14... | ...56 |
| 21... | ...55 | 12... | ...34 |
| 30... | ...91 | 20... | ...44 |
| Total....262 | | Total......179 | |

After the regular match was shot Mr. Murray and Mr. Allen shot a match of sixty arrows at 30 yards. Allen made 60 hits, 436 points. Mr. Murray 60 hits, 430 points. As soon as possible we will give the scores of the Eastern teams made on Thanksgiving Day.

---

## BASE BALL.

### Niantics vs. Haverlys.

The game played at the Recreation Grounds last Sunday resulted as follows:

| NIANTICS. | | | | | | HAVERLYS. | | | | | |
|---|---|---|---|---|---|---|---|---|---|---|---|
| | T B | R B P O A E | | | | | T B | R B P O A E |
| Brown, r f... | 5 | 3 | 3 | 1 | 0 | 0 | Carroll, p... | 5 | 0 | 0 | 1 | 7 | 1 |
| Morris, 2b... | 5 | 2 | 3 | 4 | 1 | 0 | Levy, l f... | 4 | 1 | 1 | 0 | 1 | 1 |
| Denny, 3b... | 5 | 1 | 3 | 4 | 1 | McDonald, 3b. | 4 | 1 | 0 | 2 | 1 | 3 |
| Sweeny, p... | 5 | 1 | 3 | 0 | 12 | 0 | McCord, 1 b... | 4 | 0 | 0 | 12 | 0 | 0 |
| Angus, 1 f... | 4 | 2 | 0 | 1 | 0 | Lawton, s s... | 4 | 0 | 0 | 2 | 6 | 2 |
| Incell, s f... | 4 | 0 | 0 | 0 | 0 | Gregus, 2b... | 4 | 0 | 0 | 3 | 1 |
| Egan, 1 b... | 4 | 1 | 1 | 12 | 0 | Henry, 3b... | 4 | 0 | 0 | 1 | 1 |
| Flinn, c... | 4 | 1 | 0 | 9 | 0 | Barnes, c f... | 4 | 1 | 0 | 0 | 0 |
| Donahue, c f... | 4 | 1 | 1 | 2 | 1 | Haren, c... | 4 | 1 | 0 | 3 | 1 |
| Totals...... | 41 | 13 | 10 | 27 | 14 | 6 | Totals...... | 36 | 6 | 2 | 27 | 17 | 11 |

| Innings............. | 1 | 2 | 3 | 4 | 5 | 6 | 7 | 8 | 9 |
|---|---|---|---|---|---|---|---|---|---|
| Niantics............. | 0 | 3 | 0 | 0 | 3 | 1 | 5 | 2—13 |
| Haverlys............. | 1 | 0 | 0 | 1 | 1 | 2 | 0 | 1—6 |

Earned runs, Niantics 2. Bases on balls, Niantics 3, Haverlys 1. Struck out, Niantics 6, Haverlys 8. Passed balls, Lawton 5, Flinn 1. Two-base hits, Morris 3, Denny 1. Three-base hit, Denny. Time of game, 1¾ hours. Umpire, Start of the Renos.

### Howards vs. Redingtons.

A game was played at the Olympic Club Grounds, Oakland, Sunday, with the following result:

| HOWARDS. | | | | | | REDINGTONS. | | | | | |
|---|---|---|---|---|---|---|---|---|---|---|---|
| | T B | R B P O A E | | | | | T B | R B P O A E |
| Conn, p... | 5 | 1 | 2 | 0 | 15 | 3 | Arnold, 2b... | 5 | 1 | 2 | 1 | 4 | 1 |
| Jacobus, 1 f... | 5 | 2 | 1 | 0 | 0 | 1 | Moran, s f... | 5 | 1 | 0 | 1 | 0 | 1 |
| Hardie, c... | 5 | 2 | 3 | 10 | 3 | 0 | Bennett, 3b g | 4 | 0 | 0 | 1 | 1 | 3 |
| Fitzgerald, 1b. | 5 | 1 | 0 | 11 | 0 | Lewis, s s... | 4 | 1 | 0 | 7 | 0 |
| Royce, 3b... | 5 | 0 | 1 | 1 | 4 | 2 | Watt, p g 3b. | 5 | 1 | 1 | 3 | 9 |
| Swain, c f... | 4 | 0 | 1 | 0 | 0 | Van Bergen, 1 f | 4 | 1 | 1 | 0 | 0 |
| McCord, s s... | 5 | 0 | 0 | 2 | 1 | Lemen, 1b... | 4 | 0 | 0 | 14 | 0 |
| Van Court, 2b. | 5 | 1 | 2 | 3 | 0 | Mullen, c f... | 4 | 0 | 0 | 0 | 0 |
| Adams, r f... | 4 | 0 | 1 | 1 | 0 | Dillon, c f... | 4 | 0 | 0 | 0 | 0 |
| Totals...... | 41 | 7 | 9 | 27 | 26 | 6 | Totals...... | 37 | 4 | 2 | 27 | 18 | 9 |

| Innings............. | 1 | 2 | 3 | 4 | 5 | 6 | 7 | 8 | 9 |
|---|---|---|---|---|---|---|---|---|---|
| Howards............. | 3 | 0 | 2 | 0 | 0 | 0 | 0 | 1 | 1—7 |
| Redingtons......... | 0 | 0 | 0 | 2 | 0 | 0 | 0 | 2 | 0—4 |

Balls called off. Conn 66, Pratt 69, Bennett 30. Strikes off, Bennett 17, Pratt 97, Conn 55. Passed balls, Hardie 2, Lewis 5, Moran 2. Two-base hits, Conn and Hardie. Double play, Pratt and Lemen. Earned runs, Conn. Struck out, Howards 9, Redingtons 12. First base on errors, Redingtons 5, Howards 6. Left on bases, Redingtons 7, Howards 7. Time of game, 2 hours. Scorer, C. A. Toll. Umpire, E. Sumner of the Olympics.

---

THE PHYLLOXERA IN SPAIN.—The Minister of agriculture of Spain has adopted a very radical mode of dealing with the phylloxera in that country. He has determined upon the complete destruction of all infected vines. On the other hand he has originated a very conservative mode of treatment for the owners of vines that have to be destroyed on account of the disease. By law such owners are to be compensated in a small degree for the vines destroyed in accordance with the law of the land. This compensation is to be such and such only as will save the owners from complete ruin and financial wreck. The Minister of Agriculture has formed an insurance company among vine owners, for the insurance of the vines of all against the disease. By the terms of the insurance, when the vines are condemned to destruction by law, then the insurance company—composed of those who still have vines in good health—comes forward and pays who still have vines in good health—comes forward and pays the owner of their loss, or in other words, pays the owner of the condemned vines for their loss, or so much as is agreed upon in the policy of insurance. This plan divides the loss and equalizes it among a large number of people, instead of allowing it to fall so heavy on the few. This plan also insures the faithful execution of the law to prevent the spread of the disease, by taking away the motive for concealing the fact of the existence of the disease in any particular vineyard by the owner. Why would not a plan something like this be a good one to adopt in this country?—*Riverside Press.*

## THE KENNEL.

### The Gilroy Field Trials.

The Second Annual Field Trials of the Gilroy Rod and Gun Club commenced on Monday, the 27th inst. The weather was fine and birds somewhat scarce. Some thirty or forty spectators were present, including many well known sportsmen from San Francisco. The judges were H. H. Briggs, of San Francisco, and Messrs. Horton and D. M. Pyle of Gilroy. The all-age stake, with seven entries, was commenced by Leavesley's Don, a liver Belton setter, two and a half years old, by Knox's Belton Belle handled by D. Gilroy, and H. M. Briggs' Count Warwick, two and a half years old, by Gause's Warwick Belle handled by E. Leavesley. Some very fine points and backs were made by both dogs, and the spectators, many of whom had never seen the performance of thoroughbred hunting dogs, were highly pleased at the exhibition of statuary beauty exhibited by the dogs on point. The heat was awarded to Count Warwick. The next race put down was Leavesley's Juno, two and a half years, Belton-Belle, liver and white, handled by owner, and H. H. Briggs' Belle, Red Irish setter, three years, handled by owner. Juno, a double prize winner of last year, was not in good form, and did not hunt with her accustomed vim, and the heat was awarded to Belle. The next brace put down was W. H. Whittier's lemon and white setter Rock, four years by Luther Adair's Rock-Sibyll, handled by T. Hildebrand, and Leavesley's Daisy. Blue Belton bitch by Carlowitz-Trux, six years, owned and handled by D. M. Pyle. The action of the two dogs was very animated and much admired by all present. Rock's brilliant action and Daisy's caution added to her energy and fine style were well contrasted. The old bitch, originally Waddington's Daisy from Iowa, appeared to think that the honor of the East was represented in her, she being a prize winner both in quail and prairie chickens, and let herself out in grand style, and was finally awarded the heat. Next came a bye, Wm. Henderson's Jim, a Gordon setter by Pestolise's Spirit and Welch's Quail, handled by Leavesley, and Daisy, handled by Pyle. The shadows of evening coming on, the dogs were taken up to be put down next day.

#### Tuesday.

The day was a repetition of yesterday, bright and clear, and Mr. James Murphy's ranch, some nine miles from Gilroy, was selected to continue the trials. The grounds hunted on yesterday being too full of strong-scented weeds. Plenty of birds were soon found and the first brace put down was Belle and Count Warwick. Jim, the Gordon setter, whose unfinished heat was to have been settled, and who had his red ribbon still attached to his neck, appeared to entertain the idea that he had beaten Daisy, and was so anxious to get home to exhibit his trophy that on the door of his box stall being opened in the morning he made a bee line for Leavesley's ranch, and arrived there with colors flying, to the great admiration and wonder of ten or twenty puppies, who greeted him with many anxious inquiries as to his success at the trial. But on observing Jim's red ribbon, a bit of jealousy seemed to poison them, for they all pitched on to him, and he was only too glad to divide honors with them. Worse still, he unfortunately lost his chances in the trials. After some good work Belle was given the heat. It now only remained for Belle and Daisy to decide the winner of the first prize. Daisy showed phenomenal power of hunting and scent for her age and won easily. Her last point settled the business, and Daisy was awarded the heat, winning first prize, besides a silver cup, a special prize, given by Senator Traylor, for the best dog in the trials.

#### Puppy Stakes.

The first brace put down was F. G. Abell's Scott Gordon setter by Max-Jip, twenty-two months, and J. L. Nichle's eighteen months King, by C. Miller's Joe-Farmer's Queen, liver and white. Scott handled by D. Gilroy, King by T. Hildebrand. Some very fine work was done by these two dogs, and they were so nearly matched, that after running two heats, the judges could not decide upon the merits so they were ordered to be put down again next day.

#### Wednesday.

Scott and King being called to finish their heat, it was found that King was sick and had been withdrawn by T. Hildebrand.

The next brace was Leavesley's Duke, two and one-half years, blue Belton setter, C. Miller's Joe and Farmer's Queen and H. E. Bytea's Portland, Oregon, Fourkill, red and white Irish setter, Ben–Ruby, 21 months. Duke won the heat. Duke and Silk ran next and Duke won.

Scott and Mollie Daily, English setter by Treanor's Ben, and D. Vaul's Beauty, next ran. Scott won.

Red Bess, a bye, was then run against Duke who won. The concluding heat for first prize was then run by Duke and Scott and Scott won.

A special prize, silver cup, presented by W. F. Whittier to owner of best brace of puppies run at the trials, to Duke and Mollie Daily owned by E. Leavesley.

Special prize of a pointer puppy, value $25, presented by G. A. Bassford of Colusa, for best dog not placed, to Rock. The trials were a grand success and it is the intention of the Gilroy Club to import Bob Whites and plant them out in a piece of reserved ground with our own quail, for next years' trials, so as to insure plenty of birds. Two amateurs entered dogs and handled them well, and it is to be hoped that their example will be followed next year by many others as it is the intention of the Gilroy Club to leave nothing undone to make these trials better every year, both as to their management and the selection and preservation of suitable ground, well stocked with birds to run off the heats quietly and with satisfaction to all parties concerned. Some of the decisions of the judges were commented upon freely by outsiders, but upon the whole their decisions were received with much satisfaction.

---

COURSING IN MARYLAND.—The popularity of the ancient sport of coursing in the old country can be judged from the fact that 32 first-class matches were run during the month of November.

## THE BULLDOG.

### Lord Macaulay as an Authority.—The Bulldog as a Retriever—Etc.

This unique species of the canine race derives his name from his almost universal employment in bull baiting in England up to the middle of the present century. The satisfaction with which he entered upon that congenial work was the principal reason for the passage of laws prohibiting bull baiting with dogs, for as Lord Macaulay says: "The Puritans opposed bull baiting, not because it gave the bull pain but because it afforded pleasure to the dogs." Thus we see that it is dangerous even for dogs to evince pleasure in anything, for had the bulldog gone at his work in a reluctant manner and not until forcibly urged on by his master these long-faced interferers with the course of nature would not have stopped bull baiting and thereby signed the death warrant of one of the noblest breeds of animals that ever graced this earth. Previous writers on the dog have sadly libeled this meritorious breed and it is felt that at this late day some tribute should be paid to the few remaining representatives of a once great and noble race. Even the learned Youatt went out of his way to slander the bulldog by saying that he was not capable of education and was fit for nothing but ferocity and combat. Now the truth is that the bulldog is a very intellectual animal as dogs go and were so much attention paid to his education and training as falls to the lot of the setter, pointer or spaniel he would be found as tractable as any of them. I once owned a bulldog named Bill whom I trained to do all the tricks commonly performed by pet dogs. Bill was the ugliest brindled animal that ever lived but there was a look of rugged honesty in his face and a general air of bold, manly determination about him that made one much attached to him. When he was six months old he was so fearfully underfoot—his front teeth and tusks protruded like those of a wild boar—that he was the general terror of all the females about the place and it was to convince a favorite sister that he was not as bad as he looked that I undertook to educate him in all the acts that go to make up a perfect house dog. First I taught him not to tear, fight or chase his natural enemies, the cats. Four the tortoise-shell kittens were offered up as a sacrifice to his natural instincts, but in less than ten weeks Bill had learned to leave cats alone, and even to treat them with courtesy. When he once understood that cat's meat was a prohibited luxury, no amount of temptation could induce him to forget his lessons, and I have seen him allow a cat that had recently become a mother, to scratch his face until it lied without any resentment. It took about half an hour to teach Bill to retrieve, and when once he knew what was meant no distance was too long for him to fetch any designated article. Right here his gameness came in to a remarkable extent. When sent for anything he would never let go of it until he placed it in my hand, and when he grew to be of mature age I won dozens of bets that the article he was bringing could not be taken away from him. He was an invaluable dog at a pigeon shoot. Send him after a dead bird, he might not get there ahead of the other dogs, but it was dollars to cents he would lay for them on the return trip and take the game away from the lucky, or rather unlucky, animal that had secured it. If there was ever any dispute as to who killed a bird, when my boyish companions and myself were out shooting, I was always ready to leave the question for the dogs to decide, being sure that Bill would get the game if he had to kill every dog in the field to do it. Though a smooth haired dog, Bill was one of the best water retrievers I ever saw and no water was too cold nor swim too long to keep him from dead game. I taught him to sit on his hind legs, beg, lie down as if dead with his fore feet in the air, and carry a small toy gun in his fore legs while he walked around a room upon his hind ones. He would follow me up a ladder using his teeth to hold on while his legs moved up to a higher step. No doubt was he with our family that the girls at last adopted the ugly brute for their own and never thought of taking a walk unless Bill was along for an escort. The large city in which our family lived was not free from male loafers but Bill was a better and a surer protection to the girls than any masculine human friend and on one occasion when a friend of the family touched my younger sister on the arm in the street to attract her attention he was reminded of his breach of etiquette which teeth fastened in the calf of his leg. Father used to say that he was dead sure no young man would come fooling around the girls when Bill was along. Bill died long ago but his memory lives and is a standing denial to those who claim that the bulldog is incapable of culture. I hope that this digression will be pardoned and will try to atone for it by getting right down to the general features of bulldog character and wasting no more space in giving particular instances. When one looks a bulldog in the face the first and last thing he notices is an appearance of stolid courage. The staunch Moslem who throws himself into the hottest of the fray with no thought but of victory or a place in Paradise with green robed houris to minister to his pleasures has just such a look. The old masters gave their pictures of heroes just such a look; all brave men have it habitually and all men act naturally brave when they have made up their minds to a brave or desperate action have the same appearance. But with men there is this difference, they combine intelligence of results with a regardlessness of them, while the bulldog shows by his appearance that he has no the slightest expectation of any ill or hurt befalling him. His is not a sensitive nature and in that respect he is immeasurably inferior to the lowest type of man. The tortured Indian, like the bulldog, will not cry aloud for mercy, but the Indian is away ahead of the dog because while his courage makes him keep down the howl of pain the dog feels little or no pain and consequently has no great desire to howl. The game bulldog in a fight will never quit, but allow his blood to cool and his wounds to become sore to the touch, my word for it he will decline a second encounter. So even the bitterest of bulldog courage the courage man is afraid. One of the chiefest values of the bulldog is his faculty of transmitting gameness to his progeny no matter what the character of the maternal relative. On this account nearly all the best strains of the greyhound have been crossed with the bull and the result is the progeny, even though subsequent breeding has left no trace of the bull's shape and but the merest trace of his blood, will run after their game until they drop dead from exhaustion. The bulldog is undoubtedly bred from the mastiff, which is an original breed peculiar to the British Islands. He has more intelligence and a finer scent than the mastiff. But the whole trouble with the bulldog is that he has been relegated to the company of fighters, loafers, and ruffians for so long that he has imbibed their bad traits to a considerable extent. He is also kept too much on the chain and is not given as much human society as is necessary to rescue any breed of the dog from its natural and wolfish savageness and foxish cunning.   EDWIN.

### Arizona Correspondence.

The following letter from an Arizona gentleman contains something of interest to every sportsman's club in the State. There is an abundance of such dogs as Mr. Jones describes in and around San Francisco and doubtless many are for sale.

TOMBSTONE, Arizona.

EDITOR BREEDER AND SPORTSMAN, SAN FRANCISCO: A constant and appreciative reader of your delightful paper takes the liberty to ask your advice and assistance. I want to procure a pair of Setter pups (Irish preferred), dog and bitch, of the purest strain and pure field trial winners. The dogs must be like Cæsar's wife, above suspicion, and I take the liberty to ask you to recommend me to some one in whom implicit reliance can be had. It will cost me a good deal to get them here and then considering the trouble of breaking them I want to feel that the pups I get are worth the trouble. I don't believe there is a pure blooded, well-broken pointer or setter in this benighted Territory, and having in by-gone days enjoyed the blessing of good dogs I propose to have them again if I can accomplish it. By the way, Mr. Editor, the quail most common to this vicinity is the most beautiful game bird I have ever seen and to distinguish it from the black plume California quail, and for want of better knowledge, we call it the gray quail. The bird is a little larger than the California quail (which we also have in great abundance), with rich grey plumage, speckled breast and most beautiful top-knot with snow-white plume. I am not sure but have been told that it is peculiar to Arizona and New Mexico and is found at times forty miles from water. As you approach the watercourses the California quail seem to take precedence. I would like to know the true name of this bird if any meager description will furnish you an idea of what it is.

I have a few dozen pair that I caught when quite young and have them in large pens where they have become quite tame, and I believe from their docility that they will be easily domesticated.

If any of your readers are half as enthusiastic as I am on the question of game, bird and field sports, and care to try the experiment, I will ship them a few pairs of these birds, and they can see what they are. I live upward of 400 feet above to stock a place I will send them all they want, in exchange for a pair of pups as I described.   HARRY P. JONES.

### Eastern Field Trials.

HIGH POINT, N. C., Nov. 20, 1882.

Very heavy frost covered the earth, bushes and grass this morning; the sky was cloudy, the atmosphere chilly and raw, and there was very little wind. The birds were wild and would not lie to the dogs, but ran, rendering it almost impossible to get points on them. Peg and Countess were first put down to conclude their heat, and after a run of one hour and forty-five minutes, during which more flushes than points were made, Peg was awarded the heat. Immediately after Don and Peg were put down to decide the winner of the cup. The sun was now shining and speedily melted the frost, while the atmosphere was warmer and altogether it was more favorable for good work, but Peg had become rattled by the running birds in her previous heat and was very unsteady. Both pointed simultaneously, Don standing and Peg flat. The voices of the crowd caused the bevy, which was in front of Peg, to move, when she also moved a step or two, and the bevy flushed wild. Don soon after made another point which Peg refused to back, but dashed ahead of him, flushed a single bird and then drew to a point on those remaining. The judges ordered the heat up and awarded the heat and cup to Don.

The all-aged stake—The running for the all-aged stakes commenced with the first brace, Croxteth and Monarch, which was won by Croxteth in fifteen minutes. The other went in grand style, without an error, on a scattering bevy. The next brace, Rab and Bravo, were sent down and this was won by Rab, after a heat of nearly two hours, during which very few birds were found, although a very large extent of territory was gone over. Lalla Rookh and Lady Dufferin were then put down. The heat was won in thirty-four minutes by Lalla Rookh, a wonderful puppy for her age—scarcely a month. Croxteth and Rob were then cast off. After a very long and tedious heat, occupying two hours and eight minutes, during which an immense amount of ground was gone over and very few birds were found, and the majority of these wild, Croxteth was awarded the heat. Both dogs did some excellent work for the opportunities they had, Croxteth and Lalla Rookh then came together to decide the winner of the special pointer prize, and were taken up at the expiration of seventeen minutes on account of its growing dark and the distance from home. During that time nothing further was done beyond Croxteth making a false point and Lalla Rookh a back. The birds are very scarce indeed, and the places in which they are found render good work very difficult.

It is a very grave question whether there will be birds enough to run the trials out on, as the starters in the Derby promise to be very large.—New York World.

### Hard Biting Dogs.

A correspondent writes to us to know the best way to break a dog of the vicious habit of biting his birds when retrieving, and he further asks that as many other young sportsmen are equally benighted we will publish a reply.

Nearly every dog trainer has some favorite plan for the correction of this abuse. Old dog complained of be an old offender, with whom several plans have been found to fail, as a last resort he can be bitted. A good bit can easily be made of stout iron wire bent so that it has a flat base and a rounded arch at the top. Place the flat base of the arch in the dog's mouth and pull the rounded part over his ears. Then secure the arrangement by a piece of buckskin tied, not too tightly, around the throat. The wire in the mouth will not hurt if it is put behind the tushes.

A young dog can generally be cured of the riot by being set to retrieve a dead bird through which a number of blunt pieces of wire have been passed in different directions. After he has hurt his mouth a few times he will handle a dead bird as gingerly as though it were glass and he was afraid to break it. A little patience and close watching at the commencement of a dog's education will equip all desire to mouth or bite. In case both of the methods suggested fail with an old offender the best plan is to send him to the sausage factory.

Mr. Robinson of England, former owner of the well-known Laverack setter Aldersbot, has purchased the dog from Mr. E. A. Herzberg of Brooklyn.

### Coursing at Newark.

Last Sunday at Dugan's Newark Coursing Grounds a match was run off between C. Johnson's Delebute and W. Dugan's Lady Plaice. The match was for $50, best two courses in three. Mr. Sellery was selected as judge. The first course was won by Lady Plaice. Delebute won the second. The third run resulted in a tie. During the first part of the fourth and final course it looked as if Delebute had it all her own way. She opened a wide gap from slips and made two more points before Lady Plaice got her nose in. But in her eagerness in pressing the hare she got an ugly fall in a squirrel hole which stunned her and allowed Lady Plaice to roll up points all alone. When Delebute did recover, the course was all but over. She managed to get in to help kill but Lady Plaice won the course and match by one point. The losers took their defeat in good part but to show that they have not lost confidence in their dog they now offer to make the match over again for $100 a side, the match to be run off at Merced next spring when the Pacific Coast Coursing club hold their spring meeting and to be judged by whoever is selected to judge for the club or any person who can be mutually agreed upon.

Delebute is a little stiff from her accident, but has sustained no serious injury.

### Eastern Field Trials.

The annual field trials of the National Kennel Club began Dec., 4. For the All-Ages stakes Drew's American Dan beat Don't, winner of the Members' cup at the Eastern trials; Press beat Cavalier (pointer); Gladstone beat King Dash; Sue beat Baden Baden; Carrie J. beat Gulderoy. Peep o' Day beat Philus. In the second trial Starke beat Grouse (Gordon); Spot beat Bessie Lee.

The second day found the conditions very unfavorable. In the final heat, first round, Count Noble beat Biz. In the second round American Dan beat Gladso Drann, Sue beat Bess, Carrie J beat Startle, Peep o' Day beat Scot and Count Noble beat Abbie. In the third round American Dan beat Count Noble, Sue beat Carrie J, Peep o' Day beat Abbie. In the fourth round Peep o' Day beat American Dan. The latter was a very long and close heat.

Low Prices for Dogs.—On Saturday last, says an exchange, twenty sporting dogs belonging to Dr. H. S. Strickland were sold at the American Horse Exchange, New York. Few fanciers were present, and the prices were very low. Hugo, a well bred setter, two years old, well broke and of full pedigree, got no bid and was retired. Duke, a lemon and white setter, fifteen months old, was bought by Daniel Connelly for $13; Jumbo, a setter, seven months old, was bought by Mr. Lansing for $9; Rye, a blue Belton setter, one year old, brought $5; Bessie, a lemon and white sétter, eighteen months old, was sold to Mr. Preston for $25; Lena, of the same color and age, was bought by Mr. Roach for $9; Speck, a setter, eighteen months old, full pedigree, went to Mr. Preston for $17; Juno, a black setter, fourteen months old, was sold to Mr. Stone for $13, and twelve Irish setter pups, of full pedigree, went at prices varying between $1 and $3 each.

We publish this week a complete report of the Gilroy Field Trials whi was unfortunately received too late for insertion last week. The trials were a success though not as largely attended as was expected, but as yet the number of real sporting enthusiasts in California is small.

Match at Newark.—On Sunday (to-morrow) a coursing match will be run at Newark between Chris Johnson's b d b Delebute and the be and w b Lady Plaice. The match is for $50 and will doubtless prove very interesting.

## ATHLETICS.

### Six-Day Pedestrianism.

The following sketch of the pedestrian performance of C. A. Harriman has been handed us for publication, and as will be learned from the perusal, there may be an effort made to inaugurate a "six-day go-as-you-please" contest. We were never favorably impressed with these long, dragging bouts, and think that they have an injurious effect on legitimate athletic sport. For a time there was a furore, and thousands indorsed them by their presence as spectators. They certainly proved that men had far greater powers of endurance than heretofore had been accredited, and eclipsed the old-time doings when the training was not so well understood. Further than this there was nothing gained, and we hope that the result of the last match in New York will be accepted as a token that their day has passed. Walking matches, fair "heel and toe," are interesting, but when the graceful action of O'Leary, and the easy, long stride of Harriman are replaced by the shambling dog trot of Weston or the slouching run of others who have gained distinction in this field there is nothing pleasing in the display:

An effort is being made by several of the leading pedestrians of this city to arrange a six-day contest for the Cotton diamond belt.. A meeting was held last Monday evening at Harry Maynard's rooms, for the purpose of considering the matter, but nothing definite was decided upon. It is said that Mrs. Cotton wants $500 for the belt and that those who are making overtures for it do not look favorably upon procuring it at that figure. C. A. Harriman, the champion pedestrian, who is now in this city, and who will remain until after the holidays, expresses a willingness to take part in a six-day go-as-you-please contest or a square heel and toe walk if such is held in this city before his departure.

C. A. Harriman, the renowned pedestrian, arrived in this city last week on his way to Australia. He is a young man, appearing to be about twenty-five or thirty years of age, of fine figure and a bright, vivacious talker. In a talk with the writer of this brief sketch he mentioned the principal events in which he has taken part: "In '79," he said, "I was in Baltimore. I entered there in a six-day go-as-you-please race against eight or nine competitors. I won the race. The next time I walked was at Providence, R. I., in the August following, against forty-two men in a seventy-five-hour go-as-you-please match. I walked it out and got about $250. In October I was at Newark, N. J., and entered for a six-day heel-and-toe walk; I won first place, making 342 miles. In the spring of '80 Chicago, at the Bellevue, I was in a percentage race, seven days, twelve hours each day. Vint got in first in this and I was next. This proved greatly to my benefit financially. In the spring of '80 I won a fifty-hour race at Jamestown, N. Y., against twenty-two men. It was a go-as-you-please race. From Jamestown I went to Philadelphia and entered for a twelve-hour-a-day go-as-you-please match in the Industrial Art Hall. I got in fourth, those leading me being Albert, Hughes and Reading. In this race I got four prizes—the fourth money, the costume prize, awarded to the best dressed contestant, the trainer's scarf pin and the silver cup for covering the most miles in the last four hours. I then made arrangements for a walk in Cincinnati; the contest was in a tent and after I had completed 305 miles I was drowned out by the rain. I then had an easy walk in Syracuse in which I cleared about four hundred dollars. I walked against George Root in a fifty-consecutive-hour race.

From Syracuse I went to Cincinnati for a six-day, twelve-hours-a-day walk. John Shory took first, myself second, Krohn third and Tracy fourth. I went in a twelve-hour race next at Pawtucket. In the spring of '81 at the Exposition building, New York, I made 530 miles in 142 consecutive hours in a six-day heel-and-toe walk, beating all the records of the world for heel and toe walking. Tracy took second with 523 miles and Krohn made 520 miles. This was in May, 1881. George Littlewood has since beaten the time I made then. I walked a seventy-five-hour contest at the Aquarium, New York, next and won it. I then issued a challenge to the world, (this was in October of '81,) which was never accepted. I had $1,000 on deposit until November the 7th, challenging any and all men to walk a go-as-you-please for two days or six days for from $1,000 to $5,000, the winner to take all the sweepstake money and gate money and in case the receipts were not sufficient the privilege would be given to take down my deposit to make good any deficiency. I did not get any one to take up my proposition. Walton, the plunger, backed me in my race in New York in the spring of '81. I did not come to California to walk and cannot say what I will do while I am here."

### The Last Race of George and Myers.

The New York *World* gives the following account of the final race between George and Myers, on Thanksgiving Day:

Myers was the first to make his appearance and as he passed the grand stand on his way to the starting point he was greeted with boisterous applause and cries of "Lick him to-day Lon!" Without p yi g any attention to this friendly advice he went to the starting-post, where he was shortly joined by Gerorge, whose appearance was a signal for another round of cheers. When the men met at the mark they cordially shook hands, and in answer to George's question Myrick replied: "Oh, I am pretty well to-day, thank you, how are you?" George responded: "Well, indeed, thank you; but the weather is not fine is it, I say?" A warning from the starter caused them to get ready on their mark at the start, which for the "three-quarter" is near the club house on the One Hundred and Tenth street side. George had the inside position. He was dressed in a blue jersey and black satin trunks, and looked decidedly in better health and trim than his dark, small antagonist, whose white silk uniform was in strange contrast to his swarthy complexion. At the crack of the pistol both men dashed away. George started away and made the pace astonishingly rapid. Time-keepers had been stationed at each "twelfth" of a mile, and as the men passed the first of these George's time was 19 4-5s., Myers being one yard behind and running so easily that his friends, who previously to the start were betting "even," now made the "little wonder" a favorite at five to four. When one-sixth of a mile had been passed George still led by a yard, the time being at this point 39¼s. At the "quarter" George's time was 1:1 2-5, with Myers 1-5 of a second behind. Myers after passing this point closed up some of the gap, but just before reaching the third-of-a-mile post he had dropped back, the respeqtive times being—George 4:22; Myers, 1:22¼. Going to the "five-twelfths" Myers made another spurt, and when they passed that post he was but two yards behind George, the latter's time being 1:42; Cries of "Myers wins easily," were now freqnent and loud. The half-mile was done by George in 2:02¾, Myers being ½ s. behind. His fine style and easy carriage, coupled with his closeness to George, who was seemingly straining every nerve, led his friends to make renewed offers of bets that he would win. The 7-12 of a mile was done by George in 2:26, with Myers three yards behind. At this point Myers prepared to make his final effort. Eeight-twelfths of a mile were done by George in 2:58 1-5. Meyers' time being 2:48½. Immediately after passing that point Myers with a grand burst of speed reached George's shoulder and thus they ran for many yards, amid the cheers and cries of the crowd, who now seemed bereft of all reason and broke the ropes which separated them from the track, upon which they flocked, pushing and cheering, yet leaving sufficient room for the runners. Tom McEwan, who could not bear to see his favorite beaten, got by his side, and, waving his hat in the air, shouted words of encouragement in the ears of the now drooping champion. The men as they crossed the score were caught by willing arms, who aided them to their rooms, where, after a short repose, they emerged, seemingly none the worse for their severe race. George's time for the race was 3:10½, and Meyers, though beaten but five yards, was timed in 3:13. George's time is now the best on record in this country, but is 2 1-10s slower then his English record for this distance. The track on which this race was run was soft and mdddy.

At the Olympic Club meeting on Thanksgiving Day, the baseball game between the Redingtons and Olympics was won easily by the first named club, the Olympics, before the best audience of the season, becoming thoroughly demoralized early in the game. The club trophy is now on exhibition at 529 Market street. Bobby Robinson, of the University, won the 100-yards in 10¾, C. H. Slater second. Slater got a slow start and ran on the heaviest part of the track, but closed up rapidly on the finish, and is still confident that he can beat Bobby at that distance. The 880-yards handicap was a game struggle between V. C. Driffield (O. A. C.) 40 yards, J. T. Gorevan (G. G. A. C.) 20 yards, and J. K. Lynch (O. A. C.) 35 yards, the finish being in the order named. Time, 2:11. The 220-yards handicap was another struggle between Slater and Robinson, both starting scratch. Slater was again the last to leave the scratch, but immediately set the pace, and in a few strides gained a commanding lead of Robinson. The handicap men were nowhere, and Robinson's desperate spurt on the finish was useless, as Slater was watching him over his shoulder, and beat him out for first easily. Time, 24 1-5 seconds.

The *Examiner* says that it did not accuse McIntyre of running a job race with Davis, but in the same article acknowledges that he was named as the fraud, when it should have been Guerrero, and then immediately insinuates that McIntyre did run a job race, but that time was suppressed at the request of Davis. What's the spite?

## YACHTING.

Yachts and Registry Laws.—It is probable that, as a result of the report of the Joint Congressional Committee, which recently met in this city, a change will be made in the registry laws of the United States, and that if there be any yachtmen who desire cutter, they will be able to buy them in England much cheaper than they can build them here. We presume that by taking off the lead keel, a thirty-ton cutter might be brought on the deck of a steamer, and those of a larger size can sail over. The experience of the next season will demonstrate whether such boats are best suited to the yachting needs of this country or not, and, as we have before remarked, there are enough of them now to speak for themselves. Much ink has been spilled and some little temper has been manifested by the cutter men becanse all Americans do not see the advantages of the cutter model as they do, and in the controversy the *Spirit* has remained neutral, with the exception that we have warned our friends against the extremely narrow type of British racing yachts that have been thus narrowed, not from choice, but from necessity. In all other respects we have had no particular partiality for one type of boat or another, not deeming it any of our business to dictate to gentlemen as to what their choice shall be, and only desirous that each shall have the boat that best suits him. We rejoiced in the Oriva's performance last season, although it falsified our predictions, and shall be extremely sorry to find ourselves mistaken next year in the peformance of the Bedouin and Wenonah. Thus much for the cutter, as an introduction to the yachting season of 1882—the cutter season.—*Spirit*.

The New York Yacht Club, says the *Spirit*, has not heretofore done anything on Decoration Day, but if the project now on foot for a club-house takes shape, it, too, will probably have its Decoration Day sail, and we hope to see the time when the New York, Seawanhaka, Atlantic and Larchmont clubs will have together a scrub race on that day; no prizes, no time allowance, the boats classified by length only, and the combined fleets divided into about four classes. Here is a chance where all could meet on common ground, and with all the boats in apple-pie order, as they always are at this date, a most interesting race would result, making a course from Bay Ridge, around the Scotland light ship, and return. It would be very exciting. Next year the Atlantic club is to have additions of at least two fast schooners, and the New York club will probably have as many. The Seawanhaka has already some cutters that are to be troublesome next year, for, although the owners of both the Bedouin and Wenonah belong to the New York club, the proper home of this class of yacht is with the Seawanhaka Corinthians. The Larchmont club has some small craft that are flyers, and no doubt would be fitly represented, and an annual pageant, such as these combined fleets would make, would in a few years attract an outside attention such as the annual regatta of the New York Yacht club used to attract. We don't expect to see this just yet, but at any rate the suggestion is worth thinking about, and if it could be put in practice it would be a step in the direction of a National Yatching association, which is one of the things that must come sooner or later.

Clem Uhler, who used to own the Emerald and was one of the most enthusiastic members of the S. F. Y. C. has been on a 400-mile cruise in a little cutter-rigged yacht. He has written up his adventures in the *Forest and Stream* and seems to be one of the few who have been converted to the cutter. He confesses, however, that he would prefer the yawl if he had the choice, yet he thinks a keel boat the best.

It looks as if the next season would be a more lively one than that which has just passed. Last season was the dullest we ever had, considering the number of yachts in commission. Too many people seemed to be pulling in different directions.

The little Marcia which was built by Jack Purvis and afterwards sold to Alex. Delmar, has been sold and shipped up to Vancouvers island. She was a fast little craft.

The worst part of the year for yachting is with us now. The days are short and there is no wind. Very few of the yachts are in commission.

Few of the yachtsmen seem to go over to Saucalito compared with the number which used to frequent the place.

George Farmer has nearly completed a new plunger for Smith of Lake Merritt.

The Frolic has been up the Carquinez Straits for a few days.

The stevedores yacht is in commission and seems to work well.

Stone is working away on that little 40-ft. schooner.

Purvis will launch his little schooner in a few days.

Work is slowly progressing on the Spreckels yacht.

The Chispa is still in commission.

The Clara has not been laid up.

## ROWING.

The reorganization of the Golden Gate senior crew has for some time been talked of in the club-house. The proposition which seems to be the most favored is to put Dennis Griffin, the shell rower, in the bow, give Charles Rogers forward waist, put Supervisor J. D. Griffin in the after waist (his old oar in the barge) and John F. Walthour at stroke. The shell crew thus organized is a strong one and with careful training meantime would make the next contest for the Breeder and Sportsman cup even more interesting than that on Thanksgiving Day.

The Golden City are considering the matter of procuring a a four-oared shell either of paper or wood, but it is doubtful if they will obtain what they require unless they send East for it. The Alerts of Vallejo have a boat which the Brown crew think would suit them. Whether they will dispose of it or not at what the crew think a reasonable figure is yet unanswerable.

There are two sets of amateurs of game fowls. One looks only to beauty of plumage, etc., the other, careless of feather, scans closely those points that will tell in a fight.

The poulterer will find it necessary at every season in the case of fowls in confinement to give them a little animal food as a compenstion for worms, grubs, etc.

# FISH.

Tickling Trout.—Mr. Beecher told a pretty hard "fish story" to his people at the Plymouth prayer meeting one evening recently. He said that whenever his father went down to Guilford, Conn., to visit his wife's relatives, he used to think of nothing but finding a good place to catch trout. In a certain pool there was a particularly large trout, and for several years the old gentleman vainly tried to hook him. Finally, during one of his annual visits, he saw the old trout's fins sticking out of the water in a shady spot under the bank. The reverend angler bethought him that he had heard or read that fish could be tickled and captured with the hand. He softly slipped a hand into the water under the motionless fish and slightly tickled its belly with his finger tips. It shot a little distance off, but returned almost immediately, and Pere Beecher moved his hand lightly along his scales until approaching the gill he slipped his forefinger in and jerked the surprised trout high and dry upon the bank. Mr. Beecher told this story with such dramatic force, and so cleverly imitated the old gentleman peering into the pool and reaching his arm down into the water, that when he pulled it up a rustle of excitement was noticeable in the meeting.

A New Fish-Trap.—The *Enterprise* says that an Idaho man has invented an apparatus on which is fastened a regular network of hooks. He catches trout whether or not they are in the humor to bite. He hooks them in the mouth, gills, tails and bellies, and brags that he can catch a ton a day with his machine. It seems to be an apparatus worthy of the attention of the Fish Commissioners. It is an apparatus that would be a real blessing to many of the fishermen along the Truckee and down about Pyramid lake. They would find it much safer than giant powder. Any person who will make use of such a contrivance as the one above mentioned ought to have lived in the Middle Ages when to destroy everything inferior in strength was man's principal object. The boast of the ability of the inventor to capture a ton of this beautiful game fish shows his desire so to do and such wanton destruction is inexcusable, even in one who sells to the market.

Catfish and Eels.—The Tuscarora *Times-Review* says: The catfish which were received from Fish Commissioner Parker about two years ago, and deposited in the waters of the Owyhee, it seems, deserted that stream and have taken up their residence in Bull Run creek, between the Old Peak ranch, now Dave Griffith's, and its junction with the Owyhee. In many places the water remains in holes or eddies to the depth of ten feet. Here the catfish make their home. Another species of fish caught this season in Bull Run is the eel. There has been to our knowledge no plant of that species made in these waters, and unless they came from the Columbia into the Snake, the Snake into the Owyhee and the Owyhee into Bull Run, the Darwin system of evolution has been verified, and the Bull Run eels have come from snakes.

Decided.—The case of People vs. Samuel Taylor of Marin county for violating one of the fish laws which has been dragged through all the courts has been decided. The Supreme Court has denied the petition for a writ of certiorari. Sammy will now have to pay his fine or go to jail.

Phil Caduc was out on Thanksgiving Day and caught 125 pounds off Yellow Bluff. He went out on the Saturday following and had good luck but did not get as many as he did the day previous.

A sea turtle weighing 800 pounds was recently captured in a weir off Cape Cod, the largest ever taken in those waters.

## The Model Farmer and his Sons.

J. M. Stahl, in the *Ohio Farmer*, in an article on "Model Farmers," notes one of the peculiarities of the class as follows:

"The model farmer encourages the boys. A good many people wonder why so many boys leave the farm; the wonder is why so many stick to it. A farmer boy is treated in just the right way to make him dislike his occupation. He is given worn-out tools, and is expected to do a big day's work with them. He is expected to run all the errands, carry away the refuse vegetables from the house, turn the grindstone and slop the hogs while the men are resting at dinner. He is thanked in scoldings and paid in foul dealings. This picture is not overdrawn. Farmer boys have a long, hard row to hoe, and a dull, heavy, rusty hoe to do it with. The model farmer recognizes this fact and encourages his sons—and his daughters, too, for that matter. He gives the boys a few hogs or calves to feed, and does not pocket the money, either, when he sells them. We have known farmers frequently to do that, and it is the meanest thing they can be guilty of to give one of their children a motherless lamb or a runty pig, tell them it is their own and when they, by superior care, have made a good animal out of it, to sell it and pocket the proceeds. It is lying and cheating combined, and the model farmer does not do it. On the contrary, he lets the boys purchase with their money, and thus by safe bargains make a little money for themselves. And it is a fact worthy of note that his boys are good workers and till the parental acres when they become men. The model farmer is mighty good to the boys."

# BICYCLING.

Thanksgiving Day, fortunately for those interested in out-door sports, proved to be pleasant, and the games at the grounds of the Olympic Athletic Club in Oakland were witnessed by a good number of spectators. The bicyclers were represented in two events, a one-mile race against time, and a one-mile scratch race. In the first event H. C. Finkler undertook to beat the Pacific Coast record, 3:15½, made by H. C. Eggers one year ago on the mile track at the Bay District Park. This he failed to do, partly from lack of condition, but principally on account of the heavy track, which had not dried out since the previous rains. His time for the full mile was 3:24½. The scratch race brought out the starters W. F. Fisher, G. R. Butler and Edwin Mohrig. At pistol fire Butler made a good start and took the lead, increasing it for the first two laps to about a dozen yards. In the next lap both Fisher and Mohrig drew up to him, and at the beginning of the fourth lap Fisher went to the front with a rush. The three kept close company during this lap, Butler making renewed efforts to again pass Fisher, lapping his wheel but not succeeding in heading him. Coming down the homestretch in the last lap Butler made a final effort and drew up to within a yard or two of Fisher, who crossed the line in 3:33. Mohrig showed symptoms of tiring in the fourth lap and finally gave up about the middle of the fifth without finishing. It is only fair to say that owing to the previous unfavorable weather none of the riders had been in practice and they were consequently not in good condition.

Advice to Bicyclists.—Wynter Blyth, medical officer of health for Marylebone, London, writes in the *Sanitary Record*: "I have studied the diets recorded as in use, and find that those who have done long journeys successfully have used that class of diet which science has shown most suitable for muscular exertion, viz.: one of a highly nitrogenized character, plenty of meat, eggs, and milk, with bread, but not much butter, and no alcohol. I have cycled for over fifty miles, taking frequent draughts of beer, and in these circumstances, although there has been no alcoholic effect, it has caused great physical depression. The experience of others is the same. However much it may stimulate for a little while, a period of well marked depression follows. I attribute this in part to the salts of potash which some beers contain, in part to injurious bitters, and in part to the alcohol. My own experience as to the best drink when on the road is most decidedly in favor of tea. Tea appears to rouse both the nervous and muscular system, with, so far as I can discover, no after depressing effect."

Two tricyclists, W. Bourdon and H. Martin, both of Bromley, England, left that town September 23, on a double tricycle, and rode to Land's End, arriving October 4, covering three hundred and sixty-five miles. Returning, at Penzance Mr. Martin's business necessitated his returning home by rail, and Mr. J. Snow, also of Bromley, took his place on the Sociable, and he and Mr. Bourdon completed the return journey, arriving the 14th, the whole route covering seven hundred and nineteen miles, being the longest "sociable" ride on record.

*Vanity Fair* says: "The chairman of the Faure Accumulator Company has been experimenting at Brighton in using electricty as a motor for tricycles, and with considerable success, the only drawback being the weight of the accumulator. This inordinate weight at present seems inseparable from the storage of electricty, owing to the lead plates employed. Get rid of this lead and find a suitable substitute, and there would seem to be scarcely any limit to the employment of electricity as a propellant for trains, omnibuses, cabs, boats and tricycles."

The Boston *Courier* says: "The president of the Women's Social Science Association of California, one object of which is the physical development of women and girls, has become goatly interested in the use of tricycles as a means of promoting health and strength, and is negotiating for the purchase of one for her own use. She expects good physical results from their daily use by the members of the association.

A reverend gentleman in Massachusetts of bicycling proclivities was recently favored by his parishioners with a donation party. Among the barrels of flour, potatoes and other useful articles, he found a new bicycle saddle, which he immediately proceeded to adjust and test, losing all interest for the time in the other presents.

It is said that the postmaster of Washington has asked to be allowed to purchase a number of tricycles for the use of carriers, claiming that at least one hour will be saved thereby in the collection and distribution of mail matter, and that collections can thus be made more frequently, and delayed to nearer the hour of dispatching the mails.

Several members of the S. F. Bicycling Club have made the run to San Jose recently, returning in one instance by the road on the eastern side of the bay to Oakland. They report the roads upon the western side somewhat rough and very heavy from repairs, but the eastern road as excellent.

Bicycling can hardly be said to be on the decline yet. It is stated that one bicycle firm has done business during the past year amounting to $1,000,000.

Both the Oakland and S. F. Clubs have developed considerable artistic talent in amateur photography and members may often be seen perpetuating some of the beautiful scenery to be found upon many of their trips.

About 250 cycles are in use by the English government in the police and postal departments, although the number has been erroneously stated at a much higher figure—up among the thousands, in fact.

## The Profits of Grape Culture.

Much has been said about the profits of grape growing, and some are inclined to doubt that they are sufficient to justify the very high values that lands have attained at St. Helena. The best argument we can present to such is the following list of crop values from lands in the vicinity of Pine station the present year, as furnished us by our wide-awake and intelligent correspondent at that place: Charles Wheeler, 30 acres, 285 tons, worth $9,125, or over $300 an acre. He picked from several Zinfandel vines two vineyard boxes; or about 90 pounds each, leaving a heavy second crop on the vine. He often filled three boxes from two vines of Zinfandel varieties. The yield, taken to the cellar, was eighteen tons to the acre, and Mr. Wheeler says that at least three tons per acre was left on account of frost. R. M. Wheeler, 12 acres of two-year-old vines, 47 tons, $1,645. H. M. Pond, five acres, two-year-old vines, 15 tons, worth $480. There are ten acres in the tract; but about half of it was set last year. I. J. Newkirk, 30 acres, two-year-old vines, 105 tons, worth $3,000—all that the land cost two years ago. F. W. Loeber, 27 acres, 2,700 vines, some of them young. Over ten tons per acre, worth $868. W. A. Field picked from three-year-old vines 40 pounds to the vine, or three vineyard boxes full from three vines, the same being the vines noted some time since; also at about the rate of twelve tons per acre for old vines. N. Sawyer, from eight acres, two, three and five-year-old vines, 45 tons, worth $1,600. Martin Furstenfeld harvested 234 tons, worth $4,155, from 24 to 26 acres. J. G. Norton harvested over 100 tons, worth nearly $4,000. J. W. Williams harvested from 15 acres, 100 tons, valued at $3,100. About a quarter of these are young vines, two and three years old. Captain William Peterson harvested from 35 acres, 210 tons, worth $6,000. The captain says he might have picked 15 tons more, but thinks he got enough.—*St. Helena Star.*

## One of Jack Campbell's Yarns.

The Truckee *Republican* tells this: No man ever lived in Sierra county who enjoyed a good story or a joke better than Jack Campbell. Two years ago, while he was keeping the Hot Spring Hotel, he got off the following yarn: J. Y. Johnson, Forest City went to the springs to rusticate.

"Any hunting around here?" asked Johnson the morning after his arrival, of Jack Campbell.

"Lots of it," replied mine hosl. "Plenty of ducks, geese, quail and rabbit."

"Lend me your gun," said Johnson; "guess I'll go out and kill a mess of duck."

Campbell went into the house and brought out an old bored-out musket, not an inch less than six feet long. Johnson looked incredulously at the thing a moment and inquired:

"Will it shoot?"

"Shoot! hell, yes; las' summer I was down in the modder, an' I saw a flock o' duck about seventy yards away. I raised up that 'ere gun an' took deadly aim an' blazed away. The pesky thing snapped. I looked down the barrel an' saw the charge comin', so quicker than lightnin' I took aim again an' killed six ducks. Fact—take suthin?"

The Migration of Birds.—Familiar as the migration of birds is to us, there is, perhaps, no question in zoology more obscure. The long flights they take, and the unerring certainty with which they wing their way between the most distant places, arriving and departing at the same period, year by year, are points in the history of birds of passage as mysterious as they are interesting. We know that most migrants fly after sundown, though many of them elect a moonlight night to cross the Mediterranean. But that their meteorological instinct is not unerring is proved by the fact that thousands are every year drowned in their flights over the Atlantic and other oceans. Northern Africa and Western Asia are chosen as winter quarters by most of them, and they may be noticed on their way thither to hang over towns at night, puzzled in spite of their experience, by the shifting lights of the streets and houses. The swallow and nightingale may sometimes be delayed by unexpected circumstances. Yet it is rarely that they arrive or depart many days sooner or later one year than another. Prof. Newton considered that were sea-fowl satellites, revolving round the earth, their arrival could hardly be more surely calculated by an astronomer. Foul weather or fair, heat or cold, the puffins repair to some of their stations punctually on a given day, as if their movements were regulated by clock-work. The swiftness of flight which characterizes most birds enables them to cover a vast space in a brief time. The common black swift can fly 276 miles an hour—a speed which, if it could be maintained for less than half a day, would carry the bird from its winter to its summer quarters. The large purple swift of America is capable of even greater speed on the wing. The chimney swallow is slower, ninety miles per hour being the limit of its power; but the passenger pigeon of the United States can accomplish a journey of 1,000 miles between sunrise and sunset.

The Plum Weevil.—A. Cadwell informs us that an old friend from Illinois who recently visited him here gave the following novel but simple remedy for the curculio or plum weevil. A lady neighbor of the Illinois farmer had tried it for two years with most satisfactory results. She boiled corn cobs in sweetened water and tied them up end-wise around the body of the tree. The insect lived on the sweetened matter in the cob and deposited its eggs there; the result was a full crop of fruit. Last year she tried it again and informed her neighbors of the success of her experiment. They too tried it and also succeeded. Now if the fruit raisers of Illinois after twenty years of experiment have been able with this simple remedy of sweetened cobs to check the ravages of the curculio, may it not be possible with some just as simple remedy to protect our orchards in California against the codling moth? Mr. Cadwell thinks the State should offer a liberal reward for a remedy against this fruit pest, and if the State can't do it, he suggests that the fruit raisers make up a purse for that purpose, and as an inducement offers fifty dollars for his part.—*Petaluma Courier.*

## Market Report.

FLOUR—We quote: Best City Extra, $5 37½@$5 50; Superfine, $4 50@$4 75; Interior Extra, $4 75@$5 25; Interior Superfine $3 65@$4 ⅌ bbl.

WHEAT—Considerable business transacted during the last week in the Produce Exchange. Recent sales of No. 1 White December brought $1 73@1 73½. Same quality January, $1 73½. Spot lots, No. 1, $1 70@$1 71½.

BARLEY—Market quiet. Recent sales No. 1 feed January, $1 43@1 43½; Brewing, $1 45@$1 55 ⅌ ctl.

OATS—Fair Feed, $1 70@$1 75; Good, $1 75@$1 80; Choice, $1 85@$1 90 ⅌ ctl. Milling $1 95@$2 ⅌ ctl.

RYE—Quotable at $2 12½@$2 25 for No. 1, and $1 75@$1 90 per ctl for No. 2 grade.

FEED—Ground Barley, $1 ⅌ ton; Cracked Corn, $37 ⅌ ton. Shorts, $20 ⅌ ton. Oilcake meal the oilworks sell to the trade at $32 50 ⅌ ton, less the usual discount. Middlings, $27@$28 ⅌ ton for lots at the mill.

HAY—Alfalfa, $13@$14 50; Wheat $16 50@$17 50; Wild Oat, $15@$16; Mixed $12@$16 ⅌ ton.

PROVISIONS—Eastern Hams, 19½@21c; California Hams, 16½@16¾c for plain, 16½@17c for sugar-cured canvased; Eastern Breakfast Bacon, 16½@17c; California Smoked Bacon 15½@15¾c for heavy and medium, and 16½@16¾c for light and extra light; Clear Sides, 16@16½c; Pork, $21 50@$22 for Extra Prime, $24@25 for Prime Mess, $25@25 50 for Mess, $27 for clear and $28@28 50 for extra Clear; Pigs' Feet, $16@$18 ⅌ bbl; Mess beef, $16, for bbls and $8,50 for hf bbls; Extra Mess Beef, $17 for bbls and $8 50 for half bls; Family Beef, $18@18 90 ⅌ bbl; California Smoked Beef, 13½@14c ⅌ lb.

FRUIT—We quote: Apples, 30@50c for common and 75c@$1 ⅌ bx for good; Pears, 50c@1 25 ⅌ bx. Figs, 80c@$1 ⅌ box; Grapes, 75c@1 per box; Lemons, $6@$7 ⅌ box for Sicily and $5 50@$6 for Malaga; California Lemons, $2 50 per box; Limes, $5@$6 50 per box for Mexican; Bananas, $2@$3 50 ⅌ bunch; Mexican Oranges $22 50@$25 ⅌ thousand; California $2 25@$2 75 ⅌ box; New crop Western Cranberries are offering at $15@$17 ⅌ bbl.

VEGETABLES—We quote: Marrowfat Squash, $8@$10 ⅌ ton; Carrots, 30c; Turnips, 75c@$1; Cauliflower, 75c@$1 ⅌ dozen; Cabbage, 50@75c ⅌ ctl; Garlic, 4c ⅌ lb; Green Peas, 7@8c ⅌ lb; Green Peppers, 50c@$1 ⅌ box; Tomatoes, 75c ⅌ box; Celery, 50c ⅌ doz; Mushrooms, 10@12½c per lb; Okra, 75c@1 00; Dried Okra, 18c; Dry Peppers, 15@18c ⅌ lb.

POTATOES—River Red, 45@55c; Early Rose, 60c@90c; Garnet Chile, $1@$1 10; Humboldt, 90c@$1; Tomales and Petaluma, 87½c@$1; Peerless $1.

ONIONS—Quotable at 60@70c for good and 25@40 ⅌ sack for poor.

BEANS—Bayes $3 75@$4; Butter, $3@$3 10 for small and $3 20@$3 30 for large; Lima, $3 75@$4; Pea, $3 20@$3 30; Pink, $2 75@$3; Red, $2 75@$3; small White, $3 20@$3 30; large White, $2 75@$3 ⅌ ctl.

BUTTER—We quote jobbing lots: Fancy, 35c; choice, 30@32½; fair to good, 25@28c; inferior lots from country stores, 22@25c; firkin, 27@28c for good to choice, and 25@26c for ordinary; pickled roll, 25@27½; Eastern, 18@22c ⅌ lb.

CHEESE—Fairly steady. California, 14@15c for choice; 11@13 for fair to good; do, factory, in boxes, $15@16; Eastern, 16@17c; Western, 8@12½c per lb.

EGGS—California choice, 40@42½c; Eastern, 30@35c. Lime, 27½@30c per doz.

POULTRY—Live Turkeys, gobblers, 15@17c; do Hens, 15@17c; do dressed, 16@18c; Roosters, $5 50@$6 for old and $5@$7 for young; Hens $6@$7 50; Broilers, $5@$5 50, according to size; Ducks $6 50@$8 50 ⅌ dozen; Geese, $1 50@$2 ⅌ pair.

GAME—Prices unchanged. Quail, $1@ ⅌ dozen; Mallard Ducks, $3 50@$4; Sprigs, $2 25@2 50; Canvasback, $3 50@$4; Brandt, $1 50@$2; Gray Geese $2 50@$3 50; White Geese, $1 25@$1 50; Honkers, $5@$6; Snipe, $1 25@$1 50 for English and 50@75c for common; Teal, $1@$1 25; Widgeon, $1 25@$1 50; Hare, $1 75@$2 25; Rabbits, $1 25@$1 75.

WOOL—Trade limited to small local orders. We quote fall: San Joaquin and coast, 10@12c; San Joaquin and coast Lamb, good, 11@12c; Northern Fall, free, 15@20c; Northern Fall, defective, 11@15c; Northern fall, Lamb, 15@20c; Free Mountain, 13@16c.

HIDES AND SKINS—Dry hides, usual selection, 19½@20c ⅌ lb; culls one third less, and Mexican Hides 1c ⅌ lb less. Dry Kip, 20c; Dry Calf, 21@22c; Salted Steers, over 55 lbs, 11c ⅌ lb; Steers and Cows, medium, 10c; light do, 9c; Salted Kip, 15 to 30 lbs. 11c; Salted Calf, 14@15c ⅌ lb; Dairy Calf 70@80c each; Sheep Skins, 25@30c for Shearlings; 30@50c for short, 60@90c for medium, and $1@$1 35 apeice for long wool and wool skins. Butchertown Green Skins bring higher prices.

TALLOW—Quotable at 9c@9½c ⅌ lb for rendered and 11½@12½c for refined, both in shipping order.

MEATS—Following are rates for whole carcasses from slaughterers to dealers:

BEEF—Prime, 8½@9c; medium grade, 6½@7c; inferior, 5½@6c ⅌ lb.

VEAL—Large Calves, 7½@8½c; small ones, 9@10c ⅌ lb.

MUTTON—Wethers are quotable at 4@4½c and Ewes at 4@4½c ⅌ lb, according to quality.

LAMB—Quotable at 6½@7c ⅌ lb.

PORK—Live Hogs, 6½@6¾c for hard and 6¼c@6½c for soft; dressed do 9½@10c ⅌ lb for hard grain hogs.

A new paper from the Pacific Coast makes its appearance here, the San Francisco Basanan and Sportsman, the first number of which was issued July 1st. It is well got up and printed, and, although taking general notice of sporting matters, is devoted largely to breeding and trotting interests. The Toronto correspondent of the Basanas is Mr. James Lang, who is well qualified to attend to its interests.—Toronto Mail.

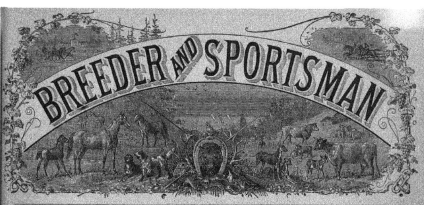

BREEDER AND SPORTSMAN

Vol. I. No. 24.
NO. 28 MONTGOMERY STREET.
SAN FRANCISCO, SATURDAY, DECEMBER 16, 1882.
SUBSCRIPTION
FIVE DOLLARS A YEAR.

## THE STABLE.

### Guards Against Concussion.

In all animals which have to progress with any degree of celerity on pedal extremities, nature has provided guards against the injurious effects of concussion. In considering the proper manner of keeping effective the natural provision in the foot of the horse, a brief comparison with other quadrupeds will not be out of place. In all are contrivances, admirable and complete, in a state of nature, for the intended uses, and valuable lessons will reward the investigator in this department of animal economy. In former papers I have alluded to the foot of the greyhound, and now the antithesis of that fleet courser will come under review. There could scarcely be two animals selected which are more dissimilar than the greyhound and elephant—the former a type of grace, agility, lightness, the other massive in its hugeness—so ponderous as to awaken a feeling of awe in a person who has not been accustomed to seeing them.

The skeleton of the greyhound differs from that of the horse, in there being a sharper angle between the shoulderblade (scapula) and the bone of the upper arm (humerus). From the elbow to the knee is far longer in proportion in the dog, and the cannon, or metacarpals, correspondingly shorter. In place of the lower pastern shuttle navicular, or bone, and the coffin bone, the dog has digits similar to those of the human hand, and these are in nearly a horizontal position. The spring of these digits, and the cushion of the sole, together with the angle of the scapula and humerus, are effective guards against the jar which follows the striking the earth after the bound. I do not intend to go into an analysis of the stride and action of the greyhound until I have studied the last series of photographs taken at Palo Alto. That it will vary from that of the horse, I feel confident, from the configuration being so different; but without that light there would be just as much liability to error as there has been in regard to the action of the horse in a fast gallop. More so, as there is fully as much speed, with quicker movements, so that the limb is still more troubled to retain the posture which is yet more transitory. For the following account of the elephant we are indebted to the Asian, a newspaper published in Calcutta, India, and as a chronicle of "sport, shikar, the turf, garden, tea, indigo, whist, chess, etc.," full of interesting matter. Published in a country where the elephant is utilized, dependence can be placed on its accuracy, particularly as the author, R. A. Sterndale, F.R.G.S., has been a resident of India long enough to give him an intimate knowledge of the subject. As it is only a small portion of the essay which we have pirated, and bearing as it does so intimately on the topic under consideration; and then, again, being so far away, the acknowledged capture may be pardoned:

The elephant has seven cervical vertebræ, the atlas much resembling the human form of the thoracic and lumbar vertebræ the number is twenty-three, of which nineteen or twenty bear ribs; the caudal vertebræ are thirty-one, of a simple character, without chevron bones.

The pelvis is peculiar in some points, such as the form of the ilium, and the arrangement of its surfaces resembling the human pelvis.

The limbs in the skeleton of the elephant are disposed in a manner differing from most other mammalia. The humerus is remarkable for the great development of the supinator ridge. "The ulna and radius are quite distinct and permanently crossed; the upper end of the latter is small, while the ulna not only contributes its principal part of the articular surface for the humerus but has its lower end actually larger than that of the radius—a condition almost unique among mammals."—(Prof. Flower.)

On looking at the skeleton of the elephant one of the first things that strike the student of comparative anatomy is the perpendicular column of the limbs; in all other animals the bones composing these supports are set at certain angles, by which a direct shock in the action of galloping and leaping is avoided. Take the skeleton of a horse and you will observe that the scapula and humerus are set almost at right angles with each other. It is so in most other animals; but in the elephant, which requires greater solidity and columnar strength, it not being given to bounding about, and having enormous bulk to be supported, the scapula, humerus, ulna and radius are almost in a perpendicular line. Owing to this rigid formation the elephant cannot spring. No greater hoax was ever perpetrated on the public than that in one of our illustrated papers which gave a picture of an elephant hurdle race. Mr. Sanderson, in his most interesting book, says: "He is physically incapable of making the smallest spring, either in vertical height or horizontal distance. Thus a trench seven feet wide is impassable to an elephant, though the step of a large one in full stride is about six and a half feet."

The hind limbs are also peculiarly formed and bear some resemblance to the arrangement of the human bones, and in these the same perpendicular disposition is to be observed; the pelvis is set nearly vertically to the vertebral column, and the femur and tibia are in almost a direct line. The fibula, or small bone of the leg, which is subject to great variation amongst animals (it being merely rudimentary in the horse, for instance), is distinct in the elephant, and is considerably enlarged at the lower end. The tarsal bones are short, and the digits have the usual number of phalanges, the unguial, or nail-bearing one, being small and rounded.

Another thing that strikes every one is the noiseless tread of this huge beast. To describe the mechanism of the foot of the elephant concisely and simply, I am going to give a few extracts from the observations of Professor W. Boyd Dawkins and Messrs. Oakley, Miall and Greenwood: "It stands on the ends of its five toes, each of which is terminated by comparatively small hoofs, and the heel bone is a little distance from the ground. Beneath comes the wonderful cushion composed of membranes, fat, nerves and blood-vessels, besides muscles, which constitutes the sole of the foot."—(W. B. D. and H. G.)—of the foot as a whole, and this remark applies to both fore and hind extremities, the separate mobility of the parts is greater than would be suspected from an external inspection, and much greater than in most ungulates. The palmar and plantar soles, though thick and tough, are not rigid boxes like hoofs, but may be made to bend, even by human fingers. The large development of muscles acting upon the capes and tarsus, and the separate existence of flexors and extensors of individual digits, is further proof that the elephant's foot is far from being a solid, unalterable mass. There are, as has been pointed out, tendinous or ligamentous attachments, which restrain the independent action of some of these muscles, but anatomical examinations would lead us to suppose that the living animal could at all events accurately direct any part of the circumference of the foot by itself on the ground. The mesocarpal and metatarsal bones form a considerable angle with the surface of the sole, while the digits, when supporting the weight of the body, are nearly horizontal.—(M. and G.) This formation would naturally give elasticity to the foot and, with the soft cushion spoken of by Professor Dawkins, would account for the noiselessness of the elephant's tread.

On one occasion, a friend and myself marched our elephant up to a sleeping tiger without disturbing the latter's slumbers.

It is a curious fact that twelve round an elephant's foot to his height it may be as much one way or the other, but still sufficiently near to make an estimate.

It is evident that there must be provided something more than is found in the foot of the dog and the horse to counteract the force of the immense weight sustained by the massive, perpendicular columns. The cushion composed of the tissues the best adapted to give softness and elasticity, is spread out to an immense size, to increase its effectiveness. "Twice round" the foot of a horse would lack several inches of reaching the elbow; and in a majority of thoroughbreds, the proportion would be nearly as one to five in measuring the height. It is also evident that the smaller foot is one of the elements of speed; and to prove this, it is only necessary to compare that of the swift horse with the pedals of the racer. The foot of the dog is much larger in comparison with the size, especially the weight, and, hence a softer cushion is admissable. To withstand the increased striction, the material must be harder, and in lieu of the indurated sole of the foot of the dog, there is the still firmer frog. But as has been partially explained heretofore, the frog is a reinforcement, aiding the parts which have stood the hardest shock of the battle. The first charge has been met with the wall, and the foreign avoided.

the wall apart, made possible by the commixure, given th frog the opportunity to play its part. It is astonishing that this should be so persistently ignored, when all but one crazy theorist, and, perhaps, a few of his disciples, admit the importance of allowing the frog to perform the part Nature intended.

A general who would shut up his reserves in a space where there could not be a chance for the least exercise, who left them there until the muscles were wasted away and the nervous force entirely lost; who went into an engagement in which he was defeated entirely from neglecting this important part of his command, offers a parallel to those who still cling to the old-time absurdities. Ignoring the functions of the frog is not the only injury which follows the common system of shoeing. The spreading of the heel is stopped, and both of the pedal guards against concussion are nullified. That the spring which is afforded by the spreading of the "quarters" is of vast importance I am well satisfied, and also that it is nearly, if not quite, as serviceable in keeping the foot sound, as anything in the mechanism of the foot, and all the contrivances to palliate the evils of a full shoe are nearly worthless.

Where the writer lived when a boy, oxen did the largest proportion of the work of the farm. It was a hilly country, heavily timbered, rocky in many places, and all the soil was nearly covered with stones. In the winter time, shoes with sharp calkins were a necessity to keep the animal from falling down on the ice-covered roads. Those which were used much in the woods in the summer needed a guard to protect the thin horn. There were two shoes on each foot—the toe portion being wide, the heel narrowed to a width of scarcely half an inch. They were fastened with very small nails, and the sharer of the ox certainly exhibited far more sense than he did when the horse was the subject. To have followed the plan pursued with the latter, he should have made one in place of two shoes for each foot, and in lieu of the narrow thin heel, put iron enough in it to raise the pad so it could never touch the ground. He could see the importance of not interfering with the cleft in the toe; the fissures in the heel of the horse were completely overlooked, and the palpable object entirely unheeded. By putting a round shoe on the cloven foot of the ox, securely nailing it to as to completely bind both portions together, there would be a proper analogy to the systems, and the ox crippled, as well as his co-laborer.—Advance Sheets Tips and Toe Weights.

### Large Shipment of Stock.

On the 28th inst., Tracy & Wilson shipped in the charge of Wm. Perrin, for Col. F. Garcia, Piedras Negras, Mexico, eighty-four head of stock as follows:

Ch c Wendover 3 y o by Bellтом, dam Experiment by Phaeton.

B c Woolley 3 y o by Bob Wooley, dam Lapwing by Lightning.

Lexington Hambletonian, b s 9 y o by Curtis Hambletonian, dam by Grey Eagle.

Charley Fole b s 4 y o by Lakeland Abdallah, dam Lou by Lexington Chief.

B f 5 y o by Waveland Chief, dam Lou by Lexington Chief.

B f 2 y o by Waveland Chief, dam Lou by Lexington Chief.

Lucy Clay 4 y o by American Clay, dam Lucy Smith by Brignolia.

Michelina b f 4 y o by Mambrino Hambletonian, dam Nicola (Dream's dam) by Neville.

Neville Walker b f 4 y o by Charley Walker, dam by Bourbon Chief.

Susie Taylor b f 3 y o by Charley Walker, dam by Bourbon Chief.

Nannie Bush br f 4 y o by Tom Bush, dam by Mambrino Pilot.

Kate br f 3 y o by Smuggler, dam by Nichols Edwin Forrest.

Eight thoroughbred bulls, one jack, four jennets, twenty-six heifers, seven cows, two calves and twenty-four mares.—Kentucky Live Stock Record.

## TURF AND TRACK.

### New York Blue Laws.

The New York *World* a short time ago, before the law came into force, published the following showing to what straits it would lead if literally enforced. Now that the police force has been diligent in prosecuting offenders there is scarcely a doubt that the obnoxious features will be repealed soon after the legislature is convened.

The bigots appear to have gone completely daft in their efforts to resuscitate the laws of a couple of centuries ago, and, if there was no balance wheel in the shape of the good sense of the people who are willing to wait for a legislative correction of the evil, would precipitate the country into revolution:

Under the Penal Code, which will become the law of the state of New York on December 1, it may become virtually impossible to legally race, either on the road or on inclosed tracks. Although racing under "special laws" is recognized in one section of the code, it will be impossible to race on any of the principal race-tracks in this state if the provisions of section 147 are enforced. The section reads as follows:

"A person concerned in any racing, running or other trial of speed between horses or other animals, within one mile of the place where a court is actually sitting, is guilty of misdemeanor."

With this section enforced it is possible to prevent any racing at Jerome Park, Sheepshead Bay, Saratoga or at any of the great trotting tracks at Buffalo, Rochester, Utica or Poughkeepsie, for even if there is not a court or court-house within a mile of any of the tracks named, police magistrates or justices of the peace can open such a court if they so choose. Even the trials of speed between private teams on the up-town avenues of this city may be brought within the provisions of the above section. Even admitting that such "trials of speed" are not meant to be covered by the above section, they certainly cannot well escape the scoop-net conditions of section 352, as follows:

"All racing or trial of speed between horses or other animals for any bet, stake or reward, except such as is allowed by special laws, is a public nuisance, and every person, on acting or aiding therein or making or being interested in any such bet, stake or reward is guilty of a misdemeanor, and, in addition to the penalty prescribed therefor, he forfeits to the people of this state all title or interest in any animal used with his privity in such race or trial of speed and in any sum of money or other property betted or staked upon the result thereof."

Under the above condition it will be impossible for the members of the Gentlemen's Driving Association to enjoy their afternoon "brushes" on the roads leading to the Driving Park, for if the stakes should amount to only the usual "bottle," or, as on special occasions, "a basket," they are liable to have their horses forfeited to the State (because they do not race "under special laws") and are liable besides to imprisonment in a penitentiary or county jail for not more than a year or to a fine of not more than $500, or both. From all of this it will be seen that, while "special laws" may allow trotting at the Driving Park, yet if there is a court actually sitting "within one mile, then all engaged are guilty of misdemeanor.

The code is as severe on betting, especially in the matter of holding stakes, and it will be virtually impossible for any one having any self respect and any respect for the laws of the State to hold the stakes for a match, be it running, trotting, or even a yacht or boat race. As to betting between individuals, the act in itself is a misdemeanor, even if it is done without recording the bet in any book or making any written evidence of the same, which is made as much a crime as the selling of pools or the making of a book, as will be seen by reading the following section:

"Section 351. A person who keeps any room, shed, tenement, tent, booth or building or any part thereof, or who occupies any place upon any public or private grounds within this State, with books, apparatus or paraphernalia, for the purpose of recording or registering bets of wagers or selling pools, and any person who records or registers bets or wagers or sells pools upon the result of any trial or contest of skill, speed or power of endurance of man or beast, or upon the result of any political nomination, appointment or election, or being the owner, lessee or occupant of any room, shed, tenement, tent, booth, building or part thereof, knowingly permits the same to be used or occupied for any of these purposes, or therein keeps, exhibits or employs any device or apparatus for the purpose of recording or registering such bets or wagers or the selling of such pools, or becomes the custodian or depositary for hire or reward of any money, property or thing of value betted or pledged upon any such result, is punishable by imprisonment for one year or by fine not exceeding $2,000, or both."

The adoption of the above laws and their enforcement produces a vast difference of opinion. The present law against "pool-selling," which was passed by the Legislature in 1877, is enforced only in the city and county of New York, while at all other racing centers it is considered "dead" and no efforts are made to enforce it. What will be done with the new code thus wide, when, but it is safe to say that outside of New York City the above proscriptive laws will not be enforced, and, as heretofore, no one will more willfully violate them than many of the legislators who voted for them, saying, as they have, heretofore, that they voted for the code knowing that the laws against betting or racing would not be enforced in their "deestricts." As to the city of New York, they say that the law ought to be enforced, and that then those who want to bet will go elsewhere, or, in other words, they will go into the outside "deestricts." But it is to be hoped that when the new Legislature meets in January, while it may not wish to repeal the above laws, it will so modify them as to exempt the regular chartered organizations from the specially obnoxious provisions.

STOCKTON, Dec. 11, 1882.
EDITOR BREEDER AND SPORTSMAN, *Dear Sir:* The Bo'd of Directors of the San Joaquin Valley Agricultural Association held their annual meeting this afternoon, and named the 20th to the 24th inclusive of September as the time for holding their next fair. They also decided to have their yearling and two-year-old State trotting stakes close Feb. 1st, '83. Due notice relative to the same will be given. Our fair for 1882 proved successful, the net earnings being 4,000.

Respectfully,    FRED ARNOLD.

MATCH RACE.—Sage Brush Sammy and Red Jacket have been matched to run a half-mile dash for $1,000 a side, race to come off at Prineville on the 5th of May next.—*Rural Spirit.*

### THE QUEEN OF THE TURF.

### She Will not do for her Millionaire Owner What She Will for His Trainer.

The queen of the turf has returned to her old quarters at Chester Park. Again she occupies the spacious apartment that is adorned with the card in the shape of a horse shoe, once divided between her and St. Julien, at Rochester, when they made the record of 2:11½, and afterwards, reunited into one lengue of honor, when they made the record of 2:10½, the same season, at Chicago. Although she has lowered the record only a fraction of the second, yet no other horse has been able to win the trophy from her. Still, the performances of Clingstone and Trinket and Black Cloud and Jerome Eddy and a host of others who have trotted in rapid succession low down into the teens, have apparently threatened to eclipse her time at no distant day. But threatening to equal or surpass her record is far from the actual performance. St. Julien has made no respectable effort in that way for the past year, and now he has gone to the life-restoring climate of the Pacific slope, to recover his enfeebled energies. Clingstone and Edwin Thorne and Black Cloud may train on next year, and approach still nearer the charmed record, but the probabilities are that they will become disabled in the effort, before they accomplish the feat. They have all been trotting-longer, have received the grand preparations more frequently, and have appeared in prime form in more campaigns than Maud S ever profited by, before she ever came out, comparatively as a novice, to show the turf community trotting speed that surpassed the sanguine predictions of the most enthusiastic prophets. It is very fortunate in the career of Maud S that she has enjoyed alternate years of retirement from the turf. After her unequaled performance of 2:17½, in her four-year-old form, she was generously wintered, her complaining limbs severely blistered, and then given to the charge of Carl Burr to handle the succeeding season. With him she did nothing. Mr. Vanderbilt urged him to trot her in the Circuit, but for prudential reasons he declined. Whether pressing engagements with other patrons, or incapability to drive the mare up to her record speed, was the actual objection, one thing is certain, that when she was returned to Mr. Bair, in the fall, she pulled and fought on the bit, as if all the high-mettled determination she had shown in colthood to battle against any attempt to curb her imperiousness by the mere application of brute force, had been again aroused. After months of gentle caressing, almost human, womanly affection to a petted child, Mr. Bair succeeded in curbing the fire of her flaming eyes and nostrils, and is persuading her to move again up to her marvelous speed, with her smooth, steady, evenly-balanced stroke that to all educated horsemen has been regarded as the type of perfect trotting action. With this victory over the unruly passions of her nature, Mr. Bair lowered her great record the fraction of a second, and in an actual race showed the fastest three heats in succession ever trotted in public or private on a mile course. Again her princely owner sent for her to minister to his pride and pleasure as a road horse in Gotham. Every horseman who knew the mare and the man was satisfied the experiment would prove a signal failure. Mr. Vanderbilt can manipulate men with imperious hauteur, but he can no more successfully apply the same dogmatic, distatorial rudeness to Maud S, and of persuade her submissive docility, than Canute could hope to cause the advancing waves of the ocean to recede at his futile command. Maud S was unconscious whether her driver possessed the millions of a railroad magnate, or the pride of the poor widow of Holy Writ. What she had shown in former years she again demonstrated to him—that reliable speed could not be forced from her by brute force, or arbitrary treatment, but was only the reward of kindness, gentleness, and skillful manipulation.

Mr. Vanderbilt has driven her, more or less, throughout the entire season, and the result is a total failure. He has harnessed her in double harness with the swiftest and most reliable pole horses in his famous stable, one after another in succession, and the result has been a signal failure. He has appeared on the course of the Gentlemen's Driving Park in New York with her frequently, and the faces of many a hard-fought battle among the bustling hosts of bulls and bears in Wall street has never been able to exhibit controlling power over Maud S, even when hooked single to his delicate road wagon. On one occasion he had her unblanketed and led from the sheds, and then he mounted into the wagon and jogged her around the course, warming her up as if preparing for a great exhibition of speed. Meantime the outspoken owners of Dick Swiveller and Edward and other noted roadsters sat on the grand stand, their watches in hand, the embodiment of great expectations. After thus jogging her a few times around the course, during which Maud S plainly showed that she was not on the best of terms with her driver, she was tamely driven out of the gate, and slowly jogged home. The bluff roadsters, in terms remarkable for strength, rather than polish, indignantly demanded why his rival should induce them to oil their watches for a great feat; if he was only rich enough to own, but not actually skilful enough to speed, the Queen of the Turf.

Still Mr. Vanderbilt is proud of the ownership of Maud S. He had her sent to Saratoga, last season, with his other noted horses, and occasionally would appear behind her and made to the pole. But these appearances were more to gratify his vanity as the owner of the peerless mare, than for any great pleasure he derived from her speed. In that regard she has always disappointed him, while her striving, unsteady action and willful unruliness. She would break and gallop, and buck and jump, in the most disgraceful manner, till the annoyance of her owner at her ugliness of temper became the gossip in turf circles at Saratoga.

It's mood of disgust he summoned her old trainer from the West. The golden wand quickly brought Mr. Bair to his side. He found the mare too high in flesh and devoid of speed. The vital fire that unapproachable queen made in 2:09, and in less than three weeks, although still too trusty and fat, she showed a full mile in 2:23, without a break. Almost at once she recognized her friend and companion, and almost instantly she yielded to the winning power of his patient kindness. But the season was well past again, and the storms of winter were brewing too visibly, in canyons of the Rocky Mountains, to sweep, like the eagle from his eyrie, over the plains to the Eastern ocean, to admit of her being reduced to trotting condition for a great performance before the sun again returns to bring us the genial spring. But she showed the same graceful, gliding action, the same rush of speed, without any evidence of overwrought muscular action, that made her the marvel of trotting performers in former years. Thus twice has Maud S been taken away from her successful trainer, and twice has she been restored to him. While with him she has made her most remarkable exhibitions of speed and steadiness and endurance. While away from him she has proved just no signal a failure in all these respects. She furnishes an instance of striking refutation of the often quoted horse saying, that it is well to exchange drivers with the best of horses, for they will drive better.

the change; or that other equally unwise saying, that a trained trotter will go as fast for one driver as for another, provided that they are equally skillful. Higher, subtler than these superficial maxims, is the profound law of affinities. Some horses, like devoted dogs, take a fancy for one master, and a dislike for all others, that can no more be eradicated than logic can destroy the freaks of human affection. There is a strange magnetism between Mr. Bair and Maud S. She instantly recognizes him, and he is brighter and more contented in her company. This is no mere vagary. It has often been observed and remarked by the *habitues* of Chester Park. Unless this strange, magnetic affection exists between man and horse, neither one exerts himself to the full extent of his powers. It is a community of identical interests, and nothing less than this affinity can account for the success of Mr. Bair with Maud S. Upon no other hypothesis could his power to reclaim the better elements of her nature, after the rebellious passions had thus been twice inflamed by unsympathetic hands, be explained. Upon any other hypothesis she would have been forever ruined. Some one queried of the cunning Dan Mace, whether he would not like to pilot Maud S for the coming season." "No," responded the master reinsman, with mingled wisdom and malevolence, "she has a greater fondness for her country driver than for any one else."

Her driver is not a countryman, unless every citizen beyond the confines of Gotham is provincial. But if countrymen have such exceptional success, it would be well for the veteran trainers of New York to move at once to the rural districts. Independently of this question, it is very questionable whether Maud S would ever become a first-class road horse. She has now become conscious of her speed. Her swiftness would be plainly handicapped by the greater draft burdens to be overcome as a roadster. The extra weight, the unevenness of the road, the want of superb condition, and the frequent starting and checking so incident to road driving, would all serve to irritate and ruin her temper. It must be remembered that in speed, intelligence, and conscious superiority, she is no ordinary organization. She requires superior treatment, in the way of condition and opportunities and manipulation. She could not receive all of these necessities as a roadster in the hands of her princely owner. To all New York roadsters the fact is obvious, that Mr. Vanderbilt is not painfully solicitous of the future welfare of his horses. Therefore his interest in horses is fostered, not so much by the love of the horse, as by the personal gratification and physical pleasure they administer to him. Such a man is never born a horseman. Such a man never feels the exquisite pleasure of that magnetic affinity that exists between himself and his favorite horse. Such a roadster never avoids all that treatment that militates against the comfort and soundness of his horse, when the discrimination would lessen to any extent his own personal gratification.

For instance; He is known to drive his horses over the hard pavements at a rate that must be injurious to their feet and limbs for fast work, but he sends them along as if the gold in his thimbleless coffers can readily buy more when these are disabled. Thus his treatment of Early Rose and Aldine, that came to him from their circuit campaign with muscles hard as iron, and in perfect condition, already begins to show that soreness that results from rough usage. Very different is the considerate handling of his great roadite rival, the owner of Dick Swiveller and Rate. He has a team, both of whom have records better than 2:26, namely Bill Thunder and John W. Hall. These he calls his "banging team" and he sends them over the pavements and drives of Central Park with much more abandon than he drives Edward and Swiveller. They are handled with extreme caution. The agony stones of the hard roads never punish them. They are walked and slowly jogged till they reach the long graded, unpaved speeding places of the road, or the more are fully prepared stretches of the racecourse, where they are given their rapid work only when they are ready and greedy for the same. Then their feet and limbs receive the most skillful nursing. As a natural consequence, they are not only in racehorse condition throughout the season, but their limbs and feet are as sound as though they were never driven faster than for healthful exercise.

This depreciation is made to point a meral. Maud S has been again returned to Mr. Bair to winter, and then in the spring to prepare for great single and double performances. She has been regarded, from this season's trials, as in a different pace horse. Mr. Bair, on the contrary, has always contended that a better one never looked through a bridle. Her mate is to be Early Rose. When he drove her and Aldine a full mile, at Hartford, to the pole, in 2:16½, he thought that Aldine at first possessed the greater speed. But, rapid as she is, before the half-mile was passed Early Rose was leading her, and actually came home at her marvelous breath of speed, carrying both the wagon and the mate in her train. Early Rose has therefore been deemed a worthy mate for Maud S to the pole. May she be preserved from severe treatment till the warm sunshine of the coming summer will enable her to startle the turf community by her performances to the pole with the Queen of the Turf.—*S. T. F.* in *National Live Stock Journal.*

Bellfounder Girl, foaled 1871, the property of Capt. Sorenson of this city, died of typhoid influenza on the 14th inst. She was by old Bellfounder; her dam by Waterloo. Bellfounder Girl was unquestionably one of the best bred brood mares ever bred in this county. Capt. Sorenson's loss is considerably mitigated by her having left him two valuable colts—one a very handsome sorrel filly by Hambletonian Mambrino, the other a weanling chestnut stud colt by Kisber. Parties who have seen this colt say that it is the most perfect and handsome colt that Kisber ever got.—*Rural Spirit.*

The Ukiah *Press says:* On Tuesday morning Mr. Jesse Thomson, of Little Lake, passed through town, on his way home from Greenville, where he went to bring home a fine Norman stallion he had purchased. As he was coming home, driving his horse and leading the stallion, he stopped at McClure's ranch, and had only been there a few minutes when the stallion dropped dead.

RACE MEETING.—Lou Remillard, of Union county, who is now here on a visit, gives notice that the fall race meeting for 1883 over his course near Union will commence Sept. 5th. In a short time he will furnish this paper with the posed programme. One of the attractions will be the Stallion Stake, $500 entrance with $500 added.—*Rural Spirit.*

CAME BACK.—Lee Knott returned on the last steamer from California, where he has been attending the fall meeting of the P. B. H. A. Mr. Knott brought back Renwick, by Joe Hooker—Big... must see fun ahead.—*Rural Sp.*

## Racing and Trotting in Oregon.

From the *North Pacific Rural Spirit* we copy the following account of the first meeting of the Eastern Oregon Fine Stock Association:

Owing to delays occasioned by the absence of one of the parties interested in the recent meeting of the Eastern Oregon Fine Stock Association, we have been delayed in receiving copy of proceedings of the late meeting until this time. We hereunto append a report that will doubtless, even at this late date, prove of interest to our readers:

FIRST DAY.

REMILLARD'S RACE COURSE. UNION, Oct. 10, 1882.—Novelty race, mile dash, for two-year-olds; $50 to $185 at half-mile, $60 at three-quarters, and $60 at end of mile.

Wm. Claypool names Maxurka, ALEX. LeBuff Chester, and F. T. Gilman Cap Wilson. Cap Wilson fell out the way to near the half-mile pole, where he was passed by Maxurka, who took all the prizes; time. 2.04. Track very heavy.

Same day—Trotting race, free for all two-year-olds; mile heats, two in three.

| | | |
|---|---|---|
| Jcon Cavinaes names Laura C. | 1 | 1 |
| Dr. Mack names (by B. Croswell) Au Revoir | 2 | 2 |
| F. T. Gilman names Henry Clay Jr. | 0 | 0 |

Time—2.28, 2.26, 2.28.

SECOND DAY.

Three-mintile trot; purse $100.

| | | |
|---|---|---|
| M. Starling names Anvil | 1 | 1 |
| D. A. McAllister names Dead Shot | 2 | 2 |
| C. A. Hogeboom names Nettie Gray | 3 | dis. |

Time—2.40, 2.22½

Same Day—Purse for three year old running-did not fill.

THIRD DAY.

Half mile heats, 2 in 3.

| | | |
|---|---|---|
| Jo Kinney names Policy | 3 | 1 |
| John Furman names Ross B. | 1 | 0 |
| John Young names Daisey A. | 0 | 0 |
| Jo Lamar names Jo Lamar | 0 | 0 |
| F. T. Gilman names Maj. Anderson | 0 | 0 |

Time—0.50½, 0.51½, 0.53½.

FOURTH DAY.

Running race, free for all horses bred in Eastern Oregon, Idaho and Washington; purse $150.

| | | |
|---|---|---|
| Jo Kinney names Policy | 1 | 1 |
| John Young names Daisey | 0 | 0 |
| John Furman names Ruby Brown | 0 | 0 |
| Alex. LeBuff names Queen | 0 | 0 |

Time—1.50½; 1.51½

Same Day—Trotting for three-year-olds and under; mile heats, 2 in 3.

| | | |
|---|---|---|
| Dr. Mack names Au Revoir (? years) | 3 | 1 |
| L. A. McAllister named Harry (3) | 1 | 2 |
| C. A. Hogeboom names Pointsetter (3) | 2 | 0 |
| F. T. Gilman names Jeff (3) | 0 | 0 |

Time—2.34, 2.33, 2.31.

Fifth Day—Two-forty-five trot, 3 in 5; purse $150. D. A. McAllister ns Lemont; Baxter, Greenback; C. A. Hogeboom, Nellie Gray.

Greenback won, Lemont second best. Time, 2.42½.

Same Day—Running, free for all; mile heats, 3 in 5. Ordnance, Policy, Bank Roll and Billy Coombs were the starters. In the pools Billy Coombs sold for $20, Ordnance realized $15, Bank Roll $3 and Policy $2. Here is the

SUMMARY.

| | | | |
|---|---|---|---|
| Ordnance | 1 | 1 | 1 |
| Policy | 4 | 2 | 3 |
| Billy Coombs | 2 | 3 | 2 |
| Bank Roll | 3 | 4 | dis |

Time—1.47, 1.16½, 1.47.

Sixth Day—Trotting race, free for all two-year-olds aged by Anvil, Dead Shot, Gen. Sprague, Bashaw Jr., Tippo Clay, Nesby, Patchen and St. Charles, that had not been trained prior to July 1; purse $100. Nominations—D. A. McAllister's Harry, by Dead Shot; John Cavines' Laura C, by Anvil; Ben Brown's Lady Poole, by Bashaw Jr.; the starters were Harry and Laura C.

| | | |
|---|---|---|
| Harry | 1 | 1 |
| Laura C. | 2 | 2 |

Time—2.34, 2.24.

Same Day—Running, free for all, dash 1½ miles. Wm. Claypool named Maxurka, 2; John Gran named Danger, aged; A. LeBuff named Billy, 4; Wm. Logan named Day Johnny, aged; Ross named Mollie, 4. Maxurka won. The purse was $50.

The races were so conducted as to give general satisfaction, again adding to the reputation of Mr. Remillard's track for fair and honorable dealing.

---

## Sale of Six Trotting Fillies.

Mr. B. J. Treacy, Ashland Park Stock Farm, Lexington, Ky., has sold to Col. F. Garcia, Piedras Negras, Mexico, the following six head of young trotting fillies:

Nannie Bush, br f, four years old, by Tom Bush (son of Mambrino Patchen), dam by Mambrino Pilot.

Lucy Clay, b f, four years old, by American Clay, dam Lucy Smith by Brignoli; second dam Lucy Garnett by Endorser, third dam Lucy Fowler by imported Albion, fourth dam by imported Leviathan, fifth dam by Pacolet, etc. Bred to Gov. Sprague.

Nicolina, b f, four years old, by Mambrino Hambletonian, dam Nicola (dam of Dream, 2.26½), by Reveille (son of Mambrino Chief); second dam thoroughbred. Bred to Banker.

Nellie Walker, b f, four years old, by Charley Walker, dam by Bourbon Chief; second dam by Gill's Vermont, third dam by Bonner's Grey Eagle. Bred to Red Wilkes.

Susie Taylor, b f, three years old, by Charley Walker, dam by Bourbon Chief; second dam by Gill's Vermont, third dam by Bonner's Grey Eagle. Bred to Young Jim.

Lydia Cook, br f, three years old, by Smuggler, dam by Nichols' Edwin Forrest; second dam by old Tom Crowder. Bred to Mambrino Patchen.—*Kentucky Live Stock Record.*

---

Archer's failure to score in either of the chief events at Shrewsbury was a sad blow to his adherents. Lowland Chief's inglorious exhibition on Tuesday is one of those things which no fellow could understand, were it not that a week or so before the close of the season it is customary to see public form put completely in the shade by a series of "unexpected developments." Although Faldirk was second to Experiment in the Shropshire Handicap, he was so far behind at the finish that his friends could hardly have felt sanguine about his success on the morrow. That he did win then we all know now, and we can only in this way account for it, as it would be like tossing for money were he and his two companions set the same task again. Likely enough odds would be laid on Walamstein, who is said to have suffered in the scratching finish. Playing at bumps with Frederick Archer suggests carrying the war into the enemy's own country, challenging the challenger, drawing the dragon's teeth, or doing any other of the deeds representative of desperate valor or no less desperate inexperience. Woodburn, who rode the winner, must be as astonished as anyone at his own temerity. Frederick the Great's indignation knew no bounds; and while b protest was only discussed by the stewards, backers of Faldirk would have taken a bit less than their former entitled to, so as to make certain.—*Pendragon in the Referee.*

---

## SPORTING NOTIONS.

### Pleasantly Related by Pendragon in the London "Referee."

Although only fourteen years have elapsed since Julius retirement from the turf, the news of his death carries us back to what, judged by events since, might well be a couple of generations. Everything seems altered since the Duke of Newcastle's colors went down before Mandrake in the Doncaster Cup of 1868. We no longer believe in the limits that used to be then set on the best obtained capacity. Our ideas of the possible and the impossible have been altered times without number since last Julius was placed in charge of the starter. This is, though, only one of many changes that have taken place during the last fourteen years. Changes in our wagering process have been as remarkable and as numerous as changes in other and perhaps far less important directions. The name of Julius takes us back at once to the time when as much money could be won and lost over a really big race as can now be won and lost in the course of an important meeting. It takes us back to the time when forthcoming event betting was the principal feature of racing, and had an existence entirely unknown to such as began their experiences within the past ten years or so. Julius was owned by one of three noblemen whose career upon the turf may be fairly said to represent a distinct epoch, and who were each of them remarkable for their ill-fortune. What was done then had much to do with the alteration in betting's business. The plunging era, though profitable beyond all previous conception to the bookmaking fraternity, sounded the knell of a period during which their makings were immeasurable.

About the time that Julius came upon the turf, training intelligence was first published in the sporting papers. Until then nothing was known about the various candidates for greater or lesser races, except that they figured in the betting lists. Many a horse has been prominent in the market for weeks—I might almost say for months—after he had broken down hopelessly. Horses have been favorites for races which were to be run within a few hours that had not been outside their stables for a long while, that were perhaps dead or turned out of training. Touts were then employed exclusively by the brokers, or by such owners and trainers as wished to know what was being done by other owners and trainers. The publication of reports from the various stables came like a thunderclap not only upon the leading spirits of such stables, but upon the bookmakers and the others who had hitherto done so well, and who had never suspected the mine's existence until it was sprung upon them. This is not all. The innovation was looked upon as an innovation, and despised accordingly by those in whose interest it had been arranged. Those who were to benefit most by it shook their heads sagaciously, and said it would never do. Owners and trainers resented it bitterly, and the great Jockey Club itself was stirred from its then chronic lethargy, and almost began to think of exterminating the newspaper which had dared to so discredit the history, not alone of the turf, but of turf journalism.

Many and violent were the articles written against such a breach of press etiquette—etiquette which until now had remained unsullied and unsuspected through all temptation; and more than one old-established sporting paper pointed with pride to the fact that it had never dreamed of interfering in such a contemptible manner with the rights and privileges of others. But there was no doubting the importance of the step nor its healthful action so far as the public was concerned. As soon as it had time to assert itself, and as soon as the public had also had time to understand what was being done for it—directly it was found that backers and bookmakers alike subscribed largely to the then one and only paper which printed stable secrets—other papers had to descend from their pedestals of purity, cease to ride the high horse of conservatism, and to do what was necessary to retain their positions. Although the touts connected with the sporting papers, like the touts connected with the bookmaking firms and training establishments, make frequent mistakes, the result as we find it now is that it is no longer possible to lay against "corpses" and "wrong 'uns" unless they are such because of owners' and trainers' intentions rather than because of their own physical infirmity.

I would be a hard thing to say that the turf is in any way purer now than it was in the days when the Marquis of Hastings, the Duke of Hamilton, and the Duke of Newcastle's names were on all men's lips, but we are certainly saved many of the scandals that were then common. Men ruin themselves now, I suppose, as much as ever they did. Still, there was a probity about the way in which the Marquis of Hastings ruined himself, and an opportunity given to sickly sentimentality by the ghastly and made by him, that has happily since been avoided. No one can think of Julius without thinking also of the time when three young noblemen came into possession, as we then reported, of immense estate, princely revenues, and large accommodations, and did their best and their worst to make ducks and drakes of their fortunes, and to show what a hideous anachronism, and how wide of all wisdom, is the great and still existent principle of primogeniture. It is customary to speak of the Marquis of Hastings as the greatest sufferer the world has known among unsuccessful gamesters. I should think this is about as wrong as wrong can be. As long as gaming has had an existence there have always been times when it has been the foremost fashionable folly, and when it has swallowed up fortune after fortune. Therefore it is unfair to give racing a discredit which should at the worst be borne by its common with Crockford's and the minor gaming hells. Many a man has sat down in a club and lost all he one sitting more than the Marquis of Hastings ever lost during three or four days of a big race meeting, and the outer world knew nothing whatever about the transaction. Even now, although such sensational wagering as that associated with Hermit, Le', Elizabeth, Julius, Lecturer, and many another is unknown, there are places at the West where the rattling of the dice-box and the shuffling of the baccarat cards are perpetual, and where ruin to golden youth comes much more easily than ever it came to Epsom or Ascot, Doncaster or Newmarket. The public do not know a great deal about the Marquis of Hastings because he was a weak and hysterical young fman who whimpered and wailed, and made a great sensation d he himself did nothing to make profit out of, which he cost away so recklessly. Had he been satisfied with turf transactions and with turf transactions only he might now have been alive and solvent. He was a sorry pigeon,at best; one who possessed neither the courage nor the capacity which has led

others of his kind to turn and rend those who first played hawk with them. But, taking him as we may, the chief way of accounting for his ruin and consequent death—death of a broken heart, so it was said at the time and currently believed—was because he had not the necessary sinews of war with which to enter upon so ruthless and undergoing a campaign as that he had mapped out for himself. The sentimentalists who sorrowed over this victim of the turf clean forgot that what he did was done of his own free will; that it was he who sent forth the fiery cross and invoked the war of extermination which ultimately ended in his ruin. As it was, he had ample opportunities of getting his own back again did, in fact, two or three times stand in as good a position as that he stood in when he started; but he would never let well alone, and therefore fell an easy prey to the vultures who constantly surrounded him.

I never myself could comprehend why sympathy was so freely and publicly shed upon the Marquis of Hastings. He was, like most other gulls of the kind, greedy and short-sighted to a degree. As a gull he stood almost without rival, although the bend-roll of the turf and the gaming-table in this particular offers us a choice such as can be found in no other direction. If the true story of Lord Hastings' life had been told, the men who were so ready to weep over him and his misfortunes could not have felt other than contempt for one who by his own act sadly marred prospects which had been arranged for him with special favor by fortune—fortune, who every day passes over unnoticed thousands of deserving suppliants. As it was those whose sorrow for him was loudest and most public were those who took him as a text from which to prove how deadly a thing is the turf in all its ramifications. Had he lost ten such fortunes as his by means of Stock Exchange speculations, had he then howled ten times as much as he did, and had he wound up with any sort of lamentable end that can be imagined, the gentry who were so anxious to point the moral and adorn the tale of his career would never have said one single word about him. The Duke of Newcastle, who owned the horse whose death arouses so many dormant recollections, must have suffered far more than the Marquis of Hastings suffered, but he never became an object of popular sympathy. His state was probably the more gracious. God help the man who becomes the recipient of public sympathy—and who requires it. He went through the Bankruptcy Court, was subjected to examination, put his property in the hands of receivers, retired into private life in a plain, straightforward, and methodical manner, and wound up his career by dying as quietly as he had lived for the past decade nearly four years ago.

Singular is it, but none the less true, that neither of these young noblemen—neither the Duke of Newcastle nor the Marquis of Hastings—lost as much, if both their losses had been counted together, as was lost by another young nobleman who is still alive, still young, and still to all outward seeming as jolly as in the days of hot youth and gambling pursuits. Enough of the man who becomes the recipient; had it got it. If it could be put on paper what was the amount of money lost by the Duke of Hamilton during the plunging period, not only lost to the bookmakers and the bone-rattlers and the card-sharpers, but lost to his own business managers as headed by the late lamented Spider, what a mouth-watering sum would have to be mentioned! But the Duke of Hamilton took his gruel with an amount of indifference which was little less than stoical. Curiously enough, although the fact is undoubted, nobody—that is, nobody among the moralists—from that day to this ever appears to suspect that of the three victims of the plunging era the one about whom the most noise was made was the smallest loser—was in reality the one least worthy of sympathy.

Quite independent of its class, Julius' career was nothing short of remarkable—it was a miracle of ill-wad-outism. Had he flourished in these days it is likely enough Sir John Astley or someone else who had backed him when he lost and laid against him when he won would have wanted the services of the jockey club to inquire into the contradictions offered by his public running. Julius did nothing worth talking about, if we except his running third in the Leger with one plate off and another twisted, until he carried off the Cesarewitch from a fairly good field, under the then extraordinary and all but unprecedented weight of 9st. But he was utterly unable to help his fluctuations. He lost races that he ought to have won, won races that he ought to have lost, and got third, close up in the Leger, despite difficulties described, after having been beaten all to pieces in the Two Thousand Guineas and Derby. Then he made his mark on the handicaps of the age by the Cesarewitch performance under 9st, a feat which should have ended his three-year-old career in a blaze of triumph. He won easily by four lengths from a field which contained many highly-tried and comparatively insanely treated performers. Although beaten by Lady Elizabeth in their memorable match directly afterwards, the performance was one that stamped Julius as first class, as at the time the filly was the wonder of the age, and was fondly regarded by the then authority as a horse of any number for centuries. Still, as a proof of what sort of a filly Lady Elizabeth was, it deserves to be put upon record now that, according to the weight for age and sex table, she was giving Julius, who on public form was as good as the best of his year, 19 pounds. Elizabeth then could beat us again closed against Julius; he was destined once more to show the glorious uncertainty of the turf by running a dead heat with Palmer for the Free Handicap at Newmarket Houghton, for which he started at about the fifth the price of his antagonist. This was the final event of his three-year-old career. By means of it, when added to his defeat by the two-year-old, all those who had insisted that his performance in the Cesarewitch was merely another proof that the best handicap form was always inferior to the best weight-for-age form found plenteous opportunity of proving their words during the dullness of winter.

If Julius' form was contradictory as a three-year-old, what is to be said about it a year later? The story is of itself so interesting and answers the question I have asked so satisfactorily that perhaps it would be as well to let it speak for itself. Julius made his first appearance as a four-year-old at Newmarket Craven, 1868, where, in the Ninth Biennial, he beat Hermit, the previous year's Derby winner. Hermit was supposed to be not altogether himself, in addition to which he was conceding 7 pounds. The race was not won without such a struggle as led Mr. Chaplin and his late adviser to believe that at even weights the decision would be reversed. Julius' people thought otherwise; indeed, they went to the length of offering one pound, and accordingly, at the Newmarket First Spring, the pair again met over the two middle miles in a match for £1,000 a side, Julius carrying 9st 10 pounds, and Hermit 8st 9 pounds, according to agreement. This time Julius, with 11 to 10 laid on him, ran up to his character, and won much more easily than he had won in the previous encounter. At the Bath and Somerset County meeting in the May following, Julius added to his already great reputation by beating Achievement in the Beaufort Cup. Achievement was, however, running under 9st 2 pounds, while Julius had to put on but 8st 10 pounds.

fore he must have been, according to the then measurement, in receipt of something like 11 pounds. It is worthy of note here, as showing what was the reputation of Colonel Pearson's flying filly, that, although he had so decisively beaten Hermit, Achievement was backed at evens, while six to four was on offer against Julius, notwithstanding the handicap. He won with so much ease that the wisdom which cometh after an event pointed out to all whom it most concerned that he would have beaten Achievement had they run on even terms—that is, allowed her weight for sex.

By this time it appeared as if Julius had all weight-for-age prizes for which he was entered at its mercy, and it is little wonder that at Ascot on the opening day, when he started for the Vase, 3 to 1 should have been laid on him. He was, however, easily beaten by Blinkbonnie, who, according to previous show, should not have had a look-in, and was not thought worth backing at 12 to 1, although there were but four runners altogether. A significant feature of this race is that had Julius won it he would have been disqualified, as, though he incurred a 4lb penalty, he failed to put it up. At Stockbridge, which is now but the shadow of its former self, even if it is that, Julius met with another reverse, and one that was still more extraordinary. The Hurstbourne Cup was looked upon as a walk over for him, only Gomera and Birdseeker forming the opposition; any price could have been obtained about the pair coupled. The official quotation in 20 to 1 on Julius, but 100 to 1 was laid on him—certainly it was offered during the running. Gomera, who, if I remember aright, was trained in Julius' stable, won by a head. Something like a panic ensued after this; the result was regarded as a fluke, and nothing else. Presently we find Julius once again a hot favorite for no less a race than the Goodwood Cup. At the slightest odds he was backed against the field, which numbered five—Speculum, Blueskin, Tabareh, Julius and Suffolk. This was how the judge placed them at the finish, so it will be seen that Julius was nearer last than first. In the Warwick Cup, getting on towards back-end, he succeeded in beating two outsiders—Tertullius and Vertigern—and again the cry of fluke of the century was raised about him. The sustaining effect of victory, no matter how many defeats may have preceded it, is shown by his starting a warm favorite on his next public appearance—in the Doncaster Cup. Again he blasted the hopes of his supporters, being somewhat easily beaten by Mandrake. This was Julius' last appearance on the racecourse, and in 1869 he was advertised as a stud horse.

Judging from the remarkable failures that have been made by some of our greatest and grandest and most consistent gallopers when placed at the stud, Julius ought to have been a tremendous success as a stock-getter. He was, however, still more disappointing as a sire than he was as a racehorse; he never begot anything worth troubling about now. When we contrast the position held by Hermit as a stallion with that occupied by Julius, it will perhaps be admitted that the sensational Derby winner of 1867 has since amply avenged himself for the two beatings he received from his extremely uncertain opponent in 1868. No new lesson is to be learnt from the further career of Julius, as times without number it has been shown that within fair and legitimate limits success of the want of it as a stallion. As Julius was in his time a sensational Cesarewitch winner, and won carrying what was then regarded as a phenomenal weight, considering the company, it may be as well to explicit the doubts and difficulties of stock-getting by means of another Cesarewitch winner of reputation. This is Robert the Devil, the offspring of about as unfashionable a union, the son of about as disastrously disappointing a sire and as unpromising a dam, as it is easy to imagine.

This looks like being a week remembered as much because of the opportunities it offered to the moralist as on any other count. The dead have full attention paid them; now we may in due course turn to the living. Wallenstein had, in the Shrewsbury Cup, such another narrow escape of winning as must have made his former proprietors smile—as must have made those who own him now think their success of some time back of American trainers a trifle premature. The one American who stood by the cast-off of his nation, depending upon the joint skill and ability of the brothers Archer, must have had an agony deserving of special mention. Those who about this time last year were driven frantic by the successes of the Yankee plunger had ample satisfaction on the field where Falstaff did battle with the men in buckram. The reference is by no means out of place if we remember the swashbuckling business which happened last back-end and in which Mr. Walton and an English baronet fought one another, in imagination, until both were killed several times over. This exhibition of modern chivalry was not given at Shrewsbury, 'tis true; but it formed a stock subject of conversation there, as did the then marvelous successes of the new plunger. How different was the story told by the side of the events this time!

Plungers are for all the world like flies; they may lead themselves with "sugar" once, mayhap twice, and get safely away; but woe betide them if they, overdone with the courage which comes of too much success, rashly give way to further temptation. In an other particular they are again like flies; they never know when they have had enough, and the result is, in ninety-nine cases out of every hundred, as inevitable as it is to them disastrous. Mr. Walton, when he went home last year, gorged for the time being to satiety with English plunder, had no intention of giving his victims a chance of getting their own again. For a while he determined to settle down in his own country, leaving, like a wise man, the chances of the turf to be encountered byothers. But time after time he read of successes in which he would have shared, of failures which he would have avoided, or which would have helped to still more enrich him. At last he could no longer bear the idea that he was allowing the potentiality of wealth beyond the dreams of avarice to slip through his fingers, and in due course he came back with the avowed intention of conquering all before him. But intention is one thing, result another. At first Mr. Walton had a moderately fair share of success—for a plunger—but presently the tide took a very decisive turn, and his losses began to be serious. Had Wallenstein won either of the races he only lost by the breadth of a man's head lately, all might yet have been well with Walton. Had he won both of them—though that, by the way, would not have been possible—the American might have chartered a ship and freighted it with English "bullion." But fate was inexorable, and fortune once again decided to show she was at the beck and call of no one. Result, disaster to Walton, who, like every backer that has preceded him had only to win long enough among the layers to let go all the money they had previously "lent" him. It is very much to be regretted that, admirable a winner as Walton has shown himself, he is anything but an admirable loser. More than once recently he has proven very disrespectfully of those who took his money; what is far worse, he has deeply, darkly, dangerously hinted that once or twice affairs had been "riddled" for him. Ha! ha! As if such an operation were possible among high-souled English racists!

## KNIGHTS OF THE RIBBONS.

### "Old Batch" and His Peculiarities—Gen. John Turner's Prominent Characteristics.

How many great trotters have been the artificial product of patient skill and industry triumphing over defective mental and physical organization; and how many phenomenal trotters have been checked in their successful career by the ugly tempers, pig-headed notions, indolence or even honest mistakes of their drivers, can never be accurately known. Suppose that nervous flighty mare, Goldsmith Maid, had stopped in her career before the memorable race at Buffalo, where she first began to show some signs of good sense, her name to-day would simply recall to the horseman such mental comment as is now bestowed upon Catch Fly, Queen of the West and a host of other speedy but unreliable trotters. Who can say but that the same possibilities existed with each one of them as with the Maid? The reformation of such a nature requires, however, the almost undivided attention, in fact, the whole heart and soul of a man whose capabilities are nearly allied to those of the great poet or the great painter; for this reason few such animals are rescued from oblivion. The dictionary has all the words; master pieces in literature are not plenty; canvas and pigment abound the world over— the world knows but few great pictures; each generation knows but one king or queen of the turf. The union of sensitive, highly-wrought, nervous organization, on the part of equine and human, requires for its delicate balance an opposition of sex, therefore the queen is greater than the king; for this reason the wildest stallions are often quiet and docile to the magic touch of a woman's hand upon the lines; and should such a woman as Middy Morgan devote her life's best efforts to the cultivation of a stallion's speed, the king would be greater than the queen. The control of great speed is a sympathetic magnetism, and the organizations that act in accord must, for the acme of great results, be mutually receptive; for this reason the extreme limit of speed thus far, belonging to the famous mares of olden time, Lady Suffolk and Flora Temple, has been reached by mares of highly-wrought, nervous temperament; or, in other words, electric batteries of tremendous power, whose efforts have been stimulated by the ardent sympathy and magnetic control of some man who has given the very best of his life to the purpose. Thus, Flora was the master-piece of "Old Blocks," of his friends fondly termed him; Goldsmith Maid the supreme effort of Budd Doble's life; Maud S of Blair's.

With this somewhat discursive prologue I will now proceed to the business on hand, which, briefly stated, is to record my personal impressions and opinions of some of the men who drive the trotters of America. I shall in no instance make any attempt at a biographical sketch, or even the turf history of a driver; but simply present my impressions of the methods, skill, characteristics and peculiarities of some of the drivers I have seen. I shall first mention them in the order of their rank or popularity, but hap-hazard, as incidents regarding them occur to me. The public judgment of a driver is often far from being in accord with the professional opinion of his capacity, while both are sometimes strongly tinged with prejudice. The whim or caprice of a wealthy gentleman sometimes, as in the past season, elevates the order of talent that nature designed for no higher employment than the manipulation of foot-book, bandages and rub rags to the management of great trotters. Such cases require the mantle of charity for the driver, as the error is that of the employer, rather than the employee.

As a beginning for my sketches, the name of one of the oldest and most eccentric drivers occurs to me, Uncle Jack Batchelor, of Georgia, a thin, weasened, withered old man, with old-fashioned steel-bowed specs, which he wears in the sulky. Dressed in the plainest attire, with a light-colored cotton blouse, that as it flutters to the wind behind the rapid strides of Mattie Graham reminds one of a night-shirt, he altogether presents exactly the opposite of one's ideal of the driver of a racehorse. But those who know him never forget that he is a driver, and that behind those old specs a keen glance often spies the way to victory. Neither do the other drivers ever forget that the slight old man is a game chicken and a thoroughbred in whose throat never rises the slightest taint of cowardice. Some years ago, in the Illinois circuit, when Mattie was first beginning to be considered, the judge at a certain place thought she might trot some faster and undertook to change drivers. Uncle Jack said: "This mare is mine and I will drive her where I please; you put a man behind her and if he drives her to the front I will shoot the ———— out of the sulky." No change was made. Last July, in the evening after Mattie had trotted a good game race at Chicago, Uncle Jack wended his way to the Sherman House to recuperate his wasted energies; the old man's plain attire and unimposing physique did not impress the lordly waiter at table with the notion that he would pay for prompt looking after. The writer was at the same table, and noticing the long delay, engaged Uncle Jack in talking about Mattie, but even this interesting topic would not serve always to allay the pangs of hunger. At last, after vain efforts to attract the attention of a waiter, he suddenly got up, as if delivering an admonition to his mare to go along when in a close pace, exploded with "I'll have some supper or I'll have something else," which brought him serviform in plenty. The first one handed him a bill of fare, which the old man dashed aside, and said: "Bring me some supper." He got a good one and the most obsequious attention. At first sight one would not think that the old man could drive a race at all, or that it would be safe for him to sit in a sulky; but he drives very well indeed, uses good judgment, knows his place and keeps it, does not squeal and is rarely ever complained of by others. From present reports he will likely manage more trotters next season, all his own, however. The flaming specs and flowing night-shirt are liable in the future, as in the past, to be the oriflamme of victory, and the indices by which tenderfoot reporters can tell where Mattie Graham is in the race. Uncle Jack will pardon me for great familiarity with his idiosyncrasies; it is the date of fame to be dealt with by garrulous scribblers.

John E. Turner, alias "the general," is a small, compactly-built, neatly-dressed, middle-aged man, who would pass anywhere for a staid and sedate broker or bank officer; he is reputed to be the wealthiest driver in the country; and these two facts have some relative significance. His applies to the racetrack his natural aptitude for business. In the sulky, with his brilliant colors, he looks aged; a more subdued shade than bright green would be appropriate to his venerable and dignified demeanor, but possibly not more in accord with his resolute and unsubdued spirit. Turner is a thoughtful and astute man, his methods in the sulky are rigid and mechanical, but usually well timed and effective; he sets bolt upright and carries his whip like the baton of a field marshal. Turner's name is intimately associated with the career of many of our great trotters, but the two T's will be longest remembered, Thorne and Turner. Turner and Thorne. Hannis, Trinket and the rest, game and speedy

trotters though they be, fade into the background beside the nonpareil of racehorses, Thorne. The acme of Turner's success has been reached with this trotter, or will be when Thorne drops his record. Fortune can not have in store for man many such prizes. Thorne could not down the record, but he could, by determined effort, down the " gang " in 1882. I doubt whether Turner's taste or capacity runs in the way of successfully manipulating horses with which he is not familiar; doubtless he can master the mysteries of such trotters as he undertakes to study, but his talent is not the superficial one of miscellaneous adaptability. Therein partially lies the secret of his momentary success. A good one in his hands, well stuck to becomes more than good. Neither has he, on the other hand, the organization that would be in perfect sympathy with mares possessing the highest form of nervous temperament, and his success has not been linked with the names of such animals.—*M. T. Grattan in Breeder's Gazette.*

### Australian Racers.

Some idea of the growth of the Australian racing interests may be obtained from the following synopsis of the list of winning sires for the season of 1881-82. The champion stallion is Panic, by Alarm, from Queen of Beauty, who has been dead some years, but still his name appears first. This season he has thirty winners, who won sixty-four races, valued at £8,417. Maribyrnong ranks second, with half as many winners, who only won twenty-six races of the value £5,820. Then comes the great New South Wales defunct sire Yattendon, with twenty winners and thirty-eight and a half races won, worth £5,447. There were no less than twenty-two other stallions, the progeny of which won upward of £1,000, namely: Kelpie (dead), £4,608; Robinson Crusoe, £3,830 (first year); Barbarian, £3,762; the Peer (dead), £3,547; Epigram, £2,798; Hawthornden, £2,728; Grand Forward, £2,481; Bethnal Green (dead), £2,228; The Drummer, £1,850; Fireworks (dead), £1,789; Tubal Cain, £1,700; King of the Ring, £1,670; Slanderer, £1,625; Tim Whiffler, £1,586; Lord of Linne (dead), one winner, two races, of the value of £1,537; Conrad, £1,444; Countryman (dead), £1,382; Gemma di Vergy (by Gemma di Vergy), £1,272; Bluegown (dead), £1,254; John Bull, £1,217; Argus Scandal, £1,211, and Snowden (dead), £1,011. Altogether there were 363 winning horses, who won 782 races, of the value of £70,000. Such an enormous sum as this speaks volumes for the success of racing in Australia. Of the 145 gentlemen who have won prizes from £4,087 down to £100 to less than seventy-one hail from Victoria, fifty-two from New South Wales and twenty from South Australia. Among the twenty principal winners Mr. De Mestre is top of the tree with £4,687, Mr. Dakin coming next with £3,100; New South Wales (nine owners), £19,110; Victoria (ten owners) £16,964; South Australia (Sir Thomas Elder), £2,406. Mr. Edward Lee, of New South Wales, who was so successful in 1878, when he carried off the rich Maribyrnong Plate, Sydney Derby and the A. J. C. Sires' Produce Stakes, has to be satisfied with a single win, and that only to the value of £100.

Will St. Julian trot again? is an interesting question to many horsemen. Some good judges claim that he has lost his speed and others, claiming to be equally long-headed, assert that his retirement the past season is a part of a deep-laid scheme. They assert that Hickok, finding there was no profitable engagements for the horse, adopted the course as that of persistently claiming him to be "off," so as to secure a series of races for the season of 1883.

The glanders is quite prevalent in some portions of Colusa county. Several horses have died of it, and others have been killed by their owners to prevent the spread of the disease. In some instances it was mistaken for horse distemper and was treated as such until the disease showed its true character, and that it was at a stage so advanced as to be incurable. Glanders is always fatal.—*Plumas National.*

RACES.—Nov. 30th, at Prineville, Widow Dun, Billy Manson and Jim Blakely were started in the half-mile repeat race, two in three. The mare won in two straight heats, Billy second, Jim being distanced in first heat; time, 0:56, 0:53¾.— *Rural Spirit.*

## CORRESPONDENCE.

### New York Letter.

NEW YORK, Dec. 16, 1882.

EDITOR BREEDER AND SPORTSMAN: Since I last wrote nothing of transcendent importance has occurred in this vicinity as regards out-door sports, and if the athletic games at the grounds on Thanksgiving Day be excepted, I have to chronicle a perfect dearth of sporting news, as befits indeed our arctic season of ice and snow, now fairly inaugurated. For over a week past, since Nov. 30, the metropolis has indulged in the unusual luxury, so early in the winter, of fine sleighing and our Central Park as well as all the roads in the upper districts of Manhattan have rung at all hours of the day and night with laughing voices and the merry ringing of the bells. And at this first installment of " earth's white coverlet" come in dry and not wet we are likely to have a plethora of it before spring, if the old-time weather prophets are to be believed.

Week before last death marked for his own the oldest jockey in the country, the widely known Gilpatrick or " Gill" as he was familiarly called. Born sixty-five years ago on the banks of the upper Hudson, this famous knight of the pigskin, has ridden and won a great many races, but not a tithe of the ridiculous number credited to him in some statements of our New York dailies, some of which are in the habit of publishing sporting items that would put to the blush an Eli Perkins or Tom Ochiltree, who both enjoy the enviable distinction of champions of the "long bow." Gilpatrick was never very well provided with this world's goods, or if he was, he quickly got rid of them, and since he rode his last races for Eugene at Brighton Beach three years ago, has lived in comparative poverty from hand to mouth, as it were. Still the old veteran was never allowed to actually want, nor ever around as spry and active as most men over three score generally are until the election day's racing at Fordham on Nov. 7th last, when exposure led to a bad cold, and resulting in that grim enemy of the medical profession, pneumonia, finished his earthly career. His old employer, Wm

Eugeman, with his characteristic benevolence and liberality, at once forwarded a liberal sum to the widow, and she will no doubt be provided for in the future.

The result of the International foot-race on last Thursday is doubtless an old story to your readers. the wires having told you the leading features of this notable contest, which was, considering the attendant circumstances, a very great performance on the part of both men, the American in spite of all interested stories of sickness, loss of form, etc., running fully up to the expectations of his party, as he best, on this occasion, his previous record at three-quarters of a mile by five seconds. But the faster Myers ran George seemed able at the critical moment to let out still another link, and his tall sable-costumed form made the pace from the crack of the pistol as he did in both the other races. In vain did the representative of Manhattan strive to head the black phantom in front of him; it was Albion's day on this occasion, and the American, if he ever gets in another race with his late adversary, will have learned sufficient to tell him to keep within his distance, five-eighths of a mile being as far as he cares to go, evidently. George has gone on a visit to the Falls of Niagara, but will return in time to run in a handicap race, Dec. 13, at Madison Square Garden, in this city, after which he will return to England. Notwithstanding all stories to the contrary, he is well liked here, since it has leaked out how much more he was sinned against than sinning in the late unpleasant controversy between the two men and their partisans, prior to the late race. Myers' running on last Thanksgiving Day clearly showed that there was "a nigger in the fence somewhere," for such exceedingly quick recuperation after being as badly off as was claimed for him is very seldom heard of, although it might have been possible. George at the time was universally censured for claiming that Myers was not as sick as he and his party declared, but the sequel rather bears him (George) out. Speculation was very heavy on the race, opening at $100 to $80 on Myers (rather peculiar odds on a convalescent (?) athlete), and closing at $100 to $80 on George, the public supporting the Englishman to a man, leaving the "knowing(?) ones" to back the American champion, and as happens very frequently on the turf, the posted division got "left," sadder but wiser men.

A new market for puss thoroughbred races has developed in this city of late, in the demand created for saddle-stock, particularly in our metropolitan riding-schools or, as the Avenue does fondly term them, equestrian academies. Little do most of the fair patrons of these establishments imagine that the quiet hack that carries them in no staid a fashion has perchance won turf honors at Jerome, Monmouth, Sheepshead, or, "perish the exciting thought," been one of the mighty brigade of "beach-comers " by the sad sea wave of Brighton. If the fair burdens of these aristocratic steeds are wise and will heed a warning they will do well to keep each fiery Bucephalus for from the madding crowd in the vicinity of any of these race-courses of ours, or the result might cause disaster should the warhorse "scent the battle from afar," or sighting the starter's falling flag, as he send, off on their journey some old comrades of many a hard-fought fray, take a notion of having a hand too, whether his fair rider will it or not.

Mr. Wm. Engeman to-day telegraphed from New Orleans that his arrangements for a five year lease of the grounds of the Louisiana Jockey Club were all completed. A new association has been formed with R. W. Simmons of the L. J. C. as president and Mr. Engeman as general manager, etc. The lease is for six years (of winters) the first season (Dec. 1882-May 1883) free, second a rental of $1,000, third $2,000, fourth $3,000, fifth $4,000 and sixth $5,000. Racing is to begin in about two weeks (Dec. 23rd) and it is calculated to give three days' racing each week until about May, it is said, but April is probably meant. The success of the venture is certainly problematical with the chances in its favor, but the projector is energy personified, and if any man can make the enterprise profitable, he will.

Our news from Albion's rock-bound isle is, of course, very meager as regards anything of great interest. The plunger (Walton) has returned from thitherward, and denies that he lost $125,000, on his recent visit, all the English sporting weeklies to the contrary notwithstanding. James Roe, the trainer of Blackburn, Hindoo Geo. Kenny, Bunnyreade, etc., has gone over some two weeks since to learn what he can about training methods in the old country.

Pincus and Tom Puryear, the trainer and manager respectively of the Lorillard English contingent, came back a few days since and reports that Iroquois has not broken down, and may run again, that the last Rancocas shipment abroad, comprising the celebrated Pinafore, Parthenia and others, arrived out in fair order, and that the Crawford two-year-old Blackheath is a very great colt much sounder than most persons think. They expect him to stand training next year. Both look hale and hearty and express themselves as glad to get home once more.

Ex-Governor Stanford has made another important purchase here for his Palo Alto stud farm.' He has bought of the Bonners the gray mare, Midnight, the dam of the great trotters, Noontide, 2:20¼, and Jay Eye See, 2:19. The latter was truly,a phenomenon last season. Cyrus Holloway the jockey is with you I see. Mr. Baldwin engaged him at Baltimore in October, and there are few more capable and honest performers in the saddle. Cyrus rode old Glenmore when he beat Lexa Blackburn for the Long Island Cup in 1881, and his thorough knowledge of his art was very conspicuous on that memorable occasion. He has earned success and certainly deserves well of his new employer.     PACIFIC.

Smiths & Powell of Syracuse, N. Y., write that they have just completed some butter tests of their Holstein cows. Eight and Netherland Queen, five years old. "They were not fed with the idea of making records, but records were made upon their regular feed, without change in quantity or quality. Eight made in seven consecutive days eighteen pounds two ounces of butter, and Netherland Queen in seven consecutive days made twenty pounds of butter. The butter was weighed after working and before salting. Netherland Queen is one of the famous Netherland family, which is second only to the Aaggie family as milk producers.—Cultivator.

A Kansas City dispatch dated Dec. 13 says: An association of unusual strength and significance, to be known as the "American Land and Cattle Syndicate," was organized here to-day. It consists of thirty members, including some of the most influential business men of this city, bankers, land and cattle owners, both United States Senators and the Governor of the State. The syndicate is preparing to control large interests in the Territories and in the Southwest, with branch offices in Texas, New York and London. A meeting is to be held later to complete the organization, when further details will be made public.

During the last ten years cattle in New South Wales have increased very little, but sheep have gone from 16,000,000 to 33,000,000.

## HERD AND SWINE.

### The Cattle Market.

Several of the daily papers have commented upon the high price of beef—and some of the views expressed would lead a person to believe that California and Nevada had been entirely drained of cattle. Had the subject been given due attention the writers would have discovered that without going to Montana we are fully able to supply the demand. While it is true that at the present there exists a scarcity of marketable beeves, there is no immediate cause of alarm for the future output of our stock ranges.

For the present and until next fall beef undoubtedly will command a price considerably above that which has ruled for several years past. This has been brought about partially by the hard winter a year ago killing many of the calves on the ranges, and principally by the stockmen during a depression of the market on this coast letting go of many of their herds to large home and Eastern buyers—men who are always ready and have the means necessary to take the advantage of all bargains during dull periods.

To still better show that parties posted are not afraid of any great scarcity after the coming year, we have only to look at the price which Messrs. Miller, Lux and other large holders and stock raisers are selling their calves for. The price of veal is no better in our market to-day than at any time during the last two or three years, while at the same time these men are buying all the cattle offered for sale at anything below the ruling price.

Viewing the movements of men who are experienced in this business, and thoroughly acquainted with the breeding ranges of this coast, we will be governed in our views by their actions, which go to show that although for the season coming beef may command a considerable advance over previous ones, yet in the future, while we may never see beef selling as low as formerly, we will be blessed with all that our requirements may need at rates that will pay the breeder and butcher yet still not harass the consumer.

While the present position of the market may be a hard one on a great many in this city, it is none the less so on our country neighbors for they have to pay higher prices for what they use than we, while many of them have their "radiced covered with their own dressing." From this fact we expect to see the experiences taken advantage of in the future, and then we will find ourselves supplied with an abundance and that of a quality far superior to what we now are compelled to use. The largest stock man on the plains to-day cannot go out and find all his beef cattle in one branch but with his herders he first finds some in the valley, and more in the sands; thus he works until he gathers his thousand or so of beef.

So it would be in our grain counties did the farmers give it the attention which the present wants of our population demand—not only with the benefit which they would confer on their city neighbors but with considerable profit to themselves.

There is scarcely a farmer on this coast who does not let go to waste or destroy enough provender to fatten several head of cattle and sheep when they, after curing or removing enough to supply their own household during the winter, would by selling the remainder be well recompensed for the time and labor devoted to their fastening. When the time comes that they fully appreciate the fact we will then see our drovers gathering their hundreds and even thousands of beeves in the most likely settled grain counties, and as ten head of cattle fastened on the farm are fully equal to fifteen of the average grass cattle, we will find that our markets will be bountifully supplied by a quantity and quality far better, and entirely independent of the millionaire stock raiser.

### Diseases of the Hog.

Colman's Rural World says:

So far as we have been able to learn, either by reading or by practical experience, there is as little known of the various diseases of swine and the methods called for to successfully treat them as of any other one thing. In the treatment of disease, whether in the biped or the quadruped, we seldom, if ever, stop to ascertain the cause, and even more seldom ask the question: "What is disease!"

We find an animal sick and immediately jump at a conclusion; the disease is this or that, and calls for such and such remedies. These are at hand,· or obtained, and applied at times with indifferent success; but successfully or not, the magazine is blind one, and the treatment as "the blind leading the blind."

The disease called hog cholera is found all over the country, and like the papers the newspapers; but the indications of the disease are as varied as the causes are abundant, and yet we have remedies, advertised by otherwise reputable newspapers, proclaimed as a specific and sure cure. To believe any such stuff and nonsense is to make ourselves the tool and toy of the quack, and to blind ourselves to the first problem to be solved, viz: what is the cause of the disease? Having found this, the remedy will suggest itself.

The following from the Henry County (Mo.) Democrat is suggestive in this connection:

Although there is no hog cholera reported in the county yet farmers should keep the fact prominently before them that its appearance at any time is not impossible. Hogs are scarce, and high in price. Hogs sleeping in a pile of old and rotting heated straw, is one cause of hog cholera. Such bedding is warm and comfortable, but the poison generated by their heat is a fruitful cause of disease and death. We have no doubt but that impure, bad water has often had the same effect. Keeping hogs night and day by filthy pens is the worst kind of treatment for such stock, though we have seen hogs treated in this way where the owners seemed to think that it was a natural enough way to treat this kind of stock. It is pretty certain that in a general way hogs need a good deal better treatment than they get at the hands of those that have the care of them. In the winter season, hogs, like most other kinds of live stock, are often seriously injured by being improperly watered. Cutting a hole in the ice to obtain water is a bad way to water any kind of stock. It is especially so with hogs, as where they are made to drink a full supply of ice cold water, they are invariably injured by it to a greater or less extent. Hogs should at all times have pure well or spring water at a temperature of about 60 degrees.

Of the desirous qualities in a pig vigorous appetite is of the first importance, the next in importance is quietness in disposition.

### Silos and Ensilage.

W. M. Vilas, Burlington, Vi., has a silo which is a lean-to to the barn. Cow stables for sixty head are about on the level of the bottom of the silo. The dimensions of the silo are twenty-five feet by forty feet with a depth of twenty-five feet. The wall on the bank end of the silo is twenty-two feet high and three feet thick. It is partially walled on two sides to protect it from the earth. Matched ⅝ inch spruce boards were used in other parts of the walls of the silo. The walls were painted and plastered with cement. The cover of the silo is of rough two-inch plank. The ensilage is weighted with stone to the thickness of twelve to eighteen inches. Corn was planted in drills 3½ to four feet apart, about twenty-five quarts to the acre. Smoothing harrow was used until the corn was ten to twelve inches high, after which cultivator was used. The produce of fodder was from ten to fifteen tons to the acre, or an average of twelve tons. The fodder was cut ¼ and ⅜ inch long with two-horse power. Very little was cut as short as ⅛ inch as it made very slow work. In filling the silo it is important to have the fodder spread evenly and well packed as it is put in. If from six inches to one foot in depth is stored each day no damage will occur. The silo was opened about two months after filling; the ensilage was found in excellent condition, having a sweet smell similar to that of hominy. Mr. Vilas states that where the ensilage has been cut down and allowed to stand exposed to the air for three or four weeks it will mould two or three inches into the fodder, yet the cows will eat it clean.

"Ensilage is better than anything else to winter cows on," says Mr. Vilas, "and perhaps the same is the case for summer feeding, but the latter remains to be tested. I fed ensilage from the middle of November until about the tenth of April. In a day or two after the latest date, my cows complained that the cows were not giving enough milk for my regular customers, and even by doubling and tripling the quantity of grain, we were not able to keep up the previous flow of milk. All my other stock, as well as my cows, were eager to eat ensilage. The quantity consumed per head was from fifty to eighty pounds, my method of feeding was to give ensilage once a day, with from four to six quarts of bran and hay twice a day. When, another season, I have enough ensilage, I shall feed it twice a day, and hay but once. As to the condition of my stock it never looked as well as when feeding on ensilage. With no other grain than bran, seventy-five per cent. of my ensilage-fed cows could have been sold for beef and yet most of them were milked all winter. Whatever is grown for ensilage should be quite near the silo, since the former is too heavy to haul a long distance. Storing and feeding ensilage will pay better on a large scale than in a small way. The silo I used last year held only about 160 tons. This year I have enlarged its capacity to about 500 tons."

James S. Chaffee, Wassaic, N. Y., has a silo by the side of and parallel with his barn, and so arranged that the ensilage comes from the silo to the floor, directly over the animals to be fed. The silo is fourteen feet long, nineteen feet wide and six feet deep. It has its sides and one end lined with boards, and the other end placed on the upper side. The dimensions of the silo are 19 feet by 50½ feet with a depth of 16 feet. The walls of the silo are concrete, of hydraulic cement, gravel and cobble-stones; the cover was made of 1½-inch spruce boards, placed crosswise, and fitting loosely to the sides of the silo. The ensilage was weighted with stone, seventy-five pounds to the square foot. Including the roof the cost of the silo was $350. Corn was the only crop used for ensilage, sown in drills three feet apart, and cut when fully tasselled and before any of the juices dried up or were appropriated for the formation of the ear. Mr. Chaffee produced from sixteen to thirty tons of green corn per acre, twenty tons being his average yield. Blount's Prolific proved the best for ensilage, and White Southern next best. The fodder was cut in one-half-inch lengths by a cutter driven by a five-horse steam engine. In filling the silo, the ensilage should be distributed evenly in the silo and packed as thoroughly as possible, putting in from twenty-five to thirty tons per day. After the silo is full a few inches of straw should be added before placing the covering planks. Eighty cents was the cost of filling per ton of fodder put in.

In this case two months elapsed before opening the silo. Mr. Chaffee writes: The ensilage loses its green color, but retains form and consistency, with no appreciable loss of moisture; has a slightly acid taste and alcoholic smell, with sometimes a very small loss at top from mould and decay. There was no deterioration in the quality of the ensilage after opening the silo. In feeding milch cows ensilage effects a saving of grain and forage, while cows thrive better under its use than without it. The milk is richer and pleasanter to the taste—more like produce from pasture than from hay and grain. I fed fifty pounds ensilage per day to each cow, some times alone in the feeding, but usually in connection with hay and grain. While feeding ensilage I noticed a decided gain in flesh, appetite better, hair sleek and glossy, and eyes bright. The excellent condition of my stock has attracted the attention and admiration of numberless visitors on the subject of ensilage. The profitableness of ensilage lies mainly in the fact that it can be made to double the stock-carrying capacity of our Eastern farms, and that too at a very small comparative cost. The advantages to the sale-milk dairymen are incalculable, and I see no reason why they should be less to butter and cheese producers. Dairy farmers who have used silos two years have already added fifty per cent. to their former stock.

GOOD POINTS IN SHORTHORNS.—A correspondent asks us to name points of excellence of Shorthorns. Mr. Allen, in his book on cattle, a standard authority, says: Muzzle fine and yellowish or drab in color, face, slightly dishing or concave; eye full and bright, forehead broad, horns, no black except on tips, and standing wide at base, short oval shaped and spreading gracefully out, and then curving in with a downward inclination, or turning upward with a stiffer spread, of a waxy color and somewhat darker at tips; the throat clean, without dewlap; the ear sizeable, thin and quickly moving; the neck full, setting well into the shoulders and breast, with a slight pendulous hanging of the skin (not a dewlap), just at the brisket; the shoulders nearly straight, and wide at the tops, the shoulder-points or neck-vein wide and full; the brisket broad, low, and projecting well forward, sometimes so much as almost to appear a deformity; the arm gracefully tapering to the knees and below that a leg of fine bone, ending with a rounded foot; the ribs round and full (giving free play to vigorous lungs), and running back well from the shoulders to the hips; the hip uncommonly wide, and level with the back and loins loin full and level; rump wide; the tail set on a level with the back and gaily and tapering; the thigh full and heavily fleshed; flank low and full; the hock standing straight, (as in the horse) or nearly so; the hind leg, like the fore one, clean and sinewy, and the foot small.

Texas sheep raisers are agitating the project of sh——ing mutton North and East by means of refrigerator car——

## How Milk is Made.

That the animal organism is capable, under certain conditions, of converting various food elements into milk is one of the most familiar facts of nature. How the milk-producing glands perform their work remains to a great extent a puzzle. The later investigations and theories in this connection are clearly set forth by Dr. G. C. Caldwell in a recent issue of the New York Weekly Tribune, in answer to the question: "How is milk made?" He says:

The essential milk-producing part of the udder is made up of a series of ducts or tubes branching out from reservoirs at the head of the teats, joining one another at little sub-reservoirs, and separating and uniting again, till finally they end within minute organs called vesicles or follicles. Both Dr. Sturtevant, of the New York Experiment Station and Mr. Arnold have traced these ducts to their sources. These follicles are the fountain heads whence the milk is collected by the ducts and carried through one reservoir after another to the teat.

The three essential ingredients of the milk, beside the water, are the fat, in the form of minute globules suspended in the liquid; the caseine, partly in solution in the water of the milk, and partly in solid grains suspended in the liquid; and the sugar, only in solution. Nearly all authorities agree that the formation of the milk is attended with a rapid production of new cells, very rich in fat, in the follicles; and the most generally adopted view is that these cells drop off and fall to pieces by what is called fatty degeneration, and that their investing membranes or cell-walls become dissolved; thus, especially, the fat of the milk is produced; and some think that all the constituents of the milk are really nothing but cell ruins, taken up by the water that must come directly from the blood, even if nothing else does, and conveyed away through the ducts and reservoirs to the teats.

But Dr. Sturtevant maintains that the fat globules of the milk are really the cells themselves that are so rapidly multiplied in the follicles—that each globule began as a bud on a parent cell in the follicle, grew and then dropped off, and was taken up and washed along by the water containing the caseine and the milk sugar in solution, which has been transuded from the tissues. With him Mr. Arnold agrees. This theory requires that each milk globule shall consist of a membrane enclosing fat; but the existence of such a membrane or envelope around the fat globule is almost universally disbelieved by microscopists, for nearly all who have given the subject their careful attention failed to find satisfactory evidence thereof. It will be, therefore, a battle of a few against a multitude to establish the fact of such a structure of the milk-fat globule; but in a battle fought with such weapons the victory is not always with the party that is strongest in numbers.

Fleischmann, than whom there is no better authority on matters pertaining to milk, is not entirely satisfied with the theory that the milk is made up of cell ruins alone. He shows that if this were so, in the case of a good milch cow, the dry weight of cell substance broken down every day would be not less than 3.5 pounds, or more than twice the weight of the dry substance of the milk glands of a well-developed udder. While allowing that there is much strength in the position of those who argue for milk production by cell destruction, he claims that there must be some secretion or straining through, as it were, of a part of the substance of the milk, directly from the blood which circulates freely and abundantly through the glands.

But even with this partial acceptance of both explanations, we are not yet altogether enlightened as to the manner in which the milk is produced. Unquestionably, however, an important and a peculiar work is done in these glands; there is produced that mixture of the three essential ingredients of food—the albuminoids, the fat and the carbohydrates, which makes milk the type of a perfect food, and there originate those substances peculiar to butter fat, the butyrine and its associate, which are not found anywhere else in the animal body. They distinguish this fat in a marked manner from any other fat, whether animal or vegetable, and enable the chemist to tell with unerring directness whether a sample called butter is butter or something else.

## Food For Milk.

In every question pertaining to milk the cow should be recognized as all important. Since science has settled the question that milk is simply liquefied cells, and not a secretion from the blood, the capacity and excellence of the machine have become prominent. It has also simplified the question of profitable food for the cow during the milking period.

The supply of milk depends essentially upon the rapid growth of new cells in the milk glands. These cells consist largely of proteine. The caseine and fats (cheese and butter elements) are formed from the proteine; hence profitable dairying must depend largely on the amount of proteine contained in the food and made on cheap food; where rations rich in proteine, are fed, such as clover and oil meal, the following results may be noticed:

1. A decided increase in the quantity of milk and very little shrinkage for a long time.

2. Considerable gain in the solid matter of the milk, as shown by chemical test, or by the increased butter and cheese production.

3. A gain in the proportion of the milk where fodders rich in carbohydrates and fats are given; the slight increase in quantity and richness of the milk is not due to any direct action these have, but to the assistance they afford the proteine in preventing its oxydation. Animals fed mainly on sugar beets, potatoes or corn will give considerable milk, but it is done at the expense of the proteine of the body, and after a while the animal will suddenly waste away.

In view of these well-established facts, what shall be the economical milk ration for farmers? Calculated upon the basis of the amount of proteine contained in each, and taking corn as the unit of value, when corn is worth fifty cents per hundred pounds, the following articles will approximately be worth per hundred: Corn, 50 cents; oats, 60 cents; barley, 55 cents; wheat, 65 cents; wheat bran, 70 cents; oil meal, $1.45; clover hay, 80 cents; timothy, 50 cents; potatoes, 12 cents.

This is not absolutely correct, because the carbohydrates and fat in some of these would materially aid the proteine and hence would be worth relatively more than above represented.

It is, however, sufficiently correct to show that the cheap foods for milk in Iowa are well-cured clover hay, wheat-bran with a little corn meal and oatmeal added.—Prof. S. A. Knapp, in Iowa Homestead.

J. S. Coffin of Fort Dodge, Iowa, a well-known sheep-breeder of experience, asserts that the sheep sold at the late Fat Stock Show by M. H. Cochrane of Canada were affected with foot-rot. Mr. Cochrane has not yet heard from on the subject.

## CONCERNING CREAMERIES.

### One of the Most Successful American Dairymen Gives some Valuable Information.

To those who are contemplating the building of a creamery and desire to know the cost and methods of construction, as well as the system of management, the following article by Prof. L. B. Arnold in the Rural Home contains many points of interest:

The first consideration in starting a creamery is a good, cool spring of water. A well will answer, but it is not so convenient, and it costs something to pump the water; besides it only runs when power is applied, while the spring is continuous night and day. Refrigeration is at the base of all creamery operations. Milk must be cooled, but the amount of refrigeration need not be as great as is often employed, though the lower the cooling the sooner the cream rises; it does not require an ice-cold temperature to separate cream successfully. The water from a cold spring of forty to fifty degrees is all that is required to cream milk while it continues sweet, and to do it perfectly. The water which would pass through an inch pipe ten rods long, with two feet fall, would do for 500 cows. More would be desirable, but even less would answer.

Two courses are pursued in creameries: One consists in making both butter and cheese, and the other in making butter only. The former is the creamery proper, and the latter more properly is a butter factory, but both establishments are almost indifferently called creameries. The plan of the building and the cost of outfit will be varied according to the work to be done. In the West, particularly in Iowa, most of the creameries make only butter. In the East, both butter and cheese are generally made. The latter, as a rule, is the more profitable course. Since the adoption of the system of cold setting, the milk when skimmed is perfectly sweet and sound, and is a fine condition for cheese making or any other use.

Skim cheese has shared in the recent improvements in cheese manufacture, and an article greatly superior to what was formerly supposed possible can now be made. A cheese in every respect better than the average whole-milk cheese, made in factories ten years ago, can now be made with the cream half out. A wholesome and fairly palatable and marketable cheese can be made out of average milk, from which three pounds of butter to the 100 pounds of milk have been taken, and more than four-fifths of the fat retained. I would be fully retained in the skim cheese than it does to make full-milk cheese is made. It requires more skill to make skim cheese than it does to make full-cream cheese, and if the maker has the skill and can make first-class butter also, he will be in a position to make a success of the creamery. Where the three pounds of butter are taken from a hundred pounds of milk, a fancy article of butter can be made that will generally bring as much as all that would be made from full skimming, as the best part of the cream that comes up is inferior and depreciates the butter.

The profit of running a creamery, as in most other kinds of business, lies in making only first-class goods of its kind. The cost of buildings will vary according to the material used in their construction, and the locality and the finish upon them. In most parts of our Eastern States buildings for the accommodating of 500 cows ought, if made of good wood, to be put up for $1,000. They may be made to easily cost more, and possibly might be made for less. A room must be provided for setting the milk, the temperature of which can be controlled in all seasons, with a floor elevated at least three feet above the manufacturing rooms, so that the milk can be spouted to the vats for making cheese; an apartment for the cheese vats and presses; and a third for making butter, all of which must be on the first floor. A second story will afford room for curing cheese, and a cellar below for storing butter, but butter can be kept on the first floor if proper refrigeration is provided. If there is plenty of cold water, ice will not be necessary, but if not an ice house will be required. Ice is generally needed.

The expense for apparatus will vary with the mode of operation adopted. The best plan will call for an outlay about equal to the cost of a building, and will include a steamer and power for churning. If cheese is not to be made, the cost both of building and apparatus will be about one-fourth less.

The best mode of raising cream is not necessarily the quickest one. Cream need not necessarily be sour to make the best butter, but it must have some age and airing. If raised in twelve hours and churned at once, it will have neither the finest flavor nor the best keeping quality, but if the cooling is not lower than is required to bring the cream up in thirty-six hours, it may be churned when first skimmed, while sweet, and the fanciest butter, with the best keeping quality, will result. If any souring is to be done, nothing more than acidity enough to be faintly perceptible should be allowed.

The best plan for raising cream, and the one which most perfectly accords with the science and philosophy of butter-making, is the following: The milk is set in tin vats twenty inches deep but no more than sixteen inches wide, with the length variable as may be convenient. The upper half of each vat is surrounded by an envelope of water ten inches perpendicularly, and two or three horizontally. The water is run into the envelope at one end of the vat and passes equally along on both sides running out at the other end. The lower half of the vat is only surrounded with air, and it is all the better if the air is not very cool. This does the cooling at the top of the milk where it should always be done. The law discovered and published by me several years ago, that cream rises best when the temperature is falling, is now recognized and adopted by all careful-observing butter makers. When milk has reached a low temperature and it ceases to vary, the cream ceases to rise. The temperature of the milk must therefore be kept changing. These vats are perfectly adapted to this law. If the milk becomes reduced to the temperature of the water flowing round it, the vats are arranged to warm the milk a little at the bottom, either by steam or water, sending the warmest part up to the top to be again cooled and precipitated, leaving the cream at the surface. The changing temperature can thus be kept up indefinitely without the necessity of extreme refrigeration, which is unfavorable to the production of the best keeping and finest delicacy of flavor. Refrigeration is all important in butter making, but we may here too much of a good thing. Aeration is essential to cream while spread out on the milk, but airing does little or no good if the temperature is very low.

For churning, too, must be philosophically done. The cream must all be acted on at once and alike, as when it falls from end to end in a barrel revolving endwise, and the butter must be freed from buttermilk by washing it in a granular form, instead of working it out. These are points which must not be missed, if the best results are to be reached. No others pay; if the manager is posted in respect to the latest

improvements in both butter and cheese making, the erection of a creamery is a good dairy district is a good and safe enterprise, but if second-rate butter and white oak cheese are to be the products, a creamery is a good thing to let alone.

One other thing not generally customary in New York is important. This is in respect to delivering the milk. It makes patrons a great deal of trouble, generally, to deliver their milk, each one making a journey twice a day. These having small dairies cannot afford to do it, and those having large ones are often so situated that they cannot conveniently attend to it, and if they are to begin with, changes are liable to occur, and the creamery loses its best patrons. A creamery or a cheese factory is always in jeopardy from the difficulty of patrons in getting their milk to it. To avoid this, the manager of the creamery should haul the milk and be allowed a reasonable sum for doing it.

These are the outlines, or salient points, to be kept in mind in the construction of a creamery. To enable one to give details the location, extent and kind of goods decided upon must be known. As a word of caution it may be remarked that the location and arrangement of the building should be made with special reference to convenience and cleanliness and pure air. Every needless step taken and every moment of time lost swell the cost of manufacture and militate against the success of the enterprise; hence, how to accomplish the most with the least labor and time, should ever be kept before the mind's eye of the designer. It is just as important to build well as to work well, and to do either successfully one must be familiar with the entire business, so that he can see in advance just what is wanted. If he has not knowledge from experience the next best thing is to visit establishments of the kind he proposes to erect, and study general structures and details.

Among the things to be avoided are the pail and pool system and the large pan system, as being too laborious and unsatisfactory; also all nooks and corners in which filth can lodge to swell the labor of cleaning or render the air of the building impure; and lastly, a site so level that a ready drainage is neither impossible nor difficult. It would be better to pump water from a well in a well-drained, dry and airy location, than to have the best spring imaginable with the creamery in a low, sunken and wet hole, always increasing in impurities and defiling everything with its contaminating emanations. Let the site by all means be on an inclined surface.

## The Fat Stock Show.

The Fat Stock Show has been all that its best wishes could desire in the way of being a capital exhibition and attracting a large amount of patronage. In all the departments this year there was a most excellent display. The cattle department, perhaps, always draws the most universal attention and excites the most universal interest, and usually, we think, the competition results in the least general satisfaction to the exhibitors. There is a settled conviction on the part of a certain class of breeders that they have the best cattle in the world, and that any award that does not recognize this fact is evidence of deplorable ignorance or doubtful honesty. Such people cannot be made to see, and the most appropriate thing that can be said of them is that they are joined to their idols and must be left alone. Then there is another class that always think that the chances are against the recognition of the merits of their breeds, because, perhaps, their cattle are not so numerous as those of other breeds are. This class will never think of being satisfied with the result of any competition which is not clearly in its favor. And so the results of the competition in cattle exhibitions are far from being satisfactory to exhibitors. But the great public is not burdened with the prejudices that breeders are, and it studies all the circumstances and figures calmly, and gets pretty close to the accurate conclusion.

One thing ought to be a source of satisfaction to the cattle exhibitors at the late show, and that is that all the stock was sufficiently fine to make its breeders feel proud of it. The Herefords and Shorthorns were, as was expected, pitted against each other with all the energy that the belief of their respective breeders that each was the best would stimulate. The Shorthorn certainly showed at its best. The Hereford men had prodded the Shorthorn men to do all that their excellent breed would enable them to do, and we do not believe that the show of Shorthorns could be excelled in this or any other country. Those who saw it saw the best Shorthorns that can now be raised. The Hereford breeders were just as confident of the alleged superior innate merits of their cattle as they ever were, and claimed that on the butcher's block there is more to be left to tell the story of merit and profit. That the best may win is our wish, and we know that we are entirely free from prejudice.

The Polled Angus, several of which were on exhibition, attracted general attention, and furnished the first opportunity which many had had of examining the breed. The oddity of their appearance was pleasant to some, and not to others. They have before them just such a contest as other new breeds have or have had. Their breeders must expect that they will have to encounter prejudice and the influence of larger numbers in other cattle, which is often a serious obstacle to the progress of new breeds. Breeds that have been longest in the country present the opportunity to select from a very large number, while the new breeds have few individuals, comparatively, and it is not always possible to make from them the most representative selections. The Polled Angus, however, we believe, have a good future before them.

The sheep, as noticed in another department of this issue, were very fine, and the exhibition of swine was excellent, consisting of all the various breeds, including the Jersey Red, which is a hog that we have always thought possessed considerable merit. Our readers are aware that they are a large breed, of red color, and the color is really the greatest objection that we have heard urged against them, and that is merely a matter of taste.—Western Rural.

Dr. schmidt, Mentheim, has investigated the nitrogenous bodies in cow's milk about which so much diversity of opinion has hitherto prevailed. He says that three albuminoid substances are regularly present in the milk, viz: caseine, albumen and pepton. The average of seven analyses gave 2.43 per cent. of caseine, 0.38 per cent. of albumen and 0.13 per cent. of peptons. Under certain circumstances the amount of peptons may increase until it equals that of the caseine. The pepton is formed from the caseine by a fermentative process; the ferment is destroyed by a boiling temperature, but its activity is not destroyed by salicylic or carbolic acid, so that in this respect it resembles the ferment that digests the albuminoids. Since milk, on long standing, may lose ten per cent. or more of its conversion into peptons, it should be made use of as fresh as possible when employed for making cheese.

Canned meat weighing not over four pounds can be sent through the mails as fourth-class matter.

## The Shorthorn Sales of 1882.

That Shorthorns are holding their own in this country, as ill as that the past has been a prosperous year, is evidenced the fact that while the Shorthorn sales in 1881 averaged 58 per head the average price this year has been over $192 er head. The last public sale of the year was that at Dexr Park, Nov. 24. The sales for the year were as follows:

### SALES MADE IN ILLINOIS.

| | | |
|---|---|---|
| on. M. H Cochrane | 33 head sold for | $45,860 |
| Anada-West J S. Am'n | 25 " | 10,186 |
| m. B. Dodge | 12 " | 2,460 |
| ichard & John Gibson | 40 " | 29,920 |
| S. Latimer & Son | 58 " | 14,080 |
| Givens | 64 " | 16,085 |
| A. Cruce & Son | 73 " | 5,655 |
| ook & Brown | 51 " | 6,905 |
| rother & Smith | 54 " | 10,476 |
| eo. A. Dean | 96 " | 5,970 |
| arther & Clark | 38 " | 5,028 |
| icknell, Thomas & Smith | 69 " | 16,880 |
| mith & Jonas | 52 " | 7,715 |
| J. Streeter & Son | 40 " | 14,416 |
| Henry Meredith | 38 " | 7,995 |
| Dijah Den | 38 " | 3,485 |
| B. Haston & Son | 37 " | 9,400 |
| eo. L. Burrus & Son | 43 " | 6,295 |
| Doming Bros | 43 " | 6,745 |
| urtis & Harrison | 43 " | 7,838 |
| eo. Lavenes & Son | 34 " | 8,740 |
| H. Potts & Son | 29 " | 9,580 |
| S. P. & S. D. Orell | 80 " | 13,090 |
| Prewitt & Day | 94 " | 11,758 |
| Dunaway & Jackson | 39 " | 3,850 |
| F. Houston | 27 " | 2,597 |
| | 1,173 " | $270,397 |

An average of $229 68.

### SALES MADE IN KENTUCKY.

| | | |
|---|---|---|
| J. Alexander | 53 head sold for | $41,870 |
| W. W. Hamilton | 33 " | 8,150 |
| Prewitt & Cunningham | 79 " | 16,640 |
| Van Meter & Hamilton | 69 " | 27,380 |
| The Hamiltons | 46 " | 18,975 |
| T. C. Anderson | 44 " | 13,458 |
| W. Bigstaff and others | 80 " | 12,980 |
| B. R & B. F. Woods | 20 " | 1,900 |
| Van Meter & Burkley | 69 " | 4,600 |
| Burgess & Lines | 62 " | 7,085 |
| The Hamiltons | 33 " | 6,315 |
| T. J. Megibben | 35 " | 26,100 |
| Mrs. Chenault | 31 " | 3,905 |
| Walter Handly | 43 " | 9,784 |
| J. M. Russell | 47 " | 4,555 |
| Josh Barton | 60 " | 4,188 |
| J. W. Livar | 46 " | 4,418 |
| B. Bartti | 45 " | 3,747 |
| C. F. Scott | 35 " | 3,100 |
| | 1,001 " | $216,346 |

An average of $216 03.

### SALES MADE IN OTHER STATES.

| | | |
|---|---|---|
| M. E. Platt (Mo.) | 66 head sold for | $7,005 |
| Barclay, Traer & Nichols (Ia.) | 88 " | 8,985 |
| Miller, Smith, Judd & J. B. Brown (Ia.) | 81 " | 7,650 |
| Chase, Morgan et al. (Ia.) | 69 " | 3,940 |
| John R. Craig (Ont.) | 14 " | 4,482 |
| J. H. Kissinger (Mo.) | 47 " | 10,480 |
| E. B. Healy & Sons (Ia.) | 71 " | 7,176 |
| The Hamiltons (Mo.) | 91 " | 13,097 |
| John Burrous et al. (Mo.) | 32 " | 2,545 |
| Estate David Selsor (O.) | 62 " | 15,365 |
| Jackson Co. (Mo.) Breeders | 100 " | 19,735 |
| Wilson & Smith (Kan.) | 49 " | 7,890 |
| Brown & Clark (Minn.) | 37 " | 6,193 |
| C. O. Platter (Ia.) | 49 " | 4,495 |
| C. H. Williams (Wis.) | 12 " | 1,390 |
| B. Hunter (Ia.) | 70 " | 7,600 |
| W. Wilson (Ia.) | 80 " | 9,025 |
| C. M. Gifford & Sons & The Hamiltons (Kan.) | 32 " | 4,075 |
| F. McHardy (Kan.) | 13 " | 1,795 |
| L. D. Mason et al. (Kan.) | 42 " | 6,800 |
| J. H. Reeper & Son (Ind.) | 6 " | 1,100 |
| J. W. Maureen & Son (Ind.) | 47 " | 6,000 |
| Chas. E. Clint (Kan.) | 57 " | 2,900 |
| J. C. Stone Jr. (Kan.) | 64 " | 6,010 |
| Jas. R. Terrill (O.) | 44 " | 5,340 |
| | 1,361 " | $169,365 |

An average of $125 67.

| | | |
|---|---|---|
| Grand Total | 8,420 " | $656,990 |

An average of $193 10.

The Breeder's Gazette, which compiles the above table, remarks: We are aware that the above is not absolutely complete. There have been in the course of the year probably a half-dozen minor sales, of which we have been unable to obtain reports. Were they all included probably the grand average would be slightly lowered. They constitute, however, a mere "drop in the bucket" as compared with the list above given, and could not possibly cause any material changes.

## Feeding Pigs.

There is a popular idea that almost anything will do to feed pigs with, refuse of every kind being thrown to the pigsty. The wisdom of this course was illustrated in an action tried at the Swindon county court, England. Lord Boling-broke's head keeper kept pigs, two of which he sold through an agent to a man in the village in which he resided. The flesh—the pigs were sold dead, by the carcass—appeared perfectly satisfactory, and was cured in a manner which was admitted to be proper, but when converted into bacon the produce had a most extraordinary smell and appearance, resembling, to use the language of some of the witnesses, the appearance and taste of tallow, and when exposed to the air turned yellow. It was not disputed that the pigs were well fed, and it was proved that they had been fattened on barley meal, but it was also admitted that the paunches of a large number of rabbits had been thrown to them, the result being that the flesh was impregnated with the peculiar odor attaching to rabbits and ground game generally. The learned judge was of the opinion that there had been no attempt to deceive in the matter, that the owner of the pigs had fed them upon the supposition that this kind of refuse would do them no harm. The result, however, proved the contrary, and the purchaser was recouped for his loss by a verdict of £4, being about half the original price. This should prove a warning to those who entertain the idea that any kind of food is fit for swine.—English Exchange.

It is a dangerous operation to cut off a cow's horns, especially to cut them off near her head. While the hemorrhage may not be such as to cause death, there are other dangerous results liable to happen from sawing off the horns at their base. The bony projections from the head, which form the support of the horns and reach far up into these, are hollow, that is, honey-combed, and these cavities connect with the cavities or sinuses of the forehead. Not only may serious catarrh of these sinuses result from thus being exposed, but the blood escaping into the cavities, and closing them up, may, by subsequent dissolution, cause troublesome chronic inflammation and alteration of the delicate lining membrane, as well as of the bony structure.

An occasional application of a mixture of equal parts of kerosene, vinegar and fish-oil will eradicate the lice from swine.

## THE DAIRYMEN'S CONVENTION.

### California Naturally a Foremost Dairy State— Butter vs. Oleomargarine.

The BREEDER AND SPORTSMAN takes an interest in whatever affects the interests of breeders of good stock: The making of the best quality of butter—the making of any butter at all at a profit—depends upon having good neat stock, and the more profitable dairying becomes the more attention will be devoted to the breeding of high grade or pure bred kine. No state in the Union has better natural advantages for dairying than California. Her soil is so fertile as to make this the garden of the world, her climate free from the months of biting zero weather of the Eastern winter as well as from the melting, sweltering midsummer weather which, in the East, continues day after day and night after night, until the heavens seem of burnished brass and the earth a smoking furnace. Nutritious grains and grasses grow in almost tropical luxuriance, and the cost of feeding and caring for stock is reduced to the minimum, while the even temperature is exactly adapted to caring for and manufacturing milk, cream, butter and cheese. Gilt-edged butter can be produced the year round with 25 per cent. less labor and expense than in the finest dairies of Vermont or of the celebrated Orange county, New York. And it is so produced. California butter will stand comparison with the product of those crack dairy regions of New York and New England, and will not come off second best. While the bulk even of the best dairy butter of the East is shipped in firkins, the climate making it too expensive to ship in rolls, California butter almost invariably arrives in the market in rolls, put up the same as the celebrated "gilt-edged" butter of Orange county or Vermont which heads the New York and Watertown markets. All this is true, though the dairying interest in this State is yet in its infancy, and though Eastern butter is constantly being received in our markets. Yet in the matter of pure bred neat stock California can already claim a front rank, and it requires no enthusiast to predict that in a few years the balance of the butter trade between California and the East will be transferred to the other side of the ledger.

It is estimated that 6,000 men are employed in the dairy business of this State, that $15,000,000 is invested, and that the annual net income is $900,000. That is six per cent. on the money invested. There are a great many branches of industry that do not yield as much, and some that yield more, but nobody who has canvassed the subject can doubt that this net income may be doubled by intelligent improvement in breeding, feeding and caring for stock, in the manufacture of the best quality of products, and in skill and judgment in marketing them. Combination, association and interchange of ideas, and practice among dairymen, as with the increasing attention given the subject by the press, will in time produce this result, and dairying will in a few years from now be one of the most profitable branches of business in this State. The idea would be preposterous that with our advantages of soil and climate we must long continue paying the Eastern farmer for butter and cheese which can be made at less cost here, and, added to this, the transportation charges on the same.

The dairying interest being, then, of such present and prospective importance in the State, the establishment of an oleomargarine factory in this city has aroused an interest and a discussion throughout the commonwealth. Nobody questions the right of the manufacturers to prepare clean, wholesome fats in any way they may see fit and place them upon the market under their right name. To put forth the manufactured article as dairy butter would, of course, be a fraud, and those States where it has been manufactured heretofore have passed laws requiring each roll and package to be plainly marked with the name of the article. The manufacturers in this city assert that they do so mark all their product, and that they have no desire that it shall do otherwise than stand or fall entirely upon its merits. But oleomargarine, after leaving the factory under the proper stamp and labels, may in a variety of ways be fraudulently imposed upon the public. the New York Tribune asserts that considerable quantities are sold to farmers in that state, by whom it is incorporated with genuine butter and the compound shipped to market as pure dairy butter. And certainly in a community like San Francisco, where the majority of people take their meals at restaurants, no law can be passed which will protect consumers from imposition if restaurant keepers see fit to buy the manufactured article, stamped and labeled though it be, and cut it into slices and serve it to their customers. Legislation is powerless here, and each individual must rely upon the protection furnished by nature in the organ of taste. That a large amount of oleomargarine is manufactured and put upon the market the manufacturers testify. Very few people can be found who knowingly consume any. But it must be consumed, and how ? Surely by being eaten by parties who suppose they are eating dairy butter. This conclusion establishes two points: First, that it is no less dairy butter as to, to frequently mistaken for it by the consumer; second, that it is thus becoming a dangerous competitor of the dairymen.

To devise plans for meeting this competition the State Dairymen's Convention met in San Francisco last Tuesday. The delegates present were as follows:

San Luis Obispo, M. B. Mac, O. A. Tognazzini, L. Warden; Monterey, J. F. Dixon; San Mateo, H. Ashbruner; Fresno, B. Marks; Marin, B. F. McClure, C. H. Smith, O. A. Hussey, A. H. Stinson, J. Riccioni, W. H. Abbott, F. C. De Long, Dr. Lyford; Sacramento, J. B. Green, Wm. Johnson; Sonoma, Godfrey Taylor; Del Norte, G. H. Kellogg, J. H. Hagler; Alameda, Judge John A. Stanley; Santa Clara, Wm. Quinn, M. M. Caholan, Rush McComas; Santa Cruz, D. M. Pyle, E. A. Davison, H. Gushee, D. D. Wilder, J. Recipina, W. V. Gaffey and B. W. Reeve.

Mr. Gaffey called the meeting to order and John A. Stanley was chosen temporary chairman.

Mr. Stanley on taking the chair stated that he favored the passage of a State law prohibiting the incorporation of any company manufacturing any article which could be sold as the natural product of the dairy.

A motion was carried that all dairymen and all having an interest in the dairy business should be entitled to take part in the deliberations.

The temporary officers were made permanent, as follows: John A. Stanley President, E. J. Wickson Secretary, E. Ashbruner Treasurer, and the following Vice Presidents: Santa Cruz, Horace Gushee; Santa Clara, Colonel Younger; Mendocino, W McClure; Fresno, B. Marks; San Luis Obispo, M B. Mac; Monterey, John Hitchcock; Marin, William H. Abbott; Sacramento, William Johnston; Yolo, J. B. Green; San Mateo, Robert Ashbruner; Stanislaus, Samuel Miller; Del Norte, G. H Kellogg; Sonoma, Hollis Hitchcock; Santa Barbara, A. Tognazzini; Humboldt, John W. Rodgers.

The following Committee on Legislation was appointed: Santa Cruz, J Recipina; Santa Clara, Rush McComas; Mendocino, D. F. McClure; Fresno, C. Marks; San Luis Obispo, L. M. Warden; Monterey, J. F. Dixon; Marin, F. C. De Long; Sacramento, William Johnston; San Mateo. Robert Ashbruner; Stanislaus, S. Miller; Yolo, S. B. Hinsdale; Del Norte, J. B. Hagler; Sonoma, Hollis Hitchcock; Santa Barbara, A. Tognazzini, with Judge Stanley of Alameda as Chairman.

Theoretically the butter coming to market is in two-pound rolls. In practice, however, it is always two ounces short of the weight, and dealers will not purchase butter from the dairymen unless it is thus short as they would have to pay the dairyman by the pound in bulk and sell by the roll in competition with those selling short-weight rolls. A very sensible resolution, and one which it is to be hoped will be adopted and enforced, was offered by Mr. Gaffey, as follows:

"Resolved, That the Legislature shall be asked to enact a law that the true weight shall be stamped on all rolled natural butter offered for sale to the public."

Such a resolution is very appropriate, coming from a convention whose object is to compel the oleomargarine men to properly stamp their products. It will come up for action at the next meeting.

After discussion it was decided that the meetings should be open to press reporters.

Mr. James Wilson, interested in the manufacture of oleomargarine, addressed the meeting by invitation, claiming the product to be very similar to butter and asserting that the manufacturers desired it to stand or fall on its merits, and had no disposition to put it forth under false colors.

The meeting adjourned to 9 a. m. Wednesday.

On Wednesday the following persons paid the annual fee of $1 each and signed the membership roll: John A. Stanley, San Francisco; Robert Ashbruner, Baden, San Mateo; Coleman Younger, San José; M. B. Mac, San Luis Obispo; M. M. Cahalan, San Jose; Rush McComas, Santa Clara; D. M. Pyle, Santa Cruz; E. A. Davison, Gilroy; O. Harvey, Sacramento; Horace Gushee, Santa Cruz; D. D. Wilder, Santa Cruz; William Johnson, Richland, Sacramento; J. Respini, Santa Cruz; W. V. Gaffey, Watsonville; B. F. McClure, Point Reyes; J. F. Dixon, Salinas; W H. Abbott, Olema, Marin; F. C. De Long, Novato, Marin; Dr. B. F. Lyford, Marin; A. Lagnazzini, Santa Barbara; C. H. Smith, Point Reyes; Hollis Hitchcock, Valley Ford; G. A. Hussey, Point Reyes; C. H. Abbott, Point Reyes; Samuel Miller, Stanislaus; G. H. Kellogg, Crescent City; J. M. Greene, Richland, Sacramento; Joseph Bloom, Olema, Marin; John Hitchcock, Monterey; J. W. Grigsby, Napa; J. Mitchell, Marin; N. Musoe, Nicasio, Marin; J. R. Hebbron, J. D. Carr, H. Mayers, Monterey; Charles L. Estee, Marin.

The following draft of an act was adopted and the Legislative Committee, which consists of one member from each county represented, was continued in office and directed to use its endeavors to have it made a law by the Legislature at its next session:

"Section 1. It shall be unlawful for any person or corporation in this State, in the manufacture of the article or substance commonly known as 'Oleomargarine' or 'Oleomargarine Butter,' to mix or incorporate therewith any part or portion of butter, the legitimate product of the cow; or to put upon the market, or sell or offer to sell, any of such substance commonly known as 'Oleomargarine' or 'Oleomargarine Butter,' in the form of rolls or cakes commonly used in this State by dairymen for the marketing of butter.

"Sec. 2. Every person who shall manufacture for sale or who shall offer or expose for sale any article or substance in semblance of butter, not the legitimate product of the dairy and not made exclusively of milk or cream, but into which the oil or fat of animals not produced from milk enters as a component part, or into which melted butter or any oil therefrom has been introduced to take the place of cream, shall distinctly brand, stamp or mark in some conspicuous place upon every package of such article or substance the words 'Oleomargarine,' in plain letters, not less than one-fourth of one inch square each; and in case of retail sale of such article or substance in parcels or otherwise, the seller shall, in all cases, deliver therewith to the purchaser a printed label, bearing the plainly printed words 'Oleomargarine,' the said words to be printed with type, each letter of which shall not be less than one-fourth of one inch square.

"Sec. 3. Every person dealing, whether by wholesale or retail, in the article or substance described in Section 2 of this Act, and every hotel or restaurant keeper, or boardinghouse keeper, in whose hotel, or restaurant, or boardinghouse, such article or substance is used, shall continuously keep conspicuously posted up, in not less than three exposed positions in and about their respective places of business, a printed notice in the following words, viz, 'Oleomargarine sold here,' the said notice to be plainly printed, with letters not less than one-half of one inch square each.

"And each and every hotel keeper and restaurant keeper, boarding house keeper or proprietor of other places where meals are furnished for pay, who may use in their respective places of business any of the article or substance described in the second section of this Act, shall, upon the furnishing of the same to his guests or customers, cause each and every guest or customer to be distinctly informed that said article is not butter, the genuine production of the dairy, but is 'Oleomargarine.'

"Sec. 4. Every person, or driver, trustee, officer, or agent of any corporation, who may violate any provision of this Act, shall be guilty of a misdemeanor, and upon conviction thereof shall be punished by a fine of not less than fifty dollars nor more than five hundred dollars, or by imprisonment for not more than three months, or by both such fine and imprisonment; and it shall be the duty of the Court trying said offense to order the payment of one-half of the fine imposed to the person giving the information upon which the prosecution was based and the conviction had, and such fine may be collected by execution, as in civil causes."

A resolution to boycott all dealers in oleomargarine was tabled.

A committee was appointed to confer with dealers and see if the present charge of half a cent per pound for casing cannot be done away with.

Mr. Gaffey's resolution to ask for a law compelling makers to stamp the weight on each roll of butter was amended to sell for the use of a uniform mould. The amended resolution was then tabled.

After an executive session the convention adjourned, subject to the call of the chair.

THE
# Breeder and Sportsman.
PUBLISHED WEEKLY BY THE
BREEDER AND SPORTSMAN PUBLISHING CO.
THE TURF AND SPORTING AUTHORITY OF THE PACIFIC COAST.
OFFICE, 508 MONTGOMERY STREET
P. O. Box 1338.

*Five dollars a year; three dollars for six months; one dollar and a half for three months. Strictly in advance.*

MAKE ALL CHECKS, MONEY ORDERS, ETC., PAYABLE TO ORDER OF BREEDER AND SPORTSMAN PUBLISHING CO.

*Money should be sent by postal order, draft or by registered letter, addressed to the "Breeder and Sportsman Publishing Company, San Francisco, Cal."*

*Communications must be accompanied by the writer's name and address, not necessarily for publication, but as a private guarantee of good faith*

JOSEPH CAIRN SIMPSON, - - - EDITOR

ADVERTISING RATES.—Displayed $1 50 per inch each insertion or pro rata for less pace. Reading Notices set in brevier type and having no foot marks, 20 cents per line each insertion. Lines will average ten words. A discount of 10 per cent. will be allowed on 3 months, 20 per cent. on 6 months and 30 per cent. on 12 months contracts. No extra rate charged for cuts or cutting of column rules. No reading notice take for less than 60 cents each insertion.

San Francisco, Saturday, December 16, 1882.

Mr. M. J. Henley is a duly authorized traveling agent and correspondent for the "Breeder and Sportsman."

## ROMERO AND OVERMAN.

This afternoon on the Bay District Course will decide the match between Romero and Overman, and whichever of these famous cracks can win the necessary three heats will be rewarded by a large sum of money.

It is conceded that these two flyers will make a closer contest than any others in this State, and there is a great diversity of opinion among the experts as to which will gain the victory. So far the betting has been so nearly even that there is no pronounced favorite, and though Romero had "slightly the call" at the opening of the pool sales on Wednesday night, this arose from a majority of the speculators being better acquainted with his late performances than the doings of Overman. There is only a second difference in the record of the two, that being in favor of the grey. Still 2:19½ and 2:20½ are so near the same notch that the difference is overcome by the slightest shade of good or bad luck. One thing in favor of Romero is his capacity to go at a great rate of speed as soon as the word is given, and this enables him to choose a position if the lottery that governs the placing at the start is adverse. But even that entails extra effort, and when a horse has to trot around another on the turn, if even he has sufficient speed to "take the pole," there is a strain which the luckier has not to endure.

There is no question regarding the capacity of Overman to wind up the mile fast, and at Buffalo in two different heats he came from the half-mile pole in 1:07 and 1:07½. In all his races from the opening of the "grand circuit" he close of the season he showed to be a good horse. At Cleveland he won the fourth and fifth heats in 2:24½ and 2:25, coming from the half in the fourth heat in 1:10, and at Buffalo, after losing the first heat to Abe Downing in 2:20¾, he won the others in 2:20½, 2:23½, 2:24½. Then he won at Rochester, beating Abe Downing, Yellow Dock and others, and at Poughkeepsie he won a hard race of six heats, one of which was "dead" between himself and Independence. The culmination of his very successful Eastern campaign was the winning of his match against Helene at the Gentlemen's Driving Park, New York. He was also matched against J. P. Morris for $2,500 a side, but Morris paid forfeit, and at that time Veritas of the New York *Spirit of the Times* thus described him:

> Overman is a lofty chestnut gelding, a year younger than Morris; he stands 16¼ hands, a very resolute trotter, with a daisy-cutting stride, and little knee action. He was bred in California, and brought East with St. Julien, but change of climate and an attack of pinkeye threw him out of condition in 1881, and he suffered from a recurrence of the pink-eye last spring, but, recovering his form in the Grand Circuit, he showed such speed and strong finishes that good judges said he was then fit to trot in 2:17 or 2:18. He was beaten only a neck in 2:20¾ at Buffalo and won the next heat in 2:20½ and the race in 2:23½, 2:24½ as he pleased, over a large field of horses. His last race was at Belmont Park, Philadelphia, on Thursday last; he won it easily in straight heats. Time, 2:22¼, 2:26¼, 2:26.

It is scarcely necessary to refer to the races of Romero in this connection further than to say that he has given evidence of steady progression, so much so that those who have watched him the most closely are of the opinion that he can trot as fast as Veritas claims for Overman. He is certainly a wonderful young horse, and should no mishap befall him is very likely to take the first place in the stallion record. It is also sure that no horse ever trotted so fast under the same circumstances, as in the early part of his life he was subjected to treatment which was not well calculated to give him a fair chance. That history, kindly furnished by his breeder, H. M. Johnson, appeared in the *Breeder and Sportsman* some time ago, and in it can be found all of the particulars.

No one who has the least fancy for the sports of the track can afford to miss witnessing this match. Unfortunately before it was consummated we made an engagement to be in Sacramento on Saturday and therefore our absence is compulsory. There is another feature of the match which will add to the interest, that being, Hickok and Goldsmith will be the pilots. With speed in the horses and the best talent in the sulkies, the race cannot fail to be highly interesting.

## NEW YEAR'S NUMBER.

We shall publish on Saturday, the 30th instant, an illustrated number of the *Breeder and Sportsman*. That is there will be two very fine illustrations, one of them a colored lithograph of the celebrated young trotting stallion Albert W, and a lithographic copy from the original painting of "Boys in Trouble," by our artist, E. Wyttenbach.

We have not the least hesitation in promising that both of these will be superior to anything offered by any other paper of this class, and will be "works of art" in every respect. The painting has elicited warm ecomiums by every one who has seen it, and we were so highly pleased that we induced Mr. Wyttenbach to delay sending it to New York until the copy was made. There is no necessity of informing those who have seen the *Breeder and Sportsman* since the commencement that Mr. Wyttenbach has a remarkable talent for portraying the horse. In our estimation he has not a superior and scarcely an equal in that line, and he is equally happy in depicting all kinds of animals.

The painting also shows that he is a fine colorist, though the great charm, at least to us, is the remarkable fidelity with which he has delineated the horse, dogs and boys. It is not the intention, however, at present, to give a description of the picture, though we can assure our readers that the lithograph will be cherished by all who receive it.

The chromo of Albert W is by another San Francisco artist, Buchler, and is further proof of the talent that is met on this side of the continent. It is a capital representation of the famous colt, and as it will be accompanied by a full description of both sides of his genealogical tree it will be a sort of epitome of the doings of the Electioneers and Trustees on this coast.

The letter press of the New Year's number will be, in the main, peculiarly Californian. At the present time it is difficult to say exactly what the subjects will be. A story of the early days has been secured, and it has the merit of having a solid foundation of facts to sustain the interest.

Then it will be near enough the close of the year so that one can give a review of what our horses have done, and though 1882 may not have supplied the the sensational events of last year, there is enough to justify the claim that the Pacific Coast is sure to take the first place in the race for the great prize in breeding fine and fast horses. This view we have persistently adhered to, even when those who had lived among the advantages a score of years before our advent were dubious about it, and to have the correctness proved is not only flattering to what our old and good friend "H. B." terms the satisfaction of saying "I told you so," but it also gives the people now a better appreciation of what they should be thankful for. Again, the 30th of December will bring to a close the first volume of this paper. A circumstance of unusual occurrence connected with it is the fact that in this half-yearly volume are twenty-seven numbers.

The first volume is an era in the life of a newspaper. It is a mark of virility, a token of a healthy life, an indication of vitality which augurs a healthy future. We are pleased to state that so far we have met with a support that may be termed enthusiastic. The paper has found friends in all sections, and from every quarter come words of encouragement. But we are anticipating the greeting that more appropriately belongs to the "New Year," and with the assurance that we cordially and sincerely thank those who have taken so much interest in our venture, and that we are determined to do everything in our power to merit a continuation of their favors, we defer further remarks.

## OLD THAD.

As will be learned from an advertisement in the appropriate column, Thad Stevens will be located the coming season at Agricultural Park, Sacramento. This horse has always been a favorite of ours, and it will be singular if he does not prove a successful sire. A third heat in 1:43½, and a second heat of four miles in 7:30, is a guarantee that the progny will be likely to excel, and then his blood is an element of value not to be overlooked.

## FINE PHOTOS OF CATTLE.

Last week we published a letter from Orestes Pierce, of Saddleback, East Baldwin, Maine, in which he alluded to photographs of his Jersey cattle.

These pictures have been received, and they are without exception the best specimens of the art of cattle picturing we have ever seen, when the sun and camera were called into requisition. They are remarkably lifelike, and though Belle of Middlefield is the subject from which was taken a capital wood cut published in the *Rural New Yorker*, it is scarcely as pleasing a picture as those that have the benefit of the contrast in colors.

As Mr. Pierce writes, "it is considered in New York one of the best wood cuts of an animal yet printed. You will see that it is not as fine as yours." It is well worthy of the encomiums bestowed, and to have the illustrations in the *Breeder and Sportsman* pronounced superior is praise enough. The Jerseys are good subjects for photographic illustrations, and though there has been a craze in the last few years for those of "whole colors" our preferences are for those which are relieved by patch-of white. There are strange conceits regarding white in horses, and this may be one cause why the cattle fanciers have fallen into the same fancies.

The old jingle, "one white foot buy, two white feet try, three white feet go without him, four white feet and a white nose, cut off his head and feed him to the crows," has probably prevented many a first-class animal from having a chance to display his merits. Lexington, and scores of others, have proved the fallacy on the racecourse, and some of the greatest animals, in milk and butter producing qualities, are well marked with white. There are five of the pictures, two of them apparently dark fawn with light muzzles Belle of Middlefield is of the light fawn, and "Mother" and "Son" have a good proportion of white. The work is done by Schreiber & Sons, and is assuredly a fine specimen of that kind of art.

## APPOINTMENT OF L. J. ROSE, DISTRICT BOARD OF APPEALS.

We are much pleased to learn of the election by the Board of Review of L. J. Rose to fill the vacancy in District Board No. 5, occasioned by the death of Colonel W. Wilson, of San Jose. In our estimation Mr. Rose is in every respect well qualified for the place. He is identified with the trotting interests of California, and has done his share to place the stock of this State in the prominent position it now occupies. He has a clear understanding of the rules and a logical turn of mind, which will enable him to see through the petifogging schemes that are sometimes brought into play to secure a wrong decision. There will be no favoritism in his awards, and the poor have an equal show with those of high station. Then it was eminently proper that the southern portion of the State should have a representative in the Board; and while this is granted, the drawback of non-attendance at the meetings is obviated, as the business of Mr. Rose compels frequent visits to San Francisco, and the meetings of the Board can be timed so as to take place during his sojourns in the city.

That there will be general satisfaction over the election of Mr. Rose is beyond question, and he and the Chairman will give a confidence heretofore completely lost. Although there has been a long delay, now that there is a chance for fair ruling, the lessons of the past may be beneficial.

## A HUNTING SKETCH FOR NEW YEAR'S.

We have the promise of a hunting story from Dr. E. H. Pardee, which will be one of the most pleasing features of the New Year's number. The doctor is as much at home among the mountains and woods as he is in the scientific department of rifle shooting, and the story of his trips will be an exceedingly interesting history of California sport. He is so much attached to his annual shooting vacation that he could not be persuaded to take the place of President of the Golden Gate Association for the third year, as the time he had to give to the business of the society interfered with his summer excursion. At any other time of the year he was willing to give "time and money" to further the interests of the association, but to break into his "life in the woods" could not be endured, and to be compelled to leave the forests and streams when the game was the most plentiful, and the salmon and trout in the best condition, was not to be thought of. Dr. Pardee being a "pioneer," he has an acquaintance with the field sports of California complete and thorough, and this joined to just as complete a knowledge, scientific and practical, of the rifle, makes whatever he writes interesting and instructive.

## ON. JAMES McM. SHAFTER AGAIN.

Now that the Honorable James McMillan Shafter s seen fit to turn the discussion as to the propriety of t retaining his place on the Board of Appeals, known the title of District Board No. 5, into a personal at-:k upon us, he has given the opportunity to state more phatically the objections there are to his retaining t position. Heretofore we have confined the charges incompatibility, unfitness arising from his peculiar tem- irment, a domineering, arbitrary disposition. Syco- :antic in one case, overbearing in another, either unable comprehend the most simple rules or with a determin- ation to twist them to suit his own views. His late ronnuciamento absolves us from restricting the con- deration to the manifest want of ability to perform the uties of a judge or arbiter, to take broader ground, and :om his past conduct prove that he is also unfit from his onnection with doings which a man of any honor would born to be partner in.

It is unnecessary to go over the ground previously ar- ed. No amount of legal sophistry, a whole page of lsehoods will not remove the load of opprobrium he bors under. While we would have preferred to have mited the accusations to his delinquencies immediately nnected with trotting affairs, our duty compels us to ing other matters forward to make his unfitness so pal- ibly apparent that no one can mistake the bearing. e has set the example of bringing personalities into the gument, and though we cannot afford to surrender the guilty of position in the manner he has, we should se- em it a culpable dereliction if we fail to show how ut- rly unworthy he is of the place he occupies. The elfare of the sports of the turf and track is the ruling motive. This being of far greater importance than the gratification of private feelings, and to accomplish the object it is necessary to show that his attack in all the major points is totally devoid of truth. In the first place we will give some more illustrations of what he has done. and after that direct some queries to him individually.

The only instance we are acquainted with of his taking a part in the rulings of District Board No. 5, before the late Embryos, was the case of Bonnie in the Stanford Stake. The facts curtly stated are as follows: Palo Alto named five colts in the Stanford Stakes, which closed the first of January, 1881. To make good the nomination, another $100 was due on the first January, 1882. Acting as secretary pro tem, we received a letter dated Palo Alto, Dec. 26, 1881, as follows:

Palo Alto makes second payment in Stanford Stakes of 1882 on Ismia, Hattie Crocker, Clay, Benefit.
H. R. COVEY, Superintendent.

The envelope also contained nominations in the Stan- ford Stake of 1882, and was postmarked San Francisco, Dec. 30, 7 a. m., 1881. Bonnie was one of the original nominations, and on the third of January we received a letter of which the following is a copy :

PALO ALTO, Jan. 1, 1882.
J. C. SIMPSON, SECRETARY OF STANFORD STAKES, Dear Sir : Palo Alto makes second payment on Bonnie in Stanford Stake to be trotted 1882. H. R. COVEY, Sup't.
This was in a Wells, Fargo envelope stamped Menlo Park, Jan. 2.

On the 6th of January we went to the office of Capt. Smith, and presented a list of those who had made the second payment, explaining to him the status of the Bonnie entry. He at once decided that it should be re- jected and so it was indorsed. Beside the four from Palo Alto these remained in: E. A. Miller Jr.'s Adair, J. B. McDonald's Brigade, A. Waldstein's Nellie W and Jos. Cairn Simpson's Anteeo. The list was published in the California Spirit of the Times of January 14, and in the article accompanying it was the following sentence: " There are some singular circumstances in connection with this stake. Palo Alto had five nominations and four of these are left in and it was only by a mistake in not including in the communication the other that the was left out. The absentee is actually the fastest of the five, but a rigid construction of the rule was considered enough to bar her."

Thus the matter was disposed of until some time in June when we received a letter from Mr. Covey in re- gard to the eligibility of Bonnie, and it was answered that the entry had been rejected, and the only way to remedy it was to bring the question before the District Board. We also notified the chairman of the Board when the meeting was called to discuss the question to let us know, and we would notify the parties interested, viz: E. H. Miller Jr., J. B. McDonald and A. Wald- stein, and bring the letters and papers in relation to the case. The first intelligence was the following letter:

SAN FRANCISCO, July 10, 1882.
MR. JOS. CAIRN SIMPSON, Dear Sir : In the matter of the appeal in the case of the bay filly Bonnie, wherein the second payment in the Stanford Stakes was refused, the Board of Appeals met July 10th, there being present Mr. J. McM. Shafter and N. T. Smith, and on the presentation of the facts of the case it was decided that the payment must be received and that the entry is not forfeited.
The facts as shown were that the second payment was due

onthe 1st of January, 1882, that the Treasurer received the letter dated January 1st, making the second payment on the morning of the 2d of January, and the Secretary received a letter dated January 1st on the 2d of January, that according to the custom and the law of this State, where an obligation matures on Sunday or a holiday it may be performed on the first business day thereafter.

All the evidence showed that the intention of the payment was real and manifest, within the legitimate time, and must be so decided.

The Treasurer was instructed to receive the money and give notice to the owner of the filly Bonnie that the entry still stands good. Yours truly, N. T. SMITH.

All the papers were in our hands, and so the above de- cision was reached without even an ex parte statement to base the award on.

We acquainted Governor Stanford that we should en- ter a protest against the starting of Bonnie, and though at first he was inclined to place a good deal of weight on Mr Shafter's opinion, as soon as the true state of the case was made apparent he acquiesced in the view which Captain Smith and we had taken at the time, or within a few days after—the 6th of January—and started Clay in the stake. We were delighted with the manner with which Governor Stanford acted. Annoyed at first that there should be anything in the way of his fastest colt starting in the stake, the most important of any in Cali- fornia, when made acquainted with the objections he cheerfully surrendered the point although it was sus- tained by " forty-two years practice at the bar."

It is only necessary to copy the rules bearing on this question to show how entirely at variance the decision was with the code, and when a person who claims to be particularly well posted makes such a ruling there can only be one inference.

The rule which governed at the time is Sec. 2, Rule 2. The convention that met in February last, amended that rule so that it is now different though, of course, the amendment cannot be held retroactive.

Sec. 2. All entries not actually received by the member as aforesaid, at the hour of closing, shall be ineligible, except entries by registered letter bearing postmark not later than the day of closing, or entries notified by telegraph, the telegram to be actually received at the office of sending at or before the hour of closing, such telegram to state the color, sex, and name of the horse, and the class to be entered, also to give the name and residence of the party making the entry.

Having occupied so much space to give a clear under- standing of the Bonnie case, we will defer the rest of the showing. Our friends, however, need not think that we are shirking the task. Although it is unpleasant we will give the history of the Haddington race at the half-mile track, the action of the State Board when Mr. Shafter was president, the Santa Cruz decision, the San Jose troubles, as all have a bearing on the question at issue.

Those directly and emphatically point to his unfitness for the office he holds, and as far as the personal matters we shall clearly show who is the one to make statements " known to be untrue.''

### EDITORIAL NOTES.

A New Blind Bridle will be found among the adver- tisements, and having given it thorough trial we are satisfied that it is really " an improvement." The line of vision is con- trolled and that without interfering with the eye; with an ordi- nary blind there is continued trouble. On one side it will flap against the eye, on the other it will stand at right angles to the cheek. The horse will look over or under it, and should he raise the bit in his mouth the " cheek pieces" will be thrown up and a vacant space be left. From experiments we are also satisfied that the action can be modulated by a change of the blinds. The straps attached give the power to regulate, and by turning the winker up something of the same effect is produced as by blindness. The animal cannot see the ground and lifts the feet higher to avoid mishaps. It may be that a contrary method will induce less knee-action, though we have never had the opportunity to test it, as all our horses have little bending of the knee.

The Big Match on the Bay District Course this afternoon between Romero and Overman continues to be the absorbing topic of conversation among all those who have the slight- est fondness for the sports of the track. The excitement is brisk, and there is likely to be more money finding than there has been on any trotting match since the "days of old." Wednesday night Powers was slightly the favorite, Thursday night Overman had the pride of place with the bettors. Not the least attraction will be the presence of the Princess Louise and the Marquis of Lorne, as there has been an announce- ment that these august personages will honor the track by witnessing this peculiarly American sport. The whole of Europe might be ransacked without finding two such horses, and it is nearly as safe to assert that the whole of the United States cannot show two that are likely to show a more excit- ing contest.

The Palo Alto Youngsters have returned safely from the victorious campaign on the other side of the big hills. They return without a single defeat to dim the luster of their fame, and only one heat to charge to the debit side of the account. It is stated that the Kentuckians are mak- ing vigorous preparations to give them a warm welcome next year, and though there is no fear of unpleasness on the part of those who have the honor of California to sustain, it is also certain that the enterprising breeders of the blue grass coun-

try will improve on their past records. This is just as we would have it. There are hard fights in the future; the harder the better, as victory in that case is not an empty name.

The Choice of the Bettors is not to be relied upon as a true augury of how the race will terminate. The amount of money is the regulator, and if there are ten thousand dol- lars to be put on one horse, and twice that sum on another, the odds must finally be adapted to circumstances. That there will be changes before the race is concluded is almost positive, and it may be startling changes. There are, at times, stampedes and a desire to "get out" of what appears to be a "bad fix," and at such times men are apt to lose their judgment. Pool-selling intensifies the demoralizations, as the excitement of bidding, heightened by the auctioneer, has a dramatic force unknown to "out of hand" wagering.

A Good Idea is that of Col. Lewis M. Clark, Presi- dent of the Louisville Jockey Club, who is adding a "straight run in" of three-quarters of a mile to the course at that place. Men are engaged in the grading, so that it will be in readiness for the spring meeting. It is also contemplated to extend the new course to 1¼ miles, the additional half mile being on an easy curve. The Turf, Rod and Gun, published at Louisville, says that the ground is admirably adapted for the purpose, and this being the case the new course will certainly be a "grand improvement" for the decision of the dashes within the distances embraced.

Our New York Letter gives the latest intelligence from the metropolis, and though at this season "sporting matters" of nearly every description are at a stand-still in the land of frost and snow, our correspondent handles the little there is in an entertaining style; he lived for some time in San Francisco, and is in a position to know what will be of the most interest to Californians, and is so situated as to ob- tain the most reliable intelligence of whatever is going on in that busy hive.

## YACHTING.

The Chicago club is one of the youngest in America, but has made advancing strides in the past season that would satisfy any lover of yachting and yacht clubs. A complete organization, with officers thoroughly awake and pushing, caused the good results. The club has secured a fine club house for their quarters, located on the "lake front," with a commanding view of the basin and the lake. A flagstaff en- ables the club to work one of the most perfect systems of signals yet seen, and add usefulness to its beauty as yachting headquarters. Three of the best schooner yachts on the lake, among the being the famed Countess of Dufferin, and a num- ber of first, second and third-class sloops, with several small schooners, make up the fleet.

Work on the Spreckels yacht is rapidly progressing. Half a dozen joiners are at work in the cabin which will be the finest finished of any on the coast. All but the ceiling will be in hard woods of rare varieties and the ceiling will be carved work. No money is being spared on this yacht.

The big yacht Mdistata which showed so much speed last season was a new yacht. She made the best time over the N. Y. Y. C. course ever made. It seems, therefore, that the charge that Americans were on the back track in yacht build- ing was not true.

In the proposed race to the Sandwich Islands between the two large yachts now being built, there will be really two trials, one off the wind, down, and the other a beat back. There will be two prizes, one for each run.

There is again talk about a National Yachting Association. When one was organized two years ago the right people did not seem to get hold of it so it failed to be a permanent in- stitution.

The N. Y. Y. C. has for the present given up all idea of a club house near the water. They have fine club rooms in New York city.

The mast saddle, jaws for gaffs and booms, box for whe l and all the blocks on the Spreckels yacht are made of tomano wood.

The forty-foot schooner being built by Stone is all planked up and it will not be very long before she will be ready.

Farmer has finished a new plunger for Lake Merritt. She has a low freeboard but it is a fine looking little craft.

The Larchmont Clat is to have a yawl among its yachts. The rig is slowly being recognized in the East.

Very little is going on among the yachtsmen now, the days being short and the winds very light.

They are building Mr. Tevis' new yacht at a yard on Chan- Street near Capt. Turner's place.

A number of new members have been taken into the San Francisco Yacht Club lately.

The Lotus Club is going to have the Whitewing next sea- son, so it is said.

Edward Hanlan of Toronto, champion oarsman of the world, and John A. Kennedy of Portland, Me., met at the office of Turf, Field and Farm last Thursday afternoon and signed articles of agreement to row a three-mile-with-a-turn race for $2,500 a side. They deposited $1,000 forfeit with Hamilton Busby of the Turf, Field and Farm, and $1,000 more will be put up on May 1st next, when a referee and the place of contest will be agreed upon. The final $500 is to be put up on May 25th. In case no referee can be agreed upon the stakeholder will act. All the moneys deposited will be forfeited in case either fails to fulfil the articles of agreement, which are ironclad. Kennedy returned to his home on the train to-night. Hanlan returns to Toronto on Monday.

Dr. Protheroe's ostriches have arrived, and it is under- stood they are to be established on Mr. Sayer's ranch in Fresno county, instead of in San Bernardino county, as stated last week, though the arrangements are not yet com- plete. The cost of the twenty-two birds—ten males and twelve females—laid down in San Francisco is $20,000. It is expected that they will begin to yield an income from sale of feathers in about two years.

## THE GUN.

### Preservation of Game.

We are not personally and individually interested in the preservation of game. There will be plenty of game long after this writer shall have gone to a better world. But we like logic. Therefore we speak as we now do. There is, it is alleged, a line somewhere in one of the Codes which authorizes Supervisors of counties to make regulations to preserve game in their respective counties. It is claimed that said line in said Code has been repealed by an act of the Legislature passed subsequently to the adoption of the Code. But many Boards of Supervisors are acting as if there had been no repeal of that Code line, and such Boards are protecting game, each in its own county, and each in its own way. The Supervisors of Nevada and El Dorado counties protect deer by extending the time that such game may be killed for one month; from the first of November to the first of December. The Supervisors of Plumas county go still further in protecting—mind you "protecting"—deer by extending the slaughter season until the first of January, or two months in each year. The Supervisors of Calaveras county are more liberal still in protecting deer, for the killing in that county can be continued until the first of February. The Plumas county and the Calaveras county sportsmen can have a good time shooting the burdened doe, and El Dorado county and Nevada county shootists are put to a disadvantage in this matter of deer killing. We do not like to see Nevada county placed in the background, and if it is lawful to extend the open season one month, it must be lawful to extend the same two months, or even indefinitely for that matter. If one month added to the time of the lawful slaughter of deer is a protection to that class of game, then adding the longer time gives still more protection. The logic of this business (and that is what we want vindicated) is inevitable for constant killing, if once it is granted that protecting game can be accomplished by extension of the open season. The constitution of the State does not allow the Legislature to pass special laws, and how the Supervisors can be authorized beats our understanding.—*Grass Valley Tidings.*

### The Trap at Stockton.

The members of the O'Neal Gun Club of Stockton indulged in a series of trap-shooting matches on Thanksgiving Day. The first was a single-bird match at twenty-one yards, entrance $10, and resulted as follows:

| | |
|---|---|
| O. Marshall | 1 1 1 1 1 1 1 1 1 1 1—11 |
| F. Leffler | 1 1 1 1 0 1 1 1 1 1 1—10 |
| C. J. Haas | 1 1 1 1 1 1 1 1 0 1 1—10 |
| L. H. Woods | 1 1 1 1 1 0 1 1 1 1 1—10 |
| P. White | 1 1 1 1 1 1 1 0 0 1 1— 9 |
| O. Hohenshell | 1 1 1 1 1 1 0 1 0 1 1— 9 |
| C. A. Merrill | 0 1 1 1 1 1 1 1 1 0 1— 9 |
| A. Meyers | 1 1 1 1 1 1 0 0 1 0 1— 8 |
| W. Woods | 1 1 1 0 1 0 1 1 1 1 0— 8 |
| C. A. Haas | 0 1 1 1 1 1 1 0 1 0 1— 8 |
| O. A. Bird | 1 1 1 1 0 0 1 0 0 1 1— 7 |
| B. Hohenshell | 1 1 0 0 0 1 1 1 1 0 1— 7 |
| F. N. Lartome | 1 0 1 0 0 0 1 0 0 1 0— 5 |

The next was a ten-bird match at thirty-one yards rise, Hurlingham rules, which was won by C. Rich with a clean score. Several other matches were also shot.—*Sacramento Bee.*

Another Big Bear.—R. H. Lee, the surveyor, Tom Shaw and Major Collins, while at Sawtooth last week, heard that good sport could be had at the slaughter pen any night in killing bear. They therefore provided themselves with Winchester rifles and struck out one evening, and were smoking cigars and considering the advisability of climbing upon the scaffolding, when a crackling of underbrush startled them. They got ready to fire all together at the word "three." A bear approached, and when a few yards off they all fired, and the bear, rising upon his hind legs, fell over into the creek. The bold hunters approached and poured a second volley into Mr. Bear, when they saw that it was surely dead. An examination proved that the first volley was fatal, as two bullets had struck upon its forehead and the other entered one of its eyes. Fifteen men with a sled took the bear to town, where it was weighed, and it tipped the beam at 1,400 pounds. It was of the bald-faced species, and one of the largest yet killed. Its paws were 16 inches long, and its jaws resembled a Blake ore crusher's. This is the largest bear killed this season.—*Wood River Times.*

Poisoning Coyotes.—From all directions the news has been accumulating that the coyotes are killing sheep by the wholesale. M. B. Rankin, of this city, who owns a large farm near Champoeg, has been losing both sheep and goats. Mr. Rankin was telling this to a man residing at the foot of the Cascades, and the man told him that for a few years he had killed these animals by putting strychnine in eggs and putting them on the range of the wolves. Mr. Rankin at once adopted the plan, and in a day or two three dead coyotes were found, and no more live ones had put in an appearance. Break a small hole in the shell, and put three grains of strychnine in. Try up the dogs.—*Rural Spirit, Portland, Oregon.*

Bear Fight.—The Prineville *News* says: A sportsman went out one day last week to train a couple of likely hounds. The pups soon brought a bear to bay upon a fallen tree. The sportsman fired, hitting bruin on the tip of the nose, whereupon the bear made a sortie. The hunter dropped his gun, seized each of the cubs by the tail and jumped up on a log for safety. In less than half an hour the bear bled to death.

"In the woods near Pino, Placer county, is a flock of turkeys nearly as wild as any ever seen in the forests of the West. They persistently refuse to be driven to their old home, and if unmolested by hunters may yet give us a stock of wild turkeys. Hunters should avoid killing them." The foregoing is from the Sacramento *Bee*, and the last sentence is eminently sound. But we fear by the time hunters begin to heed it those turkeys will have climbed the golden stair. Man is beast—that is most men are—and without legal protection it will be difficult to save the bacon, so to speak, of those birds.

There is to be a big shooting match at John's, in Colusa county, on the 20th inst., at which $170 in six money prizes will be distributed. The pigeon shooting is to be open to all.

The pigeon matches to be shot at Oak Hall, near Sacramento, will take place on the 24th and 25th insts. There will be one thousand strong birds on hand.

A mountain lion in the neighborhood of Calistoga is challenging the sportsmen.

A great many ducks are being shot by moonlight in the vicinity of Los Angeles.

---

## RABBIT-SHOOTING IN ENGLAND.

### Shooting in Summer—An Autumn Day's Sport—How to Muzzle a Ferret—Etc.

Though the rabbit is now a much despised little animal, and has been left by parliament to the mercy of the tenant farmers, it must truly be said in its favor that it has always afforded first-class sport with the gun. Most men can pretty well bowl over a hare, notwithstanding the speed puss puts on, but with the little grey-coated coney it is very different. "When you are clever with the rabbits," say most old sportsmen, "you are fairly well fit for anything." Of course there is rabbit shooting and you may, therefore, hear some men exclaim: "Rabbits difficult! Pooh-pooh!" Indeed, in an article on hares and rabbits in a well-known London sporting magazine not so very long ago, a writer who is great on the natural history of game said that "while his hares afforded noble sport the rabbits formed but toy targets for the schoolboy." How an old gamekeeper who had spent half his days cleaning out the hedge rows in order to do away with the growling of grumbling tenants would shake his head at such an assertion!

Taking rabbit shooting from first to last, from the opening to the close of the proper time for shooting them (they really have no close time at all), you can get some capital shots in the summer mornings and evenings after the middle of July, provided you are a good shot, and know an old doe in milch from the half-grown young, the first litter of the season. In the mornings if you saunter out between six and seven o'clock, while the dew is fresh on the grass, close to the hedge-rows of the wood-lands, you will find them scampering in from the feeding ground in all directions. Many, of course, will be out of range, and these you must not fire at, as nothing is more painful to think of than of a rabbit dragging itself all bleeding into the holes in the summer time when there are such a lot of young ones of all sizes and ages running about. When you get right opposite the main group of burrows, keep out a little, and you will find lots squatted close to the ground trying to conceal themselves behind some sheltering bunch of tay weeds, thistles or rushes. The heavy laden doe full of young, you must let go, as well as does with milch. As to the old bucks, just like old black cocks, you will find that they mostly disappeared on your approach, and are now safe in their underground retreats. The very, very young, if you mean to have a lot of sport when winter comes on, you wisely do not pull on, but the half-grown give you a good run for your powder and shot, and as they are then very tender eating, you may as well have them as not. "Be always well forward in rabbit-shooting, is a good motto, as "if your shot catches them anywhere behind the third rib, leaving the heart clear, unless the hind legs should be broken, they will go on and reach the hole, no matter how hard hit from both barrels." A rabbit with one hind leg gone, will go almost fast enough to beat a speedy retriever, and with two trailing, will make the sportsman run as fast as he can to catch him before he gets to ground.

Summer rabbit shooting is hot by any means rabbit shooting proper, and is merely indulged in by those who are very fond of the gun and find the long summer's evening wearisome. In the winter time it is enjoyed to full advantage, as the rabbits are then hardy, full of grain and full of fire. The regular rabbit catcher never cares to take them until after the first hard frost has been experienced, as the skins, till cold weather has been endured, will not stand preparation, and a penny or two per skin, though little to what was drawn in the days before silk hats were invented, has always to be considered. In the woodlands, as a rule, rabbits are softer than those grown in the open fields, hedgerows and common land; they bolt slower, and misses are less frequent. Still, interweaving trees, bits of scrub-wood, faggots laid down for pheasant shelter, all make difficulties in the way of taking the game, and not infrequently by little hops and skips he will bother the sportsman with a miss with the right barrel, which causes him to jump away at full speed, to be followed by the wildly-delivered contents of the left. Of course this applies to ferreting in the woodlands only, as when crossing open rides in front of the beaters they are very easily taken if the sportsman is at all smart.

Perhaps, however, as enjoyable a system of rabbit shooting as we could have is amongst with cover or gorse, with three or four good Scotch terriers hunting them out. As a rule you will have a great many shots, and, no matter how quick your trigger finger, a number of misses, as the rabbit will twist and wriggle about in the bushes like an eel, and you following him after he leaves your eyesight may cause you the loss of a dog. Supposing it is the month of November, and there have been a few nights' frost, sufficiently keen to raise an inch of ice on the surface of the ponds, the tops of the rabbit catcher are of no use; snares are equally ineffective, so the ferrets must be tried. Some sportsmen say that rabbit netting is most enjoyable; if so, they are welcome to their opinion, but it's a poacher's game at the best, and no more to be compared to rabbit shooting than salmon netting is to salmon angling. The ground you have got to start work upon is the roughest on the whole estate, being a couple of miles of boulder-strewn hill-face overlooking the loch. It is a weary climb upward, but after a time you reach the point at which, from time immemorial, the keeper has started the winter campaign. He has killed rabbits from the top of every rock you see around, he can tell you, and he knows every hole-mouth as well as the rabbits seem to do themselves. Moreover, he understands their relationship, and the directions in which they will always run when bolted from particular localities.

But a truce to explanation. We are out for a day's rabbiting. "Well, Donald, I suppose we start with the old familiar burrows."

"Weel, air, I suppose we could not do verra much better; it was always coot for a half dozen, and there hass not been a trap in it this year."

"Just so. Well, I can see the place where I missed my dark two years ago, and if the beggar goes that way again I'll"—

"I am afeard, sir, the beggar will not go that way any more; we cleared the place with the traps several times since then."

"All right he be grandfather or grandson, hanged if I am going to commence with the miss in talk this time, like a billiard sharp with a bit of chalk in his pocket."

Ne'er having seen a billiard table in the whole course of his life, the old keeper paid no attention to my remarks, but throwing off the empty game-bag, he laid down the ferret box, dung open the lid, when immediately four little yellow-haired, mischievous-looking little vagabonds reared their heads from amongst the loose meadow hay amongst which they had lain curled. Two of the young ones had never hunted, but the others were well up in the business. Seeing Blake, the big black retriever, standing earnestly looking at them, and, no doubt, smelling rabbit somewhere, they mizzled out as eager for the sport as setters on the morning

of the twelfth. The keeper seizes one, the biggest of the lot, in his left hand, and hands me a cobbler's wax end, which he draws from his waistcoat pocket with his right, remarking as he does so:

"I think you'll not have forgotten the way to put on a muzzle, and old Jack (the ferret) is verra clever with his teeth; the rest will do better with their mouths open."

Laing down my gun I run the usual half or weaver's knot up to the center of the "end" (this is not a conundrum—the center of a wax end is the middle), and as the keeper keeps the little villain's jaws open with a small blof pencil, I slip it over the lower one, cross it over his nos, and with a reef knot close his mouth effectually. Then, carrying the two ends up his forehead directly between the eyes, make another half knot, as a sailor would say amidships, double round the neck, and make fast. This is the real way to muzzle a ferret, and is far more effectual than the manufactured one for keeping them from killing in the hole. The little gentleman wriggles along the ground and tries to rub it off, but finding all his efforts ineffectual, commences to hunt the moment Donald puts him to the hole's mouth. The open mouthed old ferret is flung carelessly in among the locos rocks to choose a hole for itself, and, as directed, I take up my position on the top of a large boulder, from which I can command a grand view of the situation. The keeper with his old muzzle-loader crossed on his breast, stands with the dogs looking past his right leg on my left, a perfect picture for Landseer. There is a loud rumbling under ground, which makes the dog cock his ears and the keeper's eyes to glisten; then bunk, bunk, and away like a blue cock goes a rabbit. I miss him just past his stern, close as a ship with hard-up helm giving away on wrong tack, but he rounds into view, and holding well forward and sharp, he rolls over and over, tumbling half-a-dozen flying somersaults, and then with the white of his belly upward, lies dead. In a few seconds more Blake has deposited him at the heels of his master, and no sooner has he done so than bang, go a couple from different sides of the rock. The keeper's right barrel does its work, and with both barrels of my gun empty, I have the mortification of still witnessing my rabbit struggling onward. The keeper wheels to my assistance, and with a long shot almost takes it, and, with that twist so well known to rabbit catchers, wrings its neck and flings it down beside the slain.

And so we work till far on in the afternoon, when the sun has begun to sink, and the ferrets to get tired, then wend our way down hill, quite prepared to argue with any sportsman that when rabbits are plentiful and bolting well before the ferrets, there is no better sport in the world.—*Rockwood in Bell's Life.*

It is quite delightful to go out duck-hunting. The meadows are as bleak as the forty-mile desert in March; and the mud is just thick enough to make the walking abominable. The swift little teal and quacking mallard is as wild as the canvasback, and the latter is wild enough to give an indiscriminate hunter all the exercise he wants. After travelling all day and reaching your buckboard away after dark it is quite enjoyable to have the mustang kick over the singletree and fall down and break the shaft short off. What makes a hunt of that kind more enjoyable and romantic is to be in the middle of a 2,000-acre field and not know which way to go to escape sloughs and find an opening in the fence.—*Reno Gazette.*

If a man goes to a Thanksgiving turkey shoot, and takes twenty-five shots at twenty-five cents per shot, drinks thirty-six glasses of lager beer at 12½ cents per glass, and kills a cow worth $50, which stands in quite an opposite direction from where he intends to shoot, gets mad and breaks a $60 Sharp's rifle, and on arriving home gets fired out of doors by his wife, who breaks a rolling-pin worth seventy-five cents over his head for coming home without a turkey, how much is he winner in the whole operation, and how much would he have lost if he had stayed at home?—*Stockton Independent.*

Ernest Weldon of Vacaville the other day lost an index finger by the accidental discharge of his gun when in the act of loading it while out hunting.

Feathered game of all kinds is said to be plentiful in Honey Lake.

Bears are numerous and fat in Shasta county.

Sheep Farming.—The Willamette *Farmer* gives us the following of interest, not only to the people of Umatilla County, but also to those in this section: The greatest sheep range in Eastern Oregon is found in Western Umatilla county, along the base of the Blue Mountains, and all through these mountains. John Q. Wilson, formerly a resident of Salem, and in late years in Eastern Oregon, where he has been stock-raising for twenty years, now has a sheep range east of Heppner, and the other day gave us interesting particulars of his methods and success. Last spring he had 1,850 ewes, that brought him 1,700 lambs. It was a fortunate year, as he did not feed at all during the winter, and the wool yield was good. The grass came up early in the spring, lambing time was April, and lambs and ewes did well. Shearing came in May, and after paying for shearing and transporting to market, where he sold at 24 cents, he realized a full average of $1 50 per head from his wool, which gave him plenty of means to handle himself. After shearing, the sheep were driven into the mountains. The sheep and the small presses that come up very thickly through all the foot-hills; when these dry up, as happens early in the summer, the mountains are near by, and afford green grasses and tempting browse all summer. Mr. Wilson says you must put flesh on your sheep in June and July to make a success of it; so, when the foot-hill grasses begin to dry he divides his sheep in bands of 1,600, putting an experienced herder with a band of that number, and they start by easy stages, driving a few miles every day, until they get to their customary range.

Late in the autumn, about the middle of November, says the Union *Herald*, there were 35,000 boxes of cheese unsold in the northern part of the State, and 75,000 to 80,000 among the combinations in western New York. To-day, both of these regions are practically bare of cheese, and the same is true of the central part of the State. Much cheese placed in October than ever before. The result is that first-class stock not only is scarce, but is going to be more so.

In feeding sweet milk to pigs, trials made at the Wisconsin experiment farm showed that on an average four pounds of corn meal were equal to twenty pounds of sweet skim milk, if fed separately.

# THE KENNEL.

## Dog Dealing.

The breeding and sale of dogs of all varieties has within the last few years become an extensive if not lucrative business. The great increase in the number of sportsmen has brought a corresponding increase in the demand for good field dogs, and the requirements of fashion, capricious in this respect as in all else, have opened a large market for the sale of non-sporting dogs.

Scarcely a decade ago, the gentlemen who would have charged a friend or brother sportsman a money price for a puppy from his favorite bitch would have lost caste. Dog dealers of the olden time were not sportsmen, and the business was confined to a class that neither sought or expected recognition as gentlemen, while he who would have asked or received pay for the services of a fine dog would have been ostracized at once. In those days the owner of a well-bred bitch at whelping time was so much more fortunate than his brother sportsmen in having puppies to give his friends; no thought of their sale ever entered his mind. And this condition applied not alone to sporting dogs, but to the non-sporting as well.

This is all changed. We do not mean to assert that dogs are no longer presented by one friend to another, but only what was once the rule is now the exception, and he who makes such a gift at the present day intends it as a mark of high esteem, or it is the natural outcome of a close and friendly intimacy between the donor and receiver. As a rule, he who desires to possess a well-bred dog goes into the market as a purchaser, and pays a good round price, whether he buys from friend or stranger. And why should this not be so ? Me seldom give away pedigreed horses, and not often do we hear of fine cattle changing owners except by barter or sale; then why should sportsmen donate well-bred puppies with a fixed market value to a chance acquaintance or as a neighborly act ? We may sigh at the recollection of the antient liberality of the past, especially if we lack canine ownership, but we can hardly expect neighbor Jones, who is fortunate enough to own a well-bred bitch, to invite us over to take the pick of the litter at weaning time.

Dogs of the present day have a market value as well settled and determined as a racer, a trotter, a Shorthorn or a Hereford. Their numbers have increased an hundredfold over a period of twenty years ago, but the demand has more than kept pace with it. Breeding kennels are established in every state in the Union, and a large amount of capital is invested in them. Pedigrees are registered, and studied with a view to the improvement of the variety which it pleases the breeder to fancy, and large stud fees are paid to secure the services of some noted dog. These customs existed not in the olden time, neither would they to-day but for demand for the produce.

We have said that dog dealers of the olden time were not sportsmen. We write of them as a class. We do not say that all dog dealers of the present day are sportsmen, but we do believe a large majority are. A gentleman can now offer the services of a fine dog in the public stud and still retain his right to move in polite circles; he may advertise a litter of well-bred puppies for sale without forfeiting his claims to gentility, and as a result of this change from the old order of things we find gentlemen engaged in the business.

It is in this fact that the public which buys dogs finds its protection. A sportsman in Oregon desires to purchase a dog, and after deciding upon what he wishes, finds that a gentleman east of the Rocky mountains, possibly in the far East, advertises for sale a dog of the exact variety or breeding he has decided to buy. He has never seen this dealer, has no knowledge of his character, but finding his advertisements in a reputable journal takes it for granted that he must be all right, opens a correspondence, makes a purchase, receives the dog, and ninety-nine times in a hundred is perfectly satisfied. Distance is no obstacle since gentlemen commenced to deal in dogs, and the purchase or sale of one is as legitimate a transaction as the buying or selling of a horse.

Of course it is to be expected that one will find dishonest dog dealers, as well as rascals in every other business. There are dog sharps as there are horse sharps, but they soon become known and their occupation ceases. The opportunities afforded by bench shows and field trials for sportsmen from different sections who deal in dogs to become acquainted are availed of largely, and he who would perpetrate a swindle can be readily detected and exposed. It is worthy of note that but few such cases have occurred, although the transactions between parties unacquainted with each other have been numerous, and have involved thousands of dollars. It needs but the exercise of the same amount of judgment and common sense used in any other business event, to avoid loss by swindling in this. Deal only with well-known, reputable dealers, and one is no more likely to be swindled in buying dogs than in purchasing dry goods, groceries or hardware.

A PLACE FOR COURSING.—Referring to the capital sport of coursing, Mr. H. W. Huntington, of Brooklyn, New York, owner of the famous greyhounds Doubleshot, Dorothea and Clio, makes the following suggestions, which we heartily indorse: "If some plan could be adopted to induce a number of our prominent sportsmen to take up coursing as a pastime, I believe as great an interest would be awakened in it as is now felt in field trials—probably more, for the scoring of points is not only much easier understood by the general public, but the hares are quicker and more sprightly. The few who own greyhounds in the East are content, as it seems, to keep their dogs like French poodles, and let them rest idle instead of giving the necessary exercise to show their mettle." This is too true of sportsmen in the East, and we would suggest to Mr. Huntington the advisability of arranging a public coursing match as a sure method of arousing the latent enthusiasm of the thousands in Gotham and the City of Churches who need but witness an event of this kind to become convinced of the rare enjoyment which it affords.

A VALUABLE SETTER POISONED.—Mr. Emory F. Robinson, of Sydney, Ohio, in a letter bearing date of November 27, announces the death of his pure white setter bitch Queen Blanche, a fine worker on game, thoroughly ruffed grouse. Queen Blanche was a remarkably handsome dog, gentle, intelligent and thoroughly broken, and the fact that her death was caused by a malicious wretch, using poison, renders the loss doubly great. We hope that an example may be made of this poisoning fiend, in order to deter other human brutes of murderous instincts from perpetrating outrages of this kind, which are lamentably frequent.—Turf, Field and Farm.

Charles Lincoln has been chosen Superintendent of the Bench Show which will be held next March. The Princess Louise is grand patroness of the show.

## Coursing Etiquette.

The Sacramento Valley Coursing Club had a match a few days since, which was won by Lane's Blue Jacket, Welsh's Nelly second, Sally third. The principal feature of the match was the abuse showered on the judge for his rulings. It is a most painful fact to record that this practice of abusing judges at coursing matches is becoming so common as to be monotonous. It must be stopped or coursing will cease to be a popular California sport, and the thousands of dollars invested in fine dogs will be so much wasted coin. Whether a judge is right or wrong, whether his decision was based on fraud or favor or honestly given, it makes no difference. The duty alike of contestants and spectators is to hold their peace and make a formal protest in a proper manner, if they so desire.

"What, see ourselves robbed and not kick?" will be the exclamation of a dozen coursing men when they read this.

We most emphatically repeat that unless a man can see himself defrauded by a palpably unjust decision without making a fuss on the field and abusing the judge he lacks the essential quality of a gentleman's character, and the sooner he gives up coursing the better for the sport. We have seen decisions given that were palpably unjust, and the men who made them knew it as well as any one, but they happened to be in favor of the loud-voiced kickers, and the disgusted sufferers, being gentlemen, quietly withdrew from the field. We have seen an honest decision excite the wrath of some fellow who did not know the first thing about coursing, and have heard him roundly abuse the judge and denounce the sport as a steal, but we have always noticed that the vulgar kickers were men ignorant of the sport or totally deficient themselves in personal honesty. In nine cases out of ten it happens that the only man who sees the race from end to end is the judge, but the fact that they only saw half of the race never seems to deter the kickers from loudly swearing that the decision was wrong. There is another noticeable thing about the kickers. They are all men whose circumstances do not warrant their indulgence in an expensive sport like coursing and who bet on the matches more than they can afford to lose. We have seen such men bet three months' earnings on a dog and when they lost, and lost fairly, howl and scream that the judge was a thief and their opponent a scoundrel. There is a way to remedy this and at the same time put the sport on its proper basis. Let those gentlemen who can lose without kicking and who follow the sport for its own sake, get together and organize a club. Let them take more than ordinary care in the selection of a judge. It is not enough that a man be a good fellow, he must be a good rider and above all a good judge of coursing. Let the club promptly expel any man who openly impugns the judge's decision and take care to accept no nomination in open races that does not come from a man they know will respect himself and the club and abide by the judge's decision.

## Hare and Hounds.

This is how the Turf, Field and Farm writes up the meets of the Germantown Hare and Hounds Club.

It was a beautiful day for a hunt when the Germantown Hare and Hound Club met on Saturday, the 25th inst., at Walthamowes for its sixth "meet" this year. It was cool enough to make the trail hot, and hot for the few redcoats it was the best hunt of the season. Vixen and Drama had been led from the stables to the "meet," and at 3:40, when their blankets were taken off, they not only shone like new-coined gold pieces, but looked as if they could run for a man's life. At 3:40 the hares, E. and S. M. Waln, the former Vixen, the latter on Drama, started, and the first jump was a tense, then came a four-foot cedar hedge, then another fence, down a field, across a wafer jump, over a stiff fence and then back to the first jump again (the hedge) and away, all the jumps to be seen by those present. Three minutes later the hounds (?), three in number, started, and they were Mr. Smith on Rostante, Dr. Bray on Wait-a-While and Mr. Wilson on Hamlet. After taking the above jump, they, too, were away. The trail led over the fine farms of Messrs. Cook, Jones, Fisher and Emory, and, as heretofore, the hounds always stopped riding on account of the four-foot stiff timber, but as all the jumps were low and a good "take-off" was to be had it is a pity the hounds could not make a better show than they did, as it was understood the jumps were to be low and on that account there were many carriages, including Victorias, barouches, dog-carts and one tandem team. After a run of seven miles the hares made their reappearance and after taking two more fences galloped up the stretch, and as these two were blanketed to the eyes it was seen that neither was distressed. After ten minutes' waiting the hounds came in sight, and from the looks of things it recalled the picture of the monkey and parrot that had been left alone or, in other words, "had one"—or a time." Rosinante was over the jump first, coming into the meet field, then Wait-a-While, while Hamlet carried it away; at this time Mr. S. led ten lengths, with Wait-a-While second, but coming over the last leap Mr. S. was last. So when they turned into the finish Dr. Bray led (both feet out of the stirrups), Smith second, but about four lengths from the flag; Mr. S. sat down on his horse, and coming on, won by an open length from Wait-a-While, while Hamlet was last, that horse's rider also having broken his irons. As this was Drama's last hunt, and to settle a bet that he could not jump a stiff four-barred fence, Mr. Waln told his man to ride him over it, and right well did Daniel Green do it, for starting in a bad "take-off" Drama took it and cleared the space of 25 feet 8 inches, carrying 160 pounds. Too much can't be said for the riding of Green, and he was well applauded. We are sorry to learn that this is the last hunt to be had at the above-named place, but when so few turn out we are not surprised, for it does not pay one for going to the farmers and getting their leave to trespass. The next meet is at Glen Echo, on Thanksgiving Day, but cattle ground is white at this writing it may be off. There is some talk of getting over some English hounds and starting a kennel, but as there are so few gentlemen in our city to enjoy the sport, it is not known if it will be done.

SALE OF THE POINTER BITCH SPINAWAY.—Mr. John W. Munson, of St. Louis, has recently purchased of Mr. E. C. Sterling, the valuable pointer bitch, Spinaway, by Garnet out of Ranene, the litter sister purchased by the St. Louis Kennel Club at a cost of $500 in England. Spinaway is a very handsome and stylish bitch, thoroughly broken by Mr. B. Walters, and it is Mr. Munson's intention to breed her to Costeth. She is the only Garnet bitch in America, and Mr. Pilkington refused an offer of $2,500 for her sire.

# FISH.

## Disgusted Long Island Trouters.

Trouting on Long Island has had its praises chanted for many years and although we long wanted to try our luck it was not until last spring that our wishes were gratified. Fishing then (in the latter part of May) was poor in Pike county, Pa., so our party made a sudden move, on the afternoon of the 29th of May, and we soon arrived at Freeport, L. I.

After leaving our luggage at the hotel we took a stroll to get our bearings, and after supper were entertained with legends of the glories of neighboring streams. Legends they certainly must be, and extremely ancient at that, if ours was the usual luck of Long Island anglers. At daybreak the next morning we were afoot and on our way towards a neighboring "free" stream, so called to distinguish it from the many preserves in the vicinity.

Our party (four in number) covered the stream thoroughly, each man taking a certain section for his ground. As we struggled in to breakfast the score was taken, and showed the vast catch of five fingerling trout, all taken on summerchug bait, and from a stream that we, brought up on the banks of Maine's rocky, brawling brooks, deemed worthy only of catfish, suckers, and such trash. It was almost stagnant, with a muddy bottom, and absolutely impenetrable to one using a fly-rod. At table, however, our spirits were soothed and our hopes raised by promises of what was to come when we reached a free pond some five miles distant.

We bundled our traps in the wagon and started. The drive was certainly a beautiful one, and that may have restored our feelings somewhat unduly; however, "pride goeth before a fall," and what difference is it if the fall be a few feet more or less! On reaching the pond we found a detachment of the all-pervading small boy busily engaged in taking some very minute "minnies" in out of the wet. Adjusting what we considered a killing east of flies, we flung them boldly forth upon the waters, with all the delicacy and skill that laid in us: Not a rise. Perhaps, we thought, the flies do not suit the monarch (so called) of Long Island. Thereupon we changed our cast and tried again. Not a rise. And we kept changing until the resources of our fly-book were exhausted. The result was the same, so we fell back upon the long-suffering summerchug, and adopted the ways of the country (in Rome, you know, and all that) and fished.

Now, to some it may be the ultima thule of trout angling to throw over a hook and wait fifteen or twenty minutes for a bite, but for our part we prefer ours straight without any such mixture. By this time it was nearly noon, so we adjourned for lunch, and this was the greatest success of the day, for there we did get a splendid lot of bites at least. One of our number, known to you as Q——, (when essayed fishing from a boat, and glorious luck was his. For he caught three—remember the score, please—three pickerel, the combined weight of which might have been half a pound. Ye gods! what ecstasy was this! how great was his pride! We could only faintly imagine his beastified state when we heard him softly murmuring "he wondered how a man could get trout when such d. d. sharks were in the pond."

As the trout taken numbered about ten we separated, half the party trying another locality, and the rest going to a preserve where trout may be taken at the moderate cost of $1 per pound. Preserve fishing is not our weakness, and we stayed here just long enough to catch a dozen fish. On our return to Freeport we found the grand total to be thirty-nine trout, one of which (taken in the brook) weighed one and a quarter pounds. What a splendid showing for a full day's work for four full-grown men! We have never dared to figure the cost of each and every one of those trout. But when we go again we think it will be more profitable to buy outright a few ounces on the island. We have had our fling. We are satisfied. We are now prepared to drink in the most thrilling experiences of trouting on Long Island, fond without laying awake at night thinking of its charms, and without the slightest loss of appetite when we cannot participate in the mad sport.—Carleton in the American Angler.

LUKE FOR CATFISH.—"I saw in your paper some time ago an item in regard to catfish biting at a spoon-hook. I was fishing for bass a number of years ago, and had a catfish jump out of the water at my trolling spoon. The fish weighed not less than fifteen pounds. As you expressed a desire for information in this respect through your ever valuable journal, I give my individual experience." The above, from a correspondent of the Turf, Field and Farm, is only equaled by that taking of a catfish by Mr. Joseph Wilcox with a fly, which however, was done by trailing the cast about six feet under water. A "catty" springing out of water to take a lure, places the species in the order of game fishes.—Angler.

VITALITY OF THE TROUT.—The following from the American Angler shows strongly the marvelous vitality of the trout. The incident happened at Glenn's Falls, N. Y.: Recently there was a break in one of the street mains of the village water works. Upon digging down to break the, workmen found a brook trout of eight ounces, that had come through the ragged hole in the pipe. The trout was apparently as well as when he left the reservoir, 152 feet above the broken pipe. The pressure on the pipe where his troutship made his exit is 108 lbs. to the inch. The reservoir was one of the finest trout streams in the State.

An Eastern farmer, who has a half acre pond filled with fine fish in a permanent pasture, remarked that is paid in three ways: The water, being always accessible, was worth more to his cows than if the half acre was in grass; the fish were worth as much as the produce of any half acre on his farm; and, finally, the pond yielded an ice crop every winter. The pond stocked with gold fish and bullhead.

Brook trout take perfectly naturally to salt water. Some of the largest and finest trout ever shown in New York have been Long Island trout, the best of which run up from the ocean. Even in Connecticut those streams which empty into Long Island Sound furnish the largest trout that are caught in the state.—Boston Cultivator.

Two more specimens of the angel fish were taken last week by Italian fishermen off the Farallones. Both are large specimens, some three feet in length. They seem to belong to the family of skates.

Salmon trout are reported to be running the Olema creek. Salmon creek, however, has been closed by a sand bar. The water is too low to force its way through, and the fish cannot enter.

A good many boats were out after flounders at Brooklyn last Sunday, but luck was not very good, although the day was a fine one.

Off the training walls of Oakland Creek there are ⠆ that ought to furnish good fishing.

A FISHY FISH STORY.—It is related of a Chinese fisherman that not long ago he was angling in Napa river and joined up some small fish on his line. In extracting it from the hook, with mouth wide open, at the moment it was released it flopped head first into his open mouth. The Chinaman made a desperate thrust to get it out and shoved the fish further down his throat. He closed his jaws and smothered it to death, but afterwards, when attempting to get it from his mouth, the spines in its fins and along the back would be erected and present an impediment he could not overcome. In his desperation he sought the advice of his fellow-Mongolians, who concluded as the fish would not come out it must go in, and they forced it down his throat.—*Napa Reporter, Dec. 13.*

It is not known by what route the salmon come in to the shore to the Columbia river though it is conjectured that they enter up some small fish on his line. In extracting it from the spring runs gradually make their way up towards the upper tributaries. The summer runs proceed more rapidly, a large proportion of both reaching the very headwaters of the river. The fall run of salmon do not ascend so high, but frequently spawn on the sand-beds of the main river within fifty miles of the sea. The salmon do not follow a stated track every year in ascending the river, but one year they will take one course and another year a different one. Neither do they adhere to the same course during any specified year, but sometimes ascend the current and sometimes keep near the banks. A very strong current, however, they seem in the lower river to uniformly avoid.

The salmon make their first appearance off the Columbia in February, though in very small numbers. The main body arrives in May, June, and especially in July, when the run is enormous. The May salmon are largest. Perhaps the most correct view to take of the running of the salmon, is to consider all the salmon as included in one run, beginning in February, increasing in May and June, and culminating in July, though they might also be legitimately divided into three runs: The first or meager run coming in February, March and April; the second or full run in June; and the third or maximum run in July. After July they diminish very rapidly and soon almost entirely disappear from the river.

Water which has been used by factories is generally warm, and contains refuse of different kinds, such as lime, coloring matter, alkaline salts, remnants of plants, slime, etc. It will be evident that large quantities of such refuse will pollute rivers and brooks to such a degree as to render pisciculture impossible, and to make the water unfit to be used by either man or beast. An investigation of our smaller rivers and brooks would furnish proof of the growth and magnitude of this evil, and show the necessity of relief.

The George Crooks creek flows into the McCloud river about four miles above the Government fish hatchery, and it is there experiments are being made in propagating the California brook trout.

## Late Gunning Items.

A new shooting club called the Metropolitan Gun Club has been formed in this city. The members are negotiating for grounds at Alviso where there is said to be good shooting most of the season. The officers are as follows: President, Thomas Watson; Vice President, Thomas Ryan; Secretary, Walter E. Roche; Treasurer, P. Bodien; Directors, Aug. Ott, Wm. Oliver and Henry Grace. Those officers, who were elected on the 8th, will serve one year.

A friend of ours killed some white geese the other day up at Bouldin Island and left them on the marsh while he went on further in pursuit of game. When he came back two hours afterwards he found four vultures and a number of crows had taken possession of them and had two entirely eaten up. Two vultures were going in on the third. It seems unusual for vultures to go for fresh meat, in this way.

The ducks have been out in the big bays of late. They seem to understand enough of the hunters' habits to get out of the way of the ponds except after dark. When the day breaks they have flown away to the big bays where no one could get at them. The old ponds therefore are rather too vacant to please the hunters.

Lots of amateurs have been popping away at the unfortunate birds which have been foolish enough to come into Oakland creek to feed. There are very few good hunters among them and shots are fired so carelessly that the wonder is that no one has been shot.

So far this season has been a bad one from a duck hunter's point of view. The birds have not been plentiful, and they have learned to stay away further out of range than they used to. At least that is what some of the unsuccessful hunters say.

The ducks get out in the middle of the San Joaquin river these windless days and there float along down in large numbers, but no one can get near them. They fly very little.

A good many hunters spend their Sundays on the bay marshes between Alameda and Alviso. They are scattered all along where the railroad stations are convenient.

The old Iron House slough, on the San Joaquin, where there used to be free shooting, is now no longer visited. The land has been leased and the ponds have dried up.

Fred Butler shot thirty-five ducks at Teal station last Sunday, and twenty-three of them were "cans." The shooting up there has not been good of late.

The doves all along the main bay and the San Pablo bay seems to be filled with ducks. They seem to be scattered all along and sometimes in big flocks.

Some young men camped out on the San Leandro marsh last Saturday night so as to be near the ducks early Sunday morning.

Even at the preserved grounds this year there has been no very exciting sport such as there used to be.

Several new boats have been sent up to Union Island lately for the gentlemen who shoot up there.

We have heard no good reports from the Wayberry slough neighborhood this season.

The shooting on Sherman Island has not been up to the mark this season.

Prince's race with Morgan is now arranged to take place at the Institute Fair Building, December 9. The race will be for twenty miles, and Prince will allow his opponent two minutes' start. The stakes are announced as $250 a side.

## BASE BALL.

### Next Year's Team—Sketches of the Players.

From the following, which we copy from the New York *Herald*, some idea can be obtained of the rapid strides the "National game," has made in the last twenty years.

Forty years ago to have predicted that a "pitcher" or "catcher" could obtain a salary of $3,000 for the months embracing the season would have laid the prophet liable to a charge of lunacy. Had such a vaticination been made on the village green during the pending of one of the old-time matches, the seer would have raised a torrent of ridicule which the bravest would have shrunk from.

There was lively work in these old-fashioned games. On court or "general training" days, especially the latter, the Square would be crowded. The country champions would try conclusions with those of the town, and among the hills of Northern Pennsylvania there was no lack of strength and agility among the hardy youngsters. Lacking in the scientific phases of the present game, there was more life, more animation. The catcher would grip the ball before the striker could make the blow, the "throwers" hurl it so swift that it fairly whizzed through the air. Woolen yarn wound tightly round a cork, covered with woodchuck skin without being as large or as dense as the regulation, there was weight enough to permit its being thrown with precision, and then there had to be a "catch" or a "hit," and when the latter came fairly on the but of the ear there would be some ground if not lofty tumbling.

The old-time sports are things of the past, and though us old fellows with gray hair, and somewhat stiffened joints, may cherish the remembrance, the youngsters will vote that such crude ball-play was poor fun:

New York city will next season for the first time in the history of base ball place a representative professional team in the field to compete for the championship of the League. The Metropolitan club was organized on the 15th of September, 1880. They were exceedingly successful during the remainder of the season, playing almost daily up to the close of October. Their wonderful success, especially financially, led to their going into base ball more extensively the following season, when they surpassed all previous records by games played, they playing 151 games during the season, winning 80 and losing 69. The season of 1881 was also highly remunerative; in fact, it was so much so that the management of the club leased the ground at a rental of $10,000 per annum, in addition to which they erected a grand stand and free open seats, which cost $10,000. This gave the ground a seating capacity of about seven thousand. That portion of the ground immediately in front of the new grand stand was filled in and graded and the diamond changed. That nine for 1882 cost them about $12,000, and yet, in spite of all this enormous expense, over $70,000 were taken. After such a financial season as this Mr. John B. Day, the president of the Metropolitan Exhibition Company, has determined to give the New York public as fine a team as could possibly be gotten together for the campaign of 1883. There are better men in the field than some of the players engaged by the Metropolitans, but those are men who could not be reached this season. Money, however, was not spared in getting the present team together, and most likely it will be the highest salaried base ball team which has ever entered the arena, some of the men receiving over $3,000 apiece.

The following is a brief sketch of the men engaged as New York representatives in the League:

John M. Ward, who will, no doubt, have the heavy end of the pitching, is a heavy batter and one of the finest base runners in the country. In addition to his great power of manipulating the ball. He is also an excellent outfielder and a fine third baseman. Ward was born in Bellefonte, Centre county, Pa., in 1860. His height is 5 feet 8 inches and he weighs 150 pounds. He learned to play base ball while a student at the Pennsylvania State Agricultural College. On the college nine he changed between pitcher and third base-men. In 1876 and 1877 he played with semi-professional teams at Lock Haven, Renovo and Williamsport in his native State. His first engagement with a professional organization was in July, 1877, when he played a few games with the Athletics and Philadelphias, in the Quaker City. In August, 1877, he went to Janesville, Wis., and played with the Mutuals of that place until they disbanded in September. He finished the season with the Buffalos. During the early part of 1878 he played with the Crickets of Binghamton. When they disbanded in July he joined the Providence club, where he remained until the close of the season of 1882. Michael Welch, who will alternate with Ward in the pitcher's box, is an old Brooklynite. He is 5 feet 9 inches high, and weighs 160 pounds. In 1877 he played with the Volunteers, of Poughkeepsie; in 1878 with the Auburn and Holyoke clubs, and with the Troy club in 1880, 1881 and 1882. James E. O'Neil, who met with such wonderful success last season in the few games he pitched, has been retained another year. He has great speed, and was just beginning to have good command of the ball when he got a frog-bitten on his hand and was laid up the remainder of the season. O'Neil was born in Woodstock, Canada, and during the season of 1877, 1878, 1879 and 1880 played with the Actives of his native place. For several weeks in the beginning of the season of 1881 he played with the Detroit club. William Ewing, late of the Troy club, has been engaged to alternate with Clapp behind the bat, and when he is not catching he will have to cover second base. Ewing is one of the finest general players in the country, whence the great demand for his services this fall. He will undoubtedly be of great service next season. Ewing began to play ball as a professional in 1878. During that season and 1879 he played with the Mohawk Browns, champions of the southern part of Ohio. In the early part of 1880 he played with the Buck-eyes, of Cincinnati. In June of that year, however, he joined the Rochester club, where he remained until the following September, when he signed with the Troy club. He is 5 feet 10 inches high and weighs 176 pounds. He is a native of Cincinnati.

John Clapp, who caught so ably for the Metropolitans during the past season, will alternate with Ewing. Clapp has had many years' experience in base ball playing. He commenced playing in 1866 in Ithaca, his native village, with the Forest City club of that place, as an outfielder. In 1867 he pitched for the same club. He received his first salary for playing ball in 1868 and 1869, when he played with the In-

dependent club of Mansfield, Ohio, where he alternated as catcher and pitcher. In 1870, he budded forth as a short stop, playing that position with the Amateur club, of Oswego, New York. He caught for the Clippers of Ilion, N. Y. In 1872 he caught for the Mansfields, of Middletown, Conn., which was his first professional engagement. The Athletic club, of Philadelphia, secured his services during the season of 1873, 1874, and 1875. He accompanied the Athletic-Boston clubs on their famous tour to Europe in 1874. When the League was organized, in 1876, Clapp was engaged by the St. Louis Brown Stockings, who retained him until the close of 1877, paying him the highest salary ever given a ball player prior to the coming season—i. e., $3,000. He managed and captained the Cincinnati club in 1878, and did the same for Buffalo association in 1879. He captained the Cincinnati club on their California trip during the winter of 1879-80, and continued with them during the season of 1880. He captained and caught for the Cleveland club in 1881 and the Metropolitans in 1882. He is 5 feet 8 inches in height and weighs 190 pounds.

John Reilly, who played first base for the Metropolitans last season, has been engaged to fill that important post in the League team next season. Reilly was born and lived the most of his time in Cincinnati. His first experience at playing ball was with the Crickets, in 1877, a Cincinnati amateur club. He continued with amateur clubs until the fall of 1879, when the Cincinnati club engaged him as a substitute to accompany the club to San Francisco. In 1880 he was engaged to play first base for the Cincinnati League club. He is a lithographer and worked at his trade in 1881, with the exception of a few games he played during the summer for pleasure. He played first base in brilliant style last season for the Metropolitans. He is 6 feet 1½ inches high, and weighs 175 pounds.

John Troy, who at times plays most brilliantly, has been secured for second base. Troy hails from this city, is about 5 feet 5 inches in height and weighs 155 pounds. His first experience in a semi-professional club was with the Alaskas of this city in 1877. During the season of 1878 and 1879 he covered second base very acceptably for the Jersey City clubs. The Dubuque Club of Dubuque, Iowa, secured his services in 1880. In the early part of the season of 1881 he played with the Atlantics of Brooklyn. He secured his release and joined the Albany Club, and after they disbanded he joined the Detroits, with whom he closed the season. During the past season he played with the Detroits, Providence and Metropolitans.

Frank Hankinson has been re-engaged to cover third base, in which position he has few equals and no superiors. Hankinson was born in this city, where he has lived nearly all his life. He is 5 feet 11 inches high and weighs 160 pounds. His base ball career dates from the days of the Alaska Jr.'s, when they played in Central Park. The Alaskas came out as an amateur team in 1875. He continued with them until 1878, when he joined the Chicagos and remained with them until the close of 1879. He played with the Clevelands in 1880 and joined the Troys in 1881.

Edward J. Caskin has been secured as short stop, and a better short stop can scarcely be found. He was born in Danvers, Mass., where he spent the greater portion of his life. He is 5 feet 9½ inches in height and weighs 160 pounds. His first appearance on the ball field was with the General Scott Jr. club, of Danvers, Mass. He continued with them until the close of 1875, when he joined the Live Oaks of Lynn, Mass., and caught for them until they disbanded, in August, 1876, when he joined the Auburn club for the remainder of the season. He went to Rochester in 1877 and in fifty-four games that he played as catcher accepted ninety per cent. of chances offered. He played forty-six games with bases on third baseman and ranked second in that position in the International Association. In 1878 he played short stop for the Rochester club until they disbanded in August, when he joined the Troys and finished the season as catcher. In 1879 he played as utility man for the Troys, playing in every position on the nine but pitcher. In 1880 and 1881 he played short stop for the Troys.

P. Gillespie, the left fielder of the Troy club, has been engaged to play left field for the Metropolitans. He has been playing ball since 1875, when he made his debut with the Carbondale club, where his heavy batting brought him into prominence. In 1876 he played with the Honesdale club and with the Wilkesbarres in 1877. He was rather on the go in 1879, dividing the season up between the Live Oaks of Lynn, Mass., the Worcesters and Baltimores. In 1879 he played with the Holyoke club, who were dubbed the "heavy hitters," owing to their fine heavy left-handed batsman, all being exceedingly heavy hitters. Gillespie was born in Carbondale, Pa. He is 6 feet 1½ inches in height and weighs 180 pounds.

Roger Connor, the famous first baseman of the Troy club, has been engaged to play center field and alternate with Reilly at first base. Connor was born in Waterbury, Conn. He is 6 feet 2 inches high and weighs 194 pounds. His base ball career dates back to 1876, when he made his first appearance on the ball field with the amateur Monitors of Waterbury, with whom he played until the close of 1877. He played the first part of the season of 1878 with the New Bedfords and finished the season with the Holyokes. He re-engaged with the Holyokes until the close of the season of 1879. Ferguson secured him for the Troy team in 1880, and he remained with them until the close of the present season. Michael C. Dorgan, who has been engaged to go right field, is a remarkably clever player. He made his debut as a ball player in 1874, with the Clippers of Webster, Mass. The following season he joined the Graftons of Grafton, Mass. During the latter part of the season he played with the Live Oaks of Lynn, Mass. He played in such fine form with the Live Oaks that the Stars of Syracuse engaged him for the season of 1876. His brilliant playing attracted universal notice, and he was induced to join the St. Louis Brown Stockings in 1877. When the St. Louis club withdrew from the League in the fall of 1878 Dorgan joined the Stars of Syracuse, and played with them during the seasons of 1878 and 1879. He played with the Providence club in 1880. In the early part of 1881 he played with the Worcesters and closed the season with the Detroits. He did not play during the season of 1882. Dorgan was born in Middletown, Conn., is 5 feet 9½ inches high and weighs 186 pounds.

The game between the St. Mary's College club and the Redingtons Sunday, at the grounds of the College Club, resulted in a victory for the students, by a score of 11 to 4. The Redingtons were short two of their best men—Evatt and Lewis—and to this they attribute their defeat.

The game between the Howards and the Olympics on the 10th resulted in a victory for the Howards by a score of 15 to 14.

### The Sweeney Benefit.

The game between the reorganized Nationals and a picked

for the benefit of Sweeney, the Niantic pitcher, last ay at the Recreation Grounds resulted in the following

| PICKED NINE. | | | | | NATIONALS. | | | | |
|---|---|---|---|---|---|---|---|---|---|
| | TR. R. | B.H. | P.O. | A. E. | | TR. | R. | B.H. | P.O. A. E. |
| ..r f.... | 4 | 2 | 2 | 0 | Sohr, l f.... | 4 | 0 | 0 | 1 0 0 |
| lat b..... | 4 | 1 | 1 | 0 | Levy, c f.. | 3 | 1 | 0 | 3 0 1 |
| , s s..... | 4 | 0 | 1 | 2 | Morris, 3d b | 3 | 0 | 2 | 0 0 0 |
| 'ss, 3d b.. | 4 | 0 | 0 | 1 | Meegan, p.. | 3 | 1 | 1 | 3 3 0 |
| , and Law- | | | | | Carroll, s s | 3 | 0 | 1 | 6 3 3 |
| . n..... | 4 | 0 | 0 | 0 | F, Carroll, c | 3 | 0 | 0 | 2 1 0 |
| cery, p... | 4 | 3 | 2 | 0 | Moagna, r f.. | 3 | 0 | 0 | 0 0 0 |
| dale, 2d b. | 3 | 2 | 1 | 5 | Lawton and lr- | | | | |
| c f...... | 3 | 2 | 0 | 0 | vin, r f.... | 3 | 2 | 0 | 1 0 0 |
| c, l f..... | 3 | 2 | 1 | 0 | Pratt, 1st b.. | 3 | 1 | 1 | 4 0 9 |
| Totals..33 | | 11 | 7 | 14 12 4 | Totals...36 | | 4 | 7 | 21 6 13 |

one run—Sweeney. Three-base hit—Denny. Two-base hit—F cll, Brown. Firstoh balls—Nationals 3, Picked Nine 1. First on er—Nationals 1. Picked Nine 7. Struck out—Nationals 6, Picked Nine eft on bases—Nationals 7, Picked Nine 8.

## ATHLETICS.

### Crossley Defeats McQuigan.

he sprint-race between John T. Crossley of Philadelphia Frank McQuigan of Boston, for a stake of $800, which has a week past excited the attention of those interested in h affairs, took place Tuesday, the 5th inst., on the Polo unds, New York. This race was the first professional int-race that had taken place in this city since the All-ted-States Handicap, given on the same grounds in just, 1881, and this, together with the reputations of the men, induced a number of sporting men to attend. The ditions of the race were that the men were to race 120 da, the start to be by mutual consent from a fifteen-foot stch, and in case of no start being effected in an hour they uld be sent off by a pistol start. It was 3:55 o'clock when men were called to their marks, McQuigan having the in-i position. The betting was five to four on Crossley, and rge amount of money changed hands at these figures. hen the men got on their marks, they immediately made orts to make a start. After five or six breakaways, Cros-told the referee that he caught McQuigan over his mark, d claimed the stakes. This claim was not allowed, and erfour more breakaways the men went over the line to an an start, running side by side for fifty yards. At the one ndred yard post Crossley had a lead of a yard and crossed l line an easy winner by five feet in 13¼ seconds. This is w the best professional record for the distance in the coun-, and is at the very fast rate of 10:09 seconds for one hun-ed yards. As the additional thirty yards brings a much avier strain, the performance has greater merit than one indred yards in ten seconds.

THE AMERICAN RECORD LOWERED.—At the Manhattan Ath-ic club games as New York on the 12th George, the English ampion amateur runner, was defeated in a ten-mile race by .homas Delaney. Delaney had a start of three minutes, and ron by three minutes and fifty-eight seconds. Delaney's ime to-night beats the best previous American record, which ras 57 minutes 20 1-5 seconds. George's best time is 52 inutes 56 2-5 seconds. George is regarded as out of form. flyers, the American champion, won the half-mile run in :01 4-5.

A dispatch of the 13th from Nevada City says: C. A. Har-iman, the champion long-distance walker of the world, now n route to Australia to race with William Edwards, is here, nd will enter a match Friday evening in this city with A. S. hase, a local runner, for a twenty-seven-hour contest. The takes are $100 a side, the gate money to go to the winner. he conditions are that Harriman walks square heel-and-toe, rhile Chase goes as he pleases. The latter has no record be-ond recently making fifty-five miles in eleven hours.

Puyallup Valley, in Washington Territory, located about an miles east of Tacoma, is the great hop producing section f the Pacific Coast, and, I believe, of the United States. This rear there is a hop famine in Europe, and as a consequence he price has advanced four to five hundred per cent. The op growers of Puyallup are in high clover, so to speak—some f them clearing fifty thousand dollars on their crop. Before he picking season opened, they sent a messenger up the oast to notify the Indians of an advance in the price of pick-ng hops, for all the hop picking is done by Indians. This relcome news had the effect of bringing Siwashes from the orthern part of British Columbia, and when we were pass-ng from Tacoma to Seattle, the Sound was completely dotted rith their canoes, all heading for Tacoma. Each canoe con-ained from two (buck and squaw) to a dozen—children of all ges, occasionally a dog or two—in fact, the whole outfit, ousehold goods, gods and possessions of the family. Many f the canoes were loaded down almost to the water's dge. They live in these canoes by day, stopping at night on he shore at any convenient spot, cook a salmon, then repose ench a blanket, a tree, rock or anything handy. The squaws nd the children do most of the hop picking, the head of the amily considering it beneath the dignity of his lordship to abor, feeling better satisfied to indulge in the more congenial astime of loafing around and gambling. I should judge we aw not less than thirty of these canoe, and they certainly resented a very picturesque appearance as all hands paddled long the mirrored waters of the sound, reminding one very orcibly of the gondolas of Venice.—Bulletin correspondent.

The weights of produce established by the laws of Ken-neky are as follows: Wheat, sixty pounds to the bushel; helled corn, fifty-six pounds; corn on ear, seventy; corn real, fifty; rye, fifty-six; oats, thirty-three; barley, forty-ight; Irish potatoes, sixty; sweet potatoes, fifty; beans, six-; castor beans, forty-six; bran, twenty; shorts, thirty; mid-lings, forty; hominy, sixty; clover seed, sixty; timothy ed, forty-five; red top seed, fourteen; hungarian seed, rty-five; hemp seed, forty-four; flax seed, fifty-six; millet eed, fifty; osage orage seed, thirty-six; sorghum seed, forty-wo; Kentucky blue grass, fourteen; buckwheat, fifty-two; nions, fifty-seven; top onion sets, twenty-eight; peas, forty-ix; split peas, sixty, dried apples, twenty-four; dried peach-s, thirty-three; malt, thirty-four; salt, fifty; coal, eighty; urnips, fifty-seven; hay or straw per ton, 2,000; hemp per on, 2,040; tow per ton, 2,210.

"What is a yacht?" was inquired of a long, gaunt codder, rho was lounging about the wharf. "What's a yot?" said he fisherman. "Well, you gate any sort of a craft you lease, and fill her up with liquor and seegyars, and get our friends on board, and have a high old time, and that's a ot."

## JINGLING BELLS.

### How Gothamites Enjoyed Thanksgiving Day—Sleighing on the Uptown Drives.

Such are the "head lines" in the New York Herald of an article which will be found below. It was Thanksgiving Day which showed such a brilliant spectacle on the drives of the metropolis, and it was assuredly a handy knight of the pen-cil who portrayed the scene. It is also long odds that he is of an age when the blood tumbles through the body in warm gushes and will stand as much subtracted caloric as quick-silver before congelation. It is all very well to extol sleigh-riding in a country where it is either "hubby" roads, or mud and slush. Contrast it, however, with Thanksgiving Day here, and the most enthusiastic admirer of the snow-path will have to concede the superiority. Never were roads smoother than those in the neighborhood of San Francisco that are ever in this desirable condition. The park drives never were more admirable, and in place of the chilly fall of millions of snowflakes there were verdure and bloom. The air could not be more balmy, and the ocean and bay were tranquil as a mountain-framed tarn. Over in Oakland there was rac-ing, and the horses "scraped" as nicely as though it were mid-summer. The silk jackets of the jockeys were protection enough against chilliness, and the grooms were in their shirt-sleeves when handling the "knife of sweat" as the Duke of Newcastle denominated the scraper, or plied the rubbing cloth. The music of the bands from the picnic ground, where the Democrats were jubilating, came soft and harmoniously, and the cheers reverberated in echoes from the buildings. The field inside of the racecourse was fetlock deep in the nu-tritious "volu¹tscer," and the horses in it looked placidly at their straggling relatives on the track. There were freshly cut boquets in the hands of the occupants of the ladies' stand, and many gay youngsters had the lapels of their coats deco-rated with buds and blossoms.

It is all very well to talk, write and sing of the "merry sleigh bells," though when icicles are hanging from eyelashes, and the beard is frozen into a clod of arctic moseing, fingers and toes tingling in acute pain, the tintinnabulation does not make amends for the discomfort. The light wagon, the balmy air, and the smooth dirt road are more in accordance with our present desires, though the well-written account will interest our readers:

Thanksgiving Day, bright and rare and racy! A sky over-head clear as the palm of your hand, with a dome of gray and blue linings. Miles and miles of sleigh-worn roads, with the snow lying fast and compact and never a prospect of slough or puddle. What more was wanted to tempt from their homes the thousand pleasure-seekers of Gotham? Who-ever had the means to do it did not lose the chance of taking a spin upon the Boulevard yesterday. The homes of Har-lem seemed turned inside out and emptied upon the noble drives that sweep through it, and day- and nigh, the gay throng, boys and foot, went bustling along in a genuine holiday mood. Long before pious church people were done with service whips were cracking, bells were jingling and hoods were ringing merrily on the road. Along Fifth avenue and entering Central Park from a score of approaches came the noisy cavalcade. The streets heard the clamorous jangle. It mingled with the monotonous dinging of car horses and the rumble of the "L" road. It sent cheery sounds tingling to the ears of staid people in genteel parlors and poor people shut up in their tenements, and to all it brought a reminder of gruff and boisterous but bluff and honest Jack Frost's pres-ence.

Soon the avenues of the park were filled with glancing harness, tossing manes and gleaming runners. The trees, freighted with their white covering, took all sorts of fantas-tic shapes. The houses and spires which leaped into sight in the high ground and peeped in through the vista of trees seemed in the rush of the ongoing crowd to be fast whirling behind. And soon the road sweeps by old Mount St. Vin-cent and empties the clattering, laughing, emotious stream out upon the broad Boulevard. Here is an op¸n road and plenty of elbow room. How the racing spirit, dormant per-haps in many veins, awakens under the stimulus of the keen air and this intoxicating chorus of clattering hoofs, cracking whips and cheering halloos! Away they all go over the glit-tering way, reins taut, eyes sharp, hands ready. Stately an-imals, with bulky equipages behind them, lose their even pace and scamper on with the scrawny, well-worked beast fresh from the cart harness pounding the road alongside and showing every bit of game there is in his poor, shrunken car-cass. Here comes the trained roadster, known to onlookers at walk and hostelry and followed by eye and comment. How he spurns the snow and shoots the road with long-reaching footed steeds as though rejoicing in a sense of his superiori-ty. Big sleighs,and little sleighs single n¸t, glitter with varnish and ornament with costly furs, sleighs that have a bare coat of paint and wear a dreadfully strained and woe-be-gone aspect, sleighs that skim and sleighs that drag, all are out and doing their prettiest to contribute to the jollity of the day. On either side of the road lie bare fields. Dis-tant hills, flecked with white, run along on one side. On the other the housetops and steeples of Harlem shift like the spars of a ship showing in a fog. From the zenith an ashy sky, without a cloud, sweeps around till it meets a border of delicate pink; and below all, down on the horizon, a rim of the purest azure bounds the prospect. The Boulevard is a paradise for loungers. It blithes with hostelries. The fumes of hot punches mingle with the frosty breezes from the Hudson and the Harlem and doubtless serve to temper them. Every road house has its clientele, and the learned manner in which those ancient falsifiers of equine records and equine exploits discourse in front of their respective lairs would shock Ananias and Sapphira and make Munchausen regret he had given up spinning yarns before meeting them.

Now it is well in the afternoon, and every soul who has reins to handle seems to be plying them. The Boulevard has been turned into a torrent of horses, sleighs and harness. The spirit of emulation has seized horse and man and both struggle to leave their neighbors behind. Away at go such a "Hi! Ho!" "Git along!" a snapping of lashes and a jingle of harness. The bells palpitate in the cold, crisp air lc a sort of measured harmony. The hoof-beats thump a drum like accompaniment. There were clever whips sr¸r and spanking steeds before them. Here is a flutter of snow went Dan Mace in and out, in and out through the throng, now selecting an apponent for a test, now whipping back for

another. John Murphy amused himself in like fashion and a whole pack of turdites went hunting one another up and down the drive. Then the tsdolbs of track and avenue were abroad with some of their choicest stock. Messrs. Work and Lorillard, Stokes and Eastman, Harbeck and Sales, Kidder and Freeman were handling the ribbons behind some fast-going nags, and, in fact, every one who had an animal with g0 or show in him, sent him to the front at some time during the day.

From Fifty-ninth street all the way to Jerome Park there was all the afternoon an animated stream. Some went all the way to Fordham, most turned at Fleetwood Park, and old acquaintances who wanted to show the mettle of their animals before assemblies of onlookers confined themselves to the road this side of Macomb's Dam. Throughout the whole length of the avenue the sidewalks were lined and the hostel-ries did a brisk business.

When night fell and the color died out of the sky the tink-ling of bells and the voices and the clamor died away. For awhile the road was still and it seemed as though the pale fields and the dreary clusters of trees were to be left to the winter solitude with which they seemed in harmony. But it was only for a while. Gay as a sleigh ride may be in the bright sunlight and in the whirl of homes and vehicles it is jollier still when the lamps are lit in street and homestead and horse and driver speed ont upon the road in that mad, frolicsome humor which only the night begets. There were scores ont last night for a dash through the star-lit landscape. There was an air of bleakness about the whole scene which, in some paradoxical way, seemed to give a merrier jingle to the bells and a more musical ring to the laugh. The whoop and burst of laughter kept the road awake all through the night, and for hours beyond their usual time of closing the hostelries burned and lights shone hospitably from doors and windows.

Over a thousand men labored yesterday in order that the rest of the community might have a supplementary thanks-giving to-day for the blessing of clean streets. Long hours before the holiday public dreamt of leaving their comfortable couches—nay, hours before some had retired to them—the forces of the Street Cleaning Department and its contractors were struggling with the masses of snow that covered the great thoroughfares, buffeted the while by the last gusts of the expiring storm. As the Herald recorded yesterday, the close of the downfall left the streets buried in a depth of five inches—just deep enough to be a genuine embarrassment to wheeled traffic, and altogether too deep to leave any room for comfort to pedestrians. When the business population turn out to their regular avocations this morning they will find the entire line of Broadway from the Battery to Twenty-third street cleared of its wintry mantle; many of the down-town business streets will be opened, and large forces of men will be at work in all quarters of the city removing the en-cumbrance from all the leading avenues of travel.

Commissioner Coleman had all his preparations complete to begin work the moment the snow storm ceased, and at midnight Wednesday night his gangs were already proceed-ing to the scene of operations. He decided to concentrate his entire force on Broadway yesterday, as the best means of serving the business interests of the city. The regular Broad-way force was therefore strengthened by a large body of Italians; extra carts were hired, and the preliminary process of scraping, sweeping and piling the snow was begun at several points. All night the men worked, and at daybreak their numbers were reinforced by the gangs from all the ten districts into which that portion of the city under direct con-trol of the Commissioner is divided, with their foremen and their carts. The work was thoroughly well done. This great undertaking of clearing the line of Broadway in a day was literally carried ont, the work being completed about mid-night. Between seven hundred and eight hundred men were required, exclusive of those employed at the wharves, and about three hundred and fifty carts were used.

Mr. John S. Brown and Mr. T. W. Walton, the contractors for the downtown districts, also showed energy in dealing with the situation. Each put large forces of men on the streets in addition to their regular laborers, and numbers of extra carts were hired. Work was begun by both at mid-night and was continued throughout the entire day, both gen-tlemen visiting their districts personally to see that satisfac-tory progress was made.

### Use Only Thoroughbred Bulls.

We cannot too often nor too frequently recommend farmers and cattle men to use none other than thoroughbred bulls upon their herds. No matter what the breed may that is be chosen, the male should always be a purely-bred animal of the race. There is a mysterious influence, not at all under-stood, and which the ablest scientists have scarcely attempt-ed to explain, that follows the use of the thoroughbred male upon a stock of mixed blood. It shows itself in increased size, greater vigor and better feeding and milking qualities, and it is worthy of especial notice that, in general, the more purely bred the male may be, the more marked appears to be the effect of the cross.

With cattle raised especially for beef, it shows itself not only in greater weight attained from a given quantity of food, but in an improved quality as well, so that the farmer may, by the use of such a bull, not only raise more pounds of beef from the same amount of food, but at the same time produce animals that will bring a better price for the same weight than when breeding from common stock.

Grade bulls rarely possess this magical element of prepo-tency. The line has gone by when a single farmer can com-pete successfully in the markets for beef cattle, unless he uses a thoroughbred. He must use thoroughbred males only or quit the business. But we want to impress upon the minds of our readers the importance of knowing that the animal to be used is a thoroughbred. Be assured that nothing short of this will fill the requirement. Grades may look as well—even better—but when they come to be used for pur-poses of procreation they will fail to effect material improve-ment.

In view of the fact that the chief value of a bull for breed-ing purposes depends upon his being wholly what he is rep-resented to be—a thoroughbred—farmers cannot be too care-ful in making their purchases. For the pedigree, which is all important, the purchaser must rely mainly upon the integrity of the breeder. Hence the great importance of buying only from reputable and reliable breeders; and the dangers of dealing with mere traders and men that are not breeders, who have no reputation at stake and who neither know nor care how the animals they offer for sale are bred.—National Live Stock Journal.

A novel feature of the State Fair at Austin, Texas, was a roping contest between thirteen herdsmen for a prize saddle valued at $300. T. J. Morris of Caldwell county was the victor, having roped, thrown down and tied a Texas steer in one minute and forty-five seconds, while some of h ¹ocest petitors required five minutes for the feat.

# POULTRY.

## Is Ostrich Farming Profitable?

A gentleman who has been in South Africa and Buenos Ayres writes us, at some length, giving his observations of ostrich farming and adding some reasons why it can never be made profitable in California. Six years ago, he says, a pair of breeding birds were worth $1,000 in Cape Colony; in May last they could be bought for $100. The farmers who were once going into the business on a large scale are reducing their flocks to a few pairs and selling the chicks for what they can get. All this has come to pass in a region which is the home of the ostrich, which has great deserts in which it likes to live, and where it can roam at will over thousands of acres fenced in by the farmer and good for nothing else. Of ostrich farming in Buenos Ayres he has seen nothing, but has come in contact with a discouraged ostrich farmer, who had just imported some birds, a large proportion of which had died. Half the birds that cross the ocean, he says, are likely to die on the passage. These are all the objections he makes to the industry, and some of them are serious if they do not admit of explanation.

Now no one expects in California a wild fever of speculation in the ostrich like the Mississippi scheme or the tulip mania in Holland during the last century. There is reason in all things. In the early days of California potatoes were worth a fabulous price per pound. This induced a large number of men to go into potato culture. The market was overstocked, potatoes fell to a merely nominal price and a good many men were ruined. Something like this has happened in South Africa. People heard wonderful stories respecting the profits to be made in ostrich feathers, and expected to gain fortunes in a day. They forsook their legitimate industries and rushed pell-mell into this, with a result that they might reasonably have anticipated. Many, doubtless, mortgaged their farms, and as the pursuit is, from its very nature, unproductive for several years, they had to sacrifice all their property to their creditors. This naturally created a surfeit of birds and a ruinous fall in prices. The business has not continued long enough to gain a natural commercial equilibrium. Six years does not give opportunity for such an industry to test the laws of supply and demand. These farmers were at a distance from Cape Town, which is remote from the markets of Europe, so they were necessarily very much at the mercy of the middlemen. This is the universal law of speculative movements, and we can hardly suppose that ostrich farming in South Africa would prove an exception.

Our own experience is likely to be entirely different. Should any considerable number of our people decide to raise ostriches they will not recklessly rush into the business. They will not give up raising wheat, fruit, wine, cattle and sheep and turn their broad farms into ostrich ranches, stocked with birds from Africa worth $1,000 or $1,500 each. This objection, therefore, is sufficiently answered. We think that it is a foregone conclusion that the ostrich can be as easily acclimated in California as the turkey of the western forests could be distributed and domesticated all over the world. It does well in the mild climate of the coast of South Africa and also on the cold elevated plateaus of the interior. There is no reason to believe it ever lived in the deserts from choice. Being timid it sought them for safety. But if it needs deserts we have them in California in abundance. We also have in the Coast Range and the foothills of the Sierras a superabundance of that class of gravelly land which is not tilled, but is used for sheep and cattle ranges. There is no reason to conclude that because a flock of ostriches need several thousand acres of desert in Cape Colony for their sustenance they would not find a hundred, fifty, or even twenty-five sufficient in California, where grain, grass and vegetables, of which they are fond, are abundant. Nor are we justified in thinking, from what we know of their habits, that they would not thrive in a small inclosure in a fertile valley, where they are well fed and cared for.

Our climate is something more than temperate, and something more than semi-tropical. All forms of life thrive here, even the plants and animals that come from near the Arctic circle and from far within the tropics. Then why should not the ostrich be easily domesticated amid such favorable surroundings? We think it can profitably be introduced into the State, and while we deprecate speculation we shall be pleased to see this, like every other new industry, grow and prosper. Our resources of soil and climate are unlimited not only in extent, but in variety, and those who introduce and encourage a new pursuit that is legitimate are public benefactors.—*Chronicle.*

If you discover that a hen has deserted her nest during incubation, and that the eggs are cold, do not destroy them. Try to find another hen that is sitting, or one that is ready to sit, and put the deserted eggs under her, and wait until they have been set on at least twenty-two or twenty-three days, thus allowing two or more days extra time to make up for their having been chilled during the process of incubation. I have known a number of eggs in a setting to hatch after they had been deserted at least forty-eight hours. So do not give up and destroy the eggs without a fair trial.—*Niles' Poultry and Stock Book.*

## Game Fowls.

The games are good layers when allowed free range all over creation, but just because they are so active naturally they fret and chafe when confined to winter quarters, and for that reason do not make good winter layers, at least I have not found them so.

Good mothers? Well, yes; I believe that good mothers provide food for their offspring, and protect them from harm. As a provider, the game hen, with a family on her hands, excels anything else that wears feathers. She will scratch up anything that is within ten feet of the surface, and the neighbor's yards and gardens generally suffer most. One industrious game hen will keep a whole neighborhood in hot water. I know all about it for I have tried it. Why didn't I shut her up in a coop? Just you try to catch a game hen and her chicks and you will know all about it. Once I picked up one of the little chicks that seemed a little lame; he chirped after the senseless way that chicks have if you touch one of them, and the next thing that I knew there was a rush, a whir of wings, and for the next three minutes there was such a mixture of woman, sunbonnet and hen that you couldn't tell "tother from which." Don't you tell, but I did; yes, I did turn, and—ran away.

The games are hardy and the chicks are easy to raise—they are up and scratching and fighting almost as soon as they are out of the shell—but for all that, when the cholera comes along the game hens turn up their toes and die just as meekly as the Brahmas, Cochins, Rocks and all the rest of them. There is no breed of fowls in existence that is proof against chicken cholera.

In regard to the variety of games, if you conclude to keep them, get the kind that you like best. So far as useful qualities are concerned, one kind is just as good as another; and as for scratching, fighting and pure "cussedness" generally, one kind is just as bad as another. Perhaps you may think that I am rather hard on the games, but they were exceedingly hard on me in the first place. I kept them one summer and they caused me more "worriment" of mind than all the chickens that I ever had before or since. The four-foot fences that kept the other fowls in or out, they regarded with contempt. They visited the garden when they pleased, and as a natural consequence we didn't have any garden that we felt like boasting about. Our neighbors' gardens looked even worse than ours, and our neighbors' feelings were harrowed up worse than their gardens. If somebody didn't come along every morning about breakfast time and say: "Those confounded chickens have been in my garden again," we feared that some of the neighbors were seriously ill.

And that game rooster! He fought everything on the place, and between times found time to kill all the roosters in the neighborhood. I expected to pay for a rooster every week, and it was not often that I was disappointed. So long as he killed only cheap roosters I didn't mind it very much, but when he began on the five-dollar birds, my patience and pocket-book gave out, and I soon got rid of every game on the place.

If you do get games, build a fence ten or twelve feet high all around your garden, and hire an active boy with a dog to keep them out of the neighbors' gardens and away from the neighbors' roosters.—*Fannie Field in Prairie Farmer.*

## Poultry on the Pacific Coast.

Poultry keeping is a healthy and engrossing pursuit; it is an occupation pleasurable as well as profitable; it not only affords amusement and beneficial employment, but well repays for the time and labor spent while engaged in it, and nowhere can poultry be raised so economically and advantageously as on the cheap lands of the Pacific States and Territories. Notwithstanding these facts, this branch of industry has been so sadly neglected, so little cared for, that thousands of people indulge in the illusion that poultry-raising is merely a hobby and an expensive one at that, while other thousands content themselves with mongrels, taking no thought how they may improve their fowls and cause them to render a three-fold greater profit for the time and money expended thereon. It is a well-established fact that more money can be made in raising poultry, if of good quality, and producing eggs on this coast in proportion to the capital invested and the care required, than in any other branch of farming; yet it is no exaggeration to say that in California not one farmer in ten gives this industry the attention its importance deserves.

In the meantime, the daily mercantile reports of San Francisco continue to note the arrival of large consignments of eggs from Salt Lake and the Eastern States. In neither of these places are the conditions and climate so good as in our State. In the East heavy winters intervene and large expenditures are necessary for feed and buildings to protect the flocks from the inclement weather. Eastern eggs sell in our market for several cents less per dozen than California eggs. The cost of transportation and the commission also amounts to quite an item, leaving the producer, at present prices, from ten to twelve cents per dozen. Now if farmers East can afford to raise eggs at ten cents per dozen, the farmers of California, where all the advantages rest, can certainly afford to raise them at twenty and thirty and even forty cents per dozen. Eastern farmers have seen the importance of improving their flocks, and as a consequence the breeding of fine fowls there, both for fancy and profit, has attained a high degree of perfection, and it is certainly time the farmers of California should emulate their example by providing a better class of fowls, both for sale in our markets and for egg-producing. Let them bear in mind the fact that it costs no more to keep good stock than poor, while every advantage is in favor of the former.—*Niles' Poultry and Stock Book.*

POULTRY RAISING—An English contemporary gives the following facts concerning the methods of poultry raising in Sussex, England; The usual food for fattening consists of ground oats, suet and milk—skimmed or unskimmed—to which sometimes a little linseed meal is added, especially in winter. At first chickens have to be fed carefully, if not charily. Allowing them three weeks, they are as a rule kept on oatmeal (made into gruel) one week; then suet is added, and the last week they are crammed. Milk is highly valued as an addition to the ordinary diet, and one poultry breeder has used as much as $50 worth a week. Cramming is done with a machine, and the chickens have their crops filled twice a day. This process is continued for about a week, supposing a preparatory course to have been gone through. After about a fortnight the food ceases to take effect; but so long as they are not kept beyond the proper period, it is surprizing how few deaths occur in their ranks, Fowls or chickens are fattened up to any weight, two pounds, or five, or eight or more. Mr. Oliver produced one weighing thirteen pounds. There are farmers who lay themselves out for this as a specialty, fattening all the year round, and keeping their coops full. Among this class Mr. Joseph Oliver takes the lead, keeping about 200 dozen always in hand, and killing forty dozen at a time in the busy season, even 6 times a week. He uses nearly 700 sacks of oats a quarter, $800 worth of milk, and 9,800 pounds of suet, He keeps six men constantly employed, and twenty women. It is estimated that no less than $350,000 per year is realized by the sale of chickens in the small district bordering on Brighton, the queen of the English watering places.

"Brown's Bronchial Troches are excellent for the relief of hoarseness or sore throat. They are exceedingly effective."—*Christian World, London, Eng.*

## Market Report.

FLOUR—We quote: Best City Extra, $5 55@$5 70; Superfine, $4 70@$5 25; Interior Extra, $4 75@$5 25; Interior Superfine $3 75@$4 ℔ bbl.

WHEAT—The market has, at present, a very healthy tone. Quotations of recent sales are: No. 1 White, December, $1 77; do January, $1 77½@$1 78; do February, $1 83@$1 83½.

BARLEY—January has the choice of late, most of the business being confined to this particular month. Recent sales show January prices from $1 37½@$1 40 though $1 38½ seems to be the standard price. Brewing and Chevalier is hard to dispose of at $1 44.

OATS—Fair Feed, $1 70@$1 75; Good, $1 75@$1 80; Choice, $1 85@$1 90 ℔ ctl. Milling $1 95@$2 ℔ ctl.

RYE—Business dull. Quotable at $1 75@$2 ℔ ctl.

FEED—Ground Barley, $31 ℔ ton; Cracked Corn, $37 ℔ ton. Shorts, $20 ℔ ton. Oilcake meal the oilworks sell to the trade at $32 50 ℔ ton, less the usual discount. Middlings, $27@$28 ℔ ton for lots at the mill.

HAY—Alfalfa, $13@$14 50; Wheat, $15 50@$17 50; Wild Oat, $13 50@$17 50; Mixed, $12@$14 ℔ ton.

PROVISIONS—Eastern Hams, 19½@21c; California Hams, 16½@16¾c for plain, 16½@17c for sugar-cured canvased; Eastern Breakfast Bacon, 16½@17c; California Smoked Bacon 15½@15¾c for heavy and medium, and 16½@16½c for light and extra light; Clear Sides, 15½@16c; Pork, $21@$21 50 for Extra Prime, $23 50 @24 for Prime Mess, $25 50@26 for Mess, $27 for clear and $28@28 50 for extra Clear; Pigs' Feet, $16@$18 ℔ bbl; Mess beef, $16 for bbls and $8 50 for hf bbls; Extra Mess Beef, $17 for bbls and $8 75 for half bls; Family Beef, $18@18 50 ℔ bbl; California Smoked Beef, 13½@14c ℔ lb.

FRUIT—We quote: Apples, 30@50c for common and 75c@$1 ℔ bx for good; Pears, $1@$2 25 ℔ bx. Grapes, 75c@1 per box; Lemons, $6@$7 per box for Sicily and $5@$6 for Malaga; California Lemons, $2 50@$3 per box; Limes, $5@$6 50 per box for Mexican; Bananas, $2@$3 50 ℔ bunch; Mexican Oranges $22 50@$25 ℔ thousand; California $2 25 @$2 75 ℔ box; Pineapples, $6@$7 ℔ doz; New crop Western Cranberries are offering at $15@$17 ℔ bbl.

VEGETABLES—We quote: Marrowfat Squash, $8 @$10 ℔ ton; Carrots, 30c; Turnips, 75c@$1; Cauliflower, 75c@$1 ℔ dozen; Cabbage, 50@75c ℔ ctl; Garlic, 3½c ℔ lb; Green Peas, 7@8c ℔ lb; Green Peppers, 50c@$1 ℔ box; Tomatoes, 75c ℔ box; Celery, 50c ℔ doz; Mushrooms, 10@12½c per lb; Okra, 75c@1 00; Dried Okra, 18c; Dry Peppers, 12½@15c ℔ lb.

POTATOES—River Red, 50@70c; Early Rose, 60c @90c; Garnet Chile, $1@$1 10; Humboldt, 90c@$1; Tomales and Petaluma, 87½c@$1; Peerless $1. Cuffey Cove, $1 to $1 12½ ℔ ctl.

ONIONS—Quotable at 85@90c for good and 50 ℔ sack for poor.

BEANS—Bayos $3 75@$4; Butter, $3@$3 25 for small and $3 20@$3 30 for large; Lima, $3 75@$4; Pea, $3 20@$3 30; Pink, $2 90@$3 10; Red, $2 90@$3 10; small White, $3 20@$3 30; large White, $3 75@$3 ℔ ctl.

BUTTER—We quote jobbing lots: Fancy, 30@32c; choice, 27½@29; fair to good, 25@26c; inferior lots from country stores, 18@22c; firkin, 25@26c for good to choice, and 20@23c for ordinary; pickled roll, 24@27½; Eastern, 18@22c ℔ lb.

CHEESE—Fairly steady. California, 14@15c for choice; 11@13 for fair to good; do, factory, in boxes, $15@16; Eastern, 16@17c; Western, 8@12½c per lb.

EGGS—California choice, 32½@35c; Eastern, 27½@30c; Lime, 27½@30c per doz.

POULTRY—Live Turkeys, gobblers, 13@15c; do Hens, 13@15c; do dressed, 14@16c; Roosters, $6@$6 50 for old and $6@$7 for young; Hens $6 @$7 50; Broilers, $5@$6, according to size; Ducks $10@$12 ℔ dozen; Geese, $1 50@$2 ℔ pair.

GAME—Market steady. Quail, 90c@$1 ℔ dozen; Mallard Ducks, $3 25@$3 50; Sprigs, $1 25@$1 50; Canvasback, $3 25@$3 50; Brandt, $1 25@$1 50; Gray Geese $2@$3; White Geese, $1@$1 25; Honkers, $4@$4 50; Snipe, $1 25@$1 50 for English and 50@75c for common; Teal, $1@$1 12½; Widgeon, $1 25@$1 50; Hare, $1 75@$2 25; Rabbits, $1 25@$1 75.

WOOL—Trade limited to small local orders. We quote fall: San Joaquin and coast, 8@12c; San Joaquin and coast Lamb, good, 11@12c; Northern Fall, free, 15@20c; Northern Fall, defective, 11@15c; Northern fall, Lamb, 15@20c; free Mountain, 11@15c.

HIDES AND SKINS—Dry hides, usual selection, 19½@20c ℔ lb; culls one third less, and Mexican Hides 1c ℔ lb less. Dry Kip, 20c; Dry Calf, 21@22c; Salted Steers, over 55 lbs, 11c ℔ lb; Steers and Cows, medium, 10c; light do, 9c; Salted Kip, 15 to 30 lbs. 11c; Salted Calf, 14@15c ℔ lb; Dairy Calf 70 @85c each; Sheep Skins, 25@30c for Shearlings; 30 @50c for short, 60@90c for medium, and $1@$1 35 apiece for long wool and wool skins. Butchertown Green Skins bring higher prices.

TALLOW—Quotable at 9c@9½c ℔ lb for rendered and 11½@12½c for refined, both in shipping order.

MEATS—Following are rates for whole carcasses from slaughterers to dealers:

BEEF—Prime, 8½@9c; medium grade, 6½@7c; inferior, 5½@6c ℔ lb.

VEAL—Large Calves, 7½@8½c; small ones, 9@10c ℔ lb.

MUTTON—Wethers are quotable at 4½@5c and Ewes at 4½@4½c ℔ lb, according to quality.

LAMB—Quotable at 6½@7c ℔ lb.

PORK—Live Hogs, 6½@7c for hard and 6½c@6½c for soft; dressed do 9½@10c ℔ lb for hard grain hogs.

N. A. JUDD. D. HICKS.

D. HICKS & COMPANY,

Patentees Advertising Hotel Registers.

BOOK-BINDERS, *PRINTERS,* *BLANK BOOK MANUFACTURERS.*

Importers of Bookbinders' Material

Fine Antique Bindings at Eastern Rates.

*No. 508 Montgomery St., San Francisco, Cal.*

FOR SALE.

DORR, IMPORTED Gordon; winner in Nebraska Field Trials. Has been hunted on chickens, grouse, quail, woodcock and snipe in the New England States, North Carolina, Virginia, Minnesota, Nebraska, Missouri, Iowa and Indiana. Retrieves without injury (dead or alive) anything from a snipe to a goose, from land or water. V. H. C. on the bench at Boston; also several money prizes and medals as a performing dog. Is probably the best broken dog on this Coast. On account of an attack of paralysis in my legs, which will prevent my using him this winter, I offer him for sale before returning to Massachusetts.

25 FRED A. TAFT, Truckee, Cal.

THAD STEVENS.

THIS THOROUGHBRED HORSE WILL BE AT Agricultural Park, Sacramento, for the season commencing Feb. 1 and ending the 1st of July next. Good pasturage for mares will be provided at $3 per month. For terms and particulars apply to or address W. M. MURRY, Agent, Sacramento Racetrack.

IMPROVED

Blind Bridle & Winkers

FOR RACE HORSES.

Secured by Letters Patent, July 25, 1882.

Having thus described my invention, what I claim as new, and desire to secure by letters patent, is:

1. The part D, supported by the side straps of the bridle, extending back, as shown, the front having an opening into which the blind is fitted, substantially as herein described.

2. In a bridle, in combination with the extensions D, the curved blinds F, secured to said extensions, and as shaped, to give full freedom and ventilation to the eye while circumscribing the vision, substantially as herein described.

3. In a bridle, and in combination with the extensions D, blinds F, and side straps A, the screw, nut and washer E, to secure the blind and allow it to be set, substantially as herein described.

4. In a bridle, and in combination with the check-pieces D and blinds F, as shown, the straps or bands G and H, connecting the branches or extensions above and below the eyes, and having the adjusting slides or buckles, substantially as and for the purpose herein described.

5. In a bridle, and in combination with the blinds F, supported and pivoted to the bridle so as to be movable about the point of support, the adjustable front straps or bands G and H, and the rear band I and the throat-latch or lash connected with the blinds, and adjustable, substantially as herein described.

The above are the claims allowed by the patent office, and though the corresponding letters do not appear on the cut, the general principle will be understood.

It meets with universal approbation, doing away with all the objections urged against blinds, and at the same time giving complete control of the line of vision. By throwing the lower portion of the blind up something of the same effect on the action follows as is induced by toe-weights. This is especially the case when young colts are the pupils, teaching them to bend the knee without the strain of weights on the feet.

For bridles of all descriptions apply to

JOHN A. McKERRON,
No. 327 Sutter street, San Francisco.

---

## SPECIMEN OF OUR ARTIST'S HUMOR.

THE FISHMONGER.

HUNDREDS OF DELIGHTED ONES SEE, FOR THE FIRST TIME IN THEIR LIVES

**The Japanese Artist and Embroiderers**

*At work in their native costumes at*

# Ichi Ban, 22 & 24 Geary St.

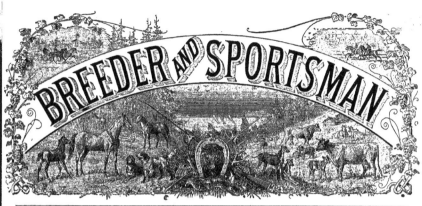

**BREEDER AND SPORTSMAN**

VOL... No. 25.
NO. 508 MONTGOMERY STREET.

SAN FRANCISCO, SATURDAY, DECEMBER 23, 1882.

SUBSCRIPTION
FIVE DOLLARS A YEAR.

## MAMBRINO WILKES—Owned by Irvin Ayres, Oakland, California.

Our old friend, Charles J. Foster, editor of the New York *Sportsman* has never wavered in his allegiance to the noted stallion who was the sire of the subject of the present illustration. From the time when he first made his acquaintance —and that was a long time ago, until he went the way of all horses, he was ready to take up the cudgels in his defense. He had predicted a glorious career, when a foal he was nourished on cow's milk with a dash of old rum to give it flavor, and gloriously the colt fulfilled the promises. He was the foremost trotting stallion of his day, and after giving due weight to the circumstances attending his life, it can be safely said that he ought to rank with the best of any day.

George Wilkes, first called Robert J. Fillingham, was bred by Harry Felter, Newburgh, N. Y. He was foaled in 1856;

by Ryadyk's Hambletonian, his dam Dolly Spanker, by Henry Clay, his second dam by Baker's Highlander. His trotting record is brilliant, obtaining a score of 2:22 in 1868, and in a well-attested trial he made two miles in 4:44. A horse of fine action, although he had a peculiar method of moving his hind legs, giving them such a long sweep that at the furthest rear extension. the foot was further back than in any other horse we ever saw. A long, easy stride, and yet with so much energy of action that there cannot be a question that with the improved training of the present time his mark would have been in the lowest notch for entire horses.

It is almost supererogatory to write of the get of George Wilkes. Nine of them dropped into " the list " this season, and from what we have heard there are others which only

require a chance to distinguish themselves. And then the second generation is giving evidence of being endowed with the prepotency. The sire of Phil Thompson and others are proving this in the most emphatic manner, and the family characteristics have become so well established that there is a greater demand for Wilkes colts than the breeders of Kentucky can supply. Mr. Corbitt in his late trip to the East had quite a long search before he could obtain one, and as he went with the determination to pay any reasonable price, and is well-known to have liberal ideas as to what really good animals are worth, the difficulty came from the general appreciation of the stock.

Our artist is always so accurate in his delineations that few written words are necessary to supplement the work of the pencil. Mambrino Wilkes is very like his sire in conformation, excepting that he is a good deal larger. He is black, with a tinge of wine; sixteen hands in height, with fine length and great substance. In fair condition he weighs over 1200 pounds, and much of this is owing to his fine muscular development. His "middle piece" is capital, showing a large girth around the chest, with corresponding length of back ribs, quarters and shoulders well clothed with muscles. He has a very handsome head and a clear eye with the kindliest expression. He was bred by B. J. Treacy, of Fayette Co., Kentucky; foaled April, 1874. His sire George Wilkes, his dam Lady Christmas by Todhunter's Mambrino, better known as Idol. His second dam was by Pilot Jr., and she from a mare of Kentucky Blue blood. This is a pedigree of the most "fashionable" kind. Hambletonian, Mambrino Chief and Pilot Jr., backed with thoroughbred, it would be an ultra hypercritical caviler who found fault with it. As has been shown, George Wilkes combined the Hambletonian and Clay. Idol by Mambrino Chief, his dam by American Eclipse, second dam by Shakespeare, third by Sir William, fourth by Orphan, and his fifth dam by imported Buzzard. Maud S, Jay-Eye-See, Noontide and others have shown the value of the Pilot Jr. blood, while the Mambrino Chief ranks as of the bluest shade in trotting pedigrees. From the form and breeding of Mambrino Wilkes it was to be expected that his colts would show merit, and those that have been trained verify the estimate. Alpheus we saw commencing his education on the Oakland course this last summer, and we were very highly impressed with his showing for future excellence. He is a very handsome colt, and of fine action, and when a two-year-old can show a half mile in 1:18, as we understand Alpheus did in Stockton, there are the best reasons to expect that he will be "fit for any company" when he has had the benefit of a little more training. The pinkeye had him in its clutches just before the trot at Stockton, and he was suffering from it at the time. We have seen others of the get of Mambrino Wilkes, which are of high form, and as those were beaten for a premium given for Wilkes' colts at the San Joaquin Valley Fair, the award made by good judges, those we have not seen must be still superior.

This is the first son of George Wilkes to come to California, and the only others we know of are the late importations of Mr. Corbitt. As soon as we have the time to spare to visit it Mr. Corbitt's breeding farm we will give a list of the prominent winners of this family, and when that appears there will be none to deny that the blood will be of vast importance to the breeding interests of this Coast.

## TURF AND TRACK.

### Coney Island Jockey Club.

The Executive Committee of the Coney Island Jockey Club announces that the following stakes, to be run in 1883, will close on the 1st prox. for the June meeting, which will begin June 12 and continue June 14, 16, 19, 21, 23, 26, 28 and 30:

The Great Two-Year-Old Post Stakes, at $500 each, half forfeit, with $1,000 added; three-quarters of a mile.

The Great Two-Year-Old Selling Sweepstakes, at $50 each, half forfeit, with $1,000 added; three-quarters of a mile.

The Seabound Stakes, for three-year-olds, at $100 each, half forfeit, only $25 if declared May 1st, 1883, with $1,500 added; non-winning allowances; mile and three furlongs.

The Coney Island Stakes, for three-year-olds and upwards, at $25 each, play or pay, with $750 added; mile and a furlong.

The Coney Island Cup, for three-year-olds and upwards, at $50 each, half forfeit, with $1,500 added; three-year-olds, 90 lbs; four-year-olds, 108 lbs; five-year-olds and upwards, 114 lbs; sex allowances; two miles and a quarter.

The following will be run during the September meeting, which is fixed to begin on Saturday, September 1, and to continue on the 4th, 6th, 8th, 11th, 13th, 15th, 18th, 20th and 22d:

The Autumn Stakes for two-year-olds, at $100 each, $25 forfeit, with $1,000 added; winning penalties, non-winning and maiden allowances; three-quarters of a mile.

September Stakes, for three-year-olds, at $100 each, $25 forfeit, with $1,000 added; winning penalties, non-winning and maiden allowances; mile and three-quarters.

Autumn Cup, a handicap sweepstakes for all ages, at $150 each, $50 forfeit if declared the day before the race, $25 only if declared spt by July 1, with $2,500 added; the weights to be announced two days before the race; three miles.

The Great Long Island Stakes, for all ages, at $250 for starters, with $2,000 added and a claim to the Woodlawn Vase; horses entered January 1, $50 forfeit, by June 1, $100 forfeit, and by September 1, $150 forfeit; three-year-olds, 95 lbs; four-year-olds, 108 lbs; five years and upwards, 114 lbs; sex allowances; four miles.

All entries should be addressed by J. G. K. Lawrence, Secretary, at the corner of East Twenty-seventh Street and Madison Avenue, who, on application, will send blank forms for entries to each of the above stakes.—*New York World.*

Savannah Jockey Club.—The annual meeting of the Savannah Jockey Club is announced for January 16, 17, 18 and 20. The events on the first list are, as follows: Two Brook Stakes, mile heats, for two-year-olds—Roderick Dhu, Mordaunt, Lady Dean and W. P. Burch. Lamar Stakes, for two-year-olds mile heats, winner of the Ten Broeck Stakes to carry five pounds extra, the same four entries. Bonaventure Stakes, mile heats, for three-year-olds—Bonnie Kate, Bantam, Homespun, Belle of Charleston and Jane Porter. Oglethorpe Stakes, mile heats, for all ages—Palmetto, Duke of Montalban, Constantina, Colonel Sprague, Vingt-et-un and Jane Foster. Savannah Cup, two miles, for all ages—Fair Count, Duke of Montalban, Colonel Sprague and Helen Wallace. In view of the Engeman movement at New Orleans it seems as if the Savannah meeting must suffer, especially if the stables of Burch and Pettingill, from which a majority of the above nominations are made, go on from Charleston to New Orleans at once.—*New York World.*

### J. R. KEENE'S HORSES IN ENGLAND.

#### A Chatty Letter Anent Horses and Trainers—Don Fulano's Leg—Etc.

The following account of Mr. Keene's horses in England is copied from the *New York Spirit of the Times*, and is the latest full intelligence regarding "the stable." It is written by the English correspondent of that popular journal, and we are pleased to learn that the quondam Californian has such good prospects. He has certainly been very successful in his ventures on the turf, and if he would send the breeding department to this State we feel sure that he would enjoy the still greater triumphs of winning with colts of his own breeding and rearing.

The pleasure of breeding winners of the big events is a more intense gratification than when the trophy is gained by an animal secured by purchase. There is the satisfaction of having, in a measure, created the champion, something akin to an author when his work has received the approbation of the critics, or, perhaps, a better illustration is that of the playwright when called before the curtain to receive the enthusiastic plaudits of the assemblage. Although Mr. Keene's chief business in California was in San Francisco, he can scarcely fail to be cognizant of the advantages "this Coast" presents for the breeding of thoroughbreds.

Those who never have visited California, but who saw the Santa Anita two-year-olds, must acknowledge that such animals as Gano and Lucky B can only be reared where everything is favorable to their growth.

It is not merely size, as the muscular development is in keeping with their stature, and in place of "gangling," overgrown breeds there is symmetry and proportion. We still hope to see Mr. Keene loosen his stud farm in this State and then, with the sires and dams he now owns, shall look for a continuation of his successes at home and abroad.

The wide expanse of down land about the village of Shipton, on the border of Wiltshire and Hampshire, has an interest for American readers, for it is here that Mr. J. R. Keene's horses are trained, and that the mighty Foxhall, who has made an unfading name for himself in the turf, underwent the preparation which enabled him to carry off, last year, the two great "back end" handicaps, the Cesarewitch and Cambridgeshire. The luxuriant herbage of these downs makes admirable galloping grounds, on which horses may do their work in safety, when the going at Newmarket, baked to brick-like consistency, is perilous to horses' legs, and this is proved by the fact that advantage is taken of this particular district by several trainers of eminence. Danebury, perhaps the most famous training ground in the country when the Matador of Hastings, the Duke of Beauford and the leading sportsman supported John Day, is within some eight or nine miles; and the Danebury gallop, from which Stockbridge race course, adjoins the grounds occupied by Tom Cannon of Houghton, the Prince of English horsemen, and as good in the capacity of trainer as of jockey (for the horses nominally trained by Olding are really trained by Cannon); while not far from here, at Kingsclere, is John Porter's stable, from which this year have come the winners of the Derby, Oaks and Ten Thousand, to which, most likely, would have been added the St. Leger, had the redoubtable Tom, who rode the winner in the other three of the five classical contests, been in the saddle. The simple story of Dutch Oven's Leger seems to be that O. Loates, a capable jockey in his way, made too sure of winning on Lord Stanford's Geheimniss, and came away too soon. Cannon, who knew more of the mare, having owned her and sold her as a two-year-old to the Earl of Stamford and Warrington, never makes too sure of anything, and though he generously protests that Loates obeyed orders implicitly, has confessed to me that he should have laid back off Geheimniss, had he been up, and thinks he might have got home.

This, however, is a digression, and in a consequent article I hope to tell the readers of the *Spirit* more of Tom Cannon and Mr. Lorillard's horses now under his charge; but the digression is a natural one, seeing that during the year—at a remaining fee higher than was ever before paid to a jockey in England—Cannon's services have been secured for Mr. Keene's horses, trained by William Day, the uncle of Mrs. Tom.

It has been said that Shipton is on the borders of Hampshire and Wiltshire, and, as a matter of fact, the Park House inn, where Foxhall stood during his handicap triumphs, before the stables at Cholderton Lodge (William Day's present residence) were completed, is so exactly on the border that a very extraordinary circumstance is recorded of it. Forty years ago a man was killed at his doors in the presence of many people, and it has never been decided in what county he died, on which day he died, or what killed him. As the clock struck twelve a blow from a drunken barrister knocked the man under the hoofs of the leader of a coach, whether was pulling up at the door of the Park House inn, and whether the blow or the horse's hoofs was the cause of death, whether or not he died before the clock finished striking, and in which county will never be known. Park House stables are now deserted, however, though on the door of the box Foxhall occupied are nailed the plates he wore in his great races, and William Day wisely continues to lease the place with the idea of using it as a sort of hospital, should any of the horses at Cholderton catch colds or show symptoms of any disease that might threaten infection.

At Cholderton Lodge itself a range of stabling has lately been completed on the admirable system set forth by William Day in his well-known book, "The Racehorse in Training." Here are roomy, well-paved boxes and stalls, in every one of which the best arrangements for ventilation and draining are made. The hot-fetid atmosphere, so common to the majority of stables, is never felt here. "William of Woodyates," as the master of Cholderton used to be called, when he continued the training ground which made his fame in the land, farms a large estate, but cannot grow corn or hay sufficiently good for thoroughbred stock, and buys all that he uses; the horse paddocks are large and convenient, the downs near at hand, and if, with every advantage which Mr. Keene's liberality and William Day's accomplished manipulation can command, the white jacket and blue spots is not often borne to victory, the fault must lie with the horses.

In writing of one who has for so long a time past occupied so prominent a place on the English turf (nearly a quarter of a century has passed since William Day rode his own colt, Promised Land, in the Derby, and finished fourth, beaten a neck from Sir Joseph Hawley's Musjid, who afterwards declared forfeit in a match with Promised Land), it is difficult

to avoid repeating some of the hundred and one anecdotes of *coups* and strokes of policy with which the name of Mr. Keene's trainer is associated. But the temptation must be resisted for the object of this paper is merely to discuss the bearers of the white, blue spots, now at Cholderton, their appearance and prospects.

During the present year, the American horses in England have not done much, though that coveted trophy, the Ascot Cup, was carried off by the famous son of King Alfonso and Jamaica, who, however, succumbed to the American 'bred Fiddler in the Alexandra Plate, run the next day; and my private opinion is that the defeat was mainly owing to the absence of a horse to lead Foxhall in his gallops. He completed his preparation by himself. Many times I have watched him tearing over the ground, his attendant Hatcher up. Hatcher was so devoted to his charge that when his wife presented him with a son, the child was christened Foxhall straightway. The great horse always seemed to go splendidly, but there can be no doubt that a horse when worked by himself does not do as much as he seems to do. He wants something to go with him, and, as it were, evoke a spirit of emulation, to make him exert himself, and the need of a schoolmaster caused the pupil to fall short at Ascot. It is very likely he might not have won the Ascot Cup, had not Martin kept Faugh-a-Ballagh, who was started to make a pace for the Duke of Beaufort's Petronel, hard at it, though on this head it is easy to fall into error. The Duke did not feel by any means confident of Petronel's success, but thought the horse had a very fair chance, and the three-year-old Faugh-a-Ballagh was merely started to make the running. Tom Cannon, on Foxhall, watched only Archer, on Petronel, and they lay behind a long way, believing that the three-year-old would have shot his bolt and been done with long before home was reached. Still, however, he kept his lead.

"I wondered when he was coming back to us," Tom Cannon said afterwards in giving me a description of the race, "and when we were in the straight it occurred to me that he wasn't coming back at all, and that I had to go on and catch him."

Catch him he did, cleverly enough, but notwithstanding that he had done all the work a horse could do by himself (and the one criticism on William Day's style of training is that he works his horses too light), Foxhall was not wound up and trained to go the long three-mile journey in the Alexandra Plate, and, with five to two on him, he was beaten by the Duke of Hamilton's son of Prestones. It was hoped that in the Champion stakes at Newmarket, for which last year Bend Or beat Iroquois, or in some of the Cup races, Foxhall would have wiped out his defeat, but an enlargement outside a joint on a foreleg stopped the horse, and necessitated blistering, the effects of which kept him at home, though now he is perfectly sound. What is to be done with the horse I cannot, of course, say. It has been rumored that his owner is willing to sell him.

Mr. Keene's luck has been bad in several particulars, and notably with regard to Don Fulano. Had this colt only kept sound he would, in all likelihood, have won a great name for himself. When unfit to run, and with 100 to 1 against him (excellent evidence of want of condition), it will be remembered that he finished third to Peregrine and Iroquois for the Two Thousand Guineas, and several good horses were behind him. When he and Foxhall were at their best there was not much more than seven pounds between them, and this means that he would have won last year's Cambridgeshire fortunate as Mr. Keene to' have such a "second string"'as Foxhall, able to win with the unprecedented weight of nine stone!) had he kept sound. A good gallop, however, after, I believe, a commission had been out to back him, settled his chances, and when I saw him a fortnight after the race he had a leg like a bolster. Brought round by William Day's skill and attention, this year he was once more going gradually, but there was always a fear lest the leg should go again, and it was impossible to wind him up and depend upon him in this year's Cambridgeshire, in which, as his trainer expected, the leg "went." The luck with Bookmaker was also very bad. In the Corinthian Plate, at Goodwood, he was not thoroughly wound up, for the reason that it had not been decided much before the meeting that he was to run, but till want of condition stopped him he was going wonderfully well, and the race was enough to show that he had a grand chance for the Cambridgeshire if leniently treated by the handicapper. He was so treated, and for a long time before the race was first favorite, but he had to be stopped in his work, and hence the failure in the contest which Mr. Peck's "hunter" Hackness carried off.

These are the four-year-olds, and, as a class, they are far superior to the threes. Golden date can gallop for three-quarters of a mile or ten. The short head beating he received from Isabel in the Summer Cup of the July meeting, at Newmarket, created a very incorrect impression on this point, for this is the longest race run on the English turf, the distance being three miles, four furlongs, one hundred and thirty-nine yards; but the horses only raced in earnest for some half mile at the end, though the time, 7:25, is far from bad. Golden Gate was made a favorite for the Derby without a penny of the owner's money being on, simply from dread of the Foxhall stable and its astute ruler, but it is to be feared that he is a bad horse, and that Rome is not much better. This colt hit his hock during a rough passage to France to run for the Grand Prix, in which Foxhall established his fame by beating off from Tristan, Fiddler, Scobell, and others, last year; but Romeo, had he been able to run, could scarcely have been dangerous. Some of Mr. Keene's horses have been handicapped with indicorou severity at some of the smaller meetings, where incompetent or dishonest handicappers play their wildest pranks.

The two-year-olds include Potosi, an own brother to Foxhall, Blue Grass, Bolero, and Crown Point, and it is quite on the cards that some of these may make a name for themselves. Potosi grows very much like his brother, but has not Foxhall's size. This colt hurt himself as a yearling, but is well enough now, and is of an improving sort. Bolero is quick, but does not seem able to stay; and probably the pick of the basket will prove to be Blue Grass. He can gallop, and such chances as Mr. Keene has of winning the Derby next year depend, I think, on Blue Grass; the chance, however, is very faint, indeed, with M. Lefevre's Ladislas, Prince Batthyany's Fulmen, Mr. W. S. Crawford's New and Energy (I cannot believe in Macbeth's power to get down the kill from Tattenham corner, brilliant as some of his performances are), Blanton's Prince, Tom Cannon's Signorpleon, Goldfield, Beau Brummel, Tyndrum, Bon Jour, and Medlock, in the way. Well placed and placing is the great art of racing, these will all win races, that's to say, three of them will, for I fear Crown Point is very bad, though he, like the rest, is a good-sized, well-framed animal, a little wanting in quality, but with overshadowing good points.

The best of the yearlings I think will prove to be Sister to Foxhall, a charming mare, with a curious resemblance to the ways of the old horse. Blue Grass does much after the style of her two brothers, is an exceedingly light-hearted filly, and playfully kicks the whole way up her first canter every morning, but it is all good nature, for she is a very kind mare. She swishes her tail just after Foxhall's fashion, and, so far as can be judged at present, is likely to do honor to her distinguished family. The young lady developed an extraordinary habit of catching mice, and on one occasion killed a young rat, but she has now adopted a kitten, a daughter of one of the two kittens of which Foxhall was so fond, and her protege will doubtless take the mousing business into her own claws. Another very promising yearling is a chestnut colt by King Alfonso—Hester, and there are a couple more, a bay colt by Virgil—Boniform, and a second bay by Monarchist—Return.

If only these are good enough, they will learn the way they should go at Cholderton, and valuable results will follow. It need hardly be said that Mr. Keene's stud could not possibly be better placed than they are; indeed, Foxhall's double victory in the two great handicaps (not to mention the Grand Duke Michael Stakes and Select Stakes) are notable triumphs for a trainer. How much Foxhall improved after leaving Newmarket, is manifested by the fact that, while in the City and Suburban Bend Or gave him two stone six pounds, and beat him a length and a half, in the Cambridgeshire Foxhall actually beat Bend Or, at even weights, and Bend Or could not have been so much off, seeing that less than a fortnight before the Cambridgeshire he had won the Champion Stakes, beating Iroquois into third place. I have on more than one occasion heard an unrivaled judge of horses and racing—the Duke of Beaufort—speak in warm terms of praise of the manner in which William Day has turned out Mr. Keene's horses, and next year no victories will be more cordially received than those of the white jacket, blue spots.

## The Plunger and Duchess.

If Theo. E. Walton was intent on obtaining notoriety he could not have affected his purpose more effectually than has been accomplished by the newspapers. His plunging propensities were not the only things to bring him prominently before the people through the medium of the press, but he is now credited with being the cause of a noble Duchess so demeaning herself on the race-course as to bring any amount of obloquy on herself and her entitled spouse. From the *Referee* of November 26th the following is taken:

A deal of mysterious paragraphing has been done recently in reference to the quarrel between her Grace of Montrose and Mr. Stirling Crawfurd of the one part, and Sherrard the trainer, and various more or less important employes of Bedford Lodge, of the other. Everybody in any way interested knows all about the quarrel, and by now knows that it arose through private information having been afforded to Walton, the plunger, during his first and most successful visit to these islands. During the time that Walton was winning large sums of money it was wondered how he could obtain the "tips" which he undoubtedly did obtain about certain horses, and all sorts of rumors were abroad, not only as to what Walton did and said, but as to what was said and done by those who considered themselves injured by his successes. The now historical quarrel between Walton and Sir John Astley arose out of Walton's having received information which should not have been accorded an outsider—information which, if my memory serves me aright, prevented the burly baronet getting nearly so good a price about his horse as he should have had, because of the forestalling which resulted from it.

Forestalling is always a dangerous game to play; irate owners have before now carried the war into the enemy's own country, and routed him with great slaughter. It was to forestalling that the suppression of public ready-money betting in London some thirteen or fourteen years ago was due. Mr. "Boy" Wright, the late leviathan commission agent, whose advertisements paid the working expenses of more than one sporting paper, took liberties similar in kind if not in degree to those taken by Walton last year, and the result was that the "through the post" men had to beat a hasty retreat across the border. Sir John Astley was satisfied to have others who suffered the smart of Walton's intrusion. These showed their indignation in a variety of ways. A large amount of the action which has made the colors of Mr. Stirling Crawfurd and the wife so unpopular on the turf is distinctly traceable to the plunger's operations.

It may be borne in mind that on Walton's reappearance here this year he commenced much the same game as he had previously played but that soon a check was put upon his progress. During the panic which his arrival here caused in certain proprietorial bosoms, the Thebais and other scratchings which led to so much popular excitement happened; it was about the same time that the Duchess of Montrose made her magnanimently conspicuous owing to the too public airing of a grievance upon the heath at Newmarket. As straws show which way the wind is blowing, so these trifling incidents made it evident that some unpleasantness was brewing between the duchess and those employed by her. Eventually the secession of Sherrard was announced, and with his secession came the news that the Duchess of Montrose and Mr. Stirling Crawfurd had received extremely valuable information as to complicity between him and that fruitful cause of all the mischief, Mr. Theodore Walton. The leading jockey of the stable was also implicated. That Walton got good information last year from somebody was not denied at the time. So far from that, he used to boast about his ability to get it. That such information was of immense value is so once shown when we contrast what he did while in receipt of it with that he did after it was withdrawn from him. Still there was no reason that can be discovered—or that is stated—for suppose ing Sherrard and the chief weaver of the all scarlet gave this information to Walton. There are always plenty of under lings in an important stable who must know sufficiently well what is going to make their news saleable. This might easily have been shown, I think, had the business of clearing up the characters of both trainer and rider been commenced judiciously.

BREEDER AND SPORTSMAN.—Our contributor, Joseph Cairn Simpson, is the editor of a new and handsome weekly entitled the BREEDER AND SPORTSMAN, published in San Francisco. The new journal aims to elevate the literature of the turf and other sports far above the plane upon which it has moved on this coast, and to present matters relating to live stock. Mr. Simpson is a very well-informed and acceptable writer, and he has associates who understand all the intricacies of outdoor sports. The new paper has our best wishes for success in its peculiar field.—*Pacific Rural Press.*

## OVERMAN AND ROMERO.

### Last Saturday's Trotting at the Bay District Course.

Saturday last there was a fine attendance on the Bay District Course to witness the match between the two cracks of the Coast, at least those which were supposed to be the champions of the tracks of the Pacific. Overman sustained his reputation, as hewon so easily that the race was no criterion of his form; Romero made the poorest exhibition of his career, and with, perhaps, the exception of his debut at Santa Rosa, never made so feeble a showing. Horses are prone to "get off," to lose condition in spite of the efforts of the trainer, and in defiance of care and the best judgment fail at the most critical period. In match races it is expected that a want of condition will be known in time so that forfeit can be declared, and the money of the backers saved. But in many instances matches are play or pay, and even when the customary "half forfeit" is the condition, the owner may hazard the other moiety in hopes that something will turn up to justify the "throwing the helve after the hatchet." The trouble, in all probability, with Romero was the long let-up after his race at Stockton, and, in fact, he has done so little this year that it is not likely he has been "keyed" to concert pitch at any time. "Let-ups" are dangerous and when Governor Stanford compared two of them to one break-down it was a forcible illustration of the mischief that arises from a cessation of exercise.

Had Romero been compelled to trot a race every week since he made his memorable performance at Stockton it is nearly certain that the "mens" would have to be reached to beat him. That is, of course, with health and freedom from accidents. It was rumored that having been lately dipped he had taken cold which caused a general stiffness of the muscles, and it is apparent that something was the matter, as in none of the heats did he show any of the fine turn of speed he surely possesses when "at himself," and even a "thirty gait" around the first turn in the first heat was enough to carry him to a break. The "muscle sore" claim appears to have some foundation inasmuch as he did better in the third heat than in any of the others.

Overman is without doubt the great horse his Eastern admirers claim him to be, and from present appearances he will have to be accredited as the champion of the Coast, always, however, leaving his stable companion, St. Julien, out of the calculation. He was always a favorite of ours, and from the time he was first harnessed we never surrendered the opinion that he was destined to take high rank in the trotting world. It is somewhat doubtful if Romero has any greater speed at his best and the action of the chestnut is preferable to keep up the rate for a distance. Still Romero has two years to catch up, and in that time if he fails to take a record much lower than his present gauge we shall be sorely disappointed.

The early portion of the afternoon was pleasant, though by the time the second heat was called the weather had changed and there were fogs and chilliness. The track was in good condition saving that the first turn was wet and soggy from the moisture seeping through the hill on the south, and this part of the track is shaded so that the sun cannot strike it.

There was more than a fine attendance, a larger concourse than has been seen since the time of the "big races," and the assemblage was composed of the foremost people of the town, while there was a large number from all parts of the State.

Now that Romero is evidently so much out of shape that he cannot be expected to make any sort of a race with Overman, we would like to see Director try his hand, and if Albert W had been kept at work his presence would add greatly to the interest. Although it is too much to expect of colts, four and five years old, to lower the colors of a horse of the capacity of Overman, a race between these three will be well worthy of a journey to the course.

The following is the account of the heats, though the race was so one-sided as to leave little chance for a description:

Before the start the pool-selling was lively, the rates being $60 on Overman to $31 on Romero. The horses were called promptly at two o'clock, and after the usual preliminary exercise to get their legs and lungs in order, they took their positions. Romero having the pole and Overman the outside. Hickok drove Overman, while Goldsmith handled Romero. After two false starts the word was given on an even start for the first heat. In rounding the first turn Overman outtrotted Romero, the latter leaving his feet on a bad break, from which he did not recover until the home stretch, six or seven lengths behind, Overman passing the quarter under a pull in 0:37½. Overman being still under a pull and Romero settling down to his work, he crept up and at the three-quarter pole had come within a length of the leader. In the stretch, however, Hickok urged his horse a little, and notwithstanding Goldsmith plied his whip and sent Romero for all that was in him, Overman crossed the wire ahead, with plenty to spare. Time, 2:24.

Second Heat—Pools sold at $200 for Overman, and $60, $57.50 and $55 for Romero. By this time the wind was blowing briskly and the sky was overcast with fog, contrasting strongly with the warm sunshine and calm that prevailed early in the afternoon. When the horses came on the track there was no time lost in sending them off, and the word was given on the second trial. The start was an even one, but Overman began to draw ahead on the turn, and from there out he increased or decreased his distance as his driver pleased, and though Romero was forced on the stretch under the whip, Hickok landed his horse an easy winner in 2:23.

Third Heat—It was so evident that Romero was over matched that the betting was dollars to dimes, and pools were sold at $100 to $10, very few backing him at that low rate at increased or decreased his distance as his driver pleased, and though Romero was forced on the stretch under the whip, Hickok landed his horse an easy winner. The word was given on the nose of the horse crossed the wire on an even line. Rounding the southern turn Overman was pulled up and Romero took the lead,

which he increased to several lengths on the back stretch, but by the time the half-mile pole was reached Overman was given his head and closed the gap very fast, passing the three-quarter pole ahead of Romero, coming in and winning the heat and race in the same easy style he had won the others. Time, 2:23½. Following is the

SUMMARY.

BAY DISTRICT COURSE, December 16, 1882.—Mile heats, best three in five, for a purse and stake of $4,000.

O. A. Hickok names s g Overman..........................1 1 1
J. A. Goldsmith names g g Romero..........................2 2 2
Time—2:24, 2:23, 2:23½.

## The End of the English Racing Season.

With the end of the official racing year in England on the 25th ult. nearly all the London dailies and sporting papers at once blossomed out with their annual contribution to racing literature in the shape of statistics and a general exultation over the failure of the "Yankee stables" to triumph, as they did in 1881. "Tavo," of the *Morning Post*, leads off by saying: "The collapse of the Yankees who were to have 'floked creation' by carrying off all our great weight-for-age prizes, if not one or more of the classic races of 1882, not only presents a striking contrast to their unparalleled triumphs of 1881—which will go down to posterity as the American year of English turf history—but supplies an equally noteworthy feature as the unprecedented series of reverses that favorites met with in almost every leading event, which will cause the season just terminated to be remembered by backers in general as one of the most disastrous on record. Foxhall's slovenly performance in the Ascot Cup, in which he only just crawled home in front of a moderate three-year-old like Fangh-a-Ballagh—mainly owing to the artistic jockeyship of Tom Cannon, who honestly earned Mr. Keene's £1,500 annual salary by that solitary ride—was the only prize of any consequence, if I except the Great Eastern Handicap, won by Aranza, that fell to the share of the two American stables during the season."

Another feature of the year in England was the general defeat of first favorites. Out of hundreds of important events they got home first in only about thirty, the failures beginning with Foxlet's success for the Lincoln Handicap, which was followed by Passaic winning the City and Suburban, Shotover and St. Marguerite, the Guineas; Prudhomme, the Chester Cup; Shotover, the Derby; Fiddler, the Alexandra Plate; Friday, the Goodwood Cup; Dutch Oven, the Doncaster St. Leger, and so on for nearly all the important autumn handicaps. Nor does the year end with anything remarkably good among the two-year-olds, for, although Macheath carried off the honors, it is very doubtful if he will stand training next spring for his three-year-old engagements, while a bet of a "thousand even" has been taken that the Derby will not be won by either Macheath, Keir, Fulmen, Prince Maurice, Galliard, Sirmophone or Ladislas, each of which, with the exception of Prince Maurice, who did not start, did fairly well as a two-year-old.

The first of the winning tables presented by the *Sportsman* is that of jockeys, which, of course, is led by Fred Archer for the ninth successive year. His record of victories this year shows 210 as against 220 last year, his total number of victories since his first on Athol Daisy in 1870 being 1,858. Second to Archer is Charley Wood with 122 victories, a position he held last year with twelve for 1882.

| | Mounts. | 1st. | 2d. | 3d. | Unplaced. | W.o. |
|---|---|---|---|---|---|---|
| F. Archer..... | 564 | 210 | 118 | 70 | 157 | 8 |
| C. Wood..... | 617 | 122 | 143 | 98 | 204 | 2 |
| G. Fordham..... | 306 | 79 | 69 | 52 | 114 | .. |
| G. Barrett..... | 411 | 73 | 65 | 65 | 205 | 1 |
| T. Cannon..... | 333 | 65 | 68 | 63 | 136 | 1 |
| T. Osborne..... | 222 | 58 | 34 | 25 | 98 | 2 |
| T. Cannon..... | 293 | 41 | 39 | 33 | 95 | 1 |
| J. Osborne..... | 269 | 40 | 16 | 35 | 118 | 2 |
| H. Custance..... | 256 | 38 | 35 | 34 | 138 | .. |
| C. Bowman..... | 182 | 37 | 16 | 18 | 101 | .. |
| W. Maidment..... | 274 | 35 | 24 | 27 | 144 | .. |
| J. Woodman..... | 236 | 30 | 33 | 42 | 132 | .. |

In regard to special honors, Tom Cannon (Mr. Pierre Lorillard's trainer) heads the list, he having ridden the winner of the 2,000 Guineas, Derby, Oaks and Ascot Gold Cup. Archer's most important success was the St. Leger, with Dutch Oven, while he also won the Chesterfield Stakes with Galliard, and the Woodcote Stakes with Bean Brummel. C. Wood was also prominent, having ridden the winners of the 1,000 Guineas, the Prince of Wales Stakes at Ascot, the Manchester Tradesmen's Cup, the Doncaster Cup, the Cesarewitch and the Middle Park Plate. Fordham's victories included the Goodwood Stakes, the Champagne Stakes, Dewhurst Plate, Queen's Vase and Hardwicke Stakes at Ascot.—*New York World.*

## Stock Sales.

W. G. Scoggin, of Dilley, Washington county, Oregon, to Maj. Magoon, of Mt. Vernon, Grant county, g c Hannibal, 3, by Hambletonian Mambrino, dam Kittie Lewis by Silver Duke. Price, $600. Mr. L. B. Lindsey regards this colt as one of the finest in Oregon, and at our suggestion promised to write a descriptive article of him for the *Rural Spirit.*

Jay Beach, proprietor of the Cascade Stock Farm, Lake county, Oregon, to Joseph Buchtel, of East Portland, b f Cascade, 2, by Altamont, dam L. B. Dyar's Kate, by Mike, a son of Vermont. This filly is nominated for the three-year-old Breeders' Stake for 1883. Mr. Macmanus arrived here this week with the filly and delivered her to Mr. Buchtel. Price, $450.

T. H. Tongue, of Hillsboro, to Hon. D. M. Gault, of this city, chestnut gelding, three years old, by Woodburn, dam Snowflake, by Volscian. Same to L. C. Triplett, Carlton, Berkshire boar, by Royal George, dam Princess Alice. Sire and dam both bred by Wm. Niles, Los Angeles, Cal. Also three sows by Royal George, and bred to Capt. Rider, No. 2969; same to R. S. Cross, Oregon City, Capt. Rider, sired by Commodore, No. 1025, the most successful prize winner ever in California.

The above items are cut from the *Rural Spirit*, Portland, Oregon, which show that there is a disposition to encourage home breeding in that State. While there is great benefit derived from the introduction of "new blood," and strains from a distance utilized, there is a disposition to carry this too far, and ignore superiority from the fact that it is a home production. We have seen several animals, for which big prices had been paid in the East and Kentucky, which were decidedly inferior in breeding, form, performances, to those which could have been bought here for less than half the cost. Still there will be advantages to follow nearly every importation, and while those who have plenty of money can gratify their penchant for foreign articles, others not so well supplied with cash can avail themselves of the chance of the same quality of goods for a moiety of the price.

## Batchelor's Invitation to the Countryman.

"I see one of your correspondents told a good story in last week's *Gazette* about Jack Batchelor—that one where he was going to shoot any driver out of the sulky that got up behind Mattie Graham—but I know a better one than that even," said a Chicago horseman the other day.

"In the summer of 1878," he continued, "there was a meeting in July at Columbus, Ohio, and among the races on the programme was one in which Proteine, Adelaide, Midnight, Deception and other good ones took part. 'Uncle Jack' was to it with his old favorite, John H, and wore the familiar white linen duster and the steel-rimmed spectacles.

"Of course it was well known that Proteine was by odds the best horse in the party, and when the boys met the day before the race to arrange the 'slate' it was decided that Proteine should win and Adelaide get second money. Midnight was known to be very fast, but he was left out of the combination, as his owner, Mr. Charles Reed, of Erie, Pa., had instructed his driver (Shillington) to always get to the front as soon as he could, and stay there as long as possible. Deception, who was driven by W. P. Kinzer, was also left out of the combination, because if the entire outfit was taken in there would be no money in the affair.

"Well, as usual in such cases, things didn't work very well. Midnight was a good deal better horse than the boys had put him up to be, and in spite of all they could do he managed to win two heats. Proteine also had a couple, and how to give Adelaide two, so that she could get second money, was the question. They finally started in to do it, however. Previous to this, Midnight had 'pinched' Adelaide a little in one or two heats, and before the start for the fifth heat Splan, who was driving the mare, notified Shillington that if any more funny business was attempted somebody would get hurt. This talk didn't alarm Shillington much, for when they got to the head of the home stretch in the sixth heat, he began crowding Adelaide to the pole again. Splan was as good as his word, though, and in an instant Midnight's sulky was overturned, the driver lying on the track and the horse running away. The rest of the horse kept on, and right under the wire Bachelor and Kinzer had a close finish for third place with John H. and Deception, the one that secured the position being entitled to fourth money, and as Deception was not in the ring, it was, of course, desirable that John H should 'get there.' When the horses came back to the stand after the heat (which was won by Proteine), Kinzer accused 'Uncle Jack' of having done some foul driving. The argument became rather warm, but finally Bachelor ended it in a very summary manner by hitting Kinzer a crack with the butt end of his whip, the driver of Deception biting the dust in less time than it takes to tell it. Kinzer lived at Columbus, and the audience was largely composed of his friends. When they saw him lying there with the blood running from a ghastly-looking wound in his head, there was trouble, and in an instant the quarter stretch was filled with an excited mass of humanity howling for Bachelor's blood.

"Seeing what a serious turn affairs had taken, some of the boys hustled Bachelor into the weighing stand, which was directly below that of the judges, hoping to keep him concealed until the storm blew over. But the crowd soon discovered what had been done and began to howl for gore again. One big countryman, who had his pants in his boots, was particularly conspicuous.

"'Let me in there,' he shouted to the men who were guarding the entrance to Bachelor's hiding place. 'Just let me get at the scoundrel once.'

"About this time somebody handed to Bachelor through the window of the weighing stand a big horse-pistol—one of the old-fashioned kind with a barrel like a gun. Just as Bachelor received the weapon, the man outside who was thirsting for gore began to howl louder than ever.

"'Let me in there,' he cried; 'I only want one chance at the villain.'

"As he ceased speaking, 'Uncle Batch's' treble voice was heard issuing from the precincts of the weighing stand:

"'Let th——in,' he said; 'I can't miss him.'

"When the ferocious countryman heard these words the one assumed a new aspect. He knew that the old man behind the spectacles would shoot, and, more than that, he knew that he 'couldn't miss him.'—*Breeder's Gazette.*

## Prescott Driving Park.

Following are summaries of the events at the winter meeting, Dec. 5, 6, 7 and 8, 1892, under the management of the Arizona Jockey Club:

First day, Dec. 5—mile heats, best two in three; purse $250; first horse $150, second horse $100; entrance ten per cent.
C. O. Palmer names b m Kansas Maid (L. C. Palmer)............ 1  1
D. C. Thorne names b g Martha's Dick (N. Beakford)......... 2  2
W. A. Smith names b g Harry Speaken........................... did not start
　　　　　　　　　　　　　　　　　　　　　　　Time—2:37.
Second day, Dec. 6—Running; half-mile heats, best three in five; purse $250; first horse $160, second horse $60; entrance ten per cent.
O'Connell & Blonger name b g Brown Dick, four years, 106 lbs. (Frabco Martin).
W. R. Campbell names b g Frenchy, aged, 116 lbs. (L. Morales)  1  1  1
D. C. Thorne names b m Kitty Stevens, 139 lbs. (J. Beckford)  2  2  2
　　　　　　　　　　　　　　　　　　Time—0:54, 0:57, 0:59½.

Kitty Stevens' jockey fouled Frenchy's jockey and the judges fined Frenchy.

Third day, Dec. 7—Running; mile dash, sweepstakes; purse $150; entrance ten per cent.
O'Connor & Blonger name Brown Dick (Fenton Mount)............... 1
D. C. Thorne names Kitty Stevens (Hercules)..................... 2
　　　　　　　　　　　　　　　　Time—1:37.
By consent horses carried two pounds under weight.
Fourth day, Dec. 8—Running; mile heats, best two in three; purse $250; entrance ten per cent; sweepstakes.
O'Connor & Blonger name Brown Dick, 105 lbs. (Fenton Mount)........
D. C. Thorne names Kitty Stevens, 100 lbs. (J. Sparks)........ 1  1
R. Schutts names Red Eye, 111 lbs. (Jeff Young)............... 2  2
　　　　　　　　　　　　　　Time—1:53¾, 1:59½.

## State Trotting—Two-Year-Old Stake.

STOCKTON, Dec. 19, 1882.
The following event will take place in September next:
Best two in three, mile heats. Nominations close February 1st, 1883; $50 entrance fee; $25 when entry is made, and $15 July 1st, or declare out. Whole of entrance money to be divided—50 per cent., 25 per cent., 15 per cent. and 10 per cent.
Four Moneys—Five hundred dollars added by the society; $100 each for the winners of moneys. One hundred dollars for the stallion whose get wins first money. Conditions same as 1882.
N.B.—This is the most liberal two-year-old trotting stake ever given. The percentage of entrance money should not exceed one per cent.
　　　　　　　　　　　　　L. U. SHIPPEE, President.
　　　　　　J. L. PHELPS, Secretary.

## Model Stables.

A visit to the Commodore Kittson farm, Erdenheim, near Chestnut Hill, a day or two ago, fully demonstrated that under Major J. B. Hubbard's management the Erdenheim stables will play an important part in the racing announced for the coming year. Since Mr. Welch sold the farm to Commodore Kittson last summer many improvements have been made, some of which are completed, while others are in progress. The most important of the improvements are a new mile track for training purposes and a stable for horses in training, which will contain box-stalls for forty-five head of horses, living accommodations for trainers, grooms and stable-boys, store-rooms for horse clothing and saddlery, feed-rooms and a veterinary room. The inside circle of the stable gives an exercising track an eighth of a mile round, which is well lighted and thoroughly protected against the weather. It is the intention to lay out, eventually, the inside plot of ground as a handsome garden, with a fountain in the center. In the matter of drainage and other necessary conveniences Major Hubbard says that the stable will be second to none, not even to Mr. Pierre Lorillard's Rancocas stable, Mr. Geo. L. Lorillard's stable at Westbrook, or Mr. Reed's stable at Saratoga. Major Hubbard also promises that the boys' quarters shall be fit for human beings, which is something rarely found with the best of stables. There will be bedrooms for boys and grooms, with bath, reading and smoking-rooms. Ample barns are to be built for the storage of hay, straw and feed, and in short, everything is to be done to afford comfort to man and beast that ingenuity can conceive or money procure. The stables are to be lighted either by gas or by electricity. In the matter of stock, although some forty head were sold a few weeks ago, the place is very much overcrowded, there being no less than 4 stallions, 32 brood mares and 28 weanlings in the breeding division under John McCloskey's care, while ready for training under Piercy Benn's superintendence there are 9 two-year-olds and 16 yearlings. The former will be three-year-olds in January and the latter two-year-olds, and as they are a well-bred lot, as will be seen below, they must play, as before said, an important part in the racing of 1883, especially in the stakes yet to close. The two-year-olds are as follows:

B f Bedotte, by Bonnie Scotland, dam Ermengarde.
B f Bric-a-brac, by Bonnie Scotland, dam Martica.
B f Corona, by Glenlyon, dam Marguerite.
Ch f Equity, by Enquirer, dam Fanny Mattingly.
Imported ch c Pocotello, by Savour, dam Lovebird.
B f Repella, by Alarm or Reform, dam Long Nine.
Br c Rretrench, by Reform, dam Kate O'Neill.
Br f Retribution, by Reform, dam Nemesis.
Ch f Temptation, by Great Tom, dam Tribulation.
Yearlings—Ch f Allene, by Alarm, dam Australind.
Ch f Alhia, by Alarm, dam Elastic.
B c Bonnie Chief, by Alarm, dam Sister of Mercy.
Imported ch c Donald A, by Scottish Chief, dam Algebra.
B f Iona, by Lyttleton, dam Iona.
Ch f Issaquena, by alarm, dam Essayez.
B c Keystone, by Alarm, dam Berisina.
B c Lewis, by Littleton, dam Nettly Fuller.
Imported Miss Easton, by Soapstone, dam Victoria.
Ch c Patrician, by Alarm, dam Delight.
Ch c Pantope, by Alarm, dam Maggie B B.
B f Rande, by Reform, dam Sue Ryder.
Ch c Rataplan, by Alarm or Reform, dam Lady Lumley.
B c Rrchiel, by Alarm or Reform, dam Sabina.
B c St. Paul, by Alarm, dam Lady Salyers.
Ch c Theodorus, by Alarm, dam Theodosia.

But little is known of the merits of the above youngsters, and as Major Hubbard is a combination of 'Airtight' Pury, year and 'Silent' Pincus, your correspondent is unable to say which of the two-year-olds he expects to win the Saratoga and Kentucky stakes, but that he expects to put the name of Norman W. Kittson on the list of winners of these stakes is certain.—*Philadelphia Correspondence New York World.*

## Racing at New Orleans.

Mr. W. A. Engeman and his party, after completing arrangements with the Louisiana Jockey Club, left New Orleans on Thursday night and arrived home late on Sunday night. Mr. Engeman says that he is more than satisfied with the outlook for a successful winter season. He was treated with the greatest courtesy by Mr. R. W. Simmons and the other officers of the club. The pitch which caused several days' delay in perfecting arrangements was that the club wanted racing suspended for thirty days previous to the beginning of the regular meeting of the Louisiana Jockey Club, which takes place soon after Easter. He objected to this part, and ten days was finally fixed upon. As to the details of management Mr. R. W. Simmons will act as presiding judge, and for the general supervision of the racing a board of governors, to consist of prominent members of the Louisiana Jockey Club, will be selected. The pools and betting privileges will remain as at Brighton Beach, under Mr. Engeman's personal supervision, while the restaurant, bar and gaming privileges will be farmed to the highest bidders. In reply to the question, "When will you start back?" Mr. Engeman said; "I shall start, if possible, on Thursday night and take some thirty or more horses now at the bench. I shall also take the most trustworthy of my summer employes and a full supply of 'mutuel' machines. Mr. McGowan will, as heretofore, act as secretary and clerk of the scales, and Mr. Battersby will have charge of the finances." As to the probable starters Mr. Engeman said he did not think there would be any lack of horses. McMahon and Caldwell, the starter, had secured some forty head from the neighborhood of Nashville, Colonel McDaniel and Dick Shea were on their way from Memphis with fourteen head, while the owners recently engaged at Columbia, Montgomery and Charleston had signified their intention to start for New Orleans at once, as also had several owners of horses already stabled on the track and several promised by Mobile owners, will make a total of over 100 horses to begin racing with on the day originally fixed, viz., Saturday, December 23. Weather favoring, he will race to-day (Christmas day) and two other days during the week.

How about racing by electric light, which, it is said, you will do?"

"Well, I may do so if I find that the people are anxious to witness it, provided it can be done with safety. I notice that the poles had been erected for some previous efforts in that line, which I believe were abandoned. But there is one thing certain—New Orleans is splendidly lit up by electricity at night. But at present I shall confine my endeavors to successfully establish racing, including steeplechasing, to which the people of New Orleans are comparative strangers."

To the question about transportation Mr. Engeman said that there was no lack of accommodations; that the horse-cars ran from Canal street direct to the track, and that he believed both lines intended to lay branches to the rear of the grand stand at once.—*New York World.*

RACING AT NEW ORLEANS.—The New Orleans *Picayune* gives the following as the conditions under which Mr. W. A. Engeman will race over the track of the Louisiana Jockey Club for the next five years: "They are to use the track this year free of charge; the second year they are to pay $2,000; third year, $3,000; fourth year, $4,000; fifth year, $5,000. They are to use the track from the first of November of each year until ten days before the spring meeting of the New Louisiana Jockey Club. After the completion of the latter event they will be allowed to resume racing and continue until about the middle of May." In an interview Mr. Engeman said he would begin racing on Saturday, the 23d instant, and continue three days each week, and that during the season he expected to offer as much as $50,000 in added money. In place of paying any rental this year he would have to make a number of improvements which would at once become the property of the jockey club. Among them is the construction of additional stables, kitchens, a field-stand and a saddling paddock. He would also have to advance considerable money for transportation of stables from Nashville and Memphis, Tenn.; Charleston, S. C.; San Antonio and Dallas, Tex., and from Baltimore, Brighton Beach, Hartford and elsewhere. Mr. Engeman and his party may be expected to arrive back to-day, and they are to reform at once with all the pool-selling and betting material used at Brighton Beach, including a small array of assistants and reporters, anxious to spend the remainder of the winter in the Sunny South.—*New York World.*

# THE STABLE.

### English Ideas of Horse-Shoeing.

Having preserved a few copies of the *Field*, the great English authority in matters pertaining to breeding domestic animals, stable management, etc., containing short articles on shoeing, with the intention of incorporating them in "Tips and Toe-Weights," we give a portion of them here. These were published in January and February, 1881, and the views in places are so similar to those which we made public some seven years ago, that it was very gratifying to find them corroborated. The Charlier method is simply an improvement on the Goodenough system, which the author introduced into England nearly twenty years ago, the improvement consisting of restricting the metal to the width or rather thickness of the wall or crust of the hoof, and using a much lighter shoe. Then it is put on with a much greater degree of nicety, the horn only being cutaway where the metal takes its place.

Should there be any necessity for a full shoe this is assuredly a better plan than incumbering the foot with a load of iron, unless there is proof that weight on the heel is a requisite for fast trotting. Although we are not yet prepared to say authoritatively that weight is not needed on the posterior portion of the foot, all of the experiments so far have led to the belief that it can be dispensed with. There may be horses which will be benefited by weight on the posterior part of the foot, and if so, a properly made bar-shoe will be the kind to use. We are satisfied that the bar, or round shoe, owes whatever merit there is in it to the pressure on the frog, when this is effected more in accordance with nature there is a greater gain.

The Charlier is superior on account of its near approach to a natural state, the whole thing being in replacing so much of the wall with a harder material. That it cramps the heel is also apparent, though far less than the ordinary shoe. The following article is from the *Field* of February 5th, 1881:

During the last fortnight of Arctic weather the state of the London streets has been a subject of interest to all and sunday, whether they walk or drive. Various feeble efforts have been made with the object of giving foothold to the unlucky horses whose mission it is to drag heavy vehicles over a surface whose quality of material varies in about every other street. Here we find a shovelful of ashes; anon we splash into a "freezing mixture" (*vide Lancet*) of salt; hard small cutting stones (called by courtesy gravel) are sent spinning along the frozen surface by the foot which they are supposed to benefit. Now, there is no sort of reason why horses should not be able to travel over the streets in safety, whatever may be their condition. It is merely a question of rational shoeing. In the ordinary mode of "roughing" a horse the heels of his shoes are turned up, and his foot is thereby prevented from sliding forward on ice, consequently he can stop or even back his load; but when he wishes to start, and the projection of this retention attempts to dig his toes into the ground, his foot fly from him in every direction, and he either falls heavily, or escapes that fate by sheer good luck. The antidote to this evil is simple enough, and why it is not universally applied is a puzzle to me. One would think that the numerous veterinary forges of London ought amongst them to be able to shoe a horse for frosty weather; but, judging from results, the contrary appears to be the case.

The whole secret of traveling over ice may be expressed in three words, viz.: "Rough the toe." A catch at the toe of each foot is perfectly effective. With three such catches, one at the toe, and one to each heel, a horse is independent of weather. Snow will ball in a foot so shod; but to prevent this a seldom a very serious consideration, as when it balls it is more or less in a state of thaw, and as a consequence disappearing; while, if it be very deep, the balling does not much matter. Snow will under no circumstances ball in a foot shod with a leather sole, nor in a foot shod with a short tip, it being the heels of the shoe that perfect this undesirable manufacture. In theory the catch at the toe may be objected to, as being likely to make the horse stumble. In practice it has not that effect, as all the horses in Canada can testify. The veterinary forges of harness and draught horses, whose toes are bound to come to the ground every time they start their load. Saddle horses take a sufficiently firm hold of the ground with short tips in front; and the hind shoes should have a catch rather on the outside of the toe, to obviate danger of tread and overreaches.

Omnibus horses should, in common with all others who drag heavy weights on slippery stones, let alone ice, have the toe of the hind shoe square, and a broad catch to it, the toe of the hoof projecting in front. The Midland Railway Company shoe their cart horses thus, and with the best results. When the foot is brought up "all standing" by a toe calk, "there it is!" When by calkins at the heel, the back sinew is too often strained. The observant will see on cab ranks many horses whose heels behind do not touch the ground at all; this contraction of the sinews is the result of the above form of sprain. My brother sportsmen must have personally experienced the difference between catching the toe, and the heel, of their shooting boot upon an unexpected obstacle. A few moments' discomfort, and, with the presence of ill-regulated minds, a possible malediction, see them through the first casualty; while the loss of a day's, or of several days' sport may be the consequence of the latter. Hunters in this sort of weather are on the straw ride; but if shod with short tips they may go anywhere on the roads.

We have lately heard a great deal about working horses without shoes, but the writers on this subject have been almost to a man theorists. If anyone had given his own experience, his testimony would have been interesting, not to say valuable. "Free Lance" appears never to have practised what he preaches in his book "Horses and Roads," although one of his correspondents used a barefooted pony. One gentleman wrote to the *Daily Telegraph* to the effect that he drives a barefooted horse eight miles daily. Now I know by experience that light work—say eight or nine miles daily—may be done by a barefooted horse, supposing his feet to be good hard ones; but that is mere exercise. Work is another thing. In no known part of the globe are horses able to work unshod, at any rate in front, on hard ground. In ancient times slippers were worn by horses and mules before shoes were invented. The want, though not supplied, made itself felt.

Nowadays we hear a great deal of South American horses, Indian ponies and the like. As a matter fact, these unshod horses inhabit districts where they never encounter a stone. Put them to work on rocky ground, and they are either shod or lamed. A friend of mine, lately returned from America, tells me that, though the horses were unshod on the plains, when a march over rocky ground (the Andes for example) was contemplated the same horses were shod with a shoe of raw ozhide. These shoes last about a week, by which time the mountains are generally crossed, and the soft plains regained. Pack mule seldom, if ever, require this protection to their feet; but even with them exceptions exist to prove the rule. And apropos of barefooted steeds, I may observe that they decidedly slip more on greasy ground with a hard substratum than horses with shoes or tips. A barefooted horse is far more pleasant to ride, to my mind, than a shod one—so long, that is to say, as he can go comfortably; but I do not know that he is more pleasant than when shod with light tips. I have not, however, yet given a fair trial to tips behind, although I mean doing so, as what experiments I have ventured on have been satisfactory.

To return to the insecure foothold of the bare foot. Example: In the beginning of the present season I was riding a horse out hunting with no shoes behind at all. The day was pouring wet after a spell of dry weather; the country, an extra-rural provincial. My troubles began at a bank, my horse's hind feet flying somewhere under his girths, and landing him on his tail, in luckily so trifling a ditch that, although we emerged with a most unbecoming scramble, we did emerge without dissolution of partnership. I tried to console myself with the thought that my flier had a soul above cramped banks and ditches; but, shortly afterwards, in crossing a common at best pace, where the other horses all slipped about very much, my steed suddenly came on to the floor bodily, and worse, on to my leg, his hind legs having again gone from under him. And this sort of thing, having gone on in a modified form all day, set me a thinking. As aforesaid, the ground was hard below, and very greasy atop. The horse is a flat-footed one, and this was, of course, "against him," as the phrase goes.

Hunters shod with short tips go so much better through dirt than when they wear full shoes, that I am compelled to believe that their heels, being free, expand on coming to the ground, and contract when the time comes for dragging them out of holding clay, etc. I have not been troubled with an overreach since I have used tips, and fancy that the fore foot gets more quickly out of the way of the hind ones when thus shod.

Miushivich asks (*Field*, Jan. 22): "What is the condition of frog which enables one horse to go with a five-inch tip, and another only with the whole shoe?" The answer is that a thrushy frog, if badly diseased and in a state of inflammation, is in too tender a state to withstand stones, etc.; and I once knew a case in which the sensitive frog was all but exposed, the horny frog, or what thrush had left of it, being worn down. The animal, a four-year-old mare, very soon recovered, and had sound frogs until a railway accident destroyed her at six years old. All sound horses will go sound in short tips; but they will not thump their feet down with the action so dear to London coachmen, as if they wished to penetrate the pavement with their legs. They will use their kneecaps, but their shoulders more. Thus shod, I have never had an instance of a horse breaking his knees on the road, with one exception, and he slipped on a piece of ice when being led at exercise. His shoes were full Charliers, and he broke his knees through his kneecaps. Had he had tips, I think he would have stood up. The full Charlier shoe is not such a safeguard against slipping as the tip, which puts the heels as well as the frog on the ground. Now I most disagree with "Miushivich's" friend as to our forefathers being experts in shoeing. The very old English shoe, worn by the "destriers" (which we should call carthorses) that carried the knights of old, was clumsy in the extreme. The great width, however, allowed some pressure to the sole, which was so far good, as experience shows that an unpared sole can stand pressure. I can only account for the horses of our grandfathers standing work at all, shod as they were, firstly, by their being nearer to their Arab ancestors, and consequently more sound in themselves, than our horses; and secondly, by the custom of turning them out to grass on every available occasion. They lost condition, went broken-winded, etc.; but their feet had a chance, or rather nature had a chance of restoring their feet; and, all the world over, there is nothing like dew and night air for anything like lever in the feet. Harness horses had no weight on their heels; those belonging to rich men were not unreasonably worked; the mail-coach horses did their stage in the allotted time, and the number of legs which they used in progression was optional with them. In many ways our horses have certainly deteriorated, and in nothing more than in unsoundness of wind.

The first carthorse I ever heard roaring caused me to turn round and make a mental note of the circumstance. Now I often hear them; and, more remarkable still, last summer a pony of the polo description cantered by me, roaring like Prince Charlie himself.

The greatest errors in the matter of shoeing history are to be found in veterinary works of a comparatively late date—say sixty years ago. What countless horses have been ruined by the theory about the descent of the sole! Our great-grandfathers and grandfathers had plenty of horses lamed by their shoeing, but they ascribed the lameness to every cause but the right one. Chronic laminitis they called "chest founder," and many a horse lame in his feet was

tortured by having his legs fired and blistered. Nor is all that practice quite changed in the present day, though much improved. To return, however, to the descent of the sole. Youatt, in "The Horse," page 418, says that, unless the sole be pared, "that portion of horn which in the unshod foot would be worn away by contact with the ground, is suffered to accumulate until the elasticity of the sole is destroyed, and it can no longer descend, and foundation is laid for corns, contraction. and navicular disease!" Fancy a man calling himself a director of public opinion about horses, and not knowing that the sole never attains more than a certain thickness, whether it be on the ground or not! When thick enough it scales away, leaving a new sole ready for any emergency below it. The sole being pared required protection, and could not even be touched by the shoe. Hence the necessity for the foot surface being beveled off; and hence contracting corns, and navicular disease.

I do not say (because I don't know it) that a horse shod with tips, and having his frog as nature made it, would never have navicular disease; but it stands to reason that he has the best chance possible of escaping it. Firstly, he minds where he is putting his feet, and does not bang them recklessly about. Secondly, the thick horny frog shields the navicular bone and performs tendon.

Otherhorms asks how Charlier shoes in front only answer? I reply, very well; but I prefer the nearest approach to nature all round, excepting for horses drawing heavy loads, and they have been discussed above. With the old-fashioned way of shoeing, only feet of medium quality, neither too strong nor too weak, had any chance of standing sound. Without shoes, sooner or later, all horses really worked on the hard will be lame. With tips, all horses can do all reasonable work, excepting those suffering from navicular disease. Tips will not make lame horses sound at once, but they give many diseases of the foot the best possible chance of righting themselves, especially if the owner of the horse possesses the quality of patience! Last season I owned a mare who had such thin feet that she could do nothing at all barefooted on the road. With short tips, however, she had, if anything, rather too much action for a hunter. At present I have a horse whose heels are quite on the ground; yet he goes better like this than he did with full shoes. Tips are no new notion. The "Ineatte" shoe of Lafosse was a tip. I do not think tips need be very narrow, unless they are let in a la Charlier. The heels, however, should always be beaten down quite thin. Clips are most useful in keeping light shoes or tips in their place; but they should on no account have a place cut out for them in the horn. Let them just be hammered on the outside of the crust. Also let the clinches be cut off and knocked down, but not rasped, as the crust is rasped with them, and a chance is given to the nails to break out. Let the sole and frog be on no account touched with a knife. Shorten the toe as much as possible on the occasion of each shoeing, with a rasp. And above all, "gentle reader!" if you don't happen to be master in yourown stable, never let the words "Charlier," "tip," or "nature" escape your lips. If, however, you are not a slave to your groom, my experiences may be of use to you, and in any case are very much at your service.

F. S.—The above remarks having been delayed in transmission, I take advantage of the opportunity to add some more last words, and to make some remarks which I hope will not be considered impertinent, on the letters written by various gentlemen re Horse Shoes which appeared in last week's *Field*. First, Waverly, who was persuaded out of the Charlier system by his farrier, says that I take for granted, for reasons which I do not attempt to explain, that grooms and smiths are opposed to Charlier shoeing. I speak from experience, as all the grooms, excepting two, with whom I have ever discussed the subject, are opposed to it, for reasons which they do not attempt to explain." As to smiths, no less than four of them have refused to shoe my horses at all on this principle; they have all been owners of superior forges. I never had my horses better shod than by a village blacksmith who did what he was told, but even he charged me 5s. per set more for tips even than for the old heavy shoe! I may say as regards Waverly *De te fabula narratur*, as Mr. Fardon's speaks his own sentiments. Had Waverly persevered with the shoeing, the discolored horn would have grown and been worn out; his horses, not being lamed by the original bruises, would not have been lamed later on, any more than mine are.

I agree with M. B. that Charlier shoes, not approaching the corn place, cannot cause corns, any more than a gag snaffle could give a sore back. I should like, however, to know whereabouts the soles of his horses were worn unduly thin, as the frog of a flat foot being always prominent, shields the part "aft" of the point thereof, and the shoe should protect the forward part, if being as impossible as undesirable to have the shoe in a very flat foot flush with the sole. Is M. B. quite sure that the soles were in a natural condition? He says he never has the frog touched with a knife, but if not absolutely watched, smiths will, under the pretense of removing "ragged dead horn," thin the sole. I am curious on this subject, as last season I possessed a hunter with absolutely punctual soles, which improved immensely in the three months that I owned him, one foot regaining the normal appearance, although in both the coffin bones had descended when I bought him, as a stop gap and as an experiment. I much regretted that I parted with him, but a severe accident was accountable for that. Capt. Gillon is of my way of thinking. Would he tell us whether the material for shoes which he mentions is procurable in England? He, like myself, has given the system a fair trial.

Snaviter in Modo also agrees with me, for his harness shoe is the modified Charlier, with which I have shod many thin-soled horses until the sole grew thick. Apropos of his remarks on curby hocks, I may say that several years ago I bought a remarkably clever young Irish mare, fired for curbs, and with curbs which appeared callous. At the end of a season of Charlier hind shoes, the enlargements were absorbed; and I sold her to a dealer at the end of the next. Finally, Mr. G. Johnson is specially happy in his remark, that in most forges "the quantity of iron employed far exceeds that of common sense." To turn from this well-worn subject to a fresh one, will H. H. kindly tell me whether his hunters can eat Goode's luncheon cake out hunting with a double bridle in their mouths? I find that I must make one more remark than the other one. Snaviter in Modo misunderstands me as regards three nails only to a shoe. I use three nails in the *tips*, of which I have a given a sketch (there is hardly room for more), and it was to these infinitesimal tips only that I referred.

Bicycling is rapidly becoming universally popular, and scarcely any section of the civilized world now is without a bicycle club. There is a flourishing organization in Port Elizabeth, Cape of Good Hope, and a club in Cape Town has about seventy members.

The lower bay has swarmed with coots lately.

## BICYCLING.

### From Oakland to San Jose and Return.

On Saturday last two Oaklanders left that village for San Francisco by the 7 a. m. boat, prepared for a bicycle trip. Skirting around the city front until the depot of the S. P. R. Was reached, the 8.30 train was taken for a few miles, to get away from the city and avoid some bad roads, after which wheels were to be used. They were joined at Valencia street by a San Francisco rider, and the trip commenced.

At Millbrae the riders turned aside to run through the grounds of the Mills, Hayward and Howard places, and, riding in a leisurely fashion, Redwood City was reached in time for an early lunch. Leaving this place by a fine road, the travelers diverged to run through the fine grounds of Flood, Doyle, Latham, Woodlawn and several others, finishing up at Palo Alto, where an hour was pleasantly spent and, thanks to the courtesy of those in charge, they were enabled to interview the famous fillies Wildflower and Hinda Rose, the noted stallions Electioneer, Piedmont and others, and see the youngsters at their work; but the declining sun of a short December day and some eighteen miles more of road warned them that they must leave, which they did with regret, reaching their destination shortly after five. A good bath, dinner, a smoke and a walk about town finished a pleasant day's work, and made beds acceptable.

The following morning was damp, disagreeable and threatening, and it was decided not to run any further south, as had been thought of, for fear of being caught in a storm; in fact, it looked as if it might even become necessary to take trains for home; but shortly after ten it was decided to start and ride as far on the return trip to Oakland as possible. The roads were in fair order, although a little heavy from dust, and the first fifteen miles were made in an hour and three-fourths, Centreville being reached in time for a capital dinner, over which and the post prandial cigar an hour and a quarter was spent. Passing through Alvarado and Mount Eden, the weather cleared until the sun appeared before San Lorenzo was reached. The remainder of the trip, through San Leandro and Brooklyn into Oakland, was completed shortly after five, and the party separated, much pleased with their two days' run of about one hundred miles.

### Rational Dress.

The Rational Dress Society of London, Eng., has offered a premium of £50 for a style of dress for women which will best accord with the following requirements: Freedom of movement; absence of pressure over any part of the body; no more weight than is necessary for warmth, and weight and warmth evenly distributed; beauty and grace combined with comfort and convenience; not departing too conspicuously from woman's ordinary dress. It also offers prizes for tricycling and other ladies' sporting costumes. Mrs. E. M. King, the secretary of the society, a tricyclienne, in a letter to the B. T. C. *Gazette*, says:

"I send leaders of the R. D. S. The dress, however, that I have devised—from practical experience—for tricycling is not the same as that described. I will explain as far as I can, and you can insert as much as you think fit of my explanation in your next issue. It will save me a great deal of trouble, as people seem always to expect that I will give them a 'full explanation' rather than the very small one I gave. I found of no use—it kept riding up—then I tried riding trousers strapped under the boot but they did not allow enough play at the knees. Knickerbockers made very loose to below the knees, and from there like riding trousers, and either kilted or braided, I found suitable and comfortable in every way, and I don't think the £10 prize will bring out anything better. For the top skirt—straight cut and narrow (without gores), with a small quantity of drapery behind, as long or as short as the wearer may desire, and braided according to taste; but the shorter the better. The jacket body to fit to the figure about as tight as a man's bicycling jacket, but not so tight as to necessitate corsets underneath. The top skirt is kept from blowing aside by a piece of elastic, which when seated is passed between the legs, so as to hold together the back and front part of the two skirts, this I also found to answer splendidly, and to do away with the necessity of the foolish plan of weighting the skirt, which I find so many ladies are taking to."—*Bicycle World*.

The two-mile bicycle race in connection with the New York Seventh Regiment games, November 25, was won by J. I. Stearns, Jr., in 6:41; F. C. Thomas second. The other starters were F. E. Davidson and Mr. Booth. Davidson, who had been in careful training for the race, went off in the lead, closely followed by Stearns, and the pair soon left the others some distance behind, but on the second lap Davidson slipped and fell at a turn, breaking a pedal so that he could not continue. This left Stearns an easy task to win. The track measured nine laps to the mile, and was chalked upon the board floor. Fully four thousand ladies and gentlemen were present, and great interest was evinced in all the games.

The meet at Washington, D. C., was not a great a success as was hoped for, partly because many preferred to spend Thanksgiving day at home, partly because of greater attractions elsewhere and partly on account of the weather, which was cold and disagreeable, with some two inches of snow upon the ground. About two hundred riders put in an appearance, however, and the programme was carried out in good style, except the racing, which was postponed until next May, when more suitable weather is expected.

An Oakland rider who has been spending some days in Redwood City reports the roads in every direction from that place to be in excellent condition, hard and smooth. Riding from that place to San Jose, he returned to Oakland by the roads upon the eastern side of the bay, making the distance, forty-five miles, between the hours of ten a. m. and three p. m., including stops. With the pleasant weather and cold bracing air of these winter months there is no finer riding season during the whole year.

Many of the English bicycle makers are extending the size of their workshops and improving their facilities for an anticipated increase of business in the spring. One firm recently received in one day export orders from three different customers for an aggregate of two hundred machines.

John Keen, formerly the English professional champion, is expected in this country shortly, and will ride one or more races against Prince while here.

# HERD AND SWINE.

## Improvements in Dairying.

The developments of civilization are spread over the civilized world with an even hand. Improvements in the arts and sciences do not accumulate exclusively in any single locality; they distribute themselves over the reading portion of the globe, with almost the readiness and equality with which water finds its level. No sooner is any important discovery or advancement made, than the press picks it up, and with the never-tiring wires of steam, spreads it out before all the nations of the globe, whose eagle-eyed intellects are trained by study and experience to snatch, from the flitting streams of passing intelligence, whatever may serve to enlighten, profit, or please. What is thus plucked from the hastily circulating current of news is scanned, weighed, and measured, and perhaps utilized by a thousand persons at the same moment.

In this equalizing tendency of the expanding novelties of the world, the dairy interest is enjoying its full share. It is interesting to look over the dairy interest of the world, and note the progress of the last score of years. A quarter of a century ago, the system of associated dairying sprang into existence in this country as if by magic. Association brought dairymen in contact with each other, and a comparison of views and study and investigation followed. The legitimate sequel to all this was improved goods, cheaper production, and larger profit. This, in turn, led to expansion in production.

An art which had been confined to a few contracted nooks and corners spread, at once, over the face of the nation with almost the velocity of news by telegraph. Improved qualities brought increased consumption and increased demand, and from this was developed a new branch of commerce, that leaped from oblivion into an importance second only to that of the food-producing cereals.

The Canadians, allied to us by contiguity and consanguinity, were at the same time stirred into activity, and built up a new industry contemporary with our own.

England and Continental Europe have also been moved to the adoption of our improved process, and to increased production and consumption. The agricultural journals of Europe have teemed with our dairy literature, and thousands of the yeomanry have read and studied and profited. The impulse given to the dairy interest of the world has not been stopped by the bounds of the continents. It has stretched out to the islands of the sea. Australia has a large and well-developed dairy industry, built up since our associated system became known, and modeled after it. They have our cheese factories and creameries. They have, also, our modes of teaching the art by organized associations, conventions, and discussions, and public reports; and the business has grown to large dimensions, and become a grand success. The far-off island of New Zealand, even, is also now rejoicing with a prosperous dairy department in her agriculture, that is furnishing her people in abundance with the choicest luxuries wrought from milk. No branch of farming is said to be more successful on the island than that of the dairy.

While we have thus been shedding light and influence upon the outside world, we have been absorbing from it in return. European practices, whether recent or hoary with age, have been freely quoted and studied by our dairymen, and from them we have gathered much that has proved useful, and worthy of adoption.

Thus do dairymen share, equally with men of other calling, in the radiation and reflection of light and intelligence, to and fro, from man to man, and nation to nation. The advancements in the dairy have been based on increased knowledge. Progressive dairymen have stepped outside the beaten track of routine and empiricism into the open channels of light and reason, and in these they must continue. The milk industry has, as yet, barely entered the field of progress. When we look back at the ground we have traveled over, it seems considerable; but when we look forward, and survey the immensely before us, the distance we have made seems as nothing. We believe there is a brilliant future open to dairymen who pursue their calling intelligently. The motto to be kept in view is, "Better goods at less cost." With this for his guiding star, he may push his way on with a speed measured by the light of his knowledge. Traditional rules have controlled in the past, but knowledge must control in the future. He who falls back on tradition will inevitably fall behind in the race. One might as well chase a steam engine with a donkey as to think of keeping up and prospering in a competition with those who avail themselves of the improvements developing for their benefit. With intelligence in command on the dairy farm, and persevering energy to do the pushing, there is no good reason for doubting that dairymen, in the future, may be much more prosperous than those of the past, or to-day.—*National Live Stock Journal.*

The Ramsaur Bros. of Florence sold car-loads of live hogs, within or about the year 1879, at the rate of $150 per car-load of 10,000 pounds. The same weight of porkers would to-day bring $950. Now, every stockgrower knows that hogs cannot be produced at $15 per 1,000 pounds, or $150 per car-load, without serious loss. However, the Ramsaur Bros. went on raising hogs upon a large scale, with implicit faith in coming remunerative prices. The reward of perseverance is now theirs. There arises here a practical lesson to those who shift and shift again with the shifting times. The shifter's bucket is apt to be bottom upwards when it does rain.—*Los Angeles Herald.*

Whatever stock is kept on the farm, the aim should be to constantly improve it as to its products. Common butter at the market price never pays. Gilt-edged butter always is in demand and at remunerative prices. The extra pound or two of wool to the fleece, and a few more cents a pound, which "Farmer Thrifty" gets above what "Farmer Slack" receives, make all the difference between profit and loss in production. A well bred and fed steer that is ready for the butcher when thirty months old pays a fine profit, while the scrub sells at a loss and is not in condition, or so large, at three and a half and four years old.—*Waldo F. Brown.*

A recent visit to the dairy farm of Mr. Walker, on Van Cycle's Island, in Suisun bay, disclosed it to be one of the finest and best arranged in the State. Mr. Walker milks on an average seventy-five cows daily, turning out 300 pounds of gilt-edge butter per week, which is delivered twice a week in San Francisco. He has a hard-finished dairy-house, with every convenience. The churn is run by horse-power. Hogs and chickens are fed with the whey and curd. The stock raised is of a fine breed, and the natural increase in it alone yields a fine revenue. The islands of the Sacramento and San Joaquin delta, when fully reclaimed, will, without doubt, become the location of the finest dairies in the State.—*Napa Register.*

---

## SHORTHORNS AND HEREFORDS.

### Facts and Figures Developed by the Chicago Fat Stock Show.

The following table shows the weight, percentage of waste, etc., as well as the breed, of the animals, entered for the premiums for dressed carcasses at the Chicago fat stock show:

[TABLE: Weights of the Various Parts of the Slaughtered Animals — illegible columnar data]

The following particulars regarding cost of productions taken from the report of the Awarding Committee, will be found of interest:

Steer, or spayed heifer, 3 and under 4 years—First premium, H. & J. Groff, on grade Shorthorn steer Canadian Champion, weighing 2,400 pounds; total cost of production, $305 70, or 8.51 cents per pound. Second premium, H. & J. Groff, on Shorthorn steer King of the West, weighing 2,335 pounds; total cost of production $209 33, or 8.96 cents per pound.

Steer, or spayed heifer, 2 and under 3 years—First premium, Leo B. Walsh, on grade Shorthorn steer Jim Blaine, weighing 1,825 pounds; total cost of production $82 96 or 4.54 cents per pound. Second premium, G. Norris & Son, on grade Hereford steer Jay, weighing 1,735 pounds; total cost of production, $111 97, or 6.42 cents per pound.

Steer, or spayed heifer, 1 and under 2 years—First premium, G. S. Burleigh, on grade Hereford heifer (spayed) Hattie, weighing 830 pounds; total cost of production $23 22 or 2.80 cents per pound. Second premium, Cobb & Phillips, on Shorthorn steer Cassius 5th, weighing 1,140 pounds; total cost of production $46 58, or 3.58 cents per pound.

The statements give some interesting data of feeding experiments, where the exhibitor evidently had in view the most rapid growth of the animal, rather than economical production. Had the latter been the chief object sought, less expensive kinds of feed would, in certain cases, have been used. The committee present the following tables, showing the comparative cost, year by year, of each animal entered. In order to make the yearly statement complete, the value of the animals at the commencement of each year is included, and based upon the actual weight certified by the exhibition at a fixed value—6 cents—per pound, live weight:

FROM BIRTH TO 12 MONTHS OF AGE.

| Names of Animals. | Total cost of twelve months. | Weight at 12 months. | Weight per month, lbs. | Cost per lb. |
|---|---|---|---|---|
| Jay | $21 30 | 600 | $36 00 | $4 72 |
| Experiment | 33 30 | 710 | 42 60 | 4 72 |
| Young Aberdeen | 24 47 | 1000 | 60 00 | 2 47 |
| King of the West | 24 67 | 1000 | 60 00 | 2 47 |
| Cassius 4th | 31 47 | 1000 | 60 00 | 3 14 |
| Cassius 5th | 38 15 | 1000 | 62 40 | 3 01 |
| Hattie | 19 76 | 700 | 42 00 | 2 82 |
| Jim Blaine | 27 30 | 960 | 57 60 | 2 84 |
| Canadian Champion | 33 67 | 1000 | 60 00 | 3 37 |

FROM 12 TO 24 MONTHS OF AGE.

| Names of Animals. | Weight at 12 months. | Weight at 24 months. | Gain in 12 months. | Total cost, 12 to 24 mos. | Cost per lb. |
|---|---|---|---|---|---|
| Jim Blaine | 960 | 887 00 | 897 00 | 1395 | $48 40 |
| Experiment | 600 | 48 00 | 30 31 | 1570 | 62 20 |
| Young Aberdeen | 1000 | 60 00 | 53 15 | 1890 | 95 00 |
| King of the West | 1000 | 60 00 | 52 13 | 1600 | 95 00 |
| Canadian Champion | 1000 | 60 00 | 52 15 | 1600 | 96 00 |

FROM 24 TO 36 MONTHS OF AGE.

| Names of Animals. | Weight at 24 months. | Weight at 36 mos. of age. | Gain. | Total cost 24 to 36 months. | Cost per lb. |
|---|---|---|---|---|---|
| Canadian Champion | 1600 | 295 | 2400 | 2350 | $118 |
| King of the West | 1600 | 295 | 2335 | 2260 | 128 |

The price of each article of food was determined on an equitable and uniform basis to all the competitors, and upon this standard the cost of the several commodities mentioned in the statements presented by exhibitors was calculated. The premiums were awarded as follows.

In the yearling ring, the animal produced at the least cost per pound was the lightest animal competing, and would not bring as much per pound in the market as the second-premium steer; and if the present market value had been considered, the awards would have been reversed. [It will be seen in the accompanying statements, that the value of a calf at birth, pasturage for each year, as well as expense for care, are the same in each case, which leaves the amount of other kinds of food consumed to determine the question of cost of production. As all the animals entered for competition were either pure bred or high grade, the amount of improved blood possessed by each would not give material advantage to any exhibitor.

As the facts are given under oath, the greatest care having been taken to secure absolute accuracy, they are of special value to all stockgrowers. Such exhibitions as the one in question, in connection with the periodical publications devoted to stockgrowing, are of more value, in the way of promoting the most desirable system and determining the most desirable breeds, than will at the first glance be realized, and we trust the time is not far distant when the agricultural fairs of this state will be productive of grand results—results, which are, indeed, already foreshadowed by what has been accomplished in a small way.

### Breeding for Desirable Points.

Breeders are often disappointed that the young things in the herd do not show an advancing tendency, as the idea holds with many that it is the province of improved breeds to move forward, rather than to stand still, gaining upon their best points and overcoming defects, from year to year. The common, familiar expression, through which we are told that animals will produce progeny like themselves, can only be depended upon to a degree. The tendency among domestic animals to vary is greater than the tendency to hold strictly to a uniform type, simply because all of our improved breeds are what the term implies, "improved," this having been done by more or less careful selection from a lot of individuals, none of which were up to our present standards. For this reason,the utmost vigilance and the highest judgment are necessary, if we would continue to gain upon the best perfect forms we have left behind us.

The law which transmits eccentricities or defects also governs the transmission of points of excellence; and as we have many examples illustrating the former, we will give a few of them, the better to show how persistent the tendency is in animals and persons to transmit marks and features to their progeny. Col. Hallam, in 1833, procured a race of two-legged pigs, the hind legs being entirely wanting. He personally had knowledge of this defect going through three generations. Nathusius describes a race of cattle on the Plata called Niatas. The forehead is very short and broad. The nasal portion of the face is short and upturned, thus leaving the lower jaw, which also curves upwards, projecting below the upper. This singular breed, undoubtedly, originated from a sport, so strongly marked as to be able to transmit this peculiarity so deeply that its propagation was continued, thus forming a breed having this ill-shaped head quite regularly planted upon the progeny, as by breeding a Niata bull to a Niata female, a Niata calf would be invariably produced. This breed originated after cattle were introduced into the country from Spain, in 1552, and it is supposed to have sprung up in the hands of the Indians south of the Plata. Mention is made by Azara of a breed which originated in South America, to which the name of Chivos was given, on account of their having straight, vertical horns. They are reported as breeding true, and, unlike the Niata, were those from a sport. So, likewise, he mention made by the same author of a breed in Corientes, having very short legs. These also must have originated from a sport, a fixed breed resulting. Hornless cattle had a foothold in South America long since, and quite generally produced offspring without horns. Thus, through variation—departure from a given form—we have most singular breeds, and a great many of these, all having sprung from two or three parent stocks. One author alone makes reference to over fifty European breeds. These, of course, are more offshoots, the results of variation, not planned and ordered, but accidental proofs of the tendency in varieties to multiply.

It is this tendency to part with one peculiarity of form, taking on another, that gives the breeder such latitude for the practice of his art; and he who learns to seize upon the advantages so offered, turning them to good account, generally proves himself an expert in his line. Peculiarities in the forms of cattle become localized, and as stated by Youatt, each locality becomes prejudiced in favor of whatever form may, through accident, have become most common. It is a very common occurrence for men to become impressed with the idea that the cows in their yards though really of inferior grade, are better than any others within their knowledge. The same fact holds good with regard to horses long bred upon the farm. In these cases every man has his own local standard. It is quite likely to be a very ordinary one, like the standard in most neighborhoods for constructing roads and bridges. Yet, in the absence of any knowledge of a better, prejudice in favor of the low type becomes very firmly fixed. Hence we see farmers and farmers' sons taking stock, of the kinds referred to, to the fairs, and they think themselves greatly wronged in not receiving awards.

The improvement of the breeds has, with men who read and observe, done away with local prejudices and attachments, and with these, improving animal forms is understood to be upon as fixed a plan as any which governs changes in form and point, of convenience of farm machinery and mechanical appliances. The same influence which, now and then, greatly changes the horn, may work marked modifications in other parts. Where these modifications amount to a betterment, they should be seized upon and used. The disappearance or modification of a defect or a gain, be it ever so slight, in a desirable feature, is not to be lightly esteemed, because only in this way are improvements wrought, and made lasting by being perpetuated.

It is within the power of any man, if he has an especial fancy for a given feature in his herd, be this a short leg, a light horn, a full bosom, a wide, level top, or other thing deemed desirable to have, to select from herds, here and there, animals having the coveted feature, breeding from both male and female of this shape, persistently, and fix any feature or combination indelibly upon his herd. We close with a hard made up by selections at sales, and counted twelve cows, standing in a row, ranging from four to seven years old, that did not vary more than three inches in height, and were almost identical in general make-up and contour. Now, with cows so selected, and bred to a bull having like characteristics deeply implanted within him, there is nothing surer than that a fixed type can, in a few years, be established in any herd.—*National Live Stock Journal.*

## Marketing Butter.

*Colman's Rural World* says : We often see quoted very high prices for the gilt-edged butter from the Jersey, York, Pennsylvania and other farms, ranging from fifty cents to over $1 per pound ; and whilst we are anxious that our Western farmers and dairymen shall make the best and get the highest prices, we are at the same time aware of the fact that the difference between the two extremes, i. e., the price there and the price realized by some of our farmers, is not all profit. The happy medium, that is, a good quality of table butter that will sell to ordinary mortals the year round readily at from twenty-five to thirty-five cents per pound, and keep good for a reasonable length of time, is in our opinion the article out of which the most profit is, under favorable circumstances, made. The following from Henry Stewart in the *Rural New Yorker* is an illustration of this fact :

Let us consider what a gilt-edge dairyman did for his customers who paid him last winter from fifty to sixty-five cents per pound for his butter. The cows, in the first place, are all pure-bred and worth from $150 to $300 each, although this is well repaid by an average yield of ten pounds of butter in the week from each. In the second place, to secure the desired quality of the product the cows are fed and watered on the best of hay and feed and pure water from a spring, curried and brushed as well as a high-mettled racer is, and are bedded in clean sawdust frequently renewed. The udders are washed and wiped with a clean towel, and so are the milkers' hands. The stable is kept clean and well swept, so that no dust can get into the milk, and the milk, as it comes from the barn to the dairy, although quite free from specks of dust and hair, is strained twice before it is set away. It is set in a milk-house or milk-room, where the temperature is kept even by a stove in the winter and ice in the summer, and no expense or labor is spared to keep all these arrangements precisely the same through all the changes of the weather. The cream is churned and the butter is managed with every care by the hands of the proprietor himself ; or if by hired help the skilled labor required is highly paid for. The butter is packed in small boxes or pails that cost from three to five cents per pound of butter, or it is moulded in a press into cakes which are wrapped in paraffine paper and then packed in a neat box at a cost of at least five cents a pound. And, lastly, it is sent to the customer at a cost of five cents a pound more for express charges.

To find a desirable market is not always easy. Location is of great importance in this respect, and the nearer the dairyman can very well afford to farm land worth $200 an acre on account of enjoying the best markets in the country and looking after them himself. It is a great advantage to have one's butter in the hands of the customer within three hours of the time it is shipped. Distant dairymen must necessarily depend upon commission agents.

The remark is sometimes made that new varieties of flowers and fruits are frequently originated and introduced in order to make trade, and keep the florists' and nurserymen's business good, as new styles of dress are established for the benefit of the milliner, dressmaker, and the tailor. But a little thought will satisfy anyone that very few plants are or can be put into the trade merely for this purpose. If it should once be learned that a horticulturist had foisted upon the public a plant of inferior value merely for the trade it might afford him, he would be so deserted by his customers, and by his professional brethren, as to lose many times what he might possibly have first gained by the operation. These men are not so reckless of their reputations ; on the contrary, they are, as a rule, very jealous of them, knowing that their ultimate success depends very greatly upon their veracity. There are exceptions, but the exceptions belong to the fag-end of the business, and have comparatively little influence. When I find a man who honestly thinks that new breeds should not be encouraged because there are plenty of breeds already established, which possess such diversity of qualities that they may fill any necessary demand, I honor his opinion, although I think he is behind the times. But I see anyone trying to put down new breeds because somebody is making "money" out of them, I see only jealousy, and I suggest, as a cure, that they drop the old breeds, which are good enough in their places, but behind the times, and nobody wants them, and take up the new breeds ; give them honest attention a few years and make a little money out of them. The popular feeling is for the new breeds, and there are not enough men in this country who breed the old and established breeds and varieties to put it down.—*Exchange.*

We have done much in two or three years past to improve the number and quality of our dairies, but we have not increased them in any proportion to the demand. We consider at this day with the market we enjoy that butter-making is the best business a man or company can enter upon. Green feed can be procured for about the entire year, and for the brief time that green grass may be short root crops are always to be had in any required abundance. And the market is simply enormous, and so largely above our supply as to astonish those who are familiar with the facts. The money paid here for butter is equal to a steady stream of gold. We are cognizant of cases facts which if aggregated would surprise our people. It is an old saying that "bread is the staff of life," and it is equally true that butter is its close companion, and it, being so, is at all times in demand by all, the blessed poor as well as the miserable rich. So those who desire a permanent, profitable business should bend their energies and invest their capital in butter-making in Los Angeles county.—*Los Angeles Mirror.*

Texas fever urgently demands consideration at the hands of our authorities. The nature of the disease and the conditions under which it is propagated appear to be but imperfectly understood even by the veterinary profession. Dr. Salmon is patiently investigating it; but a disease, so promulgated some new and startling views concerning it. There ought to be a very thorough inquiry instituted ; our very best men ought to be employed to co-operate with Dr. Salmon in his work. Hitherto but little has been done by men properly qualified to make practical investigations in this field. All have been content to follow the track of Gamgee, and to accept his conclusions as final. Dr. Salmon is the first to contest any of Gamgee's theories of the disease. Let us have more light upon this strange affection that has been no hold in various localities during the past season.—*Breeder's Gazette.*

To avoid the trouble of having dirty pigpens, a slat floor can be made and placed about two feet above the bottom of the pen. The slats can be made of scantling, 2x4 inches, and set edgewise on each other. The manure, when sufficient has accumulated, can be cleaned out by raising this grating. The floor is kept dry by this grating and will not rot. There need not be any floor underneath ; the manure will rest on the ground.

## BULL BUTTER AND THE DAIRYMEN.

## Oleomargarine's Financial Success Inevitably the Result of Fraud.

The meeting of the dairymen last week, and their organization into the State Dairymen's Association, was but the first move in a war that will be waged with bitterness between them and the manufacturers of imitation butter. This organization has been effected not too soon. The oleomargarine men have already secured a strong hold on the situation. Not only is a very large amount of imitation butter manufactured in this city and disposed of here, but great quantities are imported from the East. This great success, reported by the manufacturers, themselves, can rest only upon fraud.

Oleomargarine finds its market only through fraud. The success of its manufacturers is the result of fraud. In fact it could not be marketed at all without fraud, and the manufacturers, when they assert that they desire this product to stand or fall on its merits, and that they desire all who buy it to know just what they are buying, are putting forth a false claim. They know that only by deception on a large scale could they achieve the financial success and find the ready market of which they boast, and they know that their careful stamping and labeling of the bull butter by its right name is a farce and does nothing to accomplish the object had in view when the oleomargarine law was passed. Of the thousands of pounds put upon the market, if they be traced to their final consumers, not one per cent. is consumed by people who know that they are not eating the natural product of the cow. If such quantities are marketed there must be consumers in proportion. Yet where is the man, woman or child, in all this city, who consumes such quantities, who knows that he or she has eaten the bogus compound ? The parties who consume it are imposed upon and led to believe that they are using the natural butter of the dairy. Then of what use are your boxes and labels and stamps? The spirit of the law is evaded, though the letter be complied with. We are assured that tons of the bogus compound are disposed of in this city, and there is no ground for questioning the assertion. Where does this bull butter go ? What grocer sells it to housekeepers under its proper name ? What restaurant admits to its patrons that it serves them oleomargarine ? What hotel avows that it feeds this product to its customers ? A resolution that butter-makers refuse to consign their product to any dealer who handled oleomargarine, when offered in the convention, was promptly met with the assertion that nearly all of the dealers were handling the bogus article. That the false butter is properly stamped and labeled when it leaves the factory we do not deny. But who can trace it farther ? It is sold to half the keepers of hotels and restaurants in San Francisco and is served to their customers as the genuine article.

We do not object to any man's making any compound of grease and chemicals that he may choose to make. We do not object to any man's eating this compound if he likes it. We do not object to the Chinaman's feasting on a rat dinner or a nicely-cooked plate of roast dog. But we do object to having the chemically-compounded grease palmed off upon the guest at the hotel or the boarder at the restaurant as butter, or to having the rats and dogs disguised as sausages and fed to the customer who asks for sausage.

If every person who eats oleomargarine could know what he was eating the market for the product would be gone. It may be that the product of the factory is as good as much of the butter sold in our markets, but the great majority of people would prefer a poor quality of butter to a manufactured compound equal in quality, and if the fraud of serving oleomargarine for butter were stopped the profits of the manufacturers would vanish ; the $100,000 which has been invested in bull-butter machinery in San Francisco would prove a permanent investment and the sale of 450,000,000 pounds of bull-butter in eight years, now boastfully pointed to by the manufacturers, would not be duplicated in twenty years.

California produces good butter. Her best dairies cannot be eclipsed by any of the gilt-edge dairies of Vermont, New York, Pennsylvania or New Jersey. But her reputation for producing good butter is being damaged by the bull-butter competition. When a man finds the alleged butter in half the best restaurants in the city to be of an indifferent quality he naturally concludes that the majority of our dairymen are making an inferior article, and that the standard of dairy butter in this state is a low one. He does not know that he is judging our dairymen by a product of the San Francisco factory, and is doing them a great injustice. That there is poor butter made from cows in California we do not deny. There are incompetent, careless, slovenly and unintelligent men in every business. But the average quality of the product served as butter in San Francisco restaurants is no index of the average intelligence of our dairymen nor of the average product of the dairy in California.

Laws compelling manufacturer to stamp and label all the oleomargarine he makes will never avail. Those who buy of him know what they are buying without stamp or label. But no law can follow the manufactured article to the table and compel the waiter to stamp each piece served. The proposed law compelling restaurant, hotel and boarding-house keepers to post a conspicuous sign: "Oleomargarine sold here" if he serves any of the compound to his customers might avail but we venture the prediction that such a law will never pass our present Legislature. The influences which would oppose it are too powerful. Such a sign would drive away half the customers of any dining-room in this city in twenty-four hours. And it would result in the shutting down of the factory within a month. People can be converted, in the slow process of time, to the belief that oleomargarine is as good as ordinary butter, if such is the fact, but the conversion would be so slow that the manufacturers would have to look to the dim future for their profit. But the people can be humbugged into consuming and paying for the compound without any such slow process of wilting. Hence the oleomargarine business has been a success from the start.

There are two courses open to dairymen in combating this opposition. The first is to produce a quality of butter which no factory can imitate. This is possible. No advocate of the bull butter claims that it can equal the best quality of butter. The claim is only that it cannot be told from fair or ordinary butter. With good, healthy cows, fed on wholesome grasses and grains, drinking pure water, kept neat and housed in storms, and with the most improved system in the dairy house, a quality of butter can be produced which never goes begging for a market and which cannot be counterfeited by the manufactured article. We hope the presence of this artificial competitor will stimulate a greater percentage of the dairymen of California to the production of "gilt-edge" butter. And in the improvement of the system of dairying the establishment of creameries will probably take a conspicuous part. It has been demonstrated that the best quality of butter for the general market can be produced at the lowest cost per pound only where manufactured on a large scale. Occasionally a man may be found engaged in dairying who has the capital to conduct the business on a large scale. But the majority of buttermakers are not capitalists. The co-operative plan of making butter and cheese will meet their case, and will no doubt in time be as popular here as it is in the best dairying regions of the East.

Another means of warfare would be to ascertain to what grocery stores, restaurants, hotels and boarding-houses oleomargarine finds its devious way from the factory and to take such steps as would notify all customers of such places that oleomargarine can be had there. This would be legitimate and if the manufacturers of bull butter are sincere in their profession of a desire to let their product stand upon its merits they could not object to it. It would be simply aiding them in their professed endeavors to put their manufacture before the public under its true colors.

In this connection it may not be amiss to refer to the alleged interview with Wm. V. Gaffey, published last Sunday morning in one of the daily papers. Mr. Gaffey informs a reporter of the BREEDER AND SPORTSMAN that he is grossly misrepresented in that publication. That he was disappointed at the failure of the convention to adopt his resolution for bull weight in butter, Mr. Gaffey is free to confess, and it is probable that the association will yet adopt such a regulation. But that he is a convert to oleomargarine in any such sense as one would infer from a reading of that alleged interview he emphatically denies. What he admits is this: That he was surprised when he witnessed the working of the factory and examined its product; that the latter is equal to common grades of butter in taste, smell and appearance, and that it is only the very best grades of butter that cannot be imitated by the compound. He believes that the manufacture of a higher average grade of butter by dairymen will result. But he is as strong as ever in the spirit which led him to make the first move which resulted in the formation of the Dairymen's Association, and as earnest in desiring strict legislation to put a stop to the perpetration of the fraud by which so much of the bull butter is to-day able to find a market.

## The Growing Demand for Meat.

It really seems that the increased prices upon meats have stimulated rather than retarded consumption. During the third week in October of the present year, the receipts of cattle at the Union Stock Yards of this city were larger than at any previous time since the yards were established. Yet, right at the time of these heavy receipts, and during the height of the scare among shippers and Eastern buyers growing out of the increasing shipments of dressed beef, we find, by referring to the market report for Oct. 28th, the week following the very heavy receipts referred to, at which time the receipts were again reported as very heavy, that "shippers bought with more than ordinary freedom, anything good enough for their use being taken at an advance on the prices of the day before." It was reported that so extra cattle were in the market, but that "sales above $5 reached a larger aggregate than for any day recently." Sales at $6 and better, on the 27th, exceeded 1,000 head, and some sales were made at $6 50. Sixty head of Montana natives were sold for shipment, at $5 75. We refer to these sales because they were made immediately after the unprecedentedly large receipts.

The fact is, that no producer needs fear becoming the owner of too many cattle, or other meat-producing animals, provided he is so situated as to give them proper care and maintain a profitable growth in all seasons. The very poorest of the poor—those who formerly seldom bought meats—now swarm about the retail shops and buy shank bones, rib tips, flank pieces and all, anything that will make a broth, a stew, or swim into soup. The rapidly increasing population of our cities is made up very largely of the laborers and operators from foreign countries, a class of people who are but very little meat in their own country, many of them none at all. Increased wages, with an advantage in the price of meats here, compared to that in their own country, prompts them to eat meats and this class of consumers alone absorb an enormous amount of the lower grades of meat every day.

Under the various demands, graduated by taste and purse, the retail butchers are enabled to assort their cuts as the grocer assorts his coffee, there being ready buyers for each grade—some cuts going as readily as 20 to 25 cents as others do at 7 or 8 cents. The canning of meats opens a market for such low grades of meat as hardly any butcher, no matter who his customers are, would tolerate upon his books. This trade being, as it is constant and profitable, enables cattle growers to close out unthrifty, thin animals; getting, in the absence of any fat, the full market value for skin, shrunken muscles, tendon, bone, and offal. The accumulation of this class of stock upon the farm affects a balance too no observing farmer can fail to profit by, as he has had ample opportunity of seeing that he can now grow more good, profit-yielding meat upon the class of stock referred to, than a thrifty crop of corn upon a dry, sandy knoll.

If beef, to meet the demands of the lower grade of consumers and canners, could be produced at a cost to keeping with its selling value, then there would be some apology for growing it. The manufacturer makes a light article of cloth to meet the demand from a certain class of customers. He weaves into this fabric cheap material, makes it light, and sells by the yard, in place of selling by the pound. As a rule, he is supposed to make a higher relative profit upon the low-priced goods. But, unfortunately for the farmer, he has no low-priced material to weave in. The grass that will grow and fatten a steer at three cents, will, with greater rapidity, grow one at six cents; and what is true of grass is equally true of grain feed.—*Chicago Live Stock Journal.*

Wheat bran and oil-cake meal, combined in a proportion by weight of two of bran to one of meal, is an excellent feed for cows giving milk. A larger proportion of meal will too rapidly fatten the animals. If quantity of milk only is desired the proportion of bran may be increased.

# THE
# Breeder and Sportsman.

PUBLISHED WEEKLY BY THE

BREEDER AND SPORTSMAN PUBLISHING CO.

THE TURF AND SPORTING AUTHORITY OF THE
PACIFIC COAST.

OFFICE, 508 MONTGOMERY STREET
P. O. Box 1938.

*Five dollars a year; three dollars for six months; one dollar and a
half for three months. Strictly in advance.*

MAKE ALL CHECKS, MONEY ORDERS ETC., PAYABLE TO ORDER OF
BREEDER AND SPORTSMAN PUBLISHING CO.

*Money should be sent by postal order, draft or by registered letter, ad-
dressed to the "Breeder and Sportsman Publishing Company, San Francisco, Cal."*

*Communications must be accompanied by the writer's name and address,
not necessarily for publication, but as a private guarantee of good faith.*

JOSEPH CAIRN SIMPSON,　-　-　EDITOR

ADVERTISING RATES.—Displayed $1 50 per inch each insertion, or pro
rata for less space. Reading Notices set in brevier type and having no
flat marks, 30 cents per line each insertion. Lines will average ten
words. A discount of 10 per cent will be allowed on 1 months, 20 per cent
on 3 months and 30 per cent. on 12 months contracts. No reading notice
charged for cuts or cutting of columns &c. No reading notice take for
less than 50 cents each insertion.

San Francisco, Saturday, December 23, 1882.

Mr. M. J. Henley is a duly authorized traveling agent
and correspondent for the "Breeder and Sportsman."

## ARRAIGNED.

And now, Honorable James McMillan Shafter, we will
present further illustrations to show that the great trotting and breeding interests of the Pacific Coast demand
that you shall no longer fill the place you occupy in
District Board No. 5. Although the course you have
taken would warrant a return of personalities we shall
refrain, as far as is possible, from bringing matters of a
personal nature into the discussion.

That these cannot be entirely eliminated is unfortunate, and in order to show that you are unfitted for the
place on other grounds than incompatibility it will be
necessary to allude to circumstances, if even these should
compromise your social standing. Further than this we
have no desire to go, and though your attack would
warrant a reply in the same strain, as has been stated before, we cannot surrender the position we occupy to meet
scurrility with vituperation. Therefore, we shall write
dispassionately, although it will be necessary to use
placid language and straightforward statements. Without taking the clauses of your article—which you may
probably think are arguments—as they come we will
commence with that one where you challenge us if we
"know of any dishonorable conduct on my part of any
kind, you are quite at liberty to state it." There are
your words and we shall show that your conduct all
through has been scarcely up to the standard which
most men regard as honorable. All through your decisions and statements are errors which if you do not "know
them to be untrue" you have not the acuteness you are
generally credited with, and are far nearer imbecility than
we can possibly imagine. There is no necessity for going
over the arguments presented in previous articles, as we
have yet to meet a man who does not agree with us in
every point, excepting, of course, the member of District
Board No. 5.

You falsely state that the conversation with you in regard to the judges was before we claimed to have any
knowledge that Dawn would start. By reference to the
article in this paper of November 25th you will see that
the statement was that "we met him (Shafter) some
little time before the race was called," and in the same
article is this sentence: "Until we want to the track
shortly after 12 m. and for some time after we were
not aware that Dawn had put in an appearance." Furthermore it was explained that Antevolo was driven to
the track only in time to be " warmed up;" after that on
alighting from the sulky we learned of Dawn being
there, and as soon as the conversation was ended, and
Mr. Howes consented to act, the horses were called up.
The "convict" in this case is the "member." As to
Mr. Whitney's disagreement with the ruling in the three-
year-old the Clerk of the Course, Captain Ben E. Harris,
so stated in the presence of A. L. Hinds and others, and
we have not the least doubt of the correctness of Captain Harris' statement if it is denied by this man who
is so liberal in his accusations of falsehood. In regard
to your statement "You wished to pay ten dollars, and
as it seemed to please you to do so the President took your
money; but the decision of the Board was there was no
appeal, and that it proceeded by original jurisdiction"
is also false, whether "known to be untrue" by you or
not. The President made a demand for the money
which we got of Mr. Hinds and gave him a check on an
Oakland Bank for it, and afterwards Captain Smith
spoke of his oversight in not requiring Mr. Whitney to
pay the $20, incurred by his recorded protests or appeals

in the case of Antevolo and Sister to Honesty. As the
Board granted an adjournment on the plea of Mr. Whitney
that he desired to obtain affidavits to sustain these appeals or protests, and fixed the following Monday to
hear the evidence, it is difficult to conceive on what
grounds the denial of the appeal is based. At all events
the fee was demanded from us and paid as the Chairman
of the Board will verify.

Again there is no truth in the implication that we were
not ready to make good the stakes in the yearling and
three-year-old. We proffered them to Mr. Whitney, the
treasurer, before the race was called, and he requested us
to retain them until it was concluded.

There is no necessity to take up space in proving that
every statement we made was true. As we shall show
hereafter that Mr. Shafter is a "betting man," we proffer
him the wagers of $100 on each statement made by us
being true, and the same amount that each of his in denial is false. It is not claimed that there is any logic in
a proffered bet. All that it does prove is the sincerity of
the party making it, and that he has confidence in the
ground he takes.

A typographical error, which made "members" of
"member," was not likely to mislead anyone, as it is
well known that at the time the "board" consisted of
Captain Smith and Mr. Shafter.

And now we will "hark back" to cover ground that
comes appropriately into the discussion, and although we
do not take it upon us to say authoritatively whether
your conduct was "dishonorable" or not, it cannot be
held otherwise than prejudicial to the elevation of the
sports of the turf. You owned a horse, and probably
still own him, Haddington. Your trainer took him to
the half-mile track and there entered into a match race,
to be run on Sunday. Although in the advertisement
the name of your trainer appeared as the person
making the match, you sanctioned it with your presence, and the money put up was claimed to be yours.
At least, when the money was returned, it went into your
hands. There was a squabble at the time of the race,
and afterwards, there were charges brought before the
Pacific Coast Blood-Horse Association growing out of it.
It was proved to have been a disgraceful affair. The
trainer was punished with the utmost severity, he being
the scapegoat to carry the burden of the sin. We do not
think that you will have the effrontery to stigmatize this
brief statement as "known to be untrue." We also
think that you will for once agree with us that straightforward racing on Sunday is not the way to popularize
the turf in this country. Even if we call a decent observance of the Sabbath day bigoted prejudice, some
respect must be paid to the prejudices of the people from
whom we expect the support that will warrant the expense of breeding, rearing and training race-horses.

Occurrences like those which were a part of and followed this Sunday race on the half-mile track, and which
was won by your horse Haddington, run in your presence, and in which you did nothing in the way of exercising your prerogative of forbidding the man in your
employ to run your horse, are surely detrimental to the interest depending, and cannot be defended
from any point of view.

Such conduct, although restricted in your case to the
part indicated by the above statement, does not fit a man
to be a member of a board for the government of the
sports of the turf and track.

It may not interfere with candidacy on a platform that
calls for a rigid observance of the first day of the week,
and that denounces "recreation" on that day as something
which the Legislature must stop at all hazards. As to
that phase of the question we leave it for conventions to
determine, and the voters to pass upon; but when it has
a bearing on the interests we are pledged to do the best
in our power to protect, it comes within the legitimate
sphere of this paper. Then we must add to the previous
arraignment of J. McM. Shafter another count. By
itself we would not consider it sufficient, as there may
have been repentance that should lead to pardon. Still
it adds weight to the other charges, and until proper pen-
ance is done there cannot be absolution.

Holiness and temperance are cardinal virtues, and we
have the greatest respect for a man whose life is governed by the maxims inculcated in the Good Book.
More than that, we are not particular where the controlling influence comes so long as the actions are
in accordance with the "Golden Rule." But when the
example set is widely at variance with the precepts there
is room for doubt of the governing motive and in place
of offering advice to benefit the party, the whole aim is
to indulge a malignant disposition. Notwithstanding
that is the evident intention of the temperance homily
of Mr. Shafter it is beyond dispute well worthy of attention, and if even the preacher takes his share of Bourbon, and boasts of the number of glasses of wine he has
drank at a banquet, the good sense of the admonition is
apparent. Then again it may be a dreamy recollection
of campaign speeches made in the prohibition fight, and

a remembrance that forces itself into places that are
hardly appropriate.

There must be a general multiplication of vision regarding the propriety of Mr. Shafter filling a place in
the judges' stand, or in the Board, and in lieu of the
"seeing double" being confined to us there is a general
optical delusion accompanied with a determination to be
governed by the image on the brain. When you were
President of the State Agricultural Society the directors
appointed a committee to occupy the stand and judge the
race, leaving you out. You were indignant at the action;
although it was represented that the President might be
better employed in other duties, you could not be mollified, and by the threat of resignation compelled them to
permit your occupancy of the stand. At the late meeting of the Pacific Coast Blood Horse Association it was
difficult to induce other members to share the stand with
you, and on the first day you grossly insulted the gentlemen who differed with you in opinion although they
were clearly in the right, and from that time measures
were taken to exclude you. So general is the dissatisfaction that we have heard a large majority of those interested declare that they would not start a horse in a
race, regardless of the consequences, if you were a judge.

Although it may be in the power of a judge of a
"civil court" to send a person who is obnoxious "to
jail," there are few now wearing the ermine who give
cause for language which is in contempt.

In the days of Lord Jeffreys it was different. The wig
and gown were thought to be a warrant for usurping the
place of attorney and prosecutor, and trampling upon the
rights of those whom they wished to crush. We must say,
sir, that you show a good deal of the same temperament.
That you would like to cow into submission all those who
oppose you is evident. That your cherished arguments
are abuse and dictatorial assumption of extra knowledge is
apparent. That you have made a mistake in supposing
that we can be frightened from pursuing the course which
it is our manifest duty to follow you are liable to discover, and that wealth and "station" will not be accepted
as an excuse for wrongdoing so far as we are concerned.

## A MERRY CHRISTMAS.

The *Breeder and Sportsman* send a hearty, cordial
greeting to all.

Health, happiness, good cheer, above all contentment.
Not that kind of contentment supinely accepting whatever the conditions, but rather the complacency arising
from knowing that our duties have been tolerably well
performed, and a determination to do still better in the
future. There is much to be thankful for in the land, and
the contrast between this and the countries whose Christmas has brought its annual round of festivities for centuries is so great that we are prone to underrate the advantages.

There is an extra pleasure when yule-time can be enjoyed among flowers and green fields, and though there
is no necessity for the roaring fires, the heavy wrappings
and the fur robes, the merriment is just as heartily appreciated.

We saw an appropriate device of Christmas in California, barring the incongruity of the ice-covered lakelet. A
fair damsel, probably intended for Venus, gracefully
gliding over the smooth surface, her only habiliment being a veil of gauze of the most shadowy texture. The
skates were of the latest pattern, and an accompanying
Cupid, in just as flimsy attire, skimming along an
open length or two in advance.

That the air of Christmas day may be "soft and balmy"
enough for the comfort of the Queen (who from all accounts had a surplus of hot blood) is very likely though
the ice will have to be made with the aid of the refriger-
ating machine which is the only thing here to afford the
necessary congelation.

Notwithstanding the springtime weather of a California Christmas, there will be pleasant thoughts of those
which have been spent in days long gone. There will be
remembrances, joyous and sad, and heart yearnings for
the old friends who are so far away. There are many
breaks in the circle which surrounds the family Christmas tree, "back home," gaps that are measured by the
width of the silent river, and the shadowy banks on the
far-off side.

These are the occasion of solemn recollections, though
the more tangible interval, bounded by the Atlantic and
Pacific, is not insurmountable and there are few who do
not cherish the expectation of spending succeeding
Christmases in the land of their birth.

To the many good friends in the whole country from
ocean to ocean, to those who are still far away, we send
our sincerest wishes for their welfare, and that one and
all of our readers may spend a merry Christmas, and a
succession of them until they are ready to have the
"silver bowl broken," is our heartfelt desire.

## A SHORT VISIT TO SACRAMENTO.

Last Saturday we boarded the 8 a. m. train at 16th street, ...kland, and shortly after high twelve were doing full ...itice to a lunch at the Golden Eagle. The post-lunch...e cigar was still afire when the course was reached, ...d soon after the two-year-old Lady Viva, and the year-g, Sir Thad, were ready for a trial. It was the first ...me we ever saw them saddled. Both were broken to ...rness before being sent to Sacramento, though it was ...te in September when they were sent to join Mr. Win...r's "string." Both had a relapse of the pinkeye, the ...ly being more severely affected than the colt. She ...ent off her feed, and had to be thrown out of training on after she was broken to ride. The trials were satis...ctory; more than that, as expectations were greatly ...ceeded. These are the first thoroughbreds we have ...ed in California, and are both from our old favorite, ...dy Amanda. The filly is by Three Cheers, and though ...e colt has to be recorded as by Norfolk or Thad Stevens, ...ere is no question of the latter being the sire. We ...ust also acknowledge that successful as we have been ...n breeding a couple of trotting colts, there is a higher ...egree of pleasure attending the rearing of those of a ...lood which is more in the purple, albeit the dollars pre...ominate on the plebian side. Race-horses are luxuries, ...omething like a fine picture gallery, a yacht, or a "pala...al" residence. A "poor cuss" may indulge in a "bit of ...lood" when the others are far beyond his reach, and it ...ay be that he can make the trotting-bred help buy the ...ats for their aristocratic connections.

After the runs we accompanied Mr. Winters to his ...reeding farm, about five miles from Sacramento. All ...hat we can say at the present time is that when the im...rovements are finished it will be one of the model farms ...of the State. The location could scarcely be improved, ...and, in fact, for natural advantages it is hard to equal. Hereafter we will give a full description of it, so there is little necessity for remark now.

The stock could not look better. There is an abundance of green feed, which lasts through the whole season, and the lack of this was the great drawback at El Arroyo. The benefits are more apparent in the weanlings than the older horses, though all look well. The weanlings are the best grown lot, taken together, we ever saw, and have the size and substance now that are usually seen when six months older.

## THE OVERMAN-ROMERO TROT.

To say that there was dissatisfaction among those who witnessed the trot between Romero and Overman at the Bay District Course last Saturday, would be using mild language. There was that feeling among the regular at-tendants, and disgust in those who are not acquainted with the mishaps which horses are liable to. That the race was a poor return for the drive from the city is cer-tain; that those who made the longer pilgrimage from Los Angeles, Red Bluff, Sacramento and other places more or less remote, were disgusted with the barren re-sult of the journey is also probable.

There were great expectations of a grand race. Ro-mero in all of his previous contests had shown a flight of speed of the first class; in his work there were indications that he was fully capable of covering a portion of the ground with his accustomed velocity. The papers were unanimous in brilliant prognostications, and the knights of the quill vied with each other in warm prophesies of a "great race." There were good grounds for the vaticin-ation. Fast records closely together, drivers of es-tablished reputation, and up to the last moment there were rosy accounts of what the horses were doing.

The race was a complete fizzle; Overman could play with his antagonist and even a thirty gait was too fast at the outset for the grey to withstand. So far we have not heard a satisfactory reason for him making so poor a showing. There was an absence of his usual dash, and though in the last heat he made a better effort, the best was far behind the Romero of other days. We have no desire to offer excuses or to make charges. Not being present at the race we cannot give an opinion, founded on personal knowledge, and therefore refrain from criti-cism.

## DOG DEALING.

Inadvertently last week credit was not given the Amer-ican Field for an article under the above title which was copied in "The Kennel" department of this paper. We aim to be very exact in awarding credit whenever matter is copied, and it is somewhat mortifying to have to make the correction. The article is a very good one and a cap-ital illustration of the old methods and the new. There is a large capital now invested in dogs, and not the least reason why they should not be regarded as property the same as horses and cattle.

## MAMBRINO WILKES.

In the short history of Mambrino Wilkes we did not think that it was necessary to allude to the genuineness of the pedigree. It may be as well to state, however, that we have seen letters and certificates from Mr. Treacy which establish the correctness beyond a question. Some of these were written only a short time ago, and the identification and breeding are complete.

As it is stated, a history of the descendants of George Wilkes will be given ere long. By delaying it until after the close of the year, a great deal of labor is saved, as by that means the work of our Eastern contemporaries is utilized, and the collation, originally a work of magni-tude, relieves us of the hardest kind of a job.

## DR. PARDEE ON THE RIFLE.

Those who are not enthusiasts in rifle shooting can scarcely fail to be interested in the articles on "Ancient and Modern Arms," which Dr. E. H. Pardee is contrib-uting to the Breeder and Sportsman. It is safe to assert that when the essays are completed it will be the best practical dissertation which has yet been published.

The illustrations recall an old gun which a man pre-sented to us when a boy. The barrel was of brass and the bore was hexagonal, but without the "twist." It had a flint lock, and was evidently of ancient origin, more ancient than the time of Whitworth. We never tried it with a ball, and, boy-like, it was "traded" for a big horse pistol.

## EQUINE DENTISTRY.

We call attention to the advertisement of Mr. Wood-ruff, as a practitioner in that line will be a great benefit to the horses of the Coast. Mr. Woodruff brings recom-mendations from men who are well posted, and the work he has done here has met the approbation of those who have employed him.

# FISH.

## Carp Breeding.

There are two carp ponds of small dimensions near Bakersfield, in each of which the plant was made last spring. The fish are doing well and there are to be seen great num-bers of young fish. It cannot be long before this market will be well supplied with excellent fish. It would be well for some farmer who has half an acre of ground fitted for a pond, with a certain supply of water, to raise these fish for the household alone, as they raise fowls.

The Foothill Tidings tells of Rev. J. W. Brier, who is breeding carp some three miles from Grass Valley. He finds that 1,000 carp will live and grow finely upon what one hog will—in both cases from birth to two years old. At this age the carp would weigh 4,000 pounds, the average lot, while the average porker will weigh 250 pounds. At present prices for the two articles of food, the fish would bring $1,000, the hog, $24.

The South Coast, published at San Luis Obispo, says that Mr. McLellan, a resident of that county, recently caught 300 carp at one haul of a seine, in a small lake in that county, where only a little over two years ago ten were planted. Owing to a rest that was in his seine he thinks he did not secure more than half that were in the net. The average weight of the 300 was about one pound.

A recent foreign correspondent says: "Prince Christian assured my father that at Schleswig-Holstein the carp lakes are periodically farmed by sowing the bottom with rye grass and some other cereal, by cutting it, and afterwards turning in the water and fish, to the manifest advantage of the latter.

The good influence of this procedure has been recognized by old Gervase Markham, who, when speaking under the heading "How to Make Carp Grow to an Extraordinary Big-ness in a Pond," says: "Perceiving about the month of April that your pond begins to grow low in water, then, with an iron rake, rake off the sides of your pond where the water is falling away, then sow some hay seed and sweet fetch. By this means at the latter end of summer there will be a great growth of grass, which, when the winter comes, the pond being raised by rain to the top, will overflow all that grass. Then the carp, having water to carry them to the feed, will fill themselves, and, in a short time, become fat as the hogs that are kept for that purpose."

The difference between the directions of the old sportsman, and the German plan, as the readers will perceive, is very slight.—Kern County Gazette.

## An Imp of a Fish.

On Friday a party of young people were spending the af-ternoon at Moore's Beach. The tide was unusually low at the time, and in one of those natural aquariums, left exposed by the receding waves, a lively little specimen of the great sea monster known as the "devil fish" was found sporting around in a hole in the rocks to the evident dismay of the customary occupants of that particular pool. When in re-pose the whole animal seemed not larger than an ordinary china saucer; with its eight long legs or feelers, coiled up in regular whirls (like bundles of tape) and drawn close in to its body; or else with one or more of these long, snake-like appendages left floating lazily about its body, ready to seize with their powerful suckers upon any unfortunate mite that came within their reach. The body itself of the little "dev-il" seemed quite insignificant compared to the length of its legs, which were each about a foot long. It was about the size and shape of a large hen's egg and quite resembled one of these when denuded of its hard outside shell. Its color was a pale flesh tint, except when the creature became ex-cited, when it changed instantly to a deep blood red as if spied its prey, and darted across the pool in pursuit of it, with its long legs trailing through the water behind it. A gentleman of the party reached down into the water and grabbed hold of the little monster with the intention of bring-

ing it up for the closer inspection of the ladies, when its long pliant feelers attached themselves to his wrist by an innu-merable set of small cup-shaped valves, which extended from its body to the extreme tip of each of these snake-like exten-sions. He was now more anxious to drop his prize than he had been to exhibit it, but the little ones (his term is allow-able applied to a devil fish) hung on until others of the party came to his assistance and pulled the tightly attached suckers from his arm. The prize was then deposited in a tin can for safe transport to Santa Cruz, where it is now preserved in alcohol as a souvenir of the day.—Santa Cruz Courier-Item.

## Mountain Lakes Despoiled of Trout.

A Reno Gazette reporter is informed that immense quanti-ties of trout are being ruthlessly destroyed at Mud and Pyra-mid lakes by Indians, Italians and Chinese, the latter con-trolling the Indians so that no fish can be sold unless a certain price is obtained, no matter how much fish may be on hand. The price is seven or eight cents per pound, and the vandals "stand pat" on this unless purchasers submit to their extortion. The reporter's informant said he saw several piles of fish at Mud lake last week, aggregating a ton at least, that were rotting on the ground, and he positively knew that the perpetrators of the outrage had been offered four cents per pound for the lot before the fish spoiled. Here is a good chance for the Tar Bucket Brigade to exercise their deviltry. It is probable that there is not an American citizen among the whole band of vandals, but they have a fat thing nevertheless on Uncle Sam's domain. Destroyers of timber are punished severely, but there seems to be no way of getting at these wretches who wantonly destroy pre-cious food in order to compel purchasers to submit to their extortionate demands. Here in Reno at this time consumers have to pay fifteen cents per pound for Pyramid or Mud lake trout in order that these fish-destroyers may make money. It should not be so. A thunder clap or something else equally expressive should suddenly wean them from their destructive proclivities. A Reno dealer says he has to pay ten cents per pound for fish at Pyramid and one cent and a half freight. One hundred pounds of trout will lose twelve pounds in weight in one night after they are opened for sale, so that the dealer has not much of a chance to make large profits even at retailing them for fifteen cents. Another phase of the fishing business is this : Parties are known to go to certain places on the Truckee river, between Reno and Wadsworth, and in a few hours obtain a large quantity of trout, not by legitimate hook-and-line process, but by the use of explosives. It is probable that they bait a deep hole in an eddy and explode a cartridge of giant powder when the fish have collected in considerable numbers. Something should be done to stop this sort of work.—Bee.

THE ORCA OR WHALE-KILLER.—Captain Dan Farley, of the schooner "Fanny Gilmore," one of the oldest masters trading on this Coast, and who is said to have made more trips be-tween this port and Santa Cruz than any other Captain, on one of his recent runs up saw a dead whale nearly seventy feet long floating in the water a few miles south of the Heads. About the body were twenty orcas or "killers," as they are called by whaling captains, actively engaged in feeding. Cap-tain Farley, who many years ago pursued the leviathan in the Arctic and the Japanese Seas, says that what he saw of these rapacious fish overthrows the ideas heretofore existing regarding the manner in which they prey upon the whale. It has always been supposed that the orca kills the whale by biting it about the body, as it is provided with long sharp teeth in both jaws, similar to those of the shark. It has also a mon-strous fin upon the back, but as it contains no bone and is made only of cartilage and oil, it cuts no figure as a means of defense or assault. Among the school of orcas that sur-rounded the dead whale mentioned by Captain Farley was one thirty feet long, with a fin extending above its head ten feet high. It was observed that they operated only at the whale's mouth, and that the tongue of the animal was their food. The lips of the whale had been cut away as if with an ax, the presumption being that the orcas attacked it and caused death by a loss of blood through the lips. Once dead and the tongue eaten the whale is left by its enemies, who go thrashing through the water in search of other game. Off Half Moon Bay these fish are found in great numbers, but they have not often been seen before feeding upon their prey.—Examiner.

Sweaborg, Que., has an enterprise of which very little, hitherto, has been known, namely, the fish culture. Mr. Wm. Thornton has on his farm three fish ponds, and the fourth is under construction. The ponds will cover about two acres, and are filled with spring water. Early in the spring 15,000 fry, speckled trout and California salmon, were placed in them. The fish are growing rapidly. It is the intention of the proprietor to increase the number of ponds to twelve or fifteen, and as there is abundance of good water, there is every prospect of making the venture a pecuniary success.

## Haley and Masterson Again.

Last Thursday evening R. S. Haley, of the Olympic Club, and Joe Masterson, of the California Athletic and Lacrosse Club, of the same city, signed articles for a trophy (do-nated by C. M. Piercy of Recreation Park) costing $100, the race to be run three weeks from to-day (Jan. 13th, 1883). National Association rules to govern the event. In case of unfavorable weather, the race to be postponed until first good day and track, excepting Sunday. And either man failing to toe the mark between the hours set for race, shall pay $75 to the other's trainer for his fees attending such labor." Mr. Piercy pledges himself to prepare a perfectly level 100-yard track, and furnish five reliable fifth-second watches for the event. The men are both determined to win, and it will be a grand race. We have the agreement in our possession, and know that they are both anxious to win.

The steamer California brought back to their Oregon home R. E. Bybee's red Irish setter Sandy and F. J. Abell's Gordon setter Scott, the latter being the winner of the California field trials. Mr. Abell's Bess and Auditor and Spencer's Gem remain at Gilroy in charge of Mr. E. Leavesley, the veteran trainer. The success of the Oregon dogs speaks volumes in favor of the ability, care and attention that Mr. Leavesley bestows upon the high-bred canines confided to his care. The dogs were in good order, notwithstanding a very rough ocean voyage. Jim Renwick, the racer, also arrived on the same steamer.—Oregon Rural Press.

The Howards of the O. C. have in contemplation material for a good A 1 amateur nine next year. With the present nine they have succeeded in defeating the Redingtons and Olympics.

In selecting animals it should be borne in mind that those with small chests do not fatten readily.

## THE KENNEL.

### "Throw Physic to the Dogs."

One of the commonest troubles that beset young dog owners is the difficulty of giving medicine to their animals when they are taken sick. They try a dozen plans recommended by good-natured friends, but the result is nearly always the same; either the physic is spilt on the ground or over the operator's clothes, or else the dog, feeling that his stomach has been insulted, goes off into a corner and disgorges everything he has taken. A dog appears to have almost absolute control over his stomach, and needs no artificial emetic when he takes a notion to vomit, so it is always necessary to watch one for some time after the medicine has been administered. It is much easier and safer to fool a dog into taking physic than it is to force him into it. A pill is the easiest of all medicines to give a dog. The best plan is to coat the pill with silver paper to kill the smell, then wrap it up in a piece of meat. Throw the dog several pieces of plain meat, and when he bolts them, as most dogs will, throw him the piece containing the pill. It is a hundred to one that he will bolt it down and never know that he has been dosed. All powders, such as areca nut, iodide of potass and other drugs, given in a granulated form, can be administered in this way without the slightest trouble. Some persons mix their dog powders up in butter, which they smear on the sick animal's nose for him to lick off. Others again put the powders between two slices of bread and butter, but the meat plan is the cleanest and easiest.

It sometimes is absolutely necessary to use a moderate degree of force in giving a dog medicine. In such cases it is best to lay the dog on his back or place his head between your legs, tightly gripping his neck with the knees if he attempts to back; or else force him to a sitting position between your knees, with his fore feet in the air and his back towards you. Then make him open his mouth by forcing the thumb and fingers between his grinders, where they can come to no harm from his most frantic attempts to bite. With the other hand place the powder as far back on the tongue as possible, and then close the mouth, holding it shut with the hand. He cannot eject the dry powders, and is forced to swallow them. Try the same plan in giving control oil, holding the head well up when the dose is put in the mouth. The natural desire to relieve the mouth causes the motion of swallowing, though for the reason above stated care must be taken to see that the dog does not vomit before the medicine has had a chance to work.

In performing light surgical operations the dog should be muzzled. This can be done in the absence of a proper muzzle with a piece of wide tape tied around the nose and brought back behind the head.

An ointment or plaster must always be thoroughly covered with a bandage the dog cannot remove or he will be sure to lick it off.

A common cut or incised wound is best left to nature and the healing influence of the dog's tongue.

It often happens that in hunting, dogs, especially pointers, get a V shaped flap of skin torn which hangs with the point down. This needs to be sewn up. A glover's needle is the best to use, with waxed silk. Draw the silk through the two edges of the wound and tie it tighter, cutting off the ends so close to the skin that he cannot bite them. They can be cut out when the wound heals or if left to rot away will do no great harm.

It is not sportsman-like to cut a dog's ears, but when the job is done the cut should be made with a sharp pair of scissors always from the butt towards the point. A cap should then be put on to prevent the dog from shaking his head and if it is desired to have the ears stand erect, the points should be braced up with sticking-plaster until thoroughly healed.

Never bite a dog's tail. It is a cruel, beastly trick. If your setter has a habit of thumping the brush with his tail until it is sore take off two or three joints with a sharp knife or a heavy pair of shears. The old superstition about taking the sinew or worm out of a dog's tail to stop distemper is as idiotic as such superstitions usually are.

Do not get into the habit of giving your dog medicine for every trifling ailment. Rest, warmth and cleanliness are the best of all remedies and in most cases a change of diet will do more than a store full of drugs.

POINTERS AHEAD.—The champions of the setter should read the following from the *Turf, Field and Farm:* The result of the Eastern Field Trials has been a surprise to many of the wiseacres, not only from the fact that the crack dogs were in several instances beaten, but that the pointers carried off a large share of the honors. Croxteth won, in addition to the special pointer prize, second prize in the All-Aged Stake; while Mr. Luke White's little marvel, Lalla Rookh, divided third prize with Gladsome in the same event, and in the Derby shared the honors of the third award with Mr. Mahone's Byron. The special prize for the dog showing the finest natural abilities was awarded to Mr. A. E. Godeffroy's pointer Sefton, and second prize in the Derby fell to Tick, a young pointer dog owned by Mr. Geo. W. Foat, of Brooklyn. This is a very creditable record, especially as the proportion of pointers entered for the trials was little more than one-fifth the total number. The recent victory of Mr. Vanderwort's Don, at Fairmont, Minn., supplemented by the record at High Point, N. C., has given occasion for rejoicing among the fanciers and breeders of pointers.

ENGLISH FOX HUNTING.—There are about 190 well-known packs of fox-hounds in England, in addition to many of lesser packs of lesser. In the London *Field* records between 300 and 400 hunting appointments each week, aside from the regular meetings in Ireland and Scotland, which are also duly chronicled. The annual expenditure for the maintenance of packs and for fox hunting in Great Britain is said to exceed that of the whole civilized world beside.

On December 30th a coursing match will be held at Dixon under the management of the Dixon Coursing Club. The match is open to all dogs in the State, with an entrance fee of $5, to be sent to the Secretary of the Dixon club on or before the 28th inst. There is plenty of good coursing ground near Dixon and all the club needs to make the match a success is a judge who understands his business. Dixon judges so far have not proven a success, but we hope that this match will prove an exception to the rule.

The Pacific Coast Coursing Club will hold their regular open spring meeting at Merced on March 7 and 8.

## NEW FIELD TRIAL RULES.

### The Regulations and Restrictions which are to Apply in Future.

Following are the new Eastern Field Trial Rules arranged by Dr. Fleet S. Speir:

It shall be obligatory upon the judges to keep the scores of all dogs running, and to furnish a copy of the scores for the use of the club, to which the subscribers shall have access. Nevertheless, the distribution of all awards shall be left entirely to the discretion of the judges, subject only to Rule 7 regulating protests. The judges are expected to be governed by the running rules as closely as the circumstances will permit, but they are not bound to give the prize to the dog making the highest score unless in their judgment he has proved himself the best dog in the race. Should there be a tie in the first series of heats, the dogs making the tie shall be considered equal, and run again to decide it. In the second series of heats the dogs making a tie may divide the honors, or the judges may decide without running again.

Rule 3—A withdrawal from a heat is a withdrawal from the stake. If a dog be withdrawn from a heat after he has been called upon to start, the other dog in the heat withdraws from shall be compelled to run against a dog not in the stake, the substitute mate as above pointed out. No dog shall win a heat without running for it, except in the case of a tie in the second series of heats. The judges may suspend the running for the benefit of a dog which, having just run in a heat in the first series of heats, is obliged to run next in the second series of heats.

Rule 4—The judges shall order up the dogs as soon as they have determined which is the best according to the scale of points in Rule 5. The privilege is granted the judges of ordering up any dog or brace of dogs that have not sufficient merit, in their opinion, to get placed, but these may be put down again if there is a possible chance for them to win; the scores of these dogs shall be taken; and may be withheld or not at the option of the owners.

Rule 5—Positive points for merit: Pointing, 35; pace, 20; backing, 7; style, 6; staunchness, 6; ranging, 6; quartering, 6; obedience and disposition, 4; retrieving, 10; total, 100.

Negative points for demerit: False pointing, 1 to 7; breaking in (each offense), 3; breaking shot (each offense), 5; chasing or breaking shot and chasing (each offense), 10.

Rule 6—No person, except the judges, attendants and reporters, or officers of the club, will be permitted to accompany the handlers of dogs. Two persons will not be permitted to work one dog or a brace of dogs, unless it be agreed by all the subscribers before the start. If from any cause the handler of a dog or brace of dogs is disabled to such an extent that he cannot shoot, the judges shall appoint a person to shoot for him. The handlers of two dogs in a heat shall go together as if it were a brace of dogs, so that the dogs shall be upon an equality as to ground, opportunities for pointing, etc. No spectator, except the owners of the dogs running, will be allowed nearer than seventy yards to the rear. No person shall make any remark about the judges or the dogs in hearing of the judges. The privilege is granted the handlers to ask the judges for information or explanation that has a direct bearing upon any point at issue; pending such questions the dogs shall not be under judgment. Dogs afflicted with any contagious disease or bitches in season will not be permitted on the grounds.

Pointing fur, feather or reptiles shall not be considered making a false point. A dog making a false point and discovering it to be such without any encouragement from his handler shall not be penalized. It is desired that all dogs shall, if opportunity present, have at least two opportunities to show their behaviour on birds. The judges are requested to exercise due care in making out the score of the dogs running.

The object sought in keeping the scores of the dogs running, is to furnish each subscriber with a record of his dog's work done in the trials, a study of which it is believed will be of benefit to owners, and enable them to improve their dogs in the points where they are found to be deficient, and it will be, to some extent, a guide to the members who breed their dogs, and enable them to select suitable mates, and it will also be a means of securing for future trials a constantly improving quality in the work of the dogs.

Rule 7, Regulating Protests.—The right of subscribers to protest is recognized by the club, but only such protests shall be entertained as are based upon a breach of the running rules or matters of fact in regard to errors of entry, or the introduction of fraud or injustice.

All protests must be made on the day on which the errors occur. Protests shall come before the judges and one and other from the Board of Directors, and their decision shall be final.

Pointing—The judges will allow only those dogs the maximum that point all the birds possible for them to point under existing circumstances, a dog to earn the maximum number of points under this head, must display a first-class nose, exhibit great judgment in finding and pointing his birds, and make no flushes that a dog with the above qualities would avoid in ordinary hunting. The dogs are to be hunted in all respects as in an ordinary day's shooting. Inexcusable or willful flushes will detract from a dog's score under this head, but the character of the flush must be always taken into account in estimating the penalty, if any. They shall always consider the nature of the ground, the wind and the birds, and not penalize a dog for flushing a bird it would be impossible to point. The penalty for flushing is to be graded by the character of the offense. The judges shall not require the handlers to work their dogs down wind. Judges are allowed the discretion of declaring a dog out of the heat if absent when called.

Pace—The dog that maintains the fastest gait throughout the heat except when in cover or on game, to receive the full number of points, his competitor to be graded by him. The score for pace need not be filled out or completed until all the dogs have run.

Backing—The maximum only allowed such dogs as stand or drop promptly at sight of another dog pointing. But no dog shall be expected to back unless the dog pointing stands and is motionless. A dog shall not be said to refuse to back unless he sees the dog pointing. To get credit for a back, the dog must stop at least ten yards (when practicable) in front of the handler.

Style—The judge shall consider the dog's grace in ranging and drawing and attitude in pointing and backing.

Staunchness—The maximum allowed such dogs only as do not advance from their point when they are on game until they are ordered on.

Ranging—The maximum only allowed the dog that maintains the most killing range throughout, viz.: Wide or close, as the necessity of the case may require.

Quartering—The maximum only allowed such dogs as work at right angles with the handler, unless the nature of the ground renders such work impracticable.

Obedience and Disposition—The maximum only allowed to a dog that works promptly to the gun without noise or severity, and is obedient, prompt, cheerful and easily handled.

Retrieving—To receive the maximum under this head a dog shall go promptly and cheerfully for the bird, and deliver it to the handler without mouthing or mutilation.

False Pointing—The judges shall give the dog ample opportunity to discover whether or not he is on a true point, and the penalty shall range from one to seven for his acts throughout the heat.

Breaking In—Is when a dog, through imperfect breaking, or from excitement, leaves his position when the birds rise whether the gun is fired or not, and starts to break shot or chase, but stops within a few feet of the point from which he started of his own accord, or by command.

Breaking Shot—Is when a dog runs in when a shot is fired or not, with the intention of getting the bird, and does not stop promptly at command.

Chasing—Is when a dog follows the birds, either when the gun is fired or not, to any extent to be beyond the control of the handler, for the time being.

Puppy Stakes Rule—Dogs born prior to March 1 of preceding year will not be eligible for the Puppy Stakes. There will be no points allowed for retrieving in this stake. Rules otherwise as above.

Brace Stakes—The rules governing the Brace Stakes shall be the same as those used in the All-Aged Stakes, with the following exceptions: The maximum for ranging shall be 10 instead of 6; the maximum for quartering shall be 10 instead of 6; and the total 108 instead of 100. The brace to earn the maximum for quartering must cross each other systematically, and work independent of each other, or one dog must quarter the ground on one side of the handler, while the other dog quarters the opposite side, the dogs meeting at or near the center. Each brace will be run separately instead of running in heats, and be judged by the scale of points as laid down and explained. In case only one dog retrieves, the brace shall only be entitled to half the number of points for retrieving.

Premiums to the value of $2,000 will be offered at the Ottawa, Canada, Bench Show, which takes place March 26, 27 and 28, 1883, and a like amount of prizes will be given at the Pittsburg Dog Show, of April 3, 4 and 5, held in connection with the annual exhibition of the Western Pennsylvania Poultry society.

## Difference in Wools.

I feel somewhat like quarreling with the idea that so many have in supposing that a black gummy sheep is a sure indication of its fineness. The idea comes more forcibly to my mind in consequence of hearing so many at our late fair express their minds in that direction. One would suppose that a few ounces of the article that is sure to bring a discount when we sell our wool suddenly becomes valuable when looking at the sheep. Even awarding committees vary generally are guilty of this weakness, and you are very sure of seeing the flutter of a red ribbon in their wake, lodged near the abiding place of the blackest sheep on the ground. I have taken some pains to ascertain some of the reasons why their preference is given in that direction, and almost invariably the reason given is that an oily, gummy buck is so much better to cross on the common ewes of the country. Others claim that after using a gummy buck and getting their sheep graded up to the proper standard, they then intend to breed for longer wool. Far better would it be to try breeding to retain every particle of length that is possible, and grade to the required fineness, than to breed back and be obliged to go over the very same ground twice. It is much easier to retrograde in quality of wool than it is to advance. Short wool and coarse wool are easily produced, in fact they produce themselves if we but slacken our diligence one particle; try as best we may, some fleeces will be objectionable, and we are constantly obliged to keep turning off and weeding out in order to keep our flocks up to the proper standard. This system of keeping inferior animals when good ones could be equally well kept, and of course with a better profit, is very reprehensible; especially so when we remember the many facilities for getting good ewes and rams. To possess a fairly good flock of ewes, and a ram of good dimensions and wool, and of no chance breeding, is to have the first thing needed. But this in itself will not be sufficient if the necessary amount of forethought, energy and intelligence is not forthcoming, and it is often owing to the want of these latter qualifications that so many failures occur. It seems strange that a majority of farmers, after attending a fair and seeing first-class animals of the different breeds, can return home and again pursue the same old process of breeding without one thought of improvement put into successful practice. It seems that the old ruts in which our forefathers traveled have become so habitual to us that we are prone to follow on in the old way until some sudden jar produces an entire revolution in our plans and ideas, and then we are so thoroughly Americanized that we cannot make a gradual change like our more phlegmatic neighbors across the water, but make a pell-mell dive with mayhap both our eyes shut, and no guarantee of a safe landing.—*Cor. Ohio Farmer.*

## BASE BALL.

### The League Convention and its Work.

The legislative work accomplished by the League at its recent convention was, in some respects, the most important of any since the association was organized. The existing position of antagonism between the rival organizations of the League and the American Association was discussed and a committee of three was appointed by the League to confer with a similar committee of the American Association on the subject of 'combining together to uphold all contracts made by players with the clubs of the two associations.

The most important change made by the convention was in regard to the appointment and election of umpires. The existing laws on the subject were repealed and a law substituted authorizing the appointment of four members at a regular salary and amenable only to the established authority of the League's Secretary. The salary is $1,000 for the season of five months, with hotel and travelling expenses paid.

In regard to the playing rules but two amendments were introduced, namely, a change in the rule governing the delivery of the ball to the bat, and the abolition of the foul-bound catch. Under the new rule throwing is now legal, the only throw now prohibited being that from above the shoulder. By the new rule the pitcher has ample facility given him for an accurate aiming of the ball, and for its command in delivery. The abolition of the foul-bound catch is an improvement which has long been advocated by Harry Wright and other experienced judges of the game and its requirements. In the existing code of 1882 there were two rules which occasioned dispute in regard to their correct interpretation, namely, the rules bearing upon running back to bases on foul balls and to the running of the base-runner from home to first base. It is now decided that the umpire had not the power to decide a player out who failed to run back to his base in returning on a foul ball. In regard to the batsman running to first base after three strikes have been called, it has been held that if he fails to run to such base after the third strike has been called the umpire must decide him out. These are the chief results of the recent convention.—*New York World.*

### Olympics vs. Redingtons.

The picked nine of the O. C. succeeded in defeating the Redingtons at the O. A. C. Grounds, last Sunday. Redington was strengthened by Levy and Lawton of the Haverlys; the picked nine by Jerry Denny. The game throughout was very interesting; the batting of Denny, Conn, Van Bergen and Hardie was above the average. The fielding of Ewalt, Denny, Hardie, Lawton and Ebner was fine. The umpiring of E. Van Court was satisfactory. Boyce, the favorite third baseman of the Haverlys, being absent, Denny filled his place and played a very good game. The score was as follows:

| OLYMPIC. | TB | R | BH | PO | A | E | | REDINGTON. | TB | R | BH | PO | A | E |
|---|---|---|---|---|---|---|---|---|---|---|---|---|---|---|
| Conn, p. and c | 7 | 4 | 0 | 3 | 2 | 3 | | Arnold, 2d b | | 3 | 1 | 1 | 1 | 0 |
| Burt, 1st b | | 5 | 1 | 1 | 7 | 0 | | Lawton, c | | | 2 | 1 | 10 | 2 | 3 |
| Ebner, 3d b | | 5 | 0 | 0 | 1 | 1 | | Levy, c f | | | 4 | 0 | 2 | 1 | 1 |
| Fitzgerald, c | | 6 | 1 | 0 | 3 | 0 | | Bennett, p and 2d b | | 1 | 1 | 1 | 2 | 1 |
| Van Bergen, l f | | 5 | 2 | 0 | 0 | 0 | | Moran, s s | | | 4 | 0 | 1 | 0 | 3 |
| Hardie, c f and p | | 4 | 2 | 0 | 4 | 0 | | Lewis, 1st b | | | 4 | 0 | 1 | 3 | 0 |
| Kelly, r f | | 4 | 0 | 0 | 0 | 0 | | Lambuster, l f | | | 4 | 2 | 0 | 0 | 2 |
| Brandon, s s | | 6 | 0 | 0 | 2 | 5 | | Ewalt, 3d b and p | | | 4 | 1 | 1 | 2 | 0 |
| Denny, 2d b | | 5 | 2 | 0 | 4 | 3 | | Mullen, r f | | | 4 | 1 | 0 | 0 | 0 |
| Totals | 49 | 6 | 13 | 27 | 21 | 12 | | Totals | | 39 | 9 | 8 | 24 | 21 | 6 |

Innings ............................ 1 2 3 4 5 6 7 8 9
Olympic ........................... 1 0 0 1 3 1 0 0 *—6
Redington ......................... 0 0 1 0 1 0 0 6—9
Balls called—Bennett 8, Ewalt 58, Conn 39. Hardie 41. Strikes called Bennett 3, Ewalt 43, Conn 22, Hardie 31. Wild Pitches—Conn 1, Hardie 1, Passed balls—Fitzgerald 3, Lawton 4. Earned runs—Denny 1. Third base hit—Denny. Second base hits—Van Bergen, Denny 2, Conn 5. Lewis. Double plays—Beck and Ebner, Denny and Ebner. Time of game—2 hours. Scorer—C. A. Tetie. Umpire—E. Van Court of the Howards.

### The Riordan and McElroy Benefit.

The following is the score of the game played at the Recreation Grounds last Sunday:

| PICKED NINE. | TB | R | BU | TO | A | E | | RENOS. | TB | R | BH | PO | A | E |
|---|---|---|---|---|---|---|---|---|---|---|---|---|---|---|
| Irwin, 3d b and c | 5 | 3 | 0 | 3 | 0 | 0 | | Swanton, 1st b | | 4 | 2 | 3 | 7 | 0 | 2 |
| Finn, 2d b | | 3 | 2 | 3 | 1 | 0 | | Sweeney, p and 3d s | 4 | 1 | 1 | 1 | 1 | |
| Felix, 1st b | | 4 | 1 | 0 | 14 | 0 | | McElroy, s s and 2d s | 4 | 0 | 1 | 0 | 1 | |
| Riordan, p | | 4 | 1 | 0 | 0 | 0 | | Shirt, 2d b | | | 4 | 0 | 0 | 0 | 0 | 0 |
| Brown, l f | | 4 | 0 | 1 | 0 | 0 | | Hinton, c f | | | 3 | 0 | 0 | 0 | 0 | 0 |
| Donohue, s s | | 4 | 1 | 1 | 4 | 0 | | Sheridan, 3d b | | | 3 | 1 | 1 | 1 | 1 | 0 |
| Mitchell, r f | | 4 | 1 | 0 | 1 | 0 | | Whalen, r f | | | 3 | 0 | 1 | 0 | 10 | 0 |
| P. Carroll, c and 3d bi | 1 | 0 | 2 | 0 | | | Calloran, 1 f | | | 3 | 0 | 1 | 0 | 0 | 0 |
| Casey, c f | | 1 | 0 | 0 | 0 | 0 | | Rutledge, r f | | | 3 | 0 | 1 | 0 | 0 | 0 |
| Totals | 37 | 13 | 2 | 11 | 14 | 3 | | Totals | | 31 | 6 | 6 | 21 | 16 | 7 |

Innings ............................ 1 2 3 4 5 6 7
Picked Nine ........................ 2 1 4 1 3 0 2—13
Renos .............................. 0 2 0 0 3 0 1— 6
Three-base hit—Finn. Two-base hit—Rutledge. Base on balls—Riordan 5. Double play—McElroy and Swanton. Struck out—Renos 3, Picked Nine 3. Left on bases—Renos 1, Picked Nine 1. First base on errors—Renos 7, Picked Nine 1. Passed balls—Cregan 3, Finn 1. Wild pitch—McElroy. Umpire—Edward Taylor.

## THE RIFLE.

### Good Shooting.

There was a rifle match of three at Shell Mound Park Sunday at 1 p. m. of fifty shots at 200 yards, with a possible score of 250. The contestants were Officer Linville of the police force, and Captain P. H. McElhinney and Lieutenant Sprowl of the militia. Sergeant Nash and Colonel B. G. Beaver acted as judges, Henry Work as referee, and G. L. Graves and H. Merriweather as scorers. The following is the score:

Linville..........5 4 4 4 5 4 4 4—46
              5 4 4 4 4 4 4 5—43
              5 4 4 4 4 4 4 4—42
              5 4 4 4 4 4 5 5—44
              5 4 4 4 4 4 5 4—43

Total.................218

Sprowl............5 4 4 4 5 4 4 4—42
              4 4 5 4 4 4 4 4—40
              4 4 4 4 4 4 4 4—40
              5 4 4 4 4 4 4 4—43
              4 4 4 4 4 5 4 4—42

Total.................207

McElhinney........4 4 4 4 5 4 4 4—41
              4 4 4 4 4 4 4 4—41
              4 4 5 4 4 4 4 5—41
              4 4 3 4 4 4 5 5—41
              4 3 4 4 4 4 5 5—41

Total.................205

## ANCIENT AND MODERN ARMS.

### The Grooved Cylinder, the Elliptic Bore and the Polygonal Bore Rifles.

BY DR. E. H. PARDEE.

*(Continued from page 379.)*

In my last communication I was speaking of the necessity of the bullet fitting so closely to the groove as to prevent the escape of the gas through any portion of a groove that the bullet did not fill. The very thing caused our ancient gunmakers untold trouble; all the ingenuity of Europe was at work inventing a multiplicity of different shaped projectiles, while a continual change of rifling was taking place with a spirit of emulation among all the foremost and belligerent nations of the earth; not only individual enterprise was battling for the greater perfection of this weapon, but arsenals were erected at the government's expense, and a systematic course of experiments were conducted on the most elaborate scale.

I will attempt to give but few of the many methods of rifling for it would only be a tax on my time, and a description of the space it would occupy in your valuable paper. I will group them under three general heads, viz: the grooved cylinder, the elliptical or oval bore, and the polygonal. Rifling by grooves is a system universally adopted by gunmakers of all nations; particularly is this method of rifling used by all gunmakers that command any respect in the United States. And I believe at the present time it is adopted by all leading nations of the earth.

The oval bore is so inconsistent in its mechanical construction that I am at a loss to conceive how so intelligent a man as Mr. Lancaster, with his worldwide reputation as a gunmaker, would advocate so crazy a theory. The barrel is cut in its interior in the form of an ellipse, the difference between the major and minor axes being twelve thousandths of an inch. The only possible advantage it has is that the barrel, being a smooth bore, is easily cleaned. Cold comfort at least for an enthusiastic devotee of the rifle.

The polygonal was advocated by Mr. Whitworth, the proprietor of the celebrated Whitworth rifle, the bore being hexagonal and measuring across the flats, i. e., the minor diameter, four hundred and fifty-one thousandths of an inch, and across the angles, i. e., the major diameter, five hundred and three thousandths of an inch. Also by Westly Richards, in his breech loader, the bore which is octagonal; and by Mr. Henry of Edinburgh, the bore of whose rifle is heptagonal, with a rib in each of the angles. To make my position more clear I will make diagrams showing the three different mechanical constructions of riflings, by which the rotation is imparted to the bullet. It will demonstrate the important fact that the human mind has been at work for centuries past to devise the best method by which the projectile and rotary velocity of a bullet could be made to act in its passage or flight through the air in unison, or so that the rotary would distract from the projectile velocity but as little as possible, and at the same time to overcome what is commonly called "windage." The barrel of the old smooth-bore was little else than a bore of iron in which the ball fitted so loosely that when clean it would by its own specific gravity fall to the breech. In order to load easily it was necessary to have the bullet a little smaller than the bore of the gun, which must necessarily allow a portion of the generated gas, from the ignition of the powder, to pass by the side of the spherical ball, and not only occasion considerable loss of propelling power but also a constant changing of the ball from one side of the barrel to the other, and, as a natural result, at the instant of its leaving the muzzle of the gun it received a direction from that side of the barrel against which it was last in contact, always resulting in a defective shot; therefore, one of the principal reasons that a smooth-bored gun would never hold a ball to a common center.

Another cause of unsteady flight of the ball from the smooth-bore, was that it was almost impossible to seat a spherical ball that would be perfect and solid; a slight hollow or air cavity would be found somewhere in the interior. The center of gravity would necessarily be effected by this unequal distribution of the metal and, as there was no rotary motion to cause the ball to spin on its own axis, as a sure consequence irregularity in the flight of the projectile would take place.

This matter of "windage" has been a troublesome thing to overcome, and I must say I am in doubt that it is mastered completely at the present day with all our modern improvements and boasted superiority achieved during the past quarter of a century in gunnery.

NO. 1.      NO. 2.      NO. 3.

I do not wish to be understood that the above includes all the different devices that have been put forth for the past two hundred and fifty years, but that the above diagrams are the real principles from which thousands of different shadows have come and gone, but the principles have been left and fostered by the steady hand of science, until we begin to think we see the end approaching, not only in the perfection of gunnery, but in everything else.

It will be idle for me, in considering these different systems, to speak at length of No. 1, as it is now the only one that has stood the test of time; and with it, obstacle after obstacle, as they would come up like the heads of the hydra, has been overcome; and to-day it is recognized by all the intelligent nations of the earth to be the most simple and perfect of them all.

While I will refer to this system of rifling at some future time, and give my reasons for its preference, I am sure that a comparison with the other methods will prove it to be superior in every respect. Diagram No. 2 is a muzzle representation of the elliptic rifle and the credit is given to 'Mr. Lancaster, a celebrated gunmaker of England, but it was only a revival of a very antiquated system alluded to and most accurately described in "Scloppetaria," as a very old invention and quite obsolete, more than a century ago. I will say that this method of rifling was almost entirely confined to England although a few gunmakers in this country took the fever and the elliptic bore had the call for a short time only; while in England it has its advocates at the present time.

To show the eclat that was gotten up over the Lancaster rifle in England, I will quote from "The Rifle and How to Use It," by Hans Busk, M. A. D. L., London: "Of all the modifications of the principles of rifling that have been brought out in this country, in America, and on the continent, none can be said to excel in simplicity the one now commonly known as Mr. Lancaster's system of elliptic rifling. A problem, the solution of which has long been a scientific puzzle, has been the reduction of windage to a minimum, without even a concomitant increase of friction."

I am at a loss to reconcile myself to the fact, how a scientific man like "Hans Busk" could be so credulous as to give his support to a system so at war with the most common principles of gunnery. If reinstated the same difficulty that the old "Vererum Gaspard Zoller" in the primitive days of gunnery was trying to obviate, i. e., to cut grooves for the residuum to form in after the discharge of the gun, which was to obviate cleaning at almost every shot; it was failed with enthusiasm by the English people, when Mr. Lancaster inaugurated his system of elliptical smooth bore rifle. The barrel being smooth, a turn of this ellipsis' was given in the barrel to impart to the bullet its rotary motion; and how the "windage" was overcome in an increased ratio over a well-filled bullet, in the smooth-bore, Mr. Hans Busk forgot to tell. That it did give to the bullet a rotation and kept it spinning on its axis, no one will deny. And that there was a greater necessity of wiping every shot in order to keep the gun clean, no one who will give the subject a little thought will attempt to deny; and as there was an increased friction on account of the bullet, in its passage, constantly pressing against the spiral of the ellipsis, is surely another proof, to wipe often in order to overcome and lessen friction to a minimum.

Still there is another objection, in my opinion, of more vital importance than those already enumerated. Mr. Lancaster gave this ellipsis one turn in about 30 inches; making his bullet nearly one and a half inches long, and forced to fit the caliber of the gun, the instant of its leaving the muzzle the untrue condition would set in commotion an atmospheric disturbance that must, in the nature of things, soon take from it the rotation imparted to it on its exit in the open and unconfined atmosphere. Again, the atmosphere, coming in contact with the greatest diameter of the bullet, it must have a tendency to cause a constant deviation from its true flight.

I am inclined to the belief that most all Englishmen are clannish, and they have a desire and love to praise and eulogize the results of England; and I am charitable enough to believe that had this invention that Mr. Lancaster claims, of a spiral ellipsis, been brought forth by a Frenchman, a German, or an American, instead of its getting the support from the pen of "Mr. Hans Busk," it would have denounced it as the veriest nonsense, emanating from the bloody head of some blasted foreigner.

No. 3. The great peculiarity of this method of rifling consists in the polygonal form of the bore, and 'this the elliptic bore," it originated in the fertile brain of Mr. Whitworth, an English mechanic, and for a time it was found to meet official difficulties, and for a time it had a reputation for long-range shooting, that gave it a notoriety in all Europe.

But the inventor procured letters patent, which gave him the exclusive right to manufacture, and consequently all other gunmakers were at war with this method of rifling, and the zenith of its glory soon faded and passed away.

The great defect in the hexagonal-bored rifle is the extreme amount of friction, and consequently useless expenditure of means. Mr. Whitworth says his bullet rotates at the rate of 15,000 revolutions in a minute; the friction on the periphery of a bullet having this extreme spinning motion must very much lessen its range. If we weigh force, and carefully calculate its expenditure in 2,000 yards, we can safely estimate the periphery has made 4,000 revolutions.

Now, I ask the reader to look at No. 3 diagram, representing the muzzle of a Whitworth rifle, and estimate the friction is will undergo; bearing in mind there are about two turns in the length of the barrel, which, as Mr. Whitworth says, should be thirty-four inches long.

The bullet for the Whitworth rifle is manufactured in the most careful manner, and is composed of an alloy of lead, tin and metallic antimony, so as to render it hard enough to resist the tendency of upsetting.

The angles on the bullet must be cut with the greatest accuracy, in order to fit the groove of the barrel, possessing, in fact, a female screw of two turns in every thirty-nine inches of length.

Mr. Whitworth is deserving much credit for establishing an important fact, in his method of rifling, which has done our English cousins much good; and that is, to lessen the diameter of the caliber, increase the twist, and lengthen the bullet, in a mathematical ratio proportionate to the incline of the rifling.

All this circumstantial evidence has assisted in making up the case, which has been submitted to an intelligent Jury, consisting of some of the brightest intellects of the world, and they ask time for deliberation. Let's give it to 'em.

### Sagacity of Dogs.

A curious story of canine sagacity is reported in the Cologne journals. The owner of a number of rabbits near Barnien found that for six successive nights one of his rabbits was stolen from the house which he had made for them out of a wooden case which stood a few inches above the ground. At the top of it an opening had been made about the width of two hands, which was closed at night by a board on which heavy stones were laid.

The house having thus been secured, and as it was found each morning that only one rabbit had been stolen, and that all the rest were quite uninjured, it was considered impossible for a weasel to have effected the theft. It was, however, suspected that human hands had been at work. The owner consequently first made the opening more secure by nailing down one side of the board and covering it with grass and stones, and then hid himself in order to watch the thief.

At 1 o'clock in the morning he heard a noise at the rabbit-house and was not a little astonished to see two dogs instead of a man on top of it. One was a large dog of the neighborhood, well known to him, a cross between a St. Bernard and a large wooly collie, feared by all other dogs; the second was a stranger, a small terrier, just small enough to get through the hole into the rabbit-house.

The big dog, who on other occasions never noticed his smaller companions, had evidently come to an understanding with his little friend about the nocturnal rendezvous. The big dog scratched away all that was between the stones, dragged up the board and let the terrier jump through the hole. The latter returned in a few minutes with a rabbit in his mouth, which he presented to his great friend, and both proceeded to devour their supper undisturbed.—*Land and Water.*

A milk dealer in New York tried to ruin a rival's business by putting vinegar in the milk he had left for his customers, and was put in jail.

## THE GUN.

### My First Rhinoceros.

It is not often I take up the pen as a pastime, but I may add it is not every day I shoot a rhino, so I must sit down and send you an account of my first day's real big game shooting. The 5th of April was a wet day at B., and as I got into my howdah after five blank days, I did not feel very confident of success; however, as the mahouts said I was sure to get something to-day, I lit a pipe, a wonderful companion in wild Assam, and we started across the paddy fields for our shikar grounds; one needed to be very earnest in the pursuit of game on such a day, before venturing out of camp, for the rain came down, and soon the howdah was a sort of reservoir for the watery however, it cleared off and left the ground perfect for tracking.

We crossed a deep ravine, and got into open grass land, with only a tree here and there, and to my joy the mahout on Mukna elephant stopped, and pointed to the ground. I took Jaitra elephant to the spot, and saw the fresh tracks of a rhino. I knew he could not be very far off, for my mahout at once asked for liquor to relieve a great pain in his stomach; but Lilpoo had seen rhinos die before, and he knew that a little whisky was a great help to courage. I can almost sympathise with him, as an elephant's neck is a mighty uncomfortable seat in a scrimmage.

We soon got on rhino's tracks, and presently I saw a great black mass about 20 yards ahead of me, in jungle the height of my own elephant. I could not see what part of the body it was, but the animal seemed to take it very coolly, for he never moved, being I suppose accustomed to hearing and seeing wild elephant. I took aim at what jI guessed to be the shoulder, and fired right and left hardened ball from a double twelve bore, charged with six drachms of powder. With a loud roar rhino went straight at the small pool elephant on my left, and as all three elephants bolted trumpeting I could not help laughing to see the three individuals holding on to the pool ropes of the little one. Our friend now turned, and went northward; we followed him by the blood tracks, and again saw him moving along at about 60 yards off. I had time to give him one barrel, which hit him too high, and away he went. We now came on a boggy stream full of high grass, and with difficulty crossed it. After going for 300 yards more through dense jungle, we again saw rhino standing about 15 yards ahead. The mahout pointed in vain, I could see nothing; presently I saw a dark mass, and thinking I must finish him now, I gave him both barrels simultaneously. Some one must have whispered Scott's words to him: "Charge, Chester; charge," for with a whoof, whoof, the huge beast came at my elephant, and away went the trio again. Rhino was within five yards of me, but the howdah was rocking about in a most charming manner, and it was all I could do to hold on to my guns. Rhino suddenly turned and bolted into the jungle; we now attempted to calm the frightened elephants, for though Mukna and Jaitra were well known shikaree animals, a charge from a great brute in almost impenetrable grass is enough to alarm any hates. No power on earth could persuade Jaitra to re-enter the high grass now, and after several attempts it was decided to change the howdah to the Mukna, a magnificent young male, commonly believed to be a bit of a bidmash, but the finest shikaree I ever saw, funked nothing and smelt the battle from afar.

During the half hour it took to change the howdah I light ed a pipe, and thought of all the tales I had read about the uselessness of 12 bore rifles against large game, and how true they now appeared to me. Five bullets and 30 drachms of powder had already failed to make very much impression, as far as I could see; the whole time rhino was within 20 yards of us in thick jungle. I am glad we did not find this out till after I had mounted Mukna, as it was evidently our talking that kept him on the qui vive or he might have bolted.

Mukna now led the way, followed by the two others, and I must say it was very exciting work. We went in by a regular rhino path, and the one tusker knew there was trouble in store for him yet; for he kept tearing down the thick reeds, which were much higher than the top of the howdah, every now and again halting and then dashing on. Suddenly, with a whoof, whoof, rhino charged us from in front, and before either mahout or elephant could turn or think, the heads of the two huge brutes came clash. Mukna ran his jagged tusk two inches into rhino just below the eye; and I bent right over the mahout, and fired both barrels into him with the muzzle almost touching his spine. Rhino now rolled over on his side, and as Mukna turned to be off, for he had had enough now, I called out Hurrah! but though the end was nigh, it had not come; for I heard a crushing behind me, and saw rhino after me at full gallop. "Curse the 12 bore," was all I said as I loaded and gave rhino two more bullets. One I saw hit him off the shield, and as he rolled over I knew he had gone to the "happy hunting grounds" forever. After a race for one hundred yards, we again pulled up, and as neither force nor persuasion could get the elephants to go in again, we turned homewards, determined to return next morning. At 5 A. M., just as I was getting up, a Cachuree came in, and said rhino was lying dead; off we went, and found him about ten yards from the spot he was last-hit in; so that after getting nine bullets, backed by 54 drachms of powder, he moved again several yards before he gave in. I got on the elephant and saw the villagers cutting up the huge beast; there must have been over 200 people collected from miles around, for the Assamese prefer rhino to all other flesh, and they took away even the nails and hide to make his stew. I measured the beast on the spot. It was a very old female, though I fear I have been calling her "him" throughout. However, it makes but little difference; she was twelve feet four inches from nose to tip of tail; the horn was nineteen inches at the base, but very much worn away at the tip; and so ended my day's sport.—Royal Canadian, in Asian.

One must go away from home to learn the news. The Canadian Sportsman contains the following interesting piece of information: "California's lions and grizzlies are so numerous in parts of California that the herdsmen are banded together to destroy them. These animals have become so bold that they have advanced to the very doors of the ranchmen and killed the horses. Heretofore calves and young cattle were their only prey." We can assure our New Dominion cousin that, notwithstanding the bears and lions, there are a few horses left in California. If he don't believe it, let him bring out a few trotters and try 'em.

A Frenchman has devised a means of getting ducks at night. He puts up a pole and on this places an immense electric light. The birds swarm to the light in great numbers and are slaughtered mercilessly. This would get ahead of the birds that loaf around the pools all day out of reach and come to the feeding ponds at night when the hunters are away.

New preserves are being arranged for down near Alviso.

### Hunting in Nova Scotia.

I have lately returned from my usual fall trip moose hunting. I was out nine days and had a first rate time. I was accompanied by the veteran hunter McQ. On the day appointed McQ and I drove to Sunny Brae, eighteen miles, then packed our stuff seven miles across the barrens to the forks of Bryden's brook, on the west branch of the St. Mary's river; there we camped as we expected to get good fishing as well as hunting. The evening of the next day after we got to camp was favorable for "calling," so we tried that. We did not learn much during the day; we did not wish to disturb any game which might be near. About sunset we repaired to our calling place. On the second call we got an answer, and could hear the moose quite plainly, but he was lazy in coming up, and although we waited till past ten o'clock he did not put in an appearance; and as the night was cold and we were getting hungry we decided to return to camp. The next day we investigated and found that our moose had come up during the night to within ten feet of where we had called but had got the scent, and was off like the wind. It proved to be a young bull, and they invariably act thus; they are very shy and timid about coming to a call. If they come up boldly and find an older brother in possession of the field they are apt to get a sound threshing from the older one. Next day being Saturday we determined to go to the river and fish, so taking a light fly rod we started for the "Cameron pool," about a mile from camp. Arriving there, I got my tackle in working order and on the first cast hooked two fine sea trout. I found the fish very lively; I continued fishing till lunch time and landed about three dozen beauties and lost many fine ones forward of a net. After lunch we began fishing again and got several more.

When I began to think about reeling up and making for camp, I turned to tell Mac who was smoking quietly on the bank, that I thought it was time to go, when something broke the water, which, as I did not see it, I took by the noise to be a whale, and away went the line through the rings, and the reel keeping time at a rate of forty miles an hour. By this time it dawned upon me that I had hold of something more than I bargained for, which was no less than a salmon. No landing net nor gaff, a light hair line, and not very much of it, a single gut leader, and a "salmon." The pool was large and deep, so I determined to do my best. The fish had broken water two or three times, and I made him out to be of ten or twelve pounds, and a lively one at that. Various were the means that my good friend McQ. suggested as to the best way to land that salmon: shooting him with a rifle, a spear made out of a pointed stick, a landing net improvised out of a hat, in fact everything that he could think of, none of which appeared to me to meet the requirements of the case, so I determined to fight it out. To make along story short, after an hour and a quarter of hard work, I reeled him up to the bank, when a tap on the head from McQ. settled the business. It proved to be a fish of about eleven pounds weight. I took him with a red hackle. This was on the 30th of October, and 25 miles from the east water. The best fishing on this river is in May and June; and I have never known a salmon taken with a rod there later than July 21.

Next day it was raining and blowing a gale, and as we were camped on the open barren we had the full benefit of it, but our tent held up bravely, and beyond a little water that the high wind drove through the light canvas we did not suffer much inconvenience. The day following, as the storm had not blown over, we shifted our camp into the heavy woods, and then we were all right. We now turned our attention to hunting, and by Wednesday at noon had killed a wildcat (lynx) and a splendid big cow moose. In case some of your readers may say, why kill a cow? I ᵈᵉᵗ¹¹ to explain:" On Wednesday morning early, Mac and I came upon a good "yard." We knew by the signs there was a large bull or cow and a yearling in the "yard." We were doing our level best and were coming in well to where we thought they would most likely be feeding, when all at once we heard a loud snort and rattle of the bull's horns. This we knew at once was the signal of alarm to his family. How we had started them we were at a loss to conceive, instructed they were, sure enough. Our only chance was to run and try and get a shot, as they would have to cross a little bog about one hundred yards to our left. Run we did, and got there just in time to see the bull going out of sight in the alders, and a fine one he was, with splendid antlers. The cow was some distance behind, and as we came up I got a clear sight, and in a second a bullet was through her heart. She proved to be a very large, fat moose, and although I was much put out at losing the bull, I consoled myself with the thought that her meat would be much better eating than his.

We had scarcely come to where she fell when out walked two men who had been out looking for lumber, and they had come up directly to windward of our "yard," not knowing that the moose were there, and their approach had been the cause of alarm. Words failed to express our feelings, I can assure you, but it could not be helped, and we came to the conclusion that that bull was not intended for us anyway.

We saw one bear, but did not get a shot. They are very plentiful in these parts. Last season I killed three and wounded another, but still-hunting bears is difficult work. If we only had a couple of good dogs trained for bears what glorious sport we would have!—Globe Sight, in Forest and Stream.

A large pelican, measuring nine feet across the wings from tip to tip, was on exhibition at Fred Gates' gun shop for several days last week and attracted a good deal of attention. The bird was killed by William Nesbit, at Espinosa Lake, he wanted to hit it with a rifle at a distance of about 400 yards. It is of the species known as the American white or rough-billed pelican. The bill is about 14 inches long and the pouch attached to the under edge of the lower jaw is about 9 inches deep at the widest part, and capable of holding several gallons of water with enough fish for the dinner of half a dozen men. Pelicans do not dive for their prey, but thrust the head under the water as far as the neck will allow and swim along with only the upper mandible of the bill appear. ing above the surface; occasionaly they drive fish to shallows, where they can easily scoop them in with the pouch. As they stand upon the sand bars of lakes or rivers they have a melancholy sort of appearance, occasionally they err look, and a very ludicrous way of gaping or opening their long jaws. They destroy small fish in great numbers, several hundred minnows having been taken from the stomach and œsophagus of a single individual. When approached after a full meal, they disgorge like vultures. The flesh of pelicans is rank and fishy and unfit for food; their pouches have been used to make hats and bonnets; the sinews are said to make of them strings for musical instruments, and the Nile and other boatmen use the pouch with the lower jaw attached for baling water from their canoes.— Salinas Index.

A great many ducks are coming into the market from the Merced region.

### Fine Fun.—Messrs. F. A. Adams, W. W. Haskill, C. A. Edson

Fine Fun.—Messrs. F. A. Adams, W. W. Haskill, C. A. Edson were at the Alameda Club's preserve at Mallard Station last Saturday and had glorious sport. The day was very pleasant and the ducks stayed in on the pond all day. Two of the men would lie in the blinds while the third would walk around the lake and " stir them up" for the two behind the blinds to shoot at as they flew over. After shooting duck till they got tired the hunters went out on the marsh for snipe. The game was all in excellent condition. The result of the day's shooting was 125 ducks and several dozen snipe.

One of the best places for canvasback ducks that was ever found about this bay was at the junction of Montezuma and Suisun creeks in Suisun bay. There is a sort of shoal or split at the mouths of these creeks, and this seemed to be a favorite place for the "cans" to congregate. The Wyman boys, of Benicia, who used to shoot a great deal thereabouts, frequented this place for a long time, and it was always good for a good string. When the salmon fishing interests grew as they did a few years ago, there was established at this point a fishing station. A lot of boats are now anchored there, and the fishermen live there. The advent of the fishermen was, of course, the signal for the departure of the ducks, and now the old place is no longer sought.

W. R. Rodgers, Eli Bale, and Mr. Rodgers' two sons, spent last week hunting in the tules of Butte creek. They met with excellent luck, killing over a hundred ducks and also getting a wild hog that dressed over two hundred pounds of as nice pork as one would wish to eat—Gridley Herald.

While Con. Weber was hunting in a skiff in Twenty-one Mile slough, he discharged both barrels into a flock of ducks. The load was so heavy that he was " kicked" over and his skiff turned bottom side up. He lost his gun and his rubber boots, but brought home a teal for his day's sport.—Stockton Herald.

There are a great many young men in this city who are fond of hunting that get little chance of good bags since they do not belong to the shooting clubs which now have all the best places. If they did not preserve these tracts, however, they would have no shooting either.

On Oraycroft Hill, Sierra county, hunters have several times seen, but failed to kill or capture, an immense buck with antlers five feet long and six feet apart at the points.

The weather this week ought to bring the ducks back to the ponds again, out of the big bays, where they seem to have got in the habit of staying of late.

The season so far has not been a very good one for ducks. At a good many places where they were formerly abundant they have been pretty scarce this year.

Fifty cents' worth of gold-bearing quartz is said to have been found in the gizzard of a grouse killed the other day in Baker county, Oregon.

A good many hunters are laying out trips to last two days, on account of the holidays this week and next.

Hunters of water fowl about Sacramento report good success.

San Bernardino has a new gun club with fifty members.

### A North Carolina Venice.

Probably Morehead City is the only city in the world without a wheel in it. I do not think there is a wagon or buggy harness in the town, and very few in the country. Everything is done in boats. There is not a house in the country that a boat can get within a mile of. Not a doctor or lawyer owns a horse—they practice in boats. The people go to funerals in boats, and when they arrest a man they carry him to jail in a boat.

The main export of the town besides truck is fish, but the fish caught here embraces everything from a whale to a shrimp. Last year two or three whales were taken off this coast, and a whale is worth from $1,200 to $2,000. It is said they get between the shore and the gulf stream, and in trying to beat out to sea are sickened by the warm water. They turn in shore again and strand themselves. Along the bays and inlets mackerel are caught in large quantities in nets. But this wholesale fishing is neither picturesque nor interesting. A pretty sport practiced along the shore is' spearing flounders. A small row boat is put adrift. A man with a flambeau walks along up to his knees in water. In the bow of the boat sportsmen stand with slender gigs.

Along the bottom, by the reflection of the light, can be seen white flounders half buried in the sand. They remain perfectly still while the gig is poised over them, and never move until they are speared or missed. The only drawback to this sport is that occasionally your torch-bearer is stung by a stingaree. A stingaree is simply a long boggy whip broken out with smallpox and filled with steel springs, spur fortis and needles. When he hits you, lockjaw is the mildest result. The "little nigger" contingent about Morehead makes its living by crabbing. With a little boat, hardly bigger than a tub, they go out in the surf, and, dropping in and out like amphibia, soon come in with a bushel or so of the ugliest looking and sweetest tasting things that swim the sea.

One other very important industry of this most interesting place is the raising of " marsh tackeys." The marsh tackey is a shabby pony, hardly larger than the Shetland, light built and hardy. He lives in the water and all out on corn or hay. He is brought up on the marsh grass, which he eats between the tides. They cost literally nothing, breeding in droves as wild horses. Each drove has its leader, who selects the eating grounds and decides when the tide is coming in or going out. Once a year the owners have what is called, "pony reining." All the ponies around the coast, running into the thousands, are driven in by boats and either branded or sold. They bring from $15 to $30 apiece, and it is a tribute to their utter wildness that a "brocke" pony—that is, one that can be ridden or driven, is called a "trained tackey," and brings $70.

They are in great demand in the middle part of the state, eating little and doing a heap of work. They run down to skin and bones before they learn to eat corn or hay, but they fatten rapidly and lose the ugly reddish color the wild water gives them. There are men who buy them in large numbers, train them, and take them to the mountains and get fancy prices for them. As I write there is a drove of tackeys marching in slow and sedate procession against the horizon. The leader, bearing his responsibility with dignity, picks the way carefully, and his companions follow with a blind sense of confidence. The water, as it splashes about their legs, glistens like showered silver, and their red sides shine against the sunlike bronze. On they go, as birds beat homeward in the twilight, growing smaller and more indistinct as they plod their steady way. At last they are but specks above the water, moving dumb and patient to same well-desired goal.—New York News.

# CORRESPONDENCE.

## Simpson's Blackbird.

TISKILWA, ILLINOIS, Dec. 14, 1882.

DITOR BREEDER AND SPORTSMAN, Dear Sir: The splendid y of your paper of December 9th has made its appear- e to-day. In the article concerning Buccaneer, there ap- rs, among other good items, a reference to the stallion aphet in your own words described as "a very pretty bay né which a Mr. Wetherbee brought from the East and stood Illinois and Iowa." While you proceed to tell us that s horse was a son of Vermont Black Hawk, which is more n I have learned regarding him before, still you close aphet's history at the point where it becomes interesting to ur correspondent. Ignorance compels me to ask for more ormation regarding the bay stallion of Wetherbee's. I ve become interested in a handsome bay five-year-old gelt- ; that is the property of Sam Carter, a friend of mine who ewise belongs to the horseloving persuasion. This horse, n. K., was sired by a son of Simpson's Blackbird, while dam was by the Wetherbee horse. The sire, I have for- tten the name given him, made a circuitous season in the stthwestern portion of Whiteside and northern part of rean counties during which time the dam of Wm. K. was ated to him. One peculiarity regarding the colts sired by s son of Simpson's Blackbird was their high withers and oping hips. I would like to ask a few questions, i. e.:

1. Did the stallion familiarly known as "Simpson's Black- ird" present any unusual height at shoulder, and were is hips of the form termed sloping?
2. Were many of his get horses of this formation?
3. From what cause did he bear the distinctive title Simpson?"

The last question is to forever settle a dispute between Mr. arter and myself regarding the matter.

Please tell us where the horse Prophet made his first sason, also the year if possible? Yours Respectfully,

COLUMBUS.

Answer—As many queries have been sent us lately regard- g the form of "Simpson's Blackbird," the copy from Horse Fortraiture" a description written soon after his sath, and which is as near like him as we could picture it : the time.

Preceptor—All right, boy; give him his head; I want to ok at him from a distance first. Turn him partly around. ow run alongside of him across the yard; come a little faster : you approach me; that will do.

Well, scholar, I told you that sometime I would give you y idea of model roadster, and there stands nearer my ideal an any I have yet seen. Before going into detail of his rm, I will engage to make a trotter of him, no matter how uch he has been abused in his training. I make this prom- se not only from the fine action he exhibited while trotting cross the yard, but from that peculiar head, ear, and eye, hat all show sense. Horses have just as many degrees of ense as men, and Daniel Webster's "dome of thought" never more palpably showed his superiority over his com- peers. His head is large, yet you would not find enough meat on it to furnish a pet kitten with his supper. Look how the clearly cut nostril is just extended enough to discern the edge of the pink lining. There is an India rubber look about it that shows the orifice can be enlarged so as to admit all the air necessary to feed the lungs. The jowl appears as if carved, widening until you can thrust your clenched hand easily between the sharp jawbones. There is a correspond- ing widening of the forehead, giving plenty of room for a large brain, not alone the source of wisdom in a horse, but the center of the nerve force that wonderful something which we cannot explain, but which as surely enables the horse to do "great deeds of great renown," and places him far above his kind as it supplies the hero with the stimulus that renders him immortal. The clear hazel eyes, lustrous as a gem, shows his sagacity; and the long thin ears, placed just as I would have them, are perfection. How daintily the head is set on the neck; you could span the neck if it were detached from the throttle, which so nearly fills up the space between the jaws. Were it not that the neck is so perfectly formed is would appear too long, but the crest rises so beautifully that it requires the length to give it such a graceful curve, while the depth it displays, where joined to the body, shows a union of strength and lightness, admirable in its just propor- tions. The breast has the rabbit formation, usually seen in the first-class racehorses. The shoulder blade rises well to the top of the wither, is broad, sloping, and falls back into the sway, just as it ought to, and the point of it is well thrown forward, so that the humerus or upper bone of the leg is oblique. The elbow is properly placed, neither tied in nor standing away from the chest; this is what brings the fore- egs so truly under him. As you stand in front of them, 'hey are as true as a line, slightly converging to bring the eet squarely under the body, and the toes straight. The arm s long, the knee broad and strong, with the bony projection behind well developed. The cannon is short, the ligaments large, which gives the leg the flatness so much sought after. The fetlock joint is round, as if turned in a lathe, while the pastern is long, springy and oblique, so as to take the jar off the delicate bones below, without dropping enough to show any signs of weakness. There is no danger of ringbones or navicular disease in that formation. The feet are of a fair ize, with good heels, and horn that will never shell if the nail is placed properly. There is a great deal of truth in the old adage of "no foot, no horse;" these are not only naturally ood, but I must congratulate you on having kept them so by dicious care.

The horse is very deep through the heart. When I first aw him I should have judged him to be over fifteen hands two inches at the outside. When you stand beside him, you are satisfied that sixteen hands is, if anything, below his measurement. The barrel swells out, giving a good length of ribs, which are wide and have the right curvature. The back and loin are remarkably strong. The arch in the back is so high that it does not look as well as if a little lower, but here is a mountain of strength there when connected with the broad loin, braced with fillets as thick as your arm. The hip is long with slope enough. Were it more level, it would give him a jauntier air, but he would not be as likely to trot so well. The stifles are low, and placed the requisite distance spart to play freely, without being interfered with by the ab- domen. The hock is large and so clean that you can trace the articulation of the joint. The great width of the gaskin arises from the bone, forming the point of the hock or os-cal- sis being so long that the tendon comes up a long way before it is covered by the muscles. What was said about the can- non of the fore leg will be appropriate to describe the hind, only the flatness is more apparent. The angles, from the hip

to the foot, are just what they ought to be, to work the pro- pelling hind legs to the best advantage. His muscularity is just what I fancy, long, lean and dry; it will come as near giving you an idea of perpetual motion, as is in the power of any animal to display. If he was only a little fuller in the quarters, I believe I would like him a very little better, but as they are heavy enough, anything more would give him a cloddy appearance, that would take away from his high quali- ty. His coat is another mark of his high breeding; that and his hoofs would convince any discriminating observer that his claim to blood was well founded. He is not properly black, but dark brown, with tan-colored flank and muzzle; this I prefer to a horse that is all black. His tail is magnifi- cent. "fit for a Pacha's standard," as Willis once remarked of Lady Suffolk's but fitter to ornament such an animal as we are looking at. Some would call him too short in the body, but I think if measured you would find it equal to his height —the best proportion in my opinion, to unite speed, bottom, and that compactness of form, so essential in a procreating animal, more especially the male parent.

I have, in this cursory manner, run over the Falcon's chief points. Many, of course would differ with me as to what conjunction of these forms the best horse; but my ex- perience has led me to think a horse for fast driving on the road and track, able to keep going, up hill and down, or re- peat his heats all day, must approximate the form I have just sketched."

The great race horse Longfellow is more nearly the pattern of Blackbird than any horse we ever saw.

2. There was a great deal of the greyhound formation. There was a decided resemblance in a majority of his get, but as he died when eleven years old and his stud services restricted mainly to the last three years of his life, the number was not large.

3. To distinguish him from others of the same name. We owned him from the time he was 5 years old until his death. The only knowledge we have of Prophet is what was stated in the article referred to.

## The Judges' Decision as to Facts Final.

WOODLAND, Dec. 16, 1882.

ED. BREEDER AND SPORTSMAN, Sir: A match race came off to-day over the Woodland track between Garrotte's horse Jim and Strong's mare Lucy. The terms of the race were best three heats in five, to harness and to rule. Lucy took the first two heats and Jim took the two following. At the start of the fifth heat a slight collision of the sulkies oc- curred and the judge declared the heat a dead one on account of Jim running. The judges then reprimanded Jim's driver for running his horse, and told him that in case of a repetition they would set him back double the distance gained. In the sixth heat Jim broke twice and ran a con- siderable distance each time, coming in about two lengths ahead. The judges then declared that Lucy had won the heat, race and money. Some of Jim's backers then protested against the decision and refused to give up the money. Un- der these facts what would your decision be as to the purse, pools and outside bets. By answering the above you will oblige B. F. BRADY, H. W. HART, Judges. J. NELSON,

Answer—The decision of the judges of the race as to the facts is final, and unless something can be shown to prove absolutely that there was "collusion or fraud," their verdict must stand.

A wrong interpretation of the rules is subject to review, but in the case given above the matter was entirely in the hands of the judges. The point turns on the sixth heat, and if in the opinion of the judges Jim gained more than one length in his breaks, they were justified in declaring the heat and race to the mare. In that case the pools and bets follow the decision.

# YACHTING.

## Result of Corinthian Yachting.

In this bay all the yachtsmen are Corinthian; they all sail their own yachts, and sailing masters are unknown. It is different in the East, however, where all the large yachts have sailing masters and where many enthusiastic yachtsmen can- not sail their own boats. In this connection the following paragraph from the New York Spirit is suggestive:

Although there is little doubt that the New Jersey Yacht Club, the Atlantic, and others have had races in which the boats were sailed by their owners, to the Seawahaka Yacht Club belongs the credit of having permanently introduced Corinthian yachting into this country, and so well assured of this are they, that early in the present season they added the word Corinthian to their previous title of Seawanhaka, in order to signify that they are par excellence the Corinthi- an club of the country, and they have made the rule in rela- tion to amateurs as strict and rigid as possible. The rule reads as follows: "The yachts shall be manned by amateurs exclusively, and the sail-master and crew, if carried, shall remain below, and none of them shall, in any way, direct or assist in the management of the yacht." As a matter of fact, sailing-masters and crew are generally left on the shore, the Corinthians feeling themselves entirely competent to care for their own vessels.

Commodore C. S. Lee, the owner of the cutter Oriva, can handle her with the best of the experts, and J. Frederick Tams is far superior to the average sailing-master. Commo- dore Gautier and Secretary M. Roosevelt Schuyler can lay down the lines of the yacht for the builder, and sail her after she has been completed. We might mention many others who are experts, such as A. Cary Smith, Commodore Hyslop, the Alexander boys, etc. All this is the result of Corinthian yachting. Another result is a fondness for vessels of the cutter type as being much more easily handled than the cen- ter-board boat, and, as the club has now fitted its measure- ment to the cutter, it is probable that all of this pattern will go naturally to the Staten Island basin, the "sand-bag abor- tions," as Secretary Schuyler loves to call them, gravitating to Larchmont Manor.

We had expected when the Seawahaka Club secured the basin at Staten Island that a large fleet of sand-beggers would be moored there, and that at least two races per month would be sailed over this splendid course. Two reasons, we fancy, have prevented this: First, the cutter preference, of which we have spoken; and second, the club is rather particular as to who is selected as members, and if they do not belong to "our set" they cannot get in, and without the least disrespect

it may be said that a majority of owners of sand-bag boats are not of "our set."

An objection to Corinthian yachting is, that it is difficult to obtain the necessary crews and give them the proper pre- vious training, and this is especially the case when, as in this season's match, there are two schooners. We think that, until the club is more numerous, the entries should be re- stricted to sloops or cutters. Next season there will be two additions to the first class of sloops, the Bedouin and Weno- nah, and the schooners may well be dispensed with. Then, with crew early selected, and a month or six weeks of train- ing, we might look for more expert Corinthian work than ever before.

WHAT IS A KNOT.—The length of a nautical mile is defined ones-sixtieth part of that of a degree of a great circle of the earth. If the earth were a perfect sphere of known dimensions, the length of a nautical mile, according to the above definition, would be a definite and invariable quality. Owing, however, to the earth's compression, and the conse- quent difference in the lengths of the radii of curvature at different points of its surface, much diversity has arisen in sage and in books of reference in assigning the lengths of a nautical mile. Thus it is variously given as equal to the mean length of a minute of latitude on the meridian; the length of a minute of the meridian corresponding to the radi- us of curvature of the particular latitude, and the length of a minute of longitude on the equator; the latter definition be- ing probably due to the common use among mariners of Mercator's projection, in which the degrees of successive par- allels of latitude are equal to those on the equator. The office of the United States Coast Survey, in order to remove uncer- tainty, and to introduce uniformity, has adopted the value which resul strom considering the nautical mile as equal to the one-sixthieth part of the length of a degree on the great circle of a sphere whose surface is equal to the surface of the earth. This value, computed on Clark's spheroid, is: One nautical mile—1,853·248 meters—6,080·27ft, a value which corresponds to the adopted length of the Admiralty knot— 6,080ft.

WHAT IT COSTS TO KEEP A YACHT.—It is said that the own- er of a very successful forty-tonner is so disgusted with his yacht's success that he has advertised her for sale. The year's expenses amount, so the story goes, to £2,500. It is difficult to believe that the cost of racing a forty-tonner could be so much, even for winning thirty prizes in one season, as I am told that the new sails, spars and copper which the yacht had this season would not, or ought not to, have cost more than £500, including the recasting of lead keel; the wages of crew and extra hands £400, and the prize money £500, including bonuses to sailing master and pilot. This would make a total of £1,400, and this was the exact amount represented by the prizes won; so, from a business point of view, the accounts, on my estimate, balanced. As to the odd £1,100, surely the owner must have included his own per- sonal expenses.—London Truth.

Mr. Will Brooks of this city publishes a very creditable de- sign for a single-handed yawl in the Forest and Stream.

A 54-ft. plunger is being built by Farmer in Oakland for John L. Eckley, former owner of the Pearl.

The New York Yacht Club has given up the idea of a yacht club house by the water side.

The Lolita will remain in the marshes for another month yet and perhaps longer.

Farmer has just finished an 18-ft., plunger for Smith of Lake Merritt.

The weather of late has been very unfavorable for yacht- ing.

## San Francisco Sayings.

J. W. Murphy, proprietor of the St. George Stables, on Bush St., near Kearny, and Chief Engineer Matthew Brady, of the city Fire Department, both testify to the surpassing curative properties of the great pain-banisher, St. Jacobs Oil. The latter was completely cured of chronic and aggravated pains in the chest after a standing of four years, and after all other remedies had failed.

Mr. Murphy says that for pains, cuts, sores and swellings St. Jacobs Oil works like magic. There is nothing like it in the world; such is the experience of judges of horse-flesh.

# POULTRY.

## ABOUT KENTUCKY TURKEYS

### How they are Raised, Marketed and Packed.

What the Christmas plum pudding is to the Englishman, the haggess to a Scotchman on St. Andrew's day, or Easter eggs to the Teuton family, so is the Thanksgiving turkey to the American home. And as "Thanksgiving" is the great day of the year in every household, from the busy Atlantic to the wide Pacific, and from the Canadian Dominions to the Mexican border, the turkey is practically indispensable to the United States. The whole broad Union demands for Thanksgiving Day, will have it, as numerously and as cheaply as possible, but certainly and at any price, so that it be young, tender, fat and toothsome. It being settled that the American public must have turkey, the same American public has proceeded to supply its own requirements. When the population of the United States was chiefly agricultural nearly every farm had its few turkeys, sufficient for breeding from year to year, and for the supply of the family and a city or village friend or two, and mayhap a few birds to barter for "walker" at the corners. As occupations became more varied, and the numbers increased of those who had to purchase instead of raise their Thanksgiving turkey, some farmers with superior facilities and taste for the work increased their gobbling flocks, while others more inclined to some different branch of speculation left them the field. In this way particular portions of the country and particular farms were soon recognized as turkey raising sections and turkey farms.

The female turkey begins laying very early in the spring, and till allowed to hatch lays an egg every day. The eggs are not large considering the size of the bird, being little if any larger than an ordinary hen's egg, and more pointed at the smaller end. They are pretty thickly dotted with bright brown spots, on a rather dull white ground. The shell is thin. The hatching turkey is allowed from a dozen to fifteen eggs on which to sit. She is a most attentive incubator, seldom leaving the nest, and then only for a very short time, indeed she is one of the birds that those thin shelled eggs over which she sits will quickly grow cold; and once chilled, all vitality is gone from them. During the three weeks of her retirement the mother turkey becomes emaciated and rough of plumage, the time being with her a veritable period of fasting, if not of prayer. Only a small percentage of the eggs of turkeys are non-productive, but there is generally some loss after the young brood has left the shell, owing to the exceedingly tender nature of the newly-hatched birds. The slightest accident, or any very sudden lowering of temperature, will kill them, and the mother bird seemingly exhausts her care over the eggs, and becomes dismally indifferent toward the little family developed from them. Perhaps for this reason the young birds very soon learn to shift for themselves, but till they do the greatest watchfulness is necessary on the part of the turkey raiser, to see that they come to no harm. Once they are able to run about, they become wonderfully active in securing their own subsistence, in the shape of flies and other insects, which they greedily devour. Their increase rapidly in size and weight, and taking their places with the older birds of the flock, they march afield with the bronze battalion, apparently troubled nothing but the successive rising and setting of the sun, each intent only on his or her individual commissariat.

The turkey is eminently gregarious. From early morn till dewy eve the flock sticks close together, often wandering far from the usual roosting-place, but invariably returning to it toward sundown. While they are feeding they signal or scavenge each other by a short, peculiar call, so that a flock of turkeys can generally be heard before being seen. In the domesticated, and in the wild state, they prefer to roost on trees during the night, and if the old coverish must be accepted, they should be among the healthiest, wealthiest and wisest of the land, for they are certainly early risers. As the season advances and Thanksgiving approaches the turkey farmer takes more care in the feeding of his flock. The birds are deprived of their extended expeditions, being confined within a narrowed space, generally the farmyard. As if in return for their loss of liberty they are fed most liberally. They are not too particular as to what they eat, and accept heartily of the plentiful supply of food offered them. Thus, happily unconscious of their impending doom, they fatten and felicitate, and in a few weeks are ready for market. Sales of the birds in Kentucky, says a West ern exchange, are usually effected some time before they leave the farm, to buyers for killing and dressing houses, or to contractors for the supply of such houses. Arrangements are made for their removal, either by the farmers of the buyers, or both, and on the day set the driving begins. A company of drivers is collected, the number selected being according to the size of the flock, but always sufficient to keep all the birds together during their journey. This is the most difficult part of the driving operation, as the turkeys are prone to act on their own responsibility in straying aside, flying over fences and feeding in the fields. To control these stragglers, one or more of the driving force is almost continually in the fields on either side of the road along which the flock is being driven. The turkeys move along with heads bobbing up and down, and some of them are giving forth the peculiar turkey note every instant, so that several hundred turkeys moving in close flock have somewhat the appearance of a company of soldiers marching with music. The rate of progress is about four miles an hour. Barring their proneness to straggle, the driving of the birds is a comparatively easy task during the whole day, but on approach of sundown it is no longer possible to urge them forward, for they will go to roost, in spite of all attempts to prevent them. It is, therefore, necessary in the shades of evening to find some place to put up for the night, and for this purpose a field is usually secured. Should there be any trees in it, the lower limbs are soon literally packed with turkeys, and those who cannot get the coveted high position are forced to roost on the ground. Except from thieves, there is no danger of losing any of the birds during the night, for they will not move till morning. As soon as daylight has come they are ready to be driven forward again. Thus the journey is continued till the destination is reached. This is either some point at which the birds are to be shipped alive by rail, in cars with several decks, or the place where the turkeys are to be killed and dressed for shipment dead.

A "Turkey pens," by which name the establishments at which turkeys are received for slaughtering, dressing and shipment, have become regular institutions at many points throughout the turkey-raising sections of the country. These have of late years been carried to a remarkable degree of perfection. The first of these, now the most extensive one in Kentucky, was started by Oscar A. Gilman, of Paris, who, in the year 1867, by extensively calling the attention of farmers to the importance and profit of raising turkeys for the market, soon was able to extend his operations of both buying and selling, until now his turkey pens are known familiarly in all the regions round about, and have been heard of in all the Eastern markets, whither his shipments are made. Last year he shipped half a million pounds of turkey from two points—Paris and Flemingsburg—to Boston and New York, and this year he and two others have already shipped from Paris nearly 300,000 pounds.

The work done at the pens is highly interesting to the spectator. Each flock of turkeys on its arrival is driven up to a large scale. A large coop with a door at each end is placed on the ground, and turkeys are driven into it until it is full. It will hold say 100 birds. When filled it is placed upon the scales, and the exact weight of the birds within it being ascertained, they are paid for by the pound. The price at the present time is eight cents, being somewhat over the average. As high as eight and a half cents has been paid, and the rate has at times ranged as low as four and a half cents, though rarely is it under six cents.

After weighing the birds are driven into pens in a large yard, whence they are taken in squads of about fifty to the slaughter-house. Here they are driven into a coop from which a narrow alley leads to another room, into which it opens by a little door. In front of the door one man stands, snatching out the turkeys singly, quickly passes them over to the executioner standing behind, knife in hand. This functionary of death deftly catches each bird, long practice having made him perfect in receiving the victim in exactly the right position, and as quick as a flash he inserts the knife through the neck of the bird and passes the still quivering body to the floor. There he stands, catching with one hand and killing with the other, slaying and sparing not, the dead and dying birds piling up at his feet. The executioner at Gilman's pens has killed as many as 600 turkeys in a single day.

From the feet of the slayer the birds are removed to the picking room, in which is a low trough, occupying three sides of a square. Around this, both outside and inside, sit about seventy-five women, who receive the yet warm bodies of the turkeys and proceed to denude them of their natural covering. The scene here is quite picturesque. The pickers consist of women and girls of all shades of African descent, from the most suspicious cream color to the ebon hue which proclaims pure blood. All of them are dressed in gorgeous colors, many of them wearing turbans, thus giving them a decidedly Oriental appearance, while the variety of bright colors worn does much to brighten the effect of the living pictures. The dexterity shown by these pickers is perfectly marvelous. One of them in a very few minutes will produce from the pile of turkeys before her Aristotle's man—"a bipel without feathers." The most expert picker in Gilman's establishment, a bronze negress; has picked as high as sixty turkeys in a day. The pickers work steadily, keeping time to their own voices as they sing some good old church or plantation hymn, secular songs being entirely ignored, and so they work, filling the room with floating melody and feathers.

After leaving the picking room the turkeys are sent on to an adjoining room, where, with skillful manipulation of a small hand axe, they are decapitated and hung up and allowed to drip. From here they are sent to the cooling room, filled with racks so arranged that no one hags or overhangs the other. Here they remain for twenty-four hours to get perfectly cold. On this rack may be seen a portion of the turkeys with heads on and wing feathers, while others are the reverse. The former are for New York and the latter for Boston. Before packing the necks of the turkeys are tied to prevent blood dripping on and discoloring the bodies. This is done by drawing the skin down over the bone and tightly tying the stump, after which it is wrapped in manila paper and then packed in air-tight boxes when possible, each box holding from twenty to thirty turkeys. The covers of these boxes are tightly nailed, and they are then ready for shipment. They are, on arrival in the Eastern cities, unpacked, and either exposed for immediate sale or put away for later consumption, many of those killed at the present time not being eaten till Christmas or New Year, or even later; and epicures assert that the turkey acquires a much better flavor for being kept for some time after killing.—American Cultivator.

Those who are so situated that they can will find it beneficial to their fowls to shut them out of the poultry house and make them roost in the trees during five or six months of the year at least; they are hardier, healthier and more growthy for it, and less likely to be affected with lice. Young stock especially, as soon as left by hen, should be encouraged to roost in the trees. It is very rare that fowls thus raised are troubled with roup or snuffles.—Poultry World.

The New York Herald says that leg weakness is caused either by old age or by the size and weight of the body being more than the legs can bear. In the latter case the treatment should be such as to give strength. Climate of iron dissolved in alcohol should be added to the food, which must not be too fattening a nature. Keep plenty of lime and crushed bones in the poultry yard. In severe cases increase the limbs in cold water.

In a letter from HON. MRS. PERY, Castle Grey, Limerick, Ireland, BROWN'S BRONCHIAL TROCHES are thus referred to: "Having brought your 'Bronchial Troches' with me when I came to reside here, I found that after I had given them away to those I considered required them, the poor people will walk for miles to get a few." For Coughs, Colds and Throat Diseases they have no equal. Sold only in boxes. Price, 25 cents.

## Market Report.

FLOUR—We quote: Best City Extra, $6 50@$6 75; Superfine, $4 75@$5 00; Interior Extra, $4 75@$5 00; Superfine, $3 75@$4 00 # bbl.

WHEAT—Market fairly active with but little change in prices. The demand is for good grain, poor receive but little attention. No. 1 White, buy. ♀ December, $1 75¼; do January, $1 72⅝@$1 75¼.

BARLEY—Market steady and considerable business done. Recent sales: No. 1, Feed, December, $1 72⅝; $1 10; do January, $1 13⅝@$1 16; do February, $1 19 @$1 27; do March, $1 25@$1 34. Brewing $1 40@$1 50 according to quality.

OATS—Fair Feed, $1 70@$1 76; Good, $1 78@$1 80; Choice, $1 80@$1 90 # ctl, Eastern, $1 55 ♀ ctl.

RYE—Business dull. Quotable at $1 70@$1 80 for California ♀ ctl, and $1 80 for Eastern.

FEED—Ground Barley, $31 ♀ ton; Cracked Corn, $37 ♀ ton. Shorts, $20 ♀ ton. Oilcake meal, the oilworks sell to the trade at $33.50 ♀ ton, less the usual discount. Middlings, $27@$30 ♀ ton for sale at the mill.

HAY—Alfalfa, $13.99@$14.50; Wheat, $15 50@$17 50 Wild Oat, $11.45@$17; Mixed, $12@$14 ♀ ton.

PROVISIONS—Eastern Hams, 19½@21c; California Hams, 14@16c for plain, 16@21c for sugar-cured and fancy brands; Eastern Breakfast Bacon, 14@16½c; California Smoked Bacon, 13@16½c for heavy and medium, and 14@16½c for light and extra light; Clear Sides, 13@16½c; Pork, $22.50@$23 for Extra Prime, $23.50 for Prime Mess, $25.50@$26 for Mess; Hams, $23.50 for clear and $26@$26.50 for extra clear; Pigs' Feet, $16@$18 # bbl; Mess beef, $11 for bulk and $9.50 for half bbls; Extra mess beef, $17 for bulk and $9.75 for half bbls; Family beef, $13@$14.50; Smoked Beef, 13@14c ♀ lb.

FRUIT—We quote: Apples, 10@25c for common and 75@$2 50 # box per bushel; Pears, 50@$2.50 ♀ box; Cape Cod Cranberries, $9@$11 ♀ bbl.

VEGETABLES—Potatoes, 75@90c ♀ ctl.

PROVISIONS—Eastern Hams, etc.

POTATOES—River Red, 60@70c; Early Rose, 60@75c; Cuffey Chili, 55@65 ctl; Humboldt, 45@65 ctl; Tomales and Petalumas, 60@70 ctl; Peerless, etc.

ONIONS—Quotable at 75@90c per ctl.

BEANS—Bayos, $3 75@$4; Butter, $3.50@$3.75 for small; and $4 20@$4.50 for large; Lima, $4 75@$5; Pea, $3 30@$3.60 Pink, $3 30@$3 60 ♀ ctl; Red, $3 50@$3 75 small White, $3 50@$3 75; Large White, $3 75@$4.

BUTTER—We quote: Choice dairy, 30@32½c; choice, 27½@30c fair to good, 22@25c; interior lots from ordinary makes, 15@20c; pickling fair for good to choice, and 10@15c for ordinary; pickled roll, 16@17½c; Eastern, 16@21c # lb.

CHEESE—Fatly steady. California, 14@15c for choice; 11@13 for fair to good lots; Eastern, 15@16c; Eastern, 14@15c # lb.

EGGS—California, 37½@40c; Eastern, 30@35 per doz.

POULTRY—Live Turkeys, gobblers, 15@17c ♀ lb; Hens, 14@16c; dressed, 15@18c; Roosters, $5 00 @$6 00 for old and $6@$7 for young; Hens $5 00 @$7.50; Broilers, $3@$5, according to size; Ducks $7.00@$9 ♀ doz; Geese, $1 75@$2 ♀ pair.

GAME—In good demand. Quail, 75@90c ♀ doz; Mallard Ducks, $3@$3.50; Sprigs, $1.75@$2; Canvasbacks, $3 30@$3 75; Teal, $1 50@$2; Grey Geese, $2@$2.50 White Geese, $1 25@$1.50; Honkers, $3@$3 50; Hare, $1@$1.25; Rabbits, $1.50 for domestic and $1.25@$1.75 for tame; Venison, 8@10c.

WOOL—No change in prices. We quote: fall, San Joaquin and coast 11@15c; Northern Fall, 14c; 16@20c; Northern Fall, defective, 12@15c Southern fall, 9@16c; lamb, 20@30c; Mountain, 16@19c.

HIDES AND SKINS—Dry hides, usual selection, 18@18½c ♀ lb; culls one third less; salt Kangaroo Hides, 8 @ ½ less; Dry Kip, 17c; Dry Calf, 18@20c; salted steers, over 55 lbs, 8½c; steers and Cows, medium, 10c; light 8c, 9c; Salted Kip, 10 to 30 lbs, 8c; Salted Calf, 10@12c; Salted Veal, light 9@10c; Dairy Calf 10c; Sheepskins, shearling 25@40c, short 50@75c for medium, and 75@90 for long, pelts. Butcherskins Green hides being higher prices.

TALLOW—Quotable at 8@8½c ♀ lb for rendered and 11@11½c for refined, both in shipping order.

## INTERESTING.

THE SEMI-WEEKLY EAST OREGONIAN
With pictures of Exhibition, Conference, Wagon Cumulite City, Echo City, Pendleton and Heppner, to any address three counties, etc., six months, $1; Twelve months, $2. Sample copy of paper and picture, 5 cents.
The best and most descriptive of Umatilla county, Wallowa and other districts.
Address EAST OREGONIAN PUBLISHING COMPANY, Pendleton, Umatilla county, Oregon.

We have received Vol. 1, No. 1, of the BREEDER AND SPORTSMAN, dated July 1, 1882. This journal contains sixteen pages; is well edited by Joseph Cairn Simpson of San Francisco, where it is published; contains a clear print and is a paper that no sportsman or horseman should be without. In fact it is just what is named, the breeder and sportsman's journal. If it is desired to find anything pertaining to races, pedigrees of horses and sports of all kinds, the information can be ascertained therein, as it is the first and only authority on the Pacific Coast. We wish the paper the success that it so well deserves.—Silver City (Idaho) Avalanche.

SPECIMEN OF OUR ARTIST'S HUMOR.

THE FISHMONGER.

HUNDREDS OF DELIGHTED ONES SEE, FOR THE FIRST TIME IN THEIR LIVES

The Japanese Artist and Embroiderers

*At work in their native costumes at*

## Ichi Ban, 22 & 24 Geary St.

*The* BREEDER AND SPORTSMAN *is printed with* SHATTUCK & FLETCHER'S INK

## ALBERT W.
BY ELECTONEER. — SISTER TO AURORA BY JOHN NELSON.
OWNED BY A. WALDSTEIN, SAN FRANCISCO CAL.

## A CALIFORNIA ROMANCE.

### The Canary Bird and the Lottery Ticket—A Tale of Oakland.

A long time ago, that is a long time in California history, there lived and worked in Oakland a German shoemaker. A short, square-built man with florid complexion and small, sparkling black eyes. In the early morning, before the sun broke over the crests of the Contra Costa range, he was busily at work, and when the grand luminary was settling beneath the Pacific horizon in a haze of glory the sound of the hammer on the lapstone reverberated from the little shop. A shop not much larger than a big dry goods box, and cluttered with old boots and shoes past his skill to repair. And yet there was a neat look about it, and on the low walls hung cages of canaries and linnets, with a few wood engravings pasted on the vacant spaces. He was a cheery little man, and between the songs of the canaries and the chirping of the linnets came refrains from the tunes of the Father Land, and snatches of operas. In a cozy little room in the rear of the shop his wife was just as busy, and the few household goods, the crockery on the shelves, and the tin ware which hung by the stove were as bright as the skill of the housewife could make them. They were a happy couple notwithstanding the evident closeness of their circumstances, and the notes of the husband would be caught by the wife, and the chorus rattled off with as much zest as though they had thousands at command.

A toddling, wee bit of a girl, with the black eyes and rosy cheeks of her father, the golden hair of her mother, was the only child, and she, too, would join in the musical merriment and take part in the family concert. It was indeed a happy family, as joyous as the canaries, as cheerful as the chirping linnets.

One hot and dusty afternoon a stranger stopped before the open door of the little shop attracted by the song of the birds, and after pausing a moment, walked in. He was a fine looking young man though his clothes were worn threadbare, and his boots were broken so as to show the bare feet inside. He apologized for the intrusion, telling the shoemaker that the song of the canary was so much like that of his sister's at home, that it recalled old memories, and the old familiar faces so vividly that he could not resist the temptation of listening longer. There was moisture in his eyes as he made the brief statement and a tremor in the voice, though there was a recklessness in his demeanor which did not harmonize with the emotion he displayed. The shoemaker proffered him a seat which he accepted, and looking down at his dilapidated boots, remarked, "that if he was not dead broke he would get him to mend them."

"No matter for that" replied the little shoemaker, "you like the songs of the birds, and I will mend them for nothing."

His visitor pulled off the worn boots; while the patches were being fashioned and sewed on he gave a short account of how he came to be in the impoverished situation. He had been mining in the upper country with such success as to return to his old home, and he arrived in San Francisco a few months before with several thousand dollars in gold dust. He intimated that his life had been rather a wild one in the land of his nativity, but he felt that he would do better after the hardships he had suffered, and he especially desired to show his sister, who had often taken his part when his father was stern, that he had truly reformed. It was some time before the steamer would sail, and in the interim he had nothing to busy himself with but to walk about the town through the day, and stay at his hotel during the evening. The time hung heavily. The pinions of old father Time seemed to have big globules of mercury at the tip of every feather, and his sandals platinum soles ever so thick. From his hotel he could hear the bands playing at the gambling houses, and throngs of people were wending their way thitherwards. For many evenings he manfully withstood the temptation, and kept away from what he had good reason to think would bring evil. Gambling had led him into his worst scrapes, and he well knew the fascination there was to him in the excitement of the faro table. He had felt the keen claws of the tiger piercing through the outward integuments, rending his heart and tearing his brain, and the recollection was his safeguard.

One evening as he sat in the reading-room of the hotel, his fancy already carrying him to the scenes of his boyhood, he was startled by a man who accosted him by name, and raising his head there stood before him one of his old cronies. one of the worst of them who had been his companion in some of his wildest freaks, the instigator of what were actually crimes and which only the standing and respectability of his father saved him from the penalties attending the commission of. There was an involuntary shudder as he recognized his mephistophelean associate, though he felt pleased to see one with whom he could converse about old times, and as yet he had no misgivings about the strength of his good resolutions. After half an hour's conversation the visitor proposed a turn round the town. At first he refused, saying that he had spent several days in wandering about and all he wanted to do was to quietly spend the time until the steamer sailed.

"You do not know anything about Frisco unless you see it by gaslight." was the reply, "and I know all of the ropes and will see that no harm befalls you. We will take a short walk, and if you do not want to go to the theater, or the variety show, where there is lots of fun, or to the Mexican fandango, we will come back to the hotel."

Ashamed to refuse further the two strolled around the streets, and he was struck with the difference between the scenes of daylight and those he now witnessed. In the day-time men were hurrying in every direction evidently intent on business, the sidewalks were crowded and trucks, drays, and wagons rattling over the cobble stones. In the evening there was a far greater throng on the sidewalks, but in place of the tumult, the bustle, the clatter of the working hours, the people were leisurely sauntering along as though their only aim was to enjoy the salubrity of the evening air. It was in the early spring-time, one of those vernal, mellow evenings peculiar to California, when the air is so soft and fragrant that there is pleasure in inhaling it, and the atmosphere is filled with a voluptuous aroma, indescribable, enchanting. The jewelry, fancy goods and variety stores were ablaze with light, the windows decked with a gorgeous display of goods, crowds of people congregated before them.

They strolled through the plaza, which was also filled with people listening to the music of the bands. His companion stopped in front of a house, in the balcony of which were the musicians, proposing that they should go in and see how the games were progressing.

"I have sworn never to play again," was the response to the invitation.

"There is no law to compel you to play against your will," was the reply, given in a half mocking, half laughing tone. Ashamed to resist further, he accompanied his partner, and when over the threshold; he was astonished at the sight. In the Eastern town where he had lived the gambling houses, or club-rooms, as they were euphoniously termed, were in the rear portion of an upper story. To get there it was necessary to go through an alley, enter a back door, and after ascending the stairs, give a signal at a door which had a small aperture in it, covered by a slide. The slide would be pushed back, an eye peer through, and if the visitor was known, the bolt was slipped, and he was admitted. There was still another door to be opened, and if the Cerberus was not fully satisfied, the person would have to wait there until the proprietor had the opportunity to see if he was all right. Inside there was one table covered with faded green baize, a shabby check rack and still shabbier case. The dealing box was of plain white metal and the ivory checks stained, and some of them chipped. What a difference to walk directly from the street through wide folding doors, swung back to the full extent of the passage, into a bar-room with a long counter of rich foreign wood, the bottles and decanters of the finest cut glass, a mirror reaching from the floor to the ceiling and as long as the counter. There were several valuable oil paintings and ornaments of various kinds and the room lighted as brilliantly as a myriad of gas-jets could make it. Beyond was a still larger room, scarcely separated from the bar, the open space being nearly as wide as the space between the walls. This room was so thronged that it was difficult to find a passage way. There were two tables with the "lay out" for faro, a monte table, at which presided a large, and, in the gas-light, a fine-looking woman, her apparel blazing with diamonds; a roulette wheel, rouge-et-noir table, and back of all a billiard table, with as many as could get a place betting on rondo. There was a perfect babel of sound—English, Spanish, French, mingling in, to him, inextricable confusion. The company was as diverse as the language. Fashionably dressed men, with large gems on their shirt fronts and gloved hands, and jostling them were others clad in thick woolen shirts, coarse pants, tucked into long-legged boots, a belt round the waist, with the handles of one or two big revolvers sticking out of the cases, long hair and full beards, and complexions of a light bronze color; native Californians, wearing wide-rimmed sombreros, and many of them of such a sinister aspect as betokened treachery and cunning. Not a few women were also present, either betting on monte or watching those who did. Faro and roulette were the only kinds of play with which he was acquainted, and he and his comrade stopped in front of one of the tables. There were huge stacks of gold coin within reach of the dealer, and at his right hand was a mahogany box something like the trays used by bankers to hold specie. In this were piles of circular pieces of ivory, white, red, blue and yellow, stacked in regular order, and enough of them to nearly fill the tray. Many were in the hands of the players and distributed on a suit of thirteen cards fastened to the cloth.

"Throw in a play," remarked his associate, "and we will try our luck. You're not playing you know," he continued as he saw him hesitate; "this is my trick."

Again he was ashamed to refuse and that before so many people, so he gave him the fifty dollars to which the other added fifty from his pocket and bought a stack of twenty of the white chips. From the first he was successful. Nearly every bet he made won, and the whites were changed for reds, and the reds multiplied until there were several stacks in front of him. In the eastern town the valuation was only one-tenth as much, twenty dollars was a big bet, and fifty the limit which the dealer restricted the players to.

Here men bet a thousand dollars on the turn of a card with as much nonchalance as those at home bet ten, and frequently his partner had a stack of the red chips, or $500, down. It almost took his breath away to watch the play, and when his partner won so rapidly he became so excited he could hardly restrain himself.

Then the luck turned. He lost more rapidly than he won, and some blue chips and nearly all the reds were stacked back in the mahogany box.

"Here goes," he murmured as he put all the remaining chips on a card. It was some time before the card appeared, and the suspense was agonizing as the dealer pulled the pasteboard through the slit with the monotonous click, click, which marks the operation. It won. He left the whole amount; it won again.

It was only a short time though it seemed an age when he had regained the ground he had lost, and shoving the checks over to the dealer who returned $6,000 in bright double eagles. He pushed $3,000 of it to his partner with the remark:

"Pretty good off a hundred, we'll go back to the hotel."

To win $3,000 at one time was beyond anything he had ever thought of. It was nearly half as much as he had labored so hard and so long for in the mines, and had been considered one of the lucky ones at that. He could not sleep. The thought of the piles of gold he had seen in the gambling room, and if $6,000 could be won with a hundred, what might be done if he ventured a thousand. In several instances his partner had lost when he would have played differently, and he studied out a "system" which would be sure to make a big winning on that amount of capital. He pondered over returning to his native town with $100,000, perhaps more, and he thought how he would astonish his old neighbors with his munificence.

His sister (his mother was dead) should have the finest carriage and horses, robes fit for a queen, diamonds, everything her heart could desire. His father should have a gambling library of his favorite books, easy chairs, gold-headed canes, a watch ornamented with jewels, with an old-fashioned seal set with an emerald on which was cut his coat of arms, and a snuff-box radiant with gems. When morning came and he was up and saw the first glint of the sun's rays flickering on the ripples of the bay, he did not feel so enthusiastic. Reason took the place of fancy and he cogitated over what would be the result if he lost. He had an inordinate longing to get home, and to hazard the means of getting there was not to be thought of. So all day long there were opposing forces, and he wandered about moody and discontented. When evening came he was glad his old acquaintance did not make his appearance.

But the reading-room was never so dull, and in such a contrast to the brilliantly-lighted saloons, and the music, and the throng of gamblers, the whizz of the roulette, and the big piles of gold by the hand of the dealer. He went out thinking he would find distraction from the thoughts which tormented him by mingling with the throngs on the side walk and looking at the decorations in the blazing windows. The crowds were there, there were the same rare shows in the windows. The air was as balmy, and music swelled over the plaza as it did the night before. And yet there was a feeling of discontent he could not overcome. A strange sort of yearning, a half torture, a dread which tantalized him with its vagueness, a resolve he could not quite master. He walked down Clay street to Montgomery, turned quickly as he saw the flash of light from the open door of the gambling house, and at a rapid pace strode southward. He was on the corner of Bush ere he slackened his speed, and in place of going to Sansome street, on which was the hotel, he took the contrary direction, and once more was going north on Kearney; through the plaza again, and this time he was a little calmer.

"It is a square game, I am sure," he whispered, "and I need not play if I find I am losing."

He had come to the resolve he could not reach a few minutes before. The indefinite terror which haunted him had given way to elasticity of spirits, the dread was banished, and he complacently flattered himself over his newly found will-power. He had deposited $2,000 of the $3,000 won with his other money in the safe of the hotel. The remaining $1,000 and a hundred or two besides would be all that he could lose, and if he found his luck adverse he would quit after a stack or two of white chips were lost. He banished the thoughts of home for the time being, and this was the resolution he reached. He thought over the system he elaborated the night before, when his mind was too much occupied to sleep. The system proved correct. He played cautiously, rarely risking more than two of the checks representing $5 each, stuck closely to the plan he had marked, and after a long sitting rose from the table $1,300 better off. It was a fatal winning. Had he lost the whole of the money in his pockets, in all probability he would not have risked more, in his anxiety to revisit his home, and with his faith in the system broken.

He left the room much calmer than on the previous visit, the handling of the checks and placing the bets being something in the shape of a safety valve to relieve the excitement. And then, too, he was convinced that his plan was correct, and in lieu of $100,000, he would depart with a million to his credit. This was only one of the many big gambling houses in the town, and there was no end to the money to be won. He calculated the time it would take to a nicety, and how many steamers would sail before he was ready to depart. It is unnecessary to follow him through the varying fortunes of the next month. The inevitable result was sure to come. He became desperate as his money, the original capital, decreased, and played recklessly. When it was all gone he managed to live he scarcely knew how. An odd job on the wharves, sleeping where he could find a hole to crawl into among the bales of hay on the dock, a life ten times harder than the rough days in the mountains.

Spring-time had gone. The mellow air was followed by the trade winds and the golden autumn, with the brown hills and cooler roads. Without a definite object in view, he boarded the Oakland ferry-boat, paid his last coin for the passage, not even looking back on the city in which he had such high hopes, such bitter disappointments. Everything he possessed was on his person. Not even a blanket or an extra shirt. A farmer who lived near San Pablo asked him if he did not want a job. His affirmative answer brought instructions how to find his way there, and he was commencing the journey when the warbling of the canary bird attracted his attention. This he told in substance as the little shoemaker was sewing on the patches, though there were a good many terms beyond the comprehension of the simple-minded German, and he could not understand how a man could take the risks of squandering thousands when he was contented to labor assiduously for a trifle. But all the kindliness of his nature was aroused, and, notwithstanding the folly of a man who made such a confession, he reasoned that anyone who had stopped to listen to the song of birds, could not be utterly depraved. The boots finished, his impecunious customer commenced searching his pockets, as though there might be a stray coin somewhere, when the shoemaker said:

"Never mind, my friend, and though I have little money, I will lend you enough to get your dinner, it's a long way to San Pablo."

"Here it is," was the reply, "a lottery ticket I was foolish enough to purchase before all my money was gone. With my luck it is sure to draw a blank; in yours it may be different."

For a time the shoemaker refused it, but finally pulled out a drawer beneath his work bench and threw it in amongst a heterogeneous mass of awls, pegs, balls of thread, bunches of wax, etc. For the rest of the day the shoemaker did not carol with the birds as frequently as usual. He could not drive the gloomy thoughts away, as he pondered over the sister and her canary with the loved brother a wandering outcast.

But the next morning when the sun gilded the summits of the hills on the east, and Mount Tamalpais wore a golden crown, he was as blithe as ever. The canary trilled its most brilliant notes and the linnet chirped a softer tune. The little girl ran out and in the shop, the bright colored ringlets falling in a mess on her shoulders, and the little wife was as gleesome as the birds.

Months passed. The rains of winter had given to another spring time, and there was waving grass in the valleys and the sides of the hills decorated with the rainbow hues of the native flowers. The few gardens in Oakland were bright with blossoms, and the roses and beds of mignonettes perfumed the whole town. Busily the shoemaker worked. His only leisure time was on a Sunday when, with the wife and little daughter, they sought recreation, sometimes in the live oak grove on the Point, where the brown larkshum sang and the meadow larks twittered, and at others over in Alameda where the little one gathered bunches of wild flowers and chased the butterflies.

On one of these fragrant mornings a neighbor came into the shop and after the usual salutations inquired of the shoemaker if he had heard the news. Receiving a negative answer he remarked:

"Why, Tubal Hein, the blacksmith, bought a lottery ticket last summer, and he has drawn $1,000 on it and is over in San Francisco having a grand time over his good luck. I was foolish enough to spend ten dollars the same way, but a fool for luck, I did not get a cent, though they sent me this sheet with a list of the drawing."

Instantly he remembered the lottery ticket which he had tossed into the drawer never having given it a thought since. With some trepidation he pulled out the drawer and rather nervously poked about among the contents. He merely answered, "I have a lottery ticket," and his friend aided him in the search. Finally it was found sticking to the leather on a ball of wax, though fortunately it was the back of the ticket which adhered. Before removing it the list was consulted and neither at first could believe their eyes when it was discovered that the numbers on it corresponded with those which drew a prize of $40,000.

It could not be possible that such a stroke of fortune had followed the putting on the big patches on the stranger's boots, but his friend, better posted in these affairs, assured him that it was a reality, and that if he would go to San Francisco he could get it cashed for the usual discount.

He hocked his red cheeks in the operation of shaving, and his little wife had to button his collar and fasten his neck-tie. She was skeptical regarding the whole affair and thought it an unnecessary waste of time and money to bother about it.

When they went away, however, she became nervous, and bustled about, making a great clatter with the tinware, and to her intense disgust broke a tea cup which she was placing on the dresser. The only unconcerned inhabitants of the little domicile were the little girl and the birds, though the canary missed the accompaniment of the hammer on the lapstone, and the little girl was at a loss to know why her father had gone away without taking her mother and her with him.

All doubts were dispelled on his return. He had a certificate of deposit for the whole amount, less the usual percentage for getting the ticket cashed, and they were now rich. There was an anxious consultation that evening in the little room in the rear of the shop. His friend and his little wife sat around the little table, and the mugs of beer stood with their contents almost untouched. One thing they agreed upon, that the stranger should share the good fortune and receive half of the proceeds at least; but the trouble was to find him. As he had not given his name, there was no chance by advertisements in the papers, and though he had a faint recollection of his appearance the remembrance was too indefinite to rely upon. He had one sure means of identification, viz., the patches on the boots. He would know the patches if he boots were mixed with a thousand others, or if he saw them in any

part of the world. He had taken more pains to do a good job than if he had received payment, and the boots, apart from the break on the side, were strong, of the best leather, and would last many months of hard usage without further repairing. Then they had the clew that he was going to work on a farm at San Pablo, though it was not likely he would remain there long.

It was past midnight when the course of action was decided upon. The first thing was that the secret of the lottery ticket should be kept inviolable, and the next, that the shoemaker should go on a search for the stranger. He was the only one who could identify the boots, or who had taken notice enough of the visitor to remember him at all. A saddle-horse was hired of the livery man, the explanation that he had business "up country" and might be gone a long time being sufficient reason for making the trip. When he mounted the horse to start on his journey he did not make a very graceful appearance. His short, square figure, shoulders at right angles with the vertebrae, a straight line from shoulder to hip, there was little of Hogarth's curves in his form, and this was more apparent on horseback than when he walked. There was a good look in his face though, an honest, straightforward countenance, and on this eventful morning determination was as plainly seen in his bearing as at other times the predominant trait was good humor.

In the little hamlet of San Pablo it was easy to find traces of the person he sought. He had worked there long enough to get a little money, and some time ago started for the mines, though he had never intimated in what part of the State the mines he intended working in were situated. His employer told the shoemaker that he called himself Davidson, but that was evidently not his right name, as frequently he would pay no attention when addressed by that appellation, and as he never received a letter during his stay, there was no means of finding out. He had wrought faithfully, but it was also evident that he knew nothing about farming work, and his tasks were confined to those which only required manual strength. The shoemaker was pleased to hear that he wore away the boots, and that they were still in fair order. He also obtained a more accurate description of his appearance, and continued the journey with faith that he would be successful in the search.

It would be tiresome to follow him through all the trip. He visited various mining camps without being able to find a trace of the pseudo Davidson, and elicited many jocular replies when he described with almost microscopical minuteness the patches on the boots. He never thought of giving up the search. He felt that it was a sacred duty which he must fulfill and every fresh disappointment increased his determination. He met with many adventures, and the little was so different from that in the little shop in Oakland with his wife and little girl, and the canaries to warble, and the chirping songs of the linnets, that he, at times, thought it must be a long dream from which he would awaken. At last he found the trail. Davidson had been there but under another name, and there could not be a question, for he still wore the patched boots.

At other camps he heard of him, and if not found at one more in that part of the country the miners told him he must have gone to diggings in other regions. It might be Fraser River, it might be on the Salinas or the auriferous fields still further to the southward.

It was growing dusk when he was miles away from the point of destination, and before he got there the full moon was lighting the trail which followed the steep side of a mountain. It was so steep that trees could not get root, though there was a dense growth of chapparal, and hundreds of feet below the waters of the creek were breaking over the bowlders. The white foam seemed whiter in the moonlight and the rush of the torrent over the rocks made a seething noise, loud and hissing even as the height he was above it.

For the first time during his long journey he had misgivings. There was a despondency he could not shake off. A premonition of something dreadful to come, and he thought of his little wife and the wee girl, and the song of the canary and the linnets, as what he might never see nor hear again. There was a steep descent and at the foot of the mountain, a slight widening of the glen formed a narrow valley. A few miners' cabins skirted the edge of the ravine, and in the one nearest to him a light shone through a hole which answered for a window. Tying the halter rein of the horse to a sapling, he knocked at the door, which was partly open, and a man's voice in low tones bid him come in. On a bunk lay a man moaning, but so feebly the sounds were scarcely audible, and on a stool by the side of the couch another was seated who was fanning the sick man with a wide-brimmed Panama hat. The shoemaker moved quietly to the side of the man, who held his disengaged hand up as a token not to disturb the sleeper, and in a whisper said: " I beg pardon for the intrusion but I am in search of a man by the name of David-son, or—or—," but he could not recall the name given to him at the camp where he received the last intelligence, and completed the sentence with: "A tall, good-looking young man with a black beard, and big patches on his boots, I have good news for him."

"Your good news will come too late if I am not mistaken in your man," replied the watcher in an impressive whisper. "Just such a looking man as you describe came into this cabin about sundown, stole some bags of golddust, and when he was carrying it out, the owner here met him, raising an outcry as he clenched the thief. The rascal stabbed him twice and ran. The man was soon caught and the boys have him now on the little knoll about two hundred steps up the can-

yon, and if you hurry you may see him before they swing him off."

"My God! My God!" exclaimed the shoemaker, "six hours sooner and this would not have happened," in a tone so loud that it aroused the wounded man who partially raised up and the effort forced drops of fresh blood through a bandage which encircled his neck.

"Out of here quick" was the angry response, and he dashed out of the cabin and with a sort of instinct or intuitive knowledge of the right direction to take, he ran up the banks of the creek; he had to pause for lack of breath from the unusual exertion before he had run a hundred yards, and looking up saw a group of men on a slight elevation. It was as the miner described it a little rounded knoll covering, perhaps, an acre of ground, and on it were a few oak trees, lifeless without leaves or twigs, the scrawny, irregular branches straggling on either side of the boles. In the center of the group was a man taller than the rest, and in the bright moonlight the shoemaker could plainly see that there was a rope around his neck and thrown over one of the projecting limbs.

"Stop, for God's sake stop," he frantically shouted, again breaking with a run and continuing his exclamations until he reached the men.

Every man was looking at him and the silver mountings of pistols gleamed and glittered, some of them held within a few inches of his head.

"Who in the devil's name are you?" was the query from the man who evidently was the leader of the band.

"Oh, I am his friend," gasped the shoemaker, "I give ten, twenty, forty thousand dollars for you not to hang him."

"Not for a million" was the response in the sternest tones. "This man is a thief and a murderer and there is not money enough in California to save him from his just doom, and more than that," he continued, closely scanning the countenance of the shoemaker, "if you had not an honest face by G—d you should swing with him."

"Hang him, hang him up with him too, he must be his pard" one of the men said.

"No," returned the leader, "though it is a bad sign to acknowledge being the friend of a man like this, he may be innocent and he does not look like a scoundrel but some of you keep your eye on him, we will attend to him after we are through with the business on hand."

Undismayed at his own peril, the shoemaker broke in.

"The man he stabbed is not dead, I just saw him and he may get well."

"Nevertheless he is a murderer at heart and must suffer the penalty," was the reply. "And now boys we have spent too much time already. Man the rope; all hands of you take hold."

During this short conversation the culprit never moved or said a word. His arms were pinioned behind him, and the collar and breast of his shirt had been thrown open to admit the proper adjustment of the rope.

He was erect and almost as rigid as a statue. The moonlight was broken into bars of light and shadow by the lifeless branches above him. His face was in the full glow, every feature nearly as distinct as by daylight. It was pale but there was not a tremor, even to the twitching of an eyelid. As soon as the leader gave the order, he spoke for the first time addressing the shoemaker, there was not a particle of the emotion which he had shown in the little shop in Oakland, the eye was undimmed and his voice was calm.

"My good friend, it's no use; this is a fitting for such as I. Take good care of the canary. Don't tell my sis—,"

At this juncture the leader waved his hands, there was a quick and strong jerk on the rope, the loved name was broken ere it could be pronounced, a short gurgling sound in the throat, violent spasms in the limbs, followed by shorter convulsive twitchings, and then the body hung limp in the flecked shadows of the dead oak tree.

The shoemaker was appalled. He stood motionless, a terrible fascination compelling him to keep his gaze on the strangling victim, and though he essayed to turn away his head it was beyond his power to accomplish it.

The feet hung dangling as high as the head had been before the body was swung, and there were the well-remembered patches on the boots. The leader spoke to him, but he paid no attention, and it was only a rough shake that he seemed to be aware of what was going on.

"Now, my man, it's your turn," remarked the Captain; "let us hear what you have to say, and explain, if you can, your connection with this man, and how you came to be here on the day he committed the robbery and murder."

"Was it to aid him in getting away with the booty?"

"Let us get away from this terrible place," replied the shoemaker, " and I will tell you all about it."

"Make the line fast to that root and let the carrion hang there till morning," was the peremptory command, and that done the whole party moved towards the cabins.

The shoemaker and his questioner sat on stools fronting each other, the rest of the company standing and forming a cordon around them. There were forty or fifty of them all in the rough garb of the miners, and with beard and hair resting on their breast and shoulders.

The moon seemed to be floating directly over the canyon, illuminating every portion of it, and gave a weird, spector-like appearance to the men. When the shoemaker first essayed to speak his voice trembled so much, and he was so incoherent in his replies, that the Captain ordered one of the men to bring him a drink of whisky, remarking:

"Take plenty of time now and tell a straight story, for your life depends on what you have to say."

Revived by the stimulus the little shoemaker recounted his

first meeting with the man, the mending his boots, and as nearly as he could, repeated the history which was recited to him.

The only variation was calling the money in his hands a legacy in place of saying that it was the proceeds of a lottery ticket, and this was the sole point which seemed to puzzle the rough Court which was trying him. They could not understand why a man who had only met another once should take such a deep interest as he had exhibited, and he was closely questioned. His answer that through him he had also fallen into a fortune, and gratitude compelled him to the task of hunting him up was, as some of them expressed it, "rather too thin."

There was a long debate over the question whether they would hang him or not, but the proposition of the captain that they would postpone further action until morning was assented to, and it was, perhaps, lucky for the shoemaker that this course was followed. He was given a blanket and told to lie down on the cabin floor while two of the miners stood guard over him. The sun had risen several hours before a stray beam had found its way into the deep canyon, and by that time the trial was over. The patches on the boots corroborated that part of the story, and when a couple of pieces of leather, and shoe thread and wax were handed him his dexterity gave ample testimony that his avocation was properly given. A few were for hanging him on "general principles," as they termed it, but the captain and a large majority were convinced of his innocence, and still more so when he requested that the old patched boots be given him to carry home.

Never was any one more pleased to get home. He cried, too, when his little wife put her arms around his neck and wet his shirt collar with her tears, and the baby clung to his hand, and the canary bird warbled the clearest notes, and the linnets twittered, fluttered and hopped about the cages with quivering wings, all to welcome him back.

There was another meeting that night in the cozy little room, back of the little shop, [and there were wine glasses on the table in place of beer-mugs, and the rosy liquid was not allowed to stand untasted.

But again there were tear-drops on the cheek when he described the scene on the knoll under the oak trees, which were dead and blasted, and the dangling corpse with the wan face in the moonlight. The tears gave way to shuddering as he told of sitting on the stool before the stern questioner with the cordon of fierce-looking men surrounding them. And then the agony of the night on the hard floor of the cabin, with the measured step of the sentries before the blanket which served for a door, and he felt that if the wounded man died on that night, he would also be dangling from the gnarled, crooked branch on which yet hung the murderer. It was all over, however, and he was back—back with his wife and child and friends, and the canary bird was in full feather and would pipe a requiem for the poor unknown who came to so sad an end.

Plans were discussed and it was resolved that he would hammer and stitch in his little shop for a time, anyway. He was at his work bright and early the next morning, but the canary was disappointed when the only accompaniment was the rat-tat-tat of the hammer on the lapstone, and never a note from the tunes of the Fatherland, or a bar from an opera.

By and by it was whispered that the little shoemaker had some money to loan, which he had saved out of his earnings, and on better terms than the banks would grant. Then when more was forthcoming than could be credited to the savings from the shop, it was thought his friends in Germany were supplying the funds, and the difference between German and California rates of interest would make a rich man of him in time. After a while those who are always prying into other people's business found that deeds were recorded, the little shoemaker being the grantee, and not his rich German backers, and the description told of lots on Broadway in the center part of the city, and the recording clerk was kept busy until a whole block was thus deeded. All the time the hammer was drumming music out of the lapstone and the canary bird warbled in the little shop and the linnet chirruped, and the shoemaker joined with the old tunes.

The little wife was beginning to show that the years were telling, ever so little, for she was still bright and cheery, and the little girl had grown so that the golden curls had changed into a braid of brown hair. Workmen were busily engaged putting up a handsome residence on one of the main avenues, and every morning the little shoemaker would visit them to see how they were getting along. There was nothing grand or even stylish about it, though it was in a pleasant location, and nothing lacked for the comfort of the inmates. When finished and newly furnished from cellar to garret, the little shop and the cozy little rooms were abandoned. The birds in their cages, the wood cuts and the patched boots were about all that were taken, the other things packed in boxes and stayed away.

In course of time, when the lawn was well set in grass, the trees and shrubbery well grown, and the flowers in profusion, the little shoemaker (we will still call him so though for many years he had given up beating music out of the lapstone) surrounded his place with birds. The old canary bird had languished, drooped and died though there were lots of his descendants, not one of them, however, which could warble with the clearness and fullness of tune which attracted the wanderer in the opening of our story.

The block was covered with stores, and the owner had a bank account far exceeding the amount which the lottery ticket drew. Everything he undertook prospered, and deservedly, for he was honest and straightforward. In the midst of prosperity he often thinks of the strange occurrence which led to his good fortune, and still shudders when the retrospect carries him back to the fearful night in the canyon where the checkered shadows fell on him who gave him the lottery ticket for patching his boots.

---

## CALIFORNIA RACES IN 1851.

### Spring Meeting on the Pioneer Racecourse, Mission Dolores, Near San Francisco.

STEWARDS.

| | |
|---|---|
| Col. WILLIAM SMITH, | SAMUEL BRANNAN, Esq., |
| ALEX. WELLS, Esq., | JESSE SHEPARD. |

Hon. GEORGE McDOUGAL.

Judge—Capt. T. K. BATTELLE.
Associated Judge—Capt. B. RAY.
Honorary Secretary—Col. G. C. TURNER.
Owner of the Course—G. TREAT, Esq.

The first race over the Pioneer Course commenced on Thursday, 24th March. The uncertain appearance of the skies, and the frequent showers of rain in the morning, prevented many persons from attending, who otherwise would have done so; but, nevertheless, there was a fair number present. The appearance of the ground was very much like that of our home races; a perfect city of booths was erected, and the usual variety of games, as exhibited on such occasions, in other cities, was here less perceptible—the attention of the crowd being apparently absorbed in the excitement of the race.

The Corinthian has sent us the *Alta Californian* and the *Pacific Standard* from which we compiled the annexed report:

Thursday, March 24, 1851—Sweepstakes of $15 each, with a purse of $180 added by the Officers of San Francisco, for all horses, three-year-olds and upwards carrying 126 pounds—five-year-olds and upwards 125 pounds—horses bred in the State of California allowed five pounds. Mile-and-a-half heats.

| | |
|---|---|
| T. K. Battelle's b c Boston, 5 yrs ........................ | 1 |
| W. Foster's gr c Ito, 5 yrs ........................ | 2 dr |
| Jas. M. McDonald's b g Eclipse, 5 yrs ........................ | dis |
| Time—2:50½. | |

The horses came up well together, and got a beautiful start, Boston leading Eclipse and Ito well up and going level. They got well on to the back side, Boston still leading, but well in hand; here Ito made a brush, outfooted and passed Eclipse, and lapped the colt round the turn. They swung into the homestretch in this position. As they passed the third quarter pole, Eclipse was strikingthe behind, evidently tiring, as the pace was too sharp for him. Here the boy on the colt took him in hand, rammed home the gaffs, and made a most desperate struggle for the heat, which he won in sporting style, like a trump, by a length. Time, 1:50½.

Second heat—Ito withdrawn. Boston galloped over and received the purse and stake.

Same Day—A Silver Cup, with a sweepstakes of $10 each added, catch weights. Half-mile heats.

| | |
|---|---|
| Mr. Barton's ch f Venus ........................ | 1 1 |
| Mr. Mallet's ch g Lewis Cass ........................ | 2 2 |
| Mr. Johnson's ch g Citizen ........................ | dis |
| Mr. Taylor's b g Jenkins ........................ | dis |
| Time—8:57½, 0:55. | |

This was rather an exciting and pretty race. Venus and Cass had it all their own way, but in our opinion, condition won the race; the other horses just saving their distance in each heat. Venus evidently was in the best condition. The odds at starting were even on the mare against the field; but after the first heat the odds changed from even to a hundred to sixty on the mare against the field, and no takers.

Same Day—Napoleon Cup, with a sweepstakes of $25 each added, for backs. Mile heats.

| | |
|---|---|
| Mr. Barton's ch f Venus ........................ | 1 |
| J. H. Mallet's ch g Lewis Cass ........................ | 2 |
| Mr. Taylor's b g Jenkins ........................ | dist |
| Mr. Johnson's ch g Citizen ........................ | dist |
| Jas. M. McDonald's b g Eclipse ........................ | dist |
| Time—2:05½. Track very heavy. | |

The first heat was won by Venus.

In the second heat a false start occurred, when Cass ran off with his rider, a young boy of 12 or 13, who with much skill and nerve succeeded in getting him under control, and was coming into the course from the open country, whither the horse had taken him, when he was unexpectedly brought into collision with a horse and rider, who, it would seem, had gone to meet of him. The result was an immediate overthrow of both horses and riders. Fortunately both of the latter escaped without injury save a few bruises. One horse—the gallant little Cass—fell to rise no more. The nature of the injury received was supposed to be in the heart or loins; this incident tended to check the enjoyment in some degree; many backers of this horse were in the field and confident of his final success. In his previous contests with the mare he was over-weighted (she carrying feather weights) yet a close rival. Venus is a beautiful clean bred mare of light but powerful make and great stride. She cantered over the course the last heat after the fall of Cass without a competitor, thus realizing two cups, winning the two races. She is said to be from the Eastern States.

### Second Day.

In the grand match for $500 much sport was anticipated, from the fact that both horses are well known in this "burg," and each has troops of friends and backers. Ito, to our eye, was in tip-top condition, but owing to an accident in his stable, two days since, he showed lame in his off hind leg, and his backers were not so confident as before; however, they came up well and posted the papers to a high figure on their favorite at $100 to $90, and freely taken. It being known by the betting men that Ito was a little amiss, the mare was the favorite in starting. Mary Snow was trained by William Cummings, and stripped like a "Fashion;" her backers stuck to her like a tick, and posted their money with confidence—but the bugle sounded, and up came the horses for the

First heat—Lady Snow had the pole—Ito outside. They went off at a beautiful gait at the tap of the drum, Snow leading, and Ito two lengths behind; as they got into the back-stretch the horse let loose, when up and lapped the mare for a hundred yards. They remained in this position, until past the first quarter. As they neared the half-mile pole, Ito had opened a gap of three lengths on the mare. Time, first half-mile, 1:02. They remained in this position past the third quarter pole—1:33. Here the rider of Ito rushed home his gaffs, and took a steady pull on his horse, and continued to gain the distance to the stand—coming in amid cheers that made the welkin ring, nearly a distance ahead of the mare; and just saved her distance by half a length. Time declared, 2:04½.

Second heat—The bugle sounded, and they went off like twin bullets; a beautiful start—the mare leading as they swung into the back stretch. The mare was ahead some two lengths, when the rider of Ito, who had all the time been riding a waiting race, and confident the mare had not foot enough to win, let Ito go, to the delight of every one on the track, coming in amid tremendous cheering. First quarter 0:30; first half, 0:61; third quarter, 0:32; last quarter, 0:31; whole time—2:04.

---

Too much credit cannot be awarded Mr. Turner for the admirable manner in which he tooled his horse, bringing him to the post in splendid condition and riding in a manner becoming a "Robinson" or a "Chifney." Much credit is due Mr. Cummings for the masterly manner in which he brought his horse to the post, who unfortunately was beaten. Ito carried 146 pounds; Mary Snow 126 pounds.

Tuesday, March 26—Match for $8,000. Mile heats.

| | |
|---|---|
| W. Foster's gr g Ito, 6 yrs., 145 pounds........... | 1 1 |
| Mr. Cummings' ch f Mary Snow, 126 pounds......... | 2 2 |
| Time—2:04½, 3:04. | |

Same Day—Proprietor's Purse, $300. Mile heats.

| | |
|---|---|
| Mr. Foster's b f Black Swan, 4 yrs., 140 pounds.......... galloped over. | |
| Mr. McCauley's gr g Confidence...................... paid forfeit. | |
| Time—2:08. | |

Same Day—Purse $10, entrance $2 each, free for all, catch weights. One mile.

| | |
|---|---|
| Mr. Ellsard's b p Charley ........................ | 1 |
| Five others........................ | 0 |
| Time—2:12. | |

This was the most amusing race of the day, and presented the greatest variety of steed and rider, but all equally innocent of the "racing-mood,"—some in California gear, and some in wild Indian style, minus a saddle. When the little by-play of kicking got up among the horses to stretch their legs before the start had terminated, "Off" was given, and off they went at convenient distances, the Indian jockey rushing fiercely for a head place, which he at length secured, present closely by a ponderous animal apparently very recently emancipated from the plow—the ruck jostling each other in the distant rear. The pace was well kept up all through.

### Third Day.

The third day's racing of the first spring meeting, over the Pioneer Course, came off on Saturday, March 29, it having been postponed on account of the rain. The race was in an awful condition, nearly fetlock deep on the back side. The races being advertised to come off, rain or shine, they did come off, to the entire satisfaction of every one who visited the course. The attendance though small was composed of a number of leading merchants, including a number of spicy sporting gents, who are always willing to wade knee deep through mud and rain to witness a well-contested trial of speed between thoroughbreds.

The first race was a sweepstakes of $10 with $350 given by livery stable keepers and others. Mr. W. Foster entered Ito, Mr. T. K. Battelle entered his bay three-year-old Boston. Both horses stripped well, and showed Boston in every movement. Ito was in splendid condition, and the little pet Boston looked for all the world a winner, but being only three years old, and carrying 126 pounds on his back, it could not be expected that the knowing ones would back him to win against a five-year-old "flyer" like Ito, who, by the way, is a first rate mud horse, and had shown previously a wonderful turn of speed. In consequence there was very little betting. The bugle sounded, and up came the horses for the

First heat—They jumped off at the tap of the drum like twin rockets, a beautiful send-off, Boston leading a length, to the first turn, then both horses came near to a stand still, as they had mere to contend with than they expected, a large drove of "sporting hogs," heavy and light weights, having taken possession of the track, and were not slow to get off at the word. It must have been fifteen seconds before the horses could be let loose again, but they are now on the backstretch, and little Boston leading a length, Ito well up; as they neared the half-mile pole the grey made a rush, outlived the little horse in the mud, and opened a gap of four lengths, maintaining this position to the homestretch, when the jockey of Boston took his horse in hand and shook him up well, closing the gap to within a length. The heaviness of the track and the killing pace of the old stager put his chance back for the heat, Mr. Turner, the rider of Ito, landing his horse at the stand a winner, Boston three lengths behind.

Second heat—Both horses cooled off well and came at the first call; they went away as in the previous heat. Boston a length ahead, Ito, however, the inside; they swung round on to the backstretch and remained in this position to the half-mile pole, when Ito went up and cut the bay short on the turn, opening a gap of five lengths. On nearing the last quarter Boston closed the distance to nearly a length, but 'tis mind and weight that kills"—Ito winning the heat by a length.

Saturday, March 29—Purse $500, added to a sweepstakes of $10. Mile heats.

| | |
|---|---|
| W. Foster's gr g Ito, (Turner) ........................ | 1 1 |
| T. K. Battelle's b c Boston, (William)........... | 2 2 |

Same Day—Purse $60, added to a sweepstakes of $5, catch weights. Mile heats.

| | |
|---|---|
| J. Hatton's ch f Venus ........................ | 1 1 1 |
| Mr. Johnson's ch g Citizen ........................ | 2 3 2 |
| Mr. Foster's ch f Lady B.......... | 3 2 3 |

Same Day—Purse $50, added to a sweepstakes of $5, for all beaten horses at the meeting. Catch weights. Mile heats.

| | |
|---|---|
| Mr. Cummings' b m Mary Snow ........................ | 1 1 |
| Mr. Foster's ch f Lady B........................ | dist |

Same Day—Purse $350, presented by the residents of the Mission Dolores. Half-mile heats.

| | |
|---|---|
| Mr. Foster's b f Black Swan, 4 yrs........... | 1 1 |
| Mr. Cummings' b m Mary Snow........... | dist |
| Time—1:02. | |

Immediately after this race there were several scrubs made up; some six or eight entered for each, affording much sport for the spectators.

Last evening a match was made at the Pioneer Club House, between two celebrated horses, for $1,000 a side, for a half-mile spin; the money was deposited with Mr. T. K. Battelle, the match closed, to come off in two weeks from the 29th March. Play or pay.

---

## Haverlys vs. Olympics.

The first of a series of fourteen games of base ball which are to be played by the Haverly, Olympic and Redington clubs took place at the Recreation grounds in Oakland last Sunday between the two first-named clubs. The score is as follows:

| OLYMPICS. | T.B. | R. | B.H. | T.O. | A. | E. | HAVERLYS. | T.B. | R. | B.H. | T.O. | A. | E. |
|---|---|---|---|---|---|---|---|---|---|---|---|---|---|
| Sweeney, p........ | 5 | 0 | 1 | 10 | 0 | Levy, l f........ | 5 | 0 | 0 | 0 | 0 | 0 |
| Lewis, s s........ | 5 | 1 | 0 | 0 | 1 | Morris, 4b........ | 5 | 1 | 1 | 9 | 1 | 1 |
| Burt, 1b and l f........ | 5 | 1 | 1 | 9 | 1 | Meegan, p........ | 5 | 1 | 1 | 10 | 2 |
| Jones, c........ | 5 | 0 | 0 | 10 | 3 | Carroll, c........ | 5 | 0 | 0 | 10 | 1 |
| Emerson, c f........ | 5 | 2 | 0 | 0 | 0 | John Carroll........ | | | | | | |
| Hamilton, 3b........ | 5 | 0 | 1 | 3 | 1 | 4 | Lynch, 1b........ | 5 | 2 | 1 | 9 | 0 | 0 |
| Ebner, r f........ | 5 | 1 | 1 | 1 | 0 | Quigan, 2b........ | 5 | 1 | 2 | 2 | 1 |
| Hanly, l f and c........ | 5 | 0 | 0 | 8 | 0 | 0 | Knowles, 3b........ | 5 | 0 | 1 | 1 | 0 | 0 |
| Fitzgerald, c f........ | 4 | 1 | 1 | 3 | 0 | 1 | Lawton, r f........ | 5 | 2 | 0 | 0 | 0 |
| | | | | | | | Pratt, 2b........ | 4 | 1 | 0 | 1 | 1 |
| Total........ | 43 | 9 | 5 | 27 | 17 | 7 | Total........ | 44 | 9 | 6 | 26 | 16 | 6 |

| Innings........ | 1 | 2 | 3 | 4 | 5 | 6 | 7 | 8 | 9 |
|---|---|---|---|---|---|---|---|---|---|
| Olympics........ | 2 | 0 | 0 | 4 | 0 | 0 | 0 | 7 | 0 |
| Haverlys........ | 0 | 0 | 0 | 9 | 0 | 0 | 0 | 0 | 0 |

## The Old Days in San Francisco.

There are many, doubtless, who still have a vivid recollection of the scenes so graphically portrayed by The Corinthian, and remember Thomas K. Battello, who wrote many a good thing for the old Spirit over the above pseudonym. Comparing the account with the gambling house episode in the story, it will be seen that the writer did not draw on his imagination, and that it is really a transcript of an actual occurrence.

There can never be a repetition of these old-time doings, and it is quite as unlikely that the world will ever witness a return anything approaching the "days of forty-nine." As will be seen by the date of the letter it was written before the "spring of fifty," and therefore ranks among the "pioneers." That thirty-two years has changed things almost beyond belief is evident, and in nothing more than the changes in gambling. The "one hundred thousand dollar banks" is small comparison with the hazards which were taken a few years ago in California street, and that has given place to a comparatively "small game." Legitimate speculation is now the rule in California, and though some may still dabble in mining stocks, the fluctuations of the grain market, etc., the tendency is to employ surplus capital more in the way of production.

Luckily there is a grand field for the employment of every dollar; and with adding to the railway facilities, opening new farms, planting vineyards, stock-breeding, horticulture, commercial enterprise, manufactures, lumber, mines, etc., there are no lack of opportunities.

Faro bank, roulette and monte had their day, and after so short a space as thirty years there has come a better order of things:

### The Corinthian in California.

San Francisco, Upper California, Jan 30, 1850.

Most Potent Spirit: I promised you on my departure I would give you a few dottings of the doings in this burg, and as the bugle has sounded and everything ready, the word go given, I am off at a racing gait, and the odds is a hundred to one I am not distanced.

San Francisco, the city of "oro," at present, is dull in the extreme; very little business doing with the merchants, as the roads to the mines are stopped, the rivers and small streams are so flooded by the tremendous rains that it is entirely impossible to navigate them.

Our city at present represents one scene of rude commotion. Pedestrians are rushing through the streets clothed with oil-jackets and mud boots; now and then you see a pair of mules hooked to a wagon loaded with merchandise, anchored some three feet in the mud, with no living show to get out; and I would here remark, that our city for the last three months has been a pool of mud and water.

Feeling in good spirits last evening; I took occasion to stroll around among the principal sporting houses. On entering Crockford's, the first impression that strikes the stranger is the immense quantity of gold and silver which is to be seen on the gaming-tables, amounting to $15,000 or $30,000, and upwards of $200,000 on the several tables is not a rare sight in San Francisco. After taking a good look we passed into the Phœnix. On entering, the first table that met our observation, one of the fancy boys was seated at the game of chuck a luck A B C., etc. He is now making his game, and commences:

"Come, give me a bet, who makes the game! All sot. All can play at this game. Take no pointers here. Come, bungle 'er down! who bets this time! All in !" "Time!" (a man steps up and places his finger on a letter). "No, sir, don't take any finger bets. Come, bungle 'er down !" He throws the dice, and lifts the tin, A, E and G. "Come, give me another bet, etc."

Pass on a little further and we come to a rondo table. The game-keeper is crying out: "Come, gentlemen, who makes the bank!" Some one pops up fifty, then he commences: "Fifty in bank, who takes it !" One takes ten, and five and so on, until it is all taken, when the keeper cries out, "Come, gentlemen, hands up! The game is made—roll !" The roller makes a coolo, the bank has lost. The next is a roulette. "Come, gentlemen, give me a bet ! Let loose your gold dust. I have some tip-top scales. This is the game to win at." The ball goes round, it comes up eagle, he cries, "Eagle bird by chance!"

Here may be seen a number of miserable, ragged-looking men watching the ball, and invariably will be seen a man outside betting for a flat and capping the game; his winnings he places in a buckskin bag. Presently one of the bystanders, late from the mines and perfectly "rotten" with gold dust, will slowly draw out a long bag (his eye still on the ball, and watching the game). The game-keeper in a second has his eye on the flat, and instantly remarks, "Come down, come down !" and down goes the miner's bag.

"How much do you go on this turn, sir !"

"I go five ounces," says the flat.

All round goes the ball, and snap it comes back; the miner has lost but nothing daunted, and feeling a little excited, he pops down ten on the black. The ball goes round, it comes up black, miner wins.

At this stage of the game, drinks are ordered by the keeper, and paid for at twenty-five cents per glass, and then he cries, "Here she goes! Come, gentlemen, come down, give me a bet ! Do you bet on that figure, sir !" And here comes the flat again, he dumps down his all on the black, (that has taken his winnings back to procure). Then the game-keeper sings out, "the game is made, hand off the table!"

Round goes the ball, snap, comes up red. The gold-hunter is ruined, or in other words, broke. In a few moments he saunters out and the next day is off for the mines again.

The next is a monte bank, banked by a dark-eyed Mexican, who cries out in broken English: "Come, cabeyo, who is going to tap my bank," and so he goes on, sometimes makes a heap, and at other times he drops it all. Seated by his side is his pareda, who is his companion of his losses and winnings, who sits and deals the game for thousands with as much coolness as an omnibus driver would in New York run over an old woman.

Leaving the dark-eyed Mexican, we pass on to the next table, a thirty-six roulette-wheel, with two bars, the keeper, who, by the way, is a sharp joker (from Saratoga springs) crying out:

"Come, gentlemen, if you want to see me, you must see me now, before the steamer leaves ! Who'll give me a bet ! etc."

The next is the faro-tiger, known as the San Francisco phenomenon, owned and banked by a sportsman named M—, a New Jersey farmer, who has the largest game in California. his bank is $100,000 and no limits. A great number of "legs," who are a little out, and who usually play the game up to the handle, have been bucking at the old farmer to a high figure. I understand they raked him down to the tune of $40,000 a few evenings since. He was scotched, but not killed, and I have just been informed by a knowing one, that the farmer laid out the crowd cold, yesterday, breaking the entire party, and making up his loss, and closing the game with $36,300 in hand.

The next in rotation is a vingt-et-un table, with a dashing looking leg seated, dealing; he is one of 'em ! you instantly would perceive by his knowing look, and the graceful manner in which he throws a "natural," which is sure to come up three times in five.

Passing on we come to the bar, sixty feet long. Here may be seen a number of our leading merchants discussing business, some purchasing land, merchandise, etc., and amusing themselves over hot punches, gin toddy, etc.

Music from nine in the morning till the dead hour of the night. And now, "Tall York," you have a fair description of the principal gaming houses in San Francisco.

Please remember me to R. and the Doctor, and propel as far as Frank's and moisten your alimentary canal with such exhilarating fluid as may best suit your weak nerves, and not forget Yours, "in a horn,"
THE CORINTHIAN.

P. S.—Col. Jack Hayes of the Texas rangers, has just stepped in and grabbed me by the fives, and "you must bet your life" that we are about to off. Jack is looking like a two-year-old, and moving like a quarter nag. By the way, what has become of the "ex-Santa Fe pioneer." Has he arrived as yet ! [No, but we expect him here from Paris this month.] C.

## About Horses and Horse Feed.

Speaking of the horses of King Kama of South Africa, the author of the "Great Thirst Land," W. Gilmore, says: "Of one thing you may be certain, all of these horses can perform the most extraordinary journeys, although they know no other food than the grass of the veldt—a rarity. They are not fat nor yet lean, but in that kind of hard, serviceable condition a hunter gets towards the end of the season."

The horses of Arabia will endure enough to kill, each one, half a dozen of our own and yet are fed on little but straw. We know that the mustangs of our western prairies will in performance far surpass our horse stock. The Mongolians lope the day long on their fine horses. So do the northern Spaniards on their splendid mules. The Turks in the fifteenth century had the best cavalry in the world. They could conquer their enemies by the wonderful endurance and speed of their horses. A crusader named Brenquier returned to France through western Asia and eastern Europe, among these people who had such famous horses. He says, in a narrative of his journey that is published, that they never gave their animals food or drink by day, but at night gave them a handful of barley and some straw or other dry food, with water, and nothing else.

Southern Spain is famous for its splendid horses and mules that rival those of Arabia for speed and endurance. When we get into northern Spain, into Gallicia, we find there horses and mules no better than our own. Why is this? If we read that most interesting of all writers who ever wrote of his travels, George Borrow, in his "Bible in Spain" we will find the cause, although Borrow himself never seems to have suspected it. He says he had a splendid Andalusian stud. Slowly he ascended the mountain chain that leads into Gallicia. When he got there his first greeting was, "Ah Senor ! Why did you bring that fine entero here? " "Why not?" he asked. "Do you not know that Gallicia is fatal to horses from the south?" He learned that nearly all horses and mules brought into Gallicia get diseased and often die. "Something in the climate;" but the only food ever given to horses and mules there is Indian corn. Doubtless animals raised there endure it in a kind of way. But to strangers it is as fatal as it was to the Irish during the famine of 1846, killing off tens of thousands, as a veldt horse.

Whence came the foolish idea that high feeding and stimulating with malt or spirituous liquors are beneficial to any but hogs for fattening? The European and American world have come to the conclusion that the use of these liquors is painful. May they in time learn what the old races of Asia knew ages ago, that spare feeding is good for body and disposition.—Cor. Rural World.

## Some Thousand-Dollar Dogs.

Among the most notable of recent fashions in large dogs is the St. Bernard, which has almost suddenly pushed the way to the foreground. In England it is fast supplanting the collie, which has ruled as a prime favorite ever since the Newfoundland dog was dethroned, and perhaps as a result of this English fancy the demand for St. Bernards in this city has been asked for, "said a prominent dealer to a reporter for the Mail and Express, "yet they are very scarce. Only people of means can afford to own them, for they range in price—mind, I speak only of the genuine breed—from $500 to $1,000. Even puppies sell for $200. Now, there is a fine eighteen-month-old fellow," he said, as a large, splendid-looking dog walked majestically into the room. "That dog knows as much as a majority of men. I have a regular best for him and at night he puts his head on a pillow, I cover him up with a blanket, and he sleeps just like a baby. Worth much? I ask $2,000 for him and I'll wage his eques cannot be found on this side of the Atlantic."

There are two varieties of the St. Bernard, rough-coated and smooth-coated, both having the same characteristics except in the length of the hair. The points supposed to be the distinguishing marks of a genuine St. Bernard are a tawny or brindle color, a clearly marked line up the face, and a similar one around the neck, and a full, square head. These animals are very intelligent, and seem to be endowed with the instincts of saving life. Their attachments are very strong. They require plenty of room for exercise, and fanciers assert that a dog of this species raised in the country, where he can have plenty of exercise, will grow to a much larger stature than one raised in the city.

Among the owners of St. Bernard dogs in this city is Samuel J. Tilden, whose Askins, one of the rough-coated species, has carried away many prizes. Mrs. D. P. Foster of South Fifth avenue is the owner of Turco, a tawny-brindle rough-coated St. Bernard, five years old, who was imported from the St. Bernard Pass, and who is considered one of the best specimens of his species in this country. Herman Oelrichs is the owner of Barry, a tawny rough-coat, imported from Lucerne, who is valued at $500. H. H. Baxter of Fifth avenue owns a splendid fawn-colored smooth-coat dog, five years old, named Turk; and H. M. Hoer of East Fifty-sixth street is the owner of a tawny rough-coat, three years old, called Rover; John P. Haines of Tom's River, New Jersey, is a noted admirer of St. Bernards. His Don, an orange, tawny and white smooth-coat, is a splendid animal, gentle and playful as a kitten. His owner values him at $1,500.—New York Mail and Express.

## YACHTING.

Although the season for yachting was over some time since, and but few of the whitewinged fleet are on commission, it behooves us at this time to take a hasty backward glance to see what has been accomplished by this, one of the best patronized, locally, of our out-door sports.

Take it all in all the season was not a satisfactory one by any means. One of the clubs had no annual regatta and that given by the other was not by any means first-class. The small yacht regatta was the best attended of the year, but even that was not up to the one given last year.

The truth of the matter is, there ought to be only one club here. There are not enough yachts for two; and what is more to the purpose, there are not enough yachtsmen. Three-quarters of the people who go yachting are not yachtsmen at all, and know nothing about handling a boat under sail. One club could prosper and progress, but the rivalry of two does no special good to the amusement. Both of them are weak in some particulars.

We are told, however, that there are elements which will not mingle and thus there will be two so long as the leading spirits now controlling the respective destinies of the clubs remain with them. The worst feature of our local yachting is here hinted at. There seem to be several factions in the clubs, the rivalries of which affect the "cause" to its disadvantage. Our oldest club is specially afflicted in this way so that instead of being as prosperous as it should be under other circumstances, it does not advance. The differences should be healed as soon as may be, and mutual concessions urged, that the club itself should be able to take the position it really merits by its age and experience.

As to building of yachts some little of this is going on. Two fine large yachts are being built in this city, and one smaller one; and two small ones are in course of construction in Oakland. These will materially add to our fleet, and more are talked of. And this is the great encouraging feature, since the old boats will be bought by other people and more persons will join in the sport. A few of the old hands are dropping out and new blood is coming in, so that the yachting will not languish for want of enthusiasm.

There is no place in the world where yachting has the advantages of the weather we have here. For seven or eight months we have steady regular trade winds, which insure passages, and we seldom have drifting matches where races are called. True, our sailing grounds are somewhat limited in extent, and there is a taint of sameness. But the old hand will find many places to go which are pleasant to him, and he is always sure of "getting back," something which cannot be well counted on in other parts of the world where winds in summer are variable and light. We have to deplore the decline of small yachts among us as these furnish the yachtsmen for big ones. There are no small yachts in either club, and the tendency is now all to large ones. The owners of small yachts find they cannot keep up with the big boats on the cruises, and the time allowances give them so show in racing, so they become disgusted and want larger yachts or none. Therefore the twenty-five and thirty-foot boats have decreased in number and no new ones are being built. It seems to be agreed that thirty-six to forty feet is the smallest practicable size. The eighty and ninety-foot yachts do not build up the yachting interests of the East like the smaller ones because they cost too much to build, and what is more, cost too much to run. In a short time the owners become sensible of the constant expense, and the yacht is not so much used as would be one of less dimensions. We hope for better things next season because the yachtsmen seem to recognize the fact that there must be greater harmony among them if their favorite amusement is to prosper. If some of the more energetic will take the matter in hand and break up the cabals and factions that exist, and take hold of the interest in earnest, there is no doubt that a better record will be made next year. More cruises, more races, less brickering and talk will bring the sport to the front! The Breeder and Sportsman will do its share in the good work by faithfully chronicling all the events correctly and encouraging in every way the yachtsmen's interests.

Plenty of Yachts.—There are several yachts for sale in these waters just now. Commodore Harrison wants to sell the Frolic because he is going to Europe. Commodore MacDonough wants to sell the Aggie because he is going to Europe. Mr. Tevis will probably sell the Whitewing because he is having a larger yacht built. The Con O'Connor is for sale because the owners do not want a yacht any more. The Clara is for sale for the reason that her owner is engaged in fitting up a fine house and that takes all his time. It is rumored also that the junior might be sold so the owners could get another type of boat. The little yawl Violet is for sale, her owner having no time to use her. The little sloop Susan Nipper would change hands if a good offer was made. The yawl Emerald could be bought too as her owner wants a deep yacht. We do not believe Commodore Floyd would be averse to parting with the Ariel. So there are plenty of yachts if people want to buy. Second-hand yachts are a greatdeal the cheapest as the fittings seldom count in a sale.

Log-Line.—A correspondent wishes to know why "such an old salt like you" marked a lead-line with overhand knots instead of in the regular sea-going fashion. Because experience in sailing small yachts has taught us to use knots in preference to white and red rags, strips of leather and nothing at all for the "deeps." The knots can be counted by the touch at night and the rags require frequent renewing, while the "deeps" have to be guessed at which is not close enough work in a small yacht. We consider our plan much the more advisable, and more readily understood by casual amateurs using the line.—Forest and Stream.

Mr. Horatio Hathaway of the New Bedford Yacht Club, owner of the schooner Clio, purchased, Nov. 15, from Mr. Charles Watrous, the centerboard schooner yacht Ruth, which was built last season at Noank, by Mr. B. Palmer. She is 97 feet over all, 92 feet on water line, 23 feet 5 inches beam, 7 feet 6 inches deep, and 7 feet 9 inches draught.

## FISH.

### Trout.

Although this is not the season of year for trout to be much considered, it is just as well to remember that very shortly the Legislature will meet and that this body of representatives of the people have it in their power to look out for the fish if they so desire. It has been proposed to inflict a fine on any one exposing for sale any brook trout in this State during a term of years, as a means of preventing their total annihilation, which now appears imminent. The streams in this State which were formerly well filled are almost barren of fish and it is rarely that a good sized creel can be filled even by an expert angler.

It is to be expected of course that the creeks within any reasonable distance of the metropolis will be closely fished. And it is to be expected also that there will be men who will kill great and small alike, with more attention to the number of fish caught than the sport they may have with those large enough to show any "gamy" qualities.

The main difficulty which has to be contended with is the utter disregard of the law shown by the dwellers by the creeks. The Italians and Portuguese are the main offenders. There are many of them scattered along the small creeks, chopping wood, dairying, market gardening and the like, and they pay no more attention to the laws of the season of fish than they do to the laws of China.

They put lime in the pools or drain them, or use giant powder and hundreds of fish are sacrificed. Remonstrance is vain, and there seems to be no way to remedy the evil. Even in streams stocked with private care the fish are there killed by these vandals; they have no idea of sport; they want the fish to eat or to sell and will kill two or three hundred in mere wantonness. These facts are notoriously well known in the localities where the people of these nationalities dwell.

If the Legislature will comply with the request of the State Sportsmans' Association, it may be that in part a remedy will be supplied. The anglers themselves can greatly help also by giving information to the papers about these "trout hogs" who kill out of season or fill their creeks with fingerlings because they happen to catch them.

All interested must help to do their "level best" if any improvement is to be made. It will not do for anglers to remain passive and wait for others to begin the good work. There ought to be an anglers' association on the coast for most of the associations are devoted to the gun and not the rod. In good time we hope to see this carried out.

### Casting Tournaments.

The London *Field* says: We do not usually concern ourselves much with what are called casting tournaments, because they are, as a rule, held under such conditions and circumstances as to be of little or no practical value or test in actual fishing. Not long ago we heard a very angry discussion between two chance acquaintances, one of whom averred that he had cast twenty-seven yards (which was perfectly true, for we saw and measured it), and another gentleman who declared that he had cast twenty-two yards on one occasion, and he would be chawed into innumerable chips if anyone else could cast more; and the contention waxed high. This tournament shows, at least, that it is possible to cast thirty yards with a single-handed rod. Thirty-eight yards and two feet is a very good salmon cast; we have seen it cast before, however, and measured it; but it falls far short of Pat Hearn's famous feats, wherein he threw forty-two yards for a wager. But tournament feats are not to be put into competition with fishing casting; it is altogether a different thing.

Some time ago we heard of a competition at which the line was cast upon a large sheet of canvas, thus avoiding one of the most serious drawbacks to long casting in actual practice, viz., the friction of the line in drawing it out of the water, with all the weight of the water to weigh it down behind; the thing was absurd as a test of anything. Here we have a platform run out into a lake, raised three feet above the lake, which practically adds quite two feet to the length of the rod. Of course, the ground behind was perfectly level (at the least), and quite devoid of straws and tufts of grass, or bushes of any sort, and no doubt the fly (if any) might touch the ground even with perfect safety. Then, too, in most tournament affairs, both rod and line are picked out, and specially adapted to one another for long casting, and for nothing else. All these things are not in actual fishing. For example, the twenty-seven-yard cast we mention was with the rod, line, etc., being then fished with on the Old Barge at Winchester, the bank not a foot above the water, with high water meadow grass behind, and a rising bank. The least touch of the grass, of course, was fatal. There are no comparisons in the two things. It is no doubt a good thing to be able to make your rod do its best, and to make long casts when wanted; but it is one thing to make a long cast, and it is another to fish it. We have more than once known men who, to show their power of casting, more often than not would over-fish their cast, and then when their fish rose banged him. For all these reasons, and for the further one that we dislike anything like the introduction of competition into the art of angling, as destructive to the spirit of it, we are not inclined to attach much importance to tournaments of this sort.

THE LONDON FISHERIES EXHIBITION.—The work of gathering material for one of the most complete exhibits of fishery products ever made is now going on. Professor G. Brown Goode, who had charge of the American exhibit at Berlin in 1880, will have the care of our display at London. This is a guarantee of care in the selection and arrangement of the display. The great collection of the Smithsonian Institution and of the National Museum will be sent, together with much new material illustrating our fisheries and their products.

One of the good fishing places of the future will be the shore along Raccoon Strait and up towards California City. When the San Rafael ferry landing is at Point Tiburon, in Raccoon Strait, as it soon will be, all the shore thereabouts will be accessible. There are lots of good points to fish from, and the water is deep. Some good-sized fish are taken in this locality.

The "white fish" caught up in the tule sloughs are so bony that they are not good for food. The Chinese eat them, however.

Saucelito is not so crowded with fishermen along shore as it is in the long summer days.

They are said to be catching mackerel off Oakland wharf.

---

NEW FISH COMMISSIONER.—The Governor has appointed as State Fish Commissioner in place of J. D. Farwell, Mr. Joseph D. Redding, eldest son of the late B. B. Redding, who was for many years the leading spirit of the commission. Young Mr. Redding will bring energy and enthusiasm to his task, but if he accomplishes only half of the work his distinguished father did, it will redound to the fishing interests of the coast. The appointment is eminently a fit one, and we are glad to see so active a man come into the commission feeling sure he will do much good. Our trout fishing interests are in a bad way at present, and the commission has plenty of work before it.

With the view of ascertaining the time required to hatch out carp eggs in the latitude of Georgia, Fish Commissioner Cary made an interesting experiment, from which it was found the eggs were hatched in from five to six days. The water in which the experiment was made was of the average temperature of 69 degrees in the shade.

Bay fishing along the Saucelito shore to Point Diablo was, during the latter part of last week and part of this, very good. Messrs. Bogart and Denning were out several times lately and had excellent strings of fish. Mr. Shane and his brother were at Point Diablo last Sunday and caught some splendid black rock cod and some sea trout that weighed from two to four pounds.

A few days ago Mr. Spencer caught a large salmon trout while fishing in a boat off Lime Point. The weight of this fish was ten pounds. Though salmon trout are occasionally caught off the end of the Oakland Wharf, it is an almost unheard-of occurrence to hook one in this locality.

The Reno *Gazette* says: "Very large trout are being caught in the Truckee ten or twelve miles down the river, but the same exorbitant price is kept up by those who sell them." If the Renoites keep on catching trout out of season, they will not ere long have trout at any price.

## THE RIFLE.

### Shooting at Petaluma.

A shooting match of 100 shots each took place at the Agricultural Park range last Sunday between Lieutenant Fred. Kuhnle and Robert Wallace of this city, Kuhnle giving Wallace 50 points. The guns used were 45-caliber military rifles, and the distance 200 yards. Although the range was comparatively new to Kuhnle, the weather unfavorable for good shooting, and the bulls-eye considerably blurred, yet he succeeded in making the best score, by one point, that has been made in the State. Captain Fairbanks and J. Naylor acted as markers and R. H. Whitson as scorer. The time consumed in the match was two and one-half hours. In conversation with Lieutenant Kuhnle he stated to the writer that the rest that his score of Sunday was better than usual is the fact that the previous night he slept *well*. Wallace, although an amateur who has had but little practice, is probably above average, and will some day be a crack shot. This match is the first 100-shot contest that has taken place in the county. Following are

THE SCORES:

Kuhnle......
```
5  4  4  4  4  5  4  4  4—48
5  5  5  5  4  5  4  4  5—47
5  5  4  5  5  5  5  4  5—47
5  5  5  5  5  5  4  4  4—47
5  4  4  5  5  5  4  4  5—46
5  5  5  5  5  4  4  5  5—47
5  5  5  5  5  5  5  5  5—47
4  5  5  5  5  4  5  4  4—47
```
Total.....................467

Wallace......
```
4  5  5  5  4  4  4  5  4—44
4  5  5  3  4  4  5  3  4—40
4  4  4  4  5  5  4  5  5—40
4  4  4  4  4  5  4  4  5—41
4  3  5  5  4  4  5  5  4—41
4  5  4  5  5  4  4  5  5—45
4  4  4  4  5  5  4  4  4—42
                        50
```
Total.....................435

### The San Francisco Police Rifle Team.

This is the name of a team recently organized, and from the name one is justified in the supposition that it is composed of members of the police force of this city. This team was organized for the purpose of furnishing recreation for policemen when off duty. It is to be hoped that the movement will be approved by the principals of the department. A meeting was held last Thursday evening for the purpose of choosing a military rifle that will serve their purpose. The weapon that was chosen was the Sharp's Borchard rifle, which is a very good gun. About twelve men signified their willingness to take hold of the movement and make the team one of the best on the coast. There were Messrs. C. Nash, J. C. Lane, Harry Hook, L. Whitworth, Serg't. Fleming, P. D. Linville, D. A. Peckinpah and officers Battle, Gano and J. F. McCarthy. There are as good shots among these men as can be found anywhere; all they need is a little practice, and under tuition of Sergt. C. Nash, who is an excellent shot himself, this team ought to be one of the best on the coast, and it is to be hoped that Chief Crowley will aid, by his approbation, the new team.

CARSON CROWING.—Some funny writer for a Carson paper amuses the readers by blowing a little Christmas tin-fish-horn blast about the victory of the Carson Rifle Team in securing the bronze horse and rider, the Pacific Coast trophy! The Immortist says that the California riflemen are overhauling our hills and valleys with fine tooth combs to get together a team that will return from the next contest with the trophy. He also says that the First Regiment boys lie awake nights studying to mount back-action night wind gauges that will predict what the weather will be three days in advance, beside a great deal more nonsense. To out matters short, the California Teams is glad that the Carson Team was victorious, for if the First Regiment Team had won, though we don't wish to crow for the First, it would have been with them as it was with Alexander of old when he conquered the world, there would have been nothing more on this side of the hills to compete with. We are glad that the Carson team won the trophy and hope that the best team will win it when it is shot for again at Treadway's Park at Carson next spring.

A rifle match of 50 shots at 200 yards for a gold medal valued at $100 will take place at Shell Mound Park on the 7th of January between Officer P. D. Linville of the Police force and Mr. Geo. H. Brown. It promises to be an interesting match.

---

## National Association of Trotting Horse Breeders.

Following is the report of the Executive Committee of the National Association of Trotting Horse Breeders to the sixth annual business meeting, held at the Everett House, N. Y., at 2 p. m., Wednesday, December 13, 1882. Pursuant to the constitution your committee respectfully submit the following report:

The committee have held seven meetings, all of them in the city of New York.

At a meeting of the committee, held on the 10th of January, the following were elected for the ensuing year as a Board of Censors: Guy Miller, F. D. Norris, David Bonner, E. G. Doolittle, W. S. Tilton.

At a meeting of the committee, held on the 9th of March, the following were appointed by the President as a Committee on Trotting Rules: Chas. Backman; H. M. Whitehead; I. V. Baker Jr.; Geo. B. Alley; C. A. Willis; H. W. T. Mali, Ex-officio and President; L. D. Packer, Ex-officio and Secretary.

The result of the committee's action, together with certain proposed amendments to the constitution submitted by the President, having been laid before the committee at a meeting held this day, and duly approved, are herewith appended, and recommended for your favorable consideration.

Of the action of the committee relative to the stakes opened, nominations and several payments therein, together with the location and results of the introductory and sixth annual trotting meetings, you have been duly informed by circular letters addressed to each member and through the public press. Eighteen stakes were decided, amounting to $13,545, and the meetings were characterized by a greater number of starters in each stake, closer contests, lower records and better financial results than ever before within the history of the society. In the eleven stakes already closed and yet to be trotted, there are 318 nominations, involving the sum of $16,785, as follows:

In the National Trotting Stallion Stakes, for foals of 1880, there is $1,015, and 24 nominations from whom will be due a second payment of $15 May 1st next, and a final payment of $60 each from starters twenty days before the annual trotting meeting of 1883, when the stake will be trotted for.

In the "Fourth Renewal of the Annual Nursery Stakes," for foals of 1880, there is $530, and 53 nominations, from whom there will be due a second payment of $15 each July 1st next and a final payment of $25 each due from starters twenty days before the annual trotting meeting of 1883, when the stakes will be trotted for.

In the Mali Stakes, for foals of 1880, there are 24 nominations, amounting to $1,700, with $500 added by Mr. H. W. T. Mali; a second payment of $50 each will be due May 1st next, and a final payment of $150 each due from starters twenty days before the trotting meeting of 1883, when the stakes will be trotted for.

In the National Trotting Stallion Stakes, for foals of 1881, there are 38 nominations, whose payments, together with the subscriptions of the owners of the sires named, amount to $1,065; a second payment of $15 each will be due May 1st next, and additional payment of $15 each will be due May 1st, 1884, and a final payment, of $60 each twenty days before the meeting of 1884, when the stake will be trotted for.

In the Wilson Stakes, for foals of 1880, there are 49 nominations, and the stake now involves the sum of $9,100, to which will be added a final payment of $50 each, due from starters twenty days before the meeting of 1880, when the stakes will be trotted for.

In the Produce Stakes, for foals of 1881, there are 19 nominations whose payments, together with the subscriptions of the owners of the mares named, amount to $1,725, to which will be added a second payment of $50 each, May 1st next, and a final payment of $50 each twenty days before the meeting of 1884, when the stakes will be trotted for.

In the Juvenile Stakes, for foals of 1881, by stallions whose get have never beaten 2:30 at three years old or under, there are forty nominations, amounting to $400, to which will be added a second payment of $25 each, due May 1st next and an additional payment of $25 each, May 1st, 1884, and a final payment of $40 each due from starters twenty days before the meeting of 1884, when the stake will be trotted for.

In the Everett House Stakes, for foals of 1881, by stallions whose get have never beaten 2:45 at three years old or under, there are twenty-five nominations, amounting to $250, to which will be added a second payment of $25 each, due May 1st next, an additional payment of $60 each, due from starters twenty days before the meeting of 1884, when the stake will be trotted for.

In the National Trotting Stallion Stakes, which closed for sires May 1st, 1882, and will close for their get (foals of 1882) May 1st, 1883, there were 12 sires named whose owners subscribed for each their season's service fee (for 1882), amounting to $650.

In the Matron Stakes, for foals of 1881, the subscriptions of the owners of ten mares named, amounting to $250, whose produce (foals of 1882) are eligible to entry, May 1st, 1883, at $150 each, $50 declaration.

In the Annual Nursery Stakes, for foals of 1881, there are twenty-four nominations, amounting to $600, to which will be added a second payment of $25 each, due May 1st, 1883, an additional payment of $25 each, due May 1st, 1884, and a final payment of $75 each, due from starters twenty days before the meeting of 1884, when the stake will be trotted for.

The association has lost by death during the past year one member; one has resigned; nine have been dropped from the rolls for non-payment of dues; thirty-five members have been elected and have duly qualified, and the society now numbers 135 members.

A vast amount of capital and labor is now involved in the breeding and development of trotting horses. With what intelligence and skill this is all being directed, the brilliant records of each season's turf campaign bear ample and significant testimony.

In that department of the trotting turf to which it has been the special purpose and province of this organization to confine itself, the development and exhibition of the younger rather than the aged class, the achievements have been so remarkable as to excite universal admiration and astonishment, and foreshadow how great are the possibilities of the trotting horse of the future.

Thus far the history of this association records no backward step; its advance has been steady but sure. If the results of the past, particularly those of last year, showing, as they do, the society free from debt, with a handsome balance in the treasury, a largely increased membership, and a list of trotting stakes never before equaled in character, value and proportions, are any criterion of the future, then may we well consider it as already executed.

L. D. PACKER, Secretary.

## Albert W.

On the first page there is so good a representation of this famous young stallion that it is scarcely necessary to supplement it with a written description. The ears are a trifle short in the picture, and the head a shade too "clumpy," but in every other respect it is a faithful delineation, and gives promise of future excellence in animal portraiture by the artist, Fred U. Buehler.

Albert W was bred by his present owner, who purchased his dam from Mr. E. R. Pond. He was foaled June 7th, 1878, and therefore would be considered a "late colt" even in eastern regions. He was broken to harness in March, 1880, so that he did not have the advantage of an "early education" in the sense that is now given to the instruction of trotting colts, and it was well along in the season when he received his first track work. This history will show that his career has been more than successful, and when compared with that of entire horses is still more remarkable.

It is only a few years since George Wilkes trotted in 2:22 and that performance placed him first on the list of trotting stallions. At that time Ericsson had the pride of place among four-year-olds with 2:30 to his credit. Both of these were regarded as wonderful performances, and deservedly so, and now we have the pleasure of recording the same time as that of Wilkes for a California-bred four-year-old, and to emphasize the feat the 2:22 was made in a third heat, repeated in a fourth, and the fifth only a half a second slower. This would have been a creditable performance for a stallion of any age; when made by one of the age of Albert W, it takes rank with the very best and entitles him to a prominent place among the "notables" of any country.

On the same day there was a race for four-year-olds at Chicago, and the intelligence came that Jay Eye See won the first, third and fourth heats in 2:22½, 2:19, 2:19. There was an error in the statement that the winner was a stallion, as unfortunately the great colt is a eunuch. The great advantage which follows emasculation on the trotting tracks is too well known to require argument, and as is shown by the records there is only one instance where an entire horse leads, that being the five-year-old record of Santa Claus (2:18). Smuggler is five seconds behind Maud S, four in the rear of St. Julien, Rarus, Trinket, Goldsmith Maid, Clingstone and Hopeful also having better records. From this it is not out of the way to estimate that the three seconds which Jay Eye See leads Albert W does not give the gelding the preference. We do not wish to detract an iota from the well-earned fame of the son of Dictator, nor have we the least desire to give Albert W a greater prominence than he deserves. The gelding is entitled to the credit of trotting the best race which has ever been made by colts of any age, and the stallion by far the best of male performers before the "mouth was full."

To breeders the most prominent features are the lines of blood which have led to such an astonishing result, and both of them give the same answer, viz: A combination of the Hambletonian with fresh infusion of thoroughbred blood. Jay Eye See is by Dictator, his dam (the dam of Dexter) by Seely's American Star. The dam of Jay Eye See, Midnight, is by Pilot Jr., her dam, Twilight, by Lexington and thoroughbred. Midnight is also the dam of Noontide, a mare with a record of 2:20½, and as she is by Harold is nearly a sister in blood to Jay Eye See. American Star was a highly bred horse, so that the racing blood predominates in the victor at Chicago.

The dam of Albert W is a sister to Aurora, by John Nelson, and John Nelson was by imported Trustee, from the Redmond mare, by Abdallah. This pedigree has been questioned but only by those who have such a violent antipathy to the thoroughbred that it warps their judgment and forbids a candid weighing of testimony. They are ready to believe the most absurd stories when these fall in with their notions, impugn the evidence of reliable men when it runs counter to their views, and profess rather to believe the maunderings of some one overcome with the senility of over fourscore years, than proof which was accepted as correct at a contemporaneous period. We have before us an advertisement of John Nelson, published in 1860, soon after the horse was brought here, and the following is a transcript:

THE FINE TROTTING STALLION JOHN NELSON WILL STAND AT Robert Beatty's "White House" during the season beginning March 1. He is a rich, bright chestnut, with a star on the forehead, and two white hind feet and is fifteen hands high. Terms for the season, $75. John Nelson is by imported Trustee out of the Redmond mare (who trotted in 8:35), by Abdallah, he by Mambrino and he by imported Messenger. John Nelson is half brother to the celebrated trotting gelding, Trustee, who trotted twenty miles in the unprecedented time of 59:35½, and he bears the same relationship to Fashion, Revenue and Reube Rynders, all splendid four-mile racers. His half brother, Revenue, now stands at Versailles, Ky., for $150 the season. Mares left at the stables of Messrs. Porter & Flenner will receive prompt attention. Parties living at a distance, requiring the services of the horse, will please address them, or J. M. DANIELS, 194 Kearny Street, San Francisco.

Now this advertisement was published in the *California Spirit of the Times*, that exchanged with the papers of the time, and any man who had one-half of the experience of Mr. Daniels would know that a false pedigree would soon be detected. Like many others it was never questioned until it was supposed that years enough had elapsed to bring it in doubt. At all events the get of John Nelson show unmistakable signs of "blood," and many of them display the Abdallah characteristics. The double Abdallah cross is shown in many of the crack performers, and even when derived in double quantity through two strains of Rysdyk's Hambletonian. Goldsmith Maid is a notable example of the first, Clingstone of the second, and illustrations could be multiplied until tiresome of the "potency" of the dual progenitors. The get of John Nelson have taken a prominent place in the trotting calendar, and the mares by him are as sure as anything in the future can be to prove of the greatest value in the stud.

Aurora, the sister to the dam of Albert W, gained a record of 2:27 in 1872, and was supposed to be the best of her day. Ex-Governor Stanford paid a high figure for her—report says $20,000—and there cannot be a question that if she had not gone lame she would have reached a very low mark. Nerea in 1875 trotted in 2:23½, and Governor Stanford made 2:27½ in 1876. The dam of Medora is by John Nelson, and foals from Aurora and Nerea are of great promise.

The first race which Albert W took part in was at the Golden Gate Fair, September 14th. It was in a purse of $400 for three-year-olds, and he won in 2:43, 2:49, 3:23. In the last heat the drivers did not understand that "the word" had been given, and the colts were pulled up, turned to come back and again started. His next race was at Sacramento, Flight and Rowdy Boy his competitors. Flight won the first heat in 2:42¾, Albert W the others in 2:38½, 2:36½, 2:39. At Stockton he was again successful, winning the first, third and fourth heats in 2:37, 2:35, 2:32½, Flight the second in 2:35. At San Jose he was beaten by Sweetheart in 2:30, 2:25½, 2:26, and he trotted in 2:28 the last heat although he got a bad start.

In 1882 his first race was at Santa Rosa, and a very hotly contested one it was. The colt had not recovered from the "pinkeye," and he had to meet Inca, Poscora Hayward and Blackmore. Inca won the first and third heats in 2:27, 2:27¾, Albert W the second in 2:27; the fourth was a dead heat with Poscora Hayward in 2:28½, and he won the fifth and sixth in 2:29½, 2:32. His second race was at Petaluma, where he defeated Poscora Hayward, Inca and Blackmore in "straight heats" in 2:27, 2:26½, 2:24¾, and his third was at Oakland, and again he had a hard struggle of seven heats which is well worthy of the full

SUMMARY.

Sept. 5—2:30 class, purse $800, $480 to first, $240 to second, $80 to third horse, mile heats, three in five:

| | | | | | | | |
|---|---|---|---|---|---|---|---|
| A. Waldstein's b s Albert W, by Electioneer | 3 | 3 | 3 | 1 | 2 | 1 | 1 |
| S. Sperry's ch m Nellie R, by Gen. McClellan | 2 | 2 | 1 | 3 | 1 | 2 | 2 |
| J. A. Goldsmith's b m Sweetness, by Volunteer | 1 | 1 | 2 | 2 | dis | | |
| W. D. Hammond's gr Poscora Hayward, by Billy Hayward | dis | | | | | | |

Time—2:22, 2:24½, 2:23½, 2:28½, 2:26½, 2:25, 2:26½.

This was a great race for a four-year-old, and an unfortunate one for Poscora Hayward, who broke down so badly that it was with difficulty he could be brought back to his stall.

His first and only defeat in 1882 was at Sacramento. The race was won by Sweetness in 2:24, 2:21¾, 2:22½, Albert W only beaten a length in the fastest heat.

The races at Stockton and San Jose were brilliant finishes of the season; so brilliant that we copy them entire from the reports at the time, with the remark that the "3 in 5" is the race referred to near the opening of this history. Still the heats of two miles, in our estimation, is the greatest performance, not only ranking within two and a half seconds of the fastest, as it is also the fastest for any entire horse, and within half a second of that of Flora Temple, which for so long a time was the best on record. At Stockton the race closed with nine entries, but with some disqualified and some drawn the starters were reduced to three, Sweetness, Nellie R and Albert W. Sweetness was a great favorite in betting circles, partly from the manner in which she had won her race in Sacramento, and partly from the prestige that attaches to Goldsmith and Mr. Salisbury's stable in these later meetings of the circuit. Pools sold before the start ran: Sweetness $50, Nellie R $18, Albert W $12. In the lottery for positions Albert W drew the first prize, with Sweetness second and Nellie R outside. Scoring for the word in the first heat was somewhat tedious through the rank behavior of Albert W, who acted as though there was lax discipline in the school where he studied. When the bell did tap they were all in good shape, but the colt broke at the sound and commenced the service with a sharp run. Sweetness took the lead at once, with Nellie R on her wheel, and thus they went to the quarter in 36. At that point Nellie B broke up and Albert W took the second place, Sweetness in the meantime opening a gap of three lengths. Before the half was reached Albert W again left his feet and Nellie R sped around the turn after the leader, leaving the colt eight lengths in the rear. Nellie closed the gap rapidly and at the three-quarter pole was at Sweetness' wheel, Albert having also shortened the interval a couple of lengths. In the trot up the stretch, Nellie pushed Sweetness to a break and came to the wire first in a jog, Sweetness second, Albert W third. Time 2:22½. It appeared from this trial that Sweetness was not herself, and the speculators who had backed her heavily in the pools made haste to secure themselves by putting in large sums on the big chestnut, an operation that proved to be a repetition of the old story of out of the frying-pan into the fire. The first pool sold was Nellie R $150, Sweetness $70, Albert W $27, and the last one before the start was Nellie R $40, Sweetness $16, Albert W $14.

Second heat—There was less difficulty in starting for this mile, Sweetness getting away first, but Nellie R showing such a measure of speed that she was taken back and brought to the work gradually. Albert had overcome his disposition to break and was trotting squarely close in the trail. At the quarter in 35½ Sweetness showed in front, but at the half in 1:10 Nellie R was neck and neck with her, Albert five lengths behind. Around the turn was without change, and in the home work Goldsmith, with whip and voice, urged his mare to her utmost, but Nellie was in her happiest mood and she came under the wire without hard driving, winner by half a length, Albert W third. Time, 2:20. The rush to "get out" was greater than ever. The first pool sold was Nellie R, $200; Sweetness, $27; Albert, $25, but as the selling progressed the excited speculators cooled somewhat, and the last pool was Nellie R, $110; Albert W, $30; Sweetness, $10.

Third heat—They got away together and at the quarter in 36 Nellie R was in front and Albert W behind, but all lapped. In the backstretch the colt skipped and found himself the last member in the line by a length, Nellie R drawing away slightly from Sweetness. They reached the half in 1:10½. Around the turn they came in a string, but at the three-quarter mark Sweetness broke up and the colt began his chase after Nellie R. Sperry heard the long, steady stroke behind him and knew what was in the wind. He struck his mare two or three sharp blows with his whip, but she was done. Her speed and heart had both left her and Albert W swept past at a pace he had not before shown in the race, passing the stand winner by three open lengths, Nellie R second, Sweetness third. Time 2:22.

There was another revolution in betting. Nothing could be plainer to the habitue of the tracks than that the colt had the race cornered. In the pools it was three to one on Albert W against the field.

Fourth heat—Albert W showed the way to the quarter in 36½, but in the straight work broke up, and at the half in 1:11 there was a bunch with Sweetness first and Albert last. Around the turn he worked into second place and up the stretch beat Sweetness handily by three lengths, Nellie R third. Time 2:22½.

Fifth heat—Albert W went off first with Sweetness close up, Nellie R breaking badly at the first turn. At the quarter in 36½ and the half in 1:10½ the colt was leading with Sweetness on his wheel, Nellie R ten lengths behind. From there home the colt came at a steady clip, being practically alone in the race. He won the heat by six lengths, Sweetness second, Nellie B third. Time 2:24.

SUMMARY.

Saturday, September 23.—Pacific Coast trotting; 2:22 class; purse $1,000, and $200 added if more than ten entries. Four moneys.

| | | | | | |
|---|---|---|---|---|---|
| A. Waldstein names b s Albert W, by Electioneer—by John Nelson | 3 | 3 | 1 | 1 | 1 |
| S. Sperry names ch m Nellie R, by General McClellan Jr. | 1 | 1 | 2 | 3 | 3 |
| J. A. Goldsmith names b m Sweetness, by Volunteer | 2 | 2 | 3 | 2 | 2 |

D. McCarty's b g Hancock, H. R. Covey's b g Capt. Smith, G. Bernard's g g Allen Roy, D. Mara's ch g Tump Winston, J. A. Goldsmith's blk s Director and W. D. Hammond's Poscora Hayward drawn.

Time—2:22½, 2:20, 2:22, 2:22½, 2:24.

The heats of two miles was for a purse of $500, for the 2:30 class, in which Bullet, Freestone and Tump Winston were withdrawn, leaving the contest to Albert W and Vanderlynn, the betting being $100 to $30 in favor of the former horse. Vanderlynn took the lead and held it well to the half-mile post, when he got off his feet and commenced a succession of breaks that destroyed his chances, as on each occasion when he was getting down to his gait and diminishing the gap between himself and the leader, he would get again on the run, and thus enabled Albert W to jog in an easy winner in 5:04¾.

In the second heat Vanderlynn was much steadier in his gait and he trotted the first mile without a skip in 2:24½, and passed the wire an open length ahead of Albert W, but on the first turn he made a break at the quarter. Albert W was in the lead, but near the half-mile post he made a break and resigned his position to Vanderlynn, who, on the homestretch, trotting very squarely, looking like a winner, but Albert W came up with a fine burst of speed and carried Vanderlyn off his feet near the draw-gate, winning the heat and race in 4:51. This is another fine performance on the part of Ablert W, and many good judges thought that with a good track this promisng son of Electioneer would lower the best record at the distance, namely that of Steve Maxwell, 4:48½, made at Rochester in August, 1880.

SUMMARY.

San Jose, October 2.—Trotting for the 2:30 class, heats of two miles; for a purse of $800.

| | | |
|---|---|---|
| A. Waldstein names b s Albert W, by Electioneer, dam by John Nelson | 1 | 1 |
| P. Farrel names b h Vanderlynn, by George M. Patchen, dam by Joseph | 2 | 2 |

Bullet, Freestone and Tump Winston were entered but did not start.

Time—5:04¾, 4:51.

Although some of the following matter has been printed before, the history of Albert W would not be complete without a more extended history of the paternal side of the house.

Though Electioneer has never trotted in public, he gave evidence of possessing his share of the well-known speed of the family, and it was only the "worst run of bad luck" imaginable which prevented him from leading the noted progeny of Green Mountain Maid, great as the feats of Prospero, Dame Trot, Elaine, etc., have been. Probabilities, however, are not required, and the glory which Electioneer has obtained through his progeny is far beyond what individual capacity would merit, though that capacity were of the highest class. Individual merit in horses ends with the active life of the performer. He who has the faculty of perpetuating the desired qualities lives in future generations, and in the case of the horse under consideration there are already so many of his sons and daughters which are endowed, that it is sure he will take the place of a founder of a family, and the Electioneers be known through several generations by this distinctive appellation. Even when broken up into several branches the "head of the clan" will be remembered as the founder of the dynasty, and the banner emblazoned with the colors of the chieftain. As has been stated, there was a succession of prodigies to his credit after the fruits of his first season in California came upon the track. Though he had made some seasons in the East, he was so completely overshadowed, in the estimation of his former owner, by his stable companion, Messenger Duroc, that he occupied an inferior position. Not so humiliating as the Godolphin Arab occupied at Gog Magog, but restricted in his opportunities and his colts given no chance.

When Governor Stanford visited Stony Ford and the stallions were paraded for his inspection, his companions were enthusiastic over the fancy of the owner. Messenger Duroc was the only horse in the world, and to show another after he had been on the stage was like displaying the daubs of a village pothouse in juxtaposition to a gallery of the grand masters of the art. He was not to be misled, however, by the acclamations. First he saw that the form of Electioneer was superior—much superior, according to his idea—and then the next thing to consider was the breeding. Both were by the same sire. Messenger Duroc's dam Satinet, by Roe's Abdallah Chief, and the dam of Electioneer was Green Mountain Maid by Harry Clay.

Messenger Duroc, at that time, owed all of his celebrity to Prospero and Dame Trot, both from the dam of Electioneer, and to Hogarth, the dam of which was also by Harry Clay. To a man who had a knowledge of breeding, in the habit of forming his opinions from his own knowledge, and not easily influenced by the enthusiastic notions of others, there could be little question when a choice had to be made, and though the "big horse" was priced at a figure at least four times as much as the other, the more highly formed and better bred was taken. Price had nothing to do with the choice. The intention was to buy the best, regardless of cost, and, fortunately for the breeding interests of California, the son of Green Mountain Maid was the selection. It is supererogatory to say anything of the size of Electioneer, Rysdyk's Hambletonian. His fame is so great, and so deservedly great, that it cannot be questioned with any logical argument to support the questioner. His dam, Green Mountain Maid, stands so nearly at the head of the list of trotting broodmares that Miss Russell is the only one which can dispute the claim that she should be the premier. Prospero (2:20) Elaine (2:20) and Dame Trot (2:22) are a trio of jewels of which the highest might be proud. There are assuredly "speed lines" enough here to suit the most fastidious sticklers for this essential part of a pedigree, and to add still greater force we find that the second generation is likely, and we believe sure, to better the showing. We have not the least doubt that there will be grandsons and grand-daughters of Green Mountain Maid which will show far faster, and of this sort not a few.

For the present, a brief recapitulation of what has already been done will be all that is necessary, and with that we will rest the case : On the Bay District Course, November 13, 1880, Fred Crocker was matched against 2:30. He then was a two-year-old, and had trotted a race in Sacramento, when he was beaten by Sweetheart in 2:31½, 2:32½. This he won very handily in 2:28½. One week afterwards he was again asked to beat his own time, and he accomplished it with a margin of 3½ seconds, placing 2:25½ on the blackboard. Sweetheart had trotted in 2:26½, and the performances by two California-bred two-year-olds set the Eastern world ablaze. The fastest time for years, and it still ranks the fastest time in that section, was 2:31, and to have it lowered so much was scarcely to be credited. There were chapters upon chapters in the Eastern papers. Some questioned the accuracy in the timing, others the length of the track, and never before was there such a hubbub unless, perhaps, when Goldsmith Maid trotted 2:17 in Milwaukee. Anno Domini 1881 increased the surprise, or rather so completely established the superiority of the California colts that the Eastern breeders were in dismay. At a meeting of an association, composed of the prominent breeders of the East, it was gravely debated whether the Occidentals should be barred, handicapped, or some other plan adopted which would save from impending danger. A resolution was offered that the distance should be increased to 220 yards in colt races, and then an amendment was offered that it should be 150 yards. The cause for all this tribulation was the trotting of another lot of two-year-olds, and was as follows: At the State Fair at Sacramento there was a stake for two-year-olds, the starters Wildflower by Electioneer, and Eva by Sultan. The latter was a sister to Sweetheart, Wildflower nearly a sister in blood to Fred Crocker, both of their dams being by St. Clair. Eva won the first heat in 2:33½, Wildflower the second and third in 2:33, 2:37. This was good, if not up to the standard of the preceding year, but the owners were well aware that it was well within the rate of the two fillies, and means were taken to put it to a test. The race at Sacramento was on September 22d, and on the Bay District Course on October 22d there were two prizes given for two-year-olds to beat the once celebrated time of So-So, 2:31. The track was in good order and the day fair. The attendance was good, a large number of those who take delight in the sports of the track, but who are-prone to verify the time of the judges with their own watches. Wildflower came out first. She moved up and down the stretch a few times to "warm up," going so smoothly and easily that it was evident that 2:31 was nowhere, and some were sanguine enough to predict that the time of Fred Crocker might be equaled.

She started with the daisy-cutting stride for which she is noted, and the very best judge of speed, with his eye merely to guide, would have thought that a "forty gait" was about the measure. Thirty-five and a quarter seconds was the tale told by the watches when the quarter pole was made, and there were many of those who held timing watches who doubted the accuracy of the report and thought that their "old reliables" had failed them at a critical moment. Acting as Clerk of the course, which gave the best opportunity to see every portion of the track, and the position of the fractional posts being such that there is no difficulty in "catching the time " correctly, with as good a split-second watch as ever came from the hands of the best maker, we are prepared to be accurate, and from our coigne of advantage were prepared to verify the official time. Each of the judges had a watch, and the figures of the regular timers, stationed immediately opposite the judges' stand, agreed with ours as to

the fractions, and there was a remarkable unanimity in officials and "outsiders" regarding the time. But this break in the description in very different from the trotting of Wildflower. She swept down the backstretch at such a flight of speed that the galloper which accompanied her was put to a racing stride, and at the half mile 1:09 was the record. This was surely far too fast, and any animal not yet forty months old could not withstand the strain. There was a slight slackening of the speed around the further turn, whether owing to tiring, which appeared inevitable, or strategy on the part of the driver in order to enable her to come home, was, of course, unknown to the spectators. With all the evident slowing, she reached the three-quarters in 1:44½, and yet there was not the rush which marked her progress in the backstretch. Mr. Covey ran up the track shouting and signaling her driver to come on. He did not understand the mandate until nearly opposite the 150-yard mark, when for the first time she was touched with the whip. The response was such an acceleration of the rate-that the "teaser" was forced to extend herself for the rest of the journey, and she swept under the wire in 2:21. The explanation of the slackening on the upper turn and down the stretch was this: Frank Covey drove the galloper, carrying a chronograph in his hand. When he saw that the half mile was made in 1:09 he was startled, and fearful that a break might render all that had been done of no avail. He was satisfied that any previous two-year-old time would be beaten easily if there was no mishap, and very judiciously he directed McGregory to "take a pull." It is unnecessary to speculate what would have resulted from a different course, and it is sufficient that the best time of the East had been beaten ten seconds, and when that time was "hung out " there was a shout which might have been heard in the city. There are few men who would have started another filly after such an exhibition of speed, but Mr. Rose, with the feeling of a true sportsman, determined that Eva should fulfil her part of the programme and a grand effort be made, accomplishing the mile in 2:26. On the 5th day of November there was another wonderful exhibition of speed by the youngsters. There were special prizes for yearlings, and after what the two-year-olds had shown, some were sanguine enough to predict that the time of Memento would be beaten. This grand record for a yearling was held so superlatively good that cavil and esteemed friend H. B., of the Turf, Field and Farm, wrote that "it would be a long time before we saw such a wonderful baby trotter." Doctor Hicks' bay filly Pride, by Buccaneer, made the first essay, and led the Kentucky time 12½ seconds behind, trotting in 2:44½. This was a "hard stent," and as in the preceding day it took some nerve to make a trial after such a "breaking of the record." Mr. Covey, however, was not easily discouraged, and Hinda Rose, by Electioneer, her dam Beautiful Bells by The Moor, was selected to battle for Palo Alto. She proved victorious by the small margin of a second, 2:43½ being the mark. This disposed of the question that Electioneer could only get trotters from St. Clair mares, and when Arol, another yearling by him, with a still different cross in the dam, trotted a quarter in 41½ seconds, the "prepotency " of the sire was established.

On the same day there was a further exhibition of the quality of the stock of Sunny Slope and Palo Alto. Eva trotted a mile in 2:26½, and her two-year-old sister, Sweetheart, a mile in 2:22, only one second below that of the champion, Fred Thompson. We venture to say, quoting our old friend again, that it will be a long time before we will see sisters two and three years old which will show such time on the same day, or for that matter in the same season.

Five of the Palo Alto two-year-olds made an exhibition of a quarter of a mile. Three by Electioneer, two by General Benton. The two Bentons, Bonnie and Bertha, each made the quarter in 36 seconds, and the Electioneers as follows: Eros, 37 seconds; Bonita, 32½ seconds; Wildflower, 32 seconds.

It is not surprising that the Eastern people doubted the length of the track, the accuracy of the watches, the age of the colts. The wonder is that they did not set the whole thing down as a fiction, a moon hoax story, akin to the travel-sprightly strains of that all Californians were in conspiracy of humbug which tales which underrate the common sense of any one who would give them credit for truth.

But on the 24th day of November was accomplished in, our opinion, the greatest feat of them all. Two medals were offered, the first being for a yearling that would beat 2:43½, the second for a two-year-old to rub out any record for that age, save that of Wildflower. The figures are the most eloquent commentary. The yearling, Hinda Rose, went to the quarter in 40½ seconds, to the half-mile pole in 1:18½, and made the mile in 2:36½. She made a break on the home stretch and the "middle half" was trotted in 1:15½. That a filly taking rank as a yearling, lacking several months of being two years old, should show so much speed and endurance, and speed especially, is the most marvelous illustration of the improvement of the American trotter which has ever been shown.

These were the doings prior to 1882, and though there may not have been quite as sensational feats as those in the record of 1881, enough was done to sustain the reputation of the tribe. Wildflower and Hinda Rose went East, winning their stakes in New York and Kentucky with comparative ease. In this country, outside of the doings of Albert W, were some notable performances. All of the starters in the Stanford stake were none of Electioneer, and Adair from a daughter of Culver's Black Hawk was the winner, in the very fair time for a three-year-old of 2:34½. Clay won the second heat in 2:36½, so that both of these earned the title of trotters. In

the Embryo stake for yearlings Antevolo, by Electioneer, was second to Dawn by Nutwood. The winner made 2:59, the fastest time ever made by a yearling in an actual race, and the fastest record for a stallion colt. Antevolo is a late colt, having been foaled the 12th of May, and he was trotted barefooted. He was timed as the second horse in 3:02, which for a colt with only a little work and without shoes, tips, weights or boots cannot be called a bad showing. Since the date of the Embryo, and still barefooted, he has shown quarters at a "fifty gait," and a half mile in 1:28. Finishing with this short sketch, we must say that we have great expectations of the Electioneers in the future, and feel confident that they are likely to reach the topmost round in the ladder of fame.

## English Opinions of the George-Myers Contest;

The London *Referee* thus discourses of the races between the English and American Champions:

George and Myers ran their three-quarter mile race on Thursday, with the result already foreshadowed in these columns. For some little while another postponement had been anticipated, not this time because of the unfitness or unwillingness of either man, but because of the unfavorable weather. On Wednesday New York was favored with a heavy snowfall, besides which the cold was intense. A wire sent by George to his friends in Birmingham states that there were twelve inches of snow on the ground last Wednesday; therefore no one on this side need have thought that upon the news of the race having to wait a more favorable opportunity. But our American cousins are an energetic and courageous people, and they at once set to work to get the track laid in good a condition as possible. Notwithstanding this, one of my advices states that the men ran on nearly half a foot of snow. How this was, unless the fall continued right up to within an hour or so of the race, must be left for the next mail to explain. What we know will serve for the present, and will enable us to understand why, although the contest was for a good part of the way close and exciting, the time was nothing near that which has been talked about. I have been credibly informed during the week that what has been already stated here is perfectly correct, and that George can, given a good day and fair condition, run three-quarters of a mile in 3:4. Also those who know most about him feel certain that under the excitement of a public race—an excitement which always makes a really good man better than he is in his best trial—he would, if pushed by a worthy opponent, get well inside these figures. The time on Thursday was 3:10½, a result which, if it does nothing else, will help to show how much the excellence of modern cinder paths has to do with latter-day developments.

Men who used to run anything over a sprint twenty or thirty years ago might have thought the track on which George and Myers contested good enough for the purpose, notwithstanding the snow which lay so thick upon it. On the other hand, the clocking was in the days of Planous and Seward as loose and untrustworthy as the tracks themselves, and whenever required was as much in the man's favor as the ground was against him. Still, 3:4 is very marvelous, especially when it is remembered that the present professional record was made in comparatively recent days upon a ground which was considered a very miracle of excellence; that the man who made the record was undoubtedly well served by the distance, and just as undoubtedly the best man of his day at it; and that he was "all out" at the finish. Next year perhaps George may be induced to give us in London a display of his best quality at three-quarters of a mile, unless he disgusted at what has happened to him in America, retires from pedestrianism altogether. Should he elect to continue his career he will have a good opportunity given him of showing us what he can do. Myers has expressed great anxiety to come here again, and, properly trained, reconnoitre conditions with George. What is more, one of Myers' staunchest supporters has pledged himself to pay all expenses, travel with him, and carefully look after his interests.

Notwithstanding his victories, George's recollections of America are bound to be anything but pleasant. When it was first stated that he had definitely determined to go out and meet Myers on his own ground, I foreshadowed the unpleasantness that was imminent, and have since been grossly abused for my pains. Yet I never for one moment imagined there could be anything like the unpleasantness which has actually resulted. George having spoken his mind too freely when Myers declined to run the three-quarter mile race as originally arranged, was pulled up with a round turn. He all at once discovered he was in a country where freedom of speech is only allowed those who belong to the establishment. A week ago the *Referee* informed its readers that George had, in messages to his friends on this side, expressed a strong and undoubted opinion about Myers' treatment of him. To his intense astonishment, the following morning there appeared in the black and white of the leading New York newspaper the words which he had used in a moment of indignation—words which he would probably never have uttered had he weighed them over. The day afterwards George issued a denial, the spirit of which was that first he did not use the words attributed to him; and second, if he did, he did not mean them to be taken in the foot of the letter. The effect was the same nevertheless, and the Manhattan Club having taken serious umbrage, sternly refused George's offer to run Myers on Thanksgiving Day (the 30th) unless he apologized unconditionally. They said: We have conceded Mr. George the medal which he so much required, and now we will have no more of him. Among the wicked expressions George had to admit having made use to the effect that he did not believe that Myers was ill, as he was out and about, and looked as well as ever. Another charge against him, and one he could not evade either, was that he had called the members of the Manhattan Club "a mean and unmanly lot."

A new horse disease has made its appearance at Stockton which baffles all the veterinary surgeons. One man who lost several head of horses had the body of one of them examined and found a bucketful of pure sand in the paunch. Others were then examined, with a like result. The early rains started the grass and the subsequent drought has made feed short, so that, in nipping it off, sand has been taken up by these horses in such quantities as to cause death.

There are still large areas in Texas near the Mexican border that are not inhabited except as they are ranged over by stock men with their herds. These men are, however, up with the times in securing the best blooded Shorthorn stock to improve their cattle.

## THE
# Breeder and Sportsman.

### PUBLISHED WEEKLY BY THE
### BREEDER AND SPORTSMAN PUBLISHING CO.

THE TURF AND SPORTING AUTHORITY OF THE
PACIFIC COAST.

**OFFICE, 508 MONTGOMERY STREET**
P. O. Box 2603

*Five dollars a year; three dollars for six months; one dollar and a half for three months. Strictly in advance*

MAKE ALL CHECKS, MONEY ORDERS ETC., PAYABLE TO ORDER OF
BREEDER AND SPORTSMAN PUBLISHING CO.

*Money should be sent by postal order, draft or by registered letter, addressed to the "Breeder and Sportsman Publishing Company, San Francisco, Cal."*

*Communications must be accompanied by the writer's name and address, not necessarily for publication, but as a private guarantee of good faith.*

JOSEPH CAIRN SIMPSON, - - - EDITOR

ADVERTISING RATES.—Displayed $1 50 per inch each insertion or pro rata for less space. Reading Notices set in brevier type and having no foot marks, 25 cents per line each insertion. Lines will average ten words. A discount of 10 per cent. will be allowed on 3 months, 20 per cent. on 6 months and 30 per cent. on 12 months contracts. No extra rate charged for cuts or cutting of columns rules. No reading notice take for less than 50 cents each insertion.

San Francisco, Saturday, December 30, 1882.

Mr. M. J. Henley is a duly authorized traveling agent and correspondent for the "Breeder and Sportsman."

## A HAPPY NEW YEAR.

That there may be prosperity, prime condition, physical and mental, philosophic determination to make the best of every situation, looking for the bright lining in every cloud, however somber the hue of that which is visible, many, very many happy years without a break from January until January again to all of our readers, and every one else for that matter, is the sincere desire of the *Breeder and Sportsman.*

At this time, the starting point for another year, it may not be out of place to declare our intentions, and to indicate what will be the course in the future. Assured of the aid of friends who have done so much in the past, and with the potent auxiliaries of the corps to assist, we have not the least fear of the capacity being wanting to make a good race. The course we have marked is in some respects different from any other journal in this country.

While legitimate sports of all kinds receive attention, it is not the purpose that these shall exclude other matters. The turf and track are important in more respects than offering the means of recreation, although they are well worthy of being sustained on this account alone. The history of the world teaches that out-door sports are a protection against habits which are sure to demoralize communities as well as individuals, and the downfall of nations commences when the people become too effeminate to enjoy and take part in the pastimes that can only be indulged in the open air. Racing, and in America trotting, carry more with them than the witnessing of contests. There is not merely a great moneyed interest at stake, not only the welfare of the breeder to guard, as the community is more or less interested. Every man or woman who rides or drives has a direct interest in the improvement of the animals they use, and it is generally admitted that the course and track are absolute necessities to guide the breeder in his choice of sires and dams the best adapted to produce the highest types of the horse. Racing and trotting in themselves receive the sanction and are upheld by the best and the wisest, and it is only the excesses that are denounced. It is true that there are bigots who see vice in any amusement, and who are so austere and fanatical they rail against everything which is above their gloomy comprehension. They hate the sunshine and revel in gloom. They prefer the fogs to the dew as it sparkles on the grass, and they would blacken the hue of the rainbow so that it might be in accordance with their somber ideas. Their journey through life is like a pilgrimage in a cypress swamp, loathing the bright paths where the sun brings verdure and flowers, to wade in malarial pools, dark and dismal as their hearts.

To them the great Creator erred when he made this earth so beautiful, and they picture a Deity who delights in human suffering, and who frowns at any enjoyment, and punishes the gratification of desires, however innocent, remorselessly.

For this class we do not labor. But for the other which fortunately is growing larger as the gloom of bigotry, intolerance and superstition gives way before the light of progress, we are willing to do all in our power to remove the incumbrances. Cheerfully, gaily we will bend to the work to aid in eliminating every objectionable feature from the most popular of all recreations, and h[i]lfsafter, as in the past, the *Breeder and Sportsman* will do its utmost to elevate the sports the people take delight in. Although there is not a tithe of the rascality

that is supposed to mar the pleasures of turf sports, there are occasional wrong-doings, and not as high a standard of morality among some who are prominent. Our aim shall be to castigate, irrespective of position, those who are found to be guilty, and inculcate to the best of our ability the importance of being guided by the most ultra-"old-fashioned" ideas of honor in those who participate. We would have a loftier plane observed than honesty. A line of conduct in all pertaining to the turf, that shall be akin to that which was the governing motive in men of the halcyon days when the thought of a dishonorable action was too revolting to be entertained for a moment.

When a violation is followed by complete ostracism from the society of the "good and true" there will be no repining over the "decadence of the turf." There will be thousands to attend the meetings in place of hundreds, and in lieu of obloquy attending the ownership of horses kept for track uses, it will be part of the state and equipage of a gentleman to support a stable for the gratification of the public.

While, as has been stated before, due prominence will be given to the actual trials on course and track, the breeding interest will not be overlooked. In fact, we hold this of paramount importance, and shall do our utmost to make this journal an ally to the breeder which he can welcome. Breeding, rearing and training horses is an art, and to be successful the subject must be studied. Every department of horse breeding comes under this head, and whether for the course, the track, the road, "all-work," or heavy draft the breeder who reads, thinks, and who practices what he has derived from reading and study will be far in advance of the one who depends on chance to help him out.

To aid us in teaching this important branch of rural economy are the admirable correspondents in all sections of the country and an exchange list containing nearly every prominent paper of the class printed in the English language. An experience of thirty years gives us confidence, and though it may appear egotistical to make the claim of possessing rather more than a fair knowledge of whatever pertains to the horse, it could hardly be otherwise than that the lessons following practical results should have taught us things an acquaintance with which may benefit others. In that time we have bred, reared and trained race-horses, trotters and roadsters with a fair degree of success, and we have closely watched and carefully studied the methods of others. Following a natural bent it has been the main study of life, to the exclusion of nearly everything else, and the mysteries of breeding, stable economy, training, etc., pondered over for more than a score of years. During that long time many experiments have been tried, and very many of them were failures; the failures added to the store of available knowledge, and the success demonstrated the value of forsaking the old grooves. But fortunately we are not confined to personal knowledge. The correspondents of the *Breeder and Sportsman* are practical, intelligent men and peculiarly "well up" in what they write about.

Our exchange list gives us the benefit of the accumulated wisdom of more than one hemisphere. We draw largely on that source, and our readers have expressed a general satisfaction with the articles copied. There is an immense field from which to select, and one that has almost boundless resources. It is far more extensive than an individual would suppose. Westward the Hawaiian Islands, Sydney, Melbourne, and other portions of Australia, and still on to Calcutta, East India. Eastward across the American continent, Great Britain and Ireland. On the north it extends to the Arctic, south to the Gulf of Mexico. In making use of the advantages which this chance for selection gives it practically affords our readers the benefits of hundreds of papers, and while, of course, we present a large amount of original matter, we are not restrained from copying whatever is of the right stamp.

The *Breeder and Sportsman* is not confined to any one "speciality." Though the breeding of horses of the various grades is one of the most important of the pursuits of the agriculturist, every department of breeding cattle, swine, sheep, poultry, will receive due attention, and whatever is of interest to the farmer in all of these branches will have the fullest consideration. The grand object is to make this paper a welcome visitor to country, city and village, and the path that we have marked lies entirely in that direction.

All of the sports of field and water are embraced, and the scope is sufficient to cover whatever is legitimate in these fascinating recreations. A reference to the index to volume first, published in this number, will give an idea of what has been done, and with the assurance that there shall be no lack hereafter in these essential departments.

The aim is to publish a paper, in many respects, different from any other in the United States. Not entirely a turf paper, or journal of sport, but a combination of recreation and instruction, an upholder of that which is conducive to true sporting interests, and a castigator of those that would lower them to a grade which would insure the disapprobation of the right sort of people. The intention may be epitomized into a few words, and these are that no pains will be spared to make the *Breeder and Sportsman* essentially such a paper as the name implies, and without a line which will be repugnant to "good breeding" or honest purpose.

## TIPS—ORIENTAL AND OCCIDENTAL NO-
## TIONS.

On this side of the continent trainers who have seen tips tried are willing to admit that they are an advantage to the feet and legs but they claim that they are a drawback to trotting speed. From the following copied from the *Turf, Field and Farm* of December 15th, it will be seen that Hamilton Busbey does not agree with this view. This is the extract:

After reading the card and promising to publish we asked to see Algath. She stepped from her box with shoes partially off, and under the standard she was 16 hands. She is a bay with snip and white hind ankles and was foaled April 18, 1879. Her sire was Onyler and her dam Haroldine, by Harold; second dam Missouri, by Mambrino Chief, and third dam by thoroughbred Woodford. She is a rangy and somewhat leggy young mare, with good countenance and is easily controlled. She wore tips on her fore feet in all of her races, and it is a wonder that they did not break her down, because they are the worst thing that a trotter, young or old, can wear, especially on a hard track. Mr. Davis thinks that she would have trotted in 2:20 at Chicago, the day she made her record of 2:25½, had weather and track been good. On her return to Glenview she was timed a half mile in 1:08. It will be worth something to see her in a race with Wildflower and Alroy next year.

It is evident that when a three-year-old filly obtains a public record of 2:25½, and makes half a mile in 1:08, wearing tips, the California estimate will not hold good, so that one or other must be in error. We have the fullest faith that either view is erroneous, and are satisfied beyond the shadow of doubt that "H. B." is wrong. There is certainly nothing in theory to substantiate the ground that there is a liability to break down, in fact reasoning from a pathological position there is not nearly so much strain on the tendons, and, consequently not nearly so much danger of lesions or ruptures of the sheathing. That is when tips are properly "set." With the tip or lunette shoe, whichever name is used, imbedded into the horn so as to give the proper and equal bearing, there is a closer following after nature, an adaptation of her teachings, while at the same time we guard against an undue wear of the horn. The only chance to have an argument on anything like tenable grounds would be that the extra weight on the anterior portion of the foot entailed a risk. That does not follow. A full shoe, of average weight for a trotter or road horse, say sixteen ounces, will have three-quarters of the weight in the section corresponding to a tip, such as we use, so that there will be an excess of weight of eight ounces over the part which is posterior. Then after allowing for the balance of the rear four ounces, there will be a surplus greater than the whole weight of the tip, as seven ounces is the heaviest we have used for some time, and most of them under six ounces, some that were only four ounces.

But practice is of more value than theory though that sustains the hypothesis of greater safety emphatically so far as our experiment extends.

Anteeo has never worn a shoe on his fore feet. Tips were put on when he was fourteen and a half months old, and owing to his peculiar disposition his work has been of a nature to be very trying on his feet and legs. Now at three years and a half his legs are as "clean" as can be, and his feet are simply perfect. As we will continue his history from the time of the last illustration, giving a full account of his work, showing, etc, it is unnecessary to give it so briefly as it would be to be done at present, and then it will be known that, if tips were likely to cause breaking down, he should have succumbed long ago. We are greatly pleased to learn that Algath so substantially indorses our views regarding the use of tips on trotting colts.

The nearly universal practice of training race horses barefooted demonstrates that in the case of the galloper, shoes are superfluous and not only superfluous but dangerous as more "break-downs" were met with than at present. With both theory and practice to prove to the contrary, the claim that "it is a wonder that they did not break her down, because they are the worst things that a trotter, young or old, can wear, especially on a hard track," would be absurd were it not that so little is known about tips and the effects which follow the use of them. As Algath has done so well, however, it is not likely that Mr. McFerran will give them up until there are more than predictions against the usefulness.

## THE STANFORD STAKE FOR 1883.

The second payment of $100 in the Stanford Stake of 1883, must be made on or before the first of January next. A failure will be a forfeiture of the previous payment.

The race is fixed for the third Saturday in October, 1883, on the Bay District Course, and should that track be not obtainable at that date, the managers will select another of which due notice will be given. In case the "day and track" are not good on the day selected, the trot shall come off on the first Saturday thereafter when the day and track are good, unless that should be the first Saturday in November, when the Embryo Stakes are to be trotted.

### H. M. LA RUE.

Although ignoring a majority of questions that may be termed political, it certainly comes within the scope of the *Breeder and Sportsman* to support everything which has a tendency to benefit the breeder, farmer, horticulturist, etc. There are questions of vital importance to all of these classes arising at every session of the Legislature, some of them of the greatest moment. The Speaker of the House is in a position to be of the greatest service and believing that the interests depending will have a staunch supporter in H. M. La Rue, a candidate for the place, we take pleasure in doing what we can to aid in his election. He is a true farmer, practical, thoroughly acquainted with everything pertaining to the business in California, and with a clear comprehension of the effects of legislation. He has proved himself to be a man of executive ability in his management of the California State Agricultural Society, and his integrity is not disputed even by those who are in opposition. There may be other aspirants having equal claims, but of all the members elect of the next Assembly with whom we are acquainted, Mr. La Rue is our first choice.

We also learn that Edwin F. Smith, the efficient secretary of the California State Agricultural Society, is a candidate for Secretary of the Senate. There could not be a better man for the same position, and we sincerely trust that California will be fortunate enough to secure the services of these gentlemen.

### OCCIDENT AND STOCKTON STAKES.

There also close on the first of January the Occident Stakes, and on February 1st, 1883, the stake for two-year-olds to be trotted at the San Joaquin Fair. The Occident is for foals of 1881 to be trotted when three-year-olds, the Stockton for foals of the same year to be trotted when two years old. The Occident is $100 each, $25 to accompany nomination, $25 on the first of January 1884 and the remaining $50 thirty days before the time fixed for trotting.

The same amount must accompany the nomination in the Stockton Stakes, $25 additional to be paid July 1st. In the Occident a gold cup of the value of $400 is added; at Stockton $500 in money is added to the stake, $100 of which is awarded the stallion whose get wins first money. Thus there are two stakes closing on the first of January next for foals of 1881, viz: Stanford and Occident, and the Stockton Stakes, as stated before, on the 1st of February. Inasmuch as the latter has no distinctive name, we would suggest that it be named after the first winner of the stake. There is little necessity for urging the owners of colts to enter into engagements, as the advantages are now generally recognized. The advertisements of the Stanford and Occident Stakes give full particulars.

### THE FIRST RACE MEETING IN SAN FRANCISCO.

There is scarcely a doubt that the meeting, an account of which will be found on another page, was the first ever held in California. It may have been that there was a prior meeting in Sacramento, as we have seen a notice that one would be held in October, 1850, though we have been unable to find any account of it. A discrepancy will be noticed in the distance and time of the first race. In the "summary" the distance is given "mile-and-a-half heats and the time 1:50½. If the distance is correct 2:50½ must have been the time; if the time is right, heats of a mile must have been the distance. The Fall meeting on the same course commenced on August 7th, and on September 18th, 20th, and 21st, there was a meeting on the Brighton Course, Sacramento. At that there was a match of $10,000 between Iro and Black Swan, the former being the winner. The race was heats of a mile, though the time is not given, Black Swan drawn after the first heat. There were races at Stockton the same fall though a match for $600, in which Sam Gustine beat Blue Crane in 1:52½ is the only record at hand.

When there is more time to go over the old files and space to do justice to the subject we will continue the history of the turf and track in California. There are interesting episodes in the early days of these sports on this coast which cannot fail to be attractive to old residents and new-comers. There is a great deal of the romantic in anything pertaining to the "good old days," and the sports of Turf, Track, Field and Flood were not exceptional in this respect.

### FROM AUSTRALIA.

In addition to the news from our "regular correspondent" at Sydney we have received several private letters, all of them containing a good deal of sporting and other news of interest to our readers. We will make these the subject of an article in the paper of next week, and at the present time return our sincere thanks for the good wishes expressed. It will be seen that Honesty arrived

safely at Sydney, and that he stood the voyage "like a trump." As the big trotting race has been postponed until March, there is plenty of time to make other shipments with a chance to participate. California breeders will lose a favorable chance if they omit to do all in their power to further trotting interests in that country.

### THE STANFORD STAKE FOR 1884.

This popular trotting stake for foals of 1881 will close on the first of January next, and there are so many promising colts of the age in California that there should be a full list of nominations.

The conditions are $300 each, $100 of which must accompany the nomination, $100 on the first day of January, 1884, and the remaining $100 thirty days previous to the day set for trotting the race. That is to be heats of a mile, best three in five in harness, the day not earlier than the latter part of August, the day to be fixed on or before the first of January of the year of trotting.

That the colts and nines which have shown so well will be engaged, and these reinforced by the dark division, will present an array of names, and the potential backing of the right sort of breeding, assures a large amount to the winner. A yearling of promise that secures an engagement in this stake is increased in value to as extent that will warrant the outlay, and therefore it can scarcely be otherwise than that there will be a liberal response.

Nominations can either be made to N. T. Smith, Fourth and Townsend streets, Treasurer, or to Jos. Cairn Simpson, 508 Montgomery street, Secretary. Under the new rules adopted by the National Trotting Association the last convention, a letter containing the nomination, legibly postmarked, not later than the day of closing, will be eligible. The description and pedigree should also be given.

### EDITORIAL NOTES.

The difference between the drivers of trotters is well exemplified in the *Breeder's Gazette*. A series of articles appeared in that journal written by F. V. Johnson and not long ago we took pleasure in complimenting the author. They showed a manly, straightforward motive and were readable and instructive. In the same paper there is in course of publication something of the same kind of articles by George W. Saunders, and we are forced to take very different ground. He writes: "At the first named place (Freeport) I got second money with Newborn, Matt Kirkwood winning the race, although my horse could trot all around him that day. The next week I started Newborn at Prophetstown, and on the day of the race he could fairly fly, and I tried to knock down all of the posts on the outside railing of the track to keep from winning. I did not want a record on the horse just then." A self-convicted swindler, and his astonishing that such should ever have horses put in their charge. The National Trotting Association must adopt a rule at the next convention barring this man out and to that sort of writing or talk. Whenever a driver claims to have lost a race purposely, that he could have won, expel him and keep him expelled. If he is guilty as he pleads he certainly deserves punishment; if he falsifies he is richly entitled to the penalty for doing all in his power to bring the sport into disrepute. We shall insist that in order to relieve the track of such a dead weight the association take cognizance of this. If it falls a premium is awarded to rascality, and it makes itself a party to the fraud.

**Boys in Trouble.**—The lithograph from the original painting by E. Wyttenbach is so expressive that it does not require a word of comment. It is, in fact, so admirable that we think our readers will heartily agree with us in this estimate.

### Trotting Rules.

The following code of rules was approved by the annual business meeting of the National Association of Trotting Horse Breeders, held December 13, 1882:

Rule I—Sec. 1. All nominations shall be in writing, in the name of the owner, addressed to the Treasurer, inclosed in a sealed envelope, and plainly marked "Nominations," with a bank draft, postal order, or certified check for the amount of first payment; which envelope must bear the post mark of not later than the day upon which the Stake closes. A nomination by telegraph received by the Treasurer before the hour of closing, and confirmed by a properly written entry, as above prescribed, posted not later than the following, shall be deemed valid.

Sec. 2. The number of nominations by one owner is unlimited, but only one can start in a race.

Sec. 3. Nominations shall state the name, color, marks, age and sex, whether horse, gelding or mare, and the names of the sire and dam if known, and the sire if known.

Sec. 4. Nominations shall follow the ownership of the horse, provided notice of change of ownership shall be forthwith filed with the Secretary.

Sec. 5. All entries shall close at midnight of the day named, at the office of the Treasurer, unless otherwise provided.

Sec. 6. Only horses owned or bred by members, or the get of stallions owned or stood by members, shall be eligible to entry.

Rule II, Races—Sec. 1. All races to be in harness, mile

heats, best three in five, except for three years old and under, which are to be mile heats, unless otherwise provided in the first announcement of the Stake.

Rule IV, Division of Money—Sec. 1. If three or more horses start in a Stake race, two-thirds of the Stake shall be awarded to the winner, two-ninths to the second horse, and one-ninth to the third horse, except otherwise provided in the published conditions of the race. If not more than two horses start, only first and second money shall be awarded; and in case of walks-over only the first money shall be awarded, and it shall be optional with the Executive Committee whether the horse shall or shall not appear.

Rule V, Distance—Sec. 1. A horse distancing the field shall only be entitled to so much of the money as the starters in the race could have won.

Sec. 2. In all races best two in three, the distance shall be eighty yards; and in all races best three in five, the distance shall be 100 yards; except in heats wherein eight or more horses start, and therein the distance shall be 150 yards.

Rule VI, Judges—Sec. 1. The Executive Committee shall appoint three Judges of each race, who shall give notice from the stand ten minutes before starting the race, and five minutes before each heat thereafter.

Sec. 2. No person except the Judges, the Clerk of the course, his assistants and the timers of the race, shall be allowed in the stand during the pendency of a heat.

Sec. 3. The Executive Committee shall appoint a District Judge, and whenever requested by the Judge of the race, shall select one or more patrols.

Sec. 4. The Judge of the race shall have power and control to determine all matters in respect to the scoring and driving of the race, and its conduct after the appearance of the horses upon the course; and may for the violation of their orders, or for any unfair or improper conduct on the part of the owner, driver or his assistants, impose fines and punishments as hereinafter prescribed; and may charge the rider or driver of any horse which in their judgment is not being ridden or driven to win.

Rule VII, Fines and Punishments—Sec. 1. For failure to obey the directions of the Judges during the progress of the race, a fine of not more than $100 nor less than $5 for each offense, to be paid at once.

Sec. 2. For foul driving, disorderly conduct, profane, abusive or vulgar language, and for collusive or fraudulent driving, a fine as above limited; distance, suspension and expulsion, or any or all of such punishments.

Sec. 3. No suspension or expulsion shall be valid, unless the ground thereof shall be at the time recorded by the Clerk of the course, in the record of the race, and signed by the Judges.

Rule VIII, Timers—Sec. 1. Three or more persons shall be appointed by the Executive Committee as timers of each race, who shall time the first and second horse in each heat; and the time of the winner of each heat shall be duly recorded; the time of the winners of a dead heat shall also be duly recorded, and the time of the second horse shall be recorded for reference.

Rule IX, Starters in Heats—Sec. 1. In races of heats best two in three, a horse not winning once in three, nor making a dead heat, shall not start for a fourth; in races of heats, best three in five, a horse not winning a heat in five, nor making a dead heat, shall not start for the sixth; and a horse not placed at the finish of a race shall win no part of the stake.

Sec. 2. Whenever each of the horses making a dead heat would have been entitled to terminate the race had he won said dead heat, they only shall start again.

Sec. 3. A horse prevented from starting by this rule shall not be distanced but ruled out, and shall be entitled to a share in the stake according to his rank at the close of his last heat.

Rule X, Time between Heats—Sec. 1. The time between mile heats shall be twenty minutes, and in mile heats, best three in five, twenty-five minutes; in two mile heats, thirty minutes; in three mile heats, thirty-five minutes, and in four mile heats, forty minutes.

Rule XI, Progress of Races—Sec. 1. Only two races shall be in progress at one time.

Rule XII, Placing Horses—Sec. 1. In deciding the rank of horses other than the winner, their relative positions in each heat shall be conclusive, except when two or more appear equal in the race, their rank shall be determined by their position in the last heat.

Rule XIII, Postponement—Sec. 1. In case of storm or darkness the Executive Committee or the Judge of the race shall have power to postpone the same until the next good day and track, either before or after the race has commenced.

Rule XIV, Weights and Weighing—Sec. 1. The weight in races shall be 150 pounds, and shall be ascertained before and after each heat by the Clerk of the course, and no rider or driver shall dismount without the permission of the Judge; and any rider or driver not carrying the required weight shall be distanced, except the omission shall be fraudulent or shall be caused by some accident during the heat or through the error of the Clerk of the course.

Rule XV, Length of Whips—Sec. 1. For saddle, two feet ten inches; sulky, four feet eight inches; wagon, five feet ten inches; teams, eight feet six inches.

Rule XVI, Starting Positions—Sec. 1. The positions of horses starting in a race shall be assigned by the Judges as ascertained by lot, and thereafter according to their position at the finish of each heat.

Sec. 2. Positions may be changed during the heat in the discretion of the driver, provided such change shall cause no interference, except that after the horses shall have taken their position in the homestretch, they shall not be changed unless to pass another.

In case of accidental interference with another horse, by change of position, the horse so interfering shall be penalized by loss of the heat or of his position, and in case of intentional interference, the horse so interfering shall be distanced and the driver shall be punished.

Rule XVII, Breaking—Sec. 1. No horse shall go in a race any other gait than a trot; if through the fault of the driver the horse takes any other gait, he shall be distanced; if without the fault of the driver, the horse so often takes another gait than a trot, or on taking it continues it so far as to render the contest unfair, such horse shall be distanced.

Rule XVIII, Age—Sec. 1. The age of a horse shall be reckoned from the 1st of January of the year of foaling.

Rule XIX, Appeal—Sec. 1. Any party aggrieved by a suspension or expulsion may appeal from the decision of the Judge or Executive Committee. Such appeal may be taken by serving a written notice, within ten days after the event, upon the Secretary of the Association, specifying the matter sought to be reviewed and the error complained of; provided, a written protest shall have been filed with the Clerk of the Course within fifteen minutes after the conclusion of the race, and provided also one member of the Executive Committee shall certify in writing upon the notice of appeal, that in his judgment there is good ground

## THE KENNEL.

### National Club Field Trials.

The fourth annual field trials of the National American Kennel Club commenced at Grand Junction, Tenn., Monday morning, December 4, at 9:33, and terminated on Thursday afternoon, December 7, at 3:15—just four days, the shortest time in which a field trial, with the same number of entries, has been run.

The same ground was run over as last year, and although twice as many bevies of birds had been located previous to the trials as last year, yet they were more difficult to find this year, in consequence of the very thick cover, owing to the rank growth of weeds and grass, produced by the frequent and heavy rains during the summer, and the late frost in the fall. Moreover, the weather, taken as a whole, was very unfavorable for good scent; consequently the test of nose was severe.

Mr. Wilson having been prevented by business engagements from being present, Major J. M. Taylor, of Lexington, Ky., was substituted for him, to judge with Dr. Young, of Corinth, Miss., and Captain W. H. Key, of Florence, Ala. On Tuesday night, Major Taylor was compelled to go home in consequence of the illness of one of his children, and Captain Henry was substituted for him, to judge with Dr. Young and Captain Key the unfinished heats of the Free For All, and the Derby.

Some very fine points came up for decision during the trials which could be correctly decided only by men educated up to the highest standard of field work, which the Judges proved themselves to be, by deciding promptly and correctly in each instance.

The Free For All had eighteen entries, and was won by D. Bryson's black, white and tan setter bitch, Sue, by Druid—Heiler's Ruby. Druid by Prince—Dora; Ruby, by Rake—Fanny; (Rake by Llewellin's Dan (Duke—Rhoebe) out of Ruby, by Statter's Fred—Rhoebe; Fred by Rock—Belle II. Fanny, the dam of Ruby, is by Leicester—Dart; Leicester by Dan (Duke—Rhoebe) out of Lill II, (Dash II, Old Blue Dash—Lill I) Dash II by Sting—Cora II; Lill I by Rock—Belle II. Dart, by Prince (Dash II; Old Blue Dash—Moll III) out of Dora, (Duke—Rhoebe, Moll III by Fred I—Belle II. This is Sue's second appearance in public, she having first run in the Free For All Stake of the National American Kennel Club's field trials on prairie chickens, at Fairmont, Minn., last September, when she was awarded four-fifths of the second prize, Dashing Novice receiving the other fifth, the first prize having been won, by the pointer dog, Don. Sue has not a bench show record, never having been exhibited. The second place was won by Peep o'Day, (the winner of the stake last year also the property of D. Bryson, Memphis, Tenn. Peep o'Day is a blue Belton setter bitch, whelped April 26, 1879, and is by Gladstone—Clip; Gladstone, by Dan (Duke—Rhoebe) out of Petrel; Petrel, by Prince (Dash II, Old Blue Dash—Moll III) out of Lill II (Dash II, Old Blue Dash—Lill I) Clip is by Leicester—Dart. For the full pedigree of Leicester and Dart refer to Sue's pedigree above. This is the third time Peep o'Day has run, and each time she has been placed. When a puppy she ran in the First American Derby, at Vincennes, Ind., 1880, when she divided third with Count Nailer, May Laverack and Bruce, Count Noble winning first and Daisy Laverack second. She next ran in the Free For All of Grand Junction, last year, which she won, Sanborn's Nellie winning second, and Breckenridge and Ladd dividing third. Peep o'Day's bench show winnings are: Native English setter bitch class, St. Louis, 1880; champion English setter bitch class, Pittsburgh, 1881, and 1882. The third place in the stake was divided between Carrie J and American Dan. Carrie J is a good sized and good looking blue Belton setter bitch, owned by W. B. Gates, Memphis, Tenn., and is by Count Noble—Peep o' Day. Count Noble is by Count Wind'em—Nora; Count Wind'em is by Count Dick—Phantom; Count Dick is by Dan (Duke—Rhoebe) out of Countess (Dash II, old Blue Dash—Moll III); Phantom is by Prince—Lill I; for pedigrees of Prince and Lill I, see pedigree of Sue. Nora is by Dan, the sire of Count Dick, out of Nellie, sister of Countess and Prince. This is the first time Carrie J has run in public. She won first in English setter bitch puppy class, Pittsburgh, last March. American Dan is rather a large dog, black, white and tan, and very handsome. In style and action he resembles very much his illustrious sire, Lincoln, and in markings, his grandsire, Llewellin's Dan. American Dan is by Lincoln—Daisy Dean; Lincoln is a brother of Leicester, to whose pedigree above refer for Lincoln's pedigree. Daisy Dean is by Pride of the Border out of Ruby, imported by Dr. J. H. Gautier of New York, the first Laverack setter imported into America, and afterwards owned by Mr. Charles H. Raymond, Morris Plains, N. J., who bred Daisy Dean. Ruby was red, but the distinctive shape of an English setter, and not that of an Irish setter; she was by Mystery out of Cora; Mystery by Jet (Fred I—Belle II) out of Duchess (Sting—Cora); Cora by Dash II, Old Blue Dash (Sting—Cora II) out of Moll II (Fred I—Belle II). This is American Dan's second appearance, having first run in the American Field Derby, on prairie chickens, Fairmont, Minn., last September, in which he won third, Prince Noble winning first, Fink B second.

The Third American Derby was won by Carrie J, whose pedigree is given above. Pink B won second place, and Bessie A third place. Pink B is owned by W. P. Mallory, Memphis, Tenn.; is a black and white setter dog, and is by Gladstone out of Countess Key. As mentioned above, he won second in the American Field Derby, Fairmont, Minn., last September. Bessie A is owned by J. M. Avent, Hickory Valley, Tenn.; is a white and lemon setter bitch, small but very fast, and is by Dashing Lion—Armida. Dashing Lion is by Dash II (Blue Prince—John Armstrong's Kate) out of Leda, sister of Leicester and Lincoln. Bins Prince, by Pride of the Border—Nellie, sister to Countess; John Armstrong's Kate is by old Blue Dash, out of Edward Armstrong's Kate, sister to Duke. Armida is by Leicester—Pocahontas, she by Adams' Rock out of Dora (Duke—Rhoebe) Rock by Field's Bruce (Dash II, old Blue Dash—Rhoebe) out of Llewellin's Daisy (Dash II, old Blue Dash—Moll III).

We have taken great care in tracing the pedigrees of the winners, considering they afford one of the most thoroughly practical lessons in setter breeding possible, as it will be seen how they trace back through different sires and dams, and grand sires and grand dams to the same ancestors.

The dogs were all in good condition, especially those handled by Mr. Short, who was remarkably successful, as having handled Sue, Peep o'Day and Carrie J, the winner of first, second and half of third in the Free For All, and of Carrie J and Pink B, winners of first and second in the Derby.—American Field.

### COURSING IN CALIFORNIA.

### Reminiscences of Early Days—History of the Sport's Growth on the Coast.

New Year's Day is the time for retrospect and anticipation the time when we look back over the doings of the years that have passed and look forward to the bright and happy times we hope to enjoy in the future, and it was this custom that doubtless inspired the chief editor of the Breeder and Sportsman to demand of his admiring subordinate, the Kennel editor, as a New Year's contribution, a few lines about the past history of coursing in California and our anticipations for the future of that noble sport. We commenced to argue against the shortness of the notice, the lack of reliable data and our utter unfitness for the task of historian, but were cut short by the remark: "I have decided on the subject and you must do the best you can." So to do the best we can is all we aim at and we hope that our many shortcomings will be pardoned.

Naturally enough coursing in California commenced when the first greyhound that was brought here first caught sight of his natural game, a hare, or as they are called here, a jack rabbit. That is, always supposing that the greyhound was loose when the hare crossed his line of sight. Whether the first course in California resulted in a "kill" or not we do not know but incline to the belief that it did not, for the greyhound was probably too high in flesh or too low in strength after his long trip across the plains or around Cape Horn to be able to catch a cottontail, let alone a full grown hare. We are equally ignorant about the name of the first greyhound, or his owner, or the place where the first course was run and what troubles us more than our own ignorance is the fact that no one else appears to be any wiser. Along about the year 1854 greyhounds began to get quite common here and informal coursing matches were frequently held around the neighborhood of Dublin, Alameda, Newark and other places easy of access to San Francisco. These matches were run without much regard to rule or coursing etiquette, but were pleasant social gatherings, hugely enjoyed by those who took part. Among the earliest of California coursing men were John Scarlett, Nat Curry the gunsmith, and ex-Sheriff James Adams. Shortly afterwards there came on the scene Clem Dixon, who with a Scotchman's natural love of order, though Clem is really a North of England man with Scottish education, set about organizing the sport of coursing under the regular rules of the sport. When it came to making out the rules for judging, Clem found that there was not a copy on the Coast, and from memory prepared a set as near in conformity with the National Rules of England as a good memory and a deep love of the sport could make them, under these rules the first regular coursing match in California was run near San Jose, Nov. 30, 1867, under the auspices of the Pioneer Coursing Club of California No. 1, James Adams President, Clem Dixon Secretary. The hunt took place at Hastings' Ranch near Bay Point in the presence of about forty spectators and the record of the match is as follows:

N. Curry's Harkaway beat C. L. Place's Golden.
N. Curry's Sweep beat C. L. Place's Nelly.
Clem Dixon's Voucher beat T. Bird's Bummer.
N. Curry's Fly beat Sam Tedow's Dash Jr.
Clem Dixon's Bonnie Doon beat T. C. Mack's Belle.
C. Harley's Yankee Jim beat J. Lang's Fanny.
James Adams' Fanny Grey beat C. L. Place's Prince.
Second Ties—Sweep beat Harkaway.
Voucher beat Fly.
Yankee Jim beat Bonnie Doon.
Fanny Grey ran a bye.
Third ties—Voucher beat Sweep.
Fanny Grey beat Yankee Jim.
Final Tie—James Adams' Fanny Grey beat Voucher and won the Challenge Collar.
The Battle Royal was won by N. Curry's Harkaway.
M. H. Kelly was judge of the match.

The next regular match was run at Pacheco, Contra Costa County, by the same club, the same dogs being engaged. In the final James Adams' Fanny Grey beat Clem Dixon's Voucher again and thus got possession of the Challenge Collar. The result of these two matches is a fair indication that James Adams at that time owned the best dogs in California, and then Clem Dixon for a time had to take the second place.

On November 20 and 21, 1868, a match was run at Suisun in which a puppy and old dog stake were contested. In the puppy stake the result was as follows:

James Adams' King Cob beat N. Curry's Sweep.
N. Curry's Harkaway beat C. L. Place's Jack
Sam Felton's Dash Jr. beat C. L. Place's Prince.
Robinson's Jennie Dean and T. H. Mark's Juno were both drawn.
S. Trumbull's California Lass ran a bye.
Second Ties—King Cob beat California Lass.
Dash Jr. beat Harkaway.

In the final tie James Adams' King Cob beat Dash Jr. and won the cup, thus making Adams winner of the first three regular matches ever run in the state.

The old old stake had to be postponed on account of rain. The next event of importance in the annals of coursing was the formation of the Sacramento Coursing Club on January 13, 1870. At the preliminary meeting in the Golden Eagle Hotel James W. Hawkins acted as Chairman and L. Wells as Secretary. The Club then extended a challenge to the Pioneer Club of San Francisco for twenty of its members to visit Sacramento and run a friendly match of five dogs from each club. In case the San Franciscans win all their bills of expenses to be paid by the Sacramento Club. In accordance with that agreement a match was run at Whitcomb's ranch, Sacramento, early in the spring.

San Francisco was represented by Dr. Sharkey's Molly, N. Curry's Harkaway, R. Warwick's Spring, J. Hardy's Tip, James Adams' Bamford, James Cue's Sport, John Scarlett's Fly and Clem Dixon's Belle of the Cottage.

Sacramento was represented by D. E. Callahan's Clay, J. Hawkins' Abe, J. Hawkins' Sweep, E. M. Skagg's Frank, J. Coulan's Gipsy, W. Richard's Black Nose, J. Hawkins' Queen and J. Hawkins' Prince. The dogs were paired off in the order named.

San Francisco won the two first races and the fifth, Sacramento won the third, fourth, sixth, seventh and eighth. There was much complaint at the decision of the judge. The Sacramento Club claimed the match by five wins to three. The San Franciscans demanded that the match be run off until only one dog was left, as is the regular rule of coursing matches. This was denied and the matter was never finally settled.

On Dec. 16, 1869, the Pioneer Club ran its third match, the match the year before having been put off on account of bad weather. The place selected was Pacheco. James Adams, N. Curry, M. H. Kelly, J. K. Orr, R. Warwick, E. T. Buckman, P. McCue, C. L. Place and Clem Dixon had dogs entered.

The match was won by M. H. Kelly's Irish Boy, the runner up being P. McCue's Sport. N. Curry's Sweep and R. Warwick's Spring divided the beaten dog stake. The puppy stake was won by W. Tagus's Fly, the runner up being Tom Tunstead's Jennie Grant.

The next match gotten up by the old Pioneer Club was run at Ellis Station, March 30, 1870. J. W. Walsh, judge, and Tom Tunstead, slipper. Clem Dixon's Belle of the Cottage won the match, the "runner up " being J. H. Lord's Lightfoot. Belle of the Cottage was imported from the North of England by Clem Dixon and was by Ingomar, a celebrated Waterloo Cup winner. In honor of the victory Charles Barr of San Jose gave a dinner to the participants in the match.

From this time out the Pioneer Club held matches regularly twice a year in places near San Francisco until the increase of plowed land forced them farther afield, and they were forced to visit Merced, which is not likely to be closed out against coursers for some years to come. Many new men came into the club and imported dogs from England, the representation being seen at the match held in Merced, Nov. 16, 1876, which for its great interest we give rather fully. Wilson Davidson acted as judge and Dominick Shannon as slipper. The first ties were as follows:

James Adams' Ruler beat W. Davidson's Sandy.
Dominick Shannon's Empress beat Jerome Deasy's Bally Kearns.
J. Searles' Lady Belle beat Tom Tunstead's Moll Pitcher.
N. Curry's Fly beat J. A. Colvin's Belfast Boy.
W. H. Orr's Ben Franklin beat William Nyan's Yellow Rammer.
C. L. Place's Minetta beat J. A. Colvin's Lady Coote.
D. W. White's Gentleman Jones beat J. Douglas Thornhill.
D. Shannon's Mutaleer beat D. W. White's Lady Jones.
N. Curry's "Stub and Twist" beat D. W. White's Souter Johnny.
J. Franklin's Lucy beat Charles Barr's Fleet.
J. Kyle's Belfast Maid beat J. A. Collin's Pedro.
C. L. Place's Blanche beat T. Tunstead's Ethan Allen.
Dr. Sharkey's Master Joe beat Charles Barr's San Jose Belle.

The match was won by Place's Blanche, the runner up being Dominick Shannon's Empress, King Cobb third, Thornhill fourth.

The Puppy Stake was won by Searle's Kitty Clover, the runner up being Mountain View Bell.

The next three matches in succession, the first prize was won by Tom Tunstead's Minnehaha, who was beaten in the fourth match by James Adams' Ruler.

The same year that this happened the Pacific Coast Coursing Club was organized, with Mark Devlin for President, Mr. Bryan for Secretary, Charles Rowe, Treasurer. This club is one of the most energetic and prosperous in the State to-day. The first match was run at Modesto, Judge Pennie's Jemima winning with Place's Blanche second and gone are often spoken of in terms of kindly remembrance by those whose dogs vied with theirs for supremacy in many a well-run course on the San Joaquin plains. Who of all the old coursemen of the Pioneer Coursing Club will ever forget Captain Place? He was an enthusiast in the sport and owned some good dogs, notably Gentleman Jones and Branch. He never failed to attend every coursing match that took place within 200 miles of San Francisco and though he often lost and generally growled a little at his luck, there was no malice in his heart nor sting in his words. He enjoyed the sport hugely. Standing high in his wagon, he would watch every turn and point the dogs made, and how the old man would yell when his dog gained an advantage." He went to a coursing match for fun and from the time he left the city until his return he was always awake and always devising some joke or bit of fun. The only one of his jokes not appreciated was his attempts to sing, for he had a most dismal voice and not the slightest idea of time or tune. One night at Point of Timbers Hotel on the eve of a private match between Monarch and Kitty Clover he kept the whole house awake for four hours while he was attempting to sing a song, the only line of which he knew was:

"Did you ever see a wild goose sailing o'er the ocean?"

This he kept repeating until finally Tunstead and others could bear it no longer and he was kindly but firmly suppressed.

Then there was Mr. Searles, a kindly modest gentleman, who won the heart of every man he met. He imported several dogs from England and was a valuable patron of the sport, sadly missed when he died.

Dave White, as he was familiarly called, is another of the

In the spring of 1881 the California Coursing Club was organized with Dr. Sharkey as President, J. Murphy as Secretary and J. Carroll as Treasurer. Their first match was held at Merced, November 15, 1881; J. C. Murphy was judge and T. T. Williams slipper. Carroll's Monarch took first prize, the runner up being A. Jackson's Stonewall Jackson. Merced Maid won the Puppy Stakes.

The last matches of this and the other clubs are too fresh to need recapitulation.

For the last two years the Pioneer Coursing Club has fallen behind owing to the loss of some members and the waning interest of others. Some have left the club because they lost a match and others are dead or have left the city. But we hear that an effort is about to be made to put Club No. 1 in the front rank once more and shoot a dozen well-to-do lovers of the sport are talking about joining the club. Such an infusion of new blood would do wonders and we must say that there is room for the old club and a howling demand for gentlemen who can attend a match, enjoy the sport and leave the field with good nature whether they win or lose. Writing of old coursing matches brings to our mind's eye the familiar figures of those who were past masters in the sport ere we were born and whose dogs and gone are often spoken of in terms of kindly remembrance.

old guard who have passed away. He was a thorough sportsman and a genial gentleman.

Poor old Philosopher Pickett, though not a coursing man in the true sense, sometimes attended the matches. He was remarkable for the good nature with which he could take a joke, and many a rough one was played on him. Once the boys cut the cinch of his horse, crossed the lines and tied his coat to the saddle, and had it not been for Tom Tunstead the old gentleman would have been seriously hurt. But he never complained nor did he "kick" at the end of the day when he had worn a device on his back announcing that he was blind. But we must not dwell too long on those who are gone and shortened space warns us to close, with the hope that the future of coursing in California may be as bright as we wish it, and to the extent of our good wishes there is no limit.

## RACING IN AUSTRALIA.

### Victoria Racing Club Spring Meeting—Cup Day—Tuesday, October 31.

When the racing began, and Belmont won the Maiden Plate with comparative ease from Calma, the backers of Mistaken felt truly cock-a-whoop, for it showed that the St. Albans stable was in good form. Then Boolka bowled over his field in the Railway Stakes, and the favorite Lady Jervois landed the Kensington Stakes with Halifax second, all three of the above having been boldly foretold by the *Sportsman*. But "a change had come over the spirit of the dream" as the time approached for the Melbourne Cup to be decided, and a bitterer, wetter, or more blusterous hour was never known on the Saltwater Flat than that during which the preparation and the running for the Great Annual Handicap took place. Calculations were upset; cumes sounded loud and deep; and not a contented visage could be selected among the assembled thousands. A detailed description of the parody of a contest we shall not attempt to give in this place. Suffice it to say that the Tasmanian-owned Stockwell made the pace, and his more immediate attendants from almost the commencement of the higgledy-piggledy fray were The Assyrian and Gudars. In such a pitiless storm blowing full in the face of horse and rider—and with the mud dying back from the leaders—it was almost hopeless to expect even the gamest of the racers to forge to the front; and therefore these three held their own throughout. Nearing home Stockwell had out-run himself, and The Assyrian therefore beat him in the final set-to, whilst Gudars finished a very fair third, followed by his stable mate Sweet William, the heavy-weighted Darebin, and the still more severely treated Segenhoe. The slow time of 3-40 sufficiently tells that the race was "all wrong." The Darling Stakes won by Essex, and the Van Izen Stakes by Stockwell's mate Bagot, concluded a miserable afternoon, although the clouds had cleared away soon after doing the irremediable mischief.

Melbourne Cup—A handicap sweepstakes of 20 sovs. each, 10ft., or 5 only if declared before 7th August, with 900 added. The handicap weight of the winner of the A. J. C. or V. R. C. Derby to be not less than 4st 12lb, and the winner of any handicap race of the value of 100 sovs., after the declaration of the weights, to carry 3 lb extra, of any such race of the value of 200 sovs., 5 lb extra; of any such race of the value of 300 sovs., 7 lb extra. Penalties not cumulative. The second horse to receive 300 sovs. and the third 100 sovs. out of the stake. Two miles. (136 subs.)

Mr. J. J. Saville's br h The Assyrian, 4 yrs., by Countryman—Tindate, 1116s (Hutchins) ........................................... 1
Mr. T. Reiby's ch h Stockwell, 4 yrs., by St. Albans—Edella, 108 lbs. ..................................................................... 2
Mr. F. de Mestre's br b Gudars, 4 yrs., 109 lbs. (Gaunsford) ....... 3
Twenty-two others ran unplaced.

Betting, 4 to 1 against Sweet William; 5 to 1, Mistaken; 6 to 1, Little Jack; 12 to 1, Odd Trick; 15 to 1, Stockwell; 16 to 1 each Sting, King of the Vale and Darebin; 16 to 1, Assyrian, 20 to 1 each Lord Lisgar, Sylvanus, Savanaka, Ounnamulla; 25 to 1, Pollio; 30 to 1 each Jessie, Gudars, Drummer; 40 to 1, Santa Claus; 50 to 1 each Lord Burghley, First Water; 100 to 1, Segenhoe.

Mr. George Watson did not dispatch the field until after a couple of attempts, the principal trouble at the post being Ounnamulla, who seemed full of bad temper and kicked viciously at any horse coming near him. Consequently he was ordered to the extreme outside, and when the flag fell the twenty-five starters appeared to get away on fair terms. Owing to heavy rain and high wind it was almost impossible to satisfactorily distinguish the commencement of the race, but Sting and Gudars were the first to be recognized, and after crossing the tan Flying Jib assumed command till past the stand, Stockwell, Gudars, Mistake, Santa Claus, Brunette, Segenhoe and Sweet William being the foremost of the main body. Savanaka, First Water and Drummer in the rear, Lord Burghley a long last. At the river bend Stockwell took up the running, Gudars, Flying Jib and Brunette next; then a cluster consisting of Mistaken, Sweet William, Assyrian, Darebin, Little Jack and Ounnamulla. Along the opposite side of the course Stockwell carried on his lead, Gudars and Assyrian chasing him at the sharp turn into the straight. Darebin, Little Jack and Ounnamulla. Along the opposite side of the course Stockwell carried on his lead, Gudars and Assyrian chasing him at the abattoirs, and Mistaken running so boldly into third place on approaching the scraping-sheds as to look most dangerous, but then suddenly tailing back as if losing his feet. Lord Lisgar's colors now showed amongst the leaders for a moment and then Darebin got near to Gudars, but Assyrian tackled him and shook him off. Approaching the important turn into the long run home, Stockwell looked very dangerous, having a commanding advantage. Assyrian, however, going grandly into his wake, and Gudars holding his own, though Darebin, Segenhoe and Sweet William each had a turn of being forward. Nearing home joined the front division in the straight, and at the distance post the race remained entirely between Stockwell and The Assyrian, the latter lasting the best he reached the winning chair two-thirds of a length in front without much trouble, Gudars finishing a tolerable third, Sweet William fourth, Darebin fifth, Segenhoe sixth, Sylvanus seventh and the stable companions, Pollio and Sting, last. Time, 3-40. Value of stakes, £1,710.

### Incidents and Coincidences.

"The Assyrian came down like a wolf on the fold.
And the backers last/lost being 'skinned' as of old."
—Byron (paraphrased).

According to common report no less than 50,000 people, with one simultaneous consent, quoted Byron's well-known lines within five minutes of the Cup upset through the Adelaide outsider; and, on the strength of the Rev. Rowland Hill's assertion that "the Devil has no right to the best tunes"—which opinion caused him to have many of the hymns at his famous Tabernacle sung to opera airs—the right is now claimed of paraphrasing the words so peculiarly adapted to the present article. Moreover, the play on the words as to "skinning the lamb"—an operation so dear to the bookmaking fraternity—is all our own, besides being muchly to the purpose. But to business. When deciding on the title of to-day's contribution to the leading columns, the original intent was to dwell at length on the many incidents and coincidences connected with the running of the time-honored Melbourne Cup; but severe pressure on the

*Sportsman's* space, added to more than a suspicion that readers prefer "good goods dense up in small parcels," has caused us to give instead a terse but highly interesting resume of several noteworthy facts connected with the history of this important handicap. There have been 22 Cups run, the first having been in the year 1861; and the proportion into which they have been divided amongst the several colonies is 11 (exactly one-half) for New South Wales, 10 for Victoria, and one (that is just over) for South Australia. This calculation, however, refers only to the ownership of the winner, and if the breeding-place of the horses be taken into account (as it justly might) the sister colonies are each entitled to another unit, for Warrior hailed from Sydney, and Adelaide claimed the honor of Don Juan's nativity. Strange to say, also, each of these animals made the fortunes of the metallicians who "went a perisher" on their chances, viz., Mr. Austin Saqui the one, and Mr. Jos Thompson the other. The relative figures would therefore be, in respect to equine merits, 12 for New South Wales, 8 for Victoria, and 2 for South Australia. Those persons, then, who set down the Assyrian's win as the first credited to our Southern neighbors, are scarcely correct in the assertion; nor does the Northern colony receive in due honor unless a round dozen triumphs are placed on its roll of turf fame.

The intuitive politeness of the French nation teaches them to render *place aux dames* as an invariable rule, and the duty of racing scribes is to so far follow this polite regulation as to give the *pas* to the noble home when discussing such matters as the present, and then pass on to the owner. Preceding then from quadrupeds to bipeds we find that Mr. De Mestre has trained five winners, viz., Archer twice, and then Tim Whiffler, Chester and Calamia. Both times that Archer came in first it is a singular fact that Mr. F. Keighran's Mormon finished second; and it is also strange that the same gentleman should subsequently have run second and third with Exile in successive years. Mr. John Tait—"honest John" of the popular yellow jacket and black cap—ranks next to the "black and all black" of the Terrara squire, having had four firsts at Flemington with Barb, Glencoe, Pearl and Quack. Mr. James Wilson, despite the number of times he has contested the Cup, and the many justifiable favorites he has brought to the post, only counts two successes in Don Juan and Briseis. On the other hand, no trainer or owner ever had the series of ill luck which has attended him of St. Albans, no less than six disappointing seconds having been hoisted on the signal boards—to wit, Musidora, leading (who lost by half a head in Nimbletoot's year after slipping his round-horse at the turn home), Romula, Protos, Savanaka, and Progress. It is well known, moreover, to those "behind the scenes," that Melita and Duchess were "morals" but for female reasons; and that the highly tried Mistaken could hardly have lost last Tuesday had the ground been dry. This truthful and unprejudiced statement shows that Mr. Wilson had he not met with an extra-average of contretemps, might have scored exactly one-half of the past Cups. As a salve for these failures it may be mentioned that Briseis, with whom he pulled off the double Derby and Cup in the sensational Newminster season, was out of his favorite mare Musidora, who ran second in 1863, and thus time "worked the revenge." No older owner ever won more than once.

Outsiders only upset the favorites on five occasions, the nags to thus do the ring a turn being Toryboy, Pearl, Darriwell, Zulu and The Assyrian, the latter time being the slowest of any except Toryboy.

But one mare has ever been returned victrix, this being Mr. Wilson's beautiful Briseis, bred by himself. Musidora and Exile of Denmark, however, ran second and third to Banker, Queen of Hearts second to Tim Whiffler, Romula second to Pearl, and Sybil second to Briseis home.

Coming again to biped records we find that only two jockeys have had the winning mounts twice, Johnny Cutts having steered Archer on each occasion, whilst Piper had the double honor of Haricot and Chester. Among the erstwhile light weights who have figured in the pigskin for Melbourne, but have now attained the position of able and respectable trainers, may be named Morrison, Chifney, T. Brown, Piggot and Batty.

Finally, it is deserving of note, as proving how utterly all calculations in favor of our Victorian representatives for the cup were upset by the terrible weather last Tuesday, that the first horse was an Adelaidian, the second a Tasmanian, and the third, fourth and fifth New South Wales. In a future article on the recent V. R. C. Meeting we may relate other "incidents and coincidences" of similar import.—*The Sportsman, Melbourne, Australia.*

A Vermont farmer says: "Cows giving milk and growing stock require some variation in the quality of the food. Contrary to the belief of some, roots should not be fed with straw or poor hay, as they are too much alike in composition. Feed the roots with clover or good hay, and give the more concentrated food with the straw. It requires more skill to be successful in feeding poor than rich kinds of food. Corn fodder may be made more palatable for stock by being preserved in a silo, but hardly is added to the nutritive qualities. Sheep require a greater proportion of food according to weight than cattle, as also will the smaller animals, as there is the greatest loss of heat in the last. Corn meal and wheat bran mixed for the production of milk will be better than either alone. Horses weighing 1,000 pounds require twenty-two pounds of good hay per day. Too much of hay and too little of concentrated food is given to horses. Would advise feeding clover hay to sheep, good hay to cows and hay and grain to horses. Good corn fodder, well cured, are about equal to hay for milch cows. If grain is needed would feed cotton-seed meal or bran, or both mixed. Would not advise feeding much grain to cows when dry. Properly fed, apples make a good food for cows, say about one-half bushel each day at first."

In some parts of Spain, where butter is a rare article of merchandise, it is sold not by the pound but by the yard. It is brought from the mountain district in sheep's intestines, like sausages that are "tied off" with strings in lengths as required by the buyer. To travelers butter by the inch seems rather curious bargaining; the produce is usually neither palatable nor particularly clean.

A cross of the Jersey with the Ayrshire should make a desirable cow for ordinary farm purposes. The Ayrshire has more size than the Jersey, gives a larger flow of milk and the addition of Jersey blood will create a disposition to rich cream and gilt-edged butter.—*Cultivator.*

The competition in beef has forced Eastern butchers to build large cold-storage houses at various points in New England and New York, so that they can furnish to their customers a superior article and at a price not higher than the Chicago-dressed beef.

The Minneapolis *Tribune* says that goats are the best land cleaners known. It mentions that a herd of 1,000 entirely cleared a piece of brush land consisting of 500 acres in three years. So complete was the work that not a vestige of undergrowth was left.

## THE GUN.

### Gunning Along the Sacramento.

A correspondent of *Forest and Stream*, in a letter to that journal from Sacramento, says:

On my way I had to pass around the outskirts of a strip of young timber, principally sycamores, willows and cottonwoods, and in so doing surprised myself by blundering right into a covey of quails, which immediately took a bee line into the air and settled themselves among the topmost branches of the tallest sycamores. (I stopped one of the towerers, however, before he got there.) Failing to get the birds out I went on, and after emerging from the brush (this was only a mile and a half from a city of 25,000 inhabitants) found another covey out in the short grass. Being between them and their favorite hiding place, and knowing their habits quite well, I fired a shot at once to make them scatter and hide in the grass, which they did. This was very near the edge of a slough along the edge of which was a thin fringe of high tule, or flags, which hid the water from my view, and I did not know that there were ducks there. But there were, and of course they took wing, but did not get out of range before I brought down a couple of fine, plump bluebills with my left barrel, which was loaded with only No. 8 shot. Then I went after the quail, and before they got back to the brush I had bagged six of them. The afternoon was bright and the ducks scarce, so I went to another slough which is lined with springy, boggy banks, where I had often found English snipe, and they were there then. Having a fair supply of No. 9 cartridges with me, I went for the long-billed fellows, and by the time the sun had begun to gild with its gorgeous crimson and golden hues the neighboring snow-clad summits of the Sierras, I found I had thirteen big, fat snipe, seven quail, two ducks and a cottontail.

This was pretty good for a short afternoon's hunt but I was not quite satisfied. I believed there would be a fair flight of ducks in the evening from the marshes that lay a few miles to the west, so I waited by one of the sloughs until the great oak trees cast broad and forbidding shadows over the plains; and then, just as I began to grow chilly and disappointed, the dusky fowls put in an appearance. First came the teal, skimming low above the ground in their swift, erratic flight, and I had to empty a great many shells at the little fellows to get half a dozen of them. Soon the widgeon came along in big flocks, but too high, and, occasionally a pair of mallards for a choice place to feed, while above them all I could occasionally hear the rushing noise made by a big body of canvas backs, but could not get a chance at them, as they knew where they were going, and it was to some place other than shallow sloughs. It soon became too dark to see the teal, which I knew must have come within ten or fifteen yards of me, and I set out for town, which I reached in half an hour. My bag counted, when I reached home, four mallards and seven teal, besides the two other ducks, seven quails, thirteen snipe and a rabbit before mentioned. I thought that a pretty successful four hours' shoot, within almost gunshot of a city that turns out every week about as many game-guns as any place of its size in the Union. This illustrates the variety of sport that is to be had in many parts of this State.

### From the Hunting Grounds.

Up the river the hunting is very poor; in fact it has nearly come to a stand still. Though a few fair bags have recently been made at the Teal Station preserve the general report is that the best sport is over. The ducks have nearly all deserted the ponds and they now spend the most of their time out on the bay and rivers, or else in following flocks of geese around over the bald marshes. These geese it is said dig and tear up the soft ground like so many hogs and the ducks following close get the benefit of the others' labor. As these bald marshes are open the hunters have great difficulty in getting near enough to the game to warrant shooting. The best hunting around the marshes is by sculling around in the sloughs and shooting stray birds as they rise. There has been considerable hunting done by moonlight by the hunters from the towns in the vicinity of the preserves and this too has driven away a great deal of the game, as nothing will frighten water fowls from a locality quicker than the flash of guns on dark or moonlight nights. The sprig, mallard and teal that come in from up the river, are in rather poor condition, though the cans are said to be fat and palatable.

From the other direction the case is altogether different, sportsmen going to Alviso and Alvarado return generally well laden with game and all in good condition. If the hunters could be content overcold weather how long the game would last, but every Sunday the numbers do not decrease, nor does the size of the game bags of the hunters as they return in the evening.

From along the line of the narrow gauge railroad the hunting has given out.

SIDE HUNTS.—The valuation of game adopted by the Gulf City Gun Club, Mobile, Ala., for their annual hunt, held Nov., 19 and 20, was as follows: Bear 500, wildcat 150, deer—buck 125, doe 100; fox 100, rabbit 12, squirrel 7, goose 75, turkey—gobbler 60, hen 50, chicken hawk 25, owl 20, sparrow hawk 10, woodcock 20, quail 7, wild-pigeon 10, Wilson's snipe 5, plover 5, papabot 10, dove 4, robin 1, lark 1, rail 1, poule d'eau 1, king rail 2, gallinule 2, ducks—canvas back 25, black mallard 20, mallard 10, chick cock 3, pintail 8, widgeon 8, redhead 3, teal 5, all other ducks 5.

A gentleman who has been traveling in the valley to the west of Oroville says that there is an abundance of wild ducks—mostly mallards—all along the line of the Spring Valley debris canal. East of the canal there were a great many Canada geese—honkers; while on the west side there were millions of white and gray braadt.

Messrs. C. D. Ladd, E. H. Ladd, Mr. Brown and Mr. Gould were at the Alvarado marshes and got the best bag that has been made lately. Though they worked hard they were rewarded by obtaining eighty ducks, fifteen snipe rail and fifteen plover. There were but few hunters on the marshes.

Last Sunday Messrs. Stack, Spencer and Hoefling killed 145 ducks on the Alviso marshes. Thirty of these birds were canvasbacks. It is a rare occurrence for so many cans to be flying down in that vicinity.

Gun-making is one of the foremost industries in Syracuse, N. Y. The sales of guns manufactured there during the past year are said to have been $200,000, based on a capital of only $95,000.—*Rev.*

We are sorry to hear that Mr. R. N. Brooks, a member of the Cosmopolitan Club and an enthusiastic hunter, is very sick just now, but we hope he will speedily recover.

## Wild Fowl Shooting.

It must be said that the shooting for water fowl has not been this year what it formerly was. The absence of birds is not noticeable in one locality alone but in many. No doubt the gradual increase of population and the settling up of localities near the former feeding grounds of the birds has much to do with it. Then again the mud hens and the white geese are in a sense "preserved" as no one cares to shoot them much, and they thrive and increase, while a war of extermination is carried on against the ducks. And the mud hens get away with a good deal of feed.

At none of the usual sporting grounds has there been as good shooting as there used to be. In the Suisun marshes, where there are several preserves of shooting clubs, the sport has been so poor that the shooters are discouraged. They attribute the scarcity of game to the presence of the railroad. Of course ducks do not take kindly to the railway cars but this is not alone the cause. It is more probably because the tule islands, many of them, remain overflowed and the birds go to the ponds upon them in preference to remaining on the salt marshes. At all events the shooting is not good nor has it been this season.

Several of the tule islands have been in a measure preserved; that is portions of them that were accessible have been looked after by shooting clubs.

A feature of this wild fowl shooting of late in this State has been the formation of clubs and the preservation of grounds for the exclusive use of the members. A few years ago no such thing was heard of in California. Now, however, if men fond of wild fowl shooting want to be insured good sport they must not only preserve the grounds but sow seed and bait the ponds. This is all very well for the shooter with money but it is rather rough on the one who has not. Still if the grounds were not here and there preserved we should be in a little while without any place at all to shoot ducks.

All the available parts of the Suisun marshes are preserved and several of the tule islands like Sherman Island are preserved in such parts as are readily accessible. There are several places kept by preserves along the shore of the bay and the Alviso and Petaluma Creek grounds will soon be kept apart in the same way.

It strikes us that the heavy bags which used to be taken by shooters will never be so frequent as of yore, and people will have to be satisfied that they have had a good day's shoot if they kill half what they used to. Still if more and more ground is set apart as preserves, it may be that in a season or so the birds will become more numerous.

## A Christmas Ghost.

Last Monday morning two hunters came in from the Alvarado marshes on the early train. From their general appearance one would judge that something was wrong. Their faces wore a deadly milk-and-water look and their hair had not the usual smooth lay. On a promise of the closest secrecy the writer found out the cause of their disturbance. "We saw a ghost on the marshes last night," said hunter No. 1, with a shudder. "Yes, a real ghost," echoed No. 2 and the blonde of the first and the black hair of the second speaker assumed a perpendicular position as the thought called to mind their night's experience. Said No. 1: "We were hunting by moonlight on the marshes and had had pretty fine luck till half past eleven when the ducks began flying very high and seemed very much disturbed. As we were sitting behind our blind at about twelve o'clock we saw out on the marshes a white object that every now and then threw up its white arms in a threatening manner. Slowly and with a gliding even motion it circled around us two or three times. We were both much scared and did not think of either calling out or shooting at the apparation; but at last on the end of my hair which stood out straight, while my companion went on his knees in the mud and started in something like 'Now I lay me down to sleep,' when he suddenly broke off with 'D——h, its nothing but a white crane; what a pair of fools we are!' The explanation was sufficient but we afterwards pulled at a suspicious, ugly looking black bottle to steady our nerves." "Some low or other," said No. 1, stroking his blonde head, "my hair does'nt stay down smooth this morning." "Yes," said hunter No. 2 as he pulled at his raven mustache, "some how or other though the ducks did fly well after that we could'nt seem to hit any. It does'nt take much to upset a man. What will you have? For gracious sake don't give this away." We promised we would not, but the ashy-hued lips and the mud on the one's knees convinced us that they both had been scared.

The is good sport "sailing for mallards" in the sloughs now-a-days, but is is hard work on the wrists to keep a duck-boat moving all day with one oar. The mallards are "jumpers up" at the bends and turns of the sloughs in twos and threes, and a quick shot will have very good sport. It is much warmer work than getting in a blind before daylight waiting for birds to fly in.

The Lolita, the yacht the Cordelia Shooting Club have had at their preserves in Suisun marsh all winter, will be brought down on January 16, the contract being up then. The shooting is now so poor that it is not probable the club will do any more shooting there after the date mentioned this season.

There was but little hunting done on Christmas, as most of the boys preferred to stay at home and shoot champagne corks with their friends rather than to wade around in a cold marsh after ducks.

Mr. Jas. Payne and W. W. Traylor recently bagged fifty-eight ducks at the Teal Station preserve, Mr. Crittenden Robinson killed thirty ducks at the same place.

Mr. Whipple and his brother from Dakota shot thirty-five ducks and quite a number of snipe on the Alvarado marshes last Sunday.

Hunters who have been up along the line of the narrow gauge railroad of late have come home "skunked."

There are a great many hunters going to the Alviso and Alvarado marshes for a New Year's shooting.

The other day Mr. W. W. Traylor killed 55 ducks at the Teal Station preserve.

Charlie Dalle recently brought home 25 ducks from his hunting Sherman Island.

Mr. Autl was down at the Bridges last Sunday, and killed 24 ducks.

James Payne is going to start a preserve at the Petaluma marshes for next season. This is a place easy of access and where there might be good sport. Petaluma is the Indian dialect means "duck kill." There used to be more ducks about there than anywhere else on the

Up at Suisun the other day Ben Stickney killed 16 geese with two barrels, No. 8 shot. He crawled up on the birds and let them have both barrels. This is a goose yarn we have the papers for since Ben brought in the geese.

Two good shots tried the marsh lands last. Sunday down near San Mateo. One shot a mallard and the other got two "mud-larks." They haven't said much about their "string."

More "cans" have been shot on Grand Island than anywhere else this season. But there have been lots of hunters up there.

There are lots of geese and small ducks in the Suisun marshes just now, but very few "cans" or mallards.

James Payne is no longer connected with the Teal Shooting Club, his contract with them expiring this month.

There are quantities of coots and other poor ducks in the lower bays just now.

A good many hunters find sport on the Alvarado marshes every Sunday.

Mr. Tristan Burges of San Francisco has lost by death his Champion Llewellin setter bitch, Queen Mab, from blood-poisoning, the result of whelping. Champion Queen Mab was bred and trained by R. Ll. P. Llewellin, Ashby de la Zouch, England; imported by Arnold Burges, Hillsdale, Michigan. Whelped August 24, 1874; by the celebrated Dan out of Nelly. Registered No. 8223, English Kennel Club Stud Book. Registered No. 495, National American Kennel Club Stud Book.

Winner of the following prizes:

First and champion, Chicago, 1876.

First and champion, and special for Best Brace, with Druid, St. Louis, 1878.

First and champion, and special for Best Brace, with Druid, Detroit, 1879.

First and champion, and special for Best Brace, with Druid, St. Louis, 1879.

First and champion, New York, 1880.

First in class, and special for 'most perfect specimen of dog or bitch in show," San Francisco, 1881.

## Answers to Correspondents.

EDITOR BREEDER AND SPORTSMAN: Which horse was the sire of Lodi, owned by the late Nathan Coombs of Napa, and what horse was the sire of Monday?    ARIZONA.

Answer—The sire of Lodi was imported Yorkshire. The sire of Monday was Colton. Lodi and Colton were from the same mare, Topaz by imported Glencoe, Colton being by Lexington.

## CORRESPONDENCE.

### New South Wales Sporting News.

SYDNEY, Nov. 27, 1882.

TO THE EDITOR OF THE BREEDER AND SPORTSMAN: In my last letter to you I left off in the midst of the spring carnival held on Flemington racecourse, Victoria, and therein was contained an account of the cup contest. The third day, Nov. 2, commenced enjoyably, indeed it is rarely that Oaks Day, for such is the third day termed, meets with rather than "Queen's weather," while the attendance numbered about 4,000. The ball was set rolling with a hurdle race for which eleven saddled up. The value of the prize was $1,110; distance about three miles. Betting, 2 to 1 against Lord or Clyde, who never gained a situation, 7 to 1 against Lothair, 8 to 1 against Basilisto and Sportsman. Mr. Huvie's b h Lothair by Epigram from Legend won easily by two lengths, carrying 168lbs, completing the journey in 5.44. The same horse as a three-year-old ran fourth in the Melbourne Cup, won by Grand Flaneur, and has won several good hurdle races of late. In the weight-for-age races, considerable discussion had taken place relative to the merits of Darebin and Commotion; I have always maintained that the latter, a son of Panic, was the better over a mile and a half, and this belief has been fully indorsed by the meetings in the Canterbury Plate, in the fourth place. In the Royal Park Stakes of two miles, weight-for-age, Darebin won by a dozen lengths from Lord Burghley. The disappointed, Maribyrnong Plate. Kingsdale recouped his owner by winning the Flying Handicap from St. Lawrence. The Spring Handicap of one mile and a quarter fell to the North Australian colt, Standard Bearer, by Greywagle, beating Lesbia and The Czar. The race was a magnificent one, and fought out from the distance, eventuating in a head win, half a length between second and third. The principal event of the day, "the Oaks." The prize is a sweep of $125 each, $25 forfeit, with $1,500; for three-year-old fillies, 8 st. 10lbs, one mile and a half (61 subs). The winner turned out in Mr. F. Wentworth's b f Vancluse, by Rapid Bay—Chrysolite, while Mr. E. De Mestre's filly Solitude, who had remained the winter favorite, was easily defeated. This is to be accounted for by Eva, who ran third, taking up the running at such a cracking pace and the favorite taking up the allowing; Vancluse, a long lead was never able to get on anything like terms. The day was concluded by the Veteran Stakes, of one mile and a half. Here Commotion, with the heavy impost of 131lbs, beat the cup winner, Assyrian, 126 lbs, by three lengths, the time occupying 2.38½. In this race very good proof was given of Assyrian's merits and his second to Commotion goes a long way to prove that winning the Melbourne Cup was no fluke.

Fourth day, Saturday, Nov. 4—The last day proved perhaps the most enjoyable of the four, while the ladies turned out en masse with very choice and handsome spring toilets as if it were to make amends for the "Cup day," which with the moistness of the elements gave their handsome costumes a hue and tinge never dreamt of by the fair wearers. The scene on the

lawn surpassed anything seen during the previous three days. The racing opened with the Flemington Stakes, for which 25 horses sported silk. The race was for two-year-olds and fell to the Hon. Jas. White's br colt, Middlemarch, by Maribyrnong—Housemaid, followed home by D. S. Wallace's gr f Duranna, by Lecturer. In the race it shows how disappointing private trials are as Middlemarch in the Maribyrnong Plate of five furlongs, the similar distance, was unable to obtain a place in 1.04½ while he won the race easily in three lengths in 1.03½. Segenhoe, the great winter favorite for the V. R. C. Derby, again disappointed his stable. In the Mares' Produce Stakes, one mile and a quarter, Mr. D. S. Wallace's colt Galen, three years, by Yattendon from London Pride, defeated Boolka and Segenhoe by a length, the latter pair running a dead heat for second honors, time, 2.11½. The V. R. C. Handicap of one mile and a quarter produced one of the best and most exciting finishes of the reunion between Mr. E. De Mestre's br h Gudara, by Yattendon, carrying 110 lbs., Wm. Forrester's blk h Gipsy Cooper, 108 lbs, T. Ivory's br h Lord Burghley, 116lbs. A considerable amount of speculation ensued over this race from the fact that a number of disappointed Cup horses took part in the race which resulted in a short half length won for Gudara from Gipsy Cooper, the time occupied in running the journey was fast, 3.06. Quite a surprise was in store for backers in the steeplechase; Corrigan had the mount on Left Bower, who was weighted at 162lbs and was supposed to possess one of his usual "good things," but the heavy impost told its tale at the finish, and the outsider Kanaka, 136lbs, won by a length from Sailor, 140 lbs; time 6.51½. Considerable interest was manifested by the different admirers of Commotion, Darebin, and The Assyrian meeting at weight-for-age in the Canterbury Plate, distance two and one-quarter miles. Betting, 6 to 4 on Darebin, 7 tos against Commotion, 6 to 1 against the other. The favorites made the pace very merry and before a mile and a half had been covered Commotion took up the running and appeared from the pace he was going to make "every post a winning post." He led into the homestretch by three lengths and maintained the advantage to the end; Darebin second and Sweet William third. Time 4.00½. Each horse carried 126 lbs. The Free Handicap, one mile and a half, brought to a close one of the best meetings held on Flemington, and one which has fully illustrated the glorious uncertainty attached to racing. An outsider was "served up" for the "Free" in Plunger, starting at 3 to 1 against him, with large sums invested on him the night before the race and during the day, must have won for his party, about $30,000. The New South Wales horses secured the largest amount of prize money, for of the total £12,534 paid away; Messrs. De Mestre, Coy, Wentworth, Stewart and White received no less than £6,287. The largest winner was Mr. E. De Mestre, who received £1,205 as first money in the Derby, his total being £1,879. The Hon. E. K. Cox comes next with £1,785 for the win of Navine in the Maribyrnong Plate. Mr. J. E. Saville took £1,715, comprising £1,710 for the Melbourne Cup, and £5 as second in the Veteran Stakes. Amongst the other winners were Mr. R. Howie as first in the Steeple and Hurdle events, £310; Mr. E. Wentworth, £760; Mr. W. Pearson, £711; Mr. D. S. Wallace, £605; Mr. J. H. Hill, £495; Mr. J. Stewart, £478; Mr. F. F. Dakin, £445; Mr. W. Branch, £424; the Hon. E. Reiby, £420; the Hon. J. White, £385; Mr. F. Jordan, £346; Mr. J. Paterson, £333, and Mr. J. Redfearn, £350.

The Queensland Turf Club held a two days' gathering commencing on Nov. 6. Goldfinder won the Derby and Mares' Produce Stakes, while Czar won the principal handicap.

On the same date the Parramatta Jockey Club held a two days' meeting. Willow and Eva winning the principal races. Since the above the only meeting of any importance has been the Murrumbridge Turf Club spring meeting, held on the banks of the Murrumbridge river. The spot is better known as Wagga Wagga, famous for the Tichborne claimant. The meeting was rather protracted, extending over four days, and coming so quickly after the V. R. C. Spring carnivals proves too much for horse-owners and visitors, consequently they obtain but a few second-class animals to compete, mixed up with the second country platers. The Wagga Cup fell to Mr. W. R. Hall's br h Connamulla, by Maribyrnong, carrying 126 lbs. Willow, 114 lbs., second on what not Gipsy Cooper, 114 lbs., ran off at the home turn, a much better race would have resulted. Guineas and Gipsy Cooper were each 4t to 1 in the betting but both failed to gain a situation. Jessie won the Maiden Plate, and Eva, whose chance was greatly fancied for the Cup, won the Grand Stand Handicap in good style. St. Lawrence, by imported Glorious, won with consummate ease both the Sires' and Mares' Produce Stakes.

The events set down for decision during our summer months are the Summer Cup, run for under the auspices of the A. J. C., and the Tattersalls Club Cup, with $1,000 added money.

Trotting does not make any strides in New South Wales; the horse owners appear to possess a decided antipathy to it; not so in Victoria, but even there it has been found advisable to keep up the track, and likewise defray expenses, to introduce running races.

Yachting is in full swing and the harbor presents quite a picture with its numerous craft scudding along before the breeze. Poor Ned Trickett appears to have lost all rowing powers, and last week suffered an easy defeat over the Parramatta river, from Clifford, a sculler from the southern district.

There has been a great deal of talk about a match between M. Rush and Laycock for $1,000. The former wishes to pull on the Clarence river where he resides, while Elias wants it on the Parramatta river, but I fancy Laycock will accede to his request and should beat him.

The cricketing world is all astir just now, through the arrival of the Hon. Ivo Bligh's team of cricketers. They have met with an excellent acceptance; so have the Australians, banquets and torchlight processions being the order of the day. So far the Englishmen have won and had drawn in their favor the three matches played by them. Our team is a strong batting one, but weak in the bowling element.

To-day being our general election day (the Government having dissolved), I am exceedingly busy and must close my letter sooner than otherwise.

SYDNEY, Nov. 24, 1882.

MR. SIMPSON, Dear Sir: We arrived in Sydney on the 19th. We had a very pleasant trip and Honesty came through in the best possible shape.

The people here think he is a very fine horse. De Weir came over from Melbourne yesterday. He seemed very much pleased to see us, and to find Honesty looking so well. We will go on to Melbourne with him to-morrow night. We are going to-night but the Doctor said if we would wait till tomorrow night he would go with us.

Hoping to be back to California in two or three months we remain yours respectfully,
W. H. PAREZE,
J. H. WHITING.

**The Breeder and Sportsman.**

## New York Letter.

NEW YORK, Dec. 20, 1882.

EDITOR BREEDER AND SPORTSMAN: Last week's defeat of Albion's champion amateur runner was somewhat of a surprise to athletic circles hereabouts, for since George's successive victorie over Myers, and his stamina and ability to go on, his late valedictory exhibition at Madison Square garden was regarded by the general public in the light of a comparative "walk over," especially when he is credited with the best on record at the distance, ten miles, in 52:56 2-5, made at Lillie Bridge, England. Then the large field that started against him on this occasion number but few runners known to fame, only three or four being thought of any special account, and the handicappers evidently considered that most of them would be coming back long before the end of the trip, judging by the start that George was required to give each opponent, varying from three to fifteen minutes. When it is considered that each minute represents about 300 yards actual distance, one readily sees what a herculean task was set the young Englishman should his opponents turn out to be anything above the grade of mediocrity. But the betting (what little there was) foreshadowed the presumed easy task of the scratch man, it being three to one on him against the field. George evidently must have taken this view of the case himself, for his form was not as good as shown in his races at the Polo grounds, and he had evidently been indulged a trifle, though his party made no excuse for him on the score of condition. Some runners, however, prefer competing in the open air to racing in a closed building where the atmosphere becomes of necessity more or less vitiated from tobacco smoke and natural causes, even on a winter night such as this one was. What is "sauce for the goose, however, is sauce for the gander," and the writer does not wish to be understood as attempting to belittle the victory of young Delaney, who, though only about twenty years of age, went off like a hero and, never faltering from the word go, outstayed in the gamiest possible manner his doughty opponent, beating him nearly a sixth of a mile, exclusive of his time allowance. Delaney ran the last lap of the race like a scared deer, showing much better stamina than George, who must have been a trifle off on this occasion, his present performance being such a long ways behind his best record at the distance. But among the 3,000 or 4,000 spectators who witnessed Delaney's fine showing, few would have been found that evening to dissent from the popular verdict, that the victor can get away with his noted opponent again, and in much faster time than he showed, for Delaney ran within himself the whole journey, the last part at a sprinting pace. George sailed for home by the Servia the next morning. His intentions are, it is said, to become a member of the medical profession, although if Myers or Delaney go to England next year they will probably find him ready to accommodate them.

Last Friday evening a special train left the Pennsylvania Railroad depot at Jersey City, with the Brighton Beach contingent of men and horses en route for New Orleans. The first day's racing under the new regime is Saturday next, the 23d; and the results of the several contests on that day will have been wired to your coast before this letter reaches its destination. Likely enough the Crescent City will be exceedingly lively this winter, for besides Engeman's racing venture, the Louisianians, Creoles and representatives from every nation of the globe which comprise the mixed population will have Hanlan and other oarsmen in a projected regatta, the great "chicken dispute" of the National Gamecock Breeders Association early in February and the usual Mardigras festivities, which of themselves always attract immense crowds of visitors from all parts of the country.

But in view of this new racing enterprise and the extended programmes already issued for the early spring meetings at Memphis, Nashville, Lexington, Louisville, Cincinnati, Covington, St. Louis, Chicago, etc., in addition to those at Washington, Baltimore, and the regular Eastern racing circuit, the question of the hour is "where are all the horses to come from?" At most of the later meetings of 1882, with perhaps the exception of that at Sheepshead Bay, small fields were the rule rather than the exception, and when this gets to be the case the public interest quickly falls off, for the great mass of race-goers do not care to see races with only three or four contestants. It seems to be the prevalent opinion that in view of this probable scarcity of racing material for 1883, the racing associations named above, who have, most of them, added rather extravagantly large sums to their several stakes and purses, will, some of them, get badly left, as far as any profit is concerned, and no one accuses them of racing for fun! Unless there are more young horses in training than was the case this year the sequel is almost sure to be as outlined, for the number of races run in 1882 was greatly in excess of 1881, and 1883, with the several new Rockaway, Latonia, and other associations added to the field, must certainly very largely increase these totals. Some persons, however, think that race-horses are made of iron instead of only bone and sinew, and such generally come to grief before they find out the truth. The new Latonia Jockey Club, or rather Agricultural Association of Forkopolis, has adopted the novel and pleasing feature of giving to their stakes now open the names of celebrated racers, and on their list of fixtures to be run for this spring, at their new track at Covington, Ky., directly opposite Cincinnati, we find the Hindoo, Sensation, Himyar, Ripple, Clipsetta, Harold, Gildelia Stakes, etc., following the clever precedent of the Saratoga Association last summer, when they opened two events for 1884, called the Foxhall and Iroquois Stakes respectively. This is a good idea, tending to perpetuate the memory of famous animals long after accident or death has removed them from the racing arena, and old Parole, Checkmate, Bend Or, Blackburn and Ferida, Girofle, Glenmore and other noted good ones at all distances should, and doubtless will, also have their turn. Racing stallions seem to be a drug in the market just now. Tom Bowling, Vistor, Narragansett, and other sires of winners and first-class racers themselves go begging for want of purchasers. Only this week Catoctin, by Vauxhall—Weatherbell, a fine three-year-old performer in 1881, running Hindoo to a length and a half for the Travers Stake in very fast time at high weights, was sold at auction for next to no price at all, when his breeding, size and speed is considered. But Rayon D'Or, Sensation, Hindoo, Falsetto and other untried sires, together with the three Kentuckians, Ten Broeck, Great Tom and King Ban, whose get first appeared this year, and with such great success, command, with Virgil, Glenelg, Billet, the Illused, Catesby, Lever, Wanderer, Monarchist, Alarm, King Ernest, and others of the old guard, almost the exclusive attention of horsemen.

Capt. Conner's game mare Glidelia, the victress in so many great races, and as true a bit of horseflesh as ever was seen, will be bred to Rayon D'Or. The produce should race "by a large majority," at the Hon. Bardwell Slote, M. F., would say. The December meeting of the South Carolina Jockey Club was held last week at Charleston and four days' racing was had, lifted of interest being developed, however, and the meeting was financially or from a racing point of view. From over the water comes news of the dispersion of a great English stud on New Year Day, when the great Isonomy and others will be sold to the highest bidder.

Then a cable dispatch of yesterday brought the information of the rumors afloat for some time regarding the future connection of Mr. Keene's Day, the famous trainer, with stable in England. The previous reports were generally discredited in this city, as few thought that one who had done as well as Day, with the material he has had at hand, and who has been instrumental in winning so many honors for his patron and this country would be thrown overboard because he did not repeat in 1882 the great victories of the previous year. Why, there are owners of horses in England now who have grown gray in the pursuit of turf honors, and have yet to attain even in a single season a tithe of the successes of the white and blue spots, last year. The American stakes in England have surely won too much honor and profit on the English turf lately to bring on themselves ridicule at this late day.

R. Marsh is now the mentor of Foxhall and his stable companions, and we shall see the coming season what he can do with them.

Tom Cannon reports the Lorillard stables as doing well in the main and there are great hopes that the cherry and black will in 1883 duplicate some of the victories of 1881.

Iroquois is said to be still sound, all reports to the contrary notwithstanding, and he may win some more races yet the coming season.

Ex. Gov. Stanford is still culling some of the choicest blooded stock for his unequaled stud farm at Palo Alto. A lot recently purchased from C. S. Green's place at Babylon include Lutie (2:18), May Queen (2:20), Mattie (2:20½), and Gazalle (2:21), a very select coterie of stud matrons, indeed. And while on this subject we look for some entries in Eastern stakes this spring from the Stanford stable. The filly by Lever—Precious must be a good one and one doubtless more than pay her way East the coming year, and Palo Alto has others perhaps as good as on your horses, Messrs. Baldwin, Winters, Stanford, etc., and you shall have a fair field and no favor. Yours, PACIFIC.

Plymouth Rock fowls are probably the best general purpose fowls for farmers. They are not so exacting and destructive as lighter breeds, are good layers through the year, good mothers and the chicks are unusually hardy, and come early to maturity. They are the only variety with which a late hatched setting in the fall is not a misfortune. But with all their virtues they are not popular with fanciers, who prefer breeds with a few strong points rather than general excellence.

## Market Report.

FLOUR—We quote: Best City Extra, $6 60@$6 75; Superfine, $4@$5 25; Interior Extra, $4 75@$5 25; Interior Superfine, $5 75@$4 50 bbl.

WHEAT—The demand for this grain is not very firm. We hear of a few good trades; Sound in No. 1 White at $1 76; A choice lot of Milling recently changed hands at $1 75½, which is the highest figure paid for a long time.

BARLEY—The market is quite dull at present. Recent sales are: No. 1 Feed, $1 30@$1 20; do Feeding, $1 30; do Malt, $1 45@$1 87.

OATS—Fair Feed, $1 70@$1 75; Good, $1 75@$1 80; Choice, $1 90@$1 95 ^@ cwt. Eastern, $1 65 ^@ cwt.

RYE—Business dull. Quotable at $1 78@$1 90 for California ^@ ctl, and $1 75@$1 80 ^@ ctl for Eastern.

FEED—Ground Barley, $28@$30 ^@ ton; Cracked Corn, $27 ^@ ton. Shorts, $20 ^@ ton. Oilcake meal, the oilworks sell to the trade at $30 80 ^@ ton, less the usual discount. Middlings, $27@$28 ^@ ton for lots at the mill.

HAY—Alfalfa, $12@$14 50; Wheat, $14@$17 50 Wild Oat, $13 50@$16 50; Mixed, $13 50@$15 ^@ ton.

PROVISIONS—Eastern Hams, $19@$21c; California Hams, $15@$16½c for light; and extra light; Clear sides, $15@$16c; Pork, $18@$20; Extra Prime, $16 50 ^@ bbl for Prime Mess, $22 50@$24 50 for Mess; and $23 50 ^@ bbl for Clear. Pork; Bacon, $14@$16c for heavy; and $17 for Medium and $18 75 for light; California Smoked Beef, $18½@$14c ^@ ib.

FRUIT—We quote: Apples, $0@$80c for common; and 75@$1 25 ^@ for good; Pears, $1@$1 25 ^@ box; Lemons, $7@$8 per box for Sicily and $6@$8 for California Oranges, $2 60 for $40@$50 per box; Limes, $10 ^@ box for Mexican; Bananas, $2 50@$3 ^@ bunch; Mexican Oranges, $60 box for good; California, $3 50@$5 50 per large, and $3 50@$3 80 for small boxes; Pineapples, $6@$8 ^@ doz. New crop Western Cranberries are offering at $12@$13 ^@ bbl.

VEGETABLES—We quote: Marrowfat Squash, $8 ^@ ton; Onions, 80c; Turnips, 75c@$1; Cauliflower, 75c@$1 ^@ dozen; Cabbage, 50@75c ^@ ctl; Garlic, 8½c ^@ ib; Green Peas, 7@$9 ^@ ib; Celery 60c ^@ doz; Mushrooms, 10@16c per ib; Okra 7@9c ^@ ib; Dried Okra, 20c; Dry Peppers, 18@20c ib ^@ ib.

POTATOES—River Red, 80@75c; Early Rose, 80c@$1 ^@ ctl; Tomales Garlic, 85@$1 10; Humboldt, $1@$1 10; Tomales and Petaluma, 85@$1; Peerless $1; Cutley Cove, $1 10 to $1 15 ^@ ctl; Sweets, 2c ^@ ib.

ONIONS—Quotable at 90@95c ^@ sack.

BEANS—Bayos 6c; Yellows, Butter, $3@$3 55 for small, and $3 50@$3 60 for large; Limas, $3 55@$4; Pea, $3 30@$3 50; Pink, $2 90@$3 10; Red, $3 40@$3 60; small White, $3 40@$3 60; large White, $5 30@$3 60 ^@ ctl.

BUTTER—We quote pickled rolls Fancy, 35@30c; choice, 30@27c fair to good; 25@18c; inferior lots from country stores, 17@22c; firkin, 36@35c for good to choice, and 25@20c for ordinary; pickled rolls, 34@34c ^@ ib; fancy, 35@38c for English and 80@37½c for common; Tub, 33@37½c ^@ ib.

EGGS—California, 37½@40c; Eastern, 30@32½ per doz.

POULTRY—Live Turkeys, gobblers, 18@22c; do Hens, 20@22c; do dressed, 19@22c; Roosters, $6@$6 50 for old and $7@$9 for young; Hens $6@$7 per dozen; Broilers, according to size; Ducks $8@$11 ^@ dozen; Geese, $1 75@$2 ^@ pair.

GAME—In good demand: Quail, $1 ^@ dozen; Mallard Ducks, $3 50@$4 per dozen; Sprigs, $2@$2 50 per Canvasback, $6 ^@ dozen; Sneal, $1 25; Gray Geese $2@$3; White Geese, $1 25@$1 75; Brant $2@$3; Hare, 75c@$1; Cottontail or Jack Rabbits, $1@$1 50 per doz; Snipe, $3 50@$4 for English and $1@$1 25c for common; Teal, $2@$2 50; Widgeon, $1 50@$2; Venison, 8c; Bear, 12½@15c ^@ ib.

WOOL—No change in prices. We quote fall: San Joaquin and north, 14@16c for good and coast Lamb, good, 11@13c; Northern Fall free, 16@20c; Northern Fall, defective, 11@14c; Northern Lamb, 11@20c; free Mountain, 13@14c.

HIDES AND SKINS—Dry trade, quotable at 19@20c ^@ ib; culls one third less, and Mexican 14@16c ^@ ib. Dry Kip, 17c; Dry Calf, 21@23c; salted Steers, over 56 lbs, 11c ^@ ib; Steers and Cows, medium, 11c; light do, 9c; Salted Kip, 10 to 86 lbs, 10c; Salted Calf, 14@15c ^@ ib; Dairy Calf 10½@12c per ib for English and 11@12½c for common; Tall, salted, 13@14c for Widgeon, $1 50@$2; Veal, 8c; Dry Sheepskins, shearlings, 15@25c each; medium 50@70c; and long wool, $1@$1 25 each.

TALLOW—Quotable at 6c@6½c ^@ ib for rendered and 11@12½c for tried in shipping order.

MEATS—Following are our wholesale prices from slaughterers to dealers: BEEF—Prime, 9@9½c; medium grade, 7½@8c; inferior, 5½@6½c ^@ ib.

VEAL—Large Calves, 8½@9c; small ones, 9@10c ^@ ib.

MUTTON—Wethers are quotable at 8@9c and Ewes and Lambs, 7@8c ^@ ib.

HOGS—Live Hogs, 6@7c for large and 6½@8½c for soft; dressed do 9@9½c ^@ ib for hard grain hogs.

---

SPECIMEN OF OUR ARTIST'S HUMOR

THE FISHMONGER.

HUNDREDS OF DELIGHTED ONES SEE, FOR THE FIRST TIME IN THEIR LIVES

The Japanese Artist and Embroiderers

At work in their native costumes at

## Ichi Ban, 22 & 24 Geary St.

The BREEDER AND SPORTSMAN is printed with SHATTUCK & FLETCHER'S INK

Fifty-five laying hens, belonging to Mrs. E. Turner, in Alexander Valley, produced, during October, 843 eggs, which were sold for $57 40, an example of what any attentive and industrious housewife can do.—*Russian River Flag.*

In Great Britain the demand for poultry and eggs exceeds the supply.

After chicks are a month old cracked corn and wheat screenings are better for them than dough.

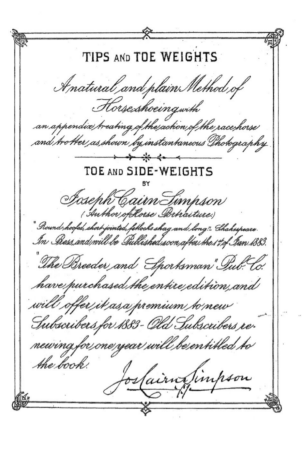

## TIPS AND TOE WEIGHTS

*A natural and plain Method of Horse-shoeing with an appendix treating of the action of the race-horse and trotter, as shown by instantaneous Photography*

### TOE AND SIDE-WEIGHTS

BY

*Joseph Cairn Simpson*

*(Author of Horse Portraiture.)*

"Round-hoofed, short-jointed, fetlocks shag and long." Shakespeare.

In Press, and will be Published soon after the 1st of Jan. 1883.

"The Breeder and Sportsman" Pub. Co. have purchased the entire edition, and will offer it as a premium to new Subscribers for 1883. Old Subscribers renewing for one year will be entitled to the book.

*Jos Cairn Simpson*

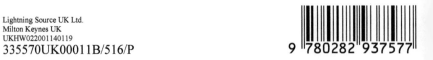